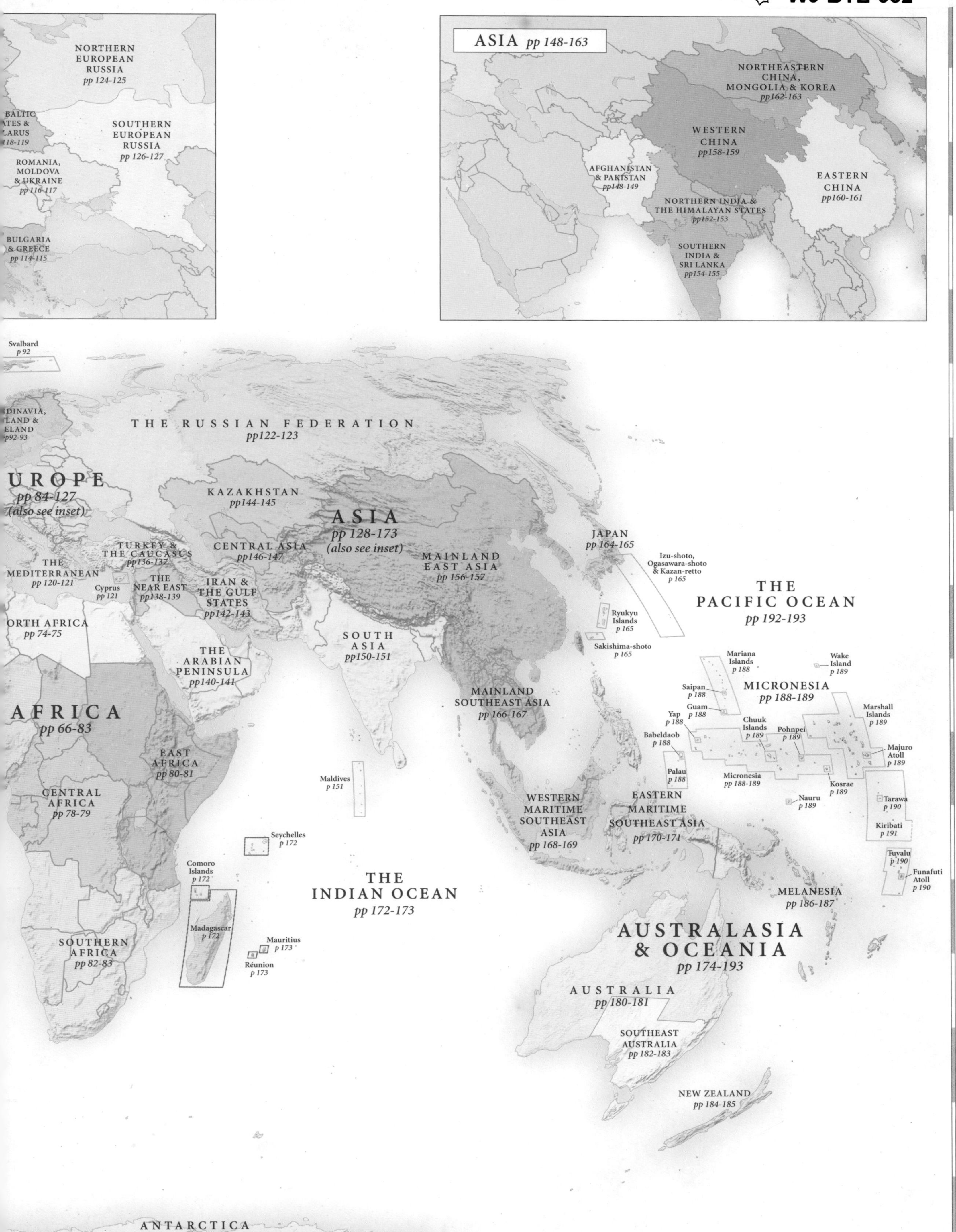
NORTHERN EUROPEAN RUSSIA pp 124-125
BALTIC
ATES &
LARUS
18-119
SOUTHERN EUROPEAN RUSSIA pp 126-127
ROMANIA, MOLDOVA & UKRAINE pp 116-117
BULGARIA & GREECE pp 114-115
ASIA pp 148-163
NORTHEASTERN CHINA, MONGOLIA & KOREA pp162-163
WESTERN CHINA pp158-159
AFGHANISTAN & PAKISTAN pp148-149
EASTERN CHINA pp160-161
NORTHERN INDIA & THE HIMALAYAN STATES pp152-153
SOUTHERN INDIA & SRI LANKA pp154-155
Svalbard p 92
DINAVIA,
LAND &
ELAND
p92-93
THE RUSSIAN FEDERATION pp122-123
UROPE pp 84-127 (also see inset)
KAZAKHSTAN pp144-145
ASIA pp 128-173 (also see inset)
CENTRAL ASIA pp146-147
TURKEY & THE CAUCASUS pp136-137
THE MEDITERRANEAN pp 120-121
Cyprus p 121
THE NEAR EAST pp138-139
IRAN & THE GULF STATES pp142-143
MAINLAND EAST ASIA pp 156-157
JAPAN pp 164-165
Izu-shoto, Ogasawara-shoto & Kazan-retto p 165
THE PACIFIC OCEAN pp 192-193
Ryukyu Islands p 165
Sakishima-shoto p 165
ORTH AFRICA pp 74-75
THE ARABIAN PENINSULA pp140-141
SOUTH ASIA pp150-151
Mariana Islands p 188
Wake Island p 189
Saipan p 188
MICRONESIA pp 188-189
Guam p 188
Marshall Islands p 189
MAINLAND SOUTHEAST ASIA pp 166-167
Yap p 188
Chuuk Islands p 189
Pohnpei p 189
Babeldaob p 188
Majuro Atoll p 189
AFRICA pp 66-83
EAST AFRICA pp 80-81
Palau p 188
Micronesia pp 188-189
Kosrae p 189
Maldives p 151
CENTRAL AFRICA pp 78-79
WESTERN MARITIME SOUTHEAST ASIA pp 168-169
EASTERN MARITIME SOUTHEAST ASIA pp 170-171
Nauru p 189
Tarawa p 190
Kiribati p 191
Seychelles p 172
Tuvalu p 190
Funafuti Atoll p 190
Comoro Islands p 172
THE INDIAN OCEAN pp 172-173
MELANESIA pp 186-187
Madagascar p 172
AUSTRALASIA & OCEANIA pp 174-193
Mauritius p 173
Réunion p 173
SOUTHERN AFRICA pp 82-83
AUSTRALIA pp 180-181
SOUTHEAST AUSTRALIA pp 182-183
NEW ZEALAND pp 184-185
ANTARCTICA pp 194-195

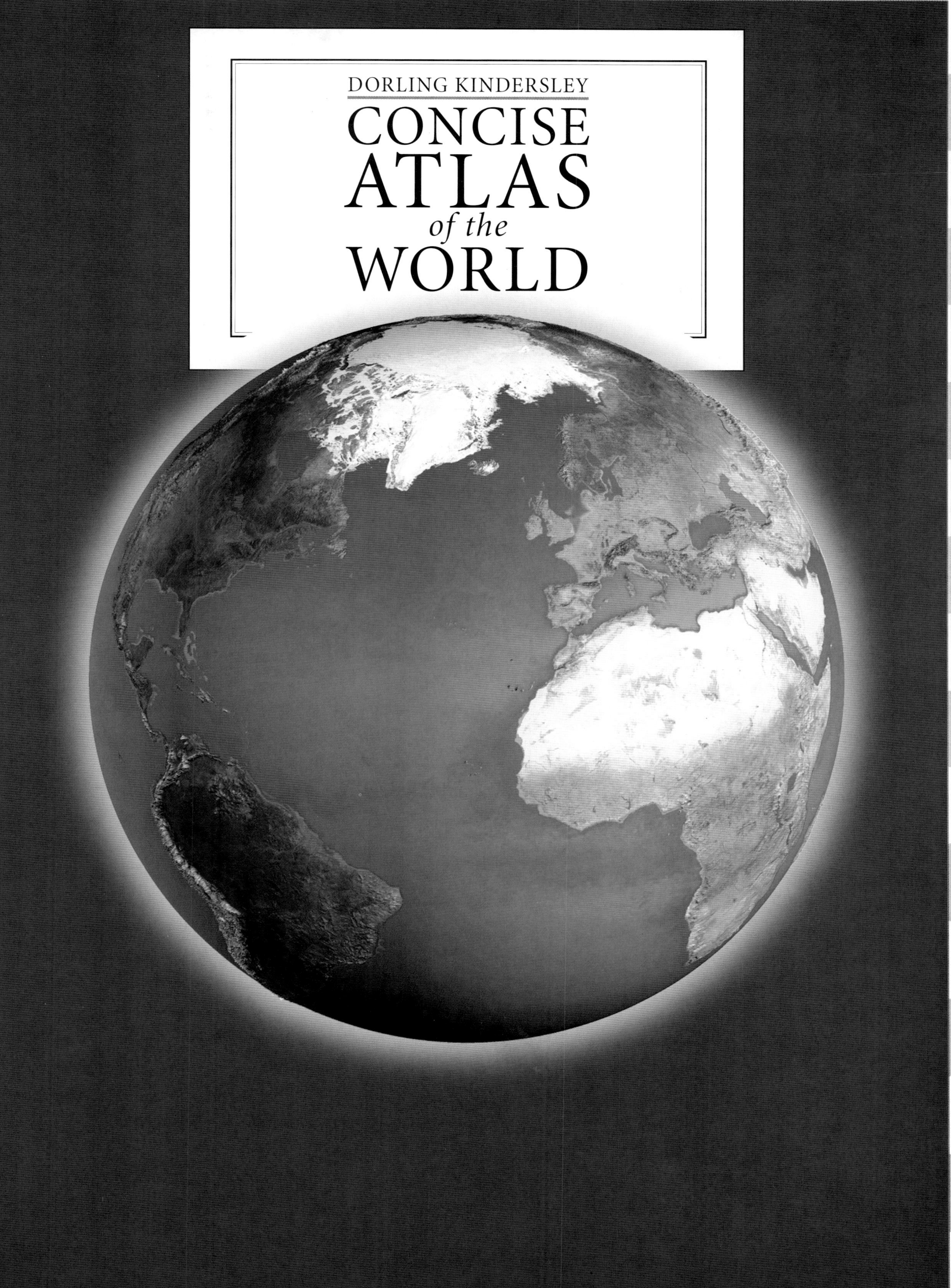
DORLING KINDERSLEY
CONCISE
ATLAS
of the
WORLD

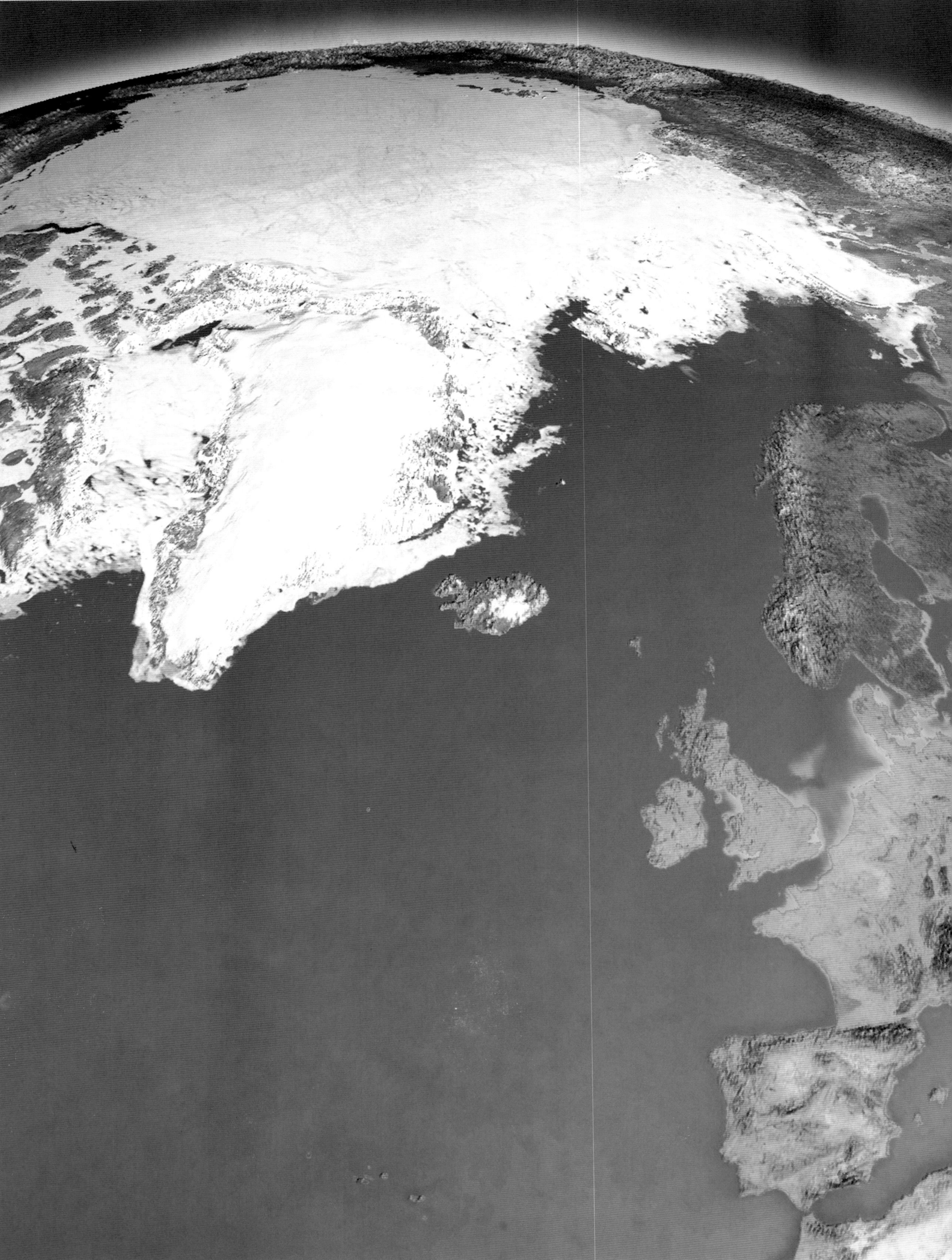

DORLING KINDERSLEY

CONCISE ATLAS *of the* WORLD

A Dorling Kindersley Book

LONDON, NEW YORK, DELHI, PARIS,
MUNICH, AND JOHANNESBURG

GENERAL GEOGRAPHICAL CONSULTANTS

PHYSICAL GEOGRAPHY • Denys Brunsden, Emeritus Professor, Department of Geography, King's College, London

HUMAN GEOGRAPHY • Professor J Malcolm Wagstaff, Department of Geography, University of Southampton

PLACE NAMES • Caroline Burgess, Permanent Committee on Geographical Names, London

BOUNDARIES • International Boundaries Research Unit, Mountjoy Research Centre, University of Durham

DIGITAL MAPPING CONSULTANTS

DK Cartopia developed by George Galfalvi and XMap Ltd, London

Professor Jan-Peter Muller, Department of Photogrammetry and Surveying, University College, London

Cover globes, planets and information on the Solar System provided by Philip Eales and Kevin Tildsley, Planetary Visions Ltd, London

REGIONAL CONSULTANTS

NORTH AMERICA • Dr David Green, Department of Geography, King's College, London
Jim Walsh, Head of Reference, Wessell Library, Tufts University, Medford, Massachussetts

SOUTH AMERICA • Dr David Preston, School of Geography, University of Leeds

EUROPE • Dr Edward M Yates, formerly of the Department of Geography, King's College, London

AFRICA • Dr Philip Amis, Development Administration Group, University of Birmingham
Dr Ieuan L Griffiths, Department of Geography, University of Sussex
Dr Tony Binns, Department of Geography, University of Sussex

CENTRAL ASIA • Dr David Turnock, Department of Geography, University of Leicester

SOUTH AND EAST ASIA • Dr Jonathan Rigg, Department of Geography, University of Durham

AUSTRALASIA AND OCEANIA • Dr Robert Allison, Department of Geography, University of Durham

ACKNOWLEDGMENTS

Digital terrain data created by Eros Data Center, Sioux Falls, South Dakota, USA. Processed by GVS Images Inc, California, USA and Planetary Visions Ltd, London, UK • CIRCA Research and Reference Information, Cambridge, UK • Digitization by Robertson Research International, Swanley, UK • Peter Clark

---

EDITOR-IN-CHIEF
Andrew Heritage

MANAGING EDITOR
Lisa Thomas

SENIOR MANAGING ART EDITOR
Philip Lord

SENIOR CARTOGRAPHIC MANAGER
David Roberts

MANAGING CARTOGRAPHER
Roger Bullen

SENIOR CARTOGRAPHIC EDITOR
Simon Mumford

DATABASE MANAGER
Simon Lewis

CARTOGRAPHERS
Pamela Alford • James Anderson • Sarah Baker-Ede • Caroline Bowie • Dale Buckton Tony Chambers • Jan Clark • Tom Coulson • Bob Croser • Martin Darlison • Claire Ellam • Sally Gable • Jeremy Hepworth • Geraldine Horner • Chris Jackson • Christine Johnston • Julia Lunn • Michael Martin • James Mills-Hicks • John Plumer • Rob Stokes • John Scott • Ann Stephenson • Julie Turner • Iorwerth Watkins • Jane Voss • Scott Wallace • Bryony Webb • Alan Whitaker • Peter Winfield

EDITORS
Debra Clapson • Thomas Heath • Wim Jenkins • Jane Oliver
Siobhán Ryan • Elizabeth Wyse

DESIGNERS
Scott David • Carol Ann Davis • David Douglas
Rhonda Fisher • Karen Gregory • Nicola Liddiard • Paul Williams

EDITORIAL RESEARCH
Helen Dangerfield • Andrew Rebeiro-Hargrave

ILLUSTRATIONS
Ciárán Hughes • Advanced Illustration, Congleton, UK

ADDITIONAL EDITORIAL ASSISTANCE
Margaret Hynes • Robert Damon • Ailsa Heritage • Constance Novis • Jayne Parsons • Chris Whitwell

PICTURE RESEARCH
Melissa Albany • James Clarke • Anna Lord • Christine Rista • Sarah Moule • Louise Thomas

EDITORIAL DIRECTION • Louise Cavanagh

ART DIRECTION • Chez Picthall

SYSTEMS COORDINATOR Phil Rowles

PRODUCTION Michelle Thomas

DIGITAL MAPS CREATED IN DK CARTOPIA BY
Tom Coulson • Thomas Robertshaw
Philip Rowles • Rob Stokes

PLACENAMES DATABASE TEAM
Natalie Clarkson • Ruth Duxbury • Caroline Falce • John Featherstone • Dan Gardiner
Ciárán Hynes • Margaret Hynes • Helen Rudkin • Margaret Stevenson • Annie Wilson

Published in the United States by
Dorling Kindersley Publishing Inc.
95 Madison Avenue, New York, New York 10016

First American Edition, 2001
2 4 6 8 10 9 7 5 3 1

A CIP catalog record for this book is available from the Library of Congress/ ISBN: 0-7894-7437-9

Reproduction by Colourscan, Singapore. Printed and bound by Graficas Estella, Spain.

Introduction

For many, the outstanding legacy of the twentieth century was the way in which the Earth shrank. As we enter the third millennium, it is increasingly important for us to have a clear vision of the World in which we live. The human population has increased fourfold since 1900. The last scraps of *terra incognita* – the polar regions and ocean depths – have been penetrated and mapped. New regions have been colonized, and previously hostile realms claimed for habitation. The advent of aviation technology and mass tourism allows many of us to travel further, faster, and more frequently than ever before. In doing so we are given a bird's-eye view of the Earth's surface denied to our forebears.

At the same time, the amount of information about our World has grown enormously. Telecommunications can span the greatest distances in fractions of a second: our multimedia environment hurls uninterrupted streams of data at us, on the printed page, through the airwaves, and across our television and computer screens; events from all corners of the globe reach us instantaneously, and are witnessed as they unfold. Our sense of stability and certainty has been eroded; instead, we are aware that the World is in a constant state of flux and change. Natural disasters, manmade cataclysms, and conflicts between nations remind us daily of the enormity and fragility of our domain.

Our current "global" culture has made the need greater than ever before for everyone to possess an atlas. This atlas has been conceived to meet this need. At its core, like all atlases, it seeks to define where places are, to describe their main characteristics, and to locate them in relation to other places. Every attempt has been made to make the information on the maps as clear and accessible as possible. In addition, each page of the atlas provides a wealth of further information, bringing the maps to life. Using photographs, diagrams, "at-a-glance" thematic maps, introductory texts, and captions, the atlas builds up a detailed portrait of those features – cultural, political, economic, and geomorphological – which make each region unique, and which are also the main agents of change.

These words, which formed the introduction to the first edition of the *DK World Atlas* in 1997, remain as true today as they were then. This *Concise Edition* incorporates thousands of revisions and updates affecting every map and every page, and features a new typographic design for the maps. The *Concise Edition* has been created to bring all these benefits to a new audience, in a handier format and at a more affordable price.

Andrew Heritage
Editor-in-Chief

Contents

Introduction v

Contents .... vi–vii

How to use this Atlas .... viii–ix

THE WORLD TODAY

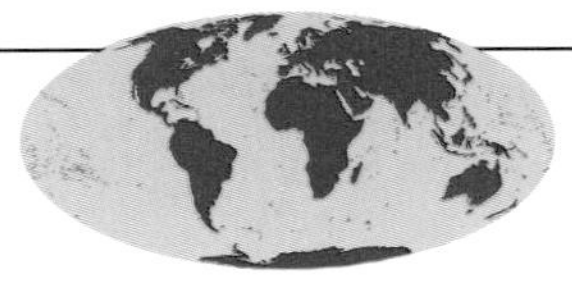

The Solar System .... x–xi

The Physical World .... xii–xiii

Structure of the Earth ...... xiv–xv

Shaping the Landscape ...... xvi–xvii

The World's Oceans .... xviii–xix

The Global Climate .... xx–xxi

Life on Earth .... xxii–xxiii

Population and Settlement .... xxiv–xxv

The Economic System ...... xxvi–xxvii

The Political World ...... xxviii–xxix

States and Boundaries ...... xxx–xxxi

International Disputes xxxii

ATLAS OF THE WORLD

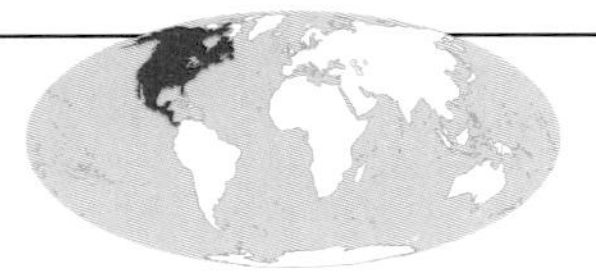

North America

NORTH AMERICA 1

PHYSICAL NORTH AMERICA 2–3

POLITICAL NORTH AMERICA 4–5

NORTH AMERICAN RESOURCES 6–7

Canada 8–9

Canada: Western Provinces 10–11
Alberta, British Columbia, Manitoba, Saskatchewan, Yukon

Canada: Eastern Provinces 12–13
New Brunswick, Newfoundland & Labrador, Nova Scotia, Ontario, Prince Edward Island, Québec, St Pierre & Miquelon

Southeastern Canada 14–15
Southern Ontario, Southern Québec

United States of America 16–17

USA: Northeastern States 18–19
Connecticut, Maine, Massachussetts, New Hampshire, New Jersey, New York, Pennsylvania, Rhode Island, Vermont

USA: Mid-Eastern States 20–21
Delaware, District of Columbia, Kentucky, Maryland, North Carolina, South Carolina, Tennessee, Virginia, West Virginia

USA: Southern States 22–23
Alabama, Florida, Georgia, Louisiana, Mississippi

USA: Texas 24–25

USA: South Midwestern States ... 26–27
Arkansas, Kansas, Missouri, Oklahoma

USA: Upper Plains States 28–29
Iowa, Minnesota, Nebraska, North Dakota, South Dakota

USA: Great Lakes States 30–31
Illinois, Indiana, Michigan, Ohio, Wisconsin

USA: North Mountain States 32–33
Idaho, Montana, Oregon, Washington, Wyoming

USA: California & Nevada 34–35

USA: South Mountain States 36–37
Arizona, Colorado, New Mexico, Utah

USA: Hawaii & Alaska 38–39

Mexico 40–41

Central America 42–43
Belize, Costa Rica, El Salvador, Guatemala, Honduras, Nicaragua, Panama

The Caribbean 44–45
Anguilla, Antigua & Barbuda, Aruba, Bahamas, Barbados, British Virgin Islands, Cayman Islands, Cuba, Dominica, Dominican Republic, Grenada, Guadeloupe, Haiti, Jamaica, Martinique, Montserrat, Navassa Island, Netherlands Antilles, Puerto Rico, St. Kitts & Nevis, St. Lucia, St. Vincent & the Grenadines, Trinidad & Tobago, Turks & Caicos Islands, Virgin Islands (US)

South America

SOUTH AMERICA 46–47

PHYSICAL SOUTH AMERICA 48–49

POLITICAL SOUTH AMERICA 50–51

SOUTH AMERICAN RESOURCES 52–53

Northern South America 54–55
Colombia, French Guiana, Guyana, Suriname, Venezuela

Western South America 56–57
Bolivia, Ecuador, Peru

Brazil 58–59

Eastern South America 60–61
Southeast Brazil, Northeast Argentina, Uruguay

Southern South America 62–63
Argentina, Chile, Paraguay

The Atlantic Ocean 64–65

Africa

AFRICA 66–67

PHYSICAL AFRICA 68–69

POLITICAL AFRICA 70–71

AFRICAN RESOURCES 72–73

North Africa 74–75
Algeria, Egypt, Libya, Morocco, Tunisia, Western Sahara

West Africa 76–77
Benin, Burkina, Cape Verde, Gambia, Ghana, Guinea, Guinea-Bissau, Ivory Coast, Liberia, Mali, Mauritania, Niger, Nigeria, Senegal, Sierra Leone, Togo

Central Africa 78–79
Cameroon, Central African Republic, Chad, Congo, Dem. Rep. Congo (Zaire), Equatorial Guinea, Gabon, Sao Tome & Principe

East Africa 80–81
Burundi, Djibouti, Eritrea, Ethiopia, Kenya, Rwanda, Somalia, Sudan, Tanzania, Uganda

Southern Africa 82–83
Angola, Botswana, Lesotho, Malawi, Mozambique, Namibia, South Africa, Swaziland, Zambia, Zimbabwe

Europe

EUROPE 84–85

PHYSICAL EUROPE 86–87

POLITICAL EUROPE 88–89

EUROPEAN RESOURCES 90–91

SCANDINAVIA, FINLAND, & ICELAND . 92–93
Denmark, Finland, Iceland, Norway, Svalbard, Sweden

SOUTHERN SCANDINAVIA 94–95
Denmark, Faeroe Islands, Southern Norway, Southern Sweden

THE BRITISH ISLES 96–97
Channel Islands, Isle of Man, Republic of Ireland, United Kingdom

THE LOW COUNTRIES 98–99
Belgium, Luxembourg, Netherlands

GERMANY 100–101

FRANCE 102–103
France, Monaco

THE IBERIAN PENINSULA 104–105
Andorra, Gibraltar, Portugal, Spain

THE ITALIAN PENINSULA 106–107
Italy, San Marino, Vatican City

THE ALPINE STATES 108–109
Austria, Liechtenstein, Slovenia, Switzerland

CENTRAL EUROPE 110–111
Czech Republic, Hungary, Poland, Slovakia

SOUTHEAST EUROPE 112–113
Albania, Bosnia & Herzegovina, Croatia, Macedonia, Yugoslavia

BULGARIA & GREECE 114–115
(including European Turkey)

ROMANIA, MOLDOVA, & UKRAINE 116–117

THE BALTIC STATES & BELARUS 118–119
Belarus, Estonia, Latvia, Lithuania, Kaliningrad

THE MEDITERRANEAN 120–121

THE RUSSIAN FEDERATION 122–123

NORTHERN EUROPEAN RUSSIA 124–125

SOUTHERN EUROPEAN RUSSIA 126–127

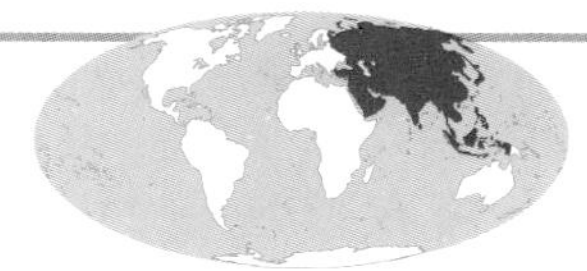

Asia

ASIA 128–129

PHYSICAL ASIA 130–131

POLITICAL ASIA 132–133

ASIAN RESOURCES 134–135

TURKEY & THE CAUCASUS 136–137
Armenia, Azerbaijan, Georgia, Turkey

THE NEAR EAST 138–139
Iraq, Israel, Jordan, Lebanon, Syria

THE ARABIAN PENINSULA 140–141
Bahrain, Kuwait, Oman, Qatar, Saudi Arabia, United Arab Emirates, Yemen

IRAN & THE GULF STATES 142–143
Bahrain, Iran, Kuwait, Qatar, United Arab Emirates

KAZAKHSTAN 144–145

CENTRAL ASIA 146–147
Kyrgyzstan, Tajikistan, Turkmenistan, Uzbekistan

AFGHANISTAN & PAKISTAN 148–149

SOUTH ASIA 150–151
Bangladesh, Bhutan, India, Maldives, Nepal, Pakistan, Sri Lanka

NORTHERN INDIA & THE HIMALAYAN STATES 152–153
Bangladesh, Bhutan, Nepal, Northern India

SOUTHERN INDIA & SRI LANKA 154–155

MAINLAND EAST ASIA 156–157
China, Mongolia, North Korea, South Korea, Taiwan

WESTERN CHINA 158–159

EASTERN CHINA 160–161
Eastern China, Taiwan

NORTHEASTERN CHINA, MONGOLIA & KOREA 162–163
Mongolia, Northeastern China, North Korea, South Korea

JAPAN 164–165

MAINLAND SOUTHEAST ASIA 166–167
Myanmar, Cambodia, Laos, Paracel Islands, Philippines, Spratly Islands, Thailand, Vietnam

WESTERN MARITIME SOUTHEAST ASIA 168–169
Brunei, Indonesia, Malaysia, Singapore

EASTERN MARITIME SOUTHEAST ASIA 170–171
East Timor, Indonesia, Philippines

THE INDIAN OCEAN 172–173

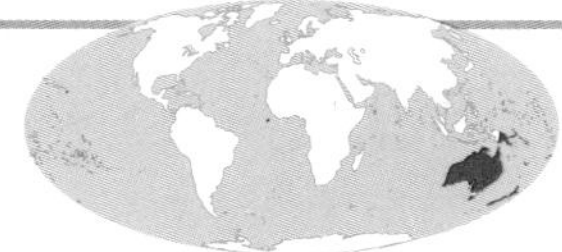

Australasia and Oceania

AUSTRALASIA & OCEANIA 174–175

POLITICAL AUSTRALASIA & OCEANIA 176–177

AUSTRALASIAN & OCEANIAN RESOURCES 178–179

AUSTRALIA 180–181

SOUTHEAST AUSTRALIA 182–183
New South Wales, South Australia, Tasmania, Victoria

NEW ZEALAND 184–185

MELANESIA 186–187
Papua New Guinea, Fiji, Solomon Islands, Vanuatu, New Caledonia

MICRONESIA 188–189
Guam, Marshall Islands, Micronesia, Nauru, Northern Mariana Islands, Palau, Wake Island

POLYNESIA 190–191
Cook Islands, Easter Island, French Polynesia, Kiribati, Niue, Pitcairn Islands, Tokelau, Tuvalu, Wallis & Futuna

THE PACIFIC OCEAN 192–193

ANTARCTICA 194–195

THE ARCTIC 196–197

INDEX-GAZETTEER

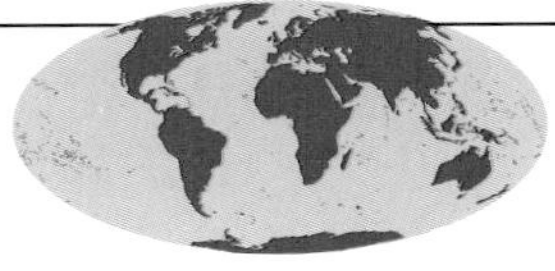

GEOGRAPHICAL COMPARISONS 198–199

COUNTRIES OF THE WORLD
including World Timezones 200–207

GEOGRAPHICAL GLOSSARY 208–210

GEOGRAPHICAL NAMES 211

INDEX 212–349

CREDITS/ACKNOWLEDGEMENTS .. 350

KEY TO REGIONAL MAPS

PHYSICAL FEATURES

elevation

6000m / 19,686ft
4000m / 13,124ft
3000m / 9843ft
2000m / 6562ft
1000m / 3281ft
500m / 1640ft
250m / 820ft
100m / 328ft
sea level
below sea level

▲ elevation above sea level (mountain height)
volcano
pass
▼ elevation below sea level (depression depth)

sand desert
lava flow
coastline
reef
atoll

sea depth

sea level
-250m / -820ft
-500m / -1640ft
-1000m / -3281ft
-2000m / -6562ft
-3000m / -9843ft

▲ seamount / guyot symbol
▼ undersea spot depth

DRAINAGE FEATURES

main river
secondary river
tertiary river
minor river
main seasonal river
secondary seasonal river
canal
waterfall
rapids
dam
perennial lake
seasonal lake
perennial salt lake
seasonal salt lake
reservoir
salt flat / salt pan
marsh / salt marsh
mangrove
wadi
spring / well / waterhole / oasis

ICE FEATURES

ice cap / sheet
ice shelf
glacier / snowfield
summer pack ice limit
winter pack ice limit

COMMUNICATIONS

highway
highway (under construction)
major road
minor road
tunnel (road)
main line
minor line
tunnel (railroad)
international airport

BORDERS

full international border
undefined international border
disputed *de facto* border
disputed territorial claim border
indication of country extent (Pacific only)
indication of dependent territory extent (Pacific only)
demarcation/ cease-fire line
autonomous / federal region border
2nd order internal administrative border
3rd order internal administrative border

SETTLEMENTS

built-up area

settlement population symbols

more than 5 million
1 million to 5 million
500,000 to 1 million
100,000 to 500,000
50,000 to 100,000
10,000 to 50,000
fewer than 10,000

country/dependent territory capital city
autonomous / federal region / 2nd order internal administrative center
3rd order internal administrative center

MISCELLANEOUS FEATURES

ancient wall
site of interest
scientific station

GRATICULE FEATURES

lines of latitude and longitude / Equator
Tropics / Polar circles
45° degrees of longitude / latitude

TYPOGRAPHIC KEY

PHYSICAL FEATURES

landscape features	*Namib Desert* *Massif Central* *ANDES*
headland	*Nordkapp*
elevation / volcano / pass	Mount Meru 4556 m
drainage features	*Lake Rudolf*
rivers / canals spring / well / waterhole / oasis / waterfall / rapids / dam	*Mekong*
ice features	*Vatnajökull*
sea features	*Golfe de Lion* *Andaman Sea* *INDIAN OCEAN*
undersea features	*Barracuda Fracture Zone*

REGIONS

country	ARMENIA
dependent territory with parent state	NIUE (to NZ)
region outside feature area	ANGOLA
autonomous / federal region	MINAS GERAIS
2nd order internal administrative region	MINSKAYA VOBLASTS'
3rd order internal administrative region	Vaucluse
cultural region	New England

SETTLEMENTS

capital city	BEIJING
dependent territory capital city	FORT-DE-FRANCE
other settlements	Chicago Adana Tizi Ozou Yonezawa Farnham

MISCELLANEOUS

sites of interest / miscellaneous	Valley of the Kings
Tropics / Polar circles	*Antarctic Circle*

HOW TO USE THIS ATLAS

THE ATLAS IS ORGANIZED BY CONTINENT, moving eastward from the International Dateline. The opening section describes the world's structure, systems, and its main features. The Atlas of the World that follows, is a continent-by-continent guide to today's world, starting with a comprehensive insight into the physical, political, and economic structure of each continent, followed by integrated mapping and descriptions of each region or country.

THE WORLD

THE INTRODUCTORY SECTION of the Atlas deals with every aspect of the planet, from physical structure to human geography, providing an overall picture of the world we live in. Complex topics such as the landscape of the Earth, climate, oceans, population, and economic patterns are clearly explained with the aid of maps and diagrams drawn from the latest information.

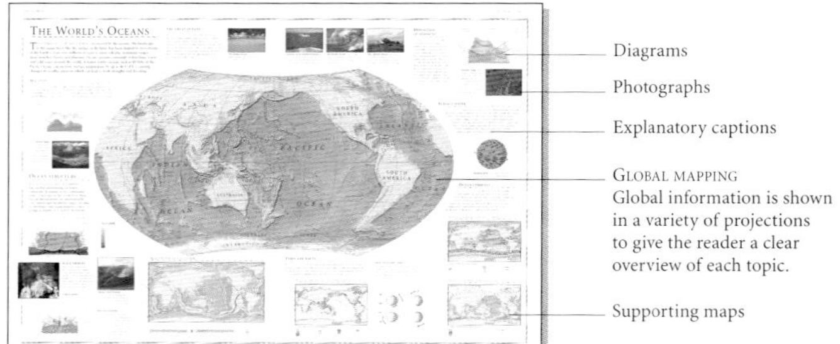
THE WORLD'S OCEANS

Diagrams
Photographs
Explanatory captions
GLOBAL MAPPING Global information is shown in a variety of projections to give the reader a clear overview of each topic.
Supporting maps

THE POLITICAL CONTINENT

THE POLITICAL PORTRAIT of the continent is a vital reference point for every continental section, showing the position of countries relative to one another, and the relationship between human settlement and geographic location. The complex mosaic of languages spoken in each continent is mapped, as is the effect of communications networks on the pattern of settlement.

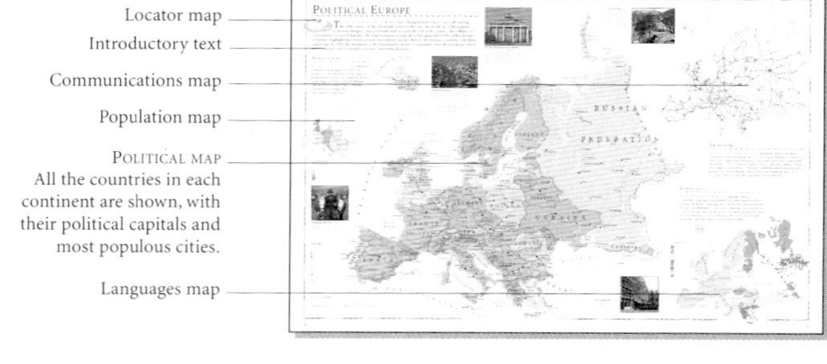
POLITICAL EUROPE

Locator map
Introductory text
Communications map
Population map
POLITICAL MAP All the countries in each continent are shown, with their political capitals and most populous cities.
Languages map

CONTINENTAL RESOURCES

THE EARTH'S RICH NATURAL RESOURCES, including oil, gas, minerals, and fertile land, have played a key role in the development of society. These pages show the location of minerals and agricultural resources on each continent, and how they have been instrumental in dictating industrial growth and the varieties of economic activity across the continent.

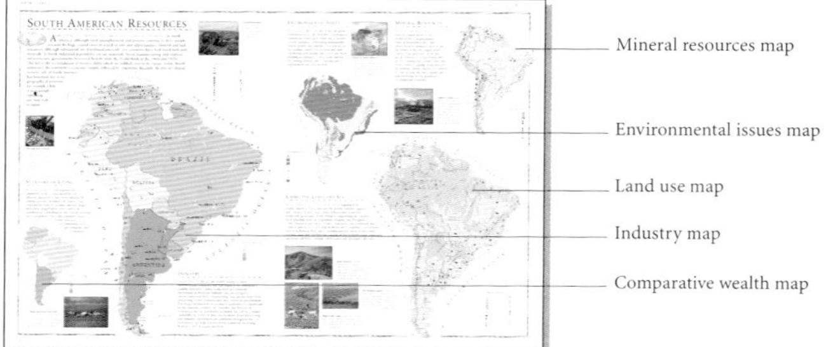
SOUTH AMERICAN RESOURCES

Mineral resources map
Environmental issues map
Land use map
Industry map
Comparative wealth map

The Physical Continent

The astonishing variety of landforms, and the dramatic forces that created and continue to shape the landscape, are explained in the continental physical spread. Cross-sections, illustrations, and terrain maps highlight the different parts of the continent, showing how nature's forces have produced the landscapes we see today.

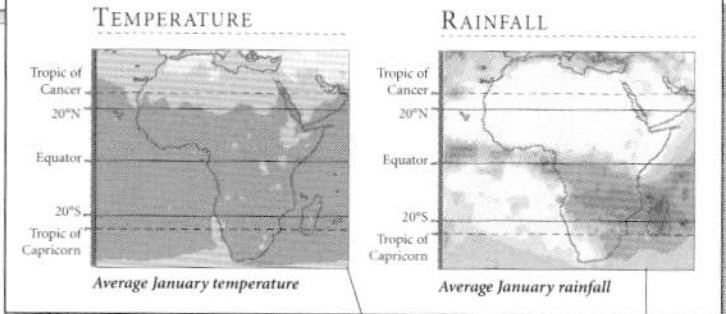
Temperature
Rainfall
Average January temperature
Average January rainfall

Climate charts
Rainfall and temperature charts clearly show the continental patterns of rainfall and temperature.

Climate map
Climatic regions vary across each continent. The map displays the differing climatic regions, as well as daily hours of sunshine at selected weather stations.

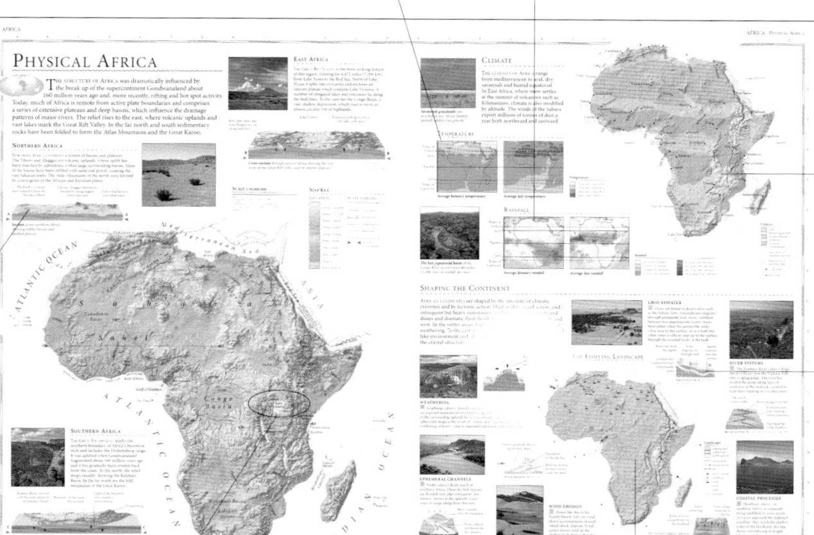
Physical Africa

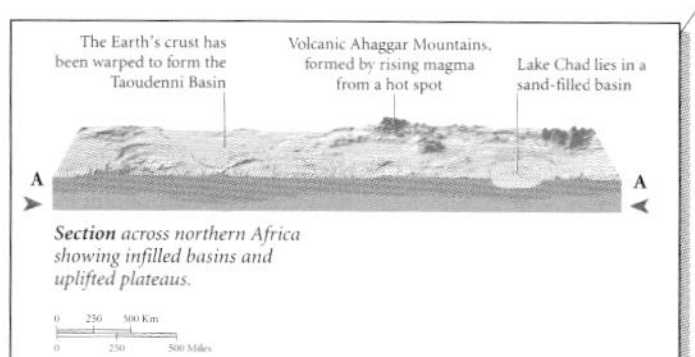
The Earth's crust has been warped to form the Taoudenni Basin
Volcanic Ahaggar Mountains, formed by rising magma from a hot spot
Lake Chad lies in a sand-filled basin
Section across northern Africa showing infilled basins and uplifted plateaus.

Cross-sections
Detailed cross-sections through selected parts of the continent show the underlying geomorphic structure.

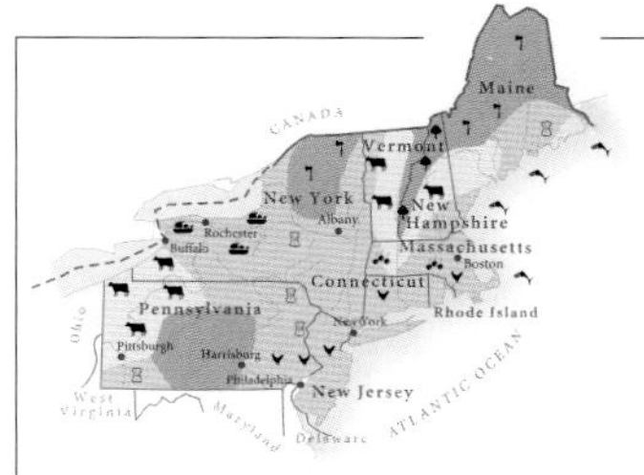
Rainwater feeds the aquifer
Water migrates up through fault
Aquifer exposed near the surface
Groundwater trapped between impermeable strata
Groundwater: Replenishment of an oasis

Landform diagrams
The complex formation of many typical landforms is summarized in these easy-to-understand illustrations.

Albert
Lake Victoria
Great Rift Valley
Kilimanjaro 5895m
Lake Tanganyika
Pemba Island
Zanzibar

Main physical map
Detailed satellite data has been used to create an accurate and visually striking picture of the surface of the continent.

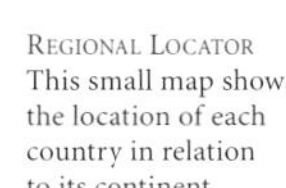

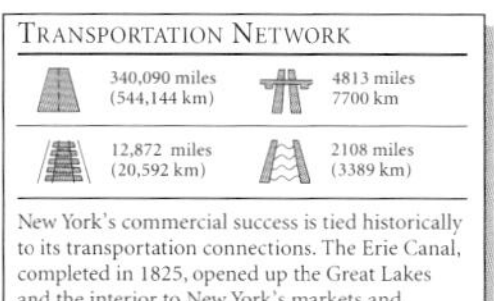

Photographs
A wide range of beautiful photographs bring the world's regions to life.

Landscape evolution map
The physical shape of each continent is affected by a variety of forces which continually sculpt and modify the landscape. This map shows the major processes which affect different parts of the continent.

Regional Mapping

The main body of the Atlas is a unique regional map set, with detailed information on the terrain, the human geography of the region and its infrastructure. Around the edge of the map, additional 'at-a-glance' maps, give an instant picture of regional industry, land use and agriculture. The detailed terrain map (shown in perspective), focuses on the main physical features of the region, and is enhanced by annotated illustrations, and photographs of the physical structure.

Regional Locator
This small map shows the location of each country in relation to its continent.

Transportation Network

340,090 miles (544,144 km)		4813 miles 7700 km	
12,872 miles (20,592 km)		2108 miles (3389 km)	

New York's commercial success is tied historically to its transportation connections. The Erie Canal, completed in 1825, opened up the Great Lakes and the interior to New York's markets and carried a stream of immigrants into the Midwest.

Transportation network
The differing extent of the transportation network for each region is shown here, along with key facts about the transportation system.

Key to main map
A key to the population symbols and land heights accompanies the main map.

World locator
This locates the continent in which the region is found on a small world map.

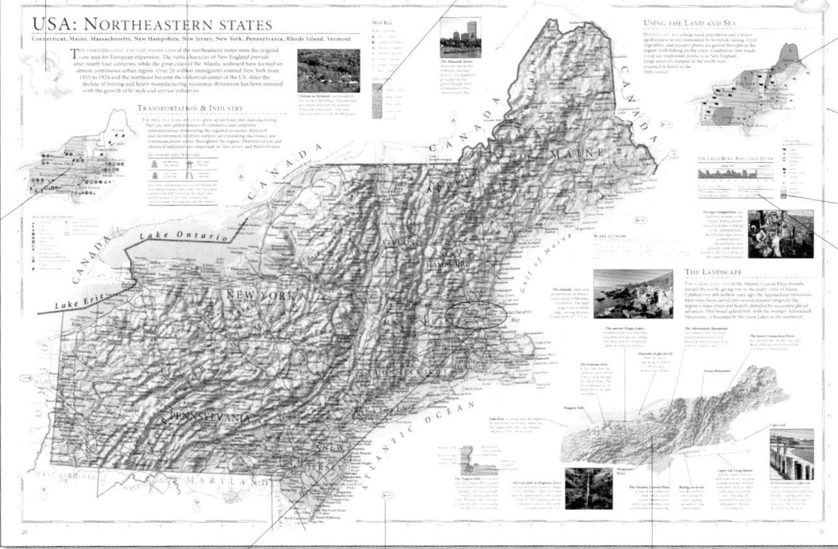
USA: Northeastern States

Land use map
This shows the different types of land use which characterize the region, as well as indicating the principal agricultural activities.

Grid reference
The framing grid provides a location reference for each place listed in the Index.

Map keys
Each supporting map has its own key.

Maine
Vermont
New Hampshire
Massachusetts
New York
Connecticut
Rhode Island
Pennsylvania
New Jersey
Atlantic Ocean

Transportation and industry map
The main industrial areas are mapped, and the most important industrial and economic activities of the region are shown.

The Urban/Rural Population Divide

urban 78% — rural 22%

Population Density	Total Land Area
306 people per sq mile (118 people per sq km)	161,096 sq miles (417,222 sq km)

Urban/rural population divide
The proportion of people in the region who live in urban and rural areas, as well as the overall population density and land area are clearly shown in these simple graphics.

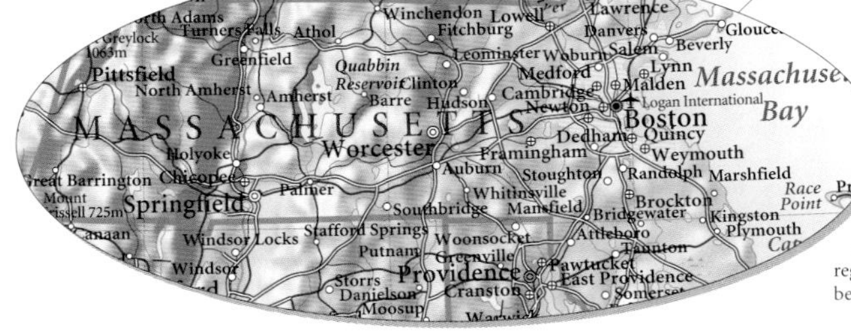
Massachusetts
Pittsfield
Springfield
Worcester
Boston
Lowell
Providence
Bay

Continuation symbols
These symbols indicate where adjacent maps can be found.

Landscape map
The computer-generated terrain model accurately portrays an oblique view of the landscape. Annotations highlight the most important geographic features of the region.

Main regional map
A wealth of information is displayed on the main map, building up a rich portrait of the interaction between the physical landscape and the human and political geography of each region. The key to the regional maps can be found on page viii.

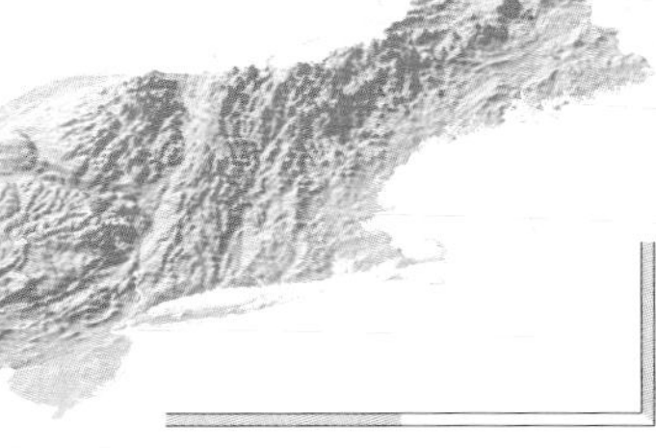

The Solar System

Nine major planets, their satellites, and countless minor planets (asteroids) orbit the Sun to form the Solar System. The Sun, our nearest star, creates energy from nuclear reactions deep within its interior, providing all the light and heat which make life on Earth possible. The Earth is unique in the Solar System in that it supports life: its size, gravitational pull and distance from the Sun have all created the optimum conditions for the evolution of life. The planetary images seen here are composites derived from actual spacecraft images (not shown to scale).

Jupiter

- **Diameter:** 88,846 miles (142,984 km)
- **Mass:** 1,900,000 million million million tons
- **Temperature:** -153°C (extremes not available)
- **Distance from Sun:** 483 million miles (778 million km)
- **Length of day:** 9.84 hours
- **Length of year:** 11.86 earth years
- **Surface gravity:** 1 kg = 2.53 kg

Mars

- **Diameter:** 4,217 miles (6,786 km)
- **Mass:** 642 million million million tons
- **Temperature:** -137 to 37°C
- **Distance from Sun:** 142 million miles (228 million km)
- **Length of day:** 24.623 hours
- **Length of year:** 1.88 earth years
- **Surface gravity:** 1 kg = 0.38 kg

Earth

- **Diameter:** 7,926 miles (12,756 km)
- **Mass:** 5,976 million million million tons
- **Temperature:** -70 to 55°C
- **Distance from Sun:** 93 million miles (150 million km)
- **Length of day:** 23.92 hours
- **Length of year:** 365.25 earth days
- **Surface gravity:** 1 kg = 1 kg

Venus

- **Diameter:** 7,520 miles (12,102 km)
- **Mass:** 4,870 million million million tons
- **Temperature:** 457°C (extremes not available)
- **Distance from Sun:** 67 million miles (108 million km)
- **Length of day:** 243.01 earth days
- **Length of year:** 224.7 earth days
- **Surface gravity:** 1 kg = 0.88 kg

Mercury

- **Diameter:** 3,031 miles (4,878 km)
- **Mass:** 330 million million million tons
- **Temperature:** -173 to 427°C
- **Distance from Sun:** 36 million miles (58 million km)
- **Length of day:** 58.65 earth days
- **Length of year:** 87.97 earth days
- **Surface gravity:** 1 kg = 0.38 kg

The Sun

- **Diameter:** 864,948 miles (1,392,000 km)
- **Mass:** 1990 million million million million tons

The Sun was formed when a swirling cloud of dust and gas contracted, pulling matter into its center. When the temperature at the center rose to 1,000,000°C, nuclear fusion – the fusing of hydrogen into helium, creating energy – occurred, releasing a constant stream of heat and light.

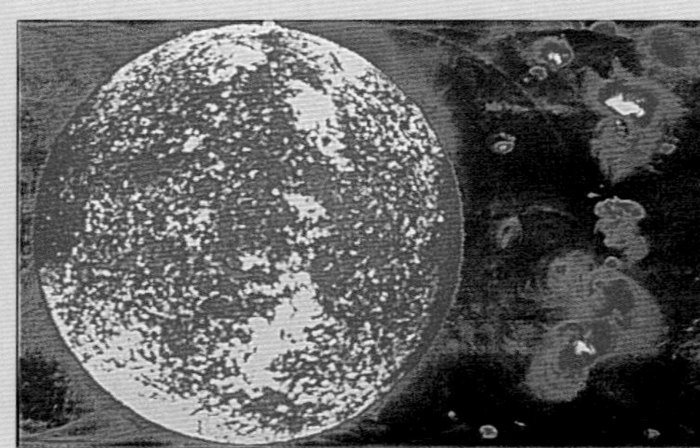

Solar flares are sudden bursts *of energy from the Sun's surface. They can be 125,000 miles (200,000 km) long.*

The formation of the Solar System

The cloud of dust and gas thrown out by the Sun during its formation cooled to form the Solar System. The smaller planets nearest the Sun are formed of minerals and metals. The outer planets were formed at lower temperatures, and consist of swirling clouds of gases.

The Milankovitch cycle

The amount of radiation from the Sun which reaches the Earth is affected by variations in the Earth's orbit and the tilt of the Earth's axis, as well as by "wobbles" in the axis. These variations cause three separate cycles, corresponding with the durations of recent ice ages.

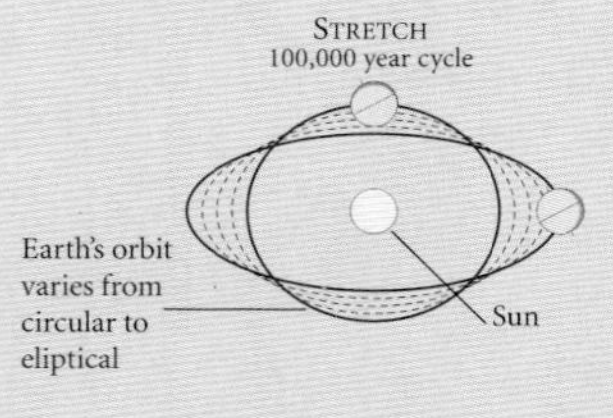
Stretch
100,000 year cycle
Earth's orbit varies from circular to eliptical
Sun

Tilt
41,000 year cycle
Sun
Angle of tilt varies by 2.4°

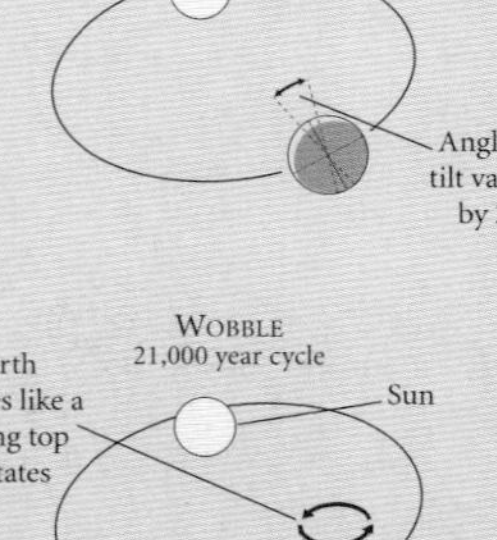
Wobble
21,000 year cycle
The Earth wobbles like a spinning top as it rotates
Sun

Saturn

- **Diameter:** 74,974 miles (120,660 km)
- **Mass:** 570,000 million million million tons
- **Temperature:** -185°C (extremes not available)
- **Distance from Sun:** 887 million miles (1,427 million km)
- **Length of day:** 10.23 hours
- **Length of year:** 29.46 earth years
- **Surface gravity:** 1 kg = 1.07 kg

Uranus

- **Diameter:** 31,763 miles (51,118 km)
- **Mass:** 86,800 million million million tons
- **Temperature:** -214°C (extremes not available)
- **Distance from Sun:** 1,783 million miles (2,870 million km)
- **Length of day:** 17.9 hours
- **Length of year:** 84.01 earth years
- **Surface gravity:** 1 kg = 0.92 kg

Space Debris

Millions of objects, remnants of planetary formation, circle the Sun in a zone lying between Mars and Jupiter: the asteroid belt. Fragments of asteroids break off to form meteoroids, which can reach the Earth's surface. Comets, composed of ice and dust, originated outside our Solar System. Their elliptical orbit brings them close to the Sun and into the inner Solar System.

Meteor Crater in Arizona *is 4200 ft (1300 m) wide and 660 ft (200 m) deep. It was formed over 10,000 years ago.*

Meteoroids

Meteoroids are fragments of asteroids which hurtle through space at great velocity. Although millions of meteoroids enter the Earth's atmosphere, the vast majority burn up on entry, and fall to the Earth as a meteor or shooting star. Large meteoroids traveling at speeds of 155,000 mph (250,000 kmph) can sometimes withstand the atmosphere and hit the Earth's surface with tremendous force, creating large craters on impact.

Possible and actual meteorite craters

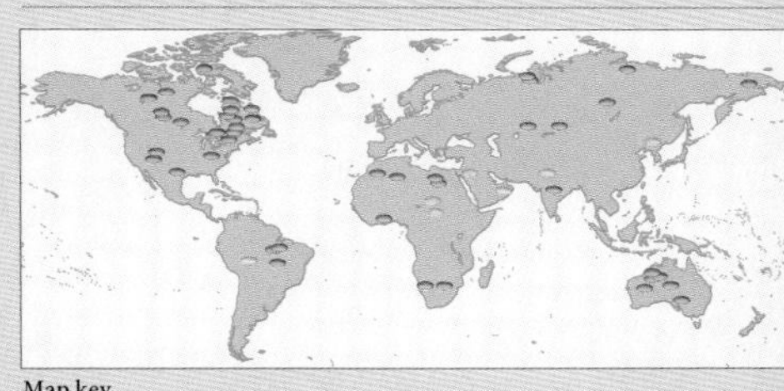

Map key
Possible impact craters   Meteorite impact craters

The orbit of Halley's Comet *brings it close to the Earth every 76 years. It last visited in 1986.*

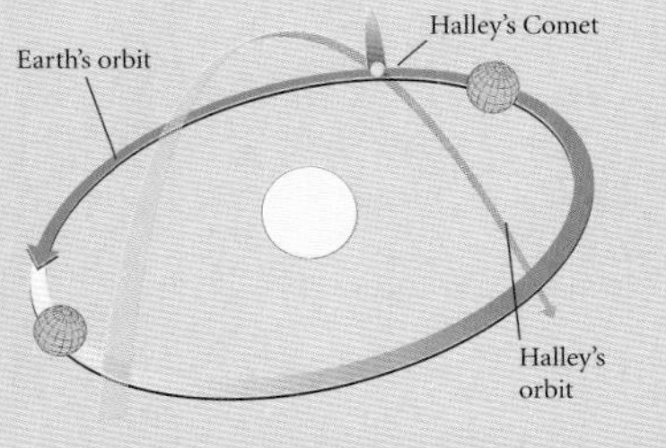

Halley's Comet
Earth's orbit
Halley's orbit

Orbit of Halley's Comet around the Sun

Neptune

- **Diameter:** 30,775 miles (49,528 km)
- **Mass:** 102,000 million million million tons
- **Temperature:** -225°C (extremes not available)
- **Distance from Sun:** 2794 million miles (4497 million km)
- **Length of day:** 19.2 hours
- **Length of year:** 164.79 earth years
- **Surface gravity:** 1 kg = 1.18 kg

The Earth's Atmosphere

During the early stages of the Earth's formation, ash, lava, carbon dioxide, and water vapor were discharged onto the surface of the planet by constant volcanic eruptions. The water formed the oceans, while carbon dioxide entered the atmosphere or was dissolved in the oceans. Clouds, formed of water droplets, reflected some of the Sun's radiation back into space. The Earth's temperature stabilized and early life forms began to emerge, converting carbon dioxide into life-giving oxygen.

It is thought *that the gases that make up the Earth's atmosphere originated deep within the interior, and were released many millions of years ago during intense volcanic actvity, similar to this eruption at Mount St. Helens.*

Pluto

- **Diameter:** 1,429 miles (2,300 km)
- **Mass:** 13 million million million tons
- **Temperature:** -236°C (extremes not available)
- **Distance from Sun:** 3,666 million miles (5,900 million km)
- **Length of day:** 6.39 hours
- **Length of year:** 248.54 earth years
- **Surface gravity:** 1 kg = 0.30 kg

Order and relative distance from the Sun of planets

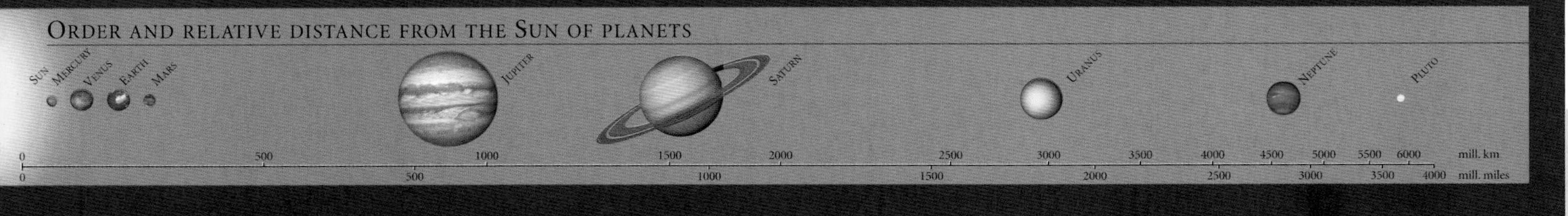
Sun
Mercury
Venus
Earth
Mars
Jupiter
Saturn
Uranus
Neptune
Pluto
0 500 1000 1500 2000 2500 3000 3500 4000 4500 5000 5500 6000 mill. km
0 500 1000 1500 2000 2500 3000 3500 4000 mill. miles

THE PHYSICAL WORLD

THE EARTH'S SURFACE is constantly being transformed: it is uplifted, folded and faulted by tectonic forces; weathered and eroded by wind, water, and ice. Sometimes change is dramatic, the spectacular results of earthquakes or floods. More often it is a slow process lasting millions of years. A physical map of the world represents a snapshot of the ever-evolving architecture of the Earth. This terrain map shows the whole surface of the Earth, both above and below the sea.

THE WORLD IN SECTION

These cross-sections around the Earth, one in the northern hemisphere; one straddling the Equator, reveal the limited areas of land above sea level in comparison with the extent of the sea floor. The greater erosive effects of weathering by wind and water limit the upward elevation of land above sea level, while the deep oceans retain their dramatic mountain and trench profiles.

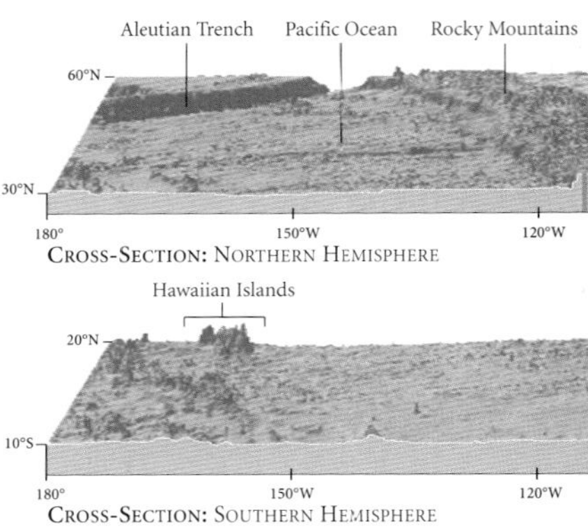

Aleutian Trench
Pacific Ocean
Rocky Mountains
60°N
30°N
180°
150°W
120°W
Hawaiian Islands
20°N
10°S

CROSS-SECTION: NORTHERN HEMISPHERE

CROSS-SECTION: SOUTHERN HEMISPHERE

MAP KEY

GEOGRAPHICAL REGIONS

- ice
- tundra
- needleleaf forest
- broadleaf forest
- cultivated land
- hot desert
- cold desert
- tropical grassland
- tropical rainforest
- mountain
- submarine regions

SCALE 1:73,000,000
(projection: Wagner VII)

Km 0 250 500 1,000 1,500 2,000

Miles 0 250 500 1,000 1,500 2,000

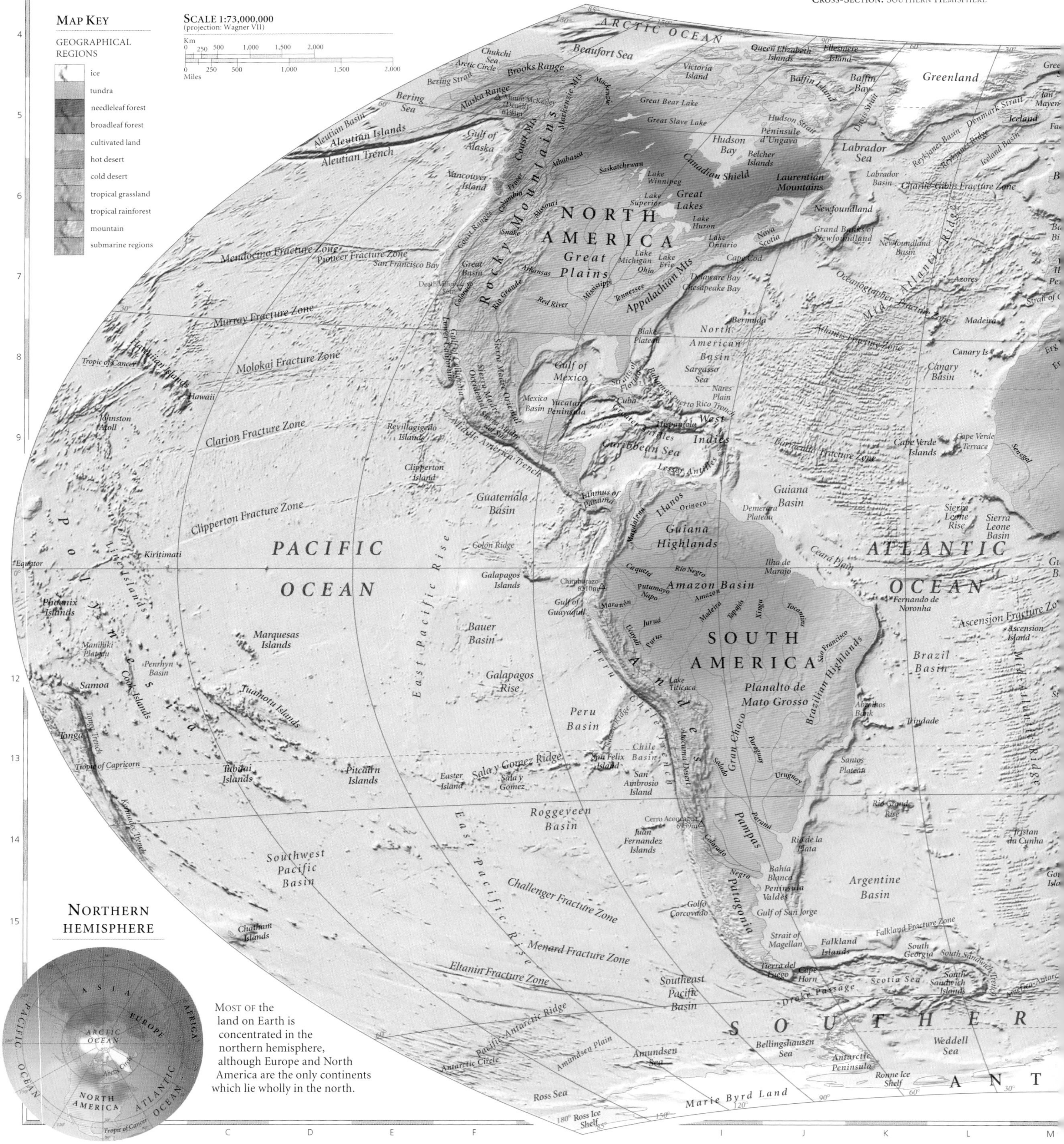

NORTHERN HEMISPHERE

MOST OF the land on Earth is concentrated in the northern hemisphere, although Europe and North America are the only continents which lie wholly in the north.

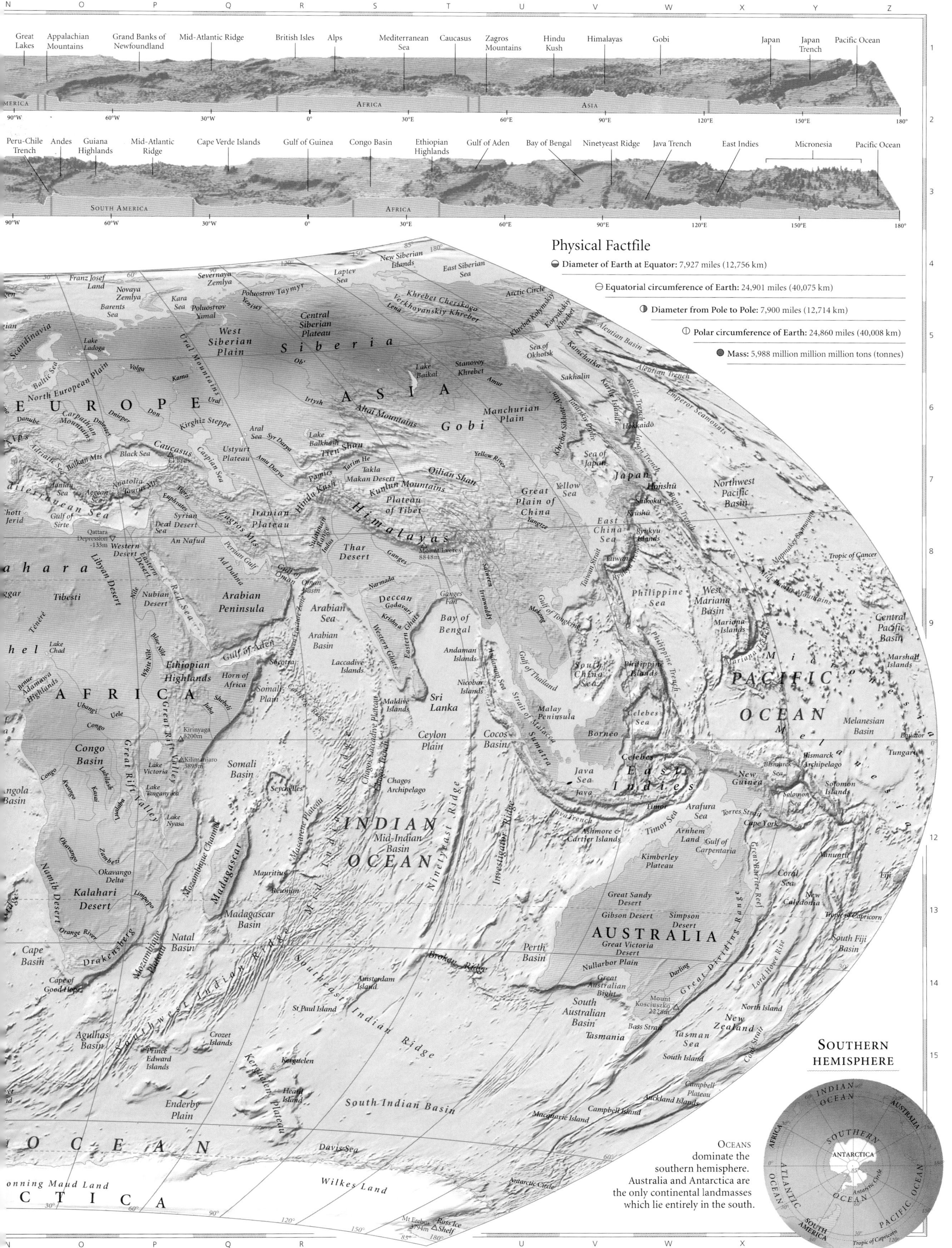
Great Lakes
Appalachian Mountains
Grand Banks of Newfoundland
Mid-Atlantic Ridge
British Isles
Alps
Mediterranean Sea
Caucasus
Zagros Mountains
Hindu Kush
Himalayas
Gobi
Japan
Japan Trench
Pacific Ocean
AFRICA
ASIA
Peru-Chile Trench
Andes
Guiana Highlands
Mid-Atlantic Ridge
Cape Verde Islands
Gulf of Guinea
Congo Basin
Ethiopian Highlands
Gulf of Aden
Bay of Bengal
Ninetyeast Ridge
Java Trench
East Indies
Micronesia
Pacific Ocean
SOUTH AMERICA
AFRICA
EUROPE
ASIA
Siberia
West Siberian Plain
Central Siberian Plateau
Ural Mountains
Caspian Sea
Black Sea
Arabian Peninsula
Iranian Plateau
Plateau of Tibet
Himalayas
Mount Everest 8848m
Thar Desert
Deccan
Arabian Sea
Bay of Bengal
Gobi
Manchurian Plain
Great Plain of China
Sea of Japan
Japan
East China Sea
Philippine Sea
South China Sea
Borneo
Sumatra
Java
East Indies
New Guinea
AFRICA
Sahara
Libyan Desert
Ethiopian Highlands
Congo Basin
Great Rift Valley
Kirinyaga 5200m
Kilimanjaro 5895m
Lake Victoria
Lake Tanganyika
Lake Nyasa
Madagascar
Kalahari Desert
Namib Desert
Drakensberg
Cape of Good Hope
INDIAN OCEAN
Mid-Indian Basin
Ninetyeast Ridge
Southeast Indian Ridge
Southwest Indian Ridge
Kerguelen
South Indian Basin
AUSTRALIA
Great Sandy Desert
Gibson Desert
Simpson Desert
Great Victoria Desert
Nullarbor Plain
Great Dividing Range
Mount Kosciuszko 2228m
Tasmania
Tasman Sea
New Zealand
PACIFIC OCEAN
Northwest Pacific Basin
Central Pacific Basin
Micronesia
Melanesia
Tropic of Cancer
Equator
Tropic of Capricorn
Arctic Circle
Antarctic Circle
Wilkes Land
Davis Sea
Mt Erebus 3794m
Ross Ice Shelf
SOUTHERN HEMISPHERE
INDIAN OCEAN
AUSTRALIA
SOUTHERN
ANTARCTICA
AFRICA
ATLANTIC OCEAN
PACIFIC OCEAN
SOUTH AMERICA

Physical Factfile

Diameter of Earth at Equator: 7,927 miles (12,756 km)

Equatorial circumference of Earth: 24,901 miles (40,075 km)

Diameter from Pole to Pole: 7,900 miles (12,714 km)

Polar circumference of Earth: 24,860 miles (40,008 km)

Mass: 5,988 million million million tons (tonnes)

OCEANS dominate the southern hemisphere. Australia and Antarctica are the only continental landmasses which lie entirely in the south.

Structure of the Earth

THE EARTH AS IT IS TODAY is just the latest phase in a constant process of evolution which has occurred over the past 4.5 billion years. The Earth's continents are neither fixed nor stable; over the course of the Earth's history, propelled by currents rising from the intense heat at its center, the great plates on which they lie have moved, collided, joined together, and separated. These processes continue to mold and transform the surface of the Earth, causing earthquakes and volcanic eruptions and creating oceans, mountain ranges, deep ocean trenches, and island chains.

Inside the Earth

THE EARTH'S HOT INNER CORE is made up of solid iron, while the outer core is composed of liquid iron and nickel. The mantle nearest the core is viscous, whereas the rocky upper mantle is fairly rigid. The crust is the rocky outer shell of the Earth. Together, the upper mantle and the crust form the lithosphere.

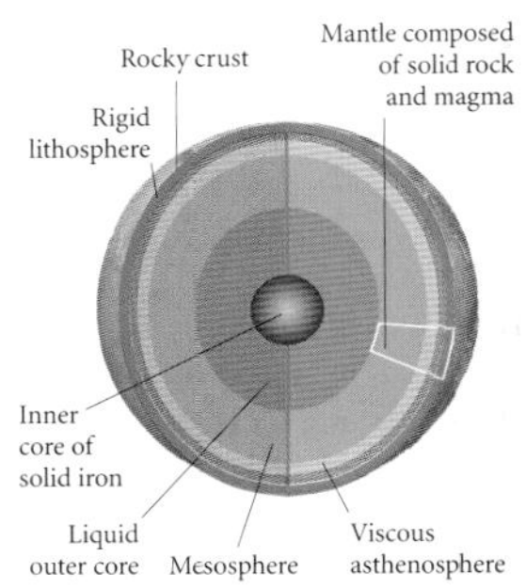
Rocky crust
Mantle composed of solid rock and magma
Rigid lithosphere
Inner core of solid iron
Liquid outer core
Mesosphere
Viscous asthenosphere

The Dynamic Earth

THE EARTH'S CRUST is made up of eight major (and several minor) rigid continental and oceanic tectonic plates, which fit closely together. The positions of the plates are not static. They are constantly moving relative to one another. The type of movement between plates affects the way in which they alter the structure of the Earth. The oldest parts of the plates, known as shields, are the most stable parts of the Earth and little tectonic activity occurs here.

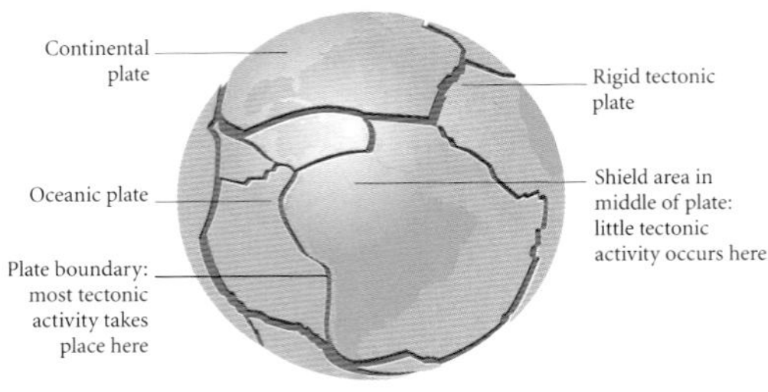
Continental plate
Oceanic plate
Plate boundary: most tectonic activity takes place here
Rigid tectonic plate
Shield area in middle of plate: little tectonic activity occurs here

Convection Currents

DEEP WITHIN THE EARTH, at its inner core, temperatures may exceed 8,100°F (4,500°C). This heat warms rocks in the mesosphere which rise through the partially molten mantle, displacing cooler rocks just below the solid crust, which sink, and are warmed again by the heat of the mantle. This process is continuous, creating convection currents which form the moving force beneath the Earth's crust.

Inner core
Outer core
Subduction zone
Ocean crust
Movement of plate
Mid-ocean ridge
Lithosphere
Asthenosphere
Mesosphere
Continental crust

Plate Boundaries

THE BOUNDARIES BETWEEN THE PLATES are the areas where most tectonic activity takes place. Three types of movement occur at plate boundaries: the plates can either move toward each other, move apart, or slide past each other. The effect this has on the Earth's structure depends on whether the margin is between two continental plates, two oceanic plates, or an oceanic and continental plate.

The Mid-Atlantic Ridge *rises above sea level in Iceland, producing geysers and volcanoes.*

Mid-Ocean Ridges

Mid-ocean ridges are formed when two adjacent oceanic plates pull apart, allowing magma to force its way up to the surface, which then cools to form solid rock. Vast amounts of volcanic material are discharged at these mid-ocean ridges which can reach heights of 10,000 ft (3,000 m).

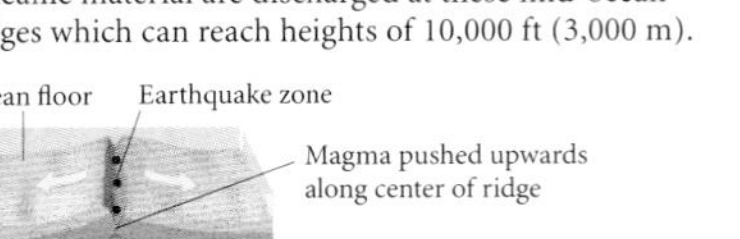
Ocean floor
Earthquake zone
Magma pushed upwards along center of ridge
Solid mantle

FORMATION OF A MID-OCEAN RIDGE

Mount Pinatubo *is an active volcano, lying on the Pacific "Ring of Fire."*

Ocean Plates Meeting

Oceanic crust is denser and thinner than continental crust; on average it is 3 miles (5 km) thick, while continental crust averages 18–24 miles (30–40 km). When oceanic plates of similar density meet, the crust is contorted as one plate overrides the other, forming deep sea trenches and volcanic island arcs above sea level.

Overriding plate
Chain of islands
Ocean trench
Diving plate
Volcanic activity

OCEAN PLATES MEETING TO FORM AN ISLAND ARC

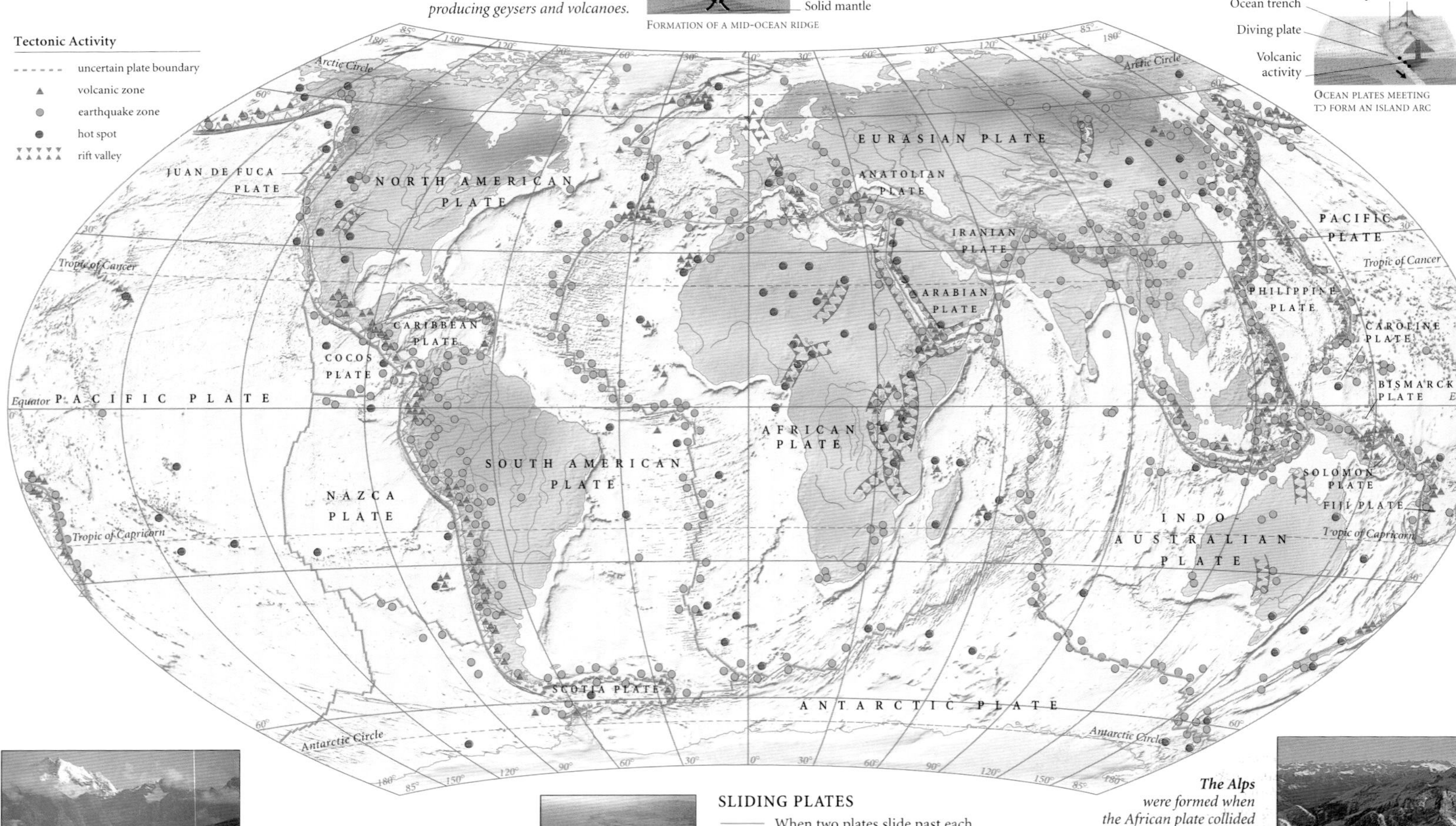
Tectonic Activity
uncertain plate boundary
volcanic zone
earthquake zone
hot spot
rift valley
Arctic Circle
Tropic of Cancer
Equator
Tropic of Capricorn
Antarctic Circle
JUAN DE FUCA PLATE
NORTH AMERICAN PLATE
EURASIAN PLATE
ANATOLIAN PLATE
IRANIAN PLATE
ARABIAN PLATE
PACIFIC PLATE
PHILIPPINE PLATE
CAROLINE PLATE
BISMARCK PLATE
CARIBBEAN PLATE
COCOS PLATE
SOUTH AMERICAN PLATE
NAZCA PLATE
AFRICAN PLATE
SOLOMON PLATE
FIJI PLATE
INDO AUSTRALIAN PLATE
SCOTIA PLATE
ANTARCTIC PLATE

Diving Plates

When an oceanic and a continental plate meet, the denser oceanic plate is driven underneath the continental plate, which is crumpled by the collision to form mountain ranges. As the ocean plate plunges downward, it heats up, and molten rock (magma) is forced up to the surface.

The Andean mountain *chain is the typical result of the impact of a diving plate.*

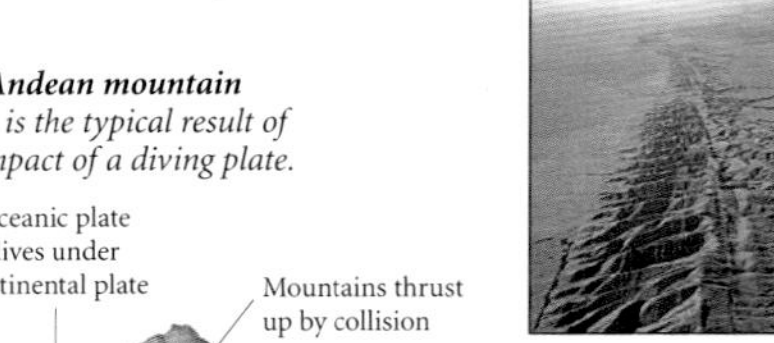
Oceanic plate dives under continental plate
Mountains thrust up by collision
Earthquake zone
Continental plate

DIVING PLATE

The deep fracture *caused by the sliding plates of the San Andreas Fault can be clearly seen in parts of California.*

Sliding Plates

When two plates slide past each other, friction is caused along the fault line which divides them. The plates do not move smoothly, and the uneven movement causes earthquakes.

Plate
Plate
Fault line
Earthquake zone

SLIDING PLATES

The Alps *were formed when the African plate collided with the Eurasian Plate, about 65 million years ago.*

Plate buckles as it collides
Mountains thrust upwards
Earthquake zone
Crust thickens in response to the impact

CONTINENTAL PLATES COLLIDING TO FORM A MOUNTAIN RANGE

Colliding Plates

When two continental plates collide, great mountain chains are thrust upward as the crust buckles and folds under the force of the impact.

CONTINENTAL DRIFT

ALTHOUGH THE PLATES which make up the Earth's crust move only a few inches in a year, over the millions of years of the Earth's history, its continents have moved many thousands of miles, to create new continents, oceans, and mountain chains.

LAURENTIA
Greenland
BALTICA
North America
Siberia
India
Arabia
Northern Europe
Africa
Australia
Antarctica
South America
GONDWANALAND

1: CAMBRIAN PERIOD

570–510 million years ago. *Most continents are in tropical latitudes. The supercontinent of Gondwanaland reaches the South Pole.*

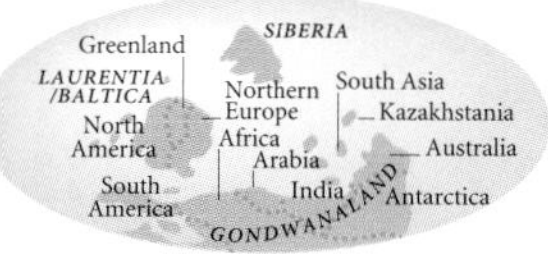
Greenland
SIBERIA
LAURENTIA /BALTICA
North America
Northern Europe
Africa
Arabia
South America
South Asia
Kazakhstania
Australia
India
Antarctica
GONDWANALAND

2: DEVONIAN PERIOD

408–362 million years ago. *The continents of Gondwanaland and Laurentia are drifting northward.*

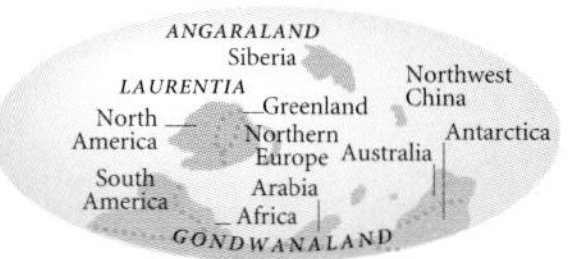
ANGARALAND
Siberia
LAURENTIA
North America
Greenland
Northern Europe
Northwest China
Australia
Antarctica
South America
Arabia
Africa
GONDWANALAND

3: CARBONIFEROUS PERIOD

362–290 million years ago. *The Earth is dominated by three continents; Laurentia, Angaraland, and Gondwanaland.*

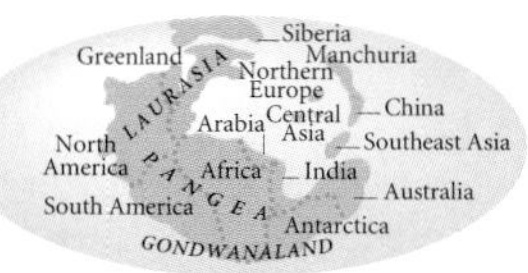
Greenland
Siberia
Manchuria
Northern Europe
Arabia
Central Asia
China
North America
Southeast Asia
Africa
India
South America
Australia
Antarctica
LAURASIA
PANGEA
GONDWANALAND

4: TRIASSIC PERIOD

245–208 million years ago. *All three major continents have joined to form the super-continent of Pangea.*

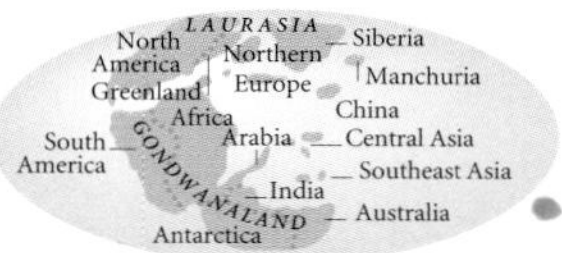
LAURASIA
North America
Greenland
Northern Europe
Siberia
Manchuria
China
Africa
Arabia
Central Asia
Southeast Asia
South America
India
Australia
Antarctica
GONDWANALAND

5: JURASSIC PERIOD

208–145 million years ago. *The super-continent of Pangea begins to break up, causing an overall rise in sea levels.*

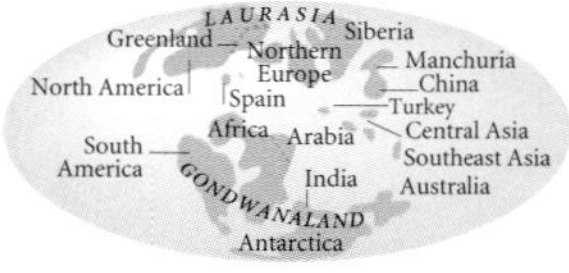
LAURASIA
Greenland
Siberia
Northern Europe
Manchuria
China
North America
Spain
Turkey
Africa
Arabia
Central Asia
Southeast Asia
South America
India
Australia
GONDWANALAND
Antarctica

6: CRETACEOUS PERIOD

145–65 million years ago. *Warm, shallow seas cover much of the land: sea levels are about 80 ft (25 m) above present levels.*

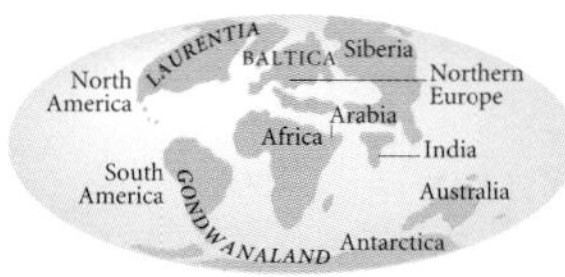
LAURENTIA
BALTICA
Siberia
North America
Northern Europe
Arabia
Africa
India
South America
Australia
Antarctica
GONDWANALAND

7: TERTIARY PERIOD

65–2 million years ago. *Although the world's geography is becoming more recognizable, major events such as the creation of the Himalayan mountain chain, are still to occur during this period.*

CONTINENTAL SHIELDS

THE CENTERS OF THE EARTH'S CONTINENTS, known as shields, were established between 2500 and 500 million years ago; some contain rocks over three billion years old. They were formed by a series of turbulent events: plate movements, earthquakes, and volcanic eruptions. Since the Pre-Cambrian period, over 570 million years ago, they have experienced little tectonic activity, and today, these flat, low-lying slabs of solidified molten rock form the stable centers of the continents. They are bounded or covered by successive belts of younger sedimentary rock.

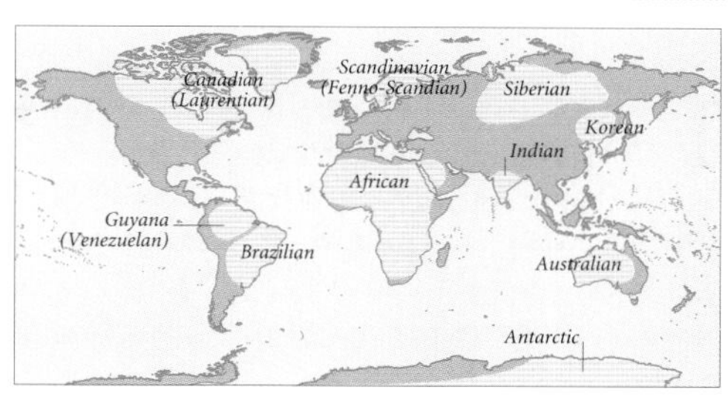
Canadian (Laurentian)
Scandinavian (Fenno-Scandian)
Siberian
Korean
Indian
African
Guyana (Venezuelan)
Brazilian
Australian
Antarctic

CREATION OF THE HIMALAYAS

BETWEEN 10 AND 20 MILLION YEARS AGO, the Indian subcontinent, part of the ancient continent of Gondwanaland, collided with the continent of Asia. The Indo-Australian Plate continued to move northward, displacing continental crust and uplifting the Himalayas, the world's highest mountain chain.

MOVEMENTS OF INDIA

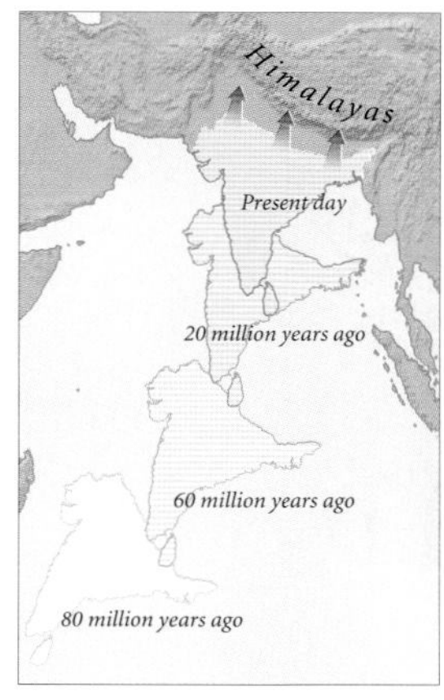
Himalayas
Present day
20 million years ago
60 million years ago
80 million years ago

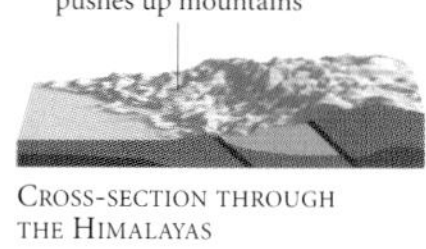
Force of collision pushes up mountains

CROSS-SECTION THROUGH THE HIMALAYAS

The Himalayas *were uplifted when the Indian subcontinent collided with Asia.*

THE HAWAIIAN ISLAND CHAIN

A HOT SPOT lying deep beneath the Pacific Ocean pushes a plume of magma from the Earth's mantle up through the Pacific Plate to form volcanic islands. While the hot spot remains stationary, the plate on which the islands sit is moving slowly. A long chain of islands has been created as the plate passes over the hot spot.

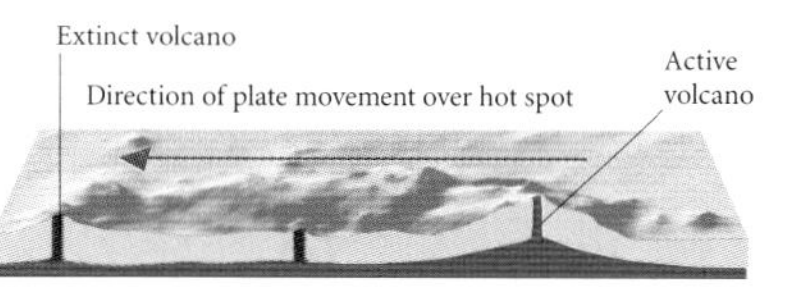
Extinct volcano
Direction of plate movement over hot spot
Active volcano

CROSS-SECTION THROUGH THE HAWAIIAN ISLANDS

EVOLUTION OF THE HAWAIIAN ISLANDS

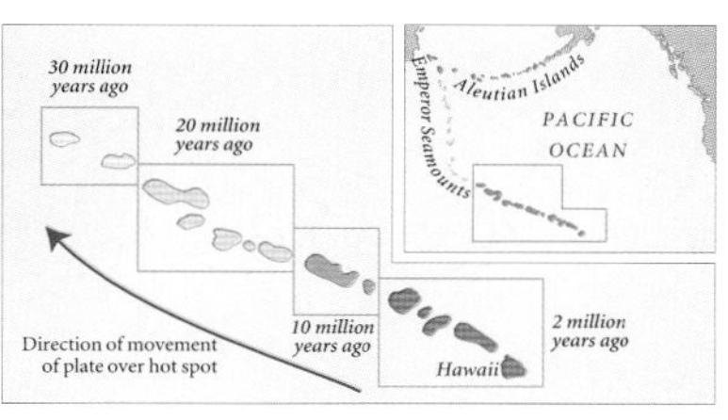
30 million years ago
20 million years ago
10 million years ago
2 million years ago
Hawaii
Direction of movement of plate over hot spot
Emperor Seamounts
Aleutian Islands
PACIFIC OCEAN

THE EARTH'S GEOLOGY

THE EARTH'S ROCKS are created in a continual cycle. Exposed rocks are weathered and eroded by wind, water and chemicals and deposited as sediments. If they pass into the Earth's crust they will be transformed by high temperatures and pressures into metamorphic rocks or they will melt and solidify as igneous rocks.

Gneiss *formations in Norway's Jotunheimen Mountains.*

GNEISS

1 Gneiss is a metamorphic rock made at great depth during the formation of mountain chains, when intense heat and pressure transform sedimentary or igneous rocks.

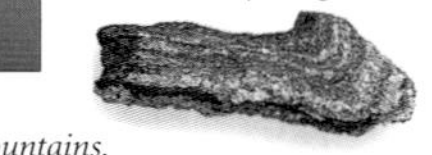

Basalt *columns at Giant's Causeway, Northern Ireland, UK.*

BASALT

2 Basalt is an igneous rock, formed when small quantities of magma lying close to the Earth's surface cool rapidly.

LIMESTONE

3 Limestone is a sedimentary rock, which is formed mainly from the calcite skeletons of marine animals which have been compressed into rock.

Limestone hills*, Guilin, China.*

SANDSTONE

8 Sandstones are sedimentary rocks formed mainly in deserts, beaches, and deltas. Desert sandstones are formed of grains of quartz which have been well rounded by wind erosion.

Rock stacks *of desert sandstone, at Bryce Canyon National Park, Utah.*

THE WORLD'S MAJOR GEOLOGICAL REGIONS

Geological Regions
- continental shield
- sedimentary cover
- coral formation
- igneous rock types

Mountain Ranges
- Alpine (new)
- Hercynian (old)
- Caledonian (ancient)

CORAL

4 Coral reefs are formed from the skeletons of millions of individual corals.

Great Barrier Reef*, Australia.*

Extrusive igneous rocks *are formed during volcanic eruptions, as here in Hawaii.*

ANDESITE

7 Andesite is an extrusive igneous rock formed from magma which has solidified on the Earth's crust after a volcanic eruption.

SCHIST

6 Schist is a metamorphic rock formed during mountain building, when temperature and pressure are comparatively high. Both mudstones and shales reform into schist under these conditions.

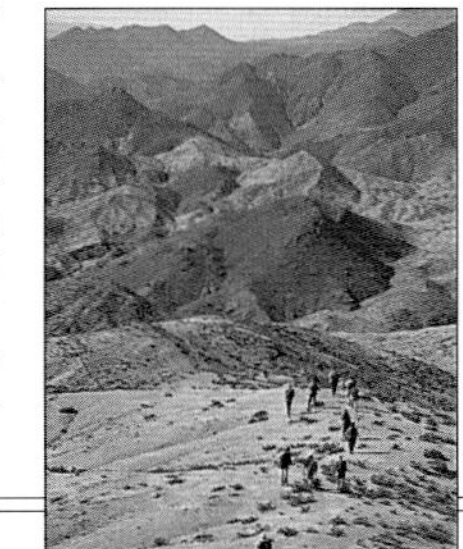

Schist formations *in the Atlas Mountains, northwestern Africa.*

GRANITE

5 Granite is an intrusive igneous rock formed from magma which has solidified deep within the Earth's crust. The magma cools slowly, producing a coarse-grained rock.

Namibia's *Namaqualand Plateau is formed of granite.*

Shaping the Landscape

The basic material of the Earth's surface is solid rock: valleys, deserts, soil, and sand are all evidence of the powerful agents of weathering, erosion, and deposition which constantly shape and transform the Earth's landscapes. Water, either flowing continually in rivers or seas, or frozen and compacted into solid sheets of ice, has the most clearly visible impact on the Earth's surface. But wind can transport fragments of rock over huge distances and strip away protective layers of vegetation, exposing rock surfaces to the impact of extreme heat and cold.

Water

Less than 2% of the world's water is on the land, but it is the most powerful agent of landscape change. Water, as rainfall, groundwater, and rivers, can transform landscapes through both erosion and deposition. Eroded material carried by rivers forms the world's most fertile soils.

***Waterfalls such as the Iguaçu Falls** on the border between Argentina and southern Brazil, erode the underlying rock, causing the falls to retreat.*

Coastal water

The world's coastlines are constantly changing; every day, tides deposit, sift and sort sand and gravel on the shoreline. Over longer periods, powerful wave action erodes cliffs and headlands and carves out bays.

***A low, wide sandy beach** on South Africa's Cape Peninsula is continually re-shaped by the action of the Atlantic waves.*

***The sheer chalk cliffs** at Seven Sisters in southern England are constantly under attack from waves.*

Groundwater

In regions where there are porous rocks such as chalk, water is stored underground in large quantities; these reservoirs of water are known as aquifers. Rain percolates through topsoil into the underlying bedrock, creating an underground store of water. The limit of the saturated zone is called the water table.

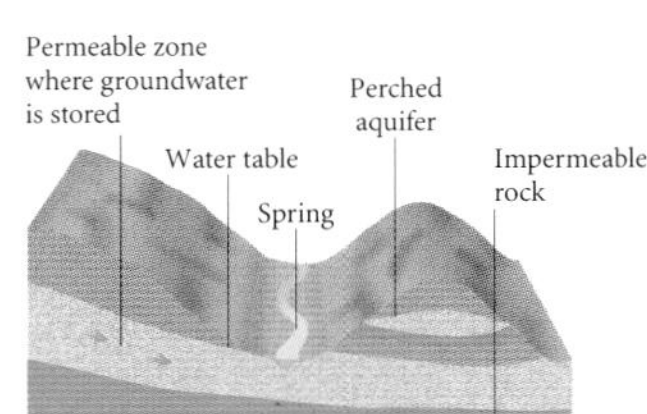
Permeable zone where groundwater is stored
Perched aquifer
Water table
Spring
Impermeable rock

Storage of groundwater in an aquifer

World river systems
drainage basin
World river systems:
Sediment deposited annually per drainage basin
tons per sq mile per year
9120
2400
6080
1600
1520
760
400
200 and less
tonnes per sq km per year
Arctic Circle
Yukon
Mackenzie
Nelson
Columbia
St. Lawrence
Mississippi/ Missouri
Colorado
Rio Grande
Tropic of Cancer
ARCTIC OCEAN
Rhine
Danube
Volga
Ob'
Yenisey
Lena
Amur
Yellow River
Tigris/ Euphrates
Indus
Ganges/ Brahmaputra
Yangtze
Mekong
ATLANTIC OCEAN
PACIFIC OCEAN
Equator
Orinoco
Amazon
São Francisco
Paraná
Niger
Nile
Congo
Zambezi
Orange
INDIAN OCEAN
Murray/ Darling
Tropic of Capricorn
Antarctic Circle

Rivers

Rivers erode the land by grinding and dissolving rocks and stones. Most erosion occurs in the river's upper course as it flows through highland areas. Rock fragments are moved along the river bed by fast-flowing water and deposited in areas where the river slows down, such as flat plains, or where the river enters seas or lakes.

River valleys

Over long periods of time rivers erode uplands to form characteristic V-shaped valleys with smooth sides.

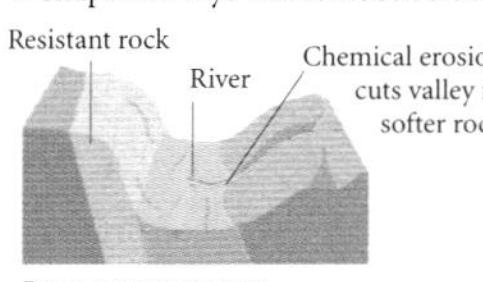
Resistant rock
River
Chemical erosion cuts valley in softer rock

River valley erosion

Meanders

In their lower courses, rivers flow slowly. As they flow across the lowlands, they form looping bends called meanders.

***The Mississippi River** forms meanders as it flows across the southern US.*

***The meanders** of Utah's San Juan River have become deeply incised.*

Deltas

When a river deposits its load of silt and sediment (alluvium) on entering the sea, it may form a delta. As this material accumulates, it chokes the mouth of the river, forcing it to create new channels to reach the sea.

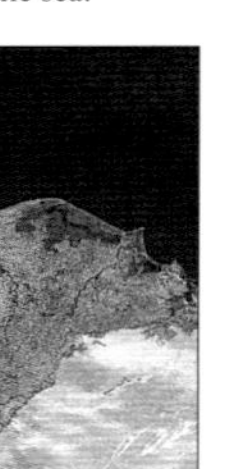

***The Nile** forms a broad delta as it flows into the Mediterranean.*

***Mud is** deposited by China's Yellow River in its lower course.*

Deposition

When rivers have deposited large quantities of fertile alluvium, they are forced to find new channels through the alluvium deposits, creating braided river systems.

Drainage basins

The drainage basin is the area of land drained by a major trunk river and its smaller branch rivers or tributaries. Drainage basins are separated from one another by natural boundaries known as watersheds.

Watershed · Major trunk river · Alps · Apennines · Tributary river · Delta · River mouth · Po Valley · Dolomites

***The drainage basin** of the Po River, northern Italy.*

Landslides

Heavy rain and associated flooding on slopes can loosen underlying rocks, which crumble, causing the top layers of rock and soil to slip.

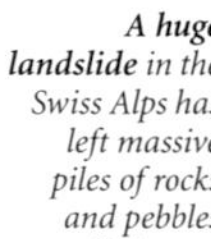

***A huge landslide** in the Swiss Alps has left massive piles of rocks and pebbles called scree.*

Gullies

In areas where soil is thin, rainwater is not effectively absorbed, and may flow overland. The water courses downhill in channels, or gullies, and may lead to rapid erosion of soil.

***A deep gully** in the French Alps caused by the scouring of upper layers of turf.*

ICE

DURING ITS LONG HISTORY, the Earth has experienced a number of glacial episodes when temperatures were considerably lower than today. During the last Ice Age, 18,000 years ago, ice covered an area three times larger than it does today. Over these periods, the ice has left a remarkable legacy of transformed landscapes.

GLACIERS

GLACIERS ARE FORMED by the compaction of snow into "rivers" of ice. As they move over the landscape, glaciers pick up and carry a load of rocks and boulders which erode the landscape they pass over, and are eventually deposited at the end of the glacier.

A massive glacier *advancing down a valley in southern Argentina.*

GLACIAL VALLEYS

GLACIERS CAN ERODE much more powerfully than rivers. They form steep-sided, flat-bottomed valleys with a typical U-shaped profile. Valleys created by tributary glaciers, whose floors have not been eroded to the same depth as the main glacial valley floor, are called hanging valleys.

The U-shaped profile *and piles of morainic debris are characteristic of a valley once filled by a glacier.*

A series of hanging valleys *high up in the Chilean Andes.*

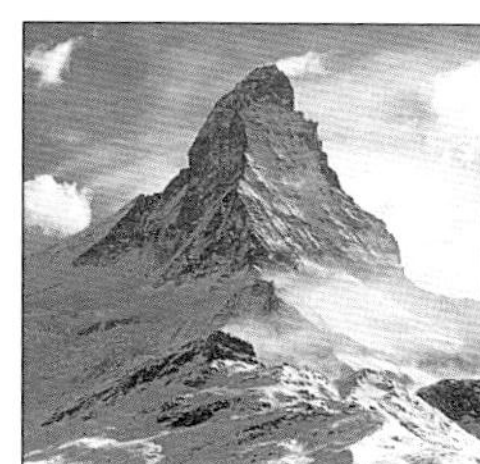

The profile *of the Matterhorn has been formed by three cirques lying "back-to-back."*

CIRQUES

Cirques are basin-shaped hollows which mark the head of a glaciated valley. Where neighboring cirques meet, they are divided by sharp rock ridges called arêtes. It is these arêtes which give the Matterhorn its characteristic profile.

FJORDS

Fjords are ancient glacial valleys flooded by the sea following the end of a period of glaciation. Beneath the water, the valley floor can be 4,000 ft (1,300 m) deep.

A fjord *fills a former glacial valley in southern New Zealand.*

PAST AND PRESENT WORLD ICE-COVER AND GLACIAL FEATURES

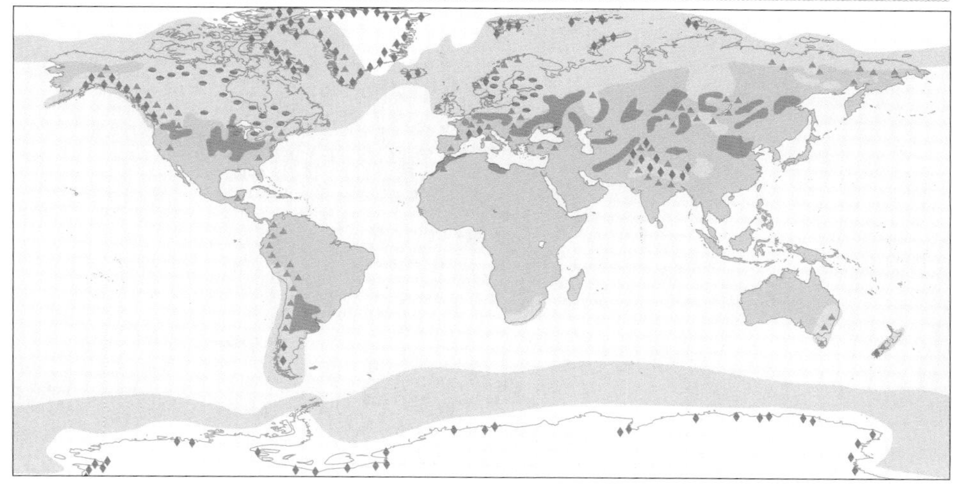

Past and present world ice cover and glacial features

extent of last Ice Age
loess deposits
post-glacial feature
glacial feature
present day ice cover
glacial field

POST-GLACIAL FEATURES

WHEN A GLACIAL EPISODE ENDS, the retreating ice leaves many features. These include depositional ridges called moraines, which may be eroded into low hills known as drumlins; sinuous ridges called eskers; kames, which are rounded hummocks; depressions known as kettle holes; and windblown loess deposits.

Kame terrace
Kettle hole
Esker
Braided river
Windblown loess
Retreating glacier
Drumlin
Terminal moraine
Glacial till
Bedrock

POST-GLACIAL LANDSCAPE FEATURES

ICE SHATTERING

Water drips into fissures in rocks and freezes, expanding as it does so. The pressure weakens the rock, causing it to crack, and eventually to shatter into polygonal patterns.

Irregular polygons *show through the sedge-grass tundra in the Yukon, Canada.*

PERIGLACIATION

Periglacial areas occur near to the edge of ice sheets. A layer of frozen ground lying just beneath the surface of the land is known as permafrost. When the surface melts in the summer, the water is unable to drain into the frozen ground, and so "creeps" downhill, a process known as solifluction

WIND

STRONG WINDS can transport rock fragments great distances, especially where there is little vegetation to protect the rock. In desert areas, wind picks up loose, unprotected sand particles, carrying them over great distances. This powerfully abrasive debris is blasted at the surface by the wind, eroding the landscape into dramatic shapes.

PREVAILING WINDS AND DUST TRAJECTORIES

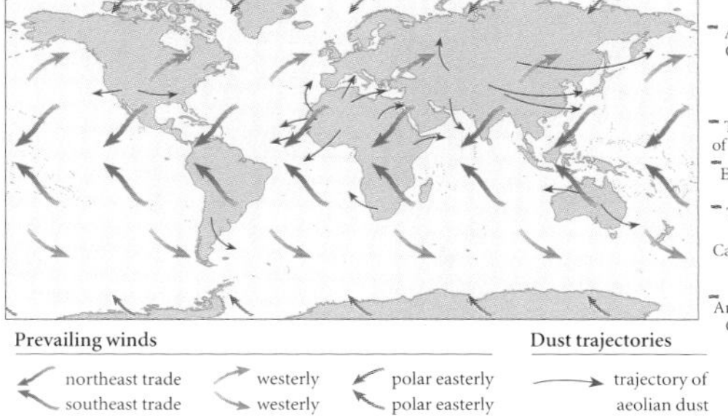
Arctic Circle
Tropic of Cancer
Equator
Tropic of Capricorn
Antarctic Circle

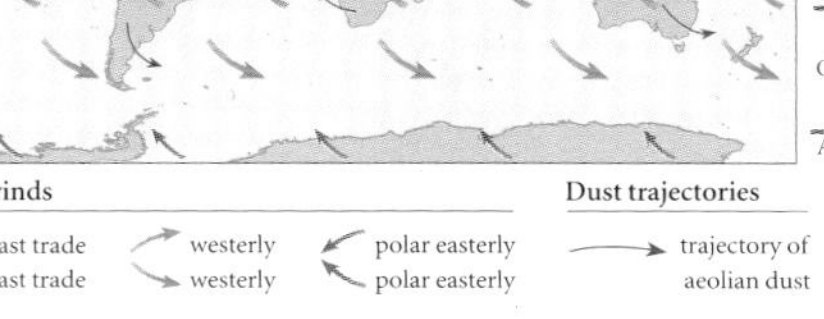

Prevailing winds: northeast trade, southeast trade; westerly, westerly; polar easterly, polar easterly
Dust trajectories: trajectory of aeolian dust

DEPOSITION

THE ROCKY, STONY FLOORS of the world's deserts are swept and scoured by strong winds. The smaller, finer particles of sand are shaped into surface ripples, dunes, or sand mountains, which rise to a height of 650 ft (200 m). Dunes usually form single lines, running perpendicular to the direction of the prevailing wind. These long, straight ridges can extend for over 100 miles (160 km).

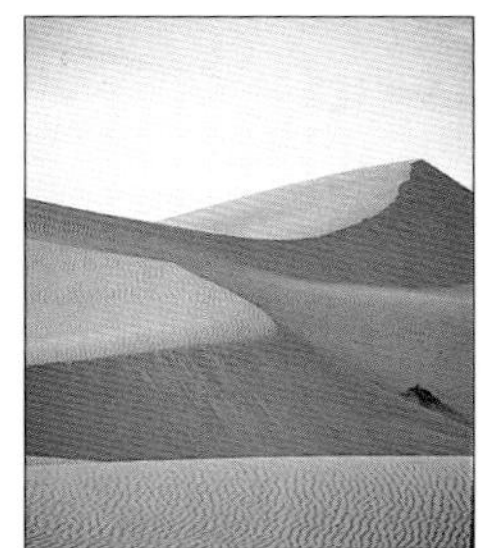

Barchan dunes *in the Arabian Desert.*

Complex dune system *in the Sahara.*

DUNES

Dunes are shaped by wind direction and sand supply. Where sand supply is limited, crescent-shaped barchan dunes are formed.

TYPES OF DUNE

wind direction
Transverse dune
Barchan dune
Linear dune
Star dune

TEMPERATURE

HOT AND COLD DESERTS

Main desert types: hot arid; semiarid; cold polar

MOST OF THE WORLD'S deserts are in the tropics. The cold deserts which occur elsewhere are arid because they are a long way from the rain-giving sea. Rock in deserts is exposed because of lack of vegetation and is susceptible to changes in temperature; extremes of heat and cold can cause both cracks and fissures to appear in the rock.

HEAT

FIERCE SUN can heat the surface of rock, causing it to expand more rapidly than the cooler, underlying layers. This creates tensions which force the rock to crack or break up. In arid regions, the evaporation of water from rock surfaces dissolves certain minerals within the water, causing salt crystals to form in small openings in the rock. The hard crystals force the openings to widen into cracks and fissures.

The cracked and parched floor *of Death Valley, California. This is one of the hottest deserts on Earth.*

DESERT ABRASION

Abrasion creates a wide range of desert landforms from faceted pebbles and wind ripples in the sand, to large-scale features such as yardangs (low, streamlined ridges), and scoured desert pavements.

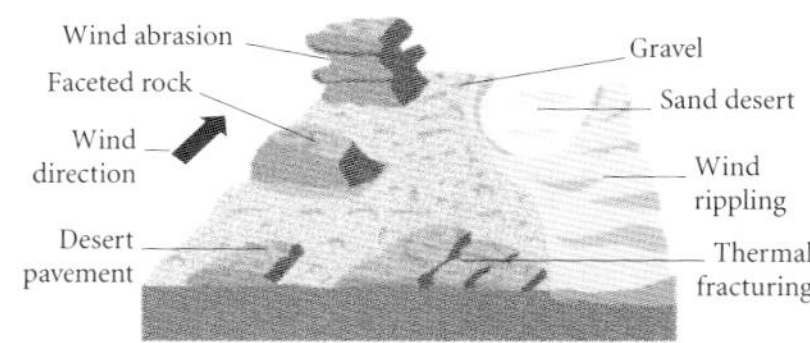
Wind abrasion
Faceted rock
Wind direction
Desert pavement
Gravel
Sand desert
Wind rippling
Thermal fracturing

FEATURES OF A DESERT SURFACE

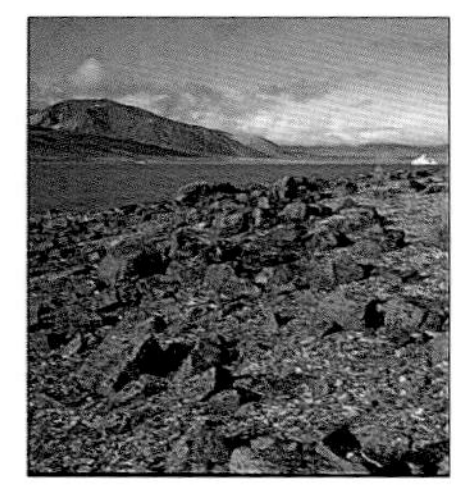

This dry valley at Ellesmere Island *in the Canadian Arctic is an example of a cold desert. The cracked floor and scoured slopes are features also found in hot deserts.*

THE WORLD'S OCEANS

TWO-THIRDS OF THE EARTH'S SURFACE is covered by the oceans. The landscape of the ocean floor, like the surface of the land, has been shaped by movements of the Earth's crust over millions of years to form volcanic mountain ranges, deep trenches, basins, and plateaus. Ocean currents constantly redistribute warm and cold water around the world. A major warm current, such as El Niño in the Pacific Ocean, can increase surface temperature by up to 46°F (8°C), causing changes in weather patterns which can lead to both droughts and flooding.

THE GREAT OCEANS

THERE ARE FIVE OCEANS on Earth: the Pacific, Atlantic, Indian, and Southern oceans, and the much smaller Arctic Ocean. These five ocean basins are relatively young, having evolved within the last 80 million years. One of the most recent plate collisions, between the Eurasian and African plates, created the present-day arrangement of continents and oceans.

***The Indian Ocean** accounts for approximately 20% of the total area of the world's oceans.*

SEA LEVEL

IF THE INFLUENCE of tides, winds, currents, and variations in gravity were ignored, the surface of the Earth's oceans would closely follow the topography of the ocean floor, with an underwater ridge 3,000 ft (915 m) high producing a rise of up to 3 ft (1 m) in the level of the surface water.

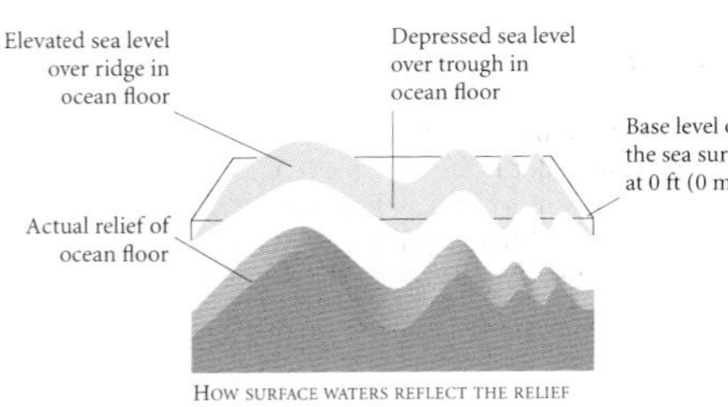
Elevated sea level over ridge in ocean floor
Depressed sea level over trough in ocean floor
Base level of the sea surface at 0 ft (0 m)
Actual relief of ocean floor

HOW SURFACE WATERS REFLECT THE RELIEF OF THE OCEAN FLOOR

***The low relief** of many small Pacific islands such as these atolls at Huahine in French Polynesia makes them vulnerable to changes in sea level.*

OCEAN STRUCTURE

THE CONTINENTAL SHELF is a shallow, flat seabed surrounding the Earth's continents. It extends to the continental slope, which falls to the ocean floor. Here, the flat abyssal plains are interrupted by vast, underwater mountain ranges, the mid-ocean ridges, and ocean trenches which plunge to depths of 35,828 ft (10,920 m).

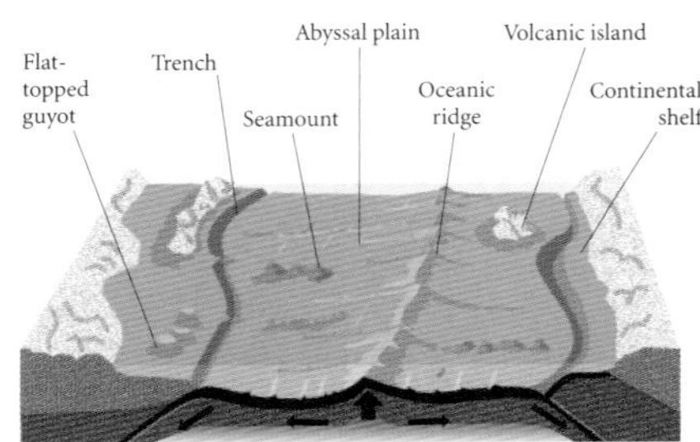
Flat-topped guyot
Trench
Seamount
Abyssal plain
Oceanic ridge
Volcanic island
Continental shelf

TYPICAL SEA-FLOOR FEATURES

Ocean depth

- Sea level
- 200m / 656ft
- 1000m / 3281ft
- 2000m / 6562ft
- 3000m / 9843ft
- 4000m / 13,124ft
- 5000m / 16,400ft
- 6000m / 19,686ft

BLACK SMOKERS

These vents in the ocean floor disgorge hot, sulfur-rich water from deep in the Earth's crust. Despite the great depths, a variety of lifeforms have adapted to the chemical-rich environment which surrounds black smokers.

***A black smoker** in the Atlantic Ocean.*

***Surtsey, near Iceland**, is a volcanic island lying directly over the Mid-Atlantic Ridge. It was formed in the 1960s following intense volcanic activity nearby.*

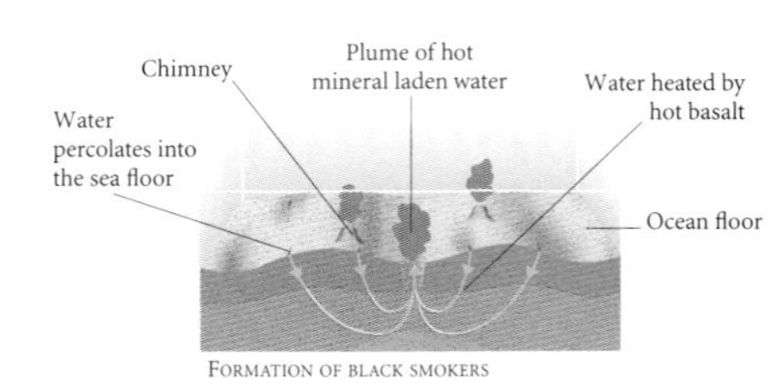
Chimney
Plume of hot mineral laden water
Water heated by hot basalt
Water percolates into the sea floor
Ocean floor

FORMATION OF BLACK SMOKERS

OCEAN FLOORS

Mid-ocean ridges are formed by lava which erupts beneath the sea and cools to form solid rock. This process mirrors the creation of volcanoes from cooled lava on the land. The ages of sea floor rocks increase in parallel bands outward from central ocean ridges.

AGES OF THE OCEAN FLOOR

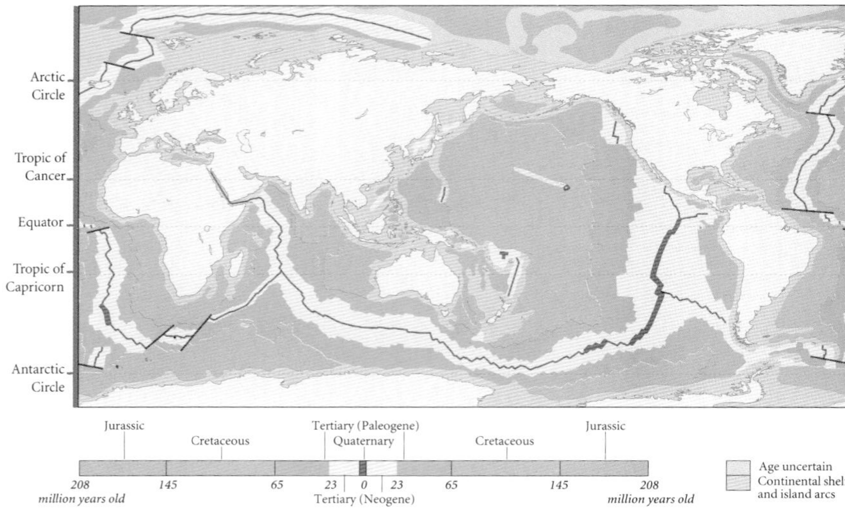
Arctic Circle
Tropic of Cancer
Equator
Tropic of Capricorn
Antarctic Circle
Jurassic
Cretaceous
Tertiary (Paleogene)
Quaternary
Cretaceous
Jurassic
208 million years old
145
65
23
0
23
65
145
208 million years old
Tertiary (Neogene)
Age uncertain
Continental shelf and island arcs

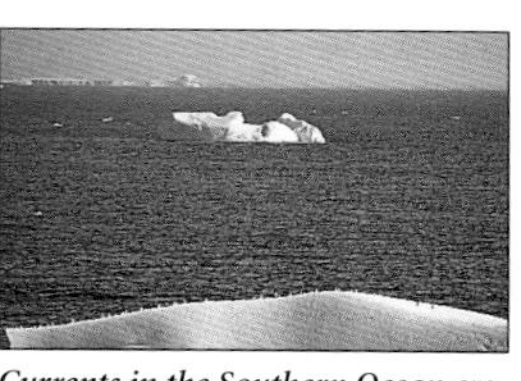

Currents in the Southern Ocean *are driven by some of the world's fiercest winds, including the Roaring Forties, Furious Fifties, and Shrieking Sixties.*

The Pacific Ocean *is the world's largest and deepest ocean, covering over one-third of the surface of the Earth.*

The Atlantic Ocean *was formed when the landmasses of the eastern and western hemispheres began to drift apart 180 million years ago.*

DEPOSITION OF SEDIMENT

STORMS, EARTHQUAKES, and volcanic activity trigger underwater currents known as turbidity currents which scour sand and gravel from the continental shelf, creating underwater canyons. These strong currents pick up material deposited at river mouths and deltas, and carry it across the continental shelf and through the underwater canyons, where it is eventually laid down on the ocean floor in the form of fans.

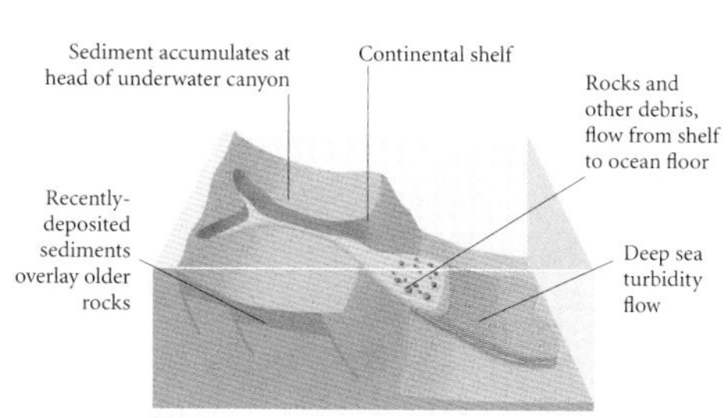
Sediment accumulates at head of underwater canyon
Continental shelf
Rocks and other debris, flow from shelf to ocean floor
Recently-deposited sediments overlay older rocks
Deep sea turbidity flow

HOW SEDIMENT IS DEPOSITED ON THE OCEAN FLOOR

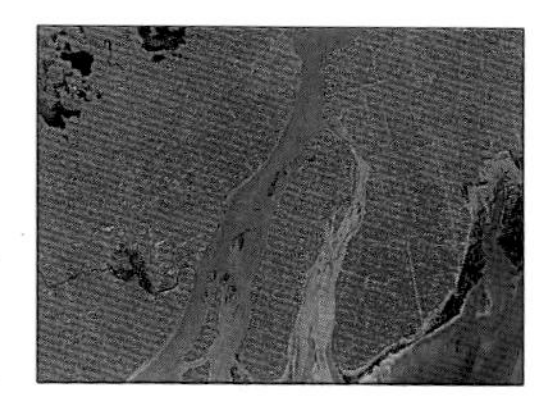

Satellite image *of the Yangtze* (Chang Jiang) *Delta, in which the land appears red. The river deposits immense quantities of silt into the East China Sea, much of which will eventually reach the deep ocean floor.*

EAN
Beaufort Sea
Baffin Bay
Greenland Sea
Arctic Circle
Davis Strait
Hudson Strait
Hudson Bay
Labrador Sea
Gulf of Alaska
Mid-Atlantic Ridge
Newfoundland Basin
NORTH AMERICA
Mendocino Fracture Zone
Murray Fracture Zone
North American Basin
Gulf of Mexico
ATLANTIC
Sargasso Sea
Canary Basin
Tropic of Cancer
Molokai Fracture Zone
Yucatan Basin
Caribbean Sea
Barracuda Fracture Zone
Clarion Fracture Zone
ACIFIC
Guatemala Basin
Clipperton Fracture Zone
Equator
East Pacific Rise
SOUTH AMERICA
Brazil Basin
Peru Basin
Nazca Ridge
Chile Basin
OCEAN
Tropic of Capricorn
Sala y Gomez Ridge
Rio Grande Rise
OCEAN
Southwest Pacific Basin
Argentine Basin
Antarctic Ridge
OCEAN
Southeast Pacific Basin
Scotia Sea
Amundsen Sea
Bellingshausen Sea
Weddell Sea
Antarctic Circle

SURFACE WATER

OCEAN CURRENTS move warm water away from the Equator toward the poles, while cold water is, in turn, moved towards the Equator. This is the main way in which the Earth distributes surface heat and is a major climatic control. Approximately 4,000 million years ago, the Earth was dominated by oceans and there was no land to interrupt the flow of the currents, which would have flowed as straight lines, simply influenced by the Earth's rotation.

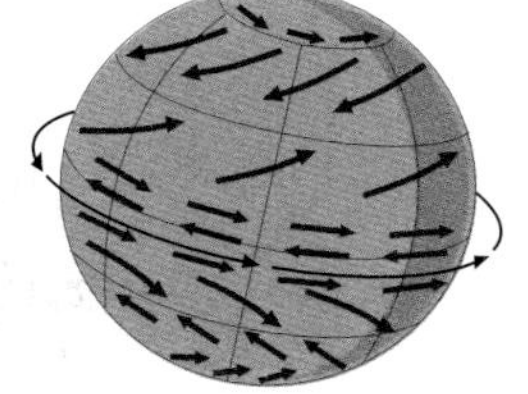

Idealized globe *showing the movement of water around a landless Earth.*

OCEAN CURRENTS

SURFACE CURRENTS are driven by the prevailing winds and by the spinning motion of the Earth, which drives the currents into circulating whirlpools, or gyres. Deep sea currents, over 330 ft (100 m) below the surface, are driven by differences in water temperature and salinity, which have an impact on the density of deep water and on its movement.

SURFACE TEMPERATURE AND CURRENTS

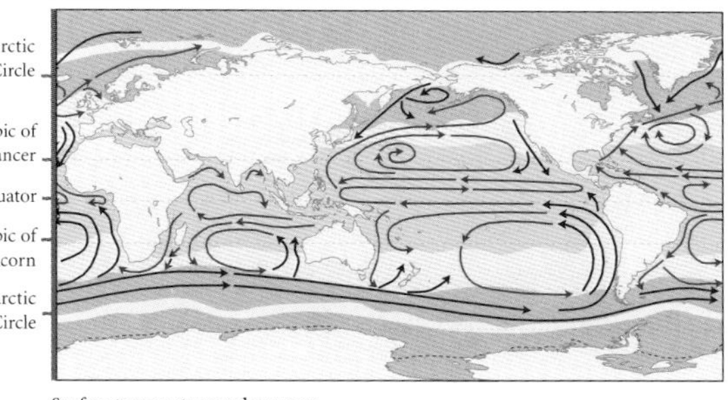
Arctic Circle
Tropic of Cancer
Equator
Tropic of Capricorn
Antarctic Circle

Surface temperature and currents

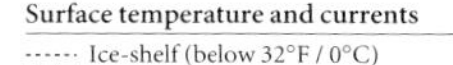
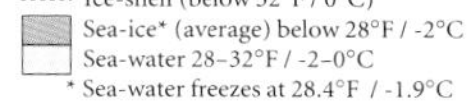
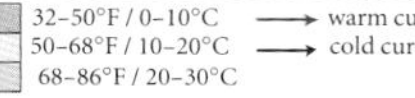
Ice-shelf (below 32°F / 0°C)
Sea-ice* (average) below 28°F / -2°C
Sea-water 28–32°F / -2–0°C
* Sea-water freezes at 28.4°F / -1.9°C
32–50°F / 0–10°C
50–68°F / 10–20°C
68–86°F / 20–30°C
warm current
cold current

TIDES AND WAVES

TIDES ARE CREATED by the pull of the Sun and Moon's gravity on the surface of the oceans. The levels of high and low tides are influenced by the position of the Moon in relation to the Earth and Sun. Waves are formed by wind blowing over the surface of the water.

TIDAL RANGE AND WAVE ENVIRONMENTS

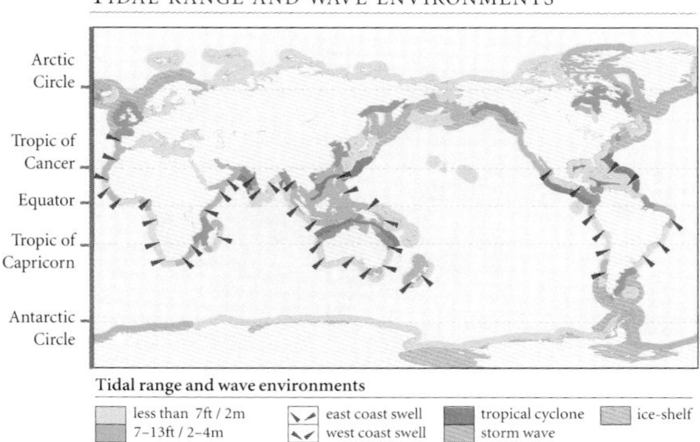
Arctic Circle
Tropic of Cancer
Equator
Tropic of Capricorn
Antarctic Circle

Tidal range and wave environments

less than 7ft / 2m
7–13ft / 2–4m
greater than 13ft / 4m
east coast swell
west coast swell
tropical cyclone storm wave
ice-shelf

HIGH AND LOW TIDES

The highest tides occur when the Earth, the Moon and the Sun are aligned *(below left)*. The lowest tides are experienced when the Sun and Moon align at right angles to one another *(below right)*.

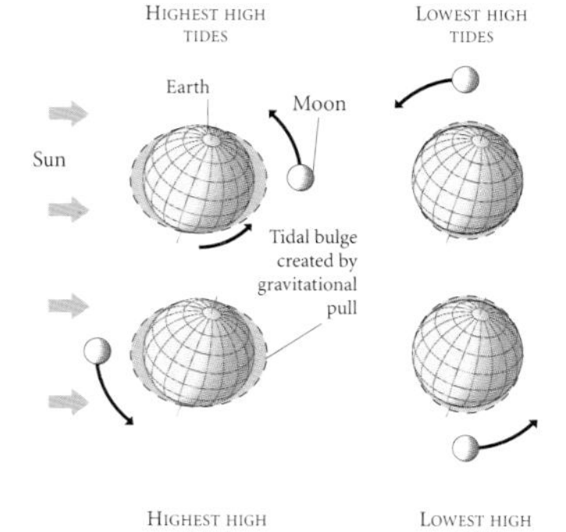
HIGHEST HIGH TIDES
LOWEST HIGH TIDES
Earth
Moon
Sun
Tidal bulge created by gravitational pull
HIGHEST HIGH TIDES
LOWEST HIGH TIDES

DEEP SEA TEMPERATURE AND CURRENTS

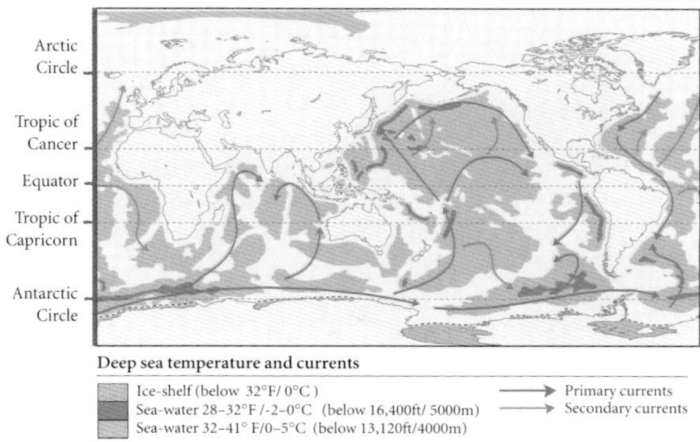
Arctic Circle
Tropic of Cancer
Equator
Tropic of Capricorn
Antarctic Circle

Deep sea temperature and currents

Ice-shelf (below 32°F/ 0°C)
Sea-water 28–32°F /-2–0°C (below 16,400ft/ 5000m)
Sea-water 32–41° F/0–5°C (below 13,120ft/4000m)
Primary currents
Secondary currents

THE GLOBAL CLIMATE

THE EARTH'S CLIMATIC TYPES CONSIST of stable patterns of weather conditions averaged out over a long period of time. Different climates are categorized according to particular combinations of temperature and humidity. By contrast, weather consists of short-term fluctuations in wind, temperature, and humidity conditions. Different climates are determined by latitude, altitude, the prevailing wind, and circulation of ocean currents. Longer-term changes in climate, such as global warming or the onset of ice ages, are punctuated by shorter-term events which comprise the day-to-day weather of a region, such as frontal depressions, hurricanes, and blizzards.

GLOBAL AIR CIRCULATION

AIR DOES NOT SIMPLY FLOW FROM THE EQUATOR TO THE POLES, it circulates in giant cells known as Hadley and Ferrel cells. As air warms it expands, becoming less dense and rising; this creates areas of low pressure. As the air rises it cools and condenses, causing heavy rainfall over the tropics and slight snowfall over the poles. This cool air then sinks, forming high pressure belts. At surface level in the tropics these sinking currents are deflected poleward as the westerlies and toward the Equator as the trade winds. At the poles they become the polar easterlies.

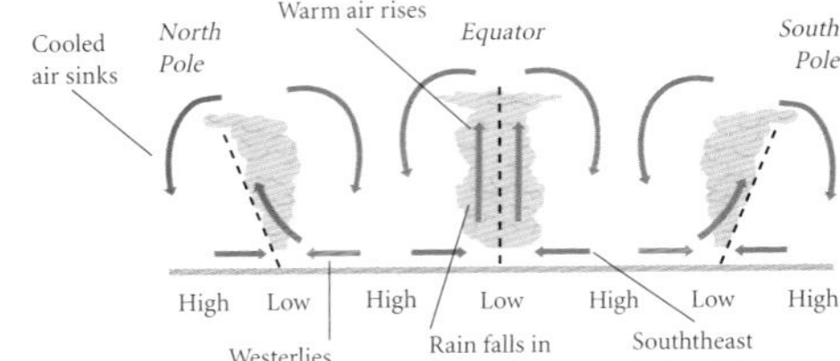
Cooled air sinks
North Pole
Warm air rises
Equator
South Pole
High
Low
High
Low
High
Low
High
Westerlies
Rain falls in the tropics
Souththeast trade winds

The Antarctic pack ice expands its area by almost seven times during the winter as temperatures drop and surrounding seas freeze.

THE ATMOSPHERE, WIND, AND WEATHER

THE EARTH'S ATMOSPHERE has been compared to a giant ocean of air which surrounds the planet. Its circulation patterns are similar to the currents in the oceans and are influenced by three factors; the Earth's orbit around the Sun and rotation about its axis, and variations in the amount of heat radiation received from the Sun. If both heat and moisture were not redistributed between the Equator and the poles, large areas of the Earth would be uninhabitable.

***Heavy fogs**, as here in southern England, form as moisture-laden air passes over cold ground.*

TEMPERATURE

THE WORLD CAN BE DIVIDED into three major climatic zones, stretching like large belts across the latitudes: the tropics which are warm; the cold polar regions and the temperate zones which lie between them. Temperatures across the Earth range from above 86°F (30°C) in the deserts to as low as -70°F (-55°C) at the poles. Temperature is also controlled by altitude; because air becomes cooler and less dense the higher it gets, mountainous regions are typically colder than those areas which are at, or close to, sea level.

AVERAGE JANUARY TEMPERATURES

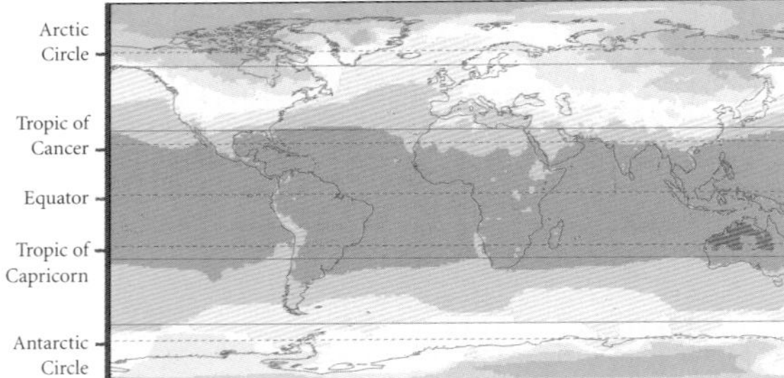
Arctic Circle
Tropic of Cancer
Equator
Tropic of Capricorn
Antarctic Circle

AVERAGE JULY TEMPERATURES

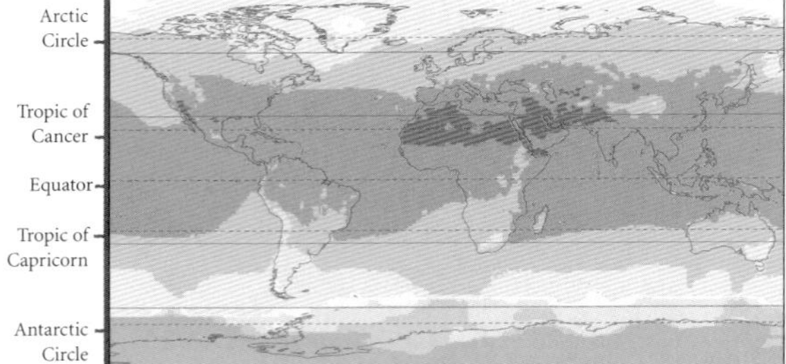
Arctic Circle
Tropic of Cancer
Equator
Tropic of Capricorn
Antarctic Circle

below -22°F (30°C) · -22 to -4°F (-30 to -20°C) · -4 to 14°F (-20 to -10°C) · 14 to 32°F (-10 to 0°C) · 32 to 50°F (0 to 10°C) · 50 to 68°F (10 to 20°C) · 68 to 86°F (20 to 30°C) · 86°F (above 30°C)

CLIMATIC CHANGE

THE EARTH IS CURRENTLY IN A WARM PHASE between ice ages. Warmer temperatures result in higher sea levels as more of the polar ice caps melt. Most of the world's population lives near coasts, so any changes which might cause sea levels to rise, could have a potentially disastrous impact.

***This ice fair**, painted by Pieter Brueghel the Younger in the 17th century, shows the Little Ice Age which peaked around 300 years ago.*

THE GREENHOUSE EFFECT

Gases such as carbon dioxide are known as "greenhouse gases" because they allow shortwave solar radiation to enter the Earth's atmosphere, but help to stop longwave radiation from escaping. This traps heat, raising the Earth's temperature. An excess of these gases, such as that which results from the burning of fossil fuels, helps trap more heat and can lead to global warming.

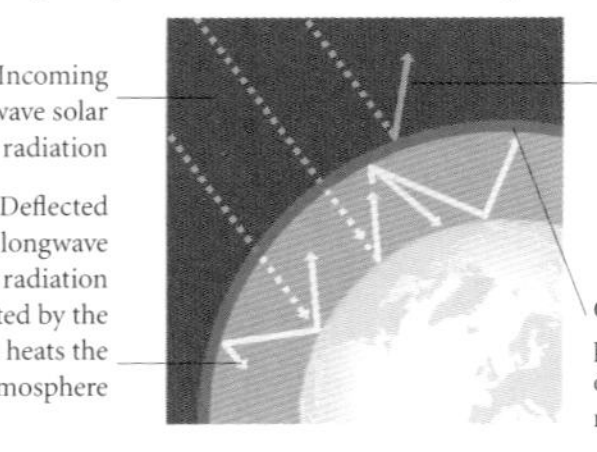
Incoming shortwave solar radiation
Deflected longwave radiation emitted by the Earth heats the atmosphere
Deflected shortwave solar radiation
Greenhouse gases prevent the escape of longwave radiation

The islands of the Caribbean, Mexico's Gulf coast and the southeastern US are often hit by hurricanes formed far out in the Atlantic.

OCEANIC WATER CIRCULATION

IN GENERAL, OCEAN CURRENTS parallel the movement of winds across the Earth's surface. Incoming solar energy is greatest at the Equator and least at the poles. So, water in the oceans heats up most at the Equator and flows poleward, cooling as it moves north or south toward the Arctic or Antarctic. The flow is eventually reversed and cold water currents move back toward the Equator. These ocean currents act as a vast system for moving heat from the Equator toward the poles and are a major influence on the distribution of the Earth's climates.

***In marginal climatic zones** years of drought can completely dry out the land and transform grassland to desert.*

TILT AND ROTATION

The tilt and rotation of the Earth during its annual orbit largely control the distribution of heat and moisture across its surface, which correspondingly controls its large-scale weather patterns. As the Earth annually rotates around the Sun, half its surface is receiving maximum radiation, creating summer and winter seasons. The angle of the Earth means that on average the tropics receive two and a half times as much heat from the Sun each day as the poles.

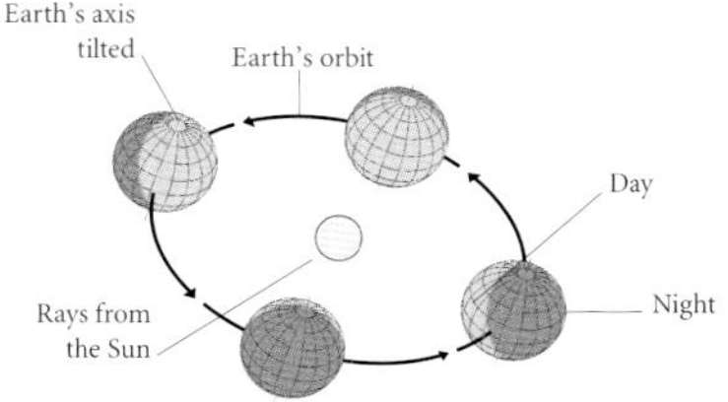

Earth's axis tilted
Earth's orbit
Day
Rays from the Sun
Night

MAP KEY

Climate zones		Ocean currents	Prevailing winds	Local winds
ice cap	mediterranean	warm	warm	warm
subarctic	semiarid	cold	cold	cold
tundra	arid			seasonal*
continental	hot humid			
temperate	humid equatorial			
warm temperate	tropical			

* (seasonal winds which can either be warm or cold)

***The wide range** of environments found in the Andes is strongly related to their altitude, which modifies climatic influences. While the peaks are snow-capped, many protected interior valleys are semitropical.*

THE CORIOLIS EFFECT

The rotation of the Earth influences atmospheric circulation by deflecting winds and ocean currents. Winds blowing in the northern hemisphere are deflected to the right and those in the southern hemisphere are deflected to the left, creating large-scale patterns of wind circulation, such as the northeast and southeast trade winds and the westerlies. This effect is greatest at the poles and least at the Equator.

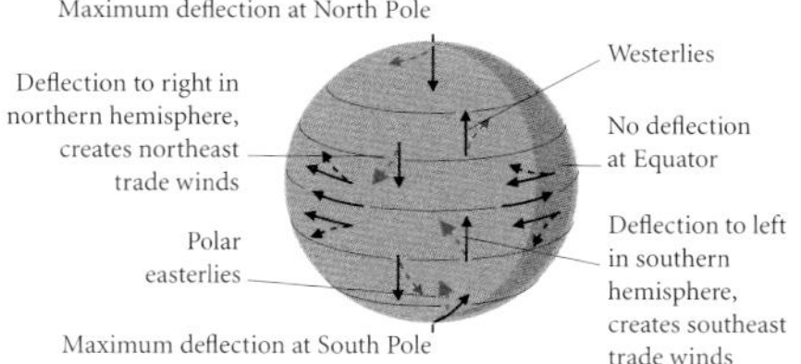

Maximum deflection at North Pole
Westerlies
Deflection to right in northern hemisphere, creates northeast trade winds
No deflection at Equator
Polar easterlies
Deflection to left in southern hemisphere, creates southeast trade winds
Maximum deflection at South Pole

PRECIPITATION

WHEN WARM AIR EXPANDS, it rises and cools, and the water vapor it carries condenses to form clouds. Heavy, regular rainfall is characteristic of the equatorial region, while the poles are cold and receive only slight snowfall. Tropical regions have marked dry and rainy seasons, while in the temperate regions rainfall is relatively unpredictable.

***Monsoon rains,** which affect southern Asia from May to September, are caused by sea winds blowing across the warm land.*

***Heavy tropical rainstorms** occur frequently in Papua New Guinea, often causing soil erosion and landslides in cultivated areas.*

AVERAGE JANUARY RAINFALL

Arctic Circle
Tropic of Cancer
Equator
Tropic of Capricorn
Antarctic Circle

AVERAGE JULY RAINFALL

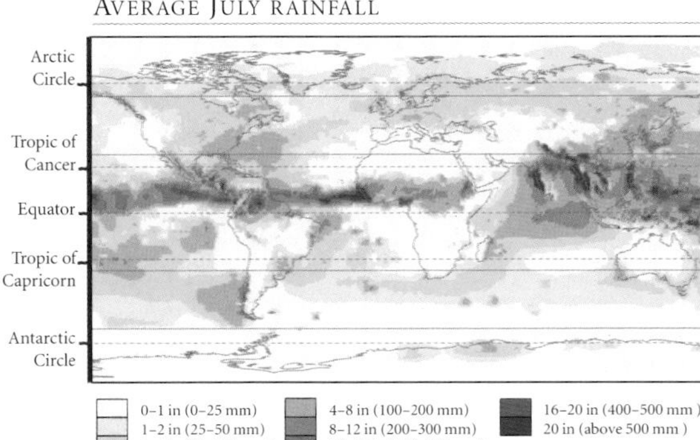

Arctic Circle
Tropic of Cancer
Equator
Tropic of Capricorn
Antarctic Circle
0–1 in (0–25 mm)
1–2 in (25–50 mm)
2–4 in (50–100 mm)
4–8 in (100–200 mm)
8–12 in (200–300 mm)
12–16 in (300–400 mm)
16–20 in (400–500 mm)
20 in (above 500 mm)

***The intensity of some blizzards** in Canada and the northern US can give rise to snowdrifts as high as 10 ft (3 m).*

***The Atacama Desert in Chile** is one of the driest places on Earth, with an average rainfall of less than 2 inches (50 mm) per year.*

***Violent thunderstorms** occur along advancing cold fronts, when cold, dry air masses meet warm, moist air, which rises rapidly, its moisture condensing into thunderclouds. Rain and hail become electrically charged, causing lightning.*

THE RAINSHADOW EFFECT

When moist air is forced to rise by mountains, it cools and the water vapor falls as precipitation, either as rain or snow. Only the dry, cold air continues over the mountains, leaving inland areas with little or no rain. This is called the rainshadow effect and is one reason for the existence of the Mojave Desert in California, which lies east of the Coast Ranges.

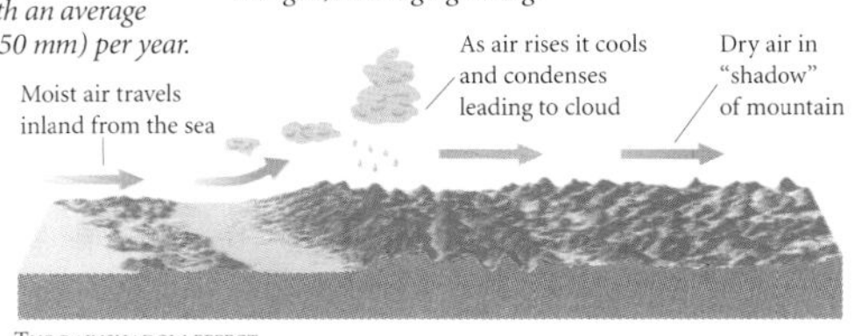

Moist air travels inland from the sea
As air rises it cools and condenses leading to cloud
Dry air in "shadow" of mountain

THE RAINSHADOW EFFECT

LIFE ON EARTH

A UNIQUE COMBINATION of an oxygen-rich atmosphere and plentiful water is the key to life on Earth. Apart from the polar ice caps, there are few areas which have not been colonized by animals or plants over the course of the Earth's history. Plants process sunlight to provide them with their energy, and ultimately all the Earth's animals rely on plants for survival. Because of this reliance, plants are known as primary producers, and the availability of nutrients and temperature of an area is defined as its primary productivity, which affects the quantity and type of animals which are able to live there. This index is affected by climatic factors – cold and aridity restrict the quantity of life, whereas warmth and regular rainfall allow a greater diversity of species.

BIOGEOGRAPHICAL REGIONS

THE EARTH CAN BE DIVIDED into a series of biogeographical regions, or biomes, ecological communities where certain species of plant and animal coexist within particular climatic conditions. Within these broad classifications, other factors including soil richness, altitude, and human activities such as urbanization, intensive agriculture, and deforestation, affect the local distribution of living species within each biome.

POLAR REGIONS

A layer of permanent ice at the Earth's poles covers both seas and land. Very little plant and animal life can exist in these harsh regions.

TUNDRA

A desolate region, with long, dark freezing winters and short, cold summers. With virtually no soil and large areas of permanently frozen ground known as permafrost, the tundra is largely treeless, though it is briefly clothed by small flowering plants in the summer months.

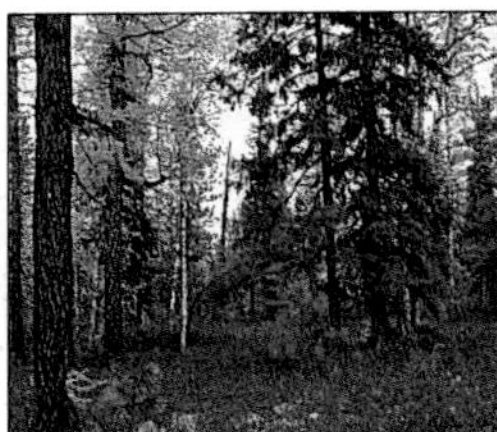

NEEDLELEAF FORESTS

With milder summers than the tundra and less wind, these areas are able to support large forests of coniferous trees.

BROADLEAF FORESTS

Much of the northern hemisphere was once covered by deciduous forests, which occurred in areas with marked seasonal variations. Most deciduous forests have been cleared for human settlement.

TEMPERATE RAIN FORESTS

In warmer wetter areas, such as southern China, temperate deciduous forests are replaced by evergreen forest.

DESERTS

Deserts are areas with negligible rainfall. Most hot deserts lie within the tropics; cold deserts are dry because of their distance from the moisture-providing sea.

MEDITERRANEAN

Hot, dry summers and short winters typify these areas, which were once covered by evergreen shrubs and woodland, but have now been cleared by humans for agriculture.

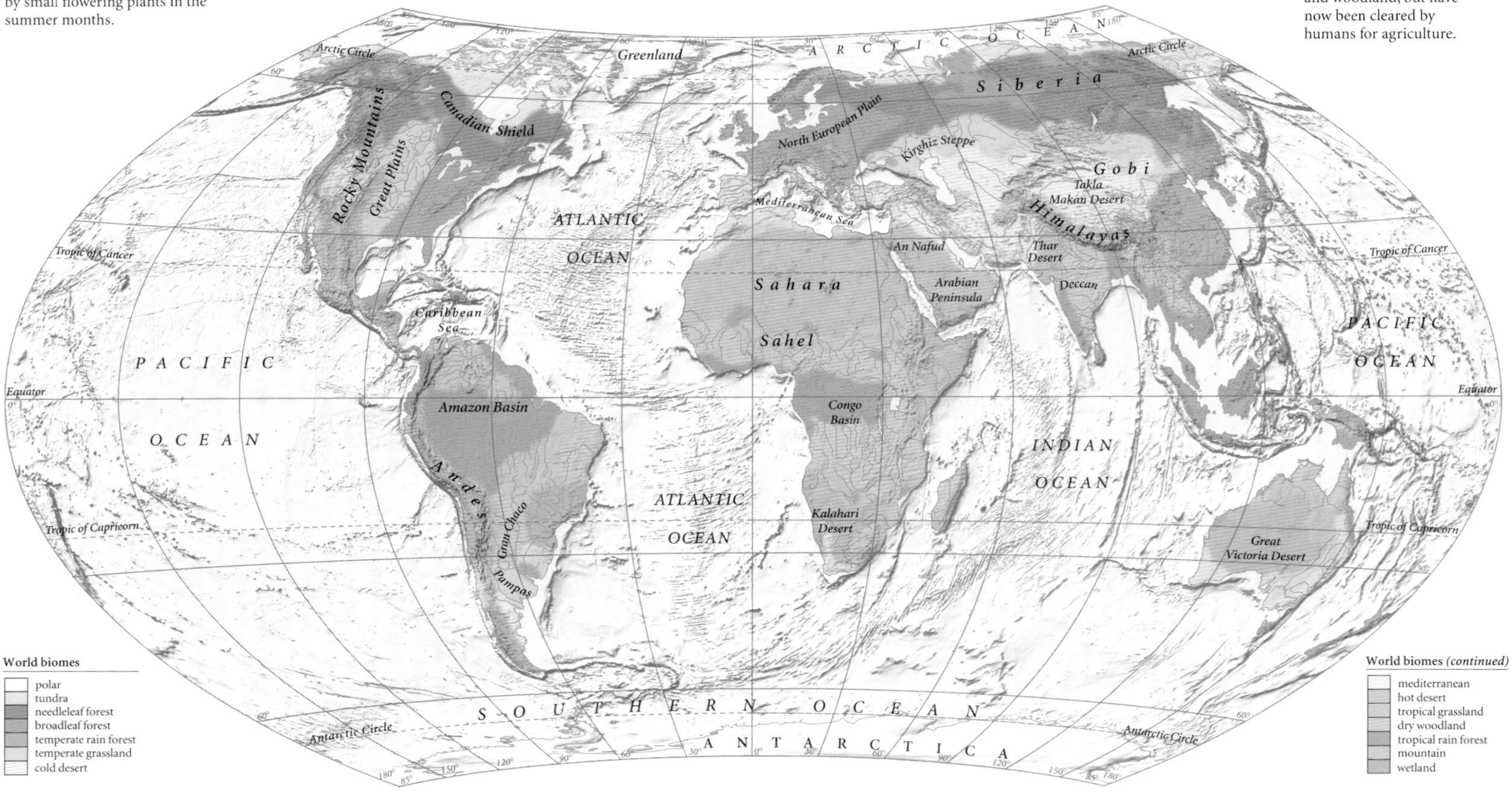

Arctic Circle
Greenland
ARCTIC OCEAN
Siberia
Rocky Mountains
Canadian Shield
Great Plains
North European Plain
Kirghiz Steppe
Gobi
Takla Makan Desert
Himalayas
Mediterranean Sea
ATLANTIC OCEAN
An Nafud
Thar Desert
Arabian Peninsula
Deccan
Tropic of Cancer
Sahara
Caribbean Sea
Sahel
PACIFIC OCEAN
Equator
Amazon Basin
Congo Basin
INDIAN OCEAN
Andes
Gran Chaco
Kalahari Desert
Tropic of Capricorn
Great Victoria Desert
Pampas
SOUTHERN OCEAN
Antarctic Circle
ANTARCTICA

World biomes

- polar
- tundra
- needleleaf forest
- broadleaf forest
- temperate rain forest
- temperate grassland
- cold desert

World biomes *(continued)*

- mediterranean
- hot desert
- tropical grassland
- dry woodland
- tropical rain forest
- mountain
- wetland

TROPICAL AND TEMPERATE GRASSLANDS

The major grassland areas are found in the centers of the larger continental landmasses. In Africa's tropical savannah regions, seasonal rainfall alternates with drought. Temperate grasslands, also known as *steppes* and *prairies* are found in the northern hemisphere, and in South America, where they are known as the *pampas*.

DRY WOODLANDS

Trees and shrubs, adapted to dry conditions, grow widely spaced from one another, interspersed by savannah grasslands.

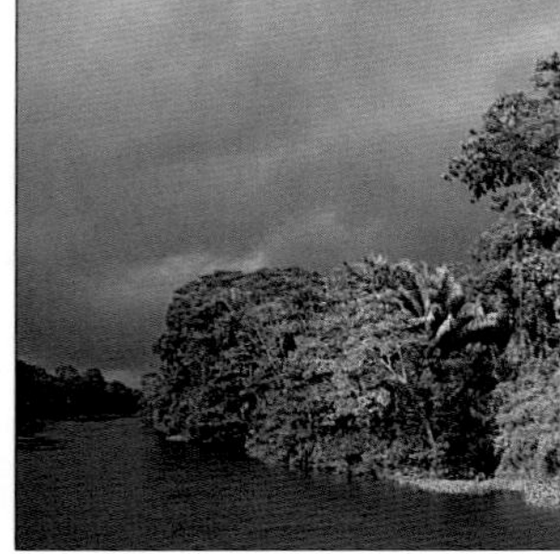

TROPICAL RAIN FORESTS

Characterized by year-round warmth and high rainfall, tropical rain forests contain the highest diversity of plant and animal species on Earth.

MOUNTAINS

Though the lower slopes of mountains may be thickly forested, only ground-hugging shrubs and other vegetation will grow above the tree line which varies according to both altitude and latitude.

WETLANDS

Rarely lying above sea level, wetlands are marshes, swamps and tidal flats. Some, with their moist, fertile soils, are rich feeding grounds for fish and breeding grounds for birds. Others have little soil structure and are too acidic to support much plant and animal life.

BIODIVERSITY

THE NUMBER OF PLANT AND ANIMAL SPECIES, and the range of genetic diversity within the populations of each species, make up the Earth's biodiversity. The plants and animals which are endemic to a region – that is, those which are found nowhere else in the world – are also important in determining levels of biodiversity. Human settlement and intervention have encroached on many areas of the world once rich in endemic plant and animal species. Increasing international efforts are being made to monitor and conserve the biodiversity of the Earth's remaining wild places.

ANIMAL ADAPTATION

THE DEGREE OF AN ANIMAL'S ADAPTABILITY to different climates and conditions is extremely important in ensuring its success as a species. Many animals, particularly the largest mammals, are becoming restricted to ever-smaller regions as human development and modern agricultural practices reduce their natural habitats. In contrast, humans have been responsible – both deliberately and accidentally – for the spread of some of the world's most successful species. Many of these introduced species are now more numerous than the indigenous animal populations.

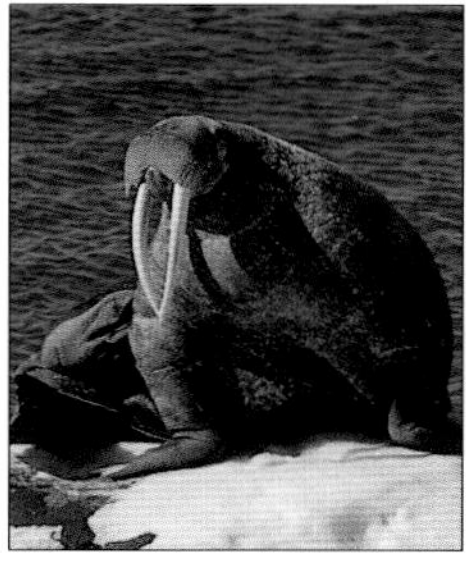

POLAR ANIMALS

The frozen wastes of the polar regions are able to support only a small range of species which derive their nutritional requirements from the sea. Animals such as the walrus *(left)* have developed insulating fat, stocky limbs, and double-layered coats to enable them to survive in the freezing conditions.

DESERT ANIMALS

Many animals which live in the extreme heat and aridity of the deserts are able to survive for days and even months with very little food or water. Their bodies are adapted to lose heat quickly and to store fat and water. The Gila monster *(above)* stores fat in its tail.

AMAZON RAINFOREST

The vast Amazon Basin is home to the world's greatest variety of animal species. Animals are adapted to live at many different levels from the treetops to the tangled undergrowth which lies beneath the canopy. The sloth *(below)* hangs upside down in the branches. Its fur grows from its stomach to its back to enable water to run off quickly.

DIVERSITY OF ANIMAL SPECIES

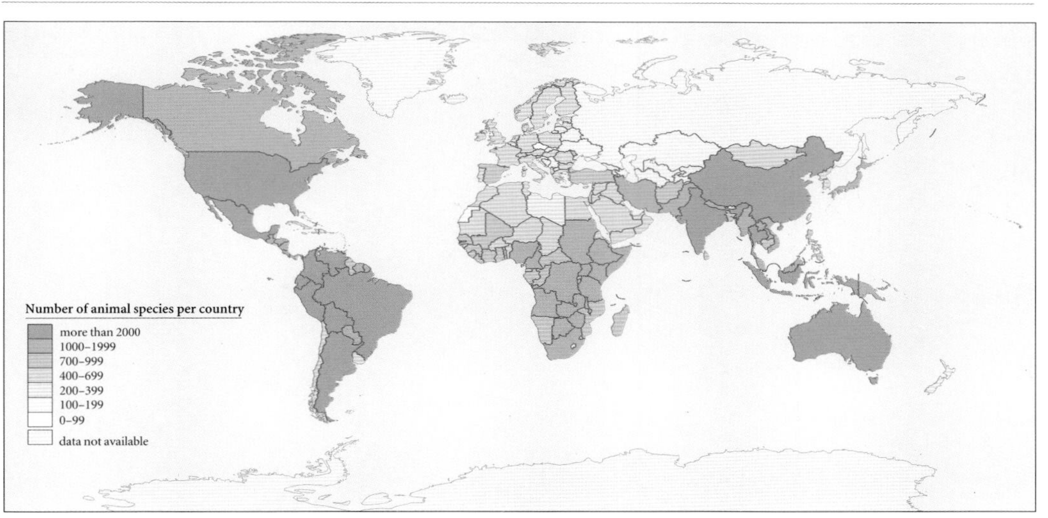
Number of animal species per country
more than 2000
1000–1999
700–999
400–699
200–399
100–199
0–99
data not available

MARINE BIODIVERSITY

The oceans support a huge variety of different species, from the world's largest mammals like whales and dolphins down to the tiniest plankton. The greatest diversities occur in the warmer seas of continental shelves, where plants are easily able to photosynthesize, and around coral reefs, where complex ecosystems are found. On the ocean floor, nematodes can exist at a depth of more than 10,000 ft (3,000 m) below sea level.

HIGH ALTITUDES

Few animals exist in the rarefied atmosphere of the highest mountains. However, birds of prey such as eagles and vultures *(above)*, with their superb eyesight can soar as high as 23,000 ft (7,000 m) to scan for prey below.

URBAN ANIMALS

The growth of cities has reduced the amount of habitat available to many species. A number of animals are now moving closer into urban areas to scavenge from the detritus of the modern city *(left)*. Rodents, particularly rats and mice, have existed in cities for thousands of years, and many insects, especially moths, quickly develop new coloring to provide them with camouflage.

ENDEMIC SPECIES

Isolated areas such as Australia and the island of Madagascar, have the greatest range of endemic species. In Australia, these include marsupials such as the kangaroo *(below)*, which carry their young in pouches on their bodies. Destruction of habitat, pollution, hunting, and predators introduced by humans, are threatening this unique biodiversity.

PLANT ADAPTATION

ENVIRONMENTAL CONDITIONS, particularly climate, soil type, and the extent of competition with other organisms, influence the development of plants into a number of distinctive forms. Similar conditions in quite different parts of the world create similar adaptations in the plants, which may then be modified by other, local, factors specific to the region.

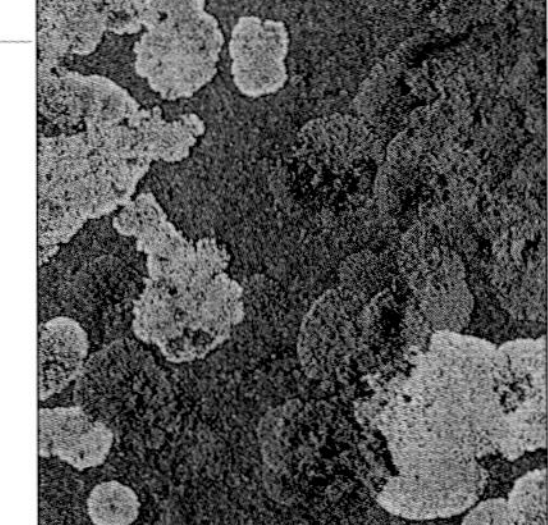

COLD CONDITIONS

In areas where temperatures rarely rise above freezing, plants such as lichens *(left)* and mosses grow densely, close to the ground.

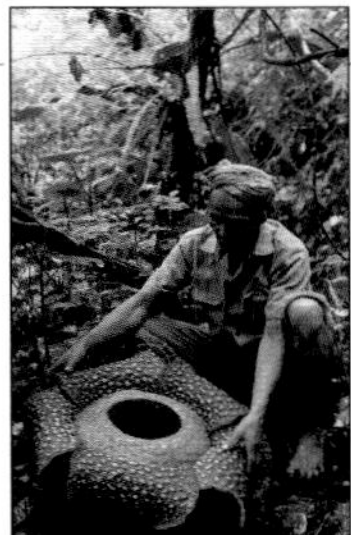

RAIN FORESTS

Most of the world's largest and oldest plants are found in rain forests; warmth and heavy rainfall provide ideal conditions for vast plants like the world's largest flower, the rafflesia *(left)*.

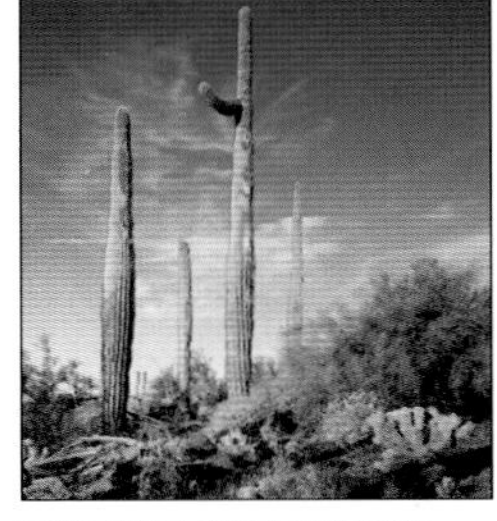

HOT, DRY CONDITIONS

Arid conditions lead to the development of plants whose surface area has been reduced to a minimum to reduce water loss. In cacti *(above)*, which can survive without water for months, leaves are minimal or not present at all.

ANCIENT PLANTS

Some of the world's most primitive plants still exist today, including algae, cycads, and many ferns *(above)*, reflecting the success with which they have adapted to changing conditions.

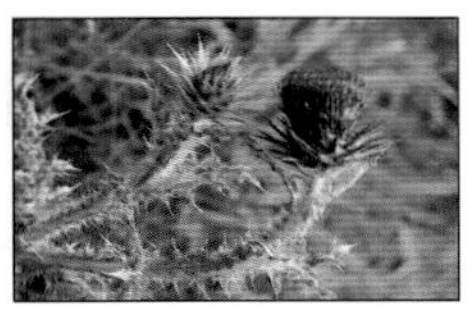

RESISTING PREDATORS

A great variety of plants have developed devices including spines *(above)*, poisons, stinging hairs, and an unpleasant taste or smell to deter animal predators.

DIVERSITY OF PLANT SPECIES

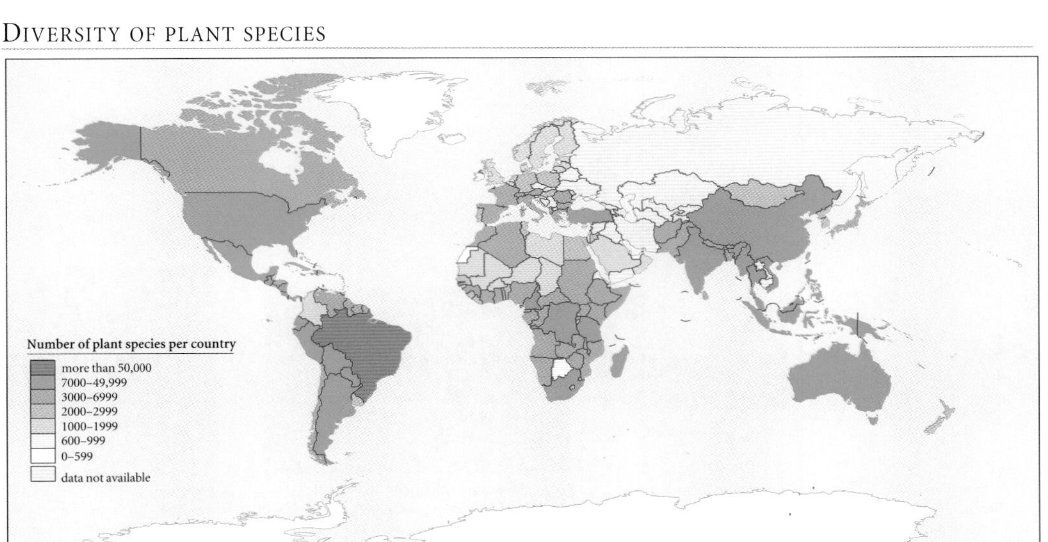
Number of plant species per country
more than 50,000
7000–49,999
3000–6999
2000–2999
1000–1999
600–999
0–599
data not available

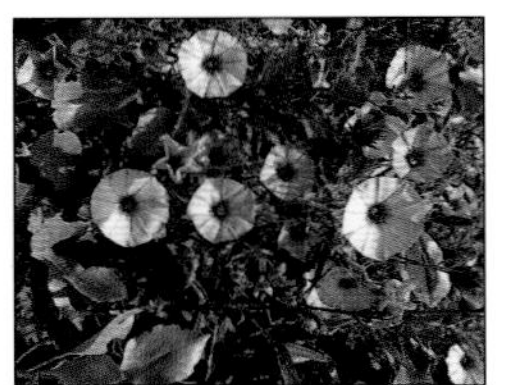

WEEDS

Weeds such as bindweed *(above)* are fast-growing, easily dispersed, and tolerant of a number of different environments, enabling them to quickly colonize suitable habitats. They are among the most adaptable of all plants.

POPULATION AND SETTLEMENT

THE EARTH'S POPULATION IS PROJECTED to rise from its current level of about 5.5 billion to reach some 10 billion by 2025. The global distribution of this rapidly growing population is very uneven, and is dictated by climate, terrain, and natural and economic resources. The great majority of the Earth's people live in coastal zones, and along river valleys. Deserts cover over 20% of the Earth's surface, but support less than 5% of the world's population. It is estimated that over half of the world's population live in cities – most of them in Asia – as a result of mass migration from rural areas in search of jobs. Many of these people live in the so-called "megacities," some with populations as great as 40 million.

PATTERNS OF SETTLEMENT

THE PAST 200 YEARS have seen the most radical shift in world population patterns in recorded history.

NOMADIC LIFE

ALL THE WORLD'S PEOPLES were hunter-gatherers 10,000 years ago. Today nomads, who live by following available food resources, account for less than 0.0001% of the world's population. They are mainly pastoral herders, moving their livestock from place to place in search of grazing land.

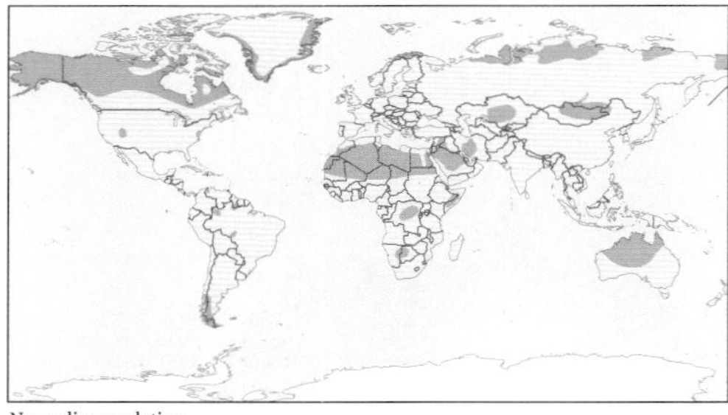

Nomadic population

Nomadic population area

THE GROWTH OF CITIES

IN 1900 there were only 14 cities in the world with populations of more than a million, mostly in the northern hemisphere. Today, as more and more people in the developing world migrate to towns and cities, there are 29 cities whose population exceeds 5 million, and around 200 "million-cities."

MILLION-CITIES IN 1900

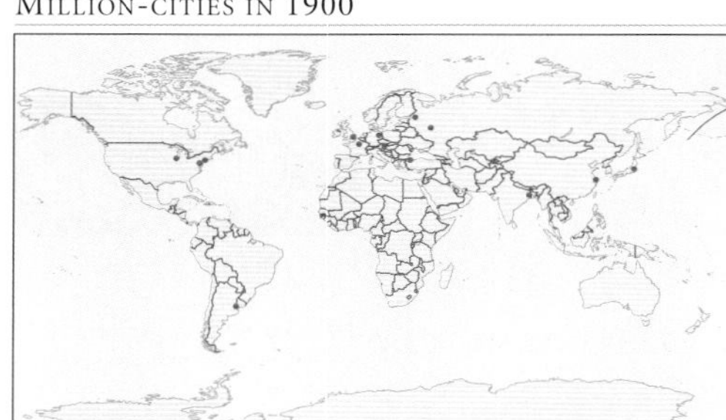

Million-cities in 1900

• Cities over 1 million population

MILLION-CITIES IN 1995

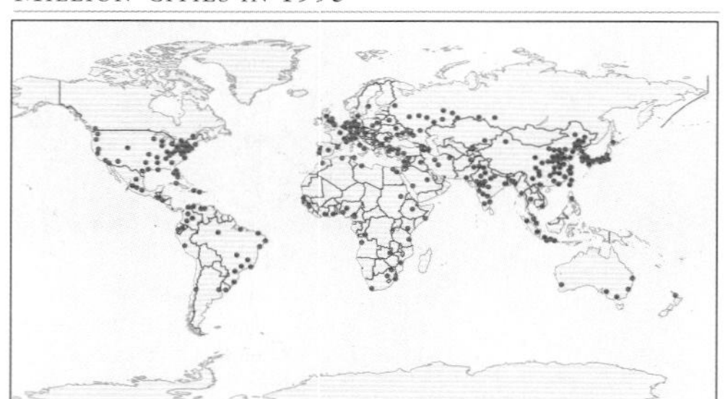

Million-cities in 1995

• Cities over 1 million population

NORTH AMERICA

THE EASTERN AND WESTERN SEABOARDS of the US, with huge expanses of interconnected cities, towns, and suburbs, are vast, densely-populated megalopolises. Central America and the Caribbean also have high population densities. Yet, away from the coasts and in the wildernesses of northern Canada the land is very sparsely settled.

***Vancouver** on Canada's west coast, grew up as a port city. In recent years it has attracted many Asian immigrants, particularly from the Pacific Rim.*

***North America's** central plains, the continent's agricultural heartland, are thinly populated and highly productive.*

EUROPE

WITH ITS TEMPERATE CLIMATE, and rich mineral and natural resources, Europe is generally very densely settled. The continent acts as a magnet for economic migrants from the developing world, and immigration is now widely restricted. Birthrates in Europe are generally low, and in some countries, such as Germany, the populations have stabilized at zero growth, with a fast-growing elderly population.

***Many European cities,** like Siena, once reflected the "ideal" size for human settlements. Modern technological advances have enabled them to grow far beyond the original walls.*

***Within** the densely-populated Netherlands the reclamation of coastal wetlands is vital to provide much-needed land for agriculture and settlement.*

Population density (inhabitants per sq mile)

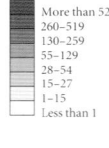

- More than 520
- 260–519
- 130–259
- 55–129
- 28–54
- 15–27
- 1–15
- Less than 1

NORTH AMERICA — Population 9%, World land area 17%

EUROPE — Population 14%, World land area 7.1%

AFRICA — Population 12%, World land area 20.2%

SOUTH AMERICA — Population 5.5%, World land area 11.8%

SOUTH AMERICA

MOST SETTLEMENT IN SOUTH AMERICA is clustered in a narrow belt in coastal zones and in the northern Andes. During the 20th century, cities such as São Paulo and Buenos Aires grew enormously, acting as powerful economic magnets to the rural population. Shantytowns have grown up on the outskirts of many major cities to house these immigrants, often lacking basic amenities.

***Many people in western** South America live at high altitudes in the Andes, both in cities and in villages such as this one in Bolivia.*

***Venezuela** is the most highly urbanized country in South America, with more than 90% of the population living in cities such as Caracas.*

AFRICA

THE ARID CLIMATE of much of Africa means that settlement of the continent is sparse, focusing in coastal areas and fertile regions such as the Nile Valley. Africa still has a high proportion of nomadic agriculturalists, although many are now becoming settled, and the population is predominantly rural.

***Cities such as Nairobi** (above), Cairo and Johannesburg have grown rapidly in recent years, although only Cairo has a significant population on a global scale.*

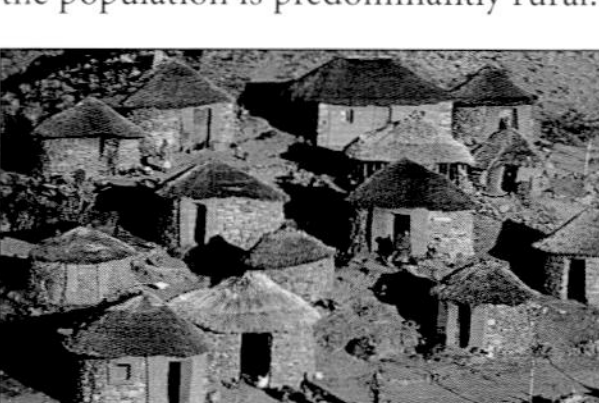

***Traditional lifestyles** and homes persist across much of Africa, which has a higher proportion of rural or village-based population than any other continent.*

ASIA

MOST ASIAN SETTLEMENT originally centered around the great river valleys such as the Indus, the Ganges, and the Yangtze. Today, almost 60% of the world's population lives in Asia, many in burgeoning cities – particularly in the economically-buoyant Pacific Rim countries. Even rural population densities are high in many countries; practices such as terracing in Southeast Asia making the most of the available land.

***Many of China's cities** are now vast urban areas with populations of more than 5 million people.*

***This stilt village in Bangladesh** is built to resist the regular flooding. Pressure on land, even in rural areas, forces many people to live in marginal areas.*

Population Structures

Population pyramids are an effective means of showing the age structures of different countries, and highlighting changing trends in population growth and decline. The typical pyramid for a country with a growing, youthful population, is broad-based *(left)*, reflecting a high birthrate and a far larger number of young rather than elderly people. In contrast, countries with populations whose numbers are stabilizing have a more balanced distribution of people in each age band, and may even have lower numbers of people in the youngest age ranges, indicating both a high life expectancy, and that the population is now barely replacing itself *(right)*. The Russian Federation *(center)* still bears the scars of World War II, reflected in the dramatically lower numbers of men than women in the 60–80+ age range.

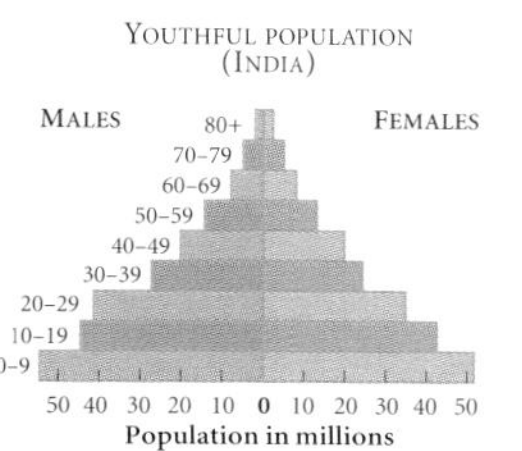
Youthful population
(India)
Males
Females
80+
70–79
60–69
50–59
40–49
30–39
20–29
10–19
0–9
50 40 30 20 10 0 10 20 30 40 50
Population in millions

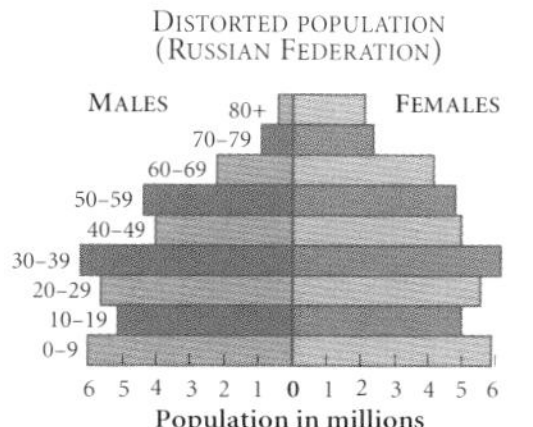
Distorted population
(Russian Federation)
Males
Females
80+
70–79
60–69
50–59
40–49
30–39
20–29
10–19
0–9
6 5 4 3 2 1 0 1 2 3 4 5 6
Population in millions

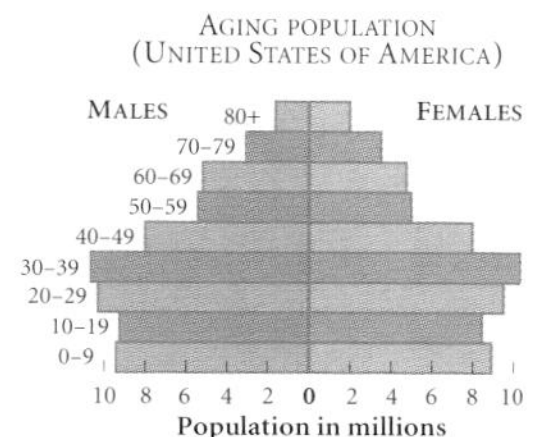
Aging population
(United States of America)
Males
Females
80+
70–79
60–69
50–59
40–49
30–39
20–29
10–19
0–9
10 8 6 4 2 0 2 4 6 8 10
Population in millions

Population Growth

Improvements in food supply and advances in medicine have both played a major role in the remarkable growth in global population, which has increased five-fold over the last 150 years. Food supplies have risen with the mechanization of agriculture and improvements in crop yields. Better nutrition, together with higher standards of public health and sanitation, have led to increased longevity and higher birthrates.

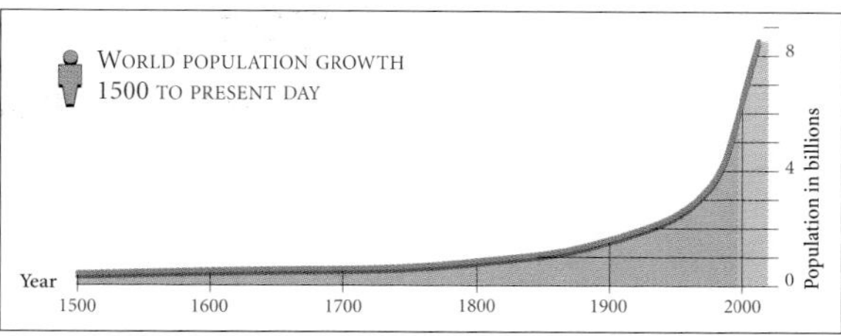
World population growth
1500 to present day
Year
1500
1600
1700
1800
1900
2000
0
4
8
Population in billions

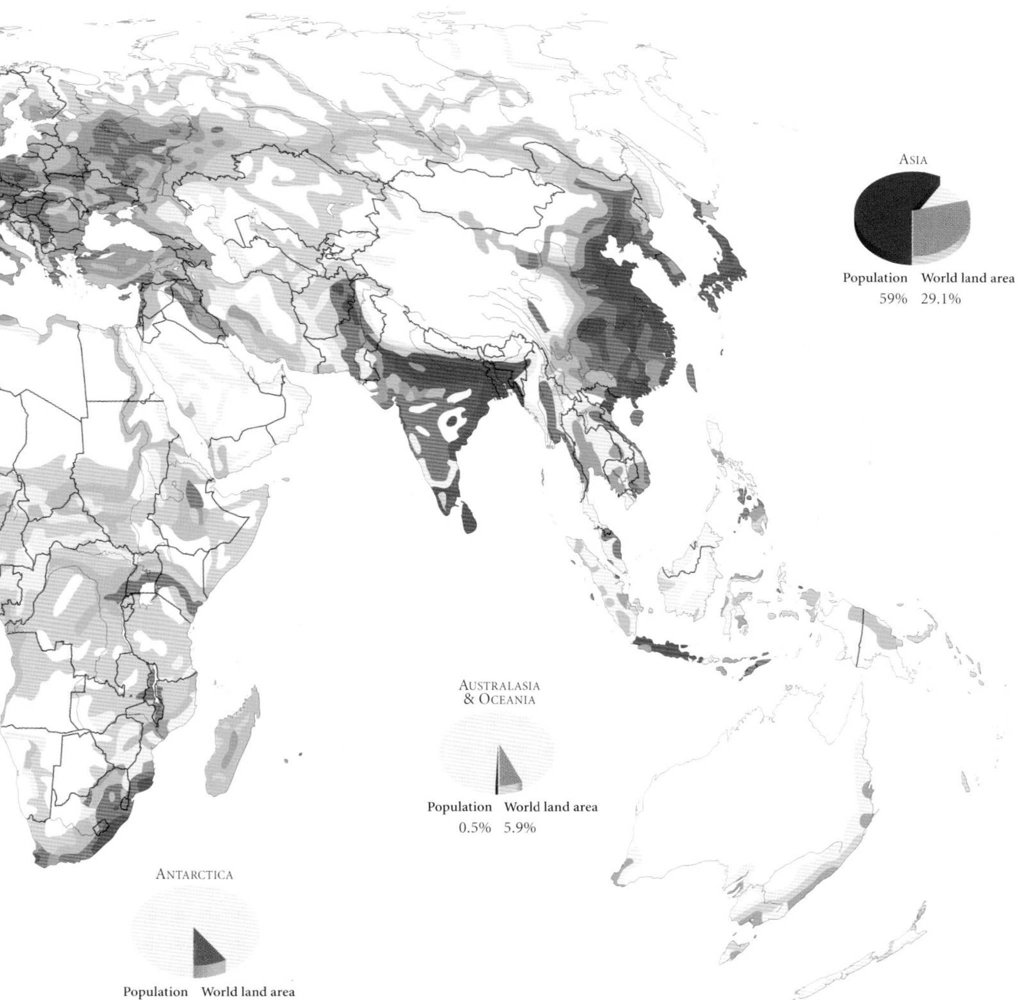
Asia
Population 59%
World land area 29.1%
Australasia & Oceania
Population 0.5%
World land area 5.9%
Antarctica
Population 0%
World land area 8.9%

World Nutrition

Two-thirds of the world's food supply is consumed by the industrialized nations, many of which have a daily calorific intake far higher than is necessary for their populations to maintain a healthy body weight. In contrast, in the developing world, about 800 million people do not have enough food to meet their basic nutritional needs.

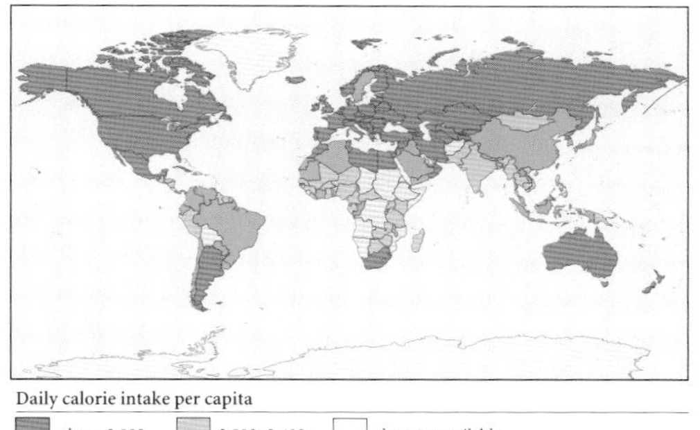

Daily calorie intake per capita

above 3,000 | 2,500–2,999 | 2,000–2,499 | below 2,000 | data not available

World Life Expectancy

Improved public health and living standards have greatly increased life expectancy in the developed world, where people can now expect to live twice as long as they did 100 years ago. In many of the world's poorest nations, inadequate nutrition and disease, means that the average life expectancy still does not exceed 45 years.

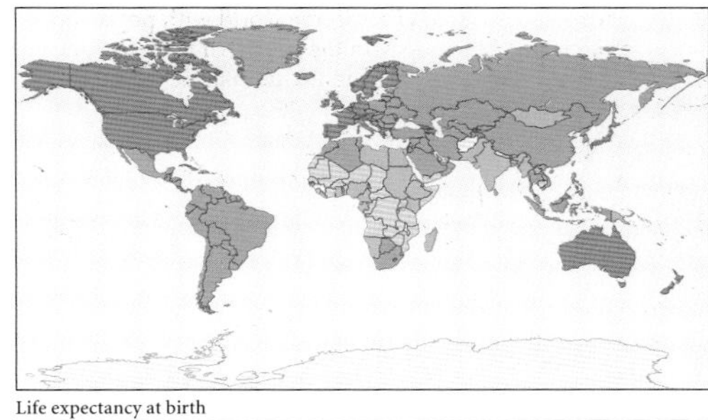

Life expectancy at birth

above 75 years | 65–74 years | 55–64 years | 45–54 years | below 44 years | data not available

Australasia & Oceania

This is the world's most sparsely settled region. The peoples of Australia and New Zealand live mainly in the coastal cities, with only scattered settlements in the arid interior. The Pacific islands can only support limited populations because of their remoteness and lack of resources.

***Brisbane**, on Australia's Gold Coast is the most rapidly expanding city in the country. The great majority of Australia's population lives in cities near the coasts.*

***The remote highlands** of Papua New Guinea are home to a wide variety of peoples, many of whom still subsist by traditional hunting and gathering.*

Average World Birthrates

Birthrates are much higher in Africa, Asia, and South America than in Europe and North America. Increased affluence and easy access to contraception are both factors which can lead to a significant decline in a country's birthrate.

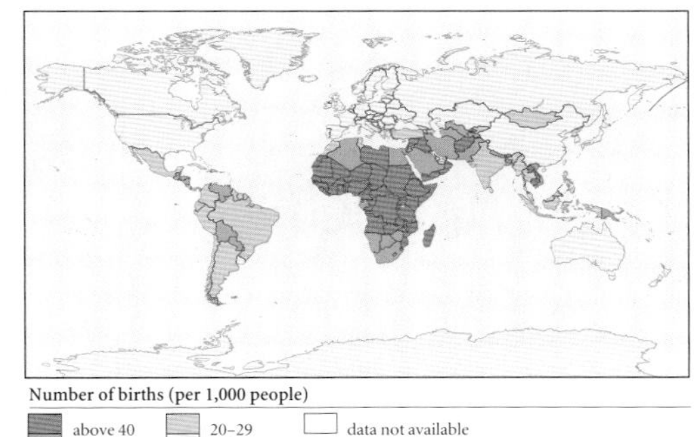

Number of births (per 1,000 people)

above 40 | 30–39 | 20–29 | below 20 | data not available

World Infant Mortality

In parts of the developing world infant mortality rates are still high; access to medical services such as immunization, adequate nutrition, and the promotion of breast-feeding have been important in combating infant mortality.

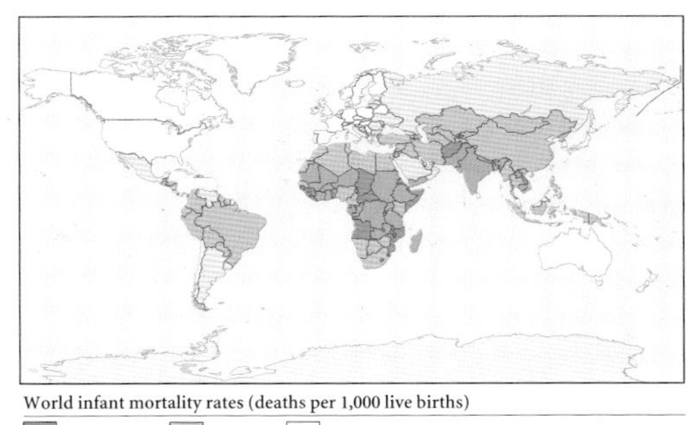

World infant mortality rates (deaths per 1,000 live births)

above 125 | 75–124 | 35–74 | 15–43 | below 15 | data not available

The Economic System

The wealthy countries of the developed world, with their aggressive, market-led economies and their access to productive new technologies and international markets, dominate the world economic system. At the other extreme, many of the countries of the developing world are locked in a cycle of national debt, rising populations, and unemployment. The state-managed economies of the former communist bloc began to be dismantled during the 1990s, and China is emerging as a major economic power following decades of isolation.

Trade blocs

EU / CACM | NAFTA / SADC | ASEAN / ECOWAS | LAIA / CEEAC

Trade Blocs

International trade blocs are formed when groups of countries, often already enjoying close military and political ties, join together to offer mutually preferential terms of trade for both imports and exports. Increasingly, global trade is dominated by three main blocs: the EU, NAFTA, and ASEAN. They are supplanting older trade blocs such as the Commonwealth, a legacy of colonialism.

International Trade Flows

World trade acts as a stimulus to national economies, encouraging growth. Over the last three decades, as heavy industries have declined, services – banking, insurance, tourism, airlines, and shipping – have taken an increasingly large share of world trade. Manufactured articles now account for nearly two-thirds of world trade; raw materials and food make up less than a quarter of the total.

SHIPPING
Ships carry 80% of international cargo, and extensive container ports, where cargo is stored, are vital links in the international transportation network.

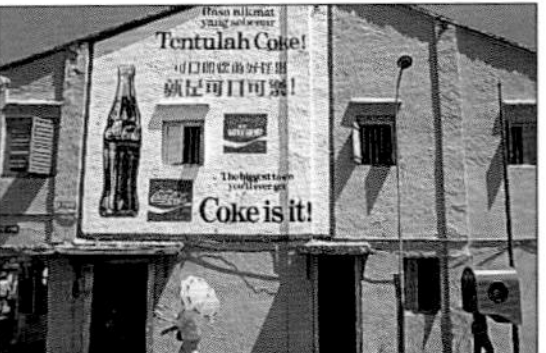
Tentulah Coke!
Coke is it!

MULTINATIONALS
Multinational companies are increasingly penetrating inaccessible markets. The reach of many American commodities is now global.

PRIMARY PRODUCTS
Many countries, particularly in the Caribbean and Africa, are still reliant on primary products such as rubber and coffee, which makes them vulnerable to fluctuating prices.

SERVICE INDUSTRIES
Service industries such as banking, tourism and insurance were the fastest-growing industrial sector in the last half of the 20th century. Lloyds of London is the center of the world insurance market.

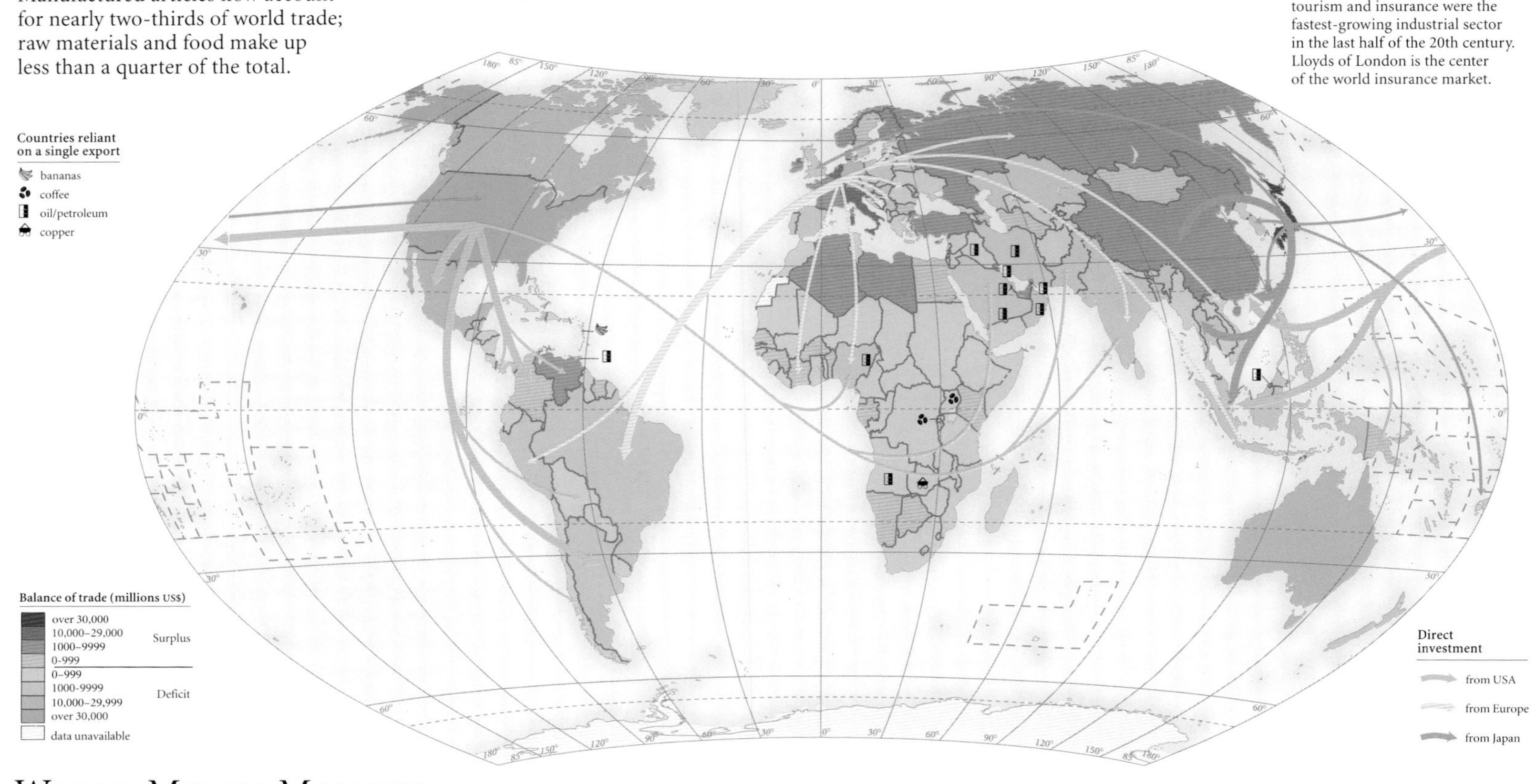
Countries reliant on a single export
bananas
coffee
oil/petroleum
copper
Balance of trade (millions US$)
Surplus
over 30,000
10,000–29,000
1000–9999
0–999
Deficit
0–999
1000–9999
10,000–29,999
over 30,000
data unavailable
Direct investment
from USA
from Europe
from Japan

World Money Markets

The financial world has traditionally been dominated by three major centers – Tokyo, New York and London, which house the headquarters of stock exchanges, multinational corporations and international banks. Their geographic location means that, at any one time in a 24-hour day, one major market is open for trading in shares, currencies, and commodities. Since the late 1980s, technological advances have enabled transactions between financial centers to occur at ever-greater speed, and new markets have sprung up throughout the world.

Major Money Markets

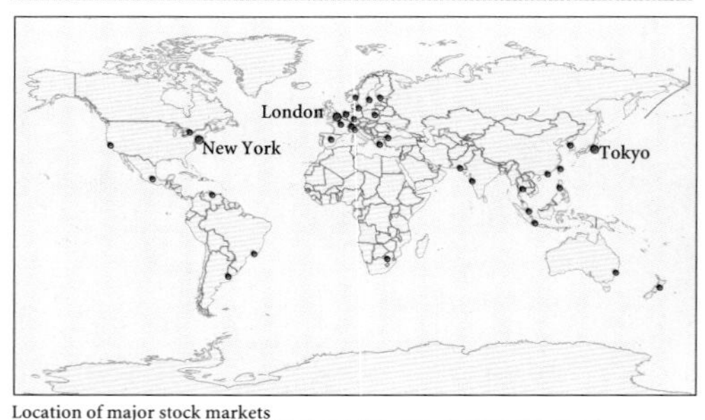
London
New York
Tokyo

Location of major stock markets

• Major stock markets

The Tokyo Stock Market crashed in 1990, leading to a slow-down in the growth of the world's most powerful economy, and a refocusing on economic policy away from export-led growth and toward the domestic market.

New Stock Markets

New stock markets are now opening in many parts of the world, where economies have recently emerged from state controls. In Moscow and Beijing, and several countries in eastern Europe, newly-opened stock exchanges reflect the transition to market-driven economies.

Dealers at the Calcutta Stock Market. *The Indian economy has been opened up to foreign investment and many multinationals now have bases there.*

The Developing World

International trade in capital and currency is dominated by the rich nations of the northern hemisphere. In parts of Africa and Asia, where exports of any sort are extremely limited, home-produced commodities are simply sold in local markets.

Markets have thrived *in communist Vietnam since the introduction of a liberal economic policy.*

World Wealth Disparity

A global assessment of Gross Domestic Product (GDP) by nation reveals great disparities. The developed world, with only a quarter of the world's population, has 80% of the world's manufacturing income. Civil war, conflict, and political instability further undermine the economic self-sufficiency of many of the world's poorest nations.

***Cities such as Detroit** have been badly hit by the decline in heavy industry.*

Urban Decay

Although the US still dominates the global economy, it faces deficits in both the federal budget and the balance of trade. Vast discrepancies in personal wealth, high levels of unemployment, and the dismantling of welfare provisions throughout the 1980s have led to severe deprivation in several of the inner cities of North America's industrial heartland.

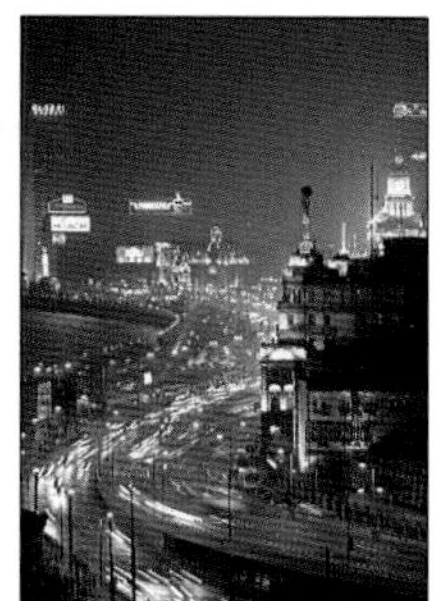

Booming Cities

Since the 1980s the Chinese government has set up special industrial zones, such as Shanghai, where foreign investment is encouraged through tax incentives. Migrants from rural China pour into these regions in search of work, creating "boomtown" economies.

***Foreign investment** has encouraged new infrastructure development in cities like Shanghai.*

Urban Sprawl

Cities are expanding all over the developing world, attracting economic migrants in search of work and opportunities. In cities such as Rio de Janeiro, housing has not kept pace with the population explosion, and squalid shanty towns *(favelas)* rub shoulders with middle-class housing.

***The favelas of Rio de Janeiro** sprawl over the hills surrounding the city.*

Comparative World Wealth

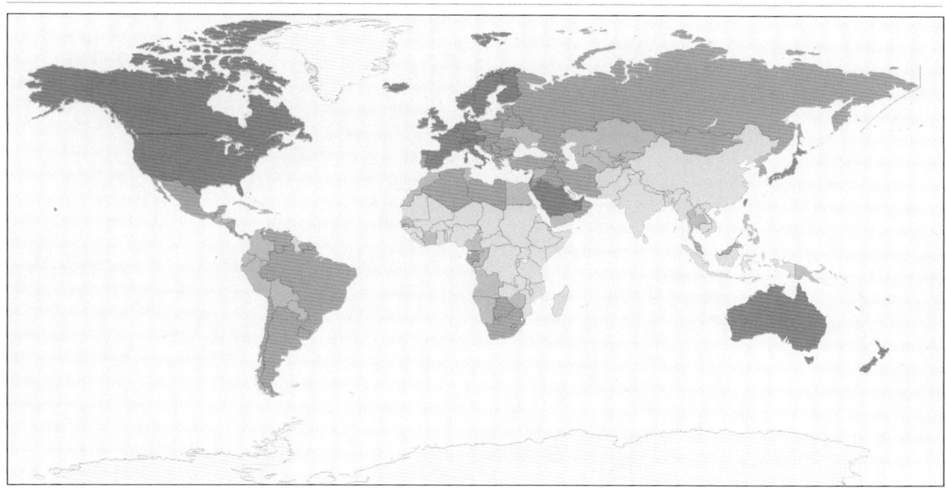

World economies
- high income
- upper-middle income
- lower-middle income
- low income
- data unavailable

Economic "Tigers"

The economic "tigers" of the Pacific Rim – Taiwan, Singapore, and South Korea – have grown faster than Europe and the US over the last decade. Their export- and service-led economies have benefited from stable government, low labor costs, and foreign investment.

***Hong Kong**, with its fine natural harbor, is one of the most important ports in Asia.*

Agricultural Economies

In parts of the developing world, people survive by subsistence farming – only growing enough food for themselves and their families. With no surplus product, they are unable to exchange goods for currency, the only means of escaping the poverty trap. In other countries, farmers have been encouraged to concentrate on growing a single crop for the export market. This reliance on cash crops leaves farmers vulnerable to crop failure and to changes in the market price of the crop.

***The Ugandan uplands** are fertile, but poor infrastructure hampers the export of cash crops.*

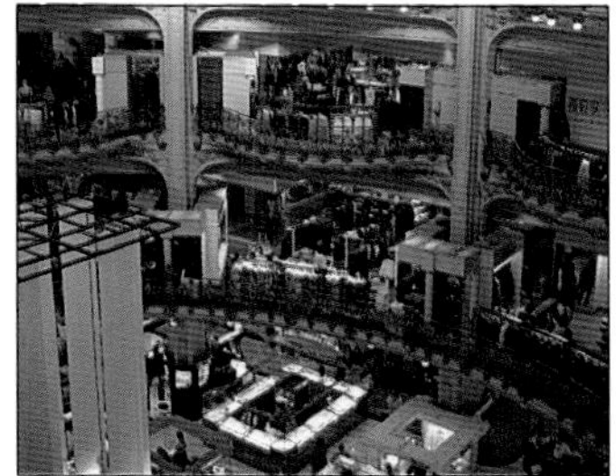

***A shopping arcade** in Paris displays a great profusion of luxury goods.*

The Affluent West

The capital cities of many countries in the developed world are showcases for consumer goods, reflecting the increasing importance of the service sector, and particularly the retail sector, in the world economy. The idea of shopping as a leisure activity is unique to the western world. Luxury goods and services attract visitors, who in turn generate tourist revenue.

Tourism

In 1995, there were 567 million tourists worldwide. Tourism is now the world's biggest single industry, employing 127 million people, though frequently in low-paid unskilled jobs. While tourists are increasingly exploring inaccessible and less-developed regions of the world, the benefits of the industry are not always felt at a local level. There are also worries about the environmental impact of tourism, as the world's last wildernesses increasingly become tourist attractions.

***Botswana's Okavango Delta** is an area rich in wildlife. Tourists go on safaris to the region, but the impact of tourism is controlled.*

Money Flows

Foreign investment in the developing world during the 1970s led to a global financial crisis in the 1980s, when many countries were unable to meet their debt repayments. The International Monetary Fund (IMF) was forced to reschedule the debts and, in some cases, write them off completely. Within the developing world, austerity programs have been initiated to cope with the debt, leading in turn to high unemployment and galloping inflation. In many parts of Africa, stricken economies are now dependent on international aid.

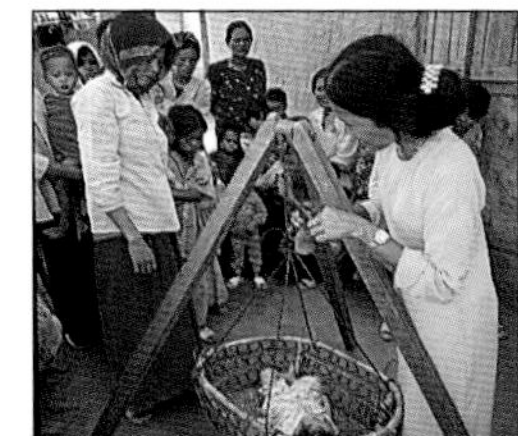

***In rural Southeast Asia**, babies are given medical checks by UNICEF as part of a global aid program sponsored by the UN.*

Tourist Arrivals

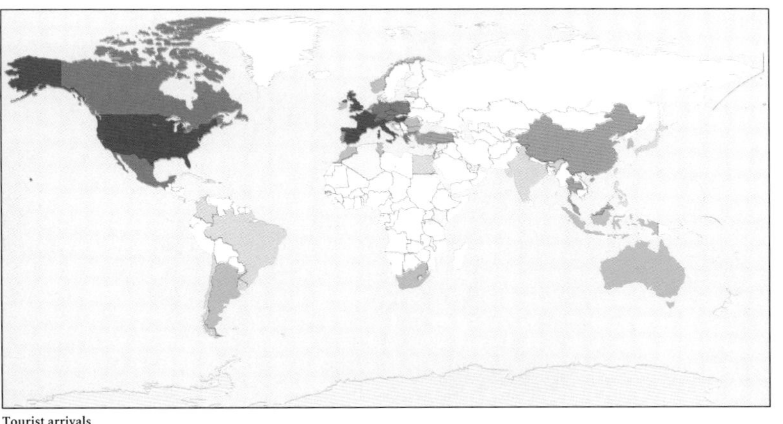

Tourist arrivals
- over 20 million
- 10–20 million
- 5–10 million
- 2.5–5 million
- 1–2.5 million
- 700,000–999,000
- under 700,000
- data unavailable

International Debt: Donors and Receivers

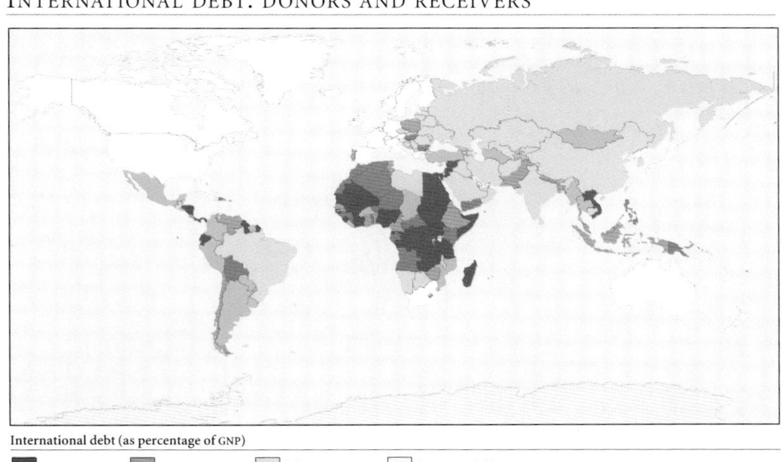

International debt (as percentage of GNP)
- over 100%
- 70–90%
- 50–69%
- 30–49%
- below 30
- negligible
- data unavailable

The Political World

There are 192 independent countries in the world today. With the exception of Antarctica, where territorial claims have been deferred by international treaty, every land area of the Earth's surface either belongs to, or is claimed by, one country or another. The largest country in the world is the Russian Federation, the smallest is Vatican City. Some 60 overseas dependent territories remain, administered variously by France, Australia, Denmark, New Zealand, Norway, Portugal, the UK, the US, and the Netherlands.

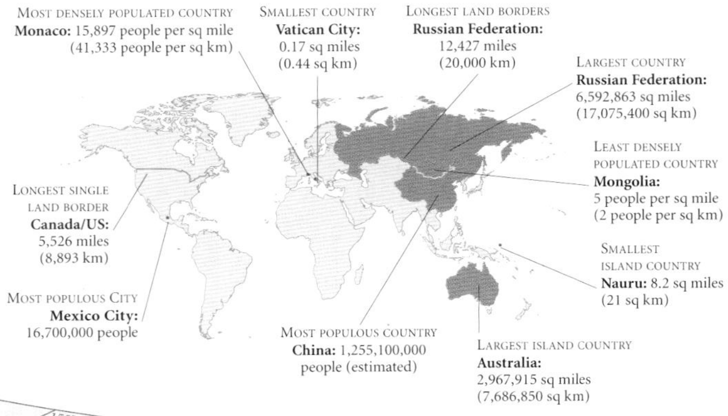

Most densely populated country
Monaco: 15,897 people per sq mile (41,333 people per sq km)

Smallest country
Vatican City: 0.17 sq miles (0.44 sq km)

Longest land borders
Russian Federation: 12,427 miles (20,000 km)

Largest country
Russian Federation: 6,592,863 sq miles (17,075,400 sq km)

Least densely populated country
Mongolia: 5 people per sq mile (2 people per sq km)

Smallest island country
Nauru: 8.2 sq miles (21 sq km)

Longest single land border
Canada/US: 5,526 miles (8,893 km)

Most populous city
Mexico City: 16,700,000 people

Most populous country
China: 1,255,100,000 people (estimated)

Largest island country
Australia: 2,967,915 sq miles (7,686,850 sq km)

International Borders

The map shows three main types of boundary between states. Full borders represent internationally agreed and recognized territorial boundaries. Undefined borders exist where no fixed boundary between states has been demarcated; the boundaries indicated in this way show approximate areas of sovereignty. A disputed border is indicated where a *de facto* territorial boundary exists, which is not agreed or is subject to arbitration.

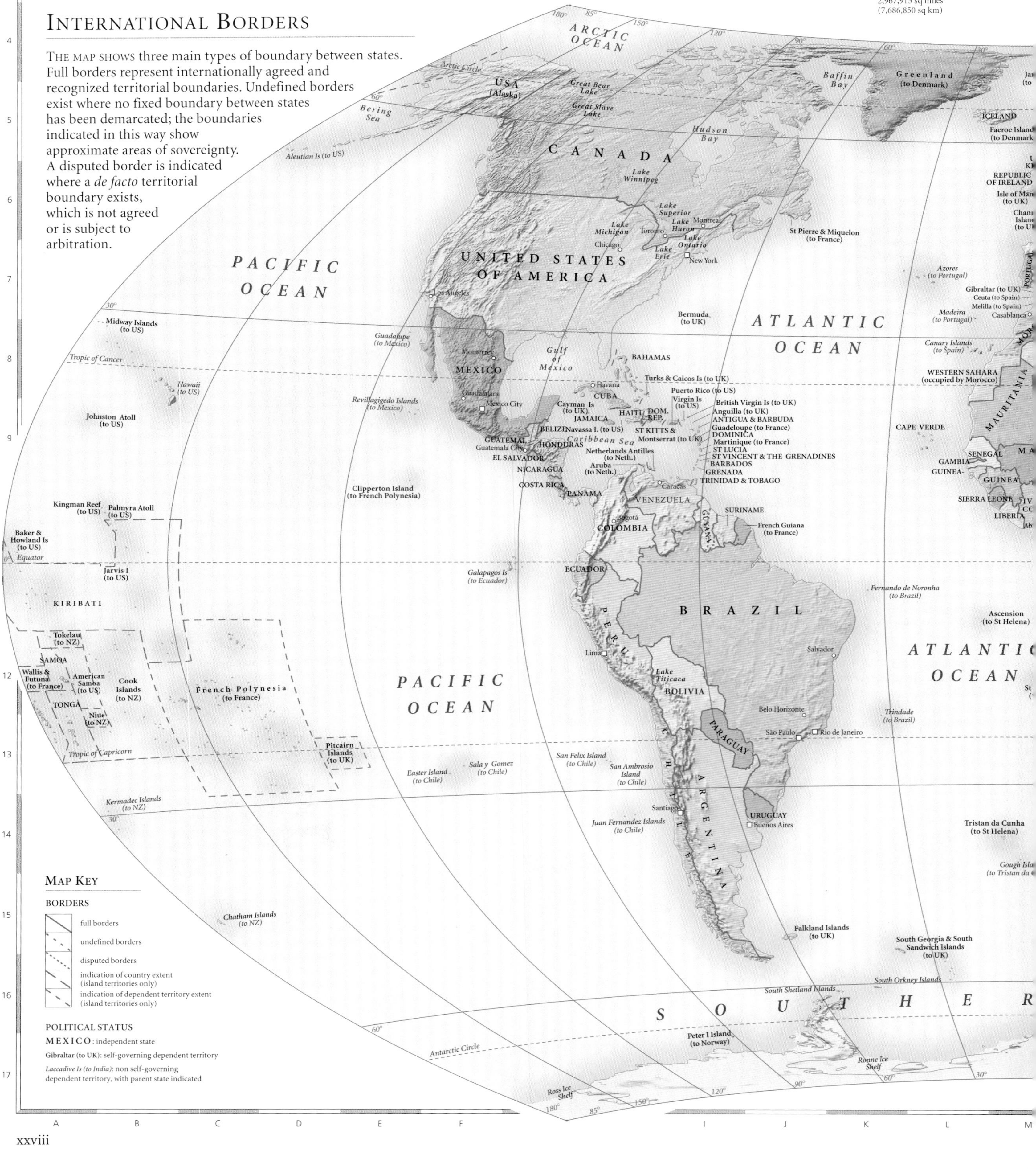

Map Key

BORDERS

- full borders
- undefined borders
- disputed borders
- indication of country extent (island territories only)
- indication of dependent territory extent (island territories only)

POLITICAL STATUS

MEXICO: independent state

Gibraltar (to UK): self-governing dependent territory

Laccadive Is (to India): non self-governing dependent territory, with parent state indicated

The World in 1914

The early years of the 20th century saw the mainly European colonial empires reaching their greatest extents by 1914. Two world wars inaugurated their disintegration, but even in 1950 there were only 82 independent countries. Since then, over 100 have gained their independence, culminating in the breakup of the Soviet Union and former Yugoslavia in the early 1990s.

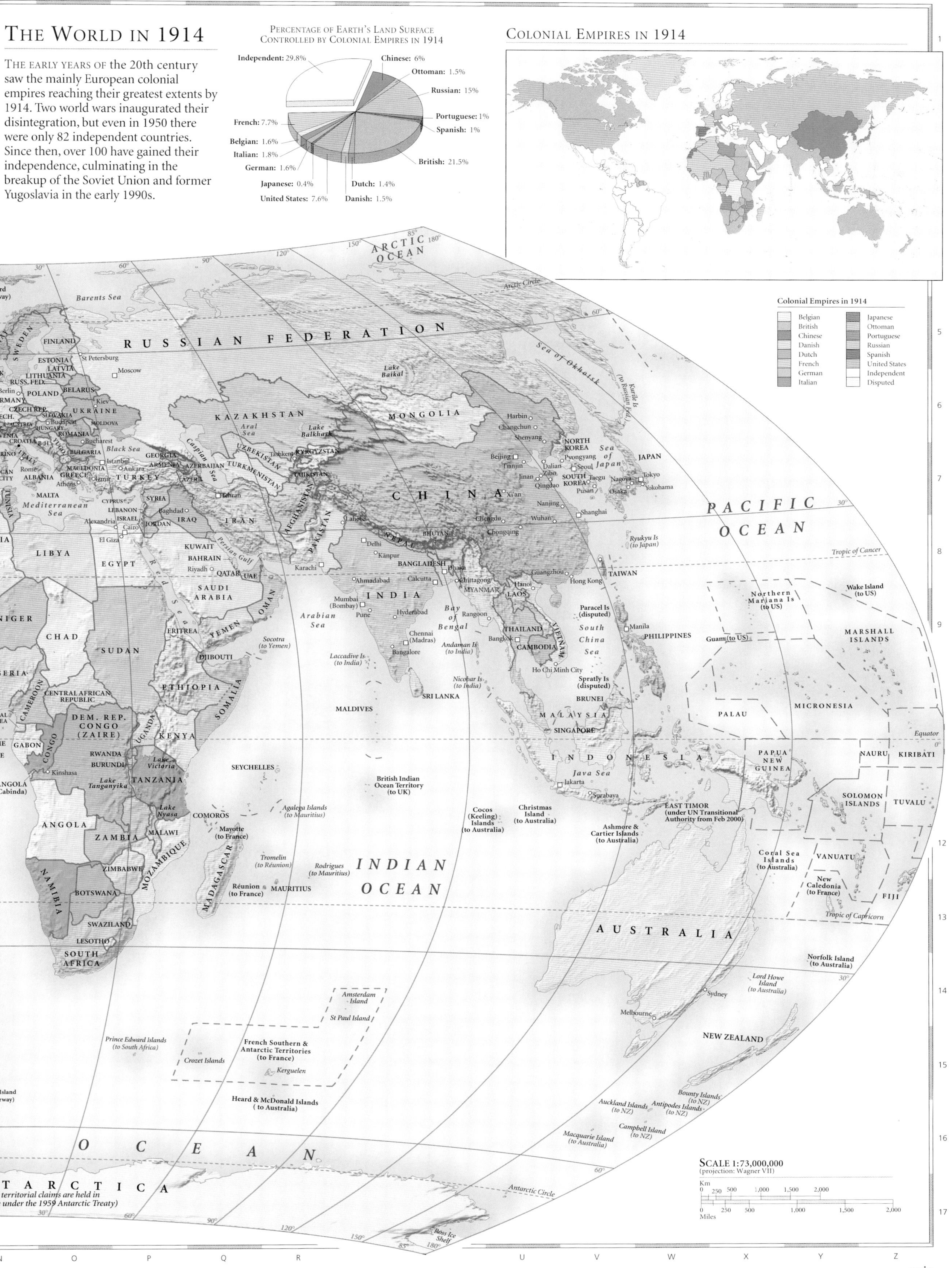

N O P Q R S T U V W X Y Z
Percentage of Earth's Land Surface Controlled by Colonial Empires in 1914
Independent: 29.8%
Chinese: 6%
Ottoman: 1.5%
Russian: 15%
Portuguese: 1%
Spanish: 1%
British: 21.5%
French: 7.7%
Belgian: 1.6%
Italian: 1.8%
German: 1.6%
Japanese: 0.4%
United States: 7.6%
Dutch: 1.4%
Danish: 1.5%
Colonial Empires in 1914
Colonial Empires in 1914
Belgian
British
Chinese
Danish
Dutch
French
German
Italian
Japanese
Ottoman
Portuguese
Russian
Spanish
United States
Independent
Disputed
1
5
6
7
8
9
12
13
14
15
16
17
ARCTIC OCEAN
Arctic Circle
Barents Sea
RUSSIAN FEDERATION
FINLAND
SWEDEN
ESTONIA
LATVIA
LITHUANIA
RUSS. FED.
St Petersburg
Moscow
POLAND
BELARUS
Berlin
Kiev
UKRAINE
CZECH REP.
SLOVAKIA
AUSTRIA
HUNGARY
Budapest
MOLDOVA
ROMANIA
CROATIA
B.-H.
YUGO.
Bucharest
BULGARIA
Black Sea
ITALY
Rome
MACEDONIA
ALBANIA
GREECE
Athens
Istanbul
Ankara
Izmir
TURKEY
GEORGIA
ARMENIA
AZERBAIJAN
AZERB.
MALTA
Mediterranean Sea
TUNISIA
CYPRUS
SYRIA
LEBANON
ISRAEL
Baghdad
IRAQ
JORDAN
Alexandria
Cairo
El Giza
LIBYA
EGYPT
Tehran
IRAN
KUWAIT
BAHRAIN
Persian Gulf
Riyadh
QATAR
UAE
SAUDI ARABIA
OMAN
YEMEN
Red Sea
KAZAKHSTAN
Aral Sea
Caspian Sea
UZBEKISTAN
TURKMENISTAN
Lake Balkhash
Tashkent
KYRGYZSTAN
TAJIKISTAN
AFGHANISTAN
PAKISTAN
Lahore
Delhi
Kanpur
NEPAL
BHUTAN
BANGLADESH
Dhaka
Karachi
Ahmadabad
Calcutta
Chittagong
INDIA
Mumbai (Bombay)
Pune
Hyderabad
Arabian Sea
Bay of Bengal
Chennai (Madras)
Bangalore
Laccadive Is (to India)
Andaman Is (to India)
Nicobar Is (to India)
SRI LANKA
MALDIVES
Socotra (to Yemen)
Lake Baikal
MONGOLIA
CHINA
Harbin
Changchun
Shenyang
Beijing
Tianjin
Dalian
Jinan
Zibo
Qingdao
Xi'an
Nanjing
Shanghai
Wuhan
Chengdu
Chongqing
Guangzhou
Hong Kong
TAIWAN
NORTH KOREA
Pyongyang
Seoul
SOUTH KOREA
Taegu
Pusan
Sea of Japan
JAPAN
Nagoya
Tokyo
Yokohama
Osaka
Sea of Okhotsk
Kurile Is (to Russian Fed.)
Ryukyu Is (to Japan)
MYANMAR
Rangoon
Hanoi
LAOS
THAILAND
Bangkok
CAMBODIA
VIETNAM
Ho Chi Minh City
Paracel Is (disputed)
South China Sea
Spratly Is (disputed)
Manila
PHILIPPINES
BRUNEI
MALAYSIA
SINGAPORE
INDONESIA
Java Sea
Jakarta
Surabaya
EAST TIMOR (under UN Transitional Authority from Feb 2000)
Ashmore & Cartier Islands (to Australia)
Christmas Island (to Australia)
Cocos (Keeling) Islands (to Australia)
PACIFIC OCEAN
Tropic of Cancer
Northern Mariana Is (to US)
Wake Island (to US)
Guam (to US)
MARSHALL ISLANDS
PALAU
MICRONESIA
Equator
PAPUA NEW GUINEA
NAURU
KIRIBATI
SOLOMON ISLANDS
TUVALU
VANUATU
Coral Sea Islands (to Australia)
New Caledonia (to France)
FIJI
Tropic of Capricorn
AUSTRALIA
Norfolk Island (to Australia)
Lord Howe Island (to Australia)
Sydney
Melbourne
NEW ZEALAND
Bounty Islands (to NZ)
Antipodes Islands (to NZ)
Auckland Islands (to NZ)
Campbell Island (to NZ)
Macquarie Island (to Australia)
NIGER
CHAD
SUDAN
ERITREA
DJIBOUTI
ETHIOPIA
SOMALIA
CAMEROON
CENTRAL AFRICAN REPUBLIC
GABON
CONGO
DEM. REP. CONGO (ZAIRE)
UGANDA
KENYA
RWANDA
BURUNDI
Lake Victoria
TANZANIA
Kinshasa
Lake Tanganyika
ANGOLA (Cabinda)
ANGOLA
Lake Nyasa
ZAMBIA
MALAWI
MOZAMBIQUE
ZIMBABWE
NAMIBIA
BOTSWANA
SWAZILAND
LESOTHO
SOUTH AFRICA
COMOROS
Mayotte (to France)
MADAGASCAR
SEYCHELLES
Agalega Islands (to Mauritius)
Tromelin (to Réunion)
Rodrigues (to Mauritius)
Réunion (to France)
MAURITIUS
British Indian Ocean Territory (to UK)
INDIAN OCEAN
Amsterdam Island
St Paul Island
Prince Edward Islands (to South Africa)
French Southern & Antarctic Territories (to France)
Crozet Islands
Kerguelen
Heard & McDonald Islands (to Australia)
OCEAN
ANTARCTICA
All territorial claims are held in abeyance under the 1959 Antarctic Treaty
Antarctic Circle
Ross Ice Shelf
SCALE 1:73,000,000
(projection: Wagner VII)
Km
0 250 500 1,000 1,500 2,000
0 250 500 1,000 1,500 2,000
Miles

States and Boundaries

There are over 190 sovereign states in the world today; in 1950 there were only 82. Over the last half-century national self-determination has been a driving force for many states with a history of colonialism and oppression. As more borders are added to the world map, the number of international border disputes increases.

In many cases, where the impetus toward independence has been religious or ethnic, disputes with minority groups have also caused violent internal conflict. While many newly-formed states have moved peacefully toward independence, successfully establishing government by multi-party democracy, dictatorship by military regime or individual despot is often the result of the internal power-struggles which characterize the early stages in the lives of new nations.

The Nature of Politics

Democracy is a broad term: it can range from the ideal of multiparty elections and fair representation to, in countries such as Singapore and Indonesia, a thin disguise for single-party rule. In despotic regimes, on the other hand, a single, often personal authority has total power; institutions such as parliament and the military are mere instruments of the dictator.

The stars and stripes of the US flag are a potent symbol of the country's status as a federal democracy.

The Changing World Map

Decolonization

In 1950, large areas of the world remained under the control of a handful of European countries (*page xxviii*). The process of decolonization had begun in Asia, where, following World WarII, much of southern and southeastern Asia sought and achieved self-determination. In the 1960s, a host of African states achieved independence, so that by 1965, most of the larger tracts of the European overseas empires had been substantially eroded. The final major stage in decolonization came with the breakup of the Soviet Union and the Eastern bloc after 1990. The process continues today as the last toeholds of European colonialism, often tiny island nations, press increasingly for independence.

Icons of communism, including statues of former leaders such as Lenin and Stalin, were destroyed when the Soviet bloc was dismantled in 1989, creating several new nations.

New nations 1945–1965

New nations 1965–1996

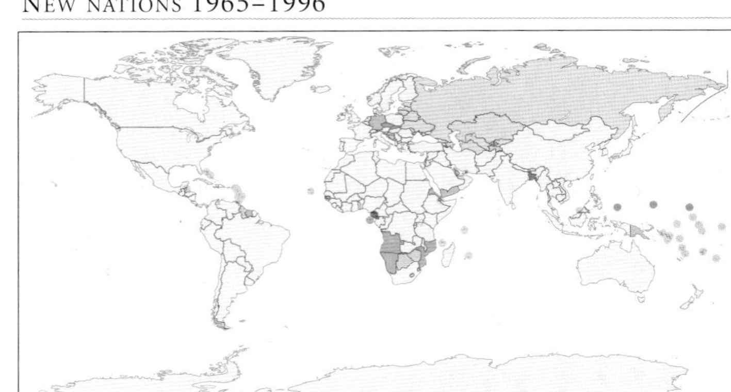

Administration at the time of independence

- Australia
- Aust/NZ/UK
- Belgium
- China
- Czechoslovakia
- Egypt/UK
- Ethiopia
- France
- France/UK
- Italy
- Japan
- Malaysia
- Netherlands
- New Zealand
- Pakistan
- Portugal
- South Africa
- Spain
- UK
- Unified country
- USA
- USSR
- Yugoslavia

Iran is one of the world's true theocracies; Islam has an impact on every aspect of political life.

North Korea is an independent communist republic. Power is concentrated in the hands of Kim Jong Il.

Saddam Hussein overthrew his predecessor in 1979. Since then he has promoted an extreme personality cult, with autocratic control over 21.8 million Iraqis.

South Africa became a democracy in 1994, when elections ended over a century of white minority rule.

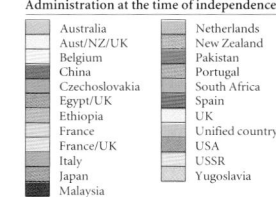

In Brunei the Sultan has ruled by decree since 1962; power is closely tied to the royal family. The Sultan's brothers are responsible for finance and foreign affairs.

Types of government

- Multiparty democracy for more than 10 yrs
- Multiparty/transitional democracy within last 10 yrs
- Single-party government
- Military regime
- Theocracy
- Absolute monarchy
- Current civil unrest

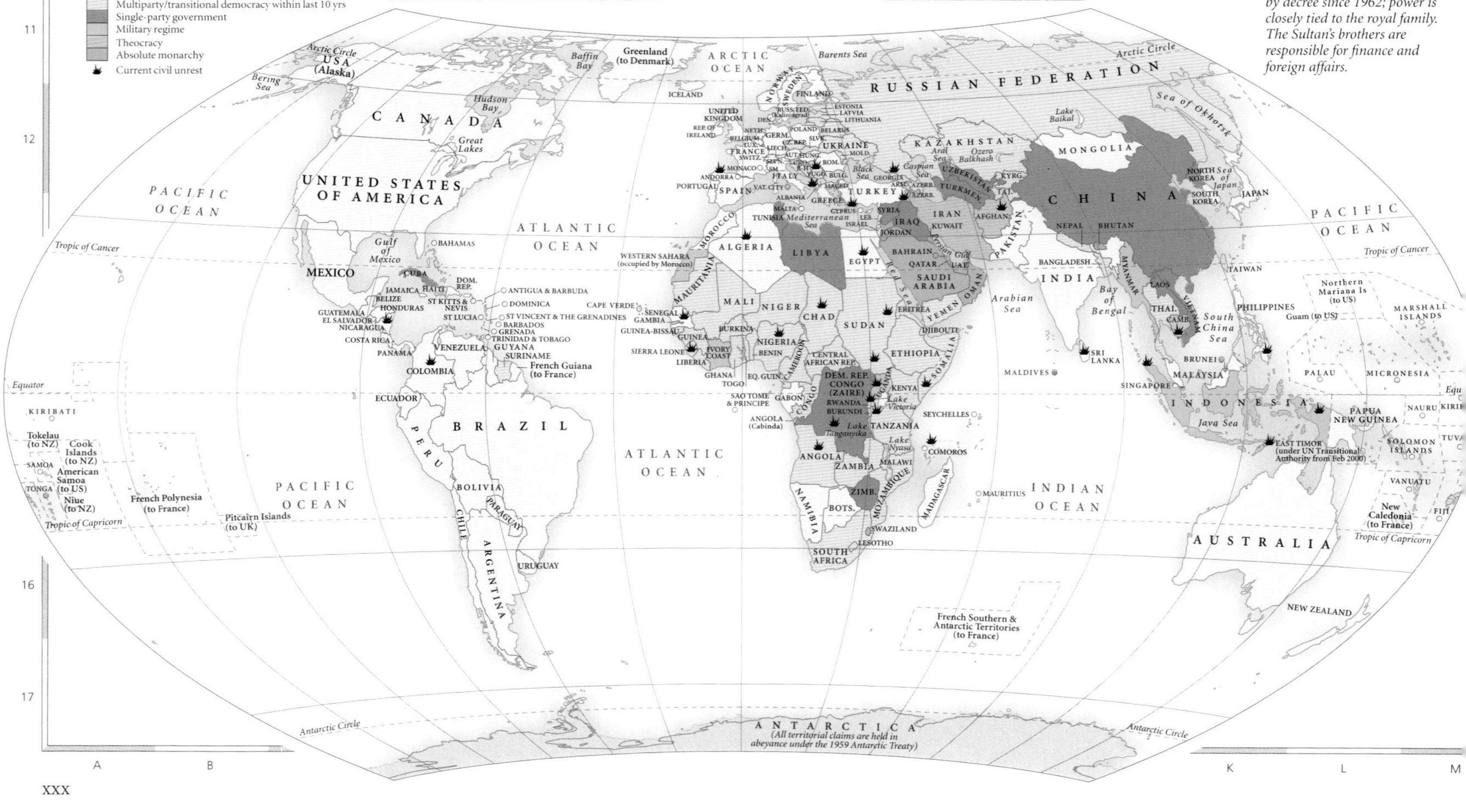

Lines on the Map

The determination of international boundaries can use a variety of criteria. Many of the borders between older states follow physical boundaries; some mirror religious and ethnic differences; others are the legacy of complex histories of conflict and colonialism, while others have been imposed by international agreements or arbitration.

Post-colonial borders

When the European colonial empires in Africa were dismantled during the second half of the 20th century, the outlines of the new African states mirrored colonial boundaries. These boundaries had been drawn up by colonial administrators, often based on inadequate geographical knowledge. Such arbitrary boundaries were imposed on people of different languages, racial groups, religions, and customs. This confused legacy often led to civil and international war.

WESTERN SAHARA
ALGERIA
MAURITANIA
MALI

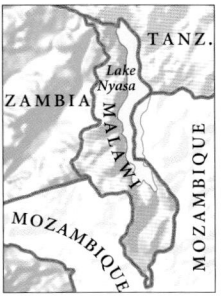

The conflict that has plagued many African countries since independence has caused millions of people to become refugees.

Physical borders

Many of the world's countries are divided by physical borders: lakes, rivers, mountains. The demarcation of such boundaries can, however, lead to disputes. Control of waterways, water supplies, and fisheries are frequent causes of international friction.

Enclaves

The shifting political map over the course of history has frequently led to anomalous situations. Parts of national territories may become isolated by territorial agreement, forming an enclave. The West German part of the city of Berlin, which until 1989 lay several hundred miles within East German territory, was a famous example.

Baltic Sea
ESTONIA
RUSSIAN FEDERATION
LATVIA
LITHUANIA
RUSS. FED. (Kaliningrad)
BELARUS
POLAND

Since the independence of Lithuania and Belarus, the peoples of the Russian enclave of Kaliningrad have become physically isolated.

Antarctica

When Antarctic exploration began a century ago, seven nations, Australia, Argentina, Britain, Chile, France, New Zealand, and Norway, laid claim to the new territory. In 1961 the Antarctic Treaty, signed by 39 nations, agreed to hold all territorial claims in abeyance.

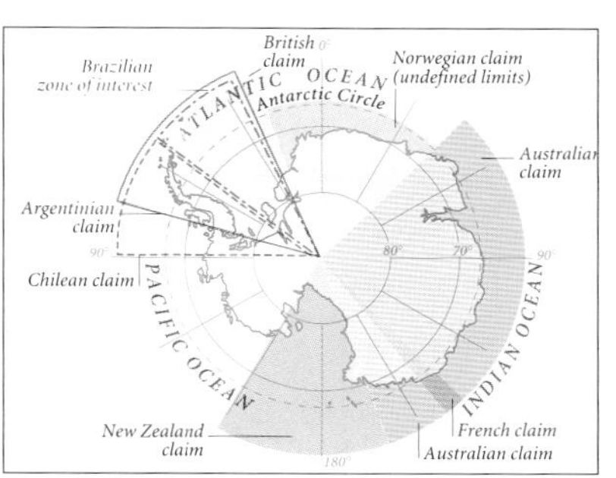
Brazilian zone of interest
British claim
Norwegian claim (undefined limits)
ATLANTIC OCEAN
Antarctic Circle
Australian claim
Argentinian claim
Chilean claim
PACIFIC OCEAN
INDIAN OCEAN
New Zealand claim
French claim
Australian claim

Geometric borders

Straight lines and lines of longitude and latitude have occasionally been used to determine international boundaries; and indeed the world's longest international boundary, between Canada and the USA follows the 49th Parallel for over one-third of its course. Many Canadian, American and Australian internal administrative boundaries are similarly determined using a geometric solution.

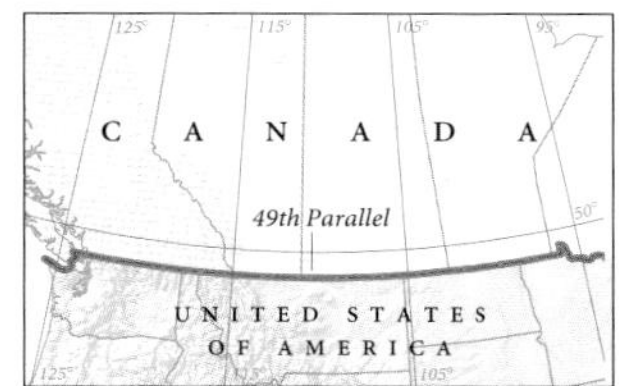
CANADA
49th Parallel
UNITED STATES OF AMERICA

Different farming techniques in Canada and the US clearly mark the course of the international boundary in this satellite map.

World boundaries

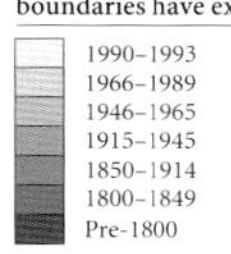
Dates from which current boundaries have existed
1990–1993
1966–1989
1946–1965
1915–1945
1850–1914
1800–1849
Pre-1800

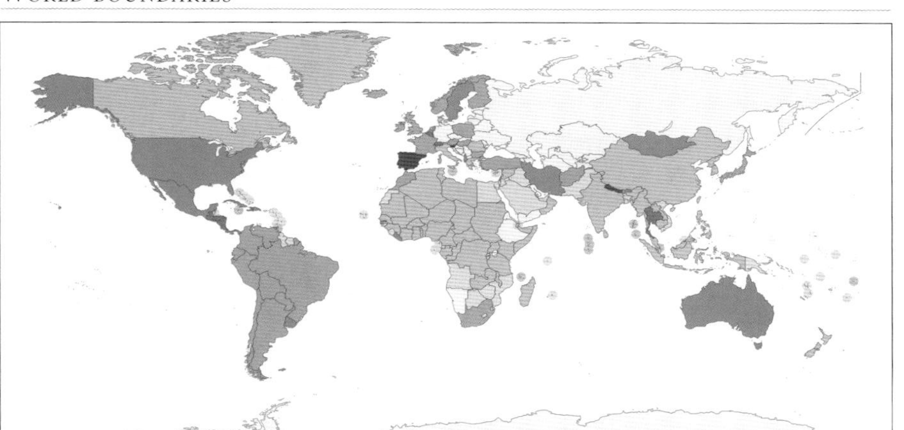

Lake borders

Countries which lie next to lakes usually fix their borders in the middle of the lake. Unusually the Lake Nyasa border between Malawi and Tanzania runs along Tanzania's shore.

TANZ.
Lake Nyasa
ZAMBIA
MALAWI
MOZAMBIQUE
MOZAMBIQUE

Complicated agreements between colonial powers led to the awkward division of Lake Nyasa.

River borders

Rivers alone account for one-sixth of the world's borders. Many great rivers form boundaries between a number of countries. Changes in a river's course and interruptions of its natural flow can lead to disputes, particularly in areas where water is scarce. The center of the river's course is the nominal boundary line.

GERMANY
Danube
UKRAINE
SLOVAKIA
AUSTRIA
HUNGARY
ROMANIA
CROATIA
Danube
YUGOSLAVIA
BULGARIA

The Danube forms all or part of the border between nine European nations.

Mountain borders

Mountain ranges form natural barriers and are the basis for many major borders, particularly in Europe and Asia. The watershed is the conventional boundary demarcation line, but its accurate determination is often problematic.

FRANCE
Pyrenees
ANDORRA
SPAIN

The Pyrenees form a natural mountain border between France and Spain.

Shifting boundaries – Poland

Borders between countries can change dramatically over time. The nations of eastern Europe have been particularly affected by changing boundaries. Poland is an example of a country whose boundaries have changed so significantly that it has literally moved around Europe. At the start of the 16th century, Poland was the largest nation in Europe. Between 1772 and 1795, it was absorbed into Prussia, Austria, and Russia, and it effectively ceased to exist. After World War I, Poland became an independent country once more, but its borders changed again after World War II following invasions by both Soviet Russia and Nazi Germany.

Moscow
POLAND
Warsaw
Kiev
In 1634, Poland was the largest nation in Europe, its eastern boundary reaching toward Moscow.

Moscow
PRUSSIA
Warsaw
RUSSIA
Kiev
AUSTRIA
From 1772–1795, Poland was gradually partitioned between Austria, Russia, and Prussia. Its eastern boundary receded by over 100 miles (160 km).

Moscow
POLAND
Warsaw
Kiev
Following World War I, Poland was reinstated as an independent state, but it was less than half the size it had been in 1634.

Moscow
POLAND
Warsaw
Kiev
After World War II, the Baltic Sea border was extended westward, but much of the eastern territory was annexed by Russia.

International disputes

There are more than 60 disputed borders or territories in the world today. Although many of these disputes can be settled by peaceful negotiation, some areas have become a focus for international conflict. Ethnic tensions have been a major source of territorial disagreement throughout history, as has the ownership of, and access to, valuable natural resources. The turmoil of the postcolonial era in many parts of Africa is partly a result of the 19th century "carve-up" of the continent, which created potential for conflict by drawing often arbitrary lines through linguistic and cultural areas.

Jammu and Kashmir

Disputes over Jammu and Kashmir have caused three serious wars between India and Pakistan since 1947. Pakistan wishes to annex the largely Muslim territory, while India refuses to cede any territory or to hold a referendum, and also lays claim to the entire territory. Most international maps show the "line of control" agreed in 1972 as the *de facto* border. In addition, both Pakistan and India have territorial disputes with neighboring China. The situation is further complicated by a Kashmiri independence movement, active since the late 1980s.

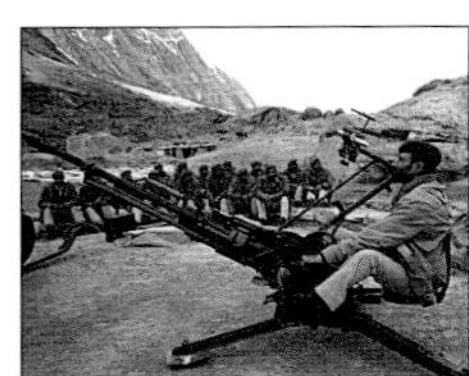

Indian army troops *maintain their positions in the mountainous terrain of northern Kashmir.*

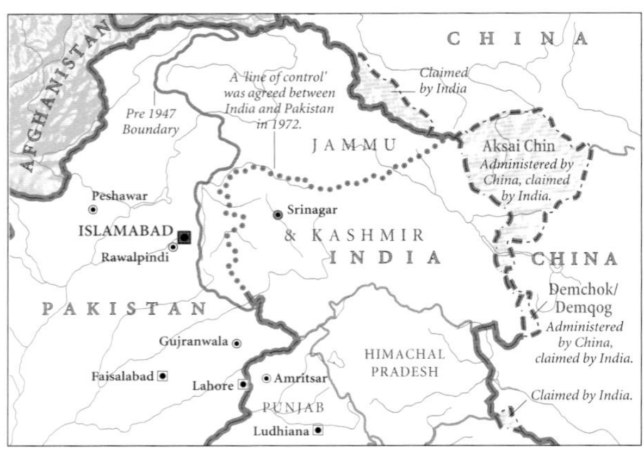

CHINA
AFGHANISTAN
Pre 1947 Boundary
A 'line of control' was agreed between India and Pakistan in 1972.
Claimed by India
JAMMU
& KASHMIR
Aksai Chin
Administered by China, claimed by India.
Peshawar
ISLAMABAD
Rawalpindi
Srinagar
INDIA
CHINA
Demchok/ Demqog
Administered by China, claimed by India.
PAKISTAN
Gujranwala
Faisalabad
Lahore
Amritsar
HIMACHAL PRADESH
PUNJAB
Ludhiana
Claimed by India.

North and South Korea

Since 1953, the *de facto* border between North and South Korea has been a ceasefire line which straddles the 38th Parallel and is designated as a demilitarized zone. Both countries have heavy fortifications and troop concentrations behind this zone.

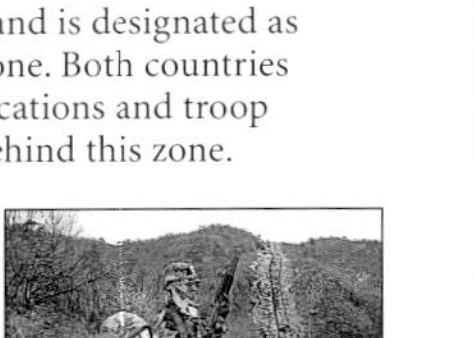

Heavy fortifications *on the border between North and South Korea.*

Cyprus

Cyprus was partitioned in 1974, following an invasion by Turkish troops. The south is now the Greek Cypriot Republic of Cyprus, while the self-proclaimed Turkish Republic of Northern Cyprus is recognized only by Turkey.

FREEDOM FOR CY

The so-called 'green line' *divides Cyprus into Greek and Turkish sectors.*

TURKISH REPUBLIC OF NORTHERN CYPRUS
Mediterranean Sea
Kyrenia Mountains
Karpasia
NICOSIA
CYPRUS
Troödos
UK Sovereign Base Area
Lárnaka
UK Sovereign Base Area
Lemesós (Limassol)
Mediterranean Sea

Disputed territories and borders

- Countries involved in active territorial or border disputes
- Disputed borders
- Undefined borders
- Disputed territories

The Falkland Islands

The British Dependent Territory of the Falkland Islands was invaded by Argentina in 1982, sparking a full-scale war with the UK. In 1995, the UK and Argentina reached an agreement on the exploitation of oil reserves around the islands.

***British** warships in Falkland Sound during the 1982 war with Argentina.*

Israel

Israel was created in 1948 following the 1947 UN Resolution (147) on Palestine. Until 1979 Israel had no borders, only ceasefire lines from a series of wars in 1948, 1967 and 1973. Treaties with Egypt in 1979 and Jordan in 1994 led to these borders being defined and agreed. Negotiations over Israeli settlements in disputed territories such as the West Bank, and the issue of self-government for the Palestinians, continue.

- Israeli settlement
- Major settlement
- Palestinian settlement
- Area under Palestinian control

Barbed-wire fences *surround a settlement in the Golan Heights.*

Yugoslavia

Following the disintegration in 1991 of the communist state of Yugoslavia, the breakaway states of Croatia and Bosnia-Herzegovina came into conflict with the "parent" state (consisting of Serbia and Montenegro). Warfare focused on ethnic and territorial ambitions in Bosnia. The tenuous Dayton Accord of 1995 sought to recognize the post-1990 borders, whilst providing for ethnic partition and required international peace-keeping troops to maintain the terms of the peace.

CROATIA
Sava
Bihać
Brčko
SERBIA
Banja Luka
Tuzla
Jajce
BOSNIA-
HERZEGOVINA
Srebrenica
Drina
Gornji Vakuf
Goražde
Split
SARAJEVO
Mostar
YUGOSLAVIA
Adriatic Sea
Dubrovnik
MONTENEGRO
Republika Srpska
Federacija Bosna i Hercegovina

The Spratly Islands

The site of potential oil and natural gas reserves, the Spratly Islands in the South China Sea have been claimed by China, Vietnam, Taiwan, Malaysia, and the Philippines since the Japanese gave up a wartime claim in 1951.

***Most claimant** states have small military garrisons on the Spratly Islands.*

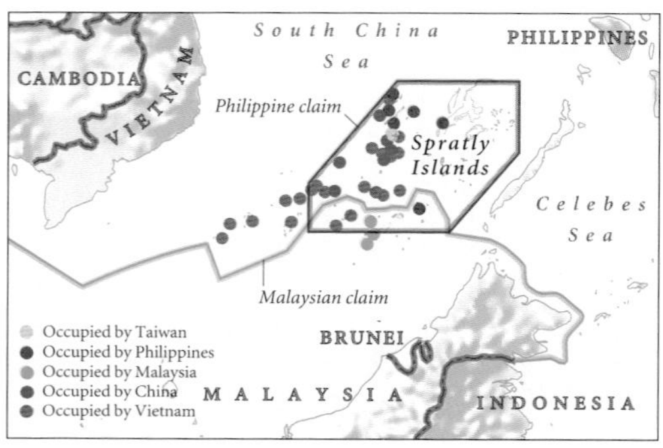

South China Sea
PHILIPPINES
CAMBODIA
VIETNAM
Philippine claim
Spratly Islands
Celebes Sea
Malaysian claim
BRUNEI
Occupied by Taiwan
Occupied by Philippines
Occupied by Malaysia
Occupied by China
Occupied by Vietnam
MALAYSIA
INDONESIA

ATLAS OF THE WORLD

The maps in this atlas are arranged continent by continent, starting from the International Date Line, and moving eastward. The maps provide a unique view of today's world, combining traditional cartographic techniques with the latest remote-sensed and digital technology.

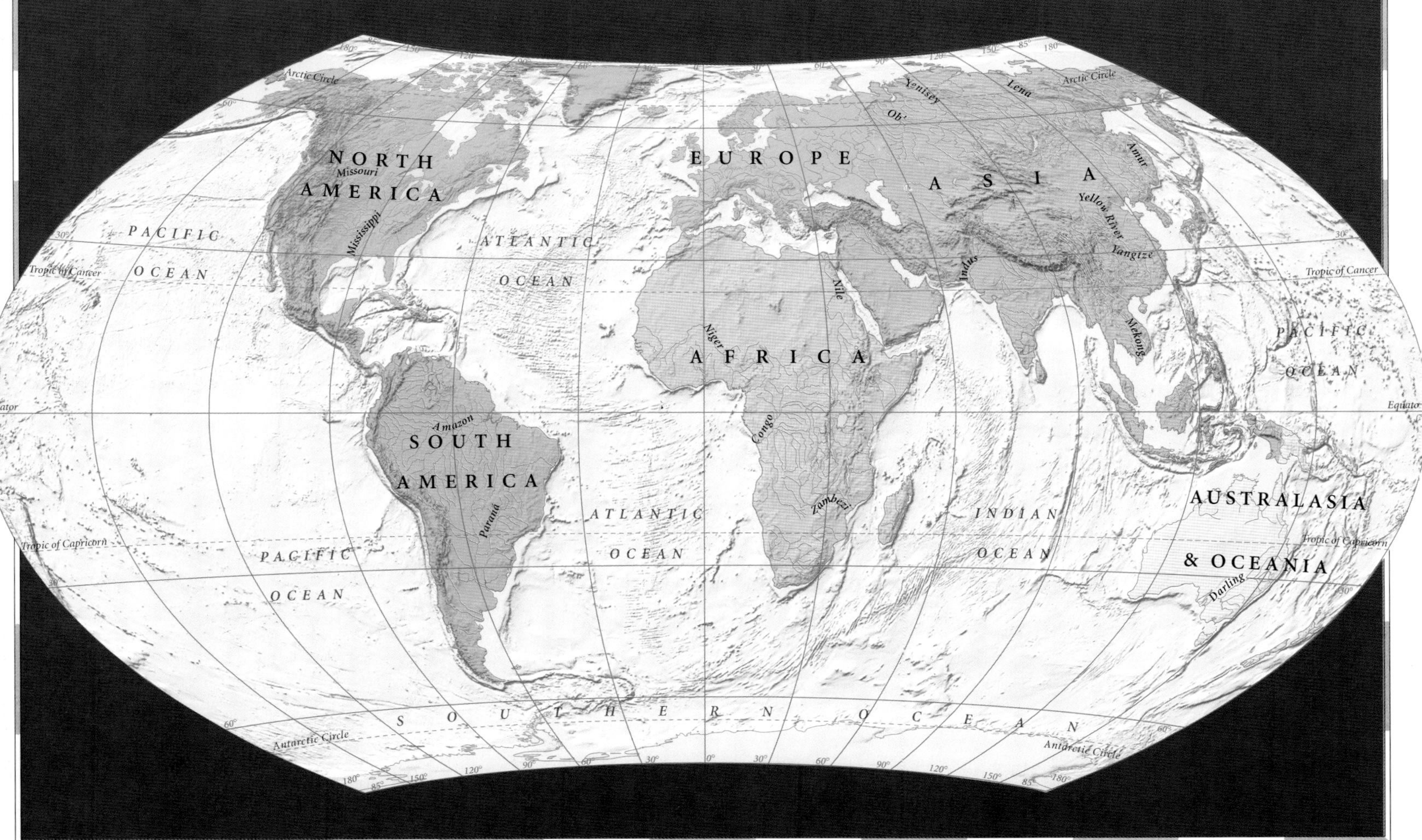

Arctic Circle
NORTH AMERICA
Missouri
Mississippi
PACIFIC OCEAN
Tropic of Cancer
ATLANTIC OCEAN
EUROPE
ASIA
Yenisey
Ob'
Lena
Amur
Yellow River
Yangtze
Indus
Mekong
Nile
Niger
AFRICA
Congo
Zambezi
Equator
SOUTH AMERICA
Amazon
Paraná
ATLANTIC OCEAN
INDIAN OCEAN
PACIFIC OCEAN
AUSTRALASIA & OCEANIA
Darling
Tropic of Capricorn
SOUTHERN OCEAN
Antarctic Circle

A B C D E F G H I J K L

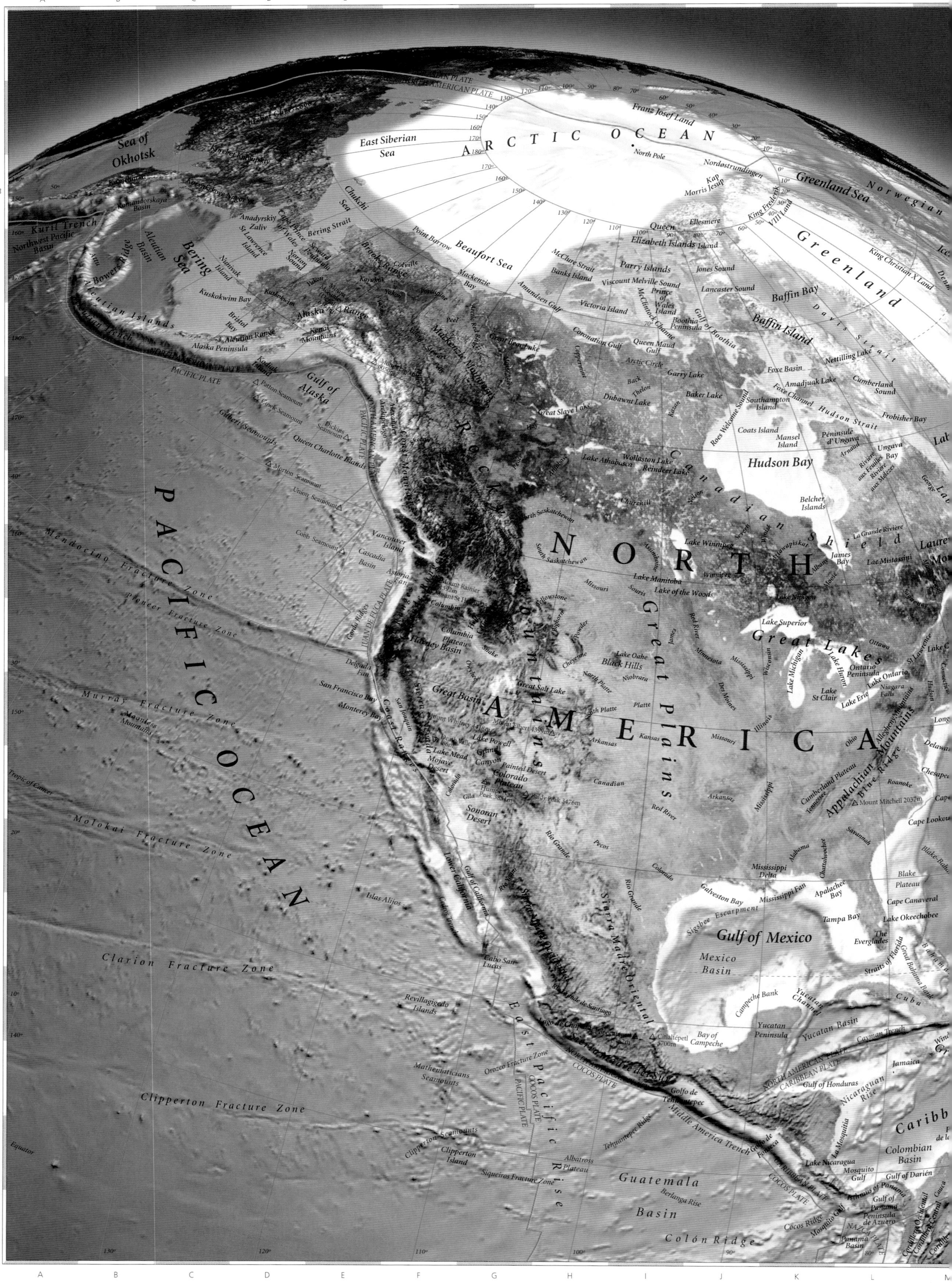

1 2 3 4 5 6 7 8 9 10 11 12 13 14 15 16 17

ARCTIC OCEAN
North Pole
Franz Josef Land
East Siberian Sea
Sea of Okhotsk
Nordøstrundingen
Kap Morris Jesup
Greenland Sea
Norwegian
Greenland
King Frederik VIII Land
King Christian X Land
Chukchi Sea
Beaufort Sea
Point Barrow
Queen Elizabeth Islands
Ellesmere Island
Anadyrskiy Zaliv
Bering Strait
Kuril Trench
Northwest Pacific Basin
Komandorskaya Basin
Aleutian Basin
Bering Sea
Bowers Ridge
St Lawrence Island
Nunivak Island
Seward Peninsula
Norton Sound
Brooks Range
Colville
Yukon
Kuskokwim Bay
Kuskokwim
Aleutian Islands
Aleutian Trench
Bristol Bay
Aleutian Range
Alaska Peninsula
Alaska Range
Kenai Mountains
Kodiak Island
PACIFIC PLATE
NORTH AMERICAN PLATE
Gulf of Alaska
Patton Seamount
Mackenzie Bay
Mackenzie
Mackenzie Mountains
Peel
Amundsen Gulf
McClure Strait
Banks Island
Parry Islands
Viscount Melville Sound
Prince of Wales Island
McClintock Channel
Victoria Island
Jones Sound
Lancaster Sound
Baffin Bay
Davis Strait
Baffin Island
Boothia Peninsula
Gulf of Boothia
Coronation Gulf
Queen Maud Gulf
Great Bear Lake
Coppermine
Arctic Circle
Garry Lake
Back
Thelon
Dubawnt Lake
Baker Lake
Foxe Basin
Nettilling Lake
Amadjuak Lake
Cumberland Sound
Foxe Channel
Southampton Island
Roes Welcome Sound
Hudson Strait
Frobisher Bay
Great Slave Lake
Hay
Coats Island
Mansel Island
Péninsule d'Ungava
Ungava Bay
Hudson Bay
Gilbert Seamount
Queen Charlotte Islands
Dickins Seamount
Rocky
Lake Athabasca
Wollaston Lake
Reindeer Lake
Canadian
Shield
Churchill
Nelson
Belcher Islands
Morton Seamount
Union Seamount
PACIFIC OCEAN
North Saskatchewan
South Saskatchewan
Mendocino Fracture Zone
Cobb Seamount
Vancouver Island
Cascadia Basin
Lake Winnipeg
James Bay
La Grande Riviere
Lac Mistassini
NORTH
AMERICA
Lake Manitoba
Lake of the Woods
Winnipeg
Missouri
Souris
Pioneer Fracture Zone
JUAN DE FUCA PLATE
Gorda Ridge
Columbia
Yellowstone
Lake Nipigon
Columbia Plateau
Harney Basin
Snake
Powder
Great Plains
Lake Superior
Great Lakes
Ottawa
Lake Oahe
Black Hills
Cheyenne
Red River
Minnesota
Mississippi
Wisconsin
Delgada Fan
San Francisco Bay
Great Salt Lake
North Platte
Niobrara
Lake Huron
Lake Michigan
Ontario Peninsula
Lake Ontario
Lake St Clair
Lake Erie
Niagara Falls
Great Basin
Monterey Bay
Platte
Des Moines
Murray Fracture Zone
San Joaquin
Lake Powell
Lake Mead
Mojave Desert
Grand Canyon
Painted Desert
Colorado Plateau
Arkansas
Kansas
Missouri
Illinois
Ohio
Allegheny Mountains
Appalachian Mountains
Blue Ridge
Cumberland Plateau
Tennessee
Roanoke
Mount Mitchell 2037m
Canadian
Arkansas
Red River
Gila
Sonoran Desert
Colorado
Rio Grande
Pecos
Tropic of Cancer
Molokai Fracture Zone
Alabama
Chattahoochee
Savannah
Cape Lookout
Mississippi Delta
Mississippi Fan
Apalachee Bay
Blake Plateau
Cape Canaveral
Galveston Bay
Gulf of California
Lower California
Islas Alijos
Sierra Madre Oriental
Sigsbee Escarpment
Tampa Bay
Lake Okeechobee
The Everglades
Straits of Florida
Gulf of Mexico
Mexico Basin
Clarion Fracture Zone
Cabo San Lucas
Campeche Bank
Yucatan Channel
Cuba
Revillagigedo Islands
Yucatan Peninsula
Yucatan Basin
Cayman Trench
Bay of Campeche
Citlaltépetl 5700m
East Pacific Rise
Orozco Fracture Zone
Mathematicians Seamounts
COCOS PLATE
CARIBBEAN PLATE
NORTH AMERICAN PLATE
Jamaica
Gulf of Honduras
Nicaraguan Rise
Clipperton Fracture Zone
Golfo de Tehuantepec
Middle America Trench
Tehuantepec Ridge
Golfo de Fonseca
Caribbean
Colombian Basin
Clipperton Seamounts
Clipperton Island
Siqueiros Fracture Zone
Albatross Plateau
Lake Nicaragua
Mosquito Gulf
Gulf of Darién
Isthmus of Panama
Gulf of Panama
Península de Azuero
Guatemala Basin
Berlanga Rise
Equator
Cocos Ridge
Colón Ridge
NAZCA PLATE
Panama Basin

A B C D E F G H I J K L

NORTH AMERICA

NORTH AMERICA IS THE WORLD'S THIRD LARGEST CONTINENT WITH A TOTAL AREA OF 9,358,340 SQ MILES (24,238,000 SQ KM) INCLUDING GREENLAND AND THE CARIBBEAN ISLANDS. IT LIES WHOLLY WITHIN THE NORTHERN HEMISPHERE.

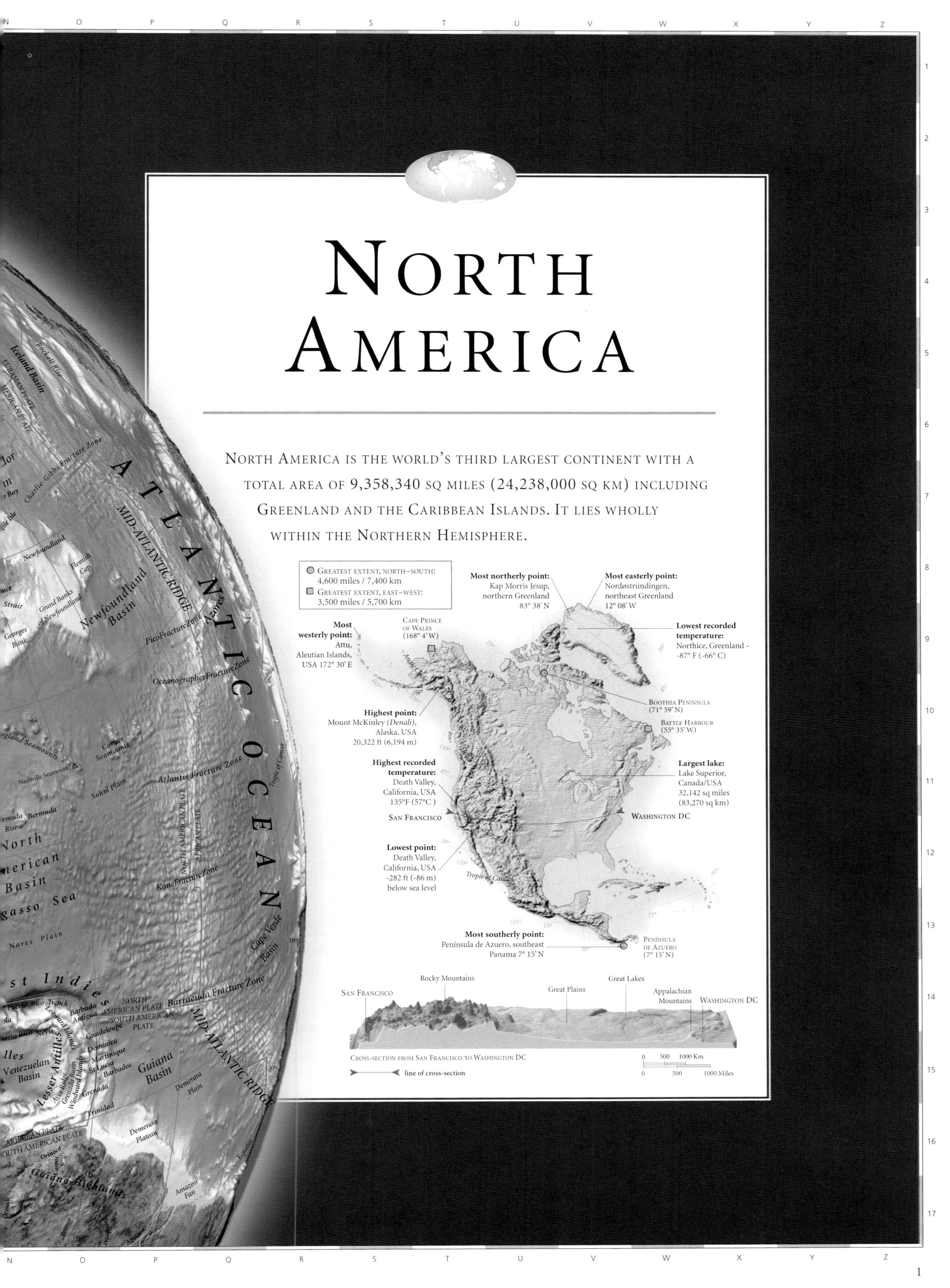

GREATEST EXTENT, NORTH–SOUTH: 4,600 miles / 7,400 km
GREATEST EXTENT, EAST–WEST: 3,500 miles / 5,700 km
Most northerly point: Kap Morris Jesup, northern Greenland 83° 38' N
Most easterly point: Nordøstrundingen, northeast Greenland 12° 08' W
Most westerly point: Attu, Aleutian Islands, USA 172° 30' E
CAPE PRINCE OF WALES (168° 4' W)
Lowest recorded temperature: Northice, Greenland -87° F (-66° C)
BOOTHIA PENINSULA (71° 59' N)
BATTLE HARBOUR (55° 35' W)
Highest point: Mount McKinley (Denali), Alaska, USA 20,322 ft (6,194 m)
Highest recorded temperature: Death Valley, California, USA 135°F (57°C)
Largest lake: Lake Superior, Canada/USA 32,142 sq miles (83,270 sq km)
SAN FRANCISCO
WASHINGTON DC
Lowest point: Death Valley, California, USA -282 ft (-86 m) below sea level
Tropic of Cancer
Arctic Circle
Most southerly point: Península de Azuero, southeast Panama 7° 15' N
PENÍNSULA DE AZUERO (7° 15' N)
SAN FRANCISCO
Rocky Mountains
Great Plains
Great Lakes
Appalachian Mountains
WASHINGTON DC
CROSS-SECTION FROM SAN FRANCISCO TO WASHINGTON DC
line of cross-section
0 500 1000 Km
0 500 1000 Miles
ATLANTIC OCEAN
MID-ATLANTIC RIDGE
Newfoundland Basin
Azores
Sargasso Sea
North American Basin
West Indies
Lesser Antilles
Guiana Basin
Guiana Highlands

Physical North America

The North American continent can be divided into a number of major structural areas: the Western Cordillera, the Canadian Shield, the Great Plains, and Central Lowlands, and the Appalachians. Other smaller regions include the Gulf Atlantic Coastal Plain which borders the southern coast of North America from the southern Appalachians to the Great Plains. This area includes the expanding Mississippi Delta. A chain of volcanic islands, running in an arc around the margin of the Caribbean Plate, lie to the east of the Gulf of Mexico.

The Canadian Shield

Spanning northern Canada and Greenland, this geologically stable plain forms the heart of the continent, containing rocks more than two billion years old. A long history of weathering and repeated glaciation has scoured the region, leaving flat plains, gentle hummocks, numerous small basins and lakes, and the bays and islands of the Arctic.

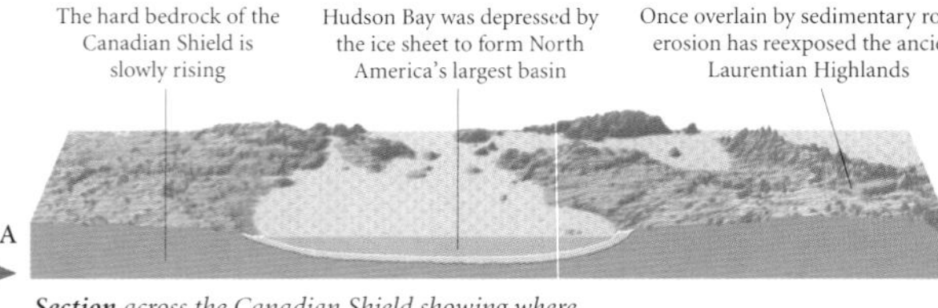
The hard bedrock of the Canadian Shield is slowly rising
Hudson Bay was depressed by the ice sheet to form North America's largest basin
Once overlain by sedimentary rocks, erosion has reexposed the ancient Laurentian Highlands
A
A
0 100 200 Km
0 100 200 Miles

Section across the Canadian Shield showing where the ice sheet has depressed the underlying rock and formed bays and islands.

The Western Cordillera

About 80 million years ago the Pacific and North American plates collided, uplifting the Western Cordillera. This consists of the Aleutian, Coast, Cascade and Sierra Nevada mountains, and the inland Rocky Mountains. These run parallel from the Arctic to Mexico.

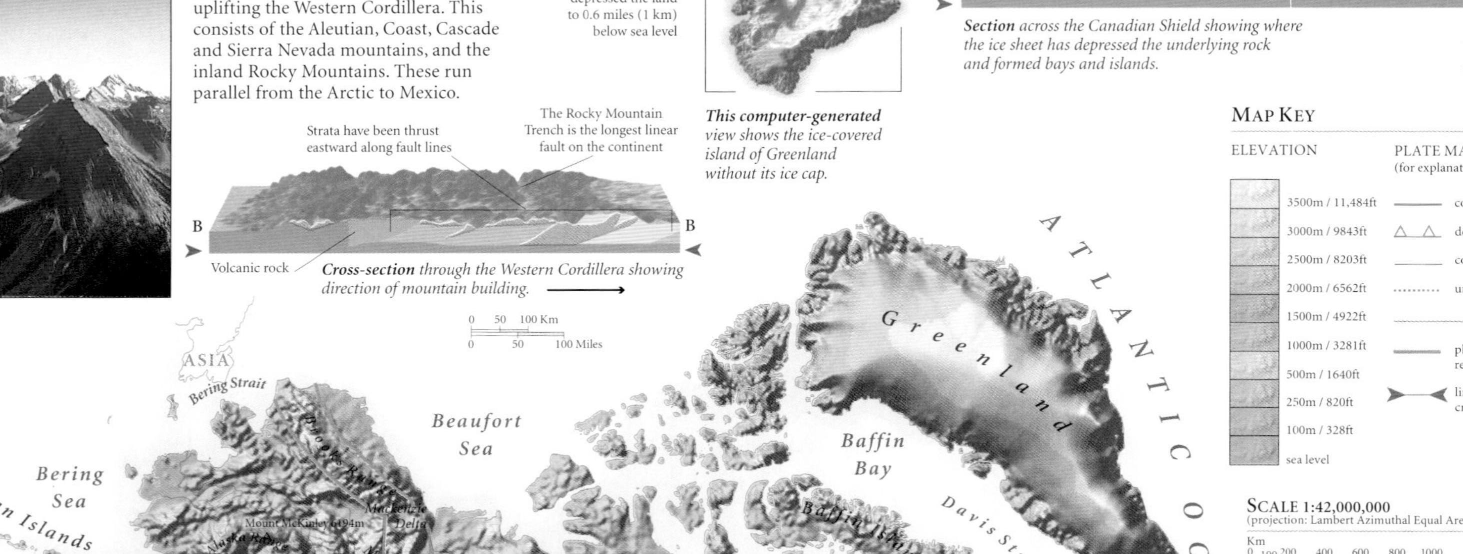
Strata have been thrust eastward along fault lines
The Rocky Mountain Trench is the longest linear fault on the continent
B
B
Volcanic rock
0 50 100 Km
0 50 100 Miles
The weight of the ice sheet, 1.8 miles (3 km) thick, has depressed the land to 0.6 miles (1 km) below sea level

***Cross-section** through the Western Cordillera showing direction of mountain building.*

***This computer-generated** view shows the ice-covered island of Greenland without its ice cap.*

Map Key

ELEVATION

3500m / 11,484ft
3000m / 9843ft
2500m / 8203ft
2000m / 6562ft
1500m / 4922ft
1000m / 3281ft
500m / 1640ft
250m / 820ft
100m / 328ft
sea level

PLATE MARGINS (for explanation see page xiv)

constructive
destructive
conservative
uncertain
physiographic regions
line of cross-section

SCALE 1:42,000,000 (projection: Lambert Azimuthal Equal Area)

Km 0 100 200 400 600 800 1000
Miles 0 50 100 200 300 400 500 600 700 800 900 1000

ASIA
Bering Strait
Bering Sea
Aleutian Islands
Beaufort Sea
Baffin Bay
Greenland
ATLANTIC OCEAN
Davis Strait
Foxe Basin
Hudson Strait
Labrador Sea
Hudson Bay
Gulf of Alaska
NORTH AMERICAN PLATE
PACIFIC PLATE
Great Bear Lake
Great Slave Lake
Lake Athabasca
Reindeer Lake
CANADIAN SHIELD
ROCKY MOUNTAINS
CENTRAL LOWLANDS
GREAT PLAINS
Lake Winnipeg
Lake Manitoba
Laurentian Mountains
Newfoundland
Nova Scotia
St Lawrence
Lake Superior
Lake Huron
Lake Ontario
Lake Michigan
Lake Erie
Great Lakes
Cape Cod
Missouri
Mississippi
Ohio
Arkansas
Great Basin
San Andreas Fault
Death Valley
Sonoran Desert
Gulf of California
Rio Grande
APPALACHIAN MOUNTAINS
GULF ATLANTIC COASTAL PLAIN
Mississippi Delta
Gulf of Mexico
Yucatan Peninsula
Volcán Pico de Orizaba
West Indies
Greater Antilles
Lesser Antilles
Caribbean Sea
CARIBBEAN PLATE
COCOS PLATE
SOUTH AMERICAN PLATE
Isthmus of Panama
SOUTH AMERICA
PACIFIC OCEAN

The Appalachians

The Appalachian Mountains, uplifted about 400 million years ago, are some of the oldest in the world. They have been lowered and rounded by erosion and now slope gently toward the Atlantic across a broad coastal plain.

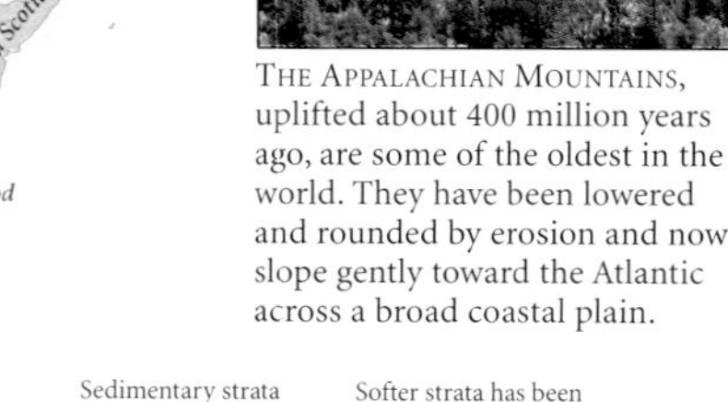
Horizontal strata
Sedimentary strata folded and faulted into ridges and valleys
Softer strata has been crumpled against the harder basement rock
Hard basement rock
C
C
0 50 100 Km
0 50 100 Miles

***Cross-section** through the Appalachians showing the numerous folds, which have subsequently been weathered to create a rounded relief.*

The Great Plains & Central Lowlands

Deposits left by retreating glaciers and rivers have made this vast flat area very fertile. In the north this is the result of glaciation, with deposits up to one mile (1.7 km) thick, covering the basement rock. To the south and west, the massive Missouri/Mississippi river system has for centuries deposited silt across the plains, creating broad, flat floodplains and deltas.

Sedimentary layers overlay domed basement rock

Upland rivers drain south toward the Mississippi Basin

Confluence of the Missouri and Mississippi Rivers

D D

0 200 400 Km
0 200 400 Miles

***Section** across the Great Plains and Central Lowlands showing river systems and structure.*

"Tornado alley" in the Mississippi Valley suffers frequent tornadoes.

CLIMATE

NORTH AMERICA'S climate includes extremes ranging from freezing Arctic conditions in Alaska and Greenland, to desert in the southwest, and tropical conditions in southeastern Florida, the Caribbean, and Central America. Central and southern regions are prone to severe storms including tornadoes and hurricanes.

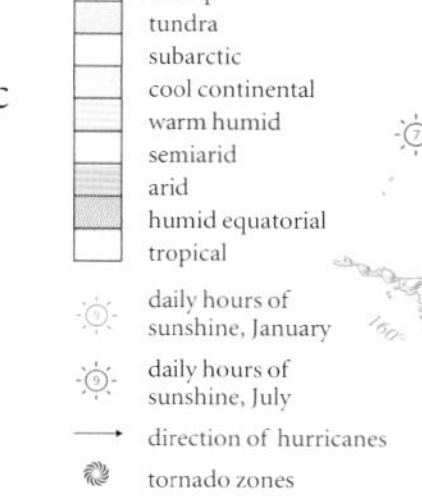
Climate
ice cap
tundra
subarctic
cool continental
warm humid
semiarid
arid
humid equatorial
tropical

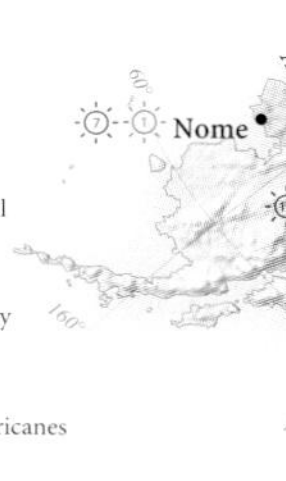
daily hours of sunshine, January
daily hours of sunshine, July
direction of hurricanes
tornado zones

Arctic Circle
Nome
Fairbanks
Aklavik
Resolute
Eismitte
Coppermine
Frobisher Bay
Haines Junction
Juneau
Fort Vermillon
Fort St John
Churchill
Happy Valley - Goose Bay
Torbay

Vancouver
Medicine Hat
Winnipeg
Montréal
Toronto
Boise
Sioux City
New York
Salt Lake City
Denver
San Francisco
Las Vegas
Phoenix
Cape Hatteras
Los Angeles
Little Rock
Atlanta
Guaymas
Houston
Chihuahua
New Orleans
Miami
Nassau
Tropic of Cancer
Santo Domingo
Fort-de-France
Mérida
Kingston
Acapulco
San Salvador
San José

Much of the southwest is semi-desert; receiving less than 12 inches (300 mm) of rainfall a year.

TEMPERATURE

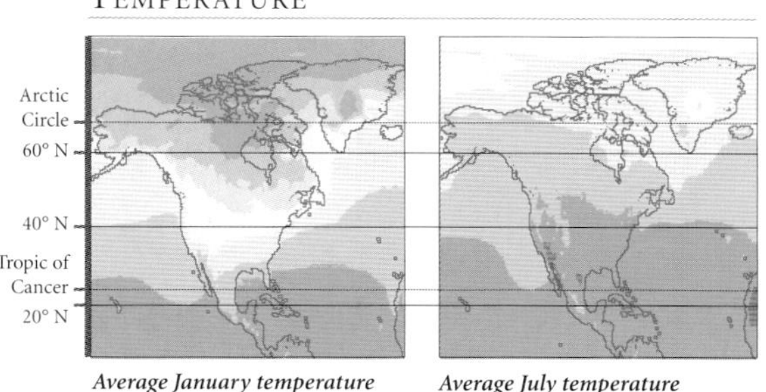
Arctic Circle
60° N
40° N
Tropic of Cancer
20° N

Average January temperature *Average July temperature*

Temperature

- below -30°C (-22°F)
- -30 to -20°C (-22 to -4°F)
- -20 to -10°C (-4 to 14°F)
- -10 to 0°C (14 to 32°F)
- 0 to 10°C (32 to 50° F)
- 10 to 20°C (50 to 68°F)
- 20 to 30°C (68 to 86°F)
- above 30°C (86° F)

RAINFALL

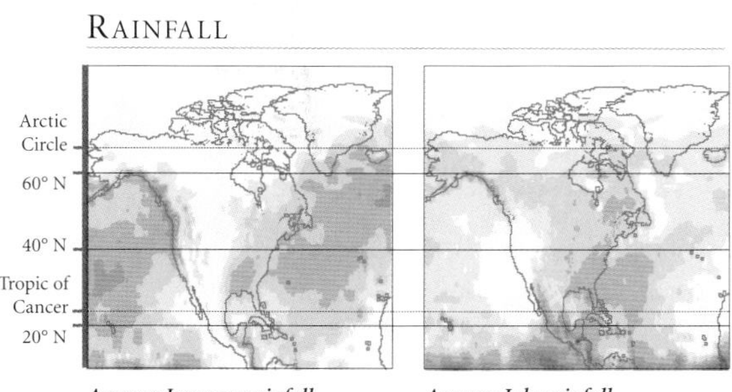
Arctic Circle
60° N
40° N
Tropic of Cancer
20° N

Average January rainfall *Average July rainfall*

Rainfall

- 0–25 mm (0–1 in)
- 25–50 mm (1–2 in)
- 50–100 mm (2–4 in)
- 100–200 mm (4–8 in)
- 200–300 mm (8–12 in)
- 300–400 mm (12–16 in)
- 400–500 mm (16–20 in)
- more than 500 mm (20 in)

The lush, green mountains of the Lesser Antilles receive annual rainfalls of up to 360 inches (9,000 mm).

SHAPING THE CONTINENT

GLACIAL PROCESSES affect much of northern Canada, Greenland and the Western Cordillera. Along the western coast of North America, Central America, and the Caribbean, underlying plates moving together lead to earthquakes and volcanic eruptions. The vast river systems, fed by mountain streams, constantly erode and deposit material along their paths.

VOLCANIC ACTIVITY

1 Mount St. Helens volcano *(right)* in the Cascade Range erupted violently in May 1980, killing 57 people and leveling large areas of forest. The lateral blast filled a valley with debris for 15 miles (25 km).

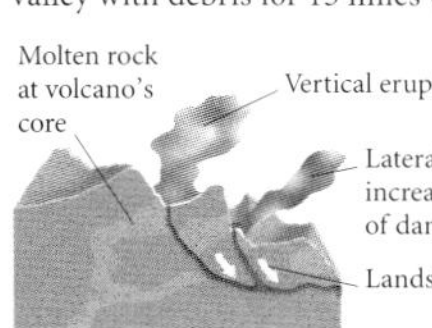
Molten rock at volcano's core
Vertical eruption
Lateral explosion increases extent of damage
Landslide fills valley

VOLCANIC ACTIVITY: ERUPTION OF MOUNT ST. HELENS

PERIGLACIATION

2 The ground in the far north is nearly always frozen: the surface thaws only in summer. This freeze-thaw process produces features such as pingos *(left)*; formed by the freezing of groundwater. With each successive winter ice accumulates producing a mound with a core of ice.

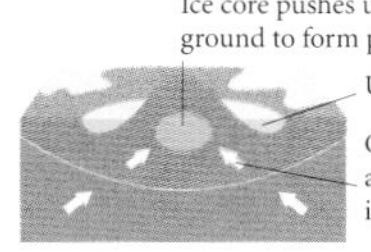
Ice core pushes up ground to form pingo
Unfrozen lake
Groundwater attracted to ice core

PERIGLACIATION: FORMATION OF A PINGO IN THE MACKENZIE DELTA

POST-GLACIAL LAKES

3 A chain of lakes from Great Bear Lake to the Great Lakes *(above)* was created as the ice retreated northward. Glaciers scoured hollows in the softer lowland rock. Glacial deposits at the lip of the hollows, and ridges of harder rock, trapped water to form lakes.

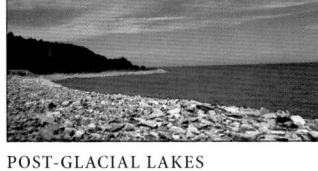

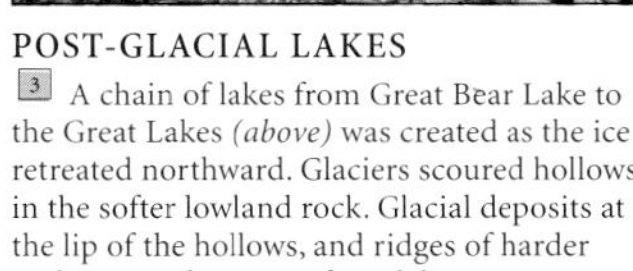
Retreating glacier
Ice-scoured hollow filled with glacial meltwater to form a lake
Harder rock creates a barrier between lakes
Softer lowland rock

POST-GLACIAL LAKES: FORMATION OF THE GREAT LAKES

THE EVOLVING LANDSCAPE

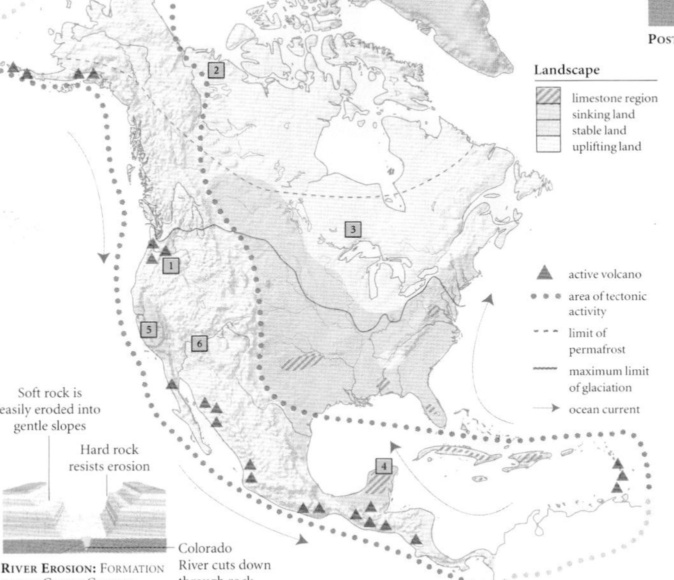
Landscape
limestone region
sinking land
stable land
uplifting land
active volcano
area of tectonic activity
limit of permafrost
maximum limit of glaciation
ocean current

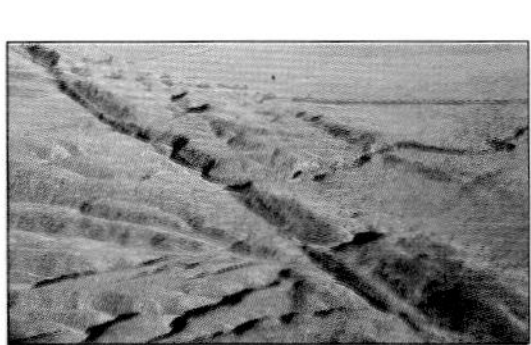

SEISMIC ACTIVITY

5 The San Andreas Fault *(above)* places much of the North America's west coast under constant threat from earthquakes. It is caused by the Pacific Plate grinding past the North American Plate at a faster rate, though in the same direction.

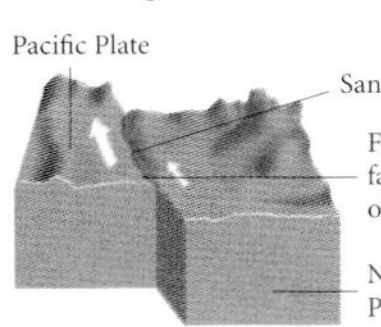
Pacific Plate
San Andreas Fault
Fault is caused by faster movement of Pacific Plate
North American Plate

SEISMIC ACTIVITY: ACTION OF THE SAN ANDREAS FAULT

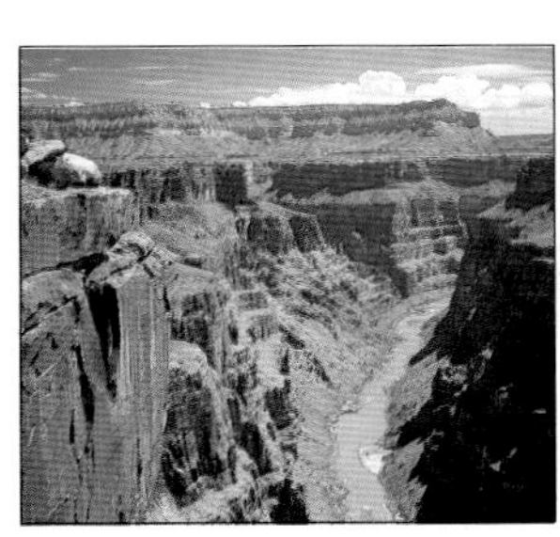

RIVER EROSION

6 The Grand Canyon *(above)* in the Colorado Plateau was created by the downward erosion of the Colorado River, combined with the gradual uplift of the plateau, over the past 30 million years. The contours of the canyon formed as the softer rock layers eroded into gentle slopes, and the hard rock layers into cliffs. The depth varies from 3,855–6,560 ft (1,175–2,000 m).

Soft rock is easily eroded into gentle slopes

Hard rock resists erosion

Colorado River cuts down through rock

RIVER EROSION: FORMATION OF THE GRAND CANYON

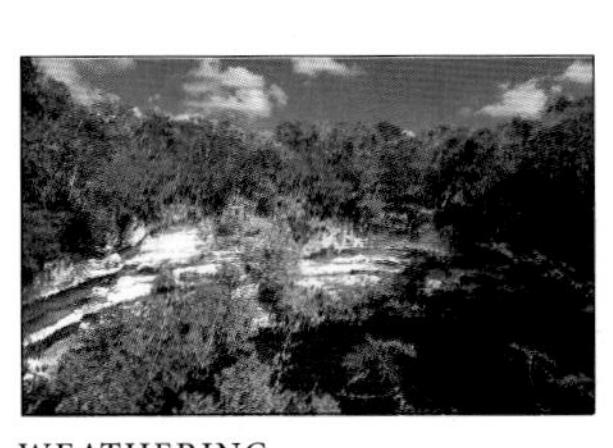

WEATHERING

4 The Yucatan Peninsula is a vast, flat limestone plateau in southern Mexico. Weathering action from both rainwater and underground streams has enlarged fractures in the rock to form caves and hollows, called sinkholes *(above)*.

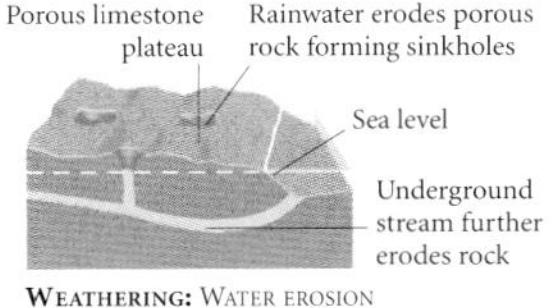
Porous limestone plateau
Rainwater erodes porous rock forming sinkholes
Sea level
Underground stream further erodes rock

WEATHERING: WATER EROSION ON THE YUCATAN PENINSULA

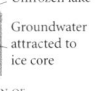

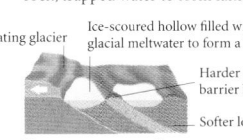

Political North America

Democracy is well established in some parts of the continent but is a recent phenomenon in others. The economically dominant nations of Canada and the US have a long democratic tradition but elsewhere, notably in the countries of Central America, political turmoil has been more common. In Nicaragua and Haiti, harsh dictatorships have only recently been superseded by democratically-elected governments. North America's largest countries, Canada, Mexico, and the US have federal state systems, sharing political power between national and state governments. The US has intervened militarily on several occasions in Central America and the Caribbean to protect its strategic interests.

Transportation

In the 19th century, railroads opened up the North American continent. Air transportation is now more common for long distance passenger travel, although railroads are still extensively used for bulk freight transportation. Waterways like the Mississippi River are important for the transportation of bulk materials, and the Panama Canal is a vital link between the Pacific and Atlantic Oceans. In the 20th century, road transportation increased massively, with the introduction of cheap, mass-produced motor cars and extensive highway construction.

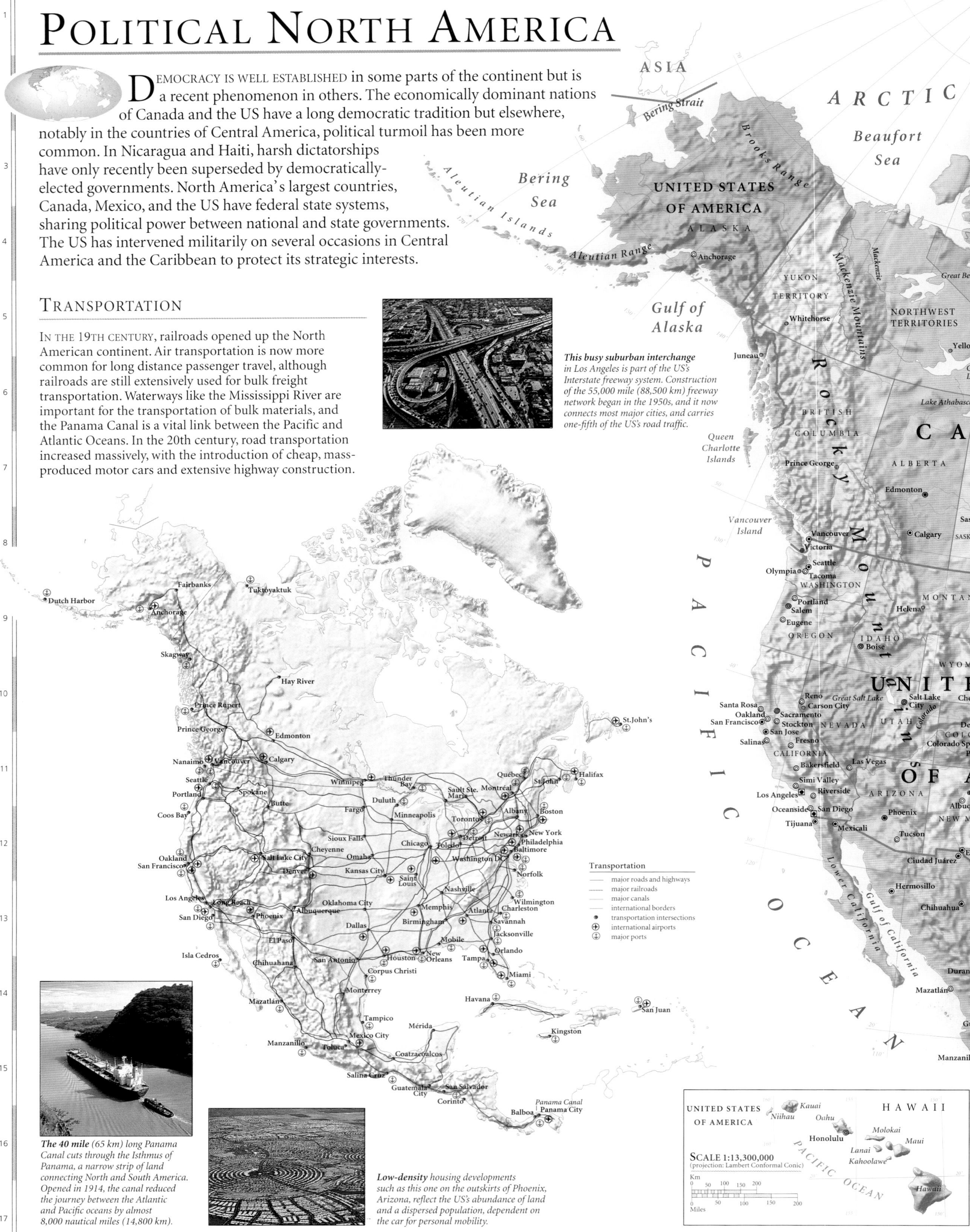
ASIA
Bering Strait
ARCTIC
Beaufort Sea
Brooks Range
Bering Sea
Aleutian Islands
Aleutian Range
UNITED STATES OF AMERICA
ALASKA
Anchorage
YUKON TERRITORY
Whitehorse
Mackenzie Mountains
NORTHWEST TERRITORIES
Great Bear
Gulf of Alaska
Juneau
Rocky Mountains
BRITISH COLUMBIA
Queen Charlotte Islands
Prince George
ALBERTA
Edmonton
Lake Athabasca
Vancouver Island
Vancouver
Victoria
Calgary
Seattle
Olympia
Tacoma
WASHINGTON
Portland
Salem
Eugene
OREGON
Helena
MONTANA
IDAHO
Boise
PACIFIC OCEAN
Reno
Great Salt Lake
Salt Lake City
Santa Rosa
Carson City
Oakland
Sacramento
San Francisco
Stockton
NEVADA
UTAH
San Jose
Fresno
Salinas
CALIFORNIA
Bakersfield
Las Vegas
Simi Valley
Los Angeles
Riverside
ARIZONA
Oceanside
San Diego
Tijuana
Mexicali
Phoenix
Tucson
Ciudad Juárez
Hermosillo
Chihuahua
Lower California
Gulf of California
Durango
Mazatlán
Manzanillo
Transportation
major roads and highways
major railroads
major canals
international borders
transportation intersections
international airports
major ports
UNITED STATES OF AMERICA
HAWAII
Kauai
Niihau
Oahu
Honolulu
Molokai
Maui
Lanai
Kahoolawe
Hawaii
PACIFIC OCEAN
SCALE 1:13,300,000
(projection: Lambert Conformal Conic)
Km
Miles

This busy suburban interchange in Los Angeles is part of the US's Interstate freeway system. Construction of the 55,000 mile (88,500 km) freeway network began in the 1950s, and it now connects most major cities, and carries one-fifth of the US's road traffic.

The 40 mile (65 km) long Panama Canal cuts through the Isthmus of Panama, a narrow strip of land connecting North and South America. Opened in 1914, the canal reduced the journey between the Atlantic and Pacific oceans by almost 8,000 nautical miles (14,800 km).

Low-density housing developments such as this one on the outskirts of Phoenix, Arizona, reflect the US's abundance of land and a dispersed population, dependent on the car for personal mobility.

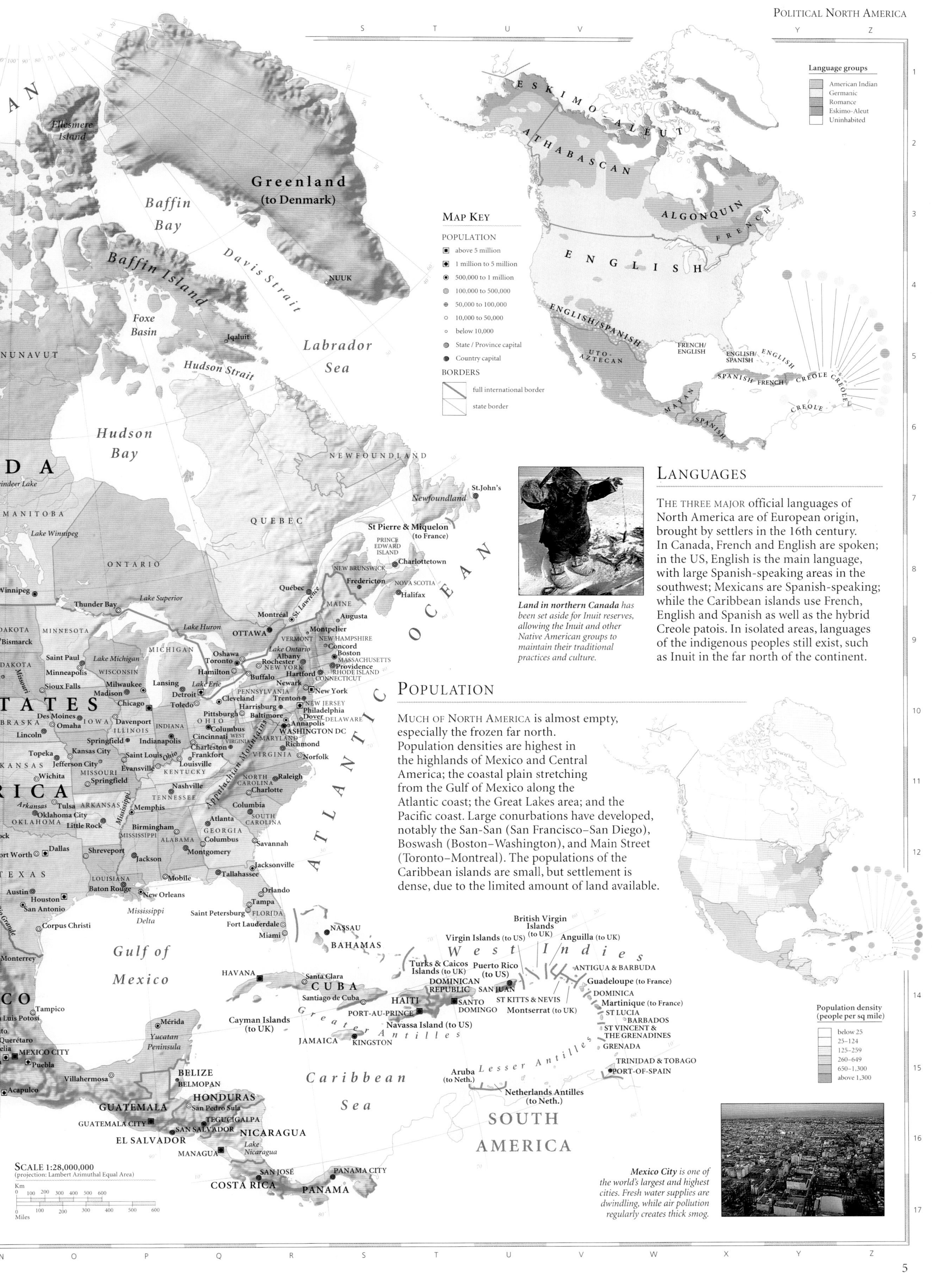

Greenland (to Denmark)
Baffin Bay
Baffin Island
Davis Strait
NUUK
Foxe Basin
Iqaluit
Labrador Sea
Hudson Strait
NUNAVUT
Hudson Bay
NEWFOUNDLAND
Newfoundland
St.John's
QUEBEC
St Pierre & Miquelon (to France)
PRINCE EDWARD ISLAND
Charlottetown
NEW BRUNSWICK
Fredericton
NOVA SCOTIA
Halifax
ONTARIO
MANITOBA
Lake Winnipeg
Winnipeg
Thunder Bay
Lake Superior
Québec
Montréal
OTTAWA
Lake Huron
Toronto
Hamilton
Lake Ontario
Lake Erie
Lake Michigan
ATLANTIC OCEAN
Gulf of Mexico
Caribbean Sea
West Indies
Greater Antilles
Lesser Antilles
BAHAMAS
NASSAU
CUBA
HAVANA
Santa Clara
Santiago de Cuba
Cayman Islands (to UK)
JAMAICA
KINGSTON
HAITI
PORT-AU-PRINCE
Navassa Island (to US)
DOMINICAN REPUBLIC
SANTO DOMINGO
Puerto Rico (to US)
SAN JUAN
Turks & Caicos Islands (to UK)
Virgin Islands (to US)
British Virgin Islands (to UK)
Anguilla (to UK)
ANTIGUA & BARBUDA
ST KITTS & NEVIS
Montserrat (to UK)
Guadeloupe (to France)
DOMINICA
Martinique (to France)
ST LUCIA
BARBADOS
ST VINCENT & THE GRENADINES
GRENADA
TRINIDAD & TOBAGO
PORT-OF-SPAIN
Aruba (to Neth.)
Netherlands Antilles (to Neth.)
SOUTH AMERICA
BELIZE
BELMOPAN
HONDURAS
San Pedro Sula
TEGUCIGALPA
GUATEMALA
GUATEMALA CITY
EL SALVADOR
SAN SALVADOR
NICARAGUA
MANAGUA
Lake Nicaragua
COSTA RICA
SAN JOSÉ
PANAMA
PANAMA CITY
MEXICO CITY
Puebla
Acapulco
Villahermosa
Mérida
Yucatan Peninsula
Tampico
Monterrey
Appalachian Mountains
Mississippi Delta
SCALE 1:28,000,000
(projection: Lambert Azimuthal Equal Area)
MAP KEY
POPULATION
above 5 million
1 million to 5 million
500,000 to 1 million
100,000 to 500,000
50,000 to 100,000
10,000 to 50,000
below 10,000
State / Province capital
Country capital
BORDERS
full international border
state border
Language groups
American Indian
Germanic
Romance
Eskimo-Aleut
Uninhabited
ESKIMO-ALEUT
ATHABASCAN
ALGONQUIN
FRENCH
ENGLISH
ENGLISH/SPANISH
UTO-AZTECAN
FRENCH/ENGLISH
ENGLISH/SPANISH
SPANISH
MAYAN
CREOLE
Population density (people per sq mile)
below 25
25–124
125–259
260–649
650–1,300
above 1,300

LANGUAGES

THE THREE MAJOR official languages of North America are of European origin, brought by settlers in the 16th century. In Canada, French and English are spoken; in the US, English is the main language, with large Spanish-speaking areas in the southwest; Mexicans are Spanish-speaking; while the Caribbean islands use French, English and Spanish as well as the hybrid Creole patois. In isolated areas, languages of the indigenous peoples still exist, such as Inuit in the far north of the continent.

Land in northern Canada has been set aside for Inuit reserves, allowing the Inuit and other Native American groups to maintain their traditional practices and culture.

POPULATION

MUCH OF NORTH AMERICA is almost empty, especially the frozen far north. Population densities are highest in the highlands of Mexico and Central America; the coastal plain stretching from the Gulf of Mexico along the Atlantic coast; the Great Lakes area; and the Pacific coast. Large conurbations have developed, notably the San-San (San Francisco–San Diego), Boswash (Boston–Washington), and Main Street (Toronto–Montreal). The populations of the Caribbean islands are small, but settlement is dense, due to the limited amount of land available.

Mexico City is one of the world's largest and highest cities. Fresh water supplies are dwindling, while air pollution regularly creates thick smog.

North American Resources

The two northern countries of Canada and the US are richly endowed with natural resources that have helped to fuel economic development. The US is the world's largest economy, although today it is facing stiff competition from the Far East. Mexico has relied on oil revenues but there are hopes that the North American Free Trade Agreement (NAFTA), will encourage trade growth with Canada and the US. The poorer countries of Central America and the Caribbean depend largely on cash crops and tourism.

Standard of Living

The US and Canada have one of the highest overall standards of living in the world. However, many people still live in poverty, especially in urban ghettos and some rural areas. Central America and the Caribbean are markedly poorer than their wealthier northern neighbors. Haiti is the poorest country in the western hemisphere.

Standard of Living
(UN Human Development Index)

high

low

Industry

The modern, industrialized economies of the US and Canada contrast sharply with those of Mexico, Central America, and the Caribbean. Manufacturing is especially important in the US; vehicle production is concentrated around the Great Lakes, while electronic and hi-tech industries are increasingly found in the western and southern states. Mexico depends on oil exports and assembly work, taking advantage of cheap labor. Many Central American and Caribbean countries rely heavily on agricultural exports.

After its purchase from Russia in 1867, Alaska's frozen lands were largely ignored by the US. Oil reserves similar in magnitude to those in eastern Texas were discovered in Prudhoe Bay, Alaska in 1968. Freezing temperatures and a fragile environment hamper oil extraction.

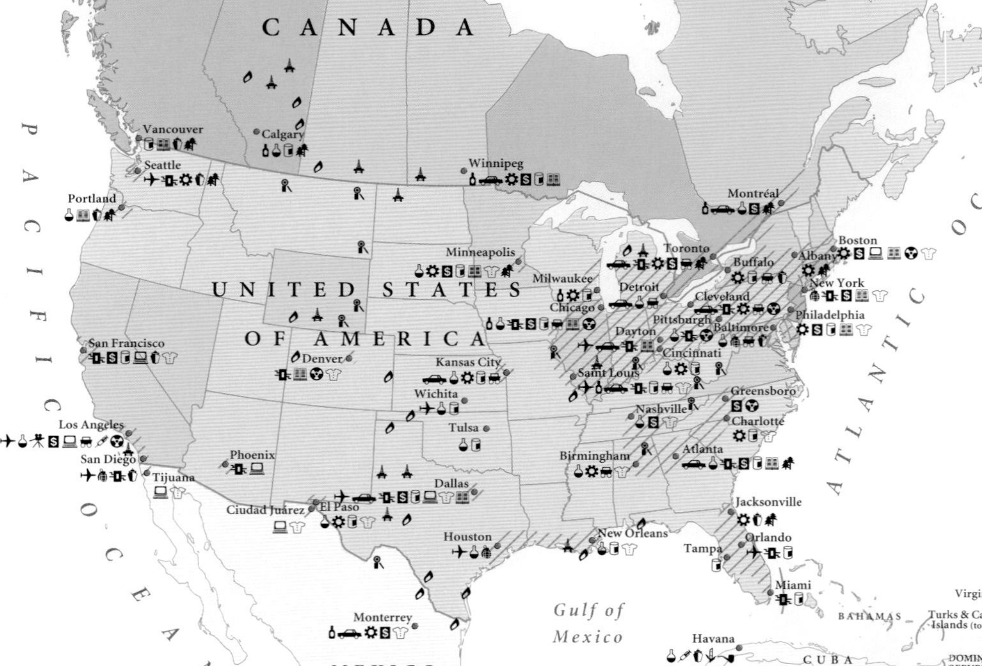
ARCTIC OCEAN
RUSS. FED.
Bering Strait
Bering Sea
Beaufort Sea
Prudhoe Bay
USA
Baffin Bay
Greenland (to Denmark)
Labrador Sea
Gulf of Alaska
Hudson Strait
Hudson Bay
CANADA
Vancouver
Calgary
Seattle
Winnipeg
Portland
Montréal
PACIFIC OCEAN
ATLANTIC OCEAN
Minneapolis
Toronto
Boston
Buffalo
Albany
Milwaukee
Detroit
New York
UNITED STATES OF AMERICA
Chicago
Cleveland
Philadelphia
Pittsburgh
Baltimore
Dayton
San Francisco
Denver
Kansas City
Cincinnati
Saint Louis
Wichita
Greensboro
Nashville
Charlotte
Los Angeles
Tulsa
San Diego
Atlanta
Phoenix
Birmingham
Tijuana
Dallas
Ciudad Juárez
El Paso
Jacksonville
New Orleans
Houston
Orlando
Tampa
Miami
Gulf of Mexico
Monterrey
MEXICO
Guadalajara
Mexico City
BAHAMAS
Havana
CUBA
West Indies
Virgin Islands (to US)
British Virgin Islands (to UK)
Turks & Caicos Islands (to UK)
Puerto Rico (to US)
Anguilla (to UK)
ST KITTS & NEVIS
ANTIGUA & BARBUDA
Montserrat
Guadeloupe
DOMINICA
Martinique
ST LUCIA
BARBADOS
ST VINCENT & THE GRENADINES
GRENADA
TRINIDAD & TOBAGO
Port-of-Spain
DOMINICAN REPUBLIC
HAITI
Port-au-Prince
San Juan
Santo Domingo
Cayman Islands (to UK)
JAMAICA
Greater Antilles
Navassa Island (to US)
Lesser Antilles
Caribbean Sea
Aruba (to Neth.)
Netherlands Antilles (to Neth.)
VENEZUELA
BELIZE
GUATEMALA
Guatemala City
HONDURAS
Tegucigalpa
EL SALVADOR
San Salvador
NICARAGUA
Managua
San José
COSTA RICA
Panama City
PANAMA
COLOMBIA

Fish such as cod, flounder, and plaice are caught in the Grand Banks, off the Newfoundland coast, and processed in many North Atlantic coastal settlements.

South of San Francisco, "Silicon Valley" is both a national and international center for hi-tech industries, electronic industries, and research institutions.

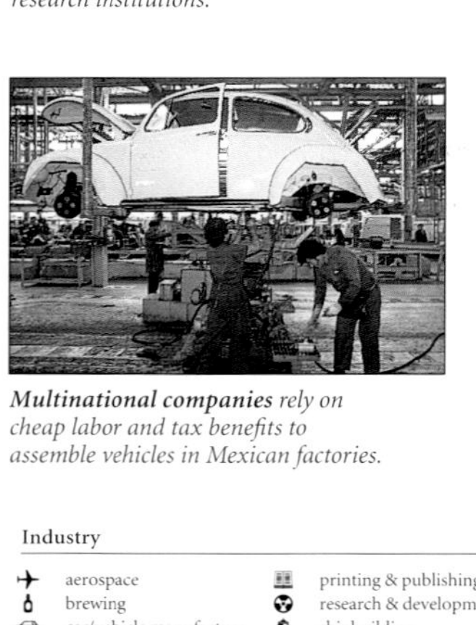

Multinational companies rely on cheap labor and tax benefits to assemble vehicles in Mexican factories.

The twin towers of the World Trade Center dominate the Manhattan skyline. New York is one of the world's leading trade and finance centers.

Industry

- aerospace
- brewing
- car/vehicle manufacture
- chemicals
- defense
- electronics
- engineering
- movie industry
- finance
- food processing
- hi-tech industry
- iron & steel
- pharmaceuticals
- printing & publishing
- research & development
- shipbuilding
- sugar processing
- textiles
- timber processing
- tobacco processing
- coal
- oil
- gas
- industrial cities
- major industrial areas

GNP per capita (US$)

- 0–1999
- 2000–4999
- 5000–9999
- 10,000–19,999
- 20,000–24,999
- 25,000+

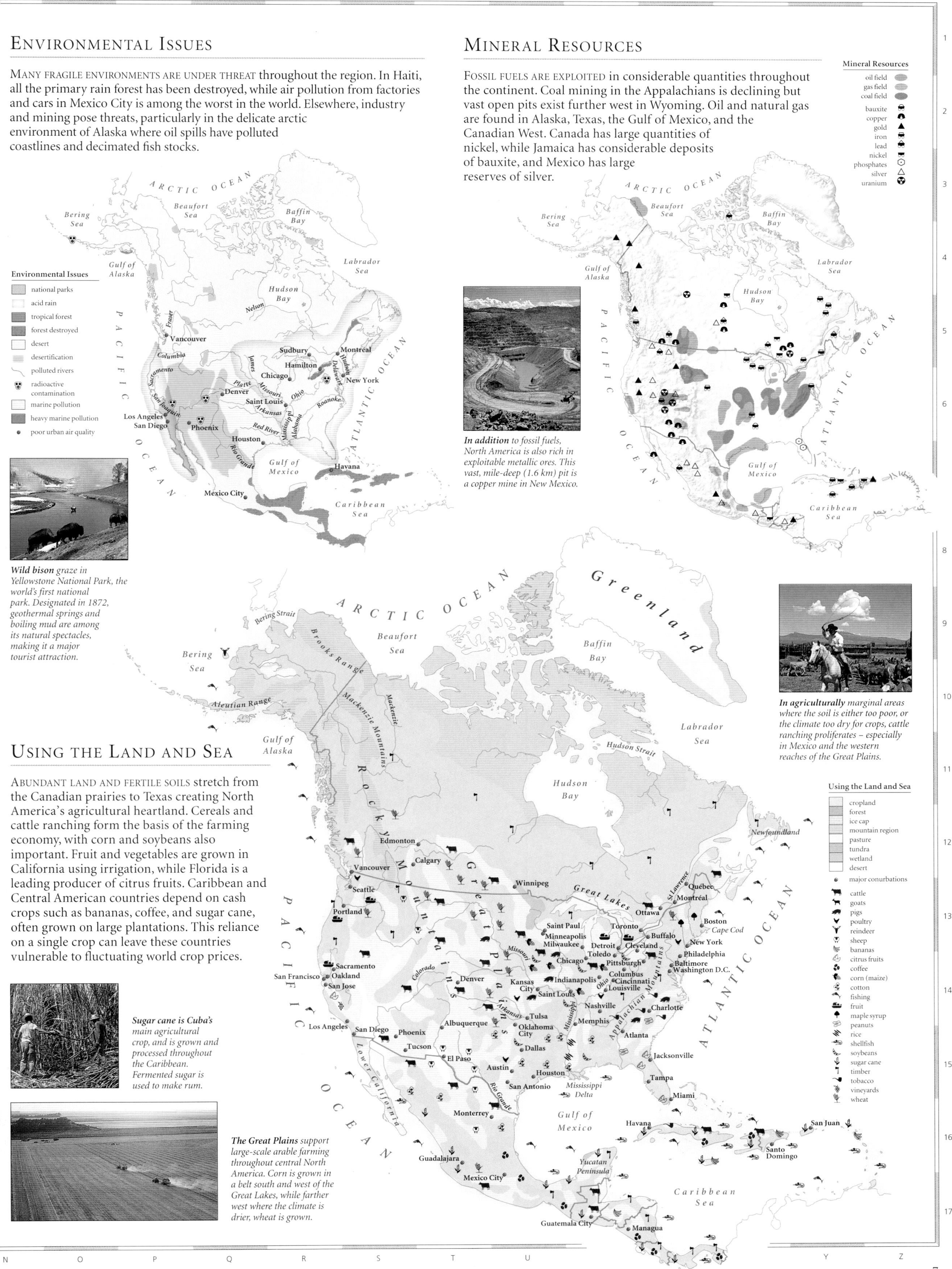

Environmental Issues
national parks
acid rain
tropical forest
forest destroyed
desert
desertification
polluted rivers
radioactive contamination
marine pollution
heavy marine pollution
poor urban air quality
Mineral Resources
oil field
gas field
coal field
bauxite
copper
gold
iron
lead
nickel
phosphates
silver
uranium
Using the Land and Sea
cropland
forest
ice cap
mountain region
pasture
tundra
wetland
desert
major conurbations
cattle
goats
pigs
poultry
reindeer
sheep
bananas
citrus fruits
coffee
corn (maize)
cotton
fishing
fruit
maple syrup
peanuts
rice
shellfish
soybeans
sugar cane
timber
tobacco
vineyards
wheat

Environmental Issues

Many fragile environments are under threat throughout the region. In Haiti, all the primary rain forest has been destroyed, while air pollution from factories and cars in Mexico City is among the worst in the world. Elsewhere, industry and mining pose threats, particularly in the delicate arctic environment of Alaska where oil spills have polluted coastlines and decimated fish stocks.

***Wild bison** graze in Yellowstone National Park, the world's first national park. Designated in 1872, geothermal springs and boiling mud are among its natural spectacles, making it a major tourist attraction.*

Mineral Resources

Fossil fuels are exploited in considerable quantities throughout the continent. Coal mining in the Appalachians is declining but vast open pits exist further west in Wyoming. Oil and natural gas are found in Alaska, Texas, the Gulf of Mexico, and the Canadian West. Canada has large quantities of nickel, while Jamaica has considerable deposits of bauxite, and Mexico has large reserves of silver.

***In addition** to fossil fuels, North America is also rich in exploitable metallic ores. This vast, mile-deep (1.6 km) pit is a copper mine in New Mexico.*

***In agriculturally** marginal areas where the soil is either too poor, or the climate too dry for crops, cattle ranching proliferates – especially in Mexico and the western reaches of the Great Plains.*

Using the Land and Sea

Abundant land and fertile soils stretch from the Canadian prairies to Texas creating North America's agricultural heartland. Cereals and cattle ranching form the basis of the farming economy, with corn and soybeans also important. Fruit and vegetables are grown in California using irrigation, while Florida is a leading producer of citrus fruits. Caribbean and Central American countries depend on cash crops such as bananas, coffee, and sugar cane, often grown on large plantations. This reliance on a single crop can leave these countries vulnerable to fluctuating world crop prices.

***Sugar cane is Cuba's** main agricultural crop, and is grown and processed throughout the Caribbean. Fermented sugar is used to make rum.*

***The Great Plains** support large-scale arable farming throughout central North America. Corn is grown in a belt south and west of the Great Lakes, while farther west where the climate is drier, wheat is grown.*

CANADA

CANADA IS THE THIRD LARGEST COUNTRY in the world, and with only about one-tenth of its land area inhabited, it is one of the most sparsely populated. Canada became a confederation in 1867, though Newfoundland did not join until 1949. As a founding member of the UN and of the Commonwealth, Canada has played an important role in international affairs. A constitutional crisis, focusing on the French-speaking Québécois, and Inuit and Native American land rights, dominated politics in the 1990s. In 1999, part of the Northwest Territories, Nunavut, became a self-governing homeland for the Inuit.

***The Selwyn Mountains** in northwestern Canada form part of the Rocky Mountains. The highest point, Keele Peak, rises to 9,750 ft (2,972 m).*

TRANSPORTATION & INDUSTRY

ABUNDANT ENERGY in the form of coal, oil, natural gas, and hydroelectric power underpins Canadian industry. Over 75% of manufacturing is concentrated in the Great Lakes–St. Lawrence region, including prospering aerospace, transportation and hi-tech industries. Across Canada as a whole, manufacturing has developed around a diversified, high-quality resource base and a wide range of metallic and nonmetallic minerals.

***Canada** has one of the world's highest rates of energy consumption per person. It is endowed with vast hydroelectric potential from which more than 60% of its electricity requirements are generated.*

Major industry and infrastructure

- aerospace
- car manufacture
- chemicals
- engineering
- food processing
- hi-tech industry
- hydroelectric power
- oil & gas
- mining
- timber processing
- capital cities
- major towns
- international airports
- major roads
- major industrial areas

TRANSPORTATION NETWORK

566,352 miles (912,000 km)	15,189 miles (24,459 km)
8,755 miles (14,098 km)	2,341 miles (3,769 km)

In recent years the road network has been expanded, especially links to remote areas. Meanwhile, for long-distance travel, air transportation now supersedes the declining rail network, which focuses mainly on east–west routes.

USING THE LAND AND SEA

MOST AGRICULTURAL LAND is found in the prairies, which cover 140 million acres (57 million ha) and support wheat and grain-fed cattle. More specialized crops, such as fruit and vegetables, are grown in pockets of land in the east and west. Of Canada's many islands, only Prince Edward Island has notable farmland. Further north, boreal forests, exploited for timber, run in an almost unbroken arc, giving way to uncultivable tundra and ice sheets in the far north.

THE URBAN/RURAL POPULATION DIVIDE

urban 77% — rural 23%

0 10 20 30 40 50 60 70 80 90 100

POPULATION DENSITY	TOTAL LAND AREA
8 people per sq mile (3 people per sq km)	3,559,294 sq miles (9,220,970 sq km)

Land use and agricultural distribution

- cattle
- cereals
- fishing
- fruit
- timber
- capital cities
- major towns
- pasture
- cropland
- forest
- wetland
- mountain region
- barren
- tundra

***The climate and topography** of the prairies makes them ideally suited to farming. Long summer days, moderate temperatures, limited rainfall, and flat plains provide excellent conditions for wheat farming.*

196
16
192
16

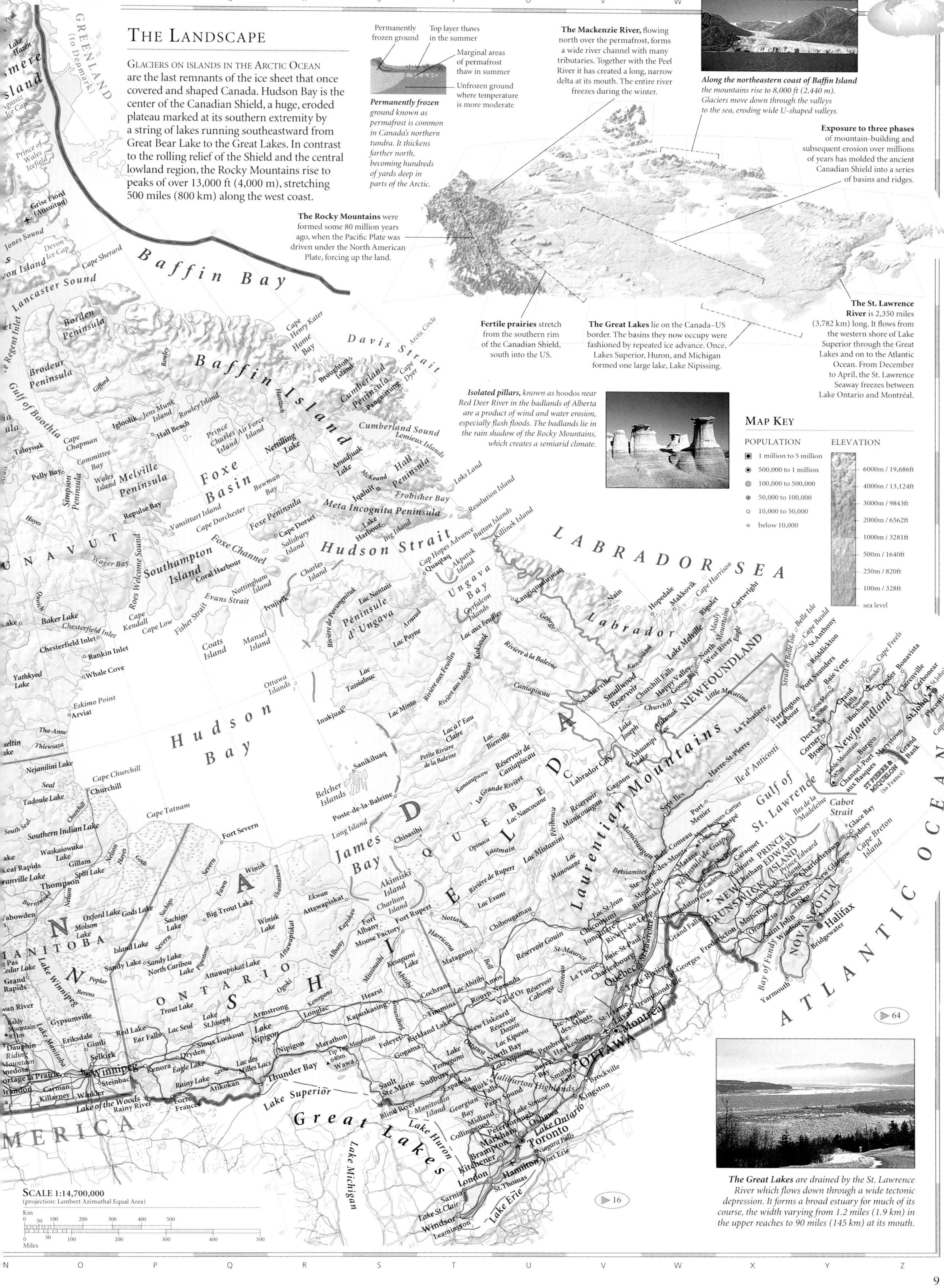

196

THE LANDSCAPE

GLACIERS ON ISLANDS IN THE ARCTIC OCEAN are the last remnants of the ice sheet that once covered and shaped Canada. Hudson Bay is the center of the Canadian Shield, a huge, eroded plateau marked at its southern extremity by a string of lakes running southeastward from Great Bear Lake to the Great Lakes. In contrast to the rolling relief of the Shield and the central lowland region, the Rocky Mountains rise to peaks of over 13,000 ft (4,000 m), stretching 500 miles (800 km) along the west coast.

Permanently frozen ground

Top layer thaws in the summer

Marginal areas of permafrost thaw in summer

Unfrozen ground where temperature is more moderate

Permanently frozen *ground known as permafrost is common in Canada's northern tundra. It thickens farther north, becoming hundreds of yards deep in parts of the Arctic.*

The Mackenzie River, flowing north over the permafrost, forms a wide river channel with many tributaries. Together with the Peel River it has created a long, narrow delta at its mouth. The entire river freezes during the winter.

Along the northeastern coast of Baffin Island *the mountains rise to 8,000 ft (2,440 m). Glaciers move down through the valleys to the sea, eroding wide U-shaped valleys.*

Exposure to three phases of mountain-building and subsequent erosion over millions of years has molded the ancient Canadian Shield into a series of basins and ridges.

The Rocky Mountains were formed some 80 million years ago, when the Pacific Plate was driven under the North American Plate, forcing up the land.

Fertile prairies stretch from the southern rim of the Canadian Shield, south into the US.

The Great Lakes lie on the Canada–US border. The basins they now occupy were fashioned by repeated ice advance. Once, Lakes Superior, Huron, and Michigan formed one large lake, Lake Nipissing.

The St. Lawrence River is 2,350 miles (3,782 km) long. It flows from the western shore of Lake Superior through the Great Lakes and on to the Atlantic Ocean. From December to April, the St. Lawrence Seaway freezes between Lake Ontario and Montréal.

Isolated pillars, *known as* hoodoos *near Red Deer River in the badlands of Alberta are a product of wind and water erosion, especially flash floods. The badlands lie in the rain shadow of the Rocky Mountains, which creates a semiarid climate.*

MAP KEY

POPULATION	ELEVATION
1 million to 5 million	6000m / 19,686ft
500,000 to 1 million	4000m / 13,124ft
100,000 to 500,000	3000m / 9843ft
50,000 to 100,000	2000m / 6562ft
10,000 to 50,000	1000m / 3281ft
below 10,000	500m / 1640ft
	250m / 820ft
	100m / 328ft
	sea level

64

The Great Lakes *are drained by the St. Lawrence River which flows down through a wide tectonic depression. It forms a broad estuary for much of its course, the width varying from 1.2 miles (1.9 km) in the upper reaches to 90 miles (145 km) at its mouth.*

16

SCALE 1:14,700,000
(projection: Lambert Azimuthal Equal Area)

Km 0 50 100 200 300 400 500
Miles 0 50 100 200 300 400 500

CANADA: WESTERN PROVINCES

Alberta, British Columbia, Manitoba, Saskatchewan, Yukon Territory

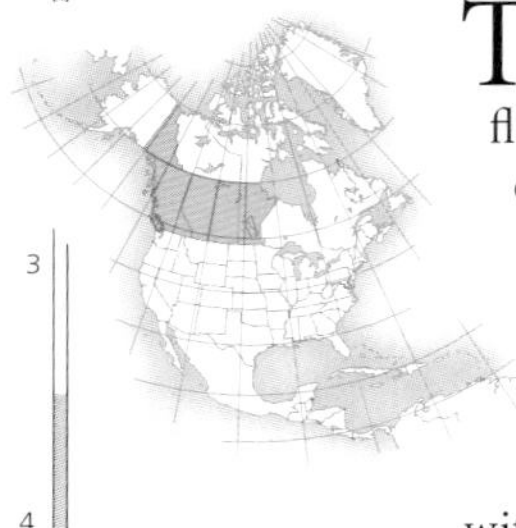

THE MOUNTAINS OF THE WEST COAST, incorporating British Columbia and the Yukon Territory, descend into the vast, flat prairies of Alberta, Saskatchewan, and Manitoba. The empty lands and fertile soils of the prairie provinces attracted migrants, and the descendants of early European immigrants still make up a large proportion of the population. The mechanization of agriculture has reduced the need for labor, and rural population densities remain low. The majority of the people live within 100 miles (160 km) of the southern Canada–US border, and in British Columbia, one of the leading Canadian provinces in terms of economic wealth. The Yukon Territory, in the far north, remains a relatively unspoiled wilderness, containing large, untapped mineral reserves. This province has a significant population of Native Americans people, many of whom maintain a traditional lifestyle.

USING THE LAND AND SEA

WHEAT FARMING IS THE ECONOMIC MAINSTAY of Alberta, Manitoba, and Saskatchewan, which contain 82% of farmland in Canada. Cattle are also raised on the prairies. Forestry and fishing are the most prominent resource-based industries in British Columbia. Despite the mountainous terrain, fruit and specialized grains can be grown in the Okanagan and Fraser valleys.

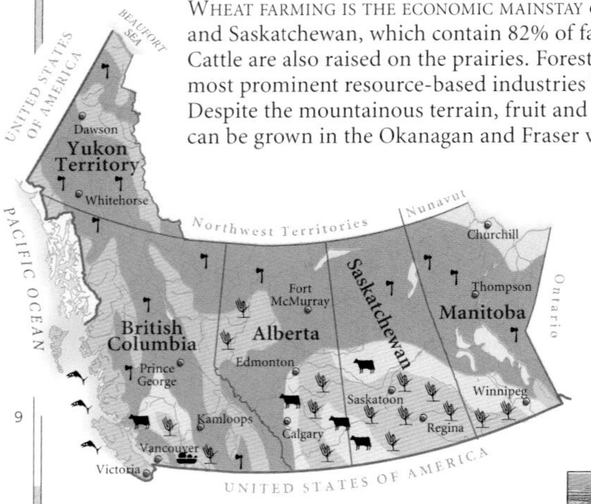

Land use and agricultural distribution

- cattle
- cereals
- fishing
- fruit
- timber
- major towns
- pasture
- cropland
- forest
- wetland
- barren
- tundra

THE URBAN/RURAL POPULATION DIVIDE

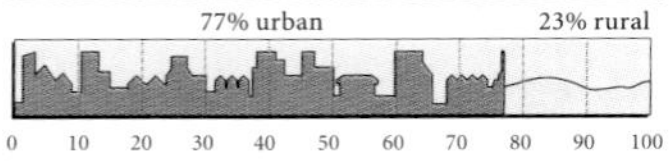

77% urban — 23% rural

0 10 20 30 40 50 60 70 80 90 100

POPULATION DENSITY	TOTAL LAND AREA
7 people per sq mile (3 people per sq km)	1,224,449 sq miles (3,172,150 sq km)

Large, highly-mechanized and often very specialized farms, requiring huge investment but little labor, characterize modern farming in the prairies.

TRANSPORTATION & INDUSTRY

THE WESTERN PROVINCES contain a wealth of mineral resources. Alberta holds the bulk of Canada's fossil fuels; the other provinces contain reserves of metallic ores, such as zinc, lead, and silver. Isolation from markets has slowed the development of manufacturing, restricting it to the large cities like Vancouver, Winnipeg, and Calgary. Hydroelectric power is widely exploited, although there is increasing concern about potential ecological damage.

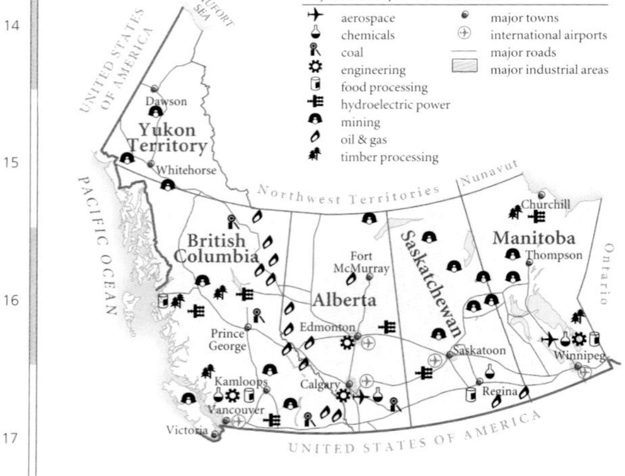

Major industry and infrastructure

- aerospace
- chemicals
- coal
- engineering
- food processing
- hydroelectric power
- mining
- oil & gas
- timber processing
- major towns
- international airports
- major roads
- major industrial areas

TRANSPORTATION NETWORK

82,438 miles (135,145 km)
6,459 miles (10,401 km)
10,811 miles (17,410 km)
None

The transportation network of the western provinces is dominated by east–west routes that weave through mountain passes and spread across the plains. Access to some northern areas is restricted to air travel.

Much of the Yukon Territory is uninhabited tundra. Industry is based on the extraction of mineral resources, and to a lesser extent, on the scattered forests of the south.

***The Fraser River valley** is a major area of settlement in British Columbia. Railraods cross the Rocky Mountains via this valley.*

***Established in 1907**, Jasper National Park lies in the heart of the Rocky Mountains. It is noted for its spectacular alpine scenery and contains part of the large Columbia Icefield.*

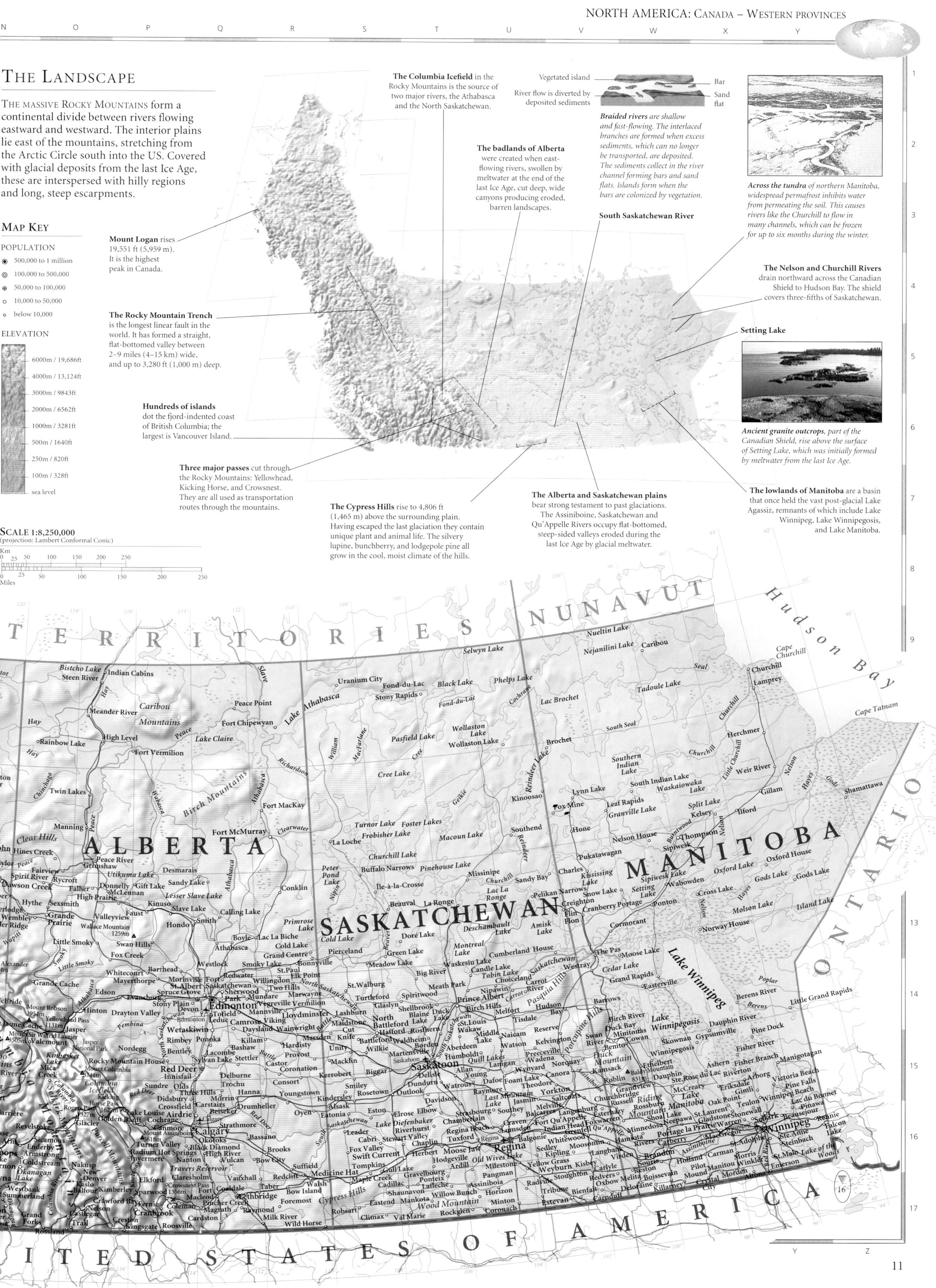

N O P Q R S T U V W X Y
1 2 3 4 5 6 7 8 9 13 14 15 16 17
Y Z

THE LANDSCAPE

THE MASSIVE ROCKY MOUNTAINS form a continental divide between rivers flowing eastward and westward. The interior plains lie east of the mountains, stretching from the Arctic Circle south into the US. Covered with glacial deposits from the last Ice Age, these are interspersed with hilly regions and long, steep escarpments.

MAP KEY
POPULATION
500,000 to 1 million
100,000 to 500,000
50,000 to 100,000
10,000 to 50,000
below 10,000
ELEVATION
6000m / 19,686ft
4000m / 13,124ft
3000m / 9843ft
2000m / 6562ft
1000m / 3281ft
500m / 1640ft
250m / 820ft
100m / 328ft
sea level

SCALE 1:8,250,000
(projection: Lambert Conformal Conic)
Km 0 25 50 100 150 200 250
Miles 0 25 50 100 150 200 250

Mount Logan rises 19,551 ft (5,959 m). It is the highest peak in Canada.
The Rocky Mountain Trench is the longest linear fault in the world. It has formed a straight, flat-bottomed valley between 2–9 miles (4–15 km) wide, and up to 3,280 ft (1,000 m) deep.
Hundreds of islands dot the fjord-indented coast of British Columbia; the largest is Vancouver Island.
Three major passes cut through the Rocky Mountains: Yellowhead, Kicking Horse, and Crowsnest. They are all used as transportation routes through the mountains.
The Columbia Icefield in the Rocky Mountains is the source of two major rivers, the Athabasca and the North Saskatchewan.
The badlands of Alberta were created when east-flowing rivers, swollen by meltwater at the end of the last Ice Age, cut deep, wide canyons producing eroded, barren landscapes.
The Cypress Hills rise to 4,806 ft (1,465 m) above the surrounding plain. Having escaped the last glaciation they contain unique plant and animal life. The silvery lupine, bunchberry, and lodgepole pine all grow in the cool, moist climate of the hills.
Vegetated island
River flow is diverted by deposited sediments
Bar
Sand flat
Braided rivers are shallow and fast-flowing. The interlaced branches are formed when excess sediments, which can no longer be transported, are deposited. The sediments collect in the river channel forming bars and sand flats. Islands form when the bars are colonized by vegetation.
South Saskatchewan River
The Alberta and Saskatchewan plains bear strong testament to past glaciations. The Assiniboine, Saskatchewan and Qu'Appelle Rivers occupy flat-bottomed, steep-sided valleys eroded during the last Ice Age by glacial meltwater.
***Across the tundra** of northern Manitoba, widespread permafrost inhibits water from permeating the soil. This causes rivers like the Churchill to flow in many channels, which can be frozen for up to six months during the winter.*
The Nelson and Churchill Rivers drain northward across the Canadian Shield to Hudson Bay. The shield covers three-fifths of Saskatchewan.
Setting Lake
***Ancient granite outcrops**, part of the Canadian Shield, rise above the surface of Setting Lake, which was initially formed by meltwater from the last Ice Age.*
The lowlands of Manitoba are a basin that once held the vast post-glacial Lake Agassiz, remnants of which include Lake Winnipeg, Lake Winnipegosis, and Lake Manitoba.

TERRITORIES
NUNAVUT
Hudson Bay
ALBERTA
SASKATCHEWAN
MANITOBA
ONTARIO
UNITED STATES OF AMERICA
Lake Athabasca
Lake Winnipeg
Lake Winnipegosis
Reindeer Lake
Lesser Slave Lake
Edmonton
Calgary
Regina
Saskatoon
Winnipeg
Red Deer
Lethbridge
Medicine Hat
Prince Albert
Brandon
Moose Jaw
Fort McMurray
Churchill
Thompson
Flin Flon
Grande Prairie
Lloydminster
North Battleford
Cypress Hills
Wood Mountain
Birch Mountains
Caribou Mountains
Clear Hills
Pasquia Hills
Porcupine Hills
Duck Mountain
Riding Mountain
Turtle Mountain
Cape Churchill
Cape Tatnam
Nueltin Lake
Selwyn Lake
Wollaston Lake
Southern Indian Lake
Cedar Lake
Lake Manitoba
Lake of the Woods

CANADA: EASTERN PROVINCES

New Brunswick, Newfoundland, Nova Scotia, Ontario, Prince Edward Island, Quebec, *St. Pierre & Miquelon* (to France)

COLONIZED BY BOTH THE ENGLISH AND THE FRENCH during the 16th century, Canada's eastern provinces are still marked by their dual influences. They contain the last fragment of once-sizeable French territories, the islands of St. Pierre and Miquelon. French remains Canada's second official language and Quebec's first language. The population of the eastern provinces is highly concentrated in the south, especially along the border with the US. A recent decline in fishing in the Atlantic provinces has encouraged a steady flow of westerly migration to more properous regions. The north, around Hudson Bay, remains snow-covered for most of the year and the indigenous Inuit people make up the bulk of its sparse population.

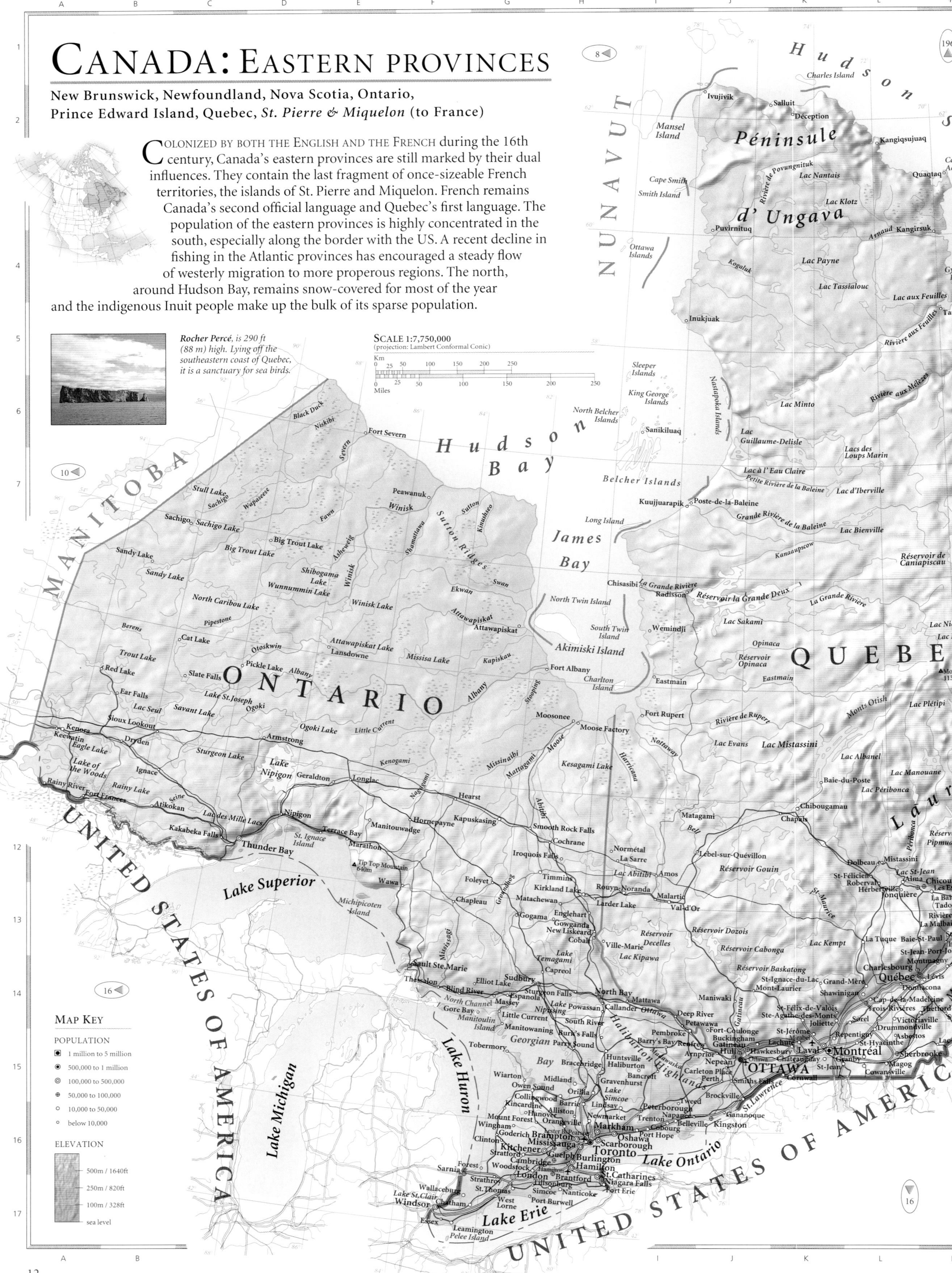

Rocher Percé, is 290 ft (88 m) high. Lying off the southeastern coast of Quebec, it is a sanctuary for sea birds.
SCALE 1:7,750,000
(projection: Lambert Conformal Conic)
Km 0 25 50 100 150 200 250
Miles 0 25 50 100 150 200 250
MAP KEY
POPULATION
1 million to 5 million
500,000 to 1 million
100,000 to 500,000
50,000 to 100,000
10,000 to 50,000
below 10,000
ELEVATION
500m / 1640ft
250m / 820ft
100m / 328ft
sea level
NUNAVUT
MANITOBA
ONTARIO
QUEBEC
UNITED STATES OF AMERICA
Hudson Bay
James Bay
Péninsule d'Ungava
Lake Superior
Lake Michigan
Lake Huron
Lake Erie
Lake Ontario
Georgian Bay
Lake Nipigon
OTTAWA
Toronto
Montréal
Québec
Hamilton
London
Windsor
Sudbury
Thunder Bay
Sault Ste. Marie
Kingston

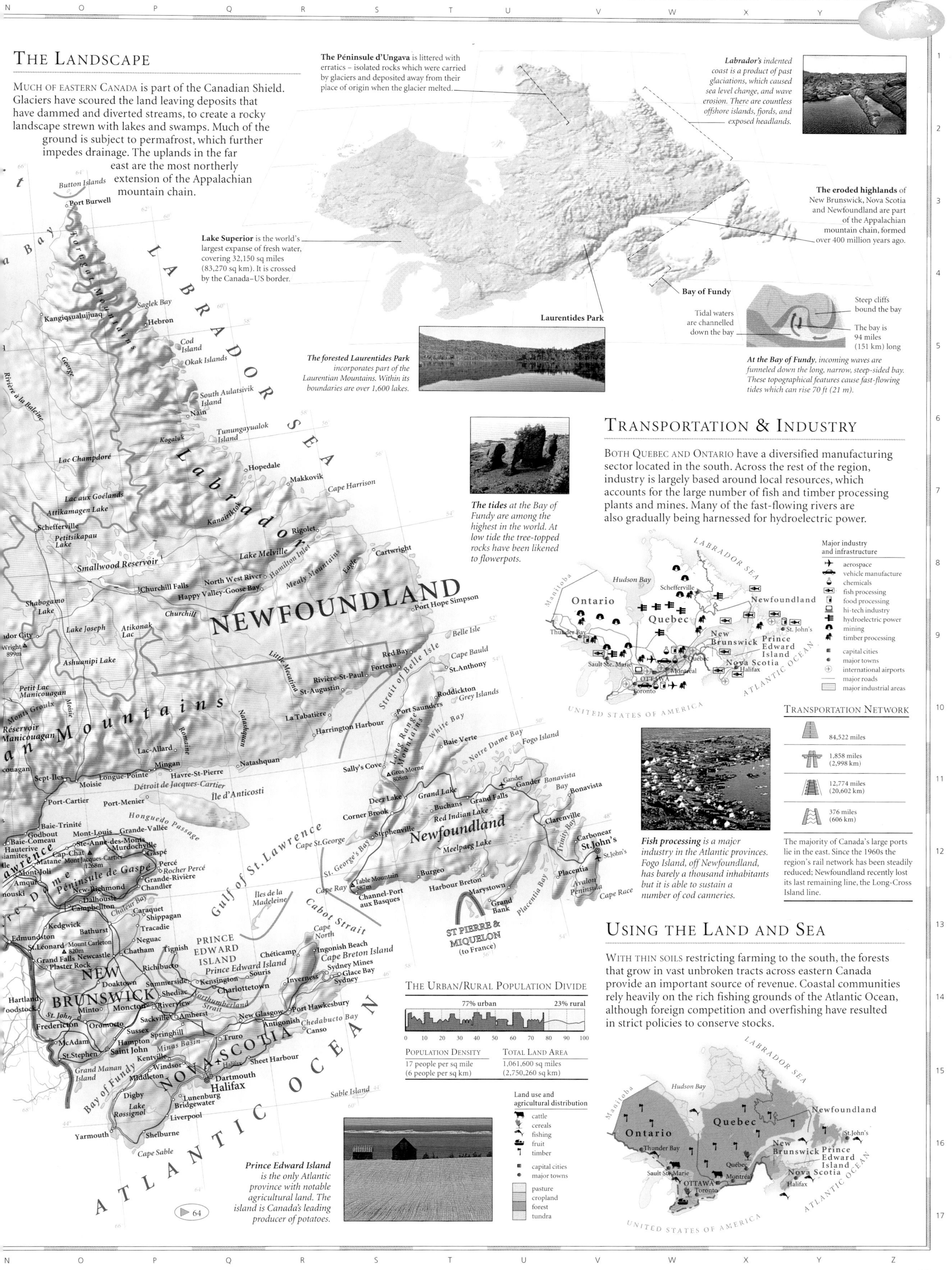

N O P Q R S T U V W X Y Z
1 2 3 4 5 6 7 8 9 10 11 12 13 14 15 16 17
LABRADOR SEA
Labrador
NEWFOUNDLAND
Newfoundland
Button Islands
Port Burwell
Torngat Mountains
Saglek Bay
Hebron
Kangiqsualujjuaq
Cod Island
Okak Islands
South Aulatsivik Island
Nain
Tunungayualok Island
Kogaluk
Lac Champdoré
Hopedale
Makkovik
Cape Harrison
Lac aux Goélands
Attikamagen Lake
Kanairiktok
Schefferville
Petitsikapau Lake
Rigolet
Cartwright
Lake Melville
Hamilton Inlet
Mealy Mountains
Eagle
Smallwood Reservoir
North West River
Churchill Falls
Happy Valley-Goose Bay
Port Hope Simpson
Churchill
Shabogamo Lake
Lake Joseph
Atikonak Lac
Ashuanipi Lake
Belle Isle
Cape Bauld
St.Anthony
Red Bay
Forteau
Strait of Belle Isle
Little Mecatina
Rivière-St-Paul
St-Augustin
Petit Lac Manicouagan
Monts Groulx
Moisie
Natashquan
Romaine
Réservoir Manicouagan
Mountains
La Tabatière
Harrington Harbour
Roddickton
Grey Islands
Port Saunders
White Bay
Long Range Mountains
Baie Verte
Notre Dame Bay
Fogo Island
Lac-Allard
Mingan
Natashquan
Sept-Iles
Longue-Pointe
Havre-St-Pierre
Moisie
Détroit de Jacques-Cartier
Île d'Anticosti
Sally's Cove
Gros Morne 806m
Gander
Bonavista Bay
Bonavista
Port-Cartier
Port-Menier
Honguedo Passage
Deer Lake
Grand Lake
Buchans
Grand Falls
Red Indian Lake
Corner Brook
Clarenville
Trinity Bay
Carbonear
St.John's
Baie-Trinité
Godbout
Baie-Comeau
Hauterive
Mont-Louis
Grande-Vallée
Ste-Anne-des-Monts
Murdochville
Cap-Chat
Matane
Mont Jacques-Cartier 1268m
Gaspé
Percé
Rocher Percé
Grande-Rivière
Chandler
Péninsule de Gaspé
New-Richmond
Mont-Joli
Amqui
Dalhousie
Campbellton
Chaleur Bay
Caraquet
Shippagan
Tracadie
Bathurst
Kedgwick
Edmundston
St.Léonard
Mount Carleton 820m
Neguac
Chatham
Grand Falls
Newcastle
Plaster Rock
Gulf of St. Lawrence
Cape St.George
Stephenville
St. George's Bay
Table Mountain 587m
Cape Ray
Channel-Port aux Basques
Meelpaeg Lake
Burgeo
Harbour Breton
Marystown
Grand Bank
Placentia Bay
Placentia
Avalon Peninsula
Cape Race
ST PIERRE & MIQUELON (to France)
Cabot Strait
Cape North
Iles de la Madeleine
PRINCE EDWARD ISLAND
Prince Edward Island
Tignish
Chéticamp
Ingonish Beach
Cape Breton Island
Sydney Mines
Glace Bay
Sydney
Inverness
Souris
Kensington
Charlottetown
Summerside
Richibucto
NEW BRUNSWICK
Doaktown
Shediac
Riverview
Moncton
Minto
Northumberland Strait
Hartland
Woodstock
Fredericton
Oromocto
St. John
Sackville
Amherst
New Glasgow
Antigonish
Port Hawkesbury
Chedabucto Bay
Canso
Sussex
Springhill
Truro
NOVA SCOTIA
McAdam
Hampton
Saint John
Minas Basin
St.Stephen
Kentville
Windsor
Sheet Harbour
Grand Manan Island
Middleton
Dartmouth
Halifax
Bay of Fundy
Digby
Lunenburg
Bridgewater
Lake Rossignol
Liverpool
Sable Island
Yarmouth
Shelburne
Cape Sable
ATLANTIC OCEAN
Laurentides Park
Bay of Fundy
Tidal waters are channelled down the bay
Steep cliffs bound the bay
The bay is 94 miles (151 km) long
LABRADOR SEA
Hudson Bay
Manitoba
Ontario
Quebec
Schefferville
Newfoundland
Thunder Bay
St. John's
New Brunswick
Prince Edward Island
Nova Scotia
Halifax
Sault Ste. Marie
Québec
Montréal
OTTAWA
Toronto
ATLANTIC OCEAN
UNITED STATES OF AMERICA
Major industry and infrastructure
aerospace
vehicle manufacture
chemicals
fish processing
food processing
hi-tech industry
hydroelectric power
mining
timber processing
capital cities
major towns
international airports
major roads
major industrial areas
Transportation Network
84,522 miles
1,858 miles (2,998 km)
12,774 miles (20,602 km)
376 miles (606 km)
The Urban/Rural Population Divide
77% urban
23% rural
0 10 20 30 40 50 60 70 80 90 100
Land use and agricultural distribution
cattle
cereals
fishing
fruit
timber
capital cities
major towns
pasture
cropland
forest
tundra

The Landscape

Much of eastern Canada is part of the Canadian Shield. Glaciers have scoured the land leaving deposits that have dammed and diverted streams, to create a rocky landscape strewn with lakes and swamps. Much of the ground is subject to permafrost, which further impedes drainage. The uplands in the far east are the most northerly extension of the Appalachian mountain chain.

The Péninsule d'Ungava is littered with erratics – isolated rocks which were carried by glaciers and deposited away from their place of origin when the glacier melted.

Labrador's indented coast is a product of past glaciations, which caused sea level change, and wave erosion. There are countless offshore islands, fjords, and exposed headlands.

Lake Superior is the world's largest expanse of fresh water, covering 32,150 sq miles (83,270 sq km). It is crossed by the Canada–US border.

The eroded highlands of New Brunswick, Nova Scotia and Newfoundland are part of the Appalachian mountain chain, formed over 400 million years ago.

The forested Laurentides Park incorporates part of the Laurentian Mountains. Within its boundaries are over 1,600 lakes.

At the Bay of Fundy, incoming waves are funneled down the long, narrow, steep-sided bay. These topographical features cause fast-flowing tides which can rise 70 ft (21 m).

***The tides** at the Bay of Fundy are among the highest in the world. At low tide the tree-topped rocks have been likened to flowerpots.*

Transportation & Industry

Both Quebec and Ontario have a diversified manufacturing sector located in the south. Across the rest of the region, industry is largely based around local resources, which accounts for the large number of fish and timber processing plants and mines. Many of the fast-flowing rivers are also gradually being harnessed for hydroelectric power.

***Fish processing** is a major industry in the Atlantic provinces. Fogo Island, off Newfoundland, has barely a thousand inhabitants but it is able to sustain a number of cod canneries.*

The majority of Canada's large ports lie in the east. Since the 1960s the region's rail network has been steadily reduced; Newfoundland recently lost its last remaining line, the Long-Cross Island line.

Population Density	Total Land Area
17 people per sq mile (6 people per sq km)	1,061,600 sq miles (2,750,260 sq km)

Using the Land and Sea

With thin soils restricting farming to the south, the forests that grow in vast unbroken tracts across eastern Canada provide an important source of revenue. Coastal communities rely heavily on the rich fishing grounds of the Atlantic Ocean, although foreign competition and overfishing have resulted in strict policies to conserve stocks.

***Prince Edward Island** is the only Atlantic province with notable agricultural land. The island is Canada's leading producer of potatoes.*

▶ 64

SOUTHEASTERN CANADA

Southern Ontario, Southern Quebec

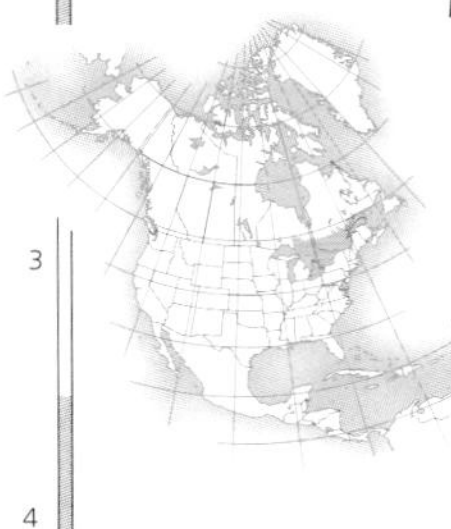

THE SOUTHERN PARTS of Quebec and Ontario form the economic heart of Canada. The two provinces are divided by their language and culture; in Quebec, French is the main language, whereas English is spoken in Ontario. Separatist sentiment in Quebec has led to a provincial referendum on the question of a sovereignty association with Canada. The region contains Canada's capital, Ottawa and its two largest cities: Toronto, the center of commerce and Montréal, the cultural and administrative heart of French Canada.

The port at Montréal is situated on the St. Lawrence Seaway. A network of 16 locks allows sea-going vessels access to routes once plied by fur-trappers and early settlers.

Niagara Falls lies on the border between Canada and the US. It comprises a system of two falls: American Falls, in New York, is separated from Horseshoe Falls, in Ontario, by Goat Island. Horseshoe Falls, seen here, plunges 184 ft (56 m) and is 2,500 ft (762 m) wide.

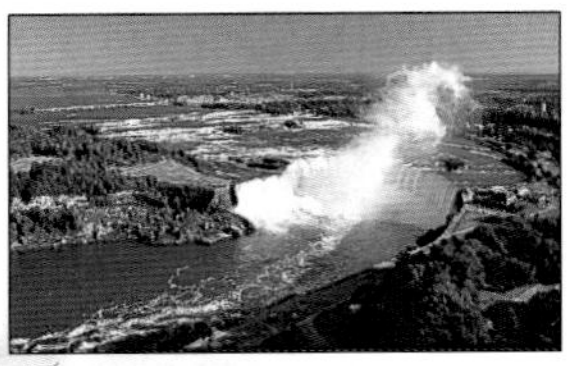

TRANSPORTATION & INDUSTRY

THE CITIES OF SOUTHERN QUEBEC AND ONTARIO, and their hinterlands, form the heart of Canadian manufacturing industry. Toronto is Canada's leading financial center, and Ontario's motor and aerospace industries have developed around the city. A major center for nickel mining lies to the north of Toronto. Most of Quebec's industry is located in Montréal, the oldest port in North America. Chemicals, paper manufacture, and the construction of transportation equipment are leading industrial activities.

Sault Ste.Marie
North Bay
Quebec
Québec
Gaspé
New Brunswick
Lake Huron
Ontario
Montréal
OTTAWA
Toronto
Lake Ontario
Lake Erie
UNITED STATES OF AMERICA

Major industry and infrastructure

- car manufacture
- chemicals
- engineering
- finance
- food processing
- hi-tech industry
- mining
- iron & steel
- textiles
- paper industry
- timber processing
- capital cities
- major towns
- international airports
- major roads
- major industrial areas

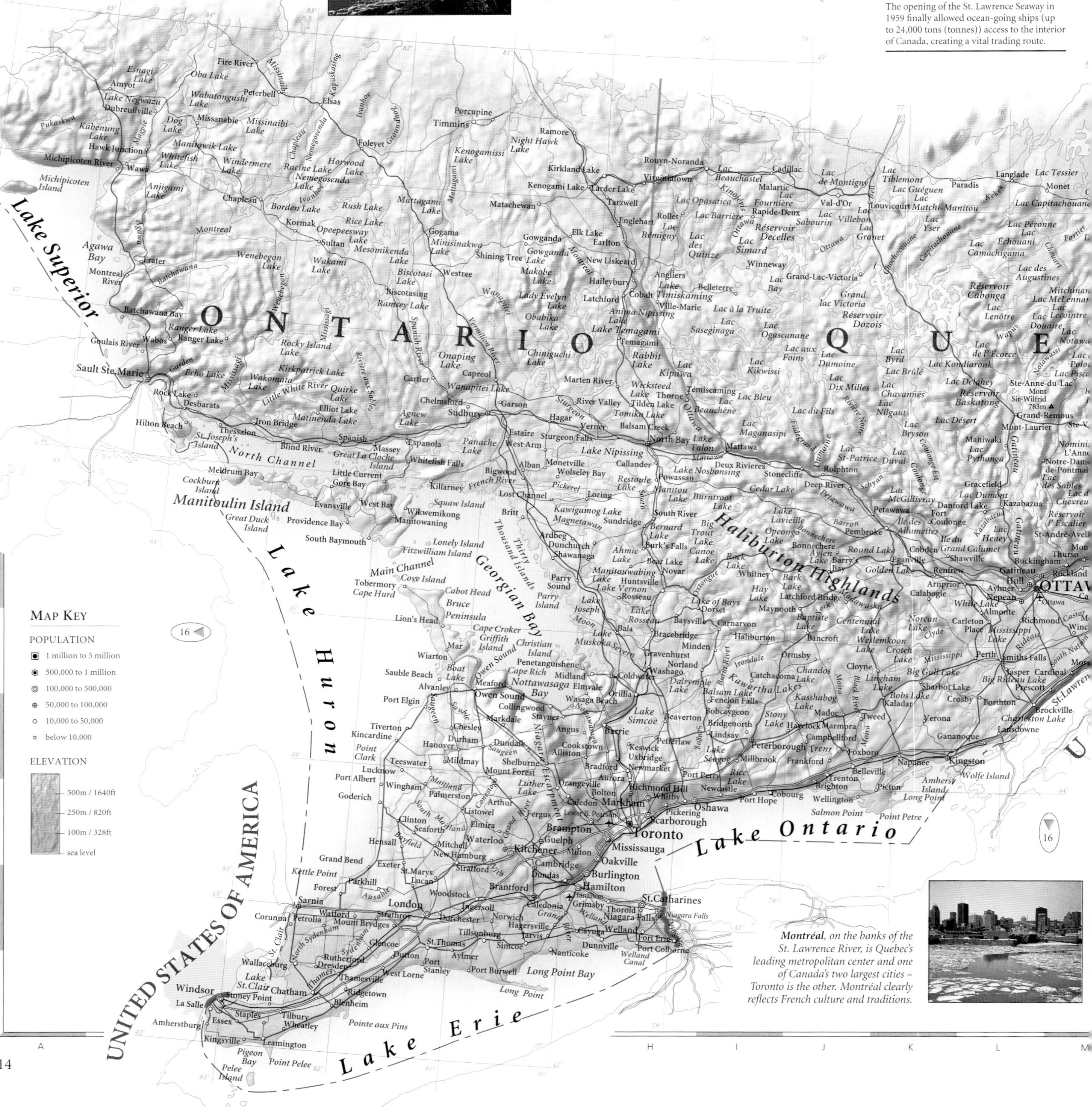

TRANSPORTATION NETWORK

The opening of the St. Lawrence Seaway in 1959 finally allowed ocean-going ships (up to 24,000 tons (tonnes)) access to the interior of Canada, creating a vital trading route.

MAP KEY

POPULATION

- 1 million to 5 million
- 500,000 to 1 million
- 100,000 to 500,000
- 50,000 to 100,000
- 10,000 to 50,000
- below 10,000

ELEVATION

- 500m / 1640ft
- 250m / 820ft
- 100m / 328ft
- sea level

Montréal, on the banks of the St. Lawrence River, is Quebec's leading metropolitan center and one of Canada's two largest cities – Toronto is the other. Montréal clearly reflects French culture and traditions.

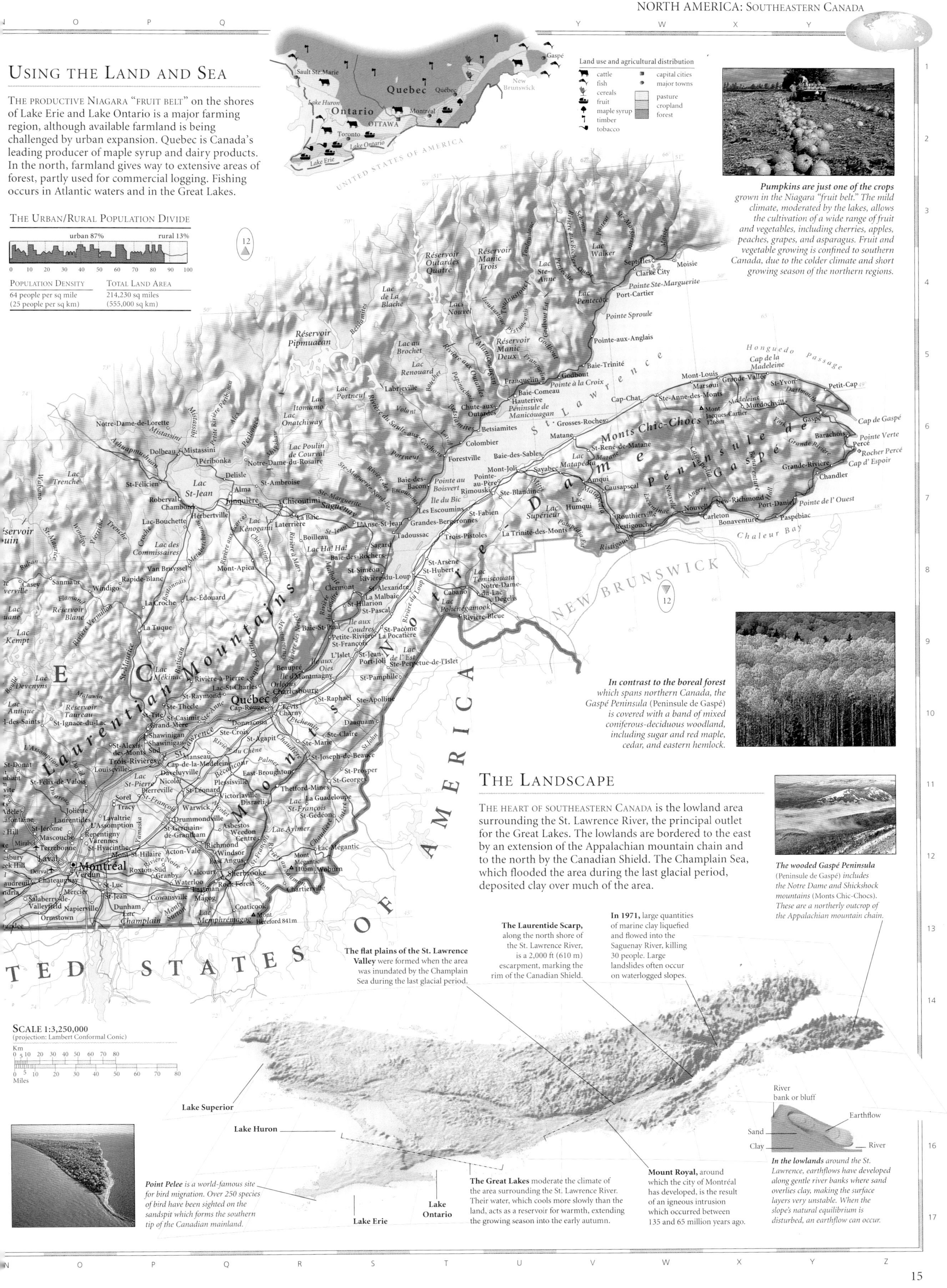
Land use and agricultural distribution
cattle
fish
cereals
fruit
maple syrup
timber
tobacco
capital cities
major towns
pasture
cropland
forest
Quebec
Ontario
OTTAWA
Toronto
Montreal
Sault Ste.Marie
Lake Huron
Lake Erie
Lake Ontario
New Brunswick
Gaspé
UNITED STATES OF AMERICA
urban 87%
rural 13%
0 10 20 30 40 50 60 70 80 90 100
Laurentian Mountains
Monts Notre-Dame
Péninsule de Gaspé
Monts Chic-Chocs
St. Lawrence
NEW BRUNSWICK
UNITED STATES OF AMERICA
Québec
Montréal
Chaleur Bay
Honguedo Passage
SCALE 1:3,250,000
(projection: Lambert Conformal Conic)
Lake Superior
Lake Huron
Lake Erie
Lake Ontario
River bank or bluff
Earthflow
Sand
Clay
River

Using the Land and Sea

The productive Niagara "fruit belt" on the shores of Lake Erie and Lake Ontario is a major farming region, although available farmland is being challenged by urban expansion. Quebec is Canada's leading producer of maple syrup and dairy products. In the north, farmland gives way to extensive areas of forest, partly used for commercial logging. Fishing occurs in Atlantic waters and in the Great Lakes.

The Urban/Rural Population Divide

Population Density	Total Land Area
64 people per sq mile (25 people per sq km)	214,230 sq miles (555,000 sq km)

***Pumpkins are just one of the crops** grown in the Niagara "fruit belt." The mild climate, moderated by the lakes, allows the cultivation of a wide range of fruit and vegetables, including cherries, apples, peaches, grapes, and asparagus. Fruit and vegetable growing is confined to southern Canada, due to the colder climate and short growing season of the northern regions.*

***In contrast to the boreal forest** which spans northern Canada, the Gaspé Peninsula (Peninsule de Gaspé) is covered with a band of mixed coniferous-deciduous woodland, including sugar and red maple, cedar, and eastern hemlock.*

The Landscape

The heart of southeastern Canada is the lowland area surrounding the St. Lawrence River, the principal outlet for the Great Lakes. The lowlands are bordered to the east by an extension of the Appalachian mountain chain and to the north by the Canadian Shield. The Champlain Sea, which flooded the area during the last glacial period, deposited clay over much of the area.

***The wooded Gaspé Peninsula** (Peninsule de Gaspé) includes the Notre Dame and Shickshock mountains (Monts Chic-Chocs). These are a northerly outcrop of the Appalachian mountain chain.*

The Laurentide Scarp, along the north shore of the St. Lawrence River, is a 2,000 ft (610 m) escarpment, marking the rim of the Canadian Shield.

In 1971, large quantities of marine clay liquefied and flowed into the Saguenay River, killing 30 people. Large landslides often occur on waterlogged slopes.

The flat plains of the St. Lawrence Valley were formed when the area was inundated by the Champlain Sea during the last glacial period.

Point Pelee is a world-famous site for bird migration. Over 250 species of bird have been sighted on the sandspit which forms the southern tip of the Canadian mainland.

The Great Lakes moderate the climate of the area surrounding the St. Lawrence River. Their water, which cools more slowly than the land, acts as a reservoir for warmth, extending the growing season into the early autumn.

Mount Royal, around which the city of Montréal has developed, is the result of an igneous intrusion which occurred between 135 and 65 million years ago.

***In the lowlands** around the St. Lawrence, earthflows have developed along gentle river banks where sand overlies clay, making the surface layers very unstable. When the slope's natural equilibrium is disturbed, an earthflow can occur.*

THE UNITED STATES OF AMERICA

CONTERMINOUS USA (FOR ALASKA AND HAWAII SEE PAGES 38–39)

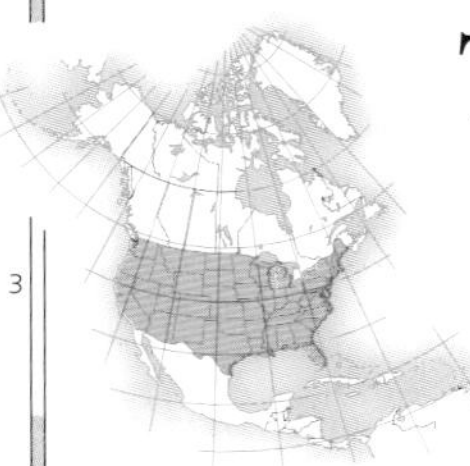

THE US'S PROGRESSION FROM FRONTIER TERRITORY to economic and political superpower has taken less than 200 years. The 48 conterminous states, along with the outlying states of Alaska and Hawaii, are part of a federal union, held together by the guiding principles of the US Constitution, which embodies the ideals of democracy and liberty for all. Abundant fertile land and a rich resource-base fueled and sustained US economic development. With the spread of agriculture and the growth of trade and industry came the need for a larger workforce, which was supplied by millions of immigrants, many seeking an escape from poverty and political or religious persecution. Immigration continues today, particularly from Central America and Asia.

***Washington D.C.** was established as the nation's capital in 1790. It is home to the seat of national government, on Capitol Hill, as well as the President's official residence, the White House.*

SCALE 1: 12,700,000
(projection: Lambert Azimuthal Equal Area)

***Mount Rainier** is a dormant volcano in the Cascade Range, Washington. This 14,090 ft (4392 m) peak is flanked by the most extensive glacier outside Alaska.*

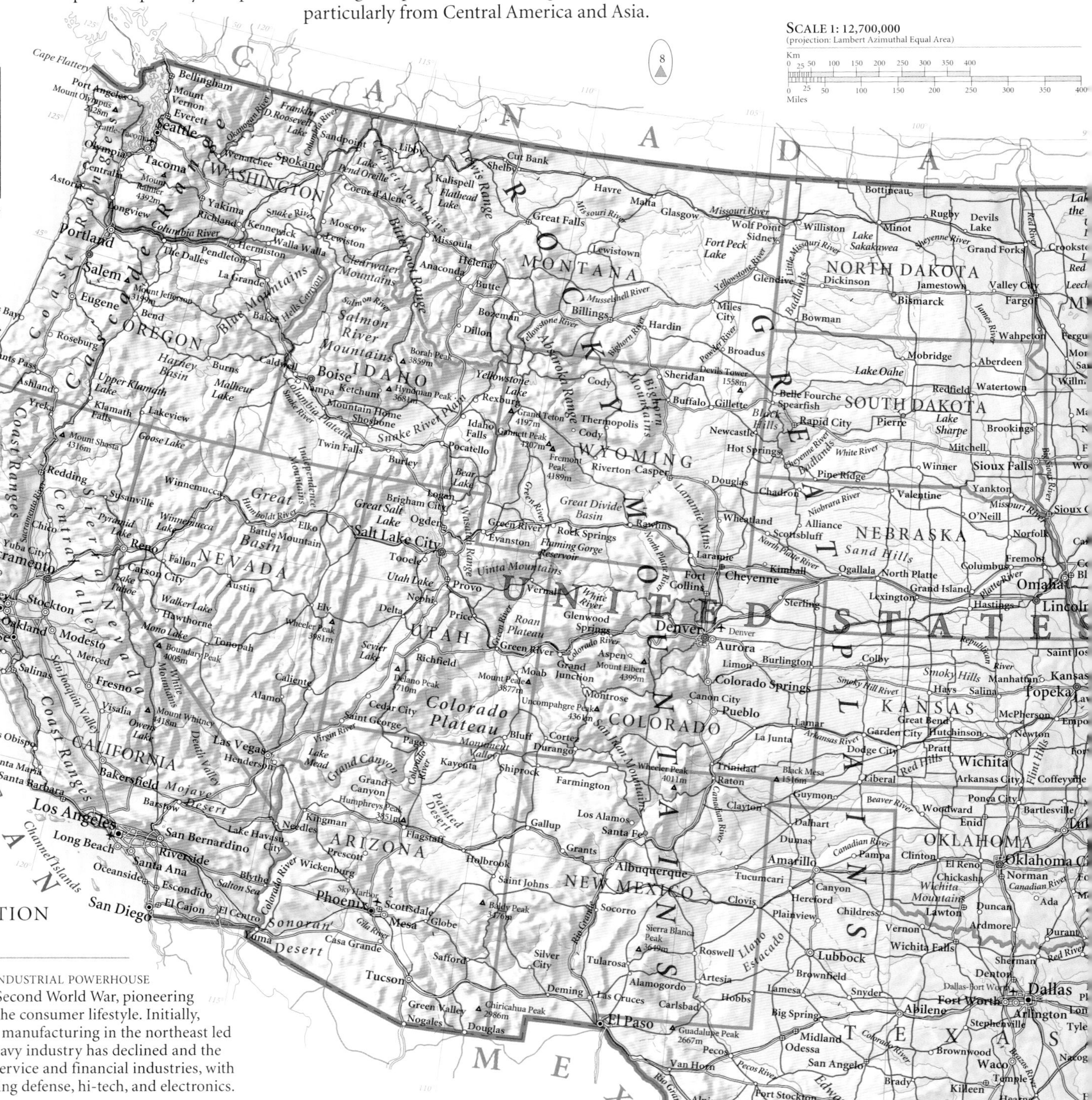

TRANSPORTATION & INDUSTRY

THE US HAS BEEN THE INDUSTRIAL POWERHOUSE of the world since the Second World War, pioneering mass-production and the consumer lifestyle. Initially, heavy engineering and manufacturing in the northeast led the economy. Today, heavy industry has declined and the economy is driven by service and financial industries, with the most important being defense, hi-tech, and electronics.

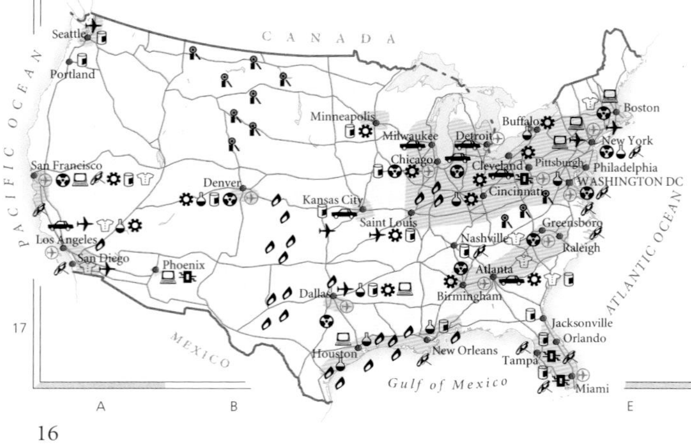

TRANSPORTATION NETWORK

3,875,040 miles (6,240,000 km)	52,388 miles (84,361 km)
148,308 miles (235,238 km)	25,467 miles (41,009 km)

Transportation in the US is dominated by the car which, with the extensive Interstate Highway system, allows great personal mobility. Today, internal air flights between major cities provide the most rapid cross-country travel.

Major industry and infrastructure

- aerospace
- car manufacture
- chemicals
- coal
- electronics
- engineering
- food processing
- hi-tech industry
- oil & gas
- research & development
- textiles
- tourism
- capital cities
- major towns
- international airports
- major roads
- major industrial areas

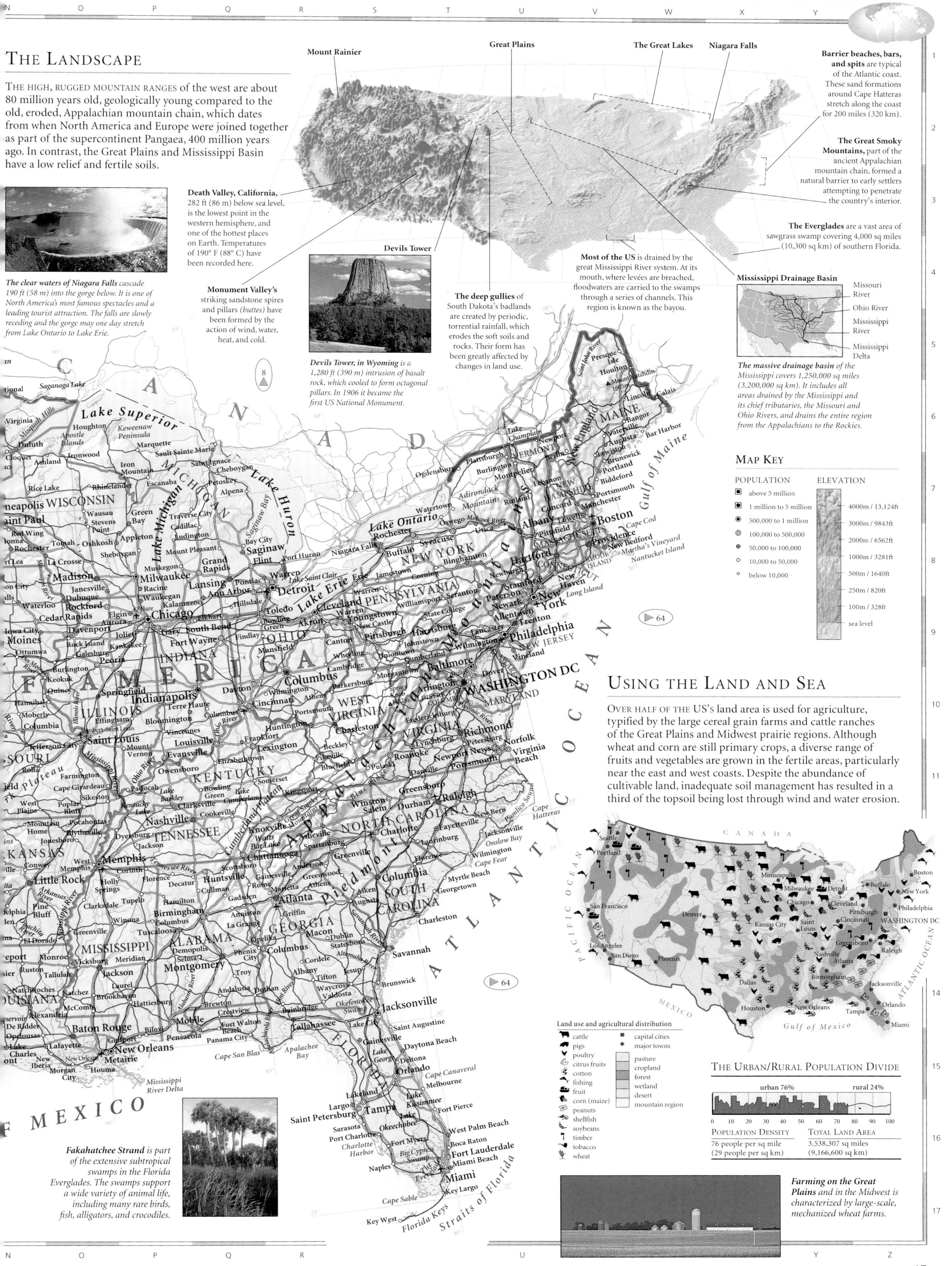

THE LANDSCAPE

THE HIGH, RUGGED MOUNTAIN RANGES of the west are about 80 million years old, geologically young compared to the old, eroded, Appalachian mountain chain, which dates from when North America and Europe were joined together as part of the supercontinent Pangaea, 400 million years ago. In contrast, the Great Plains and Mississippi Basin have a low relief and fertile soils.

Mount Rainier
Great Plains
The Great Lakes
Niagara Falls
Barrier beaches, bars, and spits are typical of the Atlantic coast. These sand formations around Cape Hatteras stretch along the coast for 200 miles (320 km).
The Great Smoky Mountains, part of the ancient Appalachian mountain chain, formed a natural barrier to early settlers attempting to penetrate the country's interior.
The Everglades are a vast area of sawgrass swamp covering 4,000 sq miles (10,300 sq km) of southern Florida.
Death Valley, California, 282 ft (86 m) below sea level, is the lowest point in the western hemisphere, and one of the hottest places on Earth. Temperatures of 190° F (88° C) have been recorded here.
Monument Valley's striking sandstone spires and pillars (*buttes*) have been formed by the action of wind, water, heat, and cold.
Devils Tower
The deep gullies of South Dakota's badlands are created by periodic, torrential rainfall, which erodes the soft soils and rocks. Their form has been greatly affected by changes in land use.
Most of the US is drained by the great Mississippi River system. At its mouth, where levées are breached, floodwaters are carried to the swamps through a series of channels. This region is known as the bayou.
Mississippi Drainage Basin
Missouri River
Ohio River
Mississippi River
Mississippi Delta

The clear waters of Niagara Falls cascade 190 ft (58 m) into the gorge below. It is one of North America's most famous spectacles and a leading tourist attraction. The falls are slowly receding and the gorge may one day stretch from Lake Ontario to Lake Erie.

***Devils Tower,* in Wyoming is a 1,280 ft (390 m) intrusion of basalt rock, which cooled to form octagonal pillars. In 1906 it became the first US National Monument.**

***The massive drainage basin** of the Mississippi covers 1,250,000 sq miles (3,200,000 sq km). It includes all areas drained by the Mississippi and its chief tributaries, the Missouri and Ohio Rivers, and drains the entire region from the Appalachians to the Rockies.*

MAP KEY

POPULATION
above 5 million
1 million to 5 million
500,000 to 1 million
100,000 to 500,000
50,000 to 100,000
10,000 to 50,000
below 10,000
ELEVATION
4000m / 13,124ft
3000m / 9843ft
2000m / 6562ft
1000m / 3281ft
500m / 1640ft
250m / 820ft
100m / 328ft
sea level
CANADA
AMERICA
ATLANTIC OCEAN
MEXICO
Gulf of Maine
Lake Superior
Lake Michigan
Lake Huron
Lake Erie
Lake Ontario
WASHINGTON DC
Appalachian Mountains
Piedmont
Straits of Florida

USING THE LAND AND SEA

OVER HALF OF THE US's land area is used for agriculture, typified by the large cereal grain farms and cattle ranches of the Great Plains and Midwest prairie regions. Although wheat and corn are still primary crops, a diverse range of fruits and vegetables are grown in the fertile areas, particularly near the east and west coasts. Despite the abundance of cultivable land, inadequate soil management has resulted in a third of the topsoil being lost through wind and water erosion.

Land use and agricultural distribution
cattle
pigs
poultry
citrus fruits
cotton
fishing
fruit
corn (maize)
peanuts
shellfish
soybeans
timber
tobacco
wheat
capital cities
major towns
pasture
cropland
forest
wetland
desert
mountain region
PACIFIC OCEAN
ATLANTIC OCEAN
Gulf of Mexico

THE URBAN/RURAL POPULATION DIVIDE

urban 76%
rural 24%
0 10 20 30 40 50 60 70 80 90 100

POPULATION DENSITY	TOTAL LAND AREA
76 people per sq mile (29 people per sq km)	3,538,307 sq miles (9,166,600 sq km)

***Fakahatchee Strand** is part of the extensive subtropical swamps in the Florida Everglades. The swamps support a wide variety of animal life, including many rare birds, fish, alligators, and crocodiles.*

***Farming on the Great Plains** and in the Midwest is characterized by large-scale, mechanized wheat farms.*

USA: Northeastern States

Connecticut, Maine, Massachusetts, New Hampshire, New Jersey, New York, Pennsylvania, Rhode Island, Vermont

THE INDENTED COAST AND VAST WOODLANDS of the northeastern states were the original core area for European expansion. The rustic character of New England prevails after nearly four centuries, while the great cities of the Atlantic seaboard have formed an almost continuous urban region. Over 20 million immigrants entered New York from 1855 to 1924 and the northeast became the industrial center of the US. After the decline of mining and heavy manufacturing, economic dynamism has been restored with the growth of hi-tech and service industries.

Chelsea in Vermont, surrounded by trees in their fall foliage. Tourism and agriculture dominate the economy of this self-consciously rural state, where no town exceeds 30,000 people.

Transportation & Industry

THE PRINCIPAL SEABOARD CITIES grew up on trade and manufacturing. They are now global centers of commerce and corporate administration, dominating the regional economy. Research and development facilities support an expanding electronics and communications sector throughout the region. Pharmaceutical and chemical industries are important in New Jersey and Pennsylvania.

Transportation Network

340,090 miles (544,144 km)	4813 miles 7700 km
12,872 miles (20,592 km)	2108 miles (3389 km)

New York's commercial success is tied historically to its transportation connections. The Erie Canal, completed in 1825, opened up the Great Lakes and the interior to New York's markets and carried a stream of immigrants into the Midwest.

Major industry and infrastructure

- chemicals
- coal
- defense
- electronics
- engineering
- finance
- hi-tech industry
- iron & steel
- pharmaceuticals
- printing & publishing
- research & development
- textiles
- timber processing
- major towns
- international airports
- major roads
- major industrial area

Map Key

POPULATION

- above 5 million
- 1 million to 5 million
- 500,000 to 1 million
- 100,000 to 500,000
- 50,000 to 100,000
- 10,000 to 50,000
- below 10,000

ELEVATION

- 1000m / 3281ft
- 500m / 1640ft
- 250m / 820ft
- 100m / 328ft
- sea level

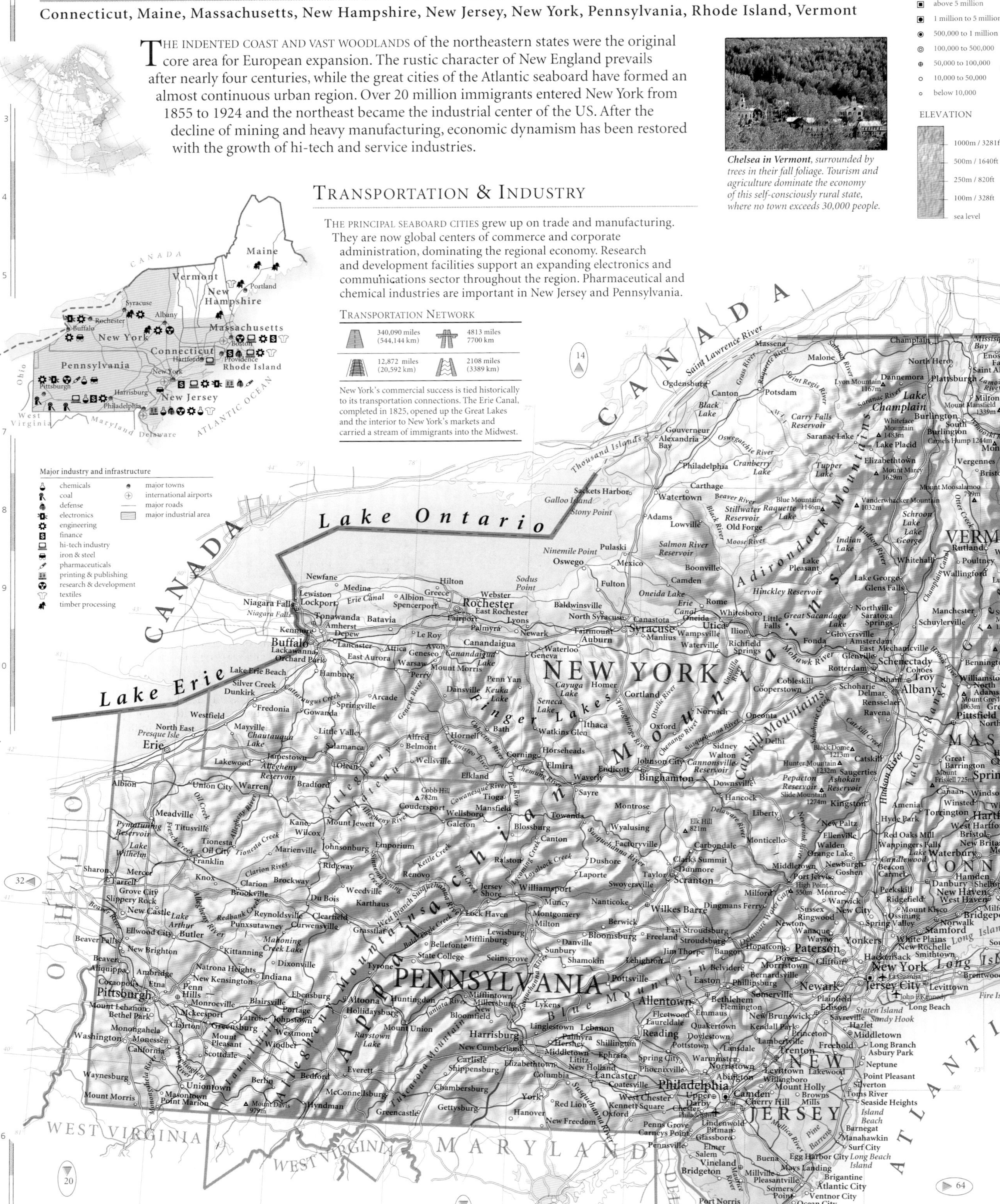
CANADA
Maine
Vermont
New Hampshire
Massachusetts
Connecticut
Rhode Island
New York
Pennsylvania
New Jersey
Ohio
West Virginia
Maryland
Delaware
ATLANTIC OCEAN
Lake Ontario
Lake Erie
NEW YORK
PENNSYLVANIA
NEW JERSEY
VERMONT
MASS
CONNE
WEST VIRGINIA
MARYLAND
DELAWARE
OHIO
ATLANTIC
Adirondack Mountains
Appalachian Mountains
Allegheny Plateau
Allegheny Mountains
Catskill Mountains
Finger Lakes
Blue Mountain
Lake Champlain
Saint Lawrence River
Thousand Islands
Delaware Bay
Long Island
Buffalo
Rochester
Syracuse
Albany
Binghamton
Pittsburgh
Harrisburg
Philadelphia
Allentown
Scranton
Erie
Newark
New York
Jersey City
Trenton
Camden
Atlantic City
Burlington
Plattsburgh
Utica
Ithaca
Elmira
Reading
Lancaster
York
Wilkes Barre
Paterson
Yonkers
Cape May

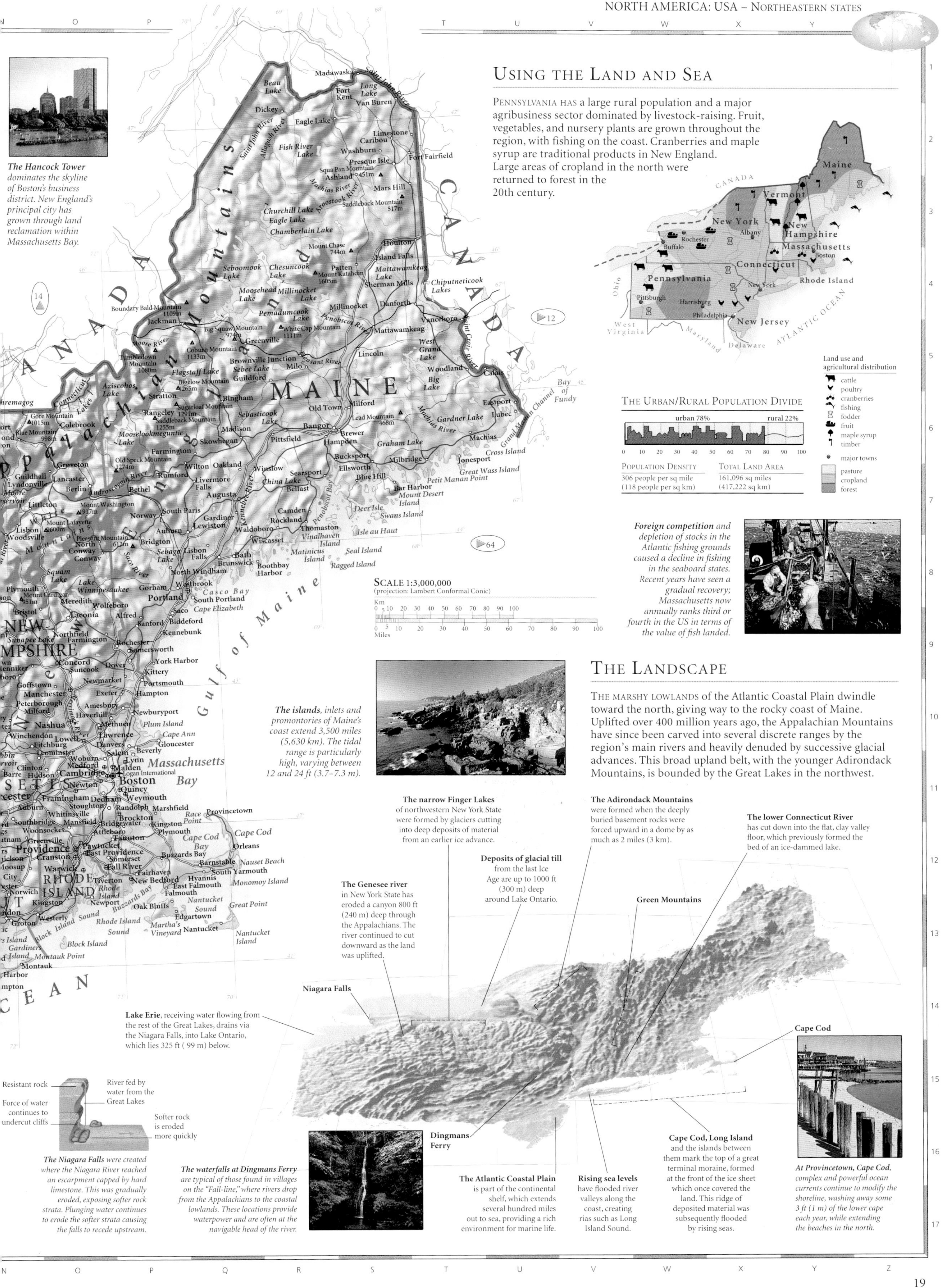

N O P T U V W X Y
1 2 3 4 5 6 7 8 9 10 11 12 13 14 15 16 17
CANADA
MAINE
Appalachian Mountains
Gulf of Maine
Bay of Fundy
Casco Bay
Massachusetts Bay
Cape Cod Bay
Nantucket Sound
Rhode Island Sound
Block Island Sound
Buzzards Bay
NEW HAMPSHIRE
Massachusetts
RHODE ISLAND
Madawaska
Fort Kent
Long Lake
Van Buren
Saint John River
Beau Lake
Dickey
Eagle Lake
Fish River Lake
Limestone
Caribou
Washburn
Fort Fairfield
Presque Isle
Squa Pan Mountain
Ashland
Mars Hill
Saddleback Mountain 517m
Churchill Lake
Eagle Lake
Chamberlain Lake
Mount Chase 744m
Houlton
Island Falls
Patten
Mount Katahdin 1605m
Mattawamkeag Lake
Chiputneticook Lakes
Sherman Mills
Seboomook Lake
Chesuncook Lake
Moosehead Lake
Millinocket Lake
Millinocket
Danforth
Boundary Bald Mountain 1109m
Jackman
Pemadumcook Lake
Penobscot River
Mattawamkeag
Vanceboro
Big Squaw Mountain 974m
White Cap Mountain 1111m
Greenville
Coburn Mountain 1133m
Tumbledown Mountain 1080m
Brownville Junction
Milo
Lincoln
West Grand Lake
Woodland
Calais
Flagstaff Lake
Sebec Lake
Guilford
Bigelow Mountain 1265m
Aziscohos Lake
Stratton
Bingham
Sugarloaf Mountain 1291m
Rangeley
Saddleback Mountain 1255m
Big Lake
Old Town
Milford
Lead Mountain 466m
Eastport
Lubec
Grand Manan Channel
Gardner Lake
Machias River
Machias
Sebasticook Lake
Madison
Bangor
Brewer
Hampden
Pittsfield
Mooselookmeguntic Lake
Skowhegan
Graham Lake
Cross Island
Jonesport
Great Wass Island
Petit Manan Point
Farmington
Bucksport
Ellsworth
Milbridge
Blue Hill
Bar Harbor
Mount Desert Island
Old Speck Mountain 1274m
Wilton
Oakland
Winslow
Searsport
China Lake
Belfast
Rumford
Livermore Falls
Bethel
Augusta
Camden
Rockland
Deer Isle
Swans Island
Isle au Haut
Mount Washington 1917m
Mount Lafayette 1600m
South Paris
Norway
Gardiner
Lewiston
Auburn
Waldoboro
Wiscasset
Thomaston
Vinalhaven Island
Matinicus Island
Seal Island
Ragged Island
Pleasant Mountain 612m
Bridgton
North Conway
Conway
Sebago Lake
Lisbon Falls
Bath
Brunswick
Boothbay Harbor
North Windham
Squam Lake
Lake Winnipesaukee
Gorham
Westbrook
Portland
South Portland
Cape Elizabeth
Meredith
Wolfeboro
Laconia
Alfred
Sanford
Biddeford
Saco
Kennebunk
Northfield
Farmington
Sunapee Lake
Rochester
Somersworth
York Harbor
Kittery
Portsmouth
Concord
Suncook
Dover
Newmarket
Exeter
Hampton
Goffstown
Manchester
Peterborough
Milford
Nashua
Amesbury
Haverhill
Newburyport
Plum Island
Methuen
Lawrence
Cape Ann
Gloucester
Lowell
Danvers
Salem
Beverly
Winchendon
Fitchburg
Leominster
Woburn
Medford
Lynn
Malden
Logan International
Boston
Cambridge
Clinton
Hudson
Newton
Quincy
Weymouth
Framingham
Dedham
Stoughton
Randolph
Marshfield
Brockton
Whitinsville
Southbridge
Mansfield
Bridgewater
Kingston
Plymouth
Provincetown
Race Point
Attleboro
Woonsocket
Taunton
Cape Cod
Orleans
Providence
Pawtucket
East Providence
Cranston
Warwick
Somerset
Fall River
Barnstable
Nauset Beach
South Yarmouth
Fairhaven
Tiverton
New Bedford
Hyannis
East Falmouth
Falmouth
Monomoy Island
Rhode Island
Newport
Kingston
Oak Bluffs
Great Point
Edgartown
Westerly
Martha's Vineyard
Nantucket
Nantucket Island
Block Island
Gardiners Island
Montauk Point
Montauk
12
64
14
SCALE 1:3,000,000
(projection: Lambert Conformal Conic)
Km 0 5 10 20 30 40 50 60 70 80 90 100
Miles 0 5 10 20 30 40 50 60 70 80 90 100

The Hancock Tower dominates the skyline of Boston's business district. New England's principal city has grown through land reclamation within Massachusetts Bay.

Using the Land and Sea

PENNSYLVANIA HAS a large rural population and a major agribusiness sector dominated by livestock-raising. Fruit, vegetables, and nursery plants are grown throughout the region, with fishing on the coast. Cranberries and maple syrup are traditional products in New England. Large areas of cropland in the north were returned to forest in the 20th century.

CANADA
Maine
Vermont
New Hampshire
New York
Massachusetts
Connecticut
Rhode Island
Pennsylvania
New Jersey
West Virginia
Maryland
Delaware
Ohio
ATLANTIC OCEAN
Rochester
Buffalo
Albany
Boston
New York
Pittsburgh
Harrisburg
Philadelphia
Land use and agricultural distribution
cattle
poultry
cranberries
fishing
fodder
fruit
maple syrup
timber
major towns
pasture
cropland
forest

The Urban/Rural Population Divide

urban 78% — rural 22%

0 10 20 30 40 50 60 70 80 90 100

Population Density	Total Land Area
306 people per sq mile (118 people per sq km)	161,096 sq miles (417,222 sq km)

Foreign competition and depletion of stocks in the Atlantic fishing grounds caused a decline in fishing in the seaboard states. Recent years have seen a gradual recovery; Massachusetts now annually ranks third or fourth in the US in terms of the value of fish landed.

The Landscape

THE MARSHY LOWLANDS of the Atlantic Coastal Plain dwindle toward the north, giving way to the rocky coast of Maine. Uplifted over 400 million years ago, the Appalachian Mountains have since been carved into several discrete ranges by the region's main rivers and heavily denuded by successive glacial advances. This broad upland belt, with the younger Adirondack Mountains, is bounded by the Great Lakes in the northwest.

The islands, inlets and promontories of Maine's coast extend 3,500 miles (5,630 km). The tidal range is particularly high, varying between 12 and 24 ft (3.7–7.3 m).

The narrow Finger Lakes of northwestern New York State were formed by glaciers cutting into deep deposits of material from an earlier ice advance.
The Adirondack Mountains were formed when the deeply buried basement rocks were forced upward in a dome by as much as 2 miles (3 km).
The lower Connecticut River has cut down into the flat, clay valley floor, which previously formed the bed of an ice-dammed lake.
Deposits of glacial till from the last Ice Age are up to 1000 ft (300 m) deep around Lake Ontario.
The Genesee river in New York State has eroded a canyon 800 ft (240 m) deep through the Appalachians. The river continued to cut downward as the land was uplifted.
Green Mountains
Niagara Falls
Lake Erie, receiving water flowing from the rest of the Great Lakes, drains via the Niagara Falls, into Lake Ontario, which lies 325 ft (99 m) below.
Cape Cod
Dingmans Ferry
The Atlantic Coastal Plain is part of the continental shelf, which extends several hundred miles out to sea, providing a rich environment for marine life.
Rising sea levels have flooded river valleys along the coast, creating rias such as Long Island Sound.
Cape Cod, Long Island and the islands between them mark the top of a great terminal moraine, formed at the front of the ice sheet which once covered the land. This ridge of deposited material was subsequently flooded by rising seas.
Resistant rock
Force of water continues to undercut cliffs
River fed by water from the Great Lakes
Softer rock is eroded more quickly

The Niagara Falls were created where the Niagara River reached an escarpment capped by hard limestone. This was gradually eroded, exposing softer rock strata. Plunging water continues to erode the softer strata causing the falls to recede upstream.

The waterfalls at Dingmans Ferry are typical of those found in villages on the "Fall-line," where rivers drop from the Appalachians to the coastal lowlands. These locations provide waterpower and are often at the navigable head of the river.

At Provincetown, Cape Cod, complex and powerful ocean currents continue to modify the shoreline, washing away some 3 ft (1 m) of the lower cape each year, while extending the beaches in the north.

USA: Mid-Eastern States

Delaware, District of Columbia, Kentucky, Maryland, North Carolina, South Carolina, Tennessee, Virginia, West Virginia

Key events in American history took place in this diverse region, which became the front line between the North and the South during the Civil War of the 1860s. Strong regional contrasts exist between the fertile coastal plains, the isolated upcountry of the Appalachian Mountains, and the cotton-growing areas of the Mississippi lowlands to the west. While coal mining, a traditional industry in the Appalachians, has declined in recent years leaving much rural poverty, service industries elsewhere have increased, especially in Washington D.C, the nation's capital.

Map Key

POPULATION
- 500,000 to 1 million
- 100,000 to 500,000
- 50,000 to 100,000
- 10,000 to 50,000
- below 10,000

ELEVATION
- 6000m / 19,686ft
- 4000m / 13,124ft
- 3000m / 9843ft
- 2000m / 6562ft
- 1000m / 3281ft
- 500m / 1640ft
- 250m / 820ft
- 100m / 328ft
- sea level

SCALE 1:3,250,000
(projection: Lambert Conformal Conic)

The Bluegrass region of Kentucky centers on the town of Lexington. This exceptionally fertile rolling plain is well known for its thoroughbred horse-breeding ranches.

Transportation & Industry

In the urbanized northeast, manufacturing remains important, alongside a burgeoning service sector. North Carolina is a major center for industrial research and development. Traditional industries include Tennessee whiskey and textiles in South Carolina. The decline of open-cast coal mining in the Appalachians has been hastened by environmental controls, although adventure-tourism is a flourishing new industry.

Major industry and infrastructure
- adventure-tourism
- car manufacture
- coal
- electronics
- engineering
- finance
- food processing
- hi-tech industry
- mining
- research & development
- textiles
- capital cities
- major towns
- international airports
- major roads
- major industrial areas

Transportation Network

452,218 miles (723,548 km)	5,737 miles (8,267 km)
18,336 miles (29,503 km)	4,404 miles (7,081 km)

Tennessee's rivers are part of an important inland bulk-transportation network. Memphis connects with New Orleans in the south, and with cities as distant as Minneapolis, Sioux City, Chicago, and Pittsburgh, via the Mississippi and its tributaries.

The Landscape

The eastern tributaries of the Mississippi drain the interior lowlands. The Cumberland Plateau and the parallel ranges of the Appalachians have been successively uplifted and eroded over time, with the eastern side reduced to a series of foothills known as the Piedmont. The broad coastal plain gradually falls away into salt marshes, lagoons, and offshore bars, broken by flooded estuaries along the shores of the Atlantic.

Natural Bridge in eastern Kentucky is an arch 78 ft (26 m) long and 65 ft (20 m) high. It has been shaped from resistant sandstone by gradual weathering processes, which removed the softer rock lying underneath.

The Allegheny Mountains form the northwestern edge of the Appalachian mountain chain. Continuous folding has formed rich seams of bituminous coal.

Farmland on the eastern shores of Chesapeake Bay is sustained by artificial drainage. The area also provides refuge for a variety of waterfowl.

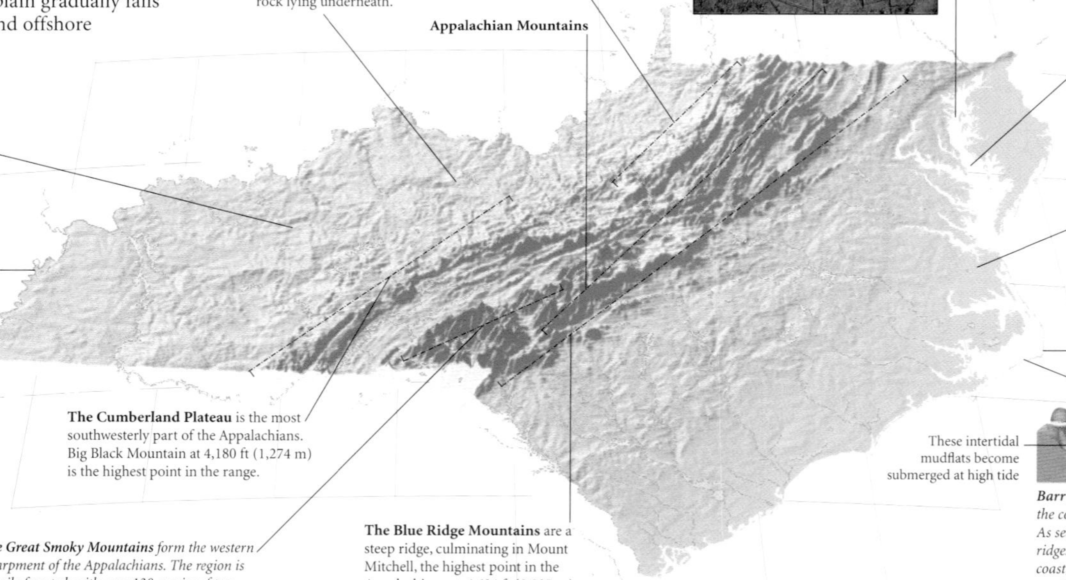

The many inlets of Chesapeake Bay are the flooded tributaries of the main river valley, which have been inundated by rising sea levels.

Appalachian Mountains

Salt marshes such as Great Dismal Swamp, develop where the coast is sheltered. Vast areas of such marshland have been reclaimed for farmland and settlement.

The Mammoth Cave is part of an extensive cave system in the limestone region of southwestern Kentucky. It stretches for over 300 miles (485 km) on five different levels and contains three rivers and three lakes.

The Mississippi River and its tributary the Ohio River form the western border of the region.

Cape Hatteras is the easternmost point of an offshore barrier island; a wave-deposited sand-bar which has become permanent, establishing its own vegetation.

Barrier islands

Tidal inlet

Barrier island

These intertidal mudflats become submerged at high tide

The Cumberland Plateau is the most southwesterly part of the Appalachians. Big Black Mountain at 4,180 ft (1,274 m) is the highest point in the range.

Barrier islands are common along the coasts of North and South Carolina. As sea levels rise, wave action builds up ridges of sand and pebbles parallel to the coast, separated by lagoons or intertidal mudflats, which are flooded at high tide.

The Great Smoky Mountains form the western escarpment of the Appalachians. The region is heavily forested, with over 130 species of tree.

The Blue Ridge Mountains are a steep ridge, culminating in Mount Mitchell, the highest point in the Appalachians, at 6,684 ft (2,037 m).

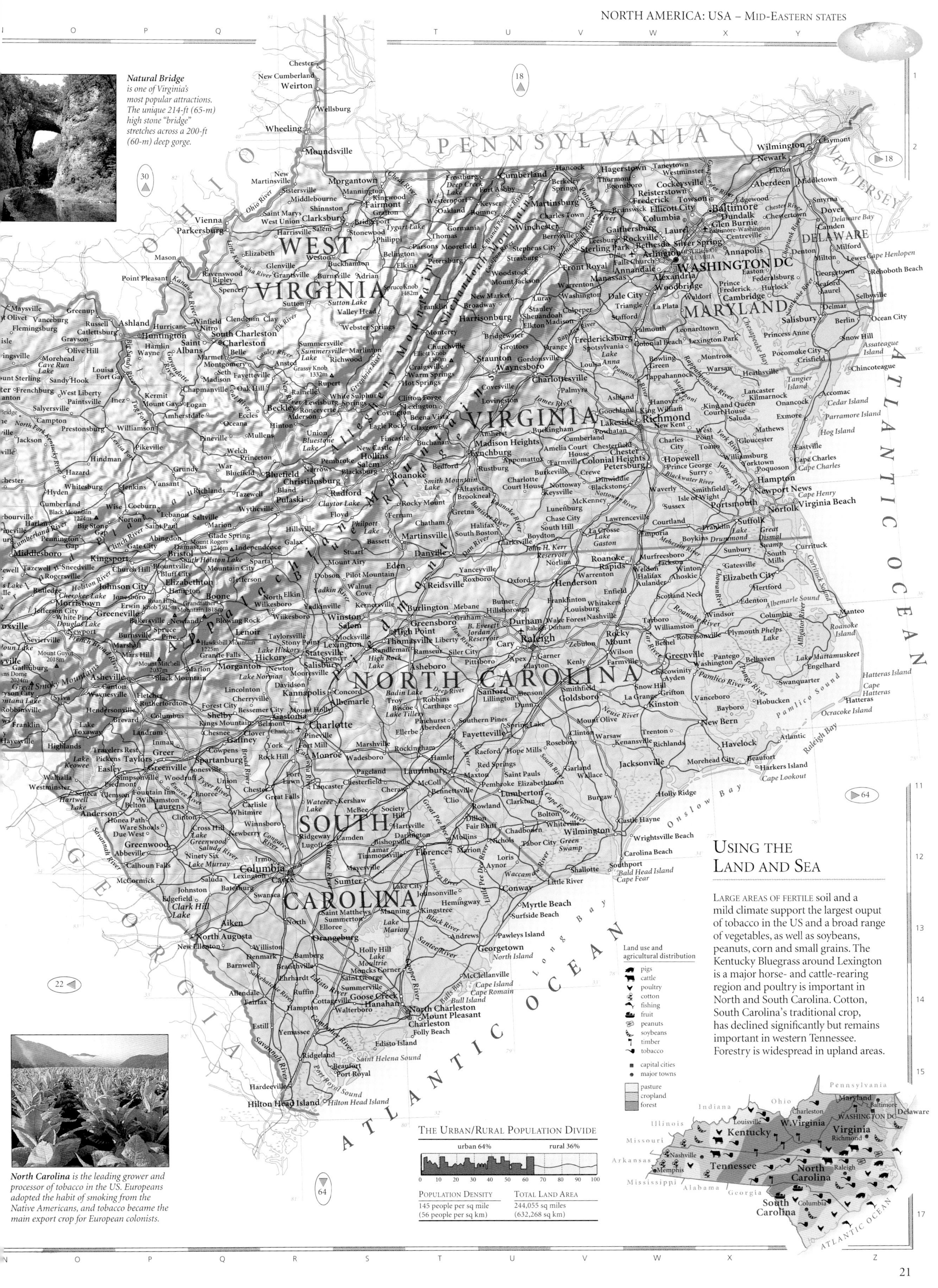
PENNSYLVANIA
OHIO
WEST VIRGINIA
VIRGINIA
MARYLAND
DELAWARE
NEW JERSEY
WASHINGTON DC
NORTH CAROLINA
SOUTH CAROLINA
GEORGIA
ATLANTIC OCEAN
Appalachian Mountains
Allegheny Mountains
Blue Ridge Mountains
Shenandoah Mountains
Piedmont
Great Smoky Mountains
Onslow Bay
Long Bay
Pamlico Sound
Albemarle Sound
Land use and agricultural distribution
pigs
cattle
poultry
cotton
fishing
fruit
peanuts
soybeans
timber
tobacco
capital cities
major towns
pasture
cropland
forest
The Urban/Rural Population Divide
urban 64%
rural 36%
0 10 20 30 40 50 60 70 80 90 100

Natural Bridge *is one of Virginia's most popular attractions. The unique 214-ft (65-m) high stone "bridge" stretches across a 200-ft (60-m) deep gorge.*

USING THE LAND AND SEA

LARGE AREAS OF FERTILE soil and a mild climate support the largest ouput of tobacco in the US and a broad range of vegetables, as well as soybeans, peanuts, corn and small grains. The Kentucky Bluegrass around Lexington is a major horse- and cattle-rearing region and poultry is important in North and South Carolina. Cotton, South Carolina's traditional crop, has declined significantly but remains important in western Tennessee. Forestry is widespread in upland areas.

THE URBAN/RURAL POPULATION DIVIDE

POPULATION DENSITY
145 people per sq mile
(56 people per sq km)

TOTAL LAND AREA
244,055 sq miles
(632,268 sq km)

North Carolina *is the leading grower and processor of tobacco in the US. Europeans adopted the habit of smoking from the Native Americans, and tobacco became the main export crop for European colonists.*

USA: Southern states

Alabama, Florida, Georgia, Louisiana, Mississippi

THE SOUTH HAS MAINTAINED a separate identity and outlook throughout the history of the US. Defeat in the Civil War (1861–65) brought chronic poverty to the former confederate states, while the subsequent liberation of four million slaves began a struggle not resolved until the 1960s, when the Civil Rights movement achieved an end to legal racial segregation. Many parts of the South have experienced rapid change. Tourism and retirement communities, together with agriculture, have fueled growth in Florida, while defense-related industries have boosted the growth of cities such as Miami and Atlanta. Many people retain a strong attachment to their history and culture, evidenced by Creole-speaking Cajuns in Louisiana and Hispanic communities in South Florida.

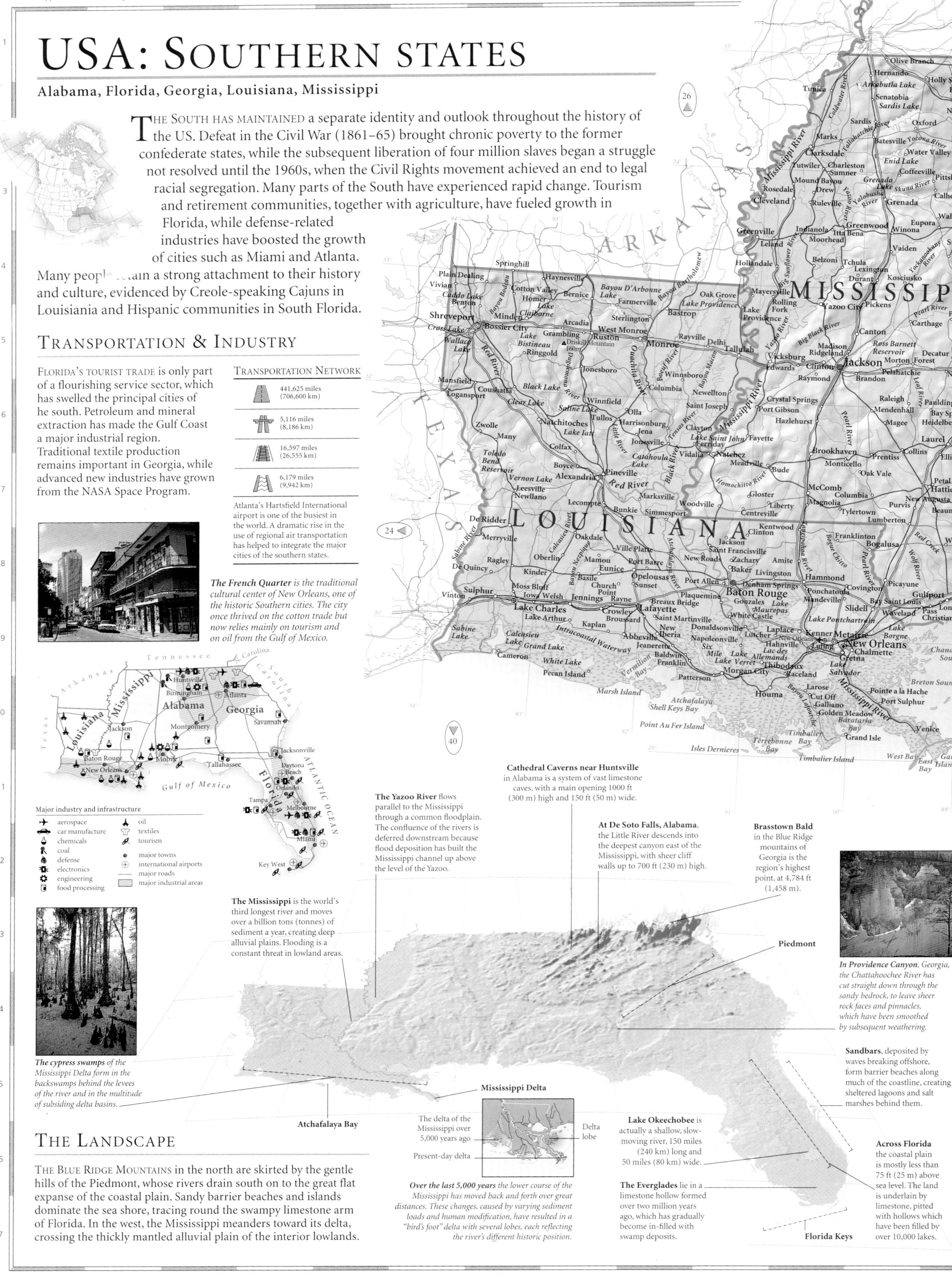

ARKANSAS
MISSISSIPPI
LOUISIANA
TEXAS
Shreveport
Monroe
Alexandria
Lake Charles
Lafayette
Baton Rouge
New Orleans
Jackson
Vicksburg
Natchez
Gulfport
Houma
Mississippi River
Red River
Mississippi Delta
Atchafalaya Bay
Piedmont
Florida Keys
Major industry and infrastructure
aerospace
car manufacture
chemicals
coal
defense
electronics
engineering
food processing
oil
textiles
tourism
major towns
international airports
major roads
major industrial areas

Transportation & Industry

FLORIDA'S TOURIST TRADE is only part of a flourishing service sector, which has swelled the principal cities of he south. Petroleum and mineral extraction has made the Gulf Coast a major industrial region. Traditional textile production remains important in Georgia, while advanced new industries have grown from the NASA Space Program.

Transportation Network

441,625 miles (706,600 km)
5,116 miles (8,186 km)
16,597 miles (26,555 km)
6,179 miles (9,942 km)

Atlanta's Hartsfield International airport is one of the busiest in the world. A dramatic rise in the use of regional air transportation has helped to integrate the major cities of the southern states.

***The French Quarter** is the traditional cultural center of New Orleans, one of the historic Southern cities. The city once thrived on the cotton trade but now relies mainly on tourism and on oil from the Gulf of Mexico.*

***The cypress swamps** of the Mississippi Delta form in the backswamps behind the levees of the river and in the multitude of subsiding delta basins.*

The Landscape

THE BLUE RIDGE MOUNTAINS in the north are skirted by the gentle hills of the Piedmont, whose rivers drain south on to the great flat expanse of the coastal plain. Sandy barrier beaches and islands dominate the sea shore, tracing round the swampy limestone arm of Florida. In the west, the Mississippi meanders toward its delta, crossing the thickly mantled alluvial plain of the interior lowlands.

The Mississippi is the world's third longest river and moves over a billion tons (tonnes) of sediment a year, creating deep alluvial plains. Flooding is a constant threat in lowland areas.

The Yazoo River flows parallel to the Mississippi through a common floodplain. The confluence of the rivers is deferred downstream because flood deposition has built the Mississippi channel up above the level of the Yazoo.

Cathedral Caverns near Huntsville in Alabama is a system of vast limestone caves, with a main opening 1000 ft (300 m) high and 150 ft (50 m) wide.

At De Soto Falls, Alabama, the Little River descends into the deepest canyon east of the Mississippi, with sheer cliff walls up to 700 ft (230 m) high.

Brasstown Bald in the Blue Ridge mountains of Georgia is the region's highest point, at 4,784 ft (1,458 m).

*In **Providence Canyon**, Georgia, the Chattahoochee River has cut straight down through the sandy bedrock, to leave sheer rock faces and pinnacles, which have been smoothed by subsequent weathering.*

Sandbars, deposited by waves breaking offshore, form barrier beaches along much of the coastline, creating sheltered lagoons and salt marshes behind them.

Mississippi Delta

The delta of the Mississippi over 5,000 years ago

Present-day delta

Delta lobe

***Over the last 5,000 years** the lower course of the Mississippi has moved back and forth over great distances. These changes, caused by varying sediment loads and human modification, have resulted in a "bird's foot" delta with several lobes, each reflecting the river's different historic position.*

Lake Okeechobee is actually a shallow, slow-moving river, 150 miles (240 km) long and 50 miles (80 km) wide.

The Everglades lie in a limestone hollow formed over two million years ago, which has gradually become in-filled with swamp deposits.

Across Florida the coastal plain is mostly less than 75 ft (25 m) above sea level. The land is underlain by limestone, pitted with hollows which have been filled by over 10,000 lakes.

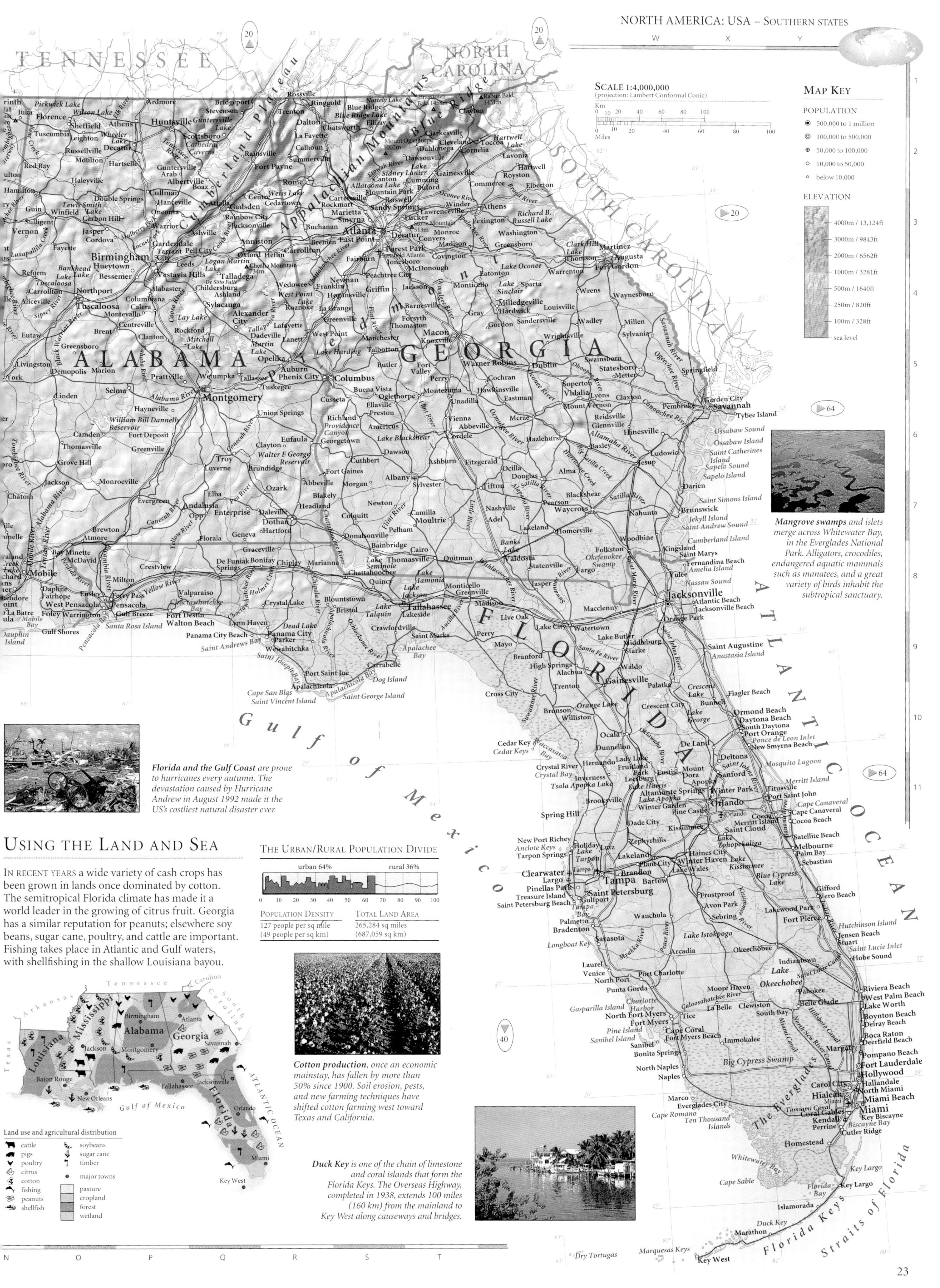
TENNESSEE
NORTH CAROLINA
SOUTH CAROLINA
ALABAMA
GEORGIA
FLORIDA
Gulf of Mexico
ATLANTIC OCEAN
Straits of Florida
Florida Keys
Cumberland Plateau
Appalachian Mountains
Blue Ridge
Piedmont
SCALE 1:4,000,000
(projection: Lambert Conformal Conic)
Km
Miles
MAP KEY
POPULATION
500,000 to 1 million
100,000 to 500,000
50,000 to 100,000
10,000 to 50,000
below 10,000
ELEVATION
4000m / 13,124ft
3000m / 9843ft
2000m / 6562ft
1000m / 3281ft
500m / 1640ft
250m / 820ft
100m / 328ft
sea level
Birmingham
Montgomery
Mobile
Atlanta
Columbus
Macon
Savannah
Augusta
Tallahassee
Jacksonville
Orlando
Tampa
Saint Petersburg
Miami
Key West
Land use and agricultural distribution
cattle
pigs
poultry
citrus
cotton
fishing
peanuts
shellfish
soybeans
sugar cane
timber
major towns
pasture
cropland
forest
wetland
THE URBAN/RURAL POPULATION DIVIDE
urban 64%
rural 36%
0 10 20 30 40 50 60 70 80 90 100
POPULATION DENSITY
127 people per sq mile
(49 people per sq km)
TOTAL LAND AREA
265,284 sq miles
(687,059 sq km)

***Mangrove swamps** and islets merge across Whitewater Bay, in the Everglades National Park. Alligators, crocodiles, endangered aquatic mammals such as manatees, and a great variety of birds inhabit the subtropical sanctuary.*

***Florida and the Gulf Coast** are prone to hurricanes every autumn. The devastation caused by Hurricane Andrew in August 1992 made it the US's costliest natural disaster ever.*

USING THE LAND AND SEA

IN RECENT YEARS a wide variety of cash crops has been grown in lands once dominated by cotton. The semitropical Florida climate has made it a world leader in the growing of citrus fruit. Georgia has a similar reputation for peanuts; elsewhere soy beans, sugar cane, poultry, and cattle are important. Fishing takes place in Atlantic and Gulf waters, with shellfishing in the shallow Louisiana bayou.

***Cotton production**, once an economic mainstay, has fallen by more than 50% since 1900. Soil erosion, pests, and new farming techniques have shifted cotton farming west toward Texas and California.*

***Duck Key** is one of the chain of limestone and coral islands that form the Florida Keys. The Overseas Highway, completed in 1938, extends 100 miles (160 km) from the mainland to Key West along causeways and bridges.*

USA: Texas

First explored by Spaniards moving north from Mexico in search of gold, Texas was controlled by Spain and then by Mexico, before becoming an independent republic in 1836, and joining the Union of States in 1845. During the 19th century, many migrants who came to Texas raised cattle on the abundant land; in the 20th century, they were joined by prospectors attracted by the promise of oil riches. Today, although natural resources, especially oil, still form the basis of its wealth, the diversified Texan economy includes thriving hi-tech and financial industries. The major urban centers, home to 80% of the population, lie in the south and east, and include Houston, the "oil-city," and Dallas Fort Worth. Hispanic influences remain strong, especially in southern and western Texas.

***Dallas was founded** in 1841 as a prairie trading post and its development was stimulated by the arrival of railroads. Cotton and then oil funded the town's early growth. Today, the modern, high-rise skyline of Dallas reflects the city's position as a leading center of banking, insurance, and the petroleum industry in the southwest.*

Using the Land

Cotton production and livestock-raising, particularly cattle, dominate farming, although crop failures and the demands of local markets have led to some diversification. Following the introduction of modern farming techniques, cotton production spread out from the east to the plains of western Texas. Cattle ranches are widespread, while sheep and goats are raised on the dry Edwards Plateau.

Land use and agricultural distribution: cattle, goats, sheep, cereals, cotton, major towns; pasture, cropland, forest, barren

The Urban/Rural Population Divide

urban 80% — rural 20%

Population Density	Total Land Area
73 people per sq mile (28 people per sq km)	267,338 sq miles (692,402 sq km)

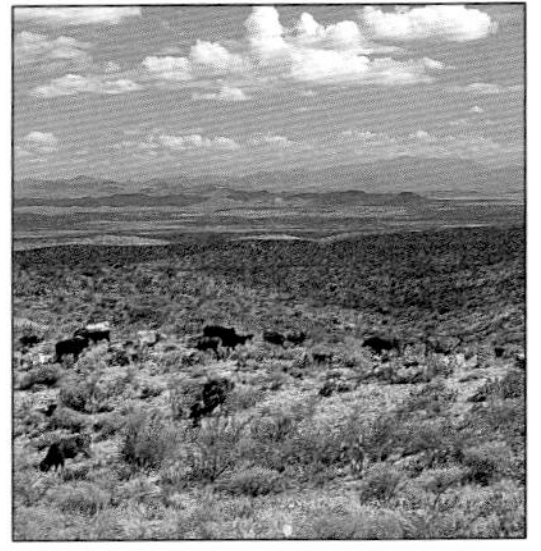

***The huge cattle ranches of Texas** developed during the 19th century when land was plentiful and could be acquired cheaply. Today, more cattle and sheep are raised in Texas than in any other state.*

The Landscape

Texas is made up of a series of massive steps descending from the mountains and high plains of the west and northwest to the coastal lowlands in the southeast. Many of the state's borders are delineated by water. The Rio Grande flows from the Rocky Mountains to the Gulf of Mexico, marking the border with Mexico.

***Cap Rock Escarpment** juts out from the plains, running 200 miles (320 km) from north to south. Its height varies from 300 ft (90 m) rising to sheer cliffs up to 1,000 ft (300 m).*

The Llano Estacado or Staked Plain in northern Texas is known for its harsh environment. In the north, freezing winds carrying ice and snow sweep down from the Rocky Mountains. To the south, sandstorms frequently blow up, scouring anything in their paths. Flash floods, in the wide, flat riverbeds that remain dry for most of the year, are another hazard.

The Red River flows for 1300 miles (2090 km), marking most of the northern border of Texas. A dam and reservoir along its course provide vital irrigation and hydro-electric power to the surrounding area.

The Guadalupe Mountains lie in the southern Rocky Mountains. They incorporate Guadalupe Peak, the highest in Texas, rising 8,749 ft (2,667 m).

Sabine River

Extensive forests of pine and cypress grow in the eastern corner of the coastal lowlands where the average rainfall is 45 inches (1145 mm) a year. This is higher than the rest of the state and over twice the average in the west.

The Rio Grande flows from the Rocky Mountains through semi-arid land, supporting sparse vegetation. The river actually shrinks along its course, losing more water through evaporation and seepage than it gains from its tributaries and rainfall.

In the coastal lowlands of southeastern Texas the Earth's crust is warping, causing the land to subside and allowing the sea to invade. Around Galveston, the rate of downward tilting is 6 inches (15 cm) per year. Erosion of the coast is also exacerbated by hurricanes.

Big Bend National Park

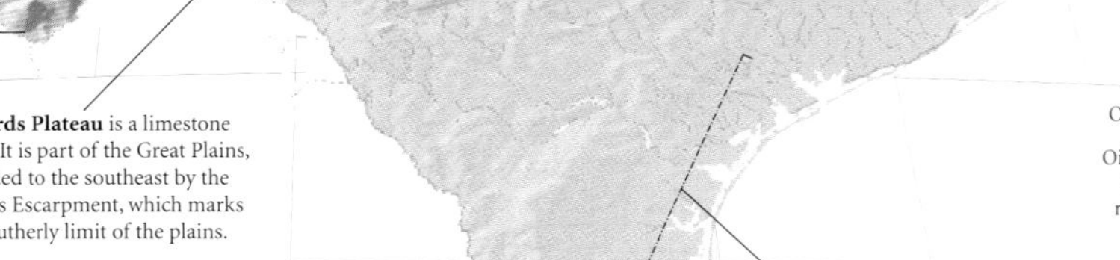

Flowing through 1,500 ft (450 m) high gorges, the shallow, muddy Rio Grande makes a 90° bend. This marks the southern border of Big Bend National Park, and gives it its name. The area is a mixture of forested mountains, deserts, and canyons.

Edwards Plateau is a limestone outcrop. It is part of the Great Plains, bounded to the southeast by the Balcones Escarpment, which marks the southerly limit of the plains.

Padre Island

Laguna Madre in southern Texas has been almost completely cut off from the sea by Padre Island. This sand bank was created by wave action, carrying and depositing material along the coast. The process is known as longshore drift.

Oil deposits

Oil trapped by fault
Oil deposits migrate through reservoir rocks such as shale
Oil accumulates beneath impermeable cap rock
Impermeable rock strata
Salt dome

***Oil deposits** are found beneath much of Texas. They collect as oil migrates upward through porous layers of rock until it is trapped, either by a cap of rock above a salt dome, or by a fault line which exposes impermeable rock through which the oil cannot rise.*

36
40

TRANSPORTATION & INDUSTRY

INDUSTRY IN THE 20TH CENTURY was largely concentrated on the processing of local raw materials, especially oil – deposits were discovered under 65% of the state's area. The technological demands of the oil industry and defense-related institutions, particularly NASA, have stimulated the development of numerous electronics and hi-tech firms which, alongside many national corporate headquarters, are based in Dallas–Fort Worth and Houston.

Major industry and infrastructure

- chemicals
- defense
- engineering
- finance
- food processing
- gas
- hi-tech industry
- mining
- oil
- textiles
- major towns
- international airports
- major roads
- major industrial areas

TRANSPORTATION NETWORK

293,509 miles (496,614 km)	3,229 miles (5,166 km)
10,681 miles (17,089 km)	845 miles (1,359 km)

The sheer size of Texas promoted the development of an extensive road and rail network. The highway system, although well-developed, is concentrated in the east.

Padre Island *is a sand bank. It extends 113 miles (182 km) along the southern coast of Texas.*

The Texas hill country *is the most southerly extension of the Great Plains. Although farming is the primary source of income, the beautiful hills, valleys, and lakes are a major tourist attraction.*

MAP KEY

POPULATION

- 1 million to 5 million
- 500,000 to 1 million
- 100,000 to 500,000
- 50,000 to 100,000
- 10,000 to 50,000
- below 10,000

ELEVATION

- 2000m / 6562ft
- 1000m / 3281ft
- 500m / 1640ft
- 250m / 820ft
- 100m / 328ft
- sea level

SCALE 1:3,500,000
(projection: Lambert Conformal Conic)

USA: South Midwestern States

Arkansas, Kansas, Missouri, Oklahoma

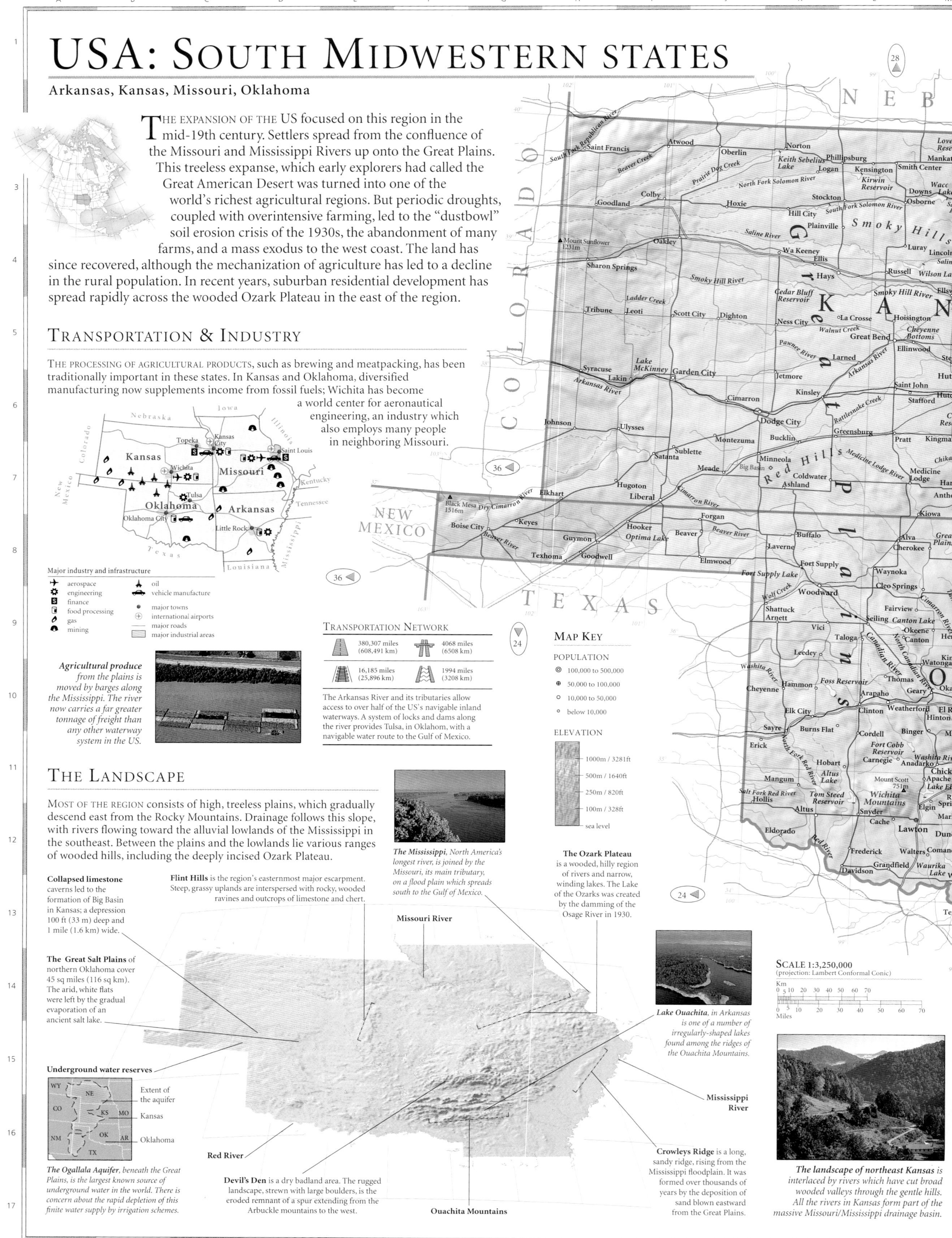

The expansion of the US focused on this region in the mid-19th century. Settlers spread from the confluence of the Missouri and Mississippi Rivers up onto the Great Plains. This treeless expanse, which early explorers had called the Great American Desert was turned into one of the world's richest agricultural regions. But periodic droughts, coupled with overintensive farming, led to the "dustbowl" soil erosion crisis of the 1930s, the abandonment of many farms, and a mass exodus to the west coast. The land has since recovered, although the mechanization of agriculture has led to a decline in the rural population. In recent years, suburban residential development has spread rapidly across the wooded Ozark Plateau in the east of the region.

Transportation & Industry

The processing of agricultural products, such as brewing and meatpacking, has been traditionally important in these states. In Kansas and Oklahoma, diversified manufacturing now supplements income from fossil fuels; Wichita has become a world center for aeronautical engineering, an industry which also employs many people in neighboring Missouri.

Major industry and infrastructure
aerospace
engineering
finance
food processing
gas
mining
oil
vehicle manufacture
major towns
international airports
major roads
major industrial areas

Agricultural produce from the plains is moved by barges along the Mississippi. The river now carries a far greater tonnage of freight than any other waterway system in the US.

Transportation Network

380,307 miles (608,491 km)	4068 miles (6508 km)	16,185 miles (25,896 km)	1994 miles (3208 km)

The Arkansas River and its tributaries allow access to over half of the US's navigable inland waterways. A system of locks and dams along the river provides Tulsa, in Oklahom, with a navigable water route to the Gulf of Mexico.

Map Key

POPULATION
100,000 to 500,000
50,000 to 100,000
10,000 to 50,000
below 10,000
ELEVATION
1000m / 3281ft
500m / 1640ft
250m / 820ft
100m / 328ft
sea level

The Landscape

Most of the region consists of high, treeless plains, which gradually descend east from the Rocky Mountains. Drainage follows this slope, with rivers flowing toward the alluvial lowlands of the Mississippi in the southeast. Between the plains and the lowlands lie various ranges of wooded hills, including the deeply incised Ozark Plateau.

The Mississippi, North America's longest river, is joined by the Missouri, its main tributary, on a flood plain which spreads south to the Gulf of Mexico.

The Ozark Plateau is a wooded, hilly region of rivers and narrow, winding lakes. The Lake of the Ozarks was created by the damming of the Osage River in 1930.

Collapsed limestone caverns led to the formation of Big Basin in Kansas; a depression 100 ft (33 m) deep and 1 mile (1.6 km) wide.

Flint Hills is the region's easternmost major escarpment. Steep, grassy uplands are interspersed with rocky, wooded ravines and outcrops of limestone and chert.

Missouri River

The Great Salt Plains of northern Oklahoma cover 45 sq miles (116 sq km). The arid, white flats were left by the gradual evaporation of an ancient salt lake.

Underground water reserves

Extent of the aquifer
Kansas
Oklahoma

The Ogallala Aquifer, beneath the Great Plains, is the largest known source of underground water in the world. There is concern about the rapid depletion of this finite water supply by irrigation schemes.

Red River

Devil's Den is a dry badland area. The rugged landscape, strewn with large boulders, is the eroded remnant of a spur extending from the Arbuckle mountains to the west.

Ouachita Mountains

Lake Ouachita, in Arkansas is one of a number of irregularly-shaped lakes found among the ridges of the Ouachita Mountains.

Mississippi River

Crowleys Ridge is a long, sandy ridge, rising from the Mississippi floodplain. It was formed over thousands of years by the deposition of sand blown eastward from the Great Plains.

SCALE 1:3,250,000 (projection: Lambert Conformal Conic)

The landscape of northeast Kansas is interlaced by rivers which have cut broad wooded valleys through the gentle hills. All the rivers in Kansas form part of the massive Missouri/Mississippi drainage basin.

Gateway Arch, in Saint Louis, Missouri, is 634 ft (192 m) high. The huge steel arch symbolizes the city's historic role as the "Gateway to the West".

Using the Land

The problems of a harsh continental climate, with severe winters and hot, dry summers, are partially offset by the rich soils of the plains. Kansas is a major cereal crop producer, ranking first in US production of wheat and sorghum. Rainfall increases toward the east, favoring the cultivation of soybeans, cotton, and rice, with corn concentrated in Missouri. Huge herds of cattle are raised in Oklahoma, Kansas, and Missouri.

A combine harvester works the land on the great plains. A hundred years ago this region, also known as the prairies – the French word for pasture – was covered with tall, wild grasses.

The Urban/Rural Population Divide

urban 65% | rural 35%

0 10 20 30 40 50 60 70 80 90 100

Population Density	Total Land Area
50 people per sq mile (19 people per sq km)	274,900 sq miles (712,177 sq km)

Land use and agricultural distribution

- cattle
- poultry
- cereals
- corn (maize)
- cotton
- fodder
- rice
- soya beans
- major towns
- pasture
- cropland
- forest

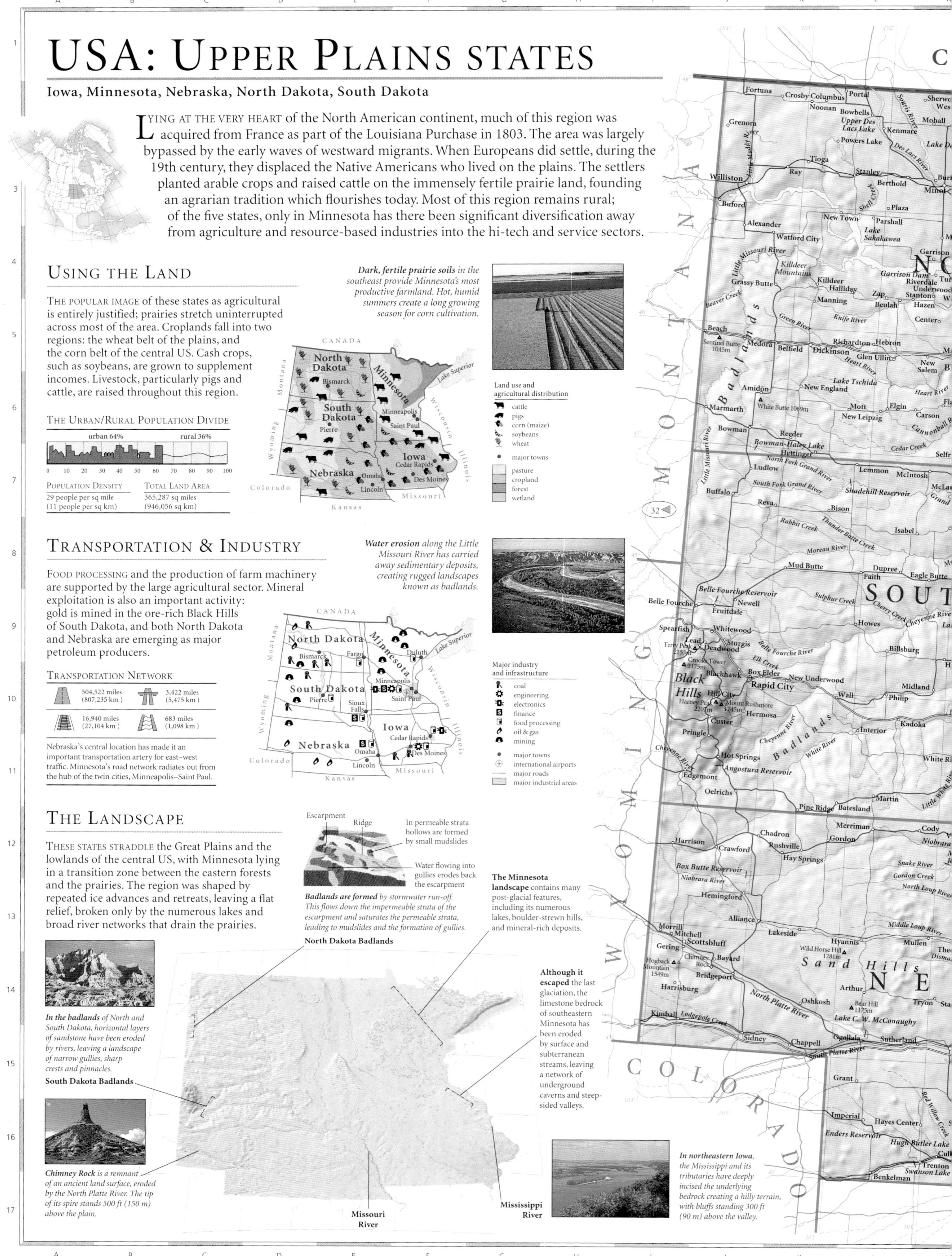

USA: Upper Plains States

Iowa, Minnesota, Nebraska, North Dakota, South Dakota

Lying at the very heart of the North American continent, much of this region was acquired from France as part of the Louisiana Purchase in 1803. The area was largely bypassed by the early waves of westward migrants. When Europeans did settle, during the 19th century, they displaced the Native Americans who lived on the plains. The settlers planted arable crops and raised cattle on the immensely fertile prairie land, founding an agrarian tradition which flourishes today. Most of this region remains rural; of the five states, only in Minnesota has there been significant diversification away from agriculture and resource-based industries into the hi-tech and service sectors.

Using the Land

The popular image of these states as agricultural is entirely justified; prairies stretch uninterrupted across most of the area. Croplands fall into two regions: the wheat belt of the plains, and the corn belt of the central US. Cash crops, such as soybeans, are grown to supplement incomes. Livestock, particularly pigs and cattle, are raised throughout this region.

The Urban/Rural Population Divide

urban 64% | rural 36%

Population Density	Total Land Area
29 people per sq mile (11 people per sq km)	365,287 sq miles (946,056 sq km)

***Dark, fertile prairie soils** in the southeast provide Minnesota's most productive farmland. Hot, humid summers create a long growing season for corn cultivation.*

Land use and agricultural distribution: cattle, pigs, corn (maize), soybeans, wheat, major towns, pasture, cropland, forest, wetland

Transportation & Industry

Food processing and the production of farm machinery are supported by the large agricultural sector. Mineral exploitation is also an important activity: gold is mined in the ore-rich Black Hills of South Dakota, and both North Dakota and Nebraska are emerging as major petroleum producers.

Transportation Network

504,522 miles (807,235 km)	3,422 miles (5,475 km)
16,940 miles (27,104 km)	683 miles (1,098 km)

Nebraska's central location has made it an important transportation artery for east–west traffic. Minnesota's road network radiates out from the hub of the twin cities, Minneapolis–Saint Paul.

***Water erosion** along the Little Missouri River has carried away sedimentary deposits, creating rugged landscapes known as badlands.*

Major industry and infrastructure: coal, engineering, electronics, finance, food processing, oil & gas, mining, major towns, international airports, major roads, major industrial areas

The Landscape

These states straddle the Great Plains and the lowlands of the central US, with Minnesota lying in a transition zone between the eastern forests and the prairies. The region was shaped by repeated ice advances and retreats, leaving a flat relief, broken only by the numerous lakes and broad river networks that drain the prairies.

Escarpment · Ridge · In permeable strata hollows are formed by small mudslides · Water flowing into gullies erodes back the escarpment

***Badlands are formed** by stormwater run-off. This flows down the impermeable strata of the escarpment and saturates the permeable strata, leading to mudslides and the formation of gullies.*

The Minnesota landscape contains many post-glacial features, including its numerous lakes, boulder-strewn hills, and mineral-rich deposits.

North Dakota Badlands

In the badlands of North and South Dakota, horizontal layers of sandstone have been eroded by rivers, leaving a landscape of narrow gullies, sharp crests and pinnacles.

South Dakota Badlands

***Chimney Rock** is a remnant of an ancient land surface, eroded by the North Platte River. The tip of its spire stands 500 ft (150 m) above the plain.*

Missouri River

Mississippi River

Although it escaped the last glaciation, the limestone bedrock of southeastern Minnesota has been eroded by surface and subterranean streams, leaving a network of underground caverns and steep-sided valleys.

In northeastern Iowa, the Mississippi and its tributaries have deeply incised the underlying bedrock creating a hilly terrain, with bluffs standing 300 ft (90 m) above the valley.

32

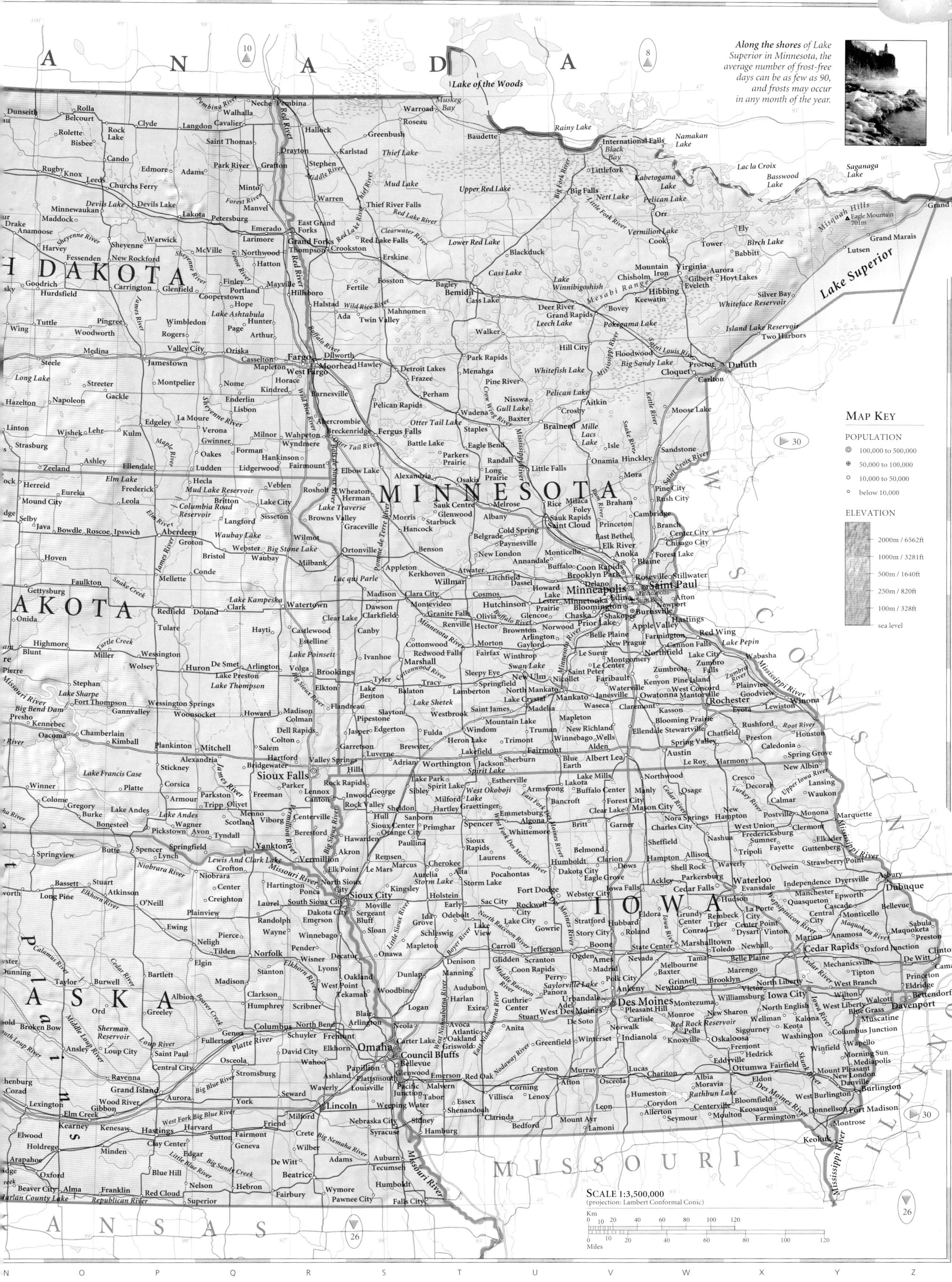

Along the shores of Lake Superior in Minnesota, the average number of frost-free days can be as few as 90, and frosts may occur in any month of the year.

MAP KEY

POPULATION
- 100,000 to 500,000
- 50,000 to 100,000
- 10,000 to 50,000
- below 10,000

ELEVATION
- 2000m / 6562ft
- 1000m / 3281ft
- 500m / 1640ft
- 250m / 820ft
- 100m / 328ft
- sea level

SCALE 1:3,500,000
(projection: Lambert Conformal Conic)

USA: GREAT LAKES STATES

Illinois, Indiana, Michigan, Ohio, Wisconsin

THE STATES BORDERING THE GREAT LAKES developed rapidly in the second half of the 19th century as a result of improvements in communications: railroads to the west and waterways to the south and east. Fertile land and good links with growing eastern seaboard cities encouraged the development of agriculture and food processing. Migrants from Europe and other parts of the US flooded into the region and for much of the 20th century the region's economy boomed. However, in recent years heavy industry has declined, earning the region the unwanted label the "Rustbelt."

TRANSPORTATION & INDUSTRY

THE GREAT LAKES REGION IS THE CENTER of the US car industry. Since the early part of the 20th century, its prosperity has been closely linked to the fortunes of automobile manufacturing. Iron and steel production has expanded to meet demand from this industry. In the 1970s, nationwide recession, cheaper foreign competition in the automobile sector, pollution in and around the Great Lakes, and the collapse of the meatpacking industry, centered on Chicago, forced these states to diversify their industrial base. New industries have emerged, notably electronics, service, and finance industries.

Major industry and infrastructure

- car manufacture
- coal
- electronics
- engineering
- finance
- food processing
- iron & steel
- oil
- research & development
- textiles
- major towns
- international airports
- major roads
- major industrial areas

TRANSPORTATION NETWORK

540,682 miles (865,091 km)	6,550 miles (10,480 km)
24,928 miles (39,884 km)	2,330 miles (3,748 km)

Few areas of the US have a comparable system. Chicago is a principal transportation terminus with a dense network of roads, railroads, and Interstate freeways that radiates out from the city.

***Ever since Ransom Olds** and Henry Ford started mass-producing automobiles in Detroit early in the 20th century, the city's name has become synonymous with the American automotive industry.*

THE LANDSCAPE

MUCH OF THIS REGION shows the impact of glaciation which lasted until about 10,000 years ago, and extended as far south as Illinois and Ohio. Although the relief of the region slopes toward the Great Lakes, because the ice sheets blocked northerly drainage, most of the rivers today flow southward, forming part of the massive Mississippi/Missouri drainage basin.

***The dunes** near Sleeping Bear Point rise 400 ft (120 m) from the banks of Lake Michigan. They are constantly being resculpted by wind action.*

The many lakes and marshes of Wisconsin and Michigan are the result of glacial erosion and deposition which occurred during the last Ice Age.

Lake Michigan

Lake Erie is the shallowest of the five Great Lakes. Its average depth is about 62 ft (19 m). Storms sweeping across from Canada erode its shores and cause the silting of its harbors.

Southwestern Wisconsin is known as a "driftless" area. Unlike most of the region, low hills protected it from erosion by the advancing ice sheet.

Most of the water used in northern Illinois is pumped from underground reservoirs. Due to increased demand, many areas now face a water shortage. Around Joliet, the water table was lowered by more than 700 ft (210 m) over the last century.

The Appalachian plateau stretches eastward from Ohio. It is dissected by streams flowing west into the Mississippi and Ohio Rivers.

Illinois plains

***The plains of Illinois** are characteristic of drift landscapes, scoured and flattened by glacial erosion and covered with fertile glacial deposits.*

Mississippi River

Relict landforms from the last glaciation, such as shallow basins and ridges, cover all but the south of this region. Ridges, known as moraines, up to 300 ft (100 m) high, lie to the south of Lake Michigan.

Ohio River

Unlike the level prairie to the north, southern Indiana is relatively rugged. Limestone in the hills has been dissolved by water, producing features such as sinkholes and underground caves.

Glacial till

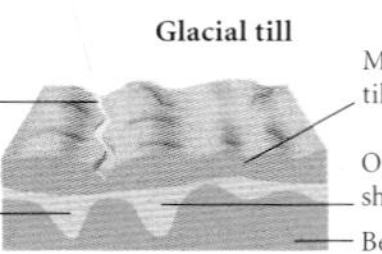
Present-day river or stream
Channels caused by outwash from melting glacier
Most recent till deposits
Older till sheet
Bedrock

***As a result of successive** glacial depositions, the total depth of till along the former southern margin of the Laurentide ice sheet can exceed 1,300 ft (400 m).*

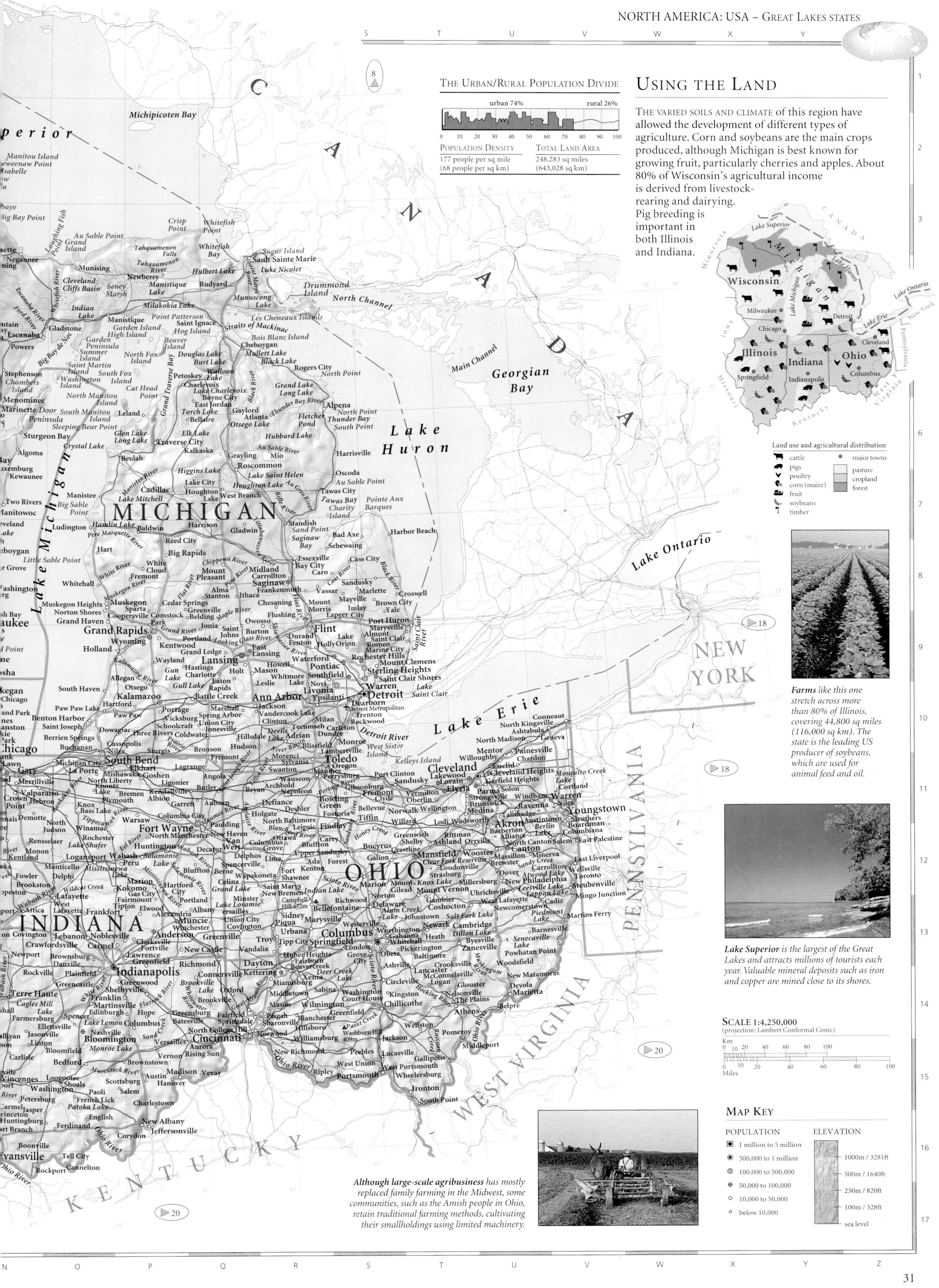
THE URBAN/RURAL POPULATION DIVIDE
urban 74%
rural 26%
0 10 20 30 40 50 60 70 80 90 100
POPULATION DENSITY
177 people per sq mile
(68 people per sq km)
TOTAL LAND AREA
248,283 sq miles
(643,028 sq km)
Land use and agricultural distribution
cattle
pigs
poultry
corn (maize)
fruit
soybeans
timber
major towns
pasture
cropland
forest
SCALE 1:4,250,000
(projection: Lambert Conformal Conic)
MAP KEY
POPULATION
1 million to 5 million
500,000 to 1 million
100,000 to 500,000
50,000 to 100,000
10,000 to 50,000
below 10,000
ELEVATION
1000m / 3281ft
500m / 1640ft
250m / 820ft
100m / 328ft
sea level
MICHIGAN
OHIO
INDIANA
PENNSYLVANIA
WEST VIRGINIA
KENTUCKY
NEW YORK
CANADA
Lake Michigan
Lake Huron
Lake Erie
Lake Ontario
Georgian Bay

USING THE LAND

THE VARIED SOILS AND CLIMATE of this region have allowed the development of different types of agriculture. Corn and soybeans are the main crops produced, although Michigan is best known for growing fruit, particularly cherries and apples. About 80% of Wisconsin's agricultural income is derived from livestock-rearing and dairying. Pig breeding is important in both Illinois and Indiana.

Farms like this one stretch across more than 80% of Illinois, covering 44,800 sq miles (116,000 sq km). The state is the leading US producer of soybeans, which are used for animal feed and oil.

Lake Superior is the largest of the Great Lakes and attracts millions of tourists each year. Valuable mineral deposits such as iron and copper are mined close to its shores.

Although large-scale agribusiness has mostly replaced family farming in the Midwest, some communities, such as the Amish people in Ohio, retain traditional farming methods, cultivating their smallholdings using limited machinery.

USA: North Mountain states

Idaho, Montana, Oregon, Washington, Wyoming

The remoteness of the northwestern states, coupled with the rugged landscape, ensured that this was one of the last areas settled by Europeans in the 19th century. Fur-trappers and gold-prospectors followed the Snake River westward as it wound its way through the Rocky Mountains. The states of the northwest have pioneered many conservationist policies, with the first US National Park opened at Yellowstone in 1872. More recently, the Cascades and Rocky Mountains have become havens for adventure tourism. The mountains still serve to isolate the western seaboard from the rest of the continent. This isolation has encouraged West Coast cities to expand their trade links with countries of the Pacific Rim.

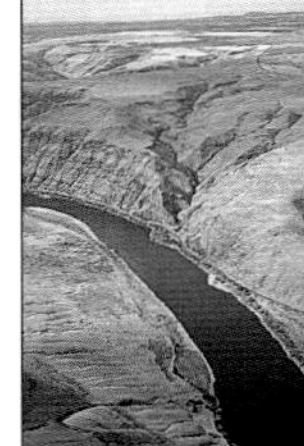

***The Snake River** has cut down into the basalt of the Columbia Basin to form Hells Canyon, the deepest in the US, with cliffs up to 7,900 ft (2,408 m) high.*

Map Key

POPULATION

- 500,000 to 1 million
- 100,000 to 500,000
- 50,000 to 100,000
- 10,000 to 50,000
- below 10,000

ELEVATION

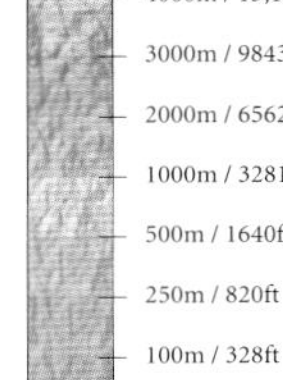

4000m / 13,124ft
3000m / 9843ft
2000m / 6562ft
1000m / 3281ft
500m / 1640ft
250m / 820ft
100m / 328ft
sea level

***Fine-textured, volcanic soils** in the hilly Palouse region of eastern Washington are susceptible to erosion.*

Using the Land

Wheat farming in the east gives way to cattle ranching as rainfall decreases. Irrigated farming in the Snake River valley produces large yields of potatoes and other vegetables. Dairying and fruit-growing take place in the wet western lowlands between the mountain ranges.

The Urban/Rural Population Divide

urban 70% | rural 30%

0 10 20 30 40 50 60 70 80 90 100

Population Density	Total Land Area
23 people per sq mile (9 people per sq km)	493,782 sq miles (1,278,846 sq km)

Scale 1:4,250,000
(projection: Lambert Conformal Conic)

Land use and agricultural distribution: cattle, poultry, cereals, fruit, potatoes, timber, major towns, pasture, cropland, forest

192

Transportation & Industry

Minerals and timber are extremely important in this region. Uranium, precious metals, copper, and coal are all mined, the latter in vast open-cast pits in Wyoming; oil and natural gas are extracted further north. Manufacturing, notably related to the aerospace and electronics industries, is important in western cities.

Transportation Network

- 347,857 miles (556,571 km)
- 4,200 miles (6,720 km)
- 12,354 miles (19,766 km)
- 1,108 miles (1,782 km)

The Union Pacific Railroad has been in service across Wyoming since 1867. The route through the Rocky Mountains is now shared with the Interstate 80, a major east–west highway.

Major industry and infrastructure: adventure tourism, aerospace, coal, chemicals, electronics, food processing, mining, oil & gas, timber processing, major towns, international airports, major roads, major industrial areas

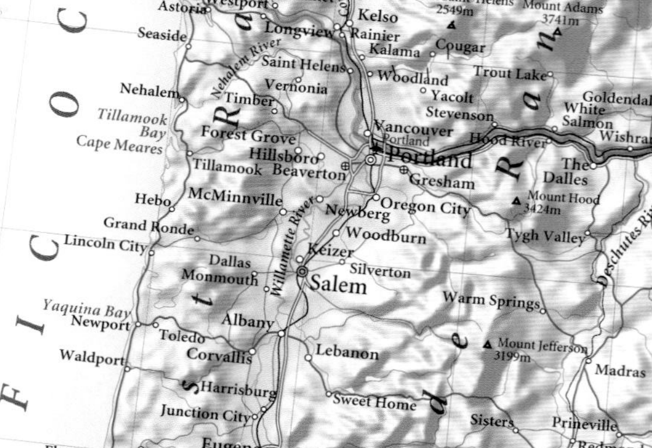

***Seattle lies** in one of Puget Sound's many inlets. The city receives oil and other resources from Alaska, and benefits from expanding trade across the Pacific.*

***Crater Lake, Oregon,** is 6 miles (10 km) wide and 1,800 ft (600 m) deep. It marks the site of a volcanic cone, which collapsed after an eruption within the last 7,000 years.*

THE LANDSCAPE

THE ROCKY MOUNTAINS are flanked by lower parallel ranges, which spread onto the Great Plains in the east and surmount the broad lava plateau which extends westward. The Cascade Range divides the Columbia Basin from the coastlands, where the low areas around Puget Sound are broken by the steep, volcanic Olympic Mountains and the wooded hills of the Coast Ranges.

Glacial valleys on the seaward side of the Olympic Mountains receive about 142 inches (3,600 mm) of rain per year, supporting the only true rain forest of the northern hemisphere.

Mount St. Helens erupted in 1980, killing 57 people and devastating a huge area.

Puget Sound

Columbia Basin

Grand Coulee and the lesser *coulées* (ravines) were cut by cataclysmic floods, from the release of an ice-dammed lake, at the end of the last ice age.

The Continental Divide, or watershed, crosses the Lewis Range. From here, rivers flow east to Hudson Bay, south to the Gulf of Mexico and west to the Pacific Ocean.

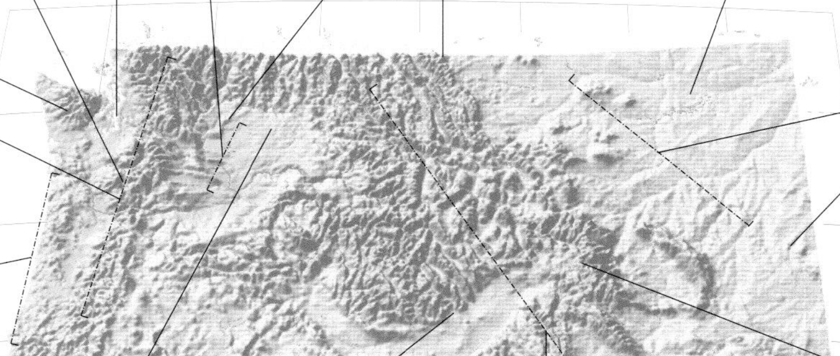

Piney Buttes *are the remnants of an older, higher land surface gradually weathered and eroded into isolated outcrops with flat tops and steep sides.*

Great Plains

Devil's Tower

The Cascades are glacially scoured volcanic mountains, the highest of which is Mount Rainier, a dormant volcano at 14,409 ft (4,392 m).

Coast Ranges

Molten rock cools, forming parallel columns

Surrounding strata eroded away

Molten rock wells up from the Earth's core

Devil's Tower in Wyoming *is an igneous intrusion, formed below the Earth's surface. Molten rock intruded through cracks in the overlying strata and cooled. Over time, the softer rock layers have been eroded away, leaving only the tower standing.*

The plateaus of the Columbia and Snake Rivers represent one of the world's largest accumulations of lava. Over 5 million years ago, successive flows of molten basalt buried the existing land surface by up to 450 ft (150 m).

The contorted rock shapes at "Craters of the Moon" National Monument in Idaho were left 2,000 years ago by the sporadic upwelling of viscous lava from fissures in the basalt plateau.

Rocky Mountains

Water from the hot springs *in Yellowstone National Park deposits minerals as it cools in rock pools. Long periods of deposition have created these rock terraces.*

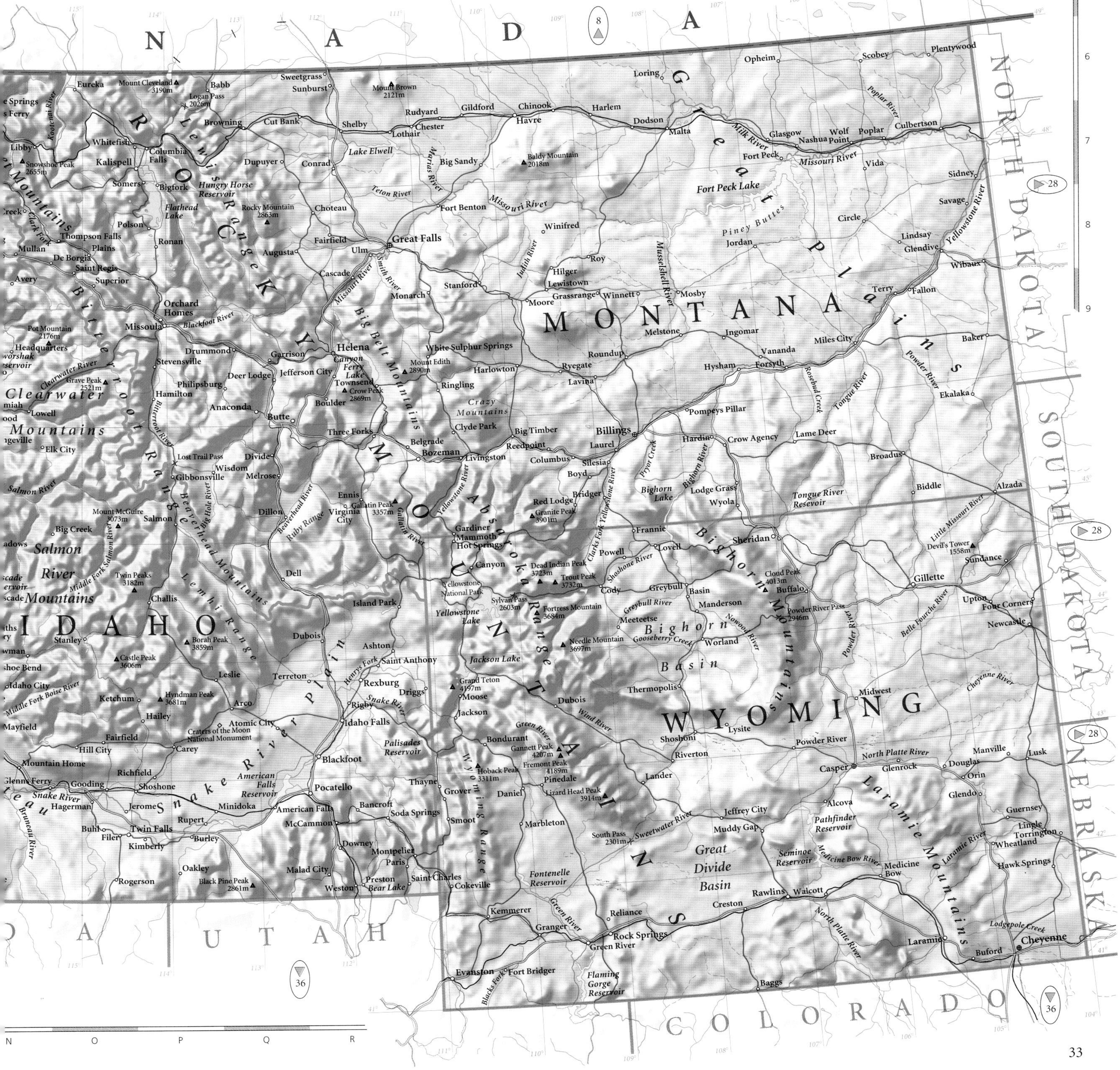

NORTH DAKOTA

SOUTH DAKOTA

NEBRASKA

MONTANA

WYOMING

IDAHO

UTAH

COLORADO

USA: California & Nevada

The Gold Rush of 1849 attracted the first major wave of European settlers to the West Coast. The pleasant climate, beautiful scenery and dynamic economy continue to attract immigrants – despite the ever-present danger of earthquakes – and California has become the US's most populous state. The overwhelmingly urban population is concentrated in the vast conurbations of Los Angeles, San Francisco, and San Diego; new immigrants include people from South Korea, the Philippines, Vietnam, and Mexico. Nevada's arid lands were initially exploited for minerals; in recent years, revenue from mining has been superseded by income from the tourist and gambling centers of Las Vegas and Reno.

Map Key

POPULATION

- 1 million to 5 million
- 500,000 to 1 million
- 100,000 to 500,000
- 50,000 to 100,000
- 10,000 to 50,000
- below 10,000

ELEVATION

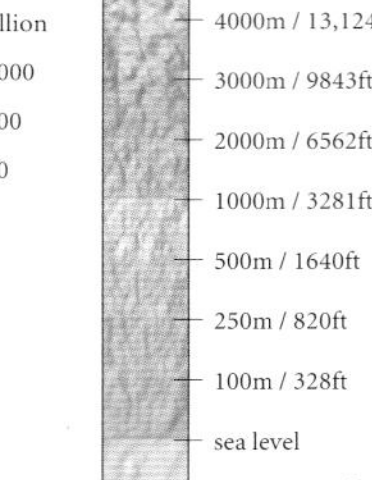

4000m / 13,124ft
3000m / 9843ft
2000m / 6562ft
1000m / 3281ft
500m / 1640ft
250m / 820ft
100m / 328ft
sea level

SCALE 1:3,250,000
(projection: Lambert Conformal Conic)

Km 0 5 10 20 30 40 50 60 70 80
Miles 0 5 10 20 30 40 50 60 70 80

Transportation & Industry

Nevada's rich mineral reserves ushered in a period of mining wealth which has now been replaced by revenue generated from gambling. California supports a broad set of activities including defense-related industries and research and development facilities. "Silicon Valley," near San Francisco, is a world leading center for microelectronics, while tourism and the Los Angeles film industry also generate large incomes.

Gambling was legalized in Nevada in 1931. Las Vegas has since become the center of this multimillion dollar industry.

Oregon
Idaho
Utah
Nevada
Reno
Carson City
Ely
Sacramento
Oakland
San Francisco
San Jose
California
Las Vegas
Bakersfield
PACIFIC OCEAN
Arizona
Los Angeles
San Diego
MEXICO

Major industry and infrastructure

- aerospace
- car manufacture
- defense
- movie industry
- finance
- food processing
- gambling
- hi-tech industry
- mining
- pharmaceuticals
- research & development
- textiles
- tourism
- major towns
- international airports
- major roads
- major industrial areas

Transportation Network

211,459 miles (338,334 km)	
2,944 miles (4,710 km)	
7,872 miles (12,595 km)	
190 miles (306 km)	

In California, the motor vehicle is a vital part of daily life, and an extensive freeway system runs throughout the state, which has a greater *per capita* car ownership than anywhere else in the world.

The Landscape

The broad Central Valley divides California's coastal mountains from the Sierra Nevada. The San Andreas Fault, running beneath much of the state, is the site of frequent earth tremors and sometimes more serious earthquakes. East of the Sierra Nevada, the landscape is characterized by the basin and range topography with stony deserts and many salt lakes.

Rising molten rock causes stretching of the Earth's crust

Extensive cracking (faulting) uplifted a series of ridges

As ridges are eroded they fill intervening valleys with sediments

***Molten rock** (magma) welling up to form a dome in the Earth's interior, causes the brittle surface rocks to stretch and crack. Some areas were uplifted to form mountains (ranges), while others sunk to form flat valleys (basins).*

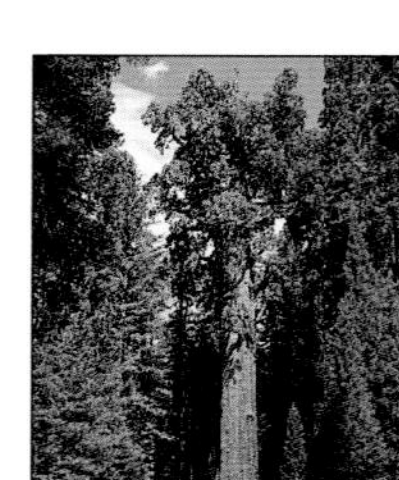

***The General Sherman** sequoia tree in Sequoia National Park is 3000 years old and at 275 ft (84 m) is one of the largest living things on earth.*

Most of California's agriculture is confined to the fertile and extensively irrigated Central Valley, running between the Coast Ranges and the Sierra Nevada. It incorporates the San Joaquin and Sacramento valleys.

The dramatic granitic rock formations of Half Dome and El Capitan, and the verdant coniferous forests, attract millions of visitors annually to Yosemite National Park in the Sierra Nevada.

The Great Basin dominates most of Nevada's topography containing large open basins, punctuated by eroded features such as *buttes* and *mesas*. River flow tends to be seasonal, dependent upon spring showers and winter snow melt.

Sierra Nevada

Wheeler Peak is home to some of the world's oldest trees, bristlecone pines, which live for up to 5,000 years.

When the Hoover Dam across the Colorado River was completed in 1936, it created Lake Mead, one of the largest artificial lakes in the world, extending for 115 miles (285 km) upstream.

The San Andreas Fault is a transverse fault which extends for 650 miles (1,050 km) through California. Major earthquakes occur when the land either side of the fault moves at different rates. San Francisco was devastated by an earthquake in 1906.

Death Valley

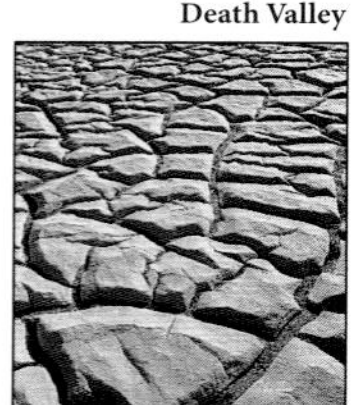

***Named by migrating settlers** in 1849, Death Valley is the driest, hottest place in North America, as well as being the lowest point on land in the western hemisphere, at 282 ft (86 m) below sea level.*

The sparsely populated Mojave Desert receives less than 8 inches (200 mm) of rainfall a year. It is used extensively for testing weapons and other military purposes.

The Salton Sea was created accidentally between 1905 and 1907 when an irrigation channel from the Colorado River broke out of its banks and formed this salty 300 sq mile (777 sq km), landlocked lake.

Amargosa Desert

***The Sierra Nevada** create a "rainshadow," preventing rain from reaching much of Nevada. Pacific air masses, passing over the mountains, are stripped of their moisture.*

Using the Land

California is the leading agricultural producer in the US, although low rainfall makes irrigation essential. The long growing season and abundant sunshine allow many crops to be grown in the fertile Central Valley including grapes, citrus fruits, vegetables, and cotton. Almost 17 million acres (6.8 million hectares) of California's forests are used commercially. Nevada's arid climate and poor soil are largely unsuitable for agriculture; 85% of its land is state owned and large areas are used for underground testing of nuclear weapons.

Land use and agricultural distribution

- cattle
- citrus fruits
- fruit
- irrigation
- timber
- vineyards
- major towns
- pasture
- cropland
- forest
- desert

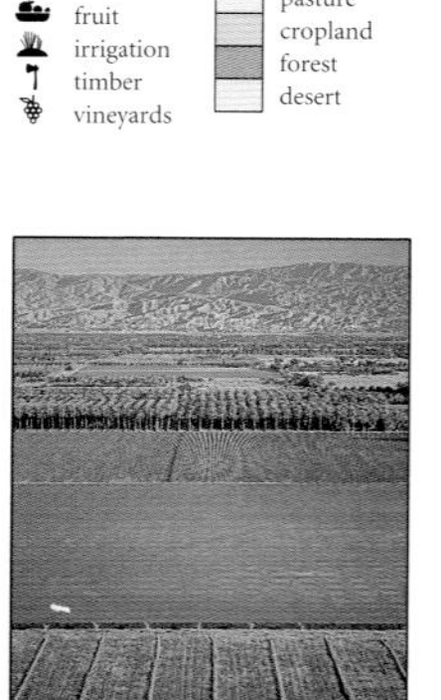

***Without considerable** irrigation, this fertile valley at Palm Springs would still be part of the Sonoran Desert. California's farmers account for about 80% of the state's total water usage.*

Oregon
Idaho
Utah
Nevada
Reno
Sacramento
San Francisco
California
Las Vegas
PACIFIC OCEAN
Arizona
Los Angeles
San Diego
MEXICO

The Urban/Rural Population Divide

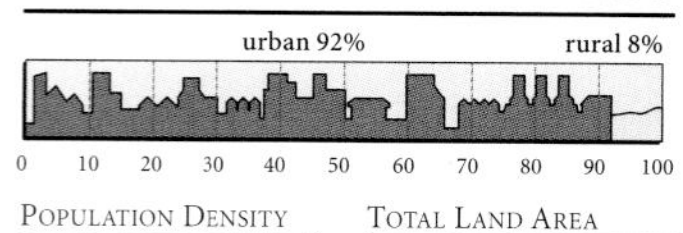

urban 92%
rural 8%
0 10 20 30 40 50 60 70 80 90 100

Population Density	Total Land Area
126 people per sq mile (49 people per sq km)	269,233 sq miles (697,286 sq km)

Smith River, Crescent City, Klamath, Orick, Mckinleyville, Arcata, Eureka, Humboldt Bay, Blue Lake, Ferndale, Fortuna, Rio Dell, Scotia, Cape Mendocino, Weott, Garberville, Weaverville, Hayfork, Orleans, Salmon Mountains, Happy Camp, Siskiyou Mountains, Klamath River, Mad River, Eel River, Van Duzen River, Trinity River, Covelo, Laytonville, Fort Bragg, Mendocino, Willits, Ukiah, Lakeport, Boonville, Hopland, Point Arena, Gualala, Cloverdale, Healdsburg, Santa, Sebastop, Bodega Head, Point Reyes, San Fra, PACIFIC

192

OREGON

IDAHO

UTAH

ARIZONA

MEXICO

NEVADA

CALIFORNIA

Great Basin

Sierra Nevada

San Joaquin Valley

California Coast Ranges

Mojave Desert

Sonoran Desert

Death Valley

Salton Sea

PACIFIC OCEAN

Channel Islands

Major places (selection):

Dorris, Tulelake, Lower Klamath Lake, Goose Lake, Clear Lake Reservoir, Fort Bidwell, Upper Lake, Alkali Lake, Catnip Mountain 2223m, Trident Peak 2558m, McDermitt, Owyhee, Mountain City, Jackpot, Matterhorn 3304m

Mount Shasta 4310m, Mount Shasta Mccloud, Dunsmuir, Alturas, Canby, Cedarville, Middle Alkali Lake, Massacre Lake, Duffer Peak 2864m, Granite Peak 2966m, Paradise Valley, McAfee Peak 3182m, Montello

Burney, Fall River Mills, Adin, Bieber, Madeline, Eagle Peak 3015m, Big Mountain, Lower Lake, King Lear Peak 2720m, Winnemucca, Golconda, Carlin, Elko, Lamoille, Spring Creek, Snow Water Lake, Ruby Dome 3471m, Spruce Mountain 3128m, Tuscarora

Los Molinos, Corning, Orland, Chico, Paradise, Lassen Peak 3187m, Susanville, Hot Springs Peak 2341m, Observation Peak 2427m, Gerlach, Empire, Kumiva Peak 2511m, Winnemucca Lake, Humboldt, Star Peak 2997m, Mount Tobin 2979m, Battle Mountain, Beowawe, Emigrant Pass, Ruby Mountains, Franklin Lake, Ruby Lake, Becky Peak 2840m

Willows, Biggs, Gridley, Oroville, Lake Oroville, Downieville, Sierra City, Chester, Westwood, Lake Almanor, Quincy, Honey Lake, Herlong, Doyle, Pyramid Lake, Nixon, Carson Sink, Humboldt Lake, Humboldt Salt Marsh, Roberts Creek Mountain 3089m, Alkali Flat, Newark Lake, North Schell Peak 3622m, Mount Moriah 3673m

Colusa, Yuba City, Marysville, Olivehurst, Grass Valley, Nevada City, Truckee, Donner Pass 2160m, Reno, Sparks, Hazen, Fernley, Fallon, Lahontan Reservoir, Austin, Summit Mountain 3189m, Eureka, Mount Callaghan 3105m, Diamond Peak 3235m, Mcgill, Ely, Connors Pass 2355m, Wheeler Peak 3981m

Live Oak, Lincoln, Roseville, Auburn, Rocklin, Citrus Heights, Folsom, Placerville, Tahoe City, Lake Tahoe, South Lake Tahoe, Carson City, Minden, Gardnerville, Markleeville, Freel Peak 3317m, Echo Summit 2249m, Virginia City, Yerington, Schurz, Gabbs, Round Mountain, Mount Jefferson 3642m, Ruth, Lund, Currant Mountain 3509m, Currant

Sacramento, Woodland, Davis, Dixon, Fairfield, Rio Vista, Lodi, Galt, Ione, Jackson, West Point, Arnold, San Andreas, Murphys, Columbia, Sonora, Hawthorne, Luning, Mina, Arc Dome 3588m, Tonopah, Warm Springs, Kawich Peak 2866m, Worthington Peak 2697m, Pioche, Panaca, Caliente, Mount Irish 2664m

Napa, Vallejo, Concord, Walnut Creek, Stockton, Oakland, Mount Diablo 1173m, Hayward, Fremont, Manteca, Riverbank, Oakdale, Coulterville, El Portal, El Capitan 2483m, Yosemite National Park, Bridgeport, Eagle Peak 3610m, Matterhorn Peak 3738m, Mono Lake, Lee Vining, Tioga Pass 3031m, Mount Dana 3978m, June Lake, Half Dome 2900m, Mount Ritter 4010m, Columbus Salt Marsh, Montgomery Pass 2183m, Boundary Peak 4005m, Lone Mountain, Goldfield, Cactus Peak 2281m, Mount Whitney, Caliente, Elgin, Alamo

San Jose, Morgan Hill, Gilroy, Patterson, Modesto, Turlock, Livingston, Atwater, Merced, Le Grand, Chowchilla, Madera, Friant, Clovis, Fresno, Bishop, Mount Humphreys 4263m, Big Pine, North Palisade 4341m, Inyo Mountains, Lake Crowley, Merced Peak 3574m, Mariposa, Gustine, Los Banos, Dos Palos, Pine Flat Lake, Independence, Owens River, Pahute Mesa, Groom Lake, Mormon Peak 2260m, Mesquite

Santa Cruz, Watsonville, Castroville, Marina, Salinas, Gonzales, Soledad, Greenfield, King City, Hollister, San Juan Bautista, San Luis Reservoir, Mendota, Sanger, Reedley, Dinuba, Woodlake, Visalia, Exeter, Lindsay, Strathmore, Lone Pine, Olancha Peak 3695m, Olancha, Haiwee Reservoir, Owens Lake, Daylight Pass 1316m, Towne Pass 1511m, Badwater Basin −86m, Telescope Peak 3368m, Hayford Peak 3021m, Indian Springs, Charleston Peak 3632m, Las Vegas, North Las Vegas, Logandale, Overton, Muddy Peak 1635m, Echo Bay, Jumbo Peak 1757m, Lake Mead

Monterey, Seaside, Carmel, Point Sur, Santa Lucia Range, Coalinga, Lemoore, Hanford, Tulare, Corcoran, Tipton, Pixley, Porterville, Sequoia National Park, Johnsondale, Kernville, Isabella Lake, Inyokern, Ridgecrest, Trona, Death Valley, Kingston Peak 2232m, Clark Mountain 2417m, Ivanpah Lake, Pahrump, East Las Vegas, Henderson, Hoover Dam, Boulder City, Colorado River

Paso Robles, Cambria, Atascadero, Morro Bay, San Luis Obispo, Black Mountain 1104m, Avenal, Alpaugh, Earlimart, Delano, Mcfarland, Wasco, Shafter, Buttonwillow, Oildale, Bakersfield, Lamont, Arvin, Johannesburg, California City, Mojave Desert, Soda Lake, Baker, Devils Playground, Providence Mountains, New York Mountains, Mountain Pass 1455m, Searchlight, Lake Mohave

Pismo Beach, Grover City, Arroyo Grande, Nipomo, Guadalupe, Santa Maria, Los Alamos, Lompoc, Ford City, Taft, Maricopa, Buena Vista Lake Bed, Tehachapi, Mojave, Boron, Rosamond, Rosamond Lake, Lancaster, Palmdale, Oro Grande, Victorville, Apple Valley, Hesperia, Barstow, Yermo, Harper Lake, Rogers Lake, Ord Mountain 1923m, Ludlow, Amboy, Bristol Lake, Cadiz Lake, Danby Lake, Needles, Lake Havasu, Parker Dam

Point Arguello, Point Conception, Goleta, Santa Barbara, Carpinteria, Ojai, Fillmore, Santa Paula, Ventura, Oxnard, Simi Valley, San Fernando, Burbank, Glendale, Pasadena, Mount San Antonio 3067m, Wrightwood, San Bernardino, San Gorgonio Mountain, Yucca Valley, Joshua Tree, Twentynine Palms, Mount Pinos 2692m, Tejon Pass 1273m, Lebec, Big Pine Mountain 2081m, Santa Ynez River, San Rafael Mountains

Los Angeles, Thousand Oaks, Beverly Hills, Santa Monica, Inglewood, Torrance, Long Beach, Huntington Beach, Alhambra, Whittier, Pomona, Fullerton, Anaheim, Santa Ana, Ontario, Redlands, Riverside, Corona, San Jacinto, Hemet, Banning, Palm Springs, Cathedral City, Indio, Coachella, Mecca, Desert Hot Springs, Mount San Jacinto 3293m, Desert Center, Palen Dry Lake, Blythe, Palo Verde, Colorado River

Laguna Beach, San Clemente, Fallbrook, Temecula, Oceanside, Carlsbad, Encinitas, Escondido, Vista, Ramona, Julian, Poway, Santee, Lakeside, El Cajon, La Mesa, National City, Chula Vista, Coronado, San Diego, Imperial, El Centro, Calexico, Holtville, Calipatria, Niland, Westmorland, Brawley, Salton Sea, Chocolate Mountains, Coachella Canal, Imperial Dam, Laguna Dam, Tero Peak 2657m

San Miguel Island, Santa Rosa Island, Santa Cruz Island, Anacapa Island, San Nicolas Island, Santa Barbara Island, Santa Catalina Island, Avalon, San Clemente Island, Gulf of Santa Catalina, Outer Santa Barbara Passage, San Pedro Channel

The towering granite cliff *of El Capitan typifies the Yosemite Valley, which is often choked with tourists during the summer months.*

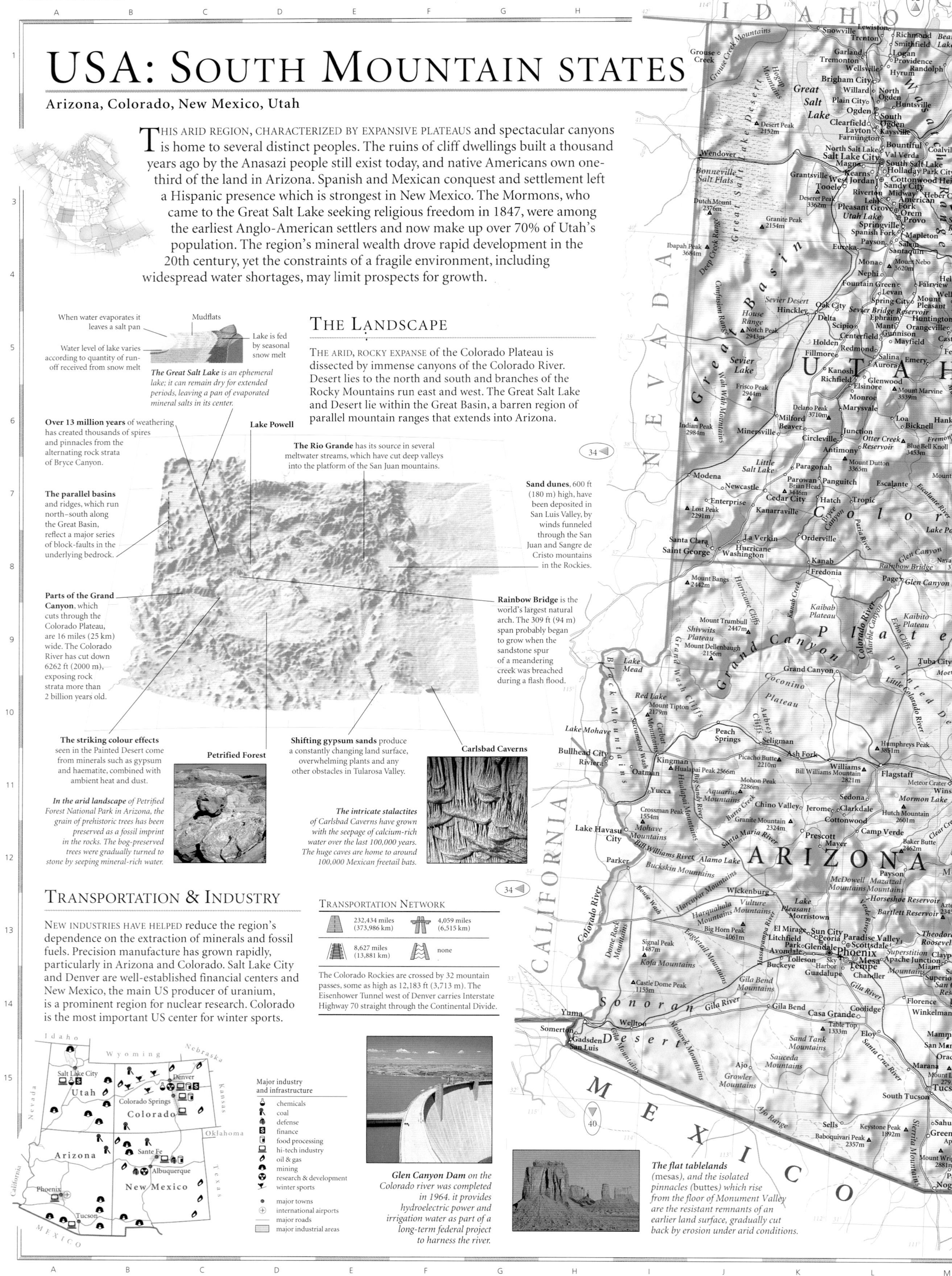

USA: South Mountain states

Arizona, Colorado, New Mexico, Utah

This arid region, characterized by expansive plateaus and spectacular canyons is home to several distinct peoples. The ruins of cliff dwellings built a thousand years ago by the Anasazi people still exist today, and native Americans own one-third of the land in Arizona. Spanish and Mexican conquest and settlement left a Hispanic presence which is strongest in New Mexico. The Mormons, who came to the Great Salt Lake seeking religious freedom in 1847, were among the earliest Anglo-American settlers and now make up over 70% of Utah's population. The region's mineral wealth drove rapid development in the 20th century, yet the constraints of a fragile environment, including widespread water shortages, may limit prospects for growth.

The Landscape

The arid, rocky expanse of the Colorado Plateau is dissected by immense canyons of the Colorado River. Desert lies to the north and south and branches of the Rocky Mountains run east and west. The Great Salt Lake and Desert lie within the Great Basin, a barren region of parallel mountain ranges that extends into Arizona.

When water evaporates it leaves a salt pan

Mudflats

Lake is fed by seasonal snow melt

Water level of lake varies according to quantity of run-off received from snow melt

The Great Salt Lake is an ephemeral lake; it can remain dry for extended periods, leaving a pan of evaporated mineral salts in its center.

Over 13 million years of weathering has created thousands of spires and pinnacles from the alternating rock strata of Bryce Canyon.

Lake Powell

The Rio Grande has its source in several meltwater streams, which have cut deep valleys into the platform of the San Juan mountains.

The parallel basins and ridges, which run north–south along the Great Basin, reflect a major series of block-faults in the underlying bedrock.

Sand dunes, 600 ft (180 m) high, have been deposited in San Luis Valley, by winds funneled through the San Juan and Sangre de Cristo mountains in the Rockies.

Parts of the Grand Canyon, which cuts through the Colorado Plateau, are 16 miles (25 km) wide. The Colorado River has cut down 6262 ft (2000 m), exposing rock strata more than 2 billion years old.

Rainbow Bridge is the world's largest natural arch. The 309 ft (94 m) span probably began to grow when the sandstone spur of a meandering creek was breached during a flash flood.

The striking colour effects seen in the Painted Desert come from minerals such as gypsum and haematite, combined with ambient heat and dust.

Petrified Forest

In the arid landscape of Petrified Forest National Park in Arizona, the grain of prehistoric trees has been preserved as a fossil imprint in the rocks. The bog-preserved trees were gradually turned to stone by seeping mineral-rich water.

Shifting gypsum sands produce a constantly changing land surface, overwhelming plants and any other obstacles in Tularosa Valley.

Carlsbad Caverns

The intricate stalactites of Carlsbad Caverns have grown with the seepage of calcium-rich water over the last 100,000 years. The huge caves are home to around 100,000 Mexican freetail bats.

Transportation & Industry

New industries have helped reduce the region's dependence on the extraction of minerals and fossil fuels. Precision manufacture has grown rapidly, particularly in Arizona and Colorado. Salt Lake City and Denver are well-established financial centers and New Mexico, the main US producer of uranium, is a prominent region for nuclear research. Colorado is the most important US center for winter sports.

Transportation Network

232,434 miles (373,986 km)	4,059 miles (6,515 km)
8,627 miles (13,881 km)	none

The Colorado Rockies are crossed by 32 mountain passes, some as high as 12,183 ft (3,713 m). The Eisenhower Tunnel west of Denver carries Interstate Highway 70 straight through the Continental Divide.

Major industry and infrastructure

- chemicals
- coal
- defense
- finance
- food processing
- hi-tech industry
- oil & gas
- mining
- research & development
- winter sports
- major towns
- international airports
- major roads
- major industrial areas

Glen Canyon Dam on the Colorado river was completed in 1964. it provides hydroelectric power and irrigation water as part of a long-term federal project to harness the river.

The flat tablelands (mesas), and the isolated pinnacles (buttes) which rise from the floor of Monument Valley are the resistant remnants of an earlier land surface, gradually cut back by erosion under arid conditions.

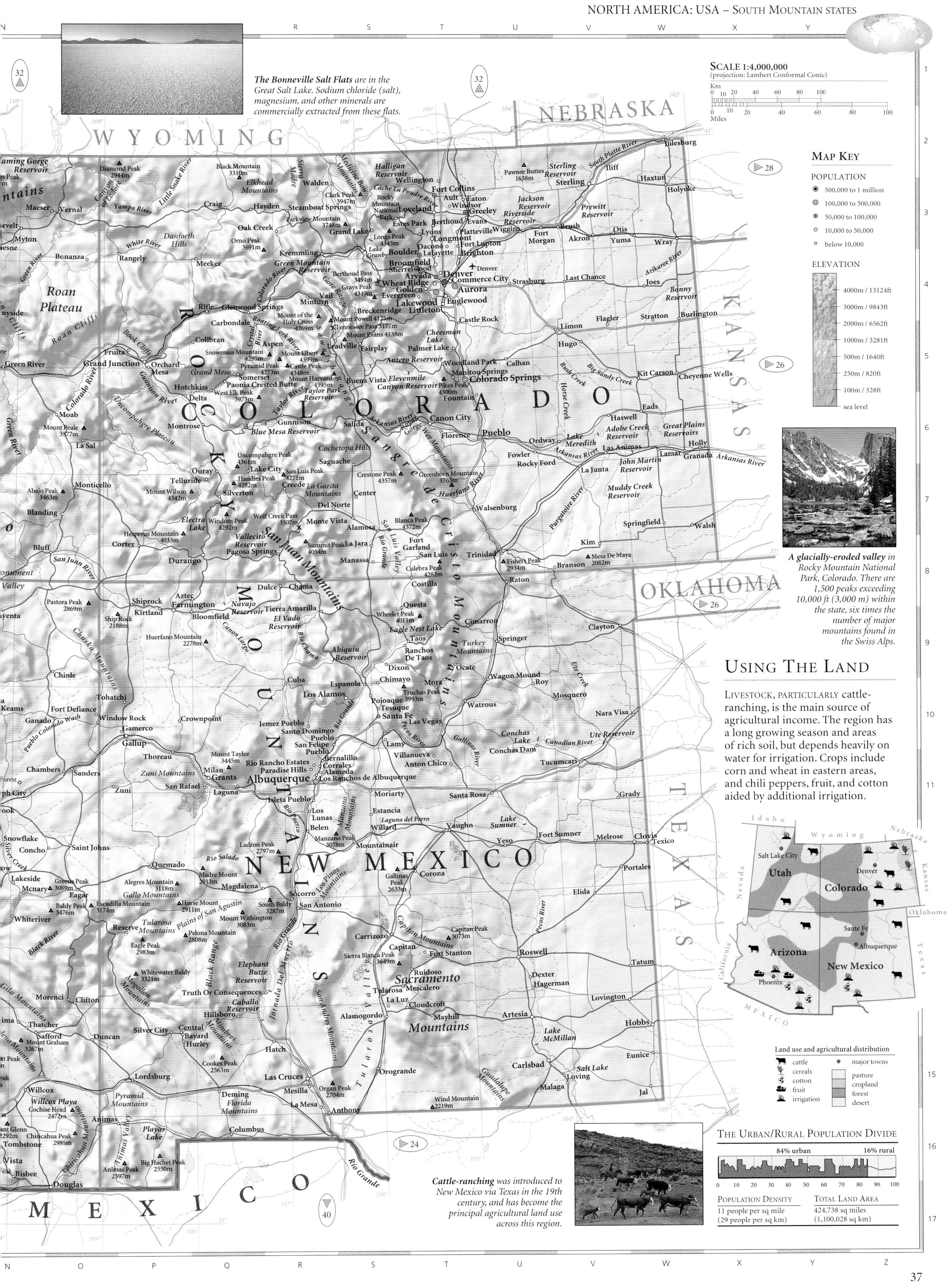

SCALE 1:4,000,000
(projection: Lambert Conformal Conic)
Km
Miles
MAP KEY
POPULATION
500,000 to 1 million
100,000 to 500,000
50,000 to 100,000
10,000 to 50,000
below 10,000
ELEVATION
4000m / 13124ft
3000m / 9843ft
2000m / 6562ft
1000m / 3281ft
500m / 1640ft
250m / 820ft
100m / 328ft
sea level
WYOMING
NEBRASKA
KANSAS
OKLAHOMA
TEXAS
COLORADO
NEW MEXICO
MEXICO
ROCKY MOUNTAINS
Sangre de Cristo Mountains
San Juan Mountains
Sacramento Mountains
Denver
Colorado Springs
Pueblo
Albuquerque
Santa Fe
Las Cruces
Grand Junction
Fort Collins
Boulder
Roswell
Carlsbad
Farmington
Durango
Rio Grande
Arkansas River
Land use and agricultural distribution
cattle
cereals
cotton
fruit
irrigation
major towns
pasture
cropland
forest
desert
Idaho
Wyoming
Nebraska
Kansas
Oklahoma
Texas
Nevada
California
MEXICO
Salt Lake City
Utah
Colorado
Denver
Arizona
Phoenix
Santa Fe
Albuquerque
New Mexico
THE URBAN/RURAL POPULATION DIVIDE
84% urban
16% rural
0 10 20 30 40 50 60 70 80 90 100
POPULATION DENSITY
11 people per sq mile
(29 people per sq km)
TOTAL LAND AREA
424,738 sq miles
(1,100,028 sq km)

The Bonneville Salt Flats are in the Great Salt Lake. Sodium chloride (salt), magnesium, and other minerals are commercially extracted from these flats.

A glacially-eroded valley in Rocky Mountain National Park, Colorado. There are 1,500 peaks exceeding 10,000 ft (3,000 m) within the state, six times the number of major mountains found in the Swiss Alps.

USING THE LAND

LIVESTOCK, PARTICULARLY cattle-ranching, is the main source of agricultural income. The region has a long growing season and areas of rich soil, but depends heavily on water for irrigation. Crops include corn and wheat in eastern areas, and chili peppers, fruit, and cotton aided by additional irrigation.

Cattle-ranching was introduced to New Mexico via Texas in the 19th century, and has become the principal agricultural land use across this region.

USA: Hawaii

THE 122 ISLANDS of the Hawaiian archipelago – which are part of Polynesia – are the peaks of the world's largest volcanoes. They rise approximately 6 miles (9.7 km) from the floor of the Pacific Ocean. The largest, the island of Hawaii, remains highly active. Hawaii became the US's 50th state in 1959. A tradition of receiving immigrant workers is reflected in the islands' ethnic diversity, with peoples drawn from around the rim of the Pacific. Only 2% of the current population are native Polynesians.

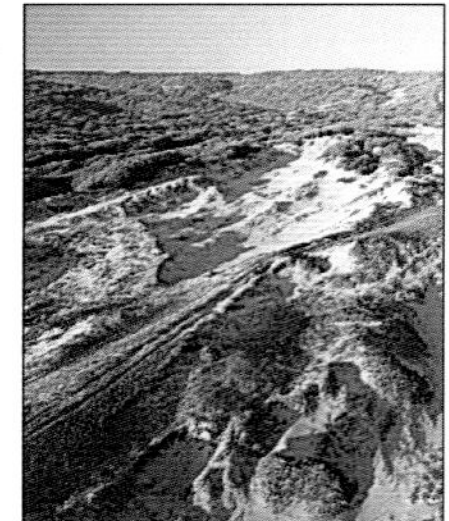

The island of Molokai is formed from volcanic rock. Mature sand dunes cover the rocks in coastal areas.

Transportation & Industry

TOURISM DOMINATES the economy, with over half of the population employed in services. The naval base at Pearl Harbor is also a major source of employment. Industry is concentrated on the island of Oahu and relies mostly on imported materials, while agricultural produce is processed locally.

Major industry and infrastructure

- food processing
- military base
- textiles
- tourism
- major towns
- international airports
- major roads
- major industrial areas

Transportation Network

4,102 miles (6,600 km)		43 miles (69 km)	
none		none	

Hawaii relies on ocean-surface transportation. Honolulu is the main focus of this network, bringing foreign trade and the markets of mainland US to Hawaii's outer islands.

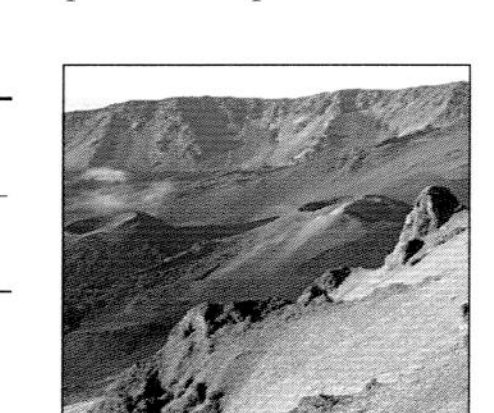

Haleakala's extinct volcanic crater is the world's largest. The giant caldera, containing many secondary cones, is 2,000 ft (600 m) deep and 20 miles (32 km) in circumference.

SCALE 1:4,000,000
(projection: Lambert Conformal Conic)

Map Key

POPULATION

- 100,000 to 500,000
- 50,000 to 100,000
- 10,000 to 50,000
- below 10,000

ELEVATION

- 4000m / 13,124ft
- 3000m / 9843ft
- 2000m / 6562ft
- 1000m / 3281ft
- 500m / 1640ft
- 250m / 820ft
- 100m / 328ft
- sea level

Using the Land and Sea

THE VOLCANIC SOILS are extremely fertile and the climate hot and humid on the lower slopes, supporting large commercial plantations growing sugar cane, bananas, pineapples, and other tropical fruit, as well as nursery plants and flowers. Some land is given to pasture, particularly for beef and dairy cattle.

Land use and agricultural distribution

- cattle
- fishing
- fruit
- sugar cane
- major towns
- pasture
- cropland
- forest
- mountain region

The island of Kauai is one of the wettest places in the world, receiving some 450 inches (11,500 mm) of rain a year.

The Urban/Rural Population Divide

urban 89% — rural 11%

Population Density	Total Land Area
183 people per sq mile (71 people per sq km)	6,423 sq miles (16,636 sq km)

Using the Land and Sea

THE ICE-FREE COASTLINE of Alaska provides access to salmon fisheries and more than 5.5 million acres (2.2 million ha) of forest. Most of Alaska is uncultivable, and around 90% of food is imported. Barley, hay, and hothouse products are grown around Anchorage, where dairy farming is also concentrated.

The Urban/Rural Population Divide

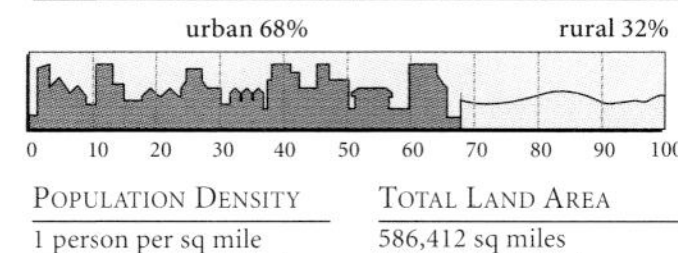
urban 68%
rural 32%

Population Density	Total Land Area
1 person per sq mile (0.4 people per sq km)	586,412 sq miles (1,518,800 sq km)

A raft of timber from the Tongass forest is hauled by a tug, bound for the pulp mills of the Alaskan coast between Juneau and Ketchikan.

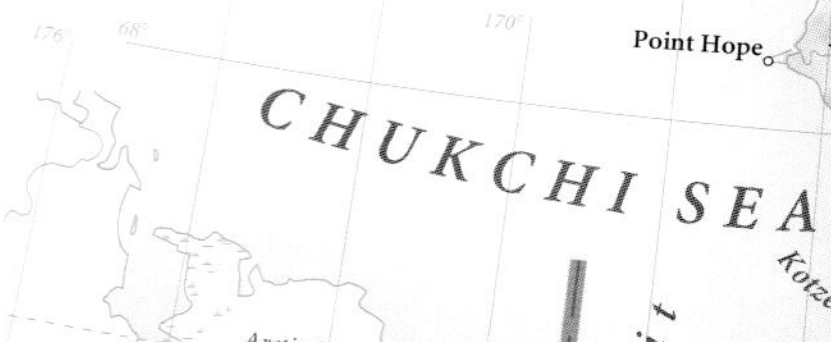

Map Key

POPULATION

- 100,000 to 500,000
- 50,000 to 100,000
- 10,000 to 50,000
- below 10,000

ELEVATION

- 4000m / 13,124ft
- 3000m / 9843ft
- 2000m / 6562ft
- 1000m / 3281ft
- 500m / 1640ft
- 250m / 820ft
- 100m / 328ft
- sea level

SCALE 1:9,000,000
(projection: Lambert Conformal Conic)

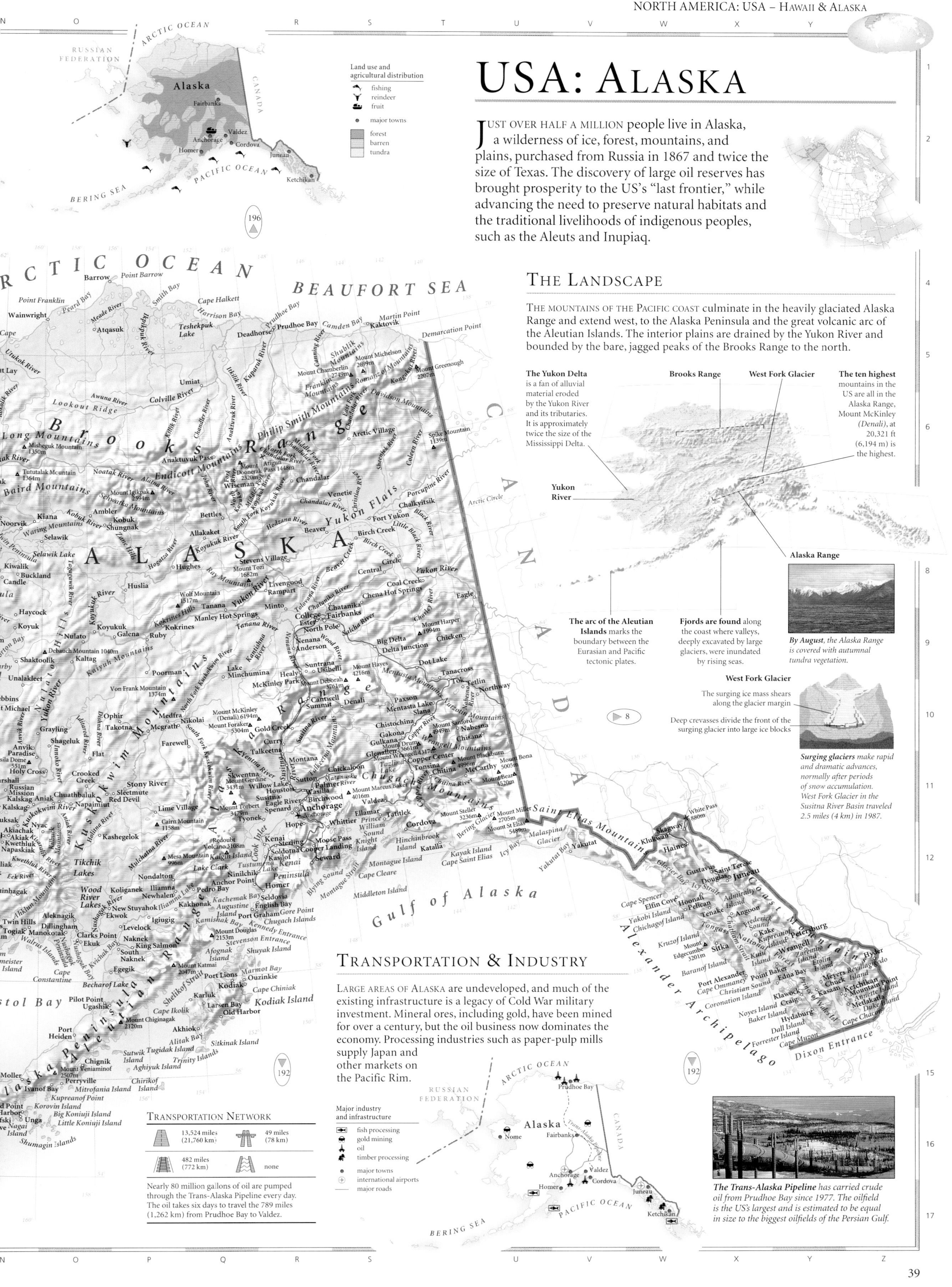
Land use and agricultural distribution
fishing
reindeer
fruit
major towns
forest
barren
tundra
ARCTIC OCEAN
BEAUFORT SEA
BERING SEA
PACIFIC OCEAN
Gulf of Alaska
Brooks Range
Alaska Range
Alexander Archipelago
The Yukon Delta is a fan of alluvial material eroded by the Yukon River and its tributaries. It is approximately twice the size of the Mississippi Delta.
Brooks Range
West Fork Glacier
The ten highest mountains in the US are all in the Alaska Range, Mount McKinley (Denali), at 20,321 ft (6,194 m) is the highest.
Yukon River
Alaska Range
The arc of the Aleutian Islands marks the boundary between the Eurasian and Pacific tectonic plates.
Fjords are found along the coast where valleys, deeply excavated by large glaciers, were inundated by rising seas.
West Fork Glacier
The surging ice mass shears along the glacier margin
Deep crevasses divide the front of the surging glacier into large ice blocks
Major industry and infrastructure
fish processing
gold mining
oil
timber processing
major towns
international airports
major roads

USA: Alaska

Just over half a million people live in Alaska, a wilderness of ice, forest, mountains, and plains, purchased from Russia in 1867 and twice the size of Texas. The discovery of large oil reserves has brought prosperity to the US's "last frontier," while advancing the need to preserve natural habitats and the traditional livelihoods of indigenous peoples, such as the Aleuts and Inupiaq.

The Landscape

The mountains of the Pacific coast culminate in the heavily glaciated Alaska Range and extend west, to the Alaska Peninsula and the great volcanic arc of the Aleutian Islands. The interior plains are drained by the Yukon River and bounded by the bare, jagged peaks of the Brooks Range to the north.

By August, the Alaska Range is covered with autumnal tundra vegetation.

***Surging glaciers** make rapid and dramatic advances, normally after periods of snow accumulation. West Fork Glacier in the Susitna River Basin traveled 2.5 miles (4 km) in 1987.*

Transportation & Industry

Large areas of Alaska are undeveloped, and much of the existing infrastructure is a legacy of Cold War military investment. Mineral ores, including gold, have been mined for over a century, but the oil business now dominates the economy. Processing industries such as paper-pulp mills supply Japan and other markets on the Pacific Rim.

Transportation Network

	13,524 miles (21,760 km)		49 miles (78 km)
	482 miles (772 km)		none

Nearly 80 million gallons of oil are pumped through the Trans-Alaska Pipeline every day. The oil takes six days to travel the 789 miles (1,262 km) from Prudhoe Bay to Valdez.

***The Trans-Alaska Pipeline** has carried crude oil from Prudhoe Bay since 1977. The oilfield is the US's largest and is estimated to be equal in size to the biggest oilfields of the Persian Gulf.*

SCALE 1:7,000,000
(projection: Lambert Conformal Conic)

The rugged, desert landscape *of the Sierra Madre del Sur is a product of complex tectonic processes, where the fold mountains in western North America, running north–south, meet the Caribbean mountain arc which runs east–west.*

Wave action *has cut steep cliffs into the igneous rocks of Isla Cedros, off the Pacific coast of Baja California. The island is home to sea lions, reptiles, and deer.*

MEXICO

MEXICO POSSESSES rich mineral resources, limited agricultural land and the world's largest and fastest growing Spanish-speaking population. Most Mexicans are *mestizo*, although Amerindian communities still exist in the south, 400 years after Spain destroyed the Aztec empire at its height. Much of the arid north is sparsely inhabited, while Mexico City is becoming the world's most populous city. Conflict with the US has long overshadowed Mexico's development, but the North American Free Trade Agreement offers the chance for a more benign relationship, which may help to offset Mexico's problems of hyperinflation, foreign debt, unequal wealth distribution and political instability.

USING THE LAND AND SEA

CORN OCCUPIES much of the cultivated area. Commercial plantations of coffee, sugar, vanilla, and cotton are found along the Gulf coastal plain and in irrigated parts of the arid north, which is otherwise used for extensive ranching. Fishing is important, particularly shellfish for export. A soaring population has created the need for grain imports since 1980.

THE URBAN/RURAL POPULATION DIVIDE

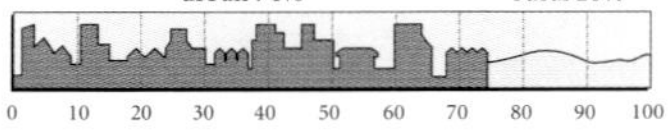

urban 74% / rural 26%

POPULATION DENSITY	TOTAL LAND AREA
130 people per sq mile (50 people per sq km)	755,865 sq miles (1,958,200 sq km)

Land use and agricultural distribution: cattle, coffee, corn (maize), cotton, fishing, shellfish, sugar cane, timber, vanilla; capital cities, major towns; pasture, cropland, forest, desert

Coffee beans *spread out to dry in the sun. Coffee, grown mainly on the Gulf coastal plain, is Mexico's most valuable export crop.*

MEXICO: ADMINISTRATIVE REGIONS

① DISTRITO FEDERAL

MAP KEY

POPULATION: above 5 million; 1 million to 5 million; 500,000 to 1 million; 100,000 to 500,000; 50,000 to 100,000; 10,000 to 50,000; below 10,000

ELEVATION: 4000m / 13,124ft; 3000m / 9843ft; 2000m / 6562ft; 1000m / 3281ft; 500m / 1640ft; 250m / 820ft; 100m / 328ft; sea level

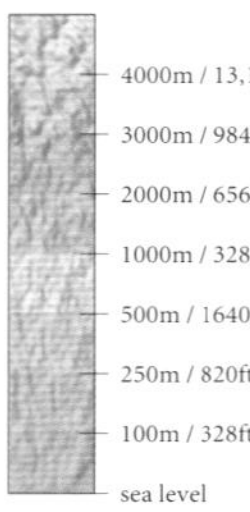

THE LANDSCAPE

THE GREAT CENTRAL PLATEAU rises gently southward from the Rio Grande, isolated from the coastal plains by the Sierra Madre Oriental and Occidental. The two ranges converge from east and west respectively, culminating in high volcanic peaks around Mexico City. Further ranges of the Sierra Madre rise to the south of the Balsas Basin, skirted by the low-lying Isthmus of Tehuantepec *(Istmo de Tehuantepec)* and Yucatan Peninsula.

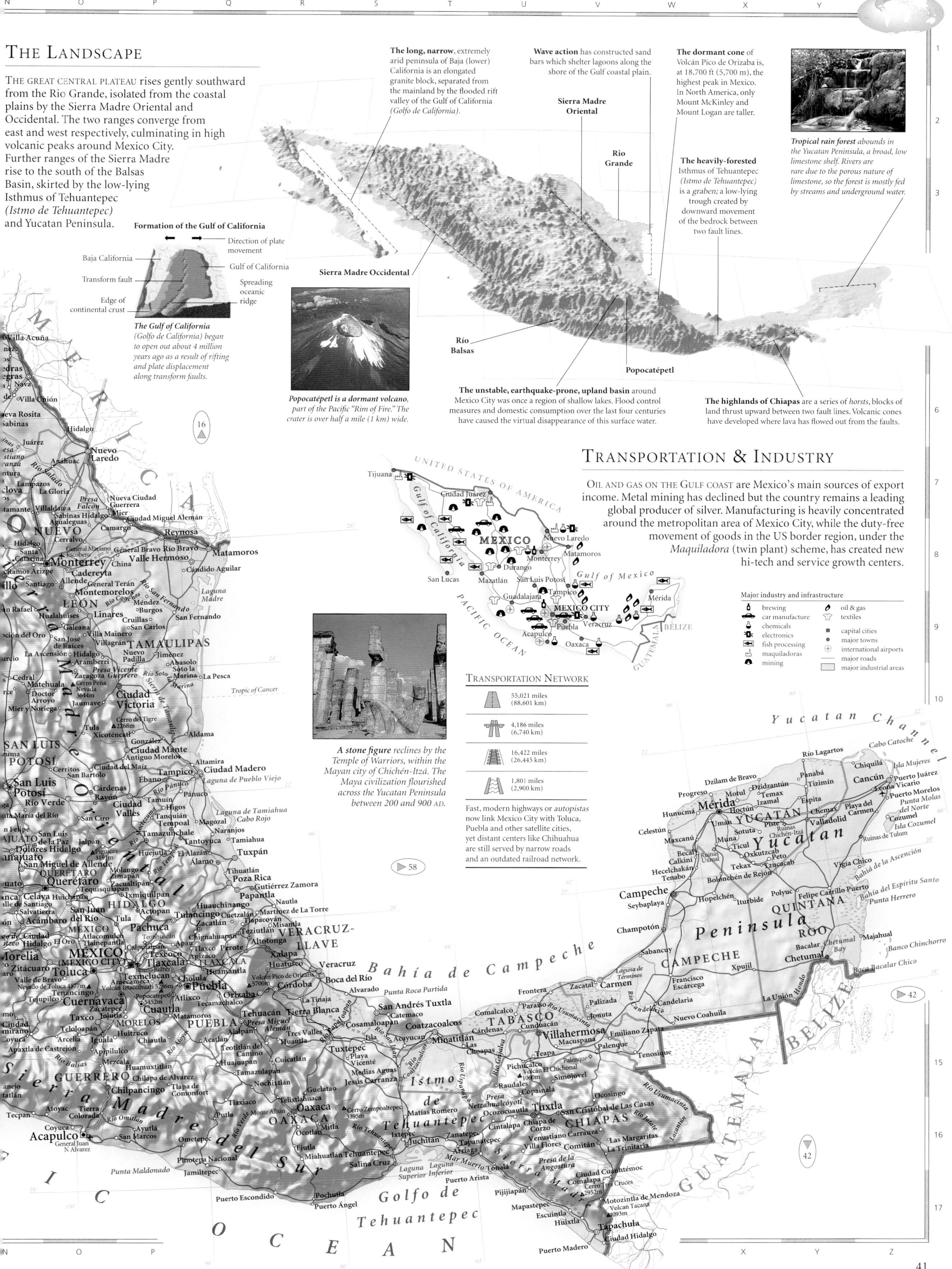

Formation of the Gulf of California
Direction of plate movement
Baja California
Gulf of California
Transform fault
Spreading oceanic ridge
Edge of continental crust
The long, narrow, extremely arid peninsula of Baja (lower) California is an elongated granite block, separated from the mainland by the flooded rift valley of the Gulf of California (Golfo de California).
Wave action has constructed sand bars which shelter lagoons along the shore of the Gulf coastal plain.
The dormant cone of Volcán Pico de Orizaba is, at 18,700 ft (5,700 m), the highest peak in Mexico. In North America, only Mount McKinley and Mount Logan are taller.
Sierra Madre Oriental
Rio Grande
The heavily-forested Isthmus of Tehuantepec (Istmo de Tehuantepec) is a graben; a low-lying trough created by downward movement of the bedrock between two fault lines.
Sierra Madre Occidental
Río Balsas
Popocatépetl
The unstable, earthquake-prone, upland basin around Mexico City was once a region of shallow lakes. Flood control measures and domestic consumption over the last four centuries have caused the virtual disappearance of this surface water.
The highlands of Chiapas are a series of horsts, blocks of land thrust upward between two fault lines. Volcanic cones have developed where lava has flowed out from the faults.
Major industry and infrastructure
brewing
car manufacture
chemicals
electronics
fish processing
maquiladoras
mining
oil & gas
textiles
capital cities
major towns
international airports
major roads
major industrial areas

The Gulf of California (Golfo de California) began to open out about 4 million years ago as a result of rifting and plate displacement along transform faults.

Tropical rain forest abounds in the Yucatan Peninsula, a broad, low limestone shelf. Rivers are rare due to the porous nature of limestone, so the forest is mostly fed by streams and underground water.

Popocatépetl is a dormant volcano, part of the Pacific "Rim of Fire." The crater is over half a mile (1 km) wide.

TRANSPORTATION & INDUSTRY

OIL AND GAS ON THE GULF COAST are Mexico's main sources of export income. Metal mining has declined but the country remains a leading global producer of silver. Manufacturing is heavily concentrated around the metropolitan area of Mexico City, while the duty-free movement of goods in the US border region, under the *Maquiladora* (twin plant) scheme, has created new hi-tech and service growth centers.

A stone figure reclines by the Temple of Warriors, within the Mayan city of Chichén-Itzá. The Maya civilization flourished across the Yucatan Peninsula between 200 and 900 AD.

TRANSPORTATION NETWORK

Roads	55,021 miles (88,601 km)
Highways	4,186 miles (6,740 km)
Railways	16,422 miles (26,445 km)
Waterways	1,801 miles (2,900 km)

Fast, modern highways or *autopistas* now link Mexico City with Toluca, Puebla and other satellite cities, yet distant centers like Chihuahua are still served by narrow roads and an outdated railroad network.

16 58 42 42

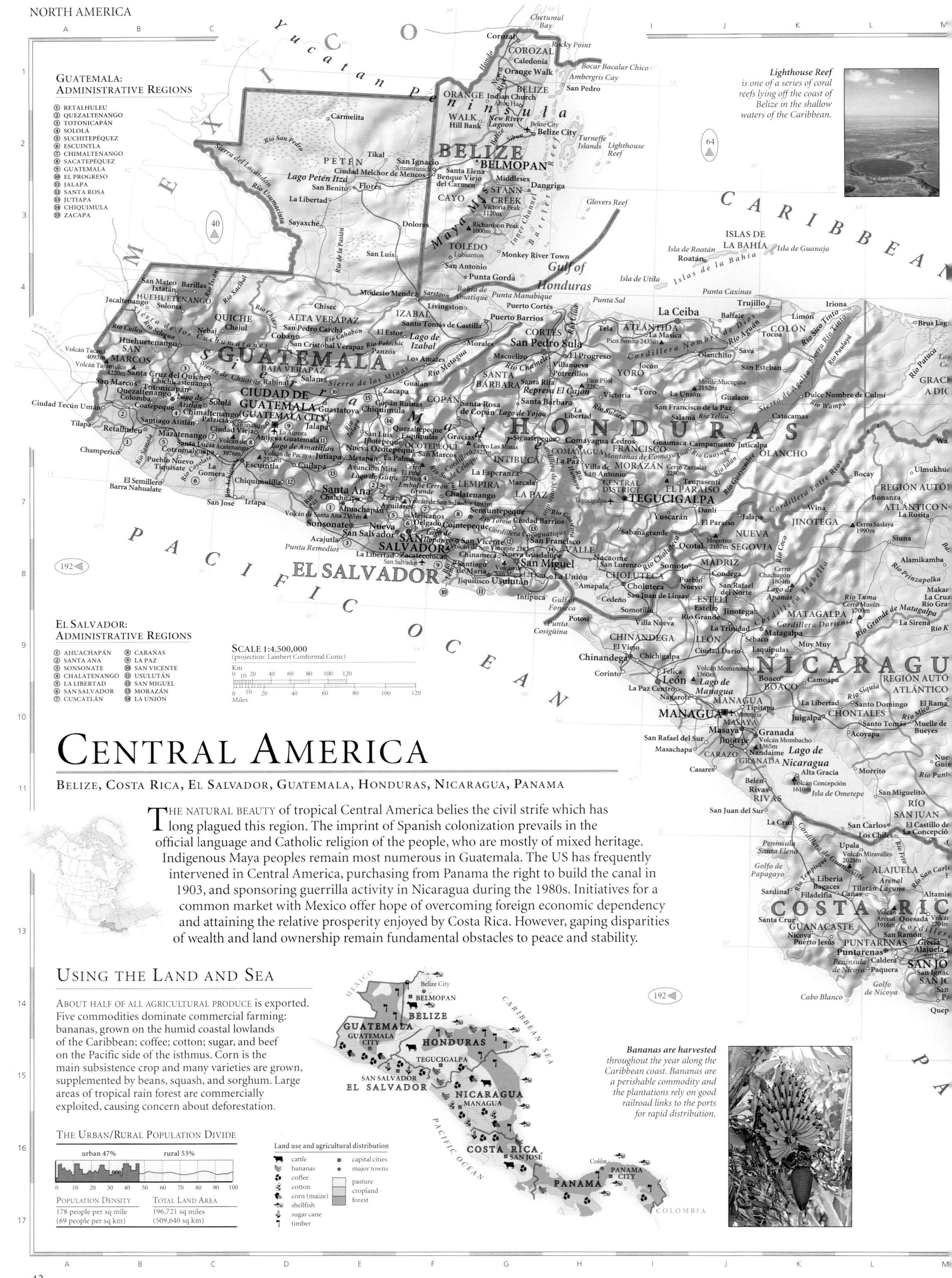
GUATEMALA: ADMINISTRATIVE REGIONS
① RETALHULEU
② QUEZALTENANGO
③ TOTONICAPÁN
④ SOLOLÁ
⑤ SUCHITEPÉQUEZ
⑥ ESCUINTLA
⑦ CHIMALTENANGO
⑧ SACATEPÉQUEZ
⑨ GUATEMALA
⑩ EL PROGRESO
⑪ JALAPA
⑫ SANTA ROSA
⑬ JUTIAPA
⑭ CHIQUIMULA
⑮ ZACAPA
EL SALVADOR: ADMINISTRATIVE REGIONS
① AHUACHAPÁN
② SANTA ANA
③ SONSONATE
④ CHALATENANGO
⑤ LA LIBERTAD
⑥ SAN SALVADOR
⑦ CUSCATLÁN
⑧ CABAÑAS
⑨ LA PAZ
⑩ SAN VICENTE
⑪ USULUTÁN
⑫ SAN MIGUEL
⑬ MORAZÁN
⑭ LA UNIÓN
SCALE 1:4,500,000
(projection: Lambert Conformal Conic)
MEXICO
Yucatan Peninsula
CARIBBEAN
PACIFIC OCEAN
BELIZE
BELMOPAN
GUATEMALA
CIUDAD DE GUATEMALA (GUATEMALA CITY)
HONDURAS
TEGUCIGALPA
EL SALVADOR
SAN SALVADOR
NICARAGUA
MANAGUA
COSTA RICA
Gulf of Honduras
Lago de Nicaragua
Lago de Managua

Lighthouse Reef is one of a series of coral reefs lying off the coast of Belize in the shallow waters of the Caribbean.

Central America

Belize, Costa Rica, El Salvador, Guatemala, Honduras, Nicaragua, Panama

THE NATURAL BEAUTY of tropical Central America belies the civil strife which has long plagued this region. The imprint of Spanish colonization prevails in the official language and Catholic religion of the people, who are mostly of mixed heritage. Indigenous Maya peoples remain most numerous in Guatemala. The US has frequently intervened in Central America, purchasing from Panama the right to build the canal in 1903, and sponsoring guerrilla activity in Nicaragua during the 1980s. Initiatives for a common market with Mexico offer hope of overcoming foreign economic dependency and attaining the relative prosperity enjoyed by Costa Rica. However, gaping disparities of wealth and land ownership remain fundamental obstacles to peace and stability.

Using the Land and Sea

ABOUT HALF OF ALL AGRICULTURAL PRODUCE is exported. Five commodities dominate commercial farming: bananas, grown on the humid coastal lowlands of the Caribbean; coffee; cotton; sugar, and beef on the Pacific side of the isthmus. Corn is the main subsistence crop and many varieties are grown, supplemented by beans, squash, and sorghum. Large areas of tropical rain forest are commercially exploited, causing concern about deforestation.

The Urban/Rural Population Divide

urban 47% — rural 53%

Population Density	Total Land Area
178 people per sq mile (69 people per sq km)	196,721 sq miles (509,640 sq km)

Land use and agricultural distribution: cattle, bananas, coffee, cotton, corn (maize), shellfish, sugar cane, timber, capital cities, major towns, pasture, cropland, forest

Bananas are harvested throughout the year along the Caribbean coast. Bananas are a perishable commodity and the plantations rely on good railroad links to the ports for rapid distribution.

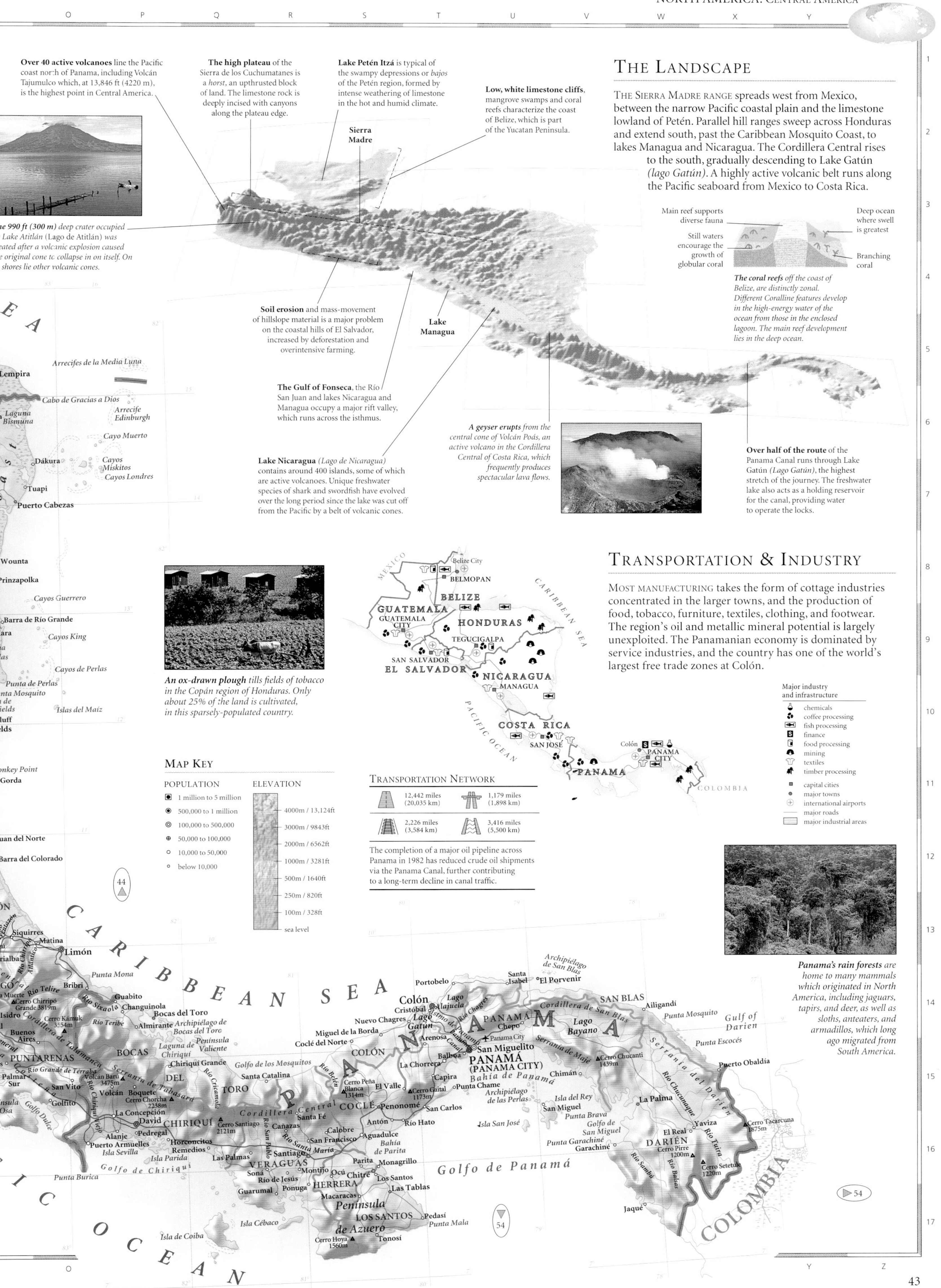
N O P Q R S T U V W X Y
1 2 3 4 5 6 7 8 9 10 11 12 13 14 15 16 17
Sierra Madre
Lake Managua
Main reef supports diverse fauna
Still waters encourage the growth of globular coral
Deep ocean where swell is greatest
Branching coral
MEXICO
Belize City
BELMOPAN
BELIZE
GUATEMALA
GUATEMALA CITY
HONDURAS
TEGUCIGALPA
SAN SALVADOR
EL SALVADOR
NICARAGUA
MANAGUA
COSTA RICA
SAN JOSÉ
Colón
PANAMA CITY
PANAMA
COLOMBIA
CARIBBEAN SEA
PACIFIC OCEAN
Arrecifes de la Media Luna
Lempira
Cabo de Gracias a Dios
Laguna Bismuna
Arrecife Edinburgh
Cayo Muerto
Dákura
Cayos Miskitos
Cayos Londres
Tuapi
Puerto Cabezas
Wounta
Prinzapolka
Cayos Guerrero
Barra de Río Grande
Kara
Cayos King
Cayos de Perlas
Punta de Perlas
Punta Mosquito
Islas del Maíz
Bluff
Monkey Point
San Juan del Norte
Barra del Colorado
Siquirres
Matina
Limón
Punta Mona
Bribri
Guabito
Changuinola
Bocas del Toro
Archipiélago de Bocas del Toro
Almirante
Península Valiente
Laguna de Chiriquí
Chiriquí Grande
BOCAS DEL TORO
PUNTARENAS
Golfo de los Mosquitos
Santa Catalina
Cerro Chirripó Grande 3819m
Cerro Kamuk 3554m
Volcán Barú 3475m
Volcán
Boquete
Cerro Chorcha 2238m
San Vito
Golfito
Golfo Dulce
La Concepción
David
Alanje
Pedregal
CHIRIQUÍ
Cerro Santiago 2121m
Puerto Armuelles
Horconcitos
Remedios
Isla Sevilla
Isla Parida
Golfo de Chiriquí
Punta Burica
Las Palmas
VERAGUAS
Soná
Río de Jesús
Guarumal
Ponuga
Montijo
Ocú
Chitré
Santiago
Cañazas
Santa Fé
Cordillera Central
Calobre
San Francisco
Aguadulce
Bahía de Parita
Parita
Monagrillo
Los Santos
Las Tablas
HERRERA
Macaracas
Península de Azuero
LOS SANTOS
Pedasí
Punta Mala
Tonosí
Cerro Hoya 1560m
Isla Cébaco
Isla de Coiba
COCLÉ
Penonomé
Antón
Río Hato
San Carlos
Cerro Peña Blanca 1314m
El Valle
Cerro Gaital 1173m
COLÓN
Coclé del Norte
Miguel de la Borda
Nuevo Chagres
Colón
Cristóbal
Lago Gatún
Portobelo
Lago Alajuela
Arenosa
Balboa
La Chorrera
Capira
Punta Chame
San Miguelito
PANAMÁ (PANAMA CITY)
Panama City
Chepo
Bahía de Panamá
Archipiélago de las Perlas
Chimán
Isla del Rey
San Miguel
Punta Brava
Golfo de San Miguel
Punta Garachiné
Garachiné
Isla San José
Golfo de Panamá
Santa Isabel
Archipiélago de San Blas
El Porvenir
SAN BLAS
Cordillera de San Blas
Lago Bayano
Serranía de Majé
Cerro Chucanti 1439m
Aligandí
Punta Mosquito
Gulf of Darien
Punta Escocés
Puerto Obaldía
Serranía del Darién
La Palma
Yaviza
Cerro Tacarcuna 1875m
El Real
DARIÉN
Cerro Pirre 1200m
Cerro Setetule 1220m
Jaqué
COLOMBIA
CARIBBEAN SEA
PACIFIC OCEAN
44
54
54

Over 40 active volcanoes line the Pacific coast north of Panama, including Volcán Tajumulco which, at 13,846 ft (4220 m), is the highest point in Central America.

The high plateau of the Sierra de los Cuchumatanes is a *horst*, an upthrusted block of land. The limestone rock is deeply incised with canyons along the plateau edge.

Lake Petén Itzá is typical of the swampy depressions or *bajos* of the Petén region, formed by intense weathering of limestone in the hot and humid climate.

Low, white limestone cliffs, mangrove swamps and coral reefs characterize the coast of Belize, which is part of the Yucatan Peninsula.

The 990 ft (300 m) deep crater occupied by Lake Atitlán (Lago de Atitlán) was created after a volcanic explosion caused the original cone to collapse in on itself. On its shores lie other volcanic cones.

Soil erosion and mass-movement of hillslope material is a major problem on the coastal hills of El Salvador, increased by deforestation and overintensive farming.

The Gulf of Fonseca, the Río San Juan and lakes Nicaragua and Managua occupy a major rift valley, which runs across the isthmus.

Lake Nicaragua *(Lago de Nicaragua)* contains around 400 islands, some of which are active volcanoes. Unique freshwater species of shark and swordfish have evolved over the long period since the lake was cut off from the Pacific by a belt of volcanic cones.

A geyser erupts from the central cone of Volcán Poás, an active volcano in the Cordillera Central of Costa Rica, which frequently produces spectacular lava flows.

Over half of the route of the Panama Canal runs through Lake Gatún *(Lago Gatún)*, the highest stretch of the journey. The freshwater lake also acts as a holding reservoir for the canal, providing water to operate the locks.

The Landscape

The Sierra Madre range spreads west from Mexico, between the narrow Pacific coastal plain and the limestone lowland of Petén. Parallel hill ranges sweep across Honduras and extend south, past the Caribbean Mosquito Coast, to lakes Managua and Nicaragua. The Cordillera Central rises to the south, gradually descending to Lake Gatún *(lago Gatún)*. A highly active volcanic belt runs along the Pacific seaboard from Mexico to Costa Rica.

***The coral reefs** off the coast of Belize, are distinctly zonal. Different Coralline features develop in the high-energy water of the ocean from those in the enclosed lagoon. The main reef development lies in the deep ocean.*

Transportation & Industry

Most manufacturing takes the form of cottage industries concentrated in the larger towns, and the production of food, tobacco, furniture, textiles, clothing, and footwear. The region's oil and metallic mineral potential is largely unexploited. The Panamanian economy is dominated by service industries, and the country has one of the world's largest free trade zones at Colón.

Major industry and infrastructure
- chemicals
- coffee processing
- fish processing
- finance
- food processing
- mining
- textiles
- timber processing
- capital cities
- major towns
- international airports
- major roads
- major industrial areas

***An ox-drawn plough** tills fields of tobacco in the Copán region of Honduras. Only about 25% of the land is cultivated, in this sparsely-populated country.*

Map Key

POPULATION
- 1 million to 5 million
- 500,000 to 1 million
- 100,000 to 500,000
- 50,000 to 100,000
- 10,000 to 50,000
- below 10,000

ELEVATION
- 4000m / 13,124ft
- 3000m / 9843ft
- 2000m / 6562ft
- 1000m / 3281ft
- 500m / 1640ft
- 250m / 820ft
- 100m / 328ft
- sea level

Transportation Network

12,442 miles (20,035 km)	1,179 miles (1,898 km)
2,226 miles (3,584 km)	3,416 miles (5,500 km)

The completion of a major oil pipeline across Panama in 1982 has reduced crude oil shipments via the Panama Canal, further contributing to a long-term decline in canal traffic.

Panama's rain forests are home to many mammals which originated in North America, including jaguars, tapirs, and deer, as well as sloths, anteaters, and armadillos, which long ago migrated from South America.

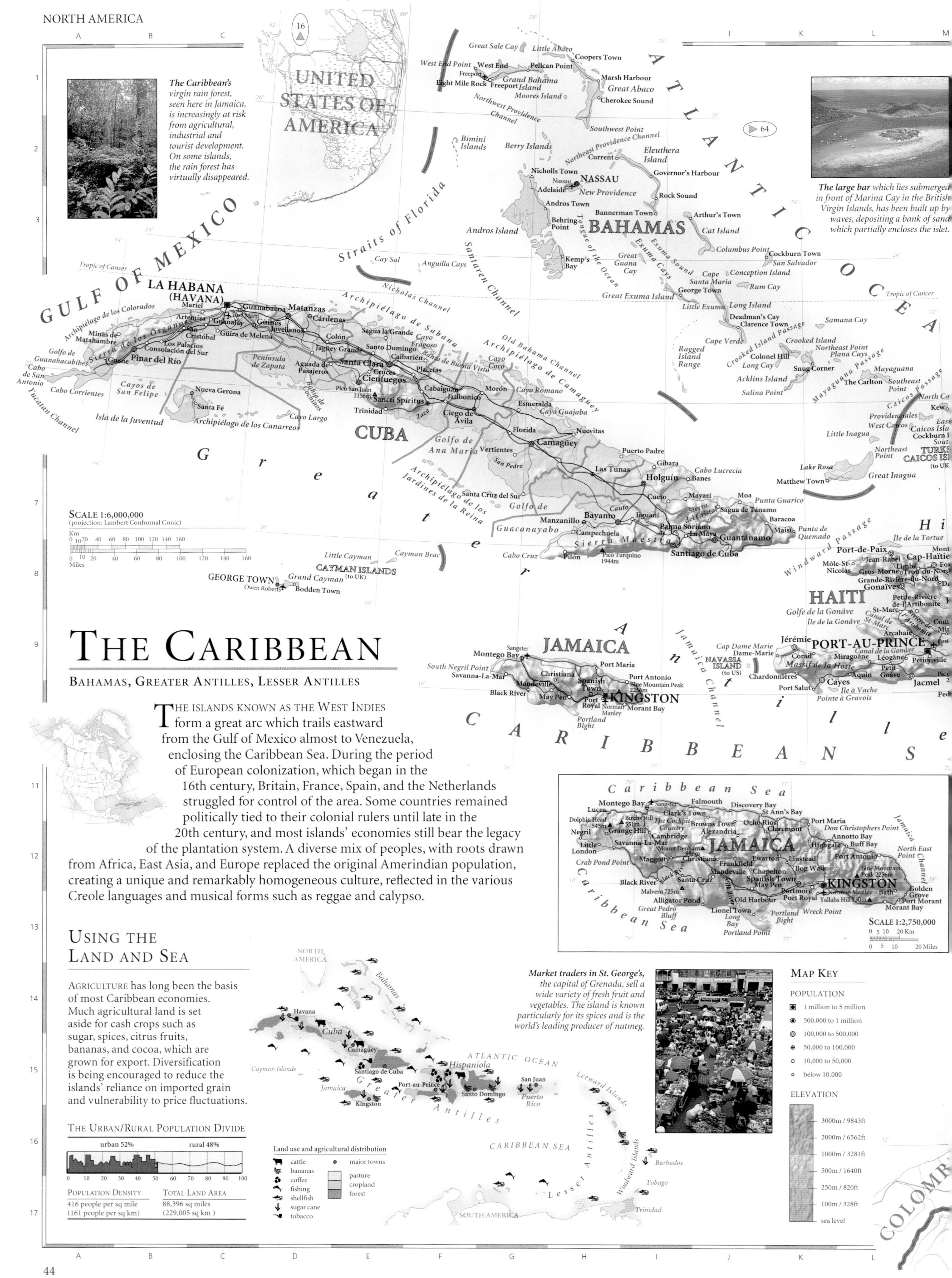
UNITED STATES OF AMERICA
GULF OF MEXICO
ATLANTIC OCEAN
Straits of Florida
BAHAMAS
NASSAU
New Providence
Grand Bahama
Great Abaco
Eleuthera Island
Andros Island
Cat Island
LA HABANA (HAVANA)
CUBA
Isla de la Juventud
Yucatan Channel
CAYMAN ISLANDS (to UK)
GEORGE TOWN
JAMAICA
KINGSTON
HAITI
PORT-AU-PRINCE
TURKS CAICOS ISLANDS (to UK)
NAVASSA ISLAND (to US)
Windward Passage
Jamaica Channel
Greater Antilles
CARIBBEAN SEA
SCALE 1:6,000,000
(projection: Lambert Conformal Conic)
SCALE 1:2,750,000

The Caribbean's virgin rain forest, seen here in Jamaica, is increasingly at risk from agricultural, industrial and tourist development. On some islands, the rain forest has virtually disappeared.

The large bar which lies submerged in front of Marina Cay in the British Virgin Islands, has been built up by waves, depositing a bank of sand which partially encloses the islet.

The Caribbean

Bahamas, Greater Antilles, Lesser Antilles

The islands known as the West Indies form a great arc which trails eastward from the Gulf of Mexico almost to Venezuela, enclosing the Caribbean Sea. During the period of European colonization, which began in the 16th century, Britain, France, Spain, and the Netherlands struggled for control of the area. Some countries remained politically tied to their colonial rulers until late in the 20th century, and most islands' economies still bear the legacy of the plantation system. A diverse mix of peoples, with roots drawn from Africa, East Asia, and Europe replaced the original Amerindian population, creating a unique and remarkably homogeneous culture, reflected in the various Creole languages and musical forms such as reggae and calypso.

Using the Land and Sea

Agriculture has long been the basis of most Caribbean economies. Much agricultural land is set aside for cash crops such as sugar, spices, citrus fruits, bananas, and cocoa, which are grown for export. Diversification is being encouraged to reduce the islands' reliance on imported grain and vulnerability to price fluctuations.

The Urban/Rural Population Divide

urban 52% — rural 48%

Population Density
416 people per sq mile (161 people per sq km)

Total Land Area
88,396 sq miles (229,005 sq km)

Land use and agricultural distribution: cattle, bananas, coffee, fishing, shellfish, sugar cane, tobacco, major towns, pasture, cropland, forest

Market traders in St. George's, the capital of Grenada, sell a wide variety of fresh fruit and vegetables. The island is known particularly for its spices and is the world's leading producer of nutmeg.

Map Key

Population: 1 million to 5 million; 500,000 to 1 million; 100,000 to 500,000; 50,000 to 100,000; 10,000 to 50,000; below 10,000

Elevation: 3000m / 9843ft; 2000m / 6562ft; 1000m / 3281ft; 500m / 1640ft; 250m / 820ft; 100m / 328ft; sea level

TRANSPORTATION & INDUSTRY

CARIBBEAN INDUSTRY remains, with few exceptions, agricultural, and export-led, or service-based, supporting the flourishing tourist industry. However, several countries including Jamaica, Barbados, Trinidad and Tobago, and Puerto Rico have developed important mineral industries, and Cuba is attempting to diversify its economy by importing capital goods to start up new manufacturing businesses.

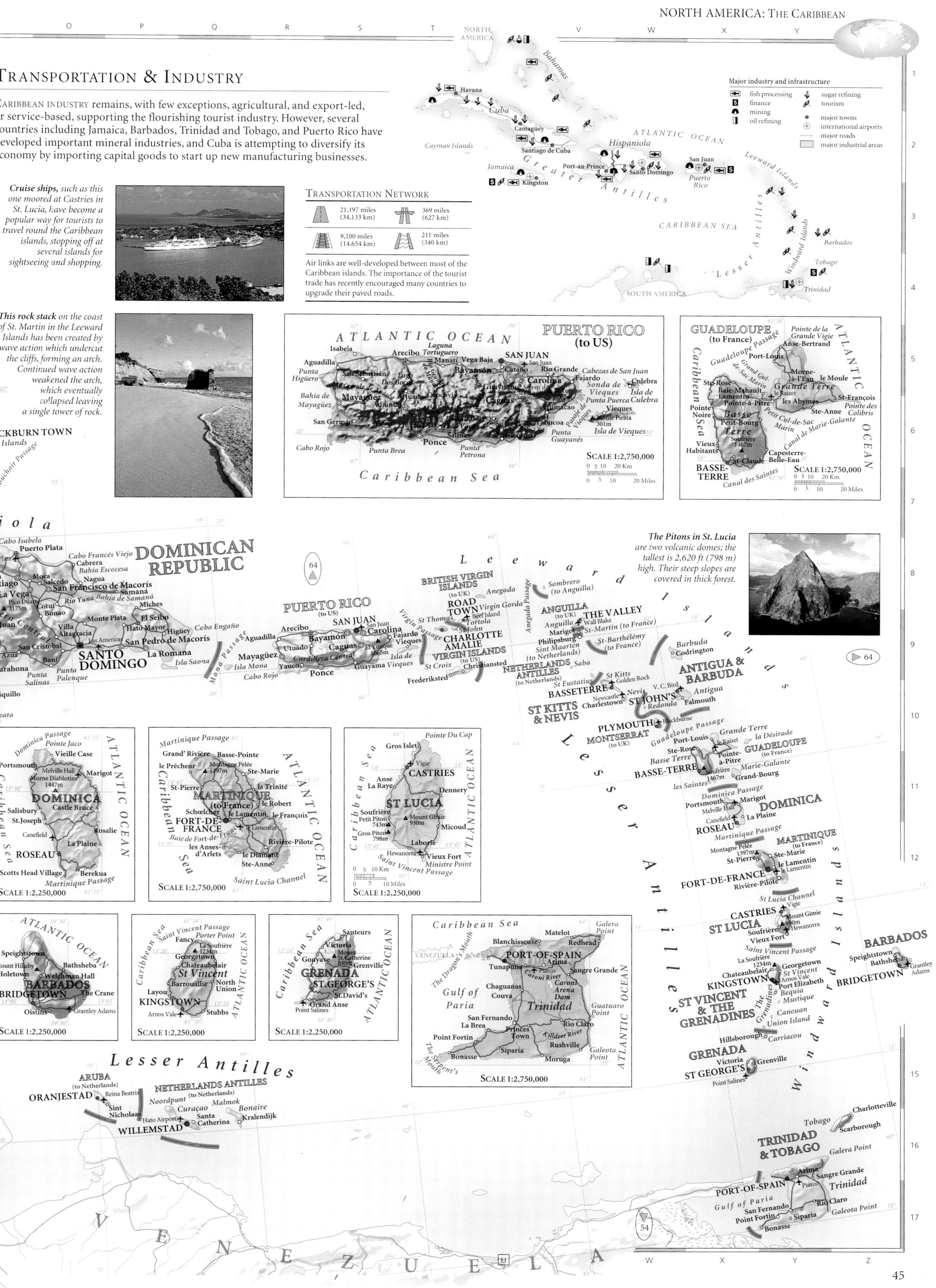

Major industry and infrastructure
fish processing
finance
mining
oil refining
sugar refining
tourism
major towns
international airports
major roads
major industrial areas
ATLANTIC OCEAN
CARIBBEAN SEA
Greater Antilles
Lesser Antilles
Leeward Islands
Windward Islands
PUERTO RICO (to US)
SCALE 1:2,750,000
GUADELOUPE (to France)
DOMINICAN REPUBLIC
SANTO DOMINGO
DOMINICA
MARTINIQUE (to France)
ST LUCIA
BARBADOS
St Vincent
GRENADA
Trinidad
TRINIDAD & TOBAGO
ANTIGUA & BARBUDA
ST KITTS & NEVIS
ST VINCENT & THE GRENADINES
NETHERLANDS ANTILLES (to Netherlands)
ARUBA (to Netherlands)
VENEZUELA

Cruise ships, such as this one moored at Castries in St. Lucia, have become a popular way for tourists to travel round the Caribbean islands, stopping off at several islands for sightseeing and shopping.

TRANSPORTATION NETWORK

21,197 miles (34,133 km)	369 miles (627 km)
9,100 miles (14,654 km)	211 miles (340 km)

Air links are well-developed between most of the Caribbean islands. The importance of the tourist trade has recently encouraged many countries to upgrade their paved roads.

This rock stack on the coast of St. Martin in the Leeward Islands has been created by wave action which undercut the cliffs, forming an arch. Continued wave action weakened the arch, which eventually collapsed leaving a single tower of rock.

The Pitons in St. Lucia are two volcanic domes; the tallest is 2,620 ft (798 m) high. Their steep slopes are covered in thick forest.

South America

Reaching from the humid tropics down into the cold South Atlantic, South America has an area of 6,886,000 sq miles (17,835,000 sq km). There are 12 separate countries, with the largest, Brazil, covering almost half the continent.

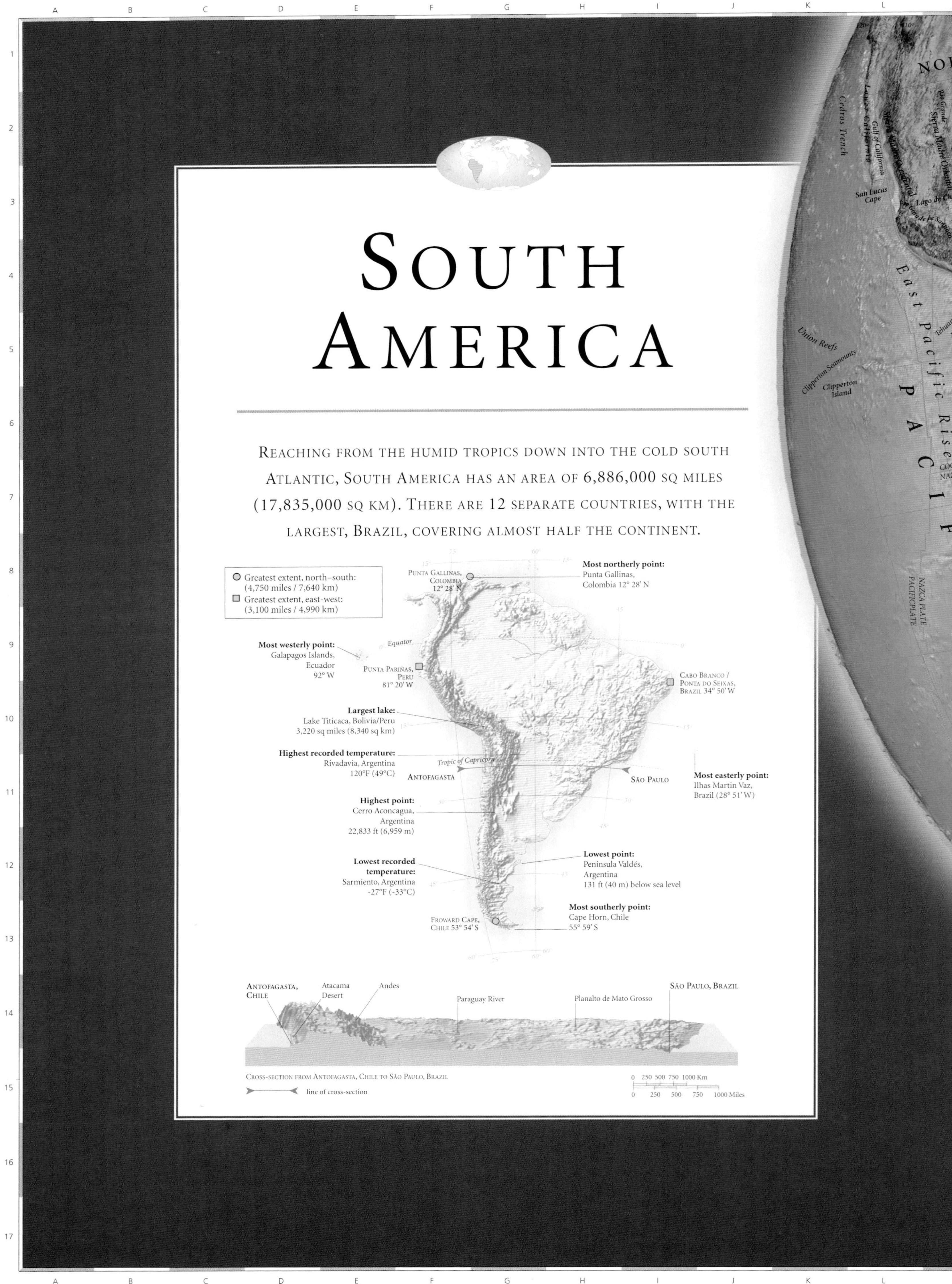

Greatest extent, north–south: (4,750 miles / 7,640 km)
Greatest extent, east-west: (3,100 miles / 4,990 km)
Punta Gallinas, Colombia 12° 28' N
Most northerly point: Punta Gallinas, Colombia 12° 28' N
Equator
Most westerly point: Galapagos Islands, Ecuador 92° W
Punta Pariñas, Peru 81° 20' W
Cabo Branco / Ponta do Seixas, Brazil 34° 50' W
Largest lake: Lake Titicaca, Bolivia/Peru 3,220 sq miles (8,340 sq km)
Highest recorded temperature: Rivadavia, Argentina 120°F (49°C)
Tropic of Capricorn
Antofagasta
São Paulo
Most easterly point: Ilhas Martin Vaz, Brazil (28° 51' W)
Highest point: Cerro Aconcagua, Argentina 22,833 ft (6,959 m)
Lowest recorded temperature: Sarmiento, Argentina -27°F (-33°C)
Lowest point: Peninsula Valdés, Argentina 131 ft (40 m) below sea level
Most southerly point: Cape Horn, Chile 55° 59' S
Froward Cape, Chile 53° 54' S
Antofagasta, Chile
Atacama Desert
Andes
Paraguay River
Planalto de Mato Grosso
São Paulo, Brazil
Cross-section from Antofagasta, Chile to São Paulo, Brazil
line of cross-section
0 250 500 750 1000 Km
0 250 500 750 1000 Miles
Cedros Trench
Gulf of California
San Lucas Cape
East Pacific Rise
Union Reefs
Clipperton Seamounts
Clipperton Island
PACIF
NAZCA PLATE
PACIFIC PLATE

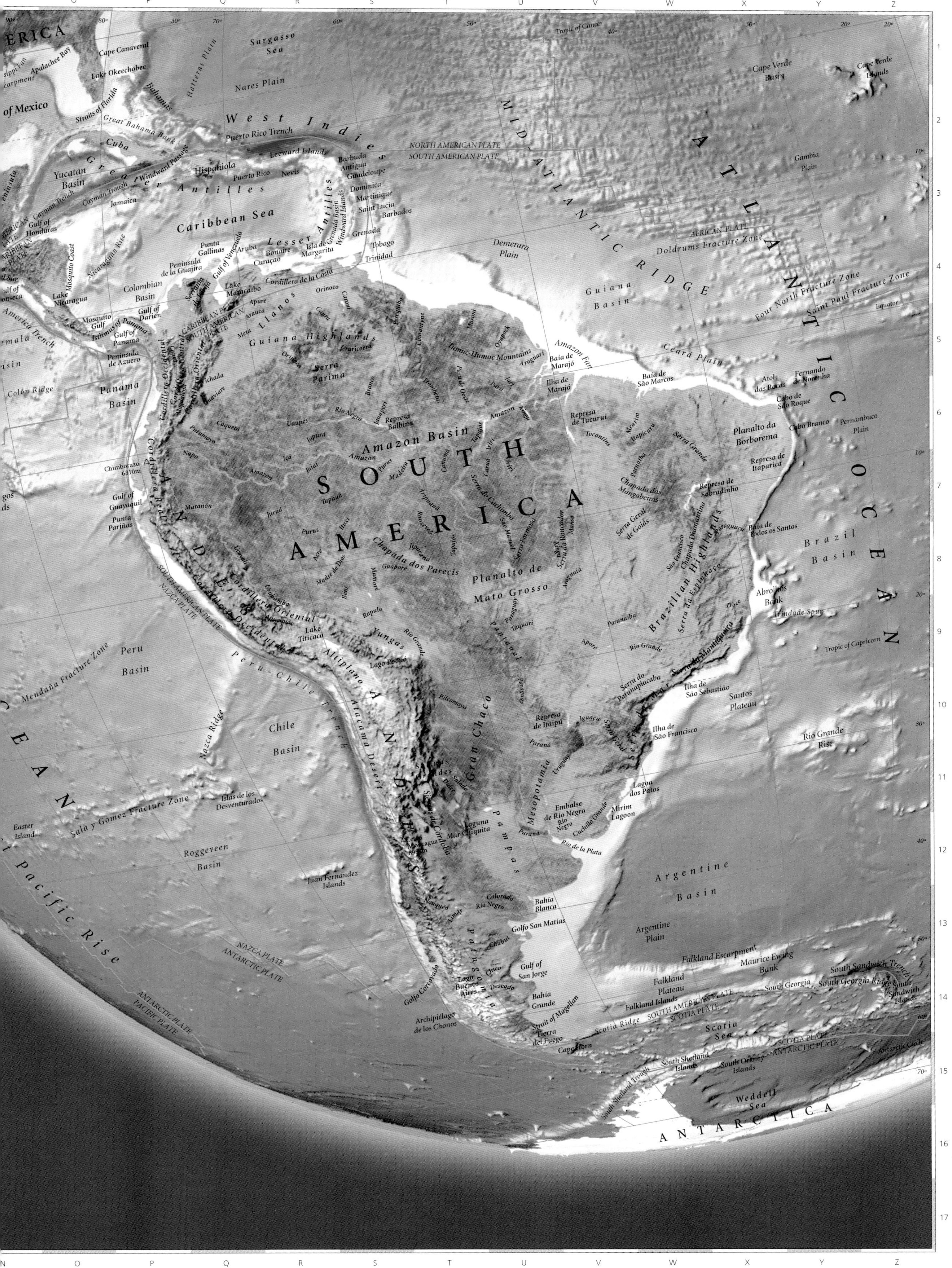

SOUTH AMERICA
ATLANTIC OCEAN
MID-ATLANTIC RIDGE
West Indies
Greater Antilles
Lesser Antilles
Caribbean Sea
Sargasso Sea
Nares Plain
Hatteras Plain
Cape Canaveral
Lake Okeechobee
Apalachee Bay
Gulf of Mexico
Straits of Florida
Great Bahama Bank
Bahamas
Cuba
Puerto Rico Trench
Leeward Islands
Hispaniola
Puerto Rico
Nevis
Barbuda
Antigua
Guadeloupe
Dominica
Martinique
Saint Lucia
Barbados
Grenada
Tobago
Trinidad
Windward Islands
Grenada Basin
Yucatan Basin
Cayman Trench
Cayman Trough
Windward Passage
Jamaica
Gulf of Honduras
Nicaraguan Rise
Mosquito Coast
Lake Nicaragua
Colombian Basin
Península de la Guajira
Punta Gallinas
Aruba
Bonaire
Curaçao
Isla de Margarita
Gulf of Venezuela
Lake Maracaibo
Cordillera de la Costa
Gulf of Darien
Mosquito Gulf
Isthmus of Panama
Gulf of Panama
Península de Azuero
Panama Basin
Colón Ridge
Orinoco
Caroní
Apure
Arauca
Meta
Llanos
Guaviare
Guiana Highlands
Uraricoera
Serra Parima
Tumuc-Humac Mountains
Araguari
Baía de Marajó
Ilha de Marajó
Amazon Fan
Demerara Plain
Guiana Basin
NORTH AMERICAN PLATE
SOUTH AMERICAN PLATE
AFRICAN PLATE
CARIBBEAN PLATE
Doldrums Fracture Zone
Four North Fracture Zone
Saint Paul Fracture Zone
Equator
Cape Verde Basin
Cape Verde Islands
Gambia Plain
Ceará Plain
Baía de São Marcos
Atol das Rocas
Fernando de Noronha
Cabo de São Roque
Cabo Branco
Pernambuco Plain
Planalto da Borborema
Represa de Itaparica
Represa de Sobradinho
Baía de Todos os Santos
Brazil Basin
Abrolhos Bank
Trindade Spur
Tropic of Capricorn
Tropic of Cancer
Amazon Basin
Amazon
Represa Balbina
Rio Negro
Uaupés
Japurá
Caquetá
Putumayo
Napo
Marañón
Juruá
Purus
Madeira
Tapajós
Xingu
Iriri
Tocantins
Araguaia
Represa de Tucuruí
Serra do Cachimbo
Serra Formosa
Serra do Roncador
Chapada das Mangabeiras
Serra Geral de Goiás
Serra Grande
Chapada dos Parecis
Planalto de Mato Grosso
Pantanal
Brazilian Highlands
Chapada Diamantina
Serra do Espinhaço
Serra da Mantiqueira
Serra do Paranapiacaba
São Francisco
Paranaíba
Rio Grande
Doce
Ilha de São Sebastião
Santos Plateau
Ilha de São Francisco
Rio Grande Rise
Represa de Itaipu
Iguaçu
Paraná
Uruguay
Mesopotamia
Embalse de Río Negro
Cuchilla Grande
Lagoa dos Patos
Mirim Lagoon
Río de la Plata
Pampas
Gran Chaco
Pilcomayo
Paraguay
Mamoré
Beni
Guaporé
Madre de Dios
Ucayali
Urubamba
Cordillera Oriental
Cordillera Occidental
Cordillera Real
ANDES
Chimborazo 6310m
Gulf of Guayaquil
Punta Pariñas
Lake Titicaca
Yungas
Altiplano
Lago Poopó
Atacama Desert
Peru-Chile Trench
SOUTH AMERICAN PLATE
NAZCA PLATE
Peru Basin
Mendaña Fracture Zone
Nazca Ridge
Chile Basin
Islas de los Desventurados
Sala y Gomez Fracture Zone
Easter Island
Roggeveen Basin
Juan Fernandez Islands
East Pacific Rise
Aconcagua
Laguna Mar Chiquita
Sierras de Córdoba
Salado
Colorado
Río Negro
Neuquén
Limay
Chubut
Patagonia
Bahía Blanca
Golfo San Matías
Gulf of San Jorge
Lago Buenos Aires
Deseado
Golfo Corcovado
Archipiélago de los Chonos
Bahía Grande
Strait of Magellan
Tierra del Fuego
Cape Horn
Argentine Basin
Argentine Plain
Falkland Escarpment
Falkland Plateau
Falkland Islands
Maurice Ewing Bank
South Georgia
South Georgia Ridge
South Sandwich Trench
South Sandwich Islands
Scotia Ridge
Scotia Sea
SCOTIA PLATE
ANTARCTIC PLATE
PACIFIC PLATE
South Shetland Islands
South Shetland Trough
South Orkney Islands
Weddell Sea
Antarctic Circle
ANTARCTICA

Physical South America

Three major physiographic regions characterize South America. The oldest, the ancient Brazilian Shield and the smaller Guyana and Patagonian shields, form the stable core of the continent. Stretching along the entire west coast are the younger Andean fold mountains with many summits rising to 20,000 ft (6,100 m). These two diverse regions are separated by a number of sedimentary basins carrying South America's large river systems to the sea. These include the massive Amazon Basin and the basin of the Gran Chaco.

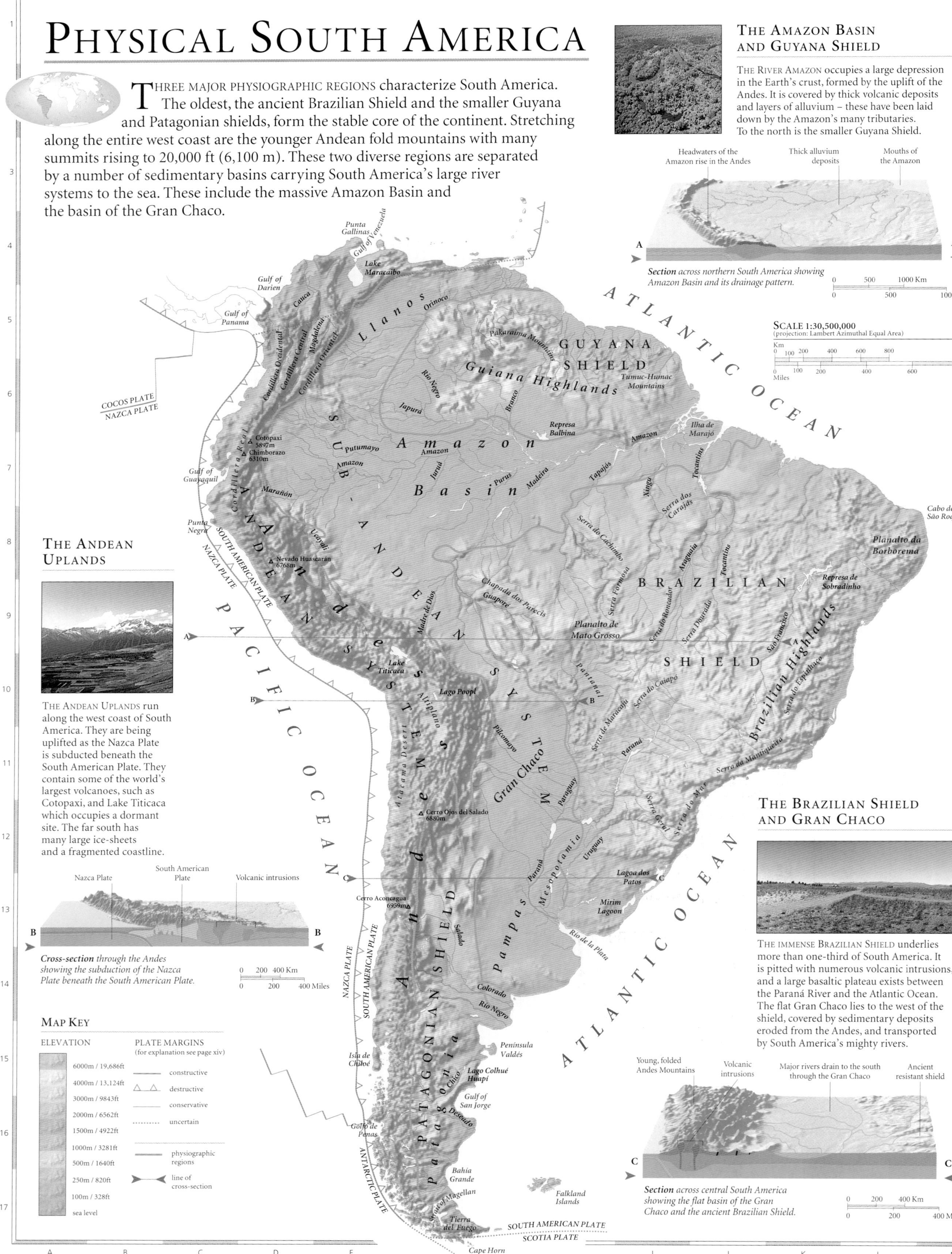

Punta Gallinas
Gulf of Venezuela
Lake Maracaibo
Gulf of Darien
Gulf of Panama
Cauca
Cordillera Occidental
Cordillera Central
Magdalena
Cordillera Oriental
Llanos
Orinoco
Pakaraima Mountains
GUYANA SHIELD
Guiana Highlands
Tumuc-Humac Mountains
Rio Negro
Japurá
Branco
COCOS PLATE
NAZCA PLATE
Cotopaxi 5897m
Chimborazo 6310m
Cordillera Real
Putumayo
Amazon
Amazon Basin
Represa Balbina
Ilha de Marajó
Gulf of Guayaquil
Marañon
Juruá
Purus
Madeira
Tapajós
Xingu
Tocantins
Serra dos Carajás
ATLANTIC OCEAN
Cabo de São Roque
Punta Negra
SOUTH AMERICAN PLATE
NAZCA PLATE
Nevado Huascarán 6768m
Ucayali
SUB-ANDEAN SYSTEM
Serra do Cachimbo
Planalto da Borborema
Represa de Sobradinho
Chapada dos Parecis
Guaporé
Madre de Dios
Serra Formosa
Araguaia
Tocantins
BRAZILIAN SHIELD
Planalto de Mato Grosso
Serra do Roncador
Serra Dourada
São Francisco
Brazilian Highlands
Serra do Espinhaço
PACIFIC OCEAN
Lake Titicaca
Lago Poopó
Altiplano
Pantanal
Serra do Caiapó
Serra de Maracaju
Pilcomayo
Atacama Desert
Paraná
Gran Chaco
Serra da Mantiqueira
Paraguay
Serra Geral
Serra do Mar
Cerro Ojos del Salado 6880m
Uruguay
Mesopotamia
Paraná
Lagoa dos Patos
Mirim Lagoon
Cerro Aconcagua 6959m
Salado
Pampas
Río de la Plata
ATLANTIC OCEAN
NAZCA PLATE
SOUTH AMERICAN PLATE
PATAGONIAN SHIELD
Colorado
Río Negro
Andes
Peninsula Valdés
Isla de Chiloé
Patagonia
Chico
Lago Colhué Huapí
Gulf of San Jorge
Deseado
Golfo de Penas
ANTARCTIC PLATE
Bahía Grande
Falkland Islands
Strait of Magellan
Tierra del Fuego
SOUTH AMERICAN PLATE
SCOTIA PLATE
Cape Horn

The Amazon Basin and Guyana Shield

The River Amazon occupies a large depression in the Earth's crust, formed by the uplift of the Andes. It is covered by thick volcanic deposits and layers of alluvium – these have been laid down by the Amazon's many tributaries. To the north is the smaller Guyana Shield.

Headwaters of the Amazon rise in the Andes
Thick alluvium deposits
Mouths of the Amazon
A
A
0 500 1000 Km
0 500 1000

***Section** across northern South America showing Amazon Basin and its drainage pattern.*

Scale 1:30,500,000
(projection: Lambert Azimuthal Equal Area)

Km
0 100 200 400 600 800
0 100 200 400 600
Miles

The Andean Uplands

The Andean Uplands run along the west coast of South America. They are being uplifted as the Nazca Plate is subducted beneath the South American Plate. They contain some of the world's largest volcanoes, such as Cotopaxi, and Lake Titicaca which occupies a dormant site. The far south has many large ice-sheets and a fragmented coastline.

Nazca Plate
South American Plate
Volcanic intrusions
B
B
0 200 400 Km
0 200 400 Miles

***Cross-section** through the Andes showing the subduction of the Nazca Plate beneath the South American Plate.*

Map Key

ELEVATION
6000m / 19,686ft
4000m / 13,124ft
3000m / 9843ft
2000m / 6562ft
1500m / 4922ft
1000m / 3281ft
500m / 1640ft
250m / 820ft
100m / 328ft
sea level
PLATE MARGINS
(for explanation see page xiv)
constructive
destructive
conservative
uncertain
physiographic regions
line of cross-section

The Brazilian Shield and Gran Chaco

The immense Brazilian Shield underlies more than one-third of South America. It is pitted with numerous volcanic intrusions, and a large basaltic plateau exists between the Paraná River and the Atlantic Ocean. The flat Gran Chaco lies to the west of the shield, covered by sedimentary deposits eroded from the Andes, and transported by South America's mighty rivers.

Young, folded Andes Mountains
Volcanic intrusions
Major rivers drain to the south through the Gran Chaco
Ancient resistant shield
C
C
0 200 400 Km
0 200 400 Miles

***Section** across central South America showing the flat basin of the Gran Chaco and the ancient Brazilian Shield.*

N O P Q R S T U X Y Z

Climate

The climate of South America is influenced by three principal factors: the seasonal shift of high pressure air masses over the tropics, cold ocean currents along the western coast, affecting temperature and precipitation, and the mountain barrier produced by by the Andes, which creates a rain shadow over much of the south.

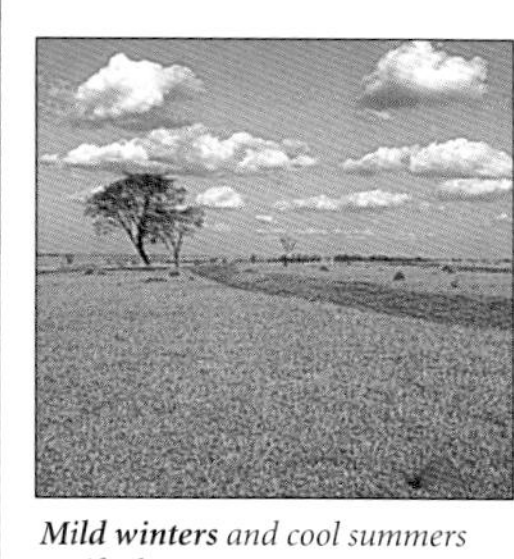

***Mild winters** and cool summers typify the extensive Pampas grasslands of Argentina.*

Chile's hyperarid *Atacama Desert is renowned as one of the driest places on Earth.*

Climate
- tundra
- cool continental
- warm humid
- semiarid
- arid
- humid equatorial
- tropical
- daily hours of sunshine, January
- daily hours of sunshine, July
- cold wind

Maracaibo, Caracas, Georgetown, Cayenne, Bogotá, Quito, Equator, Belém, Manaus, Altos, Recife, Lima, Brasília, La Paz, Santa Cruz, Belo Horizonte, La Quiaca, Tropic of Capricorn, Antofagasta, Rio de Janeiro, Asunción, Porto Alegre, Cordoba, Santiago, Buenos Aires, Montevideo, Concepción, Pamperos, Stanley

Temperature

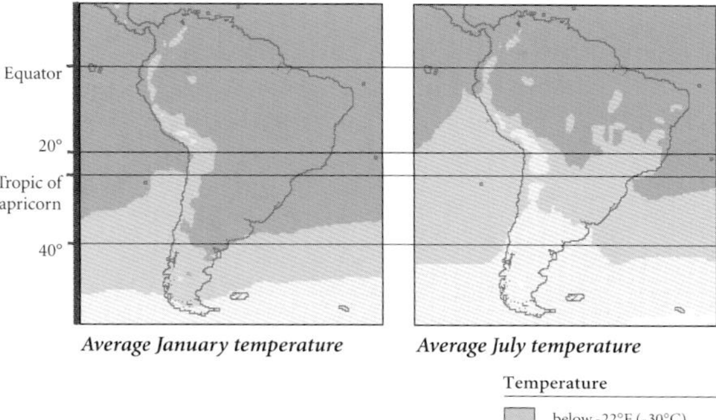

Equator
20°
Tropic of Capricorn
40°

Average January temperature

Average July temperature

Temperature
- below -22°F (-30°C)
- -22 to -4°F (-30 to -20°C)
- -4 to 14°F (-20 to -10°C)
- 14 to 32°F (-10 to 0°C)
- 32 to 50°F (0 to 10°C)
- 50°F (10 to 20°C)
- 68 to 86°F (20 to 30°C)
- above 86°F (30°C)

Rainfall

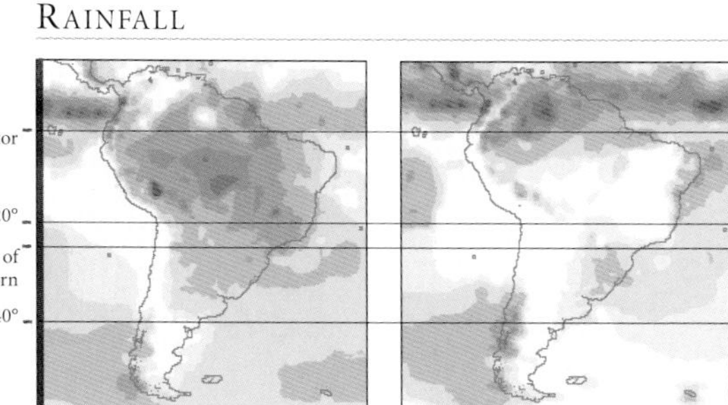

Equator
20°
Tropic of Capricorn
40°

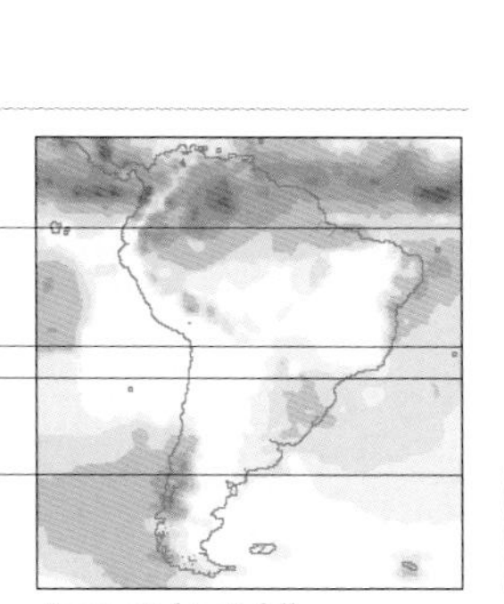

Average January rainfall

Average July rainfall

Rainfall
- 0–1 in (0–25 mm)
- 1–2 in (25–50 mm)
- 2–4 in (50–100 mm)
- 4–8 in (100–200 mm)
- 8–12 in (200–300 mm)
- 12–16 in (300–400 mm)
- 16–20 in (400–500 mm)
- more than 20 in (500 mm)

***Tropical conditions** are found across over half of South America. When both rainfall and temperatures are high, hot humid rain forests prevail.*

Shaping the Continent

South America's active tectonic belt has been extensively folded over millions of years; landslides are still frequent in the mountains. The large river systems that erode the mountains flow across resistant shield areas, depositing sediment. Present-day glaciation affects the distinctive landscape of the far south.

Mass Movement

6 Debris slides are common in the highlands of South America *(left)*. They occur where soil on a slope is saturated by rainwater and therefore less stable. The actual slides are often triggered by earthquakes.

Scarp face left after soil has moved to the base of the slope

Failure plane

Toe of debris slide

Mass movement: A section of a debris slide

Chemical Weathering

1 Table mountains *(left)* are the eroded remnants of an ancient upland. As water percolates along cracks in these high, flat-topped mountains it forms intricate cave systems. Chemical weathering also isolates large blocks which then collapse, accumulating as rockfalls at the foot of scarp slopes.

Smooth summit dissected by deep gorges

Rainfall

Runoff surges down caverns as waterfalls

Chemical weathering: Erosion of the Guyana Shield

The Evolving Landscape

River Systems

2 Along the Amazon *(above)* there is a great variation in rates of erosion. As the headwaters of the Amazon flow down from the Andes, they erode and transport vast quantities of sediment, and are known as whitewaters. Across the shield areas erosion rates are very low. These rivers, carrying rotting vegetation, are called blackwaters.

Whitewater river

Blackwater river

Little erosion in shield areas

Confluence of whitewater with blackwater

River systems: Suspended sediments in the Amazon

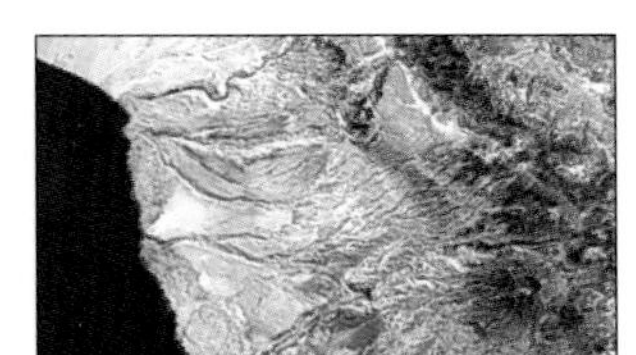

Folding

5 Folding occurs beneath the surface under high temperatures and pressures. Rocks become sufficiently malleable to flow and not fracture as tectonic plates collide. In the Valley of the Moon in Chile *(above)*, anticlines (or upfolds) and synclines (or troughs) have been exploited by erosion.

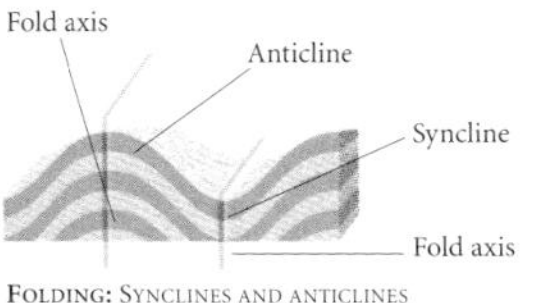

Fold axis
Anticline
Syncline
Fold axis

Folding: Synclines and anticlines

Deposition

4 Large alluvial fans are found extensively across South America *(above)*. Confined mountain rivers, carrying large quantities of eroded material, emerge from a mountain gorge onto the plains, where they deposit their load in huge fans.

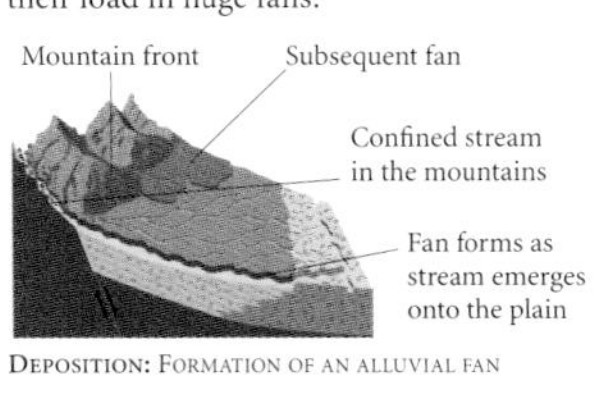

Mountain front
Subsequent fan
Confined stream in the mountains
Fan forms as stream emerges onto the plain

Deposition: Formation of an alluvial fan

Landscape
- uplifting land
- stable land
- sinking land
- glacier
- ocean current
- aluvial fan
- inselberg
- river

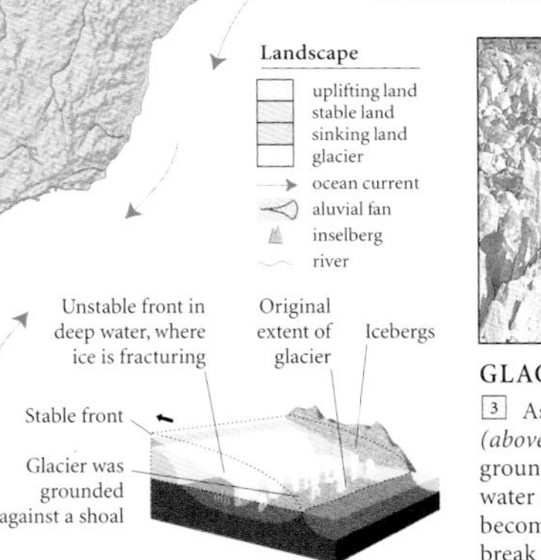

Unstable front in deep water, where ice is fracturing
Original extent of glacier
Icebergs
Stable front
Glacier was grounded against a shoal

Glaciation: Retreating glacier in Patagonia

Glaciation

3 As fjord glaciers in Patagonia *(above)* retreat, they become grounded on shoals. In deeper water the base of the glacier becomes unstable, and icebergs break off (calve) until the glacier snout grounds once more.

N O P Q R S T U V W X Y Z

POLITICAL SOUTH AMERICA

MODERN SOUTH AMERICA'S POLITICAL BOUNDARIES have their origins in the territorial endeavors of explorers during the 16th century, who claimed almost the entire continent for Portugal and Spain. The Portuguese land in the east later evolved into the federal state of Brazil, while the Spanish vice-royalties eventually emerged as separate independent nation-states in the early 19th century. South America's growing population has become increasingly urbanized, with the growth of coastal cities into large conurbations like Rio de Janeiro and Buenos Aires. In Brazil, Argentina, Chile and Uruguay, a succession of military dictatorships has given way to fragile, but strengthening, democracies.

***Europe retains** a small foothold in South America. Kourou in French Guiana was the site chosen by the European Space Agency to launch the Ariane rocket. As a result of its status as a French overseas department, French Guiana is actually part of the European Union.*

SCALE 1:24,000,000
(projection: Lambert Azimuthal Equal Area)

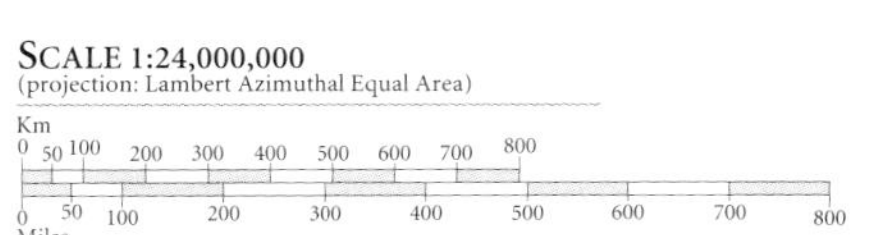
Km
0 50 100 200 300 400 500 600 700 800
0 50 100 200 300 400 500 600 700 800
Miles

TRANSPORTATION

MOST MAJOR ROAD AND RAIL ROUTES are confined to the coastal regions by the forbidding natural barriers of the Andes Mountains and the Amazon Basin. Few major cross-continental routes exist, although Buenos Aires serves as a transportation center for the main rail links to La Paz and Valparaíso, while the construction of the Trans-Amazon and Pan-American Highways have made direct road travel possible from Recife to Lima and from Puerto Montt up the coast into central America. A new waterway project is proposed to transform the River Paraguay into a major shipping route, although it involves considerable wetland destruction.

South America's most extensive rail network is centered on the Argentinian capital, Buenos Aires. The construction of new rail lines outward from this important port, allowed the colonization of the Pampas lands for agriculture.

Transportation
- major roads and highways
- major railroads
- international borders
- transportation intersections
- international airports
- major ports

LANGUAGES

PRIOR TO EUROPEAN EXPLORATION in the 16th century, a diverse range of indigenous languages were spoken across the continent. With the arrival of Iberian settlers, Spanish became the dominant language, with Portuguese spoken in Brazil, and Native American languages such as Quechua and Guaraní, becoming concentrated in the continental interior. Today this pattern persists, although successive European colonization has led to Dutch being spoken in Suriname, English in Guyana, and French in French Guiana, while in large urban areas, Japanese and Chinese are increasingly common.

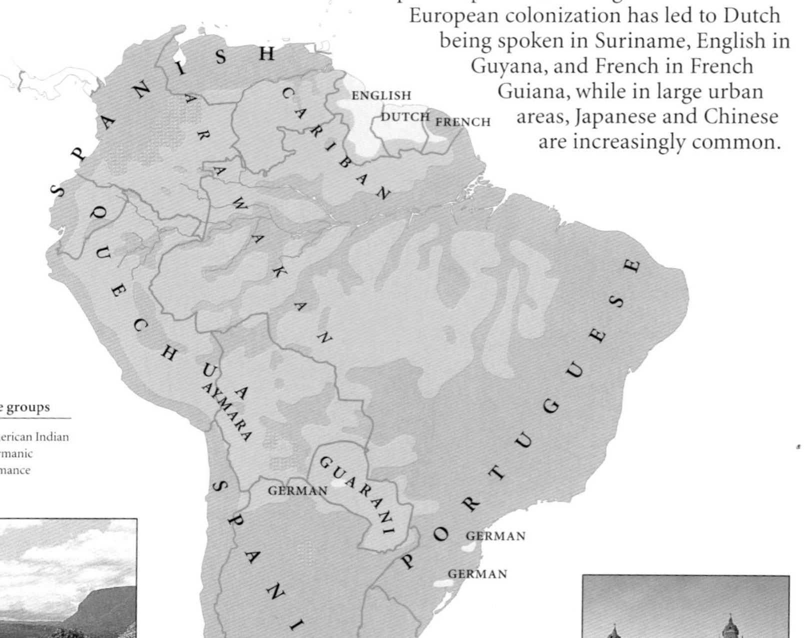

Language groups
- American Indian
- Germanic
- Romance

***Chile's main port, Valparaíso,** is a vital national shipping center, in addition to playing a key role in the growing trade with Pacific nations. The country's awkward, elongated shape means that sea transportation is frequently used for internal travel and communications in Chile.*

***Indigenous South American** lifestyles have not been totally submerged by European cultures and languages. The continental interior, and particularly the Amazon Basin, is still home to many different ethnic peoples.*

***Lima's magnificent** cathedral reflects South America's colonial past with its unmistakably Spanish style. In July 1821, Peru became the last Spanish colony on the mainland to declare independence.*

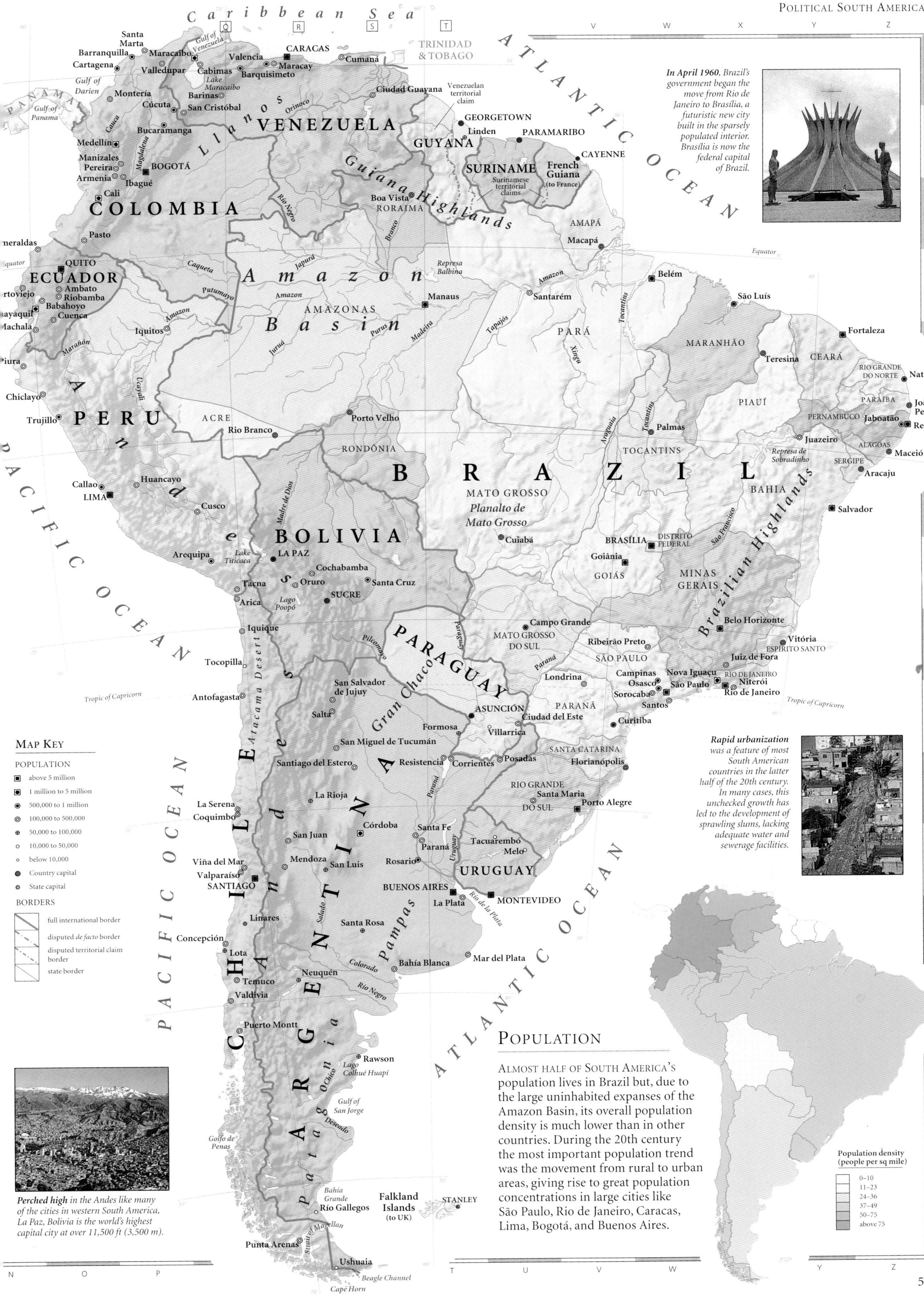

In April 1960, Brazil's government began the move from Rio de Janeiro to Brasília, a futuristic new city built in the sparsely populated interior. Brasília is now the federal capital of Brazil.

Rapid urbanization was a feature of most South American countries in the latter half of the 20th century. In many cases, this unchecked growth has led to the development of sprawling slums, lacking adequate water and sewerage facilities.

MAP KEY

POPULATION

- above 5 million
- 1 million to 5 million
- 500,000 to 1 million
- 100,000 to 500,000
- 50,000 to 100,000
- 10,000 to 50,000
- below 10,000
- Country capital
- State capital

BORDERS

- full international border
- disputed *de facto* border
- disputed territorial claim border
- state border

***Perched high** in the Andes like many of the cities in western South America, La Paz, Bolivia is the world's highest capital city at over 11,500 ft (3,500 m).*

POPULATION

ALMOST HALF OF SOUTH AMERICA'S population lives in Brazil but, due to the large uninhabited expanses of the Amazon Basin, its overall population density is much lower than in other countries. During the 20th century the most important population trend was the movement from rural to urban areas, giving rise to great population concentrations in large cities like São Paulo, Rio de Janeiro, Caracas, Lima, Bogotá, and Buenos Aires.

Population density (people per sq mile)

- 0–10
- 11–23
- 24–36
- 37–49
- 50–75
- above 75

South American Resources

Agriculture still provides the largest single form of employment in South America, although rural unemployment and poverty continue to drive people toward the huge coastal cities in search of jobs and opportunities. Mineral and fuel resources, although substantial, are distributed unevenly; few countries have both fossil fuels and minerals. To break industrial dependence on raw materials, boost manufacturing, and improve infrastructure, governments borrowed heavily from the World Bank in the 1960s and 1970s. This led to the accumulation of massive debts which are unlikely ever to be repaid. Today, Brazil dominates the continent's economic output, followed by Argentina. Recently, the less-developed western side of South America has benefited due to its geographical position; for example Chile is increasingly exporting raw materials to Japan.

Ciudad Guayana is a planned industrial complex in eastern Venezuela, built as an iron and steel centre to exploit the nearby iron ore reserves.

The cold Peru Current flows north from the Antarctic along the Pacific coast of Peru, providing rich nutrients for one of the world's largest fishing grounds. Overexploitation has severely reduced Peru's anchovy catch.

Industry
- aerospace
- brewing
- car/vehicle manufacture
- chemicals
- electronics
- engineering
- finance
- fish processing
- food processing
- hi-tech industry
- iron & steel
- meat processing
- metal refining
- narcotics
- pharmaceuticals
- printing & publishing
- shipbuilding
- sugar processing
- textiles
- timber processing
- tobacco processing
- wine
- oil
- gas
- industrial cities
- major industrial areas

Caribbean Sea
Barranquilla
Cartagena
Maracaibo
Barquisimeto
Caracas
Valencia
Ciudad Guayana
PANAMA
Gulf of Panama
VENEZUELA
Medellín
Bogotá
Cali
COLOMBIA
Georgetown
GUYANA
Paramaribo
SURINAME
French Guiana (to France)
ATLANTIC OCEAN
Quito
ECUADOR
Guayaquil
Iquitos
Amazon Basin
Manaus
Belém
Fortaleza
Natal
Recife
Maceió
Salvador
BRAZIL
Chiclayo
Chimbote
PERU
Lima
Cusco
Arequipa
PACIFIC OCEAN
BOLIVIA
La Paz
Santa Cruz
Sucre
Brasília
Arica
Iquique
Chuquicamata
Belo Horizonte
PARAGUAY
Antofagasta
Asunción
Ciudad del Este
São Paulo
Rio de Janeiro
Curitiba
San Miguel de Tucumán
Corrientes
Porto Alegre
Córdoba
Santa Fe
Rosario
Mendoza
URUGUAY
Rio Grande
Valparaíso
Santiago
Buenos Aires
Montevideo
Talca
Concepción
CHILE
ARGENTINA
Bahía Blanca
Neuquén
Valdivia
Comodoro Rivadavia
Gulf of San Jorge
Bahía Grande
Falkland Islands (to UK)
Punta Arenas
Strait of Magellan
Cape Horn

GNP per capita (US$)
- 0–499
- 500–999
- 1000–1499
- 1500–2999
- 3000–5999
- 6000+

Standard of Living

Wealth disparities throughout the continent create a wide gulf between affluent landowners and the chronically poor in inner-city slums. The illicit production of cocaine, and the hugely influential drug barons who control its distribution, contribute to the violent disorder and corruption which affect northwestern South America, de-stabilizing local governments and economies.

Standard of Living (UN Human Development Index)
- low
- high

Both Argentina and Chile are now exploring the southernmost tip of the continent in search of oil. Here in Punta Arenas, a drilling rig is being prepared for exploratory drilling in the Strait of Magellen.

Industry

Argentina and Brazil are South America's most industrialized countries and São Paulo is the continent's leading industrial center. Long-term government investment in Brazilian industry has encouraged a diverse industrial base; engineering, steel production, food processing, textile manufacture, and chemicals predominate. The illegal production of cocaine is economically significant in the Andean countries of Colombia and Bolivia. In Venezuela, the oil-dominated economy has left the country vulnerable to world oil price fluctuations. Food processing and mineral exploitation are common throughout the less industrially developed parts of the continent, including Bolivia, Chile, Ecuador, and Peru.

Environmental Issues

The Amazon Basin is one of the last great wilderness areas left on Earth. The tropical rain forests which grow there are a valuable genetic resource, containing innumerable unique plants and animals. The forests are increasingly under threat from new and expanding settlements and "slash and burn" farming techniques, which clear land for the raising of beef cattle, causing land degradation and soil erosion.

***Clouds of smoke billow** from the burning Amazon rain forest. Over 25,000 sq miles (60,000 sq km) of virgin rain forest are being cleared annually, destroying an ancient, irreplaceable, natural resource and biodiverse habitat.*

Environmental Issues

- national parks
- tropical forest
- forest destroyed
- desert
- desertification
- polluted rivers
- marine pollution
- heavy marine pollution
- poor urban air quality

Mineral Resources

Over a quarter of the world's known copper reserves are found at the Chuquicamata mine in northern Chile, and other metallic minerals such as tin are found along the length of the Andes. The discovery of oil and gas at Venezuela's Lake Maracaibo in 1917 turned the country into one of the world's leading oil producers. In contrast, South America is virtually devoid of coal, the only significant deposit being on the peninsula of Guajira in Colombia.

***Copper is Chile's** largest export, most of which is mined at Chuquicamata. Along the length of the Andes, metallic minerals like copper and tin are found in abundance, formed by the excessive pressures and heat involved in mountain-building.*

Mineral Resources

- oil field
- gas field
- coal field
- bauxite
- copper
- diamonds
- gold
- iron
- lead
- silver
- tin

Using the Land and Sea

Many foods now common worldwide originated in South America. These include the potato, tomato, squash, and cassava. Today, large herds of beef cattle roam the temperate grasslands of the Pampas, supporting an extensive meatpacking trade in Argentina, Uruguay and Paraguay. Corn (maize) is grown as a staple crop across the continent and coffee is grown as a cash crop in Brazil and Colombia. Coca plants grown in Bolivia, Peru, and Colombia provide most of the world's cocaine. Fish and shellfish are caught off the western coast, especially anchovies off Peru, shrimps off Ecuador and pilchards off Chile.

***South America,** and Brazil in particular, now leads the world in coffee production, mainly growing Coffea Arabica in large plantations. Coffee beans are harvested, roasted, and brewed to produce the world's second most popular drink, after tea.*

***High in the Andes,** hardy alpacas graze on the barren land. Alpacas are thought to have been domesticated by the Incas, whose nobility wore robes made from their wool. Today, they are still reared and prized for their soft, warm fleeces.*

***The Pampas region** of southeast South America is characterized by extensive, flat plains, and populated by cattle and ranchers (gauchos). Argentina is a major world producer of beef, much of which is exported to the US for use in hamburgers.*

Using the Land and Sea

- barren land
- cropland
- desert
- forest
- mountain region
- pasture
- major conurbations
- cattle
- pigs
- sheep
- bananas
- corn
- citrus fruits
- cocoa
- cotton
- coffee
- fishing
- oil palms
- peanuts
- rubber
- shellfish
- soybeans
- sugar cane
- vineyards
- wheat

Northern South America

Colombia, Guyana, Suriname, Venezuela, ***French Guiana*** **(to France)**

FRINGED BY THE PACIFIC AND ATLANTIC OCEANS and the Caribbean Sea, South America's northern region has a rich range of natural resources, some exploited for centuries by colonial powers including the Spanish, French, Dutch, and British, others still to be fully explored. The prospects for further economic development in Colombia, Guyana and Suriname are blighted by drug-related violence and political instability. Venezuela, despite huge incomes from its oil reserves, remains less developed in other industrial sectors.

French Guiana is an overseas *département* of France, now seeking greater autonomy. Most of the major population centers, such as Bogotá, have grown up in the temperate conditions of the high Andes or, like Caracas, at strategic points along the Caribbean coast.

***Flowers** grown in Colombia are exported all over the world, and include fine carnations and roses. Here, workers are cutting roses which have been grown in plastic greenhouses.*

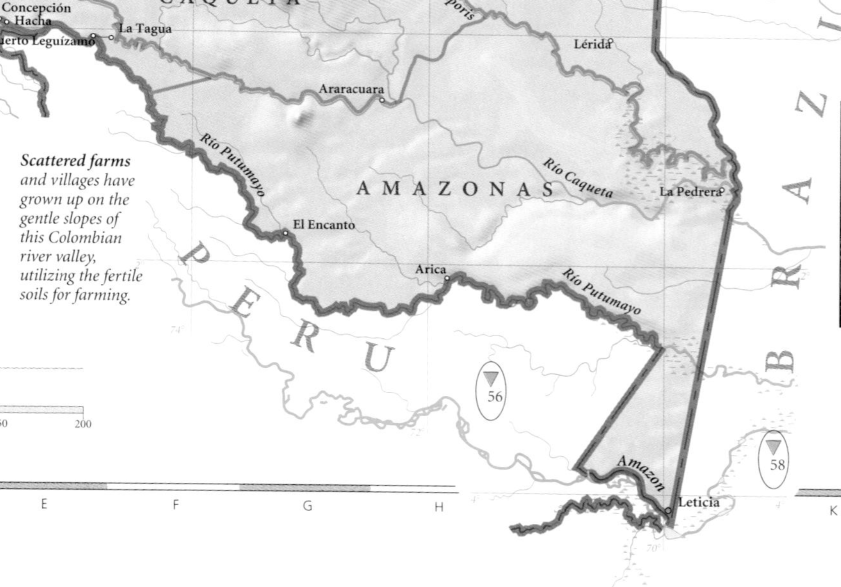

Map Key

POPULATION

- 1 million to 5 million
- 500,000 to 1 million
- 100,000 to 500,000
- 50,000 to 100,000
- 10,000 to 50,000
- below 10,000

ELEVATION

- 4000m / 13,124ft
- 3000m / 9843ft
- 2000m / 6562ft
- 1000m / 3281ft
- 500m / 1640ft
- 250m / 820ft
- 100m / 328ft
- sea level

***Large open squares** like the Plaza Bolivia in Bogotá are characteristic of many cities founded by the Spanish.*

***Scattered farms** and villages have grown up on the gentle slopes of this Colombian river valley, utilizing the fertile soils for farming.*

SCALE 1:7,250,000
(projection: Lambert Azimuthal Equal Area)

***The River Orinoco** flows from its source in the southern Guiana Highlands to form a broad delta on Venezuela's Atlantic coast. One of its distributary channels opens into a wide bay called the Serpent's Mouth.*

TRANSPORTATION & INDUSTRY

MANY MINERAL RESOURCES are mined in Colombia, including fuels, gold, and precious and semiprecious stones. Revenues from coffee and exports of illegal narcotics are crucial to the economy. Venezuela's major economic activity is the oil industry around Lake Maracaibo (*Lago de Maracaibo*). Sugar and bauxite are exported from Guyana and Suriname.

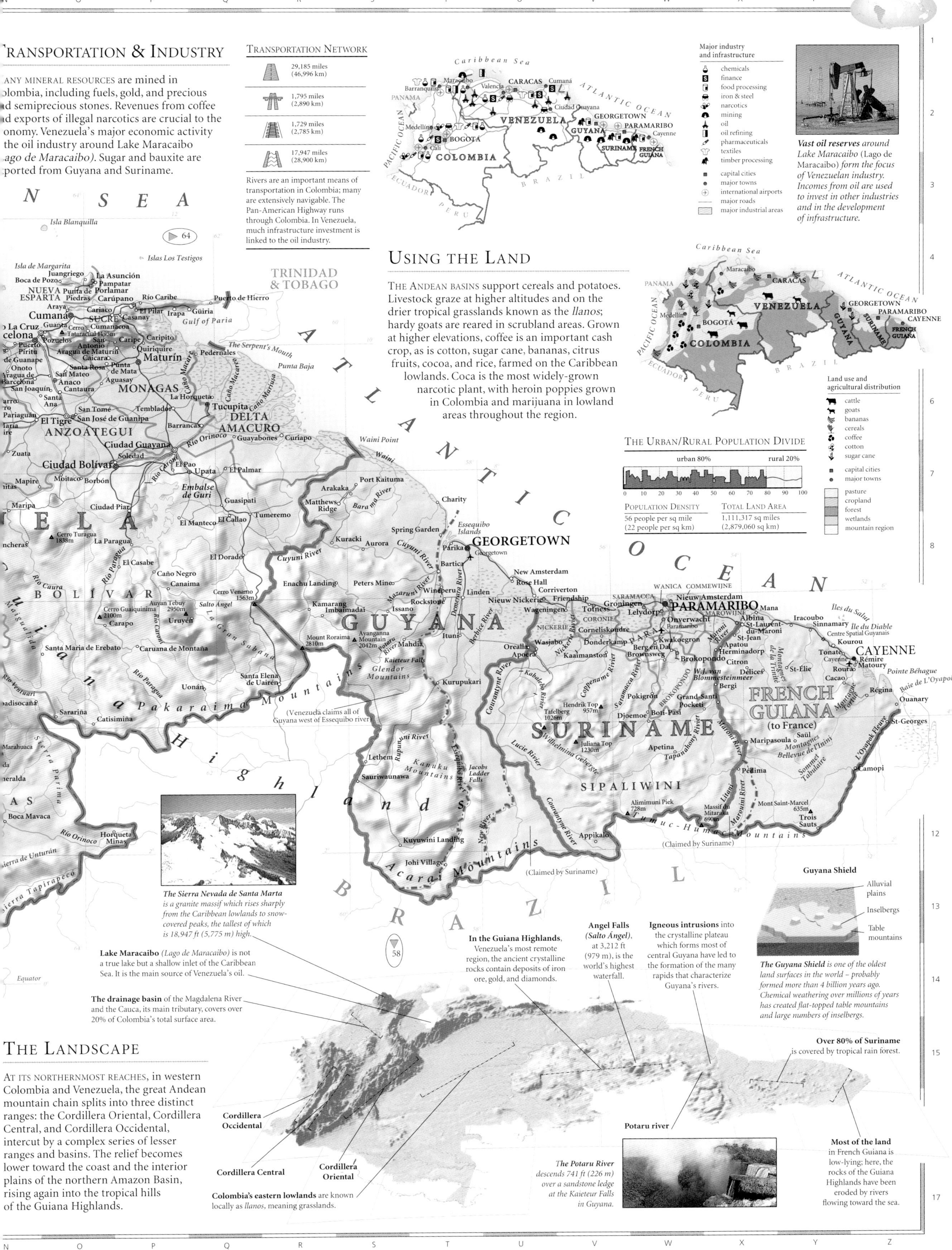

TRANSPORTATION NETWORK
29,185 miles (46,996 km)
1,795 miles (2,890 km)
1,729 miles (2,785 km)
17,947 miles (28,900 km)
Major industry and infrastructure
chemicals
finance
food processing
iron & steel
narcotics
mining
oil
oil refining
pharmaceuticals
textiles
timber processing
capital cities
major towns
international airports
major roads
major industrial areas
Land use and agricultural distribution
cattle
goats
bananas
cereals
coffee
cotton
sugar cane
capital cities
major towns
pasture
cropland
forest
wetlands
mountain region
THE URBAN/RURAL POPULATION DIVIDE
urban 80%
rural 20%
POPULATION DENSITY
56 people per sq mile (22 people per sq km)
TOTAL LAND AREA
1,111,317 sq miles (2,879,060 sq km)
ATLANTIC OCEAN
GEORGETOWN
PARAMARIBO
CAYENNE
GUYANA
SURINAME
FRENCH GUIANA (to France)
Guiana Highlands
Guyana Shield
Alluvial plains
Inselbergs
Table mountains
Cordillera Occidental
Cordillera Central
Cordillera Oriental
Potaru river

Rivers are an important means of transportation in Colombia; many are extensively navigable. The Pan-American Highway runs through Colombia. In Venezuela, much infrastructure investment is linked to the oil industry.

***Vast oil reserves** around Lake Maracaibo* (Lago de Maracaibo) *form the focus of Venezuelan industry. Incomes from oil are used to invest in other industries and in the development of infrastructure.*

USING THE LAND

THE ANDEAN BASINS support cereals and potatoes. Livestock graze at higher altitudes and on the drier tropical grasslands known as the *llanos*; hardy goats are reared in scrubland areas. Grown at higher elevations, coffee is an important cash crop, as is cotton, sugar cane, bananas, citrus fruits, cocoa, and rice, farmed on the Caribbean lowlands. Coca is the most widely-grown narcotic plant, with heroin poppies grown in Colombia and marijuana in lowland areas throughout the region.

64

58

***The Sierra Nevada de Santa Marta** is a granite massif which rises sharply from the Caribbean lowlands to snow-covered peaks, the tallest of which is 18,947 ft (5,775 m) high.*

Lake Maracaibo (*Lago de Maracaibo*) is not a true lake but a shallow inlet of the Caribbean Sea. It is the main source of Venezuela's oil.

The drainage basin of the Magdalena River and the Cauca, its main tributary, covers over 20% of Colombia's total surface area.

In the Guiana Highlands, Venezuela's most remote region, the ancient crystalline rocks contain deposits of iron ore, gold, and diamonds.

Angel Falls (*Salto Ángel*), at 3,212 ft (979 m), is the world's highest waterfall.

Igneous intrusions into the crystalline plateau which forms most of central Guyana have led to the formation of the many rapids that characterize Guyana's rivers.

***The Guyana Shield** is one of the oldest land surfaces in the world – probably formed more than 4 billion years ago. Chemical weathering over millions of years has created flat-topped table mountains and large numbers of inselbergs.*

Over 80% of Suriname is covered by tropical rain forest.

THE LANDSCAPE

AT ITS NORTHERNMOST REACHES, in western Colombia and Venezuela, the great Andean mountain chain splits into three distinct ranges: the Cordillera Oriental, Cordillera Central, and Cordillera Occidental, intercut by a complex series of lesser ranges and basins. The relief becomes lower toward the coast and the interior plains of the northern Amazon Basin, rising again into the tropical hills of the Guiana Highlands.

Colombia's eastern lowlands are known locally as *llanos*, meaning grasslands.

***The Potaru River** descends 741 ft (226 m) over a sandstone ledge at the Kaieteur Falls in Guyana.*

Most of the land in French Guiana is low-lying; here, the rocks of the Guiana Highlands have been eroded by rivers flowing toward the sea.

Western South America

Bolivia, Ecuador, Peru

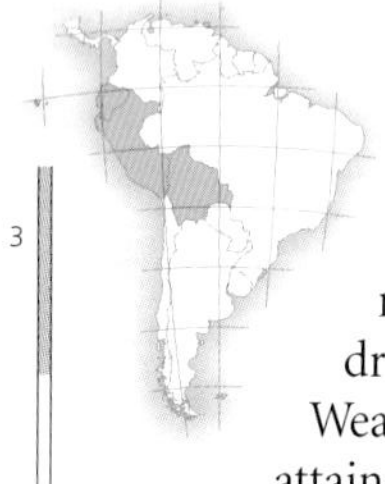

The three states of Western South America share a similar geography and recent history. Dominated by the Inca empire until Spanish conquest in the 16th century, they achieved independence from Spain in the early 19th century. The precipitous terrain of the Andes presents severe difficulties for overland transportation and continues to be a barrier to national unity and stability. Although Ecuador is now a relatively stable democracy, the military is highly influential in Peru and Bolivia, while the drug trade and associated corruption discourages external aid and economic progress. Wealth and power are still largely concentrated in the hands of a small elite of families, who attained their position during the Spanish colonial period. Land rights and political recognition for the indigenous peoples are becoming increasingly important issues, particularly in Ecuador.

*Ecuador's capital city, **Quito**, lies high in the Andes, nestling between snowcapped peaks. At 9,350 ft (2,850 m), Quito is the second highest capital in the world – La Paz in Bolivia is the highest.*

The Landscape

Bolivia, Peru, and Ecuador each possess a high Andean mountain region and an eastern region consisting of tropical lowlands and the Andean slope leading down to them. Toward the south of the region, the mountains widen to form the high plateau of the Altiplano. Peru and Ecuador also have fertile, lowland coastal plains. A wide variety of environments include *selva* (tropical rain forest), *montaña* (mountain forest), and grassland.

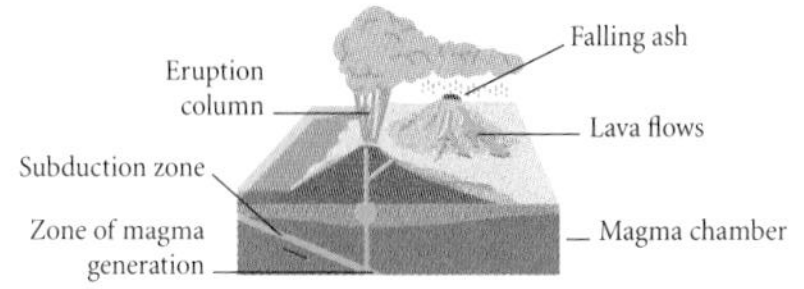

Eruption column – Falling ash – Lava flows – Subduction zone – Zone of magma generation – Magma chamber

***There are many large** and active volcanoes in the Andes. Magma generated in the heart of the volcano erupts in a huge cloud of ash. Ash-fall deposits are common throughout the Andes and the rock produced is known as andesite. This is rapidly soaked by heavy rain, causing massive debris flows.*

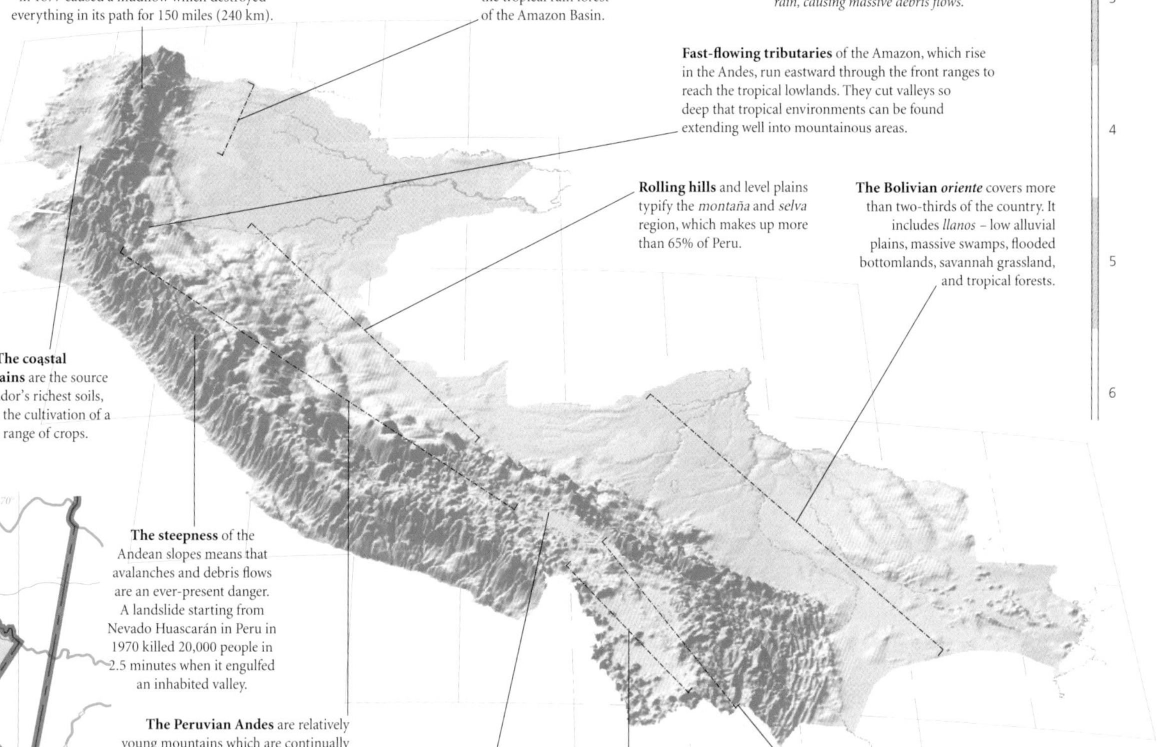

Cotopaxi is the world's highest active volcano, with a peak 19,347 ft (5,897 m) high. A massive eruption in 1877 caused a mudflow which destroyed everything in its path for 150 miles (240 km).

Much of eastern Ecuador is covered by the tropical rain forest of the Amazon Basin.

Fast-flowing tributaries of the Amazon, which rise in the Andes, run eastward through the front ranges to reach the tropical lowlands. They cut valleys so deep that tropical environments can be found extending well into mountainous areas.

Rolling hills and level plains typify the *montaña* and *selva* region, which makes up more than 65% of Peru.

The Bolivian *oriente* covers more than two-thirds of the country. It includes *llanos* – low alluvial plains, massive swamps, flooded bottomlands, savannah grassland, and tropical forests.

The coastal floodplains are the source of Ecuador's richest soils, enabling the cultivation of a wide range of crops.

The steepness of the Andean slopes means that avalanches and debris flows are an ever-present danger. A landslide starting from Nevado Huascarán in Peru in 1970 killed 20,000 people in 2.5 minutes when it engulfed an inhabited valley.

The Peruvian Andes are relatively young mountains which are continually being uplifted, making the area very unstable, with frequent earthquakes. The transportation difficulties that they present continue to form a barrier to national unity.

Lake Titicaca

***Lake Titicaca**, which forms part of the border between Peru and Bolivia, is the largest lake in South America and the highest significant body of water in the world at an altitude of 12,507 ft (3,812 m).*

The Altiplano is a flat, high plateau lying between the Cordillera Oriental and the Cordillera Occidental at a height of up to 12,500 ft (3,800 m). At its margins lie many spurs and alluvial fans.

Bolivian Andes

***Nevado de Illampu and Nevado de Ancohuma**, at 21,275 ft (6,485 m) and 21,490 ft (6,550 m) respectively, form Illampu, the highest mountain in the Bolivian Andes.*

Map Key

POPULATION	ELEVATION
above 5 million	6000m / 19,686ft
1 million to 5 million	4000m / 13,124ft
500,000 to 1 million	3000m / 9843ft
100,000 to 500,000	2000m / 6562ft
50,000 to 100,000	1000m / 3281ft
10,000 to 50,000	500m / 1640ft
below 10,000	250m / 820ft
	100m / 328ft
	sea level

SCALE 1:8,500,000 (projection: Lambert Azimuthal Equal Area)

Ecuadorean Administrative Regions

1. CARCHI
2. TUNGURAHUA
3. BOLÍVAR
4. CHIMBORAZO
5. ZAMORA CHINCHIPE

192 ◀ 54 ▲ ▶ 58

COLOMBIA ECUADOR PERU BRAZIL

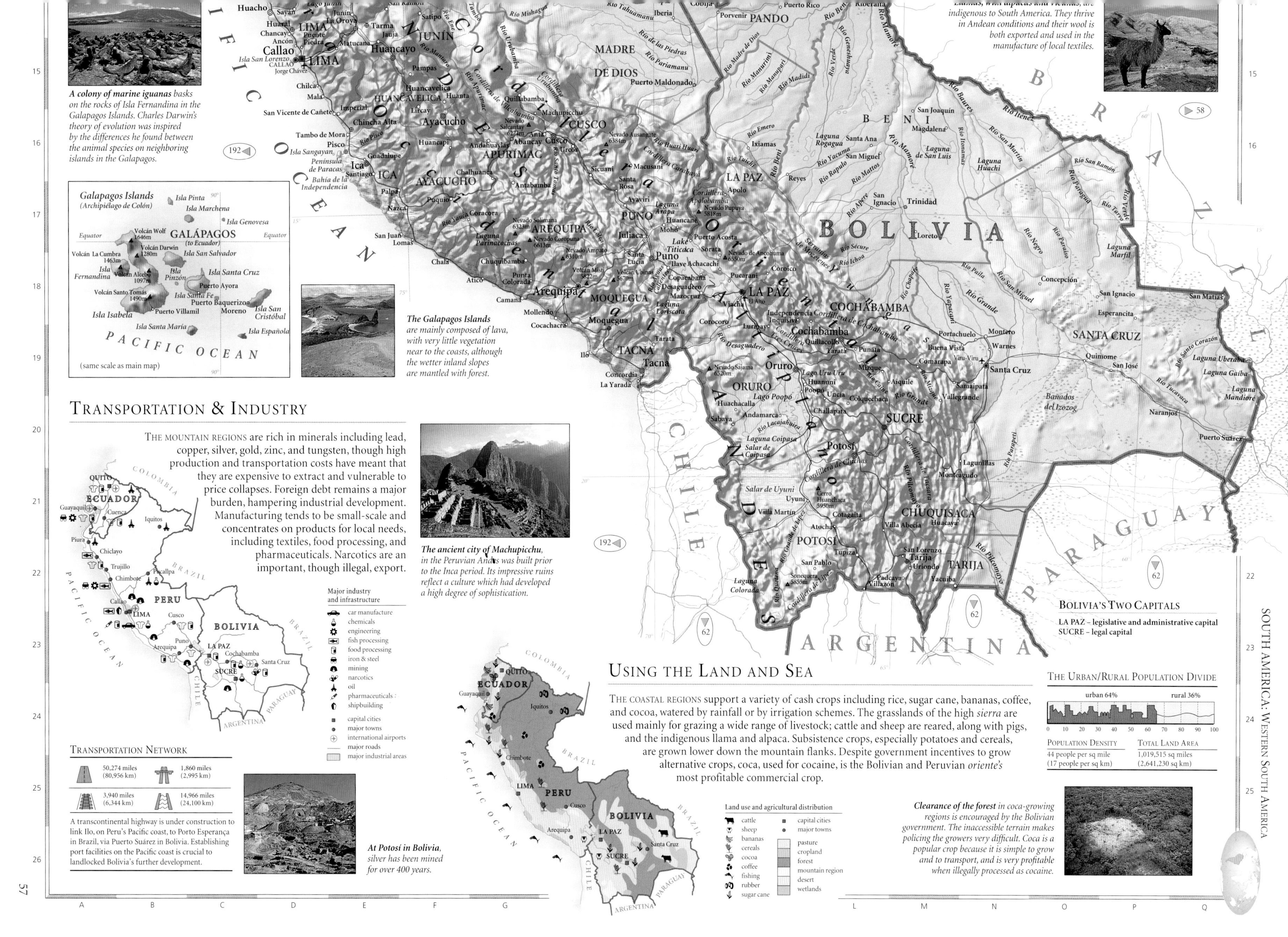

indigenous to South America. They thrive in Andean conditions and their wool is both exported and used in the manufacture of local textiles.

A colony of marine iguanas *basks on the rocks of Isla Fernandina in the Galapagos Islands. Charles Darwin's theory of evolution was inspired by the differences he found between the animal species on neighboring islands in the Galapagos.*

The Galapagos Islands are mainly composed of lava, with very little vegetation near to the coasts, although the wetter inland slopes are mantled with forest.

Bolivia's Two Capitals

LA PAZ – legislative and administrative capital
SUCRE – legal capital

Transportation & Industry

The mountain regions are rich in minerals including lead, copper, silver, gold, zinc, and tungsten, though high production and transportation costs have meant that they are expensive to extract and vulnerable to price collapses. Foreign debt remains a major burden, hampering industrial development. Manufacturing tends to be small-scale and concentrates on products for local needs, including textiles, food processing, and pharmaceuticals. Narcotics are an important, though illegal, export.

The ancient city of Machupicchu, *in the Peruvian Andes was built prior to the Inca period. Its impressive ruins reflect a culture which had developed a high degree of sophistication.*

Major industry and infrastructure
car manufacture
chemicals
engineering
fish processing
food processing
iron & steel
mining
narcotics
oil
pharmaceuticals
shipbuilding
capital cities
major towns
international airports
major roads
major industrial areas

Transportation Network

50,274 miles (80,956 km)	1,860 miles (2,995 km)
3,940 miles (6,344 km)	14,966 miles (24,100 km)

A transcontinental highway is under construction to link Ilo, on Peru's Pacific coast, to Porto Esperança in Brazil, via Puerto Suárez in Bolivia. Establishing port facilities on the Pacific coast is crucial to landlocked Bolivia's further development.

At Potosí in Bolivia, *silver has been mined for over 400 years.*

Using the Land and Sea

The coastal regions support a variety of cash crops including rice, sugar cane, bananas, coffee, and cocoa, watered by rainfall or by irrigation schemes. The grasslands of the high *sierra* are used mainly for grazing a wide range of livestock; cattle and sheep are reared, along with pigs, and the indigenous llama and alpaca. Subsistence crops, especially potatoes and cereals, are grown lower down the mountain flanks. Despite government incentives to grow alternative crops, coca, used for cocaine, is the Bolivian and Peruvian *oriente's* most profitable commercial crop.

Land use and agricultural distribution
cattle
sheep
bananas
cereals
cocoa
coffee
fishing
rubber
sugar cane
capital cities
major towns
pasture
cropland
forest
mountain region
desert
wetlands

The Urban/Rural Population Divide

urban 64% rural 36%

Population Density	Total Land Area
44 people per sq mile (17 people per sq km)	1,019,515 sq miles (2,641,230 sq km)

Clearance of the forest *in coca-growing regions is encouraged by the Bolivian government. The inaccessible terrain makes policing the growers very difficult. Coca is a popular crop because it is simple to grow and to transport, and is very profitable when illegally processed as cocaine.*

Brazil

Brazil is the largest country in South America, with a population of over 165 million – greater than the combined total for the whole of the rest of the continent. The 26 states which make up the federal republic of Brazil are administered from the purpose-built capital, Brasília. Tropical rain forest, covering more than one-third of the country, contains rich natural resources, but great tracts are sacrificed to agriculture, industry and urban expansion on a daily basis. Most of Brazil's multiethnic population now live in cities, some of which are vast areas of urban sprawl; São Paulo is one of the world's biggest conurbations, with more than 17 million inhabitants. Although prosperity is a reality for some, many people still live in great poverty, and mounting foreign debts continue to damage Brazil's prospects of economic advancement.

Using the Land

Brazil has immense natural resources, including minerals and hardwoods, many of which are found in the fragile rain forest. Brazil is the world's leading coffee grower and a major producer of livestock, sugar, and orange juice concentrate. Soybeans for animal feed, particularly for poultry feed, have become the country's most significant crop.

The Urban/Rural Population Divide

urban 78% — rural 22%

Population Density	Total Land Area
50 people per sq mile (19 people per sq km)	3,286,472 sq miles (8,511,970 sq km)

Land use and agricultural distribution: cattle, pigs, sheep, citrus fruits, coffee, cotton, soya beans, sugar cane, timber, capital cities, major towns, pasture, cropland, forest

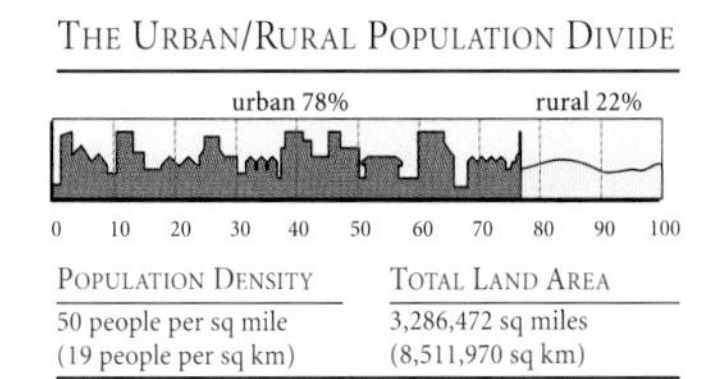

The fecundity of parts of Brazil's rain forest results from exceptionally high levels of rainfall and the quantities of silt deposited by the Amazon River system.

The Landscape

The Amazon Basin, containing the largest area of tropical rain forest on Earth, covers nearly half of Brazil. It is bordered by two shield areas: in the south by the Brazilian Highlands, and in the north by the Guiana Highlands. The east coast is dominated by a great escarpment which runs for 1,600 miles (2,565 km).

Guiana Highlands
Pantanal swamps

Brazil's highest mountain is the Pico da Neblina which was only discovered in 1962. It is 9,888 ft (3,014 m) high.

The floodplains which border the Amazon River are made up of a variety of different features including shallow lakes and swamps, mangrove forests in the tidal delta area, and fertile levées on river banks and point bars.

The Pantanal region in the south of Brazil is an extension of the Gran Chaco plain. The swamps and marshes of this area are renowned for their beauty, and abundant and unique wildlife, including wildfowl and these caimans, a type of crocodile.

The Iguaçu River surges over the spectacular Iguaçu Falls (Saltos do Iguaçu) *toward the Paraná River. Falls like these are increasingly under pressure from large-scale hydroelectric projects such as that at Itaipú.*

The Amazon Basin is the largest river basin in the world. The Amazon River and over a thousand tributaries drain an area of 2,375,000 sq miles (6,150,000 sq km) and carry one-fifth of the world's fresh water out to sea.

The ancient Brazilian Highlands have a varied topography. Their plateaus, hills, and deep valleys are bordered by highly-eroded mountains containing important mineral deposits. They are drained by three great river systems, the Amazon, the Paraguay–Paraná, and the São Francisco.

The São Francisco Basin has a climate unique in Brazil. Known as the "drought polygon," it has almost no rain during the dry season, leading to regular disastrous droughts.

The northeastern scrublands are known as the *caatinga*, a virtually impenetrable thorny woodland, sometimes intermixed with cacti where water is scarce.

The famous Sugar Loaf Mountain (*Pão de Açúcar*) which overlooks Rio de Janeiro is a fine example of a volcanic plug a domed core of solidified lava left after the slopes of the original volcano have eroded away.

Deep natural harbors such as Baia de Guanabara were created where the steep slopes of the Serra da Mantiqueira plunge directly into the ocean.

Hillslope gullying

Rainfall — Direction of growth — Water seeps through hillslope — Overland water flow — Gully

Large-scale gullies are common in Brazil, particularly on hillslopes from which vegetation has been removed. Gullies grow headwards (up the slope), aided by a combination of erosion through water seepage and rainwater runoff.

Map Key

Population	Elevation
above 5 million	3000m / 9843ft
1 million to 5 million	2000m / 6562ft
500,000 to 1 million	1000m / 3281ft
100,000 to 500,000	500m / 1640ft
50,000 to 100,000	250m / 820ft
10,000 to 50,000	100m / 328ft
below 10,000	sea level

BRAZIL
ACRE
RONDÔNIA
MATO GROSSO
MATO GROSSO DO SUL
TOCANTINS
PIAUÍ
BAHIA
GOIÁS
DISTRITO FEDERAL
MINAS GERAIS
ESPÍRITO SANTO
RIO DE JANEIRO
SÃO PAULO
PARANÁ
SANTA CATARINA
RIO GRANDE DO SUL
SERGIPE
ALAGOAS
PERNAMBUCO
PARAÍBA
RIO GRANDE DO NORTE
PERU
BOLIVIA
PARAGUAY
ARGENTINA
URUGUAY
ATLANTIC OCEAN
Planalto Central
(Brazilian Highlands)
Planalto de Mato Grosso
Pantanal
Chapada Diamantina
Espigão Mestre
Serra do Cachimbo
Chapada dos Parecis
Serra Geral
Serra do Mar
Tropic of Capricorn
Brasília
Rio de Janeiro
São Paulo
Salvador
Belo Horizonte
Curitiba
Porto Alegre
Recife
Natal
Fortaleza
Goiânia
Campo Grande
Cuiabá
Porto Velho
Rio Branco
Florianópolis
Vitória
Maceió
Aracaju
João Pessoa
56
60
62
64
SCALE 1:14,250,000
(projection: Lambert Azimuthal Equal Area)
Km
Miles

TRANSPORTATION & INDUSTRY

BRAZILIAN INDUSTRY is diverse and well developed, in part as a result of past government incentives, including the prohibition of imports. Industries which have benefited include car manufacture, petrochemicals, and microelectronics. Textiles, clothing, and footwear are among Brazil's most successful exports. The country's services and tourism sectors are also expanding rapidly.

BRAZIL
ATLANTIC OCEAN
Manaus
Belém
Fortaleza
Recife
Salvador
BRASÍLIA
Belo Horizonte
Rio de Janeiro
São Paulo
Curitiba
Porto Alegre
COLOMBIA
VENEZUELA
GUYANA
SURINAME
FRENCH GUIANA
PERU
BOLIVIA
PARAGUAY
ARGENTINA
URUGUAY

TRANSPORTATION NETWORK

139,351 miles (224,397 km)

3,105 miles (5,000 km)

18,865 miles (30,379 km)

31,050 miles (50,000 km)

An extensive new road network is being built to link Brazil's main centers. Investment is needed to update the antiquated railroad system. In São Paulo, the subway system is being extended to accommodate the expanding population.

Major industry and infrastructure

car manufacture, chemicals, electronics, finance, food processing, iron & steel, mining, oil, printing & publishing, textiles, timber processing, tourism, capital cities, major towns, international airports, major roads, major industrial areas

***Brazil's urban population** has grown by over 6% per year since the mid-1970s – at current population levels a rate of nearly 6 million people annually. In Rio de Janeiro prosperous neighborhoods exist alongside over 450 shantytowns or favelas, some of which house as many as 250,000 people.*

__A gaucho__ in traditional costume herds beef cattle on the grasslands of the Rio Grande do Sul in southern Brazil.

***Picinguaba Beach** lies in Serra do Mar State Park in São Paulo state. São Paulo's beaches stretch for 386 miles (622 km) along the Atlantic coast.*

Eastern South America

Uruguay, Northeast Argentina, Southeast Brazil

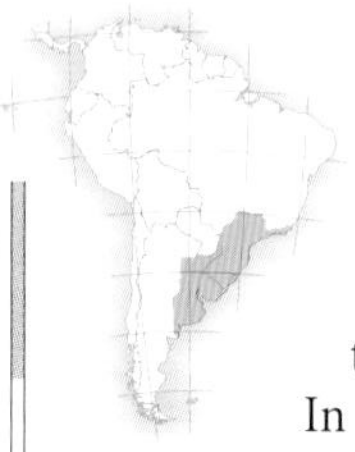

The vast conurbations of Rio de Janeiro, São Paulo, and Buenos Aires form the core of South America's highly-urbanized eastern region. São Paulo state, with almost 35 million inhabitants, is among the world's 20 most powerful economies, and São Paulo is the fastest growing city on the continent. Rio de Janeiro and Buenos Aires, transformed in the last hundred years from port cities to great metropolitan areas each with more than 10 million inhabitants, typify the unstructured growth and wealth disparities of South America's great cities. In Uruguay, over half of the population lives in the capital, Montevideo, which faces Buenos Aires across the Plate River *(Río de la Plata)*. Immigration from the countryside has created severe pressure on the urban infrastructure, particularly on available housing, leading to a profusion of crowded shanty settlements *(favelas or barrios)*.

Transportation & Industry

Southeast Brazil is home to much of the important motor and capital goods industry, largely based around São Paulo; iron and steel production is also concentrated in this region. Uruguay's economy continues to be based mainly on the export of livestock products including meat and leather goods. Buenos Aires is Argentina's chief port, and the region has a varied and sophisticated economic base including service-based industries such as finance and publishing, as well as primary processing.

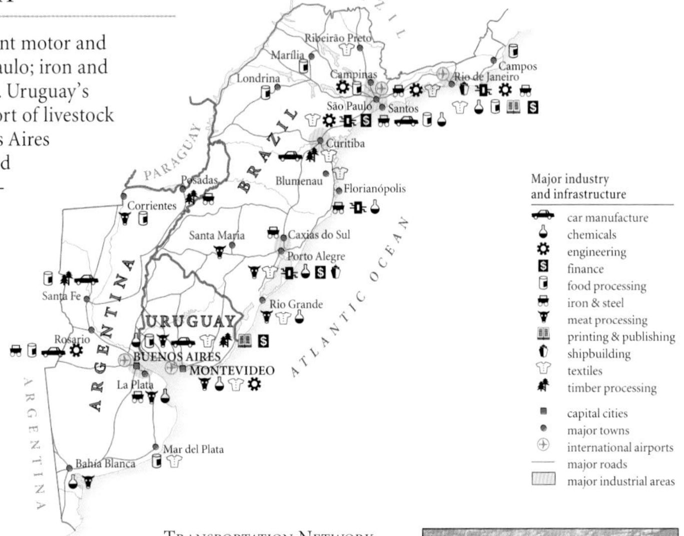

Major industry and infrastructure
- car manufacture
- chemicals
- engineering
- finance
- food processing
- iron & steel
- meat processing
- printing & publishing
- shipbuilding
- textiles
- timber processing
- capital cities
- major towns
- international airports
- major roads
- major industrial areas

Map Key

POPULATION
- above 5 million
- 1 million to 5 million
- 500,000 to 1 million
- 100,000 to 500,000
- 50,000 to 100,000
- 10,000 to 50,000
- below 10,000

ELEVATION
- 2000m / 6562ft
- 1000m / 3281ft
- 500m / 1640ft
- 250m / 820ft
- 100m / 328ft
- sea level

Transportation Network

Throughout the region, road networks need to be expanded to cope with urban development. Plans are underway to build a bridge over the Plate River *(Río de la Plata)* to link Colonia and Buenos Aires.

***The Itaipú dam** on the Paraná River is one of the largest hydroelectric projects in the world, jointly financed by Brazil and Paraguay.*

Using the Land

Most of Uruguay and the Pampas of northern Argentina are devoted to the rearing of livestock, especially cattle and sheep, which are central to both countries' economies. Soybeans, first produced in Brazil's Rio Grande do Sul, are now more widely grown for large-scale export, as are cereals, sugar cane, and grapes. Subsistence crops, including potatoes, corn and sugar beets, are grown on the remaining arable land.

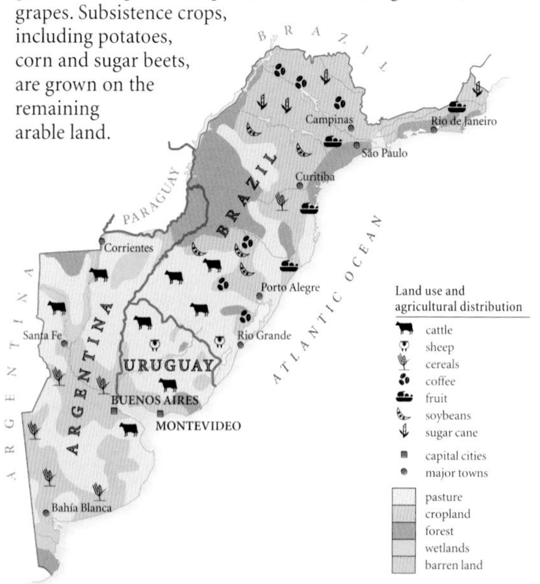

Land use and agricultural distribution
- cattle
- sheep
- cereals
- coffee
- fruit
- soybeans
- sugar cane
- capital cities
- major towns
- pasture
- cropland
- forest
- wetlands
- barren land

Scale 1:7,000,000
(projection: Lambert Azimuthal Equal Area)

***Soybeans are harvested**, pressed, and processed into soycake, which is used as animal feed. The cake is fed mainly to chickens on large-scale factory farms, and the growth in soy production has been an important factor in the expansion of the Brazilian poultry trade.*

***The rolling grasslands** of Uruguay are ideally suited to the rearing of cattle, which are concentrated in great herds throughout the region.*

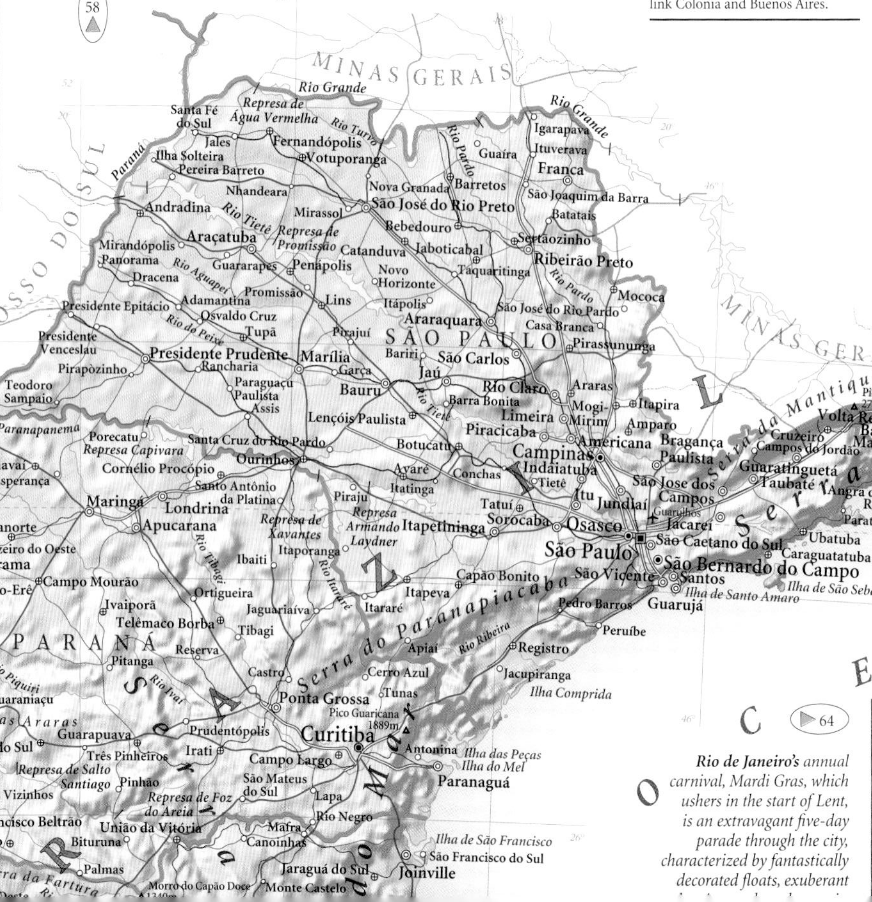

***Rio de Janeiro's** annual carnival, Mardi Gras, which ushers in the start of Lent, is an extravagant five-day parade through the city, characterized by fantastically decorated floats, exuberant*

58
62
64

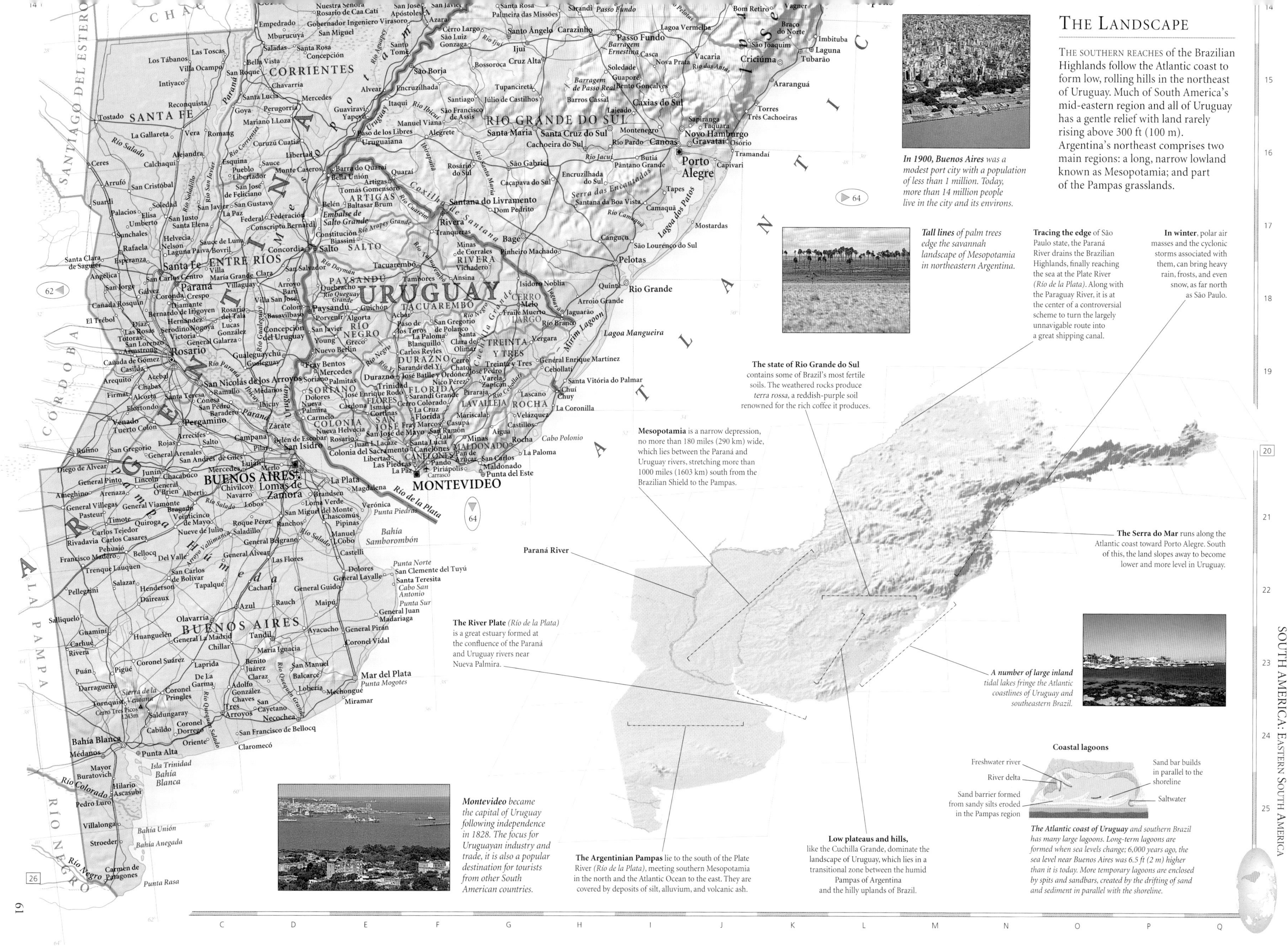
ARGENTINA
URUGUAY
ATLANTIC
SANTA FE
CORRIENTES
ENTRE RÍOS
BUENOS AIRES
RIO GRANDE DO SUL
MONTEVIDEO
BUENOS AIRES
Porto Alegre
Rosario
Paraná
Santa Fe
Mar del Plata
Bahía Blanca
Pelotas
Rio Grande
Lagoa dos Patos
Lagoa Mirim
Río de la Plata
Pampa Húmeda
Mesopotamia
SANTIAGO DEL ESTERO
CÓRDOBA
LA PAMPA
RÍO NEGRO
PAYSANDÚ
SALTO
ARTIGAS
RIVERA
TACUAREMBÓ
CERRO LARGO
TREINTA Y TRES
ROCHA
LAVALLEJA
MALDONADO
CANELONES
FLORIDA
DURAZNO
FLORES
SORIANO
COLONIA
SAN JOSÉ
RÍO NEGRO
Cuchilla Grande
Cuchilla de Santana
Coastal lagoons
Freshwater river
River delta
Sand barrier formed from sandy silts eroded in the Pampas region
Sand bar builds in parallel to the shoreline
Saltwater
Paraná River
62
64
64
26
20

The Landscape

The southern reaches of the Brazilian Highlands follow the Atlantic coast to form low, rolling hills in the northeast of Uruguay. Much of South America's mid-eastern region and all of Uruguay has a gentle relief with land rarely rising above 300 ft (100 m). Argentina's northeast comprises two main regions: a long, narrow lowland known as Mesopotamia; and part of the Pampas grasslands.

In 1900, ***Buenos Aires*** *was a modest port city with a population of less than 1 million. Today, more than 14 million people live in the city and its environs.*

Tall lines *of palm trees edge the savannah landscape of Mesopotamia in northeastern Argentina.*

Tracing the edge of São Paulo state, the Paraná River drains the Brazilian Highlands, finally reaching the sea at the Plate River (*Río de la Plata*). Along with the Paraguay River, it is at the center of a controversial scheme to turn the largely unnavigable route into a great shipping canal.

In winter, polar air masses and the cyclonic storms associated with them, can bring heavy rain, frosts, and even snow, as far north as São Paulo.

The state of Rio Grande do Sul contains some of Brazil's most fertile soils. The weathered rocks produce *terra rossa*, a reddish-purple soil renowned for the rich coffee it produces.

Mesopotamia is a narrow depression, no more than 180 miles (290 km) wide, which lies between the Paraná and Uruguay rivers, stretching more than 1000 miles (1603 km) south from the Brazilian Shield to the Pampas.

The Serra do Mar runs along the Atlantic coast toward Porto Alegre. South of this, the land slopes away to become lower and more level in Uruguay.

The River Plate (*Río de la Plata*) is a great estuary formed at the confluence of the Paraná and Uruguay rivers near Nueva Palmira.

A number of large inland *tidal lakes fringe the Atlantic coastlines of Uruguay and southeastern Brazil.*

Montevideo *became the capital of Uruguay following independence in 1828. The focus for Uruguayan industry and trade, it is also a popular destination for tourists from other South American countries.*

The Argentinian Pampas lie to the south of the Plate River (*Río de la Plata*), meeting southern Mesopotamia in the north and the Atlantic Ocean to the east. They are covered by deposits of silt, alluvium, and volcanic ash.

Low plateaus and hills, like the Cuchilla Grande, dominate the landscape of Uruguay, which lies in a transitional zone between the humid Pampas of Argentina and the hilly uplands of Brazil.

The Atlantic coast of Uruguay *and southern Brazil has many large lagoons. Long-term lagoons are formed when sea levels change; 6,000 years ago, the sea level near Buenos Aires was 6.5 ft (2 m) higher than it is today. More temporary lagoons are enclosed by spits and sandbars, created by the drifting of sand and sediment in parallel with the shoreline.*

SOUTHERN SOUTH AMERICA

ARGENTINA, CHILE, PARAGUAY

SOUTH AMERICA'S CONE-SHAPED SOUTHERN REGION is shared by Argentina and Chile, two overwhelmingly urbanized nations whose populations live mainly in or around the capital cities, Buenos Aires and Santiago. The people are largely *mestizo* or of European origin; in the early 20th century Argentina absorbed waves of new European immigrants, many from Italy and Germany. Paraguay is far less urbanized than its neighbors, with a homogeneous population of mixed Spanish and Guaraní origin, who retain their Indian roots through the Guaraní language. Though most Paraguayans live in the southeast, near Asunción, the indigenous Indians live in the sparsely populated Gran Chaco. The Gran Chaco is also home to some of Argentina's minority indigenous peoples, who otherwise live mainly in Andean regions. Chile's estimated 800,000 Mapauche Indians live almost exclusively in the south.

TRANSPORTATION & INDUSTRY

FOOD PROCESSING AND AGRICULTURAL EXPORTS remain a fundamental part of Argentina's economy. The growth of manufacturing is regularly hampered by hyper-inflation and massive foreign debts. The world's most important copper-producer and one of the top ten gold producers, Chile also has a thriving wine and grape industry. Most Paraguayan exports involve primary processing, although domestic goods are produced for home markets.

Chuquicamata copper mine*, lies on a desert plateau near Calama in the Andes of northern Chile. It is the world's largest open-pit copper mine.*

Major industry and infrastructure

- chemicals
- engineering
- food processing
- meat processing
- mining
- oil
- textiles
- timber processing
- capital cities
- major towns
- international airports
- major roads
- major industrial areas

TRANSPORTATION NETWORK

- 89,104 miles (143,485 km)
- 2,809 miles (4,523 km)
- 23,107 miles (37,210 km)
- 9,206 miles (14,825 km)

Argentina's state transportation system is undergoing privatization, though the outmoded rail network requires updating. Paraguay requires foreign investment to upgrade its roads and railroads. Essential internal air routes, especially across the Andes, are well developed in all three countries.

Boiling water *and steam emerge from a volcanic vent, one of the Tatio geysers which lie at the foot of Cerro de Tocorpuri near Chile's border with Bolivia.*

Floodwaters cover *the land in the Gran Chaco, partly submerging its vegetation of fan palms and hyacinths.*

56

58

MAP KEY

POPULATION

- 1 million to 5 million
- 500,000 to 1 million
- 100,000 to 500,000
- 50,000 to 100,000
- 10,000 to 50,000
- below 10,000

ELEVATION

- 6000m / 19,686ft
- 4000m / 13,124ft
- 3000m / 9843ft
- 2000m / 6562ft
- 1000m / 3281ft
- 500m / 1640ft
- 250m / 820ft
- 100m / 328ft

THE LANDSCAPE

THE ANDES RUN FROM NORTH TO SOUTH, forming a precipitous natural border between Chile and Argentina. East of the Andes are the scrublands of the Gran Chaco and the plains of the Pampas, which extend northward toward Paraguay. In the far southwest, Chile's indented Pacific coastline has many features typical of areas which have been affected by glaciation.

The Atacama Desert (Desierto de Atacama) *in Chile is one of the driest places on Earth where some areas have never recorded any rain. It contains a number of salt lakes.*

Landlocked Paraguay relies on its river system for access to the sea and to produce hydroelectric power. The most important river system is the Paraguay–Paraná which provides links into neighboring countries including Brazil, Uruguay, and Argentina.

The Gran Chaco combines poor drainage, extremely hot temperatures and thorn-infested scrub to make it one of South America's most inhospitable regions.

Most of the highest mountains in Chile's northern Andes are volcanoes like Volcán Lascar and Volcán Rutana.

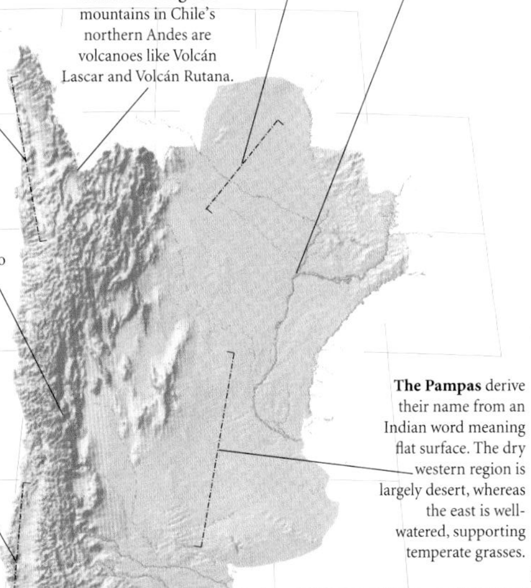

Cerro Aconcagua in the central Andes is the tallest mountain in the whole chain, rising to 22,834 ft (6,959 m).

Alluvial deposits from the many rivers in central Chile have created rich soils, ideal for a wide range of agriculture.

The Pampas derive their name from an Indian word meaning flat surface. The dry western region is largely desert, whereas the east is well-watered, supporting temperate grasses.

Andes

Patagonia divides into two zones, with the Andes in the west, and the lower main plateau, extending east toward the Atlantic. It is a desolate area with climatic extremes; dark lava fields scattered with light bunchgrass give a "leopard skin" effect to the landscape.

The Andean mountain system, *which forms Argentina's western border, was created by folding and faulting, following the convergence of the Nazca and South American tectonic plates.*

The Patagonian ice sheet is the world's third largest ice field, covering 6,560 sq miles (17,000 sq km). Patagonia also contains many typical features from past glaciations. These include glacial lakes, U-shaped valleys, fjords, and deep-cut channels.

Cape Horn is the most southerly point of South America. The severity of the "Roaring Forties" winds makes the Horn one of the world's most treacherous shipping regions.

Argentinian Pampas

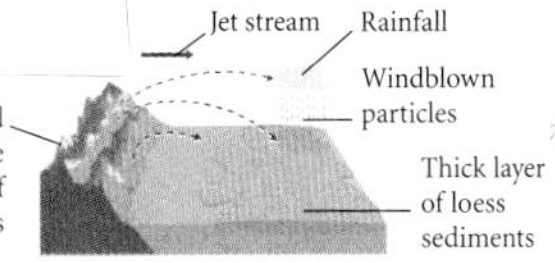

Jet stream
Rainfall
Windblown particles
Ice-capped Andes are source of loess
Thick layer of loess sediments

A thick, fertile layer *of loess lies in the basin underlying the Argentinian Pampas. It has been laid down following successive periods of glaciation. The minute loess particles are transported as dust and deposited by a downward air motion, or following rainfall.*

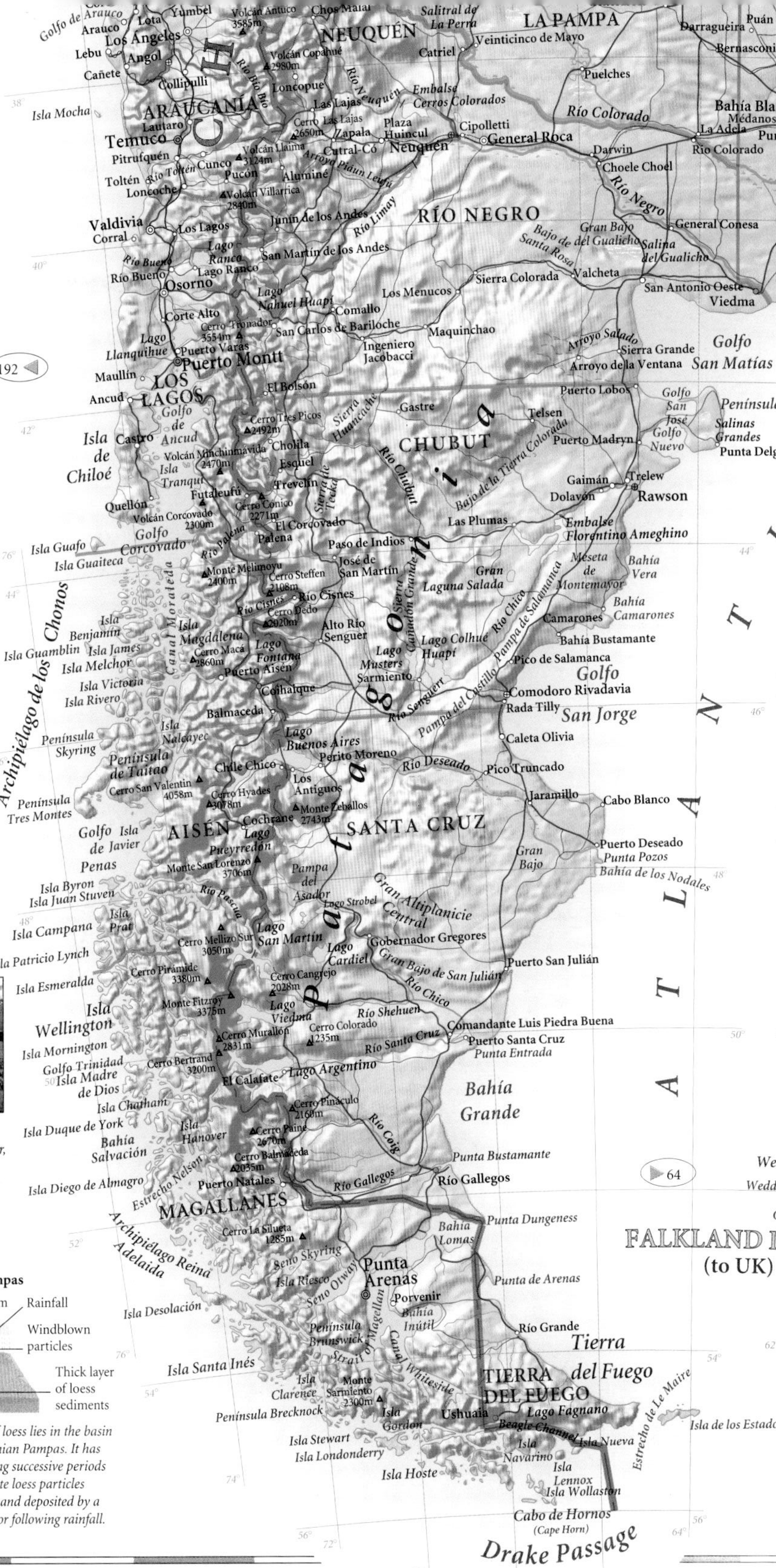

192

64

FALKLAND ISLANDS (to UK)

Drake Passage

Great blocks of ice *break away from the jagged blue peaks of these ice mountains to form icebergs off the coast of Patagonia, Argentina's most southerly region.*

USING THE LAND AND SEA

THE RICH PLAINS OF THE PAMPAS support massive herds of cattle, producing meat, milk, and hides essential to the domestic and export markets of both Argentina and Paraguay. Wheat and fruit are Argentina's other major agricultural products. A wide range of soft fruits, citrus fruits, and more specialized crops such as walnuts, and grapes for wine and the table, are grown in Chile's fertile Central Valley, while the landscape to the south is dominated by forestry, mainly growing commercial radiata pine. Paraguay is self-sufficient in wheat and other staples. Cotton, coffee, tobacco, and oil sources such as soybeans, are the major export crops.

THE URBAN/RURAL POPULATION DIVIDE

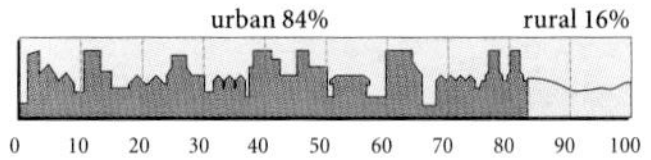

urban 84% | rural 16%

0 10 20 30 40 50 60 70 80 90 100

POPULATION DENSITY
37 people per sq mile
(14 people per sq km)

TOTAL LAND AREA
1,498,757 sq miles
(3,882,790 sq km)

Land use and agricultural distribution

cattle
sheep
cereals
fruit
grapes
timber
fishing
capital cities
major towns
pasture
cropland
forest
barren land
mountain region
desert

Charred tree stumps *surround a cattle enclosure on the island of Tierra del Fuego in southern Argentina. Forest clearance to provide grazing land for cattle is of major environmental concern.*

SCALE 1:9,750,000
(projection: Lambert Azimuthal Equal Area)

THE ATLANTIC OCEAN

THE ATLANTIC IS THE YOUNGEST OF THE WORLD'S OCEANS, formed about 180 million years ago when the landmasses of the eastern and western hemispheres separated. Its underwater topography is dominated by the Mid-Atlantic Ridge, a huge mountain system running north to south along the center of the ocean. Although most of the ridge's peaks lie below the sea, some emerge as volcanic islands, like Iceland and the Azores. The Atlantic contains a wealth of resources, including substantial oil and gas reserves and rich fishing grounds. Until the 1950s, the north Atlantic was the world's busiest shipping route; cheaper air transportation and alternative routes have shifted patterns of world trade.

RESOURCES

DEVELOPMENT OF THE OIL AND GAS RESERVES in the Atlantic began in the 1940s around the Gulf of Mexico. Since then other areas have been exploited, including the North Sea, the west coast of Africa and the area east of Newfoundland and Nova Scotia. There is also extensive mining of sand, gravel, and shell deposits by the US and UK. For centuries, the north Atlantic's fishing grounds have been utilized more heavily than other oceans, leading to a serious decline in many fish stocks.

Resources (including wildlife)
- fish
- whales
- aggregates
- oil & gas
- major towns
- major ports

Surtsey near Iceland, lies on the Mid-Atlantic Ridge. The island was formed in 1963 following a volcanic eruption caused by sea-floor spreading.

Fishing in the seas around northwestern Europe dates back over 1,500 years. The high nutrient content of the seas makes them ideal breeding grounds for many species of fish.

On January 5 1993, the oil tanker Braer ran aground in the Shetland Islands, spilling 83,660 tons (85,000 tonnes) of light crude oil into the ocean, devastating the local marine ecosystem.

SCALE 1:48,000,000 (projection: Mollweide)

AZORES (to Portugal) — SCALE 1:6,500,000

MADEIRA (to Portugal) — SCALE 1:2,500,000

ISLAS CANARIAS (CANARY ISLANDS) (to Spain) — SCALE 1:6,500,000

BERMUDA (to UK) — SCALE 1:500,000

THE LANDSCAPE

THE FLOOR OF THE ATLANTIC is spreading by about one inch (2.5 cm) a year. The South American and African plates are moving apart drawing molten rock up from the Earth's core. The Mid-Atlantic Ridge lies along the boundary of the two plates, forming the world's longest mountain range and dividing the Atlantic floor into two parallel troughs. These troughs are subdivided into numerous smaller basins by transform faults. Most of the oceanic islands in the Atlantic are volcanic in origin; either part of the Mid-Atlantic Ridge or the Caribbean arc.

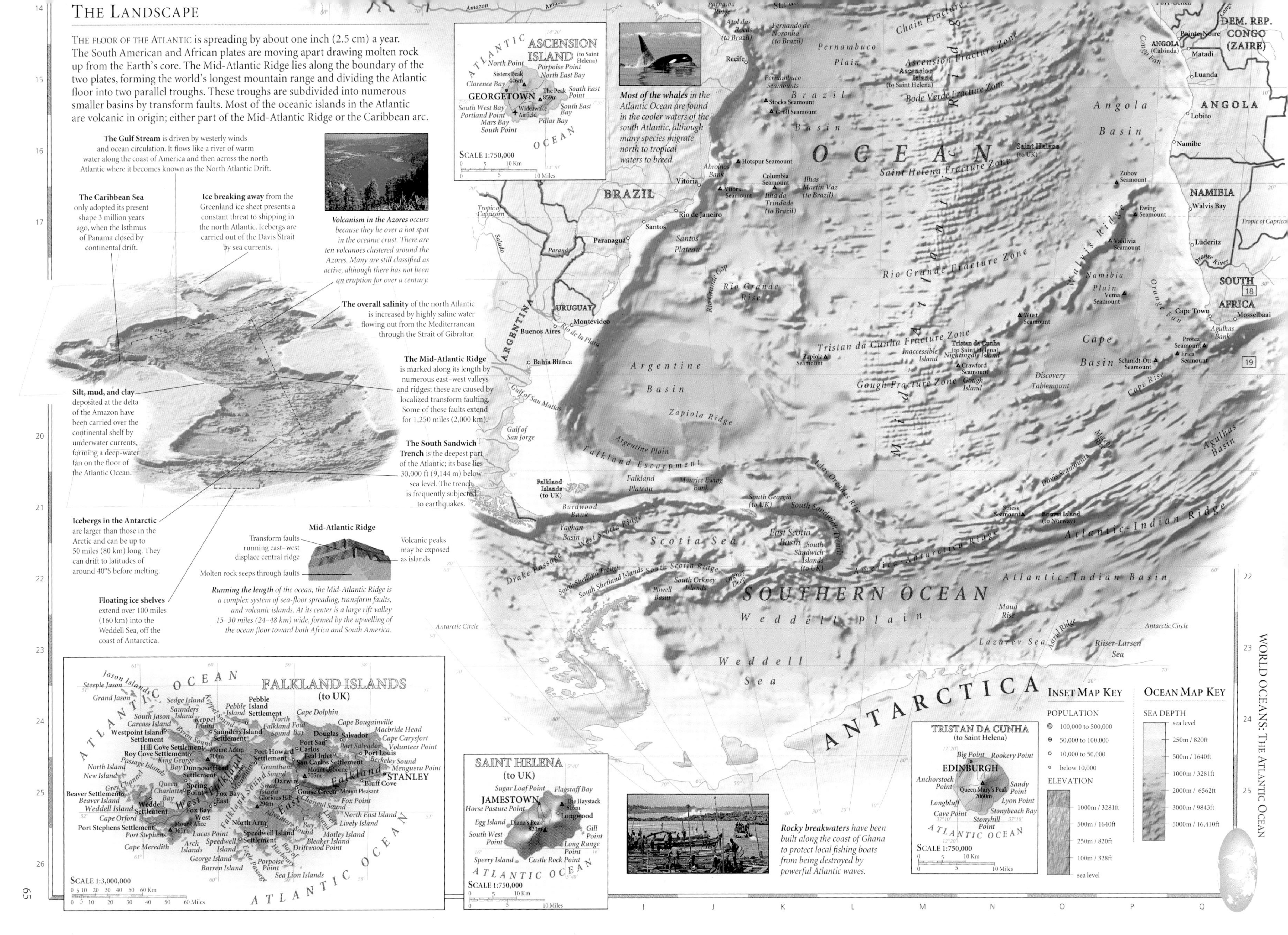

The Gulf Stream is driven by westerly winds and ocean circulation. It flows like a river of warm water along the coast of America and then across the north Atlantic where it becomes known as the North Atlantic Drift.
The Caribbean Sea only adopted its present shape 3 million years ago, when the Isthmus of Panama closed by continental drift.
Ice breaking away from the Greenland ice sheet presents a constant threat to shipping in the north Atlantic. Icebergs are carried out of the Davis Strait by sea currents.
Volcanism in the Azores occurs because they lie over a hot spot in the oceanic crust. There are ten volcanoes clustered around the Azores. Many are still classified as active, although there has not been an eruption for over a century.
The overall salinity of the north Atlantic is increased by highly saline water flowing out from the Mediterranean through the Strait of Gibraltar.
The Mid-Atlantic Ridge is marked along its length by numerous east–west valleys and ridges; these are caused by localized transform faulting. Some of these faults extend for 1,250 miles (2,000 km).
Silt, mud, and clay deposited at the delta of the Amazon have been carried over the continental shelf by underwater currents, forming a deep-water fan on the floor of the Atlantic Ocean.
The South Sandwich Trench is the deepest part of the Atlantic; its base lies 30,000 ft (9,144 m) below sea level. The trench is frequently subjected to earthquakes.
Icebergs in the Antarctic are larger than those in the Arctic and can be up to 50 miles (80 km) long. They can drift to latitudes of around 40°S before melting.
Mid-Atlantic Ridge
Transform faults running east–west displace central ridge
Volcanic peaks may be exposed as islands
Molten rock seeps through faults
Floating ice shelves extend over 100 miles (160 km) into the Weddell Sea, off the coast of Antarctica.
Running the length of the ocean, the Mid-Atlantic Ridge is a complex system of sea-floor spreading, transform faults, and volcanic islands. At its center is a large rift valley 15–30 miles (24–48 km) wide, formed by the upwelling of the ocean floor toward both Africa and South America.
ASCENSION ISLAND (to Saint Helena)
GEORGETOWN
SCALE 1:750,000
Most of the whales in the Atlantic Ocean are found in the cooler waters of the south Atlantic, although many species migrate north to tropical waters to breed.
BRAZIL
ARGENTINA
URUGUAY
ANGOLA
NAMIBIA
SOUTH AFRICA
DEM. REP. CONGO (ZAIRE)
OCEAN
SOUTHERN OCEAN
ANTARCTICA
Argentine Basin
Brazil Basin
Angola Basin
Cape Basin
Scotia Sea
Weddell Sea
Weddell Plain
Mid-Atlantic Ridge
Walvis Ridge
Rio Grande Rise
Atlantic-Indian Ridge
Atlantic-Indian Basin
Agulhas Basin
South Sandwich Trench
FALKLAND ISLANDS (to UK)
STANLEY
SCALE 1:3,000,000
SAINT HELENA (to UK)
JAMESTOWN
SCALE 1:750,000
TRISTAN DA CUNHA (to Saint Helena)
EDINBURGH
SCALE 1:750,000
Rocky breakwaters have been built along the coast of Ghana to protect local fishing boats from being destroyed by powerful Atlantic waves.

North Point
Porpoise Point
North East Bay
Sisters Peak
Clarence Bay
The Peak ▲859m
Wideawake ◆ + Airfield
South East Bay
South East Point
South West Bay
Portland Point
Mars Bay
Pillar Bay
South Point

Queen Mary's Peak Point ▲2060m
Sandy Point
Anchorstock Point
Longbluff
Cave Point
Stonybeach Bay
Stonyhill Point
South West Point

Sugar Loaf Point
Flagstaff Bay
The Haystack
Rupert's
Horse Pasture Point
Longwood
Diana's Peak ▲823m
Gill Point
Egg Island
Long Range Point
Sandy Bay
South West Point
Speery Island
Castle Rock Point

Jason Islands
Steeple Jason
Grand Jason
South Jason
Carcass Island
Sedge Island
Saunders Island
Keppel Island
Pebble Island
Cape Dolphin
Cape Bougainville
Cape Carysfort
Macbride Head
Cape Dolphin
Fox Bay
West Point Island
Westpoint Island
Roy Cove Settlement
Port Howard Settlement
Port San Carlos
Douglas Salvador
Port Louis
Berkeley Sound
Mengeary Point
Volunteer Point
Port San Carlos
San Carlos Settlement
Mount Pleasant
Darwin
Goose Green Settlement
Fitzroy
Bluff Cove
Fox Bay
North Arm
Adventure Sound
Port Stephens Settlement
Speedwell Island
Bleaker Island
George Island
Barren Island
Sea Lion Islands
Motley Island
Beaver Settlement
Weddell Island

INSET MAP KEY
POPULATION
100,000 to 500,000
50,000 to 100,000
10,000 to 50,000
below 10,000
ELEVATION
1000m / 3281ft
500m / 1640ft
250m / 820ft
100m / 328ft
sea level
OCEAN MAP KEY
SEA DEPTH
sea level
250m / 820ft
500m / 1640ft
1000m / 3281ft
2000m / 6562ft
3000m / 9843ft
5000m / 16,410ft

AFRICA

The world's second largest continent, Africa covers an area of 11,712,434 sq miles (30,335,000 sq km). It has 53 separate countries, including Madagascar in the Indian Ocean – the highest number of any continent.

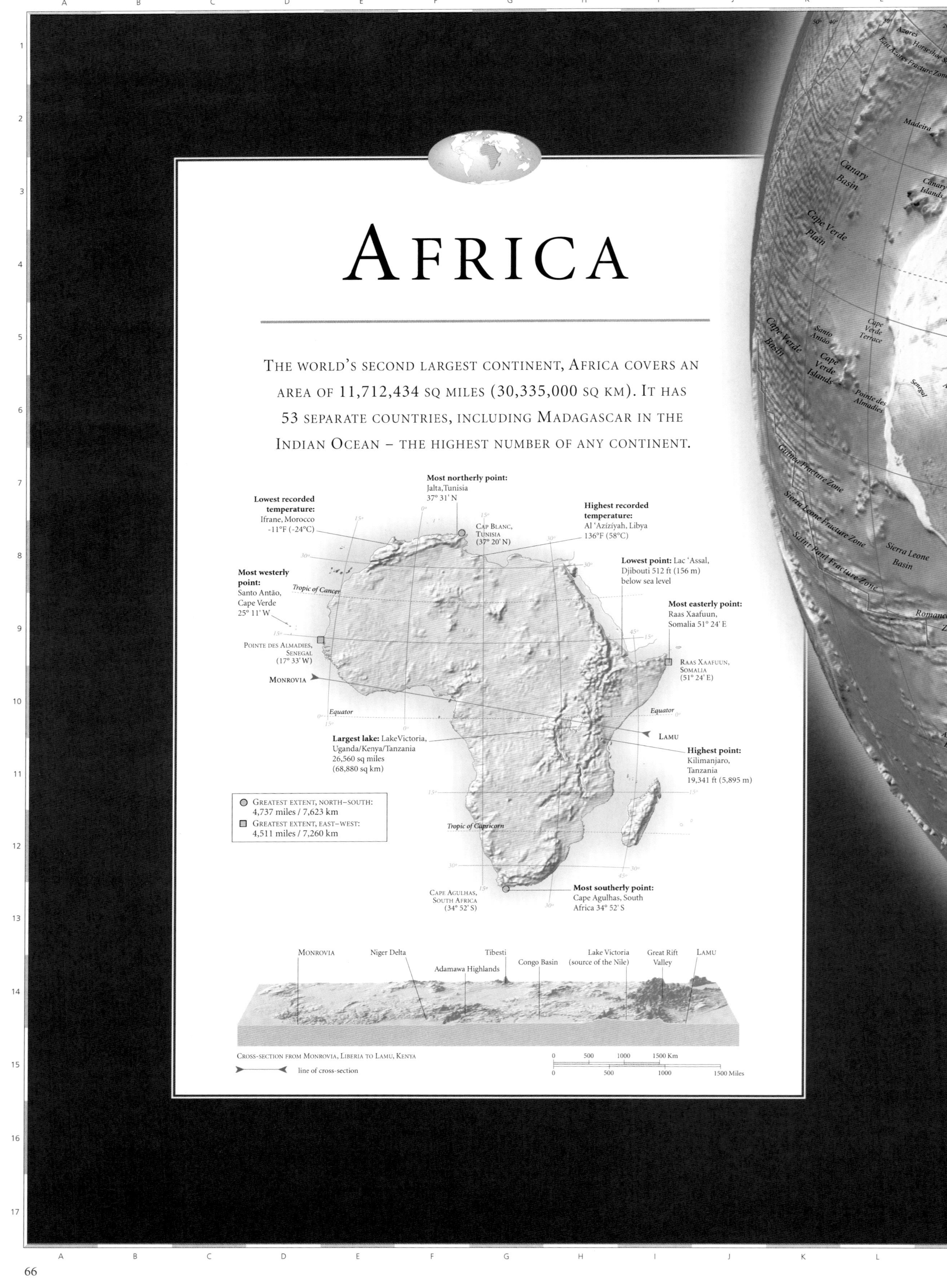

Most northerly point:
Jalta, Tunisia
37° 31' N
Lowest recorded temperature:
Ifrane, Morocco
-11°F (-24°C)
Cap Blanc, Tunisia (37° 20' N)
Highest recorded temperature:
Al 'Azízíyah, Libya
136°F (58°C)
Lowest point: Lac 'Assal, Djibouti 512 ft (156 m) below sea level
Most westerly point:
Santo Antão, Cape Verde
25° 11' W
Tropic of Cancer
Most easterly point:
Raas Xaafuun, Somalia 51° 24' E
Pointe des Almadies, Senegal (17° 33' W)
Raas Xaafuun, Somalia (51° 24' E)
Monrovia
Equator
Lamu
Largest lake: Lake Victoria, Uganda/Kenya/Tanzania
26,560 sq miles (68,880 sq km)
Highest point:
Kilimanjaro, Tanzania
19,341 ft (5,895 m)
Greatest extent, north–south: 4,737 miles / 7,623 km
Greatest extent, east–west: 4,511 miles / 7,260 km
Tropic of Capricorn
Cape Agulhas, South Africa (34° 52' S)
Most southerly point:
Cape Agulhas, South Africa 34° 52' S
Monrovia
Niger Delta
Tibesti
Adamawa Highlands
Congo Basin
Lake Victoria (source of the Nile)
Great Rift Valley
Lamu
Cross-section from Monrovia, Liberia to Lamu, Kenya
line of cross-section
0 500 1000 1500 Km
0 500 1000 1500 Miles
Azores
Madeira
Canary Basin
Canary Islands
Cape Verde Plain
Cape Verde Terrace
Santo Antão
Cape Verde Islands
Cape Verde Basin
Pointe des Almadies
Senegal
Guinea Fracture Zone
Sierra Leone Fracture Zone
Saint Paul Fracture Zone
Sierra Leone Basin

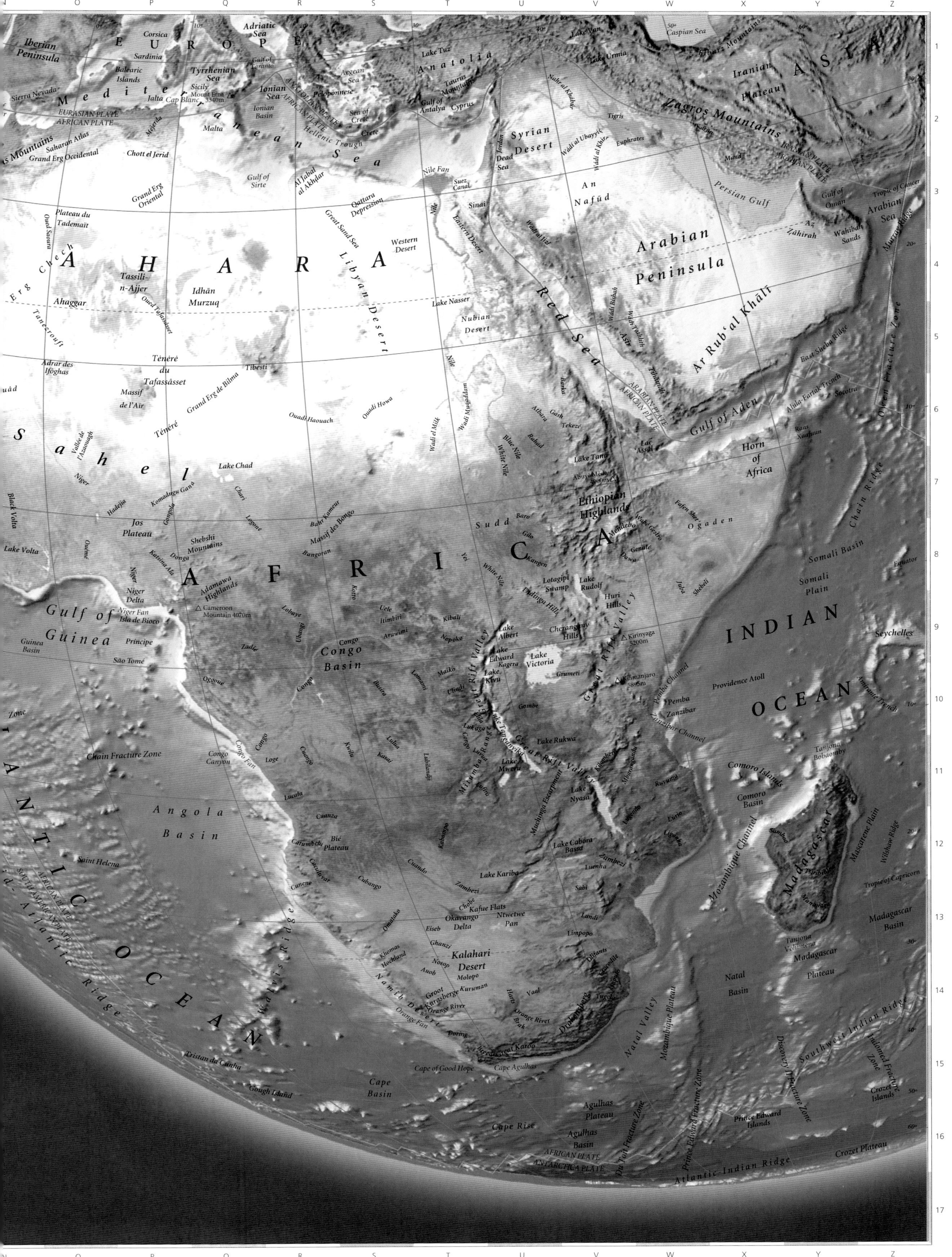

N O P Q R S T U V W X Y Z
1 2 3 4 5 6 7 8 9 10 11 12 13 14 15 16 17
Iberian Peninsula
Corsica
E U R O P E
Adriatic Sea
Sardinia
Balearic Islands
Tyrrhenian Sea
Gulf of Taranto
Sierra Nevada
Sicily
Mount Etna 3340m
Ialta
Cap Blanc
Ionian Sea
Ionian Basin
EURASIAN PLATE
AFRICAN PLATE
Malta
Mediterranean Sea
Aegean Sea
Peloponnese
Sea of Crete
Crete
Hellenic Trough
Lake Tuz
Anatolia
Taurus Mountains
Gulf of Antalya
Cyprus
Lake Van
Lake Urmia
Caspian Sea
Elburz Mountains
Iranian Plateau
ASIA
Zagros Mountains
Tigris
Euphrates
Syrian Desert
Jordan
Dead Sea
Saharan Atlas
Grand Erg Occidental
Chott el Jerid
Gulf of Sirte
Al Jabal al Akhdar
Nile Fan
Suez Canal
Sinai
An Nafūd
Persian Gulf
Gulf of Oman
Tropic of Cancer
Arabian Sea
Grand Erg Oriental
Qattara Depression
Plateau du Tademaït
Oued Saoura
Great Sand Sea
Western Desert
Nile
Eastern Desert
Arabian Peninsula
Az Zāhirah
Wahibah Sands
SAHARA
Erg Chech
Tassili-n-Ajjer
Idhān Murzuq
Ahaggar
Libyan Desert
Lake Nasser
Nubian Desert
Red Sea
Ar Rub' al Khālī
Tanezrouft
Ténéré du Tafassâsset
Tibesti
Adrar des Ifôghas
Massif de l'Aïr
Grand Erg de Bilma
Ténéré
Sahel
Ouadi Haouach
Ouadi Howa
Wadi al Milk
Wadi Muqaddam
ARABIAN PLATE
AFRICAN PLATE
Gulf of Aden
East Sheba Ridge
Socotra
Alula-Fartak Trench
Owen Fracture Zone
Horn of Africa
Lake Assal
Lake Tana
Ethiopian Highlands
Lake Chad
Niger
Black Volta
Lake Volta
Jos Plateau
Shebshi Mountains
Sudd
Ogaden
Somali Basin
Somali Plain
Chain Ridge
Equator
AFRICA
Adamawa Highlands
Niger Delta
Niger Fan
Isla de Bioco
Cameroon Mountain 4070m
Gulf of Guinea
Príncipe
São Tomé
Guinea Basin
Lotagipi Swamp
Lake Rudolf
Huri Hills
Lake Albert
Lake Edward
Lake Victoria
Lake Kivu
Kirinyaga 5200m
Kilimanjaro 5895m
Great Rift Valley
INDIAN OCEAN
Seychelles
Congo Basin
Congo
Pemba
Zanzibar
Zanzibar Channel
Providence Atoll
Amirante Trench
Lake Tanganyika
Lake Rukwa
Lake Mweru
Chain Fracture Zone
Congo Canyon
Congo Fan
Comoro Islands
Comoro Basin
Lake Nyasa
Angola Basin
Bié Plateau
Saint Helena
Lake Cabora Bassa
Zambezi
Lake Kariba
Mozambique Channel
Madagascar
Mascarene Plain
Tropic of Capricorn
ATLANTIC OCEAN
Okavango Delta
Ntwetwe Pan
Kalahari Desert
Limpopo
Namib Desert
Orange River
Madagascar Basin
Madagascar Plateau
Natal Basin
Walvis Ridge
Drakensberg
Natal Valley
Mozambique Plateau
Southwest Indian Ridge
Tristan da Cunha
Cape of Good Hope
Cape Agulhas
Cape Basin
Gough Island
Agulhas Plateau
Agulhas Basin
Cape Rise
Prince Edward Islands
Crozet Islands
Crozet Plateau
AFRICAN PLATE
ANTARCTICA PLATE
Atlantic-Indian Ridge

A B C D E F G H I J K L M

PHYSICAL AFRICA

THE STRUCTURE OF AFRICA was dramatically influenced by the break up of the supercontinent Gondwanaland about 160 million years ago and, more recently, rifting and hot spot activity. Today, much of Africa is remote from active plate boundaries and comprises a series of extensive plateaus and deep basins, which influence the drainage patterns of major rivers. The relief rises to the east, where volcanic uplands and vast lakes mark the Great Rift Valley. In the far north and south sedimentary rocks have been folded to form the Atlas Mountains and the Great Karoo.

EAST AFRICA

THE GREAT RIFT VALLEY is the most striking feature of this region, running for 4,475 miles (7,200 km) from Lake Nyasa to the Red Sea. North of Lake Nyasa it splits into two arms and encloses an interior plateau which contains Lake Victoria. A number of elongated lakes and volcanoes lie along the fault lines. To the west lies the Congo Basin, a vast, shallow depression, which rises to form an almost circular rim of highlands.

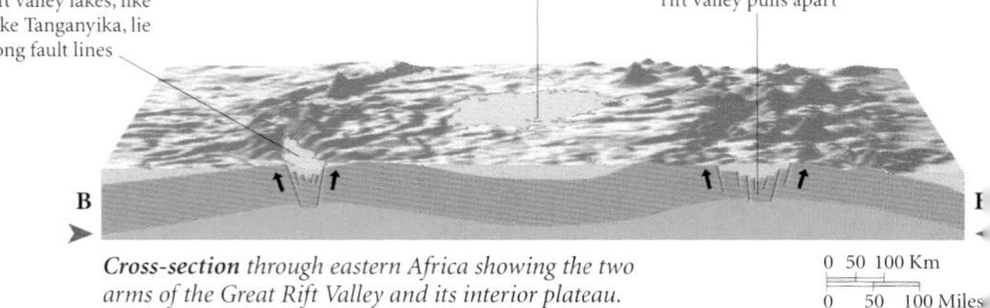
Rift valley lakes, like Lake Tanganyika, lie along fault lines
Lake Victoria
Extensive faulting occurs as rift valley pulls apart
B
B
0 50 100 Km
0 50 100 Miles

***Cross-section** through eastern Africa showing the two arms of the Great Rift Valley and its interior plateau.*

NORTHERN AFRICA

NORTHERN AFRICA COMPRISES a system of basins and plateaus. The Tibesti and Ahaggar are volcanic uplands, whose uplift has been matched by subsidence within large surrounding basins. Many of the basins have been infilled with sand and gravel, creating the vast Saharan lands. The Atlas Mountains in the north were formed by convergence of the African and Eurasian plates.

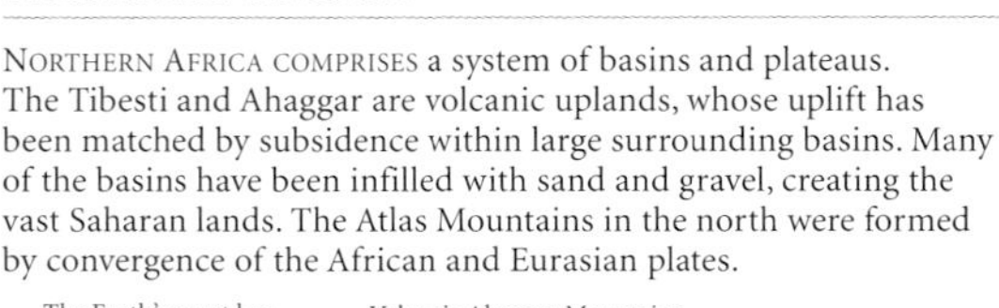
The Earth's crust has been warped to form the Taoudenni Basin
Volcanic Ahaggar Mountains, formed by rising magma from a hot spot
Lake Chad lies in a sand-filled basin
A
A

***Section** across northern Africa showing infilled basins and uplifted plateaus.*

0 250 500 Km
0 250 500 Miles

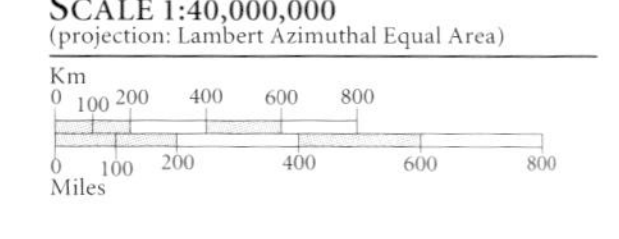
SCALE 1:40,000,000
(projection: Lambert Azimuthal Equal Area)
Km 0 100 200 400 600 800
Miles 0 100 200 400 600 800

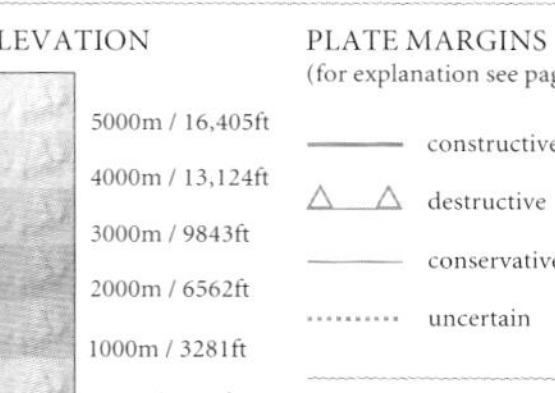
MAP KEY
ELEVATION
5000m / 16,405ft
4000m / 13,124ft
3000m / 9843ft
2000m / 6562ft
1000m / 3281ft
500m / 1640ft
250m / 820ft
100m / 328ft
sea level
below sea level
PLATE MARGINS
(for explanation see page xiv)
constructive
destructive
conservative
uncertain
line of cross-section

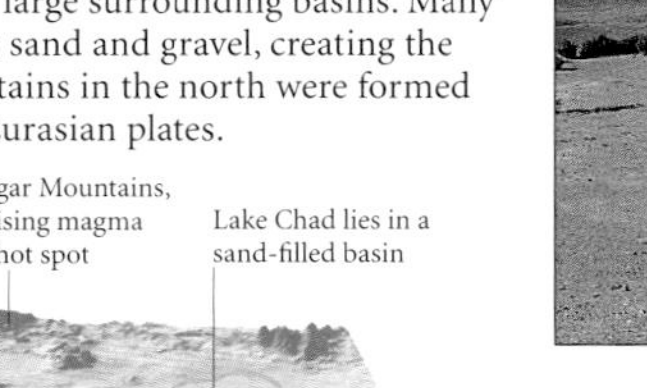

Mediterranean Sea
EURASIAN PLATE
AFRICAN PLATE
ANATOLIAN PLATE
ARABIAN PLATE
Atlas Mountains
Chott el Jerid
Gulf of Sirte
Grand Erg Occidental
Grand Erg Oriental
Erg Iguidi
Erg Chech
Qattara Depression
Nile Delta
Great Sand Sea
Western Desert
Libyan Desert
Eastern Desert
Red Sea
ASIA
ATLANTIC OCEAN
Ahaggar
Tibesti
Sahara
Lake Nasser
Nubian Desert
Cape Verde Islands
Senegal
Taoudenni Basin
Niger
Massif de l'Aïr
Ténéré
Sahel
White Volta
Blue Nile
White Nile
Lake Tana
Gulf of Aden
Horn of Africa
Ethiopian Highlands
Lake Volta
Benue
Sudd
Massif des Bongo
Grain Coast
Ivory Coast
Gold Coast
Slave Coast
Bight of Benin
Niger Delta
Adamawa Highlands
Cameroon Mountain 4070m
Ubangi
Shebeli
Lake Rudolf
Juba
Gulf of Guinea
São Tomé
Congo
Congo Basin
Great Rift Valley
Lake Albert
Lake Victoria
Kilimanjaro 5895m
Seychelles
Pemba Island
Zanzibar
Lake Tanganyika
Mitumba Mountains
Bié Plateau
Lake Nyasa
Comoro Islands
Zambezi
Mozambique Channel
Madagascar
Okavango Delta
Kalahari Basin
Kalahari Desert
Namib Desert
Limpopo
Mauritius
Réunion
INDIAN OCEAN
Orange River
Drakensberg
Great Karoo
Cape of Good Hope
C
C

SOUTHERN AFRICA

THE GREAT ESCARPMENT marks the southern boundary of Africa's basement rock and includes the Drakensberg range. It was uplifted when Gondwanaland fragmented about 160 million years ago and it has gradually been eroded back from the coast. To the north, the relief drops steadily, forming the Kalahari Basin. In the far south are the fold mountains of the Great Karoo.

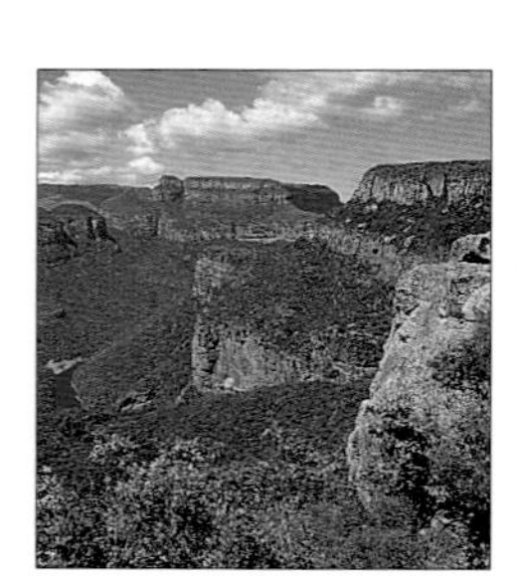
Kalahari Basin, covered with the sandy plains of the Kalahari Desert
Boundary of the Great Escarpment
Uplift of the basement rock created a raised plateau
Drakensberg
C
C

***Cross-section** through southern Africa showing the boundary of the Great Escarpment.*

0 100 200 Km
0 100 200 Miles

A B C D E F J K L M

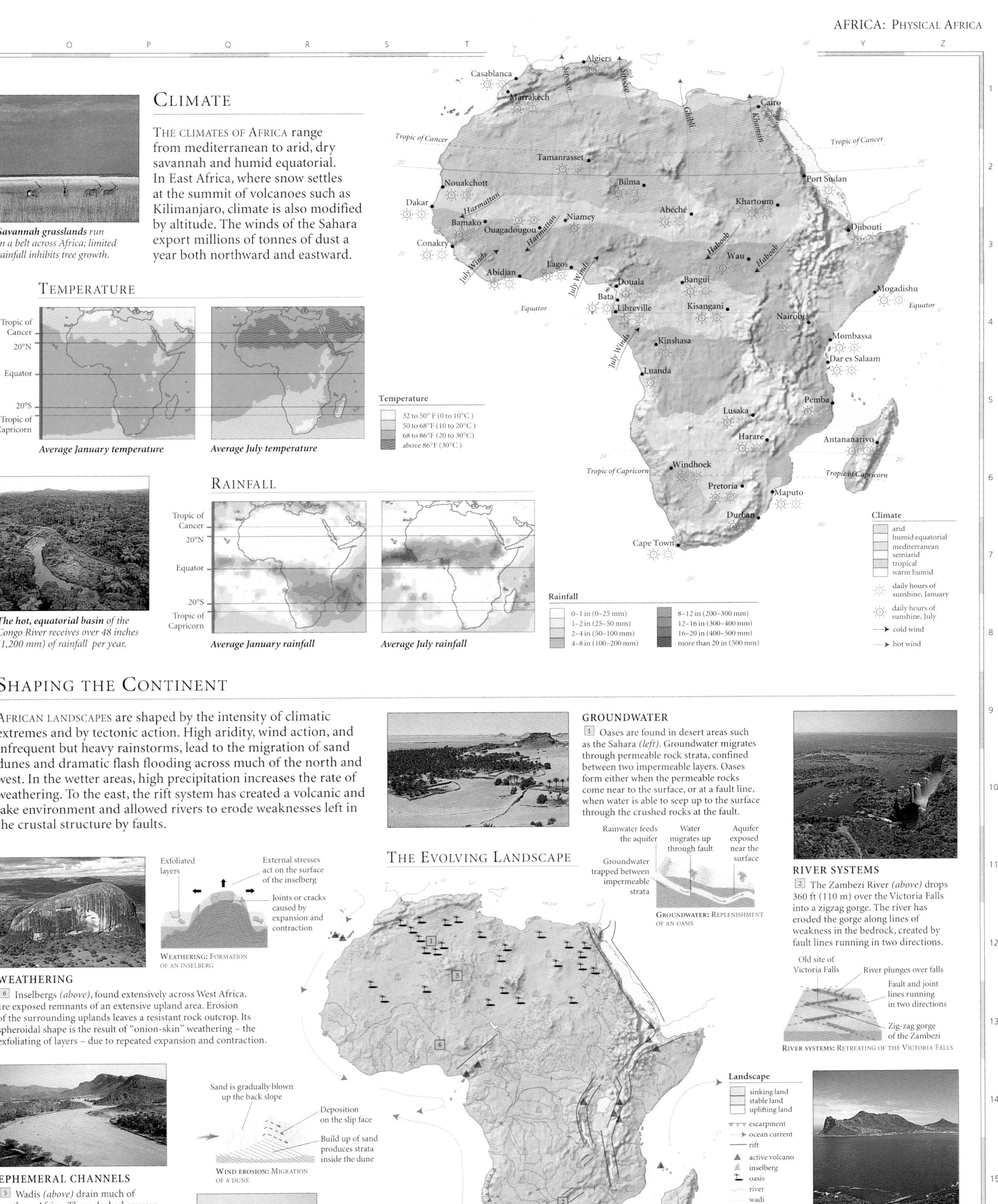

Casablanca
Algiers
Marrakech
Sirocco
Sirocco
Cairo
Ghibli
Khamsin
Tropic of Cancer
Tropic of Cancer
Tamanrasset
Nouakchott
Bilma
Port Sudan
Dakar
Harmattan
Khartoum
Abéché
Bamako
Niamey
Harmattan
Ouagadougou
Djibouti
Conakry
Haboob
Haboob
Wau
July Winds
Lagos
Abidjan
July Winds
Douala
Bangui
Bata
Mogadishu
Equator
Libreville
Kisangani
Equator
Nairobi
Kinshasa
Mombassa
July Winds
Dar es Salaam
Luanda
Pemba
Lusaka
Harare
Antananarivo
Windhoek
Tropic of Capricorn
Tropic of Capricorn
Pretoria
Maputo
Durban
Cape Town
Climate
arid
humid equatorial
mediterranean
semiarid
tropical
warm humid
daily hours of sunshine, January
daily hours of sunshine, July
cold wind
hot wind
Tropic of Cancer
20°N
Equator
20°S
Tropic of Capricorn
Temperature
32 to 50° F (0 to 10°C)
50 to 68°F (10 to 20°C)
68 to 86°F (20 to 30°C)
above 86°F (30°C)
Average January temperature
Average July temperature
Tropic of Cancer
20°N
Equator
20°S
Tropic of Capricorn
Rainfall
0–1 in (0–25 mm)
1–2 in (25–50 mm)
2–4 in (50–100 mm)
4–8 in (100–200 mm)
8–12 in (200–300 mm)
12–16 in (300–400 mm)
16–20 in (400–500 mm)
more than 20 in (500 mm)
Average January rainfall
Average July rainfall

Climate

Savannah grasslands run in a belt across Africa; limited rainfall inhibits tree growth.

THE CLIMATES OF AFRICA range from mediterranean to arid, dry savannah and humid equatorial. In East Africa, where snow settles at the summit of volcanoes such as Kilimanjaro, climate is also modified by altitude. The winds of the Sahara export millions of tonnes of dust a year both northward and eastward.

Temperature

Average January temperature

Average July temperature

Rainfall

The hot, equatorial basin of the Congo River receives over 48 inches (1,200 mm) of rainfall per year.

Average January rainfall

Average July rainfall

Shaping the Continent

AFRICAN LANDSCAPES are shaped by the intensity of climatic extremes and by tectonic action. High aridity, wind action, and infrequent but heavy rainstorms, lead to the migration of sand dunes and dramatic flash flooding across much of the north and west. In the wetter areas, high precipitation increases the rate of weathering. To the east, the rift system has created a volcanic and lake environment and allowed rivers to erode weaknesses left in the crustal structure by faults.

GROUNDWATER

1 Oases are found in desert areas such as the Sahara *(left)*. Groundwater migrates through permeable rock strata, confined between two impermeable layers. Oases form either when the permeable rocks come near to the surface, or at a fault line, when water is able to seep up to the surface through the crushed rocks at the fault.

Rainwater feeds the aquifer
Water migrates up through fault
Aquifer exposed near the surface
Groundwater trapped between impermeable strata

GROUNDWATER: REPLENISHMENT OF AN OASIS

RIVER SYSTEMS

2 The Zambezi River *(above)* drops 360 ft (110 m) over the Victoria Falls into a zigzag gorge. The river has eroded the gorge along lines of weakness in the bedrock, created by fault lines running in two directions.

Old site of Victoria Falls
River plunges over falls
Fault and joint lines running in two directions
Zig-zag gorge of the Zambezi

RIVER SYSTEMS: RETREATING OF THE VICTORIA FALLS

The Evolving Landscape

Landscape
sinking land
stable land
uplifting land
escarpment
ocean current
rift
active volcano
inselberg
oasis
river
wadi
waterfall

Exfoliated layers
External stresses act on the surface of the inselberg
Joints or cracks caused by expansion and contraction

WEATHERING: FORMATION OF AN INSELBERG

WEATHERING

6 Inselbergs *(above)*, found extensively across West Africa, are exposed remnants of an extensive upland area. Erosion of the surrounding uplands leaves a resistant rock outcrop. Its spheroidal shape is the result of "onion-skin" weathering – the exfoliating of layers – due to repeated expansion and contraction.

Sand is gradually blown up the back slope
Deposition on the slip face
Build up of sand produces strata inside the dune

WIND EROSION: MIGRATION OF A DUNE

EPHEMERAL CHANNELS

5 Wadis *(above)* drain much of northern Africa. These drybed courses are flooded only after infrequent, but intense, storms in the uplands cause water to surge along their channels.

Heavy rainfall runs off mountains
Water collects and floods the dry channel

EPHEMERAL CHANNELS: FLASH FLOODING OF A WADI

WIND EROSION

4 Dunes like this in the Namib Desert *(left)* are wind-blown accumulations of sand, which slowly migrate. Wind action moves sand up the shallow back slope; when the sand reaches the crest of the dune it is deposited on the slip face.

Waves refracting
Wave energy dispersed in the bay
Force of waves concentrates on the headland
The sea bed is deeper opposite the bay than at the headland

COASTAL PROCESSES: EROSION OF A BAY

COASTAL PROCESSES

3 Houtbaai *(above)*, in southern Africa, is constantly being modified by wave action. As waves approach the indented coastline, they reach the shallow water of the headland, slowing down and reducing in length. This causes them to bend or refract, concentrating their erosive force at the headlands.

Political Africa

The political map of modern Africa only emerged following the end of the Second World War. Over the next half-century, all of the countries formerly controlled by European powers gained independence from their colonial rulers – only Liberia and Ethiopia were never colonized. The postcolonial era has not been an easy period for many countries, but there have been moves toward multiparty democracy in much of West Africa, and in Zambia, Tanzania, and Kenya. In South Africa, democratic elections replaced the internationally-condemned apartheid system only in 1994. Other countries have still to find political stability; corruption in government, and ethnic tensions are serious problems. National infrastructures, based on the colonial transportation systems built to exploit Africa's resources, are often inappropriate for independent economic development.

Berber, Arabic, Tuareg, Fulani, Mandingo, Mosi, Teda, Hausa, Kanuri, Akan, Yoruba, Ewe, Ibo, Azande, Dinka, Beja, Tigrai, Amhara, Galla, Somali, Masai, Swahili, Bantu, Malagasy, San, Khoi, Afrikaans

Language groups
- Afro-Asiatic (Hamito-Semitic)
- Niger-Congo
- Nilo-Saharan
- Khoisan
- Indo-European
- Austronesian

Languages

Three major world languages act as *lingua francas* across the African continent: Arabic in North Africa; English in southern and eastern Africa and Nigeria; and French in Central and West Africa, and in Madagascar. A huge number of African languages are spoken as well – over 2,000 have been recorded, with more than 400 in Nigeria alone – reflecting the continuing importance of traditional cultures and values. In the north of the continent, the extensive use of Arabic reflects Middle Eastern influences while Bantu is widely-spoken across much of southern Africa.

Official African languages

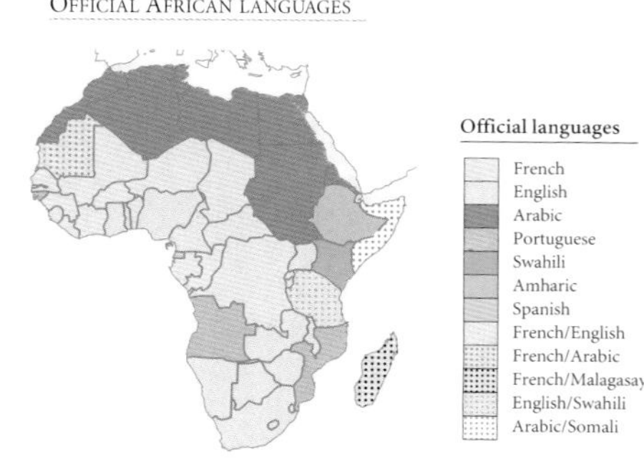
Official languages
French
English
Arabic
Portuguese
Swahili
Amharic
Spanish
French/English
French/Arabic
French/Malagasy
English/Swahili
Arabic/Somali

Madeira (to Portugal)
Canary Islands (to Spain)
MOROCCO
Agadir
LAÂYOUNE
Western Sahara (Occupied by Morocco)
Tropic of Cancer
CAPE VERDE
PRAIA
MAURITANIA
NOUAKCHOTT
Senegal
SENEGAL
DAKAR
Kaolack
GAMBIA
BANJUL
GUINEA-BISSAU
BISSAU
BAMAKO
GUINEA
CONAKRY
FREETOWN
Koidu
SIERRA LEONE
YAMOUSSOUKRO
MONROVIA
LIBERIA

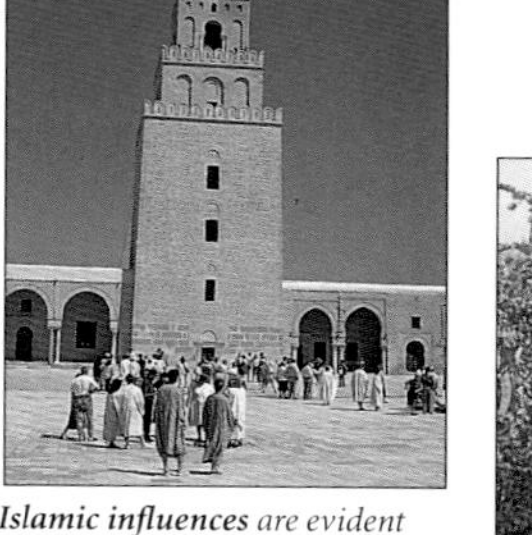

Islamic influences are evident throughout North Africa. The Great Mosque at Kairouan, Tunisia, is Africa's holiest Islamic place.

In northeastern Nigeria, people speak Kanuri – a dialect of the Saharan language group.

Transportation

African railroads were built to aid the exploitation of natural resources, and most offer passage only from the interior to the coastal cities, leaving large parts of the continent untouched – five landlocked countries have no railroads at all. The Congo, Nile, and Niger River networks offer limited access to land within the continental interior, but have a number of waterfalls and cataracts which prevent navigation from the sea. Many roads were developed in the 1960s and 1970s, but economic difficulties are making the maintenance and expansion of the networks difficult.

South Africa has the largest concentration of railroads in Africa. Over 20,000 miles (32,000 km) of routes have been built since 1870.

Traditional means of transportation, such as the camel, are still widely used across the less accessible parts of Africa.

The Congo River, though not suitable for river transportation along its entire length, forms a vital link for people and goods in its navigable inland reaches.

Ceuta (to Spain)
Tanger
Rabat
Casablanca
Algiers
Skikda
Tunis
Oran
Agadir
Tripoli
Alexandria
Port Said
Suez Canal
Cairo
Suez
Aswân
Tamanrasset
Nouâdhibou
Nouakchott
Wadi Halfa
Port Sudan
Agadez
Dakar
Banjul
Bissau
Bamako
Niamey
Ouagadougou
Kano
Maiduguri
Ndjamena
Nyala
Massawa
Khartoum
Assab
Djibouti
Conakry
Freetown
Monrovia
Abidjan
Accra
Cotonou
Lomé
Lagos
Addis Ababa
Warri
Douala
Malabo
Bangui
Yaoundé
Libreville
Port-Gentil
Kisangani
Kampala
Mogadishu
Nairobi
Bukavu
Brazzaville
Kinshasa
Pointe-Noire
Matadi
Kananga
Kalemie
Mombasa
Dodoma
Dar es Salaam
Luanda
Mbeya
Lobito
Lubumbashi
Namibe
Lusaka
Nampula
Livingstone
Harare
Tsumeb
Bulawayo
Beira
Antananarivo
Toamasina
Walvis Bay
Windhoek
Pretoria
Keetmanshoop
Johannesburg
Maputo
Durban
Cape Town
Port Elizabeth
Transportation
major roads and highways
major railroads
major canal
international borders
transportation intersections
international airports
major ports

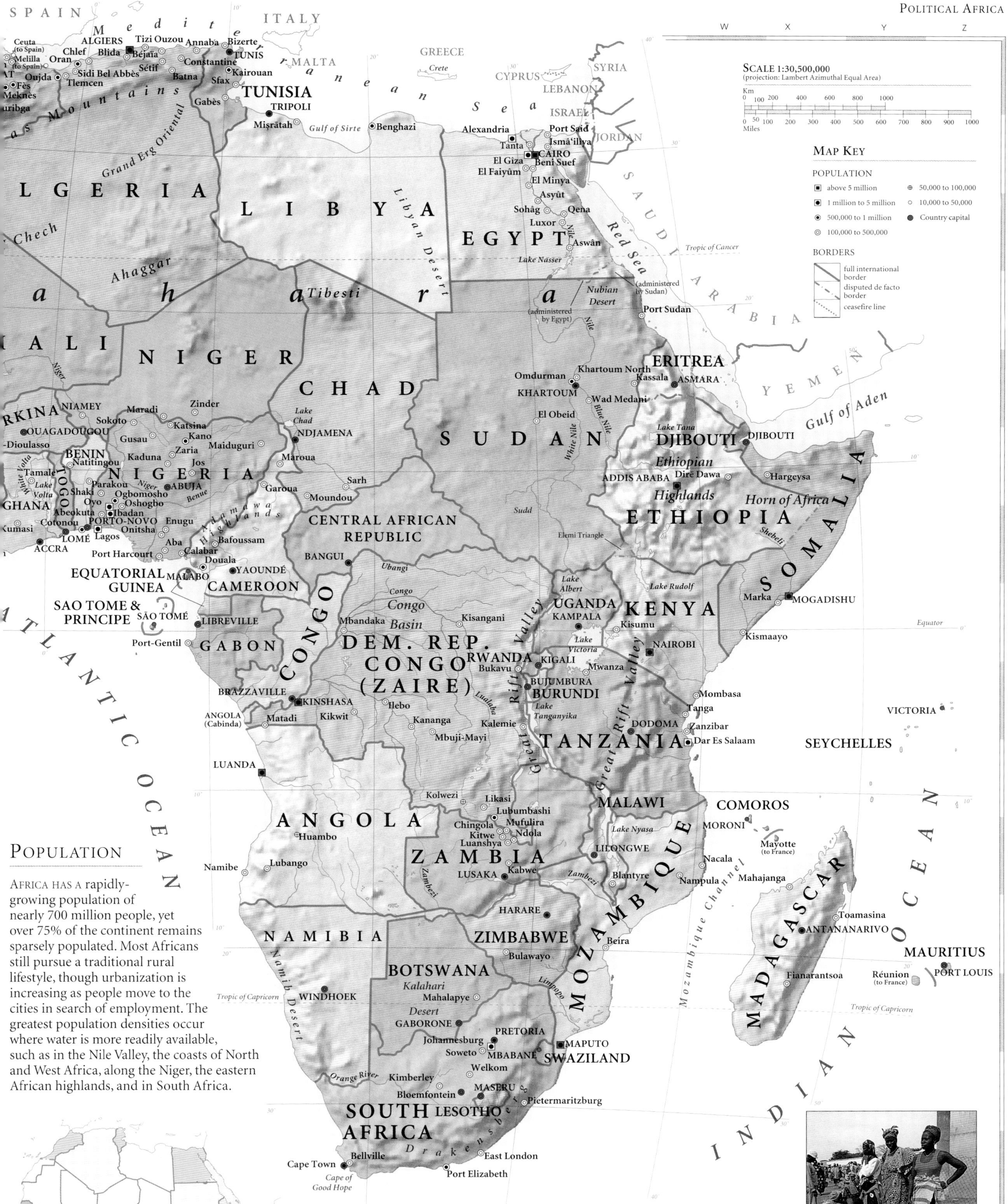

SCALE 1:30,500,000
(projection: Lambert Azimuthal Equal Area)

MAP KEY

POPULATION

- above 5 million
- 1 million to 5 million
- 500,000 to 1 million
- 100,000 to 500,000
- 50,000 to 100,000
- 10,000 to 50,000
- Country capital

BORDERS

- full international border
- disputed de facto border
- ceasefire line

POPULATION

AFRICA HAS A rapidly-growing population of nearly 700 million people, yet over 75% of the continent remains sparsely populated. Most Africans still pursue a traditional rural lifestyle, though urbanization is increasing as people move to the cities in search of employment. The greatest population densities occur where water is more readily available, such as in the Nile Valley, the coasts of North and West Africa, along the Niger, the eastern African highlands, and in South Africa.

Population density (people per sq mile)

- below 130
- 130–259
- 260–379
- 380–519
- 520–780
- above 780

***A thin layer of smog** blankets the dusty streets of Cairo, Africa's most populous city and home to over six million people. In the 1990s Cairo grew at a rate of about 1,500 people per day.*

***Thriving street markets** in Gambia's capital, Banjul, trade a variety of locally-grown produce. Africa's population is still predominantly rural.*

African Resources

The economies of most African countries are dominated by subsistence and cash crop agriculture, with limited industrialization. Manufacturing is largely confined to South Africa. Many countries depend on a single resource, such as copper or gold, or a cash crop, such as coffee, for export income, which can leave them vulnerable to fluctuations in world commodity prices. In order to diversify their economies and develop a wider industrial base, investment from overseas is being actively sought by many African governments.

Industry

Many African industries concentrate on the extraction and processing of raw materials. These include the oil industry, food processing, mining, and textile production. South Africa accounts for over half of the continent's industrial output with much of the remainder coming from the countries along the northern coast. Over 60% of Africa's workforce is employed in agriculture.

The unspoiled natural splendor of wildlife reserves, like the Serengeti National Park in Tanzania, attract tourists to Africa from around the globe. The tourist industry in Kenya and Tanzania is particularly well developed, where it accounts for almost 10% of GNP.

Standard of Living

Since the 1960s most countries in Africa have seen significant improvements in life expectancy, healthcare and education. However, 18 of the 20 most deprived countries in the world are African, and the continent as a whole lies well behind the rest of the world in terms of meeting many basic human needs.

Standard of Living
(UN Human Development Index)

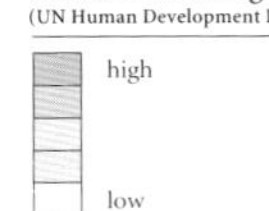

high

low

GNP per capita (US$)

- 0–199
- 200–399
- 400–599
- 600–899
- 900–1999
- 2000+

Industry

- brewing
- car/vehicle manufacture
- cement
- chemicals
- coffee processing
- electronics
- engineering
- finance
- fish processing
- food processing
- iron & steel
- mining
- palm oil processing
- peanut processing
- pharmaceuticals
- rice milling
- shipbuilding
- sugar processing
- tea processing
- textiles
- timber processing
- tobacco processing
- coal
- oil
- gas
- industrial cities
- major industrial areas

***The discovery of oil** in the swampy Niger Delta during the 1960s made Nigeria one of Africa's richer nations. As world oil prices fell in the 1980s, the Nigerian economy faltered.*

***Exotic rugs** and brightly-colored textiles are sold in a street market along the banks of the Nile River in Luxor, Egypt.*

***The Rössing uranium** mines in Namibia are the largest in the world. Africa and the US produce over half the world's uranium ore, used to fuel nuclear power plants. Elsewhere, South Africa and Niger also mine uranium on a large scale.*

Environmental Issues

One of Africa's most serious environmental problems occurs in marginal areas such as the Sahel where scrub and forest clearance, often for cooking fuel, combined with overgrazing, are causing desertification. Game reserves in southern and eastern Africa have helped to preserve many endangered animals, although the needs of growing populations have led to conflict over land use, and poaching is a serious problem.

Environmental Issues

- national parks
- tropical forest
- forest destroyed
- desert
- desertification
- polluted rivers
- radioactive contamination
- marine pollution
- heavy marine pollution
- poor urban air quality

The Sahel's delicate natural equilibrium is easily destroyed by the clearing of vegetation, drought, and overgrazing. This causes the Sahara to advance south, engulfing the savannah grasslands.

Mineral Resources

Africa's ancient plateaus contain some of the world's most substantial reserves of precious stones and metals. About 30% of the world's gold is mined in South Africa; Zambia has great copper deposits; and diamonds are mined in Botswana, Dem. Rep. Congo (Zaire), and South Africa. Oil has brought great economic benefits to Algeria, Libya, and Nigeria.

Mineral Resources

- oil field
- gas field
- coal field
- bauxite
- copper
- diamonds
- gold
- iron
- phosphates
- tin
- uranium

***North and West Africa** have large deposits of white phosphate minerals, which are used in making fertilizers. Morocco, Senegal, and Tunisia are the continent's leading producers.*

***Workers on a tea plantation** gather one of Africa's most important cash crops, providing a valuable source of income. Coffee, rubber, bananas, cotton, and cocoa are also widely grown as cash crops.*

***Surrounded by desert,** the fertile floodplains of the Nile Valley and Delta have been extensively irrigated, farmed, and settled since 3,000 BC.*

Using the Land and Sea

- cropland
- desert
- forest
- pasture
- wetland
- major conurbations
- cattle
- goats
- cereals
- sheep
- bananas
- corn (maize)
- citrus fruits
- cocoa
- cotton
- coffee
- dates
- fishing
- fruit
- oil palms
- olives
- peanuts
- rice
- rubber
- shellfish
- sugar cane
- tea
- tobacco
- vineyards
- wheat

Using the Land and Sea

Some of Africa's most productive agricultural land is found in the eastern volcanic uplands, where fertile soils support a wide range of valuable export crops including vegetables, tea, and coffee. The most widely-grown grain is corn and peanuts are particularly important in West Africa. Without intensive irrigation, cultivation is not possible in desert regions and unreliable rainfall in other areas limits crop production. Pastoral herding is most commonly found in these marginal lands. Substantial local fishing industries are found along coasts and in vast lakes such as Lake Nyasa and Lake Victoria.

North Africa

Algeria, Egypt, Libya, Morocco, Tunisia, Western Sahara

Fringed by the Mediterranean along the northern coast and by the arid Sahara in the south, North Africa reflects the influence of many invaders, both European and, most importantly, Arab, giving the region an almost universal Islamic flavor and a common Arabic language. The countries lying to the west of Egypt are often referred to as the Maghreb, an Arabic term for "west." Today, Morocco and Tunisia exploit their culture and landscape for tourism, while rich oil and gas deposits aid development in Libya and Algeria, despite political turmoil. Egypt, with its fertile, Nile-watered agricultural land and varied industrial base, is the most populous nation.

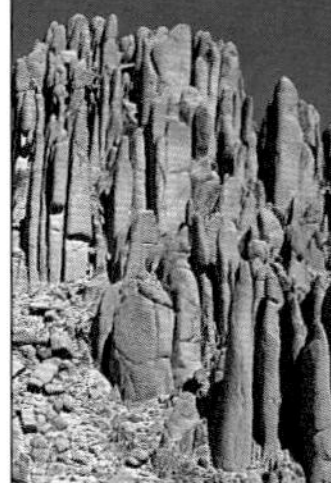

***These rock piles** in Algeria's Ahaggar Mountains are the result of weathering caused by extremes of temperature. Great cracks or joints appear in the rocks, which are then worn and smoothed by the wind.*

The Landscape

The Atlas Mountains, which extend across much of Morocco, northern Algeria, and Tunisia, are part of the fold mountain system which also runs through much of southern Europe. They recede to the south and east, becoming a steppe landscape before meeting the Sahara desert which covers more than 90% of the region. The sediments of the Sahara overlie an ancient plateau of crystalline rock, some of which is more than four billion years old.

Map Key

POPULATION
- above 5 million
- 1 million to 5 million
- 500,000 to 1 million
- 100,000 to 500,000
- 50,000 to 100,000
- 10,000 to 50,000
- below 10,000

ELEVATION
- 4000m / 13,124ft
- 3000m / 9843ft
- 2000m / 6562ft
- 1000m / 3281ft
- 500m / 1640ft
- 250m / 820ft
- 100m / 328ft
- sea level

SCALE 1:12,250,000
(projection: Lambert Azimuthal Equal Area)

The town of Tiznit, Morocco, lies in an oasis in the desert. Crops and trees grow on the fertile land surrounding the town.

***The Grand Erg Occidental** is one of Algeria's great Saharan sand seas. Wind force and direction determines the nature of landforms such as the linear or seif dunes in the foreground.*

Using the Land and Sea

Sheltered valleys in the Atlas Mountains, the Nile Valley and Delta, and the Mediterranean coast are the main sources of good farming land. A wide variety of valuable crops including cereals, rice, and cotton, and woods such as cedar and cork, are grown. Typical Mediterranean crops such as olives, figs, dates, and citrus fruits also thrive in these areas. The Nile Valley is particularly fertile, and most of Egypt's population lives close to the river. Elsewhere, irrigation is essential to improve crop yields on the desert margins.

Land use and agricultural distribution
- goats
- sheep
- cereals
- citrus fruits
- cork
- cotton
- dates
- fishing
- olives
- vineyards
- capital cities
- major towns
- pasture
- cropland
- forest
- desert

The Urban/Rural Population Divide

urban 50% / rural 50%

Population Density
62 people per sq mile (24 people per sq km)

Total Land Area
2,215,020 sq miles (5,738,394 sq km)

***Many North African nomads,** such as the Bedouin, maintain a traditional pastoral lifestyle on the desert fringes, moving their herds of sheep, goats, and camels from place to place – crossing country borders in order to find sufficient grazing land.*

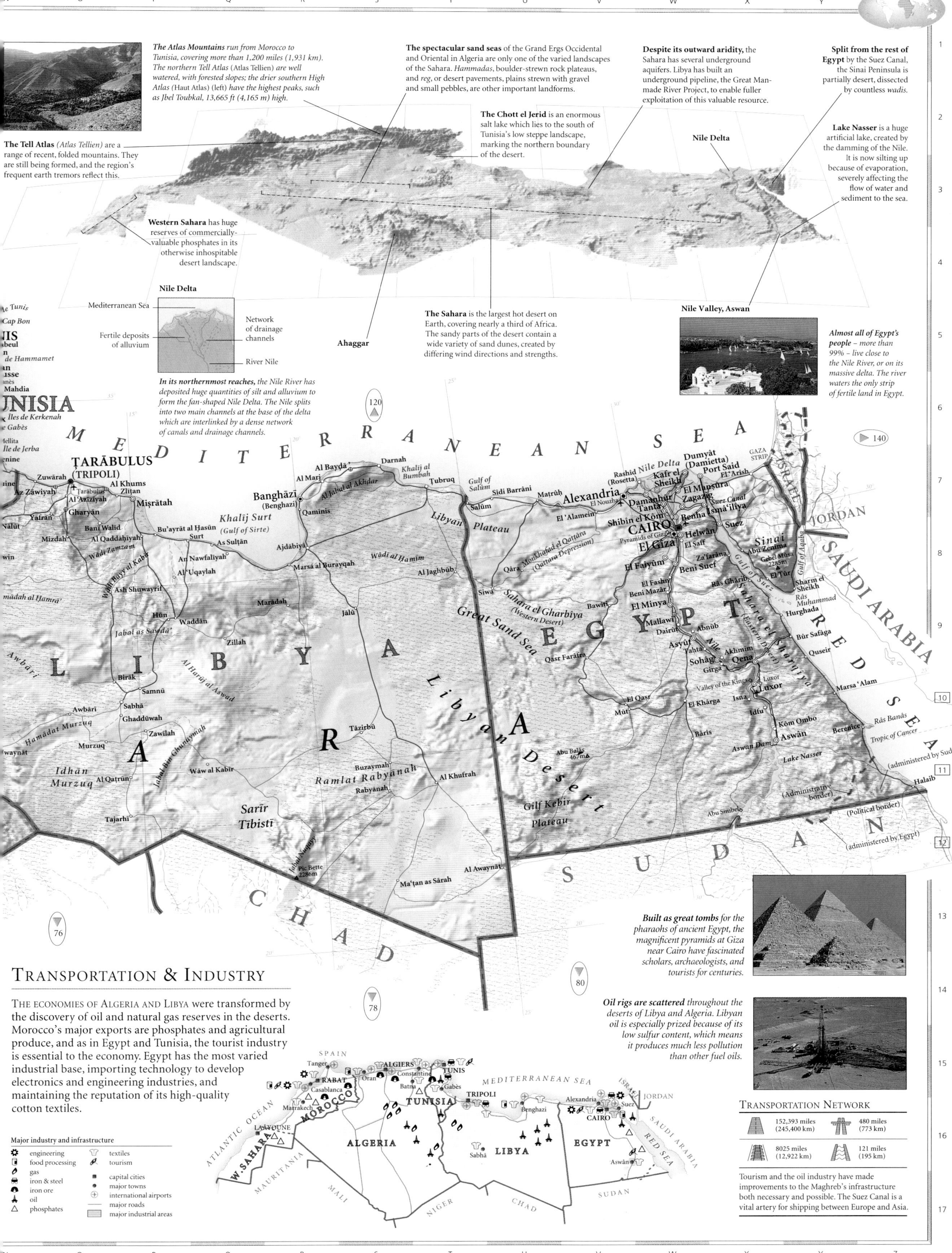
Nile Delta
Mediterranean Sea
Fertile deposits of alluvium
Network of drainage channels
River Nile
Ahaggar
Nile Valley, Aswan
MEDITERRANEAN SEA
ṬARĀBULUS (TRIPOLI)
Banghāzī (Benghazi)
Khalij Surt (Gulf of Sirte)
Alexandria
CAIRO
El Giza
Suez Canal
Sinai
LIBYA
EGYPT
Great Sand Sea
Libyan Desert
Libyan Plateau
Sahara el Gharbîya (Western Desert)
Sahara el Sharqîya (Eastern Desert)
Lake Nasser
Aswân
Luxor
RED SEA
SAUDI ARABIA
JORDAN
ISRAEL
SUDAN
CHAD
Tropic of Cancer
Ramlat Rabyānah
Sarīr Tibistī
Gilf Kebir Plateau
Pic Bette 2286m
Major industry and infrastructure
engineering
food processing
gas
iron & steel
iron ore
oil
phosphates
textiles
tourism
capital cities
major towns
international airports
major roads
major industrial areas

The Atlas Mountains *run from Morocco to Tunisia, covering more than 1,200 miles (1,931 km). The northern Tell Atlas (*Atlas Tellien*) are well watered, with forested slopes; the drier southern High Atlas (*Haut Atlas*) (left) have the highest peaks, such as Jbel Toubkal, 13,665 ft (4,165 m) high.*

The spectacular sand seas of the Grand Ergs Occidental and Oriental in Algeria are only one of the varied landscapes of the Sahara. *Hammadas*, boulder-strewn rock plateaus, and *reg*, or desert pavements, plains strewn with gravel and small pebbles, are other important landforms.

Despite its outward aridity, the Sahara has several underground aquifers. Libya has built an underground pipeline, the Great Man-made River Project, to enable fuller exploitation of this valuable resource.

Split from the rest of Egypt by the Suez Canal, the Sinai Peninsula is partially desert, dissected by countless *wadis*.

The Tell Atlas *(Atlas Tellien)* are a range of recent, folded mountains. They are still being formed, and the region's frequent earth tremors reflect this.

The Chott el Jerid is an enormous salt lake which lies to the south of Tunisia's low steppe landscape, marking the northern boundary of the desert.

Lake Nasser is a huge artificial lake, created by the damming of the Nile. It is now silting up because of evaporation, severely affecting the flow of water and sediment to the sea.

Western Sahara has huge reserves of commercially-valuable phosphates in its otherwise inhospitable desert landscape.

The Sahara is the largest hot desert on Earth, covering nearly a third of Africa. The sandy parts of the desert contain a wide variety of sand dunes, created by differing wind directions and strengths.

In its northernmost reaches, *the Nile River has deposited huge quantities of silt and alluvium to form the fan-shaped Nile Delta. The Nile splits into two main channels at the base of the delta which are interlinked by a dense network of canals and drainage channels.*

Almost all of Egypt's people *– more than 99% – live close to the Nile River, or on its massive delta. The river waters the only strip of fertile land in Egypt.*

Built as great tombs *for the pharaohs of ancient Egypt, the magnificent pyramids at Giza near Cairo have fascinated scholars, archaeologists, and tourists for centuries.*

Oil rigs are scattered *throughout the deserts of Libya and Algeria. Libyan oil is especially prized because of its low sulfur content, which means it produces much less pollution than other fuel oils.*

Transportation & Industry

THE ECONOMIES OF ALGERIA AND LIBYA were transformed by the discovery of oil and natural gas reserves in the deserts. Morocco's major exports are phosphates and agricultural produce, and as in Egypt and Tunisia, the tourist industry is essential to the economy. Egypt has the most varied industrial base, importing technology to develop electronics and engineering industries, and maintaining the reputation of its high-quality cotton textiles.

Transportation Network

152,393 miles (245,400 km)	480 miles (773 km)
8025 miles (12,922 km)	121 miles (195 km)

Tourism and the oil industry have made improvements to the Maghreb's infrastructure both necessary and possible. The Suez Canal is a vital artery for shipping between Europe and Asia.

West Africa

Benin, Burkina, Cape Verde, Gambia, Ghana, Guinea, Guinea-Bissau, Ivory Coast, Liberia, Mali, Mauritania, Niger, Nigeria, Senegal, Sierra Leone, Togo

West Africa is an immensely diverse region, encompassing the desert landscapes and mainly Muslim populations of the southern Saharan countries, and the tropical rain forests of the more humid south, with a great variety of local languages and cultures. The rich natural resources and accessibility of the area were quickly exploited by Europeans; most of the Africans taken by slave traders came from this region, causing serious depopulation. The very different influences of West Africa's leading colonial powers, Britain and France, remain today, reflected in the languages and institutions of the countries they once governed.

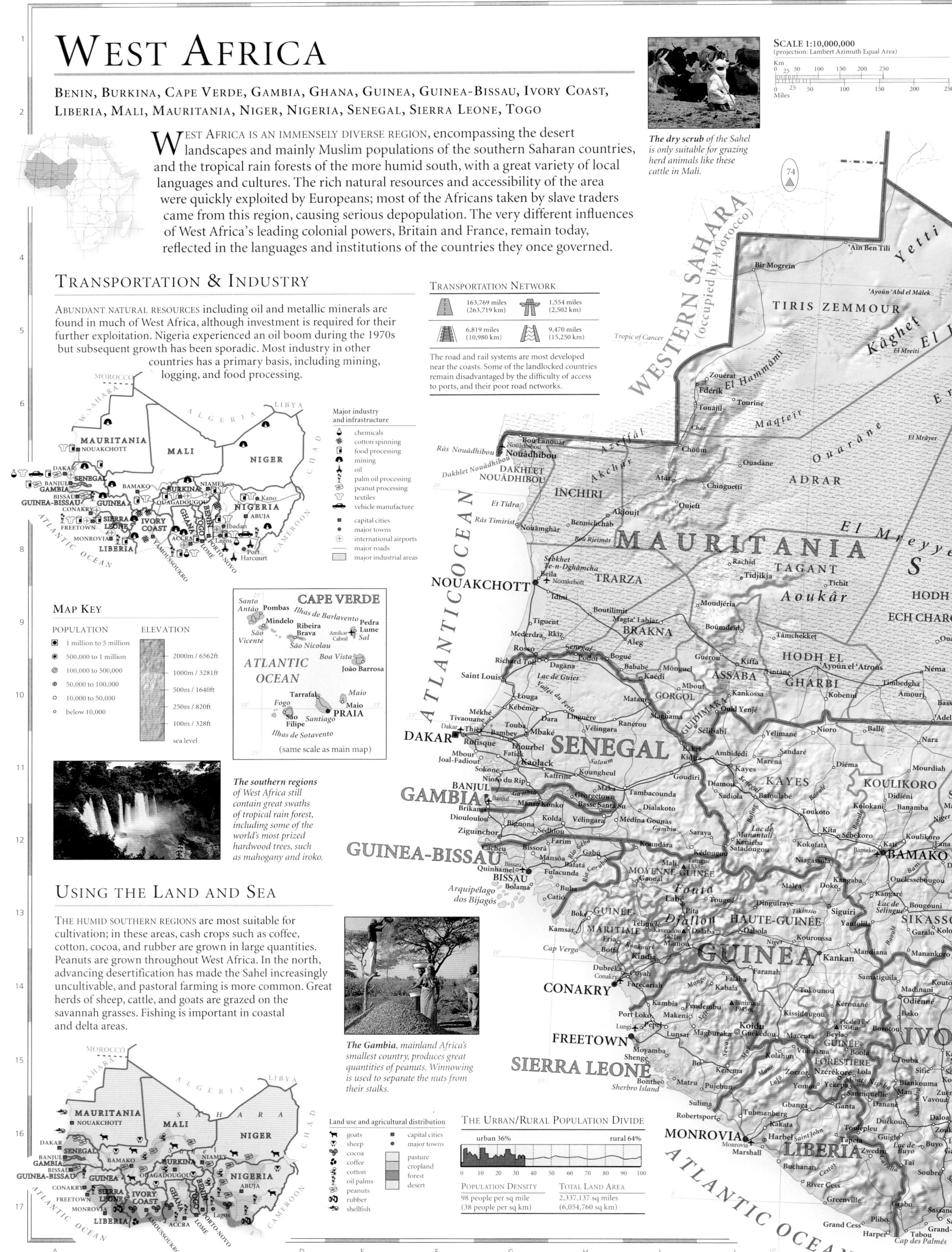

SCALE 1:10,000,000
(projection: Lambert Azimuth Equal Area)
Km 0 25 50 100 150 200 250
Miles 0 25 50 100 150 200 250
WESTERN SAHARA (occupied by Morocco)
MAURITANIA
SENEGAL
GAMBIA
GUINEA-BISSAU
GUINEA
SIERRA LEONE
LIBERIA
ATLANTIC OCEAN
NOUAKCHOTT
DAKAR
BANJUL
BISSAU
CONAKRY
FREETOWN
MONROVIA
BAMAKO
Nouâdhibou
Saint Louis
Kaolack
Ziguinchor
TIRIS ZEMMOUR
ADRAR
INCHIRI
DAKHLET NOUÂDHIBOU
TRARZA
BRAKNA
TAGANT
ASSABA
GORGOL
GUIDIMAKA
HODH EL GHARBI
KAYES
KOULIKORO
SIKASSO
HAUTE-GUINÉE
GUINÉE-MARITIME
MOYENNE-GUINÉE
GUINÉE FORESTIÈRE
Fouta Djallon
Tropic of Cancer

The dry scrub of the Sahel is only suitable for grazing herd animals like these cattle in Mali.

Transportation & Industry

Abundant natural resources including oil and metallic minerals are found in much of West Africa, although investment is required for their further exploitation. Nigeria experienced an oil boom during the 1970s but subsequent growth has been sporadic. Most industry in other countries has a primary basis, including mining, logging, and food processing.

Transportation Network

163,769 miles (263,719 km)
1,554 miles (2,502 km)
6,819 miles (10,980 km)
9,470 miles (15,250 km)

The road and rail systems are most developed near the coasts. Some of the landlocked countries remain disadvantaged by the difficulty of access to ports, and their poor road networks.

Major industry and infrastructure: chemicals, cotton spinning, food processing, mining, oil, palm oil processing, peanut processing, textiles, vehicle manufacture, capital cities, major towns, international airports, major roads, major industrial areas

Map Key

POPULATION
- 1 million to 5 million
- 500,000 to 1 million
- 100,000 to 500,000
- 50,000 to 100,000
- 10,000 to 50,000
- below 10,000

ELEVATION
2000m / 6562ft
1000m / 3281ft
500m / 1640ft
250m / 820ft
100m / 328ft
sea level

CAPE VERDE (same scale as main map)

The southern regions of West Africa still contain great swaths of tropical rain forest, including some of the world's most prized hardwood trees, such as mahogany and iroko.

Using the Land and Sea

The humid southern regions are most suitable for cultivation; in these areas, cash crops such as coffee, cotton, cocoa, and rubber are grown in large quantities. Peanuts are grown throughout West Africa. In the north, advancing desertification has made the Sahel increasingly uncultivable, and pastoral farming is more common. Great herds of sheep, cattle, and goats are grazed on the savannah grasses. Fishing is important in coastal and delta areas.

The Gambia, mainland Africa's smallest country, produces great quantities of peanuts. Winnowing is used to separate the nuts from their stalks.

Land use and agricultural distribution: goats, sheep, cocoa, coffee, cotton, oil palms, peanuts, rubber, shellfish, capital cities, major towns, pasture, cropland, forest, desert

The Urban/Rural Population Divide

urban 36% — rural 64%

Population Density	Total Land Area
98 people per sq mile (38 people per sq km)	2,337,137 sq miles (6,054,760 sq km)

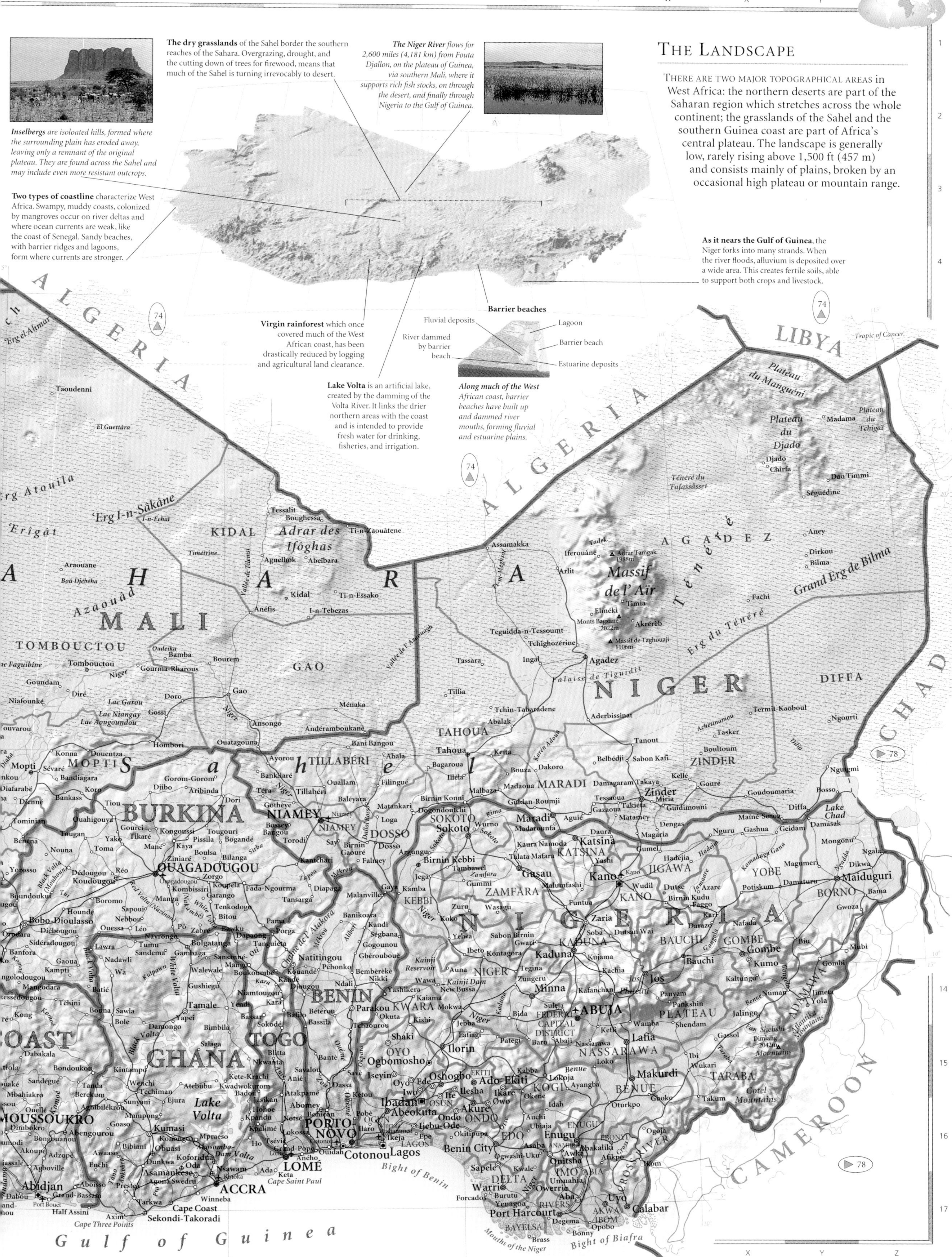
ALGERIA
LIBYA
MALI
NIGER
CHAD
BURKINA
GHANA
TOGO
BENIN
NIGERIA
CAMEROON
Sahara
Sahel
Gulf of Guinea
Bight of Benin
Bight of Biafra
Mouths of the Niger
Lake Volta
Lake Chad
Massif de l'Aïr
Grand Erg de Bilma
Ténéré
Adrar des Ifôghas
Plateau du Djado
Plateau du Manguéni
Tropic of Cancer
NIAMEY
OUAGADOUGOU
ABUJA
ACCRA
LOMÉ
PORTO-NOVO
Lagos
Cotonou
Kano
Agadez
Tombouctou
Gao
Fluvial deposits
Lagoon
River dammed by barrier beach
Barrier beach
Estuarine deposits

The Landscape

There are two major topographical areas in West Africa: the northern deserts are part of the Saharan region which stretches across the whole continent; the grasslands of the Sahel and the southern Guinea coast are part of Africa's central plateau. The landscape is generally low, rarely rising above 1,500 ft (457 m) and consists mainly of plains, broken by an occasional high plateau or mountain range.

Inselbergs are isolated hills, formed where the surrounding plain has eroded away, leaving only a remnant of the original plateau. They are found across the Sahel and may include even more resistant outcrops.

The dry grasslands of the Sahel border the southern reaches of the Sahara. Overgrazing, drought, and the cutting down of trees for firewood, means that much of the Sahel is turning irrevocably to desert.

The Niger River *flows for 2,600 miles (4,181 km) from Fouta Djallon, on the plateau of Guinea, via southern Mali, where it supports rich fish stocks, on through the desert, and finally through Nigeria to the Gulf of Guinea.*

Two types of coastline characterize West Africa. Swampy, muddy coasts, colonized by mangroves occur on river deltas and where ocean currents are weak, like the coast of Senegal. Sandy beaches, with barrier ridges and lagoons, form where currents are stronger.

As it nears the Gulf of Guinea, the Niger forks into many strands. When the river floods, alluvium is deposited over a wide area. This creates fertile soils, able to support both crops and livestock.

Virgin rainforest which once covered much of the West African coast, has been drastically reduced by logging and agricultural land clearance.

Lake Volta is an artificial lake, created by the damming of the Volta River. It links the drier northern areas with the coast and is intended to provide fresh water for drinking, fisheries, and irrigation.

Barrier beaches

Along much of the West *African coast, barrier beaches have built up and dammed river mouths, forming fluvial and estuarine plains.*

Central Africa

Cameroon, Central African Republic, Chad, Congo, Dem. Rep. Congo (Zaire), Equatorial Guinea, Gabon, Sao Tome & Principe

The great rain forest basin of the Congo River embraces most of remote Central Africa. The interior was largely unknown to Europeans until late in the 19th century, when its tribal kingdoms were split – principally between France and Belgium – with Sao Tome and Principe the lone Portuguese territory, and Equatorial Guinea controlled by Spain. Open democracy and regional economic integration are important goals for these nations – several of which have only recently emerged from restrictive regimes – and investment is needed to improve transportation infrastructures. Many of the small, but fast-growing and increasingly urban population, speak French, the regional *lingua franca*, along with several hundred Pygmy, Bantu, and Sudanic dialects.

Transportation & Industry

Large reserves of valuable minerals are found in Central Africa: copper, cobalt, zinc, and tin are mined in Dem. Rep. Congo (Zaire) and Cameroon; diamonds in the Central African Republic, and manganese in Gabon. Congo, Cameroon, Gabon, and Dem. Rep. Congo (Zaire) have oil deposits and oil has also been recently discovered in Chad. Goods such as palm oil and rubber are processed for export.

***The ancient rocks** of Dem. Rep. Congo (Zaire) hold immense and varied mineral reserves. This open pit copper mine is at Kolwezi in the far south.*

Major industry and infrastructure
- brewing
- chemicals
- cobalt
- copper
- diamonds
- food processing
- manganese
- oil
- palm oil processing
- textiles
- tin
- capital cities
- major towns
- international airports
- major roads
- major industrial areas

Transportation Network

124,349 miles (200,240 km)	342 miles (550 km)
3,830 miles (6,167 km)	15,261 miles (24,575 km)

The Trans-Gabon railroad, which began operating in 1987, has opened up new sources of timber and manganese. Elsewhere, much investment is needed to update and improve road, rail, and water transportation.

The Landscape

Lake Chad lies in a desert basin bounded by the volcanic Tibesti Mountains in the north, plateaus in the east and, in the south, the broad watershed of the Congo Basin. The vast circular depression of the Congo is isolated from the coastal plain by the granite Massif du Chaillu. To the northwest, the volcanoes and fold mountains of the Cameroon Ridge (*Dorsale Camerounaise*) extend as islands into the Gulf of Guinea. The high fold mountains fringing the east of the Congo Basin fall steeply to the lakes of the Great Rift Valley.

***A plug of resistant lava,** at the southwestern end of the Cameroon Ridge (Dorsale Camerounaise), is all that remains of an eroded volcano.*

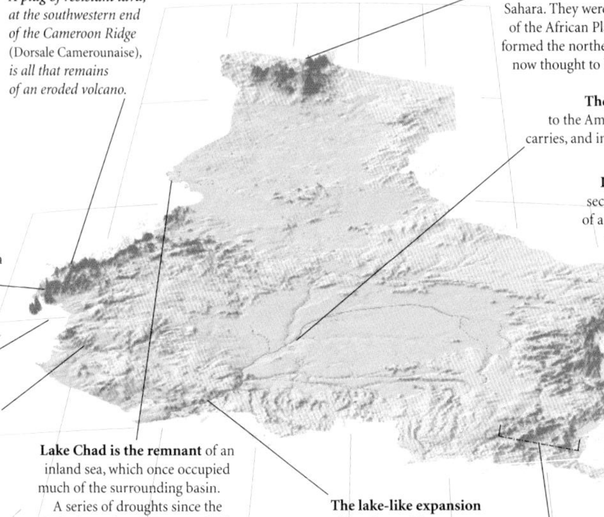

The volcanic massif of Cameroon Mountain occupies an area which remains volcanically active.

Gulf of Guinea

Massif du Chaillu

Lake Chad is the remnant of an inland sea, which once occupied much of the surrounding basin. A series of droughts since the 1970s has reduced the area of this shallow freshwater lake to about 1,000 sq miles (2,599 sq km).

The lake-like expansion of the Congo River at Stanley Pool is the lowest point of the interior basin, although the river still descends more than 1,000 ft (300 m) to reach the sea.

Rich mineral deposits in the "Copper Belt" of Dem. Rep. Congo (Zaire) were formed under intense heat and pressure when the ancient African Shield was uplifted to form the region's mountains.

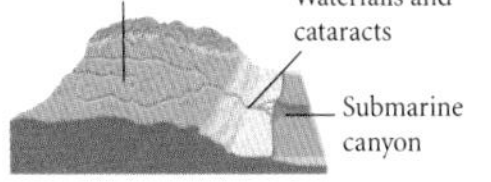

The Tibesti Mountains are the highest in the Sahara. They were pushed up by the movement of the African Plate over a hot spot, which first formed the northern Ahaggar Mountains and is now thought to lie under the Great Rift Valley.

The Congo River is second only to the Amazon in the volume of water it carries, and in the size of its drainage basin.

Lake Tanganyika, the world's second deepest lake, is the largest of a series of linear "ribbon" lakes occupying a trench within the Great Rift Valley.

Broad, shallow basin
Waterfalls and cataracts
Submarine canyon

***The Congo River** flows sluggishly through the rain forest of the interior basin. Toward the coast, the river drops steeply in a series of waterfalls and cataracts. At this point, the erosional power of the river becomes so great that it has formed a deep submarine canyon offshore.*

***Virgin tropical rain forest** covers the Ruwenzori range on the borders of Dem. Rep. Congo and Uganda.*

***The vast sandflats** surrounding Lake Chad were once covered by water. Changing climatic patterns caused the lake to shrink, and desert now covers much of its previous area.*

Map Key

Population
- 1 million to 5 million
- 500,000 to 1 million
- 100,000 to 500,000
- 50,000 to 100,000
- 10,000 to 50,000
- below 10,000

Elevation
- 4000m / 13,124ft
- 3000m / 9843ft
- 2000m / 6562ft
- 1000m / 3281ft
- 500m / 1640ft
- 250m / 820ft
- 100m / 328ft

Scale 1:10,500,000
(projection: Lambert Azimuthal Equal Area)

74
76

CENTRAL AFRICAN REPUBLIC
CAMEROON
EQUATORIAL GUINEA
SAO TOME & PRINCIPE
GABON
CONGO
DEM. REP. CONGO (ZAIRE)
ANGOLA
ANGOLA (CABINDA)
ZAMBIA
TANZANIA
UGANDA
RWANDA
BURUNDI
ATLANTIC OCEAN
Gulf of Guinea
Bight of Biafra
Congo Basin
Lake Tanganyika
Lake Kivu
Lake Albert
Lake Edward
Lake Mweru
Great Rift Valley
BANGUI
YAOUNDÉ
MALABO
LIBREVILLE
SÃO TOMÉ
BRAZZAVILLE
KINSHASA
Douala
Port-Gentil
Pointe-Noire
Matadi
Kisangani
Mbandaka
Kananga
Mbuji-Mayi
Lubumbashi
Bukavu
Goma
Kindu
Bandundu
Equator
64
80
82
Land use and agricultural distribution
cattle
cocoa
coffee
cotton
palms
peanuts
rubber
timber
capital cities
major towns
pasture
cropland
forest
desert
CHAD
NDJAMENA
THE URBAN/RURAL POPULATION DIVIDE
urban 33%
rural 67%
0 10 20 30 40 50 60 70 80 90 100
POPULATION DENSITY
39 people per sq mile
(15 people per sq km)
TOTAL LAND AREA
2,023,939 sq miles
(5,243,364 sq km)

The great Congo River *forms part of the border between Congo and Dem. Rep. Congo (Zaire). The river is fast-flowing, and a series of falls and rapids means that it is only partly navigable.*

USING THE LAND

CASH CROPS FOR EXPORT include cocoa, coffee, and rubber. Shifting cultivation is widely practiced, and plantains are the staple food of the equatorial region, grown with yam and taro. Cassava, guinea corn (sorghum), and millet are the main subsistence crops in savannah areas. Cattle farming is limited to areas free of tsetse fly, and fish from the interior rivers are an important protein source.

***High-quality timber** is floated to Port-Gentil, Gabon, via the Ogooué River. Timber provides important export revenue for several countries, although there has been concern about the uncontrolled logging of rare tropical woods.*

East Africa

Burundi, Djibouti, Eritrea, Ethiopia, Kenya, Rwanda, Somalia, Sudan, Tanzania, Uganda

The countries of East Africa divide into two distinct cultural regions. Sudan and the "Horn" nations have been influenced by the Middle East; Ethiopia was the home of one of the earliest Christian civilizations, and Sudan reflects both Muslim and Christian influences. The southern countries share a closer cultural affinity with other sub-Saharan nations. Some of Africa's most densely populated countries lie in this region, and the needs of a growing number of people have put pressure on marginal lands and fragile environments. Although most East African economies remain strongly agricultural, Kenya has developed a varied industrial base.

The Landscape

East Africa's most significant landscape feature is the Great Rift Valley, which formed during the most recent phase of continental movement when the rigid basement rocks cracked and buckled. Great blocks of land were raised and lowered, creating huge flat-bottomed valleys and steep escarpments, sometimes covered by volcanic extrusions in highland areas.

This dome at Gonder, in Ethiopia, is a volcanic intrusion, formed when molten rock pushed up the surface of the Earth and then solidified, leaving an outcrop of igneous rock.

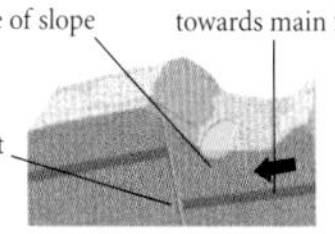

Ephemeral lake forms at far edge of slope

Central block slopes towards main fault

Boundary fault

***The eastern arm** of the Great Rift Valley is gradually being pulled apart; however the forces on one side are greater than the other causing the land to slope. This affects regional drainage which migrates down the slope.*

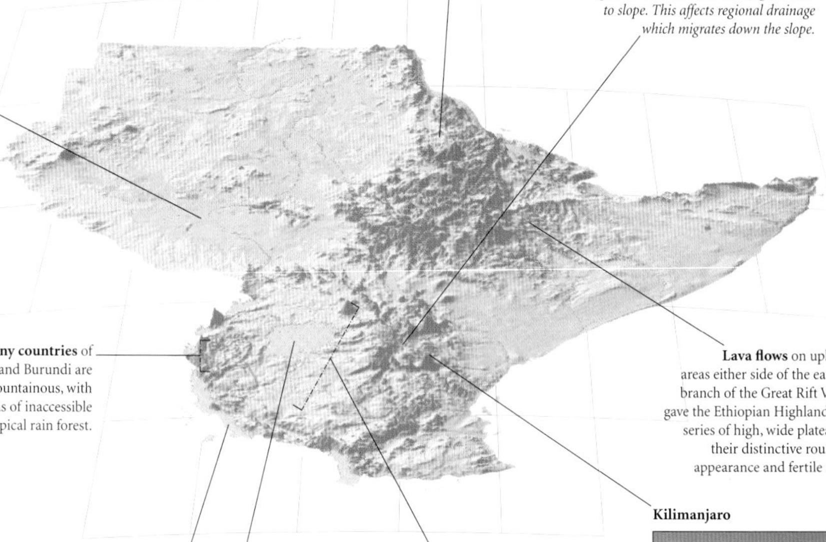

Much of northern Sudan is covered by desert. However, in the tropical wetlands of the southern Sudd region, annual rainfall can sometimes exceed 40 inches (1,000 mm).

The tiny countries of Rwanda and Burundi are mainly mountainous, with large areas of inaccessible tropical rain forest.

Lava flows on uplifted areas either side of the eastern branch of the Great Rift Valley gave the Ethiopian Highlands – a series of high, wide plateaus – their distinctive rounded appearance and fertile soils.

Kilimanjaro

Lake Tanganyika lies 8,202 ft (2,500 m) above sea level. It has a depth of nearly 4,700 ft (1,435 m). The lake traces the valley floor for some 400 miles (644 km) of the western arm of the Great Rift Valley.

Lake Victoria occupies a vast basin between the two arms of the Great Rift Valley. It is the world's second largest lake in terms of surface area, extending 26,560 sq miles (68,880 sq km). The lake contains numerous islands and coral reefs.

A vast plateau lies between the eastern and western rift valleys in Kenya, Uganda, and western Tanzania. It has been leveled by long periods of erosion to form a peneplain, but is dotted with inselbergs – outcrops of more resistant rocks.

***An extinct volcano,** Kilimanjaro is Africa's highest mountain, rising 19,340 ft (5,895 m). It is one of the few places in Africa where snow settles, allowing glacier ice to form.*

***The Kassala region** in eastern Sudan is watered by the Atbara River, an important tributary of the Nile. Most of the population is engaged in agriculture, growing cotton and cereals.*

74

78

140

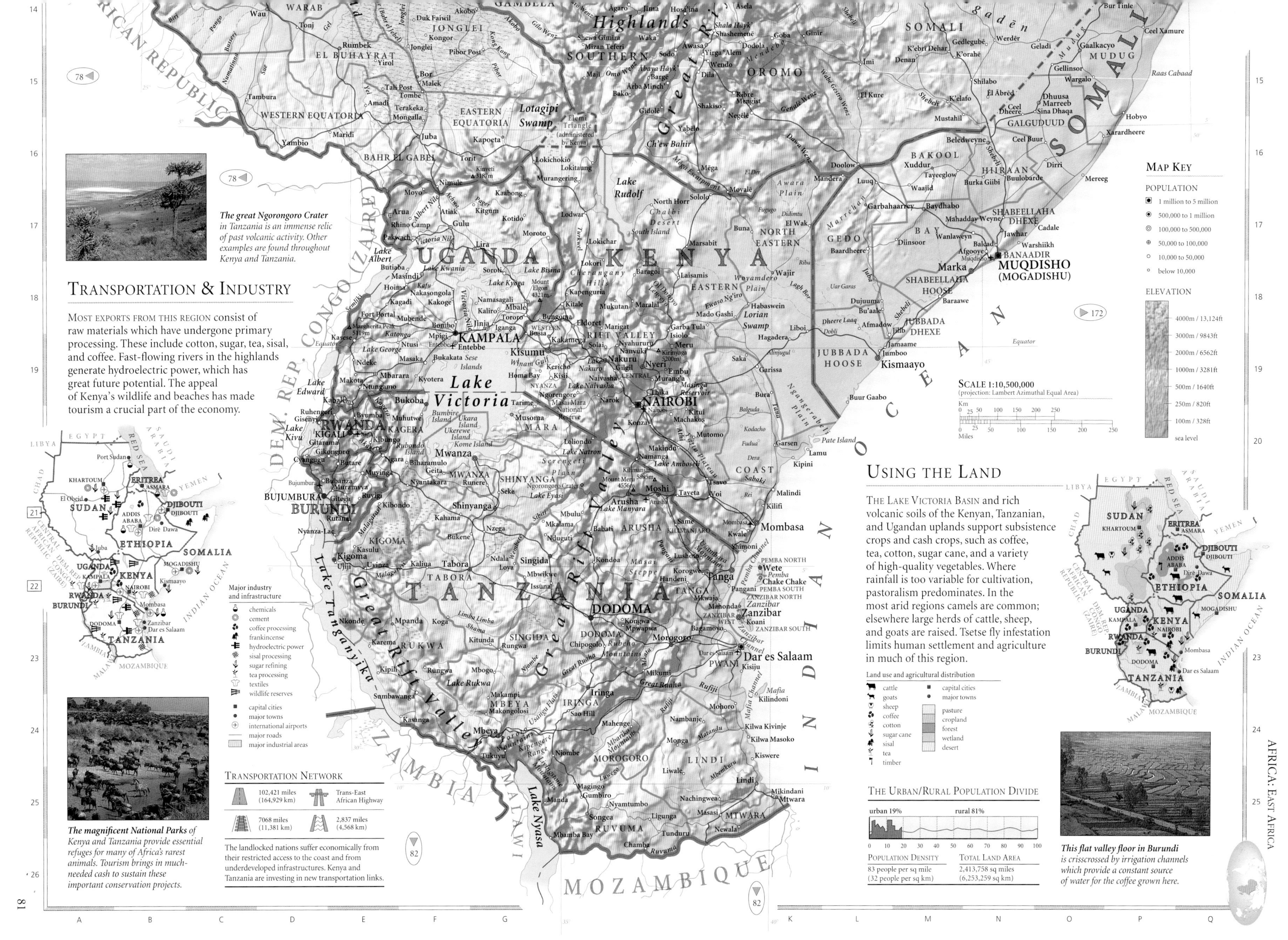
MAP KEY
POPULATION
1 million to 5 million
500,000 to 1 million
100,000 to 500,000
50,000 to 100,000
10,000 to 50,000
below 10,000
ELEVATION
4000m / 13,124ft
3000m / 9843ft
2000m / 6562ft
1000m / 3281ft
500m / 1640ft
250m / 820ft
100m / 328ft
sea level
SCALE 1:10,500,000
(projection: Lambert Azimuthal Equal Area)
Major industry and infrastructure
chemicals
cement
coffee processing
frankincense
hydroelectric power
sisal processing
sugar refining
tea processing
textiles
wildlife reserves
capital cities
major towns
international airports
major roads
major industrial areas
Land use and agricultural distribution
cattle
goats
sheep
coffee
cotton
sugar cane
sisal
tea
timber
capital cities
major towns
pasture
cropland
forest
wetland
desert
UGANDA
KENYA
TANZANIA
Lake Victoria
Lake Tanganyika
Lake Nyasa
INDIAN OCEAN
MOZAMBIQUE
ZAMBIA
MALAWI
SOMALIA
ETHIOPIA
SUDAN
DEM. REP. CONGO (ZAIRE)
NAIROBI
KAMPALA
DODOMA
MUQDISHO (MOGADISHU)
Dar es Salaam
Mombasa
Great Rift Valley

The great Ngorongoro Crater *in Tanzania is an immense relic of past volcanic activity. Other examples are found throughout Kenya and Tanzania.*

Transportation & Industry

Most exports from this region consist of raw materials which have undergone primary processing. These include cotton, sugar, tea, sisal, and coffee. Fast-flowing rivers in the highlands generate hydroelectric power, which has great future potential. The appeal of Kenya's wildlife and beaches has made tourism a crucial part of the economy.

***The magnificent National Parks** of Kenya and Tanzania provide essential refuges for many of Africa's rarest animals. Tourism brings in much-needed cash to sustain these important conservation projects.*

Transportation Network

102,421 miles (164,929 km)	Trans-East African Highway
7068 miles (11,381 km)	2,837 miles (4,568 km)

The landlocked nations suffer economically from their restricted access to the coast and from underdeveloped infrastructures. Kenya and Tanzania are investing in new transportation links.

Using the Land

The Lake Victoria Basin and rich volcanic soils of the Kenyan, Tanzanian, and Ugandan uplands support subsistence crops and cash crops, such as coffee, tea, cotton, sugar cane, and a variety of high-quality vegetables. Where rainfall is too variable for cultivation, pastoralism predominates. In the most arid regions camels are common; elsewhere large herds of cattle, sheep, and goats are raised. Tsetse fly infestation limits human settlement and agriculture in much of this region.

The Urban/Rural Population Divide

urban 19% — rural 81%

Population Density	Total Land Area
83 people per sq mile (32 people per sq km)	2,413,758 sq miles (6,253,259 sq km)

***This flat valley floor in Burundi** is crisscrossed by irrigation channels which provide a constant source of water for the coffee grown here.*

Southern Africa

ANGOLA, BOTSWANA, LESOTHO, MALAWI, MOZAMBIQUE, NAMIBIA, SOUTH AFRICA, SWAZILAND, ZAMBIA, ZIMBABWE

AFRICA'S VAST SOUTHERN PLATEAU has been a contested homeland for disparate peoples for many centuries. The European incursion began with the slave trade and quickened in the 19th century, when the discovery of enormous mineral wealth secured South Africa's regional economic dominance. The struggle against white minority rule led to strife in Namibia, Zimbabwe, and the former Portuguese territories of Angola and Mozambique. South Africa's notorious apartheid laws, which denied basic human rights to more than 75% of the people, led to the state being internationally ostracized until 1994, when the first fully democratic elections inaugurated a new era of racial justice.

Transportation & Industry

SOUTH AFRICA, the world's largest exporter of gold, has a varied economy which generates about 75% of the region's income and draws migrant labor from neighboring states. Angola exports petroleum; Botswana and Namibia rely on diamond mining; and Zambia is seeking to diversify its economy to compensate for declining copper reserves.

Almost all new mining ventures in Zimbabwe are now subject to government control. This mine at Bindura in northeastern Zimbabwe produces nickel, one of the country's top three minerals in terms of economic value.

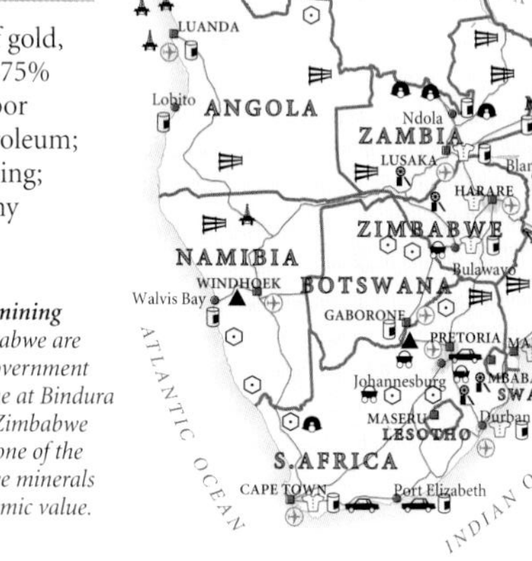

DEM. REP. CONGO (ZAIRE)
TANZANIA
LUANDA
Lobito
ANGOLA
ZAMBIA
Ndola
LUSAKA
MALAWI
LILONGWE
Blantyre
MOZAMBIQUE
HARARE
ZIMBABWE
Beira
Bulawayo
NAMIBIA
Walvis Bay
WINDHOEK
BOTSWANA
GABORONE
PRETORIA
MAPUTO
MBABANE
SWAZILAND
Johannesburg
MASERU
LESOTHO
Durban
S.AFRICA
CAPE TOWN
Port Elizabeth
ATLANTIC OCEAN
INDIAN OCEAN

Major industry and infrastructure

car manufacture	gold	capital cities
coal	oil	major towns
copper	textiles	international airports
diamonds	uranium	major roads
food processing	wildlife reserves	major industrial areas

The Landscape

MOST OF SOUTHERN AFRICA rests on a concave plateau comprising the Kalahari basin and a mountainous fringe, skirted by a coastal plain which widens out in Mozambique. The plateau extends north, toward the Planalto de Bié in Angola, the Congo Basin and the lake-filled troughs of the Great Rift Valley. The eastern region is drained by the Zambezi and Limpopo Rivers, and the Orange is the major western river.

Thousands of years of evaporating water have produced the Etosha Pan, one of the largest salt flats in the world. Lake and river sediments in the area indicate that the region was once less arid.

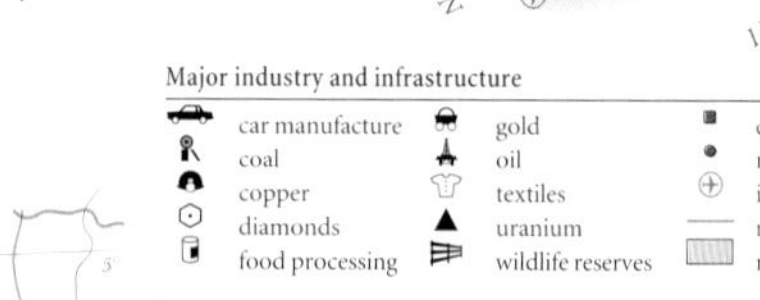

Finger Rock, near Khorixas, Namibia *is a remnant of a former land surface, which has been denuded by erosion over the last 5 million years. These occasional stacks of partially weathered rocks interrupt the plains of the dry southern interior.*

Transportation Network

84,213 miles (135,609 km)		746 miles (1,202 km)	
23,208 miles (37,372 km)		3,815 miles (6,144 km)	

Southern Africa's Cape-gauge rail network is by far the largest in the continent. About two-thirds of the 20,000 mile (32,000 km) system lies within South Africa. Lines such as the Harare–Bulawayo route have become corridors for industrial growth.

Following a series of droughts, *this baobab tree in Zimbabwe now stands alone in a field once filled by sugar cane. The thick trunk and small leaves of the baobab help it to conserve water, enabling it to survive even in drought conditions.*

At Victoria Falls, the Zambezi River has cut a spectacular gorge taking advantage of large joints in the basalt, which were first formed as the lava cooled and contracted.

The Okavango/Cubango River flows from the Planalto de Bié to the swamplands of the Okavango Delta, one of the world's largest inland deltas, where it divides into countless distributary channels, feeding out into the desert.

The fast-flowing *Zambezi River cuts a deep, wide channel as it flows along the Zimbabwe/Zambia border.*

Lake Nyasa occupies one of the deep troughs of the Great Rift Valley, where the land has been displaced downward by as much as 3,000 ft (920 m).

Planalto de Bié

Khorixas, Namibia

Namib Desert

Great Rift Valley

Bushveld intrusion

Limpopo River

Volcanic lava, over 250 million years old, caps the peaks of the Drakensberg range, which lie on the mountainous rim of southern Africa's interior plateau.

Broad, flat-topped mountains characterize the Great Karoo, which have been cut from level rock strata under extremely arid conditions.

The Kalahari Desert is the largest continuous sand surface in the world. Iron oxide gives a distinctive red color to the windblown sand, which, in eastern areas covers the bedrock by over 200 ft (60 m).

The Orange River, one of the longest in Africa, rises in Lesotho and is the only major river in the south which flows westward, rather than to the east coast.

The mountains of the Little Karoo are composed of sedimentary rocks which have been substantially folded and faulted.

Bushveld intrusion

Gabbro and peridotite

Magnetite

Platinum minerals

Granite

Chromite

The Bushveld intrusion *lies on South Africa's high "veld." Molten magma intruded into the Earth's crust creating a saucer-shaped feature, more than 180 miles (300 km) across, containing regular layers of precious minerals, overlain by a dome of granite.*

SCALE 1:10,500,000
(projection: Lambert Azimuthal Equal Area)

Km 0 25 50 100 150 200 250 300
Miles 0 25 50 100 150 200 250 300

Map Key

POPULATION
- 1 million to 5 million
- 500,000 to 1 million
- 100,000 to 500,000
- 50,000 to 100,000
- 10,000 to 50,000
- below 10,000

ELEVATION
- 3000m / 9843ft
- 2000m / 6562ft
- 1000m / 3281ft
- 500m / 1640ft
- 250m / 820ft
- 100m / 328ft
- sea level

South Africa's Three Capitals

PRETORIA – administrative capital
CAPE TOWN – legislative capital
BLOEMFONTEIN – judicial capital

78
80

CONGO
CABINDA (To Angola)
DEM. REP. CONGO (ZAIRE)
ANGOLA
TANZANIA
LUANDA
ZAIRE
UIGE
BENGO
CUANZA NORTE
MALANJE
LUNDA NORTE
LUNDA SUL
CUANZA SUL
Lake Tanganyika
Lake Mweru
LUAPULA
NORTHERN
Lake Nyasa
Great Rift

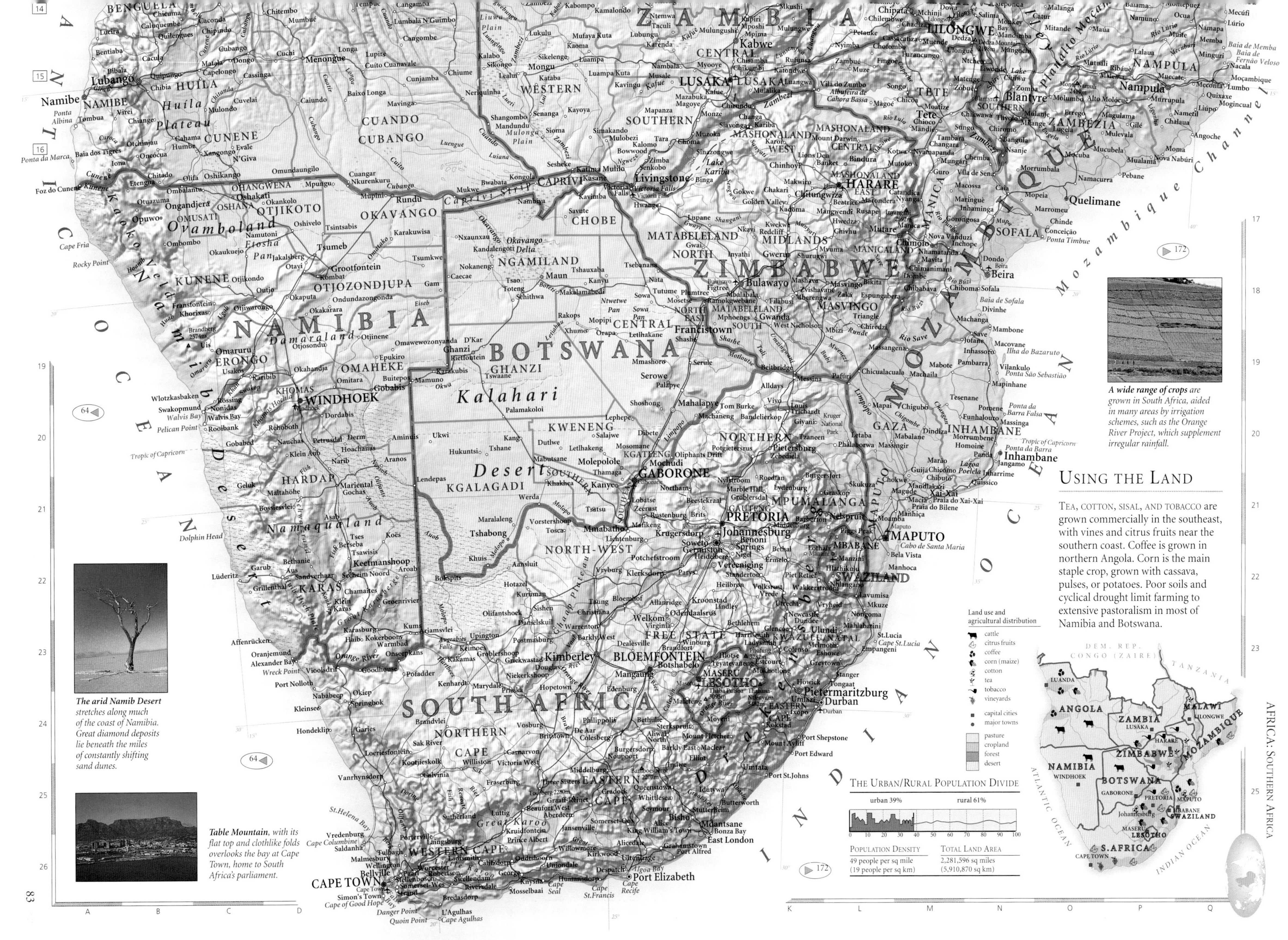
ZAMBIA
LUSAKA
NAMIBIA
WINDHOEK
BOTSWANA
GABORONE
ZIMBABWE
HARARE
MOZAMBIQUE
MAPUTO
SOUTH AFRICA
PRETORIA
CAPE TOWN
BLOEMFONTEIN
LESOTHO
MASERU
SWAZILAND
MBABANE
LILONGWE
Kalahari
Desert
Namib Desert
ATLANTIC OCEAN
INDIAN OCEAN
Mozambique Channel
Tropic of Capricorn
Johannesburg
Durban
Port Elizabeth
East London
Kimberley
Bulawayo
Beira
Quelimane
Nampula
Blantyre
Lubango
Namibe
Walvis Bay
Lüderitz
Inhambane
Pietermaritzburg
Livingstone
Victoria Falls
Okavango Delta
Etosha Pan
Cape of Good Hope
Cape Agulhas
172
64

The arid Namib Desert stretches along much of the coast of Namibia. Great diamond deposits lie beneath the miles of constantly shifting sand dunes.

Table Mountain, with its flat top and clothlike folds overlooks the bay at Cape Town, home to South Africa's parliament.

A wide range of crops are grown in South Africa, aided in many areas by irrigation schemes, such as the Orange River Project, which supplement irregular rainfall.

Using the Land

Tea, cotton, sisal, and tobacco are grown commercially in the southeast, with vines and citrus fruits near the southern coast. Coffee is grown in northern Angola. Corn is the main staple crop, grown with cassava, pulses, or potatoes. Poor soils and cyclical drought limit farming to extensive pastoralism in most of Namibia and Botswana.

Land use and agricultural distribution

- cattle
- citrus fruits
- coffee
- corn (maize)
- cotton
- tea
- tobacco
- vineyards
- capital cities
- major towns
- pasture
- cropland
- forest
- desert

The Urban/Rural Population Divide

urban 39% — rural 61%

0 10 20 30 40 50 60 70 80 90 100

Population Density	Total Land Area
49 people per sq mile (19 people per sq km)	2,281,596 sq miles (5,910,870 sq km)

ARCTIC OCEAN
North Pole
Ellesmere Island
Greenland
King Frederik VIII Land
King Christian X Land
Greenland Sea
Laptev Sea
Severnaya Zemlya
Ostrov Rudol'fa
Franz Josef Land
Poluostrov Taymyr
Kara Sea
Mys Zhelaniya
Spitsbergen
NORTH AMERICAN PLATE
EURASIAN PLATE
Barents Sea
Novaya Zemlya
Poluostrov Yamal
Baydaratskaya Guba
Yenisey
Gulf of Ob
Bjørnøya
Barents Trough
Jan Mayen Fracture Zone
Jan Mayen
Jan Mayen Ridge
Denmark Strait
Kolbeinsey Ridge
Arctic Circle
Iceland Plateau
Norwegian Sea
Norwegian Basin
Vøring Plateau
Tromsøflaket
North Cape
Nordkinn
Murmansk Rise
Kara Strait
Ostrov Kolguyev
Poluostrov Kanin
Fugløya Bank
Vesterålen
Lofoten
Kola Peninsula
White Sea
Pechora
Ural Mountains
West Siberian Plain
ASIA
Ob'
Bjargtangar
Iceland
Vatnajökull
Reykjanes Ridge
Faeroe-Iceland Ridge
Iceland Basin
Faeroe Islands
Bill Baileys Bank
Faeroe-Shetland Trough
Shetland Islands
Hatton Ridge
Viking Bank
Traena Bank
Kebnekaise 2117m
Scandinavia
Gulf of Bothnia
Lake Ladoga
Lake Onega
Timanskiy Kryazh
Northern Dvina
Onega Bay
Ozero Vygozero
Rybinsk Reservoir
Orkney Islands
Outer Hebrides
Rockall Rise
Feni Ridge
Rockall Trough
ATLANTIC OCEAN
Ben Nevis 1343m
Grampian Mountains
North Channel
North Sea
Jutland Bank
Skagerrak
Kattegat
Great Fisher Bank
Jylland
Sjælland
Åland
Gulf of Finland
Lake Peipus
Lake Ilmen
Lake Pskov
Gulf of Riga
Gotland
Vänern
Vättern
Baltic Sea
North European Plain
Western Dvina
Volga Upland
British Isles
Ireland
Irish Sea
Great Britain
Snowdon 1085m
Pennines
Dogger Bank
Frisian Islands
Porcupine Plain
Shannon
St. George's Channel
Celtic Sea
Celtic Shelf
Bristol Channel
Severn
Thames
The Fens
Strait of Dover
Land's End
English Channel
Channel Islands
Elbe
Oder
Vistula
Warta
Neman
Bug
Pripet Marshes
Desna
Dnieper
Central Russian Upland
Don
EUROPE
Ardennes
Rhine
Harz
Meuse
Moselle
Marne
Seine
Loire
Vosges
Black Forest
Danube
Lake Constance
Kiev Reservoir
Kremenchuk Reservoir
Dnieper Lowlands
Dniester
Podil's'ka Vysochina
Pivdennyy Buh
Carpathian Mountains
Tisza
Tsimlyansk Reservoir
Kirghiz Steppe
Yergeni
Manych
Black Sea Lowland
Sea of Azov
Crimea
Kerch Strait
Black Sea
Bay of Biscay
Biscay Plain
Charcot Seamounts
Azores-Biscay Rise
Massif Central
Lake Geneva
Alps
Lake Garda
Bakony
Lake Balaton
Great Hungarian Plain
Transylvanian Alps
Garonne
Dordogne
Lot
Galicia Bank
Iberian Plain
Iberian Peninsula
Cordillera Cantábrica
Miño
Duero
Douro
Ebro
Sistema Central
Sistema Ibérico
Pyrenees
Aneto 3404m
Gulf of Lion
Ligurian Sea
Adriatic Sea
Corno Grande 2912m
Apennines
Dinaric Alps
Balkan Mountains
Bosporus
Sea of Marmara
Adriatic Basin
Corsica
Strait of Bonifacio
Sardinia
Tyrrhenian Sea
Tyrrhenian Basin
Gulf of Taranto
Strait of Otranto
Lake Ohrid
Aegean Sea
Anatolia
Cabo da Roca
Tagus
Tagus Plain
Guadiana
Sierra Morena
Guadalquivir
Júcar
Gulf of Valencia
Balearic Islands
Algerian Basin
Mediterranean Sea
Gorringe Ridge
Cape Saint Vincent
Horseshoe Seamounts
Punta de Tarifa
Sistemas Béticos
Sierra Nevada
Strait of Gibraltar
Ampère Seamount
Alboran Sea
Oued Chelif
EURASIAN PLATE
AFRICAN PLATE
Tell Atlas
Mount Etna 3340m
Strait of Sicily
Sicily
Malta
Ionian Sea
Ionian Basin
Peloponnese
Mirtoan Sea
Sea of Crete
Crete
Karpathos Strait
Rhodes Basin
Gulf of Antalya
Taurus Mountains
Cyprus
Cyprus Basin
Seine Plain
Seine Seamount
Madeira
Rif
Sebou
Moulouya
Oum er Rbia
Middle Atlas
Atlas Mountains
High Atlas
Saharan Atlas
Chott el Jerid
Mediterranean Ridge
Gavdos
Levantine Basin
Nile Fan
Suez Canal
Nile
Dacia Seamount
Agadir Canyon
Canary Islands
Gulf of Sirte
Grand Erg Occidental
Grand Erg Oriental
Qattara Depression -133m
Western Desert
Libyan Desert
'Erg Iguidi
Erg Chech
AFRICA
SAHARA

EUROPE

EUROPE IS THE WORLD'S SECOND SMALLEST CONTINENT, COVERING 4,053,309 SQ MILES (10,498,000 SQ KM). IT COMPRISES 44 SEPARATE COUNTRIES, INCLUDING TURKEY AND THE RUSSIAN FEDERATION, ALTHOUGH THE GREATER PARTS OF THESE NATIONS LIE IN ASIA.

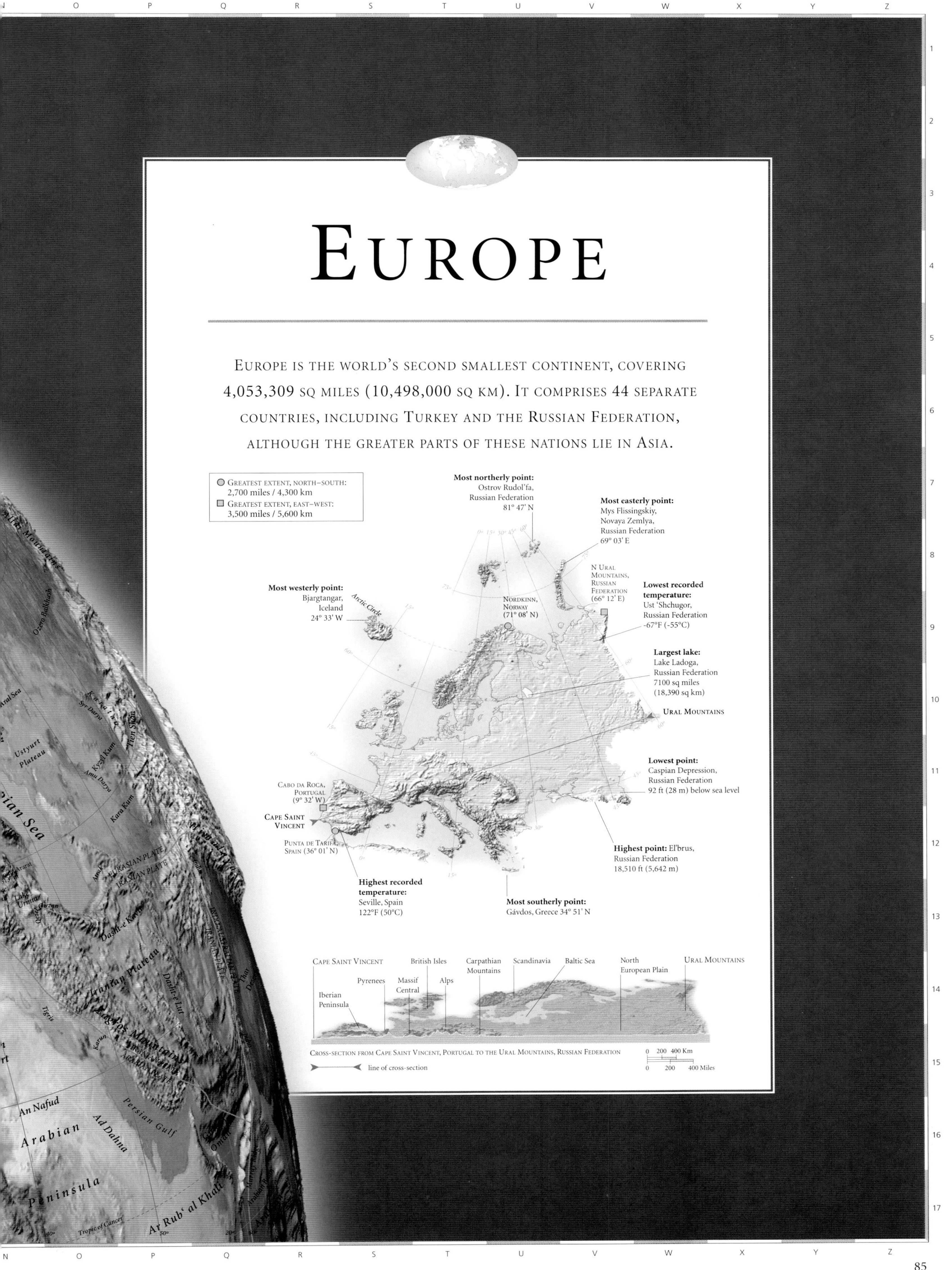

GREATEST EXTENT, NORTH–SOUTH: 2,700 miles / 4,300 km
GREATEST EXTENT, EAST–WEST: 3,500 miles / 5,600 km
Most northerly point: Ostrov Rudol'fa, Russian Federation 81° 47' N
Most easterly point: Mys Flissingskiy, Novaya Zemlya, Russian Federation 69° 03' E
N URAL MOUNTAINS, RUSSIAN FEDERATION (66° 12' E)
Lowest recorded temperature: Ust 'Shchugor, Russian Federation -67°F (-55°C)
Most westerly point: Bjargtangar, Iceland 24° 33' W
Arctic Circle
NORDKINN, NORWAY (71° 08' N)
Largest lake: Lake Ladoga, Russian Federation 7100 sq miles (18,390 sq km)
URAL MOUNTAINS
Lowest point: Caspian Depression, Russian Federation 92 ft (28 m) below sea level
CABO DA ROCA, PORTUGAL (9° 32' W)
CAPE SAINT VINCENT
PUNTA DE TARIFA, SPAIN (36° 01' N)
Highest recorded temperature: Seville, Spain 122°F (50°C)
Most southerly point: Gávdos, Greece 34° 51' N
Highest point: El'brus, Russian Federation 18,510 ft (5,642 m)
CAPE SAINT VINCENT
British Isles
Carpathian Mountains
Scandinavia
Baltic Sea
North European Plain
URAL MOUNTAINS
Pyrenees
Massif Central
Alps
Iberian Peninsula
CROSS-SECTION FROM CAPE SAINT VINCENT, PORTUGAL TO THE URAL MOUNTAINS, RUSSIAN FEDERATION
line of cross-section
0 200 400 Km
0 200 400 Miles
Aral Sea
Syr Darya
Ustyurt Plateau
Kyzyl Kum
Amu Darya
Kara Kum
Caspian Sea
EURASIAN PLATE
IRANIAN PLATE
Iranian Plateau
Dasht-e Lut
Dasht-e Kavir
Zagros Mountains
Tigris
Karun
Persian Gulf
An Nafud
Ad Dahna
Arabian Peninsula
Ar Rub' al Khali
Tropic of Cancer
Oman
Ozero Balkhash

Physical Europe

The physical diversity of Europe belies its relatively small size. To the northwest and south it is enclosed by mountains. The older, rounded Atlantic Highlands of Scandinavia and the British Isles lie to the north and the younger, rugged peaks of the Alpine Uplands to the south. In between lies the North European Plain, stretching 2,485 miles (4,000 km) from The Fens in England to the Ural Mountains in Russia. South of the plain lies a series of gently folded sedimentary rocks separated by ancient plateaus, known as massifs.

The North European Plain

Rising less than 1,000 ft (300 m) above sea level, the North European Plain strongly reflects past glaciation. Ridges of both coarse moraine and finer, wind-blown deposits have accumulated over much of the region. The ice sheet also diverted a number of river channels from their original courses.

Glacial lakes

Rivers were diverted from their original course by the ice sheet

A layer of glacial sediments covers the North European Plain

Section across the North European Plain showing its low relief and drainage.

The Atlantic Highlands

The Atlantic Highlands were formed by compression against the Scandinavian Shield during the Caledonian mountain-building period over 500 million years ago. The highlands were once part of a continuous mountain chain, now divided by the North Sea and a submerged rift valley.

The Atlantic Highlands continue in the British Isles

Rift valley buried by sediments

North Sea

Atlantic Highlands in Norway

Rocks affected by ancient mountain-building

Scandinavian Shield

Cross-section through northeastern Europe showing the continuous mountain chain and rift valley system.

SCALE 1:25,500,000
(projection: Lambert Azimuthal Equal Area)

MAP KEY

ELEVATION

4000m / 13,124ft
3000m / 9843ft
2000m / 6562ft
1000m / 3281ft
500m / 1640ft
250m / 820ft
100m / 328ft
sea level

PLATE MARGINS
(for explanation see page xiv)

constructive
destructive
conservative
uncertain

physiographic regions

line of cross-section

The Plateaus and Lowlands

The uplifted plateaus or massifs of southern central Europe are the result of long-term erosion, later followed by uplift. They are the source areas of many of the rivers which drain Europe's lowlands. In some of the higher reaches, fractures have enabled igneous rocks from deep in the Earth to reach the surface.

The Alpine Uplands

The collision of the African and European continents, which began about 65 million years ago, folded and then uplifted a series of mountain ranges running across southern Europe and into Asia. Two major lines of folding can be traced: one includes the Pyrenees, the Alps, and the Carpathian Mountains; the other incorporates the Apennines and the Dinaric Alps.

European basement rock

Alps

Weak sedimentary strata have been folded

African Plate moved northward

The Apennines

Cross-section through the Alps showing folding and faulting caused by plate tectonics.

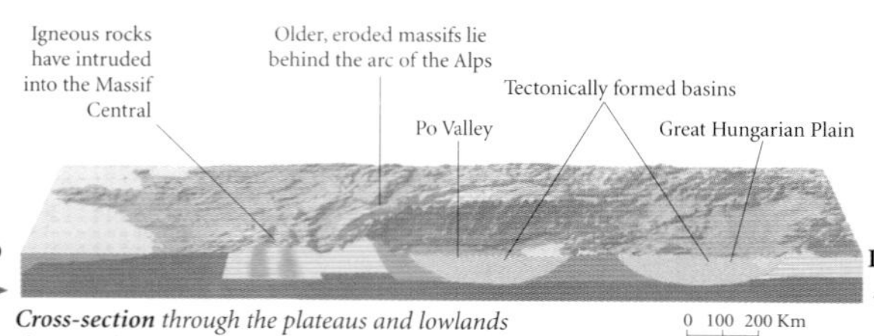
Igneous rocks have intruded into the Massif Central
Older, eroded massifs lie behind the arc of the Alps
Tectonically formed basins
Po Valley
Great Hungarian Plain
D
D

Cross-section through the plateaus and lowlands showing the lower elevation of the ancient massifs.

CLIMATE

Frost grips northern and eastern Europe during the long cold winters. Lakes and rivers frequently freeze.

EUROPE EXPERIENCES few extremes in either rainfall or temperature, with the exception of the far north and south. Along the west coast, the warm currents of the North Atlantic Drift moderate temperatures. Although east–west air movement is relatively unimpeded by relief, the Alpine Uplands halt the progress of north–south air masses, protecting most of the Mediterranean from cold, north winds.

Arctic Circle
Reykjavík
Karasjok
Murmansk
Bodø
Pajala
Pechora
Hoyvík
Kajaani
Archangel
Härnösand
Sveg
Bergen
Oslo
Helsinki
St Petersburg
Kirov
Malin Head
Dundee
Stockholm
Tallinn
Ufa
Vestervig
Gothenburg
Shannon
Morecambe
Riga
Moscow
Malmö
Exeter
London
Hamburg
Minsk
Berlin
Brussels
Warsaw
Paris
Prague
Kharkiv
Astrakhan'
Munich
A Coruña
Zürich
Rostov-na-Donu
Bordeaux
Vienna
Bratislava
Lyon
Toulouse
Milan
Zagreb
Simferopol'
Mistral
Bora
Lisbon
Madrid
Monaco
Belgrade
Bucharest
Sarajevo
Constanța
Barcelona
Sofia
Palma
Naples
Tirana
İstanbul
Gibraltar
Cagliari
Salonica
Sirocco
Messina
Athens

TEMPERATURE

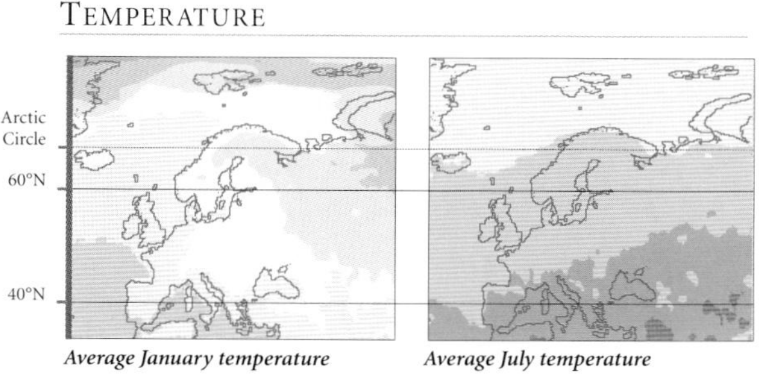

Arctic Circle
60°N
40°N

Average January temperature

Average July temperature

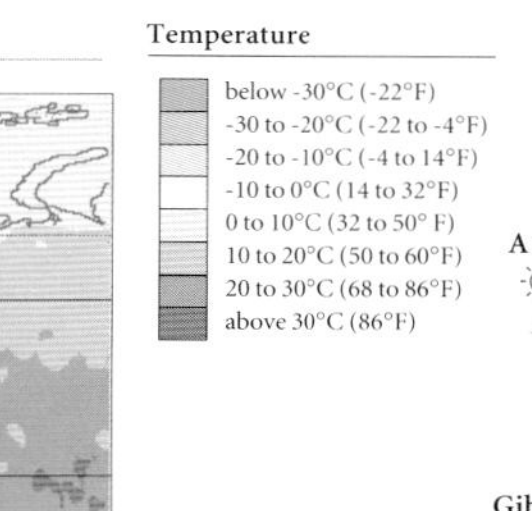

Temperature
below -30°C (-22°F)
-30 to -20°C (-22 to -4°F)
-20 to -10°C (-4 to 14°F)
-10 to 0°C (14 to 32°F)
0 to 10°C (32 to 50° F)
10 to 20°C (50 to 68°F)
20 to 30°C (68 to 86°F)
above 30°C (86°F)

Mild temperatures and frequent rainfall contribute to the fertile farming land found over much of northwestern Europe.

RAINFALL

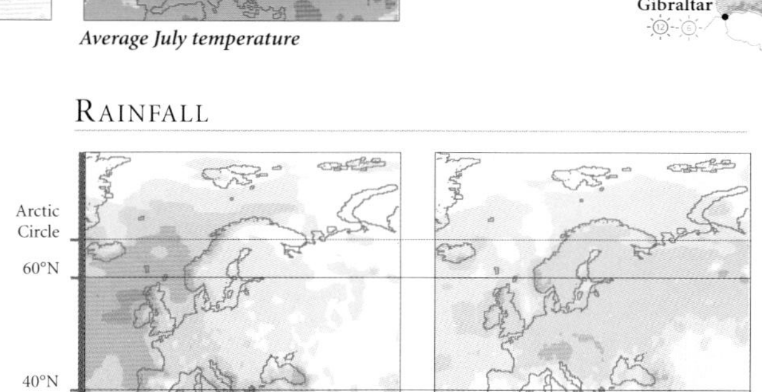

Arctic Circle
60°N
40°N

Average January rainfall

Average July rainfall

Rainfall
0–25 mm (0–1 in)
25–50 mm (1–2 in)
50–100 mm (2–4 in)
100–200 mm (4–8 in)
200–300 mm (8–12 in)
300–400 mm (12–16 in)
400–500 mm (16–20 in)
more than 500 mm (20 in)

Dusty Sirocco winds from Africa help create the semiarid scrubland common across the Mediterranean coastlands of southern Europe.

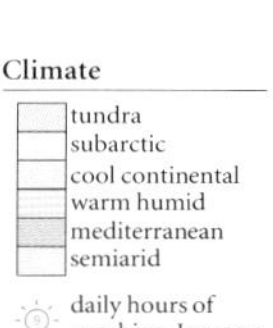

Climate
tundra
subarctic
cool continental
warm humid
mediterranean
semiarid
daily hours of sunshine, January
daily hours of sunshine, July
cold wind
hot wind

SHAPING THE CONTINENT

SUCCESSIVE ICE AGES have left many relict landforms across Europe. Present glaciers continue to carve peaks and valleys in the northern Atlantic Highlands and Alpine Uplands. Tectonic activity, both past and present, has shaped southern Europe and Iceland. Active volcanoes and earthquakes still occur in Italy and Greece. Europe's extensive coastline, particularly in the northwest, is constantly modified by wave action and fluvial deposits.

GLACIATION

1 Valley glaciers, such as this one *(left)* in Iceland, form in hollows at the top of valleys and flow downward, drawn by gravity. Their growth is dynamic; new snowfall constantly accumulates at the head of the glacier, while the snout melts, depositing material eroded and carried by the glacier.

Snow accumulates at the head of glacier
Glacier movement erodes valley
Glacier snout melts depositing eroded debris

GLACIATION: DEVELOPMENT OF A GLACIER

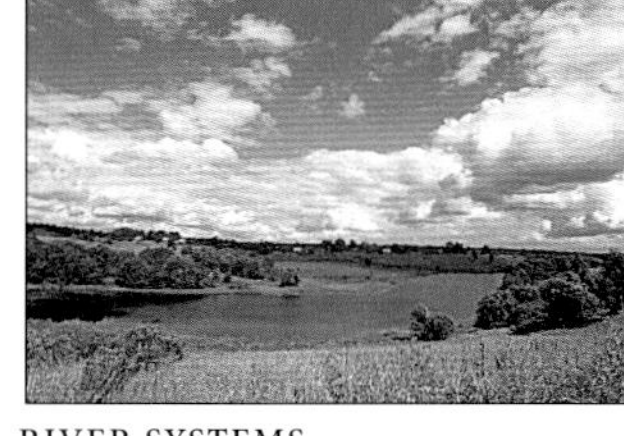

RIVER SYSTEMS

2 Rivers are continuously transporting eroded material toward the sea. Slow-moving, low-gradient rivers, like this one in western Russia *(above)*, deposit their alluvium load, infilling valleys creating a floodplain. Subsequent climatic and tectonic fluctuations may erode the floodplain to form terraces.

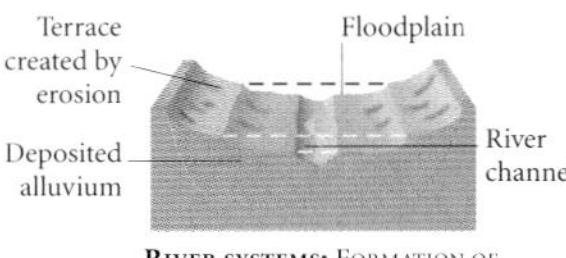

Terrace created by erosion
Floodplain
Deposited alluvium
River channel

RIVER SYSTEMS: FORMATION OF A FLOODPLAIN AND TERRACES

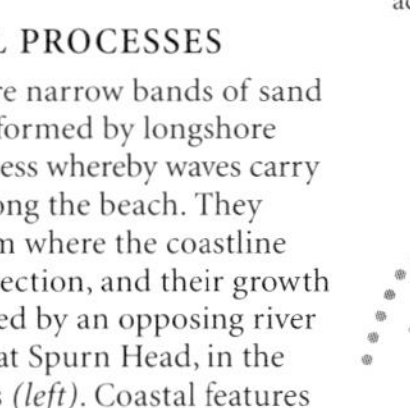

COASTAL PROCESSES

5 Spits are narrow bands of sand or shingle, formed by longshore drift; a process whereby waves carry material along the beach. They usually form where the coastline changes direction, and their growth is then halted by an opposing river current, as at Spurn Head, in the British Isles *(left)*. Coastal features such as these are constantly being created and destroyed.

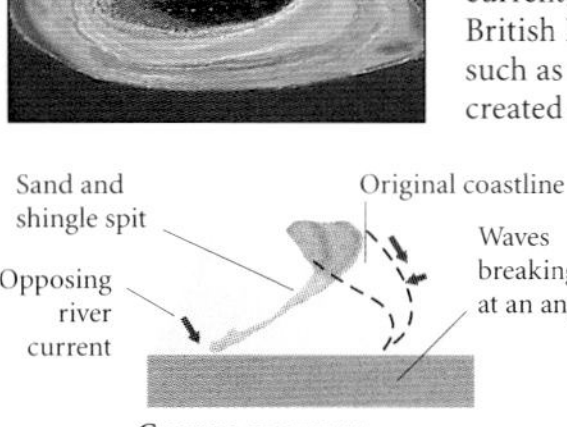

Sand and shingle spit
Original coastline
Waves breaking at an angle
Opposing river current

COASTAL PROCESSES: FORMATION OF A SPIT

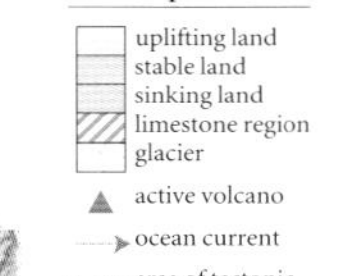

Landscape
uplifting land
stable land
sinking land
limestone region
glacier
active volcano
ocean current
area of tectonic activity
maximum limit of glaciation

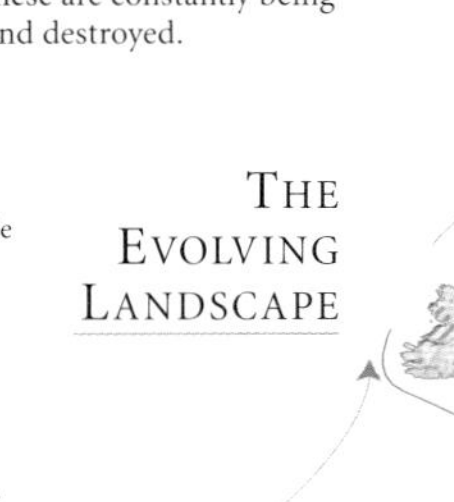

THE EVOLVING LANDSCAPE

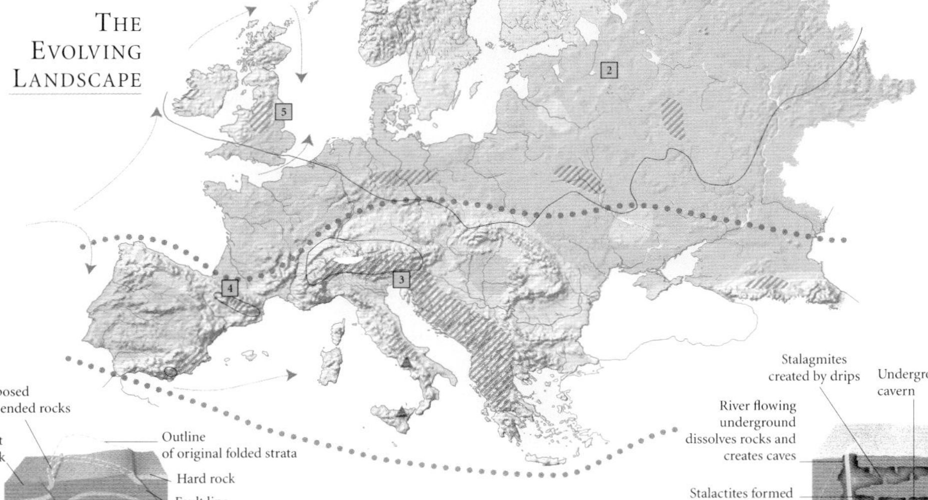

1
2
3
4
5

EROSION AND WEATHERING

4 Much of Europe was once subjected to folding and faulting, exposing hard and soft rock layers. Subsequent erosion and weathering has worn away the softer strata, leaving up-ended layers of hard rock as in the French Pyrenees *(above)*.

Exposed up-ended rocks

Soft rock

Outline of original folded strata

Hard rock

Fault line

Folded rock strata

EROSION AND WEATHERING: MODIFICATION OF A FOLD

Stalagmites created by drips

Underground cavern

River flowing underground dissolves rocks and creates caves

Stalactites formed by seeping water

WEATHERING: FORMATION OF A CAVE

WEATHERING

3 As surface water filters through permeable limestone, the rock dissolves to form underground caves, like Postojna in the Karst region of Slovenia *(above)*. Stalactites grow downward as lime-enriched water seeps from roof fractures; stalagmites grow upward where drips splash down.

Political Europe

THE POLITICAL BOUNDARIES OF EUROPE have changed many times, especially during the 20th century in the aftermath of two world wars, the breakup of the empires of Austria-Hungary, Nazi Germany and, toward the end of the century, the collapse of communism in eastern Europe. The fragmentation of Yugoslavia has again altered the political map of Europe, highlighting a trend toward nationalism and devolution. In contrast, economic federalism is growing. In 1958, the formation of the European Economic Community (now the European Union or EU) started a move toward economic and political union.

The Brandenburg Gate in Berlin *is a potent symbol of German reunification. From 1961, the road beneath it ended in a wall, built to stop the flow of refugees to the West. It was opened again in 1989 when the wall was destroyed and East and West Germany were reunited.*

Population

EUROPE IS A DENSELY POPULATED, urbanized continent; in Belgium over 90% of people live in urban areas. The highest population densities are found in an area stretching east from southern Britain and northern France, into Germany. The northern fringes are only sparsely populated.

Demand for space *in densely populated European cities like London has led to the development of high-rise offices and urban sprawl.*

Denmark Strait
Arctic Circle
REYKJAVÍK
ICELAND
Norwegian Sea
Faeroe Islands (to Denmark)
ATLANTIC OCEAN
Shetland Islands
Orkney Islands
Outer Hebrides
SCOTLAND
Aberdeen
Dundee
Glasgow
Edinburgh
NORTHERN IRELAND
Belfast
REPUBLIC OF IRELAND
DUBLIN
Isle of Man (to UK)
Newcastle upon Tyne
UNITED KINGDOM
Leeds
Liverpool
Manchester
Sheffield
WALES
Birmingham
ENGLAND
Cardiff
Thames
LONDON
Southampton
North Sea
Channel Islands (to UK)
English Channel
le Havre
Seine
Rennes
PARIS
St-Nazaire
Nantes
Loire
Orléans
Bay of Biscay
FRANCE
Limoges
A Coruña
Bordeaux
Bilbao
Toulouse
Pyrenees
Porto
Duero
Valladolid
Ebro
PORTUGAL
Tagus
LISBON
Setúbal
MADRID
Zaragoza
ANDORRA LA VELLA
ANDORRA
Barcelona
SPAIN
Valencia
Seville
Córdoba
Cádiz
Málaga
Murcia
Gibraltar (to UK)
Ceuta (to Spain)
Melilla (to Spain)
Mallorca
Menorca
Eivissa
Palma
Balearic Islands
Mediterranean Sea
Marseille
Nice
MONACO
Lyon
Rhône
Geneva
Alps
Corsica
Sardinia
Cagliari

NORWAY
SWEDEN
FINLAND
Trondheim
Gulf of Bothnia
Tampere
Bergen
Stavanger
OSLO
Kristiansand
Uppsala
Vänern
Örebro
STOCKHOLM
Åland
Turku
HELSINKI
TALLINN
ESTONIA
St Pet
Vättern
Jönköping
Gothenburg
Ålborg
DENMARK
Gotland
Ventspils
LATVIA
RIGA
Western Dvina
Liepāja
COPENHAGEN
Helsingborg
Malmö
Odense
Baltic Sea
LITHUANIA
Kaunas
VILNIUS
RUSS. FED. (Kaliningrad)
Kaliningrad
Gdańsk
Vitsyebsk
MINSK
Babruysk
BELARUS
Groningen
Hamburg
Elbe
Oder
AMSTERDAM
NETH.
THE HAGUE
Rotterdam
Bremen
Nijmegen
Hannover
BERLIN
Bydgoszcz
Vistula
Poznań
Antwerp
BELGIUM
BRUSSELS
Düsseldorf
GERMANY
Liège
Bonn
Rhine
Leipzig
Dresden
WARSAW
Łódź
Brest
POLAND
Wrocław
LUXEMBOURG
Frankfurt am Main
PRAGUE
CZECH REPUBLIC
Kraków
L'viv
UK
Nuremberg
Strasbourg
Stuttgart
Munich
Salzburg
Danube
VIENNA
BRATISLAVA
SLOVAKIA
Chernivtsi
Dniester
MOLD.
Zürich
BERN
SWITZERLAND
Innsbruck
AUSTRIA
Győr
Miskolc
BUDAPEST
LIECHTENSTEIN
HUNGARY
Cluj-Napoca
CHIŞINĂU
ROMANIA
Braşov
Milan
LJUBLJANA
SLOVENIA
Turin
Verona
Po
Venice
Trieste
ZAGREB
Genoa
Bologna
CROATIA
BELGRADE
Florence
SAN MARINO
BOS. & HERZ.
SARAJEVO
Mostar
SERBIA
BUCHAREST
Constanța
Danube
Ruse
Pisa
Adriatic Sea
ITALY
YUGOSLAVIA
MONTENEGRO
BULGARIA
SOFIA
Stara Zagora
VATICAN CITY
ROME
Naples
Bari
TIRANA
SKOPJE
MACEDONIA
ALBANIA
Salonica
Tyrrhenian Sea
Cosenza
Lárisa
Aegean Sea
GREECE
Palermo
Messina
Sicily
Catania
Piraeus
ATHENS
Ionian Sea
MALTA
VALLETTA
Iráklelo
Crete

Population density (people per sq mile)
- below 130
- 130–259
- 260–379
- 380–519
- 520–780
- above 780

Traditional lifestyles *still persist in many remote and rural parts of Europe, especially in the south, east, and in the far north.*

Map Key

POPULATION
- above 5 million
- 1 million to 5 million
- 500,000 to 1 million
- 100,000 to 500,000
- 50,000 to 100,000
- 10,000 to 50,000
- Country capital

BORDERS
- full international border

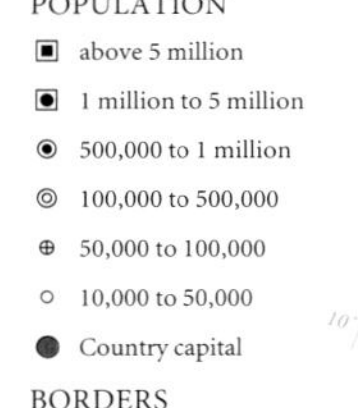

SCALE 1:17,250,000
(projection: Lambert Azimuthal Equal Area)

Km 0 50 100 200 300 400 500 600 700 800 900 1000
Miles 0 50 100 200 300 400 500 600 700

Overcoming natural barriers, the Brenner Autobahn, one of the main routes across the Alps, links Innsbruck in Austria with Verona in Italy.

TRANSPORTATION

DESPITE ITS FRAGMENTED GEOGRAPHY and many natural frontiers, communications in Europe are well developed. Extensive highway links allow rapid road transportation. High-speed rail connections like France's TGV *(Train à Grande Vitesse)*, and the Channel Tunnel have improved rail travel. Outdated communication infrastructures in parts of eastern Europe, and insufficient transportation links across the Alps, however, remain weak parts of the network.

LANGUAGES

THERE ARE THREE MAIN EUROPEAN language groups: Germanic languages predominate in central and northern Europe; Romance languages in western and Mediterranean Europe and Romania; while Slavic languages are spoken in eastern Europe and the Russian Federation. Isolated pockets of local languages, such as Basque and Gaelic, persist and frequently provide a focus for national identity.

The architecture of the Grand Place lies at the heart of Brussels – home city to one of the eu headquarters.

European Resources

Europe's large tracts of fertile, accessible land, combined with its generally temperate climate, have allowed a greater percentage of land to be used for agricultural purposes than in any other continent. Extensive coal and iron ore deposits were used to create steel and manufacturing industries during the 19th and 20th centuries. Today, although natural resources have been widely exploited, and heavy industry is of declining importance, the growth of hi-tech and service industries has enabled Europe to maintain its wealth.

Industry

Europe's wealth was generated by the rise of industry and colonial exploitation during the 19th century. The mining of abundant natural resources made Europe the industrial center of the world. Adaptation has been essential in the changing world economy, and a move to service-based industries has been widespread except in eastern Europe, where heavy industry still dominates.

***Countries like Hungary** are still struggling to modernize inefficient factories left over from extensive, centrally-planned industrialization during the communist era.*

***Frankfurt am Main** is an example of a modern service-based city. The skyline is dominated by headquarters from the worlds of banking and commerce.*

***Other power sources** are becoming more attractive as fossil fuels run out; 16% of Europe's electricity is now provided by hydroelectric power.*

Standard of Living

Living standards in western Europe are among the highest in the world, although there is a growing sector of homeless, jobless people. Eastern Europeans have lower overall standards of living – a legacy of stagnated economies.

Standard of Living
(UN Human Development Index)
low
high

***Skiing brings millions** of tourists to the slopes each year, which means that even unproductive, marginal land is used to create wealth in the French, Swiss, Italian, and Austrian Alps.*

Novaya Zemlya
Ostrov Kolguyev
Barents Sea
Murmansk
Archangel
RUSSIAN FEDERATION
Perm'
St Petersburg
Cherepovets
Yaroslavl'
Ivanovo
Nizhniy Novgorod
Kazan'
Ufa
Moscow
Tol'yatti
Samara
Ryazan'
Tula
Saratov
Voronezh
Kursk
Volgograd
KAZAKHSTAN
Caspian Sea
GEORGIA
AZERBAIJAN
Rostov-na-Donu
GNP per capita (US$)
below 1999
2000–4999
5000–9999
10,000–19,999
20,000–24,999
above 25,000
Industry
aerospace
brewing
car/vehicle manufacture
chemicals
defense
electronics
engineering
finance
food processing
hi-tech industry
iron & steel
pharmaceuticals
printing & publishing
shipbuilding
textiles
timber processing
wine
coal
oil
gas
industrial cities
major industrial areas

ICELAND
Reykjavík
Faeroe Islands (to Denmark)
Norwegian Sea
ATLANTIC OCEAN
NORWAY
SWEDEN
FINLAND
Gulf of Bothnia
Trondheim
Bergen
Oslo
Stockholm
Gothenburg
Malmö
Turku
Helsinki
Tallinn
ESTONIA
LATVIA
Riga
LITHUANIA
Vilnius
RUSS. FED. (Kaliningrad)
Baltic Sea
DENMARK
Copenhagen
North Sea
REPUBLIC OF IRELAND
Dublin
Belfast
Isle of Man (to UK)
UNITED KINGDOM
Glasgow
Newcastle upon Tyne
Liverpool
Manchester
Birmingham
Cardiff
London
Channel Islands (to UK)
NETH.
Amsterdam
Rotterdam
Antwerp
Brussels
BELG.
Essen
Cologne
Liège
LUX.
Lille
Rouen
Paris
Metz
Strasbourg
Nantes
FRANCE
Bay of Biscay
Bordeaux
Lyon
Toulouse
Marseille
ANDORRA
MONACO
GERMANY
Hamburg
Berlin
Leipzig
Dresden
Frankfurt am Main
Stuttgart
Munich
Zürich
SWITZ.
LIECH.
AUSTRIA
Linz
Vienna
CZECH REP.
Prague
POLAND
Gdańsk
Poznań
Łódź
Warsaw
Katowice
Kraków
SLOVAKIA
Bratislava
Budapest
HUNGARY
BELARUS
Minsk
UKRAINE
Kiev
Kharkiv
Dnipropetrovs'k
Donets'k
Kryvyy Rih
Odesa
MOLDOVA
ROMANIA
Ploeşti
Bucharest
Constanţa
Black Sea
BULGARIA
Sofia
Varna
Istanbul
TURKEY
SPAIN
PORTUGAL
A Coruña
Bilbao
Porto
Lisbon
Madrid
Barcelona
Seville
Gibraltar (to UK)
Ceuta (to Spain)
Melilla (to Spain)
MOROCCO
Balearic Islands
Mediterranean Sea
Corsica
Sardinia
Sicily
MALTA
ITALY
Turin
Milan
Genoa
Venice
Bologna
SAN MARINO
VATICAN CITY
Rome
Naples
Taranto
Palermo
Tyrrhenian Sea
Adriatic Sea
Ionian Sea
SLVN.
Zagreb
CROATIA
BOSNIA & HERZ.
YUGOSLAVIA
Belgrade
ALBANIA
MACED.
GREECE
Salonica
Piraeus
Athens
Aegean Sea
Crete

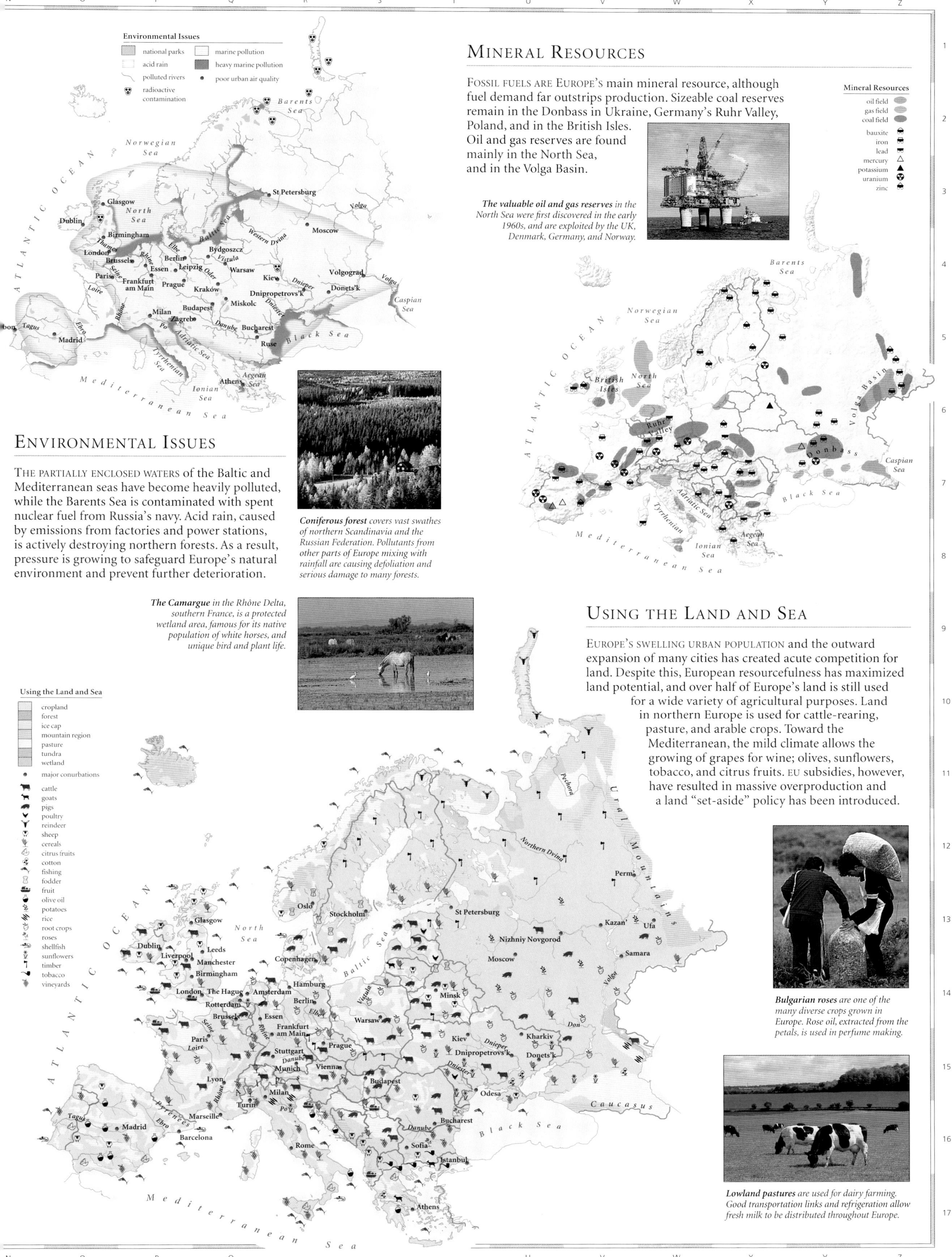
Environmental Issues
national parks
acid rain
polluted rivers
radioactive contamination
marine pollution
heavy marine pollution
poor urban air quality
Mineral Resources
oil field
gas field
coal field
bauxite
iron
lead
mercury
potassium
uranium
zinc
Using the Land and Sea
cropland
forest
ice cap
mountain region
pasture
tundra
wetland
major conurbations
cattle
goats
pigs
poultry
reindeer
sheep
cereals
citrus fruits
cotton
fishing
fodder
fruit
olive oil
potatoes
rice
root crops
roses
shellfish
sunflowers
timber
tobacco
vineyards

Mineral Resources

Fossil fuels are Europe's main mineral resource, although fuel demand far outstrips production. Sizeable coal reserves remain in the Donbass in Ukraine, Germany's Ruhr Valley, Poland, and in the British Isles. Oil and gas reserves are found mainly in the North Sea, and in the Volga Basin.

***The valuable oil and gas reserves** in the North Sea were first discovered in the early 1960s, and are exploited by the UK, Denmark, Germany, and Norway.*

Environmental Issues

The partially enclosed waters of the Baltic and Mediterranean seas have become heavily polluted, while the Barents Sea is contaminated with spent nuclear fuel from Russia's navy. Acid rain, caused by emissions from factories and power stations, is actively destroying northern forests. As a result, pressure is growing to safeguard Europe's natural environment and prevent further deterioration.

***Coniferous forest** covers vast swathes of northern Scandinavia and the Russian Federation. Pollutants from other parts of Europe mixing with rainfall are causing defoliation and serious damage to many forests.*

***The Camargue** in the Rhône Delta, southern France, is a protected wetland area, famous for its native population of white horses, and unique bird and plant life.*

Using the Land and Sea

Europe's swelling urban population and the outward expansion of many cities has created acute competition for land. Despite this, European resourcefulness has maximized land potential, and over half of Europe's land is still used for a wide variety of agricultural purposes. Land in northern Europe is used for cattle-rearing, pasture, and arable crops. Toward the Mediterranean, the mild climate allows the growing of grapes for wine; olives, sunflowers, tobacco, and citrus fruits. EU subsidies, however, have resulted in massive overproduction and a land "set-aside" policy has been introduced.

***Bulgarian roses** are one of the many diverse crops grown in Europe. Rose oil, extracted from the petals, is used in perfume making.*

***Lowland pastures** are used for dairy farming. Good transportation links and refrigeration allow fresh milk to be distributed throughout Europe.*

Scandinavia, Finland & Iceland

Denmark, Norway, Sweden, Finland, Iceland

JUTTING INTO THE ARCTIC CIRCLE, this northern swath of Europe has some of the continent's harshest environments, but benefits from great reserves of oil, gas, and natural evergreen forests. While most early settlers came from the south, migrants to Finland came from the east, giving it a distinct language and culture. Since the late 19th century, the Scandinavian states have developed strong egalitarian traditions. Today, their welfare benefits systems are among the most extensive in the world, and standards of living are high. The Lapps, or Sami, maintain their traditional lifestyle in the northern regions of Norway, Sweden, and Finland.

The Landscape

GLACIERS UP TO 10,000 ft (3,000 m) deep covered most of Scandinavia and Finland during the last Ice Age. The effects of glaciation mark the entire landscape, from the mountains to the lowlands, across the tundra landscape of Lapland, and the lake districts of Sweden and Finland.

Halti Mountain is Finland's highest point, at 4,356 ft (1,328 m).

Lapland, north of the Arctic Circle, is an area of undulating fells and plains known as tundra. The subsoil is permanently frozen and therefore impermeable. There are many peat bogs. Pools reappear in the summer when the surface thaws.

The Lofoten Islands were one of the first areas exposed as the ice sheet melted.

Geysers are a by-product of Iceland's volcanic activity. Geysir, Iceland's largest spring, gives them their name.

Oulujärvi

Finland's landscape was fashioned by ice action. Glaciers gouged out its distinctive shallow lake basins, such as Oulujärvi, and left debris called moraines in their wake.

Fjords

Sjælland coast

Area of maximum yearly uplift 0.3 in/yr (9 mm/yr)

Slower rates of uplift 0.1 in/yr (3 mm/yr)

Scandinavia is still recovering from the last Ice Age, when ice depressed the land by 2,000 ft (600 m). This gradual uplift is known as isostatic rebound.

The fjords on the western coast of Norway were once gentle river valleys. Their deep floors and steep sides were carved out by glaciers during the last Ice Age, and they

On the coast of Sjælland, these cliffs have been eroded by the sea, exposing layers

SCALE 1:9,000,000
(projection: Lambert Conformal Conic)

(same scale as main map)

Using the Land and Sea

THE COLD CLIMATE, short growing season, poorly developed soil, steep slopes, and exposure to high winds across northern regions means that most agriculture is concentrated, with the population, in the south. Most of Finland and much of Norway and Sweden are covered by dense forests of pine, spruce and birch, which supply the timber industries.

ICELAND
REYKJAVIK
NORWAY
SWEDEN
FINLAND
DENMARK
OSLO
STOCKHOLM
HELSINKI
COPENHAGEN
RUSSIAN FEDERATION
NORTH SEA
BALTIC SEA
GERMANY

Land use and agricultural distribution
fishing, pigs, reindeer, sheep, cereals, timber
capital cities, major towns
pasture, cropland, forest, mountain region, tundra

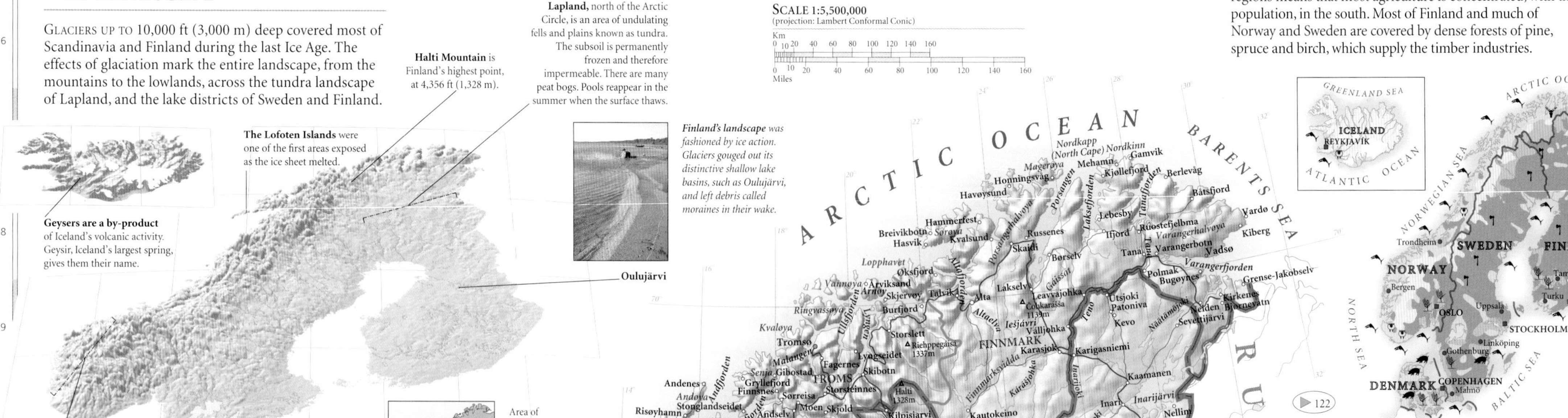
ARCTIC OCEAN
BARENTS SEA
RUSSIAN FE
Lapland
FINNMARK
TROMS
NORDLAND

SCALE 1:5,500,000
(projection: Lambert Conformal Conic)

122

The Urban/Rural Population Divide

urban 77% rural 23%

POPULATION DENSITY
20 people per sq mile
(51 people per sq km)

TOTAL LAND AREA
473,970 sq miles
(1,227,610 sq km)

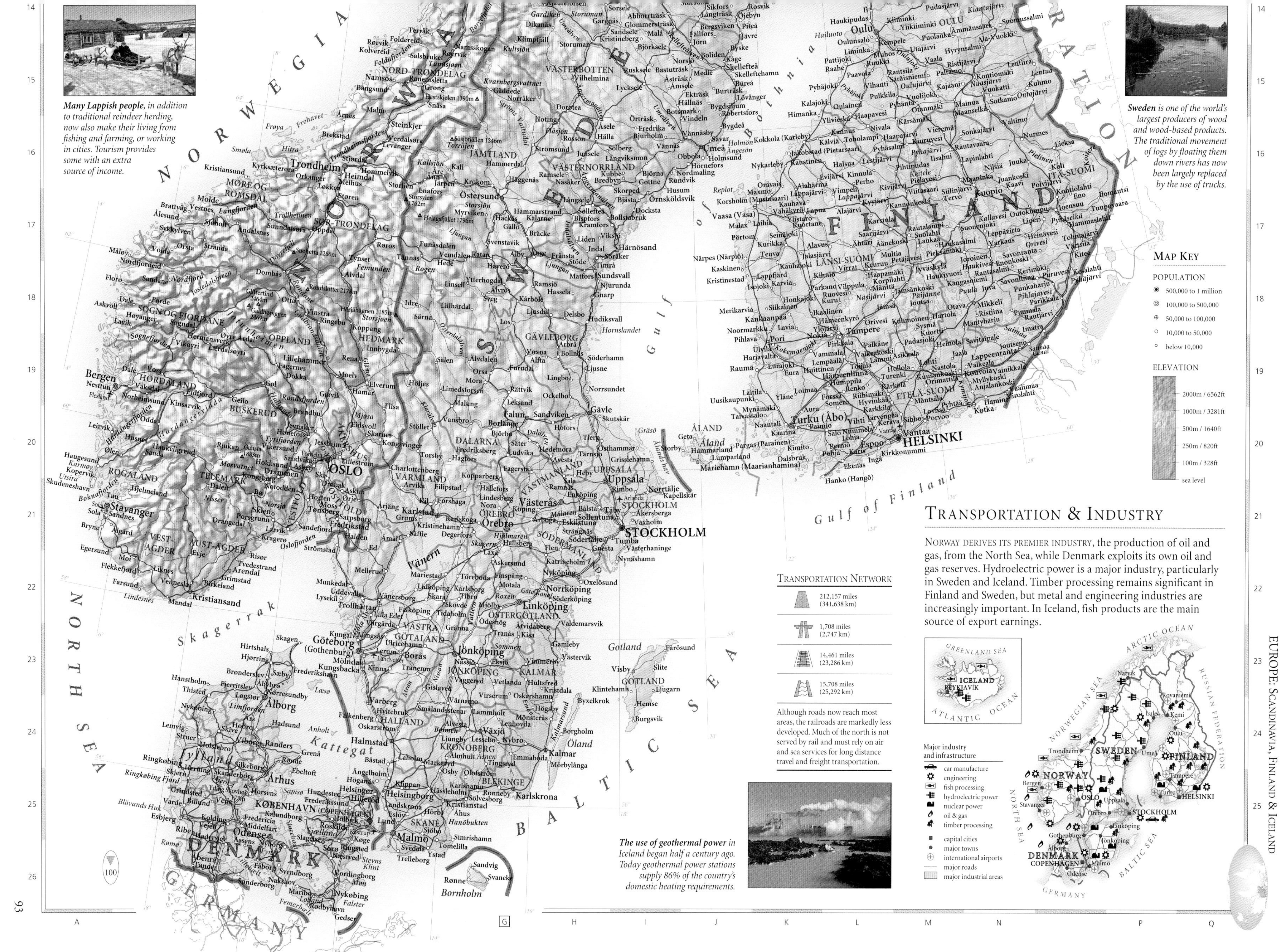
NORWEGIAN SEA
NORWAY
SWEDEN
FINLAND
DENMARK
GERMANY
NORTH SEA
BALTIC SEA
Gulf of Bothnia
Gulf of Finland
Skagerrak
Kattegat
OSLO
STOCKHOLM
HELSINKI
KØBENHAVN (COPENHAGEN)
ÅLAND
Gotland
Öland
Bornholm
MAP KEY
POPULATION
500,000 to 1 million
100,000 to 500,000
50,000 to 100,000
10,000 to 50,000
below 10,000
ELEVATION
2000m / 6562ft
1000m / 3281ft
500m / 1640ft
250m / 820ft
100m / 328ft
sea level
100

Many Lappish people, *in addition to traditional reindeer herding, now also make their living from fishing and farming, or working in cities. Tourism provides some with an extra source of income.*

Sweden *is one of the world's largest producers of wood and wood-based products. The traditional movement of logs by floating them down rivers has now been largely replaced by the use of trucks.*

Transportation & Industry

Norway derives its premier industry, the production of oil and gas, from the North Sea, while Denmark exploits its own oil and gas reserves. Hydroelectric power is a major industry, particularly in Sweden and Iceland. Timber processing remains significant in Finland and Sweden, but metal and engineering industries are increasingly important. In Iceland, fish products are the main source of export earnings.

GREENLAND SEA
ICELAND
REYKJAVIK
ATLANTIC OCEAN
ARCTIC OCEAN
RUSSIAN FEDERATION
NORWEGIAN SEA
NORTH SEA
BALTIC SEA
GERMANY
NORWAY
SWEDEN
FINLAND
DENMARK
OSLO
STOCKHOLM
HELSINKI
COPENHAGEN
Major industry and infrastructure
car manufacture
engineering
fish processing
hydroelectric power
nuclear power
oil & gas
timber processing
capital cities
major towns
international airports
major roads
major industrial areas

Transportation Network

Roads	212,157 miles (341,638 km)
Motorways	1,708 miles (2,747 km)
Railways	14,461 miles (23,286 km)
Inland waterways	15,708 miles (25,292 km)

Although roads now reach most areas, the railroads are markedly less developed. Much of the north is not served by rail and must rely on air and sea services for long distance travel and freight transportation.

***The use of geothermal power** in Iceland began half a century ago. Today geothermal power stations supply 86% of the country's domestic heating requirements.*

Southern Scandinavia

Southern Norway, Southern Sweden, Denmark

Scandinavia's economic and political hub is the more habitable and accessible southern region. Many of the area's major cities are on the southern coasts, including Oslo and Stockholm, the capitals of Norway and Sweden. In Denmark, most of the population and the capital, Copenhagen, are located on its many islands. A cultural unity links the three Scandinavian countries. Their main languages, Danish, Swedish, and Norwegian, are mutually intelligible, and they all retain their monarchies, although the parliaments have legislative control.

Using the Land

Agriculture in southern Scandinavia is highly mechanized although farms are small. Denmark is the most intensively farmed country and its western pastureland is used mainly for pig farming. Cereal crops including wheat, barley, and oats, predominate in eastern Denmark and in the far south of Sweden. Southern Norway, and Sweden have large tracts of forest which are exploited for logging.

The Urban/Rural Population Divide

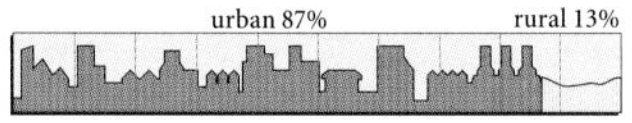

urban 87% — rural 13%

Population Density	Total Land Area
152 people per sq mile (61 people per sq km)	173,487 sq miles (456,564 sq km)

Land use and agricultural distribution: cattle, pigs, sheep, cereals, fodder, root crops, timber; capital cities, major towns; pasture, cropland, forest, mountain region

In Norway winters are longer and colder inland than in coastal areas, where the warm current of the North Atlantic Drift moderates the climate.

The Landscape

Southern Scandinavia, with the exception of Norway, has a flatter terrain than the rest of the region. Denmark and southern Sweden are both extensions of the North European Plain. In this area, because of glacial deposition rather than erosion, the soils are deeper and more fertile.

In the past, glaciers such as this one in Olden, Norway, were much larger. Today, many are retreating to yield the spectacular glacial scenery.

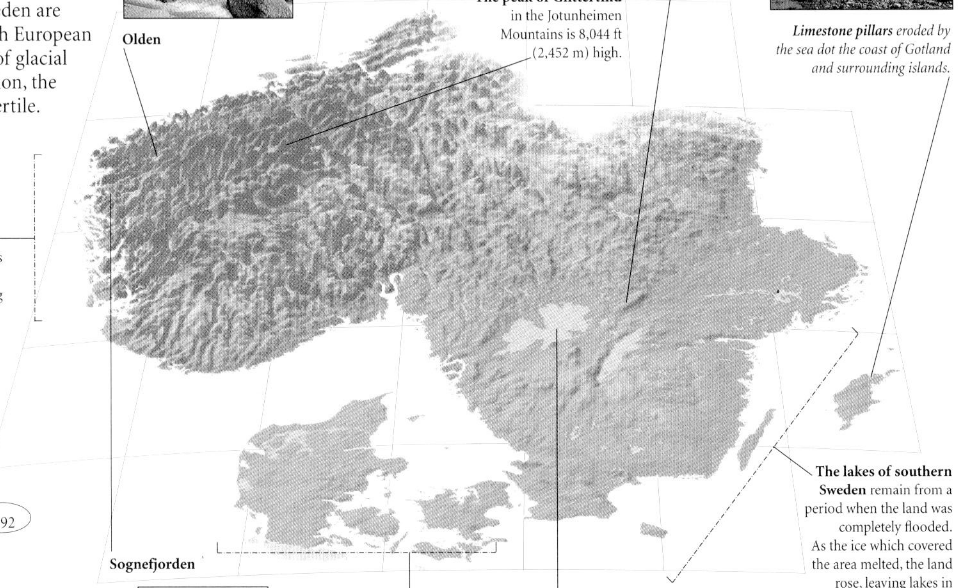

Distinctive low ridges, called eskers, are found across southern Sweden. They are formed from sand and gravel deposits left by retreating glaciers.

Limestone pillars eroded by the sea dot the coast of Gotland and surrounding islands.

The peak of Glittertind in the Jotunheimen Mountains is 8,044 ft (2,452 m) high.

Olden

Acid rain, caused by industrial pollution carried north from elsewhere in Europe, harms plant and animal life in Scandinavian forests and lakes. The region's surface rocks lack lime to neutralize the acid, so making the problem more serious.

Sognefjorden

Erosion by glaciers deepened existing river valleys

Sea level

When the ice retreated the valley was flooded by the sea

Old valley floor

Sognefjorden is the deepest of Norway's many fjords. It drops to 4,291 ft (1,308 m) below sea level.

Vänern in Sweden is the largest lake in Scandinavia. It covers an area of 2,080 sq miles (5,390 sq km).

Denmark's flat and fertile soils are formed on glacial deposits between 100–160 ft (30–50 m) deep.

The lakes of southern Sweden remain from a period when the land was completely flooded. As the ice which covered the area melted, the land rose, leaving lakes in shallow, ice-scoured depressions. Sweden has over 90,000 lakes.

Scale 1:3,250,000 (projection: Lambert Conformal Conic)

Map Key

Population: 500,000 to 1 million; 100,000 to 500,000; 50,000 to 100,000; 10,000 to 50,000; below 10,000

Elevation: 2000m / 6562ft; 1000m / 3281ft; 500m / 1640ft; 250m / 820ft; 100m / 328ft; sea level

92
96
92

NORTH SEA
Skagerrak
Kattegat
BALTIC SEA
Hanöbukten
SWEDEN
DENMARK
GERMANY
FINLAND
HORDALAND
ROGALAND
TELEMARK
VEST-AGDER
AUST-AGDER
BUSKERUD
AKERSHUS
ØSTFOLD
VESTFOLD
OSLO
VÄRMLAND
VÄSTMANLAND
UPPSALA
STOCKHOLM
ÖREBRO
SÖDERMANLAND
ÖSTERGÖTLAND
VÄSTRA GÖTALAND
JÖNKÖPING
KALMAR
HALLAND
KRONOBERG
BLEKINGE
SKÅNE
Götaland
Småland
Gotland
Öland
Bornholm
NORDJYLLAND
VIBORG
RINGKØBING
ÅRHUS
VEJLE
RIBE
SØNDERJYLLAND
FYN
VESTSJÆLLAND
STORSTRØM
KØBENHAVN
Jylland
Sjælland
Vänern
Vättern
96
100
110
FAEROE ISLANDS (to Denmark)
TÓRSHAVN
ATLANTIC OCEAN
(same scale as main map)
NORWEGIAN SEA
NORWAY
Major industry and infrastructure
car manufacture
electronics
engineering
furniture industry
iron & steel
shipbuilding
food processing
capital cities
major towns
international airports
major roads
major industrial areas
TRANSPORTATON NETWORK
133,712 miles (215,666 km)
1160 miles (1872 km)
8180 miles (13,195 km)
3668 miles (5197 km)
Major additions to the transportation network in this region are the new bridge and tunnel projects under construction, which will connect Denmark's main islands and forge links with Sweden and Germany.

Shipbuilding in Gothenburg *has declined in recent years as manufacturers in other sectors have come to the fore. One of these is the car firm, Volvo, a major employer in Gothenburg.*

TRANSPORTATION & INDUSTRY

IN DENMARK AND NORWAY food processing is a major industry. Swedish iron and steel production supports car manufacturers such as Saab and Volvo. Nearly half of Norway's income comes from North Sea oil and gas reserves. Denmark's successful hi-tech, high-profit electronics and light engineering industries largely use imported raw materials.

More than half the land *in Denmark is used for agriculture. Grains, particularly wheat and barley, are the main crops cultivated.*

Sand deposited by glaciers *at the end of the last Ice Age, has been fashioned by wind and waves into dunes, creating heathlands along the northwestern coast of Jylland.*

THE BRITISH ISLES

UNITED KINGDOM, REPUBLIC OF IRELAND

THE BRITISH ISLES have for centuries played a central role in European and world history. England, Wales, Scotland, and Northern Ireland together form the United Kingdom (UK), while the southern portion of Ireland is an independent country, self-governing since 1921. Although England has tended to be the politically and economically dominant partner in the UK, the Scots, Welsh and Irish maintain independent cultures, distinct national identities and languages. Southeastern England is the most densely populated part of this crowded region, with over nine million people living in and around the London area.

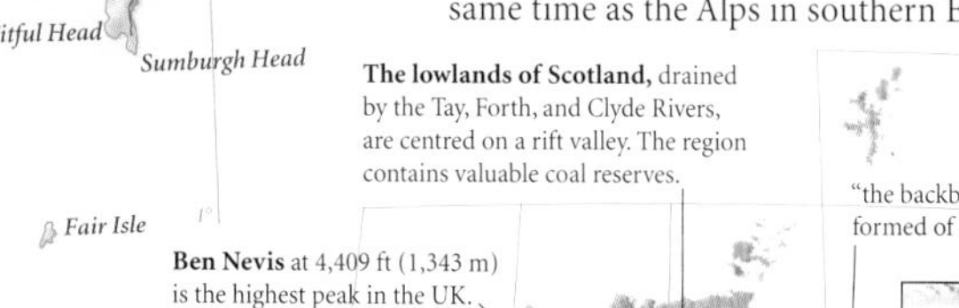

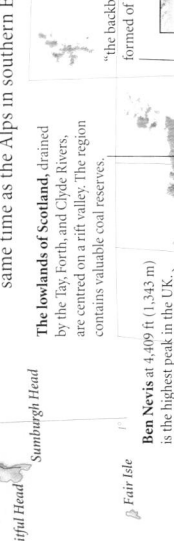

The valley of Glen Coe in the Scottish Highlands is a U-shaped valley, typical of the north and west of the British Isles, where glaciers shaped much of the landscape.

TRANSPORT AND INDUSTRY

THE BRITISH ISLES' INDUSTRIAL BASE was founded primarily on coal, iron and textiles, based largely in the north. Today, the most productive sectors include hi-tech industries clustered mainly in southeastern England, chemicals, finance and the service sector, particularly tourism.

Major industry and infrastructure

- car manufacture
- chemicals
- engineering
- hi-tech industry
- iron & steel
- tourism
- capital cities
- major towns
- international airports
- major roads
- major industrial areas

TRANSPORTATION NETWORK

288,330 miles (464,300 km)	2,046 miles (3,295 km)
11,874 miles (19,121 km)	3,806 miles (6,129 km)

The UK's congested roads have become a major focus of environmental concern in recent years. No longer an island, the UK was finally linked to continental Europe by the Channel Tunnel in 1994.

Clew Bay in western Ireland, is characteristic of the heavily indented west coast, where deep wide-mouthed bays separate the mountains of Mayo, Donegal, and Kerry as they thrust out into the Atlantic Ocean.

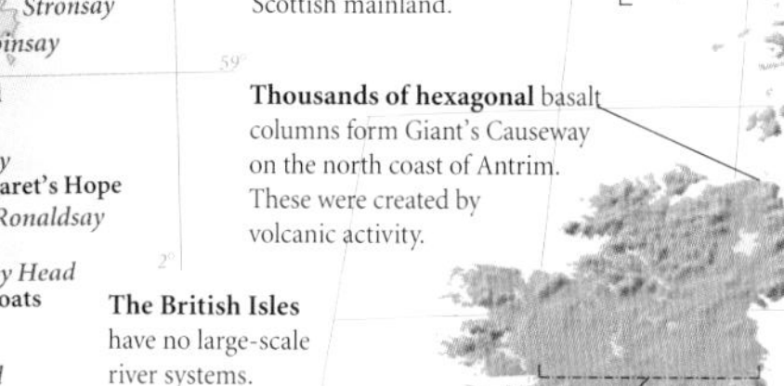

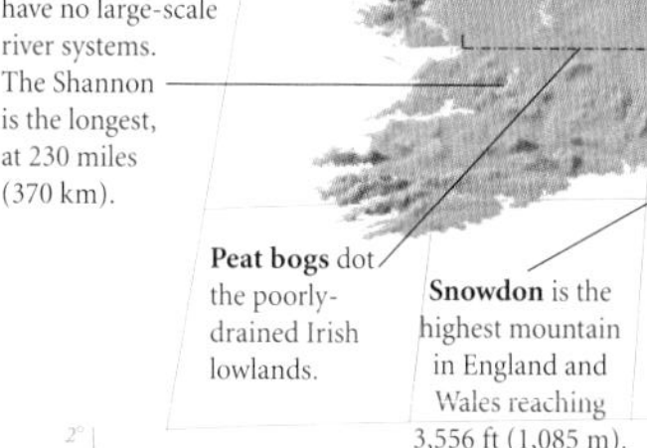

ATLANTIC OCEAN
NORTH SEA
SCOTLAND
Outer Hebrides
Inner Hebrides
Sea of the Hebrides
Orkney Islands
Shetland Islands
Isle of Lewis
Isle of Skye
Isle of Mull
Grampian Mountains
North West Highlands
Edinburgh
Glasgow
Aberdeen
Dundee
Inverness
Fort William
Oban
Stornoway
Kirkwall
Lerwick
Thurso
Wick
Perth
Stirling
St Andrews
Ben Nevis 1343m
Cairn Gorm 1245m
Ben Macdui 1309m
Sula Sgeir
North Rona
St Kilda
Fair Isle
Cape Wrath
Dunnet Head
Duncansby Head
John o'Groats
Pentland Firth
Moray Firth
Firth of Forth
Firth of Lorn
Firth of Tay
The Minch
The Little Minch
Loch Ness
Loch Lomond
Loch Tay
Mull of Oa
Islay
Jura
Tiree
Coll
Barra
Barra Head
Flannan Isles
Monach Islands
64
92

Dartmoor, studded with tors, is an exposed part of a vast granite dome, formed when molten rock intruded into the Earth's crust.

Black Ven, Lyme Regis
Water
Mudslide
Sea
Cracks
Sandstone
Clay
Limestone

Much of the south coast is subject to landslides. Following rain, porous sandstones feed water into the underlying, less permeable clays which then crumble and slide into the sea.

THE LANDSCAPE

RUGGED UPLANDS dominate the landscape of Scotland, Wales, and northern England. All the peaks in the British Isles over 4,000 ft (1,219 m) lie in highland Scotland. Lowland England rises into several ranges of rolling hills, including the older Mendips, and the Cotswolds and the Chilterns, which were formed at the same time as the Alps in southern Europe.

The lowlands of Scotland, drained by the Tay, Forth, and Clyde Rivers, are centred on a rift valley. The region contains valuable coal reserves.

The Pennines, sometimes called "the backbone of England," are formed of limestones and grits.

Ben Nevis at 4,409 ft (1,343 m) is the highest peak in the UK.

Over 600 islands, mostly uninhabited, lie west and north of the Scottish mainland.

Ullswater in the Lake District fills a deep valley formed by glacial erosion.

Thousands of hexagonal basalt columns form Giant's Causeway on the north coast of Antrim. These were created by volcanic activity.

The Fens are a low-lying area reclaimed from the sea.

The British Isles have no large-scale river systems. The Shannon is the longest, at 230 miles (370 km).

Lake District

Peat bogs dot the poorly-drained Irish lowlands.

Snowdon is the highest mountain in England and Wales reaching 3,556 ft (1,085 m).

Mendip Hills

Chiltern Hills

The Cotswold Hills are characterized by a series of limestone ridges overlooking clay vales.

Durdle Door

Coastal erosion around the British Isles forms striking features such as this limestone arch, Durdle Door in Dorset.

MAP KEY

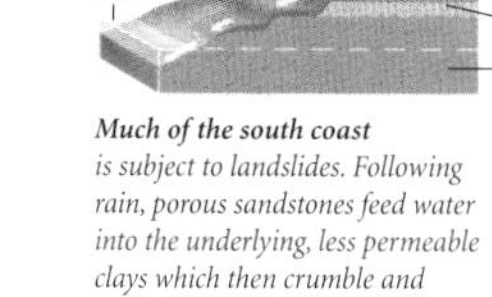

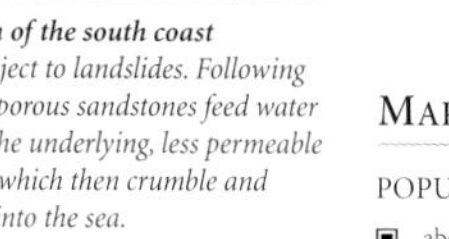

POPULATION

- above 5 million
- 1 million to 5 million
- 500,000 to 1 million
- 100,000 to 500,000
- 50,000 to 100,000
- 10,000 to 50,000
- below 10,000

ELEVATION

- 1000m / 3281ft
- 500m / 1640ft
- 250m / 820ft
- 100m / 328ft
- sea level

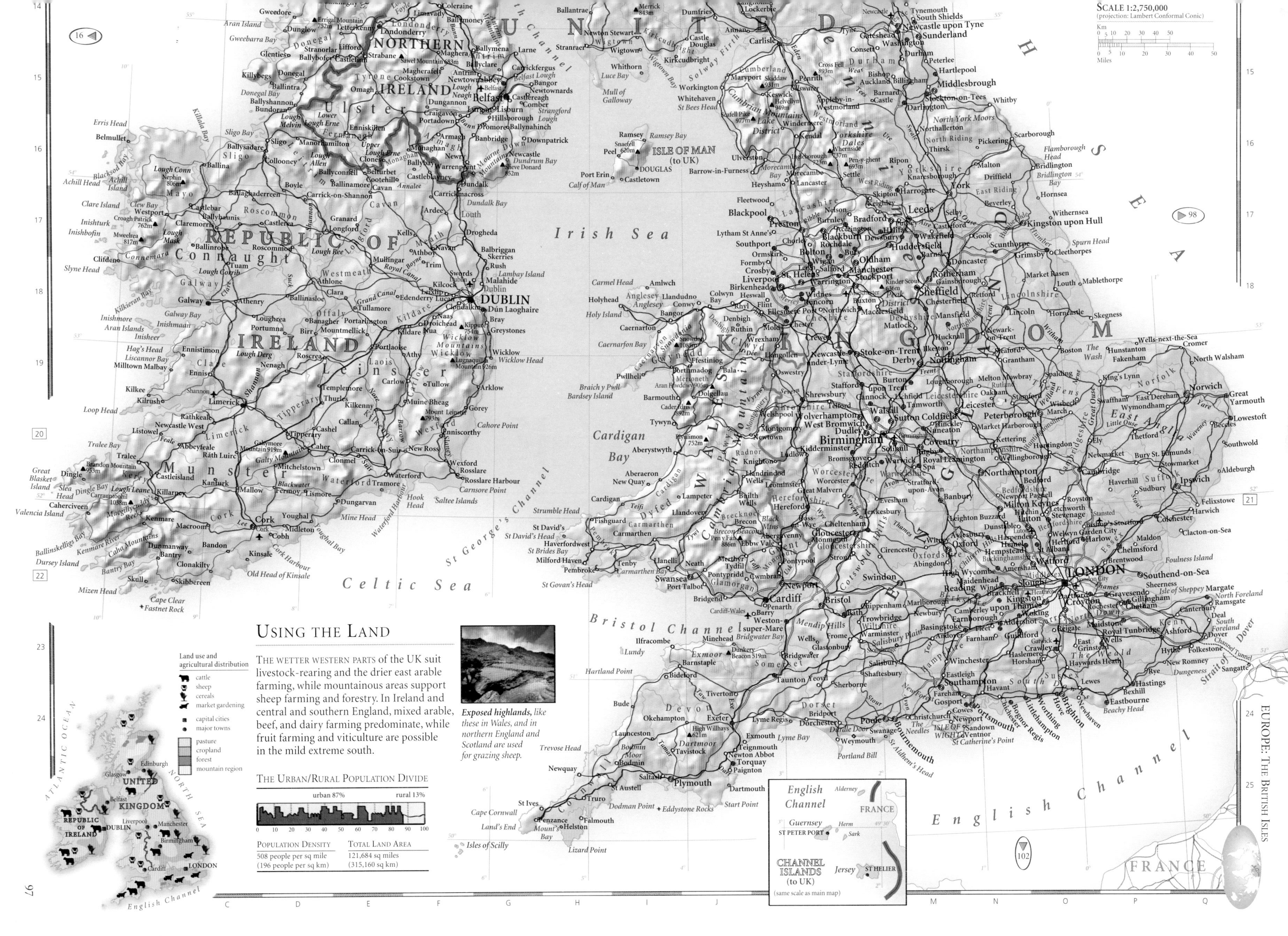
SCALE 1:2,750,000
(projection: Lambert Conformal Conic)
UNITED KINGDOM
REPUBLIC OF IRELAND
NORTHERN IRELAND
Irish Sea
Celtic Sea
NORTH SEA
English Channel
Bristol Channel
St George's Channel
Cardigan Bay
ISLE OF MAN (to UK)
CHANNEL ISLANDS (to UK)
(same scale as main map)
FRANCE
LONDON
DUBLIN
ATLANTIC OCEAN
Land use and agricultural distribution
cattle
sheep
cereals
market gardening
capital cities
major towns
pasture
cropland
forest
mountain region

USING THE LAND

THE WETTER WESTERN PARTS of the UK suit livestock-rearing and the drier east arable farming, while mountainous areas support sheep farming and forestry. In Ireland and central and southern England, mixed arable, beef, and dairy farming predominate, while fruit farming and viticulture are possible in the mild extreme south.

Exposed highlands, like these in Wales, and in northern England and Scotland are used for grazing sheep.

THE URBAN/RURAL POPULATION DIVIDE

urban 87% rural 13%

0 10 20 30 40 50 60 70 80 90 100

POPULATION DENSITY	TOTAL LAND AREA
508 people per sq mile (196 people per sq km)	121,684 sq miles (315,160 sq km)

The Low Countries

Belgium, Luxembourg, Netherlands

One of northwestern Europe's strategic crossroads, the Low Countries are united by a common history in which they have often been a battleground in European wars. For over a thousand years they were ruled by foreign powers. Even after they achieved independence, the three countries maintained close links, later forming the world's first totally free labor and goods market, the Benelux Economic Union, which became the core of the European Community (now the European Union or EU). These states have remained at the forefront of wider European cooperation; Brussels, The Hague, and Luxembourg are hosts to major institutions of the EU.

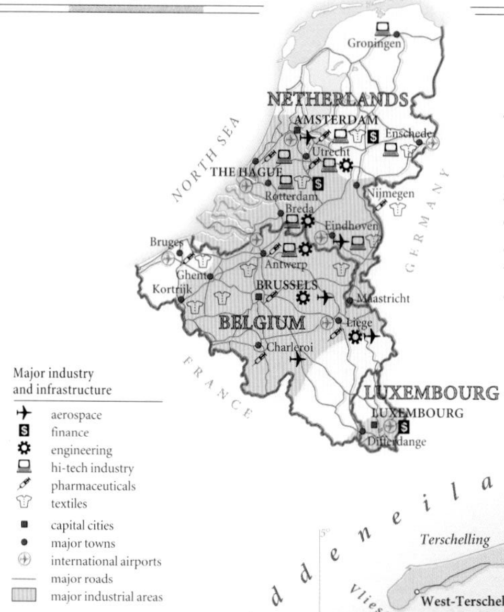

Transportation & Industry

In the western Netherlands, a massive, sprawling industrialized zone encompasses many new hi-tech and service industries. Belgium's central region has emerged as the country's light manufacturing and services center. Luxembourg city is home to more than 160 banks and the European headquarters of many international companies.

Transportation Network

280,630 miles (451,900 km)
2,536 miles (4,083 km)
4,037 miles (6,501 km)
4,366 miles (7,031 km)

The Low Countries hold a key position on the North Sea, containing Europe's two largest ports, Rotterdam and Antwerp, which are connected to a comprehensive system of inland waterways.

Major industry and infrastructure: aerospace; finance; engineering; hi-tech industry; pharmaceuticals; textiles; capital cities; major towns; international airports; major roads; major industrial areas

The Landscape

The main geographical regions of the Netherlands are the northern glacial heathlands, the low-lying lands of the Rhine and Maas/Meuse, the reclaimed polders, and the dune coast and islands. Belgium includes part of the Ardennes, together with the coalfields on its northern flanks, and the fertile Flanders Plain.

Dune system – Sea – Polder – Drainage ditch

Extensive sand dune systems *along the coast have prevented flooding of the land. Behind the dunes, marshy land is drained to form polders, usable land suitable for agriculture.*

Sand dunes

Since the Middle Ages the people of the Netherlands have used ditches and drainage dykes to reclaim land from the sea. These reclaimed areas are known as polders.

The loess soils of the Flanders Plain in western Belgium provide excellent conditions for arable farming.

Ardennes

Uplifted and folded *220 million years ago, the Ardennes have since been reduced to relatively level plateaus, then sharply incised by rivers such as the Maas/Meuse.*

Schoorl

Heathlands, *like these at Schoorl, are found along the coast of the Netherlands. Much of the coast was breached by the sea in the 5th century, creating its distinctive inlets and islands.*

One-third of the Netherlands *lies below sea level and flooding is a constant threat. Barrages have been built across the mouths of many rivers to contain floodwaters.*

The parallel valleys of the Maas/Meuse and Rhine Rivers were created when the Rhine was deflected from its previous course by the ice sheet which formed during the last Ice Age.

Silts and sands eroded by the Rhine throughout its course are deposited to form a delta on the west coast of the Netherlands.

Hautes Fagnes is the highest part of Belgium. The bogs and streams in this upland region result from high rainfall and low temperatures.

NETHERLANDS · 'S-GRAVENHAGE (THE HAGUE) · AMSTERDAM · Waddenzee · IJsselmeer · Waddeneilanden · NORTH SEA · GERMANY

▶ 100

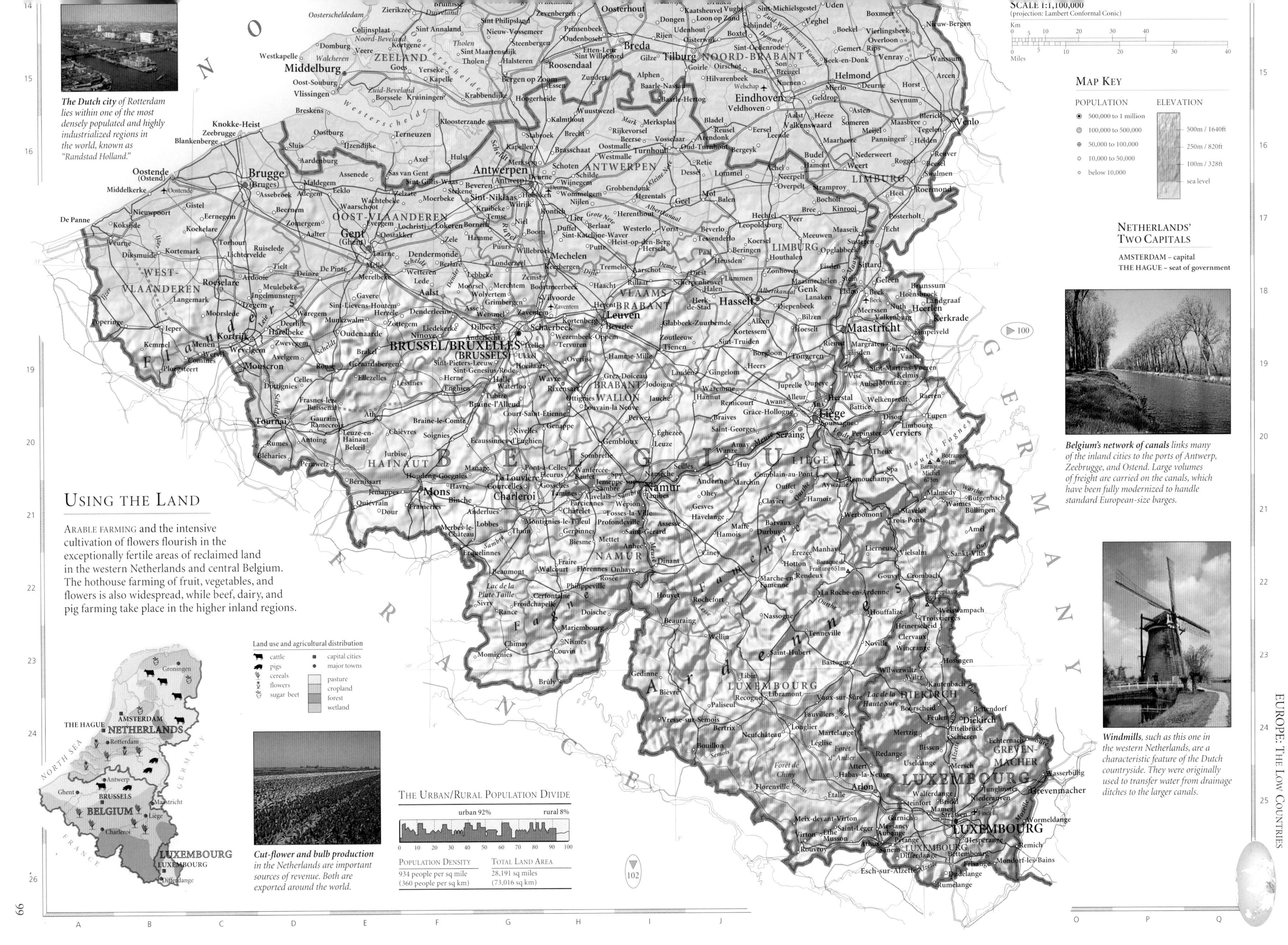
SCALE 1:1,100,000
(projection: Lambert Conformal Conic)
Km 0 5 10 20 30 40
Miles 0 5 10 20 30 40
MAP KEY
POPULATION
500,000 to 1 million
100,000 to 500,000
50,000 to 100,000
10,000 to 50,000
below 10,000
ELEVATION
500m / 1640ft
250m / 820ft
100m / 328ft
sea level
NETHERLANDS' TWO CAPITALS
AMSTERDAM – capital
THE HAGUE – seat of government
NORTH SEA
GERMANY
FRANCE
BELGIUM
LUXEMBOURG
ZEELAND
NOORD-BRABANT
LIMBURG
WEST-VLAANDEREN
OOST-VLAANDEREN
ANTWERPEN
VLAAMS BRABANT
BRABANT WALLON
HAINAUT
NAMUR
LIÈGE
DIEKIRCH
GREVENMACHER
Flanders
Ardennes
Famenne
Fagne
100
102
Land use and agricultural distribution
cattle
pigs
cereals
flowers
sugar beet
capital cities
major towns
pasture
cropland
forest
wetland
THE HAGUE
AMSTERDAM
NETHERLANDS
Groningen
Rotterdam
Antwerp
Ghent
BRUSSELS
BELGIUM
Maastricht
Liège
Charleroi
LUXEMBOURG
Differdange
NORTH SEA
GERMANY
FRANCE
THE URBAN/RURAL POPULATION DIVIDE
urban 92%
rural 8%
0 10 20 30 40 50 60 70 80 90 100
POPULATION DENSITY
934 people per sq mile
(360 people per sq km)
TOTAL LAND AREA
28,191 sq miles
(73,016 sq km)

The Dutch city of Rotterdam lies within one of the most densely populated and highly industrialized regions in the world, known as "Randstad Holland."

USING THE LAND

ARABLE FARMING and the intensive cultivation of flowers flourish in the exceptionally fertile areas of reclaimed land in the western Netherlands and central Belgium. The hothouse farming of fruit, vegetables, and flowers is also widespread, while beef, dairy, and pig farming take place in the higher inland regions.

Cut-flower and bulb production in the Netherlands are important sources of revenue. Both are exported around the world.

Belgium's network of canals links many of the inland cities to the ports of Antwerp, Zeebrugge, and Ostend. Large volumes of freight are carried on the canals, which have been fully modernized to handle standard European-size barges.

Windmills, such as this one in the western Netherlands, are a characteristic feature of the Dutch countryside. They were originally used to transfer water from drainage ditches to the larger canals.

GERMANY

DESPITE THE DEVASTATION of its industry and infrastructure during the Second World War and its separation from eastern Germany during the Cold War, West Germany made a rapid recovery in the following generation to become Europe's most formidable economic power. When the Berlin Wall was dismantled in 1989, the two halves of Germany were politically united for the first time in 40 years. Complete social and economic unity remain a longer term goal, as East German industry and society adapt to a free market. Germany has been a key player in the creation of the European Union (EU) and in moves toward a single European currency.

USING THE LAND

GERMANY has a large, efficient agricultural sector, and produces more than three-quarters of its own food. The major crops grown are cereals and sugar beet on the more fertile soils, and root crops, rye, oats, and fodder on the poorer soils of the northern plains and central uplands. Southern Germany is also a principal producer of high quality wines. Vineyards cover the slopes surrounding the Rhine and its tributaries.

Land use and agricultural distribution

- cattle
- pigs
- cereals
- sugar beet
- vineyards
- capital cities
- major towns
- pasture
- cropland
- forest

THE URBAN/RURAL POPULATION DIVIDE

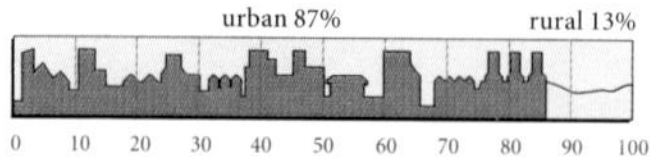

urban 87% | rural 13%

POPULATION DENSITY	TOTAL LAND AREA
598 people per sq mile (231 people per sq km)	13,804 sq miles (356,910 sq km)

The Moselle River flows through the Rhine State Uplands (Rheinisches Schiefergebirge). *During a period of uplift, preexisting river meanders were deeply incised, to form its present dramatic contours.*

THE LANDSCAPE

THE PLAINS OF NORTHERN GERMANY, the volcanic plateaus and mountains of the central uplands, and the Bavarian Alps are the three principal geographic regions in Germany. North to south the land rises steadily from barely 300 ft (90 m) in the plains to 6,500 ft (2,000 m) in the Bavarian Alps, which are a small but distinct region in the far south.

***The heathlands** of northern Germany are covered by glacial deposits of sandy outwash soil which makes them largely infertile. They support only sheep and solitary trees.*

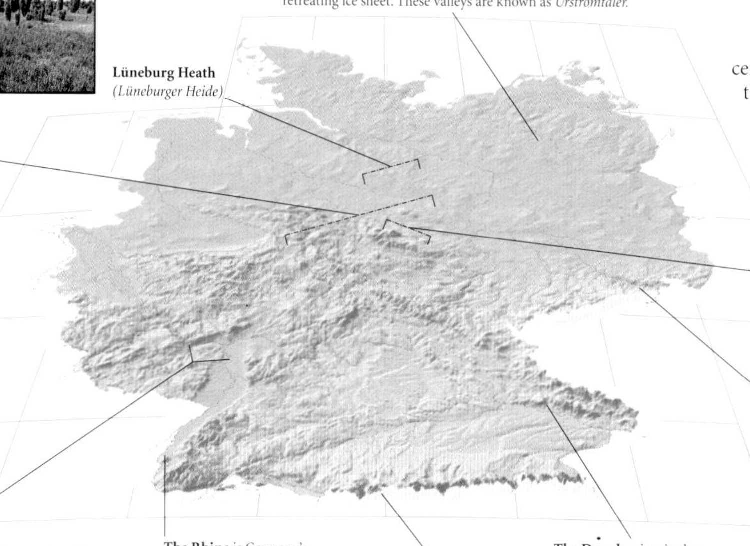

Lüneburg Heath (*Lüneburger Heide*)

Müritz lake covers 45 sq miles (117 sq km), but is only 1,08 ft (33 m) deep. It lies in a shallow valley formed by meltwater flowing out from a retreating ice sheet. These valleys are known as *Urstromtäler*.

Much of the landscape of northern Germany has been shaped by glaciation. During the last Ice Age, the ice sheet advanced as far the northern slopes of the central uplands.

The Harz Mountains were formed 300 million years ago. They are block-faulted mountains, formed when a section of the Earth's crust was thrust up between two faults.

Fault lines

Rhine

Downfaulted block

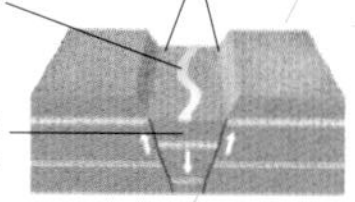

***Part of the floor** of the Rhine Rift Valley was let down between two parallel faults in the Earth's crust.*

Rhine Rift Valley

Elbe River

***The Elbe flows** in wide meanders across the north German plain to the North Sea. At its mouth it is 10 miles (16 km) wide.*

The Rhine is Germany's principal waterway and one of Europe's longest rivers, flowing 820 miles (1,320 km).

Zugspitze, the highest peak in Germany at 9,719 ft (2,962 m), was formed during the Alpine mountain-building period, 30 million years ago.

The Danube rises in the Black Forest (*Schwarzwald*) and flows east, across a wide valley, on its course to the Black Sea.

SCALE 1:2,500,000
(projection: Lambert Conformal Conic)

MAP KEY
POPULATION
1 million to 5 million
500,000 to 1 million
100,000 to 500,000
50,000 to 100,000
10,000 to 50,000
below 10,000
ELEVATION
2000m / 6562ft
1000m / 3281ft
500m / 1640ft
250m / 820ft
100m / 328ft
sea level
GERMANY
CZECH REPUBLIC
AUSTRIA
SWITZERLAND
FRANCE
LUXEMBOURG
BELGIUM
Lake Constance
Bavarian Alps
Major industry and infrastructure
car manufacture
chemicals
hi-tech industry
iron & steel
mining
precision engineering
research & development
shipbuilding
capital cities
major towns
international airports
major roads
major industrial areas

Transportation Network

393,093 miles (633,000 km)	
6949 miles (11,190 km)	
23,877 miles (38,450 km)	
4,595 miles (7,400 km)	

Germany has a complex network of inland waterways. The Rhine and Danube are at the center of a vast canal system which links central and eastern Europe to the north.

Transportation & Industry

Today, the main industries which contribute to Germany's economic power are industrial machine building, electronics, chemicals, and car manufacture, including the famous Mercedes and BMW firms. While the introduction of a free market in the east has forced the closure of many less efficient companies there, west German manufacturers have moved in to set up new plants and businesses.

***The Bavarian Alps** straddle the country's southern border at an average height of 6,500 ft (2,000 m).*

***In the Black Forest** (Schwarzwald), in southwestern Germany, woodland cloaks sandstone and granite hills, which contain rich mineral springs.*

FRANCE

FRANCE, MONACO

EUROPE'S SECOND LARGEST nation and the founder of modern Republican government, France is a major center of culture and fashion, and a leading producer of both agricultural and industrial goods. It has played a leading role in European events for centuries, and remains a key player in the push toward European unity. The Paris Basin is the most highly populated area; Île de France is home to over nine million people. Large parts of France remain thinly populated, particularly the mountainous Massif Central, Pyrennees, and southern Alps.

The chalk cliffs of Normandy (Normandie) *and southeastern England form part of a single geological region, now divided in two by the English Channel.*

THE LANDSCAPE

FRANCE'S LANDSCAPE was fashioned by two phases of mountain-building. The northwestern peninsula, the Massif Central, and the Vosges date from 220 million years ago. The complex folds of the Alps and Pyrenees, the gently-folded Jura, and the low-lying sedimentary areas of the Paris, Garonne, and Rhône basins started to form 65 million years ago.

The coast of Brittany *(Bretagne)* is highly indented where deep valleys in the northwestern peninsula were drowned by the sea.

The Normandy *(Normandie)* coastline is characterized by high chalk cliffs.

The coastline of France is 2,141 miles (3,427 km) long.

***The Paris Basin** consists of a layered sequence of sedimentary rocks. Fertile soils over much of the area make good agricultural land.*

The gently rounded summits of the Vosges are over 200 million years old.

The folded Jura form low ridges and long narrow valleys.

The Alps were forced up during several phases of mountain-building beginning 65 million years ago.

The Biscay coast, like the Mediterranean, is characterized by flat sandy beaches, interspersed with lagoons.

Garonne Basin

Rhône Basin

The Dordogne region contains spectacular examples of limestone scenery including caves and gorges.

The Pyrenees form a natural border between France and Spain.

The ancient Massif Central, disturbed by the formation of the Alps, was subject to volcanism that only ceased during the last 10,000 years.

Rhône Delta

Rhône

Delta plain

The marshes of the Camargue

***Deposition in the Rhône Delta** is wave-dominated. Sea currents carry river sediments extending the delta plain westwards.*

Corsica's northeastern peninsula has dramatic cliffs of folded limestone.

The volcanic landscape of the Auvergne where the cones of its extinct volcanoes have worn away to leave "plugs" of lava.

TRANSPORTATION & INDUSTRY

TODAY THE MAIN FRENCH GROWTH INDUSTRIES are hi-tech, including microelectronics, telecommunications, and aerospace. Other important sectors are the nuclear industry, only rivalled in scale by that of the USA, car manufacture, dominated by the giants Renault and Peugeot and a highly diversified tourist industry.

Major industry and infrastructure

- aerospace industry
- car manufacture
- chemicals
- engineering
- hi-tech industry
- nuclear power
- tourism
- capital cities
- major towns
- international airports
- major roads
- major industrial areas

TRANSPORTATION NETWORK

599,017 miles (964,600 km)	5,900 miles (9,500 km)
19,761 miles (31,821 km)	5,279 miles (8,500 km)

The French TGV (*Train à Grande Vitesse*) leads the world in high-speed train technology, and provides a service which is faster, door-to-door, than air travel.

64

104

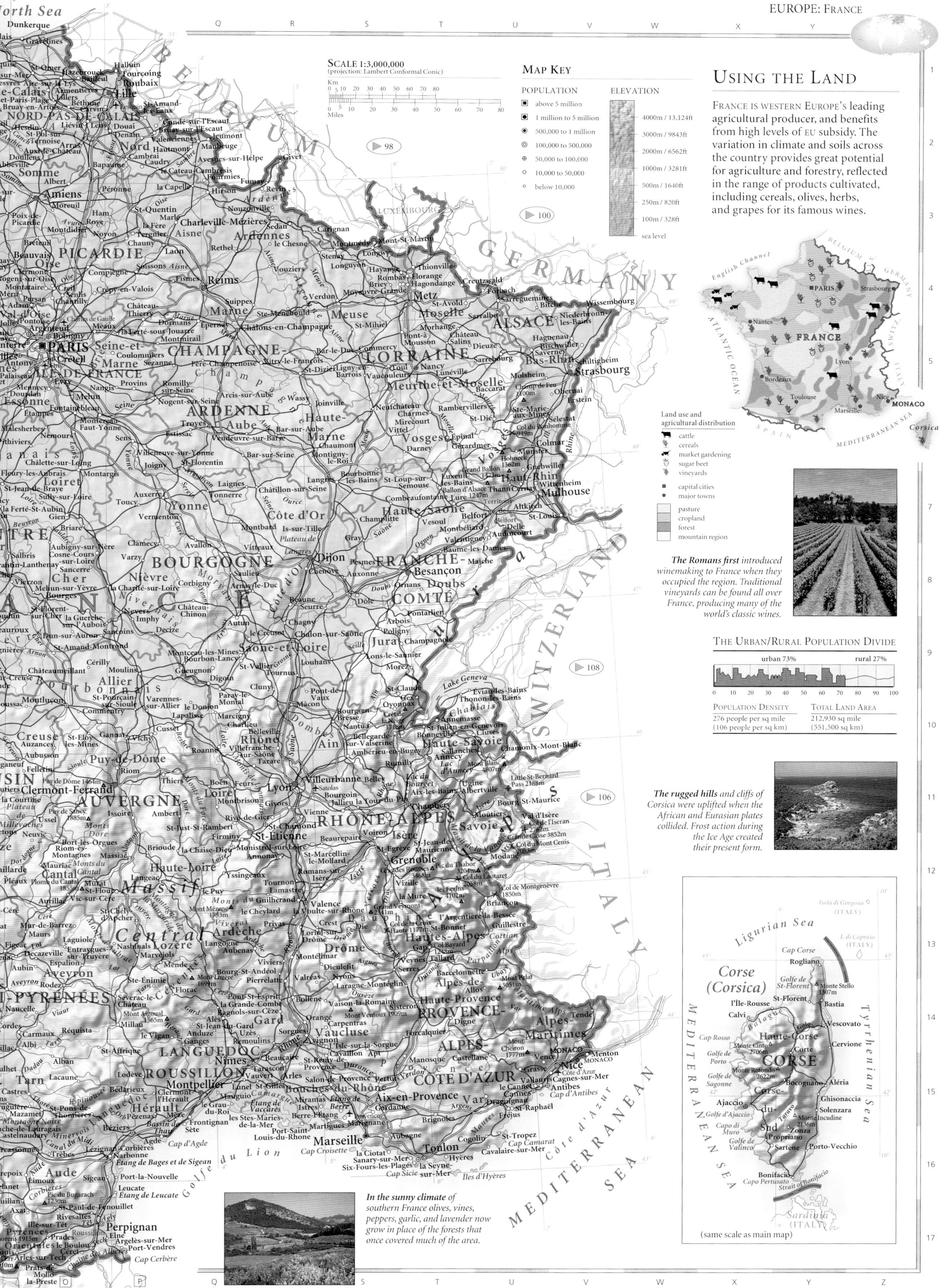
SCALE 1:3,000,000
(projection: Lambert Conformal Conic)
Km
Miles
MAP KEY
POPULATION
above 5 million
1 million to 5 million
500,000 to 1 million
100,000 to 500,000
50,000 to 100,000
10,000 to 50,000
below 10,000
ELEVATION
4000m / 13,124ft
3000m / 9843ft
2000m / 6562ft
1000m / 3281ft
500m / 1640ft
250m / 820ft
100m / 328ft
sea level
North Sea
BELGIUM
LUXEMBOURG
GERMANY
SWITZERLAND
ITALY
MEDITERRANEAN SEA
Golfe du Lion
PARIS
Land use and agricultural distribution
cattle
cereals
market gardening
sugar beet
vineyards
capital cities
major towns
pasture
cropland
forest
mountain region
Corse (Corsica)
Ligurian Sea
Tyrrhenian Sea
(same scale as main map)

USING THE LAND

FRANCE IS WESTERN EUROPE'S leading agricultural producer, and benefits from high levels of EU subsidy. The variation in climate and soils across the country provides great potential for agriculture and forestry, reflected in the range of products cultivated, including cereals, olives, herbs, and grapes for its famous wines.

***The Romans first** introduced winemaking to France when they occupied the region. Traditional vineyards can be found all over France, producing many of the world's classic wines.*

THE URBAN/RURAL POPULATION DIVIDE

urban 73% — rural 27%

POPULATION DENSITY	TOTAL LAND AREA
276 people per sq mile (106 people per sq km)	212,930 sq mile (551,500 sq km)

***The rugged hills** and cliffs of Corsica were uplifted when the African and Eurasian plates collided. Frost action during the Ice Age created their present form.*

***In the sunny climate** of southern France olives, vines, peppers, garlic, and lavender now grow in place of the forests that once covered much of the area.*

THE IBERIAN PENINSULA

ANDORRA, GIBRALTAR, PORTUGAL, SPAIN *(Azores, Canary Islands, Madeira on p.64)*

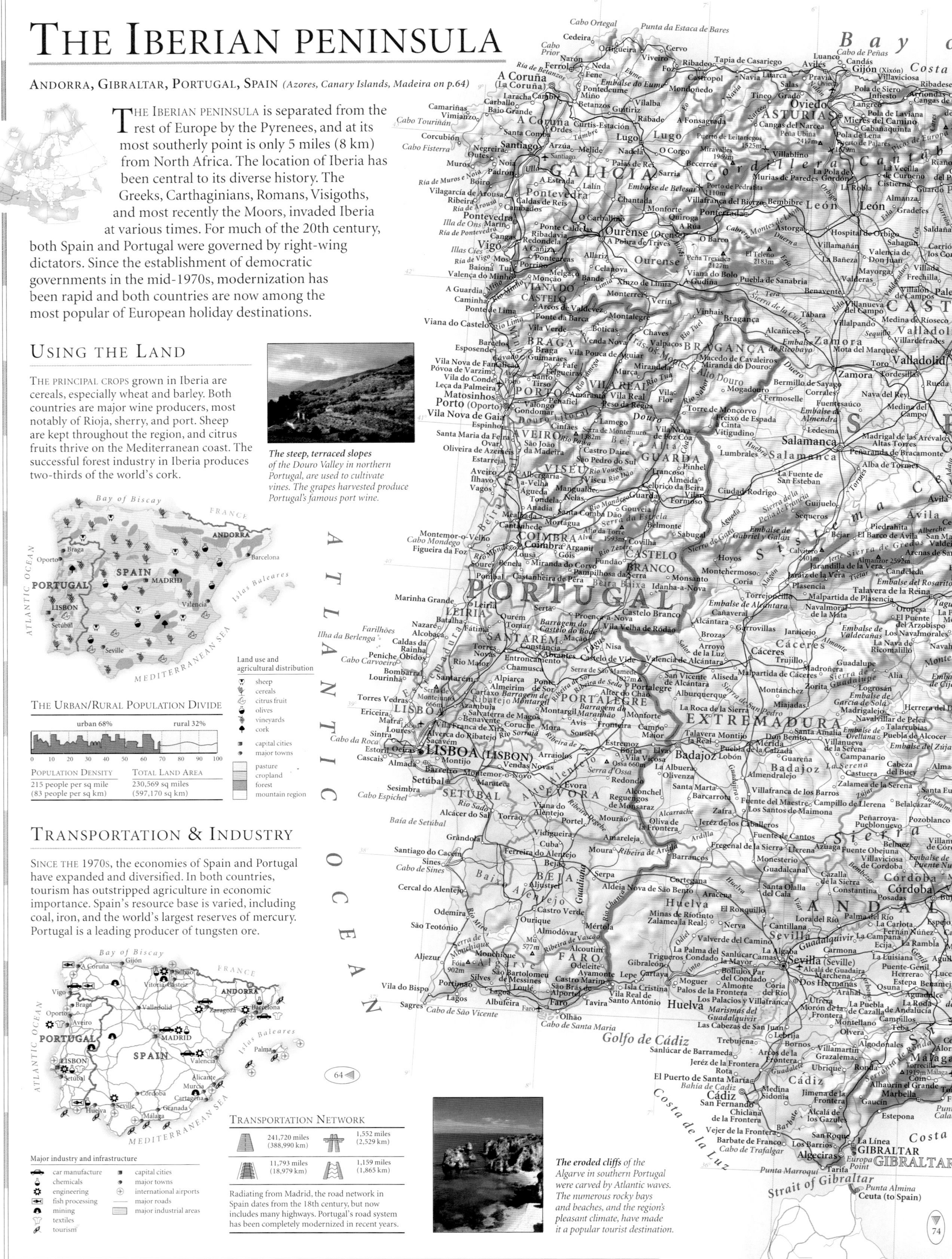

THE IBERIAN PENINSULA is separated from the rest of Europe by the Pyrenees, and at its most southerly point is only 5 miles (8 km) from North Africa. The location of Iberia has been central to its diverse history. The Greeks, Carthaginians, Romans, Visigoths, and most recently the Moors, invaded Iberia at various times. For much of the 20th century, both Spain and Portugal were governed by right-wing dictators. Since the establishment of democratic governments in the mid-1970s, modernization has been rapid and both countries are now among the most popular of European holiday destinations.

USING THE LAND

THE PRINCIPAL CROPS grown in Iberia are cereals, especially wheat and barley. Both countries are major wine producers, most notably of Rioja, sherry, and port. Sheep are kept throughout the region, and citrus fruits thrive on the Mediterranean coast. The successful forest industry in Iberia produces two-thirds of the world's cork.

The steep, terraced slopes of the Douro Valley in northern Portugal, are used to cultivate vines. The grapes harvested produce Portugal's famous port wine.

Land use and agricultural distribution: sheep, cereals, citrus fruit, olives, vineyards, cork, capital cities, major towns, pasture, cropland, forest, mountain region

THE URBAN/RURAL POPULATION DIVIDE

urban 68% — rural 32%

POPULATION DENSITY	TOTAL LAND AREA
215 people per sq mile (83 people per sq km)	230,569 sq miles (597,170 sq km)

TRANSPORTATION & INDUSTRY

SINCE THE 1970s, the economies of Spain and Portugal have expanded and diversified. In both countries, tourism has outstripped agriculture in economic importance. Spain's resource base is varied, including coal, iron, and the world's largest reserves of mercury. Portugal is a leading producer of tungsten ore.

Major industry and infrastructure: car manufacture, chemicals, engineering, fish processing, mining, textiles, tourism, capital cities, major towns, international airports, major roads, major industrial areas

TRANSPORTATION NETWORK

241,720 miles (388,990 km)	1,552 miles (2,529 km)
11,793 miles (18,979 km)	1,159 miles (1,865 km)

Radiating from Madrid, the road network in Spain dates from the 18th century, but now includes many highways. Portugal's road system has been completely modernized in recent years.

The eroded cliffs of the Algarve in southern Portugal were carved by Atlantic waves. The numerous rocky bays and beaches, and the region's pleasant climate, have made it a popular tourist destination.

64

74

The climate in northwestern Spain is milder in both summer and winter than in the rest of the country, creating a verdant environment, more commonly associated with northwestern Europe.
MAP KEY
POPULATION
1 million to 5 million
500,000 to 1 million
100,000 to 500,000
50,000 to 100,000
10,000 to 50,000
below 10,000
ELEVATION
3000m / 9843ft
2000m / 6562ft
1000m / 3281ft
500m / 1640ft
250m / 820ft
100m / 328ft
sea level
SCALE 1:3,000,000
(projection: Lambert Conformal Conic)
FRANCE
Pyrenees
MEDITERRANEAN SEA
Islas Baleares (Balearic Islands)
Golfo de Valencia
Costa Brava
Costa Blanca
Costa del Sol
Costa del Azahar
Golf de Sant Jordi
Golfo de Mazarrón
Barcelona
Valencia
Zaragoza
Bilbao
Murcia
Alicante
Granada
Almería
Cartagena
Palma
Mallorca (Majorca)
Menorca (Minorca)
Eivissa (Ibiza)
Formentera
ANDORRA
ANDORRA LA VELLA
The Pyrenees form Iberia's northeastern boundary, running for 270 miles (440 km), dividing the peninsula from the rest of Europe.
Cordillera Cantábrica
Douro/Duero River
The Meseta plateau averages 1,970 ft (600 m) in height and is now largely dry and treeless.
Tagus River
Mountain front
Pediment
Weathered material
Pediments are characteristic of semi-arid lands across Iberia. A pediment is a flat, low-lying, eroded platform, cut into the bedrock. Weathered material is transported by streams and deposited in broad fan shapes on the pediment.
The Guadalquivir River brings vital irrigation water to the plains, and like many of Iberia's rivers, is prone to flooding.
Sierra Morena
The Sierra Nevada in southern Spain contain Iberia's highest peak, Mulhacén, which rises 11,418 ft (3,481 m).
In the Sierra de los Filabres deforestation and overgrazing, which cause soil erosion, have created semidesert badlands.
The Ebro River has formed the peninsula's largest delta. Recently, sediment flows have been seriously disturbed by nearby reservoirs.
On the northeastern coast sea level changes are evident from wave-cut beaches which rise up to 200 ft (60 m) above the present sea level.
The Balearic Islands (Islas Baleares) are characterized by jagged limestones and plains.

THE LANDSCAPE

A VAST PLATEAU, the Meseta dominates the centre of the peninsula, enclosed by the Cordillera Cantábrica to the north and the Sierra Morena to the south. It is drained by three major rivers, the Douro/Duero, the Tagus, and the Guadalquivir. The peninsula experiences great variations in climate and rainfall, both regionally and locally.

The Italian Peninsula

Italy, San Marino, Vatican City

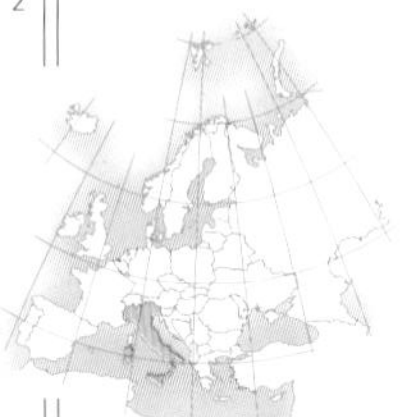

The Italian peninsula is a land of great contrasts. Until unification in 1861, Italy was a collection of independent states, whose competitiveness during the Renaissance resulted in the architectural and artistic magnificence of cities such as Rome, Florence, and Venice. The majority of Italy's population and economic activity is concentrated in the north, centered on the sophisticated industrial city of Milan. Southern Italy, the *Mezzogiorno*, has a harsh terrain, and remains far less developed than the north. Attempts to attract industry and investment in the south are frequently deterred by the entrenched network of organized crime and corruption.

The Landscape

The mainly mountainous and hilly Italian peninsula took its present form following a collision between the African and Eurasian tectonic plates. The Alps in the northwest rise to a high point of 15,772 ft (4,807 m) at Mont Blanc *(Monte Bianco)* on the French border, while the Apennines *(Appennino)* form a rugged backbone, running along the entire length of the country.

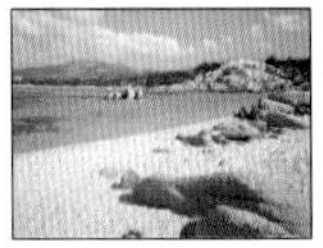

The island of Sardinia is an ancient land mass; an uplifted section of very old igneous rocks. Its rugged mountainous regions provide pasture for sheep and goats, while its valleys support some agriculture.

Costa Smeralda

Mont Blanc *(Monte Bianco)*

***The Dolomites** (Alpi Dolomitiche) are formed of thick limestones, overlying weaker marine strata. They have distinctive serrated peaks and many massive landslides occur.*

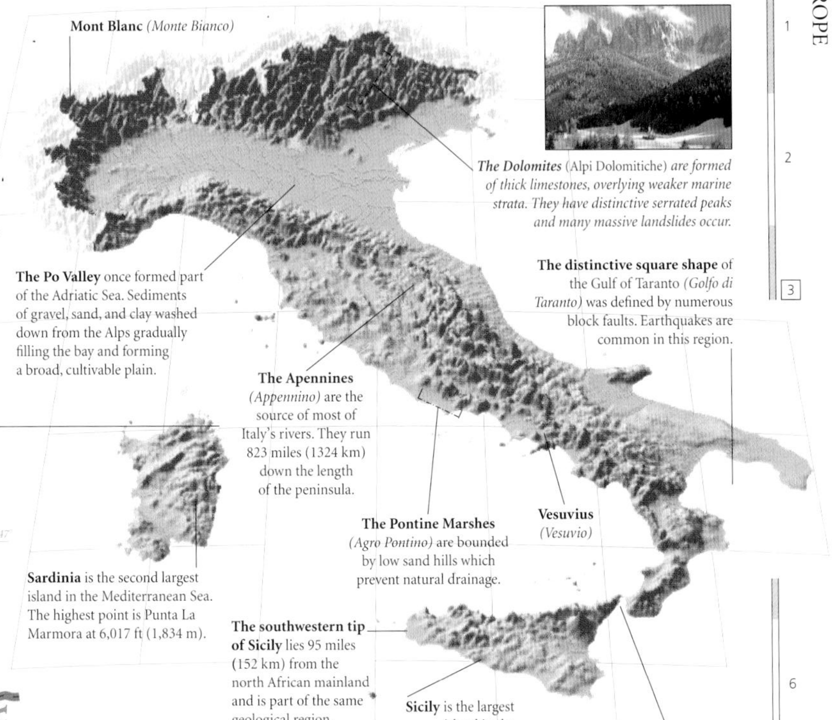

The Po Valley once formed part of the Adriatic Sea. Sediments of gravel, sand, and clay washed down from the Alps gradually filling the bay and forming a broad, cultivable plain.

The distinctive square shape of the Gulf of Taranto *(Golfo di Taranto)* was defined by numerous block faults. Earthquakes are common in this region.

The Apennines *(Appennino)* are the source of most of Italy's rivers. They run 823 miles (1324 km) down the length of the peninsula.

Sardinia is the second largest island in the Mediterranean Sea. The highest point is Punta La Marmora at 6,017 ft (1,834 m).

The Pontine Marshes *(Agro Pontino)* are bounded by low sand hills which prevent natural drainage.

Vesuvius *(Vesuvio)*

The southwestern tip of Sicily lies 95 miles (152 km) from the north African mainland and is part of the same geological region.

Sicily is the largest island in the Mediterranean at 9,926 sq miles (25,708 sq km).

The Strait of Messina *(Stretto di Messina)* is between 2 and 12 miles (3–19 km) wide, and is a rich fishing ground.

Vesuvius *(Vesuvio)*

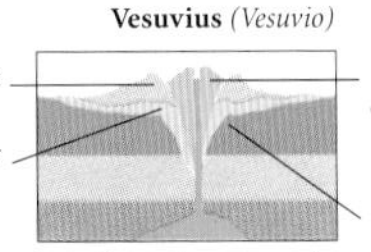

Monte Somma
Old crater
Present-day crater has developed within the old crater of Monte Somma
Old crater

***There have been four volcanoes** on the site of Vesuvius since volcanic activity began here more than 10,000 years ago.*

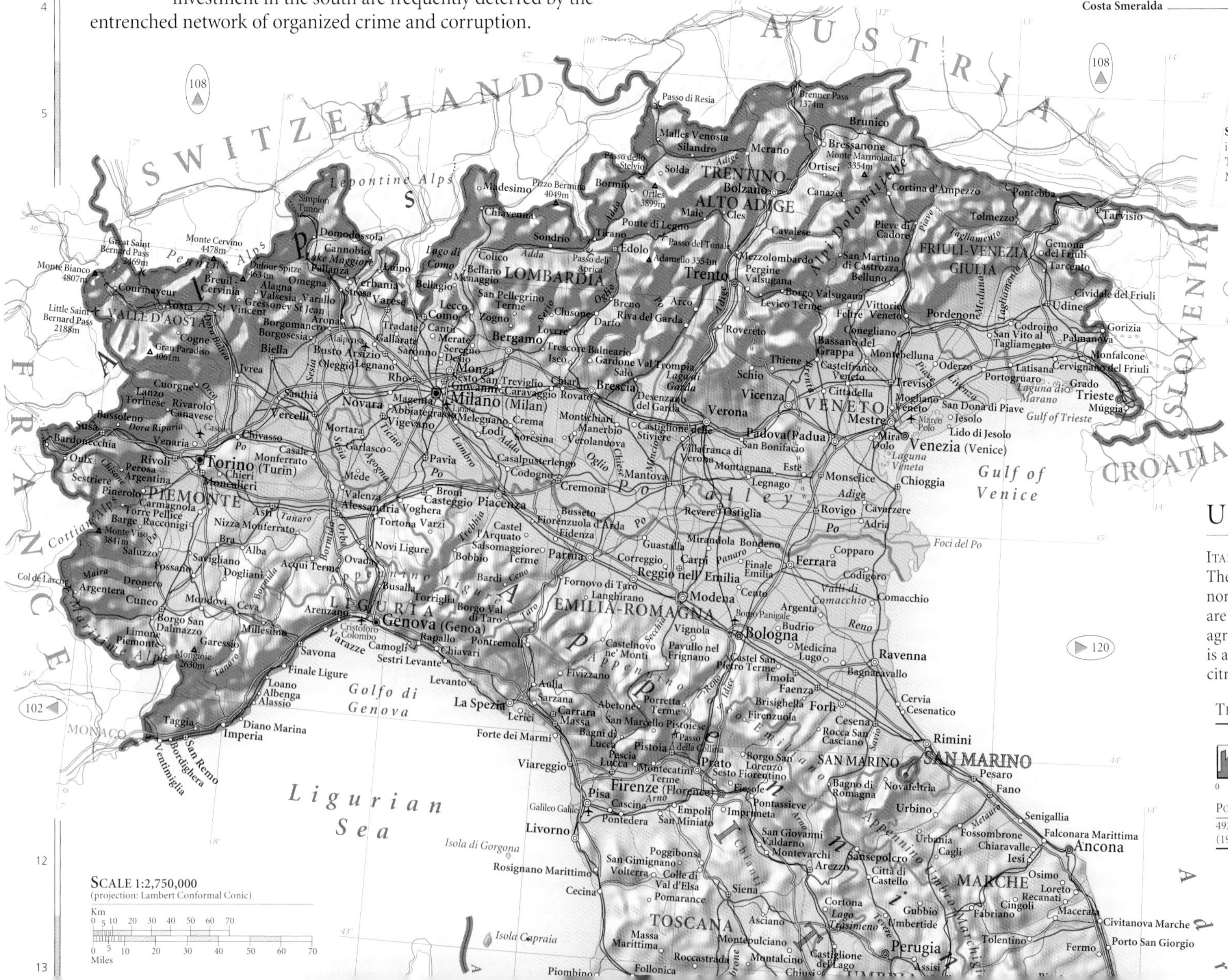

Using the Land

Italy produces 95% of its own food. The best farming land is in the Po Valley in northern Italy, where soft wheat and rice are grown. Irrigation is essential to agriculture in much of the south. Italy is a major producer and exporter of citrus fruits, olives, tomatoes, and wine.

The Urban/Rural Population Divide

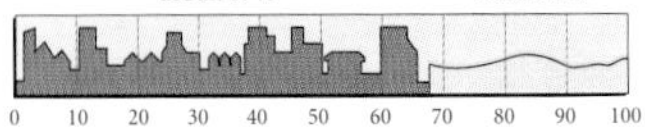

urban 67%
rural 33%
0 10 20 30 40 50 60 70 80 90 100

Population Density	Total Land Area
492 people per sq mile (190 people per sq km)	116,320 sq miles (301,270 sq km)

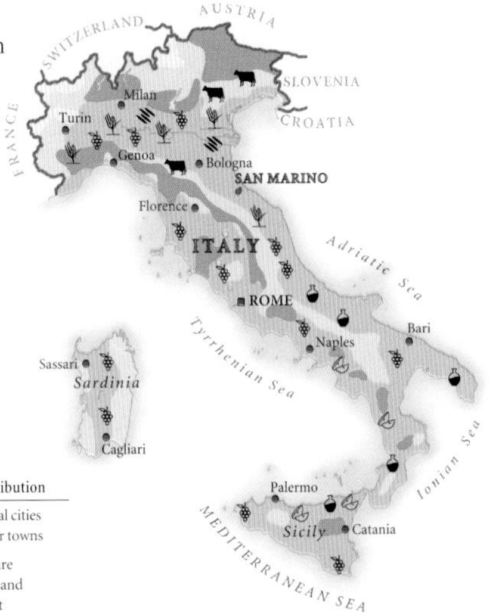

Land use and agricultural distribution
cattle
cereals
citrus fruits
olive oil
rice
vineyards
capital cities
major towns
pasture
cropland
forest
mountain region
AUSTRIA
SWITZERLAND
SLOVENIA
CROATIA
FRANCE
SAN MARINO
ITALY
ROME
Milan
Turin
Genoa
Bologna
Florence
Naples
Bari
Sassari
Sardinia
Cagliari
Palermo
Sicily
Catania
Adriatic Sea
Tyrrhenian Sea
Ionian Sea
MEDITERRANEAN SEA

SWITZERLAND
AUSTRIA
SLOVENIA
CROATIA
FRANCE
MONACO
Ligurian Sea
Golfo di Genova
Gulf of Venice
Milano (Milan)
Torino (Turin)
Genova (Genoa)
Venezia (Venice)
Bologna
Firenze (Florence)
SAN MARINO

SCALE 1:2,750,000
(projection: Lambert Conformal Conic)

108 ▲ 108 ▲ ▶ 108 ▶ 112 ▶ 120 102 ◀

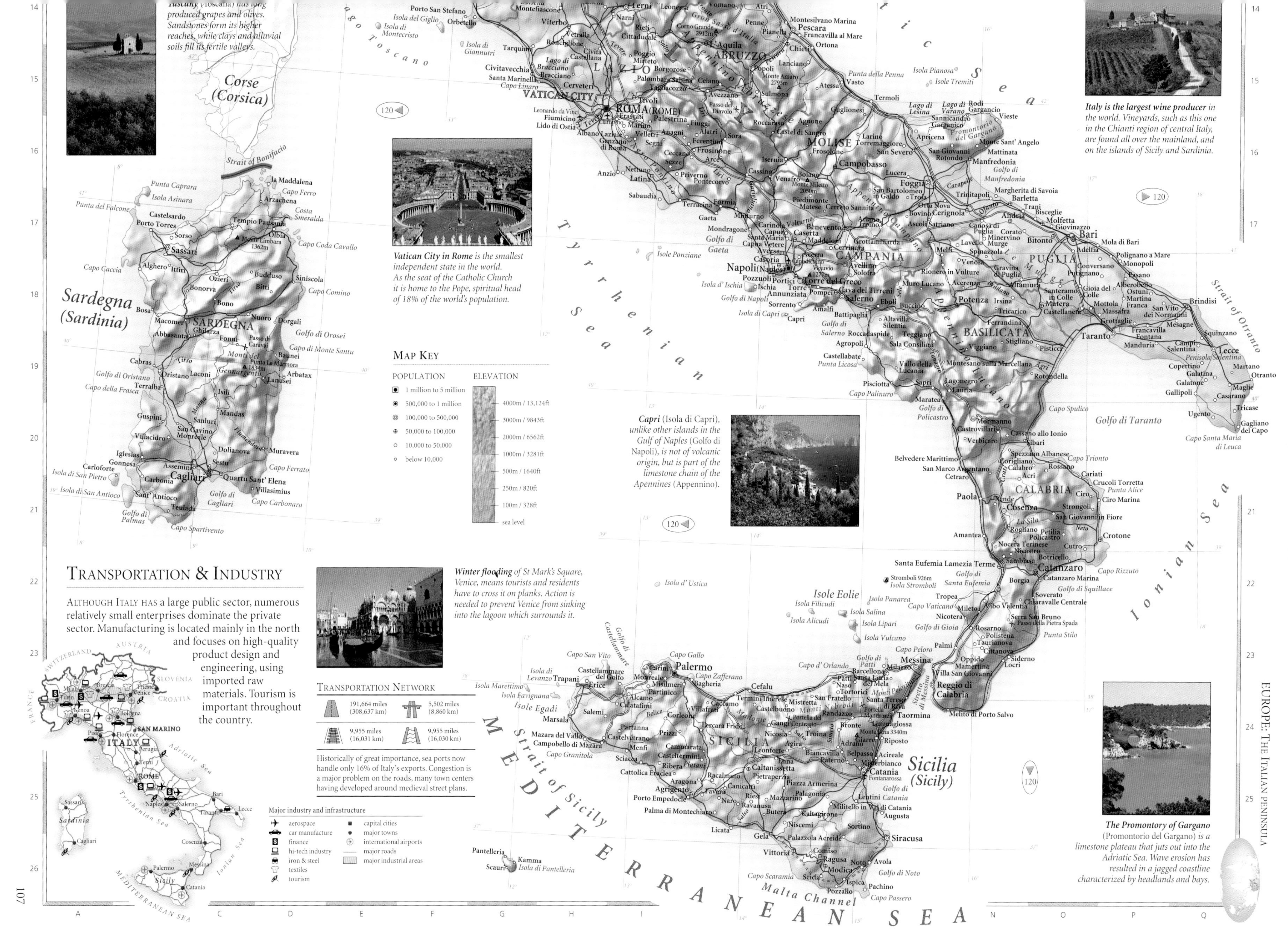
Corse (Corsica)
Sardegna (Sardinia)
SARDEGNA
Strait of Bonifacio
Tyrrhenian Sea
Adriatic Sea
Ionian Sea
MEDITERRANEAN SEA
Strait of Sicily
Strait of Otranto
Malta Channel
Golfo di Taranto
Sicilia (Sicily)
SICILIA
Isole Eolie
Isole Egadi
LAZIO
ABRUZZO
MOLISE
CAMPANIA
PUGLIA
BASILICATA
CALABRIA
VATICAN CITY
ROMA (ROME)
Napoli
Bari
Taranto
Palermo
Messina
Catania
Cagliari
Sassari
Reggio di Calabria

Tuscany (Toscana) has long produced grapes and olives. Sandstones form its higher reaches, while clays and alluvial soils fill its fertile valleys.

Italy is the largest wine producer *in the world. Vineyards, such as this one in the Chianti region of central Italy, are found all over the mainland, and on the islands of Sicily and Sardinia.*

Vatican City in Rome *is the smallest independent state in the world. As the seat of the Catholic Church it is home to the Pope, spiritual head of 18% of the world's population.*

Capri *(Isola di Capri), unlike other islands in the Gulf of Naples (Golfo di Napoli), is not of volcanic origin, but is part of the limestone chain of the Apennines (Appennino).*

Winter flooding *of St Mark's Square, Venice, means tourists and residents have to cross it on planks. Action is needed to prevent Venice from sinking into the lagoon which surrounds it.*

The Promontory of Gargano *(Promontorio del Gargano) is a limestone plateau that juts out into the Adriatic Sea. Wave erosion has resulted in a jagged coastline characterized by headlands and bays.*

Map Key

Population

- 1 million to 5 million
- 500,000 to 1 million
- 100,000 to 500,000
- 50,000 to 100,000
- 10,000 to 50,000
- below 10,000

Elevation

- 4000m / 13,124ft
- 3000m / 9843ft
- 2000m / 6562ft
- 1000m / 3281ft
- 500m / 1640ft
- 250m / 820ft
- 100m / 328ft
- sea level

Transportation & Industry

ALTHOUGH ITALY HAS a large public sector, numerous relatively small enterprises dominate the private sector. Manufacturing is located mainly in the north and focuses on high-quality product design and engineering, using imported raw materials. Tourism is important throughout the country.

Transportation Network

- 191,664 miles (308,637 km)
- 5,502 miles (8,860 km)
- 9,955 miles (16,031 km)
- 9,955 miles (16,030 km)

Historically of great importance, sea ports now handle only 16% of Italy's exports. Congestion is a major problem on the roads, many town centers having developed around medieval street plans.

Major industry and infrastructure

- aerospace
- car manufacture
- finance
- hi-tech industry
- iron & steel
- textiles
- tourism
- capital cities
- major towns
- international airports
- major roads
- major industrial areas

THE ALPINE STATES

AUSTRIA, LIECHTENSTEIN, SLOVENIA, SWITZERLAND

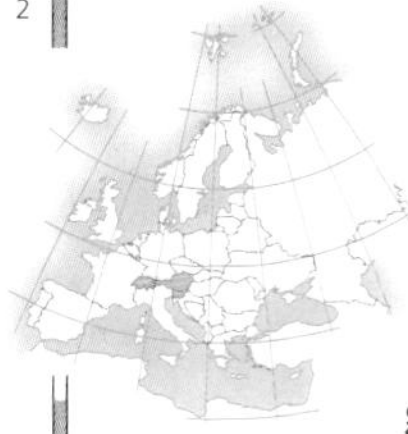

THE ALPINE COUNTRIES of Austria, Switzerland, Liechtenstein, and Slovenia form a narrow strip across western Europe's geographical core, lying on the main north–south trading routes across the Alps. Switzerland, politically neutral since 1815, is an important international meeting place and houses one of the headquarters of the United Nations, although not itself a member. Austria, once at the heart of the great Habsburg Empire has been a fully independent nation since 1955, and maintains a deserved reputation as an international center of culture. Slovenia declared independence from the former Yugoslavia in 1991 and despite initial economic hardship, is now starting to achieve the prosperity enjoyed by its Alpine neighbors.

USING THE LAND

THE ALPINE REGION'S mountainous terrain discourages cultivation over much of the land area. The primary agricultural activity is the raising of dairy and beef cattle on the pasture land of the lower mountain slopes. Austria is self-supporting in grains, and crops such as wheat, barley, and grapes are grown on the east Austrian lowlands. Woodlands are more prevalent in the eastern Alps; both Austria and Slovenia have large tracts of forest.

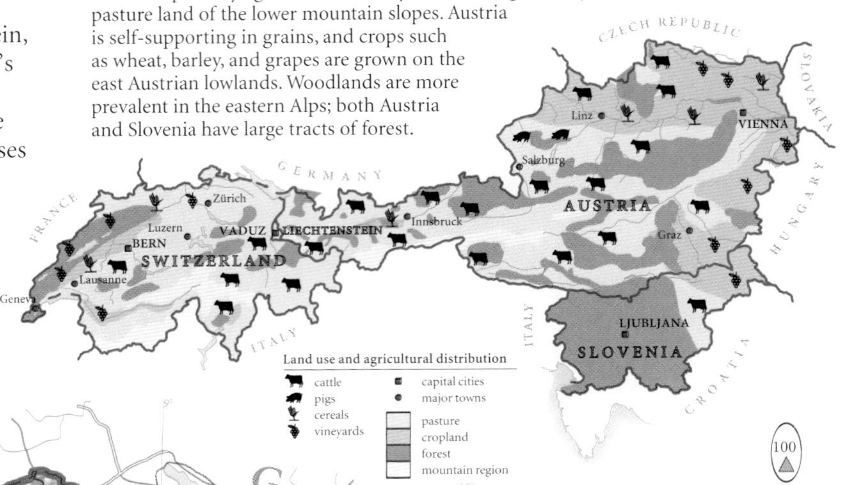

Land use and agricultural distribution
cattle
pigs
cereals
vineyards
capital cities
major towns
pasture
cropland
forest
mountain region

The Matterhorn*, on the Swiss-Italian border, is one of the highest mountains in the Alps, at 14,692 ft (4,478 m). The term "horn" refers to its distinctive peak, formed by three glaciers eroding hollows, known as cirques, in each of its sides.*

THE LANDSCAPE

THE ALPS OCCUPY THREE-FIFTHS OF SWITZERLAND, most of southern Austria and the northwest of Slovenia. They were formed by the collision of the African and Eurasian tectonic plates, which began 65 million years ago. Their complex geology is reflected in the differing heights and rock types of the various ranges. The Rhine flows along Liechtenstein's border with Switzerland, creating a broad floodplain in the north and west of Liechtenstein. In the far northeast and east are a number of lowland regions, including the Vienna Basin, Burgenland, and the plain of the Danube. Slovenia's major rivers flow across the lower eastern regions; in the west, the rivers flow underground through the limestone Karst region.

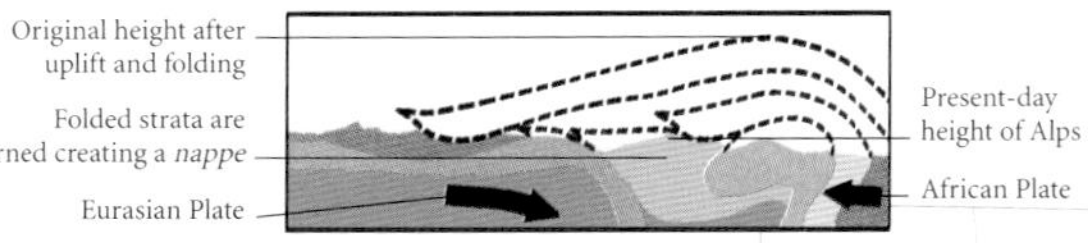

Original height after uplift and folding
Folded strata are overturned creating a *nappe*
Eurasian Plate
Present-day height of Alps
African Plate

The convergence of the African and Eurasian plates *compressed and folded huge masses of rock strata. As the plates continued to move together, the folded strata were overturned, creating complex nappes. Much of the rock strata has since been eroded, resulting in the current topography of the Alps.*

Constricted as it cuts through *ridges in the Alps, the Danube meanders across the lowlands, where uplift combined with river erosion has deepened meanders.*

The Vienna Basin lies mainly below 390 ft (120 m). It gradually subsided and filled with sediment as the Alps were uplifted.

Neusiedler See straddles the border of Austria and Hungary; the area around it provides some of the best wine-growing land in Austria.

The mountains of the Jura form a natural border between Switzerland and France. Their marine limestones date from over 200 million years ago. When the Alps were formed the Jura were folded into a series of parallel ridges and troughs.

The first road through the Brenner Pass was built in 1772, although it has been used as a mountain route since Roman times. It is the lowest of the main Alpine passes at 4,298 ft (1374 m).

The Austrian Alps comprise three distinct mountain ranges, separated by deep trenches. The northern and southern ranges are rugged limestones, while the Tauern range is formed of crystalline rocks.

Tectonic activity has resulted in dramatic changes in land height over very short distances. Lake Geneva, lying at 1,221 ft (372 m) is only 43 miles (70 km) away from the 15,772 ft (4,807 m) peak of Mont Blanc, on the France–Italy border.

The Bernese Alps *(Berner Alpen)* contain the Aletsch, which at 15 miles (24 km) is the longest Alpine glacier.

The Rhine, like other major Alpine rivers, follows a broad, flat trough between the mountains. Along part of its course, the Rhine forms the boundary between Switzerland and Liechtenstein.

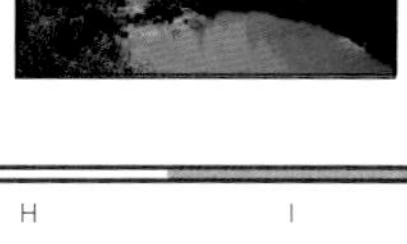

The deep, blue lakes *of the Karst region are part of a drainage network which runs largely underground through this limestone area.*

Karst region

The limestone cave system at Postojna extends for more than 10 miles (16 km) and includes caverns reaching 125 ft (40 m) in height and width.

The Tauern range in the central Austrian Alps contains the highest mountain in Austria, the towering Grossglockner, rising 12,461 ft (3,798 m).

THE URBAN/RURAL POPULATION DIVIDE

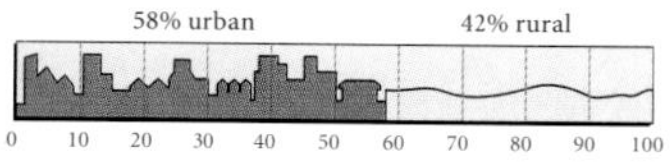

58% urban | 42% rural

0 10 20 30 40 50 60 70 80 90 100

POPULATION DENSITY	TOTAL LAND AREA
310 people per sq mile (120 people per sq km)	56,135 sq miles (145,390 sq km)

In this mountainous *region, the flatter, more accessible areas are often used for both cattle grazing and recreation.*

These converging glaciers *are marked by dark lines of moraine. This eroded material is carried by glaciers, and deposited as the ice melts.*

SCALE 1:2,000,000
rojection: Lambert Conformal Conic)

The Austrian Tirol *contains some of the most spectacular Alpine scenery. Snow cover is a permanent feature in the highest reaches.*

MAP KEY

POPULATION

- 1 million to 5 million
- 500,000 to 1 million
- 100,000 to 500,000
- 50,000 to 100,000
- 10,000 to 50,000
- below 10,000

ELEVATION

- 4000m / 13,124ft
- 3000m / 9843ft
- 2000m / 6562ft
- 1000m / 3281ft
- 500m / 1640ft
- 250m / 820ft
- 100m / 328ft
- sea level

TRANSPORTATION & INDUSTRY

LL FOUR NATIONS concentrate on high-quality manufacturing and services. ustrian iron and steel production is complemented by construction industries; nd Slovenia, traditionally the industrial powerhouse of the western Balkans has ncreasingly diversified industries. Liechtenstein and Switzerland, lacking raw aterials, produce pharmaceuticals and precision instruments, such as watches, nd act as international banking centers. The spectacular scenery of the region ncourages tourism all year round.

RANSPORTATION NETWORK

119,805 miles (192,923 km)	2044 miles (3292 km)
6227 miles (10,028 km)	984 miles (1584 km)

innels and passes through the Alps are an nportant feature of this region. The NEAT project, oviding two new high-speed rail links between isel and Milan, was given approval in 1992.

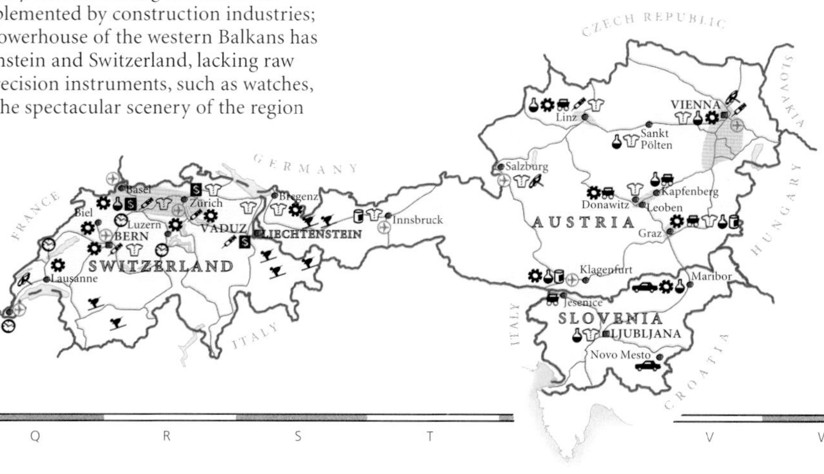

Major industry and infrastructure

- car manufacture
- chemicals
- engineering
- finance
- food processing
- iron & steel
- pharmaceuticals
- textiles
- tourism
- watch making
- winter sports
- capital cities
- major towns
- international airports
- major roads
- major industrial areas

The Schönbrunn Palace *in Vienna was the summer residence of the Habsburg monarchy. Today, it is a major tourist attraction.*

Central Europe

Czech Republic, Hungary, Poland, Slovakia

When Slovakia and the Czech Republic became separate countries in 1993, they joined Hungary and Poland in a new role as independent nation states, following centuries of shifting boundaries and imperial strife. This turbulent history bequeathed the region a rich cultural heritage, shared through the works of its many great writers and composers, and celebrated in the vibrant historic capitals of Prague, Budapest, and Warsaw. Having shaken off Soviet domination in 1989, these states are facing up to the challenge of winning commercial investment to modernize outmoded industry, while bearing the severe environmental impact from forty years of large-scale industrialization.

The Landscape

The forested Carpathian Mountains, uplifted with the Alps, lie southeast of the older Bohemian massif, which contains the Sudeten and Krušné Hory *(Erzgebirge)* ranges. They divide the fertile plains of the Danube to the south and the Vistula *(Wisła)*, which flows north across vast expanses of glacial deposits into the Baltic Sea.

Hot mineral springs occur where geothermally heated water wells up through faults and fractures in the rocks of the Sudeten Mountains.

Pomerania is a sandy coastal region of glacially-formed lakes stretching west from the Vistula *(Wisła)*.

Longshore currents moving east along the Baltic coast have built a 40 mile (65 km) spit composed of material from the Vistula *(Wisła)* River.

***The Biebrza River** has left meanders and oxbow lakes as it flows across low-lying ground.*

Gerlachovský štít, in the Tatra Mountains, is Slovakia's highest mountain, at 8,711ft (2,655 m).

Carpathian Mountains

Danube River

Krušnd Hory *(Erzgebirge)*

Bohemian Massif

***The Berounka River** cuts through the precipitous wooded landscape of the Bohemian massif, banked by a broad floodplain.*

The Slovak Ore Mountains *(Slovenské Rudohorie)* are noted for their mineral resources, including high-grade iron ore.

The Great Hungarian Plain formed by the floodplain of the Danube is a mixture of steppe and cultivated land, covering nearly half of Hungary's total area.

Bluff — Slip-off slope — Direction of flow

***Meanders** form as rivers flow across plains at a low gradient. A steep cliff or bluff, forms on the outside curve, and a gentler slip-off slope on the inside bend.*

Transportation & Industry

Heavy industry has dominated postwar life in Central Europe. Poland has large coal reserves, having inherited the Silesian coalfield from Germany after the Second World War, allowing the export of large quantities of coal, along with other minerals. Hungary specializes in consumer goods and services, while Slovakia's industrial base is still relatively small. The Czech Republic's traditional glassworks and breweries bring some stability to its precarious Soviet-built manufacturing sector.

Major industry and infrastructure

- car manufacture
- chemicals
- engineering
- food processing
- mining
- shipbuilding
- tourism
- capital cities
- major towns
- international airports
- major roads
- major industrial areas

Transportation Network

213,997 miles (344,600 km)	817 miles (1,315 km)
27,479 miles (44,249 km)	3,784 miles (6,094 km)

The huge growth of tourism and business has prompted major investment in the transportation infrastructure, with new roadbuilding schemes within and between the main cities of the region.

***Budapest, the capital of Hungary,** straddles the Danube. It comprises the historic towns of Buda, on the west bank, and Pest, which contains the Parliament*

BALTIC SEA — Gulf of Danzig — Pomeranian Bay — RUSSIAN FEDERATION (Kaliningrad) — LITHUANIA — BELARUS — POLAND

▶ 118

▶ 118

CZECH REPUBLIC
POLAND
SLOVAKIA
HUNGARY
UKRAINE
ROMANIA
YUGOSLAVIA
CROATIA
SLOVENIA
AUSTRIA
GERMANY
BRATISLAVA
BUDAPEST
PRAHA (PRAGUE)
Carpathian Mountains
Great Hungarian Plain
Little Alföld
Bohemian Forest
Slovenské rudohorie
Tatra Mountains
Danube (Duna)
MAP KEY
POPULATION
1 million to 5 million
500,000 to 1 million
100,000 to 500,000
50,000 to 100,000
10,000 to 50,000
below 10,000
ELEVATION
2000m / 6562ft
1000m / 3281ft
500m / 1640ft
250m / 820ft
100m / 328ft
sea level
SCALE 1:2,750,000
(projection: Lambert Conformal Conic)
Km
Miles
100
108
112
116
16

USING THE LAND

CEREALS, SUGAR BEET, AND POTATOES are Central Europe's main crops, along with hops for the Czech breweries, sweet peppers for paprika, sunflowers and vines in milder areas. The plains of Poland and Hungary are well-suited to livestock-rearing, while forestry is important in the mountains of Slovakia.

Land use and agricultural distribution

cattle, pigs, cereals, potatoes, root crops, timber, vineyards

capital cities, major towns

pasture, cropland, forest

Hay, used to feed livestock, *is one of the major crops grown on the fertile foothills of Slovakia's Tatra Mountains.*

THE URBAN/RURAL POPULATION DIVIDE

urban 65% — rural 35%

POPULATION DENSITY	TOTAL LAND AREA
312 people per sq mile (120 people per sq km)	201,561 sq miles (522,180 sq km)

***The upper Dunajec River** of Poland and eastern Slovakia forms a gorge through the Pieniny range of the Carpathian Mountains.*

Southeast Europe

Albania, Bosnia & Herzegovina, Croatia, Macedonia, Yugoslavia

For 46 years the federation of Yugoslavia held together the most diverse ethnic region in Europe, along the picturesque mountain hinterland of the Dalmatian coast. Economic collapse resulted in internal tensions. In the early 1990s, civil war broke out in both Croatia and Bosnia as the ethnic populations struggled to establish their own exclusive territories. Peace was only restored by the UN after NATO launched air strikes in 1995. In the province of Kosovo, attempts to gain autonomy from Yugoslavia in 1998 were crushed by the Serbian government. The slaughter of ethnic Albanians in Kosovo provoked the West to launch NATO air strikes yet again in the region, and Yugoslav forces withdrew. The flood of refugees from Kosovo has severely strained Albania.

The Landscape

The Tisza, Sava, and Drava Rivers drain the broad northern lowland, meeting the Danube after it crosses the Hungarian border. In the west, the Dinaric Alps divide the Adriatic Sea from the interior. Mainland valleys and elongated islands run parallel to the steep Dalmatian *(Dalmacija)* coastline, following alternating bands of resistant limestone.

At least 70% of the fresh water in the Western Balkans drains eastward into the Black Sea, mostly via the Danube *(Dunav)*.
The river floodplains of the Pannonian Basin are flanked by terraces of gravel and wind-blown glacial deposits known as loess.
Poljes in the Kosovo region
Underground drainage along joints in the rock
Spring at foot of cliff
Sheer limestone walls enclose all sides
Flat *polje* floor
***Rain and underground water** dissolve limestone along massive vertical joints (cracks). This creates poljes: depressions several miles across with steep walls and broad, flat floors.*
Drava River
Tisza River
Sava River
At Iron Gate *(derdap)*, on the border with Romania, the Danube narrows and cuts through foothills of the Balkan and Carpathian mountains, forming the deepest gorge in Europe.
The elongated islands, promontories and straits of the Dalmatian *(Dalmacija)* coast were formed as the Adriatic Sea rose to flood valleys running parallel to the shore.
A major earthquake at Skopje, Macedonia, in 1963 killed 1,000 people. The whole region lies on an active crustal plate margin.
Dalmatian *(Dalmacija)* coast
A series of river valleys breaking through the Dinaric Alps from the lowlands of western Albania, give access to the interior.
Lake Ohrid
SCALE 1:2,750,000
(projection: Lambert Conformal Conic)
SLOVENIA
HUNGARY
ROMANIA
CROATIA
BOSNIA & HERZEGOVINA
SERBIA
YUGO
VOJVODINA
ZAGREB
BEOGRAD (BELGRADE)
Novi Sad
Osijek
Rijeka
Zadar
Banja Luka

***Limestone cliffs** along the Dalmatian (Dalmacija) shoreline are heavily eroded, as salt water dissolves the rock along existing horizontal cracks, or joints. This tends to form a platform of rock at the foot of the cliff.*

***Lake Ohrid** borders Albania and Macedonia. Ohrid is the deepest lake in the Western Balkans, reaching depths of 938 ft (286 m).*

***Hot, dry summers and mild winters** offer excellent conditions for viticulture in Montenegro. The precipitous Dinaric Alps have kept this region relatively isolated for centuries.*

108
110
116

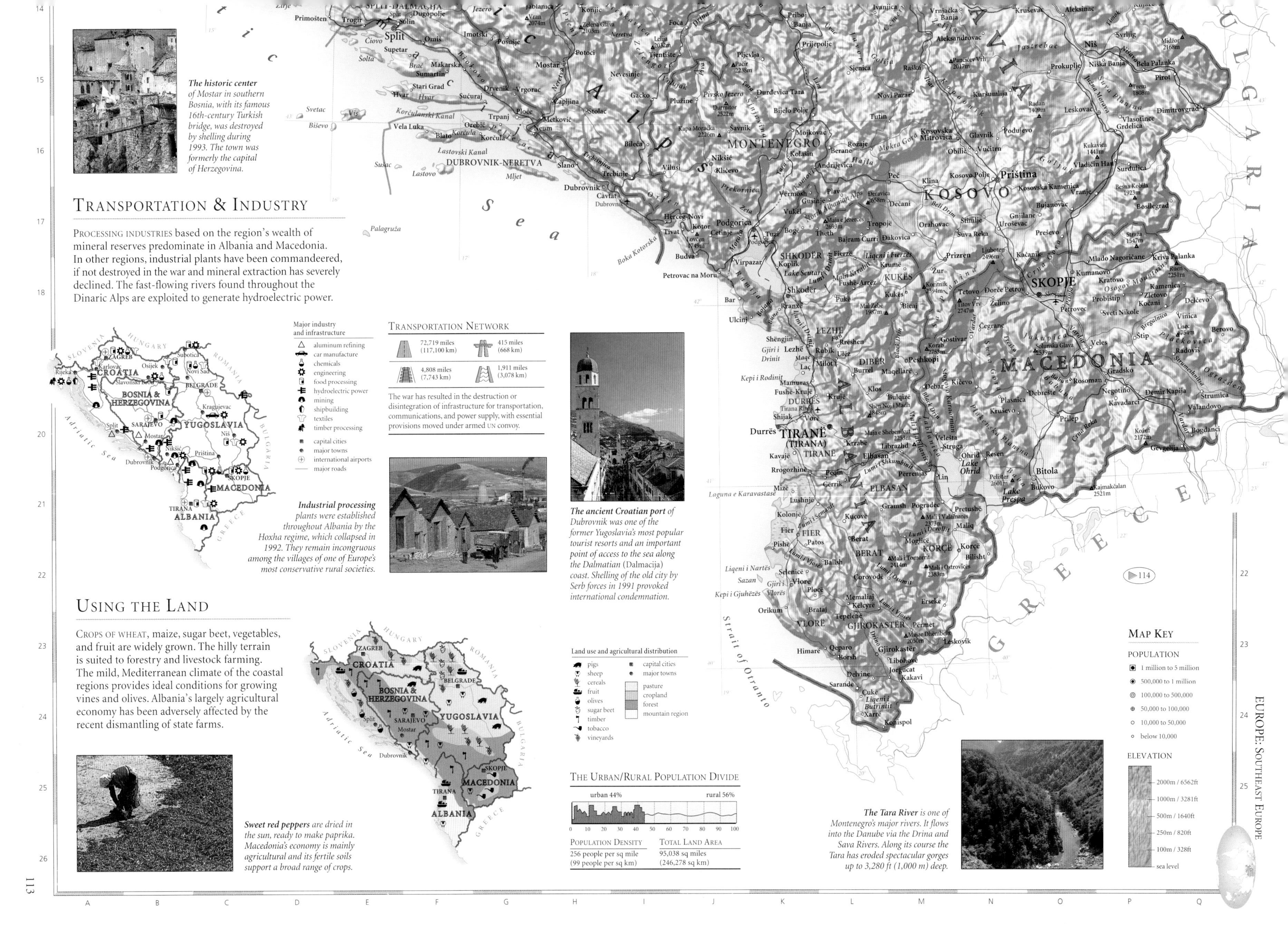
BULGARIA
MONTENEGRO
KOSOVO
MACEDONIA
ALBANIA
GREECE
SKOPJE
TIRANË (TIRANA)
Strait of Otranto
▶114

The historic center of Mostar in southern Bosnia, with its famous 16th-century Turkish bridge, was destroyed by shelling during 1993. The town was formerly the capital of Herzegovina.

Transportation & Industry

Processing industries based on the region's wealth of mineral reserves predominate in Albania and Macedonia. In other regions, industrial plants have been commandeered, if not destroyed in the war and mineral extraction has severely declined. The fast-flowing rivers found throughout the Dinaric Alps are exploited to generate hydroelectric power.

Major industry and infrastructure: aluminum refining; car manufacture; chemicals; engineering; food processing; hydroelectric power; mining; shipbuilding; textiles; timber processing; capital cities; major towns; international airports; major roads

Transportation Network

72,719 miles (117,100 km)		415 miles (668 km)	
4,808 miles (7,743 km)		1,911 miles (3,078 km)	

The war has resulted in the destruction or disintegration of infrastructure for transportation, communications, and power supply, with essential provisions moved under armed UN convoy.

Industrial processing plants were established throughout Albania by the Hoxha regime, which collapsed in 1992. They remain incongruous among the villages of one of Europe's most conservative rural societies.

The ancient Croatian port *of Dubrovnik was one of the former Yugoslavia's most popular tourist resorts and an important point of access to the sea along the Dalmatian (Dalmacija) coast. Shelling of the old city by Serb forces in 1991 provoked international condemnation.*

Using the Land

Crops of wheat, maize, sugar beet, vegetables, and fruit are widely grown. The hilly terrain is suited to forestry and livestock farming. The mild, Mediterranean climate of the coastal regions provides ideal conditions for growing vines and olives. Albania's largely agricultural economy has been adversely affected by the recent dismantling of state farms.

Land use and agricultural distribution: pigs; sheep; cereals; fruit; olives; sugar beet; timber; tobacco; vineyards; capital cities; major towns; pasture; cropland; forest; mountain region

Sweet red peppers *are dried in the sun, ready to make paprika. Macedonia's economy is mainly agricultural and its fertile soils support a broad range of crops.*

The Urban/Rural Population Divide

urban 44% — rural 56%

Population Density	Total Land Area
256 people per sq mile (99 people per sq km)	95,038 sq miles (246,278 sq km)

The Tara River *is one of Montenegro's major rivers. It flows into the Danube via the Drina and Sava Rivers. Along its course the Tara has eroded spectacular gorges up to 3,280 ft (1,000 m) deep.*

Map Key

Population: 1 million to 5 million; 500,000 to 1 million; 100,000 to 500,000; 50,000 to 100,000; 10,000 to 50,000; below 10,000

Elevation: 2000m / 6562ft; 1000m / 3281ft; 500m / 1640ft; 250m / 820ft; 100m / 328ft; sea level

BULGARIA & GREECE

Including EUROPEAN TURKEY

GREECE IS RENOWNED as the original hearth of Western civilization. The rugged terrain and numerous islands have profoundly affected its development, creating a strong agricultural and maritime tradition. In the past 50 years, this formerly rural society has rapidly urbanized, with more than half the population now living in the capital, Athens, and in the northern city of Salonica. Bulgaria, dominated for centuries by the Ottoman Turks, became part of the eastern bloc after the Second World War, only slowly emerging from Soviet influence in 1989. Moves toward democracy have led to some political instability and Bulgaria has been slow to align its economy with the rest of Europe.

THE LANDSCAPE

BULGARIA'S BALKAN MOUNTAINS divide the Danubian Plain *(Dunavska Ravnina)* and Maritsa Basin, meeting the Black Sea in the east along sandy beaches. The steep Rhodope Mountains form a natural barrier with Greece, while the younger Pindus form a rugged central spine which descends into the Aegean Sea to give a vast archipelago of over 2000 islands, the largest of which is Crete.

The Danube, Europe's second longest river, forms most of Bulgaria's northern border. The Danubian Plain *(Dunavska Ravnina)*, extending from the southern bank, is extremely fertile.

Balkan Mountains

Maritsa Basin

Rhodope Mountains

Pindus Mountains

Kythira

Crete

Karpathos

Rhodes

Corinth Canal *(Dioryga Korinthou)*

Mount Olympus is the mythical home of the Greek Gods and, at 9,570 ft (2,917 m), is the highest mountain in Greece.

Limestone rocks exposed by erosion of metamorphic rocks

Mount Olympus

Younger limestones created in shallow seas

Ancient metamorphic rock, formed miles below the surface

Mount Olympus is a composite of rocks formed by two major tectonic events. First the older metamorphic rocks were thrust over the limestones, then two million years ago regional warping and subsequent erosion, reexposed the limestone.

The Peloponnese consist of several mountainous peninsulas, linked to the mainland by the Isthmus of Corinth. The Corinth Canal *(Dioryga Korinthou)*, built in 1893, cuts through the isthmus, linking the Aegean and Ionian Seas.

***The Arda river** cuts through the Rhodope mountains in rugged, rocky gorges.*

The islands of Crete, Kythira, Karpathos, and Rhodes are part of an arc which bends southeastward from the Peloponnese, forming the southern boundary of the Aegean.

***Layers of black volcanic ash** still cover the island of Thira. This volcano last erupted 3,500 years ago, but still shows signs of volcanic activity.*

TRANSPORTATION & INDUSTRY

SOVIET INVESTMENT introduced heavy industry into Bulgaria, and the processing of agricultural produce, such as tobacco, is important throughout the country. Both countries have substantial shipyards and Greece has one of the world's largest merchant fleets. Many small craft workshops, producing textiles and processed foods, are clustered around Greek cities. The service and construction sectors have profited from the successful tourist industry.

Major industry and infrastructure

- chemicals
- engineering
- food processing
- shipbuilding
- textiles
- tourism
- capital cities
- major towns
- international airports
- major roads
- major industrial areas

ROMANIA, BULGARIA, SOFIA, Pleven, Ruse, Varna, Burgas, Stara Zagora, Plovdiv, BLACK SEA, TURKEY, Istanbul, YUGOSLAVIA, MACEDONIA, ALBANIA, GREECE, Salonica, Larisa, Volos, Aegean Sea, ATHENS, Patra, Corinth, Ionian Sea, Irakleio, MEDITERRANEAN SEA

TRANSPORTATION NETWORK

Roads	103,930 miles (167,630 km)
Motorways	345 miles (557 km)
Railways	4,346 miles (6,995 km)
Waterways	294 miles (474 km)

Bulgaria's railroads require investment to revive an outdated infrastructure. In Greece, despite a developing road network, ferry-boats remain the most effective form of transportation in many areas.

***A towering pinnacle** at Metéora in central Greece is home to the monastery of Roussanou. The 24 rock towers which dominate the plain of Thessaly (Thessalía) are remnants of an old plateau. Long-term weathering along fissures in the rock has worn*

112

116

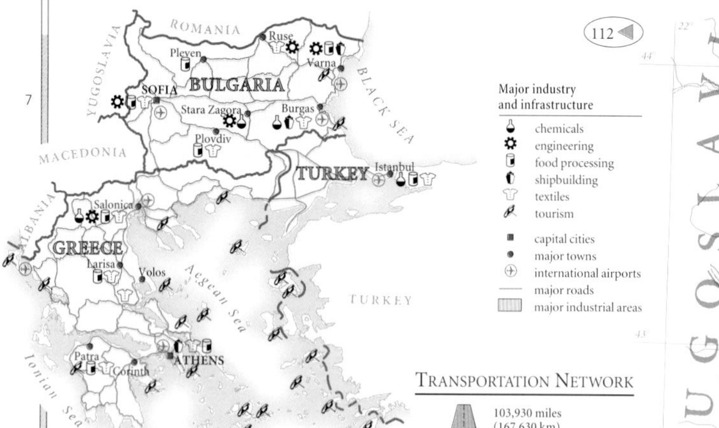

BULGARIA
ROMANIA
YUGOSLAVIA
MACEDONIA
TURKEY
BLACK SEA
Dunavska Ravnina
Balkan Mountains
Rhodope Mountains
SOFIYA
Plovdiv
Stara Zagora
Burgas
Varna
Ruse
Edirne
İstanbul

SCALE 1:2,750,000 (projection: Lambert Conformal Conic)

112

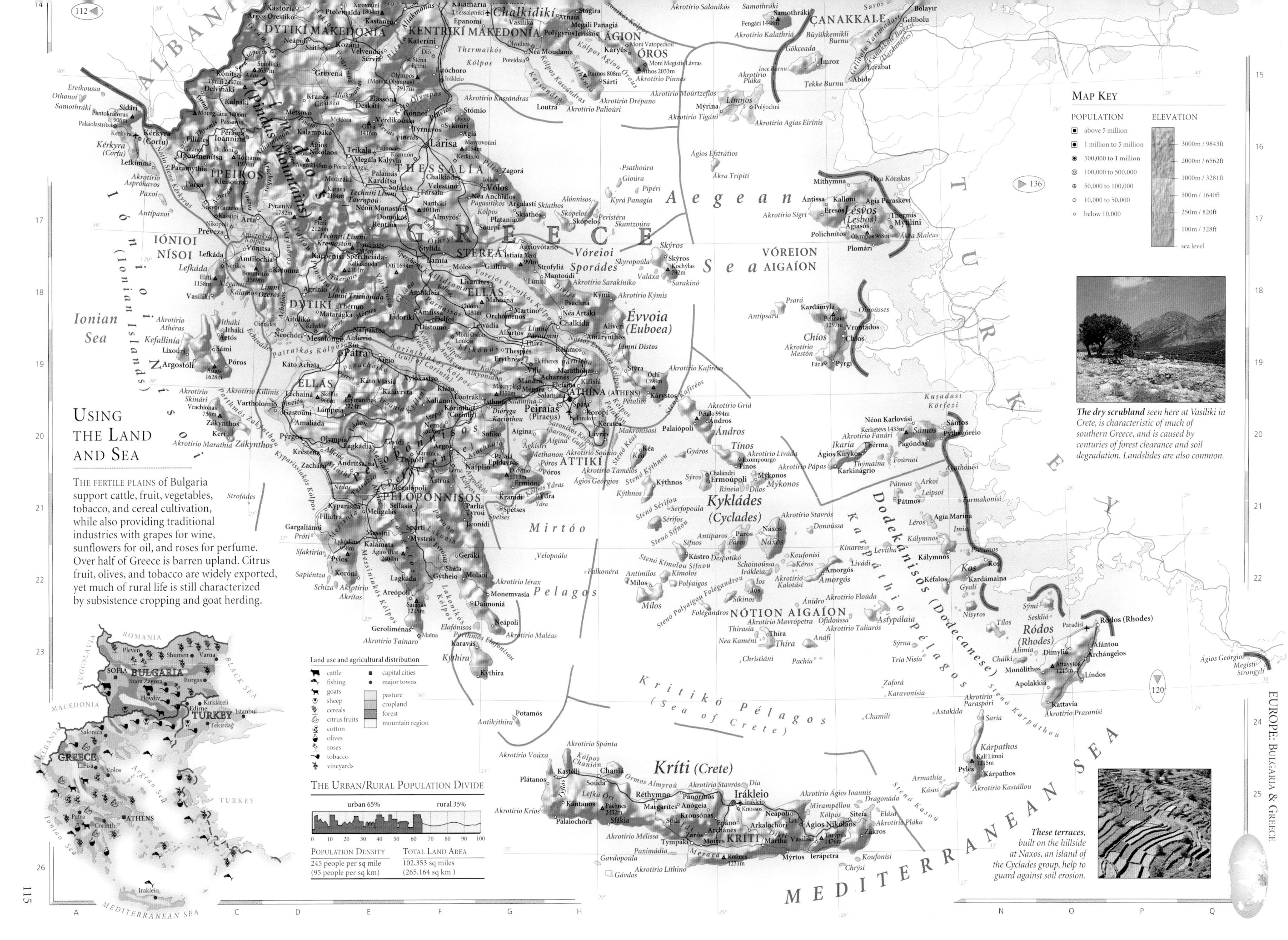
MAP KEY
POPULATION
above 5 million
1 million to 5 million
500,000 to 1 million
100,000 to 500,000
50,000 to 100,000
10,000 to 50,000
below 10,000
ELEVATION
3000m / 9843ft
2000m / 6562ft
1000m / 3281ft
500m / 1640ft
250m / 820ft
100m / 328ft
sea level
Land use and agricultural distribution
cattle
fishing
goats
sheep
cereals
citrus fruits
cotton
olives
roses
tobacco
vineyards
capital cities
major towns
pasture
cropland
forest
mountain region
THE URBAN/RURAL POPULATION DIVIDE
urban 65%
rural 35%
0 10 20 30 40 50 60 70 80 90 100
POPULATION DENSITY
245 people per sq mile
(95 people per sq km)
TOTAL LAND AREA
102,353 sq miles
(265,164 sq km)
ROMANIA
BULGARIA
SOFIA
TURKEY
GREECE
ATHENS
BLACK SEA
MEDITERRANEAN SEA
Aegean Sea
Ionian Sea
GREECE
Aegean Sea
Ionian Sea
MEDITERRANEAN SEA
TURKEY

USING THE LAND AND SEA

THE FERTILE PLAINS of Bulgaria support cattle, fruit, vegetables, tobacco, and cereal cultivation, while also providing traditional industries with grapes for wine, sunflowers for oil, and roses for perfume. Over half of Greece is barren upland. Citrus fruit, olives, and tobacco are widely exported, yet much of rural life is still characterized by subsistence cropping and goat herding.

***The dry scrubland** seen here at Vasiliki in Crete, is characteristic of much of southern Greece, and is caused by centuries of forest clearance and soil degradation. Landslides are also common.*

***These terraces**, built on the hillside at Naxos, an island of the Cyclades group, help to guard against soil erosion.*

112 ◀

▶ 136

▼ 120

Romania, Moldova & Ukraine

The industrial, social, and cultural make-up of Romania and the former Soviet states of Moldova and Ukraine still bear the imprint of their communist past. As part of the USSR, Ukraine was a leading agricultural, industrial, and energy producer. These industries, like those in Moldova and Romania, are now being reoriented more firmly toward Western markets. As a result of shifting borders, and Soviet policy actively encouraging Russian immigration into other Soviet states like Ukraine and Moldova, all three countries now contain large numbers of foreign nationals. Moldovans and Romanians are still close in terms of language and culture, although Moldova is striving to remain an independent nation.

110
110
112
114
POLAND
SLOVAKIA
HUNGARY
YUGOSLAVIA
BULGARIA
ROMANIA

Using the Land

The fertile black soils of Ukraine, often called "the breadbasket of Europe," have enabled the cultivation of a variety of cereals and vegetables, which are widely exported. Romania and Moldova also grow cereals, sunflowers, and vegetables, and are noted for the quality of their wines.

The fertile lands and tolerant climate of Moldova are ideally suited to growing grapes for wine.

Land use and agricultural distribution

- cattle
- pigs
- poultry
- sheep
- cereals
- cotton
- sugar beet
- sunflowers
- vineyards
- capital cities
- major towns
- pasture
- cropland
- forest
- wetland

The Urban/Rural Population Divide

urban 65% | rural 35%

0 10 20 30 40 50 60 70 80 90 100

Population Density	Total Land Area
232 people per sq mile (89 people per sq km)	334,947 sq miles (867,740 sq km)

***Glacial lakes** are found throughout the Transylvanian Alps (Carpații Meridionali), although the mountains no longer have any permanent snow cover.*

Transportation & Industry

Heavy industry using local raw materials characterizes much of this region. The industrial heartland of Ukraine, specializing in metal and machine-building industries, is based around its vast mineral reserves in the Donbass region. In Moldova, food processing draws on produce from its agricultural sector. Romanian industry relies both on local raw materials and imported iron, steel, and oil.

Major industry and infrastructure

- car manufacture
- chemicals
- coal
- engineering
- food processing
- mining
- oil & gas
- textiles
- tourism
- capital cities
- major towns
- international airports
- major roads
- major industrial areas

Transportation Network

151,089 miles (243,300 km)	70 miles (113 km)
21,889 miles (35,248 km)	3803 miles (6124 km)

Increased industrialization has necessitated the upgrading of road and rail networks in all three countries. Modernization has tended to focus only on major cities and industrial areas.

***During the 1960s and 1970s,** many industries, like this carbon factory, developed using the mineral resources on the flanks of the Transylvanian Alps (Carpații Meridionali).*

SCALE 1:3,500,000
(projection: Lambert Conformal Conic)
MAP KEY
POPULATION
1 million to 5 million
500,000 to 1 million
100,000 to 500,000
50,000 to 100,000
10,000 to 50,000
below 10,000
ELEVATION
2000m / 6562ft
1000m / 3281ft
500m / 1640ft
250m / 820ft
100m / 328ft
sea level
RUSSIAN FEDERATION
UKRAINE
BLACK SEA
Sea of Azov
Gulf of Taganrog
Black Sea Lowland
The Swallow's Nest castle at Yalta is one of many tourist resorts on the Crimean (Krym) coast, dubbed the "Russian Riviera."
Old glaciated valley
Water has eroded a new post-glacial valley
Balkas are common throughout Ukraine. They are large U-shaped valleys, formed during the last Ice Age, which contain narrower, deep valleys. These were incised by a sudden flow of water, following an ice melt.
Counterclockwise currents have created the sandspits which fringe the Sea of Azov.
Uplifted and folded at the same time as the Alps, some 250 miles (400 km) of the eastern Carpathian Mountains contain ancient volcanic cones and craters.
The Codrii Hills dominate the landscape of central Moldova; they are intersected by deep, flat valleys and ravines.
Steppe landscape covers two-thirds of Ukraine. These flat, treeless grasslands extend from central Europe to central Asia.
Most of the major rivers in southeastern Europe, like the Danube, the Dniester and Dnieper flow south and east to the Black Sea.
The Apuseni Mountains (Munţii Apuşeni) are rich in mineral deposits, including gold and iron ore.
Transylvanian Alps (Carpaţii Meridionali)
The Danube forms a natural border between Romania and Bulgaria.
The three branches of the Danube Delta (Delta Dunării) form a triangle of wetlands covering some 1,950 sq miles (5,050 sq km).
At Kryms'ki Hory, three flat-topped, parallel limestone ridges run 80 miles (128 km) along the southern coast of the Crimean (Krym) Peninsula.

THE LANDSCAPE

VAST FLAT LOWLANDS and gently rolling hills cover most of southeastern Europe. In the southwest, the Carpathian Mountains form a gentle arc. To the south of the Carpathian Mountains lies the Danube Plain, across which the Danube River flows to the Black Sea. To the north and east, the hills of Moldova level out into low plains, running east to the steppes of Ukraine.

Divided into crystalline massifs, the southern arm of the Carpathian Mountains, the Transylvanian Alps (Carpaţii Meridionali), *extend 170 miles (274 km) across southwestern Romania.*

The Baltic States & Belarus

Belarus, Estonia, Latvia, Lithuania, Kaliningrad

Occupying Europe's main corridor to Russia, the four distinct cultures of Estonia, Latvia, Lithuania, and Belarus share a history of struggle for nationhood against the interests of more powerful neighbors. As the first republics to declare their independence from the Soviet Union in 1990–91, the Baltic states of Estonia, Latvia, and Lithuania have sought an economic role in the EU, while reaffirming their European cultural roots through the church and a strong musical tradition. Meanwhile, Belarus has shown economic and political allegiance to Russia by joining the Commonwealth of Independent States.

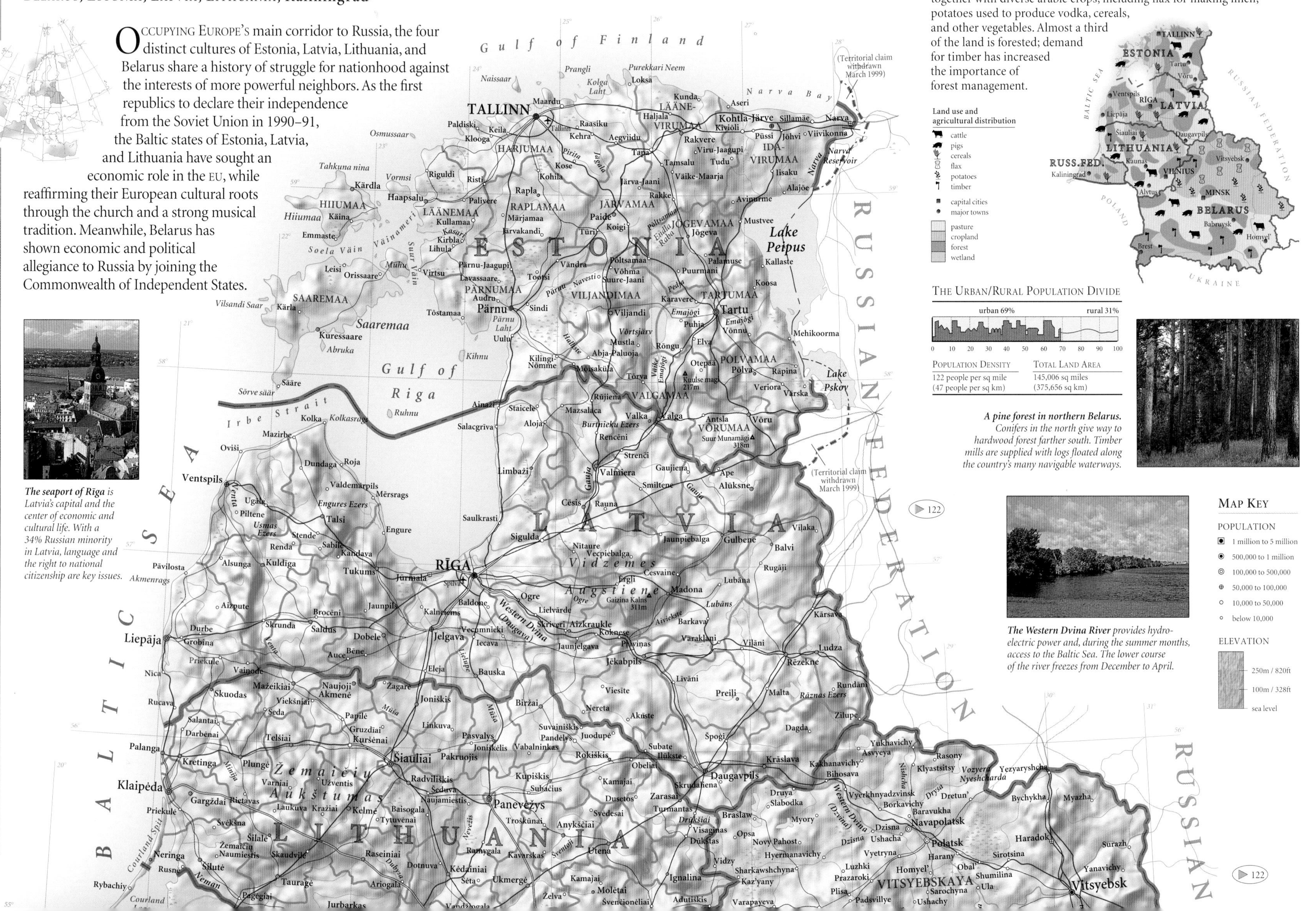
Gulf of Finland
Gulf of Riga
BALTIC SEA
RUSSIAN FEDERATION
ESTONIA
LATVIA
LITHUANIA
TALLINN
RĪGA
Lake Peipus
Lake Pskov
Irbe Strait
Narva Bay
(Territorial claim withdrawn March 1999)
122

The seaport of Rīga is Latvia's capital and the center of economic and cultural life. With a 34% Russian minority in Latvia, language and the right to national citizenship are key issues.

Using The Land

Across the four nations cattle and pig farming are widespread, together with diverse arable crops, including flax for making linen, potatoes used to produce vodka, cereals, and other vegetables. Almost a third of the land is forested; demand for timber has increased the importance of forest management.

Land use and agricultural distribution: cattle, pigs, cereals, flax, potatoes, timber, capital cities, major towns, pasture, cropland, forest, wetland

The Urban/Rural Population Divide

urban 69% — rural 31%

0 10 20 30 40 50 60 70 80 90 100

Population Density	Total Land Area
122 people per sq mile (47 people per sq km)	145,006 sq miles (375,656 sq km)

A pine forest in northern Belarus. *Conifers in the north give way to hardwood forest farther south. Timber mills are supplied with logs floated along the country's many navigable waterways.*

The Western Dvina River *provides hydro-electric power and, during the summer months, access to the Baltic Sea. The lower course of the river freezes from December to April.*

Map Key

POPULATION
- 1 million to 5 million
- 500,000 to 1 million
- 100,000 to 500,000
- 50,000 to 100,000
- 10,000 to 50,000
- below 10,000

ELEVATION
- 250m / 820ft
- 100m / 328ft
- sea level

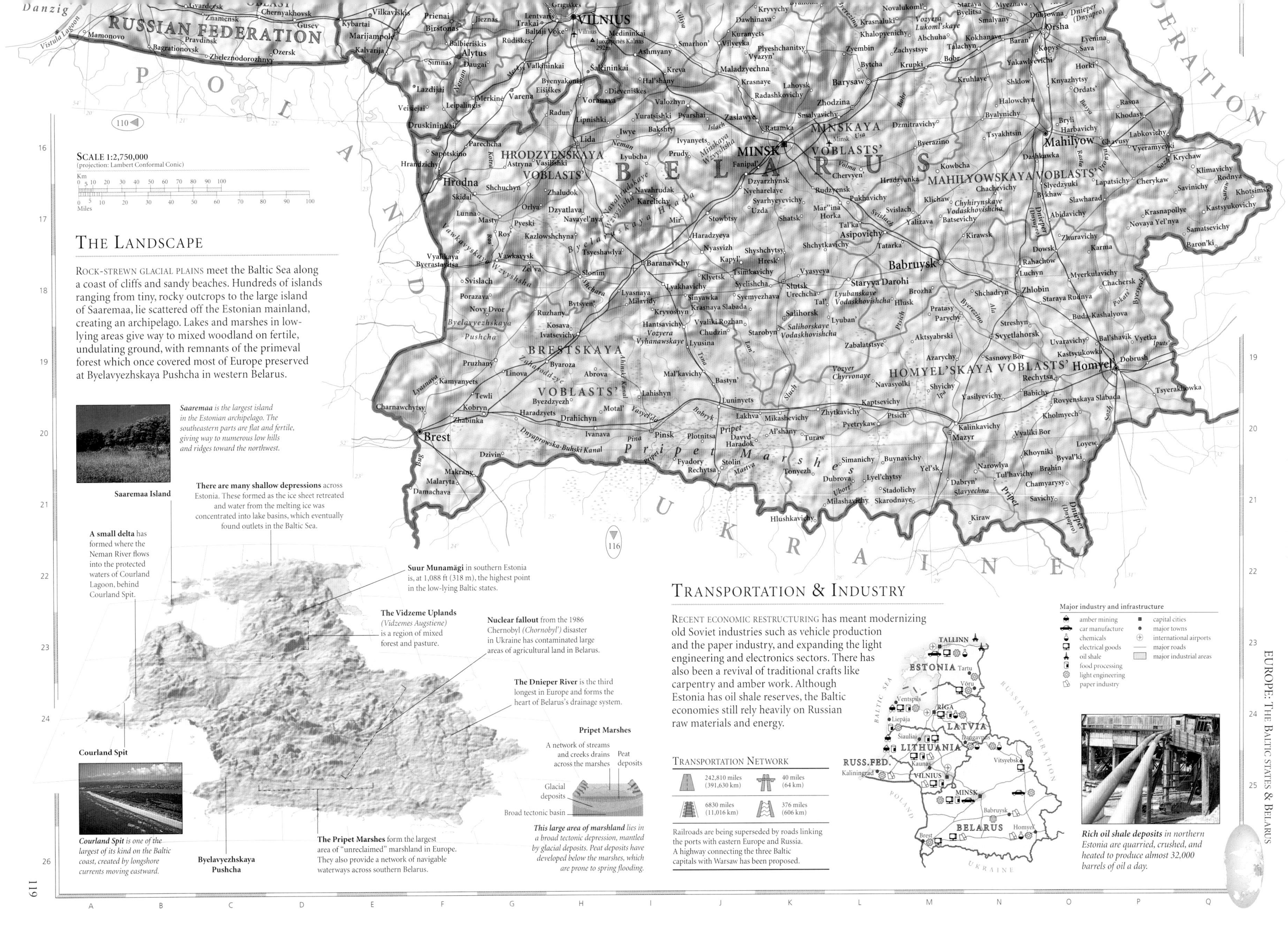
RUSSIAN FEDERATION
POLAND
BELARUS
UKRAINE
FEDERATION
VILNIUS
MINSK
Hrodna
Brest
Babruysk
Homyel'
Mahilyow
Orsha
Barysaw
Baranavichy
Pinsk
Mazyr
HRODZYENSKAYA VOBLASTS'
MINSKAYA VOBLASTS'
MAHILYOWSKAYA VOBLASTS'
BRESTSKAYA VOBLASTS'
HOMYEL'SKAYA VOBLASTS'
Pripet Marshes
Dnieper (Dnyapro)
Pripet
Byelavyezhskaya Pushcha
Danzig
Vistula Lagoon
Juozapinės Kalnas 292m
110
116
SCALE 1:2,750,000
(projection: Lambert Conformal Conic)
Km
Miles

The Landscape

ROCK-STREWN GLACIAL PLAINS meet the Baltic Sea along a coast of cliffs and sandy beaches. Hundreds of islands ranging from tiny, rocky outcrops to the large island of Saaremaa, lie scattered off the Estonian mainland, creating an archipelago. Lakes and marshes in low-lying areas give way to mixed woodland on fertile, undulating ground, with remnants of the primeval forest which once covered most of Europe preserved at Byelavyezhskaya Pushcha in western Belarus.

Saaremaa is the largest island in the Estonian archipelago. The southeastern parts are flat and fertile, giving way to numerous low hills and ridges toward the northwest.

Saaremaa Island

There are many shallow depressions across Estonia. These formed as the ice sheet retreated and water from the melting ice was concentrated into lake basins, which eventually found outlets in the Baltic Sea.

A small delta has formed where the Neman River flows into the protected waters of Courland Lagoon, behind Courland Spit.

Suur Munamägi in southern Estonia is, at 1,088 ft (318 m), the highest point in the low-lying Baltic states.

The Vidzeme Uplands *(Vidzemes Augstiene)* is a region of mixed forest and pasture.

Nuclear fallout from the 1986 Chernobyl *(Chornobyl')* disaster in Ukraine has contaminated large areas of agricultural land in Belarus.

The Dnieper River is the third longest in Europe and forms the heart of Belarus's drainage system.

Pripet Marshes

A network of streams and creeks drains across the marshes

Peat deposits

Glacial deposits

Broad tectonic basin

***This large area of marshland** lies in a broad tectonic depression, mantled by glacial deposits. Peat deposits have developed below the marshes, which are prone to spring flooding.*

Courland Spit

***Courland Spit** is one of the largest of its kind on the Baltic coast, created by longshore currents moving eastward.*

Byelavyezhskaya Pushcha

The Pripet Marshes form the largest area of "unreclaimed" marshland in Europe. They also provide a network of navigable waterways across southern Belarus.

Transportation & Industry

RECENT ECONOMIC RESTRUCTURING has meant modernizing old Soviet industries such as vehicle production and the paper industry, and expanding the light engineering and electronics sectors. There has also been a revival of traditional crafts like carpentry and amber work. Although Estonia has oil shale reserves, the Baltic economies still rely heavily on Russian raw materials and energy.

Transportation Network

242,810 miles (391,630 km)	40 miles (64 km)
6830 miles (11,016 km)	376 miles (606 km)

Railroads are being superseded by roads linking the ports with eastern Europe and Russia. A highway connecting the three Baltic capitals with Warsaw has been proposed.

Major industry and infrastructure
amber mining
car manufacture
chemicals
electrical goods
oil shale
food processing
light engineering
paper industry
capital cities
major towns
international airports
major roads
major industrial areas
TALLINN
ESTONIA
Tartu
Võru
Ventspils
RIGA
LATVIA
Liepāja
Daugavpils
Šiauliai
LITHUANIA
Kaunas
VILNIUS
RUSS.FED.
Kaliningrad
Vitsyebsk
MINSK
Babruysk
Homyel'
Brest
BELARUS
BALTIC SEA
RUSSIAN FEDERATION
POLAND
UKRAINE

***Rich oil shale deposits** in northern Estonia are quarried, crushed, and heated to produce almost 32,000 barrels of oil a day.*

THE MEDITERRANEAN

THE MEDITERRANEAN SEA stretches over 2,500 miles (4,000 km) east to west, separating Europe from Africa. At its westernmost point it is connected to the Atlantic Ocean through the Strait of Gibraltar. In the east, the Suez Canal, opened in 1869, gives passage to the Indian Ocean. In the northeast, linked by the Sea of Marmara, lies the Black Sea. Throughout history the Mediterranean has been a focal area for many great empires and civilizations, reflected in the variety of cultures found in the 28 states and territories that border its shores. Since the 1960s, development along the southern coast of Europe has expanded rapidly to accommodate increasing numbers of tourists and to enable the exploitation of oil and gas reserves. This has resulted in rising levels of pollution, threatening the future of the sea.

***Monte Carlo in Monaco** is just one of the luxurious resorts scattered along the Riviera, which stretches along the coast from Cannes in France to La Spezia in Italy. The region's mild winters and hot summers have attracted wealthy tourists since the early 19th century.*

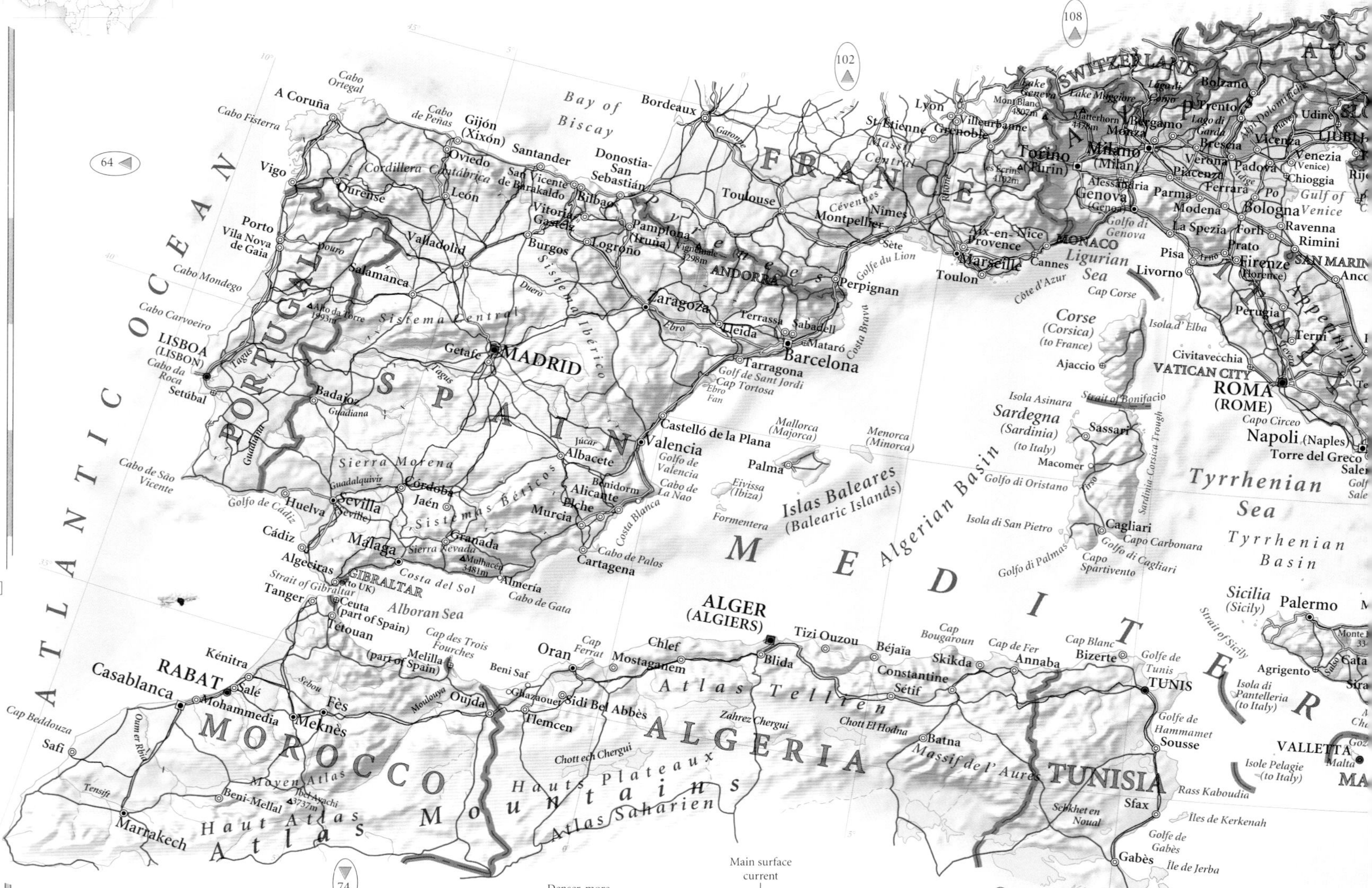

THE LANDSCAPE

THE MEDITERRANEAN SEA IS ALMOST TOTALLY LANDLOCKED, joined to the Atlantic Ocean through the Strait of Gibraltar, which is only 8 miles (13 km) wide. Lying on an active plate margin, sea floor movements have formed a variety of basins, troughs, and ridges. A submarine ridge running from Tunisia to Sicily divides the sea into two distinct basins. The western basin is characterized by broad, smooth abyssal (or ocean) plains. In contrast, the eastern basin is dominated by a large ridge system, running east to west.

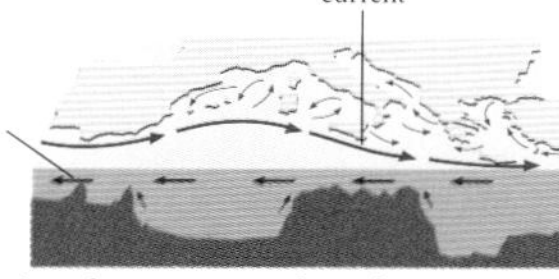

Denser, more saline currents flow back to Atlantic

Main surface current

***Atlantic surface water** enters the Mediterranean Sea via the Straits of Gibraltar and generally flows eastward, becoming progressively more saline and dense as water evaporates. This denser water sinks and at depths below 280 ft (80 m), flows back to the Atlantic Ocean.*

Industrial pollution flowing from the Dnieper and Danube Rivers has destroyed a large proportion of the fish population that used to inhabit the upper layers of the Black Sea.

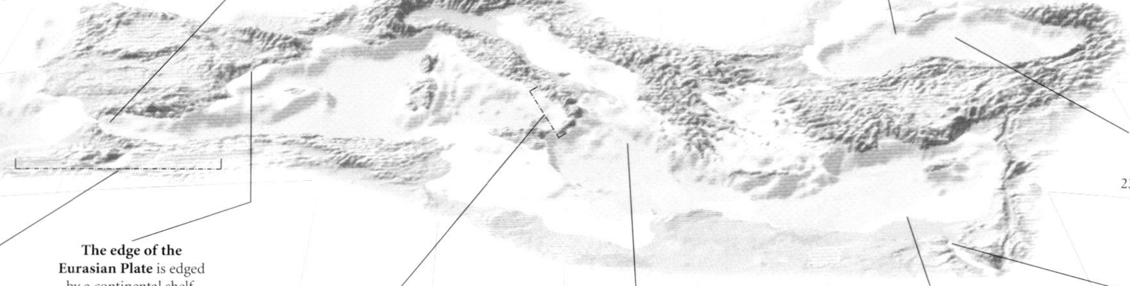

Oxygen in the Black Sea is dissolved only in its upper layers; at depths below 230–300 ft (70–100 m) the sea is "dead" and can support no life-forms other than specially-adapted bacteria.

***The Atlas Mountains** are a range of fold mountains that lie in Morocco and Algeria. They run parallel to the Mediterranean, forming a topographical and climatic divide between the Mediterranean coast and the western Sahara.*

The edge of the Eurasian Plate is edged by a continental shelf. In the Mediterranean Sea this is widest at he Ebro Fan where it extends 60 miles (96 km).

An arc of active submarine, island, and mainland volcanoes, including Etna and Vesuvius, lie in and around southern Italy. The area is also susceptible to earthquakes and landslides.

The Ionian Basin is the deepest in the Mediterranean, reaching depths of 16,800 ft (5,121 m).

Nutrient flows into the eastern Mediterranean, and sediment flows to the Nile Delta have been severely lowered by the building of the Aswan Dam across the Nile in Egypt. This is causing the delta to shrink.

The Suez Canal, opened in 1869, extends 100 miles (160 km) from Port Said to the Gulf of Suez.

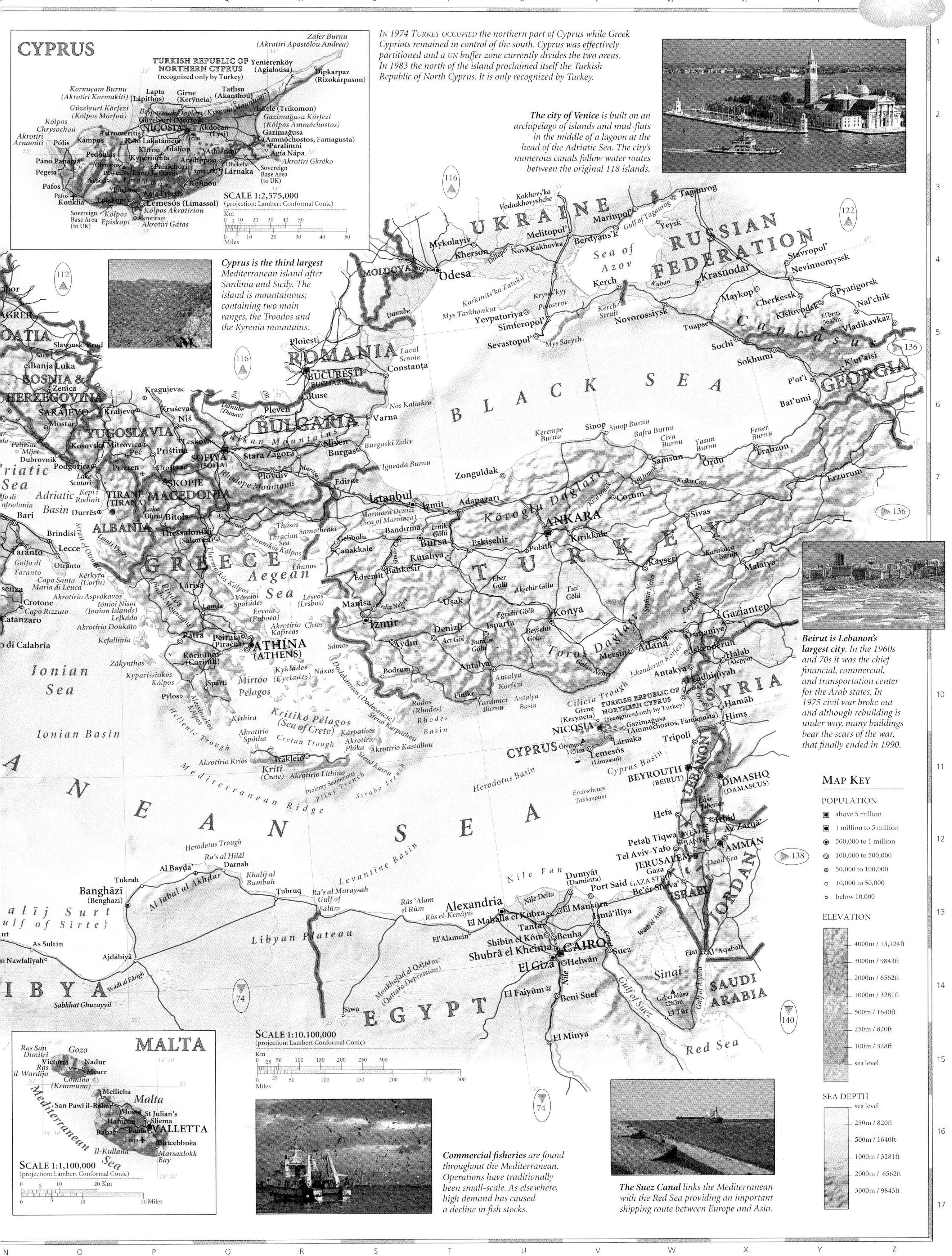
N O P Q R S T U V W X Y Z
1 2 3 4 5 6 7 8 9 10 11 12 13 14 15 16 17
CYPRUS
TURKISH REPUBLIC OF NORTHERN CYPRUS (recognized only by Turkey)
Zafer Burnu (Akrotiri Apostólou Andréa)
Yenierenköy (Agialoúsa)
Dipkarpaz (Rizokárpason)
Kornuçam Burnu (Akrotiri Kormakíti)
Lapta (Lápithos)
Girne (Kerýneia)
Tatlısu (Akanthoú)
Güzelyurt Körfezi (Kólpos Mórfou)
İskele (Tríkomon)
Gazimağusa Körfezi (Kólpos Ammóchostos)
Gazimağusa (Ammóchostos, Famagusta)
Kólpos Chrysochoú
Akrotiri Arnaoúti
Pólis
NICOSIA
Paralímni
Agia Nápa
Akrotiri Gkréko
Páno Panagiá
Pégeia
Páfos
Lárnaka
Dhekélia Sovereign Base Area (to UK)
Lemesós (Limassol)
Kólpos Akrotiriou
Akrotiri Gátas
Sovereign Base Area (to UK)
Episkopí
Koúklia
SCALE 1:2,575,000
(projection: Lambert Conformal Conic)
Km
Miles
UKRAINE
RUSSIAN FEDERATION
MOLDOVA
ROMANIA
BUCUREŞTI (BUCHAREST)
BULGARIA
SOFIYA (SOFIA)
YUGOSLAVIA
MACEDONIA
SKOPJE
ALBANIA
TIRANË (TIRANA)
GREECE
ATHÍNA (ATHENS)
TURKEY
ANKARA
İstanbul
GEORGIA
SYRIA
DIMASHQ (DAMASCUS)
LEBANON
BEYROUTH (BEIRUT)
CYPRUS
NICOSIA
ISRAEL
JERUSALEM
JORDAN
'AMMĀN
SAUDI ARABIA
EGYPT
CAIRO
Alexandria
LIBYA
BLACK SEA
Sea of Azov
Aegean Sea
Ionian Sea
Adriatic Sea
MEDITERRANEAN SEA
Red Sea
Sinai
Caucasus
Balkan Mountains
Rhodope Mountains
Toros Dağları
Köroğlu Dağları
Libyan Plateau
SCALE 1:10,100,000
(projection: Lambert Conformal Conic)
Km
Miles
MALTA
Gozo
Victoria
Comino (Kemmuna)
Malta
VALLETTA
Mediterranean Sea
SCALE 1:1,100,000
(projection: Lambert Conformal Conic)
MAP KEY
POPULATION
above 5 million
1 million to 5 million
500,000 to 1 million
100,000 to 500,000
50,000 to 100,000
10,000 to 50,000
below 10,000
ELEVATION
4000m / 13,124ft
3000m / 9843ft
2000m / 6562ft
1000m / 3281ft
500m / 1640ft
250m / 820ft
100m / 328ft
sea level
SEA DEPTH
sea level
250m / 820ft
500m / 1640ft
1000m / 3281ft
2000m / 6562ft
3000m / 9843ft

IN 1974 TURKEY OCCUPIED *the northern part of Cyprus while Greek Cypriots remained in control of the south. Cyprus was effectively partitioned and a UN buffer zone currently divides the two areas. In 1983 the north of the island proclaimed itself the Turkish Republic of North Cyprus. It is only recognized by Turkey.*

***The city of Venice** is built on an archipelago of islands and mud-flats in the middle of a lagoon at the head of the Adriatic Sea. The city's numerous canals follow water routes between the original 118 islands.*

***Cyprus is the third largest** Mediterranean island after Sardinia and Sicily. The island is mountainous; containing two main ranges, the Troodos and the Kyrenia mountains.*

***Beirut is Lebanon's largest city.** In the 1960s and 70s it was the chief financial, commercial, and transportation center for the Arab states. In 1975 civil war broke out and although rebuilding is under way, many buildings bear the scars of the war, that finally ended in 1990.*

***Commercial fisheries** are found throughout the Mediterranean. Operations have traditionally been small-scale. As elsewhere, high demand has caused a decline in fish stocks.*

***The Suez Canal** links the Mediterranean with the Red Sea providing an important shipping route between Europe and Asia.*

The Russian Federation

The Cold War era of global relations was concluded in 1991 with the formal dissolution of the Soviet Union. The Russian Federation declared its separate sovereignty from the foundering communist empire following independence declarations from a number of former Soviet republics. As the leading member of the Commonwealth of Independent States, the Russian Federation has a central role in the development of post-Soviet Eurasia. Crossing 11 time zones, the Russian Federation is almost twice the size of the US, and with more than 150 ethnic minorities and 21 autonomous republics, regionalist dissent within its own territory remains a danger.

***Summer beds of moss and lichen** scatter a 90% surface cover of ice across the islands of Franz Josef Land (Zemlya Frantsa-Iosifa), the northernmost land in the eastern hemisphere.*

The Russian Federation: Administrative Regions

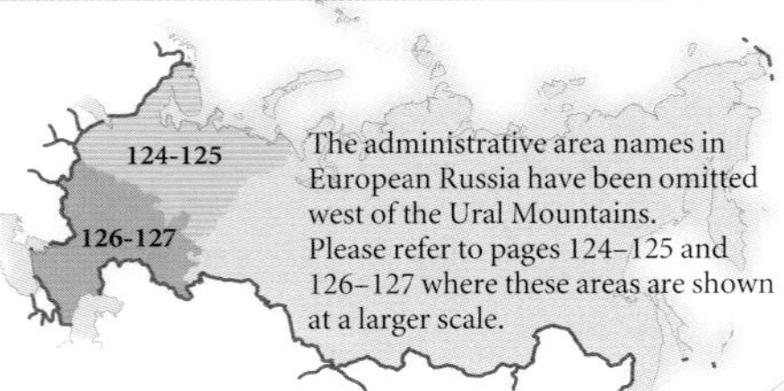

124-125

126-127

The administrative area names in European Russia have been omitted west of the Ural Mountains. Please refer to pages 124–125 and 126–127 where these areas are shown at a larger scale.

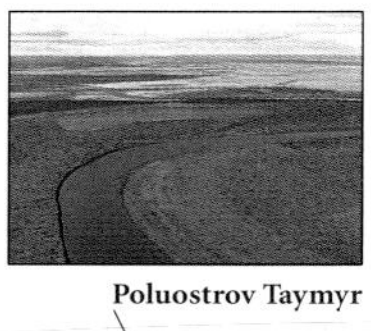

92 118 110 118 116 144 136 162

BARENTS SEA

ARCTIC

Karskoye More

KAZAKHSTAN

RUSSIAN FEDERATION

The Landscape

The Ural Mountains *(Ural'skiye Gory)* divide the fertile North European Plain from the West Siberian Plain *(Zapadno-Sibirskaya Ravnina)*, the world's largest area of flat ground, crossed by giant rivers flowing north to the Kara Sea *(Karskoye More)*. The land rises to the Central Siberian Plateau *(Srednesibirskoye Ploskogor'ye)* and becomes more mountainous to the southeast. These immense topographic regions intersect with latitudinal vegetation bands. The tundra of the extreme north gives way to a vast area of coniferous woodland, which is known as *taiga*, larger than the Amazon rain forest. This belt turns to mixed forest and then steppe grasslands towards the south.

The North European Plain is marked by huge moraine ridges left by the Scandinavian Ice Sheet and by long intermoraine drainage channels, known as *Urstromtäler*.

***The Khatanga River** meanders slowly across the Poluostrov Taymyr, a low-lying tundra landscape which floods in the spring thaw, until the water can escape to the sea.*

Poluostrov Taymyr

Kara Sea *(Karskoye More)*

Yukagirskoye Ploskogor'ye is a rolling plain with isolated drumlins, dome-like features resulting from glacial deposition.

The mountains of Verkhoyanskiy Khrebet were formed by movement between the Eurasian and North American plates, during the same period of folding that created the Urals.

Permanent ice wedges up to 16 ft (5 m) deep

Polygon shapes create patterned ground

Permafrost

The Ural Mountains *(Ural'skiye Gory)* extend 1,550 miles (2,500 km). They were formed over 280 million years ago, folded as the East European and Siberian plates moved closer together.

The Yenisey is one of the world's longest rivers, and also among the most languid, dropping only 500 ft (152 m) over 1,200 miles (2,000 km).

***Lake Baikal** (Ozero Baykal), occupies a rift valley and is the world's deepest lake, over 1 mile (1.6 km) in depth. It is fed by over 300 rivers and drained by just one, the Angara.*

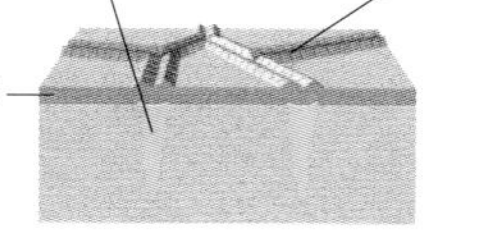

***Patterned ground** is a permafrost feature found extensively across northern Russia. Seasonal contraction of the permafrost creates polygonal cracks, which are filled by ice wedges.*

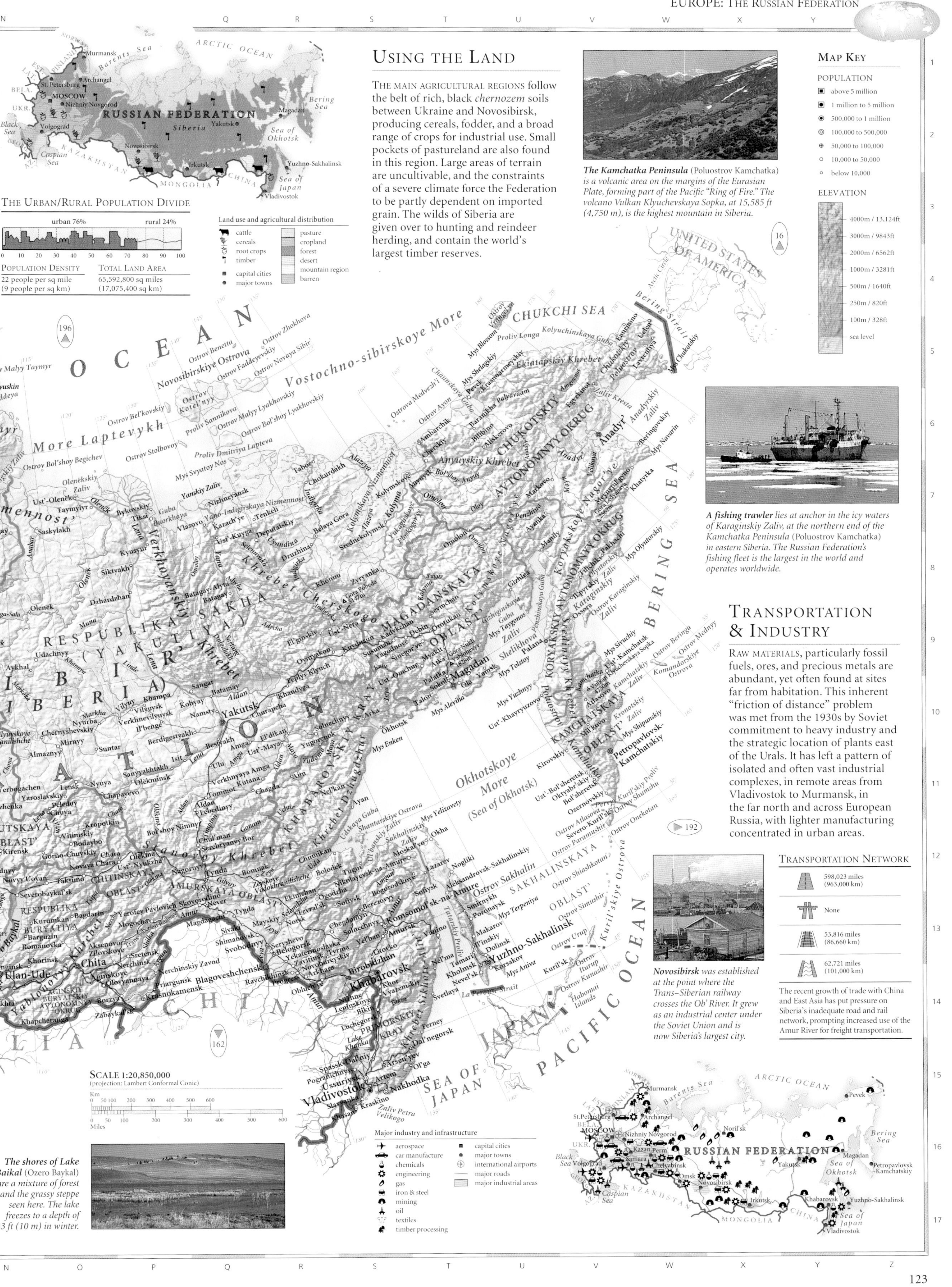

THE URBAN/RURAL POPULATION DIVIDE
urban 76%
rural 24%
0 10 20 30 40 50 60 70 80 90 100
POPULATION DENSITY
22 people per sq mile
(9 people per sq km)
TOTAL LAND AREA
65,592,800 sq miles
(17,075,400 sq km)
Land use and agricultural distribution
cattle
cereals
root crops
timber
capital cities
major towns
pasture
cropland
forest
desert
mountain region
barren
MAP KEY
POPULATION
above 5 million
1 million to 5 million
500,000 to 1 million
100,000 to 500,000
50,000 to 100,000
10,000 to 50,000
below 10,000
ELEVATION
4000m / 13,124ft
3000m / 9843ft
2000m / 6562ft
1000m / 3281ft
500m / 1640ft
250m / 820ft
100m / 328ft
sea level
TRANSPORTATION NETWORK
598,023 miles (963,000 km)
None
53,816 miles (86,660 km)
62,721 miles (101,000 km)
SCALE 1:20,850,000
(projection: Lambert Conformal Conic)
Major industry and infrastructure
aerospace
car manufacture
chemicals
engineering
gas
iron & steel
mining
oil
textiles
timber processing
capital cities
major towns
international airports
major roads
major industrial areas

USING THE LAND

THE MAIN AGRICULTURAL REGIONS follow the belt of rich, black *chernozem* soils between Ukraine and Novosibirsk, producing cereals, fodder, and a broad range of crops for industrial use. Small pockets of pastureland are also found in this region. Large areas of terrain are uncultivable, and the constraints of a severe climate force the Federation to be partly dependent on imported grain. The wilds of Siberia are given over to hunting and reindeer herding, and contain the world's largest timber reserves.

The Kamchatka Peninsula (Poluostrov Kamchatka) *is a volcanic area on the margins of the Eurasian Plate, forming part of the Pacific "Ring of Fire." The volcano Vulkan Klyuchevskaya Sopka, at 15,585 ft (4,750 m), is the highest mountain in Siberia.*

A fishing trawler *lies at anchor in the icy waters of Karaginskiy Zaliv, at the northern end of the Kamchatka Peninsula (Poluostrov Kamchatka) in eastern Siberia. The Russian Federation's fishing fleet is the largest in the world and operates worldwide.*

TRANSPORTATION & INDUSTRY

RAW MATERIALS, particularly fossil fuels, ores, and precious metals are abundant, yet often found at sites far from habitation. This inherent "friction of distance" problem was met from the 1930s by Soviet commitment to heavy industry and the strategic location of plants east of the Urals. It has left a pattern of isolated and often vast industrial complexes, in remote areas from Vladivostok to Murmansk, in the far north and across European Russia, with lighter manufacturing concentrated in urban areas.

Novosibirsk *was established at the point where the Trans-Siberian railway crosses the Ob' River. It grew as an industrial center under the Soviet Union and is now Siberia's largest city.*

The recent growth of trade with China and East Asia has put pressure on Siberia's inadequate road and rail network, prompting increased use of the Amur River for freight transportation.

The shores of Lake Baikal *(Ozero Baykal) are a mixture of forest and the grassy steppe seen here. The lake freezes to a depth of 33 ft (10 m) in winter.*

Northern European Russia

Reaching into the Arctic Circle, this region of lakeland, forest, and tundra is historically bound to Europe by St. Petersburg, the old imperial capital of Tsarist Russia and home to a third of the region's population. Communist rule from Moscow left the north politically marginalized, contributing to the present problems of outmoded industry, poor infrastructure, and serious environmental neglect. However, with borders embracing Finland, Norway, the Baltic, and the northern sea route to the Atlantic, the region's success in foreign trade is now of prime importance to the Russian economy.

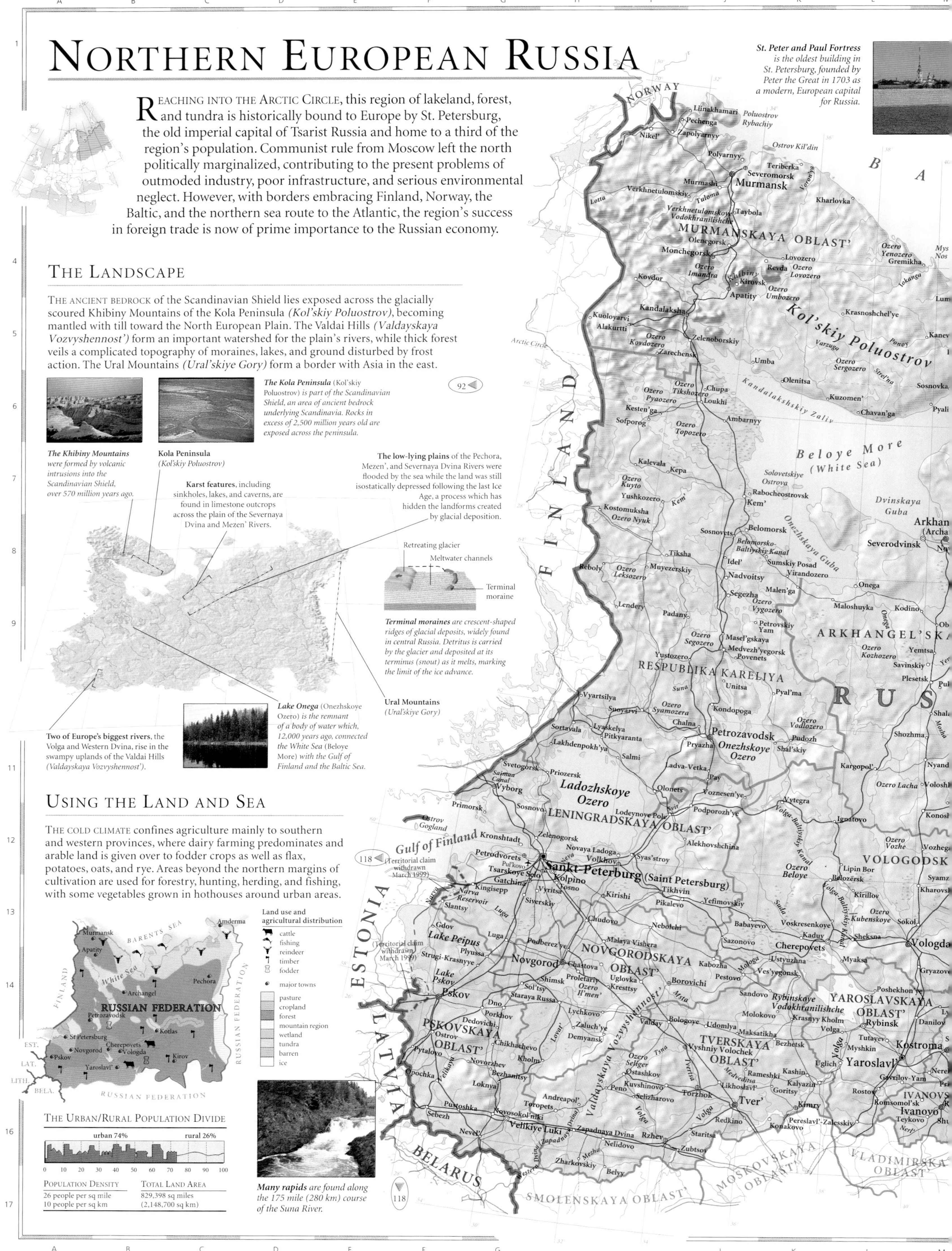

NORWAY
FINLAND
ESTONIA
LATVIA
BELARUS
Murmansk
MURMANSKAYA OBLAST'
Kol'skiy Poluostrov
Beloye More (White Sea)
ARKHANGEL'SKAYA
RESPUBLIKA KARELIYA
Petrozavodsk
Onezhskoye Ozero
Ladozhskoye Ozero
LENINGRADSKAYA OBLAST'
Gulf of Finland
Sankt-Peterburg (Saint Petersburg)
Lake Peipus
Novgorod
NOVGORODSKAYA OBLAST'
Pskov
PSKOVSKAYA OBLAST'
VOLOGODSKAYA
Vologda
Cherepovets
YAROSLAVSKAYA OBLAST'
Yaroslavl'
Kostroma
TVERSKAYA OBLAST'
Tver'
SMOLENSKAYA OBLAST'
MOSKOVSKAYA OBLAST'
VLADIMIRSKAYA OBLAST'
Arctic Circle

St. Peter and Paul Fortress is the oldest building in St. Petersburg, founded by Peter the Great in 1703 as a modern, European capital for Russia.

The Landscape

The ancient bedrock of the Scandinavian Shield lies exposed across the glacially scoured Khibiny Mountains of the Kola Peninsula *(Kol'skiy Poluostrov)*, becoming mantled with till toward the North European Plain. The Valdai Hills *(Valdayskaya Vozvyshennost')* form an important watershed for the plain's rivers, while thick forest veils a complicated topography of moraines, lakes, and ground disturbed by frost action. The Ural Mountains *(Ural'skiye Gory)* form a border with Asia in the east.

***The Khibiny Mountains** were formed by volcanic intrusions into the Scandinavian Shield, over 570 million years ago.*

Kola Peninsula *(Kol'skiy Poluostrov)*

***The Kola Peninsula** (Kol'skiy Poluostrov) is part of the Scandinavian Shield, an area of ancient bedrock underlying Scandinavia. Rocks in excess of 2,500 million years old are exposed across the peninsula.*

Karst features, including sinkholes, lakes, and caverns, are found in limestone outcrops across the plain of the Severnaya Dvina and Mezen' Rivers.

The low-lying plains of the Pechora, Mezen', and Severnaya Dvina Rivers were flooded by the sea while the land was still isostatically depressed following the last Ice Age, a process which has hidden the landforms created by glacial deposition.

Retreating glacier
Meltwater channels
Terminal moraine

***Terminal moraines** are crescent-shaped ridges of glacial deposits, widely found in central Russia. Detritus is carried by the glacier and deposited at its terminus (snout) as it melts, marking the limit of the ice advance.*

Ural Mountains *(Ural'skiye Gory)*

***Lake Onega** (Onezhskoye Ozero) is the remnant of a body of water which, 12,000 years ago, connected the White Sea (Beloye More) with the Gulf of Finland and the Baltic Sea.*

Two of Europe's biggest rivers, the Volga and Western Dvina, rise in the swampy uplands of the Valdai Hills (Valdayskaya Vozvyshennost').

Using the Land and Sea

The cold climate confines agriculture mainly to southern and western provinces, where dairy farming predominates and arable land is given over to fodder crops as well as flax, potatoes, oats, and rye. Areas beyond the northern margins of cultivation are used for forestry, hunting, herding, and fishing, with some vegetables grown in hothouses around urban areas.

Land use and agricultural distribution

cattle
fishing
reindeer
timber
fodder
major towns
pasture
cropland
forest
mountain region
wetland
tundra
barren
ice

The Urban/Rural Population Divide

urban 74% | rural 26%

0 10 20 30 40 50 60 70 80 90 100

Population Density	Total Land Area
26 people per sq mile	829,398 sq miles
10 people per sq km	(2,148,700 sq km)

***Many rapids** are found along the 175 mile (280 km) course of the Suna River.*

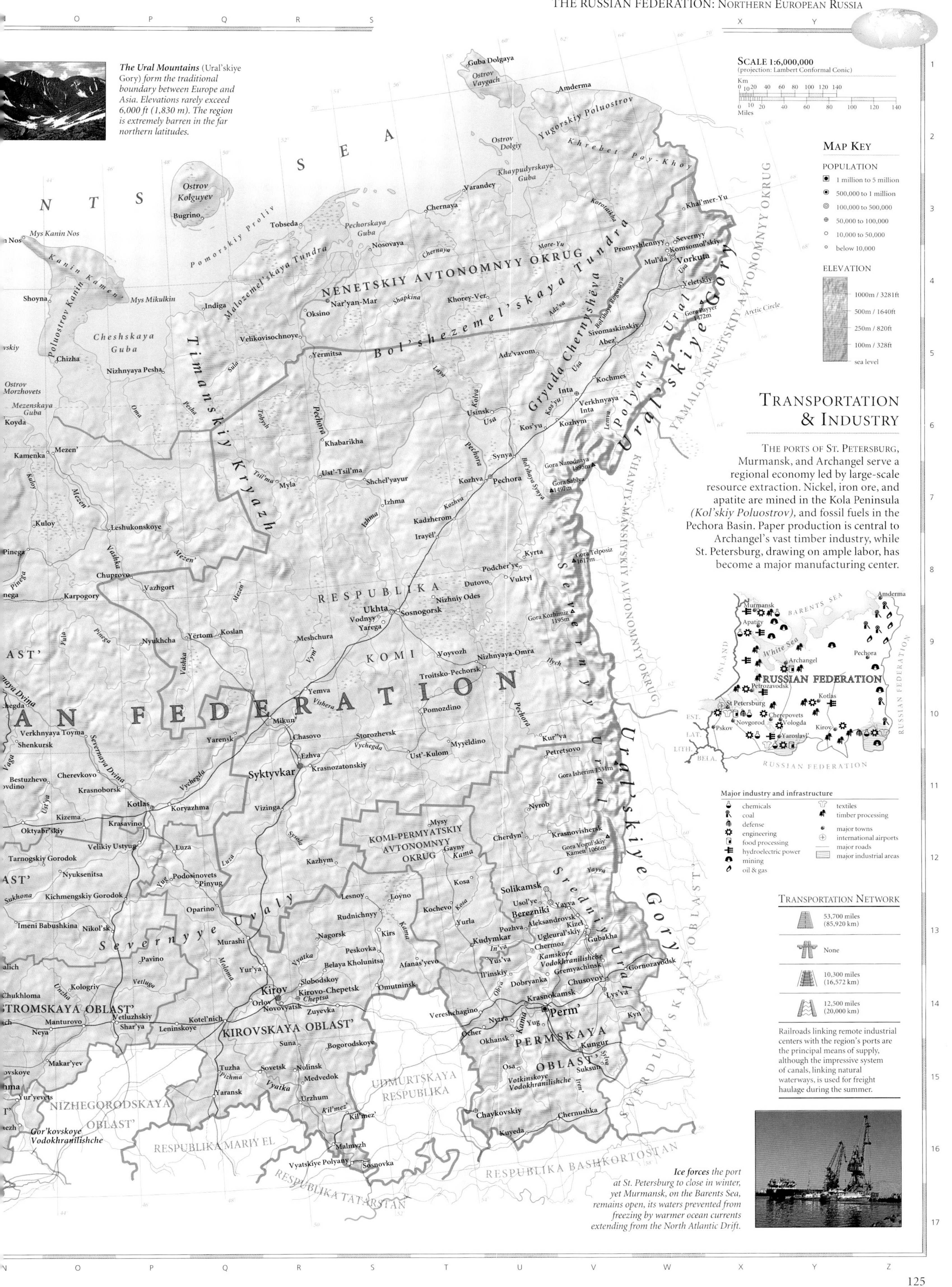
O P Q R S X Y
SCALE 1:6,000,000
(projection: Lambert Conformal Conic)
Km 0 10 20 40 60 80 100 120 140
Miles 0 10 20 40 60 80 100 120 140
MAP KEY
POPULATION
1 million to 5 million
500,000 to 1 million
100,000 to 500,000
50,000 to 100,000
10,000 to 50,000
below 10,000
ELEVATION
1000m / 3281ft
500m / 1640ft
250m / 820ft
100m / 328ft
sea level
BARENTS SEA
Ostrov Kolguyev
Bugrino
Mys Kanin Nos
Kanin Kamen'
Mys Mikulkin
Shoyna
Poluostrov Kanin
Cheshskaya Guba
Chizha
Nizhnyaya Pesha
Ostrov Morzhovets
Mezenskaya Guba
Koyda
Kamenka
Mezen'
Pomorskiy Proliv
Tobseda
Pechorskaya Guba
Nosovaya
Chernaya
Varandey
Khaypudyrskaya Guba
Guba Dolgaya
Ostrov Vaygach
Amderma
Ostrov Dolgiy
Yugorskiy Poluostrov
Khrebet Pay-Khoy
Khal'mer-Yu
Severnyy
Komsomol'skiy
Vorkuta
Promyshlennyy
Mul'da
Yeletskiy
Gora Payyer 1472m
Arctic Circle
Sivomaskinskiy
Abez'
NENETSKIY AVTONOMNYY OKRUG
Nar'yan-Mar
Oksino
Shapkina
Khorey-Ver
Malozemel'skaya Tundra
Bol'shezemel'skaya Tundra
Indiga
Velikovisochnoye
Yermitsa
Adz'vavom
Timanskiy Kryazh
Gryada Chernyshëva
Polyarnyy Ural
Ural'skiye Gory
YAMALO-NENETSKIY AVTONOMNYY OKRUG
KHANTY-MANSIYSKIY AVTONOMNYY OKRUG
Kochmes
Inta
Verkhnyaya Inta
Kozhym
Kos'yu
Usinsk
Usa
Khabarikha
Synya
Gora Narodnaya 1895m
Gora Sablya 1497m
Pechora
Kozhva
Ust'-Tsil'ma
Myla
Shchel'yayur
Izhma
Kadzherom
Irayel'
Kuloy
Leshukonskoye
Pinega
Chuprovo
Vazhgort
Karpogory
Kyrta
Gora Telposiz 1617m
Podcher'ye
Vuktyl
Dutovo
Nizhniy Odes
RESPUBLIKA KOMI
Ukhta
Sosnogorsk
Vodnyy
Yarega
Gora Kozhimiz 1195m
Severnyy Ural
Nyukhcha
Yertom
Koslan
Meshchura
Voyvozh
Nizhnyaya-Omra
Troitsko-Pechorsk
Ilych
RUSSIAN FEDERATION
Yemva
Vishera
Pomozdino
Mikun'
Yarensk
Chasovo
Storozhevsk
Vychegda
Ust'-Kulom
Myyeldino
Kur'ya
Petretsovo
Gora Isherim 1331m
Verkhnyaya Toyma
Shenkursk
Severnaya Dvina
Ezhva
Syktyvkar
Krasnozatonskiy
Bestuzhevo
Cherevkovo
Krasnoborsk
Kotlas
Koryazhma
Vizinga
Nyrob
Kizema
Krasavino
Oktyabr'skiy
Velikiy Ustyug
Luza
KOMI-PERMYATSKIY AVTONOMNYY OKRUG
Mysy
Gayny
Kama
Cherdyn'
Krasnovishersk
Gora Vogul'skiy Kamen' 1066m
Tarnogskiy Gorodok
Nyuksenitsa
Kazhym
Podosinovets
Pinyug
Yayva
Sukhona
Kichmengskiy Gorodok
Kosa
Solikamsk
Usol'ye
Berezniki
Lesnoy
Loyno
Oparino
Severnyye Uvaly
Rudnichnyy
Kochevo
Yurla
Pozhva
Aleksandrovsk
Kizel
Ugleural'skiy
Gubakha
Sredniy Ural
Imeni Babushkina
Nikol'sk
Murashi
Nagorsk
Kirs
Kudymkar
In'va
Chermoz
Peskovka
Yus'va
Kamskoye Vodokhranilishche
Gremyachinsk
Gornozavodsk
Pavino
Yur'ya
Belaya Kholunitsa
Afanas'yevo
Il'inskiy
Dobryanka
Chusovoy
Kologriv
Vetluga
Kirov
Slobodskoy
Kirovo-Chepetsk
Cheptsa
Omutninsk
Krasnokamsk
Lys'va
Chukhloma
Orlov
Novovyatsk
Zuyevka
Vereshchagino
Nytva
Perm'
Kyn
KOSTROMSKAYA OBLAST'
Vetluzhskiy
Shar'ya
Kotel'nich
Manturovo
Neya
Leninskoye
KIROVSKAYA OBLAST'
Ocher
Okhansk
Yug
PERMSKAYA OBLAST'
Kungur
Sylva
Suksun
Suna
Bogorodskoye
Makar'yev
Tuzha
Pizhma
Sovetsk
Nolinsk
Medvedok
Vyatka
UDMURTSKAYA RESPUBLIKA
Osa
Votkinskoye Vodokhranilishche
Iren'
SVERDLOVSKAYA OBLAST'
Yur'yevets
NIZHEGORODSKAYA OBLAST'
Yaransk
Urzhum
Kil'mez'
Chaykovskiy
Chernushka
Gor'kovskoye Vodokhranilishche
RESPUBLIKA MARIY EL
Malmyzh
Kuyeda
Vyatskiye Polyany
Sosnovka
RESPUBLIKA BASHKORTOSTAN
RESPUBLIKA TATARSTAN
Murmansk
Apatity
BARENTS SEA
Amderma
White Sea
Archangel
Pechora
FINLAND
RUSSIAN FEDERATION
Petrozavodsk
St Petersburg
Novgorod
Cherepovets
Vologda
Kotlas
Pskov
Yaroslavl'
Kirov
EST.
LAT.
LITH.
BELA.
Major industry and infrastructure
chemicals
coal
defense
engineering
food processing
hydroelectric power
mining
oil & gas
textiles
timber processing
major towns
international airports
major roads
major industrial areas
TRANSPORTATION NETWORK
53,700 miles (85,920 km)
None
10,300 miles (16,572 km)
12,500 miles (20,000 km)
N O P Q R S T U V W X Y Z

The Ural Mountains (Ural'skiye Gory) *form the traditional boundary between Europe and Asia. Elevations rarely exceed 6,000 ft (1,830 m). The region is extremely barren in the far northern latitudes.*

TRANSPORTATION & INDUSTRY

THE PORTS OF ST. PETERSBURG, Murmansk, and Archangel serve a regional economy led by large-scale resource extraction. Nickel, iron ore, and apatite are mined in the Kola Peninsula *(Kol'skiy Poluostrov)*, and fossil fuels in the Pechora Basin. Paper production is central to Archangel's vast timber industry, while St. Petersburg, drawing on ample labor, has become a major manufacturing center.

Railroads linking remote industrial centers with the region's ports are the principal means of supply, although the impressive system of canals, linking natural waterways, is used for freight haulage during the summer.

Ice forces *the port at St. Petersburg to close in winter, yet Murmansk, on the Barents Sea, remains open, its waters prevented from freezing by warmer ocean currents extending from the North Atlantic Drift.*

BALTIC SEA
LITHUANIA
POLAND
KALININGRADSKAYA OBLAST'
Kaliningrad
BELARUS
UKRAINE
RUSSIA
MOSKVA (MOSCOW)
Smolensk
Bryansk
Orel
Tula
Kursk
Voronezh
Belgorod
Rostov-na-Donu
Krasnodar
Sea of Azov
BLACK SEA
Sochi

Kaliningrad *has been a Russian enclave since 1945. The port is an important center for the Russian Federation's Baltic fishing fleet.*

St Basil's Cathedral, *completed in 1561, stands in Moscow's Red Square next to the Kremlin; the original fortified stronghold of the city.*

SOUTHERN EUROPEAN RUSSIA

THIS REGION, DIVIDED FROM ASIA by desert, seas, and mountains, has exerted a powerful influence both east and west since the 13th century. Over 70 years of Communist rule produced a highly urbanized, industrial society dominated by Moscow, which was the capital of the Soviet Union until 1991. Almost two-thirds of the Russian Federation's population live in this core area, with a relatively high *per capita* share of its wealth. However, the rapid growth of a market economy has caused great social upheaval, with rising crime and political instability.

THE LANDSCAPE

ANCIENT FOLDS in the deep sedimentary strata of the North European Plain have created a sequence of high and low regions. The Central Russian Upland *(Srednerusskaya Vozvyshennost')* in the west is deeply incised by rivers draining into the lowland of the Oka and Don Rivers. In the east the Volga, Europe's longest river flows south to the Caspian Sea, dividing the Volga Uplands *(Privolzhskaya Vozvyshennost')* from the foothills of the Ural Mountains *(Ural'skiye Gory)*. The Caucasus Mountains and the Black Sea form a natural border to the southwest.

A plantation of Scots pine helps consolidate the loose sandy soils of the Meshchera Lowland (Meshcherskaya Nizina), *which lies on the bed of an old glacial lake.*

The Smolensk-Moscow Upland *(Smolensko-Moskovskaya Vozvyshennost')* is a series of terminal moraine ridges marking the southern extent of the last glaciation.

Glacial till covers the bedrock to the north of the North European Plain, giving a gentle surface relief.

The lowland of the Oka and Don Rivers lies over a broad trough, between the upfolds of the Volga Uplands *(Privolzhskaya Vozvyshennost')* to the east, and the Central Russian Upland *(Srednerusskaya Vozvyshennost')* to the west.

The southern Ural Mountains *(Ural'skiye Gory)* consist of several parallel ranges of ancient fold mountains running from north to south.

Central Russian Upland *(Srednerusskaya Vozvyshennost').*

The floodplain of the Volga forms a long oasis of verdant vegetation, contrasting with the aridity of the surrounding Caspian hinterland.

The marshlands of the Volga Delta are visited by over 260 species of bird each year, migrating between South Africa and Arctic Siberia.

The Caspian Depression is a large downfold (or syncline) which became flooded, forming the Caspian Sea. The shoreline is 98 ft (30 m) below sea level.

The Caucasus Mountains *run from the Black Sea to the Caspian Sea. They include El'brus which, at 18,511 ft (5,642 m), is the highest point in Europe. It is still uplifting at a rate of 0.4 inches (10 mm/yr).*

Drifting sand occupies large areas of the south, forming dunes up to 50 ft (15 m) high.

Salt dome

Salt dome is forced up and through the rock strata
Sedimentary strata
Salts are forced upwards by denser overlying strata

Salt domes*, rounded hills up to 500 ft (150 m) high, are produced as less dense rock salts are displaced under the extreme pressure of denser, overlying strata and forced up toward the surface creating domes. They are widespread in the Caspian Depression.*

SCALE 1:6,000,000
(projection: Lambert Conformal Conic)

Km 0 10 20 40 60 80 100 120 140
Miles 0 10 20 40 60 80 100 120 140

MAP KEY

POPULATION
- above 5 million
- 1 million to 5 million
- 500,000 to 1 million
- 100,000 to 500,000
- 50,000 to 100,000
- 10,000 to 50,000
- below 10,000

ELEVATION
- 4000m / 13,124ft
- 3000m / 9843ft
- 2000m / 6562ft
- 1000m / 3281ft
- 500m / 1640ft
- 250m / 820ft
- 100m / 328ft
- sea level

USING THE LAND

IN THE COLD, HUMID NORTH and in the southern Urals *(Ural'skiye Gory)*, small grains, potatoes and flax are commonly rotated with legumes which support livestock farming. The rich chernozem (or black earth) areas support diverse crops such as sugar beet, hemp, sunflowers, millet and vegetables. Further south, aridity restricts husbandry to extensive grazing, with intensive fruit and rice cultivation along the oasis of the Volga.

THE URBAN/RURAL POPULATION DIVIDE

urban 65% rural 35%

0 10 20 30 40 50 60 70 80 90 100

POPULATION DENSITY	TOTAL LAND AREA
119 people per sq mile (46 people per sq km)	705,916 sq miles (1,828,800 sq km)

Land use and agricultural distribution
- sheep
- flax
- potatoes
- rice
- sunflowers
- sugar beet
- timber
- capital cities
- major towns
- pasture
- cropland
- forest
- wetland
- mountain region
- tundra

TRANSPORTATION & INDUSTRY

MANUFACTURING is largely based around Moscow and the Volga region, which became a major industrial area during the Second World War. Both Moscow and Nizhniy Novgorod are centers of skilled labor for light manufacturing and engineering. Most of Russia's main chemical plants are located along the Volga, and one of the world's largest car factories was recently opened in Tol'yatti. Processing and machine construction plants use oil, gas, and hydroelectric power from the Volga Basin and metallic minerals from the Urals *(Ural'skiye Gory)* and Kursk.

Industrial plants are massed along the Volga. Environmental stress from decades of unbridled industrial development has prompted widespread concern about pollution levels.

TRANSPORTATION NETWORK

250,000 miles (402,000 km)	None
28,000 miles (44,800 km)	16,300 miles (26,080 km)

Seventy private and national flag airlines have been created from the reorganization of the state airline Aeroflot, which maintained the world's largest fleet of aircraft during the Soviet era.

Major industry and infrastructure
- aerospace
- car manufacture
- chemicals
- defense
- electronics
- engineering
- gas
- mining
- oil
- textiles
- capital cities
- major towns
- international airports
- major roads
- major industrial areas

144
136
136

Asia

Asia, the world's largest continent, covers 16,838,365 sq miles (43,608,000 sq km). It comprises 48 separate countries, including 97% of Turkey and 72% of the Russian Federation. Almost 60% of the world's population lives in Asia.

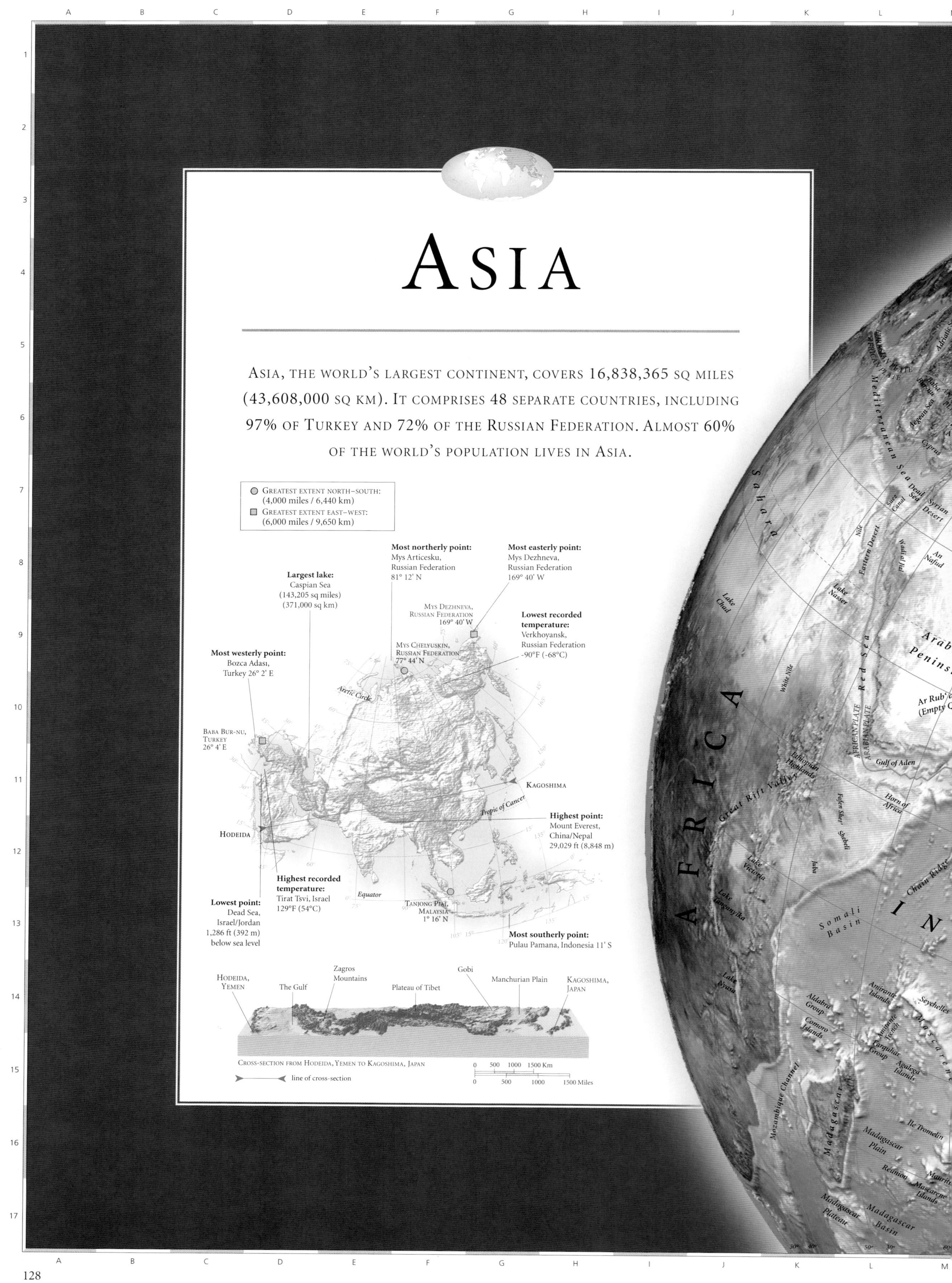

Greatest extent north–south: (4,000 miles / 6,440 km)
Greatest extent east–west: (6,000 miles / 9,650 km)
Most northerly point: Mys Articesku, Russian Federation 81° 12' N
Most easterly point: Mys Dezhneva, Russian Federation 169° 40' W
Largest lake: Caspian Sea (143,205 sq miles) (371,000 sq km)
Mys Dezhneva, Russian Federation 169° 40' W
Lowest recorded temperature: Verkhoyansk, Russian Federation -90°F (-68°C)
Mys Chelyuskin, Russian Federation 77° 44' N
Most westerly point: Bozca Adası, Turkey 26° 2' E
Arctic Circle
Baba Bur-nu, Turkey 26° 4' E
Kagoshima
Tropic of Cancer
Highest point: Mount Everest, China/Nepal 29,029 ft (8,848 m)
Hodeida
Highest recorded temperature: Tirat Tsvi, Israel 129°F (54°C)
Equator
Tanjong Piai, Malaysia 1° 16' N
Lowest point: Dead Sea, Israel/Jordan 1,286 ft (392 m) below sea level
Most southerly point: Pulau Pamana, Indonesia 11' S
Hodeida, Yemen
The Gulf
Zagros Mountains
Plateau of Tibet
Gobi
Manchurian Plain
Kagoshima, Japan
Cross-section from Hodeida, Yemen to Kagoshima, Japan
line of cross-section
0 500 1000 1500 Km
0 500 1000 1500 Miles
Africa
Sahara
Mediterranean Sea
Aegean Sea
Cyprus
Dead Sea
Suez Canal
Syrian Desert
Nile
Eastern Desert
An Nafud
Lake Nasser
Lake Chad
Red Sea
Arabian Peninsula
White Nile
Ar Rub' al Khali (Empty Quarter)
African Plate
Arabian Plate
Gulf of Aden
Ethiopian Highlands
Great Rift Valley
Horn of Africa
Shebeli
Lake Victoria
Lake Tanganyika
Somali Basin
Lake Nyasa
Aldabra Group
Comoro Islands
Amirante Islands
Seychelles
Farquhar Group
Agalega Islands
Mozambique Channel
Madagascar
Madagascar Plain
Madagascar Plateau
Madagascar Basin
Île Tromelin
Réunion
Mascarene Islands

ARCTIC OCEAN
A S I A
Siberia
Gobi
Himalayas
Plateau of Tibet
Bay of Bengal
South China Sea
Philippine Sea
PACIFIC OCEAN
East Indies
Greater Sunda Islands
AUSTRALIA

Physical Asia

The natural landscape of Asia can be divided into two distinct physical regions; one covers the north, while the other spans the south. Northern Asia consists of old mountain chains like the Ural Mountains, plateaus, including the vast Plateau of Tibet, shields, and basins. In contrast, the landscapes of the south are much younger, formed by tectonic activity beginning c. 65 million years ago, leading to an almost continuous mountain chain running from Europe, across much of Asia, and culminating in the mighty Himalayan mountains. North of the mountains lies a belt of deserts. In the far south, tectonic activity has formed narrow island arcs. To the west lies the Arabian Shield, once part of the African Plate. As it was rifted apart from Africa, the Arabian Plate collided with the Eurasian Plate, uplifting the Zagros Mountains.

Coastal Lowlands and Island Arcs

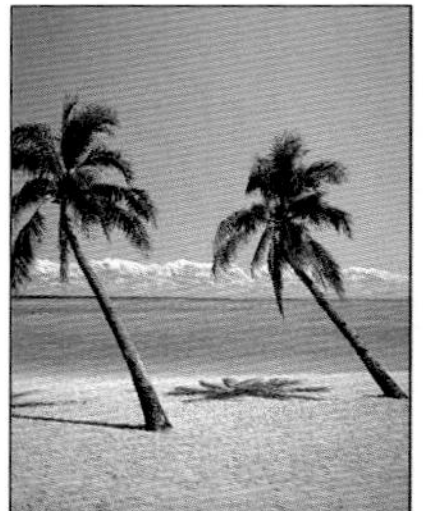

The coastal plains that fringe Southeast Asia contain many large delta systems, caused by high levels of rainfall and erosion of the Himalayas, the Plateau of Tibet, and relict loess deposits. To the south is an extensive island archipelago, lying on the drowned Sunda Shelf. Most of these islands are volcanic in origin, caused by the subduction of the Indo-Australian Plate beneath the Eurasian Plate.

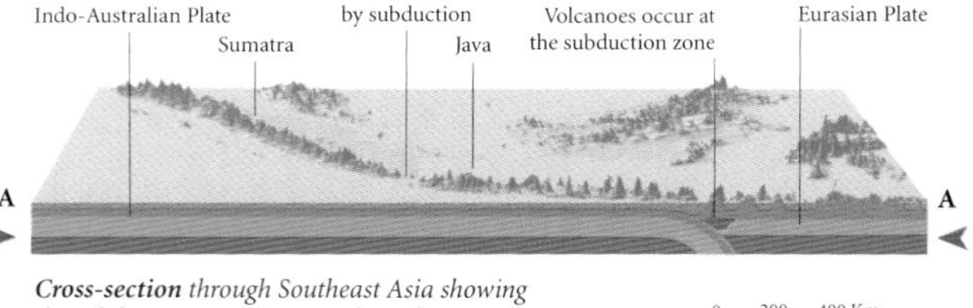
Indo-Australian Plate
Sumatra
Island arc caused by subduction
Java
Volcanoes occur at the subduction zone
Eurasian Plate
A
A

Cross-section through Southeast Asia showing the subduction zone between the Indo-Australian and Eurasian plates and the island arc.

0 200 400 Km
0 200 400 Miles

The Arabian Shield and Iranian Plateau

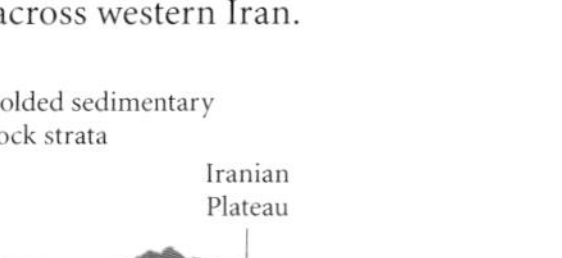

Approximately five million years ago, rifting of the continental crust split the Arabian Plate from the African Plate and flooded the Red Sea. As this rift spread, the Arabian Plate collided with the Eurasian Plate, transforming part of the Tethys seabed into the Zagros Mountains which run northwest-southeast across western Iran.

The confluence of the Tigris and Euphrates on the Mesopotamian Depression
Folded sedimentary rock strata
Zagros Mountains
Iranian Plateau
B
B

Cross-section through southwestern Asia, showing the Mesopotamian Depression, the folded Zagros Mountains and the Iranian Plateau.

0 50 100 Km
0 50 100 Miles

East Asian Plains and Uplands

Several, small, isolated shield areas, such as the Shandong Peninsula, are found in east Asia. Between these stable shield areas, large river systems like the Yangtze and the Yellow River have deposited thick layers of sediment, forming extensive alluvial plains. The largest of these is the Great Plain of China, the relief of which does not rise above 300 ft (100 m).

Map Key

Elevation

- 6000m / 19,686ft
- 4000m / 13,124ft
- 3000m / 9843ft
- 2000m / 6562ft
- 1000m / 3281ft
- 500m / 1640ft
- 250m / 820ft
- 100m / 328ft
- sea level

Plate margins (for explanation see page xiv)

- constructive
- destructive
- conservative
- uncertain
- physiographic regions
- line of cross-section

The Indian Shield and Himalayan System

The large shield area beneath the Indian subcontinent is between 2.5 and 3.5 billion years old. As the floor of the southern Indian Ocean spread, it pushed the Indian Shield north. This was eventually driven beneath the Plateau of Tibet. This process closed up the ancient Tethys Sea and uplifted the world's highest mountain chain, the Himalayas. Much of the uplifted rock strata was from the seabed of the Tethys Sea, partly accounting for the weakness of the rocks and the high levels of erosion found in the Himalayas.

Indo-Gangetic Depression
Crushed sediment from seabed of the Tethys Sea
Himalayas
Thrust zone
Plateau of Tibet
C
C

Cross-section through the Himalayas showing thrust faulting of the rock strata.

0 50 100 Km
0 50 100 Miles

Scale 1:63,000,000
(projection: Lambert Azimuthal Equal Area)

Km 0 250 500 1000 1500
Miles 0 250 500 1000 1500

Climate

The Gobi desert experiences major extremes in climate, with winter temperatures sometimes falling below -40°C (-40°F) and summer temperatures exceeding 45°C (113°F).

ASIA'S CLIMATE exhibits marked differences from region to region, with polar conditions in the north, hot and cold deserts in central regions and subtropical conditions in the south. Monsoon winds cause alternate wet and dry seasons across the south. These air masses moving north from the ocean are stripped of their moisture over the Himalayas causing arid conditions across the Plateau of Tibet. Both the south and east are susceptible to cyclones or typhoons.

Climate

- tundra
- subarctic
- cool continental
- warm humid
- mediterranean
- semiarid
- arid
- humid equatorial
- tropical
- daily hours of sunshine, January
- daily hours of sunshine, July
- cyclone
- typhoon
- cold/dry monsoon
- warm/wet monsoon
- cold wind

Temperature

Arctic Circle
60°N
40°N
Tropic of Cancer
20°N
Equator
20°S
Tropic of Capricorn
40°S

Average January temperature

Average July temperature

Temperature

- below -30°C (-22°F)
- -30 to -20°C (-22 to -4°F)
- -20 to -10°C (-4 to 14°F)
- -10 to 0°C (14 to 32°F)
- 0 to 10°C (32 to 50°F)
- 10 to 20°C (50°F)
- 20 to 30°C (68 to 86°F)
- above 30°C (86°F)

Tropical cyclones occur principally during late summer and early autumn. The intense winds and heavy rainfall can devastate entire villages.

Rainfall

Arctic Circle
60°N
40°N
Tropic of Cancer
20°N
Equator
20°S
Tropic of Capricorn
40°S

Average January rainfall

Average July rainfall

Rainfall

- 0–25 mm (0–1 in)
- 25–50 mm (1–2 in)
- 50–100 mm (2–4 in)
- 100–200 mm (4–8 in)
- 200–300 mm (8–12 in)
- 300–400 mm (12–16 in)
- 400–500 mm (16–20 in)
- more than 500 mm (20 in)

Through India, the southwest monsoon, which brings heavy rainfall from May to September, accounts for 80% of annual precipitation.

Shaping the Landscape

IN THE NORTH, melting of extensive permafrost leads to typical periglacial features such as thermokarst. In the arid areas wind action transports sand creating extensive dune systems. An active tectonic margin in the south causes continued uplift, and volcanic and seismic activity, but also high rates of weathering and erosion. Across the continent, huge rivers erode and transport vast quantities of sediment depositing it on the plains or forming large deltas.

River systems

1 Vast river systems flow across Asia, many originating in the Himalayas and the Plateau of Tibet. Seasonal melting of snow and monsoon rains swell the river flow leading to flooding and erosion. The Yellow River *(left)* gets its color from the high level of eroded material from the loess plateau.

Snow melt
Monsoon rains
Yellow River dissects loess plateau
Carries large sediment load

RIVER SYSTEMS: EROSION OF THE LOESS PLATEAU BY THE YELLOW RIVER

Sedimentation

4 The Ganges/Brahmaputra is a tide-dominated delta *(left)*. The two rivers transport huge quantities of mountain sediment, which is deposited on the delta plain. This debris is then redistributed by tidal currents, to form extensions to the bars, beach ridges, and deltaic deposits.

Distributary channels
Ganges/Brahmaputra River
Delta plain
Redistributed sediment
Sea level at high tide

SEDIMENTATION: THE DESTRUCTION OF A DELTA

The Evolving Landscape

Landscape

- limestone region
- sinking land
- stable land
- uplifting land
- active volcano
- area of tectonic activity
- limit of permafrost
- ocean current

Chemical weathering

2 Tower karsts are widespread across south China *(above)* and Vietnam. It is thought the karstic towers were formed under a soil cover, where small depressions in the limestone bedrock began to be weathered by soil water acids, eventually creating larger hollows. This process continued over millions of years, deepening the hollows and leaving steep-sided limestone hills.

Limestone hills
Old soil cover
Hollow being eroded by soil water acidity
Eroded hollow

CHEMICAL WEATHERING: FORMATION OF TOWER KARST

Volcanic activity

3 Volcanic eruptions occur frequently across Southeast Asia's island arcs *(below)*. Low-level eruptions occur when groundwater, superheated by underlying magma, becomes pressurized, forcing hot fluid and rocks up through cracks in the volcanic cone. This is known as a phreatic eruption.

Eruption within volcanic cone
Heat rising from the magma chamber
Fluid and rocks rising under pressure
Heated groundwater

VOLCANIC ACTIVITY: A PHREATIC ERUPTION

Political Asia

Asia is the world's largest continent, encompassing many different and discrete realms, from the desert Arab lands of the southwest to the subtropical archipelago of Indonesia; from the vast barren wastes of Siberia to the fertile river valleys of China and South Asia, seats of some of the world's most ancient civilizations. The collapse of the Soviet Union has fragmented the north of the continent into the Siberian portion of the Russian Federation, and the new republics of Central Asia. Strong religious traditions heavily influence the politics of South and Southwest Asia. Hindu and Muslim rivalries threaten to upset the political equilibrium in South Asia where India – in terms of population – remains the world's largest democracy. Communist China is the last great world empire; a population giant, but still relatively closed to the western world, while on its doorstep, the economically progressive and dynamic Pacific Rim countries, led by Japan, continue to assert their worldwide economic force.

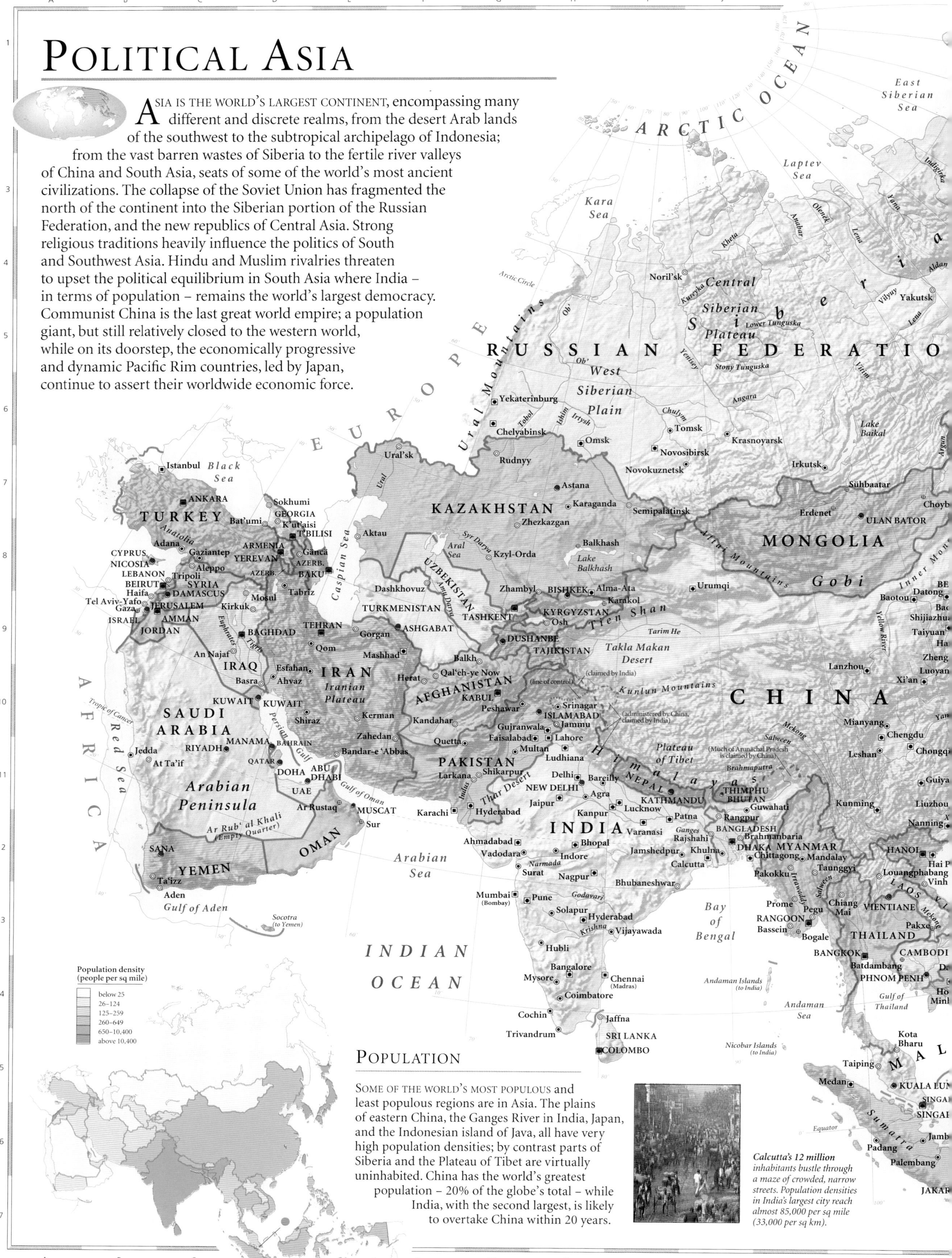

ARCTIC OCEAN
East Siberian Sea
Laptev Sea
Kara Sea
Arctic Circle
RUSSIAN FEDERATION
Central Siberian Plateau
West Siberian Plain
Siberia
EUROPE
Ural Mountains
Noril'sk
Yakutsk
Yekaterinburg
Chelyabinsk
Omsk
Tomsk
Novosibirsk
Krasnoyarsk
Novokuznetsk
Irkutsk
Lake Baikal
Ural'sk
Rudnyy
Astana
Karaganda
Semipalatinsk
KAZAKHSTAN
Zhezkazgan
Balkhash
Lake Balkhash
Aral Sea
Kzyl-Orda
Sühbaatar
Erdenet
ULAN BATOR
MONGOLIA
Altai Mountains
Gobi
Istanbul
Black Sea
ANKARA
TURKEY
Anatolia
Bat'umi
Sokhumi
GEORGIA
K'ut'aisi
T'BILISI
ARMENIA
YEREVAN
AZERB.
BAKU
Gänca
Aktau
Caspian Sea
CYPRUS
NICOSIA
Adana
Gaziantep
Aleppo
LEBANON
Tripoli
BEIRUT
SYRIA
Haifa
DAMASCUS
Tel Aviv-Yafo
JERUSALEM
Gaza
ISRAEL
AMMAN
JORDAN
Kirkuk
Mosul
Tabriz
BAGHDAD
IRAQ
An Najaf
Basra
KUWAIT
TEHRAN
Qom
Esfahan
Ahvaz
IRAN
Iranian Plateau
Kerman
Shiraz
Zahedan
Bandar-e 'Abbas
Gorgan
Mashhad
Dashkhovuz
TURKMENISTAN
ASHGABAT
UZBEKISTAN
TASHKENT
Zhambyl
BISHKEK
Alma-Ata
Karakol
KYRGYZSTAN
Osh
DUSHANBE
TAJIKISTAN
Tien Shan
Urumqi
Takla Makan Desert
Kunlun Mountains
Balkh
Herat
Qal'eh-ye Now
AFGHANISTAN
KABUL
Kandahar
Peshawar
Srinagar
ISLAMABAD
Jammu
Gujranwala
Faisalabad
Lahore
Quetta
Multan
Ludhiana
PAKISTAN
Larkana
Shikarpur
Thar Desert
Karachi
Hyderabad
Delhi
NEW DELHI
Bareilly
Agra
Jaipur
Kanpur
Lucknow
NEPAL
KATHMANDU
Himalaya
Plateau of Tibet
THIMPHU
BHUTAN
Guwahati
CHINA
Lanzhou
Xi'an
Mianyang
Chengdu
Leshan
Kunming
SAUDI ARABIA
RIYADH
Jedda
At Ta'if
MANAMA
BAHRAIN
QATAR
DOHA
ABU DHABI
UAE
MUSCAT
Sur
Ar Rustaq
OMAN
Arabian Peninsula
Ar Rub' al Khali (Empty Quarter)
SANA
YEMEN
Ta'izz
Aden
Gulf of Aden
Socotra (to Yemen)
Red Sea
AFRICA
Tropic of Cancer
Persian Gulf
Gulf of Oman
Arabian Sea
INDIAN OCEAN
INDIA
Ahmadabad
Vadodara
Surat
Bhopal
Indore
Nagpur
Varanasi
Patna
Jamshedpur
Calcutta
Bhubaneshwar
Mumbai (Bombay)
Pune
Solapur
Hyderabad
Vijayawada
Hubli
Bangalore
Mysore
Chennai (Madras)
Coimbatore
Cochin
Trivandrum
Jaffna
SRI LANKA
COLOMBO
Bay of Bengal
Andaman Islands (to India)
Nicobar Islands (to India)
Andaman Sea
BANGLADESH
DHAKA
Rajshahi
Khulna
Chittagong
MYANMAR
Mandalay
Taunggyi
Pakokku
Prome
Pegu
RANGOON
Bassein
Bogale
THAILAND
BANGKOK
Chiang Mai
VIENTIANE
LAOS
HANOI
Gulf of Thailand
PHNOM PENH
Kota Bharu
Taiping
Medan
KUALA LUMPUR
Sumatra
Padang
Palembang
Equator
Population density (people per sq mile)
below 25
26–124
125–259
260–649
650–10,400
above 10,400

Population

Some of the world's most populous and least populous regions are in Asia. The plains of eastern China, the Ganges River in India, Japan, and the Indonesian island of Java, all have very high population densities; by contrast parts of Siberia and the Plateau of Tibet are virtually uninhabited. China has the world's greatest population – 20% of the globe's total – while India, with the second largest, is likely to overtake China within 20 years.

Calcutta's 12 million *inhabitants bustle through a maze of crowded, narrow streets. Population densities in India's largest city reach almost 85,000 per sq mile (33,000 per sq km).*

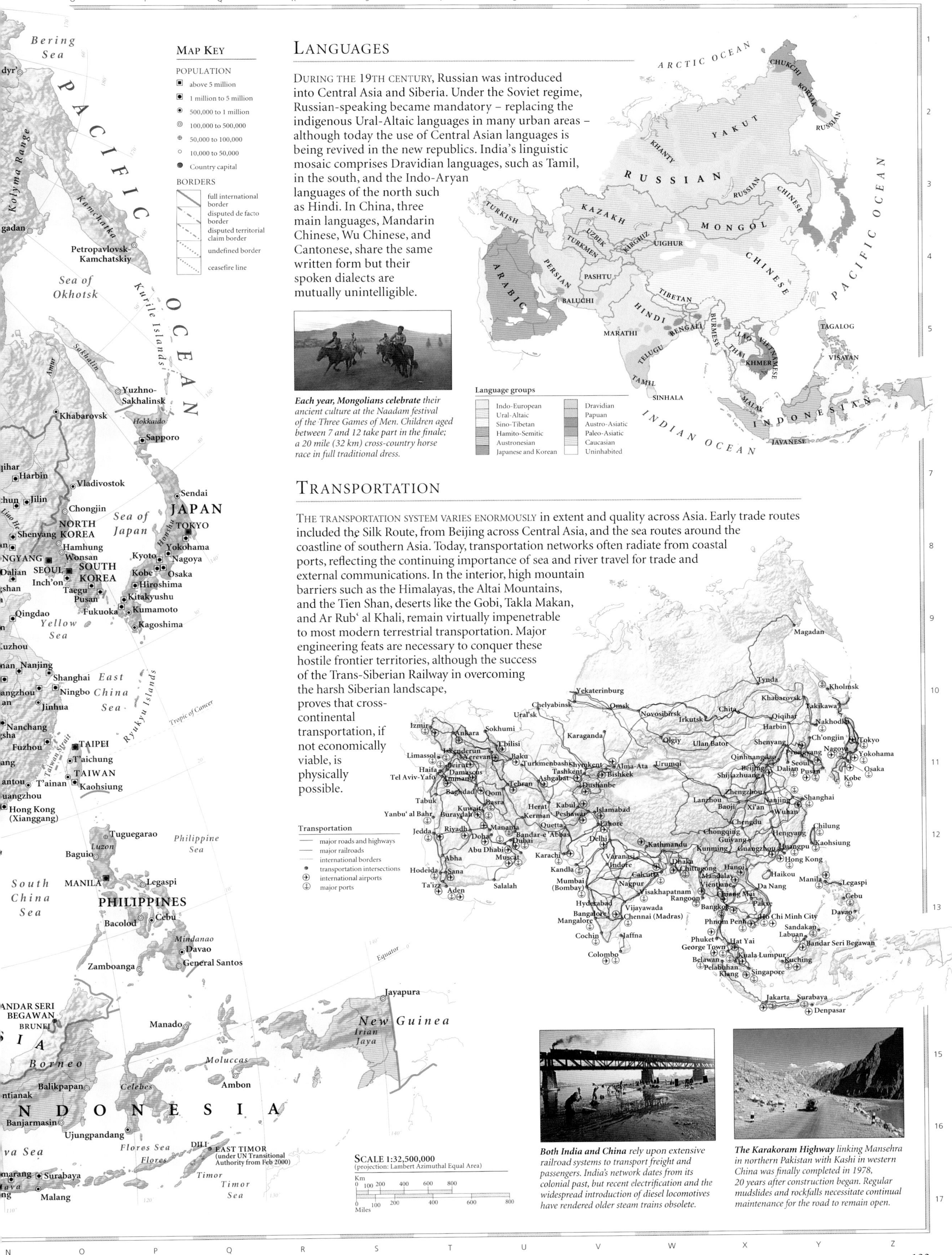
MAP KEY
POPULATION
above 5 million
1 million to 5 million
500,000 to 1 million
100,000 to 500,000
50,000 to 100,000
10,000 to 50,000
Country capital
BORDERS
full international border
disputed de facto border
disputed territorial claim border
undefined border
ceasefire line
Language groups
Indo-European
Ural-Altaic
Sino-Tibetan
Hamito-Semitic
Austronesian
Japanese and Korean
Dravidian
Papuan
Austro-Asiatic
Paleo-Asiatic
Caucasian
Uninhabited
Transportation
major roads and highways
major railroads
international borders
transportation intersections
international airports
major ports
SCALE 1:32,500,000
(projection: Lambert Azimuthal Equal Area)

LANGUAGES

DURING THE 19TH CENTURY, Russian was introduced into Central Asia and Siberia. Under the Soviet regime, Russian-speaking became mandatory – replacing the indigenous Ural-Altaic languages in many urban areas – although today the use of Central Asian languages is being revived in the new republics. India's linguistic mosaic comprises Dravidian languages, such as Tamil, in the south, and the Indo-Aryan languages of the north such as Hindi. In China, three main languages, Mandarin Chinese, Wu Chinese, and Cantonese, share the same written form but their spoken dialects are mutually unintelligible.

***Each year, Mongolians celebrate** their ancient culture at the Naadam festival of the Three Games of Men. Children aged between 7 and 12 take part in the finale; a 20 mile (32 km) cross-country horse race in full traditional dress.*

TRANSPORTATION

THE TRANSPORTATION SYSTEM VARIES ENORMOUSLY in extent and quality across Asia. Early trade routes included the Silk Route, from Beijing across Central Asia, and the sea routes around the coastline of southern Asia. Today, transportation networks often radiate from coastal ports, reflecting the continuing importance of sea and river travel for trade and external communications. In the interior, high mountain barriers such as the Himalayas, the Altai Mountains, and the Tien Shan, deserts like the Gobi, Takla Makan, and Ar Rub' al Khali, remain virtually impenetrable to most modern terrestrial transportation. Major engineering feats are necessary to conquer these hostile frontier territories, although the success of the Trans-Siberian Railway in overcoming the harsh Siberian landscape, proves that cross-continental transportation, if not economically viable, is physically possible.

***Both India and China** rely upon extensive railroad systems to transport freight and passengers. India's network dates from its colonial past, but recent electrification and the widespread introduction of diesel locomotives have rendered older steam trains obsolete.*

***The Karakoram Highway** linking Mansehra in northern Pakistan with Kashi in western China was finally completed in 1978, 20 years after construction began. Regular mudslides and rockfalls necessitate continual maintenance for the road to remain open.*

Asian Resources

Although agriculture remains the economic mainstay of most Asian countries, the number of people employed in agriculture has steadily declined, as new industries have been developed during the past 30 years. China, Indonesia, Malaysia, Thailand, and Turkey have all experienced far-reaching structural change in their economies, while the breakup of the Soviet Union has created a new economic challenge in the Central Asian republics. The countries of the Persian Gulf illustrate the rapid transformation from rural nomadism to modern, urban society which oil wealth has brought to parts of the continent. Asia's most economically dynamic countries, Japan, Singapore, South Korea, and Taiwan, fringe the Pacific Ocean and are known as the Pacific Rim. In contrast, other Southeast Asian countries like Laos and Cambodia remain both economically and industrially underdeveloped.

Standard of Living

Despite Japan's high standards of living, and Southwest Asia's oil-derived wealth, immense disparities exist across the continent. Afghanistan remains one of the world's most underdeveloped nations, as do the mountain states of Nepal and Bhutan. Further rapid population growth is exacerbating poverty and overcrowding in many parts of India and Bangladesh.

Standard of Living (UN Human Development Index)

- low
- high

Industry

Japanese industry leads the continent in both productivity and efficiency; electronics, hi-tech industries, car manufacture and shipbuilding are important. In recent years, the so-called economic "tigers" of the Pacific Rim such as Taiwan and South Korea are now challenging Japan's economic dominance. Heavy industries such as engineering, chemicals, and steel typify the industrial complexes along the corridor created by the Trans-Siberian Railway, the Fergana Valley in Central Asia, and also much of the huge industrial plain of east China. The discovery of oil in the Persian Gulf has brought immense wealth to countries that previously relied on subsistence agriculture on marginal desert land.

Industry

- aerospace
- brewing
- car/vehicle manufacture
- cement
- chemicals
- electronics
- engineering
- finance
- fish processing
- food processing
- hi-tech industry
- iron & steel
- pharmaceuticals
- printing & publishing
- shipbuilding
- sugar processing
- tea processing
- textiles
- timber processing
- tobacco processing
- coal
- oil
- gas
- industrial cities
- major industrial areas

GNP per capita (US$)

- 0–499
- 500–999
- 1000–4999
- 5000–9999
- 10000–19999
- 20000+

***On a small island** at the southern tip of the Malay Peninsula lies Singapore, one of the Pacific Rim's most vibrant economic centers. Multinational banking and finance form the core of the city's wealth.*

***Iron and steel**, engineering, and shipbuilding typify the heavy industry found in eastern China's industrial cities, especially the nation's leading manufacturing center, Shanghai.*

***Traditional industries** are still crucial to many rural economies across Asia. Here, on the Vietnamese coast, salt has been extracted from seawater by evaporation and is being loaded into a van to take to market.*

ENVIRONMENTAL ISSUES

THE TRANSFORMATION OF UZBEKISTAN by the former Soviet Union into the world's second largest producer of cotton led to the diversion of several major rivers for irrigation. Starved of this water, the Aral Sea diminished in volume by over 50% in 30 years, irreversibly altering the ecology of the area. Heavy industries in eastern China have polluted coastal waters, rivers, and urban air, while in Myanmar, Malaysia, and Indonesia, ancient hardwood rain forests are felled faster than they can regenerate.

Environmental Issues
- tropical forest
- forest destroyed
- desert
- desertification
- acid rain
- polluted rivers
- marine pollution
- heavy marine pollution
- radioactive contamination
- poor urban air quality

The long-term environmental impact of the Gulf War (1991) is still uncertain. As Iraqi troops left Kuwait, equipment was abandoned to rust and thousands of oil wells were set alight, pouring crude oil into the Persian Gulf.

MINERAL RESOURCES

AT LEAST 60% OF THE WORLD'S known oil and gas deposits are found in Asia; notably the vast oil fields of the Persian Gulf, and the less-exploited oil and gas fields of the Ob' Basin in west Siberia. Immense coal reserves in Siberia and China have been utilized to support large steel industries. Southeast Asia has some of the world's largest deposits of tin, found in a belt running down the Malay Peninsula to Indonesia.

***Although Siberia** remains a quintessentially frozen, inhospitable wasteland, vast untapped mineral reserves – especially the oil and gas of the West Siberian Plain – have lured industrial development to the area since the 1950s and 1960s.*

Mineral Resources
- oil field
- gas field
- coal field
- chromite
- copper
- gold
- iron
- lead
- nickel
- platinum
- tin
- wolfram

USING THE LAND AND SEA

VAST AREAS OF ASIA REMAIN UNCULTIVATED as a result of unsuitable climatic and soil conditions. In favorable areas such as river deltas, farming is intensive. Rice is the staple crop of most Asian countries, grown in paddy fields on waterlogged alluvial plains and terraced hillsides, and often irrigated for higher yields. Across the black earth region of the Eurasian steppe in southern Siberia and Kazakhstan, wheat farming is the dominant activity. Cash crops, like tea in Sri Lanka and dates in the Arabian Peninsula, are grown for export, and provide valuable income. The sovereignty of the rich fishing grounds in the South China Sea is disputed by China, Malaysia, Taiwan, the Philippines, and Vietnam, because of potential oil reserves.

***Date palms** have been cultivated in oases throughout the Arabian Peninsula since antiquity. In addition to the fruit, palms are used for timber, fuel, rope, and for making vinegar, syrup, and a liquor known as arrack.*

***Rice terraces** blanket the landscape across the small Indonesian island of Bali. The large amounts of water needed to grow rice have resulted in Balinese farmers organizing water-control cooperatives.*

Using the Land and Sea
- cropland
- desert
- forest
- mountain region
- pasture
- tundra
- wetland
- major conurbations
- cattle
- pigs
- goats
- sheep
- coconuts
- corn
- cotton
- dates
- fishing
- fruit
- jute
- peanuts
- rice
- rubber
- shellfish
- soybeans
- sugar beet
- sugar cane
- tea
- timber
- wheat

Turkey & the Caucasus

Armenia, Azerbaijan, Georgia, Turkey

This region occupies the fragmented junction between Europe, Asia, and the Russian Federation. Sunni Islam provides a common identity for the secular state of Turkey, which the revered leader Kemal Atatürk established from the remnants of the Ottoman Empire after the First World War. Turkey has a broad resource base and expanding trade links with Europe, but the east is relatively undeveloped and strife between the state and a large Kurdish minority has yet to be resolved. Georgia is similarly challenged by ethnic separatism, while the Christian state of Armenia and the mainly Muslim and oil-rich Azerbaijan are locked in conflict over the territory of Nagornyy Karabakh.

Using the Land and Sea

Turkey is largely self-sufficient in food. The irrigated Black Sea coastlands have the world's highest yields of hazelnuts. Tobacco, cotton, sultanas, tea, and figs are the region's main cash crops and a great range of fruit and vegetables are grown. Wine grapes are among the labor-intensive crops which allow full use of limited agricultural land in the Caucasus. Sturgeon fishing is particularly important in Azerbaijan.

RUSSIAN FEDERATION
BULGARIA
BLACK SEA
CASPIAN SEA
GREECE
Istanbul
GEORGIA
T'BILISI
ARMENIA
BAKU
AZERBAIJAN
YEREVAN
Samsun
ANKARA
TURKEY
Izmir
Konya
Diyarbakir
IRAN
Antalya
Adana
IRAQ
SYRIA
MEDITERRANEAN SEA

Land use and agricultural distribution

- cattle
- goats
- cotton
- fishing
- fruit
- hazelnuts
- olives
- sugar beet
- tobacco
- vineyards
- capital cities
- major towns
- pasture
- cropland
- forest

The Urban/Rural Population Divide

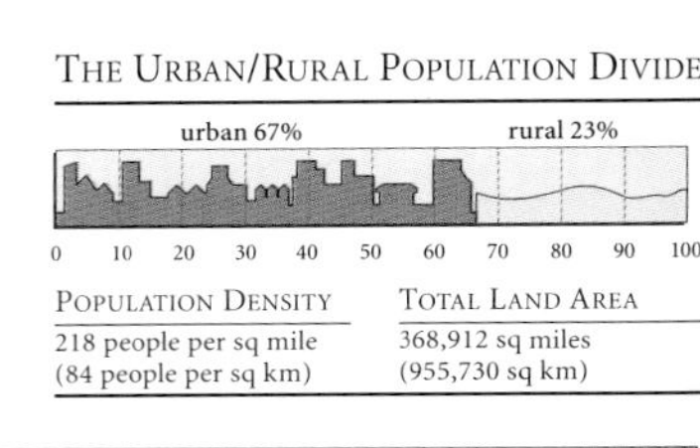

urban 67%
rural 23%
0
10
20
30
40
50
60
70
80
90
100

Population Density	Total Land Area
218 people per sq mile (84 people per sq km)	368,912 sq miles (955,730 sq km)

***For many centuries,** Istanbul has held tremendous strategic importance as a crucial gateway between Europe and Asia. Founded by the Greeks as Byzantium, the city became the center of the East Roman Empire and was known as Constantinople to the Romans. From the 15th century onward the city became the center of the great Ottoman Empire.*

Transportation & Industry

Turkey leads the region's well-diversified economy. Petrochemicals, textiles, engineering, and food processing are the main industries. Azerbaijan is able to export oil, while the other states rely heavily on hydro-electric power and imported fuel. Georgia produces precision machinery. War and earthquake damage have devastated Armenia's infrastructure.

***Azerbaijan** has substantial oil reserves, located in and around the Caspian Sea. They were some of the earliest oilfields in the world to be exploited.*

BULGARIA, BLACK SEA, RUSSIAN FEDERATION, CASPIAN SEA, GREECE, Istanbul, Izmit, Bursa, Samsun, K'ut'aisi, GEORGIA, T'BILISI, Bat'umi, ARMENIA, YEREVAN, BAKU, AZERBAIJAN, ANKARA, Sivas, Erzurum, Izmir, TURKEY, Kayseri, Konya, Diyarbakir, IRAN, Antalya, Gaziantep, Adana, Iskenderun, IRAQ, SYRIA, MEDITERRANEAN SEA

Major industry and infrastructure

- carpet weaving
- cement
- chemicals
- coal
- engineering
- food processing
- oil
- textiles
- tourism
- vehicle manufacture
- capital cities
- major towns
- international airports
- major roads
- major industrial areas

Transportation Network

- 76,289 miles (122,849 km)
- 7,74 miles (1,246 km)
- 9,047 miles (14,569 km)
- 745 miles (1,200 km)

Physical and political barriers have severely limited communications between Armenia, Georgia and Azerbaijan. Turkey has a relatively well-developed transportation network.

BULGARIA
GREECE
BLACK SEA
Aegean Sea
MEDITERRANEAN SEA
Edirne
Kırklareli
Tekirdağ
İstanbul
Marmara Denizi (Sea of Marmara)
Çanakkale
Bursa
İzmit
Adapazarı
Zonguldak
Bartın
Karabük
Kastamonu
Sinop
Samsun
Bolu
Çankırı
Çorum
Amasya
Tokat
Sivas
Eskişehir
ANKARA
Kırıkkale
Yozgat
Balıkesir
Kütahya
Manisa
İzmir
Uşak
Afyon
Kırşehir
Nevşehir
Kayseri
Aydın
Denizli
Isparta
Burdur
Konya
Aksaray
Niğde
Muğla
Antalya
Karaman
Mersin
Adana
Osmaniye
Kahramanmaraş
Gaziantep
Kilis
İskenderun
Antakya
Köroğlu Dağları
Anatolia
Toros Dağları
Tuz Gölü
114
120

THE LANDSCAPE

THE DEEPLY ERODED HILLS and salty basins of the Anatolian Plateau are bordered by several mountain ranges along the Black Sea coast, and the limestone Taurus Mountains *(Toros Dağları)* in the south. A lowland trough divides the Caucasus and the Lesser Caucasus, which form a formidable barrier of peaks in the north.

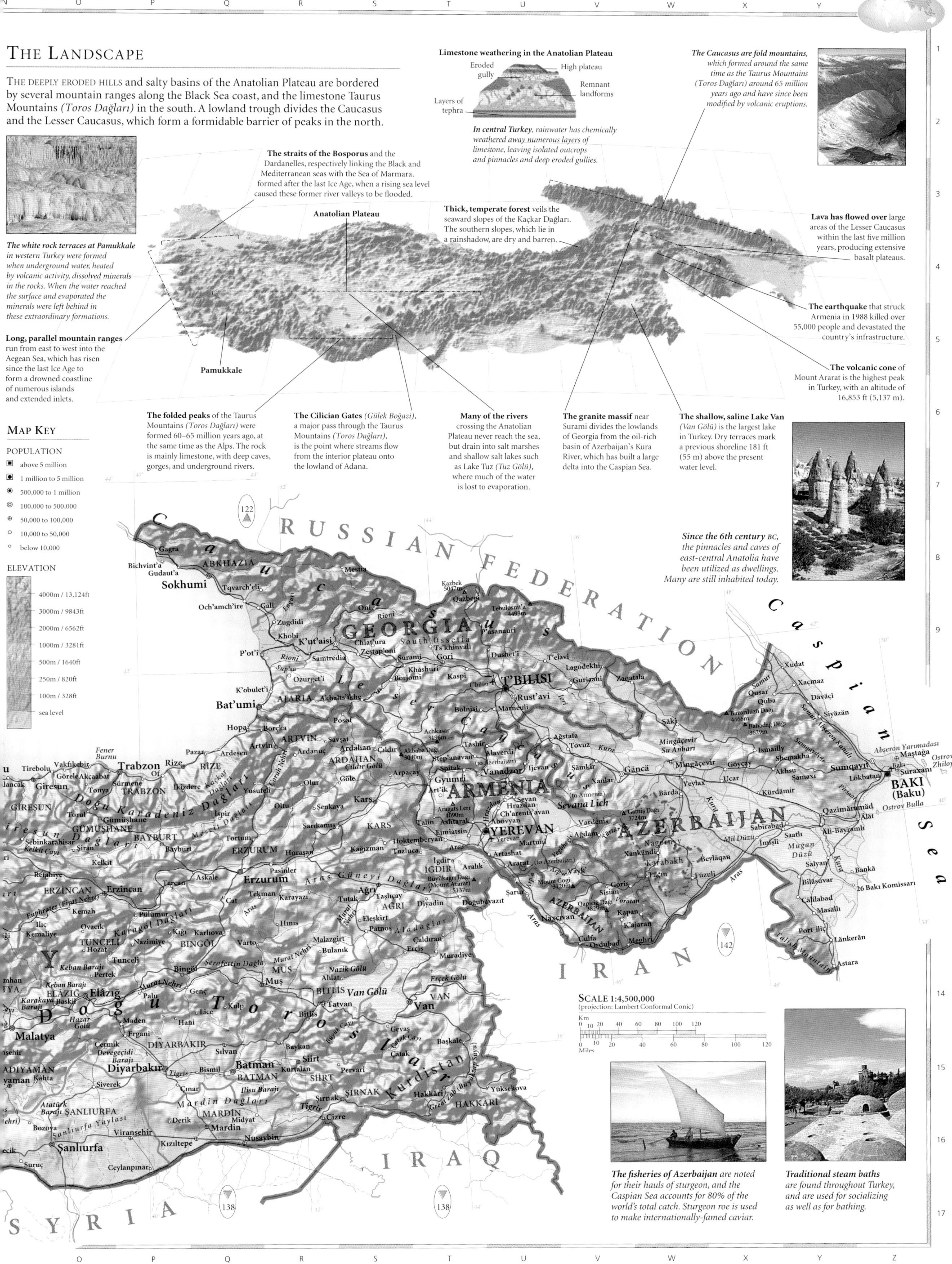

Limestone weathering in the Anatolian Plateau
Eroded gully
High plateau
Remnant landforms
Layers of tephra
Anatolian Plateau
Pamukkale
RUSSIAN FEDERATION
GEORGIA
ARMENIA
AZERBAIJAN
IRAN
IRAQ
SYRIA
Caspian Sea

The white rock terraces at Pamukkale in western Turkey were formed when underground water, heated by volcanic activity, dissolved minerals in the rocks. When the water reached the surface and evaporated the minerals were left behind in these extraordinary formations.

The straits of the Bosporus and the Dardanelles, respectively linking the Black and Mediterranean seas with the Sea of Marmara, formed after the last Ice Age, when a rising sea level caused these former river valleys to be flooded.

***In central Turkey**, rainwater has chemically weathered away numerous layers of limestone, leaving isolated outcrops and pinnacles and deep eroded gullies.*

***The Caucasus are fold mountains**, which formed around the same time as the Taurus Mountains (Toros Dağları) around 65 million years ago and have since been modified by volcanic eruptions.*

Thick, temperate forest veils the seaward slopes of the Kaçkar Dağları. The southern slopes, which lie in a rainshadow, are dry and barren.

Lava has flowed over large areas of the Lesser Caucasus within the last five million years, producing extensive basalt plateaus.

Long, parallel mountain ranges run from east to west into the Aegean Sea, which has risen since the last Ice Age to form a drowned coastline of numerous islands and extended inlets.

The earthquake that struck Armenia in 1988 killed over 55,000 people and devastated the country's infrastructure.

The volcanic cone of Mount Ararat is the highest peak in Turkey, with an altitude of 16,853 ft (5,137 m).

The folded peaks of the Taurus Mountains *(Toros Dağları)* were formed 60–65 million years ago, at the same time as the Alps. The rock is mainly limestone, with deep caves, gorges, and underground rivers.

The Cilician Gates *(Gülek Boğazi)*, a major pass through the Taurus Mountains *(Toros Dağları)*, is the point where streams flow from the interior plateau onto the lowland of Adana.

Many of the rivers crossing the Anatolian Plateau never reach the sea, but drain into salt marshes and shallow salt lakes such as Lake Tuz *(Tuz Gölü)*, where much of the water is lost to evaporation.

The granite massif near Surami divides the lowlands of Georgia from the oil-rich basin of Azerbaijan's Kura River, which has built a large delta into the Caspian Sea.

The shallow, saline Lake Van *(Van Gölü)* is the largest lake in Turkey. Dry terraces mark a previous shoreline 181 ft (55 m) above the present water level.

Since the 6th century BC, the pinnacles and caves of east-central Anatolia have been utilized as dwellings. Many are still inhabited today.

MAP KEY

POPULATION

- above 5 million
- 1 million to 5 million
- 500,000 to 1 million
- 100,000 to 500,000
- 50,000 to 100,000
- 10,000 to 50,000
- below 10,000

ELEVATION

- 4000m / 13,124ft
- 3000m / 9843ft
- 2000m / 6562ft
- 1000m / 3281ft
- 500m / 1640ft
- 250m / 820ft
- 100m / 328ft
- sea level

SCALE 1:4,500,000
(projection: Lambert Conformal Conic)

The fisheries of Azerbaijan are noted for their hauls of sturgeon, and the Caspian Sea accounts for 80% of the world's total catch. Sturgeon roe is used to make internationally-famed caviar.

Traditional steam baths are found throughout Turkey, and are used for socializing as well as for bathing.

TURKEY
SYRIA
LEBANON
ISRAEL
JORDAN
MEDITERRANEAN SEA
EGYPT
Syrian Desert
Halab (Aleppo)
Hamāh
Hims (Homs)
Al Lādhiqīyah (Latakia)
Tarṭūs
Tripoli
BEYROUTH (BEIRUT)
DIMASHQ (DAMASCUS)
Hefa (Haifa)
Tel Aviv-Yafo
JERUSALEM
'AMMĀN
Az Zarqā'
Irbid
Be'ér Sheva
Gaza Strip
Dead Sea
Lake Tiberias Sea of Galilee
Golan Heights
West Bank
Ma'ān
Al 'Aqabah
Elat
Gulf of Aqaba
Tudmur (Palmyra)
Ar Raqqa
Great Rift Valley
Wādī Mūsá (Petra)
Al Karak
At Tafīlah
136
120
140

The Near East

Iraq, Israel, Jordan, Lebanon, Syria

Some of the world's oldest civilizations developed in this region – the Fertile Crescent – which is venerated by Jews, Muslims, and Christians, but torn by competing religious, ethnic, and national claims to the land. Turkish Ottoman rule ended with World War I and the region was divided into areas administered by Britain and France. The UN endorsed calls for a Jewish homeland in what was then Palestine and in 1948 the state of Israel was declared. Hostility towards the Jewish state led to a series of wars but since 1977, and especially since 1993, a peace process between Israel and her neighbors has been evolving. Since independence, Syria has played a leading role in Middle Eastern politics. The once-prosperous state of Lebanon is emerging from a ruinous factional war, while Iraq's great oil wealth has funded military campaigns against Iran and Kuwait, and the stifling of internal dissent, leading to international ostracization.

Using the Land and Sea

Water scarcity limits cropland to the north and to areas watered principally by the Tigris, Euphrates, and Jordan Rivers. In Israel, new irrigation techniques are allowing cultivation in the arid Negev. Wheat is the chief grain and large areas of scrub support livestock herding. Commercial produce includes dates, tobacco, citrus fruits, olives, grapes, and cotton, which is Syria's main export crop. Fishing is still important in the Mediterranean.

The Urban/Rural Population Divide

urban 70% — rural 30%

Population Density	Total Land Area
163 people per sq mile (63 people per sq km)	325,460 sq miles (843,160 sq km)

Land use and agricultural distribution: sheep, cereals, citrus fruits, cotton, dates, fishing, rice, tobacco, capital cities, major towns, pasture, cropland, wetland, desert

Transportation & Industry

The petrochemical industry is well established, and central to the economies of Syria and Iraq, which was the world's second largest oil exporter before the war with Iran which began in 1980. Lebanon has traditionally been a center for commerce, while Israel has a well-diversified economy with an expanding tourist industry, despite few natural resources.

Transportation Network

- 75,427 miles (121,461 km)
- 1,468 miles (2,364 km)
- 3,271 miles (5,267 km)
- 498 miles (802 km)

Jordan's seaport of Al 'Aqabah is connected to Damascus in Syria by road and rail. This route to the Red Sea provides for large exports of phosphate and trade with states in The Persian Gulf.

Major industry and infrastructure: car manufacture, cement, chemicals, electronics, finance, food processing, iron & steel, oil, oil refining, textiles, capital cities, major towns, international airports, major roads, major industrial areas

The Dome of the Rock in Jerusalem is a magnificent mosque, revered by Muslims. Close by is the Wailing Wall, the city's most sacred Jewish landmark and the Church of the Holy Sepulchre, a famous Christian place of worship.

The city of Petra, carved from spectacular rose-colored limestone, lies deep within a canyon in southern Jordan. Revenues from the spice trade funded the construction of the city which was built by the Nabatean people in about 400 BC.

Water and wind erosion over thousands of years have created the Canyon of the Oasis at En 'Avedat in the Negev Desert (HaNegev). Extreme diurnal temperature fluctuations, coupled with wind erosion, have caused layers of rock to crack and peel away.

The Landscape

The Al Jazirah plateau divides the Euphrates and Tigris Rivers, which cross the Mesopotamian plain to reach their confluence in the southeast. The rocky Syrian Desert extends west to the northern extremity of the Great Rift Valley, which runs from the mountains of Lebanon to the Gulf of Aqaba. The River Jordan flows south along this trough into the Dead Sea, divided from the Mediterranean coastal plain by a steep-sided plateau.

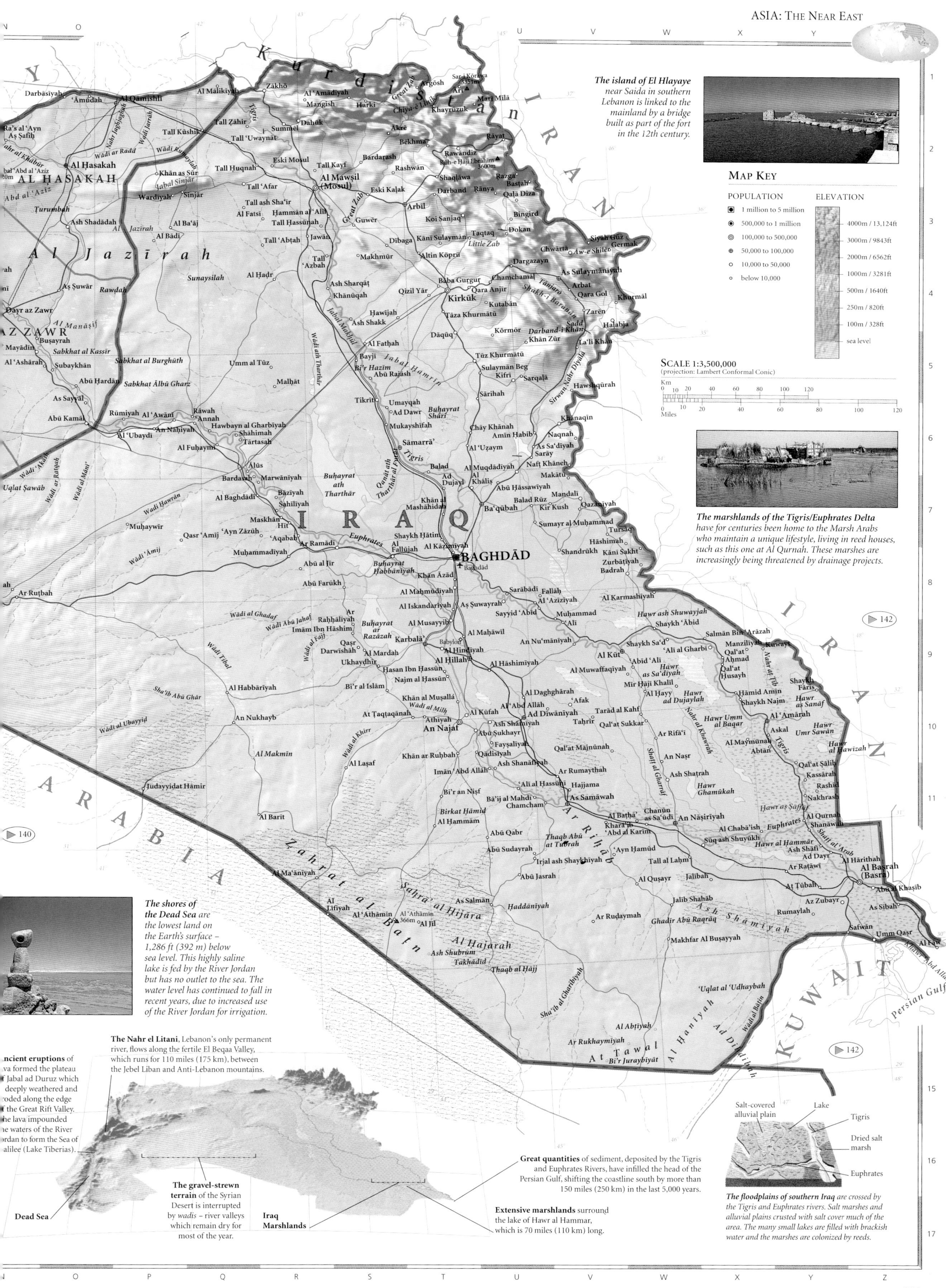
MAP KEY
POPULATION
1 million to 5 million
500,000 to 1 million
100,000 to 500,000
50,000 to 100,000
10,000 to 50,000
below 10,000
ELEVATION
4000m / 13,124ft
3000m / 9843ft
2000m / 6562ft
1000m / 3281ft
500m / 1640ft
250m / 820ft
100m / 328ft
sea level
SCALE 1:3,500,000
(projection: Lambert Conformal Conic)
IRAQ
BAGHDĀD
IRAN
KUWAIT
ARABIA
Kurdistan
Al Jazīrah
Al Mawṣil (Mosul)
Kirkūk
Arbīl
Al Başrah (Basra)
An Najaf
Karbalā'
Persian Gulf
Tigris
Euphrates
Salt-covered alluvial plain
Lake
Tigris
Dried salt marsh
Euphrates
Dead Sea
Iraq Marshlands

***The island of El Hlayaye** near Saida in southern Lebanon is linked to the mainland by a bridge built as part of the fort in the 12th century.*

***The marshlands of the Tigris/Euphrates Delta** have for centuries been home to the Marsh Arabs who maintain a unique lifestyle, living in reed houses, such as this one at Al Qurnah. These marshes are increasingly being threatened by drainage projects.*

***The shores of the Dead Sea** are the lowest land on the Earth's surface – 1,286 ft (392 m) below sea level. This highly saline lake is fed by the River Jordan but has no outlet to the sea. The water level has continued to fall in recent years, due to increased use of the River Jordan for irrigation.*

The Nahr el Litani, Lebanon's only permanent river, flows along the fertile El Beqaa Valley, which runs for 110 miles (175 km), between the Jebel Liban and Anti-Lebanon mountains.

…ncient eruptions of …va formed the plateau …f Jabal ad Duruz which …deeply weathered and …oded along the edge …f the Great Rift Valley. …he lava impounded …e waters of the River …rdan to form the Sea of …alilee (Lake Tiberias).

The gravel-strewn terrain of the Syrian Desert is interrupted by *wadis* – river valleys which remain dry for most of the year.

Great quantities of sediment, deposited by the Tigris and Euphrates Rivers, have infilled the head of the Persian Gulf, shifting the coastline south by more than 150 miles (250 km) in the last 5,000 years.

Extensive marshlands surround the lake of Hawr al Hammar, which is 70 miles (110 km) long.

***The floodplains of southern Iraq** are crossed by the Tigris and Euphrates rivers. Salt marshes and alluvial plains crusted with salt cover much of the area. The many small lakes are filled with brackish water and the marshes are colonized by reeds.*

▶ 142
▶ 140

The Arabian Peninsula

Bahrain, Kuwait, Oman, Qatar, Saudi Arabia, United Arab Emirates (UAE), Yemen

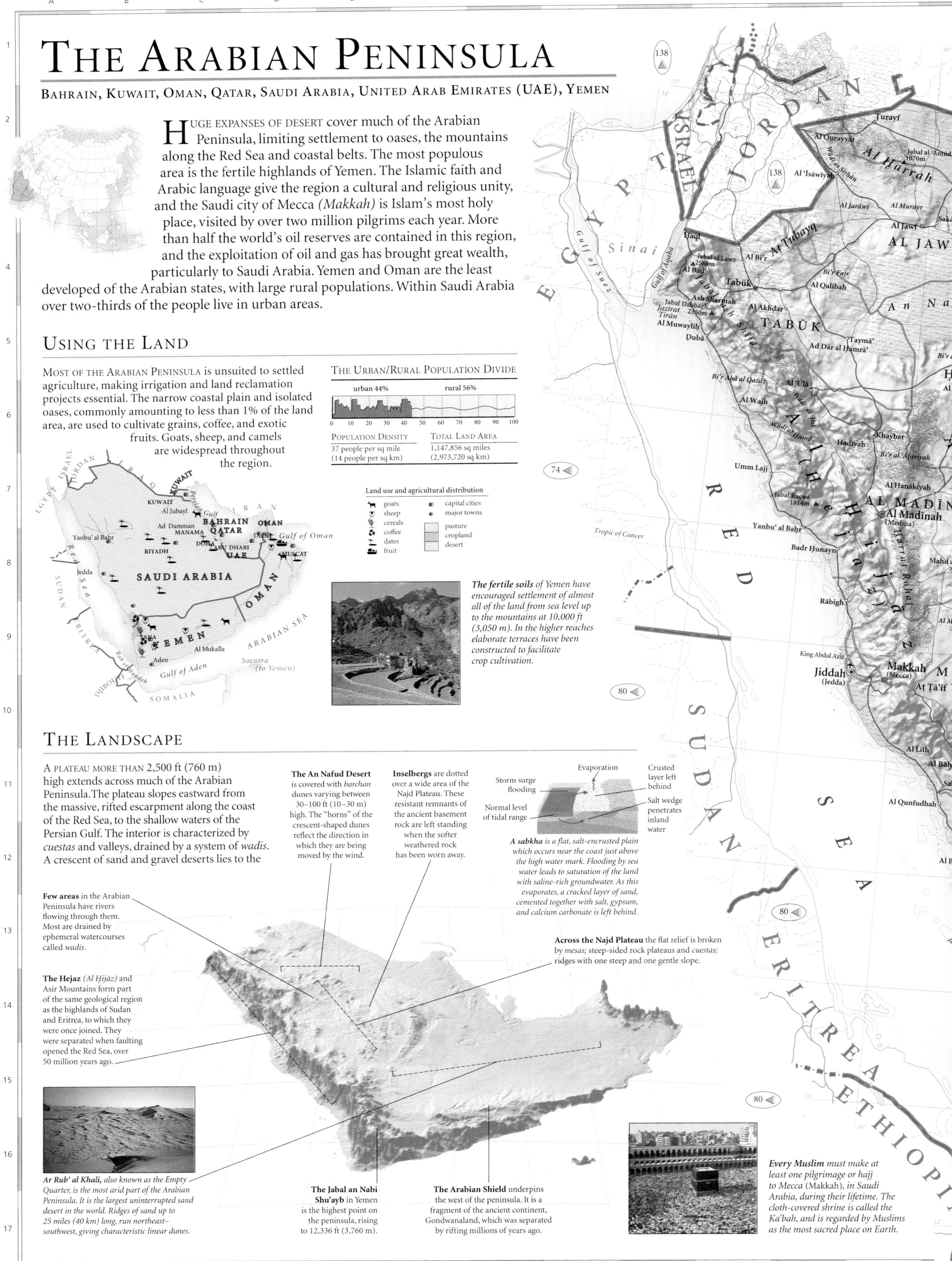

A B C D E F G H I J K L M
1 2 3 4 5 6 7 8 9 10 11 12 13 14 15 16 17
138
138
74
80
80
80
EGYPT
ISRAEL
JORDAN
Sinai
Gulf of Suez
Gulf of Aqaba
Haql
Jabal al Lawz 2580m
Al Bad'
Al Bi'r
At Tubayq
Tabūk
Al Qalibah
Bi'r Fajr
Jabal Dabbagh 2350m
Jazīrat Tīrān
Ash Sharmah
Al Muwaylih
Dubā
Al Akhdar
TABŪK
Taymā'
Ad Dār al Hamrā'
Turayf
Al Qurayyat
Wadi as Sirhan
Jabal al 'Amud 1070m
Al Harrah
Al 'Isāwīyah
Al Jarāwī
Al Murayr
Al Jawf
Sakak
AL JAWF
An Na
Bi'r Abā al Qazaz
Al 'Ulā
Al Wajh
Al Hejaz
Wādī al Hamd
Hadiyah
Khaybar
Bi'r al 'Afariyah
Umm Lajj
Al Hanākīyah
Jabal Radwa 1814m
AL MADĪNAH
Al Madinah (Medina)
Yanbu' al Bahr
Badr Hunayn
Harrat Rahat
Mahd adh
Rābigh
Tropic of Cancer
RED SEA
King Abdul Aziz
Jiddah (Jedda)
Makkah (Mecca)
At Tā'if
Al Lith
Al Bāha
Al Qunfudhah
SUDAN
ERITREA
ETHIOPIA

Huge expanses of desert cover much of the Arabian Peninsula, limiting settlement to oases, the mountains along the Red Sea and coastal belts. The most populous area is the fertile highlands of Yemen. The Islamic faith and Arabic language give the region a cultural and religious unity, and the Saudi city of Mecca *(Makkah)* is Islam's most holy place, visited by over two million pilgrims each year. More than half the world's oil reserves are contained in this region, and the exploitation of oil and gas has brought great wealth, particularly to Saudi Arabia. Yemen and Oman are the least developed of the Arabian states, with large rural populations. Within Saudi Arabia over two-thirds of the people live in urban areas.

Using the Land

Most of the Arabian Peninsula is unsuited to settled agriculture, making irrigation and land reclamation projects essential. The narrow coastal plain and isolated oases, commonly amounting to less than 1% of the land area, are used to cultivate grains, coffee, and exotic fruits. Goats, sheep, and camels are widespread throughout the region.

The Urban/Rural Population Divide

urban 44%
rural 56%
0 10 20 30 40 50 60 70 80 90 100

Population Density	Total Land Area
37 people per sq mile (14 people per sq km)	1,147,856 sq miles (2,973,720 sq km)

Land use and agricultural distribution
goats
sheep
cereals
coffee
dates
fruit
capital cities
major towns
pasture
cropland
desert
KUWAIT
Al Jubayl
Ad Damman
MANAMA
BAHRAIN
QATAR
DOHA
ABU DHABI
UAE
Dubai
MUSCAT
OMAN
RIYADH
SAUDI ARABIA
Yanbu' al Bahr
Jedda
Red Sea
YEMEN
Aden
Al Mukalla
Gulf of Aden
Socotra (to Yemen)
ARABIAN SEA
Gulf of Oman
Persian Gulf
IRAN
IRAQ
JORDAN
ISRAEL
EGYPT
SUDAN
ERITREA
DJIBOUTI
SOMALIA
Bab el Mandeb

The fertile soils of Yemen have encouraged settlement of almost all of the land from sea level up to the mountains at 10,000 ft (3,050 m). In the higher reaches elaborate terraces have been constructed to facilitate crop cultivation.

The Landscape

A plateau more than 2,500 ft (760 m) high extends across much of the Arabian Peninsula. The plateau slopes eastward from the massive, rifted escarpment along the coast of the Red Sea, to the shallow waters of the Persian Gulf. The interior is characterized by *cuestas* and valleys, drained by a system of *wadis*. A crescent of sand and gravel deserts lies to the

The An Nafud Desert is covered with *barchan* dunes varying between 30–100 ft (10–30 m) high. The "horns" of the crescent-shaped dunes reflect the direction in which they are being moved by the wind.

Inselbergs are dotted over a wide area of the Najd Plateau. These resistant remnants of the ancient basement rock are left standing when the softer weathered rock has been worn away.

Evaporation
Storm surge flooding
Normal level of tidal range
Crusted layer left behind
Salt wedge penetrates inland water

A sabkha is a flat, salt-encrusted plain which occurs near the coast just above the high water mark. Flooding by sea water leads to saturation of the land with saline-rich groundwater. As this evaporates, a cracked layer of sand, cemented together with salt, gypsum, and calcium carbonate is left behind.

Few areas in the Arabian Peninsula have rivers flowing through them. Most are drained by ephemeral watercourses called *wadis*.

Across the Najd Plateau the flat relief is broken by *mesas*; steep-sided rock plateaus and *cuestas*; ridges with one steep and one gentle slope.

The Hejaz *(Al Ḩijāz)* and Asir Mountains form part of the same geological region as the highlands of Sudan and Eritrea, to which they were once joined. They were separated when faulting opened the Red Sea, over 50 million years ago.

Ar Rub' al Khali, *also known as the Empty Quarter, is the most arid part of the Arabian Peninsula. It is the largest uninterrupted sand desert in the world. Ridges of sand up to 25 miles (40 km) long, run northeast–southwest, giving characteristic linear dunes.*

The Jabal an Nabi Shu'ayb in Yemen is the highest point on the peninsula, rising to 12,336 ft (3,760 m).

The Arabian Shield underpins the west of the peninsula. It is a fragment of the ancient continent, Gondwanaland, which was separated by rifting millions of years ago.

Every Muslim *must make at least one pilgrimage or hajj to Mecca (Makkah), in Saudi Arabia, during their lifetime. The cloth-covered shrine is called the Ka'bah, and is regarded by Muslims as the most sacred place on Earth.*

TRANSPORTATION & INDUSTRY

THE EXTRACTION AND REFINING OF OIL AND GAS are the major industrial activities in the Arabian Peninsula. The region also has an active construction sector, with many Arab cities reflecting the wealth generated by the oil industry. The service sector is dominated by financial and technical institutions, which, like the construction sector, mainly serve the oil industry. Traditional handicrafts such as carpet-weaving are found in rural areas.

***Saudi Arabia** contains the world's largest oil reserves, lying mainly along the Persian Gulf coast. Each day the region produces 8.3 million barrels of oil. Here, in the desert, excess oil is being burnt off.*

TRANSPORTATION NETWORK

65,239 miles (105,054 km)	2,071 miles (3,333 km)
864 miles (1,392 km)	none

Internal surface transportation is poorly developed across the peninsula. Along the coast, commercial routes have developed, but connections between bordering states rely on major airports.

Major industry and infrastructure

- cement
- chemicals
- iron & steel
- oil
- oil refining
- food processing
- capital cities
- major towns
- international airports
- major roads
- major industrial areas

***Seasonal watercourses** or wadis drain much of the interior of the Arabian Peninsula. Although they remain dry for much of the year, they are prone to flash floods after heavy rains.*

MAP KEY

POPULATION

- 1 million to 5 million
- 500,000 to 1 million
- 100,000 to 500,000
- 50,000 to 100,000
- 10,000 to 50,000
- below 10,000

ELEVATION

- 3000m / 9843ft
- 2000m / 6562ft
- 1000m / 3281ft
- 500m / 1640ft
- 250m / 820ft
- 100m / 328ft
- sea level

SCALE 1:8,250,000
(projection: Lambert Conformal Conic)

Iran & the Gulf States

Bahrain, Iran, Kuwait, Qatar, United Arab Emirates (UAE)

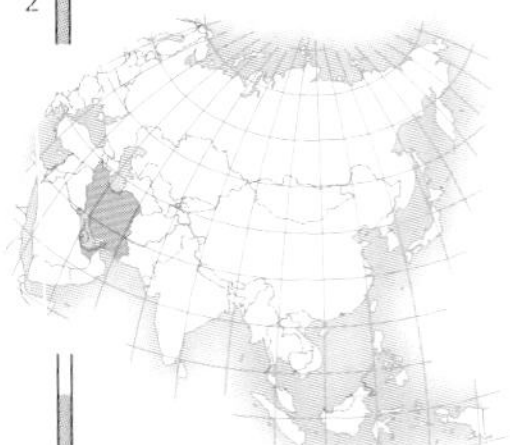

The discovery of oil in the Persian Gulf in the 1930s brought great wealth to the surrounding states. The revenue was largely used to modernize industry and infrastructure, initiating great social change in these formerly agrarian countries. Today, over 80% of the people in the Gulf states live in urban areas, and foreign nationals make up a sizeable proportion of the population in Kuwait, Qatar ,and the United Arab Emirates. The importance of control of the oil reserves has led to a number of territorial disputes, including most recently the Iran–Iraq War and the Gulf War. Islam is practiced almost exclusively throughout the region and two distinct strands are found; Sunni Muslims in Qatar, Kuwait, and UAE, and Shi'a Muslims in Iran and Bahrain. In 1979 Iran became the world's largest theocracy.

The Landscape

The land rises steeply from the fragmented coastal lowlands bordering the Persian Gulf, to reach Iran's interior plateau, bounded by heavily-eroded mountain chains. An unstable plate boundary runs northwest to southeast across Iran causing frequent earthquakes. On the sandy west coast of the Persian Gulf, the relief is generally flat, with patches of salt marsh. Bahrain consists of two groups of islands, which are mostly small and rocky.

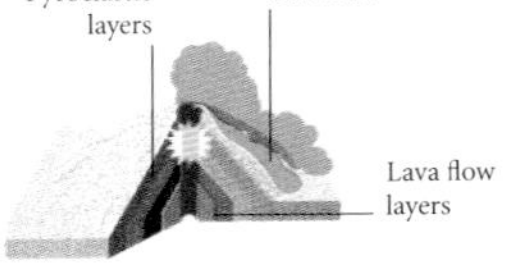

Pyroclastic layers
Lava flow
Lava flow layers

Qolleh-ye Damavand in the Elburz Mountains is a composite volcano. It comprises layers of lava and pyroclasts fragmentary rocks which accumulate on the slopes of the volcano after being ejected into the air.

***Marine sediments** from deep beneath the ancient Tethys Sea have been uplifted to form the Elburz Mountains, which stretch along the shores of the Caspian Sea, northern Iran.*

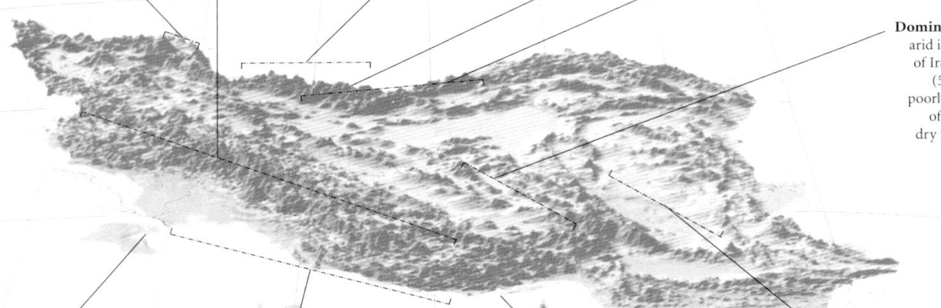

Lava and ash from previous volcanic activity covers a 200-mile (320-km) stretch from the border with Azerbaijan to the Caspian Sea.

Iran's two mountain chains, the Zagros and Elburz, were uplifted at the same time as the Alps in Europe, when the African Plate collided with the Eurasian Plate.

Caspian Sea

Qolleh-ye Damavand

Dominated by a vast, semi-arid interior plateau, most of Iran lies above 1,640 ft (500 m). The region is poorly drained with many of its basins remaining dry for months at a time.

The fierce Shamal wind affects much of this region. Every summer it blows dust south from the flood plains of the Tigris and Euphrates, reducing visibility to such an extent that Kuwait International Airport is frequently forced to close.

Prolific springs tapping artesian water make cultivation possible across the north of Bahrain's main island. This provides a sharp contrast to the sandy plains in the south and west.

The oilfields of The Gulf are formed from marine shale deposits lying in sedimentary basins at the margins of the Zagros Mountains.

Numerous islands lie along the southern coast of the Persian Gulf. Some of these are salt domes, created when less dense salts were displaced and forced up to the surface by denser, overlying strata.

Autumn winds blowing across The Gulf can reach speeds of up to 95 mph (150 kmph) causing severe storms, squalls, and waterspouts.

The Dasht-e Lut

***The Dasht-e Lut** covers a large portion of eastern Iran with its dry, wind-eroded plain of scattered sandstone pillars and salty depressions. During the summer, temperatures soar, making it one of the world's hottest, driest places.*

Using the Land and Sea

Along the coast of the Caspian Sea, desalinated water allows fruits and vegetables to be produced, although water shortages and desert soils still limit farming. Sheep are the most important livestock raised in Iran and commercial forests cover the northwest of the country. Shrimp stocks were decimated by pollution during the Gulf War, but fishing remains important for domestic and export markets.

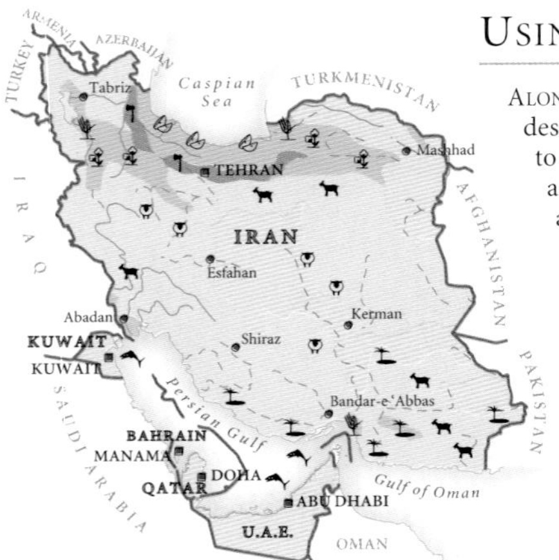

All of the Gulf states have commercial fishing fleets. Before the discovery of oil, fishing was the region's leading industry.

Land use and agricultural distribution

goats, sheep, cereals, citrus fruits, cotton, dates, fishing, timber, capital cities, major towns, pasture, cropland, forest, desert, wetland

The Urban/Rural Population Divide

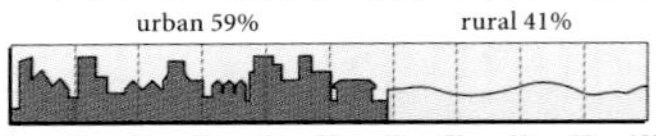

urban 59% | rural 41%

Population Density	Total Land Area
118 people per sq mile (46 people per sq km)	642,883 sq miles (1,665,500 sq km)

***The Kuwait Towers** in the centre of Kuwait are symbols of the vast wealth oil has brought to the country. Before 1960, the city had only one main street and was surrounded by a mud wall.*

136 138 140

N O P Q R S T U V W X Y
Many volcanoes lie in Iran's 1,200 mile (1930 km) volcanic belt, including the country's highest peak, the now-extinct Qolleh-ye Damavand at 18,600 ft (5,671 m).
146
Extensive oil and gas exploitation in the Gulf region has allowed the economic transformation of the Gulf states. Kuwait and the United Arab Emirates today have the highest per capita incomes in the world.
TRANSPORTATION & INDUSTRY
BOTH ONSHORE AND OFFSHORE oil reserves are exploited throughout the region. Kuwait not only extracts but also refines 80% of its oil. Bahrain has diversified its economy to become the main commercial and financial center in the Persian Gulf. Iran produces a wide range of products: textile mills are widespread and carpet weaving is an important export industry.
Caspian Sea
TURKMENISTAN
IRAN
IRAQ
KUWAIT
SAUDI ARABIA
BAHRAIN
QATAR
U.A.E.
OMAN
AFGHANISTAN
PAKISTAN
Persian Gulf
Gulf of Oman
Tabriz
Rasht
Gorgan
Mashhad
TEHRAN
Qom
Bakhtaran
Esfahan
Birjand
Ahvaz
Abadan
Kerman
Shiraz
Zahedan
Bandar-e Bushehr
Bandar-e 'Abbas
MANAMA
DOHA
Dubai
ABU DHABI
Major industry and infrastructure
carpet manufacture
chemicals
finance
food processing
oil
oil refining
textiles
capital city
major towns
international airports
major roads
major industrial areas
TRANSPORTATION NETWORK
50,340 miles (81,063 km)
466 miles (750 km)
3723 miles (5995 km)
81 miles (130 km)
Major towns and neighboring countries are linked by adequate road networks, although rural areas are less well served. Bahrain is linked to the mainland by a 15 mile (25 km) long causeway.
MAP KEY
POPULATION
above 5 million
1 million to 5 million
500,000 to 1 million
100,000 to 500,000
50,000 to 100,000
10,000 to 50,000
below 10,000
ELEVATION
4000m / 13,124ft
3000m / 9843ft
2000m / 6562ft
1000m / 3281ft
500m / 1640ft
250m / 820ft
100m / 328ft
sea level
SCALE 1:6,000,000
(projection: Lambert Conformal Conic)
Km
Miles
148
TURKMENISTAN
Caspian Sea
IRAN
AFGHANISTAN
PAKISTAN
OMAN
QATAR
UNITED ARAB EMIRATES
BAHRAIN
GOLESTĀN
MĀZANDARĀN
SEMNĀN
KHORĀSĀN
EŞFAHĀN
YAZD
KERMĀN
FĀRS
HORMOZGĀN
SĪSTĀN VA BALŪCHESTĀN
TEHRĀN
QOM
Kopet Dagh
Reshteh-ye Alborz (Elburz Mountains)
Dasht-e Kavīr
Iranian Plateau
Dasht-e Lūt
Zagros Mountains
Makran Coast
Gulf of Oman
Strait of Hormuz
Trucial Coast
Tehrān
Mashhad
Gorgān
Sārī
Qā'emshahr
Bābol
Āmol
Semnān
Shāhrūd
Dāmghān
Neyshābūr
Sabzevār
Torbat-e Ḩeydarīyeh
Kāshmar
Bojnūrd
Qūchān
Sarakhs
Qom
Kāshān
Eşfahān
Yazd
Shīrāz
Kermān
Zāhedān
Bam
Bandar-e 'Abbās
Bandar-e Būshehr
Sīrjān
Rafsanjān
Zābol
Chābahār
Jāsk
Bīrjand
Ţabas
Nā'īn
Ardakān
Qeshm
Ra's al Khaymah
Umm al Qaywayn
'Ajmān
Ash Shāriqah
Dubayy (Dubai)
Al Fujayrah
Khawr Fakkān
Ad Dawḩah (Doha)
Al Khawr
Al Wakrah
Umm Sa'īd
Abū Z̧aby (Abu Dhabi)
Al 'Ayn
Al Buraymī
Mafraq
Ar Ruways
Liwā
Ar Ruways
Tropic of Cancer
Qolleh-ye Damāvand 5671m
Kūh-e Hazārān 4420m
Kūh-e Taftān 4042m
Dena 4432m

Kazakhstan

Abundant natural resources lie in the immense steppe grasslands, deserts, and central plateau of the former Soviet republic of Kazakhstan. An intensive program of industrial and agricultural development to exploit these resources during the Soviet era resulted in catastrophic industrial pollution, including fallout from nuclear testing and the shrinkage of the Aral Sea. Since independence, the government has encouraged foreign investment and liberalized the economy to promote growth. The adoption of Kazakh as the national language is intended to encourage a new sense of national identity in a state where living conditions for the majority remain harsh, both in cramped urban centers and impoverished rural areas.

Transportation & Industry

The single most important industry in Kazakhstan is mining, based around extensive oil deposits near the Caspian Sea, the world's largest chromium mine, and vast reserves of iron ore. Recent foreign investment has helped to develop industries including food processing and steel manufacture, and to expand the exploitation of mineral resources. The Russian space program is still based at Baykonur, near Zhezkazgan in central Kazakhstan.

Major industry and infrastructure

- chemicals
- engineering
- fish processing
- food processing
- iron & steel
- metallurgy
- mining
- oil
- capital cities
- major towns
- international airports
- major roads
- major industrial areas

Transportation Network

Roads	87,561 miles (141,000 km)
Motorways	none
Railways	8,483 miles (13,660 km)
Waterways	none

Industrial areas in the north and east are well-connected to Russia. Air and rail links with Germany and China have been established through foreign investment. Better access to Baltic ports is being sought.

An open-cast coal mine in Kazakhstan. Foreign investment is being actively sought by the Kazakh government in order to fully exploit the potential of the country's rich mineral reserves.

Map Key

POPULATION

- 1 million to 5 million
- 500,000 to 1 million
- 100,000 to 500,000
- 50,000 to 100,000
- 10,000 to 50,000
- below 10,000

ELEVATION

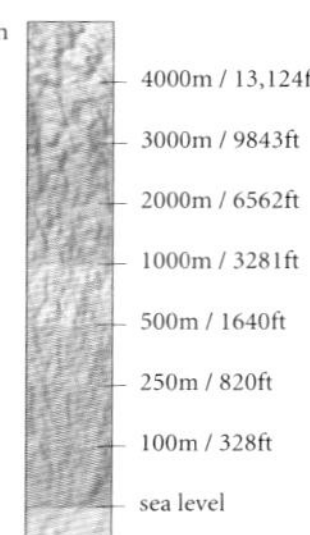
4000m / 13,124ft
3000m / 9843ft
2000m / 6562ft
1000m / 3281ft
500m / 1640ft
250m / 820ft
100m / 328ft
sea level

Using the Land and Sea

The rearing of large herds of sheep and goats on the steppe grasslands forms the core of Kazakh agriculture. Arable cultivation and cotton-growing in pasture and desert areas was encouraged during the Soviet era, but relative yields are low. The heavy use of fertilizers and the diversion of natural water sources for irrigation has degraded much of the land.

The Urban/Rural Population Divide

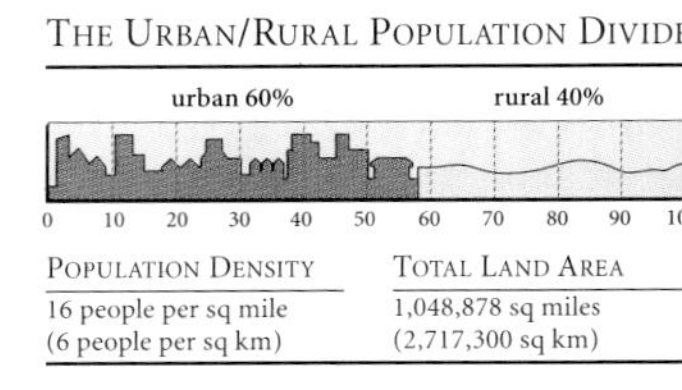
urban 60%
rural 40%
0 10 20 30 40 50 60 70 80 90 100

Population Density	Total Land Area
16 people per sq mile (6 people per sq km)	1,048,878 sq miles (2,717,300 sq km)

Land use and agricultural distribution

- cattle
- goats
- sheep
- cotton
- fishing
- wheat
- capital cities
- major towns
- pasture
- cropland
- forest
- mountain region
- desert

RUSSIAN FEDERATION
Ural'sk
Rudnyy
ASTANA
Ust'-Kamenogorsk
Semipalatinsk
Karaganda
Atyrau
KAZAKHSTAN
Aktau
Aral Sea
Kzyl-Orda
Taldykorgan
Alma-Ata
Shymkent
UZBEKISTAN
TURKMENISTAN
KYRGYZSTAN
CHINA
Caspian Sea

The nomadic peoples who moved their herds around the steppe grasslands are now largely settled, although echoes of their traditional lifestyle, in particular their superb riding skills, remain.

RUSSIA
122

Caspian Depression
ATYRAU
Atyrau
Makhambet
Makat
Dossor
Akkystau
Ganyushkino
Komsomol'skiy
Kul'sary
Koschagyl
Karaton
Opornyy
Sarykamys
AKTYUBINSK
Zharkamys
Chelkar
Emba
Gory Mugodzhary
Plato Shagyray
Peski Bol'shiye Barsuki
Severnyy Chink Ustyurta
Aral'sk
Saksaul'skiy
Sagiz
Caspian Sea

Ustyurt Plateau
MANGISTAU
Plato Mangyshlak
Aktau
Zhetybay
Zhanaozen
Kuryk
Sor Metvyy Kultuk
Beyneu
Say-Utës
Zharmysh
TURKMENISTAN
UZBEKISTAN
146

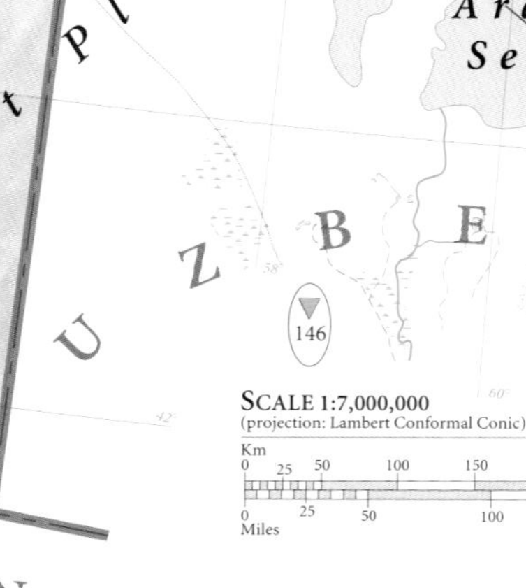
Aral Sea
Ostrov Vozrozhdeniya
KYZYLORDA
Uyaly
SCALE 1:7,000,000
(projection: Lambert Conformal Conic)
Km
Miles

THE LANDSCAPE

STRETCHING MORE THAN 1,250 MILES (2,000 km) from the Caspian Sea in the west to China in the east, more than 40% of Kazakhstan is covered by steppe grasslands which give way to barren desert in the south. The land rises eastward towards the mineral-rich central plateau, to form the Altai Mountains.

1960
1996
2010
Altai Mountains
Tien Shan
Khrebet Kanchingiz
Aral Sea

***Since 1960, the Aral Sea** has shrunk by 40%, become extremely saline, and lost all but five of its once-abundant fish species. Factors in this ecological disaster include the excessive use of fertilizers, defoliants and the diversion of its main source rivers for the irrigation of desert lands.*

The Caspian Sea is the largest body of inland water in the world.

The desert of Peski Bol'shiye Barsuki is mainly sandy, displaying a number of classic dune formations. Groundwater supports a small amount of vegetation.

A large number of salt lakes fill depressions in the rolling uplands of central Kazakhstan.

***The Altai Mountains** lie on Kazakhstan's eastern borders with China and the Russian Federation. Cold and largely barren, they are the source of many of the rivers which flow across the steppe.*

Its waters taken for industry and irrigation, the Syr Darya, one of Kazakhstan's major rivers, now barely reaches the Aral Sea which it used to fill. Like many Kazakh rivers it has been heavily polluted with chemicals and its flow has been restricted by up to 60%.

The waters of Lake Balkhash *(Ozero Balkhash)*, unlike those of the Aral Sea, are still able to support a fishing industry.

The central Kazakh Uplands *(Kazakhskiy Melkosopochnik)* contain much of the country's mineral riches. The landscape is largely flat with occasional rocky outcrops and hillocks.

***Immense stretches of steppe grasslands** characterize much of the Kazakh landscape. These lowland areas have been used for arable cultivation in recent years, although problems with irrigation have meant that much of the land is being allowed to revert to its natural vegetation and pastoral usage.*

***Rows of pine trees** edge this valley near Alma-Ata. The snow-covered slopes in the background are used for skiing.*

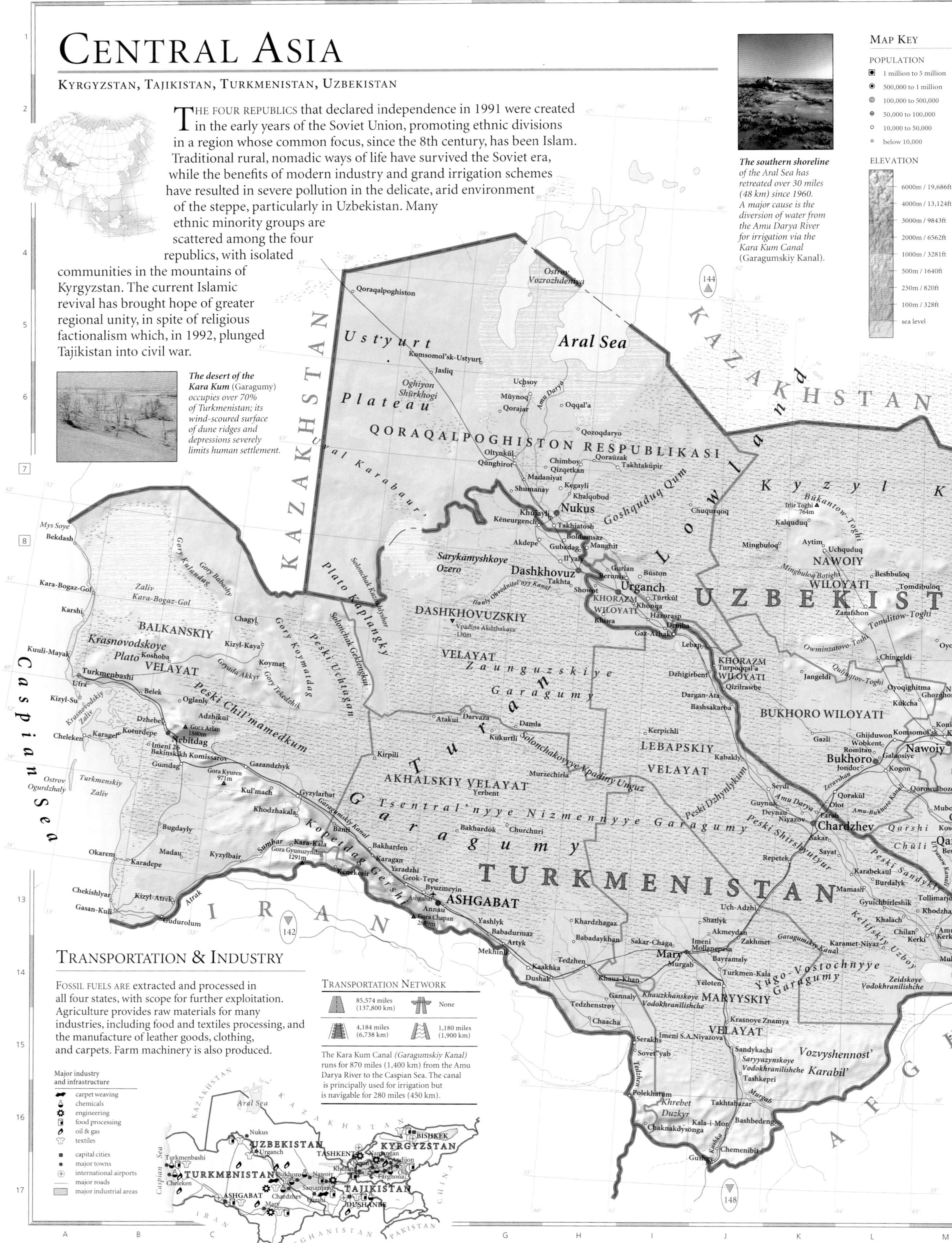
MAP KEY
POPULATION
1 million to 5 million
500,000 to 1 million
100,000 to 500,000
50,000 to 100,000
10,000 to 50,000
below 10,000
ELEVATION
6000m / 19,686ft
4000m / 13,124ft
3000m / 9843ft
2000m / 6562ft
1000m / 3281ft
500m / 1640ft
250m / 820ft
100m / 328ft
sea level
KAZAKHSTAN
UZBEKISTAN
TURKMENISTAN
IRAN
Caspian Sea
Aral Sea
ASHGABAT
Major industry and infrastructure
carpet weaving
chemicals
engineering
food processing
oil & gas
textiles
capital cities
major towns
international airports
major roads
major industrial areas

CENTRAL ASIA

KYRGYZSTAN, TAJIKISTAN, TURKMENISTAN, UZBEKISTAN

THE FOUR REPUBLICS that declared independence in 1991 were created in the early years of the Soviet Union, promoting ethnic divisions in a region whose common focus, since the 8th century, has been Islam. Traditional rural, nomadic ways of life have survived the Soviet era, while the benefits of modern industry and grand irrigation schemes have resulted in severe pollution in the delicate, arid environment of the steppe, particularly in Uzbekistan. Many ethnic minority groups are scattered among the four republics, with isolated communities in the mountains of Kyrgyzstan. The current Islamic revival has brought hope of greater regional unity, in spite of religious factionalism which, in 1992, plunged Tajikistan into civil war.

***The desert of the Kara Kum** (Garagumy) occupies over 70% of Turkmenistan; its wind-scoured surface of dune ridges and depressions severely limits human settlement.*

***The southern shoreline** of the Aral Sea has retreated over 30 miles (48 km) since 1960. A major cause is the diversion of water from the Amu Darya River for irrigation via the Kara Kum Canal* (Garagumskiy Kanal).

TRANSPORTATION & INDUSTRY

FOSSIL FUELS ARE extracted and processed in all four states, with scope for further exploitation. Agriculture provides raw materials for many industries, including food and textiles processing, and the manufacture of leather goods, clothing, and carpets. Farm machinery is also produced.

TRANSPORTATION NETWORK

85,574 miles (137,800 km)	None
4,184 miles (6,738 km)	1,180 miles (1,900 km)

The Kara Kum Canal *(Garagumskiy Kanal)* runs for 870 miles (1,400 km) from the Amu Darya River to the Caspian Sea. The canal is principally used for irrigation but is navigable for 280 miles (450 km).

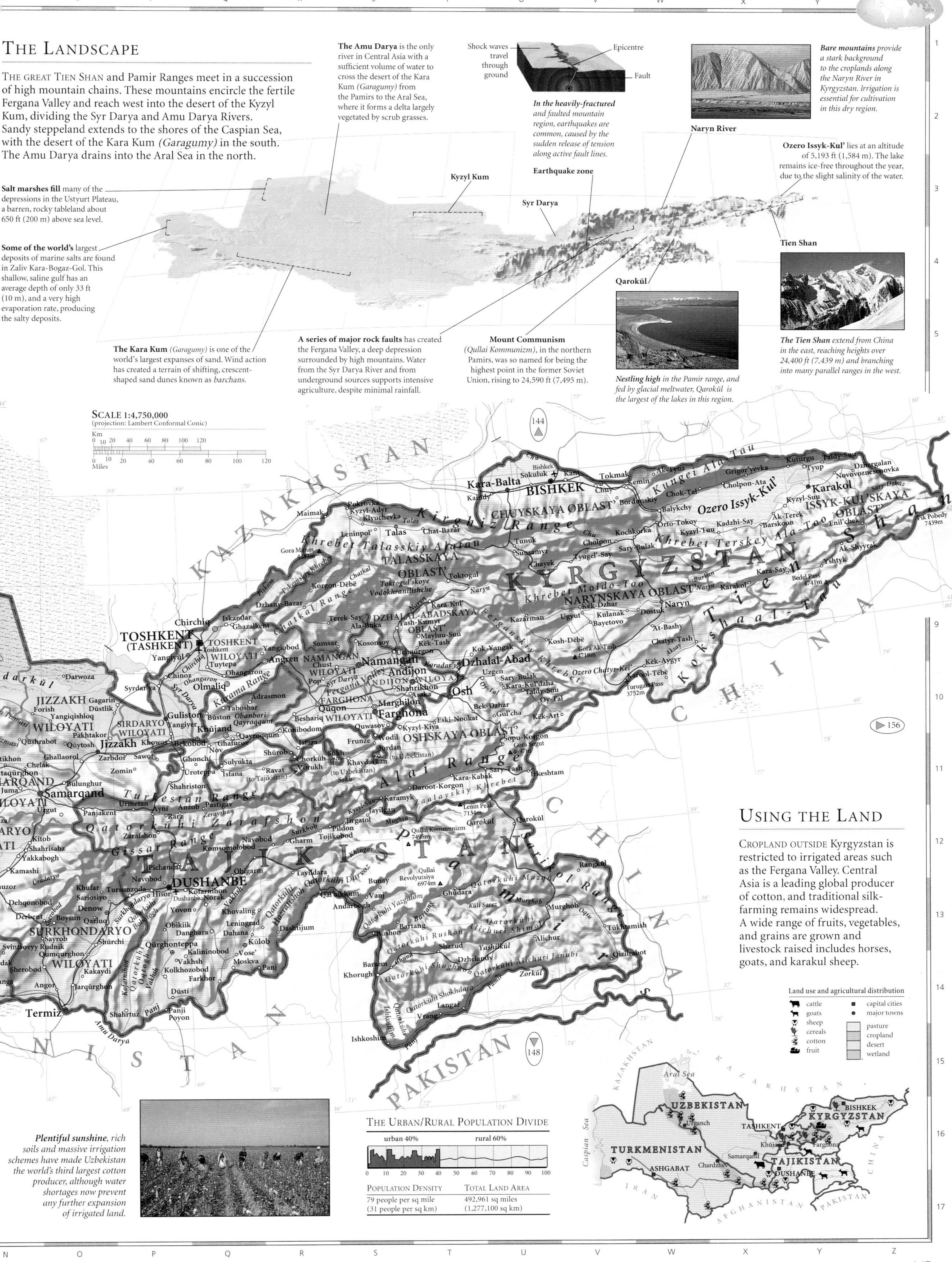
N O P Q R S T U V W X Y
1 2 3 4 5 9 10 11 12 13 14 15 16 17
Shock waves travel through ground
Epicentre
Fault
Kyzyl Kum
Earthquake zone
Syr Darya
Naryn River
Tien Shan
Qarokŭl
SCALE 1:4,750,000
(projection: Lambert Conformal Conic)
Km
Miles
KAZAKHSTAN
KYRGYZSTAN
TAJIKISTAN
CHINA
PAKISTAN
BISHKEK
TOSHKENT (TASHKENT)
DUSHANBE
Samarqand
Osh
Andijon
Namangan
Farghona
Khŭjand
Jizzakh
Termiz
Karakol
Naryn
Ozero Issyk-Kul'
Tien Shan
Alai Range
Pamirs
Lenin Peak 7134m
Qullai Kommunizm 7495m
Pik Pobedy 7439m
Amu Darya
144
156
148
Land use and agricultural distribution
cattle
goats
sheep
cereals
cotton
fruit
capital cities
major towns
pasture
cropland
desert
wetland
UZBEKISTAN
TURKMENISTAN
KYRGYZSTAN
TAJIKISTAN
ASHGABAT
TASHKENT
BISHKEK
DUSHANBE
Aral Sea
Caspian Sea
IRAN
AFGHANISTAN
PAKISTAN
CHINA
KAZAKHSTAN

The Landscape

The great Tien Shan and Pamir Ranges meet in a succession of high mountain chains. These mountains encircle the fertile Fergana Valley and reach west into the desert of the Kyzyl Kum, dividing the Syr Darya and Amu Darya Rivers. Sandy steppeland extends to the shores of the Caspian Sea, with the desert of the Kara Kum *(Garagumy)* in the south. The Amu Darya drains into the Aral Sea in the north.

The Amu Darya is the only river in Central Asia with a sufficient volume of water to cross the desert of the Kara Kum *(Garagumy)* from the Pamirs to the Aral Sea, where it forms a delta largely vegetated by scrub grasses.

In the heavily-fractured *and faulted mountain region, earthquakes are common, caused by the sudden release of tension along active fault lines.*

Bare mountains *provide a stark background to the croplands along the Naryn River in Kyrgyzstan. Irrigation is essential for cultivation in this dry region.*

Ozero Issyk-Kul' lies at an altitude of 5,193 ft (1,584 m). The lake remains ice-free throughout the year, due to the slight salinity of the water.

Salt marshes fill many of the depressions in the Ustyurt Plateau, a barren, rocky tableland about 650 ft (200 m) above sea level.

Some of the world's largest deposits of marine salts are found in Zaliv Kara-Bogaz-Gol. This shallow, saline gulf has an average depth of only 33 ft (10 m), and a very high evaporation rate, producing the salty deposits.

The Kara Kum *(Garagumy)* is one of the world's largest expanses of sand. Wind action has created a terrain of shifting, crescent-shaped sand dunes known as *barchans*.

A series of major rock faults has created the Fergana Valley, a deep depression surrounded by high mountains. Water from the Syr Darya River and from underground sources supports intensive agriculture, despite minimal rainfall.

Mount Communism *(Qullai Kommunizm)*, in the northern Pamirs, was so named for being the highest point in the former Soviet Union, rising to 24,590 ft (7,495 m).

Nestling high *in the Pamir range, and fed by glacial meltwater, Qarokŭl is the largest of the lakes in this region.*

The Tien Shan *extend from China in the east, reaching heights over 24,400 ft (7,439 m) and branching into many parallel ranges in the west.*

Using the Land

Cropland outside Kyrgyzstan is restricted to irrigated areas such as the Fergana Valley. Central Asia is a leading global producer of cotton, and traditional silk-farming remains widespread. A wide range of fruits, vegetables, and grains are grown and livestock raised includes horses, goats, and karakul sheep.

Plentiful sunshine, *rich soils and massive irrigation schemes have made Uzbekistan the world's third largest cotton producer, although water shortages now prevent any further expansion of irrigated land.*

The Urban/Rural Population Divide

urban 40% | rural 60%

0 10 20 30 40 50 60 70 80 90 100

Population Density	Total Land Area
79 people per sq mile (31 people per sq km)	492,961 sq miles (1,277,100 sq km)

Afghanistan & Pakistan

TURKMENISTAN
UZBEKISTAN
TAJIKISTAN
CHINA
IRAN
INDIA
ARABIAN SEA
AFGHANISTAN
PAKISTAN
Mazar-e Sharif
Herat
KABUL
Peshawar
ISLAMABAD
Rawalpindi
Kandahar
Lahore
Faisalabad
Quetta
Multan
Bahawalpur
Sukkur
Karachi
Hyderabad
Hunza River
Hindu Kush
Himalayas
Glacis covered by coarse-grained sediment
Sediments washed down from mountains accumulate on glacis slopes
Bedrock
Fine sediments deposited on salt flats are removed by wind erosion.
146
142
TURKMEN
IRAN
AFGH
ARABIAN
Bālā Morghāb
Kārīz-e Elyās
Towraghoudi
Qarah Bāgh
Kūshk
Harīrūd
BĀDGHĪS
Qal'eh-ye Now
Qādes
Eslām Qal'eh
Kūhestān
Dasht-e Hamdam Āb
Zendeh Jān
Ghūriān
Selseleh-ye Sefīd Kūh
Herāt
HERĀT
Namakzar
GHOW
Farāh Rūd
Kūh-e Chehel Abdāl
Shīndand
Dak
Dasht-e Bābūs
FARĀH
Anār Darreh
Farāh Rūd
Farāh
Delārām
Now Z
Hāmūn-e Şāberī
Dasht-e Khāsh
Hāmūn-e Pūzak
NIMRŪZ
Chakhānsūr
Shelleh-ye Pūdeh Tal
Gereshk
Lashkar Gāh
Zaranj
Dasht-e Mārgow
Darvīshān
Kūchnay Darwey
HELMAND
Deh Shū
Daryā-ye Helmand
Dasht-e Gowd-e Zereh
Chāgai Hills
Nok Kundi
Yakmach
Dālbandin
Dasht-i Tāhlāb
Tāhlāb
Hāmūn-i Māshkel
Kamarod
Siāhān Range
Panjgūr
Central Makran
Ispikān
Nihing
Mand
Nasirābād
Kech
Hoshāb
Kolwa
Turbat
Dasht
Suntsar
Khor Kalmat
Jīwani
Gwādar
Gwādar West Bay
Gwādar East Bay
Pasni
Astola Island
Ormāra
SCALE 1:5,000,000
(projection: Lambert Conformal Conic)
Km
Miles

Pakistan was created by the partition of British India in 1947, becoming the western arm of a new Islamic state for Indian Muslims; the eastern sector, in Bengal, seceded to become the separate country of Bangladesh in 1971. Over half of Pakistan's 147 million people live in the Punjab, at the fertile head of the great Indus Basin. The river sustains a national economy based on irrigated agriculture, including cotton for the vital textiles industry. Afghanistan, a mountainous, landlocked country, with an ancient and independent culture, has been wracked by war since 1979, when calls for help from a beleaguered government led to a Soviet invasion. Despite the Soviet withdrawal, factional strife continues and five million Afghan refugees remain over the border in Pakistan.

The town of Bamian lies high in the Hindu Kush, 250 miles (420 km) west of the Afghan capital, Kabul. It contains two huge statues of Buddha and a number of sanctuaries and cells carved in the rock. In 1222, the ancient city was destroyed by Chinghiz Khan.

Transportation & Industry

Pakistan is highly dependent on the cotton textiles industry, although diversified manufacture is expanding around cities such as Karachi and Lahore. Afghanistan's limited industry is based mainly on the processing of agricultural raw materials and includes traditional crafts such as carpet weaving.

Major industry and infrastructure

carpet weaving	capital cities
chemicals	major towns
engineering	international airports
finance	major roads
food processing	major industrial areas
iron & steel	
oil & gas	
textiles	

Transportation Network

141,340 miles (227,600 km)
211 miles (340 km)
4,852 miles (7,814 km)
745 miles (1,200 km)

The Karakoram Highway was completed after 20 years of construction in 1978. It breaches the Himalayan mountain barrier providing a commercial motor route linking lowland Pakistan and China.

***The Karakoram Highway** is one of the highest major roads in the world. It took over 24,000 workers almost 20 years to complete.*

The Landscape

Afghanistan's topography is dominated by the mountains of the Hindu Kush, which spread south and west into numerous mountain spurs. The dry plateau of southwestern Afghanistan extends into Pakistan and the hills which overlook the great Indus Basin. In northern Pakistan the Hindu Kush, Himalayan and Karakoram ranges meet to form one of the world's highest mountain regions.

***The Hunza River** rises in the northern Karakoram Range, running for 120 miles (193 km) before joining the Gilgit River.*

***The arid Hindu Kush** makes much of Afghanistan uninhabitable, with over 50% of the land lying above 6,500 ft (2,000 m).*

The plains and foothills which extend from the northern slopes of the Hindu Kush are part of the great grassy steppe lands of Central Asia.

K2 (Mount Godwin Austen), in the Karakoram Range, is the second highest mountain in the world, at an altitude of 28,251 ft (8,611 m).

Some of the largest glaciers outside the polar regions are found in the Karakoram Range, including Siachen Glacier *(Siachen Muztagh)*, which is 40 miles (72 km) long.

Frequent earthquakes mean that mountain-building processes are continuing in this region, as the Indo-Australian Plate drifts northward, colliding with the Eurasian Plate.

Mountain chains running southwest from the Hindu Kush into Pakistan form a barrier to the humid winds which blow from the Indian Ocean, creating arid conditions across southern Afghanistan.

The soils of the Punjab Plain are nourished by enormous quantities of sediment, carried from the Himalayas by the five tributaries of the Indus River.

The Indus Basin is part of the Indus-Ganges lowland, a vast depression which has been filled with layers of sediment over the last 50 million years. These deposits are estimated to be over 16,400 ft (5,000 m) deep.

The Indus Delta is prone to heavy flooding and high levels of salinity. It remains a largely uncultivated wilderness area.

***Glacis are gentle**, debris-covered slopes which lead into saltflats or deserts. They typically occur at the base of mountains in arid regions such as Afghanistan.*

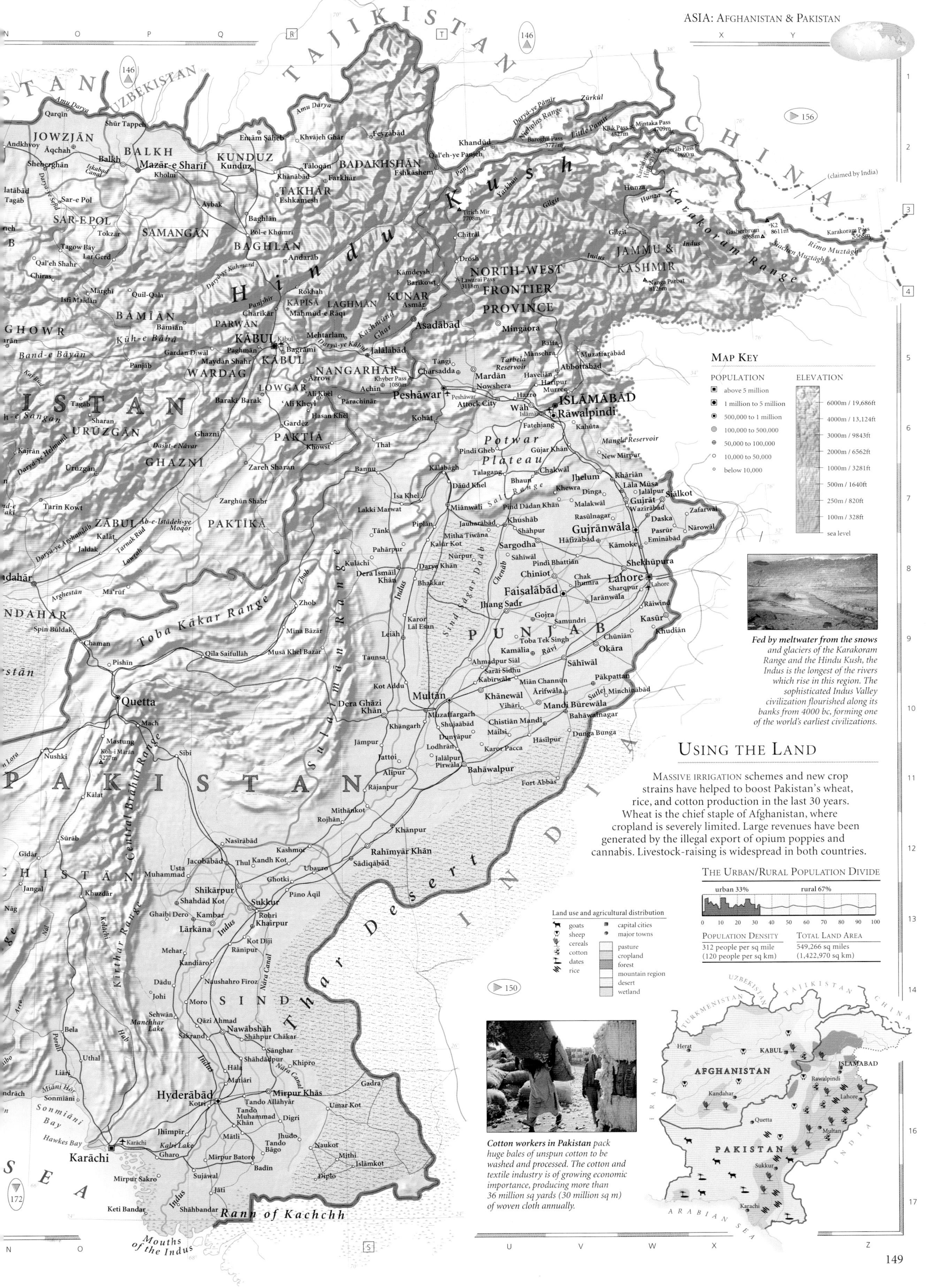
TAJIKISTAN
UZBEKISTAN
CHINA
INDIA
PAKISTAN
AFGHANISTAN
SEA
Hindu Kush
Karakoram Range
Thar Desert
Toba Kākar Range
Sulaimān Range
Kīrthar Range
Central Brahui Range
Potwar Plateau
PUNJAB
SIND
NORTH-WEST FRONTIER PROVINCE
JAMMU & KASHMIR
(claimed by India)
BADAKHSHĀN
TAKHĀR
KUNDUZ
BALKH
JOWZJĀN
SAR-E POL
SAMANGĀN
BAGHLĀN
BĀMĪĀN
PARWĀN
KĀPĪSĀ
LAGHMĀN
KUNAR
NANGARHĀR
LOWGAR
WARDAG
KĀBUL
PAKTĪĀ
PAKTĪKĀ
GHAZNĪ
URŪZGĀN
ZĀBUL
GHOWR
Kābul
Islāmābād
Rāwalpindi
Peshāwar
Lahore
Faisalābād
Multān
Quetta
Hyderābād
Karāchi
Mazār-e Sharīf
Jalālābād
Gujrānwāla
Sukkur
Bahāwalpur
Indus
Rann of Kachchh
Mouths of the Indus
K2 8611m
Nanga Parbat 8126m
Tirich Mir 7708m
Khyber Pass 1080m
MAP KEY
POPULATION
above 5 million
1 million to 5 million
500,000 to 1 million
100,000 to 500,000
50,000 to 100,000
10,000 to 50,000
below 10,000
ELEVATION
6000m / 19,686ft
4000m / 13,124ft
3000m / 9843ft
2000m / 6562ft
1000m / 3281ft
500m / 1640ft
250m / 820ft
100m / 328ft
sea level
Land use and agricultural distribution
goats
sheep
cereals
cotton
dates
rice
capital cities
major towns
pasture
cropland
forest
mountain region
desert
wetland
THE URBAN/RURAL POPULATION DIVIDE
urban 33%
rural 67%
0 10 20 30 40 50 60 70 80 90 100
POPULATION DENSITY
312 people per sq mile
(120 people per sq km)
TOTAL LAND AREA
549,266 sq miles
(1,422,970 sq km)
TURKMENISTAN
IRAN
ARABIAN SEA

Fed by meltwater from the snows *and glaciers of the Karakoram Range and the Hindu Kush, the Indus is the longest of the rivers which rise in this region. The sophisticated Indus Valley civilization flourished along its banks from 4000 bc, forming one of the world's earliest civilizations.*

USING THE LAND

MASSIVE IRRIGATION schemes and new crop strains have helped to boost Pakistan's wheat, rice, and cotton production in the last 30 years. Wheat is the chief staple of Afghanistan, where cropland is severely limited. Large revenues have been generated by the illegal export of opium poppies and cannabis. Livestock-raising is widespread in both countries.

Cotton workers in Pakistan *pack huge bales of unspun cotton to be washed and processed. The cotton and textile industry is of growing economic importance, producing more than 36 million sq yards (30 million sq m) of woven cloth annually.*

South Asia

Bangladesh, Bhutan, India, Maldives, Nepal, Pakistan, Sri Lanka

More than one-fifth of the world's population lives in the south Asian subcontinent. Great cultural diversity has come from a long succession of foreign invaders, including Hindu Aryans, Islamic Moguls, and the British, whose empire incorporated the princely states of the Maharajas and extended to the borders of Nepal and Bhutan in the Himalayas. Half a century after independence, India is the world's largest democracy, and at the current rate of growth, may overtake China as the world's most populous country within the next century. There are points of tension in the region over claims for independence by the Sikhs in the Indian Punjab and the Tamil separatists in Sri Lanka, and the long-standing dispute with Pakistan over Jammu and Kashmir in the north.

The towering Karakoram and Hindu Kush ranges, formed at the same time as the Himalayas, dominate Pakistan's northern borders. K2 on the border of northern Pakistan is the second highest mountain on Earth, at 28,251 ft (8,611 m).

The Landscape

South Asia is effectively isolated from the rest of Asia by desert along the western flank of Pakistan, and a continuous wall of mountains, dominated by the Himalayas, to the north and east. The great basins of the Indus and Ganges separate this mountain fringe from the rolling plateau of the Indian peninsula, which is bordered by a line of coastal hills, the Eastern and Western Ghats.

The Indus River flows more than 1,970 miles (3,180 km) from southwestern Tibet to its mouth on the Arabian Sea. It has an estimated catchment area of 450,000 sq miles (1,165,500 sq km).

The coast of western Pakistan is a staircase of folded rock strata caused by successive periods of rapid uplift.

The Indus Valley near Skardu in northern Pakistan has been partially infilled by great quantities of eroded sediment. Most of this is carried from the region's bare slopes by swollen rivers during the spring thaw and mass movement activity.

The Himalayas are the highest and most extensive mountain system in the world. They were formed when the Indo-Australian Plate collided with the Eurasian Plate about 40 million years ago, thrusting up huge masses of land and creating a "ripple" effect, which formed lesser mountain ranges in Tibet and Southeast Asia. Mount Everest is the world's tallest mountain at 29,028 ft (8,848 m).

Almost all of Bangladesh lies in the immense delta formed by the Ganges and the Brahmaputra which merge and flow out into the Bay of Bengal.

Bharatpur

Ganges Delta

Deccan Plateau

Eastern Ghats

Rivers flowing from the Himalayas into a broad depression in northern India have formed marshes around Bharatpur. They are now a sanctuary for numerous bird species.

Layers of volcanic basalt

Stepped valleys or 'traps'

***The Deccan Plateau** covers an area of more than 123,553 sq miles (320,000 sq km). It is formed of deep layers of volcanic basalt, reaching thicknesses of more than 9,800 ft (3,000 m) toward the coast. Distinctive stepped valleys cut in the basalt plateau by rivers are known as "traps."*

The Western Ghats are formed by a fault scarp which runs unbroken for more than 930 miles (1,500 km). They reach their highest point at the southern Cardamon Hills.

Trivandrum in southern India normally receives the first of the monsoon rains, which are essential to south Asian agriculture and moderate the extreme summer heat. The monsoon then moves northward over a period of about two months.

Coastal deposition has formed many typical features along the western coast of Sri Lanka. These include spits and bars, sometimes enclosing lagoons.

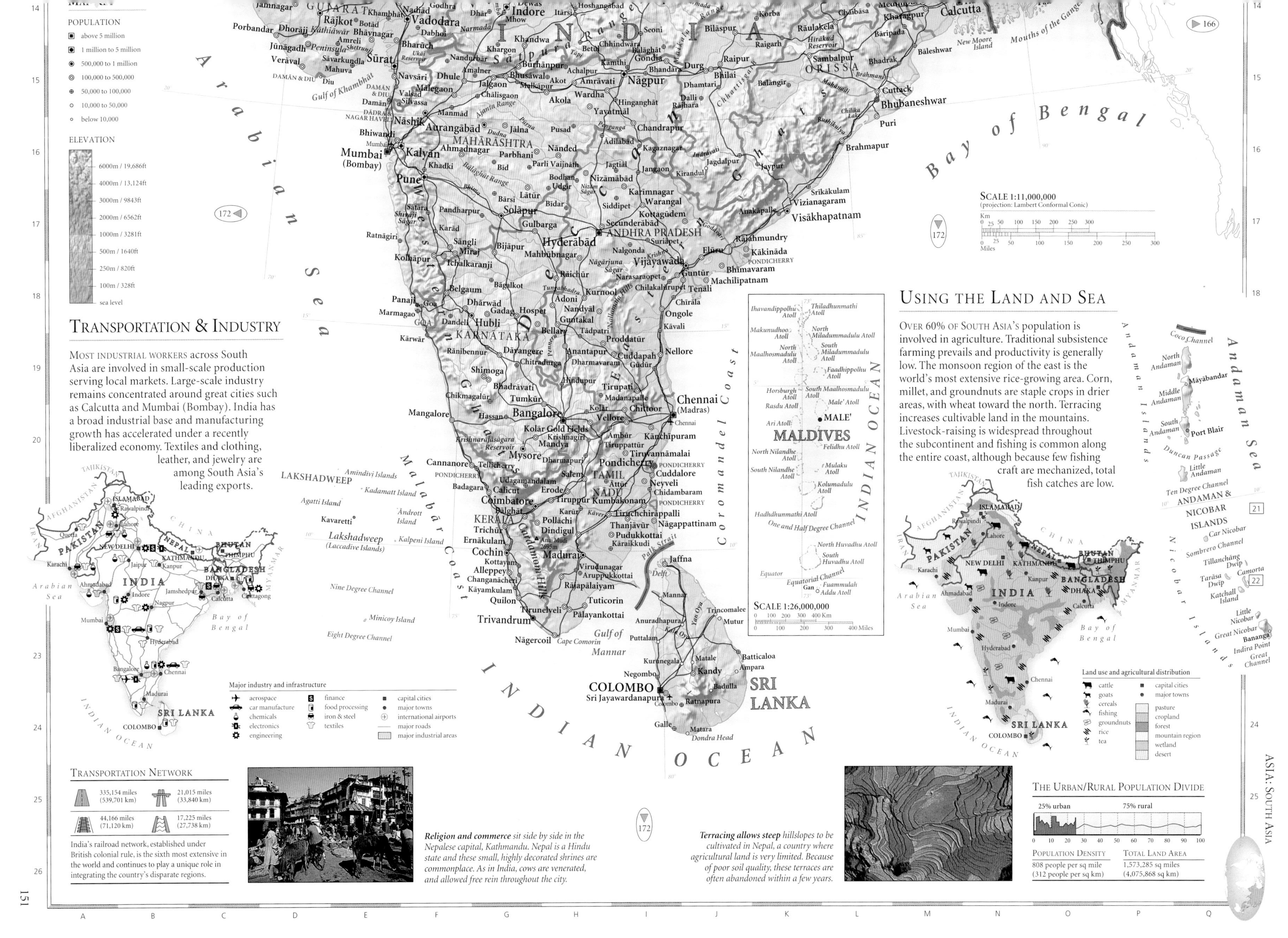
POPULATION
above 5 million
1 million to 5 million
500,000 to 1 million
100,000 to 500,000
50,000 to 100,000
10,000 to 50,000
below 10,000
ELEVATION
6000m / 19,686ft
4000m / 13,124ft
3000m / 9843ft
2000m / 6562ft
1000m / 3281ft
500m / 1640ft
250m / 820ft
100m / 328ft
sea level
SCALE 1:11,000,000
(projection: Lambert Conformal Conic)
Arabian Sea
Bay of Bengal
INDIAN OCEAN
Andaman Sea
INDIA
SRI LANKA
MALDIVES
LAKSHADWEEP
ANDAMAN & NICOBAR ISLANDS
Mumbai (Bombay)
Calcutta
Chennai (Madras)
Hyderābād
Bangalore
COLOMBO
Sri Jayawardanapura
MALE'
Malabār Coast
Coromandel Coast
Gulf of Mannar
Palk Strait
Lakshadweep (Laccadive Islands)
Andaman Islands
Nicobar Islands
SCALE 1:26,000,000
Major industry and infrastructure
aerospace
car manufacture
chemicals
electronics
engineering
finance
food processing
iron & steel
textiles
capital cities
major towns
international airports
major roads
major industrial areas
Land use and agricultural distribution
cattle
goats
cereals
fishing
groundnuts
rice
tea
capital cities
major towns
pasture
cropland
forest
mountain region
wetland
desert

Transportation & Industry

Most industrial workers across South Asia are involved in small-scale production serving local markets. Large-scale industry remains concentrated around great cities such as Calcutta and Mumbai (Bombay). India has a broad industrial base and manufacturing growth has accelerated under a recently liberalized economy. Textiles and clothing, leather, and jewelry are among South Asia's leading exports.

Using the Land and Sea

Over 60% of South Asia's population is involved in agriculture. Traditional subsistence farming prevails and productivity is generally low. The monsoon region of the east is the world's most extensive rice-growing area. Corn, millet, and groundnuts are staple crops in drier areas, with wheat toward the north. Terracing increases cultivable land in the mountains. Livestock-raising is widespread throughout the subcontinent and fishing is common along the entire coast, although because few fishing craft are mechanized, total fish catches are low.

Transportation Network

335,154 miles (539,701 km)	21,015 miles (33,840 km)
44,166 miles (71,120 km)	17,225 miles (27,738 km)

India's railroad network, established under British colonial rule, is the sixth most extensive in the world and continues to play a unique role in integrating the country's disparate regions.

***Religion and commerce** sit side by side in the Nepalese capital, Kathmandu. Nepal is a Hindu state and these small, highly decorated shrines are commonplace. As in India, cows are venerated, and allowed free rein throughout the city.*

***Terracing allows steep** hillslopes to be cultivated in Nepal, a country where agricultural land is very limited. Because of poor soil quality, these terraces are often abandoned within a few years.*

The Urban/Rural Population Divide

25% urban | 75% rural

Population Density	Total Land Area
808 people per sq mile (312 people per sq km)	1,573,285 sq miles (4,075,868 sq km)

NORTHERN INDIA & THE HIMALAYAN STATES

BANGLADESH, BHUTAN, NEPAL, Arunachal Pradesh, Assam, Bihar, Chandigarh, Delhi, Haryana, Himachal Pradesh, Jammu & Kashmir, Manipur, Meghalaya, Mizoram, Nagaland, Punjab, Rajasthan, Sikkim, Tripura, Uttar Pradesh, West Bengal

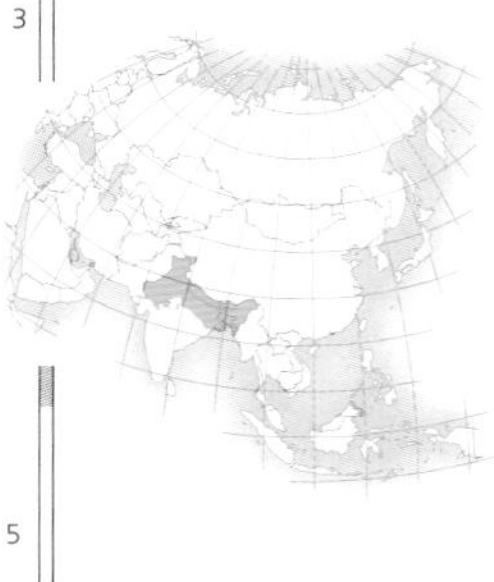

THE GANGES AND BRAHMAPUTRA river basins and the massive mountain barrier of the Himalayas define this region's landscape and have served to reinforce potent cultural and religious differences among its people. Hinduism pervades most aspects of national life and is a growing political force within India, a secular country which also encompasses the center of Sikhism at Amritsar and the world's largest Muslim minority. Nepal is a crowded mountain state, which faces severe ecological problems from deforestation, while the tiny Himalayan Buddhist kingdom of Bhutan is emerging from long-term isolation, to welcome selected visitors. The Muslim state of Bangladesh, formerly East Pakistan, is one of the world's most densely populated countries and one of the poorest, with more than 120 million people living largely on the massive Ganges/Brahmaputra Delta. Many Bangladeshis live under threat of repeated, catastrophic floods.

The Golden Temple in Amritsar, the most sacred shrine of the Sikh religion, was the scene of violent clashes between Sikh separatists and government forces in 1984.

SCALE 1:6,500,000
(projection: Lambert Conformal Conic)

MAP KEY

POPULATION
- 1 million to 5 million
- 500,000 to 1 million
- 100,000 to 500,000
- 50,000 to 100,000
- 10,000 to 50,000
- below 10,000

ELEVATION
- 6000m / 19,686ft
- 4000m / 13,124ft
- 3000m / 9843ft
- 2000m / 6562ft
- 1000m / 3281ft
- 500m / 1640ft
- 250m / 820ft
- 100m / 328ft
- sea level

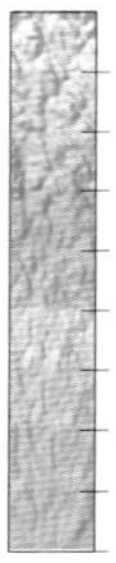

TRANSPORTATION & INDUSTRY

TEXTILES, ENGINEERING, chemicals, and electronics are leading industries in north India. The plateau of Chota Nagpur provides ore for iron and steel production in the major industrial region northeast of Calcutta. Bangladesh processes jute and Nepal has a small manufacturing sector based on agricultural produce, while Bhutan's limited industry is concentrated in the southern lowland area.

Major industry and infrastructure
- adventure tourism
- car manufacture
- chemicals
- coal
- electronics
- engineering
- finance
- food processing
- iron & steel
- jute processing
- oil
- tea processing
- textiles
- capital cities
- major towns
- international airports
- major roads
- major industrial areas

TRANSPORTATION NETWORK

Over 60% of Bangladesh's internal trade is carried by boat. The country has a very disjointed land transportation network, with no bridges over the Brahmaputra and few road crossings on the Ganges River.

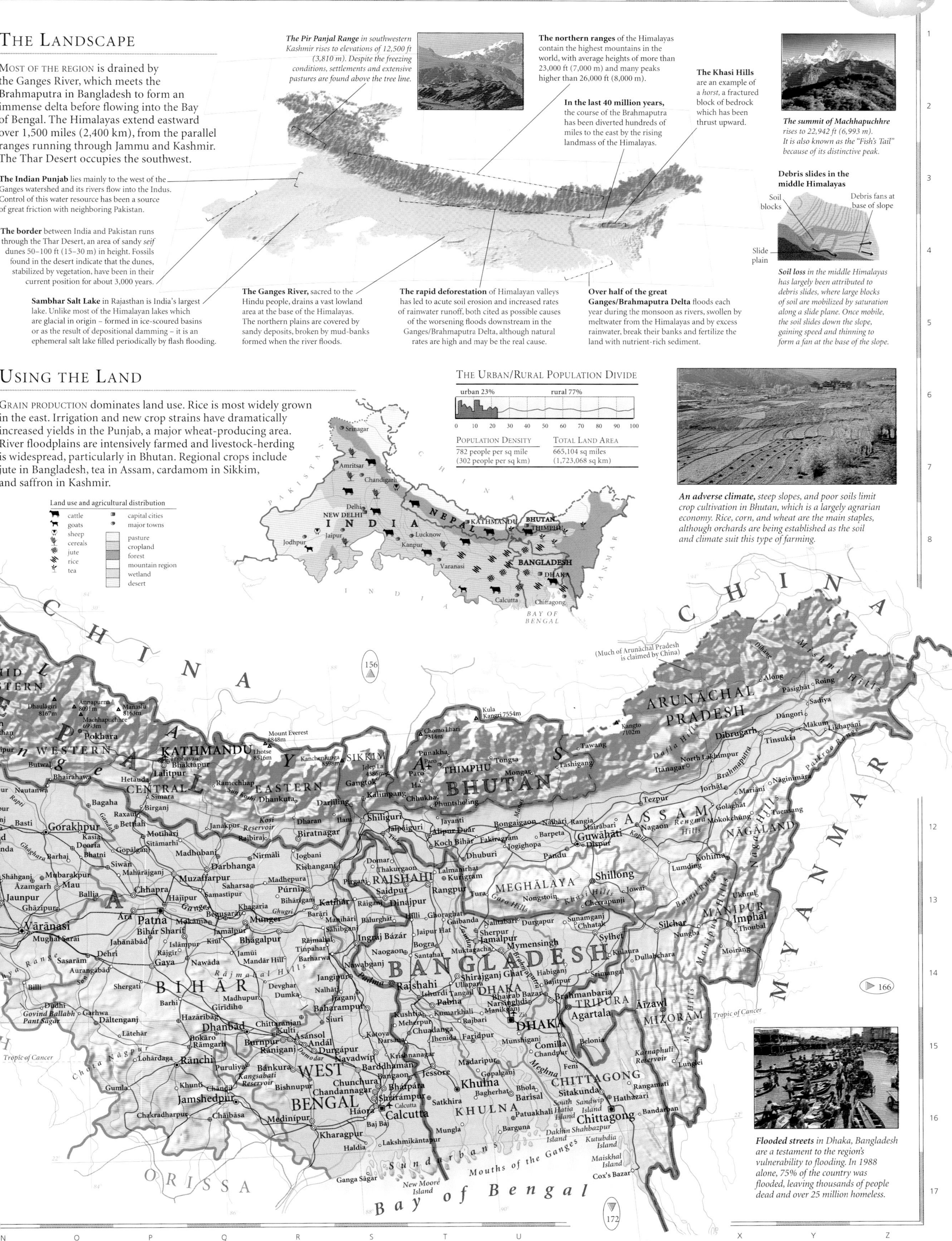

THE LANDSCAPE

MOST OF THE REGION is drained by the Ganges River, which meets the Brahmaputra in Bangladesh to form an immense delta before flowing into the Bay of Bengal. The Himalayas extend eastward over 1,500 miles (2,400 km), from the parallel ranges running through Jammu and Kashmir. The Thar Desert occupies the southwest.

The Pir Panjal Range in southwestern Kashmir rises to elevations of 12,500 ft (3,810 m). Despite the freezing conditions, settlements and extensive pastures are found above the tree line.

The northern ranges of the Himalayas contain the highest mountains in the world, with average heights of more than 23,000 ft (7,000 m) and many peaks higher than 26,000 ft (8,000 m).

In the last 40 million years, the course of the Brahmaputra has been diverted hundreds of miles to the east by the rising landmass of the Himalayas.

The Khasi Hills are an example of a *horst*, a fractured block of bedrock which has been thrust upward.

The summit of Machhapuchhre *rises to 22,942 ft (6,993 m). It is also known as the "Fish's Tail" because of its distinctive peak.*

The Indian Punjab lies mainly to the west of the Ganges watershed and its rivers flow into the Indus. Control of this water resource has been a source of great friction with neighboring Pakistan.

The border between India and Pakistan runs through the Thar Desert, an area of sandy *seif* dunes 50–100 ft (15–30 m) in height. Fossils found in the desert indicate that the dunes, stabilized by vegetation, have been in their current position for about 3,000 years.

Sambhar Salt Lake in Rajasthan is India's largest lake. Unlike most of the Himalayan lakes which are glacial in origin – formed in ice-scoured basins or as the result of depositional damming – it is an ephemeral salt lake filled periodically by flash flooding.

The Ganges River, sacred to the Hindu people, drains a vast lowland area at the base of the Himalayas. The northern plains are covered by sandy deposits, broken by mud-banks formed when the river floods.

The rapid deforestation of Himalayan valleys has led to acute soil erosion and increased rates of rainwater runoff, both cited as possible causes of the worsening floods downstream in the Ganges/Brahmaputra Delta, although natural rates are high and may be the real cause.

Over half of the great Ganges/Brahmaputra Delta floods each year during the monsoon as rivers, swollen by meltwater from the Himalayas and by excess rainwater, break their banks and fertilize the land with nutrient-rich sediment.

Debris slides in the middle Himalayas

Soil blocks
Debris fans at base of slope
Slide plain

Soil loss *in the middle Himalayas has largely been attributed to debris slides, where large blocks of soil are mobilized by saturation along a slide plane. Once mobile, the soil slides down the slope, gaining speed and thinning to form a fan at the base of the slope.*

USING THE LAND

GRAIN PRODUCTION dominates land use. Rice is most widely grown in the east. Irrigation and new crop strains have dramatically increased yields in the Punjab, a major wheat-producing area. River floodplains are intensively farmed and livestock-herding is widespread, particularly in Bhutan. Regional crops include jute in Bangladesh, tea in Assam, cardamom in Sikkim, and saffron in Kashmir.

Land use and agricultural distribution
cattle
goats
sheep
cereals
jute
rice
tea
capital cities
major towns
pasture
cropland
forest
mountain region
wetland
desert

THE URBAN/RURAL POPULATION DIVIDE

urban 23%
rural 77%
0 10 20 30 40 50 60 70 80 90 100

POPULATION DENSITY	TOTAL LAND AREA
782 people per sq mile (302 people per sq km)	665,104 sq miles (1,723,068 sq km)

An adverse climate, *steep slopes, and poor soils limit crop cultivation in Bhutan, which is a largely agrarian economy. Rice, corn, and wheat are the main staples, although orchards are being established as the soil and climate suit this type of farming.*

Flooded streets *in Dhaka, Bangladesh are a testament to the region's vulnerability to flooding. In 1988 alone, 75% of the country was flooded, leaving thousands of people dead and over 25 million homeless.*

156
166
172

Southern India & Sri Lanka

Sri Lanka, Andhra Pradesh, Dadra & Nagar Haveli, Daman & Diu, Goa, Gujarat, Karnataka, Kerala, Lakshadweep, Madhya Pradesh, Maharashtra, Orissa, Pondicherry, Tamil Nadu

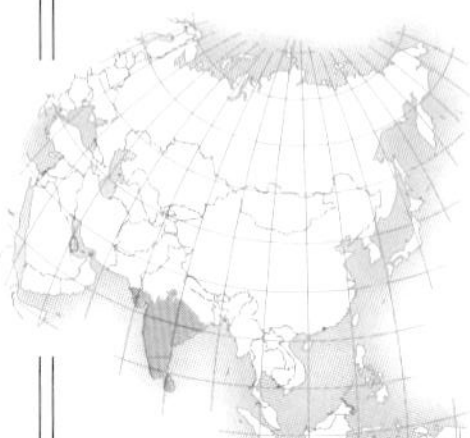

The unique and highly independent southern states reflect the diverse and decentralized nature of India, which has fourteen official languages. The southern half of the peninsula lay beyond the reach of early invaders from the north and retained the distinct and ancient culture of Dravidian peoples such as the Tamils, whose language is spoken in preference to Hindi throughout southern India. The interior plateau of southern India is less densely populated than the coastal lowlands, where the European colonial imprint is strongest. Urban and industrial growth is accelerating, but southern India's vast population remains predominantly rural. The island of Sri Lanka has two distinct cultural groups; the mainly Buddhist Sinhalese majority, and the Tamil minority whose struggle for a homeland in the northeast has led to prolonged civil war.

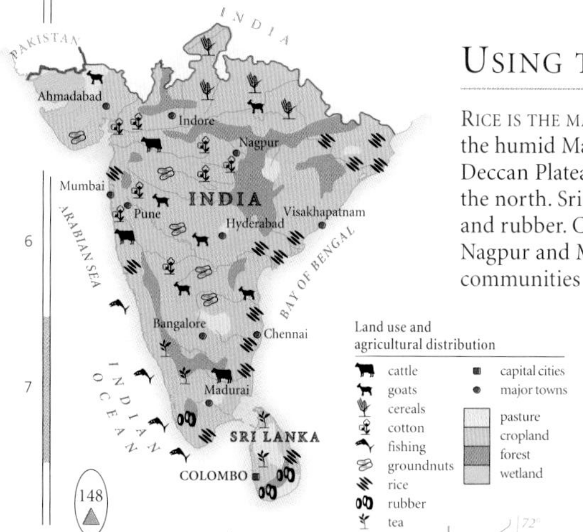

Using the Land and Sea

Rice is the main staple in the east, in Sri Lanka and along the humid Malabar Coast. Peanuts are grown on the Deccan Plateau, with wheat, corn, and chickpeas, toward the north. Sri Lanka is a leading exporter of tea, coconuts and rubber. Cotton plantations supply local mills around Nagpur and Mumbai (Bombay). Fishing supports many communities in Kerala and the Laccadive Islands.

Land use and agricultural distribution

- cattle
- goats
- cereals
- cotton
- fishing
- groundnuts
- rice
- rubber
- tea
- capital cities
- major towns
- pasture
- cropland
- forest
- wetland

Commercial plantations, growing tea, (seen here), cardamom, coffee, coconuts, and rubber, occupy about half the agricultural land in Kerala, necessitating food imports for local consumption.

The Urban/Rural Population Divide

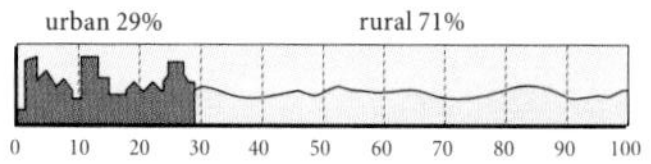

urban 29% — rural 71%

Population Density	Total Land Area
715 people per sq mile (276 people per sq km)	698,295 sq miles (1,809,054 sq km)

The Landscape

The undulating Deccan Plateau underlies most of southern India; it slopes gently down toward the east and is largely enclosed by the Ghats coastal hill ranges. The Western Ghats run continuously along the Arabian Sea coast, while the Eastern Ghats are interrupted by rivers which follow the slope of the plateau and flow across broad lowlands into the Bay of Bengal. The plateaus and basins of Sri Lanka's central highlands are surrounded by a broad plain.

Along the northern boundary of the Deccan Plateau, old basement rocks are interspersed with younger sedimentary strata. This creates spectacular scarplands, cut by numerous waterfalls along the softer sedimentary strata.

The Rann of Kachchh tidal marshes encircle the low-lying Kachchh Peninsula. For several months during the rainy season the water level of the marshes rises and Kachchh becomes an island.

The Konkan coast, which runs between Daman and Goa, is characterized by rocky headlands, and bays with crescent-shaped beaches. Flooded river valleys known as *rias* extend inland.

The interior uplands of southern India are broadly known as the Deccan Plateau. River erosion of the plateau's volcanic rock has created distinctive stepped valleys called *traps.*

The Western Ghats run north–south marking the western boundary of the Deccan Plateau. Their height rises to the south where their summits reach altitudes of 8,000 ft (2,500 m).

Deep layers of river sediment have created a broad lowland plain along the eastern coast, with rivers such as the Krishna forming extensive deltas.

The island of Sri Lanka is essentially an extension of the Deccan Plateau. It lies on the Indian continental shelf and is composed of the same hard, crystalline rocks.

Adam's Bridge

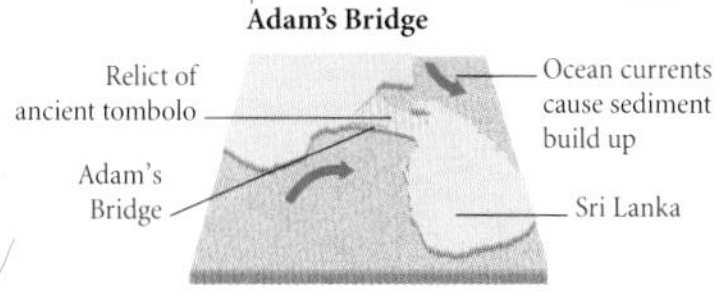

Relict of ancient tombolo — Ocean currents cause sediment build up — Adam's Bridge — Sri Lanka

***Adam's Bridge (Rama's Bridge)** is a chain of sandy shoals lying about 4 ft (1.2 m) under the sea between India and Sri Lanka. They once formed the world's longest tombolo, or land bridge, before the sea level began to rise several thousand years ago.*

148 150 150 150 172

MAP KEY

POPULATION

- above 5 million
- 1 million to 5 million
- 500,000 to 1 million
- 100,000 to 500,000
- 50,000 to 100,000
- 10,000 to 50,000
- below 10,000

ELEVATION

- 2000m / 6562ft
- 1000m / 3281ft
- 500m / 1640ft
- 250m / 820ft
- 100m / 328ft
- sea level

Sea pencils *thrive on the coral reefs around the coast of the Laccadive Islands and Sri Lanka. The reefs support an amazing diversity of marine life, but are increasingly under threat from growing coastal populations.*

Local fisheries around Sri Lanka *afford great potential for exploitation, but development has been hampered by technological constraints. Most fishermen live on the coastal fringes and operate on a small scale.*

The great triumphal arch *of Charminar, built in 1591, epitomizes the fine Islamic architecture which the Moghuls brought from the north to Hyderabad, the capital of Andhra Pradesh.*

TRANSPORTATION & INDUSTRY

SOUTH INDIA HAS a broad industrial base, with three leading regions. Around Mumbai, Bangalore, and Ahmadabad, cotton mills and chemical plants make use of cheap hydroelectric power generated in the Western Ghats. Light engineering and textiles are well established to the south and west of Chennai (Madras). Sri Lanka's industry is based mainly on the processing of agricultural products.

Major industry and infrastructure

- aerospace
- car manufacture
- chemicals
- electronics
- engineering
- food processing
- iron & steel
- pharmaceuticals
- printing & publishing
- shipbuilding
- tea processing
- textiles
- tobacco processing
- capital cities
- major towns
- international airports
- major roads
- major industrial areas

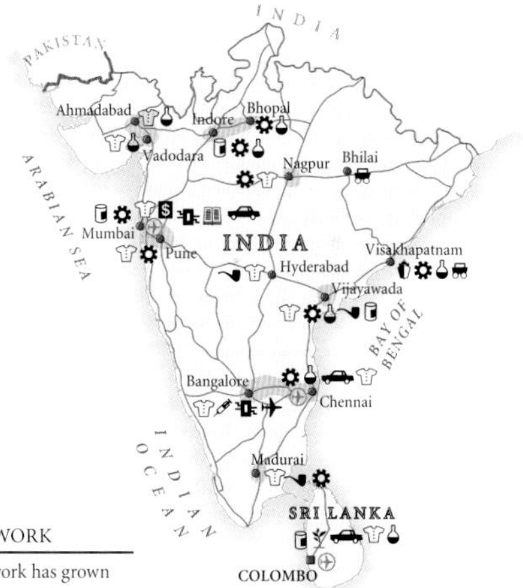

TRANSPORTATION NETWORK

India's hard-surfaced road network has grown almost tenfold since independence, yet many villages are still only accessible on foot, even in densely populated rural areas.

Mumbai *is one of the largest and most densely-populated cities in the world. It is the center of India's textile trade and has important finance and commerce sectors.*

SCALE 1: 7,000,000
(projection: Lambert Conformal Conic)

Km 0 25 50 100 150 200 250 300
Miles 0 25 50 100 150 200 250 300

Mainland East Asia

China, Mongolia, North Korea, South Korea, Taiwan

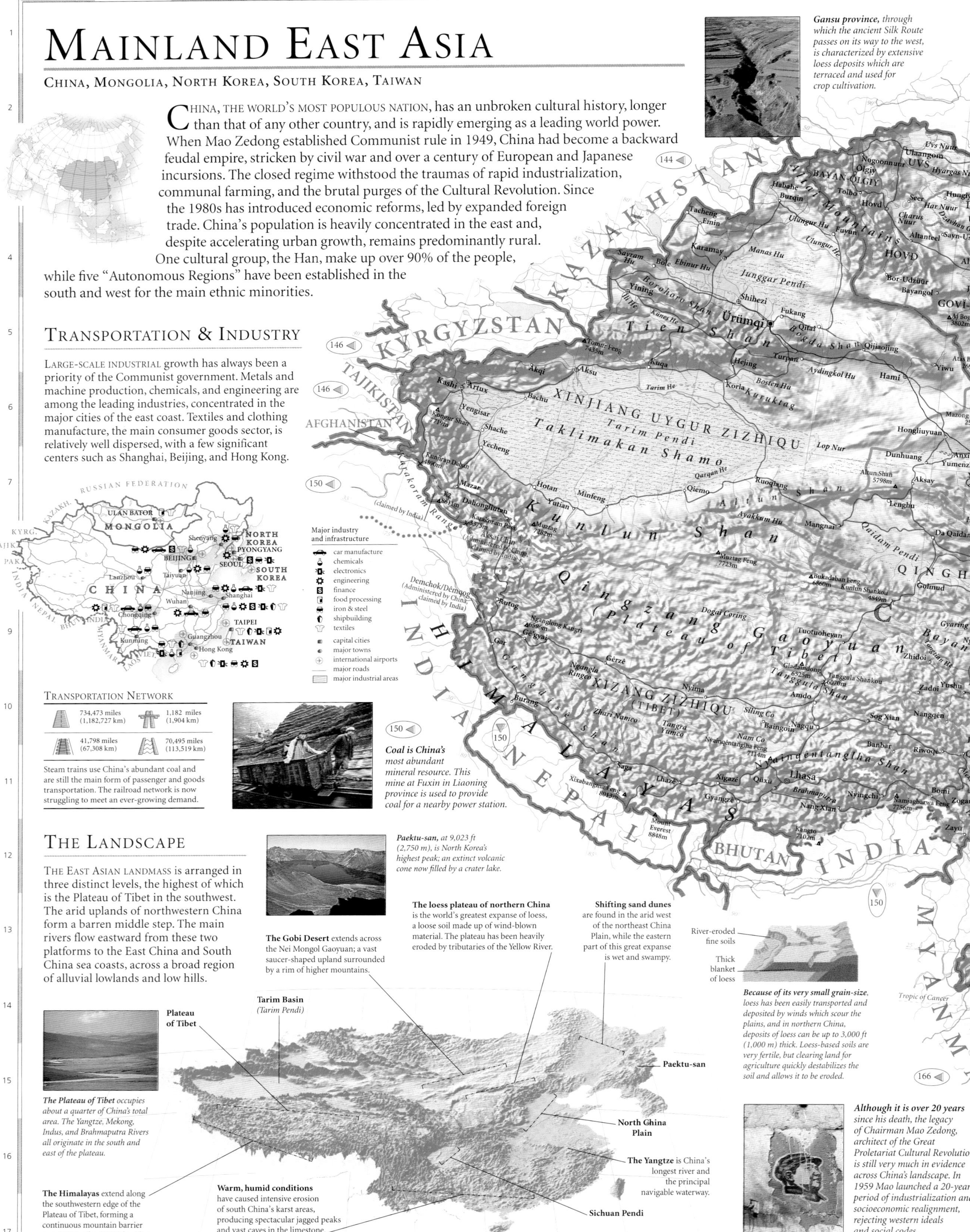

KAZAKHSTAN
KYRGYZSTAN
TAJIKISTAN
AFGHANISTAN
BHUTAN
INDIA
NEPAL
MYANMAR
XINJIANG UYGUR ZIZHIQU
Taklimakan Shamo
Tarim Pendi
Junggar Pendi
Tien Shan
Kunlun Shan
Qingzang Gaoyuan (Plateau of Tibet)
XIZANG ZIZHIQU (TIBET)
HIMALAYAS
Altay Mountains
Ürümqi
Kashi
Hotan
Lhasa
Shigatse
Mount Everest 8848m
Muztag Feng 7723m
Tropic of Cancer

CHINA, THE WORLD'S MOST POPULOUS NATION, has an unbroken cultural history, longer than that of any other country, and is rapidly emerging as a leading world power. When Mao Zedong established Communist rule in 1949, China had become a backward feudal empire, stricken by civil war and over a century of European and Japanese incursions. The closed regime withstood the traumas of rapid industrialization, communal farming, and the brutal purges of the Cultural Revolution. Since the 1980s has introduced economic reforms, led by expanded foreign trade. China's population is heavily concentrated in the east and, despite accelerating urban growth, remains predominantly rural. One cultural group, the Han, make up over 90% of the people, while five "Autonomous Regions" have been established in the south and west for the main ethnic minorities.

Gansu province, through which the ancient Silk Route passes on its way to the west, is characterized by extensive loess deposits which are terraced and used for crop cultivation.

Transportation & Industry

LARGE-SCALE INDUSTRIAL growth has always been a priority of the Communist government. Metals and machine production, chemicals, and engineering are among the leading industries, concentrated in the major cities of the east coast. Textiles and clothing manufacture, the main consumer goods sector, is relatively well dispersed, with a few significant centers such as Shanghai, Beijing, and Hong Kong.

RUSSIAN FEDERATION
ULAN BATOR
MONGOLIA
NORTH KOREA
PYONGYANG
BEIJING
SEOUL
SOUTH KOREA
CHINA
Shenyang
Lanzhou
Taiyuan
Nanjing
Shanghai
Wuhan
Chongqing
Kunming
Guangzhou
Hong Kong
TAIPEI
TAIWAN
Major industry and infrastructure
car manufacture
chemicals
electronics
engineering
finance
food processing
iron & steel
shipbuilding
textiles
capital cities
major towns
international airports
major roads
major industrial areas

Transportation Network

734,473 miles (1,182,727 km)	1,182 miles (1,904 km)
41,798 miles (67,308 km)	70,495 miles (113,519 km)

Steam trains use China's abundant coal and are still the main form of passenger and goods transportation. The railroad network is now struggling to meet an ever-growing demand.

Coal is China's most abundant mineral resource. This mine at Fuxin in Liaoning province is used to provide coal for a nearby power station.

The Landscape

THE EAST ASIAN LANDMASS is arranged in three distinct levels, the highest of which is the Plateau of Tibet in the southwest. The arid uplands of northwestern China form a barren middle step. The main rivers flow eastward from these two platforms to the East China and South China sea coasts, across a broad region of alluvial lowlands and low hills.

Paektu-san, at 9,023 ft (2,750 m), is North Korea's highest peak; an extinct volcanic cone now filled by a crater lake.

The loess plateau of northern China is the world's greatest expanse of loess, a loose soil made up of wind-blown material. The plateau has been heavily eroded by tributaries of the Yellow River.

Shifting sand dunes are found in the arid west of the northeast China Plain, while the eastern part of this great expanse is wet and swampy.

The Gobi Desert extends across the Nei Mongol Gaoyuan; a vast saucer-shaped upland surrounded by a rim of higher mountains.

River-eroded fine soils
Thick blanket of loess

Because of its very small grain-size, loess has been easily transported and deposited by winds which scour the plains, and in northern China, deposits of loess can be up to 3,000 ft (1,000 m) thick. Loess-based soils are very fertile, but clearing land for agriculture quickly destabilizes the soil and allows it to be eroded.

Tarim Basin *(Tarim Pendi)*

Plateau of Tibet

Paektu-san

North China Plain

The Plateau of Tibet occupies about a quarter of China's total area. The Yangtze, Mekong, Indus, and Brahmaputra Rivers all originate in the south and east of the plateau.

The Yangtze is China's longest river and the principal navigable waterway.

Sichuan Pendi

The Himalayas extend along the southwestern edge of the Plateau of Tibet, forming a continuous mountain barrier over 1,500 miles (2,500 km) long.

Warm, humid conditions have caused intensive erosion of south China's karst areas, producing spectacular jagged peaks and vast caves in the limestone.

Although it is over 20 years since his death, the legacy of Chairman Mao Zedong, architect of the Great Proletariat Cultural Revolution is still very much in evidence across China's landscape. In 1959 Mao launched a 20-year period of industrialization and socioeconomic realignment, rejecting western ideals and social codes.

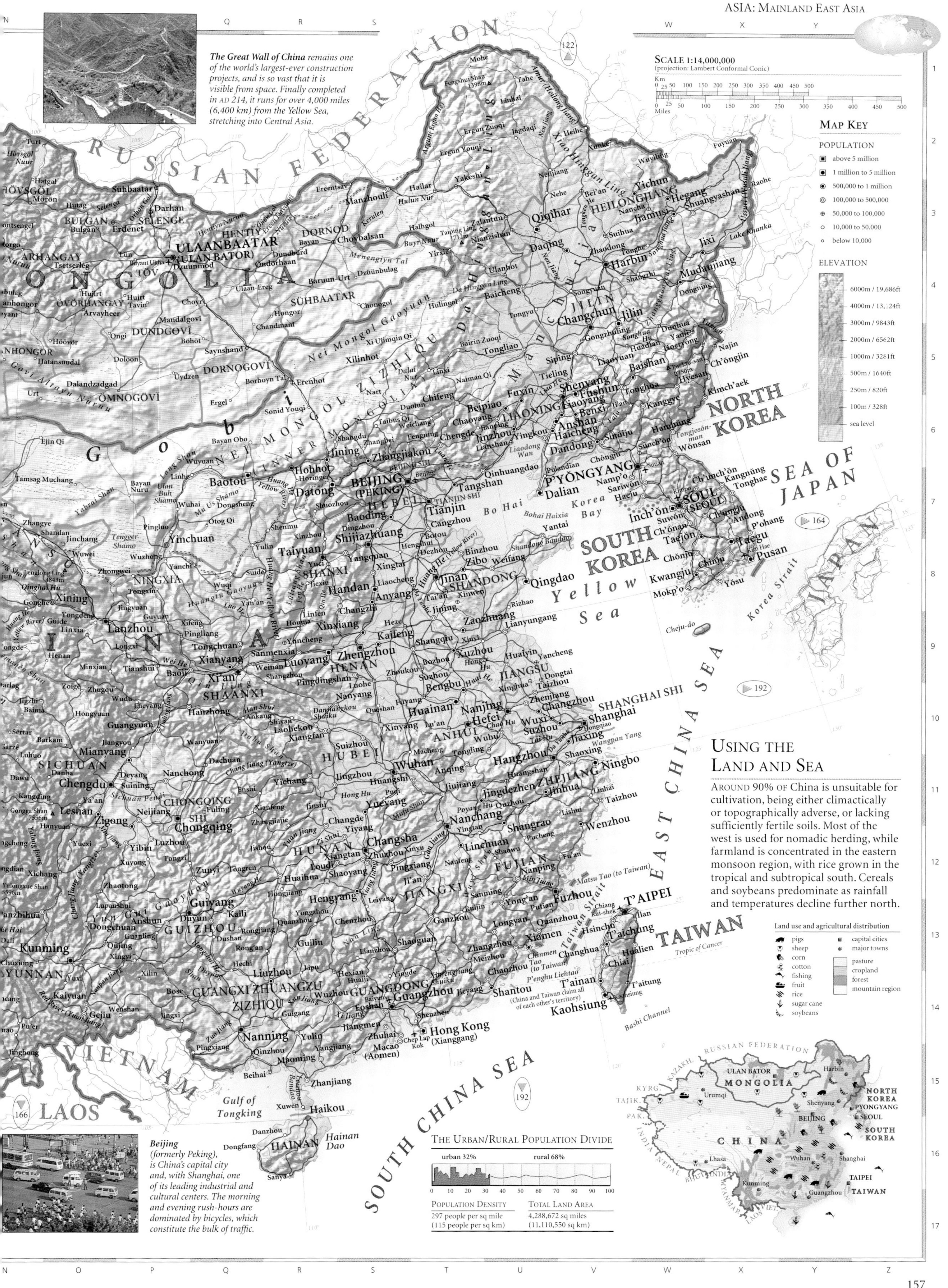
SCALE 1:14,000,000
(projection: Lambert Conformal Conic)
Km
Miles
MAP KEY
POPULATION
above 5 million
1 million to 5 million
500,000 to 1 million
100,000 to 500,000
50,000 to 100,000
10,000 to 50,000
below 10,000
ELEVATION
6000m / 19,686ft
4000m / 13,124ft
3000m / 9843ft
2000m / 6562ft
1000m / 3281ft
500m / 1640ft
250m / 820ft
100m / 328ft
sea level
RUSSIAN FEDERATION
MONGOLIA
ULAANBAATAR (ULAN BATOR)
CHINA
BEIJING (PEKING)
NORTH KOREA
P'YONGYANG
SOUTH KOREA
SOUL (SEOUL)
JAPAN
SEA OF JAPAN
Yellow Sea
Korea Bay
Bo Hai
EAST CHINA SEA
SOUTH CHINA SEA
TAIWAN
T'AIPEI
Taiwan Strait
Korea Strait
Bashi Channel
Tropic of Cancer
Gulf of Tongking
VIETNAM
LAOS
HAINAN
Hainan Dao
Gobi
Hong Kong (Xianggang)
Macao (Aomen)
Shanghai
SHANGHAI SHI
Tianjin
Harbin
HEILONGJIANG
JILIN
LIAONING
HEBEI
SHANXI
SHANDONG
HENAN
JIANGSU
ANHUI
HUBEI
ZHEJIANG
JIANGXI
FUJIAN
HUNAN
GUANGDONG
GUANGXI ZHUANGZU ZIZHIQU
GUIZHOU
YUNNAN
SICHUAN
CHONGQING SHI
SHAANXI
NINGXIA
NEI MONGOL ZIZHIQU (INNER MONGOLIA)
(China and Taiwan claim all of each other's territory)
Land use and agricultural distribution
pigs
sheep
corn
cotton
fishing
fruit
rice
sugar cane
soybeans
capital cities
major towns
pasture
cropland
forest
mountain region

The Great Wall of China *remains one of the world's largest-ever construction projects, and is so vast that it is visible from space. Finally completed in AD 214, it runs for over 4,000 miles (6,400 km) from the Yellow Sea, stretching into Central Asia.*

USING THE LAND AND SEA

AROUND 90% OF China is unsuitable for cultivation, being either climactically or topographically adverse, or lacking sufficiently fertile soils. Most of the west is used for nomadic herding, while farmland is concentrated in the eastern monsoon region, with rice grown in the tropical and subtropical south. Cereals and soybeans predominate as rainfall and temperatures decline further north.

THE URBAN/RURAL POPULATION DIVIDE

urban 32% | rural 68%

POPULATION DENSITY	TOTAL LAND AREA
297 people per sq mile (115 people per sq km)	4,288,672 sq miles (11,110,550 sq km)

Beijing *(formerly Peking), is China's capital city and, with Shanghai, one of its leading industrial and cultural centers. The morning and evening rush-hours are dominated by bicycles, which constitute the bulk of traffic.*

Western China

Gansu, Ningxia, Qinghai, Tibet, Xinjiang

The plateaus and basins of China's dry, desolate western domain are sparsely populated and largely undeveloped, although they have rich mineral reserves; they also form a critical buffer zone for China, in a geographically important and culturally sensitive part of the Asian continent. Across most of the west, the Han Chinese are outnumbered by a range of cultural groups, including the Uygur, the largest group of the various seminomadic Muslim peoples from Central Asia. The remote, inhospitable Plateau of Tibet is the world's coldest and highest plateau. It has been occupied by the Chinese since 1950. Tibet is one of western China's five "Autonomous Regions," but its reclusive Buddhist culture has been systematically undermined by the Chinese government.

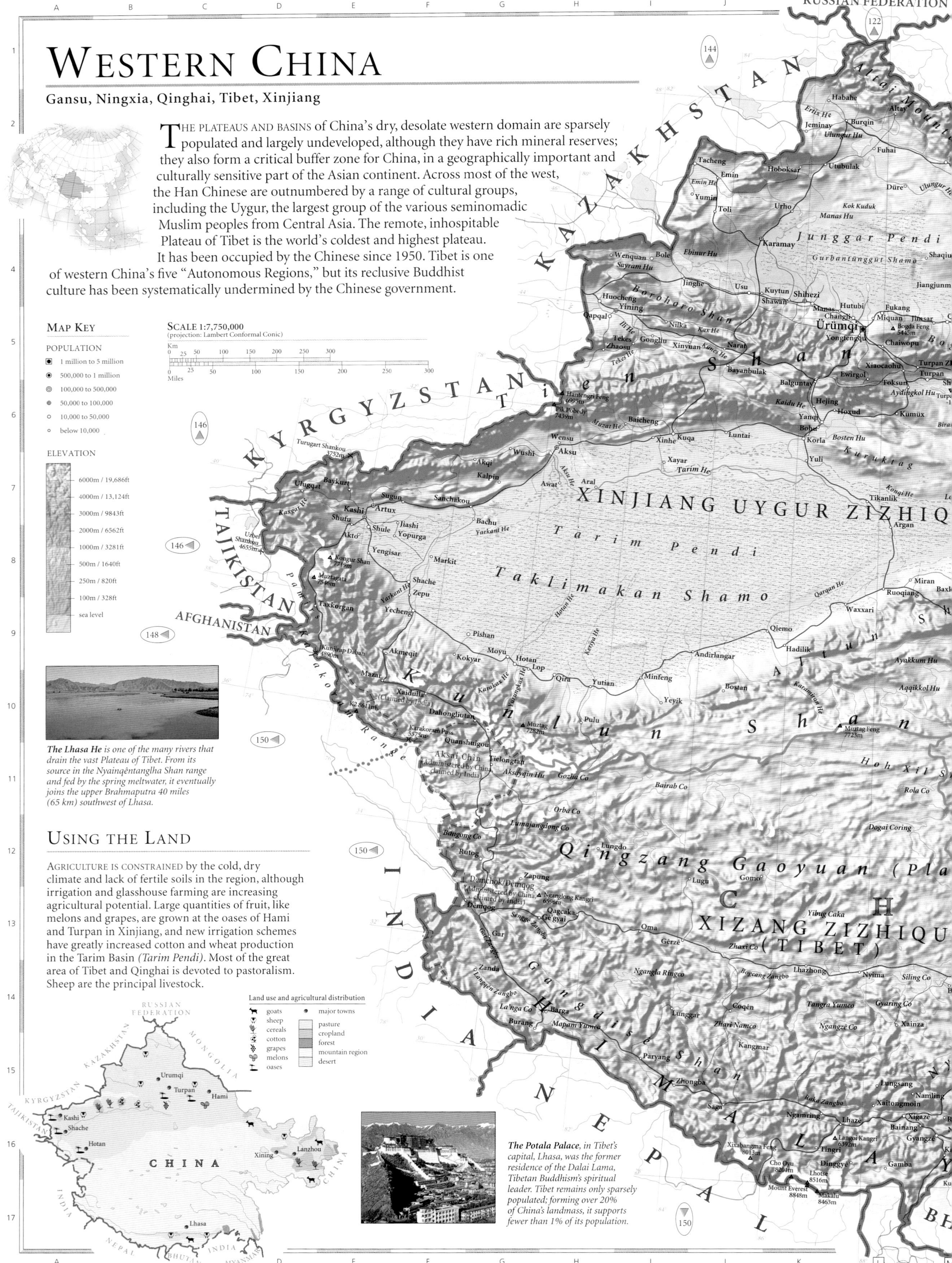
Map Key
Population
1 million to 5 million
500,000 to 1 million
100,000 to 500,000
50,000 to 100,000
10,000 to 50,000
below 10,000
Elevation
6000m / 19,686ft
4000m / 13,124ft
3000m / 9843ft
2000m / 6562ft
1000m / 3281ft
500m / 1640ft
250m / 820ft
100m / 328ft
sea level
Scale 1:7,750,000
(projection: Lambert Conformal Conic)
Km 0 25 50 100 150 200 250 300
Miles 0 25 50 100 150 200 250 300
RUSSIAN FEDERATION
KAZAKHSTAN
KYRGYZSTAN
TAJIKISTAN
AFGHANISTAN
INDIA
NEPAL
XINJIANG UYGUR ZIZHIQU
XIZANG ZIZHIQU (TIBET)
Tarim Pendi
Taklimakan Shamo
Junggar Pendi
Tien Shan
Kunlun Shan
Altun Shan
Qingzang Gaoyuan (Plateau of Tibet)
Gangdisê Shan
Himalaya
Karakoram Range
Pamirs
Ürümqi
Kashi
Hotan
Aksu
Yining
Karamay
Turpan
Shache
Yecheng
Korla
Tacheng
Altay
Pik Pobedy 7439m
Hantengri Feng 6995m
K2 8611m
Mount Everest 8848m
Muztag Feng 7723m
Aksai Chin (Administered by China, claimed by India)
Land use and agricultural distribution
goats
sheep
cereals
cotton
grapes
melons
oases
major towns
pasture
cropland
forest
mountain region
desert
CHINA
Urumqi
Turpan
Hami
Kashi
Shache
Hotan
Xining
Lanzhou
Lhasa
MONGOLIA
BHUTAN
MYANMAR

The Lhasa He is one of the many rivers that drain the vast Plateau of Tibet. From its source in the Nyainqêntanglha Shan range and fed by the spring meltwater, it eventually joins the upper Brahmaputra 40 miles (65 km) southwest of Lhasa.

Using the Land

Agriculture is constrained by the cold, dry climate and lack of fertile soils in the region, although irrigation and glasshouse farming are increasing agricultural potential. Large quantities of fruit, like melons and grapes, are grown at the oases of Hami and Turpan in Xinjiang, and new irrigation schemes have greatly increased cotton and wheat production in the Tarim Basin *(Tarim Pendi)*. Most of the great area of Tibet and Qinghai is devoted to pastoralism. Sheep are the principal livestock.

***The Potala Palace**, in Tibet's capital, Lhasa, was the former residence of the Dalai Lama, Tibetan Buddhism's spiritual leader. Tibet remains only sparsely populated; forming over 20% of China's landmass, it supports fewer than 1% of its population.*

THE LANDSCAPE

THE HIMALAYAS MARK the southwestern edge of the Plateau of Tibet, an extreme mountain wilderness which occupies nearly a quarter of China's total area. A large structural depression, the Qaidam Pendi, lies at its northeastern edge. The Kunlun mountain chain isolates the plateau from the desert to the north, where the Tien Shan range forms a spur between the Tarim Basin *(Tarim Pendi)* and Dzungarian Basin *(Junggar Pendi)*.

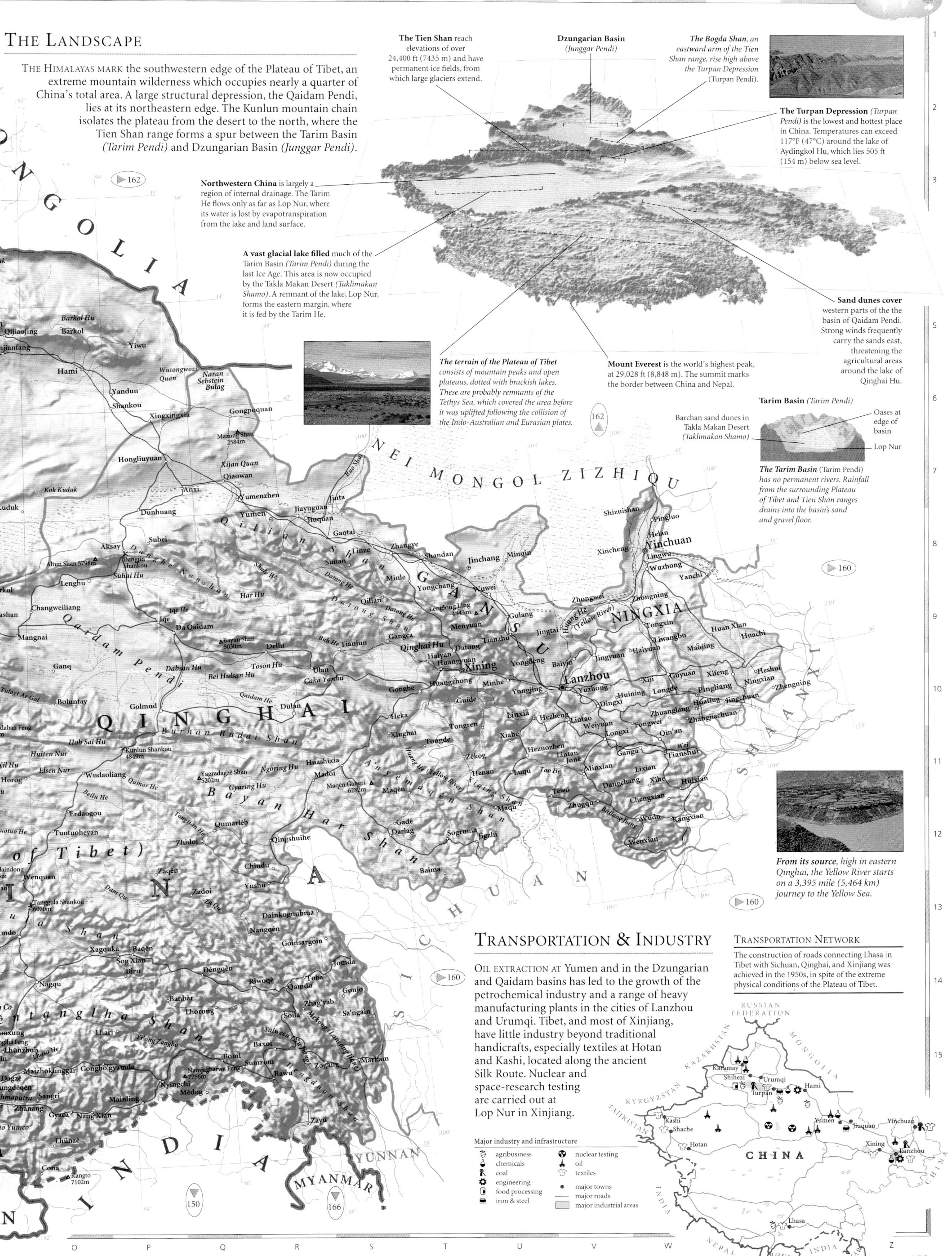

O P Q R S T U V W X Y
1 2 3 5 6 7 8 9 10 11 12 13 14 15
Dzungarian Basin (Junggar Pendi)
Tarim Basin (Tarim Pendi)
Barchan sand dunes in Takla Makan Desert (Taklimakan Shamo)
Oases at edge of basin
Lop Nur
MONGOLIA
NEI MONGOL ZIZHIQU
GANSU
NINGXIA
QINGHAI
SICHUAN
SHAANXI
YUNNAN
MYANMAR
INDIA
Qaidam Pendi
Qilian Shan
Burhan Budai Shan
Bayan Har Shan
A'nyêmaqên Shan
Tanggula Shan
Nyainqêntanglha Shan
Plateau of Tibet
Xining
Lanzhou
Yinchuan
Golmud
Yumen
Dunhuang
Hami
Qinghai Hu
Huang He (Yellow River)
Mekong (Lancang Jiang)
Salween (Nu Jiang)
162
160
150
166
Major industry and infrastructure
agribusiness
chemicals
coal
engineering
food processing
iron & steel
nuclear testing
oil
textiles
major towns
major roads
major industrial areas
RUSSIAN FEDERATION
KAZAKHSTAN
MONGOLIA
KYRGYZSTAN
TAJIKISTAN
CHINA
INDIA
NEPAL
BHUTAN
MYANMAR
Karamay
Shihezi
Urumqi
Turpan
Hami
Kashi
Shache
Hotan
Yumen
Jiuquan
Yinchuan
Xining
Lanzhou
Lhasa

The Tien Shan reach elevations of over 24,400 ft (7435 m) and have permanent ice fields, from which large glaciers extend.

The Bogda Shan, an eastward arm of the Tien Shan range, rise high above the Turpan Depression (Turpan Pendi).

The Turpan Depression *(Turpan Pendi)* is the lowest and hottest place in China. Temperatures can exceed 117°F (47°C) around the lake of Aydingkol Hu, which lies 505 ft (154 m) below sea level.

Northwestern China is largely a region of internal drainage. The Tarim He flows only as far as Lop Nur, where its water is lost by evapotranspiration from the lake and land surface.

A vast glacial lake filled much of the Tarim Basin *(Tarim Pendi)* during the last Ice Age. This area is now occupied by the Takla Makan Desert *(Taklimakan Shamo)*. A remnant of the lake, Lop Nur, forms the eastern margin, where it is fed by the Tarim He.

Sand dunes cover western parts of the the basin of Qaidam Pendi. Strong winds frequently carry the sands east, threatening the agricultural areas around the lake of Qinghai Hu.

The terrain of the Plateau of Tibet *consists of mountain peaks and open plateaus, dotted with brackish lakes. These are probably remnants of the Tethys Sea, which covered the area before it was uplifted following the collision of the Indo-Australian and Eurasian plates.*

Mount Everest is the world's highest peak, at 29,028 ft (8,848 m). The summit marks the border between China and Nepal.

The Tarim Basin (Tarim Pendi) *has no permanent rivers. Rainfall from the surrounding Plateau of Tibet and Tien Shan ranges drains into the basin's sand and gravel floor.*

From its source, *high in eastern Qinghai, the Yellow River starts on a 3,395 mile (5,464 km) journey to the Yellow Sea.*

TRANSPORTATION & INDUSTRY

OIL EXTRACTION AT Yumen and in the Dzungarian and Qaidam basins has led to the growth of the petrochemical industry and a range of heavy manufacturing plants in the cities of Lanzhou and Urumqi. Tibet, and most of Xinjiang, have little industry beyond traditional handicrafts, especially textiles at Hotan and Kashi, located along the ancient Silk Route. Nuclear and space-research testing are carried out at Lop Nur in Xinjiang.

TRANSPORTATION NETWORK

The construction of roads connecting Lhasa in Tibet with Sichuan, Qinghai, and Xinjiang was achieved in the 1950s, in spite of the extreme physical conditions of the Plateau of Tibet.

Eastern China

Taiwan, Anhui, Beijing, Fujian, Guangdong, Guangxi, Guizhou, Hainan, Hebei, Henan, Hubei, Hunan, Jiangsu, Jiangxi, Shaanxi, Shandong, Shanghai, Shanxi, Sichuan, Tianjin, Yunnan, Zhejiang

The east is China's heartland. Massive industrial development since 1949 has transformed much of the densely populated rural landscape, in a region still prone to flooding and drought. Over 20 cities have populations of over a million, including the giant metropolis of Shanghai and the capital Beijing, which has been China's cultural and political center since the 13th century. The ethnically diverse southwest and the oil-rich interior provinces of Sichuan and Shaanxi have largely missed out on the remarkable economic growth occurring in designated free-trade areas along the coasts of the South and East China seas. The republic of Taiwan was established in 1949 by Chinese nationalists ousted from the mainland by the victorious Communist forces. Taiwan now has one of the strongest economies in the world but its sovereignty is not recognized by China. Hong Kong provides a major international trade link for China; a 99-year "lease" period of British control was concluded in 1997.

North of the Qin Ling range in Shaanxi province, is an agriculturally fertile region covered with fine, wind-blown deposits and known as the loess plateau. The loose sediments are vulnerable to water erosion.

Using the Land and Sea

This is a region of intensive cultivation. Wheat, millet, sorghum, and cotton are the main crops of the Yellow River basin. South from Sichuan, rice becomes the principal crop, grown with wheat, corn, and cotton along the Yangtze River. Tea is produced in the hills and sugar cane along the coast of the southeast, where flat land is limited. Pigs and poultry are raised in great numbers.

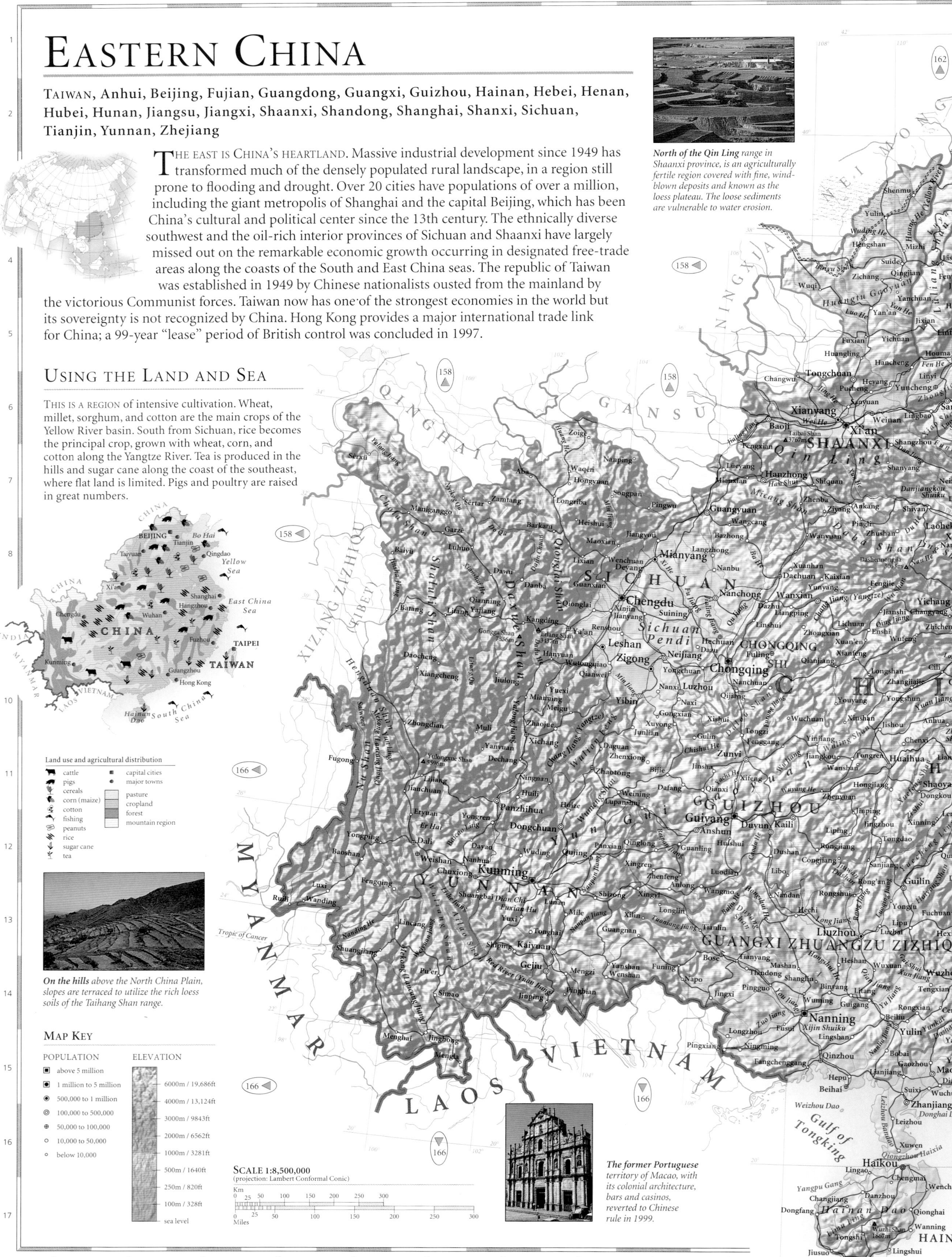

Land use and agricultural distribution
cattle
pigs
cereals
corn (maize)
cotton
fishing
peanuts
rice
sugar cane
tea
capital cities
major towns
pasture
cropland
forest
mountain region
MAP KEY
POPULATION
above 5 million
1 million to 5 million
500,000 to 1 million
100,000 to 500,000
50,000 to 100,000
10,000 to 50,000
below 10,000
ELEVATION
6000m / 19,686ft
4000m / 13,124ft
3000m / 9843ft
2000m / 6562ft
1000m / 3281ft
500m / 1640ft
250m / 820ft
100m / 328ft
sea level
SCALE 1:8,500,000
(projection: Lambert Conformal Conic)

On the hills above the North China Plain, slopes are terraced to utilize the rich loess soils of the Taihang Shan range.

The former Portuguese territory of Macao, with its colonial architecture, bars and casinos, reverted to Chinese rule in 1999.

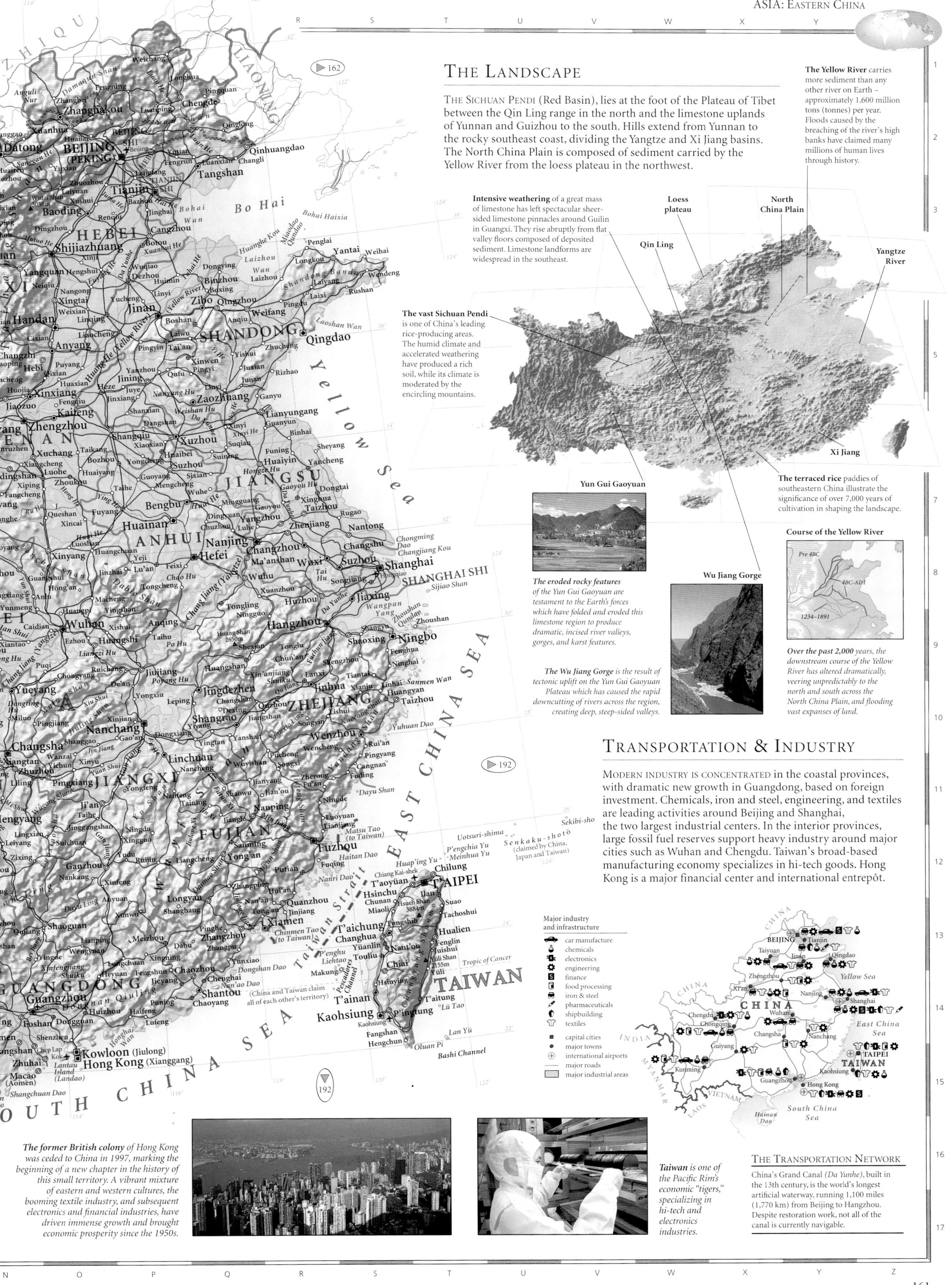
Loess plateau
North China Plain
Qin Ling
Yangtze River
Xi Jiang
Yun Gui Gaoyuan
Wu Jiang Gorge
Course of the Yellow River
Pre 4BC
4BC-AD1
1234-1891
Major industry and infrastructure
car manufacture
chemicals
electronics
engineering
finance
food processing
iron & steel
pharmaceuticals
shipbuilding
textiles
capital cities
major towns
international airports
major roads
major industrial areas
SHANGHAI SHI
TAIWAN
East China Sea
South China Sea
Yellow Sea
Taiwan Strait

The Landscape

The Sichuan Pendi (Red Basin), lies at the foot of the Plateau of Tibet between the Qin Ling range in the north and the limestone uplands of Yunnan and Guizhou to the south. Hills extend from Yunnan to the rocky southeast coast, dividing the Yangtze and Xi Jiang basins. The North China Plain is composed of sediment carried by the Yellow River from the loess plateau in the northwest.

The Yellow River carries more sediment than any other river on Earth – approximately 1,600 million tons (tonnes) per year. Floods caused by the breaching of the river's high banks have claimed many millions of human lives through history.

Intensive weathering of a great mass of limestone has left spectacular sheer-sided limestone pinnacles around Guilin in Guangxi. They rise abruptly from flat valley floors composed of deposited sediment. Limestone landforms are widespread in the southeast.

The vast Sichuan Pendi is one of China's leading rice-producing areas. The humid climate and accelerated weathering have produced a rich soil, while its climate is moderated by the encircling mountains.

The terraced rice paddies of southeastern China illustrate the significance of over 7,000 years of cultivation in shaping the landscape.

The eroded rocky features of the Yun Gui Gaoyuan are testament to the Earth's forces which have folded and eroded this limestone region to produce dramatic, incised river valleys, gorges, and karst features.

The Wu Jiang Gorge is the result of tectonic uplift on the Yun Gui Gaoyuan Plateau which has caused the rapid downcutting of rivers across the region, creating deep, steep-sided valleys.

Over the past 2,000 years, the downstream course of the Yellow River has altered dramatically, veering unpredictably to the north and south across the North China Plain, and flooding vast expanses of land.

Transportation & Industry

Modern industry is concentrated in the coastal provinces, with dramatic new growth in Guangdong, based on foreign investment. Chemicals, iron and steel, engineering, and textiles are leading activities around Beijing and Shanghai, the two largest industrial centers. In the interior provinces, large fossil fuel reserves support heavy industry around major cities such as Wuhan and Chengdu. Taiwan's broad-based manufacturing economy specializes in hi-tech goods. Hong Kong is a major financial center and international entrepôt.

The former British colony of Hong Kong was ceded to China in 1997, marking the beginning of a new chapter in the history of this small territory. A vibrant mixture of eastern and western cultures, the booming textile industry, and subsequent electronics and financial industries, have driven immense growth and brought economic prosperity since the 1950s.

Taiwan is one of the Pacific Rim's economic "tigers," specializing in hi-tech and electronics industries.

The Transportation Network

China's Grand Canal *(Da Yunhe)*, built in the 13th century, is the world's longest artificial waterway, running 1,100 miles (1,770 km) from Beijing to Hangzhou. Despite restoration work, not all of the canal is currently navigable.

Northeastern China, Mongolia & Korea

Mongolia, North Korea, South Korea, Heilongjiang, Inner Mongolia, Jilin, Liaoning

This northerly region has been a domain of shifting borders and competing colonial powers for centuries. Mongolia was the heartland of Chinghiz Khan's vast Mongol empire in the 13th century, while northeastern China was home to the Manchus, China's last ruling dynasty (1644–1911). The mineral and forest wealth of the northeast helped make this China's principal region of heavy industry, although the outdated state factories now face decline. South Korea's state-led market economy has grown dramatically and Seoul is now one of the world's largest cities. The austere communist regime of North Korea has isolated itself from the expanding markets of the Pacific Rim and faces continuing economic stagnation.

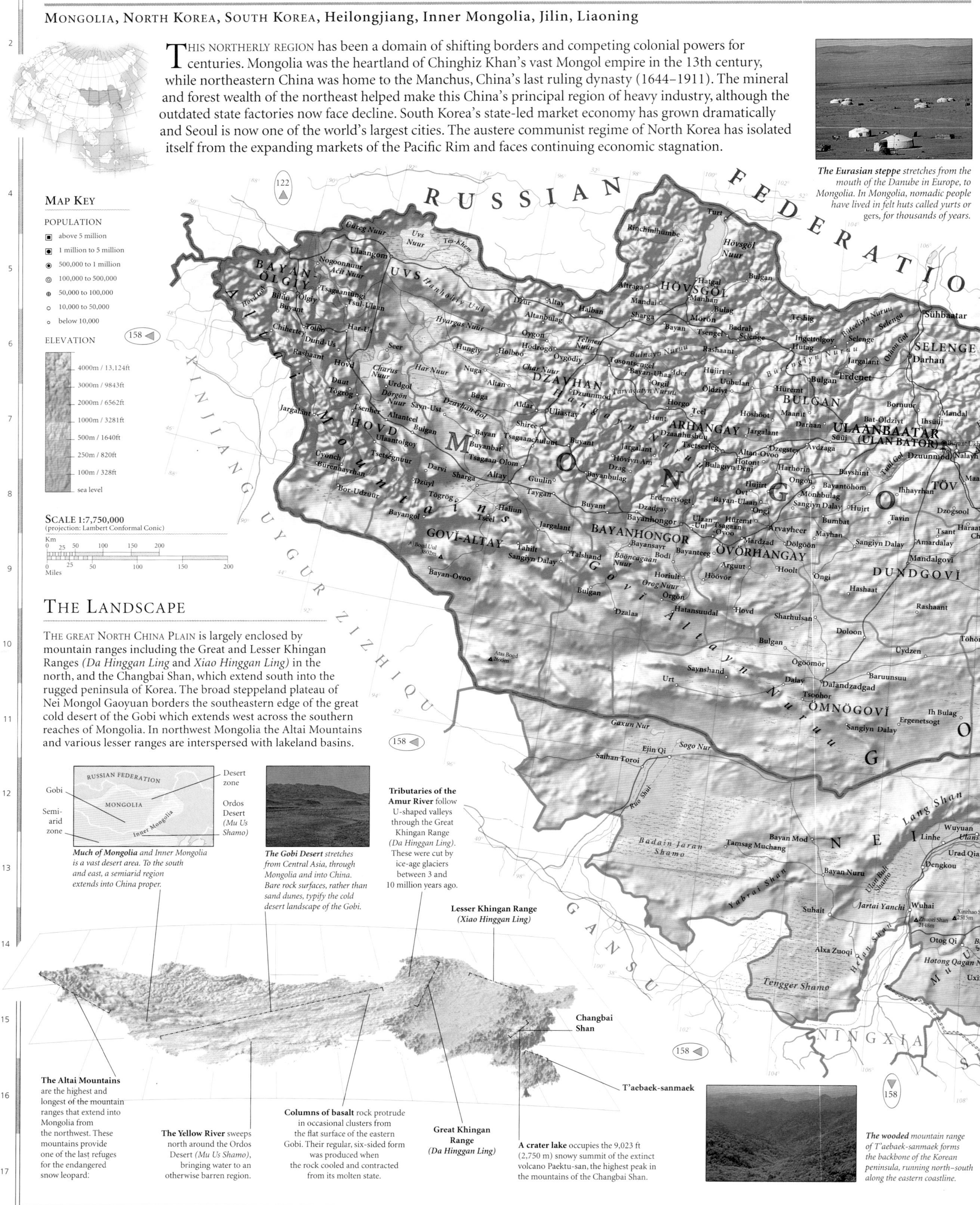

RUSSIAN FEDERATION
MONGOLIA
XINJIANG UYGUR ZIZHIQU
GANSU
NINGXIA
NEI MONGOL
BAYAN-ÖLGIY
UVS
HOVD
GOVĬ-ALTAY
DZAVHAN
HÖVSGÖL
ARHANGAY
BULGAN
SELENGE
BAYANHONGOR
ÖVÖRHANGAY
TÖV
DUNDGOVĬ
ÖMNÖGOVĬ
ULAANBAATAR (ULAN BATOR)
Altai Mountains
Govĭ Altayn Nuruu
Hangayn Nuruu
Hövsgöl Nuur
Uvs Nuur
Har-Us Nuur
Hyargas Nuur
Badain Jaran Shamo
Tengger Shamo
Mu Us Shamo
Gaxun Nur
Sogo Nur
Ulaangom
Ölgiy
Hovd
Uliastay
Altay
Darhan
Erdenet
Sühbaatar
Mörön
Bulgan
Tsetserleg
Arvayheer
Dalandzadgad
Mandalgovĭ
Saynshand
Ejin Qi
Wuhai

Map Key

POPULATION
- above 5 million
- 1 million to 5 million
- 500,000 to 1 million
- 100,000 to 500,000
- 50,000 to 100,000
- 10,000 to 50,000
- below 10,000

ELEVATION
- 4000m / 13,124ft
- 3000m / 9843ft
- 2000m / 6562ft
- 1000m / 3281ft
- 500m / 1640ft
- 250m / 820ft
- 100m / 328ft
- sea level

SCALE 1:7,750,000
(projection: Lambert Conformal Conic)

The Eurasian steppe stretches from the mouth of the Danube in Europe, to Mongolia. In Mongolia, nomadic people have lived in felt huts called yurts or gers, for thousands of years.

The Landscape

The great North China Plain is largely enclosed by mountain ranges including the Great and Lesser Khingan Ranges *(Da Hinggan Ling* and *Xiao Hinggan Ling)* in the north, and the Changbai Shan, which extend south into the rugged peninsula of Korea. The broad steppeland plateau of Nei Mongol Gaoyuan borders the southeastern edge of the great cold desert of the Gobi which extends west across the southern reaches of Mongolia. In northwest Mongolia the Altai Mountains and various lesser ranges are interspersed with lakeland basins.

Much of Mongolia and Inner Mongolia is a vast desert area. To the south and east, a semiarid region extends into China proper.

The Gobi Desert stretches from Central Asia, through Mongolia and into China. Bare rock surfaces, rather than sand dunes, typify the cold desert landscape of the Gobi.

Tributaries of the Amur River follow U-shaped valleys through the Great Khingan Range *(Da Hinggan Ling)*. These were cut by ice-age glaciers between 3 and 10 million years ago.

Lesser Khingan Range *(Xiao Hinggan Ling)*

Changbai Shan

T'aebaek-sanmaek

The Altai Mountains are the highest and longest of the mountain ranges that extend into Mongolia from the northwest. These mountains provide one of the last refuges for the endangered snow leopard.

The Yellow River sweeps north around the Ordos Desert *(Mu Us Shamo)*, bringing water to an otherwise barren region.

Columns of basalt rock protrude in occasional clusters from the flat surface of the eastern Gobi. Their regular, six-sided form was produced when the rock cooled and contracted from its molten state.

Great Khingan Range *(Da Hinggan Ling)*

A crater lake occupies the 9,023 ft (2,750 m) snowy summit of the extinct volcano Paektu-san, the highest peak in the mountains of the Changbai Shan.

The wooded mountain range of T'aebaek-sanmaek forms the backbone of the Korean peninsula, running north–south along the eastern coastline.

TRANSPORTATION & INDUSTRY

NORTH KOREA'S CENTRALLY-PLANNED ECONOMY is strongly oriented toward heavy industry, while South Korea has a broad manufacturing base which includes textiles, steel, electronics, and one of the world's largest shipbuilding industries. Mongolia and Inner Mongolia's great mineral resource potential is largely undeveloped. The heavy industrial region around Shenyang produces iron, steel, chemicals, and cement on a massive scale.

Ulan Bator, *the Mongolian capital bears many of the hallmarks of Soviet-style central planning, the result of economic and industrial assistance from the Soviet Union following Mongolian independence in 1921.*

TRANSPORTATION NETWORK

Liaoning has China's most comprehensive railroad network, the legacy of the Japanese occupation of Manchuria in the 20th century. The railroads are used primarily for freight transportation.

Major industry and infrastructure

- car manufacture
- chemicals
- coal
- electronics
- engineering
- finance
- food processing
- iron & steel
- pharmaceuticals
- shipbuilding
- textiles
- capital cities
- major towns
- international airports
- major roads
- major industrial areas

***While North Korea** has remained politically and economically isolated from the rest of the world, South Korea has enjoyed immense economic growth. It has benefited considerably from US economic aid in the aftermath of the Korean war of 1950–1953.*

USING THE LAND AND SEA

MONGOLIA AND INNER MONGOLIA rely heavily on livestock farming, with only about 1% of the land area cultivated. Northeastern China produces wheat, corn, soybeans, and sugar beet. The cool climate limits the range of crops and large upland areas of the northeast remain forested. Rice is the staple food of North and South Korea. The latter has become a leading ocean-fishing nation.

Land use and agricultural distribution

- goats
- pigs
- sheep
- corn
- fishing
- rice
- soybeans
- sugar beet
- wheat
- capital cities
- major towns
- pasture
- cropland
- forest
- mountain region
- desert

JAPAN

IN THE YEARS SINCE THE END of the Second World War, Japan has become the world's most dynamic industrial nation. The country comprises a string of over 4,000 islands which lie in a great northeast to southwest arc in the northwest Pacific. Four major islands: Hokkaido, Honshu, Shikoku, and Kyushu are home to the great majority of Japan's population of 125.9 million people, although the mountainous terrain of the central region means that most cities are situated on the coast. A densely populated industrial belt stretches along much of Honshu's southern coast, including Japan's crowded capital, Tokyo. Alongside its spectacular economic growth and the increasing westernization of its cities, Japan still maintains a most singular culture, reflected in its traditional food, formal behavioural codes, unique Shinto religion, and the reverence for the emperor, who is officially regarded as a god.

THE LANDSCAPE

THE ISLANDS OF JAPAN LIE on the Pacific "Ring of Fire," and form a series of clearly defined arcs. The largely mountainous landscape was formed very recently in geological terms. Volcanic eruptions and earthquakes continue to reshape the terrain and to shake the country's complex infrastructure. There is no one continuous mountain range; the mountains divide into many small land blocks separated by lowlands and dissected by numerous river valleys.

Sea of Japan
Active volcanic island
Japan Trench (subduction zone)

***Japan is part of** an arc of volcanic islands, formed by the Pacific Plate diving under the Eurasian Plate. This process generates intense stress which is periodically released as earthquakes.*

In much of Kyushu the coast is subsiding, giving a highly indented coastline. In some places, former hilltops are barely visible above the current sea level.

The Inland Sea (Seto-naikai) has resulted from the depression of faulted blocks which has allowed sea water to invade the region between northern Shikoku and western Honshu.

Biwa-ko is the largest lake in Japan, covering 260 sq miles (673 sq km) in central Honshu. The depression in which it lies was created by recent faulting of the underlying rocks.

A number of rivers which emerge from the volcanic parts of northeastern Honshu are so highly acidic that their water is unsuitable for irrigation and consumption.

There are over 60 active volcanoes like Asahi-dake, Hokkaido's highest peak – throughout Japan. This accounts for more than 10% of the world's total.

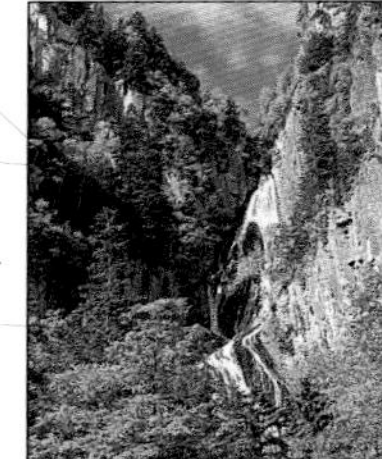

***Trees cling to the sheer slopes** of the waterfalls on the northern island of Hokkaido. The island's climate is similar to that in northern Europe, with long, cold winters and short, warm summers.*

Strong northwesterly winds blowing onshore during the winter create sand dunes which extend for miles along the western coasts.

Mount Fuji

Rising land on the Pacific coast of Honshu leads to typical features such as raised beaches, some lying over 1,000 ft (300 m) above sea level.

***Mount Fuji** is Japan's highest mountain, rising 12,388 ft (3,776 m) above the Kanto Plain in the central region of Honshu. The flat land below is suitable for growing crops such as tea. Like many Japanese mountains, it is revered as a sacred site.*

TRANSPORTATION & INDUSTRY

JAPAN IS THE WORLD'S second largest market economy, outranked only by the US. Technological development, particularly of computers, electronic goods, cars, and motorcycles is second to none. Japanese industry invests in its workforce, and in long-term research and development to maintain the high standard of its products, and a reputation for innovation. Japanese businesses are now global both in their manufacturing bases and in the distribution of goods.

Major industry and infrastructure
- brewing
- car manufacture
- chemicals
- hi-tech industry
- engineering
- finance
- iron & steel
- research & development
- shipbuilding
- textiles
- winter sports
- capital cities
- major towns
- international airports
- major roads
- major industrial areas

TRANSPORTATION NETWORK

roads	720,360 miles (1,160,000 km)	expressways	6,070 miles (12,529 km)
railways	12,529 miles (20,175 km)	waterways	1,099 miles (1,770 km)

Japanese road construction traditionally lagged behind that of its extensive and technologically advanced railroad network. The network's relative lack of development has led to severe urban congestion, although expressways have now been built in some cities.

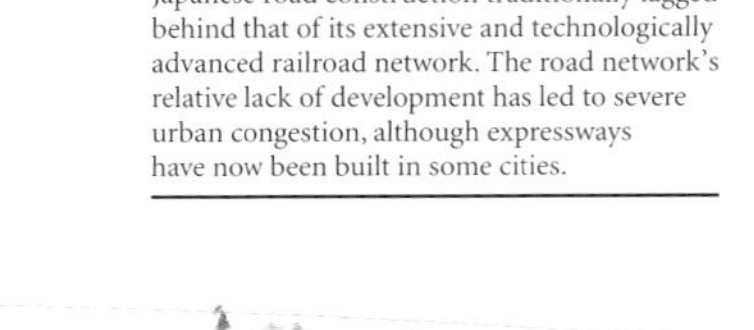

***Known in the west** as the "bullet train," the Shinkansen is the second-fastest train in the world. It speeds past the snow-capped peak of Mount Fuji between the cities of Tokyo and Osaka.*

157

***Autumnal trees** near Gifu, on central Honshu, create a spectacular display. Native trees on this island include camphor, pasania, Japanese evergreen oak, camellia, and holly.*

***The 1995 Kobe earthquake** highlighted Japan's vulnerability to earthquakes, despite technological advances. It shattered much of the infrastructure of this important port. More than 5,000 people died as buildings and overhead highways collapsed and fires broke out.*

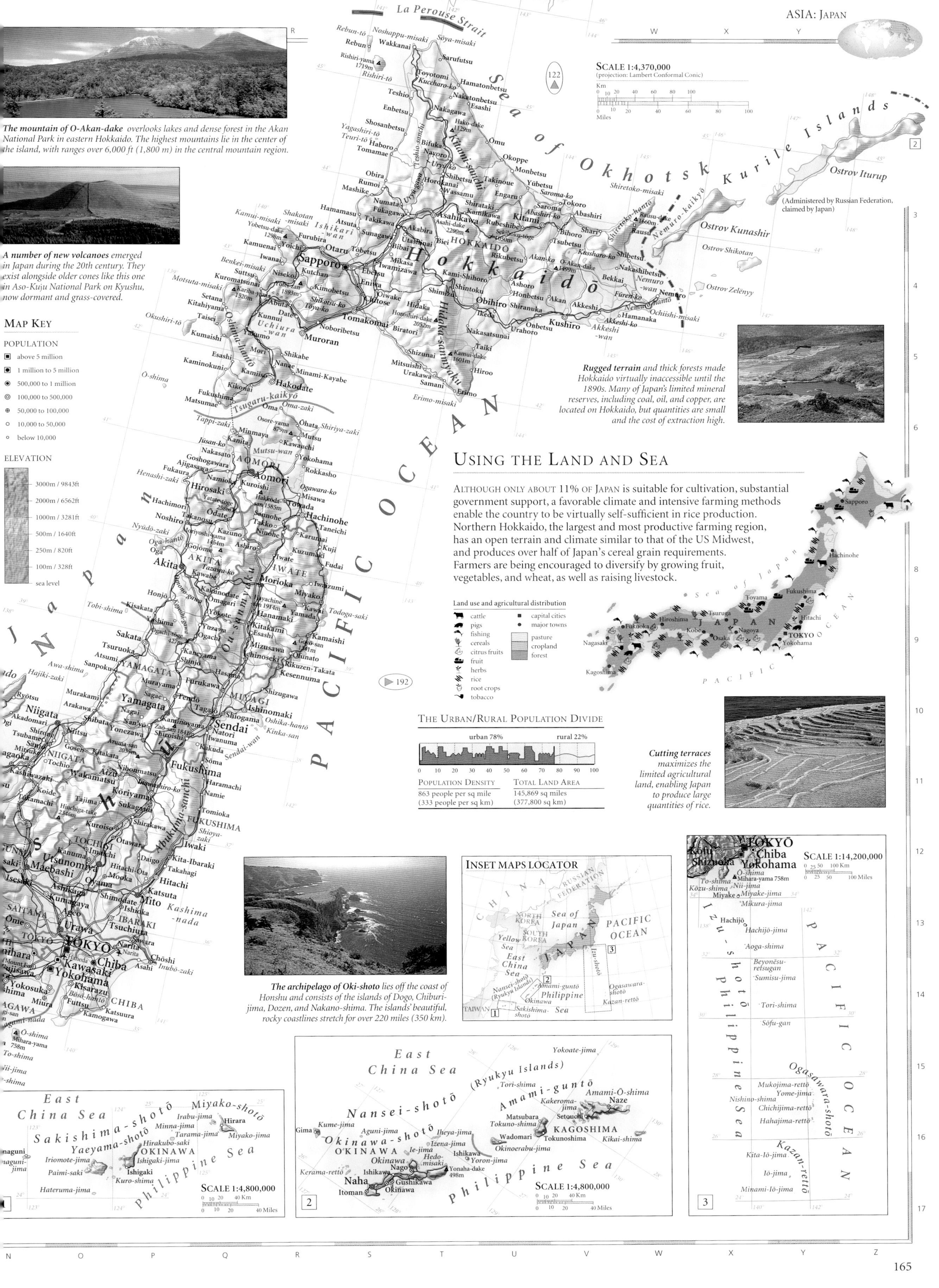
La Perouse Strait
Sea of Okhotsk
Kurile Islands
Ostrov Iturup
(Administered by Russian Federation, claimed by Japan)
Ostrov Kunashir
Ostrov Shikotan
Ostrov Zelënyy
Hokkaidō
Sapporo
Asahikawa
Hakodate
Muroran
Obihiro
Kushiro
Tomakomai
Tsugaru-kaikyō
Aomori
Hachinohe
Morioka
Akita
Sendai
Yamagata
Fukushima
Niigata
Utsunomiya
Maebashi
Mito
Chiba
Kawasaki
Yokohama
TOKYO
Sea of Japan
Honshu
PACIFIC OCEAN
SCALE 1:4,370,000
(projection: Lambert Conformal Conic)
MAP KEY
POPULATION
above 5 million
1 million to 5 million
500,000 to 1 million
100,000 to 500,000
50,000 to 100,000
10,000 to 50,000
below 10,000
ELEVATION
3000m / 9843ft
2000m / 6562ft
1000m / 3281ft
500m / 1640ft
250m / 820ft
100m / 328ft
sea level
Land use and agricultural distribution
cattle
pigs
fishing
cereals
citrus fruits
fruit
herbs
rice
root crops
tobacco
capital cities
major towns
pasture
cropland
forest
THE URBAN/RURAL POPULATION DIVIDE
urban 78%
rural 22%
POPULATION DENSITY
863 people per sq mile
(333 people per sq km)
TOTAL LAND AREA
145,869 sq miles
(377,800 sq km)
INSET MAPS LOCATOR
East China Sea
Nansei-shotō (Ryukyu Islands)
Sakishima-shotō
Okinawa
Naha
Philippine Sea
SCALE 1:4,800,000
Izu-shotō
Ogasawara-shotō
Kazan-rettō
SCALE 1:14,200,000
192
122

The mountain of O-Akan-dake overlooks lakes and dense forest in the Akan National Park in eastern Hokkaido. The highest mountains lie in the center of the island, with ranges over 6,000 ft (1,800 m) in the central mountain region.

A number of new volcanoes emerged in Japan during the 20th century. They exist alongside older cones like this one in Aso-Kuju National Park on Kyushu, now dormant and grass-covered.

Rugged terrain and thick forests made Hokkaido virtually inaccessible until the 1890s. Many of Japan's limited mineral reserves, including coal, oil, and copper, are located on Hokkaido, but quantities are small and the cost of extraction high.

Using the Land and Sea

Although only about 11% of Japan is suitable for cultivation, substantial government support, a favorable climate and intensive farming methods enable the country to be virtually self-sufficient in rice production. Northern Hokkaido, the largest and most productive farming region, has an open terrain and climate similar to that of the US Midwest, and produces over half of Japan's cereal grain requirements. Farmers are being encouraged to diversify by growing fruit, vegetables, and wheat, as well as raising livestock.

Cutting terraces maximizes the limited agricultural land, enabling Japan to produce large quantities of rice.

The archipelago of Oki-shoto lies off the coast of Honshu and consists of the islands of Dogo, Chiburi-jima, Dozen, and Nakano-shima. The islands' beautiful, rocky coastlines stretch for over 220 miles (350 km).

Mainland Southeast Asia

Cambodia, Laos, Myanmar, Thailand, Vietnam

Thickly forested mountains, intercut by the broad valleys of five great rivers characterize the landscape of Southeast Asia's mainland countries. Agriculture remains the main activity for much of the population, which is concentrated in the river flood plains and deltas. Linked ethnic and cultural roots give the region a distinct identity. Most people on the mainland are Theravada Buddhists. Foreign intervention began in the 16th century with the opening of the spice trade; Cambodia, Laos, and Vietnam were French colonies until the end of the Second World War, Myanmar was under British control. Only Thailand was never colonized. Today, Thailand is poised to play a leading role in the economic development of the Pacific Rim, and Laos and Vietnam have begun to mend the devastation of the Vietnam War, and to develop their economies. With continuing political instability and a shattered infrastructure, Cambodia faces an uncertain future, while Myanmar is seeking investment and the ending of its 38-year isolation from the world community.

The Irrawaddy River is Myanmar's vital central artery, watering the ricefields and providing a rich source of fish, as well as an important transportation link, particularly for local traffic.

The coastline of the Isthmus of Kra

Longshore drift
Spit
Eroded coastline
Lagoon
Wave attack

The east and west coasts of the Isthmus of Kra differ greatly. The tectonically uplifting west coast is exposed to the harsh south-westerly monsoon and is heavily eroded. On the east coast, longshore currents produce depositional features such as spits and lagoons.

The Landscape

A series of mountain ranges runs north–south through the mainland, formed as the result of the collision between the Eurasian Plate and the Indian subcontinent, which created the Himalayas. They are interspersed by the valleys of a number of great rivers. On their passage to the sea these rivers have deposited sediment, forming huge, fertile floodplains and deltas.

Hkakabo Razi is the highest point in mainland Southeast Asia. It rises 19,300 ft (5,885 m) at the border between China and Myanmar.

Mountains dominate the Laotian landscape with more than 90% of the land lying more than 600 ft (180 m) above sea level. The mountains of the Chaine Annamitique form the country's eastern border.

The Irrawaddy River runs virtually north–south, draining Myanmar. The Irrawaddy Delta is the country's main rice-growing area.

The Red River Delta in northern Vietnam is fringed to the north by steep-sided, round-topped limestone hills, typical of karst scenery.

Salween River

Mekong River

The fast-flowing waters of the Mekong River cascade over this waterfall in Champasak province in Laos. The force of the water erodes rocks at the base of the fall.

Isthmus of Kra

The coast of the Isthmus of Kra, in southeast Thailand has many small, precipitous islands like these, formed by chemical erosion on limestone, which is weathered along vertical cracks. The humidity of the climate in Southeast Asia increases the rate of weathering.

Malay Peninsula

Tonle Sap, a freshwater lake, drains into the Mekong Delta via the Mekong River. It is the largest lake in Southeast Asia.

The Mekong River flows through southern China and Myanmar, then for much of its length forms the border between Laos and Thailand, flowing through Cambodia before terminating in a vast delta on the southern Vietnamese coast.

Using the Land and Sea

The fertile floodplains of rivers such as the Mekong and Salween, and the humid climate, enable the production of rice throughout the region. Cambodia, Myanmar, and Laos still have substantial forests, producing hardwoods such as teak and rosewood. Cash crops include tropical fruits such as coconuts, bananas, and pineapples, rubber, oil palm, sugar cane and the jute substitute, kenaf. Pigs and cattle are the main livestock raised. Large quantities of marine and freshwater fish are caught throughout the region.

Commercial logging – still widespread in Myanmar – has now been stopped in Thailand because of overexploitation of the tropical rain forest.

The Urban/Rural Population Divide

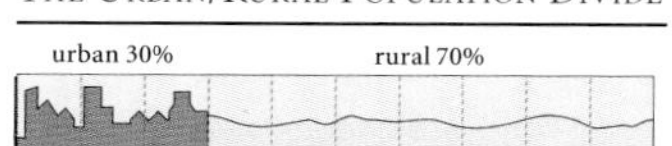

urban 30%
rural 70%
0 10 20 30 40 50 60 70 80 90 100

Population Density	Total Land Area
322 people per sq mile (124 people per sq km)	733,828 sq miles (1,901,110 sq km)

Land use and agricultural distribution

cattle
pigs
bananas
coconuts
fishing
oil palms
rice
rubber
sugar cane
timber
capital cities
major towns
pasture
cropland
forest
wetland

TRANSPORTATION & INDUSTRY

INDUSTRIAL MANUFACTURING has become increasingly important in Thailand and Vietnam in recent years. The assembling of component-based electrical and electronic goods is becoming more common throughout this region, with foreign companies benefiting from low labor costs and the upgrading of technology. The economies of Myanmar and Cambodia are still based on agricultural produce and the processing of raw materials. Tin is the region's most important metal, and nickel, copper, and chromite are also mined, although the quantities produced are not significant on a global scale. Thailand's successful tourist industry is the country's highest earner of foreign exchange.

Major industry and infrastructure
- chemicals
- electronics
- engineering
- food processing
- iron & steel
- oil & gas
- mining
- shipbuilding
- textiles
- timber processing
- capital cities
- major towns
- international airports
- major roads
- major industrial areas

TRANSPORTATION NETWORK

- 131,566 miles (211,845 km)
- 267 miles (430 km)
- 7,785 miles (12,536 km)
- 28,393 miles (45,722 km)

Transportation development has concentrated on the building of road networks. Water and sea transportation remain important, although air links have improved, particularly in Thailand.

***Opium poppies** are destroyed under army supervision in Thailand. This action is part of a government-sponsored initiative to reduce the trade in drugs such as heroin, which is derived from these plants. Drug trafficking is a major problem throughout the region; the area is known as the "Golden Triangle," and Laos is the third-largest producer of opium poppies in the world.*

SCALE 1:8,611,000
(projection: Lambert Conformal Conic)

***The city of Hue** in central Vietnam was the country's capital under the 13 emperors of the Nguyen dynasty from 1802 to 1945. It is the site of a number of religious monuments, including the Thien-Mu Pagoda.*

MAP KEY

POPULATION
- above 5 million
- 1 million to 5 million
- 500,000 to 1 million
- 100,000 to 500,000
- 50,000 to 100,000
- 10,000 to 50,000
- below 10,000

ELEVATION
- 4000m / 13,124ft
- 3000m / 9843ft
- 2000m / 6562ft
- 1000m / 3281ft
- 500m / 1640ft
- 250m / 820ft
- 100m / 328ft
- sea level

160
170
168

Western Maritime Southeast Asia

Indonesia, Malaysia, Brunei, Singapore

The world's largest archipelago, Indonesia's myriad islands stretch 3,100 miles (5,000 km) eastwards across the Pacific, from the Malay Peninsula to western New Guinea. Only about 1,500 of the 13,677 islands are inhabited and the huge, predominently Muslim population is unevenly distributed, with some two-thirds crowded onto the western islands of Java, Madura, and Bali. The national government is trying to resettle large numbers of people from these islands to other parts of the country to reduce population pressure there. Malaysia, split between the mainland and the east Malaysian states of Sabah and Sarawak on Borneo, has a diverse population, as well as a fast-growing economy, although the pace of its development is still far outstripped by that of Singapore. This small island nation is the financial and commercial capital of Southeast Asia. The Sultanate of Brunei in northern Borneo, one of the world's last princely states, has an extremely high standard of living, based on its oil revenues.

Ranks of gleaming skyscrapers, *new highways, and infrastructure construction reflect the investment that is pouring into Southeast Asian cities like the Malaysian capital, Kuala Lumpur. Many of the city's inhabitants subsist at a level far removed from the prosperity implied by its outward modernity.*

Transportation Network

160,350 miles (258,213 km)

188 miles (302 km)

5,482 miles (8,828 km)

8,827 miles (14,207,075 km)

Singapore's subway system is among the most efficient in the world. Malaysia has several fast, modern highways and most roads are paved. Java, Madura, and Sumatra have by far the most develope[d] land transportation networks in Indonesia.

Major industry and infrastructure

- aerospace
- copra processing
- chemicals
- electronics
- engineering
- finance
- food processing
- iron & steel
- oil
- ship building
- timber processing
- textiles
- capital cities
- major towns
- international airports
- major roads
- major industrial areas

SCALE 1:8,750,000 (projection: Mercator)

Km 0 25 50 100 150 200

0 25 50 100 150 200 Miles

166

172

The Landscape

Indonesia's western islands are characterized by rugged volcanic mountains cloaked with dense tropical forest, which slope down to coastal plains covered by thick alluvial swamps. The Sunda Shelf, an extension of the Eurasian Plate, lies between Java, Bali, Sumatra, and Borneo. These islands' mountains rise from a base below the sea, and they were once joined together by dry land, which has since been submerged by rising sea levels.

Danau (lake) Toba in Sumatra fills an enormous caldera 18 miles (30 km) wide and 62 miles (100 km) long – the largest in the world. It was formed through a combination of volcanic action and tectonic activity.

Borneo

Malay Peninsula

Sumatra

Drowned rivers

Broad, shallow valleys on sea floor

Present sea level

Quaternary sea level, 460 ft (140 m) below present sea level

The Sunda Shelf underlies this whole region. *It is one of the largest submarine shelves in the world, covering an area of 714,285 sq miles (1,850,000 sq km). During the early Quaternary period, when sea levels were lower, the shelf was exposed.*

Malay Peninsula has a rugged east coast, but the west coast, fronting the Strait of Malacca, has many sheltered beaches and bays. The two coasts are divided by the Banjaran Titiwangsa, which run the length of the peninsula.

The third largest island in the world, Borneo has a total area of 292,222 sq miles (757,050 sq km). Although mountainous, it is one of the most stable of the Indonesian islands, with little volcanic activity.

Gunung Kinabalu is the highest peak in Malaysia, rising 13,455 ft (4,101 m)

Much of eastern Sumatra is a low-lying swampy forest that is difficult to penetrate, seriously impeding the development of the inland area.

Sungai Mahakam River

The island of Krakatau (Palau Rakata), lying between Sumatra and Java, was all but destroyed in 1883, when the volcano erupted. The release of gas and dust into the atmosphere disrupted cloud cover and global weather patterns for several years.

Indonesia has around 220 active volcanoes and hundreds more that are considered extinct. They are strung out along the island arc from Sumatra and Java, then through the Lesser Sunda Islands and into the Moluccas and Sulawesi (see pages 170–171).

A large part of Borneo is drained by navigable rivers, the main, and often the only, lifelines of trade and commerce. The river of Sungai Mahakam cuts through the island's central highlands.

TRANSPORTATION & INDUSTRY

SINGAPORE HAS a thriving economy based on international trade and finance. Annual trade through the port is among the highest of any in the world. Indonesia's western islands still depend on natural resources, particularly petroleum, gas, and wood, although the economy is rapidly diversifying with manufactured exports including garments, consumer electronics, and footwear. A high-profile aircraft industry has developed in Bandung on Java. Malaysia has a fast-growing and varied manufacturing sector, although oil, gas, and timber remain important resource-based industries.

USING THE LAND AND SEA

Rice is the most important arable crop in Indonesia and Malaysia, and both countries manage to meet almost all of their domestic demand. Malaysian rubber accounts for 25% of world production and is the main cash crop, grown on plantations and small farms, along with oil palms and copra. Timber is exported from both Malaysia and Indonesia. Modern agricultural techniques enable Singapore to produce fruits and vegetables despite a shortage of suitable land.

Land use and agricultural distribution: coconuts, fishing, oil palms, rice, rubber, shellfish, sugar cane, timber; capital cities, major towns; pasture, cropland, forest, wetland

Spiral cuts in the bark of this rubber palm show where it has been tapped. Sophisticated cloning techniques mean that trees that produce consistently high quantities of rubber can be easily reproduced.

THE URBAN/RURAL POPULATION DIVIDE

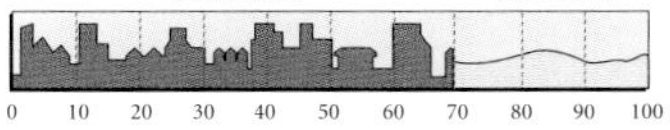

urban 70% — rural 30%

POPULATION DENSITY	TOTAL LAND AREA
196 people per sq mile (122 people per sq km)	922,807 sq miles (1,485,118 sq km)

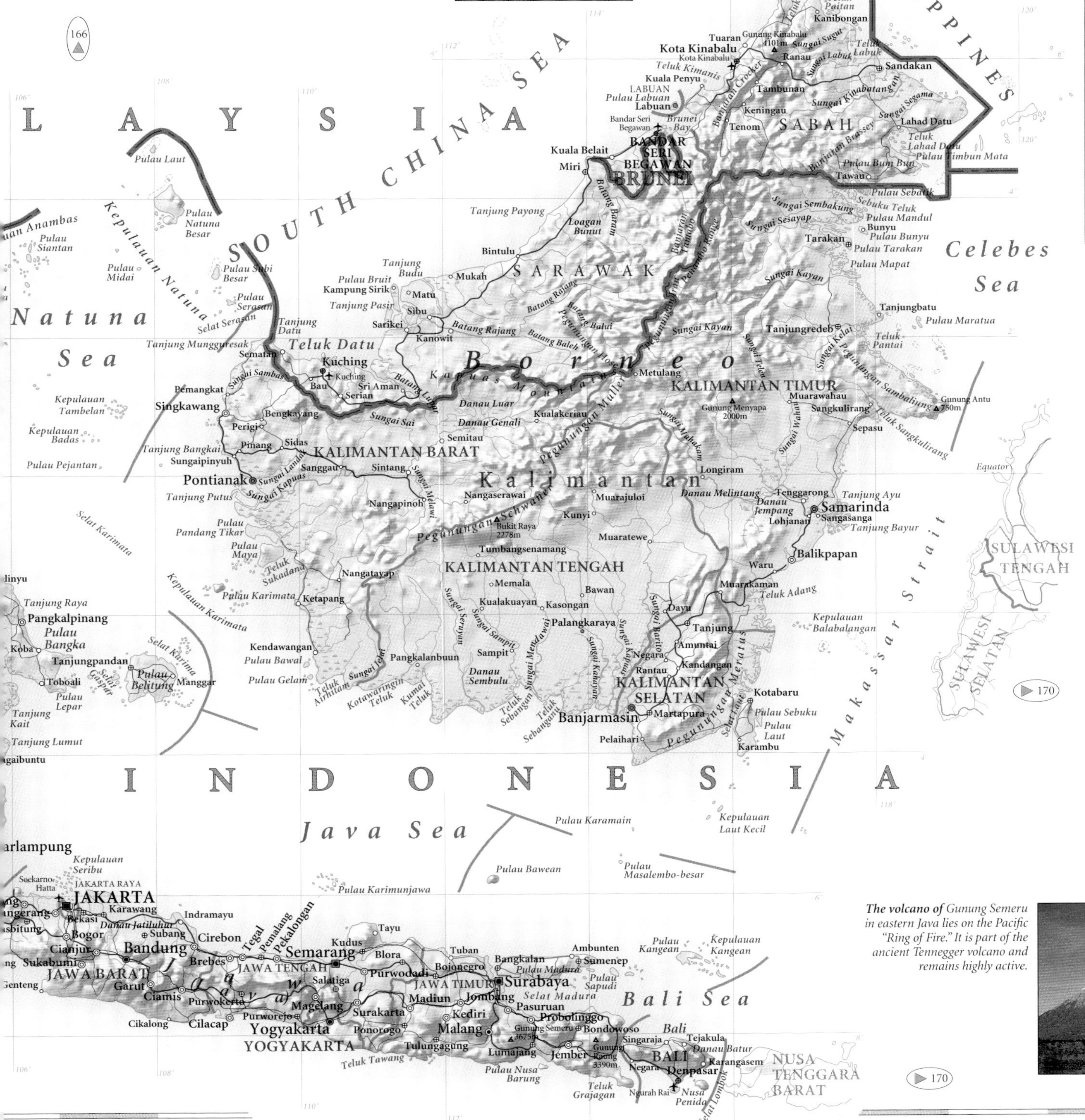

This tiny island near Kota Kinabulu, in Sabah, eastern Malaysia, is part of a designated national park. Thickly forested, it is surrounded by broad, sandy beaches and shallow inland seas.

MAP KEY

POPULATION: above 5 million; 1 million to 5 million; 500,000 to 1 million; 100,000 to 500,000; 50,000 to 100,000; 10,000 to 50,000; below 10,000

ELEVATION: 4000m / 13,124ft; 3000m / 9843ft; 2000m / 6562ft; 1000m / 3281ft; 500m / 1640ft; 250m / 820ft; 100m / 328ft; sea level

The volcano of Gunung Semeru in eastern Java lies on the Pacific "Ring of Fire." It is part of the ancient Tennegger volcano and remains highly active.

166
170

Eastern Maritime Southeast Asia

Indonesia, East Timor, Philippines

The Philippines takes its name from Philip II of Spain who was king when the islands were colonized during the 16th century. Almost 400 years of Spanish, and later US, rule have left their mark on the country's culture; English is widely spoken and over 90% of the population is Christian. The Philippines' economy is agriculturally based – inadequate infrastructure and electrical power shortages have so far hampered faster industrial growth. Indonesia's eastern islands are less economically developed than the rest of the country. Irian Jaya, which constitutes the western portion of New Guinea, is one of the world's last great wildernesses. It accounts for more than 20% of Indonesia's total area but less than 1% of its population.

***The traditional** boat-shaped houses of the Toraja people in Sulawesi. Although now Christian, the Toraja still practice the animist traditions and rituals of their ancestors. They are famous for their elaborate funeral ceremonies and burial sites in cliffside caves.*

The Landscape

Located on the Pacific "Ring of Fire" the Philippines' 7,100 islands are subject to frequent earthquakes and volcanic activity. Their terrain is largely mountainous, with narrow coastal plains and interior valleys and plains. Luzon and Mindanao are by far the largest islands and comprise roughly 66% of the country's area. Indonesia's eastern islands are mountainous and dotted with volcanoes, both active and dormant.

***Lake Taal** on the Philippines island of Luzon lies within the crater of an immense volcano that erupted twice in the 20th century, first in 1911 and again in 1965, causing the deaths of more than 3200 people.*

***Bohol in the southern Philippines** is famous for its so-called "chocolate hills." There are more than 1,000 of these regular mounds on the island. The hills are limestone in origin, the smoothed remains of an earlier cycle of erosion. Their brown appearance in the dry season gives them their name.*

The four-pronged island of Sulawesi is the product of complex tectonic activity that ruptured and then reattached small fragments of the Earth's crust to form the island's many peninsulas.

Mindanao has five mountain ranges many of which have large numbers of active volcanoes. Lying just west of the Philippines Trench, which forms the boundary between the colliding Philippine and Eurasian plates, the entire island chain is subject to earthquakes and volcanic activity.

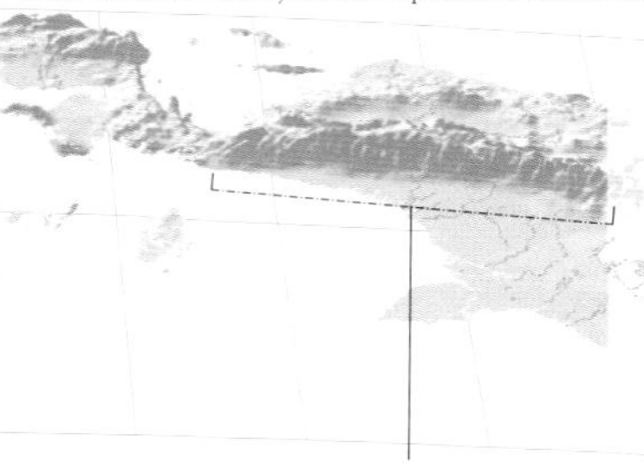

Coral islands such as Timor show evidence of very recent and dramatic movements of the Earth's plates. Reefs in Timor have risen by as much as 4,000 ft (1,300 m) in the last million years.

The 1,000 islands of the Moluccas are the fabled Spice Islands of history, whose produce attracted traders from around the globe. Most of the northern and central Moluccas have dense vegetation and rugged mountainous interiors where elevations often exceed 3,000 feet (9,144 m).

The Pegunungan Maoke range in central Irian Jaya contains the world's highest range of limestone mountains, some with peaks more than 16,400 ft (5,000 m) in height. Heavy rainfall and high temperatures, which promote rapid weathering, have led to the creation of large underground caves and river systems such as the river of Sungai Baliem.

Transportation & Industry

The Philippines' economy is primarily a mixture of agriculture and light industry. The manufacturing sector is still developing; many factories are licensees of foreign companies producing finished goods for export. Mining is also important – the country's chromite, nickel, and copper deposits are among the largest in the world. Agriculture is the main activity in eastern Indonesia. Most industry has a primary basis, including logging, food-processing, and mining. Nickel, the most important metal, is produced on Sulawesi, in Irian Jaya, and in the Moluccas.

crissa
EGO

***Manila is** the Philippines' chief port and transportation center, and the focus of the country's commercial, industrial, and cultural activities. Much of the city lies below sea level, and it suffers from floods during the rainy summer season.*

Luzon Strait
Luzon
MANILA
Philippine Sea
South China Sea
PHILIPPINES
Cebu
Sulu Sea
Zamboanga
Mindanao
Davao
MALAYSIA
PACIFIC OCEAN
Celebes Sea
Manado
Halmahera
Maluku (Moluccas)
Celebes
Ceram
Jayapura
Ujungpandang
Banda Sea
New Guinea
PAPUA NEW GUINEA
INDONESIA
Arafura Sea
Lombok
Sumbawa
Flores
DILI
EAST TIMOR
Sumba
Timor
Kupang
Timor Sea
INDIAN OCEAN

Major industry and infrastructure
- copra processing
- chemicals
- finance
- food processing
- mining
- oil
- timber processing
- textiles
- capital cities
- major towns
- international airports
- major roads
- major industrial areas

Transportation Network

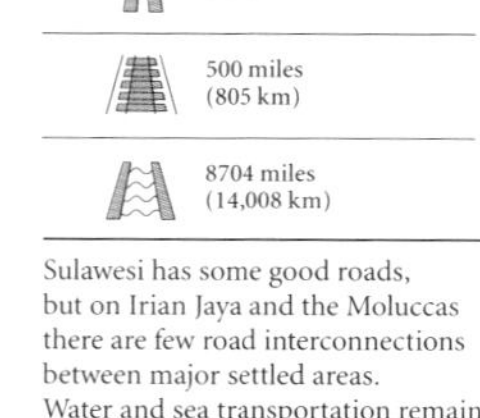

Roads	16,652 miles (26,800 km)
Motorways	None
Railways	500 miles (805 km)
Waterways	8704 miles (14,008 km)

Sulawesi has some good roads, but on Irian Jaya and the Moluccas there are few road interconnections between major settled areas. Water and sea transportation remain important although air links have improved in the Philippines.

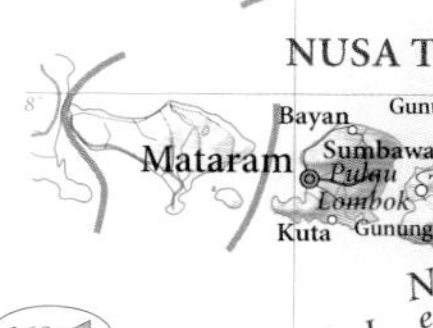
NUSA TENGG
Mataram
Bayan
Sumbawabesar
Taliwang
Kuta

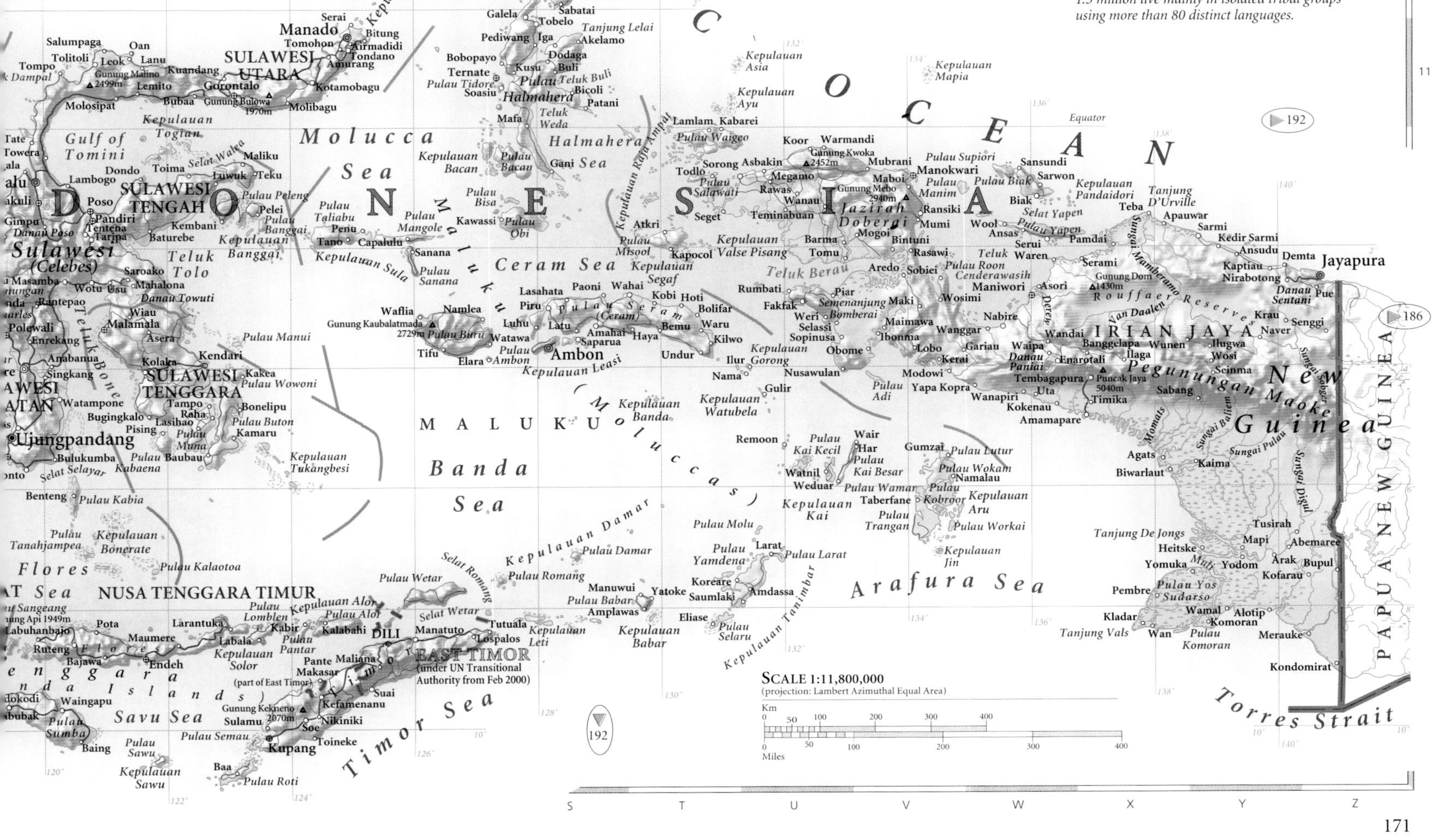

USING THE LAND AND SEA

INDONESIA'S EASTERN ISLANDS are less intensively cultivated than those in the west. Coconuts, coffee, and spices such as cloves and nutmeg are the major commercial crops while rice, corn, and soybeans are grown for local consumption. The Philippines' rich, fertile soils support year-round production of a wide range of crops. The country is one of the world's largest producers of coconuts and a major exporter of coconut products, including one-third of the world's copra. Although much of the arable land is given over to rice and corn, the main staple food crops, tropical fruits such as bananas, pineapples, and mangos, and sugar cane are also grown for export.

The terracing of land to restrict soil erosion and create flat surfaces for agriculture is a common practice throughout Southeast Asia, particularly where land is scarce. These terraces are on Luzon in the Philippines.

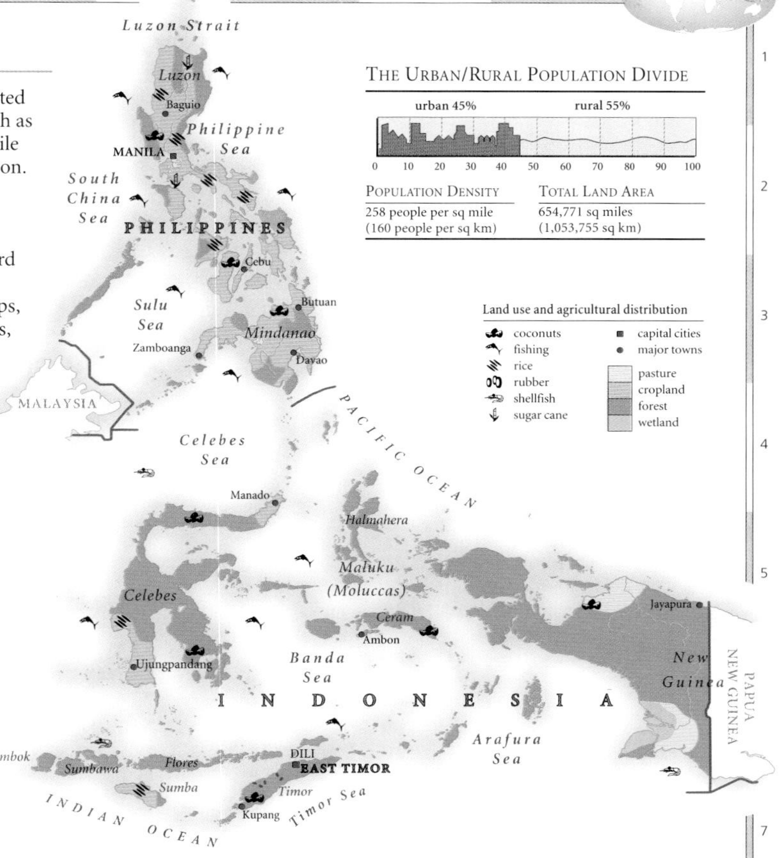

THE URBAN/RURAL POPULATION DIVIDE

urban 45% | rural 55%

POPULATION DENSITY	TOTAL LAND AREA
258 people per sq mile (160 people per sq km)	654,771 sq miles (1,053,755 sq km)

Land use and agricultural distribution: coconuts, fishing, rice, rubber, shellfish, sugar cane, capital cities, major towns, pasture, cropland, forest, wetland

More than two-thirds of Irian Jaya's land area is heavily forested and the population of around 1.5 million live mainly in isolated tribal groups using more than 80 distinct languages.

MAP KEY

POPULATION
- 1 million to 5 million
- 500,000 to 1 million
- 100,000 to 500,000
- 50,000 to 100,000
- 10,000 to 50,000
- below 10,000

ELEVATION
- 4000m / 13,124ft
- 3000m / 9843ft
- 2000m / 6562ft
- 1000m / 3281ft
- 500m / 1640ft
- 250m / 820ft
- 100m / 328ft
- sea level

SCALE 1:11,800,000 (projection: Lambert Azimuthal Equal Area)

THE INDIAN OCEAN

Despite being the smallest of the three major oceans, the evolution of the Indian Ocean was the most complex. The ocean basin was formed during the breakup of the supercontinent Gondwanaland, when the Indian subcontinent moved northeast, Africa moved west and Australia separated from Antarctica. Like the Pacific Ocean, the warm waters of the Indian Ocean are punctuated by coral atolls and islands. About one-fifth of the world's population – over a billion people – live on its shores. Those people living along the northern coasts are constantly threatened by flooding and typhoons caused by the monsoon winds.

THE LANDSCAPE

The Indian Ocean began forming about 150 million years ago, but in its present form it is relatively young, only about 36 million years old. Along the three subterranean mountain chains of its mid-ocean ridge the seafloor is still spreading. The Indian Ocean has fewer trenches than other oceans and only a narrow continental shelf around most of its surrounding land.

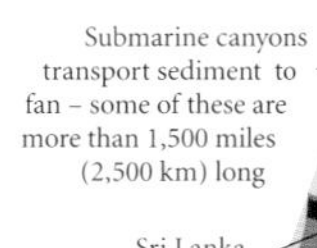
Sediments come from Ganges/Brahmaputra river system
Submarine canyons transport sediment to fan – some of these are more than 1,500 miles (2,500 km) long
Sri Lanka

The mid-oceanic ridge runs from the Arabian Sea. It diverges east of Madagascar. One arm runs southwest to join the Mid-Atlantic Ridge, the other branches southeast, joining the Pacific-Antarctic Ridge, southeast of Tasmania.

The Ninetyeast Ridge takes its name from the line of longitude it follows. It is the world's longest and straightest under-sea ridge.

Two of the world's largest rivers flow into the Indian Ocean; the Indus and the Ganges/Brahmaputra. Both have deposited enormous fans of sediment.

The Ganges Fan is one of the world's largest submarine accumulations of sediment, extending far beyond Sri Lanka. It is fed by the Ganges/Brahmaputra River system, whose sediment is carried through a network of underwater canyons at the edge of the continental shelf.

Indus River

A large proportion of the coast of Thailand, on the Isthmus of Kra, is stabilized by mangrove thickets. They act as an important breeding ground for wildlife.

The Java Trench is the world's longest, it runs 1,600 miles (2,570 km) from the southwest of Java, but is only 50 miles (80 km) wide.

The relief of Madagascar rises from a low-lying coastal strip in the east, to the central plateau. The plateau is also a major watershed separating Madagascar's three main river basins.

The central group of the Seychelles are mountainous, granite islands. They have a narrow coastal belt and lush, tropical vegetation cloaks the highlands.

The Kerguelen Islands in the Southern Ocean were created by a hot spot in the Earth's crust. The islands were formed in succession as the Antarctic Plate moved slowly over the hot spot.

The circulation in the northern Indian Ocean is controlled by the monsoon winds. Biannually these winds reverse their pattern, causing a reversal in the surface currents and alternative high and low pressure conditions over Asia and Australia.

MADAGASCAR

SCALE 1:12,250,000

RESOURCES

Many of the small islands in the Indian Ocean rely exclusively on tuna-fishing and tourism to maintain their economies. Most fisheries are artisanal, although large-scale tuna-fishing does take place in the Seychelles, Mauritius and the western Indian Ocean. Nonliving resources include oil in the Persian Gulf, pearls in the Red Sea, and tin from deposits off the shores of Myanmar, Thailand, and Indonesia.

Resources (including wildlife)

- fish
- penguins
- shellfish
- whales
- oil & gas
- tin deposits
- tourism
- major towns
- major ports

COMOROS

SCALE 1:5,000,000

SEYCHELLES

SCALE 1:2,250,000

The recent use of large dragnets for tuna-fishing has not only threatened the livelihoods of many small-scale fisheries, but also caused widespread environmental concern about the potential impact on other marine species.

Coral reefs support an enormous diversity of animal and plant life. Many species of tiny tropical fish, like these squirrel fish, live and feed around the profusion of reefs and atolls in the Indian Ocean.

***The steeper eastern side of Madagascar** is drained by numerous short, fast-flowing rivers. In contrast, larger, more languid rivers flow across the west. Both erode huge quantities of Madagascar's reddish soil.*

***There are over 1,300 small coral islands** in the Maldives, but only about 200 are inhabited. They are based around an ancient submerged volcanic mountain range and all the islands are low-lying, none rising more than 6 ft (1.8 m) above sea level.*

SCALE 1:47,000,000
(projection: Mollweide)

Km 0 200 400 600 800 1000
Miles 0 200 400 600 800 1000

INDIAN OCEAN

SOUTHERN OCEAN

ANTARCTICA

***The island of Mauritius** is volcanic in origin. Its central plateau is bounded by mountains which may once have formed the rim of a volcanic crater.*

RÉUNION (to France)

SCALE 1:2,250,000
0 5 10 20 30 Km
0 5 10 20 30 Miles

INSET MAP KEY

POPULATION

- 500,000 to 1 million
- 100,000 to 500,000
- 50,000 to 100,000
- 10,000 to 50,000
- below 10,000

ELEVATION

- 3000m / 9843ft
- 2000m / 6562ft
- 1000m / 3281ft
- 500m / 1640ft
- 250m / 820ft
- 100m / 328ft
- sea level

OCEAN MAP KEY

SEA DEPTH

- sea level
- 250m / 820ft
- 500m / 1640ft
- 1000m / 3281ft
- 2000m / 6562ft
- 3000m / 9843ft

MAURITIUS

SCALE 1:2,250,000
0 5 10 20 30 Km
0 5 10 20 30 Miles

AUSTRALASIA AND OCEANIA

AUSTRALASIA AND OCEANIA, COVERING A LAND AREA OF 3,285,048 SQ MILES (8,508,238 SQ KM), TAKES IN 14 COUNTRIES INCLUDING THE CONTINENT OF AUSTRALIA, NEW ZEALAND, PAPUA NEW GUINEA, AND MANY ISLAND GROUPS SCATTERED ACROSS THE PACIFIC OCEAN.

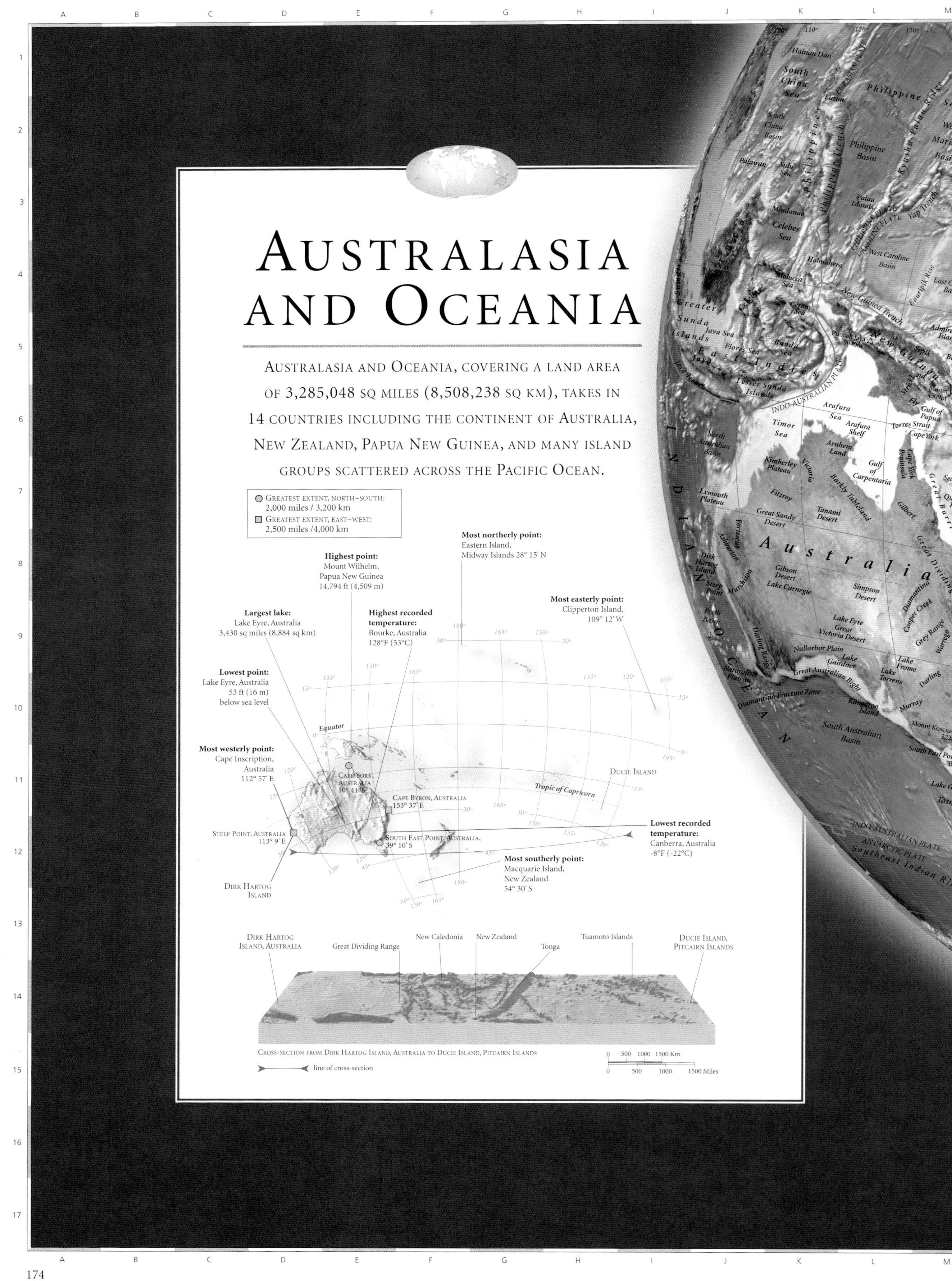

GREATEST EXTENT, NORTH–SOUTH: 2,000 miles / 3,200 km
GREATEST EXTENT, EAST–WEST: 2,500 miles /4,000 km
Most northerly point: Eastern Island, Midway Islands 28° 15' N
Highest point: Mount Wilhelm, Papua New Guinea 14,794 ft (4,509 m)
Most easterly point: Clipperton Island, 109° 12' W
Largest lake: Lake Eyre, Australia 3,430 sq miles (8,884 sq km)
Highest recorded temperature: Bourke, Australia 128°F (53°C)
Lowest point: Lake Eyre, Australia 53 ft (16 m) below sea level
Equator
Most westerly point: Cape Inscription, Australia 112° 57' E
CAPE YORK, AUSTRALIA 10° 41' S
CAPE BYRON, AUSTRALIA 153° 37' E
DUCIE ISLAND
Tropic of Capricorn
STEEP POINT, AUSTRALIA 113° 9' E
SOUTH EAST POINT, AUSTRALIA, 39° 10' S
Lowest recorded temperature: Canberra, Australia -8°F (-22°C)
Most southerly point: Macquarie Island, New Zealand 54° 30' S
DIRK HARTOG ISLAND
DIRK HARTOG ISLAND, AUSTRALIA
Great Dividing Range
New Caledonia
New Zealand
Tonga
Tuamoto Islands
DUCIE ISLAND, PITCAIRN ISLANDS
CROSS-SECTION FROM DIRK HARTOG ISLAND, AUSTRALIA TO DUCIE ISLAND, PITCAIRN ISLANDS
line of cross-section
0 500 1000 1500 Km
0 500 1000 1500 Miles
South China Sea
Philippine Sea
Philippine Basin
Celebes Sea
Molucca Sea
Java Sea
Flores Sea
Banda Sea
Arafura Sea
Timor Sea
Gulf of Carpentaria
Arnhem Land
Kimberley Plateau
Great Sandy Desert
Tanami Desert
Gibson Desert
Lake Carnegie
Simpson Desert
Great Victoria Desert
Lake Eyre
Nullarbor Plain
Great Australian Bight
Kangaroo Island
South Australian Basin
INDIAN OCEAN
Australia
INDO-AUSTRALIAN PLATE

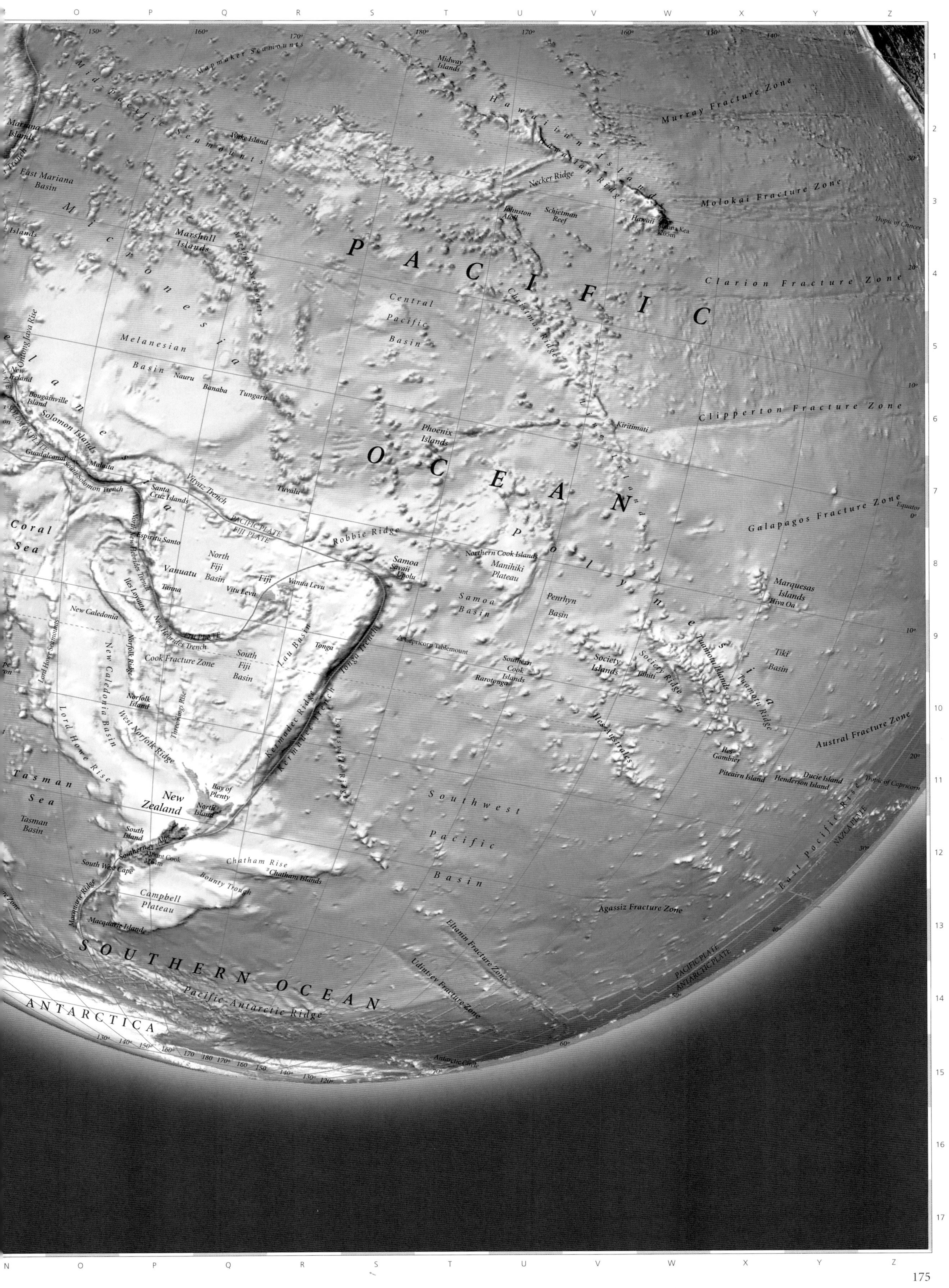
PACIFIC OCEAN
SOUTHERN OCEAN
ANTARCTICA
Mapmaker Seamounts
Mid-Pacific Seamounts
Midway Islands
Hawaiian Islands
Hawaiian Ridge
Murray Fracture Zone
Molokai Fracture Zone
Necker Ridge
Wake Island
Mariana Islands
East Mariana Basin
Johnston Atoll
Schjetman Reef
Hawaii
Mauna Kea
Tropic of Cancer
Marshall Islands
Marshall Seamounts
Micronesia
Clarion Fracture Zone
Central Pacific Basin
Christmas Ridge
Ontong Java Rise
Melanesian Basin
Melanesia
Nauru
Banaba
Tungaru
New Ireland
Bougainville Island
Solomon Islands
Clipperton Fracture Zone
Kiritimati
Line Islands
Phoenix Islands
Guadalcanal
Malaita
South Solomon Trench
Vityaz Trench
Santa Cruz Islands
Tuvalu
Coral Sea
PACIFIC PLATE
FIJI PLATE
Robbie Ridge
Galapagos Fracture Zone
Equator
Espiritu Santo
North New Hebrides Trench
North Fiji Basin
Vanuatu
Fiji
Vanua Levu
Viti Levu
Tanna
Iles Loyauté
Samoa
Savaii
Upolu
Northern Cook Islands
Manihiki Plateau
Polynesia
Marquesas Islands
Hiva Oa
New Caledonia
Samoa Basin
Penrhyn Basin
New Hebrides Trench
Lau Basin
Tonga
Tonga Trench
Capricorn Tablemount
Norfolk Ridge
Cook Fracture Zone
South Fiji Basin
Southern Cook Islands
Rarotonga
Society Islands
Tahiti
Society Ridge
Tuamotu Islands
Tuamotu Ridge
Tiki Basin
Lord Howe Seamounts
New Caledonia Basin
Norfolk Island
Three Kings Rise
West Norfolk Ridge
Kermadec Ridge
Kermadec Trench
Louisville Ridge
Iles Australes
Iles Gambier
Austral Fracture Zone
Lord Howe Rise
Tasman Sea
Tasman Basin
Pitcairn Island
Henderson Island
Ducie Island
Tropic of Capricorn
Bay of Plenty
New Zealand
North Island
South Island
Southern Alps
Mount Cook
South West Cape
Southwest Pacific Basin
East Pacific Rise
NAZCA PLATE
Chatham Rise
Chatham Islands
Bounty Trough
Campbell Plateau
Macquarie Ridge
Macquarie Island
Agassiz Fracture Zone
Eltanin Fracture Zone
Udintsev Fracture Zone
PACIFIC PLATE
ANTARCTIC PLATE
Pacific-Antarctic Ridge
Antarctic Circle

POLITICAL AUSTRALASIA AND OCEANIA

VAST EXPANSES OF OCEAN separate this geographically fragmented realm, characterized more by each country's isolation than by any political unity. Australia's and New Zealand's traditional ties with the United Kingdom, as members of the Commonwealth, are now being called into question as Australasian and Oceanian nations are increasingly looking to forge new relationships with neighboring Asian countries like Japan. External influences have featured strongly in the politics of the Pacific Islands; the various territories of Micronesia were largely under US control until the late 1980s, and France, New Zealand, the US, and the UK still have territories under colonial rule in Polynesia. Nuclear weapons-testing by Western superpowers was widespread during the Cold War period, but has now been discontinued.

Western Australia's mineral wealth has transformed its state capital, Perth, into one of Australia's major cities. Perth is one of the world's most isolated cities – over 2,500 miles (4,000 km) from the population centers of the eastern seaboard.

POPULATION

DENSITY OF SETTLEMENT in the region is generally low. Australia is one of the least densely populated countries on Earth with over 80% of its population living within 25 miles (40 km) of the coast – mostly in the southeast of the country. New Zealand, and the island groups of Melanesia, Micronesia, and Polynesia, are much more densely populated, although many of the smaller islands remain uninhabited.

Population density (people per sq mile)
- below 10
- 10-62
- 63-130
- 131-259
- 260-519
- 520-780
- above 780

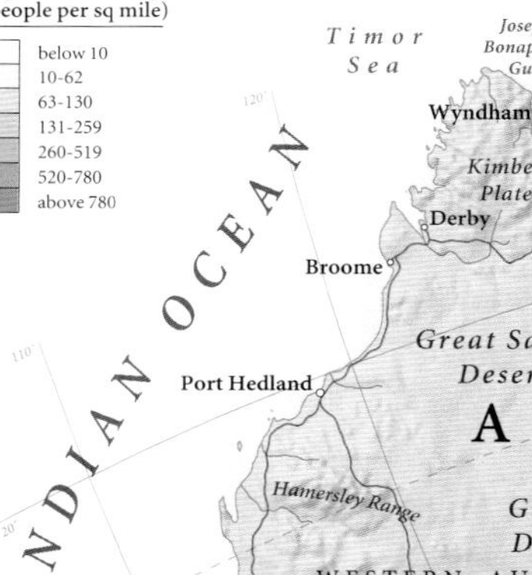

The myriad of small coral islands that are scattered across the Pacific Ocean are often uninhabited, as they offer little shelter from the weather, often no fresh water, and only limited food supplies.

The planes of the Australian Royal Flying Doctor Service are able to cover large expanses of barren land quickly, bringing medical treatment to the most inaccessible and far-flung places.

Philippine Sea
Northern Mariana Islands (to US)
Mariana Islands
Saipan
Guam (to US)
HAGÅTNA
Micronesia
MICRONESIA
Caroline Islands
Yap
Chuuk
Pohnpei
PALIKIR
Kosrae
Bikini Atoll
Babeldaob
OREOR
PALAU
Melanesia
NAURU
PAPUA NEW GUINEA
Bismarck Sea
New Ireland
Wewak
New Britain
Rabaul
Madang
Lae
Ubai
Arawa
Bougainville Island
Solomon Islands
SOLOMON ISLANDS
New Guinea
Mount Hagen
Solomon Sea
Tapini
PORT MORESBY
New Georgia Islands
HONIARA
Guadalcanal
Santa Cruz Islands
Arafura Sea
Torres Strait
VANUATU
Espiritu Santo
Malekula
Coral Sea
Coral Sea Islands (to Australia)
New Caledonia (to France)
NOUMÉA
Darwin
Arnhem Land
Gulf of Carpentaria
Cape York Peninsula
Joseph Bonaparte Gulf
Katherine
Timor Sea
Cairns
Great Barrier Reef
Normanton
Wyndham
Kimberley Plateau
Townsville
NORTHERN TERRITORY
Hughenden
Mackay
Derby
Tennant Creek
Tanami Desert
Mount Isa
Broome
QUEENSLAND
Rockhampton
Barcaldine
Great Dividing Range
INDIAN OCEAN
Great Sandy Desert
Alice Springs
Simpson Desert
Charleville
Miles
Brisbane
Port Hedland
Toowoomba
AUSTRALIA
Cunnamulla
Grafton
Hamersley Range
Gibson Desert
Lake Eyre North
Grey Range
Bourke
Barwon
Darling
Flinders Ranges
SOUTH AUSTRALIA
Wilcannia
NEW SOUTH WALES
Dubbo
Newcastle
WESTERN AUSTRALIA
Lake Torrens
Sydney
Carnavon
Great Victoria Desert
Lake Everard
Port Augusta
Campbelltown
Wollongong
Tropic of Capricorn
Lake Gairdner
Murray
CANBERRA
AUSTRALIAN CAPITAL TERRITORY
Mount Magnet
Nullarbor Plain
Ceduna
Whyalla
Wagga Wagga
Kalgoorlie
Great Australian Bight
Adelaide
Bendigo
Geraldton
Kangaroo Island
Horsham
VICTORIA
Ballarat
Melbourne
Geelong
Mount Gambier
Perth
Esperance
Bass Strait
Launceston
Albany
TASMANIA
Tasmania
Hobart
Tasman Sea
Lord Howe Island (to Australia)
Equator
SOUTHE

Languages

English is spoken throughout Australia and New Zealand. In Australia, English has been superimposed on a mosaic of Aboriginal languages. In New Zealand, the indigenous language, Maori, is the official language besides Polynesian. In Papua New Guinea, Melanesian Pidgin has become a *lingua franca* alongside several hundred indigenous languages. Across the region, the indigenous languages can be grouped into (1) the Aboriginal languages of Australia, (2) the Papuan languages spoken mostly inland in Papua New Guinea, and (3) the widely dispersed Austronesian, which includes coastal languages of Papua New Guinea, New Zealand Maori and languages of Oceania.

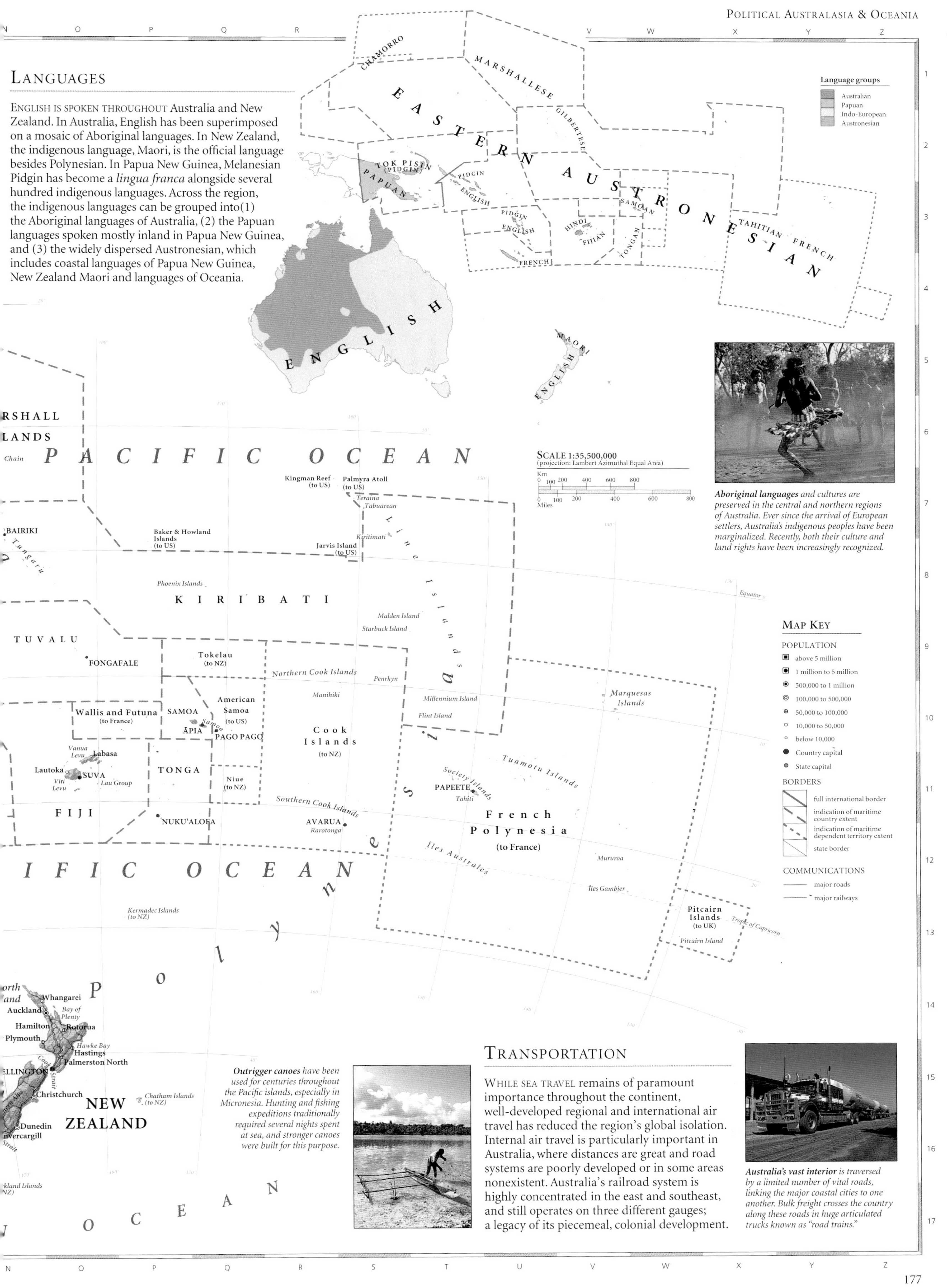

Language groups
Australian
Papuan
Indo-European
Austronesian
CHAMORRO
MARSHALLESE
GILBERTESE
EASTERN AUSTRONESIAN
TOK PISIN (PIDGIN)
PAPUAN
PIDGIN
ENGLISH
HINDI
FIJIAN
TONGAN
SAMOAN
FRENCH
TAHITIAN
FRENCH
ENGLISH
MAORI
ENGLISH
PACIFIC OCEAN
SCALE 1:35,500,000
(projection: Lambert Azimuthal Equal Area)
Km
Miles
Kingman Reef (to US)
Palmyra Atoll (to US)
Teraina
Tabuarean
Kiritimati
Line Islands
Baker & Howland Islands (to US)
Jarvis Island (to US)
BAIRIKI
Tungaru
Phoenix Islands
KIRIBATI
Malden Island
Starbuck Island
Equator
TUVALU
FONGAFALE
Tokelau (to NZ)
Northern Cook Islands
Penrhyn
Manihiki
Millennium Island
Flint Island
Marquesas Islands
Wallis and Futuna (to France)
SAMOA
Samoa
ĀPIA
American Samoa (to US)
PAGO PAGO
Cook Islands (to NZ)
Vanua Levu
Labasa
Lautoka
SUVA
Viti Levu
Lau Group
TONGA
Niue (to NZ)
Society Islands
PAPEETE
Tahiti
Tuamotu Islands
FIJI
NUKU'ALOFA
Southern Cook Islands
AVARUA
Rarotonga
French Polynesia (to France)
Iles Australes
Mururoa
Iles Gambier
Kermadec Islands (to NZ)
Pitcairn Islands (to UK)
Pitcairn Island
Tropic of Capricorn
Polynesia
Whangarei
Auckland
Bay of Plenty
Hamilton
Rotorua
Plymouth
Hawke Bay
Hastings
Palmerston North
Cook Strait
Christchurch
NEW ZEALAND
Chatham Islands (to NZ)
Dunedin
MAP KEY
POPULATION
above 5 million
1 million to 5 million
500,000 to 1 million
100,000 to 500,000
50,000 to 100,000
10,000 to 50,000
below 10,000
Country capital
State capital
BORDERS
full international border
indication of maritime country extent
indication of maritime dependent territory extent
state border
COMMUNICATIONS
major roads
major railways

Aboriginal languages and cultures are preserved in the central and northern regions of Australia. Ever since the arrival of European settlers, Australia's indigenous peoples have been marginalized. Recently, both their culture and land rights have been increasingly recognized.

***Outrigger canoes** have been used for centuries throughout the Pacific islands, especially in Micronesia. Hunting and fishing expeditions traditionally required several nights spent at sea, and stronger canoes were built for this purpose.*

Transportation

While sea travel remains of paramount importance throughout the continent, well-developed regional and international air travel has reduced the region's global isolation. Internal air travel is particularly important in Australia, where distances are great and road systems are poorly developed or in some areas nonexistent. Australia's railroad system is highly concentrated in the east and southeast, and still operates on three different gauges; a legacy of its piecemeal, colonial development.

***Australia's vast interior** is traversed by a limited number of vital roads, linking the major coastal cities to one another. Bulk freight crosses the country along these roads in huge articulated trucks known as "road trains."*

Australasian and Oceanian Resources

Natural resources are of major economic importance throughout Australasia and Oceania. Australia in particular is a major world exporter of raw materials such as coal, iron ore, and bauxite, while New Zealand's agricultural economy is dominated by sheep-raising. Trade with western Europe has declined significantly in the last 20 years, and the Pacific Rim countries of Southeast Asia are now the main trading partners, as well as a source of new settlers to the region. Australasia and Oceania's greatest resources are its climate and environment; tourism increasingly provides a vital source of income for the whole continent.

***The largely unpolluted** waters of the Pacific Ocean support rich and varied marine life, much of which is farmed commercially. Here, oysters are gathered for market off the coast of New Zealand's South Island.*

***Huge flocks of sheep** are a common sight in New Zealand, where they outnumber people by 20 to 1. New Zealand is one of the world's largest exporters of wool and frozen lamb.*

Standard of Living

In marked contrast to its neighbor, Australia, with one of the world's highest life expectancies and standards of living, Papua New Guinea is one of the world's least developed countries. In addition, high population growth and urbanization rates throughout the Pacific islands contribute to overcrowding. In Australia and New Zealand, the Aboriginal and Maori people have been isolated, although recently their traditional land ownership rights have begun to be legally recognized in an effort to ease their social and economic isolation, and to improve living standards.

Environmental Issues

The prospect of rising sea levels poses a threat to many low-lying islands in the Pacific. The testing of nuclear weapons, once common throughout the region, was finally discontinued in 1996. Australia's ecological balance has been irreversibly altered by the introduction of alien species. Although it has the world's largest underground water reserve, the Great Artesian Basin, the availability of fresh water in Australia remains critical. Periodic droughts combined with overgrazing lead to desertification and increase the risk of devastating bush fires, and occasional flash floods.

Environmental Issues
national parks
tropical forest
forest destroyed
desert
desertification
polluted rivers
radioactive contamination
marine pollution
heavy marine pollution
poor urban air quality

***In 1946 Bikini Atoll,** in the Marshall Islands, was chosen as the site for Operation Crossroads – investigating the effects of atomic bombs upon naval vessels. Further nuclear tests continued until the early 1990s. The long-term environmental effects are unknown.*

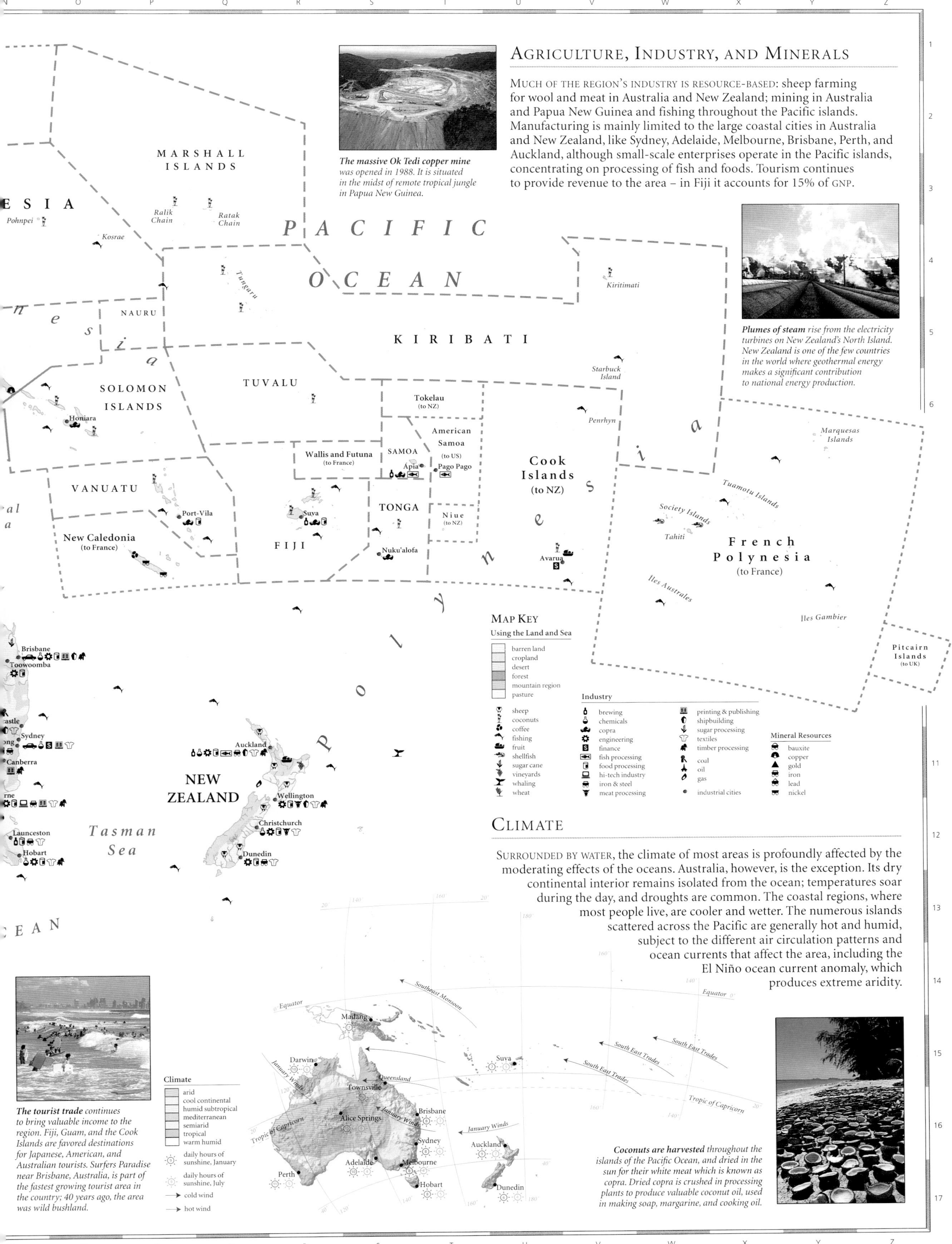

N O P Q R S T U V W X Y Z
MARSHALL ISLANDS
Pohnpei
Kosrae
Ralik Chain
Ratak Chain
PACIFIC OCEAN
Tungaru
Kiritimati
NAURU
KIRIBATI
SOLOMON ISLANDS
Honiara
TUVALU
Starbuck Island
Tokelau (to NZ)
Penrhyn
American Samoa (to US)
Pago Pago
Wallis and Futuna (to France)
SAMOA
Apia
Marquesas Islands
Cook Islands (to NZ)
Tuamotu Islands
VANUATU
Port-Vila
Suva
TONGA
Niue (to NZ)
Society Islands
Tahiti
French Polynesia (to France)
New Caledonia (to France)
FIJI
Nuku'alofa
Avarua
Îles Australes
Îles Gambier
Pitcairn Islands (to UK)
Polynesia
Brisbane
Toowoomba
Sydney
Canberra
Auckland
NEW ZEALAND
Wellington
Christchurch
Dunedin
Launceston
Hobart
Tasman Sea
OCEAN
MAP KEY
Using the Land and Sea
barren land
cropland
desert
forest
mountain region
pasture
sheep
coconuts
coffee
fishing
fruit
shellfish
sugar cane
vineyards
whaling
wheat
Industry
brewing
chemicals
copra
engineering
finance
fish processing
food processing
hi-tech industry
iron & steel
meat processing
printing & publishing
shipbuilding
sugar processing
textiles
timber processing
coal
oil
gas
industrial cities
Mineral Resources
bauxite
copper
gold
iron
lead
nickel
Equator
Southeast Monsoon
Madang
Darwin
January Winds
Queensland
Townsville
Alice Springs
Tropic of Capricorn
Brisbane
Sydney
Adelaide
Melbourne
Perth
Hobart
Auckland
Dunedin
Suva
South East Trades
Climate
arid
cool continental
humid subtropical
mediterranean
semiarid
tropical
warm humid
daily hours of sunshine, January
daily hours of sunshine, July
cold wind
hot wind

AGRICULTURE, INDUSTRY, AND MINERALS

MUCH OF THE REGION'S INDUSTRY IS RESOURCE-BASED: sheep farming for wool and meat in Australia and New Zealand; mining in Australia and Papua New Guinea and fishing throughout the Pacific islands. Manufacturing is mainly limited to the large coastal cities in Australia and New Zealand, like Sydney, Adelaide, Melbourne, Brisbane, Perth, and Auckland, although small-scale enterprises operate in the Pacific islands, concentrating on processing of fish and foods. Tourism continues to provide revenue to the area – in Fiji it accounts for 15% of GNP.

The massive Ok Tedi copper mine *was opened in 1988. It is situated in the midst of remote tropical jungle in Papua New Guinea.*

Plumes of steam *rise from the electricity turbines on New Zealand's North Island. New Zealand is one of the few countries in the world where geothermal energy makes a significant contribution to national energy production.*

CLIMATE

SURROUNDED BY WATER, the climate of most areas is profoundly affected by the moderating effects of the oceans. Australia, however, is the exception. Its dry continental interior remains isolated from the ocean; temperatures soar during the day, and droughts are common. The coastal regions, where most people live, are cooler and wetter. The numerous islands scattered across the Pacific are generally hot and humid, subject to the different air circulation patterns and ocean currents that affect the area, including the El Niño ocean current anomaly, which produces extreme aridity.

The tourist trade *continues to bring valuable income to the region. Fiji, Guam, and the Cook Islands are favored destinations for Japanese, American, and Australian tourists. Surfers Paradise near Brisbane, Australia, is part of the fastest growing tourist area in the country; 40 years ago, the area was wild bushland.*

Coconuts are harvested *throughout the islands of the Pacific Ocean, and dried in the sun for their white meat which is known as copra. Dried copra is crushed in processing plants to produce valuable coconut oil, used in making soap, margarine, and cooking oil.*

AUSTRALIA

Uluru (Ayers Rock), *the world's largest free-standing rock, is a massive outcrop of red sandstone in Australia's desert center. Wind and sandstorms have ground the rock into the smooth curves seen here. Uluru is revered as a sacred site by many aboriginal peoples.*

AUSTRALIA IS THE WORLD'S smallest continent, a stable landmass lying between the Indian and Pacific oceans. Previously home to its aboriginal peoples only, since the end of the 18th century immigration has transformed the face of the country. Initially settlers came mainly from western Europe, particularly the UK, and for years Australia remained wedded to its British colonial past. More recent immigrants have come from eastern Europe, and from Asian countries such as Japan, South Korea, and Indonesia. Australia is now forging strong trading links with these "Pacific Rim" countries and its economic future seems to lie with Asia and the Americas, rather than Europe, its traditional partner.

SCALE 1:11,500,000
(projection: Lambert Conformal Conic)

Map Key

POPULATION
- 1 million to 5 million
- 500,000 to 1 million
- 100,000 to 500,000
- 50,000 to 100,000
- 10,000 to 50,000
- below 10,000

ELEVATION
- 2000m / 6562ft
- 1000m / 3281ft
- 500m / 1640ft
- 250m / 820ft
- 100m / 328ft
- sea level

154

Using the Land

OVER 165 MILLION SHEEP are dispersed in vast herds around the country, contributing to a major export industry. Cattle-ranching is important, particularly in the west. Wheat, and grapes for Australia's wine industry, are grown mainly in the south. Much of the country is desert, unsuitable for agriculture unless irrigation is used.

The Urban/Rural Population Divide

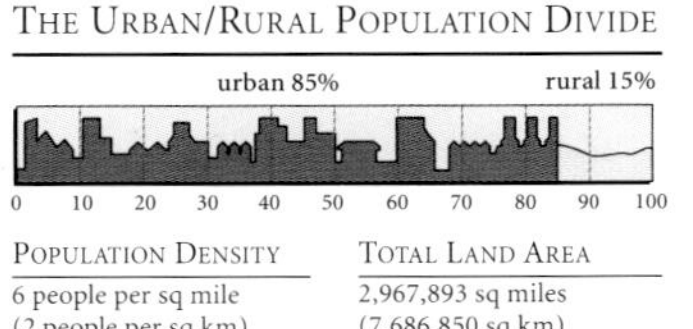

urban 85%
rural 15%
0 10 20 30 40 50 60 70 80 90 100

Population Density	Total Land Area
6 people per sq mile (2 people per sq km)	2,967,893 sq miles (7,686,850 sq km)

Land use and agricultural distribution: cattle, sheep, cereals, sugar cane, timber, vineyards, capital cities, major towns, pasture, cropland, forest, desert, mountain region

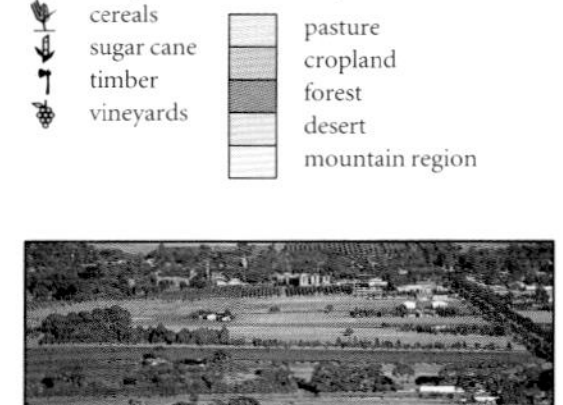

Lines of ripening vines stretch for miles in Barossa Valley, a major wine-growing region near Adelaide.

The Landscape

AUSTRALIA CONSISTS OF MANY ERODED PLATEAUS, lying firmly in the middle of the Indo-Australian Plate. It is the world's flattest continent, and the driest, after Antarctica. The coasts tend to be more hilly and fertile, especially in the east. The mountains of the Great Dividing Range form a natural barrier between the eastern coastal areas and the flat, dry plains and desert regions of the Australian "outback."

The Great Barrier Reef is the world's largest area of coral islands and reefs. It runs for about 1,240 miles (2,000 km) along the Queensland coast.

The Pinnacles are a series of rugged sandstone pillars. Their strange shapes have been formed by water and wind erosion.

The ancient Kimberley Plateau is the source of some of Australia's richest mineral deposits, including diamonds.

Arnhem Land

Uluru (Ayers Rock)

The tropical rainforest of the Cape York Peninsula contains more than 600 different varieties of tree.

Great Artesian Basin

The Great Dividing Range forms a watershed between east- and west-flowing rivers. Erosion has created deep valleys, gorges, and waterfalls where rivers tumble over escarpments on their way to the sea.

More than half of Australia rests on a uniform shield over 600 million years old. It is one of the Earth's original geological plates.

The Nullarbor Plain is a low-lying limestone plateau which is so flat that the Trans-Australian Railway runs through it in a straight line for more than 300 miles (483 km).

The Simpson Desert has a number of large salt pans, created by the evaporation of past rivers and now sourced by seasonal rains. Some are crusted with gypsum, but most are covered by common salt crystals.

The Lake Eyre basin, lying 51 ft (16 m) below sea level, is one of the largest inland drainage systems in the world, covering an area of more than 500,000 sq miles (1,300,000 sq km).

Australian Alps

Tasmania has the same geological structure as the Australian Alps. During the last period of glaciation, 18,000 years ago, sea levels were some 300 ft (100 m) lower and it was joined to the mainland.

Great Artesian Basin

Rainwater replenishes aquifer · Aquifers from which artesian water is obtained · Underground water movements · Lake Eyre

The Great Artesian Basin underlies nearly 20% of the total area of Australia, providing a valuable store of underground water, essential to Australian agriculture. The ephemeral rivers which drain the northern part of the basin have highly braided courses and, in consequence, the area is known as "channel country."

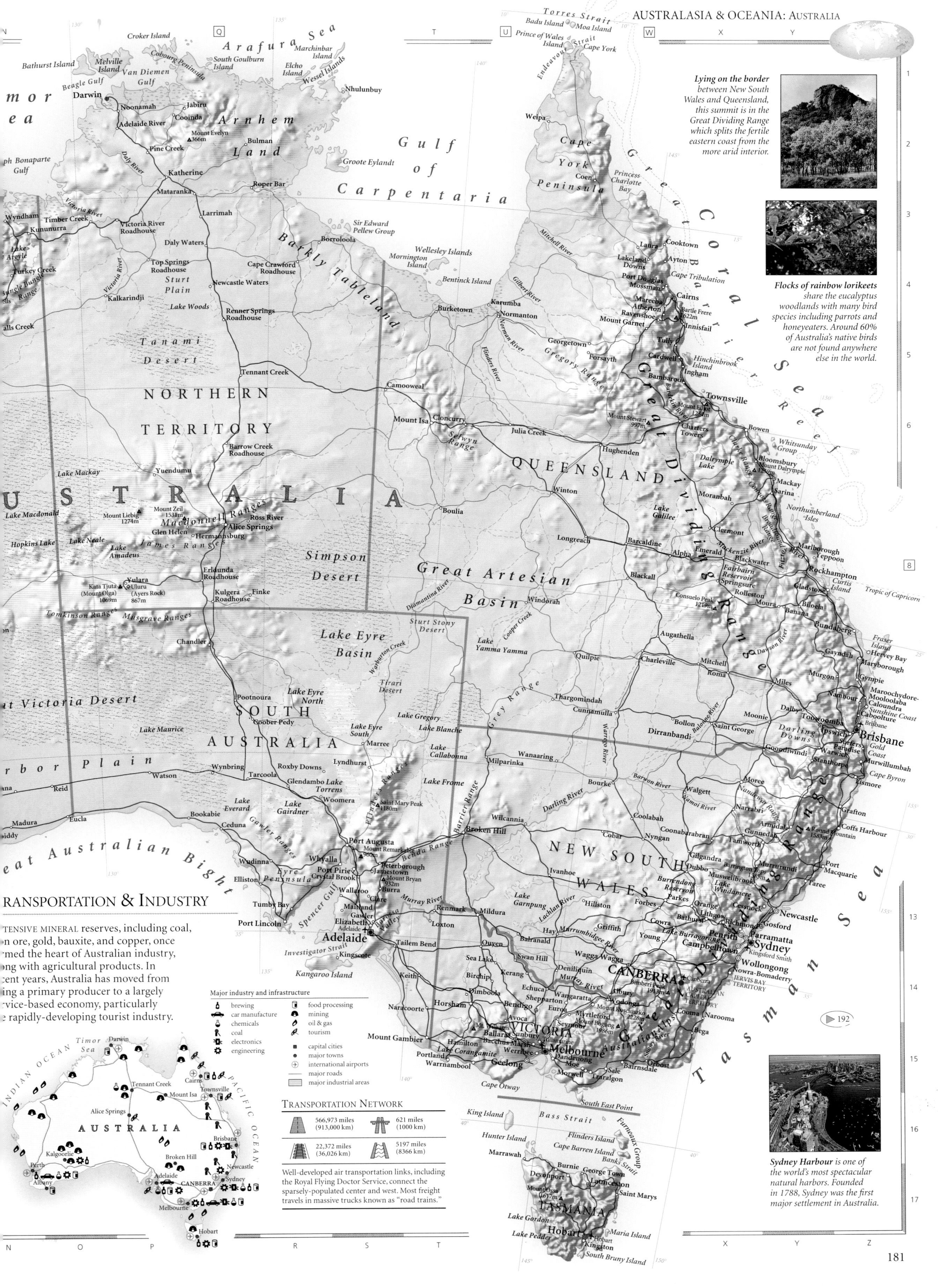
Arafura Sea
Gulf of Carpentaria
Torres Strait
Cape York Peninsula
Great Barrier Reef
Coral Sea
Tasman Sea
Great Australian Bight
Bass Strait
Arnhem Land
Barkly Tableland
Tanami Desert
Simpson Desert
Great Artesian Basin
Lake Eyre Basin
Great Victoria Desert
Great Dividing Range
NORTHERN TERRITORY
QUEENSLAND
SOUTH AUSTRALIA
NEW SOUTH WALES
VICTORIA
TASMANIA
AUSTRALIA
CANBERRA
Darwin
Katherine
Alice Springs
Tennant Creek
Mount Isa
Cairns
Townsville
Mackay
Rockhampton
Bundaberg
Brisbane
Newcastle
Sydney
Wollongong
Melbourne
Geelong
Adelaide
Port Augusta
Broken Hill
Hobart
Launceston
Uluru (Ayers Rock) 867m
Kata Tjuta (Mount Olga) 1069m
Lake Eyre North
Lake Eyre South
Tropic of Capricorn
Kangaroo Island
King Island
Flinders Island
Major industry and infrastructure
brewing
car manufacture
chemicals
coal
electronics
engineering
food processing
mining
oil & gas
tourism
capital cities
major towns
international airports
major roads
major industrial areas
TRANSPORTATION NETWORK
566,973 miles (913,000 km)
621 miles (1000 km)
22,372 miles (36,026 km)
5197 miles (8366 km)
INDIAN OCEAN
PACIFIC OCEAN
Timor Sea

Lying on the border between New South Wales and Queensland, this summit is in the Great Dividing Range which splits the fertile eastern coast from the more arid interior.

Flocks of rainbow lorikeets share the eucalyptus woodlands with many bird species including parrots and honeyeaters. Around 60% of Australia's native birds are not found anywhere else in the world.

Sydney Harbour is one of the world's most spectacular natural harbors. Founded in 1788, Sydney was the first major settlement in Australia.

RANSPORTATION & INDUSTRY

TENSIVE MINERAL reserves, including coal, n ore, gold, bauxite, and copper, once rmed the heart of Australian industry, ng with agricultural products. In cent years, Australia has moved from ing a primary producer to a largely rvice-based economy, particularly e rapidly-developing tourist industry.

Well-developed air transportation links, including the Royal Flying Doctor Service, connect the sparsely-populated center and west. Most freight travels in massive trucks known as "road trains."

192

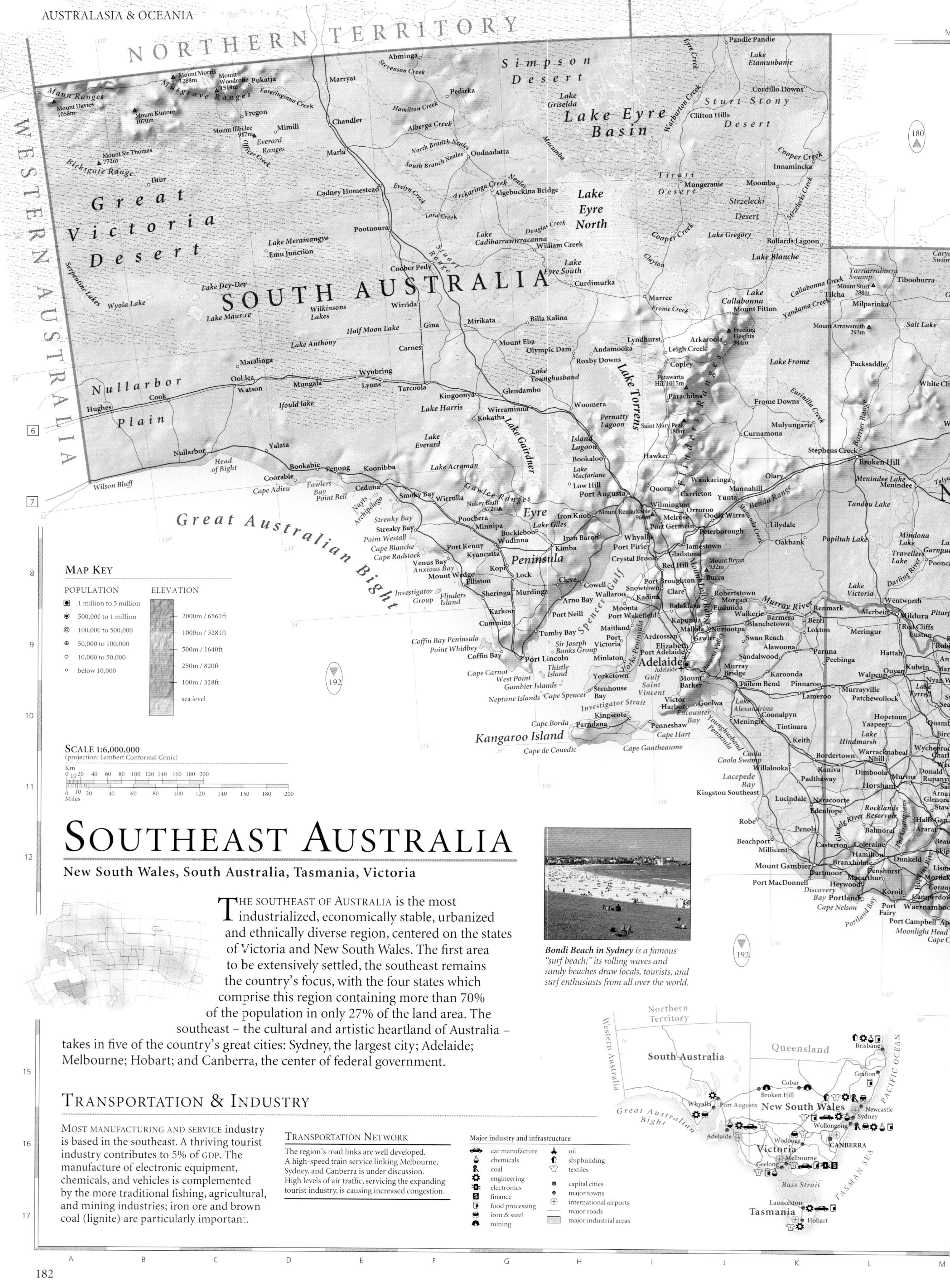
MAP KEY
POPULATION
1 million to 5 million
500,000 to 1 million
100,000 to 500,000
50,000 to 100,000
10,000 to 50,000
below 10,000
ELEVATION
2000m / 6562ft
1000m / 3281ft
500m / 1640ft
250m / 820ft
100m / 328ft
sea level
SCALE 1:6,000,000
(projection: Lambert Conformal Conic)
SOUTH AUSTRALIA
Great Australian Bight
Kangaroo Island
Adelaide

SOUTHEAST AUSTRALIA

New South Wales, South Australia, Tasmania, Victoria

THE SOUTHEAST OF AUSTRALIA is the most industrialized, economically stable, urbanized and ethnically diverse region, centered on the states of Victoria and New South Wales. The first area to be extensively settled, the southeast remains the country's focus, with the four states which comprise this region containing more than 70% of the population in only 27% of the land area. The southeast – the cultural and artistic heartland of Australia – takes in five of the country's great cities: Sydney, the largest city; Adelaide; Melbourne; Hobart; and Canberra, the center of federal government.

***Bondi Beach in Sydney** is a famous "surf beach;" its rolling waves and sandy beaches draw locals, tourists, and surf enthusiasts from all over the world.*

TRANSPORTATION & INDUSTRY

MOST MANUFACTURING AND SERVICE industry is based in the southeast. A thriving tourist industry contributes to 5% of GDP. The manufacture of electronic equipment, chemicals, and vehicles is complemented by the more traditional fishing, agricultural, and mining industries; iron ore and brown coal (lignite) are particularly important.

TRANSPORTATION NETWORK

The region's road links are well developed. A high-speed train service linking Melbourne, Sydney, and Canberra is under discussion. High levels of air traffic, servicing the expanding tourist industry, is causing increased congestion.

Major industry and infrastructure
car manufacture
chemicals
coal
engineering
electronics
finance
food processing
iron & steel
mining
oil
shipbuilding
textiles
capital cities
major towns
international airports
major roads
major industrial areas

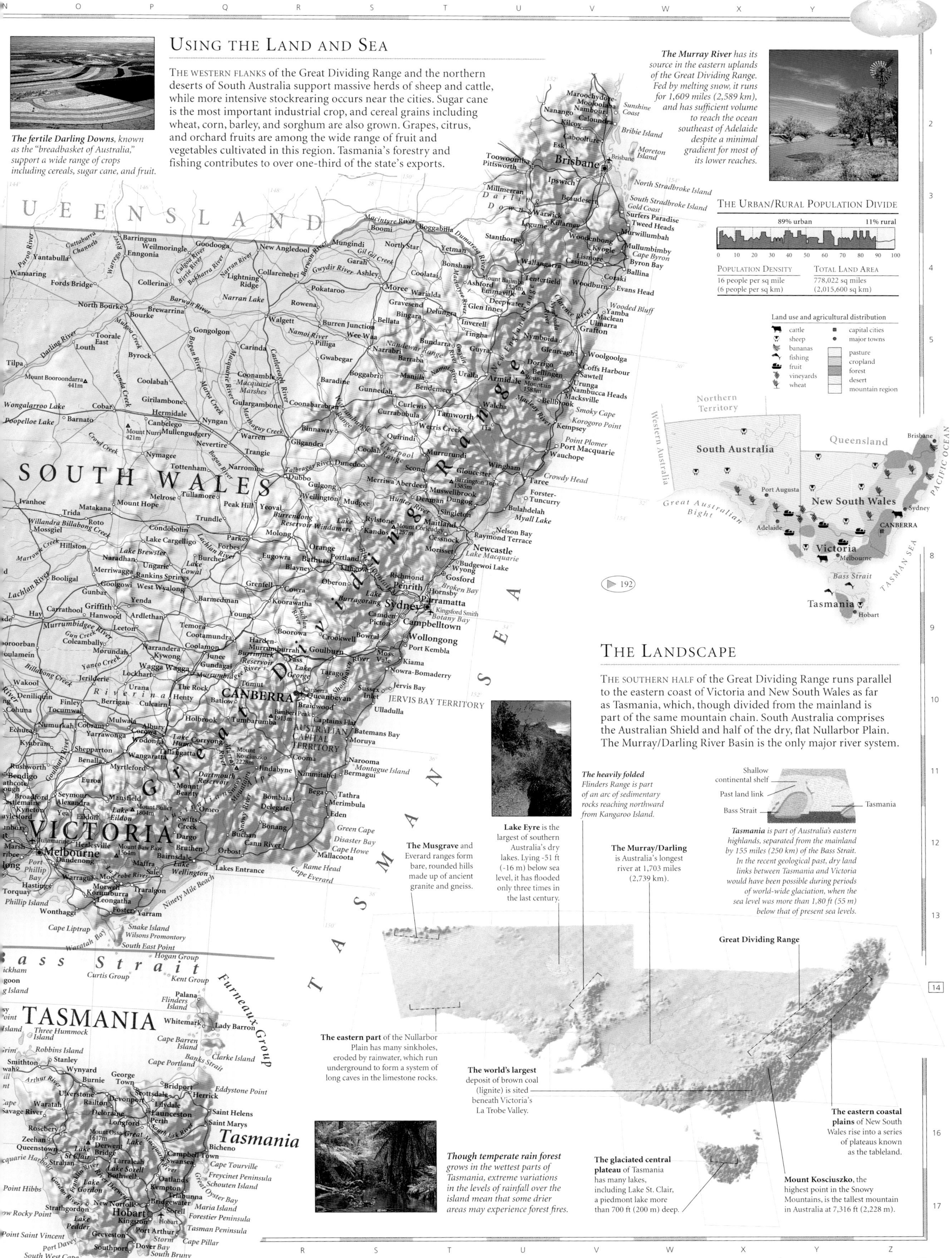

N O P Q R S T U V W X Y
1 2 3 4 5 8 9 10 11 12 13 14 16 17
R S T U V W X Y Z
QUEENSLAND
NEW SOUTH WALES
VICTORIA
TASMANIA
Bass Strait
TASMAN SEA
Great Dividing Range
Darling Downs
Brisbane
Sydney
CANBERRA
Melbourne
Hobart
Newcastle
Wollongong
Tamworth
Dubbo
Wagga Wagga
Albury
Launceston
AUSTRALIAN CAPITAL TERRITORY
JERVIS BAY TERRITORY
Mount Kosciuszko 2228m
Furneaux Group
192
The Urban/Rural Population Divide
89% urban
11% rural
0 10 20 30 40 50 60 70 80 90 100
Population Density
16 people per sq mile
(6 people per sq km)
Total Land Area
778,022 sq miles
(2,015,600 sq km)
Land use and agricultural distribution
cattle
sheep
bananas
fishing
fruit
vineyards
wheat
capital cities
major towns
pasture
cropland
forest
desert
mountain region
Northern Territory
Western Australia
South Australia
Queensland
New South Wales
Victoria
Tasmania
Great Australian Bight
Port Augusta
Adelaide
Bass Strait
PACIFIC OCEAN
TASMAN SEA
Shallow continental shelf
Past land link
Bass Strait
Tasmania
Great Dividing Range

Using the Land and Sea

The western flanks of the Great Dividing Range and the northern deserts of South Australia support massive herds of sheep and cattle, while more intensive stockrearing occurs near the cities. Sugar cane is the most important industrial crop, and cereal grains including wheat, corn, barley, and sorghum are also grown. Grapes, citrus, and orchard fruits are among the wide range of fruit and vegetables cultivated in this region. Tasmania's forestry and fishing contributes to over one-third of the state's exports.

***The fertile Darling Downs,** known as the "breadbasket of Australia," support a wide range of crops including cereals, sugar cane, and fruit.*

***The Murray River** has its source in the eastern uplands of the Great Dividing Range. Fed by melting snow, it runs for 1,609 miles (2,589 km), and has sufficient volume to reach the ocean southeast of Adelaide despite a minimal gradient for most of its lower reaches.*

The Landscape

The southern half of the Great Dividing Range runs parallel to the eastern coast of Victoria and New South Wales as far as Tasmania, which, though divided from the mainland is part of the same mountain chain. South Australia comprises the Australian Shield and half of the dry, flat Nullarbor Plain. The Murray/Darling River Basin is the only major river system.

***The heavily folded** Flinders Range is part of an arc of sedimentary rocks reaching northward from Kangaroo Island.*

Lake Eyre is the largest of southern Australia's dry lakes. Lying -51 ft (-16 m) below sea level, it has flooded only three times in the last century.

The Musgrave and Everard ranges form bare, rounded hills made up of ancient granite and gneiss.

The Murray/Darling is Australia's longest river at 1,703 miles (2,739 km).

***Tasmania** is part of Australia's eastern highlands, separated from the mainland by 155 miles (250 km) of the Bass Strait. In the recent geological past, dry land links between Tasmania and Victoria would have been possible during periods of world-wide glaciation, when the sea level was more than 1,80 ft (55 m) below that of present sea levels.*

The eastern part of the Nullarbor Plain has many sinkholes, eroded by rainwater, which run underground to form a system of long caves in the limestone rocks.

The world's largest deposit of brown coal (lignite) is sited beneath Victoria's La Trobe Valley.

The eastern coastal plains of New South Wales rise into a series of plateaus known as the tableland.

***Though temperate rain forest** grows in the wettest parts of Tasmania, extreme variations in the levels of rainfall over the island mean that some drier areas may experience forest fires.*

The glaciated central plateau of Tasmania has many lakes, including Lake St. Clair, a piedmont lake more than 700 ft (200 m) deep.

Mount Kosciuszko, the highest point in the Snowy Mountains, is the tallest mountain in Australia at 7,316 ft (2,228 m).

New Zealand

Lying 1,500 miles east-southeast of Australia, New Zealand was originally settled by the Maori people of Polynesia. It was visited by Europeans for the first time only as recently as the 1770s. The islands' rugged topography means that most settlement has concentrated in coastal areas. People of European origin make up more than 85% of the population of 3.7 million, following immigration which began in the 1920s. Many recent settlers have come from Asia, including India and China, and a number of the Pacific islands. The Maori now make up a minority of less than half a million. Their ancient claims to at least half of national territory, however, are gaining increasing legal credence.

Clouds of steam *rise from White Island, an active, offshore volcano lying in the Bay of Plenty, off the northern coast of North Island.*

The Landscape

New Zealand comprises two large islands and many scattered smaller islands. On South Island the Alpine Fault marks the boundary between the Pacific and Indo-Australian plates. Tectonic activity has strongly influenced the formation of the Southern Alps, snowcapped mountains with several peaks over 9,800 ft (3,000 m). North Island has a lower and less extensive mountain region, containing forested hills, a central volcanic plateau, and downlands.

Mountain-building in the Southern Alps

The Southern Alps *have been formed by "slip" faulting. The Indo-Australian and Pacific plates run in opposite directions along the Alpine Fault. Although they slide past each other, they are also being thrust over one another, causing the continental crust of the Pacific Plate to be uplifted to form the Alps.*

The Northland region *is characterized by many coastal inlets. These are lined by mangrove swamps, signaling the change to a subtropical climate in the far north of the island.*

The Rotorua and Taupo valleys *have some of the largest and most spectacular thermal springs in New Zealand. These occur when superheated groundwater rises to the surface through joints in the rocks.*

Mount Taranaki, rising 8,261 ft (2,518 m) is an isolated, dormant volcano.

The boundary between the Indo-Australian Plate and the Pacific Plate runs through the center of North Island, leading to many typical volcanic features. The plateau which rises from the slopes of Lake Taupo contains a string of active volcanoes.

Lake Taupo is New Zealand's largest inland lake. It occupies the crater of an extinct volcano.

The Southern Alps run for more than 300 miles, (483 km) forming the backbone of South Island. They were uplifted following the collision of the Pacific and Indo-Australian plates.

Probable location of Alpine Fault

Fiordland, in the far south west, contains a large number of flooded glacial valleys.

Sutherland Falls

The Tasman Glacier, the largest glacier in New Zealand, flows for 18 miles (29 km) down the slopes of New Zealand's highest mountain, Mount Cook.

The coastal Canterbury Plains are the result of glacial outwash. They are the only major flat area in New Zealand.

The Southern Alps contain more than 360 glaciers, including the Murchison, Mueller, and Godley glaciers on the eastern slopes and the Fox and Franz Josef glaciers to the west.

High levels of rainfall and a steep topography has made New Zealand's rivers swift-running. In the southern reaches of both islands, rivers such as the Mokoreta form broad, braided streams.

SCALE 1:3,000,000 (projection: Lambert Conformal Conic)

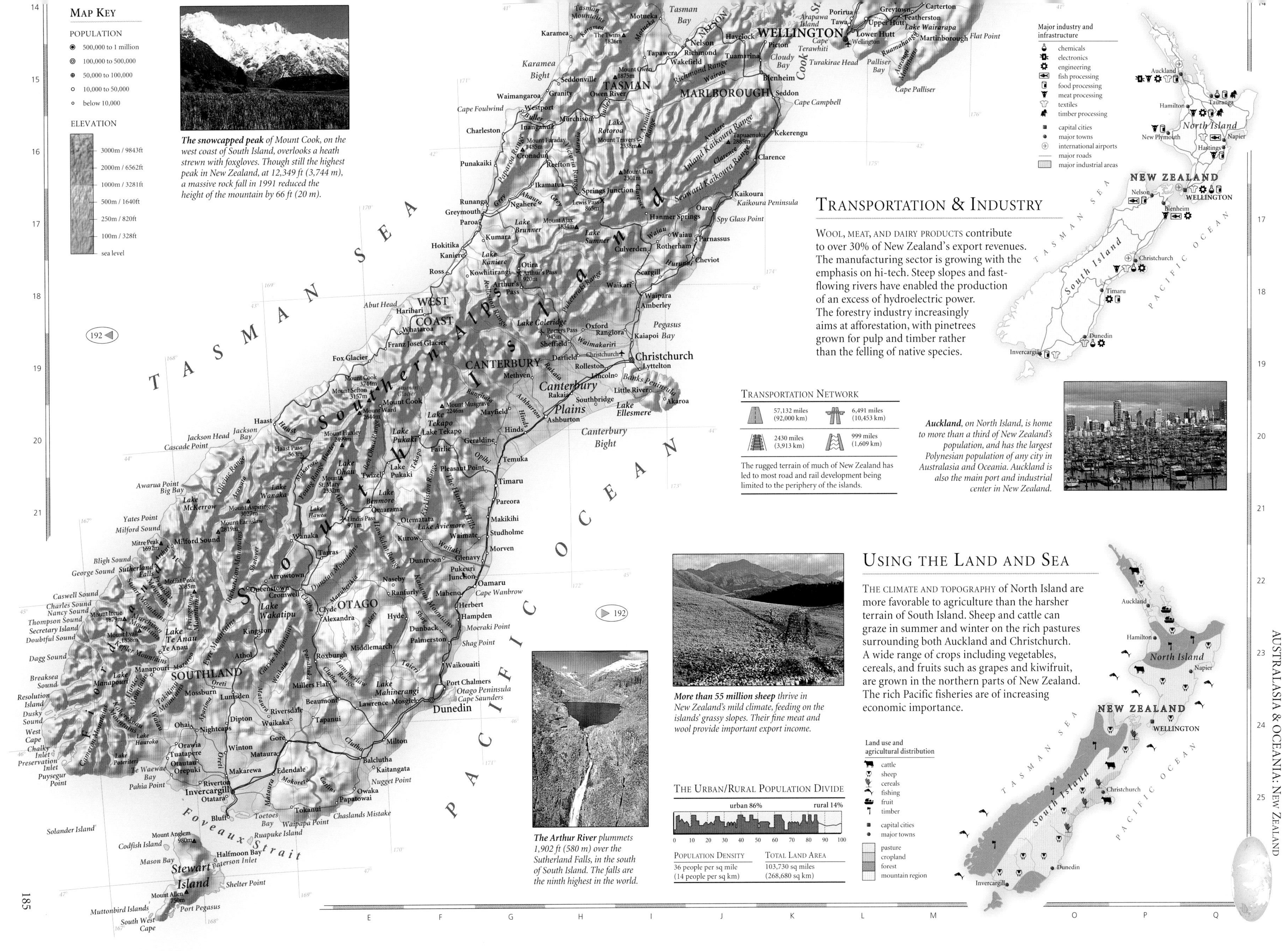

MAP KEY
POPULATION
500,000 to 1 million
100,000 to 500,000
50,000 to 100,000
10,000 to 50,000
below 10,000
ELEVATION
3000m / 9843ft
2000m / 6562ft
1000m / 3281ft
500m / 1640ft
250m / 820ft
100m / 328ft
sea level
TASMAN SEA
PACIFIC OCEAN
Major industry and infrastructure
chemicals
electronics
engineering
fish processing
food processing
meat processing
textiles
timber processing
capital cities
major towns
international airports
major roads
major industrial areas
Land use and agricultural distribution
cattle
sheep
cereals
fishing
fruit
timber
capital cities
major towns
pasture
cropland
forest
mountain region

The snowcapped peak of Mount Cook, on the west coast of South Island, overlooks a heath strewn with foxgloves. Though still the highest peak in New Zealand, at 12,349 ft (3,744 m), a massive rock fall in 1991 reduced the height of the mountain by 66 ft (20 m).

Transportation & Industry

Wool, meat, and dairy products contribute to over 30% of New Zealand's export revenues. The manufacturing sector is growing with the emphasis on hi-tech. Steep slopes and fast-flowing rivers have enabled the production of an excess of hydroelectric power. The forestry industry increasingly aims at afforestation, with pinetrees grown for pulp and timber rather than the felling of native species.

Transportation Network

57,132 miles (92,000 km)	6,491 miles (10,453 km)
2430 miles (3,913 km)	999 miles (1,609 km)

The rugged terrain of much of New Zealand has led to most road and rail development being limited to the periphery of the islands.

***Auckland**, on North Island, is home to more than a third of New Zealand's population, and has the largest Polynesian population of any city in Australasia and Oceania. Auckland is also the main port and industrial center in New Zealand.*

***The Arthur River** plummets 1,902 ft (580 m) over the Sutherland Falls, in the south of South Island. The falls are the ninth highest in the world.*

***More than 55 million sheep** thrive in New Zealand's mild climate, feeding on the islands' grassy slopes. Their fine meat and wool provide important export income.*

The Urban/Rural Population Divide

urban 86% — rural 14%

0 10 20 30 40 50 60 70 80 90 100

Population Density	Total Land Area
36 people per sq mile (14 people per sq km)	103,730 sq miles (268,680 sq km)

Using the Land and Sea

The climate and topography of North Island are more favorable to agriculture than the harsher terrain of South Island. Sheep and cattle can graze in summer and winter on the rich pastures surrounding both Auckland and Christchurch. A wide range of crops including vegetables, cereals, and fruits such as grapes and kiwifruit, are grown in the northern parts of New Zealand. The rich Pacific fisheries are of increasing economic importance.

MELANESIA

PAPUA NEW GUINEA, FIJI, SOLOMON ISLANDS, VANUATU, *New Caledonia* (to France)

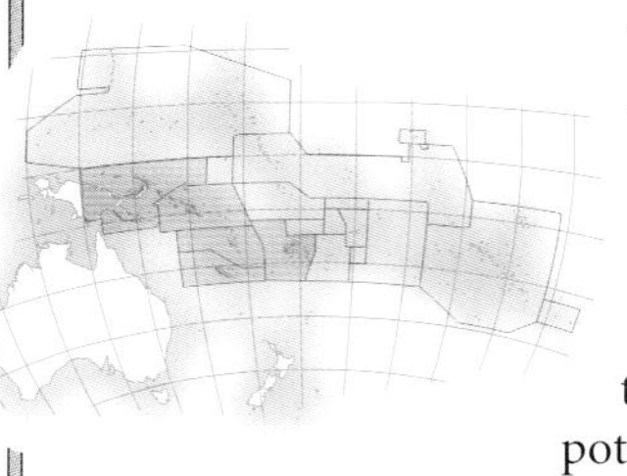

LYING IN THE SOUTHWEST PACIFIC OCEAN, northeast of Australia and south of the Equator, the islands of Melanesia form one of the three geographic divisions (along with Polynesia and Micronesia) of Oceania. Melanesia's name derives from the Greek *melas*, "black," and *nesoi*, "islands." Most of the larger islands are volcanic in origin. The smaller islands tend to be coral atolls and are mainly uninhabited. Rugged mountains, covered by dense rain forest, take up most of the land area. Melanesian's cultivate yams, taro, and sweet potatoes for local consumption and live in small, usually dispersed, homesteads.

***Huli tribesmen** from Southern Highlands Province in Papua New Guinea parade in ceremonial dress, their powdered wigs decorated with exotic plumage and their faces and bodies painted with coloured pigments.*

MAP KEY

POPULATION

- 100,000 to 500,000
- 50,000 to 100,000
- 10,000 to 50,000
- below 10,000

ELEVATION

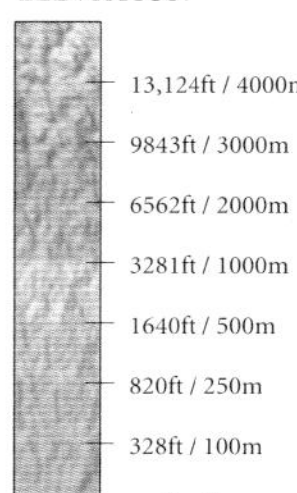
13,124ft / 4000m
9843ft / 3000m
6562ft / 2000m
3281ft / 1000m
1640ft / 500m
820ft / 250m
328ft / 100m
sea level

***Lying close to the banks** of the Sepik River in northern Papua New Guinea, this building is known as the Spirit House. It is constructed from leaves and twigs, ornately woven and trimmed into geometric patterns. The house is decorated with a mask and topped by a carved statue.*

***On one of Vanuatu's many islands**, simple beach houses stand at the water's edge, surrounded by coconut palms and other tropical vegetation. The unspoilt beaches and tranquillity of its islands are drawing ever-larger numbers of tourists to Vanuatu.*

TRANSPORTATION & INDUSTRY

The processing of natural resources generates significant export revenue for the countries of Melanesia. The region relies mainly on copra, tuna, and timber exports, with some production of cocoa and palm oil. The islands have substantial mineral resources including the world's largest copper reserves on Bougainville Island; gold, and potential oil and natural gas. Tourism has become the fastest growing sector in most of the countries' economies.

TRANSPORTATION NETWORK

- 1,236 miles (1,990 km)
- None
- 370 miles (595 km)
- 6,924 miles (11,143 km)

As most of the islands of Melanesia lie off the major sea and air routes, services to and from the rest of the world are infrequent. Transportation by road on rugged terrain is difficult and expensive.

***On New Caledonia's main island,** relatively high interior plateaus descend to coastal plains. Nickel is the most important mineral resource, but the hills also harbor metallic deposits including chrome, cobalt, iron, gold, silver, and copper.*

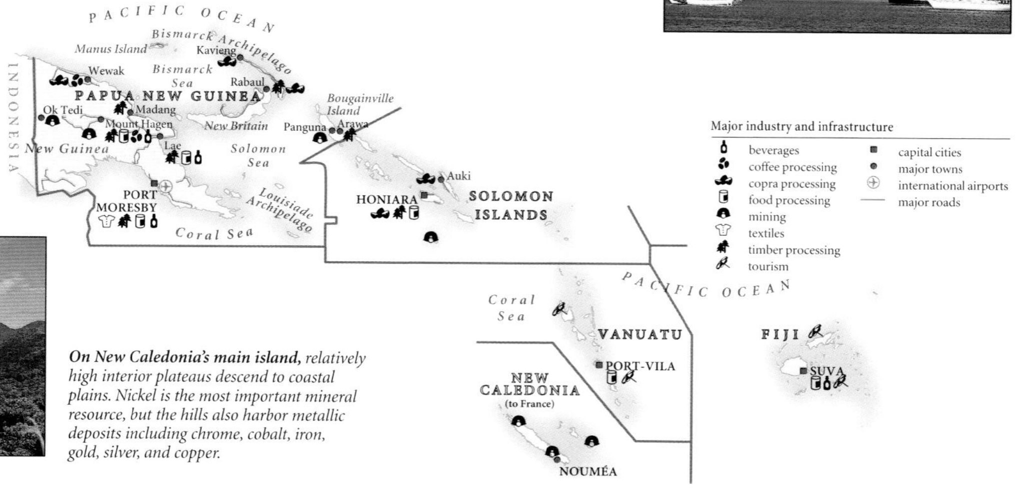

Major industry and infrastructure

- beverages
- coffee processing
- copra processing
- food processing
- mining
- textiles
- timber processing
- tourism
- capital cities
- major towns
- international airports
- major roads

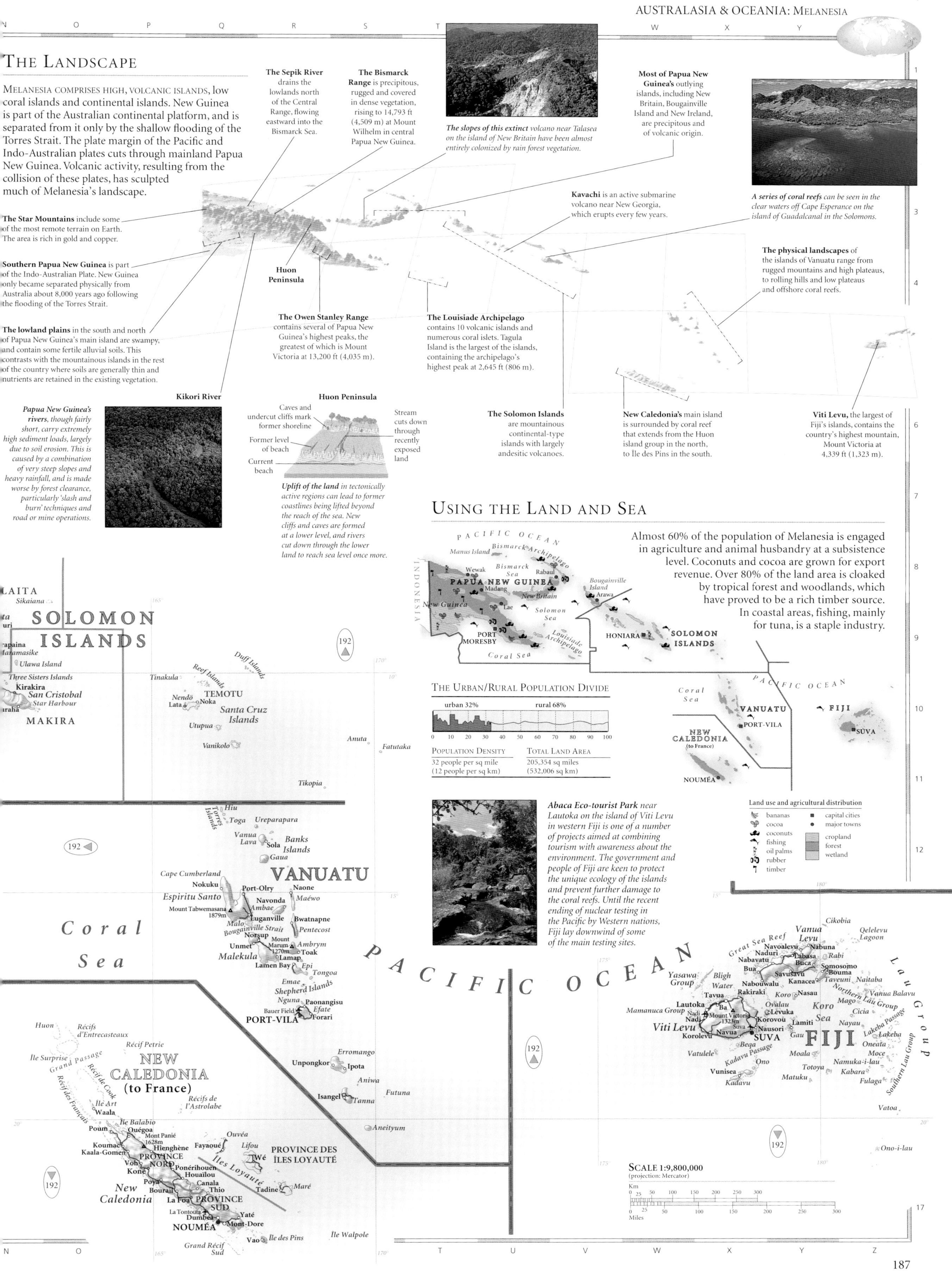

THE LANDSCAPE

MELANESIA COMPRISES HIGH, VOLCANIC ISLANDS, low coral islands and continental islands. New Guinea is part of the Australian continental platform, and is separated from it only by the shallow flooding of the Torres Strait. The plate margin of the Pacific and Indo-Australian plates cuts through mainland Papua New Guinea. Volcanic activity, resulting from the collision of these plates, has sculpted much of Melanesia's landscape.

The Star Mountains include some of the most remote terrain on Earth. The area is rich in gold and copper.

Southern Papua New Guinea is part of the Indo-Australian Plate. New Guinea only became separated physically from Australia about 8,000 years ago following the flooding of the Torres Strait.

The lowland plains in the south and north of Papua New Guinea's main island are swampy, and contain some fertile alluvial soils. This contrasts with the mountainous islands in the rest of the country where soils are generally thin and nutrients are retained in the existing vegetation.

The Sepik River drains the lowlands north of the Central Range, flowing eastward into the Bismarck Sea.

The Bismarck Range is precipitous, rugged and covered in dense vegetation, rising to 14,793 ft (4,509 m) at Mount Wilhelm in central Papua New Guinea.

The slopes of this extinct volcano near Talasea on the island of New Britain have been almost entirely colonized by rain forest vegetation.

Most of Papua New Guinea's outlying islands, including New Britain, Bougainville Island and New Ireland, are precipitous and of volcanic origin.

A series of coral reefs can be seen in the clear waters off Cape Esperance on the island of Guadalcanal in the Solomons.

Kavachi is an active submarine volcano near New Georgia, which erupts every few years.

The physical landscapes of the islands of Vanuatu range from rugged mountains and high plateaus, to rolling hills and low plateaus and offshore coral reefs.

Huon Peninsula

The Owen Stanley Range contains several of Papua New Guinea's highest peaks, the greatest of which is Mount Victoria at 13,200 ft (4,035 m).

The Louisiade Archipelago contains 10 volcanic islands and numerous coral islets. Tagula Island is the largest of the islands, containing the archipelago's highest peak at 2,645 ft (806 m).

The Solomon Islands are mountainous continental-type islands with largely andesitic volcanoes.

New Caledonia's main island is surrounded by coral reef that extends from the Huon island group in the north, to Île des Pins in the south.

Viti Levu, the largest of Fiji's islands, contains the country's highest mountain, Mount Victoria at 4,339 ft (1,323 m).

Kikori River

Papua New Guinea's rivers, though fairly short, carry extremely high sediment loads, largely due to soil erosion. This is caused by a combination of very steep slopes and heavy rainfall, and is made worse by forest clearance, particularly 'slash and burn' techniques and road or mine operations.

Huon Peninsula
Caves and undercut cliffs mark former shoreline
Former level of beach
Current beach
Stream cuts down through recently exposed land

Uplift of the land in tectonically active regions can lead to former coastlines being lifted beyond the reach of the sea. New cliffs and caves are formed at a lower level, and rivers cut down through the lower land to reach sea level once more.

USING THE LAND AND SEA

Almost 60% of the population of Melanesia is engaged in agriculture and animal husbandry at a subsistence level. Coconuts and cocoa are grown for export revenue. Over 80% of the land area is cloaked by tropical forest and woodlands, which have proved to be a rich timber source. In coastal areas, fishing, mainly for tuna, is a staple industry.

PACIFIC OCEAN
Manus Island
Bismarck Archipelago
Bismarck Sea
Wewak
Rabaul
PAPUA NEW GUINEA
Madang
New Britain
INDONESIA
New Guinea
Lae
Solomon Sea
Bougainville Island
Arawa
PORT MORESBY
Louisiade Archipelago
Coral Sea
HONIARA
SOLOMON ISLANDS
Coral Sea
PACIFIC OCEAN
VANUATU
PORT-VILA
FIJI
SUVA
NEW CALEDONIA (to France)
NOUMÉA
Land use and agricultural distribution
bananas
cocoa
coconuts
fishing
oil palms
rubber
timber
capital cities
major towns
cropland
forest
wetland

THE URBAN/RURAL POPULATION DIVIDE

urban 32%
rural 68%
0 10 20 30 40 50 60 70 80 90 100

POPULATION DENSITY	TOTAL LAND AREA
32 people per sq mile (12 people per sq km)	205,354 sq miles (532,006 sq km)

Abaca Eco-tourist Park near Lautoka on the island of Viti Levu in western Fiji is one of a number of projects aimed at combining tourism with awareness about the environment. The government and people of Fiji are keen to protect the unique ecology of the islands and prevent further damage to the coral reefs. Until the recent ending of nuclear testing in the Pacific by Western nations, Fiji lay downwind of some of the main testing sites.

SOLOMON ISLANDS
MALAITA
Sikaiana
Ulawa Island
Three Sisters Islands
Kirakira
San Cristobal
Star Harbour
MAKIRA
Tinakula
Reef Islands
Duff Islands
Nendö
Lata
Noka
TEMOTU
Santa Cruz Islands
Utupua
Vanikolo
Anuta
Fatutaka
Tikopia
Torres Islands
Hiu
Toga
Ureparapara
Vanua Lava
Sola
Banks Islands
Gaua
VANUATU
Cape Cumberland
Nokuku
Port-Olry
Naone
Espiritu Santo
Mount Tabwemasana 1879m
Navonda
Ambae
Maéwo
Luganville
Malo
Bougainville Strait
Bwatnapne
Pentecost
Norsup
Unmet
Mount Marum 1270m
Ambrym
Malekula
Toak
Lamap
Lamen Bay
Epi
Tongoa
Emae
Shepherd Islands
Nguna
Paonangisu
Bauer Field
Efate
PORT-VILA
Forari
Erromango
Unpongkor
Ipota
Aniwa
Isangel
Tanna
Futuna
Aneityum
Coral Sea
PACIFIC OCEAN
Huon
Récifs d'Entrecasteaux
Récif Petrie
Île Surprise
Grand Passage
NEW CALEDONIA (to France)
Récif de Cook
Récifs des Français
Île Art
Waala
Récifs de l'Astrolabe
Île Balabio
Ouégoa
Poum
Mont Panié 1628m
Koumac
Hienghène
Kaala-Gomen
PROVINCE NORD
Voh
Koné
Ponérihouen
Houailou
Poya
Canala
Bourail
Thio
La Foa
PROVINCE SUD
New Caledonia
La Tontouta
Dumbéa
Yaté
NOUMÉA
Mont-Dore
Vao
Île des Pins
Grand Récif Sud
Ouvéa
Fayaoué
Lifou
Wé
PROVINCE DES ÎLES LOYAUTÉ
Îles Loyauté
Tadine
Maré
Île Walpole
FIJI
Cikobia
Vanua Levu
Qelelevu Lagoon
Great Sea Reef
Navoalevu
Nabuna
Naduri
Labasa
Rabi
Nabavatu
Buca
Somosomo
Bua
Savusavu
Bouma
Taveuni
Naitaba
Yasawa Group
Bligh Water
Nabouwalu
Kanacea
Northern Lau Group
Vanua Balavu
Rakiraki
Koro
Nasau
Tavua
Mago
Lautoka
Ba
Ovalau
Koro Sea
Cicia
Mamanuca Group
Nadi
Levuka
Mount Victoria 1323m
Korovou
Lamiti
Nayau
Lakeba Passage
Viti Levu
Navua
Nausori
Suva
SUVA
Gau
Lakeba
Korolevu
Beqa
Oneata
Vatulele
Kadavu Passage
Moala
Moce
Ono
Totoya
Namuka-i-lau
Vunisea
Kabara
Kadavu
Matuku
Fulaga
Southern Lau Group
Lau Group
Vatoa
Ono-i-lau
SCALE 1:9,800,000
(projection: Mercator)
Km
0 25 50 100 150 200 250 300
0 25 50 100 150 200 250 300
Miles

192

MICRONESIA

MARSHALL ISLANDS, MICRONESIA, NAURU, PALAU,
Guam, Northern Mariana Islands, Wake Island

THE MICRONESIAN ISLANDS lie in the western reaches of the Pacific Ocean and are all part of the same volcanic zone. The Federated States of Micronesia is the largest group, with more than 600 atolls and forested volcanic islands in an area of more than 1,120 sq miles (2,900 sq km). Micronesia is a mixture of former colonies, overseas territories, and dependencies. Most of the region still relies on aid and subsidies to sustain economies limited by resources, isolation, and an emigrating population, drawn to New Zealand and Australia by the attractions of a western lifestyle.

PALAU

PALAU IS AN ARCHIPELAGO OF OVER 200 ISLANDS, only eight of which are inhabited. It was the last remaining UN trust territory in the Pacific, controlled by the US until 1994, when it became independent. The economy operates on a subsistence level, with coconuts and cassava the principal crops. Fishing licenses and tourism provide foreign currency.

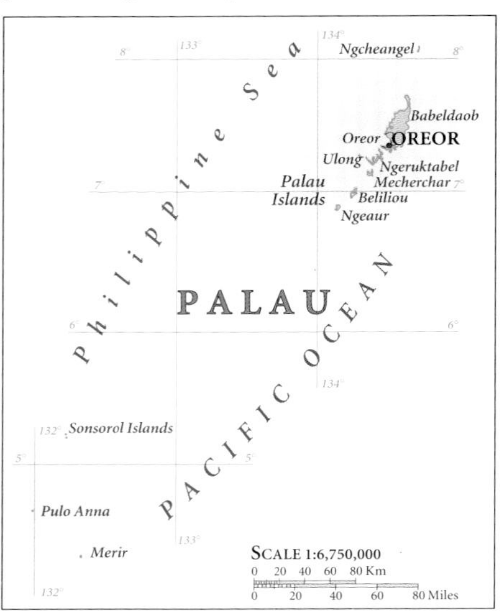
Philippine Sea
Ngcheangel
Babeldaob
Oreor OREOR
Ulong
Ngeruktabel
Mecherchar
Palau Islands
Beliliou
Ngeaur
PALAU
PACIFIC OCEAN
Sonsorol Islands
Pulo Anna
Merir
SCALE 1:6,750,000
0 20 40 60 80 Km
0 20 40 60 80 Miles

SCALE 1:825,000
0 2.5 5 10 Km
0 2.5 5 10 Miles
Philippine Sea
Ngaregur
Ollei
Chol
Aiwokako Passage
Ngardmau Bay
Chelab
Ulimang
Ngetbong
Ngkeklau
Ngermechau
Imeong
West Passage
Namai Bay
Babeldaob
Ibobang
Melekeok
Ngchemiangel
Ngerkeai
Komebail Lagoon
Namekakl Passage
Arakabesan
Ngetkip
Airai
Oikuul
OREOR
Oreor
PACIFIC OCEAN

NORTHERN MARIANA ISLANDS (to US)

A US COMMONWEALTH TERRITORY, the Northern Marianas comprise the whole of the Mariana archipelago except for Guam. The islands retain their close links with the US and continue to receive American aid. Tourism, though bringing in much-needed revenue, has speeded the decline of the traditional subsistence economy. Most of the population lives on Saipan.

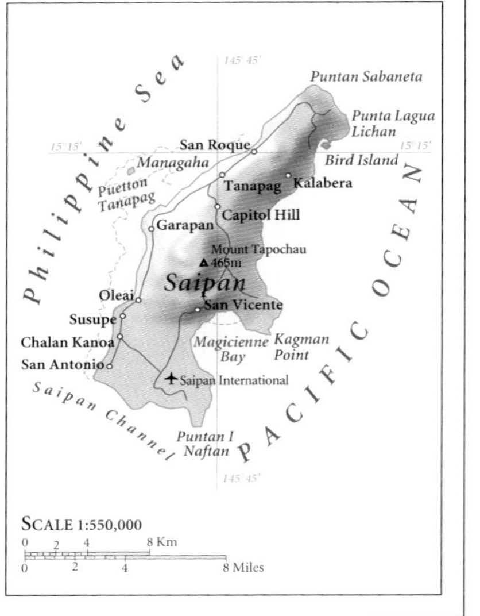
Philippine Sea
Puntan Sabaneta
Punta Lagua Lichan
San Roque
Managaha
Bird Island
Puetton Tanapag
Tanapag
Kalabera
Capitol Hill
Garapan
Mount Tapochau 466m
Saipan
Olei
San Vicente
Susupe
Chalan Kanoa
Magicienne Bay
Kagman Point
San Antonio
Saipan International
Saipan Channel
Puntan I Naftan
PACIFIC OCEAN
SCALE 1:550,000
0 2 4 8 Km
0 2 4 8 Miles

Farallon de Pajaros
Supply Reef
PACIFIC OCEAN
Maug Islands
Asuncion Island
NORTHERN MARIANA ISLANDS
(to US)
Agrihan
Pagan
Alamagan
Guguan
Zealandia Bank
Sarigan
Anatahan
Farallon de Medinilla
Philippine Sea
Mariana Islands

The Palau Islands have numerous hidden lakes and lagoons. These sustain their own ecosystems which have developed in isolation. This has produced adaptations in the animals and plants that are often unique to each lake.

Saipan
Susupe
San Jose
Tinian
Aguijan
Rota
PACIFIC OCEAN
GUAM
(to US)
HAGÅTÑA
(AGANA)
Dededo

MICRONESIA

A MIXTURE OF HIGH VOLCANIC ISLANDS and low-lying coral atolls, the Federated States of Micronesia include all the Caroline Islands except Palau. Pohnpei, Kosrae, Chuuk, and Yap are the four main island cluster states, each of which has its own language, with English remaining the official language. Nearly half the population is concentrated on Pohnpei, the largest island. Independent since 1986, the islands continue to receive considerable aid from the US which supplements an economy based primarily on fishing and copra processing.

GUAM (to US)

LYING AT THE SOUTHERN END of the Mariana Islands, Guam is an important US military base and tourist destination. Social and political life is dominated by the indigenous Chamorro, who make up just under half the population, although the increasing prevalence of western culture threatens Guam's traditional social stability.

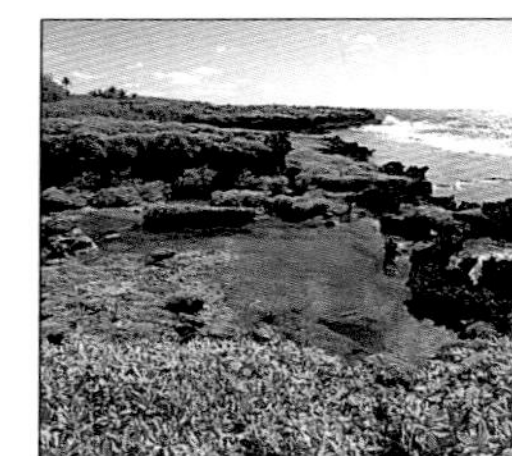

***The tranquillity** of these coastal lagoons, at Inarajan in southern Guam, belies the fact that the island lies in a region where typhoons are common.*

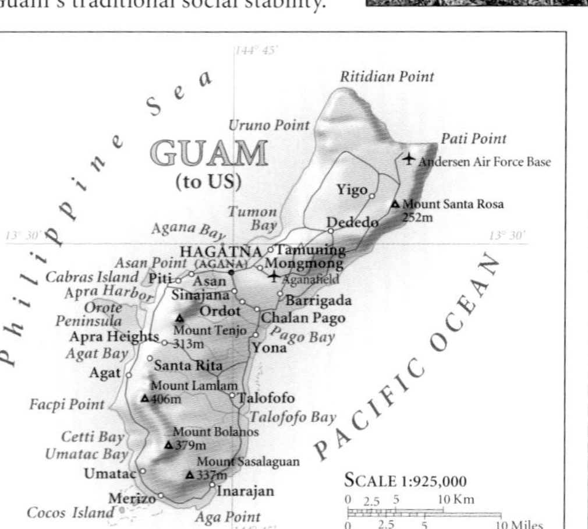
Philippine Sea
Ritidian Point
Uruno Point
GUAM
(to US)
Pati Point
Andersen Air Force Base
Yigo
Mount Santa Rosa 252m
Tumon Bay
Dededo
Agana Bay
HAGÅTÑA (AGANA)
Tamuning
Mongmong
Asan Point
Cabras Island
Piti
Asan
Apra Harbor
Sinajana
Orote Peninsula
Ordot
Barrigada
Mount Tenjo
Chalan Pago
Apra Heights 313m
Pago Bay
Yona
Agat Bay
Santa Rita
Agat
Mount Lamlam 406m
Talofofo
Facpi Point
Talofofo Bay
Cetti Bay
Mount Bolanos 379m
Umatac Bay
Mount Sasalaguan 332m
Umatac
Inarajan
Merizo
Cocos Island
Aga Point
PACIFIC OCEAN
SCALE 1:925,000
0 2.5 5 10 Km
0 2.5 5 10 Miles

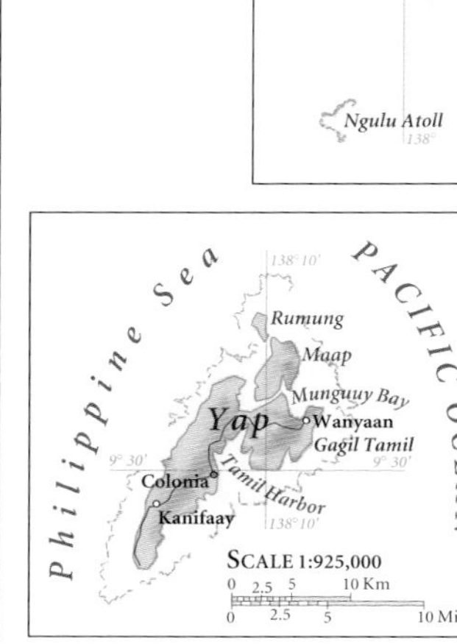
Philippine Sea
PACIFIC OCEAN
Rumung
Maap
Munguuy Bay
Yap
Wanyaan
Gagil Tamil
Colonia
Tamil Harbor
Kanifaay
SCALE 1:925,000
0 2.5 5 10 Km
0 2.5 5 10 Miles

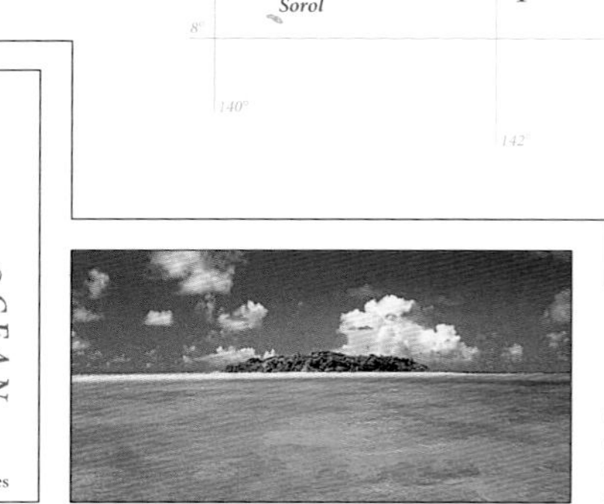

***Ulithi Atoll**, lying in the state of Yap, the most westerly part of Micronesia, is a typical coral island, with a series of reefs enclosing a large lagoon.*

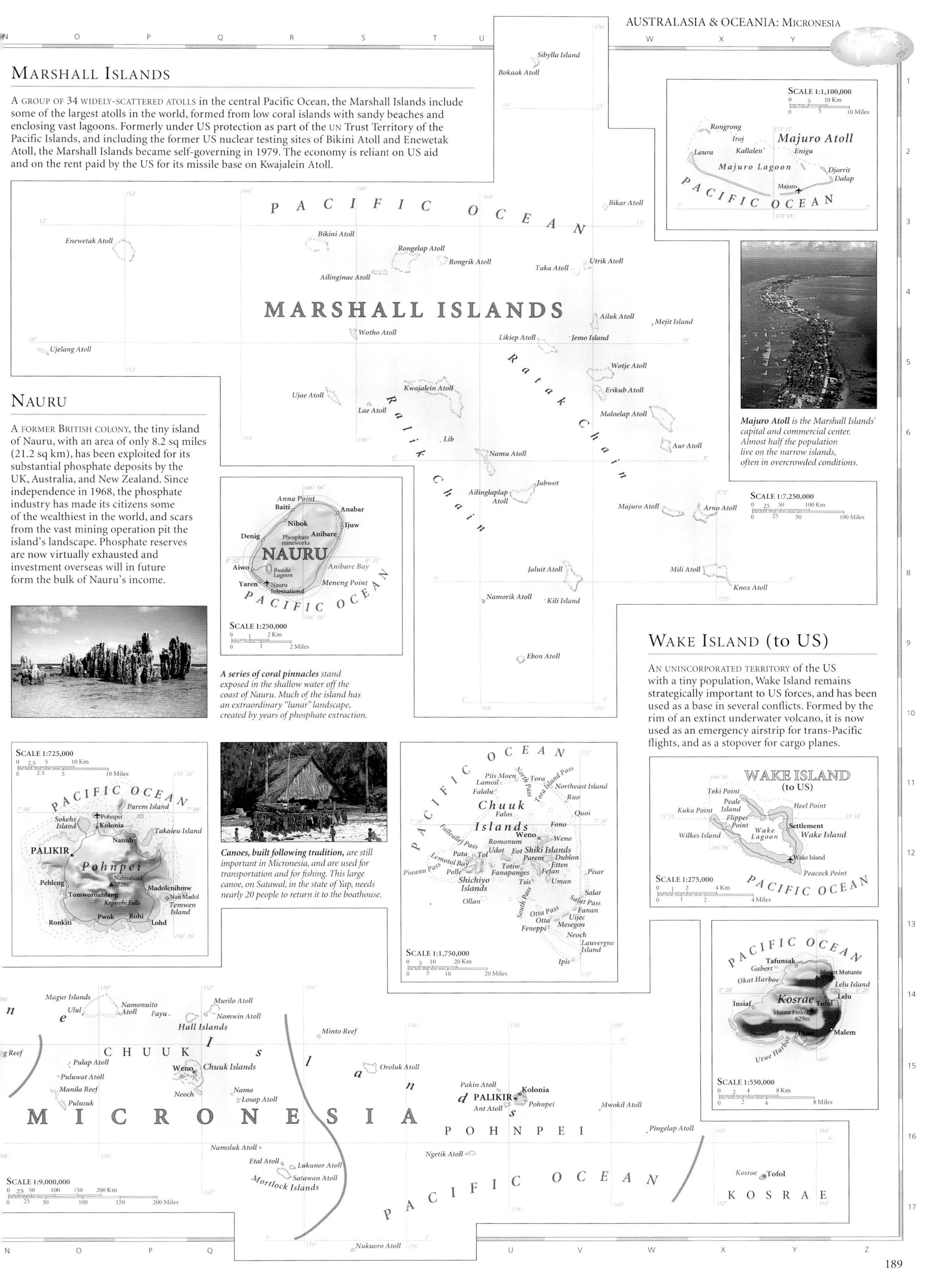

Sibylla Island
Bokaak Atoll
PACIFIC OCEAN
Bikar Atoll
Enewetak Atoll
Bikini Atoll
Rongelap Atoll
Rongrik Atoll
Ailinginae Atoll
Taka Atoll
Utrik Atoll
MARSHALL ISLANDS
Ailuk Atoll
Mejit Island
Wotho Atoll
Likiep Atoll
Jemo Island
Ujelang Atoll
Ratak Chain
Wotje Atoll
Kwajalein Atoll
Ujae Atoll
Erikub Atoll
Lae Atoll
Ralik Chain
Maloelap Atoll
Lib
Aur Atoll
Namu Atoll
Jabwot
Ailinglaplap Atoll
Majuro Atoll
Arno Atoll
Jaluit Atoll
Mili Atoll
Knox Atoll
Namorik Atoll
Kili Island
Ebon Atoll
SCALE 1:1,100,000
Rongrong
Iroj
Majuro Atoll
Laura
Kallalen
Enigu
Majuro Lagoon
Djarrit
Dalap
Majuro
PACIFIC OCEAN
SCALE 1:7,250,000
Anna Point
Baiti
Anabar
Nibok
Ijuw
Denig
Phosphate mineworks
Anibare
NAURU
Aiwo
Buada Lagoon
Anibare Bay
Yaren
Nauru International
Meneng Point
PACIFIC OCEAN
SCALE 1:250,000
SCALE 1:725,000
PACIFIC OCEAN
Parem Island
Sokehs Island
Pohnpei
Kolonia
Takaieu Island
Nanuh
PALIKIR
Pohnpei
Nahnalaud 772m
Pehleng
Madolenihmw
Nan Madol
Tomworoahlang
Kepirohi Falls
Temwen Island
Pwok
Rohi
Ronkiti
Lohd
OCEAN
PACIFIC
North Pass
Piis Moen
Tora
Tora Island Pass
Lamoil
Northeast Island
Falalu
Ruo
Chuuk Islands
Falos
Quoi
Fono
Falleallej Pass
Weno
Weno
Romanum
Udot
Eot
Shiki Islands
Pata
Tol
Parem
Dublon
Lemotol Bay
Etten
Piaanu Pass
Polle
Totiw
Fefan
Pisar
Shichiyo Islands
Fanapanges
Tsis
Uman
South Pass
Salat
Ollan
Salat Pass
Otta Pass
Fanan
Otta
Uijec
Feneppi
Mesegon
Neoch
Lauvergne Island
Ipis
SCALE 1:1,750,000
WAKE ISLAND (to US)
Toki Point
Peale Island
Kuku Point
Heel Point
Flipper Point
Wake Lagoon
Settlement
Wilkes Island
Wake Island
Wake Island
Peacock Point
PACIFIC OCEAN
SCALE 1:275,000
PACIFIC OCEAN
Tafunsak
Gabert
Mount Mutunte
Okat Harbor
Lelu Island
Insiaf
Kosrae
Tofol
Lelu
Mount Finkol 629m
Malem
Utwe Harbor
SCALE 1:550,000
Magur Islands
Namonuito Atoll
Murilo Atoll
Ulul
Fayu
Nomwin Atoll
Hall Islands
Minto Reef
CHUUK
Pulap Atoll
Weno
Chuuk Islands
Oroluk Atoll
Puluwat Atoll
Manila Reef
Neoch
Nama
Losap Atoll
Pakin Atoll
Kolonia
Pulusuk
PALIKIR
Pohnpei
Ant Atoll
Mwokil Atoll
MICRONESIA
Caroline Islands
POHNPEI
Pingelap Atoll
Namoluk Atoll
Ngetik Atoll
Etal Atoll
Lukunor Atoll
Satawan Atoll
Mortlock Islands
Kosrae
Tofol
SCALE 1:9,000,000
PACIFIC OCEAN
KOSRAE
Nukuoro Atoll

Marshall Islands

A group of 34 widely-scattered atolls in the central Pacific Ocean, the Marshall Islands include some of the largest atolls in the world, formed from low coral islands with sandy beaches and enclosing vast lagoons. Formerly under US protection as part of the UN Trust Territory of the Pacific Islands, and including the former US nuclear testing sites of Bikini Atoll and Enewetak Atoll, the Marshall Islands became self-governing in 1979. The economy is reliant on US aid and on the rent paid by the US for its missile base on Kwajalein Atoll.

Majuro Atoll *is the Marshall Islands' capital and commercial center. Almost half the population live on the narrow islands, often in overcrowded conditions.*

Nauru

A former British colony, the tiny island of Nauru, with an area of only 8.2 sq miles (21.2 sq km), has been exploited for its substantial phosphate deposits by the UK, Australia, and New Zealand. Since independence in 1968, the phosphate industry has made its citizens some of the wealthiest in the world, and scars from the vast mining operation pit the island's landscape. Phosphate reserves are now virtually exhausted and investment overseas will in future form the bulk of Nauru's income.

A series of coral pinnacles *stand exposed in the shallow water off the coast of Nauru. Much of the island has an extraordinary "lunar" landscape, created by years of phosphate extraction.*

Canoes, built following tradition, *are still important in Micronesia, and are used for transportation and for fishing. This large canoe, on Satawal, in the state of Yap, needs nearly 20 people to return it to the boathouse.*

Wake Island (to US)

An unincorporated territory of the US with a tiny population, Wake Island remains strategically important to US forces, and has been used as a base in several conflicts. Formed by the rim of an extinct underwater volcano, it is now used as an emergency airstrip for trans-Pacific flights, and as a stopover for cargo planes.

Polynesia

Kiribati, Tuvalu, *Cook Islands, Easter Island, French Polynesia, Niue, Pitcairn Islands, Tokelau, Wallis & Futuna*

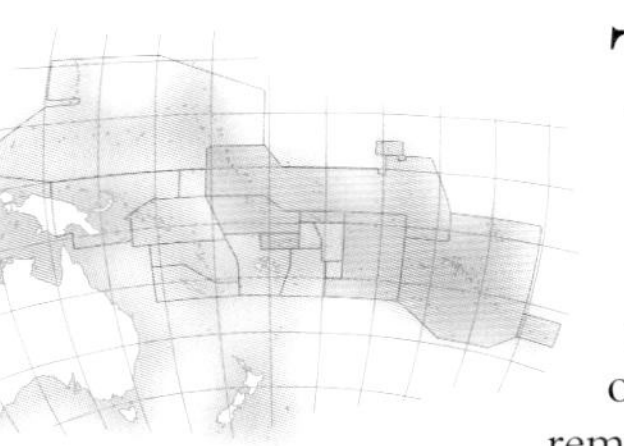

The numerous island groups of Polynesia lie to the east of Australia, scattered over a vast area in the south Pacific. The islands are a mixture of low-lying coral atolls, some of which enclose lagoons, and the tips of great underwater volcanoes. The populations on the islands are small, and most people are of Polynesian origin, as are the Maori of New Zealand. Local economies remain simple, relying mainly on subsistence crops, mineral deposits, many now exhausted, fishing, and tourism.

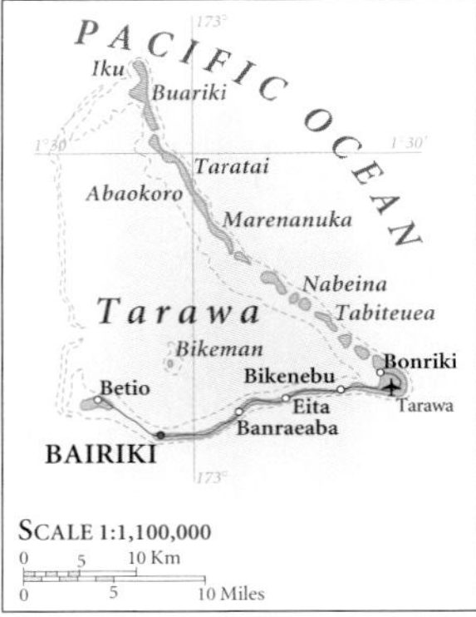

PACIFIC OCEAN
Iku
Buariki
Taratai
Abaokoro
Marenanuka
Nabeina
Tabiteuea
Tarawa
Bikeman
Bonriki
Betio
Bikenebu
Eita
Tarawa
Banraeaba
BAIRIKI
SCALE 1:1,100,000
0 5 10 Km
0 5 10 Miles

Kiribati

A former British colony, Kiribati became independent in 1979. Banaba's phosphate deposits ran out in 1980, following decades of exploitation by the British. Economic development remains slow and most agriculture is at a subsistence level, though coconuts provide export income, and underwater agriculture is being developed.

***With the exception of Banaba** all the islands in Kiribati's three groups are low-lying, coral atolls. This aerial view shows the sparsely vegetated islands, intercut by many small lagoons.*

Tuvalu

A chain of nine coral atolls, 360 miles (579 km) long with a land area of just over 9 sq miles (23 sq km), Tuvalu is one of the world's smallest and most isolated states. As the Ellice Islands, Tuvalu was linked to the Gilbert Islands (now part of Kiribati) as a British colony until independence in 1978. Politically and socially conservative, Tuvaluans live by fishing and subsistence farming.

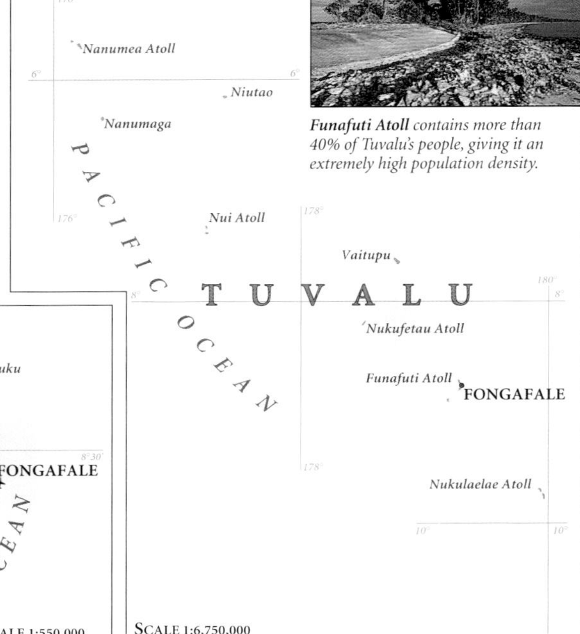

Nanumea Atoll
Niutao
Nanumaga
PACIFIC OCEAN
Nui Atoll
Vaitupu
TUVALU
Nukufetau Atoll
Funafuti Atoll
FONGAFALE
Nukulaelae Atoll
Niulakita
SCALE 1:6,750,000
0 10 20 40 60 80 Km
0 10 20 40 60 80 Miles

***Funafuti Atoll** contains more than 40% of Tuvalu's people, giving it an extremely high population density.*

Fualifeke
Te Ava I Te Lape
Amatuku
Tepuka
Fualopa
Fongafale
Fuafatu
Funafuti Atoll
FONGAFALE
Funafuti
Te Ava Fuagea
Vasafua
Funangongo
Fatato
Fuagea
Te Ava Pua Pua
Falefatu
Tefala
Funafara
Teafuafou
Telele
PACIFIC OCEAN
SCALE 1:550,000
0 2 4 Km
0 2 4 Miles

Tokelau (to New Zealand)

A low-lying coral atoll, Tokelau is a dependent territory of New Zealand with few natural resources. Although a 1990 cyclone destroyed crops and infrastructure, a tuna cannery and the sale of fishing licenses have raised revenue and a catamaran link between the islands has increased their tourism potential. Tokelau's small size and economic weakness makes independence from New Zealand unlikely.

***Fishermen cast their nets** to catch small fish in the shallow waters off Atafu Atoll, the most westerly island in Tokelau.*

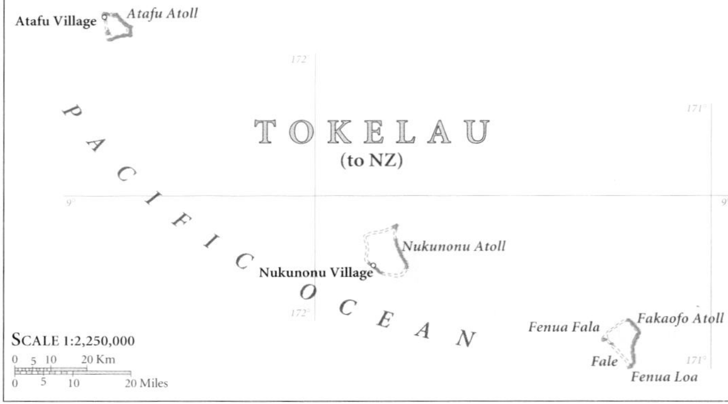

Atafu Village
Atafu Atoll
TOKELAU
(to NZ)
PACIFIC OCEAN
Nukunonu Atoll
Nukunonu Village
Fenua Fala
Fakaofo Atoll
Fale
Fenua Loa
SCALE 1:2,250,000
0 5 10 20 Km
0 5 10 20 Miles

Wallis & Futuna (to France)

In contrast to other French overseas territories in the south Pacific, the inhabitants of Wallis and Futuna have shown little desire for greater autonomy. A subsistence economy produces a variety of tropical crops, while foreign currency remittances come from expatriates and from the sale of licenses to Japanese and Korean fishing fleets.

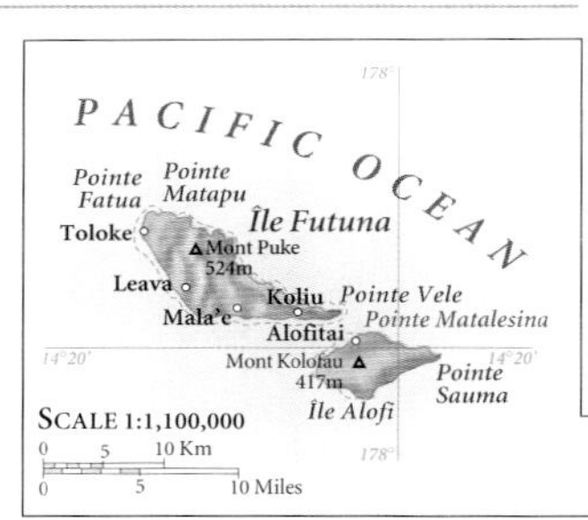

PACIFIC OCEAN
Pointe Fatua
Pointe Matapu
Île Futuna
Toloke
Mont Puke 524m
Leava
Koliu
Pointe Vele
Mala'e
Pointe Matalesina
Alofitai
Mont Kolofau 417m
Pointe Sauma
Île Alofi
SCALE 1:1,100,000
0 5 10 Km
0 5 10 Miles

PACIFIC OCEAN
Nukuloa
Nukutapu
Hihifo
Vaitupu
Îles Wallis
Baie de l'Ouest
Alele
Île Luaniva
Ahoa
Île Uvea
MATĀ'UTU
Baie de Matā'utu
Nukuhifala
Mala'atoli
Halalo
Tepa
Nukuatea
Pointe Matala'a
Île Fenuafo'ou
Île Faioa
SCALE 1:1,100,000
0 5 10 Km
0 5 10 Miles

Cook Islands (to New Zealand)

A mixture of coral atolls and volcanic peaks, the Cook Islands achieved self-government in 1965 but exist in free association with New Zealand. A diverse economy includes pearl and giant clam farming, and an ostrich farm, plus tourism and banking. A 1991 friendship treaty with France provides for French surveillance of territorial waters.

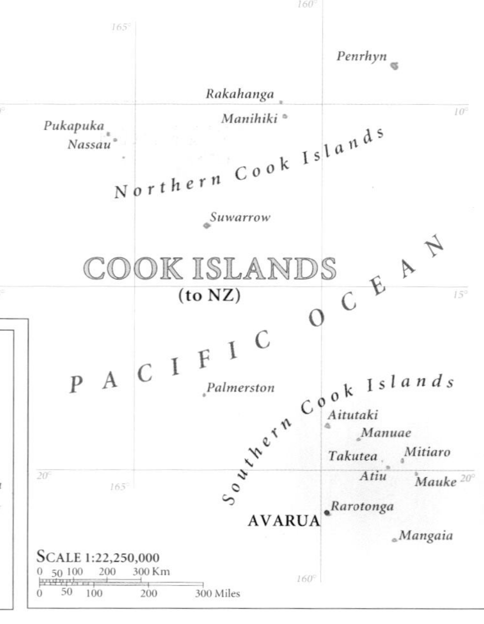

Penrhyn
Rakahanga
Manihiki
Pukapuka
Nassau
Northern Cook Islands
Suwarrow
COOK ISLANDS
(to NZ)
PACIFIC OCEAN
Palmerston
Southern Cook Islands
Aitutaki
Manuae
Takutea
Mitiaro
Atiu
Mauke
Rarotonga
AVARUA
Mangaia
SCALE 1:22,250,000
0 50 100 200 300 Km
0 50 100 200 300 Miles

Niue (to New Zealand)

Niue, the world's largest coral island, is self-governing but exists in free association with New Zealand. Tropical fruits are grown for local consumption; tourism and the sale of postage stamps provide foreign currency. The lack of local job prospects has led more than 10,000 Niueans to emigrate to New Zealand, which has now invested heavily in Niue's economy in the hope of reversing this trend.

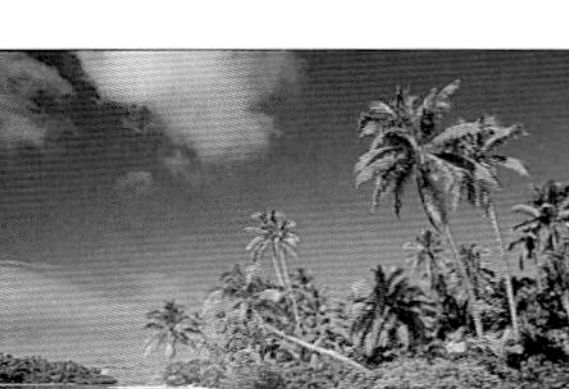

***Palm trees fringe** the white sands of a beach on Aitutaki in the Southern Cook Islands, where tourism is of increasing economic importance.*

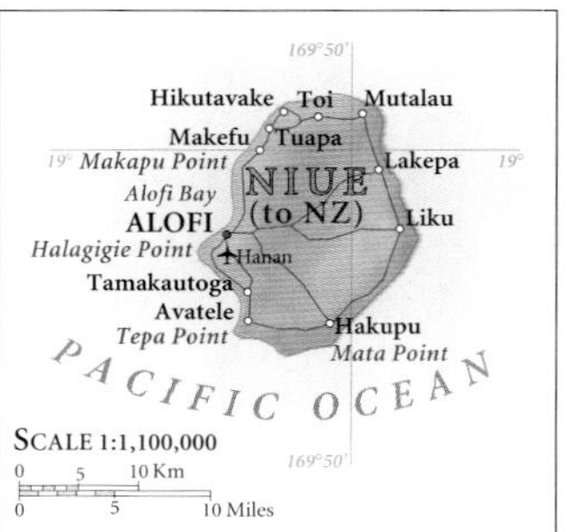

Hikutavake
Toi
Mutalau
Makefu
Tuapa
Makapu Point
Lakepa
Alofi Bay
NIUE
(to NZ)
ALOFI
Liku
Halagigie Point
Hanan
Tamakautoga
Avatele
Tepa Point
Hakupu
Mata Point
PACIFIC OCEAN
SCALE 1:1,100,000
0 5 10 Km
0 5 10 Miles

***Waves have cut back** the original coastline, exposing a sandy beach, near Mutalau in the northeast corner of Niue.*

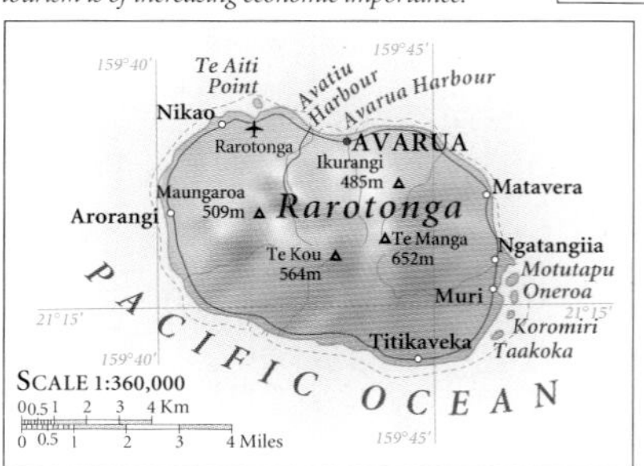

Te Aiti Point
Avatiu Harbour
Avarua Harbour
Nikao
Rarotonga
AVARUA
Ikurangi 485m
Matavera
Arorangi
Maungaroa 509m
Rarotonga
Te Manga 652m
Te Kou 564m
Ngatangiia
Motutapu
Oneroa
Muri
Koromiri
Titikaveka
Taakoka
PACIFIC OCEAN
SCALE 1:360,000
0 0.5 1 2 3 4 Km
0 0.5 1 2 3 4 Miles

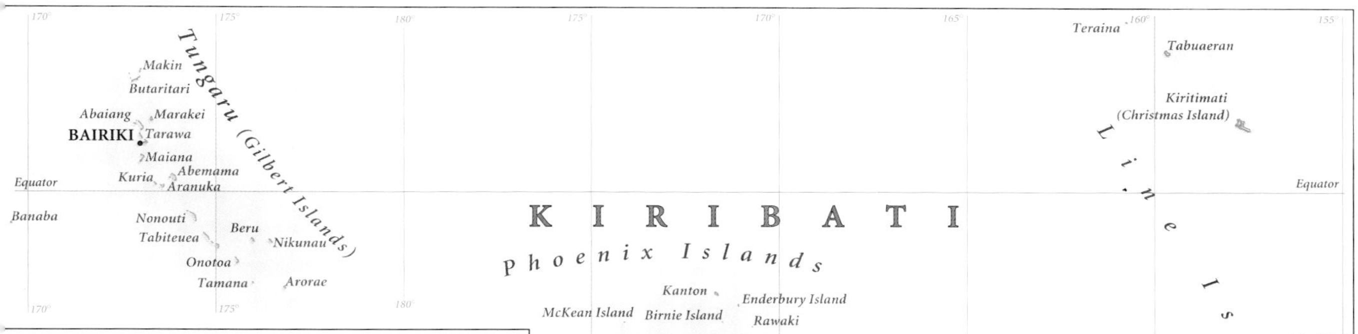

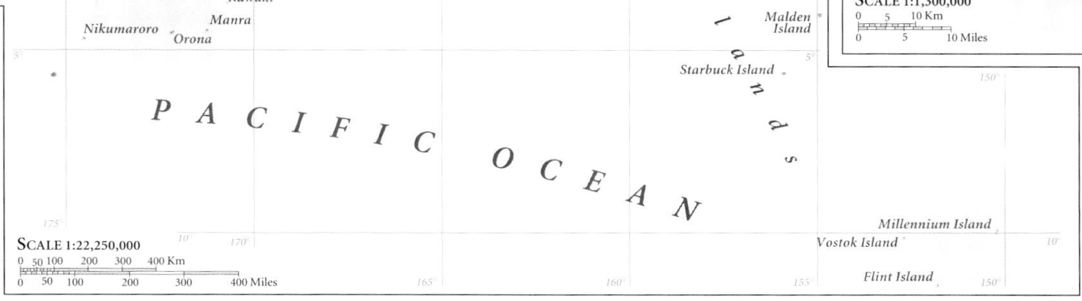

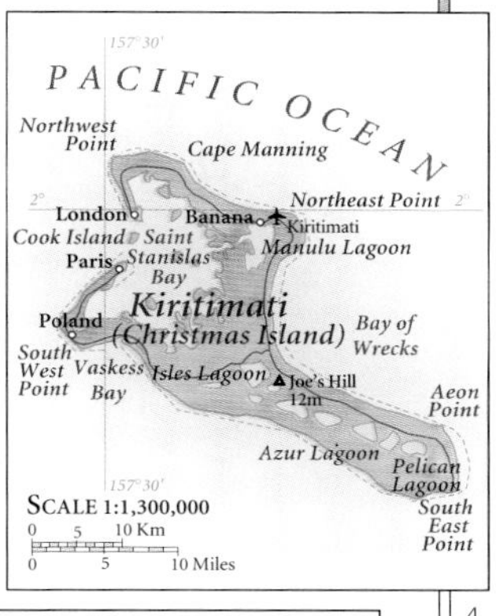

French Polynesia (to France)

The 130 islands of French Polynesia cover 4 million sq miles (10.5 million sq km). Nearly 75% of the people live on Tahiti. The use of Mururoa as a nuclear testing site by the French military transformed the economy, creating many jobs. The end of testing led to calls from the Polynesian majority for greater autonomy from France, the rebuilding of indigenous trade, and a reduction in tourism to stop the erosion of the islands' traditional culture.

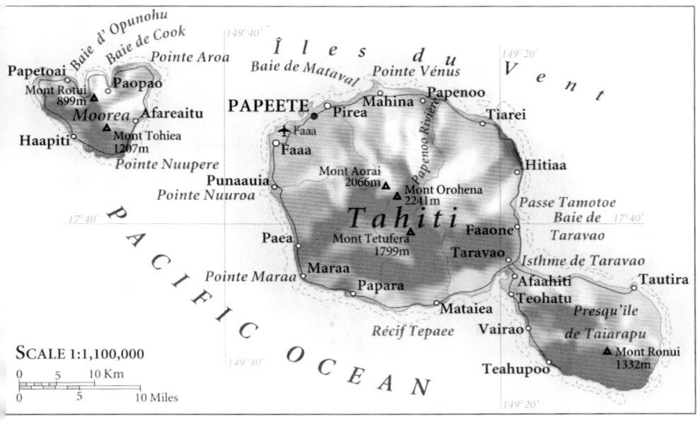

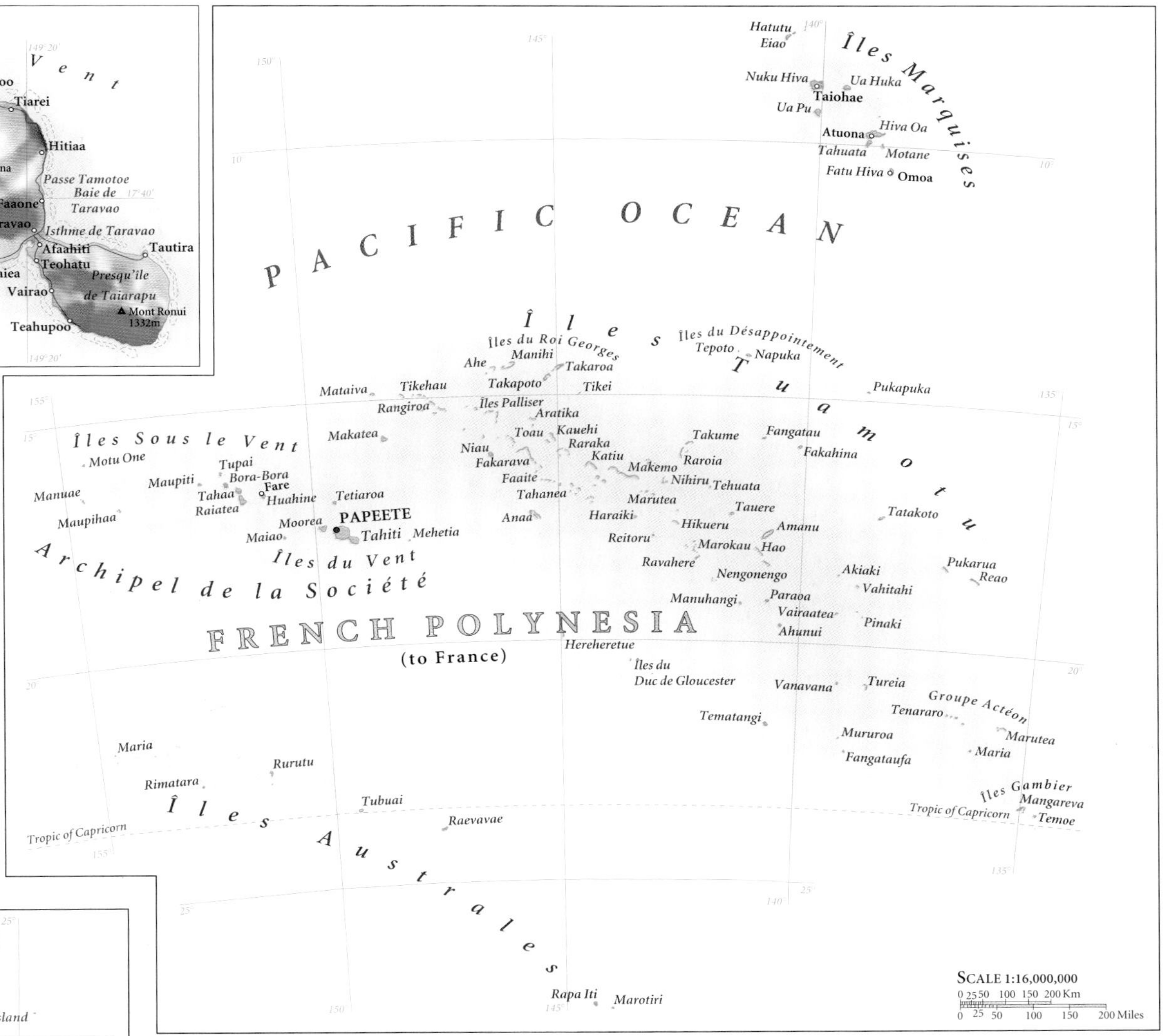

The traditional Tahitian welcome for visitors, who are greeted by parties of canoes, has become a major tourist attraction.

Pitcairn Islands (to UK)

Britain's most isolated dependency, Pitcairn Island was first populated by mutineers from the HMS *Bounty* in 1790. Emigration is further depleting the already limited gene pool of the island's inhabitants, with associated social and health problems. Barter, fishing, and subsistence farming form the basis of the economy although postage stamp sales provide foreign currency earnings, and offshore mineral exploitation may boost the economy in future.

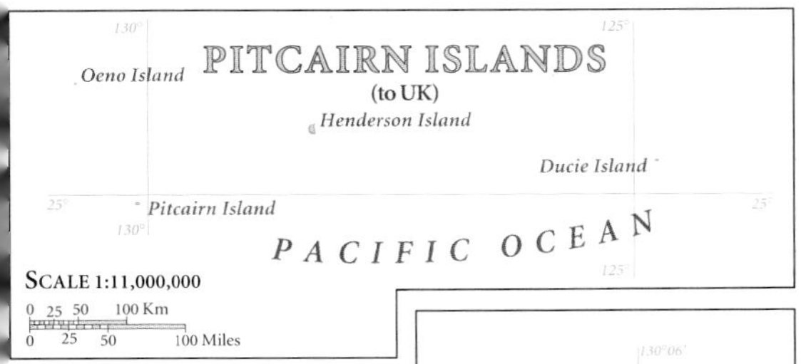

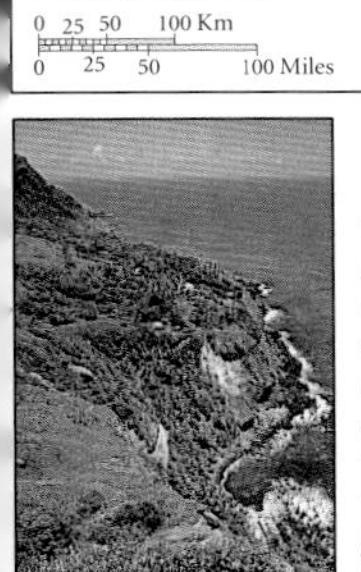

***The Pitcairn Islanders** rely on regular airdrops from New Zealand and periodic visits by supply vessels to provide them with basic commodities.*

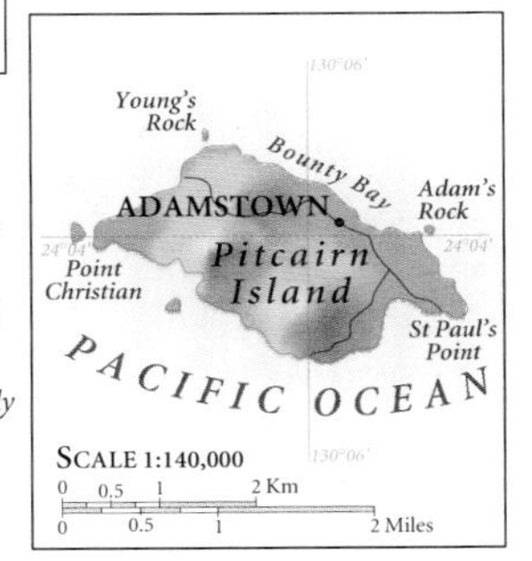
Young's Rock
Bounty Bay
Adam's Rock
ADAMSTOWN
Pitcairn Island
Point Christian
St Paul's Point
PACIFIC OCEAN
SCALE 1:140,000

Easter Island (to Chile)

One of the most easterly islands in Polynesia, Easter Island *(Isla de Pascua)* – also known as Rapa Nui, is part of Chile. The mainly Polynesian inhabitants support themselves by farming, which is mainly of a subsistence nature, and includes cattle rearing and crops such as sugar cane, bananas, corn, gourds, and potatoes. In recent years, tourism has become the most important source of income and the island sustains a small commercial airport.

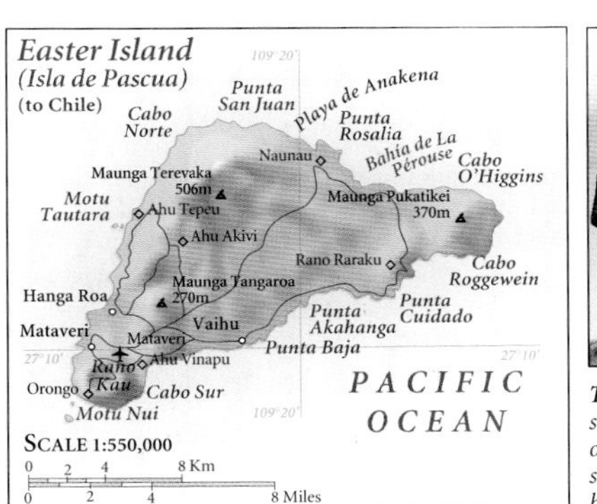
Easter Island (Isla de Pascua) (to Chile)
Cabo Norte
Punta San Juan
Playa de Anakena
Punta Rosalia
Bahía de La Pérouse
Cabo O'Higgins
Maunga Terevaka 506m
Motu Tautara
Ahu Tepeu
Naunau
Maunga Pukatikei 370m
Ahu Akivi
Rano Raraku
Cabo Roggewein
Hanga Roa
Maunga Tangaroa 270m
Vaihu
Punta Akahanga
Punta Cuidado
Mataveri
Ahu Vinapu
Punta Baja
Orongo
Rano Kau
Cabo Sur
Motu Nui
PACIFIC OCEAN
SCALE 1:550,000

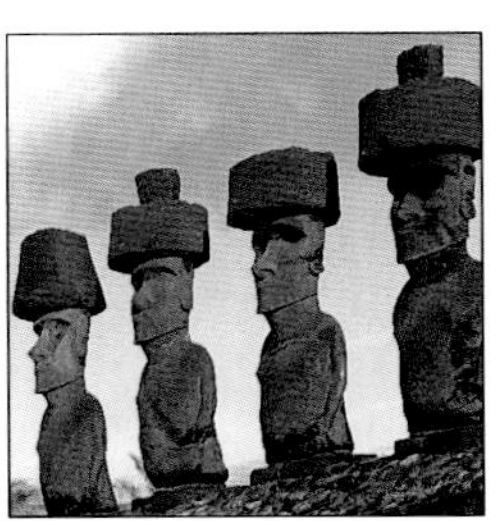

***The Naunau**, a series of huge stone statues overlook Playa de Anakena, on Easter Island. Carved from a soft volcanic rock, they were erected between 400 and 900 years ago.*

Pacific Ocean

The Pacific is the world's largest and deepest ocean. It is nearly twice the area of the Atlantic and contains almost three times as much water. The ocean is dotted with islands and surrounded by some of the world's most populous states; over half the world's population lives on its shores. The Pacific is bordered by active plate margins known as the "Ring of Fire," causing earthquakes and tsunamis, and creating volcanic islands and subterranean mountain chains. The largest underwater mountains break the surface as island arcs. The fisheries of the Pacific are some of the most productive in the world and provide a vital resource for many of the Pacific islands. Since the Second World War there has been a shift in trading patterns, with a considerable growth in trade between the United States and the countries of the Pacific Rim.

The Ring of Fire

The active plate margins surrounding the Pacific have created numerous land and island volcanoes along its border. The actual basin of the Pacific is made up of a number of separate tectonic plates which move away from each other, colliding with other plates. When they collide, the oceanic plates, being thinner, are forced beneath the thicker continental plates, forming deep ocean trenches and high ridges. These collision zones are known as subduction zones and are characterized by intense seismic and volcanic activity.

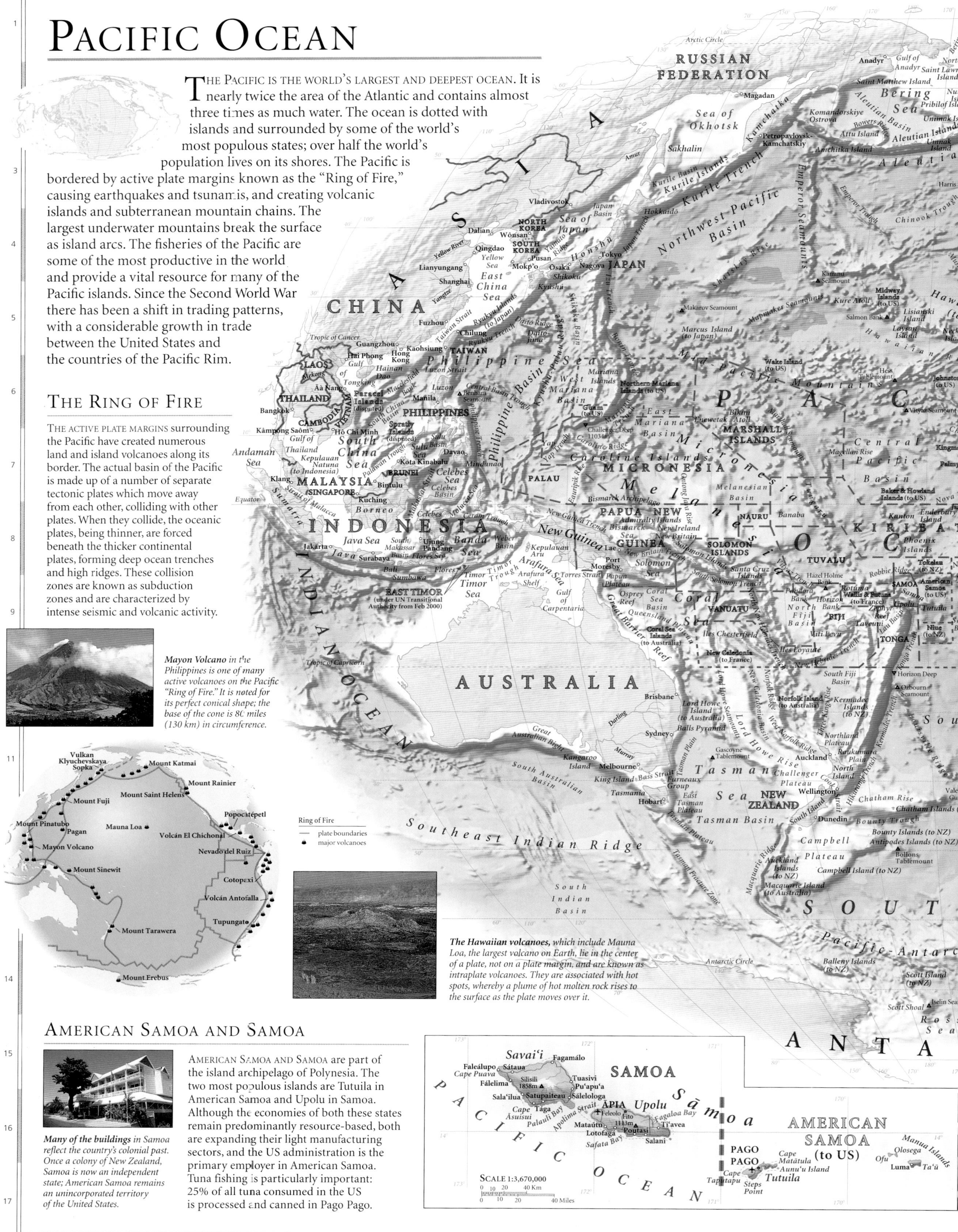

RUSSIAN FEDERATION
ASIA
CHINA
Sea of Okhotsk
Sea of Japan
Yellow Sea
East China Sea
NORTH KOREA
SOUTH KOREA
JAPAN
TAIWAN
PHILIPPINES
South China Sea
MALAYSIA
SINGAPORE
INDONESIA
Java Sea
Banda Sea
Celebes Sea
PALAU
MICRONESIA
MARSHALL ISLANDS
PAPUA NEW GUINEA
SOLOMON ISLANDS
NAURU
VANUATU
TUVALU
FIJI
TONGA
SAMOA
KIRIBATI
AUSTRALIA
Coral Sea
Tasman Sea
NEW ZEALAND
INDIAN OCEAN
Southeast Indian Ridge
South Indian Basin
Philippine Basin
Northwest Pacific Basin
Central Pacific Basin
Bering Sea
Aleutian Islands
Kurile Trench
Emperor Seamounts
Hawaiian Ridge
Mid-Pacific Mountains
Mariana Trench
Challenger Deep 11034m
Tasman Basin
Campbell Plateau
Chatham Rise
Arafura Sea
Timor Sea
Gulf of Carpentaria
Great Australian Bight
Tropic of Cancer
Tropic of Capricorn
Equator
Antarctic Circle
Arctic Circle
EAST TIMOR (under UN Transitional Authority from Feb 2000)
ANTARCTICA
Ross Sea
Vulkan Klyuchevskaya Sopka
Mount Katmai
Mount Rainier
Mount Saint Helens
Mount Fuji
Mount Pinatubo
Pagan
Mauna Loa
Popocatépetl
Volcán El Chichonal
Mayon Volcano
Nevado del Ruiz
Mount Sinewit
Cotopaxi
Volcán Antofalla
Tupungato
Mount Tarawera
Mount Erebus
Ring of Fire
plate boundaries
major volcanoes
Savai'i
Upolu
SAMOA
APIA
AMERICAN SAMOA (to US)
PAGO PAGO
Tutuila
Manua Islands
PACIFIC OCEAN
SCALE 1:3,670,000

Mayon Volcano in the Philippines is one of many active volcanoes on the Pacific "Ring of Fire." It is noted for its perfect conical shape; the base of the cone is 80 miles (130 km) in circumference.

The Hawaiian volcanoes, which include Mauna Loa, the largest volcano on Earth, lie in the center of a plate, not on a plate margin, and are known as intraplate volcanoes. They are associated with hot spots, whereby a plume of hot molten rock rises to the surface as the plate moves over it.

American Samoa and Samoa

Many of the buildings in Samoa reflect the country's colonial past. Once a colony of New Zealand, Samoa is now an independent state; American Samoa remains an unincorporated territory of the United States.

American Samoa and Samoa are part of the island archipelago of Polynesia. The two most populous islands are Tutuila in American Samoa and Upolu in Samoa. Although the economies of both these states remain predominantly resource-based, both are expanding their light manufacturing sectors, and the US administration is the primary employer in American Samoa. Tuna fishing is particularly important: 25% of all tuna consumed in the US is processed and canned in Pago Pago.

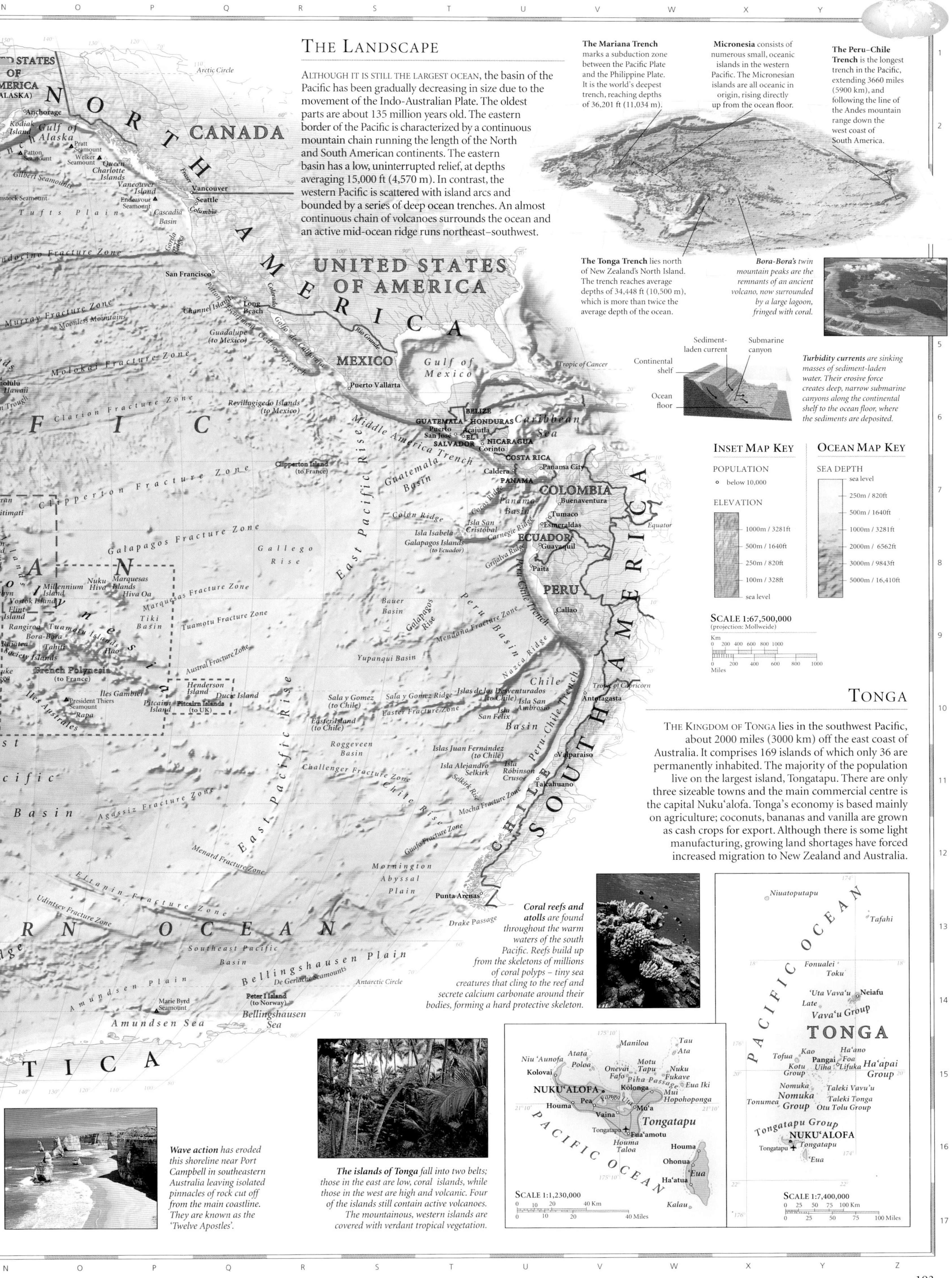

CANADA
NORTH AMERICA
UNITED STATES OF AMERICA
MEXICO
Gulf of Mexico
Caribbean Sea
GUATEMALA
BELIZE
HONDURAS
EL SALVADOR
NICARAGUA
COSTA RICA
PANAMA
COLOMBIA
ECUADOR
PERU
SOUTH AMERICA
CHILE
Anchorage
Gulf of Alaska
Kodiak Island
Vancouver
Seattle
San Francisco
Long Beach
Puerto Vallarta
Panama City
Buenaventura
Tumaco
Esmeraldas
Guayaquil
Paita
Callao
Antofagasta
Valparaíso
Talcahuano
Punta Arenas
Drake Passage
Tropic of Cancer
Equator
Tropic of Capricorn
Arctic Circle
Antarctic Circle
Middle America Trench
Guatemala Basin
East Pacific Rise
Peru-Chile Trench
Peru Basin
Nazca Ridge
Chile Basin
Chile Rise
Galapagos Fracture Zone
Clipperton Fracture Zone
Clarion Fracture Zone
Molokai Fracture Zone
Murray Fracture Zone
Mendocino Fracture Zone
Marquesas Fracture Zone
Tuamotu Fracture Zone
Austral Fracture Zone
Easter Fracture Zone
Challenger Fracture Zone
Agassiz Fracture Zone
Menard Fracture Zone
Eltanin Fracture Zone
Udintsev Fracture Zone
Mendana Fracture Zone
Mocha Fracture Zone
Guafo Fracture Zone
Galapagos Islands (to Ecuador)
Clipperton Island (to France)
Revillagigedo Islands (to Mexico)
Guadalupe (to Mexico)
Easter Island (to Chile)
Sala y Gomez (to Chile)
Islas Juan Fernández (to Chile)
Pitcairn Islands (to UK)
French Polynesia (to France)
Marquesas Islands
Tahiti
Tuamotu Islands
Iles Australes
Iles Gambier
Henderson Island
Ducie Island
Bauer Basin
Yupanqui Basin
Roggeveen Basin
Tiki Basin
Panama Basin
Gallego Rise
Mornington Abyssal Plain
Southeast Pacific Basin
Bellingshausen Plain
Bellingshausen Sea
Amundsen Plain
Amundsen Sea
Peter I Island (to Norway)
Marie Byrd Seamount
Tufts Plain
Cascadia Basin
SOUTHERN OCEAN
ANTARCTICA
Sediment-laden current
Submarine canyon
Continental shelf
Ocean floor
Inset Map Key
POPULATION
below 10,000
ELEVATION
1000m / 3281ft
500m / 1640ft
250m / 820ft
100m / 328ft
sea level
Ocean Map Key
SEA DEPTH
sea level
250m / 820ft
500m / 1640ft
1000m / 3281ft
2000m / 6562ft
3000m / 9843ft
5000m / 16,410ft
SCALE 1:67,500,000
(projection: Mollweide)
PACIFIC OCEAN
TONGA
Niuatoputapu
Tafahi
Fonualei
Toku
Vava'u Group
Neiafu
Ha'apai Group
Tongatapu Group
NUKU'ALOFA
Tongatapu
'Eua
SCALE 1:7,400,000
SCALE 1:1,230,000

The Landscape

Although it is still the largest ocean, the basin of the Pacific has been gradually decreasing in size due to the movement of the Indo-Australian Plate. The oldest parts are about 135 million years old. The eastern border of the Pacific is characterized by a continuous mountain chain running the length of the North and South American continents. The eastern basin has a low, uniform relief, at depths averaging 15,000 ft (4,570 m). In contrast, the western Pacific is scattered with island arcs and bounded by a series of deep ocean trenches. An almost continuous chain of volcanoes surrounds the ocean and an active mid-ocean ridge runs northeast–southwest.

The Mariana Trench marks a subduction zone between the Pacific Plate and the Philippine Plate. It is the world's deepest trench, reaching depths of 36,201 ft (11,034 m).

Micronesia consists of numerous small, oceanic islands in the western Pacific. The Micronesian islands are all oceanic in origin, rising directly up from the ocean floor.

The Peru–Chile Trench is the longest trench in the Pacific, extending 3660 miles (5900 km), and following the line of the Andes mountain range down the west coast of South America.

The Tonga Trench lies north of New Zealand's North Island. The trench reaches average depths of 34,448 ft (10,500 m), which is more than twice the average depth of the ocean.

Bora-Bora's twin mountain peaks are the remnants of an ancient volcano, now surrounded by a large lagoon, fringed with coral.

***Turbidity currents** are sinking masses of sediment-laden water. Their erosive force creates deep, narrow submarine canyons along the continental shelf to the ocean floor, where the sediments are deposited.*

Tonga

The Kingdom of Tonga lies in the southwest Pacific, about 2000 miles (3000 km) off the east coast of Australia. It comprises 169 islands of which only 36 are permanently inhabited. The majority of the population live on the largest island, Tongatapu. There are only three sizeable towns and the main commercial centre is the capital Nuku'alofa. Tonga's economy is based mainly on agriculture; coconuts, bananas and vanilla are grown as cash crops for export. Although there is some light manufacturing, growing land shortages have forced increased migration to New Zealand and Australia.

***Coral reefs and atolls** are found throughout the warm waters of the south Pacific. Reefs build up from the skeletons of millions of coral polyps – tiny sea creatures that cling to the reef and secrete calcium carbonate around their bodies, forming a hard protective skeleton.*

***Wave action** has eroded this shoreline near Port Campbell in southeastern Australia leaving isolated pinnacles of rock cut off from the main coastline. They are known as the 'Twelve Apostles'.*

***The islands of Tonga** fall into two belts; those in the east are low, coral islands, while those in the west are high and volcanic. Four of the islands still contain active volcanoes. The mountainous, western islands are covered with verdant tropical vegetation.*

ANTARCTICA

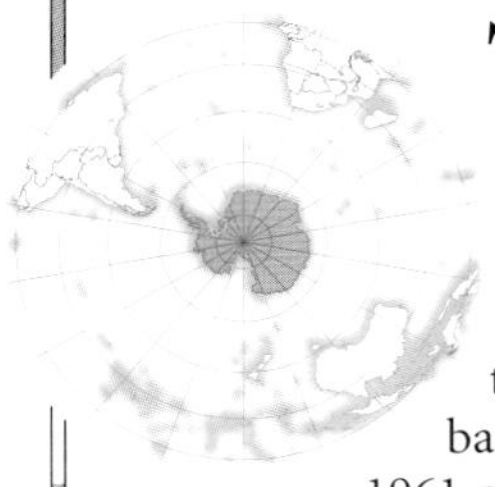

THE ICE-COVERED CONTINENT of Antarctica, which is the Earth's most southerly region, has drawn explorers and entrepreneurs seeking challenge and riches in its wintry lands for over 200 years. The extreme climate has deterred any large-scale settlement of the continent, and though commercial hunters built outposts in the past, habitation is now limited to scientific bases. The Antarctic Treaty, which came into force in 1961, provides for international governance and scientific cooperation in place of potential territorial conflict.

RESOURCES

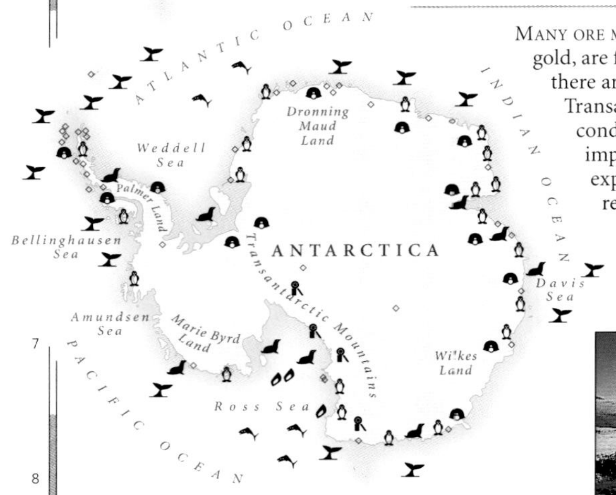

MANY ORE MINERALS, including iron and gold, are found in the Antarctic, and there are also coal reserves in the Transantarctic Mountains. The severe conditions and environmental importance of the region mean that exploitation of potential mineral resources is both uneconomic and undesirable. The unique wildlife and landscape draw a small number of tourists annually.

Atlantic Ocean
Indian Ocean
Pacific Ocean
Weddell Sea
Dronning Maud Land
Palmer Land
Bellinghausen Sea
ANTARCTICA
Transantarctic Mountains
Davis Sea
Amundsen Sea
Marie Byrd Land
Wilkes Land
Ross Sea

Resources (including wildlife)

- coal
- fish
- minerals
- oil & gas
- penguins
- seals
- whales
- polar research base

Most settlements in Antarctica are research bases such as this one at Rothera on Adelaide Island, although there is a small Chilean settlement on King George Island.

THE LANDSCAPE

THERE ARE TWO DISTINCT PARTS to Antarctica: Lesser Antarctica, a series of ice-covered, mountainous islands, joined together by the ice; and the high plateau of Greater Antarctica. The Ross Sea and the Weddell Sea are outliers of the Atlantic and Pacific oceans – deep bays partially covered by thick ice shelves.

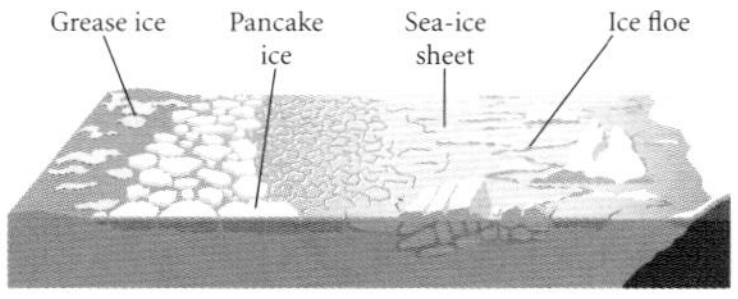

On Elephant Island, the coast is edged by glaciers, although the land is not permanently covered by ice.

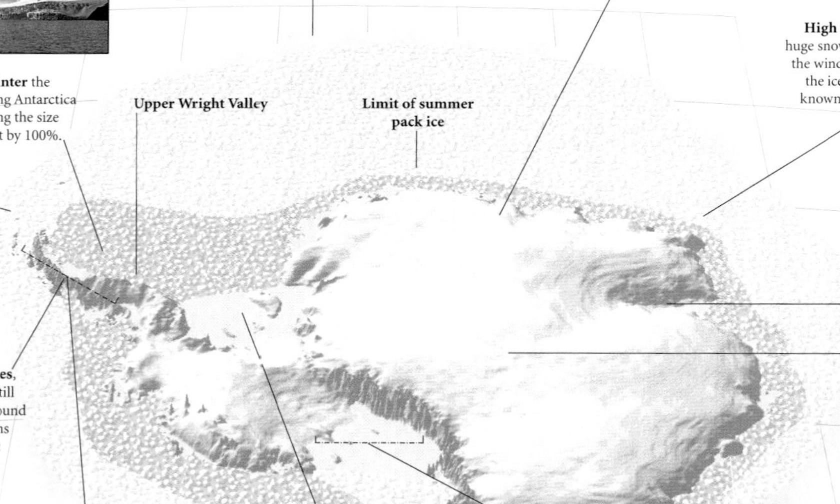

Grease ice
Pancake ice
Sea-ice sheet
Ice floe

***Pack ice forms out at sea** in freezing temperatures. At the outer limits, grease ice congeals on the surface of the ocean. This is then spun around by wind and waves into irregular "pancakes," freezing and breaking up several times before bonding together again to form sea-ice sheets, which finally cement into enormous ice floes.*

Limit of winter pack ice

Upper Wright Valley

Limit of summer pack ice

Elephant Island

During the winter the seas surrounding Antarctica freeze, increasing the size of the continent by 100%.

High winds carrying snow form huge snowdrifts. The erosive power of the wind-borne snow can also sculpt the ice sheet to produce landforms known as sastrugi which align with the direction of the wind.

The Lambert Glacier is the largest glacier system in the world, up to 50 miles (80 km) wide at its seaward limit, and reaching 180 miles (300 km) into the interior by way of the Prince Charles Mountains.

Many volcanoes, some of them still active, can be found in the mountains of the Antarctic Peninsula.

Antarctica is the highest continent on Earth, because of the great thickness of ice which overlays the land. In places the ice alone can reach up to 15,700 ft (4,800 m) thick. Much of the basement rock of west Antarctica lies below sea level, pushed down by the weight of the ice.

The mountainous Antarctic Peninsula is formed of rocks 65–225 million years old, overlain by more recent rocks and glacial deposits. It is connected to the Andes in South America by a submarine ridge.

Nearly half – 44% – of the Antarctic coastline is bounded by ice shelves, like the Ronne Ice Shelf, which float on the Ocean. These are joined to the inland ice sheet by dome-shaped ice "rises."

More than 30% of Antarctic ice is contained in the Ross Ice Shelf.

***The barren, flat-bottomed** Upper Wright Valley was once filled by a glacier, but is now dry, strewn with boulders and pebbles. In some dry valleys, there has been no rain for over 2 million years.*

***Large colonies of seabirds** live in the extremely harsh Antarctic climate. The Emperor penguins seen here, the smaller Adélie penguin, the Antarctic petrel and the South Polar skua are the only birds that breed exclusively on the continent.*

South Orkney Islands
Laurie Island
Orcadas (to Argentina)
Coronation Island
Signy (to UK)

Research Stations on King George Island

- Arctowski (to Poland)
- Artigas (to Uruguay)
- Bellingshausen (to Russian Federation)
- Comandante Ferraz (to Brazil)
- Great Wall (to China)
- Jubany (to Argentina)
- King Sejong (to South Korea)
- Teniente Rodolfo Marsh (to Chile)

TERRITORIAL CLAIMS

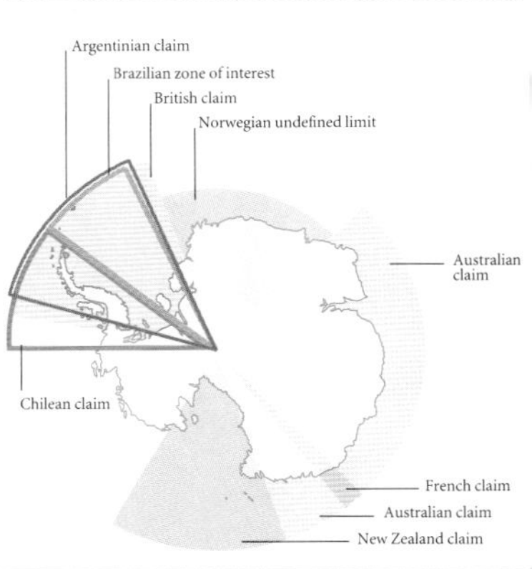

Argentinian claim
Brazilian zone of interest
British claim
Norwegian undefined limit
Australian claim
Chilean claim
French claim
Australian claim
New Zealand claim

Scotia Sea
Drake Passage
Weddell Sea
Bellingshausen Sea
Amundsen Sea
Ronne Ice Shelf
Ellsworth Land
Antarctic Peninsula
Palmer Land
Marie Byrd Land
PACIFIC OCEAN

192

ATLANTIC OCEAN
INDIAN OCEAN
ANTARCTICA
Greater Antarctica
Dronning Maud Land
Princess Astrid Kyst
Prinsesse Ragnhild Kyst
Kronprinsesse Märtha Kyst
Prins Harald Kyst
Kronprins Olav Kyst
Riiser-Larsen Peninsula
Lützow Holmbukta
Syowa (to Japan)
Molodezhnaya (to Russian Federation)
Casey Bay
Amundsen Bay
Cape Batterbee
Napier Mountains
Mount Elkins 2300m
Nye Mountains
Enderby Land
Dismal Mountains
Edward VIII Gulf
Law Promontory
Kemp Land
Hansen Mountains
Mawson Coast
Mawson (to Australia)
Gustav Bull Mountains
Lars Christensen Coast
Cape Darnley
Mac. Robertson Land
Mount Menzies 3355m
Prince Charles Mountains
Lambert Glacier
Amery Ice Shelf
Gillock Island
Mackenzie Bay
Ingrid Christensen Coast
Zhongshan (to China)
Prydz Bay
Davis (to Australia)
Princess Elizabeth Land
West Ice Shelf
King Leopold and Queen Astrid Land
Mikhaylov Island
Philippi Glacier
Wilhelm II Land
Wilhelm II Coast
Davis Sea
Mirny (to Russian Federation)
Queen Mary Coast
Masson Island
Northcliffe Glacier
Denman Glacier
Shackleton Ice Shelf
Scott Glacier
Mill Island
Bowman Island
Knox Coast
Vincennes Bay
Wilkes Land
Casey (to Australia)
Budd Coast
Cape Poinsett
Cape Waldron
Sabrina Coast
Dalton Iceberg Tongue
Banzare Coast
Cape Goodenough
Porpoise Bay
Terre Adélie
Wilkes Coast
Cape Keltie
Dibble Iceberg Tongue
Adélie Coast
Dumont d'Urville (to France)
Cape Gray
Mertz Glacier
Ninnis Glacier
George V Coast
George V Land
Cape Freshfield
Cape Hudson
Dumont d'Urville Sea
Leningradskaya (to Russian Federation)
Cape Cheetham
Oates Land
Rennick Glacier
Mount Minto 4163m
Cape Adare
Borchgrevink Coast
Coulman Island
Ross Sea
Balleny Islands
Scott Island
Victoria Land
Drygalski Ice Tongue
Scott Coast
Mount Erebus 3794m
Ross Island
Scott Base (to NZ)
McMurdo Base (to US)
Mount Lister 4026m
Hillary Coast
Mount McClintock 3492m
Byrd Glacier
Shackleton Coast
Nimrod Glacier
Mount Markham 4351m
Mount Kirkpatrick 4528m
Beardmore Glacier
Dufek Coast
Queen Maud Mountains
Amundsen Coast
Gould Coast
Transantarctic Mountains
Watson Escarpment
Horlick Mountains
Siple Coast
Ross Ice Shelf
Roosevelt Island
Shirase Coast
Edward VII Peninsula
Sulzberger Bay
South Pole
Amundsen-Scott (to US)
Vostok (to Russian Federation)
South Geomagnetic Pole
Pensacola Mountains
Foundation Ice Stream
Support Force Glacier
Recovery Glacier
Coats Land
Theron Mountains
Slessor Glacier
Belgrano II (to Argentina)
Luitpold Coast
Caird Coast
Stancomb-Wills Glacier
Brunt Ice Shelf
Maudheimvidda
Riiser-Larsen Ice Shelf
Riiser-Larsen Sea
Cape Norvegia
Georg von Neumayer (to Germany)
Sanae (to South Africa)
Fimbul Ice Shelf
Maitri (to India)
Novolazarevskaya (to Russian Federation)
Borg Massif
Mühlig-Hofmann Mountains
Fimbulheimen
Wohlthat Mountains
Asuka (to Japan)
Sør Rondane Mountains
Belgica Mountains
Mount Victor 2588m
Thorshavnheiane
Thyer Glacier
Antarctic Circle
Limit of summer pack ice
MAP KEY
ELEVATION
ice cap
ice shelf
exposed land
SCALE 1:16,500,000
(projection: Lambert Azimuthal Equal Area)

The sun sets over the Antarctic Peninsula for more than six months during the winter. However, there are more hours of sunshine during the brief Antarctic summer than most equatorial countries experience in a whole year.

Immense, flat-topped icebergs are formed when blocks of ice break away from the main ice sheet. Though the exposed area is enormous, the volume of ice concealed beneath the water may be many times greater.

THE ARCTIC

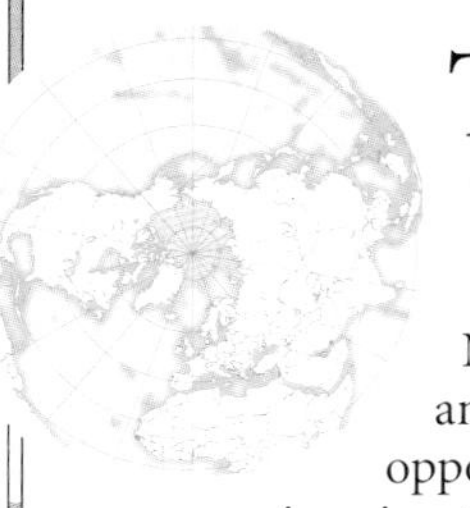

THREE CONTINENTS, ASIA, NORTH AMERICA, AND EUROPE, reach into the Arctic Circle at their northernmost limits, almost entirely encircling the Arctic Ocean. Despite the region's extraordinarily harsh climate, it has been inhabited for thousands of years by peoples such as the European Lapps, the Russian Nenet, and the North American Inuit, who draw a living from fishing, herding, and hunting. More recently, particularly in the Russian Arctic, opportunities to exploit oil and other mineral reserves have encouraged immigration. Pollution of the Arctic's unique ecology and damage to the traditional lifestyles of many native peoples have been the unfortunate results of this activity, and international cooperation is needed to safeguard the future of the region.

MAP KEY

POPULATION
- above 5 million
- 1 million to 5 million
- 500,000 to 1 million
- 100,000 to 500,000
- 50,000 to 100,000
- 10,000 to 50,000
- below 10,000

SEA DEPTH
- sea level
- 250m / 820ft
- 500m / 1640ft
- 1000m / 3281ft
- 2000m / 6562ft
- 3000m / 9843ft

SCALE 1:23,500,000
(projection: Lambert Azimuthal Equal Area)

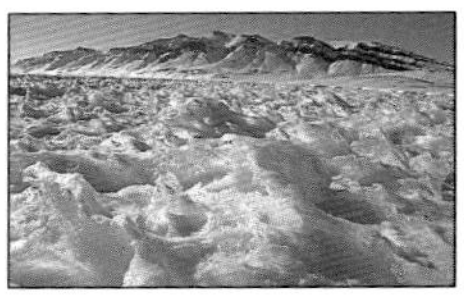

Windblown snow etches deep patterns in the ice sheet known as sastrugi. They align with the direction of the wind

RESOURCES

LARGE QUANTITIES of coal, oil, and natural gas are to be found in the basins of the Arctic Ocean, and in northern Canada, Alaska and the Russian Federation. The cost and difficulty of extraction and, more recently, awareness of damage to the environment, have limited exploitation to coastal regions. The unfrozen waters have stocks of fish including cod, flounder, and haddock. Quotas have now been put in place to restrict the number of fish caught annually. Reindeer are herded in large numbers by many of the native Arctic peoples. Most grain and vegetables are imported from elsewhere.

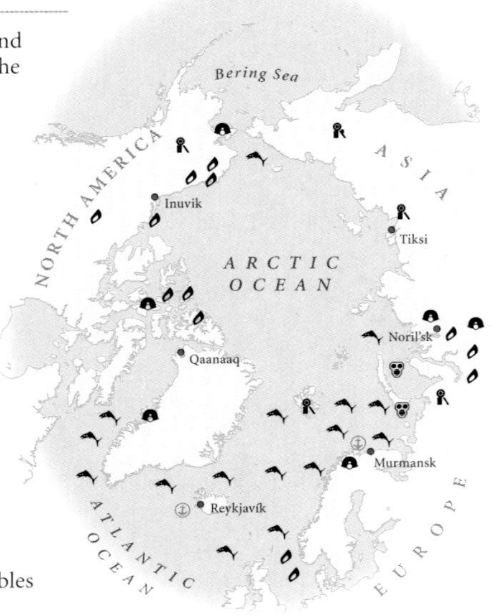

Bering Sea
NORTH AMERICA
ASIA
ARCTIC OCEAN
Inuvik
Tiksi
Noril'sk
Qaanaaq
Murmansk
Reykjavík
ATLANTIC OCEAN
EUROPE

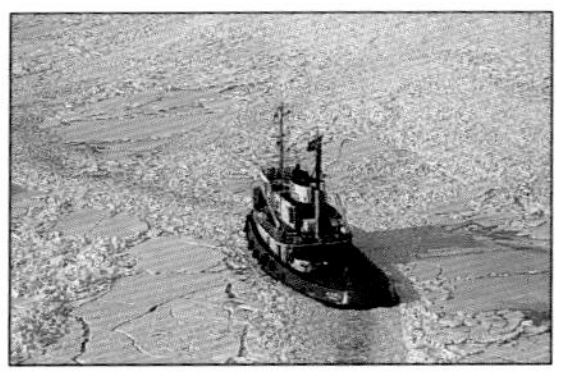

Resources
- coal
- fish
- mining
- oil & gas
- radioactive contamination
- major towns
- major ports

Icebreakers are ships with specially strengthened hulls, designed to break a path through the ice. They are used to keep important routes open during the winter, when falling temperatures cause much of the Arctic Ocean to freeze over.

THE LANDSCAPE

THE ARCTIC OCEAN comprises two large ocean basins divided by three submarine ridges, the greatest of which, the Lomonosov Ridge, is a huge underwater mountain range which has an average height of more than 10,000 ft (3,000 m). The lands which encircle the Arctic Ocean are underlain by great shield areas of ancient rocks, which were heavily glaciated during the last Ice Age.

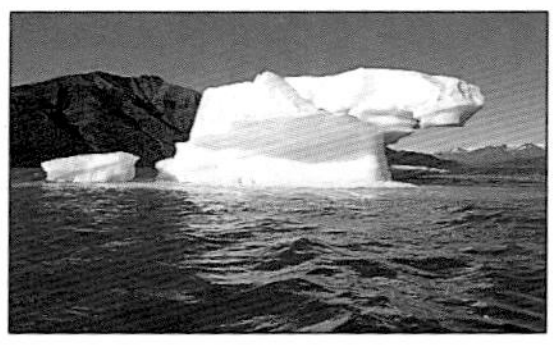

Icebergs are constantly broken up and reshaped by wind and the oceans. This flat-topped iceberg has been undercut, leaving a craggy ice cliff.

A complex and ancient mountain system, extending from the Queen Elizabeth Islands to eastern Greenland was formed more than 245 million years ago.

The Canadian Shield underlies almost all of the Canadian Arctic. It is a very stable plateau of ancient rock, now covered by glacial lakes and sediment, which supports tundra vegetation.

The Arctic Ocean is the world's smallest ocean with a total area of 5,440,000 sq miles (15,100,000 sq km).

At a latitude of more than 75° N, the Arctic Ocean is almost permanently covered by pack-ice, though high winds and the movement of the seas may cause the ice to crack and break up.

In the more southerly reaches of the Arctic, like Siberia, much of the land is covered by permafrost. In the summer, higher temperatures warm the frozen ground, causing a number of typical phenomena. These include solifluction, the fast downhill movement of top soil layers; freeze/thaw activity, which patterns the ground into regular polygonal shapes, and the formation of large domes with a frozen ice core, known as pingos.

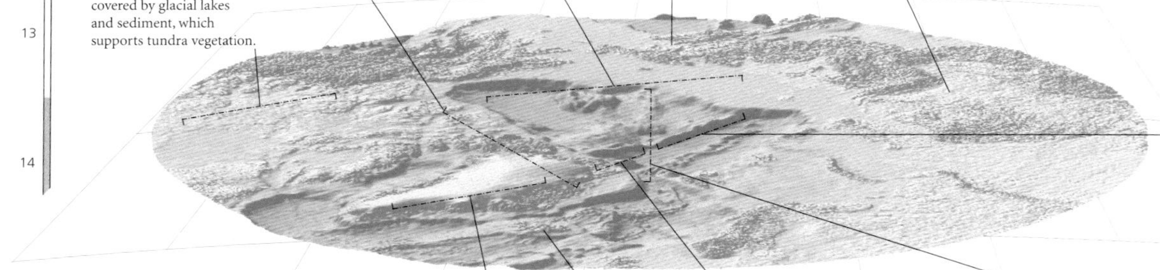

Lomonosov Ridge

Lomonosov Ridge

Arctic ice shelf

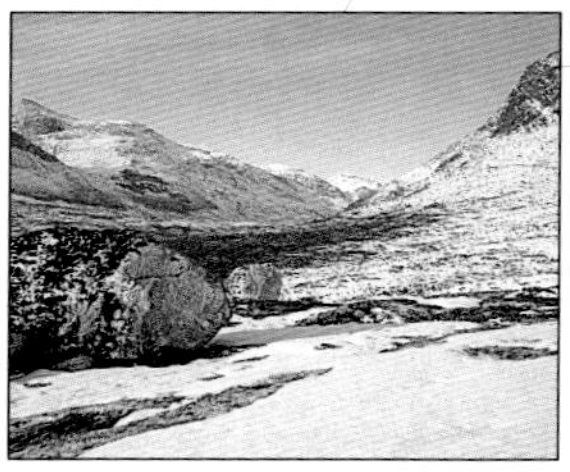

Much of Greenland is covered by a massive ice sheet more than 650,000 sq miles (1,683,400 sq km) in extent. The weight of the ice has depressed the central land area to form a basin lying more than 1,000 ft (300 m) below sea level. Only at the edges of the island is bare rock visible.

Iceland has five major glaciers, sustained by heavy snowfall. Parts of the ice cap cover active volcanoes, such as Bárdharbunga, which periodically erupt causing the melted ice to form a great lake at the glacier margins.

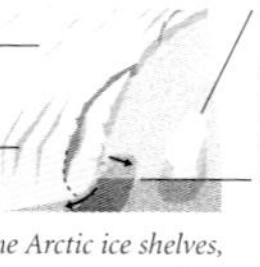

Ice sheet
Iceberg
Crevasses occur at the edge of the ice sheet
Sea water melts the edge of the ice sheet

***At the boundary** of the Arctic ice shelves, sea water flows under the ice causing melting and forming crevasses on the surface. This eventually weakens blocks of ice which break away as icebergs. This process is known as calving.*

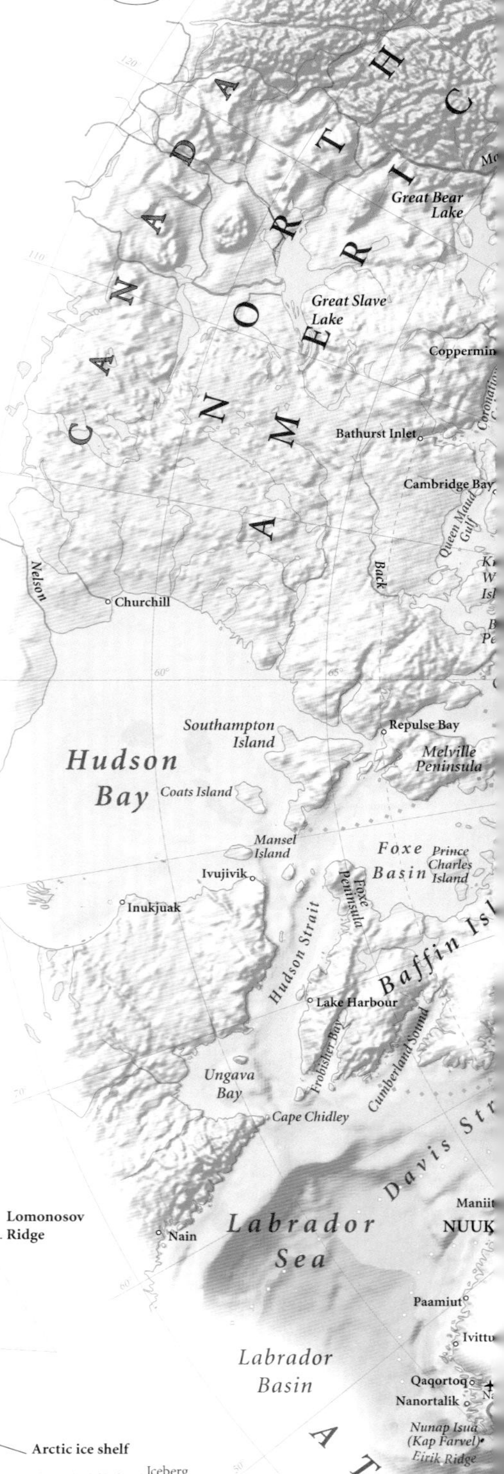

CANADA
NORTH AMERICA
Great Bear Lake
Great Slave Lake
Coppermine
Bathurst Inlet
Cambridge Bay
Churchill
Nelson
Hudson Bay
Southampton Island
Coats Island
Repulse Bay
Melville Peninsula
Mansel Island
Ivujivik
Inukjuak
Foxe Basin
Prince Charles Island
Hudson Strait
Lake Harbour
Baffin Island
Ungava Bay
Cape Chidley
Davis Strait
Nain
Labrador Sea
Maniitsoq
NUUK
Paamiut
Ivittuut
Labrador Basin
Qaqortoq
Nanortalik
Nunap Isua (Kap Farvel)
Eirik Ridge
ATLANTIC

The aurora borealis *or Northern Lights are colored bands of light which appear in northern latitudes. Light is emitted when dust particles from the Sun react with gases in the Earth's atmosphere.*

Polar bears *range for great distances over the Arctic pack-ice in search of food. They are formidable hunters that live mainly on seals. In December and January, mother bears give birth to their cubs in dens dug deep beneath the snow.*

Geographical Comparisons

Largest Countries

Russian Federation	6,592,800 sq miles	(17,075,400 sq km)
Canada	3,851,788 sq miles	(9,976,140 sq km)
USA	3,681,760 sq miles	(9,372,610 sq km)
China	3,600,292 sq miles	(9,326,410 sq km)
Brazil	3,286,472 sq miles	(8,511,970 sq km)
Australia	2,967,893 sq miles	(7,686,850 sq km)
India	1,269,338 sq miles	(3,287,590 sq km)
Argentina	1,068,296 sq miles	(2,766,890 sq km)
Kazakhstan	1,049,150 sq miles	(2,717,300 sq km)
Sudan	967,493 sq miles	(2,505,815 sq km)

Smallest Countries

Vatican City	0.17 sq miles	(0.44 sq km)
Monaco	0.75 sq miles	(1.95 sq km)
Nauru	8.2 sq miles	(21.2 sq km)
Tuvalu	10 sq miles	(26 sq km)
San Marino	24 sq miles	(61 sq km)
Liechtenstein	62 sq miles	(160 sq km)
Marshall Islands	70 sq miles	(181 sq km)
Seychelles	108 sq miles	(280 sq km)
Maldives	116 sq miles	(300 sq km)
Malta	124 sq miles	(320 sq km)

Largest Islands

(to the nearest 1,000 - or 100,000 for the largest)

Greenland	849,400 sq miles	(2,200,000 sq km)
New Guinea	312,000 sq miles	(808,000 sq km)
Borneo	292,222 sq miles	(757,050 sq km)
Madagascar	229,300 sq miles	(594,000 sq km)
Sumatra	202,300 sq miles	(524,000 sq km)
Baffin Island	183,800 sq miles	(476,000 sq km)
Honshu	88,800 sq miles	(230,000 sq km)
Britain	88,700 sq miles	(229,800 sq km)
Victoria Island	81,900 sq miles	(212,000 sq km)
Ellesmere Island	75,700 sq miles	(196,000 sq km)

Richest Countries

(GNP per capita, in US$)

Luxembourg	45,360
Switzerland	44,350
Japan	40,940
Liechtenstein	40,000
Norway	34,510
Denmark	32,100
Singapore	30,550
Germany	28,870
Austria	28,110
USA	28,020

Poorest Countries

(GNP per capita, in US$)

Mozambique	80
Somalia	100
Ethiopia	100
Eritrea	100
Congo (Zaire)	130
Chad	160
Tanzania	170
Burundi	170
Malawi	180
Rwanda	190
Sierra Leone	200
Niger	200

Most Populous Countries

China	1,255,100,000
India	935,700,000
USA	263,300,000
Indonesia	197,600,000
Brazil	165,800,000
Russian Federation	147,000,000
Pakistan	140,500,000
Japan	125,100,000
Bangladesh	120,400,000
Nigeria	111,700,000

Least Populous Countries

Vatican City	1,000
Tuvalu	9,000
Nauru	10,000
Palau	16,200
San Marino	24,000
Liechtenstein	30,630
Monaco	31,000
St Kitts & Nevis	44,000
Marshall Islands	52,000
Andorra	64,000
Dominica	71,000
Seychelles	73,000

Most Densely Populated Countries

Monaco	41,332 people per sq mile	(15,897 per sq km)
Singapore	11,894 people per sq mile	(4,590 per sq km)
Vatican City	5,890 people per sq mile	(2,273 per sq km)
Malta	3,239 people per sq mile	(1,250 per sq km)
Maldives	2,591 people per sq mile	(1,000 per sq km)
Bangladesh	2,330 people per sq mile	(899 per sq km)
Bahrain	2,286 people per sq mile	(882 per sq km)
Barbados	1,809 people per sq mile	(698 per sq km)
Taiwan	1,682 people per sq mile	(649 per sq km)
Mauritius	1,542 people per sq mile	(595 per sq km)

Most Sparsely Populated Countries

Australia	5 people per sq mile	(2 per sq km)
Mauritania	5 people per sq mile	(2 per sq km)
Mongolia	5 people per sq mile	(2 per sq km)
Namibia	5 people per sq mile	(2 per sq km)
Suriname	5 people per sq mile	(2 per sq km)
Botswana	8 people per sq mile	(3 per sq km)
Canada	8 people per sq mile	(3 per sq km)
Iceland	8 people per sq mile	(3 per sq km)
Libya	8 people per sq mile	(3 per sq km)
Guyana	10 people per sq mile	(4 per sq km)

Most Widely Spoken Languages

1. Chinese (Mandarin)	6. Arabic
2. English	7. Bengali
3. Hindi	8. Portuguese
4. Spanish	9. Malay-Indonesian
5. Russian	10. French

Countries With The Most Land Borders

14: China *(Afghanistan, Bhutan, Mynamar, India, Kazakhstan, Kyrgyzstan, Laos, Mongolia, Nepal, North Korea, Pakistan, Russian Federation, Tajikistan, Vietnam)*

14: Russian Federation *(Azerbaijan, Belarus, China, Estonia, Finland, Georgia, Kazakhstan, Latvia, Lithuania, Mongolia, North Korea, Norway, Poland, Ukraine)*

10: Brazil *(Argentina, Bolivia, Colombia, French Guiana, Guyana, Paraguay, Peru, Suriname, Uruguay, Venezuela)*

9: Congo (Zaire) *(Angola, Burundi, Central African Republic, Congo, Rwanda, Sudan, Tanzania, Uganda, Zambia)*

9: Germany *(Austria, Belgium, Czech Republic, Denmark, France, Luxembourg, Netherlands, Poland, Switzerland)*

9: Sudan *(Central African Republic, Chad, Congo (Zaire), Egypt, Eritrea, Ethiopia, Kenya, Libya, Uganda)*

8: Austria *(Czech Republic, Germany, Hungary, Italy, Liechtenstein, Slovakia, Slovenia, Switzerland)*
8: France *(Andorra, Belgium, Germany, Italy, Luxembourg, Monaco, Spain, Switzerland)*
8: Tanzania *(Burundi, Congo (Zaire), Kenya, Malawi, Mozambique, Rwanda, Uganda, Zambia)*
8: Turkey *(Armenia, Azerbaijan, Bulgaria, Georgia, Greece, Iran, Iraq, Syria)*
8: Zambia *(Angola, Botswana, Congo (Zaire), Malawi, Mozambique, Namibia, Tanzania, Zimbabwe)*

Longest Rivers

Nile (NE Africa)	4,160 miles	(6,695 km)
Amazon (South America)	4,049 miles	(6,516 km)
Yangtze (China)	3,915 miles	(6,299 km)
Mississippi/Missouri (USA)	3,710 miles	(5,969 km)
Ob'-Irtysh (Russian Federation)	3,461 miles	(5,570 km)
Yellow River (China)	3,395 miles	(5,464 km)
Congo (Central Africa)	2,900 miles	(4,667 km)
Mekong (Southeast Asia)	2,749 miles	(4,425 km)
Lena (Russian Federation)	2,734 miles	(4,400 km)
Mackenzie (Canada)	2,640 miles	(4,250 km)
Yenisey (Russian Federation)	2,541 miles	(4,090km)

Highest Mountains

(HEIGHT ABOVE SEA LEVEL)

Everest	29,030 ft	(8,848 m)
K2	28,253 ft	(8,611 m)
Kanchenjunga I	28,210 ft	(8,598 m)
Makalu I	27,767 ft	(8,463 m)
Cho Oyu	26,907 ft	(8,201 m)
Dhaulagiri I	26,796 ft	(8,167 m)
Manaslu I	26,783 ft	(8,163 m)
Nanga Parbat I	26,661 ft	(8,126 m)
Annapurna I	26,547 ft	(8,091 m)
Gasherbrum I	26,471 ft	(8,068 m)

Largest Bodies of Inland Water

(WITH AREA AND DEPTH)

Caspian Sea	143,243 sq miles (371,000 sq km)	3,215 ft (980 m)
Lake Superior	31,151 sq miles (83,270 sq km)	1,289 ft (393 m)
Lake Victoria	26,828 sq miles (69,484 sq km)	328 ft (100 m)
Lake Huron	23,436 sq miles (60,700 sq km)	751 ft (229 m)
Lake Michigan	22,402 sq miles (58,020 sq km)	922 ft (281 m)
Lake Tanganyika	12,703 sq miles (32,900 sq km)	4,700 ft (1435 m)
Great Bear Lake	12,274 sq miles (31,790 sq km)	1,047 ft (319 m)
Lake Baikal	11,776 sq miles (30,500 sq km)	5,712 ft (1741 m)
Great Slave Lake	10,981 sq miles (28,440 sq km)	459 ft (140 m)
Lake Erie	9,915 sq miles (25,680 sq km)	197 ft (60 m)

Deepest Ocean Features

Challenger Deep, Marianas Trench (Pacific)	36,201 ft	(11,034 m)
Vityaz III Depth, Tonga Trench (Pacific)	35,704 ft	(10,882 m)
Vityaz Depth, Kurile-Kamchatka Trench (Pacific)	34,588 ft	(10,542 m)
Cape Johnson Deep, Philippine Trench (Pacific)	34,441 ft	(10,497 m)
Kermadec Trench (Pacific)	32,964 ft	(10,047 m)
Ramapo Deep, Japan Trench (Pacific)	32,758 ft	(9,984 m)
Milwaukee Deep, Puerto Rico Trench (Atlantic)	30,185 ft	(9,200 m)
Argo Deep, Torres Trench (Pacific)	30,070 ft	(9,165 m)
Meteor Depth, South Sandwich Trench (Atlantic)	30,000 ft	(9,144 m)
Planet Deep, New Britain Trench (Pacific)	29,988 ft	(9,140 m)

Greatest Waterfalls

(MEAN FLOW OF WATER)

Boyoma (Congo (Zaire))	600,400 cu. ft/sec	(17,000 cu.m/sec)
Khône (Laos/Cambodia)	410,000 cu. ft/sec	(11,600 cu.m/sec)
Niagara (USA/Canada)	195,000 cu. ft/sec	(5,500 cu.m/sec)
Grande (Uruguay)	160,000 cu. ft/sec	(4,500 cu.m/sec)
Paulo Afonso (Brazil)	100,000 cu. ft/sec	(2,800 cu.m/sec)
Urubupunga (Brazil)	97,000 cu. ft/sec	(2,750 cu.m/sec)
Iguaçu (Argentina/Brazil)	62,000 cu. ft/sec	(1,700 cu.m/sec)
Maribondo (Brazil)	53,000 cu. ft/sec	(1,500 cu.m/sec)
Victoria (Zimbabwe)	39,000 cu. ft/sec	(1,100 cu.m/sec)
Kabalega (Uganda)	42,000 cu. ft/sec	(1,200 cu.m/sec)
Churchill (Canada)	35,000 cu. ft/sec	(1,000 cu.m/sec)
Cauvery (India)	33,000 cu. ft/sec	(900 cu.m/sec)

Highest Waterfalls

Angel (Venezuela)	3,212 ft	(979 m)
Tugela (South Africa)	3,110 ft	(948 m)
Utigard (Norway)	2,625 ft	(800 m)
Mongefossen (Norway)	2,539 ft	(774 m)
Mtarazi (Zimbabwe)	2,500 ft	(762 m)
Yosemite (USA)	2,425 ft	(739 m)
Ostre Mardola Foss (Norway)	2,156 ft	(657 m)
Tyssestrengane (Norway)	2,119 ft	(646 m)
***Cuquenan** (Venezuela)	2,001 ft	(610 m)
Sutherland (New Zealand)	1,903 ft	(580 m)
***Kjellfossen** (Norway)	1,841 ft	(561 m)

** indicates that the total height is a single leap*

Largest Deserts

Sahara	3,450,000 sq miles	(9,065,000 sq km)
Gobi	500,000 sq miles	(1,295,000 sq km)
Ar Rub al Khali	289,600 sq miles	(750,000 sq km)
Great Victorian	249,800 sq miles	(647,000 sq km)
Sonoran	120,000 sq miles	(311,000 sq km)
Kalahari	120,000 sq miles	(310,800 sq km)
Kara Kum	115,800 sq miles	(300,000 sq km)
Takla Makan	100,400 sq miles	(260,000 sq km)
Namib	52,100 sq miles	(135,000 sq km)
Thar	33,670 sq miles	(130,000 sq km)

NB – Most of Antarctica is a polar desert, with only 50mm of precipitation annually

Hottest Inhabited Places

Djibouti (Djibouti)	86° F	(30 °C)
Timbouctou (Mali)	84.7° F	(29.3 °C)
Tirunelveli (India)		
Tuticorin (India)		
Nellore (India)	84.5° F	(29.2 °C)
Santa Marta (Colombia)		
Aden (Yemen)	84° F	(28.9 °C)
Madurai (India)		
Niamey (Niger)		
Hodeida (Yemen)	83.8° F	(28.8 °C)
Ouagadougou (Burkina)		
Thanjavur (India)		
Tiruchchirappalli (India)		

Driest Inhabited Places

Aswân (Egypt)	0.02 in	(0.5 mm)
Luxor (Egypt)	0.03 in	(0.7 mm)
Arica (Chile)	0.04 in	(1.1 mm)
Ica (Peru)	0.1 in	(2.3 mm)
Antofagasta (Chile)	0.2 in	(4.9 mm)
El Minya (Egypt)	0.2 in	(5.1 mm)
Asyût (Egypt)	0.2 in	(5.2 mm)
Callao (Peru)	0.5 in	(12.0 mm)
Trujillo (Peru)	0.55 in	(14.0 mm)
El Faiyûm (Egypt)	0.8 in	(19.0 mm)

Wettest Inhabited Places

Buenaventura (Colombia)	265 in	(6,743 mm)
Monrovia (Liberia)	202 in	(5,131 mm)
Pago Pago (American Samoa)	196 in	(4,990 mm)
Moulmein (Burma)	191 in	(4,852 mm)
Lae (Papua New Guinea)	183 in	(4,645 mm)
Baguio (Luzon Island, Philippines)	180 in	(4,573 mm)
Sylhet (Bangladesh)	176 in	(4,457 mm)
Padang (Sumatra, Indonesia)	166 in	(4,225 mm)
Bogor (Java, Indonesia)	166 in	(4,225 mm)
Conakry (Guinea)	171 in	(4,341 mm)

THE TIME ZONES

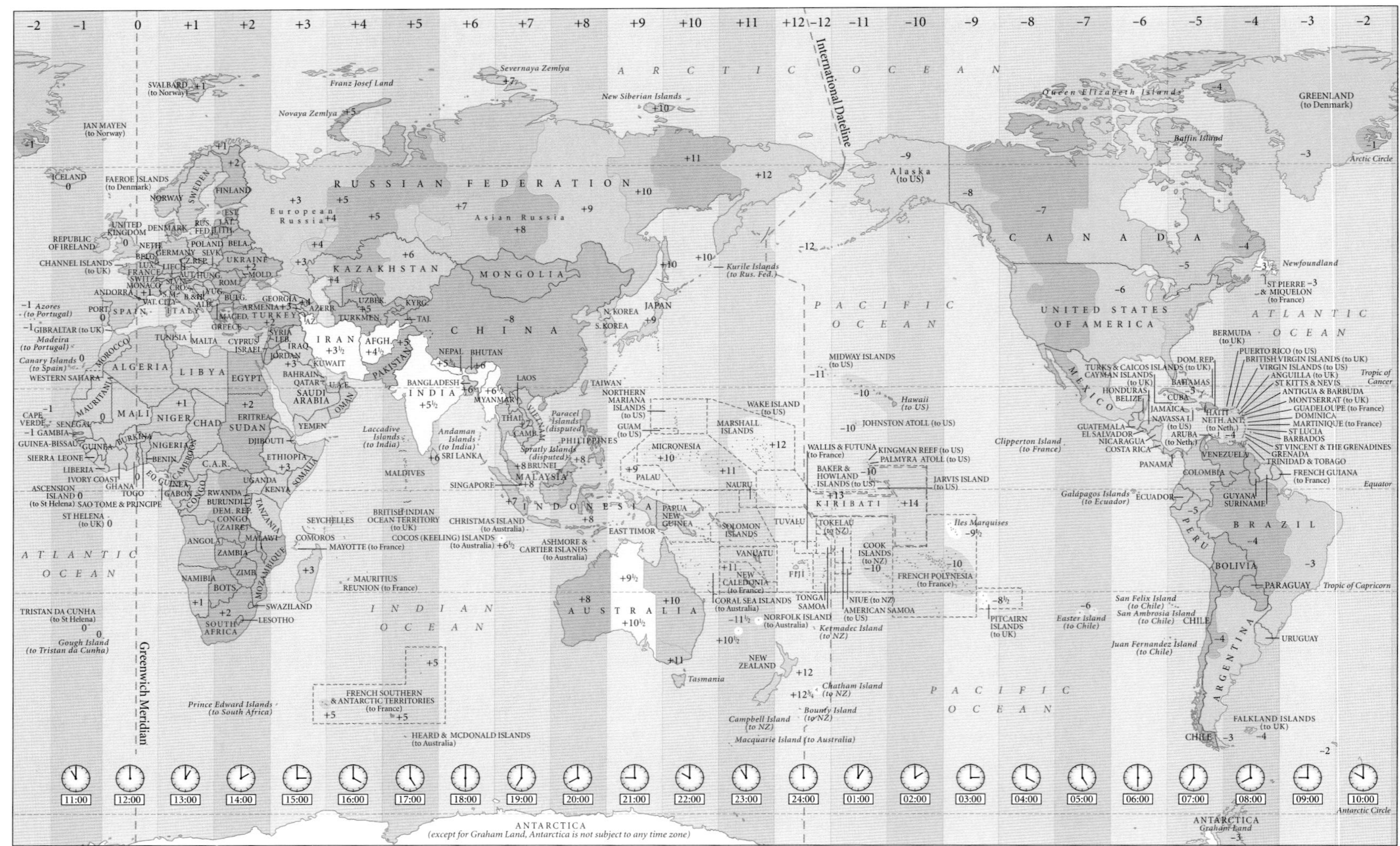

-2 -1 0 +1 +2 +3 +4 +5 +6 +7 +8 +9 +10 +11 +12 -12 -11 -10 -9 -8 -7 -6 -5 -4 -3 -2
International Dateline
Greenwich Meridian
ARCTIC OCEAN
ATLANTIC OCEAN
INDIAN OCEAN
PACIFIC OCEAN
RUSSIAN FEDERATION
KAZAKHSTAN
MONGOLIA
CHINA
INDIA
IRAN
ALGERIA
LIBYA
EGYPT
MALI
NIGER
CHAD
SUDAN
AUSTRALIA
NEW ZEALAND
KIRIBATI
CANADA
UNITED STATES OF AMERICA
MEXICO
BRAZIL
BOLIVIA
ARGENTINA
GREENLAND (to Denmark)
Alaska (to US)
Hawaii (to US)
Arctic Circle
Tropic of Cancer
Equator
Tropic of Capricorn
Antarctic Circle
ANTARCTICA (except for Graham Land, Antarctica is not subject to any time zone)
11:00 12:00 13:00 14:00 15:00 16:00 17:00 18:00 19:00 20:00 21:00 22:00 23:00 24:00 01:00 02:00 03:00 04:00 05:00 06:00 07:00 08:00 09:00 10:00

The numbers at the top of the map indicate the number of hours each time zone is ahead or behind Greenwich Mean Time (GMT). The clocks and 24-hour times given at the bottom of the map show the time in each time zone when it is 12:00 hours noon GMT.

TIME ZONES

The present system of international timekeeping divides the world into 24 time zones by means of 24 standard meridians of longitude, each 15° apart. Time is measured in each zone as so many hours ahead or behind the time at the Greenwich Meridian (GMT). Countries, or parts of countries, falling in the vicinity of each zone, adopt its time as shown on the map above. Therefore, using the map, when it is 12:00 noon GMT, it will be 2:00 pm in Zambia; similarly, when it is 4:30 pm GMT, it will be 11:30 am in Peru.

GREENWICH MEAN TIME (GMT)

Greenwich Mean Time (or Universal Time, as it is more correctly called) has been the internationally accepted basis for calculating solar time – measured in relation to the Earth's rotation around the Sun – since 1884. Greenwich Mean Time is specifically the solar time at the site of the former Royal Observatory in the London Borough of Greenwich, United Kingdom. The Greenwich Meridian is an imaginary line around the world that runs through the North and South poles. It corresponds to 0° of longitude, which lies on this site at Greenwich. Time is measured around the world in relation to the official time along the Meridian.

STANDARD TIME

Standard time is the official time, designated by law, in any specific country or region. Standard time was initiated in 1884, after it became apparent that the practice of keeping various systems of local time was causing confusion – particularly in the US and Canada, where several railroad routes passed through scores of areas which calculated local time by different rules. The standard time of a particular region is calculated in reference to the longitudinal time zone in which it falls. In practice, these zones do not always match their longitudinal position; in some places the area of the zone has been altered in shape for the convenience of inhabitants, as can be seen in the map. For example, whilst Greenland occupies three time zones, the majority of the territory uses a standard time of -3 hours GMT. Similarly China, which spans five time zones, is standardized at -8 hours GMT.

THE INTERNATIONAL DATELINE

The International Dateline is an imaginary line that extends from pole to pole, and roughly corresponds to a line of 180° longitude for much of its length. This line is the arbitrary marker between calendar days. By moving from east to west across the line, a traveler will need to set their calendar back one day, whilst those traveling in the opposite direction will need to add a day. This is to compensate for the use of standard time around the world, which is based on the time at noon along the Greenwich Meridian, approximately halfway around the world. Wide deviations from 180° longitude occur through the Bering Strait – to avoid dividing Siberia into two separate calendar days – and in the Pacific Ocean – to allow certain Pacific islands the same calendar day as New Zealand. Changes were made to the International Dateline in 1995 that made Millennium Island (formerly Caroline Island) in Kiribati the first land area to witness the beginning of the year 2000.

DAYLIGHT SAVING TIME

Also known as summer time, daylight saving is a system of advancing clocks in order to extend the waking day during periods of later daylight hours. This normally means advancing clocks by one hour in early spring, and reverting back to standard time in early autumn. The system of daylight saving is used throughout much of Europe, the US, Australia, and many other countries worldwide, although there are no standardized dates for the changeover to summer time due to the differences in hours of daylight at different latitudes. Daylight saving was first introduced in certain countries during the First World War, to decrease the need for artificial light and heat – the system stayed in place after the war, as it proved practical. During the Second World War, some countries went so far as to keep their clocks an hour ahead of standard time continuously, and the UK temporarily introduced "double summer time," which advanced clocks two hours ahead of standard time during the summer months.

COUNTRIES OF THE WORLD

THERE ARE CURRENTLY 192 independent countries in the world – more than at any previous time – and 59 dependencies. Antarctica is the only land area on Earth that is not officially part of, and does not belong to, any single country.

In 1950, the world comprised 82 countries. In the decades following, many more states came into being as they achieved independence from their former colonial rulers. Most recently, the breakup of the former Soviet Union in 1991, and the former Yugoslavia in 1992, swelled the ranks of independent states.

COUNTRY FACTFILE KEY

Formation Date of independence / date current borders were established
Population Total population / population density – based on total *land* area / percentage of urban-based population
Languages An asterisk (*) denotes the official language(s)
Calorie consumption Average number of calories consumed daily per person

AFGHANISTAN
Central Asia

Official name Islamic State of Afghanistan
Formation 1919 / 1919
Capital Kabul
Population 23.4 million / 93 people per sq mile (36 people per sq km) / 20%
Total area 251,770 sq miles (652,090 sq km)
Languages Persian*, Pashtu*, Dari, Uzbek, Turkmen
Religions Sunni Muslim 84%, Shi'a Muslim 15%, other 1%
Ethnic mix Pashtun 38%, Tajik 25%, Hazara 19%, Uzbek 6%, other 12%
Government Mujahideen coalition
Currency Afghani = 100 puls
Literacy rate 31%
Calorie consumption 1,523 kilocalories

ALBANIA
Southeastern Europe

Official name Republic of Albania
Formation 1912 / 1921
Capital Tiranë
Population 3.4 million / 321 people per sq mile (124 people per sq km) / 37%
Total area 11,100 sq miles (28,750 sq km)
Languages Albanian*, Greek, Macedonian
Religions Muslim 70%, Greek Orthodox 20%, Roman Catholic 10%
Ethnic mix Albanian 96%, Greek 2%, other (including Macedonian) 2%
Government Multiparty republic
Currency Lek = 100 qindars
Literacy rate 85%
Calorie consumption 2,605 kilocalories

ALGERIA
Northern Africa

Official name Democratic and Popular Republic of Algeria
Formation 1962 / 1962
Capital Algiers
Population 27.9 million / 33 people per sq mile (13 people per sq km) / 56%
Total area 919,590 sq miles (2,381,740 sq km)
Languages Arabic*, Berber, French
Religions Muslim 99%, Christian and Jewish 1%
Ethnic mix Arab and Berber 99%, European 1%
Government Multiparty republic
Currency Dinar = 100 centimes
Literacy rate 60%
Calorie consumption 2,897 kilocalories

ANDORRA
Southwestern Europe

Official name Principality of Andorra
Formation 1278 / 1278
Capital Andorra la Vella
Population 65,000 / 359 people per sq mile (139 people per sq km) / 63%
Total area 181 sq miles (468 sq km)
Languages Catalan*, Spanish, French, Portuguese
Religions Roman Catholic 94%, other 6%
Ethnic mix Catalan 61%, Spanish Castilian 30%, other 9%
Government Parliamentary democracy
Currency French franc, Spanish peseta
Literacy rate 100%
Calorie consumption 3,708 kilocalories

ANGOLA
Southern Africa

Official name Republic of Angola
Formation 1975 / 1975
Capital Luanda
Population 12 million / 25 people per sq mile (10 people per sq km) / 32%
Total area 481,551 sq miles (1,246,700 sq km)
Languages Portuguese*, Umbundu, Kimbundu, Kongo
Religions Roman Catholic / Protestant 64%, traditional beliefs 34%, other 2%
Ethnic mix Ovimbundu 37%, Mbundu 25%, Bakongo 13%, other 25%
Government Multiparty republic
Currency Readjusted kwanza = 100 lwei
Literacy rate 45%
Calorie consumption 1,839 kilocalories

ANTIGUA & BARBUDA
West Indies

Official name Antigua and Barbuda
Formation 1981 / 1981
Capital St John's
Population 66,000 / 389 people per sq mile (150 people per sq km) / 36%
Total area 170 sq miles (440 sq km)
Languages English*, English patios
Religions Protestant 86%, Roman Catholic 10%, other 4%
Ethnic mix Black 98%, other 2%
Government Parliamentary democracy
Currency E. Caribbean dollar = 100 cents
Literacy rate 95%
Calorie consumption 2,458 kilocalories

ARGENTINA
South America

Official name Republic of Argentina
Formation 1816 / 1816
Capital Buenos Aires
Population 36.1 million / 34 people per sq mile (13 people per sq km) / 87%
Total area 1,068,296 sq miles (2,766,890 sq km)
Languages Spanish*, Italian, English, German, French, Amerindian languages
Religions Roman Catholic 90%, Jewish 2%, other 8%
Ethnic mix European 85%, other (including *mestizo* and Indian) 15%
Government Multiparty republic
Currency Peso = 100 centavos
Literacy rate 96%
Calorie consumption 2,880 kilocalories

ARMENIA
Southwestern Asia

Official name Republic of Armenia
Formation 1991 / 1991
Capital Yerevan
Population 3.6 million / 313 people per sq mile (121 people per sq km) / 69%
Total area 11,505 sq miles (29,000 sq km)
Languages Armenian*, Azerbaijani, Russian, Kurdish
Religions Armenian Apostolic 90%, other Christian and Muslim 10%
Ethnic mix Armenian 93%, Azeri 3%, other 4%
Government Multiparty republic
Currency Dram = 100 louma
Literacy rate 99%
Calorie consumption NOT AVAILABLE

AUSTRALIA
Australasia & Oceania

Official name Commonwealth of Australia
Formation 1901 / 1901
Capital Canberra
Population 18.5 million / 6 people per sq mile (2 people per sq km) / 85%
Total area 2,967,893 sq miles (7,686,850 sq km)
Languages English*, Greek, Italian, Vietnamese, Aboriginal languages
Religions Protestant 38%, Roman Catholic 26%, other 36%
Ethnic mix European 95%, Asian 4%, Aboriginal and other 1%
Government Parliamentary democracy
Currency Australian dollar = 100 cents
Literacy rate 99%
Calorie consumption 3,179 kilocalories

AUSTRIA
Central Europe

Official name Republic of Austria
Formation 1918 / 1919
Capital Vienna
Population 8.2 million / 257 people per sq mile (99 people per sq km) / 56%
Total area 32,375 sq miles (83,850 sq km)
Languages German*, Croat, Slovene
Religions Roman Catholic 78%, Protestant 5%, other (including Jewish and Muslim) 17%
Ethnic mix German 93%, Croat, Slovene, Hungarian 6%, other 1%
Government Multiparty republic
Currency Austrian Schilling = 100 groschen
Literacy rate 99%
Calorie consumption 3,497 kilocalories

AZERBAIJAN
Southwestern Asia

Official name Azerbaijani Republic
Formation 1991 / 1991
Capital Baku
Population 7.7 million / 230 people per sq mile (89 people per sq km) / 56%
Total area 33,436 sq miles (86,600 sq km)
Languages Azerbaijani*, Russian, Armenian
Religions Muslim 83%, Armenian Apostolic and Russian Orthodox 17%
Ethnic mix Azeri 83%, Armenian 6%, Russian 5%, Daghestani 3%, other 3%
Government Multiparty republic
Currency Manat = 100 gopik
Literacy rate 96%
Calorie consumption NOT AVAILABLE

BAHAMAS
West Indies

Official name Commonwealth of the Bahamas
Formation 1973 / 1973
Capital Nassau
Population 293,000 / 76 people per sq mile (29 people per sq km)/ 87%
Total area 5,359 sq miles (13,880 sq km)
Languages English*, English Creole,
Religions Protestant 64%, Roman Catholic 19%, other 17%
Ethnic mix Black 85%, White 15%
Government Parliamentary democracy
Currency Bahamian dollar = 100 cents
Literacy rate 96%
Calorie consumption 2,624 kilocalories

BAHRAIN
Southwestern Asia

Official name State of Bahrain
Formation 1971 / 1971
Capital Manama
Population 594,000 / 2,262 people per sq mile (874 people per sq km) / 90%
Total area 263 sq miles (680 sq km)
Languages Arabic*, English, Urdu
Religions Muslim (Shi'a majority) 85%, Christian 7%, other 8%
Ethnic mix Bahraini 70%, Iranian, Indian, Pakistani 24%, other Arab 4%, European 2%
Government Absolute monarchy (emirate)
Currency Bahrain dinar = 1,000 fils
Literacy rate 86%
Calorie consumption NOT AVAILABLE

BANGLADESH
Southern Asia

Official name People's Republic of Bangladesh
Formation 1971 / 1971
Capital Dhaka
Population 124 million / 2,400 people per sq mile (926 people per sq km) / 18%
Total area 55,598 sq miles (143,998 sq km)
Languages Bengali*, Urdu, Chakma, Marma, Garo, Khasi, Santhali, Tripuri, Mro
Religions Muslim 87%, Hindu 12%, other 1%
Ethnic mix Bengali 98%, other 2%
Government Multiparty republic
Currency Taka = 100 paisa
Literacy rate 40%
Calorie consumption 2,019 kilocalories

BARBADOS
West Indies

Official name Barbados
Formation 1966 / 1966
Capital Bridgetown
Population 263,000 / 1,584 people per sq mile (612 people per sq km) / 47%
Total area 166 sq miles (430 sq km)
Languages English*, English Creole
Religions Protestant 55%, Roman Catholic 4%, other 41%
Ethnic mix Black 80%, mixed 15%, White 4%, other 1%
Government Parliamentary democracy
Currency Barbados dollar = 100 cents
Literacy rate 97%
Calorie consumption 3,207 kilocalories

BELARUS
Eastern Europe

Official name Republic of Belarus
Formation 1991 / 1991
Capital Minsk
Population 10.3 million / 129 people per sq mile (50 people per sq km) / 68%
Total area 80,154 sq miles (207,600 sq km)
Languages Belarusian*, Russian*
Religions Russian Orthodox 60%, Roman Catholic 8%, other 32%
Ethnic mix Belarusian 78%, Russian 13%, Polish 4%, other 5%
Government Multiparty republic
Currency Belarusian rouble = 100 kopeks
Literacy rate 99%
Calorie consumption NOT AVAILABLE

BELGIUM
Northwestern Europe

Official name Kingdom of Belgium
Formation 1830 / 1919
Capital Brussels
Population 10.2 million / 805 people per sq mile (311 people per sq km) / 97%
Total area 12,780 sq miles (33,100 sq km)
Languages Flemish*, French*, German*
Religions Roman Catholic 88%, other 12%
Ethnic mix Fleming 58%, Walloon 33%, other 9%
Government Constitutional monarchy
Currency Belgian franc = 100 centimes
Literacy rate 99%
Calorie consumption: 3,681 kilocalories

BELIZE
Central America

Official name Belize
Formation 1981 / 1981
Capital Belmopan
Population 200,000 /23 people per sq mile (9 people per sq km) / 47%
Total area 8,865 sq miles (22,960 sq km)
Languages English*, English Creole, Spanish
Religions Christian 87%, other 13%
Ethnic mix *Mestizo* 44%, Creole 30%, Maya 11%, Asian Indian 4%, Garifuna 7%, other 4%
Government Parliamentary democracy
Currency Belizean dollar =100 cents
Literacy rate 75%
Calorie consumption 2,662 kilocalories

BENIN
Western Africa

Official name Republic of Benin
Formation 1960 / 1960
Capital Porto-Novo
Population 5.9 million / 138 people per sq mile (53 people per sq km) / 31%
Total area 43,480 sq miles (112,620 sq km)
Languages French*, Fon, Bariba, Yoruba, Adja
Religions Traditional beliefs 70%, Muslim 15%, Christian 15%
Ethnic mix Fon 39%, Yoruba 12%, Adja 10%, other 39%
Government Multiparty republic
Currency CFA franc = 100 centimes
Literacy rate 34%
Calorie consumption 2,532 kilocalories

BHUTAN
Southeastern Asia

Official name Kingdom of Bhutan
Formation 1656 / 1865
Capital Thimphu
Population 1.9 million / 105 people per sq mile (40 people per sq km) / 6%
Total area 18,147 sq miles (47,000 sq km)
Languages Dzongkha*, Nepali, Assamese
Religions Mahayana Buddhism 70%, Hindu 24%, Muslim 5%, other 1%
Ethnic mix Bhutia 61%, Gurung 15%, Assamese 13%, other 11%
Government Constitutional monarchy
Currency Ngultrum = 100 chetrum
Literacy rate 44%
Calorie consumption 2,553 kilocalories

BOLIVIA
South America

Official name Republic of Bolivia
Formation 1825 / 1938
Capitals Sucre (official)/La Paz (administrative)
Population 8 million / 19 people per sq mile (7 people per sq km) / 61%
Total area 424,162 sq miles (1,098,580 sq km)
Languages Spanish*, Quechua*, Aymará*
Religions Roman Catholic 93%, other 7%
Ethnic mix Quechua 37%, Aymará 32%, mixed 13%, European 10%, other 8%
Government Multiparty republic
Currency Boliviano = 100 centavos
Literacy rate 84%
Calorie consumption 2,094 kilocalories

BOSNIA & HERZEGOVINA
Southeastern Europe

Official name Republic of Bosnia and Herzegovina
Formation 1992 / 1992
Capital Sarajevo
Population 4 million / 203 people per sq mile (78 people per sq km) / 49%
Total area 19,741 sq miles (51,130 sq km)
Languages Serbian*, Croatian*
Religions Muslim 40%, Serbian Orthodox 31%, Roman Catholic 15%, other 14%
Ethnic mix Bosnian 44%, Serb 31%, Croat 17%, other 8%
Government Multiparty republic
Currency Maraka = 100 pfenniga
Literacy rate 93%
Calorie consumption NOT AVAILABLE

BOTSWANA
Southern Africa

Official name Republic of Botswana
Formation 1966 / 1966
Capital Gaborone
Population 1.6 million / 7 people per sq mile (3 people per sq km) / 28%
Total area 224,600 sq miles (581,730 sq km)
Languages English*, Tswana, Shona, San
Religions Traditional beliefs 50%, Christian 50%
Ethnic mix Tswana 98%, other 2%
Government Multiparty republic
Currency Pula = 100 thebe
Literacy rate 74%
Calorie consumption 2,266 kilocalories

BRAZIL
South America

Official name Federative Republic of Brazil
Formation 1822 / 1889
Capital Brasília
Population 165.2 million / 51 people per sq mile (20 people per sq km) / 78%
Total area 3,286,472 sq miles (8,511,970 sq km)
Languages Portuguese*, German, Italian
Religions Roman Catholic 89%, other 11%
Ethnic mix White (Portuguese, Italian, German, Japanese) 66%, mixed 22%, Black 12%
Government Multiparty republic
Currency Real = 100 centavos
Literacy rate 84%
Calorie consumption 2,824 kilocalories

BRUNEI
Southeastern Asia

Official name Sultanate of Brunei
Formation 1984 / 1984
Capital Bandar Seri Begawan
Population 313,000 / 154 people per sq mile (57 people per sq km) / 59%
Total area 2,228 sq miles (5,770 sq km)
Languages Malay*, English, Chinese
Religions Muslim 63%, Buddhist 14%, Christian 10%, other 13%
Ethnic mix Malay 67%, Chinese 16%, other 17%
Government Absolute monarchy
Currency Brunei dollar = 100 cents
Literacy rate 90%
Calorie consumption 2,745 kilocalories

BULGARIA
Southeastern Europe

Official name Republic of Bulgaria
Formation 1908 / 1947
Capital Sofia
Population 8.4 million / 197 people per sq mile (76 people per sq km) / 71%
Total area 42,822 sq miles (110,910 sq km)
Languages Bulgarian*, Turkish, Macedonian, Romany, Armenian, Russian
Religions Christian 85%, Muslim 13%, Jewish 1%, other 1%
Ethnic mix Bulgarian 85%, Turkish 9%, Macedonian 3%, Romany 3%
Government Multiparty republic
Currency Lev = 100 stoninki
Literacy rate 98%
Calorie consumption 2,831 kilocalories

BURKINA
Western Africa

Official name Burkina Faso
Formation 1960 / 1960
Capital Ouagadougou
Population 11.4 million / 108 people per sq mile (42 people per sq km) / 27%
Total area 105,870 sq miles (274,200 sq km)
Languages French*, Mossi, Fulani
Religions Indigenous beliefs 55%, Muslim 35%, Christian 10%
Ethnic mix Mossi 45%, Mande 10%, Fulani 10%, other 35%
Government Multiparty republic
Currency CFA franc = 100 centimes
Literacy rate 21%
Calorie consumption 2,387 kilocalories

Burundi
Central Africa

Official name Republic of Burundi
Formation 1962 / 1962
Capital Bujumbura
Population 6.6 million / 666 people per sq mile (257 people per sq km) / 7%
Total area 10,750 sq miles (27,830 sq km)
Languages Kirundi*, French*, Swahili
Religions Christian 68%, Traditional beliefs 32%
Ethnic mix Hutu 85%, Tutsi 14%, Twa pygmy 1%
Government Multiparty republic
Currency Burundi franc = 100 centimes
Literacy rate 45%
Calorie consumption 1,941 kilocalories

Cambodia
Southeastern Asia

Official name Kingdom of Cambodia
Formation 1953 / 1953
Capital Phnom Penh
Population 10.8 million / 158 people per sq mile (61 people per sq km) / 21%
Total area 69,000 sq miles (181,040 sq km)
Languages Khmer*, French, Chinese, Vietnamese
Religions Theravada Buddhist 88%, Muslim 2%, other 10%
Ethnic mix Khmer 94%, Chinese 4%, other 2%
Government Constitutional monarchy
Currency Riel = 100 sen
Literacy rate 66%
Calorie consumption 2,021 kilocalories

Cameroon
Central Africa

Official name Republic of Cameroon
Formation 1960 / 1961
Capital Yaoundé
Population 14.3 million / 80 people per sq mile (31 people per sq km) / 45%
Total area 183,570 miles (475,440 sq km)
Languages English*, French*, Fang, Bulu, Yaundé, Duala
Religions Traditional beliefs 25%, Christian 53%, Muslim 22%
Ethnic mix Bamileke and Manum 20%, Fang 19%, other 61%
Government Multiparty republic
Currency CFA franc = 100 centimes
Literacy rate 72%
Calorie consumption 1,981 kilocalories

Canada
North America

Official name Canada
Formation 1867 / 1949
Capital Ottawa
Population 30.2 million / 8 people per sq mile (3 people per sq km) / 77%
Total area 3,851,788 sq miles (9,976,140 sq km)
Languages English*, French*, Chinese, Italian, German, Portuguese, Inuit
Religions Roman Catholic 47%, Protestant 41%, other 12%
Ethnic mix British origin 44%, French origin 25%, other European 20%, other 11%
Government Parliamentary democracy
Currency Canadian dollar = 100 cents
Literacy rate 99%
Calorie consumption 3,094 kilocalories

Cape Verde
Atlantic Ocean

Official Name Republic of Cape Verde
Formation 1975 / 1975
Capital Praia
Population 417,000 / 268 people per sq mile (103 people per sq km) / 54%
Total area 1,556 sq miles (4,030 sq km)
Languages Portuguese*, Creole
Religions Roman Catholic 98%, Protestant 2%
Ethnic mix Mestico 60%, African 30%, other 10%
Government Multiparty republic
Currency Cape Verde escudo = 100 centavos
Literacy rate 71%
Calorie consumption 2,805 kilocalories

Central African Republic
Central Africa

Official name Central African Republic
Formation 1960 / 1960
Capital Bangui
Population 3.5 million / 15 people per sq mile (6 people per sq km) / 39%
Total area 240,530 sq miles (622,980 sq km)
Languages French*, Sango, Banda, Gbaya
Religions Christian 50%, traditional beliefs 27%, Muslim 15%, other 8%
Ethnic mix Baya 34%, Banda 27%, Mandjia 21%, other 18%
Government Multiparty republic
Currency CFA franc = 100 centimes
Literacy rate 42%
Calorie consumption 1,690 kilocalories

Chad
Central Africa

Official name Republic of Chad
Formation 1960 / 1960
Capital N'Djamena
Population 6.9 million / 14 people per sq mile (5 people per sq km) / 21%
Total area 495,752 sq miles (1,284,000 sq km)
Languages French*, Sara, Maba
Religions Muslim 50%, Traditional beliefs 43%, Christian 7%
Ethnic mix Bagirmi, Sara and Kreish 31%, Sudanic Arab 26%, Teda 7%, other 36%
Government Multiparty republic
Currency CFA franc = 100 centimes
Literacy rate 50%
Calorie consumption 1,989 kilocalories

Chile
South America

Official name Republic of Chile
Formation 1818 / 1883
Capital Santiago
Population 14.8 million / 51 people per sq mile (20 people per sq km) / 84%
Total area 292,258 sq miles (756,950 sq km)
Languages Spanish*, Indian languages
Religions Roman Catholic 80%, Protestant and other 20%
Ethnic mix *Mestizo* and European 90%, Indian 10%
Government Multiparty republic
Currency Chilean peso = 100 centavos
Literacy rate 95%
Calorie consumption 2,582 kilocalories

China
Eastern Asia

Official name People's Republic of China
Formation 1949 / 1999
Capital Beijing
Population 1.3 billion / 349 people per sq mile (135 people per sq km) / 30%
Total area 3,628,166 sq miles (9,396,960 sq km)
Languages Mandarin*, Wu, Cantonese, Hsiang, Min, Hakka, Kan
Religions Nonreligious 59%, Traditional beliefs 20%, Buddhist 6%, other 15%
Ethnic mix Han 93%, Zhaung 1%, other 6%
Government Single-party republic
Currency Yuan = 10 jiao = 100 fen
Literacy rate 84%
Calorie consumption 2,727 kilocalories

Colombia
South America

Official name Republic of Colombia
Formation 1819 / 1922
Capital Bogotá
Population 37.7 million / 94 people per sq mile (36 people per sq km) / 73%
Total area 439,733 sq miles (1,138,910 sq km)
Languages Spanish*, Amerindian languages, English Creole
Religions Roman Catholic 95%, other 5%
Ethnic mix *Mestizo* 58%, White 20%, European-African 14%, other 8%
Government Multiparty republic
Currency Colombian peso = 100 centavos
Literacy rate 91%
Calorie consumption 2,677 kilocalories

Comoros
Indian Ocean

Official name Federal Islamic Republic of the Comoros
Formation 1975 / 1975
Capital Moroni
Population 672,000 / 780 people per sq mile (301 people per sq km) / 29%
Total area 861 sq miles (2,230 sq km)
Languages Arabic*, French*, Comoran
Religions Muslim 98%, Roman Catholic 1%, other 1%
Ethnic mix Comorian 96%, other 4%
Government Islamic republic
Currency Comoros franc = 100 centimes
Literacy rate 55%
Calorie consumption 1,897 kilocalories

Congo
Central Africa

Official name Republic of the Congo
Formation 1960 / 1960
Capital Brazzaville
Population 2.8 million / 21 people per sq km (8 people per sq km) / 59%
Total area 132,040 sq miles (342,000 sq km)
Languages French*, Kongo, Teke, Lingala
Religions Roman Catholic 50%, Traditional beliefs 48%, other 2%
Ethnic mix Bakongo 48%, Sangha 20%, Teke 17%, Mbochi 12%, other 3%
Government Multiparty republic
Currency CFA franc = 100 centimes
Literacy rate 77%
Calorie consumption 2,296 kilocalories

Congo, Dem. Rep. (Zaire)
Central Africa

Official name Democratic Republic of the Congo
Formation 1960 / 1960
Capital Kinshasa
Population 49.2 million / 56 people per sq mile (22 people per sq km) / 29%
Total area 905,563 sq miles (2,345,410 sq km)
Languages French*, Kiswahili, Tshiluba, Lingala
Religions Traditional beliefs 50%, Roman Catholic 37%, Protestant 13%
Ethnic mix Bantu 23%, Hamitic 23%, other 54%
Government Single-party republic
Currency Congolese franc = 100 centimes
Literacy rate 77%
Calorie consumption 2,060 kilocalories

Costa Rica
Central America

Official name Republic of Costa Rica
Formation 1821 / 1838
Capital San José
Population 3.7 million / 188 people per sq mile (72 people per sq km) / 50%
Total area 19,730 miles (51,100 sq km)
Languages Spanish*, English Creole, Bribri, Cabecar
Religions Roman Catholic 76%, other 24%
Ethnic mix White and *mestizo* 96%, Black 2%, Indian 2%
Government Multiparty republic
Currency Costa Rica colón = 100 centimos
Literacy rate 95%
Calorie consumption 2,883 kilocalories

Croatia
Southeastern Europe

Official name Republic of Croatia
Formation 1991 / 1991
Capital Zagreb
Population 4.5 million / 206 people per sq mile (80 people per sq km) / 64%
Total area 21,830 sq miles (56,540 sq km)
Languages Croatian*, Serbian, Hungarian (Magyar), Slovenian
Religions Roman Catholic 76%, Eastern Orthodox 11%, Protestant 1%, Muslim 1%, other 10%
Ethnic mix Croat 80%, Serb 12%, Hungarian, Slovenian, other 8%
Government Multiparty republic
Currency Kuna = 100 lipa
Literacy rate 98%
Calorie consumption NOT AVAILABLE

Cuba
West Indies

Official name Republic of Cuba
Formation 1902 / 1898
Capital Havana
Population 11.1 million / 259 people per sq mile (100 people per sq km) / 76%
Total area 42,803 sq miles (110,860 sq km)
Languages Spanish*, English, French
Religions Nonreligious **55%**, Roman Catholic 40%, other 5%
Ethnic mix White 66%, European-African 22%, Black 12%
Government Socialist republic
Currency Cuban peso = 100 centavos
Literacy rate 96%
Calorie consumption 2,833 kilocalories

Cyprus
Southeastern Europe

Official name Republic of Cyprus
Formation 1960 / 1983
Capital Nicosia
Population 766,000 / 218 people per sq mile (84 people per sq km) / 54%
Total area 3,572 sq miles (9,251 sq km)
Languages Greek*, Turkish, English
Religions Greek Orthodox 77%, Muslim 18%, other 5%
Ethnic mix Greek 77%, Turkish 18%, other (mainly British) 5%
Government Multiparty republic
Currency Cyprus pound / Turkish lira
Literacy rate 96%
Calorie consumption 3,779 kilocalories

Czech Republic
Central Europe

Official name Czech Republic
Formation 1993 / 1993
Capital Prague
Population 10.2 million / 335 people per sq mile (129 people per sq km) / 65%
Total area 30,260 sq miles (78,370 sq km)
Languages Czech*, Slovak, Romany, Hungarian (Magyar)
Religions Roman Catholic 39%, nonreligious 40%, other 21%
Ethnic mix Czech 85%, Moravian 13%, other 2%
Government Multiparty republic
Currency Czech koruna = 100 halura
Literacy rate 99%
Calorie consumption 3,156 kilocalories

Denmark
Northern Europe

Official name Kingdom of Denmark
Formation AD 960 / 1920
Capital Copenhagen
Population 5.3 million / 324 people per sq mile (125 people per sq km) / 85%
Total area 16,629 sq miles (43,069 sq km)
Languages Danish*, Faeroese, Inuit
Religions Evangelical Lutheran 89% other Christian 11%
Ethnic mix Danish 96%, Faeroese & Inuit 1%, other 3%
Government Constitutional monarchy
Currency Danish krone = 100 øre
Literacy rate 100%
Calorie consumption 3,664 kilocalories

Djibouti
Eastern Africa

Official name Republic of Djibouti
Formation 1977 / 1977
Capital Djibouti
Population 652,000 / 73 people per sq mile (28 people per sq km) /83%
Total area 8,958 sq miles (23,200 sq km)
Languages Arabic*, French*, Somali, Afar
Religions Christian 87%, other 13%
Ethnic mix Issa 60%, Afar 35%, other 5%
Government Multiparty republic
Currency Djibouti franc = 100 centimes
Literacy rate 48%
Calorie consumption 2,338 kilocalories

Dominica
West Indies

Official name Commonwealth of Dominica
Formation 1978 / 1978
Capital Roseau
Population 74,000 / 256 people per sq mile (99 people per sq km)/ 69%
Total area 290 sq miles (750 sq km)
Languages English*, French Creole, Carib, Cocoy
Religions Roman Catholic 77%, Protestant 15%, other 8%
Ethnic mix Black 98%, Indian 2%
Government Multiparty republic
Currency East Caribbean dollar = 100 cents
Literacy rate 94%
Calorie consumption 2,778 kilocalories

Dominican Republic
West Indies

Official name Dominican Republic
Formation 1865 / 1865
Capital Santo Domingo
Population 8.2 million / 439 people per sq mile (169 people per sq km) / 65%
Total area 18,815 sq miles (48,730 sq km)
Languages Spanish*, French Creole
Religions Roman Catholic 92%, other 8%
Ethnic mix European-African 73%, White 16%, Black 11%
Government Multiparty republic
Currency Dom. Republic peso = 100 centavos
Literacy rate 83%
Calorie consumption 2,286 kilocalories

Ecuador
South America

Official name Republic of Ecuador
Formation 1830 / 1941
Capital Quito
Population 12.2 million / 114 people per sq mile (44 people per sq km) / 58%
Total area 109,483 sq miles (283,560 sq km)
Languages Spanish*, Quechua, other Amerindian languages
Religions Roman Catholic 95%, other 5%
Ethnic mix *Mestizo* 55%, Indian 25%, Black 10%, White 10%
Government Multiparty republic
Currency Sucre = 100 centavos
Literacy rate 91%
Calorie consumption 2,583 kilocalories

Egypt
Northern Africa

Official name Arab Republic of Egypt
Formation 1936 / 1982
Capital Cairo
Population 65.7 million / 171 people per sq mile (66 people per sq km) / 45%
Total area 386,660 sq miles (1,001,450 sq km)
Languages Arabic*, French, English, Berber, Greek, Armenian
Religions Muslim 94%, other 6%
Ethnic mix Eastern Hamitic 90%, other (including Greek, Armenian) 10%
Government Multiparty republic
Currency Egyptian pound = 100 piastres
Literacy rate 53%
Calorie consumption 3,335 kilocalories

El Salvador
Central America

Official name Republic of El Salvador
Formation 1856 / 1838
Capital San Salvador
Population 6.1 million / 763 people per sq mile (294 people per sq km) /45%
Total area 8,124 sq miles (21,040 sq km)
Languages Spanish*, Nahua
Religions Roman Catholic 80%, other 20%
Ethnic mix *Mestizo* 89%, Indian 10%, White 1%
Government Multiparty republic
Currency Salvadorean colón = 100 centavos
Literacy rate 73%
Calorie consumption 2,663 kilocalories

Equatorial Guinea
Central Africa

Official name Republic of Equatorial Guinea
Formation 1968 / 1968
Capital Malabo
Population 430,000 / 40 people per sq mile (15 people per sq km) / 42%
Total area 10,830 sq miles (28,050 sq km)
Languages Spanish*, Fang, Bubi
Religions Christian 90%, other 10%
Ethnic mix Fang 72%, Bubi 14%, Duala 3%, other 11%
Government Multiparty republic
Currency CFA franc = 100 centimes
Literacy rate 80%
Calorie consumption NOT AVAILABLE

Eritrea
Eastern Africa

Official name State of Eritrea
Formation 1993 / 1993
Capital Asmara
Population 3.5 million / 97 people per sq mile (37 people per sq km) / 17%
Total area 36,170 sq miles (93,680 sq km)
Languages Tigrinya*, Arabic*, Tigre
Religions Christian 45%, Muslim 45%, other 10%
Ethnic mix Nine main ethnic groups
Government Provisional military government
Currency Nakfa = 100 cents
Literacy rate 25%
Calorie consumption 1,610 kilocalories

Estonia
Northeastern Europe

Official name Republic of Estonia
Formation 1991 / 1991
Capital Tallinn
Population 1.4 million / 80 people per sq mile (31 people per sq km) / 73%
Total area 17,423 sq miles (45,125 sq km)
Languages Estonian*, Russian
Religions Evangelical Lutheran 98%, Eastern Orthodox, Baptist 2%
Ethnic mix Russian 62%, Estonian 30%, Ukrainian 3%, other 5%
Government Multiparty republic
Currency Kroon = 100 cents
Literacy rate 99%
Calorie consumption NOT AVAILABLE

Ethiopia
Eastern Africa

Official name Federal Democratic Republic of Ethiopia
Formation 1896 / 1993
Capital Addis Ababa
Population 62.1 million / 146 people per sq mile (56 people per sq km) / 13%
Total area 435,605 sq miles (1,128,221 sq km)
Languages Amharic*, English, Arabic
Religions Muslim 40%, Christian 40%, Traditional beliefs 15%, other 5%
Ethnic mix Oromo 40%, Amhara 25%, Sidamo 9%, Somali 6%, other 20%
Government Multiparty republic
Currency Ethiopian birr = 100 cents
Literacy rate 35%
Calorie consumption 1,610 kilocalories

Fiji
Australasia & Oceania

Official name Sovereign Democratic Republic of Fiji
Formation 1970 / 1970
Capital Suva
Population 822,000 / 117 people per sq mile (45 people per sq km) / 40%
Total area 7,054 sq miles (18,270 sq km)
Languages English*, Fijian, Hindu, Urdu
Religions Christian 46%, Hindu 38%, Muslim 8%, other 8%
Ethnic mix Native Fijian 49%, Indo-Fijian 46%, other 5%
Government Multiparty republic
Currency Fiji dollar = 100 cents
Literacy rate 92%
Calorie consumption 3,089 kilocalories

FINLAND
Northern Europe

Official name Republic of Finland
Formation 1917 / 1947
Capital Helsinki
Population 5.2 million / 44 people per sq mile (17 people per sq km) / 63%
Total area 130,552 sq miles (338,130 sq km)
Languages Finnish*, Swedish*, Lappish
Religions Evangelical Lutheran 89%, Finnish Orthodox 1%, other 10%
Ethnic mix Finnish 93%, Swedish 6%, other (including Sami) 1%
Government Multiparty republic
Currency Markka = 100 pennia
Literacy rate 99%
Calorie consumption 3,018 kilocalories

FRANCE
Western Europe

Official name French Republic
Formation 486 / 1919
Capital Paris
Population 58.7 million / 276 people per sq mile (107 people per sq km) / 73%
Total area 212,930 sq miles (551,500 sq km)
Languages French*, Provençal, Breton, Catalan, Basque
Religions Roman Catholic 88%, Muslim 8%, other 4%
Ethnic mix French 90%, North African 6%, German 2%, Breton 1%, other 1%
Government Multiparty republic
Currency Franc = 100 centimes
Literacy rate 99%
Calorie consumption 3,633 kilocalories

GABON
Central Africa

Official name Gabonese Republic
Formation 1960 / 1960
Capital Libreville
Population 1.2 million / 12 people per sq mile (5 people per sq km) / 50%
Total area 103,347 sq miles (267,670 sq km)
Languages French*, Fang, Punu, Sira, Nzebi, Mpongwe
Religions Christian 96%, Muslim 2%, other 2%
Ethnic mix Fang 3%, Eshira 25%, other Bantu 25%, European and other African 9%
Government Multiparty republic
Currency CFA franc = 100 centimes
Literacy rate 66%
Calorie consumption 2,500 kilocalories

GAMBIA
Western Africa

Official name Republic of the Gambia
Formation 1965 / 1965
Capital Banjul
Population 1.9 million / 309 people per sq mile (119 people per sq km) / 26%
Total area 4,363 sq miles (11,300 sq km)
Languages English*, Mandinka, Fulani, Wolof, Diola, Soninke
Religions Muslim 85%, Christian 9%, Traditional beliefs 6%
Ethnic mix Mandingo 42%, Fulani 18% Wolof 16%, Jola 10%, Serahuli 9%, other 5%
Government Multiparty republic
Currency Dalasi = 100 butut
Literacy rate 33%
Calorie consumption 2,360 kilocalories

GEORGIA
Southwestern Asia

Official name Republic of Georgia
Formation 1991 / 1991
Capital Tbilisi
Population 5.4 million / 201 people per sq mile (77 people per sq km) / 58%
Total area 26,911 sq miles (69,700 sq km)
Languages Georgian*, Russian
Religions Georgian Orthodox 70%, Russian Orthodox 10%, other 20%
Ethnic mix Georgian 70%, Armenian 8%, Russian 6%, Azeri 6%, other 10%
Government Multiparty republic
Currency Lari = 100 tetri
Literacy rate 99%
Calorie consumption NOT AVAILABLE

GERMANY
Northern Europe

Official name Federal Republic of Germany
Formation 1871 / 1990
Capital Berlin
Population 82.4 million / 611 people per sq mile (236 people per sq km) / 87%
Total area 137,800 sq miles (356,910 sq km)
Languages German*, Sorbian, Turkish
Religions Protestant 36%, Roman Catholic 35%, Muslim 2%, other 27%
Ethnic mix German 92%, other 8%
Government Multiparty republic
Currency Deutsche Mark = 100 pfennigs
Literacy rate 99%
Calorie consumption 3,344 kilocalories

GHANA
Western Africa

Official name Republic of Ghana
Formation 1957 / 1957
Capital Accra
Population 18.9 million / 213 people per sq mile (82 people per sq km) / 36%
Total area 92,100 sq miles (238,540 sq km)
Languages English*, Akan, Mossi, Ewe
Religions Traditional beliefs 38%, Christian 43%, Muslim 11%, other 8%
Ethnic mix Akan 52%, Mossi 15%, Ewe 12%, Ga 8%, other 13%
Government Multiparty republic
Currency Cedi = 100 pesewas
Literacy rate 66%
Calorie consumption 2,199 kilocalories

GREECE
Southeastern Europe

Official name Hellenic Republic
Formation 1829 / 1947
Capital Athens
Population 10.6 million / 210 people per sq mile (81 people per sq km) / 65%
Total area 50,961 sq miles (131,990 sq km)
Languages Greek*, Turkish, Albanian, Macedonian
Religions Greek Orthodox 98%, Muslim 1%, other 1%
Ethnic mix Greek 98%, other 2%
Government Multiparty republic
Currency Drachma = 100 lepta
Literacy rate 96%
Calorie consumption 3,815 kilocalories

GRENADA
West Indies

Official name Grenada
Formation 1974 / 1974
Capital St George's
Population 98,600 / 751 people per sq mile (290 people per sq km) / 37%
Total area 131 sq miles (340 sq km)
Languages English*, English Creole
Religions Roman Catholic 68%, Anglican 17%, other 15%
Ethnic mix Black 84%, European-African 13%, South Asian 3%
Government Parliamentary democracy
Currency East Caribbean dollar = 100 cents
Literacy rate 98%
Calorie consumption 2,402 kilocalories

GUATEMALA
Central America

Official name Republic of Guatemala
Formation 1838 / 1838
Capital Guatemala City
Population 11.6 million / 277 people per sq mile (107 people per sq km) / 41%
Total area 42,043 sq miles (108,890 sq km)
Languages Spanish*, Quiché, Mam, Kekchí
Religions Christian 99%, other 1%
Ethnic mix Indian 60%, *mestizo* 30%, other 10%
Government Multiparty republic
Currency Quetzal = 100 centavos
Literacy rate 66%
Calorie consumption 2,255 kilocalories

GUINEA
Western Africa

Official name Republic of Guinea
Formation 1958 / 1958
Capital Conakry
Population 7.7 million / 81 people per sq mile (31 people per sq km) / 30%
Total area 94,926 sq miles (245,860 sq km)
Languages French*, Fulani, Malinke, Soussou, Kissi
Religions Muslim 85%, Christian 8%, Traditional beliefs 7%
Ethnic mix Fila (Fulani) 30%, Malinke 30%, Soussou 15%, Kissi 10% other 20%
Government Multiparty republic
Currency Franc = 100 centimes
Literacy rate 37%
Calorie consumption 2,389 kilocalories

GUINEA-BISSAU
Western Africa

Official name Republic of Guinea-Bissau
Formation 1974 / 1974
Capital Bissau
Population 1.1 million / 101 people per sq mile (39 people per sq km) / 22%
Total area 13,940 sq miles (36,120 sq km)
Languages Portuguese*, Balante, Fulani, Malinke
Religions Traditional beliefs 52%, Muslim 40%, Christian 8%
Ethnic mix Balante 30%, Fila (Fulani) 22%, Malinke 12%, other 36%
Government Multiparty republic
Currency Guinea peso = 100 centavos
Literacy rate 33%
Calorie consumption 2,556 kilocalories

GUYANA
South America

Official name Cooperative Republic of Guyana
Formation 1966 / 1966
Capital Georgetown
Population 856,000 / 11 people per sq mile (4 people per sq km) / 36%
Total area 83,000 sq miles (214,970 sq km)
Languages English*, English Creole, Hindi, Tamil, English
Religions Christian 57%, Hindu 33%, Muslim 9%, other 1%
Ethnic mix East Indian 52%, Black African 38%, Indian 4%, other 6%
Government Multiparty republic
Currency Guyana dollar =100 cents
Literacy rate 98%
Calorie consumption 2,384 kilocalories

HAITI
West Indies

Official name Republic of Haiti
Formation 1804 / 1844
Capital Port-au-Prince
Population 7.5 million / 705 people per sq mile (272 people per sq km) / 32%
Total area 10,714 sq miles (27,750 sq km)
Languages French*, French Creole*,
Religions Roman Catholic 80%, Protestant 16%, other 4%
Ethnic mix Black 95%, European-African 5%
Government Multiparty republic
Currency Gourde = 100 centimes
Literacy rate 45%
Calorie consumption 1,706 kilocalories

HONDURAS
Central America

Official name Republic of Honduras
Formation 1838 / 1838
Capital Tegucigalpa
Population 6.1 million / 141 people per sq mile (55 people per sq km) / 44%
Total area 43,278 sq miles (112,090 sq km)
Languages Spanish*, English Creole, Garifuna, Indian languages
Religions Roman Catholic 97%, other 3%
Ethnic mix *Mestizo* 90%, Black African 5%, Indian 4%, White 1%
Government Multiparty republic
Currency Lempira = 100 centavos
Literacy rate 70%
Calorie consumption 2,305 kilocalories

HUNGARY
Central Europe

Official name Republic of Hungary
Formation 1918 / 1947
Capital Budapest
Population 9.9 million / 278 people per sq mile (107 people per sq km) / 65%
Total area 35,919 sq miles (93,030 sq km)
Languages Hungarian (Magyar)*, German, Slovak
Religions Roman Catholic 64%, Protestant 27%, other 7%
Ethnic mix Hungarian (Magyar) 90%, German 2%, other 8%
Government Multiparty republic
Currency Forint = 100 filler
Literacy rate 99%
Calorie consumption 3,503 kilocalories

ICELAND
Northwestern Europe

Official name Republic of Iceland
Formation 1944 / 1944
Capital Reykjavík
Population 277,000 / 7 people per sq mile (3 people per sq km) / 92%
Total area 39,770 sq miles (103,000 sq km)
Languages Icelandic*, English
Religions Evangelical Lutheran 93%, nonreligious 6%, other Christian 1%
Ethnic mix Icelandic (Norwegian-Celtic descent) 98%, other 2%
Government Constitutional republic
Currency New Icelandic króna = 100 aurar
Literacy rate 99%
Calorie consumption 3,058 kilocalories

INDIA
Southern Asia

Official name Republic of India
Formation 1947 / 1947
Capital New Delhi
Population 976 million / 850 people per sq mile (328 people per sq km) / 27%
Total area 1,269,338 sq miles (3,287,590 sq km)
Languages Hindi*, English*, Urdu, Bengali, Marathi, Telugu, Tamil, Bihari
Religions Hindu 83%, Muslim 11%, Christian 2%, Sikh 2%, other 2%
Ethnic mix Indo-Aryan 72%, Dravidian 25%, Mongoloid and other 3%
Government Multiparty republic
Currency Rupee = 100 paisa
Literacy rate 53%
Calorie consumption 2,395 kilocalories

INDONESIA
Southeastern Asia

Official name Republic of Indonesia
Formation 1949 / 1963
Capital Jakarta
Population 206.5 million / 295 people per sq mile (114 people per sq km) / 35%
Total area 735,555 sq miles (1,904,570 sq km)
Languages Bahasa Indonesia*, 250 (est.) languages or dialects
Religions Muslim 87%, Christian 9%, Hindu 2%, Buddhist 1%, other 1%
Ethnic mix Javanese 45%, Sundanese 14%, Madurese 8%, Coastal Malays 8%, other 25%
Government Multiparty republic
Currency Rupiah = 100 sen
Literacy rate 82%
Calorie consumption 2,752 kilocalories

IRAN
Southwestern Asia

Official name Islamic Republic of Iran
Formation 1906 / 1906
Capital Tehran
Population 73.1 million / 116 people per sq mile (45 people per sq km) / 59%
Total area 636,293 sq miles (1,648,000 sq km)
Languages Farsi (Persian)*, Azerbaijani, Gilaki, Mazanderani, Kurdish, Baluchi, Arabic
Religions Shi'a Muslim 95%, Sunni Muslim 4%, other 1%
Ethnic mix Persian 50%, Azeri 20%, Lur and Bakhtiari 10%, Kurd 8%, Arab 2%, other 10%
Government Islamic Republic
Currency Iranian rial = 100 dinars
Literacy rate 73%
Calorie consumption 2,860 kilocalories

IRAQ
Southwestern Asia

Official name Republic of Iraq
Formation 1932 / 1991
Capital Baghdad
Population 21.8 million / 129 people per sq mile (50 people per sq km) / 75%
Total area 169,235 sq miles (438,320 sq km)
Languages Arabic*, Kurdish, Armenian, Assyrian
Religions Shi'a ithna Muslim 62%, Sunni Muslim 33%, other 5%
Ethnic mix Arab 79%, Kurdish 16%, Persian 3%, Turkoman 2%
Government Single-party republic
Currency Iraqi dinar = 1000 fils
Literacy rate 58%
Calorie consumption 2,121 kilocalories

IRELAND
Northwestern Europe

Official name Republic of Ireland
Formation 1922 / 1922
Capital Dublin
Population 3.6 million / 135 people per sq mile (52 people per sq km) / 57%
Total area 27,155 sq miles (70,280 sq km)
Languages English*, Irish Gaelic*
Religions Roman Catholic 88%, Protestant 3%, other 9%
Ethnic mix Irish 95%, other 5%
Government Multiparty republic
Currency Punt = 100 pence
Literacy rate 99%
Calorie consumption 3,847 kilocalories

ISRAEL
Southwestern Asia

Official name State of Israel
Formation 1948 / 1994
Capital Jerusalem
Population 5.9 million / 752 people per sq mile (290 people per sq km) / 91%
Total area 7,992 sq miles (20,700 sq km)
Languages Hebrew*, Arabic*, Yiddish
Religions Jewish 82%, Muslim 14%, Christian 2%, Druze and other 2%
Ethnic mix Jewish 82%, Arab 18%
Government Multiparty republic
Currency New Israeli shekel = 100 agorat
Literacy rate 95%
Calorie consumption 3,050 kilocalories

ITALY
Southern Europe

Official name Italian Republic
Formation 1871 / 1954
Capital Rome
Population 57.2 million / 504 people per sq mile (195 people per sq km) / 67%
Total area 116,320 sq miles (301,270 sq km)
Languages Italian*, German, French, Rhaeto-Romanic, Sardinian
Religions Roman Catholic 83%, other 17%
Ethnic mix Italian 94%, other 6%
Government Multiparty republic
Currency Lira = 100 centesimi
Literacy rate 98%
Calorie consumption 3,561 kilocalories

IVORY COAST
Western Africa

Official name Republic of the Ivory Coast
Formation 1960 / 1960
Capital Yamoussoukro
Population 14.6 million / 119 people per sq mile (45 people per sq km) / 42%
Total area 124,503 sq miles (322,463 sq km)
Languages French*, Akran, Kru, Voltaic
Religions Traditional beliefs 63%, Muslim 25%, Christian 12%
Ethnic mix Baoulé 23%, Bété 18%, Kru 17%, Malinke 15%, other 27%
Government Multiparty republic
Currency CFA franc = 100 centimes
Literacy rate 54%
Calorie consumption 2,491 kilocalories

JAMAICA
West Indies

Official name Jamaica
Formation 1962 / 1962
Capital Kingston
Population 2.5 million / 598 people per sq mile (231 people per sq km) / 54%
Total area 4,243 sq miles (10,990 sq km)
Languages English*, English Creole
Religions Christian 55%, other 45%
Ethnic mix Black 75%, mixed 15%, South Asian 5%, other 5%
Government Parliamentary democracy
Currency Jamaican dollar = 100 cents
Literacy rate 85%
Calorie consumption 2,607 kilocalories

JAPAN
Eastern Asia

Official name Japan
Formation 1600 / 1972
Capital Tokyo
Population 125.9 million / 866 people per sq mile (334 people per sq km) / 78%
Total area 145,869 sq miles (377,800 sq km)
Languages Japanese*, Korean, Chinese
Religions Shinto and Buddhist 76%, Buddhist 16%, other 8%
Ethnic mix Japanese 99%, other 1%
Government Constitutional monarchy
Currency Yen = 100 sen
Literacy rate 99%
Calorie consumption 2,903 kilocalories

JORDAN
Southwestern Asia

Official name Hashemite Kingdom of Jordan
Formation 1946 / 1976
Capital Amman
Population 6 million / 175 people per sq mile (67 people per sq km) / 71%
Total area 34,440 sq miles (89,210 sq km)
Languages Arabic*
Religions Muslim 95%, Christian 5%
Ethnic mix Arab 98%, (40% Palestinian), Armenian 1%, Circassian 1%
Government Constitutional monarchy
Currency Jordanian dinar = 1,000 fils
Literacy rate 87%
Calorie consumption 3,022 kilocalories

KAZAKHSTAN
Central Asia

Official Name Republic of Kazakhstan
Formation 1991 / 1991
Capital Astana
Population 16.9 million / 16 people per sq mile (6 people per sq km) / 60%
Total area 1,049,150 sq miles (2,717,300 sq km)
Languages Kazakh*, Russian, German
Religions Muslim 47%, other 53% (mostly Russian Orthodox and Lutheran)
Ethnic mix Kazakh 44%, Russian 38%, Ukrainian 6%, German 2%, other 14%
Government Multiparty republic
Currency Tenge = 100 tein
Literacy rate 99%
Calorie consumption NOT AVAILABLE

KENYA
East Africa

Official name Republic of Kenya
Formation 1963 / 1963
Capital Nairobi
Population 29 million / 132 people per sq mile (51 people per sq km) / 28%
Total area 224,081 sq miles (580,370 sq km)
Languages Swahili*, English, Kikuyu, Luo, Kamba
Religions Christian 60%, Traditional beliefs 25%, Muslim 6%, other 9%
Ethnic mix Kikuyu 21%, Luhya 14%, Luo 13%, Kalenjin 11% other 41%
Government Multiparty republic
Currency Kenya shilling = 100 cents
Literacy rate 79%
Calorie consumption 2,075 kilocalories

KIRIBATI
Australasia & Oceania

Official Name Republic of Kiribati
Formation 1979 / 1979
Capital Bairiki
Population 78,000 / 284 people per sq mile (110 people per sq km) / 36%
Total area 274 sq miles (710 sq km)
Languages English*, Kiribati
Religions Roman Catholic 53%, Protestant 39%, other 8%
Ethnic mix I-Kiribati 98%, other 2%
Government Multiparty republic
Currency Australian dollar = 100 cents
Literacy rate 98%
Calorie consumption 2,651 kilocalories

KUWAIT
Southwestern Asia

Official name State of Kuwait
Formation 1961 / 1961
Capital Kuwait
Population 1.8 million / 262 people per sq mile (101 people per sq km) / 97%
Total area 6,880 sq miles (17,820 sq km)
Languages Arabic*, English
Religions Muslim 92%, Christian 6%, other 2%
Ethnic mix Kuwaiti 45%, other Arab 35%, South Asian 9%, Iranian 4%, other 7%
Government Constitutional monarchy
Currency Dinar = 1,000 fils
Literacy rate 80%
Calorie consumption 2,523 kilocalories

KYRGYZSTAN
Central Asia

Official name Kyrgyz Republic
Formation 1991 / 1991
Capital Bishkek
Population 4.5 million / 59 people per sq mile (23 people per sq km) / 39%
Total area 76,640 sq miles (198,500 sq km)
Languages Kyrgyz*, Russian*, Uzbek
Religions Muslim 65%, other (mostly Russian Orthodox) 35%
Ethnic mix Kyrgyz 57%, Russian 19%, Uzbek 13%, Tatar, Ukrainian, other 11%
Government Multiparty republic
Currency Som =100 teen
Literacy rate 97%
Calorie consumption NOT AVAILABLE

LAOS
Southeastern Asia

Official name Lao People's Democratic Republic
Formation 1953 / 1953
Capital Vientiane
Population 5.4 million / 61 people per sq mile (23 people per sq km) / 22%
Total area 91,428 sq miles (236,800 sq km)
Languages Lao*, Miao, Yao
Religions Buddhist 85%, other (including Traditional beliefs) 15%
Ethnic mix Lao Loum 56%, Lao Theung 34%, Lao Soung 9%, other 1%
Government Single-party republic
Currency New kip = 100 cents
Literacy rate 58%
Calorie consumption 2,259 kilocalories

LATVIA
Northeastern Europe

Official name Republic of Latvia
Formation 1991 / 1991
Capital Riga
Population 2.4 million / 96 people per sq mile (37 people per sq km) / 73%
Total area 24,938 sq miles (64,589 sq km)
Languages Latvian*, Russian
Religions Evangelical Lutheran 85%, other Christian 15%
Ethnic mix Latvian 52%, Russian 34%, Belarusian 5%, Ukrainian 4%, other 5%
Government Multiparty republic
Currency Lats = 100 santimi
Literacy rate 99%
Calorie consumption NOT AVAILABLE

LEBANON
Southwestern Asia

Official name Republic of Lebanon
Formation 1944 / 1944
Capital Beirut
Population 3.2 million / 810 people per sq mile (313 people per sq km) / 87%
Total area 4015 sq miles (10,400 sq km)
Languages Arabic*, French, Armenian,
Religions Muslim (mainly Shi'a) 70%, Christian (mainly Maronite) 30%
Ethnic mix Arab 93% (Lebanese 83%, Palestinian 10%), other 7%
Government Multiparty republic
Currency Lebanese pound = 100 piastres
Literacy rate 84%
Calorie consumption 3,317 kilocalories

LESOTHO
Southern Africa

Official name Kingdom of Lesotho
Formation 1966 / 1966
Capital Maseru
Population 2.2 million / 188 people per sq mile (72 people per sq km) / 23%
Total area 11,718 sq miles (30,350 sq km)
Languages English*, Sesotho*, Zulu
Religions Christian 93%, other 7%
Ethnic mix Basotho 97%, European and Asian 3%
Government Constitutional monarchy
Currency Loti = 100 lisente
Literacy rate 82%
Calorie consumption 2,201 kilocalories

LIBERIA
Western Africa

Official name Republic of Liberia
Formation 1847 / 1947
Capital Monrovia
Population 2.7 million / 73 people per sq mile (28 people per sq km) / 45%
Total area 43,000 sq miles (111,370 sq km)
Languages English*, Kpelle, Bassa, Vai, Kru, Grebo, Kissi, Gola
Religions Traditional beliefs 70%, Muslim 20%, Christian 10%
Ethnic mix Indigenous tribes (16 main groups) 95%, Americo-Liberians 4%
Government Multiparty republic
Currency Liberian dollar = 100 cents
Literacy rate 38%
Calorie consumption 1,640 kilocalories

LIBYA
Northern Africa

Official name The Great Socialist People's Libyan Arab Jamahiriya
Formation 1951 / 1951
Capital Tripoli
Population 6 million / 9 people per sq mile (3 people per sq km) / 86%
Total area 679,358 sq miles (1,759,540 sq km)
Languages Arabic*, Tuareg
Religions Muslim (mainly Sunni) 97%, other 3%
Ethnic mix Arab and Berber 95%, other 5%
Government Single-party state
Currency Libyan dinar = 1,000 dirhams
Literacy rate 76%
Calorie consumption 3,308 kilocalories

LIECHTENSTEIN
Western Europe

Official name Principality of Liechtenstein
Formation 1719 / 1719
Capital Vaduz
Population 31,000 / 504 people per sq mile (195 people per sq km) / 87%
Total area 62 sq miles (160 sq km)
Languages German*, Alemannish, Italian
Religions Roman Catholic 81%, Protestant 7%, other 12%
Ethnic mix Liechtensteiner 63%, Swiss 15%, German 9%, other 13%
Government Constitutional monarchy
Currency Swiss franc = 100 centimes
Literacy rate 99%
Calorie consumption NOT AVAILABLE

LITHUANIA
Northeastern Europe

Official name Republic of Lithuania
Formation 1991 / 1991
Capital Vilnius
Population 3.7 million / 147 people per sq mile (57 people per sq km) / 72%
Total area 25,174 sq miles (65,200 sq km)
Languages Lithuanian*, Russian
Religions Roman Catholic 87%, Russian Orthodox 10%, other 3%
Ethnic mix Lithuanian 80%, Russian 9%, Polish 7%, Belarusian 2%, other 2%
Government Multiparty republic
Currency Litas = 100 centas
Literacy rate 98%
Calorie consumption NOT AVAILABLE

LUXEMBOURG
Northwest Europe

Official name Grand Duchy of Luxembourg
Formation 1867 / 1867
Capital Luxembourg
Population 422,000 / 423 people per sq mile (163 people per sq km) / 89%
Total area 998 sq miles (2,586 sq km)
Languages Letzeburgish*, French*, German*
Religions Roman Catholic 97%, other 3%
Ethnic mix Luxemburger 72%, Portuguese 9%, Italian 5%, other 14%
Government Constitutional monarchy
Currency Franc = 100 centimes
Literacy rate 99%
Calorie consumption 3,681 kilocalories

MACEDONIA
Southeastern Europe

Official name Former Yugoslav Republic of Macedonia
Formation 1991 / 1991
Capital Skopje
Population 2.2 million / 222 people per sq mile (86 people per sq km) / 60%
Total area 9,929 sq miles (25,715 sq km)
Languages Macedonian*, Serbo-Croatian
Religions Christian 80%, Muslim 20%
Ethnic mix Macedonian 67%, Albanian 23%, Turkish 4%, Serb 2%, Romany 2%, other 2%
Government Multiparty republic
Currency Macedonian denar = 100 deni
Literacy rate 89%
Calorie consumption NOT AVAILABLE

MADAGASCAR
Indian Ocean

Official name Democratic Republic of Madagascar
Formation 1960 / 1960
Capital Antananarivo
Population 16.3 million / 73 people per sq mile (28 people per sq km) / 27%
Total area 226,660 sq miles (587,040 sq km)
Languages Malagasy*, French*
Religions Traditional beliefs 52%, Christian 41%, Muslim 7%
Ethnic mix Merina 26%, Betsimisaraka 15%, Betsileo 12%, other 47%
Government Multiparty republic
Currency Franc = 100 centimes
Literacy rate 81%
Calorie consumption 2,135 kilocalories

MALAWI
Southern Africa

Official name Republic of Malawi
Formation 1964 / 1964
Capital Lilongwe
Population 10.4 million / 286 people per sq mile (111 people per sq km) / 14%
Total area 45,745 sq miles (118,480 sq km)
Languages English*, Chewa, Lomwe, Yao
Religions Christian 75%, Muslim 20% traditional beliefs 5%
Ethnic mix Maravi 55%, Lomwe 17%, Yao 13%, other 15%
Government Multiparty republic
Currency Malawi kwacha = 100 tambala
Literacy rate 57%
Calorie consumption 1,825 kilocalories

MALAYSIA
Southeastern Asia

Official name Malaysia
Formation 1963 / 1965
Capital Kuala Lumpur
Population 21.5 million / 169 people per sq mile (65 people per sq km) / 54%
Total area 127,317 sq miles (329,750 sq km)
Languages Malay*, English*, Chinese, Tamil
Religions Muslim 53%, Buddhist 19%, Chinese faiths 12%, Christian 7%, other 9%
Ethnic mix Malay 47%, Chinese 32%, Indigenous tribes 12%, Indian 8%, other 1%
Government Federal constitutional monarchy
Currency Ringgit = 100 cents
Literacy rate 85%
Calorie consumption 2,888 kilocalories

MALDIVES
Indian Ocean

Official name Republic of Maldives
Formation 1965 / 1965
Capital Male'
Population 282,000 / 2,435 people per sq mile (940 people per sq km) / 26%
Total area 116 sq miles (300 sq km)
Languages Dhivehi (Maldivian)*, Sinhala, Tamil
Religions Sunni Muslim 100%
Ethnic mix Maldivian 99%, other 1%
Government Republic
Currency Rufiyaa = 100 laari
Literacy rate 91%
Calorie consumption 2,580 kilocalories

MALI
Western Africa

Official name Republic of Mali
Formation 1960 / 1960
Capital Bamako
Population 11.8 million / 25 people per sq mile (10 people per sq km) / 27%
Total area 478,837 sq miles (1,240,190 sq km)
Languages French*, Bambara, Fulani, Senufo, Soninké
Religions Muslim 80%, Traditional beliefs 18%, Christian 2%
Ethnic mix Bambara 31%, Fulani 13%, Senufo 12%, other 44%
Government Multiparty republic
Currency CFA franc = 100 centimes
Literacy rate 35%
Calorie consumption 2,278 kilocalories

MALTA
Southern Europe

Official name Republic of Malta
Formation 1964 / 1964
Capital Valletta
Population 374,000 / 3,027 people per sq mile (1,169 people per sq km) / 89%
Total area 124 sq miles (320 sq km)
Languages Maltese*, English*
Religions Roman Catholic 98%, other (mostly Anglican) 2%
Ethnic mix Maltese (mixed Arab, Sicilian, Norman, Spanish, Italian, English) 98%, other 2%
Government Multiparty republic
Currency Maltese lira = 100 cents
Literacy rate 91%
Calorie consumption 3,486 kilocalories

MARSHALL ISLANDS
Australasia & Oceania

Official name Republic of the Marshall Islands
Formation 1986 / 1986
Capital Majuro
Population 59,000 / 848 people per sq mile (327 people per sq km) / 69%
Total area 70 sq miles (181 sq km)
Languages English*, Marshallese*
Religions Protestant 80%, Roman Catholic 15%, other 5%
Ethnic mix Micronesian 97%, other 3%
Government Multiparty republic
Currency US dollar = 100 cents
Literacy rate 91%
Calorie consumption NOT AVAILABLE

MAURITANIA
West Africa

Official name Islamic Republic of Mauritania
Formation 1960 / 1960
Capital Nouakchott
Population 2.5 million / 6 people per sq mile (2 people per sq km) / 54%
Total area 395,953 sq miles (1,025,520 sq km)
Languages French*, Arabic*, Wolof
Religions Muslim 100%
Ethnic mix Maure 80%, Wolof 7%, Tukulor 5%, other 8%
Government Multiparty republic
Currency Ouguiya = 5 khoums
Literacy rate 38%
Calorie consumption 2,685 kilocalories

MAURITIUS
Indian Ocean

Official name Republic of Mauritius
Formation 1968 / 1968
Capital Port Louis
Population 1.2 million / 1,680 people per sq mile (649 people per sq km) / 41%
Total area 718 sq miles (1,860 sq km)
Languages English*, French Creole, Hindi, Urdu, Tamil, Chinese
Religions Hindu 52%, Roman Catholic, 26%, Muslim 17%, other 5%
Ethnic mix Creole 55%, South Asian 40%, Chinese 3%, other 2%
Government Multiparty republic
Currency Mauritian rupee = 100 cents
Literacy rate 83%
Calorie consumption 2,690 kilocalories

MEXICO
North America

Official name United Mexican States
Formation 1836 / 1848
Capital Mexico City
Population 95.8 million / 130 people per sq mile (50 people per sq km) / 75%
Total area 756,061 sq miles (1,958,200 sq km)
Languages Spanish*, Mayan dialects
Religions Roman Catholic 95%, Protestant 1%, other 4%
Ethnic mix *Mestizo* 55%, Indigenous Indian 20%, European 16%, other 9%
Government Multiparty republic
Currency Mexican peso = 100 centavos
Literacy rate 90%
Calorie consumption 3,146 kilocalories

MICRONESIA
Australasia & Oceania

Official name Federated States of Micronesia
Formation 1986 / 1986
Capital Palikir
Population 109,000 / 403 people per sq mile (156 people per sq km) / 28%
Total area 1,120 sq miles (2,900 sq km)
Languages English*, Trukese, Pohnpeian, Mortlockese, Kosrean
Religions Roman Catholic 50%, Protestant 48%, other 2%
Ethnic mix Micronesian 99%, other 1%
Government Republic
Currency US dollar = 100 cents
Literacy rate 90%
Calorie consumption NOT AVAILABLE

MOLDOVA
Southeastern Europe

Official name Republic of Moldova
Formation 1991 / 1991
Capital Chişinău
Population 4.5 million / 346 people per sq mile (134 people per sq km) / 52%
Total area 13,000 sq miles (33,700 sq km)
Languages Romanian*, Moldovan, Russian
Religions Romanian Orthodox 98%, Jewish 1%, other 1%
Ethnic mix Moldovan 65%, Ukrainian 14%, Russian 13%, Gagauz 4%, other 4%
Government Multiparty republic
Currency Moldovan leu = 100 bani
Literacy rate 98%
Calorie consumption NOT AVAILABLE

MONACO
Southern Europe

Official name Principality of Monaco
Formation 1861 / 1861
Capital Monaco
Population 32,000 / 42,503 people per sq mile (16,410 people per sq km) / 100%
Total area 0.75 sq miles (1.95 sq km)
Languages French*, Italian, Monégasque, English
Religions Roman Catholic 89%, other 11%
Ethnic mix French 47%, Monégasque 17%, Italian 16%, other 20%
Government Constitutional monarchy
Currency French franc = 100 centimes
Literacy rate 99%
Calorie consumption NOT AVAILABLE

MONGOLIA
Eastern Asia

Official name Mongolia
Formation 1924 / 1924
Capital Ulan Bator
Population 2.6 million / 4 people per sq mile (2 people per sq km) / 61%
Total area 604,247 sq miles (1,565,000 sq km)
Languages Khalkha Mongol*, Turkic, Russian, Chinese
Religions Predominantly Tibetan Buddhist, with a Muslim minority
Ethnic mix Mongol 90%, Kazakh 4%, Chinese 2%, Russian 2%, other 2%
Government Multiparty republic
Currency Tughrik (togrog) = 100 möngös
Literacy rate 84%
Calorie consumption 1,899 kilocalories

MOROCCO
Northern Africa

Official name Kingdom of Morocco
Formation 1956 / 1956
Capital Rabat
Population 28 million / 162 people per sq mile (63 people per sq km) / 48%
Total area 269,757 sq miles (698,670 sq km)
Religions Muslim 98%, Jewish 1%, Christian 1%
Ethnic mix Arab and Berber 99%, European 1%
Government Constitutional monarchy
Currency Moroccan dirham = 100 centimes
Literacy rate 45%
Calorie consumption 2,984 kilocalories

MOZAMBIQUE
Southern Africa

Official name Republic of Mozambique
Formation 1975 / 1975
Capital Maputo
Population 18.7 million / 62 people per sq mile (24 people per sq km) / 34%
Total area 309,493 sq miles (801,590 sq km)
Languages Portuguese*, Makua, Tsonga, Sena
Religions Traditional beliefs 60%, Christian 30%, Muslim 10%
Ethnic mix Makua-Lomwe 47%, Thonga 23%, Malawi 12%, Shona 11%, Yao 4%, other 3%
Government Multiparty republic
Currency Metical = 100 centavos
Literacy rate 40%
Calorie consumption 1,680 kilocalories

MYANMAR
Southeastern Asia

Official name Union of Myanmar
Formation 1948 / 1948
Capital Rangoon
Population 47.6 million / 187 people per sq mile (72 people per sq km) / 26%
Total area 261,200 sq miles (676,550 sq km)
Languages Burmese*, Karen, Shan, Mon
Religions Buddhist 87%, Christian 6%, Muslim 4%, other 3%
Ethnic mix Burman 68%, Shan 9%, Karen 6%, Rakhine 4%, other 13%
Government Military regime
Currency Kyat = 100 pyas
Literacy rate 84%
Calorie consumption 2,598 kilocalories

NAMIBIA
Southern Africa

Official name Republic of Namibia
Formation 1990 / 1994
Capital Windhoek
Population 1.7 million / 5 people per sq mile (2 people per sq km) / 37%
Total area 318,260 sq miles (824,290 sq km)
Languages English*, Afrikaans, Ovambo, Kavango, Bergdama
Religions Christian 90%, other 10%
Ethnic mix Ovambo 50%, Kavango 9%, Herero 8%, Damara 8%, other 25%
Government Multiparty republic
Currency Namibian dollar = 100 cents
Literacy rate 79%
Calorie consumption 2,134 kilocalories

NAURU
Australasia & Oceania

Official name Republic of Nauru
Formation 1968 / 1968
Capital No official capital
Population 11,000 / 1332 people per sq mile (514 people per sq km) / 100%
Total area 8.2 sq miles (21.2 sq km)
Languages Nauruan*, English, Kiribati, Chinese, Tuvaluan
Religions Christian 95%, other 5%
Ethnic mix Nauruan 62%, other Pacific islanders 25%, Chinese 8%, European 5%
Government Parliamentary democracy
Currency Australian dollar = 100 cents
Literacy rate 99%
Calorie consumption NOT AVAILABLE

NEPAL
Southern Asia

Official name Kingdom of Nepal
Formation 1769 / 1769
Capital Kathmandu
Population 23.2 million / 439 people per sq mile (170 people per sq km) / 14%
Total area 54,363 sq miles (140,800 sq km)
Languages Nepali*, Maithilli, Bhojpuri
Religions Hindu 90%, Buddhist 4%, Muslim 3%, Christian 1%, other 2%
Ethnic mix Nepalese 58%, Bihari 19%, Tamang 6%, other 17%
Government Constitutional monarchy
Currency Nepalese rupee = 100 paisa
Literacy rate 38%
Calorie consumption 1,957 kilocalories

NETHERLANDS
Northwest Europe

Official name Kingdom of the Netherlands
Formation 1815 / 1839
Capitals Amsterdam, The Hague
Population 15.7 million / 1,199 people per sq mile (463 people per sq km) / 89%
Total area 14,410 sq miles (37,330 sq km)
Languages Dutch*, Frisian
Religions Roman Catholic 36%, Protestant 27%, Muslim 3%, other 34%
Ethnic mix Dutch 96%, other 4%
Government Constitutional monarchy
Currency Netherland guilder = 100 cents
Literacy rate 99%
Calorie consumption 3,222 kilocalories

NEW ZEALAND
Australasia & Oceania

Official name New Zealand
Formation 1947 / 1947
Capital Wellington
Population 3.7 million / 36 people per sq mile (14 people per sq km) / 86%
Total area 103,730 sq miles (268,680 sq km)
Languages English*, Maori
Religions Protestant 47%, Roman Catholic 15%, other 38%
Ethnic mix European 82%, Maori 9%, Pacific Islanders 3%, other 6%
Government Constitutional monarchy
Currency NZ dollar = 100 cents
Literacy rate 99%
Calorie consumption 3,669 kilocalories

NICARAGUA
Central America

Official name Republic of Nicaragua
Formation 1838 / 1838
Capital Managua
Population 4.5 million / 98 people per sq mile (38 people per sq km) / 63%
Total area 50,193 sq miles (130,000 sq km)
Languages Spanish*, English Creole, Miskito
Religions Roman Catholic 95%, other 5%
Ethnic mix *Mestizo* 69%, White 14%, Black 8%, Indigenous Indian 5%, Zambos 4%
Government Multiparty republic
Currency Córdoba ora = 100 pence
Literacy rate 63%
Calorie consumption 2,293 kilocalories

NIGER
Western Africa

Official name Republic of Niger
Formation 1960 / 1960
Capital Niamey
Population 10.1 million / 21 people per sq mile (8 people per sq km) / 17%
Total area 489,188 sq miles (1,267,000 sq km)
Languages French*, Hausa, Djerma, Fulani, Tuareg, Teda
Religions Muslim 85%, traditional beliefs 14%, Christian 1%
Ethnic mix Hausa 54%, Djerma and Songhal 21%, Fulani 10%, Tuareg 9%, other 6%
Government Multiparty republic
Currency CFA franc = 100 centimes
Literacy rate 14%
Calorie consumption 2,257 kilocalories

NIGERIA
Western Africa

Official name Federal Republic of Nigeria
Formation 1960 / 1961
Capital Abuja
Population 122 million / 346 people per sq mile (123 people per sq km) / 34%
Total area 356,668 sq miles (923,770 sq km)
Languages English*, Hausa, Yoruba, Ibo
Religions Muslim 50%, Christian 40%, Traditional beliefs 10%
Ethnic mix Hausa 21%, Yoruba 21%, Ibo 18%, Fulani 11%, other 29%
Government Multiparty republic
Currency Naira = 100 kobo
Literacy rate 59%
Calorie consumption 2,124 kilocalories

NORTH KOREA
Eastern Asia

Official name Democratic People's Republic of Korea
Formation 1948 / 1953
Capital Pyongyang
Population 23.2 million / 499 people per sq mile (193 people per sq km) / 61%
Total area 46,540 sq miles (120,540 sq km)
Languages Korean*, Chinese
Religions Traditional beliefs 16%, Ch'ondogyo 14%, Buddhist 2%, nonreligious 68%
Ethnic mix Korean 99%, other 1%
Government Single-party republic
Currency North Korean Won = 100 chon
Literacy rate 99%
Calorie consumption 2,833 kilocalories

NORWAY
Northern Europe

Official name Kingdom of Norway
Formation 1905 / 1905
Capital Oslo
Population 4.4 million / 37 people per sq mile (14 people per sq km) / 73%
Total area 125,060 sq miles (323,900 sq km)
Languages Norwegian* (Bokmal and *Nynorsk*), Lappish, Finnish
Religions Evangelical Lutheran 89%, Roman Catholic 1%, other and nonreligious 10%
Ethnic mix Norwegian 95%, Lapp 1%, other 4%
Government Constitutional monarchy
Currency Norwegian krone = 100 øre
Literacy rate 99%
Calorie consumption 3,244 kilocalories

OMAN
Southwestern Asia

Official name Sultanate of Oman
Formation 1951 / 1951
Capital Muscat
Population 2.5 million / 30 people per sq mile (12 people per sq km) / 13%
Total area 82,030 sq miles (212,460 sq km)
Languages Arab*, Baluchi
Religions Ibadi Muslim 75%, other Muslim 11%, Hindu 14%
Ethnic mix Arab 75%, Baluchi 15%, other 15%
Government Monarchy with Consultative Council
Currency Omani rial = 1,000 baizas
Literacy rate 67%
Calorie consumption 3,013 kilocalories

PAKISTAN
Southern Asia

Official name Islamic Republic of Pakistan
Formation 1947 / 1947
Capital Islamabad
Population 147.8 million / 497 people per sq mile (192 people per sq km) / 35%
Total area 307,374 sq miles (796,100 sq km)
Main languages Urdu*, Punjabi, Sindhi, Pashtu, Baluchi
Religions Sunni Muslim 77%, Shi'a Muslim 20%, Hindu 2%, Christian 1%
Ethnic mix Punjabi 50%, Sindhi 15%, Pashtu 15%, Mohajir 8%, Baluch 5%, other 7%
Government Multiparty republic
Currency Pakistani rupee = 100 paisa
Literacy rate 40%
Calorie consumption 2,315 kilocalories

PALAU
Australasia & Oceania

Official name Palau
Formation 1994 / 1994
Capital Oreor
Population 17,700 /90 people per sq mile (35 people per sq km) / 29%
Total area 192 sq miles (497 sq km)
Languages Palauan*, English*, Japanese
Religions Roman Catholic 66%, Modekngei 34%
Ethnic mix Palauan 99%, other 1%
Government Multiparty republic
Currency US dollar = 100 cents
Literacy rate 92%
Calorie consumption NOT AVAILABLE

PANAMA
Central America

Official name Republic of Panama
Formation 1903 / 1903
Capital Panama City
Population 2.8 million / 95 people per sq mile (37 people per sq km) / 53%
Total area 29,761 sq miles (77,080 sq km)
Languages Spanish*, English Creole, Indian languages
Religions Roman Catholic 93%, other 7%
Ethnic mix *Mestizo* 60%, White 14%, Black 12%, Indigenous Indian 8%, other 6%
Government Multiparty republic
Currency Balboa = 100 centesimos
Literacy rate 91%
Calorie consumption 2,242 kilocalories

PAPUA NEW GUINEA
Australasia & Oceania

Official name Independent State of Papua New Guinea
Formation 1975 / 1975
Capital Port Moresby
Population 4.6 million / 26 people per sq mile (10 people per sq km) / 16%
Total area 178,700 sq miles (462, 840 sq km)
Languages English*, Pidgin English, Papuan, Motu, 750 (estimated) native languages
Religions Christian 62%, Traditional beliefs 38%
Ethnic mix Papuan 85%, other 15%
Government Parliamentary democracy
Currency Kina = 100 toea
Literacy rate 73%
Calorie consumption 2,613 kilocalories

PARAGUAY
South America

Official name Paraguay
Formation 1811 / 1938
Capital Asunción
Population 5.2 million / 34 people per sq mile (13 people per sq km) / 53%
Total area 157,046 sq miles (406,750 sq km)
Languages Spanish*, Guaraní
Religions Roman Catholic 90%, other 10%
Ethnic mix *Mestizo* 90%, Indigenous Indian 2%, other 8%
Government Multiparty republic
Literacy rate 92%
Calorie consumption 2,670 kilocalories

PERU
South America

Official name Republic of Peru
Formation 1824 / 1941
Capital Lima
Population 24.8 million / 50 people per sq mile (19 people per sq km) / 72%
Total area 496,223 sq miles (1,285,220 sq km)
Languages Spanish*, Quechua*, Aymará
Religions Roman Catholic 95%, other 5%
Ethnic mix Indigenous Indian 54%, *mestizo* 32%, White 12%, other 2%
Government Multiparty republic
Currency New sol = 100 centimos
Literacy rate 88%
Calorie consumption 1,882 kilocalories

PHILIPPINES
Southwestern Asia

Official name Republic of the Philippines
Formation 1946 / 1946
Capital Manila
Population 72.2 million / 627 people per sq mile (242 people per sq km) / 54%
Total area 115,831 sq miles (300,000 sq km)
Languages Filipino*, English*, Cebuano, Hiligaynon, Samaran, Bikol, Ilocano
Religions Roman Catholic 83%, Protestant 9%, Muslim 5%, other 3%
Ethnic mix Malay 50%, Indonesian and Polynesian 30%, Chinese 10%, other 10%
Government Multiparty republic
Currency Philippine peso = 100 centavos
Literacy rate 94%
Calorie consumption 2,257 kilocalories

POLAND
Northern Europe

Official name Republic of Poland
Formation 1918 / 1945
Capital Warsaw
Population 38.7 million / 329 people per sq mile (127 people per sq km) / 65%
Total area 120,720 sq miles (312,680 sq km)
Languages Polish*, German
Religions Roman Catholic 93%, Eastern Orthodox 2%, other and nonreligious 5%
Ethnic mix Polish 98%, German 1%, other 1%
Government Multiparty republic
Currency Zloty = 100 groszy
Literacy rate 99%
Calorie consumption 3,301 kilocalories

PORTUGAL
Southwestern Europe

Official name Republic of Portugal
Formation 1140 / 1640
Capital Lisbon
Population 9.8 million / 276 people per sq mile (107 people per sq km) / 36%
Total area 35,670 sq miles (92,390 sq km)
Languages Portuguese*
Religions Roman Catholic 97%, Protestant 1%, other 2%
Ethnic mix Portuguese 99%, African 1%
Government Multiparty republic
Currency Escudo = 100 centavos
Literacy rate 90%
Calorie consumption 3,634 kilocalories

QATAR
Southwestern Asia

Official name State of Qatar
Formation 1971 / 1971
Capital Doha
Population 600,000 / 136 people per sq mile (53 people per sq km) / 91%
Total area 4,247 sq miles (11,000 sq km)
Languages Arabic*, Farsi (Persian), Urdu, Hindi, English
Religions Sunni Muslim 86%, Hindu 10%, Christian 4%
Ethnic mix Arab 40%, Pakistani 18%, Iranian 10% Indian 18%, other 14%
Government Absolute monarchy
Currency Qatar riyal = 100 dirhams
Literacy rate 80%
Calorie consumption NOT AVAILABLE

ROMANIA
Southeastern Europe

Official name Romania
Formation 1878 / 1947
Capital Bucharest
Population 22.6 million /254 people per sq mile (98 people per sq km) / 55%
Total area 91,700 sq miles (237,500 sq km)
Languages Romanian*, Hungarian,
Religions Romanian Orthodox 70%, Roman Catholic 5%, Protestant 4%, other 21%
Ethnic mix Romanian 89%, Magyar 9%, Romany 1%, other 1%
Government Multiparty republic
Currency Leu = 100 bani
Literacy rate 97%
Calorie consumption 3,051 kilocalories

RUSSIAN FEDERATION
Europe / Asia

Official name Russian Federation
Formation 1991 / 1991
Capital Moscow
Population 147.2 million /22 people per sq mile (9 people per sq km) / 76%
Total area 6,592,800 sq miles (17,075,400 sq km)
Languages Russian*, Tatar, Ukrainian
Religions Russian Orthodox 75%, other (including Jewish, Muslim) 25%
Ethnic mix Russian 82%, Tatar 4%, Ukrainian 3%, Chuvash 1%, other 10%
Currency Rouble = 100 kopeks
Literacy rate 99%
Calorie consumption NOT AVAILABLE

RWANDA
Central Africa

Official name Rwandese Republic
Formation 1962 / 1962
Capital Kigali
Population 6.5 million / 675 people per sq mile (261 people per sq km) / 6%
Total area 10,170 sq miles (26,340 sq km)
Languages Kinyarwanda*, French*, Kiswahili, English
Religions Christian 74%, Traditional beliefs 25%, other 1%
Ethnic mix Hutu 90%, Tutsi 8%, Twa pygmy 2%
Government Multiparty republic
Currency Rwanda franc = 100 centimes
Literacy rate 63%
Calorie consumption 1,821 kilocalories

SAINT KITTS & NEVIS
West Indies

Official name Federation of Saint Christopher and Nevis
Formation 1983 / 1983
Capital Basseterre
Population 41,000 / 295 people per sq mile (114 people per sq km) / 42%
Total area 139 sq miles (360 sq km)
Languages English*, English Creole
Religions Protestant 71%, Roman Catholic 7%, other 22%
Ethnic mix Black 95%, mixed 5%
Government Parliamentary democracy
Currency E. Caribbean dollar = 100 cents
Literacy rate 90%
Calorie consumption 2,419 kilocalories

SAINT LUCIA
West Indies

Official name Saint Lucia
Formation 1979 / 1979
Capital Castries
Population 142,000 / 603 people per sq mile (233 people per sq km) / 48%
Total area 239 sq miles (620 sq km)
Languages English*, French Creole, Hindi, Urdu
Religions Roman Catholic 90%, other 10%
Ethnic mix Black 90%, African-European 6%, South Asian 4%
Government Parliamentary democracy
Currency E. Caribbean dollar = 100 cents
Literacy rate 93%
Calorie consumption 2,588 kilocalories

SAINT VINCENT & THE GRENADINES *West Indies*

Official name Saint Vincent and the Grenadines
Formation 1979 / 1979
Capital Kingstown
Population 111,000 / 846 people per sq mile (327 people per sq km) / 46%
Total area 131 sq miles (340 sq km)
Languages English*, English Creole
Religions Protestant 62% Roman Catholic 19%, other 19%
Ethnic mix Black 82%, mixed 14%, White 3%, South Asian 1%
Government Parliamentary democracy
Currency E. Caribbean dollar = 100 cents
Literacy rate 82%
Calorie consumption 2,347 kilocalories

SAMOA
Australasia & Oceania

Official name Independent State of Samoa
Formation 1962 / 1962
Capital Apia
Population 170,000 / 156 people per sq mile (60 people per sq km) / 21%
Total area 1,027 sq miles (2,840 sq km)
Languages Samoan*, English*
Religions Protestant 74%, Roman Catholic 26%
Ethnic mix Samoan 90%, other 10%
Government Parliamentary state
Currency Tala = 100 sene
Literacy rate 98%
Calorie consumption 2,828 kilocalories

SAN MARINO
Southern Europe

Official name Republic of San Marino
Formation AD 301 / 301
Capital San Marino
Population 25,000 / 1,061 people per sq mile (410 people per sq km) / 94%
Total area 24 sq miles (61 sq km)
Languages *Italian
Religions Roman Catholic 93%, other and nonreligious 7%
Ethnic mix Sammarinese 95%, other 5%
Government Multiparty republic
Currency Lira = 100 centesimi
Literacy rate 96%
Calorie consumption 3,561 kilocalories

SAO TOME & PRINCIPE
Western Africa

Official name Democratic Republic of Sao Tome and Principe
Formation 1975 / 1975
Capital São Tomé
Population 131,000 / 354 people per sq mile (137 people per sq km) / 46%
Total area 372 sq miles (964 sq km)
Languages *Portuguese, Portuguese Creole
Religions Roman Catholic 90%, other Christian 10%
Ethnic mix Black 90%, Portuguese and Creole 10%
Government Multiparty republic
Currency Dobra = 100 centimos
Literacy rate 75%
Calorie consumption 2,129 kilocalories

Saudi Arabia
Southwestern Asia

Official name Kingdom of Saudi Arabia
Formation 1932 / 1935
Capital Riyadh
Population 20.2 million / 24 people per sq mile (8 people per sq km) / 80%
Total area 829,995 sq miles (2,149,690 sq km)
Languages Arabic*
Religions Sunni Muslim 85%, Shi'a Muslim 15%
Ethnic mix Arab 90%, Afroasian 10%
Government Absolute monarchy
Currency Saudi riyal = 100 malalah
Literacy rate 73%
Calorie consumption 2,735 kilocalories

Senegal
Western Africa

Official name Republic of Senegal
Formation 1960 / 1960
Capital Dakar
Population 9 million /121 people per sq mile (47 people per sq km) / 42%
Total area 75,950 sq miles (196,720 sq km)
Languages *French, Wolof, Fulani, Serer
Religions Muslim 90%, Traditional beliefs 5%, Christian 5%
Ethnic mix Wolof 46%, Fulani 25%, Serer 16%, other 13%
Government Multiparty republic
Currency CFA franc = 100 centimes
Literacy rate 35%
Calorie consumption 2,262 kilocalories

Seychelles
Indian Ocean

Official name Republic of Seychelles
Formation 1976 / 1976
Capital Victoria
Population 75,000 / 722 people per sq mile (279 people per sq km) / 54%
Total area 108 sq miles (280 sq km)
Languages *French Creole, French, English
Religions Roman Catholic 90%, other 10%
Ethnic mix Seychellois (mixed African, South Asian and European) 95%, Chinese and South Asian 5%
Government Multiparty republic
Currency Seychelles rupee = 100 cents
Literacy rate 84%
Calorie consumption 2,287 kilocalories

Sierra Leone
Western Africa

Official name Republic of Sierra Leone
Formation 1961 / 1961
Capital Freetown
Population 4.6 million / 166 people per sq mile (64 people per sq km) / 36%
Total area 27,699 sq miles (71,740 sq km)
Languages English*, Krio (Creole), Mende, Temne
Religions Traditional beliefs 52%, Muslim 40%, Christian 8%
Ethnic mix Mende 35%, Temne 32%, Limba 8%, Kuranko 4%, other 21%
Government Multiparty republic
Currency Leone = 100 cents
Literacy rate 33%
Calorie consumption 1,694 kilocalories

Singapore
Southeastern Asia

Official name Republic of Singapore
Formation 1965 / 1965
Capital Singapore
Population 3.5 million / 14,861 people per sq mile (5,738 people per sq km) / 100%
Total area 239 sq miles (620 sq km)
Languages Malay*, Chinese*, Tamil*, English*
Religions Buddhist 30%, Christian 20%, Muslim 17%, other 33%
Ethnic mix Chinese 78%, Malay 14%, Indian 6%, other 2%
Government Multiparty republic
Currency Singapore dollar = 100 cents
Literacy rate 91%
Calorie consumption 3,128 kilocalories

Slovakia
Central Europe

Official name Slovak Republic
Formation 1993 / 1993
Capital Bratislava
Population 5.4 million / 285 people per sq mile (110 people per sq km) / 59%
Total area 19,100 sq miles (49,500 sq km)
Languages Slovak*, Hungarian (Magyar), Romany, Czech
Religions Roman Catholic 60%, Atheist 10%, Protestant 8%, Orthodox 4%, other 18%
Ethnic mix Slovak 85%, Hungarian 9%, Czech 1%, other 5%
Government Multiparty republic
Currency Koruna = 100 halierov
Literacy rate 99%
Calorie consumption 3,156 kilocalories

Slovenia
Central Europe

Official name Republic of Slovenia
Formation 1991 / 1991
Capital Ljubljana
Population 1.9 million / 243 people per sq mile (94 people per sq km) / 64%
Total area 7,820 sq miles (20,250 sq km)
Languages Slovene*, Serbian, Croatian
Religions Roman Catholic 96%, Muslim 1%, other 3%
Ethnic mix Slovene 88%, Croat 3%, Serb 2%, Bosniak 1%, other 4%
Government Multiparty republic
Currency Tolar = 100 stotins
Literacy rate 99%
Calorie consumption NOT AVAILABLE

Solomon Islands
Australasia & Oceania

Official name Solomon Islands
Formation 1978 / 1978
Capital Honiara
Population 417,000 / 39 people per sq mile (15 people per sq km) / 17%
Total area 10,954 sq miles (28,370 sq km)
Languages English*, Pidgin English, Melanesian Pidgin
Religions Christian 91%, other 9%
Ethnic mix Melanesian 94%, other 6%
Government Parliamentary democracy
Currency Solomon Islands dollar = 100 cents
Literacy rate 62%
Calorie consumption 2,173 kilocalories

Somalia
Eastern Africa

Official name Somali Democratic Republic
Formation 1960 / 1960
Capital Mogadishu
Population 10.7 million / 39 people per sq mile (15 people per sq km) / 25%
Total area 246,200 sq miles (637,660 sq km)
Languages Somali*, Arabic*, English
Religions Sunni Muslim 98%, other (including Christian) 2%
Ethnic mix Somali 98%, Bantu, Arab and other 2%
Government Transitional
Currency Somaili shilling = 100 cents
Literacy rate 24%
Calorie consumption 1,499 kilocalories

South Africa
Southern Africa

Official name Republic of South Africa
Formation 1934 / 1994
Capitals Pretoria/Cape Town/Bloemfontein
Population 44.3 million / 94 people per sq mile (36 people per sq km) / 51%
Total area 471,443 sq miles (1,221,040 sq km)
Languages Afrikaans*, English*, 11 African languages
Religions Protestant 55%, Roman Catholic 9%, Hindu 1%, Muslim 1%, other 34%
Ethnic mix Other Black 38%, White 16%, Zulu 23%, mixed 10%, Xhosa 9%, other 4%
Government Multiparty republic
Currency Rand = 100 cents
Literacy rate 82%
Calorie consumption 2,695 kilocalories

South Korea
Eastern Asia

Official name Republic of Korea
Formation 1948 / 1953
Capital Seoul
Population 46.1 million / 1209 people per sq mile (467 people per sq km) / 81%
Total area 38,232 sq miles (99,020 sq km)
Languages Korean*, Chinese
Religions Mahayana Buddhist 47%, Protestant 38%, Roman Catholic 11%, Confucianist 3%, other 1%
Ethnic mix Korean 100%
Government Multiparty republic
Currency Won = 100 chon
Literacy rate 97%
Calorie consumption 3,285 kilocalories

Spain
Southwestern Europe

Official name Kingdom of Spain
Formation 1492 / 1713
Capital Madrid
Population 39.8 million / 206 people per sq mile (80 people per sq km) / 76%
Total area 194,900 sq miles (504,780 sq km)
Languages Castilian Spanish*, Catalan*, Galician*, Basque*
Religions Roman Catholic 96%, other 4%
Ethnic mix Castilian Spanish 72%, Catalan 17%, Galician 6%, other 5%
Government Constitutional monarchy
Currency Spanish Peseta = 100 céntimos
Literacy rate 95%
Calorie consumption 3,708 kilocalories

Sri Lanka
Southern Asia

Official name Democratic Socialist Republic of Sri Lanka
Formation 1948 / 1948
Capital Colombo
Population 18.5 million / 740 people per sq mile (286 people per sq km) / 22%
Total area 25,332 sq miles (65,610 sq km)
Languages Sinhala*, Tamil, English
Religions Buddhist 70%, Hindu 15%, Christian 8%, Muslim 7%
Ethnic mix Sinhalese 74%, Tamil 18%, other 8%
Government Multiparty republic
Currency Sri Lanka rupee = 100 cents
Literacy rate 90%
Calorie consumption 2,273 kilocalories

Sudan
Eastern Africa

Official name Republic of Sudan
Formation 1956 / 1956
Capital Khartoum
Population 28.5 million / 31 people per sq mile (12 people per sq km) / 25%
Total area 967,493 sq miles (2,505,815 sq km)
Languages Arabic*, Dinka, Nuer, Nubian, Beja, Zande, Bari, Fur
Religions Muslim 70%, Traditional beliefs 20%, Christian 9%, other 1%
Ethnic mix Arab 51%, Dinka 13%, Nuba 9%, Beja 7%, other 20%
Government Military regime
Currency Sudanese pound or dinar = 100 piastres
Literacy rate 53%
Calorie consumption 2,202 kilocalories

Suriname
South America

Official name Republic of Suriname
Formation 1975 / 1975
Capital Paramaribo
Population 442,000 / 7 people per sq mile (3 people per sq km) / 50%
Total area 63,039 sq miles (163,270 sq km)
Languages Dutch*, Pidgin English (Taki-Taki), Hindi, Javanese, Carib
Religions Christian 48%, Hindu 27%, Muslim 20%, other 5%
Ethnic mix Hindustani 34%, Creole 34%, Javanese 18%, Black 9%, other 5%
Government Multiparty republic
Currency Suriname guilder = 100 cents
Literacy rate 93%
Calorie consumption 2547 kilocalories

Swaziland
Southern Africa

Official name Kingdom of Swaziland
Formation 1968 / 1968
Capital Mbabane
Population 900,000 / 140 people per sq mile (54 people per sq km) / 29%
Total area 6,703 sq miles (17,360 sq km)
Languages Siswati*, English*, Zulu
Religions Christian 60%, Traditional beliefs 40%
Ethnic mix Swazi 95%, other 5%
Government Executive monarchy
Currency Lilangeni = 100 cents
Literacy rate 77%
Calorie consumption 2,706 kilocalories

Sweden
Northern Europe

Official name Kingdom of Sweden
Formation 1809 / 1905
Capital Stockholm
Population 8.9 million / 56 people per sq mile (22 people per sq km) / 83%
Total area 173,730 sq miles (449,960 sq km)
Languages Swedish*, Finnish, Lappish,
Religions Evangelical Lutheran 89%, Roman Catholic 2%, Muslim 1%, other 8%
Ethnic mix Swedish 91%, other European 6%, Finnish and Lapp 3%
Government Constitutional monarchy
Currency Swedish krona = 100 öre
Literacy rate 99%
Calorie consumption 2,972 kilocalories

Switzerland
Central Europe

Official name Swiss Confederation
Formation 1291 / 1815
Capital Bern
Population 7.3 million / 475 people per sq mile (184 people per sq km) / 61%
Total area 15,940 sq miles (41,290 sq km)
Languages German*, French*, Italian*, Romansch
Religions Roman Catholic 48%, Protestant 44%, other 8%
Ethnic mix German 65%, French 18%, Italian 10%, other 7%
Government Federal republic
Currency Franc = 100 centimes
Literacy rate 99%
Calorie consumption 3,379 kilocalories

Syria
Southwest Asia

Official name Syrian Arab Republic
Formation 1946 / 1967
Capital Damascus
Population 15.3 million / 215 people per sq mile (83 people per sq km) / 52%
Total area 71,500 sq miles (185,180 sq km)
Languages Arabic*, French, Kurdish
Religions Sunni Muslim 74%, other Muslim 16%, Christian 10%
Ethnic mix Arab 89%, Kurdish 6%, Armenian, Turkmen, Circassian 2%, other 3%
Government Single-party republic
Currency Syrian pound = 100 piastres
Literacy rate 71%
Calorie consumption 3175 kilocalories

Taiwan
East Asia

Official name Republic of China
Formation 1949 / 1949
Capital Taipei
Population 21.5 million / 1724 people per sq mile (666 people per sq km) / 69%
Total area 13,969 sq miles (36,179 sq km)
Languages Mandarin Chinese*, Amoy Chinese, Hakka Chinese
Religions Buddhist, Confucianist, Taoist 93%, Christian 5%, other 2%
Ethnic mix Indigenous Chinese, Mainland Chinese 14%, Aborigine 2%
Government Multiparty republic
Currency Taiwan dollar = 100 cents
Literacy rate 94%
Calorie consumption NOT AVAILABLE

Tajikistan
Central Asia

Official name Republic of Tajikistan
Formation 1991 / 1991
Capital Dushanbe
Population 6.2 million / 112 people per sq mile (43 people per sq km) / 32%
Total area 55,251 sq miles (143,100 sq km)
Main languages Tajik*, Uzbek, Russian
Religions Sunni Muslim 80%, Shi'a Muslim 5%, other 15%
Ethnic mix Tajik 62%, Uzbek 24%, Russian 4%, Tatar 2%, other 8%
Government Multiparty republic
Currency Tajik rouble = 100 kopeks
Literacy rate 99%
Calorie consumption NOT AVAILABLE

Tanzania
East Africa

Official name United Republic of Tanzania
Formation 1961 / 1964
Capital Dodoma
Population 32.2 million / 94 people per sq mile (36 people per sq km) / 24%
Total area 364,900 sq miles (945,090 sq km)
Languages English*, Swahili*, Sukuma, Chagga, Nyamwezi, Hehe, Makonde
Religions Muslim 33%, Christian 33%, Traditional beliefs 30%, other 4%
Ethnic mix 120 small ethnic Bantu groups 99%, other 1%
Government Multiparty republic
Currency Tanzanian shilling = 100 cents
Literacy rate 71%
Calorie consumption 2018 kilocalories

Thailand
Southeastern Asia

Official name Kingdom of Thailand
Formation 1782 / 1907
Capital Bangkok
Population 59.6 million / 302 people per sq mile (117 people per sq km) / 20%
Total area 198,116 sq miles (513,120 sq km)
Languages Thai*, Chinese, Malay, Khmer, Mon, Karen
Religions Buddhist 95%, other 5%
Ethnic mix Thai 80%, Chinese 12%, Malay 4%, Khmer and other 4%
Government Constitutional monarchy
Currency Baht = 100 stangs
Literacy rate 94%
Calorie consumption 2432 kilocalories

Togo
Western Africa

Official name Togolese Republic
Formation 1960 / 1960
Capital Lomé
Population 4.4 million /210 people per sq mile (81 people per sq km) / 31%
Total area 21,927 sq miles (56,790 sq km)
Languages French*, Ewe, Kabye, Gurma
Religions Traditional beliefs 50%, Christian 35%, Muslim 15%
Ethnic mix Ewe 43%, Kabye 26%, Gurma 16%, other 15%
Government Multiparty republic
Currency CFA franc = 100 centimes
Literacy rate 53%
Calorie consumption 2242 kilocalories

Tonga
Australasia & Oceania

Official name Kingdom of Tonga
Formation 1970 / 1970
Capital Nuku'alofa
Population 97,000 / 351 people per sq mile (135 people per sq km) / 21%
Total area 290 sq miles (750 sq km)
Languages Tongan*, English*
Religions Protestant 64%, Roman Catholic 15%, other 21%
Ethnic mix Tongan 98%, other 2%
Government Constitutional monarchy
Currency Pa'anga = 100 seniti
Literacy rate 99%
Calorie consumption 2,946 kilocalories

Trinidad & Tobago
West Indies

Official name Republic of Trinidad and Tobago
Formation 1962 / 1962
Capital Port-of-Spain
Population 1.3 million / 656 people per sq mile (253 people per sq km) / 72%
Total area 1,981 sq miles (5,130 sq km)
Languages English*, English Creole, Hindi, French, Spanish
Religions Christian 58%, Hindu 30%, Muslim 8%, other 4%
Ethnic mix Black 43%, Asian 40%, mixed 19%, White and Chinese 1%
Government Multiparty republic
Currency Trinidad & Tobago dollar = 100 cents
Literacy rate 98%
Calorie consumption 2,585 kilocalories

Tunisia
Northern Africa

Official name Republic of Tunisia
Formation 1956 / 1956
Capital Tunis
Population 9.5 million / 158 people per sq mile (61 people per sq km) / 57%
Total area 63,170 sq miles (163,610 sq km)
Languages Arabic*, French
Religions Muslim 98%, Christian 1%, Jewish 1%
Ethnic mix Arab and Berber 98%, European 1%, other 1%
Government Multiparty republic
Currency Tunisian dinar = 1,000 millimes
Literacy rate 67%
Calorie consumption 3,330 kilocalories

Turkey
Asia / Europe

Official name Republic of Turkey
Formation 1923 / 1939
Capital Ankara
Population 63.8 million / 215 people per sq mile (83 people per sq km) / 69%
Total area 300,950 sq miles (779,450 sq km)
Languages Turkish*, Kurdish, Arabic, Circassian, Armenian
Religions Muslim 99%, other 1%
Ethnic mix Turkish 70%, Kurdish 20%, other 8%, Arab 2%
Government Multiparty republic
Currency Turkish lira = 100 krural
Literacy rate 83%
Calorie consumption 3,429 kilocalories

Turkmenistan
Central Asia

Official name Turkmenistan
Formation 1991 / 1991
Capital Ashgabat
Population 4.3 million / 23 people per sq mile (9 people per sq km) / 45%
Total area 188,455 sq miles (488,100 sq km)
Languages Turkmen*, Uzbek, Russian
Religions Muslim 87%, Eastern Orthodox 11%, other 2%
Ethnic mix Turkmen 72%, Russian 9%, Uzbek 9%, other 10%
Government Multiparty republic
Currency Manat = 100 tenge
Literacy rate 98%
Calorie consumption NOT AVAILABLE

Tuvalu
Australasia & Oceania

Official name Tuvalu
Formation 1978 / 1978
Capital Fongafale
Population 9000 / 976 people per sq mile (377 people per sq km) / 46%
Total area 10 sq miles (26 sq km)
Languages Tuvaluan*, Kiribati, English
Religions Protestant 97%, other 3%
Ethnic mix Polynesian 95% other 5%
Government Constitutional monarchy
Currency Australian dollar = 100 cents
Literacy rate 95%
Calorie consumption NOT AVAILABLE

Uganda
Eastern Africa

Official name Republic of Uganda
Formation 1962 / 1962
Capital Kampala
Population 21.3 million / 276 people per sq mile (107 people per sq km) / 13%
Total area 91,073 sq miles (235,880 sq km)
Languages English*, Luganda, Nkole, Chiga, Lango, Acholi, Teso
Religions Christian 71%, Traditional beliefs 13%, Muslim 5%, other (including Hindu) 11%
Ethnic mix Buganda 18%, Banyoro 14%, Teso 9%, other 59%
Government Multiparty republic
Currency New Uganda shilling = 100 cents
Literacy rate 64%
Calorie consumption 2,159 kilocalories

Ukraine
Eastern Europe

Official name Ukraine
Formation 1991 / 1991
Capital Kiev
Population 51.2 million / 220 people per sq mile (85 people per sq km) / 70%
Total area 223,090 sq miles (603,700 sq km)
Languages Ukrainian*, Russian, Tatar
Religions Mostly Ukrainian Orthodox, with Roman Catholic, Protestant and Jewish minorities
Ethnic mix Ukrainian 73%, Russian 22%, other (including Tatar) 5%
Government Multiparty republic
Currency Hryvna = 100 kopiykas
Literacy rate 98%
Calorie consumption NOT AVAILABLE

United Arab Emirates
Southwestern Asia

Official name United Arab Emirates
Formation 1971 / 1971
Capital Abu Dhabi
Population 2.4 million / 7 people per sq mile (29 people per sq km) / 84%
Total area 32,278 sq miles (83,600 sq km)
Languages Arabic*, Farsi (Persian), Urdu, Hindi, English
Religions Sunni Muslim 77%, Shi'a Muslim 19%, other 4%
Ethnic mix Asian 50%, Emirian 19%, other Arab 23%, other 8%
Government Federation of monarchs
Currency UAE dirham = 100 fils
Literacy rate 79%
Calorie consumption 3,384 kilocalories

United Kingdom
Northwestern Europe

Official name United Kingdom of Great Britain and Northern Ireland
Formation 1707 / 1922
Capital London
Population 58.2 million / 624 people per sq mile (241 people per sq km) / 89%
Total area 94,550 sq miles (244,880 sq km)
Languages English*, Welsh*, Scottish, Gaelic
Religions Protestant 52%, Roman Catholic 9%, Muslim 3%, other 36%
Ethnic mix English 80%, Scottish 10%, Northern Irish 4%, Welsh 2%, West Indian, Asian 4%
Government Constitutional monarchy
Currency Pound sterling = 100 pence
Literacy rate 99%
Calorie consumption 3,317 kilocalories

United States
North America

Official name United States of America
Formation 1787 / 1959
Capital Washington DC
Population 273.8 million / 77 people per sq mile (30 people per sq km) / 76%
Total area 3,681,760 sq miles (9,372,610 sq km)
Languages English*, Spanish, Italian, German, French, Polish, Chinese, Greek
Religions Protestant 61%, Roman Catholic 25%, Jewish 2%, other 12%
Ethnic mix White (including Hispanic) 84%, Black 12%, Chinese 1%, other 3%
Government Multiparty republic
Currency US dollar = 100 cents
Literacy rate 99%
Calorie consumption 3,732 kilocalories

Uruguay
South America

Official name Oriental Republic of Uruguay
Formation 1828 / 1828
Capital Montevideo
Population 3.2 million / 47 people per sq mile (18 people per sq km) / 90%
Total area 67,494 sq miles (174,810 sq km)
Languages Spanish*
Religions Roman Catholic 66%, Protestant 2%, Jewish 2%, other 30%
Ethnic mix White 90%, *mestizo* 6% Black 4%
Government Multiparty republic
Currency Uruguayan peso = 100 centimes
Literacy rate 97%
Calorie consumption 2,750 kilocalories

Uzbekistan
Central Asia

Official name Republic of Uzbekistan
Formation 1991 / 1991
Capital Tashkent
Population 24.1 million / 140 people per sq mile (54 people per sq km) / 41%
Total area 172,741 sq miles (447,400 sq km)
Languages Uzbek*, Russian
Religions Muslim 88%, other (mostly Eastern Orthodox) 9%, other 3%
Ethnic mix Uzbek 71%, Russian 8%, Tajik 5%, Kazakh 4%, other 12%
Government Multiparty republic
Currency Sum = 100 teen
Literacy rate 99%
Calorie consumption NOT AVAILABLE

Vanuatu
Australasia & Oceania

Official name Republic of Vanuatu
Formation 1980 / 1980
Capital Port-Vila
Population 200,000 / 42 people per sq mile (16 people per sq km) / 19%
Total area 4706 sq miles (12,190 sq km)
Languages Bislama*, English*, French*
Religions Protestant 77%, Roman Catholic 15%, Traditional beliefs 8%
Ethnic mix ni-Vanuatu 94%, other 6%
Government Multiparty republic
Currency Vatu = 100 centimes
Literacy rate 64%
Calorie consumption 2,739 kilocalories

Vatican City
Southern Europe

Official name Vatican City State
Formation 1929 / 1929
Capital Not applicable
Population 1,000 / 5,886 people per sq mile (2,273 people per sq km) /100%
Total area 0.17 sq miles (0.44 sq km)
Languages Italian*, Latin*
Religions Roman Catholic 100%
Ethnic mix Italian 90%, Swiss 10% (including the Swiss Guard, which is responsible for papal security)
Government Papal Commission
Currency Italian lira = 100 centesimi
Literacy rate 99%
Calorie consumption 3,561 kilocalories

Venezuela
South America

Official name Republic of Venezuela
Formation 1821 / 1930
Capital Caracas
Population 23.2 million / 68 people per sq mile (26 people per sq km) / 93%
Total area 352,143 sq miles (912,050 sq km)
Languages Spanish*, Indian languages *
Religions Roman Catholic 89%, Protestant and other 11%
Ethnic mix *Mestizo* 69%, White 20%, Black 9%, Indian 2%
Government Multiparty republic
Currency Bolívar = 100 centimos
Literacy rate 92%
Calorie consumption 2,618 kilocalories

Vietnam
Southeastern Asia

Official name Socialist Republic of Vietnam
Formation 1976 / 1976
Capital Hanoi
Population 77.9 million / 620 people per sq mile (239 people per sq km) / 21%
Total area 127,243 sq miles (329,560 sq km)
Languages Vietnamese*, Chinese, Thai, Khmer, Muong
Religions Buddhist 55%, Christian 7%, other and nonreligious 38%
Ethnic mix Vietnamese 88%, Chinese 4%, Thai 2%, other 6%
Government Single-party republic
Currency Dong = 10 hao = 100 xu
Literacy rate 91%
Calorie consumption 2,250 kilocalories

Yemen
Southwestern Asia

Official name Republic of Yemen
Formation 1990 / 1990
Capital Sana
Population 16.9 million / 82 people per sq mile (32 people per sq km) / 34%
Total area 203,849 sq miles (527,970 sq km)
Languages Arabic*, Hindi, Tamil, Urdu
Religions Shi'a Muslim 55%, Sunni Muslim 42%, Christian, Hindu, Jewish 3%
Ethnic mix Arab 95%, Afro-Arab 3%, Indian, Somali, European 2%
Government Multiparty republic
Currency Rial (North), Dinar (South) – both are legal currency
Literacy rate 42%
Calorie consumption 2,203 kilocalories

Yugoslavia (Serbia & Montenegro)
Europe

Official name Federal Republic of Yugoslavia
Formation 1992 / 1992
Capital Belgrade
Population 10.4 million / 264 people per sq mile (102 people per sq km) / 57%
Total area 39,449 sq miles (102,173 sq km)
Languages Serbo-croat*, Albanian
Religions Roman Catholic, Eastern Orthodox 69%, Muslim 19%, Protestant 1%, other 11%
Ethnic mix Serb 62%, Albanian 17%, Montenegrin 5%, Magyar 3%, other 13%
Government Multiparty republic
Currency Dinar = 100 para
Literacy rate 93%
Calorie consumption NOT AVAILABLE

Zambia
Southern Africa

Official name Republic of Zambia
Formation 1964 / 1964
Capital Lusaka
Population 8.7 million / 30 people per sq mile (12 people per sq km) / 43%
Total area 285,992 sq miles (740,720 sq km)
Languages English*, Bemba, Nyanja, Tonga, Kaonde, Lunda
Religions Christian 63%, Traditional beliefs 36%, other 1%
Ethnic mix Bemba 36%, Maravi 18%, Tonga 15%, other 31%
Government Multiparty republic
Currency Kwacha = 100 ngwee
Literacy rate 75%
Calorie consumption 1,931 kilocalories

Zimbabwe
Southern Africa

Official name Republic of Zimbabwe
Formation 1980 / 1980
Capital Harare
Population 11.9 million / 80 people per sq mile (21 people per sq km) / 32%
Total area 150,800 sq miles (390,580 sq km)
Languages English*, Shona, Ndebele
Religions Syncretic (Christian and traditional beliefs) 50%, Christian 26%, Traditional beliefs 24%
Ethnic mix Shona 71%, Ndebele 16%, other African 11%, White, Asian 2%
Government Multiparty republic
Currency Zimbabwe dollar = 100 cents
Literacy rate 90%
Calorie consumption 1,985 kilocalories

Glossary

THIS GLOSSARY lists all geographical, technical, and foreign language terms that appear in the text, followed by a brief definition of the term. Any acronyms used in the text are also listed in full. Terms in italics are for cross-reference and indicate that the word is separately defined in the glossary.

A

Aboriginal The original (*indigenous*) inhabitants of a country or continent. Especially used with reference to Australia.

Abyssal plain A broad *plain* found in the depths of the ocean, more than 10,000 ft (3,000 m) below sea level.

Acid rain Rain, sleet, snow, or mist which has absorbed waste gases from fossil-fueled power stations and vehicle exhausts, becoming more acid. It causes severe environmental damage.

Adaptation The gradual evolution of plants and animals so that they become better suited to survive and reproduce in their *environment*.

Afforestation The planting of new forest in areas that were once forested but have been cleared.

Agribusiness A term applied to activities such as the growing of crops, rearing of animals, or the manufacture of farm machinery, which eventually leads to the supply of agricultural produce at market.

Air mass A huge, homogeneous mass of air, within which horizontal patterns of temperature and *humidity* are consistent. Air masses are separated by *fronts*.

Alliance An agreement between two or more states, to work together to achieve common purposes.

Alluvial fan A large fan-shaped deposit of fine sediments deposited by a river as it emerges from a narrow, mountain valley onto a broad, open *plain*.

Alluvium Material deposited by rivers. Nowadays usually only applied to finer particles of silt and clay.

Alpine Mountain *environment*, between the *treeline* and the level of permanent snow cover.

Alpine mountains Ranges of mountains formed between 30 and 65 million years ago, by *folding*, in western and central Europe.

Amerindian A term applied to people *indigenous* to North, Central, and South America.

Animal husbandry The business of rearing animals.

Antarctic circle The parallel which lies at *latitude* of 66° 32' S.

Anticline A geological *fold* that forms an arch shape, curving upward in the rock *strata*.

Anticyclone An area of relatively high atmospheric pressure.

Aquaculture Collective term for the farming of produce derived from the sea, including fish-farming, the cultivation of shellfish, and plants such as seaweed.

Aquifer A body of rock that can absorb water. Also applied to any rock strata that have sufficient porosity to yield *groundwater* through wells or springs.

Arable Land which has been plowed and is being used, or is suitable, for growing crops.

Archipelago A group or chain of islands.

Arctic Circle The parallel that lies at a *latitude* of 66° 32' N.

Arête A thin, jagged mountain ridge that divides two adjacent *cirques*, found in regions where *glaciation* has occurred.

Arid Dry. An area of low rainfall, where the rate of *evaporation* may be greater than that of *precipitation*. Often defined as those areas that receive less than one inch (25 mm) of rain a year. In these areas only drought-resistant plants can survive.

Artesian well A naturally occurring source of underground water, stored in an *aquifer*.

Artisanal Small-scale, manual operation, such as fishing, using little or no machinery.

ASEAN Association of Southeast Asian Nations. Established in 1967 to promote economic, social, and cultural cooperation. Its members include Brunei, Indonesia, Malaysia, Philippines, Singapore, and Thailand.

Aseismic A region where *earthquake* activity has ceased.

Asteroid A minor planet circling the Sun, mainly between the orbits of Mars and Jupiter.

Asthenosphere A zone of hot, partially melted rock, which underlies the *lithosphere*, within the Earth's *crust*.

Atmosphere The envelope of odorless, colorless and tasteless gases surrounding the Earth, consisting of *oxygen* (23%), *nitrogen* (75%), argon (1%), *carbon dioxide* (0.03%), as well as tiny proportions of other gases.

Atmospheric pressure The pressure created by the action of gravity on the gases surrounding the Earth.

Atoll A ring-shaped island or *coral reef* often enclosing a *lagoon* of sea water.

Avalanche The rapid movement of a mass of snow and ice down a steep slope. Similar movements of other materials are described as *rock avalanches* or *landslides* and *sand avalanches*.

B

Badlands A landscape that has been heavily eroded and dissected by rainwater, and which has little or no vegetation.

Back slope The gentler windward slope of a sand *dune* or gentler slope of a *cuesta*.

Bajos An *alluvial fan* deposited by a river at the base of mountains and hills that encircle *desert* areas.

Bar, coastal An offshore strip of sand or shingle, either above or below the water. Usually parallel to the shore but sometimes crescent-shaped or at an oblique angle.

Barchan A crescent-shaped sand *dune*, formed where wind direction is very consistent. The horns of the crescent point downwind and where there is enough sand the barchan is mobile.

Barrio A Spanish term for the shantytowns – settlements of shacks – that are clustered around many South and Central American cities (*see also Favela*).

Basalt Dark, fine-grained *igneous rock* that is formed near the Earth's surface from fast-cooling *lava*.

Base level The level below which flowing water cannot erode the land.

Basement rock A mass of ancient rock often of *PreCambrian age*, covered by a layer of more recent *sedimentary rocks*. Commonly associated with *shield* areas.

Beach Lake or sea shore where waves break and there is an accumulation of loose sand, mud, gravel, or pebbles.

Bedrock Solid, consolidated and relatively unweathered rock, found on the surface of the land or just below a layer of soil or *weathered* rock.

Biodiversity The quantity of animal or plant species in a given area.

Biomass The total mass of organic matter – plants and animals – in a given area. It is usually measured in kilogrammes per square meter. Plant biomass is proportionally greater than that of animals, except in cities.

Biosphere The zone just above and below the Earth's surface, where all plants and animals live.

Blizzard A severe windstorm with snow and sleet. Visibility is often severely restricted.

Bluff The steep bank of a *meander*, formed by the erosive action of a river.

Boreal forest Tracts of mainly coniferous forest found in northern *latitudes*.

Breccia A type of rock composed of sharp fragments, cemented by a fine-grained material such as clay.

Butte An isolated, flat-topped hill with steep or vertical sides, buttes are the eroded remnants of a former land surface.

C

Caatinga Portuguese (Brazilian) term for thorny woodland growing in areas of pale granitic soils.

CACM Central American Common Market. Established in 1960 to further economic ties between its members, which are Costa Rica, El Salvador, Guatemala, Honduras, and Nicaragua.

Calcite Hexagonal crystals of calcium carbonate.

Caldera A huge volcanic vent, often containing a number of smaller vents, and sometimes a crater lake.

Carbon cycle The transfer of carbon to and from the *atmosphere*. This occurs on land through *photosynthesis*. In the sea, *carbon dioxide* is absorbed, some returning to the air and some taken up into the bodies of sea creatures.

Carbon dioxide A colorless, odorless gas (CO_2) that makes up 0.03% of the *atmosphere*.

Carbonation The process whereby rocks are broken down by carbonic acid. Carbon dioxide in the air dissolves in rainwater, forming carbonic acid. *Limestone* terrain can be rapidly eaten away.

Cash crop A single crop grown specifically for export sale, rather than for local use. Typical examples include coffee, tea, and citrus fruits.

Cassava A type of grain meal, used to produce tapioca. A staple crop in many parts of Africa.

Castle kopje Hill or rock outcrop, especially in southern Africa, where steep sides, and a summit composed of blocks, give a castle-like appearance.

Cataracts A series of stepped waterfalls created as a river flows over a band of hard, resistant rock.

Causeway A raised route through marshland or a body of water.

CEEAC Economic Community of Central African States. Established in 1983 to promote regional cooperation and if possible, establish a common market between 16 Central African nations.

Chemical weathering The chemical reactions leading to the decomposition of rocks. Types of chemical weathering include *carbonation*, *hydrolysis*, and *oxidation*.

Chernozem A fertile soil, also known as "black earth" consisting of a layer of dark topsoil, rich in decaying vegetation, overlying a lighter chalky layer.

Cirque Armchair-shaped basin, found in mountain regions, with a steep back, or rear, wall and a raised rock lip, often containing a lake (or *tarn*). The cirque floor has been eroded by a *glacier*, while the back wall is eroded both by the *glacier* and by *weathering*.

Climate The average weather conditions in a given area over a period of years, sometimes defined as 30 years or more.

Cold War A period of hostile relations between the US and the Soviet Union and their allies after the Second World War.

Composite volcano Also known as a strato-volcano, the volcanic cone is composed of alternating deposits of *lava* and *pyroclastic* material.

Compound A substance made up of *elements* chemically combined in a consistent way.

Condensation The process whereby a gas changes into a liquid. For example, water vapor in the *atmosphere* condenses around tiny airborne particles to form droplets of water.

Confluence The point at which two rivers meet.

Conglomerate Rock composed of large, water-worn or rounded pebbles, held together by a natural cement.

Coniferous forest A forest type containing trees which are generally, but not necessarily, *evergreen* and have slender, needlelike leaves. Coniferous trees reproduce by means of seeds contained in a cone.

Continental drift The theory that the continents of today are fragments of one or more prehistoric *supercontinents* which have moved across the Earth's surface, creating ocean basins. The theory has been superseded by a more sophisticated one – *plate tectonics*.

Continental shelf An area of the continental crust, below sea level, which slopes gently. It is separated from the deep ocean by a much more steeply inclined *continental slope*.

Continental slope A steep slope running from the edge of the *continental shelf* to the ocean floor.

Conurbation A vast metropolitan area created by the expansion of towns and cities into a virtually continuous urban area.

Cool continental A rainy *climate* with warm summers [warmest month below 76°F (22°C)] and often severe winters [coldest month below 32°F (0°C)].

Copra The dried, white kernel of a coconut, from which coconut oil is extracted.

Coral reef An underwater barrier created by colonies of the coral polyp. Polyps secrete a protective skeleton of calcium carbonate, and reefs develop as live polyps build on the skeletons of dead generations.

Core The center of the Earth, consisting of a dense mass of iron and nickel. It is thought that the outer core is molten or liquid, and that the hot inner core is solid due to extremely high pressures.

Coriolis effect A deflecting force caused by the rotation of the Earth. In the northern hemisphere a body, such as an *air mass* or ocean current, is deflected to the right, and in the southern hemisphere to the left. This prevents winds from blowing straight from areas of high to low pressure.

Coulées A US / Canadian term for a ravine formed by river *erosion*.

Craton A large block of the Earth's *crust* which has remained stable for a long period of *geological time*. It is made up of ancient *shield* rocks.

Cretaceous A period of *geological time* beginning about 145 million years ago and lasting until about 65 million years ago.

Crevasse A deep crack in a *glacier*.

Crust The hard, thin outer shell of the Earth. The crust floats on the *mantle*, which is softer and more dense. Under the oceans (oceanic crust) the crust is 3.7–6.8 miles (6–11 km) thick. Continental crust averages 18–24 miles (30–40 km).

Crystalline rock Rocks formed when molten *magma* crystallizes (*igneous rocks*) or when heat or pressure cause re-crystallization (*metamorphic rocks*). Crystalline rocks are distinct from *sedimentary rocks*.

Cuesta A hill which rises into a steep slope on one side but has a gentler gradient on its other slope.

Cyclone An area of low *atmospheric pressure*, occurring where the air is warm and relatively low in density, causing low level winds to spiral. *Hurricanes* and *typhoons* are tropical cyclones.

D

De facto
1 Government or other activity that takes place, or exists in actuality if not by right.
2 A border, which exists in practice, but which is not officially recognized by all the countries it adjoins.

Deciduous forest A forest of trees that shed their leaves annually at a particular time or season. In *temperate* climates the fall of leaves occurs in the autumn. Some *coniferous* trees, such as the larch, are deciduous. Deciduous vegetation contrasts with *evergreen*, which keeps its leaves for more than a year.

Defoliant Chemical spray used to remove foliage (leaves) from trees.

Deforestation The act of cutting down and clearing large areas of forest for human activities, such as agricultural land or urban development.

Delta Low-lying, fan-shaped area at a river mouth, formed by the *deposition* of successive layers of *sediment*. Slowing as it enters the sea, a river deposits sediment and may, as a result, split into numerous smaller channels, known as *distributaries*.

Denudation The combined effect of *weathering*, *erosion*, and *mass movement*, which, over long periods, exposes underlying rocks.

Deposition The laying down of material that has accumulated:
(*1*) after being *eroded* and then transported by physical forces such as wind, ice, or water;
(*2*) as organic remains, such as coal and coral;
(*3*) as the result of *evaporation* and chemical *precipitation*.

Depression
1 In climatic terms it is a large low pressure system.
2 A complex *fold*, producing a large valley, which incorporates both a *syncline* and an *anticline*.

Desert An *arid* region of low rainfall, with little vegetation or animal life, which is adapted to the dry conditions. The term is now applied not only to hot tropical and subtropical regions, but to arid areas of the continental interiors and to the ice deserts of the *Arctic* and *Antarctic*.

Desertification The gradual extension of *desert* conditions in *arid* or *semiarid* regions, as a result of climatic change or human activity, such as over-grazing and *deforestation*.

Despot A ruler with absolute power. Despots are often associated with oppressive regimes.

Detritus Piles of rock deposited by an erosive agent such as a river or *glacier*.

Distributary A minor branch of a river, which does not rejoin the main stream, common at *deltas*.

Diurnal Daily, something that occurs each day. Diurnal temperature refers to the variation in temperature over the course of a full day and night.

Divide A US term describing the area of high ground separating two *drainage basins*.

Donga A steep-sided *gully*, resulting from *erosion* by a river or by floods.

Dormant A term used to describe a *volcano* which is not currently erupting. They differ from extinct volcanoes as dormant volcanoes are still considered likely to erupt in the future.

Drainage basin The area drained by a single river system, its boundary is marked by a *watershed* or *divide*.

Drought A long period of continuously low rainfall.

Drumlin A long, streamlined hillock composed of material deposited by a *glacier*. They often occur in groups known as swarms.

Dune A mound or ridge of sand, shaped, and often moved, by the wind. They are found in hot *deserts* and on low-lying coasts where onshore winds blow across sandy beaches.

Dyke A wall constructed in low-lying areas to contain floodwaters or protect from high tides.

E

Earthflow The rapid movement of soil and other loose surface material down a slope, when saturated by water. Similar to a mudflow but not as fast-flowing, due to a lower percentage of water.

Earthquake Sudden movements of the Earth's *crust*, causing the ground to shake. Frequently occurring at *tectonic plate* margins. The shock, or series of shocks, spreads out from an *epicenter*.

EC The European Community (*see* EU).

Ecosystem A system of living organisms – plants and animals – interacting with their *environment*.

ECOWAS Economic Community of West African States. Established in 1975, it incorporates 16 West African states and aims to promote closer regional and economic cooperation.

Element
1 A constituent of the *climate* – *precipitation*, *humidity*, temperature, *atmospheric pressure*, or wind.
2 A substance that cannot be separated into simpler substances by chemical means.

El Niño A climatic phenomenon, the El Niño effect occurs about 14 times each century and leads to major shifts in global air circulation. It is associated with unusually warm currents off the coasts of Peru, Ecuador and Chile. The anomaly can last for up to two years.

Environment The conditions created by the surroundings (both natural and artificial) within which an organism lives. In human geography the word includes the surrounding economic, cultural, and social conditions.

Eon (aeon) Traditionally a long, but indefinite, period of *geological time*.

Ephemeral A nonpermanent feature, often used in connection with seasonal rivers or lakes in dry areas.

Epicenter The point on the Earth's surface directly above the underground origin – or focus – of an *earthquake*.

Equator The line of *latitude* which lies equidistant between the North and South Poles.

Erg An extensive area of sand *dunes*, particularly in the Sahara Desert.

Erosion The processes which wear away the surface of the land. *Glaciers*, wind, rivers, waves, and currents all carry debris which causes *erosion*. Some definitions also include *mass movement* due to gravity as an agent of erosion.

Escarpment A steep slope at the margin of a level, upland surface. In a landscape created by *folding*, escarpments (or scarps) frequently lie behind a more gentle backward slope.

Esker A narrow, winding ridge of sand and gravel deposited by streams of water flowing beneath or at the edge of a *glacier*.

Erratic A rock transported by a *glacier* and deposited some distance from its place of origin.

Eustacy A world-wide fall or rise in ocean levels.

EU The European Union. Established in 1965, it was formerly known as the EEC (European Economic Community) and then the EC (European Community). Its members are Austria, Belgium, Denmark, Finland, France, Germany, Greece, Ireland, Italy, Luxembourg, Netherlands, Portugal, Spain, Sweden, and UK. It seeks to establish an integrated European common market and eventual federation.

Evaporation The process whereby a liquid or solid is turned into a gas or vapor. Also refers to the diffusion of water vapor into the *atmosphere* from exposed water surfaces such as lakes and seas.

Evapotranspiration The loss of moisture from the Earth's surface through a combination of *evaporation*, and *transpiration* from the leaves of plants.

Evergreen Plants with long-lasting leaves, which are not shed annually or seasonally.

Exfoliation A kind of *weathering* whereby scalelike flakes of rock are peeled or broken off by the development of salt crystals in water within the rocks. *Groundwater*, which contains dissolved salts, seeps to the surface and evaporates, precipitating a film of salt crystals, which expands causing fine cracks. As these grow, flakes of rock break off.

Extrusive rock *Igneous* rock formed when molten material (*magma*) pours forth at the Earth's surface and cools rapidly. It usually has a glassy texture.

F

Factionalism The actions of one or more minority political group acting against the interests of the majority government.

Fault A fracture or crack in rock, where strains (*tectonic* movement) have caused blocks to move, vertically or laterally, relative to each other.

Fauna Collective name for the animals of a particular period of time, or region.

Favela Brazilian term for the shantytowns or temporary huts that have grown up around the edge of many South and Central American cities.

Ferrel cell A component in the global pattern of air circulation, which rises in the colder *latitudes* (60° N and S) and descends in warmer *latitudes* (30° N and S). The Ferrel cell forms part of the world's three-cell air circulation pattern, with the *Hadley* and Polar cells.

Fissure A deep crack in a rock or a *glacier*.

Fjord A deep, narrow inlet, created when the sea inundates the *U-shaped valley* created by a *glacier*.

Flash flood A sudden, short-lived rise in the water level of a river or stream, or surge of water down a dry river channel, or *wadi*, caused by heavy rainfall.

Flax A plant used to make linen.

Floodplain The broad, flat part of a river valley, adjacent to the river itself, formed by *sediment* deposited during flooding.

Flora The collective name for the plants of a particular period of time or region.

Flow The movement of a river within its banks, particularly in terms of the speed and volume of water.

Fold A bend in the rock *strata* of the Earth's *crust*, resulting from compression.

Fossil The remains, or traces, of a dead organism preserved in the Earth's *crust*.

Fossil dune A *dune* formed in a once-*arid* region which is now wetter. *Dunes* normally move with the wind, but in these cases vegetation makes them stable.

Fossil fuel Fuel – coal, natural gas or oil – composed of the fossilized remains of plants and animals.

Front The boundary between two *air masses*, which contrast sharply in temperature and *humidity*.

Frontal depression An area of low pressure caused by rising warm air. They are generally 600–1,200 miles (1,000–2,000 km) in diameter. Within *depressions* there are both warm and cold fronts.

Frost shattering A form of *weathering* where water freezes in cracks, causing expansion. As temperatures fluctuate and the ice melts and refreezes, it eventually causes the rocks to shatter and fragments of rock to break off.

G

Gaucho South American term for a stock herder or cowboy who works on the grassy *plains* of Paraguay, Uruguay, and Argentina.

Geological timescale The chronology of the Earth's history as revealed in its rocks. Geological time is divided into a number of periods: *eon*, era, period, epoch, age, and chron (the shortest). These units are not of uniform length.

Geosyncline A concave fold (*syncline*) or large depression in the Earth's *crust*, extending hundreds of miles. This basin contains a deep layer of sediment, especially at its center, from the land masses around it.

Geothermal energy Heat derived from hot rocks within the Earth's *crust* and resulting in hot springs, steam, or hot rocks at the surface. The energy is generated by rock movements, and from the breakdown of radioactive elements occurring under intense pressure.

GDP Gross Domestic Product. The total value of goods and services produced by a country excluding income from foreign countries.

Geyser A jet of steam and hot water that intermittently erupts from vents in the ground in areas that are, or were, *volcanic*. Some geysers occasionally reach heights of 196 ft (60 m).

Ghetto An area of a city or region occupied by an overwhelming majority of people from one racial or religious group, who may be subject to persecution or containment.

Glaciation The growth of *glaciers* and *ice sheets*, and their impact on the landscape.

Glacier A body of ice moving downslope under the influence of gravity and consisting of compacted and frozen snow. A glacier is distinct from an *ice sheet*, which is wider and less confined by features of the landscape.

Glacio-eustacy A world-wide change in the level of the oceans, caused when the formation of *ice sheets* takes up water or when their melting returns water to the ocean. The formation of ice sheets in the *Pleistocene* epoch, for example, caused sea level to drop by about 320 ft (100 m).

Glaciofluvial To do with glacial *meltwater*, the landforms it creates and its processes; *erosion*, transportation, and *deposition*. Glaciofluvial effects are more powerful and rapid where they occur within or beneath the *glacier*, rather than beyond its edge.

Glacis A gentle slope or *pediment*.

Global warming An increase in the average temperature of the Earth. At present the *greenhouse effect* is thought to contribute to this.

GNP Gross National Product. The total value of goods and services produced by a country.

Gondwanaland The *supercontinent* thought to have existed over 200 million years ago in the southern hemisphere. Gondwanaland is believed to have comprised today's Africa, Madagascar, Australia, parts of South America, *Antarctica*, and the Indian subcontinent.

Graben A block of rock let down between two parallel *faults*. Where the graben occurs within a valley, the structure is known as a *rift valley*.

Grease ice Slicks of ice which form in *Antarctic* seas, when ice crystals are bonded together by wind and wave action.

Greenhouse effect A change in the temperature of the *atmosphere*. Short-wave solar radiation travels through the *atmosphere* unimpeded to the Earth's surface, whereas outgoing, long-wave terrestrial radiation is absorbed by materials that reradiate it back to the Earth. Radiation trapped in this way, by water vapor, carbon dioxide, and other "greenhouse gases," keeps the Earth warm. As more *carbon dioxide* is released into the atmosphere by the burning of *fossil fuels*, the greenhouse effect may cause a global increase in temperature.

Groundwater Water that has seeped into the pores, cavities, and cracks of rocks or into soil and water held in an *aquifer*.

Gully A deep, narrow channel eroded in the landscape by *ephemeral* streams.

Guyot A small, flat-topped submarine mountain, formed as a result of subsidence which occurs during *sea-floor spreading*.

Gypsum A soft mineral *compound* (hydrated calcium sulphate), used as the basis of many forms of plaster, including plaster of Paris.

H

Hadley cell A large-scale component in the global pattern of air circulation. Warm air rises over the *Equator* and blows at high altitude toward the poles, sinking in subtropical regions (30° N and 30° S) and creating high pressure. The air then flows at the surface toward the *Equator* in the form of trade winds. There is one cell in each hemisphere. Named after G. Hadley, who published his theory in 1735.

Hamada An Arabic word for a plateau of bare rock in a *desert*.

Hanging valley A tributary valley that ends suddenly, high above the bed of the main valley. The effect is found where the main valley has been more deeply eroded by a *glacier*, than has the tributary valley. A stream in a hanging valley will descend to the floor of the main valley as a waterfall or *cataract*.

Headwards The action of a river eroding back upstream, as opposed to the normal process of downstream *erosion*. Headwards erosion is often associated with *gullying*.

Hoodos Pinnacles of rock that have been worn away by *weathering* in *semiarid* regions.

Horst A block of the Earth's *crust* which has been left upstanding by the sinking of adjoining blocks along fault lines.

Hot spot A region of the Earth's *crust* where high thermal activity occurs, often leading to volcanic eruptions. Hot spots often occur far from plate boundaries, but their movement is associated with *plate tectonics*.

Humid equatorial Rainy *climate* with no winter, where the coolest month is generally above 64°F (18°C).

Humidity The relative amount of moisture held in the Earth's *atmosphere*.

Hurricane
1 A tropical *cyclone* occurring in the Caribbean and western North Atlantic.
2 A wind of more than 65 knots (75 kmph).

Hydroelectric power Energy produced by harnessing the rapid movement of water down steep mountain slopes to drive turbines to generate electricity.

Hydrolysis The chemical breakdown of rocks in reaction with water, forming new compounds.

I

Ice Age A period in the Earth's history when surface temperatures in the temperate *latitudes* were much lower and *ice sheets* expanded considerably. There have been *ice ages* from *Pre-Cambrian* times onward. The most recent began two million years ago and ended 10,000 years ago.

Ice cap A permanent dome of ice in highland areas. The term ice cap is often seen as distinct from *ice sheet*, which denotes a much wider covering of ice; and is also used refer to the very extensive polar and Greenland ice caps.

Ice floe A large, flat mass of ice floating free on the ocean surface. It is usually formed after the break-up of winter ice by heavy storms.

Ice sheet A continuous, very thick layer of ice and snow. The term is usually used of ice masses which are continental in extent.

Ice shelf A floating mass of ice attached to the edge of a coast. The seaward edge is usually a sheer cliff up to 100 ft (30 m) high.

Ice wedge Massive blocks of ice up to 6.5 ft (2 m) wide at the top and extending 32 ft (10 m) deep. They are found in cracks in *polygonally-patterned* ground in *periglacial* regions.

Iceberg A large mass of ice in a lake or a sea, which has broken off from a floating *ice sheet* (an *ice shelf*) or from a *glacier*.

Igneous rock Rock formed when molten material, *magma*, from the hot, lower layers of the Earth's *crust*, cools, solidifies, and crystallizes, either within the Earth's *crust* (*intrusive*) or on the surface (*extrusive*).

IMF International Monetary Fund. Established in 1944 as a UN agency, it contains 182 members around the world and is concerned with world monetary stability and economic development.

Incised meander A *meander* where the river, following its original course, cuts deeply into *bedrock*. This may occur when a mature, meandering river begins to erode its bed much more vigorously after the surrounding land has been uplifted.

Indigenous People, plants, or animals native to a particular region.

Infrastructure The communications and services – roads, railroads, and telecommunications – necessary for the functioning of a country or region.

Inselberg An isolated, steep-sided hill, rising from a low *plain* in *semiarid* and *savannah* landscapes. Inselbergs are usually composed of a rock, such as granite, which resists *erosion*.

Interglacial A period of global *climate*, between two *ice ages*, when temperatures rise and *ice sheets* and *glaciers* retreat.

Intraplate volcano A *volcano* which lies in the centre of one of the Earth's *tectonic plates*, rather than, as is more common, at its edge. They are thought to have been formed by a *hot spot*.

Intrusion (intrusive igneous rock) Rock formed when molten material, *magma*, penetrates existing rocks below the Earth's surface before cooling and solidifying. These rocks cool more slowly than extrusive rock and therefore tend to have coarser grains.

Irrigation The artificial supply of agricultural water to dry areas, often involving the creation of canals and the diversion of natural watercourses.

Island arc A curved chain of islands. Typically, such an arc fringes an ocean trench, formed at the margin between two *tectonic plates*. As one plate overrides another, *earthquakes* and volcanic activity are common and the islands themselves are often volcanic cones.

Isostasy The state of equilibrium that the Earth's *crust* maintains as its lighter and heavier parts float on the denser underlying mantle.

Isthmus A narrow strip of land connecting two larger landmasses or islands.

J

Jet stream A narrow belt of westerly winds in the *troposphere*, at altitudes above 39,000 ft (12,000 m). Jet streams tend to blow more strongly in winter and include: the subtropical jet stream; the *polar* front jet stream in mid-*latitudes*; the *Arctic* jet stream; and the polar-night jet stream.

Joint A crack in a rock, formed where blocks of rock have not shifted relative to each other, as is the case with a *fault*. Joints are created by *folding*; by shrinkage in *igneous rock* as it cools or *sedimentary rock* as it dries out; and by the release of pressure in a rock mass when overlying materials are removed by *erosion*.

Jute A plant fiber used to make coarse ropes, sacks, and matting.

K

Kame A mound of stratified sand and gravel with steep sides, deposited in a *crevasse* by *meltwater* running over a *glacier*. When the ice retreats, this forms an undulating terrain of hummocks.

Karst A barren *limestone* landscape created by carbonic acid in streams and rainwater, in areas where *limestone* is close to the surface. Typical features include caverns, towerlike hills, *sinkholes*, and flat limestone pavements.

Kettle hole A round hollow formed in a glacial deposit by a detached block of glacial ice, which later melted. They can fill with water to form kettle-lakes.

L

Lagoon A shallow stretch of coastal salt-water behind a partial barrier such as a sandbank or *coral reef*. Lagoon is also used to describe the water encircled by an *atoll*.

LAIA Latin American Integration Association. Established in 1980, its members are Argentina, Bolivia, Brazil, Chile, Colombia, Ecuador, Mexico, Paraguay, Peru, Uruguay, and Venezuala. It aims to promote economic cooperation between member states.

Landslide The sudden downslope movement of a mass of rock or earth on a slope, caused either by heavy rain; the impact of waves; an *earthquake* or human activity.

Laterite A hard red deposit left by *chemical weathering* in tropical conditions, and consisting mainly of oxides of iron and aluminium.

Latitude The angular distance from the *Equator*, to a given point on the Earth's surface. Imaginary lines of *latitude* running parallel to the Equator encircle the Earth, and are measured in degrees north or south of the Equator. The Equator is 0°, the poles 90° South and North respectively. Also called parallels.

Laurasia In the theory of *continental drift*, the northern part of the great *supercontinent* of *Pangaea*. Laurasia is said to consist of N America, Greenland and all of Eurasia north of the Indian subcontinent.

Lava The molten rock, *magma*, which erupts onto the Earth's surface through a *volcano*, or through a *fault* or crack in the Earth's *crust*. Lava refers to the rock both in its molten and in its later, solidified form.

Leaching The process whereby water dissolves minerals and moves them down through layers of soil or rock.

Levée A raised bank alongside the channel of a river. Levées are either human-made or formed in times of flood when the river overflows its channel, slows and deposits much of its *sediment* load.

Lichen An organism which is the symbiotic product of an algae and a fungus. Lichens form in tight crusts on stones and trees, and are resistant to extreme cold. They are often found in tundra regions.

Lignite Low-grade coal, also known as brown coal. Found in large deposits in eastern Europe.

Limestone A porous *sedimentary* rock formed from carbonate materials.

Lingua franca The language adopted as the common language between speakers whose native languages are different. This is common in former colonial states.

Lithosphere The rigid upper layer of the Earth, comprising the *crust* and the upper part of the *mantle*.

Llanos Vast grassland *plains* of northern South America.

Loess Fine-grained, yellow deposits of unstratified silts and sands. Loess is believed to be wind-carried *sediment* created in the last *Ice Age*. Some deposits may later have been redistributed by rivers. Loess-derived soils are of high quality, fertile, and easy to work.

Longitude A division of the Earth which pinpoints how far east or west a given place is from the Prime Meridian (0°) which runs through the Royal Observatory at Greenwich, England (UK). Imaginary lines of longitude are drawn around the world from pole to pole. The world is divided into 360 degrees.

Longshore drift The movement of sand and silt along the coast, carried by waves hitting the beach at an angle.

M

Magma Underground, molten rock, which is very hot and highly charged with gas. It is generated at great pressure, at depths 10 miles (16 km) or more below the Earth's surface. It can issue as *lava* at the Earth's surface or, more often, solidify below the surface as *intrusive igneous rock*.

Mantle The layer of the Earth between the *crust* and the *core*. It is about 1,800 miles (2,900 km) thick. The uppermost layer of the mantle is the soft, 125-mile (200 km) thick *asthenosphere* on which the more rigid *lithosphere* floats.

Maquiladoras Factories on the Mexico side of the Mexico/US border, that are allowed to import raw materials and components duty-free and use low-cost labor to assemble the goods, finally exporting them for sale in the US.

Market gardening The intensive growing of fruit and vegetables close to large local markets.

Mass movement Downslope movement of weathered materials such as rock, often helped by rainfall or glacial *meltwater*. Mass movement may be a gradual process or rapid, as in a *landslide* or rockfall.

Massif A single very large mountain or an area of mountains with uniform characteristics and clearly-defined boundaries.

Meander A looplike bend in a river, which is found typically in the lower, mature reaches of a river but can form wherever the valley is wide and the slope gentle.

Mediterranean climate A temperate *climate* of hot, dry summers and warm, damp winters. This is typical of the western fringes of the world's continents in the warm temperate regions between *latitudes* of 30° and 40° (north and south).

Meltwater Water resulting from the melting of a *glacier* or *ice sheet*.

Mesa A broad, flat-topped hill, characteristic of *arid* regions.

Mesosphere A layer of the Earth's *atmosphere*, between the *stratosphere* and the *thermosphere*. Extending from about 25–50 miles (40–80 km) above the surface of the Earth.

Mestizo A person of mixed *Amerindian* and European origin.

Metallurgy The refining and working of metals.

Metamorphic rocks Rocks that have been altered from their original form, in terms of texture, composition, and structure by intense heat, pressure, or by the introduction of new chemical substances – or a combination of more than one of these.

Meteor A body of rock, metal or other material, that travels through space at great speeds. Meteors are visible as they enter the Earth's *atmosphere* as shooting stars and fireballs.

Meteorite The remains of a *meteor* that has fallen to Earth.

Meteoroid A *meteor* that is still traveling in space, outside the Earth's *atmosphere*.

Mezzogiorno A term applied to the southern portion of Italy.

Milankovitch hypothesis A theory suggesting that there are a series of cycles that slightly alter the Earth's position when rotating about the Sun. The cycles identified all affect the amount of *radiation* the Earth receives at different *latitudes*. The theory is seen as a key factor in the cause of *ice ages*.

Millet A grain-crop, forming part of the staple diet in much of Africa.

Mistral A strong, dry, cold northerly or north-westerly wind, which blows from the Massif Central of France to the Mediterranean Sea. It is common in winter and its cold blasts can cause crop damage in the Rhône Delta, in France.

Mohorovičić discontinuity (Moho) The structural divide at the margin between the Earth's *crust* and the *mantle*. On average it is 20 miles (35 km) below the continents and 6 miles (10 km) below the oceans. The different densities of the *crust* and the mantle cause *earthquake* waves to accelerate at this point.

Monarchy A form of government in which the head of state is a single hereditary monarch. The monarch may be a mere figurehead, or may retain significant authority.

Monsoon A wind that changes direction biannually. The change is caused by the reversal of pressure over landmasses and the adjacent oceans. Because the inflowing moist winds bring rain, the term monsoon is also used to refer to the rains themselves. The term is derived from and most commonly refers to the seasonal winds of south and east Asia.

Montaña Mountain areas along the west coast of South America.

Moraine Debris, transported and deposited by a *glacier* or *ice sheet* in unstratified, mixed, piles of rock, boulders, pebbles, and clay.

Mountain-building The formation of *fold* mountains by tectonic activity. Also known as orogeny, mountain-building often occurs on the margin where two *tectonic plates* collide. The periods when most mountain-building occurred are known as orogenic phases and lasted many millions of years.

Mudflow An *avalanche* of mud that occurs when a mass of soil is drenched by rain or melting snow. It is a type of *mass movement*, faster than an *earthflow* because it is lubricated by water.

N

Nappe A mass of rocks which has been overfolded by repeated thrust *faulting*.

NAFTA The North American Free Trade Association. Established in 1994 between Canada, Mexico, and the US to set up a free-trade zone.

NASA The North American Space Agency. It is a government body, established in 1958 to develop manned and unmanned space programs.

NATO The North Atlantic Treaty Organization. Established in 1949 to promote mutual defense and cooperation between its members, which are Belgium, Canada, Czech Republic, Denmark, France, Germany, Greece, Iceland, Italy, Luxembourg, the Netherlands, Norway, Portugal, Poland, Spain, Turkey, UK, and US.

Nitrogen The odorless, colorless gas that makes up 78% of the atmosphere. Within the soil, it is a vital nutrient for plants.

Nomads (nomadic) Wandering communities that move around in search of suitable pasture for their herds of animals.

Nuclear fusion A technique used to create a new nucleus by the merging of two lighter ones, resulting in the release of large quantities of energy.

O

Oasis A fertile area in the midst of a *desert*, usually watered by an underground *aquifer*.

Oceanic ridge A mid-ocean ridge formed, according to the theory of *plate tectonics*, when plates drift apart and hot *magma* pours through to form new oceanic *crust*.

Oligarchy The government of a state by a small, exclusive group of people – such as an elite class or a family group.

Onion-skin weathering The *weathering* away or *exfoliation* of a rock or outcrop by the peeling off of surface layers.

Oriente A flatter region lying to the east of the Andes in South America.

Outwash plain *Glaciofluvial* material (typically clay, sand, and gravel) carried beyond an ice sheet by *meltwater* streams, forming a broad, flat deposit.

Oxbow lake A crescent-shaped lake formed on a river *floodplain* when a river erodes the outside bend of a *meander*, making the neck of the *meander* narrower until the river cuts across the neck. The meander is cut off and is dammed off with sediment, creating an oxbow lake. Also known as a cut-off or mortlake.

Oxidation A form of *chemical weathering* where *oxygen* dissolved in water reacts with minerals in rocks – particularly iron – to form oxides. Oxidation causes brown or yellow staining on rocks, and eventually leads to the break down of the rock.

Oxygen A colorless, odorless gas which is one of the main constituents of the Earth's *atmosphere* and is essential to life on Earth.

Ozone layer A layer of enriched *oxygen* (O_3) within the stratosphere, mostly between 18–50 miles (30–80 km) above the Earth's surface. It is vital to the existence of life on Earth because it absorbs harmful shortwave ultraviolet radiation, while allowing beneficial longer wave ultraviolet radiation to penetrate to the Earth's surface.

P

Pacific Rim The name given to the economically-dynamic countries bordering the Pacific Ocean.

Pack ice Ice masses more than 10 ft (3 m) thick that form on the sea surface and are not attached to a landmass.

Pancake ice Thin discs of ice, up to 8 ft (2.4 m) wide which form when slicks of *grease ice* are tossed together by winds and stormy seas.

Pangaea In the theory of continental drift, Pangaea is the original great land mass which, about 190 million years ago, began to split into Gondwanaland in the south and Laurasia in the north, separated by the Tethys Sea.

Pastoralism Grazing of livestock – usually sheep, goats, or cattle. Pastoralists in many drier areas have traditionally been *nomadic*.

Parallel *see Latitude.*

Peat Ancient, partially-decomposed vegetation found in wet, boggy conditions where there is little *oxygen*. It is the first stage in the development of coal and is often dried for use as fuel. It is also used to improve soil quality.

Pediment A gently-sloping ramp of *bedrock* below a steeper slope, often found at mountain edges in *desert* areas, but also in other climatic zones. Pediments may include depositional elements such as *alluvial fans*.

Peninsula A thin strip of land surrounded on three of its sides by water. Large examples include Florida and Korea.

Per capita Latin term meaning "for each person."

Periglacial Regions on the edges of *ice sheets* or *glaciers* or, more commonly, cold regions experiencing intense frost action, *permafrost* or both. Periglacial climates bring long, freezing winters and short, mild summers.

Permafrost Permanently frozen ground, typical of *Arctic* regions. Although a layer of soil above the permafrost melts in summer, the melted water does not drain through the permafrost.

Permeable rocks Rocks through which water can seep, because they are either porous or cracked.

Pharmaceuticals The manufacture of medicinal drugs.

Phreatic eruption A volcanic eruption which occurs when *lava* combines with *groundwater*, superheating the water and causing a sudden emission of steam at the surface.

Physical weathering (mechanical weathering) The breakdown of rocks by physical, as opposed to chemical, processes. Examples include: changes in pressure or temperature; the effect of windblown sand; the pressure of growing salt crystals in cracks within rock; and the expansion and contraction of water within rock as it freezes and thaws.

Pingo A dome of earth with a core of ice, found in *tundra* regions. Pingos are formed either when *groundwater* freezes and expands, pushing up the land surface, or when trapped, freezing water in a lake expands and pushes up lake *sediments* to form the pingo dome.

Placer A belt of mineral-bearing rock *strata* lying at or close to the Earth's surface, from which minerals can be easily extracted.

Plain A flat, level region of land, often relatively low-lying.

Plateau A highland tract of flat land.

Plate *see Tectonic plates.*

Plate tectonics The study of *tectonic plates*, that helps to explain *continental drift*, mountain formation and volcanic activity. The movement of tectonic plates may be explained by the currents of rock rising and falling from within the Earth's *mantle*, as it heats up and then cools. The boundaries of the plates are known as plate margins and most mountains, *earthquakes*, and *volcanoes* occur at these margins. Constructive margins are moving apart; destructive margins are crunching together and conservative margins are sliding past one another.

Pleistocene A period of *geological time* spanning from about 5.2 million years ago to 1.6 million years ago.

Plutonic rock *Igneous* rocks found deep below the surface. They are coarse-grained because they cooled and solidified slowly.

Polar The zones within the *Arctic* and *Antarctic* circles.

Polje A long, broad *depression* found in *karst* (*limestone*) regions.

Polygonal patterning Typical ground patterning, found in areas where the soil is subject to severe frost action, often in *periglacial* regions.

Porosity A measure of how much water can be held within a rock or a soil. Porosity is measured as the percentage of holes or pores in a material, compared to its total volume. For example, the porosity of slate is less than 1%, whereas that of gravel is 25–35%.

Prairies Originally a French word for grassy *plains* with few or no trees.

Pre-Cambrian The earliest period of *geological time* dating from over 570 million years ago.

Precipitation The fall of moisture from the *atmosphere* onto the surface of the Earth, whether as dew, hail, rain, sleet, or snow.

Pyramidal peak A steep, isolated mountain summit, formed when the back walls of three or more *cirques* are cut back and move toward each other. The cliffs around such a horned peak, or horn, are divided by sharp *arêtes*. The Matterhorn in the Swiss Alps is an example.

Pyroclasts Fragments of rock ejected during volcanic eruptions.

Q

Quaternary The current period of *geological time*, which started about 1.6 million years ago.

R

Radiation The emission of energy in the form of particles or waves. Radiation from the sun includes heat, light, ultraviolet rays, gamma rays, and X-rays. Only some of the solar energy radiated into space reaches the Earth.

Rainforest Dense forests in tropical zones with high rainfall, temperature and *humidity*. Strictly, the term applies to the equatorial rain forest in tropical lowlands with constant rainfall and no seasonal change. The Congo and Amazon basins are examples. The term is applied more loosely to lush forest in other climates. Within rain forests organic life is dense and varied: at least 40% of all plant and animal species are found here and there may be as many as 100 tree species per hectare.

Rainshadow An area which experiences low rainfall, because of its position on the leeward side of a mountain range.

Reg A large area of stony *desert*, where tightly-packed gravel lies on top of clayey sand. A reg is formed where the wind blows away the finer sand.

Remote-sensing Method of obtaining information about the *environment* using unmanned equipment, such as a satellite, that relays the information to a point where it is collected and used.

Resistance The capacity of a rock to resist *denudation*, by processes such as *weathering* and *erosion*.

Ria A flooded *V-shaped river valley* or estuary, flooded by a rise in sea level (*eustacy*) or sinking land. It is shorter than a *fjord* and gets deeper as it meets the sea.

Rift valley A long, narrow depression in the Earth's *crust*, formed by the sinking of rocks between two *faults*.

River channel The trough which contains a river and is molded by the flow of water within it.

Roche moutonée A rock found in a glaciated valley. The side facing the flow of the *glacier* has been smoothed and rounded, while the other side has been left more rugged because the *glacier*, as it flows over it, has plucked out frozen fragments and carried them away.

Runoff Water draining from a land surface by flowing across it.

S

Sabkha The floor of an isolated *depression* that occurs in an *arid environment* – usually covered by salt deposits and devoid of vegetation.

SADC Southern African Development Community. Established in 1992 to promote economic integration between its member states, which are Angola, Botswana, Lesotho, Malawi, Mauritius, Mozambique, Namibia, South Africa, Swaziland, Tanzania, Zambia, and Zimbabwe.

Salt plug A rounded hill produced by the upward doming of rock *strata* caused by the movement of salt or other evaporite deposits under intense pressure.

Sastrugi Ice ridges formed by wind action. They lie parallel to the direction of the wind.

Savannah Open grassland found between the zone of *deserts*, and that of tropical *rain forests* in the tropics and subtropics. Scattered trees and shrubs are found in some kinds of savannah. A savannah *climate* usually has wet and dry seasons.

Scarp *see Escarpment.*

Scree Piles of rock fragments beneath a cliff or rock face, caused by mechanical *weathering*, especially *frost shattering*, where the expansion and contraction of freezing and thawing water within the rock, gradually breaks it up.

Sea-floor spreading The process whereby *tectonic plates* move apart, allowing hot *magma* to erupt and solidify. This forms a new sea floor and, ultimately, widens the ocean.

Seamount An isolated, submarine mountain or hill, probably of volcanic origin.

Season A period of time linked to regular changes in the weather, especially the intensity of solar *radiation*.

Sediment Grains of rock transported and deposited by rivers, sea, ice, or wind.

Sedimentary rocks Rocks formed from the debris of preexisting rocks or of organic material. They are found in many *environments* – on the ocean floor, on beaches, rivers, and *deserts*. Organically-formed sedimentary rocks include coal and chalk. Other sedimentary rocks, such as flint, are formed by chemical processes. Most of these rocks contain *fossils*, which can be used to date them.

Seif A sand *dune* which lies parallel to the direction of the prevailing wind. Seifs form steep-sided ridges, sometimes extending for miles.

Seismic activity Movement within the Earth, such as an *earthquake* or *tremor*.

Selva A region of wet forest found in the Amazon Basin.

Semiarid, semidesert The *climate* and landscape which lies between *savannah* and *desert* or between savannah and a *mediterranean* climate. In semiarid conditions there is a little more moisture than in a true *desert*; and more patches of drought-resistant vegetation can survive.

Shale (marine shale) A compacted *sedimentary rock*, with fine-grained particles. Marine shale is formed on the seabed. Fuel such as oil may be extracted from it.

Sheetwash Water that runs downhill in thin sheets without forming channels. It can cause *sheet erosion*.

Sheet erosion The washing away of soil by a thin film or sheet of water, known as *sheetwash*.

Shield A vast stable block of the Earth's *crust*, which has experienced little or no *mountain-building*.

Sierra The Spanish word for mountains.

Sinkhole A circular *depression* in a *limestone* region. They are formed by the collapse of an underground cave system or the *chemical weathering* of the *limestone*.

Sisal A plant-fiber used to make matting.

Slash and burn A farming technique involving the cutting down and burning of scrub forest, to create agricultural land. After a number of seasons this land is abandoned and the process is repeated. This practice is common in Africa and South America.

Slip face The steep leeward side of a sand *dune* or slope. Opposite side to a *back slope*.

Soil A thin layer of rock particles mixed with the remains of dead plants and animals. This occurs naturally on the surface of the Earth and provides a medium for plants to grow.

Soil creep The very gradual downslope movement of rock debris and soil, under the influence of gravity. This is a type of *mass movement*.

Soil erosion The wearing away of soil more quickly than it is replaced by natural processes. Soil can be carried away by wind as well as by water. Human activities, such as over-grazing and the clearing of land for farming, accelerate the process in many areas.

Solar energy Energy derived from the Sun. Solar energy is converted into other forms of energy. For example, the wind and waves, as well as the creation of plant material in photosynthesis, depend on solar energy.

Solifluction A kind of *soil creep*, where water in the surface layer has saturated the soil and rock debris which slips slowly downhill. It often happens where frozen top-layer deposits thaw, leaving frozen layers below them.

Sorghum A type of grass found in South America, similar to sugar cane. When refined it is used to make molasses.

Spit A thin linear deposit of sand or shingle extending from the sea shore. Spits are formed as angled waves shift sand along the beach, eventually extending a ridge of sand beyond a change in the angle of the coast. Spits are common where the coastline bends, especially at estuaries.

Squash A type of edible gourd.

Stack A tall, isolated pillar of rock near a coastline, created as wave action erodes away the adjacent rock.

Stalactite A tapering cylinder of mineral deposit, hanging from the roof of a cave in a *karst* area. It is formed by calcium carbonate, dissolved in water, which drips through the roof of a *limestone* cavern.

Stalagmite A cone of calcium carbonate, similar to a *stalactite*, rising from the floor of a *limestone* cavern and formed when drops of water fall from the roof of a *limestone* cave. If the water has dripped from a *stalactite* above the stalagmite, the two may join to form a continuous pillar.

Staple crop The main crop on which a country is economically and or physically reliant. For example, the major crop grown for large-scale local consumption in South Asia is rice.

Steppe Large areas of dry grassland in the northern hemisphere – particularly found in southeast Europe and central Asia.

Strata The plural of stratum, a distinct, virtually horizontal layer of deposited material, lying parallel to other layers.

Stratosphere A layer of the *atmosphere*, above the *troposphere*, extending from about 7–30 miles (11–50 km) above the Earth's surface. In the lower part of the stratosphere, the temperature is relatively stable and there is little moisture.

Strike-slip fault Occurs where plates move sideways past each other and blocks of rocks move horizontally in relation to each other, not up or down as in normal *faults*.

Subduction zone A region where two *tectonic plates* collide, forcing one beneath the other. Typically, a dense oceanic plate dips below a lighter continental plate, melting in the heat of the *asthenosphere*. This is why the zone is also called a destructive margin (*see Plate tectonics*). These zones are characterized by *earthquakes*, volcanoes, *mountain-building*, and the development of oceanic trenches and *island arcs*.

Submarine canyon A steep-sided valley, that extends along the *continental shelf* to the ocean floor. Often formed by *turbidity currents*.

Submarine fan Deposits of silt and *alluvium*, carried by large rivers forming great fan-shaped deposits on the ocean floor.

Subsistence agriculture An agricultural practice in which enough food is produced to support the farmer and his dependents, but not providing any surplus to generate an income.

Subtropical A term applied loosely to *climates* which are nearly tropical or tropical for a part of the year – areas north or south of the *tropics* but outside the *temperate zone*.

Supercontinent A large continent that breaks up to form smaller continents or that forms when smaller continents merge. In the theory of *continental drift*, the supercontinents are *Pangaea*, *Gondwanaland*, and *Laurasia*.

Sustainable development An approach to development, especially applied to economies across the world which exploit natural resources without destroying them or the *environment*.

Syncline A basin-shaped downfold in rock *strata*, created when the *strata* are compressed, for example where *tectonic plates* collide.

T

Tableland A highland area with a flat or gently undulating surface.

Taiga The belt of *coniferous* forest found in the north of Asia and North America. The conifers are adapted to survive low temperatures and long periods of snowfall.

Tarn A Scottish term for a small mountain lake, usually found at the head of a *glacier*.

Tectonic plates Plates, or tectonic plates, are the rigid slabs which form the Earth's outer shell, the *lithosphere*. Eight big plates and several smaller ones have been identified.

Temperate A moderate *climate* without extremes of temperature, typical of the mid-*latitudes* between the *tropics* and the *polar* circles.

Theocracy A state governed by religious laws – today Iran is the world's largest theocracy.

Thermokarst Subsidence created by the thawing of ground ice in *periglacial* areas, creating depressions.

Thermosphere A layer of the Earth's *atmosphere* which lies above the *mesophere*, about 60–300 miles (100–500 km) above the Earth

Terraces Steps cut into steep slopes to create flat surfaces for cultivating crops. They also help reduce soil *erosion* on unconsolidated slopes. They are most common in heavily-populated parts of Southeast Asia.

Till Unstratified glacial deposits or drift left by a *glacier* or *ice sheet*. Till includes mixtures of clay, sand, gravel, and boulders.

Topography The typical shape and features of a given area such as land height and terrain.

Tombolo A large sand *spit* which attaches part of the mainland to an island.

Tornado A violent, spiraling windstorm, with a center of very low pressure. Wind speeds reach 200 mph (320 kmph) and there is often thunder and heavy rain.

Transform fault In *plate tectonics*, a *fault* of continental scale, occurring where two plates slide past each other, staying close together for example, the San Andreas Fault, USA. The jerky, uneven movement creates *earthquakes* but does not destroy or add to the Earth's *crust*

Transpiration The loss of water vapor through the pores (or stomata) of plants. The process helps to return moisture to the *atmosphere*.

Trap An area of fine-grained *igneous rock* that has been extruded and cooled on the Earth's surface in stages, forming a series of steps or terraces.

Treeline The line beyond which trees cannot grow, dependent on *latitude* and altitude, as well as local factors such as soil.

Tremor A slight *earthquake*.

Trench (oceanic trench) A long, deep trough in the ocean floor, formed, according to the theory of *plate tectonics*, when two plates collide and one dives under the other, creating a *subduction zone*.

Tropics The zone between the *Tropic of Cancer* and the *Tropic of Capricorn* where the *climate* is hot. Tropical climate is also applied to areas rather further north and south of the *Equator* where the climate is similar to that of the true tropics.

Tropic of Cancer A line of *latitude* or imaginary circle round the Earth, lying at 23° 28' N.

Tropic of Capricorn A line of *latitude* or imaginary circle round the Earth, lying at 23° 28' S.

Troposphere The lowest layer of the Earth's *atmosphere*. From the surface, it reaches a height of between 4–10 miles (7–16 km). It is the most turbulent zone of the atmosphere and accounts for the generation of most of the world's weather. The layer above it is called the *stratosphere*.

Tsunami A huge wave created by shock waves from an *earthquake* under the sea. Reaching speeds of up to 600 mph (960 kmph), the wave may increase to heights of 50 ft (15 m) on entering coastal waters; and it can cause great damage.

Tundra The treeless *plains* of the *Arctic Circle*, found south of the *polar* region of permanent ice and snow, and north of the belt of *coniferous* forests known as *taiga*. In this region of long, very cold winters, vegetation is usually limited to mosses, *lichens*, sedges, and rushes, although flowers and dwarf shrubs blossom in the brief summer.

Turbidity current An oceanic feature. A turbidity current is a mass of *sediment*-laden water that has substantial erosive power. Turbidity currents are thought to contribute to the formation of *submarine canyons*.

Typhoon A kind of *hurricane* (or tropical cyclone) bringing violent winds and heavy rain, a typhoon can do great damage. They occur in the South China Sea, especially around the Philippines.

U

U-shaped valley A river valley that has been deepened and widened by a *glacier*. They are characteristically flat-bottomed and steep-sided and generally much deeper than river valleys.

UN United Nations. Established in 1945, it contains 188 nations and aims to maintain international peace and security, and promote cooperation over economic, social, cultural, and humanitarian problems.

UNICEF United Nations Children's Fund. A UN organization set up to promote family and child related programs.

Urstromtäler A German word used to describe *meltwater* channels that flowed along the front edge of the advancing *ice sheet* during the last Ice Age, 18,000–20,000 years ago.

V

V-shaped valley A typical valley eroded by a river in its upper course.

Virgin rain forest Tropical *rain-forest* in its original state, untouched by human activity such as logging, clearance for agriculture, settlement, or roadbuilding.

Viticulture The cultivation of grapes for wine.

Volcano An opening or vent in the Earth's *crust* where molten rock, *magma*, erupts. Volcanoes tend to be conical but may also be a crack in the Earth's surface or a hole blasted through a mountain. The magma is accompanied by other materials such as gas, steam, and fragments of rock, or *pyroclasts*. They tend to occur on destructive or constructive tectonicplate margins.

W–Z

Wadi The dry bed left by a torrent of water. Also classified as a *ephemeral* stream, found in *arid* and *semiarid* regions, which are subject to sudden and often severe flash flooding.

Warm humid climate A rainy climate with warm summers and mild winters.

Water cycle The continuous circulation of water between the Earth's surface and the *atmosphere*. The processes include *evaporation* and *transpiration* of moisture into the atmosphere, and its return as *precipitation*, some of which flows into lakes and oceans.

Water table The upper level of *groundwater* saturation in permeable rock *strata*.

Watershed The dividing line between one *drainage basin* – an area where all streams flow into a single river system – and another. In the US, watershed also means the whole drainage basin of a single river system – its catchment area.

Waterspout A rotating column of water in the form of cloud, mist, and spray which form on open water. Often has the appearance of a small *tornado*.

Weathering The decay and breakup of rocks at or near the Earth's surface, caused by water, wind, heat or ice, organic material, or the *atmosphere*. *Physical weathering* includes the effects of frost and temperature changes. Biological weathering includes the effects of plant roots, burrowing animals and the acids produced by animals, especially as they decay after death. *Carbonation* and *hydrolysis* are among many kinds of *chemical weathering*.

Geographical Names

The following glossary lists all geographical terms occurring on the maps and in main-entry names in the Index-Gazetteer. These terms may precede, follow or be run together with the proper element of the name; where they precede it the term is reversed for indexing purposes – thus Poluostrov Yamal is indexed as Yamal, Poluostrov.

Key

Geographical term *Language*, Term

A

Å *Danish, Norwegian*, River
Āb *Persian*, River
Adrar *Berber*, Mountains
Agía, Ágios *Greek*, Saint
Air *Indonesian*, River
Ákra *Greek*, Cape, point
Alpen *German*, Alps
Alt- *German*, Old
Altiplanicie *Spanish*, Plateau
Älve(en) *Swedish*, River
-ån *Swedish*, River
Anse *French*, Bay
'Aqabat *Arabic*, Pass
Archipiélago *Spanish*, Archipelago
Arcipelago *Italian*, Archipelago
Arquipélago *Portuguese*, Archipelago
Arrecife(s) *Spanish*, Reef(s)
Aru *Tamil*, River
Augstiene *Latvian*, Upland
Aukštuma *Lithuanian*, Upland
Aust- *Norwegian*, Eastern
Avtonomnyy Okrug *Russian*, Autonomous district
Āw *Kurdish*, River
'Ayn *Arabic*, Spring, well
'Ayoûn *Arabic*, Wells

B

Baelt *Danish*, Strait
Bahía *Spanish*, Bay
Baḩr *Arabic*, River
Baía *Portuguese*, Bay
Baie *French*, Bay
Bañado *Spanish*, Marshy land
Bandao *Chinese*, Peninsula
Banjaran *Malay*, Mountain range
Barajı *Turkish*, Dam
Barragem *Portuguese*, Reservoir
Bassin *French*, Basin
Batang *Malay*, Stream
Beinn, Ben *Gaelic*, Mountain
-berg *Afrikaans, Norwegian*, Mountain
Besar *Indonesian, Malay*, Big
Birkat, Birket *Arabic*, Lake, well,
Boğazi *Turkish*, Lake
Boka *Serbo-Croatian*, Bay
Bol'sh-aya, -iye, -oy, -oye *Russian*, Big
Botigh(i) *Uzbek*, Depression basin
-bre(en) *Norwegian*, Glacier
Bredning *Danish*, Bay
Bucht *German*, Bay
Bugt(en) *Danish*, Bay
Buḩayrat *Arabic*, Lake, reservoir
Buḩeiret *Arabic*, Lake
Bukit *Malay*, Mountain
-bukta *Norwegian*, Bay
bukten *Swedish*, Bay
Bulag *Mongolian*, Spring
Bulak *Uighur*, Spring
Burnu *Turkish*, Cape, point
Buuraha *Somali*, Mountains

C

Cabo *Portuguese*, Cape
Caka *Tibetan*, Salt lake
Canal *Spanish*, Channel
Cap *French*, Cape
Capo *Italian*, Cape, headland
Cascada *Portuguese*, Waterfall
Cayo(s) *Spanish*, Islet(s), rock(s)
Cerro *Spanish*, Mountain
Chaîne *French*, Mountain range
Chapada *Portuguese*, Hills, upland
Chau *Cantonese*, Island
Chāy *Turkish*, River
Chhâk *Cambodian*, Bay
Chhu *Tibetan*, River
-chŏsuji *Korean*, Reservoir
Chott *Arabic*, Depression, salt lake
Chŭli *Uzbek*, Grassland, steppe
Ch'ün-tao *Chinese*, Island group
Chuŏr Phnum *Cambodian*, Mountains
Ciudad *Spanish*, City, town
Co *Tibetan*, Lake
Colline(s) *French*, Hill(s)
Cordillera *Spanish*, Mountain range
Costa *Spanish*, Coast
Côte *French*, Coast
Coxilha *Portuguese*, Mountains
Cuchilla *Spanish*, Mountains

D

Daban *Mongolian, Uighur*, Pass
Daği *Azerbaijani, Turkish*, Mountain
Dağlari *Azerbaijani, Turkish*, Mountains
-dake *Japanese*, Peak
-dal(en) *Norwegian*, Valley
Danau *Indonesian*, Lake
Dao *Chinese*, Island
Đao *Vietnamese*, Island
Daryā *Persian*, River
Daryācheh *Persian*, Lake
Dasht *Persian*, Desert, plain
Dawḩat *Arabic*, Bay
Denizi *Turkish*, Sea
Dere *Turkish*, Stream
Desierto *Spanish*, Desert
Dili *Azerbaijani*, Spit
-do *Korean*, Island
Dooxo *Somali*, Valley
Düzü *Azerbaijani*, Steppe
-dwīp *Bengali*, Island

E

-eilanden *Dutch*, Islands
Embalse *Spanish*, Reservoir
Ensenada *Spanish*, Bay
Erg *Arabic*, Dunes
Estany *Catalan*, Lake
Estero *Spanish*, Inlet
Estrecho *Spanish*, Strait
Étang *French*, Lagoon, lake
-ey *Icelandic*, Island
Ezero *Bulgarian, Macedonian*, Lake
Ezers *Latvian*, Lake

F

Feng *Chinese*, Peak
Fjord *Danish*, Fjord
-fjord(en) *Danish, Norwegian, Swedish*, fjord
-fjørdhur *Faeroese*, Fjord
Fleuve *French*, River
Fliegu *Maltese*, Channel
-fljór *Icelandic*, River
-flói *Icelandic*, Bay
Forêt *French*, Forest

G

-gan *Japanese*, Rock
-gang *Korean*, River
Ganga *Hindi, Nepali, Sinhala*, River
Gaoyuan *Chinese*, Plateau
Garagumy *Turkmen*, Sands
-gawa *Japanese*, River
Gebel *Arabic*, Mountain
-gebirge *German*, Mountain range
Ghadīr *Arabic*, Well
Ghubbat *Arabic*, Bay
Gjiri *Albanian*, Bay
Gol *Mongolian*, River
Golfe *French*, Gulf
Golfo *Italian, Spanish*, Gulf
Göl(ü) *Turkish*, Lake
Golyam, -a *Bulgarian*, Big
Gora *Russian, Serbo-Croatian*, Mountain
Góra *Polish*, Mountain
Gory *Russian*, Mountain
Gryada *Russian*, Ridge
Guba *Russian*, Bay
-gundo *Korean*, Island group
Gunung *Malay*, Mountain

H

Ḩadd *Arabic*, Spit
-haehyŏp *Korean*, Strait
Haff *German*, Lagoon
Hai *Chinese*, Bay, lake, sea
Haixia *Chinese*, Strait
Hamada *Arabic*, Plateau
Ḩammādat *Arabic*, Plateau
Hāmūn *Persian*, Lake
-hantō *Japanese*, Peninsula
Har, Haré *Hebrew*, Mountain
Ḩarrat *Arabic*, Lava-field
Hav(et) *Danish, Swedish*, Sea
Hawr *Arabic*, Lake
Hāyk' *Amharic*, Lake
He *Chinese*, River
-hegység *Hungarian*, Mountain range
Heide *German*, Heath, moorland
Helodrano *Malagasy*, Bay
Higashi- *Japanese*, East(ern)
Ḩişā' *Arabic*, Well
Hka *Burmese*, River
-ho *Korean*, Lake
Hô *Korean*, Reservoir
Ḩolot *Hebrew*, Dunes
Hora *Belorussian, Czech*, Mountain
Hrada *Belorussian*, Mountain, ridge
Hsi *Chinese*, River
Hu *Chinese*, Lake
Huk *Danish*, Point

I

Île(s) *French*, Island(s)
Ilha(s) *Portuguese*, Island(s)
Ilhéu(s) *Portuguese*, Islet(s)
Imeni *Russian*, In the name of
Inish- *Gaelic*, Island
Insel(n) *German*, Island(s)
Irmağı, Irmak *Turkish*, River
Isla(s) *Spanish*, Island(s)
Isola (Isole) *Italian*, Island(s)

J

Jabal *Arabic*, Mountain
Jāl *Arabic*, Ridge
-järv *Estonian*, Lake
-järvi *Finnish*, Lake
Jazā'ir *Arabic*, Islands
Jazīrat *Arabic*, Island
Jazīreh *Persian*, Island
Jebel *Arabic*, Mountain
Jezero *Serbo-Croatian*, Lake
Jezioro *Polish*, Lake
Jiang *Chinese*, River
-jima *Japanese*, Island
Jižní *Czech*, Southern
-jõgi *Estonian*, River
-joki *Finnish*, River
-jökull *Icelandic*, Glacier
Jūn *Arabic*, Bay
Juzur *Arabic*, Islands

K

Kaikyō *Japanese*, Strait
-kaise *Lappish*, Mountain
Kali *Nepali*, River
Kalnas *Lithuanian*, Mountain
Kalns *Latvian*, Mountain
Kang *Chinese*, Harbor
Kangri *Tibetan*, Mountain(s)
Kaôh *Cambodian*, Island
Kapp *Norwegian*, Cape
Káto *Greek*, Lower
Kavīr *Persian*, Desert
K'edi *Georgian*, Mountain range
Kediet *Arabic*, Mountain
Kepi *Albanian*, Cape, point
Kepulauan *Indonesian, Malay*, Island group
Khalig, Khalīj *Arabic*, Gulf
Khawr *Arabic*, Inlet
Khola *Nepali*, River
Khrebet *Russian*, Mountain range
Ko *Thai*, Island
-ko *Japanese*, Inlet, lake
Kólpos *Greek*, Bay
-kopf *German*, Peak
Körfäzi *Azerbaijani*, Bay
Körfezi *Turkish*, Bay
Kõrgustik *Estonian*, Upland
Kosa *Russian, Ukrainian*, Spit
Koshi *Nepali*, River
Kou *Chinese*, River-mouth
Kowtal *Persian*, Pass
Kray *Russian*, Region, territory
Kryazh *Russian*, Ridge
Kuduk *Uighur*, Well
Kūh(hā) *Persian*, Mountain(s)
-kul' *Russian*, Lake
Kŭl(i) *Tajik, Uzbek*, Lake
-kundo *Korean*, Island group
-kysten *Norwegian*, Coast
Kyun *Burmese*, Island

L

Laaq *Somali*, Watercourse
Lac *French*, Lake
Lacul *Romanian*, Lake
Lagh *Somali*, Stream
Lago *Italian, Portuguese, Spanish*, Lake
Lagoa *Portuguese*, Lagoon
Laguna *Italian, Spanish*, Lagoon, lake
Laht *Estonian*, Bay
Laut *Indonesian*, Bay
Lembalemba *Malagasy*, Plateau
Lerr *Armenian*, Mountain
Lerrnashght'a *Armenian*, Mountain range
Les *Czech*, Forest
Lich *Armenian*, Lake
Liehtao *Chinese*, Island group
Liqeni *Albanian*, Lake
Límni *Greek*, Lake
Ling *Chinese*, Mountain range
Llano *Spanish*, Plain, prairie
Lumi *Albanian*, River
Lyman *Ukrainian*, Estuary

M

Madīnat *Arabic*, City, town
Mae Nam *Thai*, River
-mägi *Estonian*, Hill
Maja *Albanian*, Mountain
Mal *Albanian*, Mountains
Mal-aya, -oye, -yy, *Russian*, Small
-man *Korean*, Bay
Mar *Spanish*, Lake
Marios *Lithuanian*, Lake
Massif *French*, Mountains
Meer *German*, Lake
-meer *Dutch*, Lake
Melkosopochnik *Russian*, Plain
-meri *Estonian*, Sea
Mifraz *Hebrew*, Bay
Minami- *Japanese*, South(ern)
-misaki *Japanese*, Cape, point
Monkhafad *Arabic*, Depression
Montagne(s) *French*, Mountain(s)
Montañas *Spanish*, Mountains
Mont(s) *French*, Mountain(s)
Monte *Italian, Portuguese*, Mountain
More *Russian*, Sea
Mörön *Mongolian*, River
Mys *Russian*, Cape, point

N

-nada *Japanese*, Open stretch of water
Nagor'ye *Russian*, Upland
Naḩal *Hebrew*, River
Nahr *Arabic*, River
Nam *Laotian*, River
Namakzār *Persian*, Salt desert
Né-a, -on, -os *Greek*, New
Nedre- *Norwegian*, Lower
-neem *Estonian*, Cape, point
Nehri *Turkish*, River
-nes *Norwegian*, Cape, point
Nevado *Spanish*, Mountain (snow-capped)
Nieder- *German*, Lower
Nishi- *Japanese*, West(ern)
-nísi *Greek*, Island
Nisoi *Greek*, Islands
Nizhn-eye, -iy, -iye, -yaya *Russian*, Lower
Nizmennost' *Russian*, Lowland, plain
Nord *Danish, French, German*, North
Norte *Portuguese, Spanish*, North
Nos *Bulgarian*, Point, spit
Nosy *Malagasy*, Island
Nov-a, -i, *Bulgarian, Serbo-Croatian*, New
Nov-aya, -o, -oye, -yy, -yye *Russian*, New
Now-a, -e, -y *Polish*, New
Nur *Mongolian*, Lake
Nuruu *Mongolian*, Mountains
Nuur *Mongolian*, Lake
Nyzovyna *Ukrainian*, Lowland, plain

O

-ø *Danish*, Island
Ober- *German*, Upper
Oblast' *Russian*, Province
Órmos *Greek*, Bay
Orol(i) *Uzbek*, Island
Øster- *Norwegian*, Eastern
Ostrov(a) *Russian*, Island(s)
Otok *Serbo-Croatian*, Island
Oued *Arabic*, Watercourse
-oy *Faeroese*, Island
-øy(a) *Norwegian*, Island
Oya *Sinhala*, River
Ozero *Russian, Ukrainian*, Lake

P

Passo *Italian*, Pass
Pegunungan *Indonesian, Malay*, Mountain range
Pélagos *Greek*, Sea
Pendi *Chinese*, Basin
Penisola *Italian*, Peninsula
Pertuis *French*, Strait
Peski *Russian*, Sands
Phanom *Thai*, Mountain
Phou *Laotian*, Mountain
Pi *Chinese*, Point
Pic *Catalan, French*, Peak
Pico *Portuguese, Spanish*, Peak
-piggen *Danish*, Peak
Pik *Russian*, Peak
Pivostriv *Ukrainian*, Peninsula
Planalto *Portuguese*, Plateau
Planina, Planini *Bulgarian, Macedonian, Serbo-Croatian*, Mountain range
Plato *Russian*, Plateau
Ploskogor'ye *Russian*, Upland
Poluostrov *Russian*, Peninsula
Ponta *Portuguese*, Point
Porthmós *Greek*, Strait
Pótamos *Greek*, River
Presa *Spanish*, Dam
Prokhod *Bulgarian*, Pass
Proliv *Russian*, Strait
Pulau *Indonesian, Malay*, Island
Pulu *Malay*, Island
Punta *Spanish*, Point
Pushcha *Belarussian*, Forest
Puszcza *Polish*, Forest

Q

Qā' *Arabic*, Depression
Qalamat *Arabic*, Well
Qatorkŭh(i) *Tajik*, Mountain
Qiuling *Chinese*, Hills
Qolleh *Persian*, Mountain
Qu *Tibetan*, Stream
Quan *Chinese*, Well
Qulla(i) *Tajik*, Peak
Qundao *Chinese*, Island group

R

Raas *Somali*, Cape
-rags *Latvian*, Cape
Ramlat *Arabic*, Sands
Ra's *Arabic*, Cape, headland, point
Ravnina *Bulgarian, Russian*, Plain
Récif *French*, Reef
Recife *Portuguese*, Reef
Reka *Bulgarian*, River
Represa (Rep.) *Portuguese, Spanish*, Reservoir
Reshteh *Persian*, Mountain range
Respublika *Russian*, Republic, first-order administrative division
Respublika(si) *Uzbek*, Republic, first-order administrative division
-retsugan *Japanese*, Chain of rocks
-rettō *Japanese*, Island chain
Riacho *Spanish*, Stream
Riban' *Malagasy*, Mountains
Rio *Portuguese*, River
Río *Spanish*, River
Riu *Catalan*, River
Rivier *Dutch*, River
Rivière *French*, River
Rowd *Pashtu*, River
Rt *Serbo-Croatian*, Point
Rūd *Persian*, River
Rūdkhāneh *Persian*, River
Rudohorie *Slovak*, Mountains
Ruisseau *French*, Stream

S

-saar *Estonian*, Island
-saari *Finnish*, Island
Sabkhat *Arabic*, Salt marsh
Sāgar(a) *Hindi*, Lake, reservoir
Şaḩrā' *Arabic*, Desert
Saint, Sainte *French*, Saint
Salar *Spanish*, Salt-pan
Salto *Portuguese, Spanish*, Waterfall
Samudra *Sinhala*, Reservoir
-san *Japanese, Korean*, Mountain
-sanchi *Japanese*, Mountains
-sandur *Icelandic*, Beach
Sankt *German, Swedish*, Saint
-sanmaek *Korean*, Mountain range
-sanmyaku *Japanese*, Mountain range
San, Santa, Santo *Italian, Portuguese, Spanish*, Saint
São *Portuguese*, Saint
Sarīr *Arabic*, Desert
Sebkha, Sebkhet *Arabic*, Depression, salt marsh
Sedlo *Czech*, Pass
See *German*, Lake
Selat *Indonesian*, Strait
Selatan *Indonesian*, Southern
-selkä *Finnish*, Lake, ridge
Selseleh *Persian*, Mountain range
Serra *Portuguese*, Mountain
Serranía *Spanish*, Mountain
-seto *Japanese*, Channel, strait
Sever-naya, -noye, -nyy, -o *Russian*, Northern
Sha'īb *Arabic*, Watercourse
Shākh *Kurdish*, Mountain
Shamo *Chinese*, Desert
Shan *Chinese*, Mountain(s)
Shankou *Chinese*, Pass
Shanmo *Chinese*, Mountain range
Shaţţ *Arabic*, Distributary
Shet' *Amharic*, River
Shi *Chinese*, Municipality
-shima *Japanese*, Island
Shiqqat *Arabic*, Depression
-shotō *Japanese*, Group of islands
Shuiku *Chinese*, Reservoir
Shūrkhog(i) *Uzbek*, Salt marsh
Sierra *Spanish*, Mountains
Sint *Dutch*, Saint
-sjø(en) *Norwegian*, Lake
-sjön *Swedish*, Lake
Solonchak *Russian*, Salt lake
Solonchakovyye Vpadiny *Russian*, Salt basin, wetlands
Sơn *Vietnamese*, Mountain
Sông *Vietnamese*, River
Sør- *Norwegian*, Southern
-spitze *German*, Peak
Star-á, -é *Czech*, Old
Star-aya, -oye, -yy, -yye *Russian*, Old
Stenó *Greek*, Strait
Step' *Russian*, Steppe
Štít *Slovak*, Peak
Stœng *Cambodian*, River
Stolovaya Strana *Russian*, Plateau
Stredné *Slovak*, Middle
Střední *Czech*, Middle
Stretto *Italian*, Strait
Su Anbari *Azerbaijani*, Reservoir
-suidō *Japanese*, Channel, strait
Sund *Swedish*, Sound, strait
Sungai *Indonesian, Malay*, River
Suu *Turkish*, River

T

Tal *Mongolian*, Plain
Tandavan' *Malagasy*, Mountain range
Tangorombohitr' *Malagasy*, Mountain massif
Tanjung *Indonesian, Malay*, Cape, point
Tao *Chinese*, Island
Ţaraq *Arabic*, Hills
Tassili *Berber*, Mountain, plateau
Tau *Russian*, Mountain(s)
Taungdan *Burmese*, Mountain range
Techníti Límni *Greek*, Reservoir
Tekojärvi *Finnish*, Reservoir
Teluk *Indonesian, Malay*, Bay
Tengah *Indonesian*, Middle
Terara *Amharic*, Mountain
Timur *Indonesian*, Eastern
-tind(an) *Norwegian*, Peak
Tizma(si) *Uzbek*, Mountain range, ridge
-tō *Japanese*, Island
Tog *Somali*, Valley
-tōge *Japanese*, Pass
Togh(i) *Uzbek*, Mountain
Tônlé *Cambodian*, Lake
Top *Dutch*, Peak
-tunturi *Finnish*, Mountain
Ţurāq *Arabic*, Hills
Tur'at *Arabic*, Channel

U

Udde(n) *Swedish*, Cape, point
'Uqlat *Arabic*, Well
Utara *Indonesian*, Northern
Uul *Mongolian*, Mountains

V

Väin *Estonian*, Strait
Vallée *French*, Valley
-vatn *Icelandic*, Lake
-vatnet *Norwegian*, Lake
Velayat *Turkmen*, Province
-vesi *Finnish*, Lake
Vestre- *Norwegian*, Western
-vidda *Norwegian*, Plateau
-vík *Icelandic*, Bay
-viken *Swedish*, Bay, inlet
Vinh *Vietnamese*, Bay
Víztárloló *Hungarian*, Reservoir
Vodaskhovishcha *Belarussian*, Reservoir
Vodokhranilishche (Vdkhr.) *Russian*, Reservoir
Vodoskhovyshche (Vdskh.) *Ukrainian*, Reservoir
Volcán *Spanish*, Volcano
Vostochn-o, yy *Russian*, Eastern
Vozvyshennost' *Russian*, Upland, plateau
Vozyera *Belarussian*, Lake
Vpadina *Russian*, Depression
Vrchovina *Czech*, Mountains
Vrha *Macedonian*, Peak
Vychodné *Slovak*, Eastern
Vysochyna *Ukrainian*, Upland
Vysočina *Czech*, Upland

W

Waadi *Somali*, Watercourse
Wādī *Arabic* Watercourse
Wāḩat, Wâhat *Arabic*, Oasis
Wald *German*, Forest
Wan *Chinese*, Bay
Way *Indonesian*, River
Webi *Somali*, River
Wenz *Amharic*, River
Wiloyat(i) *Uzbek*, Province
Wyżyna *Polish*, Upland
Wzgórza *Polish*, Upland
Wzvyshsha *Belarussian*, Upland

X

Xé *Laotian*, River
Xi *Chinese*, Stream

Y

-yama *Japanese*, Mountain
Yanchi *Chinese*, Salt lake
Yang *Chinese*, Bay
Yanhu *Chinese*, Salt lake
Yarımadası *Azerbaijani, Turkish*, Peninsula
Yaylası *Turkish*, Plateau
Yazovir *Bulgarian*, Reservoir
Yoma *Burmese*, Mountains
Ytre- *Norwegian*, Outer
Yü *Chinese*, Island
Yunhe *Chinese*, Canal
Yuzhn-o, -yy *Russian*, Southern

Z

-zaki *Japanese*, Cape, point
Zaliv *Bulgarian, Russian*, Bay
-zan *Japanese*, Mountain
Zangbo *Tibetan*, River
Zapadn-aya, -o, -yy *Russian*, Western
Západné *Slovak*, Western
Západní *Czech*, Western
Zatoka *Polish, Ukrainian*, Bay
-zee *Dutch*, Sea
Zemlya *Russian*, Earth, land
Zizhiqu *Chinese*, Autonomous region

Index

Glossary of Abbreviations

This glossary provides a comprehensive guide to the abbreviations used in this Atlas, and in the Index.

A
abbrev. abbreviated
AD Anno Domini
Afr. Afrikaans
Alb. Albanian
Amh. Amharic
anc. ancient
approx. approximately
Ar. Arabic
Arm. Armenian
ASEAN Association of South East Asian Nations
ASSR Autonomous Soviet Socialist Republic
Aust. Australian
Az. Azerbaijani
Azerb. Azerbaijan

B
Basq. Basque
BC before Christ
Bel. Belorussian
Ben. Bengali
Ber. Berber
B-H Bosnia-Herzegovina
bn billion (one thousand million)
BP British Petroleum
Bret. Breton
Brit. British
Bul. Bulgarian
Bur. Burmese

C
C central
C. Cape
°C degrees Centigrade
CACM Central America Common Market
Cam. Cambodian
Cant. Cantonese
CAR Central African Republic
Cast. Castilian
Cat. Catalan
CEEAC Central America Common Market
Chin. Chinese
CIS Commonwealth of Independent States
cm centimeter(s)
Cro. Croat
Cz. Czech
Czech Rep. Czech Republic

D
Dan. Danish
Div. Divehi
Dom. Rep. Dominican Republic
Dut. Dutch

E
E east
EC *see* EU
EEC *see* EU
ECOWAS Economic Community of West African States
ECU European Currency Unit
EMS European Monetary System
Eng. English
est estimated
Est. Estonian
EU European Union (previously European Community [EC], European Economic Community [EEC])

F
°F degrees Fahrenheit
Faer. Faeroese
Fij. Fijian
Fin. Finnish
Fr. French
Fris. Frisian
ft foot/feet
FYROM Former Yugoslav Republic of Macedonia

G
g gram(s)
Gael. Gaelic
Gal. Galician
GDP Gross Domestic Product (the total value of goods and services produced by a country excluding income from foreign countries)
Geor. Georgian
Ger. German
Gk Greek
GNP Gross National Product (the total value of goods and services produced by a country)

H
Heb. Hebrew
HEP hydroelectric power
Hind. Hindi
hist. historical
Hung. Hungarian

I
I. Island
Icel. Icelandic
in inch(es)
In. Inuit (Eskimo)
Ind. Indonesian
Intl International
Ir. Irish
Is Islands
It. Italian

J
Jap. Japanese

K
Kaz. Kazakh
kg kilogram(s)
Kir. Kirghiz
km kilometer(s)
km² square kilometer (singular)
Kor. Korean
Kurd. Kurdish

L
L. Lake
LAIA Latin American Integration Association
Lao. Laotian
Lapp. Lappish
Lat. Latin
Latv. Latvian
Liech. Liechtenstein
Lith. Lithuanian
Lux. Luxembourg

M
m million/meter(s)
Mac. Macedonian
Maced. Macedonia
Mal. Malay
Malg. Malagasy
Malt. Maltese
mi. mile(s)
Mong. Mongolian
Mt. Mountain
Mts Mountains

N
N north
NAFTA North American Free Trade Agreement
Nep. Nepali
Neth. Netherlands
Nic. Nicaraguan
Nor. Norwegian
NZ New Zealand

P
Pash. Pashtu
PNG Papua New Guinea
Pol. Polish
Poly. Polynesian
Port. Portuguese
prev. previously

R
Rep. Republic
Res. Reservoir
Rmsch Romansch
Rom. Romanian
Rus. Russian
Russ. Fed. Russian Federation

S
S south
SADC Southern Africa Development Community
SCr. Serbian/Croatian
Sinh. Sinhala
Slvk Slovak
Slvn. Slovene
Som. Somali
Sp. Spanish
St., St Saint
Strs Straits
Swa. Swahili
Swe. Swedish
Switz. Switzerland

T
Taj. Tajik
Th. Thai
Thai. Thailand
Tib. Tibetan
Turk. Turkish
Turkm. Turkmenistan

U
UAE United Arab Emirates
Uigh. Uighur
UK United Kingdom
Ukr. Ukrainian
UN United Nations
Urd. Urdu
US/USA United States of America
USSR Union of Soviet Socialist Republics
Uzb. Uzbek

V
var. variant
Vdkhr. Vodokhranilishche (Russian for reservoir)
Vdskh. Vodoskhovyshche (Ukrainian for reservoir)
Vtn. Vietnamese

W
W west
Wel. Welsh

Y
Yugo. Yugoslavia

This index lists all the placenames and features shown on the regional and continental maps in this Atlas. Placenames are referenced to the largest scale map on which they appear. The policy followed throughout the Atlas is to use the local spelling or local name at regional level; commonly-used English language names may occasionally be added (in parentheses) where this is an aid to identification e.g. Firenze (Florence). English names, where they exist, have been used for all international features e.g. oceans and country names; they are also used on the continental maps and in the introductory World Today section; these are then fully cross-referenced to the local names found on the regional maps. The index also contains commonly-found alternative names and variant spellings, which are also fully cross-referenced.

All main entry names are those of settlements unless otherwise indicated by the use of italicized definitions or representative symbols, which are keyed at the foot of each page.

1

25 de Mayo *see* Veinticinco de Mayo
137 *Y13* **26** *Bakı Komissarı* ***Rus.*** Imeni 26 *Bakinskikh Komissarov. SE Azerbaijan*
26 *Baku Komissarlary Adyndaky see* Imeni 26 *Bakinskikh Komissarov*
10 *M16* **100** *Mile House* **var.** Hundred Mile House. British Columbia, SW Canada

A

Aa *see* Gauja
Aabenraa *see* Åbenrå
Aabybro *see* Åbybro
101 *C16* **Aachen** ***Dut.*** Aken, ***Fr.*** Aix-la-Chapelle; ***anc.*** Aquae Grani, Aquisgranum. Nordrhein-Westfalen, W Germany
Aaiún *see* Laâyoune
Aakirkeby *see* Åkirkeby
Aalborg *see* Ålborg
Aalborg Bugt *see* Ålborg Bugt
101 *J21* **Aalen** Baden-Württemberg, S Germany
Aalestrup *see* Ålestrup
98 *I11* **Aalsmeer** Noord-Holland, C Netherlands
99 *F18* **Aalst** ***Fr.*** Alost. Oost-Vlaanderen, C Belgium
99 *K18* **Aalst** Noord-Brabant, S Netherlands
98 *O12* **Aalten** Gelderland, E Netherlands
99 *D17* **Aalter** Oost-Vlaanderen, NW Belgium
Aanaar *see* Inari
Aanaarjävri *see* I narijärvi
93 *M17* **Äänekoski** Länsi-Suomi, W Finland
138 *H7* **Aanjar** ***var.*** 'Anjar. C Lebanon
83 *G21* **Aansluit** Northern Cape, N South Africa
Aar *see* Aare
108 *F7* **Aarau** Aargau, N Switzerland
108 *D8* **Aarberg** Bern, W Switzerland
99 *D16* **Aardenburg** Zeeland, SW Netherlands
108 *D8* **Aare** ***var.*** Aar. ≈ W Switzerland
108 *F7* **Aargau** ***Fr.*** Argovie. ◈ *canton* N Switzerland
Aarhus *see* Århus
Aarlen *see* Arlon
Aars *see* Års
99 *I17* **Aarschot** Vlaams Brabant, C Belgium
Aassi, Nahr el *see* Orontes
Aat *see* Ath
160 *G7* **Aba** ***prev.*** Ngawa. Sichuan, C China
77 *V17* **Aba** Abia, S Nigeria
79 *P16* **Aba** Orientale, NE Dem. Rep. Congo (Zaire)
140 *J6* **Abā al Qazāz, Bi'r** *well* NW Saudi Arabia
Abā as Su'ūd *see* Najrān
59 *G14* **Abacaxis, Rio** ≈ NW Brazil
Abaco Island *see* Great Abaco/Little Abaco
Abaco Island *see* Great Abaco, N Bahamas
142 *K10* **Ābādān** Khūzestān, SW Iran
143 *O10* **Ābādeh** Fārs, C Iran
74 *H8* **Abadla** W Algeria
59 *M20* **Abaeté** Minas Gerais, SE Brazil
163 *Q10* **Abag Qi** ***var.*** Xin Hot. Nei Mongol Zizhiqu, N China
62 *P7* **Abaí** Caazapá, S Paraguay
191 *O2* **Abaiang** ***var.*** Apia; ***prev.*** Charlotte Island. *atoll* Tungaru, W Kiribati
Abaj *see* Abay
77 *U15* **Abaji** Federal Capital District, C Nigeria
37 *O7* **Abajo Peak** ▲ Utah, W USA
77 *V16* **Abakaliki** Ebonyi, SE Nigeria
122 *K13* **Abakan** Respublika Khakasiya, S Russian Federation
77 *S11* **Abala** Tillabéri, SW Niger
77 *U11* **Abalak** Tahoua, C Niger
119 *N14* **Abalyanka** ***Rus.*** Obolyanka. ≈ N Belarus
122 *L12* **Aban** Krasnoyarskiy Kray, S Russian Federation
143 *P9* **Āb Anbār-e Kān Sorkh** Yazd, C Iran
57 *G16* **Abancay** Apurímac, SE Peru
190 *H2* **Abaokoro** *atoll* Tungaru, W Kiribati
Abariringa *see* Kanton
143 *P10* **Abarkū** Yazd, C Iran
165 *V3* **Abashiri** ***var.*** Abasiri. Hokkaidō, NE Japan
165 *U3* **Abashiri-ko** ◎ Hokkaidō, NE Japan
Abasiri *see* Abashiri
41 *P10* **Abasolo** Tamaulipas, C Mexico
186 *F9* **Abau** Central, S PNG
145 *R10* **Abay** ***var.*** Abaj. Karaganda, C Kazakhstan
81 *I15* **Ābaya Hāyk'** ***Eng.*** Lake Margherita, ***It.*** Abbaia. ◎ SW Ethiopia
Ābay Wenz *see* Blue Nile
122 *K13* **Abaza** Respublika Khakasiya, S Russian Federation
Abbaia *see* Ābaya Hāyk'
143 *Q13* **Āb Bārīk** Fārs, S Iran
107 *C18* **Abbasanta** Sardegna, Italy, C Mediterranean Sea
Abbatis Villa *see* Abbeville
30 *M3* **Abbaye, Point** *headland* Michigan, N USA
Abbazia *see* Opatija
Abbé, Lake *see* Abhe, Lake
103 *N2* **Abbeville** ***anc.*** Abbatis Villa. Somme, N France
23 *R7* **Abbeville** Alabama, S USA
23 *U6* **Abbeville** Georgia, SE USA
22 *I9* **Abbeville** Louisiana, S USA
21 *P12* **Abbeville** South Carolina, SE USA
97 *B20* **Abbeyfeale** ***Ir.*** Mainistir na Féile. SW Ireland
106 *D8* **Abbiategrasso** Lombardia, NW Italy
93 *I14* **Abborrträsk** Norrbotten, N Sweden
194 *J9* **Abbot Ice Shelf** *ice shelf* Antarctica
10 *M17* **Abbotsford** British Columbia, SW Canada
30 *K6* **Abbotsford** Wisconsin, N USA
149 *U5* **Abbottābād** North-West Frontier Province, NW Pakistan
119 *M14* **Abchuha** ***Rus.*** Obchuga. Minskaya Voblasts', NW Belarus
98 *I10* **Abcoude** Utrecht, C Netherlands
139 *N2* **'Abd al 'Azīz, Jabal** ▲ NE Syria
141 *U17* **'Abd al Kūrī** *island* SE Yemen
139 *Z13* **'Abd Allāh, Khawr** *bay* Iraq/Kuwait
129 *U6* **Abdulino** Orenburgskaya Oblast', W Russian Federation
78 *J10* **Abéché** ***var.*** Abécher, Abeshr. Ouaddaï, SE Chad
Abécher *see* Abéché
143 *S8* **Āb-e Garm va Sard** Khorāsān, E Iran
77 *R8* **Abeïbara** Kidal, NE Mali
105 *P5* **Abejar** Castilla-León, N Spain
54 *E9* **Abejorral** Antioquia, W Colombia
Abela *see* Ávila
Abellinum *see* Avellino
92 *Q2* **Abeløya** *island* Kong Karls Land, E Svalbard
80 *I13* **Ābeltī** Oromo, C Ethiopia
191 *O2* **Abemama** ***var.*** Apamama; ***prev.*** Roger Simpson Island. *atoll* Tungaru, W Kiribati
171 *Y15* **Abemaree** ***var.*** Abemarre. Irian Jaya, E Indonesia
77 *O16* **Abengourou** E Ivory Coast
95 *G24* **Åbenrå** ***var.*** Aabenraa, ***Ger.*** Apenrade. Sønderjylland, SW Denmark
101 *L22* **Abens** ≈ SE Germany
77 *S16* **Abeokuta** Ogun, SW Nigeria
97 *I20* **Aberaeron** SW Wales, UK
Aberbrothock *see* Arbroath
Abercorn *see* Mbala
29 *R6* **Abercrombie** North Dakota, N USA
183 *T7* **Aberdeen** New South Wales, SE Australia
11 *T15* **Aberdeen** Saskatchewan, S Canada
83 *H25* **Aberdeen** Eastern Cape, S South Africa
96 *L9* **Aberdeen** ***anc.*** Devana. NE Scotland, UK
21 *X2* **Aberdeen** Maryland, NE USA
23 *N3* **Aberdeen** Mississippi, S USA
21 *T10* **Aberdeen** North Carolina, SE USA
29 *P8* **Aberdeen** South Dakota, N USA
32 *F8* **Aberdeen** Washington, NW USA
96 *K9* **Aberdeen** *cultural region* NE Scotland, UK
8 *L8* **Aberdeen Lake** ◎ Nunavut, NE Canada
96 *J10* **Aberfeldy** C Scotland, UK
97 *K21* **Abergavenny** ***anc.*** Gobannium. SE Wales, UK
Abergwaun *see* Fishguard
Abermarre *see* Abemaree
25 *N5* **Abernathy** Texas, SW USA
Abersee *see* Wolfgangsee
Abertawe *see* Swansea
Aberteifi *see* Cardigan
32 *I15* **Abert, Lake** ◎ Oregon, NW USA
97 *I20* **Aberystwyth** W Wales, UK
Abeshr *see* Abéché
106 *F10* **Abetone** Toscana, C Italy
127 *V5* **Abez'** Respublika Komi, NW Russian Federation
142 *M5* **Āb Garm** Qazvin, N Iran
141 *N12* **Abhā** 'Asīr, SW Saudi Arabia
142 *M5* **Abhar** Zanjān, NW Iran
Abhé Bad/Ābhē Bid Hāyk' *see* Abhe, Lake
80 *K12* **Abhe, Lake** ***var.*** Lake Abbé, ***Amh.*** Ābhē Bid Hāyk', ***Som.*** Abhé Bad. ◎ Djibouti/Ethiopia
77 *V17* **Abia** ◈ *state* SE Nigeria
139 *V9* **'Abīd 'Alī** E Iraq
119 *O17* **Abidavichy** ***Rus.*** Obidovichi. Mahilyowskaya Voblasts', E Belarus
115 *L15* **Abide** Çanakkale, NW Turkey
77 *N17* **Abidjan** S Ivory Coast
Āb-i-Istāda *see* Īstādeh-ye Moqor, Āb-e-
27 *N4* **Abilene** Kansas, C USA
25 *Q7* **Abilene** Texas, SW USA
Abindonia *see* Abingdon
97 *M21* **Abingdon** ***anc.*** Abindonia. S England, UK
30 *K12* **Abingdon** Illinois, N USA
21 *P8* **Abingdon** Virginia, NE USA
Abingdon *see* Pinta, Isla
18 *J15* **Abington** Pennsylvania, NE USA
128 *K14* **Abinsk** Krasnodarskiy Kray, SW Russian Federation
37 *R9* **Abiquiu Reservoir** ▣ New Mexico, SW USA
92 *I10* **Abisko** Norrbotten, N Sweden
12 *G12* **Abitibi** ≈ Ontario, S Canada
12 *H12* **Abitibi, Lac** ◎ Ontario/Quebec, S Canada
80 *J10* **Ābīy Ādī** Tigray, N Ethiopia
118 *H6* **Abja-Paluoja** Viljandimaa, S Estonia
137 *Q8* **Abkhazia** ◈ *autonomous republic* NW Georgia
182 *F1* **Abminga** South Australia
75 *W9* **Abnûb** C Egypt
Åbo *see* Turku
152 *G9* **Abohar** Punjab, N India
77 *O17* **Aboisso** SE Ivory Coast
78 *H5* **Abo, Massif d'** ▲ NW Chad
77 *R16* **Abomey** S Benin
79 *F16* **Abong Mbang** Est, SE Cameroon
111 *L23* **Abony** Pest, C Hungary
78 *J11* **Abou-Déïa** Salamat, SE Chad
Aboudouhour *see* Abū aḍ Ḍuhūr
Abou Kémal *see* Abū Kamāl
Abou Simbel *see* Abu Simbel
137 *T12* **Abovyan** C Armenia
171 *O2* **Abra** ≈ Luzon, N Philippines
141 *P15* **Abrād, Wādī** *seasonal river* W Yemen
Abraham Bay *see* The Carlton
104 *G10* **Abrantes** ***var.*** Abrántes. Santarém, C Portugal
62 *J4* **Abra Pampa** Jujuy, N Argentina
Abrashlare *see* Brezovo
54 *G7* **Abrego** Norte de Santander, N Colombia
Abrene *see* Pytalovo
40 *C7* **Abreojos, Punta** *headland* W Mexico
65 *J16* **Abrolhos Bank** *undersea feature* W Atlantic Ocean
119 *H19* **Abrova** ***Rus.*** Obrovo. Brestskaya Voblasts', SW Belarus
116 *G11* **Abrud** ***Ger.*** Gross-Schlatten, ***Hung.*** Abrudbánya. Alba, SW Romania
Abrudbánya *see* Abrud
118 *E6* **Abruka** *island* SW Estonia
107 *J15* **Abruzzese, Appennino** ▲ C Italy
107 *J14* **Abruzzo** ◈ *region* C Italy
141 *N14* **'Abs** ***var.*** Sūq 'Abs. W Yemen
33 *T12* **Absaroka Range** ▲ Montana/Wyoming, NW USA
137 *Z11* **Abşeron Yarımadası** ***Rus.*** Apsheronskiy Poluostrov. *peninsula* E Azerbaijan
143 *N6* **Āb Shīrīn** Eşfahān, C Iran
139 *X10* **Abtān** SE Iraq
109 *R6* **Abtenau** Salzburg, NW Austria
164 *E12* **Abu** Yamaguchi, Honshū, SW Japan
152 *E14* **Ābu** Rājasthān, N India
138 *I4* **Abū aḍ Ḍuhūr** ***Fr.*** Aboudouhour. Idlib, NW Syria
143 *P17* **Abū al Abyaḍ** *island* C UAE
138 *K10* **Abū al Ḥuṣayn, Khabrat** ◎ N Jordan
139 *R8* **Abū al Jīr** C Iraq
139 *Y12* **Abū al Khaṣīb** ***var.*** Abul Khasib. SE Iraq
139 *U12* **Abū at Tubrah, Thaqb** *well* S Iraq
75 *V11* **Abu Balâs** ▲ SW Egypt
Abu Dhabi *see* Abū Ẓaby
139 *R8* **Abū Farūkh** C Iraq
80 *C12* **Abu Gabra** Southern Darfur, W Sudan
139 *P10* **Abū Ghār, Sha'īb** *dry watercourse* S Iraq
80 *G7* **Abu Hamed** River Nile, N Sudan
139 *O5* **Abū Ḥardān** ***var.*** Hajîne. Dayr az Zawr, E Syria
139 *T7* **Abū Ḥāssawīyah** E Iraq
138 *K10* **Abū Ḥifnah, Wādī** *dry watercourse* N Jordan
77 *V15* **Abuja** ● (Nigeria) Federal Capital District, C Nigeria
139 *R9* **Abū Jahaf, Wādī** *dry watercourse* C Iraq
56 *F12* **Abujao, Río** ≈ E Peru
139 *U12* **Abū Jasrah** S Iraq
139 *O6* **Abū Kamāl** ***Fr.*** Abou Kémal. Dayr az Zawr, E Syria
165 *P12* **Abukuma-sanchi** ▲ Honshū, C Japan
Abula *see* Ávila
Abul Khasib *see* Abū al Khaṣīb
79 *K16* **Abumombazi** ***var.*** Abumonbazi. Equateur, N Dem. Rep. Congo (Zaire)
Abumonbazi *see* Abumombazi
59 *D15* **Abunã** Rondônia, W Brazil
56 *K13* **Abunã, Rio** ***var.*** Río Abuná. ≈ Bolivia/Brazil
138 *G10* **Abū Nuşayr** ***var.*** Abu Nuseir. 'Ammān, W Jordan
Abu Nuseir *see* Abū Nuşayr
139 *T12* **Abū Qabr** S Iraq
138 *K5* **Abū Raḥbah, Jabal** ▲ C Syria
139 *S5* **Abū Rajāsh** N Iraq

◆ Country ● Country Capital ◇ Dependent Territory ○ Dependent Territory Capital ◈ Administrative Region ✈ International Airport ▲ Mountain ▲ Mountain Range Volcano ≈ River ◎ Lake ▣ Reservoir

139 W13 **Abū Raqrāq, Ghadīr** *well* S Iraq
152 E14 **Ābu Road** Rājasthān, N India
80 I6 **Abu Shagara, Ras** *headland* NE Sudan
75 W12 **Abu Simbel** *var.* Abou Simbel, Abū Sunbul. *ancient monument* S Egypt
139 U12 **Abū Sudayrah** S Iraq
139 T10 **Abū Şukhayr** S Iraq
Abū Sunbul *see* Abu Simbel
165 R4 **Abuta** Hokkaidō, NE Japan
185 E18 **Abut Head** *headland* South Island, NZ
80 E9 **Abu 'Urug** Northern Kordofan, C Sudan
80 K12 **Ābuyē Mēda** ▲ C Ethiopia
80 D11 **Abu Zabad** Western Kordofan, C Sudan
Abū Ẓabī *see* Abū Ẓaby
143 P16 **Abū Ẓaby** *var.* Abū Ẓabī, *Eng.* Abu Dhabi. ● (UAE) Abū Ẓaby, C UAE
75 X8 **Abu Zenima** E Egypt
95 N17 **Åby** Östergötland, S Sweden
Abyaḍ, Al Baḥr al *see* White Nile
95 G20 **Åbybro** *var.* Aabybro. Nordjylland, N Denmark
80 D13 **Abyei** Western Kordofan, S Sudan
Abyla *see* Ávila
Abymes *see* les Abymes
Abyssinia *see* Ethiopia
Açâba *see* Assaba
54 F11 **Acacias** Meta, C Colombia
58 L13 **Açailandia** Maranhão, E Brazil
Acaill *see* Achill Island
42 E8 **Acajutla** Sonsonate, W El Salvador
79 D17 **Acalayong** SW Equatorial Guinea
41 N13 **Acámbaro** Guanajuato, C Mexico
54 C6 **Acandí** Chocó, NW Colombia
104 H4 **A Cañiza** *var.* La Cañiza. Galicia, NW Spain
40 J11 **Acaponeta** Nayarit, C Mexico
40 J11 **Acaponeta, Río de** ≈ C Mexico
41 O16 **Acapulco** *var.* Acapulco de Juárez. Guerrero, S Mexico
Acapulco de Juárez *see* Acapulco
55 T13 **Acarai Mountains** *Sp.* Serra Acaraí. ▲ Brazil/Guyana
Acaraí, Serra *see* Acarai Mountains
58 O13 **Acaraú** Ceará, NE Brazil
54 J6 **Acarigua** Portuguesa, N Venezuela
42 C6 **Acatenango, Volcán de** ※ S Guatemala
41 Q15 **Acatlán** *var.* Acatlán de Osorio. Puebla, S Mexico
Acatlán de Osorio *see* Acatlán
41 S15 **Acayucan** *var.* Acayucán. Veracruz-Llave, E Mexico
Accho *see* 'Akko
21 Y5 **Accomac** Virginia, NE USA
77 Q17 **Accra** ● (Ghana) SE Ghana
97 L17 **Accrington** NW England, UK
61 B19 **Acebal** Santa Fe, C Argentina
101 H8 **Aceh** *off.* Daerah Istimewa Aceh, *var.* Acheen, Achin, Atchin, Atjeh. ◐ *autonomous district* NW Indonesia
107 M18 **Acerenza** Basilicata, S Italy
107 K17 **Acerra** *anc.* Acerrae. Campania, S Italy
Acerrae *see* Acerra
Ach'asar Lerr *see* Achkasar
57 J17 **Achacachi** La Paz, W Bolivia
54 K7 **Achaguas** Apure, C Venezuela
154 H12 **Achalpur** *prev.* Elichpur, Ellichpur. Mahārāshtra, C India
61 F18 **Achar** Tacuarembó, C Uruguay
115 H19 **Acharnés** *var.* Aharnes; *prev.* Akharnaí. Attikí, C Greece
Acheen *see* Aceh
99 K16 **Achel** Limburg, NE Belgium
115 D16 **Achelóos** *var.* Akhelóös, Aspropótamos; *anc.* Achelous. ≈ W Greece
Achelous *see* Achelóos
163 W8 **Acheng** Heilongjiang, NE China
109 N6 **Achenkirch** Tirol, W Austria
101 L24 **Achenpass** *pass* Austria/Germany
109 N7 **Achensee** ◎ W Austria
101 F22 **Achern** Baden-Württemberg, SW Germany
115 C16 **Acherón** ≈ W Greece
77 W11 **Achétinamou** ≈ S Niger
152 J12 **Achhnera** Uttar Pradesh, N India
42 C7 **Achiguate, Río** ≈ S Guatemala
97 A16 **Achill Head** *Ir.* Ceann Acla. *headland* W Ireland
97 A16 **Achill Island** *Ir.* Acaill. *island* W Ireland
100 H11 **Achim** Niedersachsen, NW Germany
149 S5 **Achīn** Nangarhār, E Afghanistan
Achin *see* Aceh
122 K12 **Achinsk** Krasnoyarskiy Kray, S Russian Federation
162 E5 **Achit Nuur** ◎ NW Mongolia
137 T11 **Achkasar** *Arm.* Ach'asar Lerr. ▲ Armenia/Georgia
128 K13 **Achuyevo** Krasnodarskiy Kray, SW Russian Federation
81 F16 **Achwa** *var.* Aswa. ≈ N Uganda
136 E15 **Acıgöl** *salt lake* SW Turkey
107 L24 **Acireale** Sicilia, Italy, C Mediterranean Sea
Aciris *see* Agri
25 N7 **Ackerly** Texas, SW USA
22 M4 **Ackerman** Mississippi, S USA
29 W13 **Ackley** Iowa, C USA
44 J5 **Acklins Island** *island* SE Bahamas
Acla, Ceann *see* Achill Head
62 H11 **Aconcagua, Cerro** ▲ W Argentina
Açores/Açores, Arquipélago dos/Açores, Ilhas dos *see* Azores
104 G2 **A Coruña** *Cast.* La Coruña. ◐ *province* Galicia, NW Spain
104 H2 **A Coruña** *Cast.* La Coruña, *Eng.* Corunna; *anc.* Caronium. Galicia, NW Spain
42 L10 **Acoyapa** Chontales, S Nicaragua
106 H13 **Acquapendente** Lazio, C Italy
106 J13 **Acquasanta Terme** Marche, C Italy
106 I13 **Acquasparta** Lazio, C Italy
106 C9 **Acqui Terme** Piemonte, NW Italy
Acrae *see* Palazzola Acreide
182 F7 **Acraman, Lake** *salt lake* South Australia
59 A15 **Acre** *off.* Estado do Acre. ◐ *state* W Brazil
Acre *see* 'Akko
59 C16 **Acre, Rio** ≈ W Brazil
107 N20 **Acri** Calabria, SW Italy
Acte *see* Ágion Óros
191 Y12 **Actéon, Groupe** *island group* Îles Tuamotu, SE French Polynesia
15 P12 **Acton-Vale** Quebec, SE Canada
41 P13 **Actopan** *var.* Actopán. Hidalgo, C Mexico
59 P14 **Açu** *var.* Assu. Rio Grande do Norte, E Brazil
Acunum Acusio *see* Montélimar
77 Q17 **Ada** SE Ghana
29 R5 **Ada** Minnesota, N USA
31 R12 **Ada** Ohio, N USA
27 O12 **Ada** Oklahoma, C USA
112 L8 **Ada** Serbia, N Yugoslavia
Ada Bazar *see* Adapazarı
40 D3 **Adair, Bahía de** *bay* NW Mexico
104 M7 **Adaja** ≈ N Spain
38 H17 **Adak Island** *island* Aleutian Islands, Alaska, USA
Adalia *see* Antalya
Adalia, Gulf of *see* Antalya Körfezi
141 X9 **Adam** N Oman
Adama *see* Nazrēt
60 I8 **Adamantina** São Paulo, S Brazil
79 E14 **Adamaoua** *Eng.* Adamawa. ◐ *province* N Cameroon
68 F11 **Adamaoua, Massif d'** *Eng.* Adamawa Highlands. *plateau* NW Cameroon
77 Y14 **Adamawa** ◐ *state* E Nigeria
Adamawa *see* Adamaoua
Adamawa Highlands *see* Adamaoua, Massif d'
106 F6 **Adamello** ▲ N Italy
81 J14 **Ādamī Tulu** Oromo, C Ethiopia
63 M23 **Adam, Mount** *var.* Monte Independencia. ▲ West Falkland, Falkland Islands
29 R16 **Adams** Nebraska, C USA
18 H8 **Adams** New York, NE USA
29 Q3 **Adams** North Dakota, N USA
155 I23 **Adam's Bridge** *chain of shoals* NW Sri Lanka
32 H10 **Adams, Mount** ▲ Washington, NW USA
Adam's Peak *see* Sri Pada
191 R16 **Adam's Rock** *island* Pitcairn Island, Pitcairn Islands
191 P16 **Adamstown** ○ (Pitcairn Islands) Pitcairn Island, Pitcairn Islands
20 G10 **Adamsville** Tennessee, S USA
25 S9 **Adamsville** Texas, SW USA
141 O17 **'Adan** *Eng.* Aden. SW Yemen
136 K16 **Adana** *var.* Seyhan. Adana, S Turkey
136 K16 **Adana** *var.* Seyhan. ◐ *province* S Turkey
Adâncata *see* Horlivka
169 V12 **Adang, Teluk** *bay* Borneo, C Indonesia
136 F11 **Adapazarı** *prev.* Ada Bazar. Sakarya, NW Turkey
80 H8 **Adarama** River Nile, NE Sudan
195 Q16 **Adare, Cape** *headland* Antarctica
106 E6 **Adda** *anc.* Addua. ≈ N Italy
80 A13 **Adda** ≈ W Sudan
143 Q17 **Ad Dab'iyah** Abū Ẓaby, C UAE
143 O18 **Ad Dafrah** *desert* S UAE
141 Q6 **Ad Dahnā'** *desert* E Saudi Arabia
74 A11 **Ad Dakhla** *var.* Dakhla. SW Western Sahara
Ad Dalanj *see* Dilling
Ad Damar *see* Ed Damer
Ad Damazīn *see* Ed Damazin
Ad Dāmir *see* Ed Damer
173 N2 **Ad Dammām** *desert* NE Saudi Arabia
141 R6 **Ad Dammān** *var.* Dammām. Ash Sharqīyah, NE Saudi Arabia
Ad Dāmūr *see* Damoûr
140 K5 **Ad Dār al Ḥamrā'** Tabūk, NW Saudi Arabia
140 M13 **Ad Darb** Jīzān, SW Saudi Arabia
141 O8 **Ad Dawādimī** Ar Riyāḍ, C Saudi Arabia
143 N16 **Ad Dawḥah** *Eng.* Doha. ● (Qatar) C Qatar
143 N16 **Ad Dawḥah** *Eng.* Doha. × C Qatar
139 S6 **Ad Dawr** N Iraq
139 Y12 **Ad Dayr** *var.* Dayr, Shahbān. E Iraq
Addi Arkay *see* Ādī Ārk'ay
139 X15 **Ad Dibdibah** *physical region* Iraq/Kuwait
Ad Diffah *see* Libyan Plateau
Addis Ababa *see* Ādīs Ābeba
Addison *see* Webster Springs
139 U10 **Ad Dīwānīyah** *var.* Diwaniyah. C Iraq
Addua *see* Adda
151 K22 **Addu Atoll** *atoll* S Maldives
Ad Dujail *see* Ad Dujayl
139 T7 **Ad Dujayl** *var.* Ad Dujail. N Iraq
Ad Duwaym/Ad Duwēm *see* Ed Dueim
99 D16 **Adegem** Oost-Vlaanderen, NW Belgium
23 U7 **Adel** Georgia, SE USA
29 U14 **Adel** Iowa, C USA
182 I9 **Adelaide** *state capital* South Australia
44 H2 **Adelaide** New Providence, N Bahamas
182 I9 **Adelaide** × South Australia
194 H6 **Adelaide Island** *island* Antarctica
181 P2 **Adelaide River** Northern Territory, N Australia
76 M10 **'Adel Bagrou** Hodh ech Chargui, SE Mauritania
186 D6 **Adelbert Range** ▲ N PNG
180 K3 **Adele Island** *island* Western Australia
107 O17 **Adelfia** Puglia, SE Italy
195 V16 **Adélie Coast** *physical region* Antarctica
195 V14 **Adélie, Terre** *physical region* Antarctica
Adelnau *see* Odolanów
Adelsberg *see* Postojna
Aden *see* 'Adan
141 Q17 **Aden, Gulf of** *gulf* SW Arabian Sea
77 V10 **Aderbissinat** Agadez, C Niger
Adhaim *see* Al 'Uẓaym
143 R16 **Adh Dhayd** *var.* Al Dhaid. Ash Shāriqah, NE UAE
140 M4 **'Adhfā'** *spring/well* NW Saudi Arabia
138 I13 **'Ādhriyāt, Jabāl al** ▲ S Jordan
80 I10 **Ādī Ārk'ay** *var.* Addi Arkay. Amhara, N Ethiopia
182 C7 **Adieu, Cape** *headland* South Australia
106 H8 **Adige** *Ger.* Etsch. ≈ N Italy
80 J10 **Ādīgrat** Tigray, N Ethiopia
154 I13 **Ādilabād** *var.* Ādilābād. Andhra Pradesh, C India
35 P2 **Adin** California, W USA
171 V14 **Adi, Pulau** *island* E Indonesia
18 K8 **Adirondack Mountains** ▲ New York, NE USA
80 J13 **Ādīs Ābeba** *Eng.* Addis Ababa. ● (Ethiopia) Ādīs Ābeba, C Ethiopia
80 J13 **Ādīs Ābeba** × Ādīs Ābeba, C Ethiopia
80 I11 **Ādīs Zemen** Amhara, N Ethiopia
Adi Ugri *see* Mendefera
137 N15 **Adıyaman** Adıyaman, SE Turkey
137 N15 **Adıyaman** ◐ *province* S Turkey
116 L11 **Adjud** Vrancea, E Romania
45 T6 **Adjuntas** C Puerto Rico
Adjuntas, Presa de las *see* Vicente Guerrero, Presa
Ādkup *see* Erikub Atoll
128 L15 **Adler** Krasnodarskiy Kray, SW Russian Federation
Adler *see* Orlice
108 G7 **Adliswil** Zürich, NW Switzerland
32 G7 **Admiralty Inlet** *inlet* Washington, NW USA
39 X13 **Admiralty Island** *island* Alexander Archipelago, Alaska, USA
186 E5 **Admiralty Islands** *island group* N PNG
136 B14 **Adnan Menderes** × (İzmir) İzmir, W Turkey
37 V6 **Adobe Creek Reservoir** ▣ Colorado, C USA
77 T16 **Ado-Ekiti** Ekiti, SW Nigeria
Adola *see* Kibre Mengist
61 C23 **Adolfo González Chaues** Buenos Aires, E Argentina
155 H17 **Ādoni** Andhra Pradesh, C India
102 K15 **Adour** *anc.* Aturus. ≈ SW France
Adowa *see* Ādwa
105 O15 **Adra** Andalucía, S Spain
107 L24 **Adrano** Sicilia, Italy, C Mediterranean Sea
74 I9 **Adrar** C Algeria
76 K7 **Adrar** ◐ *region* C Mauritania
74 L11 **Adrar** ▲ SE Algeria
74 A12 **Adrar Souttouf** ▲ SW Western Sahara
Adrasman *see* Adrasmon
147 Q10 **Adrasmon** *Rus.* Adrasman. NW Tajikistan
78 K10 **Adré** Ouaddaï, E Chad
106 H9 **Adria** *anc.* Atria, Hadria, Hatria. Veneto, NE Italy
31 R10 **Adrian** Michigan, N USA
29 S11 **Adrian** Minnesota, N USA
27 R5 **Adrian** Missouri, C USA
24 M2 **Adrian** Texas, SW USA
21 S4 **Adrian** West Virginia, NE USA
Adrianople/Adrianopolis *see* Edirne
121 P7 **Adriatic Basin** *undersea feature* Adriatic Sea, N Mediterranean Sea
Adriatico, Mare *see* Adriatic Sea
106 L13 **Adriatic Sea** *Alb.* Deti Adriatik, *It.* Mare Adriatico, *SCr.* Jadransko More, *Slvn.* Jadransko Morje. *sea* N Mediterranean Sea
Adriatik, Deti *see* Adriatic Sea
Adua *see* Ādwa
Aduana del Sásabe *see* El Sásabe
79 O17 **Adusa** Orientale, NE Dem. Rep. Congo (Zaire)
118 J13 **Adutiškis** Švenčionys, E Lithuania
27 Y7 **Advance** Missouri, C USA
65 D25 **Adventure Sound** *bay* East Falkland, Falkland Islands
80 J10 **Ādwa** *var.* Adowa, *It.* Adua. Tigray, N Ethiopia
123 Q8 **Adycha** ≈ NE Russian Federation
128 L14 **Adygeya, Respublika** ◐ *autonomous republic* SW Russian Federation
146 C11 **Adzhikui** *Turkm.* Ajyguyy. Balkanskiy Velayat, W Turkmenistan
77 N17 **Adzopé** SE Ivory Coast
127 U4 **Adz'va** ≈ NW Russian Federation
127 U5 **Adz'vavom** Respublika Komi, NW Russian Federation
Ædua *see* Autun
115 K19 **Aegean Islands** *island group* Greece/Turkey
Aegean North *see* Vóreion Aigaíon
115 I17 **Aegean Sea** *Gk.* Aigaíon Pélagos, Aigaío Pélagos, *Turk.* Ege Denizi. *sea* NE Mediterranean Sea
Aegean South *see* Nótion Aigaíon
118 H3 **Aegviidu** *Ger.* Charlottenhof. Harjumaa, NW Estonia
Aegyptus *see* Egypt
Aelana *see* Al 'Aqabah
Aelok *see* Ailuk Atoll
Aelōninae *see* Ailinginae Atoll
Aelōnlaplap *see* Ailinglaplap Atoll
Æmilia *see* Emilia-Romagna
Æmilianum *see* Millau
Aemona *see* Ljubljana
Aenaria *see* Ischia
Aeolian Islands *see* Eolie, Isole
191 Z3 **Aeon Point** *headland* Kiritimati, NE Kiribati
95 G24 **Ærø** *Ger.* Arrö. *island* C Denmark
95 H24 **Ærøskøbing** Fyn, C Denmark
Æsernia *see* Isernia
104 G3 **A Estrada** Galicia, NW Spain
115 C18 **Aetós** Itháki, Iónioi Nísoi, Greece, C Mediterranean Sea
191 Q8 **Afaahiti** Tahiti, W French Polynesia
139 U10 **'Afak** C Iraq
Afanasjevo *see* Afanas'yevo
127 T14 **Afanas'yevo** *var.* Afanasjevo. Kirovskaya Oblast', NW Russian Federation
Afándou *see* Afántou
115 O23 **Afántou** *var.* Afándou. Ródos, Dodekánisos, Greece, Aegean Sea
Afar Depression *see* Danakil Desert
80 K11 **Afar** ◐ *region* NE Ethiopia
191 O7 **Afareaitu** Moorea, W French Polynesia
140 L7 **'Afarīyah, Bi'r al** *well* NW Saudi Arabia
Afars et des Issas, Territoire Français des *see* Djibouti
83 D22 **Affenrücken** Karas, SW Namibia
Afghānestān, Dowlat-e Eslāmī-ye *see* Afghanistan
148 M6 **Afghanistan** *off.* Islamic State of Afghanistan, *Per.* Dowlat-e Eslāmī-ye Afghānestān; *prev.* Republic of Afghanistan. ◆ *Islamic state* C Asia
Afgoi *see* Afgooye
81 N17 **Afgooye** *It.* Afgoi. Shabeellaha Hoose, S Somalia
141 N8 **'Afīf** Ar Riyāḍ, C Saudi Arabia
77 V17 **Afikpo** Ebonyi, SE Nigeria
Afiun Karahissar *see* Afyon
94 H7 **Åfjord** Sør-Trøndelag, C Norway
109 V6 **Aflenz Kurort** Steiermark, E Austria
74 J6 **Aflou** N Algeria
81 L18 **Afmadow** Jubbada Hoose, S Somalia
39 Q14 **Afognak Island** *island* Alaska, USA
104 J2 **A Fonsagrada** Galicia, NW Spain
186 E9 **Afore** Northern, S PNG
59 O15 **Afrânio** Pernambuco, E Brazil
68-69 **Africa** *continent*
68 L11 **Africa, Horn of** *physical region* Ethiopia/Somalia
172 K11 **Africana Seamount** *undersea feature* SW Indian Ocean
86 A14 **African Plate** *tectonic feature*
138 I2 **'Afrīn** Ḥalab, N Syria
136 M15 **Afşin** Kahramanmaraş, C Turkey
98 J7 **Afsluitdijk** *dam* N Netherlands
29 U15 **Afton** Iowa, C USA
29 W9 **Afton** Minnesota, N USA
27 R8 **Afton** Oklahoma, C USA
136 F14 **Afyon** *prev.* Afyonkarahisar. Afyon, W Turkey
136 F14 **Afyon** *var.* Afiun Karahissar, Afyonkarahisar. ◐ *province* W Turkey
Afyonkarahisar *see* Afyon
Agadès *see* Agadez
77 V10 **Agadez** *prev.* Agadès. Agadez, C Niger
77 W8 **Agadez** ◐ *department* N Niger
74 E8 **Agadir** SW Morocco
64 M9 **Agadir Canyon** *undersea feature* SE Atlantic Ocean
145 R12 **Agadyr'** Zhezkazgan, C Kazakhstan
173 O7 **Agalega Islands** *island group* N Mauritius
42 K6 **Agalta, Sierra de** ▲ E Honduras
122 I10 **Agan** ≈ C Russian Federation
Agana/Agaña *see* Hagåtña
188 B15 **Agana Bay** *bay* NW Guam
188 C16 **Agana Field** × (Agana) C Guam
171 Kk13 **Agano-gawa** ≈ Honshū, C Japan
188 B17 **Aga Point** *headland* S Guam
154 G9 **Agar** Madhya Pradesh, C India
81 I14 **Āgaro** Oromo, C Ethiopia
153 V15 **Agartala** Tripura, NE India
194 I5 **Agassiz, Cape** *headland* Antarctica
9 N2 **Agassiz Ice Cap** *ice feature* Nunavut, N Canada
175 V13 **Agassiz Fracture Zone** *tectonic feature* S Pacific Ocean
188 B16 **Agat** W Guam
188 B16 **Agat Bay** *bay* W Guam
145 P13 **Agat, Gory** *hill* C Kazakhstan
Agatha *see* Agde
115 M20 **Agathónisi** *island* Dodekánisos, Greece, Aegean Sea
171 X14 **Agats** Irian Jaya, E Indonesia
155 C21 **Agatti Island** *island* Lakshadweep, India, N Indian Ocean
38 D16 **Agattu Island** *island* Aleutian Islands, Alaska, USA
38 D16 **Agattu Strait** *strait* Aleutian Islands, Alaska, USA
14 B8 **Agawa** ≈ Ontario, S Canada
14 B8 **Agawa Bay** *lake bay* Ontario, S Canada
77 N17 **Agboville** SE Ivory Coast
137 V12 **Ağdam** *Rus.* Agdam. SW Azerbaijan
103 P16 **Agde** *anc.* Agatha. Hérault, S France
103 P16 **Agde, Cap d'** *headland* S France
Agedabia *see* Ajdābiyā
102 L14 **Agen** *anc.* Aginnum. Lot-et-Garonne, SW France
Agendicum *see* Sens
165 O13 **Ageo** Saitama, Honshū, S Japan
109 R5 **Ager** ≈ N Austria
Agere Hiywet *see* Hāgere Hiywet
108 G8 **Ägerisee** ◎ W Switzerland
142 M10 **Āghā Jārī** Khūzestān, SW Iran
39 P15 **Aghiyuk Island** *island* Alaska, USA
74 B12 **Aghouinit** SE Western Sahara
Aghri Dagh *see* Büyükağrı Dağı
74 B10 **Aghzoumal, Sebkhet** *var.* Sebjet Agsumal. *salt lake* E Western Sahara
115 F15 **Agiá** *var.* Ayiá. Thessalía, C Greece
40 G7 **Agiabampo, Estero de** *estuary* NW Mexico
121 P3 **Agía Fýlaxis** *var.* Ayia Phyla. S Cyprus
Agialoúsa *see* Yenierenköy
115 M21 **Agía Marína** Léros, Dodekánisos, Greece, Aegean Sea
121 Q2 **Agía Nápa** *var.* Ayia Napa. E Cyprus
115 L16 **Agía Paraskeví** Lésvos, E Greece
115 J15 **Agías Eirínis, Akrotírio** *headland* Límnos, E Greece
115 L17 **Agiasós** *var.* Ayiásos, Ayiássos. Lésvos, E Greece
Aginnum *see* Agen
123 O14 **Aginskiy Buryatskiy Avtonomnyy Okrug** ◐ *autonomous district* S Russian Federation
123 O14 **Aginskoye** Aginskiy Buryatskiy Avtonomnyy Okrug, S Russian Federation
115 I14 **Ágion Óros** *Eng.* Mount Athos. ◐ *monastic republic* NE Greece
115 H14 **Ágion Óros** *var.* Akte, Aktí; *anc.* Acte. *peninsula* NE Greece
114 D13 **Ágios Achílleios** *religious building* Dytikí Makedonía, N Greece
115 J16 **Ágios Efstrátios** *var.* Áyios Evstrátios, Hagios Evstrátios. *island* E Greece
115 H20 **Ágios Geórgios** *island* Kykládes, Greece, Aegean Sea
115 Q23 **Ágios Geórgios** *island* SE Greece
115 E21 **Ágios Ilías** ▲ S Greece
115 K25 **Ágios Ioannis, Akrotírio** *headland* Kríti, Greece, E Mediterranean Sea
115 L20 **Ágios Kírykos** *var.* Áyios Kírikos. Ikaría, Dodekánisos, Greece, Aegean Sea
115 D16 **Ágios Nikolaos** Thessalía, C Greece
115 K25 **Ágios Nikólaos** *var.* Áyios Nikólaos. Kríti, Greece, E Mediterranean Sea
115 H14 **Agíou Órous, Kólpos** *gulf* N Greece
107 K24 **Agira** *anc.* Agyrium. Sicilia, Italy, C Mediterranean Sea
115 G20 **Agkístri** *island* S Greece
114 G12 **Agkístro** *var.* Angistro. ▲ NE Greece
103 O17 **Agly** ≈ S France
Agnetheln *see* Agnita
14 E10 **Agnew Lake** ◎ Ontario, S Canada
77 O16 **Agnibilékrou** E Ivory Coast
116 I11 **Agnita** *Ger.* Agnetheln, *Hung.* Szentágota. Sibiu, SW Romania
107 K15 **Agnone** Molise, C Italy
164 K14 **Ago** Mie, Honshū, SW Japan
106 C8 **Agogna** ≈ N Italy
Agoitz *see* Aoiz-Agoitz
77 P17 **Agona Swedru** *var.* Swedru. SE Ghana
Agordat *see* Akurdet
Agosta *see* Augusta
103 N15 **Agout** ≈ S France
152 J12 **Āgra** Uttar Pradesh, N India
Agra and Oudh, United Provinces of *see* Uttar Pradesh
Agram *see* Zagreb
105 U5 **Agramunt** Cataluña, NE Spain
105 Q5 **Agreda** Castilla-León, N Spain
137 S13 **Ağrı** *var.* Karaköse; *prev.* Karakılısse. Ağrı, NE Turkey
137 S13 **Ağrı** ◐ *province* NE Turkey
107 N19 **Agri** *anc.* Aciris. ≈ S Italy
Agri Dagi *see* Büyükağrı Dağı
107 J24 **Agrigento** *Gk.* Akragas; *prev.* Girgenti. Sicilia, Italy, C Mediterranean Sea
188 K4 **Agrihan** *island* N Northern Mariana Islands
115 D18 **Agrínio** *prev.* Agrinion. Dytikí Ellás, W Greece
Agrinion *see* Agrínio
115 G17 **Agriovótano** Évvoia, C Greece
107 L18 **Agropoli** Campania, S Italy
129 T3 **Agryz** Udmurtskaya Respublika, NW Russian Federation
137 U11 **Ağstafa** *Rus.* Akstafa. NW Azerbaijan
Agsumal, Sebjet *see* Aghzoumal, Sebkhet
40 J11 **Agua Brava, Laguna** *lagoon* W Mexico
54 F7 **Aguachica** Cesar, N Colombia
59 J20 **Água Clara** Mato Grosso do Sul, SW Brazil
44 D5 **Aguada de Pasajeros** Cienfuegos, C Cuba
54 J5 **Aguada Grande** Lara, N Venezuela
45 S5 **Aguadilla** W Puerto Rico
43 S16 **Aguadulce** Coclé, S Panama
104 L14 **Aguadulce** Andalucía, S Spain
41 O8 **Agualeguas** Nuevo León, NE Mexico
40 L9 **Aguanaval, Río** ≈ C Mexico
42 J5 **Aguán, Río** ≈ N Honduras
25 R16 **Agua Nueva** Texas, SW USA
60 J8 **Aguapeí, Rio** ≈ S Brazil
61 E14 **Aguapey, Río** ≈ NE Argentina
40 G3 **Agua Prieta** Sonora, NW Mexico
104 G5 **A Guardia** *var.* Laguardia, La Guardia. Galicia, NW Spain
56 E6 **Aguarico, Río** ≈ Ecuador/Peru
55 O6 **Aguasay** Monagas, NE Venezuela
40 M12 **Aguascalientes** Aguascalientes, C Mexico
40 L12 **Aguascalientes** ◐ *state* C Mexico
57 I18 **Aguas Calientes, Río** ≈ S Peru
105 R7 **Aguasvivas** ≈ NE Spain
60 J7 **Água Vermelha, Represa de** ▣ S Brazil
56 E12 **Aguaytía** Ucayali, C Peru
104 I5 **A Gudiña** *var.* La Gudiña. Galicia, NW Spain
104 G7 **Águeda** Aveiro, N Portugal
104 J8 **Águeda** ≈ Portugal/Spain
77 Q8 **Aguelhok** Kidal, NE Mali
77 V12 **Aguié** Maradi, S Niger
188 K8 **Aguijan** *island* S Northern Mariana Islands
104 M14 **Aguilar** *var.* Aguilar de la Frontera. Andalucía, S Spain
104 M3 **Aguilar de Campóo** Castilla-León, N Spain
Aguilar de la Frontera *see* Aguilar
42 F7 **Aguilares** San Salvador, C El Salvador
105 Q14 **Aguilas** Murcia, SE Spain
40 L15 **Aguililla** Michoacán de Ocampo, SW Mexico
Agulhas *see* L'Agulhas
172 J11 **Agulhas Bank** *undersea feature* SW Indian Ocean
172 K11 **Agulhas Basin** *undersea feature* SW Indian Ocean
83 F26 **Agulhas, Cape** *Afr.* Kaap Agulhas. *headland* SW South Africa
Agulhas, Kaap *see* Agulhas, Cape
60 O9 **Agulhas Negras, Pico das** ▲ SE Brazil
172 K11 **Agulhas Plateau** *undersea feature* SW Indian Ocean
165 S16 **Aguni-jima** *island* Nansei-shotō, SW Japan
Agurain *see* Salvatierra
54 G5 **Agustín Codazzi** *var.* Codazzi. Cesar, N Colombia
Agyrium *see* Agira
74 L12 **Ahaggar** *high plateau region* SE Algeria
Ahal Welayaty *see* Akhalskiy Velayat
142 K2 **Ahar** Āzarbāyjān-e Khāvarī, NW Iran
Aharnes *see* Acharnés
138 J3 **Aḥaṣ, Jabal** ▲ NW Syria
138 J3 **Aḥaṣ, Jebal** ▲ W Syria
185 G16 **Ahaura** ≈ South Island, NZ
100 E13 **Ahaus** Nordrhein-Westfalen, NW Germany
191 U9 **Ahe** *atoll* Îles Tuamotu, C French Polynesia
184 N10 **Ahimanawa Range** ▲ North Island, NZ
119 I19 **Ahinski Kanal** *Rus.* Oginskiy Kanal. *canal* SW Belarus
186 G10 **Ahioma** SE PNG
184 I2 **Ahipara** Northland, North Island, NZ
184 I2 **Ahipara Bay** *bay* SE Tasman Sea
39 N13 **Ahklun Mountains** ▲ Alaska, USA
137 R14 **Ahlat** Bitlis, E Turkey
101 F14 **Ahlen** Nordrhein-Westfalen, W Germany
154 D10 **Ahmadābād** *var.* Ahmedabad. Gujarāt, W India
143 R10 **Ahmadābād** Kermān, C Iran
Ahmadi *see* Al Aḥmadī
Ahmad Khel *see* Ḥasan Khēl
155 F14 **Ahmadnagar** *var.* Ahmednagar. Mahārāshtra, W India
149 T9 **Ahmadpur Siāl** Punjab, E Pakistan
77 N5 **Aḥmar, 'Erg el** *desert* N Mali
80 K13 **Ahmar Mountains** ▲ C Ethiopia
Ahmedabad *see* Ahmadābād
Ahmednagar *see* Ahmadnagar
114 N12 **Ahmetbey** Kırklareli, NW Turkey
14 H12 **Ahmic Lake** ◎ Ontario, S Canada
190 G12 **Ahoa** Île Uvea, E Wallis and Futuna
40 G8 **Ahomé** Sinaloa, C Mexico
21 X8 **Ahoskie** North Carolina, SE USA
101 D17 **Ahr** ≈ W Germany
143 N12 **Ahram** *var.* Ahrom. Būshehr, S Iran
100 J9 **Ahrensburg** Schleswig-Holstein, N Germany
Ahrom *see* Ahram
93 L17 **Ähtäri** Länsi-Suomi, W Finland
40 K12 **Ahuacatlán** Nayarit, C Mexico
42 E7 **Ahuachapán** Ahuachapán, W El Salvador
42 A9 **Ahuachapán** ◐ *department* W El Salvador
191 V16 **Ahu Akivi** *var.* Siete Moai. *ancient monument* Easter Island, Chile, E Pacific Ocean

191 W11 **Ahunui** *atoll* Îles Tuamotu, C French Polynesia
185 E20 **Ahuriri** South Island, NZ
95 L22 **Åhus** Skåne, S Sweden
Ahu Tahira *see* Ahu Vinapu
191 V16 **Ahu Tepeu** *ancient monument* Easter Island, Chile, E Pacific Ocean
191 V17 **Ahu Vinapu** *var.* Ahu Tahira. *ancient monument* Easter Island, Chile, E Pacific Ocean
142 L9 **Ahvāz** *var.* Ahwāz; *prev.* Nāsiri. Khūzestān, SW Iran
Ahvenanmaa *see* Åland
141 Q16 **Aḥwar** SW Yemen
Ahwāz *see* Ahvāz
Aibak *see* Āybak
101 K22 **Aichach** Bayern, SE Germany
164 L14 **Aichi** *off.* Aichi-ken, *var.* Aiti. ◆ *prefecture* Honshū, SW Japan
Aïdin *see* Aydın
Aidussina *see* Ajdovščina
Aifir, Clochán an *see* Giant's Causeway
Aigaíon Pélagos/Aigaío Pélagos *see* Aegean Sea
109 S3 **Aigen im Mülkreis** Oberösterreich, N Austria
115 G20 **Aígina** *var.* Aíyina, Egina. Aígina, C Greece
115 G20 **Aígina** *island* S Greece
115 E18 **Aígio** *var.* Egio; *prev.* Aíyion. Dytikí Ellás, S Greece
108 C10 **Aigle** Vaud, SW Switzerland
103 P14 **Aigoual, Mont** ▲ S France
173 O16 **Aigrettes, Pointe des** *headland* W Réunion
61 G19 **Aiguá** *var.* Aigua. Maldonado, S Uruguay
103 S13 **Aigues** SE France
103 N10 **Aigurande** Indre, C France
Ai-hun *see* Heihe
165 N10 **Aikawa** Niigata, Sado, C Japan
21 Q13 **Aiken** South Carolina, SE USA
25 N4 **Aiken** Texas, SW USA
160 F13 **Ailao Shan** ▲ SW China
43 W14 **Ailigandí** San Blas, NE Panama
189 R4 **Ailinginae Atoll** *var.* Aelōninae. *atoll* Ralik Chain, SW Marshall Islands
189 T7 **Ailinglaplap Atoll** *var.* Aelōnlaplap. *atoll* Ralik Chain, S Marshall Islands
Aillionn, Loch *see* Allen, Lough
96 H13 **Ailsa Craig** *island* SW Scotland, UK
189 V5 **Ailuk Atoll** *var.* Aelok. *atoll* Ratak Chain, NE Marshall Islands
123 R11 **Aim** Khabarovskiy Kray, E Russian Federation
103 R11 **Ain** ◆ *department* E France
103 S10 **Ain** E France
118 G7 **Ainaži** *Est.* Heinaste, *Ger.* Hainasch. Limbaži, N Latvia
74 L6 **Aïn Beida** NE Algeria
76 K4 **'Aïn Ben Tili** Tiris Zemmour, N Mauritania
74 J5 **Aïn Defla** *var.* Aïn Eddefla. N Algeria
Aïn Eddefla *see* Aïn Defla
74 L5 **Aïn El Bey** ✕ (Constantine) NE Algeria
115 C19 **Aínos** ▲ Kefallinía, Iónioi Nísoi, Greece, C Mediterranean Sea
105 T4 **Ainsa** Aragón, NE Spain
74 I7 **Aïn Sefra** NW Algeria
29 N13 **Ainsworth** Nebraska, C USA
Aintab *see* Gaziantep
74 H5 **Aïn Témouchent** N Algeria
186 C6 **Aiome** Madang, N PNG
Aïoun el Atrous/Aïoun el Atroûss *see* 'Ayoûn el 'Atroûs
54 E11 **Aipe** Huila, C Colombia
56 D9 **Aipena, Río** N Peru
57 L19 **Aiquile** Cochabamba, C Bolivia
Aïr *see* Aïr, Massif de l'
188 E10 **Airai** Babeldaob, C Palau
188 E10 **Airai** ✕ (Oreor) Babeldaob, N Palau
168 I11 **Airbangis** Sumatera, NW Indonesia
11 Q16 **Airdrie** Alberta, SW Canada
96 I12 **Airdrie** S Scotland, UK
Air du Azbine *see* Aïr, Massif de l'
97 M17 **Aire** N England, UK
102 K15 **Aire-sur-l'Adour** Landes, SW France
103 O1 **Aire-sur-la-Lys** Pas-de-Calais, N France
9 Q6 **Air Force Island** *island* Baffin Island, Nunavut, NE Canada
169 Q13 **Airhitam, Teluk** *bay* Borneo, C Indonesia
171 Q11 **Airmadidi** Sulawesi, N Indonesia
77 V8 **Aïr, Massif de l'** *var.* Aïr, Air du Azbine, Asben. ▲ NC Niger
108 G10 **Airolo** Ticino, S Switzerland
102 K9 **Airvault** Deux-Sèvres, W France
101 K19 **Aisch** S Germany
63 G20 **Aisén** *off.* Región Aisén del General Carlos Ibañez del Campo, *var.* Aysen. ◆ *region* S Chile
10 H7 **Aishihik Lake** ◎ Yukon Territory, W Canada
103 P3 **Aisne** ◆ *department* N France
103 R4 **Aisne** NE France
109 T4 **Aist** N Austria
114 K13 **Aisými** Anatolikí Makedonía kai Thráki, NE Greece
105 S11 **Aitana** ▲ E Spain
186 B5 **Aitape** *var.* Eitape. Sandaun, NW PNG
Aiti *see* Aichi
29 V6 **Aitkin** Minnesota, N USA
115 D18 **Aitolikó** *var.* Etoliko; *prev.* Aitolikón. Dytikí Ellás, C Greece
Aitolikón *see* Aitolikó
190 L15 **Aitutaki** *island* S Cook Islands
116 H11 **Aiud** *Ger.* Strassburg, *Hung.* Nagyenyed; *prev.* Engeten. Alba, SW Romania
118 I9 **Aiviekste** C Latvia
189 Q8 **Aiwo** SW Nauru
188 E8 **Aiwokako Passage** *passage* Babeldaob, N Palau
Aix *see* Aix-en-Provence
103 S15 **Aix-en-Provence** *var.* Aix; *anc.* Aquae Sextiae. Bouches-du-Rhône, SE France
Aix-la-Chapelle *see* Aachen
103 T11 **Aix-les-Bains** Savoie, E France
186 A6 **Aiyang, Mount** ▲ NW PNG
Aíyina *see* Aígina
Aíyion *see* Aígio
153 W15 **Āīzawl** Mizoram, NE India
118 H9 **Aizkraukle** Aizkraukle, S Latvia
118 C9 **Aizpute** Liepāja, W Latvia
165 O11 **Aizu-Wakamatsu** *var.* Aizuwakamatu. Fukushima, Honshū, C Japan
Aizuwakamatu *see* Aizu-Wakamatsu
103 X15 **Ajaccio** Corse, France, C Mediterranean Sea
103 X15 **Ajaccio, Golfe d'** *gulf* Corse, France, C Mediterranean Sea
41 Q15 **Ajalpán** Puebla, S Mexico
154 F13 **Ajanta Range** ▲ C India
137 R10 **Ajaria** ◆ *autonomous republic* SW Georgia
Ajastan *see* Armenia
93 G14 **Ajaureforsen** Västerbotten, N Sweden
185 H17 **Ajax, Mount** ▲ South Island, NZ
162 F9 **Aj Bogd Uul** ▲ SW Mongolia
75 R8 **Ajdābiyā** *var.* Agedabia, Ajdābiyah. NE Libya
Ajdābiyah *see* Ajdābiyā
109 S12 **Ajdovščina** *Ger.* Haidenschaft, *It.* Aidussina. W Slovenia
165 Q7 **Ajigasawa** Aomori, Honshū, C Japan
Ajjinena *see* El Geneina
111 H23 **Ajka** Veszprém, W Hungary
138 G9 **'Ajlūn** Irbid, N Jordan
138 H9 **'Ajlūn, Jabal** ▲ W Jordan
143 R15 **'Ajmān** *var.* Ajman, 'Ujmān. 'Ajmān, NE UAE
152 G12 **Ajmer** *var.* Ajmere. Rājasthān, N India
36 J15 **Ajo** Arizona, SW USA
105 N2 **Ajo, Cabo de** *headland* N Spain
36 J16 **Ajo Range** ▲ Arizona, SW USA
Ajyguyy *see* Adzhikui
Akaba *see* Al 'Aqabah
165 T3 **Akabira** Hokkaidō, NE Japan
165 N10 **Akadomari** Niigata, Sado, C Japan
81 E20 **Akagera** *var.* Kagera. Rwanda/Tanzania *see also* Kagera
191 W16 **Akahanga, Punta** *headland* Easter Island, Chile, E Pacific Ocean
80 J13 **Āk'ak'i** Oromo, C Ethiopia
155 G15 **Akalkot** Mahārāshtra, W India
Akamagaseki *see* Shimonoseki
165 U4 **Akan** Hokkaidō, NE Japan
165 U4 **Akan-ko** ◎ Hokkaidō, NE Japan
Akanthoú *see* Tatlısu
185 I19 **Akaroa** Canterbury, South Island, NZ
80 E6 **Akasha** Northern, N Sudan
164 I13 **Akashi** *var.* Akasi. Hyōgo, Honshū, SW Japan
139 N7 **'Akāsh, Wādī** *var.* Wādī 'Ukash. *dry watercourse* W Iraq
Akasi *see* Akashi
92 K11 **Äkäsjokisuu** Lappi, N Finland
137 S11 **Akbaba Dağı** ▲ Armenia/Turkey
136 B15 **Akbük Limanı** *bay* W Turkey
129 V8 **Akbulak** Orenburgskaya Oblast', W Russian Federation
137 O11 **Akçaabat** Trabzon, NE Turkey
137 N15 **Akçadağ** Malatya, C Turkey
136 G11 **Akçakoca** Bolu, NW Turkey
Akchakaya, Vpadina *see* Akdzhakaya, Vpadina
76 H7 **Akchâr** *desert* W Mauritania
145 S12 **Akchatau** *Kaz.* Aqshataū. Zhezkazgan, C Kazakhstan
136 L13 **Akdağlar** ▲ C Turkey
136 E17 **Ak Dağları** ▲ SW Turkey
136 K13 **Akdağmadeni** Yozgat, C Turkey
146 G8 **Akdepe** *prev.* Ak-Tepe, Leninsk, *Turkm.* Lenin. Dashkhovuzskiy Velayat, N Turkmenistan
Ak-Dere *see* Byala
121 P2 **Akdoğan** *Gk.* Lýsi. C Cyprus
122 D14 **Ak-Dovurak** Respublika Tyva, S Russian Federation
146 F9 **Akdzhakaya, Vpadina** *var.* Vpadina Akchakaya. *depression* N Turkmenistan
171 S11 **Akelamo** Pulau Halmahera, E Indonesia
Aken *see* Aachen
Akermanceaster *see* Bath
95 P15 **Åkersberga** Stockholm, C Sweden
95 H15 **Akershus** ◆ *county* S Norway
79 L16 **Aketi** Orientale, N Dem. Rep. Congo (Zaire)
Akgyr Erezi *see* Gryada Akkyr
146 E12 **Akhalskiy Velayat** *Turkm.* Ahal Welayaty. ◆ *province* C Turkmenistan
137 S10 **Akhalts'ikhe** SW Georgia
Akhangaran *see* Ohangaron
Akharnaí *see* Acharnés
75 R7 **Akhḍar, Al Jabal al** *hill range* NE Libya
Akhelóös *see* Achelóos
39 Q15 **Akhiok** Kodiak Island, Alaska, USA
136 C13 **Akhisar** Manisa, W Turkey
75 X10 **Akhmîm** *anc.* Panopolis. C Egypt
152 H6 **Akhnūr** Jammu and Kashmir, NW India
129 P11 **Akhtuba** SW Russian Federation
129 P11 **Akhtubinsk** Astrakhanskaya Oblast', SW Russian Federation
Akhtyrka *see* Okhtyrka
164 H14 **Aki** Kōchi, Shikoku, SW Japan
39 N12 **Akiachak** Alaska, USA
39 N12 **Akiak** Alaska, USA
191 X11 **Akiaki** *atoll* Îles Tuamotu, E French Polynesia
12 H9 **Akimiski Island** *island* Nunavut, C Canada
136 K17 **Akıncı Burnu** *headland* S Turkey
Akıncılar *see* Selçuk
117 U10 **Akinovka** Zaporiz'ka Oblast', S Ukraine
95 M24 **Åkirkeby** *var.* Aakirkeby. Bornholm, E Denmark
165 P8 **Akita** Akita, Honshū, C Japan
165 Q8 **Akita** *off.* Akita-ken. ◆ *prefecture* Honshū, C Japan
76 H8 **Akjoujt** *prev.* Fort-Repoux. Inchiri, W Mauritania
92 H11 **Akkajaure** ◎ N Sweden
Akkala *see* Oqqal'a
155 L25 **Akkaraipattu** Eastern Province, E Sri Lanka
92 H11 **Akkavare** ▲ N Sweden
145 P13 **Akkense** Zhezkazgan, C Kazakhstan
Akkerman *see* Bilhorod-Dnistrovs'kyy
129 W8 **Akkermanovka** Orenburgskaya Oblast', W Russian Federation
165 V4 **Akkeshi** Hokkaidō, NE Japan
165 V4 **Akkeshi-ko** ◎ Hokkaidō, NE Japan
165 V5 **Akkeshi-wan** *bay* NW Pacific Ocean
138 F8 **'Akko** *Eng.* Acre, *Fr.* Saint-Jean-d'Acre; *Bibl.* Accho, Ptolemaïs. Northern, N Israel
145 Q8 **Akkol'** *Kaz.* Aqköl; *prev.* Alekseyevka, *Kaz.* Alekseevka. Akmola, C Kazakhstan
145 T14 **Akkol'** *Kaz.* Aqköl. Almaty, SE Kazakhstan
145 Q16 **Akkol'** *Kaz.* Aqköl. Zhambyl, S Kazakhstan
144 M11 **Akkol', Ozero** *prev.* Ozero Zhaman-Akkol'. ◎ C Kazakhstan
98 L6 **Akkrum** Friesland, N Netherlands
145 U8 **Akku** *prev.* Lebyazh'ye. Pavlodar, NE Kazakhstan
144 F12 **Akkystau** *Kaz.* Aqqystaū. Atyrau, SW Kazakhstan
8 G6 **Aklavik** Northwest Territories, NW Canada
118 B9 **Akmenrags** *headland* W Latvia
158 E9 **Akmeqit** Xinjiang Uygur Zizhiqu, NW China
146 J14 **Akmeydan** Maryyskiy Velayat, C Turkmenistan
Akmola *see* Astana
145 P9 **Akmola** *off.* Akmolinskaya Oblast', *Kaz.* Aqmola Oblysy; *prev.* Tselinogradskaya Oblast. ◆ *province* C Kazakhstan
Akmolinsk *see* Astana
Akmolinskaya Oblast' *see* Akmola
Aknavásár *see* Târgu Ocna
118 I11 **Aknīste** Jēkabpils, S Latvia
81 G14 **Akobo** Jonglei, SE Sudan
81 G14 **Akobo** *var.* Ākobowenz. Ethiopia/Sudan
Ākobowenz *see* Akobo
154 H12 **Akola** Mahārāshtra, C India
Akordat *see* Akurdet
77 Q16 **Akosombo Dam** *dam* SE Ghana
154 H12 **Akot** Mahārāshtra, C India
77 N16 **Akoupé** SE Ivory Coast
12 M3 **Akpatok Island** *island* Nunavut, E Canada
158 G7 **Akqi** Xinjiang Uygur Zizhiqu, NW China
138 I2 **Akrād, Jabal al** ▲ N Syria
Akragas *see* Agrigento
92 H3 **Akranes** Vesturland, W Iceland
139 S2 **Ākrē** *Ar.* 'Aqrah. N Iraq
95 C16 **Åkrehamn** Rogaland, S Norway
77 V9 **Akrérèb** Agadez, C Niger
115 D22 **Akrítas, Akrotírio** *headland* S Greece
37 V3 **Akron** Colorado, C USA
29 R12 **Akron** Iowa, C USA
31 U12 **Akron** Ohio, N USA
Akrotiri *see* Akrotírion
Akrotiri Bay *see* Akrotírion, Kólpos
121 P3 **Akrotírion** *var.* Akrotiri. *UK air base* S Cyprus
121 P3 **Akrotírion, Kólpos** *var.* Akrotiri Bay. *bay* S Cyprus
121 O3 **Akrotiri Sovereign Base Area** *UK military installation* S Cyprus
158 F11 **Aksai Chin** *Chin.* Aksayqin. *disputed region* China/India
Aksaj *see* Aksay
136 I15 **Aksaray** Aksaray, C Turkey
136 I15 **Aksaray** ◆ *province* C Turkey
159 P8 **Aksay** *var.* Aksay Kazakzu Zizhixian. Gansu, N China
144 G8 **Aksay** *var.* Aksaj, *Kaz.* Aqsay. Zapadnyy Kazakhstan, NW Kazakhstan
129 O11 **Aksay** Volgogradskaya Oblast', SW Russian Federation
147 W10 **Aksay** *var.* Toxkan He. China/Kyrgyzstan
Aksay Kazakzu Zizhixian *see* Aksay
Aksayqin *see* Aksai Chin
158 G11 **Aksayqin Hu** ◎ NW China
136 G14 **Akşehir** Konya, W Turkey
136 G14 **Akşehir Gölü** ◎ C Turkey
136 G16 **Akseki** Antalya, SW Turkey
123 P13 **Aksenovo-Zilovskoye** Chitinskaya Oblast', S Russian Federation
145 V11 **Akshatau, Khrebet** ▲ E Kazakhstan
147 Y8 **Ak-Shyyrak** Issyk-Kul'skaya Oblast', E Kyrgyzstan
Akstafa *see* Ağstafa
158 H7 **Aksu** Xinjiang Uygur Zizhiqu, NW China
145 R8 **Aksu** *Kaz.* Aqsū. Akmola, N Kazakhstan
145 W13 **Aksu** *Kaz.* Aqsū. Almaty, SE Kazakhstan
145 V13 **Aksu** *Kaz.* Aqsū. SE Kazakhstan
145 X11 **Aksuat** *Kaz.* Aqsūat. Vostochnyy Kazakhstan, E Kazakhstan
145 Y11 **Aksuat** *Kaz.* Aqsūat. Vostochnyy Kazakhstan, SE Kazakhstan
129 S4 **Aksubayevo** Respublika Tatarstan, W Russian Federation
158 H7 **Aksu He** *Rus.* Sary-Dzhaz. China/Kyrgyzstan *see also* Sary-Dzhaz
80 J10 **Āksum** Tigray, N Ethiopia
145 O12 **Aktas** *Kaz.* Aqtas. Zhezkazgan, C Kazakhstan
Aktash *see* Oqtosh
147 V9 **Ak-Tash, Gora** ▲ C Kyrgyzstan
145 R10 **Aktau** *Kaz.* Aqtaū. Karaganda, C Kazakhstan
144 E11 **Aktau** *Kaz.* Aqtaū; *prev.* Shevchenko. Mangistau, W Kazakhstan
Aktau, Khrebet *see* Oqtogh, SW Tajikistan
Aktau, Khrebet *see* Oqtow Tizmasi, C Uzbekistan
Akte *see* Ágion Óros
Ak-Tepe *see* Akdepe
147 X7 **Ak-Terek** Issyk-Kul'skaya Oblast', E Kyrgyzstan
Aktí *see* Ágion Óros
158 E8 **Akto** Xinjiang Uygur Zizhiqu, NW China
145 V12 **Aktogay** *Kaz.* Aqtoghay. Vostochnyy Kazakhstan, E Kazakhstan
145 T12 **Aktogay** *Kaz.* Aqtoghay. Zhezkazgan, C Kazakhstan
119 M18 **Aktsyabrski** *Rus.* Oktyabr'skiy; *prev.* Karpilovka. Homyel'skaya Voblasts', SE Belarus
144 I10 **Aktyubinsk** *Kaz.* Aqtöbe. Aktyubinsk, NW Kazakhstan
144 H11 **Aktyubinsk** *off.* Aktyubinskaya Oblast', *Kaz.* Aqtöbe Oblysy. ◆ *province* W Kazakhstan
147 W7 **Ak-Tyuz** *var.* Aktyuz. Chuyskaya Oblast', N Kyrgyzstan
79 J17 **Akula** Equateur, NW Dem. Rep. Congo (Zaire)
164 C15 **Akune** Kagoshima, Kyūshū, SW Japan
38 L16 **Akun Island** *island* Aleutian Islands, Alaska, USA
80 J9 **Akurdet** *var.* Agordat, Akordat. C Eritrea
77 T16 **Akure** Ondo, SW Nigeria
92 J2 **Akureyri** Nordhurland Eystra, N Iceland
38 L17 **Akutan** Akutan Island, Alaska, USA
38 K17 **Akutan Island** *island* Aleutian Islands, Alaska, USA
77 V17 **Akwa Ibom** ◆ *state* SE Nigeria
Akyab *see* Sittwe
129 W7 **Ak"yar** Respublika Bashkortostan, W Russian Federation
145 Y11 **Akzhar** *Kaz.* Aqzhar. Vostochnyy Kazakhstan, E Kazakhstan
94 F13 **Ål** Buskerud, S Norway
119 N18 **Ala** *Rus.* Ola. SE Belarus
20 H11 **Alabama** *off.* State of Alabama; also known as Camellia State, Heart of Dixie, The Cotton State, Yellowhammer State. ◆ *state* S USA
23 P6 **Alabama River** Alabama, S USA
23 P4 **Alabaster** Alabama, S USA
139 U10 **Al 'Abd Allāh** *var.* Al Abdullah. S Iraq
Al Abdullah *see* Al 'Abd Allāh
139 W14 **Al Abṭīyah** *well* S Iraq
147 S9 **Ala-Buka** Dzhalal-Abadskaya Oblast', W Kyrgyzstan
136 J12 **Alaca** Çorum, N Turkey
136 K10 **Alaçam** Samsun, N Turkey
Alacant *see* Alicante
23 V9 **Alachua** Florida, SE USA
137 S13 **Aladağlar** ▲ W Turkey
136 K15 **Ala Dağları** ▲ C Turkey
129 O16 **Alagir** Respublika Severnaya Osetiya, SW Russian Federation
106 B6 **Alagna Valsesia** Valle d'Aosta, NW Italy
103 P12 **Alagnon** C France
59 P16 **Alagoas** *off.* Estado de Alagoas. ◆ *state* E Brazil
59 P17 **Alagoinhas** Bahia, E Brazil
105 R5 **Alagón** Aragón, NE Spain
104 J9 **Alagón** W Spain
93 K16 **Alahärmä** Länsi-Suomi, W Finland
al Ahdar *see* Al Akhḍar
142 K12 **Al Aḥmadī** *var.* Ahmadi. E Kuwait
Al Ain *see* Al 'Ayn
105 Z8 **Alaior** *prev.* Alayor. Menorca, Spain, W Mediterranean Sea
147 T11 **Alai Range** *Rus.* Alayskiy Khrebet. ▲ Kyrgyzstan/Tajikistan
Alais *see* Alès
141 X11 **Al 'Ajā'iz** E Oman
141 X11 **Al 'Ajā'iz** *oasis* SE Oman
93 L16 **Alajärvi** Länsi-Suomi, W Finland
118 K4 **Alajõe** Ida-Virumaa, NE Estonia
42 M13 **Alajuela** Alajuela, C Costa Rica
42 L12 **Alajuela** *off.* Provincia de Alajuela. ◆ *province* N Costa Rica
43 T14 **Alajuela, Lago** ◎ C Panama
38 M11 **Alakanuk** Alaska, USA
140 K5 **Al Akhḍar** *var.* Al Ahdar. Tabūk, NW Saudi Arabia
Alaköl *see* Alakol', Ozero
145 X13 **Alakol', Ozero** *Kaz.* Alaköl. ◎ SE Kazakhstan
126 I5 **Alakurtti** Murmanskaya Oblast', NW Russian Federation
38 F10 **Alalakeiki Channel** *channel* Hawaii, USA, C Pacific Ocean
Al 'Alamayn *see* El 'Alamein
139 R1 **Al 'Amādīyah** N Iraq
188 K5 **Alamagan** *island* C Northern Mariana Islands
139 X10 **Al 'Amārah** *var.* Amara. E Iraq
80 J11 **Ālamat'ā** Tigray, N Ethiopia
37 R11 **Alameda** New Mexico, SW USA
121 T13 **'Alam el Rûm, Râs** *headland* N Egypt
Alamícamba *see* Alamikamba
42 M8 **Alamikamba** *var.* Alamícamba. Región Autónoma Atlántico Norte, NE Nicaragua
24 K11 **Alamito Creek** Texas, SW USA
40 M8 **Alamitos, Sierra de los** ▲ NE Mexico
35 X9 **Alamo** Nevada, W USA
20 F9 **Alamo** Tennessee, S USA
41 Q12 **Álamo** Veracruz-Llave, C Mexico
37 S14 **Alamogordo** New Mexico, SW USA
36 J12 **Alamo Lake** ▣ Arizona, SW USA
40 H7 **Alamos** Sonora, NW Mexico
37 S7 **Alamosa** Colorado, C USA
93 J20 **Åland** *var.* Aland Islands, *Fin.* Ahvenanmaa. ◆ *province* SW Finland
93 J19 **Åland** *Fin.* Ahvenanmaa. *island* SW Finland
88 K9 **Åland** *var.* Aland Islands, *Fin.* Ahvenanmaa. *island group* SW Finland
Aland Islands *see* Åland
Aland Sea *see* Ålands Hav
95 Q14 **Ålands Hav** *var.* Aland Sea. *strait* Baltic Sea/Gulf of Bothnia
43 P16 **Alanje** Chiriquí, SW Panama
25 O2 **Alanreed** Texas, SW USA
136 G17 **Alanya** Antalya, S Turkey
23 U7 **Alapaha River** Florida/Georgia, SE USA
122 G10 **Alapayevsk** Sverdlovskaya Oblast', C Russian Federation
Alappuzha *see* Alleppey
138 F14 **Al 'Aqabah** *var.* Akaba, 'Aqaba; *anc.* Aelana, Elath. Ma'ān, SW Jordan
Al 'Arabīyah as Su'ūdīyah *see* Saudi Arabia
al Araïch *see* Larache
105 Q10 **Alarcón** Castilla-La Mancha, C Spain
105 Q9 **Alarcón, Embalse de** ▣ C Spain
138 J2 **Al 'Arīmah** *Fr.* Arime. Ḥalab, N Syria
Al 'Arīsh *see* El 'Arîsh
141 P6 **Al Arṭāwīyah** Ar Riyāḍ, N Saudi Arabia
Alasca, Golfo de *see* Alaska, Gulf of
136 D14 **Alaşehir** Manisa, W Turkey
139 N5 **Al 'Ashārah** *var.* Ashara. Dayr az Zawr, E Syria
Al Ashkhara *see* Al Ashkharah
141 Z9 **Al Ashkharah** *var.* Al Ashkhara. NE Oman
39 P8 **Alaska** *off.* State of Alaska; also known as Land of the Midnight Sun, The Last Frontier, Seward's Folly; *prev.* Russian America. ◆ *state* NW USA
39 T13 **Alaska, Gulf of** *var.* Golfo de Alasca. *gulf* Canada/USA
39 O15 **Alaska Peninsula** *peninsula* Alaska, USA
39 Q11 **Alaska Range** ▲ Alaska, USA
Al-Asnam *see* Chlef
106 B10 **Alassio** Liguria, NW Italy
Alat *see* Olot
137 Y12 **Älät** *Rus.* Alyat; *prev.* Alyaty-Pristan'. SE Azerbaijan
139 S13 **Al 'Athāmīn** S Iraq
39 P7 **Alatna River** Alaska, USA
107 J15 **Alatri** Lazio, C Italy
Alattio *see* Alta
129 P5 **Alatyr'** Chuvashskaya Respublika, W Russian Federation
56 C7 **Alausí** Chimborazo, C Ecuador
105 O3 **Álava** *Basq.* Araba. ◆ *province* País Vasco, N Spain
137 T11 **Alaverdi** N Armenia
Alavo *see* Alavus
93 N14 **Ala-Vuokki** Oulu, E Finland
93 K17 **Alavus** *Swe.* Alavo. Länsi-Suomi, W Finland
Al 'Awābī *see* Awābī
139 P6 **Al 'Awānī** W Iraq
75 U12 **Al Awaynāt** SE Libya
Al Awaynāt *see* Al 'Uwaynāt
182 K9 **Alawoona** South Australia
Alaykel'/Alay-Kuu *see* Këk-Art
143 R17 **Al 'Ayn** *var.* Al Ain. Abū Ẓaby, E UAE
143 R17 **Al 'Ayn** *var.* Al Ain. ✕ Abū Ẓaby, E UAE
138 G12 **Al 'Aynā** Al Karak, W Jordan
Alayor *see* Alaior
Alayskiy Khrebet *see* Alai Range
123 S6 **Alazeya** NE Russian Federation
139 U8 **Al 'Azīzīyah** *var.* Aziziya. E Iraq
120 M12 **Al 'Azīzīyah** NW Libya
138 I10 **Al Azraq al Janūbī** Az Zarqā', N Jordan
106 B9 **Alba** *anc.* Alba Pompeia. Piemonte, NW Italy
25 V6 **Alba** Texas, SW USA
116 G11 **Alba** ◆ *county* W Romania
139 P3 **Al Ba'āj** N Iraq
138 J2 **Al Bāb** Ḥalab, N Syria
116 G10 **Albac** *Hung.* Fehérvölgy; *prev.* Álbák. Alba, SW Romania
105 Q11 **Albacete** Castilla-La Mancha, C Spain
105 P11 **Albacete** ◆ *province* Castilla-La Mancha, C Spain
140 J4 **Al Bad'** Tabūk, NW Saudi Arabia
104 L7 **Alba de Tormes** Castilla-León, N Spain
139 P3 **Al Bādī** N Iraq
141 V8 **Al Badī'ah** ✕ (Abū Ẓaby) Abū Ẓaby, C UAE
143 P17 **Al Badī'ah** *var.* Al Bedei'ah. *spring/well* C UAE
139 Q7 **Al Baghdādī** *var.* Khān al Baghdādī. SW Iraq
Al Bāha *see* Al Bāḥah
140 M11 **Al Bāḥah** *var.* Al Bāha. Al Bāḥah, SW Saudi Arabia
140 M11 **Al Bāḥah** *off.* Minṭaqat al Bāḥah. ◆ *province* W Saudi Arabia
Al Baḥrayn *see* Bahrain
105 S11 **Albaida** País Valenciano, E Spain
116 H11 **Alba Iulia** *Ger.* Weissenburg, *Hung.* Gyulafehérvár; *prev.* Bălgrad, Karlsburg, Károly-Fehérvár. Alba, W Romania
Álbák *see* Albac
138 G10 **Al Balqā'** *off.* Muḥāfaẓat al Balqā', *var.* Balqā'. ◆ *governorate* NW Jordan
14 F11 **Alban** Ontario, S Canada
103 O15 **Alban** Tarn, S France
12 K11 **Albanel, Lac** ◎ Quebec, SE Canada
113 L20 **Albania** *off.* Republic of Albania, *Alb.* Republika e Shqipërisë, Shqipëria; *prev.* People's Socialist Republic of Albania. ◆ *republic* SE Europe
Albania *see* Aubagne
107 H15 **Albano Laziale** Lazio, C Italy
180 J14 **Albany** Western Australia
23 S7 **Albany** Georgia, SE USA
31 P13 **Albany** Indiana, N USA
20 L8 **Albany** Kentucky, S USA
29 U7 **Albany** Minnesota, N USA
27 R2 **Albany** Missouri, C USA
18 L10 **Albany** *state capital* New York, NE USA
32 G12 **Albany** Oregon, NW USA
25 Q6 **Albany** Texas, SW USA
12 F10 **Albany** Ontario, S Canada
Alba Pompeia *see* Alba
Alba Regia *see* Székesfehérvár
138 J6 **Al Bāridah** *var.* Bāridah. Ḥimṣ, C Syria
139 Q11 **Al Barīt** S Iraq
105 R8 **Albarracín** Aragón, NE Spain
139 Y12 **Al Baṣrah** *Eng.* Basra; *hist.* Busra, Bussora. SE Iraq
139 V11 **Al Baṭḥā'** SE Iraq
141 X8 **Al Bāṭinah** *var.* Batinah. *coastal region* N Oman
(0) H16 **Albatross Plateau** *undersea feature* E Pacific Ocean
Al Batrūn *see* Batroûn
121 Q12 **Al Bayḍā'** *var.* Beida. NE Libya
141 P16 **Al Bayḍā'** *var.* Al Beida. SW Yemen
Al Bedei'ah *see* Al Badī'ah
Al Beida *see* Al Bayḍā'
21 S10 **Albemarle** *var.* Albermarle. North Carolina, SE USA
Albemarle Island *see* Isabela, Isla
21 N8 **Albemarle Sound** *inlet* W Atlantic Ocean
106 B10 **Albenga** Liguria, NW Italy
104 L8 **Alberche** C Spain
103 O17 **Albères, Chaîne des** *var.* les Albères, Montes Albères. ▲ France/Spain
Albères, Montes *see* Albères, Chaîne des
182 F2 **Alberga Creek** *seasonal river* South Australia
104 G7 **Albergaria-a-Velha** Aveiro, N Portugal
105 S10 **Alberic** País Valenciano, E Spain
Albermarle *see* Albemarle
107 P18 **Alberobello** Puglia, SE Italy
108 J7 **Alberschwende** Vorarlberg, W Austria
103 O3 **Albert** Somme, N France
11 O12 **Alberta** ◆ *province* SW Canada
Albert Edward Nyanza *see* Edward, Lake
61 C20 **Alberti** Buenos Aires, E Argentina
111 K23 **Albertirsa** Pest, C Hungary
99 I16 **Albertkanaal** *canal* N Belgium
79 P17 **Albert, Lake** *var.* Albert Nyanza, Lac Mobutu Sese Seko. ◎ Uganda/Dem. Rep. Congo (Zaire)
29 V11 **Albert Lea** Minnesota, N USA
81 F16 **Albert Nile** NW Uganda
Albert Nyanza *see* Albert, Lake
103 T11 **Albertville** Savoie, E France
23 Q2 **Albertville** Alabama, S USA
Albertville *see* Kalemie
103 N15 **Albi** *anc.* Albiga. Tarn, S France
29 W15 **Albia** Iowa, C USA
Albiga *see* Albi
55 X9 **Albina** Marowijne, NE Suriname
83 A15 **Albina, Ponta** *headland* SW Angola
30 M16 **Albion** Illinois, N USA
31 P11 **Albion** Indiana, N USA
29 P14 **Albion** Nebraska, C USA
18 E9 **Albion** New York, NE USA
18 B12 **Albion** Pennsylvania, NE USA
Al Biqā' *see* El Beqaa
140 J4 **Al Bi'r** *var.* Bi'r Ibn Hirmās. Tabūk, NW Saudi Arabia
140 M12 **Al Birk** Makkah, SW Saudi Arabia
141 Q9 **Al Biyāḍ** *desert* C Saudi Arabia
98 H13 **Alblasserdam** Zuid-Holland, SW Netherlands

◆ COUNTRY ● COUNTRY CAPITAL ◇ DEPENDENT TERRITORY ○ DEPENDENT TERRITORY CAPITAL ◆ ADMINISTRATIVE REGION ✕ INTERNATIONAL AIRPORT ▲ MOUNTAIN ▲ MOUNTAIN RANGE VOLCANO RIVER ◎ LAKE ▣ RESERVOIR

105 *T8* **Albocácer** *var.* Albocasser. País Valenciano, E Spain
Albocasser *see* Albocácer
95 *H19* **Ålbæk** Nordjylland, N Denmark
Albona *see* Labin
105 *O17* **Alborán, Isla de** *island* S Spain
Alborán, Mar de *see* Alboran Sea
105 *N17* **Alboran Sea** *Sp.* Mar de Alborán. *sea* SW Mediterranean Sea
95 *G20* **Ålborg** *var.* Aalborg, Ålborg-Nørresundby; *anc.* Alburgum. Nordjylland, N Denmark
95 *H21* **Ålborg Bugt** *var.* Aalborg Bugt. *bay* N Denmark
Ålborg-Nørresundby *see* Ålborg
143 *O5* **Alborz, Reshteh-ye Kūhhā-ye** *Eng.* Elburz Mountains. ⛰ N Iran
105 *Q14* **Albox** Andalucía, S Spain
101 *H23* **Albstadt** Baden-Württemberg, SW Germany
104 *G14* **Albufeira** Beja, S Portugal
139 *P5* **Ālbū Gharz, Sabkhat** ◎ W Iraq
105 *O15* **Albuñol** Andalucía, S Spain
37 *Q11* **Albuquerque** New Mexico, SW USA
141 *W8* **Al Buraymī** *var.* Buraimi. N Oman
143 *R17* **Al Buraymī** *var.* Buraimi. *spring/well* Oman/UAE
Al Burayqah *see* Marsá al Burayqah
Alburgum *see* Ålborg
104 *I10* **Alburquerque** Extremadura, W Spain
181 *V14* **Albury** New South Wales, SE Australia
141 *T14* **Al Buzūn** SE Yemen
93 *G17* **Alby** Västernorrland, C Sweden
Albyn, Glen *see* Mor, Glen
104 *G12* **Alcácer do Sal** Setúbal, W Portugal
Alcalá de Chisvert *see* Alcalá de Chivert
105 *T8* **Alcalá de Chivert** *var.* Alcalá de Chisvert. País Valenciano, E Spain
104 *K14* **Alcalá de Guadaira** Andalucía, S Spain
105 *O8* **Alcalá de Henares** *Ar.* Alkal'a; *anc.* Complutum. Madrid, C Spain
104 *K16* **Alcalá de los Gazules** Andalucía, S Spain
105 *N14* **Alcalá La Real** Andalucía, S Spain
107 *I23* **Alcamo** Sicilia, Italy, C Mediterranean Sea
105 *T4* **Alcanadre** ≈ NE Spain
105 *T8* **Alcanar** Cataluña, NE Spain
104 *J5* **Alcañices** Castilla-León, N Spain
105 *T7* **Alcañiz** Aragón, NE Spain
104 *I9* **Alcántara** Extremadura, W Spain
104 *J9* **Alcántara, Embalse de** ▣ W Spain
105 *R13* **Alcantarilla** Murcia, SE Spain
105 *P11* **Alcaraz** Castilla-La Mancha, C Spain
105 *P12* **Alcaraz, Sierra de** ⛰ C Spain
104 *I12* **Alcarrache** ≈ SW Spain
105 *T6* **Alcarràs** Cataluña, NE Spain
105 *N14* **Alcaudete** Andalucía, S Spain
Alcázar *see* Ksar-el-Kebir
105 *O10* **Alcázar de San Juan** *anc.* Alce. Castilla-La Mancha, C Spain
Alcazarquivir *see* Ksar-el-Kebir
Alce *see* Alcázar de San Juan
57 *B17* **Alcebo, Volcán** ✱ Galapagos Islands, Ecuador, E Pacific Ocean
139 *X12* **Al Chabā'ish** *var.* Al Kaba'ish. SE Iraq
117 *Y7* **Alchevs'k** *prev.* Kommunarsk, Voroshilovsk. Luhans'ka Oblast', E Ukraine
Alcira *see* Alzira
21 *N9* **Alcoa** Tennessee, S USA
104 *F9* **Alcobaça** Leiria, C Portugal
105 *N8* **Alcobendas** Madrid, C Spain
Alcoi *see* Alcoy
105 *P7* **Alcolea del Pinar** Castilla-La Mancha, C Spain
104 *I11* **Alconchel** Extremadura, W Spain
105 *S9* **Alcora** País Valenciano, E Spain
105 *N8* **Alcorcón** Madrid, C Spain
105 *S7* **Alcorisa** Aragón, NE Spain
61 *B19* **Alcorta** Santa Fe, C Argentina
104 *H14* **Alcoutim** Faro, S Portugal
33 *W15* **Alcova** Wyoming, C USA
105 *S11* **Alcoy** *var.* Alcoi. País Valenciano, E Spain
105 *Y9* **Alcúdia, Badia d'** *bay* Mallorca, Spain, W Mediterranean Sea
172 *M7* **Aldabra Group** *island group* SW Seychelles
139 *U10* **Al Daghghārah** C Iraq
40 *J5* **Aldama** Chihuahua, N Mexico
41 *P11* **Aldama** Tamaulipas, C Mexico
123 *Q11* **Aldan** Respublika Sakha (Yakutiya), NE Russian Federation
123 *Q10* **Aldan** ≈ NE Russian Federation
162 *G7* **Aldar** Dzavhan, W Mongolia
al Dar al Baida *see* Rabat
97 *Q20* **Aldeburgh** E England, UK
105 *P5* **Aldehuela de Calatañazor** Castilla-León, N Spain
Aldeia Nova *see* Aldeia Nova de São Bento
104 *H13* **Aldeia Nova de São Bento** *var.* Aldeia Nova. Beja, S Portugal
29 *V11* **Alden** Minnesota, N USA
184 *N6* **Aldermen Islands, The** *island group* N NZ
97 *L25* **Alderney** *island* Channel Islands
97 *N22* **Aldershot** S England, UK
21 *R6* **Alderson** West Virginia, NE USA
Al Dhaid *see* Adh Dhayd
30 *J11* **Aledo** Illinois, N USA
76 *H9* **Aleg** Brakna, SW Mauritania
64 *Q10* **Alegranza** *island* Islas Canarias, Spain, NE Atlantic Ocean
37 *P12* **Alegres Mountain** ▲ New Mexico, SW USA
61 *F15* **Alegrete** Rio Grande do Sul, S Brazil
61 *C16* **Alejandra** Santa Fe, C Argentina
193 *T11* **Alejandro Selkirk, Isla** *island* Islas Juan Fernández, Chile, E Pacific Ocean
126 *I12* **Alekhovshchina** Leningradskaya Oblast', NW Russian Federation
39 *O13* **Aleknagik** Alaska, USA
Aleksandriya *see* Oleksandriya
Aleksandropol' *see* Gyumri
128 *L3* **Aleksandrov** Vladimirskaya Oblast', W Russian Federation
113 *N14* **Aleksandrovac** Serbia, C Yugoslavia
129 *R9* **Aleksandrov Gay** Saratovskaya Oblast', W Russian Federation
129 *U6* **Aleksandrovka** Orenburgskaya Oblast', W Russian Federation
Aleksandrovka *see* Oleksandrivka
114 *J8* **Aleksandrovo** Lovech, N Bulgaria
127 *V13* **Aleksandrovsk** Permskaya Oblast', NW Russian Federation
Aleksandrovsk *see* Zaporizhzhya
129 *N14* **Aleksandrovskoye** Stavropol'skiy Kray, SW Russian Federation
123 *T12* **Aleksandrovsk-Sakhalinskiy** Ostrov Sakhalin, Sakhalinskaya Oblast', SE Russian Federation
110 *J10* **Aleksandrów Kujawski** Kujawskio-pomorskie, C Poland
110 *K12* **Aleksandrów Łódzki** Łódzkie, C Poland
Alekseevka *see* Akkol'/Alekseyevka
126 *L9* **Alekseyevka** Belgorodskaya Oblast', W Russian Federation
145 *P7* **Alekseyevka** *Kaz.* Alekseevka. Severnyy Kazakhstan, N Kazakhstan
145 *Z10* **Alekseyevka** *Kaz.* Alekseevka. Vostochnyy Kazakhstan, E Kazakhstan
129 *S7* **Alekseyevka** Samarskaya Oblast', W Russian Federation
Alekseyevka *see* Akkol'
129 *R4* **Alekseyevskoye** Respublika Tatarstan, W Russian Federation
128 *K5* **Aleksin** Tul'skaya Oblast', W Russian Federation
113 *O14* **Aleksinac** Serbia, SE Yugoslavia
190 *G11* **Alele** Île Uvea, E Wallis and Futuna
95 *N20* **Ålem** Kalmar, S Sweden
102 *L6* **Alençon** Orne, N France
58 *I12* **Alenquer** Pará, NE Brazil
38 *G10* **Alenuihaha Channel** *channel* Hawaii, USA, C Pacific Ocean
Alep/Aleppo *see* Ḩalab
103 *Y15* **Aléria** Corse, France, C Mediterranean Sea
197 *Q11* **Alert** Ellesmere Island, Nunavut, N Canada
103 *Q14* **Alès** *prev.* Alais. Gard, S France
116 *G9* **Aleşd** *Hung.* Élesd. Bihor, SW Romania
106 *C9* **Alessandria** *Fr.* Alexandrie. Piemonte, N Italy
95 *G21* **Ålestrup** *var.* Aalestrup. Viborg, NW Denmark
94 *D9* **Ålesund** Møre og Romsdal, S Norway
108 *E10* **Aletschhorn** ▲ SW Switzerland
197 *S1* **Aleutian Basin** *undersea feature* Bering Sea
38 *H17* **Aleutian Islands** *island group* Alaska, USA
39 *P14* **Aleutian Range** ⛰ Alaska, USA
(0) *B5* **Aleutian Trench** *undersea feature* S Bering Sea
123 *T10* **Alevina, Mys** *headland* E Russian Federation
15 *Q6* **Alex** ≈ Quebec, SE Canada
28 *J3* **Alexander** North Dakota, N USA
39 *W14* **Alexander Archipelago** *island group* Alaska, USA
Alexanderbaai *see* Alexander Bay
83 *D23* **Alexander Bay** *Afr.* Alexanderbaai. Northern Cape, W South Africa
23 *Q5* **Alexander City** Alabama, S USA
194 *J6* **Alexander Island** *island* Antarctica
Alexander Range *see* Kirghiz Range
183 *O12* **Alexandra** Victoria, SE Australia
185 *D22* **Alexandra** Otago, South Island, NZ
115 *F14* **Alexándreia** *var.* Alexándria. Kentrikí Makedonía, N Greece
Alexandretta *see* İskenderun
Alexandretta, Gulf of *see* İskenderun Körfezi
15 *N13* **Alexandria** Ontario, SE Canada
121 *U13* **Alexandria** *Ar.* Al Iskandarīyah. N Egypt
44 *J12* **Alexandria** C Jamaica
116 *J15* **Alexandria** Teleorman, S Romania
31 *P13* **Alexandria** Indiana, N USA
20 *M4* **Alexandria** Kentucky, S USA
22 *H7* **Alexandria** Louisiana, S USA
29 *T7* **Alexandria** Minnesota, N USA
29 *Q11* **Alexandria** South Dakota, N USA
21 *W4* **Alexandria** Virginia, NE USA
Alexándria *see* Alexándreia
18 *I7* **Alexandria Bay** New York, NE USA
Alexandrie *see* Alessandria
182 *J10* **Alexandrina, Lake** ◎ South Australia
114 *K13* **Alexandroúpoli** *var.* Alexandroúpolis, *Turk.* Dedeagaç, Dedeagach. Anatolikí Makedonía kai Thráki, NE Greece
Alexandroúpolis *see* Alexandroúpoli
10 *L15* **Alexis Creek** British Columbia, SW Canada
122 *I13* **Aleysk** Altayskiy Kray, S Russian Federation
8 *L15* **Alexis Creek** British Columbia, SW Canada
122 *I13* **Aleysk** Altayskiy Kray, S Russian Federation
139 *S8* **Al Fallūjah** *var.* Falluja. C Iraq
105 *R8* **Alfambra** ≈ E Spain
Al Faqa *see* Faq'
141 *R15* **Al Farḍah** C Yemen
105 *Q4* **Alfaro** La Rioja, N Spain
105 *U5* **Alfarràs** Cataluña, NE Spain
Al Fāshir *see* El Fasher
Al Fashn *see* El Fashn
114 *M7* **Alfatar** Silistra, NE Bulgaria
139 *S5* **Al Fatḩah** C Iraq
139 *Q3* **Al Fatsī** N Iraq
139 *Z13* **Al Fāw** *var.* Fao. SE Iraq
Al Fayyūm *see* El Faiyûm
115 *D20* **Alfeiós** *prev.* Alfiós, *anc.* Alpheius, Alpheus. ≈ S Greece
100 *I13* **Alfeld** Niedersachsen, C Germany
Alfiós *see* Alfeiós
Alföld *see* Great Hungarian Plain
94 *C11* **Ålfotbreen** *glacier* S Norway
19 *P9* **Alfred** Maine, NE USA
18 *F11* **Alfred** New York, NE USA
61 *K14* **Alfredo Vagner** Santa Catarina, S Brazil
94 *M12* **Alfta** Gävleborg, C Sweden
140 *K12* **Al Fuḩayḩīl** *var.* Fahaheel. SE Kuwait
139 *Q6* **Al Fuḩaymī** C Iraq
143 *S16* **Al Fujayrah** *Eng.* Fujairah. Al Fujayrah, NE UAE
143 *S16* **Al Fujayrah** *Eng.* Fujairah. ✕ Al Fujayrah, NE UAE
Al Furāt *see* Euphrates
144 *I10* **Alga** *Kaz.* Algha. Aktyubinsk, NW Kazakhstan
144 *G9* **Algabas** Zapadnyy Kazakhstan, NW Kazakhstan
95 *C17* **Ålgård** Rogaland, S Norway
104 *G14* **Algarve** *cultural region* S Portugal
182 *G3* **Algebuckina Bridge** South Australia
104 *K16* **Algeciras** Andalucía, SW Spain
105 *S10* **Algemesí** País Valenciano, E Spain
Al-Genain *see* El Geneina
120 *F9* **Alger** *var.* Algiers, El Djazaïr, Al Jazair. ● (Algeria) N Algeria
74 *H9* **Algeria** *off.* Democratic and Popular Republic of Algeria. ◆ *republic* N Africa
120 *J8* **Algerian Basin** *var.* Balearic Plain *undersea feature* W Mediterranean Sea
Algha *see* Alga
138 *I4* **Al Ghāb** ◎ NW Syria
141 *X10* **Al Ghābah** *var.* Ghaba. C Oman
141 *U14* **Al Ghayḍah** E Yemen
140 *M6* **Al Ghazālah** Ḩā'il, NW Saudi Arabia
107 *B17* **Alghero** Sardegna, Italy, C Mediterranean Sea
95 *M20* **Älghult** Kronoberg, S Sweden
Al Ghurdaqah *see* Hurghada
Algiers *see* Alger
105 *S10* **Alginet** País Valenciano, E Spain
83 *I26* **Algoa Bay** *bay* S South Africa
104 *L15* **Algodonales** Andalucía, S Spain
105 *N9* **Algodor** ≈ C Spain
Al Golea *see* El Goléa
31 *N6* **Algoma** Wisconsin, N USA
29 *U12* **Algona** Iowa, C USA
20 *L8* **Algood** Tennessee, S USA
105 *O2* **Algorta** País Vasco, N Spain
61 *E18* **Algorta** Río Negro, W Uruguay
Al Haba *see* Haba
139 *Q10* **Al Habbārīyah** S Iraq
Al Hadhar *see* Al Ḩaḑr
139 *Q4* **Al Ḩaḑr** *var.* Al Hadhar; *anc.* Hatra. NW Iraq
139 *T13* **Al Ḩajarah** *desert* S Iraq
141 *W8* **Al Ḩajār al Gharbī** ⛰ N Oman
141 *Y8* **Al Ḩajar ash Sharqī** ⛰ NE Oman
141 *R15* **Al Hajarayn** C Yemen
138 *L10* **Al Ḩamād** *desert* Jordan/Saudi Arabia
Al Hamad *see* Syrian Desert
75 *N9* **Al Ḩamādah al Ḩamrā'** *var.* Al Ḩamrā'. *desert* NW Libya
105 *N15* **Alhama de Granada** Andalucía, S Spain
105 *R13* **Alhama de Murcia** Murcia, SE Spain
35 *T15* **Alhambra** California, W USA
139 *T12* **Al Ḩammām** S Iraq
141 *X8* **Al Ḩamrā'** NE Oman
Al Ḩamrā' *see* Al Ḩamādah al Ḩamrā'
141 *O6* **Al Ḩamūdīyah** *spring/well* N Saudi Arabia
140 *M7* **Al Ḩanākīyah** Al Madīnah, W Saudi Arabia
139 *W14* **Al Ḩanīyah** *escarpment* Iraq/Saudi Arabia
139 *Y12* **Al Hārithah** SE Iraq
140 *L3* **Al Ḩarrah** *desert* NW Saudi Arabia
75 *Q10* **Al Harūj al Aswad** *desert* C Libya
Al Hasaifin *see* Al Ḩusayfīn
139 *N2* **Al Ḩasakah** *var.* Al Hasijah, El Haseke, *Fr.* Hassetché. Al Ḩasakah, NE Syria
139 *O2* **Al Ḩasakah** *off.* Muḩāfaẓat al Ḩasakah, *var.* Al Hasakah, Āl Hasakah, Hasakah, Hassakeh. ◈ *governorate* NE Syria
139 *T9* **Al Hāshimīyah** C Iraq
138 *G13* **Al Hāshimīyah** Ma'ān, S Jordan
Al Hasijah *see* Al Ḩasakah
104 *M15* **Alhaurín el Grande** Andalucía, S Spain
141 *Q16* **Al Ḩawrā** S Yemen
139 *V10* **Al Ḩayy** *var.* Kut al Hai, Kūt al Ḩayy. E Iraq
141 *U11* **Al Ḩibāk** *desert* E Saudi Arabia
138 *H8* **Al Hījānah** *var.* Hejanah, Hijanah. Dimashq, W Syria
140 *K7* **Al Ḩijāz** *Eng.* Hejaz. *physical region* NW Saudi Arabia
Al Hilbeh *see* 'Ulayyānīyah, Bi'r al
139 *T9* **Al Ḩillah** *var.* Hilla. C Iraq
139 *T9* **Al Hindīyah** *var.* Hindiya. C Iraq
138 *G12* **Al Ḩisā** Aţ Ţafīlah, W Jordan
74 *G5* **Al-Hoceïma** *var.* al Hoceima, Al-Hoceima, Alhucemas; *prev.* Villa Sanjurjo. N Morocco
Alhucemas *see* Al-Hoceïma
105 *N17* **Alhucemas, Peñon de** *island group* S Spain
141 *N15* **Al Ḩudaydah** *Eng.* Hodeida. W Yemen
141 *N15* **Al Ḩudaydah** *Eng.* Hodeida. ✕ W Yemen
140 *M4* **Al Ḩudūd ash Shamālīyah** *var.* Minţaqat al Ḩudūd ash Shamālīyah, *Eng.* Northern Border Region. ◈ *province* N Saudi Arabia
141 *S7* **Al Hufūf** *var.* Hofuf. Ash Sharqīyah, NE Saudi Arabia
al-Hurma *see* Al Khurmah
141 *X7* **Al Ḩusayfīn** *var.* Al Hasaifin. N Oman
138 *G9* **Al Ḩuşn** *var.* Husn. Irbid, N Jordan
139 *U9* **'Alī** E Iraq
104 *L10* **Alia** Extremadura, W Spain
143 *P9* **'Alīābād** Yazd, C Iran
'Alīābad *see* Qā'emshahr
105 *S7* **Aliaga** Aragón, NE Spain
136 *B13* **Aliağa** İzmir, W Turkey
Aliákmon *see* Aliákmonas
115 *F14* **Aliákmonas** *prev.* Aliákmon, *anc.* Haliacmon. ≈ N Greece
139 *W9* **'Alī al Gharbī** E Iraq
139 *U11* **'Alī al Ḩassūnī** S Iraq
115 *G18* **Alíartos** Stereá Ellás, C Greece
137 *Y12* **Äli-Bayramlı** *Rus.* Ali-Bayramly. SE Azerbaijan
Ali-Bayramly *see* Äli-Bayramlı
114 *P12* **Alibey Barajı** ▣ NW Turkey
77 *S13* **Alibori** ≈ N Benin
112 *M10* **Alibunar** Serbia, NE Yugoslavia
105 *S12* **Alicante** *Cat.* Alacant; *Lat.* Lucentum. País Valenciano, SE Spain
105 *S12* **Alicante** ◈ *province* País Valenciano, SE Spain
105 *S12* **Alicante** ✕ Murcia, E Spain
83 *I25* **Alice** Eastern Cape, S South Africa
25 *S14* **Alice** Texas, SW USA
83 *I25* **Alicedale** Eastern Cape, S South Africa
65 *B25* **Alice, Mount** *hill* West Falkland, Falkland Islands
107 *P20* **Alice, Punta** *headland* S Italy
181 *Q7* **Alice Springs** Northern Territory, C Australia
23 *N4* **Aliceville** Alabama, S USA
147 *U13* **Alichur** SE Tajikistan
147 *U14* **Alichuri Janubí, Qatorkŭhi** *Rus.* Yuzhno-Alichurskiy Khrebet. ⛰ SE Tajikistan
147 *U13* **Alichuri Shimolí, Qatorkŭhi** *Rus.* Severo-Alichurskiy Khrebet. ⛰ SE Tajikistan
107 *K22* **Alicudi, Isola** *island* Isole Eolie, S Italy
152 *J11* **Alīgarh** Uttar Pradesh, N India
142 *M7* **Alīgūdarz** Lorestān, W Iran
(0) *F12* **Alijos, Islas** *island group* California, SW USA
149 *R6* **'Alī Kbel** *Pash.* 'Alī Khēl. Paktīkā, E Afghanistan
Ali Khel *see* 'Alī Kheyl, Paktīā, Afghanistan
'Alī Khēl *see* 'Alī Kbel, Paktīkā, Afghanistan
149 *R6* **'Alī Kheyl** *var.* Ali Khel, Jajı. Paktīā, SE Afghanistan
141 *V17* **Al Ikhwān** *island group* SE Yemen
Aliki *see* Alykí
79 *H19* **Alima** ≈ C Congo
Al Imārāt al 'Arabīyah al Muttaḩidah *see* United Arab Emirates
115 *N23* **Alimía** *island* Dodekánisos, Greece, Aegean Sea
55 *V12* **Alimimuni Piek** ▲ S Suriname
79 *K15* **Alindao** Basse-Kotto, S Central African Republic
95 *J18* **Alingsås** Västra Götaland, S Sweden
81 *K18* **Alinjugul** *spring/well* E Kenya
149 *S11* **Alīpur** Punjab, E Pakistan
153 *T12* **Alīpur Duār** West Bengal, NE India
18 *B14* **Aliquippa** Pennsylvania, NE USA
80 *L12* **'Ali Sabieh** *var.* 'Alī Sabīḩ. S Djibouti
'Alī Sabīḩ *see* 'Ali Sabieh
140 *K3* **Al 'Īsāwīyah** Al Jawf, NW Saudi Arabia
104 *J10* **Aliseda** Extremadura, W Spain
139 *T8* **Al Iskandarīyah** C Iraq
Al Iskandarīyah *see* Alexandria
123 *T6* **Aliskerovo** Chukotskiy Avtonomnyy Okrug, NE Russian Federation
114 *H13* **Alistráti** Kentrikí Makedonía, NE Greece
39 *P15* **Alitak Bay** *bay* Kodiak Island, Alaska, USA
Al Ittiḩād *see* Madīnat ash Sha'b
115 *H18* **Alivéri** *var.* Alivérion. Évvoia, C Greece
Alivérion *see* Alivéri
Aliwal-Noord *see* Aliwal North
83 *I24* **Aliwal North** *Afr.* Aliwal-Noord. Eastern Cape, SE South Africa
121 *Q13* **Al Jabal al Akhḑar** ⛰ NE Libya
138 *H13* **Al Jafr** Ma'ān, S Jordan
75 *T8* **Al Jaghbūb** NE Libya
142 *K11* **Al Jahrā'** *var.* Al Jahrah, Jahra. C Kuwait
Al Jahrah *see* Al Jahrā'
Al Jamāhīrīyah al 'Arabīyah al Lībīyah ash Sha'bīyah al Ishtirāk *see* Libya
140 *K3* **Al Jarāwī** *spring/well* NW Saudi Arabia
141 *X11* **Al Jawārah** *oasis* SE Oman
140 *L3* **Al Jawf** *var.* Jauf. Al Jawf, NW Saudi Arabia
140 *L4* **Al Jawf** *off.* Minţaqat al Jawf. ◈ *province* N Saudi Arabia
Al Jawlān *see* Golan Heights
Al Jazair *see* Alger
139 *N4* **Al Jazīrah** *physical region* Iraq/Syria
104 *F14* **Aljezur** Faro, S Portugal
139 *S13* **Al Jīl** S Iraq
138 *G11* **Al Jīzah** *var.* Jiza. 'Ammān, N Jordan
Al Jīzah *see* El Gîza
Al Jubail *see* Al Jubayl
141 *S6* **Al Jubayl** *var.* Al Jubail. Ash Sharqīyah, NE Saudi Arabia
141 *T10* **Āl Juḩaysh, Qalamat** *well* SE Saudi Arabia
143 *N15* **Al Jumaylīyah** N Qatar
Al Junaynah *see* El Geneina
104 *G13* **Aljustrel** Beja, S Portugal
Al Kaba'ish *see* Al Chabā'ish
Al-Kadhimain *see* Al Kāẓimīyah
Al Kāf *see* El Kef
Alkal'a *see* Alcalá de Henares
35 *W4* **Alkali Flat** *salt flat* Nevada, W USA
35 *Q1* **Alkali Lake** ◎ Nevada, W USA
141 *Z9* **Al Kāmil** NE Oman
138 *G11* **Al Karak** *var.* El Kerak, Karak, Kerak; *anc.* Kir Moab, Kir of Moab. Al Karak, W Jordan
138 *G12* **Al Karak** *off.* Muḩāfaẓat al Karak. ◈ *governorate* W Jordan
139 *W8* **Al Karmashīyah** E Iraq
Al-Kashaniya *see* Al Qash'ānīyah
Al-Kasr al-Kebir *see* Ksar-el-Kebir
139 *T8* **Al Kāẓimīyah** *var.* Al-Kadhimain, Kadhimain. C Iraq
99 *J18* **Alken** Limburg, NE Belgium
141 *X8* **Al Khābūrah** *var.* Khabura. N Oman
Al Khalīl *see* Hebron
139 *T7* **Al Khāliş** C Iraq
Al Khaluf *see* Khalūf
Al Khārijah *see* El Khârga
141 *Q8* **Al Kharj** Ar Riyāḑ, C Saudi Arabia
141 *W6* **Al Khaşab** *var.* Khasab. N Oman
Al Khaur *see* Al Khawr
143 *N15* **Al Khawr** *var.* Al Khaur, Al Khor. N Qatar
142 *K12* **Al Khīrān** *var.* Al Khiran. SE Kuwait
141 *W9* **Al Khīrān** *spring/well* NW Oman
Al Khiyām *see* El Khiyam
Al-Khobar *see* Al Khubar
Al Khor *see* Al Khawr
141 *S6* **Al Khubar** *var.* Al-Khobar. Ash Sharqīyah, NE Saudi Arabia
75 *T11* **Al Khufrah** SE Libya
120 *M12* **Al Khums** *var.* Homs, Khoms, Khums. NW Libya
141 *R15* **Al Khuraybah** C Yemen
140 *M9* **Al Khurmah** *var.* al-Hurma. Makkah, W Saudi Arabia
141 *V9* **Al Kidan** *desert* NE Saudi Arabia
98 *H9* **Alkmaar** Noord-Holland, NW Netherlands
139 *T10* **Al Kūfah** *var.* Kufa. S Iraq
141 *T10* **Al Kursū'** *desert* E Saudi Arabia
139 *V9* **Al Kūt** *var.* Kūt al 'Amārah, Kut al Imara. E Iraq
Al-Kuwait *see* Al Kuwayt
Al Kuwayr *see* Guwēr
142 *K11* **Al Kuwayt** *var.* Al-Kuwait, *Eng.* Kuwait, Kuwait City; *prev.* Qurein. ● (Kuwait) E Kuwait
142 *K11* **Al Kuwayt** ✕ C Kuwait
115 *G19* **Alkyonidón, Kólpos** *gulf* C Greece
141 *N4* **Al Labbah** *physical region* N Saudi Arabia
138 *G4* **Al Lādhiqīyah** *Eng.* Latakia, *Fr.* Lattaquié; *anc.* Laodicea, Laodicea ad Mare. Al Lādhiqīyah, W Syria
138 *H4* **Al Lādhiqīyah** *off.* Muḩāfaẓat al Ļādhiqīyah, *var.* Al Lathqiyah, Latakia, Lattakia. ◈ *governorate* W Syria
19 *R2* **Allagash River** ≈ Maine, NE USA
152 *M13* **Allahābād** Uttar Pradesh, N India
143 *S3* **Allāh Dāgh, Reshteh-ye** ⛰ NE Iran
39 *Q8* **Allakaket** Alaska, USA
11 *T15* **Allan** Saskatchewan, S Canada
166 *L6* **Allanmyo** Magwe, C Myanmar
83 *I22* **Allanridge** Free State, C South Africa
104 *H4* **Allariz** Galicia, NW Spain
139 *R11* **Al Laşaf** *var.* Al Lussuf. S Iraq
Al Lathqiyah *see* Al Lādhiqīyah
23 *S2* **Allatoona Lake** ▣ Georgia, SE USA
83 *J19* **Alldays** Northern, NE South Africa
Alle *see* Łyna
31 *P10* **Allegan** Michigan, N USA
18 *E14* **Allegheny Mountains** ⛰ NE USA
18 *E12* **Allegheny Plateau** ⛰ New York/Pennsylvania, NE USA
18 *D11* **Allegheny Reservoir** ▣ New York/Pennsylvania, NE USA
18 *E12* **Allegheny River** ≈ New York/Pennsylvania, NE USA
22 *K9* **Allemands, Lac des** ◎ Louisiana, S USA
25 *U6* **Allen** Texas, SW USA
21 *R14* **Allendale** South Carolina, SE USA
41 *N6* **Allende** Coahuila de Zaragoza, NE Mexico
41 *O9* **Allende** Nuevo León, NE Mexico
97 *D16* **Allen, Lough** *Ir.* Loch Aillionn. ◎ NW Ireland
185 *B26* **Allen, Mount** ▲ Stewart Island, Southland, SW NZ
109 *V2* **Allensteig** Niederösterreich, N Austria
Allenstein *see* Olsztyn
18 *I14* **Allentown** Pennsylvania, NE USA
155 *G23* **Alleppey** *var.* Alappuzha; *prev.* Alleppi. Kerala, SW India
Alleppi *see* Alleppey
100 *J12* **Aller** ≈ NW Germany
29 *V16* **Allerton** Iowa, C USA
99 *K19* **Alleur** Liège, E Belgium
101 *J25* **Allgäuer Alpen** ⛰ Austria/Germany
28 *J13* **Alliance** Nebraska, C USA
31 *U12* **Alliance** Ohio, N USA
103 *O10* **Allier** ◈ *department* N France
139 *R13* **Al Līfīyah** S Iraq
44 *J13* **Alligator Pond** C Jamaica
21 *Y9* **Alligator River** ≈ North Carolina, SE USA
29 *W12* **Allison** Iowa, C USA
14 *G14* **Alliston** Ontario, S Canada
140 *L11* **Al Līth** Makkah, SW Saudi Arabia
Al Liwā' *see* Līwā
96 *J12* **Alloa** C Scotland, UK
103 *U14* **Allos** Alpes-de-Haute-Provence, SE France
108 *D6* **Allschwil** Basel-Land, NW Switzerland
Al Lubnān *see* Lebanon
141 *N14* **Al Luḩayyah** W Yemen
14 *K12* **Allumettes, Île des** *island* Quebec, SE Canada
Al Lussuf *see* Al Laşaf
109 *S5* **Alm** ≈ N Austria
15 *Q7* **Alma** Quebec, SE Canada
27 *S10* **Alma** Arkansas, C USA
23 *V7* **Alma** Georgia, SE USA
27 *P4* **Alma** Kansas, C USA
31 *Q8* **Alma** Michigan, N USA
29 *O17* **Alma** Nebraska, C USA
30 *I7* **Alma** Wisconsin, N USA
139 *R12* **Al Ma'ānīyah** S Iraq
Alma-Ata *see* Almaty
Alma-Atinskaya Oblast' *see* Almaty
Almacellas *see* Almacelles
105 *T5* **Almacelles** *var.* Almacellas. Cataluña, NE Spain
104 *F11* **Almada** Setúbal, W Portugal
104 *L11* **Almadén** Castilla-La Mancha, C Spain
66 *L6* **Almadies, Pointe des** *headland* W Senegal
140 *L7* **Al Madīnah** *Eng.* Medina. Al Madīnah, W Saudi Arabia
140 *L7* **Al Madīnah** *off.* Minţaqat al Madīnah. ◈ *province* W Saudi Arabia
138 *H9* **Al Mafraq** *var.* Mafraq. Al Mafraq, N Jordan
138 *J10* **Al Mafraq** *off.* Muḩāfaẓat al Mafraq. ◈ *governorate* NW Jordan
141 *R15* **Al Maghārīm** C Yemen
105 *N11* **Almagro** Castilla-La Mancha, C Spain
Al Maḩallah al Kubrá *see* El Maḩalla el Kubra
139 *T9* **Al Maḩāwīl** *var.* Khān al Maḩāwīl. C Iraq
Al Mahdīyah *see* Mahdia
139 *T8* **Al Maḩmūdīyah** *var.* Mahmudiya. C Iraq
141 *T14* **Al Mahrah** ⛰ E Yemen
141 *P7* **Al Majma'ah** Ar Riyāḑ, C Saudi Arabia
139 *Q11* **Al Makmīn** *well* S Iraq
139 *Q1* **Al Mālikīyah** *var.* Malkiye. Al Ḩasakah, N Syria
Almalyk *see* Olmaliq
Al Mamlakah al Urdunīyah al Hāshimīyah *see* Jordan
Al Mamlakah *see* Morocco
143 *Q18* **Al Manādir** *var.* Al Manadir. *desert* Oman/UAE
142 *L15* **Al Manāmah** *Eng.* Manama. ● (Bahrain) N Bahrain
139 *O5* **Al Manāşif** ⛰ E Syria
35 *O4* **Almanor, Lake** ▣ California, W USA
105 *R11* **Almansa** Castilla-La Mancha, C Spain
Al Manşūrah *see* El Manşûra
104 *L3* **Almanza** Castilla-León, N Spain
104 *L8* **Almanzor** ▲ W Spain
105 *P14* **Almanzora** ≈ SE Spain
139 *S9* **Al Mardah** C Iraq
Al-Mariyya *see* Almería
75 *R7* **Al Marj** *var.* Barka, *It.* Barce. NE Libya
138 *L2* **Al Mashrafah** Ar Raqqah, N Syria
141 *X8* **Al Maşna'ah** *var.* Al Muşana'a. NE Oman
105 *T9* **Almassora** País Valenciano, E Spain
Almatinskaya Oblast' *see* Almaty
145 *U15* **Almaty** *var.* Alma-Ata. Almaty, SE Kazakhstan
145 *S14* **Almaty** *off.* Almatinskaya Oblast', *Kaz.* Almaty Oblysy; *prev.* Alma-Atinskaya Oblast'. ◈ *province* SE Kazakhstan
145 *U15* **Almaty** ✕ Almaty, SE Kazakhstan
Almaty Oblysy *see* Almaty
al-Mawailih *see* Al Muwayliḩ
139 *R3* **Al Mawşil** *Eng.* Mosul. N Iraq

◆ Country
● Country Capital
◇ Dependent Territory
○ Dependent Territory Capital
◈ Administrative Region
✕ International Airport
▲ Mountain
⛰ Mountain Range
✱ Volcano
≈ River
◎ Lake
▣ Reservoir

139 N5 **Al Mayādīn** var. Mayadin, Fr. Meyadine. Dayr az Zawr, E Syria
139 X10 **Al Maymūnah** var. Maimuna. SE Iraq
141 N5 **Al Mayyāh** Ḥā'il, N Saudi Arabia
Al Ma'zam see Al Ma'zim
105 P6 **Almazán** Castilla-León, N Spain
141 W8 **Al Ma'zim** var. Al Ma'zam. NW Oman
123 N11 **Almaznyy** Respublika Sakha (Yakutiya), NE Russian Federation
Al Mazra' see Al Mazra'ah
138 G11 **Al Mazra'ah** var. Al Mazra', Mazra'a. Al Karak, W Jordan
101 G15 **Alme** ≈ W Germany
104 I7 **Almeida** Guarda, N Portugal
104 G10 **Almeirim** Santarém, C Portugal
98 O10 **Almelo** Overijssel, E Netherlands
105 S9 **Almenara** País Valenciano, E Spain
105 P12 **Almenaras** ▲ S Spain
105 P5 **Almenar de Soria** Castilla-León, N Spain
104 J6 **Almendra, Embalse de** ▣ Castilla-León, NW Spain
104 J11 **Almendralejo** Extremadura, W Spain
98 J10 **Almere** var. Almere-stad. Flevoland, C Netherlands
98 J10 **Almere-Buiten** Flevoland, C Netherlands
98 J10 **Almere-Haven** Flevoland, C Netherlands
Almere-stad see Almere
105 P15 **Almería** Ar. Al-Mariyya; anc. Unci, Lat. Portus Magnus. Andalucía, S Spain
105 P14 **Almería** ◈ province Andalucía, S Spain
105 P15 **Almería, Golfo de** gulf S Spain
129 S5 **Al'met'yevsk** Respublika Tatarstan, W Russian Federation
95 L21 **Älmhult** Kronoberg, S Sweden
141 U9 **Al Miḥrāḍ** desert NE Saudi Arabia
Al Mīnā' see El Mina
104 L17 **Almina, Punta** headland Ceuta, Spain, N Africa
Al Minyā see El Minya
Al Miqdādīyah see Al Muqdādīyah
43 P14 **Almirante** Bocas del Toro, NW Panama
Almirós see Almyrós
140 M9 **Al Mislaḥ** spring/well W Saudi Arabia
Almissa see Omiš
104 G13 **Almodôvar** var. Almodóvar. Beja, S Portugal
104 M11 **Almodóvar del Campo** Castilla-La Mancha, C Spain
105 Q9 **Almodóvar del Pinar** Castilla-La Mancha, C Spain
31 S9 **Almont** Michigan, N USA
14 L13 **Almonte** Ontario, SE Canada
104 J14 **Almonte** Andalucía, S Spain
104 K9 **Almonte** ≈ W Spain
152 K9 **Almora** Uttar Pradesh, N India
104 M8 **Almorox** Castilla-La Mancha, C Spain
141 S7 **Al Mubarraz** Ash Sharqīyah, E Saudi Arabia
Al Muḍaibī see Al Muḍaybī
138 G15 **Al Mudawwarah** Ma'ān, SW Jordan
141 Y9 **Al Muḍaybī** var. Al Muḍaibī. NE Oman
Almudébar see Almudévar
105 S5 **Almudévar** var. Almudébar. Aragón, NE Spain
141 S15 **Al Mukallā** var. Mukalla. SE Yemen
141 N16 **Al Mukhā** Eng. Mocha. SW Yemen
105 N15 **Almuñécar** Andalucía, S Spain
139 U7 **Al Muqdādīyah** var. Al Miqdādīyah. C Iraq
140 L3 **Al Murayr** spring/well NW Saudi Arabia
136 M12 **Almus** Tokat, N Turkey
Al Muṣana'a see Al Maṣna'ah
139 T9 **Al Musayyib** var. Musaiyib. C Iraq
139 V9 **Al Muwaffaqīyah** S Iraq
138 H10 **Al Muwaqqar** var. El Muwaqqar. 'Ammān, W Jordan
140 J5 **Al Muwayliḥ** var. al-Mawailih. Tabūk, NW Saudi Arabia
115 F17 **Almyrós** var. Almirós. Thessalía, C Greece
115 I24 **Almyroú, Órmos** bay Kríti, Greece, E Mediterranean Sea
Al Nūwfalīyah see An Nawfalīyah
96 L13 **Alnwick** N England, UK
Al Obayyid see El Obeid
Al Odaid see Al 'Udayd
190 B16 **Alofi** ○ (Niue) W Niue
190 A16 **Alofi Bay** bay W Niue, C Pacific Ocean
190 E13 **Alofi, Île** island S Wallis and Futuna
190 E13 **Alofitai** Île Alofi, W Wallis and Futuna
Aloha State see Hawaii
118 G7 **Aloja** Limbaži, N Latvia
153 X10 **Along** Arunāchel Pradesh, NE India
115 H16 **Alónnisos** island Vóreioi Sporádes, Greece, Aegean Sea
104 M15 **Álora** Andalucía, S Spain
171 Q16 **Alor, Kepulauan** island group E Indonesia
171 Q16 **Alor, Pulau** prev. Ombai. island Kepulauan Alor, E Indonesia
168 I7 **Alor Setar** var. Alor Star, Alur Setar. Kedah, Peninsular Malaysia
Alost see Aalst
154 F9 **Ālot** Madhya Pradesh, C India
186 G10 **Alotau** Milne Bay, SE PNG
171 Y16 **Alotip** Irian Jaya, E Indonesia
Al Oued see El Oued
35 R12 **Alpaugh** California, W USA
Alpen see Alps
31 R6 **Alpena** Michigan, N USA
Alpes see Alps
103 S14 **Alpes-de-Haute-Provence** ◈ department SE France
103 U14 **Alpes-Maritimes** ◈ department SE France
181 W8 **Alpha** Queensland, E Australia
197 R9 **Alpha Cordillera** var. Alpha Ridge. undersea feature Arctic Ocean
Alpha Ridge see Alpha Cordillera
Alpheius see Alfeiós
99 I15 **Alphen** Noord-Brabant, S Netherlands
98 H11 **Alphen aan den Rijn** var. Alphen. Zuid-Holland, C Netherlands
Alpheus see Alfeiós
Alpi see Alps
104 G10 **Alpiarça** Santarém, C Portugal
24 K10 **Alpine** Texas, SW USA
108 F8 **Alpnach** Unterwalden, W Switzerland
108 D11 **Alps** Fr. Alpes, Ger. Alpen, It. Alpi. ▲ C Europe
141 W8 **Al Qābil** var. Qabil. N Oman
Al Qaḍārif see Gedaref
75 P8 **Al Qaddāḥīyah** N Libya
Al Qāhirah see Cairo
140 K4 **Al Qalībah** Tabūk, NW Saudi Arabia
139 O1 **Al Qāmishlī** var. Kamishli, Qamishly. Al Ḥasakah, NE Syria
138 I6 **Al Qaryatayn** var. Qaryatayn, Fr. Qariateïne. Ḥimṣ, C Syria
142 K11 **Al Qash'ānīyah** var. Al-Kashaniya. NE Kuwait
141 N7 **Al Qaṣīm** off. Minṭaqat Qaṣīm, Qassim. ◈ province C Saudi Arabia
138 J5 **Al Qaṣr** Ḥimṣ, C Syria
Al Qaṣr see El Qaṣr
Al Qaṣrayn see Kasserine
141 S6 **Al Qaṭīf** Ash Sharqīyah, NE Saudi Arabia
138 G11 **Al Qaṭrānah** var. El Qatrani, Qatrana. Al Karak, W Jordan
75 P11 **Al Qaṭrūn** SW Libya
Al Qayrawān see Kairouan
Al-Qsar al-Kbir see Ksar-el-Kebir
Al Qubayyāt see Qoubaïyât
Al Quds/Al Quds ash Sharīf see Jerusalem
138 G8 **Al Qunayṭirah** var. El Kuneitra, El Quneitra, Kuneitra, Qunaytra. Al Qunayṭirah, SW Syria
138 G8 **Al Qunayṭirah** off. Muḥāfaẓat al Qunayṭirah, var. El Q'unaytirah, Qunaytirah, Fr. Kuneitra. ◈ governorate SW Syria
140 M11 **Al Qunfudhah** Makkah, SW Saudi Arabia
140 K2 **Al Qurayyāt** Al Jawf, NW Saudi Arabia
139 Y11 **Al Qurnah** var. Kurna. SE Iraq
139 V12 **Al Quṣayr** S Iraq
138 I6 **Al Quṣayr** var. El Quseir, Quṣayr, Fr. Kousseir. Ḥimṣ, W Syria
Al Quṣayr see Quseir
138 H7 **Al Quṭayfah** var. Quṭayfah, Qutayfe, Quteife, Fr. Kouteifé. Dimashq, W Syria
141 P8 **Al Quwayīyah** Ar Riyāḍ, C Saudi Arabia
Al Quwayr see Guwêr
138 F14 **Al Quwayrah** var. El Quweira. Ma'ān, SW Jordan
Al Rayyan see Ar Rayyān
Al Ruweis see Ar Ruways
95 G24 **Als** Ger. Alsen. island SW Denmark
103 U5 **Alsace** Ger. Elsass; anc. Alsatia. ◈ region NE France
11 R16 **Alsask** Saskatchewan, S Canada
Alsasua see Altsasu
Alsatia see Alsace
101 C16 **Alsdorf** Nordrhein-Westfalen, W Germany
10 G8 **Alsek** ≈ Canada/USA
Alsen see Als
101 F19 **Alsenz** ≈ W Germany
101 H17 **Alsfeld** Hessen, C Germany
119 K20 **Al'shany** Rus. Ol'shany. Brestskaya Voblasts', SW Belarus
Alsókubin see Dolný Kubín
118 C9 **Alsunga** Kuldīga, W Latvia
Alt see Olt
92 K9 **Alta** Fin. Alattio. Finnmark, N Norway
29 T12 **Alta** Iowa, C USA
108 I7 **Altach** Vorarlberg, W Austria
92 K9 **Altaelva** ≈ N Norway
92 J8 **Altafjorden** fjord NE Norwegian Sea
62 K10 **Alta Gracia** Córdoba, C Argentina
42 K11 **Alta Gracia** Rivas, SW Nicaragua
54 H4 **Altagracia** Zulia, NW Venezuela
54 M5 **Altagracia de Orituco** Guárico, N Venezuela
Altai see Altai Mountains
131 T7 **Altai Mountains** var. Altai, Chin. Altay Shan, Rus. Altay. ▲ Asia/Europe
23 V6 **Altamaha River** ≈ Georgia, SE USA
58 J13 **Altamira** Pará, NE Brazil
54 D12 **Altamira** Huila, S Colombia
42 M13 **Altamira** Alajuela, N Costa Rica
41 Q11 **Altamira** Tamaulipas, C Mexico
30 L15 **Altamont** Illinois, N USA
27 Q7 **Altamont** Kansas, C USA
32 H16 **Altamont** Oregon, NW USA
20 K10 **Altamont** Tennessee, S USA
23 X11 **Altamonte Springs** Florida, SE USA
107 O17 **Altamura** anc. Lupatia. Puglia, SE Italy
40 H9 **Altamura, Isla** island C Mexico
162 G7 **Altan** Dzavhan, W Mongolia
162 G6 **Altanbulag** Dzavhan, N Mongolia
Altan Emel see Xin Barag Youqi
162 J8 **Altan-Ovoo** Arhangay, C Mongolia
162 E7 **Altanteel** Hovd, W Mongolia
40 F3 **Altar** Sonora, NW Mexico
40 D2 **Altar, Desierto de** var. Sonoran Desert. desert Mexico/USA see also Sonoran Desert
105 Q8 **Alta, Sierra** ▲ N Spain
40 H9 **Altata** Sinaloa, C Mexico
42 D4 **Alta Verapaz** off. Departamento de Alta Verapaz. ◈ department C Guatemala
107 L18 **Altavilla Silentia** Campania, S Italy
21 T7 **Altavista** Virginia, NE USA
158 L2 **Altay** Xinjiang Uygur Zizhiqu, NW China
162 G5 **Altay** Dzavhan, N Mongolia
162 F8 **Altay** Govĭ-Altay, W Mongolia
Altay see Altai Mountains
122 J14 **Altay, Respublika** var. Gornyy Altay; prev. Gorno-Altayskaya Respublika. ◈ autonomous republic S Russian Federation
Altay Shan see Altai Mountains
123 I13 **Altayskiy Kray** ◈ territory S Russian Federation
Altbetsche see Bečej
101 L20 **Altdorf** Bayern, SE Germany
108 G8 **Altdorf** var. Altorf. Uri, C Switzerland
105 T11 **Altea** País Valenciano, E Spain
100 L10 **Alte Elde** ≈ N Germany
101 M16 **Altenburg** Thüringen, E Germany
Altenburg see București, Romania
Altenburg see Baia de Criş, Romania
100 P12 **Alte Oder** ≈ NE Germany
104 H10 **Alter do Chão** Portalegre, C Portugal
92 I10 **Altevatnet** ◎ N Norway
27 V12 **Altheimer** Arkansas, C USA
109 T9 **Althofen** Kärnten, S Austria
114 H7 **Altimir** Vratsa, NW Bulgaria
136 K11 **Altınkaya Barajı** ▣ N Turkey
139 S3 **Altin Köprü** var. Altun Kupri. N Iraq
136 E13 **Altıntaş** Kütahya, W Turkey
57 K18 **Altiplano** physical region W South America
Altkanischa see Kanjiža
103 U7 **Altkirch** Haut-Rhin, NE France
Altlublau see Stará Ľubovňa
100 L12 **Altmark** cultural region N Germany
Altmoldowa see Moldova Veche
25 W8 **Alto** Texas, SW USA
104 H11 **Alto Alentejo** physical region S Portugal
59 I19 **Alto Araguaia** Mato Grosso, C Brazil
58 L12 **Alto Bonito** Pará, NE Brazil
83 O15 **Alto Molócuè** Zambézia, NE Mozambique
30 K15 **Alton** Illinois, N USA
27 W8 **Alton** Missouri, C USA
11 X17 **Altona** Manitoba, S Canada
18 E14 **Altoona** Pennsylvania, NE USA
30 J6 **Altoona** Wisconsin, N USA
62 N3 **Alto Paraguay** off. Departamento del Alto Paraguay. ◈ department N Paraguay
59 L17 **Alto Paraíso de Goiás** Goiás, S Brazil
62 P6 **Alto Paraná** off. Departamento del Alto Paraná. ◈ department E Paraguay
Alto Paraná see Paraná
59 L15 **Alto Parnaíba** Maranhão, E Brazil
56 H13 **Alto Purús, Río** ≈ E Peru
Altorf see Altdorf
63 H19 **Alto Río Senguer** var. Alto Río Senguerr. Chubut, S Argentina
41 Q13 **Altotonga** Veracruz-Llave, E Mexico
101 N23 **Altötting** Bayern, SE Germany
Altpasua see Stara Pazova
162 I5 **Altraga** Hövsgöl, N Mongolia
Alt-Schwanenburg see Gulbene
105 P3 **Altsasu** Cast. Alsasua. Navarra, N Spain
Altsohl see Zvolen
108 I7 **Altstätten** Sankt Gallen, NE Switzerland
42 G1 **Altun Ha** ruins Belize, N Belize
Altun Kupri see Altin Köprü
158 D8 **Altun Shan** ▲ C China
158 L9 **Altun Shan** var. Altyn Tagh. ▲ NW China
35 P2 **Alturas** California, W USA
26 K12 **Altus** Oklahoma, C USA
26 K11 **Altus Lake** ▣ Oklahoma, C USA
Altvater see Praděd
Altyn Tagh see Altun Shan
Alu see Shortland Island
al-'Ubaila see Al 'Ubaylah
139 O6 **Al 'Ubaydī** W Iraq
141 T9 **Al 'Ubaylah** var. al-'Ubaila. Ash Sharqīyah, E Saudi Arabia
141 T9 **Al 'Ubaylah** spring/well E Saudi Arabia
Al Ubayyiḍ see El Obeid
141 T7 **Al 'Udayd** var. Al Odaid. Abū Ẓaby, W UAE
118 J8 **Alūksne** Ger. Marienburg. Alūksne, NE Latvia
140 K6 **Al 'Ulā** Al Madīnah, NW Saudi Arabia
173 N4 **Alula-Fartak Trench** var. Illaue Fartak Trench. undersea feature W Indian Ocean
138 I11 **Al 'Umarī** 'Ammān, E Jordan
31 S13 **Alum Creek Lake** ▣ Ohio, N USA
63 H15 **Aluminé** Neuquén, C Argentina
95 O14 **Alunda** Uppsala, C Sweden
117 T14 **Alupka** Respublika Krym, S Ukraine
75 P8 **Al 'Uqaylah** N Libya
Al Uqṣur see Luxor
Al Urdunn see Jordan
168 J9 **Alur Panal** bay Sumatera, W Indonesia
141 V10 **Al 'Urūq al Mu'tariḍah** salt lake SE Saudi Arabia
139 Q7 **Ālūs** C Iraq
117 T13 **Alushta** Respublika Krym, S Ukraine
75 N11 **Al 'Uwaynāt** var. Al Awaynāt. SW Libya
139 T6 **Al 'Uẓaym** var. Adhaim. E Iraq
26 L8 **Alva** Oklahoma, C USA
104 H8 **Alva** ≈ N Portugal
95 J18 **Älvängen** Västra Götaland, S Sweden
14 F14 **Alvanley** Ontario, S Canada
41 S14 **Alvarado** Veracruz-Llave, E Mexico
25 T7 **Alvarado** Texas, SW USA
58 D13 **Alvarães** Amazonas, NW Brazil
40 G6 **Alvaro Obregón, Presa** ▣ W Mexico
94 H10 **Alvdal** Hedmark, S Norway
94 K12 **Älvdalen** Dalarna, C Sweden
61 E15 **Alvear** Corrientes, NE Argentina
104 F10 **Alverca do Ribatejo** Lisboa, C Portugal
95 L20 **Alvesta** Kronoberg, S Sweden
94 D13 **Ålvik** Hordaland, S Norway
25 W12 **Alvin** Texas, SW USA
95 O13 **Älvkarleby** Uppsala, C Sweden
25 S5 **Alvord** Texas, SW USA
93 G18 **Älvros** Jämtland, C Sweden
92 J13 **Älvsbyn** Norrbotten, N Sweden
142 K12 **Al Wafrā'** SE Kuwait
140 J6 **Al Wajh** Tabūk, NW Saudi Arabia
143 N16 **Al Wakrah** var. Wakra. C Qatar
138 M8 **al Walaj, Sha'īb** dry watercourse W Iraq
152 I11 **Alwar** Rājasthān, N India
141 Q5 **Al Wari'ah** Ash Sharqīyah, N Saudi Arabia
155 G22 **Alwaye** Kerala, SW India
162 K14 **Alxa Zuoqi** var. Ehen Hudag. Nei Mongol Zizhiqu, N China
Al Yaman see Yemen
138 G9 **Al Yarmūk** Irbid, N Jordan
Alyat/Alyaty-Pristan' see Älät
115 I14 **Alykí** var. Aliki. Thásos, N Greece
119 F14 **Alytus** Pol. Olita. Alytus, S Lithuania
101 N23 **Alz** ≈ SE Germany
33 Y11 **Alzada** Montana, NW USA
122 L12 **Alzamay** Irkutskaya Oblast', S Russian Federation
99 M25 **Alzette** ≈ S Luxembourg
105 S10 **Alzira** var. Alcira ; anc. Saetabicula, Suero. País Valenciano, E Spain
Al Zubair see Az Zubayr
181 O8 **Amadeus, Lake** seasonal lake Northern Territory, C Australia
81 E15 **Amadi** Western Equatoria, SW Sudan
9 R7 **Amadjuak Lake** ◎ Baffin Island, Nunavut, N Canada
95 J23 **Amager** island E Denmark
165 N14 **Amagi-san** ▲ Honshū, S Japan
171 S13 **Amahai** var. Masohi. Pulau Seram, E Indonesia
38 M16 **Amak Island** island Alaska, USA
164 B14 **Amakusa-nada** gulf Kyūshū, SW Japan
95 J16 **Åmål** Västra Götaland, S Sweden
54 E8 **Amalfi** Antioquia, N Colombia
107 L18 **Amalfi** Campania, S Italy
115 D19 **Amaliáda** var. Amaliás. Dytikí Ellás, S Greece
Amaliás see Amaliáda
154 F12 **Amalner** Mahārāshtra, C India
171 W14 **Amamapare** Irian Jaya, E Indonesia
59 H21 **Amambaí, Serra de** var. Cordillera de Amambay, Serra de Amambay. ▲ Brazil/Paraguay see also Amambay, Cordillera de
62 P4 **Amambay** off. Departamento del Amambay. ◈ department E Paraguay
62 P5 **Amambay, Cordillera de** var. Serra de Amambaí, Serra de Amambay. ▲ Brazil/Paraguay see also Amambaí, Serra de
Amambay, Serra de see Amambaí, Serra de/Amambay, Cordillera de
165 U16 **Amami-guntō** island group SW Japan
165 V15 **Amami-Ō-shima** island S Japan
186 A5 **Amanab** Sandaun, NW PNG
106 J13 **Amandola** Marche, C Italy
107 N21 **Amantea** Calabria, SW Italy
191 W10 **Amanu** island Îles Tuamotu, C French Polynesia
58 J10 **Amapá** Amapá, NE Brazil
58 J11 **Amapá** off. Estado de Amapá; prev. Território de Amapá. ◈ state NE Brazil
42 H8 **Amapala** Valle, S Honduras
Amara see Al 'Amārah
104 H6 **Amarante** Porto, N Portugal
166 M5 **Amarapura** Mandalay, C Myanmar
162 L9 **Amardalay** Dundgovĭ, C Mongolia
104 I12 **Amareleja** Beja, S Portugal
35 V11 **Amargosa Range** ▲ California, W USA
25 N2 **Amarillo** Texas, SW USA
Amarinthos see Amárynthos
107 K15 **Amaro, Monte** ▲ C Italy
115 H18 **Amárynthos** var. Amarinthos. Évvoia, C Greece
Amasia see Amasya
136 K12 **Amasya** anc. Amasia. Amasya, N Turkey
136 K11 **Amasya** ◈ province N Turkey
42 F4 **Amatique, Bahía de** bay Gulf of Honduras, W Caribbean Sea
42 D6 **Amatitlán, Lago de** ◎ S Guatemala
107 J14 **Amatrice** Lazio, C Italy
190 C8 **Amatuku** atoll C Tuvalu
99 J20 **Amay** Liège, E Belgium
48 F7 **Amazon** Sp. Amazonas. ≈ Brazil/Peru
59 C14 **Amazonas** off. Estado do Amazonas. ◈ state N Brazil
54 G15 **Amazonas** off. Comisaria del Amazonas. ◈ province SE Colombia
56 C10 **Amazonas** off. Departamento de Amazonas. ◈ department N Peru
54 M12 **Amazonas** off. Territorio Amazonas. ◈ federal territory S Venezuela
Amazonas see Amazon
48 F7 **Amazon Basin** basin N South America
47 V5 **Amazon Fan** undersea feature W Atlantic Ocean
58 K11 **Amazon, Mouths of the** delta NE Brazil
187 R13 **Ambae** var. Aoba, Omba. island C Vanuatu
152 I9 **Ambāla** Haryāna, NW India
155 J26 **Ambalangoda** Southern Province, SW Sri Lanka
155 K26 **Ambalantota** Southern Province, S Sri Lanka
172 I6 **Ambalavao** Fianarantsoa, C Madagascar
54 E10 **Ambalema** Tolima, C Colombia
79 E17 **Ambam** Sud, S Cameroon
172 J2 **Ambanja** Antsiranana, N Madagascar
123 T6 **Ambarchik** Respublika Sakha (Yakutiya), NE Russian Federation
62 K9 **Ambargasta, Salinas de** salt lake C Argentina
126 J6 **Ambarnyy** Respublika Kareliya, NW Russian Federation
56 C7 **Ambato** Tungurahua, C Ecuador
172 I5 **Ambatolampy** Antananarivo, C Madagascar
172 H4 **Ambatomainty** Mahajanga, W Madagascar
172 J4 **Ambatondrazaka** Toamasina, C Madagascar
101 L20 **Amberg** var. Amberg in der Oberpfalz. Bayern, SE Germany
Amberg in der Oberpfalz see Amberg
42 H1 **Ambergris Cay** island NE Belize
103 S11 **Ambérieu-en-Bugey** Ain, E France
185 I18 **Amberley** Canterbury, South Island, NZ
103 P11 **Ambert** Puy-de-Dôme, C France
Ambianum see Amiens
76 J11 **Ambidédi** Kayes, SW Mali
154 M10 **Ambikāpur** Madhya Pradesh, C India
172 J2 **Ambilobe** Antsiranana, N Madagascar
39 O7 **Ambler** Alaska, USA
Amblève see Amel
Ambo see Hägere Hiywet
172 I8 **Amboasary** Toliara, S Madagascar
172 J4 **Ambodifotatra** var. Ambodifototra. Toamasina, E Madagascar
Amboenten see Ambunten
172 I5 **Ambohidratrimo** Antananarivo, C Madagascar
172 I6 **Ambohimahasoa** Fianarantsoa, SE Madagascar
172 K3 **Ambohitralanana** Antsiranana, NE Madagascar
Amboina see Ambon
102 M8 **Amboise** Indre-et-Loire, C France
171 S13 **Ambon** prev. Amboina, Amboyna. Pulau Ambon, E Indonesia
171 S13 **Ambon, Pulau** island E Indonesia
81 I20 **Amboseli, Lake** ◎ Kenya/Tanzania
172 I6 **Ambositra** Fianarantsoa, SE Madagascar
172 I8 **Ambovombe** Toliara, S Madagascar
35 W14 **Amboy** California, W USA
30 L11 **Amboy** Illinois, N USA
Amboyna see Ambon
Ambracia see Árta
18 B14 **Ambridge** Pennsylvania, NE USA
Ambrim see Ambrym
Ambrizete see N'Zeto
187 R13 **Ambrym** var. Ambrim. island C Vanuatu
8 K3 **Amund Ringnes Island** island Nunavut, N Canada
169 T16 **Ambunten** prev. Amboenten. Pulau Madura, E Indonesia
186 B6 **Ambunti** East Sepik, NW PNG
155 I20 **Āmbūr** Tamil Nādu, SE India
38 E17 **Amchitka Island** island Aleutian Islands, Alaska, USA
38 F17 **Amchitka Pass** strait Aleutian Islands, Alaska, USA
141 R15 **'Amd** C Yemen
78 J10 **Am Dam** Ouaddaï, E Chad
171 U16 **Amdassa** Pulau Yamdena, E Indonesia
127 U1 **Amderma** Nenetskiy Avtonomnyy Okrug, NW Russian Federation
159 N14 **Amdo** Xizang Zizhiqu, W China
40 K13 **Ameca** Jalisco, SW Mexico
41 P14 **Amecameca** var. Amecameca de Juárez. México, C Mexico
Amecameca de Juárez see Amecameca
61 A20 **Ameghino** Buenos Aires, E Argentina
99 M21 **Amel** Fr. Amblève. Liège, E Belgium
98 K4 **Ameland** Fris. It Amelân. island Waddeneilanden, N Netherlands
Amelân, It see Ameland
107 H14 **Amelia** Umbria, C Italy
21 V6 **Amelia Court House** Virginia, NE USA
23 W8 **Amelia Island** island Florida, SE USA
18 L12 **Amenia** New York, NE USA
America see United States of America
65 M21 **America-Antarctica Ridge** undersea feature S Atlantic Ocean
America in Miniature see Maryland
60 L9 **Americana** São Paulo, S Brazil
33 Q15 **American Falls** Idaho, NW USA
33 Q15 **American Falls Reservoir** ▣ Idaho, NW USA
36 L3 **American Fork** Utah, W USA
192 K16 **American Samoa** ◇ US unincorporated territory W Polynesia
23 S6 **Americus** Georgia, SE USA
98 K12 **Amerongen** Utrecht, C Netherlands
98 K11 **Amersfoort** Utrecht, C Netherlands
97 N21 **Amersham** SE England, UK
30 I5 **Amery** Wisconsin, N USA
195 W6 **Amery Ice Shelf** ice shelf Antarctica
29 V13 **Ames** Iowa, C USA
19 P10 **Amesbury** Massachusetts, NE USA
Amestratus see Mistretta
115 F18 **Amfíkleia** var. Amfíklia. Stereá Ellás, C Greece
Amfíklia see Amfíkleia
115 D17 **Amfilochía** var. Amfilokhía. Dytikí Ellás, C Greece
Amfilokhía see Amfilochía
114 H13 **Amfípoli** anc. Amphipolis. site of ancient city Kentrikí Makedonía, NE Greece
115 F18 **Ámfissa** Stereá Ellás, C Greece
123 Q10 **Amga** Respublika Sakha (Yakutiya), NE Russian Federation
123 Q11 **Amga** ≈ NE Russian Federation
Amgalang see Xin Barag Zuoqi
123 V5 **Amguema** ≈ NE Russian Federation
123 S12 **Amgun'** ≈ SE Russian Federation
80 J12 **Amhara** ◈ region N Ethiopia
13 P15 **Amherst** Nova Scotia, SE Canada
18 M11 **Amherst** Massachusetts, NE USA
18 D10 **Amherst** New York, NE USA
24 M4 **Amherst** Texas, SW USA
21 U6 **Amherst** Virginia, NE USA
Amherst see Kyaikkami
14 C18 **Amherstburg** Ontario, S Canada
21 Q6 **Amherstdale** West Virginia, NE USA
14 K15 **Amherst Island** island Ontario, SE Canada
Amida see Diyarbakır
28 J6 **Amidon** North Dakota, N USA
103 O3 **Amiens** anc. Ambianum, Samarobriva. Somme, N France
139 P8 **'Āmij, Wādī** var. Wadi 'Amīq. dry watercourse W Iraq
136 L17 **Amik Ovası** ◎ S Turkey
76 E9 **Amilcar Cabral** × Sal, NE Cape Verde
Amilḥayt, Wādī see Umm al Ḥayt, Wādī
Amíndaion/Amindeo see Amýntaio
155 C21 **Amīndīvi Islands** island group Lakshadweep, India, N Indian Ocean
139 U6 **Āmin Ḥabīb** E Iraq
83 E20 **Aminuis** Omaheke, E Namibia
'Amīq, Wadi see 'Āmij, Wādī
142 J7 **Amīrābād** Īlām, NW Iran
Amirante Bank see Amirante Ridge
173 N6 **Amirante Basin** undersea feature W Indian Ocean
173 N6 **Amirante Islands** var. Amirantes Group. island group C Seychelles
173 N7 **Amirante Ridge** var. Amirante Bank. undersea feature W Indian Ocean
Amirantes Group see Amirante Islands
173 N7 **Amirante Trench** undersea feature W Indian Ocean
11 U13 **Amisk Lake** ◎ Saskatchewan, C Canada
Amistad, Presa de la see Amistad Reservoir
25 O12 **Amistad Reservoir** var. Presa de la Amistad. ▣ Mexico/USA
Amisus see Samsun
22 K8 **Amite** var. Amite City. Louisiana, S USA
Amite City see Amite
27 T12 **Amity** Arkansas, C USA
154 H11 **Amla** prev. Amulla. Madhya Pradesh, C India
38 I17 **Amlia Island** island Aleutian Islands, Alaska, USA
97 I18 **Amlwch** NW Wales, UK
Ammaia see Portalegre
138 H10 **'Ammān** var. Amman; anc. Philadelphia, Bibl. Rabbah Ammon, Rabbath Ammon. ● (Jordan) 'Ammān, NW Jordan

◆ Country ● Country Capital ◇ Dependent Territory ○ Dependent Territory Capital ◈ Administrative Region × International Airport ▲ Mountain ▲ Mountain Range Volcano ≈ River ◎ Lake ▣ Reservoir

138 H10 **'Ammān** *off.* Muḩāfaẓat 'Ammān. ◆ *governorate* NW Jordan
93 N14 **Ämmänsaari** Oulu, E Finland
92 H13 **Ammarnäs** Västerbotten, N Sweden
197 O15 **Ammassalik** *var.* Angmagssalik. Tunu, S Greenland
101 K24 **Ammer** ≈ SE Germany
101 K24 **Ammersee** ◎ SE Germany
98 J13 **Ammerzoden** Gelderland, C Netherlands
Ammóchostos *see* Gazimağusa
Ammóchostos, Kólpos *see* Gazimağusa Körfezi
Amnok-kang *see* Yalu
Amoea *see* Portalegre
Amoentai *see* Amuntai
Amoerang *see* Amurang
143 O4 **Āmol** *var.* Amul. Māzandarān, N Iran
115 K21 **Amorgós** Amorgós, Kykládes, Greece, Aegean Sea
115 K22 **Amorgós** *island* Kykládes, Greece, Aegean Sea
23 N3 **Amory** Mississippi, S USA
12 I13 **Amos** Quebec, SE Canada
95 G15 **Åmot** Buskerud, S Norway
95 E15 **Åmot** Telemark, S Norway
95 J15 **Åmotfors** Värmland, C Sweden
76 L10 **Amourj** Hodh ech Chargui, SE Mauritania
Amoy *see* Xiamen
172 H7 **Ampanihy** Toliara, SW Madagascar
155 L25 **Ampara** *var.* Amparai. Eastern Province, E Sri Lanka
172 J4 **Amparafaravola** Toamasina, E Madagascar
Amparai *see* Ampara
60 M9 **Amparo** São Paulo, S Brazil
172 J5 **Ampasimanolotra** Toamasina, E Madagascar
57 H17 **Ampato, Nevado** ▲ S Peru
101 L23 **Amper** ≈ SE Germany
64 M9 **Ampère Seamount** *undersea feature* E Atlantic Ocean
Amphipolis *see* Amfipoli
167 X10 **Amphitrite Group** *island group* N Paracel Islands
171 T16 **Amplawas** *var.* Emplawas. Pulau Babar, E Indonesia
105 U7 **Amposta** Cataluña, NE Spain
15 V7 **Amqui** Quebec, SE Canada
141 O14 **'Amrān** W Yemen
Amraoti *see* Amrāvati
154 H12 **Amrāvati** *prev.* Amraoti. Mahārāshtra, C India
154 C11 **Amreli** Gujarāt, W India
108 H6 **Amriswil** Thurgau, NE Switzerland
138 H5 **'Amrīt** *ruins* Ṭarṭūs, W Syria
152 H7 **Amritsar** Punjab, N India
152 J10 **Amroha** Uttar Pradesh, N India
100 G7 **Amrum** *island* NW Germany
93 I15 **Åmsele** Västerbotten, N Sweden
98 I10 **Amstelveen** Noord-Holland, C Netherlands
98 I10 **Amsterdam** ● (Netherlands) Noord-Holland, C Netherlands
18 K10 **Amsterdam** New York, NE USA
173 Q11 **Amsterdam Fracture Zone** *tectonic feature* S Indian Ocean
173 R11 **Amsterdam Island** *island* NE French Southern and Antarctic Territories
109 U4 **Amstetten** Niederösterreich, N Austria
78 J11 **Am Timan** Salamat, SE Chad
146 L12 **Amu-Bukhoro Kanali** *var.* Aral-Bukhorskiy Kanal. *canal* C Uzbekistan
139 O1 **'Āmūdah** *var.* Amude. Al Ḩasakah, N Syria
146 M14 **Amu-Dar'ya** Lebapskiy Velayat, NE Turkmenistan
147 O15 **Amu Darya** *Rus.* Amudar'ya, *Taj.* Dar"yoi Amu, *Turkm.* Amyderya, *Uzb.* Amudaryo; *anc.* Oxus. ≈ C Asia
Amudar'ya/Amudaryo/Amu, Dar"yoi *see* Amu Darya
Amude *see* 'Āmūdah
140 L3 **'Amūd, Jabal al** ▲ NW Saudi Arabia
38 J17 **Amukta Island** *island* Aleutian Islands, Alaska, USA
38 I17 **Amukta Pass** *strait* Aleutian Islands, Alaska, USA
Amul *see* Āmol
Amulla *see* Amla
Amundsen Basin *see* Fram Basin
195 X3 **Amundsen Bay** *bay* Antarctica
195 P10 **Amundsen Coast** *physical region* Antarctica
8 I6 **Amundsen Gulf** *gulf* Northwest Territories, N Canada
193 O14 **Amundsen Plain** *undersea feature* S Pacific Ocean
195 Q9 **Amundsen-Scott** *US research station* Antarctica
194 J11 **Amundsen Sea** *sea* S Pacific Ocean
94 M12 **Amungen** ◎ C Sweden
169 U13 **Amuntai** *prev.* Amoentai. Borneo, C Indonesia
131 W6 **Amur** *Chin.* Heilong Jiang. ≈ China/Russian Federation
171 Q11 **Amurang** *prev.* Amoerang. Sulawesi, C Indonesia
105 O3 **Amurrio** País Vasco, N Spain
123 S13 **Amursk** Khabarovskiy Kray, SE Russian Federation
123 Q12 **Amurskaya Oblast'** ◆ *province* SE Russian Federation
80 G7 **'Amur, Wadi** ≈ NE Sudan
115 C17 **Amvrakikós Kólpos** *gulf* W Greece
Amvrosiyevka *see* Amvrosiyivka
117 X8 **Amvrosiyivka** *Rus.* Amvrosiyevka. Donets'ka Oblast', SE Ukraine
Amyderya *see* Amu Darya
114 E13 **Amýntaio** *var.* Amindeo; *prev.* Amíndaion. Dytikí Makedonía, N Greece
14 B6 **Amyot** Ontario, S Canada
191 U10 **Anaa** *atoll* Îles Tuamotu, C French Polynesia
Anabanoea *see* Anabanua
171 N14 **Anabanua** *prev.* Anabanoea. Sulawesi, C Indonesia
189 R8 **Anabar** NE Nauru
123 N8 **Anabar** ≈ NE Russian Federation
An Abhainn Mhór *see* Blackwater
55 O6 **Anaco** Anzoátegui, NE Venezuela
33 Q10 **Anaconda** Montana, NW USA
32 H7 **Anacortes** Washington, NW USA
26 M11 **Anadarko** Oklahoma, C USA
114 N12 **Ana Dere** ≈ NW Turkey
104 G8 **Anadia** Aveiro, N Portugal
Anadolu Dağları *see* Doğu Karadeniz Dağları
123 V6 **Anadyr'** Chukotskiy Avtonomnyy Okrug, NE Russian Federation
123 V6 **Anadyr'** ≈ NE Russian Federation
Anadyr, Gulf of *see* Anadyrskiy Zaliv
131 X4 **Anadyrskiy Khrebet** *var.* Chukot Range. ▲ NE Russian Federation
123 W6 **Anadyrskiy Zaliv** *Eng.* Gulf of Anadyr. *gulf* NE Russian Federation
115 K22 **Anáfi** *anc.* Anaphe. *island* Kykládes, Greece, Aegean Sea
107 J15 **Anagni** Lazio, C Italy
'Ānah *see* 'Annah
35 T15 **Anaheim** California, W USA
10 L15 **Anahim Lake** British Columbia, SW Canada
38 B8 **Anahola** Kauai, Hawaii, USA, C Pacific Ocean
25 X11 **Anahuac** Texas, SW USA
41 O7 **Anáhuac** Nuevo León, NE Mexico
155 G22 **Anai Mudi** ▲ S India
Anaiza *see* 'Unayzah
155 M15 **Anakāpalle** Andhra Pradesh, E India
191 W15 **Anakena, Playa de** *beach* Easter Island, Chile, E Pacific Ocean
39 Q7 **Anaktuvuk Pass** Alaska, USA
39 Q6 **Anaktuvuk River** ≈ Alaska, USA
172 J3 **Analalava** Mahajanga, NW Madagascar
44 F6 **Ana María, Golfo de** *gulf* C Cuba
Anambas Islands *see* Anambas, Kepulauan
169 N8 **Anambas, Kepulauan** *var.* Anambas Islands *island group* W Indonesia
77 U17 **Anambra** ◆ *state* SE Nigeria
29 N4 **Anamoose** North Dakota, N USA
29 Y13 **Anamosa** Iowa, C USA
136 H17 **Anamur** İçel, S Turkey
136 H17 **Anamur Burnu** *headland* S Turkey
154 O12 **Anandadur** Orissa, E India
155 H18 **Anantapur** Andhra Pradesh, S India
152 H5 **Anantnāg** *var.* Islamabad. Jammu and Kashmir, NW India
Ananyev *see* Anan'yiv
117 O9 **Anan'yiv** *Rus.* Ananyev. Odes'ka Oblast', SW Ukraine
128 J14 **Anapa** Krasnodarskiy Kray, SW Russian Federation
Anaphe *see* Anáfi
59 K18 **Anápolis** Goiás, C Brazil
143 R10 **Anār** Kermān, C Iran
Anār *see* Inari
143 P7 **Anārak** Eşfahān, C Iran
Anar Dara *see* Anār Darreh
148 J7 **Anār Darreh** *var.* Anar Dara. Farāh, W Afghanistan
Anárjohka *see* Inarijoki
23 X9 **Anastasia Island** *island* Florida, SE USA
188 K7 **Anatahan** *island* C Northern Mariana Islands
130 M6 **Anatolia** *plateau* C Turkey
86 F14 **Anatolian Plate** *tectonic feature* Asia/Europe
114 H13 **Anatolikí Makedonía kai Thráki** *Eng.* Macedonia East and Thrace. ◆ *region* NE Greece
Anatom *see* Aneityum
62 L8 **Añatuya** Santiago del Estero, N Argentina
An Baile Meánach *see* Ballymena
An Bhearú *see* Barrow
An Bhóinn *see* Boyne
An Blascaod Mór *see* Great Blasket Island
An Cabhán *see* Cavan
An Caisleán Nua *see* Newcastle
An Caisleán Riabhach *see* Castlereagh, Northern Ireland, UK
An Caisleán Riabhach *see* Castlerea, Ireland
56 C13 **Ancash** *off.* Departamento de Ancash. ◆ *department* W Peru
An Cathair *see* Caher
102 J8 **Ancenis** Loire-Atlantique, NW France
An Chanáil Ríoga *see* Royal Canal
An Cheacha *see* Caha Mountains
39 R11 **Anchorage** Alaska, USA
39 R12 **Anchorage** ✕ Alaska, USA
39 Q13 **Anchor Point** Alaska, USA
An Chorr Chríochach *see* Cookstown
65 M24 **Anchorstack Point** *headland* W Tristan da Cunha
An Clár *see* Clare
An Clochán *see* Clifden
An Clochán Liath *see* Dunglow
23 U12 **Anclote Keys** *island group* Florida, SE USA
An Cóbh *see* Cobh
57 J17 **Ancohuma, Nevado de** ▲ W Bolivia
An Comar *see* Comber
57 D14 **Ancón** Lima, W Peru
106 J12 **Ancona** Marche, C Italy
Ancuabe *see* Ancuabi
82 Q13 **Ancuabi** *var.* Ancuabe. Cabo Delgado, NE Mozambique
63 F17 **Ancud** *prev.* San Carlos de Ancud. Los Lagos, S Chile
63 G17 **Ancud, Golfo de** *gulf* S Chile
Ancyra *see* Ankara
163 V8 **Anda** Heilongjiang, NE China
57 G16 **Andahuaylas** Apurímac, S Peru
An Daingean *see* Dingle
153 R15 **Andāl** West Bengal, NE India
94 E9 **Åndalsnes** Møre og Romsdal, S Norway
104 K13 **Andalucía** *Eng.* Andalusia. ◆ *autonomous community* S Spain
23 P7 **Andalusia** Alabama, S USA
Andalusia *see* Andalucía
151 Q21 **Andaman and Nicobar Islands** *var.* Andamans and Nicobars. ◆ *union territory* India, NE Indian Ocean
173 T4 **Andaman Basin** *undersea feature* NE Indian Ocean
151 P19 **Andaman Islands** *island group* India, NE Indian Ocean
173 T4 **Andaman Sea** *sea* NE Indian Ocean
57 K19 **Andamarca** Oruro, C Bolivia
182 H5 **Andamooka** South Australia
141 Y9 **'Andām, Wādī** *seasonal river* NE Oman
172 J3 **Andapa** Antsirañana, NE Madagascar
149 R4 **Andarāb** *var.* Banow. Baghlān, NE Afghanistan
Andarbag *see* Andarbogh
147 S13 **Andarbogh** *Rus.* Andarbag, Anderbak. S Tajikistan
109 Z5 **Andau** Burgenland, E Austria
108 I10 **Andeer** Graubünden, S Switzerland
92 H9 **Andenes** Nordland, C Norway
99 J20 **Andenne** Namur, SE Belgium
77 S11 **Andéramboukane** Gao, E Mali
Anderbak *see* Andarbogh
99 G18 **Anderlecht** Brussels, C Belgium
99 G21 **Anderlues** Hainaut, S Belgium
108 G9 **Andermatt** Uri, C Switzerland
101 E17 **Andernach** *anc.* Antunnacum. Rheinland-Pfalz, SW Germany
188 D15 **Andersen Air Force Base** *air base* NE Guam
39 R9 **Anderson** Alaska, USA
35 N4 **Anderson** California, W USA
31 P13 **Anderson** Indiana, N USA
27 R8 **Anderson** Missouri, C USA
21 P11 **Anderson** South Carolina, SE USA
25 V10 **Anderson** Texas, SW USA
95 K20 **Anderstorp** Jönköping, S Sweden
54 D9 **Andes** Antioquia, W Colombia
47 P7 **Andes** ▲ W South America
29 P12 **Andes, Lake** ◎ South Dakota, N USA
92 H9 **Andfjorden** *fjord* E Norwegian Sea
155 H16 **Andhra Pradesh** ◆ *state* E India
98 J8 **Andijk** Noord-Holland, NW Netherlands
147 S10 **Andijon** *Rus.* Andizhan. Andijon Wiloyati, E Uzbekistan
147 S10 **Andijon Wiloyati** *Rus.* Andizhanskaya Oblast'. ◆ *province* E Uzbekistan
Andikíthira *see* Antikýthira
172 J4 **Andilamena** Toamasina, C Madagascar
142 L8 **Andīmeshk** *var.* Andimishk; *prev.* Salehābād. Khūzestān, SW Iran
Andimishk *see* Andīmeshk
Andipáros *see* Antíparos
Andipaxi *see* Antípaxoi
Andípsara *see* Antípsara
136 L16 **Andırın** Kahramanmaraş, S Turkey
158 J8 **Andirlangar** Xinjiang Uygur Zizhiqu, NW China
Andírrion *see* Antírrio
Ándissa *see* Ántissa
Andizhan *see* Andijon
Andizhanskaya Oblast' *see* Andijon Wiloyati
149 N2 **Andkhvoy** Fāryāb, N Afghanistan
105 Q2 **Andoain** País Vasco, N Spain
163 Y15 **Andong** *Jap.* Antō. E South Korea
109 R4 **Andorf** Oberösterreich, N Austria
105 S7 **Andorra** Aragón, NE Spain
105 V4 **Andorra** *off.* Principality of Andorra, *Cat.* Valls d'Andorra, *Fr.* Vallée d'Andorre. ◆ *monarchy* SW Europe
Andorra *see* Andorra la Vella
105 V4 **Andorra la Vella** *var.* Andorra, *Fr.* Andorre la Vielle, *Sp.* Andorra la Vieja. ● (Andorra) C Andorra
Andorra la Vieja *see* Andorra la Vella
Andorra, Valls d'/Andorre, Vallée d' *see* Andorra
Andorre la Vielle *see* Andorra la Vella
97 M22 **Andover** S England, UK
27 N6 **Andover** Kansas, C USA
92 G10 **Andøya** *island* C Norway
60 I8 **Andradina** São Paulo, S Brazil
39 N10 **Andreafsky River** ≈ Alaska, USA
38 H17 **Andreanof Islands** *island group* Aleutian Islands, Alaska, USA
126 H16 **Andreapol'** Tverskaya Oblast', W Russian Federation
Andreas, Cape *see* Zafer Burnu
Andreevka *see* Kabanbay
21 N10 **Andrews** North Carolina, SE USA
21 T13 **Andrews** South Carolina, SE USA
24 M7 **Andrews** Texas, SW USA
173 N5 **Andrew Tablemount** *var.* Gora Andryu. *undersea feature* W Indian Ocean
Andreyevka *see* Kabanbay
107 N17 **Andria** Puglia, SE Italy
113 K16 **Andrijevica** Montenegro, SW Yugoslavia
115 E20 **Andrítsaina** Pelopónnisos, S Greece
An Droichead Nua *see* Newbridge
Andropov *see* Rybinsk
115 J19 **Ándros** Ándros, Kykládes, Greece, Aegean Sea
115 J20 **Ándros** *island* Kykládes, Greece, Aegean Sea
19 O7 **Androscoggin River** ≈ Maine/New Hampshire, NE USA
44 F3 **Andros Island** *island* NW Bahamas
129 R7 **Androsovka** Samarskaya Oblast', W Russian Federation
44 G3 **Andros Town** Andros Island, NW Bahamas
155 D21 **Āndrott Island** *island* Lakshadweep, India, N Indian Ocean
117 N5 **Andrushivka** Zhytomyrs'ka Oblast', N Ukraine
111 K17 **Andrychów** Małopolskie, S Poland
Andryu, Gora *see* Andrew Tablemount
92 I10 **Andselv** Troms, N Norway
79 O17 **Andudu** Orientale, NE Dem. Rep. Congo (Zaire)
105 N13 **Andújar** *anc.* Illiturgis. Andalucía, SW Spain
82 C12 **Andulo** Bié, W Angola
103 Q14 **Anduze** Gard, S France
An Earagail *see* Errigal Mountain
95 L19 **Aneby** Jönköping, S Sweden
Anécho *see* Aného
77 Q9 **Anéfis** Kidal, NE Mali
45 U8 **Anegada** *island* NE British Virgin Islands
61 B25 **Anegada, Bahía** *bay* E Argentina
45 U9 **Anegada Passage** *passage* Anguilla/British Virgin Islands
77 R17 **Aného** *var.* Anécho; *prev.* Petit-Popo. S Togo
197 D17 **Aneityum** *var.* Anatom; *prev.* Kéamu. *island* S Vanuatu
117 N10 **Anenii Noi** *Rus.* Novyye Aneny. C Moldova
186 F7 **Anepmete** New Britain, E PNG
105 U4 **Aneto** ▲ NE Spain
Ānew *see* Annau
Ānewetak *see* Enewetak Atoll
77 Y8 **Aney** Agadez, NE Niger
An Fheoir *see* Nore
122 L12 **Angara** ≈ C Russian Federation
122 M13 **Angarsk** Irkutskaya Oblast', S Russian Federation
93 G17 **Ånge** Västernorrland, C Sweden
Angel *see* Úhlava
40 D4 **Ángel de la Guarda, Isla** *island* NW Mexico
171 O3 **Angeles** *off.* Angeles City. Luzon, N Philippines
Angeles City *see* Angeles
Angel Falls *see* Ángel, Salto
95 J22 **Ängelholm** Skåne, S Sweden
61 A17 **Angélica** Santa Fe, C Argentina
25 W8 **Angelina River** ≈ Texas, SW USA
55 Q9 **Ángel, Salto** *Eng.* Angel Falls. *waterfall* E Venezuela
95 M15 **Ängelsberg** Västmanland, C Sweden
35 P8 **Angels Camp** California, W USA
109 W7 **Anger** Steiermark, SE Austria
Angerapp *see* Ozersk
Angerburg *see* Węgorzewo
93 H15 **Ångermanälven** ≈ N Sweden
100 P11 **Angermünde** Brandenburg, NE Germany
102 K7 **Angers** *anc.* Juliomagus. Maine-et-Loire, NW France
15 W7 **Angers** ≈ Quebec, SE Canada
93 J16 **Ängesön** *island* N Sweden
Angistro *see* Ágkistro
114 H13 **Angítis** ≈ NE Greece
167 R13 **Ângk Tasaôm** *prev.* Angtassom. Takêv, S Cambodia
185 C25 **Anglem, Mount** ▲ Stewart Island, Southland, SW NZ
97 I18 **Anglesey** *cultural region* NW Wales, UK
97 I18 **Anglesey** *island* NW Wales, UK
102 I15 **Anglet** Pyrénées-Atlantiques, SW France
25 W12 **Angleton** Texas, SW USA
Anglia *see* England
14 H9 **Angliers** Quebec, SE Canada
Anglo-Egyptian Sudan *see* Sudan
Angmagssalik *see* Ammassalik
167 Q7 **Ang Nam Ngum** ◎ C Laos
79 N16 **Ango** Orientale, N Dem. Rep. Congo (Zaire)
83 Q15 **Angoche** Nampula, E Mozambique
63 G14 **Angol** Araucanía, C Chile
31 Q11 **Angola** Indiana, N USA
82 A9 **Angola** *off.* Republic of Angola; *prev.* People's Republic of Angola, Portuguese West Africa. ◆ *republic* SW Africa
65 P15 **Angola Basin** *undersea feature* E Atlantic Ocean
39 X13 **Angoon** Admiralty Island, Alaska, USA
147 O14 **Angor** Surkhondaryo Wiloyati, S Uzbekistan
Angora *see* Ankara
186 C6 **Angoram** East Sepik, NW PNG
40 H8 **Angostura** Sinaloa, C Mexico
Angostura *see* Ciudad Bolívar
41 U17 **Angostura, Presa de la** ⊠ SE Mexico
28 J11 **Angostura Reservoir** ⊠ South Dakota, N USA
102 L11 **Angoulême** *anc.* Iculisma. Charente, W France
102 K11 **Angoumois** *cultural region* W France
64 O2 **Angra do Heroísmo** Terceira, Azores, Portugal, NE Atlantic Ocean
60 O10 **Angra dos Reis** Rio de Janeiro, SE Brazil
Angra Pequena *see* Lüderitz
147 Q10 **Angren** Toshkent Wiloyati, E Uzbekistan
Angtassom *see* Ângk Tasaôm
167 O10 **Ang Thong** *var.* Angthong. Ang Thong, C Thailand
79 M16 **Angu** Orientale, N Dem. Rep. Congo (Zaire)
105 S5 **Angüés** Aragón, NE Spain
45 U9 **Anguilla** ◇ *UK dependent territory* E West Indies
45 V9 **Anguilla** *island* E West Indies
44 F4 **Anguilla Cays** *islets* SW Bahamas
Angul *see* Anugul
161 N1 **Anguli Nur** ◎ E China
79 O18 **Angumu** Orientale, E Dem. Rep. Congo (Zaire)
14 G14 **Angus** Ontario, S Canada
96 J10 **Angus** *cultural region* E Scotland, UK
59 K19 **Anhangüera** Goiás, S Brazil
99 I21 **Anhée** Namur, S Belgium
95 I21 **Anholt** *island* C Denmark
160 M11 **Anhua** *prev.* Dongping. Hunan, S China
161 P8 **Anhui** *var.* Anhui Sheng, Anhwei, Wan. ◆ *province* E China
Anhui Sheng/Anhwei *see* Anhui
39 O11 **Aniak** Alaska, USA
39 O12 **Aniak River** ≈ Alaska, USA
An Iarmhí *see* Westmeath
189 R8 **Anibare** E Nauru
189 R8 **Anibare Bay** *bay* E Nauru, W Pacific Ocean
Anicium *see* le Puy
115 K22 **Ánidro** *island* Kykládes, Greece, Aegean Sea
77 R15 **Anié** C Togo
77 Q15 **Anié** ≈ C Togo
102 J16 **Anie, Pic d'** ▲ SW France
129 Y7 **Anikhovka** Orenburgskaya Oblast', W Russian Federation
14 G9 **Anima Nipissing Lake** ◎ Ontario, S Canada
37 O16 **Animas** New Mexico, SW USA
37 P16 **Animas Peak** ▲ New Mexico, SW USA
37 P16 **Animas Valley** *valley* New Mexico, SW USA
116 F13 **Anina** *Ger.* Steierdorf, *Hung.* Stájerlakanina; *prev.* Ştaierdorf-Anina, Steierdorf-Anina, Steyerlak-Anina. Caraş-Severin, SW Romania
29 U14 **Anita** Iowa, C USA
123 U14 **Aniva, Mys** *headland* Ostrov Sakhalin, SE Russian Federation
187 S15 **Aniwa** *island* S Vanuatu
93 M19 **Anjalankoski** Etelä-Suomi, S Finland
'Anjar *see* Aanjar
Anjiangying *see* Luanping
14 B8 **Anjigami Lake** ◎ Ontario, S Canada
164 K14 **Anjō** *var.* Anzyô. Aichi, Honshū, SW Japan
102 J8 **Anjou** *cultural region* NW France
172 I13 **Anjouan** *var.* Nzwani, Johanna Island. *island* SE Comoros
172 J4 **Anjozorobe** Antananarivo, C Madagascar
163 W13 **Anju** W North Korea
98 M5 **Anjum** *Fris.* Eanjum. Friesland, N Netherlands
172 G6 **Ankaboa, Tanjona** *headland* W Madagascar
160 L7 **Ankang** *prev.* Xing'an. Shaanxi, C China
136 I12 **Ankara** *prev.* Angora, *anc.* Ancyra. ● (Turkey) Ankara, C Turkey
136 H12 **Ankara** ◆ *province* C Turkey
95 N19 **Ankarsrum** Kalmar, S Sweden
172 H6 **Ankazoabo** Toliara, SW Madagascar
172 I4 **Ankazobe** Antananarivo, C Madagascar
29 V14 **Ankeny** Iowa, C USA
167 U11 **An Khê** Gia Lai, C Vietnam
100 O9 **Anklam** Mecklenburg-Vorpommern, NE Germany
80 K13 **Ānkober** Amhara, N Ethiopia
77 O17 **Ankobra** ≈ S Ghana
79 N22 **Ankoro** Katanga, SE Dem. Rep. Congo (Zaire)
99 L24 **Anlier, Forêt d'** *forest* SE Belgium
160 I13 **Anlong** Guizhou, S China
An Longfort *see* Longford
167 R11 **Ânlong Vêng** Siĕmréab, NW Cambodia
An Lorgain *see* Lurgan
161 N8 **Anlu** Hubei, C China
An Mhí *see* Meath
An Mhuir Cheilteach *see* Celtic Sea
An Muileann gCearr *see* Mullingar
93 F16 **Ånn** Jämtland, C Sweden
128 M8 **Anna** Voronezhskaya Oblast', W Russian Federation
30 L17 **Anna** Illinois, N USA
25 U5 **Anna** Texas, SW USA
74 L5 **Annaba** *prev.* Bône. NE Algeria
An Nabatīyah at Taḩtā *see* Nabatîyé
101 N17 **Annaberg-Buchholz** Sachsen, E Germany
109 T9 **Annabichl** ✕ (Klagenfurt) Kärnten, S Austria
140 M5 **An Nafūd** *desert* NW Saudi Arabia
139 P6 **'Annah** *var.* 'Ānah. NW Iraq
139 P6 **An Nāḩiyah** W Iraq
139 T10 **An Najaf** *var.* Najaf. S Iraq
21 V5 **Anna, Lake** ⊠ Virginia, NE USA
97 F16 **Annalee** ≈ N Ireland
167 S9 **Annamitique, Chaîne** ▲ C Laos
97 J14 **Annan** S Scotland, UK
29 U8 **Annandale** Minnesota, N USA
21 W4 **Annandale** Virginia, NE USA
189 Q7 **Anna Point** *headland* N Nauru
21 X3 **Annapolis** *state capital* Maryland, NE USA
188 A10 **Anna, Pulo** *island* S Palau
153 O10 **Annapurna** ▲ C Nepal
An Nāqūrah *see* En Nâqoûra
31 R10 **Ann Arbor** Michigan, N USA
An Nás *see* Naas
139 W12 **An Nāṣirīyah** *var.* Nasiriya. SE Iraq
139 W11 **An Naṣr** E Iraq
146 F13 **Annau** *Turkm.* Ānew. Akhalskiy Velayat, C Turkmenistan
121 O13 **An Nawfalīyah** *var.* Al Nūwfalīyah. N Libya
19 P10 **Ann, Cape** *headland* Massachusetts, NE USA
180 I10 **Annean, Lake** ◎ Western Australia
Anneciacum *see* Annecy
103 T11 **Annecy** *anc.* Anneciacum. Haute-Savoie, E France
103 T11 **Annecy, Lac d'** ◎ E France
103 T10 **Annemasse** Haute-Savoie, E France
39 Z14 **Annette Island** *island* Alexander Archipelago, Alaska, USA
An Nhon *see* Binh Ðinh
An Nīl al Abyaḑ *see* White Nile
An Nīl al Azraq *see* Blue Nile
23 Q3 **Anniston** Alabama, S USA
79 A19 **Annobón** *island* W Equatorial Guinea
103 R12 **Annonay** Ardèche, E France
44 K12 **Annotto Bay** C Jamaica
141 R5 **An Nu'ayrīyah** *var.* Nariya. Ash Sharqīyah, NE Saudi Arabia
182 M9 **Annuello** Victoria, SE Australia
139 Q10 **An Nukhayb** S Iraq
139 U9 **An Nu'mānīyah** E Iraq
Áno Arkhánai *see* Epáno Archánes
115 J25 **Anógeia** *var.* Anogia, Anóyia. Kríti, Greece, E Mediterranean Sea
Anogia *see* Anógeia
29 V8 **Anoka** Minnesota, N USA
An Ómaigh *see* Omagh
172 I1 **Anorontany, Tanjona** *headland* N Madagascar
172 J5 **Anosibe An'Ala** Toamasina, E Madagascar
Anóyia *see* Anógeia
An Pointe *see* Warrenpoint
161 P9 **Anqing** Anhui, E China
161 Q5 **Anqiu** Shandong, E China
An Ráth *see* Ráth Luirc
An Ribhéar *see* Kenmare River
An Ros *see* Rush
99 K19 **Ans** Liège, E Belgium
Anṣāb *see* Niṣāb
171 W12 **Ansas** Irian Jaya, E Indonesia
101 J20 **Ansbach** Bayern, SE Germany
An Sciobairín *see* Skibbereen
An Scoil *see* Skull
An Seancheann *see* Old Head of Kinsale
45 Y5 **Anse-Bertrand** Grande Terre, N Guadeloupe
172 H17 **Anse Boileau** Mahé, NE Seychelles
45 S11 **Anse La Raye** NW Saint Lucia
54 D9 **Anserma** Caldas, W Colombia
109 T4 **Ansfelden** Oberösterreich, N Austria
163 U12 **Anshan** Liaoning, NE China
160 J12 **Anshun** Guizhou, S China
61 F17 **Ansina** Tacuarembó, C Uruguay
29 O15 **Ansley** Nebraska, C USA
25 P6 **Anson** Texas, SW USA
77 Q10 **Ansongo** Gao, E Mali
An Srath Bán *see* Strabane
21 R5 **Ansted** West Virginia, NE USA
171 Y13 **Ansudu** Irian Jaya, E Indonesia
57 G15 **Anta** Cusco, S Peru
57 G16 **Antabamba** Apurímac, C Peru
Antafalva *see* Kovačica
136 L17 **Antakya** *anc.* Antioch, Antiochia. Hatay, S Turkey
172 K3 **Antalaha** Antsirañana, NE Madagascar
136 F17 **Antalya** *prev.* Adalia, *anc.* Attaleia, *Bibl.* Attalia. Antalya, SW Turkey
136 F17 **Antalya** ◆ *province* SW Turkey
136 F16 **Antalya** ✕ Antalya, SW Turkey
121 U10 **Antalya Basin** *undersea feature* E Mediterranean Sea
Antalya, Gulf of *see* Antalya Körfezi
136 F16 **Antalya Körfezi** *var.* Gulf of Adalia, *Eng.* Gulf of Antalya. *gulf* SW Turkey
172 J5 **Antanambao Manampotsy** Toamasina, E Madagascar
172 I5 **Antananarivo** *prev.* Tananarive. ● (Madagascar) Antananarivo, C Madagascar

◆ Country ● Country Capital ◇ Dependent Territory ○ Dependent Territory Capital ◆ Administrative Region ✕ International Airport ▲ Mountain ▲ Mountain Range ⊼ Volcano ≈ River ◎ Lake ⊠ Reservoir

172 I4 **Antananarivo** ❖ *province* C Madagascar
172 J5 **Antananarivo** × Antananarivo, C Madagascar
An tAonach *see* Nenagh
204-205 **Antarctica** *continent*
194 I5 **Antarctic Peninsula** *peninsula* Antarctica
61 J15 **Antas, Rio das** ≈ S Brazil
189 U16 **Ant Atoll** *atoll* Caroline Islands, E Micronesia
An Teampall Mór *see* Templemore
Antep *see* Gaziantep
104 M15 **Antequera** *anc.* Anticaria, Antiquaria. Andalucía, S Spain
Antequera *see* Oaxaca
37 S5 **Antero Reservoir** ⊡ Colorado, C USA
26 M7 **Anthony** Kansas, C USA
37 R16 **Anthony** New Mexico, SW USA
182 D5 **Anthony, Lake** *salt lake* South Australia
74 E8 **Anti-Atlas** ▲ SW Morocco
103 U15 **Antibes** *anc.* Antipolis. Alpes-Maritimes, SE France
103 U15 **Antibes, Cap d'** *headland* SE France
Anticaria *see* Antequera
13 Q11 **Anticosti, Île d'** *Eng.* Anticosti Island. *island* Quebec, E Canada
Anticosti Island *see* Anticosti, Île d'
102 K3 **Antifer, Cap d'** *headland* N France
30 L6 **Antigo** Wisconsin, N USA
13 Q15 **Antigonish** Nova Scotia, SE Canada
64 P11 **Antigua** Fuerteventura, Islas Canarias, NE Atlantic Ocean
45 X10 **Antigua** *island* S Antigua and Barbuda, Leeward Islands
Antigua *see* Antigua Guatemala
45 W9 **Antigua and Barbuda** ◆ *commonwealth republic* E West Indies
42 C6 **Antigua Guatemala** *var.* Antigua. Sacatepéquez, SW Guatemala
41 P11 **Antiguo Morelos** *var.* Antiguo-Morelos. Tamaulipas, C Mexico
115 F19 **Antíkyras, Kólpos** *gulf* C Greece
115 G24 **Antikýthira** *var.* Andikíthira. *island* S Greece
138 I7 **Anti-Lebanon** *var.* Jebel esh Sharqi, *Ar.* Al Jabal ash Sharqī, *Fr.* Anti-Liban. ▲ Lebanon/Syria
Anti-Liban *see* Anti-Lebanon
115 I22 **Antímilos** *island* Kykládes, Greece, Aegean Sea
36 L6 **Antimony** Utah, W USA
An tInbhear Mór *see* Arklow
30 M10 **Antioch** Illinois, N USA
Antioch *see* Antakya
102 I10 **Antioche, Pertuis d'** *inlet* W France
Antiochia *see* Antakya
54 D8 **Antioquia** Antioquia, C Colombia
54 E8 **Antioquia** *off.* Departamento de Antioquia. ❖ *province* C Colombia
115 J21 **Antíparos** *var.* Andipáros. *island* Kykládes, Greece, Aegean Sea
115 B17 **Antípaxoi** *var.* Andipaxi. *island* Iónioi Nísoi, Greece, C Mediterranean Sea
122 J8 **Antipayuta** Yamalo-Nenetskiy Avtonomnyy Okrug, N Russian Federation
192 L12 **Antipodes Islands** *island group* S NZ
Antipolis *see* Antibes
115 J18 **Antípsara** *var.* Andípsara. *island* E Greece
Antiquaria *see* Antequera
15 N10 **Antique, Lac** ◎ Quebec, SE Canada
115 E18 **Antírrio** *var.* Andírrion. Dytikí Ellás, C Greece
115 K16 **Ántissa** *var.* Ándissa. Lésvos, E Greece
An tIúr *see* Newry
Antivari *see* Bar
56 C6 **Antizana** ▲ N Ecuador
27 Q13 **Antlers** Oklahoma, C USA
93 J14 **Antnäs** Norrbotten, N Sweden
Antō *see* Andong
62 G5 **Antofagasta** Antofagasta, N Chile
62 G6 **Antofagasta** *off.* Región de Antofagasta. ❖ *region* N Chile
62 I7 **Antofalla, Salar de** *salt lake* NW Argentina
99 D20 **Antoing** Hainaut, SW Belgium
24 M5 **Anton** Texas, SW USA
43 S16 **Antón** Coclé, C Panama
37 T11 **Anton Chico** New Mexico, SW USA
60 K12 **Antonina** Paraná, S Brazil
103 O5 **Antony** Hauts-de-Seine, N France
Antratsit *see* Antratsyt
117 Y8 **Antratsyt** *Rus.* Antratsit. Luhans'ka Oblast', E Ukraine
97 G15 **Antrim** *Ir.* Aontroim. NE Northern Ireland, UK
97 G14 **Antrim** *Ir.* Aontroim. *cultural region* NE Northern Ireland, UK
97 G14 **Antrim Mountains** ▲ NE Northern Ireland, UK
172 H5 **Antsalova** Mahajanga, W Madagascar
Antserana *see* Antsirañana
An tSionainn *see* Shannon
172 J2 **Antsirañana** *var.* Antserana; *prev.* Antsirane, Diégo-Suarez. Antsirañana, N Madagascar
172 J2 **Antsirañana** ❖ *province* N Madagascar
Antsirane *see* Antsirañana
An tSiúir *see* Suir
118 I7 **Antsla** *Ger.* Anzen. Võrumaa, SE Estonia
An tSláine *see* Slaney
172 J3 **Antsohihy** Mahajanga, NW Madagascar
63 G14 **Antuco, Volcán** ▲ C Chile
169 W10 **Antu, Gunung** ▲ Borneo, N Indonesia
An Tullach *see* Tullow
An-tung *see* Dandong
Antunnacum *see* Andernach
Antwerp *see* Antwerpen
99 G16 **Antwerpen** *Eng.* Antwerp, *Fr.* Anvers. Antwerpen, N Belgium
99 H16 **Antwerpen** *Eng.* Antwerp. ❖ *province* N Belgium
An Uaimh *see* Navan
154 N12 **Anugul** *var.* Angul. Orissa, E India
152 F9 **Anūpgarh** Rājasthān, NW India
154 K10 **Anūppur** Madhya Pradesh, C India
155 K24 **Anuradhapura** North Central Province, C Sri Lanka
187 S11 **Anuta** *island*, E Soloman Islands
Anvers *see* Antwerpen
194 G4 **Anvers Island** *island* Antarctica
39 N11 **Anvik** Alaska, USA
39 N10 **Anvik River** ≈ Alaska, USA
38 F17 **Anvil Peak** ▲ Semisopochnoi Island, Alaska, USA
159 P7 **Anxi** Gansu, N China
182 F8 **Anxious Bay** *bay* South Australia
161 O5 **Anyang** Henan, C China
159 S11 **A'nyêmaqên Shan** ▲ C China
118 H12 **Anykščiai** Anykščiai, E Lithuania
161 P13 **Anyuan** Jiangxi, S China
123 T7 **Anyuysk** Chukotskiy Avtonomnyy Okrug, NE Russian Federation
123 T7 **Anyuyskiy Khrebet** ▲ NE Russian Federation
54 D8 **Anza** Antioquia, C Colombia
Anzen *see* Antsla
107 I16 **Anzio** Lazio, C Italy
55 O6 **Anzoátegui** *off.* Estado Anzoátegui. ❖ *state* NE Venezuela
147 P12 **Anzob** W Tajikistan
Anzyô *see* Anjō
165 X13 **Aoga-shima** *island* Izu-shotō, SE Japan
163 T12 **'Aohan Qi** Nei Mongol Zizhiqu, N China
Aoiz *see* Aoiz-Agoitz
105 R3 **Aoiz-Agoitz** *var.* Agoitz, Aoiz. Navarra, N Spain
186 M9 **Aola** *var.* Tenaghau. Guadalcanal, C Solomon Islands
166 M15 **Ao Luk Nua** Krabi, SW Thailand
Aomen *see* Macao
172 N8 **Aomori** Aomori, Honshū, C Japan
165 Q6 **Aomori** *off.* Aomori-ken. ❖ *prefecture* Honshū, C Japan
Aontroim *see* Antrim
117 C15 **Aóos** *var.* Vijosa, Vijosë, *Alb.* Lumi i Vjosës,. ≈ Albania/Greece *see also* Vjosës, Lumi i
191 Q7 **Aorai, Mont** ▲ Tahiti, W French Polynesia
Aoraki *see* Cook, Mount
178 I13 **Aôral, Phnum** *prev.* Phnom Aural. ▲ W Cambodia
Aorangi *see* Cook, Mount
193 L15 **Aorangi Mountains** ▲ North Island, NZ
184 H13 **Aorere** ≈ South Island, NZ
106 A7 **Aosta** *anc.* Augusta Praetoria. Valle d'Aosta, NW Italy
77 O11 **Aougoundou, Lac** ◎ S Mali
76 K9 **Aoukâr** *var.* Aouker. *plateau* C Mauritania
78 J13 **Aouk, Bahr** ≈ Central African Republic/Chad
Aouker *see* Aoukâr
74 B11 **Aousard** SE Western Sahara
164 H12 **Aoya** Tottori, Honshū, SW Japan
78 H5 **Aozou** Borkou-Ennedi-Tibesti, N Chad
26 M11 **Apache** Oklahoma, C USA
36 L14 **Apache Junction** Arizona, SW USA
24 J9 **Apache Mountains** ▲ Texas, SW USA
36 M16 **Apache Peak** ▲ Arizona, SW USA
116 H10 **Apahida** Cluj, NW Romania
23 T9 **Apalachee Bay** *bay* Florida, SE USA
23 T3 **Apalachee River** ≈ Georgia, SE USA
23 S10 **Apalachicola** Florida, SE USA
23 S10 **Apalachicola Bay** *bay* Florida, SE USA
23 R9 **Apalachicola River** ≈ Florida, SE USA
Apam *see* Apan
Apamama *see* Abemama
41 P14 **Apan** *var.* Apam. Hidalgo, C Mexico
42 J8 **Apanás, Lago de** ◎ NW Nicaragua
54 H14 **Apaporis, Río** ≈ Brazil/Colombia
185 C23 **Aparima** ≈ South Island, NZ
171 O1 **Aparri** Luzon, N Philippines
112 J9 **Apatin** Serbia, NW Yugoslavia
126 J4 **Apatity** Murmanskaya Oblast', NW Russian Federation
55 X9 **Apatou** NW French Guiana
40 M14 **Apatzingán** *var.* Apatzingán de la Constitución. Michoacán de Ocampo, SW Mexico
171 X12 **Apauwar** Irian Jaya, E Indonesia
Apaxtla *see* Apaxtla de Castrejón
41 O15 **Apaxtla de Castrejón** *var.* Apaxtla. Guerrero, S Mexico
118 J7 **Ape** Alūksne, NE Latvia
98 L11 **Apeldoorn** Gelderland, E Netherlands
Apennines *see* Appennino
Apenrade *see* Åbenrå
57 L17 **Apere, Río** ≈ C Bolivia
55 W11 **Apetina** Sipaliwini, SE Suriname
21 U9 **Apex** North Carolina, SE USA
79 M16 **Api** Orientale, N Dem. Rep. Congo (Zaire)
152 M9 **Api** ▲ NW Nepal
Apia *see* Abaiang
192 H16 **Āpia** ● (Samoa) Upolu, SE Samoa
60 K11 **Apiaí** São Paulo, S Brazil
170 M16 **Api, Gunung** ▲ Pulau Sangeang, S Indonesia
187 N9 **Apio** Maramasike Island, N Solomon Islands
41 O15 **Apipilulco** Guerrero, S Mexico
41 P14 **Apizaco** Tlaxcala, S Mexico
104 I4 **A Pobla de Trives** *Cast.* Puebla de Trives. Galicia, NW Spain
55 U9 **Apoera** Sipaliwini, NW Suriname
115 O23 **Apolakkiá** Ródos, Dodekánisos, Greece, Aegean Sea
101 L16 **Apolda** Thüringen, C Germany
192 H16 **Apolima Strait** *strait* C Pacific Ocean
182 M13 **Apollo Bay** Victoria, SE Australia
Apollonia *see* Sozopol
57 J16 **Apolo** La Paz, W Bolivia
57 J16 **Apolobamba, Cordillera** ▲ Bolivia/Peru
171 Q8 **Apo, Mount** ▲ Mindanao, S Philippines
23 W11 **Apopka** Florida, SE USA
23 W11 **Apopka, Lake** ◎ Florida, SE USA
59 I19 **Aporé, Rio** ≈ SW Brazil
30 K2 **Apostle Islands** *island group* Wisconsin, N USA
Apostolas Andreas, Cape *see* Zafer Burnu
61 F14 **Apóstoles** Misiones, NE Argentina
Apostólou Andréa, Akrotíri *see* Zafer Burnu
117 S9 **Apostolove** *Rus.* Apostolovo. Dnipropetrovs'ka Oblast', E Ukraine
Apostolovo *see* Apostolove
17 S10 **Appalachian Mountains** ▲ E USA
95 K14 **Äppelbo** Dalarna, C Sweden
98 N7 **Appelscha** *Fris.* Appelskea. Friesland, N Netherlands
Appelskea *see* Appelscha
106 G11 **Appennino** *Eng.* Apennines. ▲ Italy/San Marino
107 L17 **Appennino Campano** ▲ C Italy
108 I7 **Appenzell** Appenzell, NW Switzerland
108 H7 **Appenzell** ❖ *canton* NE Switzerland
55 V12 **Appikalo** Sipaliwini, S Suriname
98 O5 **Appingedam** Groningen, NE Netherlands
25 X8 **Appleby** Texas, SW USA
97 L15 **Appleby-in-Westmorland** NW England, UK
30 K10 **Apple River** ≈ Illinois, N USA
30 I5 **Apple River** ≈ Wisconsin, N USA
25 W9 **Apple Springs** Texas, SW USA
29 S8 **Appleton** Minnesota, N USA
30 M7 **Appleton** Wisconsin, N USA
27 S5 **Appleton City** Missouri, C USA
35 U14 **Apple Valley** California, W USA
29 V9 **Apple Valley** Minnesota, N USA
21 U6 **Appomattox** Virginia, NE USA
188 B16 **Apra Harbour** *harbour* W Guam
188 B16 **Apra Heights** W Guam
106 F6 **Aprica, Passo dell'** *pass* N Italy
107 M15 **Apricena** *anc.* Hadria Picena. Puglia, SE Italy
128 L14 **Apsheronsk** Krasnodarskiy Kray, SW Russian Federation
Apsheronskiy Poluostrov *see* Abşeron Yarımadası
103 S15 **Apt** *anc.* Apta Julia. Vaucluse, SE France
Apta Julia *see* Apt
38 H12 **Apua Point** *headland* Hawaii, USA, C Pacific Ocean
60 I10 **Apucarana** Paraná, S Brazil
Apulia *see* Puglia
54 K8 **Apure** *off.* Estado Apure. ❖ *state* C Venezuela
54 J7 **Apure, Río** ≈ W Venezuela
57 F16 **Apurímac** *off.* Departamento de Apurímac. ❖ *department* C Peru
57 F15 **Apurímac, Río** ≈ S Peru
116 G10 **Apuseni, Munţii** ▲ W Romania
Aqaba/'Aqaba *see* Al 'Aqabah
138 F15 **Aqaba, Gulf of** *var.* Gulf of Elat, *Ar.* Khalīj al 'Aqabah; *anc.* Sinus Aelaniticus. *gulf* NE Red Sea
139 R7 **'Aqabah** C Iraq
'Aqabah, Khalīj al *see* Aqaba, Gulf of
149 O2 **Āqchah** *var.* Āqcheh. Jowzjān, N Afghanistan
Āqcheh *see* Āqchah
Aqköl *see* Akkol'
Aqmola *see* Astana
Aqmola Oblysy *see* Akmola
158 L10 **Aqqikkol Hu** ◎ NW China
Aqqystaū *see* Akkystau
'Aqrah *see* Ākrē
Aqsay *see* Aksay
Aqshataū *see* Akchatau
Aqsū *see* Aksu
Aqsūat *see* Aksuat
Aqtas *see* Aktas
Aqtaū *see* Aktau
Aqtöbe/Aqtöbe Oblysy *see* Aktyubinsk
Aqtoghay *see* Aktogay
Aquae Augustae *see* Dax
Aquae Calidae *see* Bath
Aquae Flaviae *see* Chaves
Aquae Grani *see* Aachen
Aquae Panoniae *see* Baden
Aquae Sextiae *see* Aix-en-Provence
Aquae Solis *see* Bath
Aquae Tarbelicae *see* Dax
36 J11 **Aquarius Mountains** ▲ Arizona, SW USA
62 O5 **Aquidabán, Río** ≈ E Paraguay
59 H20 **Aquidauana** Mato Grosso do Sul, S Brazil
40 L15 **Aquila** Michoacán de Ocampo, S Mexico
Aquila/Aquila degli Abruzzi *see* L'Aquila
25 T8 **Aquilla** Texas, SW USA
44 L9 **Aquin** S Haiti
Aquisgranum *see* Aachen
102 J13 **Aquitaine** ❖ *region* SW France
Aqzhar *see* Akzhar
153 P13 **Āra** *prev.* Arrah. Bihār, N India
105 S4 **Ara** ≈ NE Spain
23 P2 **Arab** Alabama, S USA
Araba *see* Álava
138 G12 **'Arabah, Wādī al** *Heb.* Ha'Arava. *dry watercourse* Israel/Jordan
117 U12 **Arabats'ka Strilka, Kosa** *spit* S Ukraine
117 U12 **Arabats'ka Zatoka** *gulf* S Ukraine
'Arab, Baḩr al *see* Arab, Bahr el
80 C12 **Arab, Bahr el** *var.* Baḩr al 'Arab. ≈ S Sudan
56 E7 **Arabela, Río** ≈ N Peru
173 O4 **Arabian Basin** *undersea feature* N Arabian Sea
Arabian Desert *see* Sahara el Sharqîya
141 N9 **Arabian Peninsula** *peninsula* SW Asia
85 P15 **Arabian Plate** *tectonic feature* Africa/Asia/Europe
141 W14 **Arabian Sea** *sea* NW Indian Ocean
Arabicus, Sinus *see* Red Sea
'Arabī, Khalīj al *see* Persian Gulf
Arabistan *see* Khūzestān
'Arabīyah as Su'ūdīyah, Al Mamlakah al *see* Saudi Arabia
'Arabīyah Jumhūrīyah, Mişr al *see* Egypt
138 I9 **'Arab, Jabal al** ▲ S Syria
Arab Republic of Egypt *see* Egypt
Arabs Gulf *see* 'Arab, Khalīg el
139 Y12 **'Arab, Shaţţ al** *Eng.* Shatt al Arab, *Per.* Arvand Rūd. ≈ Iran/Iraq
136 I11 **Araç** Kastamonu, N Turkey
59 P16 **Aracaju** *state capital* Sergipe, E Brazil
54 F5 **Aracataca** Magdalena, N Colombia
58 P13 **Aracati** Ceará, E Brazil
60 J8 **Araçatuba** São Paulo, S Brazil
104 J13 **Aracena** Andalucía, S Spain
115 F20 **Arachnaío** ▲ S Greece
115 D16 **Árachthos** *var.* Arta; *prev.* Árakhthos, *anc.* Arachthus. ≈ W Greece
Arachthus *see* Árachthos
59 N19 **Araçuai** Minas Gerais, SE Brazil
136 I11 **Araç Çayı** ≈ N Turkey
138 F11 **'Arad** Southern, S Israel
116 F11 **Arad** Arad, W Romania
116 F11 **Arad** ❖ *county* W Romania
78 J9 **Arada** Biltine, NE Chad
143 P18 **'Arādah** Abū Z̧aby, S UAE
Aradhippou *see* Aradíppou
121 Q3 **Aradíppou** *var.* Aradhippou. SE Cyprus
174 K6 **Arafura Sea** *Ind.* Laut Arafuru. *sea* W Pacific Ocean
174 L6 **Arafura Shelf** *undersea feature* C Arafura Sea
Arafuru, Laut *see* Arafura Sea
59 J18 **Aragarças** Goiás, C Brazil
Aragats, Gora *see* Aragats Lerr
137 T12 **Aragats Lerr** *Rus.* Gora Aragats. ▲ W Armenia
32 E14 **Arago, Cape** *headland* Oregon, NW USA
105 R6 **Aragón** ❖ *autonomous community* E Spain
105 Q4 **Aragón** ≈ NE Spain
107 I24 **Aragona** Sicilia, Italy, C Mediterranean Sea
105 Q7 **Aragoncillo** ▲ C Spain
54 L5 **Aragua** *off.* Estado Aragua. ❖ *state* N Venezuela
55 N6 **Aragua de Barcelona** Anzoátegui, NE Venezuela
55 O5 **Aragua de Maturín** Monagas, NE Venezuela
59 K15 **Araguaia, Río** *var.* Araguaya. ≈ C Brazil
59 K19 **Araguari** Minas Gerais, SE Brazil
58 J11 **Araguari, Rio** ≈ SW Brazil
Araguaya *see* Araguaia, Río
104 K14 **Arahal** Andalucía, S Spain
165 N11 **Arai** Niigata, Honshū, C Japan
Árainn *see* Inishmore
Árainn Mhór *see* Aran Island
Ara Jovis *see* Aranjuez
74 J11 **Arak** C Algeria
171 Y15 **Arak** Irian Jaya, E Indonesia
142 M7 **Arāk** *prev.* Sultānābād. Markazī, W Iran
188 D10 **Arakabesan** *island* Palau Islands, N Palau
55 S7 **Arakaka** NW Guyana
166 K6 **Arakan State** *var.* Rakhine State. ❖ *state* W Myanmar
166 K5 **Arakan Yoma** ▲ W Myanmar
165 O10 **Arakawa** Niigata, Honshū, C Japan
Árakhthos *see* Árachthos
Araks/Arak's *see* Aras
158 H7 **Aral** Xinjiang Uygur Zizhiqu, NW China
Aral *see* Aral'sk, Kazakhstan
Aral *see* Vose', Tajikistan
Aral-Bukhorskiy Kanal *see* Amu-Bukhoro Kanali
137 T12 **Aralik** Iğdır, E Turkey
146 H5 **Aral Sea** *Kaz.* Aral Tengizi, *Rus.* Aral'skoye More, *Uzb.* Orol Dengizi. *inland sea* Kazakhstan/Uzbekistan
144 L13 **Aral'sk** *Kaz.* Aral. Kzylorda, SW Kazakhstan
Aral'skoye More/Aral Tengizi *see* Aral Sea
41 O10 **Aramberri** Nuevo León, NE Mexico
186 B8 **Aramia** ≈ SW PNG
143 N6 **Ārān** *var.* Golārā. Eşfahān, C Iran
105 N5 **Aranda de Duero** Castilla-León, N Spain
112 M12 **Aranđelovac** *prev.* Arandjelovac. Serbia, C Yugoslavia
Arandjelovac *see* Aranđelovac
97 J19 **Aran Fawddwy** ▲ NW Wales, UK
97 C14 **Aran Island** *Ir.* Árainn Mhór. *island* NW Ireland
97 A18 **Aran Islands** *island group* W Ireland
105 N9 **Aranjuez** *anc.* Ara Jovis. Madrid, C Spain
83 E20 **Aranos** Hardap, SE Namibia
25 U14 **Aransas Bay** *inlet* Texas, SW USA
25 T14 **Aransas Pass** Texas, SW USA
191 O3 **Aranuka** *prev.* Nanouki. *atoll* Tungaru, W Kiribati
167 Q11 **Aranyaprathet** Prachin Buri, S Thailand
Aranyosasztal *see* Zlatý Stôl
Aranyosgyéres *see* Câmpia Turzii
Aranyosmarót *see* Zlaté Moravce
164 C14 **Arao** Kumamoto, Kyūshū, SW Japan
77 O8 **Araouane** Tombouctou, N Mali
26 L10 **Arapaho** Oklahoma, C USA
29 N16 **Arapahoe** Nebraska, C USA
57 I16 **Arapa, Laguna** ◎ SE Peru
185 K14 **Arapawa Island** *island* C NZ
61 E17 **Arapey Grande, Río** ≈ N Uruguay
59 P16 **Arapiraca** Alagoas, E Brazil
140 M3 **'Ar'ar** Al Ḩudūd ash Shamālīyah, NW Saudi Arabia
54 G15 **Araracuara** Caquetá, S Colombia
61 K15 **Ararangúa** Santa Catarina, S Brazil
60 L8 **Araraquara** São Paulo, S Brazil
59 O13 **Araras** Ceará, E Brazil
58 I14 **Araras** Pará, N Brazil
60 L9 **Araras** São Paulo, S Brazil
60 H11 **Araras, Serra das** ▲ S Brazil
137 U12 **Ararat** S Armenia
182 M12 **Ararat** Victoria, SE Australia
Ararat, Mount *see* Büyükağrı Dağı
140 M3 **'Ar'ar, Wādī** *dry watercourse* Iraq/Saudi Arabia
131 N7 **Aras** *Arm.* Arak's, *Az.* Araz Nehri, *Per.* Rūd-e Aras, *Rus.* Araks; *prev.* Araxes. ≈ SW Asia
105 R9 **Aras de Alpuente** País Valenciano, E Spain
137 S13 **Aras Güneyi Dağları** ▲ NE Turkey
Aras, Rūd-e *see* Aras
191 U9 **Aratika** *atoll* Îles Tuamotu, C French Polynesia
Aratürük *see* Yiwu
54 I8 **Arauca** Arauca, NE Colombia
54 I8 **Arauca** *off.* Intendencia de Arauca. ❖ *province* NE Colombia
63 G15 **Araucanía** *off.* Región de la Araucanía. ❖ *region* C Chile
54 L7 **Arauca, Río** ≈ Colombia/Venezuela
63 F14 **Arauco** Bío Bío, C Chile
63 F14 **Arauco, Golfo de** *gulf* S Chile
54 H8 **Arauquita** Arauca, C Colombia
Arausio *see* Orange
152 F13 **Arāvali Range** ▲ N India
186 J7 **Arawa** Bougainville Island, NE PNG
185 C20 **Arawata** ≈ South Island, NZ
186 F7 **Arawe Islands** *island group* E PNG
59 L20 **Araxá** Minas Gerais, SE Brazil
Araxes *see* Aras
55 O5 **Araya** Sucre, N Venezuela
105 R4 **Arba** ≈ N Spain
81 I15 **Ārba Minch'** Southern, S Ethiopia
139 U4 **Arbat** NE Iraq
107 D19 **Arbatax** Sardegna, Italy, C Mediterranean Sea
Arbe *see* Rab
Arbela *see* Arbīl
139 S3 **Arbīl** *var.* Erbil, Irbīl, *Kurd.* Hawlēr; *anc.* Arbela. N Iraq
95 M16 **Arboga** Västmanland, C Sweden
95 M16 **Arbogaån** ≈ C Sweden
103 S9 **Arbois** Jura, E France
54 D6 **Arboletes** Antioquia, NW Colombia
11 X15 **Arborg** Manitoba, S Canada
94 N12 **Arbrå** Gävleborg, C Sweden
96 K10 **Arbroath** *anc.* Aberbrothock. E Scotland, UK
35 N6 **Arbuckle** California, W USA
27 N12 **Arbuckle Mountains** ▲ Oklahoma, C USA
Arbuzinka *see* Arbyzynka
117 Q8 **Arbyzynka** *Rus.* Arbuzinka. Mykolayivs'ka Oblast', S Ukraine
103 U12 **Arc** ≈ E France
102 J13 **Arcachon** Gironde, SW France
102 J13 **Arcachon, Bassin d'** *inlet* SW France
18 E10 **Arcade** New York, NE USA
23 W14 **Arcadia** Florida, SE USA
22 H5 **Arcadia** Louisiana, S USA
30 J7 **Arcadia** Wisconsin, N USA
Arcae Remorum *see* Châlons-en-Champagne
44 L9 **Arcahaie** C Haiti
34 K3 **Arcata** California, W USA
35 U6 **Arc Dome** ▲ Nevada, W USA
107 J16 **Arce** Lazio, C Italy
41 O15 **Arcelia** Guerrero, S Mexico
99 M15 **Arcen** Limburg, SE Netherlands
Archangel *see* Arkhangel'sk
Archangel Bay *see* Chëshskaya Guba
115 O23 **Archángelos** *var.* Arhangelos, Arkhángelos. Ródos, Dodekánisos, Greece, Aegean Sea
114 F7 **Archar** ≈ NW Bulgaria
31 R11 **Archbold** Ohio, N USA
105 R12 **Archena** Murcia, SE Spain
25 R5 **Archer City** Texas, SW USA
104 M14 **Archidona** Andalucía, S Spain
65 B25 **Arch Islands** *island group* SW Falkland Islands
106 G13 **Arcidosso** Toscana, C Italy
103 Q5 **Arcis-sur-Aube** Aube, N France
182 F3 **Arckaringa Creek** *seasonal river* South Australia
106 G7 **Arco** Trentino-Alto Adige, N Italy
33 Q14 **Arco** Idaho, NW USA
30 M14 **Arcola** Illinois, N USA
105 P6 **Arcos de Jalón** Castilla-León, N Spain
104 K15 **Arcos de la Frontera** Andalucía, S Spain
104 G5 **Arcos de Valdevez** Viana do Castelo, N Portugal
59 P15 **Arcoverde** Pernambuco, E Brazil
102 H5 **Arcovest, Pointe de l'** *headland* NW France
Arctic-Mid Oceanic Ridge *see* Nansen Cordillera
197 R8 **Arctic Ocean** *ocean*
8 G7 **Arctic Red River** ≈ Northwest Territories/Yukon Territory, NW Canada
Arctic Red River *see* Tsiigehtchic
39 S6 **Arctic Village** Alaska, USA
194 H1 **Arctowski** *Polish research station* South Shetland Islands, Antarctica
114 I12 **Arda** *var.* Ardhas, *Gk.* Ardas. ≈ Bulgaria/Greece *see also* Ardas
142 L2 **Ardabīl** *var.* Ardebil. Ardabīl, NW Iran
142 L2 **Ardabīl** *off.* Ostān-e Ardabīl. ❖ *province* NW Iran
137 R11 **Ardahan** Ardahan, NE Turkey
137 S11 **Ardahan** ❖ *province* NE Turkey
143 P8 **Ardakān** Yazd, C Iran
94 E12 **Årdalstangen** Sogn og Fjordane, S Norway
137 R11 **Ardanuç** Artvin, NE Turkey
114 L12 **Ardas** *var.* Ardhas, *Bul.* Arda. ≈ Bulgaria/Greece *see also* Arda
138 I13 **Arḑ aş Şawwān** *var.* Ardh es Suwwān. *plain* S Jordan
129 P5 **Ardatov** Respublika Mordoviya, W Russian Federation
14 G12 **Ardbeg** Ontario, S Canada
Ardeal *see* Transylvania
Ardebil *see* Ardabīl
103 Q13 **Ardèche** ≈ C France
103 Q13 **Ardèche** ❖ *department* E France
97 F17 **Ardee** *Ir.* Baile Átha Fhirdhia. NE Ireland
103 Q3 **Ardennes** ❖ *department* NE France
99 J23 **Ardennes** *physical region* Belgium/France
137 Q11 **Ardeşen** Rize, NE Turkey
143 O7 **Ardestān** *var.* Ardistan. Eşfahān, C Iran
108 J9 **Ardez** Graubünden, SE Switzerland
Ardhas *see* Arda/Ardas
Ardh es Suwwān *see* Arḑ aş Şawwān
104 I12 **Ardila, Ribeira de** *Sp.* Ardilla. ≈ Portugal/Spain *see also* Ardilla
11 T17 **Ardill** Saskatchewan, S Canada
104 I12 **Ardilla** *Port.* Ribeira de Ardila. ≈ Portugal/Spain *see also* Ardila, Ribeira de
40 M11 **Ardilla, Cerro la** ▲ C Mexico
114 J12 **Ardino** Kŭrdzhali, S Bulgaria
Ardistan *see* Ardestān
183 P9 **Ardlethan** New South Wales, SE Australia
Ard Mhacha *see* Armagh
23 P1 **Ardmore** Alabama, S USA
27 N13 **Ardmore** Oklahoma, C USA
20 J10 **Ardmore** Tennessee, S USA
96 G10 **Ardnamurchan, Point of** *headland* N Scotland, UK
99 C17 **Ardooie** West-Vlaanderen, W Belgium
182 I9 **Ardrossan** South Australia
116 H9 **Ardusat** *Hung.* Erdőszáda. Maramureş, N Romania
93 F16 **Åre** Jämtland, C Sweden
79 P16 **Arebi** Orientale, NE Dem. Rep. Congo (Zaire)
45 T5 **Arecibo** C Puerto Rico
171 V13 **Aredo** Irian Jaya, E Indonesia
59 P14 **Areia Branca** Rio Grande do Norte, E Brazil
119 O14 **Arekhawsk** *Rus.* Orekhovsk. Vitsyebskaya Voblasts', N Belarus
Arel *see* Arlon
Arelas/Arelate *see* Arles
Arenal, Embalse de *see* Arenal Laguna
42 L12 **Arenal Laguna** *var.* Embalse de Arenal. ◎ NW Costa Rica
42 L13 **Arenal, Volcán** ▲ NW Costa Rica
34 K6 **Arena, Point** *headland* California, W USA
59 H17 **Arenápolis** Mato Grosso, W Brazil
40 G10 **Arena, Punta** *headland* W Mexico
104 L8 **Arenas de San Pedro** Castilla-León, N Spain

◆ Country ● Country Capital ◇ Dependent Territory ○ Dependent Territory Capital ❖ Administrative Region × International Airport ▲ Mountain ▲ Mountain Range ▲ Volcano ≈ River ◎ Lake ⊡ Reservoir

63 I24 **Arenas, Punta de** *headland* S Argentina
61 B20 **Arenaza** Buenos Aires, E Argentina
95 F17 **Arendal** Aust-Agder, S Norway
99 J16 **Arendonk** Antwerpen, N Belgium
43 T15 **Arenosa** Panamá, N Panama
Arensburg *see* Kuressaare
105 W5 **Arenys de Mar** Cataluña, NE Spain
106 C9 **Arenzano** Liguria, NW Italy
115 F22 **Areópoli** *prev.* Areópolis. Pelopónnisos, S Greece
Areópolis *see* Areópoli
57 H18 **Arequipa** Arequipa, SE Peru
57 G17 **Arequipa** *off.* Departamento de Arequipa. ◈ *department* SW Peru
61 B19 **Arequito** Santa Fe, C Argentina
104 M7 **Arévalo** Castilla-León, N Spain
106 H12 **Arezzo** *anc.* Arretium. Toscana, C Italy
105 Q4 **Arga** ≈ N Spain
Argaeus *see* Erciyes Dağı
115 G17 **Argalastí** Thessalía, C Greece
105 O10 **Argamasilla de Alba** Castilla-La Mancha, C Spain
158 L8 **Argan** Xinjiang Uygur Zizhiqu, NW China
105 O8 **Arganda** Madrid, C Spain
104 H8 **Arganil** Coimbra, N Portugal
171 P6 **Argao** Cebu, C Philippines
153 V15 **Argartala** Tripura, NE India
123 N9 **Arga-Sala** ≈ NE Russian Federation
103 P17 **Argelès-sur-Mer** Pyrénées-Orientales, S France
103 T15 **Argens** ≈ SE France
106 H9 **Argenta** Emilia-Romagna, N Italy
102 K5 **Argentan** Orne, N France
103 N12 **Argentat** Corrèze, C France
106 A9 **Argentera** Piemonte, NE Italy
103 N5 **Argenteuil** Val-d'Oise, N France
62 K13 **Argentina** *off.* Republic of Argentina. ◆ *republic* S South America
Argentina Basin *see* Argentine Basin
Argentine Abyssal Plain *see* Argentine Plain
65 I19 **Argentine Basin** *var.* Argentina Basin. *undersea feature* SW Atlantic Ocean
65 I20 **Argentine Plain** *var.* Argentine Abyssal Plain. *undersea feature* SW Atlantic Ocean
Argentine Rise *see* Falkland Plateau
63 H22 **Argentino, Lago** ◎ S Argentina
102 K8 **Argenton-Château** Deux-Sèvres, W France
102 M9 **Argenton-sur-Creuse** Indre, C France
Argentoratum *see* Strasbourg
116 I12 **Argeş** ◈ *county* S Romania
116 K14 **Argeş** ≈ S Romania
149 O8 **Arghandāb, Daryā-ye** ≈ SE Afghanistan
Arghastān *see* Arghestān
149 O8 **Arghestān** *Pash.* Arghastān. ≈ SE Afghanistan
Argirocastro *see* Gjirokastër
80 E7 **Argo** Northern, N Sudan
173 P7 **Argo Fracture Zone** *tectonic feature* C Indian Ocean
115 F20 **Argolikós Kólpos** *gulf* S Greece
103 R4 **Argonne** *physical region* NE France
115 F20 **Árgos** Pelopónnisos, S Greece
139 S1 **Argōsh** N Iraq
115 D14 **Árgos Orestikó** Dytikí Makedonía, N Greece
115 B19 **Argostóli** *var.* Argostólion. Kefallinía, Iónioi Nísoi, Greece, C Mediterranean Sea
Argostólion *see* Argostóli
Argovie *see* Aargau
35 O14 **Arguello, Point** *headland* California, W USA
129 P16 **Argun** Chechenskaya Respublika, SW Russian Federation
157 T2 **Argun** *Chin.* Ergun He, *Rus.* Argun'. ≈ China/Russian Federation
77 T12 **Argungu** Kebbi, NW Nigeria
162 J9 **Arguut** Övörhangay, C Mongolia
181 N3 **Argyle, Lake** *salt lake* Western Australia
96 G12 **Argyll** *cultural region* W Scotland, UK
Argyrokastron *see* Gjirokastër
162 I7 **Arhangay** ◈ *province* C Mongolia
Arhangelos *see* Archángelos
95 P14 **Arholma** Stockholm, C Sweden
95 G22 **Århus** *var.* Aarhus. Århus, C Denmark
95 G22 **Århus** ◈ *county* C Denmark
139 T1 **Ārī** E Iraq
Aria *see* Herāt
83 F22 **Ariamsvlei** Karas, SE Namibia
107 L17 **Ariano Irpino** Campania, S Italy
54 F11 **Ariari, Río** ≈ C Colombia
151 K19 **Ari Atoll** *atoll* C Maldives
77 P11 **Aribinda** N Burkina
62 G2 **Arica** *hist.* San Marcos de Arica. Tarapacá, N Chile
54 H16 **Arica** Amazonas, S Colombia
62 G2 **Arica** ✈ Tarapacá, N Chile
114 E13 **Aridaía** *var.* Aridea, Aridhaía. Dytikí Makedonía, N Greece
Aridea *see* Aridaía
172 I15 **Aride, Île** *island* Inner Islands, NE Seychelles
Aridhaía *see* Aridaía
103 N17 **Ariège** ◈ *department* S France
102 M16 **Ariège** *var.* la Riege. ≈ Andorra/France
116 H11 **Arieş** ≈ W Romania
149 U10 **Ārifwāla** Punjab, E Pakistan
Ariguaní *see* El Difícil
138 G11 **Arīhā** Al Karak, W Jordan
138 I3 **Arīhā** *var.* Arīhā. Idlib, W Syria
Arīhā *see* Jericho
37 W4 **Arikaree River** ≈ Colorado/Nebraska, C USA
164 B14 **Arikawa** Nagasaki, Nakadōri-jima, SW Japan
112 L13 **Arilje** Serbia, W Yugoslavia
45 U14 **Arima** Trinidad, Trinidad and Tobago
Arime *see* Al 'Arīmah
Ariminum *see* Rimini
59 H16 **Arinos, Rio** ≈ W Brazil
40 M14 **Ario de Rosales** *var.* Ario de Rosáles. Michoacán de Ocampo, SW Mexico
118 F12 **Ariogala** Raseiniai, C Lithuania
47 T7 **Aripuanā** ≈ W Brazil
59 E15 **Ariquemes** Rondônia, W Brazil
121 W13 **'Arīsh, Wādi el** ≈ NE Egypt
54 K6 **Arismendi** Barinas, C Venezuela
10 J14 **Aristazabal Island** *island* SW Canada
60 F13 **Aristóbulo del Valle** Misiones, NE Argentina
172 I5 **Arivonimamo** ✈ (Antananarivo) Antananarivo, C Madagascar
Arixang *see* Wenquan
105 Q6 **Ariza** Aragón, NE Spain
62 I6 **Arizaro, Salar de** *salt lake* NW Argentina
62 K13 **Arizona** San Luis, C Argentina
36 J12 **Arizona** *off.* State of Arizona; *also known as* Copper State, Grand Canyon State. ◈ *state* SW USA
40 G4 **Arizpe** Sonora, NW Mexico
95 J16 **Årjäng** Värmland, C Sweden
143 P8 **Arjenān** Yazd, C Iran
92 I13 **Arjeplog** Norrbotten, N Sweden
54 E5 **Arjona** Bolívar, N Colombia
105 N13 **Arjona** Andalucía, S Spain
123 S10 **Arka** Khabarovskiy Kray, E Russian Federation
22 L2 **Arkabutla Lake** ⊞ Mississippi, S USA
129 O7 **Arkadak** Saratovskaya Oblast', W Russian Federation
27 T13 **Arkadelphia** Arkansas, C USA
115 J25 **Arkalochóri** *prev.* Arkalohori, Arkalokhórion. Kríti, Greece, E Mediterranean Sea
Arkalohori/Arkalokhórion *see* Arkalochóri
145 O10 **Arkalyk** *Kaz.* Arqalyq. Kostanay, N Kazakhstan
27 U10 **Arkansas** *off.* State of Arkansas; *also known as* The Land of Opportunity. ◈ *state* S USA
27 W14 **Arkansas City** Arkansas, C USA
27 O7 **Arkansas City** Kansas, C USA
16 K11 **Arkansas River** ≈ C USA
182 J5 **Arkaroola** South Australia
Arkhángelos *see* Archángelos
126 L8 **Arkhangel'sk** *Eng.* Archangel. Arkhangel'skaya Oblast', NW Russian Federation
126 L9 **Arkhangel'skaya Oblast'** ◈ *province* NW Russian Federation
129 O14 **Arkhangel'skoye** Stavropol'skiy Kray, SW Russian Federation
123 R14 **Arkhara** Amurskaya Oblast', S Russian Federation
97 G19 **Arklow** *Ir.* An tInbhear Mór. SE Ireland
115 M20 **Arkoí** *island* Dodekánisos, Greece, Aegean Sea
27 R11 **Arkoma** Oklahoma, C USA
100 O7 **Arkona, Kap** *headland* NE Germany
95 N17 **Arkösund** Östergötland, S Sweden
122 J6 **Arkticheskogo Instituta, Ostrova** *island* N Russian Federation
95 O15 **Arlanda** ✈ (Stockholm) Stockholm, C Sweden
146 C11 **Arlan, Gora** ▲ W Turkmenistan
105 O5 **Arlanza** ≈ N Spain
105 N5 **Arlanzón** ≈ N Spain
103 R15 **Arles** *var.* Arles-sur-Rhône; *anc.* Arelas, Arelate. Bouches-du-Rhône, SE France
Arles-sur-Rhône *see* Arles
103 O17 **Arles-sur-Tech** Pyrénées-Orientales, S France
29 U9 **Arlington** Minnesota, N USA
29 R15 **Arlington** Nebraska, C USA
32 J11 **Arlington** Oregon, NW USA
29 R10 **Arlington** South Dakota, N USA
20 E10 **Arlington** Tennessee, S USA
25 T6 **Arlington** Texas, SW USA
21 W4 **Arlington** Virginia, NE USA
32 H7 **Arlington** Washington, NW USA
30 M10 **Arlington Heights** Illinois, N USA
77 U8 **Arlit** Agadez, C Niger
99 L24 **Arlon** *Dut.* Aarlen, *Ger.* Arel; *Lat.* Orolaunum. Luxembourg, SE Belgium
27 R7 **Arma** Kansas, C USA
97 F16 **Armagh** *Ir.* Ard Mhacha. S Northern Ireland, UK
97 F16 **Armagh** *cultural region* S Northern Ireland, UK
102 K15 **Armagnac** *cultural region* S France
103 Q7 **Armançon** ≈ C France
60 K10 **Armando Laydner, Represa** ⊞ S Brazil
115 M24 **Armathía** *island* SE Greece
128 M14 **Armavir** Krasnodarskiy Kray, SW Russian Federation
54 E10 **Armenia** Quindío, W Colombia
137 T12 **Armenia** *off.* Republic of Armenia, *var.* Ajastan, *Arm.* Hayastani Hanrapetut'yun; *prev.* Armenian Soviet Socialist Republic. ◆ *republic* SW Asia
Armenierstadt *see* Gherla
103 O1 **Armentières** Nord, N France
40 K14 **Armería** Colima, SW Mexico
183 T5 **Armidale** New South Wales, SE Australia
29 P11 **Armour** South Dakota, N USA
61 B18 **Armstrong** Santa Fe, C Argentina
11 N16 **Armstrong** British Columbia, SW Canada
12 D11 **Armstrong** Ontario, S Canada
29 U11 **Armstrong** Iowa, C USA
25 S16 **Armstrong** Texas, SW USA
117 S11 **Armyans'k** *Rus.* Armyansk. Respublika Krym, S Ukraine
115 H14 **Arnaía** *var.* Arnea. Kentrikí Makedonía, N Greece
121 N2 **Arnaoúti, Akrotíri** *var.* Arnaoútis, Cape Arnaouti. *headland* W Cyprus
Arnaouti, Cape/Arnaoútis *see* Arnaoúti, Akrotíri
12 L4 **Arnaud** ≈ Quebec, E Canada
103 Q8 **Arnay-le-Duc** Côte d'Or, C France
Arnea *see* Arnaía
105 Q4 **Arnedo** La Rioja, N Spain
95 I14 **Årnes** Akershus, S Norway
93 E15 **Årnes** Sør-Trøndelag, S Norway
26 K9 **Arnett** Oklahoma, C USA
98 L12 **Arnhem** Gelderland, SE Netherlands
181 Q2 **Arnhem Land** *physical region* Northern Territory, N Australia
106 F11 **Arno** ≈ C Italy
Arno *see* Arno Atoll
189 W7 **Arno Atoll** *var.* Arno. *atoll* Ratak Chain, NE Marshall Islands
182 H8 **Arno Bay** South Australia
35 Q8 **Arnold** California, W USA
27 X5 **Arnold** Missouri, C USA
29 N15 **Arnold** Nebraska, C USA
109 R10 **Arnoldstein** *Slvn.* Pod Klošter. Kärnten, S Austria
103 N9 **Arnon** ≈ C France
45 P14 **Arnos Vale** ✈ (Kingstown) Saint Vincent, SE Saint Vincent and the Grenadines
92 I8 **Arnøy** *island* N Norway
14 L12 **Arnprior** Ontario, SE Canada
101 G15 **Arnsberg** Nordrhein-Westfalen, W Germany
101 K16 **Arnstadt** Thüringen, C Germany
Arnswalde *see* Choszczno
54 K5 **Aroa** Yaracuy, N Venezuela
83 E21 **Aroab** Karas, SE Namibia
115 E19 **Aroania** ▲ S Greece
191 O6 **Aroa, Pointe** *headland* Moorea, W French Polynesia
Aroe Islands *see* Aru, Kepulauan
101 H15 **Arolsen** Niedersachsen, C Germany
106 C7 **Arona** Piemonte, NE Italy
19 R3 **Aroostook River** ≈ Canada/USA
Arop Island *see* Long Island
38 M12 **Aropuk Lake** ◎ Alaska, USA
191 P4 **Arorae** *atoll* Tungaru, W Kiribati
190 G16 **Arorangi** Rarotonga, S Cook Islands
108 I9 **Arosa** Graubünden, S Switzerland
104 F4 **Arousa, Ría de** *estuary* E Atlantic Ocean
184 P8 **Arowhana** ▲ North Island, NZ
137 V12 **Arp'a** *Az.* Arpaçay. ≈ Armenia/Azerbaijan
137 S11 **Arpaçay** Kars, NE Turkey
Arpaçay *see* Arp'a
Arqalyq *see* Arkalyk
149 N14 **Arra** ≈ SW Pakistan
Arrabona *see* Győr
Arrah *see* Āra
Ar Rahad *see* Er Rahad
139 R9 **Ar Raḩḩālīyah** C Iraq
60 Q10 **Arraial do Cabo** Rio de Janeiro, SE Brazil
104 H11 **Arraiolos** Évora, S Portugal
139 R8 **Ar Ramādī** *var.* Ramadi, Rumadiya. SW Iraq
138 J6 **Ar Rāmī** Ḩimş, C Syria
Ar Rams *see* Rams
138 H9 **Ar Ramthā** *var.* Ramtha. Irbid, N Jordan
96 H13 **Arran, Isle of** *island* SW Scotland, UK
138 L3 **Ar Raqqah** *var.* Rakka; *anc.* Nicephorium. Ar Raqqah, N Syria
138 L3 **Ar Raqqah** *off.* Muḩāfaẓat al Raqqah, *var.* Raqqah, *Fr.* Rakka. ◈ *governorate* N Syria
103 O2 **Arras** *anc.* Nemetocenna. Pas-de-Calais, N France
Arrasate *see* Mondragón
138 G12 **Ar Rashādīyah** Aṭ Ṭafīlah, W Jordan
138 I5 **Ar Rastān** *var.* Rastâne. Ḩimş, W Syria
139 X12 **Ar Raṭāwī** E Iraq
102 L15 **Arrats** ≈ S France
141 N10 **Ar Rawḑah** Makkah, S Saudi Arabia
141 Q15 **Ar Rawḑah** S Yemen
142 K11 **Ar Rawḑatayn** *var.* Raudhatain. N Kuwait
143 N16 **Ar Rayyān** *var.* Al Rayyan. C Qatar
102 L17 **Arreau** Hautes-Pyrénées, S France
64 Q11 **Arrecife** *var.* Arrecife de Lanzarote, Puerto Arrecife. Lanzarote, Islas Canarias, NE Atlantic Ocean
Arrecife de Lanzarote *see* Arrecife
43 P6 **Arrecife Edinburgh** *reef* NE Nicaragua
61 C19 **Arrecifes** Buenos Aires, E Argentina
102 F6 **Arrée, Monts d'** ▲ NW France
Ar Refā'ī *see* Ar Rifā'ī
Arretium *see* Arezzo
Arriaca *see* Guadalajara
109 S9 **Arriach** Kärnten, S Austria
41 T16 **Arriaga** Chiapas, SE Mexico
41 N12 **Arriaga** San Luis Potosí, C Mexico
139 W10 **Ar Rifā'ī** *var.* Ar Refā'ī. SE Iraq
139 V12 **Ar Riḩāb** *salt flat* S Iraq
104 L2 **Arriondas** Asturias, N Spain
141 Q7 **Ar Riyāḑ** *Eng.* Riyadh. ● (Saudi Arabia) Ar Riyāḑ, C Saudi Arabia
141 O8 **Ar Riyāḑ** *off.* Minţaqat ar Riyāḑ. ◈ *province* C Saudi Arabia
141 S15 **Ar Riyān** S Yemen
Arrö *see* Ærø
61 H18 **Arroio Grande** Rio Grande do Sul, S Brazil
102 K15 **Arros** ≈ S France
103 Q9 **Arroux** ≈ C France
25 R5 **Arrowhead, Lake** ⊞ Texas, SW USA
182 L5 **Arrowsmith, Mount** *hill* New South Wales, SE Australia
185 D21 **Arrowtown** Otago, South Island, NZ
61 D17 **Arroyo Barú** Entre Ríos, E Argentina
104 J10 **Arroyo de la Luz** Extremadura, W Spain
63 J16 **Arroyo de la Ventana** Río Negro, SE Argentina
35 P13 **Arroyo Grande** California, W USA
Ar Ru'ays *see* Ar Ruways
141 R11 **Ar Rub' al Khālī** *Eng.* Empty Quarter, Great Sandy Desert. *desert* SW Asia
139 V13 **Ar Rudaymah** S Iraq
61 A16 **Arrufó** Santa Fe, C Argentina
138 I7 **Ar Ruḩaybah** *var.* Ruhaybeh, *Fr.* Rouhaïbé. Dimashq, W Syria
139 V15 **Ar Rukhaymīyah** *well* S Iraq
139 U11 **Ar Rumaythah** *var.* Rumaitha. S Iraq
141 X8 **Ar Rustāq** *var.* Rostak, Rustaq. N Oman
139 N8 **Ar Ruṭbah** *var.* Rutba. SW Iraq
140 M3 **Ar Rūthīyah** *spring/well* NW Saudi Arabia
ar-Ruwaida *see* Ar Ruwayḑah
141 O8 **Ar Ruwayḑah** *var.* ar-Ruwaida. Jīzān, C Saudi Arabia
143 N15 **Ar Ruways** *var.* Al Ruweis, Ar Ru'ays, Ruwais. N Qatar
143 O17 **Ar Ruways** *var.* Ar Ru'ays, Ruwaisv. Abū Ẓaby, W UAE
95 G21 **Års** *var.* Aars. Nordjylland, N Denmark
Arsanias *see* Murat Nehri
123 S15 **Arsen'yev** Primorskiy Kray, SE Russian Federation
155 G19 **Arsikere** Karnātaka, W India
129 R3 **Arsk** Respublika Tatarstan, W Russian Federation
94 N10 **Årskogen** Gävleborg, C Sweden
121 O3 **Ársos** C Cyprus
94 N13 **Årsunda** Gävleborg, C Sweden
Arta *see* Árachthos
115 C17 **Árta** *anc.* Ambracia. Ípeiros, W Greece
137 T12 **Artashat** S Armenia
40 M15 **Arteaga** Michoacán de Ocampo, SW Mexico
123 S15 **Artem** Primorskiy Kray, SE Russian Federation
44 C4 **Artemisa** La Habana, W Cuba
117 W7 **Artemivs'k** Donets'ka Oblast', E Ukraine
122 K13 **Artemovsk** Krasnoyarskiy Kray, S Russian Federation
105 U5 **Artesa de Segre** Cataluña, NE Spain
37 U14 **Artesia** New Mexico, SW USA
25 Q14 **Artesia Wells** Texas, SW USA
108 G8 **Arth** Schwyz, C Switzerland
14 F15 **Arthur** Ontario, S Canada
30 M14 **Arthur** Illinois, N USA
28 L14 **Arthur** Nebraska, C USA
29 Q5 **Arthur** North Dakota, N USA
185 B21 **Arthur** ≈ South Island, NZ
18 B13 **Arthur, Lake** ⊞ Pennsylvania, NE USA
183 N15 **Arthur River** ≈ Tasmania, SE Australia
185 G18 **Arthur's Pass** Canterbury, South Island, NZ
185 G17 **Arthur's Pass** *pass* South Island, NZ
44 I3 **Arthur's Town** Cat Island, C Bahamas
44 M9 **Artibonite, Rivière de l'** ≈ C Haiti
61 E16 **Artigas** *prev.* San Eugenio, San Eugenio del Cuareim. Artigas, N Uruguay
61 E16 **Artigas** ◈ *department* N Uruguay
194 H1 **Artigas** *Uruguayan research station* Antarctica
137 T11 **Art'ik** W Armenia
187 O16 **Art, Île** *island* Îles Belep, W New Caledonia
103 O2 **Artois** *cultural region* N France
136 L12 **Artova** Tokat, N Turkey
105 Y9 **Artrutx, Cap d'** *var.* Cabo Dartuch. *headland* Menorca, Spain, W Mediterranean Sea
Artsiz *see* Artsyz
117 N11 **Artsyz** *Rus.* Artsiz. Odes'ka Oblast', SW Ukraine
158 E7 **Artux** Xinjiang Uygur Zizhiqu, NW China
137 R11 **Artvin** Artvin, NE Turkey
137 R11 **Artvin** ◈ *province* NE Turkey
146 G14 **Artyk** Akhalskiy Velayat, C Turkmenistan
79 Q16 **Aru** Orientale, NE Dem. Rep. Congo (Zaire)
104 I4 **A Rúa** *var.* La Rúa. Galicia, NW Spain
81 E17 **Arua** NW Uganda
Aruângua *see* Luangwa
45 O15 **Aruba** *var.* Oruba. ◇ *Dutch autonomous region* S West Indies
47 Q4 **Aruba** *island* Aruba, Lesser Antilles
Aru Islands *see* Aru, Kepulauan
171 W15 **Aru, Kepulauan** *Eng.* Aru Islands; *prev.* Aroe Islands. *island group* E Indonesia
153 W10 **Arunāchal Pradesh** *prev.* North East Frontier Agency, North East Frontier Agency of Assam. ◈ *state* NE India
163 U7 **Arun Qi** Nei Mongol Zizhiqu, N China
155 H23 **Aruppukkottai** Tamil Nādu, SE India
81 I20 **Arusha** Arusha, N Tanzania
81 I21 **Arusha** ◈ *region* E Tanzania
81 I20 **Arusha** ✈ Arusha, N Tanzania
54 C9 **Arusí, Punta** *headland* NW Colombia
155 J23 **Aruvi Aru** ≈ NW Sri Lanka
79 M17 **Aruwimi** *var.* Ituri (upper course). ≈ NE Dem. Rep. Congo (Zaire)
Árva *see* Orava
37 T4 **Arvada** Colorado, C USA
Arvand Rūd *see* 'Arab, Shaṭṭ al
162 J8 **Arvayheer** Övörhangay, C Mongolia
9 O10 **Arviat** *prev.* Eskimo Point. Nunavut, C Canada
93 I14 **Arvidsjaur** Norrbotten, N Sweden
95 J15 **Arvika** Värmland, C Sweden
92 I8 **Årviksand** Troms, N Norway
35 S13 **Arvin** California, W USA
145 P7 **Arykbalyk** *Kaz.* Aryqbalyq. Severnyy Kazakhstan, N Kazakhstan
Aryqbalyq *see* Arykbalyk
145 P17 **Arys'** *Kaz.* Arys. Yuzhnyy Kazakhstan, S Kazakhstan
Arys *see* Orzysz
Arys Köli *see* Arys, Ozero
145 O14 **Arys, Ozero** *Kaz.* Arys Köli. ◎ C Kazakhstan
107 D16 **Arzachena** Sardegna, Italy, C Mediterranean Sea
129 O4 **Arzamas** Nizhegorodskaya Oblast', W Russian Federation
141 V13 **Arzāt** S Oman
104 H3 **Arzúa** Galicia, NW Spain
111 A16 **Aš** *Ger.* Asch. Karlovarský Kraj, W Czech Republic
95 H15 **Ås** Akershus, S Norway
95 H20 **Aså** Nordjylland, N Denmark
83 E21 **Asab** Karas, S Namibia
77 U16 **Asaba** Delta, S Nigeria
149 S4 **Asadābād** *var.* Asadābād; *prev.* Chaghasarāy. Kunar, E Afghanistan
138 K3 **Asad, Buḩayrat al** ◎ N Syria
63 H20 **Asador, Pampa del** *plain* S Argentina
165 P14 **Asahi** Chiba, Honshū, S Japan
164 M11 **Asahi** Toyama, Honshū, SW Japan
165 T3 **Asahi-dake** ▲ Hokkaidō, N Japan
165 T3 **Asahikawa** Hokkaidō, N Japan
147 S10 **Asaka** *Rus.* Assake; *prev.* Leninsk. Andijon Wiloyati, E Uzbekistan
77 P17 **Asamankese** SE Ghana
188 B15 **Asan** W Guam
188 B15 **Asan Point** *headland* W Guam
153 R15 **Āsānsol** West Bengal, NE India
80 K12 **Āsayita** Afar, NE Ethiopia
171 T12 **Asbakin** Irian Jaya, E Indonesia
Asben *see* Aïr, Massif de l'
15 Q12 **Asbestos** Quebec, SE Canada
29 Y13 **Asbury** Iowa, C USA
18 K15 **Asbury Park** New Jersey, NE USA
41 Z12 **Ascención, Bahiá de la** *bay* NW Caribbean Sea
40 I3 **Ascensión** Chihuahua, N Mexico
65 M14 **Ascension Fracture Zone** *tectonic feature* C Atlantic Ocean
65 G14 **Ascension Island** ◇ *dependency of St. Helena* C Atlantic Ocean
65 N16 **Ascension Island** *island* C Atlantic Ocean
Asch *see* Aš
109 S3 **Aschach an der Donau** Oberösterreich, N Austria
101 H18 **Aschaffenburg** Bayern, SW Germany
101 F14 **Ascheberg** Nordrhein-Westfalen, W Germany
101 L14 **Aschersleben** Sachsen-Anhalt, C Germany
106 G12 **Asciano** Toscana, C Italy
106 J13 **Ascoli Piceno** *anc.* Asculum Picenum. Marche, C Italy
107 M17 **Ascoli Satriano** *anc.* Asculub, Asculum Apulum. Puglia, SE Italy
108 G11 **Ascona** Ticino, S Switzerland
Asculub *see* Ascoli Satriano
Asculum Picenum *see* Ascoli Piceno
80 L11 **Aseb** *var.* Assab, *Amh.* Āseb. SE Eritrea
95 M20 **Åseda** Kronoberg, S Sweden
129 T6 **Asekeyevo** Orenburgskaya Oblast', W Russian Federation
81 J14 **Āsela** *var.* Asella, Aselle, Asselle. Oromo, C Ethiopia
93 H15 **Åsele** Västerbotten, N Sweden
Asella/Aselle *see* Āsela
94 K12 **Åsen** Dalarna, C Sweden
114 J11 **Asenovgrad** *prev.* Stanimaka. Plovdiv, C Bulgaria
171 O13 **Asera** Sulawesi, C Indonesia
95 E17 **Åseral** Vest-Agder, S Norway
118 J3 **Aseri** *var.* Asserien, *Ger.* Asserin. Ida-Virumaa, NE Estonia
40 J10 **Aserradero** Durango, W Mexico
95 H16 **Åsgårdstrand** Vestfold, S Norway
Ashara *see* Al 'Ashārah
23 T6 **Ashburn** Georgia, SE USA
185 G19 **Ashburton** Canterbury, South Island, NZ
185 G19 **Ashburton** ≈ South Island, NZ
180 H8 **Ashburton River** ≈ Western Australia
145 V10 **Ashchysu** ≈ E Kazakhstan
10 M16 **Ashcroft** British Columbia, SW Canada
138 E10 **Ashdod** *anc.* Azotos, *Lat.* Azotus. Central, W Israel
27 S14 **Ashdown** Arkansas, C USA
21 T9 **Asheboro** North Carolina, SE USA
11 X15 **Ashern** Manitoba, S Canada
21 P10 **Asheville** North Carolina, SE USA
12 E8 **Asheweig** ≈ Ontario, C Canada
27 V9 **Ash Flat** Arkansas, C USA
183 T4 **Ashford** New South Wales, SE Australia
97 P22 **Ashford** SE England, UK
36 K11 **Ash Fork** Arizona, SW USA
146 F13 **Ashgabat** *prev.* Ashkhabad, Poltoratsk. ● (Turkmenistan) Akhalskiy Velayat, C Turkmenistan
146 F13 **Ashgabat** ✈ Akhalskiy Velayat, C Turkmenistan
27 T7 **Ash Grove** Missouri, C USA
165 O12 **Ashikaga** *var.* Asikaga. Tochigi, Honshū, S Japan
165 Q8 **Ashiro** Iwate, Honshū, C Japan
164 F15 **Ashizuri-misaki** *headland* Shikoku, SW Japan
Ashkelon *see* Ashqelon
Ashkhabad *see* Ashgabat
23 Q4 **Ashland** Alabama, S USA
26 K7 **Ashland** Kansas, C USA
21 P5 **Ashland** Kentucky, S USA
19 S2 **Ashland** Maine, NE USA
22 M1 **Ashland** Mississippi, S USA
27 U4 **Ashland** Missouri, C USA
29 S15 **Ashland** Nebraska, C USA
31 T12 **Ashland** Ohio, N USA
32 G15 **Ashland** Oregon, NW USA
21 W6 **Ashland** Virginia, NE USA
30 K3 **Ashland** Wisconsin, N USA
20 I8 **Ashland City** Tennessee, S USA
183 S4 **Ashley** New South Wales, SE Australia
29 O7 **Ashley** North Dakota, N USA
173 W7 **Ashmore and Cartier Islands** ◇ *Australian external territory* E Indian Ocean
119 I14 **Ashmyany** *Rus.* Oshmyany. Hrodzyenskaya Voblasts', W Belarus
18 K12 **Ashokan Reservoir** ⊞ New York, NE USA
165 U4 **Ashoro** Hokkaidō, NE Japan
138 E10 **Ashqelon** *var.* Ashkelon. Southern, C Israel
Ashraf *see* Behshahr
139 O3 **Ash Shadādah** *var.* Ash Shaddādah, Jisr ash Shadadi, Shaddādī, Shedadi, Tell Shedadi. Al Ḩasakah, NE Syria
Ash Shaddādah *see* Ash Shadādah
139 Y12 **Ash Shāfī** E Iraq
139 R4 **Ash Shakk** *var.* Shaykh. C Iraq
Ash Sham/Ash Shām *see* Dimashq
139 T10 **Ash Shāmīyah** *var.* Shamiya. C Iraq
139 Y13 **Ash Shāmīyah** *var.* Al Bādiyah al Janūbīyah. *desert* S Iraq
139 T11 **Ash Shanāfīyah** *var.* Ash Shināfīyah. S Iraq
138 G13 **Ash Sharāh** *var.* Esh Sharā. ▲ W Jordan
143 R16 **Ash Shāriqah** *Eng.* Sharjah. Ash Shāriqah, NE UAE
143 R16 **Ash Shāriqah** *var.* Sharjah. ✈ Ash Shāriqah, NE UAE
140 I4 **Ash Sharmah** *var.* Šarma. Tabūk, NW Saudi Arabia
139 R4 **Ash Sharqāṭ** NW Iraq
141 S10 **Ash Sharqīyah** *off.* Al Minṭaqah ash Sharqīyah, *Eng.* Eastern Region. ◈ *province* E Saudi Arabia
139 W11 **Ash Shaṭrah** *var.* Shatra. SE Iraq
138 G13 **Ash Shawbak** Ma'ān, W Jordan
138 L5 **Ash Shaykh Ibrāhīm** Ḩimş, C Syria
141 O17 **Ash Shaykh 'Uthmān** SW Yemen
141 S15 **Ash Shiḩr** SE Yemen
Ash Shināfīyah *see* Ash Shanāfīyah
141 V12 **Ash Shişar** *var.* Shisur. SW Oman
139 S13 **Ash Shubrūm** *well* S Iraq
141 R10 **Ash Shuqqān** *desert* E Saudi Arabia
75 O9 **Ash Shuwayrif** *var.* Ash Shwayrif. N Libya
Ash Shwayrif *see* Ash Shuwayrif
31 U10 **Ashtabula** Ohio, N USA
29 Q5 **Ashtabula, Lake** ⊞ North Dakota, N USA
137 T12 **Ashtarak** W Armenia
142 M6 **Āshtīān** *var.* Āshtiyān. Markazī, W Iran
Āshtiyān *see* Āshtīān
33 R13 **Ashton** Idaho, NW USA
13 O10 **Ashuanipi Lake** ◎ Newfoundland, E Canada
15 P6 **Ashuapmushuan** ≈ Quebec, SE Canada
23 Q3 **Ashville** Alabama, S USA
31 S14 **Ashville** Ohio, N USA
30 K3 **Ashwabay, Mount** *hill* Wisconsin, N USA
171 T11 **Asia, Kepulauan** *island group* E Indonesia
154 N13 **Āsika** Orissa, E India

Asikaga see Ashikaga
93 M18 **Asikkala** var. Vääksy. Etelä-Suomi, S Finland
74 G5 **Asilah** N Morocco
'Aṣī, Nahr al see Orontes
107 B16 **Asinara, Isola** island W Italy
122 J12 **Asino** Tomskaya Oblast', C Russian Federation
119 O14 **Asintorf** Rus. Osintorf. Vitsyebskaya Voblasts', N Belarus
119 L17 **Asipovichy** Rus. Osipovichi. Mahilyowskaya Voblasts', C Belarus
141 N12 **'Asīr** off. Minṭaqat 'Asīr. ◆ province SW Saudi Arabia
140 M11 **'Asīr** Eng. Asir. ▲ SW Saudi Arabia
139 X10 **Askal** E Iraq
137 P13 **Aşkale** Erzurum, NE Turkey
117 T11 **Askaniya-Nova** Khersons'ka Oblast', S Ukraine
95 H15 **Asker** Akershus, S Norway
95 L17 **Askersund** Örebro, C Sweden
Askī Kalak see Eski Kaļak
95 I15 **Askim** Østfold, S Norway
129 V3 **Askino** Respublika Bashkortostan, W Russian Federation
115 D14 **Áskio** ▲ N Greece
152 L9 **Askot** Uttar Pradesh, N India
94 C12 **Askvoll** Sogn og Fjordane, S Norway
136 A13 **Aslan Burnu** headland W Turkey
136 L16 **Aslantaş Barajı** ⊠ S Turkey
149 S4 **Asmār** var. Bar Kunar. Kunar, E Afghanistan
80 I9 **Asmara** Amh. Āsmera. ● (Eritrea) C Eritrea
Āsmera see Asmara
95 L21 **Åsnen** ◎ S Sweden
115 F19 **Asopós** ↝ S Greece
171 W13 **Asori** Irian Jaya, E Indonesia
80 G12 **Āsosa** Benishangul, W Ethiopia
32 M10 **Asotin** Washington, NW USA
Aspadana see Eşfahān
Aspang see Aspang Markt
109 X6 **Aspang Markt** var. Aspang. Niederösterreich, E Austria
105 S12 **Aspe** País Valenciano, E Spain
37 R5 **Aspen** Colorado, C USA
25 P6 **Aspermont** Texas, SW USA
Asphaltites, Lacus see Dead Sea
Aspinwall see Colón
185 C20 **Aspiring, Mount** ▲ South Island, NZ
115 B16 **Asprókavos, Akrotírio** headland Kérkyra, Iónioi Nísoi, Greece, C Mediterranean Sea
Aspropótamos see Achelóos
Assab see Aseb
76 J10 **Assaba** var. Açâba. ◆ region S Mauritania
138 L4 **As Sabkhah** var. Sabkha. Ar Raqqah, NE Syria
139 U6 **As Sa'dīyah** E Iraq
Assad, Lake see Asad, Buḩayrat al
138 I8 **Aş Şafā** ▲ S Syria
138 I10 **Aş Şafāwī** Al Mafraq, N Jordan
Aş Şaff see El Şaff
139 N2 **Aş Şafīḩ** Al Ḩasakah, N Syria
Aş Şaḩrā' al Gharbīyah see Sahara el Gharbîya
Aş Şaḩrā' ash Sharqīyah see Sahara el Sharqîya
Assake see Asaka
As Salamīyah see Salamīyah
141 Q4 **As Sālimī** var. Salemy. SW Kuwait
67 W7 **'Assal, Lac** ◎ C Djibouti
As Sallūm see Salûm
139 T13 **As Salmān** S Iraq
138 G10 **As Salṭ** var. Salt. Al Balqā', NW Jordan
142 M16 **As Salwā** var. Salwa, Salwah. S Qatar
153 V12 **Assam** ◆ state NE India
Assamaka see Assamakka
77 T8 **Assamakka** var. Assamaka. Agadez, NW Niger
139 U11 **As Samāwah** var. Samawa. S Iraq
As Saqia al Hamra see Saguia al Hamra
138 J4 **Aş Şā'rān** Ḩamāh, C Syria
138 G9 **Aş Şarīḩ** Irbid, N Jordan
21 Z5 **Assateague Island** island Maryland, NE USA
139 O6 **As Sayyāl** var. Sayyāl. Dayr az Zawr, E Syria
99 G18 **Asse** Vlaams Brabant, C Belgium
99 D16 **Assebroek** West-Vlaanderen, NW Belgium
Asselle see Āsela
107 C20 **Assemini** Sardegna, Italy, C Mediterranean Sea
98 N7 **Assen** Drenthe, NE Netherlands
99 E16 **Assenede** Oost-Vlaanderen, NW Belgium
95 G24 **Assens** Fyn, C Denmark
Asserien/Asserin see Aseri
121 J21 **Assesse** Namur, SE Belgium
141 Y8 **As Sīb** var. Seeb. NE Oman
139 Z13 **As Sībah** var. Sibah. SE Iraq
11 T17 **Assiniboia** Saskatchewan, S Canada
11 V15 **Assiniboine** ↝ Manitoba, S Canada
11 P16 **Assiniboine, Mount** ▲ Alberta/British Columbia, SW Canada
Assiout see Asyût
60 J9 **Assis** São Paulo, S Brazil
106 I13 **Assisi** Umbria, C Italy
Assiut see Asyût
Assling see Jesenice
Assouan see Aswân
Assu see Açu
Assuan see Aswân
142 K12 **Aş Şubayḩīyah** var. Subiyah. S Kuwait
141 R16 **As Sufāl** S Yemen
138 L5 **As Sukhnah** var. Sukhne, Fr. Soukhné. Ḩimş, C Syria
139 U4 **As Sulaymānīyah** var. Sulaimaniya, Kurd. Slēmānī. NE Iraq
141 P11 **As Sulayyil** Ar Riyāḑ, S Saudi Arabia
121 O13 **As Sulṭān** N Libya
141 Q5 **Aş Şummān** desert N Saudi Arabia
141 Q16 **Aş Şurrah** SW Yemen
139 N4 **Aş Şuwār** var. Şuwār. Dayr az Zawr, E Syria
138 H9 **As Suwaydā'** var. El Suweida, Es Suweida, Suweida, Fr. Soueida. As Suwaydā', SW Syria
138 H9 **As Suwaydā'** off. Muḩāfaẓat as Suwaydā', var. As Suwaydā, Suwaydá, Suweida, Fr. Soueida. ◆ governorate S Syria
141 Z9 **As Suwayḩ** NE Oman
141 X8 **As Suwayq** var. Suwaik. N Oman
139 T8 **Aş Şuwayrah** var. Suwaira. E Iraq
As Suways see Suez
Asta Colonia see Asti
Astacus see İzmit
115 M23 **Astakída** island SE Greece
145 Q9 **Astana** prev. Akmola, Akmolinsk, Tselinograd, Aqmola. ● (Kazakhstan) Akmola, N Kazakhstan
142 M3 **Āstāneh** Gīlān, NW Iran
Asta Pompeia see Asti
137 Y14 **Astara** S Azerbaijan
Astarabad see Gorgān
99 L15 **Asten** Noord-Brabant, SE Netherlands
Asterābād see Gorgān
106 C8 **Asti** anc. Asta Colonia, Asta Pompeia, Hasta Colonia, Hasta Pompeia. Piemonte, NW Italy
Astigi see Ecija
Astipálaia see Astypálaia
148 L16 **Astola Island** island SW Pakistan
152 H4 **Astor** Jammu and Kashmir, NW India
104 K4 **Astorga** anc. Asturica Augusta. Castilla-León, N Spain
32 F10 **Astoria** Oregon, NW USA
(0) F8 **Astoria Fan** undersea feature E Pacific Ocean
95 J22 **Åstorp** Skåne, S Sweden
Astrabad see Gorgān
129 Q13 **Astrakhan'** Astrakhanskaya Oblast', SW Russian Federation
Astrakhan-Bazar see Cälilabad
129 Q11 **Astrakhanskaya Oblast'** ◆ province SW Russian Federation
93 J15 **Åsträsk** Västerbotten, N Sweden
Astrida see Butare
65 O22 **Astrid Ridge** undersea feature S Atlantic Ocean
187 P15 **Astrolabe, Récifs de l'** reef C New Caledonia
121 P2 **Astromerítis** N Cyprus
115 F20 **Ástros** Pelopónnisos, S Greece
119 G16 **Astryna** Rus. Ostryna. Hrodzyenskaya Voblasts', W Belarus
104 J2 **Asturias** ◆ autonomous community NW Spain
Asturias see Oviedo
Asturica Augusta see Astorga
115 L22 **Astypálaia** var. Astipálaia, It. Stampalia. island Kykládes, Greece, Aegean Sea
192 G16 **Āsuisui, Cape** headland Savai'i, W Samoa
195 S2 **Asuka** Japanese research station Antarctica
62 O6 **Asunción** ● (Paraguay) Central, S Paraguay
62 O6 **Asunción** ✕ Central, S Paraguay
188 K3 **Asuncion Island** island N Northern Mariana Islands
42 E6 **Asunción Mita** Jutiapa, SE Guatemala
Asunción Nochixtlán see Nochixtlán
40 E3 **Asunción, Río** ↝ NW Mexico
95 M18 **Åsunden** ◎ S Sweden
118 K11 **Asvyeya** Rus. Osveya. Vitsyebskaya Voblasts', N Belarus
Aswa see Achwa
75 X11 **Aswân** var. Assouan, Assuan; anc. Syene. SE Egypt
75 X11 **Aswân High Dam** dam SE Egypt
75 W9 **Asyût** var. Assiout, Assiut, Siut; anc. Lycopolis. C Egypt
193 W15 **Ata** island Tongatapu Group, SW Tonga
62 G8 **Atacama** off. Región de Atacama. ◆ region C Chile
Atacama Desert see Atacama, Desierto de
62 H4 **Atacama, Desierto de** Eng. Atacama Desert. desert N Chile
62 I6 **Atacama, Puna de** ▲ NW Argentina
62 I5 **Atacama, Salar de** salt lake N Chile
54 E11 **Ataco** Tolima, C Colombia
190 H8 **Atafu Atoll** island NW Tokelau
190 H8 **Atafu Village** Atafu Atoll, NW Tokelau
74 K12 **Atakor** ▲ SE Algeria
77 R14 **Atakora, Chaîne de l'** var. Atakora Mountains. ▲ N Benin
Atakora Mountains see Atakora, Chaîne de l'
77 R16 **Atakpamé** C Togo
146 F11 **Atakui** Akhalskiy Velayat, C Turkmenistan
58 B13 **Atalaia do Norte** Amazonas, N Brazil
76 I7 **Atâr** Adrar, W Mauritania
162 G10 **Atas Bogd** ▲ SW Mongolia
35 P12 **Atascadero** California, W USA
25 S13 **Atascosa River** ↝ Texas, SW USA
145 R11 **Atasu** Zhezkazgan, C Kazakhstan
145 R12 **Atasu** ↝ C Kazakhstan
193 V15 **Atata** island Tongatapu Group, S Tonga
136 H10 **Atatürk** ✕ (İstanbul) Istanbul, NW Turkey
137 N16 **Atatürk Barajı** ⊠ S Turkey
Atax see Aude
80 G8 **Atbara** var. 'Aṭbārah. River Nile, NE Sudan
80 H8 **Atbara** var. Nahr 'Aṭbarah. ↝ Eritrea/Sudan
'Aṭbārah/'Aṭbarah, Nahr see Atbara
145 P9 **Atbasar** Akmola, N Kazakhstan
At-Bashi see At-Bashy
147 W9 **At-Bashy** var. At-Bashi. Narynskaya Oblast', C Kyrgyzstan
22 I10 **Atchafalaya Bay** bay Louisiana, S USA
22 I8 **Atchafalaya River** ↝ Louisiana, S USA
Atchin see Aceh
27 Q3 **Atchison** Kansas, C USA
77 P16 **Atebubu** C Ghana
105 Q6 **Ateca** Aragón, NE Spain
40 K11 **Atengo, Río** ↝ C Mexico
Aternum see Pescara
107 K15 **Atessa** Abruzzo, C Italy
Ateste see Este
99 E19 **Ath** var. Aat. Hainaut, SW Belgium
11 Q13 **Athabasca** Alberta, SW Canada
11 Q12 **Athabasca** var. Athabaska. ↝ Alberta, SW Canada
11 R10 **Athabasca, Lake** ◎ Alberta/Saskatchewan, SW Canada
Athabaska see Athabasca
115 C16 **Athamánon** ▲ C Greece
97 F17 **Athboy** Ir. Baile Átha Buí. E Ireland
Athenae see Athína
97 C18 **Athenry** Ir. Baile Átha an Rí. W Ireland
23 P2 **Athens** Alabama, S USA
23 T3 **Athens** Georgia, SE USA
31 T14 **Athens** Ohio, N USA
20 M10 **Athens** Tennessee, S USA
25 V7 **Athens** Texas, SW USA
Athens see Athína
115 B18 **Athéras, Akrotírio** headland Kefallinía, Iónioi Nísoi, Greece, C Mediterranean Sea
181 W4 **Atherton** Queensland, NE Australia
81 I19 **Athi** ↝ S Kenya
121 Q2 **Athíenou** SE Cyprus
115 H19 **Athína** Eng. Athens; prev. Athínai, anc. Athenae. ● (Greece) Attikí, C Greece
Athínai see Athína
139 S10 **Athīyah** C Iraq
97 D18 **Athlone** Ir. Baile Átha Luain. C Ireland
155 F16 **Athni** Karnātaka, W India
185 C23 **Athol** Southland, South Island, NZ
19 N11 **Athol** Massachusetts, NE USA
115 I15 **Áthos** ▲ NE Greece
Athos, Mount see Ágion Óros
Ath Thawrah see Madīnat ath Thawrah
141 P5 **Ath Thumāmī** spring/well N Saudi Arabia
99 L25 **Athus** Luxembourg, SE Belgium
97 E19 **Athy** Ir. Baile Átha Í. C Ireland
78 I10 **Ati** Batha, C Chad
81 F16 **Atiak** NW Uganda
57 G17 **Atico** Arequipa, SW Peru
105 O6 **Atienza** Castilla-La Mancha, C Spain
39 Q6 **Atigun Pass** pass Alaska, USA
12 B12 **Atikokan** Ontario, S Canada
13 O9 **Atikonak Lac** ◎ Newfoundland, E Canada
42 C6 **Atitlán, Lago de** ◎ W Guatemala
190 L16 **Atiu** island S Cook Islands
Atjeh see Aceh
123 T9 **Atka** Magadanskaya Oblast', E Russian Federation
38 H17 **Atka** Atka Island, Alaska, USA
38 H17 **Atka Island** island Aleutian Islands, Alaska, USA
129 O7 **Atkarsk** Saratovskaya Oblast', W Russian Federation
27 U11 **Atkins** Arkansas, C USA
29 O13 **Atkinson** Nebraska, C USA
171 T12 **Atkri** Irian Jaya, E Indonesia
41 O13 **Atlacomulco** var. Atlacomulco de Fabela. México, C Mexico
Atlacomulco de Fabela see Atlacomulco
23 S3 **Atlanta** state capital Georgia, SE USA
31 R6 **Atlanta** Michigan, N USA
25 X6 **Atlanta** Texas, SW USA
29 T15 **Atlantic** Iowa, C USA
21 Y10 **Atlantic** North Carolina, SE USA
23 W8 **Atlantic Beach** Florida, SE USA
18 J17 **Atlantic City** New Jersey, NE USA
172 L14 **Atlantic-Indian Basin** undersea feature SW Indian Ocean
172 K13 **Atlantic-Indian Ridge** undersea feature SW Indian Ocean
54 E4 **Atlántico** off. Departamento del Atlántico. ◆ province NW Colombia
66-67 **Atlantic Ocean** ocean
42 K7 **Atlántico Norte, Región Autónoma** prev. Zelaya Norte. ◆ autonomous region NE Nicaragua
42 L10 **Atlántico Sur, Región Autónoma** prev. Zelaya Sur. ◆ autonomous region SE Nicaragua
42 I5 **Atlántida** ◆ department N Honduras
77 Y15 **Atlantika Mountains** ▲ E Nigeria
64 J10 **Atlantis Fracture Zone** tectonic feature NW Atlantic Ocean
74 H7 **Atlas Mountains** ▲ NW Africa
123 V11 **Atlasova, Ostrov** island SE Russian Federation
123 V10 **Atlasovo** Kamchatskaya Oblast', E Russian Federation
120 G11 **Atlas Saharien** var. Saharan Atlas. ▲ Algeria/Morocco
Atlas, Tell see Atlas Tellien
120 H10 **Atlas Tellien** Eng. Tell Atlas. ▲ N Algeria
10 I9 **Atlin** British Columbia, W Canada
10 I9 **Atlin Lake** ◎ British Columbia, W Canada
41 P14 **Atlixco** Puebla, S Mexico
94 B11 **Atløyna** island S Norway
155 I17 **Ātmakūr** Andhra Pradesh, C India
23 O8 **Atmore** Alabama, S USA
101 J20 **Atmühl** ↝ S Germany
94 H11 **Atna** ↝ S Norway
164 E13 **Atō** Yamaguchi, Honshū, SW Japan
57 L21 **Atocha** Potosí, S Bolivia
27 P12 **Atoka** Oklahoma, C USA
27 O12 **Atoka Lake** var. Atoka Reservoir. ⊠ Oklahoma, C USA
Atoka Reservoir see Atoka Lake
33 Q14 **Atomic City** Idaho, NW USA
40 L10 **Atotonilco** Zacatecas, C Mexico
40 M13 **Atotonilco el Alto** var. Atotonilco. Jalisco, SW Mexico
77 N7 **Atouila, 'Erg** desert N Mali
41 N16 **Atoyac** var. Atoyac de Alvarez. Guerrero, S Mexico
Atoyac de Alvarez see Atoyac
41 P15 **Atoyac, Río** ↝ S Mexico
39 O5 **Atqasuk** Alaska, USA
146 C13 **Atrak** Per. Rūd-e Atrak, Rus. Atrek, Turk. Etrek. ↝ Iran/Turkmenistan
Atrak, Rūd-e see Atrak
95 J20 **Ätran** ↝ S Sweden
54 C7 **Atrato, Río** ↝ NW Colombia
Atrek see Atrak
107 K14 **Atri** Abruzzo, C Italy
Atria see Adria
165 P9 **Atsumi** Yamagata, Honshū, C Japan
165 S3 **Atsuta** Hokkaidō, NE Japan
143 Q17 **Aṭ Ṭaff** desert C UAE
138 G12 **Aṭ Ṭafīlah** var. Et Tafila, Tafila. Aṭ Ṭafīlah, W Jordan
138 G12 **Aṭ Ṭafīlah** off. Muḩāfaẓat aṭ Ṭafīlah. ◆ governorate W Jordan
140 L10 **Aṭ Ṭā'if** Makkah, W Saudi Arabia
Attaleia/Attalia see Antalya
23 Q3 **Attalla** Alabama, S USA
138 L2 **At Tall al Abyaḑ** var. Tall al Abyaḑ, Tell Abyad, Fr. Tell Abiad. Ar Raqqah, N Syria
138 L7 **Aṭ Ṭanf** Ḩimş, S Syria
Attapu see Samakhixai
139 S10 **At Taqṭaqānah** C Iraq
115 O23 **Attávytos** ▲ Ródos, Dodekánisos, Greece, Aegean Sea
139 V15 **At Tawal** desert Iraq/Saudi Arabia
12 G9 **Attawapiskat** Ontario, C Canada
12 F9 **Attawapiskat** ↝ Ontario, S Canada
12 D9 **Attawapiskat Lake** ◎ Ontario, C Canada
At Taybé see Ţayyibah
101 F16 **Attendorn** Nordrhein-Westfalen, W Germany
109 R5 **Attersee** Salzburg, NW Austria
109 R5 **Attersee** ◎ N Austria
99 L24 **Attert** Luxembourg, SE Belgium
138 M4 **At Tibnī** var. Tibnī. Dayr az Zawr, NE Syria
31 N13 **Attica** Indiana, N USA
18 E10 **Attica** New York, NE USA
Attica see Attikí
13 N7 **Attikamagen Lake** ◎ Newfoundland, E Canada
115 H20 **Attikí** Eng. Attica. ◆ region C Greece
19 O12 **Attleboro** Massachusetts, NE USA
109 R5 **Attnang** Oberösterreich, N Austria
149 U6 **Attock City** Punjab, E Pakistan
Attopeu see Samakhixai
25 X8 **Attoyac River** ↝ Texas, SW USA
38 D16 **Attu** Attu Island, Alaska, USA
139 Y12 **Aṭ Ṭūbah** E Iraq
140 K4 **Aṭ Ṭubayq** plain Jordan/Saudi Arabia
38 C16 **Attu Island** island Aleutian Islands, Alaska, USA
Aṭ Ṭūr see El Ṭûr
155 I21 **Āttūr** Tamil Nādu, SE India
141 N17 **At Turbah** SW Yemen
62 I12 **Atuel, Río** ↝ C Argentina
Atugi see Atsugi
191 X7 **Atuona** Hiva Oa, NE French Polynesia
Aturus see Adour
95 M18 **Åtvidaberg** Östergötland, S Sweden
35 P9 **Atwater** California, W USA
29 T8 **Atwater** Minnesota, N USA
26 I2 **Atwood** Kansas, C USA
31 U12 **Atwood Lake** ⊠ Ohio, N USA
129 P5 **Atyashevo** Respublika Mordoviya, W Russian Federation
144 F12 **Atyrau** prev. Gur'yev. Atyrau, W Kazakhstan
144 E11 **Atyrau** off. Atyrauskaya Oblast', var. Kaz. Atyraū Oblysy; prev. Gur'yevskaya Oblast'. ◆ province W Kazakhstan
Atyraū Oblysy/Atyrauskaya Oblast' see Atyrau
108 J7 **Au** Vorarlberg, NW Austria
186 B4 **Aua Island** island NW PNG
103 S16 **Aubagne** anc. Albania. Bouches-du-Rhône, SE France
99 L25 **Aubange** Luxembourg, SE Belgium
103 Q6 **Aube** ◆ department N France
103 R6 **Aube** ↝ N France
99 L19 **Aubel** Liège, E Belgium
103 Q13 **Aubenas** Ardèche, E France
103 O8 **Aubigny-sur-Nère** Cher, C France
103 O13 **Aubin** Aveyron, S France
103 O13 **Aubrac, Monts d'** ▲ S France
36 J10 **Aubrey Cliffs** cliff Arizona, SW USA
23 R5 **Auburn** Alabama, S USA
35 P6 **Auburn** California, W USA
30 K14 **Auburn** Illinois, N USA
31 Q11 **Auburn** Indiana, N USA
20 J7 **Auburn** Kentucky, S USA
19 P8 **Auburn** Maine, NE USA
19 N11 **Auburn** Massachusetts, NE USA
29 S16 **Auburn** Nebraska, C USA
18 H10 **Auburn** New York, NE USA
32 H8 **Auburn** Washington, NW USA
103 N11 **Aubusson** Creuse, C France
118 E10 **Auce** Ger. Autz. Dobele, SW Latvia
102 L15 **Auch** Lat. Augusta Auscorum, Elimberrum. Gers, S France
77 U16 **Auchi** Edo, S Nigeria
23 T9 **Aucilla River** ↝ Florida/Georgia, SE USA
184 L6 **Auckland** Auckland, North Island, NZ
184 K5 **Auckland** off. Auckland Region. ◆ region North Island, NZ
184 L6 **Auckland** ✕ Auckland, North Island, NZ
192 J12 **Auckland Islands** island group S NZ
103 O16 **Aude** ◆ department S France
103 N16 **Aude** anc. Atax. ↝ S France
Audenarde see Oudenaarde
Audern see Audru
102 E6 **Audierne** Finistère, NW France
102 E6 **Audierne, Baie d'** bay NW France
103 U7 **Audincourt** Doubs, E France
118 G5 **Audru** Ger. Audern. Pärnumaa, SW Estonia
29 T14 **Audubon** Iowa, C USA
101 N17 **Aue** Sachsen, E Germany
100 H12 **Aue** ↝ NW Germany
100 L9 **Auerbach** Bayern, SE Germany
101 M17 **Auerbach** Sachsen, E Germany
108 I10 **Auererrhein** ↝ SW Switzerland
101 N17 **Auersberg** ▲ E Germany
181 W9 **Augathella** Queensland, E Australia
31 Q12 **Auglaize River** ↝ Ohio, N USA
83 F22 **Augrabies Falls** waterfall W South Africa
31 R7 **Au Gres River** ↝ Michigan, N USA
Augsbourg see Augsburg
101 K22 **Augsburg** Fr. Augsbourg; anc. Augusta Vindelicorum. Bayern, S Germany
180 I14 **Augusta** Western Australia
107 L25 **Augusta** It. Agosta. Sicilia, Italy, C Mediterranean Sea
27 W11 **Augusta** Arkansas, C USA
23 V3 **Augusta** Georgia, SE USA
27 O6 **Augusta** Kansas, C USA
19 Q7 **Augusta** state capital Maine, NE USA
33 Q8 **Augusta** Montana, NW USA
Augusta see London
Augusta Auscorum see Auch
Augusta Emerita see Mérida
Augusta Praetoria see Aosta
Augusta Suessionum see Soissons
Augusta Trajana see Stara Zagora
Augusta Treverorum see Trier
Augusta Vangionum see Worms
Augusta Vindelicorum see Augsburg
95 G24 **Augustenborg** Ger. Augustenburg. Sønderjylland, SW Denmark
Augustenburg see Augustenborg
39 Q13 **Augustine Island** island Alaska, USA
14 L9 **Augustines, Lac des** ◎ Quebec, SE Canada
Augustobona Tricassium see Troyes
Augustodunum see Autun
Augustodurum see Bayeux
Augustoritum Lemovicensium see Limoges
110 O8 **Augustów** Rus. Avgustov. Podlaskie, NE Poland
Augustow Canal see Augustowski, Kanał
110 O8 **Augustowski, Kanał** Eng. Augustow Canal, Rus. Avgustovskiy Kanal. canal NE Poland
180 I9 **Augustus, Mount** ▲ Western Australia
186 M9 **Auki** Malaita, N Solomon Islands
21 W8 **Aulander** North Carolina, SE USA
180 L7 **Auld, Lake** salt lake Western Australia
Aulie Ata/Auliye-Ata see Taraz
106 E10 **Aulla** Toscana, C Italy
102 F6 **Aulne** ↝ NW France
Aulong see Ulong
37 T3 **Ault** Colorado, C USA
103 N3 **Aumale** Seine-Maritime, N France
Auminzatau, Gory see Owminzatovo-Toshi
77 T14 **Auna** Niger, W Nigeria
95 H21 **Auning** Århus, C Denmark
192 K17 **Aunu'u Island** island W American Samoa
83 E20 **Auob** var. Oup. ↝ Namibia/South Africa
93 K19 **Aura** Länsi-Suomi, W Finland
109 R5 **Aurach** ↝ N Austria
Aural, Phnom see Aôral, Phnum
153 O14 **Aurangābād** Bihār, N India
154 F13 **Aurangābād** Mahārāshtra, C India
189 V7 **Aur Atoll** atoll E Marshall Islands
102 G7 **Auray** Morbihan, NW France
94 G13 **Aurdal** Oppland, S Norway
94 F8 **Aure** Møre og Romsdal, S Norway
29 T12 **Aurelia** Iowa, C USA
Aurelia Aquensis see Baden-Baden
Aurelianum see Orléans
120 J10 **Aurès, Massif de l'** ▲ NE Algeria
100 F10 **Aurich** Niedersachsen, NW Germany
103 O13 **Aurillac** Cantal, C France
Aurine, Alpi see Zillertaler Alpen
Aurium see Ourense
14 H15 **Aurora** Ontario, S Canada
55 S8 **Aurora** NW Guyana
37 T4 **Aurora** Colorado, C USA
30 M11 **Aurora** Illinois, N USA
31 Q15 **Aurora** Indiana, N USA
29 W4 **Aurora** Minnesota, N USA
27 S8 **Aurora** Missouri, C USA
29 P16 **Aurora** Nebraska, C USA
36 J5 **Aurora** Utah, W USA
Aurora see Maéwo, Vanuatu
Aurora see San Francisco, Philippines
94 F10 **Aursjøen** ◎ S Norway
94 I9 **Aursunden** ◎ S Norway
83 D21 **Aus** Karas, SW Namibia
Ausa see Vic
14 E16 **Ausable** ↝ Ontario, S Canada
31 O3 **Au Sable Point** headland Michigan, N USA
31 S7 **Au Sable Point** headland Michigan, N USA
31 R6 **Au Sable River** ↝ Michigan, N USA
57 H16 **Ausangate, Nevado** ▲ C Peru
Auschwitz see Oświęcim
Ausculum Apulum see Ascoli Satriano
105 Q4 **Ausejo** La Rioja, N Spain
Aussig see Ústí nad Labem
95 F17 **Aust-Agder** ◆ county S Norway
92 P2 **Austfonna** glacier NE Svalbard
31 P15 **Austin** Indiana, N USA
29 W11 **Austin** Minnesota, N USA
35 U5 **Austin** Nevada, W USA
25 S10 **Austin** state capital Texas, S USA
180 J10 **Austin, Lake** salt lake Western Australia
31 V11 **Austintown** Ohio, N USA
25 V9 **Austonio** Texas, SW USA
Australes, Archipel des see Australes, Îles
Australes et Antarctiques Françaises, Terres see French Southern and Antarctic Territories
191 T14 **Australes, Îles** var. Archipel des Australes, Îles Tubuai, Tubuai Islands, Eng. Austral Islands. island group SW French Polynesia
175 Y11 **Austral Fracture Zone** tectonic feature S Pacific Ocean
181 O7 **Australia** off. Commonwealth of Australia. ◆ commonwealth republic
174 M8 **Australia** continent
183 Q12 **Australian Alps** ▲ SE Australia
183 R11 **Australian Capital Territory** prev. Federal Capital Territory. ◆ territory SE Australia
Australie, Bassin Nord de l' see North Australian Basin
Austral Islands see Australes, Îles
Austrava see Ostrov
109 T6 **Austria** off. Republic of Austria, Ger. Österreich. ◆ republic C Europe
92 K3 **Austurland** ◆ region SE Iceland
92 G10 **Austvågøya** island C Norway
Ausuituq see Grise Fiord
58 G13 **Autazes** Amazonas, N Brazil
102 M16 **Auterive** Haute-Garonne, S France
Autesiodorum see Auxerre
103 N2 **Authie** ↝ N France
Autissiodorum see Auxerre
40 K14 **Autlán** var. Autlán de Navarro. Jalisco, SW Mexico
Autlán de Navarro see Autlán
Autricum see Chartres
103 Q9 **Autun** anc. Ædua, Augustodunum. Saône-et-Loire, C France
Autz see Auce
99 H20 **Auvelais** Namur, S Belgium
103 P11 **Auvergne** ◆ region C France
102 M12 **Auvézère** ↝ W France
103 P7 **Auxerre** anc. Autesiodorum, Autissiodorum. Yonne, C France
103 N2 **Auxi-le-Château** Pas-de-Calais, N France
103 S8 **Auxonne** Côte d'Or, C France
55 P9 **Auyan Tebuy** ▲ SE Venezuela
103 O10 **Auzances** Creuse, C France
27 U8 **Ava** Missouri, C USA
142 M5 **Āvaj** Qazvīn, N Iran
95 C15 **Avaldsnes** Rogaland, S Norway
103 Q8 **Avallon** Yonne, C France
102 K6 **Avaloirs, Mont des** ▲ NW France
35 S16 **Avalon** Santa Catalina Island, California, W USA
18 J17 **Avalon** New Jersey, NE USA
13 V13 **Avalon Peninsula** peninsula Newfoundland, E Canada
197 Q11 **Avannaarsua** ◆ province N Greenland
60 K10 **Avaré** São Paulo, S Brazil
Avaricum see Bourges
190 H16 **Avarua** ○ (Cook Islands) Rarotonga, S Cook Islands
190 H16 **Avarua Harbour** harbour Rarotonga, S Cook Islands
Avasfelsőfalu see Negrești-Oaș
38 L17 **Avatanak Island** island Aleutian Islands, Alaska, USA
190 B16 **Avatele** S Niue
190 H16 **Avatiu** Rarotonga, S Cook Islands

◆ Country ● Country Capital ◇ Dependent Territory ○ Dependent Territory Capital ◆ Administrative Region ✕ International Airport ▲ Mountain ▲ Mountain Range ⛰ Volcano ↝ River ◎ Lake ⊠ Reservoir

190 *H15* **Avatiu Harbour** *harbour* Rarotonga, S Cook Islands
Avdeyevka *see* Avdiyivka
114 *J13* **Ávdira** Anatolikí Makedonía kai Thráki, NE Greece
117 *X8* **Avdiyivka** ***Rus.*** Avdeyevka. Donets'ka Oblast', SE Ukraine
162 *K7* **Avdzaga** C Mongolia
104 *G6* **Ave** ≈ N Portugal
104 *G7* **Aveiro** ***anc.*** Talabriga. Aveiro, W Portugal
104 *G7* **Aveiro** ◈ *district* N Portugal
Avela *see* Ávila
99 *D18* **Avelgem** West-Vlaanderen, W Belgium
61 *D20* **Avellaneda** Buenos Aires, E Argentina
107 *L17* **Avellino** ***anc.*** Abellinum. Campania, S Italy
35 *Q12* **Avenal** California, W USA
Avenio *see* Avignon
94 *E8* **Averoya** *island* S Norway
107 *K17* **Aversa** Campania, S Italy
33 *N9* **Avery** Idaho, NW USA
25 *W5* **Avery** Texas, SW USA
Aves, Islas de *see* Las Aves, Islas
Avesnes *see* Avesnes-sur-Helpe
103 *Q2* **Avesnes-sur-Helpe** ***var.*** Avesnes. Nord, N France
64 *G12* **Aves Ridge** *undersea feature* SE Caribbean Sea
95 *M14* **Avesta** Dalarna, C Sweden
103 *O14* **Aveyron** ◈ *department* S France
103 *N14* **Aveyron** ≈ S France
107 *J15* **Avezzano** Abruzzo, C Italy
115 *D16* **Avgó** ▲ C Greece
Avgustov *see* Augustów
Avgustovskiy Kanal *see* Augustowski, Kanał
96 *J9* **Aviemore** N Scotland, UK
185 *F21* **Aviemore, Lake** ◎ South Island, NZ
103 *R15* **Avignon** ***anc.*** Avenio. Vaucluse, SE France
104 *M7* **Ávila** ***var.*** Avila; ***anc.*** Abela, Abula, Abyla, Avela. Castilla-León, C Spain
104 *L8* **Ávila** ◈ *province* Castilla-León, C Spain
104 *K2* **Avilés** Asturias, NW Spain
118 *J4* **Avinurme** ***Ger.*** Awwinorm. Ida-Virumaa, NE Estonia
104 *H10* **Avis** Portalegre, C Portugal
95 *F22* **Avlum** Ringkøbing, C Denmark
182 *M11* **Avoca** Victoria, SE Australia
29 *T14* **Avoca** Iowa, C USA
182 *M11* **Avoca River** ≈ Victoria, SE Australia
107 *L25* **Avola** Sicilia, Italy, C Mediterranean Sea
18 *F10* **Avon** New York, NE USA
29 *P12* **Avon** South Dakota, N USA
97 *M23* **Avon** ≈ S England, UK
97 *L20* **Avon** ≈ C England, UK
66 *K13* **Avondale** Arizona, SW USA
23 *X13* **Avon Park** Florida, SE USA
102 *J5* **Avranches** Manche, N France
103 *O3* **Avre** ≈ N France
186 *M6* **Avuavu** ***var.*** Kolotambu. Guadalcanal, C Solomon Islands
Avveel *see* Ivalo, Finland
Avveel *see* Ivalojoki, Finland
Avvil *see* Ivalo
77 *O17* **Awaaso** ***var.*** Awaso. SW Ghana
141 *X8* **Awābī** ***var.*** Al 'Awābī. NE Oman
184 *L9* **Awakino** Waikato, North Island, NZ
142 *M15* **'Awālī** C Bahrain
99 *K19* **Awans** Liège, E Belgium
184 *I2* **Awanui** Northland, North Island, NZ
148 *M14* **Awārān** Baluchistān, SW Pakistan
81 *K16* **Awara Plain** *plain* NE Kenya
80 *M13* **Āwarē** Somali, E Ethiopia
138 *M6* **'Awāriḍ, Wādī** *dry watercourse* E Syria
185 *B20* **Awarua Point** *headland* South Island, NZ
81 *J14* **Āwasa** Southern, S Ethiopia
80 *K13* **Āwash** Afar, NE Ethiopia
80 *K12* **Āwash** ***var.*** Hawash. ≈ C Ethiopia
Awaso *see* Awaaso
158 *H7* **Awat** Xinjiang Uygur Zizhiqu, NW China
185 *J15* **Awatere** ≈ South Island, NZ
75 *O10* **Awbārī** SW Libya
75 *N9* **Awbāri, Idhān** ***var.*** Edeyen d'Oubari. *desert* Algeria/Libya
80 *C13* **Aweil** Northern Bahr el Ghazal, SW Sudan
96 *H11* **Awe, Loch** ◎ W Scotland, UK
77 *U16* **Awka** Anambra, SW Nigeria
39 *O6* **Awuna River** ≈ Alaska, USA
Awwinorm *see* Avinurme
Ax *see* Dax
Axarfjördhur *see* Öxarfjördhur
103 *N17* **Axat** Aude, S France
99 *F16* **Axel** Zeeland, SW Netherlands
8 *M2* **Axel Heiberg Island** ***var.*** Axel Heiburg. *island* Nunavut, N Canada
Axel Heiburg *see* Axel Heiberg Island
77 *O17* **Axim** S Ghana
114 *F13* **Axiós** ***var.*** Vardar. ≈ Greece/FYR Macedonia ***see also*** Vardar
103 *N17* **Ax-les-Thermes** Ariège, S France
120 *D11* **Ayachi, Jbel** ▲ C Morocco
61 *D22* **Ayacucho** Buenos Aires, E Argentina
57 *F15* **Ayacucho** Ayacucho, S Peru
57 *E16* **Ayacucho** ***off.*** Departamento de Ayacucho. ◈ *department* SW Peru
145 *W11* **Ayagoz** ***var.*** Ayaguz, ***Kaz.*** Ayaköz; ***prev.*** Sergiopol. Vostochnyy Kazakhstan, E Kazakhstan
145 *V12* **Ayagoz** ***var.*** Ayaguz, ***Kaz.*** Ayaköz. ≈ E Kazakhstan
Ayaguz *see* Ayagoz
Ayakagytma *see* Oyoqighitma
Ayakkuduk *see* Oyoqquduq
158 *L10* **Ayakkum Hu** ◎ NW China
Ayaköz *see* Ayagoz
104 *H14* **Ayamonte** Andalucía, S Spain
123 *S11* **Ayan** Khabarovskiy Kray, E Russian Federation
136 *J10* **Ayancık** Sinop, N Turkey
55 *S9* **Ayanganna Mountain** ▲ C Guyana
77 *U16* **Ayangba** Kogi, C Nigeria
123 *U7* **Ayanka** Koryakskiy Avtonomnyy Okrug, E Russian Federation
54 *E7* **Ayapel** Córdoba, NW Colombia
136 *H12* **Ayaş** Ankara, N Turkey
57 *I16* **Ayaviri** Puno, S Peru
149 *P3* **Āybak** ***var.*** Aibak, Haibak; ***prev.*** Samangān. Samangān, NE Afghanistan
147 *N10* **Aydarkŭl** ***Rus.*** Ozero Aydarkul'. ◎ C Uzbekistan
Aydarkul', Ozero *see* Aydarkŭl
21 *W10* **Ayden** North Carolina, SE USA
136 *C15* **Aydın** ***var.*** Aïdin; ***anc.*** Tralles. Aydın, SW Turkey
136 *C15* **Aydın** ***var.*** Aïdin. ◈ *province* SW Turkey
136 *I17* **Aydıncık** İçel, S Turkey
136 *C15* **Aydın Dağları** ▲▲ W Turkey
158 *L6* **Aydingkol Hu** ◎ NW China
129 *X7* **Aydyrlinskiy** Orenburgskaya Oblast', W Russian Federation
105 *S4* **Ayerbe** Aragón, NE Spain
Ayers Rock *see* Uluru
Ayeyarwady *see* Irrawaddy
Ayiá *see* Agiá
Ayia Napa *see* Agía Nápa
Ayia Phyla *see* Agía Fýlaxis
Ayiásos/Ayiássos *see* Agiasós
Áyios Evstrátios *see* Ágios Efstrátios
Áyios Kírikos *see* Ágios Kírykos
Áyios Nikólaos *see* Ágios Nikólaos
Ayios Seryios *see* Yeniboğaziçi
80 *I11* **Āykel** Amhara, N Ethiopia
123 *N9* **Aykhal** Respublika Sakha (Yakutiya), NE Russian Federation
14 *J12* **Aylen Lake** ◎ Ontario, SE Canada
97 *N21* **Aylesbury** SE England, UK
105 *O6* **Ayllón** Castilla-León, N Spain
14 *F17* **Aylmer** Ontario, S Canada
14 *L12* **Aylmer** Quebec, SE Canada
15 *R12* **Aylmer, Lac** ◎ Quebec, SE Canada
8 *L9* **Aylmer Lake** ◎ Northwest Territories, NW Canada
145 *V14* **Aynabulak** Almaty, SE Kazakhstan
138 *K2* **'Ayn al 'Arab** Ḥalab, N Syria
Aynayn *see* 'Aynīn
139 *V12* **'Ayn Ḥamūd** S Iraq
147 *P12* **Ayní** ***prev. Rus.*** Varzimanor Ayni. W Tajikistan
140 *M10* **'Aynīn** ***var.*** Aynayn. *spring/well* SW Saudi Arabia
21 *U12* **Aynor** South Carolina, SE USA
139 *Q7* **'Ayn Zāzūh** C Iraq
153 *N12* **Ayodhya** Uttar Pradesh, N India
123 *S6* **Ayon, Ostrov** *island* NE Russian Federation
105 *R11* **Ayora** País Valenciano, E Spain
77 *Q11* **Ayorou** Tillabéri, W Niger
79 *E16* **Ayos** Centre, S Cameroon
76 *L5* **'Ayoûn 'Abd el Mâlek** *well* N Mauritania
76 *K10* **'Ayoûn el 'Atroûs** ***var.*** Aïoun el Atrous, Aïoun el Atroûss. Hodh el Gharbi, SE Mauritania
96 *I13* **Ayr** W Scotland, UK
96 *I13* **Ayr** ≈ W Scotland, UK
96 *I13* **Ayrshire** *cultural region* SW Scotland, UK
Aysen *see* Aisén
80 *L12* **Āysha** Somali, E Ethiopia
144 *L14* **Ayteke Bi** ***Kaz.*** Zhangaqazaly ***prev.*** Novokazalinsk. Kyzylorda, SW Kazakhstan
146 *K8* **Aytim** Nawoiy Wiloyati, N Uzbekistan
181 *W4* **Ayton** Queensland, NE Australia
114 *M9* **Aytos** Burgas, E Bulgaria
171 *T11* **Ayu, Kepulauan** *island group* E Indonesia
A Yun Pa *see* Cheo Reo
169 *V11* **Ayu, Tanjung** *headland* Borneo, N Indonesia
40 *K13* **Ayutla** Jalisco, C Mexico
41 *P16* **Ayutlá** ***var.*** Ayutla de los Libres. Guerrero, S Mexico
Ayutla de los Libres *see* Ayutlá
167 *O11* **Ayutthaya** ***var.*** Phra Nakhon Si Ayutthaya. Phra Nakhon Si Ayutthaya, C Thailand
136 *B13* **Ayvalık** Balıkesir, W Turkey
99 *L20* **Aywaille** Liège, E Belgium
141 *R13* **'Aywat aş Şay'ar, Wādī** *seasonal river* N Yemen
Azaffal *see* Azeffâl
105 *T9* **Azahar, Costa del** *coastal region* E Spain
105 *S6* **Azaila** Aragón, NE Spain
104 *F10* **Azambuja** Lisboa, C Portugal
153 *N13* **Āzamgarh** Uttar Pradesh, N India
77 *O9* **Azaouâd** *desert* C Mali
77 *S10* **Azaouagh, Vallée de l'** ***var.*** Azaouak. ≈ W Niger
Azaouak *see* Azaouagh, Vallée de l'
61 *F14* **Azara** Misiones, NE Argentina
142 *K3* **Āzarān** Āžarbāyjān-e Khāvarī, N Iran
Azärbaycan/Azärbaycan Respublikası *see* Azerbaijan
Āžarbāyjān-e Bākhtarī *see* Āžarbāyjān-e Gharbī
142 *I4* **Āžarbāyjān-e Gharbī** ***off.*** Ostān-e Āžarbāyjān-e Gharbī ***Eng.*** West Azerbaijan ***prev.*** Āžarbāyjān-e Bākhtarī . ◈ *province* NW Iran
Āžarbāyjān-e Khāvarī *see* Āžarbāyjān-e Sharqī
142 *J3* **Āžarbāyjān-e Sharqī** ***off.*** Ostān-e Āžarbāyjān-e Sharqī, ***Eng.*** East Azerbaijan; ***prev.*** Āžarbāyjān-e Sharqī. ◈ *province* NW Iran
77 *W13* **Azare** Bauchi, N Nigeria
119 *M19* **Azarychy** ***Rus.*** Ozarichi. Homyel'skaya Voblasts', SE Belarus
102 *L8* **Azay-le-Rideau** Indre-et-Loire, C France
138 *I2* **A'zāz** Ḥalab, NW Syria
76 *H7* **Azeffâl** ***var.*** Azaffal. *desert* Mauritania/Western Sahara
137 *V12* **Azerbaijan** ***off.*** Azerbaijani Republic, ***Az.*** Azärbaycan, Azärbaycan Respublikası; ***prev.*** Azerbaijan SSR. ◆ *republic* SE Asia
145 *T7* **Azhbulat, Ozero** ◎ NE Kazakhstan
74 *F7* **Azilal** C Morocco
Azimabad *see* Patna
19 *O6* **Aziscohos Lake** ⊠ Maine, NE USA
Azizbekov *see* Vayk'
Azizie *see* Telish
Aziziya *see* Al 'Azīzīyah
129 *T4* **Aznakayevo** Respublika Tatarstan, W Russian Federation
56 *C8* **Azogues** Cañar, S Ecuador
64 *N2* **Azores** ***var.*** Açores, Ilhas dos Açores, ***Port.*** Arquipélago dos Açores. *island group* Portugal, NE Atlantic Ocean
64 *L8* **Azores-Biscay Rise** *undersea feature* E Atlantic Ocean
Azotos/Azotus *see* Ashdod
78 *K11* **Azoum, Bahr** *seasonal river* SE Chad
128 *L12* **Azov** Rostovskaya Oblast', SW Russian Federation
128 *J13* **Azov, Sea of** ***Rus.*** Azovskoye More, ***Ukr.*** Azovs'ke More. *sea* NE Black Sea
Azovs'ke More/Azovskoye More *see* Azov, Sea of
138 *I10* **Azraq, Wāḥat al** *oasis* N Jordan
Āzro *see* Āzrow
74 *G6* **Azrou** C Morocco
149 *R5* **Āzrow** ***var.*** Āzro. Lowgar, E Afghanistan
37 *P8* **Aztec** New Mexico, SW USA
36 *M13* **Aztec Peak** ▲ Arizona, SW USA
45 *N9* **Azua** ***var.*** Azua de Compostela. S Dominican Republic
Azua de Compostela *see* Azua
104 *K12* **Azuaga** Extremadura, W Spain
56 *B8* **Azuay** ◈ *province* W Ecuador
164 *C13* **Azuchi-Ō-shima** *island* SW Japan
105 *O11* **Azuer** ≈ C Spain
43 *S17* **Azuero, Península de** *peninsula* S Panama
62 *I6* **Azufre, Volcán** ***var.*** Volcán Lastarria. ▲ N Chile
116 *J12* **Azuga** Prahova, SE Romania
61 *C22* **Azul** Buenos Aires, E Argentina
62 *I8* **Azul, Cerro** ▲ NW Argentina
56 *E12* **Azul, Cordillera** ▲▲ C Peru
165 *P11* **Azuma-san** ▲ Honshū, C Japan
103 *V15* **Azur, Côte d'** *coastal region* SE France
191 *Z3* **Azur Lagoon** ◎ Kiritimati, E Kiribati
'Azza *see* Gaza
Az Zāb al Kabīr *see* Great Zab
138 *H7* **Az Zabdānī** ***var.*** Zabadani. Dimashq, W Syria
141 *W8* **Aẓ Ẓāhirah** *desert* NW Oman
141 *S6* **Aẓ Ẓahrān** ***Eng.*** Dhahran. Ash Sharqīyah, NE Saudi Arabia
141 *R6* **Aẓ Ẓahrān al Khubar** ***var.*** Dhahran Al Khobar. ✕ Ash Sharqīyah, NE Saudi Arabia
Az Zaqāzīq *see* Zagazig
138 *H10* **Az Zarqā'** ***var.*** Zarqa. Az Zarqā', NW Jordan
138 *I11* **Az Zarqā'** ***off.*** Muḥāfaẓat az Zarqā', ***var.*** Zarqa. ◈ *governorate* N Jordan
75 *O7* **Az Zāwiyah** ***var.*** Zawia. NW Libya
141 *N15* **Az Zaydīyah** W Yemen
74 *I11* **Azzel Matti, Sebkha** ***var.*** Sebkra Azz el Matti. *salt flat* C Algeria
141 *P6* **Az Zilfī** Ar Riyāḍ, N Saudi Arabia
139 *Y13* **Az Zubayr** ***var.*** Al Zubair. SE Iraq
Az Zuqur *see* Jabal Zuuqar, Jazīrat

B

187 *X15* **Ba** ***prev.*** Mba. Viti Levu, W Fiji
Ba *see* Đa Răng
171 *P17* **Baa** Pulau Rote, C Indonesia
138 *H7* **Baalbek** ***var.*** Ba'labakk; ***anc.*** Heliopolis. E Lebanon
108 *G8* **Baar** Zug, N Switzerland
81 *L17* **Baardheere** ***var.*** Bardere, ***It.*** Bardera. Gedo, SW Somalia
80 *Q12* **Baargaal** Bari, NE Somalia
99 *I15* **Baarle-Hertog** Antwerpen, N Belgium
99 *I15* **Baarle-Nassau** Noord-Brabant, S Netherlands
98 *J11* **Baarn** Utrecht, C Netherlands
114 *D13* **Baba** ***var.*** Buševa, ***Gk.*** Varnoús. ▲▲ FYR Macedonia/Greece
76 *H10* **Bababé** Brakna, W Mauritania
136 *G10* **Baba Burnu** *headland* NW Turkey
117 *N13* **Babadag** Tulcea, SE Romania
137 *X10* **Babadağ Dağı** ▲ NE Azerbaijan
Babadayhan *see* Babadaykhan
146 *H14* **Babadaykhan** ***Turkm.*** Babadayhan; ***prev.*** Kirovsk. Akhalskiy Velayat, C Turkmenistan
146 *G14* **Babadurmaz** Akhalskiy Velayat, C Turkmenistan
114 *M12* **Babaeski** Kırklareli, NW Turkey
139 *T4* **Bāba Gurgur** N Iraq
56 *B7* **Babahoyo** ***prev.*** Bodegas. Los Ríos, C Ecuador
149 *P5* **Bābā, Kūh-e** ▲▲ C Afghanistan
171 *N12* **Babana** Sulawesi, C Indonesia
171 *Q12* **Babar, Kepulauan** *island group* E Indonesia
171 *T12* **Babar, Pulau** *island* Kepulauan Babar, E Indonesia
152 *G4* **Bābāsar Pass** *pass* India/Pakistan
146 *C9* **Babashy** ▲▲ W Turkmenistan
168 *M13* **Babat** Sumatera, W Indonesia
Babatag, Khrebet *see* Bobotogh, Qatorkŭhi
81 *H21* **Babati** Arusha, NE Tanzania
126 *J13* **Babayevo** Vologodskaya Oblast', NW Russian Federation
129 *Q15* **Babayurt** Respublika Dagestan, SW Russian Federation
33 *P6* **Babb** Montana, NW USA
29 *X4* **Babbitt** Minnesota, N USA
188 *E9* **Babeldaob** ***var.*** Babeldaop, Babelthuap. *island* N Palau
Babeldaop *see* Babeldaob
141 *N17* **Bab el Mandeb** *strait* Gulf of Aden/Red Sea
Babelthuap *see* Babeldaob
111 *K17* **Babia Góra** ***var.*** Babia Hora. ▲ Slovakia/Poland
Babia Hora *see* Babia Góra
Babian Jiang *see* Black River
Babichi *see* Babichy
119 *N19* **Babichy** ***Rus.*** Babichi. Homyel'skaya Voblasts', SE Belarus
112 *I10* **Babina Greda** Vukovar-Srijem, E Croatia
10 *K13* **Babine Lake** ◎ British Columbia, SW Canada
143 *O4* **Bābol** ***var.*** Babul, Balfrush, Barfrush; ***prev.*** Barfurush. Māzandarān, N Iran
143 *O4* **Bābolsar** ***var.*** Babulsar; ***prev.*** Meshed-i-Sar. Māzandarān, N Iran
36 *L16* **Baboquivari Peak** ▲ Arizona, SW USA
79 *G15* **Baboua** Nana-Mambéré, W Central African Republic
119 *M17* **Babruysk** ***Rus.*** Bobruysk. Mahilyowskaya Voblasts', E Belarus
Babu *see* Hexian
Babul *see* Bābol
Babulsar *see* Bābolsar
113 *O19* **Babuna** ≈ C FYR Macedonia
113 *O19* **Babuna** ▲▲ C FYR Macedonia
148 *K7* **Bābūs, Dasht-e** ***Pash.*** Bebas, Dasht-i. ▲▲ W Afghanistan
171 *O1* **Babuyan Channel** *channel* N Philippines
171 *O1* **Babuyan Island** *island* N Philippines
139 *T9* **Babylon** *site of ancient city* C Iraq
112 *J9* **Bač** ***Ger.*** Batsch. Serbia, NW Yugoslavia
58 *M13* **Bacabal** Maranhão, E Brazil
41 *Y14* **Bacalar** Quintana Roo, SE Mexico
41 *Y14* **Bacalar Chico, Boca** *strait* SE Mexico
171 *Q12* **Bacan, Kepulauan** *island group* E Indonesia
171 *S12* **Bacan, Pulau** ***prev.*** Batjan. *island* Maluku, E Indonesia
116 *L10* **Bacău** ***Hung.*** Bákó. Bacău, NE Romania
116 *K11* **Bacău** ◈ *county* E Romania
Băc Bô, Vinh *see* Tongking, Gulf of
167 *T5* **Băc Can** Băc Thai, N Vietnam
103 *T5* **Baccarat** Meurthe-et-Moselle, NE France
183 *N12* **Bacchus Marsh** Victoria, SE Australia
40 *H4* **Bacerac** Sonora, NW Mexico
116 *L10* **Băceşti** Vaslui, E Romania
167 *T6* **Băc Giang** Ha Băc, N Vietnam
54 *I5* **Bachaquero** Zulia, NW Venezuela
Bacher *see* Pohorje
118 *M13* **Bacheykava** ***Rus.*** Bocheykovo. Vitsyebskaya Voblasts', N Belarus
40 *I5* **Bachíniva** Chihuahua, N Mexico
158 *G8* **Bachu** Xinjiang Uygur Zizhiqu, NW China
9 *N8* **Back** ≈ Nunavut, N Canada
112 *K10* **Bačka Palanka** ***prev.*** Palanka. Serbia, NW Yugoslavia
112 *K8* **Bačka Topola** ***Hung.*** Topolya; ***prev. Hung.*** Bácstopolya. Serbia, N Yugoslavia
95 *J17* **Bäckefors** Västra Götaland, S Sweden
Bäckermühle Schulzenmühle *see* Żywiec
95 *L16* **Bäckhammar** Värmland, C Sweden
112 *K9* **Bački Petrovac** ***Hung.*** Petrőcz; ***prev.*** Petrovac, Petrovácz. Serbia, NW Yugoslavia
101 *I21* **Backnang** Baden-Württemberg, SW Germany
167 *S15* **Bac Liêu** ***var.*** Vinh Loi. Minh Hai, S Vietnam
167 *T6* **Băc Ninh** Ha Băc, N Vietnam
40 *G4* **Bacoachi** Sonora, NW Mexico
171 *P6* **Bacolod** ***off.*** Bacolod City. Negros, C Philippines
171 *O4* **Baco, Mount** ▲ Mindoro, N Philippines
111 *K25* **Bácsalmás** Bács-Kiskun, S Hungary
Bácsjózseffalva *see* Žednik
111 *J24* **Bács-Kiskun** ***off.*** Bács-Kiskun Megye. ◈ *county* S Hungary
Bácsszenttamás *see* Srbobran
Bácstopolya *see* Bačka Topola
Bactra *see* Balkh
155 *F21* **Badagara** Kerala, SW India
101 *M24* **Bad Aibling** Bayern, SE Germany
162 *I13* **Badain Jaran Shamo** *desert* N China
104 *I11* **Badajoz** ***anc.*** Pax Augusta. Extremadura, W Spain
104 *J11* **Badajoz** ◈ *province* Extremadura, W Spain
149 *S2* **Badakhshān** ◈ *province* NE Afghanistan
105 *W6* **Badalona** ***anc.*** Baetulo. Cataluña, E Spain
154 *O11* **Bādāmapāhārh** Orissa, E India
152 *K8* **Badarīnāth** ▲ N India
169 *O10* **Badas, Kepulauan** *island group* W Indonesia
109 *S6* **Bad Aussee** Salzburg, E Austria
31 *S8* **Bad Axe** Michigan, N USA
101 *G16* **Bad Berleburg** Nordrhein-Westfalen, W Germany
101 *L17* **Bad Blankenburg** Thüringen, C Germany
Bad Borseck *see* Borsec
101 *G18* **Bad Camberg** Hessen, W Germany
100 *L8* **Bad Doberan** Mecklenburg-Vorpommern, N Germany
101 *N14* **Bad Düben** Sachsen, E Germany
109 *X4* **Baden** ***var.*** Baden bei Wien; ***anc.*** Aquae Panoniae, Thermae Pannonicae. Niederösterreich, NE Austria
108 *F9* **Baden** Aargau, N Switzerland
101 *G21* **Baden-Baden** ***anc.*** Aurelia Aquensis. Baden-Württemberg, SW Germany
Baden bei Wien *see* Baden
101 *G22* **Baden-Württemberg** ***Fr.*** Bade-Wurtemberg. ◈ *state* SW Germany
112 *A10* **Baderna** Istra, NW Croatia
Bade-Wurtemberg *see* Baden-Württemberg
101 *H20* **Bad Fredrichshall** Baden-Württemberg, S Germany
100 *P11* **Bad Freienwalde** Brandenburg, NE Germany
109 *Q8* **Badgastein** ***var.*** Gastein. Salzburg, NW Austria
Badger State *see* Wisconsin
148 *L4* **Bādghīs** ◈ *province* NW Afghanistan
109 *T5* **Bad Hall** Oberösterreich, N Austria
101 *J14* **Bad Harzburg** Niedersachsen, C Germany
101 *I16* **Bad Hersfeld** Hessen, C Germany
98 *I10* **Badhoevedorp** Noord-Holland, C Netherlands
109 *Q8* **Bad Hofgastein** Salzburg, NW Austria
Bad Homburg *see* Bad Homburg vor der Höhe
101 *G18* **Bad Homburg vor der Höhe** ***var.*** Bad Homburg. Hessen, W Germany
101 *E17* **Bad Honnef** Nordrhein-Westfalen, W Germany
149 *Q17* **Badīn** Sind, SE Pakistan
21 *S10* **Badin Lake** ⊠ North Carolina, SE USA
40 *I8* **Badiraguato** Sinaloa, C Mexico
109 *R6* **Bad Ischl** Oberösterreich, N Austria
Badjawa *see* Bajawa
101 *J18* **Bad Kissingen** Bayern, SE Germany
Bad Königswart *see* Lázně Kynžvart
101 *F19* **Bad Kreuznach** Rheinland-Pfalz, SW Germany
101 *F24* **Bad Krozingen** Baden-Württemberg, SW Germany
101 *G16* **Bad Laasphe** Nordrhein-Westfalen, W Germany
28 *J6* **Badlands** *physical region* North Dakota, N USA
101 *K16* **Bad Langensalza** Thüringen, C Germany
109 *T3* **Bad Leonfelden** Oberösterreich, N Austria
101 *I20* **Bad Mergentheim** Baden-Württemberg, SW Germany
101 *H17* **Bad Nauheim** Hessen, W Germany
101 *E17* **Bad Neuenahr-Arhweiler** Rheinland-Pfalz, W Germany
Bad Neustadt *see* Bad Neustadt an der Saale
101 *J18* **Bad Neustadt an der Saale** ***var.*** Bad Neustadt. Berlin, C Germany
Badnur *see* Betūl
100 *H13* **Bad Oeynhausen** Nordrhein-Westfalen, NW Germany
100 *J9* **Bad Oldesloe** Schleswig-Holstein, N Germany
77 *Q16* **Badou** C Togo
Bad Polzin *see* Połczyn-Zdrój
100 *H13* **Bad Pyrmont** Niedersachsen, C Germany
109 *X9* **Bad Radkersburg** Steiermark, SE Austria
139 *V8* **Badrah** E Iraq
162 *J6* **Badrah** Hövsgöl, N Mongolia
101 *N24* **Bad Reichenhall** Bayern, SE Germany
140 *K8* **Badr Ḥunayn** Al Madīnah, W Saudi Arabia
28 *M10* **Bad River** ≈ South Dakota, N USA
30 *K4* **Bad River** ≈ Wisconsin, N USA
100 *H13* **Bad Salzuflen** Nordrhein-Westfalen, NW Germany
101 *J16* **Bad Salzungen** Thüringen, C Germany
109 *V8* **Bad Sankt Leonhard im Lavanttal** Kärnten, S Austria
100 *K9* **Bad Schwartau** Schleswig-Holstein, N Germany
101 *L24* **Bad Tölz** Bayern, SE Germany
181 *U1* **Badu Island** *island* Queensland, NE Australia
155 *K25* **Badulla** Uva Province, C Sri Lanka
109 *X5* **Bad Vöslau** Niederösterreich, NE Austria
101 *I24* **Bad Waldsee** Baden-Württemberg, S Germany
35 *U11* **Badwater Basin** *depression* California, W USA
101 *J20* **Bad Windsheim** Bayern, C Germany
101 *J23* **Bad Wörishofen** Bayern, S Germany
100 *G10* **Bad Zwischenahn** Niedersachsen, NW Germany
104 *M13* **Baena** Andalucía, S Spain
Baeterrae/Baeterrae Septimanorum *see* Béziers
Baetic Cordillera/Baetic Mountains *see* Béticos, Sistemas
Baetulo *see* Badalona
57 *K18* **Baeza** Napo, NE Ecuador
105 *N13* **Baeza** Andalucía, S Spain
79 *D15* **Bafang** Ouest, W Cameroon
76 *H12* **Bafatá** C Guinea-Bissau
149 *U5* **Baffa** North-West Frontier Province, NW Pakistan
197 *O11* **Baffin Basin** *undersea feature* N Labrador Sea
197 *N12* **Baffin Bay** *bay* Canada/Greenland
25 *T15* **Baffin Bay** *inlet* Texas, SW USA
196 *M12* **Baffin Island** *island* Nunavut, NE Canada
79 *E15* **Bafia** Centre, C Cameroon
77 *R14* **Bafilo** NE Togo
76 *J12* **Bafing** ≈ W Africa
76 *J12* **Bafoulabé** Kayes, W Mali
79 *D15* **Bafoussam** Ouest, W Cameroon
143 *R9* **Bāfq** Yazd, C Iran
136 *L10* **Bafra** Samsun, N Turkey
136 *L10* **Bafra Burnu** *headland* N Turkey
143 *S12* **Bāft** Kermān, S Iran
79 *N18* **Bafwabalinga** Orientale, NE Dem. Rep. Congo (Zaire)
79 *N18* **Bafwaboli** Orientale, NE Dem. Rep. Congo (Zaire)
79 *N17* **Bafwasende** Orientale, NE Dem. Rep. Congo (Zaire)
42 *K13* **Bagaces** Guanacaste, NW Costa Rica
153 *O12* **Bagaha** Bihār, N India
155 *F16* **Bāgalkot** Karnātaka, W India
81 *J22* **Bagamoyo** Pwani, E Tanzania
168 *J8* **Bagan Datuk** ***var.*** Bagan Datok. Perak, Peninsular Malaysia
171 *R7* **Baganga** Mindanao, S Philippines
168 *J9* **Bagansiapiapi** ***var.*** Pasirpangarayan. Sumatera, W Indonesia
Bagaria *see* Bagheria
77 *T11* **Bagaroua** Tahoua, W Niger
79 *I20* **Bagata** Bandundu, W Dem. Rep. Congo (Zaire)
Bagdad *see* Baghdād
123 *O13* **Bagdarin** Respublika Buryatiya, S Russian Federation
61 *G17* **Bagé** Rio Grande do Sul, S Brazil
Bagenalstown *see* Muine Bheag
Bagerhat *see* Bagherhat
103 *P16* **Bages et de Sigean, Étang de** ◎ S France
33 *W17* **Baggs** Wyoming, C USA
154 *F11* **Bāgh** Madhya Pradesh, C India
139 *T8* **Baghdād** ***var.*** Bagdad, ***Eng.*** Baghdad. ● (Iraq) C Iraq
139 *T8* **Baghdād** ✕ C Iraq
153 *T16* **Bagherhat** ***var.*** Bagerhat. Khulna, S Bangladesh
107 *J23* **Bagheria** ***var.*** Bagaria. Sicilia, Italy, C Mediterranean Sea
143 *S10* **Bāghīn** Kermān, C Iran
149 *Q3* **Baghlān** Baghlān, NE Afghanistan
149 *Q3* **Baghlān** ***var.*** Bāghlān. ◈ *province* NE Afghanistan
148 *M7* **Bāghrān** Helmand, S Afghanistan
29 *T4* **Bagley** Minnesota, N USA
106 *H10* **Bagnacavallo** Emilia-Romagna, C Italy
102 *K16* **Bagnères-de-Bigorre** Hautes-Pyrénées, S France
102 *L17* **Bagnères-de-Luchon** Hautes-Pyrénées, S France
106 *F11* **Bagni di Lucca** Toscana, C Italy
106 *H11* **Bagno di Romagna** Emilia-Romagna, C Italy
103 *R14* **Bagnols-sur-Cèze** Gard, S France
162 *M14* **Bag Nur** ◎ N China
171 *P6* **Bago** ***off.*** Bago City. Negros, C Philippines
Bago *see* Pegu
76 *M13* **Bagoé** ≈ Ivory Coast/Mali
Bagrāmē *see* Bagrāmī
149 *R5* **Bagrāmī** ***var.*** Bagrāmē. Kābul, E Afghanistan
119 *B14* **Bagrationovsk** ***Ger.*** Preussisch Eylau. Kaliningradskaya Oblast', W Russian Federation
Bagrax *see* Bohu
Bagrax Hu *see* Bosten Hu
56 *C10* **Bagua** Amazonas, NE Peru
171 *O2* **Baguio** ***off.*** Baguio City. Luzon, N Philippines
77 *V9* **Bagzane, Monts** ▲ N Niger
Bāḥah, Minṭaqat al *see* Al Bāḥah
Bahama Islands *see* Bahamas
44 *H3* **Bahamas** ***off.*** Commonwealth of the Bahamas. ◆ *commonwealth republic* N West Indies
(0) *L13* **Bahamas** ***var.*** Bahama Islands. *island group* N West Indies
153 *S15* **Baharampur** ***prev.*** Berhampore. West Bengal, NE India
149 *U10* **Bahāwalnagar** Punjab, E Pakistan
149 *T11* **Bahāwalpur** Punjab, E Pakistan
136 *L16* **Bahçe** Osmaniye, S Turkey

◆ Country
● Country Capital
◇ Dependent Territory
○ Dependent Territory Capital
◈ Administrative Region
✕ International Airport
▲ Mountain
▲▲ Mountain Range
Volcano
≈ River
◎ Lake
⊠ Reservoir

160 J8 **Ba He** ≈ C China
Bäherden see Bakharden
59 N16 **Bahia** off. Estado da Bahia. ◈ state E Brazil
61 B24 **Bahía Blanca** Buenos Aires, E Argentina
40 L15 **Bahía Bufadero** Michoacán de Ocampo, SW Mexico
63 J19 **Bahía Bustamante** Chubut, SE Argentina
40 D5 **Bahía de los Ángeles** Baja California, NW Mexico
40 C6 **Bahía de Tortugas** Baja California Sur, W Mexico
42 J4 **Bahía, Islas de la** Eng. Bay Islands. island group N Honduras
40 E5 **Bahía Kino** Sonora, NW Mexico
40 E9 **Bahía Magdalena** var. Puerto Magdalena. Baja California Sur, W Mexico
54 C8 **Bahía Solano** var. Ciudad Mutis, Solano. Chocó, W Colombia
80 I11 **Bahir Dar** var. Bahr Dar, Bahrdar Giyorgis. Amhara, N Ethiopia
141 X8 **Bahlā'** var. Bahlah, Bahlat. NW Oman
Bāhla see Bālān
Bahlah/Bahlat see Bahlā'
152 M11 **Bahraich** Uttar Pradesh, N India
143 M14 **Bahrain** off. State of Bahrain, Dawlat al Bahrayn, Ar. Al Baḥrayn; prev. Bahrein, anc. Tylos or Tyros. ◆ monarchy SW Asia
142 M14 **Bahrain** ✕ C Bahrain
142 M15 **Bahrain, Gulf of** gulf Persian Gulf, NW Arabian Sea
138 I7 **Baḥrat Mallāḥah** ◎ W Syria
Bahrayn, Dawlat al see Bahrain
Bahr Dar/Bahrdar Giyorgis see Bahir Dar
Bahrein see Bahrain
81 E16 **Bahr el Gabel** ◈ state S Sudan
80 E13 **Bahr ez Zaref** ≈ C Sudan
67 R8 **Bahr Kameur** ≈ N Central African Republic
Bahr Tabariya, Sea of see Tiberias, Lake
143 W15 **Bāhū Kalāt** Sīstān va Balūchestān, SE Iran
118 N13 **Bahushewsk** Rus. Bogushëvsk. Vitsyebskaya Voblasts', NE Belarus
Bai see Tagow Bāy
116 G13 **Baia de Aramă** Mehedinţi, SW Romania
116 G11 **Baia de Criş** Ger. Altenburg, Hung. Körösbánya. Hunedoara, SW Romania
83 A16 **Baia dos Tigres** Namibe, SW Angola
82 A13 **Baia Farta** Benguela, W Angola
116 H9 **Baia Mare** Ger. Frauenbach, Hung. Nagybánya; prev. Neustadt. Maramureş, NW Romania
116 H8 **Baia Sprie** Ger. Mittelstadt, Hung. Felsőbánya. Maramureş, NW Romania
78 G13 **Baïbokoum** Logone-Oriental, SW Chad
160 F12 **Baicao Ling** ▲▲ SW China
163 U9 **Baicheng** var. Pai-ch'eng; prev. T'aon-an. Jilin, NE China
158 I6 **Baicheng** var. Bay. Xinjiang Uygur Zizhiqu, NW China
116 J13 **Băicoi** Prahova, SE Romania
Baidoa see Baydhabo
15 U6 **Baie-Comeau** Quebec, SE Canada
15 T7 **Baie-des-Bacon** Quebec, SE Canada
15 S8 **Baie-des-Rochers** Quebec, SE Canada
15 U6 **Baie-des-Sables** Quebec, SE Canada
12 K11 **Baie-du-Poste** Quebec, SE Canada
172 H17 **Baie Lazare** Mahé, NE Seychelles
45 Y5 **Baie-Mahault** Basse Terre, C Guadeloupe
15 R9 **Baie-St-Paul** Quebec, SE Canada
15 V5 **Baie-Trinité** Quebec, SE Canada
13 T11 **Baie Verte** Newfoundland, SE Canada
163 X11 **Baihe** prev. Erdaobaihe. Jilin, NE China
Baiguan see Shangyu
139 U11 **Bā'ij al Mahdī** S Iraq
Baiji see Bayjī
Baikal, Lake see Baykal, Ozero
Bailādila see Kirandul
Baile an Chaistil see Ballycastle
Baile an Róba see Ballinrobe
Baile an tSratha see Ballintra
Baile Átha an Rí see Athenry
Baile Átha Buí see Athboy
Baile Átha Cliath see Dublin
Baile Átha Fhirdhia see Ardee
Baile Átha Í see Athy
Baile Átha Luain see Athlone
Baile Átha Troim see Trim
Baile Brigín see Balbriggan
Baile Easa Dara see Ballysadare
116 I13 **Băile Govora** Vâlcea, SW Romania
116 F13 **Băile Herculane** Ger. Herkulesbad, Hung. Herkulesfürdő. Caraş-Severin, SW Romania
Baile Locha Riach see Loughrea
Baile Mhistéala see Mitchelstown
Baile Monaidh see Ballymoney
105 N12 **Bailén** Andalucía, S Spain
Baile na hInse see Ballynahinch
Baile na Lorgan see Castleblayney
Baile na Mainistreach see Newtownabbey
Baile Nua na hArda see Newtownards
116 I12 **Băile Olăneşti** Vâlcea, SW Romania
116 H14 **Băileşti** Dolj, SW Romania
Bailingmiao see Darhan Muminggan Lianheqi
58 K11 **Bailique, Ilha** island NE Brazil
103 O1 **Bailleul** Nord, N France
78 H12 **Ba Illi** Chari-Baguirmi, SW Chad
159 V12 **Bailong Jiang** ≈ C China
82 C13 **Bailundo** Port. Vila Teixeira da Silva. Huambo, C Angola
159 T13 **Baima** var. Sêraitang. Qinghai, C China
186 C8 **Baimuru** Gulf, S PNG
158 M16 **Bainang** Xizang Zizhiqu, W China
23 S8 **Bainbridge** Georgia, SE USA
171 O17 **Baing** Pulau Sumba, SE Indonesia
158 M14 **Baingoin** Xizang Zizhiqu, W China
104 G2 **Baio Grande** Galicia, NW Spain
104 G4 **Baiona** Galicia, NW Spain
163 V7 **Baiquan** Heilongjiang, NE China
Bā'ir see Bāyir
158 I11 **Bairab Co** ◎ W China
25 Q7 **Baird** Texas, SW USA
39 N7 **Baird Mountains** ▲▲ Alaska, USA
Baireuth see Bayreuth
190 H3 **Bairiki** ● (Kiribati) Tarawa, NW Kiribati
163 S11 **Bairin Youqi** var. Daban. Nei Mongol Zizhiqu, N China
163 S10 **Bairin Zuoqi** var. Lindong. Nei Mongol Zizhiqu, N China
145 P17 **Bairkum** Kaz. Bayyrqum. Yuzhnyy Kazakhstan, S Kazakhstan
183 P12 **Bairnsdale** Victoria, SE Australia
171 P6 **Bais** Negros, S Philippines
102 L15 **Baïse** var. Baise. ≈ S France
163 W11 **Baishan** prev. Hunjiang. Jilin, NE China
118 F12 **Baisogala** Radviliškis, C Lithuania
189 Q7 **Baiti** N Nauru
104 G13 **Baixo Alentejo** physical region S Portugal
64 P5 **Baixo, Ilhéu de** island Madeira, Portugal, NE Atlantic Ocean
83 E15 **Baixo Longa** Cuando Cubango, SE Angola
159 V10 **Baiyin** Gansu, C China
160 E8 **Baiyü** Sichuan, C China
161 N14 **Baiyun** ✕ (Guangzhou) Guangdong, S China
160 K4 **Baiyu Shan** ▲▲ C China
111 J25 **Baja** Bács-Kiskun, S Hungary
40 C4 **Baja California** ◈ state NW Mexico
40 C4 **Baja California** Eng. Lower California. peninsula NW Mexico
40 E9 **Baja California Sur** ◈ state W Mexico
Bājah see Béja
Bajan see Bayan
191 V16 **Baja, Punta** headland Easter Island, Chile, E Pacific Ocean
40 B4 **Baja, Punta** headland NW Mexico
55 R5 **Baja, Punta** headland NE Venezuela
42 D5 **Baja Verapaz** off. Departamento de Baja Verapaz. ◈ department C Guatemala
171 N16 **Bajawa** prev. Badjawa. Flores, S Indonesia
153 S16 **Baj Baj** prev. Budge-Budge. West Bengal, E India
141 N15 **Bājil** W Yemen
183 U4 **Bajimba, Mount** ▲ New South Wales, SE Australia
112 K13 **Bajina Bašta** Serbia, W Yugoslavia
153 U14 **Bajitpur** Dhaka, E Bangladesh
112 K8 **Bajmok** Serbia, NW Yugoslavia
Bajo Boquete see Boquete
113 L17 **Bajram Curri** Kukës, N Albania
79 J14 **Bakala** Ouaka, C Central African Republic
129 T4 **Bakaly** Respublika Bashkortostan, W Russian Federation
Bakan see Shimonoseki
145 U14 **Bakanas** Kaz. Baqanas. Almaty, SE Kazakhstan
145 V12 **Bakanas** Kaz. Baqanas. ≈ E Kazakhstan
145 U14 **Bakbakty** Kaz. Baqbaqty. Almaty, SE Kazakhstan
122 J12 **Bakchar** Tomskaya Oblast', C Russian Federation
76 I11 **Bakel** E Senegal
35 W13 **Baker** California, W USA
22 J8 **Baker** Louisiana, S USA
33 Y9 **Baker** Montana, NW USA
32 L12 **Baker** Oregon, NW USA
192 L7 **Baker and Howland Islands** ◇ US unincorporated territory W Polynesia
36 L12 **Baker Butte** ▲ Arizona, SW USA
39 X15 **Baker Island** island Alexander Archipelago, Alaska, USA
9 N9 **Baker Lake** Nunavut, N Canada
9 N9 **Baker Lake** ◎ Nunavut, N Canada
32 H6 **Baker, Mount** ▲ Washington, NW USA
35 R13 **Bakersfield** California, W USA
24 M9 **Bakersfield** Texas, SW USA
21 P9 **Bakersville** North Carolina, SE USA
Bakhābī see Bū Khābī
146 E12 **Bakharden** Turkm. Bäherden; prev. Bakherden. Akhalskiy Velayat, C Turkmenistan
146 F12 **Bakhardok** Turkm. Bokurdak. Akhalskiy Velayat, C Turkmenistan
143 U5 **Bākharz, Kuhhā-ye** ▲▲ NE Iran
152 D13 **Bākhāsar** Rājasthān, NW India
Bakhchisaray see Bakhchysaray
117 T13 **Bakhchysaray** Rus. Bakhchisaray. Respublika Krym, S Ukraine
Bakherden see Bakharden
117 R3 **Bakhmach** Chernihivs'ka Oblast', N Ukraine
142 K6 **Bākhtarān** prev. Kermānshāh, Qahremānshahr. Kermānshāh, W Iran
Bākhtarān see Kermānshāh
143 Q11 **Bakhtegān, Daryācheh-ye** ◎ C Iran
145 X12 **Bakhty** Vostochnyy Kazakhstan, E Kazakhstan
137 Z11 **Bakı** Eng. Baku. ● (Azerbaijan) E Azerbaijan
137 Z11 **Bakı** ✕ E Azerbaijan
136 C13 **Bakır Çayı** ≈ W Turkey
92 L1 **Bakkafjördhur** Austurland, NE Iceland
92 L1 **Bakkaflói** sea area W Norwegian Sea
81 I15 **Bako** Southern, S Ethiopia
76 L15 **Bako** NW Ivory Coast
Bákó see Bacău
111 H23 **Bakony** Eng. Bakony Mountains, Ger. Bakonywald. ▲▲ W Hungary
Bakony Mountains/Bakonywald see Bakony
81 M16 **Bakool** off. Gobolka Bakool. ◈ region W Somalia
79 L15 **Bakouma** Mbomou, SE Central African Republic
129 N15 **Baksan** Kabardino-Balkarskaya Respublika, SW Russian Federation
119 J16 **Bakshty** Hrodzyenskaya Voblasts', W Belarus
Baku see Bakı
194 K12 **Bakutis Coast** physical region Antarctica
Bakwanga see Mbuji-Mayi
145 O15 **Bakyrly** Yuzhnyy Kazakhstan, S Kazakhstan
14 H13 **Bala** Ontario, S Canada
97 J19 **Bala** NW Wales, UK
136 I13 **Balâ** Ankara, C Turkey
170 L7 **Balabac Island** island W Philippines
Balabac, Selat see Balabac Strait
169 V5 **Balabac Strait** var. Selat Balabac. strait Malaysia/Philippines
Ba'labakk see Baalbek
187 P16 **Balabio, Île** island Province Nord, W New Caledonia
116 I14 **Balaci** Teleorman, S Romania
139 S7 **Balad** N Iraq
139 U7 **Balad Rūz** E Iraq
154 J11 **Bālāghāt** Madhya Pradesh, C India
155 F14 **Bālāghāt Range** ▲▲ W India
103 X14 **Balagne** physical region Corse, France, C Mediterranean Sea
105 U5 **Balaguer** Cataluña, NE Spain
105 S3 **Balaïtous** var. Pic de Balaïtous. ▲ France/Spain
Balaïtous, Pic de see Balaïtous
129 O3 **Balakhna** Nizhegorodskaya Oblast', W Russian Federation
122 L12 **Balakhta** Krasnoyarskiy Kray, S Russian Federation
182 I9 **Balaklava** South Australia
Balakleya see Balakliya
117 V6 **Balakliya** Rus. Balakleya. Kharkivs'ka Oblast', E Ukraine
129 Q7 **Balakovo** Saratovskaya Oblast', W Russian Federation
83 P14 **Balama** Cabo Delgado, N Mozambique
169 U6 **Balambangan, Pulau** island East Malaysia
148 L3 **Bālā Morghāb** Laghmān, NW Afghanistan
152 E11 **Bālān** prev. Bāhla. Rājasthān, NW India
116 J10 **Bălan** Hung. Balánbánya. Harghita, C Romania
Balánbánya see Bălan
171 O3 **Balanga** Luzon, N Philippines
154 M12 **Balāngīr** prev. Bolangir. Orissa, E India
129 N8 **Balashov** Saratovskaya Oblast', W Russian Federation
Balasore see Bāleshwar
111 K21 **Balassagyarmat** Nógrád, N Hungary
29 S10 **Balaton** Minnesota, N USA
111 H24 **Balaton** var. Lake Balaton, Ger. Plattensee. ◎ W Hungary
111 I23 **Balatonfüred** var. Füred. Veszprém, W Hungary
Balaton, Lake see Balaton
116 I11 **Bălăuşeri** Ger. Bladenmarkt, Hung. Balavásár. Mureş, C Romania
Balavásár see Bălăuşeri
105 Q11 **Balazote** Castilla-La Mancha, C Spain
Balázsfalva see Blaj
119 F14 **Balbieriškis** Prienai, S Lithuania
186 J7 **Balbi, Mount** ▲ Bougainville Island, NE PNG
58 F11 **Balbina, Represa** ▣ NW Brazil
43 T15 **Balboa** Panamá, C Panama
97 G17 **Balbriggan** Ir. Baile Brigín. E Ireland
Balbunar see Kubrat
81 N17 **Balcad** Shabeellaha Dhexe, C Somalia
61 D23 **Balcarce** Buenos Aires, E Argentina
11 U16 **Balcarres** Saskatchewan, S Canada
114 O8 **Balchik** Dobrich, NE Bulgaria
185 E24 **Balclutha** Otago, South Island, NZ
25 Q12 **Balcones Escarpment** escarpment Texas, SW USA
18 F14 **Bald Eagle Creek** ≈ Pennsylvania, NE USA
Baldenburg see Biały Bór
21 V12 **Bald Head Island** island North Carolina, SE USA
27 W10 **Bald Knob** Arkansas, C USA
30 K17 **Bald Knob** hill Illinois, N USA
Baldohn see Baldone
118 G9 **Baldone** Ger. Baldohn. Rīga, W Latvia
22 I9 **Baldwin** Louisiana, S USA
31 P7 **Baldwin** Michigan, N USA
27 Q4 **Baldwin City** Kansas, C USA
39 N8 **Baldwin Peninsula** headland Alaska, USA
18 H9 **Baldwinsville** New York, NE USA
23 N2 **Baldwyn** Mississippi, S USA
11 W15 **Baldy Mountain** ▲ Manitoba, S Canada
33 T7 **Baldy Mountain** ▲ Montana, NW USA
37 O13 **Baldy Peak** ▲ Arizona, SW USA
Bâle see Basel
105 X9 **Baleares** ◈ autonomous community E Spain
105 X11 **Baleares, Islas** Eng. Balearic Islands. island group Spain, W Mediterranean Sea
Baleares Major see Mallorca
Balearic Islands see Baleares, Islas
Balearic Plain see Algerian Basin
Balearis Minor see Menorca
169 S9 **Baleh, Batang** ≈ East Malaysia
12 J8 **Baleine, Grande Rivière de la** ≈ Quebec, E Canada
12 K7 **Baleine, Petite Rivière de la** ≈ Quebec, SE Canada
13 N6 **Baleine, Rivière à la** ≈ Quebec, E Canada
99 J16 **Balen** Antwerpen, N Belgium
171 O3 **Baler** Luzon, N Philippines
154 P11 **Bāleshwar** prev. Balasore. Orissa, E India
77 S12 **Baléyara** Tillabéri, W Niger
129 T1 **Balezino** Udmurtskaya Respublika, NW Russian Federation
42 J4 **Balfate** Colón, N Honduras
11 O17 **Balfour** British Columbia, SW Canada
29 N3 **Balfour** North Dakota, N USA
Balfrush see Bābol
122 L14 **Balgazyn** Respublika Tyva, S Russian Federation
11 U16 **Balgonie** Saskatchewan, S Canada
Bălgrad see Alba Iulia
81 J19 **Balguda** spring/well S Kenya
158 K6 **Balguntay** Xinjiang Uygur Zizhiqu, NW China
141 R16 **Balḥāf** S Yemen
152 F13 **Bāli** Rājasthān, N India
169 U17 **Bali** ◈ province S Indonesia
169 T17 **Bali** island C Indonesia
111 K16 **Balice** ✕ (Kraków) Małopolskie, S Poland
171 Y14 **Baliem, Sungai** ≈ Irian Jaya, E Indonesia
136 C12 **Balıkesir** Balıkesir, W Turkey
136 C12 **Balıkesir** ◈ province NW Turkey
138 L3 **Balīkh, Nahr** ≈ N Syria
169 V12 **Balikpapan** Borneo, C Indonesia
Bali, Laut see Bali Sea
171 N9 **Balimbing** Tawitawi, SW Philippines
186 B8 **Balimo** Western, SW PNG
Bálinc see Balinţ
101 H23 **Balingen** Baden-Württemberg, SW Germany
116 F11 **Balinţ** Hung. Bálinc. Timiş, W Romania
171 O1 **Balintang Channel** channel N Philippines
138 K3 **Bālis** Ḥalab, N Syria
169 T16 **Bali Sea** Ind. Laut Bali. sea C Indonesia
98 K7 **Balk** Friesland, N Netherlands
121 R6 **Balkan Mountains** Bul./SCr. Stara Planina. ▲▲ Bulgaria/Yugoslavia
146 B9 **Balkanskiy Velayat** Turkm. Balkan Welaýaty. ◈ province W Turkmenistan
Balkan Welaýaty see Balkanskiy Velayat
145 P8 **Balkashino** Akmola, N Kazakhstan
149 O2 **Balkh** anc. Bactra. Balkh, N Afghanistan
149 P2 **Balkh** ◈ province N Afghanistan
145 T13 **Balkhash** Kaz. Balqash. Zhezkazgan, SE Kazakhstan
Balkhash, Lake see Balkhash, Ozero
145 T13 **Balkhash, Ozero** Eng. Lake Balkhash, Kaz. Balqash. ◎ SE Kazakhstan
Balla Balla see Mbalabala
96 H10 **Ballachulish** N Scotland, UK
180 M12 **Balladonia** Western Australia
97 C16 **Ballaghaderreen** Ir. Bealach an Doirín. C Ireland
92 H10 **Ballangen** Nordland, NW Norway
97 H14 **Ballantrae** W Scotland, UK
183 N12 **Ballarat** Victoria, SE Australia
180 K11 **Ballard, Lake** salt lake Western Australia
Ballari see Bellary
76 L11 **Ballé** Koulikoro, W Mali
40 D7 **Ballenas, Bahía de** bay W Mexico
40 D5 **Ballenas, Canal de** channel NW Mexico
195 R17 **Balleny Islands** island group Antarctica
40 J7 **Balleza** var. San Pablo Balleza. Chihuahua, N Mexico
114 M13 **Ballı** Tekirdağ, NW Turkey
153 O13 **Ballia** Uttar Pradesh, N India
183 V4 **Ballina** New South Wales, SE Australia
97 C16 **Ballina** Ir. Béal an Átha. W Ireland
97 D16 **Ballinamore** Ir. Béal an Átha Móir. NW Ireland
97 D18 **Ballinasloe** Ir. Béal Átha na Sluaighe. W Ireland
25 P8 **Ballinger** Texas, SW USA
97 C17 **Ballinrobe** Ir. Baile an Róba. W Ireland
97 A21 **Ballinskelligs Bay** Ir. Bá na Scealg. inlet SW Ireland
97 D15 **Ballintra** Ir. Baile an tSratha. NW Ireland
103 T7 **Ballon d'Alsace** ▲ NE France
Ballon de Guebwiller see Grand Ballon
113 K21 **Ballsh** var. Ballshi. Fier, SW Albania
Ballshi see Ballsh
98 K4 **Ballum** Friesland, N Netherlands
97 F16 **Ballybay** Ir. Béal Átha Beithe. N Ireland
97 E14 **Ballybofey** Ir. Bealach Féich. NW Ireland
97 G14 **Ballycastle** Ir. Baile an Chaistil. N Northern Ireland, UK
97 G15 **Ballyclare** Ir. Bealach Cláir. E Northern Ireland, UK
97 E16 **Ballyconnell** Ir. Béal Átha Conaill. N Ireland
97 C17 **Ballyhaunis** Ir. Beál Átha hAmhnais. W Ireland
97 G14 **Ballymena** Ir. An Baile Meánach. NE Northern Ireland, UK
97 F14 **Ballymoney** Ir. Baile Monaidh. NE Northern Ireland, UK
97 G15 **Ballynahinch** Ir. Baile na hInse. SE Northern Ireland, UK
97 D16 **Ballysadare** Ir. Baile Easa Dara. NW Ireland
97 D15 **Ballyshannon** Ir. Béal Átha Seanaidh. NW Ireland
63 H19 **Balmaceda** Aisén, S Chile
63 G23 **Balmaceda, Cerro** ▲ S Chile
111 N22 **Balmazújváros** Hajdú-Bihar, E Hungary
108 E10 **Balmhorn** ▲ SW Switzerland
182 L12 **Balmoral** Victoria, SE Australia
24 K9 **Balmorhea** Texas, SW USA
Balneario Claromecó see Claromecó
Balochistān see Baluchistān
82 B13 **Balombo** Port. Norton de Matos, Vila Norton de Matos. Benguela, W Angola
82 B13 **Balombo** ≈ W Angola
181 X10 **Balonne River** ≈ Queensland, E Australia
152 E13 **Bālotra** Rājasthān, N India
145 V14 **Balpyk Bi** prev. Kirovskiy Kaz. Kirov. Almaty, SE Kazakhstan
Balqā'/Balqā', Muḥāfaẓat al see Al Balqā'
Balqash see Balkhash/Balkhash, Ozero
152 M12 **Balrāmpur** Uttar Pradesh, N India
182 M9 **Balranald** New South Wales, SE Australia
116 H14 **Balş** Olt, S Romania
14 H11 **Balsam Creek** Ontario, S Canada
30 I5 **Balsam Lake** Wisconsin, N USA
14 I14 **Balsam Lake** ◎ Ontario, SE Canada
59 M14 **Balsas** Maranhão, E Brazil
40 M15 **Balsas, Río** var. Río Mexcala. ≈ S Mexico
43 W16 **Balsas, Río** ≈ SE Panama
119 O18 **Bal'shavik** Rus. Bol'shevik. Homyel'skaya Voblasts', SE Belarus
95 O15 **Bålsta** Uppsala, C Sweden
108 E7 **Balsthal** Solothurn, NW Switzerland
117 O8 **Balta** Odes'ka Oblast', SW Ukraine
119 H14 **Baltaji Voke** Vilnius, SE Lithuania
105 N5 **Baltanás** Castilla-León, N Spain
61 E16 **Baltasar Brum** Artigas, N Uruguay
116 M9 **Bălţi** Rus. Bel'tsy. N Moldova
Baltic Port see Paldiski
118 B10 **Baltic Sea** Ger. Ostee, Rus. Baltiskoye More. sea N Europe
21 X3 **Baltimore** Maryland, NE USA
31 T13 **Baltimore** Ohio, N USA
21 X3 **Baltimore-Washington** ✕ Maryland, E USA
Baltischport/Baltiski see Paldiski
Baltiskoye More see Baltic Sea
119 A14 **Baltiysk** Ger. Pillau. Kaliningradskaya Oblast', W Russian Federation
Baltkrievija see Belarus
Balūchestān va Sīstān see Sīstān va Balūchestān
148 M12 **Baluchistān** var. Balochistān, Beluchistan. ◈ province SW Pakistan
171 P5 **Balud** Masbate, N Philippines
169 T9 **Balui, Batang** ≈ East Malaysia
153 S13 **Bālurghat** West Bengal, NE India
118 J8 **Balvi** Balvi, NE Latvia
147 W7 **Balykchy** Kir. Ysyk-Köl; prev. Issyk-Kul', Rybach'ye. Issyk-Kul'skaya Oblast', NE Kyrgyzstan
56 B7 **Balzar** Guayas, W Ecuador
108 I8 **Balzers** S Liechtenstein
143 T12 **Bam** Kermān, SE Iran
77 Y13 **Bama** Borno, NE Nigeria
76 L12 **Bamako** ● (Mali) Capital District, SW Mali
77 P10 **Bamba** Gao, C Mali
42 M8 **Bambana, Río** ≈ NE Nicaragua
79 J15 **Bambari** Ouaka, C Central African Republic
181 W5 **Bambaroo** Queensland, NE Australia
101 K19 **Bamberg** Bayern, SE Germany
21 R14 **Bamberg** South Carolina, SE USA
79 M16 **Bambesa** Orientale, N Dem. Rep. Congo (Zaire)
76 G11 **Bambey** W Senegal
79 H16 **Bambio** Sangha-Mbaéré, SW Central African Republic
83 I24 **Bamboesberge** ▲ S South Africa
79 D14 **Bamenda** Nord-Ouest, W Cameroon
10 K17 **Bamfield** Vancouver Island, British Columbia, SW Canada
146 E12 **Bami** Turkm. Bamy. Akhalskiy Velayat, C Turkmenistan
149 P4 **Bāmīān** var. Bāmiān. Bāmīān, NE Afghanistan
149 O4 **Bāmīān** ◈ province C Afghanistan
79 J14 **Bamingui** Bamingui-Bangoran, C Central African Republic
78 J13 **Bamingui** ≈ N Central African Republic
78 J13 **Bamingui-Bangoran** ◈ prefecture N Central African Republic
143 V13 **Bampūr** Sīstān va Balūchestān, SE Iran
186 C8 **Bamu** ≈ SW PNG
Bamy see Bami
Bán see Bánovce nad Bebravou
81 N17 **Banaadir** off. Gobolka Banaadir. ◈ region S Somalia
191 N3 **Banaba** var. Ocean Island. island Tungaru, W Kiribati
59 O14 **Banabuiú, Açude** ▣ NE Brazil
57 O19 **Bañados del Izozog** salt lake SE Bolivia
97 D18 **Banagher** Ir. Beannchar. C Ireland
79 M17 **Banalia** Orientale, N Dem. Rep. Congo (Zaire)
76 L12 **Banamba** Koulikoro, W Mali
40 G4 **Banámichi** Sonora, NW Mexico
181 Y9 **Banana** Queensland, E Australia
191 Z2 **Banana** prev. Main Camp. Kiritimati, E Kiribati
59 K16 **Bananal, Ilha do** island C Brazil
23 Y12 **Banana River** lagoon Florida, SE USA
151 Q22 **Bananga** Andaman and Nicobar Islands, India, NE Indian Ocean
Banaras see Vārānasi
114 N13 **Banarlı** Tekirdağ, NW Turkey
152 H12 **Banās** ≈ N India
75 Z11 **Banâs, Râs** headland E Egypt
112 N10 **Banatski Karlovac** Serbia, NE Yugoslavia
141 P16 **Banā, Wādī** dry watercourse SW Yemen
136 E14 **Banaz** Uşak, W Turkey
136 E14 **Banaz Çayı** ≈ W Turkey
159 P14 **Banbar** Xizang Zizhiqu, W China
97 G15 **Banbridge** Ir. Droichead na Banna. SE Northern Ireland, UK
Ban Bua Yai see Bua Yai
97 M21 **Banbury** S England, UK
167 O7 **Ban Chiang Dao** Chiang Mai, NW Thailand
96 K9 **Banchory** NE Scotland, UK
14 J13 **Bancroft** Ontario, SE Canada
33 R15 **Bancroft** Idaho, NW USA
29 U11 **Bancroft** Iowa, C USA
154 I9 **Banda** Madhya Pradesh, C India
152 L13 **Bānda** Uttar Pradesh, N India
168 F7 **Bandaaceh** var. Banda Atjeh; prev. Koetaradja, Kutaradja, Kutaraja. Sumatera, W Indonesia
Banda Atjeh see Bandaaceh
171 S14 **Banda, Kepulauan** island group E Indonesia
Banda, Laut see Banda Sea
77 N17 **Bandama** var. Bandama Fleuve. ≈ S Ivory Coast
77 N15 **Bandama Blanc** ≈ C Ivory Coast
Bandama Fleuve see Bandama
Bandar 'Abbās see Bandar-e 'Abbās
153 W16 **Bandarban** Chittagong, SE Bangladesh
80 Q13 **Bandarbeyla** var. Bender Beila, Bender Beyla. Bari, NE Somalia
143 R14 **Bandar-e 'Abbās** var. Bandar 'Abbās; prev. Gombroon. Hormozgān, S Iran
142 M3 **Bandar-e Anzalī** Gīlān, NW Iran
143 N12 **Bandar-e Būshehr** var. Būshehr, Eng. Bushire. Būshehr, S Iran
142 M11 **Bandar-e Gonāveh** var. Ganāveh; prev. Gonāveh. Būshehr, SW Iran
143 R14 **Bandar-e Khamīr** Hormozgān, S Iran
143 Q14 **Bandar-e Langeh** var. Bandar-e Lengeh, Lingeh. Hormozgān, S Iran
Bandar-e Lengeh see Bandar-e Langeh
142 L10 **Bandar-e Māhshahr** var. Māh-Shahr; prev. Bandar-e Ma'shūr. Khūzestān, SW Iran
Bandar-e Ma'shūr see Bandar-e Māhshahr
143 O14 **Bandar-e Nakhīlū** Hormozgān, S Iran
Bandar-e Shāh see Bandar-e Torkaman
143 P4 **Bandar-e Torkaman** var. Bandar-e Torkeman, Bandar-e Torkman; prev. Bandar-e Shāh. Golestān, N Iran
Bandar-e Torkeman/Bandar-e Torkman see Bandar-e Torkaman
Bandar Kassim see Boosaaso
168 M15 **Bandarlampung** prev. Tanjungkarang, Teloekbetoeng, Telukbetung. Sumatera, W Indonesia
Bandar Maharani see Muar
Bandar Masulipatnam see Machilīpatnam
Bandar Penggaram see Batu Pahat
169 T7 **Bandar Seri Begawan** prev. Brunei Town. ● (Brunei) N Brunei

◆ Country ● Country Capital ◇ Dependent Territory ○ Dependent Territory Capital ◈ Administrative Region ✕ International Airport ▲ Mountain ▲▲ Mountain Range Volcano ≈ River ◎ Lake ▣ Reservoir

169 T7 **Bandar Seri Begawan** ✕ N Brunei
171 R15 **Banda Sea** var. Laut Banda. sea E Indonesia
104 H5 **Bande** Galicia, NW Spain
59 G15 **Bandeirantes** Mato Grosso, W Brazil
59 N20 **Bandeira, Pico da** ▲ SE Brazil
83 K19 **Bandelierkop** Northern, NE South Africa
62 L8 **Bandera** Santiago del Estero, N Argentina
25 Q11 **Bandera** Texas, SW USA
40 J13 **Banderas, Bahía de** bay W Mexico
77 O11 **Bandiagara** Mopti, C Mali
152 I12 **Bāndīkūi** Rājasthān, N India
136 C11 **Bandırma** var. Penderma. Balıkesir, NW Turkey
Bandjarmasin see Banjarmasin
Bandoeng see Bandung
97 C21 **Bandon** Ir. Droicheadna Bandan. SW Ireland
32 E14 **Bandon** Oregon, NW USA
167 R8 **Ban Dong Bang** Nong Khai, E Thailand
167 Q6 **Ban Donkon** Oudômxai, N Laos
172 J14 **Bandrélé** SE Mayotte
79 H20 **Bandundu** prev. Banningville. Bandundu, W Dem. Rep. Congo (Zaire)
79 I21 **Bandundu** off. Région de Bandundu. ◈ region W Dem. Rep. Congo (Zaire)
169 O16 **Bandung** prev. Bandoeng. Jawa, C Indonesia
116 L15 **Băneasa** Constanţa, SW Romania
142 J4 **Bāneh** Kordestān, N Iran
44 I7 **Banes** Holguín, E Cuba
11 P16 **Banff** Alberta, SW Canada
96 K8 **Banff** NE Scotland, UK
96 K8 **Banff** cultural region NE Scotland, UK
Bánffyhunyad see Huedin
77 N14 **Banfora** SW Burkina
155 H19 **Bangalore** Karnātaka, S India
153 S16 **Bangaon** West Bengal, NE India
79 L15 **Bangassou** Mbomou, SE Central African Republic
186 D7 **Bangeta, Mount** ▲ C PNG
171 P12 **Banggai, Kepulauan** island group C Indonesia
177 Q12 **Banggai, Pulau** island Kepulauan Banggai, N Indonesia
171 X13 **Banggelapa** Irian Jaya, E Indonesia
Banggi see Banggi, Pulau
169 V6 **Banggi, Pulau** var. Banggi. island East Malaysia
121 P13 **Banghāzī** Eng. Bengazi, Benghazi, It. Bengasi. NE Libya
Bang Hieng see Xé Banghiang
169 P11 **Bangkai, Tanjung** var. Bankai. headland Borneo, N Indonesia
169 S16 **Bangkalan** Pulau Madura, C Indonesia
169 N12 **Bangka, Pulau** island W Indonesia
169 N13 **Bangka, Selat** strait Sumatera, W Indonesia
168 J11 **Bangkinang** Sumatera, W Indonesia
168 K12 **Bangko** Sumatera, W Indonesia
Bangkok see Krung Thep
Bangkok, Bight of see Krung Thep, Ao
153 T14 **Bangladesh** off. People's Republic of Bangladesh; prev. East Pakistan. ◆ republic S Asia
167 V13 **Ba Ngoi** Khanh Hoa, S Vietnam
152 K5 **Bangong Co** var. Pangong Tso. ◎ China/India see also Pangong Tso
97 G15 **Bangor** Ir. Beannchar. E Northern Ireland, UK
97 I18 **Bangor** NW Wales, UK
19 R6 **Bangor** Maine, NE USA
18 I14 **Bangor** Pennsylvania, NE USA
67 R8 **Bangoran** ≈ S Central African Republic
Bang Phra see Trat
Bang Pla Soi see Chon Buri
25 Q8 **Bangs** Texas, SW USA
167 N13 **Bang Saphan** var. Bang Saphan Yai. Prachuap Khiri Khan, SW Thailand
Bang Saphan Yai see Bang Saphan
36 I8 **Bangs, Mount** ▲ Arizona, SW USA
93 E15 **Bangsund** Nord-Trøndelag, C Norway
171 O2 **Bangued** Luzon, N Philippines
79 I15 **Bangui** ● (Central African Republic) Ombella-Mpoko, SW Central African Republic
79 I15 **Bangui** ✕ Ombella-Mpoko, SW Central African Republic
83 N16 **Bangula** Southern, S Malawi
Bangwaketse see Southern
82 K12 **Bangweulu, Lake** var. Lake Bengweulu. ◎ N Zambia
Banhā see Benha
Ban Hat Yai see Hat Yai
167 Q7 **Ban Hin Heup** Viangchan, C Laos
Ban Houayxay/Ban Houei Sai see Houayxay
167 O12 **Ban Hua Hin** var. Hua Hin. Prachuap Khiri Khan, SW Thailand
79 L14 **Bani** Haute-Kotto, E Central African Republic
77 N12 **Bani** ≈ S Mali
45 O9 **Baní** S Dominican Republic
Banias see Bāniyās
77 S11 **Bani Bangou** Tillabéri, SW Niger
76 M12 **Banifing** var. Ngorolaka. ≈ Burkina/Mali
77 R13 **Banikoara** N Benin
Banī Mazār see Beni Mazâr
114 K8 **Baniski Lom** ≈ N Bulgaria
21 U7 **Banister River** ≈ Virginia, NE USA
Banī Suwayf see Beni Suef
75 O8 **Banī Walīd** NW Libya
138 H5 **Bāniyās** var. Banias, Baniyas, Paneas. Tarṭūs, W Syria
113 K14 **Banja** Serbia, W Yugoslavia
Banjak, Kepulauan see Banyak, Kepulauan
112 J12 **Banja Koviljača** Serbia, W Yugoslavia
112 G11 **Banja Luka** Republika Srpska, NW Bosnia and Herzegovina
169 T13 **Banjarmasin** prev. Bandjarmasin. Borneo, C Indonesia
76 F11 **Banjul** prev. Bathurst. ● (Gambia) W Gambia
76 F11 **Banjul** ✕ W Gambia
Bank see Bankä
137 Y13 **Bankä** Rus. Bank. SE Azerbaijan
167 S11 **Ban Kadian** var. Ban Kadiene. Champasak, S Laos
Ban Kadiene see Ban Kadian
Bankai see Bangkai, Tanjung
166 M14 **Ban Kam Phuam** Phangnga, SW Thailand
Ban Kantang see Kantang
77 O11 **Bankass** Mopti, S Mali
95 L19 **Bankeryd** Jönköping, S Sweden
83 K16 **Banket** Mashonaland West, N Zimbabwe
167 T11 **Ban Khamphô** Attapu, S Laos
23 O4 **Bankhead Lake** ▣ Alabama, S USA
77 Q11 **Bankilaré** Tillabéri, SW Niger
Banks, Îles see Banks Islands
10 I14 **Banks Island** island British Columbia, SW Canada
187 R12 **Banks Islands** Fr. Îles Banks. island group N Vanuatu
23 U8 **Banks Lake** ◎ Georgia, SE USA
32 K8 **Banks Lake** ▣ Washington, NW USA
185 I19 **Banks Peninsula** peninsula South Island, NZ
183 Q15 **Banks Strait** strait SW Tasman Sea
Ban Kui Nua see Kui Buri
153 R16 **Bānkura** West Bengal, NE India
167 S8 **Ban Lakxao** var. Lak Sao. Bolikhamxai, C Laos
167 O16 **Ban Lam Phai** Songkhla, SW Thailand
Ban Mae Sot see Mae Sot
Ban Mae Suai see Mae Suai
Ban Mak Khaeng see Udon Thani
166 M3 **Banmauk** Sagaing, N Burma
Banmo see Bhamo
167 T10 **Ban Mun-Houamuang** S Laos
97 F14 **Bann** var. Lower Bann, Upper Bann. ≈ N Northern Ireland, UK
167 S10 **Ban Nadou** Salavan, S Laos
167 S9 **Ban Nakala** Savannakhét, S Laos
167 Q8 **Ban Nakha** Viangchan, C Laos
167 S9 **Ban Nakham** Khammouan, S Laos
167 P7 **Ban Namoun** Xaignabouli, N Laos
167 O17 **Ban Nang Sata** Yala, SW Thailand
167 N15 **Ban Na San** Surat Thani, SW Thailand
167 R7 **Ban Nasi** Xiangkhoang, N Laos
44 I3 **Bannerman Town** Eleuthera Island, C Bahamas
35 V15 **Banning** California, W USA
Banningville see Bandundu
167 S11 **Ban Nongsim** Champasak, S Laos
149 S7 **Bannu** prev. Edwardesabad. North-West Frontier Province, NW Pakistan
Bañolas see Banyoles
56 C7 **Baños** Tungurahua, C Ecuador
Bánovce see Bánovce nad Bebravou
111 I19 **Bánovce nad Bebravou** var. Bánovce, Hung. Bán. Trenčiansky Kraj, W Slovakia
112 I12 **Banovići** Federacija Bosna I Hercegovina, E Bosnia and Herzegovina
Banow see Andarāb
Ban Pak Phanang see Pak Phanang
167 O7 **Ban Pan Nua** Lampang, NW Thailand
167 Q9 **Ban Phai** Khon Kaen, E Thailand
167 T9 **Ban Phou A Douk** Khammouan, C Laos
167 Q8 **Ban Phu** Uthai Thani, W Thailand
167 O11 **Ban Pong** Ratchaburi, W Thailand
190 I3 **Banraeaba** Tarawa, W Kiribati
167 N10 **Ban Sai Yok** Kanchanaburi, W Thailand
Ban Sattahip/Ban Sattahipp see Sattahip
Ban Sichon see Sichon
Ban Si Racha see Siracha
111 J19 **Banská Bystrica** Ger. Neusohl, Hung. Besztercebánya. Banskobystrický Kraj, C Slovakia
111 K20 **Banskobystrický Kraj** ◈ region C Slovakia
167 R8 **Ban Sôppheung** Bolikhamxai, C Laos
Ban Sop Prap see Sop Prap
152 G15 **Bānswāra** Rājasthān, N India
167 N15 **Ban Ta Khun** Surat Thani, SW Thailand
Ban Takua Pa see Takua Pa
167 S8 **Ban Talak** Khammouan, C Laos
77 R15 **Bantè** W Benin
167 Q8 **Ban Thabôk** Bolikhamxai, C Laos
167 T9 **Ban Tôp** Savannakhét, S Laos
97 B21 **Bantry** Ir. Beanntraí. SW Ireland
97 A21 **Bantry Bay** Ir. Bá Bheanntraí. bay SW Ireland
155 F19 **Bantvāl** var. Bantwāl. Karnātaka, E India
Bantwāl see Bantvāl
114 N9 **Banya** Burgas, E Bulgaria
168 G10 **Banyak, Kepulauan** prev. Kepulauan Banjak. island group NW Indonesia
105 U8 **Banya, La** headland E Spain
79 E14 **Banyo** Adamaoua, NW Cameroon
105 X4 **Banyoles** var. Bañolas. Cataluña, NE Spain
167 N16 **Ban Yong Sata** Trang, SW Thailand
195 X14 **Banzare Coast** physical region Antarctica
173 Q14 **Banzare Seamounts** undersea feature S Indian Ocean
Banzart see Bizerte
Baochang see Taibus Qi
161 O3 **Baoding** var. Pao-ting; prev. Tsingyuan. Hebei, E China
Baoebaoe see Baubau
Baoi, Oileán see Dursey Island
160 J6 **Baoji** var. Pao-chi, Paoki. Shaanxi, C China
186 L8 **Baolo** Santa Isabel, N Solomon Islands
167 U13 **Bao Lôc** Lâm Đông, S Vietnam
163 Z7 **Baoqing** Heilongjiang, NE China
Baoqing see Shaoyang
79 H15 **Baoro** Nana-Mambéré, W Central African Republic
160 E12 **Baoshan** var. Pao-shan. Yunnan, SW China
163 N13 **Baotou** var. Pao-t'ou, Paotow. Nei Mongol Zizhiqu, N China
76 L14 **Baoulé** ≈ S Mali
76 K12 **Baoulé** ≈ W Mali
103 O2 **Bapaume** Pas-de-Calais, N France
14 J13 **Baptiste Lake** ◎ Ontario, SE Canada
Baqanas see Bakanas
Baqbaqty see Bakbakty
159 P14 **Baqên** var. Dartang. Xizang Zizhiqu, W China
138 F14 **Bāqir, Jabal** ▲ S Jordan
139 T7 **Ba'qūbah** var. Qubba. C Iraq
62 H5 **Baquedano** Antofagasta, N Chile
116 M6 **Bar** Vinnyts'ka Oblast', C Ukraine
113 J18 **Bar** It. Antivari. Montenegro, SW Yugoslavia
80 E10 **Bara** Northern Kordofan, C Sudan
81 M18 **Baraawe** It. Brava. Shabeellaha Hoose, S Somalia
152 M12 **Bāra Banki** Uttar Pradesh, N India
30 L8 **Baraboo** Wisconsin, N USA
30 K8 **Baraboo Range** hill range Wisconsin, N USA
Baracaldo see San Vicente de Barakaldo
15 Y6 **Barachois** Quebec, SE Canada
44 J7 **Baracoa** Guantánamo, E Cuba
61 C19 **Baradero** Buenos Aires, E Argentina
183 R6 **Baradine** New South Wales, SE Australia
Baraf Daja Islands see Damar, Kepulauan
154 M12 **Baragarh** Orissa, E India
81 I17 **Baragoi** Rift Valley, W Kenya
45 N9 **Barahona** SW Dominican Republic
153 W13 **Barail Range** ▲ NE India
80 I9 **Baraka** var. Barka, Ar. Khawr Barakah. seasonal river Eritrea/Sudan
80 G10 **Barakat** Gezira, C Sudan
Barakī see Barakī Barak
149 Q6 **Barakī Barak** var. Barakī, Baraki Rajan. Lowgar, E Afghanistan
Baraki Rajan see Barakī Barak
154 N11 **Barākot** Orissa, E India
55 S7 **Barama River** ≈ N Guyana
155 E14 **Bārāmati** Mahārāshtra, W India
152 H5 **Bāramūla** Jammu and Kashmir, NW India
119 N14 **Baran'** Vitsyebskaya Voblasts', NE Belarus
152 I14 **Bārān** Rājasthān, N India
139 U4 **Barānān, Shākh-i** ▲ E Iraq
119 I17 **Baranavichy** Pol. Baranowicze, Rus. Baranovichi. Brestskaya Voblasts', SW Belarus
123 T6 **Baranikha** Chukotskiy Avtonomnyy Okrug, NE Russian Federation
116 M4 **Baranivka** Zhytomyrs'ka Oblast', N Ukraine
39 W14 **Baranof Island** island Alexander Archipelago, Alaska, USA
Baranovichi/ Baranowicze see Baranavichy
111 N15 **Baranów Sandomierski** Podkarpackie, SE Poland
111 I26 **Baranya** off. Baranya Megye. ◈ county S Hungary
153 R13 **Barāri** Bihār, NE India
22 L10 **Barataria Bay** bay Louisiana, S USA
Barat Daya, Kepulauan see Damar, Kepulauan
118 L12 **Baravukha** Rus. Borovukha. Vitsyebskaya Voblasts', N Belarus
54 E11 **Baraya** Huila, C Colombia
59 M21 **Barbacena** Minas Gerais, SE Brazil
54 B13 **Barbacoas** Nariño, SW Colombia
54 L6 **Barbacoas** Aragua, N Venezuela
45 Z13 **Barbados** ◆ commonwealth republic SE West Indies
47 S3 **Barbados** island Barbados
105 U11 **Barbaria, Cap de** var. Cabo de Berberia. headland Formentera, E Spain
114 N13 **Barbaros** Tekirdağ, NW Turkey
74 A11 **Barbas, Cap** headland S Western Sahara
105 T5 **Barbastro** Aragón, NE Spain
104 K16 **Barbate** ≈ SW Spain
104 K16 **Barbate de Franco** Andalucía, S Spain
9 N1 **Barbeau Peak** ▲ Nunavut, N Canada
83 K21 **Barberton** Mpumalanga, NE South Africa
31 U12 **Barberton** Ohio, N USA
102 K12 **Barbezieux-St-Hilaire** Charente, W France
54 G9 **Barbosa** Santander, C Colombia
21 N7 **Barbourville** Kentucky, S USA
45 W9 **Barbuda** island N Antigua and Barbuda
181 W8 **Barcaldine** Queensland, E Australia
Barcarozsnyó see Râşnov
104 I11 **Barcarrota** Extremadura, W Spain
Barcău see Berettyó
Barce see Al Marj
107 L23 **Barcellona** var. Barcellona Pozzo di Gotto. Sicilia, Italy, C Mediterranean Sea
Barcellona Pozzo di Gotto see Barcellona
105 W6 **Barcelona** anc. Barcino, Barcinona. Cataluña, E Spain
55 N5 **Barcelona** Anzoátegui, NE Venezuela
105 S5 **Barcelona** ◈ province Cataluña, NE Spain
105 W6 **Barcelona** ✕ Cataluña, E Spain
103 U14 **Barcelonnette** Alpes-de-Haute-Provence, SE France
58 E12 **Barcelos** Amazonas, N Brazil
104 G5 **Barcelos** Braga, N Portugal
110 I10 **Barcin** Ger. Bartschin. Kujawski-pomorskie, C Poland
Barcino/Barcinona see Barcelona
Barcoo see Cooper Creek
111 H26 **Barcs** Somogy, SW Hungary
137 W11 **Bärdä** Rus. Barda. C Azerbaijan
78 H5 **Bardaï** Borkou-Ennedi-Tibesti, N Chad
139 R2 **Bardaṛash** N Iraq
139 Q7 **Bardasah** SW Iraq
153 S16 **Barddhamān** West Bengal, NE India
111 N18 **Bardejov** Ger. Bartfeld, Hung. Bártfa. Prešovský Kraj, E Slovakia
105 R4 **Bárdenas Reales** physical region N Spain
Bardera/Bardere see Baardheere
Bardesīr see Bardsīr
92 K3 **Bárdharbunga** ▲ C Iceland
Bardhë, Drini i see Beli Drim
106 E9 **Bardi** Emilia-Romagna, C Italy
106 A8 **Bardonecchia** Piemonte, W Italy
97 H19 **Bardsey Island** island NW Wales, UK
143 S11 **Bardsīr** var. Bardesīr, Mashīz. Kermān, C Iran
20 L6 **Bardstown** Kentucky, S USA
Barduli see Barletta
20 G7 **Bardwell** Kentucky, S USA
152 K11 **Bareilly** var. Bareli. Uttar Pradesh, N India
Bareli see Bareilly
98 H13 **Barendrecht** Zuid-Holland, SW Netherlands
102 M3 **Barentin** Seine-Maritime, N France
92 N3 **Barentsburg** Spitsbergen, W Svalbard
Barentsevo More/Barents Havet see Barents Sea
92 O3 **Barentsøya** island E Svalbard
197 T11 **Barents Plain** undersea feature N Barents Sea
127 P3 **Barents Sea** Nor. Barents Havet, Rus. Barentsevo More. sea Arctic Ocean
197 U14 **Barents Trough** undersea feature SW Barents Sea
80 I9 **Barentu** W Eritrea
102 J3 **Barfleur** Manche, N France
102 J3 **Barfleur, Pointe de** headland N France
Barfrush/Barfurush see Bābol
158 H14 **Barga** Xizang Zizhiqu, W China
105 N9 **Bargas** Castilla-La Mancha, C Spain
81 I15 **Bargē** Southern, S Ethiopia
106 A9 **Barge** Piemonte, NE Italy
153 U16 **Barguna** Khulna, S Bangladesh
Bärguşad see Vorotan
123 N13 **Barguzin** Respublika Buryatiya, S Russian Federation
153 O13 **Barhaj** Uttar Pradesh, N India
183 N10 **Barham** New South Wales, SE Australia
152 J12 **Barhan** Uttar Pradesh, N India
19 S7 **Bar Harbor** Mount Desert Island, Maine, NE USA
153 R14 **Barharwa** Bihār, NE India
153 P15 **Barhi** Bihār, N India
107 O17 **Bari** var. Bari delle Puglie; anc. Barium. Puglia, SE Italy
80 P12 **Bari** off. Gobolka Bari. ◈ region NE Somalia
167 T14 **Ba Ria** Ba Ria-Vung Tau, S Vietnam
Bāridah see Al Bāridah
Bari delle Puglie see Bari
Barikot see Barīkowṭ
149 T4 **Barīkowṭ** var. Barikot. Kunar, NE Afghanistan
42 C4 **Barillas** var. Santa Cruz Barillas. Huehuetenango, NW Guatemala
54 J6 **Barinas** Barinas, W Venezuela
54 I7 **Barinas** off. Estado Barinas; prev. Zamora. ◈ state C Venezuela
54 I6 **Barinitas** Barinas, NW Venezuela
154 P11 **Bāripada** Orissa, E India
60 K9 **Bariri** São Paulo, S Brazil
75 W11 **Bârîs** S Egypt
152 G14 **Bari Sādri** Rājasthān, N India
153 U16 **Barisal** Khulna, S Bangladesh
168 I10 **Barisan, Pegunungan** ▲ Sumatera, W Indonesia
169 T12 **Barito, Sungai** ≈ Borneo, C Indonesia
Barium see Bari
Barka see Baraka
Barka see Al Marj
160 H8 **Barkam** Sichuan, C China
118 J9 **Barkava** Madona, C Latvia
10 M15 **Barkerville** British Columbia, SW Canada
14 J12 **Bark Lake** ◎ Ontario, SE Canada
20 H7 **Barkley, Lake** ▣ Kentucky/Tennessee, S USA
10 K17 **Barkley Sound** inlet British Columbia, W Canada
83 J24 **Barkly East** Afr. Barkly-Oos. Eastern Cape, SE South Africa
Barkly-Oos see Barkly East
181 S4 **Barkly Tableland** plateau Northern Territory/Queensland, N Australia
Barkly-Wes see Barkly West
83 H22 **Barkly West** Afr. Barkly-Wes. Northern Cape, N South Africa
159 O5 **Barkol** var. Barkol Kazak Zizhixian. Xinjiang Uygur Zizhiqu, NW China
159 O5 **Barkol Hu** ◎ NW China
Barkol Kazak Zizhixian see Barkol
30 J3 **Bark Point** headland Wisconsin, N USA
25 P11 **Barksdale** Texas, SW USA
Bar Kunar see Asmār
116 L11 **Bârlad** prev. Bîrlad. Vaslui, E Romania
116 M11 **Bârlad** prev. Bîrlad. ≈ E Romania
76 D9 **Barlavento, Ilhas de** var. Windward Islands. island group N Cape Verde
103 R5 **Bar-le-Duc** var. Bar-sur-Ornain. Meuse, NE France
180 K11 **Barlee, Lake** ◎ Western Australia
180 H8 **Barlee Range** ▲ Western Australia
107 N16 **Barletta** anc. Barduli. Puglia, SE Italy
110 E10 **Barlinek** Ger. Berlinchen. Zachodniopomorskie, NW Poland
27 S11 **Barling** Arkansas, C USA
171 U12 **Barma** Irian Jaya, E Indonesia
183 Q9 **Barmedman** New South Wales, SE Australia
Barmen-Elberfeld see Wuppertal
152 D12 **Bārmer** Rājasthān, NW India
182 K9 **Barmera** South Australia
97 I19 **Barmouth** NW Wales, UK
154 F10 **Barnagar** Madhya Pradesh, C India
152 H9 **Barnāla** Punjab, NW India
97 L15 **Barnard Castle** N England, UK
183 O6 **Barnato** New South Wales, SE Australia
122 I13 **Barnaul** Altayskiy Kray, C Russian Federation
109 V8 **Bärnbach** Steiermark, SE Austria
18 K16 **Barnegat** New Jersey, NE USA
23 S4 **Barnesville** Georgia, SE USA
29 R6 **Barnesville** Minnesota, N USA
31 U13 **Barnesville** Ohio, N USA
98 K11 **Barneveld** var. Barnveld. Gelderland, C Netherlands
25 O9 **Barnhart** Texas, SW USA
27 P8 **Barnsdall** Oklahoma, C USA
97 M17 **Barnsley** N England, UK
19 Q12 **Barnstable** Massachusetts, NE USA
97 I23 **Barnstaple** SW England, UK
Barnveld see Barneveld
21 Q14 **Barnwell** South Carolina, SE USA
67 U8 **Baro** var. Baro Wenz. ≈ Ethiopia/Sudan
77 U15 **Baro** Niger, C Nigeria
Baro see Baro Wenz
Baroda see Vadodara
149 U2 **Baroghil Pass** var. Kowtal-e Barowghīl. pass Afghanistan/Pakistan
119 Q17 **Baron'ki** Rus. Boron'ki. Mahilyowskaya Voblasts', E Belarus
182 J9 **Barossa Valley** valley South Australia
Baroui see Salisbury
81 H14 **Baro Wenz** var. Baro, Nahr Barū. ≈ Ethiopia/Sudan
153 U12 **Barpeta** Assam, NE India
31 S7 **Barques, Pointe Aux** headland Michigan, N USA
54 I5 **Barquisimeto** Lara, NW Venezuela
59 N16 **Barra** Bahia, E Brazil
96 E9 **Barra** island NW Scotland, UK
183 T5 **Barraba** New South Wales, SE Australia
60 L9 **Barra Bonita** São Paulo, S Brazil
64 J12 **Barracuda Fracture Zone** var. Fifteen Twenty Fracture Zone. tectonic feature SW Atlantic Ocean
64 G11 **Barracuda Ridge** undersea feature N Atlantic Ocean
43 N12 **Barra del Colorado** Limón, NE Costa Rica
43 N9 **Barra de Río Grande** Región Autónoma Atlántico Sur, E Nicaragua
82 A11 **Barra do Cuanza** Luanda, NW Angola
60 O9 **Barra do Piraí** Rio de Janeiro, SE Brazil
61 D16 **Barra do Quaraí** Rio Grande do Sul, SE Brazil
59 G14 **Barra do São Manuel** Pará, N Brazil
83 N19 **Barra Falsa, Ponta da** headland S Mozambique
96 E10 **Barra Head** headland NW Scotland, UK
Barram see Baram, Batang
60 O9 **Barra Mansa** Rio de Janeiro, SE Brazil
57 D14 **Barranca** Lima, W Peru
54 F8 **Barrancabermeja** Santander, N Colombia
54 H4 **Barrancas** La Guajira, N Colombia
54 J6 **Barrancas** Barinas, NW Venezuela
55 Q6 **Barrancas** Monagas, NE Venezuela
54 F6 **Barranco de Loba** Bolívar, N Colombia
104 I12 **Barrancos** Beja, S Portugal
62 N7 **Barranqueras** Chaco, N Argentina
54 E4 **Barranquilla** Atlántico, N Colombia
83 N20 **Barra, Ponta da** headland S Mozambique
105 P11 **Barrax** Castilla-La Mancha, C Spain
19 N11 **Barre** Massachusetts, NE USA
18 M7 **Barre** Vermont, NE USA
59 M17 **Barreiras** Bahia, E Brazil
104 F11 **Barreiro** Setúbal, W Portugal
65 C26 **Barren Island** island S Falkland Islands
20 K7 **Barren River Lake** ▣ Kentucky, S USA
60 L7 **Barretos** São Paulo, S Brazil
11 P14 **Barrhead** Alberta, SW Canada
14 G14 **Barrie** Ontario, S Canada
11 N16 **Barrière** British Columbia, SW Canada
14 H8 **Barrière, Lac** ◎ Quebec, SE Canada
182 L6 **Barrier Range** hill range New South Wales, SE Australia
42 G3 **Barrier Reef** reef E Belize
188 C16 **Barrigada** C Guam
Barrington Island see Santa Fe, Isla
183 T7 **Barrington Tops** ▲ New South Wales, SE Australia
183 O4 **Barringun** New South Wales, SE Australia
59 K18 **Barro Alto** Goiás, S Brazil
59 N14 **Barro Duro** Piauí, NE Brazil
30 I5 **Barron** Wisconsin, N USA
14 J12 **Barron** ≈ Ontario, SE Canada
61 H15 **Barros Cassal** Rio Grande do Sul, S Brazil
45 P14 **Barrouallie** Saint Vincent, W Saint Vincent and the Grenadines
39 O4 **Barrow** Alaska, USA
97 E20 **Barrow** Ir. An Bhearú. ≈ SE Ireland
181 Q6 **Barrow Creek Roadhouse** Northern Territory, N Australia
97 J16 **Barrow-in-Furness** NW England, UK
180 G7 **Barrow Island** island Western Australia
39 O4 **Barrow, Point** headland Alaska, USA
11 V14 **Barrows** Manitoba, S Canada
97 J22 **Barry** S Wales, UK
14 J12 **Barry's Bay** Ontario, SE Canada
144 K14 **Barsakel'mes, Ostrov** island SW Kazakhstan
Baršć Łužyca see Forst
147 S14 **Barsem** S Tajikistan
145 V11 **Barshatas** Vostochnyy Kazakhstan, E Kazakhstan
155 F14 **Bārsi** Mahārāshtra, W India
100 I13 **Barsinghausen** Niedersachsen, C Germany
147 X8 **Barskoon** Issyk-Kul'skaya Oblast', E Kyrgyzstan
100 F10 **Barssel** Niedersachsen, NW Germany
35 U14 **Barstow** California, W USA
24 L8 **Barstow** Texas, SW USA
103 R6 **Bar-sur-Aube** Aube, NE France
Bar-sur-Ornain see Bar-le-Duc
103 Q6 **Bar-sur-Seine** Aube, N France
147 S13 **Bartang** S Tajikistan
147 T13 **Bartang** ≈ SE Tajikistan
Bartenstein see Bartoszyce
Bártfa/Bartfeld see Bardejov
100 N7 **Barth** Mecklenburg-Vorpommern, NE Germany
27 W13 **Bartholomew, Bayou** ≈ Arkansas/Louisiana, S USA
55 T8 **Bartica** N Guyana
136 H10 **Bartın** Bartın, NW Turkey
136 H10 **Bartın** ◈ province NW Turkey
181 W4 **Bartle Frere** ▲ Queensland, E Australia
27 P8 **Bartlesville** Oklahoma, C USA
29 P14 **Bartlett** Nebraska, C USA
20 E10 **Bartlett** Tennessee, S USA
25 T9 **Bartlett** Texas, SW USA
36 L13 **Bartlett Reservoir** ▣ Arizona, SW USA
19 N6 **Barton** Vermont, NE USA
110 L7 **Bartoszyce** Ger. Bartenstein. Warmińsko-Mazurskie, NE Poland,
23 W12 **Bartow** Florida, SE USA
Bartschin see Barcin
168 J10 **Barumun, Sungai** ≈ Sumatera, W Indonesia
Barū, Nahr see Baro Wenz
169 S17 **Barung, Nusa** island S Indonesia
168 H9 **Barus** Sumatera, NW Indonesia
162 L10 **Baruunsuu** Ömnögovĭ, S Mongolia
163 P8 **Baruun-Urt** Sühbaatar, E Mongolia
43 P15 **Barú, Volcán** var. Volcán de Chiriquí. ⛰ W Panama
99 K21 **Barvaux** Luxembourg, SE Belgium
42 M13 **Barva, Volcán** ⛰ NW Costa Rica
117 W6 **Barvinkove** Kharkivs'ka Oblast', E Ukraine
154 G11 **Barwāh** Madhya Pradesh, C India
Bärwalde Neumark see Mieszkowice
154 F11 **Barwāni** Madhya Pradesh, C India
183 P5 **Barwon River** ≈ New South Wales, SE Australia
119 L15 **Barysaw** Rus. Borisov. Minskaya Voblasts', NE Belarus
129 Q6 **Barysh** Ul'yanovskaya Oblast', W Russian Federation

◆ Country ● Country Capital ◇ Dependent Territory ○ Dependent Territory Capital ◈ Administrative Region ✕ International Airport ▲ Mountain ▲ Mountain Range ⛰ Volcano ≈ River ◎ Lake ▣ Reservoir

117 Q4 **Baryshivka** Kyyivs'ka Oblast', N Ukraine
79 J17 **Basankusu** Equateur, NW Dem. Rep. Congo (Zaire)
117 N11 **Basarabeasca** *Rus.* Bessarabka. SE Moldova
116 M14 **Basarabi** Constanţa, SW Romania
40 H6 **Basaseachic** Chihuahua, NW Mexico
105 O2 **Basauri** País Vasco, N Spain
61 D18 **Basavilbaso** Entre Ríos, E Argentina
79 F21 **Bas-Congo** *off.* Région du Bas-Congo; *prev.* Bas-Zaïre. ◆ *region* SW Dem. Rep. Congo (Zaire)
108 E6 **Basel** *Eng.* Basle, *Fr.* Bâle. Basel-Stadt, NW Switzerland
108 E7 **Basel** *Eng.* Basle, *Fr.* Bâle. ◆ *canton* NW Switzerland
143 T14 **Bashākerd, Kūhhā-ye** ▲ SE Iran
11 Q15 **Bashaw** Alberta, SW Canada
146 K16 **Bashbedeng** Maryyskiy Velayat, S Turkmenistan
161 T15 **Bashi Channel** *Chin.* Pa-shih Hai-hsia. *channel* Philippines/Taiwan
Bashkiria *see* Bashkortostan, Respublika
122 F11 **Bashkortostan, Respublika** *prev.* Bashkiria. ◆ *autonomous republic* W Russian Federation
129 N6 **Bashmakovo** Penzenskaya Oblast', W Russian Federation
146 J10 **Bashsakarba** Lebapskiy Velayat, NE Turkmenistan
117 R9 **Bashtanka** Mykolayivs'ka Oblast', S Ukraine
22 H8 **Basile** Louisiana, S USA
107 M18 **Basilicata** ◆ *region* S Italy
33 V13 **Basin** Wyoming, C USA
97 N22 **Basingstoke** S England, UK
143 U8 **Başīrān** Khorāsān, E Iran
112 B10 **Baška** *It.* Bescanuova. Primorje-Gorski Kotar, NW Croatia
137 T15 **Başkale** Van, SE Turkey
14 L10 **Baskatong, Réservoir** ⊠ Quebec, SE Canada
137 O14 **Baskil** Elazığ, E Turkey
Basle *see* Basel
154 H9 **Bāsoda** Madhya Pradesh, C India
79 L17 **Basoko** Orientale, N Dem. Rep. Congo (Zaire)
Basque Country, The *see* País Vasco
Basra *see* Al Başrah
103 U5 **Bas-Rhin** ◆ *department* NE France
Bassam *see* Grand-Bassam
9 Q16 **Bassano** Alberta, SW Canada
106 H7 **Bassano del Grappa** Veneto, NE Italy
77 Q15 **Bassar** *var.* Bassari. NW Togo
Bassari *see* Bassar
172 L9 **Bassas da India** *island group* W Madagascar
108 D7 **Bassecourt** Jura, W Switzerland
166 K8 **Bassein** *var.* Pathein. Irrawaddy, SW Myanmar
79 J15 **Basse-Kotto** ◆ *prefecture* S Central African Republic
105 V5 **Bassella** Cataluña, NE Spain
102 J5 **Basse-Normandie** *Eng.* Lower Normandy. ◆ *region* N France
45 Q11 **Basse-Pointe** N Martinique
76 H12 **Basse Santa Su** E Gambia
Basse-Saxe *see* Niedersachsen
45 X6 **Basse-Terre** ○ (Guadeloupe) Basse Terre, SW Guadeloupe
45 X6 **Basse Terre** *island* W Guadeloupe
45 V10 **Basseterre** ● (Saint Kitts and Nevis) Saint Kitts, Saint Kitts and Nevis
29 O13 **Bassett** Nebraska, C USA
21 S7 **Bassett** Virginia, NE USA
37 N15 **Bassett Peak** ▲ Arizona, SW USA
76 M10 **Bassikounou** Hodh ech Chargui, SE Mauritania
77 R15 **Bassila** W Benin
Bass, Îlots de *see* Marotiri
31 O11 **Bass Lake** Indiana, N USA
183 O14 **Bass Strait** *strait* SE Australia
100 H11 **Bassum** Niedersachsen, NW Germany
29 X3 **Basswood Lake** ⊚ Canada/USA
95 J21 **Båstad** Skåne, S Sweden
139 U2 **Baştah** E Iraq
153 N12 **Basti** Uttar Pradesh, N India
103 X14 **Bastia** Corse, France, C Mediterranean Sea
99 L23 **Bastogne** Luxembourg, SE Belgium
22 I5 **Bastrop** Louisiana, S USA
25 T11 **Bastrop** Texas, SW USA
93 J15 **Bastuträsk** Västerbotten, N Sweden
119 J19 **Bastyn'** *Rus.* Bostyn'. Brestskaya Voblasts', SW Belarus
Basuo *see* Dongfang
Basutoland *see* Lesotho
119 O15 **Basya** ≈ E Belarus
117 V8 **Basyl'kivka** Dnipropetrovs'ka Oblast', E Ukraine
79 D17 **Bata** NW Equatorial Guinea
79 D17 **Bata** × S Equatorial Guinea
Batae Coritanorum *see* Leicester
123 Q8 **Batagay** Respublika Sakha (Yakutiya), NE Russian Federation
123 P8 **Batagay-Alyta** Respublika Sakha (Yakutiya), NE Russian Federation
112 L10 **Batajnica** Serbia, N Yugoslavia
136 H15 **Bataklık Gölü** ⊚ S Turkey
114 H11 **Batak, Yazovir** ⊠ SW Bulgaria
152 H7 **Batāla** Punjab, N India
104 F9 **Batalha** Leiria, C Portugal
79 N17 **Batama** Orientale, NE Dem. Rep. Congo (Zaire)
123 Q10 **Batamay** Respublika Sakha (Yakutiya), NE Russian Federation
160 F9 **Batang** Sichuan, C China
79 I14 **Batangafo** Ouham, NW Central African Republic
171 P8 **Batangas** *off.* Batangas City. Luzon, N Philippines
Bătania *see* Battonya
171 Q10 **Batan Islands** *island group* N Philippines
60 L8 **Batatais** São Paulo, S Brazil
18 E10 **Batavia** New York, NE USA
Batavia *see* Jakarta
173 T9 **Batavia Seamount** *undersea feature* E Indian Ocean
128 L12 **Bataysk** Rostovskaya Oblast', SW Russian Federation
14 B9 **Batchawana** ≈ Ontario, S Canada
14 B9 **Batchawana Bay** Ontario, S Canada
167 Q12 **Bătdâmbâng** *prev.* Battambang. Bătdâmbâng, NW Cambodia
79 G20 **Batéké, Plateaux** *plateau* S Congo
183 S11 **Batemans Bay** New South Wales, SE Australia
21 Q13 **Batesburg** South Carolina, SE USA
28 K12 **Batesland** South Dakota, N USA
27 V10 **Batesville** Arkansas, C USA
31 Q14 **Batesville** Indiana, N USA
22 L2 **Batesville** Mississippi, S USA
25 Q13 **Batesville** Texas, SW USA
44 L13 **Bath** E Jamaica
97 L22 **Bath** *hist.* Akermanceaster, *anc.* Aquae Calidae, Aquae Solis. SW England, UK
19 Q8 **Bath** Maine, NE USA
18 F11 **Bath** New York, NE USA
Bath *see* Berkeley Springs
78 I10 **Batha** *off.* Préfecture du Batha. ◆ *prefecture* C Chad
78 I10 **Batha** *seasonal river* C Chad
141 Y8 **Baṭḥā', Wādī al** *dry watercourse* NE Oman
152 H9 **Bathinda** Punjab, NW India
98 M11 **Bathmen** Overijssel, E Netherlands
45 Z14 **Bathsheba** E Barbados
183 R8 **Bathurst** New South Wales, SE Australia
13 O13 **Bathurst** New Brunswick, SE Canada
Bathurst *see* Banjul
8 H6 **Bathurst, Cape** *headland* Northwest Territories, NW Canada
196 L8 **Bathurst Inlet** Nunavut, N Canada
8 L7 **Bathurst Inlet** *inlet* Nunavut, N Canada
8 k4 **Bathurst Island** *island* Northern Territory, N Australia
197 O9 **Bathurst Island** *island* Parry Islands, Nunavut, N Canada
77 O14 **Batié** SW Burkina
Batinah *see* Al Bāṭinah
141 Y9 **Bāṭin, Wādī al** *dry watercourse* SW Asia
15 P9 **Batiscan** ≈ Quebec, SE Canada
136 F16 **Batı Toroslar** ▲ SW Turkey
Batjan *see* Bacan, Pulau
Batlle y Ordóñez *see* José Batlle y Ordóñez
183 Q10 **Batlow** New South Wales, SE Australia
137 Q15 **Batman** *var.* Iluh. Batman, SE Turkey
137 Q15 **Batman** ◆ *province* SE Turkey
74 L6 **Batna** NE Algeria
Batoe *see* Batu, Kepulauan
162 K7 **Bat-Öldziyt** Töv, C Mongolia
22 J8 **Baton Rouge** *state capital* Louisiana, S USA
79 G15 **Batouri** Est, E Cameroon
138 G14 **Batrā', Jibāl al** ▲ S Jordan
138 G6 **Batroûn** *var.* Al Batrūn. N Lebanon
Batsch *see* Bač
Batsevichi *see* Batsevichy
119 M17 **Batsevichy** *Rus.* Batsevichi. Mahilyowskaya Voblasts', E Belarus
92 M7 **Båtsfjord** Finnmark, N Norway
Battambang *see* Bătdâmbâng
195 X3 **Batterbee, Cape** *headland* Antarctica
155 L24 **Batticaloa** Eastern Province, E Sri Lanka
99 L19 **Battice** Liège, E Belgium
107 L18 **Battipaglia** Campania, S Italy
11 R15 **Battle** ≈ Alberta/Saskatchewan, SW Canada
Battle Born State *see* Nevada
31 Q10 **Battle Creek** Michigan, N USA
27 T7 **Battlefield** Missouri, C USA
11 S15 **Battleford** Saskatchewan, S Canada
29 S6 **Battle Lake** Minnesota, N USA
35 U3 **Battle Mountain** Nevada, W USA
111 M25 **Battonya** *Rom.* Bătania. Békés, SE Hungary
168 D11 **Batu, Kepulauan** *prev.* Batoe. *island group* W Indonesia
137 Q10 **Bat'umi** W Georgia
168 K10 **Batu Pahat** *prev.* Bandar Penggaram. Johor, Peninsular Malaysia
171 O12 **Baturebe** Sulawesi, N Indonesia
122 J12 **Baturino** Tomskaya Oblast', C Russian Federation
117 R3 **Baturyn** Chernihivs'ka Oblast', N Ukraine
138 F10 **Bat Yam** Tel Aviv, C Israel
129 Q4 **Batyrevo** Chuvashskaya Respublika, W Russian Federation
Batys Qazaqstan Oblysy *see* Zapadnyy Kazakhstan
102 F5 **Batz, Île de** *island* NW France
169 Q10 **Bau** Sarawak, East Malaysia
171 N2 **Bauang** Luzon, N Philippines
171 P14 **Baubau** *var.* Baoebaoe. Pulau Buton, C Indonesia
77 W14 **Bauchi** Bauchi, NE Nigeria
77 W14 **Bauchi** ◆ *state* C Nigeria
102 H7 **Baud** Morbihan, NW France
29 T2 **Baudette** Minnesota, N USA
193 S9 **Bauer Basin** *undersea feature* E Pacific Ocean
187 R14 **Bauer Field** *var.* Port Vila. × (Port-Vila) Éfaté, C Vanuatu
13 T9 **Bauld, Cape** *headland* Newfoundland, E Canada
103 T8 **Baume-les-Dames** Doubs, E France
101 I15 **Baunatal** Hessen, C Germany
107 D18 **Baunei** Sardegna, Italy, C Mediterranean Sea
57 M15 **Baures, Río** ≈ N Bolivia
60 K9 **Bauru** São Paulo, S Brazil
Baushar *see* Bawshar
118 G10 **Bauska** *Ger.* Bauske. Bauska, S Latvia
Bauske *see* Bauska
101 Q15 **Bautzen** *Lus.* Budyšin. Sachsen, E Germany
145 Q16 **Bauyrzhan Momysh-Uly** *Kaz.* Baūyrzhan Momyshuly; *prev.* Burnoye. Zhambyl, S Kazakhstan
Bauzanum *see* Bolzano
Bavaria *see* Bayern
109 N7 **Bavarian Alps** *Ger.* Bayrische Alpen. ▲ Austria/Germany
Bavière *see* Bayern
40 H4 **Bavispe, Río** ≈ NW Mexico
129 T5 **Bavly** Respublika Tatarstan, W Russian Federation
169 P13 **Bawal, Pulau** *island* N Indonesia
169 T12 **Bawan** Borneo, C Indonesia
183 O12 **Baw Baw, Mount** ▲ Victoria, SE Australia
169 S15 **Bawean, Pulau** *island* S Indonesia
75 V9 **Bawîti** N Egypt
77 Q13 **Bawku** N Ghana
167 N7 **Bawlakè** Kayah State, C Myanmar
169 H11 **Bawo Ofuloa** Pulau Tanahmasa, W Indonesia
141 Y8 **Bawshar** *var.* Baushar. NE Oman
Ba Xian *see* Bazhou
158 M8 **Baxkorgan** Xinjiang Uygur Zizhiqu, W China
23 V6 **Baxley** Georgia, SE USA
159 R15 **Baxoi** Xizang Zizhiqu, W China
29 W14 **Baxter** Iowa, C USA
29 U6 **Baxter** Minnesota, N USA
27 R8 **Baxter Springs** Kansas, C USA
81 M17 **Bay** *off.* Gobolka Bay. ◆ *region* SW Somalia
Bay *see* Baicheng
44 H7 **Bayamo** Granma, E Cuba
45 U5 **Bayamón** E Puerto Rico
163 W8 **Bayan** Heilongjiang, NE China
170 L16 **Bayan** *prev.* Bajan. Pulau Lombok, C Indonesia
162 I6 **Bayan** Arhangay, C Mongolia
163 P7 **Bayan** Dornod, E Mongolia
163 N9 **Bayan** Dornogovĭ, SE Mongolia
162 F7 **Bayan** Govĭ-Altay, W Mongolia
163 O8 **Bayan** Hentiy, C Mongolia
152 I12 **Bayāna** Rājasthān, N India
149 N5 **Bāyān, Band-e** ▲ C Afghanistan
162 H8 **Bayanbulag** Bayanhongor, C Mongolia
163 N7 **Bayanbulag** Hentiy, C Mongolia
158 J5 **Bayanbulak** Xinjiang Uygur Zizhiqu, W China
Bayan Gol *see* Dengkou
162 F8 **Bayangol** Govĭ-Altay, SW Mongolia
159 R12 **Bayan Har Shan** *var.* Bayan Khar. ▲ C China
162 I8 **Bayanhongor** Bayanhongor, C Mongolia
162 H9 **Bayanhongor** ◆ *province* C Mongolia
Bayan Khar *see* Bayan Har Shan
168 J7 **Bayan Lepas** × (George Town) Pinang, Peninsular Malaysia
162 K13 **Bayan Mod** Nei Mongol Zizhiqu, N China
162 K13 **Bayan Nuru** Nei Mongol Zizhiqu, N China
162 N12 **Bayan Obo** Nei Mongol Zizhiqu, N China
43 V15 **Bayano, Lago** ⊚ E Panama
162 C5 **Bayan-Ölgiy** ◆ *province* NW Mongolia
162 F9 **Bayan-Ovoo** Govĭ-Altay, SW Mongolia
162 H9 **Bayansayr** Bayanhongor, C Mongolia
159 Q9 **Bayan Shan** ▲ C China
162 J9 **Bayanteeg** Övörhangay, C Mongolia
162 L8 **Bayantöhöm** Töv, C Mongolia
162 H6 **Bayan-Uhaa** Dzavhan, C Mongolia
162 J8 **Bayan-Ulaan** Övörhangay, C Mongolia
Bayan Ul Hot *see* Xi Ujimqin Qi
28 J14 **Bayard** Nebraska, C USA
37 P15 **Bayard** New Mexico, SW USA
103 T13 **Bayard, Col** *pass* SE France
163 O8 **Bayasgalant** Sühbaatar, E Mongolia
136 J12 **Bayat** Çorum, N Turkey
171 P6 **Bayawan** Negros, C Philippines
143 R10 **Bayāz** Kermān, C Iran
171 Q6 **Baybay** Leyte, C Philippines
21 X10 **Bayboro** North Carolina, SE USA
137 P12 **Bayburt** Bayburt, NE Turkey
137 P12 **Bayburt** ◆ *province* NE Turkey
31 R8 **Bay City** Michigan, N USA
25 V12 **Bay City** Texas, SW USA
122 I7 **Baydaratskaya Guba** *var.* Baydarata Bay. *bay* N Russian Federation
81 M16 **Baydhabo** *var.* Baydhowa, Isha Baydhabo, *It.* Baidoa. Bay, SW Somalia
Baydhowa *see* Baydhabo
101 N21 **Bayerischer Wald** ▲ SE Germany
101 K21 **Bayern** *Eng.* Bavaria, *Fr.* Bavière. ◆ *state* SE Germany
147 V9 **Bayetovo** Narynskaya Oblast', C Kyrgyzstan
102 K4 **Bayeux** *anc.* Augustodurum. Calvados, N France
14 E15 **Bayfield** ≈ Ontario, S Canada
145 O15 **Baygakum** *Kaz.* Bāygequm. Kzylorda, S Kazakhstan
Bāygequm *see* Baygakum
136 C14 **Bayındır** Izmir, SW Turkey
138 H12 **Bāyir** *var.* Bā'ir. Ma'ān, S Jordan
Bay Islands *see* Bahía, Islas de la
139 R5 **Bayjī** *var.* Baiji. N Iraq
Baykadam *see* Saudakent
123 N13 **Baykal, Ozero** *Eng.* Lake Baikal. ⊚ S Russian Federation
123 M14 **Baykal'sk** Irkutskaya Oblast', S Russian Federation
137 R15 **Baykan** Siirt, SE Turkey
123 L11 **Baykit** Evenkiyskiy Avtonomnyy Okrug, C Russian Federation
Baykonur *see* Baykonyr
144 M14 **Baykonyr** *var.* Baykonur *Kaz.* Bayqongyr; *prev.* Leninsk. Kyzylorda, S Kazakhstan
145 N12 **Baykonyr** *var.* Baykonur. Zhezkazgan, C Kazakhstan
158 E7 **Baykurt** Xinjiang Uygur Zizhiqu, W China
14 I9 **Bay, Lac** ⊚ Quebec, SE Canada
129 W6 **Baymak** Respublika Bashkortostan, W Russian Federation
23 O8 **Bay Minette** Alabama, S USA
143 O17 **Baynūnah** *desert* W UAE
184 O8 **Bay of Plenty** *off.* Bay of Plenty Region. ◆ *region* North Island, NZ
191 Z3 **Bay of Wrecks** *bay* Kiritimati, E Kiribati
102 I15 **Bayonne** *anc.* Lapurdum. Pyrénées-Atlantiques, SW France
22 H4 **Bayou D'Arbonne Lake** ⊠ Louisiana, S USA
23 N9 **Bayou La Batre** Alabama, S USA
Bayou State *see* Mississippi
Bayqadam *see* Saudakent
Bayqongyr *see* Baykonyr
Bayram-Ali *see* Bayramaly
146 J14 **Bayramaly** *prev.* Bayram-Ali. Maryyskiy Velayat, S Turkmenistan
101 L19 **Bayreuth** *var.* Baireuth. Bayern, SE Germany
Bayrische Alpen *see* Bavarian Alps
Bayrūt *see* Beyrouth
22 L9 **Bay Saint Louis** Mississippi, S USA
Baysān *see* Bet She'an
162 L8 **Bayshint** Töv, C Mongolia
14 H13 **Bays, Lake of** ⊚ Ontario, S Canada
22 M6 **Bay Springs** Mississippi, S USA
Bay State *see* Massachusetts
Baysun *see* Boysun
14 H13 **Baysville** Ontario, S Canada
141 N15 **Bayt al Faqīh** W Yemen
158 M4 **Baytik Shan** ▲ China/Mongolia
Bayt Laḥm *see* Bethlehem
25 W11 **Baytown** Texas, SW USA
169 V11 **Bayur, Tanjung** *headland* Borneo, N Indonesia
121 N14 **Bayy al Kabīr, Wādī** *dry watercourse* NW Libya
Bayyrqum *see* Bairkum
105 P14 **Baza** Andalucía, S Spain
137 X10 **Bazardüzü Dağı** *Rus.* Gora Bazardyuzyu. ▲ N Azerbaijan
Bazardyuzyu, Gora *see* Bazardüzü Dağı
Bazargic *see* Dobrich
83 N18 **Bazaruto, Ilha do** *island* SE Mozambique
102 K14 **Bazas** Gironde, SW France
105 O14 **Baza, Sierra de** ▲ S Spain
160 J8 **Bazhong** Sichuan, C China
161 P3 **Bazhou** *prev.* Baxian, Ba Xian. Hebei, E China
14 M9 **Bazin** ≈ Quebec, SE Canada
Bazin *see* Pezinok
139 Q7 **Bāziyah** C Iraq
138 H6 **Bcharré** *var.* Bcharreh, Bsharrī, Bsherri. NE Lebanon
Bcharreh *see* Bcharré
28 J5 **Beach** North Dakota, N USA
182 K12 **Beachport** South Australia
97 O23 **Beachy Head** *headland* SE England, UK
18 K13 **Beacon** New York, NE USA
63 J25 **Beagle Channel** *channel* Argentina/Chile
181 O1 **Beagle Gulf** *gulf* Northern Territory, N Australia
Bealach an Doirín *see* Ballaghaderreen
Bealach Cláir *see* Ballyclare
Bealach Féich *see* Ballybofey
172 J3 **Bealanana** Mahajanga, NE Madagascar
Béal an Átha *see* Ballina
Béal an Átha Móir *see* Ballinamore
Béal an Mhuirhead *see* Belmullet
Béal Átha Beithe *see* Ballybay
Béal Átha Conaill *see* Ballyconnell
Beál Átha hAmhnais *see* Ballyhaunis
Béal Átha na Sluaighe *see* Ballinasloe
Béal Átha Seanaidh *see* Ballyshannon
Bealdovuopmi *see* Peltovuoma
Béal Feirste *see* Belfast
Béal Tairbirt *see* Belturbet
Beanna Boirche *see* Mourne Mountains
Beannchar *see* Banagher, Ireland
Beannchar *see* Bangor, Northern Ireland, UK
Beanntraí *see* Bantry
23 N2 **Bear Creek** ≈ Alabama/Mississippi, S USA
30 J13 **Bear Creek** ≈ Illinois, N USA
27 U13 **Bearden** Arkansas, C USA
195 Q10 **Beardmore Glacier** *glacier* Antarctica
30 K13 **Beardstown** Illinois, N USA
28 L14 **Bear Hill** ▲ Nebraska, C USA
Bear Island *see* Bjørnøya
14 H12 **Bear Lake** Ontario, S Canada
36 M1 **Bear Lake** ⊚ Idaho/Utah, NW USA
39 U11 **Bear, Mount** ▲ Alaska, USA
102 J16 **Béarn** *cultural region* SW France
194 J11 **Bear Peninsula** *peninsula* Antarctica
152 I7 **Beās** ≈ India/Pakistan
105 P3 **Beasain** País Vasco, N Spain
105 O12 **Beas de Segura** Andalucía, S Spain
45 N10 **Beata, Cabo** *headland* SW Dominican Republic
45 N10 **Beata, Isla** *island* SW Dominican Republic
64 F11 **Beata Ridge** *undersea feature* N Caribbean Sea
29 R17 **Beatrice** Nebraska, C USA
83 L16 **Beatrice** Mashonaland East, NE Zimbabwe
11 N11 **Beatton** ≈ British Columbia, W Canada
11 N11 **Beatton River** British Columbia, W Canada
35 V10 **Beatty** Nevada, W USA
21 N6 **Beattyville** Kentucky, S USA
173 X16 **Beau Bassin** W Mauritius
103 R15 **Beaucaire** Gard, S France
14 I8 **Beauchastel, Lac** ⊚ Quebec, SE Canada
14 I10 **Beauchêne, Lac** ⊚ Quebec, SE Canada
183 V3 **Beaudesert** Queensland, E Australia
182 M12 **Beaufort** Victoria, SE Australia
21 X11 **Beaufort** North Carolina, SE USA
21 R15 **Beaufort** South Carolina, SE USA
38 M11 **Beaufort Sea** *sea* Arctic Ocean
Beaufort-Wes *see* Beaufort West
83 G25 **Beaufort West** *Afr.* Beaufort-Wes. Western Cape, SW South Africa
103 N7 **Beaugency** Loiret, C France
19 R1 **Beau Lake** ⊠ Maine, NE USA
96 I8 **Beauly** N Scotland, UK
99 G21 **Beaumont** Hainaut, S Belgium
185 E23 **Beaumont** Otago, South Island, NZ
22 M7 **Beaumont** Mississippi, S USA
25 X10 **Beaumont** Texas, SW USA
102 M15 **Beaumont-de-Lomagne** Tarn-et-Garonne, S France
102 L6 **Beaumont-sur-Sarthe** Sarthe, NW France
103 R8 **Beaune** Côte d'Or, C France
15 R9 **Beaupré** Quebec, SE Canada
102 J8 **Beaupréau** Maine-et-Loire, NW France
99 I22 **Beauraing** Namur, SE Belgium
103 R12 **Beaurepaire** Isère, E France
11 Y16 **Beausejour** Manitoba, S Canada
103 N4 **Beauvais** *anc.* Bellovacum, Caesaromagus. Oise, N France
11 S13 **Beauval** Saskatchewan, C Canada
102 I9 **Beauvoir-sur-Mer** Vendée, NW France
39 R8 **Beaver** Alaska, USA
26 J8 **Beaver** Oklahoma, C USA
18 B14 **Beaver** Pennsylvania, NE USA
36 K6 **Beaver** Utah, W USA
10 L9 **Beaver** ≈ British Columbia/Yukon Territory, W Canada
11 S13 **Beaver** ≈ Saskatchewan, C Canada
29 N17 **Beaver City** Nebraska, C USA
10 G6 **Beaver Creek** Yukon Territory, W Canada
31 R14 **Beavercreek** Ohio, N USA
39 S8 **Beaver Creek** ≈ Alaska, USA
26 H3 **Beaver Creek** ≈ Kansas/Nebraska, C USA
28 J5 **Beaver Creek** ≈ Montana/North Dakota, N USA
29 Q14 **Beaver Creek** ≈ Nebraska, C USA
25 Q4 **Beaver Creek** ≈ Texas, SW USA
30 M8 **Beaver Dam** Wisconsin, N USA
30 M8 **Beaver Dam Lake** ⊚ Wisconsin, N USA
18 B14 **Beaver Falls** Pennsylvania, NE USA
33 P12 **Beaverhead Mountains** ▲ Idaho/Montana, NW USA
33 Q12 **Beaverhead River** ≈ Montana, NW USA
65 A25 **Beaver Island** *island* W Falkland Islands
31 P5 **Beaver Island** *island* Michigan, N USA
27 S9 **Beaver Lake** ⊠ Arkansas, C USA
11 N13 **Beaverlodge** Alberta, W Canada
18 I8 **Beaver River** ≈ New York, NE USA
26 J8 **Beaver River** ≈ Oklahoma, C USA
18 B13 **Beaver River** ≈ Pennsylvania, NE USA
65 A25 **Beaver Settlement** Beaver Island, W Falkland Islands
Beaver State *see* Oregon
14 H14 **Beaverton** Ontario, S Canada
32 G11 **Beaverton** Oregon, NW USA
152 G12 **Beāwar** Rājasthān, N India
Bebas, Dasht-i *see* Bābūs, Dasht-e
60 L8 **Bebedouro** São Paulo, S Brazil
101 I16 **Bebra** Hessen, C Germany
41 W12 **Becal** Campeche, SE Mexico
15 Q11 **Bécancour** ≈ Quebec, SE Canada
97 Q19 **Beccles** E England, UK
112 L9 **Bečej** *Ger.* Altbetsche, *Hung.* Óbecse, Rácz-Becse; *prev.* Magyar-Becse, Stari Bečej. Serbia, N Yugoslavia
104 I3 **Becerreá** Galicia, NW Spain
74 H7 **Béchar** *prev.* Colomb-Béchar. W Algeria
39 O14 **Becharof Lake** ⊚ Alaska, USA
116 H15 **Bechet** *var.* Bechetu. Dolj, SW Romania
Bechetu *see* Bechet
21 R6 **Beckley** West Virginia, NE USA
101 G14 **Beckum** Nordrhein-Westfalen, W Germany
25 X7 **Beckville** Texas, SW USA
35 X4 **Becky Peak** ▲ Nevada, W USA
116 I9 **Beclean** *Hung.* Bethlen; *prev.* Betlen. Bistriţa-Năsăud, N Romania
Bécs *see* Wien
111 H18 **Bečva** *Ger.* Betschau, *Pol.* Beczwa. ≈ E Czech Republic
Beczwa *see* Bečva
103 P15 **Bédarieux** Hérault, S France
120 B10 **Beddouza, Cap** *headland* W Morocco
80 I13 **Bedelē** Oromo, C Ethiopia
147 Y8 **Bedel Pass** *Rus.* Pereval Bedel. *pass* China/Kyrgyzstan
Bedel, Pereval *see* Bedel Pass
95 H22 **Beder** Århus, C Denmark
97 N20 **Bedford** E England, UK
31 O15 **Bedford** Indiana, N USA
29 U16 **Bedford** Iowa, C USA
20 L4 **Bedford** Kentucky, S USA
18 D15 **Bedford** Pennsylvania, NE USA
21 T6 **Bedford** Virginia, NE USA
97 N20 **Bedfordshire** *cultural region* E England, UK
129 N5 **Bednodem'yanovsk** Penzenskaya Oblast', W Russian Federation
98 N5 **Bedum** Groningen, NE Netherlands
27 V11 **Beebe** Arkansas, C USA
45 T9 **Beef Island** × (Road Town) Tortola, E British Virgin Islands
Beehive State *see* Utah
99 L18 **Beek** Limburg, SE Netherlands
99 L18 **Beek** × (Maastricht) Limburg, SE Netherlands
99 K14 **Beek-en-Donk** Noord-Brabant, S Netherlands
138 F13 **Be'er Menuḥa** *var.* Be'er Menukha. Southern, S Israel
Be'er Menukha *see* Be'er Menuḥa
99 D16 **Beernem** West-Vlaanderen, NW Belgium
99 I16 **Beerse** Antwerpen, N Belgium
Beersheba *see* Be'ér Sheva'
138 E11 **Be'ér Sheva'** *var.* Beersheba, *Ar.* Bir es Saba. Southern, S Israel
98 J13 **Beesd** Gelderland, C Netherlands
99 M16 **Beesel** Limburg, SE Netherlands
83 J21 **Beestekraal** North-West, N South Africa
194 J7 **Beethoven Peninsula** *peninsula* Alexander Island, Antarctica
Beetstersweach *see* Beetsterzwaag
98 M6 **Beetsterzwaag** *Fris.* Beetstersweach. Friesland, N Netherlands
25 S13 **Beeville** Texas, SW USA
79 J18 **Befale** Equateur, NW Dem. Rep. Congo (Zaire)
Befandriana *see* Befandriana Avaratra
172 J3 **Befandriana Avaratra** *var.* Befandriana, Befandriana Nord. Mahajanga, NW Madagascar
Befandriana Nord *see* Befandriana Avaratra
79 K18 **Befori** Equateur, N Dem. Rep. Congo (Zaire)
172 I7 **Befotaka** Fianarantsoa, S Madagascar
183 R11 **Bega** New South Wales, SE Australia
102 G5 **Bégard** Côtes d'Armor, NW France
112 M9 **Begejski Kanal** *canal* NE Yugoslavia
145 V9 **Begen'** Vostochnyy Kazakhstan, E Kazakhstan
94 G13 **Begna** ≈ S Norway
Begoml' *see* Byahoml'
Begovat *see* Bekobod
153 Q13 **Begusarāi** Bihār, NE India
143 R9 **Behābād** Yazd, C Iran
Behagle *see* Laï
55 Z10 **Béhague, Pointe** *headland* E French Guiana
Behar *see* Bihār
142 M10 **Behbahān** *var.* Behbehān. Khūzestān, SW Iran
Behbehān *see* Behbahān
44 G3 **Behring Point** Andros Island, W Bahamas
143 P4 **Behshahr** *prev.* Ashraf. Māzandarān, N Iran
163 V6 **Bei'an** Heilongjiang, NE China
Beibunar *see* Sredishte
Beibu Wan *see* Tongking, Gulf of
Beida *see* Al Bayḍā'
80 H13 **Beigi** Oromo, C Ethiopia
160 L16 **Beihai** Guangxi Zhuangzu Zizhiqu, S China
159 Q10 **Bei Hulsan Hu** ⊚ C China
161 N13 **Bei Jiang** ≈ S China
161 O2 **Beijing** *var.* Pei-ching, *Eng.* Peking; *prev.* Pei-p'ing. *country/municipality capital* (China) Beijing Shi, E China
161 P2 **Beijing** × Beijing Shi, E China
Beijing *see* Beijing Shi
161 O2 **Beijing Shi** *var.* Beijing, Jing, Pei-ching, *Eng.* Peking; *prev.* Pei-p'ing. ◆ *municipality* E China

◆ Country ● Country Capital ◇ Dependent Territory ○ Dependent Territory Capital ◆ Administrative Region × International Airport ▲ Mountain ▲ Mountain Range ☒ Volcano ≈ River ⊚ Lake ⊠ Reservoir

76 G8 **Beïla** Trarza, W Mauritania
98 N7 **Beilen** Drenthe, NE Netherlands
160 L15 **Beiliu** Guangxi Zhuangzu Zizhiqu, S China
159 O12 **Beilu He** ≈ W China
Beilul see Beylul
96 H8 **Beinn Dearg** ▲ N Scotland, UK
Beinn MacDuibh see Ben Macdui
160 I12 **Beipan Jiang** ≈ S China
163 T12 **Beipiao** Liaoning, NE China
83 N17 **Beira** Sofala, C Mozambique
83 N17 **Beira** ✕ Sofala, C Mozambique
104 I7 **Beira Alta** former province N Portugal
104 H9 **Beira Baixa** former province C Portugal
104 G8 **Beira Litoral** former province N Portugal
Beirut see Beyrouth
Beisān see Bet She'an
9 Q16 **Beiseker** Alberta, SW Canada
83 K19 **Beitbridge** Matabeleland South, S Zimbabwe
116 G10 **Beiuș** Hung. Belényes. Bihor, NW Romania
163 U12 **Beizhen** Liaoning, NE China
104 H12 **Beja** anc. Pax Julia. Beja, SE Portugal
104 G13 **Beja** ◈ district S Portugal
74 M5 **Béja** var. Bājah. N Tunisia
120 I9 **Béjaïa** var. Bejaïa, Fr. Bougie; anc. Saldae. NE Algeria
104 K8 **Béjar** Castilla-León, N Spain
Bejraburi see Phetchaburi
Bekaa Valley see El Beqaa
Bekabad see Bekobod
Békás see Bicaz
169 O15 **Bekasi** Jawa, C Indonesia
Bek-Budi see Qarshi
146 A8 **Bekdash** Balkanskiy Velayat, NW Turkmenistan
147 T10 **Bek-Dzhar** Oshskaya Oblast', SW Kyrgyzstan
111 N24 **Békés** Rom. Bichiș. Békés, SE Hungary
111 M24 **Békés** off. Békés Megye. ◈ county SE Hungary
111 M24 **Békéscsaba** Rom. Bichiș-Ciaba. Békés, SE Hungary
139 S2 **Bēkhma** E Iraq
172 H7 **Bekily** Toliara, S Madagascar
165 W4 **Bekkai** Hokkaidō, NE Japan
147 Q11 **Bekobod** Rus. Bekabad; prev. Begovat. Toshkent Wiloyati, E Uzbekistan
129 O7 **Bekovo** Penzenskaya Oblast', W Russian Federation
Bél see Beliu
152 M13 **Bela** Uttar Pradesh, N India
149 N15 **Bela** Baluchistān, SW Pakistan
79 F15 **Bélabo** Est, C Cameroon
112 N10 **Bela Crkva** Ger. Weisskirchen, Hung. Fehértemplom. Serbia, W Yugoslavia
173 Y16 **Bel Air** var. Rivière Sèche. E Mauritius
104 L12 **Belalcázar** Andalucía, S Spain
113 P15 **Bela Palanka** Serbia, SE Yugoslavia
119 H16 **Belarus** off. Republic of Belarus, var. Belorussia, Latv. Baltkrievija; prev. Belorussian SSR, Rus. Belorusskaya SSR. ◆ republic E Europe
Belau see Palau
59 H21 **Bela Vista** Mato Grosso do Sul, SW Brazil
83 L21 **Bela Vista** Maputo, S Mozambique
168 I8 **Belawan** Sumatera, W Indonesia
Běla Woda see Weisswasser
129 U4 **Belaya** ≈ W Russian Federation
123 R7 **Belaya Gora** Respublika Sakha (Yakutiya), NE Russian Federation
128 M11 **Belaya Kalitva** Rostovskaya Oblast', SW Russian Federation
127 R14 **Belaya Kholunitsa** Kirovskaya Oblast', NW Russian Federation
Belaya Tserkov' see Bila Tserkva
77 V11 **Belbédji** Zinder, S Niger
110 K13 **Bełchatów** var. Belchatow. Łodzkie, C Poland
Belcher, Îles see Belcher Islands
12 H7 **Belcher Islands** Fr. Îles Belcher. island group Nunavut, SE Canada
105 S6 **Belchite** Aragón, NE Spain
29 O2 **Belcourt** North Dakota, N USA
31 P9 **Belding** Michigan, N USA
129 U5 **Belebey** Respublika Bashkortostan, W Russian Federation
81 N16 **Beledweyne** var. Belet Huen, It. Belet Uen. Hiiraan, C Somalia
146 B10 **Belek** Balkanskiy Velayat, W Turkmenistan
58 L12 **Belém** var. Pará. state capital Pará, N Brazil
65 I14 **Belém Ridge** undersea feature C Atlantic Ocean
37 R12 **Belen** New Mexico, SW USA
62 I7 **Belén** Catamarca, NW Argentina
54 G9 **Belén** Boyacá, C Colombia
42 J11 **Belén** Rivas, SW Nicaragua
62 O5 **Belén** Concepción, C Paraguay
61 D16 **Belén** Salto, N Uruguay
61 D20 **Belén de Escobar** Buenos Aires, E Argentina
114 J7 **Belene** Pleven, N Bulgaria
114 J7 **Belene, Ostrov** island N Bulgaria
43 R15 **Belén, Río** ≈ C Panama
Belényes see Beiuș
104 H3 **Belesar, Embalse de** ▣ NW Spain
Belet Huen/Belet Uen see Beledweyne
128 J5 **Belëv** Tul'skaya Oblast', W Russian Federation
97 G15 **Belfast** Ir. Béal Feirste. ◐ E Northern Ireland, UK
19 R7 **Belfast** Maine, NE USA
97 G15 **Belfast** ✕ E Northern Ireland, UK
97 G15 **Belfast Lough** Ir. Loch Lao inlet E Northern Ireland, UK
28 K5 **Belfield** North Dakota, N USA
103 U7 **Belfort** Territoire-de-Belfort, E France
Belgard see Białogard
155 E17 **Belgaum** Karnātaka, W India
Belgian Congo see Congo (Democratic Republic of)
195 T3 **Belgica Mountains** ⛰ Antarctica
België/Belgique see Belgium
99 F20 **Belgium** off. Kingdom of Belgium, Dut. België, Fr. Belgique. ◆ monarchy NW Europe
128 J8 **Belgorod** Belgorodskaya Oblast', W Russian Federation
Belgorod-Dnestrovskiy see Bilhorod-Dnistrovs'kyy
128 J8 **Belgorodskaya Oblast'** ◈ province W Russian Federation
Belgrad see Beograd
29 T8 **Belgrade** Minnesota, N USA
33 S11 **Belgrade** Montana, NW USA
Belgrade see Beograd
195 N5 **Belgrano II** Argentinian research station Antarctica
Belgrano, Cabo see Meredith, Cape
21 X9 **Belhaven** North Carolina, SE USA
107 I23 **Belice** anc. Hypsas. ≈ Sicilia, Italy, C Mediterranean Sea
Belice see Belize/Belize City
113 M16 **Beli Drim** Alb. Drini i Bardhë. ≈ Albania/Yugoslavia
Beligrad see Berat
188 C8 **Beliliou** prev. Peleliu. island S Palau
114 L8 **Beli Lom, Yazovir** ▣ NE Bulgaria
112 I8 **Beli Manastir** Hung. Pélmonostor; prev. Monostor. Osijek-Baranja, NE Croatia
102 J13 **Bélin-Béliet** Gironde, SW France
79 F17 **Bélinga** Ogooué-Ivindo, NE Gabon
21 S4 **Belington** West Virginia, NE USA
129 O6 **Belinskiy** Penzenskaya Oblast', W Russian Federation
169 N12 **Belinyu** Pulau Bangka, W Indonesia
169 O13 **Belitung, Pulau** island W Indonesia
116 F10 **Beliu** Hung. Bél. Arad, W Romania
114 I9 **Beli Vit** ≈ NW Bulgaria
42 G2 **Belize** Sp. Belice; prev. British Honduras, Colony of Belize. ◆ commonwealth republic Central America
42 F2 **Belize** Sp. Belice. ◈ district NE Belize
42 G2 **Belize** ≈ Belize/Guatemala
Belize see Belize City
42 G2 **Belize City** var. Belize, Sp. Belice. Belize, NE Belize
42 G2 **Belize City** ✕ Belize, NE Belize
Beljak see Villach
39 N16 **Belkofski** Alaska, USA
123 O6 **Bel'kovskiy, Ostrov** island Novosibirskiye Ostrova, NE Russian Federation
14 J8 **Bell** ≈ Quebec, SE Canada
10 J15 **Bella Bella** British Columbia, SW Canada
102 M10 **Bellac** Haute-Vienne, C France
10 K15 **Bella Coola** British Columbia, SW Canada
106 D6 **Bellagio** Lombardia, N Italy
31 P6 **Bellaire** Michigan, N USA
106 D6 **Bellano** Lombardia, N Italy
155 G17 **Bellary** var. Ballari. Karnātaka, S India
183 S5 **Bellata** New South Wales, SE Australia
61 D16 **Bella Unión** Artigas, N Uruguay
61 C14 **Bella Vista** Corrientes, NE Argentina
62 J7 **Bella Vista** Tucumán, N Argentina
62 P4 **Bella Vista** Amambay, C Paraguay
56 B10 **Bellavista** Cajamarca, N Peru
56 D11 **Bellavista** San Martín, N Peru
183 U6 **Bellbrook** New South Wales, SE Australia
27 V5 **Belle** Missouri, C USA
21 Q5 **Belle** West Virginia, NE USA
31 R13 **Bellefontaine** Ohio, N USA
18 F14 **Bellefonte** Pennsylvania, NE USA
28 J9 **Belle Fourche** South Dakota, N USA
28 J9 **Belle Fourche Reservoir** ▣ South Dakota, N USA
28 K9 **Belle Fourche River** ≈ South Dakota/Wyoming, N USA
103 S10 **Bellegarde-sur-Valserine** Ain, E France
23 Y14 **Belle Glade** Florida, SE USA
102 G8 **Belle Île** island NW France
13 T9 **Belle Isle** island Belle Isle, Newfoundland, E Canada
13 S10 **Belle Isle, Strait of** strait Newfoundland, E Canada
Bellenz see Bellinzona
29 W14 **Belle Plaine** Iowa, C USA
29 V9 **Belle Plaine** Minnesota, N USA
14 I9 **Belleterre** Quebec, SE Canada
14 J15 **Belleville** Ontario, SE Canada
103 R10 **Belleville** Rhône, E France
30 K15 **Belleville** Illinois, N USA
27 N3 **Belleville** Kansas, C USA
29 Z13 **Bellevue** Iowa, C USA
29 S15 **Bellevue** Nebraska, C USA
31 S11 **Bellevue** Ohio, N USA
25 S5 **Bellevue** Texas, SW USA
32 H8 **Bellevue** Washington, NW USA
55 Y11 **Bellevue de l'Inini, Montagnes** ⛰ S French Guiana
103 S11 **Belley** Ain, E France
Bellin see Kangirsuk
183 V6 **Bellingen** New South Wales, SE Australia
97 L14 **Bellingham** N England, UK
32 H6 **Bellingham** Washington, NW USA
Belling Hausen Mulde see Southeast Pacific Basin
194 H2 **Bellingshausen** Russian research station South Shetland Islands, Antarctica
Bellingshausen see Motu One
Bellingshausen Abyssal Plain see Bellingshausen Plain
196 R14 **Bellingshausen Plain** var. Bellingshausen Abyssal Plain. undersea feature SE Pacific Ocean
194 I8 **Bellingshausen Sea** sea Antarctica
98 P6 **Bellingwolde** Groningen, NE Netherlands
108 H11 **Bellinzona** Ger. Bellenz. Ticino, S Switzerland
25 T8 **Bellmead** Texas, SW USA
54 E8 **Bello** Antioquia, W Colombia
61 B21 **Bellocq** Buenos Aires, E Argentina
Bello Horizonte see Belo Horizonte
186 L10 **Bellona** var. Mungiki. island S Solomon Islands
Bellovacum see Beauvais
182 D7 **Bell, Point** headland South Australia
20 F9 **Bells** Tennessee, S USA
25 U5 **Bells** Texas, SW USA
92 N3 **Bellsund** inlet SW Svalbard
106 H6 **Belluno** Veneto, NE Italy
62 L11 **Bell Ville** Córdoba, C Argentina
83 E26 **Bellville** Western Cape, SW South Africa
25 U11 **Bellville** Texas, SW USA
104 L12 **Belmez** Andalucía, S Spain
29 V12 **Belmond** Iowa, C USA
18 E11 **Belmont** New York, NE USA
21 R10 **Belmont** North Carolina, SE USA
59 O18 **Belmonte** Bahia, E Brazil
104 I8 **Belmonte** Castelo Branco, C Portugal
105 P10 **Belmonte** Castilla-La Mancha, C Spain
42 G2 **Belmopan** ● (Belize) Cayo, C Belize
97 B16 **Belmullet** Ir. Béal an Mhuirhead. W Ireland
123 R13 **Belogorsk** Amurskaya Oblast', SE Russian Federation
Belogorsk see Bilohirs'k
114 F7 **Belogradchik** Vidin, NW Bulgaria
172 H8 **Beloha** Toliara, S Madagascar
59 M20 **Belo Horizonte** prev. Bello Horizonte. state capital Minas Gerais, SE Brazil
26 M3 **Beloit** Kansas, C USA
30 L9 **Beloit** Wisconsin, N USA
Belokorovichi see Bilokorovychi
126 J8 **Belomorsk** Respublika Kareliya, NW Russian Federation
126 J8 **Belomorsko-Baltiyskiy Kanal** Eng. White Sea-Baltic Canal, White Sea Canal. canal NW Russian Federation
153 V15 **Belonia** Tripura, NE India
Belopol'ye see Bilopillya
105 O4 **Belorado** Castilla-León, N Spain
128 L14 **Belorechensk** Krasnodarskiy Kray, SW Russian Federation
129 W5 **Beloretsk** Respublika Bashkortostan, W Russian Federation
Belorussia/Belorussian SSR see Belarus
Belorusskaya Gryada see Byelaruskaya Hrada
Belorusskaya SSR see Belarus
Beloshchel'ye see Nar'yan-Mar
114 N8 **Beloslav** Varna, E Bulgaria
Belostok see Białystok
172 H5 **Belo Tsiribihina** var. Belo-sur-Tsiribihina. Toliara, W Madagascar
Belovár see Bjelovar
Belovezhskaya Pushcha see Białowieska, Puszcza/Byelavyezhskaya Pushcha
114 H10 **Belovo** Pazardzhik, C Bulgaria
Belovodsk see Bilovods'k
122 H9 **Beloyarskiy** Khanty-Mansiyskiy Avtonomnyy Okrug, N Russian Federation
126 K7 **Beloye More** Eng. White Sea. sea NW Russian Federation
126 K13 **Beloye, Ozero** ◎ NW Russian Federation
114 J10 **Belozem** Plovdiv, C Bulgaria
126 K13 **Belozërsk** Vologodskaya Oblast', NW Russian Federation
99 E20 **Belœil** Hainaut, SW Belgium
108 D8 **Belp** Bern, W Switzerland
108 D8 **Belp** ✕ (Bern) Bern, C Switzerland
107 L24 **Belpasso** Sicilia, Italy, C Mediterranean Sea
31 U14 **Belpre** Ohio, N USA
98 M8 **Belterwijde** ◎ N Netherlands
27 R4 **Belton** Missouri, C USA
21 P11 **Belton** South Carolina, SE USA
25 T9 **Belton** Texas, SW USA
25 S9 **Belton Lake** ▣ Texas, SW USA
Bel'tsy see Bălți
97 E16 **Belturbet** Ir. Béal Tairbirt. N Ireland
Beluchistan see Baluchistān
145 Z9 **Belukha, Gora** ▲ Kazakhstan/Russian Federation
107 M20 **Belvedere Marittimo** Calabria, SW Italy
30 L10 **Belvidere** Illinois, N USA
18 J14 **Belvidere** New Jersey, NE USA
Bely see Belyy
129 V8 **Belyayevka** Orenburgskaya Oblast', W Russian Federation
Belynichi see Byalynichy
126 H17 **Belyy** var. Bely, Beyj. Tverskaya Oblast', W Russian Federation
128 I6 **Belyye Berega** Bryanskaya Oblast', W Russian Federation
122 J6 **Belyy, Ostrov** island N Russian Federation
122 J11 **Belyy Yar** Tomskaya Oblast', C Russian Federation
100 N13 **Belzig** Brandenburg, NE Germany
22 K4 **Belzoni** Mississippi, S USA
172 H4 **Bemaraha** var. Plateau du Bemaraha. ▲ W Madagascar
82 B10 **Bembe** Uíge, NW Angola
77 S14 **Bembèrèkè** var. Bimbéréké. N Benin
104 K12 **Bembézar** ≈ SW Spain
104 J3 **Bembibre** Castilla-León, N Spain
29 T4 **Bemidji** Minnesota, N USA
98 L12 **Bemmel** Gelderland, SE Netherlands
171 T13 **Bemu** Pulau Seram, E Indonesia
Benāb see Bonāb
105 T5 **Benabarre** var. Benavarn. Aragón, NE Spain
Benaco see Garda, Lago di
79 L20 **Bena-Dibele** Kasai Oriental, C Dem. Rep. Congo (Zaire)
105 R9 **Benageber, Embalse de** ▣ E Spain
183 O11 **Benalla** Victoria, SE Australia
104 M14 **Benamejí** Andalucía, S Spain
Benares see Vārānasi
Benavarn see Benabarre
104 F10 **Benavente** Santarém, C Portugal
104 K5 **Benavente** Castilla-León, N Spain
25 S15 **Benavides** Texas, SW USA
96 F8 **Benbecula** island NW Scotland, UK
Bencovazzo see Benkovac
32 H13 **Bend** Oregon, NW USA
182 K7 **Benda Range** ⛰ South Australia
183 T6 **Bendemeer** New South Wales, SE Australia
Bender see Tighina
Bender Beila/Bender Beyla see Bandarbeyla
Bender Cassim/Bender Qaasim see Boosaaso
Bendery see Tighina
183 N11 **Bendigo** Victoria, SE Australia
118 E10 **Bēne** Dobele, SW Latvia
98 K13 **Beneden-Leeuwen** Gelderland, C Netherlands
101 L24 **Benediktenwand** ▲ S Germany
Benemérita de San Cristóbal see San Cristóbal
77 N12 **Bénéna** Ségou, S Mali
172 I7 **Benenitra** Toliara, S Madagascar
Beneschau see Benešov
Beneški Zaliv see Venice, Gulf of
111 D17 **Benešov** Ger. Beneschau. Středočeský Kraj, W Czech Republic
123 Q5 **Benetta, Ostrov** island Novosibirskiye Ostrova, NE Russian Federation
107 L17 **Benevento** anc. Beneventum, Malventum. Campania, S Italy
Beneventum see Benevento
173 S3 **Bengal, Bay of** bay N Indian Ocean
79 M17 **Bengamisa** Orientale, N Dem. Rep. Congo (Zaire)
Bengasi see Banghāzī
Bengazi see Banghāzī
161 P7 **Bengbu** var. Peng-pu. Anhui, E China
32 L9 **Benge** Washington, NW USA
Benghazi see Banghāzī
168 K10 **Bengkalis** Pulau Bengkalis, W Indonesia
168 K10 **Bengkalis, Pulau** island W Indonesia
169 Q10 **Bengkayang** Borneo, C Indonesia
Bengkoelen/Bengkoeloe see Bengkulu
168 K14 **Bengkulu** prev. Bengkoeloe, Benkoelen, Benkulen. Sumatera, W Indonesia
168 J13 **Bengkulu** off. Propinsi Bengkulu; prev. Bengkoelen, Benkoelen, Benkulen. ◈ province W Indonesia
82 A11 **Bengo** ◈ province W Angola
95 J16 **Bengtsfors** Västra Götaland, S Sweden
82 B13 **Benguela** var. Benguella. Benguela, W Angola
83 A14 **Benguela** ◈ province W Angola
Benguella see Benguela
Bengweulu, Lake see Bangweulu, Lake
121 V13 **Benha** var. Banhā. N Egypt
192 F6 **Benham Seamount** undersea feature W Philippine Sea
96 H6 **Ben Hope** ▲ N Scotland, UK
79 P18 **Beni** Nord Kivu, NE Dem. Rep. Congo (Zaire)
57 L15 **Beni** var. El Beni. ◈ department N Bolivia
74 H8 **Beni Abbès** W Algeria
105 T8 **Benicarló** País Valenciano, E Spain
105 T9 **Benicasim** País Valenciano, E Spain
105 T12 **Benidorm** País Valenciano, SE Spain
75 W9 **Beni Mazâr** var. Banī Mazār. C Egypt
120 C11 **Beni-Mellal** C Morocco
77 R14 **Benin** off. Republic of Benin; prev. Dahomey. ◆ republic W Africa
77 S17 **Benin, Bight of** gulf W Africa
77 U16 **Benin City** Edo, SW Nigeria
57 K16 **Beni, Río** ≈ N Bolivia
120 F10 **Beni Saf** var. Beni-Saf. NW Algeria
80 H12 **Benishangul** ◈ region W Ethiopia
105 T11 **Benissa** País Valenciano, E Spain
121 V14 **Beni Suef** var. Banī Suwayf. N Egypt
11 V15 **Benito** Manitoba, S Canada
Benito see Uolo, Río
61 C23 **Benito Juárez** Buenos Aires, E Argentina
41 P14 **Benito Juaréz Internacional** ✕ (México) México, S Mexico
25 P5 **Benjamin** Texas, SW USA
58 B13 **Benjamin Constant** Amazonas, N Brazil
40 F4 **Benjamín Hill** Sonora, NW Mexico
63 F19 **Benjamín, Isla** island Archipiélago de los Chonos, S Chile
165 Q4 **Benkei-misaki** headland Hokkaidō, NE Japan
28 L17 **Benkelman** Nebraska, C USA
96 I7 **Ben Klibreck** ▲ N Scotland, UK
Benkoelen see Bengkulu
112 D13 **Benkovac** It. Bencovazzo. Zadar, SW Croatia
Benkulen see Bengkulu
96 I11 **Ben Lawers** ▲ C Scotland, UK
96 J9 **Ben Macdui** var. Beinn MacDuibh. ▲ C Scotland, UK
96 G11 **Ben More** ▲ W Scotland, UK
96 I11 **Ben More** ▲ C Scotland, UK
96 H7 **Ben More Assynt** ▲ N Scotland, UK
185 E20 **Benmore, Lake** ◎ South Island, NZ
98 L12 **Bennekom** Gelderland, SE Netherlands
21 T11 **Bennettsville** South Carolina, SE USA
96 H10 **Ben Nevis** ▲ N Scotland, UK
184 M9 **Benneydale** Waikato, North Island, NZ
Bennichab see Bennichchâb
76 H8 **Bennichchâb** var. Bennichab. Inchiri, W Mauritania
18 L10 **Bennington** Vermont, NE USA
185 E20 **Ben Ohau Range** ⛰ South Island, NZ
83 J21 **Benoni** Gauteng, NE South Africa
172 J2 **Be, Nosy** var. Nossi-Bé. island NW Madagascar
Bénoué see Benue
42 F2 **Benque Viejo del Carmen** Cayo, W Belize
101 G19 **Bensheim** Hessen, W Germany
37 N16 **Benson** Arizona, SW USA
29 S8 **Benson** Minnesota, N USA
21 U10 **Benson** North Carolina, SE USA
171 N15 **Benteng** Pulau Selayar, C Indonesia
83 A14 **Bentiaba** Namibe, SW Angola
181 T4 **Bentinck Island** island Wellesley Islands, Queensland, N Australia
80 E13 **Bentiu** Wahda, S Sudan
138 G8 **Bent Jbaïl** var. Bint Jubayl. S Lebanon
11 Q15 **Bentley** Alberta, SW Canada
61 I15 **Bento Gonçalves** Rio Grande do Sul, S Brazil
27 U12 **Benton** Arkansas, C USA
30 L16 **Benton** Illinois, N USA
20 H7 **Benton** Kentucky, S USA
22 G5 **Benton** Louisiana, S USA
27 Y7 **Benton** Missouri, C USA
20 M10 **Benton** Tennessee, S USA
31 O10 **Benton Harbor** Michigan, N USA
27 S9 **Bentonville** Arkansas, C USA
77 V16 **Benue** ◈ state SE Nigeria
78 F13 **Benue** Fr. Bénoué. ≈ Cameroon/Nigeria
163 V12 **Benxi** prev. Pen-ch'i, Penhsihu, Penki. Liaoning, NE China
Benyakoni see Byenyakoni
112 K10 **Beočin** Serbia, N Yugoslavia
Beodericsworth see Bury St Edmunds
112 M11 **Beograd** Eng. Belgrade, Ger. Belgrad; anc. Singidunum. ● (Yugoslavia) Serbia, N Yugoslavia
112 L11 **Beograd** Eng. Belgrade. ✕ Serbia, N Yugoslavia
76 M16 **Béoumi** C Ivory Coast
35 V3 **Beowawe** Nevada, W USA
164 E14 **Beppu** Ōita, Kyūshū, SW Japan
187 X15 **Beqa** prev. Mbengga. island W Fiji
Beqa Barrier Reef see Kavukavu Reef
45 Y14 **Bequia** island C Saint Vincent and the Grenadines
113 L16 **Berane** prev. Ivangrad. Montenegro, SW Yugoslavia
113 L21 **Berat** var. Berati, SCr. Beligrad. Berat, C Albania
113 L21 **Berat** ◈ district C Albania
Berătău see Berettyó
Berati see Berat
Beraun see Berounka, Czech Republic
Beraun see Beroun, Czech Republic
171 U13 **Berau, Teluk** var. MacCluer Gulf. bay Irian Jaya, E Indonesia
80 G8 **Berber** River Nile, NE Sudan
80 N12 **Berbera** Woqooyi Galbeed, NW Somalia
79 H16 **Berbérati** Mambéré-Kadéï, SW Central African Republic
Berberia, Cabo de see Barbaria, Cap de
55 T9 **Berbice River** ≈ NE Guyana
Berchid see Berrechid
103 N2 **Berck-Plage** Pas-de-Calais, N France
25 T13 **Berclair** Texas, SW USA
117 W10 **Berda** ≈ SE Ukraine
Berdichev see Berdychiv
123 P10 **Berdigestyakh** Respublika Sakha (Yakutiya), NE Russian Federation
122 I12 **Berdsk** Novosibirskaya Oblast', C Russian Federation
117 W10 **Berdyans'k** Rus. Berdyansk; prev. Osipenko. Zaporiz'ka Oblast', SE Ukraine
117 W10 **Berdyans'ka Kosa** spit SE Ukraine
117 V10 **Berdyans'ka Zatoka** gulf S Ukraine
117 N5 **Berdychiv** Rus. Berdichev. Zhytomyrs'ka Oblast', N Ukraine
20 M6 **Berea** Kentucky, S USA
Beregovo/Beregszász see Berehove
116 G8 **Berehove** Cz. Berehovo, Hung. Beregszász, Rus. Beregovo. Zakarpats'ka Oblast', W Ukraine
Berehovo see Berehove
186 D9 **Bereina** Central, S PNG
45 O12 **Berekua** S Dominica
77 O16 **Berekum** W Ghana
75 Y11 **Berenice** var. Mînâ Baranîs. SE Egypt
9 O14 **Berens** ≈ Manitoba/Ontario, C Canada
11 X14 **Berens River** Manitoba, C Canada
29 R12 **Beresford** South Dakota, N USA
116 J4 **Berestechko** Volyns'ka Oblast', NW Ukraine
116 M11 **Berești** Galați, E Romania
117 U6 **Berestova** ≈ E Ukraine
Beretău see Berettyó
111 N23 **Berettyó** Rom. Barcău; prev. Berătău, Beretău. ≈ Hungary/Romania
111 N23 **Berettyóújfalu** Hajdú-Bihar, E Hungary
Berëza/Bereza Kartuska see Byaroza
117 Q4 **Berezan'** Kyyivs'ka Oblast', N Ukraine
117 Q10 **Berezanka** Mykolayivs'ka Oblast', S Ukraine
116 J6 **Berezhany** Pol. Brzeżany. Ternopil's'ka Oblast', W Ukraine
Berezina see Byerezino
Berezino see Byerazino
117 P10 **Berezivka** Rus. Berezovka. Odes'ka Oblast', SW Ukraine
117 Q2 **Berezna** Chernihivs'ka Oblast', NE Ukraine
116 L3 **Berezne** Rivnens'ka Oblast', NW Ukraine
117 R9 **Bereznehuvate** Mykolayivs'ka Oblast', S Ukraine
127 N10 **Bereznik** Arkhangel'skaya Oblast', NW Russian Federation
127 U13 **Berezniki** Permskaya Oblast', NW Russian Federation
Berezovka see Berezivka
122 H9 **Berezovo** Khanty-Mansiyskiy Avtonomnyy Okrug, N Russian Federation
129 O9 **Berezovskaya** Volgogradskaya Oblast', SW Russian Federation
123 S13 **Berezovyy** Khabarovskiy Kray, E Russian Federation
83 E25 **Berg** ≈ W South Africa
Berg see Berg bei Rohrbach
105 V4 **Berga** Cataluña, NE Spain
95 N20 **Berga** Kalmar, S Sweden
136 B13 **Bergama** İzmir, W Turkey
106 E7 **Bergamo** anc. Bergomum. Lombardia, N Italy
105 P3 **Bergara** País Vasco, N Spain
109 S3 **Berg bei Rohrbach** var. Berg. Oberösterreich, N Austria
100 O6 **Bergen** Mecklenburg-Vorpommern, NE Germany
101 I11 **Bergen** Niedersachsen, NW Germany
98 H8 **Bergen** Noord-Holland, NW Netherlands
94 C13 **Bergen** Hordaland, S Norway
Bergen see Mons
55 W9 **Berg en Dal** Brokopondo, C Suriname
99 G15 **Bergen op Zoom** Noord-Brabant, S Netherlands
102 L13 **Bergerac** Dordogne, SW France
99 J16 **Bergeyk** Noord-Brabant, S Netherlands
101 D16 **Bergheim** Nordrhein-Westfalen, W Germany
55 X10 **Bergi** Sipaliwini, E Suriname
101 E16 **Bergisch Gladbach** Nordrhein-Westfalen, W Germany
101 F14 **Bergkamen** Nordrhein-Westfalen, W Germany
95 N21 **Bergkvara** Kalmar, S Sweden
Bergomum see Bergamo
98 K13 **Bergse Maas** ≈ S Netherlands
95 P15 **Bergshamra** Stockholm, C Sweden
94 N10 **Bergsjö** Gävleborg, C Sweden
93 J14 **Bergsviken** Norrbotten, N Sweden
98 L6 **Bergum** Fris. Burgum. Friesland, N Netherlands
98 M6 **Bergumer Meer** ◎ N Netherlands
94 N12 **Bergviken** ◎ C Sweden
168 M11 **Berhala, Selat** strait Sumatera, W Indonesia
Berhampore see Baharampur
123 W9 **Beringa, Ostrov** island E Russian Federation
99 J17 **Beringen** Limburg, NE Belgium
39 T12 **Bering Glacier** glacier Alaska, USA
Beringov Proliv see Bering Strait
123 W6 **Beringovskiy** Chukotskiy Avtonomnyy Okrug, NE Russian Federation

◆ Country ● Country Capital ◇ Dependent Territory ○ Dependent Territory Capital ◈ Administrative Region ✕ International Airport ▲ Mountain ⛰ Mountain Range ▲ Volcano ≈ River ◎ Lake ▣ Reservoir

192 L2 **Bering Sea** *sea* N Pacific Ocean
38 L9 **Bering Strait** *Rus.* Beringov Proliv. *strait* Bering Sea/Chukchi Sea
Berislav *see* Beryslav
105 O15 **Berja** Andalucía, S Spain
94 H9 **Berkåk** Sør-Trøndelag, S Norway
98 N11 **Berkel** ~ Germany/Netherlands
35 N8 **Berkeley** California, W USA
65 E24 **Berkeley Sound** *sound* NE Falkland Islands
21 V2 **Berkeley Springs** *var.* Bath. West Virginia, NE USA
195 N6 **Berkner Island** *island* Antarctica
114 G8 **Berkovitsa** Montana, NW Bulgaria
97 M22 **Berkshire** *cultural region* S England, UK
99 H17 **Berlaar** Antwerpen, N Belgium
Berlanga *see* Berlanga de Duero
105 P6 **Berlanga de Duero** *var.* Berlanga. Castilla-León, N Spain
(0) I16 **Berlanga Rise** *undersea feature* E Pacific Ocean
99 F17 **Berlare** Oost-Vlaanderen, NW Belgium
104 E9 **Berlenga, Ilha da** *island* C Portugal
92 M7 **Berlevåg** Finnmark, N Norway
100 O12 **Berlin** ● (Germany) Berlin, NE Germany
21 Z4 **Berlin** Maryland, NE USA
19 O7 **Berlin** New Hampshire, NE USA
18 D16 **Berlin** Pennsylvania, NE USA
30 L7 **Berlin** Wisconsin, N USA
100 O12 **Berlin** ◈ *state* NE Germany
Berlinchen *see* Barlinek
31 U12 **Berlin Lake** ▣ Ohio, N USA
183 R11 **Bermagui** New South Wales, SE Australia
40 L8 **Bermejillo** Durango, C Mexico
62 M6 **Bermejo (viejo), Río** ~ N Argentina
62 L5 **Bermejo, Río** ~ N Argentina
62 I10 **Bermejo, Río** ~ W Argentina
105 P2 **Bermeo** País Vasco, N Spain
104 K6 **Bermillo de Sayago** Castilla-León, N Spain
106 E6 **Bermina, Pizzo** *Rmsch.* Piz Bernina. ▲ Italy/Switzerland *see also* Bernina, Piz
64 A12 **Bermuda** *var.* Bermuda Islands, Bermudas; *prev.* Somers Islands. ◇ *UK crown colony* NW Atlantic Ocean
1 N11 **Bermuda** *var.* Great Bermuda, Long Island, Main Island. *island* Bermuda
Bermuda Islands *see* Bermuda
Bermuda-New England Seamount Arc *see* New England Seamounts
1 N11 **Bermuda Rise** *undersea feature* C Sargasso Sea
Bermudas *see* Bermuda
108 D8 **Bern** *Fr.* Berne. ● (Switzerland) Bern, W Switzerland
108 D9 **Bern** *Fr.* Berne. ◈ *canton* W Switzerland
37 R11 **Bernalillo** New Mexico, SW USA
14 H12 **Bernard Lake** ◎ Ontario, S Canada
61 B18 **Bernardo de Irigoyen** Santa Fe, NE Argentina
18 J14 **Bernardsville** New Jersey, NE USA
63 K14 **Bernasconi** La Pampa, C Argentina
100 O12 **Bernau** Brandenburg, NE Germany
102 L4 **Bernay** Eure, N France
101 L14 **Bernburg** Sachsen-Anhalt, C Germany
109 X5 **Berndorf** Niederösterreich, NE Austria
31 Q12 **Berne** Indiana, N USA
Berne *see* Bern
108 D10 **Berner Alpen** *var.* Berner Oberland, *Eng.* Bernese Oberland. ▲▲ SW Switzerland
Berner Oberland/Bernese Oberland *see* Berner Alpen
109 Y2 **Bernhardsthal** Niederösterreich, N Austria
22 H4 **Bernice** Louisiana, S USA
27 Y8 **Bernie** Missouri, C USA
180 G9 **Bernier Island** *island* Western Australia
Bernina Pass *see* Bernina, Passo del
108 J10 **Bernina, Passo del** *Eng.* Bernina Pass. *pass* SE Switzerland
108 J10 **Bernina, Piz** *It.* Pizzo Bermina. ▲ Italy/Switzerland *see also* Bermina, Pizzo
99 E20 **Bérnissart** Hainaut, SW Belgium
101 E18 **Bernkastel-Kues** Rheinland-Pfalz, W Germany
Beroea *see* Ḥalab
172 H6 **Beroroha** Toliara, SW Madagascar
Béroubouay *see* Gbéroubouè
111 C17 **Beroun** *Ger.* Beraun. Středočeský Kraj, W Czech Republic
111 C16 **Berounka** *Ger.* Beraun. ~ W Czech Republic
113 Q18 **Berovo** E FYR Macedonia
74 F6 **Berrechid** *var.* Berchid. W Morocco
103 R15 **Berre, Étang de** ◎ SE France
103 S15 **Berre-l'Étang** Bouches-du-Rhône, SE France
182 K9 **Berri** South Australia
31 O10 **Berrien Springs** Michigan, N USA
183 O10 **Berrigan** New South Wales, SE Australia
103 N9 **Berry** *cultural region* C France
35 N7 **Berryessa, Lake** ◎ California, W USA
44 G2 **Berry Islands** *island group* N Bahamas
27 T9 **Berryville** Arkansas, C USA
21 V3 **Berryville** Virginia, NE USA
83 D21 **Berseba** Karas, S Namibia
117 O8 **Bershad'** Vinnyts'ka Oblast', C Ukraine
28 L3 **Berthold** North Dakota, N USA
37 T3 **Berthoud** Colorado, C USA
37 S4 **Berthoud Pass** *pass* Colorado, C USA
79 F15 **Bertoua** Est, E Cameroon
25 S10 **Bertram** Texas, SW USA
63 G22 **Bertrand, Cerro** ▲ S Argentina
99 J23 **Bertrix** Luxembourg, SE Belgium
191 P3 **Beru** *var.* Peru. *atoll* Tungaru, W Kiribati
Beruni *see* Beruniy
146 I9 **Beruniy** *var.* Biruni, *Rus.* Beruni. Qoraqalpoghiston Respublikasi, W Uzbekistan
58 F13 **Beruri** Amazonas, NW Brazil
18 H14 **Berwick** Pennsylvania, NE USA
96 K12 **Berwick** *cultural region* SE Scotland, UK
96 L12 **Berwick-upon-Tweed** N England, UK
117 S10 **Beryslav** *Rus.* Berislav. Khersons'ka Oblast', S Ukraine
Berytus *see* Beyrouth
172 H4 **Besalampy** Mahajanga, W Madagascar
103 T8 **Besançon** *anc.* Besontium, Vesontio. Doubs, E France
103 P10 **Besbre** ~ C France
Bescanuova *see* Baška
Besdan *see* Bezdan
Besed' *see* Byesyedz'
147 R10 **Beshariq** *Rus.* Besharyk; *prev.* Kirovo. Farghona Wiloyati, E Uzbekistan
Besharyk *see* Beshariq
146 L9 **Beshbuloq** *Rus.* Beshulak. Nawoiy Wiloyati, N Uzbekistan
Beshenkovichi *see* Byeshankovichy
146 M13 **Beshkent** Qashqadaryo Wiloyati, S Uzbekistan
Beshulak *see* Beshbuloq
112 L10 **Beška** Serbia, N Yugoslavia
Beskra *see* Biskra
129 O16 **Beslan** Respublika Severnaya Osetiya, SW Russian Federation
113 P16 **Besna Kobila** ▲ SE Yugoslavia
137 N16 **Besni** Adıyaman, S Turkey
Besontium *see* Besançon
121 Q2 **Beşparmak Dağları** *Eng.* Kyrenia Mountains. ▲▲ N Cyprus
Bessarabka *see* Basarabeasca
92 O2 **Bessels, Kapp** *headland* C Svalbard
23 P4 **Bessemer** Alabama, S USA
30 K3 **Bessemer** Michigan, N USA
21 Q10 **Bessemer City** North Carolina, SE USA
102 M10 **Bessines-sur-Gartempe** Haute-Vienne, C France
99 K15 **Best** Noord-Brabant, S Netherlands
25 N9 **Best** Texas, SW USA
127 O11 **Bestuzhevo** Arkhangel'skaya Oblast', NW Russian Federation
123 M11 **Bestyakh** Respublika Sakha (Yakutiya), NE Russian Federation
Beszterce *see* Bistriţa
Besztercebánya *see* Banská Bystrica
172 I5 **Betafo** Antananarivo, C Madagascar
104 H2 **Betanzos** Galicia, NW Spain
104 G2 **Betanzos, Ría de** *estuary* NW Spain
79 G15 **Bétaré Oya** Est, E Cameroon
105 S9 **Bétera** País Valenciano, E Spain
77 R15 **Bétérou** C Benin
83 K21 **Bethal** Mpumalanga, NE South Africa
30 K15 **Bethalto** Illinois, N USA
83 D21 **Bethanie** *var.* Bethanien, Bethany. Karas, S Namibia
Bethanien *see* Bethanie
27 S2 **Bethany** Missouri, C USA
27 N10 **Bethany** Oklahoma, C USA
Bethany *see* Bethanie
39 N12 **Bethel** Alaska, USA
19 P7 **Bethel** Maine, NE USA
21 W9 **Bethel** North Carolina, SE USA
18 B15 **Bethel Park** Pennsylvania, NE USA
21 W3 **Bethesda** Maryland, NE USA
83 J22 **Bethlehem** Free State, C South Africa
18 I14 **Bethlehem** Pennsylvania, NE USA
138 F10 **Bethlehem** *Ar.* Bayt Laḥm, *Heb.* Bet Leḥem. C West Bank
Bethlen *see* Beclean
83 I24 **Bethulie** Free State, C South Africa
103 O1 **Béthune** Pas-de-Calais, N France
102 M3 **Béthune** ~ N France
104 M14 **Béticos, Sistemas** *var.* Sistema Penibético, *Eng.* Baetic Cordillera, Baetic Mountains. ▲▲ S Spain
54 I6 **Betijoque** Trujillo, NW Venezuela
59 M20 **Betim** Minas Gerais, SE Brazil
190 H3 **Betio** Tarawa, W Kiribati
172 H7 **Betioky** Toliara, S Madagascar
Bet Leḥem *see* Bethlehem
Betlen *see* Beclean
167 O17 **Betong** Yala, SW Thailand
79 I16 **Bétou** La Likouala, N Congo
145 P14 **Betpak-Dala** *Kaz.* Betpaqdala. *plateau* S Kazakhstan
Betpaqdala *see* Betpak-Dala
172 H7 **Betroka** Toliara, S Madagascar
Betschau *see* Bečva
138 G9 **Bet She'an** *Ar.* Baysān, Beisān; *anc.* Scythopolis. Northern, N Israel
15 T6 **Betsiamites** Quebec, SE Canada
15 T6 **Betsiamites** ~ Quebec, SE Canada
172 I4 **Betsiboka** ~ N Madagascar
99 M25 **Bettembourg** Luxembourg, S Luxembourg
99 M23 **Bettendorf** Diekirch, NE Luxembourg
29 Z14 **Bettendorf** Iowa, C USA
75 R13 **Bette, Pic** *var.* Bikkū Bīttī, *It.* Picco Bette. ▲ S Libya
Bette, Picco *see* Bette, Pic
153 P12 **Bettiah** Bihār, N India
39 Q7 **Bettles** Alaska, USA
95 N17 **Bettna** Södermanland, C Sweden
154 H11 **Betūl** *prev.* Badnur. Madhya Pradesh, C India
154 H9 **Betwa** ~ C India
101 F16 **Betzdorf** Rheinland-Pfalz, W Germany
82 C9 **Béu** Uíge, NW Angola
31 P6 **Beulah** Michigan, N USA
28 L5 **Beulah** North Dakota, N USA
98 M8 **Beulakerwijde** ◎ N Netherlands
98 L13 **Beuningen** Gelderland, SE Netherlands
Beuthen *see* Bytom
103 N7 **Beuvron** ~ C France
99 F16 **Beveren** Oost-Vlaanderen, N Belgium
21 T9 **B.Everett Jordan Reservoir** *var.* Jordan Lake. ▣ North Carolina, SE USA
97 N17 **Beverley** E England, UK
Beverley *see* Beverly
99 J17 **Beverlo** Limburg, NE Belgium
19 P11 **Beverly** Massachusetts, NE USA
32 J9 **Beverly** *var.* Beverley. Washington, NW USA
35 S15 **Beverly Hills** California, W USA
101 I14 **Beverungen** Nordrhein-Westfalen, C Germany
98 H9 **Beverwijk** Noord-Holland, W Netherlands
108 C10 **Bex** Vaud, W Switzerland
97 P23 **Bexhill** *var.* Bexhill-on-Sea. SE England, UK
Bexhill-on-Sea *see* Bexhill
136 E17 **Bey Dağları** ▲▲ SW Turkey
Beyj *see* Belyy
136 E10 **Beykoz** İstanbul, NW Turkey
76 K15 **Beyla** Guinée-Forestière, SE Guinea
137 X12 **Beyläqan** *prev.* Zhdanov. SW Azerbaijan
80 L10 **Beylul** *var.* Beilul. SE Eritrea
144 H14 **Beyneu** *Kaz.* Beyneū. Mangistau, SW Kazakhstan
Beyneū *see* Beyneu
165 X14 **Beyonësu-retsugan** *Eng.* Bayonnaise Rocks. *island group* SE Japan
136 G12 **Beypazarı** Ankara, NW Turkey
155 F21 **Beypore** Kerala, SW India
138 G7 **Beyrouth** *var.* Bayrūt, *Eng.* Beirut; *anc.* Berytus. ● (Lebanon) W Lebanon
138 G7 **Beyrouth** ✕ W Lebanon
136 G15 **Beyşehir** Konya, SW Turkey
136 G15 **Beyşehir Gölü** ◎ C Turkey
108 J7 **Bezau** Vorarlberg, NW Austria
112 J8 **Bezdan** *Ger.* Besdan, *Hung.* Bezdán. Serbia, NW Yugoslavia
Bezdezh *see* Byezdzyezh
126 G15 **Bezhanitsy** Pskovskaya Oblast', W Russian Federation
126 K15 **Bezhetsk** Tverskaya Oblast', W Russian Federation
103 P16 **Béziers** *anc.* Baeterrae, Baeterrae Septimanorum, Julia Beterrae. Hérault, S France
Bezmein *see* Byuzmeyin
Bezwada *see* Vijayawāda
154 P12 **Bhadrak** *var.* Bhadrakh. Orissa, E India
Bhadrakh *see* Bhadrak
155 F19 **Bhadra Reservoir** ▣ SW India
155 F18 **Bhadrāvati** Karnātaka, SW India
153 R14 **Bhāgalpur** Bihār, NE India
Bhairab *see* Bhairab Bazar
153 U14 **Bhairab Bazar** *var.* Bhairab. Dhaka, C Bangladesh
153 O11 **Bhairahawa** Western, S Nepal
149 S8 **Bhakkar** Punjab, E Pakistan
153 P11 **Bhaktapur** Central, C Nepal
167 N3 **Bhamo** *var.* Banmo. Kachin State, N Myanmar
Bhāmragad *see* Bhāmragarh
154 K13 **Bhāmragarh** *var.* Bhāmragad. Mahārāshtra, C India
154 J12 **Bhandāra** Mahārāshtra, C India
Bhārat *see* India
152 J12 **Bharatpur** *prev.* Bhurtpore. Rājasthān, N India
154 D11 **Bharūch** Gujarāt, W India
155 E18 **Bhatkal** Karnātaka, W India
153 O13 **Bhatni** *var.* Bhatni Junction. Uttar Pradesh, N India
Bhatni Junction *see* Bhatni
153 S16 **Bhātpāra** West Bengal, NE India
149 U7 **Bhaun** Punjab, E Pakistan
Bhaunagar *see* Bhāvnagar
154 M13 **Bhavānīpātna** Orissa, E India
155 H21 **Bhavānīsāgar Reservoir** ▣ S India
154 D11 **Bhāvnagar** *prev.* Bhaunagar. Gujarāt, W India
Bheanntraí, Bá *see* Bantry Bay
Bheara, Béal an *see* Gweebarra Bay
154 K12 **Bhilai** Madhya Pradesh, C India
152 G13 **Bhīlwāra** Rājasthān, N India
155 E14 **Bhīma** ~ S India
155 K16 **Bhīmavaram** Andhra Pradesh, E India
154 I7 **Bhind** Madhya Pradesh, C India
152 E13 **Bhīnmāl** Rājasthān, N India
Bhir *see* Bīd
154 D13 **Bhiwandi** Mahārāshtra, W India
152 H10 **Bhiwāni** Haryāna, N India
152 L13 **Bhognīpur** Uttar Pradesh, N India
153 U16 **Bhola** Khulna, S Bangladesh
154 H10 **Bhopāl** Madhya Pradesh, C India
155 J14 **Bhopālpatnam** Madhya Pradesh, C India
155 E14 **Bhor** Mahārāshtra, W India
154 O12 **Bhubaneshwar** *prev.* Bhubaneswar, Bhuvaneshwar. Orissa, E India
Bhubaneswar *see* Bhubaneshwar
154 B9 **Bhuj** Gujarāt, W India
Bhuket *see* Phuket
Bhurtpore *see* Bharatpur
Bhusaval *see* Bhusāwal
154 G12 **Bhusāwal** *prev.* Bhusaval. Mahārāshtra, C India
153 T12 **Bhutan** *off.* Kingdom of Bhutan, *var.* Druk-yul. ◆ *monarchy* S Asia
Bhuvaneshwar *see* Bhubaneshwar
143 T15 **Bīābān, Kūh-e** ▲▲ S Iran
77 V18 **Biafra, Bight of** *var.* Bight of Bonny. *bay* W Africa
171 W12 **Biak** Irian Jaya, E Indonesia
171 W12 **Biak, Pulau** *island* E Indonesia
110 P12 **Biała Podlaska** Lubelskie, E Poland
110 F7 **Białogard** *Ger.* Belgard. Zachodniopomorskie, NW Poland
110 P10 **Białowieska, Puszcza** *Bel.* Byelavyezhskaya Pushcha, *Rus.* Belovezhskaya Pushcha. *physical region* Belarus/Poland *see also* Byelavyezhskaya Pushcha
110 G8 **Biały Bór** *Ger.* Baldenburg. Zachodniopomorskie, NW Poland
110 P9 **Białystok** *Rus.* Belostok, Bielostok. Podlaskie, NE Poland
107 L24 **Biancavilla** *prev.* Inessa. Sicilia, Italy, C Mediterranean Sea
Bianco, Monte *see* Blanc, Mont
76 L15 **Biankouma** W Ivory Coast
167 R7 **Bia, Phou** *var.* Pou Bia. ▲ C Laos
Bia, Pou *see* Bia, Phou
143 R5 **Bīārjmand** Semnān, N Iran
105 P4 **Biarra** ~ NE Spain
102 I15 **Biarritz** Pyrénées-Atlantiques, SW France
108 H10 **Biasca** Ticino, S Switzerland
61 E17 **Biassini** Salto, N Uruguay
165 S3 **Bibai** Hokkaidō, NE Japan
83 B15 **Bibala** *Port.* Vila Arriaga. Namibe, SW Angola
104 I4 **Bibéi** ~ NW Spain
Biberach *see* Biberach an der Riss
101 I23 **Biberach an der Riss** *var.* Biberach, *Ger.* Biberach an der Riß. Baden-Württemberg, S Germany
108 E7 **Biberist** Solothurn, NW Switzerland
77 O16 **Bibiani** SW Ghana
112 C13 **Bibinje** Zadar, SW Croatia
Biblical Gebal *see* Jbaïl
116 I5 **Bibrka** *Pol.* Bóbrka, *Rus.* Bobrka. L'vivs'ka Oblast', NW Ukraine
117 N10 **Bic** ~ S Moldova
113 M18 **Bicaj** Kukës, NE Albania
116 K10 **Bicaz** *Hung.* Békás. Neamţ, NE Romania
183 Q16 **Bicheno** Tasmania, SE Australia
Bichiş *see* Békés
Bichiş-Ciaba *see* Békéscsaba
Bichitra *see* Phichit
137 P8 **Bichvint'a** *Rus.* Pitsunda. NW Georgia
15 T7 **Bic, Île du** *island* Quebec, SE Canada
32 J10 **Bickleton** Washington, NW USA
36 L6 **Bicknell** Utah, W USA
171 S11 **Bicoli** Pulau Halmahera, E Indonesia
111 J22 **Bicske** Fejér, C Hungary
155 F14 **Bīd** *prev.* Bhir. Mahārāshtra, W India
77 U15 **Bida** Niger, C Nigeria
155 H15 **Bīdar** Karnātaka, C India
141 Y8 **Bidbid** NE Oman
19 P9 **Biddeford** Maine, NE USA
98 L9 **Biddinghuizen** Flevoland, C Netherlands
33 X11 **Biddle** Montana, NW USA
97 J23 **Bideford** SW England, UK
82 D13 **Bié** ◈ *province* C Angola
35 O2 **Bieber** California, W USA
110 O9 **Biebrza** ~ NE Poland
165 T3 **Biei** Hokkaidō, NE Japan
108 D8 **Biel** *Fr.* Bienne. Bern, W Switzerland
100 G13 **Bielefeld** Nordrhein-Westfalen, NW Germany
108 D8 **Bieler See** *Fr.* Lac de Bienne. ◎ W Switzerland
Bielitz/Bielitz-Biala *see* Bielsko-Biała
106 C7 **Biella** Piemonte, N Italy
Bielostok *see* Białystok
111 J17 **Bielsko-Biała** *Ger.* Bielitz, Bielitz-Biala. Śląskie, S Poland
110 P10 **Bielsk Podlaski** Białystok, E Poland
Bien Bien *see* Điện Biên
Biên Đông *see* South China Sea
9 V17 **Bienfait** Saskatchewan, S Canada
167 T14 **Biên Hoa** Đông Nai, S Vietnam
Bienne *see* Biel
Bienne, Lac de *see* Bieler See
12 K8 **Bienville, Lac** ◎ Quebec, C Canada
82 D13 **Bié, Planalto do** *var.* Bié Plateau. *plateau* C Angola
Bié Plateau *see* Bié, Planalto do
108 B9 **Bière** Vaud, W Switzerland
98 O4 **Bierum** Groningen, NE Netherlands
98 I13 **Biesbos** *var.* Biesbosch. *wetland* S Netherlands
Biesbosch *see* Biesbos
99 H21 **Biesme** Namur, S Belgium
101 H21 **Bietigheim-Bissingen** Baden-Württemberg, SW Germany
99 I23 **Bièvre** Namur, SE Belgium
79 D18 **Bifoun** Moyen-Ogooué, NW Gabon
165 T2 **Bifuka** Hokkaidō, NE Japan
136 C11 **Biga** Çanakkale, NW Turkey
136 C13 **Bigadiç** Balıkesir, W Turkey
26 J7 **Big Basin** *basin* Kansas, C USA
185 B20 **Big Bay** *bay* South Island, NZ
31 O5 **Big Bay de Noc** ◎ Michigan, N USA
31 N3 **Big Bay Point** *headland* Michigan, N USA
33 R10 **Big Belt Mountains** ▲▲ Montana, NW USA
29 N10 **Big Bend Dam** *dam* South Dakota, N USA
24 K12 **Big Bend National Park** *national park* Texas, S USA
22 K5 **Big Black River** ~ Mississippi, S USA
27 O3 **Big Blue River** ~ Kansas/Nebraska, C USA
24 M10 **Big Canyon** ~ Texas, SW USA
33 N12 **Big Creek** Idaho, NW USA
23 N8 **Big Creek Lake** ▣ Alabama, S USA
23 X15 **Big Cypress Swamp** *wetland* Florida, SE USA
39 S9 **Big Delta** Alaska, USA
30 K6 **Big Eau Pleine Reservoir** ▣ Wisconsin, N USA
19 P5 **Bigelow Mountain** ▲ Maine, NE USA
29 U3 **Big Falls** Minnesota, N USA
33 P8 **Bigfork** Montana, NW USA
29 U3 **Big Fork River** ~ Minnesota, N USA
11 S15 **Biggar** Saskatchewan, S Canada
180 L3 **Bigge Island** *island* Western Australia
35 O5 **Biggs** California, W USA
32 I11 **Biggs** Oregon, NW USA
14 K13 **Big Gull Lake** ◎ Ontario, SE Canada
37 P16 **Big Hachet Peak** ▲ New Mexico, SW USA
33 P11 **Big Hole River** ~ Montana, NW USA
33 V13 **Bighorn Basin** *basin* Wyoming, C USA
33 U11 **Bighorn Lake** ◎ Montana/Wyoming, N USA
33 W13 **Bighorn Mountains** ▲▲ Wyoming, C USA
36 J13 **Big Horn Peak** ▲ Arizona, SW USA
33 V11 **Bighorn River** ~ Montana/Wyoming, NW USA
9 S7 **Big Island** *island* Nunavut, NE Canada
39 O16 **Big Koniuji Island** *island* Shumagin Islands, Alaska, USA
25 N9 **Big Lake** Texas, SW USA
19 T5 **Big Lake** ◎ Maine, NE USA
30 I3 **Big Manitou Falls** *waterfall* Wisconsin, N USA
35 R2 **Big Mountain** ▲ Nevada, W USA
108 G10 **Bignasco** Ticino, S Switzerland
29 R16 **Big Nemaha River** ~ Nebraska, C USA
76 G12 **Bignona** SW Senegal
Bigorra *see* Tarbes
Bigosovo *see* Bihosava
35 S10 **Big Pine** California, W USA
35 Q14 **Big Pine Mountain** ▲ California, W USA
27 V6 **Big Piney Creek** ~ Missouri, C USA
65 M24 **Big Point** *headland* N Tristan da Cunha
31 P8 **Big Rapids** Michigan, N USA
30 K6 **Big Rib River** ~ Wisconsin, N USA
14 L14 **Big Rideau Lake** ◎ Ontario, SE Canada
11 T14 **Big River** Saskatchewan, C Canada
27 X5 **Big River** ~ Missouri, C USA
31 N7 **Big Sable Point** *headland* Michigan, N USA
33 S7 **Big Sandy** Montana, NW USA
25 W6 **Big Sandy** Texas, SW USA
37 V5 **Big Sandy Creek** ~ Colorado, C USA
29 Q16 **Big Sandy Creek** ~ Nebraska, C USA
29 V5 **Big Sandy Lake** ◎ Minnesota, N USA
36 J11 **Big Sandy River** ~ Arizona, SW USA
21 P5 **Big Sandy River** ~ S USA
23 V6 **Big Satilla Creek** ~ Georgia, SE USA
29 R12 **Big Sioux River** ~ Iowa/South Dakota, N USA
35 U7 **Big Smoky Valley** *valley* Nevada, W USA
25 N7 **Big Spring** Texas, SW USA
19 Q5 **Big Squaw Mountain** ▲ Maine, NE USA
21 O7 **Big Stone Gap** Virginia, NE USA
29 Q8 **Big Stone Lake** ◎ Minnesota/South Dakota, N USA
22 K4 **Big Sunflower River** ~ Mississippi, S USA
33 T11 **Big Timber** Montana, NW USA
12 D8 **Big Trout Lake** Ontario, C Canada
14 I12 **Big Trout Lake** ◎ Ontario, SE Canada
35 O2 **Big Valley Mountains** ▲▲ California, W USA
25 Q13 **Big Wells** Texas, SW USA
14 F11 **Bigwood** Ontario, S Canada
112 D11 **Bihać** Federacija Bosna I Hercegovina, NW Bosnia and Herzegovina
153 P14 **Bihār** *prev.* Behar. ◈ *state* N India
Bihār *see* Bihār Sharīf
81 F20 **Biharamulo** Kagera, NW Tanzania
153 R13 **Bihārīganj** Bihār, NE India
153 P14 **Bihār Sharīf** *var.* Bihār. Bihār, N India
116 F10 **Bihor** ◈ *county* NW Romania
165 V3 **Bihoro** Hokkaidō, NE Japan
118 K11 **Bihosava** *Rus.* Bigosovo. Vitsyebskaya Voblasts', NW Belarus
Bijagos Archipelago *see* Bijagós, Arquipélago dos
76 G13 **Bijagós, Arquipélago dos** *var.* Bijagos Archipelago. *island group* W Guinea-Bissau
155 F16 **Bijāpur** Karnātaka, C India
142 K5 **Bījār** Kordestān, W Iran
112 J11 **Bijeljina** Republika Srpska, NE Bosnia and Herzegovina
113 K15 **Bijelo Polje** Montenegro, SW Yugoslavia
160 I11 **Bijie** Guizhou, S China
152 J10 **Bijnor** Uttar Pradesh, N India
152 F11 **Bīkāner** Rājasthān, NW India
189 V3 **Bikar Atoll** *var.* Pikaar. *atoll* Ratak Chain, N Marshall Islands
190 H3 **Bikeman** *atoll* Tungaru, W Kiribati
190 I3 **Bikenebu** Tarawa, W Kiribati
123 S14 **Bikin** Khabarovskiy Kray, SE Russian Federation
123 S14 **Bikin** ~ SE Russian Federation
189 R3 **Bikini Atoll** *var.* Pikinni. *atoll* Ralik Chain, NW Marshall Islands
83 L17 **Bikita** Masvingo, E Zimbabwe
Bīkkū Bīttī *see* Bette, Pic
79 I19 **Bikoro** Equateur, W Dem. Rep. Congo (Zaire)
141 Z9 **Bilād Banī Bū 'Alī** NE Oman
141 Z9 **Bilād Banī Bū Ḥasan** NE Oman
141 X9 **Bilād Manaḥ** *var.* Manaḥ. NE Oman
77 Q12 **Bilanga** C Burkina
152 F12 **Bilāra** Rājasthān, N India
152 K10 **Bilāri** Uttar Pradesh, N India
138 J5 **Bil'ās, Jabal al** ▲ C Syria
152 I8 **Bilāspur** Himāchal Pradesh, N India
154 L11 **Bilāspur** Madhya Pradesh, C India
168 J9 **Bila, Sungai** ~ Sumatera, W Indonesia
137 Y13 **Biläsuvar** *Rus.* Bilyasuvar; *prev.* Pushkino. SE Azerbaijan
117 O5 **Bila Tserkva** *Rus.* Belaya Tserkov'. Kyyivs'ka Oblast', N Ukraine
167 N11 **Bilauktaung Range** *var.* Thanintari Taungdan. ▲▲ Myanmar/Thailand
105 O2 **Bilbao** *Basq.* Bilbo. País Vasco, N Spain
Bilbo *see* Bilbao
92 H2 **Bíldudalur** Vestfirdhir, NW Iceland
113 I16 **Bileća** Republika Srpska, S Bosnia and Herzegovina
136 E12 **Bilecik** Bilecik, NW Turkey
136 F12 **Bilecik** ◈ *province* NW Turkey
116 E11 **Biled** *Ger.* Billed, *Hung.* Billéd. Timiş, W Romania
111 O15 **Biłgoraj** Lubelskie, E Poland
117 P11 **Bilhorod-Dnistrovs'kyy** *Rus.* Belgorod-Dnestrovskiy, *Rom.* Cetatea Albă; *prev.* Akkerman, *anc.* Tyras. Odes'ka Oblast', SW Ukraine
79 M16 **Bili** Orientale, N Dem. Rep. Congo (Zaire)
123 T6 **Bilibino** Chukotskiy Avtonomnyy Okrug, NE Russian Federation
166 M8 **Bilin** Mon State, S Myanmar
113 N21 **Bilisht** *var.* Bilishti. Korçë, SE Albania
Bilishti *see* Bilisht
183 N10 **Billabong Creek** *var.* Moulamein Creek. *seasonal river* New South Wales, SE Australia
182 G4 **Billa Kalina** South Australia
197 Q17 **Bill Baileys Bank** *undersea feature* N Atlantic Ocean
Billed/Billéd *see* Biled
153 N14 **Billi** Uttar Pradesh, N India
97 M15 **Billingham** N England, UK
33 U11 **Billings** Montana, NW USA
95 J16 **Billingsfors** Västra Götaland, S Sweden
Bill of Cape Clear, The *see* Clear, Cape
28 L9 **Billsburg** South Dakota, N USA
95 F23 **Billund** Ribe, W Denmark
36 L11 **Bill Williams Mountain** ▲ Arizona, SW USA
36 I12 **Bill Williams River** ~ Arizona, SW USA
77 Y8 **Bilma** Agadez, NE Niger
77 Y8 **Bilma, Grand Erg de** *desert* NE Niger
181 Y9 **Biloela** Queensland, E Australia
112 G8 **Bilo Gora** ▲▲ N Croatia
117 U13 **Bilohirs'k** *Rus.* Belogorsk; *prev.* Karasubazar. Respublika Krym, S Ukraine
116 M3 **Bilokorovychi** *Rus.* Belokorovichi. Zhytomyrs'ka Oblast', N Ukraine
117 X5 **Bilokurakine** Luhans'ka Oblast', E Ukraine
117 T3 **Bilopillya** *Rus.* Belopol'ye. Sums'ka Oblast', NE Ukraine
117 Y6 **Bilovods'k** *Rus.* Belovodsk. Luhans'ka Oblast', E Ukraine
22 M9 **Biloxi** Mississippi, S USA
117 R10 **Bilozerka** Khersons'ka Oblast', S Ukraine
117 W7 **Bilozers'ke** Donets'ka Oblast', E Ukraine
98 J11 **Bilthoven** Utrecht, C Netherlands
78 K9 **Biltine** Biltine, E Chad
78 J9 **Biltine** *off.* Préfecture de Biltine. ◈ *prefecture* E Chad
162 D5 **Bilüü** Bayan-Ölgiy, W Mongolia
Bilwi *see* Puerto Cabezas
Bilyasuvar *see* Biläsuvar
117 O11 **Bilyayivka** Odes'ka Oblast', SW Ukraine

◆ Country ● Country Capital ◇ Dependent Territory ○ Dependent Territory Capital ◈ Administrative Region ✕ International Airport ▲ Mountain ▲▲ Mountain Range Volcano ~ River ◎ Lake ▣ Reservoir

99 K18 **Bilzen** Limburg, NE Belgium
Bimbéréké *see* Bembèrèkè
183 R10 **Bimberi Peak** ▲ New South Wales, SE Australia
77 Q15 **Bimbila** E Ghana
79 I15 **Bimbo** Ombella-Mpoko, SW Central African Republic
44 F2 **Bimini Islands** *island group* W Bahamas
154 I9 **Bīna** Madhya Pradesh, C India
143 T4 **Bīnālūd, Kūh-e** ▲▲ NE Iran
99 F20 **Binche** Hainaut, S Belgium
Bindloe Island *see* Marchena, Isla
83 L16 **Bindura** Mashonaland Central, NE Zimbabwe
105 T5 **Binefar** Aragón, NE Spain
83 J16 **Binga** Matabeleland North, W Zimbabwe
183 T5 **Bingara** New South Wales, SE Australia
101 F18 **Bingen am Rhein** Rheinland-Pfalz, SW Germany
26 M11 **Binger** Oklahoma, C USA
Bingerau *see* Węgrów
Bin Ghalfān, Jazā'ir *see* Ḥalāniyāt, Juzur al
19 Q6 **Bingham** Maine, NE USA
18 H11 **Binghamton** New York, NE USA
Bin Ghanīmah, Jabal *see* Bin Ghunaymah, Jabal
75 P11 **Bin Ghunaymah, Jabal** *var.* Jabal Bin Ghanīmah. ▲▲ C Libya
139 U3 **Bingird** NE Iraq
137 P14 **Bingöl** Bingöl, E Turkey
137 P14 **Bingöl** ◈ *province* E Turkey
161 R6 **Binhai** *var.* Binhai Xian, Dongkan. Jiangsu, E China
Binhai Xian *see* Binhai
167 V11 **Binh Đinh** *var.* An Nhon. Binh Đinh, C Vietnam
167 U10 **Binh Sơn** *var.* Châu Ô. Quang Ngai, C Vietnam
Binimani *see* Bintimani
168 I8 **Binjai** Sumatera, W Indonesia
183 R6 **Binnaway** New South Wales, SE Australia
108 E6 **Binningen** Basel-Land, NW Switzerland
168 J8 **Bintang, Banjaran** ▲▲ Peninsular Malaysia
168 M10 **Bintan, Pulau** *island* Kepulauan Riau, W Indonesia
76 J14 **Bintimani** *var.* Binimani. ▲ NE Sierra Leone
Bint Jubayl *see* Bent Jbaïl
169 S9 **Bintulu** Sarawak, East Malaysia
171 V12 **Bintuni** *prev.* Steenkool. Irian Jaya, E Indonesia
163 W8 **Bin Xian** Heilongjiang, NE China
160 K14 **Binyang** Guangxi Zhuangzu Zizhiqu, S China
161 Q4 **Binzhou** Shandong, E China
63 G14 **Bío Bío** *off.* Región del Bío Bío. ◈ *region* C Chile
63 G14 **Bío Bío, Río** ≈ C Chile
79 C16 **Bioco, Isla de** *var.* Bioko, *Eng.* Fernando Po, *Sp.* Fernando Póo; *prev.* Macías Nguema Biyogo. *island* NW Equatorial Guinea
112 D13 **Biograd na Moru** *It.* Zaravecchia. Zadar, SW Croatia
Bioko *see* Bioco, Isla de
113 F14 **Biokovo** ▲▲ S Croatia
Biorra *see* Birr
Bipontium *see* Zweibrücken
143 W13 **Birag, Kūh-e** ▲▲ SE Iran
75 O10 **Birāk** *var.* Brak. C Libya
139 S10 **Bi'r al Islām** C Iraq
154 N11 **Biramitrapur** Orissa, E India
139 T11 **Bi'r an Niṣf** S Iraq
112 L12 **Birao** Vakaga, NE Central African Republic
158 M6 **Biratar Bulak** *well* NW China
153 R12 **Biratnagar** Eastern, SE Nepal
165 R5 **Biratori** Hokkaidō, NE Japan
39 S8 **Birch Creek** Alaska, USA
38 M11 **Birch Creek** ≈ Alaska, USA
11 T14 **Birch Hills** Saskatchewan, S Canada
182 M10 **Birchip** Victoria, SE Australia
29 X4 **Birch Lake** ◎ Minnesota, N USA
11 Q11 **Birch Mountains** ▲▲ Alberta, W Canada
11 V15 **Birch River** Manitoba, S Canada
44 H12 **Birchs Hill** *hill* W Jamaica
39 R11 **Birchwood** Alaska, USA
188 I5 **Bird Island** *island* S Northern Mariana Islands
137 N16 **Birecik** Şanlıurfa, S Turkey
152 M10 **Birendranagar** *var.* Surkhet. Mid Western, W Nepal
Bir es Saba *see* Be'ér Sheva'
74 A12 **Bir-Gandouz** SW Western Sahara
153 P12 **Birganj** Central, C Nepal
81 B14 **Biri** ≈ W Sudan
Bi'r Ibn Hirmās *see* Al Bi'r
143 U8 **Birjand** Khorāsān, E Iran
139 T11 **Birkat Ḥāmid** *well* S Iraq
95 F18 **Birkeland** Aust-Agder, S Norway
101 E19 **Birkenfeld** Rheinland-Pfalz, SW Germany
97 K18 **Birkenhead** NW England, UK
109 W7 **Birkfeld** Steiermark, SE Austria
182 A2 **Birksgate Range** ▲▲ South Australia
Birlad *see* Bârlad
97 K20 **Birmingham** C England, UK
23 P4 **Birmingham** Alabama, S USA
97 M20 **Birmingham** × C England, UK
Bir Moghrein *see* Bîr Mogreïn
76 J4 **Bîr Mogreïn** *var.* Bir Moghrein; *prev.* Fort-Trinquet. Tiris Zemmour, N Mauritania
191 S4 **Birnie Island** *atoll* Phoenix Islands, C Kiribati
Birni-Ngaouré *see* Birnin Gaouré
77 S12 **Birnin Gaouré** *var.* Birni-Ngaouré. Dosso, SW Niger
77 S12 **Birnin Kebbi** Kebbi, NW Nigeria
Birni-Nkonni *see* Birnin Konni
77 T12 **Birnin Konni** *var.* Birni-Nkonni. Tahoua, SW Niger
77 W13 **Birnin Kudu** Jigawa, N Nigeria
123 S16 **Birobidzhan** Yevreyskaya Avtonomnaya Oblast', SE Russian Federation
97 D18 **Birr** *var.* Parsonstown, *Ir.* Biorra. C Ireland
183 P4 **Birrie River** ≈ New South Wales/Queensland, SE Australia
108 D7 **Birse** ≈ NW Switzerland
Birsen *see* Biržai
108 E6 **Birsfelden** Basel-Land, NW Switzerland
129 U4 **Birsk** Respublika Bashkortostan, W Russian Federation
119 F14 **Birštonas** Prienai, C Lithuania
159 P14 **Biru** Xinjiang Uygur Zizhiqu, W China
Biruni *see* Beruniy
122 L12 **Biryusa** ≈ C Russian Federation
122 L12 **Biryusinsk** Irkutskaya Oblast', C Russian Federation
118 G10 **Biržai** *Ger.* Birsen. Biržai, NE Lithuania
121 P16 **Birżebbuġa** SE Malta
Bisanthe *see* Tekirdağ
171 R12 **Bisa, Pulau** *island* Maluku, E Indonesia
37 N17 **Bisbee** Arizona, SW USA
29 O2 **Bisbee** North Dakota, N USA
Biscaia, Baía de *see* Biscay, Bay of
102 I13 **Biscarrosse et de Parentis, Étang de** ◎ SW France
104 M1 **Biscay, Bay of** *Sp.* Golfo de Vizcaya, *Port.* Baía de Biscaia. *bay* France/Spain
23 Z16 **Biscayne Bay** *bay* Florida, SE USA
64 M7 **Biscay Plain** *undersea feature* SE Bay of Biscay
107 N17 **Bisceglie** Puglia, SE Italy
Bischoflack *see* Škofja Loka
Bischofsburg *see* Biskupiec
109 Q7 **Bischofshofen** Salzburg, NW Austria
101 P15 **Bischofswerda** Sachsen, E Germany
103 V5 **Bischwiller** Bas-Rhin, NE France
21 T10 **Biscoe** North Carolina, SE USA
194 G5 **Biscoe Islands** *island group* Antarctica
14 E9 **Biscotasi Lake** ◎ Ontario, S Canada
14 E9 **Biscotasing** Ontario, S Canada
54 J6 **Biscucuy** Portuguesa, NW Venezuela
114 K11 **Biser** Khaskovo, S Bulgaria
113 D15 **Biševo** *It.* Busi. *island* SW Croatia
141 N12 **Bishah, Wādī** *dry watercourse* C Saudi Arabia
147 U7 **Bishkek** *var.* Pishpek; *prev.* Frunze. ● (Kyrgyzstan) Chuyskaya Oblast', N Kyrgyzstan
147 U7 **Bishkek** × Chuyskaya Oblast', N Kyrgyzstan
153 R16 **Bishnupur** West Bengal, NE India
83 J25 **Bisho** Eastern Cape, S South Africa
35 S9 **Bishop** California, W USA
25 S15 **Bishop** Texas, SW USA
97 L15 **Bishop Auckland** N England, UK
Bishop's Lynn *see* King's Lynn
97 O21 **Bishop's Stortford** E England, UK
21 S12 **Bishopville** South Carolina, SE USA
138 M5 **Bishrī, Jabal** ▲▲ E Syria
163 U4 **Bishui** Heilongjiang, NE China
81 G17 **Bisina, Lake** *prev.* Lake Salisbury. ◎ E Uganda
Biskara *see* Biskra
74 L6 **Biskra** *var.* Beskra, Biskara. NE Algeria
110 M8 **Biskupiec** *Ger.* Bischofsburg. Warmińsko-Mazurskie, NE Poland
171 R7 **Bislig** Mindanao, S Philippines
27 X6 **Bismarck** Missouri, C USA
28 M5 **Bismarck** *state capital* North Dakota, N USA
186 D5 **Bismarck Archipelago** *island group* NE PNG
131 Z16 **Bismarck Plate** *tectonic feature* W Pacific Ocean
186 D7 **Bismarck Range** ▲▲ N PNG
186 E6 **Bismarck Sea** *sea* W Pacific Ocean
137 P15 **Bismil** Dıyarbakır, SE Turkey
43 N6 **Bismuna, Laguna** *lagoon* NE Nicaragua
Bisnulok *see* Phitsanulok
171 R10 **Bisoa, Tanjung** *headland* Pulau Halmahera, N Indonesia
28 K7 **Bison** South Dakota, N USA
93 H17 **Bispfors** Jämtland, C Sweden
79 E17 **Bitam** Woleu-Ntem, N Gabon
101 D18 **Bitburg** Rheinland-Pfalz, SW Germany
103 U4 **Bitche** Moselle, NE France
78 I11 **Bitkine** Guéra, C Chad
137 R15 **Bitlis** Bitlis, SE Turkey
137 R14 **Bitlis** ◈ *province* E Turkey
Bitoeng *see* Bitung
113 N20 **Bitola** *Turk.* Monastir; *prev.* Bitolj. S FYR Macedonia
Bitolj *see* Bitola
107 O17 **Bitonto** *anc.* Butuntum. Puglia, SE Italy
77 Q13 **Bitou** *var.* Bittou. SE Burkina
155 C20 **Bitra Island** *island* Lakshadweep, India, N Indian Ocean
101 M14 **Bitterfeld** Sachsen-Anhalt, E Germany
32 O9 **Bitterroot Range** ▲▲ Idaho/Montana, NW USA
33 P10 **Bitterroot River** ≈ Montana, NW USA
107 D18 **Bitti** Sardegna, Italy, C Mediterranean Sea
Bittou *see* Bitou
171 Q11 **Bitung** *prev.* Bitoeng. Sulawesi, C Indonesia
60 I12 **Bituruna** Paraná, S Brazil
77 Y13 **Biu** Borno, E Nigeria
Biumba *see* Byumba
164 J13 **Biwa-ko** ◎ Honshū, SW Japan
171 X14 **Biwarlaut** Irian Jaya, E Indonesia
27 P10 **Bixby** Oklahoma, C USA
122 J13 **Biya** ≈ S Russian Federation
Biy-Khem *see* Bol'shoy Yenisey
122 J13 **Biysk** Altayskiy Kray, S Russian Federation
164 H13 **Bizen** Okayama, Honshū, SW Japan
Bizerta *see* Bizerte
120 K10 **Bizerte** *Ar.* Banzart, *Eng.* Bizerta. N Tunisia
Bizkaia *see* Vizcaya
92 G2 **Bjargtangar** *headland* W Iceland
Bjärnå *see* Perniö
95 K22 **Bjärnum** Skåne, S Sweden
93 I16 **Bjästa** Västernorrland, C Sweden
113 I14 **Bjelašnica** ▲ SE Bosnia and Herzegovina
112 C10 **Bjelolasica** ▲ NW Croatia
112 F8 **Bjelovar** *Hung.* Belovár. Bjelovar-Bilogora, N Croatia
112 F8 **Bjelovar-Bilogora** *off.* Bjelovarsko-Bilogorska Županija. ◈ *province* NE Croatia
Bjelovarsko-Bilogorska Županija *see* Bjelovar-Bilogora
92 H10 **Bjerkvik** Nordland, C Norway
95 G21 **Bjerringbro** Viborg, NW Denmark
Bjeshkët e Namuna *see* North Albanian Alps
95 L14 **Björbo** Dalarna, C Sweden
95 I15 **Bjørkelangen** Akershus, S Norway
95 O14 **Björklinge** Uppsala, C Sweden
93 I14 **Björksele** Västerbotten, N Sweden
93 I16 **Björna** Västernorrland, C Sweden
95 C14 **Bjørnafjorden** *fjord* S Norway
95 L16 **Björneborg** Värmland, C Sweden
Björneborg *see* Pori
95 E14 **Bjornesfjorden** ◎ S Norway
92 M9 **Bjørnevatn** Finnmark, N Norway
197 T13 **Bjørnøya** *Eng.* Bear Island. *island* N Norway
93 I15 **Bjurholm** Västerbotten, N Sweden
95 J22 **Bjuv** Skåne, S Sweden
76 M12 **Bla** Ségou, W Mali
181 W8 **Blackall** Queensland, E Australia
29 V2 **Black Bay** *lake bay* Minnesota, N USA
27 N9 **Black Bear Creek** ≈ Oklahoma, C USA
97 K17 **Blackburn** NW England, UK
45 W10 **Blackburne** × (Plymouth) E Montserrat
39 T11 **Blackburn, Mount** ▲ Alaska, USA
35 N5 **Black Butte Lake** ⊟ California, W USA
194 J5 **Black Coast** *physical region* Antarctica
11 Q16 **Black Diamond** Alberta, SW Canada
18 K11 **Black Dome** ▲ New York, NE USA
113 L18 **Black Drin** *Alb.* Lumi i Drinit të Zi, *SCr.* Crni Drim. ≈ Albania/FYR Macedonia
12 D6 **Black Duck** ≈ Ontario, C Canada
29 U4 **Blackduck** Minnesota, N USA
33 R14 **Blackfoot** Idaho, NW USA
33 P9 **Blackfoot River** ≈ Montana, NW USA
Black Forest *see* Schwarzwald
28 J10 **Blackhawk** South Dakota, N USA
28 I10 **Black Hills** ▲▲ South Dakota/Wyoming, N USA
11 T10 **Black Lake** ◎ Saskatchewan, C Canada
31 Q5 **Black Lake** ◎ Michigan, N USA
18 I7 **Black Lake** ◎ New York, NE USA
22 G6 **Black Lake** ⊟ Louisiana, S USA
26 F7 **Black Mesa** ▲ Oklahoma, C USA
21 P10 **Black Mountain** North Carolina, SE USA
35 P13 **Black Mountain** ▲ California, W USA
37 Q2 **Black Mountain** ▲ Colorado, C USA
21 O7 **Black Mountain** ▲ Kentucky, E USA
96 K1 **Black Mountains** ▲▲ SE Wales, UK
36 H10 **Black Mountains** ▲▲ Arizona, SW USA
33 Q16 **Black Pine Peak** ▲ Idaho, NW USA
97 K17 **Blackpool** NW England, UK
37 Q14 **Black Range** ▲▲ New Mexico, SW USA
44 I12 **Black River** W Jamaica
14 J14 **Black River** ≈ Ontario, SE Canada
131 U12 **Black River** *Chin.* Babian Jiang, Lixian Jiang, *Fr.* Rivière Noire, *Vtn.* Sông Đa. ≈ China/Vietnam
44 I12 **Black River** ≈ W Jamaica
39 T7 **Black River** ≈ Alaska, USA
37 N13 **Black River** ≈ Arizona, SW USA
27 X7 **Black River** ≈ Arkansas/Missouri, C USA
22 I7 **Black River** ≈ Louisiana, S USA
31 S8 **Black River** ≈ Michigan, N USA
31 Q5 **Black River** ≈ Michigan, N USA
18 I8 **Black River** ≈ New York, NE USA
21 T13 **Black River** ≈ South Carolina, SE USA
30 J7 **Black River** ≈ Wisconsin, N USA
30 J7 **Black River Falls** Wisconsin, N USA
35 R3 **Black Rock Desert** *desert* Nevada, W USA
Black Sand Desert *see* Garagumy
21 S7 **Blacksburg** Virginia, NE USA
136 H10 **Black Sea** *var.* Euxine Sea, *Bul.* Cherno More, *Rom.* Marea Neagră, *Rus.* Chernoye More, *Turk.* Karadeniz, *Ukr.* Chorne More. *sea* Asia/Europe
117 Q10 **Black Sea Lowland** *Ukr.* Prychornomors'ka Nyzovyna. *depression* SE Europe
33 S17 **Blacks Fork** ≈ Wyoming, C USA
23 V7 **Blackshear** Georgia, SE USA
23 S6 **Blackshear, Lake** ⊟ Georgia, SE USA
97 A16 **Blacksod Bay** *Ir.* Cuan an Fhóid Duibh. *inlet* W Ireland
21 V7 **Blackstone** Virginia, NE USA
77 O14 **Black Volta** *var.* Borongo, Mouhoun, Moun Hou, *Fr.* Volta Noire. ≈ W Africa
23 O5 **Black Warrior River** ≈ Alabama, S USA
181 X8 **Blackwater** Queensland, E Australia
97 D20 **Blackwater** *Ir.* An Abhainn Mhór. ≈ S Ireland
27 T4 **Blackwater River** ≈ Missouri, C USA
21 W7 **Blackwater River** ≈ Virginia, NE USA
Blackwater State *see* Nebraska
27 N8 **Blackwell** Oklahoma, C USA
25 P7 **Blackwell** Texas, SW USA
99 J15 **Bladel** Noord-Brabant, S Netherlands
Bladenmarkt *see* Bălăuşeri
114 G11 **Blagoevgrad** *prev.* Gorna Dzhumaya. Blagoevgrad, SW Bulgaria
114 G11 **Blagoevgrad** ◈ *province* SW Bulgaria
123 Q14 **Blagoveshchensk** Amurskaya Oblast', SE Russian Federation
129 V4 **Blagoveshchensk** Respublika Bashkortostan, W Russian Federation
102 I7 **Blain** Loire-Atlantique, NW France
29 V8 **Blaine** Minnesota, N USA
32 H6 **Blaine** Washington, NW USA
11 T15 **Blaine Lake** Saskatchewan, S Canada
29 S14 **Blair** Nebraska, C USA
96 J10 **Blairgowrie** C Scotland, UK
18 C15 **Blairsville** Pennsylvania, NE USA
116 H11 **Blaj** *Ger.* Blasendorf, *Hung.* Balázsfalva. Alba, SW Romania
64 F9 **Blake-Bahama Ridge** *undersea feature* W Atlantic Ocean
23 S7 **Blakely** Georgia, SE USA
64 E10 **Blake Plateau** *var.* Blake Terrace. *undersea feature* W Atlantic Ocean
30 M1 **Blake Point** *headland* Michigan, N USA
Blake Terrace *see* Blake Plateau
61 B24 **Blanca, Bahía** *bay* E Argentina
56 C12 **Blanca, Cordillera** ▲▲ W Peru
105 T12 **Blanca, Costa** *physical region* SE Spain
37 S7 **Blanca Peak** ▲ Colorado, C USA
24 I9 **Blanca, Sierra** ▲ Texas, SW USA
120 K9 **Blanc, Cap** *headland* N Tunisia
Blanc, Cap *see* Nouâdhibou, Râs
31 R12 **Blanchard River** ≈ Ohio, N USA
182 E8 **Blanche, Cape** *headland* South Australia
182 J4 **Blanche, Lake** ◎ South Australia
31 R14 **Blanchester** Ohio, N USA
182 J9 **Blanchetown** South Australia
45 U13 **Blanchisseuse** Trinidad, Trinidad and Tobago
103 T11 **Blanc, Mont** *It.* Monte Bianco. ▲ France/Italy
25 R11 **Blanco** Texas, SW USA
42 K14 **Blanco, Cabo** *headland* NW Costa Rica
32 D14 **Blanco, Cape** *headland* Oregon, NW USA
62 H10 **Blanco, Río** ≈ W Argentina
56 F10 **Blanco, Río** ≈ NE Peru
15 O9 **Blanc, Réservoir** ⊟ Quebec, SE Canada
21 R7 **Bland** Virginia, NE USA
92 I2 **Blanda** ≈ N Iceland
37 O7 **Blanding** Utah, W USA
105 X5 **Blanes** Cataluña, NE Spain
103 N3 **Blangy-sur-Bresle** Seine-Maritime, N France
111 C18 **Blanice** *Ger.* Blanitz. ≈ SE Czech Republic
Blanitz *see* Blanice
99 C16 **Blankenberge** West-Vlaanderen, NW Belgium
101 D17 **Blankenheim** Nordrhein-Westfalen, W Germany
25 R8 **Blanket** Texas, SW USA
55 O3 **Blanquilla, Isla** *var.* La Blanquilla. *island* N Venezuela
Blanquilla, La *see* Blanquilla, Isla
61 F18 **Blanquillo** Durazno, C Uruguay
111 G18 **Blansko** *Ger.* Blanz. Brněnský Kraj, SE Czech Republic
83 N15 **Blantyre** *var.* Blantyre-Limbe. Southern, S Malawi
83 N15 **Blantyre** × Southern, S Malawi
Blantyre-Limbe *see* Blantyre
Blanz *see* Blansko
98 J10 **Blaricum** Noord-Holland, C Netherlands
Blasendorf *see* Blaj
Blatnitsa *see* Durankulak
113 F15 **Blato** *It.* Blatta. Dubrovnik-Neretva, S Croatia
Blatta *see* Blato
108 E10 **Blatten** Valais, SW Switzerland
101 J20 **Blaufelden** Baden-Württemberg, SW Germany
95 E23 **Blåvands Huk** *headland* W Denmark
102 G6 **Blavet** ≈ NW France
102 J12 **Blaye** Gironde, SW France
183 R8 **Blayney** New South Wales, SE Australia
65 D25 **Bleaker Island** *island* SE Falkland Islands
109 T10 **Bled** *Ger.* Veldes. NW Slovenia
99 D20 **Bléharies** Hainaut, SW Belgium
109 U9 **Bleiburg** *Slvn.* Pliberk. Kärnten, S Austria
101 L17 **Bleiloch-Stausee** ⊟ C Germany
98 H12 **Bleiswijk** Zuid-Holland, W Netherlands
95 L22 **Blekinge** ◈ *county* S Sweden
14 D17 **Blenheim** Ontario, S Canada
185 K15 **Blenheim** Marlborough, South Island, NZ
99 M15 **Blerick** Limburg, SE Netherlands
Blesae *see* Blois
25 V13 **Blessing** Texas, SW USA
14 I10 **Bleu, Lac** ◎ Quebec, SE Canada
Blibba *see* Blitta
120 H10 **Blida** *var.* El Boulaida, El Boulaïda. N Algeria
95 P15 **Blidö** Stockholm, C Sweden
95 K18 **Blidsberg** Västra Götaland, S Sweden
185 A21 **Bligh Sound** *sound* South Island, NZ
187 X14 **Bligh Water** *strait* NW Fiji
14 D11 **Blind River** Ontario, S Canada
31 R11 **Blissfield** Michigan, N USA
77 R15 **Blitta** *prev.* Blibba. C Togo
19 O13 **Block Island** *island* Rhode Island, NE USA
19 O13 **Block Island Sound** *sound* Rhode Island, NE USA
98 H10 **Bloemendaal** Noord-Holland, W Netherlands
83 H23 **Bloemfontein** *var.* Mangaung. ● (South Africa-judicial capital) Free State, C South Africa
83 I22 **Bloemhof** North-West, NW South Africa
102 M7 **Blois** *anc.* Blesae. Loir-et-Cher, C France
98 L8 **Blokzijl** Overijssel, N Netherlands
95 N20 **Blomstermåla** Kalmar, S Sweden
92 I2 **Blönduós** Nordhurland Vestra, N Iceland
110 L11 **Błonie** Mazowieckie, C Poland
97 C14 **Bloody Foreland** *Ir.* Cnoc Fola. *headland* NW Ireland
31 N15 **Bloomfield** Indiana, N USA
29 X16 **Bloomfield** Iowa, C USA
27 Y8 **Bloomfield** Missouri, C USA
37 P9 **Bloomfield** New Mexico, SW USA
25 U7 **Blooming Grove** Texas, SW USA
29 W10 **Blooming Prairie** Minnesota, N USA
30 L13 **Bloomington** Illinois, N USA
31 O15 **Bloomington** Indiana, N USA
29 V9 **Bloomington** Minnesota, N USA
25 U13 **Bloomington** Texas, SW USA
18 H14 **Bloomsburg** Pennsylvania, NE USA
181 X7 **Bloomsbury** Queensland, NE Australia
169 R16 **Blora** Jawa, C Indonesia
18 G12 **Blossburg** Pennsylvania, NE USA
25 V5 **Blossom** Texas, SW USA
123 T5 **Blossom, Mys** *headland* Ostrov Vrangelya, NE Russian Federation
23 R8 **Blountstown** Florida, SE USA
21 P8 **Blountville** Tennessee, S USA
21 Q9 **Blowing Rock** North Carolina, SE USA
108 J8 **Bludenz** Vorarlberg, W Austria
36 L6 **Blue Bell Knoll** ▲ Utah, W USA
23 Y12 **Blue Cypress Lake** ◎ Florida, SE USA
29 U11 **Blue Earth** Minnesota, N USA
21 Q7 **Bluefield** Virginia, NE USA
21 R7 **Bluefield** West Virginia, NE USA
43 N10 **Bluefields** Región Autónoma Atlántico Sur, SE Nicaragua
43 N10 **Bluefields, Bahía de** *bay* W Caribbean Sea
29 Z14 **Blue Grass** Iowa, C USA
Bluegrass State *see* Kentucky
Blue Hen State *see* Delaware
19 S7 **Blue Hill** Maine, NE USA
29 P16 **Blue Hill** Nebraska, C USA
30 J5 **Blue Hills** *hill range* Wisconsin, N USA
34 L3 **Blue Lake** California, W USA
Blue Law State *see* Connecticut
37 Q6 **Blue Mesa Reservoir** ⊟ Colorado, C USA
27 S12 **Blue Mountain** ▲ Arkansas, C USA
19 O6 **Blue Mountain** ▲ New Hampshire, NE USA
18 K8 **Blue Mountain** ▲ New York, NE USA
18 H15 **Blue Mountain** *ridge* Pennsylvania, NE USA
44 H10 **Blue Mountain Peak** ▲ E Jamaica
183 S8 **Blue Mountains** ▲▲ New South Wales, SE Australia
32 L11 **Blue Mountains** ▲▲ Oregon/Washington, NW USA
80 G12 **Blue Nile** ◈ *state* E Sudan
80 H12 **Blue Nile** *var.* Abai, Bahr el Azraq, *Amh.* Äbay Wenz, *Ar.* An Nīl al Azraq. ≈ Ethiopia/Sudan
8 J7 **Bluenose Lake** ◎ Nunavut, NW Canada
27 O3 **Blue Rapids** Kansas, C USA
23 S1 **Blue Ridge** Georgia, SE USA
17 S11 **Blue Ridge** *var.* Blue Ridge Mountains. ▲▲ North Carolina/Virginia, E USA
23 S1 **Blue Ridge Lake** ⊟ Georgia, SE USA
Blue Ridge Mountains *see* Blue Ridge
9 N15 **Blue River** British Columbia, SW Canada
27 O12 **Blue River** ≈ Oklahoma, C USA
27 R4 **Blue Springs** Missouri, C USA
21 R6 **Bluestone Lake** ⊟ West Virginia, NE USA
185 C25 **Bluff** Southland, South Island, NZ
37 O8 **Bluff** Utah, W USA
21 P8 **Bluff City** Tennessee, S USA
65 E24 **Bluff Cove** East Falkland, Falkland Islands
25 S7 **Bluff Dale** Texas, SW USA
183 N15 **Bluff Hill Point** *headland* Tasmania, SE Australia
31 Q12 **Bluffton** Indiana, N USA
31 R12 **Bluffton** Ohio, N USA
25 T7 **Blum** Texas, SW USA
101 G24 **Blumberg** Baden-Württemberg, SW Germany
60 K13 **Blumenau** Santa Catarina, S Brazil
29 N9 **Blunt** South Dakota, N USA
32 H15 **Bly** Oregon, NW USA
39 R13 **Blying Sound** *sound* Alaska, USA
97 M14 **Blyth** N England, UK
35 Y16 **Blythe** California, W USA
27 Y9 **Blytheville** Arkansas, C USA
117 V7 **Blyznyuky** Kharkivs'ka Oblast', E Ukraine
76 I15 **Bo** S Sierra Leone
95 G16 **Bø** Telemark, S Norway
171 O4 **Boac** Marinduque, N Philippines
42 K10 **Boaco** Boaco, S Nicaragua
42 J10 **Boaco** ◈ *department* C Nicaragua
79 I15 **Boali** Ombella-Mpoko, SW Central African Republic
Boalsert *see* Bolsward
31 V12 **Boardman** Ohio, N USA
32 J11 **Boardman** Oregon, NW USA
14 F13 **Boat Lake** ◎ Ontario, S Canada
58 F10 **Boa Vista** *state capital* Roraima, NW Brazil
76 D9 **Boa Vista** *island* Ilhas de Barlavento, E Cape Verde
23 Q2 **Boaz** Alabama, S USA
160 L15 **Bobai** Guangxi Zhuangzu Zizhiqu, S China
172 J1 **Bobaomby, Tanjona** *Fr.* Cap d'Ambre. *headland* N Madagascar
155 M14 **Bobbili** Andhra Pradesh, E India
106 D9 **Bobbio** Emilia-Romagna, C Italy
14 I14 **Bobcaygeon** Ontario, SE Canada
Bober *see* Bóbr
103 O5 **Bobigny** Seine-St-Denis, N France
77 N13 **Bobo-Dioulasso** SW Burkina
110 G8 **Bobolice** *Ger.* Bublitz. Zachodniopomorskie, NW Poland
171 R11 **Bobopayo** Pulau Halmahera, E Indonesia
147 P13 **Bobotogh, Qatorkŭhi** *Rus.* Khrebet Babatag. ▲▲ Tajikistan/Uzbekistan
114 G10 **Bobovdol** Kyustendil, W Bulgaria
119 M15 **Bobr** Minskaya Voblasts', NW Belarus
119 M15 **Bobr** ≈ C Belarus
111 E14 **Bóbr** *Eng.* Bobrawa, *Ger.* Bober. ≈ SW Poland
Bobrawa *see* Bóbr
Bobrik *see* Bobryk
Bobrinets *see* Bobrynets'
Bobrka/Bóbrka *see* Bibrka
128 L8 **Bobrov** Voronezhskaya Oblast', W Russian Federation
117 Q4 **Bobrovytsya** Chernihivs'ka Oblast', N Ukraine
Bobruysk *see* Babruysk
119 J19 **Bobryk** *Rus.* Bobrik. ≈ SW Belarus
117 Q8 **Bobrynets'** *Rus.* Bobrinets. Kirovohrads'ka Oblast', C Ukraine

◆ Country ● Country Capital ◇ Dependent Territory ○ Dependent Territory Capital ◈ Administrative Region × International Airport ▲ Mountain ▲▲ Mountain Range Volcano ≈ River ◎ Lake ⊟ Reservoir

14 K14 **Bobs Lake** ◎ Ontario, SE Canada
54 I6 **Bobures** Zulia, NW Venezuela
42 H1 **Boca Bacalar Chico** *headland* N Belize
112 G11 **Bočac** Republika Srpska, NW Bosnia and Herzegovina
41 R14 **Boca del Río** Veracruz-Llave, S Mexico
55 O4 **Boca de Pozo** Nueva Esparta, NE Venezuela
59 C15 **Boca do Acre** Amazonas, N Brazil
55 N12 **Boca Mavaca** Amazonas, S Venezuela
79 G14 **Bocaranga** Ouham-Pendé, W Central African Republic
23 Z15 **Boca Raton** Florida, SE USA
43 P14 **Bocas del Toro** Bocas del Toro, NW Panama
43 P15 **Bocas del Toro** *off.* Provincia de Bocas del Toro. ◈ *province* NW Panama
43 P15 **Bocas del Toro, Archipiélago de** *island group* NW Panama
42 L7 **Bocay** Jinotega, N Nicaragua
105 N6 **Boceguillas** Castilla-León, N Spain
Bocheykovo *see* Bacheykava
111 L17 **Bochnia** Małopolskie, SE Poland
99 K16 **Bocholt** Limburg, NE Belgium
101 D14 **Bocholt** Nordrhein-Westfalen, W Germany
101 E15 **Bochum** Nordrhein-Westfalen, W Germany
103 Y15 **Bocognano** Corse, France, C Mediterranean Sea
54 I6 **Boconó** Trujillo, NW Venezuela
116 F12 **Bocşa** *Ger.* Bokschen, *Hung.* Boksánbánya. Caraş-Severin, SW Romania
79 H15 **Boda** Lobaye, SW Central African Republic
94 L12 **Boda** Dalarna, C Sweden
95 O20 **Böda** Kalmar, S Sweden
95 L19 **Bodafors** Jönköping, S Sweden
123 O12 **Bodaybo** Irkutskaya Oblast', E Russian Federation
22 G5 **Bodcau, Bayou** *var.* Bodcau Creek. ≈ Louisiana, S USA
Bodcau Creek *see* Bodcau, Bayou
44 D8 **Bodden Town** *var.* Boddentown. Grand Cayman, SW Cayman Islands
101 K14 **Bode** ≈ C Germany
34 L7 **Bodega Head** *headland* California, W USA
Bodegas *see* Babahoyo
98 H11 **Bodegraven** Zuid-Holland, C Netherlands
78 H8 **Bodélé** *depression* W Chad
92 J13 **Boden** Norrbotten, N Sweden
Bodensee *see* Constance, Lake, C Europe
65 M15 **Bode Verde Fracture Zone** *tectonic feature* E Atlantic Ocean
155 H14 **Bodhan** Andhra Pradesh, C India
162 I9 **Bodĭ** Bayanhongor, C Mongolia
155 H22 **Bodināyakkanūr** Tamil Nādu, SE India
108 H10 **Bodio** Ticino, S Switzerland
97 I24 **Bodmin** SW England, UK
97 I24 **Bodmin Moor** *moorland* SW England, UK
92 G12 **Bodø** Nordland, C Norway
59 H20 **Bodoquena, Serra da** ▲ SW Brazil
136 B16 **Bodrum** Muğla, SW Turkey
Bodzafordulő *see* Întorsura Buzăului
99 L14 **Boekel** Noord-Brabant, SE Netherlands
Boeloekoemba *see* Bulukumba
103 Q11 **Boën** Loire, E France
79 K18 **Boende** Equateur, C Dem. Rep. Congo (Zaire)
25 R11 **Boerne** Texas, SW USA
Boeroe *see* Buru, Pulau
Boetoeng *see* Buton, Pulau
22 I5 **Boeuf River** ≈ Arkansas/Louisiana, S USA
76 H14 **Boffa** Guinée-Maritime, W Guinea
Bó Finne, Inis *see* Inishbofin
Boga *see* Bogë
166 L9 **Bogale** Irrawaddy, SW Myanmar
22 L8 **Bogalusa** Louisiana, S USA
77 Q12 **Bogandé** C Burkina
79 I15 **Bogangolo** Ombella-Mpoko, C Central African Republic
183 Q7 **Bogan River** ≈ New South Wales, SE Australia
25 W5 **Bogata** Texas, SW USA
111 D14 **Bogatynia** *Ger.* Reichenau. Dolnośląskie, SW Poland
136 K13 **Boğazlıyan** Yozgat, C Turkey
79 J17 **Bogbonga** Equateur, NW Dem. Rep. Congo (Zaire)
158 J14 **Bogcang Zangbo** ≈ W China
158 L5 **Bogda Feng** ▲ NW China
114 I9 **Bogdan** ▲ C Bulgaria
113 Q20 **Bogdanci** SE FYR Macedonia
158 M5 **Bogda Shan** *var.* Po-ko-to Shan. ▲ NW China
113 K17 **Bogë** *var.* Boga. Shkodër, N Albania
Bogendorf *see* Łuków
95 G23 **Bogense** Fyn, C Denmark
183 T3 **Boggabilla** New South Wales, SE Australia
183 S6 **Boggabri** New South Wales, SE Australia
186 D6 **Bogia** Madang, N PNG
97 N23 **Bognor Regis** SE England, UK
Bogodukhov *see* Bohodukhiv
181 V15 **Bogong, Mount** ▲ Victoria, SE Australia
169 O16 **Bogor** *Dut.* Buitenzorg. Jawa, C Indonesia
128 L5 **Bogoroditsk** Tul'skaya Oblast', W Russian Federation
129 O3 **Bogorodsk** Nizhegorodskaya Oblast', W Russian Federation
Bogorodskoje *see* Bogorodskoye
123 S12 **Bogorodskoye** Khabarovskiy Kray, SE Russian Federation
127 R15 **Bogorodskoye** *var.* Bogorodskoje. Kirovskaya Oblast', NW Russian Federation
54 F10 **Bogotá** *prev.* Santa Fe, Santa Fe de Bogotá. ● (Colombia) Cundinamarca, C Colombia
153 T14 **Bogra** Rajshahi, N Bangladesh
Bogschan *see* Boldu
122 L12 **Boguchany** Krasnoyarskiy Kray, C Russian Federation
128 M9 **Boguchar** Voronezhskaya Oblast', W Russian Federation
76 H10 **Bogué** Brakna, SW Mauritania
22 K8 **Bogue Chitto** ≈ Louisiana/Mississippi, S USA
Bogushëvsk *see* Bahushewsk
Boguslav *see* Bohuslav
44 K12 **Bog Walk** C Jamaica
161 Q3 **Bo Hai** *var.* Gulf of Chihli. *gulf* NE China
161 R3 **Bohai Haixia** *strait* NE China
161 Q3 **Bohai Wan** *bay* NE China
111 C17 **Bohemia** *Cz.* Čechy, *Ger.* Böhmen. *cultural and historical region* W Czech Republic
111 B18 **Bohemian Forest** *Cz.* Ceský Les, Šumava, *Ger.* Böhmerwald. ▲ C Europe
Bohemian-Moravian Highlands *see* Českomoravská Vrchovina
77 R16 **Bohicon** S Benin
109 S11 **Bohinjska Bistrica** *Ger.* Wocheiner Feistritz. NW Slovenia
Bohkká *see* Pokka
Böhmen *see* Bohemia
Böhmerwald *see* Bohemian Forest
Böhmisch-Krumau *see* Český Krumlov
Böhmisch-Leipa *see* Česká Lípa
Böhmisch-Mährische Höhe *see* Českomoravská Vrchovina
Böhmisch-Trübau *see* Česká Třebová
117 U5 **Bohodukhiv** *Rus.* Bogodukhov. Kharkivs'ka Oblast', E Ukraine
171 Q6 **Bohol** *island* C Philippines
171 Q7 **Bohol Sea** *var.* Mindanao Sea. *sea* S Philippines
116 I7 **Bohorodchany** Ivano-Frankivs'ka Oblast', W Ukraine
162 M9 **Böhöt** Dundgovĭ, C Mongolia
158 K6 **Bohu** *var.* Bagrax. Xinjiang Uygur Zizhiqu, NW China
111 I17 **Bohumín** *Ger.* Oderberg; *prev.* Neuoderberg, Nový Bohumín. Ostravský Kray, E Czech Republic
117 P6 **Bohuslav** *Rus.* Boguslav. Kyyivs'ka Oblast', N Ukraine
58 F11 **Boiaçu** Roraima, N Brazil
107 K16 **Boiano** Molise, C Italy
15 R8 **Boilleau** Quebec, SE Canada
59 O17 **Boipeba, Ilha de** *island* SE Brazil
104 G3 **Boiro** Galicia, NW Spain
31 Q5 **Bois Blanc Island** *island* Michigan, N USA
29 R7 **Bois de Sioux River** ≈ Minnesota, N USA
33 N14 **Boise** *var.* Boise City. *state capital* Idaho, NW USA
26 G8 **Boise City** Oklahoma, C USA
33 N14 **Boise River, Middle Fork** ≈ Idaho, NW USA
Bois, Lac des *see* Woods, Lake of the
Bois-le-Duc *see* 's-Hertogenbosch
9 W17 **Boissevain** Manitoba, S Canada
15 T7 **Boisvert, Pointe au** *headland* Quebec, SE Canada
100 K10 **Boizenburg** Mecklenburg-Vorpommern, N Germany
Bojador *see* Boujdour
113 K18 **Bojana** *Alb.* Bunë. ≈ Albania/Yugoslavia *see also* Bunë
143 S3 **Bojnūrd** *var.* Bujnurd. Khorāsān, N Iran
169 R16 **Bojonegoro** *prev.* Bodjonegoro. Jawa, C Indonesia
189 T1 **Bokaak Atoll** *var.* Bokak, Taongi. *atoll* Ratak Chain, NE Marshall Islands
Bokak *see* Bokaak Atoll
153 Q15 **Bokāro** Bihār, N India
79 I18 **Bokatola** Equateur, NW Dem. Rep. Congo (Zaire)
76 H13 **Boké** Guinée-Maritime, W Guinea
Bokhara *see* Bukhoro
183 Q4 **Bokharra River** ≈ New South Wales/Queensland, SE Australia
95 C16 **Boknafjorden** *fjord* S Norway
78 H11 **Bokoro** Chari-Baguirmi, W Chad
79 K19 **Bokota** Equateur, NW Dem. Rep. Congo (Zaire)
167 N13 **Bokpyin** Tenasserim, S Myanmar
Boksánbánya/Bokschen *see* Bocşa
83 F21 **Bokspits** Kgalagadi, SW Botswana
79 K18 **Bokungu** Equateur, C Dem. Rep. Congo (Zaire)
Bokurdak *see* Bakhardok
78 G10 **Bol** Lac, W Chad
76 G13 **Bolama** SW Guinea-Bissau
Bolangir *see* Balāngir
Bolanos *see* Bolanos, Mount, Guam
Bolaños *see* Bolaños de Calatrava, Spain
105 N11 **Bolaños de Calatrava** *var.* Bolaños. Castilla-La Mancha, C Spain
188 B17 **Bolanos, Mount** *var.* Bolanos. ▲ S Guam
40 L12 **Bolaños, Río** ≈ C Mexico
115 M14 **Bolayır** Çanakkale, NW Turkey
102 L3 **Bolbec** Seine-Maritime, N France
116 L13 **Boldu** *var.* Bogschan. Buzău, SE Romania
146 H8 **Boldumsaz** *prev.* Kalinin, Kalininsk, Porsy. Dashkhovuzskiy Velayat, N Turkmenistan
158 I4 **Bole** *var.* Bortala. Xinjiang Uygur Zizhiqu, NW China
77 O15 **Bole** NW Ghana
79 J19 **Boleko** Equateur, W Dem. Rep. Congo (Zaire)
111 E14 **Bolesławiec** *Ger.* Bunzlau. Dolnośląskie, SW Poland
129 R4 **Bolgar** *prev.* Kuybyshev. Respublika Tatarstan, W Russian Federation
77 P14 **Bolgatanga** N Ghana
Bolgrad *see* Bolhrad
117 N12 **Bolhrad** *Rus.* Bolgrad. Odes'ka Oblast', SW Ukraine
163 Y8 **Boli** Heilongjiang, NE China
79 I19 **Bolia** Bandundu, W Dem. Rep. Congo (Zaire)
93 J14 **Boliden** Västerbotten, N Sweden
171 T13 **Bolifar** Pulau Seram, E Indonesia
171 N2 **Bolinao** Luzon, N Philippines
27 T6 **Bolivar** Missouri, C USA
20 F10 **Bolivar** Tennessee, S USA
54 C12 **Bolívar** Cauca, SW Colombia
54 F7 **Bolívar** *off.* Departmento de Bolívar. ◈ *province* N Colombia
56 A13 **Bolívar** ◈ *province* C Ecuador
55 N9 **Bolívar** *off.* Estado Bolívar. ◈ *state* SE Venezuela
25 X12 **Bolivar Peninsula** *headland* Texas, SW USA
54 I6 **Bolívar, Pico** ▲ W Venezuela
57 K17 **Bolivia** *off.* Republic of Bolivia. ◆ *republic* W South America
112 O13 **Boljevac** Serbia, E Yugoslavia
Bolkenhain *see* Bolków
128 J5 **Bolkhov** Orlovskaya Oblast', W Russian Federation
111 F14 **Bolków** *Ger.* Bolkenhain. Dolnośląskie, SW Poland
182 K3 **Bollards Lagoon** South Australia
103 R14 **Bollène** Vaucluse, SE France
94 N12 **Bollnäs** Gävleborg, C Sweden
181 W10 **Bollon** Queensland, C Australia
192 L12 **Bollons Tablemount** *undersea feature* S Pacific Ocean
93 H17 **Bollstabruk** Västernorrland, C Sweden
Bolluilos de Par del Condado *see* Bollulos Par del Condado
104 J14 **Bollulos Par del Condado** *var.* Bolluilos de Par del Condado. Andalucía, S Spain
95 K21 **Bolmen** ◎ S Sweden
137 T10 **Bolnisi** S Georgia
79 H19 **Bolobo** Bandundu, W Dem. Rep. Congo (Zaire)
123 R12 **Bolodek** Khabarovskiy Kray, SE Russian Federation
106 G10 **Bologna** Emilia-Romagna, N Italy
126 I15 **Bologoye** Tverskaya Oblast', W Russian Federation
79 J18 **Bolomba** Equateur, NW Dem. Rep. Congo (Zaire)
41 X13 **Bolónchén de Rejón** *var.* Bolonchén de Rejón. Campeche, SE Mexico
114 J13 **Boloústra, Akrotírio** *headland* NE Greece
167 L8 **Bolovens, Plateau des** *plateau* S Laos
106 H13 **Bolsena** Lazio, C Italy
107 G14 **Bolsena, Lago di** ◎ C Italy
128 B3 **Bol'shakovo** *Ger.* Kreuzingen; *prev.* Gross-Skaisgirren. Kaliningradskaya Oblast', W Russian Federation
Bol'shaya Berëstovitsa *see* Vyalikaya Byerastavitsa
129 S7 **Bol'shaya Chernigovka** Samarskaya Oblast', W Russian Federation
129 S7 **Bol'shaya Glushitsa** Samarskaya Oblast', W Russian Federation
144 H9 **Bol'shaya Khobda** *Kaz.* Ülkenqobda. ≈ Kazakhstan/Russian Federation
128 M12 **Bol'shaya Martynovka** Rostovskaya Oblast', SW Russian Federation
122 K12 **Bol'shaya Murta** Krasnoyarskiy Kray, C Russian Federation
127 V4 **Bol'shaya Rogovaya** ≈ NW Russian Federation
127 U7 **Bol'shaya Synya** ≈ NW Russian Federation
145 V9 **Bol'shaya Vladimirovka** Vostochnyy Kazakhstan, E Kazakhstan
123 V11 **Bol'sheretsk** Kamchatskaya Oblast', E Russian Federation
129 W3 **Bol'sheust'ikinskoye** Respublika Bashkortostan, W Russian Federation
Bol'shevik *see* Bal'shavik
122 L5 **Bol'shevik, Ostrov** *island* Severnaya Zemlya, N Russian Federation
127 U4 **Bol'shezemel'skaya Tundra** *physical region* NW Russian Federation
144 J13 **Bol'shiye Barsuki, Peski** *desert* SW Kazakhstan
123 T7 **Bol'shoy Anyuy** ≈ NE Russian Federation
123 N7 **Bol'shoy Begichev, Ostrov** *island* NE Russian Federation
129 O4 **Bol'shoye Murashkino** Nizhegorodskaya Oblast', W Russian Federation
129 W4 **Bol'shoy Iremel'** ▲ W Russian Federation
129 R7 **Bol'shoy Irgiz** ≈ W Russian Federation
123 Q6 **Bol'shoy Lyakhovskiy, Ostrov** *island* NE Russian Federation
123 Q11 **Bol'shoy Nimnyr** Respublika Sakha (Yakutiya), NE Russian Federation
Bol'shoy Rozhan *see* Vyaliki Rozhan
144 E10 **Bol'shoy Uzen'** *Kaz.* Ülkenözen. ≈ Kazakhstan/Russian Federation
40 K6 **Bolson de Mapimi** ▲ NW Mexico
98 K6 **Bolsward** *Fris.* Boalsert. Friesland, N Netherlands
105 T4 **Boltaña** Aragón, NE Spain
14 G15 **Bolton** Ontario, S Canada
97 K17 **Bolton** *prev.* Bolton-le-Moors. NW England, UK
21 V12 **Bolton** North Carolina, SE USA
Bolton-le-Moors *see* Bolton
136 G11 **Bolu** Bolu, NW Turkey
136 G11 **Bolu** ◈ *province* NW Turkey
186 G9 **Bolubolu** Goodenough Island, S PNG
92 H1 **Bolungarvík** Vestfirdhir, NW Iceland
159 O10 **Boluntay** Qinghai, W China
136 F14 **Bolvadin** Afyon, W Turkey
114 M10 **Bolyarovo** *prev.* Pashkeni. Yambol, E Bulgaria
106 G6 **Bolzano** *Ger.* Bozen; *anc.* Bauzanum. Trentino-Alto Adige, N Italy
79 F22 **Boma** Bas-Congo, W Dem. Rep. Congo (Zaire)
183 R12 **Bombala** New South Wales, SE Australia
104 F10 **Bombarral** Leiria, C Portugal
Bombay *see* Mumbai
171 U13 **Bomberai, Semenanjung** *headland* Irian Jaya, E Indonesia
81 F18 **Bombo** S Uganda
79 I17 **Bomboma** Equateur, NW Dem. Rep. Congo (Zaire)
59 I14 **Bom Futuro** Pará, N Brazil
159 Q15 **Bomi** *var.* Bowo, Zhamo. Xizang Zizhiqu, W China
79 N17 **Bomili** Orientale, NE Dem. Rep. Congo (Zaire)
59 N17 **Bom Jesus da Lapa** Bahia, E Brazil
60 Q8 **Bom Jesus do Itabapoana** Rio de Janeiro, SE Brazil
95 C15 **Bømlafjorden** *fjord* S Norway
95 B15 **Bømlo** *island* S Norway
123 Q12 **Bomnak** Amurskaya Oblast', SE Russian Federation
79 I17 **Bomongo** Equateur, NW Dem. Rep. Congo (Zaire)
61 K14 **Bom Retiro** Santa Catarina, S Brazil
79 L15 **Bomu** *var.* Mbomou, Mbomu, M'Bomu. ≈ Central African Republic/Dem. Rep. Congo (Zaire)
142 J3 **Bonāb** *var.* Benāb, Bunab. Āžarbāyjān-e Khāvarī, N Iran
45 Q16 **Bonaire** *island* E Netherlands Antilles
39 U11 **Bona, Mount** ▲ Alaska, USA
183 Q12 **Bonang** Victoria, SE Australia
42 L7 **Bonanza** Región Autónoma Atlántico Norte, NE Nicaragua
37 O4 **Bonanza** Utah, W USA
45 O9 **Bonao** C Dominican Republic
180 L3 **Bonaparte Archipelago** *island group* Western Australia
32 K6 **Bonaparte, Mount** ▲ Washington, NW USA
39 N11 **Bonasila Dome** ▲ Alaska, USA
92 H11 **Bonåsjøen** Nordland, C Norway
45 T15 **Bonasse** Trinidad, Trinidad and Tobago
15 X7 **Bonaventure** Quebec, SE Canada
15 X7 **Bonaventure** ≈ Quebec, SE Canada
13 V11 **Bonavista** Newfoundland, SE Canada
13 U11 **Bonavista Bay** *inlet* NW Atlantic Ocean
79 E19 **Bonda** Ogooué-Lolo, C Gabon
129 N6 **Bondari** Tambovskaya Oblast', W Russian Federation
106 G9 **Bondeno** Emilia-Romagna, C Italy
30 L4 **Bond Falls Flowage** ◎ Michigan, N USA
79 L16 **Bondo** Orientale, N Dem. Rep. Congo (Zaire)
171 N17 **Bondokodi** Pulau Sumba, S Indonesia
77 O15 **Bondoukou** E Ivory Coast
Bondoukui/Bondoukuy *see* Boundoukui
169 T17 **Bondowoso** Jawa, C Indonesia
33 S14 **Bondurant** Wyoming, C USA
Bone *see* Watampone, Indonesia
Bône *see* Annaba, Algeria
30 I5 **Bone Lake** ◎ Wisconsin, N USA
171 P14 **Bonelipu** Pulau Buton, C Indonesia
171 O15 **Bonerate, Kepulauan** *var.* Macan. *island group* C Indonesia
29 O12 **Bonesteel** South Dakota, N USA
62 I8 **Bonete, Cerro** ▲ N Argentina
171 O14 **Bone, Teluk** *bay* Sulawesi, C Indonesia
108 D6 **Bonfol** Jura, NW Switzerland
153 U12 **Bongaigaon** Assam, NE India
79 K17 **Bongandanga** Equateur, NW Dem. Rep. Congo (Zaire)
78 L13 **Bongo, Massif des** *var.* Chaîne des Mongos. ▲ NE Central African Republic
78 G12 **Bongor** Mayo-Kébbi, SW Chad
77 N16 **Bongouanou** E Ivory Coast
167 V11 **Bông Sơn** *var.* Hoai Nhơn. Bình Định, C Vietnam
25 U5 **Bonham** Texas, SW USA
Bonhard *see* Bonyhád
103 U6 **Bonhomme, Col du** *pass* NE France
103 Y16 **Bonifacio** Corse, France, C Mediterranean Sea
Bonifacio, Bocche de/Bonifacio, Bouches de *see* Bonifacio, Strait of
103 Y16 **Bonifacio, Strait of** *Fr.* Bouches de Bonifacio, *It.* Bocche de Bonifacio. *strait* C Mediterranean Sea
23 Q8 **Bonifay** Florida, SE USA
Bonin Islands *see* Ogasawara-shotō
192 H5 **Bonin Trench** *undersea feature* NW Pacific Ocean
23 W15 **Bonita Springs** Florida, SE USA
42 I5 **Bonito, Pico** ▲ N Honduras
101 E17 **Bonn** Nordrhein-Westfalen, W Germany
14 J12 **Bonnechere** Ontario, SE Canada
14 J12 **Bonnechere** ≈ Ontario, SE Canada
33 N7 **Bonners Ferry** Idaho, NW USA
27 R4 **Bonner Springs** Kansas, C USA
102 L6 **Bonnétable** Sarthe, NW France
27 X6 **Bonne Terre** Missouri, C USA
10 J5 **Bonnet Plume** ≈ Yukon Territory, NW Canada
102 M6 **Bonneval** Eure-et-Loir, C France
103 T10 **Bonneville** Haute-Savoie, E France
36 J3 **Bonneville Salt Flats** *salt flat* Utah, W USA
77 U18 **Bonny** Rivers, S Nigeria
Bonny, Bight of *see* Biafra, Bight of
37 W4 **Bonny Reservoir** ▣ Colorado, C USA
11 R14 **Bonnyville** Alberta, SW Canada
107 C18 **Bono** Sardegna, Italy, C Mediterranean Sea
Bononia *see* Vidin, Bulgaria
Bononia *see* Boulogne-sur-Mer, France
107 B18 **Bonorva** Sardegna, Italy, C Mediterranean Sea
30 M15 **Bonpas Creek** ≈ Illinois, N USA
190 I3 **Bonriki** Tarawa, W Kiribati
183 T4 **Bonshaw** New South Wales, SE Australia
76 I15 **Bonthe** SW Sierra Leone
171 N2 **Bontoc** Luzon, N Philippines
25 Y9 **Bon Wier** Texas, SW USA
111 J25 **Bonyhád** *Ger.* Bonhard. Tolna, S Hungary
Bonzabaai *see* Bonza Bay
83 J25 **Bonza Bay** *Afr.* Bonzabaai. Eastern Cape, S South Africa
182 D7 **Bookabie** South Australia
182 H6 **Bookaloo** South Australia
37 P5 **Book Cliffs** *cliff* Colorado/Utah, W USA
25 P1 **Booker** Texas, SW USA
76 K15 **Boola** Guinée-Forestière, SE Guinea
183 O8 **Booligal** New South Wales, SE Australia
99 G17 **Boom** Antwerpen, N Belgium
43 N6 **Boom** *var.* Boon. Región Autónoma Atlántico Norte, NE Nicaragua
183 S3 **Boomi** New South Wales, SE Australia
Boon *see* Boom
29 V13 **Boone** Iowa, C USA
21 Q8 **Boone** North Carolina, SE USA
27 S11 **Booneville** Arkansas, C USA
21 N6 **Booneville** Kentucky, S USA
23 N2 **Booneville** Mississippi, S USA
21 V3 **Boonsboro** Maryland, NE USA
162 H9 **Bööntsagaan Nuur** ◎ S Mongolia
34 L6 **Boonville** California, W USA
31 N16 **Boonville** Indiana, N USA
27 U4 **Boonville** Missouri, C USA
18 I9 **Boonville** New York, NE USA
80 M12 **Boorama** Woqooyi Galbeed, NW Somalia
183 O6 **Booroondarra, Mount** *hill* New South Wales, SE Australia
183 N9 **Booroorban** New South Wales, SE Australia
183 R9 **Boorowa** New South Wales, SE Australia
99 H17 **Boortmeerbeek** Vlaams Brabant, C Belgium
80 P11 **Boosaaso** *var.* Bandar Kassim, Bender Qaasim, Bosaso, *It.* Bender Cassim. Bari, N Somalia
19 Q8 **Boothbay Harbor** Maine, NE USA
Boothia Felix *see* Boothia Peninsula
9 N6 **Boothia, Gulf of** *gulf* Nunavut, NE Canada
8 M6 **Boothia Peninsula** *prev.* Boothia Felix. *peninsula* Nunavut, NE Canada
79 E18 **Booué** Ogooué-Ivindo, NE Gabon
101 J21 **Bopfingen** Baden-Württemberg, S Germany
101 F18 **Boppard** Rheinland-Pfalz, W Germany
62 M4 **Boquerón** *off.* Departamento de Boquerón. ◈ *department* W Paraguay
43 P15 **Boquete** *var.* Bajo Boquete. Chiriquí, W Panama
40 J6 **Boquilla, Presa de la** ▣ N Mexico
40 L5 **Boquillas** *var.* Boquillas del Carmen. Coahuila de Zaragoza, NE Mexico
Boquillas del Carmen *see* Boquillas
81 F15 **Bor** Jonglei, S Sudan
95 L20 **Bor** Jönköping, S Sweden
136 J15 **Bor** Niğde, S Turkey
112 P12 **Bor** Serbia, E Yugoslavia
191 S10 **Bora-Bora** *island* Îles Sous le Vent, W French Polynesia
167 Q9 **Borabu** Maha Sarakham, E Thailand
33 P13 **Borah Peak** ▲ Idaho, NW USA
Boralday *see* Burunday
95 J19 **Borås** Västra Götaland, S Sweden
143 N11 **Borāzjān** *var.* Borazjān. Būshehr, S Iran
Borazjān *see* Borāzjān
58 G13 **Borba** Amazonas, N Brazil
104 H11 **Borba** Évora, S Portugal
Borbetomagus *see* Worms
55 O7 **Borbón** Bolívar, E Venezuela
59 Q15 **Borborema, Planalto da** *plateau* NE Brazil
116 M14 **Borcea, Braţul** ≈ S Romania
Borchalo *see* Marneuli
195 R15 **Borchgrevink Coast** *physical region* Antarctica
137 Q11 **Borçka** Artvin, NE Turkey
98 N11 **Borculo** Gelderland, E Netherlands
182 G10 **Borda, Cape** *headland* South Australia
102 K13 **Bordeaux** *anc.* Burdigala. Gironde, SW France
11 T15 **Borden** Saskatchewan, S Canada
14 D8 **Borden Lake** ◎ Ontario, S Canada
9 N4 **Borden Peninsula** *peninsula* Baffin Island, Nunavut, NE Canada
182 K11 **Bordertown** South Australia
92 H2 **Bordheyri** Vestfirdhir, NW Iceland
95 B18 **Bordhoy** *Dan.* Bordø *Island* Faeroe Islands
106 B11 **Bordighera** Liguria, NW Italy
74 K5 **Bordj-Bou-Arreridj** *var.* Bordj Bou Arreridj, Bordj Bou Arréridj. N Algeria
74 L10 **Bordj Omar Driss** E Algeria
143 N13 **Bord Khūn** Hormozgān, S Iran
147 V7 **Bordunskiy** Chuyskaya Oblast', N Kyrgyzstan
95 M17 **Borensberg** Östergötland, S Sweden
Borgå *see* Porvoo
92 L2 **Borgarfjördhur** Austurland, NE Iceland
92 H3 **Borgarnes** Vesturland, W Iceland
93 G14 **Børgefjellet** ▲ C Norway
98 O7 **Borger** Drenthe, NE Netherlands
25 N2 **Borger** Texas, SW USA
95 N20 **Borgholm** Kalmar, S Sweden
107 N22 **Borgia** Calabria, SW Italy
99 J18 **Borgloon** Limburg, NE Belgium
195 P2 **Borg Massif** ▲ Antarctica
22 L9 **Borgne, Lake** ◎ Louisiana, S USA
106 C7 **Borgomanero** Piemonte, NE Italy
106 G10 **Borgo Panigale** ✕ (Bologna) Emilia-Romagna, N Italy
107 J15 **Borgorose** Lazio, C Italy
106 A9 **Borgo San Dalmazzo** Piemonte, N Italy
106 G11 **Borgo San Lorenzo** Toscana, C Italy
106 C7 **Borgosesia** Piemonte, NE Italy
106 E9 **Borgo Val di Taro** Emilia-Romagna, C Italy
106 G6 **Borgo Valsugana** Trentino-Alto Adige, N Italy
163 O11 **Borhoyn Tal** Dornogovĭ, SE Mongolia
167 R8 **Borikhan** *var.* Borikhane. Bolikhamxai, C Laos
Borikhane *see* Borikhan
Borislav *see* Boryslav
129 N8 **Borisoglebsk** Voronezhskaya Oblast', W Russian Federation
Borisov *see* Barysaw
Borisovgrad *see* Pŭrvomay
Borispol' *see* Boryspil'
172 I3 **Boriziny** Mahajanga, NW Madagascar
105 Q5 **Borja** Aragón, NE Spain
Borjas Blancas *see* Les Borges Blanques
137 S10 **Borjomi** *Rus.* Borzhomi. C Georgia
118 L12 **Borkavichy** *Rus.* Borkovichi. Vitsyebskaya Voblasts', N Belarus
101 H16 **Borken** Hessen, C Germany
101 E14 **Borken** Nordrhein-Westfalen, W Germany
92 H10 **Borkenes** Troms, N Norway
78 H7 **Borkou-Ennedi-Tibesti** *off.* Préfecture du Borkou-Ennedi-Tibesti. ◈ *prefecture* N Chad
Borkovichi *see* Borkavichy
100 E9 **Borkum** *island* NW Germany
81 K17 **Bor, Lagh** *var.* Lak Bor. *dry watercourse* NE Kenya
Bor, Lak *see* Bor, Lagh
95 M14 **Borlänge** Dalarna, C Sweden
106 C9 **Bormida** ≈ NW Italy
106 F6 **Bormio** Lombardia, N Italy
101 M16 **Borna** Sachsen, E Germany
98 O10 **Borne** Overijssel, E Netherlands
99 F17 **Bornem** Antwerpen, N Belgium
169 S10 **Borneo** *island* Brunei/Indonesia/Malaysia
101 E16 **Bornheim** Nordrhein-Westfalen, W Germany
95 L24 **Bornholm** ◈ *county* E Denmark
95 L24 **Bornholm** *island* E Denmark
77 Y13 **Borno** ◈ *state* NE Nigeria
104 K15 **Bornos** Andalucía, S Spain

◆ Country ● Country Capital ◇ Dependent Territory ○ Dependent Territory Capital ◈ Administrative Region ✕ International Airport ▲ Mountain ▲ Mountain Range ⛰ Volcano ≈ River ◎ Lake ▣ Reservoir

162 L7 **Bornuur** Töv, C Mongolia
117 O4 **Borodyanka** Kyyivs'ka Oblast', N Ukraine
158 I5 **Borohoro Shan** ▲ NW China
77 O13 **Boromo** SW Burkina
35 T13 **Boron** California, W USA
Borongo see Black Volta
Boron'ki see Baron'ki
Borosjenő see Ineu
Borossebes see Sebiş
76 L15 **Borotou** NW Ivory Coast
117 W6 **Borova** Kharkivs'ka Oblast', E Ukraine
114 H8 **Borovan** Vratsa, NW Bulgaria
126 I14 **Borovichi** Novgorodskaya Oblast', W Russian Federation
Borovlje see Ferlach
112 J9 **Borovo** Vukovar-Srijem, NE Croatia
145 Q7 **Borovoye** Kaz. Būrabay. Severnyy Kazakhstan, N Kazakhstan
128 K4 **Borovsk** Kaluzhskaya Oblast', W Russian Federation
145 N7 **Borovskoy** Kostanay, N Kazakhstan
Borovukha see Baravukha
95 L23 **Borrby** Skåne, S Sweden
181 R3 **Borroloola** Northern Territory, N Australia
116 F9 **Bors** Bihor, NW Romania
116 I9 **Borşa** Hung. Borsa. Maramureş, N Romania
116 J10 **Borsec** Ger. Bad Borseck, Hung. Borszék. Harghita, C Romania
92 K8 **Børselv** Finnmark, N Norway
113 L23 **Borsh** var. Borshi. Vlorë, S Albania
Borshchev see Borshchiv
116 K7 **Borshchiv** Pol. Borszczów, Rus. Borshchev. Ternopil's'ka Oblast', W Ukraine
Borshi see Borsh
111 L20 **Borsod-Abaúj-Zemplén** off. Borsod-Abaúj-Zemplén Megye. ◈ county NE Hungary
99 E15 **Borssele** Zeeland, SW Netherlands
Borszczów see Borshchiv
Borszék see Borsec
Bortala see Bole
103 O12 **Bort-les-Orgues** Corrèze, C France
Bor u České Lípy see Nový Bor
162 E8 **Bor-Udzüür** Hovd, W Mongolia
143 N9 **Borūjen** Chahār Maḩall va Bakhtīārī, C Iran
142 L7 **Borūjerd** var. Burujird. Lorestān, W Iran
116 H6 **Boryslav** Pol. Borysław, Rus. Borislav. L'vivs'ka Oblast', NW Ukraine
Borysław see Boryslav
117 P4 **Boryspil'** Rus. Borispol'. Kyyivs'ka Oblast', N Ukraine
117 P4 **Boryspil'** Rus. Borispol'. ✕ (Kyyiv) Kyyivs'ka Oblast', N Ukraine
Borzhomi see Borjomi
117 R3 **Borzna** Chernihivs'ka Oblast', NE Ukraine
123 O14 **Borzya** Chitinskaya Oblast', S Russian Federation
107 B18 **Bosa** Sardegna, Italy, C Mediterranean Sea
112 F10 **Bosanska Dubica** var. Kozarska Dubica. Republika Srpska, NW Bosnia and Herzegovina
112 G10 **Bosanska Gradiška** var. Gradiška. Republika Srpska, N Bosnia and Herzegovina
112 F10 **Bosanska Kostajnica** var. Srpska Kostajnica. Republika Srpska, NW Bosnia and Herzegovina
112 E11 **Bosanska Krupa** var. Krupa, Krupa na Uni. Federacija Bosna I Hercegovina, NW Bosnia and Herzegovina
112 H10 **Bosanski Brod** var. Srpski Brod. Republika Srpska, N Bosnia and Herzegovina
112 E10 **Bosanski Novi** var. Novi Grad. Republika Srpska, NW Bosnia and Herzegovina
112 E11 **Bosanski Petrovac** var. Petrovac. Federacija Bosna I Hercegovina, NW Bosnia and Herzegovina
112 N12 **Bosanski Petrovac** Serbia, E Yugoslavia
112 I10 **Bosanski Šamac** var. Šamac. Republika Srpska, N Bosnia and Herzegovina
112 E12 **Bosansko Grahovo** var. Grahovo, Hrvatsko Grahovo. Federacija Bosna I Hercegovina, W Bosnia and Herzegovina
Bosaso see Boosaaso
186 B7 **Bosavi, Mount** ▲ W PNG
160 J14 **Bose** Guangxi Zhuangzu Zizhiqu, S China
161 Q5 **Boshan** Shandong, E China
113 P16 **Bosilegrad** prev. Bosiljgrad. Serbia, SE Yugoslavia
Bosiljgrad see Bosilegrad
Bösing see Pezinok
98 H12 **Boskoop** Zuid-Holland, C Netherlands
111 G18 **Boskovice** Ger. Boskowitz. Brněnský Kraj, SE Czech Republic
Boskowitz see Boskovice
112 I10 **Bosna** ≈ N Bosnia and Herzegovina
113 G14 **Bosna I Hercegovina, Federacija** ◈ republic Bosnia and Herzegovina
112 H12 **Bosnia and Herzegovina** off. Republic of Bosnia and Herzegovina. ◆ republic SE Europe
79 J16 **Bosobolo** Equateur, NW Dem. Rep. Congo (Zaire)
165 O14 **Bōsō-hantō** peninsula Honshū, S Japan
Bosora see Buşrá ash Shām
Bosphorus/Bosporus see İstanbul Boğazı
Bosporus Cimmerius see Kerch Strait
Bosporus Thracius see İstanbul Boğazı
Bosra see Buşrá ash Shām
79 H14 **Bossangoa** Ouham, C Central African Republic
Bossé Bangou see Bossey Bangou
79 I15 **Bossembélé** Ombella-Mpoko, C Central African Republic
79 H15 **Bossentélé** Ouham-Pendé, W Central African Republic
77 R12 **Bossey Bangou** var. Bossé Bangou. Tillabéri, SW Niger
22 G5 **Bossier City** Louisiana, S USA
83 D20 **Bossiesvlei** Hardap, S Namibia
77 Y11 **Bosso** Diffa, SE Niger
61 F15 **Bossoroca** Rio Grande do Sul, S Brazil
158 J10 **Bostan** Xinjiang Uygur Zizhiqu, W China
142 K3 **Bostānābād** Āžarbāyjān-e Khāvarī, N Iran
158 K6 **Bosten Hu** var. Bagrax Hu. ⊚ NW China
97 O18 **Boston** prev. St.Botolph's Town. E England, UK
19 O11 **Boston** state capital Massachusetts, NE USA
10 M17 **Boston Bar** British Columbia, SW Canada
27 T10 **Boston Mountains** ▲ Arkansas, C USA
15 P8 **Bostonnais** ≈ Quebec, SE Canada
Bostyn' see Bastyn'
112 J10 **Bosut** ≈ E Croatia
154 C11 **Botād** Gujarāt, W India
183 T9 **Botany Bay** inlet New South Wales, SE Australia
83 G18 **Boteti** var. Botletle. ≈ N Botswana
114 J9 **Botev** ▲ C Bulgaria
114 H9 **Botevgrad** prev. Orkhaniye. Sofiya, W Bulgaria
93 J16 **Bothnia, Gulf of** Fin. Pohjanlahti, Swe. Bottniska Viken. gulf N Baltic Sea
183 P17 **Bothwell** Tasmania, SE Australia
104 H5 **Boticas** Vila Real, N Portugal
55 W10 **Boti-Pasi** Sipaliwini, C Surinname
Botletle see Boteti
129 P16 **Botlikh** Chechenskaya Respublika, SW Russian Federation
117 N10 **Botna** ≈ E Moldova
116 I9 **Botoşani** Hung. Botosány. Botoşani, NE Romania
116 K8 **Botoşani** ◈ county NE Romania
Botosány see Botoşani
161 P4 **Botou** prev. Bozhen. Hebei, E China
99 M20 **Botrange** ▲ E Belgium
107 O21 **Botricello** Calabria, SW Italy
83 I23 **Botshabelo** Free State, C South Africa
93 J15 **Botsmark** Västerbotten, N Sweden
83 G19 **Botswana** off. Republic of Botswana. ◆ republic S Africa
29 N2 **Bottineau** North Dakota, N USA
Bottniska Viken see Bothnia, Gulf of
60 L9 **Botucatu** São Paulo, S Brazil
76 M16 **Bouaflé** C Ivory Coast
77 N16 **Bouaké** var. Bwake. C Ivory Coast
79 G14 **Bouar** Nana-Mambéré, W Central African Republic
74 H7 **Bouarfa** NE Morocco
111 B19 **Boubín** ▲ SW Czech Republic
79 I14 **Bouca** Ouham, W Central African Republic
15 T5 **Boucher** ≈ Quebec, SE Canada
103 R15 **Bouches-du-Rhône** ◈ department SE France
74 C9 **Bou Craa** var. Bu Craa. NW Western Sahara
77 O9 **Boû Djébéha** oasis C Mali
108 C8 **Boudry** Neuchâtel, W Switzerland
180 L2 **Bougainville, Cape** headland Western Australia
65 E24 **Bougainville, Cape** headland East Falkland, Falkland Islands
Bougainville, Détroit de see Bougainville Strait, Vanuatu
186 J7 **Bougainville Island** island NE PNG
186 Q13 **Bougainville Strait** strait N Solomon Islands
197 B12 **Bougainville Strait** Fr. Détroit de Bougainville. strait C Vanuatu
120 I9 **Bougaroun, Cap** headland NE Algeria
77 R8 **Boughessa** Kidal, NE Mali
Bougie see Béjaïa
76 L13 **Bougouni** Sikasso, SW Mali
99 J24 **Bouillon** Luxembourg, SE Belgium
74 K5 **Bouira** var. Bouïra. N Algeria
74 D8 **Bou-Izakarn** SW Morocco
74 B9 **Boujdour** var. Bojador. W Western Sahara
74 G5 **Boukhalef** ✕ (Tanger) N Morocco
Boukombé see Boukoumbé
77 R14 **Boukoumbé** var. Boukombé. C Benin
76 G6 **Boû Lanouâr** Dakhlet Nouâdhibou, W Mauritania
37 T4 **Boulder** Colorado, C USA
33 R10 **Boulder** Montana, NW USA
35 X12 **Boulder City** Nevada, W USA
181 T7 **Boulia** Queensland, C Australia
15 N10 **Boullé** ≈ Quebec, SE Canada
102 J9 **Boulogne** ≈ NW France
Boulogne see Boulogne-sur-Mer
102 L16 **Boulogne-sur-Gesse** Haute-Garonne, S France
103 N1 **Boulogne-sur-Mer** var. Boulogne; anc. Bononia, Gesoriacum, Gessoriacum. Pas-de-Calais, N France
77 Q12 **Boulsa** C Burkina
77 W11 **Boultoum** Zinder, C Niger
187 Y14 **Bouma** Taveuni, N Fiji
79 G16 **Boumba** ≈ SE Cameroon
76 J9 **Boûmdeïd** var. Boumdeït. Assaba, S Mauritania
Boumdeït see Boûmdeïd
115 C17 **Boumistós** ▲ W Greece
77 O15 **Bouna** NE Ivory Coast
19 P4 **Boundary Bald Mountain** ▲ Maine, NE USA
35 S8 **Boundary Peak** ▲ Nevada, W USA
76 M14 **Boundiali** N Ivory Coast
79 G19 **Boundji** Cuvette, C Congo
77 O13 **Boundoukui** var. Bondoukui, Bondoukuy. W Burkina
36 L2 **Bountiful** Utah, W USA
Bounty Basin see Bounty Trough
191 Q16 **Bounty Bay** bay Pitcairn Island, C Pacific Ocean
192 L12 **Bounty Islands** island group S NZ
175 Q13 **Bounty Trough** var. Bounty Basin. undersea feature S Pacific Ocean
187 P17 **Bourail** Province Sud, C New Caledonia
27 V5 **Bourbeuse River** ≈ Missouri, C USA
103 Q9 **Bourbon-Lancy** Saône-et-Loire, C France
31 N11 **Bourbonnais** Illinois, N USA
103 O10 **Bourbonnais** cultural region C France
103 S7 **Bourbonne-les-Bains** Haute-Marne, N France
Bourbon Vendée see la Roche-sur-Yon
74 M8 **Bourdj Messaouda** E Algeria
77 Q10 **Bourem** Gao, C Mali
Bourg see Bourg-en-Bresse
103 N11 **Bourganeuf** Creuse, C France
Bourgas see Burgas
Bourge-en-Bresse see Bourg-en-Bresse
103 S10 **Bourg-en-Bresse** var. Bourg, Bourge-en-Bresse. Ain, E France
103 O8 **Bourges** anc. Avaricum. Cher, C France
103 T11 **Bourget, Lac du** ⊚ E France
103 P8 **Bourgogne** Eng. Burgundy. ◈ region E France
103 S11 **Bourgoin-Jallieu** Isère, E France
103 R14 **Bourg-St-Andéol** Ardèche, E France
103 U11 **Bourg-St-Maurice** Savoie, E France
108 C11 **Bourg St.Pierre** Valais, SW Switzerland
76 H8 **Boû Rjeïmât** well W Mauritania
183 P5 **Bourke** New South Wales, SE Australia
97 M24 **Bournemouth** S England, UK
99 M23 **Bourscheid** Diekirch, NE Luxembourg
74 K6 **Bou Saâda** var. Bou Saada. N Algeria
36 I13 **Bouse Wash** ≈ Arizona, SW USA
103 N10 **Boussac** Creuse, C France
102 M16 **Boussens** Haute-Garonne, S France
78 H12 **Bousso** prev. Fort-Bretonnet. Chari-Baguirmi, S Chad
76 H9 **Boutilimit** Trarza, SW Mauritania
65 D21 **Bouvet Island** ◇ Norwegian dependency S Atlantic Ocean
77 U11 **Bouza** Tahoua, SW Niger
109 R10 **Bovec** Ger. Flitsch, It. Plezzo. NW Slovenia
98 J8 **Bovenkarspel** Noord-Holland, NW Netherlands
29 V5 **Bovey** Minnesota, N USA
32 M9 **Bovill** Idaho, NW USA
24 L4 **Bovina** Texas, SW USA
107 M17 **Bovino** Puglia, SE Italy
61 C17 **Bovril** Entre Ríos, E Argentina
28 L2 **Bowbells** North Dakota, N USA
11 Q16 **Bow City** Alberta, SW Canada
29 O8 **Bowdle** South Dakota, N USA
181 X6 **Bowen** Queensland, NE Australia
192 L2 **Bowers Ridge** undersea feature S Bering Sea
25 S5 **Bowie** Texas, SW USA
11 R17 **Bow Island** Alberta, SW Canada
Bowkān see Būkān
20 J7 **Bowling Green** Kentucky, S USA
27 V3 **Bowling Green** Missouri, C USA
31 R11 **Bowling Green** Ohio, N USA
21 W5 **Bowling Green** Virginia, NE USA
28 J6 **Bowman** North Dakota, N USA
9 Q7 **Bowman Bay** bay NW Atlantic Ocean
194 I5 **Bowman Coast** physical region Antarctica
28 J7 **Bowman-Haley Lake** ⊠ North Dakota, N USA
195 Z11 **Bowman Island** island Antarctica
Bowo see Bomi
183 S9 **Bowral** New South Wales, SE Australia
186 E8 **Bowutu Mountains** ▲ C PNG
83 I16 **Bowwood** Southern, S Zambia
28 I12 **Box Butte Reservoir** ⊠ Nebraska, C USA
28 J10 **Box Elder** South Dakota, N USA
95 M18 **Boxholm** Östergötland, S Sweden
Bo Xian/Boxian see Bozhou
161 Q4 **Boxing** Shandong, E China
99 L14 **Boxmeer** Noord-Brabant, SE Netherlands
99 J14 **Boxtel** Noord-Brabant, S Netherlands
136 J10 **Boyabat** Sinop, N Turkey
54 F9 **Boyacá** off. Departamento de Boyacá. ◈ province C Colombia
117 O4 **Boyarka** Kyyivs'ka Oblast', N Ukraine
22 H7 **Boyce** Louisiana, S USA
33 U11 **Boyd** Montana, NW USA
25 S6 **Boyd** Texas, SW USA
21 V8 **Boydton** Virginia, NE USA
Boyer Ahmadī va Kohkīlūyeh see Kohkīlūyeh va Būyer Aḩmadī
29 T13 **Boyer River** ≈ Iowa, C USA
21 W8 **Boykins** Virginia, NE USA
11 Q13 **Boyle** Alberta, SW Canada
97 D16 **Boyle** Ir. Mainistirna Búille. C Ireland
97 F17 **Boyne** Ir. An Bhóinn. ≈ E Ireland
31 Q5 **Boyne City** Michigan, N USA
23 Z14 **Boynton Beach** Florida, SE USA
147 O13 **Boysun** Rus. Baysun. Surkhondaryo Wiloyati, S Uzbekistan
Bozau see Întorsura Buzăului
136 B12 **Bozcaada** island Çanakkale, NW Turkey
136 C14 **Boz Dağları** ▲ W Turkey
33 S11 **Bozeman** Montana, NW USA
Bozen see Bolzano
79 J16 **Bozene** Equateur, NW Dem. Rep. Congo (Zaire)
161 P7 **Bozhou** var. Boxian, Bo Xian. Anhui, E China
136 H16 **Bozkır** Konya, S Turkey
136 K13 **Bozok Yaylası** plateau C Turkey
79 H14 **Bozoum** Ouham-Pendé, W Central African Republic
137 N16 **Bozova** Sanlıurfa, S Turkey
Bozrah see Buşrá ash Shām
136 E12 **Bozüyük** Bilecik, NW Turkey
106 B9 **Bra** Piemonte, NW Italy
194 G4 **Brabant Island** island Antarctica
99 I20 **Brabant Wallon** ◈ province C Belgium
113 F15 **Brač** var. Brach, It. Brazza; anc. Brattia. island S Croatia
Bracara Augusta see Braga
107 H15 **Bracciano** Lazio, C Italy
107 H14 **Bracciano, Lago di** ⊚ C Italy
14 H13 **Bracebridge** Ontario, S Canada
Brach see Brač
93 G17 **Bräcke** Jämtland, C Sweden
25 P12 **Brackettville** Texas, SW USA
97 N22 **Bracknell** S England, UK
61 K14 **Braço do Norte** Santa Catarina, S Brazil
116 G11 **Brad** Hung. Brád. Hunedoara, SW Romania
107 N18 **Bradano** ≈ S Italy
23 V13 **Bradenton** Florida, SE USA
14 H14 **Bradford** Ontario, S Canada
97 L17 **Bradford** N England, UK
27 W10 **Bradford** Arkansas, C USA
18 D12 **Bradford** Pennsylvania, NE USA
27 T15 **Bradley** Arkansas, C USA
25 P7 **Bradshaw** Texas, SW USA
25 Q9 **Brady** Texas, SW USA
25 Q9 **Brady Creek** ≈ Texas, SW USA
96 J10 **Braemar** NE Scotland, UK
116 K8 **Brăeşti** Botoşani, NW Romania
104 G5 **Braga** anc. Bracara Augusta. Braga, NW Portugal
104 G5 **Braga** ◈ district N Portugal
116 J15 **Bragadiru** Teleorman, S Romania
61 C20 **Bragado** Buenos Aires, E Argentina
104 J5 **Bragança** Eng. Braganza; anc. Julio Briga. Bragança, NE Portugal
104 I5 **Bragança** ◈ district N Portugal
60 N9 **Bragança Paulista** São Paulo, S Brazil
Braganza see Bragança
Bragin see Brahin
29 V7 **Braham** Minnesota, N USA
Brahe see Brda
Brahestad see Raahe
119 O20 **Brahin** Rus. Bragin. Homyel'skaya Voblasts', SE Belarus
153 U15 **Brahmanbaria** Chittagong, E Bangladesh
154 O12 **Brāhmani** ≈ E India
154 N13 **Brahmapur** Orissa, E India
131 S10 **Brahmaputra** var. Padma, Tsangpo, Ben. Jamuna, Chin. Yarlung Zangbo Jiang, Ind. Bramaputra, Dihang, Siang. ≈ S Asia
97 H19 **Braich y Pwll** headland NW Wales, UK
183 R10 **Braidwood** New South Wales, SE Australia
30 M11 **Braidwood** Illinois, N USA
116 M13 **Brăila** Brăila, E Romania
116 L13 **Brăila** ◈ county SE Romania
99 G19 **Braine-l'Alleud** Brabant Wallon, C Belgium
99 F19 **Braine-le-Comte** Hainaut, SW Belgium
29 U6 **Brainerd** Minnesota, N USA
99 J19 **Braives** Liège, E Belgium
83 H23 **Brak** ≈ C South Africa
Brak see Birāk
99 E18 **Brakel** Oost-Vlaanderen, SW Belgium
98 J13 **Brakel** Gelderland, C Netherlands
76 H9 **Brakna** ◈ region S Mauritania
95 J17 **Brålanda** Västra Götaland, S Sweden
Bramaputra see Brahmaputra
95 F23 **Bramming** Ribe, W Denmark
14 G15 **Brampton** Ontario, S Canada
100 F12 **Bramsche** Niedersachsen, NW Germany
116 J12 **Bran** Ger. Törzburg, Hung. Törcsvár. Braşov, S Romania
29 W8 **Branch** Minnesota, N USA
21 R14 **Branchville** South Carolina, SE USA
47 Y6 **Branco, Cabo** headland E Brazil
58 F11 **Branco, Rio** ≈ N Brazil
108 J8 **Brand** Vorarlberg, W Austria
83 B18 **Brandberg** ▲ NW Namibia
95 H14 **Brandbu** Oppland, S Norway
95 F22 **Brande** Ringkøbing, W Denmark
Brandebourg see Brandenburg
100 M12 **Brandenburg** var. Brandenburg an der Havel. Brandenburg, NE Germany
20 K5 **Brandenburg** Kentucky, S USA
100 N12 **Brandenburg** off. Freie und Hansestadt Hamburg, Fr. Brandebourg. ◈ state NE Germany
Brandenburg an der Havel see Brandenburg
83 I23 **Brandfort** Free State, C South Africa
11 W16 **Brandon** Manitoba, S Canada
23 V12 **Brandon** Florida, SE USA
22 L6 **Brandon** Mississippi, S USA
97 A20 **Brandon Mountain** Ir. Cnoc Bréanainn. ▲ SW Ireland
Brandsen see Coronel Brandsen
95 I14 **Brandval** Hedmark, S Norway
83 F24 **Brandvlei** Northern Cape, W South Africa
23 U9 **Branford** Florida, SE USA
110 K7 **Braniewo** Ger. Braunsberg. Warmińsko-Mazurskie, NE Poland
194 H3 **Bransfield Strait** strait Antarctica
37 U8 **Branson** Colorado, C USA
27 T8 **Branson** Missouri, C USA
14 G16 **Brantford** Ontario, S Canada
102 L12 **Brantôme** Dordogne, SW France
182 L12 **Branxholme** Victoria, SE Australia
Brasil see Brazil
59 C16 **Brasiléia** Acre, W Brazil
59 K18 **Brasília** ● (Brazil) Distrito Federal, C Brazil
Braslav see Braslaw
118 J12 **Braslaw** Pol. Brasław, Rus. Braslav. Vitsyebskaya Voblasts', N Belarus
116 J12 **Braşov** Ger. Kronstadt, Hung. Brassó; prev. Oraşul Stalin. Braşov, C Romania
116 I12 **Braşov** ◈ county C Romania
77 U18 **Brass** Bayelsa, S Nigeria
99 H16 **Brasschaat** var. Brasschaet. Antwerpen, N Belgium
Brasschaet see Brasschaat
169 V8 **Brassey, Banjaran** var. Brassey Range. ▲ East Malaysia
Brassey Range see Brassey, Banjaran
Brassó see Braşov
23 T1 **Brasstown Bald** ▲ Georgia, SE USA
113 K22 **Brataj** Vlorë, SW Albania
114 J10 **Bratan** var. Morozov. ▲ C Bulgaria
111 F21 **Bratislava** Ger. Pressburg, Hung. Pozsony. ● (Slovakia) Bratislavský Kraj, W Slovakia
111 H21 **Bratislavský Kraj** ◈ region W Slovakia
114 H10 **Bratiya** ▲ C Bulgaria
122 M12 **Bratsk** Irkutskaya Oblast', C Russian Federation
117 Q8 **Brats'ke** Mykolayivs'ka Oblast', S Ukraine
122 M13 **Bratskoye Vodokhranilishche** Eng. Bratsk Reservoir. ⊠ S Russian Federation
Bratsk Reservoir see Bratskoye Vodokhranilishche
Brattia see Brač
94 D9 **Brattvåg** Møre og Romsdal, S Norway
112 K12 **Bratunac** Republika Srpska, E Bosnia and Herzegovina
114 J10 **Bratya Daskalovi** prev. Grozdovo. Stara Zagora, C Bulgaria
109 U2 **Braunau** ≈ N Austria
Braunau see Braunau am Inn
109 Q4 **Braunau am Inn** var. Braunau. Oberösterreich, N Austria
Braunsberg see Braniewo
100 J13 **Braunschweig** Eng./Fr. Brunswick. Niedersachsen, N Germany
Brava see Baraawe
105 Y6 **Brava, Costa** coastal region NE Spain
43 V16 **Brava, Punta** headland E Panama
95 N17 **Bråviken** inlet S Sweden
56 B10 **Bravo, Cerro** ▲ N Peru
Bravo del Norte, Río/Bravo, Río see Grande, Rio
35 X17 **Brawley** California, W USA
97 G18 **Bray** Ir. Bré. E Ireland
59 G16 **Brazil** off. Federative Republic of Brazil, Port. República Federativa do Brasil, Sp. Brasil; prev. United States of Brazil. ◆ federal republic South America
65 K15 **Brazil Basin** var. Brazilian Basin, Brazil'skaya Kotlovina. undersea feature W Atlantic Ocean
Brazilian Basin see Brazil Basin
Brazilian Highlands see Central, Planalto
Brazil'skaya Kotlovina see Brazil Basin
25 U10 **Brazos River** ≈ Texas, SW USA
Brazza see Brač
79 G21 **Brazzaville** ● (Congo) Capital District, S Congo
79 G21 **Brazzaville** ✕ Le Pool, S Congo
112 J11 **Brčko** Republika Srpska, NE Bosnia and Herzegovina
110 H8 **Brda** Ger. Brahe. ≈ N Poland
Bré see Bray
185 A23 **Breaksea Sound** sound South Island, NZ
184 L4 **Bream Bay** bay North Island, NZ
184 L4 **Bream Head** headland North Island, NZ
Bréanainn, Cnoc see Brandon Mountain
45 S6 **Brea, Punta** headland W Puerto Rico
22 I9 **Breaux Bridge** Louisiana, S USA
116 J13 **Breaza** Prahova, SE Romania
169 P16 **Brebes** Jawa, C Indonesia
96 K10 **Brechin** E Scotland, UK
99 H15 **Brecht** Antwerpen, N Belgium
37 S4 **Breckenridge** Colorado, C USA
29 R6 **Breckenridge** Minnesota, N USA
25 R6 **Breckenridge** Texas, SW USA
97 J21 **Brecknock** cultural region SE Wales, UK
63 G25 **Brecknock, Península** headland S Chile
111 G19 **Břeclav** Ger. Lundenburg. Brněnský Kraj, SE Czech Republic
97 J21 **Brecon** E Wales, UK
97 J21 **Brecon Beacons** ▲ S Wales, UK
99 I14 **Breda** Noord-Brabant, S Netherlands
95 K20 **Bredaryd** Jönköping, S Sweden
83 F26 **Bredasdorp** Western Cape, SW South Africa
93 H16 **Bredbyn** Västernorrland, N Sweden
122 F11 **Bredy** Chelyabinskaya Oblast', C Russian Federation
99 K17 **Bree** Limburg, NE Belgium
67 T15 **Breede** ≈ S South Africa
98 I7 **Breezand** Noord-Holland, NW Netherlands
113 P18 **Bregalnica** ≈ E FYR Macedonia
108 I6 **Bregenz** anc. Brigantium. Vorarlberg, W Austria
108 J7 **Bregenzer Wald** ▲ W Austria
114 F6 **Bregovo** Vidin, NW Bulgaria
102 H5 **Bréhat, Île de** island NW France
92 H2 **Breiðhafjördhur** bay W Iceland
92 L3 **Breiðdalsvík** Austurland, E Iceland
108 H9 **Breil** Ger. Brigels. Graubünden, S Switzerland
92 J8 **Breivikbotn** Finnmark, N Norway
94 I9 **Brekken** Sør-Trøndelag, S Norway
94 G7 **Brekstad** Sør-Trøndelag, S Norway
94 B10 **Bremangerlandet** island S Norway
Brême see Bremen
100 H11 **Bremen** Fr. Brême. Bremen, NW Germany
23 R3 **Bremen** Georgia, SE USA
31 O11 **Bremen** Indiana, N USA
100 H10 **Bremen** off. Freie Hansestadt Bremen, Fr. Brême. ◈ state N Germany
100 G9 **Bremerhaven** Bremen, NW Germany
Bremersdorp see Manzini
32 G8 **Bremerton** Washington, NW USA
100 H10 **Bremervörde** Niedersachsen, NW Germany
25 U9 **Bremond** Texas, SW USA
25 U10 **Brenham** Texas, SW USA
108 M8 **Brenner** Tirol, W Austria
Brenner, Col du/Brennero, Passo del see Brenner Pass
108 M8 **Brenner Pass** var. Brenner Sattel, Fr. Col du Brenner, Ger. Brennerpass, It. Passo del Brennero. pass Austria/Italy
Brenner Sattel see Brenner Pass
108 G10 **Brenno** ≈ SW Switzerland
106 F7 **Breno** Lombardia, N Italy
23 O5 **Brent** Alabama, S USA
106 H7 **Brenta** ≈ NE Italy
97 P21 **Brentwood** E England, UK
18 L14 **Brentwood** Long Island, New York, NE USA
106 F7 **Brescia** anc. Brixia. Lombardia, N Italy
99 D15 **Breskens** Zeeland, SW Netherlands
Breslau see Dolnośląskie
106 H5 **Bressanone** Ger. Brixen. Trentino-Alto Adige, N Italy
96 M2 **Bressay** island NE Scotland, UK
102 K9 **Bressuire** Deux-Sèvres, W France
119 F20 **Brest** Pol. Brześć nad Bugiem, Rus. Brest-Litovsk; prev. Brześć Litewski. Brestskaya Voblasts', SW Belarus
102 F5 **Brest** Finistère, NW France
Brest-Litovsk see Brest
112 A10 **Brestova** Istra, NW Croatia
Brestskaya Oblast' see Brestskaya Voblasts'
119 G19 **Brestskaya Voblasts'** prev. Rus. Brestskaya Oblast'. ◈ province SW Belarus
102 G6 **Bretagne** Eng. Brittany; Lat. Britannia Minor. ◈ region NW France
116 G12 **Bretea-Română** Hung. Oláhbrettye; prev. Bretea-Romînă. Hunedoara, W Romania
Bretea-Romînă see Bretea-Română
103 O3 **Breteuil** Oise, N France
102 I10 **Breton, Pertuis** inlet W France
22 L10 **Breton Sound** sound Louisiana, S USA
184 K2 **Brett, Cape** headland North Island, NZ
101 G21 **Bretten** Baden-Württemberg, SW Germany
99 K15 **Breugel** Noord-Brabant, S Netherlands
106 B6 **Breuil-Cervinia** It. Cervinia. Valle d'Aosta, NW Italy
98 I11 **Breukelen** Utrecht, C Netherlands
21 P10 **Brevard** North Carolina, SE USA
38 L9 **Brevig Mission** Alaska, USA

◆ Country
● Country Capital
◇ Dependent Territory
○ Dependent Territory Capital
◈ Administrative Region
✕ International Airport
▲ Mountain
▲ Mountain Range
▲ Volcano
≈ River
⊚ Lake
⊠ Reservoir

95 G16 **Brevik** Telemark, S Norway
183 P5 **Brewarrina** New South Wales, SE Australia
19 R6 **Brewer** Maine, NE USA
29 T11 **Brewster** Minnesota, N USA
29 N14 **Brewster** Nebraska, C USA
31 U12 **Brewster** Ohio, N USA
183 O8 **Brewster, Lake** ◎ New South Wales, SE Australia
23 P7 **Brewton** Alabama, S USA
Brezhnev see Naberezhnyye Chelny
109 W12 **Brežice** Ger. Rann. E Slovenia
114 G9 **Breznik** Pernik, W Bulgaria
111 K19 **Brezno** Ger. Bries, Briesen, Hung. Breznóbánya; prev. Brezno nad Hronom. Banskobystrický Kraj, C Slovakia
Breznóbánya/Brezno nad Hronom see Brezno
116 I12 **Brezoi** Vâlcea, SW Romania
114 J10 **Brezovo** prev. Abrashlare. Plovdiv, C Bulgaria
79 K14 **Bria** Haute-Kotto, C Central African Republic
103 U13 **Briançon** anc. Brigantio. Hautes-Alpes, SE France
36 K7 **Brian Head** ▲ Utah, W USA
103 O7 **Briare** Loiret, C France
183 V2 **Bribie Island** island Queensland, E Australia
43 O14 **Bribrí** Limón, E Costa Rica
116 L8 **Briceni** var. Brinceni, Rus. Brichany. N Moldova
Bricgstow see Bristol
Brichany see Briceni
99 M24 **Bridel** Luxembourg, C Luxembourg
97 J22 **Bridgend** S Wales, UK
14 J14 **Bridgenorth** Ontario, SE Canada
23 Q1 **Bridgeport** Alabama, S USA
35 R8 **Bridgeport** California, W USA
18 L13 **Bridgeport** Connecticut, NE USA
31 N15 **Bridgeport** Illinois, N USA
28 J14 **Bridgeport** Nebraska, C USA
25 S6 **Bridgeport** Texas, SW USA
21 S3 **Bridgeport** West Virginia, NE USA
25 S5 **Bridgeport, Lake** ▣ Texas, SW USA
33 U11 **Bridger** Montana, NW USA
18 J17 **Bridgeton** New Jersey, NE USA
180 J14 **Bridgetown** Western Australia
45 Y14 **Bridgetown** ● (Barbados) SW Barbados
183 P17 **Bridgewater** Tasmania, SE Australia
13 P16 **Bridgewater** Nova Scotia, SE Canada
19 P12 **Bridgewater** Massachusetts, NE USA
29 Q11 **Bridgewater** South Dakota, N USA
21 U5 **Bridgewater** Virginia, NE USA
19 P8 **Bridgton** Maine, NE USA
97 K23 **Bridgwater** SW England, UK
97 K22 **Bridgwater Bay** bay SW England, UK
97 O16 **Bridlington** E England, UK
97 O16 **Bridlington Bay** bay E England, UK
183 P15 **Bridport** Tasmania, SE Australia
97 K24 **Bridport** S England, UK
103 O5 **Brie** cultural region N France
Brieg see Brzeg
Briel see Brielle
98 G12 **Brielle** var. Briel, Bril, Eng. The Brill. Zuid-Holland, SW Netherlands
108 E9 **Brienz** Bern, C Switzerland
108 E9 **Brienzer See** ◎ SW Switzerland
Bries/Briesen see Brezno
Brietzig see Brzesko
103 S4 **Briey** Meurthe-et-Moselle, NE France
108 E10 **Brig** Fr. Brigue, It. Briga. Valais, SW Switzerland
Briga see Brig
101 G24 **Brigach** ∽ S Germany
18 K17 **Brigantine** New Jersey, NE USA
Brigantio see Briançon
Brigantium see Bregenz
Brigels see Breil
25 S9 **Briggs** Texas, SW USA
36 L1 **Brigham City** Utah, W USA
14 J15 **Brighton** Ontario, SE Canada
97 O23 **Brighton** SE England, UK
37 T4 **Brighton** Colorado, C USA
30 K15 **Brighton** Illinois, N USA
103 T16 **Brignoles** Var, SE France
Brigue see Brig
105 O7 **Brihuega** Castilla-La Mancha, C Spain
112 A10 **Brijuni** It. Brioni. island group NW Croatia
76 G12 **Brikama** W Gambia
Bril see Brielle
Brill, The see Brielle
101 G15 **Brilon** Nordrhein-Westfalen, W Germany
Brinceni see Briceni
107 Q18 **Brindisi** anc. Brundisium, Brundusium. Puglia, SE Italy
27 W11 **Brinkley** Arkansas, C USA
Brioni see Brijuni
103 P12 **Brioude** anc. Brivas. Haute-Loire, C France
Briovera see St-Lô
183 U2 **Brisbane** state capital Queensland, E Australia
183 V2 **Brisbane** × Queensland, E Australia
25 P2 **Briscoe** Texas, SW USA
106 H10 **Brisighella** Emilia-Romagna, C Italy
108 G11 **Brissago** Ticino, S Switzerland
97 K22 **Bristol** anc. Bricgstow. SW England, UK
18 M12 **Bristol** Connecticut, NE USA
23 R9 **Bristol** Florida, SE USA
19 N9 **Bristol** New Hampshire, NE USA
29 Q8 **Bristol** South Dakota, N USA
21 P8 **Bristol** Tennessee, S USA
18 M8 **Bristol** Vermont, NE USA
39 N14 **Bristol Bay** bay Alaska, USA
97 I22 **Bristol Channel** inlet England/Wales, UK
35 W14 **Bristol Lake** ◎ California, W USA
27 P10 **Bristow** Oklahoma, C USA
86 C10 **Britain** var. Great Britain. island UK
Britannia Minor see Bretagne
10 L12 **British Columbia** Fr. Colombie-Britannique. ◈ province SW Canada
British Guiana see Guyana
British Honduras see Belize
173 Q7 **British Indian Ocean Territory** ◇ UK dependent territory C Indian Ocean
86 B9 **British Isles** island group NW Europe
10 I1 **British Mountains** ▲ Yukon Territory, NW Canada
British North Borneo see Sabah
British Solomon Islands Protectorate see Solomon Islands
45 S8 **British Virgin Islands** var. Virgin Islands. ◇ UK dependent territory E West Indies
83 J21 **Brits** North-West, N South Africa
83 H24 **Britstown** Northern Cape, W South Africa
14 F12 **Britt** Ontario, S Canada
29 V12 **Britt** Iowa, C USA
Brittany see Bretagne
29 Q7 **Britton** South Dakota, N USA
Briva Curretia see Brive-la-Gaillarde
Briva Isarae see Pontoise
Brivas see Brioude
Brive see Brive-la-Gaillarde
102 M12 **Brive-la-Gaillarde** prev. Brive, anc. Briva Curretia. Corrèze, C France
105 O4 **Briviesca** Castilla-León, N Spain
Brixen see Bressanone
Brixia see Brescia
145 S15 **Brlik** prev. Novotroickoje, Novotroitskoye. Zhambyl, SE Kazakhstan
111 G19 **Brněnský Kraj** ◈ region SE Czech republic
111 G18 **Brno** Ger. Brünn. Brněnský Kraj, SE Czech Republic
96 G7 **Broad Bay** bay NW Scotland, UK
25 X8 **Broaddus** Texas, SW USA
183 O12 **Broadford** Victoria, SE Australia
96 G9 **Broadford** N Scotland, UK
96 J13 **Broad Law** ▲ S Scotland, UK
23 U3 **Broad River** ∽ Georgia, SE USA
21 N8 **Broad River** ∽ North Carolina/South Carolina, SE USA
181 Y8 **Broadsound Range** ▲ Queensland, E Australia
33 X11 **Broadus** Montana, NW USA
21 U4 **Broadway** Virginia, NE USA
118 E9 **Brocēni** Saldus, SW Latvia
11 U11 **Brochet** Manitoba, C Canada
11 U10 **Brochet, Lac** ◎ Manitoba, C Canada
15 S5 **Brochet, Lac au** ◎ Quebec, SE Canada
101 K14 **Brocken** ▲ C Germany
19 O12 **Brockton** Massachusetts, NE USA
14 L14 **Brockville** Ontario, SE Canada
18 D13 **Brockway** Pennsylvania, NE USA
Brod/Bród see Slavonski Brod
9 N5 **Brodeur Peninsula** peninsula Baffin Island, Nunavut, NE Canada
96 H13 **Brodick** W Scotland, UK
Brod na Savi see Slavonski Brod
110 K9 **Brodnica** Ger. Buddenbrock. Kujawski-pomorskie, C Poland
112 G10 **Brod-Posavina** off. Brodsko-Posavska Županija. ◈ province NE Croatia
116 J5 **Brody** L'vivs'ka Oblast', NW Ukraine
95 G22 **Brædstrup** Vejle, C Denmark
98 I10 **Broek-in-Waterland** Noord-Holland, C Netherlands
32 L13 **Brogan** Oregon, NW USA
110 N10 **Brok** Mazowieckie, C Poland
27 P9 **Broken Arrow** Oklahoma, C USA
183 T9 **Broken Bay** bay New South Wales, SE Australia
29 N15 **Broken Bow** Nebraska, C USA
27 R13 **Broken Bow** Oklahoma, C USA
27 R12 **Broken Bow Lake** ▣ Oklahoma, C USA
182 L6 **Broken Hill** New South Wales, SE Australia
173 S10 **Broken Ridge** undersea feature S Indian Ocean
186 C6 **Broken Water Bay** bay W Bismarck Sea
55 W10 **Brokopondo** Brokopondo, NE Suriname
55 W10 **Brokopondo** ◈ district C Suriname
Bromberg see Bydgoszcz
95 L22 **Bromölla** Skåne, S Sweden
97 L20 **Bromsgrove** W England, UK
95 G20 **Brønderslev** Nordjylland, N Denmark
106 D8 **Broni** Lombardia, N Italy
10 K11 **Bronlund Peak** ▲ British Columbia, W Canada
93 F14 **Brønnøysund** Nordland, C Norway
23 V10 **Bronson** Florida, SE USA
31 Q11 **Bronson** Michigan, N USA
25 X8 **Bronson** Texas, SW USA
107 L24 **Bronte** Sicilia, Italy, C Mediterranean Sea
25 P8 **Bronte** Texas, SW USA
25 Y9 **Brookeland** Texas, SW USA
170 M7 **Brooke's Point** Palawan, W Philippines
27 T3 **Brookfield** Missouri, C USA
22 K7 **Brookhaven** Mississippi, S USA
32 E16 **Brookings** Oregon, NW USA
29 R10 **Brookings** South Dakota, N USA
29 W14 **Brooklyn** Iowa, C USA
29 U8 **Brooklyn Park** Minnesota, N USA
21 U7 **Brookneal** Virginia, NE USA
11 R16 **Brooks** Alberta, SW Canada
25 V11 **Brookshire** Texas, SW USA
38 L8 **Brooks Mountain** ▲ Alaska, USA
38 M11 **Brooks Range** ▲ Alaska, USA
31 O12 **Brookston** Indiana, N USA
23 V11 **Brooksville** Florida, SE USA
23 N4 **Brooksville** Mississippi, S USA
180 J13 **Brookton** Western Australia
31 Q14 **Brookville** Indiana, N USA
18 D13 **Brookville** Pennsylvania, NE USA
31 Q14 **Brookville Lake** ▣ Indiana, N USA
180 K5 **Broome** Western Australia
37 S4 **Broomfield** Colorado, C USA
Broos see Orăştie
96 J7 **Brora** N Scotland, UK
96 I7 **Brora** ∽ N Scotland, UK
95 F23 **Brørup** Ribe, W Denmark
95 L23 **Brösarp** Skåne, S Sweden
116 J9 **Broşteni** Suceava, NE Romania
102 M6 **Brou** Eure-et-Loir, C France
Broucsella see Brussel/Bruxelles
Broughton Bay see Tongjosŏn-man
9 R5 **Broughton Island** Nunavut, NE Canada
138 G7 **Broummâna** C Lebanon
22 I9 **Broussard** Louisiana, S USA
98 E13 **Brouwersdam** dam SW Netherlands
98 E13 **Brouwershaven** Zeeland, SW Netherlands
117 P4 **Brovary** Kyyivs'ka Oblast', N Ukraine
95 G20 **Brovst** Nordjylland, N Denmark
31 S8 **Brown City** Michigan, N USA
24 M6 **Brownfield** Texas, SW USA
33 Q7 **Browning** Montana, NW USA
33 R6 **Brown, Mount** ▲ Montana, NW USA
(0) M9 **Browns Bank** undersea feature NW Atlantic Ocean
31 O14 **Brownsburg** Indiana, N USA
18 J16 **Browns Mills** New Jersey, NE USA
44 J12 **Browns Town** C Jamaica
31 P15 **Brownstown** Indiana, N USA
29 R8 **Browns Valley** Minnesota, N USA
20 K7 **Brownsville** Kentucky, S USA
20 F9 **Brownsville** Tennessee, S USA
25 T17 **Brownsville** Texas, SW USA
55 W10 **Brownsweg** Brokopondo, C Suriname
29 U9 **Brownton** Minnesota, N USA
19 R5 **Brownville Junction** Maine, NE USA
25 R8 **Brownwood** Texas, SW USA
25 R8 **Brownwood Lake** ▣ Texas, SW USA
104 I9 **Brozas** Extremadura, W Spain
119 M18 **Brozha** Mahilyowskaya Voblasts', E Belarus
103 O2 **Bruay-en-Artois** Pas-de-Calais, N France
103 P2 **Bruay-sur-l'Escaut** Nord, N France
14 F13 **Bruce Peninsula** peninsula Ontario, S Canada
20 H9 **Bruceton** Tennessee, S USA
25 T9 **Bruceville** Texas, SW USA
101 G21 **Bruchsal** Baden-Württemberg, SW Germany
109 Q7 **Bruck** Salzburg, NW Austria
Bruck see Bruck an der Mur
109 Y4 **Bruck an der Leitha** Niederösterreich, NE Austria
109 V7 **Bruck an der Mur** var. Bruck. Steiermark, C Austria
101 M24 **Bruckmühl** Bayern, SE Germany
168 E7 **Brueuh, Pulau** island NW Indonesia
Bruges see Brugge
108 F6 **Brugg** Aargau, NW Switzerland
99 C16 **Brugge** Fr. Bruges. West-Vlaanderen, NW Belgium
109 R9 **Bruggen** Kärnten, S Austria
101 E16 **Brühl** Nordrhein-Westfalen, W Germany
99 F14 **Bruinisse** Zeeland, SW Netherlands
169 R9 **Bruit, Pulau** island East Malaysia
14 K10 **Brûlé, Lac** ◎ Quebec, SE Canada
30 M4 **Brule River** ∽ Michigan/Wisconsin, N USA
99 H23 **Brûly** Namur, S Belgium
59 N17 **Brumado** Bahia, E Brazil
98 M11 **Brummen** Gelderland, E Netherlands
94 H13 **Brumunddal** Hedmark, S Norway
23 Q6 **Brundidge** Alabama, S USA
Brundisium/Brundusium see Brindisi
33 N15 **Bruneau River** ∽ Idaho, NW USA
Bruneck see Brunico
169 T8 **Brunei** off. Sultanate of Brunei, Mal. Negara Brunei Darussalam. ◆ monarchy SE Asia
169 T7 **Brunei Bay** var. Teluk Brunei. bay N Brunei
Brunei, Teluk see Brunei Bay
Brunei Town see Bandar Seri Begawan
106 H5 **Brunico** Ger. Bruneck. Trentino-Alto Adige, N Italy
Brünn see Brno
185 G17 **Brunner, Lake** ◎ South Island, NZ
99 M18 **Brunssum** Limburg, SE Netherlands
23 W7 **Brunswick** Georgia, SE USA
19 Q8 **Brunswick** Maine, NE USA
21 V3 **Brunswick** Maryland, NE USA
27 T3 **Brunswick** Missouri, C USA
31 T11 **Brunswick** Ohio, N USA
Brunswick see Braunschweig
63 H24 **Brunswick, Península** headland S Chile
111 H17 **Bruntál** Ger. Freudenthal. Ostravský Kraj, E Czech Republic
195 N3 **Brunt Ice Shelf** ice shelf Antarctica
Brusa see Bursa
37 U3 **Brush** Colorado, C USA
42 M5 **Brus Laguna** Gracias a Dios, E Honduras
60 K13 **Brusque** Santa Catarina, S Brazil
Brussa see Bursa
99 E18 **Brussel** var. Brussels, Fr. Bruxelles, Ger. Brüssel; anc. Broucsella. ● (Belgium) Brussels, C Belgium see also Bruxelles
Brüssel/Brussels see Brussel/Bruxelles
117 O5 **Brusyliv** Zhytomyrs'ka Oblast', N Ukraine
183 Q12 **Bruthen** Victoria, SE Australia
Bruttium see Calabria
Brüx see Most
99 E18 **Bruxelles** var. Brussels, Dut. Brussel, Ger. Brüssel; anc. Broucsella. ● (Belgium) Brussels, C Belgium see also Brussel
54 J7 **Bruzual** Apure, W Venezuela
31 Q11 **Bryan** Ohio, N USA
25 U10 **Bryan** Texas, SW USA
194 J4 **Bryan Coast** physical region Antarctica
122 L11 **Bryanka** Krasnoyarskiy Kray, C Russian Federation
117 Y7 **Bryanka** Luhans'ka Oblast', E Ukraine
182 J8 **Bryan, Mount** ▲ South Australia
128 I6 **Bryansk** Bryanskaya Oblast', W Russian Federation
128 H6 **Bryanskaya Oblast'** ◈ province W Russian Federation
194 J5 **Bryant, Cape** headland Antarctica
27 U8 **Bryant Creek** ∽ Missouri, C USA
36 K8 **Bryce Canyon** canyon Utah, W USA
119 O15 **Bryli** Rus. Bryli. Mahilyowskaya Voblasts', E Belarus
95 C17 **Bryne** Rogaland, S Norway
25 R6 **Bryson** Texas, SW USA
21 N10 **Bryson City** North Carolina, SE USA
14 K11 **Bryson, Lac** ◎ Quebec, SE Canada
128 K13 **Bryukhovetskaya** Krasnodarskiy Kray, SW Russian Federation
111 H15 **Brzeg** Ger. Brieg; anc. Civitas Altae Ripae. Opolskie, S Poland
111 G14 **Brzeg Dolny** Ger. Dyhernfurth. Dolnośląskie, SW Poland
Brześć Litewski/Brześć nad Bugiem see Brest
111 L17 **Brzesko** Ger. Brietzig. Małopolskie, S Poland
Brzeżany see Berezhany
110 K12 **Brzeziny** Łódzkie, C Poland
Brzostowica Wielka see Vyalikaya Byerastavitsa
111 O17 **Brzozów** Podkarpackie, SE Poland
Bsharrī/Bsherri see Bcharré
187 X14 **Bua** Vanua Levu, N Fiji
95 J20 **Bua** Halland, S Sweden
82 M13 **Bua** ∽ C Malawi
Bua see Čiovo
81 L18 **Bu'aale** It. Buale. Jubbada Dhexe, SW Somalia
189 Q8 **Buada Lagoon** lagoon Nauru, C Pacific Ocean
186 M8 **Buala** Santa Isabel, E Solomon Islands
Buale see Bu'aale
190 H1 **Buariki** atoll Tungaru, W Kiribati
167 Q10 **Bua Yai** var. Ban Bua Yai. Nakhon Ratchasima, E Thailand
75 P8 **Bu'ayrāt al Ḥasūn** var. Buwayrat al Hasūn. C Libya
76 H13 **Buba** S Guinea-Bissau
171 P11 **Bubaa** Sulawesi, N Indonesia
81 D20 **Bubanza** NW Burundi
83 K18 **Bubi** prev. Bubye. ∽ S Zimbabwe
142 L11 **Būbīyan, Jazīrat** island E Kuwait
Bublitz see Bobolice
Bubye see Bubi
187 Y13 **Buca** prev. Mbutha. Vanua Levu, N Fiji
136 F16 **Bucak** Burdur, SW Turkey
54 G8 **Bucaramanga** Santander, N Colombia
107 M18 **Buccino** Campania, S Italy
116 K9 **Bucecea** Botoşani, NE Romania
116 J6 **Buchach** Pol. Buczacz. Ternopil's'ka Oblast', W Ukraine
183 Q12 **Buchan** Victoria, SE Australia
76 J17 **Buchanan** prev. Grand Bassa. SW Liberia
23 R3 **Buchanan** Georgia, SE USA
31 O11 **Buchanan** Michigan, N USA
21 T6 **Buchanan** Virginia, NE USA
25 R10 **Buchanan Dam** Texas, SW USA
25 R10 **Buchanan, Lake** ▣ Texas, SW USA
96 L8 **Buchan Ness** headland NE Scotland, UK
13 T12 **Buchans** Newfoundland, SE Canada
Bucharest see Bucureşti
101 H20 **Buchen** Baden-Württemberg, SW Germany
100 I10 **Buchholz in der Nordheide** Niedersachsen, NW Germany
108 F7 **Buchs** Aargau, N Switzerland
108 I8 **Buchs** Sankt Gallen, NE Switzerland
100 H13 **Bückeburg** Niedersachsen, NW Germany
36 K14 **Buckeye** Arizona, SW USA
Buckeye State see Ohio
21 S4 **Buckhannon** West Virginia, NE USA
25 T9 **Buckholts** Texas, SW USA
96 K8 **Buckie** NE Scotland, UK
14 M12 **Buckingham** Quebec, SE Canada
21 U6 **Buckingham** Virginia, NE USA
97 N21 **Buckinghamshire** cultural region SE England, UK
39 N8 **Buckland** Alaska, USA
182 G7 **Buckleboo** South Australia
26 K7 **Bucklin** Kansas, C USA
27 T3 **Bucklin** Missouri, C USA
36 I12 **Buckskin Mountains** ▲ Arizona, SW USA
19 R7 **Bucksport** Maine, NE USA
82 A9 **Buco Zau** Cabinda, NW Angola
Bu Craa see Bou Craa
116 K14 **Bucureşti** Eng. Bucharest, Ger. Bukarest; prev. Altenburg, anc. Cetatea Damboviţei. ● (Romania) Bucureşti, S Romania
31 S12 **Bucyrus** Ohio, N USA
Buczacz see Buchach
94 E9 **Bud** Møre og Romsdal, S Norway
25 S11 **Buda** Texas, SW USA
119 O18 **Buda-Kashalyova** Rus. Buda-Koshelëvo. Homyel'skaya Voblasts', SE Belarus
Buda-Koshelëvo see Buda-Kashalyova
166 L4 **Budalin** Sagaing, C Myanmar
111 J22 **Budapest** off. Budapest Főváros, SCr. Budimpešta. ● (Hungary) Pest, N Hungary
152 K11 **Budaun** Uttar Pradesh, N India
141 O9 **Budayyi'ah** oasis C Saudi Arabia
195 Y12 **Budd Coast** physical region Antarctica
Buddenbrock see Brodnica
107 C17 **Budduso** Sardegna, Italy, C Mediterranean Sea
97 I23 **Bude** SW England, UK
22 J7 **Bude** Mississippi, S USA
111 C18 **Budějovický Kraj** ◈ region S Czech Republic
99 K16 **Budel** Noord-Brabant, SE Netherlands
100 I8 **Büdelsdorf** Schleswig-Holstein, N Germany
129 O14 **Budënnovsk** Stavropol'skiy Kray, SW Russian Federation
116 K14 **Budeşti** Călăraşi, SE Romania
Budgewoi see Budgewoi Lake
183 T8 **Budgewoi Lake** var. Budgewoi. New South Wales, SE Australia
92 I2 **Búdhardalur** Vesturland, W Iceland
Budimpešta see Budapest
79 J16 **Budjala** Equateur, NW Dem. Rep. Congo (Zaire)
106 G10 **Budrio** Emilia-Romagna, C Italy
Budslav see Budslaw
119 K14 **Budslaw** Rus. Budslav. Minskaya Voblasts', N Belarus
Budua see Budva
169 R9 **Budu, Tanjung** headland East Malaysia
113 J17 **Budva** It. Budua. Montenegro, SW Yugoslavia
Budweis see České Budějovice
Budyšin see Bautzen
79 D16 **Buea** Sud-Ouest, SW Cameroon
103 S13 **Buëch** ∽ SE France
18 J17 **Buena** New Jersey, NE USA
62 K12 **Buena Esperanza** San Luis, C Argentina
54 C11 **Buenaventura** Valle del Cauca, W Colombia
40 I4 **Buenaventura** Chihuahua, N Mexico
57 M18 **Buena Vista** Santa Cruz, C Bolivia
40 G10 **Buenavista** Baja California Sur, W Mexico
37 S5 **Buena Vista** Colorado, C USA
23 S5 **Buena Vista** Georgia, SE USA
21 T6 **Buena Vista** Virginia, NE USA
44 F5 **Buena Vista, Bahia de** bay N Cuba
35 R13 **Buena Vista Lake Bed** ◎ California, W USA
105 P8 **Buendía, Embalse de** ▣ C Spain
63 F16 **Bueno, Río** ∽ S Chile
62 N12 **Buenos Aires** hist. Santa Maria del Buen Aire. ● (Argentina) Buenos Aires, E Argentina
43 O15 **Buenos Aires** Puntarenas, SE Costa Rica
61 C20 **Buenos Aires** off. Provincia de Buenos Aires. ◈ province E Argentina
63 H19 **Buenos Aires, Lago** var. Lago General Carrera. ◎ Argentina/Chile
54 C13 **Buesaco** Nariño, SW Colombia
29 U8 **Buffalo** Minnesota, N USA
26 T6 **Buffalo** Missouri, C USA
18 D10 **Buffalo** New York, NE USA
27 K8 **Buffalo** Oklahoma, C USA
28 J7 **Buffalo** South Dakota, N USA
25 V8 **Buffalo** Texas, SW USA
33 W12 **Buffalo** Wyoming, C USA
29 U11 **Buffalo Center** Iowa, C USA
24 M3 **Buffalo Lake** ▣ Texas, SW USA
30 K7 **Buffalo Lake** ▣ Wisconsin, N USA
11 S12 **Buffalo Narrows** Saskatchewan, C Canada
27 U9 **Buffalo River** ∽ Arkansas, C USA
29 R5 **Buffalo River** ∽ Minnesota, N USA
20 I10 **Buffalo River** ∽ Tennessee, S USA
30 J6 **Buffalo River** ∽ Wisconsin, N USA
44 L12 **Buff Bay** E Jamaica
23 T3 **Buford** Georgia, SE USA
28 J3 **Buford** North Dakota, N USA
33 Y17 **Buford** Wyoming, C USA
116 J14 **Buftea** Bucureşti, S Romania
84 I9 **Bug** Bel. Zakhodni Buh, Eng. Western Bug, Rus. Zapadnyy Bug, Ukr. Zakhidnyy Buh. ∽ E Europe
54 D11 **Buga** Valle del Cauca, W Colombia
162 F7 **Buga** Dzavhan, W Mongolia
103 O17 **Bugarach, Pic du** ▲ S France
146 B12 **Bugdayly** Balkanskiy Velayat, W Turkmenistan
Buggs Island Lake see John H.Kerr Reservoir
Bughotu see Santa Isabel
171 O14 **Bugingkalo** Sulawesi, C Indonesia
64 P6 **Bugio** island Madeira, Portugal, NE Atlantic Ocean
92 M8 **Bugøynes** Finnmark, N Norway
127 Q3 **Bugrino** Nenetskiy Avtonomnyy Okrug, NW Russian Federation
129 T5 **Bugul'ma** Respublika Tatarstan, W Russian Federation
Bügür see Luntai
129 T6 **Buguruslan** Orenburgskaya Oblast', W Russian Federation
159 R9 **Buh He** ∽ C China
33 O15 **Buhl** Idaho, NW USA
101 F22 **Bühl** Baden-Württemberg, SW Germany
116 K10 **Buhuşi** Bacău, E Romania
Buie d'Istria see Buje
97 J20 **Builth Wells** E Wales, UK
186 J8 **Buin** Bougainville Island, NE PNG
108 J9 **Buin, Piz** ▲ Austria/Switzerland
129 Q4 **Buinsk** Chuvashskaya Respublika, W Russian Federation
129 Q4 **Buinsk** Respublika Tatarstan, W Russian Federation
163 R8 **Buir Nur** Mong. Buyr Nuur. ◎ China/Mongolia see also Buyr Nuur
98 M5 **Buitenpost** Fris. Bûtenpost. Friesland, N Netherlands
Buitenzorg see Bogor
83 F19 **Buitepos** Omaheke, E Namibia
105 N7 **Buitrago del Lozoya** Madrid, C Spain
Buj see Buy
104 M13 **Bujalance** Andalucía, S Spain
113 O17 **Bujanovac** Serbia, SE Yugoslavia
105 S6 **Bujaraloz** Aragón, NE Spain
112 A9 **Buje** It. Buie d'Istria. Istra, NW Croatia
Bujnurd see Bojnūrd
81 D21 **Bujumbura** prev. Usumbura. ● (Burundi) W Burundi
81 D20 **Bujumbura** × W Burundi
159 N11 **Bukadaban Feng** ▲ C China
186 J6 **Buka Island** island NE PNG
81 F18 **Bukakata** S Uganda
79 N24 **Bukama** Katanga, SE Dem. Rep. Congo (Zaire)
142 J4 **Būkān** var. Bowkān. Āżarbāyjān-e Bākhtarī, NW Iran
Bukantau, Gory see Bŭkantow-Toghi
146 K8 **Bŭkantow-Toghi** Rus. Gory Bukantau. ▲ N Uzbekistan
Bukarest see Bucureşti
79 O19 **Bukavu** prev. Costermansville. Sud Kivu, E Dem. Rep. Congo (Zaire)
81 F21 **Bukene** Tabora, NW Tanzania
141 W8 **Bū Khābī** var. Bakhābī. NW Oman
Bukhara see Bukhoro
Bukharskaya Oblast' see Bukhoro Wiloyati
146 L11 **Bukhoro** var. Bokhara, Rus. Bukhara. Bukhoro Wiloyati, C Uzbekistan
146 J11 **Bukhoro Wiloyati** Rus. Bukharskaya Oblast'. ◈ province C Uzbekistan
168 M14 **Bukitkemuning** Sumatera, W Indonesia
168 I11 **Bukittinggi** prev. Fort de Kock. Sumatera, W Indonesia
111 L21 **Bükk** ▲ NE Hungary
81 F19 **Bukoba** Kagera, NW Tanzania
113 N20 **Bukovo** S FYR Macedonia
108 G6 **Bülach** Zürich, NW Switzerland
Bŭlaevo see Bulayevo
162 I6 **Bulag** Hövsgöl, N Mongolia
162 M7 **Bulag** Töv, C Mongolia
162 I8 **Bulagiyn Denj** Arhangay, C Mongolia
183 U7 **Bulahdelah** New South Wales, SE Australia
171 P4 **Bulan** Luzon, N Philippines

◆ Country
● Country Capital
◇ Dependent Territory
○ Dependent Territory Capital
◈ Administrative Region
× International Airport
▲ Mountain
▲ Mountain Range
Volcano
∽ River
◎ Lake
▣ Reservoir

137 N11 Bulancak Giresun, N Turkey
152 J10 Bulandshahr Uttar Pradesh, N India
137 R14 Bulanık Muş, E Turkey
129 V7 Bulanovo Orenburgskaya Oblast', W Russian Federation
83 J17 Bulawayo var. Buluwayo. Matabeleland North, SW Zimbabwe
83 J17 Bulawayo ✕ Matabeleland North, SW Zimbabwe
145 Q6 Bulayevo Kaz. Bŭlaevo. Severnyy Kazakhstan, N Kazakhstan
136 D15 Buldan Denizli, SW Turkey
154 G12 Buldāna Mahārāshtra, C India
38 E16 Buldir Island island Aleutian Islands, Alaska, USA
Buldur see Burdur
162 H9 Bulgan Bayanhongor, C Mongolia
162 K6 Bulgan Bulgan, N Mongolia
162 F7 Bulgan Hovd, W Mongolia
162 J5 Bulgan Hövsgöl, N Mongolia
162 J10 Bulgan Ömnögovĭ, S Mongolia
162 J7 Bulgan ◐ province N Mongolia
114 H10 Bulgaria off. Republic of Bulgaria, Bul. Bŭlgariya; prev. People's Republic of Bulgaria. ◆ republic SE Europe
Bŭlgariya see Bulgaria
114 L9 Bŭlgarka ▲ E Bulgaria
171 S11 Buli Pulau Halmahera, E Indonesia
171 S11 Buli, Teluk bay Pulau Halmahera, E Indonesia
160 J13 Buliu He ≈ S China
Bullange see Büllingen
104 M11 Bullaque ≈ C Spain
105 Q13 Bullas Murcia, SE Spain
80 M12 Bullaxaar Woqooyi Galbeed, NW Somalia
108 C9 Bulle Fribourg, SW Switzerland
185 G15 Buller ≈ South Island, NZ
183 P12 Buller, Mount ▲ Victoria, SE Australia
36 H11 Bullhead City Arizona, SW USA
99 N21 Büllingen Fr. Bullange. Liège, E Belgium
Bullion State see Missouri
21 T14 Bull Island island South Carolina, SE USA
182 M4 Bulloo River Overflow wetland New South Wales, SE Australia
184 M12 Bulls Manawatu-Wanganui, North Island, NZ
21 T14 Bulls Bay bay South Carolina, SE USA
27 U9 Bull Shoals Lake ▣ Arkansas/Missouri, C USA
181 Q2 Bulman Northern Territory, N Australia
162 I6 Bulnayn Nuruu ▲ N Mongolia
171 O11 Bulowa, Gunung ▲ Sulawesi, N Indonesia
Bulqiza see Bulqizë
113 L19 Bulqizë var. Bulqiza. Dibër, C Albania
Bulsar see Valsād
171 N14 Bulukumba prev. Boeloekoemba. Sulawesi, C Indonesia
147 O11 Bulunghur Rus. Bulungur; prev. Krasnogvardeysk. Samarqand Wiloyati, C Uzbekistan
79 I21 Bulungu Bandundu, SW Dem. Rep. Congo (Zaire)
Bulungur see Bulunghur
Buluwayo see Bulawayo
79 K17 Bumba Equateur, N Dem. Rep. Congo (Zaire)
121 R12 Bumbah, Khalīj al gulf N Libya
162 K8 Bumbat Övörhangay, C Mongolia
81 F19 Bumbire Island island N Tanzania
169 V8 Bum Bun, Pulau island East Malaysia
81 J17 Buna North Eastern, NE Kenya
25 Y10 Buna Texas, SW USA
Bunab see Bonāb
Bunai see M'bunai
147 S13 Bunay S Tajikistan
180 I13 Bunbury Western Australia
97 E14 Buncrana Ir. Bun Cranncha. NW Ireland
Bun Cranncha see Buncrana
181 Z9 Bundaberg Queensland, E Australia
183 T5 Bundarra New South Wales, SE Australia
100 G13 Bünde Nordrhein-Westfalen, NW Germany
152 H13 Būndi Rājasthān, N India
Bun Dobhráin see Bundoran
97 D15 Bundoran Ir. Bun Dobhráin. NW Ireland
113 K18 Bunë SCr. Bojana. ≈ Albania/Yugoslavia see also Bojana
171 Q8 Bunga ≈ Mindanao, S Philippines
168 I12 Bungalaut, Selat strait W Indonesia
167 R8 Bung Kan Nong Khai, E Thailand
181 N4 Bungle Bungle Range ▲ Western Australia
82 C10 Bungo Uíge, NW Angola
81 G18 Bungoma Western, W Kenya
164 F15 Bungo-suidō strait SW Japan
164 E14 Bungo-Takada Ōita, Kyūshū, SW Japan
100 K8 Bungsberg hill N Germany
Bungur see Bunyu
79 P17 Bunia Orientale, NE Dem. Rep. Congo (Zaire)
35 U6 Bunker Hill ▲ Nevada, W USA
22 I7 Bunkie Louisiana, S USA
23 X10 Bunnell Florida, SE USA
105 S10 Buñol País Valenciano, E Spain
98 K11 Bunschoten Utrecht, C Netherlands
136 K14 Bünyan Kayseri, C Turkey
169 W8 Bunyu var. Bungur. Borneo, N Indonesia
169 W8 Bunyu, Pulau island N Indonesia
Bunzlau see Bolesławiec
Buoddobohki see Patoniva
123 P7 Buorkhaya Guba bay N Russian Federation
171 Z15 Bupul Irian Jaya, E Indonesia
81 K19 Bura Coast, SE Kenya
80 P12 Buraan Sanaag, N Somalia
Būrabay see Borovoye
Buraida see Buraydah
Buraimi see Al Buraymī
145 Y11 Buran Vostochnyy Kazakhstan, E Kazakhstan
158 G15 Burang Xizang Zizhiqu, W China
Burao see Burco
138 H8 Burāq Dar'ā, S Syria
141 O6 Buraydah var. Buraida. Al Qaşīm, N Saudi Arabia
35 S15 Burbank California, W USA
31 N11 Burbank Illinois, N USA
183 Q8 Burcher New South Wales, SE Australia
80 N13 Burco var. Burao, Bur'o. Togdheer, NW Somalia
146 L13 Burdalyk Lebapskiy Velayat, E Turkmenistan
181 W6 Burdekin River ≈ Queensland, NE Australia
27 O7 Burden Kansas, C USA
Burdigala see Bordeaux
136 E15 Burdur var. Buldur. Burdur, SW Turkey
136 E15 Burdur var. Buldur. ◐ province SW Turkey
136 E15 Burdur Gölü salt lake SW Turkey
65 H21 Burdwood Bank undersea feature SW Atlantic Ocean
80 I12 Burē Amhara, N Ethiopia
80 H13 Burē Oromo, C Ethiopia
93 J15 Bureå Västerbotten, N Sweden
101 G14 Büren Nordrhein-Westfalen, W Germany
162 K6 Bürengiyn Nuruu ▲ N Mongolia
162 E8 Bürenhayrhan Hovd, W Mongolia
Bürewāla see Mandi Būrewāla
92 J9 Burfjord Troms, N Norway
100 L13 Burg var. Burg an der Ihle, Burg bei Magdeburg. Sachsen-Anhalt, C Germany
Burg an der Ihle see Burg
114 N10 Burgas var. Bourgas. Burgas, E Bulgaria
114 N9 Burgas ✕ Burgas, E Bulgaria
114 N10 Burgas ◐ province E Bulgaria
114 N10 Burgaski Zaliv gulf E Bulgaria
114 M10 Burgasko Ezero lagoon E Bulgaria
21 V11 Burgaw North Carolina, SE USA
Burg bei Magdeburg see Burg
108 E8 Burgdorf Bern, NW Switzerland
109 Y7 Burgenland off. Land Burgenland. ◐ state SE Austria
13 S13 Burgeo Newfoundland, SE Canada
83 I24 Burgersdorp Eastern Cape, SE South Africa
83 K20 Burgersfort Mpumalanga, NE South Africa
101 N23 Burghausen Bayern, SE Germany
139 O5 Burghūth, Sabkhat al ◎ E Syria
101 M20 Burglengenfeld Bayern, SE Germany
41 P9 Burgos Tamaulipas, C Mexico
105 N4 Burgos Castilla-León, N Spain
105 N4 Burgos ◐ province Castilla-León, N Spain
Burgstadlberg see Hradiště
95 P20 Burgsvik Gotland, SE Sweden
Burgum see Bergum
Burgundy see Bourgogne
159 Q11 Burhan Budai Shan ▲ C China
136 B12 Burhaniye Balıkesir, W Turkey
154 G12 Burhānpur Madhya Pradesh, C India
129 W7 Buribay Respublika Bashkortostan, W Russian Federation
43 O17 Burica, Punta headland Costa Rica/Panama
167 Q10 Buriram var. Buri Ram, Puriramya. Buri Ram, E Thailand
105 S10 Burjassot País Valenciano, E Spain
81 N16 Burka Giibi Hiiraan, C Somalia
147 X8 Burkan ≈ E Kyrgyzstan
25 R4 Burkburnett Texas, SW USA
29 O12 Burke South Dakota, N USA
10 K15 Burke Channel channel British Columbia, W Canada
194 J10 Burke Island island Antarctica
20 L7 Burkesville Kentucky, S USA
181 T4 Burketown Queensland, NE Australia
25 Q8 Burkett Texas, SW USA
25 Y9 Burkeville Texas, SW USA
21 V7 Burkeville Virginia, NE USA
77 O12 Burkina off. Burkina Faso; prev. Upper Volta. ◆ republic W Africa
Burkina Faso see Burkina
194 L13 Burks, Cape headland Antarctica
14 H12 Burk's Falls Ontario, S Canada
101 H23 Burladingen Baden-Württemberg, S Germany
25 T7 Burleson Texas, SW USA
33 P15 Burley Idaho, NW USA
144 G8 Burlin Zapadnyy Kazakhstan, NW Kazakhstan
14 G16 Burlington Ontario, S Canada
37 W4 Burlington Colorado, C USA
29 Y15 Burlington Iowa, C USA
27 P5 Burlington Kansas, C USA
21 T9 Burlington North Carolina, SE USA
28 M3 Burlington North Dakota, N USA
18 L7 Burlington Vermont, NE USA
30 M9 Burlington Wisconsin, N USA
27 Q1 Burlington Junction Missouri, C USA
Burma see Myanmar
10 L17 Burnaby British Columbia, SW Canada
117 O12 Burnas, Ozero ◎ SW Ukraine
25 S10 Burnet Texas, SW USA
35 O3 Burney California, W USA
183 O16 Burnie Tasmania, SE Australia
97 L17 Burnley NW England, UK
Burnoye see Bauyrzhan Momysh-Uly
153 R15 Burnpur West Bengal, NE India
32 K14 Burns Oregon, NW USA
26 K11 Burns Flat Oklahoma, C USA
20 M7 Burnside Kentucky, S USA
8 K8 Burnside ≈ Nunavut, NW Canada
32 L15 Burns Junction Oregon, NW USA
10 L13 Burns Lake British Columbia, SW Canada
29 V9 Burnsville Minnesota, N USA
21 P9 Burnsville North Carolina, SE USA
21 R4 Burnsville West Virginia, NE USA
14 I13 Burnt River ≈ Ontario, SE Canada
14 I11 Burntroot Lake ◎ Ontario, SE Canada
11 W12 Burntwood ≈ Manitoba, C Canada
Bur'o see Burco
158 L2 Burqin Xinjiang Uygur Zizhiqu, NW China
182 J8 Burra South Australia
183 S9 Burragorang, Lake ▣ New South Wales, SE Australia
96 K5 Burray island NE Scotland, UK
113 L19 Burrel var. Burreli. Dibër, C Albania
Burreli see Burrel
183 R8 Burrendong Reservoir ▣ New South Wales, SE Australia
183 R5 Burren Junction New South Wales, SE Australia
105 T9 Burriana País Valenciano, E Spain
183 R10 Burrinjuck Reservoir ▣ New South Wales, SE Australia
36 J12 Burro Creek ≈ Arizona, SW USA
40 M5 Burro, Serranías del ▲ NW Mexico
62 K7 Burruyacú Tucumán, N Argentina
136 E12 Bursa var. Brussa; prev. Brusa, anc. Prusa. Bursa, NW Turkey
136 D12 Bursa var. Brusa, Brussa. ◐ province NW Turkey
75 Y9 Būr Safāga var. Būr Safājah. E Egypt
Būr Safājah see Būr Safāga
Būr Saʿīd see Port Said
81 O14 Bur Tinle Mudug, C Somalia
31 Q5 Burt Lake ◎ Michigan, N USA
Burtnieks see Burtnieku Ezers
118 H7 Burtnieku Ezers var. Burtnieks. ◎ N Latvia
31 Q9 Burton Michigan, N USA
Burton on Trent see Burton upon Trent
97 M19 Burton upon Trent var. Burton on Trent, Burton-upon-Trent. C England, UK
93 J15 Burträsk Västerbotten, N Sweden
145 S14 Burubaytal prev. Burylbaytal. Zhambyl, SE Kazakhstan
Burujird see Borūjerd
Burultokay see Fuhai
141 R15 Burūm SE Yemen
145 U16 Burunday Kaz. Boralday. Almaty, SE Kazakhstan
81 D21 Burundi off. Republic of Burundi; prev. Kingdom of Burundi, Urundi. ◆ republic C Africa
171 R13 Buru, Pulau prev. Boeroe. island E Indonesia
77 T17 Burutu Delta, S Nigeria
10 G7 Burwash Landing Yukon Territory, W Canada
29 O14 Burwell Nebraska, C USA
97 L17 Bury NW England, UK
123 N13 Buryatiya, Respublika prev. Buryatskaya ASSR. ◐ autonomous republic S Russian Federation
Buryatskaya ASSR see Buryatiya, Respublika
Burylbaytal see Burubaytal
117 S3 Buryn' Sums'ka Oblast', NE Ukraine
97 P20 Bury St Edmunds hist. Beodericsworth. E England, UK
114 G8 Bŭrziya ≈ NW Bulgaria
106 D9 Busalla Liguria, NW Italy
139 N5 Buşayrah Dayr az Zawr, E Syria
Buševa see Baba
143 N12 Būshehr off. Ostān-e Būshehr. ◐ province SW Iran
Būshehr/Bushire see Bandar-e Būshehr
25 N2 Bushland Texas, SW USA
30 J12 Bushnell Illinois, N USA
Busi see Biševo
81 G18 Busia SE Uganda
Busiasch see Buziaş
79 K16 Businga Equateur, NW Dem. Rep. Congo (Zaire)
79 J18 Busira ≈ NW Dem. Rep. Congo (Zaire)
116 I5 Bus'k Rus. Busk. L'vivs'ka Oblast', W Ukraine
95 E14 Buskerud ◐ county S Norway
113 F14 Buško Jezero ▣ SW Bosnia and Herzegovina
111 M15 Busko-Zdrój Świętokrzyskie, C Poland
Busra see Al Başrah, Iraq
Buşrá see Buşrá ash Shām, Syria
138 H9 Buşrá ash Shām var. Bosora, Bosra, Bozrah, Buşrá. Dar'ā, S Syria
180 I13 Busselton Western Australia
81 C14 Busseri ≈ W Sudan
106 E9 Busseto Emilia-Romagna, C Italy
106 A8 Bussoleno Piemonte, NE Italy
Bussora see Al Başrah
98 J10 Bussum Noord-Holland, C Netherlands
41 N7 Bustamante Nuevo León, NE Mexico
63 I23 Bustamante, Punta headland S Argentina
Bustan see Bŭston
116 J12 Buşteni Prahova, SE Romania
106 D7 Busto Arsizio Lombardia, N Italy
147 Q10 Bŭston Rus. Buston. NW Tajikistan
146 I9 Bŭston Rus. Bustan. Qoraqalpoghiston Respublikasi, W Uzbekistan
100 H8 Büsum Schleswig-Holstein, N Germany
79 M16 Buta Orientale, N Dem. Rep. Congo (Zaire)
81 E20 Butare prev. Astrida. S Rwanda
191 O2 Butaritari atoll Tungaru, W Kiribati
Butawal see Butwal
96 H13 Bute cultural region SW Scotland, UK
162 K6 Büteeliyn Nuruu ▲ N Mongolia
10 L16 Bute Inlet fjord British Columbia, W Canada
96 H12 Bute, Island of island SW Scotland, UK
79 P18 Butembo Nord Kivu, NE Dem. Rep. Congo (Zaire)
Bûtenpost see Buitenpost
107 K25 Butera Sicilia, Italy, C Mediterranean Sea
99 M20 Bütgenbach Liège, E Belgium
Butha Qi see Zalantun
166 J5 Buthidaung Arakan State, W Myanmar
61 I16 Butiá Rio Grande do Sul, S Brazil
81 F17 Butiaba NW Uganda
23 N6 Butler Alabama, S USA
23 S5 Butler Georgia, SE USA
31 Q11 Butler Indiana, N USA
27 R5 Butler Missouri, C USA
18 B14 Butler Pennsylvania, NE USA
194 K5 Butler Island island Antarctica
21 U8 Butner North Carolina, SE USA
171 P14 Buton, Pulau var. Pulau Butung; prev. Boetoeng. island C Indonesia
Bütow see Bytów
113 L23 Butrintit, Liqeni i ◎ S Albania
23 N3 Buttahatchee River ≈ Alabama/Mississippi, S USA
33 Q10 Butte Montana, NW USA
29 O12 Butte Nebraska, C USA
168 J7 Butterworth Pinang, Peninsular Malaysia
83 J25 Butterworth var. Gcuwa. Eastern Cape, SE South Africa
13 O3 Button Islands island group Nunavut, NE Canada
35 R13 Buttonwillow California, W USA
171 Q7 Butuan off. Butuan City. Mindanao, S Philippines
Butung, Pulau see Buton, Pulau
Butuntum see Bitonto
128 M8 Buturlinovka Voronezhskaya Oblast', W Russian Federation
153 O11 Butwal var. Butawal. Western, C Nepal
101 G17 Butzbach Hessen, W Germany
100 L9 Bützow Mecklenburg-Vorpommern, N Germany
80 N13 Buuhoodle Togdheer, N Somalia
81 N16 Buulobarde var. Buulo Berde. Hiiraan, C Somalia Africa
Buulo Berde see Buulobarde
80 P12 Buuraha Cal Miskaat ▲ NE Somalia
81 L19 Buur Gaabo Jubbada Hoose, S Somalia
99 M22 Buurgplaatz ▲ N Luxembourg
Buwayrāt al Hasūn see Bu'ayrāt al Ḩasūn
100 I10 Buxtehude Niedersachsen, NW Germany
97 L18 Buxton C England, UK
126 M14 Buy var. Buj. Kostromskaya Oblast', NW Russian Federation
162 G7 Buyanbat Govĭ-Altay, W Mongolia
162 H8 Buyant Bayanhongor, C Mongolia
162 D6 Buyant Bayan-Ölgiy, W Mongolia
162 H7 Buyant Dzavhan, C Mongolia
163 N9 Buyant Hentiy, C Mongolia
163 N10 Buyant-Uhaa Dornogovĭ, SE Mongolia
162 M7 Buyant Ukha ✕ (Ulaanbaatar) Töv, N Mongolia
129 Q16 Buynaksk Respublika Dagestan, SW Russian Federation
119 L20 Buynavichy Rus. Buynovichi. Homyel'skaya Voblasts', SE Belarus
Buynovichi see Buynavichy
76 L16 Buyo SW Ivory Coast
76 L16 Buyo, Lac de ▣ W Ivory Coast
163 R7 Buyr Nuur var. Buir Nur. ◎ China/Mongolia see also Buir Nur
137 T13 Büyükağrı Dağı var. Aghri Dagh, Agri Dagi, Koh I Noh, Masis, Eng. Great Ararat, Mount Ararat. ▲ E Turkey
137 R15 Büyük Çayı ≈ NE Turkey
114 O13 Büyük Çekmece İstanbul, NW Turkey
114 N12 Büyükkarıştıran Kırklareli, NW Turkey
115 L14 Büyükkemikli Burnu headland NW Turkey
136 E15 Büyükmenderes Nehri ≈ SW Turkey
Büyükzap Suyu see Great Zab
102 M9 Buzançais Indre, C France
116 K13 Buzău Buzău, SE Romania
116 K13 Buzău ◐ county SE Romania
116 L12 Buzău ≈ E Romania
75 S11 Buzaymah var. Bzīmah. SE Libya
164 E13 Buzen Fukuoka, Kyūshū, SW Japan
116 F12 Buziaş Ger. Busiasch, Hung. Buziásfürdő; prev. Buziás. Timiş, W Romania
Buziásfürdő see Buziaş
83 M18 Búzi, Rio ≈ C Mozambique
117 Q10 Buz'kyy Lyman bay S Ukraine
Büzmeyin see Byuzmeyin
145 O8 Buzuluk Akmola, C Kazakhstan
129 T6 Buzuluk Orenburgskaya Oblast', W Russian Federation
129 N8 Buzuluk ≈ SW Russian Federation
19 P12 Buzzards Bay Massachusetts, NE USA
19 P13 Buzzards Bay bay Massachusetts, NE USA
83 G16 Bwabata Caprivi, NE Namibia
186 H10 Bwagaoia Misima Island, SE PNG
Bwake see Bouaké
187 R13 Bwatnapne Pentecost, C Vanuatu
119 K14 Byahoml' Rus. Begoml'. Vitsyebskaya Voblasts', N Belarus
114 J8 Byala Ruse, N Bulgaria
114 N9 Byala prev. Ak-Dere. Varna, E Bulgaria
Byala Reka see Erydropótamos
114 H8 Byala Slatina Vratsa, NW Bulgaria
119 N15 Byalynichy Rus. Belynichi. Mahilyowskaya Voblasts', E Belarus
119 G19 Byaroza Pol. Bereza Kartuska, Rus. Bereza. Brestskaya Voblasts', SW Belarus
Byblos see Jbaïl
111 O14 Bychawa Lubelskie, SE Poland
Bychikha see Bychykha
118 N11 Bychykha Rus. Bychikha. Vitsyebskaya Voblasts', NE Belarus
111 I14 Byczyna Ger. Pitschen. Opolskie, S Poland
110 I10 Bydgoszcz Ger. Bromberg. Kujawski-pomorskie, C Poland
119 I17 Byelaruskaya Hrada Rus. Belorusskaya Gryada. ridge N Belarus
119 G18 Byelavyezhskaya Pushcha Pol. Puszcza Białowieska, Rus. Belovezhskaya Pushcha. forest Belarus/Poland see also Białowieska, Puszcza
119 H15 Byenyakoni Rus. Benyakoni. Hrodzyenskaya Voblasts', W Belarus
119 M16 Byerazino Rus. Berezino. Minskaya Voblasts', C Belarus
118 L13 Byerazino Rus. Berezino. Vitsyebskaya Voblasts', N Belarus
119 L14 Byerazino Rus. Berezina. ≈ C Belarus
118 M13 Byeshankovichy Rus. Beshenkovichi. Vitsyebskaya Voblasts', N Belarus
31 U13 Byesville Ohio, N USA
119 P18 Byesyedz' Rus. Besed'. ≈ SE Belarus
119 H19 Byezdzyezh Rus. Bezdezh. Brestskaya Voblasts', SW Belarus
93 J15 Bygdeå Västerbotten, N Sweden
94 F12 Bygdin ◎ S Norway
93 J15 Bygdsiljum Västerbotten, N Sweden
95 E17 Bygland Aust-Agder, S Norway
95 E17 Byglandsfjord Aust-Agder, S Norway
119 N16 Bykhaw Rus. Bykhov. Mahilyowskaya Voblasts', E Belarus
Bykhov see Bykhaw
129 P9 Bykovo Volgogradskaya Oblast', SW Russian Federation
123 P7 Bykovskiy Respublika Sakha (Yakutiya), NE Russian Federation
195 R12 Byrd Glacier glacier Antarctica
14 K10 Byrd, Lac ◎ Quebec, SE Canada
183 P5 Byrock New South Wales, SE Australia
30 L10 Byron Illinois, N USA
183 V4 Byron Bay New South Wales, SE Australia
183 V4 Byron, Cape headland New South Wales, E Australia
63 F21 Byron, Isla island S Chile
Byron Island see Nikunau
65 B24 Byron Sound sound NW Falkland Islands
122 M6 Byrranga, Gory ▲ N Russian Federation
93 J14 Byske Västerbotten, N Sweden
111 K18 Bystrá ▲ N Slovakia
111 F18 Bystřice nad Pernštejnem Ger. Bistritz ober Pernstein. Jihlavský Kraj, C Czech Republic
Bystrovka see Kemin
111 G16 Bystrzyca Kłodzka Ger. Habelschwerdt. Wałbrzych, SW Poland
111 I18 Bytča Žilinský Kraj, N Slovakia
119 L15 Bytcha Rus. Bytcha. Minskaya Voblasts', NE Belarus
Byteń/Byten' see Bytsyen'
111 J16 Bytom Ger. Beuthen. Śląskie, S Poland
110 H7 Bytów Ger. Bütow. Pomorskie, N Poland
119 H18 Bytsyen' Pol. Byteń, Rus. Byten'. Brestskaya Voblasts', SW Belarus
81 E19 Byumba var. Biumba. N Rwanda
146 F13 Byuzmeyin Turkm. Büzmeyin; prev. Bezmein. Akhalskiy Velayat, C Turkmenistan
119 O20 Byval'ki Homyel'skaya Voblasts', SE Belarus
95 O20 Byxelkrok Kalmar, S Sweden
Byzantium see İstanbul
Bzīmah see Buzaymah

C

62 O6 Caacupé Cordillera, S Paraguay
62 P6 Caaguazú off. Departamento de Caaguazú. ◐ department C Paraguay
82 C13 Caála var. Kaala, Robert Williams, Port. Vila Robert Williams. Huambo, C Angola
62 P7 Caazapá Caazapá, S Paraguay
62 P7 Caazapá off. Departamento de Caazapá. ◐ department SE Paraguay
81 P15 Cabaad, Raas headland C Somalia
55 N10 Cabadisocaña Amazonas, S Venezuela
44 F5 Cabaiguán Sancti Spíritus, C Cuba
Caballeria, Cabo see Cavalleria, Cap de
37 Q14 Caballo Reservoir ▣ New Mexico, SW USA
40 L6 Caballos Mesteños, Llano de los plain N Mexico
104 L2 Cabañaquinta Asturias, N Spain
42 B9 Cabañas ◐ department E El Salvador
171 O3 Cabanatuan off. Cabanatuan City. Luzon, N Philippines
15 T8 Cabano Quebec, SE Canada
104 L11 Cabeza del Buey Extremadura, W Spain
45 V5 Cabezas de San Juan headland E Puerto Rico
105 N2 Cabezón de la Sal Cantabria, N Spain
Cabhán see Cavan
61 B23 Cabildo Buenos Aires, E Argentina
Cabillonum see Chalon-sur-Saône
54 H5 Cabimas Zulia, NW Venezuela
82 A9 Cabinda var. Kabinda. Cabinda, NW Angola
82 A9 Cabinda var. Kabinda. ◐ province NW Angola
33 N7 Cabinet Mountains ▲ Idaho/Montana, NW USA
82 B11 Cabiri Bengo, NW Angola
63 J20 Cabo Blanco Santa Cruz, SE Argentina
82 P13 Cabo Delgado off. Província de Capo Delgado. ◐ province NE Mozambique
14 L9 Cabonga, Réservoir ▣ Quebec, SE Canada
27 V7 Cabool Missouri, C USA
183 V2 Caboolture Queensland, E Australia
Cabora Bassa, Lake see Cahora Bassa, Albufeira de
40 F3 Caborca Sonora, NW Mexico
Cabo San Lucas see San Lucas
27 V11 Cabot Arkansas, C USA
14 F12 Cabot Head headland Ontario, S Canada
9 Y11 Cabot Strait strait E Canada
Cabo Verde, Ilhas do see Cape Verde
104 M14 Cabra Andalucía, S Spain
107 B19 Cabras Sardegna, Italy, C Mediterranean Sea
188 A15 Cabras Island island W Guam
45 O8 Cabrera N Dominican Republic
105 X10 Cabrera anc. Capraria. island Islas Baleares, Spain, W Mediterranean Sea
104 J4 Cabrera ≈ NW Spain
105 Q15 Cabrera, Sierra ▲ S Spain
11 S16 Cabri Saskatchewan, S Canada
105 R10 Cabriel ≈ E Spain
54 M7 Cabruta Guárico, C Venezuela
171 N2 Cabugao Luzon, N Philippines
54 G10 Cabuyaro Meta, C Colombia
60 I13 Caçador Santa Catarina, S Brazil
42 G8 Cacaguatique, Cordillera var. Cordillera. ▲ NE El Salvador
112 L13 Čačak Serbia, C Yugoslavia
55 Y10 Cacao NE French Guiana
61 H16 Caçapava do Sul Rio Grande do Sul, S Brazil
21 U3 Cacapon River ≈ West Virginia, NE USA
107 J23 Caccamo Sicilia, Italy, C Mediterranean Sea
107 A17 Caccia, Capo headland Sardegna, Italy, C Mediterranean Sea
59 G18 Cáceres Mato Grosso, W Brazil
104 J10 Cáceres Ar. Qazris. Extremadura, W Spain
104 J9 Cáceres ◐ province Extremadura, W Spain
Cachacrou see Scotts Head Village
61 C21 Cacharí Buenos Aires, E Argentina

26 L12 **Cache** Oklahoma, C USA
10 M16 **Cache Creek** British Columbia, SW Canada
35 N6 **Cache Creek** ≈ California, W USA
37 S3 **Cache La Poudre River** ≈ Colorado, C USA
Cacheo *see* Cacheu
27 W11 **Cache River** ≈ Arkansas, C USA
30 L17 **Cache River** ≈ Illinois, N USA
76 G12 **Cacheu** *var.* Cacheo. W Guinea-Bissau
59 I15 **Cachimbo** Pará, NE Brazil
59 H15 **Cachimbo, Serra do** ▲ C Brazil
82 D13 **Cachingues** Bié, C Angola
54 G7 **Cáchira** Norte de Santander, N Colombia
61 H16 **Cachoeira do Sul** Rio Grande do Sul, S Brazil
59 O20 **Cachoeiro de Itapemirim** Espírito Santo, SE Brazil
82 E12 **Cacolo** Lunda Sul, NE Angola
83 C14 **Caconda** Huíla, C Angola
82 A9 **Cacongo** Cabinda, NW Angola
35 U9 **Cactus Peak** ▲ Nevada, W USA
82 A11 **Cacuaco** Luanda, NW Angola
83 B14 **Cacula** Huíla, SW Angola
67 R12 **Caculuvar** ≈ SW Angola
59 O19 **Caçumba, Ilha** *island* SE Brazil
55 N10 **Cacuri** Amazonas, S Venezuela
81 N17 **Cadale** Shabeellaha Dhexe, E Somalia
105 X4 **Cadaqués** Cataluña, NE Spain
111 J18 **Čadca** *Hung.* Csaca. Žilinský Kraj, N Slovakia
27 P13 **Caddo** Oklahoma, C USA
25 R6 **Caddo** Texas, SW USA
25 X6 **Caddo Lake** ⊞ Louisiana/Texas, SW USA
27 S12 **Caddo Mountains** ▲ Arkansas, C USA
41 O8 **Cadereyta** Nuevo León, NE Mexico
97 J19 **Cader Idris** ▲ NW Wales, United Kingdom
182 F3 **Cadibarrawirracanna, Lake** *salt lake* South Australia
14 I7 **Cadillac** Quebec, SE Canada
11 T17 **Cadillac** Saskatchewan, S Canada
102 K13 **Cadillac** Gironde, SW France
31 P7 **Cadillac** Michigan, N USA
105 V4 **Cadí, Torre de** ▲ NE Spain
171 P5 **Cadiz** *off.* Cadiz City. Negros, C Philippines
20 H7 **Cadiz** Kentucky, S USA
31 U13 **Cadiz** Ohio, N USA
104 J15 **Cádiz** *anc.* Gades, Gadier, Gadir, Gadire. Andalucía, SW Spain
104 K15 **Cádiz** ◈ *province* Andalucía, SW Spain
104 I15 **Cadiz, Bahía de** *bay* SW Spain
Cadiz City *see* Cadiz
104 H15 **Cádiz, Golfo de** *Eng.* Gulf of Cadiz. *gulf* Portugal/Spain
Cadiz, Gulf of *see* Cádiz, Golfo de
35 X14 **Cadiz Lake** ◎ California, W USA
182 E2 **Cadney Homestead** South Australia
Cadurcum *see* Cahors
83 F17 **Caecae** Ngamiland, NW Botswana
102 K4 **Caen** Calvados, N France
Caene/Caenepolis *see* Qena
Caerdydd *see* Cardiff
Caer Glou *see* Gloucester
Caer Gybi *see* Holyhead
Caerleon *see* Chester
Caer Luel *see* Carlisle
97 I18 **Caernarfon** *var.* Caernarvon, Carnarvon. NW Wales, UK
97 H18 **Caernarfon Bay** *bay* NW Wales, UK
97 I19 **Caernarvon** *cultural region* NW Wales, UK
Caernarvon *see* Caernarfon
Caesaraugusta *see* Zaragoza
Caesarea Mazaca *see* Kayseri
Caesarobriga *see* Talavera de la Reina
Caesarodunum *see* Tours
Caesaromagus *see* Beauvais
Caesena *see* Cesena
59 N17 **Caetité** Bahia, E Brazil
62 J6 **Cafayate** Salta, N Argentina
171 O2 **Cagayan** ≈ Luzon, N Philippines
171 Q7 **Cagayan de Oro** *off.* Cagayan de Oro City. Mindanao, S Philippines
170 M8 **Cagayan de Tawi Tawi** *island* S Philippines
171 N6 **Cagayan Islands** *island group* C Philippines
31 O14 **Cagles Mill Lake** ⊞ Indiana, N USA
106 I12 **Cagli** Marche, C Italy
107 C20 **Cagliari** *anc.* Caralis. Sardegna, Italy, C Mediterranean Sea
107 C20 **Cagliari, Golfo di** *gulf* Sardegna, Italy, C Mediterranean Sea
103 U15 **Cagnes-sur-Mer** Alpes-Maritimes, SE France
54 L5 **Cagua** Aragua, N Venezuela
171 O1 **Cagua, Mount** ▲ Luzon, N Philippines
54 F13 **Caguán, Río** ≈ SW Colombia
45 U6 **Caguas** E Puerto Rico
23 P5 **Cahaba River** ≈ Alabama, S USA
42 E5 **Cahabón, Río** ≈ C Guatemala
83 B15 **Cahama** Cunene, SW Angola
97 B21 **Caha Mountains** *Ir.* An Cheacha. ▲ SW Ireland
97 D20 **Caher** *Ir.* An Cathair. S Ireland
97 A21 **Cahersiveen** *Ir.* Cathair Saidhbhín. SW Ireland
30 K15 **Cahokia** Illinois, N USA
83 L15 **Cahora Bassa, Albufeira de** *var.* Lake Cabora Bassa. ⊞ NW Mozambique
97 G20 **Cahore Point** *Ir.* Rinn Chathóir. *headland* SE Ireland
102 M14 **Cahors** *anc.* Cadurcum. Lot, S France
56 D9 **Cahuapanas, Río** ≈ N Peru
116 M12 **Cahul** *Rus.* Kagul. S Moldova
Cahul, Lacul *see* Kahul, Ozero
83 N16 **Caia** Sofala, C Mozambique
59 J19 **Caiapó, Serra do** ▲ C Brazil
44 F5 **Caibarién** Villa Clara, C Cuba
55 O5 **Caicara** Monagas, NE Venezuela
54 L5 **Caicara del Orinoco** Bolívar, C Venezuela
59 P14 **Caicó** Rio Grande do Norte, E Brazil
44 M6 **Caicos Islands** *island group* W Turks and Caicos Islands
44 L5 **Caicos Passage** *strait* Bahamas/Turks and Caicos Islands
161 O9 **Caidian** *prev.* Hanyang. Hubei, C China
Caiffa *see* Hefa
180 M12 **Caiguna** Western Australia
Cailli, Ceann *see* Hag's Head
40 J11 **Caimanero, Laguna del** *var.* Laguna del Camaronero. *lagoon* E Pacific Ocean
117 N10 **Căinari** *Rus.* Kaynary. C Moldova
57 L19 **Caine, Río** ≈ C Bolivia
Caiphas *see* Hefa
195 N4 **Caird Coast** *physical region* Antarctica
96 J9 **Cairn Gorm** ▲ C Scotland, UK
96 J9 **Cairngorm Mountains** ▲ C Scotland, UK
39 P12 **Cairn Mountain** ▲ Alaska, USA
181 W4 **Cairns** Queensland, NE Australia
121 V13 **Cairo** *Ar.* Al Qāhirah, *var.* El Qâhira. ● (Egypt) N Egypt
23 T8 **Cairo** Georgia, SE USA
30 L17 **Cairo** Illinois, N USA
75 V8 **Cairo** × C Egypt
Caiseal *see* Cashel
Caisleán an Bharraigh *see* Castlebar
Caisleán na Finne *see* Castlefinn
96 J6 **Caithness** *cultural region* N Scotland, UK
83 D15 **Caiundo** Cuando Cubango, S Angola
56 C11 **Cajamarca** *prev.* Caxamarca. Cajamarca, NW Peru
56 B11 **Cajamarca** *off.* Departamento de Cajamarca. ◈ *department* N Peru
103 N14 **Cajarc** Lot, S France
42 G6 **Cajón, Represa El** ⊞ NW Honduras
58 N12 **Caju, Ilha do** *island* NE Brazil
Cakaubalavu Reef *see* Kavukavu Reef
159 R10 **Caka Yanhu** ◎ C China
112 E7 **Čakovec** *Ger.* Csakathurn, *Hung.* Csáktornya; *prev. Ger.* Tschakathurn. Međimurje, N Croatia
77 V17 **Calabar** Cross River, S Nigeria
14 K13 **Calabogie** Ontario, SE Canada
54 L6 **Calabozo** Guárico, C Venezuela
107 N20 **Calabria** *anc.* Bruttium. ◈ *region* SW Italy
104 M16 **Calaburra, Punta de** *headland* S Spain
116 G14 **Calafat** Dolj, SW Romania
Calafate *see* El Calafate
105 Q4 **Calahorra** La Rioja, N Spain
103 N1 **Calais** Pas-de-Calais, N France
19 T5 **Calais** Maine, NE USA
Calais, Pas de *see* Dover, Strait of
Calalen *see* Kallalen
62 H4 **Calama** Antofagasta, N Chile
Calamianes *see* Calamian Group
170 M5 **Calamian Group** *var.* Calamianes. *island group* W Philippines
105 R7 **Calamocha** Aragón, NE Spain
29 N14 **Calamus River** ≈ Nebraska, C USA
116 G12 **Călan** *Ger.* Kalan, *Hung.* Pusztakalán. Hunedoara, SW Romania
105 S7 **Calanda** Aragón, NE Spain
168 F9 **Calang** Sumatera, W Indonesia
171 N4 **Calapan** Mindoro, N Philippines
Călăras *see* Călărași
116 M9 **Călărași** *var.* Călăras, *Rus.* Kalarash. C Moldova
116 L14 **Călărași** Călărași, SE Romania
116 K14 **Călărași** ◈ *county* SE Romania
54 E10 **Calarca** Quindío, W Colombia
105 Q12 **Calasparra** Murcia, SE Spain
107 I23 **Calatafimi** Sicilia, Italy, C Mediterranean Sea
105 Q6 **Calatayud** Aragón, NE Spain
171 O4 **Calauag** Luzon, N Philippines
35 P8 **Calaveras River** ≈ California, W USA
171 N4 **Calavite, Cape** *headland* Mindoro, N Philippines
171 Q8 **Calbayog** *off.* Calbayog City. Samar, C Philippines
22 G9 **Calcasieu Lake** ◎ Louisiana, S USA
22 H8 **Calcasieu River** ≈ Louisiana, S USA
56 B6 **Calceta** Manabí, W Ecuador
61 B16 **Calchaquí** Santa Fe, C Argentina
62 J6 **Calchaquí, Río** ≈ NW Argentina
58 J10 **Calçoene** Amapá, NE Brazil
153 S16 **Calcutta** West Bengal, NE India
153 S16 **Calcutta** × West Bengal, N India
54 E9 **Caldas** *off.* Departamento de Caldas. ◈ *province* W Colombia
104 F10 **Caldas da Rainha** Leiria, W Portugal
104 G3 **Caldas de Reis** *var.* Caldas de Reyes. Galicia, NW Spain
Caldas de Reyes *see* Caldas de Reis
58 F13 **Caldeirão** Amazonas, NW Brazil
62 G7 **Caldera** Atacama, N Chile
42 L14 **Caldera** Puntarenas, W Costa Rica
105 N10 **Calderina** ▲ C Spain
137 T13 **Çaldıran** Van, E Turkey
32 M14 **Caldwell** Idaho, NW USA
27 N8 **Caldwell** Kansas, C USA
14 G15 **Caledon** Ontario, S Canada
83 I23 **Caledon** *var.* Mohokare. ≈ Lesotho/South Africa
42 G1 **Caledonia** Corozal, N Belize
14 G16 **Caledonia** Ontario, S Canada
29 X11 **Caledonia** Minnesota, N USA
105 X5 **Calella** *var.* Calella de la Costa. Cataluña, NE Spain
Calella de la Costa *see* Calella
23 P4 **Calera** Alabama, S USA
63 I19 **Caleta Olivia** Santa Cruz, SE Argentina
35 X17 **Calexico** California, W USA
97 H16 **Calf of Man** *island* SW Isle of Man
11 Q16 **Calgary** Alberta, SW Canada
11 Q16 **Calgary** × Alberta, SW Canada
37 U5 **Calhan** Colorado, C USA
64 O5 **Calheta** Madeira, Portugal, NE Atlantic Ocean
23 R2 **Calhoun** Georgia, SE USA
20 I6 **Calhoun** Kentucky, S USA
22 M3 **Calhoun City** Mississippi, S USA
21 P12 **Calhoun Falls** South Carolina, SE USA
54 D11 **Cali** Valle del Cauca, W Colombia
27 V9 **Calico Rock** Arkansas, C USA
155 F21 **Calicut** *var.* Kozhikode. Kerala, SW India
35 Y9 **Caliente** Nevada, W USA
27 U5 **California** Missouri, C USA
18 B15 **California** Pennsylvania, NE USA
35 Q12 **California** *off.* State of California; also known as El Dorado, The Golden State. ◈ *state* W USA
35 P11 **California Aqueduct** *aqueduct* California, W USA
35 T13 **California City** California, W USA
40 F6 **California, Golfo de** *Eng.* Gulf of California; *prev.* Sea of Cortez. *gulf* W Mexico
California, Gulf of *see* California, Golfo de
137 Y13 **Cälilabad** *Rus.* Dzhalilabad; *prev.* Astrakhan-Bazar. S Azerbaijan
116 I12 **Călimănești** Vâlcea, SW Romania
116 J9 **Călimani, Munții** ▲ N Romania
Calinisc *see* Cupcina
35 X17 **Calipatria** California, W USA
Calisia *see* Kalisz
34 M7 **Calistoga** California, W USA
83 G25 **Calitzdorp** Western Cape, SW South Africa
41 W12 **Calkiní** Campeche, E Mexico
182 K4 **Callabonna Creek** *var.* Tilcha Creek. *seasonal river* New South Wales/South Australia
182 J4 **Callabonna, Lake** ◎ South Australia
102 G5 **Callac** Côtes d'Armor, NW France
35 U5 **Callaghan, Mount** ▲ Nevada, W USA
Callain *see* Callan
97 E19 **Callan** *Ir.* Callain. S Ireland
14 H11 **Callander** Ontario, S Canada
96 I11 **Callander** C Scotland, UK
98 H7 **Callantsoog** Noord-Holland, NW Netherlands
57 D14 **Callao** Callao, W Peru
57 D15 **Callao** *off.* Departamento del Callao. ◈ *constitutional province* W Peru
56 F11 **Callaria, Río** ≈ E Peru
Callatis *see* Mangalia
9 Q13 **Calling Lake** Alberta, W Canada
Callosa de Ensarriá *see* Callosa d'En Sarrià
105 T11 **Callosa d'En Sarrià** *var.* Callosa de Ensarriá. País Valenciano, E Spain
105 S12 **Callosa de Segura** País Valenciano, E Spain
29 X11 **Calmar** Iowa, C USA
Calmar *see* Kalmar
43 R16 **Calobre** Veraguas, C Panama
23 X14 **Caloosahatchee River** ≈ Florida, SE USA
183 V2 **Caloundra** Queensland, E Australia
105 T11 **Calpe** País Valenciano, E Spain
41 P14 **Calpulalpan** Tlaxcala, S Mexico
107 K25 **Caltagirone** Sicilia, Italy, C Mediterranean Sea
107 J24 **Caltanissetta** Sicilia, Italy, C Mediterranean Sea
82 E11 **Caluango** Lunda Norte, NE Angola
82 C12 **Calucinga** Bié, W Angola
82 B12 **Calulo** Cuanza Sul, NW Angola
83 B14 **Caluquembe** Huíla, W Angola
80 Q11 **Caluula** Bari, NE Somalia
102 K4 **Calvados** ◈ *department* N France
186 I10 **Calvados Chain, The** *island group* SE PNG
25 U9 **Calvert** Texas, SW USA
20 H7 **Calvert City** Kentucky, S USA
103 X14 **Calvi** Corse, France, C Mediterranean Sea
40 L12 **Calvillo** Aguascalientes, C Mexico
83 F24 **Calvinia** Northern Cape, W South Africa
104 K8 **Calvitero** ▲ W Spain
101 G22 **Calw** Baden-Württemberg, SW Germany
Calydon *see* Kalydón
105 N11 **Calzada de Calatrava** Castilla-La Mancha, C Spain
Cama *see* Kama
82 C11 **Camabatela** Cuanza Norte, NW Angola
64 Q5 **Camacha** Porto Santo, Madeira, Portugal, NE Atlantic Ocean
14 L8 **Camachigama, Lac** ◎ Quebec, SE Canada
40 M9 **Camacho** Zacatecas, C Mexico
82 D13 **Camacupa** *var.* General Machado, *Port.* Vila General Machado. Bié, C Angola
54 L7 **Camaguán** Guárico, C Venezuela
44 G6 **Camagüey** *prev.* Puerto Príncipe. Camagüey, C Cuba
44 G5 **Camagüey, Archipiélago de** *island group* C Cuba
40 D5 **Camalli, Sierra de** ▲ NW Mexico
57 G18 **Camana** *var.* Camaná. Arequipa, SW Peru
29 Z14 **Camanche** Iowa, C USA
35 P8 **Camanche Reservoir** ⊞ California, W USA
61 I16 **Camaquã** Rio Grande do Sul, S Brazil
61 H16 **Camaquã, Rio** ≈ S Brazil
64 P6 **Câmara de Lobos** Madeira, Portugal, NE Atlantic Ocean
103 U16 **Camarat, Cap** *headland* SE France
41 O8 **Camargo** Tamaulipas, C Mexico
103 R15 **Camargue** *physical region* SE France
104 F2 **Camariñas** Galicia, NW Spain
Camaronero, Laguna del *see* Caimanero, Laguna del
63 J18 **Camarones** Chaco, S Argentina
63 J18 **Camarones, Bahía** *bay* S Argentina
104 J14 **Camas** Andalucía, S Spain
167 S15 **Ca Mau** *prev.* Quan Long. Minh Hai, S Vietnam
82 E11 **Camaxilo** Lunda Norte, NE Angola
104 G3 **Cambados** Galicia, NW Spain
Cambay, Gulf of *see* Khambhāt, Gulf of
Camberia *see* Chambéry
97 N22 **Camberley** SE England, UK
167 R12 **Cambodia** *off.* Kingdom of Cambodia, *var.* Democratic Kampuchea, Roat Kampuchea, *Cam.* Kampuchea; *prev.* People's Democratic Republic of Kampuchea. ◆ *republic* SE Asia
102 I16 **Cambo-les-Bains** Pyrénées-Atlantiques, SW France
103 P2 **Cambrai** *Flem.* Kambryk; *prev.* Cambray, *anc.* Cameracum. Nord, N France
Cambray *see* Cambrai
104 H2 **Cambre** Galicia, NW Spain
35 O12 **Cambria** California, W USA
97 J20 **Cambrian Mountains** ▲ C Wales, UK
14 G16 **Cambridge** Ontario, S Canada
44 I12 **Cambridge** W Jamaica
184 M8 **Cambridge** Waikato, North Island, NZ
97 O20 **Cambridge** *Lat.* Cantabrigia. E England, UK
32 M12 **Cambridge** Idaho, NW USA
30 K11 **Cambridge** Illinois, N USA
21 Y4 **Cambridge** Maryland, NE USA
19 O11 **Cambridge** Massachusetts, NE USA
29 V7 **Cambridge** Minnesota, N USA
29 N16 **Cambridge** Nebraska, C USA
31 U13 **Cambridge** Ohio, NE USA
8 L7 **Cambridge Bay** Victoria Island, Nunavut, NW Canada
97 O20 **Cambridgeshire** *cultural region* E England, UK
105 U6 **Cambrils de Mar** Cataluña, NE Spain
Cambundi-Catembo *see* Nova Gaia
137 N11 **Çam Burnu** *headland* N Turkey
183 S9 **Camden** New South Wales, SE Australia
23 O6 **Camden** Alabama, S USA
27 U14 **Camden** Arkansas, C USA
21 Y3 **Camden** Delaware, NE USA
19 R7 **Camden** Maine, NE USA
18 I16 **Camden** New Jersey, NE USA
18 I9 **Camden** New York, NE USA
21 R12 **Camden** South Carolina, SE USA
20 H8 **Camden** Tennessee, S USA
25 X9 **Camden** Texas, SW USA
39 S5 **Camden Bay** *bay* S Beaufort Sea
27 U6 **Camdenton** Missouri, C USA
Camellia State *see* Alabama
18 M7 **Camels Hump** ▲ Vermont, NE USA
117 N8 **Camenca** *Rus.* Kamenka. N Moldova
Cameracum *see* Cambrai
22 G9 **Cameron** Louisiana, S USA
25 T9 **Cameron** Texas, SW USA
30 J5 **Cameron** Wisconsin, N USA
10 M12 **Cameron** ≈ British Columbia, W Canada
185 A24 **Cameron Mountains** ▲ South Island, NZ
79 D15 **Cameroon** *off.* Republic of Cameroon, *Fr.* Cameroun. ◆ *republic* W Africa
79 D15 **Cameroon Mountain** ▲ SW Cameroon
Cameroon Ridge *see* Camerounaise, Dorsale
Cameroun *see* Cameroon
79 E14 **Camerounaise, Dorsale** *Eng.* Cameroon Ridge. *ridge* NW Cameroon
171 N3 **Camiling** Luzon, N Philippines
23 T7 **Camilla** Georgia, SE USA
104 G5 **Caminha** Viana do Castelo, N Portugal
35 P7 **Camino** California, W USA
136 B15 **Çamiçi Gölü** ◎ SW Turkey
107 J24 **Cammarata** Sicilia, Italy, C Mediterranean Sea
42 K10 **Camoapa** Boaco, S Nicaragua
58 O13 **Camocim** Ceará, E Brazil
106 D10 **Camogli** Liguria, NW Italy
181 S5 **Camooweal** Queensland, C Australia
55 Y11 **Camopi** E French Guiana
151 Q22 **Camorta** *island* Nicobar Islands, India, NE Indian Ocean
42 I6 **Campamento** Olancho, C Honduras
61 D19 **Campana** Buenos Aires, E Argentina
63 F21 **Campana, Isla** *island* S Chile
104 K11 **Campanario** Extremadura, W Spain
107 L17 **Campania** *Eng.* Champagne. ◈ *region* S Italy
27 Y8 **Campbell** Missouri, C USA
185 K15 **Campbell, Cape** *headland* South Island, NZ
14 J14 **Campbellford** Ontario, SE Canada
31 R13 **Campbell Hill** *hill* Ohio, N USA
192 K13 **Campbell Island** *island* S NZ
175 P13 **Campbell Plateau** *undersea feature* SW Pacific Ocean
10 K17 **Campbell River** Vancouver Island, British Columbia, SW Canada
20 L6 **Campbellsville** Kentucky, S USA
13 O13 **Campbellton** New Brunswick, SE Canada
183 P16 **Campbell Town** Tasmania, SE Australia
183 S9 **Campbelltown** New South Wales, SE Australia
96 G13 **Campbeltown** W Scotland, UK
41 W13 **Campeche** Campeche, SE Mexico
41 W14 **Campeche** ◈ *state* SE Mexico
41 T14 **Campeche, Bahía de** *Eng.* Bay of Campeche. *bay* E Mexico
Campeche, Banco de *see* Campeche Bank
64 C11 **Campeche Bank** *Sp.* Banco de Campeche, Sonda de Campeche. *undersea feature* S Gulf of Mexico
Campeche, Bay of *see* Campeche, Bahía de
Campeche, Sonda de *see* Campeche Bank
44 H7 **Campechuela** Granma, E Cuba
182 M13 **Camperdown** Victoria, SE Australia
167 U6 **Câm Pha** Quang Ninh, N Vietnam
116 H10 **Câmpia Turzii** *Ger.* Jerischmarkt, *Hung.* Aranyosgyéres; *prev.* Cîmpia Turzii, Ghiriș, Gyéres. Cluj, NW Romania
104 K12 **Campillo de Llerena** Extremadura, W Spain
104 L15 **Campillos** Andalucía, S Spain
116 J13 **Câmpina** *prev.* Cîmpina. Prahova, SE Romania
59 Q15 **Campina Grande** Paraíba, E Brazil
60 L9 **Campinas** São Paulo, S Brazil
38 L10 **Camp Kulowiye** Saint Lawrence Island, Alaska, USA
79 D17 **Campo** *var.* Kampo. Sud, SW Cameroon
Campo *see* Ntem
59 N15 **Campo Alegre de Lourdes** Bahia, E Brazil
107 L16 **Campobasso** Molise, C Italy
107 H24 **Campobello di Mazara** Sicilia, Italy, C Mediterranean Sea
Campo Criptana *see* Campo de Criptana
105 O10 **Campo de Criptana** *var.* Campo Criptana. Castilla-La Mancha, C Spain
59 I16 **Campo de Diauarum** *var.* Pôsto Diuarum. Mato Grosso, W Brazil
54 E5 **Campo de la Cruz** Atlántico, N Colombia
105 P11 **Campo de Montiel** *physical region* C Spain
Campo dos Goitacazes *see* Campos
60 H12 **Campo Erê** Santa Catarina, S Brazil
62 L7 **Campo Gallo** Santiago del Estero, N Argentina
59 I20 **Campo Grande** *state capital* Mato Grosso do Sul, SW Brazil
60 K12 **Campo Largo** Paraná, S Brazil
58 N13 **Campo Maior** Piauí, E Brazil
104 I10 **Campo Maior** Portalegre, C Portugal
60 H10 **Campo Mourão** Paraná, S Brazil
60 Q9 **Campos** *var.* Campo dos Goitacazes. Rio de Janeiro, SE Brazil
59 L17 **Campos Belos** Goiás, S Brazil
60 N9 **Campos do Jordão** São Paulo, S Brazil
60 I13 **Campos Novos** Santa Catarina, S Brazil
59 O14 **Campos Sales** Ceará, E Brazil
25 Q9 **Camp San Saba** Texas, SW USA
21 N6 **Campton** Kentucky, S USA
116 I13 **Câmpulung** *prev.* Câmpulung-Mușcel, Cîmpulung. Argeș, S Romania
116 J9 **Câmpulung Moldovenesc** *var.* Cîmpulung Moldovenesc, *Ger.* Kimpolung, *Hung.* Hosszúmezjő. Suceava, NE Romania
Câmpulung-Mușcel *see* Câmpulung
Campus Stellae *see* Santiago
36 L12 **Camp Verde** Arizona, SW USA
25 P11 **Camp Wood** Texas, SW USA
167 V13 **Cam Ranh** Khanh Hoa, S Vietnam
11 Q15 **Camrose** Alberta, SW Canada
Camulodunum *see* Colchester
136 B12 **Çan** Çanakkale, NW Turkey
18 L12 **Canaan** Connecticut, NE USA
9 O13 **Canada** ◆ *commonwealth republic* N North America
197 P6 **Canada Basin** *undersea feature* Arctic Ocean
61 B18 **Cañada de Gómez** Santa Fe, C Argentina
197 P6 **Canada Plain** *undersea feature* Arctic Ocean
61 A18 **Cañada Rosquín** Santa Fe, C Argentina
25 P1 **Canadian** Texas, SW USA
16 K12 **Canadian River** ≈ SW USA
8 L12 **Canadian Shield** *physical region* Canada
63 I18 **Cañadón Grande, Sierra** ▲ S Argentina
55 P9 **Canaima** Bolívar, SE Venezuela
136 B11 **Çanakkale** *var.* Dardanelli; *prev.* Chanak, Kale Sultanie. Çanakkale, W Turkey
136 B12 **Çanakkale** ◈ *province* NW Turkey
136 B11 **Çanakkale Boğazı** *Eng.* Dardanelles. *strait* NW Turkey
187 Q17 **Canala** Province Nord, C New Caledonia
59 A15 **Canamari** Amazonas, W Brazil
18 G10 **Canandaigua** New York, NE USA
18 F10 **Canandaigua Lake** ◎ New York, NE USA
40 G3 **Cananea** Sonora, NW Mexico
56 B8 **Cañar** ◈ *province* C Ecuador
64 N10 **Canarias, Islas** *Eng.* Canary Islands. ◈ *autonomous community* Spain, NE Atlantic Ocean
Canaries Basin *see* Canary Basin
44 C6 **Canarreos, Archipiélago de los** *island group* W Cuba
66 K3 **Canary Basin** *var.* Canaries Basin, Monaco Basin. *undersea feature* E Atlantic Ocean
Canary Islands *see* Canarias, Islas
42 L13 **Cañas** Guanacaste, NW Costa Rica
18 I10 **Canastota** New York, NE USA
40 K9 **Canatlán** Durango, C Mexico
104 J9 **Cañaveral** Extremadura, W Spain
23 Y11 **Canaveral, Cape** *headland* Florida, SE USA
59 O18 **Canavieiras** Bahia, E Brazil
43 R16 **Cañazas** Veraguas, W Panama
106 H6 **Canazei** Trentino-Alto Adige, N Italy
183 P6 **Canbelego** New South Wales, SE Australia
183 R10 **Canberra** ● (Australia) Australian Capital Territory, SE Australia
183 R10 **Canberra** × Australian Capital Territory, SE Australia
35 P2 **Canby** California, W USA
29 S9 **Canby** Minnesota, N USA
103 N2 **Canche** ≈ N France
102 L13 **Cancon** Lot-et-Garonne, SW France
41 Z11 **Cancún** Quintana Roo, SE Mexico
104 K2 **Candás** Asturias, N Spain
102 J7 **Cande** Maine-et-Loire, NW France
41 W14 **Candelaria** Campeche, SE Mexico
24 J11 **Candelaria** Texas, SW USA
41 W15 **Candelaria, Río** ≈ Guatemala/Mexico
104 L8 **Candeleda** Castilla-León, N Spain
Candia *see* Irákleio
41 P8 **Cándido Aguilar** Tamaulipas, C Mexico
39 N8 **Candle** Alaska, USA
11 T14 **Candle Lake** Saskatchewan, C Canada
18 L13 **Candlewood, Lake** ⊞ Connecticut, NE USA
29 O3 **Cando** North Dakota, N USA
Canea *see* Chaniá
45 O12 **Canefield** × (Roseau) SW Dominica
61 F20 **Canelones** *prev.* Guadalupe. Canelones, S Uruguay
61 E20 **Canelones** ◈ *department* S Uruguay
Canendiyú *see* Canindeyú
63 F14 **Cañete** Bío Bío, C Chile
105 Q9 **Cañete** Castilla-La Mancha, C Spain
Cañete *see* San Vicente de Cañete
27 P8 **Caney** Kansas, C USA
27 P8 **Caney River** ≈ Kansas/Oklahoma, C USA

◆ Country ● Country Capital ◇ Dependent Territory ○ Dependent Territory Capital ◈ Administrative Region × International Airport ▲ Mountain ▲ Mountain Range Ж Volcano ≈ River ◎ Lake ⊞ Reservoir

105 S3 **Canfranc-Estación** Aragón, NE Spain
83 E14 **Cangamba** *Port.* Vila de Aljustrel. Moxico, E Angola
82 C12 **Cangandala** Malanje, NW Angola
104 G4 **Cangas** Galicia, NW Spain
104 J2 **Cangas del Narcea** Asturias, N Spain
104 L2 **Cangas de Onís** Asturias, N Spain
161 S11 **Cangnan** *prev.* Lingxi. Zhejiang, SE China
82 C10 **Cangola** Uíge, NW Angola
83 E14 **Cangombe** Moxico, E Angola
63 H21 **Cangrejo, Cerro** ▲ S Argentina
61 H17 **Canguçu** Rio Grande do Sul, S Brazil
161 P3 **Cangzhou** Hebei, E China
12 M7 **Caniapiscau** ≈ Quebec, E Canada
12 M8 **Caniapiscau, Réservoir de** ▣ Quebec, C Canada
107 J24 **Canicattì** Sicilia, Italy, C Mediterranean Sea
136 L11 **Canik Dağları** ⛰ N Turkey
105 P14 **Caniles** Andalucía, S Spain
59 B16 **Canindé** Acre, W Brazil
62 P6 **Canindeyú** *var.* Canendiyú, Canindiyú. ◈ *department* E Paraguay
Canindiyú *see* Canindeyú
194 J10 **Canisteo Peninsula** *peninsula* Antarctica
18 F11 **Canisteo River** ≈ New York, NE USA
40 M10 **Cañitas** *var.* Cañitas de Felipe Pescador. Zacatecas, C Mexico
Cañitas de Felipe Pescador *see* Cañitas
105 P15 **Canjáyar** Andalucía, S Spain
136 I12 **Çankırı** *var.* Chankiri; *anc.* Gangra, Germanicopolis. Çankırı, N Turkey
136 I11 **Çankırı** *var.* Chankiri. ◈ *province* N Turkey
171 P6 **Canlaon Volcano** ☗ Negros, C Philippines
11 P16 **Canmore** Alberta, SW Canada
96 F9 **Canna** *island* NW Scotland, UK
155 F20 **Cannanore** *var.* Kananur, Kannur. Kerala, SW India
31 O17 **Cannelton** Indiana, N USA
103 U15 **Cannes** Alpes-Maritimes, SE France
39 R5 **Canning River** ≈ Alaska, USA
106 C6 **Cannobio** Piemonte, NE Italy
97 L19 **Cannock** C England, UK
28 M6 **Cannonball River** ≈ North Dakota, N USA
29 W9 **Cannon Falls** Minnesota, N USA
18 I11 **Cannonsville Reservoir** ▣ New York, NE USA
183 R12 **Cann River** Victoria, SE Australia
61 I16 **Canoas** Rio Grande do Sul, S Brazil
61 I14 **Canoas, Rio** ≈ S Brazil
14 I12 **Canoe Lake** ◎ Ontario, SE Canada
60 J12 **Canoinhas** Santa Catarina, S Brazil
37 T6 **Canon City** Colorado, C USA
55 P8 **Caño Negro** Bolívar, SE Venezuela
173 X15 **Canonniers Point** *headland* N Mauritius
23 W6 **Canoochee River** ≈ Georgia, SE USA
11 V15 **Canora** Saskatchewan, S Canada
45 Y14 **Canouan** *island* S Saint Vincent and the Grenadines
13 R15 **Canso** Nova Scotia, SE Canada
104 M3 **Cantabria** ◈ *autonomous community* N Spain
104 K3 **Cantábrica, Cordillera** ⛰ N Spain
Cantabrigia *see* Cambridge
103 O12 **Cantal** ◈ *department* C France
105 N6 **Cantalejo** Castilla-León, N Spain
103 O12 **Cantal, Monts du** ⛰ C France
104 G8 **Cantanhede** Coimbra, C Portugal
Cantaño *see* Cataño
55 O6 **Cantaura** Anzoátegui, NE Venezuela
116 M11 **Cantemir** *Rus.* Kantemir. S Moldova
97 Q22 **Canterbury** *hist.* Cantwaraburh, *anc.* Durovernum, *Lat.* Cantuaria. SE England, UK
185 F19 **Canterbury** *off.* Canterbury Region. ◈ *region* South Island, NZ
185 H20 **Canterbury Bight** *bight* South Island, NZ
185 H19 **Canterbury Plains** *plain* South Island, NZ
167 S14 **Cần Thơ** Cần Thơ, S Vietnam
104 K13 **Cantillana** Andalucía, S Spain
59 N15 **Canto do Buriti** Piauí, NE Brazil
23 S2 **Canton** Georgia, SE USA
30 K12 **Canton** Illinois, N USA
22 L5 **Canton** Mississippi, S USA
27 V2 **Canton** Missouri, C USA
18 J7 **Canton** New York, NE USA
21 O10 **Canton** North Carolina, SE USA
31 U12 **Canton** Ohio, N USA
26 L9 **Canton** Oklahoma, C USA
18 G12 **Canton** Pennsylvania, NE USA
29 R11 **Canton** South Dakota, N USA
25 V7 **Canton** Texas, SW USA
Canton *see* Guangzhou
Canton Island *see* Kanton
26 L9 **Canton Lake** ▣ Oklahoma, C USA
106 D7 **Cantù** Lombardia, N Italy
Cantuaria/Cantwaraburh *see* Canterbury
39 R10 **Cantwell** Alaska, USA
59 O16 **Canudos** Bahia, E Brazil
47 T7 **Canumã, Rio** ≈ N Brazil
Canusium *see* Puglia, Canosa di
24 G7 **Canutillo** Texas, SW USA
25 N3 **Canyon** Texas, SW USA
33 S12 **Canyon** Wyoming, C USA
32 K13 **Canyon City** Oregon, NW USA
33 R10 **Canyon Ferry Lake** ◎ Montana, NW USA
25 S11 **Canyon Lake** ▣ Texas, SW USA
167 T5 **Cao Bằng** *var.* Caobang. Cao Bằng, N Vietnam
160 J12 **Caodu He** ≈ S China
167 S14 **Cao Lanh** Đông Thap, S Vietnam
82 C11 **Caombo** Malanje, NW Angola
Caorach, Cuan na g *see* Sheep Haven
Caozhou *see* Heze
171 Q12 **Capalulu** Pulau Mangole, E Indonesia
54 K8 **Capanaparo, Río** ≈ Colomiba/Venezuela
58 L12 **Capanema** Pará, NE Brazil
60 L10 **Capão Bonito** São Paulo, S Brazil
60 I13 **Capão Doce, Morro do** ▲ S Brazil
54 I4 **Capatárida** Falcón, N Venezuela
102 I15 **Capbreton** Landes, SW France
Cap-Breton, Île du *see* Cape Breton Island
15 W6 **Cap-Chat** Quebec, SE Canada
15 P11 **Cap-de-la-Madeleine** Quebec, SE Canada
103 N13 **Capdenac** Aveyron, S France
183 Q15 **Cape Barren Island** *island* Furneaux Group, Tasmania, SE Australia
65 O18 **Cape Basin** *undersea feature* S Atlantic Ocean
13 R14 **Cape Breton Island** *Fr.* Île du Cap-Breton. *island* Nova Scotia, SE Canada
23 Y11 **Cape Canaveral** Florida, SE USA
21 Y6 **Cape Charles** Virginia, NE USA
77 P17 **Cape Coast** *prev.* Cape Coast Castle. S Ghana
Cape Coast Castle *see* Cape Coast
19 Q12 **Cape Cod Bay** *bay* Massachusetts, NE USA
23 W15 **Cape Coral** Florida, SE USA
181 R4 **Cape Crawford Roadhouse** Northern Territory, N Australia
9 Q7 **Cape Dorset** Baffin Island, Nunavut, NE Canada
21 N8 **Cape Fear River** ≈ North Carolina, SE USA
27 Y7 **Cape Girardeau** Missouri, C USA
21 T14 **Cape Island** *island* South Carolina, SE USA
186 A6 **Capella** ▲ NW PNG
98 H12 **Capelle aan den IJssel** Zuid-Holland, SW Netherlands
83 C15 **Capelongo** Huíla, C Angola
18 J17 **Cape May** New Jersey, NE USA
18 J17 **Cape May Court House** New Jersey, NE USA
Cape Palmas *see* Harper
8 I6 **Cape Parry** Northwest Territories, N Canada
65 P19 **Cape Rise** *undersea feature* SW Indian Ocean
Cape Saint Jacques *see* Vung Tau
Capesterre *see* Capesterre-Belle-Eau
45 Y6 **Capesterre-Belle-Eau** *var.* Capesterre. Basse Terre, S Guadeloupe
83 D26 **Cape Town** *var.* Ekapa, *Afr.* Kaapstad, Kapstad. ● (South Africa-legislative capital) Western Cape, SW South Africa
83 E26 **Cape Town** ✕ Western Cape, SW South Africa
76 D9 **Cape Verde** *off.* Republic of Cape Verde, *Port.* Cabo Verde, Ilhas do Cabo Verde. ◆ *republic* E Atlantic Ocean
64 L11 **Cape Verde Basin** *undersea feature* E Atlantic Ocean
66 K5 **Cape Verde Islands** *island group* E Atlantic Ocean
64 L10 **Cape Verde Plain** *undersea feature* E Atlantic Ocean
Cape Verde Plateau/Cape Verde Rise *see* Cape Verde Terrace
64 L11 **Cape Verde Terrace** *var.* Cape Verde Plateau, Cape Verde Rise. *undersea feature* E Atlantic Ocean
181 V2 **Cape York Peninsula** *peninsula* Queensland, N Australia
44 M8 **Cap-Haïtien** *var.* Le Cap. N Haiti
43 T15 **Capira** Panamá, C Panama
14 K8 **Capitachouane** ≈ Quebec, SE Canada
14 L8 **Capitachouane, Lac** ◎ Quebec, SE Canada
37 T13 **Capitan** New Mexico, SW USA
194 G3 **Capitán Arturo Prat** *Chilean research station* South Shetland Islands, Antarctica
37 S13 **Capitan Mountains** ⛰ New Mexico, SW USA
62 M3 **Capitán Pablo Lagerenza** *var.* Mayor Pablo Lagerenza. Chaco, N Paraguay
37 T13 **Capitan Peak** ▲ New Mexico, SW USA
188 H5 **Capitol Hill** Saipan, S Northern Mariana Islands
60 I9 **Capivara, Represa** ▣ S Brazil
61 J16 **Capivari** Rio Grande do Sul, S Brazil
113 H15 **Čapljina** Federacija Bosna I Hercegovina, S Bosnia and Herzegovina
83 M15 **Capoche** *var.* Kapoche. ≈ Mozambique/Zambia
Capo Delgado, Província de *see* Cabo Delgado
107 K17 **Capodichino** ✕ (Napoli) Campania, S Italy
Capodistria *see* Koper
106 E12 **Capraia, Isola** *island* Archipelago Toscano, C Italy
107 B16 **Caprara, Punta** *var.* Punta dello Scorno. *headland* Isola Asinara, W Italy
Capraria, Isola di to
Capraia, Isola *see* Cabrera
14 F10 **Capreol** Ontario, S Canada
107 K18 **Capri** Campania, S Italy
175 S9 **Capricorn Tablemount** *undersea feature* W Pacific Ocean
107 J18 **Capri, Isola di** *island* S Italy
83 G16 **Caprivi** ◈ *district* NE Namibia
Caprivi Concession *see* Caprivi Strip
83 F16 **Caprivi Strip** *Ger.* Caprivizipfel; *prev.* Caprivi Concession. *cultural region* NE Namibia
Caprivizipfel *see* Caprivi Strip
25 O5 **Cap Rock Escarpment** *cliffs* Texas, SW USA
15 R10 **Cap-Rouge** Quebec, SE Canada
Cap Saint-Jacques *see* Vung Tau
38 F12 **Captain Cook** Hawaii, USA, C Pacific Ocean
183 R10 **Captains Flat** New South Wales, SE Australia
102 K14 **Captieux** Gironde, SW France
107 K17 **Capua** Campania, S Italy
54 F14 **Caquetá** *off.* Departamento del Caquetá. ◈ *province* S Colombia
54 E13 **Caquetá, Río** *var.* Rio Japurá, Yapurá. ≈ Brazil/Colombia *see also* Japurá, Rio
CAR *see* Central African Republic
Cara *see* Kara
57 I16 **Carabaya, Cordillera** ⛰ E Peru
54 K5 **Carabobo** *off.* Estado Carabobo. ◈ *state* N Venezuela
116 I14 **Caracal** Olt, S Romania
58 F10 **Caracaraí** Rondônia, W Brazil
54 L5 **Caracas** ● (Venezuela) Distrito Federal, N Venezuela
54 I5 **Carache** Trujillo, N Venezuela
60 N10 **Caraguatatuba** São Paulo, S Brazil
48 I7 **Carajás, Serra dos** ⛰ N Brazil
Caralis *see* Cagliari
54 E9 **Caramanta** Antioquia, W Colombia
171 P4 **Caramoan** Catanduanes Island, N Philippines
Caramurat *see* Mihail Kogălniceanu
116 F12 **Caransebeş** *Ger.* Karansebesch, *Hung.* Karánsebes. Caraş-Severin, SW Romania
Carapella *see* Carapelle
107 M16 **Carapelle** *var.* Carapella. ≈ SE Italy
55 O9 **Carapo** Bolívar, SE Venezuela
13 P13 **Caraquet** New Brunswick, SE Canada
Caras *see* Caraz
116 F12 **Caraşova** *Hung.* Krassóvár. Caraş-Severin, SW Romania
116 F12 **Caraş-Severin** ◈ *county* SW Romania
42 M5 **Caratasca, Laguna de** *lagoon* NE Honduras
58 C13 **Carauari** Amazonas, NW Brazil
Caravaca *see* Caravaca de la Cruz
105 Q12 **Caravaca de la Cruz** *var.* Caravaca. Murcia, SE Spain
106 E7 **Caravaggio** Lombardia, N Italy
107 C18 **Caravai, Passo di** *pass* Sardegna, Italy, C Mediterranean Sea
59 O19 **Caravelas** Bahia, E Brazil
56 C12 **Caraz** *var.* Caras. Ancash, W Peru
61 H14 **Carazinho** Rio Grande do Sul, S Brazil
42 J11 **Carazo** ◈ *department* SW Nicaragua
Carballiño *see* O Carballiño
104 G2 **Carballo** Galicia, NW Spain
11 W16 **Carberry** Manitoba, S Canada
40 F4 **Carbó** Sonora, NW Mexico
107 C20 **Carbonara, Capo** *headland* Sardegna, Italy, C Mediterranean Sea
37 Q5 **Carbondale** Colorado, C USA
30 L17 **Carbondale** Illinois, N USA
27 Q4 **Carbondale** Kansas, C USA
18 I13 **Carbondale** Pennsylvania, NE USA
13 V12 **Carbonear** Newfoundland, SE Canada
105 Q9 **Carboneras de Guadazaón** *var.* Carboneras de Guadazón. Castilla-La Mancha, C Spain
Carboneras de Guadazón *see* Carboneras de Guadazaón
23 O3 **Carbon Hill** Alabama, S USA
107 B20 **Carbonia** *var.* Carbonia Centro. Sardegna, Italy, C Mediterranean Sea
Carbonia Centro *see* Carbonia
105 S10 **Carcaixent** País Valenciano, E Spain
Carcaso *see* Carcassonne
65 B24 **Carcass Island** *island* NW Falkland Islands
103 O16 **Carcassonne** *anc.* Carcaso. Aude, S France
105 R12 **Carche** ▲ S Spain
56 A13 **Carchi** ◈ *province* N Ecuador
10 I8 **Carcross** Yukon Territory, W Canada
Cardamomes, Chaîne des *see* Krâvanh, Chuŏr Phnum
155 G22 **Cardamom Hills** ⛰ SW India
Cardamom Mountains *see* Krâvanh, Chuŏr Phnum
104 M12 **Cardeña** Andalucía, S Spain
44 D4 **Cárdenas** Matanzas, W Cuba
41 O11 **Cárdenas** San Luis Potosí, C Mexico
41 U15 **Cárdenas** Tabasco, SE Mexico
63 H21 **Cardiel, Lago** ◎ S Argentina
97 K22 **Cardiff** *Wel.* Caerdydd. ◐ S Wales, UK
97 J22 **Cardiff-Wales** ✕ S Wales, UK
97 I21 **Cardigan** *Wel.* Aberteifi. SW Wales, UK
97 I20 **Cardigan** *cultural region* W Wales, UK
97 I20 **Cardigan Bay** *bay* W Wales, UK
19 N8 **Cardigan, Mount** ▲ New Hampshire, NE USA
14 M13 **Cardinal** Ontario, SE Canada
105 V5 **Cardona** Cataluña, NE Spain
61 E19 **Cardona** Soriano, SW Uruguay
105 V4 **Cardoner** ≈ NE Spain
11 Q17 **Cardston** Alberta, SW Canada
181 W5 **Cardwell** Queensland, NE Australia
116 G8 **Carei** *Ger.* Gross-Karol, Karol, *Hung.* Nagykároly; *prev.* Careii-Mari. Satu Mare, NW Romania
Careii-Mari *see* Carei
58 F13 **Careiro** Amazonas, NW Brazil
102 J4 **Carentan** Manche, N France
104 M2 **Cares** ≈ N Spain
33 P14 **Carey** Idaho, NW USA
31 S12 **Carey** Ohio, N USA
25 P4 **Carey** Texas, SW USA
180 L11 **Carey, Lake** ◎ Western Australia
173 O8 **Cargados Carajos Bank** *undersea feature* C Indian Ocean
102 G6 **Carhaix-Plouguer** Finistère, NW France
61 A22 **Carhué** Buenos Aires, E Argentina
55 O5 **Cariaco** Sucre, NE Venezuela
107 O20 **Cariati** Calabria, SW Italy
2 H17 **Caribbean Plate** *tectonic feature*
44 I11 **Caribbean Sea** *sea* W Atlantic Ocean
11 N15 **Cariboo Mountains** ⛰ British Columbia, SW Canada
11 W9 **Caribou** Manitoba, C Canada
19 S2 **Caribou** Maine, NE USA
11 P10 **Caribou Mountains** ⛰ Alberta, SW Canada
Caribrod *see* Dimitrovgrad
40 I6 **Carichic** Chihuahua, N Mexico
103 R3 **Carignan** Ardennes, N France
183 Q5 **Carinda** New South Wales, SE Australia
105 R6 **Cariñena** Aragón, NE Spain
107 I23 **Carini** Sicilia, Italy, C Mediterranean Sea
107 K17 **Carinola** Campania, S Italy
Carinthi *see* Kärnten
55 O5 **Caripe** Monagas, NE Venezuela
55 P5 **Caripito** Monagas, NE Venezuela
15 W7 **Carleton** Quebec, SE Canada
31 S10 **Carleton** Michigan, N USA
13 O14 **Carleton, Mount** ▲ New Brunswick, SE Canada
14 L13 **Carleton Place** Ontario, SE Canada
35 V3 **Carlin** Nevada, W USA
30 K14 **Carlinville** Illinois, N USA
97 K14 **Carlisle** *anc.* Caer Luel, Luguvallium, Luguvallum. NW England, UK
27 V11 **Carlisle** Arkansas, C USA
31 N15 **Carlisle** Indiana, N USA
29 V14 **Carlisle** Iowa, C USA
21 N5 **Carlisle** Kentucky, S USA
18 F15 **Carlisle** Pennsylvania, NE USA
21 Q11 **Carlisle** South Carolina, SE USA
38 J17 **Carlisle Island** *island* Aleutian Islands, Alaska, USA
27 R7 **Carl Junction** Missouri, C USA
107 A20 **Carloforte** Sardegna, Italy, C Mediterranean Sea
Carlopago *see* Karlobag
61 B21 **Carlos Casares** Buenos Aires, E Argentina
61 E18 **Carlos Reyles** Durazno, C Uruguay
61 A21 **Carlos Tejedor** Buenos Aires, E Argentina
97 F19 **Carlow** *Ir.* Ceatharlach. SE Ireland
97 F19 **Carlow** *Ir.* Cheatharlach. *cultural region* SE Ireland
96 F7 **Carloway** NW Scotland, UK
Carlsbad *see* Karlovy Vary
35 U17 **Carlsbad** California, W USA
37 U15 **Carlsbad** New Mexico, SW USA
131 N13 **Carlsberg Ridge** *undersea feature* S Arabian Sea
Carlsruhe *see* Karlsruhe
29 W6 **Carlton** Minnesota, N USA
11 V17 **Carlyle** Saskatchewan, S Canada
30 L15 **Carlyle** Illinois, N USA
30 L15 **Carlyle Lake** ▣ Illinois, N USA
10 H7 **Carmacks** Yukon Territory, W Canada
106 B9 **Carmagnola** Piemonte, NW Italy
11 X16 **Carman** Manitoba, S Canada
Carmana/Carmania *see* Kermān
97 I21 **Carmarthen** SW Wales, UK
97 I21 **Carmarthen** *cultural region* SW Wales, UK
97 I22 **Carmarthen Bay** *inlet* SW Wales, UK
103 N14 **Carmaux** Tarn, S France
35 N11 **Carmel** California, W USA
31 O13 **Carmel** Indiana, N USA
18 L13 **Carmel** New York, NE USA
97 H18 **Carmel Head** *headland* NW Wales, UK
42 E2 **Carmelita** Petén, N Guatemala
61 D19 **Carmelo** Colonia, SW Uruguay
41 V14 **Carmen** *var.* Ciudad del Carmen. Campeche, SE México
61 A25 **Carmen de Patagones** Buenos Aires, E Argentina
40 F8 **Carmen, Isla** *island* W Mexico
40 M5 **Carmen, Sierra del** ⛰ NW Mexico
30 M16 **Carmi** Illinois, N USA
35 O7 **Carmichael** California, W USA
Carmiel *see* Karmi'él
25 U11 **Carmine** Texas, SW USA
104 K14 **Carmona** Andalucía, S Spain
Carmona *see* Uíge
Carnaro *see* Kvarner
14 I13 **Carnarvon** Ontario, SE Canada
83 G24 **Carnarvon** Northern Cape, W South Africa
Carnarvon *see* Caernarfon
180 K9 **Carnarvon Range** ⛰ Western Australia
180 G9 **Carnarvon** Western Australia
Carn Domhnach *see* Carndonagh
96 E13 **Carndonagh** *Ir.* Carn Domhnach. NW Ireland
11 V17 **Carnduff** Saskatchewan, S Canada
26 L11 **Carnegie** Oklahoma, C USA
180 L9 **Carnegie, Lake** *salt lake* Western Australia
193 U8 **Carnegie Ridge** *undersea feature* E Pacific Ocean
96 H9 **Carn Eige** ▲ N Scotland, UK
182 F5 **Carnes** South Australia
194 J12 **Carney Island** *island* Antarctica
18 H16 **Carneys Point** New Jersey, NE USA
Carniche, Alpi *see* Karnische Alpen
151 Q21 **Car Nicobar** *island* Nicobar Islands, India, NE Indian Ocean
79 H15 **Carnot** Mambéré-Kadéï, W Central African Republic
182 F10 **Carnot, Cape** *headland* South Australia
96 K11 **Carnoustie** E Scotland, UK
97 F20 **Carnsore Point** *Ir.* Ceann an Chairn. *headland* SE Ireland
8 H7 **Carnwath** ≈ Northwest Territories, NW Canada
31 R8 **Caro** Michigan, N USA
23 Z15 **Carol City** Florida, SE USA
59 L14 **Carolina** Maranhão, E Brazil
45 U5 **Carolina** E Puerto Rico
21 V12 **Carolina Beach** North Carolina, SE USA
Caroline Island *see* Millennium Island
189 N15 **Caroline Islands** *island group* C Micronesia
131 Z14 **Caroline Plate** *tectonic feature*
192 H7 **Caroline Ridge** *undersea feature* E Philippine Sea
Carolopois *see* Châlons-en-Champagne
45 V14 **Caroni Arena Dam** ▣ Trinidad, Trinidad and Tobago
Caronie, Monti *see* Nebrodi, Monti
55 P7 **Caroní, Río** ≈ E Venezuela
45 U14 **Caroni River** ≈ Trinidad, Trinidad and Tobago
Caronium *see* A Coruña
54 J5 **Carora** Lara, N Venezuela
86 F12 **Carpathian Mountains** *var.* Carpathians, *Cz./Pol.* Karpaty, *Ger.* Karpaten. ⛰ E Europe
Carpathians *see* Carpathian Mountains
Carpathos/Carpathus *see* Kárpathos
116 H12 **Carpaţii Meridionali** *var.* Alpi Transilvaniei, Carpaţii Sudici, *Eng.* South Carpathians, Transylvanian Alps, *Ger.* Südkarpaten, Transsylvanische Alpen, *Hung.* Déli-Kárpátok, Erdélyi-Havasok. ⛰ C Romania
Carpaţii Sudici *see* Carpaţii Meridionali
174 L7 **Carpentaria, Gulf of** *gulf* N Australia
Carpentoracte *see* Carpentras
103 R14 **Carpentras** *anc.* Carpentoracte. Vaucluse, SE France
106 F9 **Carpi** Emilia-Romagna, N Italy
116 E11 **Cărpiniş** *Hung.* Gyertyámos. Timiş, W Romania
35 R14 **Carpinteria** California, W USA
23 S9 **Carrabelle** Florida, SE USA
Carraig Aonair *see* Fastnet Rock
Carraig Fhearghais *see* Carrickfergus
Carraig Mhachaire Rois *see* Carrickmacross
Carraig na Siúire *see* Carrick-on-Suir
Carrantual *see* Carrauntoohil
106 E10 **Carrara** Toscana, C Italy
61 F20 **Carrasco** ✕ (Montevideo) Canelones, S Uruguay
105 P9 **Carrascosa del Campo** Castilla-La Mancha, C Spain
54 H4 **Carrasquero** Zulia, NW Venezuela
183 O9 **Carrathool** New South Wales, SE Australia
Carrauntohil *see* Carrauntoohil
97 B21 **Carrauntoohil** *Ir.* Carrantual, Carrauntohil, Corrán Tuathail. ▲ SW Ireland
45 Y15 **Carriacou** *island* N Grenada
97 G15 **Carrickfergus** *Ir.* Carraig Fhearghais. NE Northern Ireland, UK
97 F16 **Carrickmacross** *Ir.* Carraig Mhachaire Rois. N Ireland
97 D16 **Carrick-on-Shannon** *Ir.* Cora Droma Rúisc. NW Ireland
97 E20 **Carrick-on-Suir** *Ir.* Carraig na Siúire. S Ireland
182 I7 **Carrieton** South Australia
40 L7 **Carrillo** Chihuahua, N Mexico
29 O4 **Carrington** North Dakota, N USA
104 M4 **Carrión** ≈ N Spain
104 M4 **Carrión de los Condes** Castilla-León, N Spain
25 P13 **Carrizo Springs** Texas, SW USA
37 S13 **Carrizozo** New Mexico, SW USA
29 T13 **Carroll** Iowa, C USA
23 N4 **Carrollton** Alabama, S USA
23 R3 **Carrollton** Georgia, SE USA
30 K14 **Carrollton** Illinois, N USA
20 L4 **Carrollton** Kentucky, S USA
31 R8 **Carrollton** Michigan, N USA
27 T3 **Carrollton** Missouri, C USA
31 U12 **Carrollton** Ohio, N USA
25 T6 **Carrollton** Texas, SW USA
11 U14 **Carrot** ≈ Saskatchewan, S Canada
11 U14 **Carrot River** Saskatchewan, C Canada
18 J7 **Carry Falls Reservoir** ▣ New York, NE USA
136 L11 **Çarşamba** Samsun, N Turkey
28 L6 **Carson** North Dakota, N USA
35 Q6 **Carson City** *state capital* Nevada, W USA
35 R6 **Carson River** ≈ Nevada, W USA
35 S5 **Carson Sink** *salt flat* Nevada, W USA
11 Q16 **Carstairs** Alberta, SW Canada
Carstensz, Puntjak *see* Jaya, Puncak
54 E5 **Cartagena** *var.* Cartagena de los Indes. Bolívar, NW Colombia
105 R13 **Cartagena** *anc.* Carthago Nova. Murcia, SE Spain
Cartagena de los Indes *see* Cartagena
54 D10 **Cartago** Valle del Cauca, W Colombia
43 N14 **Cartago** Cartago, C Costa Rica
42 M14 **Cartago** *off.* Provincia de Cartago. ◈ *province* C Costa Rica
25 O11 **Carta Valley** Texas, SW USA
104 F10 **Cartaxo** Santarém, C Portugal
104 I14 **Cartaya** Andalucía, S Spain
Carteret Islands *see* Tulun Islands
29 S15 **Carter Lake** Iowa, C USA
23 S3 **Cartersville** Georgia, SE USA
185 M14 **Carterton** Wellington, North Island, NZ
30 J13 **Carthage** Illinois, N USA
22 L5 **Carthage** Mississippi, S USA
27 R7 **Carthage** Missouri, C USA
18 I8 **Carthage** New York, NE USA
21 T10 **Carthage** North Carolina, SE USA
20 K8 **Carthage** Tennessee, S USA
25 X7 **Carthage** Texas, SW USA
74 M5 **Carthage** ✕ (Tunis) N Tunisia
Carthago Nova *see* Cartagena
14 E10 **Cartier** Ontario, S Canada
54 E13 **Cartogena de Chaira** Caquetá, S Colombia
13 S8 **Cartwright** Newfoundland, E Canada
55 P9 **Caruana de Montaña** Bolívar, SE Venezuela
59 Q15 **Caruaru** Pernambuco, E Brazil
55 P5 **Carúpano** Sucre, NE Venezuela
Carusbur *see* Cherbourg
58 M12 **Carutapera** Maranhão, E Brazil
27 Y9 **Caruthersville** Missouri, C USA
103 O1 **Carvin** Pas-de-Calais, N France
58 E12 **Carvoeiro** Amazonas, NW Brazil
104 E10 **Carvoeiro, Cabo** *headland* C Portugal
21 U9 **Cary** North Carolina, SE USA
182 M3 **Caryapundy Swamp** *wetland* New South Wales/Queensland, SE Australia
65 E24 **Carysfort, Cape** *headland* East Falkland, Falkland Islands
74 F6 **Casablanca** *Ar.* Dar-el-Beida. NW Morocco
60 M8 **Casa Branca** São Paulo, S Brazil
36 L14 **Casa Grande** Arizona, SW USA
106 C8 **Casale Monferrato** Piemonte, NW Italy
106 E8 **Casalpusterlengo** Lombardia, N Italy
54 H10 **Casanare** *off.* Intendencia de Casanare. ◈ *province* C Colombia
55 P5 **Casanay** Sucre, NE Venezuela
24 K11 **Casa Piedra** Texas, SW USA
107 Q19 **Casarano** Puglia, SE Italy
42 J11 **Casares** Carazo, W Nicaragua
105 R10 **Casas Ibáñez** Castilla-La Mancha, C Spain
61 I14 **Casca** Rio Grande do Sul, S Brazil
172 I17 **Cascade** Mahé, NE Seychelles
33 N13 **Cascade** Idaho, NW USA
29 Y13 **Cascade** Iowa, C USA

◆ Country ● Country Capital ◇ Dependent Territory ○ Dependent Territory Capital ◈ Administrative Region ✕ International Airport ▲ Mountain ⛰ Mountain Range ☗ Volcano ≈ River ◎ Lake ▣ Reservoir

33 R9 Cascade Montana, NW USA
185 B20 Cascade Point headland South Island, NZ
32 G13 Cascade Range ▲ Oregon/Washington, NW USA
33 N12 Cascade Reservoir ⊠ Idaho, NW USA
0 E8 Cascadia Basin undersea feature NE Pacific Ocean
104 E11 Cascais Lisboa, C Portugal
15 W7 Cascapédia ≈ Quebec, SE Canada
59 I22 Cascavel Ceará, E Brazil
60 G11 Cascavel Paraná, S Brazil
106 I13 Cascia Umbria, C Italy
106 F11 Cascina Toscana, C Italy
19 Q8 Casco Bay bay Maine, NE USA
194 J7 Case Island island Antarctica
106 B8 Caselle × (Torino) Piemonte, NW Italy
107 K17 Caserta Campania, S Italy
15 N8 Casey Quebec, SE Canada
30 M14 Casey Illinois, N USA
195 Y12 Casey Australian research station Antarctica
195 W3 Casey Bay bay Antarctica
80 Q11 Caseyr, Raas headland NE Somalia
97 D20 Cashel Ir. Caiseal. S Ireland
54 G6 Casigua Zulia, W Venezuela
61 B19 Casilda Santa Fe, C Argentina
Casim see General Toshevo
183 V4 Casino New South Wales, SE Australia
Casinum see Cassino
111 E17 Čáslav Ger. Tschaslau. Střední Čechy, C Czech Republic
56 C13 Casma Ancash, C Peru
167 S7 Ca, Sông ≈ N Vietnam
107 K17 Casoria Campania, S Italy
105 T6 Caspe Aragón, NE Spain
33 X15 Casper Wyoming, C USA
84 M10 Caspian Depression Kaz. Kaspiy Mangy Oypaty, Rus. Prikaspiyskaya Nizmennost'. depression Kazakhstan/Russian Federation
138 Kk9 Caspian Sea Az. Xäzär Dänizi, Kaz. Kaspiy Tengizi, Per. Baḩr-e Khazar, Daryā-ye Khazar, Rus. Kaspiyskoye More. inland sea Asia/Europe
83 L14 Cassacatiza Tete, NW Mozambique
Cassai see Kasai
82 F13 Cassamba Moxico, E Angola
107 N20 Cassano allo Ionio Calabria, SE Italy
31 S8 Cass City Michigan, N USA
Cassel see Kassel
14 M13 Casselman Ontario, SE Canada
29 R5 Casselton North Dakota, N USA
59 M16 Cássia var. Santa Rita de Cassia. Bahia, E Brazil
10 J9 Cassiar British Columbia, W Canada
10 K10 Cassiar Mountains ▲ British Columbia, W Canada
83 C15 Cassinga Huíla, SW Angola
107 J16 Cassino prev. San Germano; anc. Casinum. Lazio, C Italy
29 T4 Cass Lake Minnesota, N USA
29 T4 Cass Lake ◎ Minnesota, N USA
31 P10 Cassopolis Michigan, N USA
31 S8 Cass River ≈ Michigan, N USA
27 S8 Cassville Missouri, C USA
Castamoni see Kastamonu
58 L12 Castanhal Pará, NE Brazil
104 G8 Castanheira de Pêra Leiria, C Portugal
41 N7 Castaños Coahuila de Zaragoza, NE Mexico
108 I10 Castasegna Graubünden, SE Switzerland
106 D8 Casteggio Lombardia, N Italy
107 K23 Castelbuono Sicilia, Italy, C Mediterranean Sea
107 K15 Castel di Sangro Abruzzo, C Italy
106 H7 Castelfranco Veneto Veneto, NE Italy
102 K14 Casteljaloux Lot-et-Garonne, SW France
107 L18 Castellabate var. Santa Maria di Castellabate. Campania, S Italy
107 I23 Castellammare del Golfo Sicilia, Italy, C Mediterranean Sea
107 H22 Castellammare, Golfo di gulf Sicilia, Italy, C Mediterranean Sea
103 U15 Castellane Alpes-de-Haute-Provence, SE France
107 O18 Castellaneta Puglia, SE Italy
106 E9 Castel l'Arquato Emilia-Romagna, C Italy
61 E21 Castelli Buenos Aires, E Argentina
105 T9 Castelló de la Plana var. Castellón. País Valenciano, E Spain
105 S8 Castellón ◈ province País Valenciano, E Spain
Castellón see Castelló de la Plana
105 S7 Castellote Aragón, NE Spain
103 N16 Castelnaudary Aude, S France
102 L16 Castelnau-Magnoac Hautes-Pyrénées, S France
106 F10 Castelnovo ne' Monti Emilia-Romagna, C Italy
Castelnuovo see Herceg-Novi
104 H9 Castelo Branco Castelo Branco, C Portugal
104 H8 Castelo Branco ◈ district C Portugal
104 I10 Castelo de Vide Portalegre, C Portugal
104 G9 Castelo do Bode, Barragem do ⊠ C Portugal
106 G10 Castel San Pietro Terme Emilia-Romagna, C Italy
107 B17 Castelsardo Sardegna, Italy, C Mediterranean Sea
102 M14 Castelsarrasin Tarn-et-Garonne, S France
107 I24 Casteltermini Sicilia, Italy, C Mediterranean Sea
107 H24 Castelvetrano Sicilia, Italy, C Mediterranean Sea
182 L12 Casterton Victoria, SE Australia
102 J15 Castets Landes, SW France
106 H12 Castiglione del Lago Umbria, C Italy
106 F13 Castiglione della Pescaia Toscana, C Italy
106 F8 Castiglione delle Stiviere Lombardia, N Italy
104 M9 Castilla-La Mancha ◈ autonomous community NE Spain
104 L5 Castilla-León var. Castillia y Leon. ◈ autonomous community NW Spain
105 N10 Castilla Nueva cultural region C Spain
105 N6 Castilla Vieja cultural region N Spain
Castilla y Leon see Castilla-León
Castillo de Locubim see Castillo de Locubín
105 N14 Castillo de Locubín var. Castillo de Locubim. Andalucía, S Spain
102 K13 Castillon-la-Bataille Gironde, SW France
63 I19 Castillo, Pampa del plain S Argentina
61 G19 Castillos Rocha, SE Uruguay
97 B16 Castlebar Ir. Caisleán an Bharraigh. W Ireland
97 F16 Castleblayney Ir. Baile na Lorgan. N Ireland
45 O11 Castle Bruce E Dominica
36 M5 Castle Dale Utah, W USA
36 I14 Castle Dome Peak ▲ Arizona, SW USA
97 J14 Castle Douglas S Scotland, UK
97 E14 Castlefinn Ir. Caisleán na Finne. NW Ireland
97 M17 Castleford N England, UK
11 O17 Castlegar British Columbia, SW Canada
64 B12 Castle Harbour inlet Bermuda, NW Atlantic Ocean
21 V12 Castle Hayne North Carolina, SE USA
97 B20 Castleisland Ir. Oileán Ciarral. SW Ireland
183 N12 Castlemaine Victoria, SE Australia
37 R5 Castle Peak ▲ Colorado, C USA
33 O13 Castle Peak ▲ Idaho, NW USA
184 N13 Castlepoint Wellington, North Island, NZ
97 D17 Castlerea Ir. An Caisleán Riabhach. W Ireland
97 G15 Castlereagh Ir. An Caisleán Riabhach. N Northern Ireland, UK
183 R6 Castlereagh River ≈ New South Wales, SE Australia
37 T5 Castle Rock Colorado, C USA
30 K7 Castle Rock Lake ⊠ Wisconsin, N USA
65 G25 Castle Rock Point headland S Saint Helena
97 I16 Castletown SE Isle of Man
29 R9 Castlewood South Dakota, N USA
11 R15 Castor Alberta, SW Canada
14 M13 Castor ≈ Ontario, SE Canada
27 X7 Castor River ≈ Missouri, C USA
Castra Albiensium see Castres
Castra Regina see Regensburg
103 N15 Castres anc. Castra Albiensium. Tarn, S France
98 H9 Castricum Noord-Holland, W Netherlands
45 S11 Castries ● (Saint Lucia) N Saint Lucia
60 J11 Castro Paraná, S Brazil
63 F17 Castro Los Lagos, W Chile
104 H7 Castro Daire Viseu, N Portugal
104 M13 Castro del Río Andalucía, S Spain
Castrogiovanni see Enna
104 H14 Castro Marim Faro, S Portugal
104 J2 Castropol Asturias, N Spain
105 O2 Castro-Urdiales var. Castro Urdiales. Cantabria, N Spain
104 G13 Castro Verde Beja, S Portugal
107 N19 Castrovillari Calabria, SW Italy
35 N10 Castroville California, W USA
25 R12 Castroville Texas, SW USA
104 K11 Castuera Extremadura, W Spain
61 F19 Casupá Florida, S Uruguay
185 A22 Caswell Sound sound South Island, NZ
137 Q13 Çat Erzurum, NE Turkey
42 K6 Catacamas Olancho, C Honduras
56 A10 Catacaos Piura, NW Peru
22 I7 Catahoula Lake ◎ Louisiana, S USA
137 S15 Çatak Van, SE Turkey
137 S15 Çatak Çayi ≈ SE Turkey
114 O12 Çatalca İstanbul, NW Turkey
114 O12 Çatalca Yarımadası physical region NW Turkey
62 H6 Catalina Antofagasta, N Chile
Catalonia see Cataluña
105 U5 Cataluña Cat. Catalunya; Eng. Catalonia. ◈ autonomous community N Spain
Catalunya see Cataluña
62 I7 Catamarca off. Provincia de Catamarca. ◈ province NW Argentina
Catamarca see San Fernando del Valle de Catamarca
83 M16 Catandica Manica, C Mozambique
171 P4 Catanduanes Island island N Philippines
60 K8 Catanduva São Paulo, S Brazil
107 L24 Catania Sicilia, Italy, C Mediterranean Sea
107 M24 Catania, Golfo di gulf Sicilia, Italy, C Mediterranean Sea
45 U5 Cataño var. Cantaño. E Puerto Rico
107 O21 Catanzaro Calabria, SW Italy
107 O22 Catanzaro Marina var. Marina di Catanzaro. Calabria, S Italy
25 Q14 Catarina Texas, SW USA
171 Q5 Catarman Samar, C Philippines
105 S10 Catarroja País Valenciano, E Spain
21 R11 Catawba River ≈ North Carolina/South Carolina, SE USA
171 Q5 Catbalogan Samar, C Philippines
14 I14 Catchacoma Ontario, SE Canada
41 S15 Catemaco Veracruz-Llave, SE Mexico
Cathair na Mart see Westport
Cathair Saidhbhín see Cahersiveen
31 P5 Cat Head Point headland Michigan, N USA
23 Q2 Cathedral Caverns cave Alabama, S USA
35 V16 Cathedral City California, W USA
24 K10 Cathedral Mountain ▲ Texas, SW USA
32 G10 Cathlamet Washington, NW USA
76 G13 Catió S Guinea-Bissau
55 O10 Catisimiña Bolívar, SE Venezuela
44 J3 Cat Island island C Bahamas
12 B9 Cat Lake Ontario, S Canada
21 P5 Catlettsburg Kentucky, S USA
185 D24 Catlins ≈ South Island, NZ
35 R1 Catnip Mountain ▲ Nevada, W USA
41 Z11 Catoche, Cabo headland SE Mexico
27 P9 Catoosa Oklahoma, C USA
41 N10 Catorce San Luis Potosí, C Mexico
63 I14 Catriel Río Negro, C Argentina
62 K13 Catriló La Pampa, C Argentina
58 F11 Catrimani Roraima, N Brazil
58 E10 Catrimani, Rio ≈ N Brazil
18 K11 Catskill New York, NE USA
18 K11 Catskill Creek ≈ New York, NE USA
18 J11 Catskill Mountains ▲ New York, NE USA
18 D11 Cattaraugus Creek ≈ New York, NE USA
Cattaro see Kotor
Cattaro, Bocche di see Kotorska, Boka
107 I24 Cattolica Eraclea Sicilia, Italy, C Mediterranean Sea
83 B14 Catumbela ≈ W Angola
83 N14 Catur Niassa, N Mozambique
82 C10 Cauale ≈ NE Angola
171 O2 Cauayan Luzon, N Philippines
54 C12 Cauca off. Departamento del Cauca. ◈ province SW Colombia
47 P5 Cauca ≈ SE Venezuela
58 P13 Caucaia Ceará, E Brazil
54 E7 Cauca, Río ≈ N Colombia
54 E7 Caucasia Antioquia, NW Colombia
137 Q8 Caucasus Rus. Kavkaz. ▲ Georgia/Russian Federation
62 I10 Caucete San Juan, W Argentina
105 R11 Caudete Castilla-La Mancha, C Spain
103 P2 Caudry Nord, N France
82 D11 Caungula Lunda Norte, NE Angola
62 G13 Cauquenes Maule, C Chile
55 N8 Caura, Río ≈ C Venezuela
15 V7 Causapscal Quebec, SE Canada
117 N10 Căușeni Rus. Kaushany. E Moldova
102 M14 Caussade Tarn-et-Garonne, S France
102 K17 Cauterets Hautes-Pyrénées, S France
8 J15 Caution, Cape headland British Columbia, SW Canada
44 H7 Cauto ≈ E Cuba
Cauvery see Kāveri
102 L3 Caux, Pays de physical region N France
107 L18 Cava dei Tirreni Campania, S Italy
104 G6 Cávado ≈ N Portugal
Cavaia see Kavajë
103 R15 Cavaillon Vaucluse, SE France
103 U16 Cavalaire-sur-Mer Var, SE France
106 G6 Cavalese Ger. Gablös. Trentino-Alto Adige, N Italy
29 Q2 Cavalier North Dakota, N USA
76 L17 Cavalla var. Cavally, Cavally Fleuve. ≈ Ivory Coast/Liberia
105 Y8 Cavalleria, Cap de var. Cabo Caballeria. headland Menorca, Spain, W Mediterranean Sea
184 K2 Cavalli Islands island group N NZ
Cavally/Cavally Fleuve see Cavalla
97 E16 Cavan Ir. Cabhán. N Ireland
97 E16 Cavan Ir. An Cabhán. cultural region N Ireland
106 H8 Cavarzere Veneto, NE Italy
27 W9 Cave City Arkansas, C USA
20 K7 Cave City Kentucky, S USA
65 M25 Cave Point headland S Tristan da Cunha
21 N5 Cave Run Lake ⊠ Kentucky, S USA
58 K11 Caviana de Fora, Ilha var. Ilha Caviana. island N Brazil
Caviana, Ilha see Caviana de Fora, Ilha
113 I16 Cavtat It. Ragusavecchia. Dubrovnik-Neretva, SE Croatia
Cawnpore see Kānpur
Caxamarca see Cajamarca
58 A13 Caxias Amazonas, W Brazil
58 N13 Caxias Maranhão, E Brazil
61 I15 Caxias do Sul Rio Grande do Sul, S Brazil
42 J4 Caxinas, Punta headland N Honduras
82 B11 Caxito Bengo, NW Angola
136 F14 Çay Afyon, W Turkey
40 L15 Cayacal, Punta var. Punta Mongrove. headland S Mexico
56 C6 Cayambe Pichincha, N Ecuador
56 C6 Cayambe ▲ N Ecuador
21 R12 Cayce South Carolina, SE USA
55 Y10 Cayenne ○ (French Guiana) NE French Guiana
55 Y10 Cayenne × NE French Guiana
44 K10 Cayes var. Les Cayes. SW Haiti
45 U6 Cayey C Puerto Rico
45 U6 Cayey, Sierra de ▲ E Puerto Rico
103 N14 Caylus Tarn-et-Garonne, S France
44 E8 Cayman Brac island E Cayman Islands
44 D8 Cayman Islands ◇ UK dependent territory W West Indies
64 D11 Cayman Trench undersea feature NW Caribbean Sea
47 O3 Cayman Trough undersea feature NW Caribbean Sea
80 O13 Caynabo Togdheer, N Somalia
42 F3 Cayo ◈ district SW Belize
Cayo see San Ignacio
43 N9 Cayos Guerrero reef E Nicaragua
43 O9 Cayos King reef E Nicaragua
44 E4 Cay Sal islet SW Bahamas
14 G16 Cayuga Ontario, S Canada
25 V8 Cayuga Texas, SW USA
18 G10 Cayuga Lake ◎ New York, NE USA
104 K13 Cazalla de la Sierra Andalucía, S Spain
116 L14 Căzănești Ialomița, SE Romania
102 M16 Cazères Haute-Garonne, S France
112 E10 Cazin Federacija Bosna I Hercegovina, NW Bosnia and Herzegovina
82 G13 Cazombo Moxico, E Angola
105 O13 Cazorla Andalucía, S Spain
Cazza see Sušac
104 L4 Cea ≈ NW Spain
Ceadâr-Lunga see Ciadîr-Lunga
Ceanannas see Kells
Ceann Toirc see Kanturk
58 O13 Ceará off. Estado do Ceará. ◈ state C Brazil
Ceará see Fortaleza
Ceara Abyssal Plain see Ceará Plain
59 Q14 Ceará Mirim Rio Grande do Norte, E Brazil
64 J13 Ceará Plain var. Ceara Abyssal Plain. undersea feature W Atlantic Ocean
64 I13 Ceará Ridge undersea feature C Atlantic Ocean
Ceatharlach see Carlow
43 Q17 Cébaco, Isla island SW Panama
40 K7 Ceballos Durango, C Mexico
61 G19 Cebollatí Rocha, E Uruguay
61 G19 Cebollatí, Río ≈ E Uruguay
105 P5 Cebollera ▲ N Spain
104 M8 Cebreros Castilla-León, N Spain
171 P6 Cebu off. Cebu City. Cebu, C Philippines
171 P6 Cebu island C Philippines
107 J16 Ceccano Lazio, C Italy
Čechy see Bohemia
106 F12 Cecina Toscana, C Italy
26 K4 Cedar Bluff Reservoir ⊠ Kansas, C USA
30 M8 Cedarburg Wisconsin, N USA
36 J7 Cedar City Utah, W USA
25 T11 Cedar Creek Texas, SW USA
28 L7 Cedar Creek ≈ North Dakota, N USA
25 U7 Cedar Creek Reservoir ⊠ Texas, SW USA
29 W13 Cedar Falls Iowa, C USA
31 N8 Cedar Grove Wisconsin, N USA
21 Y6 Cedar Island island Virginia, NE USA
23 U11 Cedar Key Cedar Keys, Florida, SE USA
23 U11 Cedar Keys island group Florida, SE USA
11 V14 Cedar Lake ◎ Manitoba, C Canada
14 I11 Cedar Lake ◎ Ontario, SE Canada
24 M6 Cedar Lake ◎ Texas, SW USA
29 X13 Cedar Rapids Iowa, C USA
29 X14 Cedar River ≈ Iowa/Minnesota, C USA
29 O14 Cedar River ≈ Nebraska, C USA
31 P8 Cedar Springs Michigan, N USA
23 R3 Cedartown Georgia, SE USA
27 O7 Cedar Vale Kansas, C USA
35 Q2 Cedarville California, W USA
104 H1 Cedeira Galicia, NW Spain
42 H8 Cedeño Choluteca, S Honduras
41 N10 Cedral San Luis Potosí, C Mexico
42 I6 Cedros Francisco Morazán, C Honduras
40 M9 Cedros Zacatecas, C Mexico
40 B5 Cedros, Isla island W Mexico
193 R5 Cedros Trench undersea feature E Pacific Ocean
182 E7 Ceduna South Australia
110 D10 Cedynia Ger. Zehden. Zachodniopomorskie, W Poland
80 P12 Ceelaayo Sanaag, N Somalia
81 O16 Ceel Buur It. El Bur; Galguduud, C Somalia
81 N15 Ceel Dheere var. Ceel Dher, It. El Dere. Galguduud, C Somalia
Ceel Dher see Ceel Dheere
81 P14 Ceel Xamure Mudug, E Somalia
80 O12 Ceerigaabo var. Erigabo, Erigavo. Sanaag, N Somalia
107 J23 Cefalu anc. Cephaloedium. Sicilia, Italy, C Mediterranean Sea
105 N6 Cega ≈ N Spain
111 K23 Cegléd prev. Czegléd. Pest, C Hungary
113 N18 Čegrane W FYR Macedonia
105 Q13 Cehegín Murcia, SE Spain
136 K12 Çekerek Yozgat, N Turkey
107 J15 Celano Abruzzo, C Italy
104 H4 Celanova Galicia, NW Spain
42 F6 Celaque, Cordillera de ▲ W Honduras
41 N13 Celaya Guanajuato, C Mexico
Celebes see Sulawesi
192 F7 Celebes Basin undersea feature SE South China Sea
192 F7 Celebes Sea Ind. Laut Sulawesi. sea Indonesia/Philippines
41 W12 Celestún Yucatán, E Mexico
31 Q12 Celina Ohio, N USA
20 L8 Celina Tennessee, S USA
25 U5 Celina Texas, SW USA
112 G11 Čelinac Donji Republika Srpska, N Bosnia and Herzegovina
109 V10 Celje Ger. Cilli. C Slovenia
111 G23 Celldömölk Vas, W Hungary
100 J12 Celle var. Zelle. Niedersachsen, N Germany
99 D19 Celles Hainaut, SW Belgium
104 I7 Celorico da Beira Guarda, N Portugal
Celovec see Klagenfurt
64 M7 Celtic Sea Ir. An Mhuir Cheilteach. sea SW British Isles
64 N7 Celtic Shelf undersea feature E Atlantic Ocean
114 L13 Çeltik Gölu ◎ NW Turkey
113 M14 Čemerno ▲ C Yugoslavia
105 Q12 Cenajo, Embalse del ⊠ S Spain
171 V13 Cenderawasih, Teluk var. Teluk Irian, Teluk Sarera. bay W Pacific Ocean
105 P4 Cenicero La Rioja, N Spain
106 E9 Ceno ≈ NW Italy
102 K13 Cenon Gironde, SW France
14 K13 Centennial Lake ◎ Ontario, SE Canada
Centennial State see Colorado
37 S7 Center Colorado, C USA
29 Q13 Center Nebraska, C USA
28 M5 Center North Dakota, N USA
25 X8 Center Texas, SW USA
29 W8 Center City Minnesota, N USA
36 L5 Centerfield Utah, W USA
20 K9 Center Hill Lake ⊠ Tennessee, S USA
29 X13 Center Point Iowa, C USA
25 R11 Center Point Texas, SW USA
29 W16 Centerville Iowa, C USA
27 W7 Centerville Missouri, C USA
29 R12 Centerville South Dakota, N USA
20 I9 Centerville Tennessee, S USA
25 V9 Centerville Texas, SW USA
40 M5 Centinela, Picacho del ▲ NE Mexico
106 G9 Cento Emilia-Romagna, N Italy
Centrafricaine, République see Central African Republic
39 S8 Central Alaska, USA
37 P15 Central New Mexico, SW USA
83 H18 Central ◈ district E Botswana
138 E10 Central ◈ district C Israel
81 I19 Central ◈ province C Kenya
82 M13 Central ◈ region C Malawi
153 P12 Central ◈ zone C Nepal
186 E9 Central ◈ province S PNG
63 I21 Central ◈ department C Paraguay
186 M9 Central off. Central Province. ◈ province S Solomon Islands
83 J14 Central ◈ province C Zambia
117 P11 Central × (Odesa) Odes'ka Oblast', SW Ukraine
Central see Centre
79 H14 Central African Republic var. République Centrafricaine, abbrev. CAR; prev. Ubangi-Shari, Oubangui-Chari, Territoire de l'Oubangui-Chari. ◆ republic C Africa
192 G6 Central Basin Trough undersea feature W Pacific Ocean
Central Borneo see Kalimantan Tengah
149 P12 Central Brāhui Range ▲ W Pakistan
Central Celebes see Sulawesi Tengah
29 Y13 Central City Iowa, C USA
20 I6 Central City Kentucky, S USA
29 P15 Central City Nebraska, C USA
48 D6 Central, Cordillera ▲ W Bolivia
54 D11 Central, Cordillera ▲ W Colombia
42 M13 Central, Cordillera ▲ C Costa Rica
45 N9 Central, Cordillera ▲ C Dominican Republic
43 R16 Central, Cordillera ▲ C Panama
45 S6 Central, Cordillera ▲ Puerto Rico
42 H7 Central District var. Tegucigalpa. ◈ district C Honduras
30 L15 Centralia Illinois, N USA
27 U4 Centralia Missouri, C USA
32 G9 Centralia Washington, NW USA
Central Indian Ridge see Mid-Indian Ridge
Central Java see Jawa Tengah
Central Kalimantan see Kalimantan Tengah
148 L14 Central Makrān Range ▲ W Pakistan
192 K7 Central Pacific Basin undersea feature C Pacific Ocean
59 M19 Central, Planalto var. Brazilian Highlands. ▲ E Brazil
32 F15 Central Point Oregon, NW USA
155 K25 Central Province ◈ province C Sri Lanka
Central Provinces and Berar see Madhya Pradesh
186 B6 Central Range ▲ NW PNG
Central Russian Upland see Srednerusskaya Vozvyshennost'
Central Siberian Plateau/Central Siberian Uplands see Srednesibirskoye Ploskogor'ye
104 K8 Central, Sistema ▲ C Spain
Central Sulawesi see Sulawesi Tengah
35 N3 Central Valley California, W USA
35 P8 Central Valley valley California, W USA
23 Q3 Centre Alabama, S USA
79 E15 Centre Eng. Central. ◈ province C Cameroon
102 M8 Centre ◈ region N France
173 Y16 Centre de Flacq E Mauritius
55 Y9 Centre Spatial Guyanais space station N French Guiana
23 O5 Centreville Alabama, S USA
21 X3 Centreville Maryland, NE USA
22 J7 Centreville Mississippi, S USA
Centum Cellae see Civitavecchia
160 M14 Cenxi Guangxi Zhuangzu Zizhiqu, S China
Ceos see Kéa
Cephaloedium see Cefalu
112 I9 Čepin Hung. Csepén. Osijek-Baranja, E Croatia
Ceram see Seram, Pulau
171 R13 Ceram Sea Ind. Laut Seram. sea E Indonesia
192 G8 Ceram Trough undersea feature W Pacific Ocean
Cerasus see Giresun
36 I10 Cerbat Mountains ▲ Arizona, SW USA
103 P17 Cerbère, Cap headland S France
104 F13 Cercal do Alentejo Setúbal, S Portugal
111 A18 Čerchov Ger. Czerkow. ▲ W Czech Republic
103 O13 Cère ≈ C France
61 A16 Ceres Santa Fe, C Argentina
59 K18 Ceres Goiás, C Brazil
Ceresio see Lugano, Lago di
103 O17 Céret Pyrénées-Orientales, S France
54 E6 Cereté Córdoba, NW Colombia
172 I17 Cerf, Île au island Inner Islands, NE Seychelles
99 G22 Cerfontaine Namur, S Belgium
Cergy-Pontoise see Pontoise
107 N16 Cerignola Puglia, SE Italy
Cerigo see Kýthira
103 O9 Cérilly Allier, C France
136 I11 Çerkeş Çankırı, N Turkey
136 D10 Çerkezköy Tekirdağ, NW Turkey
109 T12 Cerknica Ger. Zirknitz. SW Slovenia
109 S11 Cerkno W Slovenia
116 F10 Cermei Hung. Csermő. Arad, W Romania
137 O15 Çermik Diyarbakır, SE Turkey
112 I10 Cerna Vukovar-Srijem, E Croatia
Cernăuți see Chernivtsi
116 M14 Cernavodă Constanța, SW Romania
103 U7 Cernay Haut-Rhin, NE France
Černice see Schwarzach
41 O8 Cerralvo Nuevo León, NE Mexico
40 G9 Cerralvo, Isla island W Mexico
107 L16 Cerreto Sannita Campania, S Italy
113 L20 Cërrik var. Cerriku. Elbasan, C Albania
Cerriku see Cërrik
41 O11 Cerritos San Luis Potosí, C Mexico
60 K11 Cerro Azul Paraná, S Brazil
61 F18 Cerro Chato Treinta y Tres, E Uruguay
61 F19 Cerro Colorado Florida, S Uruguay
56 E13 Cerro de Pasco Pasco, C Peru
61 G18 Cerro Largo ◈ department NE Uruguay
61 G14 Cerro Largo Rio Grande do Sul, S Brazil
42 E7 Cerrón Grande, Embalse ⊠ N El Salvador
63 I14 Cerros Colorados, Embalse ◎ W Argentina
105 V5 Cervera Cataluña, NE Spain
104 M3 Cervera del Pisuerga Castilla-León, N Spain
105 Q5 Cervera del Río Alhama La Rioja, N Spain
107 H15 Cerveteri Lazio, C Italy
106 H10 Cervia Emilia-Romagna, N Italy
106 J7 Cervignano del Friuli Friuli-Venezia Giulia, NE Italy
107 L17 Cervinara Campania, S Italy
Cervinia see Breuil-Cervinia
106 B6 Cervino, Monte var. Matterhorn. ▲ Italy/Switzerland see also Matterhorn

◆ Country ● Country Capital ◇ Dependent Territory ○ Dependent Territory Capital ◈ Administrative Region × International Airport ▲ Mountain ▲ Mountain Range Volcano ≈ River ◎ Lake ⊠ Reservoir

103 Y14 **Cervione** Corse, France, C Mediterranean Sea
104 I1 **Cervo** Galicia, NW Spain
54 F5 **Cesar** *off.* Departamento del Cesar. ◈ *province* N Colombia
106 H10 **Cesena** *anc.* Caesena. Emilia-Romagna, N Italy
106 I10 **Cesenatico** Emilia-Romagna, N Italy
118 H8 **Cēsis** *Ger.* Wenden. Cēsis, C Latvia
111 D15 **Česká Lípa** *Ger.* Böhmisch-Leipa. Liberecký Kraj, N Czech Republic
Česká Republika *see* Czech Republic
111 F17 **Česká Třebová** *Ger.* Böhmisch-Trübau. Pardubický Kraj, C Czech Republic
111 D19 **České Budějovice** *Ger.* Budweis. Budějovický Kraj, S Czech Republic
111 D19 **České Velenice** Budějovický Kraj, S Czech Republic
111 E18 **Českomoravská Vrchovina** *var.* Českomoravská Vysočina, *Eng.* Bohemian-Moravian Highlands, *Ger.* Böhmisch-Mährische Höhe. ▲ S Czech Republic
Českomoravská Vysočina *see* Českomoravská Vrchovina
111 C19 **Český Krumlov** *var.* Böhmisch-Krumau, *Ger.* Krummau. Budějovický Kraj, S Czech Republic
Ceský Les *see* Bohemian Forest
112 F8 **Česma** ≈ N Croatia
136 A14 **Çeşme** İzmir, W Turkey
Cess *see* Cestos
183 T8 **Cessnock** New South Wales, SE Australia
76 K17 **Cestos** *var.* Cess. ≈ S Liberia
118 I9 **Cesvaine** Madona, E Latvia
116 G14 **Cetate** Dolj, SW Romania
Cetatea Albă *see* Bilhorod-Dnistrovs'kyy
113 J17 **Cetinje** *It.* Cettigne. Montenegro, SW Yugoslavia
107 N20 **Cetraro** Calabria, S Italy
Cette *see* Sète
188 A17 **Cetti Bay** *bay* SW Guam
Cettigne *see* Cetinje
104 L17 **Ceuta** *var.* Sebta. Ceuta, Spain, N Africa
88 C15 **Ceuta** *enclave* Spain, N Africa
106 B9 **Ceva** Piemonte, NE Italy
103 P14 **Cévennes** ▲ S France
108 G10 **Cevio** Ticino, S Switzerland
136 K16 **Ceyhan** Adana, S Turkey
136 K17 **Ceyhan Nehri** ≈ S Turkey
137 P17 **Ceylanpınar** Şanlıurfa, SE Turkey
Ceylon *see* Sri Lanka
173 R6 **Ceylon Plain** *undersea feature* N Indian Ocean
Ceyre to the Caribs *see* Marie-Galante
103 Q14 **Cèze** ≈ S France
146 H15 **Chaacha** *Turkm.* Chäche. Akhalskiy Velayat, S Turkmenistan
129 P6 **Chaadayevka** Penzenskaya Oblast', W Russian Federation
167 O12 **Cha-Am** Phetchaburi, SW Thailand
143 W15 **Chābahār** *var.* Chāh Bahār, Chahbar. Sīstān va Balūchestān, SE Iran
61 B19 **Chabas** Santa Fe, C Argentina
103 T10 **Chablais** *physical region* E France
61 B20 **Chacabuco** Buenos Aires, E Argentina
42 K8 **Chachagón, Cerro** ▲ N Nicaragua
56 C10 **Chachapoyas** Amazonas, NW Peru
Chäche *see* Chaacha
119 O18 **Chachersk** *Rus.* Chechersk. Homyel'skaya Voblasts', SE Belarus
119 N16 **Chachevichy** *Rus.* Chechevichi. Mahilyowskaya Voblasts', E Belarus
61 B14 **Chaco** *off.* Provincia de Chaco. ◈ *province* NE Argentina
Chaco *see* Gran Chaco
62 M6 **Chaco Austral** *physical region* N Argentina
62 M3 **Chaco Boreal** *physical region* N Paraguay
62 M6 **Chaco Central** *physical region* N Argentina
39 Y15 **Chacon, Cape** *headland* Prince of Wales Island, Alaska, USA
78 H9 **Chad** *off.* Republic of Chad, *Fr.* Tchad. ◆ *republic* C Africa
122 K14 **Chadan** Respublika Tyva, S Russian Federation
21 U12 **Chadbourn** North Carolina, SE USA
83 L14 **Chadiza** Eastern, E Zambia
67 Q7 **Chad, Lake** *Fr.* Lac Tchad. ◎ C Africa
28 J12 **Chadron** Nebraska, C USA
Chadyr-Lunga *see* Ciadîr-Lunga
163 W14 **Chaeryŏng** SW North Korea
105 P17 **Chafarinas, Islas** *island group* S Spain
27 Y7 **Chaffee** Missouri, C USA
148 L12 **Chāgai Hills** *var.* Chāh Gay. ▲ Afghanistan/Pakistan
123 Q11 **Chagda** Respublika Sakha (Yakutiya), NE Russian Federation
Chaghasarāy *see* Asadābād
149 N5 **Chaghcharān** *var.* Chakhcharan, Cheghcheran, Qala Āhangarān. Ghowr, C Afghanistan
103 R9 **Chagny** Saône-et-Loire, C France
173 Q7 **Chagos Archipelago** *var.* Oil Islands. *island group* British Indian Ocean Territory
131 O15 **Chagos Bank** *undersea feature* C Indian Ocean
131 O14 **Chagos-Laccadive Plateau** *undersea feature* N Indian Ocean
173 Q7 **Chagos Trench** *undersea feature* N Indian Ocean
43 T14 **Chagres, Río** ≈ C Panama
45 U14 **Chaguanas** Trinidad, Trinidad and Tobago
54 M6 **Chaguaramas** Guárico, N Venezuela
146 C9 **Chagyl** Balkanskiy Velayat, NW Turkmenistan
Chahārmahāl and Bakhtiyāri *see* Chahār Maḩall va Bakhtīārī
142 M9 **Chahār Maḩall va Bakhtīārī** *off.* Ostān-e Chahār Maḩall va Bakhtīārī, *var.* Chahārmahāl and Bakhtiyāri. ◈ *province* SW Iran
Chāh Bahār/Chahbar *see* Chābahār
143 V13 **Chāh Derāz** Sīstān va Balūchestān, SE Iran
Chāh Gay *see* Chāgai Hills
167 P10 **Chai Badan** Lop Buri, C Thailand
153 Q16 **Chāībāsa** Bihār, N India
79 E19 **Chaillu, Massif du** ▲ C Gabon
167 O10 **Chai Nat** *var.* Chainat, Jainat, Jayanath. Chai Nat, C Thailand
65 M14 **Chain Fracture Zone** *tectonic feature* E Atlantic Ocean
173 N5 **Chain Ridge** *undersea feature* W Indian Ocean
Chairn, Ceann an *see* Carnsore Point
158 L5 **Chaiwopu** Xinjiang Uygur Zizhiqu, W China
167 Q10 **Chaiyaphum** *var.* Jayabum. Chaiyaphum, C Thailand
62 N10 **Chajarí** Entre Ríos, E Argentina
42 C5 **Chajul** Quiché, W Guatemala
83 K16 **Chakari** Mashonaland West, N Zimbabwe
148 J9 **Chakhānsūr** Nīmrūz, SW Afghanistan
Chakhānsūr *see* Nīmrūz
Chakhcharan *see* Chaghcharān
149 V8 **Chak Jhumra** *var.* Jhumra. Punjab, E Pakistan
146 I16 **Chaknakdysonga** Akhalskiy Velayat, S Turkmenistan
153 P16 **Chakradharpur** Bihār, N India
152 J8 **Chakrāta** Uttar Pradesh, N India
149 U7 **Chakwāl** Punjab, NE Pakistan
57 F17 **Chala** Arequipa, SW Peru
102 K12 **Chalais** Charente, W France
108 D10 **Chalais** Valais, SW Switzerland
115 J20 **Chalándri** *var.* Halandri; *prev.* Khalándrion. *prehistoric site* Sýros, Kykládes, Greece, Aegean Sea
188 H6 **Chalan Kanoa** Saipan, S Northern Mariana Islands
188 C16 **Chalan Pago** C Guam
Chalap Dalam/Chalap Dalan *see* Chehel Abdālān, Kūh-e
42 F7 **Chalatenango** Chalatenango, N El Salvador
42 A9 **Chalatenango** ◈ *department* NW El Salvador
83 P15 **Chalaua** Nampula, NE Mozambique
81 I16 **Chalbi Desert** *desert* N Kenya
42 D7 **Chalchuapa** Santa Ana, W El Salvador
Chalcidice *see* Chalkidikí
Chalcis *see* Chalkída
103 N6 **Châlette-sur-Loing** Loiret, C France
15 X8 **Chaleur Bay** *Fr.* Baie des Chaleurs. *bay* New Brunswick/Quebec, E Canada
Chaleurs, Baie des *see* Chaleur Bay
57 G16 **Chalhuanca** Apurímac, S Peru
154 F12 **Chālisgaon** Mahārāshtra, C India
115 N23 **Chálki** *island* Dodekánisos, Greece, Aegean Sea
115 F16 **Chalkiádes** Thessalía, C Greece
115 H18 **Chalkída** *var.* Halkida; *prev.* Khalkís, *anc.* Chalcis. Evvoia, E Greece
115 G14 **Chalkidikí** *var.* Khalkidhikí; *anc.* Chalcidice. *peninsula* NE Greece
185 A24 **Chalky Inlet** *inlet* South Island, NZ
39 S7 **Chalkyitsik** Alaska, USA
102 I9 **Challans** Vendée, NW France
57 K19 **Challapata** Oruro, SW Bolivia
192 H6 **Challenger Deep** *undersea feature* W Pacific Ocean
193 S11 **Challenger Fracture Zone** *tectonic feature* SE Pacific Ocean
192 K11 **Challenger Plateau** *undersea feature* E Tasman Sea
33 P13 **Challis** Idaho, NW USA
22 L9 **Chalmette** Louisiana, S USA
126 J11 **Chalna** Respublika Kareliya, NW Russian Federation
103 Q5 **Châlons-en-Champagne** *prev.* Châlons-sur-Marne, *hist.* Arcae Remorum, *anc.* Carolopois. Marne, NE France
Châlons-sur-Marne *see* Châlons-en-Champagne
103 R9 **Chalon-sur-Saône** *anc.* Cabillonum. Saône-et-Loire, C France
Chaltel, Cerro *see* Fitzroy, Monte
143 N4 **Chālūs** Māzandarān, N Iran
102 M11 **Châlus** Haute-Vienne, C France
101 N20 **Cham** Bayern, SE Germany
108 F7 **Cham** Zug, N Switzerland
37 R8 **Chama** New Mexico, SW USA
Cha Mai *see* Thung Song
83 E22 **Chamaites** Karas, S Namibia
149 O9 **Chaman** Baluchistān, SW Pakistan
37 R9 **Chama, Rio** ≈ New Mexico, SW USA
152 I6 **Chamba** Himāchal Pradesh, N India
81 I25 **Chamba** Ruvuma, S Tanzania
150 H12 **Chambal** ≈ C India
11 U16 **Chamberlain** Saskatchewan, S Canada
29 O11 **Chamberlain** South Dakota, N USA
19 R3 **Chamberlain Lake** ◎ Maine, NE USA
39 S5 **Chamberlin, Mount** ▲ Alaska, USA
37 O11 **Chambers** Arizona, SW USA
18 F16 **Chambersburg** Pennsylvania, NE USA
31 N5 **Chambers Island** *island* Wisconsin, N USA
103 T11 **Chambéry** *anc.* Camberia. Savoie, E France
82 L12 **Chambeshi** Northern, NE Zambia
82 L12 **Chambeshi** ≈ NE Zambia
74 M6 **Chambi, Jebel** *var.* Jabal ash Sha'nabī. ▲ W Tunisia
15 Q7 **Chambord** Quebec, SE Canada
139 U11 **Chamcham** S Iraq
139 T4 **Chamchamāļ** N Iraq
40 J14 **Chamela** Jalisco, SW Mexico
42 G5 **Chamelecón, Río** ≈ NW Honduras
62 J9 **Chamical** La Rioja, C Argentina
115 L23 **Chamilí** *island* Kykládes, Greece, Aegean Sea
167 Q13 **Châmnar** Kaôh Kông, SW Cambodia
152 K9 **Chamoli** Uttar Pradesh, N India
103 U11 **Chamonix-Mont-Blanc** Haute-Savoie, E France
154 L11 **Chāmpa** Madhya Pradesh, C India
8 H8 **Champagne** Yukon Territory, W Canada
103 Q5 **Champagne** *cultural region* N France
Champagne *see* Campania
103 Q5 **Champagne-Ardenne** ◈ *region* N France
103 S9 **Champagnole** Jura, E France
30 M13 **Champaign** Illinois, N USA
167 S10 **Champasak** Champasak, S Laos
103 U6 **Champ de Feu** ▲ NE France
13 O7 **Champdoré, Lac** ◎ Quebec, NE Canada
42 B6 **Champerico** Retalhuleu, SW Guatemala
108 C11 **Champéry** Valais, SW Switzerland
18 L6 **Champlain** New York, NE USA
18 L9 **Champlain Canal** *canal* New York, NE USA
15 P13 **Champlain, Lac** ◎ Quebec, SE Canada
18 L7 **Champlain, Lake** ◎ Canada/USA
103 S7 **Champlitte** Haute-Saône, E France
41 W13 **Champotón** Campeche, SE Mexico
104 G10 **Chamusca** Santarém, C Portugal
119 O20 **Chamyarysy** *Rus.* Chemerisy. Homyel'skaya Voblasts', SE Belarus
129 P5 **Chamzinka** Respublika Mordoviya, W Russian Federation
Chanáil Mhór, An *see* Grand Canal
Chanak *see* Çanakkale
64 G7 **Chañaral** Atacama, N Chile
104 H13 **Chança, Rio** *var.* Chanza. ≈ Portugal/Spain
57 D14 **Chancay** Lima, W Peru
Chan-chiang/Chanchiang *see* Zhanjiang
64 G13 **Chanco** Maule, Chile
39 R7 **Chandalar** Alaska, USA
39 R6 **Chandalar River** ≈ Alaska, USA
152 L10 **Chandan Chauki** Uttar Pradesh, N India
153 S16 **Chandannagar** *prev.* Chandernagore. West Bengal, E India
152 K10 **Chandausi** Uttar Pradesh, N India
22 M10 **Chandeleur Islands** *island group* Louisiana, S USA
22 M9 **Chandeleur Sound** *sound* N Gulf of Mexico
152 I8 **Chandīgarh** Punjab, N India
153 Q16 **Chāndil** Bihār, NE India
182 D2 **Chandler** South Australia
15 Y7 **Chandler** Quebec, SE Canada
36 L14 **Chandler** Arizona, SW USA
27 O10 **Chandler** Oklahoma, C USA
25 V7 **Chandler** Texas, SW USA
39 Q6 **Chandler River** ≈ Alaska, USA
56 H13 **Chandles, Río** ≈ E Peru
163 N9 **Chandmanī** Dornogovī, SE Mongolia
14 J13 **Chandos Lake** ◎ Ontario, SE Canada
153 U15 **Chandpur** Chittagong, C Bangladesh
154 I13 **Chandrapur** Mahārāshtra, C India
83 J15 **Changa** Southern, S Zambia
Changan *see* Xi'an, Shaanxi, China
Chang'an *see* Rong'an, Guangxi Zhuangzu Zizhiqu, China
155 G23 **Changanācheri** Kerala, SW India
83 M19 **Changane** ≈ S Mozambique
83 M16 **Changara** Tete, NW Mozambique
163 X11 **Changbai** *var.* Changbai Chaoxianzu Zizhixian. Jilin, NE China
Changbai Chaoxianzu Zizhixian *see* Changbai
163 X11 **Changbai Shan** ▲ NE China
163 V10 **Changchun** *var.* Ch'angch'un, Ch'ang-ch'un; *prev.* Hsinking. Jilin, NE China
160 M10 **Changde** Hunan, S China
161 S13 **Changhua** *Jap.* Shōka. C Taiwan
168 L10 **Changi** ✕ (Singapore) E Singapore
158 L5 **Changji** Xinjiang Uygur Zizhiqu, NW China
157 O13 **Chang Jiang** *var.* Yangtze Kiang, *Eng.* Yangtze. ≈ C China
160 L17 **Changjiang** *prev.* Shiliu. Hainan, S China
161 S8 **Changjiang Kou** *delta* E China
167 P12 **Chang, Ko** *island* S Thailand
161 Q2 **Changli** Hebei, E China
163 V10 **Changling** Jilin, NE China
161 N11 **Changsha** *var.* Ch'angsha, Ch'ang-sha. Hunan, S China
161 Q10 **Changshan** Zhejiang, SE China
163 V14 **Changshan Qundao** *island group* NE China
161 S8 **Changshu** *var.* Ch'ang-shu. Jiangsu, E China
163 V11 **Changtu** Liaoning, NE China
43 P14 **Changuinola** Bocas del Toro, NW Panama
159 N9 **Changweiliang** Qinghai, W China
160 K6 **Changwu** Shaanxi, C China
163 U13 **Changxing Dao** *island* N China
160 M9 **Changyang** Hubei, C China
163 W14 **Changyŏn** SW North Korea
161 N5 **Changzhi** Shanxi, C China
161 R8 **Changzhou** Jiangsu, E China
115 H24 **Chaniá** *var.* Hania, Khaniá, *Eng.* Canea; *anc.* Cydonia. Kríti, Greece, E Mediterranean Sea
62 J5 **Chañi, Nevado de** ▲ NW Argentina
115 H24 **Chanión, Kólpos** *gulf* Kríti, Greece, E Mediterranean Sea
Chankiri *see* Çankırı
30 M11 **Channahon** Illinois, N USA
155 H20 **Channapatna** Karnātaka, E India
97 K26 **Channel Islands** *Fr.* Îles Normandes. *island group* S English Channel
35 R16 **Channel Islands** *island group* California, W USA
13 S13 **Channel-Port aux Basques** Newfoundland, SE Canada
Channel, The *see* English Channel
97 Q23 **Channel Tunnel** *tunnel* France/UK
24 M2 **Channing** Texas, SW USA
Chantabun/Chantaburi *see* Chanthaburi
104 H3 **Chantada** Galicia, NW Spain
167 P12 **Chanthaburi** *var.* Chantabun, Chantaburi. Chantaburi, S Thailand
103 O4 **Chantilly** Oise, N France
139 V12 **Chanūn as Sa'ūdī** S Iraq
27 Q6 **Chanute** Kansas, C USA
Chanza *see* Chança, Rio
Ch'ao-an/Chaochow *see* Chaozhou
161 P8 **Chao Hu** ◎ E China
167 P11 **Chao Phraya, Mae Nam** ≈ C Thailand
163 T8 **Chaor He** ≈ NE China
Chaouèn *see* Chefchaouen
161 P14 **Chaoyang** Guangdong, S China
163 T12 **Chaoyang** Liaoning, NE China
Chaoyang *see* Huinan, Jilin, China
Chaoyang *see* Jiayin, Heilongjiang, China
161 Q14 **Chaozhou** *var.* Chaoan, Chao'an, Ch'ao-an; *prev.* Chaochow. Guangdong, SE China
58 N13 **Chapadinha** Maranhão, E Brazil
12 K12 **Chapais** Quebec, SE Canada
40 L13 **Chapala** Jalisco, SW Mexico
40 L13 **Chapala, Lago de** ◎ C Mexico
146 F13 **Chapan, Gora** ▲ C Turkmenistan
57 M18 **Chapare, Río** ≈ C Bolivia
54 E11 **Chaparral** Tolima, C Colombia
144 F9 **Chapayevo** Zapadnyy Kazakhstan, NW Kazakhstan
123 O11 **Chapayevo** Respublika Sakha (Yakutiya), NE Russian Federation
129 R6 **Chapayevsk** Samarskaya Oblast', W Russian Federation
60 H13 **Chapecó** Santa Catarina, S Brazil
60 I13 **Chapecó, Rio** ≈ S Brazil
20 J9 **Chapel Hill** Tennessee, S USA
44 J12 **Chapelton** C Jamaica
14 C8 **Chapleau** Ontario, SE Canada
14 D7 **Chapleau** ≈ Ontario, S Canada
11 T16 **Chaplin** Saskatchewan, S Canada
128 M6 **Chaplygin** Lipetskaya Oblast', W Russian Federation
117 S11 **Chaplynka** Khersons'ka Oblast', S Ukraine
9 O6 **Chapman, Cape** *headland* Nunavut, NE Canada
25 T15 **Chapman Ranch** Texas, SW USA
Chapman's *see* Okwa
21 P5 **Chapmanville** West Virginia, NE USA
28 K15 **Chappell** Nebraska, C USA
Chapra *see* Chhapra
56 D9 **Chapuli, Río** ≈ N Peru
76 I6 **Châr** *well* N Mauritania
123 P12 **Chara** Chitinskaya Oblast', S Russian Federation
123 O11 **Chara** ≈ C Russian Federation
54 G8 **Charala** Santander, C Colombia
41 N10 **Charcas** San Luis Potosí, C Mexico
25 T13 **Charco** Texas, SW USA
194 H7 **Charcot Island** *island* Antarctica
64 M8 **Charcot Seamounts** *undersea feature* E Atlantic Ocean
Chardara *see* Shardara
145 P17 **Chardarinskoye Vodokhranilishche** ▣ S Kazakhstan
31 U11 **Chardon** Ohio, N USA
44 K9 **Chardonnières** SW Haiti
146 K12 **Chardzhev** *prev.* Chardzhou, Chardzhui, Leninsk-Turkmenski, *Turkm.* Chärjew. Lebapskiy Velayat, E Turkmenistan
Chardzhevskaya Oblast' *see* Lebapskiy Velayat
Chardzhou/Chardzhui *see* Chardzhev
102 L11 **Charente** ◈ *department* W France
102 J11 **Charente** ≈ W France
102 J10 **Charente-Maritime** ◈ *department* W France
137 U12 **Ch'arents'avan** C Armenia
78 I12 **Chari** *var.* Shari. ≈ Central African Republic/Chad
78 G11 **Chari-Baguirmi** *off.* Préfecture du Chari-Baguirmi. ◈ *prefecture* SW Chad
149 Q4 **Chārīkār** Parwān, NE Afghanistan
29 V15 **Chariton** Iowa, C USA
27 U3 **Chariton River** ≈ Missouri, C USA
55 T7 **Charity** NW Guyana
31 R7 **Charity Island** *island* Michigan, N USA
Chärjew *see* Chardzhev
Chärjew Oblasty *see* Lebapskiy Velayat
Charkhlik/Charkhliq *see* Ruoqiang
99 G20 **Charleroi** Hainaut, S Belgium
11 V12 **Charles** Manitoba, C Canada
15 R10 **Charlesbourg** Quebec, SE Canada
21 Y7 **Charles, Cape** *headland* Virginia, NE USA
29 W12 **Charles City** Iowa, C USA
21 W6 **Charles City** Virginia, NE USA
103 O5 **Charles de Gaulle** ✕ (Paris) Seine-et-Marne, N France
12 K1 **Charles Island** *island* Nunavut, NE Canada
Charles Island *see* Santa María, Isla
30 K9 **Charles Mound** *hill* Illinois, N USA
185 A22 **Charles Sound** *sound* South Island, NZ
185 G15 **Charleston** West Coast, South Island, NZ
27 S11 **Charleston** Arkansas, C USA
30 M14 **Charleston** Illinois, N USA
22 L3 **Charleston** Mississippi, S USA
27 Z7 **Charleston** Missouri, C USA
21 T15 **Charleston** South Carolina, SE USA
21 Q5 **Charleston** *state capital* West Virginia, NE USA
14 L14 **Charleston Lake** ◎ Ontario, SE Canada
35 W11 **Charleston Peak** ▲ Nevada, W USA
45 W10 **Charlestown** Nevis, Saint Kitts and Nevis
31 P16 **Charlestown** Indiana, N USA
18 M9 **Charlestown** New Hampshire, NE USA
21 V3 **Charles Town** West Virginia, NE USA
181 W9 **Charleville** Queensland, E Australia
103 R3 **Charleville-Mézières** Ardennes, N France
31 P5 **Charlevoix** Michigan, N USA
31 Q6 **Charlevoix, Lake** ◎ Michigan, N USA
39 T9 **Charley River** ≈ Alaska, USA
64 J6 **Charlie-Gibbs Fracture Zone** *tectonic feature* N Atlantic Ocean
103 Q10 **Charlieu** Loire, E France
31 Q9 **Charlotte** Michigan, N USA
21 R10 **Charlotte** North Carolina, SE USA
20 I8 **Charlotte** Tennessee, S USA
25 R13 **Charlotte** Texas, SW USA
21 R10 **Charlotte** ✕ North Carolina, SE USA
45 T9 **Charlotte Amalie** *prev.* Saint Thomas. ○ (Virgin Islands (US)) Saint Thomas, N Virgin Islands (US)
21 U7 **Charlotte Court House** Virginia, NE USA
23 W14 **Charlotte Harbor** *inlet* Florida, SE USA
Charlotte Island *see* Abaiang
95 J15 **Charlottenberg** Värmland, C Sweden
Charlottenhof *see* Aegviidu
21 U5 **Charlottesville** Virginia, NE USA
Charlotte Town *see* Roseau, Dominica
Charlotte Town *see* Gouyave, Grenada
13 Q14 **Charlottetown** Prince Edward Island, Prince Edward Island, SE Canada
45 Z16 **Charlotteville** Tobago, Trinidad and Tobago
182 M11 **Charlton** Victoria, SE Australia
12 H10 **Charlton Island** *island* Nunavut, C Canada
103 T6 **Charmes** Vosges, NE France
119 F19 **Charnawchytsy** *Rus.* Chernavchitsy. Brestskaya Voblasts', SW Belarus
15 R10 **Charny** Quebec, SE Canada
149 T5 **Chārsadda** North-West Frontier Province, NW Pakistan
146 M14 **Charshanga** *prev.* Charshangy, *Turkm.* Charshangngy. Lebapskiy Velayat, E Turkmenistan
Charshangngy/Charshangy *see* Charshanga
Charsk *see* Shar
181 W6 **Charters Towers** Queensland, NE Australia
15 R12 **Chartierville** Quebec, SE Canada
102 M6 **Chartres** *anc.* Autricum, Civitas Carnutum. Eure-et-Loir, C France
145 W15 **Charyn** *Kaz.* Sharyn. Almaty, SE Kazakhstan
61 D21 **Chascomús** Buenos Aires, E Argentina
11 N16 **Chase** British Columbia, SW Canada
21 U7 **Chase City** Virginia, NE USA
19 S4 **Chase, Mount** ▲ Maine, NE USA
118 M13 **Chashniki** *Rus.* Chashniki. Vitsyebskaya Voblasts', N Belarus
115 D15 **Chásia** ▲ C Greece
29 V9 **Chaska** Minnesota, N USA
185 D25 **Chaslands Mistake** *headland* South Island, NZ
127 R11 **Chasovo** Respublika Komi, NW Russian Federation
Chasovo *see* Vazhgort
126 H14 **Chastova** Novgorodskaya Oblast', NW Russian Federation
143 R3 **Chāt** Golestān, N Iran
Chatak *see* Chhatak
39 R9 **Chatanika** Alaska, USA
39 R9 **Chatanika River** ≈ Alaska, USA
147 T8 **Chat-Bazar** Talasskaya Oblast', NW Kyrgyzstan
45 Y14 **Chateaubelair** Saint Vincent, W Saint Vincent and the Grenadines
102 J7 **Châteaubriant** Loire-Atlantique, NW France
103 Q8 **Château-Chinon** Nièvre, C France
108 C10 **Château d'Oex** Vaud, W Switzerland
102 L7 **Château-du-Loir** Sarthe, NW France
102 M6 **Châteaudun** Eure-et-Loir, C France
102 K7 **Château-Gontier** Mayenne, NW France
15 O13 **Châteauguay** Quebec, SE Canada
102 F6 **Châteaulin** Finistère, NW France
103 N9 **Châteaumeillant** Cher, C France
102 K11 **Châteauneuf-sur-Charente** Charente, W France
102 M7 **Château-Renault** Indre-et-Loire, C France
103 N9 **Châteauroux** *prev.* Indreville. Indre, C France
103 T5 **Château-Salins** Moselle, NE France
103 P4 **Château-Thierry** Aisne, N France
99 H21 **Châtelet** Hainaut, S Belgium
Châtelherault *see* Châtellerault
102 L9 **Châtellerault** *var.* Châtelherault. Vienne, W France
29 X10 **Chatfield** Minnesota, N USA
13 O14 **Chatham** New Brunswick, SE Canada
14 D17 **Chatham** Ontario, S Canada
97 P22 **Chatham** SE England, UK
30 K14 **Chatham** Illinois, N USA
21 T7 **Chatham** Virginia, NE USA
63 F22 **Chatham, Isla** *island* S Chile
175 R12 **Chatham Island** *island* Chatham Islands, NZ
Chatham Island *see* San Cristóbal, Isla
Chatham Island Rise *see* Chatham Rise
192 L12 **Chatham Islands** *island group* NZ, SW Pacific Ocean
175 Q12 **Chatham Rise** *var.* Chatham Island Rise. *undersea feature* S Pacific Ocean
39 X13 **Chatham Strait** *strait* Alaska, USA
Chathóir, Rinn *see* Cahore Point
102 M9 **Châtillon-sur-Indre** Indre, C France
103 Q7 **Châtillon-sur-Seine** Côte d'Or, C France
147 S8 **Chatkal** *Uzb.* Chotqol. ≈ Kyrgyzstan/Uzbekistan
147 R9 **Chatkal Range** *Rus.* Chatkal'skiy Khrebet. ▲ Kyrgyzstan/Uzbekistan
Chatkal'skiy Khrebet *see* Chatkal Range
23 N7 **Chatom** Alabama, S USA
Chatrapur *see* Chhatrapur
143 S10 **Chatrūd** Kermān, C Iran
23 S2 **Chatsworth** Georgia, SE USA
Chāttagām *see* Chittagong
23 S8 **Chattahoochee** Florida, SE USA
23 R8 **Chattahoochee River** ≈ SE USA
20 L10 **Chattanooga** Tennessee, S USA
147 V10 **Chatyr-Kël', Ozero** ◎ C Kyrgyzstan
147 W9 **Chatyr-Tash** Narynskaya Oblast', C Kyrgyzstan
15 R12 **Chaudière** ≈ Quebec, SE Canada
167 S14 **Châu Đôc** *var.* Chauphu, Chau Phu. An Giang, S Vietnam
152 D13 **Chauhtan** *prev.* Chohtan. Rājasthān, NW India
115 F15 **Chauk** Magwe, W Burma
103 R6 **Chaumont** *prev.* Chaumont-en-Bassigny. Haute-Marne, N France
Chaumont-en-Bassigny *see* Chaumont
123 T5 **Chaunskaya Guba** *bay* NE Russian Federation
103 P3 **Chauny** Aisne, N France
Châu Ô *see* Binh Sơn
Chau Phu *see* Châu Đôc
102 I5 **Chausey, Îles** *island group* N France
Chausy *see* Chavusy
18 C11 **Chautauqua Lake** ◎ New York, NE USA
102 L9 **Chauvigny** Vienne, W France
126 L6 **Chavan'ga** Murmanskaya Oblast', NW Russian Federation
14 K10 **Chavannes, Lac** ◎ Quebec, SE Canada

Chavantes, Represa de *see* Xavantes, Represa de
61 D15 **Chavarría** Corrientes, NE Argentina
Chavash Respubliki *see* Chuvashskaya Respublika
104 I5 **Chaves** *anc.* Aquae Flaviae. Vila Real, N Portugal
Chávez, Isla *see* Santa Cruz, Isla
82 G13 **Chavuma** North Western, NW Zambia
119 O16 **Chavusy** *Rus.* Chausy. Mahilyowskaya Voblasts', E Belarus
145 Q16 **Chayan** Yuzhnyy Kazakhstan, S Kazakhstan
147 U8 **Chayek** Narynskaya Oblast', C Kyrgyzstan
139 T6 **Chāy Khānah** E Iraq
127 T16 **Chaykovskiy** Permskaya Oblast', NW Russian Federation
167 T12 **Chbar** Môndól Kiri, E Cambodia
23 Q4 **Cheaha Mountain** ▲ Alabama, S USA
Cheatharlach *see* Carlow
21 S2 **Cheat River** ≈ NE USA
111 A16 **Cheb** *Ger.* Eger. Karlovarský Kraj, W Czech Republic
129 Q3 **Cheboksary** Chuvashskaya Respublika, W Russian Federation
31 Q5 **Cheboygan** Michigan, N USA
Chechaouèn *see* Chefchaouen
Chechenia *see* Chechenskaya Respublika
129 O15 **Chechenskaya Respublika** *Eng.* Chechenia, Chechnia, *Rus.* Chechnya. ◈ *autonomous republic* SW Russian Federation
67 N4 **Chech, Erg** *desert* Algeria/Mali
Chechersk *see* Chachersk
Chechevichi *see* Chachevichy
Che-chiang *see* Zhejiang
Chechnia/Chechnya *see* Chechenskaya Respublika
163 Y15 **Chech'ŏn** *Jap.* Teisen. N South Korea
111 L15 **Chęciny** Świętokrzyskie, S Poland
27 Q10 **Checotah** Oklahoma, C USA
13 R15 **Chedabucto Bay** *inlet* Nova Scotia, E Canada
166 J7 **Cheduba Island** *island* W Burma
37 T5 **Cheesman Lake** ⊞ Colorado, C USA
195 S16 **Cheetham, Cape** *headland* Antarctica
74 G5 **Chefchaouen** *var.* Chaouèn, Chechaouèn, *Sp.* Xauen. N Morocco
Chefoo *see* Yantai
38 M12 **Chefornak** Alaska, USA
123 R13 **Chegdomyn** Khabarovskiy Kray, SE Russian Federation
76 M4 **Chegga** Tiris Zemmour, NE Mauritania
Cheghcheran *see* Chaghcharān
32 G9 **Chehalis** Washington, NW USA
32 G9 **Chehalis River** ≈ Washington, NW USA
148 M6 **Chehel Abdālān, Kūh-e** *var.* Chalap Dalam, *Pash.* Chalap Dalan. ▲▲ C Afghanistan
115 D14 **Cheimadítis, Límni** ◎ N Greece
103 U15 **Cheiron, Mont** ▲ SE France
163 X17 **Cheju** *Jap.* Saishū. S South Korea
163 Y17 **Cheju** × S South Korea
163 Y17 **Cheju-do** *Jap.* Saishū; *prev.* Quelpart. *island* S South Korea
163 X17 **Cheju-haehyŏp** *strait* S South Korea
Chekiang *see* Zhejiang
Chekichler *see* Chekishlyar
146 B13 **Chekishlyar** *Turkm.* Chekichler. Balkanskiy Velayat, W Turkmenistan
188 F8 **Chelab** Babeldaob, N Palau
147 N11 **Chelak** *Rus.* Chelek. Samarqand Wiloyati, C Uzbekistan
32 J7 **Chelan, Lake** ⊞ Washington, NW USA
Chelek *see* Chelak
146 A11 **Cheleken** Balkanskiy Velayat, W Turkmenistan
Chélif/Chéliff *see* Chelif, Oued
74 J5 **Chelif, Oued** *var.* Chélif, Chéliff, Chellif, Shellif. ≈ N Algeria
144 K12 **Chelkar** Aktyubinsk, W Kazakhstan
Chelkar, Ozero *see* Shalkar, Ozero
Chellif *see* Chelif, Oued
111 P14 **Chełm** *Rus.* Kholm. Lubelskie, SE Poland
110 I9 **Chełmno** *Ger.* Culm, Kulm. Kujawski-pomorskie, C Poland
14 F10 **Chelmsford** Ontario, S Canada
97 P21 **Chelmsford** E England, UK
110 J9 **Chełmża** *Ger.* Culmsee. Kujawski-pomorskie, C Poland
27 Q8 **Chelsea** Oklahoma, C USA
18 M8 **Chelsea** Vermont, NE USA
97 L21 **Cheltenham** C England, UK
105 R9 **Chelva** País Valenciano, E Spain
122 G11 **Chelyabinsk** Chelyabinskaya Oblast', C Russian Federation
122 F11 **Chelyabinskaya Oblast'** ◈ *province* C Russian Federation
123 N5 **Chelyuskin, Mys** *headland* N Russian Federation
41 Y12 **Chemax** Yucatán, SE Mexico
83 N16 **Chemba** Sofala, C Mozambique
82 J13 **Chembe** Luapula, NE Zambia
146 J17 **Chemenibit** Maryyskiy Velayat, S Turkmenistan
Chemerisy *see* Chamyarysy
116 K7 **Chemerivtsi** Khmel'nyts'ka Oblast', W Ukraine
102 J8 **Chemillé** Maine-et-Loire, NW France
173 X17 **Chemin Grenier** S Mauritius
101 N16 **Chemnitz** *prev.* Karl-Marx-Stadt. Sachsen, E Germany
Chemulpo *see* Inch'ŏn
32 H14 **Chemult** Oregon, NW USA
18 G12 **Chemung River** ≈ New York/Pennsylvania, NE USA
149 U8 **Chenāb** ≈ India/Pakistan
39 S9 **Chena Hot Springs** Alaska, USA
18 I11 **Chenango River** ≈ New York, NE USA
168 J7 **Chenderoh, Tasik** ◎ Peninsular Malaysia
15 Q11 **Chêne, Rivière du** ≈ Quebec, SE Canada
32 L8 **Cheney** Washington, NW USA
26 M6 **Cheney Reservoir** ⊞ Kansas, C USA
Chengchiatun *see* Liaoyuan
Ch'eng-chou/Chengchow *see* Zhengzhou
161 P1 **Chengde** *var.* Jehol. Hebei, E China
160 I9 **Chengdu** *var.* Chengtu, Ch'eng-tu. Sichuan, C China
161 Q14 **Chenghai** Guangdong, S China
Chenghsien *see* Zhengzhou
160 L17 **Chengmai** Hainan, S China
Chengtu/Ch'eng-tu *see* Chengdu
159 W12 **Chengxian** *var.* Cheng Xian. Gansu, C China
Chenkiang *see* Zhenjiang
155 J19 **Chennai** *prev.* Madras. Tamil Nādu, S India
155 J19 **Chennai** × Tamil Nādu, S India
103 R8 **Chenôve** Côte d'Or, C France
Chenstokhov *see* Częstochowa
160 L11 **Chenxi** Hunan, S China
Chen Xian/Chenxian/Chen Xiang *see* Chenzhou
161 N12 **Chenzhou** *var.* Chenxian, Chen Xian, Chen Xiang. Hunan, S China
167 U12 **Cheo Reo** *var.* A Yun Pa. Gia Lai, S Vietnam
114 I11 **Chepelare** Smolyan, S Bulgaria
114 I11 **Chepelarska Reka** ≈ S Bulgaria
56 B11 **Chepén** La Libertad, C Peru
62 J10 **Chepes** La Rioja, C Argentina
161 O15 **Chep Lap Kok** × (Hong Kong) S China
43 U14 **Chepo** Panamá, C Panama
Chepping Wycombe *see* High Wycombe
127 R14 **Cheptsa** ≈ NW Russian Federation
30 K3 **Chequamegon Point** *headland* Wisconsin, N USA
103 O8 **Cher** ◈ *department* C France
102 M8 **Cher** ≈ C France
Cherangani Hills *see* Cherangany Hills
81 H17 **Cherangany Hills** *var.* Cherangani Hills. ▲▲ W Kenya
21 S11 **Cheraw** South Carolina, SE USA
102 I3 **Cherbourg** *anc.* Carusbur. Manche, N France
129 R5 **Cherdakly** Ul'yanovskaya Oblast', W Russian Federation
127 U12 **Cherdyn'** Permskaya Oblast', NW Russian Federation
126 J14 **Cherekha** ≈ W Russian Federation
122 M13 **Cheremkhovo** Irkutskaya Oblast', S Russian Federation
Cheren *see* Keren
126 K14 **Cherepovets** Vologodskaya Oblast', NW Russian Federation
127 O11 **Cherevkovo** Arkhangel'skaya Oblast', NW Russian Federation
74 I6 **Chergui, Chott ech** *salt lake* NW Algeria
Cherikov *see* Cherykaw
117 P6 **Cherkas'ka Oblast'** *var.* Cherkasy, *Rus.* Cherkasskaya Oblast'. ◈ *province* C Ukraine
Cherkasskaya Oblast' *see* Cherkas'ka Oblast'
Cherkassy *see* Cherkasy
117 Q6 **Cherkasy** *Rus.* Cherkassy. Cherkas'ka Oblast', C Ukraine
Cherkasy *see* Cherkas'ka Oblast'
128 M15 **Cherkessk** Karachayevo-Cherkesskaya Respublika, SW Russian Federation
122 H12 **Cherlak** Omskaya Oblast', C Russian Federation
122 H12 **Cherlakskiy** Omskaya Oblast', C Russian Federation
127 U13 **Chermoz** Permskaya Oblast', NW Russian Federation
Chernavchitsy *see* Charnawchytsy
127 T3 **Chernaya** Nenetskiy Avtonomnyy Okrug, NW Russian Federation
127 T4 **Chernaya** ≈ NW Russian Federation
Chernigov *see* Chernihiv
Chernigovskaya Oblast' *see* Chernihivs'ka Oblast'
117 Q2 **Chernihiv** *Rus.* Chernigov. Chernihivs'ka Oblast', NE Ukraine
Chernihiv *see* Chernihivs'ka Oblast'
117 V9 **Chernihivka** Zaporiz'ka Oblast', SE Ukraine
117 P2 **Chernihivs'ka Oblast'** *var.* Chernihiv, *Rus.* Chernigovskaya Oblast'. ◈ *province* NE Ukraine
114 I9 **Cherni Osŭm** ≈ N Bulgaria
116 J8 **Chernivets'ka Oblast'** *var.* Chernivtsi, *Rus.* Chernovitskaya Oblast'. ◈ *province* W Ukraine
114 I9 **Cherni Vit** ≈ NW Bulgaria
114 G10 **Cherni Vrŭkh** ▲ W Bulgaria
116 K8 **Chernivtsi** *Ger.* Czernowitz, *Rom.* Cernăuţi, *Rus.* Chernovtsy. Chernivets'ka Oblast', W Ukraine
116 M7 **Chernivtsi** Vinnyts'ka Oblast', C Ukraine
Chernivtsi *see* Chernivets'ka Oblast'
Chernobyl' *see* Chornobyl'
Cherno More *see* Black Sea
Chernomorskoye *see* Chornomors'ke
145 T7 **Chernoretskoye** Pavlodar, NE Kazakhstan
Chernovitskaya Oblast' *see* Chernivets'ka Oblast'
Chernovtsy *see* Chernivtsi
145 U8 **Chernoye** Pavlodar, NE Kazakhstan
Chernoye More *see* Black Sea
127 U16 **Chernushka** Permskaya Oblast', NW Russian Federation
117 N4 **Chernyakhiv** *Rus.* Chernyakhov. Zhytomyrs'ka Oblast', N Ukraine
Chernyakhov *see* Chernyakhiv
119 C14 **Chernyakhovsk** *Ger.* Insterburg. Kaliningradskaya Oblast', W Russian Federation
128 K8 **Chernyanka** Belgorodskaya Oblast', W Russian Federation
127 V5 **Chernyshëva, Gryada** ▲▲ NW Russian Federation
144 J14 **Chernyshëva, Zaliv** *gulf* SW Kazakhstan
123 O10 **Chernyshevskiy** Respublika Sakha (Yakutiya), NE Russian Federation
129 P13 **Chërnyye Zemli** *plain* SW Russian Federation
Chërnyy Irtysh *see* Ertix He
129 V7 **Chernyy Otrog** Orenburgskaya Oblast', W Russian Federation
29 T12 **Cherokee** Iowa, C USA
26 M8 **Cherokee** Oklahoma, C USA
25 R9 **Cherokee** Texas, SW USA
21 O8 **Cherokee Lake** ⊞ Tennessee, S USA
Cherokees, Lake O' The *see* Grand Lake O' The Cherokees
44 H1 **Cherokee Sound** Great Abaco, N Bahamas
153 V13 **Cherrapunji** Meghālaya, NE India
28 L9 **Cherry Creek** ≈ South Dakota, N USA
18 J16 **Cherry Hill** New Jersey, NE USA
27 Q7 **Cherryvale** Kansas, C USA
21 Q10 **Cherryville** North Carolina, SE USA
Cherski Range *see* Cherskogo, Khrebet
123 T6 **Cherskiy** Respublika Sakha (Yakutiya), NE Russian Federation
123 R8 **Cherskogo, Khrebet** *var.* Cherski Range. ▲▲ NE Russian Federation
Cherso *see* Cres
128 L10 **Chertkovo** Rostovskaya Oblast', SW Russian Federation
Cherven' *see* Chervyen'
114 H8 **Cherven Bryag** Pleven, N Bulgaria
116 M4 **Chervonoarmiys'k** Zhytomyrs'ka Oblast', N Ukraine
Chervonograd *see* Chervonohrad
116 I4 **Chervonohrad** *Rus.* Chervonograd. L'vivs'ka Oblast', NW Ukraine
117 W6 **Chervonooskil's'ke Vodoskhovyshche** *Rus.* Krasnoosol'skoye Vodokhranilishche. ⊞ NE Ukraine
Chervonoye, Ozero *see* Chyrvonaye, Vozyera
117 S4 **Chervonozavods'ke** Poltavs'ka Oblast', C Ukraine
119 L16 **Chervyen'** *Rus.* Cherven'. Minskaya Voblasts', C Belarus
119 P16 **Cherykaw** *Rus.* Cherikov. Mahilyowskaya Voblasts', E Belarus
31 R9 **Chesaning** Michigan, N USA
21 X5 **Chesapeake Bay** *inlet* NE USA
Cheshevlya *see* Tsyeshawlya
97 K18 **Cheshire** *cultural region* C England, UK
127 P5 **Chëshskaya Guba** *var.* Archangel Bay, Chesha Bay, Dvina Bay. *bay* NW Russian Federation
14 F14 **Chesley** Ontario, S Canada
21 Q10 **Chesnee** South Carolina, SE USA
97 K18 **Chester** *Wel.* Caerleon; *hist.* Legeaceaster, *Lat.* Deva, Devana Castra. C England, UK
35 O4 **Chester** California, W USA
30 K16 **Chester** Illinois, N USA
33 S7 **Chester** Montana, NW USA
18 I16 **Chester** Pennsylvania, NE USA
21 R11 **Chester** South Carolina, SE USA
25 X9 **Chester** Texas, SW USA
21 W6 **Chester** Virginia, NE USA
21 R11 **Chester** West Virginia, NE USA
97 M18 **Chesterfield** C England, UK
21 S11 **Chesterfield** South Carolina, SE USA
21 W6 **Chesterfield** Virginia, NE USA
192 J9 **Chesterfield, Îles** *island group* NW New Caledonia
9 O9 **Chesterfield Inlet** Nunavut, NW Canada
9 O9 **Chesterfield Inlet** *inlet* Nunavut, N Canada
21 Y3 **Chester River** ≈ Delaware/Maryland, NE USA
21 X3 **Chestertown** Maryland, NE USA
19 R4 **Chesuncook Lake** ◎ Maine, NE USA
30 J5 **Chetek** Wisconsin, N USA
13 R14 **Chéticamp** Nova Scotia, SE Canada
27 Q8 **Chetopa** Kansas, C USA
41 Y14 **Chetumal** *var.* Payo Obispo. Quintana Roo, SE Mexico
Chetumal, Bahia/Chetumal, Bahía de *see* Chetumal Bay
42 G1 **Chetumal Bay** *var.* Bahia Chetumal, Bahía de Chetumal. *bay* Belize/Mexico
8 M13 **Chetwynd** British Columbia, W Canada
38 M11 **Chevak** Alaska, USA
36 M12 **Chevelon Creek** ≈ Arizona, SW USA
185 J17 **Cheviot** Canterbury, South Island, NZ
96 L13 **Cheviot Hills** *hill range* England/Scotland, UK
96 L13 **Cheviot, The** ▲ NE England, UK
14 M11 **Chevreuil, Lac du** ◎ Quebec, SE Canada
81 I16 **Ch'ew Bahir** *var.* Lake Stefanie. ◎ Ethiopia/Kenya
32 L7 **Chewelah** Washington, NW USA
26 K10 **Cheyenne** Oklahoma, C USA
33 Z17 **Cheyenne** *state capital* Wyoming, C USA
26 L5 **Cheyenne Bottoms** ⊞ Kansas, C USA
16 J8 **Cheyenne River** ≈ South Dakota/Wyoming, N USA
37 W5 **Cheyenne Wells** Colorado, C USA
108 C9 **Cheyres** Vaud, W Switzerland
Chezdi-Oşorheiu *see* Târgu Secuiesc
153 P13 **Chhapra** *prev.* Chapra. Bihār, N India
153 V13 **Chhatak** *var.* Chatak. Chittagong, NE Bangladesh
154 J9 **Chhatarpur** Madhya Pradesh, C India
154 N13 **Chhatrapur** *prev.* Chatrapur; Orissa, E India
154 L12 **Chhattīsgarh** *plain* C India
154 I11 **Chhindwāra** Madhya Pradesh, C India
153 T12 **Chhukha** SW Bhutan
161 S14 **Chiai** *var.* Chia-i, Chiayi, Kiayi, Jiayi, *Jap.* Kagi. C Taiwan
Chia-mu-ssu *see* Jiamusi
83 B15 **Chiange** *Port.* Vila de Almoster. Huíla, SW Angola
Chiang-hsi *see* Jiangxi
161 S12 **Chiang Kai-shek** × (T'aipei) N Taiwan
167 P8 **Chiang Khan** Loei, E Thailand
167 O7 **Chiang Mai** *var.* Chiangmai, Chiengmai, Kiangmai. Chiang Mai, NW Thailand
167 O7 **Chiang Mai** × Chiang Mai, NW Thailand
167 O6 **Chiang Rai** *var.* Chianpai, Chienrai, Muang Chiang Rai. Chiang Rai, NW Thailand
Chiang-su *see* Jiangsu
Chianning/Chian-ning *see* Nanjing
Chianpai *see* Chiang Rai
106 G12 **Chianti** *cultural region* C Italy
Chiapa *see* Chiapa de Corzo
41 U16 **Chiapa de Corzo** *var.* Chiapa. Chiapas, SE Mexico
41 V16 **Chiapas** ◈ *state* SE Mexico
106 J12 **Chiaravalle** Marche, C Italy
107 N22 **Chiaravalle Centrale** Calabria, SW Italy
106 E7 **Chiari** Lombardia, N Italy
108 H12 **Chiasso** Ticino, S Switzerland
137 S9 **Chiat'ura** C Georgia
41 P15 **Chiautla** *var.* Chiautla de Tapia. Puebla, S Mexico
Chiautla de Tapia *see* Chiautla
106 D10 **Chiavari** Liguria, NW Italy
106 E6 **Chiavenna** Lombardia, N Italy
Chiayi *see* Chiai
Chiazza *see* Piazza Armerina
165 O13 **Chiba** *var.* Tiba. Chiba, Honshū, S Japan
165 O14 **Chiba** *off.* Chiba-ken, *var.* Tiba. ◈ *prefecture* Honshū, S Japan
83 M18 **Chibabava** Sofala, C Mozambique
83 B15 **Chibia** *Port.* João de Almeida, Vila João de Almeida. Huíla, SW Angola
83 M18 **Chiboma** Sofala, C Mozambique
82 J12 **Chibondo** Luapula, N Zambia
82 K11 **Chibote** Luapula, NE Zambia
12 K12 **Chibougamau** Quebec, SE Canada
164 H11 **Chiburi-jima** *island* Oki-shotō, SW Japan
83 M20 **Chibuto** Gaza, S Mozambique
31 N11 **Chicago** Illinois, N USA
31 N11 **Chicago Heights** Illinois, N USA
15 W6 **Chic-Chocs, Monts** *Eng.* Shickshock Mountains. ▲▲ Quebec, SE Canada
39 W13 **Chichagof Island** *island* Alexander Archipelago, Alaska, USA
57 K20 **Chichas, Cordillera de** ▲▲ SW Bolivia
41 X12 **Chichén-Itzá, Ruinas** *ruins* Yucatán, SE Mexico
97 N23 **Chichester** SE England, UK
42 C5 **Chichicastenango** Quiché, W Guatemala
42 I9 **Chichigalpa** Chinandega, NW Nicaragua
Ch'i-ch'i-ha-erh *see* Qiqihar
165 X16 **Chichijima-rettō** *Eng.* Beechy Group. *island group* SE Japan
54 K4 **Chichiriviche** Falcón, N Venezuela
39 R11 **Chickaloon** Alaska, USA
20 L10 **Chickamauga Lake** ⊞ Tennessee, S USA
23 N7 **Chickasawhay River** ≈ Mississippi, S USA
26 M11 **Chickasha** Oklahoma, C USA
39 T9 **Chicken** Alaska, USA
104 J16 **Chiclana de la Frontera** Andalucía, S Spain
56 B11 **Chiclayo** Lambayeque, NW Peru
35 N5 **Chico** California, W USA
83 L15 **Chicoa** Tete, NW Mozambique
83 M20 **Chicomo** Gaza, S Mozambique
18 M11 **Chicopee** Massachusetts, NE USA
63 I19 **Chico, Río** ≈ SE Argentina
63 I21 **Chico, Río** ≈ S Argentina
27 W14 **Chicot, Lake** ◎ Arkansas, C USA
15 R7 **Chicoutimi** Quebec, SE Canada
15 Q8 **Chicoutimi** ≈ Quebec, SE Canada
83 L19 **Chicualacuala** Gaza, SW Mozambique
83 B14 **Chicuma** Benguela, C Angola
155 J21 **Chidambaram** Tamil Nādu, SE India
196 K13 **Chidley, Cape** *headland* Newfoundland, E Canada
101 N24 **Chiemsee** ◎ SE Germany
Chiengmai *see* Chiang Mai
Chienrai *see* Chiang Rai
106 B8 **Chieri** Piemonte, NW Italy
106 F8 **Chiese** ≈ N Italy
107 K14 **Chieti** *var.* Teate. Abruzzo, C Italy
99 E19 **Chièvres** Hainaut, SW Belgium
163 S12 **Chifeng** *var.* Ulanhad. Nei Mongol Zizhiqu, N China
82 F13 **Chifumage** ≈ E Angola
82 M13 **Chifunda** Eastern, NE Zambia
145 S14 **Chiganak** *var.* Čiganak. Zhambyl, SE Kazakhstan
39 P15 **Chiginagak, Mount** ▲ Alaska, USA
Chigirin *see* Chyhyryn
41 P13 **Chignahuapan** Puebla, S Mexico
39 O15 **Chignik** Alaska, USA
83 M19 **Chigombe** ≈ S Mozambique
54 D7 **Chigorodó** Antioquia, NW Colombia
83 M19 **Chigubo** Gaza, S Mozambique
162 D6 **Chihertey** Bayan-Ölgiy, W Mongolia
Chih-fu *see* Yantai
Chihli *see* Hebei
Chihli, Gulf of *see* Bo Hai
40 J6 **Chihuahua** Chihuahua, NW Mexico
40 I6 **Chihuahua** ◈ *state* N Mexico
145 O15 **Chiili** Kzylorda, S Kazakhstan
26 M7 **Chikaskia River** ≈ Kansas/Oklahoma, C USA
155 H19 **Chik Ballāpur** Karnātaka, W India
126 G15 **Chikhachevo** Pskovskaya Oblast', W Russian Federation
155 F19 **Chikmagalūr** Karnātaka, W India
131 V7 **Chikoy** ≈ C Russian Federation
83 J15 **Chikumbi** Lusaka, C Zambia
82 M13 **Chikwa** Eastern, NE Zambia
Chikwana *see* Chikwawa
83 N15 **Chikwawa** *var.* Chikwana. Southern, S Malawi
155 J16 **Chilakalūrupet** Andhra Pradesh, E India
146 L14 **Chilan** Lebapskiy Velayat, E Turkmenistan
Chilapa *see* Chilapa de Alvarez
41 P16 **Chilapa de Alvarez** *var.* Chilapa. Guerrero, S Mexico
155 J25 **Chilaw** North Western Province, W Sri Lanka
57 D15 **Chilca** Lima, W Peru
23 Q4 **Childersburg** Alabama, S USA
25 P4 **Childress** Texas, SW USA
63 G14 **Chile** *off.* Republic of Chile. ◆ *republic* SW South America
47 R10 **Chile Basin** *undersea feature* E Pacific Ocean
63 H20 **Chile Chico** Aisén, W Chile
62 I9 **Chilecito** La Rioja, NW Argentina
62 H12 **Chilecito** Mendoza, W Argentina
83 L14 **Chilembwe** Eastern, E Zambia
193 S11 **Chile Rise** *undersea feature* SE Pacific Ocean
117 N13 **Chilia Braţul** ≈ SE Romania
Chilia-Nouă *see* Kiliya
145 V15 **Chilik** Almaty, SE Kazakhstan
145 V15 **Chilik** ≈ SE Kazakhstan
154 O13 **Chilika Lake** *var.* Chilka Lake. ◎ E India
82 J13 **Chililabombwe** Copperbelt, C Zambia
Chi-lin *see* Jilin
Chilka Lake *see* Chilika Lake
8 H9 **Chilkoot Pass** *pass* British Columbia, W Canada
Chill Ala, Cuan *see* Killala Bay
62 G13 **Chillán** Bío Bío, C Chile
61 C22 **Chillar** Buenos Aires, E Argentina
Chill Chiaráin, Cuan *see* Kilkieran Bay
30 K12 **Chillicothe** Illinois, N USA
27 S3 **Chillicothe** Missouri, C USA
31 S14 **Chillicothe** Ohio, N USA
25 Q4 **Chillicothe** Texas, SW USA
10 M17 **Chilliwack** British Columbia, SW Canada
Chill Mhantáin, Ceann *see* Wicklow Head
Chill Mhantáin, Sléibhte *see* Wicklow Mountains
108 C10 **Chillon** Vaud, W Switzerland
146 C11 **Chil'mamedkum, Peski** *Turkm.* Chilmämetgum. *desert* W Turkmenistan
Chilmämetgum *see* Chil'mamedkum, Peski
63 F17 **Chiloé, Isla de** *var.* Isla Grande de Chiloé. *island* W Chile
32 H15 **Chiloquin** Oregon, NW USA
41 O16 **Chilpancingo** *var.* Chilpancingo de los Bravos. Guerrero, S Mexico
Chilpancingo de los Bravos *see* Chilpancingo
97 N21 **Chiltern Hills** *hill range* S England, UK
30 M7 **Chilton** Wisconsin, N USA
82 F11 **Chiluage** Lunda Sul, NE Angola
82 N12 **Chilumba** *prev.* Deep Bay. Northern, N Malawi
161 T12 **Chilung** *var.* Keelung, *Jap.* Kirun, Kirun'; *prev. Sp.* Santissima Trinidad. N Taiwan
83 N15 **Chilwa, Lake** *var.* Lago Chirua, Lake Shirwa. ◎ SE Malawi
167 R10 **Chi, Mae Nam** ≈ E Thailand
42 C6 **Chimaltenango** Chimaltenango, C Guatemala
42 A2 **Chimaltenango** *off.* Departamento de Chimaltenango. ◈ *department* S Guatemala
43 V15 **Chimán** Panamá, E Panama
83 M17 **Chimanimani** *prev.* Mandidzudzure, Melsetter. Manicaland, E Zimbabwe
99 G22 **Chimay** Hainaut, S Belgium
37 S10 **Chimayo** New Mexico, SW USA
Chimbay *see* Chimboy
56 A13 **Chimborazo** ◈ *province* C Ecuador
56 C7 **Chimborazo** ⛰ C Ecuador
56 C12 **Chimbote** Ancash, W Peru
146 H7 **Chimboy** *Rus.* Chimbay. Qoraqalpoghiston Respublikasi, NW Uzbekistan
186 D7 **Chimbu** ◈ *province* C PNG
54 F6 **Chimichagua** Cesar, N Colombia
Chimishliya *see* Cimişlia
Chimkent *see* Shymkent
Chimkentskaya Oblast' *see* Yuzhnyy Kazakhstan
28 I14 **Chimney Rock** *rock* Nebraska, C USA
83 M17 **Chimoio** Manica, C Mozambique
82 K11 **Chimpembe** Northern, NE Zambia
41 O8 **China** Nuevo León, NE Mexico
156 M9 **China** *off.* People's Republic of China, *Chin.* Chung-hua Jen-min Kung-ho-kuo, Zhonghua Renmin Gongheguo; *prev.* Chinese Empire. ◆ *republic* E Asia
19 Q7 **China Lake** ◎ Maine, NE USA
42 F8 **Chinameca** San Miguel, E El Salvador
Chi-nan/Chinan *see* Jinan
42 H9 **Chinandega** Chinandega, NW Nicaragua
42 H9 **Chinandega** ◈ *department* NW Nicaragua
China, People's Republic of *see* China
China, Republic of *see* Taiwan
24 J11 **Chinati Mountains** ▲▲ Texas, SW USA
Chinaz *see* Chinoz
57 E15 **Chincha Alta** Ica, SW Peru
11 N11 **Chinchaga** ≈ Alberta, SW Canada
Chin-chiang *see* Quanzhou
Chinchilla *see* Chinchilla de Monte Aragón
105 Q11 **Chinchilla de Monte Aragón** *var.* Chinchilla. Castilla-La Mancha, C Spain
54 D10 **Chinchiná** Caldas, W Colombia
105 O8 **Chinchón** Madrid, C Spain
41 Z14 **Chinchorro, Banco** *island* SE Mexico
Chin-chou/Chinchow *see* Jinzhou
21 Z5 **Chincoteague** Assateague Island, Virginia, NE USA
83 O17 **Chinde** Zambézia, NE Mozambique
163 X17 **Chin-do** *Jap.* Chin-tō. *island* SW South Korea
159 R13 **Chindu** Qinghai, C China
166 M2 **Chindwin** ≈ N Burma
Chinese Empire *see* China
146 L10 **Chingeldi** *Rus.* Chingildi. Nawoiy Wiloyati, N Uzbekistan
Ch'ing Hai *see* Qinghai Hu
Chinghai *see* Qinghai
Chingildi *see* Chingeldi
144 H9 **Chingirlau** *Kaz.* Shyngghyrlaū. Zapadnyy Kazakhstan, W Kazakhstan
82 J13 **Chingola** Copperbelt, C Zambia
Ching-Tao/Ch'ing-tao *see* Qingdao
82 C13 **Chinguar** Huambo, C Angola
76 I7 **Chinguețți** *var.* Chinguetti. Adrar, C Mauritania
163 Z16 **Chinhae** *Jap.* Chinkai. S South Korea
166 K4 **Chin Hills** ▲▲ W Burma
83 K16 **Chinhoyi** *prev.* Sinoia. Mashonaland West, N Zimbabwe
Chinhsien *see* Jinzhou
39 Q14 **Chiniak, Cape** *headland* Kodiak Island, Alaska, USA
14 G10 **Chiniguchi Lake** ◎ Ontario, S Canada
149 U8 **Chiniot** Punjab, NE Pakistan
163 Y16 **Chinju** *Jap.* Shinshū. S South Korea
Chinkai *see* Chinhae
78 M13 **Chinko** ≈ E Central African Republic
37 O9 **Chinle** Arizona, SW USA
161 R13 **Chinmen Tao** *var.* Jinmen Dao, Quemoy. *island* W Taiwan
Chinnchâr *see* Shinshār
Chinnereth *see* Tiberias, Lake
164 C12 **Chino** *var.* Tino. Nagano, Honshū, S Japan

102 L8 **Chinon** Indre-et-Loire, C France
33 T7 **Chinook** Montana, NW USA
Chinook State see Washington
192 L4 **Chinook Trough** undersea feature N Pacific Ocean
36 K11 **Chino Valley** Arizona, SW USA
147 P10 **Chinoz** Rus. Chinaz. Toshkent Wiloyati, E Uzbekistan
82 L12 **Chinsali** Northern, NE Zambia
166 K5 **Chin State** ❖ state W Burma
Chinsura see Chunchura
Chin-tō see Chin-do
54 E6 **Chinú** Córdoba, NW Colombia
99 K24 **Chiny, Forêt de** forest SE Belgium
83 M15 **Chioco** Tete, NW Mozambique
106 H8 **Chioggia** anc. Fossa Claudia. Veneto, NE Italy
114 H12 **Chionótrypa** ▲ NE Greece
115 L18 **Chíos** var. Hios, Khíos, It. Scio, Turk. Sakiz-Adasi. Chíos, E Greece
115 K18 **Chíos** var. Khíos. island E Greece
83 M14 **Chipata** prev. Fort Jameson. Eastern, E Zambia
83 C14 **Chipindo** Huíla, C Angola
23 R8 **Chipley** Florida, SE USA
155 D15 **Chiplūn** Mahārāshtra, W India
81 H22 **Chipogolo** Dodoma, C Tanzania
23 R8 **Chipola River** ⁓ Florida, SE USA
97 L22 **Chippenham** S England, UK
30 J6 **Chippewa Falls** Wisconsin, N USA
30 J4 **Chippewa, Lake** ⊠ Wisconsin, N USA
31 Q8 **Chippewa River** ⁓ Michigan, N USA
30 I6 **Chippewa River** ⁓ Wisconsin, N USA
Chipping Wycombe see High Wycombe
114 G8 **Chiprovtsi** Montana, NW Bulgaria
19 T4 **Chiputneticook Lakes** lakes Canada/USA
56 D13 **Chiquián** Ancash, W Peru
41 Y11 **Chiquilá** Quintana Roo, SE Mexico
42 E6 **Chiquimula** Chiquimula, SE Guatemala
42 A3 **Chiquimula** off. Departamento de Chiquimula. ❖ department SE Guatemala
42 D7 **Chiquimulilla** Santa Rosa, S Guatemala
54 F9 **Chiquinquirá** Boyacá, C Colombia
155 J17 **Chīrāla** Andhra Pradesh, E India
149 N4 **Chīras** Ghowr, N Afghanistan
152 H11 **Chirāwa** Rājasthān, N India
Chirchik see Chirchiq
147 Q9 **Chirchiq** Rus. Chirchik. Toshkent Wiloyati, E Uzbekistan
147 P10 **Chirchiq** ⁓ E Uzbekistan
Chire see Shire
83 L18 **Chiredzi** Masvingo, SE Zimbabwe
25 X8 **Chireno** Texas, SW USA
77 X7 **Chirfa** Agadez, NE Niger
37 O16 **Chiricahua Mountains** ▲ Arizona, SW USA
37 O16 **Chiricahua Peak** ▲ Arizona, SW USA
54 F6 **Chiriguaná** Cesar, N Colombia
39 P15 **Chirikof Island** island Alaska, USA
43 P16 **Chiriquí** off. Provincia de Chiriquí. ❖ province SW Panama
43 P17 **Chiriquí, Golfo de** Eng. Chiriqui Gulf. gulf SW Panama
43 P15 **Chiriquí Grande** Bocas del Toro, W Panama
Chiriqui Gulf see Chiriquí, Golfo de
43 P15 **Chiriquí, Laguna de** lagoon NW Panama
43 O16 **Chiriquí Viejo, Río** ⁓ W Panama
Chiriquí, Volcán de see Barú, Volcán
83 N15 **Chiromo** Southern, S Malawi
114 J10 **Chirpan** Stara Zagora, C Bulgaria
43 N14 **Chirripó Atlántico, Río** ⁓ E Costa Rica
Chirripó, Cerro see Chirripó Grande, Cerro
43 N14 **Chirripó Grande, Cerro** var. Cerro Chirripó. ▲ SE Costa Rica
43 N13 **Chirripó, Río** var. Río Chirripó del Pacífico. ⁓ NE Costa Rica
Chirua, Lago see Chilwa, Lake
83 J15 **Chirundu** Southern, S Zambia
29 W8 **Chisago City** Minnesota, N USA
83 J14 **Chisamba** Central, C Zambia
39 T10 **Chisana** Alaska, USA
82 I13 **Chisasa** North Western, NW Zambia
12 I9 **Chisasibi** Quebec, C Canada
42 D4 **Chisec** Alta Verapaz, C Guatemala
129 U5 **Chishmy** Respublika Bashkortostan, W Russian Federation
29 V4 **Chisholm** Minnesota, N USA
160 I11 **Chishui He** ⁓ C China
Chisimaio/Chisimayu see Kismaayo
117 N10 **Chişinău** Rus. Kishinev. ● (Moldova) C Moldova
117 N10 **Chişinău** ✕ S Moldova
Chişinău-Criş see Chişineu-Criş
116 F10 **Chişineu-Criş** Hung. Kşjenő; prev. Chişinău-Criş. Arad, W Romania
83 K14 **Chisomo** Central, C Zambia
106 A8 **Chisone** ⁓ NW Italy
24 K12 **Chisos Mountains** ▲ Texas, SW USA
149 U10 **Chistiān Mandi** Punjab, E Pakistan
39 T10 **Chistochina** Alaska, USA
129 R4 **Chistopol'** Respublika Tatarstan, W Russian Federation
145 O8 **Chistopol'ye** Severnyy Kazakhstan, N Kazakhstan
123 O13 **Chita** Chitinskaya Oblast', S Russian Federation
83 B16 **Chitado** Cunene, SW Angola
Chitaldroog/Chitaldrug see Chitradurga
83 C15 **Chitanda** ⁓ S Angola
Chitangwiza see Chitungwiza
82 F10 **Chitato** Lunda Norte, NE Angola
83 C14 **Chitembo** Bié, C Angola
39 T11 **Chitina** Alaska, USA
39 T11 **Chitina River** ⁓ Alaska, USA
123 O12 **Chitinskaya Oblast'** ❖ province S Russian Federation
82 M11 **Chitipa** Northern, NW Malawi
165 S4 **Chitose** var. Titose. Hokkaidō, NE Japan
155 G18 **Chitradurga** prev. Chitaldroog, Chitaldrug. Karnātaka, W India
149 T3 **Chitrāl** North-West Frontier Province, NW Pakistan
43 S16 **Chitré** Herrera, S Panama
153 V16 **Chittagong** Ben. Chāttagām. Chittagong, SE Bangladesh
153 U16 **Chittagong** ❖ division E Bangladesh
153 Q15 **Chittaranjan** West Bengal, NE India
152 G14 **Chittaurgarh** Rājasthān, N India
155 I19 **Chittoor** Andhra Pradesh, E India
155 G21 **Chittūr** Kerala, SW India
83 K16 **Chitungwiza** prev. Chitangwiza. Mashonaland East, NE Zimbabwe
62 H4 **Chiuchíu** Antofagasta, N Chile
82 F12 **Chiumbe** var. Tshiumbe. ⁓ Angola/Dem. Rep. Congo (Zaire)
83 F15 **Chiume** Moxico, E Angola
82 K13 **Chiundaponde** Northern, NE Zambia
106 H13 **Chiusi** Toscana, C Italy
54 J5 **Chivacoa** Yaracuy, N Venezuela
106 B8 **Chivasso** Piemonte, NW Italy
83 L17 **Chivhu** prev. Enkeldoorn. Midlands, C Zimbabwe
61 C20 **Chivilcoy** Buenos Aires, E Argentina
82 N12 **Chiweta** Northern, N Malawi
42 D4 **Chixoy, Río** var. Río Negro, Río Salinas. ⁓ Guatemala/Mexico
82 H13 **Chizela** North Western, NW Zambia
127 O5 **Chizha** Nenetskiy Avtonomnyy Okrug, NW Russian Federation
164 I12 **Chizu** Tottori, Honshū, SW Japan
Chkalov see Orenburg
74 J5 **Chlef** var. Ech Cheliff, Ech Chleff; prev. Al-Asnam, El Asnam, Orléansville. NW Algeria
115 G18 **Chlómo** ▲ C Greece
111 M15 **Chmielnik** Świętokrzyskie, C Poland
167 S11 **Chŏâm Khsant** Preăh Vihéar, N Cambodia
62 G10 **Choapa, Río** var. Choapo. ⁓ C Chile
Choapas see Las Choapas
Choarta see Chwārtā
83 H17 **Chobe** ❖ district NE Botswana
67 T13 **Chobe** ⁓ N Botswana
14 K8 **Chochocouane** ⁓ Quebec, SE Canada
110 E13 **Chocianów** Ger. Kotzenan. Dolnośląskie, SW Poland
54 C9 **Chocó** off. Departamento del Chocó. ❖ province W Colombia
35 X16 **Chocolate Mountains** ▲ California, W USA
21 W9 **Chocowinity** North Carolina, SE USA
27 N10 **Choctaw** Oklahoma, C USA
23 Q8 **Choctawhatchee Bay** bay Florida, SE USA
23 Q8 **Choctawhatchee River** ⁓ Florida, SE USA
Chodau see Chodov
163 V14 **Chŏ-do** island SW North Korea
Chodorów see Khodoriv
111 A16 **Chodov** Ger. Chodau. Karlovarský Kraj, W Czech Republic
110 G10 **Chodzież** Wielkopolskie, C Poland
63 J15 **Choele Choel** Río Negro, C Argentina
83 L14 **Chofombo** Tete, NW Mozambique
Chohtan see Chauhtan
11 U14 **Choiceland** Saskatchewan, C Canada
186 K8 **Choiseul** var. Lauru. island NW Solomon Islands
63 M23 **Choiseul Sound** sound East Falkland, Falkland Islands
40 H7 **Choix** Sinaloa, C Mexico
110 D10 **Chojna** Zachodniopomorskie, W Poland
110 H8 **Chojnice** Ger. Konitz. Pomorskie, N Poland
111 F14 **Chojnów** Ger. Hainau, Haynau. Dolnośląskie, SW Poland
167 Q10 **Chok Chai** Nakhon Ratchasima, C Thailand
80 I12 **Ch'ok'ē** var. Choke Mountains. ▲ NW Ethiopia
25 R13 **Choke Canyon Lake** ⊠ Texas, SW USA
Choke Mountains see Ch'ok'ē
145 T15 **Chokpar** Kaz. Shoqpar. Zhambyl, S Kazakhstan
147 W7 **Chok-Tal** var. Choktal. Issyk-Kul'skaya Oblast', E Kyrgyzstan
Chókué see Chokwé
123 R7 **Chokurdakh** Respublika Sakha (Yakutiya), NE Russian Federation
83 L20 **Chokwé** var. Chókué. Gaza, S Mozambique
188 F8 **Chol** Babeldaob, N Palau
160 E8 **Chola Shan** ▲ C China
102 J8 **Cholet** Maine-et-Loire, NW France
63 H17 **Cholila** Chubut, W Argentina
Cholo see Thyolo
147 V8 **Cholpon** Narynskaya Oblast', C Kyrgyzstan
147 X7 **Cholpon-Ata** Issyk-Kul'skaya Oblast', E Kyrgyzstan
41 P14 **Cholula** Puebla, S Mexico
42 I8 **Choluteca** Choluteca, S Honduras
42 H8 **Choluteca** ❖ department S Honduras
42 G6 **Choluteca, Río** ⁓ SW Honduras
83 I15 **Choma** Southern, S Zambia
153 T11 **Chomo Lhari** ▲ NW Bhutan
167 N7 **Chom Thong** Chiang Mai, NW Thailand
111 B15 **Chomutov** Ger. Komotau. Ústecký Kraj, NW Czech Republic
123 N11 **Chona** ⁓ C Russian Federation
163 X15 **Ch'ŏnan** Jap. Tenan. W South Korea
167 P11 **Chon Buri** prev. Bang Pla Soi. Chon Buri, S Thailand
56 B6 **Chone** Manabí, W Ecuador
163 W13 **Ch'ŏngch'ŏn-gang** ⁓ W North Korea
163 Y11 **Ch'ŏngjin** NE North Korea
163 W13 **Chŏngju** W North Korea
161 S8 **Chongming Dao** island E China
160 J10 **Chongqing** var. Ch'ung-ching, Ch'ung-ch'ing, Chungking, Pahsien, Tchongking, Yuzhou. Chongqing Shi, C China
Chŏngup see Chŏnju
161 O10 **Chongyang** Hubei, C China
163 Y16 **Chŏnju** prev. Chŏngup, Jap. Seiyu. SW South Korea
163 Y15 **Chŏnju** Jap. Zenshū. SW South Korea
Chonnacht see Connaught
163 Q9 **Chonogol** Sühbaatar, E Mongolia
63 F19 **Chonos, Archipiélago de los** island group S Chile
42 K10 **Chontales** ❖ department S Nicaragua
167 T13 **Chơn Thanh** Sông Be, S Vietnam
158 K17 **Cho Oyu** var. Qowowuyag. ▲ China/Nepal
116 G7 **Chop** Cz. Čop, Hung. Csap. Zakarpats'ka Oblast', W Ukraine
21 Y3 **Choptank River** ⁓ Maryland, NE USA
Chorcaí, Cuan see Cork Harbour
43 P15 **Chorcha, Cerro** ▲ W Panama
Chorku see Chorkŭh
147 R11 **Chorkŭh** Rus. Chorku. N Tajikistan
97 K17 **Chorley** NW England, UK
Chorne More see Black Sea
117 R5 **Chornobay** Cherkas'ka Oblast', C Ukraine
117 O3 **Chornobyl'** Rus. Chernobyl'. Kyyivs'ka Oblast', N Ukraine
117 R12 **Chornomors'ke** Rus. Chernomorskoye. Respublika Krym, S Ukraine
117 R4 **Chornukhy** Poltavs'ka Oblast', C Ukraine
Chorokh/Chorokhi see Çoruh Nehri
110 O9 **Choroszcz** Podlaskie, NE Poland
116 K6 **Chortkiv** Rus. Chortkov. Ternopil's'ka Oblast', W Ukraine
Chortkov see Chortkiv
Chorum see Çorum
110 M9 **Chorzele** Mazowieckie, C Poland
111 J16 **Chorzów** Ger. Königshütte; prev. Królewska Huta. Śląskie, S Poland
163 W12 **Ch'osan** N North Korea
Chōsen-kaikyō see Korea Strait
164 P14 **Chōshi** var. Tyôsi. Chiba, Honshū, S Japan
63 H14 **Chos Malal** Neuquén, W Argentina
Chosŏn-minjujuŭi-inmin-kanghwaguk see North Korea
110 E9 **Choszczno** Ger. Arnswalde. Zachodniopomorskie, NW Poland
153 O15 **Chota Nāgpur** plateau N India
33 R8 **Choteau** Montana, NW USA
Chotqol see Chatkal
14 M8 **Chouart** ⁓ Quebec, SE Canada
76 I7 **Choûm** Adrar, C Mauritania
27 Q9 **Chouteau** Oklahoma, C USA
21 X8 **Chowan River** ⁓ North Carolina, SE USA
35 Q10 **Chowchilla** California, W USA
163 P7 **Choybalsan** Dornod, E Mongolia
162 M9 **Choyr** Dornogovĭ, C Mongolia
185 I19 **Christchurch** Canterbury, South Island, NZ
97 M24 **Christchurch** S England, UK
185 I18 **Christchurch** ✕ Canterbury, South Island, NZ
44 J12 **Christiana** C Jamaica
83 H22 **Christiana** Free State, C South Africa
115 J23 **Christiáni** island Kykládes, Greece, Aegean Sea
Christiania see Oslo
14 G13 **Christian Island** island Ontario, S Canada
191 P16 **Christian, Point** headland Pitcairn Island, Pitcairn Islands
38 M11 **Christian River** ⁓ Alaska, USA
Christiansand see Kristiansand
21 S7 **Christiansburg** Virginia, NE USA
95 G23 **Christiansfeld** Sønderjylland, SW Denmark
Christianshåb see Qasigiannguit
39 X14 **Christian Sound** inlet Alaska, USA
45 T9 **Christiansted** Saint Croix, S Virgin Islands (US)
Christiansund see Kristiansund
25 R13 **Christine** Texas, SW USA
173 U7 **Christmas Island** ◇ Australian external territory E Indian Ocean
131 T17 **Christmas Island** island E Indian Ocean
Christmas Island see Kiritimati
192 M7 **Christmas Ridge** undersea feature C Pacific Ocean
30 L16 **Christopher** Illinois, N USA
25 P9 **Christoval** Texas, SW USA
111 E17 **Chrudim** Pardubický Kraj, C Czech Republic
115 K25 **Chrýsi** island SE Greece
121 N2 **Chrysochoú, Kólpos** var. Khrysokhou Bay. bay E Mediterranean Sea
114 I13 **Chrysoúpoli** var. Hrisoupoli; prev. Khrisoúpolis. Anatolikí Makedonía kai Thráki, NE Greece
111 K16 **Chrzanów** var. Chrzanow, Ger. Zaumgarten. Śląskie, S Poland
131 Q7 **Chu** Kaz. Shū. ⁓ Kazakhstan/Kyrgyzstan
42 C5 **Chuacús, Sierra de** ▲ W Guatemala
153 S15 **Chuadanga** Khulna, W Bangladesh
Chuan see Sichuan
Ch'uan-chou see Quanzhou
39 O11 **Chuathbaluk** Alaska, USA
Chubek see Moskva
63 I17 **Chubut** off. Provincia de Chubut. ❖ province S Argentina
63 I17 **Chubut, Río** ⁓ SE Argentina
43 V15 **Chucanti, Cerro** ▲ E Panama
Ch'u-chiang see Shaoguan
43 W15 **Chucunaque, Río** ⁓ E Panama
Chudin see Chudzin
116 M5 **Chudniv** Zhytomyrs'ka Oblast', N Ukraine
126 H13 **Chudovo** Novgorodskaya Oblast', W Russian Federation
Chudskoye Ozero see Peipus, Lake
119 J18 **Chudzin** Rus. Chudin. Brestskaya Voblasts', SW Belarus
39 Q13 **Chugach Islands** island group Alaska, USA
39 S11 **Chugach Mountains** ▲ Alaska, USA
164 G12 **Chūgoku-sanchi** ▲ Honshū, SW Japan
Chuguyev see Chuhuyiv
117 V5 **Chuhuyiv** var. Chuguyev. Kharkivs'ka Oblast', E Ukraine
61 H19 **Chuí** Rio Grande do Sul, S Brazil
Chuí see Chuy
145 S15 **Chu-Iliyskiye Gory** Kaz. Shū-Ile Taūlary. ▲ S Kazakhstan
Chukai see Cukai
Chukchi Avtonomnyy Okrug see Chukotskiy Avtonomnyy Okrug
Chukchi Peninsula see Chukotskiy Poluostrov
197 R6 **Chukchi Plain** undersea feature Arctic Ocean
197 R6 **Chukchi Plateau** undersea feature Arctic Ocean
197 R4 **Chukchi Sea** Rus. Chukotskoye More. sea Arctic Ocean
127 N14 **Chukhloma** Kostromskaya Oblast', NW Russian Federation
Chukotka see Chukotskiy Avtonomnyy Okrug
Chukot Range see Anadyrskiy Khrebet
123 V6 **Chukotskiy Avtonomnyy Okrug** var. Chukchi Avtonomnyy Okrug, Chukotka. ❖ autonomous district NE Russian Federation
123 W5 **Chukotskiy, Mys** headland NE Russian Federation
123 V5 **Chukotskiy Poluostrov** Eng. Chukchi Peninsula. peninsula NE Russian Federation
Chukotskoye More see Chukchi Sea
Chukurkak see Chuqurqoq
Chulakkurgan see Shollakorgan
35 U17 **Chula Vista** California, W USA
123 Q12 **Chul'man** Respublika Sakha (Yakutiya), NE Russian Federation
56 B9 **Chulucanas** Piura, NW Peru
122 J12 **Chulym** ⁓ C Russian Federation
152 K6 **Chumar** Jammu and Kashmir, N India
114 K9 **Chumerna** ▲ C Bulgaria
123 R12 **Chumikan** Khabarovskiy Kray, E Russian Federation
167 Q9 **Chum Phae** Khon Kaen, C Thailand
167 N13 **Chumphon** var. Jumporn. Chumphon, SW Thailand
167 O9 **Chumsaeng** var. Chum Saeng. Nakhon Sawan, C Thailand
122 L12 **Chuna** ⁓ C Russian Federation
161 R9 **Chun'an** var. Pailing. Zhejiang, SE China
161 S13 **Chunan** N Taiwan
163 Y14 **Ch'unch'ŏn** Jap. Shunsen. N South Korea
153 S16 **Chunchura** prev. Chinsura. West Bengal, NE India
145 W15 **Chundzha** Almaty, SE Kazakhstan
Ch'ung-ch'ing/Ch'ung-ching see Chongqing
Chung-hua Jen-min Kung-ho-kuo see China
163 Y15 **Ch'ungju** Jap. Chūshū. C South Korea
Chungking see Chongqing
161 T14 **Chungyang Shanmo** Chin. Taiwan Shan. ▲ C Taiwan
149 V9 **Chūniān** Punjab, E Pakistan
122 L12 **Chunskiy** Irkutskaya Oblast', S Russian Federation
122 M11 **Chunya** ⁓ C Russian Federation
126 J6 **Chupa** Respublika Kareliya, NW Russian Federation
127 P8 **Chuprovo** Respublika Komi, NW Russian Federation
57 G17 **Chuquibamba** Arequipa, SW Peru
62 H4 **Chuquicamata** Antofagasta, N Chile
57 L21 **Chuquisaca** ❖ department S Bolivia
Chuquisaca see Sucre
146 I8 **Chuqurqoq** Rus. Chukurkak. Qoraqalpoghiston Respublikasi, NW Uzbekistan
129 T2 **Chur** Udmurtskaya Respublika, NW Russian Federation
108 I9 **Chur** Fr. Coire, It. Coira, Rmsch. Cuera, Quera; anc. Curia Rhaetorum. Graubünden, E Switzerland
123 Q10 **Churapcha** Respublika Sakha (Yakutiya), NE Russian Federation
11 V16 **Churchbridge** Saskatchewan, S Canada
21 O8 **Church Hill** Tennessee, S USA
11 X9 **Churchill** Manitoba, C Canada
11 X10 **Churchill** ⁓ Manitoba/Saskatchewan, C Canada
13 P9 **Churchill** ⁓ Newfoundland, E Canada
11 Y9 **Churchill, Cape** headland Manitoba, C Canada
13 P9 **Churchill Falls** Newfoundland, E Canada
11 S12 **Churchill Lake** ◎ Saskatchewan, C Canada
19 Q3 **Churchill Lake** ⊠ Maine, NE USA
194 I5 **Churchill Peninsula** peninsula Antarctica
22 H8 **Church Point** Louisiana, S USA
29 O3 **Churchs Ferry** North Dakota, N USA
146 G12 **Churchuri** Akhalskiy Velayat, C Turkmenistan
21 T5 **Churchville** Virginia, NE USA
152 G10 **Chūru** Rājasthān, NW India
54 J4 **Churuguara** Falcón, N Venezuela
144 J12 **Chushkakul, Gory** ▲ SW Kazakhstan
Chūshū see Ch'ungju
37 O9 **Chuska Mountains** ▲ Arizona/New Mexico, SW USA
Chu, Sông see Sam, Nam
127 V14 **Chusovoy** Permskaya Oblast', NW Russian Federation
167 U11 **Chư Srê** Gia Lai, C Vietnam
147 R10 **Chust** Namangan Wiloyati, E Uzbekistan
Chust see Khust
15 U6 **Chute-aux-Outardes** Quebec, SE Canada
117 U5 **Chutove** Poltavs'ka Oblast', C Ukraine
189 O15 **Chuuk** var. Truk. ❖ state C Micronesia
189 P15 **Chuuk Islands** var. Hogoley Islands; prev. Truk Islands. island group Caroline Islands, C Micronesia
Chuvashia see Chuvashskaya Respublika
129 P4 **Chuvashskaya Respublika** var. Chavash Respubliki, Eng. Chuvashia. ❖ autonomous republic W Russian Federation
Chuwārtah see Chwārtā
Chu Xian/Chuxian see Chuzhou
160 G13 **Chuxiong** Yunnan, SW China
147 V7 **Chuy** Chuyskaya Oblast', N Kyrgyzstan
61 H19 **Chuy** var. Chuí. Rocha, E Uruguay
123 O11 **Chuya** Respublika Sakha (Yakutiya), NE Russian Federation
Chüy Oblasty see Chuyskaya Oblast'
147 U8 **Chuyskaya Oblast'** Kir. Chüy Oblasty. ❖ province N Kyrgyzstan
161 Q7 **Chuzhou** var. Chuxian, Chu Xian. Anhui, E China
139 U3 **Chwārtā** var. Choarta, Chuwārtah. NE Iraq
119 N16 **Chyhirynskaye Vodaskhovishcha** ⊠ E Belarus
117 R6 **Chyhyryn** Rus. Chigirin. Cherkas'ka Oblast', N Ukraine
Chyrvonaya Slabada see Krasnaya Slabada
119 L19 **Chyrvonaye, Vozyera** Rus. Ozero Chervonoye. ◎ SE Belarus
117 N11 **Ciadîr-Lunga** var. Ceadâr-Lunga, Rus. Chadyr-Lunga. S Moldova
169 P16 **Ciamis** prev. Tjiamis. Jawa, C Indonesia
107 I16 **Ciampino** ✕ Lazio, C Italy
169 N16 **Cianjur** prev. Tjiandjoer. Jawa, C Indonesia
60 H10 **Cianorte** Paraná, S Brazil
Ciarraí see Kerry
112 N13 **Ćićevac** Serbia, E Yugoslavia
187 Z14 **Cicia** prev. Thithia. island Lau Group, E Fiji
105 P4 **Cidacos** ⁓ N Spain
136 I10 **Cide** Kastamonu, N Turkey
110 L10 **Ciechanów** prev. Zichenau. Mazowieckie, C Poland
110 O10 **Ciechanowiec** Ger. Rudelstadt. Podlaskie, E Poland
110 J10 **Ciechocinek** Kujawsko-pomorskie, C Poland
44 F6 **Ciego de Ávila** Ciego de Ávila, C Cuba
54 F4 **Ciénaga** Magdalena, N Colombia
54 E6 **Ciénaga de Oro** Córdoba, NW Colombia
44 E5 **Cienfuegos** Cienfuegos, C Cuba
104 F4 **Cíes, Illas** island group NW Spain
111 P16 **Cieszanów** Podkarpackie, SE Poland
111 J17 **Cieszyn** Cz. Těšín, Ger. Teschen. Śląskie, S Poland
105 R12 **Cieza** Murcia, SE Spain
136 F13 **Çifteler** Eskişehir, W Turkey
105 P7 **Cifuentes** Castilla-La Mancha, C Spain
Čiganak see Chiganak
105 P9 **Cigüela** ⁓ C Spain
136 H14 **Cihanbeyli** Konya, C Turkey
136 H14 **Cihanbeyli Yaylası** plateau C Turkey
104 L10 **Cíjara, Embalse de** ⊠ C Spain
169 P16 **Cikalong** Jawa, S Indonesia
169 N16 **Cikawung** Jawa, S Indonesia
187 Y13 **Cikobia** prev. Thikombia. island N Fiji
169 P17 **Cilacap** prev. Tjilatjap. Jawa, C Indonesia
173 O16 **Cilaos** C Réunion
137 S11 **Çıldır** Ardahan, NE Turkey
137 S11 **Çıldır Gölü** ◎ NE Turkey
160 M10 **Cili** Hunan, S China
121 V10 **Cilicia Trough** undersea feature E Mediterranean Sea
Cill Airne see Killarney
Cill Chainnigh see Kilkenny
Cill Chaoi see Kilkee
Cill Choca see Kilcock
Cill Dara see Kildare
105 N3 **Cillero de Bezana** Castilla-León, N Spain
Cilli see Celje
Cill Mhantáin see Wicklow
Cill Rois see Kilrush
26 J6 **Cimarron** Kansas, C USA
37 T9 **Cimarron** New Mexico, SW USA
26 M9 **Cimarron River** ⁓ Kansas/Oklahoma, C USA
117 N11 **Cimişlia** Rus. Chimishliya. S Moldova
Cîmpia Turzii see Câmpia Turzii
Cîmpina see Câmpina
Cîmpulung see Câmpulung
Cîmpulung Moldovenesc see Câmpulung Moldovenesc
137 P15 **Çınar** Dıyarbakır, SE Turkey
54 J8 **Cinaruco, Río** ⁓ Colombia/Venezuela
Cina Selatan, Laut see South China Sea
105 T5 **Cinca** ⁓ NE Spain
112 G13 **Cincar** ▲ SW Bosnia and Herzegovina
31 Q15 **Cincinnati** Ohio, N USA
21 M4 **Cincinnati** ✕ Kentucky, S USA
Cinco de Outubro see Xá-Muteba
136 C15 **Çine** Aydın, SW Turkey
99 J21 **Ciney** Namur, SE Belgium
104 H6 **Cinfães** Viseu, N Portugal
106 J12 **Cingoli** Marche, C Italy
41 U16 **Cintalapa** var. Cintalapa de Figueroa. Chiapas, SE Mexico
Cintalapa de Figueroa see Cintalapa
103 X14 **Cinto, Monte** ▲ Corse, France, C Mediterranean Sea
Cintra see Sintra
105 Q5 **Cintruénigo** Navarra, N Spain
Cionn tSáile see Kinsale
116 K13 **Ciorani** Prahova, SE Romania
113 E14 **Čiovo** It. Bua. island S Croatia
Cipiúr see Kippure
63 I15 **Cipolletti** Río Negro, C Argentina
120 L7 **Circeo, Capo** headland C Italy
39 S8 **Circle** var. Circle City. Alaska, USA
33 X8 **Circle** Montana, NW USA
Circle City see Circle
31 S14 **Circleville** Ohio, N USA
36 K6 **Circleville** Utah, W USA
169 P16 **Cirebon** prev. Tjirebon. Jawa, S Indonesia
97 L21 **Cirencester** anc. Corinium, Corinium Dobunorum. C England, UK
Cirkvenica see Crikvenica
107 O20 **Ciro** Calabria, SW Italy
107 O20 **Ciro Marina** Calabria, S Italy
102 K14 **Ciron** ⁓ SW France
Cirquenizza see Crikvenica
25 R7 **Cisco** Texas, SW USA
116 I12 **Cisnădie** Ger. Heltau, Hung. Nagydisznód. Sibiu, SW Romania
63 G18 **Cisnes, Río** ⁓ S Chile
25 T11 **Cisco** Texas, SW USA
104 L3 **Cistierna** Castilla-León, N Spain
Citharista see la Ciotat
Citlaltépetl see Orizaba, Volcán Pico de
55 X10 **Citron** NW French Guiana
23 N7 **Citronelle** Alabama, S USA
35 O7 **Citrus Heights** California, W USA
106 H7 **Cittadella** Veneto, NE Italy
106 H13 **Città della Pieve** Umbria, C Italy
106 H12 **Città di Castello** Umbria, C Italy
107 I14 **Cittaducale** Lazio, C Italy
107 N22 **Cittanova** Calabria, SW Italy

◆ Country ● Country Capital ◇ Dependent Territory ○ Dependent Territory Capital ❖ Administrative Region ✕ International Airport ▲ Mountain ▲ Mountain Range ☒ Volcano ⁓ River ◎ Lake ⊠ Reservoir

Cittavecchia *see* Starigrad
116 *G10* **Ciucea** *Hung.* Csucsa. Cluj, NW Romania
116 *M13* **Ciucurova** Tulcea, SE Romania
Ciudad Acuña *see* Villa Acuña
41 *N15* **Ciudad Altamirano** Guerrero, S Mexico
42 *G7* **Ciudad Barrios** San Miguel, NE El Salvador
54 *I7* **Ciudad Bolívar** Barinas, NW Venezuela
55 *N7* **Ciudad Bolívar** *prev.* Angostura. Bolívar, E Venezuela
40 *K6* **Ciudad Camargo** Chihuahua, N Mexico
40 *E8* **Ciudad Constitución** Baja California Sur, W Mexico
Ciudad Cortés *see* Cortés
41 *V17* **Ciudad Cuauhtémoc** Chiapas, SE Mexico
42 *J9* **Ciudad Darío** *var.* Dario. Matagalpa, W Nicaragua
Ciudad de Dolores Hidalgo *see* Dolores Hidalgo
42 *C6* **Ciudad de Guatemala** *Eng.* Guatemala City; *prev.* Santiago de los Caballeros. ● (Guatemala) Guatemala, C Guatemala
Ciudad del Carmen *see* Carmen
62 *Q6* **Ciudad del Este** *prev.* Cuidad Presidente Stroessner, Presidente Stroessner, Puerto Presidente Stroessner. Alto Paraná, SE Paraguay
62 *K5* **Ciudad de Libertador General San Martín** *var.* Libertador General San Martín. Jujuy, C Argentina
Ciudad Delicias *see* Delicias
41 *O11* **Ciudad del Maíz** San Luis Potosí, C Mexico
Ciudad de México *see* México
54 *J7* **Ciudad de Nutrias** Barinas, NW Venezuela
Ciudad de Panamá *see* Panamá
55 *P7* **Ciudad Guayana** *prev.* San Tomé de Guayana, Santo Tomé de Guayana. Bolívar, NE Venezuela
40 *K14* **Ciudad Guzmán** Jalisco, SW Mexico
41 *V17* **Ciudad Hidalgo** Chiapas, SE Mexico
41 *N14* **Ciudad Hidalgo** Michoacán de Ocampo, SW Mexico
40 *J3* **Ciudad Juárez** Chihuahua, N Mexico
40 *L8* **Ciudad Lerdo** Durango, C Mexico
41 *Q11* **Ciudad Madero** *var.* Villa Cecilia. Tamaulipas, C Mexico
41 *P11* **Ciudad Mante** Tamaulipas, C Mexico
42 *F2* **Ciudad Melchor de Mencos** *var.* Melchor de Mencos. Petén, NE Guatemala
41 *P8* **Ciudad Miguel Alemán** Tamaulipas, C Mexico
Ciudad Mutis *see* Bahía Solano
40 *G6* **Ciudad Obregón** Sonora, NW Mexico
54 *I5* **Ciudad Ojeda** Zulia, NW Venezuela
55 *P7* **Ciudad Piar** Bolívar, E Venezuela
Ciudad Porfirio Díaz *see* Piedras Negras
Ciudad Quesada *see* Quesada
105 *N11* **Ciudad Real** Castilla-La Mancha, C Spain
105 *N11* **Ciudad Real** ◈ *province* Castilla-La Mancha, C Spain
104 *J7* **Ciudad-Rodrigo** Castilla-León, N Spain
42 *A6* **Ciudad Tecún Umán** San Marcos, SW Guatemala
Ciudad Trujillo *see* Santo Domingo
41 *P12* **Ciudad Valles** San Luis Potosí, C Mexico
41 *O10* **Ciudad Victoria** Tamaulipas, C Mexico
42 *C6* **Ciudad Vieja** Suchitepéquez, S Guatemala
116 *L8* **Ciuhuru** *var.* Reuţel. ≈ N Moldova
Ciutadella *see* Ciutadella de Menorca
105 *Z8* **Ciutadella de Menorca** *var.* Ciutadella. Menorca, Spain, W Mediterranean Sea
136 *L11* **Civa Burnu** *headland* N Turkey
106 *J7* **Cividale del Friuli** Friuli-Venezia Giulia, NE Italy
107 *H14* **Civita Castellana** Lazio, C Italy
106 *J12* **Civitanova Marche** Marche, C Italy
Civitas Altae Ripae *see* Brzeg
Civitas Carnutum *see* Chartres
Civitas Eburovicum *see* Évreux
Civitas Nemetum *see* Speyer
107 *G15* **Civitavecchia** *anc.* Centum Cellae, Trajani Portus. Lazio, C Italy
102 *L10* **Civray** Vienne, W France
136 *E14* **Çivril** Denizli, W Turkey
161 *O5* **Cixian** Hebei, E China
137 *R16* **Cizre** Şırnak, SE Turkey
Clacton *see* Clacton-on-Sea
97 *Q21* **Clacton-on-Sea** *var.* Clacton. E England, UK
22 *H5* **Claiborne, Lake** ⊟ Louisiana, S USA
102 *L10* **Clain** ≈ W France
11 *Q11* **Claire, Lake** ◎ Alberta, C Canada
25 *O6* **Clairemont** Texas, SW USA
34 *M3* **Clair Engle Lake** ⊟ California, W USA
18 *B15* **Clairton** Pennsylvania, NE USA
32 *F7* **Clallam Bay** Washington, NW USA
103 *P8* **Clamecy** Nièvre, C France
23 *P5* **Clanton** Alabama, S USA
61 *D17* **Clara** Entre Ríos, E Argentina
97 *E18* **Clara** *Ir.* Clóirtheach. C Ireland
29 *T9* **Clara City** Minnesota, N USA
61 *D23* **Claraz** Buenos Aires, E Argentina
Clár Chlainne Mhuiris *see* Claremorris
182 *I8* **Clare** South Australia
97 *C19* **Clare** *Ir.* An Clár. *cultural region* W Ireland
97 *C18* **Clare** ≈ W Ireland
97 *A16* **Clare Island** *Ir.* Cliara. *island* W Ireland
44 *J12* **Claremont** C Jamaica
29 *W10* **Claremont** Minnesota, N USA
19 *N9* **Claremont** New Hampshire, NE USA
27 *Q9* **Claremore** Oklahoma, C USA
97 *C17* **Claremorris** *Ir.* Clár Chlainne Mhuiris. W Ireland
185 *J16* **Clarence** Canterbury, South Island, NZ
185 *J16* **Clarence** ≈ South Island, NZ
65 *F15* **Clarence Bay** *bay* Ascension Island, C Atlantic Ocean
63 *H25* **Clarence, Isla** *island* S Chile
194 *H2* **Clarence Island** *island* South Shetland Islands, Antarctica
183 *V5* **Clarence River** ≈ New South Wales, SE Australia
44 *J5* **Clarence Town** Long Island, C Bahamas
27 *W12* **Clarendon** Arkansas, C USA
25 *O3* **Clarendon** Texas, SW USA
13 *U12* **Clarenville** Newfoundland, SE Canada
11 *Q17* **Claresholm** Alberta, SW Canada
29 *T16* **Clarinda** Iowa, C USA
55 *N5* **Clarines** Anzoátegui, NE Venezuela
29 *V12* **Clarion** Iowa, C USA
18 *C13* **Clarion** Pennsylvania, NE USA
193 *O6* **Clarion Fracture Zone** *tectonic feature* NE Pacific Ocean
18 *D13* **Clarion River** ≈ Pennsylvania, NE USA
29 *Q9* **Clark** South Dakota, N USA
36 *K11* **Clarkdale** Arizona, SW USA
15 *W4* **Clarke City** Quebec, SE Canada
183 *Q15* **Clarke Island** *island* Furneaux Group, Tasmania, SE Australia
181 *X6* **Clarke Range** ▲▲ Queensland, E Australia
23 *T2* **Clarkesville** Georgia, SE USA
29 *S9* **Clarkfield** Minnesota, N USA
33 *N7* **Clark Fork** Idaho, NW USA
33 *N8* **Clark Fork** ≈ Idaho/Montana, NW USA
39 *Q12* **Clark, Lake** ◎ Alaska, USA
35 *W12* **Clark Mountain** ▲ California, W USA
37 *S3* **Clark Peak** ▲ Colorado, C USA
14 *D14* **Clark, Point** *headland* Ontario, S Canada
21 *S3* **Clarksburg** West Virginia, NE USA
22 *K2* **Clarksdale** Mississippi, S USA
33 *U12* **Clarks Fork Yellowstone River** ≈ Montana/Wyoming, NW USA
21 *P13* **Clark Hill Lake** *var.* J.Storm Thurmond Reservoir. ⊟ Georgia/South Carolina, SE USA
29 *R14* **Clarkson** Nebraska, C USA
39 *O13* **Clarks Point** Alaska, USA
18 *I13* **Clarks Summit** Pennsylvania, NE USA
32 *M10* **Clarkston** Washington, NW USA
44 *J12* **Clark's Town** C Jamaica
27 *T10* **Clarksville** Arkansas, C USA
31 *P13* **Clarksville** Indiana, N USA
20 *I8* **Clarksville** Tennessee, S USA
25 *W5* **Clarksville** Texas, SW USA
21 *U8* **Clarksville** Virginia, NE USA
21 *U11* **Clarkton** North Carolina, SE USA
61 *C24* **Claromecó** *var.* Balneario Claromecó. Buenos Aires, E Argentina
25 *N3* **Claude** Texas, SW USA
Clausentum *see* Southampton
171 *O1* **Claveria** Luzon, N Philippines
99 *J20* **Clavier** Liège, E Belgium
23 *W6* **Claxton** Georgia, SE USA
21 *R4* **Clay** West Virginia, NE USA
27 *N3* **Clay Center** Kansas, C USA
29 *P16* **Clay Center** Nebraska, C USA
21 *Y2* **Claymont** Delaware, NE USA
36 *M14* **Claypool** Arizona, SW USA
23 *R6* **Clayton** Alabama, S USA
23 *T1* **Clayton** Georgia, SE USA
22 *J5* **Clayton** Louisiana, S USA
27 *X5* **Clayton** Missouri, C USA
37 *V9* **Clayton** New Mexico, SW USA
21 *V9* **Clayton** North Carolina, SE USA
27 *Q12* **Clayton** Oklahoma, C USA
182 *I4* **Clayton River** *seasonal river* South Australia
21 *R7* **Claytor Lake** ⊟ Virginia, NE USA
27 *P13* **Clear Boggy Creek** ≈ Oklahoma, C USA
97 *B22* **Clear, Cape** *var.* The Bill of Cape Clear, *Ir.* Ceann Cléire. *headland* SW Ireland
36 *M12* **Clear Creek** ≈ Arizona, SW USA
39 *S12* **Cleare, Cape** *headland* Montague Island, Alaska, USA
18 *E13* **Clearfield** Pennsylvania, NE USA
36 *L2* **Clearfield** Utah, W USA
25 *Q6* **Clear Fork Brazos River** ≈ Texas, SW USA
31 *T12* **Clear Fork Reservoir** ⊟ Ohio, N USA
11 *N12* **Clear Hills** ▲▲ Alberta, SW Canada
29 *V12* **Clear Lake** Iowa, C USA
29 *R9* **Clear Lake** South Dakota, N USA
34 *M6* **Clear Lake** ◎ California, W USA
22 *G6* **Clear Lake** ⊟ Louisiana, S USA
34 *M6* **Clearlake** California, W USA
35 *P1* **Clear Lake Reservoir** ⊟ California, W USA
11 *N16* **Clearwater** British Columbia, SW Canada
23 *U12* **Clearwater** Florida, SE USA
11 *R12* **Clearwater** ≈ Alberta/Saskatchewan, C Canada
27 *W7* **Clearwater Lake** ⊟ Missouri, C USA
33 *N10* **Clearwater Mountains** ▲▲ Idaho, NW USA
33 *N10* **Clearwater River** ≈ Idaho, NW USA
29 *S4* **Clearwater River** ≈ Minnesota, N USA
25 *T7* **Cleburne** Texas, SW USA
32 *I9* **Cle Elum** Washington, NW USA
97 *O17* **Cleethorpes** E England, UK
Cléire, Ceann *see* Clear, Cape
21 *O11* **Clemson** South Carolina, SE USA
21 *Q4* **Clendenin** West Virginia, NE USA
26 *M9* **Cleo Springs** Oklahoma, C USA
Clerk Island *see* Onotoa
181 *X8* **Clermont** Queensland, E Australia
15 *S8* **Clermont** Quebec, SE Canada
103 *O4* **Clermont** Oise, N France
29 *X12* **Clermont** Iowa, C USA
103 *P11* **Clermont-Ferrand** Puy-de-Dôme, C France
103 *Q15* **Clermont-l'Hérault** Hérault, S France
99 *M22* **Clervaux** Diekirch, N Luxembourg
106 *G6* **Cles** Trentino-Alto Adige, N Italy
182 *H8* **Cleve** South Australia
Cleve *see* Kleve
23 *T2* **Cleveland** Georgia, SE USA
22 *K3* **Cleveland** Mississippi, S USA
31 *T11* **Cleveland** Ohio, N USA
27 *O9* **Cleveland** Oklahoma, C USA
20 *L10* **Cleveland** Tennessee, S USA
25 *W10* **Cleveland** Texas, SW USA
31 *N7* **Cleveland** Wisconsin, N USA
31 *O4* **Cleveland Cliffs Basin** ◎ Michigan, N USA
31 *U11* **Cleveland Heights** Ohio, N USA
33 *P6* **Cleveland, Mount** ▲ Montana, NW USA
Cleves *see* Kleve
97 *B16* **Clew Bay** *Ir.* Cuan Mó. *inlet* W Ireland
23 *Y14* **Clewiston** Florida, SE USA
Cliara *see* Clare Island
97 *A17* **Clifden** *Ir.* An Clochán. W Ireland
37 *O14* **Clifton** Arizona, SW USA
18 *K14* **Clifton** New Jersey, NE USA
25 *S8* **Clifton** Texas, SW USA
21 *S6* **Clifton Forge** Virginia, NE USA
182 *I1* **Clifton Hills** South Australia
11 *S17* **Climax** Saskatchewan, S Canada
21 *O8* **Clinch River** ≈ Tennessee/Virginia, S USA
25 *P12* **Cline** Texas, SW USA
21 *N10* **Clingmans Dome** ▲ North Carolina/Tennessee, SE USA
24 *H8* **Clint** Texas, SW USA
10 *M16* **Clinton** British Columbia, SW Canada
14 *E15* **Clinton** Ontario, S Canada
27 *U10* **Clinton** Arkansas, C USA
30 *L10* **Clinton** Illinois, N USA
29 *Z14* **Clinton** Iowa, C USA
20 *G7* **Clinton** Kentucky, S USA
22 *J8* **Clinton** Louisiana, S USA
19 *N11* **Clinton** Massachusetts, NE USA
31 *R10* **Clinton** Michigan, N USA
22 *K5* **Clinton** Mississippi, S USA
27 *S5* **Clinton** Missouri, C USA
21 *V10* **Clinton** North Carolina, SE USA
26 *L10* **Clinton** Oklahoma, C USA
21 *Q12* **Clinton** South Carolina, SE USA
21 *M9* **Clinton** Tennessee, S USA
8 *L9* **Clinton-Colden Lake** ◎ Northwest Territories, NW Canada
10 *H5* **Clinton Creek** Yukon Territory, NW Canada
30 *L13* **Clinton Lake** ⊟ Illinois, N USA
27 *Q4* **Clinton Lake** ⊟ Kansas, N USA
21 *T11* **Clio** South Carolina, SE USA
193 *O7* **Clipperton Fracture Zone** *tectonic feature* E Pacific Ocean
193 *Q7* **Clipperton Island** ◇ *French dependency of French Polynesia* E Pacific Ocean
46 *K6* **Clipperton Island** *island* E Pacific Ocean
(0) *F16* **Clipperton Seamounts** *undersea feature* E Pacific Ocean
102 *J8* **Clisson** Loire-Atlantique, NW France
62 *K7* **Clodomira** Santiago del Estero, N Argentina
Cloich na Coillte *see* Clonakilty
Clóirtheach *see* Clara
97 *C21* **Clonakilty** *Ir.* Cloich na Coillte. SW Ireland
181 *T6* **Cloncurry** Queensland, C Australia
97 *F18* **Clondalkin** *Ir.* Cluain Dolcáin. E Ireland
97 *E16* **Clones** *Ir.* Cluain Eois. N Ireland
97 *D20* **Clonmel** *Ir.* Cluain Meala. S Ireland
100 *G11* **Cloppenburg** Niedersachsen, NW Germany
29 *W6* **Cloquet** Minnesota, N USA
37 *S14* **Cloudcroft** New Mexico, SW USA
33 *W12* **Cloud Peak** ▲ Wyoming, C USA
185 *K14* **Cloudy Bay** *inlet* South Island, NZ
21 *R10* **Clover** South Carolina, SE USA
34 *M6* **Cloverdale** California, W USA
20 *J5* **Cloverport** Kentucky, S USA
35 *Q10* **Clovis** California, W USA
37 *W12* **Clovis** New Mexico, SW USA
14 *K13* **Cloyne** Ontario, SE Canada
Cluain Dolcáin *see* Clondalkin
Cluain Eois *see* Clones
Cluainín *see* Manorhamilton
Cluain Meala *see* Clonmel
116 *H10* **Cluj** ◈ *county* NW Romania
Cluj *see* Cluj-Napoca
116 *H10* **Cluj-Napoca** *Ger.* Klausenburg, *Hung.* Kolozsvár; *prev.* Cluj. Cluj, NW Romania
Clunia *see* Feldkirch
103 *R10* **Cluny** Saône-et-Loire, C France
103 *T10* **Cluses** Haute-Savoie, E France
106 *E7* **Clusone** Lombardia, N Italy
25 *W12* **Clute** Texas, SW USA
185 *D23* **Clutha** ≈ South Island, NZ
97 *J18* **Clwyd** *cultural region* NE Wales, UK
185 *D22* **Clyde** Otago, South Island, NZ
27 *N3* **Clyde** Kansas, C USA
29 *P2* **Clyde** North Dakota, N USA
31 *S11* **Clyde** Ohio, N USA
25 *Q7* **Clyde** Texas, SW USA
14 *K13* **Clyde** ≈ Ontario, SE Canada
96 *J13* **Clyde** ≈ W Scotland, UK
96 *H12* **Clydebank** S Scotland, UK
96 *H13* **Clyde, Firth of** *inlet* S Scotland, UK
33 *S11* **Clyde Park** Montana, NW USA
104 *I7* **Côa, Rio** ≈ N Portugal
35 *W16* **Coachella** California, W USA
35 *W16* **Coachella Canal** *canal* California, W USA
40 *I9* **Coacoyole** Durango, C Mexico
25 *N7* **Coahoma** Texas, SW USA
10 *K8* **Coal** ≈ Yukon Territory, NW Canada
40 *L14* **Coalcomán** *var.* Coalcomán de Matamoros. Michoacán de Ocampo, S Mexico
Coalcomán de Matamoros *see* Coalcomán
39 *T8* **Coal Creek** Alaska, USA
11 *Q17* **Coaldale** Alberta, SW Canada
27 *P12* **Coalgate** Oklahoma, C USA
35 *P11* **Coalinga** California, W USA
10 *L9* **Coal River** British Columbia, W Canada
21 *Q6* **Coal River** ≈ West Virginia, NE USA
36 *M2* **Coalville** Utah, W USA
58 *E13* **Coari** Amazonas, N Brazil
59 *D14* **Coari, Rio** ≈ NW Brazil
81 *J20* **Coast** ◈ *province* SE Kenya
Coast *see* Pwani
8 *G12* **Coast Mountains** *Fr.* Chaîne Côtière. ▲▲ Canada/USA
16 *C7* **Coast Ranges** ▲▲ W USA
96 *I12* **Coatbridge** S Scotland, UK
42 *B6* **Coatepeque** Quezaltenango, SW Guatemala
18 *H16* **Coatesville** Pennsylvania, NE USA
15 *Q13* **Coaticook** Quebec, SE Canada
9 *P9* **Coats Island** *island* Nunavut, NE Canada
195 *O4* **Coats Land** *physical region* Antarctica
41 *T14* **Coatzacoalcos** *var.* Quetzalcoalco; *prev.* Puerto México. Veracruz-Llave, E Mexico
41 *S14* **Coatzacoalcos, Río** ≈ SE Mexico
116 *M15* **Cobadin** Constanţa, SW Romania
14 *H9* **Cobalt** Ontario, S Canada
42 *D5* **Cobán** Alta Verapaz, C Guatemala
183 *O6* **Cobar** New South Wales, SE Australia
18 *F12* **Cobb Hill** ▲ Pennsylvania, NE USA
(0) *D8* **Cobb Seamount** *undersea feature* E Pacific Ocean
14 *K12* **Cobden** Ontario, SE Canada
97 *D21* **Cobh** *Ir.* An Cóbh; *prev.* Cove of Cork, Queenstown. SW Ireland
57 *J14* **Cobija** Pando, NW Bolivia
Coblence/Coblenz *see* Koblenz
18 *J10* **Cobleskill** New York, NE USA
14 *I15* **Cobourg** Ontario, SE Canada
181 *P1* **Cobourg Peninsula** *headland* Northern Territory, N Australia
183 *O10* **Cobram** Victoria, SE Australia
82 *N13* **Cóbuè** Niassa, N Mozambique
101 *K18* **Coburg** Bayern, SE Germany
19 *Q5* **Coburn Mountain** ▲ Maine, NE USA
Coca *see* Puerto Francisco de Orellana
57 *H18* **Cocachacra** Arequipa, SW Peru
59 *J17* **Cocalinho** Mato Grosso, W Brazil
Cocanada *see* Kākināda
105 *S11* **Cocentaina** País Valenciano, E Spain
57 *L18* **Cochabamba** *hist.* Oropeza. Cochabamba, C Bolivia
57 *K18* **Cochabamba** ◈ *department* C Bolivia
57 *L18* **Cochabamba, Cordillera de** ▲▲ C Bolivia
101 *E18* **Cochem** Rheinland-Pfalz, W Germany
37 *R6* **Cochetopa Hills** ▲▲ Colorado, C USA
155 *G22* **Cochin** *var.* Kochi. Kerala, SW India
44 *D5* **Cochinos, Bahía de** *Eng.* Bay of Pigs. *bay* SE Cuba
37 *O16* **Cochise Head** ▲ Arizona, SW USA
23 *U5* **Cochran** Georgia, SE USA
11 *P16* **Cochrane** Alberta, SW Canada
12 *G12* **Cochrane** Ontario, S Canada
63 *G20* **Cochrane** Aisén, S Chile
11 *U10* **Cochrane** ≈ Manitoba/Saskatchewan, C Canada
Cochrane, Lago *see* Pueyrredón, Lago
Cocibolca *see* Nicaragua, Lago de
Cockade State *see* Maryland
44 *M6* **Cockburn Harbour** South Caicos, S Turks and Caicos Islands
14 *C11* **Cockburn Island** *island* Ontario, S Canada
44 *J3* **Cockburn Town** San Salvador, E Bahamas
21 *X2* **Cockeysville** Maryland, NE USA
181 *N12* **Cocklebiddy** Western Australia
44 *I12* **Cockpit Country, The** *physical region* W Jamaica
43 *S16* **Coclé** *off.* Provincia de Coclé. ◈ *province* C Panama
43 *S15* **Coclé del Norte** Colón, C Panama
23 *Y12* **Cocoa** Florida, SE USA
23 *Y12* **Cocoa Beach** Florida, SE USA
79 *D17* **Cocobeach** Estuaire, NW Gabon
44 *G5* **Coco, Cayo** *island* C Cuba
151 *Q19* **Coco Channel** *strait* Andaman Sea/Bay of Bengal
173 *N6* **Coco-de-Mer Seamounts** *undersea feature* W Indian Ocean
36 *K10* **Coconino Plateau** *plain* Arizona, SW USA
43 *N6* **Coco, Río** *var.* Río Wanki, Segoviao Wangkí. ≈ Honduras/Nicaragua
173 *T8* **Cocos (Keeling) Islands** ◇ *Australian external territory* E Indian Ocean
173 *T7* **Cocos Basin** *undersea feature* E Indian Ocean
188 *B17* **Cocos Island** *island* S Guam
Cocos Island Ridge *see* Cocos Ridge
131 *S17* **Cocos Islands** *island group* E Indian Ocean
(0) *G15* **Cocos Plate** *tectonic feature*
193 *T7* **Cocos Ridge** *var.* Cocos Island Ridge. *undersea feature* E Pacific Ocean
40 *K13* **Cocula** Jalisco, SW Mexico
107 *D17* **Coda Cavallo, Capo** *headland* Sardegna, Italy, C Mediterranean Sea
58 *E13* **Codajás** Amazonas, N Brazil
Codazzi *see* Agustín Codazzi
19 *Q12* **Cod, Cape** *headland* Massachusetts, NE USA
185 *B25* **Codfish Island** *island* SW NZ
106 *H9* **Codigoro** Emilia-Romagna, N Italy
13 *P5* **Cod Island** *island* Newfoundland, E Canada
116 *J12* **Codlea** *Ger.* Zeiden, *Hung.* Feketehalom. Braşov, C Romania
58 *M13* **Codó** Maranhão, E Brazil
106 *E8* **Codogno** Lombardia, N Italy
116 *M10* **Codrii** *hill range* C Moldova
45 *W9* **Codrington** Barbuda, Antigua and Barbuda
106 *J7* **Codroipo** Friuli-Venezia Giulia, NE Italy
28 *M12* **Cody** Nebraska, C USA
33 *U12* **Cody** Wyoming, C USA
21 *P7* **Coeburn** Virginia, NE USA
54 *E10* **Coello** Tolima, W Colombia
Coemba *see* Cuemba
181 *V2* **Coen** Queensland, NE Australia
101 *E14* **Coesfeld** Nordrhein-Westfalen, W Germany
32 *M8* **Coeur d'Alene** Idaho, NW USA
32 *M8* **Coeur d'Alene Lake** ⊟ Idaho, NW USA
98 *O8* **Coevorden** Drenthe, NE Netherlands
10 *H6* **Coffee Creek** Yukon Territory, W Canada
30 *L15* **Coffeen Lake** ⊟ Illinois, N USA
22 *L3* **Coffeeville** Mississippi, S USA
27 *Q8* **Coffeyville** Kansas, C USA
182 *G9* **Coffin Bay** South Australia
182 *F9* **Coffin Bay Peninsula** *peninsula* South Australia
183 *V5* **Coffs Harbour** New South Wales, SE Australia
105 *R10* **Cofrentes** País Valenciano, E Spain
Cogîlnic *see* Kohyl'nyk
102 *K11* **Cognac** *anc.* Compniacum. Charente, W France
106 *B7* **Cogne** Valle d'Aosta, NW Italy
103 *U16* **Cogolin** Var, SE France
105 *O7* **Cogolludo** Castilla-La Mancha, C Spain
Cohalm *see* Rupea
92 *L8* **Čohkará##a** *var.* Cuokkarašša. ▲ N Norway
F11 **Cohocton River** ≈ New York, NE USA
18 *L10* **Cohoes** New York, NE USA
183 *N10* **Cohuna** Victoria, SE Australia
43 *P17* **Coiba, Isla de** *island* SW Panama
63 *H23* **Coig, Río** ≈ S Argentina
63 *G19* **Coihaique** *var.* Coyhaique. Aisén, S Chile
155 *G21* **Coimbatore** Tamil Nādu, S India
104 *G8* **Coimbra** *anc.* Conimbria, Conimbriga. Coimbra, W Portugal
104 *G8* **Coimbra** ◈ *district* N Portugal
104 *L15* **Coín** Andalucía, S Spain
57 *J20* **Coipasa, Laguna** ◎ W Bolivia
57 *J20* **Coipasa, Salar de** *salt lake* W Bolivia
Coira/Coire *see* Chur
Coirib, Loch *see* Corrib, Lough
54 *K6* **Cojedes** *off.* Estado Cojedes. ◈ *state* N Venezuela
42 *F7* **Cojutepeque** Cuscatlán, C El Salvador
33 *S16* **Cokeville** Wyoming, C USA
182 *M13* **Colac** Victoria, SE Australia
59 *O20* **Colatina** Espírito Santo, SE Brazil
27 *O13* **Colbert** Oklahoma, C USA
100 *L12* **Colbitz-Letzinger Heide** *heathland* N Germany
26 *I3* **Colby** Kansas, C USA
57 *H17* **Colca, Río** ≈ SW Peru
97 *P21* **Colchester** *hist.* Colneceaste, *anc.* Camulodunum. E England, UK
19 *N13* **Colchester** Connecticut, NE USA
38 *M16* **Cold Bay** Alaska, USA
11 *R14* **Cold Lake** Alberta, SW Canada
11 *R13* **Cold Lake** ◎ Alberta/Saskatchewan, S Canada
29 *U8* **Cold Spring** Minnesota, N USA
25 *W10* **Coldspring** Texas, SW USA
11 *N17* **Coldstream** British Columbia, SW Canada
96 *L13* **Coldstream** SE Scotland, UK
14 *H13* **Coldwater** Ontario, S Canada
26 *K7* **Coldwater** Kansas, C USA
31 *Q10* **Coldwater** Michigan, N USA
25 *N1* **Coldwater Creek** ≈ Oklahoma/Texas, SW USA
22 *K2* **Coldwater River** ≈ Mississippi, S USA
183 *O9* **Coleambally** New South Wales, SE Australia
19 *O6* **Colebrook** New Hampshire, NE USA
27 *T5* **Cole Camp** Missouri, C USA
39 *T6* **Coleen River** ≈ Alaska, USA
11 *P17* **Coleman** Alberta, SW Canada
25 *Q8* **Coleman** Texas, SW USA
Çölemerik *see* Hakkâri
83 *K22* **Colenso** KwaZulu/Natal, E South Africa
182 *L12* **Coleraine** Victoria, SE Australia
97 *F14* **Coleraine** *Ir.* Cúil Raithin. N Northern Ireland, UK
185 *G18* **Coleridge, Lake** ◎ South Island, NZ
83 *H24* **Colesberg** Northern Cape, C South Africa
22 *H7* **Colfax** Louisiana, S USA
32 *L9* **Colfax** Washington, NW USA
30 *J6* **Colfax** Wisconsin, N USA
63 *I19* **Colhué Huapí, Lago** ◎ S Argentina
45 *Z6* **Colibris, Pointe des** *headland* Grande Terre, E Guadeloupe
106 *D6* **Colico** Lombardia, N Italy
99 *E14* **Colijnsplaat** Zeeland, SW Netherlands
40 *L14* **Colima** Colima, S Mexico
40 *K14* **Colima** ◈ *state* SW Mexico
40 *L14* **Colima, Nevado de** ⛰ C Mexico
59 *M14* **Colinas** Maranhão, E Brazil
96 *F10* **Coll** *island* W Scotland, UK
105 *N7* **Collado Villalba** *var.* Villalba. Madrid, C Spain
183 *R4* **Collarenebri** New South Wales, SE Australia
37 *P5* **Collbran** Colorado, C USA
106 *G12* **Colle di Val d'Elsa** Toscana, C Italy
39 *R9* **College** Alaska, USA
32 *K10* **College Place** Washington, NW USA
25 *U10* **College Station** Texas, SW USA
183 *P4* **Collerina** New South Wales, SE Australia
180 *I13* **Collie** Western Australia
180 *L4* **Collier Bay** *bay* Western Australia
21 *F10* **Collierville** Tennessee, S USA
106 *F11* **Collina, Passo della** *pass* C Italy
14 *G14* **Collingwood** Ontario, S Canada
184 *I13* **Collingwood** Tasman, South Island, NZ
22 *L7* **Collins** Mississippi, S USA
30 *K15* **Collinsville** Illinois, N USA
27 *P9* **Collinsville** Oklahoma, C USA
20 *H10* **Collinwood** Tennessee, S USA
Collipo *see* Leiria
63 *G14* **Collipulli** Araucanía, C Chile
97 *D16* **Collooney** *Ir.* Cúil Mhuine. NW Ireland
29 *R10* **Colman** South Dakota, N USA
103 *U6* **Colmar** *Ger.* Kolmar. Haut-Rhin, NE France
104 *M15* **Colmenar** Andalucía, S Spain
Colmenar *see* Colmenar de Oreja
105 *O9* **Colmenar de Oreja** *var.* Colmenar. Madrid, C Spain
105 *N7* **Colmenar Viejo** Madrid, C Spain
25 *X9* **Colmesneil** Texas, SW USA
Cöln *see* Köln
Colneceaste *see* Colchester

◆ Country
● Country Capital
◇ Dependent Territory
○ Dependent Territory Capital
◈ Administrative Region
× International Airport
▲ Mountain
▲▲ Mountain Range
⛰ Volcano
≈ River
◎ Lake
⊟ Reservoir

40 C3 **Colnet** Baja California, NW Mexico
59 G15 **Colniza** Mato Grosso, W Brazil
Cologne see Köln
42 B6 **Colomba** Quezaltenango, SW Guatemala
Colomb-Béchar see Béchar
54 E11 **Colombia** Huila, C Colombia
54 G10 **Colombia** *off.* Republic of Colombia. ◆ *republic* N South America
64 E12 **Colombian Basin** *undersea feature* SW Caribbean Sea
Colombie-Britannique see British Columbia
15 T6 **Colombier** Quebec, SE Canada
155 J25 **Colombo** ● (Sri Lanka) Western Province, W Sri Lanka
155 J25 **Colombo** × Western Province, SW Sri Lanka
29 N11 **Colome** South Dakota, N USA
61 D18 **Colon** Entre Ríos, E Argentina
61 B19 **Colón** Buenos Aires, E Argentina
44 D5 **Colón** Matanzas, C Cuba
43 T14 **Colón** *prev.* Aspinwall. Colón, C Panama
42 K5 **Colón** ◈ *department* NE Honduras
43 S15 **Colón** *off.* Provincia de Colón. ◈ *province* N Panama
57 A16 **Colón, Archipiélago de** *var.* Islas de los Galápagos, *Eng.* Galapagos Islands, Tortoise Islands. *island group* Ecuador, E Pacific Ocean
44 K5 **Colonel Hill** Crooked Island, SE Bahamas
40 B3 **Colonet, Cabo** *headland* NW Mexico
188 G14 **Colonia** Yap, W Micronesia
61 D19 **Colonia** ◈ *department* SW Uruguay
Colonia see Kolonia, Micronesia
Colonia see Colonia del Sacramento, Uruguay
Colonia Agrippina see Köln
61 D20 **Colonia del Sacramento** *var.* Colonia. Colonia, SW Uruguay
62 L8 **Colonia Dora** Santiago del Estero, N Argentina
Colonia Julia Fanestris see Fano
21 W5 **Colonial Beach** Virginia, NE USA
21 V6 **Colonial Heights** Virginia, NE USA
193 S7 **Colón Ridge** *undersea feature* E Pacific Ocean
96 F12 **Colonsay** *island* W Scotland, UK
57 K22 **Colorada, Laguna** ◎ SW Bolivia
37 R6 **Colorado** *off.* State of Colorado; also known as Centennial State, Silver State. ◈ *state* C USA
63 H22 **Colorado, Cerro** ▲ S Argentina
25 O7 **Colorado City** Texas, SW USA
36 M7 **Colorado Plateau** *plateau* W USA
61 A24 **Colorado, Río** ≈ E Argentina
43 N12 **Colorado, Río** ≈ NE Costa Rica
Colorado, Río see Colorado River
16 F12 **Colorado River** *var.* Río Colorado. ≈ Mexico/USA
16 K14 **Colorado River** ≈ Texas, SW USA
35 W15 **Colorado River Aqueduct** *aqueduct* California, W USA
44 A4 **Colorados, Archipiélago de los** *island group* NW Cuba
62 J9 **Colorados, Desagües de los** ◎ W Argentina
37 T5 **Colorado Springs** Colorado, C USA
40 L11 **Colotlán** Jalisco, SW Mexico
57 L19 **Colquechaca** Potosí, C Bolivia
23 S7 **Colquitt** Georgia, SE USA
29 R11 **Colton** South Dakota, N USA
32 M10 **Colton** Washington, NW USA
35 P8 **Columbia** California, W USA
30 K16 **Columbia** Illinois, N USA
20 L7 **Columbia** Kentucky, S USA
22 I6 **Columbia** Louisiana, S USA
21 W3 **Columbia** Maryland, NE USA
22 L7 **Columbia** Mississippi, S USA
27 U4 **Columbia** Missouri, C USA
21 Y9 **Columbia** North Carolina, SE USA
18 G16 **Columbia** Pennsylvania, NE USA
21 Q12 **Columbia** *state capital* South Carolina, SE USA
20 I9 **Columbia** Tennessee, S USA
(0) F9 **Columbia** ≈ Canada/USA
32 K9 **Columbia Basin** *basin* Washington, NW USA
197 Q10 **Columbia, Cape** *headland* Ellesmere Island, Nunavut, NE Canada
31 Q12 **Columbia City** Indiana, N USA
21 W3 **Columbia, District of** ◈ *federal district* NE USA
33 P7 **Columbia Falls** Montana, NW USA
11 O15 **Columbia Icefield** *icefield* Alberta/British Columbia, S Canada
11 O15 **Columbia, Mount** ▲ Alberta/British Columbia, SW Canada
11 N15 **Columbia Mountains** ▲ British Columbia, SW Canada
23 P4 **Columbiana** Alabama, S USA
31 V12 **Columbiana** Ohio, N USA
32 M14 **Columbia Plateau** *plateau* Idaho/Oregon, NW USA
29 P7 **Columbia Road Reservoir** ▣ South Dakota, N USA
65 K16 **Columbia Seamount** *undersea feature* C Atlantic Ocean
83 D25 **Columbine, Cape** *headland* SW South Africa
105 U9 **Columbretes, Islas** *island group* E Spain
23 R5 **Columbus** Georgia, SE USA
31 P14 **Columbus** Indiana, N USA
27 R7 **Columbus** Kansas, C USA
23 N4 **Columbus** Mississippi, S USA
33 U11 **Columbus** Montana, NW USA
29 Q15 **Columbus** Nebraska, C USA
37 Q16 **Columbus** New Mexico, SW USA
21 P10 **Columbus** North Carolina, SE USA
28 K2 **Columbus** North Dakota, N USA
31 S13 **Columbus** *state capital* Ohio, N USA
25 U11 **Columbus** Texas, SW USA
30 L8 **Columbus** Wisconsin, N USA
31 R12 **Columbus Grove** Ohio, N USA
29 Y15 **Columbus Junction** Iowa, C USA
44 J3 **Columbus Point** *headland* Cat Island, C Bahamas
35 T8 **Columbus Salt Marsh** *salt marsh* Nevada, W USA
35 N6 **Colusa** California, W USA
32 L7 **Colville** Washington, NW USA
184 M5 **Colville, Cape** *headland* North Island, NZ
184 M5 **Colville Channel** *channel* North Island, NZ
39 P6 **Colville River** ≈ Alaska, USA
97 J18 **Colwyn Bay** N Wales, UK
106 H9 **Comacchio** *var.* Commachio; *anc.* Comactium. Emilia-Romagna, N Italy
106 H9 **Comacchio, Valli di** *lagoon* Adriatic Sea, N Mediterranean Sea
Comactium see Comacchio
41 V17 **Comalapa** Chiapas, SE Mexico
41 U15 **Comalcalco** Tabasco, SE Mexico
63 H16 **Comallo** Río Negro, SW Argentina
26 M12 **Comanche** Oklahoma, C USA
25 R8 **Comanche** Texas, SW USA
194 H2 **Comandante Ferraz** *Brazilian research station* Antarctica
62 N6 **Comandante Fontana** Formosa, N Argentina
63 I22 **Comandante Luis Peidra Buena** Santa Cruz, S Argentina
59 O18 **Comandatuba** Bahia, SE Brazil
116 K11 **Comănești** *Hung.* Kománfalva. Bacău, SW Romania
57 M19 **Comarapa** Santa Cruz, C Bolivia
116 J13 **Comarnic** Prahova, SE Romania
42 H6 **Comayagua** Comayagua, W Honduras
42 H6 **Comayagua** ◈ *department* W Honduras
42 I6 **Comayagua, Montañas de** ▲ C Honduras
21 R15 **Combahee River** ≈ South Carolina, SE USA
62 G10 **Combarbalá** Coquimbo, C Chile
103 S7 **Combeaufontaine** Haute-Saône, E France
97 G15 **Comber** *Ir.* An Comar. E Northern Ireland, UK
99 K20 **Comblain-au-Pont** Liège, E Belgium
102 I6 **Combourg** Ille-et-Vilaine, NW France
44 M9 **Comendador** *prev.* Elías Piña. W Dominican Republic
Comer See see Como, Lago di
25 R11 **Comfort** Texas, SW USA
153 V15 **Comilla** *Ben.* Kumillā. Chittagong, E Bangladesh
99 B18 **Comines** Hainaut, W Belgium
121 O15 **Comino** *Malt.* Kemmuna. *island* C Malta
107 D18 **Comino, Capo** *headland* Sardegna, Italy, C Mediterranean Sea
107 K25 **Comiso** Sicilia, Italy, C Mediterranean Sea
41 V16 **Comitán** *var.* Comitán de Domínguez. Chiapas, SE Mexico
Comitán de Domínguez see Comitán
Commachio see Comacchio
Commander Islands see Komandorskiye Ostrova
103 O10 **Commentry** Allier, C France
23 T2 **Commerce** Georgia, SE USA
27 R8 **Commerce** Oklahoma, C USA
25 V5 **Commerce** Texas, SW USA
37 T4 **Commerce City** Colorado, C USA
103 S5 **Commercy** Meuse, NE France
55 W9 **Commewijne** *var.* Commewyne. ◈ *district* NE Suriname
Commewyne see Commewijne
15 P8 **Commissaires, Lac des** ◎ Quebec, SE Canada
64 A12 **Commissioner's Point** *headland* W Bermuda
9 O7 **Committee Bay** *bay* Nunavut, N Canada
106 D7 **Como** *anc.* Comum. Lombardia, N Italy
63 J19 **Comodoro Rivadavia** Chubut, SE Argentina
106 D6 **Como, Lago di** *var.* Lario, *Eng.* Lake Como, *Ger.* Comer See. ◎ N Italy
Como, Lake see Como, Lago di
40 E7 **Comondú** Baja California Sur, W Mexico
116 F12 **Comorâște** *Hung.* Komornok. Caraș-Severin, SW Romania
Comores, République Fédérale Islamique des see Comoros
155 G24 **Comorin, Cape** *headland* SE India
172 M8 **Comoro Basin** *undersea feature* SW Indian Ocean
172 I14 **Comoro Islands** *island group* W Indian Ocean
172 H13 **Comoros** *off.* Federal Islamic Republic of the Comoros, *Fr.* République Fédérale Islamique des Comores. ◆ *republic* W Indian Ocean
10 L17 **Comox** Vancouver Island, British Columbia, SW Canada
103 O4 **Compiègne** Oise, N France
Complutum see Alcalá de Henares
Compniacum see Cognac
40 K12 **Compostela** Nayarit, C Mexico
Compostella see Santiago
60 L11 **Comprida, Ilha** *island* S Brazil
117 N11 **Comrat** *Rus.* Komrat. S Moldova
25 O11 **Comstock** Texas, SW USA
31 P9 **Comstock Park** Michigan, N USA
193 N3 **Comstock Seamount** *undersea feature* N Pacific Ocean
Comum see Como
159 N17 **Cona** Xizang Zizhiqu, W China
76 H14 **Conakry** ● (Guinea) Conakry, SW Guinea
76 H14 **Conakry** × Conakry, SW Guinea
Conamara see Connemara
Conca see Cuenca
25 Q12 **Concan** Texas, SW USA
102 F6 **Concarneau** Finistère, NW France
83 O17 **Conceição** Sofala, C Mozambique
59 K15 **Conceição do Araguaia** Pará, NE Brazil
58 F10 **Conceição do Maú** Roraima, W Brazil
61 D14 **Concepción** *var.* Concepcion. Corrientes, NE Argentina
62 J8 **Concepción** Tucumán, N Argentina
57 O17 **Concepción** Santa Cruz, E Bolivia
62 G13 **Concepción** Bío Bío, C Chile
54 E14 **Concepción** Putumayo, S Colombia
62 O5 **Concepción** *var.* Villa Concepción. Concepción, C Paraguay
62 O5 **Concepción** *off.* Departamento de Concepción. ◈ *department* E Paraguay
Concepción see La Concepción
Concepción de la Vega see La Vega
41 N9 **Concepción del Oro** Zacatecas, C Mexico
61 D18 **Concepción del Uruguay** Entre Ríos, E Argentina
42 K11 **Concepción, Volcán** ⊼ SW Nicaragua
44 J4 **Conception Island** *island* C Bahamas
35 P14 **Conception, Point** *headland* California, W USA
54 H6 **Concha** Zulia, W Venezuela
60 L9 **Conchas** São Paulo, S Brazil
37 U11 **Conchas Dam** New Mexico, SW USA
37 U10 **Conchas Lake** ▣ New Mexico, SW USA
102 M5 **Conches-en-Ouche** Eure, N France
37 N12 **Concho** Arizona, SW USA
40 J5 **Conchos, Río** ≈ NW Mexico
41 O8 **Conchos, Río** ≈ C Mexico
108 C8 **Concise** Vaud, W Switzerland
35 N8 **Concord** California, W USA
19 O9 **Concord** *state capital* New Hampshire, NE USA
21 R10 **Concord** North Carolina, SE USA
61 D17 **Concordia** Entre Ríos, E Argentina
54 D9 **Concordia** Antioquia, W Colombia
40 J10 **Concordia** Sinaloa, C Mexico
57 I19 **Concordia** Tacna, SW Peru
27 N3 **Concordia** Kansas, C USA
27 S4 **Concordia** Missouri, C USA
60 I13 **Concórdia** Santa Catarina, S Brazil
167 S7 **Con Cuông** Nghê An, N Vietnam
167 T15 **Côn Đao** *var.* Con Son. *island* S Vietnam
Condate see St-Claude, Jura, France
Condate see Rennes, Ille-et-Vilaine, France
Condate see Montereau-Faut-Yonne, Seine-St-Denis, France
29 P8 **Conde** South Dakota, N USA
42 J8 **Condega** Estelí, NW Nicaragua
103 P2 **Condé-sur-l'Escaut** Nord, N France
102 K5 **Condé-sur-Noireau** Calvados, N France
Condivincum see Nantes
183 P8 **Condobolin** New South Wales, SE Australia
102 L15 **Condom** Gers, S France
32 J11 **Condon** Oregon, NW USA
54 D9 **Condoto** Chocó, W Colombia
23 P7 **Conecuh River** ≈ Alabama/Florida, SE USA
106 H7 **Conegliano** Veneto, NE Italy
61 C19 **Conesa** Buenos Aires, E Argentina
14 F15 **Conestogo** ≈ Ontario, S Canada
Confluentes see Koblenz
102 L10 **Confolens** Charente, W France
36 J4 **Confusion Range** ▲ Utah, W USA
62 N6 **Confuso, Río** ≈ C Paraguay
21 R12 **Congaree River** ≈ South Carolina, SE USA
Công Hoa Xa Hôi Chu Nghia Viêt Nam see Vietnam
160 K12 **Congjiang** *prev.* Bingmei. Guizhou, S China
79 K19 **Congo** *off.* Democratic Republic of Congo; *prev.* Zaire, Belgian Congo, Congo (Kinshasa). ◆ *republic* C Africa
79 G18 **Congo** *off.* Republic of the Congo, *Fr.* Moyen-Congo; *prev.* Middle Congo. ◆ *republic* C Africa
67 T11 **Congo** *var.* Kongo, *Fr.* Zaire. ≈ C Africa
Congo see Zaire (province, Angola)
Congo/Congo (Kinshasa) see Congo (Democratic Republic of)
79 K18 **Congo Basin** *drainage basin* W Dem. Rep. Congo (Zaire)
67 Q11 **Congo Canyon** *var.* Congo Seavalley, Congo Submarine Canyon. *undersea feature* E Atlantic Ocean
Congo Cone see Congo Fan
65 P15 **Congo Fan** *var.* Congo Cone. *undersea feature* E Atlantic Ocean
Coni see Cuneo
63 H18 **Cónico, Cerro** ▲ SW Argentina
Conimbria/Conimbriga see Coimbra
Conjeeveram see Kānchipuram
11 R13 **Conklin** Alberta, C Canada
24 M1 **Conlen** Texas, SW USA
Con, Loch see Conn, Lough
Connacht see Connaught
97 B17 **Connaught** *var.* Connacht, *Ir.* Chonnacht, Cúige. *cultural region* W Ireland
31 V10 **Conneaut** Ohio, N USA
18 L13 **Connecticut** *off.* State of Connecticut; also known as Blue Law State, Constitution State, Land of Steady Habits, Nutmeg State. ◈ *state* NE USA
19 N8 **Connecticut** ≈ Canada/USA
19 O6 **Connecticut Lakes** *lakes* New Hampshire, NE USA
32 K9 **Connell** Washington, NW USA
97 B17 **Connemara** *Ir.* Conamara. *region* W Ireland
31 Q14 **Connersville** Indiana, N USA
97 B16 **Conn, Lough** *Ir.* Loch Con. ◎ W Ireland
35 X6 **Connors Pass** *pass* Nevada, W USA
181 X7 **Connors Range** ▲ Queensland, E Australia
56 E7 **Cononaco, Río** ≈ E Ecuador
29 W13 **Conrad** Iowa, C USA
33 R7 **Conrad** Montana, NW USA
25 W10 **Conroe** Texas, SW USA
25 V10 **Conroe, Lake** ▣ Texas, SW USA
61 C17 **Conscripto Bernardi** Entre Ríos, E Argentina
59 M20 **Conselheiro Lafaiete** Minas Gerais, SE Brazil
Consentia see Cosenza
97 L14 **Consett** N England, UK
44 B5 **Consolación del Sur** Pinar del Río, W Cuba
Con Son see Côn Đao
11 R15 **Consort** Alberta, SW Canada
Constance see Konstanz
108 I6 **Constance, Lake** *Ger.* Bodensee. ◎ C Europe
104 G9 **Constância** Santarém, C Portugal
117 N14 **Constanța** *var.* Küstendje, *Eng.* Constanza, *Ger.* Konstanza, *Turk.* Küstence. Constanța, SE Romania
116 L14 **Constanța** ◈ *county* SE Romania
Constantia see Coutances, France
Constantia see Konstanz, Germany
104 K13 **Constantina** Andalucía, S Spain
74 L5 **Constantine** *var.* Qacentina, *Ar.* Qoussantîna. NE Algeria
39 O14 **Constantine, Cape** *headland* Alaska, USA
Constantinople see İstanbul
Constantiola see Oltenișa
Constanz see Konstanz
Constanza see Constanța
62 G13 **Constitución** Maule, C Chile
61 D17 **Constitución** Salto, N Uruguay
Constitution State see Connecticut
105 N10 **Consuegra** Castilla-La Mancha, C Spain
181 X9 **Consuelo Peak** ▲ Queensland, E Australia
56 E11 **Contamana** Loreto, N Peru
Contrasto, Colle del see Contrasto, Portella del
107 K23 **Contrasto, Portella del** *var.* Colle del Contrasto. *pass* Sicilia, Italy, C Mediterranean Sea
54 G8 **Contratación** Santander, C Colombia
102 M8 **Contres** Loir-et-Cher, C France
107 O17 **Conversano** Puglia, SE Italy
27 U11 **Conway** Arkansas, C USA
19 O8 **Conway** New Hampshire, NE USA
21 U13 **Conway** South Carolina, SE USA
25 N2 **Conway** Texas, SW USA
27 U11 **Conway, Lake** ▣ Arkansas, C USA
27 N7 **Conway Springs** Kansas, C USA
97 J18 **Conwy** N Wales, UK
23 T3 **Conyers** Georgia, SE USA
Coo see Kos
182 F4 **Coober Pedy** South Australia
181 P2 **Cooinda** Northern Territory, N Australia
182 B6 **Cook** South Australia
29 W4 **Cook** Minnesota, N USA
191 N6 **Cook, Baie de** *bay* Moorea, W French Polynesia
10 J16 **Cook, Cape** *headland* Vancouver Island, British Columbia, SW Canada
37 Q15 **Cookes Peak** ▲ New Mexico, SW USA
20 L8 **Cookeville** Tennessee, S USA
175 P9 **Cook Fracture Zone** *tectonic feature* S Pacific Ocean
Cook, Grand Récif de see Cook, Récif de
39 Q12 **Cook Inlet** *inlet* Alaska, USA
191 X2 **Cook Island** *island* Line Islands, E Kiribati
190 J14 **Cook Islands** ◇ *territory in free association with NZ* S Pacific Ocean
185 E19 **Cook, Mount** *prev.* Aoraki, Aorangi. ▲ South Island, NZ
187 O15 **Cook, Récif de** *var.* Grand Récif de Cook. *reef* S New Caledonia
14 G14 **Cookstown** Ontario, S Canada
97 F15 **Cookstown** *Ir.* An Chorr Chríochach. C Northern Ireland, UK
185 K14 **Cook Strait** *var.* Raukawa. *strait* NZ
181 W3 **Cooktown** Queensland, NE Australia
183 P6 **Coolabah** New South Wales, SE Australia
182 J11 **Coola Coola Swamp** *wetland* South Australia
183 S7 **Coolah** New South Wales, SE Australia
183 P9 **Coolamon** New South Wales, SE Australia
183 T4 **Coolatai** New South Wales, SE Australia
180 K12 **Coolgardie** Western Australia
36 L14 **Coolidge** Arizona, SW USA
25 U8 **Coolidge** Texas, SW USA
183 Q11 **Cooma** New South Wales, SE Australia
Coomassie see Kumasi
183 R6 **Coonabarabran** New South Wales, SE Australia
182 J10 **Coonalpyn** South Australia
183 R6 **Coonamble** New South Wales, SE Australia
Coondapoor see Kundāpura
155 G21 **Coonoor** Tamil Nādu, SE India
29 U14 **Coon Rapids** Iowa, C USA
29 V8 **Coon Rapids** Minnesota, N USA
25 V5 **Cooper** Texas, SW USA
181 U9 **Cooper Creek** *var.* Barcoo, Cooper's Creek. *seasonal river* Queensland/South Australia
39 R12 **Cooper Landing** Alaska, USA
21 T14 **Cooper River** ≈ South Carolina, SE USA
Cooper's Creek see Cooper Creek
44 H1 **Coopers Town** Great Abaco, N Bahamas
18 J10 **Cooperstown** New York, NE USA
29 P4 **Cooperstown** North Dakota, N USA
31 P9 **Coopersville** Michigan, N USA
182 D7 **Coorabie** South Australia
23 Q3 **Coosa River** ≈ Alabama/Georgia, S USA
32 E14 **Coos Bay** Oregon, NW USA
183 Q9 **Cootamundra** New South Wales, SE Australia
97 E16 **Cootehill** *Ir.* Muinchille. N Ireland
Čop see Chop
57 J17 **Copacabana** La Paz, W Bolivia
63 H14 **Copahué, Volcán** ▲ C Chile
41 U16 **Copainalá** Chiapas, SE Mexico
32 F8 **Copalis Beach** Washington, NW USA
42 F6 **Copán** ◈ *department* W Honduras
Copán see Copán Ruinas
25 T14 **Copano Bay** *bay* NW Gulf of Mexico
42 F6 **Copán Ruinas** *var.* Copán. Copán, W Honduras
Copenhagen see København
107 Q19 **Copertino** Puglia, SE Italy
62 H7 **Copiapó** Atacama, N Chile
62 G8 **Copiapó, Bahía** *bay* N Chile
62 G7 **Copiapó, Río** ≈ N Chile
114 M12 **Çöpköy** Edirne, NW Turkey
182 I5 **Copley** South Australia
106 H9 **Copparo** Emilia-Romagna, C Italy
55 V10 **Coppename Rivier** *var.* Koppename. ≈ C Suriname
25 S9 **Copperas Cove** Texas, SW USA
82 J13 **Copperbelt** ◈ *province* C Zambia
39 S11 **Copper Center** Alaska, USA
Coppermine see Kugluktuk
8 K8 **Coppermine** ≈ Northwest Territories/Nunavut, N Canada
39 T11 **Copper River** ≈ Alaska, USA
Copper State see Arizona
116 I11 **Copșa Mică** *Ger.* Kleinkopisch, *Hung.* Kiskapus. Sibiu, C Romania
158 J14 **Coqên** Xizang Zizhiqu, W China
Coquilhatville see Mbandaka
32 E14 **Coquille** Oregon, NW USA
62 G9 **Coquimbo** Coquimbo, N Chile
62 G9 **Coquimbo** *off.* Región de Coquimbo. ◈ *region* C Chile
116 I15 **Corabia** Olt, S Romania
57 F17 **Coracora** Ayacucho, SW Peru
Cora Droma Rúisc see Carrick-on-Shannon
44 K9 **Corail** SW Haiti
183 V4 **Coraki** New South Wales, SE Australia
180 G8 **Coral Bay** Western Australia
23 Y16 **Coral Gables** Florida, SE USA
9 P8 **Coral Harbour** Southampton Island, Northwest Territories, NE Canada
192 I9 **Coral Sea** *sea* SW Pacific Ocean
174 M7 **Coral Sea Basin** *undersea feature* N Coral Sea
192 H9 **Coral Sea Islands** ◇ *Australian external territory* SW Pacific Ocean
182 M12 **Corangamite, Lake** ◎ Victoria, SE Australia
Corantijn Rivier see Courantyne River
18 B14 **Coraopolis** Pennsylvania, NE USA
107 N17 **Corato** Puglia, SE Italy
103 O17 **Corbières** ▲ S France
103 P8 **Corbigny** Nièvre, C France
21 N7 **Corbin** Kentucky, S USA
104 L14 **Corbones** ≈ SW Spain
Corcaigh see Cork
35 R11 **Corcoran** California, W USA
47 T14 **Corcovado, Golfo** *gulf* S Chile
63 G18 **Corcovado, Volcán** ▲ S Chile
104 F3 **Corcubión** Galicia, NW Spain
Corcyra Nigra see Korčula
60 Q9 **Cordeiro** Rio de Janeiro, SE Brazil
23 T6 **Cordele** Georgia, SE USA
26 L11 **Cordell** Oklahoma, C USA
103 N14 **Cordes** Tarn, S France
62 O6 **Cordillera** *off.* Departamento de la Cordillera. ◈ *department* C Paraguay
182 K1 **Cordillo Downs** South Australia
62 K10 **Córdoba** Córdoba, C Argentina
41 R14 **Córdoba** Veracruz-Llave, E Mexico
104 M13 **Córdoba** *var.* Cordoba, *Eng.* Cordova; *anc.* Corduba. Andalucía, SW Spain
62 K11 **Córdoba** *off.* Provincia de Córdoba. ◈ *province* C Argentina
54 D7 **Córdoba** *off.* Departamento de Córdoba. ◈ *province* NW Colombia
104 L13 **Córdoba** ◈ *province* Andalucía, S Spain
62 K10 **Córdoba, Sierras de** ▲ C Argentina
23 O3 **Cordova** Alabama, S USA
39 S12 **Cordova** Alaska, USA
Cordova/Corduba see Córdoba
Corentyne River see Courantyne River
Corfu see Kérkyra
104 J9 **Coria** Extremadura, W Spain
104 J14 **Coria del Río** Andalucía, S Spain
183 S8 **Coricudgy, Mount** ▲ New South Wales, SE Australia
107 N20 **Corigliano Calabro** Calabria, SW Italy
Corinium/Corinium Dobunorum see Cirencester
23 N1 **Corinth** Mississippi, S USA
Corinth see Kórinthos
Corinth Canal see Dióryga Korinthou
Corinth, Gulf of/Corinthiacus Sinus see Korinthiakós Kólpos
Corinthus see Kórinthos
42 I9 **Corinto** Chinandega, NW Nicaragua
97 C21 **Cork** *Ir.* Corcaigh. S Ireland
97 C21 **Cork** *Ir.* Corcaigh. *cultural region* SW Ireland
97 C21 **Cork** × SW Ireland
97 D21 **Cork Harbour** *Ir.* Cuan Chorcaí. *inlet* SW Ireland
107 I23 **Corleone** Sicilia, Italy, C Mediterranean Sea
114 N13 **Çorlu** Tekirdağ, NW Turkey
114 N12 **Çorlu Çayı** ≈ NW Turkey
Cormaiore see Courmayeur
11 V13 **Cormorant** Manitoba, C Canada
23 T2 **Cornelia** Georgia, SE USA
60 J10 **Cornélio Procópio** Paraná, S Brazil
55 V9 **Corneliskondre** Sipaliwini, N Suriname
30 J5 **Cornell** Wisconsin, N USA
13 S12 **Corner Brook** Newfoundland, E Canada
Corner Rise Seamounts see Corner Seamounts
64 I9 **Corner Seamounts** *var.* Corner Rise Seamounts. *undersea feature* NW Atlantic Ocean
116 M9 **Cornești** *Rus.* Korneshty. C Moldova
Corneto see Tarquinia
Cornhusker State see Nebraska
27 X8 **Corning** Arkansas, C USA
35 N5 **Corning** California, W USA
29 U15 **Corning** Iowa, C USA
18 G11 **Corning** New York, NE USA
Corn Islands see Maíz, Islas del
107 J14 **Corno Grande** ▲ C Italy
15 N13 **Cornwall** Ontario, SE Canada
97 H25 **Cornwall** *cultural region* SW England, UK
97 G25 **Cornwall, Cape** *headland* SW England, UK
54 J4 **Coro** *prev.* Santa Ana de Coro. Falcón, NW Venezuela
57 J18 **Corocoro** La Paz, W Bolivia
57 K17 **Coroico** La Paz, W Bolivia
184 M5 **Coromandel** Waikato, North Island, NZ
155 K20 **Coromandel Coast** *coast* E India
184 M5 **Coromandel Peninsula** *peninsula* North Island, NZ

◆ Country ● Country Capital ◇ Dependent Territory ○ Dependent Territory Capital ◈ Administrative Region × International Airport ▲ Mountain ▲ Mountain Range ⊼ Volcano ≈ River ◎ Lake ▣ Reservoir

184 M6 **Coromandel Range** ▲ North Island, NZ
171 N5 **Coron** Busuanga Island, W Philippines
35 T15 **Corona** California, W USA
37 T12 **Corona** New Mexico, SW USA
11 U17 **Coronach** Saskatchewan, S Canada
35 U17 **Coronado** California, W USA
43 N15 **Coronado, Bahía de** *bay* S Costa Rica
11 R15 **Coronation** Alberta, SW Canada
8 K7 **Coronation Gulf** *gulf* Nunavut, N Canada
194 I1 **Coronation Island** *island* Antarctica
39 X14 **Coronation Island** *island* Alexander Archipelago, Alaska, USA
61 B18 **Coronda** Santa Fe, C Argentina
63 F14 **Coronel** Bío Bío, C Chile
61 D20 **Coronel Brandsen** *var.* Brandsen. Buenos Aires, E Argentina
62 K4 **Coronel Cornejo** Salta, N Argentina
61 B24 **Coronel Dorrego** Buenos Aires, E Argentina
62 P6 **Coronel Oviedo** Caaguazú, SE Paraguay
61 B23 **Coronel Pringles** Buenos Aires, E Argentina
61 B23 **Coronel Suárez** Buenos Aires, E Argentina
61 E22 **Coronel Vidal** Buenos Aires, E Argentina
55 V9 **Coronie** ◆ *district* NW Suriname
57 G17 **Coropuna, Nevado** ▲ S Peru
Çorovoda *see* Çorovodë
113 L22 **Çorovodë** *var.* Çorovoda. Berat, S Albania
183 P11 **Corowa** New South Wales, SE Australia
42 G1 **Corozal** Corozal, N Belize
54 E6 **Corozal** Sucre, NW Colombia
42 G1 **Corozal** ◆ *district* N Belize
25 T14 **Corpus Christi** Texas, SW USA
25 T14 **Corpus Christi Bay** *inlet* Texas, SW USA
25 R14 **Corpus Christi, Lake** ▣ Texas, SW USA
63 F16 **Corral** Los Lagos, C Chile
105 O9 **Corral de Almaguer** Castilla-La Mancha, C Spain
104 K6 **Corrales** Castilla-León, N Spain
37 R11 **Corrales** New Mexico, SW USA
Corrán Tuathail *see* Carrauntoohil
106 F9 **Correggio** Emilia-Romagna, C Italy
59 M16 **Corrente** Piauí, E Brazil
59 I19 **Correntes, Rio** ≈ SW Brazil
103 N12 **Corrèze** ◆ *department* C France
97 C17 **Corrib, Lough** *Ir.* Loch Coirib. ◎ W Ireland
61 C14 **Corrientes** Corrientes, NE Argentina
61 D15 **Corrientes** *off.* Provincia de Corrientes. ◆ *province* NE Argentina
44 A5 **Corrientes, Cabo** *headland* W Cuba
40 I13 **Corrientes, Cabo** *headland* SW Mexico
Corrientes, Provincia de *see* Corrientes
61 C16 **Corrientes, Río** ≈ NE Argentina
56 E8 **Corrientes, Río** ≈ Ecuador/Peru
25 W9 **Corrigan** Texas, SW USA
55 U9 **Corriverton** E Guyana
Corriza *see* Korçë
183 Q11 **Corryong** Victoria, SE Australia
103 Y12 **Corse** *Eng.* Corsica. ◆ *region* France, C Mediterranean Sea
103 X13 **Corse** *Eng.* Corsica. *island* France, C Mediterranean Sea
105 Y13 **Corse, Cap** *headland* Corse, France, C Mediterranean Sea
105 X15 **Corse-du-Sud** ◆ *department* Corse, France, C Mediterranean Sea
29 P11 **Corsica** South Dakota, N USA
Corsica *see* Corse
25 U7 **Corsicana** Texas, SW USA
103 Y15 **Corte** Corse, France, C Mediterranean Sea
63 G16 **Corte Alto** Los Lagos, S Chile
104 I13 **Cortegana** Andalucía, S Spain
43 N15 **Cortés** *var.* Ciudad Cortés. Puntarenas, SE Costa Rica
42 G5 **Cortés** ◆ *department* NW Honduras
37 P8 **Cortez** Colorado, C USA
Cortez, Sea of *see* California, Golfo de
106 H6 **Cortina d'Ampezzo** Veneto, NE Italy
18 H11 **Cortland** New York, NE USA
31 V11 **Cortland** Ohio, N USA
106 H12 **Cortona** Toscana, C Italy
76 H13 **Corubal, Rio** ≈ E Guinea-Bissau
104 G10 **Coruche** Santarém, C Portugal
Çoruh *see* Rize
137 R11 **Çoruh Nehri** *Geor.* Chorokhi, *Rus.* Chorokh. ≈ Georgia/Turkey
136 K12 **Çorum** *var.* Chorum. Çorum, N Turkey
136 J12 **Çorum** *var.* Chorum. ◆ *province* N Turkey
59 H19 **Corumbá** Mato Grosso do Sul, S Brazil
14 D16 **Corunna** Ontario, S Canada
Corunna *see* A Coruña
32 F12 **Corvallis** Oregon, NW USA
64 M1 **Corvo** *var.* Ilha do Corvo. *island* Azores, Portugal, NE Atlantic Ocean
Corvo, Ilha do *see* Corvo
31 O16 **Corydon** Indiana, N USA
29 V16 **Corydon** Iowa, C USA
Cos *see* Kos
40 I9 **Cosalá** Sinaloa, C Mexico
41 R15 **Cosamaloapan** *var.* Cosamaloapan de Carpio. Veracruz-Llave, E Mexico
Cosamaloapan de Carpio *see* Cosamaloapan
107 N21 **Cosenza** *anc.* Consentia. Calabria, SW Italy
31 T13 **Coshocton** Ohio, N USA
42 H9 **Cosigüina, Punta** *headland* NW Nicaragua
29 T9 **Cosmos** Minnesota, N USA
103 O8 **Cosne-sur-Loire** Nièvre, C France
108 B9 **Cossonay** Vaud, W Switzerland
Cossyra *see* Pantelleria
47 R4 **Costa, Cordillera de la** *var.* Cordillera de Venezuela. ▲ N Venezuela
42 K13 **Costa Rica** *off.* Republic of Costa Rica. ♦ *republic* Central America
43 N15 **Costeña, Fila** ▲ S Costa Rica
Costermansville *see* Bukavu
116 I14 **Costeşti** Argeş, SW Romania
37 S8 **Costilla** New Mexico, SW USA
35 O7 **Cosumnes River** ≈ California, W USA
101 O16 **Coswig** Sachsen, E Germany
101 M14 **Coswig** Sachsen-Anhalt, E Germany
Cosyra *see* Pantelleria
171 Q7 **Cotabato** Mindanao, S Philippines
56 C5 **Cotacachi** ▲ N Ecuador
57 L21 **Cotagaita** Potosí, S Bolivia
103 V15 **Côte d'Azur** *prev.* Nice. × (Nice) Alpes-Maritimes, SE France
Côte d'Ivoire *see* Ivory Coast
103 R8 **Côte d'Or** *cultural region* C France
103 R7 **Côte d'Or** ◆ *department* E France
Côte Française des Somalis *see* Djibouti
102 J4 **Cotentin** *peninsula* N France
102 G6 **Côtes d'Armor** *prev.* Côtes-du-Nord. ◆ *department* NW France
Côtes-du Nord *see* Côtes d'Armor
Cöthen *see* Köthen
Côtière, Chaîne *see* Coast Mountains
40 M13 **Cotija** *var.* Cotija de la Paz. Michoacán de Ocampo, SW Mexico
Cotija de la Paz *see* Cotija
77 R16 **Cotonou** *var.* Kotonu. S Benin
77 R16 **Cotonou** × S Benin
56 B6 **Cotopaxi** *prev.* León. ◆ *province* C Ecuador
56 C6 **Cotopaxi** ※ N Ecuador
Cotrone *see* Crotone
97 L21 **Cotswold Hills** *var.* Cotswolds. *hill range* S England, UK
Cotswolds *see* Cotswold Hills
32 F13 **Cottage Grove** Oregon, NW USA
21 S14 **Cottageville** South Carolina, SE USA
101 P14 **Cottbus** *prev.* Kottbus. Brandenburg, E Germany
27 U9 **Cotter** Arkansas, C USA
106 A9 **Cottian Alps** *Fr.* Alpes Cottiennes, *It.* Alpi Cozie. ▲ France/Italy
Cottiennes, Alpes *see* Cottian Alps
Cotton State, The *see* Alabama
22 G4 **Cotton Valley** Louisiana, S USA
36 L12 **Cottonwood** Arizona, SW USA
32 M10 **Cottonwood** Idaho, NW USA
29 S9 **Cottonwood** Minnesota, N USA
25 Q7 **Cottonwood** Texas, SW USA
27 O5 **Cottonwood Falls** Kansas, C USA
36 L3 **Cottonwood Heights** Utah, W USA
29 S10 **Cottonwood River** ≈ Minnesota, N USA
45 O9 **Cotuí** C Dominican Republic
25 Q13 **Cotulla** Texas, SW USA
Cotyora *see* Ordu
102 I11 **Coubre, Pointe de la** *headland* W France
18 E12 **Coudersport** Pennsylvania, NE USA
15 S9 **Coudres, Île aux** *island* Quebec, SE Canada
182 G11 **Couedic, Cape de** *headland* South Australia
Couentrey *see* Coventry
102 I6 **Couesnon** ≈ NW France
32 H10 **Cougar** Washington, NW USA
102 L10 **Couhé** Vienne, W France
32 K8 **Coulee City** Washington, NW USA
195 Q15 **Coulman Island** *island* Antarctica
103 P5 **Coulommiers** Seine-et-Marne, N France
14 K11 **Coulonge** ≈ Quebec, SE Canada
14 K11 **Coulonge Est** ≈ Quebec, SE Canada
35 Q9 **Coulterville** California, W USA
38 M9 **Council** Alaska, USA
32 M12 **Council** Idaho, NW USA
29 S15 **Council Bluffs** Iowa, C USA
27 O5 **Council Grove** Kansas, C USA
27 O5 **Council Grove Lake** ▣ Kansas, C USA
32 G7 **Coupeville** Washington, NW USA
55 U12 **Courantyne River** *var.* Corantijn Rivier, Corentyne River. ≈ Guyana/Suriname
99 G21 **Courcelles** Hainaut, S Belgium
108 C7 **Courgenay** Jura, NW Switzerland
128 B2 **Courland Lagoon** *Ger.* Kurisches Haff, *Rus.* Kurskiy Zaliv. *lagoon* Lithuania/Russian Federation
118 B12 **Courland Spit** *Lith.* Kuršių Nerija, *Rus.* Kurshskaya Kosa. *spit* Lithuania/Russian Federation
106 A6 **Courmayeur** *prev.* Cormaiore. Valle d'Aosta, NW Italy
108 D7 **Courroux** Jura, NW Switzerland
10 K17 **Courtenay** Vancouver Island, British Columbia, SW Canada
21 W7 **Courtland** Virginia, NE USA
25 V10 **Courtney** Texas, SW USA
30 J4 **Court Oreilles, Lac** ◎ Wisconsin, N USA
Courtrai *see* Kortrijk
99 H19 **Court-Saint-Étienne** Wallon Brabant, C Belgium
22 G6 **Coushatta** Louisiana, S USA
172 I16 **Cousin** *island* Inner Islands, NE Seychelles
172 I16 **Cousine** *island* Inner Islands, NE Seychelles
102 J4 **Coutances** *anc.* Constantia. Manche, N France
102 K12 **Coutras** Gironde, SW France
45 U14 **Couva** Trinidad, Trinidad and Tobago
108 B8 **Couvet** Neuchâtel, W Switzerland
99 H22 **Couvin** Namur, S Belgium
116 K12 **Covasna** *Ger.* Kowasna, *Hung.* Kovászna. Covasna, E Romania
116 J11 **Covasna** ◆ *county* E Romania
14 E12 **Cove Island** *island* Ontario, S Canada
34 M5 **Covelo** California, W USA
97 M20 **Coventry** *anc.* Couentrey. C England, UK
Cove of Cork *see* Cobh
21 U5 **Covesville** Virginia, NE USA
104 I8 **Covilhã** Castelo Branco, E Portugal
23 T3 **Covington** Georgia, SE USA
31 N13 **Covington** Indiana, N USA
20 M3 **Covington** Kentucky, S USA
22 K8 **Covington** Louisiana, S USA
31 Q13 **Covington** Ohio, N USA
20 F9 **Covington** Tennessee, S USA
21 S6 **Covington** Virginia, NE USA
183 Q8 **Cowal, Lake** *seasonal lake* New South Wales, SE Australia
11 W15 **Cowan** Manitoba, S Canada
18 F12 **Cowanesque River** ≈ New York/Pennsylvania, NE USA
180 L12 **Cowan, Lake** ◎ Western Australia
15 P13 **Cowansville** Quebec, SE Canada
182 H8 **Cowell** South Australia
97 M23 **Cowes** S England, UK
27 Q10 **Coweta** Oklahoma, C USA
(0) D6 **Cowie Seamount** *undersea feature* NE Pacific Ocean
32 G10 **Cowlitz River** ≈ Washington, NW USA
21 Q11 **Cowpens** South Carolina, SE USA
183 R8 **Cowra** New South Wales, SE Australia
Coxen Hole *see* Roatán
59 I19 **Coxim** Mato Grosso do Sul, S Brazil
59 I19 **Coxim, Rio** ≈ SW Brazil
Coxin Hole *see* Roatán
153 V17 **Cox's Bazar** Chittagong, S Bangladesh
76 H14 **Coyah** Conakry, W Guinea
40 K5 **Coyame** Chihuahua, N Mexico
24 L9 **Coyanosa Draw** ≈ Texas, SW USA
Coyhaique *see* Coihaique
42 C7 **Coyolate, Río** ≈ S Guatemala
Coyote State *see* South Dakota
40 I10 **Coyotitán** Sinaloa, C Mexico
41 N15 **Coyuca** *var.* Coyuca de Catalán. Guerrero, S Mexico
41 O16 **Coyuca** *var.* Coyuca de Benítez. Guerrero, S Mexico
Coyuca de Benítez/Coyuca de Catalán *see* Coyuca
29 N15 **Cozad** Nebraska, C USA
Cozie, Alpi *see* Cottian Alps
Cozmeni *see* Kitsman'
40 E3 **Cozón, Cerro** ▲ NW Mexico
41 Z12 **Cozumel** Quintana Roo, E Mexico
41 Z12 **Cozumel, Isla** *island* SE Mexico
32 K8 **Crab Creek** ≈ Washington, NW USA
44 H12 **Crab Pond Point** *headland* W Jamaica
Cracovia/Cracow *see* Małopolskie
83 I25 **Cradock** Eastern Cape, S South Africa
39 Y14 **Craig** Prince of Wales Island, Alaska, USA
37 Q3 **Craig** Colorado, C USA
97 F15 **Craigavon** C Northern Ireland, UK
21 T5 **Craigsville** Virginia, NE USA
101 J21 **Crailsheim** Baden-Württemberg, S Germany
116 H14 **Craiova** Dolj, SW Romania
10 K12 **Cranberry Junction** British Columbia, SW Canada
18 J8 **Cranberry Lake** ◎ New York, NE USA
11 V13 **Cranberry Portage** Manitoba, C Canada
11 P17 **Cranbrook** British Columbia, SW Canada
30 M5 **Crandon** Wisconsin, N USA
32 K14 **Crane** Oregon, NW USA
24 M9 **Crane** Texas, SW USA
Crane *see* The Crane
25 S8 **Cranfills Gap** Texas, SW USA
19 O12 **Cranston** Rhode Island, NE USA
Cranz *see* Zelenogradsk
59 L15 **Craolândia** Tocantins, E Brazil
102 J7 **Craon** Mayenne, NW France
195 V16 **Crary, Cape** *headland* Antarctica
Crasna *see* Kraszna
32 G14 **Crater Lake** ◎ Oregon, NW USA
33 P14 **Craters of the Moon National Monument** *national park* Idaho, NW USA
59 O14 **Crateús** Ceará, E Brazil
Crathis *see* Crati
107 N20 **Crati** *anc.* Crathis. ≈ S Italy
11 U16 **Craven** Saskatchewan, S Canada
54 I8 **Cravo Norte** Arauca, E Colombia
28 J12 **Crawford** Nebraska, C USA
25 T8 **Crawford** Texas, SW USA
11 O17 **Crawford Bay** British Columbia, SW Canada
65 M19 **Crawford Seamount** *undersea feature* S Atlantic Ocean
31 O13 **Crawfordsville** Indiana, N USA
23 S9 **Crawfordville** Florida, SE USA
97 O23 **Crawley** SE England, UK
33 S10 **Crazy Mountains** ▲ Montana, NW USA
11 T11 **Cree** ≈ Saskatchewan, C Canada
37 R7 **Creede** Colorado, C USA
40 I6 **Creel** Chihuahua, N Mexico
11 S11 **Cree Lake** ◎ Saskatchewan, C Canada
11 V13 **Creighton** Saskatchewan, C Canada
29 Q13 **Creighton** Nebraska, C USA
103 O4 **Creil** Oise, N France
106 E8 **Crema** Lombardia, N Italy
106 E8 **Cremona** Lombardia, N Italy
Creole State *see* Louisiana
112 M10 **Crepaja** *Hung.* Cserépalja. Serbia, N Yugoslavia
103 O4 **Crépy-en-Valois** Oise, N France
112 B10 **Cres** *It.* Cherso. Primorje-Gorski Kotar, NW Croatia
112 A11 **Cres** *It.* Cherso; *anc.* Crexa. *island* W Croatia
32 H14 **Crescent** Oregon, NW USA
34 K1 **Crescent City** California, W USA
23 W10 **Crescent City** Florida, SE USA
167 X10 **Crescent Group** *island group* C Paracel Islands
23 W10 **Crescent Lake** ◎ Florida, SE USA
29 X11 **Cresco** Iowa, C USA
61 B18 **Crespo** Entre Ríos, E Argentina
54 E5 **Crespo** × (Cartagena) Bolívar, NW Colombia
103 R13 **Crest** Drôme, E France
37 R5 **Crested Butte** Colorado, C USA
31 S12 **Crestline** Ohio, N USA
11 O17 **Creston** British Columbia, SW Canada
29 U15 **Creston** Iowa, C USA
33 V16 **Creston** Wyoming, C USA
37 S7 **Crestone Peak** ▲ Colorado, C USA
23 P8 **Crestview** Florida, SE USA
121 R10 **Cretan Trough** *undersea feature* Aegean Sea, C Mediterranean Sea
29 R16 **Crete** Nebraska, C USA
Crete *see* Kríti
103 O5 **Créteil** Val-de-Marne, N France
Crete, Sea of/Creticum, Mare *see* Kritikó Pélagos
105 X4 **Creus, Cap de** *headland* NE Spain
103 N10 **Creuse** ◆ *department* C France
102 L9 **Creuse** ≈ C France
103 T4 **Creutzwald** Moselle, NE France
105 S12 **Crevillente** País Valenciano, E Spain
97 L18 **Crewe** C England, UK
21 V7 **Crewe** Virginia, NE USA
Crexa *see* Cres
43 Q15 **Cricamola, Río** ≈ NW Panama
61 K14 **Criciúma** Santa Catarina, S Brazil
96 J11 **Crieff** C Scotland, UK
112 B10 **Crikvenica** *It.* Cirquenizza; *prev.* Cirkvenica, Crjkvenica. Primorje-Gorski Kotar, NW Croatia
Crimea/Crimean Oblast *see* Krym, Respublika
101 M16 **Crimmitschau** *var.* Krimmitschau. Sachsen, E Germany
116 G11 **Crişcior** *Hung.* Kristyor. Hunedoara, W Romania
21 Y5 **Crisfield** Maryland, NE USA
31 P3 **Crisp Point** *headland* Michigan, N USA
59 L19 **Cristalina** Goiás, C Brazil
44 J7 **Cristal, Sierra del** ▲ E Cuba
43 T14 **Cristóbal** Colón, C Panama
54 F4 **Cristóbal Colón, Pico** ▲ N Colombia
Cristur/Cristuru Săcuiesc *see* Cristuru Secuiesc
116 I11 **Cristuru Secuiesc** *prev.* Cristur, Cristuru Săcuiesc, Sitaş Cristuru, *Ger.* Kreutz, *Hung.* Székelykeresztúr, Szitás-Keresztúr. Harghita, C Romania
116 F10 **Crişul Alb** *var.* Weisse Kreisch, *Ger.* Weisse Körös, *Hung.* Fehér-Körös. ≈ Hungary/Romania
116 F10 **Crişul Negru** *Ger.* Schwarze Körös, *Hung.* Fekete-Körös. ≈ Hungary/Romania
116 G10 **Crişul Repede** *var.* Schnelle Kreisch, *Ger.* Schnelle Körös, *Hung.* Sebes-Körös. ≈ Hungary/Romania
117 N10 **Criuleni** *Rus.* Kriulyany. C Moldova
Crivadia Vulcanului *see* Vulcan
Crjkvenica *see* Crikvenica
113 O17 **Crna Gora** ▲ FYR Macedonia/Yugoslavia
Crna Gora *see* Montenegro
113 O20 **Crna Reka** ≈ S FYR Macedonia
Crni Drim *see* Black Drin
109 V10 **Črni Vrh** ▲ NE Slovenia
109 V13 **Črnomelj** *Ger.* Tschernembl. SE Slovenia
97 A17 **Croagh Patrick** *Ir.* Cruach Phádraig. ▲ W Ireland
112 D9 **Croatia** *off.* Republic of Croatia, *Ger.* Kroatien, *SCr.* Hrvatska. ♦ *republic* SE Europe
Croce, Picco di *see* Wilde Kreuzspitze
15 P8 **Croche** ≈ Quebec, SE Canada
169 V7 **Crocker, Banjaran** *var.* Crocker Range. ▲ East Malaysia
Crocker Range *see* Crocker, Banjaran
25 V9 **Crockett** Texas, SW USA
67 V14 **Crocodile** *var.* Krokodil. ≈ N South Africa
Crocodile *see* Limpopo
20 I7 **Crofton** Kentucky, S USA
29 Q12 **Crofton** Nebraska, C USA
Croia *see* Krujë
103 R16 **Croisette, Cap** *headland* SE France
102 G8 **Croisic, Pointe du** *headland* NW France
103 S13 **Croix Haute, Col de la** *pass* E France
15 U5 **Croix, Pointe à la** *headland* Quebec, SE Canada
14 F13 **Croker, Cape** *headland* Ontario, S Canada
181 P1 **Croker Island** *island* Northern Territory, N Australia
96 I8 **Cromarty** N Scotland, UK
99 M21 **Crombach** Liège, E Belgium
97 Q18 **Cromer** E England, UK
185 D22 **Cromwell** Otago, South Island, NZ
185 H16 **Cronadun** West Coast, South Island, NZ
39 O11 **Crooked Creek** Alaska, USA
44 K5 **Crooked Island** *island* SE Bahamas
44 J5 **Crooked Island Passage** *channel* SE Bahamas
32 I13 **Crooked River** ≈ Oregon, NW USA
29 R4 **Crookston** Minnesota, N USA
28 I10 **Crooks Tower** ▲ South Dakota, N USA
31 T14 **Crooksville** Ohio, N USA
183 R9 **Crookwell** New South Wales, SE Australia
14 L14 **Crosby** Ontario, SE Canada
97 K17 **Crosby** *var.* Great Crosby. NW England, UK
29 U6 **Crosby** Minnesota, N USA
28 K2 **Crosby** North Dakota, N USA
25 O5 **Crosbyton** Texas, SW USA
77 V16 **Cross** ≈ Cameroon/Nigeria
23 U10 **Cross City** Florida, SE USA
Crossen *see* Krosno Odrzańskie
27 V14 **Crossett** Arkansas, C USA
97 K15 **Cross Fell** ▲ N England, UK
11 P16 **Crossfield** Alberta, SW Canada
21 Q12 **Cross Hill** South Carolina, SE USA
19 U6 **Cross Island** *island* Maine, NE USA
11 X13 **Cross Lake** Manitoba, C Canada
22 F5 **Cross Lake** ▣ Louisiana, S USA
36 I12 **Crossman Peak** ▲ Arizona, SW USA
25 Q7 **Cross Plains** Texas, SW USA
77 V17 **Cross River** ◆ *state* SE Nigeria
20 L9 **Crossville** Tennessee, S USA
31 S8 **Croswell** Michigan, N USA
14 K13 **Crotch Lake** ◎ Ontario, SE Canada
Croton/Crotona *see* Crotone
107 O21 **Crotone** *var.* Cotrone; *anc.* Croton, Crotona. Calabria, SW Italy
33 V11 **Crow Agency** Montana, NW USA
183 U7 **Crowdy Head** *headland* New South Wales, SE Australia
25 Q4 **Crowell** Texas, SW USA
183 O6 **Crowl Creek** *seasonal river* New South Wales, SE Australia
22 H9 **Crowley** Louisiana, S USA
35 S9 **Crowley, Lake** ▣ California, W USA
27 X10 **Crowleys Ridge** *hill range* Arkansas, C USA
31 N11 **Crown Point** Indiana, N USA
37 P10 **Crownpoint** New Mexico, SW USA
33 R10 **Crow Peak** ▲ Montana, NW USA
11 P17 **Crowsnest Pass** *pass* Alberta/British Columbia, SW Canada
29 T6 **Crow Wing River** ≈ Minnesota, N USA
97 O22 **Croydon** SE England, UK
173 P11 **Crozet Basin** *undersea feature* S Indian Ocean
173 O12 **Crozet Islands** *island group* French Southern and Antarctic Territories
173 N12 **Crozet Plateau** *var.* Crozet Plateaus. *undersea feature* SW Indian Ocean
Crozet Plateaus *see* Crozet Plateau
102 E6 **Crozon** Finistère, NW France
Cruacha Dubha, Na *see* Macgillycuddy's Reeks
Cruach Phádraig *see* Croagh Patrick
116 M14 **Crucea** Constanţa, SE Romania
44 E5 **Cruces** Cienfuegos, C Cuba
107 O20 **Crucoli Torretta** Calabria, SW Italy
41 P9 **Cruillas** Tamaulipas, C Mexico
64 K9 **Cruiser Tablemount** *undersea feature* E Atlantic Ocean
61 G14 **Cruz Alta** Rio Grande do Sul, S Brazil
44 G8 **Cruz, Cabo** *headland* S Cuba
60 N9 **Cruzeiro** São Paulo, S Brazil
60 H10 **Cruzeiro do Oeste** Paraná, S Brazil
59 A15 **Cruzeiro do Sul** Acre, W Brazil
23 U11 **Crystal Bay** *bay* Florida, SE USA
182 I8 **Crystal Brook** South Australia
11 X17 **Crystal City** Manitoba, S Canada
27 X5 **Crystal City** Missouri, C USA
25 P13 **Crystal City** Texas, SW USA
30 M4 **Crystal Falls** Michigan, N USA
23 Q8 **Crystal Lake** Florida, SE USA
31 O6 **Crystal Lake** ◎ Michigan, N USA
23 V11 **Crystal River** Florida, SE USA
37 Q5 **Crystal River** ≈ Colorado, C USA
22 K6 **Crystal Springs** Mississippi, S USA
Csaca *see* Čadca
Csakathurn/Csáktornya *see* Čakovec
Csap *see* Chop
Csepén *see* Čepin
Cserépalja *see* Crepaja
Csermő *see* Cermei
Csíkszereda *see* Miercurea-Ciuc
111 L24 **Csongrád** Csongrád, SE Hungary
111 L24 **Csongrád** *off.* Csongrád Megye. ◆ *county* SE Hungary
111 H22 **Csorna** Győr-Moson-Sopron, NW Hungary
Csucsa *see* Ciucea
111 G25 **Csurgó** Somogy, SW Hungary
Csurog *see* Čurug
54 L5 **Cúa** Miranda, N Venezuela
82 C11 **Cuale** Malanje, NW Angola
67 T12 **Cuando** *var.* Kwando. ≈ S Africa
83 E15 **Cuando Cubango** *var.* Kuando-Kubango. ◆ *province* SE Angola
83 E16 **Cuangar** Cuando Cubango, S Angola
82 D11 **Cuango** Lunda Norte, NE Angola
82 C10 **Cuango** Uíge, NW Angola
82 C10 **Cuango** *var.* Kwango. ≈ Angola/Dem. Rep. Congo (Zaire) **see also** Kwango
Cuan, Loch *see* Strangford Lough
82 C12 **Cuanza** *var.* Kwanza. ≈ C Angola
82 B11 **Cuanza Norte** *var.* Kuanza Norte. ◆ *province* NE Angola
82 B12 **Cuanza Sul** *var.* Kuanza Sul. ◆ *province* NE Angola
61 E16 **Cuareim, Río** *var.* Rio Quaraí. ≈ Brazil/Uruguay **see also** Quaraí, Rio
83 D15 **Cuatir** ≈ S Angola
40 M7 **Cuatro Ciénegas** *var.* Cuatro Ciénegas de Carranza. Coahuila de Zaragoza, NE Mexico
Cuatro Ciénegas de Carranza *see* Cuatro Ciénegas
40 I6 **Cuauhtémoc** Chihuahua, N Mexico
41 P14 **Cuautla** Morelos, S Mexico
104 H12 **Cuba** Beja, S Portugal
27 W6 **Cuba** Missouri, C USA
37 R10 **Cuba** New Mexico, SW USA
44 E6 **Cuba** *off.* Republic of Cuba. ♦ *republic* W West Indies
47 O2 **Cuba** *island* W West Indies
82 B13 **Cubal** Benguela, W Angola
83 C15 **Cubango** *var.* Kuvango, *Port.* Vila Artur de Paiva, Vila da Ponte. Huíla, SW Angola
83 D16 **Cubango** *var.* Kavango, Kavengo, Kubango, Okavango, Okavanggo. ≈ S Africa **see also** Okavango
54 H8 **Cubará** Boyacá, N Colombia
136 I12 **Çubuk** Ankara, N Turkey
83 D14 **Cuchi** Cuando Cubango, C Angola
42 C5 **Cuchumatanes, Sierra de los** ▲ W Guatemala
Cuculaya, Rio *see* Kukalaya, Rio
82 E12 **Cucumbi** *prev.* Trás-os-Montes. Lunda Sul, NE Angola
54 G7 **Cúcuta** *var.* San José de Cúcuta. Norte de Santander, N Colombia
31 N9 **Cudahy** Wisconsin, N USA
155 J21 **Cuddalore** Tamil Nādu, SE India
155 I18 **Cuddapah** Andhra Pradesh, S India
104 M6 **Cuéllar** Castilla-León, N Spain
82 D13 **Cuemba** *var.* Coemba. Bié, C Angola
56 B8 **Cuenca** Azuay, S Ecuador
105 Q9 **Cuenca** *anc.* Conca. Castilla-La Mancha, C Spain
105 P9 **Cuenca** ◆ *province* Castilla-La Mancha, C Spain
40 L9 **Cuencamé** *var.* Cuencamé de Ceniceros. Durango, C Mexico
Cuencamé de Ceniceros *see* Cuencamé
105 Q8 **Cuenca, Serrania de** ▲ C Spain
Cuera *see* Chur
105 P5 **Cuerda del Pozo, Embalse de la** ▣ N Spain
41 O14 **Cuernavaca** Morelos, S Mexico
25 T12 **Cuero** Texas, SW USA
44 I7 **Cueto** Holguín, E Cuba
41 Q13 **Cuetzalán** *var.* Cuetzalán del Progreso. Puebla, S Mexico
Cuetzalán del Progreso *see* Cuetzalán

♦ Country
● Country Capital
◇ Dependent Territory
○ Dependent Territory Capital
◆ Administrative Region
× International Airport
▲ Mountain
▲ Mountain Range
※ Volcano
≈ River
◎ Lake
▣ Reservoir

105 Q14 **Cuevas de Almanzora** Andalucía, S Spain
105 T8 **Cuevas de Vinromá** País Valenciano, E Spain
116 H12 **Cugir** *Hung.* Kudzsir. Alba, SW Romania
59 H18 **Cuiabá** *prev.* Cuyabá. *state capital* Mato Grosso, SW Brazil
59 H19 **Cuiabá, Rio** ≈ SW Brazil
41 R15 **Cuicatlán** *var.* San Juan Bautista Cuicatlán. Oaxaca, SE Mexico
191 W16 **Cuidado, Punta** *headland* Easter Island, Chile, E Pacific Ocean
Cuidad Presidente Stroessner *see* Ciudad del Este
Cúige *see* Connaught
Cúige Laighean *see* Leinster
Cúige Mumhan *see* Munster
98 L13 **Cuijck** Noord-Brabant, SE Netherlands
Cúil an tSúdaire *see* Portarlington
42 D7 **Cuilapa** Santa Rosa, S Guatemala
42 B5 **Cuilco, Río** ≈ W Guatemala
Cúil Mhuine *see* Collooney
Cúil Raithin *see* Coleraine
83 C14 **Cuima** Huambo, C Angola
83 E16 **Cuito** *var.* Kwito. ≈ SE Angola
83 E15 **Cuíto Cuanavale** Cuando Cubango, E Angola
41 N14 **Cuitzeo, Lago de** ◎ C Mexico
27 W4 **Cuivre River** ≈ Missouri, C USA
Çuka *see* Çukë
168 L8 **Cukai** *var.* Chukai, Kemaman. Terengganu, Peninsular Malaysia
113 L23 **Çukë** *var.* Çuka. Vlorë, S Albania
Cularo *see* Grenoble
33 Y7 **Culbertson** Montana, NW USA
28 M16 **Culbertson** Nebraska, C USA
183 P10 **Culcairn** New South Wales, SE Australia
45 W5 **Culebra** *var.* Dewey. E Puerto Rico
45 W6 **Culebra, Isla de** *island* E Puerto Rico
37 T8 **Culebra Peak** ▲ Colorado, C USA
104 J5 **Culebra, Sierra de la** ▲▲ NW Spain
98 J12 **Culemborg** Gelderland, C Netherlands
137 V14 **Culfa** *Rus.* Dzhul'fa. SW Azerbaijan
183 P4 **Culgoa River** ≈ New South Wales/Queensland, SE Australia
40 I9 **Culiacán** *var.* Culiacán Rosales, Culiacán-Rosales. Sinaloa, C Mexico
Culiacán-Rosales/Culiacán Rosales *see* Culiacán
105 P14 **Cúllar-Baza** Andalucía, S Spain
105 S10 **Cullera** País Valenciano, E Spain
23 P3 **Cullman** Alabama, S USA
108 B10 **Cully** Vaud, W Switzerland
Culm *see* Chełmno
Culmsee *see* Chełmża
21 V4 **Culpeper** Virginia, NE USA
185 I17 **Culverden** Canterbury, South Island, NZ
55 N5 **Cumaná** Sucre, NE Venezuela
55 O5 **Cumanacoa** Sucre, NE Venezuela
54 C13 **Cumbal, Nevado de** *elevation* S Colombia
21 O7 **Cumberland** Kentucky, S USA
21 U2 **Cumberland** Maryland, NE USA
21 V6 **Cumberland** Virginia, NE USA
187 P12 **Cumberland, Cape** *var.* Cape Nahoi. *headland* Espiritu Santo, N Vanuatu
11 V14 **Cumberland House** Saskatchewan, C Canada
23 W8 **Cumberland Island** *island* Georgia, SE USA
20 L7 **Cumberland, Lake** ⊡ Kentucky, S USA
9 R5 **Cumberland Peninsula** *peninsula* Baffin Island, Nunavut, NE Canada
2 N9 **Cumberland Plateau** *plateau* E USA
30 L1 **Cumberland Point** *headland* Michigan, N USA
21 O7 **Cumberland River** ≈ Kentucky/Tennessee, S USA
9 S6 **Cumberland Sound** *inlet* Baffin Island, Nunavut, NE Canada
96 I12 **Cumbernauld** S Scotland, UK
97 K15 **Cumbria** *cultural region* NW England, UK
97 K15 **Cumbrian Mountains** ▲▲ NW England, UK
23 S2 **Cumming** Georgia, SE USA
Cummin in Pommern *see* Kamień Pomorski
182 G9 **Cummins** South Australia
96 I13 **Cumnock** W Scotland, UK
40 G4 **Cumpas** Sonora, NW Mexico
136 H16 **Çumra** Konya, C Turkey
63 G15 **Cunco** Araucanía, C Chile
54 E9 **Cundinamarca** *off.* Departamento de Cundinamarca. ◈ *province* C Colombia
41 U15 **Cunduacán** Tabasco, SE Mexico
83 C16 **Cunene** ◈ *province* S Angola
83 A16 **Cunene** *var.* Kunene. ≈ Angola/Namibia *see also* Kunene
106 A9 **Cuneo** *Fr.* Coni. Piemonte, NW Italy
83 E15 **Cunjamba** Cuando Cubango, E Angola
181 V10 **Cunnamulla** Queensland, E Australia
Cuokkarašša *see* Čohkarášša
106 B7 **Cuorgne** Piemonte, NE Italy
96 K11 **Cupar** E Scotland, UK
116 L8 **Cupcina** *Rus.* Kupchino; *prev.* Calinisc, Kalinisk. N Moldova
54 C8 **Cupica** Chocó, W Colombia
54 C8 **Cupica, Golfo de** *gulf* W Colombia
112 N13 **Ćuprija** Serbia, E Yugoslavia
Cura *see* Villa de Cura
45 P16 **Curaçao** *island* Netherlands Antilles
56 H13 **Curanja, Río** ≈ E Peru
56 F7 **Curaray, Río** ≈ Ecuador/Peru
116 K14 **Curcani** Călărași, SE Romania
182 H4 **Curdimurka** South Australia
103 P7 **Cure** ≈ C France
173 Y16 **Curepipe** C Mauritius
55 R6 **Curiapo** Delta Amacuro, NE Venezuela
Curia Rhaetorum *see* Chur
62 G12 **Curicó** Maule, C Chile
Curieta *see* Krk
172 I15 **Curieuse** *island* Inner Islands, NE Seychelles
59 C16 **Curitiba** Acre, W Brazil
60 K12 **Curitiba** *prev.* Curytiba. *state capital* Paraná, S Brazil
60 J13 **Curitibanos** Santa Catarina, S Brazil
183 S6 **Curlewis** New South Wales, SE Australia
182 J6 **Curnamona** South Australia
83 A15 **Curoca** ≈ SW Angola
183 T6 **Currabubula** New South Wales, SE Australia
59 Q14 **Currais Novos** Rio Grande do Norte, E Brazil
35 W7 **Currant** Nevada, W USA
35 W6 **Currant Mountain** ▲ Nevada, W USA
44 H2 **Current** Eleuthera Island, C Bahamas
27 W8 **Current River** ≈ Arkansas/Missouri, C USA
182 M14 **Currie** Tasmania, SE Australia
21 Y8 **Currituck** North Carolina, SE USA
21 Y8 **Currituck Sound** *sound* North Carolina, SE USA
39 R11 **Curry** Alaska, USA
Curtbunar *see* Tervel
116 I13 **Curtea de Argeș** *var.* Curtea-de-Arges. Argeș, S Romania
116 E10 **Curtici** *Ger.* Kurtitsch, *Hung.* Kürtös. Arad, W Romania
28 M16 **Curtis** Nebraska, C USA
104 H2 **Curtis-Estación** Galicia, NW Spain
183 O14 **Curtis Group** *island group* Tasmania, SE Australia
181 Y8 **Curtis Island** *island* Queensland, SE Australia
58 K11 **Curuá, Ilha do** *island* NE Brazil
47 U7 **Curuá, Rio** ≈ N Brazil
59 A14 **Curuçá, Rio** ≈ NW Brazil
112 L9 **Čurug** *Hung.* Csurog. Serbia, N Yugoslavia
61 D16 **Curuzú Cuatiá** Corrientes, NE Argentina
59 M19 **Curvelo** Minas Gerais, SE Brazil
18 E14 **Curwensville** Pennsylvania, NE USA
30 M3 **Curwood, Mount** ▲ Michigan, N USA
Curytiba *see* Curitiba
Curzola *see* Korčula
42 A10 **Cuscatlán** ◈ *department* C El Salvador
57 H15 **Cusco** *var.* Cuzco. Cusco, C Peru
57 H15 **Cusco** *off.* Departamento de Cusco; *var.* Cuzco. ◈ *department* C Peru
27 O9 **Cushing** Oklahoma, C USA
25 W8 **Cushing** Texas, SW USA
40 I6 **Cusihuiriachic** Chihuahua, N Mexico
103 P10 **Cusset** Allier, C France
23 S5 **Cusseta** Georgia, SE USA
28 J10 **Custer** South Dakota, N USA
Cüstrin *see* Kostrzyn
33 Q7 **Cut Bank** Montana, NW USA
Cutch, Gulf of *see* Kachchh, Gulf of
23 S6 **Cuthbert** Georgia, SE USA
11 S15 **Cut Knife** Saskatchewan, S Canada
23 Y16 **Cutler Ridge** Florida, SE USA
22 K10 **Cut Off** Louisiana, S USA
63 I15 **Cutral-Có** Neuquén, C Argentina
107 O21 **Cutro** Calabria, SW Italy
183 O4 **Cuttaburra Channels** *seasonal river* New South Wales, SE Australia
154 O12 **Cuttack** Orissa, E India
83 C15 **Cuvelai** Cunene, SW Angola
79 G18 **Cuvette** *var.* Région de la Cuvette. ◈ *province* C Congo
173 V9 **Cuvier Basin** *undersea feature* E Indian Ocean
173 U9 **Cuvier Plateau** *undersea feature* E Indian Ocean
82 B12 **Cuvo** ≈ W Angola
100 H9 **Cuxhaven** Niedersachsen, NW Germany
Cuyabá *see* Cuiabá
Cuyuni, Río *see* Cuyuni River
55 S8 **Cuyuni River** *var.* Río Cuyuni. ≈ Guyana/Venezuela
Cuzco *see* Cusco
97 K22 **Cwmbran** *Wel.* Cwmbrân. SW Wales, UK
28 K15 **C.W.McConaughy, Lake** ⊡ Nebraska, C USA
81 D20 **Cyangugu** SW Rwanda
110 D11 **Cybinka** *Ger.* Ziebingen. Lubuskie, W Poland
Cyclades *see* Kykládes
Cydonia *see* Chaniá
Cymru *see* Wales
20 M5 **Cynthiana** Kentucky, S USA
11 S17 **Cypress Hills** ▲ Alberta/Saskatchewan, SW Canada
Cypro-Syrian Basin *see* Cyprus Basin
121 U11 **Cyprus** *off.* Republic of Cyprus, *Gk.* Kypros, *Turk.* Kıbrıs, Kıbrıs Cumhuriyeti. ◆ *republic* E Mediterranean Sea
84 L14 **Cyprus** *Gk.* Kypros, *Turk.* Kıbrıs. *island* E Mediterranean Sea
121 W11 **Cyprus Basin** *var.* Cypro-Syrian Basin. *undersea feature* E Mediterranean Sea
Cythera *see* Kýthira
Cythnos *see* Kýthnos
110 F9 **Czaplinek** *Ger.* Tempelburg. Zachodniopomorskie, NW Poland
Czarna Woda *see* Wda
110 G8 **Czarne** Pomorskie, N Poland
110 G10 **Czarnków** Wielkopolskie, C Poland
111 E17 **Czech Republic** *Cz.* Česká Republika. ◆ *republic* C Europe
Czegléd *see* Cegléd
110 G12 **Czempiń** Wielkolpolskie, C Poland
Czenstochau *see* Częstochowa
Czerkow *see* Čerchov
Czernowitz *see* Chernivtsi
110 I8 **Czersk** Pomorskie, N Poland
111 J15 **Częstochowa** *Ger.* Czenstochau, Tschenstochau, *Rus.* Chenstokhov. Śląskie, S Poland
110 F10 **Człopa** *Ger.* Schloppe. Zachodniopomorskie, NW Poland
110 H8 **Człuchów** *Ger.* Schlochau. Pomorskie, NW Poland

D

163 V9 **Da'an** *var.* Dalai. Jilin, NE China
15 S10 **Daaquam** Quebec, SE Canada
Daawo, Webi *see* Dawa Wenz
54 I4 **Dabajuro** Falcón, NW Venezuela
77 N15 **Dabakala** NE Ivory Coast
Daban *see* Bairin Youqi
111 K23 **Dabas** Pest, C Hungary
160 L8 **Daba Shan** ▲▲ C China
140 J5 **Dabbāgh, Jabal** ▲ NW Saudi Arabia
54 D8 **Dabeiba** Antioquia, NW Colombia
154 E11 **Dabhoi** Gujarāt, W India
161 P8 **Dabie Shan** ▲▲ C China
76 J13 **Dabola** Haute-Guinée, C Guinea
77 N17 **Dabou** S Ivory Coast
110 P8 **Dąbrowa Białostocka** Podlaskie, NE Poland
111 M16 **Dąbrowa Tarnowska** Małopolskie, S Poland
119 M20 **Dabryn'** *Rus.* Dobryn'. Homyel'skaya Voblasts', SE Belarus
159 P10 **Dabsan Hu** ◎ C China
161 Q13 **Dabu** *prev.* Huliao. Guangdong, S China
116 H15 **Dăbuleni** Dolj, SW Romania
Dacca *see* Dhaka
101 L23 **Dachau** Bayern, SE Germany
160 K8 **Dachuan** *prev.* Daxian, Da Xian. Sichuan, C China
Dacia Bank *see* Dacia Seamount
64 M10 **Dacia Seamount** *var.* Dacia Bank. *undersea feature* E Atlantic Ocean
37 T3 **Dacono** Colorado, C USA
Đắc Tô *see* Đak Tô
Dacura *see* Dákura
23 W12 **Dade City** Florida, SE USA
152 L10 **Dadeldhura** *var.* Dandeldhura. Far Western, W Nepal
23 Q5 **Dadeville** Alabama, S USA
103 N15 **Dadou** ≈ S France
154 D12 **Dādra and Nagar Haveli** ◈ *union territory* W India
149 P14 **Dādu** Sind, SE Pakistan
167 U11 **Da Du Boloc** Kon Tum, C Vietnam
160 G9 **Dadu He** ≈ C China
Daegu *see* Taegu
Daerah Istimewa Aceh *see* Aceh
171 P4 **Daet** Luzon, N Philippines
160 I11 **Dafang** Guizhou, S China
153 W11 **Dafla Hills** ▲▲ NE India
11 U15 **Dafoe** Saskatchewan, S Canada
76 G10 **Dagana** N Senegal
Dagana *see* Dahana, Tajikistan
Dagana *see* Massakory, Chad
118 K11 **Dagda** Krāslava, SE Latvia
Dagden *see* Hiiumaa
Dagden-Sund *see* Soela Väin
129 P16 **Dagestan, Respublika** *prev.* Dagestanskaya ASSR, *Eng.* Daghestan. ◈ *autonomous republic* SW Russian Federation
Dagestanskaya ASSR *see* Dagestan, Respublika
129 R17 **Dagestanskiye Ogni** Respublika Dagestan, SW Russian Federation
185 A23 **Dagg Sound** *sound* South Island, NZ
Daghestan *see* Dagestan, Respublika
141 Y8 **Daghmar** NE Oman
Dağliq Qarabağ *see* Nagornyy Karabakh
Dagö *see* Hiiumaa
54 D11 **Dagua** Valle del Cauca, W Colombia
160 H11 **Daguan** Yunnan, SW China
171 N3 **Dagupan** *off.* Dagupan City. Luzon, N Philippines
159 N16 **Dagzê** Xizang Zizhiqu, W China
147 Q13 **Dahana** *Rus.* Dagana, Dakhana. SW Tajikistan
163 V10 **Dahei Shan** ▲ N China
163 T7 **Da Hinggan Ling** *Eng.* Great Khingan Range. ▲▲ NE China
Dahlac Archipelago *see* Dahlak Archipelago
80 K9 **Dahlak Archipelago** *var.* Dahlac Archipelago. *island group* E Eritrea
23 T2 **Dahlonega** Georgia, SE USA
101 O14 **Dahme** Brandenburg, E Germany
100 O13 **Dahme** ≈ E Germany
141 O14 **Dahm, Ramlat** *desert* NW Yemen
154 E10 **Dāhod** *prev.* Dohad. Gujarāt, W India
Dahomey *see* Benin
158 G10 **Dahongliutan** Xinjiang Uygur Zizhiqu, NW China
Dahra *see* Dara
139 R2 **Dahūk** *var.* Dohuk, *Kurd.* Dihōk. N Iraq
116 J15 **Daia** Giurgiu, S Romania
165 P12 **Daigo** Ibaraki, Honshū, S Japan
163 O13 **Dai Hai** ◎ N China
Daihoku *see* T'aipei
186 M8 **Dai Island** *island* N Solomon Islands
166 M8 **Daik-u** Pegu, SW Burma
138 H9 **Dā'īl** Dar'ā, S Syria
167 U12 **Đai Lanh** Khanh Hoa, S Vietnam
161 Q13 **Daimao Shan** ▲▲ SE China
105 N11 **Daimiel** Castilla-La Mancha, C Spain
115 F22 **Daimonía** Pelopónnisos, S Greece
Dainan *see* T'ainan
25 W6 **Daingerfield** Texas, SW USA
Daingin, Bá an *see* Dingle Bay
159 R13 **Dainkognubma** Xizang Zizhiqu, W China
164 K14 **Daiō-zaki** *headland* Honshū, SW Japan
Dairbhre *see* Valencia Island
61 B22 **Daireaux** Buenos Aires, E Argentina
Dairen *see* Dalian
75 W9 **Dairût** *var.* Dayrūṭ. C Egypt
25 X10 **Daisetta** Texas, SW USA
192 G5 **Daitō-jima** *island group* SW Japan
192 G5 **Daitō Ridge** *undersea feature* N Philippine Sea
161 N3 **Daixian** *var.* Dai Xian. Shanxi, C China
161 Q12 **Daiyun Shan** ▲▲ SE China
44 M8 **Dajabón** NW Dominican Republic
160 G8 **Dajin Chuan** ≈ C China
148 J6 **Dak** ◎ W Afghanistan
76 F11 **Dakar** ● (Senegal) W Senegal
76 F11 **Dakar** ✕ W Senegal
167 U10 **Đak Glây** Kon Tum, C Vietnam
Dakhana *see* Dahana
153 U16 **Dakhin Shahbazpur Island** *island* S Bangladesh
Dakhla *see* Ad Dakhla
76 F7 **Dakhlet Nouâdhibou** ◈ *region* NW Mauritania
Đak Lap *see* Kiến Đức
167 U13 **Đak Nông** Đắc Lắc, S Vietnam
77 U11 **Dakoro** Maradi, S Niger
29 U12 **Dakota City** Iowa, C USA
29 R13 **Dakota City** Nebraska, C USA
112 M17 **Đakovica** *var.* Djakovica, *Alb.* Gjakovë. Serbia, S Yugoslavia
112 I10 **Đakovo** *var.* Djakovo, *Hung.* Diakovár. Osijek-Baranja, E Croatia
Dakshin *see* Deccan
167 U11 **Đak Tô** *var.* Đắc Tô. Kon Tum, C Vietnam
43 N7 **Dákura** *var.* Dacura. Región Autónoma Atlántico Norte, NE Nicaragua
95 I14 **Dal** Akershus, S Norway
82 E12 **Dala** Lunda Sul, E Angola
108 J8 **Dalaas** Vorarlberg, W Austria
76 I13 **Dalaba** Moyenne-Guinée, W Guinea
Dalai *see* Da'an
Dalain Hob *see* Ejin Qi
Dalai Nor *see* Hulun Nur
163 Q11 **Dalai Nur** *salt lake* N China
Dala-Jarna *see* Järna
95 M14 **Dalälven** ≈ C Sweden
136 C16 **Dalaman** Muğla, SW Turkey
136 C16 **Dalaman** ✕ Muğla, SW Turkey
136 D16 **Dalaman Çayı** ≈ SW Turkey
162 K11 **Dalandzadgad** Ömnögovĭ, S Mongolia
95 D17 **Dalane** *physical region* S Norway
189 Z2 **Dalap-Uliga-Djarrit** *var.* Delap-Uliga-Darrit, D-U-D. *island group* Ratak Chain, SE Marshall Islands
94 J12 **Dalarna** *prev.* Kopparberg ◈ *county* C Sweden
94 L13 **Dalarna** *prev. Eng.* Dalecarlia. *cultural region* C Sweden
95 P16 **Dalarö** Stockholm, C Sweden
167 U13 **Đa Lat** Lâm Đông, S Vietnam
162 J11 **Dalay** Ömnögovĭ, S Mongolia
148 L12 **Dālbandīn** *var.* Dāl Bandin. Baluchistān, SW Pakistan
95 J17 **Dalbosjön** *lake bay* S Sweden
181 Y10 **Dalby** Queensland, E Australia
94 D13 **Dale** Hordaland, S Norway
94 C12 **Dale** Sogn og Fjordane, S Norway
32 K12 **Dale** Oregon, NW USA
25 T11 **Dale** Texas, SW USA
Dalecarlia *see* Dalarna
21 W4 **Dale City** Virginia, NE USA
20 L8 **Dale Hollow Lake** ⊡ Kentucky/Tennessee, S USA
98 O8 **Dalen** Drenthe, NE Netherlands
95 E15 **Dalen** Telemark, S Norway
166 K14 **Daletme** Chin State, W Burma
23 Q7 **Daleville** Alabama, S USA
98 M9 **Dalfsen** Overijssel, E Netherlands
24 M1 **Dalhart** Texas, SW USA
13 O13 **Dalhousie** New Brunswick, SE Canada
152 I6 **Dalhousie** Himāchal Pradesh, N India
160 F12 **Dali** *var.* Xiaguan. Yunnan, SW China
Dali *see* Idālion
163 U14 **Dalian** *var.* Dairen, Dalien, Lüda, Ta-lien, *Rus.* Dalny. Liaoning, NE China
105 O15 **Dalías** Andalucía, S Spain
Dalien *see* Dalian
Dalijan *see* Delījān
112 J9 **Dalj** *Hung.* Dalja. Osijek-Baranja, E Croatia
Dalja *see* Dalj
32 F12 **Dallas** Oregon, NW USA
25 U6 **Dallas** Texas, SW USA
25 T7 **Dallas-Fort Worth** ✕ Texas, SW USA
154 K12 **Dalli Rājhara** Madhya Pradesh, C India
39 X15 **Dall Island** *island* Alexander Archipelago, Alaska, USA
38 M12 **Dall Lake** ◎ Alaska, USA
77 S12 **Dallol Bosso** *seasonal river* W Niger
141 U7 **Dalmā** *island* W UAE
113 E14 **Dalmacija** *Eng.* Dalmatia, *Ger.* Dalmatien, *It.* Dalmazia. *cultural region* S Croatia
Dalmatia/Dalmatien/Dalmazia *see* Dalmacija
123 S15 **Dal'negorsk** Primorskiy Kray, SE Russian Federation
Dalny *see* Dalian
76 M16 **Daloa** C Ivory Coast
160 J11 **Dalou Shan** ▲▲ S China
181 X7 **Dalrymple Lake** ◎ Queensland, E Australia
14 H14 **Dalrymple Lake** ◎ Ontario, S Canada
181 X7 **Dalrymple, Mount** ▲ Queensland, E Australia
93 K20 **Dalsbruk** *Fin.* Taalintehdas. Länsi-Suomi, W Finland
95 K19 **Dalsjöfors** Västra Götaland, S Sweden
95 J17 **Dals Långed** *var.* Långed. Västra Götaland, S Sweden
153 O15 **Dāltenganj** *prev.* Daltonganj. Bihār, N India
23 R2 **Dalton** Georgia, SE USA
Daltonganj *see* Dāltenganj
195 X14 **Dalton Iceberg Tongue** *ice feature* Antarctica
92 J1 **Dalvík** Nordhurland Eystra, N Iceland
35 N8 **Daly City** California, W USA
181 P2 **Daly River** ≈ Northern Territory, N Australia
181 Q3 **Daly Waters** Northern Territory, N Australia
119 F20 **Damachava** *var.* Damachova, *Pol.* Domaczewo, *Rus.* Domachëvo. Brestskaya Voblasts', SW Belarus
Damachova *see* Damachava
77 W11 **Damagaram Takaya** Zinder, S Niger
154 D12 **Damān** Damān and Diu, W India
154 B12 **Damān and Diu** ◈ *union territory* W India
75 V7 **Damanhûr** *anc.* Hermopolis Parva. N Egypt
Damão *see* Damān
161 O1 **Damaqun Shan** ▲ E China
79 I15 **Damara** Ombella-Mpoko, S Central African Republic
83 D18 **Damaraland** *physical region* C Namibia
171 S15 **Damar, Kepulauan** *var.* Baraf Daja Islands, Kepulauan Barat Daya. *island group* C Indonesia
168 J8 **Damar Laut** Perak, Peninsular Malaysia
171 S15 **Damar, Pulau** *island* Maluku, E Indonesia
Damas *see* Dimashq
77 Y12 **Damasak** Borno, NE Nigeria
Damasco *see* Dimashq
21 Q8 **Damascus** Virginia, NE USA
Damascus *see* Dimashq
77 X13 **Damaturu** Yobe, NE Nigeria
171 R9 **Damau** Pulau Kaburuang, N Indonesia
143 O5 **Damāvand, Qolleh-ye** ▲ N Iran
82 B10 **Damba** Uíge, NW Angola
114 M12 **Dambaslar** Tekirdağ, NW Turkey
116 J13 **Dâmbovița** *prev.* Dîmbovița. ◈ *county* SE Romania
116 J13 **Dâmbovița** *prev.* Dîmbovița. ≈ S Romania
173 Y15 **D'Ambre, Île** *island* NE Mauritius
155 K24 **Dambulla** Central Province, C Sri Lanka
44 K9 **Dame-Marie** SW Haiti
44 J9 **Dame Marie, Cap** *headland* SW Haiti
143 Q4 **Dāmghān** Semnān, N Iran
Damietta *see* Dumyāṭ
138 G10 **Dāmiyā** Al Balqā', NW Jordan
146 G11 **Damla** Dashkhovuzskiy Velayat, N Turkmenistan
Dammām *see* Ad Dammān
100 G12 **Damme** Niedersachsen, NW Germany
153 R15 **Dāmodar** ≈ NE India
154 J9 **Damoh** Madhya Pradesh, C India
77 P15 **Damongo** NW Ghana
138 G7 **Damoûr** *var.* Ad Dāmūr. W Lebanon
171 N11 **Dampal, Teluk** *bay* Sulawesi, C Indonesia
180 H7 **Dampier** Western Australia
180 H6 **Dampier Archipelago** *island group* Western Australia
141 U14 **Damqawt** *var.* Damqut. E Yemen
159 O13 **Dam Qu** ≈ C China
Damqut *see* Damqawt
167 R13 **Dâmrei, Chuŏr Phnum** *Fr.* Chaîne de l'Éléphant. ▲▲ SW Cambodia
108 C7 **Damvant** Jura, NW Switzerland
Damwâld *see* Damwoude
98 L5 **Damwoude** *Fris.* Damwâld. Friesland, N Netherlands
159 N15 **Damxung** Xizang Zizhiqu, W China
80 K11 **Danakil Desert** *var.* Afar Depression, Danakil Plain. *desert* E Africa
Danakil Plain *see* Danakil Desert
35 R8 **Dana, Mount** ▲ California, W USA
76 L16 **Danané** W Ivory Coast
167 U10 **Đa Nang** *prev.* Tourane. Quang Nam-Đa Nang, C Vietnam
160 G9 **Danba** Sichuan, C China
Danborg *see* Daneborg
18 L13 **Danbury** Connecticut, NE USA
25 W12 **Danbury** Texas, SW USA
35 X15 **Danby Lake** ◎ California, W USA
194 H4 **Danco Coast** *physical region* Antarctica
82 B11 **Dande** ≈ NW Angola
Dandeldhura *see* Dadeldhura
155 E17 **Dandeli** Karnātaka, W India
183 O12 **Dandenong** Victoria, SE Australia
163 V13 **Dandong** *var.* Tan-tung; *prev.* An-tung. Liaoning, NE China
197 Q14 **Daneborg** *var.* Danborg. Tunu, N Greenland
25 V12 **Danevang** Texas, SW USA
Dänew *see* Deynau
14 L12 **Danford Lake** Quebec, SE Canada
19 T4 **Danforth** Maine, NE USA
37 P3 **Danforth Hills** ▲ Colorado, C USA
Dangara *see* Danghara
159 V12 **Dangchang** Gansu, C China
Dangchengwan *see* Subei
82 B10 **Dange** Uíge, NW Angola
Dangerous Archipelago *see* Tuamotu, Îles
83 E26 **Danger Point** *headland* SW South Africa
147 Q13 **Danghara** *Rus.* Dangara. SW Tajikistan
159 P8 **Danghe Nanshan** ▲▲ W China
80 I12 **Dangila** *var.* Dānglā. Amhara, NW Ethiopia
159 P8 **Dangjin Shankou** *pass* N China
Dangla *see* Tanggula Shan
Dānglā *see* Dangila, NW Ethiopia
Dangme Chu *see* Manās
153 Y11 **Dāngori** Assam, NE India
Dang Raek, Phanom/Dangrek, Chaîne des *see* Dângrêk, Chuŏr Phnum
167 S11 **Dângrêk, Chuŏr Phnum** *var.* Phanom Dang Raek, Phanom Dong Rak, *Fr.* Chaîne des Dangrek. ▲▲ Cambodia/Thailand
42 G3 **Dangriga** *prev.* Stann Creek. Stann Creek, E Belize
161 P6 **Dangshan** Anhui, E China
33 T15 **Daniel** Wyoming, C USA
83 H22 **Daniëlskuil** Northern Cape, N South Africa
19 N12 **Danielson** Connecticut, NE USA
126 M15 **Danilov** Yaroslavskaya Oblast', W Russian Federation
129 O9 **Danilovka** Volgogradskaya Oblast', SW Russian Federation
Danish West Indies *see* Virgin Islands (US)
160 L7 **Dan Jiang** ≈ C China
160 M7 **Danjiangkou Shuiku** ⊡ C China
141 W8 **Dank** *var.* Dhank. NW Oman
152 J7 **Dankhar** Himāchal Pradesh, N India
128 L6 **Dankov** Lipetskaya Oblast', W Russian Federation
42 J7 **Danlí** El Paraíso, S Honduras
Danmark *see* Denmark
Danmarksstraedet *see* Denmark Strait
95 O14 **Dannemora** Uppsala, C Sweden
18 L6 **Dannemora** New York, NE USA
100 K11 **Dannenberg** Niedersachsen, N Germany
184 N12 **Dannevirke** Manawatu-Wanganui, North Island, NZ
21 U8 **Dan River** ≈ Virginia, NE USA
167 P8 **Dan Sai** Loei, C Thailand
18 F10 **Dansville** New York, NE USA
Dantzig *see* Gdańsk
86 E12 **Danube** *Bul.* Dunav, *Cz.* Dunaj, *Ger.* Donau, *Hung.* Duna, *Rom.* Dunărea. ≈ C Europe
Danubian Plain *see* Dunavska Ravnina
166 L8 **Danubyu** Irrawaddy, SW Burma
Danum *see* Doncaster
19 P11 **Danvers** Massachusetts, NE USA
27 T11 **Danville** Arkansas, C USA
31 N13 **Danville** Illinois, N USA
31 O14 **Danville** Indiana, N USA
29 Y15 **Danville** Iowa, C USA
20 M6 **Danville** Kentucky, S USA
18 G14 **Danville** Pennsylvania, NE USA
21 T6 **Danville** Virginia, NE USA
Danxian/Dan Xian *see* Danzhou
160 L17 **Danzhou** *prev.* Danxian, Dan Xian, Nada. Hainan, S China
Danzig *see* Gdańsk
Danziger Bucht *see* Danzig, Gulf of
110 J6 **Danzig, Gulf of** *var.* Gulf of Gdańsk, *Ger.* Danziger Bucht, *Pol.* Zakota Gdańska, *Rus.* Gdan'skaya Bukhta. *gulf* N Poland
160 F10 **Daocheng** Sichuan, C China
Daokou *see* Huaxian
104 H7 **Dão, Rio** ≈ N Portugal
Daosa *see* Dausa
77 Y7 **Dao Timmi** Agadez, NE Niger
160 M13 **Daoxian** *var.* Dao Xian. Hunan, S China
77 Q14 **Dapaong** N Togo
23 N8 **Daphne** Alabama, S USA
171 P7 **Dapitan** Mindanao, S Philippines

◆ Country ● Country Capital ◇ Dependent Territory ○ Dependent Territory Capital ◈ Administrative Region ✕ International Airport ▲ Mountain ▲▲ Mountain Range ⚠ Volcano ≈ River ◎ Lake ⊡ Reservoir

159 P9 **Da Qaidam** Qinghai, C China
163 V8 **Daqing** Heilongjiang, NE China
163 O13 **Daqing Shan** ⛰ N China
Daqm *see* Duqm
139 T5 **Dāqūq** *var.* Tāwūq. N Iraq
76 G10 **Dara** *var.* Dahra. NW Senegal
138 H9 **Dar'ā** *var.* Der'a, *Fr.* Déraa. Dar'ā, SW Syria
138 H8 **Dar'ā** *off.* Muḥāfaẓat Dar'ā, *var.* Dará, Derá, Derrá. ◈ *governorate* S Syria
143 Q12 **Dārāb** Fārs, S Iran
116 K8 **Darabani** Botoşani, NW Romania
Daraj *see* Dirj
142 M8 **Dārān** Eşfahān, W Iran
167 U12 **Đa Răng, Sông** *var.* Ba. ∽ S Vietnam
Daraut-Kurgan *see* Daroot-Korgon
77 W13 **Darazo** Bauchi, E Nigeria
139 S3 **Darband** N Iraq
139 V4 **Darband-i Khān, Sadd** *dam* NE Iraq
139 N1 **Darbāsīyah** *var.* Derbisīye. Al Ḥasakah, N Syria
118 C11 **Darbėnai** Kretinga, NW Lithuania
153 Q13 **Darbhanga** Bihār, N India
38 M9 **Darby, Cape** *headland* Alaska, USA
112 I9 **Darda** *Hung.* Dárda. Osijek-Baranja, E Croatia
27 T11 **Dardanelle** Arkansas, C USA
27 S11 **Dardanelle, Lake** ⊠ Arkansas, C USA
Dardanelles *see* Çanakkale Boğazı
Dardanelli *see* Çanakkale
Dar-el-Beida *see* Casablanca
136 M14 **Darende** Malatya, C Turkey
81 J22 **Dar es Salaam** Dar es Salaam, E Tanzania
81 J22 **Dar es Salaam** × Pwani, E Tanzania
185 H18 **Darfield** Canterbury, South Island, NZ
106 F7 **Darfo** Lombardia, N Italy
80 B10 **Darfur** *var.* Darfur Massif. *cultural region* W Sudan
Darfur Massif *see* Darfur
146 J10 **Dargan-Ata** *var.* Darganata. Lebapskiy Velayat, NE Turkmenistan
Darganata *see* Dargan-Ata
143 T3 **Dargaz** *var.* Darreh Gaz; *prev.* Moḥammadābād. Khorāsān, NE Iran
139 U4 **Dargazayn** NE Iraq
183 P12 **Dargo** Victoria, SE Australia
162 K7 **Darhan** Bulgan, C Mongolia
163 N8 **Darhan** Hentiy, C Mongolia
162 L6 **Darhan** Selenge, N Mongolia
163 N12 **Darhan Muminggan Lianheqi** *var.* Bailingmiao. Nei Mongol Zizhiqu, N China
23 W7 **Darien** Georgia, SE USA
43 W16 **Darién** *off.* Provincia del Darién. ◈ *province* SE Panama
Darién, Golfo del *see* Darien, Gulf of
43 X14 **Darien, Gulf of** *Sp.* Golfo del Darién. *gulf* S Caribbean Sea
Darien, Isthmus of *see* Panamá, Istmo de
42 K9 **Dariense, Cordillera** ⛰ C Nicaragua
43 W15 **Darién, Serranía del** ⛰ Colombia/Panama
Dario *see* Ciudad Darío
Dariorigum *see* Vannes
Dariv *see* Darvi
Darj *see* Dirj
Darjeeling *see* Darjiling
153 S12 **Darjiling** *prev.* Darjeeling. West Bengal, NE India
Darkehnen *see* Ozersk
159 S12 **Darlag** Qinghai, C China
183 T3 **Darling Downs** *hill range* Queensland, E Australia
28 M2 **Darling, Lake** ⊠ North Dakota, N USA
180 I12 **Darling Range** ⛰ Western Australia
182 L8 **Darling River** ∽ New South Wales, SE Australia
97 M15 **Darlington** N England, UK
21 T12 **Darlington** South Carolina, SE USA
30 K9 **Darlington** Wisconsin, N USA
110 G7 **Darłowo** Zachodniopomorskie, NW Poland
101 G19 **Darmstadt** Hessen, SW Germany
75 S7 **Darnah** *var.* Dérna. NE Libya
103 S6 **Darney** Vosges, NE France
182 M7 **Darnick** New South Wales, SE Australia
195 Y6 **Darnley, Cape** *headland* Antarctica
105 R7 **Daroca** Aragón, NE Spain
147 S11 **Daroot-Korgon** *var.* Daraut-Kurgan. Oshskaya Oblast', SW Kyrgyzstan
61 A23 **Darragueira** *var.* Darregueira. Buenos Aires, E Argentina
Darregueira *see* Darragueira
Darreh Gaz *see* Dargaz
142 K7 **Darreh Shahr** *var.* Darreh-ye Shahr. Īlām, W Iran
Darreh-ye Shahr *see* Darreh Shahr
32 I7 **Darrington** Washington, NW USA
25 P1 **Darrouzett** Texas, SW USA
153 S15 **Darsana** *var.* Darshana. Khulna, N Bangladesh
Darshana *see* Darsana
100 M7 **Darss** *peninsula* NE Germany
100 M7 **Darsser Ort** *headland* NE Germany
97 J24 **Dart** ∽ SW England, UK
Dartang *see* Baqên
97 P22 **Dartford** SE England, UK
182 L12 **Dartmoor** Victoria, SE Australia
97 I24 **Dartmoor** *moorland* SW England, UK
13 Q15 **Dartmouth** Nova Scotia, SE Canada
97 J24 **Dartmouth** SW England, UK
15 Y6 **Dartmouth** ∽ Quebec, SE Canada
183 Q11 **Dartmouth Reservoir** ◎ Victoria, SE Australia
Dartuch, Cabo *see* Artrutx, Cap d'
186 C9 **Daru** Western, SW PNG
112 G9 **Daruvar** *Hung.* Daruvár. Bjelovar-Bilogora, NE Croatia
146 F10 **Darvaza** *Turkm.* Derweze. Akhalskiy Velayat, C Turkmenistan
Darvaza *see* Darwoza
Darvazskiy Khrebet *see* Darvoz, Qatorkŭhi
162 F8 **Darvi** *var.* Dariv. Govĭ-Altay, W Mongolia
148 L9 **Darvīshān** *var.* Darweshan, Garmser. Helmand, S Afghanistan
147 R13 **Darvoz, Qatorkŭhi** *Rus.* Darvazskiy Khrebet. ⛰ C Tajikistan
Darweshan *see* Darvīshān
63 J15 **Darwin** Río Negro, S Argentina
181 O1 **Darwin** *prev.* Palmerston, Port Darwin. *territory capital* Northern Territory, N Australia
65 D24 **Darwin** *var.* Darwin Settlement. East Falkland, Falkland Islands
62 H8 **Darwin, Cordillera** ⛰ N Chile
57 B17 **Darwin, Volcán** Ѫ Galapagos Islands, Ecuador, E Pacific Ocean
147 O10 **Darwoza** *Rus.* Darvaza. Jizzakh Wiloyati, C Uzbekistan
149 S8 **Darya Khān** Punjab, E Pakistan
145 O15 **Dar'yalyktakyr, Ravnina** *plain* S Kazakhstan
143 T11 **Dārzīn** Kermān, S Iran
160 L8 **Dashennongjia** ▲ C China
Dashhowuz *see* Dashkhovuz
Dashhowuz Welayaty *see* Dashkhovuzskiy Velayat
119 O16 **Dashkawka** *Rus.* Dashkovka. Mahilyowskaya Voblasts', E Belarus
146 H8 **Dashkhovuz** *Turkm.* Dashhowuz; *prev.* Tashauz. Dashkhovuzskiy Velayat, N Turkmenistan
Dashkhovuz *see* Dashkhovuzskiy Velayat
146 E9 **Dashkhovuzskiy Velayat** *var.* Dashkhovuz, *Turkm.* Dashhowuz Welayaty. ◈ *province* N Turkmenistan
Dashköpri *see* Tashkepri
Dashkovka *see* Dashkawka
148 J15 **Dasht** ∽ SW Pakistan
Dashtidzhum *see* Dashtijum
147 R13 **Dashtijum** *Rus.* Dashtidzhum. SW Tajikistan
149 W7 **Daska** Punjab, NE Pakistan
Da, Sông *see* Black River
77 R15 **Dassa** *var.* Dassa-Zoumé. S Benin
Dassa-Zoumé *see* Dassa
29 U8 **Dassel** Minnesota, N USA
149 T4 **Dastegil Sar** *var.* Disteghil Sār. ▲ N India
136 C16 **Datça** Muğla, SW Turkey
165 R4 **Date** Hokkaidō, NE Japan
154 I8 **Datia** *prev.* Duttia. Madhya Pradesh, C India
159 T10 **Datong** Qinghai, C China
161 N2 **Datong** *var.* Tatung, Ta-t'ung. Shanxi, C China
159 S9 **Datong He** ∽ C China
159 S9 **Datong Shan** ⛰ C China
169 O10 **Datu, Tanjung** *headland* Indonesia/Malaysia
Daua *see* Dawa Wenz
172 H16 **Dauban, Mount** ▲ Silhouette, NE Seychelles
149 T7 **Dāūd Khel** Punjab, E Pakistan
119 G15 **Daugai** Alytus, S Lithuania
Daugava *see* Western Dvina
118 J11 **Daugavpils** *Ger.* Dünaburg; *prev. Rus.* Dvinsk. *municipality* Daugvapils, SE Latvia
Dauka *see* Dawkah
Daulatabad *see* Malāyer
101 D18 **Daun** Rheinland-Pfalz, W Germany
155 E14 **Daund** *prev.* Dhond. Mahārāshtra, W India
166 M12 **Daung Kyun** *island* S Burma
11 W15 **Dauphin** Manitoba, S Canada
103 S13 **Dauphiné** *cultural region* E France
23 N9 **Dauphin Island** *island* Alabama, S USA
11 X15 **Dauphin River** Manitoba, S Canada
77 V12 **Daura** Katsina, N Nigeria
152 H12 **Dausa** *prev.* Daosa. Rājasthān, N India
Dauwa *see* Dawwah
137 Y10 **Däväçi** *Rus.* Divichi. NE Azerbaijan
155 F18 **Dāvangere** Karnātaka, W India
171 Q8 **Davao** *off.* Davao City. Mindanao, S Philippines
171 Q8 **Davao Gulf** *gulf* Mindanao, S Philippines
15 Q11 **Daveluyville** Quebec, SE Canada
29 Z14 **Davenport** Iowa, C USA
32 L8 **Davenport** Washington, NW USA
43 P16 **David** Chiriquí, W Panama
15 O11 **David** ∽ Quebec, SE Canada
29 R15 **David City** Nebraska, C USA
David-Gorodok *see* Davyd-Haradok
11 T16 **Davidson** Saskatchewan, S Canada
21 R10 **Davidson** North Carolina, SE USA
26 K12 **Davidson** Oklahoma, C USA
39 S6 **Davidson Mountains** ⛰ Alaska, USA
172 M8 **Davie Ridge** *undersea feature* W Indian Ocean
182 A1 **Davies, Mount** ▲ South Australia
35 O7 **Davis** California, W USA
27 N12 **Davis** Oklahoma, C USA
195 Y7 **Davis** *Australian research station* Antarctica
194 H3 **Davis Coast** *physical region* Antarctica
18 C16 **Davis, Mount** ▲ Pennsylvania, NE USA
24 K9 **Davis Mountains** ⛰ Texas, SW USA
195 Z9 **Davis Sea** *sea* Antarctica
65 O20 **Davis Seamounts** *undersea feature* S Atlantic Ocean
196 M13 **Davis Strait** *strait* Baffin Bay/Labrador Sea
129 U5 **Davlekanovo** Respublika Bashkortostan, W Russian Federation
108 J9 **Davos** *Rmsch.* Tavau. Graubünden, E Switzerland
119 J20 **Davyd-Haradok** *Pol.* Dawidgródek, *Rus.* David-Gorodok. Brestskaya Voblasts', SW Belarus
163 U12 **Dawa** Liaoning, NE China
141 O11 **Dawāsir, Wādī ad** *dry watercourse* S Saudi Arabia
81 K15 **Dawa Wenz** *var.* Daua, Webi Daawo. ∽ E Africa
Dawaymah, Birkat ad *see* Umm al Baqar, Hawr
Dawei *see* Tavoy
119 K14 **Dawhinava** *Rus.* Dolginovo. Minskaya Voblasts', N Belarus
Dawidgródek *see* Davyd-Haradok
141 V12 **Dawkah** *var.* Dauka. SW Oman
Dawlat Qaṭar *see* Qatar
24 M3 **Dawn** Texas, SW USA
140 M11 **Daws** Al Bāḥah, SW Saudi Arabia
10 H5 **Dawson** *var.* Dawson City. Yukon Territory, NW Canada
23 S6 **Dawson** Georgia, SE USA
29 S9 **Dawson** Minnesota, N USA
Dawson City *see* Dawson
11 N13 **Dawson Creek** British Columbia, W Canada
8 H7 **Dawson Range** ⛰ Yukon Territory, W Canada
181 Y9 **Dawson River** ∽ Queensland, E Australia
10 J15 **Dawsons Landing** British Columbia, SW Canada
20 I7 **Dawson Springs** Kentucky, S USA
23 S2 **Dawsonville** Georgia, SE USA
160 G8 **Dawu** Sichuan, C China
Dawu *see* Maqên
Dawukou *see* Shizuishan
141 Y10 **Dawwah** *var.* Dauwa. W Oman
102 J15 **Dax** *var.* Ax; *anc.* Aquae Augustae, Aquae Tarbelicae. Landes, SW France
Da Xian/Daxian *see* Dachuan
160 G9 **Daxue Shan** ⛰ C China
160 G12 **Dayao** Yunnan, SW China
Dayishan *see* Gaoyou
183 N12 **Daylesford** Victoria, SE Australia
35 U10 **Daylight Pass** *pass* California, W USA
61 D17 **Daymán, Río** ∽ N Uruguay
Dayr *see* Ad Dayr
138 G10 **Dayr 'Allā** *var.* Deir 'Alla. Al Balqā', N Jordan
139 N4 **Dayr az Zawr** *var.* Deir ez Zor. Dayr az Zawr, E Syria
138 M5 **Dayr az Zawr** *off.* Muḥāfaẓat Dayr az Zawr, *var.* Dayr Az-Zor. ◈ *governorate* E Syria
Dayr Az-Zor *see* Dayr az Zawr
Dayrūṭ *see* Dairûṭ
11 Q15 **Daysland** Alberta, SW Canada
31 R14 **Dayton** Ohio, N USA
20 L10 **Dayton** Tennessee, S USA
25 W11 **Dayton** Texas, SW USA
32 L10 **Dayton** Washington, NW USA
23 X10 **Daytona Beach** Florida, SE USA
169 U12 **Dayu** Borneo, C Indonesia
161 O13 **Dayu Ling** ⛰ S China
161 R7 **Da Yunhe** *Eng.* Grand Canal. *canal* E China
161 S11 **Dayu Shan** *island* SE China
160 J9 **Dazhu** Sichuan, C China
160 J9 **Dazu** Chongqing Shi, C China
83 H24 **De Aar** Northern Cape, C South Africa
194 K5 **Deacon, Cape** *headland* Antarctica
39 R5 **Deadhorse** Alaska, USA
33 T12 **Dead Indian Peak** ▲ Wyoming, C USA
23 R9 **Dead Lake** ◎ Florida, SE USA
44 J4 **Deadman's Cay** Long Island, C Bahamas
138 G11 **Dead Sea** *var.* Bahret Lut, Lacus Asphaltites, *Ar.* Al Baḥr al Mayyit, Baḥrat Lūt, *Heb.* Yam HaMelaḥ. *salt lake* Israel/Jordan
28 J9 **Deadwood** South Dakota, N USA
97 Q22 **Deal** SE England, UK
83 I22 **Dealesville** Free State, C South Africa
Dealnu *see* Tana/Teno
161 P10 **De'an** Jiangxi, S China
62 K9 **Deán Funes** Córdoba, C Argentina
194 L12 **Dean Island** *island* Antarctica
31 S10 **Dearborn** Michigan, N USA
27 R3 **Dearborn** Missouri, C USA
32 K9 **Deary** Idaho, NW USA
32 M9 **Deary** Washington, NW USA
10 J10 **Dease** ∽ British Columbia, W Canada
10 J10 **Dease Lake** British Columbia, W Canada
35 U11 **Death Valley** California, W USA
35 U11 **Death Valley** *valley* California, W USA
102 L4 **Deauville** Calvados, N France
117 X7 **Debal'tseve** *Rus.* Debal'tsevo. Donets'ka Oblast', E Ukraine
Debal'tsevo *see* Debal'tseve
113 M19 **Debar** *Ger.* Dibra, *Turk.* Debre. W FYR Macedonia
39 O9 **Debauch Mountain** ▲ Alaska, USA
De Behagle *see* Laï
25 X7 **De Berry** Texas, SW USA
129 T2 **Debesy** Udmurtskaya Respublika, NW Russian Federation
111 N16 **Dębica** Podkarpackie, SE Poland
De Bildt *see* De Bilt
98 J11 **De Bilt** *var.* De Bildt. Utrecht, C Netherlands
123 T9 **Debin** Magadanskaya Oblast', E Russian Federation
110 N13 **Dęblin** *Rus.* Ivangorod. Lubelskie, E Poland
110 D10 **Dębno** Zachodniopomorskie, NW Poland
39 S10 **Deborah, Mount** ▲ Alaska, USA
33 N8 **De Borgia** Montana, NW USA
Debra Birhan *see* Debre Birhan
Debra Marcos *see* Debre Mark'os
Debra Tabor *see* Debre Tabor
Debre *see* Debar
80 J13 **Debre Birhan** *var.* Debra Birhan. Amhara, N Ethiopia
111 N22 **Debrecen** *Ger.* Debreczin, *Rom.* Debreţin; *prev.* Debreczen. Hajdú-Bihar, E Hungary
Debreczen/Debreczin *see* Debrecen
80 I12 **Debre Mark'os** *var.* Debra Marcos. Amhara, N Ethiopia
113 N19 **Debrešte** SW FYR Macedonia
80 J11 **Debre Tabor** *var.* Debra Tabor. Amhara, N Ethiopia
Debreţin *see* Debrecen
80 J13 **Debre Zeyt** Oromo, C Ethiopia
113 L16 **Dečani** Serbia, S Yugoslavia
23 P2 **Decatur** Alabama, S USA
23 S3 **Decatur** Georgia, SE USA
30 L13 **Decatur** Illinois, N USA
31 Q12 **Decatur** Indiana, N USA
22 M5 **Decatur** Mississippi, S USA
29 S14 **Decatur** Nebraska, C USA
25 S6 **Decatur** Texas, SW USA
20 H9 **Decaturville** Tennessee, S USA
103 O13 **Decazeville** Aveyron, S France
155 H17 **Deccan** *Hind.* Dakshin. *plateau* C India
14 J8 **Decelles, Réservoir** ⊠ Quebec, SE Canada
12 K2 **Déception** Quebec, NE Canada
160 G11 **Dechang** Sichuan, C China
111 C15 **Děčín** *Ger.* Tetschen. Ústecký Kraj, NW Czech Republic
103 P9 **Decize** Nièvre, C France
98 I6 **De Cocksdorp** Noord-Holland, NW Netherlands
29 X11 **Decorah** Iowa, C USA
Dedeagaç/Dedeagach *see* Alexandroúpoli
188 C15 **Dededo** N Guam
98 N9 **Dedemsvaart** Overijssel, E Netherlands
19 O11 **Dedham** Massachusetts, NE USA
63 H19 **Dedo, Cerro** ▲ SW Argentina
77 O13 **Dédougou** W Burkina
126 G15 **Dedovichi** Pskovskaya Oblast', W Russian Federation
163 V6 **Dedu** *var.* Qingshan. Heilongjiang, NE China
155 J24 **Deduru Oya** ∽ W Sri Lanka
83 N14 **Dedza** Central, S Malawi
83 N14 **Dedza Mountain** ▲ C Malawi
97 J19 **Dee** *Wel.* Afon Dyfrdwy. ∽ England/Wales, UK
96 K9 **Dee** ∽ NE Scotland, UK
Deep Bay *see* Chilumba
21 T3 **Deep Creek Lake** ⊠ Maryland, NE USA
36 J4 **Deep Creek Range** ⛰ Utah, W USA
27 P10 **Deep Fork** ∽ Oklahoma, C USA
14 J11 **Deep River** Ontario, SE Canada
21 T10 **Deep River** ∽ North Carolina, SE USA
183 U4 **Deepwater** New South Wales, SE Australia
31 S14 **Deer Creek Lake** ◎ Ohio, N USA
23 Z15 **Deerfield Beach** Florida, SE USA
39 N8 **Deering** Alaska, USA
38 M16 **Deer Island** *island* Alaska, USA
19 S7 **Deer Isle** *island* Maine, NE USA
13 S11 **Deer Lake** Newfoundland, SE Canada
99 D18 **Deerlijk** West-Vlaanderen, W Belgium
33 Q10 **Deer Lodge** Montana, NW USA
32 L8 **Deer Park** Washington, NW USA
29 U5 **Deer River** Minnesota, N USA
Deés *see* Dej
31 R11 **Defiance** Ohio, N USA
23 Q8 **De Funiak Springs** Florida, SE USA
95 L23 **Degeberga** Skåne, S Sweden
104 H12 **Degebe, Ribeira** ∽ S Portugal
80 M13 **Degeh Bur** Somali, E Ethiopia
15 U9 **Dégelis** Quebec, SE Canada
77 U17 **Degema** Rivers, S Nigeria
95 L16 **Degerfors** Örebro, C Sweden
193 R14 **De Gerlache Seamounts** *undersea feature* SE Pacific Ocean
101 N21 **Deggendorf** Bayern, SE Germany
80 I11 **Degoma** Amhara, N Ethiopia
De Gordyk *see* Gorredijk
27 T12 **De Gray Lake** ⊠ Arkansas, C USA
180 J6 **De Grey River** ∽ Western Australia
128 M10 **Degtevo** Rostovskaya Oblast', SW Russian Federation
143 X13 **Dehak** Sīstān va Balūchestān, SE Iran
143 R9 **Deh 'Alī** Kermān, C Iran
143 S13 **Dehbārez** *var.* Rūdān. Hormozgān, S Iran
143 P10 **Deh Bīd** Fārs, C Iran
142 M10 **Deh Dasht** Kohkīlūyeh va Būyer Aḥmadī, SW Iran
75 N8 **Dehibat** SE Tunisia
Dehli *see* Delhi
142 K8 **Dehlorān** Īlām, W Iran
147 N13 **Dehqonobod** *Rus.* Dekhkanabad. Qashqadaryo Wiloyati, S Uzbekistan
152 J9 **Dehra Dūn** Uttar Pradesh, N India
153 O14 **Dehri** Bihār, N India
148 K10 **Deh Shū** *var.* Deshu. Helmand, S Afghanistan
99 D17 **Deinze** Oost-Vlaanderen, NW Belgium
Deir 'Alla *see* Dayr 'Allā
Deir ez Zor *see* Dayr az Zawr
Deirgeirt, Loch *see* Derg, Lough
116 H9 **Dej** *Hung.* Dés; *prev.* Deés. Cluj, NW Romania
95 K15 **Deje** Värmland, C Sweden
171 Y15 **De Jongs, Tanjung** *headland* Irian Jaya, SE Indonesia
De Jouwer *see* Joure
30 M10 **De Kalb** Illinois, N USA
22 M5 **De Kalb** Mississippi, S USA
25 W5 **De Kalb** Texas, SW USA
Dekéleia *see* Dhekélia
79 K20 **Dekese** Kasai Occidental, C Dem. Rep. Congo (Zaire)
Dekhkanabad *see* Dehqonobod
79 I14 **Dékoa** Kémo, 243C Central African Republic
98 H6 **De Koog** Noord-Holland, NW Netherlands
30 M9 **Delafield** Wisconsin, N USA
61 C23 **De La Garma** Buenos Aires, E Argentina
14 K10 **Delahey, Lac** ◎ Quebec, SE Canada
80 E11 **Delami** Southern Kordofan, C Sudan
23 X11 **De Land** Florida, SE USA
35 R12 **Delano** California, W USA
29 V8 **Delano** Minnesota, N USA
36 K6 **Delano Peak** ▲ Utah, W USA
Delap-Uliga-Darrit *see* Dalap-Uliga-Djarrit
148 L7 **Delārām** Farāh, SW Afghanistan
38 F17 **Delarof Islands** *island group* Aleutian Islands, Alaska, USA
30 M9 **Delavan** Wisconsin, N USA
31 S13 **Delaware** Ohio, N USA
18 I17 **Delaware** *off.* State of Delaware; *also known as* Blue Hen State, Diamond State, First State. ◈ *state* NE USA
18 I17 **Delaware Bay** *bay* NE USA
24 J8 **Delaware Mountains** ⛰ Texas, SW USA
18 I12 **Delaware River** ∽ NE USA
27 Q3 **Delaware River** ∽ Kansas, C USA
18 J14 **Delaware Water Gap** *valley* New Jersey/Pennsylvania, NE USA
101 G14 **Delbrück** Nordrhein-Westfalen, W Germany
11 Q15 **Delburne** Alberta, SW Canada
172 M12 **Del Cano Rise** *undersea feature* SW Indian Ocean
113 Q18 **Delčevo** NE FYR Macedonia
Delcommune, Lac *see* Nzilo, Lac
98 O10 **Delden** Overijssel, E Netherlands
183 R12 **Delegate** New South Wales, SE Australia
De Lemmer *see* Lemmer
108 D7 **Delémont** *Ger.* Delsberg. Jura, NW Switzerland
25 R7 **De Leon** Texas, SW USA
115 F18 **Delfoí** Stereá Ellás, C Greece
98 G12 **Delft** Zuid-Holland, W Netherlands
155 J23 **Delft** *island* NW Sri Lanka
98 O5 **Delfzijl** Groningen, NE Netherlands
(0) E9 **Delgada Fan** *undersea feature* NE Pacific Ocean
42 F7 **Delgado** San Salvador, SW El Salvador
82 Q12 **Delgado, Cabo** *headland* N Mozambique
80 E6 **Delgo** Northern, N Sudan
159 R10 **Delhi** *var.* Delingha. Qinghai, C China
152 I10 **Delhi** *var.* Dehli, *Hind.* Dilli; *hist.* Shahjahanabad. Delhi, N India
22 J5 **Delhi** Louisiana, S USA
18 J11 **Delhi** New York, NE USA
152 I10 **Delhi** ◈ *union territory* NW India
136 J17 **Deli Burnu** *headland* S Turkey
55 X10 **Délices** C French Guiana
136 J12 **Delice Çayı** ∽ C Turkey
40 J6 **Delicias** *var.* Ciudad Delicias. Chihuahua, N Mexico
143 N7 **Delījān** *var.* Dalijan, Dilijan. Markazī, W Iran
112 P12 **Deli Jovan** ⛰ E Yugoslavia
Déli-Kárpátok *see* Carpaţii Meridionali
8 I8 **Déline** *prev.* Fort Franklin. Northwest Territories, NW Canada
Delingha *see* Delhi
15 Q7 **Delisle** Quebec, SE Canada
11 T15 **Delisle** Saskatchewan, S Canada
101 M15 **Delitzsch** Sachsen, E Germany
33 Q12 **Dell** Montana, NW USA
24 I7 **Dell City** Texas, SW USA
103 U7 **Delle** Territoire-de-Belfort, E France
36 J9 **Dellenbaugh, Mount** ▲ Arizona, SW USA
29 R11 **Dell Rapids** South Dakota, N USA
21 Y4 **Delmar** Maryland, NE USA
18 K11 **Delmar** New York, NE USA
100 G11 **Delmenhorst** Niedersachsen, NW Germany
112 C9 **Delnice** Primorje-Gorski Kotar, NW Croatia
37 R7 **Del Norte** Colorado, C USA
39 N6 **De Long Mountains** ⛰ Alaska, USA
183 P16 **Deloraine** Tasmania, SE Australia
11 W17 **Deloraine** Manitoba, S Canada
31 O12 **Delphi** Indiana, N USA
31 Q12 **Delphos** Ohio, N USA
23 Z15 **Delray Beach** Florida, SE USA
25 O12 **Del Rio** Texas, SW USA
Delsberg *see* Delémont
94 N11 **Delsbo** Gävleborg, C Sweden
37 P6 **Delta** Colorado, C USA
36 K5 **Delta** Utah, W USA
77 T17 **Delta** ◈ *state* S Nigeria
55 Q6 **Delta Amacuro** *off.* Territorio Delta Amacuro. ◈ *federal district* NE Venezuela
39 S9 **Delta Junction** Alaska, USA
23 X11 **Deltona** Florida, SE USA
183 T5 **Delungra** New South Wales, SE Australia
154 C12 **Delvāda** Gujarāt, W India
61 B21 **Del Valle** Buenos Aires, E Argentina
Delvina *see* Delvinë
115 C15 **Delvináki** *var.* Dhelvinákion; *prev.* Pogónion. Ípeiros, W Greece
113 L23 **Delvinë** *var.* Delvina, *It.* Delvino. Vlorë, S Albania
Delvino *see* Delvinë
116 I7 **Delyatyn** Ivano-Frankivs'ka Oblast', W Ukraine
129 U5 **Dëma** ∽ W Russian Federation
105 O5 **Demanda, Sierra de la** ⛰ W Spain
39 T5 **Demarcation Point** *headland* Alaska, USA
79 K21 **Demba** Kasai Occidental, C Dem. Rep. Congo (Zaire)
172 H13 **Dembéni** Grande Comore, NW Comoros
79 M15 **Dembia** Mbomou, SE Central African Republic
Dembidollo *see* Dembī Dolo
80 H13 **Dembī Dolo** *var.* Dembidollo. Oromo, C Ethiopia
152 K6 **Demchok** *var.* Dêmqog. China/India *see also* Dêmqog
152 L6 **Demchok** *var.* Dêmqog. *disputed region* China/India *see also* Dêmqog
98 I12 **De Meern** Utrecht, C Netherlands
99 I17 **Demer** ∽ C Belgium
64 H12 **Demerara Plain** *undersea feature* W Atlantic Ocean
64 H12 **Demerara Plateau** *undersea feature* W Atlantic Ocean
55 T9 **Demerara River** ∽ NE Guyana
128 H3 **Demidov** Smolenskaya Oblast', W Russian Federation
37 Q15 **Deming** New Mexico, SW USA
32 H6 **Deming** Washington, NW USA
58 E10 **Demini, Rio** ∽ NW Brazil
136 D13 **Demirci** Manisa, W Turkey
113 P19 **Demir Kapija** *prev.* Železna Vrata. SE FYR Macedonia
114 N11 **Demirköy** Kırklareli, NW Turkey
100 N9 **Demmin** Mecklenburg-Vorpommern, NE Germany
23 O5 **Demopolis** Alabama, S USA
31 N11 **Demotte** Indiana, N USA
158 F13 **Dêmqog** *var.* Demchok. China/India *see also* Demchok
152 L6 **Dêmqog** *var.* Demchok. *disputed region* China/India *see also* Demchok
171 Y13 **Demta** Irian Jaya, E Indonesia
122 H11 **Dem'yanka** ∽ C Russian Federation
126 H15 **Demyansk** Novgorodskaya Oblast', W Russian Federation
122 H10 **Dem'yanskoye** Tyumenskaya Oblast', C Russian Federation
103 P2 **Denain** Nord, N France
39 S10 **Denali** Alaska, USA
Denali *see* McKinley, Mount
81 M14 **Denan** Somali, E Ethiopia
Denau *see* Denow
97 J18 **Denbigh** *Wel.* Dinbych. NE Wales, UK
97 J18 **Denbigh** *cultural region* N Wales, UK
98 I6 **Den Burg** Noord-Holland, NW Netherlands
99 F18 **Dender** *Fr.* Dendre. ∽ W Belgium
99 F18 **Denderleeuw** Oost-Vlaanderen, NW Belgium
99 F17 **Dendermonde** *Fr.* Termonde. Oost-Vlaanderen, NW Belgium
Dendre *see* Dender
194 I9 **Dendtler Island** *island* Antarctica
98 P10 **Denekamp** Overijssel, E Netherlands
77 W12 **Dengas** Zinder, S Niger
Dêngkagoin *see* Têwo
162 L13 **Dengkou** *var.* Bayan Gol. Nei Mongol Zizhiqu, N China
159 Q14 **Dêngqên** Xizang Zizhiqu, W China
Deng Xian *see* Dengzhou
160 M7 **Dengzhou** *prev.* Deng Xian. Henan, C China
Dengzhou *see* Penglai
Den Haag *see* 's-Gravenhage
98 N9 **Den Ham** Overijssel, E Netherlands
180 H10 **Denham** Western Australia
44 J12 **Denham, Mount** ▲ C Jamaica
22 J8 **Denham Springs** Louisiana, S USA

◆ Country ● Country Capital ◇ Dependent Territory ○ Dependent Territory Capital ◈ Administrative Region × International Airport ▲ Mountain ⛰ Mountain Range Ѫ Volcano ∽ River ◎ Lake ⊠ Reservoir

98 I7 **Den Helder** Noord-Holland, NW Netherlands
105 T11 **Denia** País Valenciano, E Spain
189 Q8 **Denig** W Nauru
183 N10 **Deniliquin** New South Wales, SE Australia
29 T14 **Denison** Iowa, C USA
25 U5 **Denison** Texas, SW USA
136 D15 **Denizli** Denizli, SW Turkey
136 D15 **Denizli** ◈ *province* SW Turkey
Denjong *see* Sikkim
183 S7 **Denman** New South Wales, SE Australia
195 Y10 **Denman Glacier** *glacier* Antarctica
21 R14 **Denmark** South Carolina, SE USA
95 G23 **Denmark** *off.* Kingdom of Denmark, *Dan.* Danmark; *anc.* Hafnia. ◆ *monarchy* N Europe
92 H1 **Denmark Strait** *var.* Danmarksstraedet. *strait* Greenland/Iceland
45 T11 **Dennery** E Saint Lucia
98 I7 **Den Oever** Noord-Holland, NW Netherlands
147 O13 **Denow** *Rus.* Denau. Surkhondaryo Wiloyati, S Uzbekistan
169 U17 **Denpasar** *prev.* Paloe. Bali, C Indonesia
116 E12 **Denta** Timiş, W Romania
21 Y3 **Denton** Maryland, NE USA
25 T6 **Denton** Texas, SW USA
186 G9 **D'Entrecasteaux Islands** *island group* SE PNG
37 T4 **Denver** *state capital* Colorado, C USA
16 I10 **Denver** ✕ Colorado, C USA
24 L6 **Denver City** Texas, SW USA
152 J9 **Deoband** Uttar Pradesh, N India
Deoghar *see* Devghar
154 E13 **Deolāli** Mahārāshtra, W India
154 I10 **Deori** Madhya Pradesh, C India
153 O12 **Deoria** Uttar Pradesh, N India
99 A17 **De Panne** West-Vlaanderen, W Belgium
54 M5 **Dependencia Federal** *off.* Territorio Dependencia Federal. ◈ *federal dependency* N Venezuela
Dependencia Federal, Territorio *see* Dependencia Federal
30 M7 **De Pere** Wisconsin, N USA
18 D10 **Depew** New York, NE USA
99 E17 **De Pinte** Oost-Vlaanderen, NW Belgium
25 V5 **Deport** Texas, SW USA
123 Q8 **Deputatskiy** Respublika Sakha (Yakutiya), NE Russian Federation
27 S13 **De Queen** Arkansas, C USA
22 G8 **De Quincy** Louisiana, S USA
81 J20 **Dera** *spring/well* S Kenya
Der'a/Derá/Déraa *see* Dar'ā
149 S10 **Dera Ghāzi Khān** *var.* Dera Ghāzikhān. Punjab, C Pakistan
149 S8 **Dera Ismāīl Khān** North-West Frontier Province, C Pakistan
113 L16 **Đeravica** ▲ S Yugoslavia
116 L6 **Derazhnya** Khmel'nyts'ka Oblast', W Ukraine
129 R17 **Derbent** Respublika Dagestan, SW Russian Federation
147 N13 **Derbent** Surkhondaryo Wiloyati, S Uzbekistan
Derbisīye *see* Darbāsīyah
79 M15 **Derbissaka** Mbomou, SE Central African Republic
180 L4 **Derby** Western Australia
97 M19 **Derby** C England, UK
27 N7 **Derby** Kansas, C USA
97 L18 **Derbyshire** *cultural region* C England, UK
112 O11 **Đerdap** *physical region* E Yugoslavia
Derelí *see* Gónnoi
171 W13 **Derew** ≈ Irian Jaya, E Indonesia
129 R8 **Dergachi** Saratovskaya Oblast', W Russian Federation
Dergachi *see* Derhachi
97 C19 **Derg, Lough** *Ir.* Loch Deirgeirt. ◎ W Ireland
117 V5 **Derhachi** *Rus.* Dergachi. Kharkivs'ka Oblast', E Ukraine
22 G8 **De Ridder** Louisiana, S USA
137 P16 **Derik** Mardin, SE Turkey
83 E20 **Derm** Hardap, C Namibia
144 M14 **Dermentobe** *prev.* Dyurmen'tyube. Kzylorda, S Kazakhstan
27 W14 **Dermott** Arkansas, C USA
Dérna *see* Darnah
Dernberg, Cape *see* Dolphin Head
22 J11 **Dernieres, Isles** *island group* Louisiana, S USA
Derniš *see* Drniš
102 I4 **Déroute, Passage de la** *strait* Channel Islands/France
Derrá *see* Dar'ā
Derry *see* Londonderry
Dertona *see* Tortona
Dertosa *see* Tortosa
80 H8 **Derudeb** Red Sea, NE Sudan
112 H10 **Derventa** Republika Srpska, N Bosnia and Herzegovina
183 O16 **Derwent Bridge** Tasmania, SE Australia
183 O17 **Derwent, River** ≈ Tasmania, SE Australia
Derweze *see* Darvaza
Deržavinsk *see* Derzhavinsk
145 O9 **Derzhavinsk** *var.* Deržavinsk. Akmola, C Kazakhstan
Dés *see* Dej
57 J18 **Desaguadero** Puno, S Peru
57 J18 **Desaguadero, Río** ≈ Bolivia/Peru
191 W9 **Désappointement, Îles du** *island group* Îles Tuamotu, C French Polynesia
27 W11 **Des Arc** Arkansas, C USA
14 C10 **Desbarats** Ontario, S Canada
62 H13 **Descabezado Grande, Volcán** ※ C Chile
40 B2 **Descanso** Baja California, NW Mexico
102 L9 **Descartes** Indre-et-Loire, C France
11 T13 **Deschambault Lake** ◎ Saskatchewan, C Canada
Deschnaer Koppe *see* Velká Deštná
32 I11 **Deschutes River** ≈ Oregon, NW USA
80 J12 **Desē** *var.* Desse, *It.* Dessie. Amhara, N Ethiopia
63 I20 **Deseado, Río** ≈ S Argentina
106 F8 **Desenzano del Garda** Lombardia, N Italy
36 K3 **Deseret Peak** ▲ Utah, W USA
64 P6 **Deserta Grande** *island* Madeira, Portugal, NE Atlantic Ocean
64 P6 **Desertas, Ilhas** *island group* Madeira, Portugal, NE Atlantic Ocean
35 X16 **Desert Center** California, W USA
35 V15 **Desert Hot Springs** California, W USA
14 K10 **Désert, Lac** ◎ Quebec, SE Canada
36 J2 **Desert Peak** ▲ Utah, W USA
31 R11 **Deshler** Ohio, N USA
Deshu *see* Deh Shū
Desiderii Fanum *see* St-Dizier
106 D7 **Desio** Lombardia, N Italy
115 E15 **Deskáti** *var.* Dheskáti. Dytikí Makedonía, N Greece
28 L2 **Des Lacs River** ≈ North Dakota, N USA
27 X6 **Desloge** Missouri, C USA
11 Q12 **Desmarais** Alberta, W Canada
29 Q10 **De Smet** South Dakota, N USA
29 V14 **Des Moines** *state capital* Iowa, C USA
17 N9 **Des Moines River** ≈ C USA
117 P4 **Desna** ≈ Russian Federation/Ukraine
116 G14 **Desnăţui** ≈ S Romania
63 F24 **Desolación, Isla** *island* S Chile
29 V14 **De Soto** Iowa, C USA
23 Q4 **De Soto Falls** *waterfall* Alabama, S USA
83 I25 **Despatch** Eastern Cape, S South Africa
105 N12 **Despeñaperros, Desfiladero de** *pass* S Spain
31 N10 **Des Plaines** Illinois, N USA
115 J21 **Despotikó** *island* Kykládes, Greece, Aegean Sea
112 N12 **Despotovac** Serbia, E Yugoslavia
101 M14 **Dessau** Sachsen-Anhalt, E Germany
Desse *see* Desē
99 J16 **Dessel** Antwerpen, N Belgium
Dessie *see* Desē
Desterro *see* Florianópolis
23 P9 **Destin** Florida, SE USA
Deštná *see* Velká Deštná
193 T10 **Desventurados, Islas de los** *island group* W Chile
103 N1 **Desvres** Pas-de-Calais, N France
116 E12 **Deta** *Ger.* Detta. Timiş, W Romania
101 H14 **Detmold** Nordrhein-Westfalen, W Germany
31 S10 **Detroit** Michigan, N USA
25 W5 **Detroit** Texas, SW USA
31 S10 **Detroit** ≈ Canada/USA
29 S6 **Detroit Lakes** Minnesota, N USA
31 S10 **Detroit Metropolitan** ✕ Michigan, N USA
Detta *see* Deta
167 S10 **Det Udom** Ubon Ratchathani, E Thailand
111 K20 **Detva** *Hung.* Gyeva. Banskobystrický Kraj, C Slovakia
154 G13 **Deūlgaon Rāja** Mahārāshtra, C India
99 L15 **Deurne** Noord-Brabant, SE Netherlands
99 H16 **Deurne** ✕ (Antwerpen) Antwerpen, N Belgium
Deutsch-Brod *see* Havlíčkův Brod
Deutschendorf *see* Poprad
Deutsch-Eylau *see* Iława
109 Y6 **Deutschkreutz** Burgenland, E Austria
Deutsch Krone *see* Wałcz
Deutschland/Deutschland, Bundesrepublik *see* Germany
109 V9 **Deutschlandsberg** Steiermark, SE Austria
Deutsch-Südwestafrika *see* Namibia
109 Y3 **Deutsch-Wagram** Niederösterreich, E Austria
Deux-Ponts *see* Zweibrücken
14 I11 **Deux Rivieres** Ontario, SE Canada
102 K9 **Deux-Sèvres** ◈ *department* W France
116 G11 **Deva** *Ger.* Diemrich, *Hung.* Déva. Hunedoara, W Romania
Deva *see* Chester
Devana *see* Aberdeen
Devana Castra *see* Chester
Đevđelija *see* Gevgelija
136 L12 **Deveci Dağları** ▲▲ N Turkey
137 P15 **Devegeçidi Barajı** ▣ SE Turkey
136 K15 **Develi** Kayseri, C Turkey
98 M11 **Deventer** Overijssel, E Netherlands
15 O10 **Devenyns, Lac** ◎ Quebec, SE Canada
96 K8 **Deveron** ≈ NE Scotland, UK
153 R14 **Devghar** *prev.* Deoghar. Bihār, NE India
27 R10 **Devil's Den** *plateau* Arkansas, C USA
35 R7 **Devils Gate** *pass* California, W USA
30 J2 **Devils Island** *island* Apostle Islands, Wisconsin, N USA
Devil's Island *see* Diable, Île du
29 P3 **Devils Lake** North Dakota, N USA
31 R10 **Devils Lake** ◎ Michigan, N USA
29 O3 **Devils Lake** ◎ North Dakota, N USA
35 W13 **Devils Playground** *desert* California, W USA
25 O11 **Devils River** ≈ Texas, SW USA
33 Y12 **Devils Tower** ▲ Wyoming, C USA
114 I11 **Devin** *prev.* Dovlen. Smolyan, SW Bulgaria
25 R12 **Devine** Texas, SW USA
152 H13 **Devli** Rājasthān, N India
Devne *see* Devnya
114 N8 **Devnya** *prev.* Devne. Varna, E Bulgaria
31 U14 **Devola** Ohio, N USA
Devoll *see* Devollit, Lumi i
113 M21 **Devollit, Lumi i** *var.* Devoll. ≈ SE Albania
11 Q14 **Devon** Alberta, SW Canada
97 I23 **Devon** *cultural region* SW England, UK
9 O4 **Devon Ice Cap** *ice feature* Nunavut, N Canada
8 N4 **Devon Island** *prev.* North Devon Island. *island* Parry Islands, Nunavut, NE Canada
183 O16 **Devonport** Tasmania, SE Australia
136 H11 **Devrek** Zonguldak, N Turkey
154 G10 **Dewās** Madhya Pradesh, C India
De Westerein *see* Zwaagwesteinde
27 P8 **Dewey** Oklahoma, C USA
Dewey *see* Culebra
98 M8 **De Wijk** Drenthe, NE Netherlands
27 W12 **De Witt** Arkansas, C USA
29 Z14 **De Witt** Iowa, C USA
29 R16 **De Witt** Nebraska, C USA
97 M17 **Dewsbury** N England, UK
161 Q10 **Dexing** Jiangxi, S China
27 Y8 **Dexter** Missouri, C USA
37 U14 **Dexter** New Mexico, SW USA
160 I8 **Deyang** Sichuan, C China
182 C4 **Dey-Dey, Lake** *salt lake* South Australia
143 S7 **Deyhūk** Khorāsān, E Iran
146 K12 **Deynau** *var.* Dyanev, *Turkm.* Dänew. Lebapskiy Velayat, NE Turkmenistan
142 L8 **Dezfūl** *var.* Dizful. Khūzestān, SW Iran
131 X4 **Dezhneva, Mys** *headland* NE Russian Federation
161 P4 **Dezhou** Shandong, E China
Dezh Shāhpūr *see* Marīvān
Dhahran *see* Aẓ Ẓahrān
Dhahran Al Khobar *see* Aẓ Ẓahrān al Khubar
153 U14 **Dhaka** *prev.* Dacca. ● (Bangladesh) Dhaka, C Bangladesh
153 T15 **Dhaka** ◈ *division* C Bangladesh
Dhali *see* Idálion
141 O15 **Dhamār** W Yemen
Dhambul *see* Taraz
154 K12 **Dhamtari** Madhya Pradesh, C India
153 Q15 **Dhanbād** Bihār, NE India
152 L10 **Dhangadhi** *var.* Dhangarhi. Far Western, W Nepal
Dhangarhi *see* Dhangadhi
Dhank *see* Ḍank
153 R12 **Dhankuta** Eastern, E Nepal
152 I6 **Dhaola Dhār** ▲▲ NE India
154 F10 **Dhār** Madhya Pradesh, C India
153 R12 **Dharan** *var.* Dharan Bazar. Eastern, E Nepal
155 H21 **Dhārāpuram** Tamil Nādu, SE India
155 H20 **Dharmapuri** Tamil Nādu, SE India
155 H18 **Dharmavaram** Andhra Pradesh, E India
154 M11 **Dharmjaygarh** Madhya Pradesh, C India
Dharmsāla *see* Dharmshāla
152 I7 **Dharmshāla** *prev.* Dharmsāla. Himāchal Pradesh, N India
155 F17 **Dhārwād** *prev.* Dharwar. Karnātaka, SW India
Dharwar *see* Dhārwād
153 O10 **Dhaulāgiri** ▲ C Nepal
81 L18 **Dheere Laaq** *var.* Lak Dera, *It.* Lach Dera. *seasonal river* Kenya/Somalia
121 Q3 **Dhekéleia Sovereign Base Area** *UK military installation* E Cyprus
121 Q3 **Dhekélia** *Eng.* Dhekelia. *Gk.* Dekéleia. *UK air base* SE Cyprus
Dhelvinákion *see* Delvináki
113 M22 **Dhëmbelit, Majae** ▲ S Albania
154 O12 **Dhenkānāl** Orissa, E India
Dheskáti *see* Deskáti
138 G11 **Dhībān** 'Ammān, NW Jordan
Dhidhimótikhon *see* Didymóteicho
Dhíkti Ori *see* Díkti
138 I12 **Dhirwah, Wādī adh** *dry watercourse* C Jordan
Dhístomon *see* Dístomo
Dhodhekánisos *see* Dodekánisos
Dhodhóni *see* Dodóni
Dhofar *see* Ẓufār
Dhomokós *see* Domokós
Dhond *see* Daund
155 H17 **Dhone** Andhra Pradesh, C India
154 B11 **Dhorāji** Gujarāt, W India
Dhráma *see* Dráma
154 C10 **Dhrāngadhra** Gujarāt, W India
Dhrepanon, Akrotírio *see* Drépano, Akrotírio
153 T13 **Dhuburi** Assam, NE India
154 F12 **Dhule** *prev.* Dhulia. Mahārāshtra, C India
Dhulia *see* Dhule
Dhún Dealgan, Cuan *see* Dundalk Bay
Dhún Droma, Cuan *see* Dundrum Bay
Dhún na nGall, Bá *see* Donegal Bay
Dhū Shaykh *see* Qazānīyah
80 Q13 **Dhuudo** Bari, NE Somalia
81 N15 **Dhuusa Marreeb** *var.* Dusa Marreb, *It.* Dusa Mareb. Galguduud, C Somalia
115 J24 **Día** *island* SE Greece
55 Y9 **Diable, Île du** *var.* Devil's Island. *island* N French Guiana
15 N12 **Diable, Rivière du** ≈ Quebec, SE Canada
35 N8 **Diablo, Mount** ▲ California, W USA
35 O9 **Diablo Range** ▲▲ California, W USA
24 I8 **Diablo, Sierra** ▲▲ Texas, SW USA
45 O11 **Diablotins, Morne** ▲ N Dominica
77 N11 **Diafarabé** Mopti, C Mali
77 N11 **Diaka** ≈ SW Mali
Diakovár *see* Đakovo
76 I12 **Dialakoto** S Senegal
61 B18 **Diamante** Entre Ríos, E Argentina
62 I12 **Diamante, Río** ≈ C Argentina
59 M19 **Diamantina** Minas Gerais, SE Brazil
59 N17 **Diamantina, Chapada** ▲▲ E Brazil
173 U11 **Diamantina Fracture Zone** *tectonic feature* E Indian Ocean
181 T8 **Diamantina River** ≈ Queensland/South Australia
38 D9 **Diamond Head** *headland* Oahu, Hawaii, USA, C Pacific Ocean
37 P2 **Diamond Peak** ▲ Colorado, C USA
35 W5 **Diamond Peak** ▲ Nevada, W USA
Diamond State *see* Delaware
76 J11 **Diamou** Kayes, SW Mali
95 I23 **Dianalund** Vestsjælland, C Denmark
65 G25 **Diana's Peak** ▲ C Saint Helena
160 M16 **Dianbai** Guangdong, S China
160 G13 **Dian Chi** ◎ SW China
106 B10 **Diano Marina** Liguria, NW Italy
77 R13 **Diapaga** E Burkina
Diarbekr *see* Diyarbakır
107 J15 **Diavolo, Passo del** *pass* C Italy
61 B18 **Díaz** Santa Fe, C Argentina
141 W6 **Dibā al Ḥiṣn** *var.* Dibāh, Dibba. Ash Shāriqah, NE UAE
139 S3 **Dībaga** N Iraq
Dibāh *see* Dibā al Ḥiṣn
79 L22 **Dibaya** Kasai Occidental, S Dem. Rep. Congo (Zaire)
Dibba *see* Dibā al Ḥiṣn
195 W15 **Dibble Iceberg Tongue** *ice feature* Antarctica
113 L19 **Dibër** ◈ *district* E Albania
83 I20 **Dibete** Central, SE Botswana
25 W9 **Diboll** Texas, SW USA
Dibra *see* Debar
153 X11 **Dibrugarh** Assam, NE India
54 G4 **Dibulla** La Guajira, N Colombia
25 O5 **Dickens** Texas, SW USA
19 R2 **Dickey** Maine, NE USA
30 K9 **Dickeyville** Wisconsin, N USA
28 K5 **Dickinson** North Dakota, N USA
(0) E6 **Dickins Seamount** *undersea feature* NE Pacific Ocean
27 O13 **Dickson** Oklahoma, C USA
20 I9 **Dickson** Tennessee, S USA
Dicle *see* Tigris
Dicsőszentmárton *see* Târnăveni
98 M12 **Didam** Gelderland, E Netherlands
163 Y8 **Didao** Heilongjiang, NE China
76 L12 **Didiéni** Koulikoro, W Mali
Didimo *see* Dídymo
Didimotiho *see* Didymóteicho
81 K17 **Didimtu** *spring/well* NE Kenya
67 U9 **Didinga Hills** ▲▲ S Sudan
11 Q16 **Didsbury** Alberta, SW Canada
152 G11 **Dīdwāna** Rājasthān, N India
115 G20 **Dídymo** *var.* Didimo. ▲ S Greece
114 L12 **Didymóteicho** *var.* Dhidhimótikhon, Didimotiho. Anatolikí Makedonía kai Thráki, NE Greece
103 S13 **Die** Drôme, E France
77 O13 **Diébougou** SW Burkina
Diedenhofen *see* Thionville
11 S16 **Diefenbaker, Lake** ▣ Saskatchewan, S Canada
62 H7 **Diego de Almagro** Atacama, N Chile
63 F23 **Diego de Almagro, Isla** *island* S Chile
61 A20 **Diego de Alvear** Santa Fe, C Argentina
173 Q7 **Diego Garcia** *island* S British Indian Ocean Territory
Diégo-Suarez *see* Antsirañana
99 M23 **Diekirch** Diekirch, C Luxembourg
99 L23 **Diekirch** ◈ *district* N Luxembourg
76 K11 **Diéma** Kayes, W Mali
101 H15 **Diemel** ≈ W Germany
98 I10 **Diemen** Noord-Holland, C Netherlands
Diemrich *see* Deva
167 R6 **Điện Biên** *var.* Bien Bien, Dien Bien Phu. Lai Châu, N Vietnam
Dien Bien Phu *see* Điện Biên
167 S7 **Điện Châu** Nghê An, N Vietnam
99 K18 **Diepenbeek** Limburg, NE Belgium
98 N11 **Diepenheim** Overijssel, E Netherlands
98 M10 **Diepenveen** Overijssel, E Netherlands
100 G12 **Diepholz** Niedersachsen, NW Germany
102 M3 **Dieppe** Seine-Maritime, N France
98 M12 **Dieren** Gelderland, E Netherlands
27 S13 **Dierks** Arkansas, C USA
99 J17 **Diest** Vlaams Brabant, C Belgium
108 F7 **Dietikon** Zürich, NW Switzerland
103 R13 **Dieulefit** Drôme, E France
103 T5 **Dieuze** Moselle, NE France
119 H15 **Dieveniškės** Šalčininkai, SE Lithuania
98 N7 **Diever** Drenthe, NE Netherlands
101 F17 **Diez** Rheinland-Pfalz, W Germany
77 Y12 **Diffa** Diffa, SE Niger
77 Y10 **Diffa** ◈ *department* SE Niger
99 L25 **Differdange** Luxembourg, SW Luxembourg
13 O16 **Digby** Nova Scotia, SE Canada
26 J5 **Dighton** Kansas, C USA
Dignano d'Istria *see* Vodnjan
103 T14 **Digne** *var.* Digne-les-Bains. Alpes-de-Haute-Provence, SE France
Digne-les-Bains *see* Digne
Digoel *see* Digul, Sungai
103 Q10 **Digoin** Saône-et-Loire, C France
171 Q8 **Digos** Mindanao, S Philippines
149 Q16 **Digri** Sind, SE Pakistan
171 Y14 **Digul Barat, Sungai** ≈ Irian Jaya, E Indonesia
171 Y15 **Digul, Sungai** *prev.* Digoel. ≈ Irian Jaya, E Indonesia
171 Z14 **Digul Timur, Sungai** ≈ Irian Jaya, E Indonesia
Dihang *see* Brahmaputra
153 X10 **Dihāng** ≈ NE India
Dihōk *see* Dahūk
81 L17 **Diinsoor** Bay, S Somalia
Dijlah *see* Tigris
99 H17 **Dijle** ≈ C Belgium
103 R8 **Dijon** *anc.* Dibio. Côte d'Or, C France
93 H14 **Dikanäs** Västerbotten, N Sweden
80 L12 **Dikhil** SW Djibouti
136 B13 **Dikili** İzmir, W Turkey
99 B17 **Diksmuide** *var.* Dixmuide, *Fr.* Dixmude. West-Vlaanderen, W Belgium
122 K7 **Dikson** Taymyrskiy (Dolgano-Nenetskiy) Avtonomnyy Okrug, N Russian Federation
115 K25 **Díkti** *var.* Dhíkti Ori. ▲▲ Kríti, Greece, E Mediterranean Sea
77 Z13 **Dikwa** Borno, NE Nigeria
81 J15 **Dila** Southern, S Ethiopia
99 G18 **Dilbeek** Vlaams Brabant, C Belgium
171 Q16 **Dili** *var.* Dilli, Dilly. ○ (East Timor) N East Timor
77 Y11 **Dilia** *var.* Dillia. ≈ SE Niger
Dilijan *see* Delijan
167 U13 **Di Linh** Lâm Đông, S Vietnam
101 G16 **Dillenburg** Hessen, W Germany
25 Q13 **Dilley** Texas, SW USA
Dilli *see* Delhi, India
Dilli *see* Dili, East Timor
Dillia *see* Dilia
80 E11 **Dilling** *var.* Ad Dalanj. Southern Kordofan, C Sudan
101 D20 **Dillingen** Saarland, SW Germany
Dillingen *see* Dillingen an der Donau
101 J22 **Dillingen an der Donau** *var.* Dillingen. Bayern, S Germany
39 O13 **Dillingham** Alaska, USA
33 Q12 **Dillon** Montana, NW USA
21 T12 **Dillon** South Carolina, SE USA
31 T13 **Dillon Lake** ▣ Ohio, N USA
Dilly *see* Dili
Dilman *see* Salmās
79 K24 **Dilolo** Katanga, S Dem. Rep. Congo (Zaire)
115 J20 **Dílos** *island* Kykládes, Greece, Aegean Sea
141 Y11 **Ḍil', Ra's aḍ** *headland* E Oman
29 R5 **Dilworth** Minnesota, N USA
138 H7 **Dimashq** *var.* Ash Shām, Esh Sham, *Eng.* Damascus, *Fr.* Damas, *It.* Damasco. ● (Syria) Dimashq, SW Syria
138 I8 **Dimashq** *off.* Muḥāfaẓat Dimashq, *var.* Damascus, *Ar.* Ash Sham, Ash Shām, Damasco, Esh Sham, *Fr.* Damas. ◈ *governorate* S Syria
138 I7 **Dimashq** ✕ Dimashq, S Syria
79 L21 **Dimbelenge** Kasai Occidental, C Dem. Rep. Congo (Zaire)
77 N16 **Dimbokro** E Ivory Coast
182 L11 **Dimboola** Victoria, SE Australia
Dîmboviţa *see* Dâmboviţa
Dimitrov *see* Dymytrov
114 K11 **Dimitrovgrad** Khaskovo, S Bulgaria
129 R5 **Dimitrovgrad** Ul'yanovskaya Oblast', W Russian Federation
113 Q15 **Dimitrovgrad** *prev.* Caribrod. Serbia, SE Yugoslavia
Dimitrovo *see* Pernik
Dimlang *see* Vogel Peak
24 M3 **Dimmitt** Texas, SW USA
114 F7 **Dimovo** Vidin, NW Bulgaria
59 A16 **Dimpolis** Acre, W Brazil
115 O23 **Dimyliá** Ródos, Dodekánisos, Greece, Aegean Sea
171 Q6 **Dinagat Island** *island* S Philippines
153 S13 **Dinajpur** Rajshahi, NW Bangladesh
102 I6 **Dinan** Côtes d'Armor, NW France
99 I21 **Dinant** Namur, S Belgium
136 E15 **Dinar** Afyon, SW Turkey
112 F13 **Dinara** ▲ W Croatia
Dinara *see* Dinaric Alps
102 I5 **Dinard** Ille-et-Vilaine, NW France
112 F13 **Dinaric Alps** *var.* Dinara. ▲▲ Bosnia and Herzegovina/Croatia
143 N10 **Dīnār, Kūh-e** ▲ C Iran
Dinbych *see* Denbigh
155 H22 **Dindigul** Tamil Nādu, SE India
83 M19 **Dindiza** Gaza, S Mozambique
149 V7 **Dinga** Punjab, E Pakistan
79 H21 **Dinga** Bandundu, SW Dem. Rep. Congo (Zaire)
158 L16 **Dinggyê** Xizang Zizhiqu, W China
97 A20 **Dingle** *Ir.* An Daingean. SW Ireland
97 A20 **Dingle Bay** *Ir.* Bá an Daingin. *bay* SW Ireland
18 I13 **Dingmans Ferry** Pennsylvania, NE USA
101 N22 **Dingolfing** Bayern, SE Germany
171 O1 **Dingras** Luzon, N Philippines
76 J13 **Dinguiraye** Haute-Guinée, N Guinea
96 I8 **Dingwall** N Scotland, UK
159 V10 **Dingxi** Gansu, C China
161 Q7 **Dingyuan** Anhui, E China
161 O3 **Dingzhou** *prev.* Ding Xian. Hebei, E China
167 U6 **Đinh Lâp** Lang Sơn, N Vietnam
167 T13 **Đinh Quan** Đông Nai, S Vietnam
100 E13 **Dinkel** ≈ Germany/Netherlands
101 J21 **Dinkelsbühl** Bayern, S Germany
101 D14 **Dinslaken** Nordrhein-Westfalen, W Germany
35 R11 **Dinuba** California, W USA
21 W7 **Dinwiddie** Virginia, NE USA
98 N13 **Dinxperlo** Gelderland, E Netherlands
115 F14 **Dió** *anc.* Dium. *site of ancient city* Kentrikí Makedonía, N Greece
Diófás *see* Nucet
76 M12 **Dioïla** Koulikoro, W Mali
115 G19 **Dióryga Korinthou** *Eng.* Corinth Canal. *canal* S Greece
76 G12 **Diouloulou** SW Senegal
77 N11 **Dioura** Mopti, W Mali
76 G11 **Diourbel** W Senegal
152 L10 **Dipayal** Far Western, W Nepal
121 R1 **Dipkarpaz** *Gk.* Rizokarpaso, Rizokárpason. NE Cyprus
149 R17 **Diplo** Sind, SE Pakistan
171 P7 **Dipolog** *var.* Dipolog City. Mindanao, S Philippines
185 C23 **Dipton** Southland, South Island, NZ
77 O10 **Diré** Tombouctou, C Mali
80 L13 **Dirē Dawa** Dirē Dawa, E Ethiopia
Dirfis *see* Dírfys
115 H18 **Dírfys** *var.* Dirfis. ▲ Évvioa, C Greece
75 N9 **Dirj** *var.* Daraj, Darj. W Libya
180 G10 **Dirk Hartog Island** *island* Western Australia
77 Y8 **Dirkou** Agadez, NE Niger
181 X11 **Dirranbandi** Queensland, E Australia
81 O16 **Dirri** Galguduud, C Somalia
Dirschau *see* Tczew
37 N6 **Dirty Devil River** ≈ Utah, W USA
32 E10 **Disappointment, Cape** *headland* Washington, NW USA
180 L8 **Disappointment, Lake** *salt lake* Western Australia
183 R12 **Disaster Bay** *bay* New South Wales, SE Australia
44 J11 **Discovery Bay** C Jamaica
182 K13 **Discovery Bay** *inlet* SE Australia
67 Y15 **Discovery II Fracture Zone** *tectonic feature* SW Indian Ocean
Discovery Seamount/Discovery Seamounts *see* Discovery Tablemount
65 O19 **Discovery Tablemount** *var.* Discovery Seamount, Discovery Seamounts. *undersea feature* SW Indian Ocean
108 G9 **Disentis** *Rmsch.* Mustér. Graubünden, S Switzerland
39 O10 **Dishna River** ≈ Alaska, USA
195 X4 **Dismal Mountains** ▲▲ Antarctica
28 M14 **Dismal River** ≈ Nebraska, C USA
Disna *see* Dzisna
99 L19 **Dison** Liège, E Belgium
153 V12 **Dispur** Assam, NE India
15 R11 **Disraeli** Quebec, SE Canada
115 F18 **Dístomo** *prev.* Dhístomon. Stereá Ellás, C Greece
115 H18 **Dístos, Límni** ◎ Évvoia, C Greece
59 L18 **Distrito Federal** *Eng.* Federal District. ◈ *federal district* C Brazil
41 P14 **Distrito Federal** ◈ *federal district* S Mexico
54 L4 **Distrito Federal** *off.* Territorio Distrito Federal. ◈ *federal district* N Venezuela
Distrito Federal, Territorio *see* Distrito Federal
116 J10 **Ditrău** *Hung.* Ditró. Harghita, C Romania
Ditró *see* Ditrău
154 B12 **Diu** Damān and Diu, W India
Dium *see* Dió
109 S13 **Divača** SW Slovenia
102 K5 **Dives** ≈ N France
Divichi *see* Däväçi
33 Q11 **Divide** Montana, NW USA
Divin *see* Dzivin
83 N18 **Divinhe** Sofala, E Mozambique
59 L20 **Divinópolis** Minas Gerais, SE Brazil
129 N13 **Divnoye** Stavropol'skiy Kray, SW Russian Federation
76 M17 **Divo** S Ivory Coast
Divodurum Mediomatricum *see* Metz
137 N13 **Divriği** Sivas, C Turkey
Diwaniyah *see* Ad Dīwānīyah
14 J10 **Dix Milles, Lac** ◎ Quebec, SE Canada
14 M8 **Dix Milles, Lac des** ◎ Quebec, SE Canada
Dixmude/Dixmuide *see* Diksmuide

◆ Country ◇ Dependent Territory ◈ Administrative Region ▲ Mountain ※ Volcano ◎ Lake
● Country Capital ○ Dependent Territory Capital ✕ International Airport ▲▲ Mountain Range ≈ River ▣ Reservoir

35 N7 **Dixon** California, W USA
30 L10 **Dixon** Illinois, N USA
20 I6 **Dixon** Kentucky, S USA
27 V6 **Dixon** Missouri, C USA
37 S9 **Dixon** New Mexico, SW USA
39 Y15 **Dixon Entrance** *strait* Canada/USA
18 D14 **Dixonville** Pennsylvania, NE USA
137 T13 **Diyadin** Ağrı, E Turkey
139 V5 **Diyālá, Nahr** *var.* Rudkhaneh-ye Sīrvān, Sirwan. ≈ Iran/Iraq **see also** Sīrvān, Rudkhaneh-ye
137 P15 **Diyarbakır** *var.* Diarbekr; *anc.* Amida. Diyarbakır, SE Turkey
137 P15 **Diyarbakır** *var.* Diarbekr. ◈ *province* SE Turkey
Dizful *see* Dezfūl
79 F16 **Dja** ≈ SE Cameroon
Djadié *see* Zadié
77 X7 **Djado** Agadez, NE Niger
77 X6 **Djado, Plateau du** ▲ NE Niger
Djailolo *see* Halmahera, Pulau
Djajapura *see* Jayapura
Djakarta *see* Jakarta
Djakovica *see* Đakovica
Djakovo *see* Đakovo
79 G20 **Djambala** Plateaux, C Congo
Djambi *see* Jambi
Djambi *see* Hari, Batang, Sumatera, W Indonesia
74 M9 **Djanet** E Algeria
74 M11 **Djanet** *prev.* Fort Charlet. SE Algeria
Djatiwangi *see* Jatiwangi
Djaul *see* Dyaul Island
Djawa *see* Jawa
Djéblé *see* Jablah
78 I10 **Djédaa** Batha, C Chad
74 J6 **Djelfa** *var.* El Djelfa. N Algeria
79 M14 **Djéma** Haut-Mbomou, E Central African Republic
Djeneponto *see* Jeneponto
77 N12 **Djenné** *var.* Jenné. Mopti, C Mali
Djérablous *see* Jarābulus
Djerba *see* Jerba, Île de
79 F15 **Djérem** ≈ C Cameroon
Djevdjelija *see* Gevgelija
77 P11 **Djibo** N Burkina
80 L12 **Djibouti** *var.* Jibuti. ● (Djibouti) E Djibouti
80 L12 **Djibouti** *off.* Republic of Djibouti, *var.* Jibuti; *prev.* French Somaliland, French Territory of the Afars and Issas, *Fr.* Côte Française des Somalis, Territoire Français des Afars et des Issas. ◆ *republic* E Africa
80 L12 **Djibouti** ✕ C Djibouti
Djidjel/Djidjelli *see* Jijel
55 W10 **Djoemoe** Sipaliwini, C Suriname
Djokjakarta *see* Yogyakarta
79 K21 **Djoku-Punda** Kasai Occidental, S Dem. Rep. Congo (Zaire)
79 K18 **Djolu** Equateur, N Dem. Rep. Congo (Zaire)
Djorče Petrov *see* Đorče Petrov
79 F17 **Djoua** ≈ Congo/Gabon
77 R14 **Djougou** W Benin
79 F16 **Djoum** Sud, S Cameroon
78 I8 **Djourab, Erg du** *dunes* N Chad
79 P17 **Djugu** Orientale, NE Dem. Rep. Congo (Zaire)
Djumbir *see* Ďumbier
92 L3 **Djúpivogur** Austurland, SE Iceland
94 L13 **Djura** Dalarna, C Sweden
Djurdjevac *see* Đurđevac
83 G18 **D'Kar** Ghanzi, NW Botswana
197 U6 **Dmitriya Lapteva, Proliv** *strait* N Russian Federation
128 J7 **Dmitriyev-L'govskiy** Kurskaya Oblast', W Russian Federation
Dmitriyevsk *see* Makiyivka
128 K3 **Dmitrov** Moskovskaya Oblast', W Russian Federation
Dmitrovichi *see* Dzmitravichy
128 J6 **Dmitrovsk-Orlovskiy** Orlovskaya Oblast', W Russian Federation
117 R3 **Dmytrivka** Chernihivs'ka Oblast', N Ukraine
Dnepr *see* Dnieper
Dneprodzerzhinsk *see* Dniprodzerzhyns'k
Dneprodzerzhinskoye Vodokhranilishche *see* Dniprodzerzhyns'ke Vodoskhovyshche
Dnepropetrovsk *see* Dnipropetrovs'k
Dnepropetrovskaya Oblast' *see* Dnipropetrovs'ka Oblast'
Dneprorudnoye *see* Dniprorudne
Dneprovskiy Liman *see* Dniprovs'kyy Lyman
Dneprovsko-Bugskiy Kanal *see* Dnyaprowska-Buhski, Kanal
Dnestr *see* Dniester
Dnestrovskiy Liman *see* Dnistrovs'kyy Lyman
86 H11 **Dnieper** *Bel.* Dnyapro, *Rus.* Dnepr, *Ukr.* Dnipro. ≈ E Europe
117 P3 **Dnieper Lowland** *Bel.* Prydnyaprowskaya Nizina, *Ukr.* Prydniprovs'ka Nyzovyna. *lowlands* Belarus/Ukraine
116 M8 **Dniester** *Rom.* Nistru, *Rus.* Dnestr, *Ukr.* Dnister; *anc.* Tyras. ≈ Moldova/Ukraine
Dnipro *see* Dnieper
117 T7 **Dniprodzerzhyns'k** *Rus.* Dneprodzerzhinsk; *prev.* Kamenskoye. Dnipropetrovs'ka Oblast', E Ukraine
117 T7 **Dniprodzerzhyns'ke Vodoskhovyshche** *Rus.* Dneprodzerzhinskoye Vodokhranilishche. ⊞ C Ukraine
117 U7 **Dnipropetrovs'k** *Rus.* Dnepropetrovsk; *prev.* Yekaterinoslav. Dnipropetrovs'ka Oblast', E Ukraine
117 U8 **Dnipropetrovs'k** ✕ Dnipropetrovs'ka Oblast', S Ukraine
Dnipropetrovs'k *see* Dnipropetrovs'ka Oblast'
117 T7 **Dnipropetrovs'ka Oblast'** *var.* Dnipropetrovs'k, *Rus.* Dnepropetrovskaya Oblast'. ◈ *province* E Ukraine
117 U9 **Dniprorudne** *Rus.* Dneprorudnoye. Zaporiz'ka Oblast', SE Ukraine
117 Q11 **Dniprovs'kyy Lyman** *Rus.* Dneprovskiy Liman. *bay* S Ukraine
Dnister *see* Dniester
117 O11 **Dnistrovs'kyy Lyman** *Rus.* Dnestrovskiy Liman. *inlet* S Ukraine
126 G14 **Dno** Pskovskaya Oblast', W Russian Federation
Dnyapro *see* Dnieper
119 H20 **Dnyaprowska-Buhski, Kanal** *Rus.* Dneprovsko-Bugskiy Kanal. *canal* SW Belarus
13 O14 **Doaktown** New Brunswick, SE Canada
78 H13 **Doba** Logone-Oriental, S Chad
118 E9 **Dobele** *Ger.* Doblen. Dobele, W Latvia
101 N16 **Döbeln** Sachsen, E Germany
171 U12 **Doberai, Jazirah** *Dut.* Vogelkop. *peninsula* Irian Jaya, E Indonesia
110 F10 **Dobiegniew** *Ger.* Lubuskie, W Poland
Doblen *see* Dobele
81 K18 **Dobli** *spring/well* SW Somalia
112 H11 **Doboj** Republika Srpska, N Bosnia and Herzegovina
110 L8 **Dobre Miasto** *Ger.* Guttstadt. Warmińsko-Mazurskie, NE Poland
114 N7 **Dobrich** *Rom.* Bazargic; *prev.* Tolbukhin. Dobrich, NE Bulgaria
114 N7 **Dobrich** ◈ *province* NE Bulgaria
128 M8 **Dobrinka** Lipetskaya Oblast', W Russian Federation
128 M7 **Dobrinka** Volgogradskaya Oblast', SW Russian Federation
Dobrla Vas *see* Eberndorf
111 I15 **Dobrodzień** *Ger.* Guttentag. Opolskie, S Poland
Dobrogea *see* Dobruja
117 W7 **Dobropillya** *Rus.* Dobropol'ye. Donets'ka Oblast', SE Ukraine
Dobropol'ye *see* Dobropillya
117 P8 **Dobrovelychkivka** Kirovohrads'ka Oblast', C Ukraine
Dobrudja/Dobrudzha *see* Dobruja
114 O7 **Dobruja** *var.* Dobrudja, *Bul.* Dobrudzha, *Rom.* Dobrogea. *physical region* Bulgaria/Romania
119 P19 **Dobrush** Homyel'skaya Voblasts', SE Belarus
127 U14 **Dobryanka** Permskaya Oblast', NW Russian Federation
117 P2 **Dobryanka** Chernihivs'ka Oblast', N Ukraine
Dobryn' *see* Dabryn'
21 R8 **Dobson** North Carolina, SE USA
59 N20 **Doce, Rio** ≈ SE Brazil
93 I16 **Docksta** Västernorrland, C Sweden
41 N10 **Doctor Arroyo** Nuevo León, NE Mexico
62 L4 **Doctor Pedro P. Peña** Boquerón, W Paraguay
171 S11 **Dodaga** Pulau Halmahera, E Indonesia
155 G21 **Dodda Betta** ▲ S India
Dodecanese *see* Dodekánisos
115 M22 **Dodekánisos** *var.* Nóties Sporádes, *Eng.* Dodecanese; *prev.* Dhodhekánisos. *island group* SE Greece
26 J6 **Dodge City** Kansas, C USA
30 K9 **Dodgeville** Wisconsin, N USA
97 H25 **Dodman Point** *headland* SW England, UK
81 J14 **Dodola** Oromo, C Ethiopia
81 H22 **Dodoma** ● (Tanzania) Dodoma, C Tanzania
81 H22 **Dodoma** ◈ *region* C Tanzania
115 C16 **Dodóni** *var.* Dhodhóni. *site of ancient city* Ípeiros, W Greece
33 U7 **Dodson** Montana, NW USA
25 P3 **Dodson** Texas, SW USA
98 M12 **Doesburg** Gelderland, E Netherlands
98 N12 **Doetinchem** Gelderland, E Netherlands
158 L12 **Dogai Coring** *var.* Lake Montcalm. ⊚ W China
137 N15 **Doğanşehir** Malatya, C Turkey
84 E9 **Dogger Bank** *undersea feature* C North Sea
23 S10 **Dog Island** *island* Florida, SE USA
14 C7 **Dog Lake** ⊚ Ontario, S Canada
106 B9 **Dogliani** Piemonte, NE Italy
164 H11 **Dōgo** *island* Oki-shotō, SW Japan
Do Gonbadān *see* Dow Gonbadān
77 S12 **Dogondoutchi** Dosso, SW Niger
Dogrular *see* Pravda
137 T13 **Doğubayazıt** Ağrı, E Turkey
137 P12 **Doğu Karadeniz Dağları** *var.* Anadolu Dağları. ▲ NE Turkey
Doha *see* Ad Dawḩah
Dohad *see* Dāhod
Dohuk *see* Dahūk
159 N16 **Doilungdêqên** Xizang Zizhiqu, W China
114 F12 **Doïranis, Límnis** *Bul.* Ezero Doyransko. ⊚ N Greece
Doire *see* Londonderry
99 H22 **Doische** Namur, S Belgium
59 P17 **Dois de Julho** ✕ (Salvador) Bahia, NE Brazil
60 H12 **Dois Vizinhos** Paraná, S Brazil
80 H10 **Doka** Gedaref, E Sudan
Doka *see* Kéita, Bahr
139 T3 **Dokan** *var.* Dūkān. E Iraq
94 H13 **Dokka** Oppland, S Norway
98 L5 **Dokkum** Friesland, N Netherlands
98 L5 **Dokkumer Ee** ≈ N Netherlands
76 K13 **Doko** Haute-Guinée, NE Guinea
Dokshitsy *see* Dokshytsy
118 K13 **Dokshytsy** *Rus.* Dokshitsy. Vitsyebskaya Voblasts', N Belarus
117 X8 **Dokuchayevs'k** *var.* Dokuchayevsk. Donets'ka Oblast', SE Ukraine
Dolak, Pulau *see* Yos Sudarso, Pulau
29 P9 **Doland** South Dakota, N USA
63 J18 **Dolavón** Chaco, S Argentina
15 P6 **Dolbeau** Quebec, SE Canada
102 I5 **Dol-de-Bretagne** Ille-et-Vilaine, NW France
64 J13 **Doldrums Fracture Zone** *tectonic feature* W Atlantic Ocean
103 S8 **Dôle** Jura, E France
97 J19 **Dolgellau** NW Wales, UK
Dolginovo *see* Dawhinava
Dolgi, Ostrov *see* Dolgiy, Ostrov
127 U2 **Dolgiy, Ostrov** *var.* Ostrov Dolgi. *island* NW Russian Federation
162 J9 **Dölgöön** Övörhangay, C Mongolia
107 C20 **Dolianova** Sardegna, Italy, C Mediterranean Sea
Dolina *see* Dolyna
123 T13 **Dolinsk** Ostrov Sakhalin, Sakhalinskaya Oblast', SE Russian Federation
Dolinskaya *see* Dolyns'ka
79 F21 **Dolisie** *prev.* Loubomo. Le Niari, S Congo
116 G14 **Dolj** ◈ *county* SW Romania
98 P5 **Dollard** *bay* NW Germany
194 J5 **Dolleman Island** *island* Antarctica
114 I8 **Dolni Dŭbnik** Pleven, N Bulgaria
114 F8 **Dolni Lom** Vidin, NW Bulgaria
Dolnja Lendava *see* Lendava
114 K9 **Dolno Panicherevo** *var.* Panicherevo. Sliven, C Bulgaria
111 F14 **Dolnośląskie** ◈ *province* SW Poland
111 K18 **Dolný Kubín** *Hung.* Alsókubin. Žilinský Kraj, N Slovakia
106 H8 **Dolo** Veneto, NE Italy
Dolomites/Dolomiti *see* Dolomitiche, Alpi
106 H6 **Dolomitiche, Alpi** *var.* Dolomiti, *Eng.* Dolomites. ▲ NE Italy
Dolonnur *see* Duolun
162 K10 **Doloon** Ömnögovĭ, S Mongolia
61 E21 **Dolores** Buenos Aires, E Argentina
42 E3 **Dolores** Petén, N Guatemala
171 Q5 **Dolores** Samar, C Philippines
105 S12 **Dolores** País Valenciano, E Spain
61 D19 **Dolores** Soriano, SW Uruguay
41 N12 **Dolores Hidalgo** *var.* Ciudad de Dolores Hidalgo. Guanajuato, C Mexico
8 J7 **Dolphin and Union Strait** *strait* Northwest Territories / Nunavut, N Canada
65 D23 **Dolphin, Cape** *headland* East Falkland, Falkland Islands
44 H12 **Dolphin Head** *hill* W Jamaica
83 B21 **Dolphin Head** *var.* Cape Dernberg. *headland* SW Namibia
110 G12 **Dolsk** *Ger.* Dolzig. Wielkopolskie, C Poland
167 S8 **Đô Lương** Nghê An, N Vietnam
116 I6 **Dolyna** *Rus.* Dolina. Ivano-Frankivs'ka Oblast', W Ukraine
117 R8 **Dolyns'ka** *Rus.* Dolinskaya. Kirovohrads'ka Oblast', S Ukraine
Dolzig *see* Dolsk
Domachëvo/Domaczewo *see* Damachava
117 P9 **Domanivka** Mykolayivs'ka Oblast', S Ukraine
153 S13 **Domar** Rajshahi, N Bangladesh
108 I9 **Domat/Ems** Graubünden, SE Switzerland
111 A18 **Domažlice** *Ger.* Taus. Plzeňský Kraj, W Czech Republic
129 X8 **Dombarovskiy** Orenburgskaya Oblast', W Russian Federation
94 G10 **Dombås** Oppland, S Norway
83 M17 **Dombe** Manica, C Mozambique
82 A13 **Dombe Grande** Benguela, C Angola
103 R10 **Dombes** *physical region* E France
111 I25 **Dombóvár** Tolna, S Hungary
99 D14 **Domburg** Zeeland, SW Netherlands
58 L13 **Dom Eliseu** Pará, NE Brazil
Domel Island *see* Letsôk-aw Kyun
103 O11 **Dôme, Puy de** ▲ C France
36 H13 **Dome Rock Mountains** ▲ Arizona, SW USA
Domesnes, Cape *see* Kolkasrags
62 G8 **Domeyko** Atacama, N Chile
62 H5 **Domeyko, Cordillera** ▲ N Chile
102 K5 **Domfront** Orne, N France
171 X13 **Dom, Gunung** ▲ Irian Jaya, E Indonesia
45 X11 **Dominica** *off.* Commonwealth of Dominica. ◆ *republic* E West Indies
47 S3 **Dominica** *island* Dominica
Dominica Channel *see* Martinique Passage
43 N15 **Dominical** Puntarenas, SE Costa Rica
45 Q8 **Dominican Republic** ◆ *republic* C West Indies
45 X11 **Dominica Passage** *passage* E Caribbean Sea
99 K14 **Dommel** ≈ S Netherlands
81 O14 **Domo** Somali, E Ethiopia
128 L4 **Domodedovo** ✕ (Moskva) Moskovskaya Oblast', W Russian Federation
106 C6 **Domodossola** Piemonte, NE Italy
115 F17 **Domokós** *var.* Dhomokós. Stereá Ellás, C Greece
172 I14 **Domoni** Anjouan, SE Comoros
61 G16 **Dom Pedrito** Rio Grande do Sul, S Brazil
Dompoe *see* Dompu
170 M16 **Dompu** *prev.* Dompoe. Sumbawa, C Indonesia
Domschale *see* Domžale
62 H13 **Domuyo, Volcán** Ж W Argentina
109 U11 **Domžale** *Ger.* Domschale. C Slovenia
129 O10 **Don** *var.* Duna, Tanais. ≈ SW Russian Federation
96 K9 **Don** ≈ NE Scotland, UK
182 M11 **Donald** Victoria, SE Australia
22 J9 **Donaldsonville** Louisiana, S USA
23 S8 **Donalsonville** Georgia, SE USA
Donau *see* Danube
101 G23 **Donaueschingen** Baden-Württemberg, SW Germany
101 K22 **Donaumoos** *wetland* S Germany
101 K22 **Donauwörth** Bayern, S Germany
109 U7 **Donawitz** Steiermark, SE Austria
117 X7 **Donbass** *industrial region* Russian Federation/Ukraine
104 K11 **Don Benito** Extremadura, W Spain
97 M17 **Doncaster** *anc.* Danum. N England, UK
44 K12 **Don Christophers Point** *headland* C Jamaica
55 V9 **Donderkamp** Sipaliwini, NW Suriname
82 B12 **Dondo** Cuanza Norte, NW Angola
171 O12 **Dondo** Sulawesi, N Indonesia
83 N17 **Dondo** Sofala, C Mozambique
155 K26 **Dondra Head** *headland* S Sri Lanka
Dondușani *see* Donduşeni
116 M8 **Donduşeni** *var.* Donduşani, *Rus.* Dondyushany. N Moldova
Dondyushany *see* Donduşeni
97 D15 **Donegal** *Ir.* Dún na nGall. NW Ireland
97 D14 **Donegal** *Ir.* Dún na nGall. *cultural region* NW Ireland
97 C15 **Donegal Bay** *Ir.* Bá Dhún na nGall. *bay* NW Ireland
84 K10 **Donets** ≈ Russian Federation/Ukraine
117 X8 **Donets'k** *Rus.* Donetsk; *prev.* Stalino. Donets'ka Oblast', E Ukraine
117 W8 **Donets'k** ✕ Donets'ka Oblast', E Ukraine
Donets'k *see* Donets'ka Oblast'
117 W8 **Donets'ka Oblast'** *var.* Donets'k, *Rus.* Donetskaya Oblast'; *prev. Rus.* Stalinskaya Oblast'. ◈ *province* SE Ukraine
Donetskaya Oblast' *see* Donets'ka Oblast'
67 P8 **Donga** ≈ Cameroon/Nigeria
157 O13 **Dongchuan** Yunnan, SW China
99 I14 **Dongen** Noord-Brabant, S Netherlands
160 K17 **Dongfang** *var.* Basuo. Hainan, S China
163 Z7 **Dongfanghong** Heilongjiang, NE China
163 W11 **Dongfeng** Jilin, NE China
171 N12 **Donggala** Sulawesi, C Indonesia
163 V13 **Donggou** Liaoning, NE China
161 O14 **Dongguan** Guangdong, S China
167 T9 **Đông Ha** Quang Tri, C Vietnam
Dong Hai *see* East China Sea
160 M16 **Donghai Dao** *island* S China
167 T9 **Đông Hơi** Quang Binh, C Vietnam
108 H10 **Dongio** Ticino, S Switzerland
Dongkan *see* Binhai
160 L11 **Dongkou** Hunan, S China
Dongliao *see* Liaoyuan
Dong-nai *see* Đông Nai, Sông
167 U13 **Đông Nai, Sông** *var.* Dong-nai, Dong Noi, Donnai. ≈ S Vietnam
161 O14 **Dongnan Qiuling** *plateau* SE China
163 Y9 **Dongning** Heilongjiang, NE China
Dong Noi *see* Đông Nai, Sông
83 C14 **Dongo** Huíla, C Angola
80 E7 **Dongola** *var.* Donqola, Dunqulah. Northern, N Sudan
79 I17 **Dongou** La Likouala, NE Congo
167 T13 **Đông Phu** Sông Be, S Vietnam
Dong Rak, Phanom *see* Dângrêk, Chuŏr Phnum
161 Q14 **Dongshan Dao** *island* SE China
163 N14 **Dongsheng** Nei Mongol Zizhiqu, N China
161 R7 **Dongtai** Jiangsu, E China
161 N10 **Dongting Hu** *var.* Tung-t'ing Hu. ⊚ S China
161 P10 **Dongxiang** Jiangxi, S China
161 Q4 **Dongying** Shandong, E China
27 X8 **Doniphan** Missouri, C USA
10 G7 **Donjek** ≈ Yukon Territory, W Canada
112 E11 **Donji Lapac** Lika-Senj, W Croatia
112 H8 **Donji Miholjac** Osijek-Baranja, NE Croatia
112 P12 **Donji Milanovac** Serbia, E Yugoslavia
112 G12 **Donji Vakuf** *var.* Srbobran, Federacija Bosna I Hercegovina, C Bosnia & Herzegovina
98 M6 **Donkerbroek** Friesland, N Netherlands
167 P11 **Don Muang** ✕ (Krung Thep) Nonthaburi, C Thailand
25 S17 **Donna** Texas, SW USA
15 Q10 **Donnacona** Quebec, SE Canada
Donnai *see* Đông Nai, Sông
29 Y16 **Donnellson** Iowa, C USA
11 O13 **Donnelly** Alberta, W Canada
35 H6 **Donner Pass** *pass* California, W USA
101 F19 **Donnersberg** ▲ W Germany
Donoso *see* Miguel de la Borda
105 P2 **Donostia-San Sebastián** País Vasco, N Spain
115 K21 **Donoússa** *island* Kykládes, Greece, Aegean Sea
35 P8 **Don Pedro Reservoir** ⊞ California, W USA
Donqola *see* Dongola
128 L5 **Donskoy** Tul'skaya Oblast', W Russian Federation
81 L16 **Doolow** Somali, E Ethiopia
39 Q7 **Doonerak, Mount** ▲ Alaska, USA
98 J12 **Doorn** Utrecht, C Netherlands
Doornik *see* Tournai
31 N6 **Door Peninsula** *peninsula* Wisconsin, N USA
80 P13 **Dooxo Nugaaleed** *var.* Nogal Valley. *valley* E Somalia
160 G8 **Do Qu** ≈ C China
106 B7 **Dora Baltea** *anc.* Duria Major. ≈ NW Italy
180 K7 **Dora, Lake** *salt lake* Western Australia
106 A8 **Dora Riparia** *anc.* Duria Minor. ≈ NW Italy
Dorbiljin *see* Emin
163 V8 **Dorbod** *var.* Dorbod Mongolzu Zizhixian, Talkang. Heilongjiang, NE China
Dorbod Mongolzu Zizhixian *see* Dorbod
113 N18 **Đorče Petrov** *var.* Djorče Petrov, Gorče Petrov. N FYR Macedonia
14 F16 **Dorchester** Ontario, S Canada
97 L24 **Dorchester** *anc.* Durnovaria. S England, UK
9 P7 **Dorchester, Cape** *headland* Baffin Island, Nunavut, NE Canada
83 D19 **Dordabis** Khomas, C Namibia
102 L12 **Dordogne** ◈ *department* SW France
103 N12 **Dordogne** ≈ W France
98 H13 **Dordrecht** *var.* Dordt, Dort. Zuid-Holland, SW Netherlands
Dordt *see* Dordrecht
103 P11 **Dore** ≈ C France
11 S13 **Doré Lake** Saskatchewan, C Canada
103 O12 **Dore, Monts** ▲ C France
101 M23 **Dorfen** Bayern, SE Germany
107 D18 **Dorgali** Sardegna, Italy, C Mediterranean Sea
162 F7 **Dörgön Nuur** ⊚ NW Mongolia
77 Q12 **Dori** N Burkina
83 E24 **Doring** ≈ S South Africa
101 E16 **Dormagen** Nordrhein-Westfalen, W Germany
103 P4 **Dormans** Marne, N France
108 E6 **Dornach** Solothurn, NW Switzerland
Dorna Watra *see* Vatra Dornei
108 J7 **Dornbirn** Vorarlberg, W Austria
96 I7 **Dornoch** N Scotland, UK
96 J7 **Dornoch Firth** *inlet* N Scotland, UK
163 P7 **Dornod** ◈ *province* E Mongolia
163 N10 **Dornogovĭ** ◈ *province* SE Mongolia
77 P10 **Doro** Tombouctou, S Mali
116 L14 **Dorobanțu** Călăraşi, S Romania
111 J22 **Dorog** Komárom-Esztergom, N Hungary
128 I4 **Dorogobuzh** Smolenskaya Oblast', W Russian Federation
116 K8 **Dorohoi** Botoşani, NE Romania
93 H15 **Dorotea** Västerbotten, N Sweden
Dorpat *see* Tartu
180 G10 **Dorre Island** *island* Western Australia
183 U5 **Dorrigo** New South Wales, SE Australia
35 N1 **Dorris** California, W USA
14 H13 **Dorset** Ontario, SE Canada
97 K23 **Dorset** *cultural region* S England, UK
101 E14 **Dorsten** Nordrhein-Westfalen, W Germany
Dort *see* Dordrecht
101 F15 **Dortmund** Nordrhein-Westfalen, W Germany
100 F12 **Dortmund-Ems-Kanal** *canal* W Germany
136 L17 **Dörtyol** Hatay, S Turkey
142 L7 **Do Rūd** *var.* Dow Rūd, Durud. Lorestān, W Iran
79 O15 **Doruma** Orientale, N Dem. Rep. Congo (Zaire)
15 O12 **Dorval** ✕ (Montréal) Quebec, SE Canada
45 T5 **Dos Bocas, Lago** ⊚ C Puerto Rico
104 K14 **Dos Hermanas** Andalucía, S Spain
Dospad Dagh *see* Rhodope Mountains
35 P10 **Dos Palos** California, W USA
114 I11 **Dospat** Smolyan, S Bulgaria
114 H11 **Dospat, Yazovir** ⊞ SW Bulgaria
100 M11 **Dosse** ≈ NE Germany
77 S12 **Dosso** Dosso, SW Niger
77 S12 **Dosso** ◈ *department* SW Niger
144 G12 **Dossor** Atyrau, SW Kazakhstan
147 V9 **Dostuk** Narynskaya Oblast', C Kyrgyzstan
145 X13 **Dostyk** *prev.* Druzhba. Almaty, SE Kazakhstan
23 R7 **Dothan** Alabama, S USA
39 T9 **Dot Lake** Alaska, USA
118 F12 **Dotnuva** Kėdainiai, C Lithuania
99 D19 **Dottignies** Hainaut, W Belgium
103 P2 **Douai** *prev.* Douay, *anc.* Duacum. Nord, N France
14 L9 **Douaire, Lac** ⊚ Quebec, SE Canada
79 D16 **Douala** *var.* Duala. Littoral, W Cameroon
79 D16 **Douala** ✕ Littoral, W Cameroon
102 F6 **Douarnenez** Finistère, NW France
102 E6 **Douarnenez, Baie de** *bay* NW France
Douay *see* Douai
25 O6 **Double Mountain Fork Brazos River** ≈ Texas, SW USA
23 O3 **Double Springs** Alabama, S USA
103 T8 **Doubs** ◈ *department* E France
108 C8 **Doubs** ≈ France/Switzerland
185 A22 **Doubtful Sound** *sound* South Island, NZ
184 J2 **Doubtless Bay** *bay* North Island, NZ
25 X9 **Doucette** Texas, SW USA
102 K8 **Doué-la-Fontaine** Maine-et-Loire, NW France
77 O11 **Douentza** Mopti, S Mali
65 D24 **Douglas** East Falkland, Falkland Islands
97 I16 **Douglas** ○ (Isle of Man) E Isle of Man
83 H23 **Douglas** Northern Cape, C South Africa
39 X13 **Douglas** Alexander Archipelago, Alaska, USA
37 O17 **Douglas** Arizona, SW USA
23 U7 **Douglas** Georgia, SE USA
33 Y15 **Douglas** Wyoming, C USA
38 L9 **Douglas, Cape** *headland* Alaska USA
10 J14 **Douglas Channel** *channel* British Columbia, W Canada
182 G3 **Douglas Creek** *seasonal river* South Australia
31 P5 **Douglas Lake** ⊚ Michigan, N USA
21 O9 **Douglas Lake** ⊞ Tennessee, S USA
39 Q13 **Douglas, Mount** ▲ Alaska, USA
194 I6 **Douglas Range** ▲ Alexander Island, Antarctica
121 P9 **Doukáto, Akrotírio** *headland* Lefkáda, W Greece
103 O2 **Doullens** Somme, N France
Douma *see* Dūmā
79 F15 **Doumé** Est, E Cameroon
99 E21 **Dour** Hainaut, S Belgium
59 K18 **Dourada, Serra** ▲ S Brazil
59 I21 **Dourados** Mato Grosso do Sul, S Brazil
103 N5 **Dourdan** Essonne, N France
104 I6 **Douro** *Sp.* Duero. ≈ Portugal/Spain **see also** Duero
104 G6 **Douro Litoral** *former province* N Portugal
Douvres *see* Dover
102 K15 **Douze** ≈ SW France
183 P17 **Dover** Tasmania, SE Australia
97 Q22 **Dover** *Fr.* Douvres; *Lat.* Dubris Portus. SE England, UK
17 U9 **Dover** *state capital* Delaware, NE USA
19 P9 **Dover** New Hampshire, NE USA
18 J14 **Dover** New Jersey, NE USA
31 U12 **Dover** Ohio, N USA
20 H8 **Dover** Tennessee, S USA
97 Q23 **Dover, Strait of** *var.* Straits of Dover, *Fr.* Pas de Calais. *strait* England, UK/France
Dover, Straits of *see* Dover, Strait of
Dovlen *see* Devin
94 G11 **Dovre** Oppland, S Norway
94 G10 **Dovrefjell** *plateau* S Norway
Dovsk *see* Dowsk
83 M14 **Dowa** Central, C Malawi
31 O10 **Dowagiac** Michigan, N USA
143 N10 **Dow Gonbadān** *var.* Do Gonbadān, Gonbadān. Kohkīlūyeh va Būyer Aḩmadī, SW Iran
148 M2 **Dowlatābād** Fāryāb, N Afghanistan
97 G16 **Down** *cultural region* SE Northern Ireland, UK
33 R16 **Downey** Idaho, NW USA
35 P5 **Downieville** California, W USA
97 G16 **Downpatrick** *Ir.* Dún Pádraig. SE Northern Ireland, UK
26 M3 **Downs** Kansas, C USA
18 J12 **Downsville** New York, NE USA
Dow Rūd *see* Do Rūd
29 V12 **Dows** Iowa, C USA
119 O17 **Dowsk** *Rus.* Dovsk. Homyel'skaya Voblasts', SE Belarus
35 Q4 **Doyle** California, W USA
18 I15 **Doylestown** Pennsylvania, NE USA
Doyransko, Ezero *see* Doïranis, Límnis
114 I8 **Doyrentsi** Lovech, N Bulgaria
164 G11 **Dōzen** *island* Oki-shotō, SW Japan

◆ Country
● Country Capital
◇ Dependent Territory
○ Dependent Territory Capital
◈ Administrative Region
✕ International Airport
▲ Mountain
▲ Mountain Range
Ж Volcano
≈ River
⊚ Lake
⊞ Reservoir

14 K9 **Dozois, Réservoir** ⊞ Quebec, SE Canada
74 D9 **Drâa** *seasonal river* S Morocco
Drâa, Hammada du *see* Dra, Hammada du
Drabble *see* José Enrique Rodó
117 Q5 **Drabiv** Cherkas'ka Oblast', C Ukraine
Drable *see* José Enrique Rodó
103 S13 **Drac** ∽ E France
Drač/Draç *see* Durrës
60 I8 **Dracena** São Paulo, S Brazil
98 M6 **Drachten** Friesland, N Netherlands
92 H11 **Drag** Nordland, C Norway
116 L14 **Dragalina** Călărași, SE Romania
116 J14 **Drăgănești-Vlașca** Teleorman, S Romania
116 I13 **Drăgășani** Vâlcea, SW Romania
114 G9 **Dragoman** Sofiya, W Bulgaria
115 L25 **Dragonáda** *island* SE Greece
Dragonera, Isla *see* Sa Dragonera
45 T14 **Dragon's Mouths, The** *strait* Trinidad and Tobago/Venezuela
95 J23 **Dragør** København, E Denmark
114 F10 **Dragovishitsa** Kyustendil, W Bulgaria
103 U15 **Draguignan** Var, SE France
74 E9 **Dra, Hamada du** *var.* Hammada du Drâa, Haut Plateau du Dra. *plateau* W Algeria
Dra, Haut Plateau du *see* Dra, Hamada du
119 H19 **Drahichyn** *Pol.* Drohiczyn Poleski, *Rus.* Drogichin. Brestskaya Voblasts', SW Belarus
29 N4 **Drake** North Dakota, N USA
83 K23 **Drakensberg** ▲▲ Lesotho/South Africa
194 F3 **Drake Passage** *passage* Atlantic Ocean/Pacific Ocean
114 L8 **Dralfa** Türgovishte, N Bulgaria
114 I12 **Dráma** *var.* Dhráma. Anatolikí Makedonía kai Thráki, NE Greece
Dramburg *see* Drawsko Pomorskie
95 H15 **Drammen** Buskerud, S Norway
95 H15 **Drammensfjorden** *fjord* S Norway
92 H1 **Drangajökull** ▲ NW Iceland
95 F16 **Drangedal** Telemark, S Norway
92 I2 **Drangsnes** Vestfirdhir, NW Iceland
Drann *see* Dravinja
109 T10 **Drau** *var.* Drava, *Eng.* Drave, *Hung.* Dráva. ∽ C Europe *see also* Drava
84 I11 **Drava** *var.* Drau, *Eng.* Drave, *Hung.* Dráva. ∽ C Europe *see also* Drau
Dráva *see* Drau/Drava
Drave *see* Drau/Drava
109 W10 **Dravinja** *Ger.* Drann. ∽ NE Slovenia
109 V9 **Dravograd** *Ger.* Unterdrauburg; *prev.* Spodnji Dravograd. N Slovenia
110 F10 **Drawa** ∽ NW Poland
110 F9 **Drawno** Zachodniopomorskie, NW Poland
110 F9 **Drawsko Pomorskie** *Ger.* Dramburg. Zachodniopomorskie, NW Poland
29 R3 **Drayton** North Dakota, N USA
11 P14 **Drayton Valley** Alberta, SW Canada
186 B6 **Dreikikir** East Sepik, NW PNG
Dreikirchen *see* Teiuș
98 N7 **Drenthe** ◈ *province* NE Netherlands
115 H15 **Drépano, Akrotírio** *var.* Akra Dhrepanon. *headland* N Greece
Drepanum *see* Trapani
14 D17 **Dresden** Ontario, S Canada
101 O16 **Dresden** Sachsen, E Germany
20 G8 **Dresden** Tennessee, S USA
118 M11 **Dretun'** *Rus.* Dretun'. Vitsyebskaya Voblasts', N Belarus
102 M5 **Dreux** *anc.* Drocae, Durocasses. Eure-et-Loir, C France
94 I11 **Drevsjø** Hedmark, S Norway
22 K3 **Drew** Mississippi, S USA
110 F10 **Drezdenko** *Ger.* Driesen. Lubuskie, W Poland
98 J12 **Driebergen** *var.* Driebergen-Rijsenburg. Utrecht, C Netherlands
Driebergen-Rijsenburg *see* Driebergen
Driesen *see* Drezdenko
97 N16 **Driffield** E England, UK
65 D25 **Driftwood Point** *headland* East Falkland, Falkland Islands
33 S14 **Driggs** Idaho, NW USA
Drin *see* Drinit, Lumi i
112 K12 **Drina** ∽ Bosnia and Herzegovina/Yugoslavia
Drin, Gulf of *see* Drinit, Gjiri i
113 K18 **Drinit, Gjiri i** *var.* Pellg i Drinit, *Eng.* Gulf of Drin. *gulf* NW Albania
113 L17 **Drinit, Lumi i** *var.* Drin. ∽ NW Albania
Drinit, Pellg i *see* Drinit, Gjiri i
Drinit të Zi, Lumi i *see* Black Drin
113 L22 **Dríno** *var.* Drino, Drínos Pótamos, *Alb.* Lumi i Drinos. ∽ Albania/Greece
Drinos, Lumi i/Drínos Pótamos *see* Dríno
25 S11 **Dripping Springs** Texas, SW USA
25 S15 **Driscoll** Texas, SW USA
22 H5 **Driskill Mountain** ▲ Louisiana, S USA
Drissa *see* Drysa
94 G10 **Driva** ∽ S Norway
112 E13 **Drniš** *It.* Šibenik-Knin, S Croatia
95 H15 **Drøbak** Akershus, S Norway
116 G13 **Drobeta-Turnu Severin** *prev.* Turnu Severin. Mehedinți, SW Romania
Drocae *see* Dreux
116 M8 **Drochia** *Rus.* Drokiya. N Moldova
97 F17 **Drogheda** *Ir.* Droichead Átha. NE Ireland
Drogichin *see* Drahichyn
Drogobych *see* Drohobych
Drohiczyn Poleski *see* Drahichyn
116 H6 **Drohobych** *Pol.* Drohobycz, *Rus.* Drogobych. L'vivs'ka Oblast', NW Ukraine
Drohobycz *see* Drohobych
Droichead Átha *see* Drogheda
Droicheadna Bandan *see* Bandon
Droichead na Banna *see* Banbridge
Droim Mór *see* Dromore
Drokiya *see* Drochia
103 R13 **Drôme** ◈ *department* E France
103 S13 **Drôme** ∽ E France
97 G15 **Dromore** *Ir.* Droim Mór. SE Northern Ireland, UK
106 A9 **Dronero** Piemonte, NE Italy
102 L12 **Dronne** ∽ SW France
195 Q3 **Dronning Maud Land** *physical region* Antarctica
98 K6 **Dronrijp** *Fris.* Dronryp. Friesland, N Netherlands
Dronryp *see* Dronrijp
98 L9 **Dronten** Flevoland, C Netherlands
Drontheim *see* Trondheim
102 L13 **Dropt** ∽ SW France
149 T4 **Drosh** North-West Frontier Province, NW Pakistan
Drossen *see* Ośno Lubuskie
Drug *see* Durg
146 I9 **Drujba** *Rus.* Druzhba. Khorazm Wiloyati, W Uzbekistan
118 I12 **Drūkšiai** ◎ NE Lithuania
Druk-yul *see* Bhutan
11 Q16 **Drumheller** Alberta, SW Canada
33 Q10 **Drummond** Montana, NW USA
31 R4 **Drummond Island** *island* Michigan, N USA
Drummond Island *see* Tabiteuea
21 X7 **Drummond, Lake** ◎ Virginia, NE USA
15 P12 **Drummondville** Quebec, SE Canada
39 T11 **Drum, Mount** ▲ Alaska, USA
27 O9 **Drumright** Oklahoma, C USA
99 J14 **Drunen** Noord-Brabant, S Netherlands
Druskienniki *see* Druskininkai
119 F15 **Druskininkai** *Pol.* Druskienniki. Druskininkai, S Lithuania
98 K13 **Druten** Gelderland, SE Netherlands
118 K11 **Druya** Vitsyebskaya Voblasts', NW Belarus
117 S2 **Druzhba** Sums'ka Oblast', NE Ukraine
Druzhba *see* Dostyk, Kazakhstan
Druzhba *see* Drujba, Uzbekistan
123 R7 **Druzhina** Respublika Sakha (Yakutiya), NE Russian Federation
117 X7 **Druzhkivka** Donets'ka Oblast', E Ukraine
112 E12 **Drvar** Federacija Bosna I Hercegovina, Bosnia and Herzegovina
113 G15 **Drvenik** Split-Dalmacija, SE Croatia
114 K9 **Dryanovo** Gabrovo, N Bulgaria
26 G7 **Dry Cimarron River** ∽ Kansas/Oklahoma, C USA
12 B11 **Dryden** Ontario, C Canada
24 M11 **Dryden** Texas, SW USA
195 Q14 **Drygalski Ice Tongue** *ice feature* Antarctica
118 L11 **Drysa** *Rus.* Drissa. ∽ N Belarus
23 V17 **Dry Tortugas** *island* Florida, SE USA
79 D15 **Dschang** Ouest, W Cameroon
54 J5 **Duaca** Lara, N Venezuela
Duacum *see* Douai
Duala *see* Douala
45 N9 **Duarte, Pico** ▲ C Dominican Republic
140 J5 **Ḍubā** Tabūk, NW Saudi Arabia
Dubai *see* Dubayy
117 N9 **Dubăsari** *Rus.* Dubossary. NE Moldova
117 N9 **Dubăsari Reservoir** ⊞ NE Moldova
8 M10 **Dubawnt** ∽ Nunavut, NW Canada
8 L9 **Dubawnt Lake** ◎ Northwest Territories/Nunavut, N Canada
30 L6 **Du Bay, Lake** ⊞ Wisconsin, N USA
141 U7 **Dubayy** *Eng.* Dubai. Dubayy, NE UAE
141 W7 **Dubayy** *Eng.* Dubai. × Dubayy, NE UAE
183 R7 **Dubbo** New South Wales, SE Australia
108 G7 **Dübendorf** Zürich, NW Switzerland
97 F18 **Dublin** *Ir.* Baile Átha Cliath; *anc.* Eblana. ● (Ireland), E Ireland
23 U5 **Dublin** Georgia, SE USA
25 R7 **Dublin** Texas, SW USA
97 G18 **Dublin** *Ir.* Baile Átha Cliath; *anc.* Eblana. *cultural region* E Ireland
97 G18 **Dublin Airport** × E Ireland
189 V12 **Dublon** *var.* Tonoas. *island* Chuuk Islands, C Micronesia
128 K2 **Dubna** Moskovskaya Oblast', W Russian Federation
111 G19 **Dubňany** *Ger.* Dubnian. Brněnský Kraj, SE Czech Republic
Dubnian *see* Dubňany
111 I19 **Dubnica nad Váhom** *Hung.* Máriatölgyes; *prev.* Dubnicz. Trenčiansky Kraj, W Slovakia
Dubnicz *see* Dubnica nad Váhom
116 K4 **Dubno** Rivnens'ka Oblast', NW Ukraine
18 D13 **Du Bois** Pennsylvania, NE USA
33 R13 **Dubois** Idaho, NW USA
33 T14 **Dubois** Wyoming, C USA
Dubossary *see* Dubăsari
129 O10 **Dubovka** Volgogradskaya Oblast', SW Russian Federation
76 H14 **Dubréka** Guinée-Maritime, SW Guinea
14 B7 **Dubreuilville** Ontario, S Canada
Dubris Portus *see* Dover
119 L20 **Dubrova** *Rus.* Dubrova. Homyel'skaya Voblasts', SE Belarus
128 I5 **Dubrovka** Bryanskaya Oblast', W Russian Federation
113 H16 **Dubrovnik** *It.* Ragusa. Dubrovnik-Neretva, SE Croatia
113 I16 **Dubrovnik** × Dubrovnik-Neretva, SE Croatia
113 F16 **Dubrovnik-Neretva** *off.* Dubrovačko-Neretvanska Županija. ◈ *province* SE Croatia
Dubrovno *see* Dubrowna
116 L2 **Dubrovytsya** Rivnens'ka Oblast', NW Ukraine
119 O14 **Dubrowna** *Rus.* Dubrovno. Vitsyebskaya Voblasts', N Belarus
29 Z13 **Dubuque** Iowa, C USA
118 E12 **Dubysa** ∽ C Lithuania
167 U11 **Đức Cơ** Gia Lai, C Vietnam
191 V12 **Duc de Gloucester, Îles du** *Eng.* Duke of Gloucester Islands. *island group* C French Polynesia
111 C15 **Duchcov** *Ger.* Dux. Ústecký Kraj, NW Czech Republic
37 N3 **Duchesne** Utah, W USA
191 P17 **Ducie Island** *atoll* E Pitcairn Islands
11 W15 **Duck Bay** Manitoba, S Canada
23 X17 **Duck Key** *island* Florida Keys, Florida, SE USA
11 T14 **Duck Lake** Saskatchewan, S Canada
11 V15 **Duck Mountain** ▲▲ Manitoba, S Canada
20 I9 **Duck River** ∽ Tennessee, S USA
20 M10 **Ducktown** Tennessee, S USA
167 U10 **Đức Phổ** Quang Ngai, C Vietnam
167 T8 **Đức Tho** Ha Tinh, N Vietnam
167 U13 **Đức Trong** *var.* Liên Nghia. Lâm Đồng, S Vietnam
D-U-D *see* Dalap-Uliga-Djarrit
99 M25 **Dudelange** *var.* Forge du Sud, *Ger.* Dudelingen. Luxembourg, S Luxembourg
Dudelingen *see* Dudelange
101 J15 **Duderstadt** Niedersachsen, C Germany
153 N15 **Dūdhi** Uttar Pradesh, N India
122 K8 **Dudinka** Taymyrskiy (Dolgano-Nenetskiy) Avtonomnyy Okrug, N Russian Federation
97 L20 **Dudley** C England, UK
154 G13 **Dudna** ∽ C India
76 L16 **Duékoué** W Ivory Coast
104 M5 **Dueñas** Castilla-León, N Spain
104 K4 **Duerna** ∽ NW Spain
105 O6 **Duero** *Port.* Douro. ∽ Portugal/Spain *see also* Douro
Duesseldorf *see* Düsseldorf
21 P12 **Due West** South Carolina, SE USA
195 P11 **Dufek Coast** *physical region* Antarctica
99 H17 **Duffel** Antwerpen, C Belgium
35 S2 **Duffer Peak** ▲ Nevada, W USA
187 Q9 **Duff Islands** *island group* E Solomon Islands
Dufour, Pizzo/Dufour, Punta *see* Dufour Spitze
108 E12 **Dufour Spitze** *It.* Pizzo Dufour, Punta Dufour. ▲ Italy/Switzerland
112 D9 **Duga Resa** Karlovac, C Croatia
22 H5 **Dugdemona River** ∽ Louisiana, S USA
154 J12 **Duggipar** Mahārāshtra, C India
112 B13 **Dugi Otok** *var.* Isola Grossa, *It.* Isola Lunga. *island* W Croatia
113 F14 **Dugopolje** Split-Dalmacija, S Croatia
160 L8 **Du He** ∽ C China
54 M11 **Duida, Cerro** ▲ S Venezuela
Duinekerke *see* Dunkerque
101 E15 **Duisburg** *prev.* Duisburg-Hamborn. Nordrhein-Westfalen, W Germany
Duisburg-Hamborn *see* Duisburg
99 F14 **Duiveland** *island* SW Netherlands
98 M12 **Duiven** Gelderland, E Netherlands
139 W10 **Dujaylah, Hawr ad** ◎ S Iraq
81 L18 **Dujuuma** Shabeellaha Hoose, S Somalia
Dūkān *see* Dokan
39 Z14 **Duke Island** *island* Alexander Archipelago, Alaska, USA
Dukelský Priesmy/Dukelský Průsmyk *see* Dukla Pass
Duke of Gloucester Islands *see* Duc de Gloucester, Îles du
81 F14 **Duk Faiwil** Jonglei, SE Sudan
141 T7 **Dukhān** C Qatar
Dukhan Heights *see* Dukhān, Jabal
143 N16 **Dukhān, Jabal** *var.* Dukhan Heights. *hill range* S Qatar
129 Q7 **Dukhovnitskoye** Saratovskaya Oblast', W Russian Federation
128 H4 **Dukhovshchina** Smolenskaya Oblast', W Russian Federation
Dukielska, Przełęcz *see* Dukla Pass
111 N17 **Dukla** Podkarpackie, SE Poland
Duklai Hág *see* Dukla Pass
111 N18 **Dukla Pass** *Cz.* Dukelský Průsmyk, *Ger.* Dukla-Pass, *Hung.* Duklai Hág, *Pol.* Przełęcz Dukielska, *Slvk.* Dukelský Priesmy. *pass* Poland/Slovakia
Dukou *see* Panzhihua
118 I12 **Dūkštas** Ignalina, E Lithuania
162 M8 **Dulaan** Hentiy, C Mongolia
159 R10 **Dulan** *var.* Qagan Us. Qinghai, C China
37 R8 **Dulce** New Mexico, SW USA
43 N16 **Dulce, Golfo** *gulf* S Costa Rica
Dulce, Golfo *see* Izabal, Lago de
42 K6 **Dulce Nombre de Culmí** Olancho, C Honduras
62 L9 **Dulce, Río** ∽ C Argentina
123 Q9 **Dulgalakh** ∽ NE Russian Federation
114 M8 **Dŭlgopol** Varna, E Bulgaria
153 V14 **Dullabchara** Assam, NE India
20 D3 **Dulles** × (Washington DC) Virginia, NE USA
101 E14 **Dülmen** Nordrhein-Westfalen, W Germany
114 M7 **Dulovo** Silistra, NE Bulgaria
29 W5 **Duluth** Minnesota, N USA
138 H7 **Dūmā** *Fr.* Douma. Dimashq, SW Syria
171 O8 **Dumagasa Point** *headland* Mindanao, S Philippines
171 P6 **Dumaguete** *var.* Dumaguete City. Negros, C Philippines
168 J10 **Dumai** Sumatera, W Indonesia
183 T4 **Dumaresq River** ∽ New South Wales/Queensland, SE Australia
27 W13 **Dumas** Arkansas, C USA
25 N1 **Dumas** Texas, SW USA
138 I7 **Ḍumayr** Dimashq, W Syria
96 I12 **Dumbarton** W Scotland, UK
96 I12 **Dumbarton** *cultural region* C Scotland, UK
187 Q17 **Dumbéa** Province Sud, S New Caledonia
111 K19 **Ďumbier** *Ger.* Djumbir, *Hung.* Gyömbér. ▲ C Slovakia
116 I11 **Dumbrăveni** *Ger.* Elisabethstedt, *Hung.* Erzsébetváros; *prev.* Ebesfalva, Eppeschdorf, Ibașfalău. Sibiu, C Romania
116 L12 **Dumbrăveni** Vrancea, E Romania
97 J14 **Dumfries** S Scotland, UK
97 J14 **Dumfries** *cultural region* SW Scotland, UK
153 R15 **Dumka** Bihār, NE India
Dümmer *see* Dümmersee
100 G12 **Dümmersee** *var.* Dümmer. ◎ NW Germany
14 J11 **Dumoine** ∽ Quebec, SE Canada
14 J10 **Dumoine, Lac** ◎ Quebec, SE Canada
195 V16 **Dumont d'Urville** *French research station* Antarctica
195 W15 **Dumont d'Urville Sea** S Pacific Ocean
14 K11 **Dumont, Lac** ◎ Quebec, SE Canada
75 W7 **Dumyāt** *Eng.* Damietta. N Egypt
Duna *see* Don, Russian Federation
Duna *see* Danube, C Europe
Düna *see* Western Dvina
Dünaburg *see* Daugavpils
111 J24 **Dunaföldvár** Tolna, C Hungary
Dunaj *see* Wien, Austria
Dunaj *see* Danube, C Europe
111 L18 **Dunajec** ∽ S Poland
111 H21 **Dunajská Streda** *Hung.* Dunaszerdahely. Trnavský Kraj, W Slovakia
Dunapentele *see* Dunaújváros
Dunărea *see* Danube
116 M13 **Dunărea Veche, Brațul** ∽ SE Romania
117 N13 **Dunării, Delta** *delta* SE Romania
Dunaszerdahely *see* Dunajská Streda
111 J23 **Dunaújváros** *prev.* Dunapentele, Sztálinváros. Fejér, C Hungary
Dunav *see* Danube
114 J8 **Dunavska Ravnina** *Eng.* Danubian Plain. *plain* N Bulgaria
114 G7 **Dunavtsi** Vidin, NW Bulgaria
Dunayevtsy *see* Dunayivtsi
116 L7 **Dunayivtsi** *Rus.* Dunayevtsy. Khmel'nyts'ka Oblast', NW Ukraine
185 F22 **Dunback** Otago, South Island, NZ
10 L17 **Duncan** Vancouver Island, British Columbia, SW Canada
37 O15 **Duncan** Arizona, SW USA
26 M12 **Duncan** Oklahoma, C USA
Duncan Island *see* Pinzón, Isla
151 Q20 **Duncan Passage** *strait* Andaman Sea/Bay of Bengal
96 K6 **Duncansby Head** *headland* N Scotland, UK
14 G12 **Dunchurch** Ontario, S Canada
118 D7 **Dundaga** Talsi, NW Latvia
14 G14 **Dundalk** Ontario, S Canada
97 F16 **Dundalk** *Ir.* Dún Dealgan. NE Ireland
21 X3 **Dundalk** Maryland, NE USA
97 F16 **Dundalk Bay** *Ir.* Cuan Dhún Dealgan. *bay* NE Ireland
14 G16 **Dundas** Ontario, S Canada
180 L12 **Dundas, Lake** *salt lake* Western Australia
163 O7 **Dundbürd** Hentiy, E Mongolia
Dún Dealgan *see* Dundalk
15 N13 **Dundee** Quebec, SE Canada
83 K22 **Dundee** KwaZulu/Natal, E South Africa
96 K11 **Dundee** E Scotland, UK
31 R10 **Dundee** Michigan, N USA
25 R5 **Dundee** Texas, SW USA
194 H3 **Dundee Island** *island* Antarctica
162 L9 **Dundgovĭ** ◈ *province* C Mongolia
97 G16 **Dundrum Bay** *Ir.* Cuan Dhún Droma. *inlet* NW Irish Sea
11 T15 **Dundurn** Saskatchewan, S Canada
162 E6 **Dund-Us** Hovd, W Mongolia
185 F23 **Dunedin** Otago, South Island, NZ
183 R7 **Dunedoo** New South Wales, SE Australia
97 D14 **Dunfanaghy** *Ir.* Dún Fionnachaidh. NW Ireland
96 J12 **Dunfermline** C Scotland, UK
Dún Fionnachaidh *see* Dunfanaghy
149 V10 **Dunga Bunga** Punjab, E Pakistan
97 F15 **Dungannon** *Ir.* Dún Geanainn. C Northern Ireland, UK
Dun Garbháin *see* Dungarvan
152 F15 **Dūngarpur** Rājasthān, N India
97 E21 **Dungarvan** *Ir.* Dun Garbháin. S Ireland
101 N21 **Dungau** *cultural region* SE Germany
Dún Geanainn *see* Dungannon
97 P23 **Dungeness** *headland* SE England, UK
63 I23 **Dungeness, Punta** *headland* S Argentina
Dungloe *see* Dunglow
97 D14 **Dunglow** *var.* Dungloe, *Ir.* An Clochán Liath. NW Ireland
183 T7 **Dungog** New South Wales, SE Australia
79 O16 **Dungu** Orientale, NE Dem. Rep. Congo (Zaire)
168 L8 **Dungun** *var.* Kuala Dungun. Terengganu, Peninsular Malaysia
80 I6 **Dungûnab** Red Sea, NE Sudan
15 P13 **Dunham** Quebec, SE Canada
Dunheved *see* Launceston
Dunholme *see* Durham
163 X10 **Dunhua** Jilin, NE China
159 P8 **Dunhuang** Gansu, N China
182 L12 **Dunkeld** Victoria, SE Australia
103 O1 **Dunkerque** *Eng.* Dunkirk, *Flem.* Duinekerke; *prev.* Dunquerque. Nord, N France
97 K23 **Dunkery Beacon** ▲ SW England, UK
18 C11 **Dunkirk** New York, NE USA
Dunkirk *see* Dunkerque
77 P17 **Dunkwa** SW Ghana
97 G18 **Dún Laoghaire** *Eng.* Dunleary; *prev.* Kingstown. E Ireland
29 S14 **Dunlap** Iowa, C USA
20 L10 **Dunlap** Tennessee, S USA
Dunleary *see* Dún Laoghaire
Dún Mánmhaí *see* Dunmanway
97 B21 **Dunmanway** *Ir.* Dún Mánmhaí. SW Ireland
18 I13 **Dunmore** Pennsylvania, NE USA
21 U10 **Dunn** North Carolina, SE USA
Dún na nGall *see* Donegal
23 V11 **Dunnellon** Florida, SE USA
96 J6 **Dunnet Head** *headland* N Scotland, UK
29 N14 **Dunning** Nebraska, C USA
65 B24 **Dunnose Head Settlement** West Falkland, Falkland Islands
14 G17 **Dunnville** Ontario, S Canada
Dún Pádraig *see* Downpatrick
Dunquerque *see* Dunkerque
Dunqulah *see* Dongola
96 L12 **Duns** SE Scotland, UK
29 N2 **Dunseith** North Dakota, N USA
35 N2 **Dunsmuir** California, W USA
97 N21 **Dunstable** *Lat.* Durocobrivae. E England, UK
185 D21 **Dunstan Mountains** ▲▲ South Island, NZ
103 O9 **Dun-sur-Auron** Cher, C France
185 F21 **Duntroon** Canterbury, South Island, NZ
149 T10 **Dunyāpur** Punjab, E Pakistan
163 U5 **Duobukur He** ∽ NE China
163 R12 **Duolun** *var.* Dolonnur. Nei Mongol Zizhiqu, N China
167 Q14 **Dương Đông** Kiên Giang, S Vietnam
114 G10 **Dupnitsa** *prev.* Marek, Stanke Dimitrov. Kyustendil, W Bulgaria
28 L8 **Dupree** South Dakota, N USA
33 Q7 **Dupuyer** Montana, NW USA
141 Y11 **Duqm** *var.* Daqm. E Oman
63 F23 **Duque de York, Isla** *island* S Chile
181 N4 **Durack Range** ▲▲ Western Australia
136 K10 **Durağan** Sinop, N Turkey
103 S15 **Durance** ∽ SE France
31 R9 **Durand** Michigan, N USA
30 I6 **Durand** Wisconsin, N USA
40 K10 **Durango** *var.* Victoria de Durango. Durango, W Mexico
105 P3 **Durango** País Vasco, N Spain
37 Q8 **Durango** Colorado, C USA
40 J9 **Durango** ◈ *state* C Mexico
114 O7 **Durankulak** *Rom.* Răcari; *prev.* Blatnitsa, Duranulac. Dobrich, NE Bulgaria
22 L4 **Durant** Mississippi, S USA
27 P13 **Durant** Oklahoma, C USA
Duranulac *see* Durankulak
105 N6 **Duratón** ∽ N Spain
61 E19 **Durazno** *var.* San Pedro de Durazno. Durazno, C Uruguay
61 E19 **Durazno** ◈ *department* C Uruguay
Durazzo *see* Durrës
83 K23 **Durban** *var.* Port Natal. KwaZulu/Natal, E South Africa
83 K23 **Durban** × KwaZulu/Natal, E South Africa
118 C9 **Durbe** *Ger.* Durben. Liepāja, W Latvia
Durben *see* Durbe
99 K21 **Durbuy** Luxembourg, SE Belgium
105 N15 **Dúrcal** Andalucía, S Spain
112 F8 **Đurđevac** *Ger.* Sankt Georgen, *Hung.* Szentgyörgy; *prev.* Djurdjevac, Gjurgjevac. Koprivnica-Križevci, N Croatia
113 K15 **Đurđevica Tara** Montenegro, SW Yugoslavia
97 L24 **Durdle Door** *natural arch* S England, UK
158 L3 **Düre** Xinjiang Uygur Zizhiqu, W China
101 D16 **Düren** *anc.* Marcodurum. Nordrhein-Westfalen, W Germany
154 K12 **Durg** *prev.* Drug. Madhya Pradesh, C India
153 U13 **Durgapur** Dhaka, N Bangladesh
153 R15 **Durgāpur** West Bengal, NE India
14 F14 **Durham** Ontario, S Canada
97 M14 **Durham** *hist.* Dunholme. N England, UK
21 U9 **Durham** North Carolina, SE USA
97 L15 **Durham** *cultural region* N England, UK
168 J10 **Duri** Sumatera, W Indonesia
Duria Major *see* Dora Baltea
Duria Minor *see* Dora Riparia
Durlas *see* Thurles
141 P8 **Ḍurmā** Ar Riyāḍ, C Saudi Arabia
113 J15 **Durmitor** ▲ N Yugoslavia
96 H6 **Durness** N Scotland, UK
109 Y3 **Dürnkrut** Niederösterreich, E Austria
Durnovaria *see* Dorchester
Durobrivae *see* Rochester
Durocasses *see* Dreux
Durocobrivae *see* Dunstable
Durocortorum *see* Reims
Durostorum *see* Silistra
Durovernum *see* Canterbury
113 K20 **Durrës** *var.* Durrësi, Dursi, *It.* Durazzo, *SCr.* Drač, *Turk.* Draç. Durrës, W Albania
113 K19 **Durrës** ◈ *district* W Albania
Durrësi *see* Durrës
97 A21 **Dursey Island** *Ir.* Oileán Baoi. *island* SW Ireland
Dursi *see* Durrës
Durud *see* Do Rūd
114 P12 **Durusu** İstanbul, NW Turkey
114 O12 **Durusu Gölü** ◎ NW Turkey
138 I9 **Durūz, Jabal ad** ▲ SW Syria
184 K13 **D'Urville Island** *island* C NZ
171 X12 **D'Urville, Tanjung** *headland* Irian Jaya, E Indonesia
Dusa Mareb/Dusa Marreb *see* Dhuusa Marreeb
118 I11 **Dusetos** Zarasai, NE Lithuania
146 H14 **Dushak** Akhalskiy Velayat, S Turkmenistan
160 K12 **Dushan** Guizhou, S China
147 P13 **Dushanbe** *var.* Dyushambe; *prev.* Stalinabad, *Taj.* Stalinobod. ● (Tajikistan) W Tajikistan
147 P13 **Dushanbe** × W Tajikistan
137 T9 **Dushet'i** E Georgia
18 H13 **Dushore** Pennsylvania, NE USA
185 A23 **Dusky Sound** *sound* South Island, NZ
101 E15 **Düsseldorf** *var.* Duesseldorf. Nordrhein-Westfalen, W Germany
147 P14 **Dŭsti** *Rus.* Dusti. SW Tajikistan
194 I9 **Dustin Island** *island* Antarctica
147 O10 **Dŭstlik** Jizzakh Wiloyati, C Uzbekistan
Dutch East Indies *see* Indonesia
Dutch Guiana *see* Suriname
38 L17 **Dutch Harbor** Unalaska Island, Alaska, USA
36 J3 **Dutch Mount** ▲ Utah, W USA
Dutch New Guinea *see* Irian Jaya
Dutch West Indies *see* Netherlands Antilles
83 H20 **Dutlwe** Kweneng, S Botswana
67 V16 **Du Toit Fracture Zone** *tectonic feature* SW Indian Ocean
127 U8 **Dutovo** Respublika Komi, NW Russian Federation
77 V13 **Dutsan Wai** *var.* Dutsen Wai. Kaduna, C Nigeria
77 W13 **Dutse** Jigawa, N Nigeria
Dutsen Wai *see* Dutsan Wai
Duttia *see* Datia
14 E17 **Dutton** Ontario, S Canada
36 L7 **Dutton, Mount** ▲ Utah, W USA

◆ Country ● Country Capital ◇ Dependent Territory ○ Dependent Territory Capital ◈ Administrative Region × International Airport ▲ Mountain ▲▲ Mountain Range ※ Volcano ∽ River ◎ Lake ⊞ Reservoir

162 E7 **Duut** Hovd, W Mongolia
14 K11 **Duval, Lac** ◎ Quebec, SE Canada
129 W3 **Duvan** Respublika Bashkortostan, W Russian Federation
138 L9 **Duwaykhilat Satīḥ ar Ruwayshid** seasonal river SE Jordan
Dux see Duchcov
160 J13 **Duyang Shan** ▲▲ S China
167 T14 **Duyên Hai** Tra Vinh, S Vietnam
160 K12 **Duyun** Guizhou, S China
136 G11 **Düzce** Bolu, NW Turkey
Duzdab see Zāhedān
Duzenkyr, Khrebet see Duzkyr, Khrebet
146 I16 **Duzkyr, Khrebet** prev. Khrebet Duzenkyr. ▲▲ S Turkmenistan
Dvina Bay see Chëshskaya Guba
Dvinsk see Daugavpils
126 L7 **Dvinskaya Guba** bay NW Russian Federation
112 E10 **Dvor** Sisak-Moslavina, C Croatia
117 W5 **Dvorichna** Kharkivs'ka Oblast', E Ukraine
111 F16 **Dvůr Králové nad Labem** Ger. Königinhof an der Elbe. Hradecký Kraj, NE Czech Republic
154 A10 **Dwārka** Gujarāt, W India
30 M12 **Dwight** Illinois, N USA
98 N8 **Dwingeloo** Drenthe, NE Netherlands
33 N10 **Dworshak Reservoir** ⊠ Idaho, NW USA
Dyal see Dyaul Island
Dyanev see Deynau
Dyatlovo see Dzyatlava
186 G5 **Dyaul Island** var. Djaul, Dyal. island NE PNG
20 G8 **Dyer** Tennessee, S USA
9 S5 **Dyer, Cape** headland Baffin Island, Nunavut, NE Canada
20 F8 **Dyersburg** Tennessee, S USA
29 Y13 **Dyersville** Iowa, C USA
97 I21 **Dyfed** cultural region SW Wales, UK
Dyfrdwy, Afon see Dee
Dyhernfurth see Brzeg Dolny
111 E19 **Dyje** var. Thaya. ∽ Austria/Czech Republic see also Thaya
117 T5 **Dykanska** Poltavs'ka Oblast', C Ukraine
129 N16 **Dykhtau** ▲ SW Russian Federation
111 A16 **Dyleń** Ger. Tillenberg. ▲ NW Czech Republic
110 K9 **Dylewska Góra** ▲ N Poland
117 O4 **Dymer** Kyyivs'ka Oblast', N Ukraine
117 W7 **Dymytrov** Rus. Dimitrov. Donets'ka Oblast', SE Ukraine
111 O17 **Dynów** Podkarpackie, SE Poland
29 X13 **Dysart** Iowa, C USA
Dysna see Dzisna
115 D18 **Dytikí Ellás** Eng. Greece West. ◈ region C Greece
115 C14 **Dytikí Makedonía** Eng. Macedonia West. ◈ region N Greece
Dyurmen'tyube see Dermentobe
129 U4 **Dyurtyuli** Respublika Bashkortostan, W Russian Federation
Dyushambe see Dushanbe
162 I7 **Dzaanhushuu** Arhangay, C Mongolia
Dza Chu see Mekong
162 I8 **Dzadgay** Bayanhongor, C Mongolia
162 H8 **Dzag** Bayanhongor, C Mongolia
162 H10 **Dzalaa** Bayanhongor, C Mongolia
172 J14 **Dzaoudzi** E Mayotte
Dzaudzhikau see Vladikavkaz
162 G7 **Dzavhan** ◈ province NW Mongolia
162 G7 **Dzavhan Gol** ∽ NW Mongolia
162 J7 **Dzegstey** Arhangay, C Mongolia
129 O3 **Dzerzhinsk** Nizhegorodskaya Oblast', W Russian Federation
Dzerzhinsk see Dzyarzhynsk, Belarus
Dzerzhinsk see Dzerzhyns'k, Ukraine
Dzerzhinskiy see Nar'yan-Mar
145 W13 **Dzerzhinskoye** Almaty, SE Kazakhstan
117 X7 **Dzerzhyns'k** Rus. Dzerzhinsk. Donets'ka Oblast', SE Ukraine
116 M5 **Dzerzhyns'k** Zhytomyrs'ka Oblast', N Ukraine
Dzhailgan see Jayilgan
145 N14 **Dzhalagash** Kaz. Zhalashash. Kzylorda, S Kazakhstan
147 T10 **Dzhalal-Abad** Kir. Jalal-Abad. Dzhalal-Abadskaya Oblast', W Kyrgyzstan
147 S9 **Dzhalal-Abadskaya Oblast'** Kir. Jalal-Abad Oblasty. ◈ province W Kyrgyzstan
Dzhalilabad see Cälilabad
144 G9 **Dzhambeyty** Kaz. Zhympity. Zapadnyy Kazakhstan, W Kazakhstan
Dzhambulskaya Oblast' see Zhambyl
Dzhankel'dy see Jangeldi
117 T12 **Dzhankoy** Respublika Krym, S Ukraine
145 V14 **Dzhansugurov** Kaz. Zhansügirov. Almaty, SE Kazakhstan
147 R9 **Dzhany-Bazar** var. Yangibazar. Dzhalal-Abadskaya Oblast', W Kyrgyzstan
144 D9 **Dzhanybek** Kaz. Zhänibek. Zapadnyy Kazakhstan, W Kazakhstan
123 P8 **Dzhardzhan** Respublika Sakha (Yakutiya), NE Russian Federation
Dzharkurgan see Jarqürghon
117 S11 **Dzharylhats'ka Zatoka** gulf S Ukraine
Dzhayilgan see Jayilgan
146 B11 **Dzhebel** Turkm. Jebel. Balkanskiy Velayat, W Turkmenistan
147 T14 **Dzhelandy** SE Tajikistan
147 Y7 **Dzhergalan** Kir. Jyrgalan. Issyk-Kul'skaya Oblast', NE Kyrgyzstan
144 L8 **Dzhetygara** Kaz. Zhetiqara. Kostanay, NW Kazakhstan
Dzhetysay see Zhetysay.
Dzhezkazgan see Zhezkazgan
146 J10 **Dzhigirbent** Turkm. Jigerbent. Lebapskiy Velayat, NE Turkmenistan
Dzhirgatal' see Jirgatol
Dzhizak see Jizzakh
Dzhizakskaya Oblast' see Jizzakh Wiloyati
123 P8 **Dzhugdzhur, Khrebet** ▲ E Russian Federation
Dzhul'fa see Culfa
Dzhuma see Juma
145 W14 **Dzhungarskiy Alatau** ▲▲ China/Kazakhstan
144 M14 **Dzhusaly** Kaz. Zholsaly. Kzylorda, SW Kazakhstan
146 J12 **Dzhynlykum, Peski** desert E Turkmenistan
110 L9 **Działdowo** Warmińsko-Mazurskie, C Poland
111 L16 **Działoszyce** Świętokrzyskie, C Poland
41 X11 **Dzidzantún** Yucatán, E Mexico
111 G15 **Dzierżoniów** Ger. Reichenbach. Dolnośląskie, SW Poland
41 X11 **Dzilam de Bravo** Yucatán, E Mexico
118 L12 **Dzisna** Rus. Disna. Vitsyebskaya Voblasts', N Belarus
118 K12 **Dzisna** Lith. Dysna, Rus. Disna. ∽ Belarus/Lithuania
119 G20 **Dzivin** Rus. Divin. Brestskaya Voblasts', SW Belarus
119 M15 **Dzmitravichy** Rus. Dmitrovichi. Minskaya Voblasts', C Belarus
162 M8 **Dzogsool** Töv, C Mongolia
131 S8 **Dzungaria** var. Sungaria, Zungaria. physical region W China
Dzungarian Basin see Junggar Pendi
162 G5 **Dzür** Dzavhan, W Mongolia
163 Q8 **Dzüünbulag** Dornod, E Mongolia
163 O8 **Dzüünbulag** Sühbaatar, E Mongolia
162 H7 **Dzuunmod** Dzavhan, C Mongolia
162 L8 **Dzuunmod** Töv, C Mongolia
Dzüün Soyonï Nuruu see Eastern Sayans
162 F8 **Dzüyl** Govĭ-Altay, SW Mongolia
Dzvina see Western Dvina
119 J16 **Dzyarzhynsk** Rus. Dzerzhinsk; prev. Kaydanovo. Minskaya Voblasts', C Belarus
119 H17 **Dzyatlava** Pol. Zdzięcioł, Rus. Dyatlovo. Hrodzyenskaya Voblasts', W Belarus

E

E see Hubei
Éadan Doire see Edenderry
37 W6 **Eads** Colorado, C USA
37 O13 **Eagar** Arizona, SW USA
39 T8 **Eagle** Alaska, USA
13 S8 **Eagle** ∽ Newfoundland, E Canada
10 I3 **Eagle** ∽ Yukon Territory, NW Canada
29 T7 **Eagle Bend** Minnesota, N USA
28 M8 **Eagle Butte** South Dakota, N USA
29 V12 **Eagle Grove** Iowa, C USA
19 R2 **Eagle Lake** Maine, NE USA
25 U11 **Eagle Lake** Texas, SW USA
12 A11 **Eagle Lake** ◎ Ontario, S Canada
35 P3 **Eagle Lake** ◎ California, W USA
19 R3 **Eagle Lake** ◎ Maine, NE USA
29 Y3 **Eagle Mountain** ▲ Minnesota, N USA
25 T6 **Eagle Mountain Lake** ⊠ Texas, SW USA
37 S9 **Eagle Nest Lake** ⊠ New Mexico, SW USA
25 P13 **Eagle Pass** Texas, SW USA
65 C25 **Eagle Passage** passage SW Atlantic Ocean
35 R8 **Eagle Peak** ▲ California, W USA
35 Q2 **Eagle Peak** ▲ California, W USA
37 P13 **Eagle Peak** ▲ New Mexico, SW USA
10 I4 **Eagle Plain** Yukon Territory, NW Canada
32 G15 **Eagle Point** Oregon, NW USA
186 F10 **Eagle Point** headland SE PNG
39 R11 **Eagle River** Alaska, USA
30 M2 **Eagle River** Michigan, N USA
30 L4 **Eagle River** Wisconsin, N USA
21 S6 **Eagle Rock** Virginia, NE USA
36 J13 **Eagletail Mountains** ▲▲ Arizona, SW USA
167 U12 **Ea Hleo** Đăc Lăc, S Vietnam
167 U12 **Ea Kar** Đăc Lăc, S Vietnam
Eanjum see Anjum
Eanodat see Enontekiö
12 B10 **Ear Falls** Ontario, C Canada
27 X10 **Earle** Arkansas, C USA
35 R12 **Earlimart** California, W USA
20 I6 **Earlington** Kentucky, S USA
14 H8 **Earlton** Ontario, S Canada
29 T13 **Early** Iowa, C USA
96 J11 **Earn** ∽ N Scotland, UK
185 C21 **Earnslaw, Mount** ▲ South Island, NZ
24 M4 **Earth** Texas, SW USA
21 P11 **Easley** South Carolina, SE USA
East see Est
East Açores Fracture Zone see East Azores Fracture Zone
97 P19 **East Anglia** physical region E England, UK
15 Q12 **East Angus** Quebec, SE Canada
East Antarctica see Greater Antarctica
18 E10 **East Aurora** New York, NE USA
East Australian Basin see Tasman Basin
East Azerbaijan see Āzarbāyjān-e Sharqī
64 L9 **East Azores Fracture Zone** var. East Açores Fracture Zone. tectonic feature E Atlantic Ocean
22 M11 **East Bay** bay Louisiana, S USA
25 V11 **East Bernard** Texas, SW USA
29 V8 **East Bethel** Minnesota, N USA
East Borneo see Kalimantan Timur
97 P23 **Eastbourne** SE England, UK
15 R11 **East-Broughton** Quebec, SE Canada
44 M6 **East Caicos** island E Turks and Caicos Islands
184 R7 **East Cape** headland North Island, NZ
174 M4 **East Caroline Basin** undersea feature SW Pacific Ocean
192 F4 **East China Sea** Chin. Dong Hai. sea W Pacific Ocean
97 P19 **East Dereham** E England, UK
30 J9 **East Dubuque** Illinois, N USA
11 S17 **Eastend** Saskatchewan, S Canada
193 S10 **Easter Fracture Zone** tectonic feature E Pacific Ocean
Easter Island see Pascua, Isla de
81 J18 **Eastern** ◈ province Kenya
153 Q12 **Eastern** ◈ zone E Nepal
82 L13 **Eastern** ◈ province E Zambia
83 H24 **Eastern Cape** off. Eastern Cape Province, Afr. Oos-Kaap. ◈ province SE South Africa
Eastern Desert see Sahara el Sharqîya
81 F15 **Eastern Equatoria** ◈ state SE Sudan
Eastern Euphrates see Murat Nehri
155 J17 **Eastern Ghats** ▲▲ SE India
186 E7 **Eastern Highlands** ◈ province C PNG
155 K25 **Eastern Province** ◈ province E Sri Lanka
Eastern Region see Ash Sharqīyah
122 L13 **Eastern Sayans** Mong. Dzüün Soyonï Nuruu, Rus. Vostochnyy Sayan. ▲▲ Mongolia/Russian Federation
Eastern Scheldt see Oosterschelde
Eastern Sierra Madre see Madre Oriental, Sierra
Eastern Transvaal see Mpumalanga
11 W14 **Easterville** Manitoba, C Canada
Easterwâlde see Oosterwolde
63 M23 **East Falkland** var. Isla Soledad. island E Falkland Islands
19 P12 **East Falmouth** Massachusetts, NE USA
East Fayu see Fayu
East Flanders see Oost Vlaanderen
39 S6 **East Fork Chandalar River** ∽ Alaska, USA
29 U12 **East Fork Des Moines River** ∽ Iowa/Minnesota, C USA
East Frisian Islands see Ostfriesische Inseln
18 K10 **East Glenville** New York, NE USA
29 R4 **East Grand Forks** Minnesota, N USA
97 O23 **East Grinstead** SE England, UK
18 M12 **East Hartford** Connecticut, NE USA
18 M13 **East Haven** Connecticut, NE USA
173 T9 **East Indiaman Ridge** undersea feature E Indian Ocean
131 V16 **East Indies** island group SE Asia
East Java see Jawa Timur
31 Q6 **East Jordan** Michigan, N USA
East Kalimantan see Kalimantan Timur
East Kazakhstan see Vostochnyy Kazakhstan
96 I12 **East Kilbride** S Scotland, UK
25 R7 **Eastland** Texas, SW USA
31 Q9 **East Lansing** Michigan, N USA
35 X11 **East Las Vegas** Nevada, W USA
97 M23 **Eastleigh** S England, UK
31 V12 **East Liverpool** Ohio, N USA
83 J25 **East London** Afr. Oos-Londen; prev. Emonti, Port Rex. Eastern Cape, S South Africa
96 K12 **East Lothian** cultural region SE Scotland, UK
12 I10 **Eastmain** Quebec, E Canada
12 J10 **Eastmain** ∽ Quebec, C Canada
15 P13 **Eastman** Quebec, SE Canada
23 U6 **Eastman** Georgia, SE USA
175 O3 **East Mariana Basin** undersea feature W Pacific Ocean
30 K11 **East Moline** Illinois, N USA
186 H7 **East New Britain** ◈ province E PNG
29 T15 **East Nishnabotna River** ∽ Iowa, C USA
197 V12 **East Novaya Zemlya Trough** var. Novaya Zemlya Trough. undersea feature W Kara Sea
East Nusa Tenggara see Nusa Tenggara Timur
21 X4 **Easton** Maryland, NE USA
18 I14 **Easton** Pennsylvania, NE USA
193 R16 **East Pacific Rise** undersea feature E Pacific Ocean
East Pakistan see Bangladesh
31 V12 **East Palestine** Ohio, N USA
30 L12 **East Peoria** Illinois, N USA
23 S3 **East Point** Georgia, SE USA
19 U6 **Eastport** Maine, NE USA
27 Z8 **East Prairie** Missouri, C USA
19 O12 **East Providence** Rhode Island, NE USA
20 L11 **East Ridge** Tennessee, S USA
97 N16 **East Riding** cultural region N England, UK
18 F9 **East Rochester** New York, NE USA
30 K15 **East Saint Louis** Illinois, N USA
65 K21 **East Scotia Basin** undersea feature SE Scotia Sea
East Sea see Japan, Sea of
186 B6 **East Sepik** ◈ province NW PNG
173 N4 **East Sheba Ridge** undersea feature W Arabian Sea
East Siberian Sea see Vostochno-Sibirskoye More
18 I14 **East Stroudsburg** Pennsylvania, NE USA
East Tasmanian Rise/East Tasmania Plateau/East Tasmania Rise see East Tasman Plateau
192 I12 **East Tasman Plateau** var. East Tasmanian Rise, East Tasmania Plateau, East Tasmania Rise. undersea feature SW Tasman Sea
64 L7 **East Thulean Rise** undersea feature N Atlantic Ocean
171 R16 **East Timor** var Loro Sae prev. Portuguese Timor, Timor Timur ◇ disputed territory SE Asia
21 Y6 **Eastville** Virginia, NE USA
35 R7 **East Walker River** ∽ California/Nevada, W USA
182 D1 **Eateringinna Creek** ∽ South Australia
37 T3 **Eaton** Colorado, C USA
15 Q12 **Eaton** ∽ Quebec, SE Canada
11 S16 **Eatonia** Saskatchewan, S Canada
31 Q10 **Eaton Rapids** Michigan, N USA
23 U4 **Eatonton** Georgia, SE USA
32 H9 **Eatonville** Washington, NW USA
30 J6 **Eau Claire** Wisconsin, N USA
Eau Claire, Lac à L' see St.Clair, Lake
12 J7 **Eau Claire, Lac à l'** ◎ Quebec, SE Canada
30 L6 **Eau Claire River** ∽ Wisconsin, N USA
188 J16 **Eauripik Atoll** atoll Caroline Islands, C Micronesia
192 H7 **Eauripik Rise** undersea feature W Pacific Ocean
102 K15 **Eauze** Gers, S France
41 P11 **Ébano** San Luis Potosí, C Mexico
97 K21 **Ebbw Vale** SE Wales, UK
79 E17 **Ebebiyin** NE Equatorial Guinea
95 H22 **Ebeltoft** Århus, C Denmark
109 X5 **Ebenfurth** Niederösterreich, E Austria
18 D14 **Ebensburg** Pennsylvania, NE USA
109 S5 **Ebensee** Oberösterreich, N Austria
101 H20 **Eberbach** Baden-Württemberg, SW Germany
121 U8 **Eber Gölü** salt lake C Turkey
109 U9 **Eberndorf** Slvn. Dobrla Vas. Kärnten, S Austria
109 R4 **Eberschwang** Oberösterreich, N Austria
100 O11 **Eberswalde-Finow** Brandenburg, E Germany
Ebesfalva see Dumbrăveni
165 T4 **Ebetsu** var. Ebetu. Hokkaidō, NE Japan
Ebetu see Ebetsu
Ebinayon see Evinayong
158 I4 **Ebinur Hu** ◎ NW China
138 I3 **Ebla** Ar. Tell Mardikh. site of ancient city Idlib, NW Syria
Eblana see Dublin
108 H7 **Ebnat** Sankt Gallen, NE Switzerland
107 L18 **Eboli** Campania, S Italy
79 E16 **Ebolowa** Sud, S Cameroon
79 N21 **Ebombo** Kasai Oriental, C Dem. Rep. Congo (Zaire)
189 T9 **Ebon Atoll** var. Epoon. atoll Ralik Chain, S Marshall Islands
Ebora see Évora
Eboracum see York
Eborodunum see Yverdon
101 J19 **Ebrach** Bayern, C Germany
109 X5 **Ebreichsdorf** Niederösterreich, E Austria
105 S6 **Ebro** ∽ NE Spain
105 N3 **Ebro, Embalse del** ⊠ N Spain
120 G7 **Ebro Fan** undersea feature W Mediterranean Sea
Eburacum see York
Ebusus see Eivissa
99 F20 **Écaussinnes-d'Enghien** Hainaut, SW Belgium
Ecbatana see Hamadān
21 Q6 **Eccles** West Virginia, NE USA
115 L14 **Eceabat** Çanakkale, NW Turkey
171 O2 **Echague** Luzon, N Philippines
Ech Cheliff/Ech Chleff see Chlef
Echeng see Ezhou
115 C18 **Echinádes** island group W Greece
114 J12 **Echínos** var. Ehinos, Ekhínos. Anatolikí Makedonía kai Thráki, NE Greece
164 J12 **Echizen-misaki** headland Honshū, SW Japan
Echmiadzin see Ejmiatsin
8 J8 **Echo Bay** Northwest Territories, NW Canada
35 Y11 **Echo Bay** Nevada, W USA
36 L9 **Echo Cliffs** cliff Arizona, SW USA
14 C10 **Echo Lake** ◎ Ontario, S Canada
35 Q7 **Echo Summit** ▲ California, W USA
14 L8 **Échouani, Lac** ◎ Quebec, SE Canada
99 L17 **Echt** Limburg, SE Netherlands
101 H22 **Echterdingen** ✈ (Stuttgart) Baden-Württemberg, SW Germany
99 N24 **Echternach** Grevenmacher, E Luxembourg
183 N11 **Echuca** Victoria, SE Australia
104 L14 **Ecija** anc. Astigi. Andalucía, SW Spain
Eckengraf see Viesīte
100 I7 **Eckernförde** Schleswig-Holstein, N Germany
100 J7 **Eckernförder Bucht** inlet N Germany
102 L7 **Écommoy** Sarthe, NW France
14 L10 **Écorce, Lac de l'** ◎ Quebec, SE Canada
15 Q8 **Écorces, Rivière aux** ∽ Quebec, SE Canada
56 C7 **Ecuador** off. Republic of Ecuador. ◆ republic NW South America
80 L10 **Ed** var. Edd. SE Eritrea
95 I17 **Ed** Västra Götaland, S Sweden
98 I9 **Edam** Noord-Holland, C Netherlands
96 K4 **Eday** island NE Scotland, UK
25 S17 **Edcouch** Texas, SW USA
Edd see Ed
80 C11 **Ed Da'ein** Southern Darfur, W Sudan
80 G11 **Ed Damazin** var. Ad Damazīn. Blue Nile, E Sudan
80 G8 **Ed Damer** var. Ad Damar, Ad Dāmir. River Nile, NE Sudan
80 E8 **Ed Debba** Northern, N Sudan
80 F10 **Ed Dueim** var. Ad Duwaym, Ad Duwēm. White Nile, C Sudan
183 Q16 **Eddystone Point** headland Tasmania, SE Australia
97 I25 **Eddystone Rocks** rocks SW England, UK
29 W15 **Eddyville** Iowa, C USA
20 H7 **Eddyville** Kentucky, S USA
98 L12 **Ede** Gelderland, C Netherlands
77 T16 **Ede** Osun, SW Nigeria
79 D16 **Edéa** Littoral, SW Cameroon
111 M20 **Edelény** Borsod-Abaúj-Zemplén, NE Hungary
183 R12 **Eden** New South Wales, SE Australia
21 T8 **Eden** North Carolina, SE USA
25 P9 **Eden** Texas, SW USA
97 K14 **Eden** ∽ NW England, UK
83 I23 **Edenburg** Free State, C South Africa
185 D24 **Edendale** Southland, South Island, NZ
97 E18 **Edenderry** Ir. Éadan Doire. C Ireland
182 L11 **Edenhope** Victoria, SE Australia
21 X8 **Edenton** North Carolina, SE USA
101 G16 **Eder** ∽ NW Germany
101 H15 **Edersee** ◎ W Germany
Edessa see Şanlıurfa
114 E13 **Édessa** var. Édhessa. Kentrikí Makedonía, N Greece
Edfu see Idfu
29 P16 **Edgar** Nebraska, C USA
19 P13 **Edgartown** Martha's Vineyard, Massachusetts, NE USA
39 X13 **Edgecumbe, Mount** ▲ Baranof Island, Alaska, USA
21 Q13 **Edgefield** South Carolina, SE USA
29 P6 **Edgeley** North Dakota, N USA
28 I11 **Edgemont** South Dakota, N USA
92 O3 **Edgeøya** island S Svalbard
27 Q4 **Edgerton** Kansas, C USA
29 S10 **Edgerton** Minnesota, N USA
21 X3 **Edgewood** Maryland, NE USA
25 V6 **Edgewood** Texas, SW USA
Édhessa see Édessa
29 V9 **Edina** Minnesota, N USA
27 U2 **Edina** Missouri, C USA
25 S15 **Edinburg** Texas, SW USA
65 M24 **Edinburgh** var. Settlement of Edinburgh. ○ (Tristan da Cunha) NW Tristan da Cunha
96 J12 **Edinburgh** ◉ S Scotland, UK
31 P14 **Edinburgh** Indiana, N USA
96 J12 **Edinburgh** ✈ S Scotland, UK
116 L8 **Edineț** var. Edineţi, Rus. Yedintsy. NW Moldova
Edineţi see Edineț
Edingen see Enghien
136 B9 **Edirne** Eng. Adrianople; anc. Adrianopolis, Hadrianopolis. Edirne, NW Turkey
136 B11 **Edirne** ◈ province NW Turkey
18 K15 **Edison** New Jersey, NE USA
21 S15 **Edisto Island** South Carolina, SE USA
21 R14 **Edisto River** ∽ South Carolina, SE USA
33 S10 **Edith, Mount** ▲ Montana, NW USA
27 N10 **Edmond** Oklahoma, C USA
32 H8 **Edmonds** Washington, NW USA
11 Q14 **Edmonton** Alberta, SW Canada
20 K7 **Edmonton** Kentucky, S USA
11 Q14 **Edmonton** ✈ Alberta, SW Canada
29 P3 **Edmore** North Dakota, N USA
13 N13 **Edmundston** New Brunswick, SE Canada
25 U12 **Edna** Texas, SW USA
39 X14 **Edna Bay** Kosciusko Island, Alaska, USA
77 U16 **Edo** ◈ state S Nigeria
106 F6 **Edolo** Lombardia, N Italy
64 L6 **Edoras Bank** undersea feature C Atlantic Ocean
96 G7 **Edrachillis Bay** bay NW Scotland, UK
136 B12 **Edremit** Balıkesir, NW Turkey
136 B12 **Edremit Körfezi** gulf NW Turkey
95 P14 **Edsbro** Stockholm, C Sweden
95 N18 **Edsbruk** Kalmar, S Sweden
94 M12 **Edsbyn** Gävleborg, C Sweden
11 O14 **Edson** Alberta, SW Canada
62 K13 **Eduardo Castex** La Pampa, C Argentina
58 F12 **Eduardo Gomes** ✈ (Manaus) Amazonas, NW Brazil
Edwardesabad see Bannu
67 U9 **Edward, Lake** var. Albert Edward Nyanza, Edward Nyanza, Lac Idi Amin, Lake Rutanzige. ◎ Uganda/Dem. Rep. Congo (Zaire)
Edward Nyanza see Edward, Lake
22 K5 **Edwards** Mississippi, S USA
25 O10 **Edwards Plateau** plain Texas, SW USA
30 J11 **Edwards River** ∽ Illinois, N USA
30 K15 **Edwardsville** Illinois, N USA
195 O13 **Edward VII Peninsula** peninsula Antarctica
195 X4 **Edward VIII Gulf** bay Antarctica
10 J11 **Edziza, Mount** ▲ British Columbia, W Canada
8 K10 **Edzo** prev. Rae-Edzo. Northwest Territories, NW Canada
39 N12 **Eek** Alaska, USA
99 D16 **Eeklo** var. Eekloo. Oost-Vlaanderen, NW Belgium
Eekloo see Eeklo
39 N12 **Eek River** ∽ Alaska, USA
98 N6 **Eelde** Drenthe, NE Netherlands
34 L5 **Eel River** ∽ California, W USA
31 P12 **Eel River** ∽ Indiana, N USA
Eems see Ems
98 O4 **Eemshaven** Groningen, NE Netherlands
98 O5 **Eems Kanaal** canal NE Netherlands
98 M11 **Eerbeek** Gelderland, E Netherlands
99 C17 **Eernegem** West-Vlaanderen, W Belgium
99 J15 **Eersel** Noord-Brabant, S Netherlands
Eesti Vabariik see Estonia
187 R14 **Efate** var. Éfaté, Fr. Vaté; prev. Sandwich Island. island C Vanuatu
109 S4 **Eferding** Oberösterreich, N Austria
30 M15 **Effingham** Illinois, N USA
117 N15 **Eforie-Nord** Constanța, SE Romania
117 N15 **Eforie Sud** Constanța, E Romania
Efyrnwy, Afon see Vyrnwy
163 N7 **Eg** Hentiy, N Mongolia
107 G23 **Egadi, Isole** island group S Italy
35 X6 **Egan Range** ▲▲ Nevada, W USA
14 K12 **Eganville** Ontario, SE Canada
Ege Denizi see Aegean Sea
39 O14 **Egegik** Alaska, USA
111 L21 **Eger** Ger. Erlau. Heves, NE Hungary
Eger see Cheb, Czech Republic
Eger see Ohre, Czech Republic/Germany
173 P8 **Egeria Fracture Zone** tectonic feature W Indian Ocean
95 C17 **Egersund** Rogaland, S Norway
108 J7 **Egg** Vorarlberg, NW Austria
101 H14 **Egge-gebirge** ▲ C Germany
109 Q4 **Eggelsberg** Oberösterreich, N Austria
109 W2 **Eggenburg** Niederösterreich, NE Austria
101 N22 **Eggenfelden** Bayern, SE Germany
18 J17 **Egg Harbor City** New Jersey, NE USA
65 G25 **Egg Island** island W Saint Helena
183 N14 **Egg Lagoon** Tasmania, SE Australia
99 I20 **Éghezée** Namur, C Belgium
92 L2 **Egilsstadhir** Austurland, E Iceland
Egina see Aígina
Egindibulaq see Yegindybulak
Egio see Aígio
103 N12 **Égletons** Corrèze, C France
98 H9 **Egmond aan Zee** Noord-Holland, NW Netherlands
Egmont see Taranaki, Mount
184 J10 **Egmont, Cape** headland North Island, NZ
Egoli see Johannesburg
Egri Palanka see Kriva Palanka
95 G23 **Egtved** Vejle, C Denmark
123 U5 **Egvekinot** Chukotskiy Avtonomnyy Okrug, NE Russian Federation

◆ Country ● Country Capital ◇ Dependent Territory ○ Dependent Territory Capital ◈ Administrative Region ✈ International Airport ▲ Mountain ▲▲ Mountain Range ⊼ Volcano ∽ River ◎ Lake ⊠ Reservoir

75 V9 **Egypt** *off.* Arab Republic of Egypt, *Ar.* Jumhūrīyah Miṣr al 'Arabīyah; *prev.* United Arab Republic, *anc.* Aegyptus. ◆ *republic* NE Africa
30 L17 **Egypt, Lake Of** ⊡ Illinois, N USA
Ehen Hudag *see* Alxa Zuoqi
164 F14 **Ehime** *off.* Ehime-ken. ⬖ *prefecture* Shikoku, SW Japan
101 I23 **Ehingen** Baden-Württemberg, S Germany
Ehinos *see* Echínos
21 R14 **Ehrhardt** South Carolina, SE USA
108 L7 **Ehrwald** Tirol, W Austria
191 W6 **Eiao** *island* Îles Marquises, NE French Polynesia
105 P2 **Eibar** País Vasco, N Spain
98 O11 **Eibergen** Gelderland, E Netherlands
109 V9 **Eibiswald** Steiermark, SE Austria
109 P8 **Eichham** ▲ SW Austria
101 J15 **Eichsfeld** *hill range* C Germany
101 K21 **Eichstätt** Bayern, SE Germany
100 H8 **Eider** ≈ N Germany
94 E13 **Eidfjord** Hordaland, S Norway
94 D13 **Eidfjorden** *fjord* S Norway
94 F9 **Eidsvåg** Møre og Romsdal, S Norway
95 I14 **Eidsvoll** Akershus, S Norway
92 N2 **Eidsvollfjellet** ▲ NW Svalbard
Eier-Berg *see* Suur Munamägi
101 D18 **Eifel** *plateau* W Germany
108 E9 **Eiger** ▲ C Switzerland
96 G10 **Eigg** *island* W Scotland, UK
155 D24 **Eight Degree Channel** *channel* India/Maldives
44 G1 **Eight Mile Rock** Grand Bahama Island, N Bahamas
194 J9 **Eights Coast** *physical region* Antarctica
180 K6 **Eighty Mile Beach** *beach* Western Australia
99 L18 **Eijsden** Limburg, SE Netherlands
95 G15 **Eikeren** ⊚ S Norway
Eil *see* Eyl
Eilat *see* Elat
183 O12 **Eildon** Victoria, SE Australia
183 O12 **Eildon, Lake** ⊚ Victoria, SE Australia
80 E8 **Eilei** Northern Kordofan, C Sudan
101 N15 **Eilenburg** Sachsen, E Germany
94 H13 **Eina** Oppland, S Norway
Ein 'Avedat *see* En 'Avedat
101 I14 **Einbeck** Niedersachsen, C Germany
99 K15 **Eindhoven** Noord-Brabant, S Netherlands
108 G8 **Einsiedeln** Schwyz, NE Switzerland
Eipel *see* Ipel'
Éire *see* Ireland, Republic of
Éireann, Muir *see* Irish Sea
Eirik Outer Ridge *see* Eirik Ridge
64 I6 **Eirik Ridge** *var.* Eirik Outer Ridge. *undersea feature* E Labrador Sea
92 I3 **Eiríksjökull** ▲ C Iceland
59 B14 **Eirunepé** Amazonas, N Brazil
99 L17 **Eisden** Limburg, NE Belgium
83 F18 **Eiseb** ≈ Botswana/Namibia
Eisen *see* Yŏngch'ŏn
101 J16 **Eisenach** Thüringen, C Germany
Eisenburg *see* Vasvár
109 U6 **Eisenerz** Steiermark, SE Austria
100 Q13 **Eisenhüttenstadt** Brandenburg, E Germany
109 U10 **Eisenkappel** *Slvn.* Železna Kapela. Kärnten, S Austria
Eisenmarkt *see* Hunedoara
109 Y5 **Eisenstadt** Burgenland, E Austria
Eishū *see* Yŏngju
119 H15 **Eišiškes** Šalčininkai, SE Lithuania
101 L15 **Eisleben** Sachsen-Anhalt, C Germany
190 I3 **Eita** Tarawa, W Kiribati
Eitape *see* Aitape
105 V11 **Eivissa** *var.* Iviza, *Cast.* Ibiza; *anc.* Ebusus. Eivissa, Spain, W Mediterranean Sea
105 V10 **Eivissa** *var.* Iviza, *Cast.* Ibiza; *anc.* Ebusus. *island* Islas Baleares, Spain, W Mediterranean Sea
105 R4 **Ejea de los Caballeros** Aragón, NE Spain
40 E8 **Ejido Insurgentes** Baja California Sur, W Mexico
162 I12 **Ejin Qi** *var.* Dalain Hob. Nei Mongol Zizhiqu, N China
Ejmiadzın *see* Ejmiatsin
137 T12 **Ejmiatsin** *var.* Ejmiadzın, Etchmiadzin, *Rus.* Echmiadzin. W Armenia
77 P16 **Ejura** C Ghana
41 R16 **Ejutla** *var.* Ejutla de Crespo. Oaxaca, SE Mexico
Ejutla de Crespo *see* Ejutla
33 Y10 **Ekalaka** Montana, NW USA
Ekapa *see* Cape Town
128 **Ekaterinodar** *see* Krasnodar
93 L20 **Ekenäs** *Fin.* Tammisaari. Etelä-Suomi, SW Finland
Ekerem *see* Okarem
184 M13 **Eketahuna** Manawatu-Wanganui, North Island, NZ
Ekhínos *see* Echínos
123 U5 **Ekiatapskiy Khrebet** ⛰ NE Russian Federation
145 T8 **Ekibastuz** Pavlodar, NE Kazakhstan
123 R13 **Ekimchan** Amurskaya Oblast', SE Russian Federation
95 O15 **Ekoln** ⊚ C Sweden
80 I7 **Ekowit** Red Sea, NE Sudan
95 L19 **Eksjö** Jönköping, S Sweden
93 I15 **Ekträsk** Västerbotten, N Sweden
39 O13 **Ekuk** Alaska, USA
12 F9 **Ekwan** ≈ Ontario, C Canada
39 O13 **Ekwok** Alaska, USA
166 M6 **Ela** Mandalay, C Burma
El Aaiun *see* El Ayoun
81 N15 **Ēl Ābrēd** Somali, E Ethiopia
115 F22 **Elafónisos** *island* S Greece
115 F22 **Elafonísou, Porthmós** *strait* S Greece
El-Aïoun *see* El Ayoun
75 U8 **El 'Alamein** *var.* Al 'Alamayn. N Egypt
41 Q12 **El Alazán** Veracruz-Llave, C Mexico
57 J18 **El Alto** *var.* La Paz. ✕ (La Paz) La Paz, W Bolivia
Elam *see* Īlām
El Amparo *see* El Amparo de Apure
54 I8 **El Amparo de Apure** *var.* El Amparo. Apure, C Venezuela
171 R13 **Elara** Pulau Ambelau, E Indonesia
El Araïch/El Araïche *see* Larache
40 D6 **El Arco** Baja California, NW Mexico
75 X7 **El 'Arîsh** *var.* Al 'Arīsh. NE Egypt
115 L25 **Elása** *island* SE Greece
El Asnam *see* Chlef
Elassón *see* Elassóna
115 E15 **Elassóna** *prev.* Elassón. Thessalía, C Greece
105 N2 **El Astillero** Cantabria, N Spain
138 F14 **Elat** *var.* Eilat, Elath. Southern, S Israel
Elat, Gulf of *see* Aqaba, Gulf of
Elath *see* Elat, Israel
Elath *see* Al 'Aqabah, Jordan
115 C17 **Eláti** ▲ Lefkáda, Iónioi Nísoi, Greece, C Mediterranean Sea
188 L16 **Elato Atoll** *atoll* Caroline Islands, C Micronesia
80 C7 **El'Atrun** Northern Darfur, NW Sudan
74 H6 **El Ayoun** *var.* El Aaiun, El-Aïoun, La Youne. NE Morocco
137 N14 **Elâzığ** *var.* Elâziz. Elâzığ, E Turkey
137 O14 **Elâzığ** *var.* Elâziz. ⬖ *province* C Turkey
Elâziz *see* Elâzığ
Azraq, Bahr el *see* Blue Nile
23 Q7 **Elba** Alabama, S USA
106 E13 **Elba, Isola d'** *island* Archipelago Toscano, C Italy
54 F6 **El Banco** Magdalena, N Colombia
El Barco *see* O Barco
104 L8 **El Barco de Ávila** Castilla-León, N Spain
El Barco de Valdeorras *see* O Barco
138 H7 **El Barouk, Jabal** ⛰ C Lebanon
113 L20 **Elbasan** *var.* Elbasani. Elbasan, C Albania
113 L20 **Elbasan** ⬖ *district* C Albania
Elbasani *see* Elbasan
54 K6 **El Baúl** Cojedes, C Venezuela
86 D11 **Elbe** *Cz.* Labe. ≈ Czech Republic/Germany
100 L13 **Elbe-Havel-Kanal** *canal* E Germany
100 K9 **Elbe-Lübeck-Kanal** *canal* N Germany
El Beni *see* Beni
138 H7 **El Beqaa** *var.* Al Biqā', Bekaa Valley. *valley* E Lebanon
25 R6 **Elbert** Texas, SW USA
37 R5 **Elbert, Mount** ▲ Colorado, C USA
23 U3 **Elberton** Georgia, SE USA
100 K11 **Elbe-Seiten-Kanal** *canal* N Germany
102 M4 **Elbeuf** Seine-Maritime, N France
Elbing *see* Elbląg
136 M15 **Elbistan** Kahramanmaraş, S Turkey
110 K7 **Elbląg** *var.* Elblag, *Ger.* Elbing. Warmińsko-Mazurskie, NE Poland
43 N10 **El Bluff** Región Autónoma Atlántico Sur, SE Nicaragua
63 H17 **El Bolsón** Río Negro, W Argentina
105 P11 **El Bonillo** Castilla-La Mancha, C Spain
El Bordo *see* Patía
El Boulaida/El Boulaïda *see* Blida
11 T16 **Elbow** Saskatchewan, S Canada
29 S7 **Elbow Lake** Minnesota, N USA
129 N16 **El'brus** *var.* Gora El'brus. ▲ SW Russian Federation
El'brus, Gora *see* El'brus
128 M15 **El'brusskiy** Karachayevo-Cherkesskaya Respublika, SW Russian Federation
81 D14 **El Buhayrat** *var.* Lakes State. ⬖ *state* S Sudan
El Bur *see* Ceel Buur
98 L10 **Elburg** Gelderland, E Netherlands
105 O6 **El Burgo de Osma** Castilla-León, C Spain
Elburz Mountains *see* Alborz, Reshteh-ye Kūhhā-ye
35 V17 **El Cajon** California, W USA
63 H22 **El Calafate** *var.* Calafate. Santa Cruz, S Argentina
55 Q8 **El Callao** Bolívar, E Venezuela
25 U12 **El Campo** Texas, SW USA
54 I7 **El Cantón** Barinas, W Venezuela
35 Q8 **El Capitan** ▲ California, W USA
54 H5 **El Carmelo** Zulia, NW Venezuela
62 J5 **El Carmen** Jujuy, NW Argentina
54 E5 **El Carmen de Bolívar** Bolívar, NW Colombia
55 O8 **El Casabe** Bolívar, SE Venezuela
42 M12 **El Castillo de La Concepción** Río San Juan, SE Nicaragua
El Cayo *see* San Ignacio
35 X17 **El Centro** California, W USA
55 N6 **El Chaparro** Anzoátegui, NE Venezuela
105 S12 **Elche** *var.* Elx-Elche; *anc.* Ilici, *Lat.* Illicis. País Valenciano, E Spain
105 Q12 **Elche de la Sierra** Castilla-La Mancha, C Spain
41 U15 **El Chichonal, Volcán** Ж SE Mexico
40 C2 **El Chinero** Baja California, NW Mexico
181 R1 **Elcho Island** *island* Wessel Islands, Northern Territory, N Australia
63 H18 **El Corcovado** Chubut, SW Argentina
105 R12 **Elda** País Valenciano, E Spain
100 M10 **Elde** ≈ NE Germany
98 L12 **Elden** Gelderland, E Netherlands
81 J16 **El Der** *spring/well* S Ethiopia
El Dere *see* Ceel Dheere
40 E3 **El Desemboque** Sonora, NW Mexico
54 F5 **El Difícil** *var.* Ariguaní. Magdalena, N Colombia
123 R10 **El'dikan** Respublika Sakha (Yakutiya), NE Russian Federation
El Djazaïr *see* Alger
El Djelfa *see* Djelfa
29 X15 **Eldon** Iowa, C USA
27 U5 **Eldon** Missouri, C USA
54 E13 **El Doncello** Caquetá, S Colombia
29 W13 **Eldora** Iowa, C USA
60 G12 **Eldorado** Misiones, NE Argentina
40 I9 **El Dorado** Sinaloa, C Mexico
27 U14 **El Dorado** Arkansas, C USA
30 M17 **Eldorado** Illinois, N USA
27 O6 **El Dorado** Kansas, C USA
26 K12 **Eldorado** Oklahoma, C USA
25 O9 **Eldorado** Texas, SW USA
55 Q8 **El Dorado** Bolívar, E Venezuela
54 F10 **El Dorado** ✕ (Bogotá) Cundinamarca, C Colombia
El Dorado *see* California
27 O6 **El Dorado Lake** ⊡ Kansas, C USA
27 S6 **El Dorado Springs** Missouri, C USA
81 H18 **Eldoret** Rift Valley, W Kenya
29 Z14 **Eldridge** Iowa, C USA
95 J21 **Eldsberga** Halland, S Sweden
25 R4 **Electra** Texas, SW USA
37 Q7 **Electra Lake** ⊡ Colorado, C USA
38 B8 **Eleele** *Haw.* 'Ele'ele. Kauai, Hawaii, USA, C Pacific Ocean
Elefantes *see* Olifants
115 H19 **Elefsína** *prev.* Elevsís. Attikí, C Greece
115 G19 **Eléftheres** *anc.* Eleutherae. *site of ancient city* Attikí/Stereá Ellás, C Greece
114 I13 **Eleftheroúpoli** *prev.* Elevtheroúpolis. Anatolikí Makedonía kai Thráki, NE Greece
74 F10 **El Eglab** ▲ SW Algeria
118 F10 **Eleja** Jelgava, C Latvia
Elek *see* Ilek
119 G14 **Elektrėnai** Kaišiadorys, SE Lithuania
128 L3 **Elektrostal'** Moskovskaya Oblast', W Russian Federation
81 H15 **Elemi Triangle** *disputed region* Kenya/Sudan
54 G16 **El Encanto** Amazonas, S Colombia
37 R14 **Elephant Butte Reservoir** ⊡ New Mexico, SW USA
Éléphant, Chaîne de l' *see* Dâmrei, Chuŏr Phmun
194 G2 **Elephant Island** *island* South Shetland Islands, Antarctica
Elephant River *see* Olifants
El Escorial *see* San Lorenzo de El Escorial
Élesd *see* Aleşd
114 F11 **Eleshnitsa** ≈ W Bulgaria
137 S13 **Eleşkirt** Ağrı, E Turkey
42 F5 **El Estor** Izabal, E Guatemala
Eleutherae *see* Eléftheres
44 I2 **Eleuthera Island** *island* N Bahamas
37 S5 **Elevenmile Canyon Reservoir** ⊡ Colorado, C USA
27 W8 **Eleven Point River** ≈ Arkansas/Missouri, C USA
Elevsís *see* Elefsína
Elevtheroúpolis *see* Eleftheroúpoli
75 W8 **El Faiyûm** *var.* Al Fayyūm. N Egypt
80 B10 **El Fasher** *var.* Al Fāshir. Northern Darfur, W Sudan
75 W8 **El Fashn** *var.* Al Fashn. C Egypt
El Ferrol/El Ferrol del Caudillo *see* Ferrol
39 W13 **Elfin Cove** Chichagof Island, Alaska, USA
105 W4 **El Fluvià** ≈ NE Spain
40 H7 **El Fuerte** Sinaloa, W Mexico
80 D11 **El Fula** Western Kordofan, C Sudan
El Gedaref *see* Gedaref
80 A10 **El Geneina** *var.* Ajjinena, Al-Genain, Al Junaynah. Western Darfur, W Sudan
96 J8 **Elgin** NE Scotland, UK
30 M10 **Elgin** Illinois, N USA
29 P14 **Elgin** Nebraska, C USA
35 Y9 **Elgin** Nevada, W USA
28 L6 **Elgin** North Dakota, N USA
26 M12 **Elgin** Oklahoma, C USA
25 T10 **Elgin** Texas, SW USA
123 R9 **El'ginskiy** Respublika Sakha (Yakutiya), NE Russian Federation
75 W8 **El Gîza** *var.* Al Jīzah, Gîza, Gizeh. N Egypt
74 J8 **El Goléa** *var.* Al Golea. C Algeria
40 D2 **El Golfo de Santa Clara** Sonora, NW Mexico
81 G18 **Elgon, Mount** ▲ E Uganda
94 I10 **Elgpiggen** ▲ S Norway
105 T4 **El Grado** Aragón, NE Spain
40 L6 **El Guaje, Laguna** ⊡ NE Mexico
54 H6 **El Guayabo** Zulia, W Venezuela
77 O6 **El Guettâra** *oasis* N Mali
76 J6 **El Ḥammâmi** *desert* N Mauritania
76 M5 **El Ḥank** *cliff* N Mauritania
El Haseke *see* Al Ḥasakah
80 H10 **El Hawata** Gedaref, E Sudan
El Higo *see* Higos
171 T16 **Eliase** Pulau Selaru, E Indonesia
Elías Piña *see* Comendador
25 R6 **Eliasville** Texas, SW USA
Elichpur *see* Achalpur
37 V13 **Elida** New Mexico, SW USA
115 F18 **Elikónas** ⛰ C Greece
67 T10 **Elila** ≈ W Dem. Rep. Congo (Zaire)
39 N9 **Elim** Alaska, USA
Elimberrum *see* Auch
Eliocroca *see* Lorca
61 B16 **Elisa** Santa Fe, C Argentina
Elisabethstedt *see* Dumbrăveni
Élisabethville *see* Lubumbashi
129 O13 **Elista** Respublika Kalmykiya, SW Russian Federation
182 I9 **Elizabeth** South Australia
21 Q3 **Elizabeth** West Virginia, NE USA
19 Q9 **Elizabeth, Cape** *headland* Maine, NE USA
21 Y8 **Elizabeth City** North Carolina, SE USA
21 P8 **Elizabethton** Tennessee, S USA
30 M17 **Elizabethtown** Illinois, N USA
20 K6 **Elizabethtown** Kentucky, S USA
18 L7 **Elizabethtown** New York, NE USA
21 U11 **Elizabethtown** North Carolina, SE USA
18 G15 **Elizabethtown** Pennsylvania, NE USA
74 E6 **El-Jadida** *prev.* Mazagan. W Morocco
El Jafr *see* Jafr, Qā' al
80 F11 **El Jebelein** White Nile, E Sudan
110 N8 **Ełk** *Ger.* Lyck. Warmińsko-Mazurskie, NE Poland
110 O8 **Ełk** ≈ NE Poland
29 Y12 **Elkader** Iowa, C USA
80 G9 **El Kamlin** Gezira, C Sudan
33 N11 **Elk City** Idaho, NW USA
26 K10 **Elk City** Oklahoma, C USA
27 P7 **Elk City Lake** ⊡ Kansas, C USA
34 M5 **Elk Creek** California, W USA
28 J10 **Elk Creek** ≈ South Dakota, N USA
74 M5 **El Kef** *var.* Al Kāf, Le Kef. NW Tunisia
74 F7 **El Kelâa Srarhna** *var.* Kal al Sraghna. C Morocco
El Kerak *see* Al Karak
11 P17 **Elkford** British Columbia, SW Canada
El Khalil *see* Hebron
80 E7 **El Khandaq** Northern, N Sudan
75 W10 **El Khârga** *var.* Al Khārijah. C Egypt
31 P11 **Elkhart** Indiana, N USA
26 H7 **Elkhart** Kansas, C USA
25 V8 **Elkhart** Texas, SW USA
30 M7 **Elkhart Lake** ⊚ Wisconsin, N USA
El Khartûm *see* Khartoum
37 Q3 **Elkhead Mountains** ⛰ Colorado, C USA
18 I12 **Elk Hill** ▲ Pennsylvania, NE USA
138 G8 **El Khiyam** *var.* Al Khiyām, Khiam. S Lebanon
29 S15 **Elkhorn** Nebraska, C USA
30 M9 **Elkhorn** Wisconsin, N USA
29 R14 **Elkhorn River** ≈ Nebraska, C USA
129 O16 **El'khotovo** Respublika Severnaya Osetiya, SW Russian Federation
114 L10 **Elkhovo** *prev.* Kizilagach. Yambol, E Bulgaria
21 R8 **Elkin** North Carolina, SE USA
21 S4 **Elkins** West Virginia, NE USA
195 X3 **Elkins, Mount** ▲ Antarctica
14 G8 **Elk Lake** Ontario, S Canada
31 P6 **Elk Lake** ⊚ Michigan, N USA
18 F12 **Elkland** Pennsylvania, NE USA
35 W3 **Elko** Nevada, W USA
11 R14 **Elk Point** Alberta, SW Canada
29 R12 **Elk Point** South Dakota, N USA
29 V8 **Elk River** Minnesota, N USA
20 J10 **Elk River** ≈ Alabama/Tennessee, S USA
21 R4 **Elk River** ≈ West Virginia, NE USA
20 I7 **Elkton** Kentucky, S USA
21 Y2 **Elkton** Maryland, NE USA
29 R10 **Elkton** South Dakota, N USA
20 I10 **Elkton** Tennessee, S USA
21 U5 **Elkton** Virginia, NE USA
El Kuneitra *see* Al Qunayṭirah
81 L15 **El Kure** Somali, E Ethiopia
80 D12 **El Lagowa** Western Kordofan, C Sudan
39 S12 **Ellamar** Alaska, USA
Ellás *see* Greece
23 S6 **Ellaville** Georgia, SE USA
8 I3 **Ellef Ringnes Island** *island* Nunavut, N Canada
29 V10 **Ellendale** Minnesota, N USA
29 P7 **Ellendale** North Dakota, N USA
36 M6 **Ellen, Mount** ▲ Utah, W USA
32 I9 **Ellensburg** Washington, NW USA
18 K12 **Ellenville** New York, NE USA
Ellep *see* Lib
21 T10 **Ellerbe** North Carolina, SE USA
9 N2 **Ellesmere Island** *island* Queen Elizabeth Islands, Nunavut, N Canada
185 H19 **Ellesmere, Lake** ⊚ South Island, NZ
97 K18 **Ellesmere Port** C England, UK
31 O14 **Ellettsville** Indiana, N USA
99 E19 **Ellezelles** Hainaut, SW Belgium
8 L7 **Ellice** ≈ Nunavut, NE Canada
Ellice Islands *see* Tuvalu
Ellichpur *see* Achalpur
21 W3 **Ellicott City** Maryland, NE USA
23 S2 **Ellijay** Georgia, SE USA
27 W7 **Ellington** Missouri, C USA
26 L5 **Ellinwood** Kansas, C USA
83 J24 **Elliot** Eastern Cape, SE South Africa
14 D10 **Elliot Lake** Ontario, S Canada
181 X6 **Elliot, Mount** ▲ Queensland, E Australia
21 T5 **Elliott Knob** ▲ Virginia, NE USA
26 K4 **Ellis** Kansas, C USA
182 F8 **Elliston** South Australia
22 M7 **Ellisville** Mississippi, S USA
105 V5 **El Llobregat** ≈ NE Spain
96 L9 **Ellon** NE Scotland, UK
Ellore *see* Elūru
21 S13 **Elloree** South Carolina, SE USA
26 M4 **Ellsworth** Kansas, C USA
19 S7 **Ellsworth** Maine, NE USA
30 I6 **Ellsworth** Wisconsin, N USA
26 M11 **Ellsworth, Lake** ⊡ Oklahoma, C USA
194 K9 **Ellsworth Land** *physical region* Antarctica
194 L9 **Ellsworth Mountains** ⛰ Antarctica
101 J21 **Ellwangen** Baden-Württemberg, S Germany
18 B14 **Ellwood City** Pennsylvania, NE USA
108 H8 **Elm** Glarus, NE Switzerland
32 G9 **Elma** Washington, NW USA
121 V13 **El Maḥalla el Kubra** *var.* Al Maḥallah al Kubrá, Mahalla el Kubra. N Egypt
74 E9 **El Mahbas** *var.* Mahbés. SW Western Sahara
63 H17 **El Maitén** Chubut, W Argentina
136 E16 **Elmalı** Antalya, SW Turkey
80 G10 **El Manaqil** Gezira, C Sudan
54 M12 **El Mango** Amazonas, S Venezuela
75 W7 **El Manṣûra** *var.* Al Manṣūrah, Manṣûra. N Egypt
55 P8 **El Manteco** Bolívar, E Venezuela
29 O16 **Elm Creek** Nebraska, C USA
El Mediyya *see* Médéa
77 V9 **Elméki** Agadez, C Niger
108 K7 **Elmen** Tirol, W Austria
18 I16 **Elmer** New Jersey, NE USA
138 G6 **El Mina** *var.* Al Mīnā'. N Lebanon
75 W9 **El Minya** *var.* Al Minyā, Minya. C Egypt
14 F15 **Elmira** Ontario, S Canada
18 G11 **Elmira** New York, NE USA
36 K13 **El Mirage** Arizona, SW USA
29 O7 **Elm Lake** ⊡ South Dakota, N USA
El Moján *see* San Rafael
105 N7 **El Molar** Madrid, C Spain
76 L7 **El Mrâyer** *well* C Mauritania
76 L5 **El Mreiti** *well* N Mauritania
76 L8 **El Mreyyé** *desert* E Mauritania
29 P8 **Elm River** ≈ North Dakota/South Dakota, N USA
100 I9 **Elmshorn** Schleswig-Holstein, N Germany
80 D12 **El Muglad** Western Kordofan, C Sudan
El Muwaqqar *see* Al Muwaqqar
14 G14 **Elmvale** Ontario, S Canada
30 K12 **Elmwood** Illinois, N USA
26 J8 **Elmwood** Oklahoma, C USA
103 P17 **Elne** *anc.* Illiberis. Pyrénées-Orientales, S France
54 F11 **El Nevado, Cerro** *elevation* C Colombia
171 N5 **El Nido** Palawan, W Philippines
62 I12 **El Nihuil** Mendoza, W Argentina
75 W7 **El Nouzha** ✕ (Alexandria) N Egypt
80 E10 **El Obeid** *var.* Al Obayyid, Al Ubayyiḍ. Northern Kordofan, C Sudan
41 O13 **El Oro** México, S Mexico
56 B8 **El Oro** ⬖ *province* SW Ecuador
61 B19 **Elortondo** Santa Fe, C Argentina
54 J8 **Elorza** Apure, C Venezuela
El Ouâdi *see* El Oued
74 L7 **El Oued** *var.* Al Oued, El Ouâdi, El Wad. NE Algeria
36 L15 **Eloy** Arizona, SW USA
55 Q7 **El Palmar** Bolívar, E Venezuela
40 K8 **El Palmito** Durango, W Mexico
55 P7 **El Pao** Bolívar, E Venezuela
54 K5 **El Pao** Cojedes, N Venezuela
42 J7 **El Paraíso** El Paraíso, S Honduras
42 I7 **El Paraíso** ⬖ *department* SE Honduras
30 L12 **El Paso** Illinois, N USA
24 G8 **El Paso** Texas, SW USA
24 G8 **El Paso** ✕ Texas, SW USA
105 U7 **El Perello** Cataluña, NE Spain
55 P5 **El Pilar** Sucre, NE Venezuela
42 F7 **El Pital, Cerro** ▲ El Salvador/Honduras
35 Q9 **El Portal** California, W USA
40 J3 **El Porvenir** Chihuahua, N Mexico
43 U14 **El Porvenir** San Blas, N Panama
105 W6 **El Prat de Llobregat** Cataluña, NE Spain
42 H5 **El Progreso** Yoro, NW Honduras
42 A2 **El Progreso** *off.* Departamento de El Progreso. ⬖ *department* C Guatemala
El Progreso *see* Guastatoya
104 L9 **El Puente del Arzobispo** Castilla-La Mancha, C Spain
104 J15 **El Puerto de Santa María** Andalucía, S Spain
62 I8 **El Puesto** Catamarca, NW Argentina
El Qâhira *see* Cairo
75 V10 **El Qaṣr** *var.* Al Qaṣr. C Egypt
El Qatrani *see* Al Qaṭrānah
40 I10 **El Quelite** Sinaloa, C Mexico
62 G9 **Elqui, Río** ≈ N Chile
El Quneitra *see* Al Qunayṭirah
El Quseir *see* Al Quṣayr
El Quweira *see* Al Quwayrah
141 O15 **El-Rahaba** ✕ (Ṣan'ā') W Yemen
42 M10 **El Rama** Región Autónoma Atlántico Sur, SE Nicaragua
43 W16 **El Real** *var.* El Real de Santa María. Darién, SE Panama
El Real de Santa María *see* El Real
26 M10 **El Reno** Oklahoma, C USA
40 K9 **El Rodeo** Durango, C Mexico
104 J13 **El Ronquillo** Andalucía, S Spain
11 S16 **Elrose** Saskatchewan, S Canada
30 K8 **Elroy** Wisconsin, N USA
25 S17 **Elsa** Texas, SW USA
75 W8 **El Ṣaff** *var.* Aṣ Ṣaff. N Egypt
40 J10 **El Salto** Durango, C Mexico
42 D8 **El Salvador** *off.* Republica de El Salvador. ◆ *republic* Central America
54 K7 **El Samán de Apure** Apure, C Venezuela
14 D7 **Elsas** Ontario, S Canada
40 F3 **El Sásabe** *var.* Aduana del Sásabe. Sonora, NW Mexico
Elsass *see* Alsace
40 J5 **El Sáuz** Chihuahua, N Mexico
27 W4 **Elsberry** Missouri, C USA
45 P9 **El Seibo** *var.* Santa Cruz de El Seibo, Santa Cruz del Seibo. E Dominican Republic
42 B7 **El Semillero Barra Nahualate** Escuintla, SW Guatemala
Elsene *see* Ixelles
159 N11 **Elsen Nur** ⊚ C China
36 L6 **Elsinore** Utah, W USA
Elsinore *see* Helsingør
99 L18 **Elsloo** Limburg, SE Netherlands
60 G13 **El Soberbio** Misiones, NE Argentina
55 N6 **El Socorro** Guárico, C Venezuela
54 L6 **El Sombrero** Guárico, N Venezuela
98 L10 **Elspeet** Gelderland, E Netherlands
98 L12 **Elst** Gelderland, E Netherlands
101 O15 **Elsterwerda** Brandenburg, E Germany
40 J4 **El Sueco** Chihuahua, N Mexico
El Suweida *see* As Suwaydā'
El Suweis *see* Suez
54 D12 **El Tambo** Cauca, SW Colombia
175 T13 **Eltanin Fracture Zone** *tectonic feature* SE Pacific Ocean
105 X5 **El Ter** ≈ NE Spain
184 K11 **Eltham** Taranaki, North Island, NZ
55 O6 **El Tigre** Anzoátegui, NE Venezuela
El Tigrito *see* San José de Guanipa
54 J5 **El Tocuyo** Lara, N Venezuela
129 Q10 **El'ton** Volgogradskaya Oblast', SW Russian Federation
32 K10 **Eltopia** Washington, NW USA
61 A18 **El Trébol** Santa Fe, C Argentina
40 J13 **El Tuito** Jalisco, SW Mexico
75 X8 **El Ṭûr** *var.* Aṭ Ṭūr. NE Egypt
155 K16 **Elūru** *prev.* Ellore. Andhra Pradesh, E India
118 H13 **Elva** *Ger.* Elwa. Tartumaa, SE Estonia
37 R9 **El Vado Reservoir** ⊡ New Mexico, SW USA
43 S15 **El Valle** Coclé, C Panama
104 I11 **Elvas** Portalegre, C Portugal
54 K7 **El Venado** Apure, C Venezuela
105 V6 **El Vendrell** Cataluña, NE Spain
94 I13 **Elverum** Hedmark, S Norway
42 I9 **El Viejo** Chinandega, NW Nicaragua
54 G7 **El Viejo, Cerro** ▲ C Colombia
54 H6 **El Vigía** Mérida, NW Venezuela
105 Q4 **El Villar de Arnedo** La Rioja, N Spain
59 A14 **Elvira** Amazonas, W Brazil
Elwa *see* Elva
El Wad *see* El Oued
81 K17 **El Wak** North Eastern, NE Kenya
33 R7 **Elwell, Lake** ⊡ Montana, NW USA
31 P13 **Elwood** Indiana, N USA
27 R3 **Elwood** Kansas, C USA
29 N16 **Elwood** Nebraska, C USA
Elx-Elche *see* Elche
97 O20 **Ely** E England, UK
29 X4 **Ely** Minnesota, N USA
35 X6 **Ely** Nevada, W USA
El Yopal *see* Yopal
31 T11 **Elyria** Ohio, N USA
45 S9 **El Yunque** ▲ E Puerto Rico
101 F23 **Elz** ≈ SW Germany
187 R14 **Emae** *island* Shepherd Islands, C Vanuatu
118 I5 **Emajõgi** *Ger.* Embach. ≈ SE Estonia
Emāmrūd *see* Shāhrūd
149 Q2 **Emām Ṣāḥeb** *var.* Emam Saheb, Hazarat Imam. Kunduz, NE Afghanistan
Emāmshahr *see* Shāhrūd
95 M20 **Emån** ≈ S Sweden

◆ Country ● Country Capital ◇ Dependent Territory ○ Dependent Territory Capital ⬖ Administrative Region ✕ International Airport ▲ Mountain ⛰ Mountain Range Ж Volcano ≈ River ⊚ Lake ⊡ Reservoir

144 J11 **Emba** *Kaz.* Embi. Aktyubinsk, W Kazakhstan
144 H12 **Emba** *Kaz.* Zhem. ≈ W Kazakhstan
Embach *see* Emajõgi
62 K5 **Embarcación** Salta, N Argentina
30 M15 **Embarras River** ≈ Illinois, N USA
Embi *see* Emba
81 I19 **Embu** Eastern, C Kenya
100 E10 **Emden** Niedersachsen, NW Germany
29 Q4 **Emerado** North Dakota, N USA
181 X8 **Emerald** Queensland, E Australia
Emerald Isle *see* Montserrat
57 J15 **Emero, Río** ≈ W Bolivia
11 Y17 **Emerson** Manitoba, S Canada
29 T15 **Emerson** Iowa, C USA
29 R13 **Emerson** Nebraska, C USA
36 M5 **Emery** Utah, W USA
Emesa *see* Ḩimş
183 E13 **Emet** Kütahya, W Turkey
186 B8 **Emeti** Western, SW PNG
35 V3 **Emigrant Pass** *pass* Nevada, W USA
78 I6 **Emi Koussi** ▲ N Chad
Emilia *see* Emilia-Romagna
41 V15 **Emiliano Zapata** Chiapas, SE Mexico
106 E9 **Emilia-Romagna** *prev.* Emilia, *anc.* Æmilia. ◈ *region* N Italy
158 J3 **Emin** *var.* Dorbiljin. Xinjiang Uygur Zizhiqu, NW China
149 W8 **Eminābād** Punjab, E Pakistan
21 L5 **Eminence** Kentucky, S USA
27 W7 **Eminence** Missouri, C USA
114 N9 **Emine, Nos** *headland* E Bulgaria
158 I3 **Emin He** ≈ NW China
186 G4 **Emirau Island** *island* N PNG
136 F13 **Emirdağ** Afyon, W Turkey
95 M21 **Emmaboda** Kalmar, S Sweden
118 E5 **Emmaste** Hiiumaa, W Estonia
18 I15 **Emmaus** Pennsylvania, NE USA
183 U4 **Emmaville** New South Wales, SE Australia
108 E9 **Emme** ≈ W Switzerland
98 L8 **Emmeloord** Flevoland, N Netherlands
98 O8 **Emmen** Drenthe, NE Netherlands
108 F8 **Emmen** Luzern, C Switzerland
101 F23 **Emmendingen** Baden-Württemberg, SW Germany
98 P8 **Emmer-Compascuum** Drenthe, NE Netherlands
101 D14 **Emmerich** Nordrhein-Westfalen, W Germany
29 U12 **Emmetsburg** Iowa, C USA
32 M14 **Emmett** Idaho, NW USA
38 M10 **Emmonak** Alaska, USA
Emona *see* Ljubljana
Emonti *see* East London
24 L12 **Emory Peak** ▲ Texas, SW USA
40 F6 **Empalme** Sonora, NW Mexico
83 L23 **Empangeni** KwaZulu/Natal, E South Africa
61 C14 **Empedrado** Corrientes, NE Argentina
192 K3 **Emperor Seamounts** *undersea feature* NW Pacific Ocean
192 L3 **Emperor Trough** *undersea feature* N Pacific Ocean
35 R4 **Empire** Nevada, W USA
Empire State of the South *see* Georgia
Emplawas *see* Amplawas
106 F11 **Empoli** Toscana, C Italy
27 P5 **Emporia** Kansas, C USA
21 W7 **Emporia** Virginia, NE USA
18 E13 **Emporium** Pennsylvania, NE USA
Empty Quarter *see* Ar Rub' al Khālī
100 E10 **Ems** *Dut.* Eems. ≈ NW Germany
100 F13 **Emsdetten** Nordrhein-Westfalen, NW Germany
Ems-Hunte Canal *see* Küstenkanal
100 F10 **Ems-Jade-Kanal** *canal* NW Germany
100 F11 **Emsland** *cultural region* NW Germany
182 D3 **Emu Junction** South Australia
163 T3 **Emur He** ≈ NE China
55 R8 **Enachu Landing** NW Guyana
93 F16 **Enafors** Jämtland, C Sweden
94 N11 **Enånger** Gävleborg, C Sweden
96 G7 **Enard Bay** *bay* NW Scotland, UK
Enareträsk *see* Inarijärvi
171 X14 **Enarotali** Irian Jaya, E Indonesia
138 E12 **En 'Avedat** *var.* Ein 'Avedat, *well* S Israel
165 T2 **Enbetsu** Hokkaidō, NE Japan
61 H16 **Encantadas, Serra das** ▲▲ S Brazil
40 E7 **Encantado, Cerro** ▲ NW Mexico
62 P7 **Encarnación** Itapúa, S Paraguay
40 M12 **Encarnación de Díaz** Jalisco, SW Mexico
77 O17 **Enchi** SW Ghana
25 Q14 **Encinal** Texas, SW USA
35 U17 **Encinitas** California, W USA
25 S16 **Encino** Texas, SW USA
54 H6 **Encontrados** Zulia, NW Venezuela
182 I10 **Encounter Bay** *inlet* South Australia
61 F15 **Encruzilhada** Rio Grande do Sul, S Brazil
61 H16 **Encruzilhada do Sul** Rio Grande do Sul, S Brazil
111 M20 **Encs** Borsod-Abaúj-Zemplén, NE Hungary
193 P3 **Endeavour Seamount** *undersea feature* N Pacific Ocean
181 V1 **Endeavour Strait** *strait* Queensland, NE Australia
171 O16 **Endeh** Flores, S Indonesia
95 G23 **Endelave** *island* C Denmark
191 T4 **Enderbury Island** *atoll* Phoenix Islands, C Kiribati
11 N16 **Enderby** British Columbia, SW Canada
195 W4 **Enderby Land** *physical region* Antarctica
173 N14 **Enderby Plain** *undersea feature* S Indian Ocean
29 Q6 **Enderlin** North Dakota, N USA
Endersdorf *see* Jędrzejów
28 K16 **Enders Reservoir** ⊠ Nebraska, C USA
18 H11 **Endicott** New York, NE USA
39 P7 **Endicott Mountains** ▲▲ Alaska, USA
118 I5 **Endla Raba** *wetland* C Estonia
117 T9 **Enerhodar** Zaporiz'ka Oblast', SE Ukraine
57 F14 **Ene, Río** ≈ C Peru
189 N4 **Enewetak Atoll** *var.* Ānewetak, Eniwetok. *atoll* Ralik Chain, W Marshall Islands
114 L13 **Enez** Edirne, NW Turkey
21 W8 **Enfield** North Carolina, SE USA
186 B7 **Enga** ◈ *province* W PNG
45 Q9 **Engaño, Cabo** *headland* E Dominican Republic
164 U3 **Engaru** Hokkaidō, NE Japan
138 F11 **'En Gedi** Southern, E Israel
108 F9 **Engelberg** Unterwalden, C Switzerland
21 Y9 **Engelhard** North Carolina, SE USA
129 P8 **Engel's** Saratovskaya Oblast', W Russian Federation
101 G24 **Engen** Baden-Württemberg, SW Germany
Engeten *see* Aiud
168 K15 **Enggano, Pulau** *island* W Indonesia
80 J8 **Enghershatu** ▲ N Eritrea
99 F19 **Enghien** *Dut.* Edingen. Hainaut, SW Belgium
27 V12 **England** Arkansas, C USA
97 M20 **England** *Lat.* Anglia. *national region* UK
14 H8 **Englehart** Ontario, S Canada
37 T4 **Englewood** Colorado, C USA
31 O16 **English** Indiana, N USA
39 Q13 **English Bay** Alaska, USA
English Bazar *see* Ingrāj Bāzār
97 N25 **English Channel** *var.* The Channel, *Fr.* la Manche. *channel* NW Europe
194 J7 **English Coast** *physical region* Antarctica
105 S11 **Enguera** País Valenciano, E Spain
118 E8 **Engure** Tukums, W Latvia
118 E8 **Engures Ezers** ◎ NW Latvia
137 R9 **Enguri** *Rus.* Inguri. ≈ NW Georgia
Engyum *see* Gangi
26 M9 **Enid** Oklahoma, C USA
22 L3 **Enid Lake** ⊠ Mississippi, S USA
189 Y2 **Enigu** *island* Ratak Chain, SE Marshall Islands
Enikale Strait *see* Kerch Strait
147 Z8 **Enil'chek** Issyk-Kul'skaya Oblast', E Kyrgyzstan
115 F17 **Enipéfs** ≈ C Greece
165 S4 **Eniwa** Hokkaidō, NE Japan
Eniwetok *see* Enewetak Atoll
Enkeldoorn *see* Chivhu
123 S11 **Enken, Mys** *headland* NE Russian Federation
98 J8 **Enkhuizen** Noord-Holland, NW Netherlands
109 Q4 **Enknach** ≈ N Austria
95 N15 **Enköping** Uppsala, C Sweden
107 K24 **Enna** *var.* Castrogiovanni, Henna. Sicilia, Italy, C Mediterranean Sea
80 D11 **En Nahud** Western Kordofan, C Sudan
138 F8 **En Nâqoûra** *var.* An Nāqūrah. SW Lebanon
En Nazira *see* Nazerat
78 K8 **Ennedi** *plateau* E Chad
101 E15 **Ennepetal** Nordrhein-Westfalen, W Germany
183 P4 **Enngonia** New South Wales, SE Australia
97 C19 **Ennis** *Ir.* Inis. W Ireland
33 R11 **Ennis** Montana, NW USA
25 U7 **Ennis** Texas, SW USA
97 F20 **Enniscorthy** *Ir.* Inis Córthaidh. SE Ireland
97 E15 **Enniskillen** *var.* Inniskilling, *Ir.* Inis Ceithleann. SW Northern Ireland, UK
97 B19 **Ennistimon** *Ir.* Inis Díomáin. W Ireland
109 T4 **Enns** Oberösterreich, N Austria
109 T4 **Enns** ≈ C Austria
93 O16 **Eno** Itä-Suomi, E Finland
24 M5 **Enochs** Texas, SW USA
93 N17 **Enonkoski** Isä-Suomi, E Finland
92 K10 **Enontekiö** *Lapp.* Eanodat. Lappi, N Finland
21 Q11 **Enoree** South Carolina, SE USA
21 P11 **Enoree River** ≈ South Carolina, SE USA
18 M6 **Enosburg Falls** Vermont, NE USA
171 N13 **Enrekang** Sulawesi, C Indonesia
45 N10 **Enriquillo** SW Dominican Republic
45 N9 **Enriquillo, Lago** ◎ SW Dominican Republic
98 L9 **Ens** Flevoland, N Netherlands
98 P11 **Enschede** Overijssel, E Netherlands
40 B2 **Ensenada** Baja California, NW Mexico
101 E20 **Ensheim** ✕ (Saarbrücken) Saarland, W Germany
160 L9 **Enshi** Hubei, C China
164 L14 **Enshū-nada** *gulf* SW Japan
23 O8 **Ensley** Florida, SE USA
Enso *see* Svetogorsk
81 F18 **Entebbe** S Uganda
81 F18 **Entebbe** ✕ C Uganda
101 M18 **Entenbühl** ▲ Czech Republic/Germany
98 N10 **Enter** Overijssel, E Netherlands
23 Q7 **Enterprise** Alabama, S USA
32 L11 **Enterprise** Oregon, NW USA
36 J7 **Enterprise** Utah, W USA
32 J8 **Entiat** Washington, NW USA
105 P15 **Entinas, Punta de las** *headland* S Spain
108 F8 **Entlebuch** Luzern, W Switzerland
108 F8 **Entlebuch** *valley* C Switzerland
63 I22 **Entrada, Punta** *headland* S Argentina
103 O13 **Entraygues-sur-Truyère** Aveyron, S France
187 O14 **Entrecasteaux, Récifs d'** *reef* N New Caledonia
61 C17 **Entre Ríos** *off.* Provincia de Entre Ríos. ◈ *province* NE Argentina
42 K7 **Entre Ríos, Cordillera** ▲▲ Honduras/Nicaragua
104 G9 **Entroncamento** Santarém, C Portugal
77 V16 **Enugu** Enugu, S Nigeria
77 U16 **Enugu** ◈ *state* SE Nigeria
123 V5 **Enurmino** Chukotskiy Avtonomnyy Okrug, NE Russian Federation
54 E9 **Envigado** Antioquia, W Colombia
59 B15 **Envira** Amazonas, W Brazil
Enyélé *see* Enyellé
79 I16 **Enyellé** *var.* Enyélé. La Likouala, NE Congo
101 H21 **Enz** ≈ SW Germany
165 N13 **Enzan** Yamanashi, Honshū, S Japan
104 I2 **Eo** ≈ NW Spain
Eochaill *see* Youghal
Eochaille, Cuan *see* Youghal Bay
107 K22 **Eolie, Isole** *var.* Isole Lipari, *Eng.* Aeolian Islands, Lipari Islands. *island group* S Italy
189 U12 **Eot** *island* Chuuk, C Micronesia
115 J25 **Epáno Archánes** *var.* Áno Arkhánai; *prev.* Epáno Arkhánai. Kríti, Greece, E Mediterranean Sea
Epáno Arkhánai *see* Epáno Archánes
115 G14 **Epanomí** Kentrikí Makedonía, N Greece
98 M10 **Epe** Gelderland, E Netherlands
77 S16 **Epe** Lagos, S Nigeria
79 I17 **Epéna** La Likouala, NE Congo
Eperies/Eperjes *see* Prešov
103 Q4 **Épernay** *anc.* Sparnacum. Marne, N France
36 L5 **Ephraim** Utah, W USA
18 H15 **Ephrata** Pennsylvania, NE USA
32 J8 **Ephrata** Washington, NW USA
187 R14 **Epi** *var.* Épi. *island* C Vanuatu
105 R6 **Épila** Aragón, NE Spain
103 T6 **Épinal** Vosges, NE France
Epiphania *see* Ḩamāh
Epirus *see* Ípeiros
121 P3 **Episkopí** SW Cyprus
Episkopi Bay *see* Episkopí, Kólpos
121 P3 **Episkopí, Kólpos** *var.* Episkopi Bay. *bay* SE Cyprus
Epitoli *see* Pretoria
Epoon *see* Ebon Atoll
Eporedia *see* Ivrea
Eppeschdorf *see* Dumbrăveni
101 H21 **Eppingen** Baden-Württemberg, SW Germany
83 E18 **Epukiro** Omaheke, E Namibia
29 Y13 **Epworth** Iowa, C USA
143 O10 **Eqlīd** *var.* Iqlid. Fārs, C Iran
Equality State *see* Wyoming
79 J18 **Equateur** *off.* Région de l'Equateur. ◈ *region* N Dem. Rep. Congo (Zaire)
151 K22 **Equatorial Channel** *channel* S Maldives
79 B17 **Equatorial Guinea** *off.* Republic of Equatorial Guinea. ◆ *republic* C Africa
121 V11 **Eratosthenes Tablemount** *undersea feature* E Mediterranean Sea
Erautini *see* Johannesburg
136 L12 **Erbaa** Tokat, N Turkey
101 E19 **Erbeskopf** ▲ W Germany
Erbil *see* Arbīl
121 P2 **Ercan** ✕ (Nicosia) N Cyprus
Ercegnovi *see* Herceg-Novi
137 T14 **Erçek Gölü** ◎ E Turkey
137 S14 **Erciş** Van, E Turkey
136 K14 **Erciyes Dağı** *anc.* Argaeus. ▲ C Turkey
111 J22 **Érd** *Ger.* Hanselbeck. Pest, C Hungary
Erdaobaihe *see* Baihe
159 O12 **Erdaogou** Qinghai, W China
163 X11 **Erdao Jiang** ≈ NE China
Erdăt-Săngeorz *see* Sângeorgiu de Pădure
136 C11 **Erdek** Balıkesir, NW Turkey
Erdély *see* Transylvania
Erdélyi-Havasok *see* Carpaţii Meridionali
136 J17 **Erdemli** İçel, S Turkey
162 K6 **Erdenet** Bulgan, N Mongolia
162 I8 **Erdenetsogt** Bayanhongor, C Mongolia
78 K7 **Erdi** *plateau* NE Chad
78 L7 **Erdi Ma** *desert* NE Chad
101 M23 **Erding** Bayern, SE Germany
Erdőszáda *see* Ardusat
Erdőszentgyörgy *see* Sângeorgiu de Pădure
102 I7 **Erdre** ≈ NW France
195 R13 **Erebus, Mount** ▲ Ross Island, Antarctica
61 H14 **Erechim** Rio Grande do Sul, S Brazil
163 O7 **Ereen Davaanī Nuruu** ▲▲ NE Mongolia
163 Q6 **Ereentsav** Dornod, NE Mongolia
136 I16 **Ereğli** Konya, S Turkey
136 I15 **Ereğli Gölü** ◎ W Turkey
115 A15 **Ereíkoussa** *island* Iónioi Nísoi, Greece, C Mediterranean Sea
163 O11 **Erenhot** *var.* Erlian. Nei Mongol Zizhiqu, NE China
104 M6 **Eresma** ≈ N Spain
115 K17 **Eresós** *var.* Eressós. Lésvos, E Greece
Eressós *see* Eresós
Erevan *see* Yerevan
Ereymentaū *see* Yereymentau
99 K21 **Érezée** Luxembourg, SE Belgium
74 G7 **Erfoud** SE Morocco
101 D16 **Erft** ≈ W Germany
101 K16 **Erfurt** Thüringen, C Germany
137 P15 **Ergani** Dıyarbakır, SE Turkey
163 N11 **Ergel** Dornogovĭ, SE Mongolia
Ergene Irmaği *see* Ergene Çayi
162 L11 **Ergenetsogt** Ömnögovĭ, S Mongolia
136 C10 **Ergene Çayi** *var.* Ergene Irmaği. ≈ NW Turkey
118 I9 **Ērgli** Madona, C Latvia
78 H11 **Erguig, Bahr** ≈ SW Chad
Ergun He *see* Argun
163 S5 **Ergun Youqi** Nei Mongol Zizhiqu, N China
163 T5 **Ergun Zuoqi** Nei Mongol Zizhiqu, N China
160 F12 **Er Hai** ◎ SW China
102 G4 **Er, Îles d'** *island group* NW France
106 K4 **Ería** ≈ NW Spain
80 H8 **Eriba** Kassala, NE Sudan
96 I6 **Eriboll, Loch** *inlet* NW Scotland, UK
65 Q18 **Erica Seamount** *undersea feature* SW Indian Ocean
107 H23 **Erice** Sicilia, Italy, C Mediterranean Sea
104 E10 **Ericeira** Lisboa, C Portugal
96 H10 **Ericht, Loch** ◎ C Scotland, UK
26 J11 **Erick** Oklahoma, C USA
18 B11 **Erie** Pennsylvania, NE USA
18 E9 **Erie Canal** *canal* New York, NE USA
Érié, Lac *see* Erie, Lake
31 T10 **Erie, Lake** *Fr.* Lac Érié. ◎ Canada/USA
Erigabo *see* Ceerigaabo
77 N8 **'Erigât** *desert* N Mali
Erigavo *see* Ceerigaabo
92 P2 **Erik Eriksenstretet** *strait* E Svalbard
11 X15 **Eriksdale** Manitoba, S Canada
189 V6 **Erikub Atoll** *var.* Ādkup. *atoll* Ratak Chain, C Marshall Islands
Erimanthos *see* Erýmanthos
165 T6 **Erimo** Hokkaidō, NE Japan
165 T6 **Erimo-misaki** *headland* Hokkaidō, NE Japan
20 H8 **Erin** Tennessee, S USA
96 E9 **Eriskay** *island* NW Scotland, UK
Erithraí *see* Erythrés
80 I9 **Eritrea** *off.* State of Eritrea, *Tig.* Ērtra. ◆ *transitional government* E Africa
Erivan *see* Yerevan
101 D16 **Erkelenz** Nordrhein-Westfalen, W Germany
95 P15 **Erken** ◎ C Sweden
101 K19 **Erlangen** Bayern, S Germany
160 G9 **Erlang Shan** ▲ C China
Erlau *see* Eger
109 V5 **Erlauf** ≈ NE Austria
181 Q8 **Erldunda Roadhouse** Northern Territory, N Australia
Erlian *see* Erenhot
27 T15 **Erling, Lake** ⊠ Arkansas, USA
109 O8 **Erlsbach** Tirol, W Austria
Ermak *see* Aksu
98 K10 **Ermelo** Gelderland, C Netherlands
83 K21 **Ermelo** Mpumalanga, NE South Africa
136 H17 **Ermenek** Karaman, S Turkey
Érmihályfalva *see* Valea lui Mihai
115 G20 **Ermióni** Pelopónnisos, S Greece
115 J20 **Ermoúpoli** *var.* Hermoupolis; *prev.* Ermoúpolis. Sýros, Kykládes, Greece, Aegean Sea
Ermoúpolis *see* Ermoúpoli
Ernabella *see* Pukatja
155 G22 **Ernākulam** Kerala, SW India
102 J6 **Ernée** Mayenne, NW France
61 H14 **Ernestina, Barragem** ⊠ S Brazil
54 E4 **Ernesto Cortissoz** ✕ (Barranquilla) Atlántico, N Colombia
155 H21 **Erode** Tamil Nādu, SE India
Eroj *see* Iroj
83 C19 **Erongo** ◈ *district* W Namibia
99 F21 **Erquelinnes** Hainaut, S Belgium
74 G7 **Er-Rachidia** *var.* Ksar al Soule. E Morocco
80 E11 **Er Rahad** *var.* Ar Rahad. Northern Kordofan, C Sudan
Er Ramle *see* Ramla
83 O15 **Errego** Zambézia, NE Mozambique
Errenteria *see* Rentería
Er Rif/Er Riff *see* Rif
97 D14 **Errigal Mountain** *Ir.* An Earagail. ▲ N Ireland
97 A15 **Erris Head** *Ir.* Ceann Iorrais. *headland* W Ireland
187 S15 **Erromango** *island* S Vanuatu
Error Guyot *see* Error Tablemount
173 O4 **Error Tablemount** *var.* Error Guyot. *undersea feature* W Indian Ocean
80 G11 **Er Roseires** Blue Nile, E Sudan
Erseka *see* Ersekë
113 M22 **Ersekë** *var.* Erseka, Kolonjë. Korçë, SE Albania
Érsekújvár *see* Nové Zámky
29 S4 **Erskine** Minnesota, N USA
103 V6 **Erstein** Bas-Rhin, NE France
108 G9 **Erstfeld** Uri, C Switzerland
158 M3 **Ertai** Xinjiang Uygur Zizhiqu, NW China
128 M7 **Ertil'** Voronezhskaya Oblast', W Russian Federation
Ertis *see* Irtysh, C Asia
Ertis *see* Irtyshsk, Kazakhstan
158 K2 **Ertix He** *Rus.* Chërnyy Irtysh. ≈ China/Kazakhstan
Ērtra *see* Eritrea
21 P9 **Erwin** North Carolina, SE USA
114 L12 **Erydropótamos** *Bul.* Byala Reka. ≈ Bulgaria/Greece
115 E19 **Erýmanthos** *var.* Erimanthos. ▲ S Greece
115 G19 **Erythrés** *prev.* Erithraí. Stereá Ellás, C Greece
160 F12 **Eryuan** Yunnan, SW China
109 U6 **Erzbach** ≈ W Austria
Erzerum *see* Erzurum
101 N17 **Erzgebirge** *Cz.* Krušné Hory, *Eng.* Ore Mountains. ▲▲ Czech Republic/Germany *see also* Krušné Hory
122 L14 **Erzin** Respublika Tyva, S Russian Federation
137 O13 **Erzincan** *var.* Erzinjan. Erzincan, E Turkey
137 N13 **Erzincan** *var.* Erzinjan. ◈ *province* NE Turkey
Erzinjan *see* Erzincan
Erzsébetváros *see* Dumbrăveni
137 Q13 **Erzurum** *prev.* Erzerum. Erzurum, NE Turkey
137 Q12 **Erzurum** *prev.* Erzerum. ◈ *province* NE Turkey
186 G9 **Esa'ala** Normanby Island, SE PNG
165 T2 **Esashi** Hokkaidō, NE Japan
165 Q9 **Esashi** *var.* Esasi. Iwate, Honshū, C Japan
165 Q5 **Esasho** Hokkaidō, N Japan
Esasi *see* Esashi
95 F23 **Esbjerg** Ribe, W Denmark
Esbo *see* Espoo
36 L7 **Escalante** Utah, W USA
36 M7 **Escalante River** ≈ Utah, W USA
14 L12 **Escalier, Réservoir l'** ⊠ Quebec, SE Canada
40 K7 **Escalón** Chihuahua, N Mexico
104 M8 **Escalona** Castilla-La Mancha, C Spain
23 O8 **Escambia River** ≈ Florida, SE USA
31 N5 **Escanaba** Michigan, N USA
31 N4 **Escanaba River** ≈ Michigan, N USA
105 R8 **Escandón, Puerto de** *pass* E Spain
41 W14 **Escárcega** Campeche, SE Mexico
171 O1 **Escarpada Point** *headland* Luzon, N Philippines
23 N8 **Escatawpa River** ≈ Alabama/Mississippi, S USA
103 P2 **Escaut** ≈ N France
Escaut *see* Scheldt
99 M25 **Esch-sur-Alzette** Luxembourg, S Luxembourg
101 J15 **Eschwege** Hessen, C Germany
101 D16 **Eschweiler** Nordrhein-Westfalen, W Germany
Esclaves, Grand Lac des *see* Great Slave Lake
45 O8 **Escocesa, Bahía** *bay* N Dominican Republic
43 W15 **Escocés, Punta** *headland* NE Panama
35 U17 **Escondido** California, W USA
42 M10 **Escondido, Río** ≈ SE Nicaragua
15 S7 **Escoumins, Rivière des** ≈ Quebec, SE Canada
37 O13 **Escudilla Mountain** ▲ Arizona, SW USA
40 J11 **Escuinapa** *var.* Escuinapa de Hidalgo. Sinaloa, C Mexico
Escuinapa de Hidalgo *see* Escuinapa
42 C6 **Escuintla** Escuintla, S Guatemala
41 V17 **Escuintla** Chiapas, SE Mexico
42 A2 **Escuintla** *off.* Departamento de Escuintla. ◈ *department* S Guatemala
15 W7 **Escuminac** ≈ Quebec, SE Canada
79 D16 **Eséka** Centre, SW Cameroon
136 I12 **Esenboğa** ✕ (Ankara) Ankara, C Turkey
Esenguly *see* Gasan-Kuli
136 D17 **Eşen Çayı** ≈ SW Turkey
105 T4 **Ésera** ≈ NE Spain
143 N8 **Eşfahān** *Eng.* Isfahan; *anc.* Aspadana. Eşfahān, C Iran
143 O7 **Eşfahān** *off.* Ostān-e Eşfahān. ◈ *province* C Iran
105 N5 **Esgueva** ≈ N Spain
149 Q3 **Eshkamesh** Takhār, NE Afghanistan
149 T2 **Eshkāshem** Badakhshān, NE Afghanistan
83 L23 **Eshowe** KwaZulu/Natal, E South Africa
143 T5 **'Eshqābād** Khorāsān, NE Iran
Esh Sham *see* Dimashq
Esh Sharā *see* Ash Sharāh
Esik *see* Yesik
Esil *see* Ishim, Kazakhstan/Russian Federation
Esil *see* Yesil', Kazakhstan
183 V2 **Esk** Queensland, E Australia
184 O11 **Eskdale** Hawke's Bay, North Island, NZ
Eski Dzhumaya *see* Tŭrgovishte
92 L2 **Eskifjördhur** Austurland, E Iceland
139 S3 **Eski Kaļak** *var.* Askī Kalak, Kalak. N Iraq
95 N16 **Eskilstuna** Södermanland, C Sweden
8 H6 **Eskimo Lakes** *lakes* Northwest Territories, NW Canada
0 O10 **Eskimo Point** *headland* Nunavut, E Canada
Eskimo Point *see* Arviat
139 Q2 **Eski Mosul** N Iraq
147 T10 **Eski-Nookat** *var.* Iski-Nauket. Oshskaya Oblast', SW Kyrgyzstan
136 F12 **Eskişehir** *var.* Eskishehr. Eskişehir, W Turkey
136 F13 **Eskişehir** *var.* Eski shehr. ◈ *province* NW Turkey
Eskishehr *see* Eskişehir
104 K5 **Esla** ≈ NW Spain
142 J6 **Eslāmābād** *var.* Eslāmābād-e Gharb; *prev.* Harunabad, Shāhābād. Kermānshāhān, W Iran
Eslāmābād-e Gharb *see* Eslāmābād
148 J4 **Eslām Qal'eh** *Pash.* Islam Qala. Herāt, W Afghanistan
95 K23 **Eslöv** Skåne, S Sweden
143 S12 **Esma'īlābād** Kermān, S Iran
143 U8 **Esma'īlābād** Khorāsān, E Iran
136 D14 **Eşme** Uşak, W Turkey
44 G6 **Esmeralda** Camagüey, E Cuba
63 F21 **Esmeralda, Isla** *island* S Chile
56 B5 **Esmeraldas** Esmeraldas, N Ecuador
56 B5 **Esmeraldas** ◈ *province* NW Ecuador
Esna *see* Isna
14 B6 **Esnagi Lake** ◎ Ontario, S Canada
143 V14 **Espakeh** Sīstān va Balūchestān, SE Iran
103 O13 **Espalion** Aveyron, S France
España *see* Spain
14 E11 **Espanola** Ontario, S Canada
37 S10 **Espanola** New Mexico, SW USA
57 C18 **Española, Isla** *var.* Hood Island. *island* Galapagos Islands, Ecuador, E Pacific Ocean
104 M13 **Espejo** Andalucía, S Spain
94 C13 **Espeland** Hordaland, S Norway
100 G12 **Espelkamp** Nordrhein-Westfalen, NW Germany
38 M8 **Espenberg, Cape** *headland* Alaska, USA
180 L13 **Esperance** Western Australia
186 L9 **Esperance, Cape** *headland* Guadacanal, C Solomon Islands
57 P18 **Esperancita** Santa Cruz, E Bolivia
61 B17 **Esperanza** Santa Fe, C Argentina
40 G6 **Esperanza** Sonora, NW Mexico
24 H9 **Esperanza** Texas, SW USA
194 H3 **Esperanza** *Argentinian research station* Antarctica
104 E12 **Espichel, Cabo** *headland* S Portugal
54 E10 **Espinal** Tolima, C Colombia
48 K10 **Espinhaço, Serra do** ▲▲ SE Brazil
104 G6 **Espinho** Aveiro, N Portugal
59 N18 **Espinosa** Minas Gerais, SE Brazil
103 O15 **Espinouse** ▲▲ S France
60 Q8 **Espírito Santo** *off.* Estado do Espírito Santo. ◈ *state* E Brazil
187 P13 **Espiritu Santo** *var.* Santo. *island* W Vanuatu
41 Z13 **Espíritu Santo, Bahía del** *bay* SE Mexico
40 F9 **Espíritu Santo, Isla del** *island* W Mexico
41 Y12 **Espita** Yucatán, SE Mexico
15 Y7 **Espoir, Cap d'** *headland* Quebec, SE Canada
Esponsede/Esponsende *see* Esposende
93 L20 **Espoo** *Swe.* Esbo. Etelä-Suomi, S Finland
104 G5 **Esposende** *var.* Esponsede, Esponsende. Braga, N Portugal
83 M18 **Espungabera** Manica, SW Mozambique
63 H17 **Esquel** Chubut, SW Argentina
10 L17 **Esquimalt** Vancouver Island, British Columbia, SW Canada
61 C16 **Esquina** Corrientes, NE Argentina
42 E6 **Esquipulas** Chiquimula, SE Guatemala
42 K9 **Esquipulas** Matagalpa, C Nicaragua
94 I8 **Essandjøen** ◎ S Norway
74 E7 **Essaouira** *prev.* Mogador. W Morocco
Esseg *see* Osijek
Es Semara *see* Smara
99 G15 **Essen** Antwerpen, N Belgium
101 E15 **Essen** *var.* Essen an der Ruhr. Nordrhein-Westfalen, W Germany
Essen an der Ruhr *see* Essen
74 I5 **Es Senia** ✕ (Oran) NW Algeria
55 T8 **Essequibo Islands** *island group* N Guyana
55 T11 **Essequibo River** ≈ C Guyana
14 C18 **Essex** Ontario, S Canada
29 T16 **Essex** Iowa, C USA
97 P21 **Essex** *cultural region* E England, UK
31 R8 **Essexville** Michigan, N USA
101 H22 **Esslingen** *var.* Esslingen am Neckar. Baden-Württemberg, SW Germany
Esslingen am Neckar *see* Esslingen
103 N6 **Essonne** ◈ *department* N France
Es Suweida *see* As Suwaydā'
79 F16 **Est** *Eng.* East. ◈ *province* SE Cameroon
104 I1 **Estaca de Bares, Punta** *da point* NW Spain
24 M5 **Estacado, Llano** *plain* New Mexico/Texas, SW USA
63 K25 **Estados, Isla de los** *prev. Eng.* Staten Island. *island* S Argentina
143 P12 **Eşţahbān** Fārs, S Iran
14 F11 **Estaire** Ontario, S Canada
37 S12 **Estancia** New Mexico, SW USA
59 P16 **Estância** Sergipe, E Brazil
104 G7 **Estarreja** Aveiro, N Portugal
102 M17 **Estats, Pic d'** *Sp.* Pico d'Estats. ▲ France/Spain

◆ Country ● Country Capital ◇ Dependent Territory ○ Dependent Territory Capital ◈ Administrative Region ✕ International Airport ▲ Mountain ▲▲ Mountain Range ⛰ Volcano ≈ River ◎ Lake ⊠ Reservoir

Estats, Pico d' see Estats, Pic d'
83 K23 **Estcourt** KwaZulu/Natal, E South Africa
106 H8 **Este** anc. Ateste. Veneto, NE Italy
42 J9 **Estelí** Estelí, NW Nicaragua
42 J9 **Estelí** ◆ department NW Nicaragua
Estella see Estella-Lizarra
105 Q4 **Estella-Lizarra** Bas. Lizarra var Estella Navarra, N Spain
29 R9 **Estelline** South Dakota, N USA
25 P4 **Estelline** Texas, SW USA
104 L14 **Estepa** Andalucía, S Spain
104 L16 **Estepona** Andalucía, S Spain
39 R9 **Ester** Alaska, USA
11 V16 **Esterhazy** Saskatchewan, S Canada
37 S3 **Estes Park** Colorado, C USA
11 V17 **Estevan** Saskatchewan, S Canada
29 T11 **Estherville** Iowa, C USA
21 R15 **Estill** South Carolina, SE USA
103 Q6 **Estissac** Aube, N France
15 T9 **Est, Lac de l'** ◎ Quebec, SE Canada
Estland see Estonia
11 S16 **Eston** Saskatchewan, S Canada
118 G5 **Estonia** off. Republic of Estonia, Est. Eesti Vabariik, Ger. Estland, Latv. Igaunija; prev. Estonian SSR, Rus. Estonskaya SSR. ◆ republic NE Europe
Estonskaya SSR see Estonia
104 E11 **Estoril** Lisboa, W Portugal
59 L14 **Estreito** Maranhão, E Brazil
104 I8 **Estrela, Serra da** ▲ C Portugal
40 D3 **Estrella, Punta** headland NW Mexico
Estremadura see Extremadura
104 F10 **Estremadura** cultural and historical region W Portugal
104 H11 **Estremoz** Évora, S Portugal
79 D18 **Estuaire** off. Province de l'Estuaire, var. L'Estuaire. ◆ province NW Gabon
Eszék see Osijek
111 I22 **Esztergom** Ger. Gran; anc. Strigonium. Komárom-Esztergom, N Hungary
152 K11 **Etah** Uttar Pradesh, N India
189 R17 **Etal Atoll** atoll Mortlock Islands, C Micronesia
99 K24 **Étalle** Luxembourg, SE Belgium
103 N6 **Étampes** Essonne, N France
182 J1 **Etamunbanie, Lake** salt lake South Australia
103 N1 **Étaples** Pas-de-Calais, N France
152 K12 **Etāwah** Uttar Pradesh, N India
15 R10 **Etchemin** ≈ Quebec, SE Canada
Etchmiadzin see Ejmiatsin
40 G7 **Etchojoa** Sonora, NW Mexico
93 L19 **Etelä-Suomi** ◆ province S Finland
83 B16 **Etengua** Kunene, NW Namibia
99 K25 **Éthe** Luxembourg, SE Belgium
11 W15 **Ethelbert** Manitoba, S Canada
80 H12 **Ethiopia** off. Federal Democratic Republic of Ethiopia; prev. Abyssinia, People's Democratic Republic of Ethiopia. ◆ republic E Africa
80 I13 **Ethiopian Highlands** var. Ethiopian Plateau. plateau N Ethiopia
Ethiopian Plateau see Ethiopian Highlands
34 M2 **Etna** California, W USA
18 B14 **Etna** Pennsylvania, NE USA
94 G12 **Etna** ≈ S Norway
107 L24 **Etna, Monte** Eng. Mount Etna. ▲ Sicilia, Italy, C Mediterranean Sea
Etna, Mount see Etna, Monte
95 C15 **Etne** Hordaland, S Norway
Etoliko see Aitolikó
39 Y14 **Etolin Island** island Alexander Archipelago, Alaska, USA
38 L12 **Etolin Strait** strait Alaska, USA
83 C17 **Etosha Pan** salt lake N Namibia
79 G18 **Etoumbi** Cuvette, NW Congo
20 M10 **Etowah** Tennessee, S USA
23 S2 **Etowah River** ≈ Georgia, SE USA
Etrek see Atrak
102 L3 **Étretat** Seine-Maritime, N France
114 H9 **Etropole** Sofiya, W Bulgaria
Etsch see Adige
Et Tafila see Aṭ Ṭafīlah
99 M23 **Ettelbrück** Diekirch, C Luxembourg
189 V12 **Etten** atoll Chuuk Islands, C Micronesia
99 H14 **Etten-Leur** Noord-Brabant, S Netherlands
76 G7 **Et Tîdra** var. Ile Tîdra. island Dakhlet Nouâdhibou, NW Mauritania
101 G21 **Ettlingen** Baden-Württemberg, SW Germany
102 M2 **Eu** Seine-Maritime, N France
193 W16 **'Eua** prev. Middleburg Island. island Tongatapu Group, SE Tonga
193 W15 **Eua Iki** island Tongatapu Group, S Tonga
Euboea see Évvoia
181 O12 **Eucla** Western Australia
31 U11 **Euclid** Ohio, N USA
27 W14 **Eudora** Arkansas, C USA
27 Q4 **Eudora** Kansas, C USA
182 J9 **Eudunda** South Australia
23 R6 **Eufaula** Alabama, S USA
27 Q11 **Eufaula** Oklahoma, C USA
27 Q11 **Eufaula Lake** var. Eufaula Reservoir. ⊠ Oklahoma, C USA
Eufaula Reservoir see Eufaula Lake
32 F13 **Eugene** Oregon, NW USA
40 B6 **Eugenia, Punta** headland W Mexico
183 Q8 **Eugowra** New South Wales, SE Australia
104 I2 **Eume** ≈ NW Spain
104 H2 **Eume, Embalse do** ⊠ NW Spain
Eumolpias see Plovdiv
59 O18 **Eunápolis** Bahia, SE Brazil
22 H8 **Eunice** Louisiana, S USA
37 W15 **Eunice** New Mexico, SW USA
99 M19 **Eupen** Liège, E Belgium
138 J9 **Euphrates** Ar. Al Furāt, Turk. Firat Nehri. ≈ SW Asia
138 L3 **Euphrates Dam** dam N Syria
22 M4 **Eupora** Mississippi, S USA
93 K19 **Eura** Länsi-Suomi, W Finland
93 K19 **Eurajoki** Länsi-Suomi, W Finland
84 **Eurasian Plate** tectonic feature
102 L4 **Eure** ◆ department N France
102 M4 **Eure** ≈ N France
102 M6 **Eure-et-Loir** ◆ department C France
34 K3 **Eureka** California, W USA
27 P6 **Eureka** Kansas, C USA
33 O6 **Eureka** Montana, NW USA
35 V5 **Eureka** Nevada, W USA
29 O7 **Eureka** South Dakota, N USA
36 L4 **Eureka** Utah, W USA
32 K10 **Eureka** Washington, NW USA
27 S9 **Eureka Springs** Arkansas, C USA
182 K6 **Eurinilla Creek** seasonal river South Australia
183 O11 **Euroa** Victoria, SE Australia
172 M9 **Europa** island W Madagascar
104 L3 **Europa, Picos de** ▲ N Spain
104 L16 **Europa Point** headland S Gibraltar
86-87 **Europe** continent
98 F12 **Europoort** Zuid-Holland, W Netherlands
Euskadi see País Vasco
101 D17 **Euskirchen** Nordrhein-Westfalen, W Germany
23 W11 **Eustis** Florida, SE USA
182 M9 **Euston** New South Wales, SE Australia
23 N5 **Eutaw** Alabama, S USA
100 K8 **Eutin** Schleswig-Holstein, N Germany
10 K14 **Eutsuk Lake** ⊠ British Columbia, SW Canada
Euxine Sea see Black Sea
83 C16 **Evale** Cunene, SW Angola
37 T3 **Evans** Colorado, C USA
11 P14 **Evansburg** Alberta, SW Canada
29 X13 **Evansdale** Iowa, C USA
183 V4 **Evans Head** New South Wales, SE Australia
12 J11 **Evans, Lac** ◎ Quebec, SE Canada
37 S5 **Evans, Mount** ▲ Colorado, C USA
9 Q8 Nunavut, N Canada
31 N10 **Evanston** Illinois, N USA
33 S17 **Evanston** Wyoming, C USA
14 D11 **Evansville** Manitoulin Island, Ontario, S Canada
31 N16 **Evansville** Indiana, N USA
30 L9 **Evansville** Wisconsin, N USA
25 S8 **Evant** Texas, SW USA
143 P13 **Evaz** Fārs, S Iran
29 W4 **Eveleth** Minnesota, N USA
182 E3 **Evelyn Creek** seasonal river South Australia
181 Q2 **Evelyn, Mount** ▲ Northern Territory, N Australia
122 K10 **Evenkiyskiy Avtonomnyy Okrug** ◆ autonomous district N Russian Federation
183 R13 **Everard, Cape** headland Victoria, SE Australia
182 F6 **Everard, Lake** salt lake South Australia
182 C2 **Everard Ranges** ▲ South Australia
153 R11 **Everest, Mount** Chin. Qomolangma Feng, Nep. Sagarmatha. ▲ China/Nepal
18 E15 **Everett** Pennsylvania, NE USA
32 H7 **Everett** Washington, NW USA
99 E17 **Evergem** Oost-Vlaanderen, NW Belgium
23 X16 **Everglades City** Florida, SE USA
23 Y16 **Everglades, The** wetland Florida, SE USA
23 P7 **Evergreen** Alabama, S USA
37 T4 **Evergreen** Colorado, C USA
Evergreen State see Washington
97 L21 **Evesham** C England, UK
103 T10 **Évian-les-Bains** Haute-Savoie, E France
93 K16 **Evijärvi** Länsi-Suomi, W Finland
79 D17 **Evinayong** var. Ebinayon, Evinayoung. C Equatorial Guinea
Evinayoung see Evinayong
115 E18 **Évinos** ≈ C Greece
95 E17 **Evje** Aust-Agder, S Norway
Evmolpia see Plovdiv
104 H11 **Évora** anc. Ebora, Lat. Liberalitas Julia. Évora, C Portugal
104 G11 **Évora** ◆ district S Portugal
102 M4 **Évreux** anc. Civitas Eburovicum. Eure, N France
102 K6 **Évron** Mayenne, NW France
114 L13 **Évros** Bul. Maritsa, Turk. Meriç; anc. Hebrus. ≈ SE Europe see also Maritsa/Meriç
115 F21 **Evrótas** ≈ S Greece
103 O5 **Évry** Essonne, N France
25 O8 **E.V.Spence Reservoir** ⊠ Texas, SW USA
115 I18 **Évvoia** Lat. Euboea. island C Greece
38 D9 **Ewa Beach** Oahu, Hawaii, USA, C Pacific Ocean
32 L9 **Ewan** Washington, NW USA
44 K12 **Ewarton** C Jamaica
81 J18 **Ewaso Ng'iro** var. Nyiro. ≈ C Kenya
29 P13 **Ewing** Nebraska, C USA
194 J5 **Ewing Island** island Antarctica
65 P17 **Ewing Seamount** undersea feature E Atlantic Ocean
158 L6 **Ewirgol** Xinjiang Uygur Zizhiqu, W China
79 G19 **Ewo** Cuvette, W Congo
27 S3 **Excelsior Springs** Missouri, C USA
97 J23 **Exe** ≈ SW England, UK
194 L12 **Executive Committee Range** ▲ Antarctica
14 E16 **Exeter** Ontario, S Canada
97 J24 **Exeter** anc. Isca Damnoniorum. SW England, UK
35 R11 **Exeter** California, W USA
19 P10 **Exeter** New Hampshire, NE USA
Exin see Kcynia
29 T14 **Exira** Iowa, C USA
97 J23 **Exmoor** moorland SW England, UK
21 Y6 **Exmore** Virginia, NE USA
180 G8 **Exmouth** Western Australia
97 J24 **Exmouth** SW England, UK
180 G8 **Exmouth Gulf** gulf Western Australia
173 V8 **Exmouth Plateau** undersea feature E Indian Ocean
115 J20 **Exompourgo** ancient monument Tínos, Kykládes, Greece, Aegean Sea
104 I10 **Extremadura** var. Estremadura. ◆ autonomous community W Spain
78 F12 **Extrême-Nord** Eng. Extreme North. ◆ province N Cameroon
Extreme North see Extrême-Nord
44 I3 **Exuma Cays** islets C Bahamas
44 I3 **Exuma Sound** sound C Bahamas
81 H20 **Eyasi, Lake** ◎ N Tanzania
95 F17 **Eydehavn** Aust-Agder, S Norway
96 L12 **Eyemouth** SE Scotland, UK
96 G7 **Eye Peninsula** peninsula NW Scotland, UK
80 Q13 **Eyl** It. Eil. Nugaal, E Somalia
103 N11 **Eymoutiers** Haute-Vienne, C France
Eyo (lower course) see Uolo, Río
29 X10 **Eyota** Minnesota, N USA
182 H2 **Eyre Basin, Lake** salt lake South Australia
182 I1 **Eyre Creek** seasonal river Northern Territory/South Australia
174 L9 **Eyre, Lake** salt lake South Australia
185 C22 **Eyre Mountains** ▲ South Island, NZ
182 H3 **Eyre North, Lake** salt lake South Australia
182 G7 **Eyre Peninsula** peninsula South Australia
182 H4 **Eyre South, Lake** salt lake South Australia
95 B18 **Eysturoy** Dan. Østerø Island Faeroe Islands
61 D20 **Ezeiza** ✕ (Buenos Aires) Buenos Aires, E Argentina
Ezeres see Ezeriş
116 F12 **Ezeriş** Hung. Ezeres. Caraş-Severin, W Romania
161 O9 **Ezhou** prev. Echeng. Hubei, C China
127 R11 **Ezhva** Respublika Komi, NW Russian Federation
136 B12 **Ezine** Çanakkale, NW Turkey
Ezo see Hokkaidō
Ezra/Ezraa see Izra'

F

191 P7 **Faaa** Tahiti, W French Polynesia
191 P7 **Faaa** ✕ (Papeete) Tahiti, W French Polynesia
Faaborg see Fåborg
151 K19 **Faadhippolhu Atoll** var. Fadiffolu, Lhaviyani Atoll. atoll N Maldives
191 U10 **Faaite** atoll Îles Tuamotu, C French Polynesia
191 Q8 **Faaone** Tahiti, W French Polynesia
24 H8 **Fabens** Texas, SW USA
94 H12 **Fåberg** Oppland, S Norway
95 H24 **Fåborg** var. Faaborg. Fyn, C Denmark
106 I12 **Fabriano** Marche, C Italy
145 U16 **Fabrichnyy** Almaty, SE Kazakhstan
54 F10 **Facatativá** Cundinamarca, C Colombia
77 X9 **Fachi** Agadez, C Niger
188 B16 **Facpi Point** headland W Guam
18 I13 **Factoryville** Pennsylvania, NE USA
78 K8 **Fada** Borkou-Ennedi-Tibesti, E Chad
77 Q13 **Fada-Ngourma** E Burkina
123 N6 **Faddeya, Zaliv** bay N Russian Federation
123 Q5 **Faddeyevskiy, Ostrov** island Novosibirskiye Ostrova, NE Russian Federation
141 W12 **Fadhī** S Oman
106 H10 **Faenza** anc. Faventia. Emilia-Romagna, N Italy
64 M5 **Faeroe-Iceland Ridge** undersea feature NW Norwegian Sea
64 M5 **Faeroe Islands** Dan. Færøerne, Faer. Føroyar. ◇ Danish external territory N Atlantic Ocean
86 C8 **Faeroe Islands** island group N Atlantic Ocean
Færøerne see Faeroe Islands
64 N6 **Faeroe-Shetland Trough** undersea feature NE Atlantic Ocean
104 H6 **Fafe** Braga, N Portugal
80 K13 **Fafen Shet'** ≈ E Ethiopia
193 V15 **Fafo** island Tongatapu Group, S Tonga
192 I16 **Fagaloa Bay** bay Upolu, E Samoa
192 H15 **Fagamālo** Savai'i, N Samoa
116 I12 **Făgăraş** Ger. Fogarasch, Hung. Fogaras. Braşov, C Romania
95 M20 **Fagerhult** Kalmar, S Sweden
94 G13 **Fagernes** Oppland, S Norway
92 I9 **Fagernes** Troms, N Norway
95 M14 **Fagersta** Västmanland, C Sweden
77 W13 **Faggo** var. Foggo. Bauchi, N Nigeria
Faghman see Fughmah
Fagibina, Lake see Faguibine, Lac
63 J25 **Fagnano, Lago** ◎ S Argentina
99 G22 **Fagne** hill range S Belgium
77 N10 **Faguibine, Lac** var. Lake Fagibina. ◎ NW Mali
Fahaheel see Al Fuḥayḥīl
Fahlun see Falun
143 U12 **Fahraj** Kermān, SE Iran
64 P5 **Faial** Madeira, Portugal, NE Atlantic Ocean
64 N2 **Faial** var. Ilha do Faial. island Azores, Portugal, NE Atlantic Ocean
Faial, Ilha do see Faial
108 G10 **Faido** Ticino, S Switzerland
Faifo see Hôi An
Failaka Island see Faylakah
190 G12 **Faioa, Île** island N Wallis and Futuna
181 W8 **Fairbairn Reservoir** ⊠ Queensland, E Australia
39 R9 **Fairbanks** Alaska, USA
21 U12 **Fair Bluff** North Carolina, SE USA
31 R14 **Fairborn** Ohio, N USA
23 S3 **Fairburn** Georgia, SE USA
30 M12 **Fairbury** Illinois, N USA
29 Q17 **Fairbury** Nebraska, C USA
29 T9 **Fairfax** Minnesota, N USA
27 O8 **Fairfax** Oklahoma, C USA
21 R14 **Fairfax** South Carolina, SE USA
35 N8 **Fairfield** California, W USA
33 O14 **Fairfield** Idaho, NW USA
30 M16 **Fairfield** Illinois, N USA
29 X15 **Fairfield** Iowa, C USA
33 R8 **Fairfield** Montana, NW USA
31 Q14 **Fairfield** Ohio, N USA
25 U8 **Fairfield** Texas, SW USA
27 T7 **Fair Grove** Missouri, C USA
19 P12 **Fairhaven** Massachusetts, NE USA
23 N8 **Fairhope** Alabama, S USA
96 L4 **Fair Isle** island NE Scotland, UK
185 F20 **Fairlie** Canterbury, South Island, NZ
29 U11 **Fairmont** Minnesota, N USA
29 Q16 **Fairmont** Nebraska, C USA
21 S3 **Fairmont** West Virginia, NE USA
31 P13 **Fairmount** Indiana, N USA
18 H10 **Fairmount** New York, NE USA
29 R7 **Fairmount** North Dakota, N USA
37 S5 **Fairplay** Colorado, C USA
18 F9 **Fairport** New York, NE USA
11 O12 **Fairview** Alberta, W Canada
26 L9 **Fairview** Oklahoma, C USA
36 L4 **Fairview** Utah, W USA
35 T6 **Fairview Peak** ▲ Nevada, W USA
188 H14 **Fais** atoll Caroline Islands, W Micronesia
149 U8 **Faisalābād** prev. Lyallpur. Punjab, NE Pakistan
Faisaliya see Fayşalīyah
28 L8 **Faith** South Dakota, N USA
153 N12 **Faizābād** Uttar Pradesh, N India
Faizabad/Faizābād see Feyzābād
45 S9 **Fajardo** E Puerto Rico
139 R9 **Fajj, Wādī al** dry watercourse S Iraq
140 K4 **Fajr, Bi'r** well NW Saudi Arabia
191 W10 **Fakahina** atoll Îles Tuamotu, C French Polynesia
190 L10 **Fakaofo Atoll** island SE Tokelau
191 U10 **Fakarava** atoll Îles Tuamotu, C French Polynesia
129 T2 **Fakel** Udmurtskaya Respublika, NW Russian Federation
97 P19 **Fakenham** E England, UK
171 U13 **Fakfak** Irian Jaya, E Indonesia
153 T12 **Fakīragrām** Assam, NE India
114 M10 **Fakiyska Reka** ≈ SE Bulgaria
95 J24 **Fakse** Storstrøm, SE Denmark
95 J24 **Fakse Bugt** bay SE Denmark
95 J24 **Fakse Ladeplads** Storstrøm, SE Denmark
163 V11 **Faku** Liaoning, NE China
76 J14 **Falaba** N Sierra Leone
102 K5 **Falaise** Calvados, N France
114 H12 **Falakró** ▲ NE Greece
189 T12 **Falalu** island Chuuk, C Micronesia
166 L4 **Falam** Chin State, W Burma
143 N8 **Falāvarjān** Eşfahān, C Iran
116 M11 **Fălciu** Vaslui, E Romania
54 I4 **Falcón** off. Estado Falcón. ◆ state NW Venezuela
106 J12 **Falconara Marittima** Marche, C Italy
Falcone, Capo del see Falcone, Punta del
107 A16 **Falcone, Punta del** var. Capo del Falcone. headland Sardegna, Italy, C Mediterranean Sea
11 Y16 **Falcon Lake** Manitoba, S Canada
Falcon Lake see Falcón, Presa/Falcon Reservoir
41 O7 **Falcón, Presa** var. Falcon Lake, Falcon Reservoir. ⊠ Mexico/USA see also Falcon Reservoir
25 Q16 **Falcon Reservoir** var. Falcon Lake, Presa Falcón. ⊠ Mexico/USA see also Falcón, Presa
190 L10 **Fale** island Fakaofo Atoll, SE Tokelau
192 F15 **Faleālupo** Savai'i, NW Samoa
190 B10 **Falefatu** island Funafuti Atoll, C Tuvalu
192 G15 **Fālelima** Savai'i, NW Samoa
95 N18 **Falerum** Östergötland, S Sweden
Faleshty see Fălești
116 M9 **Fălești** Rus. Faleshty. NW Moldova
25 S15 **Falfurrias** Texas, SW USA
11 O13 **Falher** Alberta, W Canada
Falkenau an der Eger see Sokolov
95 J21 **Falkenberg** Halland, S Sweden
Falkenberg see Niemodlin
Falkenburg in Pommern see Złocieniec
100 N12 **Falkensee** Brandenburg, NE Germany
96 J12 **Falkirk** C Scotland, UK
65 I20 **Falkland Escarpment** undersea feature SW Atlantic Ocean
63 K24 **Falkland Islands** var. Falklands, Islas Malvinas. ◇ UK dependent territory SW Atlantic Ocean
47 W14 **Falkland Islands** island group SW Atlantic Ocean
65 I20 **Falkland Plateau** var. Argentine Rise. undersea feature SW Atlantic Ocean
Falklands see Falkland Islands
63 M23 **Falkland Sound** var. Estrecho de San Carlos. strait C Falkland Islands
Falknov nad Ohří see Sokolov
115 H21 **Falkonéra** island S Greece
95 K18 **Falköping** Västra Götaland, S Sweden
139 U8 **Fallāḥ** E Iraq
35 U16 **Fallbrook** California, W USA
189 U12 **Falleallej Pass** passage Chuuk Islands, C Micronesia
93 J14 **Fällfors** Västerbotten, N Sweden
194 I6 **Fallières Coast** physical region Antarctica
100 I11 **Fallingbostel** Niedersachsen, NW Germany
33 X9 **Fallon** Montana, NW USA
35 S5 **Fallon** Nevada, W USA
19 O12 **Fall River** Massachusetts, NE USA
27 P6 **Fall River Lake** ⊠ Kansas, C USA
35 O3 **Fall River Mills** California, W USA
21 W4 **Falls Church** Virginia, NE USA
29 S17 **Falls City** Nebraska, C USA
25 S12 **Falls City** Texas, SW USA
Falluja see Al Fallūjah
77 S12 **Falmey** Dosso, SW Niger
45 W10 **Falmouth** Antigua, Antigua and Barbuda
44 J11 **Falmouth** W Jamaica
97 H25 **Falmouth** SW England, UK
20 M4 **Falmouth** Kentucky, S USA
19 P13 **Falmouth** Massachusetts, NE USA
21 W5 **Falmouth** Virginia, NE USA
189 U12 **Falos** island Chuuk, C Micronesia
83 E26 **False Bay** Afr. Valsbaai. bay SW South Africa
155 K17 **False Divi Point** headland E India
38 M16 **False Pass** Unimak Island, Alaska, USA
154 P12 **False Point** headland E India
105 U6 **Falset** Cataluña, NE Spain
95 I25 **Falster** island SE Denmark
95 J23 **Falsterbo** Skåne, S Sweden
116 K9 **Fălticeni** Hung. Falticsén. Suceava, NE Romania
Falticsén see Fălticeni
94 M13 **Falun** var. Fahlun. Dalarna, C Sweden
Famagusta see Gazimağusa
Famagusta Bay see Gazimağusa Körfezi
62 I8 **Famatina** La Rioja, NW Argentina
99 J21 **Famenne** physical region SE Belgium
113 D22 **Fan** var. Fani. ≈ N Albania
77 X15 **Fan** ≈ E Nigeria
76 M12 **Fana** Koulikoro, SW Mali
115 K19 **Fána** ancient harbor Chíos, SE Greece
189 V13 **Fanan** island Chuuk, C Micronesia
189 U12 **Fanapanges** island Chuuk, C Micronesia
115 L20 **Fanári, Akrotírio** headland Ikaría, Dodekánisos, Greece, Aegean Sea
45 Q13 **Fancy** Saint Vincent, Saint Vincent and the Grenadines
172 I5 **Fandriana** Fianarantsoa, SE Madagascar
167 O6 **Fang** Chiang Mai, NW Thailand
80 E13 **Fangak** Jonglei, SE Sudan
191 W10 **Fangatau** atoll Îles Tuamotu, C French Polynesia
191 X12 **Fangataufa** island Îles Tuamotu, SE French Polynesia
193 V15 **Fanga Uta** bay S Tonga
161 N7 **Fangcheng** Henan, C China
160 K15 **Fangchenggang** var. Fangcheng Gezu Zizhixian; prev. Fangcheng. Guangxi Zhuangzu Zizhiqu, S China
161 S15 **Fangshan** S Taiwan
163 X8 **Fangzheng** Heilongjiang, NE China
Fani see Fan
119 K16 **Fanipal'** Rus. Fanipol'. Minskaya Voblasts', C Belarus
Fanipol' see Fanipal'
25 T13 **Fannin** Texas, SW USA
Fanning Island see Tabuaeran
94 G8 **Fannrem** Sør-Trøndelag, S Norway
106 I11 **Fano** anc. Colonia Julia Fanestris, Fanum Fortunae. Marche, C Italy
95 E23 **Fanø** island W Denmark
167 R5 **Fan Si Pan** ▲ N Vietnam
Fanum Fortunae see Fano
Fao see Al Fāw
141 W7 **Faq'** var. Al Faqa. Dubayy, E UAE
146 K12 **Farab** Turkm. Farap. Lebapskiy Velayat, NE Turkmenistan
194 H5 **Faraday** UK research station Antarctica
185 G16 **Faraday, Mount** ▲ South Island, NZ
79 P16 **Faradje** Orientale, NE Dem. Rep. Congo (Zaire)
Faradofay see Tôlañaro
172 I7 **Farafangana** Fianarantsoa, SE Madagascar
148 J7 **Farāh** var. Farah, Fararud. Farāh, W Afghanistan
148 K7 **Farāh** ◆ province W Afghanistan
148 J7 **Farāh Rūd** ≈ W Afghanistan
188 K7 **Farallon de Medinilla** island C Northern Mariana Islands
188 J2 **Farallon de Pajaros** var. Uracas. island N Northern Mariana Islands
76 J14 **Faranah** Haute-Guinée, S Guinea
Farap see Farab
Fararud see Farāh
140 M13 **Farasān, Jazā'ir** island group SW Saudi Arabia
172 I5 **Faratsiho** Antananarivo, C Madagascar
188 K15 **Faraulep Atoll** atoll Caroline Islands, C Micronesia
99 H20 **Farciennes** Hainaut, S Belgium
105 O14 **Fardes** ≈ S Spain
191 S10 **Fare** Huahine, W French Polynesia
97 M23 **Fareham** S England, UK
39 P11 **Farewell** Alaska, USA
184 H13 **Farewell, Cape** headland South Island, NZ
Farewell, Cape see Nunap Isua
184 I13 **Farewell Spit** spit South Island, NZ
95 I17 **Färgelanda** Västra Götaland, S Sweden
147 S10 **Farghona** Rus. Fergana; prev. Novyy Margilan. Farghona Wiloyati, E Uzbekistan
Farghona Valley see Fergana Valley
147 R10 **Farghona Wiloyati** Rus. Ferganskaya Oblast'. ◆ province E Uzbekistan
Farghona, Wodii/Farghona Wodiysi see Fergana Valley
23 V8 **Fargo** Georgia, SE USA
29 R5 **Fargo** North Dakota, N USA
29 V10 **Faribault** Minnesota, N USA
152 J11 **Farīdābād** Haryāna, N India
152 H8 **Farīdkot** Punjab, NW India
153 T15 **Faridpur** Dhaka, C Bangladesh
121 P14 **Fārigh, Wādī al** ≈ N Libya
172 I4 **Farihy Alaotra** ◎ C Madagascar
94 M11 **Färila** Gävleborg, C Sweden
104 E9 **Farilhões** island C Portugal
76 G12 **Farim** NW Guinea-Bissau
Farish see Forish
141 T11 **Fāris, Qalamat** well SE Saudi Arabia
95 N21 **Färjestaden** Kalmar, S Sweden
149 R2 **Farkhār** Takhār, NE Afghanistan
147 Q14 **Farkhor** Rus. Parkhar. SW Tajikistan
116 F12 **Fârliug** prev. Fîrliug, Hung. Furluk. Caraş-Severin, SW Romania
115 M21 **Farmakonísi** island Dodekánisos, Greece, Aegean Sea
30 M13 **Farmer City** Illinois, N USA
31 N14 **Farmersburg** Indiana, N USA
25 U6 **Farmersville** Texas, SW USA
22 H5 **Farmerville** Louisiana, S USA
29 X16 **Farmington** Iowa, C USA
19 Q6 **Farmington** Maine, NE USA
29 V9 **Farmington** Minnesota, N USA
27 X6 **Farmington** Missouri, C USA
19 O9 **Farmington** New Hampshire, NE USA
37 P9 **Farmington** New Mexico, SW USA
36 L2 **Farmington** Utah, W USA
21 W9 **Farmville** North Carolina, SE USA
21 U6 **Farmville** Virginia, NE USA
97 N22 **Farnborough** S England, UK
97 N22 **Farnham** S England, UK
10 J7 **Faro** Yukon Territory, W Canada
104 G14 **Faro** Faro, S Portugal
104 G14 **Faro** ◆ district S Portugal
104 G14 **Faro** ✕ Faro, S Portugal
78 F13 **Faro** ≈ Cameroon/Nigeria
95 Q18 **Fårö** Gotland, SE Sweden
Faro, Punta del see Peloro, Capo
95 Q18 **Fårösund** Gotland, SE Sweden
173 N7 **Farquhar Group** island group S Seychelles
18 B13 **Farrell** Pennsylvania, NE USA
152 K11 **Farrukhābād** Uttar Pradesh, N India
143 P11 **Fārs** off. Ostān-e Fārs; anc. Persis. ◆ province S Iran
115 F16 **Fársala** Thessalía, C Greece
143 R4 **Fārsīān** Golestān, N Iran
Fars, Khalīj-e see The Gulf
95 G21 **Farsø** Nordjylland, N Denmark
95 D18 **Farsund** Vest-Agder, S Norway
141 U14 **Fartak, Ra's** headland E Yemen
60 H13 **Fartura, Serra da** ▲ S Brazil
Farvel, Kap see Nunap Isua
24 L4 **Farwell** Texas, SW USA
194 I9 **Farwell Island** island Antarctica

◆ Country
● Country Capital
◇ Dependent Territory
○ Dependent Territory Capital
◆ Administrative Region
✕ International Airport
▲ Mountain
▲ Mountain Range
▲ Volcano
≈ River
◎ Lake
⊠ Reservoir

152 L9 **Far Western** ◈ zone W Nepal
148 M3 **Fāryāb** ◈ province N Afghanistan
143 P12 **Fasā** Fārs, S Iran
141 U12 **Fasad, Ramlat** desert SW Oman
107 P17 **Fasano** Puglia, SE Italy
92 L3 **Fáskrúdhsfjördhur** Austurland, E Iceland
117 O5 **Fastiv** Rus. Fastov. Kyyivs'ka Oblast', NW Ukraine
97 B22 **Fastnet Rock** Ir. Carraig Aonair. island SW Ireland
Fastov see Fastiv
190 C9 **Fatato** island Funafuti Atoll, C Tuvalu
152 K12 **Fatehgarh** Uttar Pradesh, N India
149 U6 **Fatehjang** Punjab, E Pakistan
152 G11 **Fatehpur** Rājasthān, N India
152 L13 **Fatehpur** Uttar Pradesh, N India
128 J7 **Fatezh** Kurskaya Oblast', W Russian Federation
76 G11 **Fatick** W Senegal
104 G9 **Fátima** Santarém, W Portugal
136 M11 **Fatsa** Ordu, N Turkey
Fatshan see Foshan
190 D12 **Fatua, Pointe** var. Pointe Nord. headland Île Futuna, S Wallis and Futuna
191 X7 **Fatu Hiva** island Îles Marquises, NE French Polynesia
Fatunda see Fatundu
79 H21 **Fatundu** var. Fatunda. Bandundu, W Dem. Rep. Congo (Zaire)
187 S11 **Fatutaka** island, E Soloman Islands
29 O8 **Faulkton** South Dakota, N USA
116 L13 **Făurei** prev. Filimon Sîrbu. Brăila, SE Romania
92 G12 **Fauske** Nordland, C Norway
11 P13 **Faust** Alberta, W Canada
99 L23 **Fauvillers** Luxembourg, SE Belgium
107 J24 **Favara** Sicilia, Italy, C Mediterranean Sea
Faventia see Faenza
107 G23 **Favignana, Isola** island Isole Egadi, S Italy
12 D8 **Fawn** ≈ Ontario, SE Canada
Faxa Bay see Faxaflói
92 H3 **Faxaflói** Eng. Faxa Bay. bay W Iceland
78 I7 **Faya** prev. Faya-Largeau, Largeau. Borkou-Ennedi-Tibesti, N Chad
Faya-Largeau see Faya
187 Q16 **Fayaoué** Province des Îles Loyauté, C New Caledonia
138 M5 **Fayḍāt** hill range E Syria
23 O3 **Fayette** Alabama, S USA
29 X12 **Fayette** Iowa, C USA
22 J6 **Fayette** Mississippi, S USA
27 U4 **Fayette** Missouri, C USA
27 S9 **Fayetteville** Arkansas, C USA
21 U10 **Fayetteville** North Carolina, SE USA
20 J10 **Fayetteville** Tennessee, S USA
25 U11 **Fayetteville** Texas, SW USA
21 R5 **Fayetteville** West Virginia, NE USA
141 R4 **Faylakah** var. Failaka Island. island E Kuwait
139 T10 **Fayşalīyah** var. Faisaliya. S Iraq
189 P15 **Fayu** var. East Fayu. island Hall Islands, C Micronesia
152 G8 **Fāzilka** Punjab, NW India
Fdérick see Fdérik
76 I6 **Fdérik** var. Fdérick, Fr. Fort Gouraud. Tiris Zemmour, NW Mauritania
Feabhail, Loch see Foyle, Lough
97 B20 **Feale** ≈ SW Ireland
21 V12 **Fear, Cape** headland Bald Head Island, North Carolina, SE USA
35 O6 **Feather River** ≈ California, W USA
185 M14 **Featherston** Wellington, North Island, NZ
102 L3 **Fécamp** Seine-Maritime, N France
Fédala see Mohammedia
61 D17 **Federación** Entre Ríos, E Argentina
61 D17 **Federal** Entre Ríos, E Argentina
77 T15 **Federal Capital District** ◈ capital territory C Nigeria
Federal Capital Territory see Australian Capital Territory
Federal District see Distrito Federal
21 Y4 **Federalsburg** Maryland, NE USA
74 M6 **Fedjaj, Chott el** var. Chott el Fejaj, Shaṭṭ al Fijāj. salt lake C Tunisia
94 B13 **Fedje** island S Norway
144 M7 **Fedorovka** Kostanay, N Kazakhstan
129 U6 **Fedorovka** Respublika Bashkortostan, W Russian Federation
Fëdory see Fyadory
117 U11 **Fedotova Kosa** spit SE Ukraine
189 V13 **Fefan** atoll Chuuk Islands, C Micronesia
111 O21 **Fehérgyarmat** Szabolcs-Szatmár-Bereg, E Hungary
Fehér-Körös see Crişul Alb
Fehértemplom see Bela Crkva
Fehérvölgy see Albac
100 L7 **Fehmarn** island N Germany
Fehmarnbelt see Femerbælt
109 X8 **Fehring** Steiermark, SE Austria
59 B15 **Feijó** Acre, W Brazil
184 M12 **Feilding** Manawatu-Wanganui, North Island, NZ
Feira see Feira de Santana
59 O17 **Feira de Santana** var. Feira. Bahia, E Brazil
109 X7 **Feistritz** ≈ SE Austria
Feistritz see Ilirska Bistrica
161 P8 **Feixi** prev. Shangpaihe. Anhui, E China
Fejaj, Chott el see Fedjaj, Chott el
111 I23 **Fejér** off. Fejér Megye. ◈ county W Hungary
95 I24 **Fejø** island SE Denmark
136 K15 **Feke** Adana, S Turkey
Feketehalom see Codlea
Fekete-Körös see Crişul Negru
109 T3 **Feldaist** ≈ N Austria
109 W8 **Feldbach** Steiermark, SE Austria
101 F24 **Feldberg** ▲ SW Germany
116 J12 **Feldioara** Ger. Marienburg, Hung. Földvár. Braşov, C Romania
108 I7 **Feldkirch** anc. Clunia. Vorarlberg, W Austria
109 S9 **Feldkirchen in Kärnten** Slvn. Trg. Kärnten, S Austria
Félegyháza see Kiskunfélegyháza
192 H16 **Feleolo** × (Āpia) Upolu, C Samoa
104 H6 **Felgueiras** Porto, N Portugal
Felicitas Julia see Lisboa
172 J16 **Félicité** island Inner Islands, NE Seychelles
151 K20 **Felidhu Atoll** atoll C Maldives
41 Y13 **Felipe Carrillo Puerto** Quintana Roo, SE Mexico
97 Q21 **Felixstowe** E England, UK
103 N11 **Felletin** Creuse, C France
Fellin see Viljandi
Felsőbánya see Baia Sprie
Felsőmuzslya see Mužlja
Felsővisó see Vişeu de Sus
35 N10 **Felton** California, W USA
106 H7 **Feltre** Veneto, NE Italy
95 H25 **Femerbælt** Ger. Fehmarnbelt. strait Denmark/Germany
95 I24 **Femø** island SE Denmark
94 I10 **Femunden** ◎ S Norway
104 H2 **Fene** Galicia, NW Spain
14 I14 **Fenelon Falls** Ontario, SE Canada
189 U13 **Feneppi** atoll Chuuk Islands, C Micronesia
137 O11 **Fener Burnu** headland N Turkey
115 J14 **Fengári** ▲ Samothráki, E Greece
163 V13 **Fengcheng** var. Feng-cheng, Fenghwangcheng. Liaoning, NE China
160 K11 **Fenggang** prev. Longquan. Guizhou, S China
161 S9 **Fenghua** Zhejiang, SE China
Fenghwangcheng see Fengcheng
160 L9 **Fengjie** Sichuan, C China
160 M14 **Fengkai** prev. Jiankou. Guangdong, S China
161 T13 **Fenglin** Jap. Hōrin. C Taiwan
161 P1 **Fengning** prev. Dagezhen. Hebei, E China
160 E13 **Fengqing** Yunnan, SW China
161 O6 **Fengqiu** Henan, C China
161 Q2 **Fengrun** Hebei, E China
163 T4 **Fengshui Shan** ▲ NE China
161 P14 **Fengshun** Guangdong, S China
Fengtien see Liaoning, China
Fengtien see Shenyang, China
160 J7 **Fengxian** var. Feng Xian; prev. Shuangshipu. Shaanxi, C China
Fengxiang see Luobei
163 P13 **Fengzhen** Nei Mongol Zizhiqu, N China
160 M6 **Fen He** ≈ C China
153 V15 **Feni** Chittagong, E Bangladesh
186 I6 **Feni Islands** island group NE PNG
38 H17 **Fenimore Pass** strait Aleutian Islands, Alaska, USA
84 B9 **Feni Ridge** undersea feature N Atlantic Ocean
Fennern see Vändra
30 J9 **Fennimore** Wisconsin, N USA
172 J4 **Fenoarivo** Toamasina, E Madagascar
95 I24 **Fensmark** Storstrøm, SE Denmark
97 O19 **Fens, The** wetland E England, UK
31 R9 **Fenton** Michigan, N USA
190 K10 **Fenua Fala** island SE Tokelau
190 F12 **Fenuafo'ou, Île** island E Wallis and Futuna
190 L10 **Fenua Loa** island Fakaofo Atoll, E Tokelau
160 M4 **Fenyang** Shanxi, C China
117 U13 **Feodosiya** var. Kefe, It. Kaffa; anc. Theodosia. Respublika Krym, S Ukraine
94 I10 **Feragen** ◎ S Norway
74 L5 **Fer, Cap de** headland NE Algeria
31 O16 **Ferdinand** Indiana, N USA
Ferdinand see Montana, Bulgaria
Ferdinand see Mihail Kogălniceanu, Romania
Ferdinandsberg see Oţelu Roşu
143 T7 **Ferdows** var. Firdaus; prev. Tūn. Khorāsān, E Iran
103 Q5 **Fère-Champenoise** Marne, N France
Ferencz-József Csúcs see Gerlachovský štít
107 J16 **Ferentino** Lazio, C Italy
114 L13 **Féres** Anatolikí Makedonía kai Thráki, NE Greece
Fergana see Farghona
147 S10 **Fergana Valley** var. Farghona Valley, Rus. Ferganskaya Dolina, Taj. Wodii Farghona, Uzb. Farghona Wodiysi. basin Tajikistan/Uzbekistan
Ferganskaya Dolina see Fergana Valley
Ferganskaya Oblast' see Farghona Wiloyati
147 U9 **Ferganskiy Khrebet** ▲ C Kyrgyzstan
14 F15 **Fergus** Ontario, S Canada
29 S6 **Fergus Falls** Minnesota, N USA
186 G9 **Fergusson Island** var. Kaluwawa. island SE PNG
111 K22 **Ferihegy** × (Budapest) Budapest, C Hungary
Ferizaj see Uroševac
77 N14 **Ferkessédougou** N Ivory Coast
109 T10 **Ferlach** Slvn. Borovlje. Kärnten, S Austria
97 E16 **Fermanagh** cultural region SW Northern Ireland, UK
106 J13 **Fermo** anc. Firmum Picenum. Marche, C Italy
104 J6 **Fermoselle** Castilla-León, N Spain
97 D20 **Fermoy** Ir. Mainistir Fhear Maí. SW Ireland
23 W8 **Fernandina Beach** Amelia Island, Florida, SE USA
57 A17 **Fernandina, Isla** var. Narborough Island. island Galapagos Islands, Ecuador, E Pacific Ocean
47 Y5 **Fernando de Noronha** island E Brazil
Fernando Po/Fernando Póo see Bioco, Isla de
60 J7 **Fernandópolis** São Paulo, S Brazil
104 M13 **Fernán Núñez** Andalucía, S Spain
83 Q14 **Fernão Veloso, Baia de** bay NE Mozambique
34 K3 **Ferndale** California, W USA
32 H6 **Ferndale** Washington, NW USA
11 P17 **Fernie** British Columbia, SW Canada
35 R5 **Fernley** Nevada, W USA
Ferozepore see Firozpur
107 N18 **Ferrandina** Basilicata, S Italy
106 G9 **Ferrara** anc. Forum Alieni. Emilia-Romagna, N Italy
120 F9 **Ferrat, Cap** headland NW Algeria
107 D20 **Ferrato, Capo** headland Sardegna, Italy, C Mediterranean Sea
104 G12 **Ferreira do Alentejo** Beja, S Portugal
56 B11 **Ferreñafe** Lambayeque, W Peru
108 C12 **Ferret** Valais, SW Switzerland
102 I13 **Ferret, Cap** headland W France
22 I6 **Ferriday** Louisiana, S USA
Ferro see Hierro
107 D16 **Ferro, Capo** headland Sardegna, Italy, C Mediterranean Sea
104 H2 **Ferrol** var. El Ferrol; prev. El Ferrol del Caudillo. Galicia, NW Spain
56 B12 **Ferrol, Península de** peninsula W Peru
36 M5 **Ferron** Utah, W USA
21 S7 **Ferrum** Virginia, NE USA
23 O8 **Ferry Pass** Florida, SE USA
Ferryville see Menzel Bourguiba
29 S4 **Fertile** Minnesota, N USA
Fertő see Neusiedler See
98 L5 **Ferwerd** Fris. Ferwert. Friesland, N Netherlands
Ferwert see Ferwerd
74 G6 **Fès** Eng. Fez. N Morocco
79 I22 **Feshi** Bandundu, SW Dem. Rep. Congo (Zaire)
29 O4 **Fessenden** North Dakota, N USA
Festenberg see Twardogóra
27 X5 **Festus** Missouri, C USA
116 M14 **Feteşti** Ialomiţa, SE Romania
136 D17 **Fethiye** Muğla, SW Turkey
96 M1 **Fetlar** island NE Scotland, UK
95 I15 **Fetsund** Akershus, S Norway
12 L5 **Feuilles, Lac aux** ◎ Quebec, E Canada
12 L5 **Feuilles, Rivière aux** ≈ Quebec, E Canada
99 M23 **Feulen** Diekirch, C Luxembourg
103 Q11 **Feurs** Loire, E France
95 F18 **Fevik** Aust-Agder, S Norway
123 R13 **Fevral'sk** Amurskaya Oblast', SE Russian Federation
149 S2 **Feyẓābād** var. Faizabad, Faizābād, Feyzābād, Fyzabad. Badakhshān, NE Afghanistan
Fez see Fès
97 J19 **Ffestiniog** NW Wales, UK
Fhóid Duibh, Cuan an see Blacksod Bay
62 I8 **Fiambalá** Catamarca, NW Argentina
172 I6 **Fianarantsoa** Fianarantsoa, C Madagascar
172 H6 **Fianarantsoa** ◈ province SE Madagascar
78 G12 **Fianga** Mayo-Kébbi, SW Chad
Ficce see Fichē
80 J12 **Fichē** It. Ficce. Oromo, C Ethiopia
101 N17 **Fichtelberg** ▲ Czech Republic/Germany
101 M18 **Fichtelgebirge** ▲ SE Germany
101 M19 **Fichtelnaab** ≈ SE Germany
106 E9 **Fidenza** Emilia-Romagna, N Italy
113 K21 **Fier** var. Fieri. Fier, SW Albania
113 K21 **Fier** ◈ district W Albania
Fieri see Fier
Fierza see Fierzë
113 L17 **Fierzë** var. Fierza. Shkodër, N Albania
113 L17 **Fierzës, Liqeni i** ◎ N Albania
108 F10 **Fiesch** Valais, SW Switzerland
106 G11 **Fiesole** Toscana, C Italy
138 G12 **Fīfah** Aṭ Ṭafīlah, W Jordan
96 K11 **Fife** var. Kingdom of Fife. cultural region E Scotland, UK
96 K11 **Fife Ness** headland E Scotland, UK
Fifteen Twenty Fracture Zone see Barracuda Fracture Zone
103 N13 **Figeac** Lot, S France
95 N19 **Figeholm** Kalmar, SE Sweden
Figig see Figuig
83 J18 **Figtree** Matabeleland South, SW Zimbabwe
104 F8 **Figueira da Foz** Coimbra, W Portugal
105 X4 **Figueres** Cataluña, E Spain
74 H7 **Figuig** var. Figig. E Morocco
Fijāj, Shaṭṭ al see Fedjaj, Chott el
187 Y15 **Fiji** off. Sovereign Democratic Republic of Fiji, Fij. Viti. ◆ republic SW Pacific Ocean
192 K9 **Fiji** island group SW Pacific Ocean
175 Q8 **Fiji Plate** tectonic feature
105 P14 **Filabres, Sierra de los** ▲ SE Spain
83 K18 **Filabusi** Matabeleland South, S Zimbabwe
42 K13 **Filadelfia** Guanacaste, W Costa Rica
111 K20 **Fil'akovo** Hung. Fülek. Banskobystrický Kraj, C Slovakia
195 N5 **Filchner Ice Shelf** ice shelf Antarctica
14 J11 **Fildegrand** ≈ Quebec, SE Canada
33 O15 **Filer** Idaho, NW USA
Filevo see Vŭrbitsa
116 H14 **Filiaşi** Dolj, SW Romania
115 B16 **Filiátes** Ípeiros, W Greece
115 D21 **Filiatrá** Pelopónnisos, S Greece
107 K22 **Filicudi, Isola** island Isole Eolie, S Italy
141 Y10 **Filim** E Oman
Filimon Sîrbu see Făurei
77 S11 **Filingué** Tillabéri, W Niger
114 K13 **Filiouri** ≈ NE Greece
114 I13 **Filippoi** anc. Philippi. site of ancient city Anatolikí Makedonía kai Thráki, NE Greece
95 L15 **Filipstad** Värmland, C Sweden
108 I9 **Filisur** Graubünden, S Switzerland
94 E12 **Fillefjell** ▲ S Norway
35 R14 **Fillmore** California, W USA
36 K5 **Fillmore** Utah, W USA
14 J10 **Fils, Lac du** ◎ Quebec, SE Canada
136 H11 **Filyos Çayı** ≈ N Turkey
195 Q2 **Fimbulheimen** physical region Antarctica
195 Q1 **Fimbul Ice Shelf** ice shelf Antarctica
106 G9 **Finale Emilia** Emilia-Romagna, C Italy
106 C10 **Finale Ligure** Liguria, NW Italy
105 P14 **Fiñana** Andalucía, S Spain
172 I6 **Finandrahana** Fianarantsoa, SE Madagascar
21 S6 **Fincastle** Virginia, NE USA
99 M25 **Findel** × (Luxembourg) Luxembourg, C Luxembourg
96 J9 **Findhorn** ≈ N Scotland, UK
31 R12 **Findlay** Ohio, N USA
18 G11 **Finger Lakes** lakes New York, NE USA
83 L14 **Fingoè** Tete, NW Mozambique
136 E17 **Finike** Antalya, SW Turkey
102 F6 **Finistère** ◈ department NW France
186 D7 **Finisterre Range** ▲ N PNG
181 Q8 **Finke** Northern Territory, N Australia
109 S10 **Finkenstein** Kärnten, S Austria
189 Y15 **Finkol, Mount** var. Mount Crozer. ▲ Kosrae, E Micronesia
93 L17 **Finland** off. Republic of Finland, Fin. Suomen Tasavalta, Suomi. ◆ republic N Europe
126 F12 **Finland, Gulf of** Est. Soome Laht, Fin. Suomenlahti, Ger. Finnischer Meerbusen, Rus. Finskiy Zaliv, Swe. Finska Viken. gulf E Baltic Sea
10 L11 **Finlay** ≈ British Columbia, W Canada
183 O10 **Finley** New South Wales, SE Australia
29 Q4 **Finley** North Dakota, N USA
Finnischer Meerbusen see Finland, Gulf of
92 K9 **Finnmark** ◈ county N Norway
92 K9 **Finnmarksvidda** physical region N Norway
92 I9 **Finnsnes** Troms, N Norway
186 E7 **Finschhafen** Morobe, C PNG
94 E13 **Finse** Hordaland, S Norway
Finska Viken/Finskiy Zaliv see Finland, Gulf of
95 M17 **Finspång** Östergötland, S Sweden
108 F10 **Finsteraarhorn** ▲ Swtizerland
101 O14 **Finsterwalde** Brandenburg, E Germany
185 A23 **Fiordland** physical region South Island, NZ
106 E9 **Fiorenzuola d'Arda** Emilia-Romagna, C Italy
Firat Nehri see Euphrates
Firdaus see Ferdows
18 M14 **Fire Island** island New York, NE USA
106 G11 **Firenze** Eng. Florence; anc. Florentia. Toscana, C Italy
106 G10 **Firenzuola** Toscana, C Italy
14 C6 **Fire River** Ontario, S Canada
Firliug see Fârliug
61 B19 **Firmat** Santa Fe, C Argentina
103 Q12 **Firminy** Loire, E France
Firmum Picenum see Fermo
152 J12 **Fīrozābād** Uttar Pradesh, N India
152 G8 **Fīrozpur** var. Ferozepore. Punjab, NW India
First State see Delaware
143 O12 **Fīrūzābād** Fārs, S Iran
Fischamend see Fischamend Markt
109 Y4 **Fischamend Markt** var. Fischamend. Niederösterreich, NE Austria
109 W6 **Fischbacher Alpen** ▲ E Austria
Fischhausen see Primorsk
83 D21 **Fish** var. Vis. ≈ S Namibia
83 F24 **Fish** Afr. Vis. ≈ SW South Africa
11 X15 **Fisher Branch** Manitoba, S Canada
11 X15 **Fisher River** Manitoba, S Canada
19 N13 **Fishers Island** island New York, NE USA
37 U8 **Fishers Peak** ▲ Colorado, C USA
9 P9 **Fisher Strait** strait Nunavut, N Canada
97 H21 **Fishguard** Wel. Abergwaun. SW Wales, UK
19 R2 **Fish River Lake** ◎ Maine, NE USA
194 K6 **Fiske, Cape** headland Antarctica
103 P4 **Fismes** Marne, N France
104 F3 **Fisterra, Cabo** headland NW Spain
19 N11 **Fitchburg** Massachusetts, NE USA
96 L3 **Fitful Head** headland NE Scotland, UK
95 C14 **Fitjar** Hordaland, S Norway
192 H16 **Fito** ▲ Upolu, C Samoa
23 U6 **Fitzgerald** Georgia, SE USA
180 M5 **Fitzroy Crossing** Western Australia
63 G21 **Fitzroy, Monte** var. Cerro Chaltel. ▲ S Argentina
181 Y8 **Fitzroy River** ≈ Queensland, E Australia
180 L5 **Fitzroy River** ≈ Western Australia
14 E12 **Fitzwilliam Island** island Ontario, S Canada
107 J15 **Fiuggi** Lazio, C Italy
Fiume see Rijeka
107 H15 **Fiumicino** Lazio, C Italy
Fiumicino see Leonardo da Vinci
106 E10 **Fivizzano** Toscana, C Italy
79 O21 **Fizi** Sud Kivu, E Dem. Rep. Congo (Zaire)
Fizuli see Füzuli
92 I11 **Fjällåsen** Norrbotten, N Sweden
95 G20 **Fjerritslev** Nordjylland, N Denmark
F.J.S. see Franz Josef Strauss
95 L16 **Fjugesta** Örebro, C Sweden
Fladstrand see Frederikshavn
37 V5 **Flagler** Colorado, C USA
23 X10 **Flagler Beach** Florida, SE USA
36 L11 **Flagstaff** Arizona, SW USA
65 H24 **Flagstaff Bay** bay Saint Helena, C Atlantic Ocean
19 P5 **Flagstaff Lake** ◎ Maine, NE USA
94 E13 **Flåm** Sogn og Fjordane, S Norway
15 O8 **Flamand** ≈ Quebec, SE Canada
30 J5 **Flambeau River** ≈ Wisconsin, N USA
97 O16 **Flamborough Head** headland E England, UK
100 N13 **Fläming** hill range NE Germany
16 H8 **Flaming Gorge Reservoir** ⊞ Utah/Wyoming, NW USA
99 B18 **Flanders** Dut. Vlaanderen, Fr. Flandre. cultural region Belgium/France
Flandre see Flanders
29 R10 **Flandreau** South Dakota, N USA
96 D6 **Flannan Isles** island group NW Scotland, UK
28 M6 **Flasher** North Dakota, N USA
93 G15 **Flåsjön** ◎ N Sweden
39 O11 **Flat** Alaska, USA
92 H1 **Flateyri** Vestfirdhir, Nw Iceland
33 P8 **Flathead Lake** ◎ Montana, NW USA
173 Y15 **Flat Island** Fr. Île Plate. island N Mauritius
25 T11 **Flatonia** Texas, SW USA
185 M14 **Flat Point** headland North Island, NZ
27 X6 **Flat River** Missouri, C USA
31 P8 **Flat River** ≈ Michigan, N USA
31 P14 **Flatrock River** ≈ Indiana, N USA
32 E6 **Flattery, Cape** headland Washington, NW USA
64 B12 **Flatts Village** var. The Flatts Village. C Bermuda
108 H7 **Flawil** Sankt Gallen, NE Switzerland
97 N22 **Fleet** S England, UK
97 K16 **Fleetwood** NW England, UK
18 H15 **Fleetwood** Pennsylvania, NE USA
95 D18 **Flekkefjord** Vest-Agder, S Norway
21 N5 **Flemingsburg** Kentucky, S USA
18 J15 **Flemington** New Jersey, NE USA
64 I7 **Flemish Cap** undersea feature NW Atlantic Ocean
95 N16 **Flen** Södermanland, C Sweden
100 I6 **Flensburg** Schleswig-Holstein, N Germany
100 J6 **Flensburger Förde** inlet Denmark/Germany
102 K5 **Flers** Orne, N France
95 C14 **Flesland** × (Bergen) Hordaland, S Norway
Flessingue see Vlissingen
21 P10 **Fletcher** North Carolina, SE USA
31 R6 **Fletcher Pond** ◎ Michigan, N USA
102 L15 **Fleurance** Gers, S France
108 B8 **Fleurier** Neuchâtel, W Switzerland
99 H20 **Fleurus** Hainaut, S Belgium
103 N7 **Fleury-les-Aubrais** Loiret, C France
98 K10 **Flevoland** ◈ province C Netherlands
Flickertail State see North Dakota
108 H9 **Flims** Glarus, NE Switzerland
182 F8 **Flinders Island** island Investigator Group, South Australia
183 P14 **Flinders Island** island Furneaux Group, Tasmania, SE Australia
182 I6 **Flinders Ranges** ▲ South Australia
181 U5 **Flinders River** ≈ Queensland, NE Australia
11 V13 **Flin Flon** Manitoba, C Canada
97 K18 **Flint** NE Wales, UK
31 R9 **Flint** Michigan, N USA
97 J18 **Flint** cultural region NE Wales, UK
27 O7 **Flint Hills** hill range Kansas, C USA
191 Y6 **Flint Island** island Line Islands, E Kiribati
23 S4 **Flint River** ≈ Georgia, SE USA
31 R9 **Flint River** ≈ Michigan, N USA
189 X12 **Flipper Point** headland C Wake Island
94 I13 **Flisa** Hedmark, S Norway
94 I13 **Flisa** ≈ S Norway
122 J5 **Flissingskiy, Mys** headland Novaya Zemlya, NW Russian Federation
Flitsch see Bovec
105 U6 **Flix** Cataluña, NE Spain
95 J19 **Floda** Västra Götaland, S Sweden
101 O16 **Flöha** ≈ E Germany
25 O4 **Flomot** Texas, SW USA
29 V5 **Floodwood** Minnesota, N USA
30 M15 **Flora** Illinois, N USA
103 P14 **Florac** Lozère, S France
23 Q8 **Florala** Alabama, S USA
103 S4 **Florange** Moselle, NE France
Floreana, Isla see Santa María, Isla
23 O2 **Florence** Alabama, S USA
36 L14 **Florence** Arizona, SW USA
37 T6 **Florence** Colorado, C USA
27 O5 **Florence** Kansas, C USA
20 M4 **Florence** Kentucky, S USA
32 E13 **Florence** Oregon, NW USA
21 T12 **Florence** South Carolina, SE USA
25 S9 **Florence** Texas, SW USA
Florence see Firenze
54 E13 **Florencia** Caquetá, S Colombia
99 H21 **Florennes** Namur, S Belgium
Florentia see Firenze
63 J18 **Florentino Ameghino, Embalse** ◎ S Argentina
99 J24 **Florenville** Luxembourg, SE Belgium
42 E3 **Flores** Petén, N Guatemala
61 E19 **Flores** ◈ department S Uruguay
171 O16 **Flores** island Nusa Tenggara, C Indonesia
64 M1 **Flores** island Azores, Portugal, NE Atlantic Ocean
Floreshty see Floreşti
Flores, Lago de see Petén Itzá, Lago
Flores, Laut see Flores Sea
171 N15 **Flores Sea** Ind. Laut Flores. sea C Indonesia
116 M8 **Floreşti** Rus. Floreshty. N Moldova
25 S12 **Floresville** Texas, SW USA
59 N14 **Floriano** Piauí, E Brazil
61 K14 **Florianópolis** prev. Destêrro. state capital Santa Catarina, S Brazil
44 G6 **Florida** Camagüey, C Cuba
61 F19 **Florida** Florida, S Uruguay
61 F19 **Florida** ◈ department S Uruguay
23 U9 **Florida** off. State of Florida; also known as Peninsular State, Sunshine State. ◈ state SE USA
23 Y17 **Florida Bay** bay Florida, SE USA
54 G8 **Floridablanca** Santander, N Colombia
23 Y17 **Florida Keys** island group Florida, SE USA
37 Q16 **Florida Mountains** ▲ New Mexico, SW USA
64 D10 **Florida, Straits of** strait Atlantic Ocean/Gulf of Mexico
114 D13 **Flórina** var. Phlórina. Dytikí Makedonía, N Greece
27 X4 **Florissant** Missouri, C USA
94 C11 **Florø** Sogn og Fjordane, S Norway
115 L22 **Floúda, Akrotírio** headland Astypálaia, Kykládes, Greece, Aegean Sea
21 S7 **Floyd** Virginia, NE USA
25 N4 **Floydada** Texas, SW USA
Flüela Wisshorn see Weisshorn
98 K7 **Fluessen** ◎ N Netherlands
105 S5 **Flúmen** ≈ NE Spain
107 C20 **Flumendosa** ≈ Sardegna, Italy, C Mediterranean Sea
31 R9 **Flushing** Michigan, N USA
Flushing see Vlissingen
25 O6 **Fluvanna** Texas, SW USA
186 B8 **Fly** ≈ Indonesia/PNG
194 I10 **Flying Fish, Cape** headland Thurston Island, Antarctica
Flylân see Vlieland
193 Y15 **Foa** island Ha'apai Group, C Tonga
11 U15 **Foam Lake** Saskatchewan, S Canada
113 J14 **Foča** var Srbinje, Republika Srpska, Bosnia and Herzegovina
116 L12 **Focşani** Vrancea, E Romania
Fogaras/Fogarasch see Făgăraş
107 M16 **Foggia** Puglia, SE Italy
Foggo see Faggo
76 D10 **Fogo** island Ilhas de Sotavento, SW Cape Verde
13 U11 **Fogo Island** island Newfoundland, E Canada
109 U7 **Fohnsdorf** Steiermark, SE Austria
100 G7 **Föhr** island NW Germany
104 F14 **Fóia** ▲ S Portugal
14 I10 **Foins, Lac aux** ◎ Quebec, SE Canada
103 N17 **Foix** Ariège, S France
128 I5 **Fokino** Bryanskaya Oblast', W Russian Federation
Fola, Cnoc see Bloody Foreland
94 E13 **Folarskardnuten** ▲ S Norway
92 G11 **Folda** fjord C Norway
93 E14 **Foldafjorden** fjord C Norway
Földvár see Feldioara
93 F14 **Foldereid** Nord-Trøndelag, C Norway
115 J22 **Folégandros** island Kykládes, Greece, Aegean Sea
23 O9 **Foley** Alabama, S USA
29 U7 **Foley** Minnesota, N USA
14 E7 **Foleyet** Ontario, S Canada
95 D14 **Folgefonni** glacier S Norway

◆ Country ◇ Dependent Territory ◈ Administrative Region ▲ Mountain Volcano ◎ Lake
● Country Capital ○ Dependent Territory Capital × International Airport ▲ Mountain Range ≈ River ⊞ Reservoir

106 I13 **Foligno** Umbria, C Italy
97 Q23 **Folkestone** SE England, UK
23 W8 **Folkston** Georgia, SE USA
94 H10 **Folldal** Hedmark, S Norway
25 P1 **Follett** Texas, SW USA
106 F13 **Follonica** Toscana, C Italy
21 T15 **Folly Beach** South Carolina, SE USA
35 O7 **Folsom** California, W USA
116 M12 **Foltești** Galați, E Romania
172 H14 **Fomboni** Mohéli, S Comoros
18 K10 **Fonda** New York, NE USA
11 S10 **Fond-du-Lac** Saskatchewan, C Canada
30 M8 **Fond du Lac** Wisconsin, N USA
11 T10 **Fond-du-Lac** ≈ Saskatchewan, C Canada
190 C9 **Fongafale** var. Funafuti. ● (Tuvalu) Funafuti Atoll, SE Tuvalu
190 G8 **Fongafale** atoll C Tuvalu
107 C18 **Fonni** Sardegna, Italy, C Mediterranean Sea
189 V12 **Fono** island Chuuk, C Micronesia
54 G4 **Fonseca** La Guajira, N Colombia
Fonseca, Golfo de see Fonseca, Gulf of
42 H8 **Fonseca, Gulf of** Sp. Golfo de Fonseca. gulf Central America
103 O6 **Fontainebleau** Seine-et-Marne, N France
63 G19 **Fontana, Lago** ⊚ W Argentina
21 N10 **Fontana Lake** ▣ North Carolina, SE USA
107 L24 **Fontanarossa** ✕ (Catania) Sicilia, Italy, C Mediterranean Sea
11 N11 **Fontas** ≈ British Columbia, W Canada
58 D12 **Fonte Boa** Amazonas, N Brazil
102 J10 **Fontenay-le-Comte** Vendée, NW France
33 T16 **Fontenelle Reservoir** ▣ Wyoming, C USA
193 Y14 **Fonualei** island Vava'u Group, N Tonga
111 H24 **Fonyód** Somogy, W Hungary
Foochow see Fuzhou
39 Q10 **Foraker, Mount** ▲ Alaska, USA
187 R14 **Forari** Éfaté, C Vanuatu
103 U4 **Forbach** Moselle, NE France
183 Q8 **Forbes** New South Wales, SE Australia
77 T17 **Forcados** Delta, S Nigeria
103 S14 **Forcalquier** Alpes-de-Haute-Provence, SE France
101 K19 **Forchheim** Bayern, SE Germany
35 R13 **Ford City** California, W USA
94 D11 **Førde** Sogn og Fjordane, S Norway
31 N4 **Ford River** ≈ Michigan, N USA
183 O4 **Fords Bridge** New South Wales, SE Australia
20 J6 **Fordsville** Kentucky, S USA
27 U13 **Fordyce** Arkansas, C USA
76 I14 **Forécariah** Guinée-Maritime, SW Guinea
197 O14 **Forel, Mont** ▲ SE Greenland
11 R17 **Foremost** Alberta, SW Canada
14 D16 **Forest** Ontario, S Canada
22 L5 **Forest** Mississippi, S USA
31 S12 **Forest** Ohio, N USA
29 V11 **Forest City** Iowa, C USA
21 Q10 **Forest City** North Carolina, SE USA
32 G11 **Forest Grove** Oregon, NW USA
183 P17 **Forestier Peninsula** peninsula Tasmania, SE Australia
29 V8 **Forest Lake** Minnesota, N USA
23 S3 **Forest Park** Georgia, SE USA
29 Q3 **Forest River** ≈ North Dakota, N USA
15 T6 **Forestville** Quebec, SE Canada
103 Q11 **Forez, Monts du** ▲ C France
96 K10 **Forfar** E Scotland, UK
26 J8 **Forgan** Oklahoma, C USA
Forge du Sud see Dudelange
101 J24 **Forggensee** ⊚ S Germany
147 N10 **Forish** Rus. Farish. Jizzakh Wiloyati, C Uzbekistan
20 F9 **Forked Deer River** ≈ Tennessee, S USA
32 F7 **Forks** Washington, NW USA
92 N2 **Forlandsundet** sound W Svalbard
106 H10 **Forlì** anc. Forum Livii. Emilia-Romagna, N Italy
29 Q7 **Forman** North Dakota, N USA
97 K17 **Formby** NW England, UK
105 V11 **Formentera** anc. Ophiusa, Lat. Frumentum. island Islas Baleares, Spain, W Mediterranean Sea
Formentor, Cabo de see Formentor, Cap de
105 Y9 **Formentor, Cap de** var. Cabo de Formentor, Cape Formentor. headland Mallorca, Spain, W Mediterranean Sea
Formentor, Cape see Formentor, Cap de
107 J16 **Formia** Lazio, C Italy
62 O7 **Formosa** Formosa, NE Argentina
62 M6 **Formosa** off. Provincia de Formosa. ◈ province NE Argentina
Formosa/Formo'sa see Taiwan
59 I17 **Formosa, Serra** ▲ C Brazil
Formosa Strait see Taiwan Strait
95 H15 **Fornebu** ✕ (Oslo) Akershus, S Norway
25 U6 **Forney** Texas, SW USA
95 H21 **Fornæs** headland C Denmark
106 E9 **Fornovo di Taro** Emilia-Romagna, C Italy
117 T14 **Foros** Respublika Krym, S Ukraine
Føroyar see Faeroe Islands
96 J8 **Forres** NE Scotland, UK
27 X11 **Forrest City** Arkansas, C USA
39 Y15 **Forrester Island** island Alexander Archipelago, Alaska, USA
25 N7 **Forsan** Texas, SW USA
181 V5 **Forsayth** Queensland, NE Australia
95 L19 **Forserum** Jönköping, S Sweden
95 K15 **Forshaga** Värmland, C Sweden
93 L19 **Forssa** Etelä-Suomi, S Finland
101 Q14 **Forst** Lus. Baršć Łužyca. Brandenburg, E Germany
183 U7 **Forster-Tuncurry** New South Wales, SE Australia
23 T4 **Forsyth** Georgia, SE USA
27 T8 **Forsyth** Missouri, C USA
33 W10 **Forsyth** Montana, NW USA
149 U11 **Fort Abbās** Punjab, E Pakistan
12 G10 **Fort Albany** Ontario, C Canada
56 L13 **Fortaleza** Pando, N Bolivia
58 P13 **Fortaleza** prev. Ceará. state capital Ceará, NE Brazil
59 D16 **Fortaleza** Rondônia, W Brazil
56 C13 **Fortaleza, Río** ≈ W Peru
Fort-Archambault see Sarh
21 U3 **Fort Ashby** West Virginia, NE USA
96 I9 **Fort Augustus** N Scotland, UK
Fort-Bayard see Zhanjiang
33 S8 **Fort Benton** Montana, NW USA
35 Q1 **Fort Bidwell** California, W USA
34 L5 **Fort Bragg** California, W USA
31 N16 **Fort Branch** Indiana, N USA
Fort-Bretonnet see Bousso
33 T17 **Fort Bridger** Wyoming, C USA
Fort-Cappolani see Tidjikja
Fort Charlet see Djanet
Fort-Chimo see Kuujjuaq
11 R10 **Fort Chipewyan** Alberta, C Canada
Fort Cobb Lake see Fort Cobb Reservoir
26 L11 **Fort Cobb Reservoir** var. Fort Cobb Lake. ▣ Oklahoma, C USA
37 T3 **Fort Collins** Colorado, C USA
14 K12 **Fort-Coulonge** Quebec, SE Canada
Fort-Crampel see Kaga Bandoro
Fort-Dauphin see Tôlañaro
24 K10 **Fort Davis** Texas, SW USA
37 O10 **Fort Defiance** Arizona, SW USA
45 Q12 **Fort-de-France** prev. Fort-Royal. ○ (Martinique) W Martinique
45 P12 **Fort-de-France, Baie de** bay W Martinique
Fort de Kock see Bukittinggi
23 P6 **Fort Deposit** Alabama, S USA
29 U13 **Fort Dodge** Iowa, C USA
15 S10 **Forteau** Quebec, E Canada
106 E11 **Forte dei Marmi** Toscana, C Italy
14 H17 **Fort Erie** Ontario, S Canada
180 H7 **Fortescue River** ≈ Western Australia
19 S2 **Fort Fairfield** Maine, NE USA
Fort-Foureau see Kousséri
12 A11 **Fort Frances** Ontario, S Canada
Fort Franklin see Déline
23 R7 **Fort Gaines** Georgia, SE USA
37 T8 **Fort Garland** Colorado, C USA
21 P5 **Fort Gay** West Virginia, NE USA
Fort George see La Grande Rivière
27 Q10 **Fort Gibson** Oklahoma, C USA
27 Q9 **Fort Gibson Lake** ▣ Oklahoma, C USA
8 H7 **Fort Good Hope** var. Good Hope. Northwest Territories, NW Canada
23 V4 **Fort Gordon** Georgia, SE USA
Fort Gouraud see Fdérik
96 I11 **Forth** ≈ C Scotland, UK
Fort Hall see Murang'a
24 H8 **Fort Hancock** Texas, SW USA
Fort Hertz see Putao
96 K12 **Forth, Firth of** estuary E Scotland, UK
14 L14 **Forthton** Ontario, SE Canada
14 M8 **Fortier** ≈ Quebec, SE Canada
Fortín General Eugenio Garay see General Eugenio A. Garay
Fort Jameson see Chipata
Fort Johnston see Mangochi
19 R1 **Fort Kent** Maine, NE USA
Fort-Lamy see Ndjamena
23 Z15 **Fort Lauderdale** Florida, SE USA
21 R11 **Fort Lawn** South Carolina, SE USA
8 H10 **Fort Liard** var. Liard. Northwest Territories, W Canada
44 M8 **Fort-Liberté** NE Haiti
21 N9 **Fort Loudoun Lake** ▣ Tennessee, S USA
37 T3 **Fort Lupton** Colorado, C USA
11 R12 **Fort MacKay** Alberta, C Canada
11 Q17 **Fort Macleod** var. MacLeod. Alberta, SW Canada
29 Y16 **Fort Madison** Iowa, C USA
Fort Manning see Mchinji
25 P9 **Fort McKavett** Texas, SW USA
11 R12 **Fort McMurray** Alberta, C Canada
8 G7 **Fort McPherson** var. McPherson. Northwest Territories, NW Canada
21 R11 **Fort Mill** South Carolina, SE USA
Fort-Millot see Ngouri
37 U3 **Fort Morgan** Colorado, C USA
23 W14 **Fort Myers** Florida, SE USA
23 W15 **Fort Myers Beach** Florida, SE USA
10 M10 **Fort Nelson** British Columbia, W Canada
10 M10 **Fort Nelson** ≈ British Columbia, W Canada
Fort Norman see Tulita.
23 Q2 **Fort Payne** Alabama, S USA
33 W7 **Fort Peck** Montana, NW USA
33 V8 **Fort Peck Lake** ▣ Montana, NW USA
23 Y13 **Fort Pierce** Florida, SE USA
29 N10 **Fort Pierre** South Dakota, N USA
81 E18 **Fort Portal** SW Uganda
8 J10 **Fort Providence** var. Providence. Northwest Territories, W Canada
11 U16 **Fort Qu'Appelle** Saskatchewan, S Canada
Fort-Repoux see Akjoujt
8 K10 **Fort Resolution** var. Resolution. Northwest Territories, W Canada
33 T13 **Fortress Mountain** ▲ Wyoming, C USA
Fort Rosebery see Mansa
Fort-Rousset see Owando
Fort-Royal see Fort-de-France
12 I10 **Fort Rupert** prev. Rupert House. Quebec, SE Canada
8 H13 **Fort St.James** British Columbia, SW Canada
11 N12 **Fort St.John** British Columbia, W Canada
Fort Sandeman see Zhob
11 Q14 **Fort Saskatchewan** Alberta, SW Canada
27 R6 **Fort Scott** Kansas, C USA
12 E6 **Fort Severn** Ontario, C Canada
31 R12 **Fort Shawnee** Ohio, N USA
144 E14 **Fort-Shevchenko** Mangistau, W Kazakhstan
Fort-Sibut see Sibut
8 I10 **Fort Simpson** var. Simpson. Northwest Territories, W Canada
8 K11 **Fort Smith** district capital Northwest Territories, W Canada
27 R10 **Fort Smith** Arkansas, C USA
37 T13 **Fort Stanton** New Mexico, SW USA
24 L9 **Fort Stockton** Texas, SW USA
37 U12 **Fort Sumner** New Mexico, SW USA
26 K8 **Fort Supply** Oklahoma, C USA
26 K8 **Fort Supply Lake** ▣ Oklahoma, C USA
29 O10 **Fort Thompson** South Dakota, N USA
Fort-Trinquet see Bîr Mogreïn
105 R12 **Fortuna** Murcia, SE Spain
34 K3 **Fortuna** California, W USA
28 J2 **Fortuna** North Dakota, N USA
23 T5 **Fort Valley** Georgia, SE USA
11 P11 **Fort Vermilion** Alberta, W Canada
Fort Victoria see Masvingo
31 P13 **Fortville** Indiana, N USA
23 P9 **Fort Walton Beach** Florida, SE USA
31 P12 **Fort Wayne** Indiana, N USA
96 H10 **Fort William** N Scotland, UK
25 T6 **Fort Worth** Texas, SW USA
28 M7 **Fort Yates** North Dakota, N USA
39 S7 **Fort Yukon** Alaska, USA
Forum Alieni see Ferrara
Forum Julii see Fréjus
Forum Livii see Forlì
143 Q15 **Forür, Jazīreh-ye** island S Iran
94 H7 **Fosen** physical region S Norway
161 N14 **Foshan** var. Fatshan, Fo-shan, Namhoi. Guangdong, S China
Fossa Claudia see Chioggia
106 B9 **Fossano** Piemonte, NW Italy
99 H21 **Fosses-la-Ville** Namur, S Belgium
32 J12 **Fossil** Oregon, NW USA
Foss Lake see Foss Reservoir
106 I11 **Fossombrone** Marche, C Italy
26 K10 **Foss Reservoir** var. Foss Lake. ▣ Oklahoma, C USA
29 S4 **Fosston** Minnesota, N USA
183 O13 **Foster** Victoria, SE Australia
11 T12 **Foster Lakes** ⊚ Saskatchewan, C Canada
31 S12 **Fostoria** Ohio, N USA
79 D19 **Fougamou** Ngounié, C Gabon
102 J6 **Fougères** Ille-et-Vilaine, NW France
Fou-hsin see Fuxin
27 S14 **Fouke** Arkansas, C USA
96 K2 **Foula** island NE Scotland, UK
65 D24 **Foul Bay** bay East Falkland, Falkland Islands
97 P21 **Foulness Island** island SE England, UK
185 F15 **Foulwind, Cape** headland South Island, NZ
79 E15 **Foumban** Ouest, NW Cameroon
172 H13 **Foumbouni** Grande Comore, NW Comoros
195 N8 **Foundation Ice Stream** glacier Antarctica
37 T6 **Fountain** Colorado, C USA
36 L4 **Fountain Green** Utah, W USA
21 P11 **Fountain Inn** South Carolina, SE USA
27 S11 **Fourche LaFave River** ≈ Arkansas, C USA
33 Z13 **Four Corners** Wyoming, C USA
103 Q2 **Fourmies** Nord, N France
38 J17 **Four Mountains, Islands of** island group Aleutian Islands, Alaska, USA
173 P17 **Fournaise, Piton de la** ▲ SE Réunion
14 J8 **Fournière, Lac** ⊚ Quebec, SE Canada
115 L20 **Foúrnoi** island Dodekánisos, Greece, Aegean Sea
64 K13 **Four North Fracture Zone** tectonic feature W Atlantic Ocean
Fouron-Saint-Martin see Sint-Martens-Voeren
30 L3 **Fourteen Mile Point** headland Michigan, N USA
76 I13 **Fouta Djallon** var. Futa Jallon. ▲ W Guinea
185 C25 **Foveaux Strait** strait S NZ
35 Q11 **Fowler** California, W USA
37 U6 **Fowler** Colorado, C USA
31 N12 **Fowler** Indiana, N USA
182 D7 **Fowlers Bay** bay South Australia
25 R13 **Fowlerton** Texas, SW USA
142 M3 **Fowman** var. Fuman, Fumen. Gīlān, NW Iran
65 C25 **Fox Bay East** West Falkland, Falkland Islands
65 C25 **Fox Bay West** West Falkland, Falkland Islands
14 J14 **Foxboro** Ontario, SE Canada
11 O14 **Fox Creek** Alberta, W Canada
64 G5 **Foxe Basin** sea Nunavut, N Canada
64 G5 **Foxe Channel** channel Nunavut, N Canada
95 I16 **Foxen** ⊚ C Sweden
9 Q7 **Foxe Peninsula** peninsula Baffin Island, Nunavut, NE Canada
185 E19 **Fox Glacier** West Coast, South Island, NZ
38 L17 **Fox Islands** island Aleutian Islands, Alaska, USA
30 M10 **Fox Lake** Illinois, N USA
11 V12 **Fox Mine** Manitoba, C Canada
35 R3 **Fox Mountain** ▲ Nevada, W USA
65 E25 **Fox Point** headland East Falkland, Falkland Islands
30 M11 **Fox River** ≈ Illinois/Wisconsin, N USA
30 L7 **Fox River** ≈ Wisconsin, N USA
184 L13 **Foxton** Manawatu-Wanganui, North Island, NZ
11 S16 **Fox Valley** Saskatchewan, S Canada
11 W16 **Foxwarren** Manitoba, S Canada
97 E14 **Foyle, Lough** Ir. Loch Feabhail. inlet N Ireland
194 H5 **Foyn Coast** physical region Antarctica
104 I2 **Foz** Galicia, NW Spain
60 I12 **Foz do Areia, Represa de** ▣ S Brazil
59 A16 **Foz do Breu** Acre, W Brazil
83 A16 **Foz do Cunene** Namibe, SW Angola
60 G12 **Foz do Iguaçu** Paraná, S Brazil
58 C12 **Foz do Mamoriá** Amazonas, NW Brazil
105 T6 **Fraga** Aragón, NE Spain
44 F5 **Fragoso, Cayo** island C Cuba
61 G18 **Fraile Muerto** Cerro Largo, NE Uruguay
99 H21 **Fraire** Namur, S Belgium
99 L21 **Fraiture, Baraque de** hill SE Belgium
Frakštát see Hlohovec
197 S10 **Fram Basin** var. Amundsen Basin. undersea feature Arctic Ocean
99 F20 **Frameries** Hainaut, S Belgium
19 O11 **Framingham** Massachusetts, NE USA
60 L7 **Franca** São Paulo, S Brazil
187 O15 **Français, Récif des** reef W New Caledonia
107 K14 **Francavilla al Mare** Abruzzo, C Italy
107 P18 **Francavilla Fontana** Puglia, SE Italy
102 M8 **France** off. French Republic, It./Sp. Francia; prev. Gaul, Gaule, Lat. Gallia. ◆ republic W Europe
45 O8 **Francés Viejo, Cabo** headland NE Dominican Republic
79 F19 **Franceville** var. Massoukou, Masuku. Haut-Ogooué, E Gabon
79 F19 **Franceville** ✕ Haut-Ogooué, E Gabon
Francfort see Frankfurt am Main
103 T8 **Franche-Comté** ◈ region E France
Francia see France
29 O11 **Francis Case, Lake** ▣ South Dakota, N USA
60 H12 **Francisco Beltrão** Paraná, S Brazil
Francisco I. Madero see Villa Madero
61 A21 **Francisco Madero** Buenos Aires, E Argentina
42 H6 **Francisco Morazán** prev. Tegucigalpa. ◈ department C Honduras
83 J18 **Francistown** North East, NE Botswana
Franconian Forest see Frankenwald
Franconian Jura see Fränkische Alb
98 K6 **Franeker** Fris. Frjentsjer. Friesland, N Netherlands
Frankenalb see Fränkische Alb
101 H16 **Frankenberg** Hessen, C Germany
101 J20 **Frankenhöhe** hill range C Germany
31 R8 **Frankenmuth** Michigan, N USA
101 F20 **Frankenstein** hill W Germany
Frankenstein/Frankenstein in Schlesien see Ząbkowice Śląskie
101 G20 **Frankenthal** Rheinland-Pfalz, W Germany
101 L18 **Frankenwald** Eng. Franconian Forest. ▲ C Germany
44 J12 **Frankfield** C Jamaica
14 J14 **Frankford** Ontario, SE Canada
31 O13 **Frankfort** Indiana, N USA
27 O3 **Frankfort** Kansas, C USA
20 L5 **Frankfort** state capital Kentucky, S USA
Frankfort on the Main see Frankfurt am Main
Frankfurt see Słubice, Poland
Frankfurt see Frankfurt am Main, Germany
101 G18 **Frankfurt am Main** var. Frankfurt, Fr. Francfort; prev. Eng. Frankfort on the Main. Hessen, SW Germany
100 Q12 **Frankfurt an der Oder** Brandenburg, E Germany
101 L21 **Fränkische Alb** var. Frankenalb, Eng. Franconian Jura. ▲ S Germany
101 I18 **Fränkische Saale** ≈ C Germany
101 L19 **Fränkische Schweiz** hill range C Germany
23 R4 **Franklin** Georgia, SE USA
31 P14 **Franklin** Indiana, N USA
20 J7 **Franklin** Kentucky, S USA
22 I9 **Franklin** Louisiana, S USA
29 O17 **Franklin** Nebraska, C USA
21 N10 **Franklin** North Carolina, SE USA
18 C13 **Franklin** Pennsylvania, NE USA
20 J9 **Franklin** Tennessee, S USA
25 U9 **Franklin** Texas, SW USA
21 X7 **Franklin** Virginia, NE USA
21 T4 **Franklin** West Virginia, NE USA
30 M9 **Franklin** Wisconsin, N USA
8 I6 **Franklin Bay** inlet Northwest Territories, N Canada
32 K7 **Franklin D.Roosevelt Lake** ▣ Washington, NW USA
35 W4 **Franklin Lake** ⊚ Nevada, W USA
185 B22 **Franklin Mountains** ▲ South Island, NZ
39 R5 **Franklin Mountains** ▲ Alaska, USA
39 N4 **Franklin, Point** headland Alaska, USA
183 O17 **Franklin River** ≈ Tasmania, SE Australia
22 K8 **Franklinton** Louisiana, S USA
21 U9 **Franklinton** North Carolina, SE USA
Frankstadt see Frenštát pod Radhoštěm
25 V7 **Frankston** Texas, SW USA
33 U12 **Frannie** Wyoming, C USA
15 U5 **Franquelin** Quebec, SE Canada
15 U5 **Franquelin** ≈ Quebec, SE Canada
83 C18 **Fransfontein** Kunene, NW Namibia
93 H17 **Fränsta** Västernorrland, C Sweden
122 J3 **Frantsa-Iosifa, Zemlya** Eng. Franz Josef Land. island group N Russian Federation
185 E18 **Franz Josef Glacier** West Coast, South Island, NZ
Franz Josef Land see Frantsa-Iosifa, Zemlya
Franz-Josef Spitze see Gerlachovský štít
101 L23 **Franz Josef Strauss** abbrev. F.J.S. ✕ (München) Bayern, SE Germany
107 A19 **Frasca, Capo della** headland Sardegna, Italy, C Mediterranean Sea
107 I15 **Frascati** Lazio, C Italy
11 N14 **Fraser** ≈ British Columbia, SW Canada
83 G24 **Fraserburg** Western Cape, SW South Africa
96 L8 **Fraserburgh** NE Scotland, UK
181 Z9 **Fraser Island** var. Great Sandy Island. island Queensland, E Australia
10 L14 **Fraser Lake** British Columbia, SW Canada
10 L15 **Fraser Plateau** plateau British Columbia, SW Canada
184 P10 **Frasertown** Hawke's Bay, North Island, NZ
99 E19 **Frasnes-lez-Buissenal** Hainaut, SW Belgium
108 I7 **Frastanz** Vorarlberg, NW Austria
14 B8 **Frater** Ontario, S Canada
Frauenbach see Baia Mare
Frauenburg see Saldus, Latvia
Frauenburg see Frombork, Poland
108 H6 **Frauenfeld** Thurgau, NE Switzerland
109 Z5 **Frauenkirchen** Burgenland, E Austria
61 D19 **Fray Bentos** Río Negro, W Uruguay
61 F19 **Fray Marcos** Florida, S Uruguay
29 S6 **Frazee** Minnesota, N USA
104 M5 **Frechilla** Castilla-León, N Spain
30 I4 **Frederic** Wisconsin, N USA
95 G23 **Fredericia** Vejle, C Denmark
21 W3 **Frederick** Maryland, NE USA
26 L12 **Frederick** Oklahoma, C USA
29 P7 **Frederick** South Dakota, N USA
29 X12 **Fredericksburg** Iowa, C USA
25 R10 **Fredericksburg** Texas, SW USA
21 W5 **Fredericksburg** Virginia, NE USA
39 X13 **Frederick Sound** sound Alaska, USA
27 X6 **Fredericktown** Missouri, C USA
60 H13 **Frederico Westphalen** Rio Grande do Sul, S Brazil
13 O15 **Fredericton** New Brunswick, SE Canada
95 I22 **Frederiksborg** off. Frederiksborgs Amt. ◈ county E Denmark
Frederikshåb see Paamiut
95 H19 **Frederikshavn** prev. Fladstrand. Nordjylland, N Denmark
95 J22 **Frederikssund** Frederiksborg, E Denmark
45 T9 **Frederiksted** Saint Croix, S Virgin Islands (US)
95 I22 **Frederiksværk** var. Frederiksværk og Hanehoved. Frederiksborg, E Denmark
Frederiksværk og Hanehoved see Frederiksværk
54 E9 **Fredonia** Antioquia, W Colombia
36 K8 **Fredonia** Arizona, SW USA
27 P7 **Fredonia** Kansas, C USA
18 C11 **Fredonia** New York, NE USA
35 P4 **Fredonyer Pass** pass California, W USA
93 I15 **Fredrika** Västerbotten, N Sweden
95 L14 **Fredriksberg** Dalarna, C Sweden
Fredrikshald see Halden
Fredrikshamn see Hamina
95 H16 **Fredrikstad** Østfold, S Norway
30 K16 **Freeburg** Illinois, N USA
18 K15 **Freehold** New Jersey, NE USA
18 H14 **Freeland** Pennsylvania, NE USA
182 J5 **Freeling Heights** ▲ South Australia
35 Q7 **Freel Peak** ▲ California, W USA
9 Z9 **Freels, Cape** headland Newfoundland, E Canada
29 Q11 **Freeman** South Dakota, N USA
44 G1 **Freeport** Grand Bahama Island, N Bahamas
30 L10 **Freeport** Illinois, N USA
25 W12 **Freeport** Texas, SW USA
44 G1 **Freeport** ✕ Grand Bahama Island, N Bahamas
25 R14 **Freer** Texas, SW USA
83 I22 **Free State** off. Free State Province; prev. Orange Free State, Afr. Oranje Vrystaat. ◈ province C South Africa
Free State see Maryland
76 G15 **Freetown** ● (Sierra Leone) W Sierra Leone
172 J16 **Frégate** island Inner Islands, NE Seychelles
104 J12 **Fregenal de la Sierra** Extremadura, W Spain
182 C2 **Fregon** South Australia
102 H5 **Fréhel, Cap** headland NW France
94 F8 **Frei** Møre og Romsdal, S Norway
101 O16 **Freiberg** Sachsen, E Germany
101 O16 **Freiberger Mulde** ≈ E Germany
Freiburg see Fribourg, Switzerland
Freiburg see Freiburg im Breisgau, Germany
101 F23 **Freiburg im Breisgau** var. Freiburg, Fr. Fribourg-en-Brisgau. Baden-Württemberg, SW Germany
Freiburg in Schlesien see Świebodzice
Freie Hansestadt Bremen see Bremen
Freie und Hansestadt Hamburg see Brandenburg
101 L22 **Freising** Bayern, SE Germany
109 T3 **Freistadt** Oberösterreich, N Austria
Freistadtl see Hlohovec
101 O16 **Freital** Sachsen, E Germany
Freiwaldau see Jeseník
104 I6 **Freixo de Espada à Cinta** Bragança, N Portugal
103 U15 **Fréjus** anc. Forum Julii. Var, SE France
180 I13 **Fremantle** Western Australia
35 N9 **Fremont** California, W USA
31 Q11 **Fremont** Indiana, N USA
29 W15 **Fremont** Iowa, C USA
31 P8 **Fremont** Michigan, N USA
29 R15 **Fremont** Nebraska, C USA
31 S11 **Fremont** Ohio, N USA
33 T14 **Fremont Peak** ▲ Wyoming, C USA
36 M6 **Fremont River** ≈ Utah, W USA
21 O9 **French Broad River** ≈ Tennessee, S USA
21 N5 **Frenchburg** Kentucky, S USA
18 C12 **French Creek** ≈ Pennsylvania, NE USA
32 K15 **Frenchglen** Oregon, NW USA
55 Y10 **French Guiana** var. Guiana, Guyane. ◇ French overseas department N South America
French Guinea see Guinea
31 O15 **French Lick** Indiana, N USA
185 J14 **French Pass** Marlborough, South Island, NZ
191 T11 **French Polynesia** ◇ French overseas territory C Polynesia
French Republic see France
14 F11 **French River** ≈ Ontario, S Canada
French Somaliland see Djibouti
173 P12 **French Southern and Antarctic Territories** Fr. Terres Australes et Antarctiques Françaises. ◇ French overseas territory S Indian Ocean
French Sudan see Mali
French Territory of the Afars and Issas see Djibouti
French Togoland see Togo
74 J6 **Frenda** NW Algeria
111 I18 **Frenštát pod Radhoštěm** Ger. Frankstadt. Ostravský Kraj E Czech Republic
76 M17 **Fresco** S Ivory Coast
195 U16 **Freshfield, Cape** headland Antarctica
40 L10 **Fresnillo** var. Fresnillo de González Echeverría. Zacatecas, C Mexico
Fresnillo de González Echeverría see Fresnillo

◆ Country ● Country Capital ◇ Dependent Territory ○ Dependent Territory Capital ◈ Administrative Region ✕ International Airport ▲ Mountain ▲ Mountain Range Volcano ≈ River ⊚ Lake ▣ Reservoir

35 Q10 **Fresno** California, W USA
Freu, Cabo del see Freu, Cap des
105 Y9 **Freu, Cap des** var. Cabo del Freu. headland Mallorca, Spain, W Mediterranean Sea
101 G22 **Freudenstadt** Baden-Württemberg, SW Germany
Freudenthal see Bruntál
183 Q17 **Freycinet Peninsula** peninsula Tasmania, SE Australia
76 H14 **Fria** Guinée-Maritime, W Guinea
83 A17 **Fria, Cape** headland NW Namibia
35 Q10 **Friant** California, W USA
62 K8 **Frías** Catamarca, N Argentina
108 D9 **Fribourg** Ger. Freiburg. Fribourg, W Switzerland
108 C9 **Fribourg** Ger. Freiburg. ◆ canton W Switzerland
Fribourg-en-Brisgau see Freiburg im Breisgau
32 G7 **Friday Harbor** San Juan Islands, Washington, NW USA
Friedau see Ormož
101 K23 **Friedberg** Bayern, S Germany
101 H18 **Friedberg** Hessen, W Germany
Friedeberg Neumark see Strzelce Krajeńskie
Friedek-Mistek see Frýdek-Místek
Friedland see Pravdinsk
101 I24 **Friedrichshafen** Baden-Württemberg, S Germany
Friedrichstadt see Jaunjelgava
29 Q16 **Friend** Nebraska, C USA
Friendly Islands see Tonga
55 V9 **Friendship** Coronie, N Suriname
30 L7 **Friendship** Wisconsin, N USA
109 T8 **Friesach** Kärnten, S Austria
Friesche Eilanden see Frisian Islands
101 F22 **Friesenheim** Baden-Württemberg, SW Germany
Friesische Inseln see Frisian Islands
98 K6 **Friesland** ◆ province N Netherlands
60 Q10 **Frio, Cabo** headland SE Brazil
24 M3 **Friona** Texas, SW USA
42 L12 **Frío, Río** ≈ N Costa Rica
25 R13 **Frio River** ≈ Texas, SW USA
99 M25 **Frisange** Luxembourg, S Luxembourg
Frisches Haff see Vistula Lagoon
36 J6 **Frisco Peak** ▲ Utah, W USA
84 F9 **Frisian Islands** Dut. Friesche Eilanden, Ger. Friesische Inseln. island group N Europe
18 L12 **Frissell, Mount** ▲ Connecticut, NE USA
95 J19 **Fristad** Västra Götaland, S Sweden
25 N2 **Fritch** Texas, SW USA
95 J19 **Fritsla** Västra Götaland, S Sweden
101 H16 **Fritzlar** Hessen, C Germany
106 H6 **Friuli-Venezia Giulia** ◆ region NE Italy
Frjentsjer see Franeker
196 L13 **Frobisher Bay** inlet Baffin Island, Nunavut, NE Canada
Frobisher Bay see Iqaluit
11 S12 **Frobisher Lake** ⊗ Saskatchewan, C Canada
94 G7 **Frohavet** sound C Norway
Frohenbruck see Veselí nad Lužnicí
109 V7 **Frohnleiten** Steiermark, SE Austria
99 G22 **Froidchapelle** Hainaut, S Belgium
129 O9 **Frolovo** Volgogradskaya Oblast', SW Russian Federation
110 K7 **Frombork** Ger. Frauenburg. Warmińsko-Mazurskie, NE Poland
97 L22 **Frome** SW England, UK
182 I4 **Frome Creek** seasonal river South Australia
182 J6 **Frome Downs** South Australia
182 J5 **Frome, Lake** salt lake South Australia
Fronicken see Wronki
104 H10 **Fronteira** Portalegre, C Portugal
40 M7 **Frontera** Coahuila de Zaragoza, NE Mexico
41 U14 **Frontera** Tabasco, SE Mexico
40 G3 **Fronteras** Sonora, NW Mexico
103 Q16 **Frontignan** Hérault, S France
54 D8 **Frontino** Antioquia, NW Colombia
21 V4 **Front Royal** Virginia, NE USA
107 J16 **Frosinone** anc. Frusino. Lazio, C Italy
107 K16 **Frosolone** Molise, C Italy
25 U7 **Frost** Texas, SW USA
21 U2 **Frostburg** Maryland, NE USA
23 X13 **Frostproof** Florida, SE USA
Frostviken see Kvarnbergsvattnet
95 M15 **Frövi** Örebro, C Sweden
94 F7 **Frøya** island W Norway
37 P5 **Fruita** Colorado, C USA
28 J9 **Fruitdale** South Dakota, N USA
23 W11 **Fruitland Park** Florida, SE USA
Frumentum see Formentera
147 S11 **Frunze** Oshskaya Oblast', SW Kyrgyzstan
Frunze see Bishkek
117 O9 **Frunzivka** Odes'ka Oblast', SW Ukraine
Frusino see Frosinone
108 E9 **Frutigen** Bern, W Switzerland
111 I17 **Frýdek-Místek** Ger. Friedek-Mistek. Ostravský Kraj, E Czech Republic
193 V16 **Fua'amotu** Tongatapu, S Tonga
190 A9 **Fuafatu** island Funafuti Atoll, C Tuvalu
190 A9 **Fuagea** island Funafuti Atoll, C Tuvalu
190 B8 **Fualifeke** atoll C Tuvalu
190 A8 **Fualopa** island Funafuti Atoll, C Tuvalu
151 K22 **Fuammulah** var. Gnaviyani Atoll. atoll S Maldives
161 R11 **Fu'an** Fujian, SE China
Fu-chien see Fujian
Fu-chou see Fuzhou
164 G13 **Fuchū** var. Hutyû. Hiroshima, Honshū, SW Japan
160 M13 **Fuchuan** Guangxi Zhuangzu Zizhiqu, S China
165 R8 **Fudai** Iwate, Honshū, C Japan
161 S11 **Fuding** Fujian, SE China
81 J20 **Fudua** spring/well S Kenya
104 M16 **Fuengirola** Andalucía, S Spain
104 J12 **Fuente de Cantos** Extremadura, W Spain
104 J11 **Fuente del Maestre** Extremadura, W Spain
104 L12 **Fuente Obejuna** Andalucía, S Spain
104 L6 **Fuentesaúco** Castilla-León, N Spain
62 O3 **Fuerte Olimpo** var. Olimpo. Alto Paraguay, NE Paraguay
40 H8 **Fuerte, Río** ≈ C Mexico
64 Q11 **Fuerteventura** island Islas Canarias, Spain, NE Atlantic Ocean
141 S14 **Fughmah** var. Faghman, Fugma. C Yemen
92 M2 **Fuglehuken** headland W Svalbard
95 B18 **Fugloy** Dan. Fuglø Island Faeroe Islands
197 T15 **Fugløya Bank** undersea feature E Norwegian Sea
166 E11 **Fugong** Yunnang, SW China
Fugma see Fughmah
81 K16 **Fugugo** spring/well NE Kenya
158 L2 **Fuhai** var. Burultokay. Xinjiang Uygur Zizhiqu, NW China
161 P10 **Fu He** ≈ S China
Fuhkien see Fujian
100 J9 **Fuhlsbüttel** ✕ (Hamburg) Hamburg, N Germany
101 L14 **Fuhne** ≈ C Germany
Fu-hsin see Fuxin
Fujairah see Al Fujayrah
164 M14 **Fuji** var. Huzi. Shizuoka, Honshū, S Japan
161 Q12 **Fujian** var. Fu-chien, Fuhkien, Fujian Sheng, Fukien, Min. ◆ province SE China
160 I9 **Fu Jiang** ≈ C China
Fujian Sheng see Fujian
164 M14 **Fujieda** var. Huzieda. Shizuoka, Honshū, S Japan
Fuji, Mount/Fujiyama see Fuji-san
163 Y7 **Fujin** Heilongjiang, NE China
164 M13 **Fujinomiya** var. Huzinomiya. Shizuoka, Honshū, S Japan
164 N13 **Fuji-san** var. Fujiyama, Eng. Mount Fuji. ▲ Honshū, SE Japan
165 N14 **Fujisawa** var. Huzisawa. Kanagawa, Honshū, S Japan
165 T3 **Fukagawa** var. Hukagawa. Hokkaidō, NE Japan
158 L5 **Fukang** Xinjiang Uygur Zizhiqu, W China
165 P7 **Fukaura** Aomori, Honshū, C Japan
193 W15 **Fukave** island Tongatapu Group, S Tonga
Fukien see Fujian
164 J13 **Fukuchiyama** var. Hukutiyama. Kyōto, Honshū, SW Japan
164 A14 **Fukue** var. Hukue. Nagasaki, Fukue-jima, SW Japan
164 A13 **Fukue-jima** island Gotō-rettō, SW Japan
164 K12 **Fukui** var. Hukui. Fukui, Honshū, SW Japan
164 K12 **Fukui** off. Fukui-ken, var. Hukui. ◆ prefecture Honshū, SW Japan
164 D13 **Fukuoka** var. Hukuoka; hist. Najima. Fukuoka, Kyūshū, SW Japan
164 D13 **Fukuoka** off. Fukuoka-ken, var. Hukuoka. ◆ prefecture Kyūshū, SW Japan
165 P11 **Fukushima** var. Hukusima. Fukushima, Honshū, C Japan
165 Q6 **Fukushima** Hokkaidō, NE Japan
165 Q12 **Fukushima** off. Fukushima-ken, var. Hukusima. ◆ prefecture Honshū, C Japan
164 G13 **Fukuyama** var. Hukuyama. Hiroshima, Honshū, SW Japan
76 G13 **Fulacunda** C Guinea-Bissau
131 P8 **Fūlādī, Kūh-e** ▲ E Afghanistan
187 Z15 **Fulaga** island Lau Group, E Fiji
101 I17 **Fulda** Hessen, C Germany
29 S10 **Fulda** Minnesota, N USA
101 I16 **Fulda** ≈ C Germany
Fülek see Fil'akovo
Fulin see Hanyuan
160 K10 **Fuling** Chongqing Shi, C China
35 T15 **Fullerton** California, W USA
29 P15 **Fullerton** Nebraska, C USA
108 M8 **Fulpmes** Tirol, W Austria
22 G8 **Fulton** Kentucky, S USA
20 N2 **Fulton** Mississippi, S USA
27 V4 **Fulton** Missouri, C USA
18 H9 **Fulton** New York, NE USA
Fuman/Fumen see Fowman
103 R3 **Fumay** Ardennes, N France
102 M13 **Fumel** Lot-et-Garonne, SW France
190 B10 **Funafara** atoll C Tuvalu
190 C9 **Funafuti** ✕ Funafuti Atoll, C Tuvalu
Funafuti see Fongafale
190 F8 **Funafuti Atoll** atoll C Tuvalu
190 B9 **Funangongo** atoll C Tuvalu
93 F17 **Funäsdalen** Jämtland, C Sweden
64 O6 **Funchal** Madeira, Portugal, NE Atlantic Ocean
64 P5 **Funchal** ✕ Madeira, Portugal, NE Atlantic Ocean
54 F5 **Fundación** Magdalena, N Colombia
104 I8 **Fundão** var. Fundáo. Castelo Branco, C Portugal
13 O16 **Fundy, Bay of** bay Canada/USA
Fünen see Fyn
54 C13 **Fúnes** Nariño, SW Colombia
Fünfkirchen see Pécs
83 M19 **Funhalouro** Inhambane, S Mozambique
161 R6 **Funing** Jiangsu, E China
160 I14 **Funing** Yunnan, SW China
160 M7 **Funiu Shan** ▲ C China
77 U13 **Funtua** Katsina, N Nigeria
161 R12 **Fuqing** Fujian, SE China
83 M14 **Furancungo** Tete, NW Mozambique
116 J15 **Furculeşti** Teleorman, S Romania
Füred see Balatonfüred
165 W4 **Füren-ko** ⊗ Hokkaidō, NE Japan
143 R12 **Fürg** Fārs, S Iran
Furluk see Fârliug
Fürmanov/Furmanovka see Moyynkum
Furmanovo see Zhalpaktal
59 L20 **Furnas, Represa de** ⊞ SE Brazil
183 Q14 **Furneaux Group** island group Tasmania, SE Australia
Furnes see Veurne
160 J10 **Furong Jiang** ≈ S China
138 I5 **Furqlus** Ḥimṣ, W Syria
100 F12 **Fürstenau** Niedersachsen, NW Germany
109 X8 **Fürstenfeld** Steiermark, SE Austria
101 L23 **Fürstenfeldbruck** Bayern, S Germany
100 P12 **Fürstenwalde** Brandenburg, NE Germany
101 K20 **Fürth** Bayern, S Germany
109 W3 **Furth bei Göttweig** Niederösterreich, NW Austria
165 R3 **Furubira** Hokkaidō, NE Japan
94 L12 **Furudal** Dalarna, C Sweden
164 L12 **Furukawa** Gifu, Honshū, SW Japan
165 Q10 **Furukawa** var. Hurukawa. Miyagi, Honshū, C Japan
54 F10 **Fusagasugá** Cundinamarca, C Colombia
Fusan see Pusan
Fushë-Arëzi/Fushë-Arrësi see Fushë-Arrëz
113 L18 **Fushë-Arrëz** var. Fushë-Arëzi, Fushë-Arrësi. Shkodër, N Albania
Fushë-Kruja see Fushë-Krujë
113 K19 **Fushë-Krujë** var. Fushë-Kruja. Durrës, C Albania
163 V12 **Fushun** var. Fou-shan, Fu-shun. Liaoning, NE China
Fusin see Fuxin
108 G10 **Fusio** Ticino, S Switzerland
163 X11 **Fusong** Jilin, NE China
101 K24 **Füssen** Bayern, S Germany
160 K15 **Fusui** prev. Funan. Guangxi Zhuangzu Zizhiqu, S China
Futa Jallon see Fouta Djallon
63 G18 **Futaleufú** Los Lagos, S Chile
112 K10 **Futog** Serbia, NW Yugoslavia
165 O14 **Futtsu** var. Huttu. Chiba, Honshū, S Japan
187 S15 **Futuna** island S Vanuatu
190 D12 **Futuna, Île** island S Wallis and Futuna
161 Q11 **Futun Xi** ≈ SE China
160 L5 **Fuxian** var. Fu Xian. Shaanxi, C China
Fuxian see Wafangdian
160 G13 **Fuxian Hu** ⊗ SW China
163 U12 **Fuxin** var. Fou-hsin, Fu-hsin, Fusin. Liaoning, NE China
Fuxing see Wangmo
161 P7 **Fuyang** Anhui, E China
161 O4 **Fuyang He** ≈ E China
163 U7 **Fuyu** Heilongjiang, NE China
Fuyu/Fu-yü see Songyuan
163 Z6 **Fuyuan** Heilongjiang, NE China
158 M3 **Fuyun** var. Koktokay. Xinjiang Uygur Zizhiqu, NW China
111 L22 **Füzesabony** Heves, E Hungary
161 R12 **Fuzhou** var. Foochow, Fu-chou. Fujian, SE China
Fuzhou see Linchuan
137 W13 **Füzuli** Rus. Fizuli. SW Azerbaijan
119 I20 **Fyadory** Rus. Fëdory. Brestskaya Voblasts', SW Belarus
95 G24 **Fyn** off. Fyns Amt, var. Fünen. ◆ county C Denmark
95 G23 **Fyn** Ger. Fünen. island C Denmark
96 H12 **Fyne, Loch** inlet W Scotland, UK
95 E16 **Fyresvatnet** ⊗ S Norway
FYR Macedonia/FYROM see Macedonia, FYR
Fyzabad see Feyzābād

G

81 O14 **Gaalkacyo** var. Galka'yo, It. Galcaio. Mudug, C Somalia
Gabakly see Kabakly
114 H8 **Gabare** Vratsa, NW Bulgaria
102 K15 **Gabas** ≈ SW France
35 T7 **Gabbs** Nevada, W USA
82 B12 **Gabela** Cuanza Sul, W Angola
Gaberones see Gaborone
189 X14 **Gabert** island Caroline Islands, E Micronesia
74 M7 **Gabès** var. Qābis. E Tunisia
74 M6 **Gabès, Golfe de** Ar. Khalīj Qābis. gulf E Tunisia
Gablonz an der Neisse see Jablonec nad Nisou
Gablös see Cavalese
79 E18 **Gabon** off. Gabonese Republic. ◆ republic C Africa
83 I20 **Gaborone** prev. Gaberones. ● (Botswana) South East, SE Botswana
83 I20 **Gaborone** ✕ South East, SE Botswana
104 K8 **Gabriel y Galán, Embalse de** ⊞ W Spain
143 U15 **Gābrīk, Rūd-e** ≈ SE Iran
114 J9 **Gabrovo** Gabrovo, N Bulgaria
114 J9 **Gabrovo** ◆ province N Bulgaria
76 H12 **Gabú** prev. Nova Lamego. E Guinea-Bissau
29 O6 **Gackle** North Dakota, N USA
113 I15 **Gacko** Republika Srpska, Bosnia and Herzegovina
155 F17 **Gadag** Karnātaka, W India
93 G15 **Gäddede** Jämtland, C Sweden
159 S12 **Gadê** Qinghai, C China
Gades/Gadier/Gadir/Gadire see Cádiz
105 P15 **Gádor, Sierra de** ▲ S Spain
149 S15 **Gadra** Sind, SE Pakistan
23 Q3 **Gadsden** Alabama, S USA
36 H15 **Gadsden** Arizona, SW USA
Gadyach see Hadyach
79 H15 **Gadzi** Mambéré-Kadéï, SW Central African Republic
116 J13 **Găeşti** Dâmboviţa, S Romania
107 J17 **Gaeta** Lazio, C Italy
107 J17 **Gaeta, Golfo di** var. Gulf of Gaeta. gulf C Italy
188 L14 **Gaferut** atoll Caroline Islands, W Micronesia
21 Q10 **Gaffney** South Carolina, SE USA
Gäfle see Gävle
Gäfleborg see Gävleborg
74 M6 **Gafsa** var. Qafşah. W Tunisia
Gafurov see Ghafurov
128 J3 **Gagarin** Smolenskaya Oblast', W Russian Federation
147 O10 **Gagarin** Jizzakh Wiloyati, C Uzbekistan
101 G21 **Gaggenau** Baden-Württemberg, SW Germany
188 F16 **Gagil Tamil** var. Gagil-Tomil. island Caroline Islands, W Micronesia
Gagil-Tomil see Gagil Tamil
129 O4 **Gagino** Nizhegorodskaya Oblast', W Russian Federation
107 Q19 **Gagliano del Capo** Puglia, SE Italy
94 L13 **Gagnef** Dalarna, C Sweden
76 M17 **Gagnoa** C Ivory Coast
13 N10 **Gagnon** Quebec, E Canada
Gago Coutinho see Lumbala N'Guimbo
137 P8 **Gagra** NW Georgia
31 S13 **Gahanna** Ohio, N USA
143 R13 **Gahkom** Hormozgān, S Iran
Gahnpa see Ganta
57 Q19 **Gaíba, Laguna** ⊗ E Bolivia
153 T13 **Gaibanda** var. Gaibandah. Rajshahi, NW Bangladesh
Gaibandah see Gaibanda
Gaibhlte, Cnoc Mór na n see Galtymore Mountain
109 R9 **Gail** ≈ S Austria
101 I21 **Gaildorf** Baden-Württemberg, S Germany
103 N15 **Gaillac** var. Gaillac-sur-Tarn. Tarn, S France
Gaillac-sur-Tarn see Gaillac
Gaillimh see Galway
Gaillimhe, Cuan na see Galway Bay
109 Q9 **Gailtaler Alpen** ▲ S Austria
63 J17 **Gaimán** Chaco, S Argentina
20 K8 **Gainesboro** Tennessee, S USA
23 V10 **Gainesville** Florida, SE USA
23 T2 **Gainesville** Georgia, SE USA
27 U8 **Gainesville** Missouri, C USA
25 T5 **Gainesville** Texas, SW USA
109 X5 **Gainfarn** Niederösterreich, NE Austria
97 N18 **Gainsborough** E England, UK
182 G6 **Gairdner, Lake** salt lake South Australia
Gaissane see Gáissát
92 L8 **Gáissát** var. Gaissane. ▲ N Norway
43 T15 **Gaital, Cerro** ▲ C Panama
21 W3 **Gaithersburg** Maryland, NE USA
163 U13 **Gaizhou** Liaoning, NE China
Gaiziņ see Gaiziņa Kalns
118 I9 **Gaiziņa Kalns** var. Gaiziņ. ▲ E Latvia
Gajac see Villeneuve-sur-Lot
39 S10 **Gakona** Alaska, USA
Galaassiya see Galaosiye
Galāğil see Jalājil
Galam, Pulau see Gelam, Pulau
62 J6 **Galán, Cerro** ▲ NW Argentina
111 H21 **Galanta** Hung. Galánta. Trnavský Kraj, W Slovakia
146 L11 **Galaosiye** Rus. Galaassiya. Bukhoro Wiloyati, C Uzbekistan
57 B17 **Galápagos** off. Provincia de Galápagos. ◆ province Ecuador, E Pacific Ocean
193 P8 **Galapagos Fracture Zone** tectonic feature E Pacific Ocean
193 S9 **Galapagos Rise** undersea feature E Pacific Ocean
96 K13 **Galashiels** SE Scotland, UK
116 M12 **Galaţi** Ger. Galatz. Galaţi, E Romania
116 L12 **Galaţi** ◆ county E Romania
107 Q19 **Galatina** Puglia, SE Italy
107 Q19 **Galatone** Puglia, SE Italy
Galatz see Galaţi
21 R8 **Galax** Virginia, NE USA
Galaymor see Kala-i-Mor
Galcaio see Gaalkacyo
64 P11 **Gáldar** Gran Canaria, Islas Canarias, NE Atlantic Ocean
94 F11 **Galdhøpiggen** ▲ S Norway
40 I4 **Galeana** Chihuahua, N Mexico
41 O9 **Galeana** Nuevo León, NE Mexico
60 P9 **Galeão** ✕ (Rio de Janeiro) Rio de Janeiro, SE Brazil
171 R10 **Galela** Pulau Halmahera, E Indonesia
39 O9 **Galena** Alaska, USA
30 K10 **Galena** Illinois, N USA
27 R7 **Galena** Kansas, C USA
27 T8 **Galena** Missouri, C USA
45 V15 **Galeota Point** headland Trinidad, Trinidad and Tobago
105 P13 **Galera** Andalucía, S Spain
45 Y16 **Galera Point** headland Trinidad, Trinidad and Tobago
56 A5 **Galera, Punta** headland NW Ecuador
30 K12 **Galesburg** Illinois, N USA
30 J7 **Galesville** Wisconsin, N USA
18 F12 **Galeton** Pennsylvania, NE USA
116 H9 **Gâlgău** Hung. Galgó; prev. Gîlgău. Sălaj, NW Romania
Galgó see Gâlgău
Galgóc see Hlohovec
81 N15 **Galguduud** off. Gobolka Galguduud. ◆ region E Somalia
137 Q9 **Gali** W Georgia
127 N14 **Galich** Kostromskaya Oblast', NW Russian Federation
114 H7 **Galiche** Vratsa, NW Bulgaria
104 H3 **Galicia** anc. Gallaecia. ◆ autonomous community NW Spain
64 M8 **Galicia Bank** undersea feature E Atlantic Ocean
Galilee see HaGalil
181 W7 **Galilee, Lake** ⊗ Queensland, NE Australia
Galilee, Sea of see Tiberias, Lake
106 E11 **Galileo Galilei** ✕ (Pisa) Toscana, C Italy
31 S12 **Galion** Ohio, N USA
Galka'yo see Gaalkacyo
80 H11 **Gallabat** Gedaref, E Sudan
Gallaecia see Galicia
106 C7 **Gallarate** Lombardia, NW Italy
27 S2 **Gallatin** Missouri, C USA
20 J8 **Gallatin** Tennessee, S USA
33 R11 **Gallatin Peak** ▲ Montana, NW USA
33 R12 **Gallatin River** ≈ Montana/Wyoming, NW USA
155 J26 **Galle** prev. Point de Galle. Southern Province, SW Sri Lanka
105 S5 **Gállego** ≈ NE Spain
193 Q8 **Gallego Rise** undersea feature E Pacific Ocean
Gallegos see Río Gallegos
63 H23 **Gallegos, Río** ≈ Argentina/Chile
Gallia see France
22 K10 **Galliano** Louisiana, S USA
114 G13 **Gallikós** ≈ N Greece
37 S12 **Gallinas Peak** ▲ New Mexico, SW USA
54 H3 **Gallinas, Punta** headland NE Colombia
37 T11 **Gallinas River** ≈ New Mexico, SW USA
107 Q19 **Gallipoli** Puglia, SE Italy
Gallipoli see Gelibolu
Gallipoli Peninsula see Gelibolu Yarımadası
31 T15 **Gallipolis** Ohio, N USA
92 J12 **Gällivare** Norrbotten, N Sweden
109 T4 **Gallneukirchen** Oberösterreich, N Austria
105 Q7 **Gallo** ≈ C Spain
93 G17 **Gällö** Jämtland, C Sweden
107 I23 **Gallo, Capo** headland Sicilia, Italy, C Mediterranean Sea
37 P13 **Gallo Mountains** ▲ New Mexico, SW USA
18 G8 **Galloo Island** island New York, NE USA
97 H15 **Galloway, Mull of** headland S Scotland, UK
37 P10 **Gallup** New Mexico, SW USA
105 R5 **Gallur** Aragón, NE Spain
Gâlma see Guelma
35 O8 **Galt** California, W USA
74 C10 **Galtat-Zemmour** C Western Sahara
95 G22 **Galten** Århus, C Denmark
97 D20 **Galtymore Mountain** Ir. Cnoc Mór na nGaibhlte. ▲ S Ireland
97 D20 **Galty Mountains** Ir. Na Gaibhlte. ▲ S Ireland
30 K11 **Galva** Illinois, N USA
25 X12 **Galveston** Texas, SW USA
25 W11 **Galveston Bay** inlet Texas, SW USA
25 W12 **Galveston Island** island Texas, SW USA
61 B18 **Gálvez** Santa Fe, C Argentina
97 C18 **Galway** Ir. Gaillimh. W Ireland
97 B18 **Galway** Ir. Gaillimh. cultural region W Ireland
97 B18 **Galway Bay** Ir. Cuan na Gaillimhe. bay W Ireland
83 F18 **Gam** Otjozondjupa, NE Namibia
164 L14 **Gamagōri** Aichi, Honshū, SW Japan
54 F7 **Gamarra** Cesar, N Colombia
Gámas see Kaamanen
158 L17 **Gamba** Xizang Zizhiqu, W China
77 P14 **Gambaga** NE Ghana
80 G13 **Gambēla** Gambēla, W Ethiopia
83 H14 **Gambēla** ◆ region, W Ethiopia
38 K10 **Gambell** Saint Lawrence Island, Alaska, USA
76 E12 **Gambia** off. Republic of The Gambia, The Gambia. ◆ republic W Africa
76 I12 **Gambia** Fr. Gambie. ≈ W Africa
64 K12 **Gambia Plain** undersea feature E Atlantic Ocean
Gambie see Gambia
31 T13 **Gambier** Ohio, N USA
191 Y13 **Gambier, Îles** island group E French Polynesia
182 G10 **Gambier Islands** island group South Australia
79 H19 **Gamboma** Plateaux, E Congo
79 G16 **Gamboula** Mambéré-Kadéï, SW Central African Republic
37 P10 **Gamerco** New Mexico, SW USA
137 V12 **Gamiş Dağı** ▲ W Azerbaijan
Gamlakarleby see Kokkola
95 N18 **Gamleby** Kalmar, S Sweden
Gammelstad see Gammelstaden
93 J14 **Gammelstaden** var. Gammelstad. Norrbotten, N Sweden
Gammouda see Sidi Bouzid
155 J25 **Gampaha** Western Province, W Sri Lanka
155 K25 **Gampola** Central Province, C Sri Lanka
167 S5 **Gâm, Sông** ≈ N Vietnam
92 L7 **Gamvik** Finnmark, N Norway
150 H13 **Gan** Addu Atoll, C Maldives
Gan see Gansu, China
Gan see Jiangxi, China
Ganaane see Juba
37 O10 **Ganado** Arizona, SW USA
25 U12 **Ganado** Texas, SW USA
14 L14 **Gananoque** Ontario, SE Canada
Ganāveh see Bandar-e Gonāveh
137 V11 **Gäncä** Rus. Gyandzha; prev. Kirovabad, Yelisavetpol. W Azerbaijan
Ganchi see Ghonchí
Gand see Gent
82 B13 **Ganda** var. Mariano Machado, Port. Vila Mariano Machado. Benguela, W Angola
79 L22 **Gandajika** Kasai Oriental, S Dem. Rep. Congo (Zaire)
153 O12 **Gandak** Nep. Nārāyāni. ≈ India/Nepal
13 U11 **Gander** Newfoundland, SE Canada
13 U11 **Gander** ✕ Newfoundland, E Canada
100 G11 **Ganderkesee** Niedersachsen, NW Germany
105 T7 **Gandesa** Cataluña, NE Spain
154 B10 **Gāndhīdhām** Gujarāt, W India
154 D10 **Gāndhīnagar** Gujarāt, W India
154 F9 **Gāndhi Sāgar** ⊗ C India
105 T11 **Gandía** País Valenciano, E Spain
159 O10 **Gang** Qinghai, W China
152 G9 **Gangānagar** Rājasthān, NW India
152 I12 **Gangāpur** Rājasthān, N India
153 S17 **Ganga Sāgar** West Bengal, NE India
Gangavathi see Gangāwati
155 G17 **Gangāwati** var. Gangavathi. Karnātaka, C India
159 S9 **Gangca** var. Shaliuhe. Qinghai, C China
158 H14 **Gangdisê Shan** Eng. Kailas Range. ▲ W China
103 Q15 **Ganges** Hérault, S France
153 P13 **Ganges** Ben. Padma. ≈ Bangladesh/India see also Padma
Ganges Cone see Ganges Fan
173 S3 **Ganges Fan** var. Ganges Cone. undersea feature N Bay of Bengal
153 U17 **Ganges, Mouths of the** delta Bangladesh/India
107 K23 **Gangi** anc. Engyum. Sicilia, Italy, C Mediterranean Sea
152 K8 **Gangotri** Uttar Pradesh, N India
Gangra see Çankırı
153 S11 **Gangtok** Sikkim, N India
159 W11 **Gangu** Gansu, C China
163 U5 **Gan He** ≈ NE China
171 S12 **Gani** Pulau Halmahera, E Indonesia
161 O12 **Gan Jiang** ≈ S China
146 H15 **Gannaly** Akhalskiy Velayat, S Turkmenistan
163 U7 **Gannan** Heilongjiang, NE China
103 P10 **Gannat** Allier, C France
33 T14 **Gannett Peak** ▲ Wyoming, C USA
29 O10 **Gannvalley** South Dakota, N USA
109 Y3 **Gänserndorf** Niederösterreich, NE Austria
Gansos, Lago dos see Goose Lake
159 T9 **Gansu** var. Gan, Gansu Sheng, Kansu. ◆ province N China
Gansu Sheng see Gansu
76 K16 **Ganta** var. Gahnpa. NE Liberia
182 H11 **Gantheaume, Cape** headland South Australia
Gantsevichi see Hantsavichy
161 Q6 **Ganyu** var. Qingkou. Jiangsu, E China
144 D12 **Ganyushkino** Atyrau, SW Kazakhstan
161 O12 **Ganzhou** Jiangxi, S China
77 Q10 **Gao** Gao, E Mali
77 R10 **Gao** ◆ region SE Mali
161 O10 **Gao'an** Jiangxi, S China
161 N5 **Gaoping** Shanxi, C China
159 S8 **Gaotai** Gansu, N China
Gaoth Dobhair see Gweedore
77 O14 **Gaoua** SW Burkina
76 I13 **Gaoual** Moyenne-Guinée, N Guinea
Gaoxiong see Kaohsiung
161 R7 **Gaoyou** var. Dayishan. Jiangsu, E China
161 R7 **Gaoyou Hu** ⊗ E China
160 M15 **Gaozhou** Guangdong, S China
103 T13 **Gap** anc. Vapincum. Hautes-Alpes, SE France
158 G13 **Gar** var. Gar Xincun. Xizang Zizhiqu, W China
Garabekevyul/Garabekewül see Karabekaul
Garabogazköl see Kara-Bogaz-Gol

◆ COUNTRY ● COUNTRY CAPITAL ◇ DEPENDENT TERRITORY ○ DEPENDENT TERRITORY CAPITAL ◆ ADMINISTRATIVE REGION ✕ INTERNATIONAL AIRPORT ▲ MOUNTAIN ▲ MOUNTAIN RANGE ☒ VOLCANO ≈ RIVER ⊗ LAKE ⊞ RESERVOIR

43 V16 **Garachiné** Darién, SE Panama
43 V16 **Garachiné, Punta** *headland* SE Panama
Garagan *see* Karagan
54 G10 **Garagoa** Boyacá, C Colombia
Garagöl *see* Karagel'
Garagum *see* Garagumy
Garagum Kanaly *see* Garagumskiy Kanal
146 E12 **Garagumskiy Kanal** *var.* Kara Kum Canal, Karakumskiy Kanal, *Turkm.* Garagum Kanaly. *canal* C Turkmenistan
146 F12 **Garagumy** *var.* Qara Qum, *Eng.* Black Sand Desert, Kara Kum, *Turkm.* Garagum; *prev.* Peski Karakumy. *desert* C Turkmenistan
183 S4 **Garah** New South Wales, SE Australia
64 O11 **Garajonay** ▲ Gomera, Islas Canarias, NE Atlantic Ocean
114 M8 **Gara Khitrino** Shumen, NE Bulgaria
76 L13 **Garalo** Sikasso, SW Mali
Garam *see* Hron
Garamäbnyyaz *see* Karamet-Niyaz
Garamszentkereszt *see* Žiar nad Hronom
77 Q13 **Garango** S Burkina
59 Q15 **Garanhuns** Pernambuco, E Brazil
188 H5 **Garapan** Saipan, S Northern Mariana Islands
Gárassavon *see* Kaaresuvanto
78 J13 **Garba** Bamingui-Bangoran, N Central African Republic
81 L16 **Garbahaarrey** *It.* Garba Harre. Gedo, SW Somalia
Garba Harre *see* Garbahaarrey
81 J18 **Garba Tula** Eastern, C Kenya
27 N9 **Garber** Oklahoma, C USA
34 L4 **Garberville** California, W USA
100 I12 **Garbsen** Niedersachsen, N Germany
60 K9 **Garça** São Paulo, S Brazil
104 L10 **García de Solá, Embalse de** ▣ C Spain
103 Q14 **Gard** ◈ *department* S France
103 Q14 **Gard** ≈ S France
106 F7 **Garda, Lago di** *var.* Benaco, *Eng.* Lake Garda, *Ger.* Gardasee. ◎ NE Italy
Garda, Lake *see* Garda, Lago di
Gardan Divāl *see* Gardan Dīwāl
149 Q5 **Gardan Dīwāl** *var.* Gardan Divāl. Wardag, C Afghanistan
103 S15 **Gardanne** Bouches-du-Rhône, SE France
Gardasee *see* Garda, Lago di
100 L12 **Gardelegen** Sachsen-Anhalt, C Germany
14 B10 **Garden** ≈ Ontario, S Canada
23 X6 **Garden City** Georgia, SE USA
26 I6 **Garden City** Kansas, C USA
27 S5 **Garden City** Missouri, C USA
25 N8 **Garden City** Texas, SW USA
23 P3 **Gardendale** Alabama, S USA
31 P5 **Garden Island** *island* Michigan, N USA
22 M11 **Garden Island Bay** *bay* Louisiana, S USA
31 O5 **Garden Peninsula** *peninsula* Michigan, N USA
Garden State *see* New Jersey
95 I14 **Gardermoen** Akershus, S Norway
Gardeyz *see* Gardēz
149 Q6 **Gardēz** *var.* Gardeyz, Gordiaz. Paktīā, E Afghanistan
93 G14 **Gardiken** ◎ N Sweden
19 Q7 **Gardiner** Maine, NE USA
33 S12 **Gardiner** Montana, NW USA
19 N13 **Gardiners Island** *island* New York, NE USA
Gardner Island *see* Nikumaroro
19 T6 **Gardner Lake** ◎ Maine, NE USA
35 Q6 **Gardnerville** Nevada, W USA
Gardo *see* Qardho
106 F7 **Gardone Val Trompia** Lombardia, N Italy
Garegegasnjárga *see* Karigasniemi
38 F17 **Gareloi Island** *island* Aleutian Islands, Alaska, USA
106 B10 **Garessio** Piemonte, NE Italy
32 M9 **Garfield** Washington, NW USA
31 U11 **Garfield Heights** Ohio, N USA
Gargaliani *see* Gargaliánoi
115 D21 **Gargaliánoi** *var.* Gargaliani. Pelopónnisos, S Greece
107 N15 **Gargano, Promontorio del** *headland* SE Italy
108 J8 **Gargellen** Graubünden, W Switzerland
93 I14 **Gargnäs** Västerbotten, N Sweden
118 C11 **Gargždai** Gargždai, W Lithuania
154 J13 **Garhchiroli** Mahārāshtra, C India
153 O15 **Garhwa** Bihār, N India
171 V13 **Gariau** Irian Jaya, E Indonesia
83 E24 **Garies** Northern Cape, W South Africa
109 K17 **Garigliano** ≈ C Italy
81 K19 **Garissa** Coast, E Kenya
21 V11 **Garland** North Carolina, SE USA
25 T6 **Garland** Texas, SW USA
36 L1 **Garland** Utah, W USA
106 D8 **Garlasco** Lombardia, N Italy
119 F14 **Garliava** Kaunas, S Lithuania
Garm *see* Gharm
142 M9 **Garm, Āb-e** *var.* Rūd-e Khersān. ≈ SW Iran
101 K25 **Garmisch-Partenkirchen** Bayern, S Germany
143 O5 **Garmsār** *prev.* Qishlaq. Semnān, N Iran
Garmser *see* Darvīshān
29 V12 **Garner** Iowa, C USA
21 U9 **Garner** North Carolina, SE USA
27 Q5 **Garnett** Kansas, C USA
99 M25 **Garnich** Luxembourg, SW Luxembourg
182 M8 **Garnpung, Lake** *salt lake* New South Wales, SE Australia
Garoe *see* Garoowe
Garoet *see* Garut
153 U13 **Gāro Hills** *hill range* NE India
102 K13 **Garonne** *anc.* Garumna. ≈ S France
80 P13 **Garoowe** *var.* Garoe. Nugaal, N Somalia
78 F12 **Garoua** *var.* Garua. Nord, N Cameroon
79 G14 **Garoua Boulaï** Est, E Cameroon
77 O10 **Garou, Lac** ◎ C Mali
95 L16 **Garphyttan** Örebro, C Sweden
29 R11 **Garretson** South Dakota, N USA
31 Q11 **Garrett** Indiana, N USA
33 Q10 **Garrison** Montana, NW USA
28 M4 **Garrison** North Dakota, N USA
25 X8 **Garrison** Texas, SW USA
28 L4 **Garrison Dam** *dam* North Dakota, N USA
104 J9 **Garrovillas** Extremadura, W Spain
Garrygala *see* Kara-Kala
8 L8 **Garry Lake** ◎ Nunavut, N Canada
Gars *see* Gars am Kamp
109 W3 **Gars am Kamp** *var.* Gars. Niederösterreich, NE Austria
81 K20 **Garsen** Coast, S Kenya
Garshy *see* Karshi
14 F10 **Garson** Ontario, S Canada
109 T5 **Garsten** Oberösterreich, N Austria
Gartar *see* Qianning
102 M10 **Gartempe** ≈ C France
Gartog *see* Markam
Garua *see* Garoua
83 D21 **Garub** Karas, SW Namibia
Garumna *see* Garonne
169 P16 **Garut** *prev.* Garoet. Jawa, C Indonesia
185 C20 **Garvie Mountains** ▲ South Island, NZ
110 N12 **Garwolin** Mazowieckie, E Poland
25 U12 **Garwood** Texas, SW USA
Gar Xincun *see* Gar
31 N11 **Gary** Indiana, N USA
25 X7 **Gary** Texas, SW USA
158 G13 **Gar Zangbo** ≈ W China
160 F8 **Garzê** Sichuan, C China
54 E12 **Garzón** Huila, S Colombia
146 B13 **Gasan-Kuli** *var.* Esenguly. Balkanskiy Velayat, W Turkmenistan
31 P13 **Gas City** Indiana, N USA
102 K15 **Gascogne** *Eng.* Gascony. *cultural region* S France
Gascogne, Golfe de *see* Gascony, Gulf of
26 V5 **Gasconade River** ≈ Missouri, C USA
Gascony *see* Gascogne
180 H9 **Gascoyne Junction** Western Australia
173 V8 **Gascoyne Plain** *undersea feature* E Indian Ocean
180 H9 **Gascoyne River** ≈ Western Australia
192 J11 **Gascoyne Tablemount** *undersea feature* N Tasman Sea
67 U6 **Gash** *var.* Nahr al Qāsh. ≈ W Sudan
149 X3 **Gasherbrum** ▲ NE Pakistan
159 N9 **Gas Hu** ◎ C China
77 X12 **Gashua** Yobe, NE Nigeria
186 G7 **Gasmata** New Britain, E PNG
23 V14 **Gasparilla Island** *island* Florida, SE USA
169 O13 **Gaspar, Selat** *strait* W Indonesia
15 Y6 **Gaspé** Quebec, SE Canada
15 Z6 **Gaspé, Cap de** *headland* Quebec, SE Canada
15 X6 **Gaspé, Péninsule de** *var.* Péninsule de la Gaspésie. *peninsula* Quebec, SE Canada
Gaspésie, Péninsule de la *see* Gaspé, Péninsule de
77 W15 **Gassol** Taraba, E Nigeria
Gastein *see* Badgastein
21 R10 **Gastonia** North Carolina, SE USA
21 V8 **Gaston, Lake** ▣ North Carolina/Virginia, SE USA
115 D19 **Gastoúni** Dytikí Ellás, S Greece
63 I17 **Gastre** Chubut, S Argentina
Gat *see* Ghāt
105 P15 **Gata, Cabo de** *headland* S Spain
Gata, Cape *see* Gátas, Akrotíri
105 T11 **Gata de Gorgos** País Valenciano, E Spain
116 E12 **Gătaia** *Ger.* Gataja, *Hung.* Gátalja; *prev.* Găttája. Timiş, W Romania
Gataja/Gátalja *see* Gătaia
121 P3 **Gátas, Akrotíri** *var.* Cape Gata. *headland* S Cyprus
104 J8 **Gata, Sierra de** ▲ W Spain
126 G13 **Gatchina** Leningradskaya Oblast', NW Russian Federation
21 P8 **Gate City** Virginia, NE USA
97 M14 **Gateshead** NE England, UK
21 X8 **Gatesville** North Carolina, SE USA
25 S8 **Gatesville** Texas, SW USA
14 L12 **Gatineau** Quebec, SE Canada
14 L11 **Gatineau** ≈ Ontario/Quebec, SE Canada
21 N9 **Gatlinburg** Tennessee, S USA
Gatooma *see* Kadoma
Gáttája *see* Gătaia
43 T14 **Gatún, Lago** ▣ C Panama
59 N14 **Gaturiano** Piauí, NE Brazil
97 O22 **Gatwick** ✕ (London) SE England, UK
187 Y14 **Gau** *prev.* Ngau. *island* C Fiji
187 R12 **Gaua** *var.* Santa Maria, *island* Banks Islands, N Vanuatu
104 L16 **Gaucín** Andalucía, S Spain
Gauhāti *see* Guwāhāti
118 I8 **Gauja** *Ger.* Aa. ≈ Estonia/Latvia
118 J7 **Gaujiena** Alūksne, NE Latvia
Gaul/Gaule *see* France
94 H9 **Gauldalen** *valley* S Norway
21 R5 **Gauley River** ≈ West Virginia, NE USA
99 D19 **Gaurain-Ramecroix** Hainaut, SW Belgium
95 F15 **Gausta** ▲ S Norway
83 J21 **Gauteng** *off.* Gauteng Province; *prev.* Pretoria-Witwatersrand-Vereeniging. ◈ *province* NE South Africa
Gauteng *see* Germiston, South Africa
Gauteng *see* Johannesburg, South Africa
143 P14 **Gāvbandī** Hormozgān, S Iran
115 H25 **Gavdopoúla** *island* SE Greece
115 H26 **Gávdos** *island* SE Greece
102 K16 **Gave de Pau** *var.* Gave-de-Pay. ≈ SW France
Gave-de-Pay *see* Gave de Pau
102 J16 **Gave d'Oloron** ≈ SW France
99 E18 **Gavere** Oost-Vlaanderen, NW Belgium
94 N13 **Gävle** *var.* Gäfle; *prev.* Gefle. Gävleborg, C Sweden
94 M11 **Gävleborg** *var.* Gäfleborg, Gefleborg. ◈ *county* C Sweden
94 O13 **Gävlebukten** *bay* C Sweden
126 L16 **Gavrilov-Yam** Yaroslavskaya Oblast', W Russian Federation
182 I9 **Gawler** South Australia
182 G7 **Gawler Ranges** *hill range* South Australia
Gawso *see* Goaso
162 H11 **Gaxun Nur** ◎ N China
153 P14 **Gaya** Bihār, N India
77 S13 **Gaya** Dosso, SW Niger
Gaya *see* Kyjov
31 Q6 **Gaylord** Michigan, N USA
29 U9 **Gaylord** Minnesota, N USA
181 Y9 **Gayndah** Queensland, E Australia
127 T12 **Gayny** Komi-Permyatskiy Avtonomnyy Okrug, NW Russian Federation
Gaysin *see* Haysyn
Gayvorno *see* Hayvoron
138 E11 **Gaza** *Ar.* Ghazzah, *Heb.* 'Azza. NE Gaza Strip
83 L20 **Gaza** *off.* Província de Gaza. ◈ *province* SW Mozambique
146 I9 **Gaz-Achak** *Turkm.* Gazojak. Lebapskiy Velayat, NE Turkmenistan
Gazalkent *see* Ghazalkent
146 C11 **Gazandzhyk** *Turkm.* Gazanjyk; *prev.* Kazandzhik. Balkanskiy Velayat, W Turkmenistan
Gazanjyk *see* Gazandzhyk
77 V12 **Gazaoua** Maradi, S Niger
138 E11 **Gaza Strip** *Ar.* Qiṭā' Ghazzah. *disputed region* SW Asia
Gazgan *see* Ghozghon
Gazi Antep *see* Gaziantep
136 M16 **Gaziantep** *var.* Gazi Antep; *prev.* Aintab, Antep. Gaziantep, S Turkey
136 M17 **Gaziantep** *var.* Gazi Antep. ◈ *province* S Turkey
114 M13 **Gaziköy** Tekirdağ, NW Turkey
121 Q2 **Gazimağusa** *var.* Famagusta, *Gk.* Ammóchostos. E Cyprus
121 Q2 **Gazimağusa Körfezi** *var.* Famagusta Bay, *Gk.* Kólpos Ammóchostos. *bay* E Cyprus
146 K11 **Gazli** Bukhoro Wiloyati, C Uzbekistan
Gazojak *see* Gaz-Achak
79 K15 **Gbadolite** Equateur, NW Dem. Rep. Congo (Zaire)
76 K16 **Gbanga** *var.* Gbarnga. N Liberia
Gbarnga *see* Gbanga
77 S14 **Gbéroubouè** *var.* Béroubouay. N Benin
77 W16 **Gboko** Benue, S Nigeria
Gcuwa *see* Butterworth
110 J7 **Gdańsk** *Fr.* Dantzig, *Ger.* Danzig. Pomorskie, N Poland
Gdan'skaya Bukhta/Gdańsk, Gulf of *see* Danzig, Gulf of
Gdańska, Zakota *see* Danzig, Gulf of
Gdingen *see* Gdynia
126 F13 **Gdov** Pskovskaya Oblast', W Russian Federation
110 I6 **Gdynia** *Ger.* Gdingen. Pomorskie, N Poland
26 M10 **Geary** Oklahoma, C USA
Geavvú *see* Kevo
76 H12 **Gêba, Rio** ≈ C Guinea-Bissau
136 E11 **Gebze** Kocaeli, NW Turkey
80 H10 **Gedaref** *var.* Al Qaḍārif, El Gedaref. Gedaref, E Sudan
80 H10 **Gedaref** ◈ *state* E Sudan
80 B11 **Gedid Ras el Fil** Southern Darfur, W Sudan
101 I23 **Gedinne** Namur, SE Belgium
136 E13 **Gediz** Kütahya, W Turkey
136 C14 **Gediz Nehri** ≈ W Turkey
81 N14 **Gedlegubē** Somali, E Ethiopia
81 L17 **Gedo** *off.* Gobolka Gedo. ◈ *region* SW Somalia
95 I25 **Gedser** Storstrøm, SE Denmark
99 I16 **Geel** *var.* Gheel. Antwerpen, N Belgium
183 N13 **Geelong** Victoria, SE Australia
Ge'e'mu *see* Golmud
99 I14 **Geertruidenberg** Noord-Brabant, S Netherlands
100 H10 **Geeste** ≈ NW Germany
100 J10 **Geesthacht** Schleswig-Holstein, N Germany
183 P17 **Geeveston** Tasmania, SE Australia
Gefle *see* Gävle
Gefleborg *see* Gävleborg
158 G13 **Gê'gyai** Xizang Zizhiqu, W China
77 X12 **Geidam** Yobe, NE Nigeria
11 T11 **Geikie** ≈ Saskatchewan, C Canada
94 F13 **Geilo** Buskerud, S Norway
94 E10 **Geiranger** Møre og Romsdal, S Norway
101 I22 **Geislingen** *var.* Geislingen an der Steige. Baden-Württemberg, SW Germany
Geislingen an der Steige *see* Geislingen
81 F20 **Geita** Mwanza, NW Tanzania
95 G15 **Geithus** Buskerud, S Norway
160 H14 **Gejiu** *var.* Kochiu. Yunnan, S China
Gëkdepe *see* Geok-Tepe
146 E9 **Geklengkui, Solonchak** *var.* Solonchak Goklenkuy. *salt marsh* NW Turkmenistan
81 D14 **Gel** ≈ W Sudan
107 K25 **Gela** *prev.* Terranova di Sicilia. Sicilia, Italy, C Mediterranean Sea
Gěladaindong *see* Gladaindong
81 N14 **Geladī** Somali, E Ethiopia
169 P13 **Gelam, Pulau** *var.* Pulau Galam. *island* N Indonesia
98 L11 **Gelderland** *prev. Eng.* Guelders. ◈ *province* E Netherlands
98 J13 **Geldermalsen** Gelderland, C Netherlands
101 D14 **Geldern** Nordrhein-Westfalen, W Germany
99 K15 **Geldrop** Noord-Brabant, SE Netherlands
99 L17 **Geleen** Limburg, SE Netherlands
128 K14 **Gelendzhik** Krasnodarskiy Kray, SW Russian Federation
Gelib *see* Jilib
136 B11 **Gelibolu** *Eng.* Gallipoli. Çanakkale, NW Turkey
115 L14 **Gelibolu Yarımadası** *Eng.* Gallipoli Peninsula. *peninsula* NW Turkey
81 O14 **Gellinsor** Mudug, C Somalia
101 H18 **Gelnhausen** Hessen, C Germany
101 E14 **Gelsenkirchen** Nordrhein-Westfalen, W Germany
83 C20 **Geluk** Hardap, SW Namibia
99 H20 **Gembloux** Namur, Belgium
79 J16 **Gemena** Equateur, NW Dem. Rep. Congo (Zaire)
99 L14 **Gemert** Noord-Brabant, SE Netherlands
136 E11 **Gemlik** Bursa, NW Turkey
Gem of the Mountains *see* Idaho
106 J6 **Gemona del Friuli** Friuli-Venezia Giulia, NE Italy
Gem State *see* Idaho
Genalē Wenz *see* Juba
169 R10 **Genali, Danau** ◎ Borneo, N Indonesia
99 G19 **Genappe** Wallon Brabant, C Belgium
137 P14 **Genç** Bingöl, E Turkey
Genck *see* Genk
98 M9 **Genemuiden** Overijssel, E Netherlands
63 K14 **General Acha** La Pampa, C Argentina
61 C21 **General Alvear** Buenos Aires, E Argentina
62 I12 **General Alvear** Mendoza, W Argentina
61 B20 **General Arenales** Buenos Aires, E Argentina
61 D21 **General Belgrano** Buenos Aires, E Argentina
194 H3 **General Bernardo O'Higgins** *Chilean research station* Antarctica
41 O8 **General Bravo** Nuevo León, NE Mexico
62 M7 **General Capdevila** Chaco, N Argentina
General Carrera, Lago *see* Buenos Aires, Lago
41 N9 **General Cepeda** Coahuila de Zaragoza, NE Mexico
63 K15 **General Conesa** Río Negro, E Argentina
61 G18 **General Enrique Martínez** Treinta y Tres, E Uruguay
62 L3 **General Eugenio A. Garay** *var.* Fortín General Eugenio Garay; *prev.* Yrendagüé. Nueva Asunción, NW Paraguay
61 C18 **General Galarza** Entre Ríos, E Argentina
61 E22 **General Guido** Buenos Aires, E Argentina
General José F.Uriburu *see* Zárate
61 E22 **General Juan Madariaga** Buenos Aires, E Argentina
41 O16 **General Juan N Alvarez** ✕ (Acapulco) Guerrero, S Mexico
61 B22 **General La Madrid** Buenos Aires, E Argentina
61 E21 **General Lavalle** Buenos Aires, E Argentina
General Machado *see* Camacupa
62 I8 **General Manuel Belgrano, Cerro** ▲ W Argentina
41 O8 **General Mariano Escobero** ✕ (Monterrey) Nuevo León, NE Mexico
61 B20 **General O'Brien** Buenos Aires, E Argentina
62 K13 **General Pico** La Pampa, C Argentina
62 M7 **General Pinedo** Chaco, N Argentina
61 B20 **General Pinto** Buenos Aires, E Argentina
61 E22 **General Pirán** Buenos Aires, E Argentina
43 N15 **General, Río** ≈ S Costa Rica
63 I15 **General Roca** Río Negro, C Argentina
171 Q8 **General Santos** *off.* General Santos City. Mindanao, S Philippines
41 O9 **General Terán** Nuevo León, NE Mexico
114 N7 **General Toshevo** *Rom.* I.G.Duca, *prev.* Casim, Kasimköj. Dobrich, NE Bulgaria
61 B20 **General Viamonte** Buenos Aires, E Argentina
61 A20 **General Villegas** Buenos Aires, E Argentina
Gênes *see* Genova
18 E11 **Genesee River** ≈ New York/Pennsylvania, NE USA
30 K11 **Geneseo** Illinois, N USA
18 F10 **Geneseo** New York, NE USA
57 L14 **Geneshuaya, Río** ≈ N Bolivia
23 Q8 **Geneva** Alabama, S USA
30 M10 **Geneva** Illinois, N USA
29 Q16 **Geneva** Nebraska, C USA
18 G10 **Geneva** New York, NE USA
31 U10 **Geneva** Ohio, NE USA
Geneva *see* Genève
108 B10 **Geneva, Lake** *Fr.* Lac de Genève, Lac Léman, le Léman, *Ger.* Genfer See. ◎ France/Switzerland
108 A10 **Genève** *Eng.* Geneva, *Ger.* Genf, *It.* Ginevra. Genève, SW Switzerland
108 A11 **Genève** *Eng.* Geneva, *Ger.* Genf, *It.* Ginevra. ◈ *canton* SW Switzerland
108 A10 **Genève** *var.* Geneva. ✕ Vaud, SW Switzerland
Genève, Lac de *see* Geneva, Lake
Genf *see* Genève
Genfer See *see* Geneva, Lake
163 S5 **Gen He** ≈ NE China
Genichesk *see* Heniches'k
104 L14 **Genil** ≈ S Spain
99 K18 **Genk** *var.* Genck. Limburg, NE Belgium
164 C13 **Genkai-nada** *gulf* Kyūshū, SW Japan
107 C19 **Gennargentu, Monti del** ▲ Sardegna, Italy, C Mediterranean Sea
99 M14 **Gennep** Limburg, SE Netherlands
30 M10 **Genoa** Illinois, N USA
29 Q15 **Genoa** Nebraska, C USA
Genoa *see* Genova
Genoa, Gulf of *see* Genova, Golfo di
106 D10 **Genova** *Eng.* Genoa, *Fr.* Gênes; *anc.* Genua. Liguria, NW Italy
106 D10 **Genova, Golfo di** *Eng.* Gulf of Genoa. *gulf* NW Italy
57 C17 **Genovesa, Isla** *var.* Tower Island. *island* Galapagos Islands, Ecuador, E Pacific Ocean
Genshū *see* Wŏnju
99 E17 **Gent** *Eng.* Ghent, *Fr.* Gand. Oost-Vlaanderen, NW Belgium
169 N16 **Genteng** Jawa, C Indonesia
100 M12 **Genthin** Sachsen-Anhalt, E Germany
27 R9 **Gentry** Arkansas, C USA
Genua *see* Genova
107 I15 **Genzano di Roma** Lazio, C Italy
Geokchay *see* Göyçay
146 F13 **Geok-Tepe** *var.* Gëkdepe, *Turkm.* Gökdepe. Akhalskiy Velayat, C Turkmenistan
122 I3 **Georga, Zemlya** *Eng.* George Land. *island* Zemlya Frantsa-Iosifa, N Russian Federation
83 G26 **George** Western Cape, S South Africa
29 S11 **George** Iowa, C USA
AA O5 **George** ≈ Newfoundland/Quebec, E Canada
65 C25 **George Island** *island* S Falkland Islands
183 R10 **George, Lake** ◎ New South Wales, SE Australia
81 E18 **George, Lake** ◎ SW Uganda
23 W10 **George, Lake** ◎ Florida, SE USA
18 L8 **George, Lake** ▣ New York, NE USA
George Land *see* Georga, Zemlya
Georgenburg *see* Jurbarkas
George River *see* Kangiqsualujjuaq
64 G8 **Georges Bank** *undersea feature* W Atlantic Ocean
185 A21 **George Sound** *sound* South Island, NZ
65 F15 **Georgetown** ○ (Ascension Island) NW Ascension Island
181 V5 **Georgetown** Queensland, NE Australia
183 P15 **George Town** Tasmania, SE Australia
44 I4 **George Town** Great Exuma Island, C Bahamas
44 D8 **George Town** *var.* Georgetown. ○ (Cayman Islands) Grand Cayman, SW Cayman Islands
76 H12 **Georgetown** E Gambia
55 T8 **Georgetown** ● (Guyana) N Guyana
168 I7 **George Town** *var.* Penang, Pinang. Pinang, Peninsular Malaysia
45 Y14 **Georgetown** Saint Vincent, Saint Vincent and the Grenadines
21 Y4 **Georgetown** Delaware, NE USA
23 R6 **Georgetown** Georgia, SE USA
20 M5 **Georgetown** Kentucky, S USA
21 T13 **Georgetown** South Carolina, SE USA
25 S10 **Georgetown** Texas, SW USA
55 T8 **Georgetown** ✕ N Guyana
195 U16 **George V Coast** *physical region* Antarctica
195 T15 **George V Land** *physical region* Antarctica
194 J7 **George VI Ice Shelf** *ice shelf* Antarctica
194 J6 **George VI Sound** *sound* Antarctica
25 S14 **George West** Texas, SW USA
137 R9 **Georgia** *off.* Republic of Georgia, *Geor.* Sak'art'velo, *Rus.* Gruzinskaya SSR, Gruziya; *prev.* Georgian SSR. ◆ *republic* SW Asia
23 S5 **Georgia** *off.* State of Georgia; also known as Empire State of the South, Peach State. ◈ *state* SE USA
14 F12 **Georgian Bay** *lake bay* Ontario, S Canada
10 L17 **Georgia, Strait of** *strait* British Columbia, W Canada
Georgi Dimitrov *see* Kostenets
Georgi Dimitrov, Yazovir *see* Koprinka, Yazovir
114 M9 **Georgi Traykov, Yazovir** ▣ NE Bulgaria
Georgiu-Dezh *see* Liski
145 W10 **Georgiyevka** Vostochnyy Kazakhstan, E Kazakhstan
Georgiyevka *see* Korday, Kazakhstan
129 N15 **Georgiyevsk** Stavropol'skiy Kray, SW Russian Federation
100 G13 **Georgsmarienhütte** Niedersachsen, NW Germany
195 O1 **Georg von Neumayer** *German research station* Antarctica
101 M16 **Gera** Thüringen, E Germany
101 K16 **Gera** ≈ C Germany
99 E19 **Geraardsbergen** Oost-Vlaanderen, SW Belgium
115 F21 **Geráki** Pelopónnisos, S Greece
27 W5 **Gerald** Missouri, C USA
47 V8 **Geral de Goiás, Serra** ▲ E Brazil
185 G20 **Geraldine** Canterbury, South Island, NZ
180 H11 **Geraldton** Western Australia
12 E11 **Geraldton** Ontario, S Canada
60 J12 **Geral, Serra** ▲ S Brazil
103 U6 **Gérardmer** Vosges, NE France
Gerasa *see* Jarash
Gerdauen *see* Zheleznodorozhnyy
39 Q11 **Gerdine, Mount** ▲ Alaska, USA
136 H11 **Gerede** Bolu, N Turkey
136 H11 **Gerede Çayı** ≈ N Turkey
148 M8 **Gereshk** Helmand, SW Afghanistan
101 L24 **Geretsried** Bayern, S Germany
105 P14 **Gérgal** Andalucía, S Spain
28 I14 **Gering** Nebraska, C USA
35 R3 **Gerlach** Nevada, W USA
Gerlachfalvi Csúcs/Gerlachovka *see* Gerlachovský štít
111 L18 **Gerlachovský štít** *var.* Gerlachovka, *Ger.* Gerlsdorfer Spitze, *Hung.* Gerlachfalvi Csúcs; *prev.* Stalinov Štít, *Ger.* Franz-Josef Spitze, *Hung.* Ferencz-Jósef Csúcs. ▲ N Slovakia
108 E8 **Gerlafingen** Solothurn, NW Switzerland
Gerlsdorfer Spitze *see* Gerlachovský štít
139 V3 **Germak** E Iraq
German East Africa *see* Tanzania
Germanicopolis *see* Çankırı
Germanicum, Mare/German Ocean *see* North Sea
Germanovichi *see* Hyermanavichy
German Southwest Africa *see* Namibia
20 E10 **Germantown** Tennessee, S USA
101 I15 **Germany** *off.* Federal Republic of Germany, *Ger.* Bundesrepublik Deutschland, Deutschland. ◆ *federal republic* N Europe
101 L23 **Germering** Bayern, SE Germany
83 J21 **Germiston** *var.* Gauteng. Gauteng, NE South Africa
Gernika *see* Gernika-Lumo
105 P2 **Gernika-Lumo** *var.* Gernika, Guernica, Guernica y Lumo. País Vasco, N Spain
164 L12 **Gero** Gifu, Honshū, SW Japan
115 F22 **Geroliménas** Pelopónnisos, S Greece
Gerona *see* Girona
99 H21 **Gerpinnes** Hainaut, S Belgium
102 L15 **Gers** ◈ *department* S France
102 L14 **Gers** ≈ S France
Gerunda *see* Girona
136 K10 **Gerze** Sinop, N Turkey
158 I13 **Gêrzê** Xizang Zizhiqu, W China
Gesoriacum/Gessoriacum *see* Boulogne-sur-Mer
99 J21 **Gesves** Namur, SE Belgium
93 J20 **Geta** Åland, SW Finland
105 N8 **Getafe** Madrid, C Spain
95 J21 **Getinge** Halland, S Sweden
18 F16 **Gettysburg** Pennsylvania, NE USA
29 N8 **Gettysburg** South Dakota, N USA
194 K12 **Getz Ice Shelf** *ice shelf* Antarctica
137 S15 **Gevaş** Van, SE Turkey
Gevgeli *see* Gevgelija
113 Q20 **Gevgelija** *var.* Đevđelija, Djevdjelija, *Turk.* Gevgeli. SE FYR Macedonia
103 T10 **Gex** Ain, E France
92 I3 **Geysir** *physical region* SW Iceland
136 F11 **Geyve** Sakarya, NW Turkey
80 G10 **Gezira** ◈ *state* E Sudan
109 V3 **Gföhl** Niederösterreich, N Austria
83 H22 **Ghaap Plateau** *Afr.* Ghaapplato. *plateau* C South Africa
Ghaapplato *see* Ghaap Plateau
Ghaba *see* Al Ghābah
138 J8 **Ghāb, Tall** ▲ SE Syria
139 Q9 **Ghadaf, Wādī al** *dry watercourse* C Iraq
Ghadamès *see* Ghadāmis
74 M9 **Ghadāmis** *var.* Ghadamès, Rhadames. W Libya
141 Y10 **Ghadan** E Oman
75 O10 **Ghaddūwah** C Libya
147 Q11 **Ghafurov** *Rus.* Gafurov; *prev.* Sovetabad. NW Tajikistan
153 N12 **Ghāghara** ≈ S Asia
149 P13 **Ghaibi Dero** Sind, SE Pakistan

◆ COUNTRY ● COUNTRY CAPITAL ◇ DEPENDENT TERRITORY ○ DEPENDENT TERRITORY CAPITAL ◈ ADMINISTRATIVE REGION ✕ INTERNATIONAL AIRPORT ▲ MOUNTAIN ▲ MOUNTAIN RANGE ⊗ VOLCANO ≈ RIVER ◎ LAKE ▣ RESERVOIR

141 Y10 **Ghalat** E Oman
147 O11 **Ghallaorol** Jizzakh Wiloyati, C Uzbekistan
139 W11 **Ghamūkah, Hawr** ◎ S Iraq
77 P15 **Ghana** *off.* Republic of Ghana. ◆ *republic* W Africa
141 X12 **Ghānah** *spring/well* S Oman
Ghanongga *see* Ranongga
Ghansi/Ghansiland *see* Ghanzi
83 F18 **Ghanzi** *var.* Khanzi. Ghanzi, W Botswana
83 G19 **Ghanzi** *var.* Ghansi, Ghansiland, Khanzi. ◈ *district* C Botswana
67 T14 **Ghanzi** *var.* Knanzi. ≈ Botswana/South Africa
Ghap'an *see* Kapan
138 F13 **Gharandal** Ma'ān, SW Jordan
Gharbt, Jabal al *see* Liban, Jebel
74 K7 **Ghardaïa** N Algeria
139 U14 **Gharibīyah, Sha'īb al** ≈ S Iraq
147 R12 **Gharm** *Rus.* Garm. C Tajikistan
149 P17 **Gharo** Sind, SE Pakistan
139 W10 **Gharrāf, Shaṭṭ al** ≈ S Iraq
Gharvān *see* Gharyān
75 O7 **Gharyān** *var.* Gharvān. NW Libya
74 M11 **Ghāt** *var.* Gat. SW Libya
Ghawdex *see* Gozo
141 U8 **Ghayathi** Abū Ẓaby, W UAE
Ghazāl, Baḥr al *see* Ghazal, Bahr el
78 H9 **Ghazal, Bahr el** *var.* Soro. *seasonal river* C Chad
80 E13 **Ghazal, Bahr el** *var.* Baḥr al Ghazāl. ≈ S Sudan
147 Q9 **Ghazalkent** *Rus.* Gazalkent. Toshkent Wiloyati, E Uzbekistan
74 H6 **Ghazaouet** NW Algeria
152 J10 **Ghāziābād** Uttar Pradesh, N India
153 O13 **Ghāzīpur** Uttar Pradesh, N India
149 Q6 **Ghaznī** *var.* Ghazni. Ghaznī, E Afghanistan
149 P7 **Ghaznī** ◈ *province* SE Afghanistan
Ghazzah *see* Gaza
Gheel *see* Geel
Ghelizâne *see* Relizane
Ghent *see* Gent
Gheorghe Brațul *see* Sfântu Gheorghe, Brațul
Gheorghe Gheorghiu-Dej *see* Onești
116 J10 **Gheorgheni** *prev.* Gheorghieni, Sînt-Miclăuș, *Ger.* Niklasmarkt, *Hung.* Gyergyószentmiklós. Harghita, C Romania
Gheorghieni *see* Gheorgheni
116 H10 **Gherla** *Ger.* Neuschliss, *Hung.* Szamosújvár; *prev.* Armenierstadt. Cluj, NW Romania
Gheweifat *see* Ghuwayfāt
146 L11 **Ghijduwon** *Rus.* Gizhduvan. Bukhoro Wiloyati, C Uzbekistan
Ghilan *see* Gīlān
107 C18 **Ghilarza** Sardegna, Italy, C Mediterranean Sea
Ghilizane *see* Relizane
Ghimbi *see* Gīmbī
Ghiriș *see* Câmpia Turzii
103 Y15 **Ghisonaccia** Corse, France, C Mediterranean Sea
147 Q11 **Ghonchí** *Rus.* Ganchi. NW Tajikistan
Ghor *see* Ghowr
153 T13 **Ghoraghat** Rajshahi, NW Bangladesh
149 R13 **Ghotki** Sind, SE Pakistan
148 M5 **Ghowr** *var.* Ghor. ◈ *province* C Afghanistan
146 M10 **Ghozghon** *Rus.* Gazgan. Nawoiy Wiloyati, C Uzbekistan
147 T13 **Ghūdara** *var.* Gudara, *Rus.* Kudara. SE Tajikistan
153 R13 **Ghugri** ≈ N India
147 S14 **Ghund** *Rus.* Gunt. ≈ SE Tajikistan
Ghurdaqah *see* Hurghada
148 J5 **Ghūrīān** Herāt, W Afghanistan
141 T8 **Ghuwayfāt** *var.* Gheweifat. Abū Ẓaby, W UAE
121 O14 **Ghuzayyil, Sabkhat** *salt lake* N Libya
147 N13 **Ghuzor** *Rus.* Guzar. Qashqadaryo Wiloyati, S Uzbekistan
115 G17 **Giáltra** Évvoia, C Greece
Giamame *see* Jamaame
114 F13 **Giannitsá** *var.* Yiannitsá. Kentrikí Makedonía, N Greece
107 F14 **Giannutri, Isola di** *island* Archipelago Toscano, C Italy
96 F13 **Giant's Causeway** *Ir.* Clochán an Aifir. *lava flow* N Northern Ireland, UK
167 S15 **Gia Rai** Minh Hai, S Vietnam
107 L24 **Giarre** Sicilia, Italy, C Mediterranean Sea
44 I7 **Gibara** Holguín, E Cuba
29 O16 **Gibbon** Nebraska, C USA
32 K11 **Gibbon** Oregon, NW USA
33 P11 **Gibbonsville** Idaho, NW USA
64 A13 **Gibb's Hill** *hill* S Bermuda
92 I9 **Gibostad** Troms, N Norway
104 I14 **Gibraleón** Andalucía, S Spain
104 L16 **Gibraltar** ○ (Gibraltar) S Gibraltar
104 L16 **Gibraltar** ◇ *UK dependent territory* SW Europe
Gibraltar, Détroit de/Gibraltar, Estrecho de *see* Gibraltar, Strait of
104 J17 **Gibraltar, Strait of** *Fr.* Détroit de Gibraltar, *Sp.* Estrecho de Gibraltar. *strait* Atlantic Ocean/ Mediterranean Sea
31 S11 **Gibsonburg** Ohio, N USA
30 M13 **Gibson City** Illinois, N USA
180 L8 **Gibson Desert** *desert* Western Australia
10 L17 **Gibsons** British Columbia, SW Canada
149 N12 **Gīdār** Baluchistān, SW Pakistan
155 I17 **Giddalūr** Andhra Pradesh, E India
24 U10 **Giddings** Texas, SW USA
27 Y8 **Gideon** Missouri, C USA
81 I15 **Gīdolē** Southern, S Ethiopia
118 H13 **Giedraičiai** Molėtai, E Lithuania
103 O7 **Gien** Loiret, C France
101 G17 **Giessen** Hessen, W Germany
98 O6 **Gieten** Drenthe, NE Netherlands
23 Y13 **Gifford** Florida, SE USA
9 O5 **Gifford** ≈ Baffin Island, Nunavut, NE Canada
100 J12 **Gifhorn** Niedersachsen, N Germany
11 P13 **Gift Lake** Alberta, W Canada
164 K13 **Gifu** *var.* Gihu. Gifu, Honshū, SW Japan
164 L13 **Gifu** *off.* Gifu-ken, *var.* Gihu. ◈ *prefecture* Honshū, SW Japan
128 M13 **Gigant** Rostovskaya Oblast', SW Russian Federation
40 E8 **Giganta, Sierra de la** ▲▲ W Mexico
54 E12 **Gigante** Huila, S Colombia
114 I7 **Gigen** Pleven, N Bulgaria
Giggiga *see* Jijiga
96 G12 **Gigha Island** *island* SW Scotland, UK
107 E14 **Giglio, Isola del** *island* Archipelago Toscano, C Italy
Gihu *see* Gifu
104 L2 **Gijón** *var.* Xixón. Asturias, NW Spain
81 D20 **Gikongoro** SW Rwanda
36 K14 **Gila Bend** Arizona, SW USA
36 J14 **Gila Bend Mountains** ▲▲ Arizona, SW USA
37 N14 **Gila Mountains** ▲▲ Arizona, SW USA
36 I15 **Gila Mountains** ▲▲ Arizona, SW USA
142 M4 **Gīlān** *off.* Ostān-e Gīlān; *var.* Ghilan, Guilan. ◈ *province* NW Iran
Gilani *see* Gnjilane
36 L14 **Gila River** ≈ Arizona, SW USA
29 W4 **Gilbert** Minnesota, N USA
Gilbert Islands *see* Tungaru
10 L16 **Gilbert, Mount** ▲ British Columbia, SW Canada
181 U4 **Gilbert River** ≈ Queensland, NE Australia
(0) C6 **Gilbert Seamounts** *undersea feature* NE Pacific Ocean
33 S7 **Gildford** Montana, NW USA
83 P15 **Gilé** Zambézia, NE Mozambique
30 K4 **Gile Flowage** ◎ Wisconsin, N USA
182 G7 **Giles, Lake** *salt lake* South Australia
75 U12 **Gilf Kebir Plateau** *Ar.* Haḍabat al Jilf al Kabīr. *plateau* SW Egypt
183 R6 **Gilgandra** New South Wales, SE Australia
Gilgău *see* Gâlgău
81 I19 **Gilgil** Rift Valley, SW Kenya
183 S4 **Gil Gil Creek** ≈ New South Wales, SE Australia
149 V3 **Gilgit** Jammu and Kashmir, NE Pakistan
149 V3 **Gilgit** ≈ N Pakistan
11 X11 **Gillam** Manitoba, C Canada
95 J22 **Gilleleje** Frederiksborg, E Denmark
30 K14 **Gillespie** Illinois, N USA
27 W13 **Gillett** Arkansas, C USA
33 X12 **Gillette** Wyoming, C USA
97 P22 **Gillingham** SE England, UK
195 X6 **Gillock Island** *island* Antarctica
173 O16 **Gillot** ✈ (St-Denis) N Réunion
65 H25 **Gill Point** *headland* E Saint Helena
30 M12 **Gilman** Illinois, N USA
25 W6 **Gilmer** Texas, SW USA
Gilolo *see* Halmahera, Pulau
81 G14 **Gīlo Wenz** ≈ SW Ethiopia
35 O10 **Gilroy** California, W USA
123 Q12 **Gilyuy** ≈ SE Russian Federation
99 I14 **Gilze** Noord-Brabant, S Netherlands
165 R16 **Gima** Okinawa, Kume-jima, SW Japan
80 H13 **Gīmbī** *It.* Ghimbi. Oromo, C Ethiopia
45 T12 **Gimie, Mount** ▲ C Saint Lucia
11 X16 **Gimli** Manitoba, S Canada
Gimma *see* Jīma
95 O14 **Gimo** Uppsala, C Sweden
102 L15 **Gimone** ≈ S France
Gimpoe *see* Gimpu
171 N12 **Gimpu** *prev.* Gimpoe. Sulawesi, C Indonesia
182 F5 **Gina** South Australia
Ginevra *see* Genève
99 J19 **Gingelom** Limburg, NE Belgium
180 I12 **Gingin** Western Australia
171 Q7 **Gingoog** Mindanao, S Philippines
81 K14 **Gīnīr** Oromo, C Ethiopia
Giohar *see* Jawhar
107 O17 **Gioia del Colle** Puglia, SE Italy
107 M22 **Gioia, Golfo di** *gulf* S Italy
Gióna *see* Gkióna
115 I16 **Gioúra** *island* Vóreioi Sporádes, Greece, Aegean Sea
107 O17 **Giovinazzo** Puglia, SE Italy
Gipeswic *see* Ipswich
Gipuzkoa *see* Guipúzcoa
Giran *see* Ilan
30 K14 **Girard** Illinois, N USA
27 R7 **Girard** Kansas, C USA
25 O6 **Girard** Texas, SW USA
54 E10 **Girardot** Cundinamarca, C Colombia
172 M7 **Giraud Seamount** *undersea feature* SW Indian Ocean
83 A15 **Girault** ≈ SW Angola
96 L9 **Girdle Ness** *headland* NE Scotland, UK
137 N11 **Giresun** *var.* Kerasunt; *anc.* Cerasus, Pharnacia. Giresun, NE Turkey
137 N12 **Giresun** *var.* Kerasunt. ◈ *province* NE Turkey
137 N12 **Giresun Dağları** ▲▲ N Turkey
75 X10 **Girga** *var.* Girgeh, Jirjā. C Egypt
Girgeh *see* Girga
Girgenti *see* Agrigento
153 Q15 **Girīdīh** Bihār, NE India
183 P6 **Girilambone** New South Wales, SE Australia
Girin *see* Jilin
121 W10 **Girne** *Gk.* Kerýneia, Kyrenia. N Cyprus
105 X5 **Girona** *var.* Gerona; *anc.* Gerunda. Cataluña, NE Spain
105 W5 **Girona** *var.* Gerona ◈ *province* Cataluña, NE Spain
102 J12 **Gironde** ◈ *department* SW France
102 J11 **Gironde** *estuary* SW France
105 V5 **Gironella** Cataluña, NE Spain
103 N15 **Girou** ≈ S France
97 H14 **Girvan** W Scotland, UK
24 M9 **Girvin** Texas, SW USA
184 Q9 **Gisborne** Gisborne, North Island, NZ
184 P9 **Gisborne** *off.* Gisborne District. ◈ *unitary authority* North Island, NZ
Giseifu *see* Üijŏngbu
Gisenye *see* Gisenyi
81 D19 **Gisenyi** *var.* Gisenye. NW Rwanda
95 K20 **Gislaved** Jönköping, S Sweden
103 N4 **Gisors** Eure, N France
Gissar *see* Hisor
147 P12 **Gissar Range** *Rus.* Gissarskiy Khrebet. ▲▲ Tajikistan/Uzbekistan
Gissarskiy Khrebet *see* Gissar Range
99 B16 **Gistel** West-Vlaanderen, W Belgium
108 F9 **Giswil** Unterwalden, C Switzerland
115 B16 **Gitánes** *ancient monument* Ípeiros, W Greece
81 E20 **Gitarama** C Rwanda
81 E20 **Gitega** C Burundi
Githio *see* Gýtheio
108 H11 **Giubiasco** Ticino, S Switzerland
106 K13 **Giulianova** Abruzzo, C Italy
Giulie, Alpi *see* Julian Alps
Giumri *see* Gyumri
116 M13 **Giurgeni** Ialomița, SE Romania
116 J15 **Giurgiu** Giurgiu, S Romania
116 J14 **Giurgiu** ◈ *county* SE Romania
95 F22 **Give** Vejle, C Denmark
103 R2 **Givet** Ardennes, N France
103 R11 **Givors** Rhône, E France
83 K19 **Giyani** Northern, NE South Africa
80 I13 **Giyon** Oromo, C Ethiopia
Giza/Gizeh *see* El Gîza
75 V8 **Giza, Pyramids of** *ancient monument* N Egypt
Gizhduvan *see* Ghijduwon
123 U8 **Gizhiga** Magadanskaya Oblast', E Russian Federation
123 T9 **Gizhiginskaya Guba** *bay* E Russian Federation
186 K8 **Gizo** Gizo, NW Solomon Islands
110 N7 **Giżycko** *Ger.* Warmińsko-Mazurskie, NE Poland
Gízymałów *see* Hrymayliv
Gjakovë *see* Đakovica
94 F12 **Gjende** ◎ S Norway
95 F17 **Gjerstad** Aust-Agder, S Norway
Gjilan *see* Gnjilane
Gjinokastër *see* Gjirokastër
113 L23 **Gjirokastër** *var.* Gjirokastra; *prev.* Gjinokastër, *Gk.* Argyrokastron, *It.* Argirocastro. Gjirokastër, S Albania
113 L22 **Gjirokastër** ◈ *district* S Albania
8 M7 **Gjoa Haven** King William Island, Nunavut, NW Canada
94 H13 **Gjøvik** Oppland, S Norway
113 J22 **Gjuhëzës, Kepi i** *headland* SW Albania
Gjurgjevac *see* Đurđevac
115 E18 **Gkióna** *var.* Giona. ▲ C Greece
121 R3 **Gkréko, Akrotíri** *var.* Cape Greco, Pidálion. *headland* E Cyprus
99 I18 **Glabbeek-Zuurbemde** Vlaams Brabant, C Belgium
13 R14 **Glace Bay** Cape Breton Island, Nova Scotia, SE Canada
11 O16 **Glacier** British Columbia, SW Canada
39 W12 **Glacier Bay** *inlet* Alaska, USA
32 I7 **Glacier Peak** ▲ Washington, NW USA
159 N13 **Gladaindong** *var.* Gèladaindong. ▲ C China
21 Q7 **Glade Spring** Virginia, NE USA
25 W7 **Gladewater** Texas, SW USA
181 Y8 **Gladstone** Queensland, E Australia
182 I8 **Gladstone** South Australia
11 X16 **Gladstone** Manitoba, S Canada
31 O5 **Gladstone** Michigan, N USA
27 R4 **Gladstone** Missouri, C USA
31 Q7 **Gladwin** Michigan, N USA
95 J15 **Glafsfjorden** ◎ C Sweden
92 H2 **Gláma** *physical region* NW Iceland
94 I12 **Glåma** *var.* Glommen, Glomma. ≈ S Norway
112 F13 **Glamoč** Federacija Bosna I Hercegovina, NE Bosnia and Herzegovina
97 J22 **Glamorgan** *cultural region* S Wales, UK
95 G24 **Glamsbjerg** Fyn, C Denmark
171 Q8 **Glan** Mindanao, S Philippines
95 M17 **Glan** ◎ S Sweden
109 T9 **Glan** ≈ SE Austria
101 F19 **Glan** ≈ W Germany
Glaris *see* Glarus
108 H9 **Glarner Alpen** *Eng.* Glarus Alps. ▲▲ E Switzerland
108 H8 **Glarus** Glarus, E Switzerland
108 H9 **Glarus** *Fr.* Glaris. ◈ *canton* C Switzerland
Glarus Alps *see* Glarner Alpen
27 N3 **Glasco** Kansas, C USA
96 I12 **Glasgow** S Scotland, UK
20 K7 **Glasgow** Kentucky, S USA
27 T4 **Glasgow** Missouri, C USA
33 W7 **Glasgow** Montana, NW USA
21 T6 **Glasgow** Virginia, NE USA
96 I12 **Glasgow** ✈ W Scotland, UK
11 S14 **Glaslyn** Saskatchewan, S Canada
18 I16 **Glassboro** New Jersey, NE USA
24 L10 **Glass Mountains** ▲▲ Texas, SW USA
97 K23 **Glastonbury** SW England, UK
Glatz *see* Kłodzko
101 N16 **Glauchau** Sachsen, E Germany
Glavn'a Morava *see* Velika Morava
113 N16 **Glavnik** Serbia, S Yugoslavia
129 T1 **Glazov** Udmurtskaya Respublika, NW Russian Federation
Głda *see* Gwda
109 U8 **Gleinalpe** ▲▲ SE Austria
109 W8 **Gleisdorf** Steiermark, SE Austria
Gleiwitz *see* Gliwice
39 S11 **Glenallen** Alaska, USA
102 F7 **Glénan, Îles** *island group* NW France
185 G21 **Glenavy** Canterbury, South Island, NZ
10 H5 **Glenboyle** Yukon Territory, NW Canada
21 X3 **Glen Burnie** Maryland, NE USA
36 L8 **Glen Canyon** *canyon* Utah, W USA
36 L8 **Glen Canyon Dam** *dam* Arizona, SW USA
30 K15 **Glen Carbon** Illinois, N USA
14 E17 **Glencoe** Ontario, S Canada
83 K22 **Glencoe** KwaZulu/Natal, E South Africa
29 U9 **Glencoe** Minnesota, N USA
96 H10 **Glen Coe** *valley* N Scotland, UK
36 K13 **Glendale** Arizona, SW USA
35 S15 **Glendale** California, W USA
182 G5 **Glendambo** South Australia
33 Y8 **Glendive** Montana, NW USA
33 Y15 **Glendo** Wyoming, C USA
55 S10 **Glendor Mountians** ▲▲ C Guyana
182 K12 **Glenelg River** ≈ South Australia/Victoria, SE Australia
29 P4 **Glenfield** North Dakota, N USA
25 V12 **Glen Flora** Texas, SW USA
181 P7 **Glen Helen** Northern Territory, N Australia
183 U5 **Glen Innes** New South Wales, SE Australia
31 P6 **Glen Lake** ◎ Michigan, N USA
10 I7 **Glenlyon Peak** ▲ Yukon Territory, W Canada
37 N16 **Glenn, Mount** ▲ Arizona, SW USA
33 N15 **Glenns Ferry** Idaho, NW USA
23 W6 **Glennville** Georgia, SE USA
10 J10 **Glenora** British Columbia, W Canada
182 M11 **Glenorchy** Victoria, SE Australia
183 V5 **Glenreagh** New South Wales, SE Australia
33 X15 **Glenrock** Wyoming, C USA
96 K11 **Glenrothes** E Scotland, UK
18 L9 **Glens Falls** New York, NE USA
97 D14 **Glenties** *Ir.* Na Gleannta. NW Ireland
28 L5 **Glen Ullin** North Dakota, N USA
21 R4 **Glenville** West Virginia, NE USA
27 T12 **Glenwood** Arkansas, C USA
29 S15 **Glenwood** Iowa, C USA
29 T7 **Glenwood** Minnesota, N USA
36 L5 **Glenwood** Utah, W USA
30 I5 **Glenwood City** Wisconsin, N USA
37 Q4 **Glenwood Springs** Colorado, C USA
108 F10 **Gletsch** Valais, S Switzerland
Glevum *see* Gloucester
29 U14 **Glidden** Iowa, C USA
112 E9 **Glina** Sisak-Moslavina, NE Croatia
94 F11 **Glittertind** ▲ S Norway
111 J16 **Gliwice** *Ger.* Gleiwitz. Śląskie, S Poland
36 M14 **Globe** Arizona, SW USA
Globino *see* Hlobyne
108 L9 **Glockturm** ▲ SW Austria
116 L9 **Glodeni** *Rus.* Glodyany. N Moldova
109 S9 **Glödnitz** Kärnten, S Austria
Glodyany *see* Glodeni
Glogau *see* Głogów
109 W6 **Gloggnitz** Niederösterreich, E Austria
110 F13 **Głogów** *Ger.* Glogau, Glogow. Dolnośląskie, SW Poland
111 I16 **Głogówek** *Ger.* Oberglogau. Opolskie, S Poland
92 G12 **Glomfjord** Nordland, C Norway
Glommen *see* Glåma
93 I14 **Glommersträsk** Norrbotten, N Sweden
172 I1 **Glorieuses, Nosy** *island group* N Madagascar
65 C25 **Glorious Hill** *hill* East Falkland, Falkland Islands
38 J12 **Glory of Russia Cape** *headland* Saint Matthew Island, Alaska, USA
22 J7 **Gloster** Mississippi, S USA
183 U7 **Gloucester** New South Wales, SE Australia
186 F7 **Gloucester** New Britain, E PNG
97 L21 **Gloucester** *hist.* Caer Glou, *Lat.* Glevum. C England, UK
19 P10 **Gloucester** Massachusetts, NE USA
21 X6 **Gloucester** Virginia, NE USA
97 K21 **Gloucestershire** *cultural region* C England, UK
31 T14 **Glouster** Ohio, N USA
42 H3 **Glovers Reef** *reef* E Belize
18 K10 **Gloversville** New York, NE USA
110 K12 **Głowno** Łódź, C Poland
111 H16 **Głubczyce** *Ger.* Leobschütz. Opolskie, S Poland
128 L11 **Glubokiy** Rostovskaya Oblast', SW Russian Federation
145 W9 **Glubokoye** Vostochnyy Kazakhstan, E Kazakhstan
Glubokoye *see* Hlybokaye
111 H16 **Głuchołazy** *Ger.* Ziegenhais. Opolskie, S Poland
100 I9 **Glückstadt** Schleswig-Holstein, N Germany
Glukhov *see* Hlukhiv
Glushkevichi *see* Hlushkavichy
Glusk/Glussk *see* Hlusk
Glybokaya *see* Hlyboka
95 F21 **Glyngøre** Viborg, NW Denmark
129 Q9 **Gmelinka** Volgogradskaya Oblast', SW Russian Federation
109 R8 **Gmünd** Kärnten, S Austria
109 U2 **Gmünd** Niederösterreich, N Austria
Gmünd *see* Schwäbisch Gmünd
109 S5 **Gmunden** Oberösterreich, N Austria
Gmundner See *see* Traunsee
94 N10 **Gnarp** Gävleborg, C Sweden
109 W8 **Gnas** Steiermark, SE Austria
Gnesen *see* Gniezno
95 O16 **Gnesta** Södermanland, C Sweden
110 H11 **Gniezno** *Ger.* Gnesen. Wielkolpolskie, C Poland
113 O17 **Gnjilane** *var.* Gilani, *Alb.* Gjilan. Serbia, S Yugoslavia
95 K20 **Gnosjö** Jönköping, S Sweden
155 E17 **Goa** *prev.* Old Goa, Vela Goa, Velha Goa. Goa, W India
155 E17 **Goa** *var.* Old Goa. ◈ *state* W India
42 H7 **Goascorán, Río** ≈ El Salvador/Honduras
77 O16 **Goaso** *var.* Gawso. W Ghana
81 K14 **Goba** *It.* Oromo, S Ethiopia
83 C20 **Gobabed** Erongo, W Namibia
83 E19 **Gobabis** Omaheke, E Namibia
Gobannium *see* Abergavenny
64 M7 **Goban Spur** *undersea feature* NW Atlantic Ocean
Gobbà *see* Goba
63 H21 **Gobernador Gregores** Santa Cruz, S Argentina
61 F14 **Gobernador Ingeniero Virasoro** Corrientes, NE Argentina
162 L12 **Gobi** *desert* China/Mongolia
164 I14 **Gobō** Wakayama, Honshū, SW Japan
101 D14 **Goch** Nordrhein-Westfalen, W Germany
83 E20 **Gochas** Hardap, S Namibia
155 I14 **Godāvari** *var.* Godavari. ≈ C India
155 L16 **Godāvari, Mouths of the** *delta* E India
15 V5 **Godbout** Quebec, SE Canada
15 U5 **Godbout** ≈ Quebec, SE Canada
15 U5 **Godbout Est** ≈ Quebec, SE Canada
27 N6 **Goddard** Kansas, C USA
14 E15 **Goderich** Ontario, S Canada
Godhavn *see* Qeqertarsuaq
154 E10 **Godhra** Gujarāt, W India
Göding *see* Hodonín
111 K22 **Gödöllő** Pest, N Hungary
62 H11 **Godoy Cruz** Mendoza, W Argentina
11 Y11 **Gods** ≈ Manitoba, C Canada
11 Y13 **Gods Lake** Manitoba, C Canada
11 X13 **Gods Lake** ◎ Manitoba, C Canada
Godthaab/Godthåb *see* Nuuk
Godwin Austen, Mount *see* K2
Goede Hoop, Kaap de *see* Good Hope, Cape of
Goedgegun *see* Nhlangano
Goeie Hoop, Kaap die *see* Good Hope, Cape of
13 O7 **Goélands, Lac aux** ◎ Quebec, SE Canada
98 E13 **Goeree** *island* SW Netherlands
99 F15 **Goes** Zeeland, SW Netherlands
Goettingen *see* Göttingen
19 O10 **Goffstown** New Hampshire, NE USA
14 E8 **Gogama** Ontario, S Canada
30 L3 **Gogebic, Lake** ◎ Michigan, N USA
30 K3 **Gogebic Range** *hill range* Michigan/Wisconsin, N USA
137 V13 **Gogi, Mount** *Arm.* Gogi Lerr, *Az.* Küküdağ. ▲ Armenia/Azerbaijan
126 F12 **Gogland, Ostrov** *island* NW Russian Federation
111 I15 **Gogolin** Opolskie, S Poland
Gogonou *see* Gogounou
77 S14 **Gogounou** *var.* Gogonou. N Benin
152 I10 **Gohāna** Haryāna, N India
59 K18 **Goianésia** Goiás, C Brazil
59 K18 **Goiânia** *prev.* Goyania. *state capital* Goiás, C Brazil
59 K18 **Goiás** Goiás, C Brazil
59 J18 **Goiás** *off.* Estado de Goiás; *prev.* Goiaz, Goyaz. ◈ *state* C Brazil
Goiaz *see* Goiás
159 R14 **Goinsargoin** Xizang Zizhiqu, W China
60 H10 **Goio-Erê** Paraná, SW Brazil
99 I15 **Goirle** Noord-Brabant, S Netherlands
104 H8 **Góis** Coimbra, N Portugal
165 Q8 **Gojōme** Akita, Honshū, NW Japan
149 U9 **Gojra** Punjab, E Pakistan
136 A11 **Gökçeada** *var.* Imroz Adası, *Gk.* Imbros. *island* NW Turkey
Gökçeada *see* İmroz
Gökdepe *see* Geok-Tepe
136 I10 **Gökırmak** ≈ N Turkey
Goklenkuy, Solonchak *see* Geklengkui, Solonchak
136 C16 **Gökova Körfezi** *gulf* SW Turkey
136 K15 **Göksu** ≈ S Turkey
136 L15 **Göksun** Kahramanmaraş, C Turkey
136 I17 **Göksu Nehri** ≈ S Turkey
83 J16 **Gokwe** Midlands, NW Zimbabwe
94 F13 **Gol** Buskerud, S Norway
153 X12 **Golāghāt** Assam, NE India
110 H10 **Gołańcz** Wielkopolskie, C Poland
138 G8 **Golan Heights** *Ar.* Al Jawlān, *Heb.* HaGolan. ▲ SW Syria
Golārā *see* Ārān
Golaya Pristan *see* Hola Prystan'
143 T11 **Golbāf** Kermān, C Iran
136 M15 **Gölbaşı** Adıyaman, S Turkey
109 P9 **Gölbner** ▲ SW Austria
30 M17 **Golconda** Illinois, N USA
35 T3 **Golconda** Nevada, W USA
136 E11 **Gölcük** Kocaeli, NW Turkey
108 I7 **Goldach** Sankt Gallen, NE Switzerland
110 N7 **Gołdap** *Ger.* Goldap. Warmińsko-Mazurskie, NE Poland
32 E15 **Gold Beach** Oregon, NW USA
Goldberg *see* Złotoryja
68 D11 **Gold Coast** *coastal region* S Ghana
183 V3 **Gold Coast** *cultural region* Queensland, E Australia
39 R10 **Gold Creek** Alaska, USA
11 O16 **Golden** British Columbia, SW Canada
37 T4 **Golden** Colorado, C USA
184 I13 **Golden Bay** *bay* South Island, NZ
27 R7 **Golden City** Missouri, C USA
32 I11 **Goldendale** Washington, NW USA
Goldener Tisch *see* Zlatý Stôl
44 L13 **Golden Grove** E Jamaica
14 J12 **Golden Lake** ◎ Ontario, SE Canada
22 K10 **Golden Meadow** Louisiana, S USA
45 V10 **Golden Rock** ✈ (Basseterre) Saint Kitts, Saint Kitts and Nevis
Golden State, The *see* California
83 K16 **Golden Valley** Mashonaland West, N Zimbabwe
35 U9 **Goldfield** Nevada, W USA
Goldingen *see* Kuldīga
Goldmarkt *see* Zlatna
10 K17 **Gold River** Vancouver Island, British Columbia, SW Canada
21 V10 **Goldsboro** North Carolina, SE USA
24 M8 **Goldsmith** Texas, SW USA
25 R8 **Goldthwaite** Texas, SW USA
137 R11 **Göle** Ardahan, NE Turkey
Golema Ada *see* Ostrovo
114 H9 **Golema Planina** ▲▲ W Bulgaria
114 F9 **Golemi Vrŭkh** ▲ W Bulgaria
110 D8 **Goleniów** *Ger.* Gollnow. Zachodniopomorskie, NW Poland
149 R3 **Golestān** ◈ *province* N Iran
35 Q14 **Goleta** California, W USA
43 O16 **Golfito** Puntarenas, SE Costa Rica
25 T13 **Goliad** Texas, SW USA
113 L14 **Golija** ▲▲ SW Yugoslavia
113 O16 **Goljak** ▲▲ SE Yugoslavia
136 M12 **Gölköy** Ordu, N Turkey
Gollel *see* Lavumisa
109 X3 **Göllersbach** ≈ NE Austria
Gollnow *see* Goleniów
Golmo *see* Golmud
159 P10 **Golmud** *var.* Ge'e'mu, Golmo, *Chin.* Ko-erh-mu. Qinghai, C China
103 Y14 **Golo** ≈ Corse, France, C Mediterranean Sea
Golovanevsk *see* Holovanivs'k
Golovchin *see* Halowchyn
39 N9 **Golovin** Alaska, USA
142 M7 **Golpāyegān** *var.* Gulpaigan. Eşfahān, W Iran
Golshan *see* Ṭabas
Gol'shany *see* Hal'shany
96 J7 **Golspie** N Scotland, UK
112 O11 **Golubac** Serbia, NE Yugoslavia
110 J9 **Golub-Dobrzyń** Kujawski-pomorskie, C Poland
145 S7 **Golubovka** Pavlodar, N Kazakhstan
82 B11 **Golungo Alto** Cuanza Norte, NW Angola
114 M8 **Golyama Kamchiya** ≈ E Bulgaria
114 L8 **Golyama Reka** ≈ N Bulgaria
114 H11 **Golyama Syutkya** ▲ SW Bulgaria
114 I12 **Golyam Perelik** ▲ S Bulgaria
114 I11 **Golyam Persenk** ▲ S Bulgaria
79 P19 **Goma** Nord Kivu, NE Dem. Rep. Congo (Zaire)
Gomati *see* Gumti
77 X14 **Gombe** Gombe, E Nigeria
67 U10 **Gombe** *var.* Igombe. ≈ E Tanzania
77 Y14 **Gombi** Adamawa, E Nigeria
Gombroon *see* Bandar-e 'Abbās
Gomel' *see* Homyel'
Gomel'skaya Oblast' *see* Homyel'skaya Voblasts'

◆ Country ● Country Capital ◇ Dependent Territory ○ Dependent Territory Capital ◈ Administrative Region ✈ International Airport ▲ Mountain ▲▲ Mountain Range Volcano ≈ River ◎ Lake Reservoir

64 N11 **Gomera** *island* Islas Canarias, Spain, NE Atlantic Ocean
40 I5 **Gómez Farias** Chihuahua, N Mexico
40 L8 **Gómez Palacio** Durango, C Mexico
158 J13 **Gomo** Xizang Zizhiqu, W China
143 T6 **Gonābād** *var.* Gunabad. Khorāsān, NE Iran
44 L8 **Gonaïves** *var.* Les Gonaïves. N Haiti
123 Q12 **Gonam** ≈ NE Russian Federation
44 L9 **Gonâve, Canal de la** *var.* Canal de Sud. *channel* N Caribbean Sea
44 K9 **Gonâve, Golfe de la** *gulf* N Caribbean Sea
Gonāveh *see* Bandar-e Gonāveh
44 K9 **Gonâve, Île de la** *island* C Haiti
Gonbadān *see* Dow Gonbadān
143 Q3 **Gonbad-e Kāvūs** *var.* Gunbad-i-Qawus. Golestān, N Iran
152 M12 **Gonda** Uttar Pradesh, N India
Gondar *see* Gonder
80 I11 **Gonder** *var.* Gondar. Amhara, N Ethiopia
78 J13 **Gondey** Moyen-Chari, S Chad
154 J12 **Gondia** Mahārāshtra, C India
104 G6 **Gondomar** Porto, NW Portugal
136 C12 **Gönen** Balıkesir, W Turkey
136 C12 **Gönen Çayı** ≈ NW Turkey
159 O15 **Gongbo'gyamda** Xizang Zizhiqu, W China
159 N16 **Gonggar** Xizang Zizhiqu, W China
160 G9 **Gongga Shan** ▲ C China
159 T10 **Gonghe** Qinghai, C China
158 I5 **Gongliu** *var.* Tokkuztara. Xinjiang Uygur Zizhiqu, NW China
77 W14 **Gongola** ≈ E Nigeria
Gongoleh State *see* Jonglei
183 P5 **Gongolgon** New South Wales, SE Australia
159 Q6 **Gongpoquan** Gansu, N China
160 I10 **Gongxian** *var.* Gong Xian. Sichuan, C China
157 V10 **Gongzhuling** *prev.* Huaide. Jilin, NE China
159 S14 **Gonjo** Xizang Zizhiqu, W China
107 B20 **Gonnesa** Sardegna, Italy, C Mediterranean Sea
Gonni/Gónnos *see* Gónnoi
115 F15 **Gónnoi** *var.* Gonni, Gónnos; *prev.* Derelí. Thessalía, C Greece
164 C13 **Gōnoura** Nagasaki, Iki, SW Japan
35 O11 **Gonzales** California, W USA
22 J9 **Gonzales** Louisiana, S USA
25 T12 **Gonzales** Texas, SW USA
41 P11 **González** Tamaulipas, C Mexico
21 V6 **Goochland** Virginia, NE USA
195 X14 **Goodenough, Cape** *headland* Antarctica
186 F9 **Goodenough Island** *var.* Morata. *island* SE PNG
Good Hope *see* Fort Good Hope
39 N8 **Goodhope Bay** *bay* Alaska, USA
83 D26 **Good Hope, Cape of** *Afr.* Kaap de Goede Hoop, Kaap die Goeie Hoop. *headland* SW South Africa
10 K10 **Good Hope Lake** British Columbia, W Canada
83 E23 **Goodhouse** Northern Cape, W South Africa
33 O15 **Gooding** Idaho, NW USA
26 H3 **Goodland** Kansas, C USA
173 Y15 **Goodlands** NW Mauritius
20 J8 **Goodlettsville** Tennessee, S USA
39 N13 **Goodnews** Alaska, USA
25 O3 **Goodnight** Texas, SW USA
183 Q4 **Goodooga** New South Wales, SE Australia
29 N4 **Goodrich** North Dakota, N USA
25 W10 **Goodrich** Texas, SW USA
29 X10 **Goodview** Minnesota, N USA
26 H8 **Goodwell** Oklahoma, C USA
97 N17 **Goole** E England, UK
183 O8 **Goolgowi** New South Wales, SE Australia
182 I10 **Goolwa** South Australia
181 Y11 **Goondiwindi** Queensland, E Australia
98 O11 **Goor** Overijssel, E Netherlands
Goose Bay *see* Happy Valley-Goose Bay
33 V13 **Gooseberry Creek** ≈ Wyoming, C USA
21 S14 **Goose Creek** South Carolina, SE USA
63 M23 **Goose Green** *var.* Prado del Ganso. East Falkland, Falkland Islands
16 D8 **Goose Lake** *var.* Lago dos Gansos. ◎ California/Oregon, W USA
29 Q4 **Goose River** ≈ North Dakota, N USA
153 T16 **Gopalganj** Dhaka, S Bangladesh
153 O12 **Gopālganj** Bihār, N India
Gopher State *see* Minnesota
101 I22 **Göppingen** Baden-Württemberg, SW Germany
110 G13 **Góra** *Ger.* Guhrau. Dolnośląskie, SW Poland
110 M12 **Góra Kalwaria** Mazowieckie, C Poland
153 O12 **Gorakhpur** Uttar Pradesh, N India
Gorany *see* Harany
113 J14 **Goražde** Federacija Bosna I Hercegovina, Bosnia and Herzegovina
Gorbovichi *see* Harbavichy
Gorče Petrov *see* Đorče Petrov
(0) E9 **Gorda Ridges** *undersea feature* NE Pacific Ocean
Gordiaz *see* Gardēz
78 K12 **Gordil** Vakaga, N Central African Republic
23 U5 **Gordon** Georgia, SE USA
28 K12 **Gordon** Nebraska, C USA
25 R7 **Gordon** Texas, SW USA
28 L13 **Gordon Creek** ≈ Nebraska, C USA
63 I25 **Gordon, Isla** *island* S Chile
183 O17 **Gordon, Lake** ◎ Tasmania, SE Australia
183 O17 **Gordon River** ≈ Tasmania, SE Australia
21 V5 **Gordonsville** Virginia, NE USA
80 H13 **Goré** Oromo, C Ethiopia
185 D24 **Gore** Southland, South Island, NZ
78 H13 **Goré** Logone-Oriental, S Chad
14 D11 **Gore Bay** Manitoulin Island, Ontario, S Canada
25 Q5 **Goree** Texas, SW USA
137 O11 **Görele** Giresun, NE Turkey
19 N6 **Gore Mountain** ▲ Vermont, NE USA
39 R13 **Gore Point** *headland* Alaska, USA
37 R4 **Gore Range** ▲ Colorado, C USA
97 F19 **Gorey** *Ir.* Guaire. SE Ireland
143 R12 **Gorgāb** Kermān, S Iran
143 Q4 **Gorgān** *var.* Astarabad, Astrabad, Gurgan; *prev.* Asterābād, *anc.* Hyrcania. Golestān, N Iran
143 Q4 **Gorgān, Rūd-e** ≈ N Iran
76 I10 **Gorgol** ◈ *region* S Mauritania
106 D12 **Gorgona, Isola di** *island* Archipelago Toscano, C Italy
19 P8 **Gorham** Maine, NE USA
137 T10 **Gori** C Georgia
98 I13 **Gorinchem** *var.* Gorkum. Zuid-Holland, C Netherlands
137 V13 **Goris** SE Armenia
126 K16 **Goritsy** Tverskaya Oblast', W Russian Federation
106 J7 **Gorizia** *Ger.* Görz. Friuli-Venezia Giulia, NE Italy
116 G13 **Gorj** ◈ *county* SW Romania
109 W12 **Gorjanci** *var.* Uskočke Planine, Žumberak, Žumberačko Gorje, *Ger.* Uskokengebirge; *prev.* Sichelburger Gerbirge. ▲ Croatia/Slovenia *see also* Žumberačko Gorje
Görkau *see* Jirkov
Gorki *see* Horki
Gor'kiy *see* Nizhniy Novgorod
Gor'kiy Reservoir *see* Gor'kovskoye Vodokhranilishche
Gorkum *see* Gorinchem
95 I23 **Gørlev** Vestsjælland, E Denmark
111 M17 **Gorlice** Małopolskie, S Poland
101 Q15 **Görlitz** Sachsen, E Germany
Görlitz *see* Zgorzelec
Gorlovka *see* Horlivka
25 R7 **Gorman** Texas, SW USA
21 T3 **Gormania** West Virginia, NE USA
Gorna Dzhumaya *see* Blagoevgrad
114 K8 **Gorna Oryakhovitsa** Veliko Tŭrnovo, N Bulgaria
114 J8 **Gorna Studena** Veliko Tŭrnovo, N Bulgaria
Gornja Mužlja *see* Mužlja
109 X9 **Gornja Radgona** *Ger.* Oberradkersburg. NE Slovenia
112 M13 **Gornji Milanovac** Serbia, C Yugoslavia
112 G13 **Gornji Vakuf** *var.* Uskoplje. Federacija Bosna I Hercegovina, W Bosnia and Herzegovina
122 J13 **Gorno-Altaysk** Respublika Altay, S Russian Federation
Gorno-Altayskaya Respublika *see* Altay, Respublika
123 N12 **Gorno-Chuyskiy** Irkutskaya Oblast', C Russian Federation
127 V14 **Gornozavodsk** Permskaya Oblast', NW Russian Federation
122 I13 **Gornyak** Altayskiy Kray, S Russian Federation
129 R8 **Gornyy** Saratovskaya Oblast', W Russian Federation
Gornyy Altay *see* Altay, Respublika
129 O10 **Gornyy Balykley** Volgogradskaya Oblast', SW Russian Federation
80 I13 **Goroch'an** ▲ W Ethiopia
Gorodenka *see* Horodenka
129 O3 **Gorodets** Nizhegorodskaya Oblast', W Russian Federation
Gorodets *see* Haradzyets
Gorodeya *see* Haradzyeya
129 P6 **Gorodishche** Penzenskaya Oblast', W Russian Federation
Gorodishche *see* Horodyshche
Gorodnya *see* Horodnya
Gorodok *see* Haradok
Gorodok/Gorodok Yagellonski *see* Horodok
128 M13 **Gorodovikovsk** Respublika Kalmykiya, SW Russian Federation
186 D7 **Goroka** Eastern Highlands, C PNG
Gorokhov *see* Horokhiv
129 N3 **Gorokhovets** Vladimirskaya Oblast', W Russian Federation
77 Q11 **Gorom-Gorom** NE Burkina
171 U13 **Gorong, Kepulauan** *island group* E Indonesia
83 M17 **Gorongosa** Sofala, C Mozambique
171 P11 **Gorontalo** Sulawesi, C Indonesia
Gorontalo, Teluk *see* Tomini, Gulf of
110 L7 **Górowo Iławeckie** *Ger.* Landsberg. Warmińsko-Mazurskie, NE Poland,
98 M7 **Gorredijk** *Fris.* De Gordyk. Friesland, N Netherlands
84 C14 **Gorringe Ridge** *undersea feature* E Atlantic Ocean
98 M11 **Gorssel** Gelderland, E Netherlands
109 T8 **Görtschitz** ≈ S Austria
Goryn *see* Horyn'
Görz *see* Gorizia
110 E10 **Gorzów Wielkopolski** *Ger.* Landsberg, Landsberg an der Warthe. Lubuskie, W Poland
108 G9 **Göschenen** Uri, C Switzerland
165 O11 **Gosen** Niigata, Honshū, C Japan
183 T8 **Gosford** New South Wales, SE Australia
31 P11 **Goshen** Indiana, N USA
18 K13 **Goshen** New York, NE USA
Goshoba *see* Koshoba
165 Q7 **Goshogawara** *var.* Gosyogawara. Aomori, Honshū, C Japan
146 I8 **Goshquduq Qum** *var.* Tosquduq Qumlari, *Rus.* Peski Taskuduk. *desert* W Uzbekistan
101 J14 **Goslar** Niedersachsen, C Germany
27 Y9 **Gosnell** Arkansas, C USA
112 C11 **Gospić** Lika-Senj, C Croatia
97 N23 **Gosport** S England, UK
94 D9 **Gossa** *island* S Norway
108 H7 **Gossau** Sankt Gallen, NE Switzerland
99 G20 **Gosselies** *var.* Goss'lies. Hainaut, S Belgium
77 P10 **Gossi** Tombouctou, C Mali
Goss'lies *see* Gosselies
113 N18 **Gostivar** W FYR Macedonia
Gostomel' *see* Hostomel'
110 G12 **Gostyń** *var.* Gostyn. Wielkopolskie, C Poland
110 K11 **Gostynin** Mazowieckie, C Poland
Gosyogawara *see* Goshogawara
95 J18 **Göta Älv** ≈ S Sweden
95 N17 **Göta kanal** *canal* S Sweden
95 K18 **Götaland** *cultural region* S Sweden
95 H17 **Göteborg** *Eng.* Gothenburg. Västra Götaland, S Sweden
77 X16 **Gotel Mountains** ▲ E Nigeria
95 K17 **Götene** Västra Götaland, S Sweden
Gotera *see* San Francisco
101 K16 **Gotha** Thüringen, C Germany
29 N15 **Gothenburg** Nebraska, C USA
Gothenburg *see* Göteborg
77 R12 **Gothèye** Tillabéri, SW Niger
Gothland *see* Gotland
95 P19 **Gotland** *var.* Gothland, Gottland. ◈ *county* SE Sweden
95 O18 **Gotland** *island* SE Sweden
164 B13 **Gotō-rettō** *island group* SW Japan
114 H12 **Gotse Delchev** *prev.* Nevrokop. Blagoevgrad, SW Bulgaria
95 P17 **Gotska Sandön** *island* SE Sweden
101 I15 **Göttingen** *var.* Goettingen. Niedersachsen, C Germany
Gottland *see* Gotland
93 I16 **Gottne** Västernorrland, C Sweden
Gottschee *see* Kočevje
Gottwaldov *see* Zlín
Gôtu *see* Gôtsu
Goturdepe *see* Koturdepe
108 I7 **Götzis** Vorarlberg, NW Austria
98 H12 **Gouda** Zuid-Holland, C Netherlands
76 I11 **Goudiri** *var.* Goudiry. E Senegal
Goudiry *see* Goudiri
77 X12 **Goudoumaria** Diffa, S Niger
15 R9 **Gouffre, Rivière du** ≈ Quebec, SE Canada
65 M19 **Gough Fracture Zone** *tectonic feature* S Atlantic Ocean
65 M19 **Gough Island** *island* Tristan da Cunha, S Atlantic Ocean
15 N8 **Gouin, Réservoir** ⊟ Quebec, SE Canada
14 B10 **Goulais River** Ontario, S Canada
183 R9 **Goulburn** New South Wales, SE Australia
183 O11 **Goulburn River** ≈ Victoria, SE Australia
195 O10 **Gould Coast** *physical region* Antarctica
Goulimime *see* Guelmime
114 F13 **Gouménissa** Kentrikí Makedonía, N Greece
77 O10 **Goundam** Tombouctou, NW Mali
78 H12 **Goundi** Moyen-Chari, S Chad
78 G12 **Gounou-Gaya** Mayo-Kébbi, SW Chad
77 O12 **Gourci** *var.* Gourcy. NW Burkina
Gourcy *see* Gourci
102 M13 **Gourdon** Lot, S France
77 W11 **Gouré** Zinder, SE Niger
102 G6 **Gourin** Morbihan, NW France
77 P10 **Gourma-Rharous** Tombouctou, C Mali
103 N4 **Gournay-en-Bray** Seine-Maritime, N France
78 J6 **Gouro** Borkou-Ennedi-Tibesti, N Chad
104 H8 **Gouveia** Guarda, N Portugal
18 I7 **Gouverneur** New York, NE USA
99 L21 **Gouvy** Luxembourg, E Belgium
45 R14 **Gouyave** *var.* Charlotte Town. NW Grenada
Goverla, Gora *see* Hoverla, Hora
59 N20 **Governador Valadares** Minas Gerais, SE Brazil
171 R8 **Governor Generoso** Mindanao, S Philippines
44 I2 **Governor's Harbour** Eleuthera Island, C Bahamas
162 F9 **Govĭ-Altay** ◈ *province* SW Mongolia
162 I10 **Govĭ Altayn Nuruu** ▲ S Mongolia
154 L9 **Govind Ballabh Pant Sāgar** ⊟ C India
152 I7 **Govind Sāgar** ⊟ NE India
147 N14 **Govurdak** *Turkm.* Gowurdak; *prev.* Guardak. Lebapskiy Velayat, E Turkmenistan
18 D11 **Gowanda** New York, NE USA
148 J10 **Gowd-e Zereh, Dasht-e** *var.* Guad-i-Zirreh. *marsh* SW Afghanistan
14 F8 **Gowganda** Ontario, S Canada
14 G8 **Gowganda Lake** ◎ Ontario, S Canada
29 U13 **Gowrie** Iowa, C USA
Gowurdak *see* Govurdak
61 C15 **Goya** Corrientes, NE Argentina
Goyania *see* Goiânia
137 X11 **Göyçay** *Rus.* Geokchay. C Azerbaijan
Goymat *see* Koymat
Goymatdag *see* Koymatdag, Gory
136 F12 **Göynük** Bolu, NW Turkey
165 R9 **Goyō-san** ▲ Honshū, C Japan
78 K11 **Goz Beïda** Ouaddaï, SE Chad
158 H11 **Gozha Co** ◎ W China
121 O15 **Gozo** *Malt.* Ghawdex. *island* N Malta
80 H9 **Göz Regeb** Kassala, NE Sudan
Gozyō *see* Gojō
83 H25 **Graaff-Reinet** Eastern Cape, S South Africa
Graasten *see* Gråsten
76 L17 **Grabo** SW Ivory Coast
112 P11 **Grabovica** Serbia, E Yugoslavia
110 I13 **Grabów nad Prosną** Wielkopolskie, C Poland
108 I8 **Grabs** Sankt Gallen, NE Switzerland
112 D12 **Gračac** Zadar, C Croatia
112 I11 **Gračanica** Federacija Bosna I Hercegovina, NE Bosnia and Herzegovina
14 L11 **Gracefield** Quebec, SE Canada
99 K19 **Grâce-Hollogne** Liège, E Belgium
23 R8 **Graceville** Florida, SE USA
29 R8 **Graceville** Minnesota, N USA
42 G6 **Gracias** Lempira, W Honduras
Gracias *see* Lempira
42 L5 **Gracias a Dios** ◈ *department* E Honduras
43 O6 **Gracias a Dios, Cabo de** *headland* Honduras/Nicaragua
64 O2 **Graciosa** *var.* Ilha Graciosa. *island* Azores, Portugal, NE Atlantic Ocean
64 Q11 **Graciosa** *island* Islas Canarias, Spain, NE Atlantic Ocean
Graciosa, Ilha *see* Graciosa
112 I11 **Gradačac** Federacija Bosna I Hercegovina, N Bosnia and Herzegovina
59 J15 **Gradaús, Serra dos** ▲ C Brazil
104 L3 **Gradefes** Castilla-León, N Spain
Gradiška *see* Bosanska Gradiška
Gradizhsk *see* Hradyz'k
106 J7 **Grado** Friuli-Venezia Giulia, NE Italy
104 K2 **Grado** Asturias, N Spain
113 P19 **Gradsko** C FYR Macedonia
37 V11 **Grady** New Mexico, SW USA
29 T12 **Graettinger** Iowa, C USA
101 M23 **Grafing** Bayern, SE Germany
25 S6 **Graford** Texas, SW USA
183 V5 **Grafton** New South Wales, SE Australia
29 Q3 **Grafton** North Dakota, N USA
21 S3 **Grafton** West Virginia, NE USA
21 T9 **Graham** North Carolina, SE USA
25 R6 **Graham** Texas, SW USA
Graham Bell Island *see* Greem-Bell, Ostrov
10 I13 **Graham Island** *island* Queen Charlotte Islands, British Columbia, SW Canada
19 S6 **Graham Lake** ◎ Maine, NE USA
194 H4 **Graham Land** *physical region* Antarctica
37 N15 **Graham, Mount** ▲ Arizona, SW USA
Grahamstad *see* Grahamstown
83 I25 **Grahamstown** *Afr.* Grahamstad. Eastern Cape, S South Africa
Grahovo *see* Bosansko Grahovo
68 C11 **Grain Coast** *coastal region* S Liberia
169 S17 **Grajagan, Teluk** *bay* Jawa, S Indonesia
58 L14 **Grajaú** Maranhão, E Brazil
58 M13 **Grajaú, Rio** ≈ NE Brazil
110 O8 **Grajewo** Podlaskie, NE Poland
95 F24 **Gram** Sønderjylland, SW Denmark
103 N13 **Gramat** Lot, S France
22 H5 **Grambling** Louisiana, S USA
115 C14 **Grámmos** ▲ Albania/Greece
96 I9 **Grampian Mountains** ▲ C Scotland, UK
182 L12 **Grampians, The** ▲ Victoria, SE Australia
98 O9 **Gramsbergen** Overijssel, E Netherlands
113 L21 **Gramsh** *var.* Gramshi. Elbasan, C Albania
Gramshi *see* Gramsh
Gran *see* Hron, Slovakia
Gran *see* Esztergom, N Hungary
54 F11 **Granada** Meta, C Colombia
42 J10 **Granada** Granada, SW Nicaragua
105 N14 **Granada** Andalucía, S Spain
37 W6 **Granada** Colorado, C USA
42 J11 **Granada** ◈ *department* SW Nicaragua
105 N14 **Granada** ◈ *province* Andalucía, S Spain
63 I21 **Gran Altiplanicie Central** *plain* S Argentina
97 E17 **Granard** *Ir.* Gránard. C Ireland
63 J20 **Gran Bajo** *basin* S Argentina
63 J15 **Gran Bajo del Gualicho** *basin* E Argentina
63 I21 **Gran Bajo de San Julián** *basin* SE Argentina
25 S7 **Granbury** Texas, SW USA
15 P12 **Granby** Quebec, SE Canada
27 S8 **Granby** Missouri, C USA
37 S3 **Granby, Lake** ⊟ Colorado, C USA
64 O12 **Gran Canaria** *var.* Grand Canary. *island* Islas Canarias, Spain, NE Atlantic Ocean
47 T11 **Gran Chaco** *var.* Chaco. *lowland plain* South America
45 R14 **Grand Anse** SW Grenada
Grand-Anse *see* Portsmouth
44 G1 **Grand Bahama Island** *island* N Bahamas
Grand Balé *see* Tui
103 U7 **Grand Ballon** *Ger.* Ballon de Guebwiller. ▲ NE France
13 T13 **Grand Bank** Newfoundland, SE Canada
64 I7 **Grand Banks of Newfoundland** *undersea feature* NW Atlantic Ocean
Grand Bassa *see* Buchanan
77 N17 **Grand-Bassam** *var.* Bassam. SE Ivory Coast
14 E16 **Grand Bend** Ontario, S Canada
76 L17 **Grand-Bérébi** *var.* Grand-Bérréby. SW Ivory Coast
Grand-Béréby *see* Grand-Bérébi
45 X11 **Grand-Bourg** Marie-Galante, SE Guadeloupe
44 M6 **Grand Caicos** *var.* Middle Caicos. *island* C Turks and Caicos Islands
14 K12 **Grand Calumet, Île du** *island* Quebec, SE Canada
97 E18 **Grand Canal** *Ir.* An Chanáil Mhór. *canal* C Ireland
Grand Canary *see* Gran Canaria
36 K10 **Grand Canyon** Arizona, SW USA
36 J9 **Grand Canyon** *canyon* Arizona, SW USA
Grand Canyon State *see* Arizona
44 D8 **Grand Cayman** *island* SW Cayman Islands
11 R14 **Grand Centre** Alberta, SW Canada
76 L17 **Grand Cess** SE Liberia
108 D12 **Grand Combin** ▲ S Switzerland
32 K8 **Grand Coulee** Washington, NW USA
32 J8 **Grand Coulee** *valley* Washington, NW USA
45 X5 **Grand Cul-de-Sac Marin** *bay* N Guadeloupe
Grand Duchy of Luxembourg *see* Luxembourg
63 I22 **Grande, Bahía** *bay* S Argentina
11 N14 **Grande Cache** Alberta, W Canada
103 U12 **Grande Casse** ▲ E France
172 G12 **Grande Comore** *var.* Njazidja, Great Comoro. *island* NW Comoros
61 G18 **Grande, Cuchilla** *hill range* E Uruguay
45 S5 **Grande de Añasco, Río** ≈ W Puerto Rico
Grande de Chiloé, Isla *see* Chiloé, Isla de
58 J12 **Grande de Gurupá, Ilha** *river island* NE Brazil
57 K21 **Grande de Lipez, Río** ≈ SW Bolivia
45 U6 **Grande de Loíza, Río** ≈ E Puerto Rico
45 T5 **Grande de Manatí, Río** ≈ C Puerto Rico
42 L9 **Grande de Matagalpa, Río** ≈ C Nicaragua
40 K12 **Grande de Santiago, Río** *var.* Santiago. ≈ C Mexico
43 O15 **Grande de Térraba, Río** *var.* Río Térraba. ≈ SE Costa Rica
12 J9 **Grande Deux, Réservoir la** ⊟ Quebec, E Canada
60 O10 **Grande, Ilha** *island* SE Brazil
11 O13 **Grande Prairie** Alberta, W Canada
74 I8 **Grand Erg Occidental** *desert* W Algeria
74 L9 **Grand Erg Oriental** *desert* Algeria/Tunisia
59 J20 **Grande, Rio** ≈ S Brazil
2 F15 **Grande, Rio** *var.* Río Bravo, *Sp.* Río Bravo del Norte, Bravo del Norte. ≈ Mexico/USA
57 M18 **Grande, Río** ≈ C Bolivia
15 Y7 **Grande-Rivière** Quebec, SE Canada
15 Y6 **Grande Rivière** ≈ Quebec, SE Canada
44 M8 **Grande-Rivière-du-Nord** N Haiti
62 K9 **Grande, Salina** *var.* Gran Salitral. *salt lake* C Argentina
15 S7 **Grandes-Bergeronnes** Quebec, SE Canada
47 W6 **Grande, Serra** ▲ W Brazil
40 K4 **Grande, Sierra** ▲ N Mexico
103 S12 **Grandes Rousses** ▲ E France
63 K17 **Grandes, Salinas** *salt lake* E Argentina
45 Y5 **Grande Terre** *island* E West Indies
15 X5 **Grande-Vallée** Quebec, SE Canada
45 Y5 **Grande Vigie, Pointe de la** *headland* Grande Terre, N Guadeloupe
13 N14 **Grand Falls** New Brunswick, SE Canada
13 T11 **Grand Falls** Newfoundland, SE Canada
24 L9 **Grandfalls** Texas, SW USA
21 P9 **Grandfather Mountain** ▲ North Carolina, SE USA
26 L13 **Grandfield** Oklahoma, C USA
11 N17 **Grand Forks** British Columbia, SW Canada
29 R4 **Grand Forks** North Dakota, N USA
31 O9 **Grand Haven** Michigan, N USA
Grandichi *see* Hrandzichy
29 P15 **Grand Island** Nebraska, C USA
31 O3 **Grand Island** *island* Michigan, N USA
22 K10 **Grand Isle** Louisiana, S USA
65 A23 **Grand Jason** *island* Jason Islands, NW Falkland Islands
37 P5 **Grand Junction** Colorado, C USA
20 F10 **Grand Junction** Tennessee, S USA
14 J9 **Grand-Lac-Victoria** Quebec, SE Canada
14 J9 **Grand lac Victoria** ◎ Quebec, SE Canada
77 N17 **Grand-Lahou** *var.* Grand Lahu. S Ivory Coast
Grand Lahu *see* Grand-Lahou
37 S3 **Grand Lake** Colorado, C USA
13 S11 **Grand Lake** ◎ Newfoundland, E Canada
22 G9 **Grand Lake** ◎ Louisiana, S USA
31 R5 **Grand Lake** ◎ Michigan, N USA
31 Q13 **Grand Lake** ⊟ Ohio, N USA
27 R9 **Grand Lake O' The Cherokees** *var.* Lake O' The Cherokees. ⊟ Oklahoma, C USA
31 Q9 **Grand Ledge** Michigan, N USA
102 I8 **Grand-Lieu, Lac de** ◎ NW France
19 U6 **Grand Manan Channel** *channel* Canada/USA
13 O15 **Grand Manan Island** *island* New Brunswick, SE Canada
29 Y4 **Grand Marais** Minnesota, N USA
15 P10 **Grand-Mère** Quebec, SE Canada
37 P5 **Grand Mesa** ▲ Colorado, C USA
108 C10 **Grand Muveran** ▲ W Switzerland
104 G12 **Grândola** Setúbal, S Portugal
Grand Paradis *see* Gran Paradiso
187 O15 **Grand Passage** *passage* N New Caledonia
77 R16 **Grand-Popo** S Benin
29 Z3 **Grand Portage** Minnesota, N USA
25 T6 **Grand Prairie** Texas, SW USA
11 W14 **Grand Rapids** Manitoba, C Canada
31 P9 **Grand Rapids** Michigan, N USA
29 V5 **Grand Rapids** Minnesota, N USA
14 L10 **Grand-Remous** Quebec, SE Canada
14 F15 **Grand River** ≈ Ontario, S Canada
31 P9 **Grand River** ≈ Michigan, N USA
27 T3 **Grand River** ≈ Missouri, C USA
28 M7 **Grand River** ≈ South Dakota, N USA
45 Q11 **Grand' Rivière** N Martinique
32 F11 **Grand Ronde** Oregon, NW USA
32 L11 **Grand Ronde River** ≈ Oregon/Washington, NW USA
Grand-Saint-Bernard, Col du *see* Great Saint Bernard Pass
25 V6 **Grand Saline** Texas, SW USA
55 X10 **Grand-Santi** W French Guiana
Grandsee *see* Grandson
108 B9 **Grandson** *prev.* Grandsee. Vaud, W Switzerland
172 J16 **Grand Sœur** *island* Les Sœurs, NE Seychelles
33 S14 **Grand Teton** ▲ Wyoming, C USA
31 P5 **Grand Traverse Bay** *lake bay* Michigan, N USA
45 N6 **Grand Turk** ○ (Turks and Caicos Islands) Grand Turk Island, S Turks and Caicos Islands
45 N6 **Grand Turk Island** *island* SE Turks and Caicos Islands
103 S13 **Grand Veymont** ▲ E France
11 W15 **Grandview** Manitoba, S Canada
27 R4 **Grandview** Missouri, C USA
36 I10 **Grand Wash Cliffs** *cliff* Arizona, SW USA
14 J8 **Granet, Lac** ◎ Quebec, SE Canada
95 L14 **Grangärde** Dalarna, C Sweden
44 H12 **Grange Hill** W Jamaica
96 J12 **Grangemouth** C Scotland, UK
25 T10 **Granger** Texas, SW USA
32 J10 **Granger** Washington, NW USA
33 T17 **Granger** Wyoming, C USA
Granges *see* Grenchen
95 L14 **Grängesberg** Dalarna, C Sweden
33 N11 **Grangeville** Idaho, NW USA
10 K13 **Granisle** British Columbia, SW Canada
30 K15 **Granite City** Illinois, N USA
29 S9 **Granite Falls** Minnesota, N USA
21 Q9 **Granite Falls** North Carolina, SE USA
36 K12 **Granite Mountain** ▲ Arizona, SW USA
33 T12 **Granite Peak** ▲ Montana, NW USA
35 T2 **Granite Peak** ▲ Nevada, W USA
36 J3 **Granite Peak** ▲ Utah, W USA

◆ Country ● Country Capital ◇ Dependent Territory ○ Dependent Territory Capital ◈ Administrative Region ✈ International Airport ▲ Mountain ▲ Mountain Range Volcano ≈ River ◎ Lake ⊟ Reservoir

Granite State see New Hampshire
107 H24 Granitola, Capo headland Sicilia, Italy, C Mediterranean Sea
185 H15 Granity West Coast, South Island, NZ
Gran Lago see Nicaragua, Lago de
63 J18 Gran Laguna Salada ⊚ S Argentina
Gran Malvina, Isla see West Falkland
95 L18 Gränna Jönköping, S Sweden
105 W5 Granollers var. Granollérs. Cataluña, NE Spain
106 A7 Gran Paradiso Fr. Grand Paradis. ▲ NW Italy
Gran Pilastro see Hochfeiler
Gran Salitral see Grande, Salina
Gran San Bernardo, Passo di see Great Saint Bernard Pass
Gran Santiago see Santiago
107 J14 Gran Sasso d'Italia ▲ C Italy
100 N11 Gransee Brandenburg, NE Germany
28 L15 Grant Nebraska, C USA
27 R1 Grant City Missouri, C USA
97 N19 Grantham E England, UK
65 D24 Grantham Sound sound East Falkland, Falkland Islands
194 K13 Grant Island island Antarctica
45 Z14 Grantley Adams ✕ (Bridgetown) SE Barbados
35 S7 Grant, Mount ▲ Nevada, W USA
96 J9 Grantown-on-Spey N Scotland, UK
35 W8 Grant Range ▲ Nevada, W USA
37 Q11 Grants New Mexico, SW USA
30 I4 Grantsburg Wisconsin, N USA
32 F15 Grants Pass Oregon, NW USA
36 K3 Grantsville Utah, W USA
21 R4 Grantsville West Virginia, NE USA
102 I5 Granville Manche, N France
11 V12 Granville Lake ⊚ Manitoba, C Canada
25 V8 Grapeland Texas, SW USA
25 T6 Grapevine Texas, SW USA
83 K20 Graskop Mpumalanga, NE South Africa
95 P14 Gräsö Uppsala, C Sweden
93 I19 Gräsö island C Sweden
103 U15 Grasse Alpes-Maritimes, SE France
18 E14 Grassflat Pennsylvania, NE USA
33 U9 Grassrange Montana, NW USA
18 J6 Grass River ≈ New York, NE USA
35 P6 Grass Valley California, W USA
183 N14 Grassy Tasmania, SE Australia
28 K4 Grassy Butte North Dakota, N USA
21 R5 Grassy Knob ▲ West Virginia, NE USA
95 G24 Gråsten var. Graasten. Sønderjylland, SW Denmark
95 J18 Grästorp Västra Götaland, S Sweden
Gratianopolis see Grenoble
109 V8 Gratwein Steiermark, SE Austria
Gratz see Graz
108 I9 Graubünden Fr. Grisons, It. Grigioni. ⬥ canton SE Switzerland
Graudenz see Grudziądz
103 N15 Graulhet Tarn, S France
105 T4 Graus Aragón, NE Spain
61 I16 Gravataí Rio Grande do Sul, S Brazil
98 L13 Grave Noord-Brabant, SE Netherlands
11 T17 Gravelbourg Saskatchewan, S Canada
103 N1 Gravelines Nord, N France
Graven see Grez-Doiceau
14 H13 Gravenhurst Ontario, S Canada
33 O10 Grave Peak ▲ Idaho, NW USA
102 I11 Grave, Pointe de headland W France
183 S4 Gravesend New South Wales, SE Australia
97 P22 Gravesend SE England, UK
107 N17 Gravina di Puglia Eng. Gravina in Puglia. Puglia, SE Italy
Gravina in Puglia see Gravina di Puglia
103 S8 Gray Haute-Saône, E France
23 T4 Gray Georgia, SE USA
195 V16 Gray, Cape headland Antarctica
32 F9 Grayland Washington, NW USA
39 N10 Grayling Alaska, USA
31 Q6 Grayling Michigan, N USA
32 F9 Grays Harbor inlet Washington, NW USA
21 O5 Grayson Kentucky, S USA
37 S4 Grays Peak ▲ Colorado, C USA
30 M16 Grayville Illinois, N USA
109 V8 Graz prev. Gratz. Steiermark, SE Austria
104 L15 Grazalema Andalucía, S Spain
113 P15 Grdelica Serbia, SE Yugoslavia
44 H1 Great Abaco var. Abaco Island. island N Bahamas
Great Admiralty Island see Manus Island
Great Alfold see Great Hungarian Plain
Great Ararat see Büyükağrı Dağı
181 U8 Great Artesian Basin lowlands Queensland, C Australia
181 O12 Great Australian Bight bight S Australia
64 E11 Great Bahama Bank undersea feature E Gulf of Mexico
184 M4 Great Barrier Island island N NZ
181 X4 Great Barrier Reef reef Queensland, NE Australia
18 L11 Great Barrington Massachusetts, NE USA
(0) F10 Great Basin basin W USA
8 I8 Great Bear Lake Fr. Grand Lac de l'Ours. ⊚ Northwest Territories, NW Canada
Great Belt see Storebælt
26 L5 Great Bend Kansas, C USA
Great Bermuda see Bermuda
97 A20 Great Blasket Island Ir. An Blascaod Mór. island SW Ireland
Great Britain see Britain
151 Q23 Great Channel channel Andaman Sea/Indian Ocean
166 J10 Great Coco Island island SW Burma
Great Crosby see Crosby
21 X7 Great Dismal Swamp wetland North Carolina/Virginia, SE USA
33 V16 Great Divide Basin basin Wyoming, C USA
181 W7 Great Dividing Range ▲ NE Australia
14 D12 Great Duck Island island Ontario, S Canada
Great Elder Reservoir see Waconda Lake
195 V8 Greater Antarctica var. East Antarctica. physical region Antarctica
44 G8 Greater Antilles island group West Indies
131 V16 Greater Sunda Islands var. Sunda Islands. island group Indonesia
184 I1 Great Exhibition Bay inlet North Island, NZ
44 H4 Great Exuma Island island C Bahamas
33 R8 Great Falls Montana, NW USA
21 R11 Great Falls South Carolina, SE USA
84 F9 Great Fisher Bank undersea feature C North Sea
Great Glen see Mor, Glen
Great Grimsby see Grimsby
44 I4 Great Guana Cay island C Bahamas
64 I5 Great Hellefiske Bank undersea feature N Atlantic Ocean
111 L24 Great Hungarian Plain var. Great Alfold, Plain of Hungary, Hung. Alföld. plain SE Europe
44 L7 Great Inagua var. Inagua Islands. island S Bahamas
Great Indian Desert see Thar Desert
83 G25 Great Karoo var. Great Karroo, High Veld, Afr. Groot Karoo, Hoë Karoo. plateau region S South Africa
Great Karroo see Great Karoo
Great Kei see Groot-Kei
Great Khingan Range see Da Hinggan Ling
14 E11 Great La Cloche Island island Ontario, S Canada
183 P16 Great Lake ⊚ Tasmania, SE Australia
Great Lake see Tônlé Sap
9 R15 Great Lakes lakes Ontario, Canada/USA
Great Lakes State see Michigan
97 L20 Great Malvern W England, UK
184 M5 Great Mercury Island island N NZ
Great Meteor Seamount see Great Meteor Tablemount
64 K10 Great Meteor Tablemount var. Great Meteor Seamount. undersea feature E Atlantic Ocean
31 Q14 Great Miami River ≈ Ohio, N USA
151 Q24 Great Nicobar island Nicobar Islands, India, NE Indian Ocean
97 O19 Great Ouse var. Ouse. ≈ E England, UK
183 Q17 Great Oyster Bay bay Tasmania, SE Australia
44 I13 Great Pedro Bluff headland W Jamaica
21 T12 Great Pee Dee River ≈ North Carolina/South Carolina, SE USA
131 W9 Great Plain of China plain E China
(0) F12 Great Plains var. High Plains. plains Canada/USA
37 W6 Great Plains Reservoirs ⊞ Colorado, C USA
19 Q13 Great Point headland Nantucket Island, Massachusetts, NE USA
68 I13 Great Rift Valley var. Rift Valley. depression Asia/Africa
81 I23 Great Ruaha ≈ S Tanzania
18 K10 Great Sacandaga Lake ⊞ New York, NE USA
108 C12 Great Saint Bernard Pass Fr. Col du Grand-Saint-Bernard, It. Passo di Gran San Bernardo. pass Italy/Switzerland
44 F1 Great Sale Cay island N Bahamas
Great Salt Desert see Kavīr, Dasht-e
36 K1 Great Salt Lake salt lake Utah, W USA
36 J3 Great Salt Lake Desert plain Utah, W USA
26 M8 Great Salt Plains Lake ⊞ Oklahoma, C USA
75 T9 Great Sand Sea desert Egypt/Libya
180 L6 Great Sandy Desert desert Western Australia
Great Sandy Desert see Ar Rub' al Khālī
Great Sandy Island see Fraser Island
187 Y13 Great Sea Reef reef Vanua Levu, N Fiji
38 H17 Great Sitkin Island island Aleutian Islands, Alaska, USA
8 J10 Great Slave Lake Fr. Grand Lac des Esclaves. ⊚ Northwest Territories, NW Canada
21 O10 Great Smoky Mountains ▲ North Carolina/Tennessee, SE USA
10 L11 Great Snow Mountain ▲ British Columbia, W Canada
64 A12 Great Sound bay Bermuda, NW Atlantic Ocean
180 M10 Great Victoria Desert desert South Australia/Western Australia
194 H2 Great Wall Chinese research station South Shetland Islands, Antarctica
19 T7 Great Wass Island island Maine, NE USA
97 Q19 Great Yarmouth var. Yarmouth. E England, UK
139 S1 Great Zab Ar. Az Zāb al Kabīr, Kurd. Zē-i Bādīnān, Turk. Büyükzap Suyu. ≈ Iraq/Turkey
95 I17 Grebbestad Västra Götaland, S Sweden
Grebenka see Hrebinka
42 M13 Grecia Alajuela, C Costa Rica
61 E18 Greco Río Negro, W Uruguay
Greco, Cape see Gkréko, Akrotíri
104 L8 Gredos, Sierra de ▲ W Spain
18 F9 Greece New York, NE USA
115 E17 Greece off. Hellenic Republic, Gk. Ellás; anc. Hellas. ◆ republic SE Europe
Greece Central see Stereá Ellás
Greece West see Dytikí Ellás
37 T3 Greeley Colorado, C USA
29 P14 Greeley Nebraska, C USA
122 K3 Greem-Bell, Ostrov Eng. Graham Bell Island. island Zemlya Frantsa-Iosifa, N Russian Federation
30 M6 Green Bay Wisconsin, N USA
31 N6 Green Bay lake bay Michigan/Wisconsin, N USA
21 S5 Greenbrier River ≈ West Virginia, NE USA
29 S2 Greenbush Minnesota, N USA
183 R12 Green Cape headland New South Wales, SE Australia
31 O14 Greencastle Indiana, N USA
18 F16 Greencastle Pennsylvania, NE USA
27 T2 Green City Missouri, C USA
21 O9 Greeneville Tennessee, S USA
35 O11 Greenfield California, W USA
31 P14 Greenfield Indiana, N USA
29 U15 Greenfield Iowa, C USA
18 M11 Greenfield Massachusetts, NE USA
27 S7 Greenfield Missouri, C USA
31 S14 Greenfield Ohio, N USA
20 G8 Greenfield Tennessee, S USA
30 M9 Greenfield Wisconsin, N USA
27 T9 Green Forest Arkansas, C USA
37 T7 Greenhorn Mountain ▲ Colorado, C USA
Green Island see Lü Tao
186 I6 Green Islands var. Nissan Islands. island group NE PNG
11 S14 Green Lake Saskatchewan, C Canada
30 L8 Green Lake ⊚ Wisconsin, N USA
197 O14 Greenland Dan. Grønland, Inuit Kalaallit Nunaat. ◇ Danish external territory NE North America
84 D4 Greenland island NE North America
197 R13 Greenland Plain undersea feature N Greenland Sea
197 R14 Greenland Sea sea Arctic Ocean
37 R4 Green Mountain Reservoir ⊞ Colorado, C USA
18 M8 Green Mountains ▲ Vermont, NE USA
Green Mountain State see Vermont
96 H12 Greenock W Scotland, UK
39 T5 Greenough, Mount ▲ Alaska, USA
16 G10 Green River Sandaun, NW PNG
37 N5 Green River Utah, W USA
33 U17 Green River Wyoming, C USA
16 H9 Green River ≈ W USA
30 K11 Green River ≈ Illinois, N USA
20 J7 Green River ≈ Kentucky, S USA
28 K5 Green River ≈ North Dakota, N USA
37 N6 Green River ≈ Utah, W USA
33 T16 Green River ≈ Wyoming, C USA
20 L7 Green River Lake ⊞ Kentucky, S USA
23 O5 Greensboro Alabama, S USA
23 U3 Greensboro Georgia, SE USA
21 T9 Greensboro North Carolina, SE USA
31 P14 Greensburg Indiana, N USA
26 K6 Greensburg Kansas, C USA
20 L7 Greensburg Kentucky, S USA
18 C15 Greensburg Pennsylvania, NE USA
37 O13 Greens Peak ▲ Arizona, SW USA
21 V12 Green Swamp wetland North Carolina, SE USA
21 O4 Greenup Kentucky, S USA
36 M16 Green Valley Arizona, SW USA
76 K17 Greenville var. Sino, Sinoe. SE Liberia
23 P6 Greenville Alabama, S USA
23 T8 Greenville Florida, SE USA
23 S4 Greenville Georgia, SE USA
30 L15 Greenville Illinois, N USA
20 I7 Greenville Kentucky, S USA
19 Q5 Greenville Maine, NE USA
31 P9 Greenville Michigan, N USA
22 J4 Greenville Mississippi, S USA
21 W9 Greenville North Carolina, SE USA
31 Q13 Greenville Ohio, N USA
19 O12 Greenville Rhode Island, NE USA
21 P11 Greenville South Carolina, SE USA
25 U6 Greenville Texas, SW USA
31 T12 Greenwich Ohio, N USA
27 S11 Greenwood Arkansas, C USA
31 O14 Greenwood Indiana, N USA
22 K4 Greenwood Mississippi, S USA
21 P12 Greenwood South Carolina, SE USA
21 Q12 Greenwood, Lake ⊞ South Carolina, SE USA
21 P11 Greer South Carolina, SE USA
27 V10 Greers Ferry Lake ⊞ Arkansas, C USA
27 S13 Greeson, Lake ⊞ Arkansas, C USA
29 O12 Gregory South Dakota, N USA
182 J3 Gregory, Lake salt lake South Australia
180 J9 Gregory Lake ⊚ Western Australia
181 V5 Gregory Range ▲ Queensland, E Australia
Greifenberg/Greifenberg in Pommern see Gryfice
Greifenhagen see Gryfino
100 O8 Greifswald Mecklenburg-Vorpommern, NE Germany
100 O8 Greifswalder Bodden bay NE Germany
109 U4 Grein Oberösterreich, N Austria
101 M17 Greiz Thüringen, C Germany
Gremicha/Gremiha see Gremikha
126 M4 Gremikha var. Gremicha, Gremiha. Murmanskaya Oblast', NW Russian Federation
127 V14 Gremyachinsk Permskaya Oblast', NW Russian Federation
95 H21 Grenå var. Grenaa. Århus, C Denmark
Grenaa see Grenå
22 L3 Grenada Mississippi, S USA
45 W15 Grenada ◆ commonwealth republic SE West Indies
47 S4 Grenada island Grenada
47 R4 Grenada Basin undersea feature W Atlantic Ocean
22 L3 Grenada Lake ⊞ Mississippi, S USA
45 Y14 Grenadines, The island group Grenada/St Vincent and the Grenadines
108 D7 Grenchen Fr. Granges. Solothurn, NW Switzerland
183 Q9 Grenfell New South Wales, SE Australia
11 V16 Grenfell Saskatchewan, S Canada
92 J1 Grenivík Nordhurland Eystra, N Iceland
103 S12 Grenoble anc. Cularo, Gratianopolis. Isère, E France
28 J2 Grenora North Dakota, N USA
92 N8 Grense-Jakobselv Finnmark, N Norway
45 S14 Grenville E Grenada
32 G11 Gresham Oregon, NW USA
Gresk see Hresk
106 B7 Gressoney-St-Jean Valle d'Aosta, NW Italy
22 K9 Gretna Louisiana, S USA
21 T7 Gretna Virginia, NE USA
98 F13 Grevelingen inlet S North Sea
100 F13 Greven Nordrhein-Westfalen, NW Germany
115 D15 Grevená Dytikí Makedonía, N Greece
101 D16 Grevenbroich Nordrhein-Westfalen, W Germany
99 N24 Grevenmacher Grevenmacher, E Luxembourg
99 M24 Grevenmacher ⬥ district E Luxembourg
100 K9 Grevesmühlen Mecklenburg-Vorpommern, N Germany
185 H16 Grey ≈ South Island, NZ
33 V12 Greybull Wyoming, C USA
33 U13 Greybull River ≈ Wyoming, C USA
65 A24 Grey Channel sound Falkland Islands
Greyerzer See see Gruyère, Lac de la
13 T10 Grey Islands island group Newfoundland, E Canada
18 L10 Greylock, Mount ▲ Massachusetts, NE USA
185 G17 Greymouth West Coast, South Island, NZ
181 U10 Grey Range ▲ New South Wales/Queensland, E Australia
97 G18 Greystones Ir. Na Clocha Liatha. E Ireland
185 M14 Greytown Wellington, North Island, NZ
83 K23 Greytown KwaZulu/Natal, E South Africa
Greytown see San Juan del Norte
99 H19 Grez-Doiceau Dut. Graven. Wallon Brabant, C Belgium
115 J19 Griá, Akrotírio headland Ándros, Kykládes, Greece, Aegean Sea
129 N8 Gribanovskiy Voronezhskaya Oblast', W Russian Federation
78 I13 Gribingui ≈ N Central African Republic
35 O6 Gridley California, W USA
83 G23 Griekwastad Northern Cape, C South Africa
23 S4 Griffin Georgia, SE USA
183 O9 Griffith New South Wales, SE Australia
14 F13 Griffith Island island Ontario, S Canada
21 W10 Grifton North Carolina, SE USA
Grigioni see Graubünden
119 H14 Grigiškes Trakai, SE Lithuania
117 N10 Grigoriopol C Moldova
147 X7 Grigor'yevka Issyk-Kul'skaya Oblast', E Kyrgyzstan
193 U8 Grijalva Ridge undersea feature E Pacific Ocean
41 U15 Grijalva, Río var. Tabasco. ≈ Guatemala/Mexico
98 N5 Grijpskerk Groningen, NE Netherlands
83 C22 Grillenthal Karas, SW Namibia
79 J15 Grimari Ouaka, C Central African Republic
Grimaylov see Hrymayliv
99 G18 Grimbergen Vlaams Brabant, C Belgium
183 N15 Grim, Cape headland Tasmania, SE Australia
100 N8 Grimmen Mecklenburg-Vorpommern, NE Germany
14 G16 Grimsby Ontario, S Canada
97 O17 Grimsby prev. Great Grimsby. E England, UK
92 J1 Grímsey var. Grimsey. island N Iceland
11 O12 Grimshaw Alberta, W Canada
95 F18 Grimstad Aust-Agder, S Norway
92 H4 Grindavík Reykjanes, W Iceland
108 F9 Grindelwald Bern, S Switzerland
95 F23 Grindsted Ribe, W Denmark
29 W14 Grinnell Iowa, C USA
8 K4 Grinnell Peninsula peninsula Nunavut, N Canada
109 U10 Grintovec ▲ N Slovenia
9 N3 Grise Fiord var. Ausuittuq. Nunavut, N Canada
182 H1 Griselda, Lake salt lake South Australia
Grisons see Graubünden
95 P14 Grisslehamn Stockholm, C Sweden
29 T15 Griswold Iowa, C USA
102 M1 Griz Nez, Cap headland N France
112 P13 Grljan Serbia, E Yugoslavia
112 E11 Grmeč ▲ NW Bosnia and Herzegovina
99 H16 Grobbendonk Antwerpen, N Belgium
Grobin see Grobiņa
118 C10 Grobiņa Ger. Grobin. Liepāja, W Latvia
83 K20 Groblersdal Mpumalanga, NE South Africa
83 G23 Groblershoop Northern Cape, W South Africa
Gródek Jagielloński see Horodok
109 Q6 Grödig Salzburg, W Austria
111 H15 Grodków Opolskie, S Poland
Grodnenskaya Oblast' see Hrodzyenskaya Voblasts'
Grodno see Hrodna
110 L12 Grodzisk Mazowiecki Mazowieckie, C Poland
110 F12 Grodzisk Wielkopolski Wielkopolskie, C Poland
Grodzyanka see Hradzyanka
98 O12 Groenlo Gelderland, E Netherlands
83 E22 Groenrivier Karas, SE Namibia
25 U8 Groesbeck Texas, SW USA
98 L13 Groesbeek Gelderland, SE Netherlands
102 G7 Groix, Îles de island group NW France
110 M12 Grójec Mazowieckie, C Poland
65 K15 Gröll Seamount undersea feature C Atlantic Ocean
100 E13 Gronau var. Gronau in Westfalen. Nordrhein-Westfalen, NW Germany
Gronau in Westfalen see Gronau
93 F15 Grong Nord-Trøndelag, C Norway
95 N22 Grönhögen Kalmar, S Sweden
98 N5 Groningen Groningen, NE Netherlands
55 W9 Groningen Saramacca, N Suriname
98 N5 Groningen ⬥ province NE Netherlands
Grønland see Greenland
108 H11 Grono Graubünden, S Switzerland
95 M20 Grönskåra Kalmar, S Sweden
25 O2 Groom Texas, SW USA
35 W9 Groom Lake ⊚ Nevada, W USA
83 H25 Groot ≈ S South Africa
181 S2 Groote Eylandt island Northern Territory, N Australia
98 M6 Grootegast Groningen, NE Netherlands
83 D17 Grootfontein Otjozondjupa, N Namibia
83 E22 Groot Karasberge ▲ S Namibia
Groot Karoo see Great Karoo
83 J25 Groot-Kei Eng. Great Kei. ≈ S South Africa
45 T10 Gros Islet N Saint Lucia
44 L8 Gros-Morne NW Haiti
13 S11 Gros Morne ▲ Newfoundland, E Canada
103 R9 Grosne ≈ C France
45 S12 Gros Piton ▲ SW Saint Lucia
Grossa, Isola see Dugi Otok
Grossbetschkerek see Zrenjanin
Grosse Isper see Grosse Ysper
Grosse Kokel see Târnava Mare
101 M21 Grosse Laaber var. Grosse Laber. ≈ SE Germany
Grosse Laber see Grosse Laaber
Grosse Morava see Velika Morava
101 O15 Grossenhain Sachsen, E Germany
109 Y4 Grossenzersdorf Niederösterreich, NE Austria
101 O21 Grosser Arber ▲ SE Germany
101 K17 Grosser Beerberg ▲ C Germany
101 G18 Grosser Feldberg ▲ W Germany
109 O8 Grosser Löffler It. Monte Lovello. ▲ Austria/Italy
109 N8 Grosser Möseler var. Mesule. ▲ Austria/Italy
100 J8 Grosser Plöner See ⊚ N Germany
101 O21 Grosser Rachel ▲ SE Germany
Grosser Sund see Suur Väin
15 V6 Grosses-Roches Quebec, SE Canada
109 P8 Grosses Weiesbachhorn var. Wiesbachhorn. ▲ W Austria
106 F13 Grosseto Toscana, C Italy
101 M22 Grosse Vils ≈ SE Germany
109 U4 Grosse Ysper var. Grosse Isper. ≈ N Austria
101 G19 Gross-Gerau Hessen, W Germany
109 U3 Gross Gerungs Niederösterreich, N Austria
109 P8 Grossglockner ▲ W Austria
Grosskanizsa see Nagykanizsa
Gross-Karol see Carei
Grosskikinda see Kikinda
109 W9 Grossklein Steiermark, SE Austria
Grosskoppe see Velká Deštná
Grossmeseritsch see Velké Meziříčí
Grossmichel see Michalovce
101 H19 Grossostheim Bayern, C Germany
109 X7 Grosspetersdorf Burgenland, SE Austria
109 T5 Grossraming Oberösterreich, C Austria
101 P14 Grossräschen Brandenburg, E Germany
Grossrauschenbach see Revúca
Gross-Sankt-Johannis see Suure-Jaani
Gross-Schlatten see Abrud
109 V2 Gross-Siegharts Niederösterreich, N Austria
Gross-Skaisgirren see Bol'shakovo
Gross-Steffelsdorf see Rimavská Sobota
Gross Strehlitz see Strzelce Opolskie
109 O8 Grossvenediger ▲ W Austria
Grosswardein see Oradea
Gross Wartenberg see Syców
109 U11 Grosuplje C Slovenia
99 H17 Grote Nete ≈ N Belgium
94 E10 Grotli Oppland, S Norway
19 N13 Groton Connecticut, NE USA
29 P8 Groton South Dakota, N USA
107 P18 Grottaglie Puglia, SE Italy
107 L17 Grottaminarda Campania, S Italy
106 K13 Grottammare Marche, C Italy
21 U5 Grottoes Virginia, NE USA
Grou see Grouw
13 N10 Groulx, Monts ▲ Quebec, E Canada
14 E7 Groundhog ≈ Ontario, S Canada
36 J1 Grouse Creek Utah, W USA
36 J1 Grouse Creek Mountains ▲ Utah, W USA
98 L6 Grouw Fris. Grou. Friesland, N Netherlands
27 R8 Grove Oklahoma, C USA
31 S13 Grove City Ohio, N USA
18 B13 Grove City Pennsylvania, NE USA
23 O6 Grove Hill Alabama, S USA
33 S15 Grover Wyoming, C USA
35 P13 Grover City California, W USA
25 Y11 Groves Texas, SW USA
19 O7 Groveton New Hampshire, NE USA
25 W9 Groveton Texas, SW USA
36 J15 Growler Mountains ▲ Arizona, SW USA
Grozdovo see Bratya Daskalovi
129 P16 Groznyy Chechenskaya Respublika, SW Russian Federation
Grubeshov see Hrubieszów
112 G9 Grubišno Polje Bjelovar-Bilogora, NE Croatia
Grudovo see Sredets
110 J9 Grudziądz Ger. Graudenz. Kujawsko-pomorskie, C Poland
25 R17 Grulla var. La Grulla. Texas, SW USA
40 K14 Grullo Jalisco, SW Mexico
67 V10 Grumeti ≈ N Tanzania
95 K16 Grums Värmland, C Sweden
109 S5 Grünau im Almtal Oberösterreich, N Austria
101 H17 Grünberg Hessen, W Germany
Grünberg/Grünberg in Schlesien see Zielona Góra
Grünberg in Schlesien see Zielona Góra
92 H3 Grundarfjördhur Vestfirdhir, W Iceland
21 P7 Grundy Virginia, NE USA
29 W13 Grundy Center Iowa, C USA
Grüneberg see Zielona Góra
25 N1 Gruver Texas, SW USA
108 C9 Gruyère, Lac de la Ger. Greyerzer See. ⊚ SW Switzerland
108 C9 Gruyères Fribourg, W Switzerland
118 E11 Gruzdžiai Šiauliai, N Lithuania
Gruzinskaya SSR/Gruziya see Georgia
146 C10 Gryada Akkyr Turkm. Akgyr Erezi. hill range NW Turkmenistan
128 L7 Gryazi Lipetskaya Oblast', W Russian Federation
126 M14 Gryazovets Vologodskaya Oblast', NW Russian Federation
111 M17 Grybów Małopolskie, SE Poland
94 M13 Grycksbo Dalarna, C Sweden

◆ Country ● Country Capital ◇ Dependent Territory ○ Dependent Territory Capital ⬥ Administrative Region ✕ International Airport ▲ Mountain ▲ Mountain Range ✻ Volcano ≈ River ⊚ Lake ⊞ Reservoir

110 E8 **Gryfice** *Ger.* Greifenberg, Greifenberg in Pommern. Zachodniopomorskie, NW Poland
110 D9 **Gryfino** *Ger.* Greifenhagen. Zachodniopomorskie, NW Poland
92 H9 **Gryllefjord** Troms, N Norway
95 L15 **Grythyttan** Örebro, C Sweden
108 D10 **Gstaad** Bern, W Switzerland
43 P14 **Guabito** Bocas del Toro, NW Panama
44 G7 **Guacanayabo, Golfo de** *gulf* S Cuba
40 I7 **Guachochi** Chihuahua, N Mexico
104 J11 **Guadajira** ≈ SW Spain
104 M13 **Guadajoz** ≈ S Spain
40 L13 **Guadalajara** Jalisco, C Mexico
105 O8 **Guadalajara** *Ar.* Wad Al-Hajarah; *anc.* Arriaca. Castilla-La Mancha, C Spain
105 O7 **Guadalajara** ◈ *province* Castilla-La Mancha, C Spain
104 K12 **Guadalcanal** Andalucía, S Spain
186 L10 **Guadalcanal** *off.* Guadalcanal Province. ◈ *province* C Solomon Islands
186 M9 **Guadalcanal** *island* C Solomon Islands
105 O12 **Guadalén** ≈ S Spain
105 R13 **Guadalentín** ≈ SE Spain
104 K15 **Guadalete** ≈ SW Spain
105 O13 **Guadalimar** ≈ S Spain
105 P12 **Guadalmena** ≈ S Spain
104 L11 **Guadalmez** ≈ W Spain
105 S7 **Guadalope** ≈ E Spain
104 K13 **Guadalquivir** ≈ W Spain
104 J14 **Guadalquivir, Marismas del** *var.* Las Marismas. *wetland* SW Spain
40 M11 **Guadalupe** Zacatecas, C Mexico
57 E16 **Guadalupe** Ica, W Peru
104 L10 **Guadalupe** Extremadura, W Spain
36 L14 **Guadalupe** Arizona, SW USA
35 P13 **Guadalupe** California, W USA
193 P5 **Guadalupe** *island* NW Mexico
Guadalupe *see* Canelones
40 J3 **Guadalupe Bravos** Chihuahua, N Mexico
40 A4 **Guadalupe, Isla** *island* NW Mexico
37 U15 **Guadalupe Mountains** ⛰ New Mexico/Texas, SW USA
24 J8 **Guadalupe Peak** ▲ Texas, SW USA
25 R11 **Guadalupe River** ≈ SW USA
104 K10 **Guadalupe, Sierra de** ⛰ W Spain
40 K9 **Guadalupe Victoria** Durango, C Mexico
40 I8 **Guadalupe y Calvo** Chihuahua, N Mexico
105 N7 **Guadarrama** Madrid, C Spain
105 N7 **Guadarrama** ≈ C Spain
104 M7 **Guadarrama, Puerto de** *pass* C Spain
105 N9 **Guadarrama, Sierra de** ⛰ C Spain
105 Q9 **Guadazaón** ≈ C Spain
45 X10 **Guadeloupe** ◇ *French overseas department* E West Indies
47 S3 **Guadeloupe** *island group* E West Indies
45 W10 **Guadeloupe Passage** *passage* E Caribbean Sea
104 H13 **Guadiana** ≈ Portugal/Spain
105 O13 **Guadiana Menor** ≈ S Spain
105 Q8 **Guadiela** ≈ C Spain
105 O14 **Guadix** Andalucía, S Spain
Guad-i-Zirreh *see* Gowd-e Zereh, Dasht-e
193 T12 **Guafo Fracture Zone** *tectonic feature* SE Pacific Ocean
63 F18 **Guafo, Isla** *island* S Chile
42 I6 **Guaimaca** Francisco Morazán, C Honduras
54 J12 **Guainía** *off.* Comisaría del Guainía. ◈ *province* E Colombia
54 K12 **Guainía, Río** ≈ Colombia/Venezuela
55 O9 **Guaiquinima, Cerro** *elevation* SE Venezuela
62 O7 **Guairá** *off.* Departamento del Guairá. ◈ *department* S Paraguay
60 G10 **Guaíra** Paraná, S Brazil
60 L7 **Guaíra** São Paulo, S Brazil
Guaire *see* Gorey
63 F18 **Guaiteca, Isla** *island* S Chile
44 G6 **Guajaba, Cayo** *headland* C Cuba
59 D16 **Guajará-Mirim** Rondônia, W Brazil
Guajira *see* La Guajira
54 H3 **Guajira, Península de la** *peninsula* N Colombia
42 J6 **Gualaco** Olancho, C Honduras
34 L7 **Gualala** California, W USA
42 E5 **Gualán** Zacapa, C Guatemala
61 C19 **Gualeguay** Entre Ríos, E Argentina
61 D18 **Gualeguaychú** Entre Ríos, E Argentina
61 C18 **Gualeguay, Río** ≈ E Argentina
63 K16 **Gualicho, Salina del** *salt lake* E Argentina
188 B15 **Guam** ◇ *US unincorporated territory* W Pacific Ocean
63 F19 **Guamblin, Isla** *island* Archipiélago de los Chonos, S Chile
61 A22 **Guaminí** Buenos Aires, E Argentina
40 H8 **Guamúchil** Sinaloa, C Mexico
54 H4 **Guana** *var.* Misión de Guana. Zulia, NW Venezuela
44 C4 **Guanabacoa** La Habana, W Cuba
42 K13 **Guanacaste** *off.* Provincia de Guanacaste. ◈ *province* NW Costa Rica
42 K12 **Guanacaste, Cordillera de** ⛰ NW Costa Rica
40 J8 **Guanaceví** Durango, C Mexico
44 A5 **Guanahacabibes, Golfo de** *gulf* W Cuba
42 K4 **Guanaja, Isla de** *island* Islas de la Bahía, N Honduras
44 C4 **Guanajay** La Habana, W Cuba
41 N12 **Guanajuato** Guanajuato, C Mexico
40 M12 **Guanajuato** ◈ *state* C Mexico
54 J6 **Guanare** Portuguesa, N Venezuela
54 K7 **Guanare, Río** ≈ W Venezuela
54 J6 **Guanarito** Portuguesa, NW Venezuela
160 M3 **Guancen Shan** ⛰ C China
62 I9 **Guandacol** La Rioja, W Argentina
44 A5 **Guane** Pinar del Río, W Cuba
161 N14 **Guangdong** *var.* Guangdong Sheng, Kuang-tung, Kwangtung, Yue. ◈ *province* S China
Guangdong Sheng *see* Guangdong
Guanghua *see* Laohekou
Guangju *see* Kwangju
160 I13 **Guangnan** Yunnan, SW China
161 N8 **Guangshui** *prev.* Yingshan. Hubei, C China
Guangxi *see* Guangxi Zhuangzu Zizhiqu
160 K14 **Guangxi Zhuangzu Zizhiqu** *var.* Guangxi, Gui, Kuang-hsi, Kwangsi, *Eng.* Kwangsi Chuang Autonomous Region. ◈ *autonomous region* S China
160 J8 **Guangyuan** *var.* Kuang-yuan, Kwangyuan. Sichuan, C China
161 N14 **Guangzhou** *var.* Kuang-chou, Kwangchow, *Eng.* Canton. Guangdong, S China
59 N19 **Guanhães** Minas Gerais, SE Brazil
160 I12 **Guanling** *var.* Guanling Bouyeizu Miaozu Zizhixian. Guizhou, S China
Guanling Bouyeizu Miaozu Zizhixian *see* Guanling
55 N5 **Guanta** Anzoátegui, NE Venezuela
44 J8 **Guantánamo** Guantánamo, SE Cuba
160 H9 **Guanxian** *var.* Guan Xian. Sichuan, C China
161 Q6 **Guanyun** Jiangsu, E China
54 C12 **Guapí** Cauca, SW Colombia
43 N13 **Guápiles** Limón, NE Costa Rica
61 I15 **Guaporé** Rio Grande do Sul, S Brazil
47 S8 **Guaporé, Rio** *var.* Río Iténez. ≈ Bolivia/Brazil **see also** Iténez, Río
56 B7 **Guaranda** Bolívar, C Ecuador
60 H11 **Guaraniaçu** Paraná, S Brazil
59 O20 **Guarapari** Espírito Santo, SE Brazil
60 I12 **Guarapuava** Paraná, S Brazil
60 J8 **Guararapes** São Paulo, S Brazil
105 S4 **Guara, Sierra de** ⛰ NE Spain
60 N10 **Guaratinguetá** São Paulo, S Brazil
104 I7 **Guarda** Guarda, N Portugal
104 I7 **Guarda** ◈ *district* N Portugal
Guardak *see* Govurdak
104 M3 **Guardo** Castilla-León, N Spain
104 K11 **Guareña** Extremadura, W Spain
60 J11 **Guaricana, Pico** ▲ S Brazil
54 L6 **Guárico** *off.* Estado Guárico. ◈ *state* N Venezuela
44 J7 **Guarico, Punta** *headland* E Cuba
54 L7 **Guárico, Río** ≈ C Venezuela
60 M10 **Guarujá** São Paulo, SE Brazil
61 L22 **Guarulhos** × (São Paulo) São Paulo, S Brazil
43 R17 **Guarumal** Veraguas, S Panama
Guasapa *see* Guasopa
40 H8 **Guasave** Sinaloa, C Mexico
54 I8 **Guasdualito** Apure, C Venezuela
55 Q7 **Guasipati** Bolívar, E Venezuela
186 I9 **Guasopa** *var.* Guasapa. Woodlark Island, SE PNG
106 F9 **Guastalla** Emilia-Romagna, C Italy
42 D6 **Guastatoya** *var.* El Progreso. El Progreso, C Guatemala
42 D5 **Guatemala** *off.* Republic of Guatemala. ◆ *republic* Central America
42 A2 **Guatemala** *off.* Departamento de Guatemala. ◈ *department* S Guatemala
193 S7 **Guatemala Basin** *undersea feature* E Pacific Ocean
Guatemala City *see* Ciudad de Guatemala
45 V14 **Guatuaro Point** *headland* Trinidad, Trinidad and Tobago
186 B8 **Guavi** ≈ SW PNG
54 G13 **Guaviare** *off.* Comisaría Guaviare. ◈ *province* S Colombia
54 J11 **Guaviare, Río** ≈ E Colombia
61 E15 **Guaviravi** Corrientes, NE Argentina
54 G12 **Guayabero, Río** ≈ SW Colombia
45 U6 **Guayama** E Puerto Rico
42 J7 **Guayambre, Río** ≈ S Honduras
Guayanas, Macizo de las *see* Guiana Highlands
45 V6 **Guayanés, Punta** *headland* E Puerto Rico
42 J6 **Guayape, Río** ≈ C Honduras
56 B7 **Guayaquil** *var.* Santiago de Guayaquil. Guayas, SW Ecuador
Guayaquil *see* Simon Bolivar
56 A8 **Guayaquil, Golfo de** *var.* Gulf of Guayaquil. *gulf* SW Ecuador
Guayaquil, Gulf of *see* Guayaquil, Golfo de
56 A7 **Guayas** ◈ *province* W Ecuador
62 N7 **Guaycurú, Río** ≈ NE Argentina
40 F6 **Guaymas** Sonora, NW Mexico
45 U5 **Guaynabo** E Puerto Rico
80 H12 **Guba** Benishangul, W Ethiopia
146 H8 **Gubadag** *Turkm.* Tel'man; *prev.* Tel'mansk. Dashkhovuzskiy Velayat, N Turkmenistan
127 T1 **Guba Dolgaya** Nenetskiy Avtonomnyy Okrug, NW Russian Federation
127 V13 **Gubakha** Permskaya Oblast', NW Russian Federation
106 I12 **Gubbio** Umbria, C Italy
100 Q13 **Guben** *var.* Wilhelm-Pieck-Stadt. Brandenburg, E Germany
Guben *see* Gubin
110 D12 **Gubin** *Ger.* Guben. Lubuskie, W Poland
128 K8 **Gubkin** Belgorodskaya Oblast', W Russian Federation
Gudara *see* Ghŭdara
105 S8 **Gúdar, Sierra de** ⛰ E Spain
137 P8 **Gudaut'a** NW Georgia
94 G12 **Gudbrandsdalen** *valley* S Norway
95 G21 **Gudenå** *var.* Gudenaa. ≈ C Denmark
Gudenaa *see* Gudenå
129 P16 **Gudermes** Chechenskaya Respublika, SW Russian Federation
155 J18 **Gūdūr** Andhra Pradesh, E India
146 B13 **Gudurolum** Balkanskiy Velayat, W Turkmenistan
94 D13 **Gudvangen** Sogn og Fjordane, S Norway
103 U7 **Guebwiller** Haut-Rhin, NE France
Guéckédou *see* Guékédou
14 K8 **Guéguen, Lac** ◎ Quebec, SE Canada
76 J15 **Guékédou** *var.* Guéckédou. Guinée-Forestière, S Guinea
41 R16 **Guelatao** Oaxaca, SE Mexico
Guelders *see* Gelderland
78 G11 **Guélengdeng** Mayo-Kébbi, W Chad
74 L5 **Guelma** *var.* Gâlma. NE Algeria
74 D8 **Guelmime** *var.* Goulimime. SW Morocco
14 G15 **Guelph** Ontario, S Canada
102 I7 **Guémené-Penfao** Loire-Atlantique, NW France
102 I7 **Guer** Morbihan, NW France
78 I11 **Guéra** *off.* Préfecture du Guéra. ◈ *prefecture* S Chad
102 H8 **Guérande** Loire-Atlantique, NW France
78 K9 **Guéréda** Biltine, E Chad
103 N10 **Guéret** Creuse, C France
Guernica/Guernica y Lumo *see* Gernika-Lumo
33 Z15 **Guernsey** Wyoming, C USA
97 K25 **Guernsey** *island* Channel Islands, NW Europe
76 J10 **Guérou** Assaba, S Mauritania
25 R16 **Guerra** Texas, SW USA
41 O15 **Guerrero** ◈ *state* S Mexico
40 D6 **Guerrero Negro** Baja California Sur, NW Mexico
103 P9 **Gueugnon** Saône-et-Loire, C France
76 M17 **Guéyo** S Ivory Coast
107 L15 **Guglionesi** Molise, C Italy
188 K5 **Guguan** *island* C Northern Mariana Islands
Guhrau *see* Góra
Gui *see* Guangxi Zhuangzu Zizhiqu
Guiana *see* French Guiana
47 V4 **Guiana Basin** *undersea feature* W Atlantic Ocean
48 G6 **Guiana Highlands** *var.* Macizo de las Guayanas. ⛰ N South America
Guiba *see* Juba
102 I7 **Guichen** Ille-et-Vilaine, NW France
61 E18 **Guichón** Paysandú, W Uruguay
77 U12 **Guidan-Roumji** Maradi, S Niger
Guidder *see* Guider
159 T10 **Guide** Qinghai, C China
78 F12 **Guider** *var.* Guidder. Nord, N Cameroon
76 I11 **Guidimaka** ◈ *region* S Mauritania
77 W12 **Guidimouni** Zinder, S Niger
76 G10 **Guier, Lac de** *var.* Lac de Guiers. ◎ N Senegal
160 L14 **Guigang** *prev.* Guixian, Gui Xian. Guangxi Zhuangzu Zizhiqu, S China
76 L16 **Guiglo** W Ivory Coast
54 L5 **Güigüe** Carabobo, N Venezuela
83 M20 **Guijá** Gaza, S Mozambique
42 E7 **Güija, Lago de** ◎ El Salvador/Guatemala
104 K8 **Guijuelo** Castilla-León, N Spain
Guilan *see* Gīlān
97 N22 **Guildford** SE England, UK
19 R5 **Guildford** Maine, NE USA
19 O7 **Guildhall** Vermont, NE USA
103 R13 **Guilherand** Ardèche, E France
160 L13 **Guilin** *var.* Kuei-lin, Kweilin. Guangxi Zhuangzu Zizhiqu, S China
12 J6 **Guillaume-Delisle, Lac** ◎ Quebec, NE Canada
103 U13 **Guillestre** Hautes-Alpes, SE France
104 H6 **Guimarães** *var.* Guimaráes. Braga, N Portugal
58 D11 **Guimarães Rosas, Pico** ▲ NW Brazil
23 N3 **Guin** Alabama, S USA
Güina *see* Wina
76 I14 **Guinea** *off.* Republic of Guinea, *var.* Guinée; *prev.* French Guinea, People's Revolutionary Republic of Guinea. ◆ *republic* W Africa
64 N13 **Guinea Basin** *undersea feature* E Atlantic Ocean
76 E12 **Guinea-Bissau** *off.* Republic of Guinea-Bissau, *Fr.* Guinée-Bissau, *Port.* Guiné-Bissau; *prev.* Portuguese Guinea. ◆ *republic* W Africa
66 K7 **Guinea Fracture Zone** *tectonic feature* E Atlantic Ocean
64 O13 **Guinea, Gulf of** *Fr.* Golfe de Guinée. *gulf* E Atlantic Ocean
Guiné-Bissau *see* Guinea-Bissau
Guinée *see* Guinea
Guinée-Bissau *see* Guinea-Bissau
76 K15 **Guinée-Forestière** ◈ *state* SE Guinea
Guinée, Golfe de *see* Guinea, Gulf of
76 H13 **Guinée-Maritime** ◈ *state* W Guinea
44 C4 **Güines** La Habana, W Cuba
102 G5 **Guingamp** Côtes d'Armor, NW France
105 P3 **Guipúzcoa** *Basq.* Gipuzkoa. ◈ *province* País Vasco, N Spain
44 C5 **Güira de Melena** La Habana, W Cuba
74 G8 **Guir, Hamada du** *desert* Algeria/Morocco
55 P5 **Güiria** Sucre, NE Venezuela
160 L14 **Gui Shui** ≈ S China
104 H2 **Guitiriz** Galicia, NW Spain
77 N17 **Guitri** S Ivory Coast
171 Q5 **Guiuan** Samar, C Philippines
Gui Xian/Guixian *see* Guigang
160 J12 **Guiyang** *var.* Kuei-Yang, Kuei-yang, Kueyang, Kweiyang; *prev.* Kweichu. Guizhou, S China
160 J12 **Guizhou** *var.* Guizhou Sheng, Kuei-chou, Kweichow, Qian. ◈ *province* S China
Guizhou Sheng *see* Guizhou
102 J13 **Gujan-Mestras** Gironde, SW France
154 B10 **Gujarāt** *var.* Gujerat. ◈ *state* W India
149 V6 **Gūjar Khān** Punjab, E Pakistan
Gujerat *see* Gujarāt
149 V7 **Gujrānwāla** Punjab, NE Pakistan
149 V7 **Gujrāt** Punjab, E Pakistan
159 U9 **Gulang** Gansu, C China
183 R6 **Gulargambone** New South Wales, SE Australia
155 G15 **Gulbarga** Karnātaka, C India
118 J8 **Gulbene** *Ger.* Alt-Schwanenburg. Gulbene, NE Latvia
147 U10 **Gul'cha** *Kir.* Gülchö. Oshskaya Oblast', SW Kyrgyzstan
Gülchö *see* Gul'cha
173 T10 **Gulden Draak Seamount** *undersea feature* E Indian Ocean
136 J16 **Gülek Boğazı** *var.* Cilician Gates. *pass* S Turkey
186 D8 **Gulf** ◈ *province* S PNG
23 O9 **Gulf Breeze** Florida, SE USA
23 V13 **Gulfport** Florida, SE USA
22 M9 **Gulfport** Mississippi, S USA
23 O9 **Gulf Shores** Alabama, S USA
141 T5 **The Gulf** *var.* Persian Gulf *Ar.* Khalīj al 'Arabī, *Per.* Khalīj-e Fars. *gulf* SW Asia
183 R7 **Gulgong** New South Wales, SE Australia
160 I11 **Gulin** Sichuan, C China
171 U14 **Gulir** Pulau Kasiui, E Indonesia
Gulistan *see* Guliston
147 P10 **Guliston** *Rus.* Gulistan. Sirdaryo Wiloyati, E Uzbekistan
163 T6 **Guliya Shan** ▲ NE China
Gulja *see* Yining
39 S11 **Gulkana** Alaska, USA
11 S17 **Gull Lake** Saskatchewan, S Canada
31 P10 **Gull Lake** ◎ Michigan, N USA
29 T6 **Gull Lake** ◎ Minnesota, N USA
95 L16 **Gullspång** Västra Götaland, S Sweden
152 H5 **Gulmarg** Jammu and Kashmir, NW India
Gulpaigan *see* Golpāyegān
99 L18 **Gulpen** Limburg, SE Netherlands
145 S13 **Gul'shad** *Kaz.* Gulshat. Zhezkazgan, E Kazakhstan
Gulshat *see* Gul'shad
81 F17 **Gulu** N Uganda
114 K10 **Gŭlŭbovo** Stara Zagora, C Bulgaria
114 I7 **Gulyantsi** Pleven, N Bulgaria
Gulyaypole *see* Hulyaypole
Guma *see* Pishan
79 K16 **Gumba** Equateur, NW Dem. Rep. Congo (Zaire)
Gumbinnen *see* Gusev
81 H24 **Gumbiro** Ruvuma, S Tanzania
146 B11 **Gumdag** *prev.* Kum-Dag. Balkanskiy Velayat, W Turkmenistan
77 W12 **Gumel** Jigawa, N Nigeria
105 N5 **Gumiel de Hizán** Castilla-León, N Spain
Gumire *see* Gumine
153 P16 **Gumla** Bihār, N India
Gumma *see* Gunma
101 F16 **Gummersbach** Nordrhein-Westfalen, W Germany
77 T13 **Gummi** Zamfara, NW Nigeria
Gumpolds *see* Humpolec
153 N13 **Gumti** *var.* Gomati. ≈ N India
Gümülcine/Gümüljina *see* Komotiní
Gümüşane *see* Gümüşhane
137 O12 **Gümüşhane** *var.* Gümüşane, Gumushkhane. Gümüşhane, NE Turkey
137 O12 **Gümüşhane** *var.* Gümüşane, Gumushkhane. ◈ *province* NE Turkey
Gumushkhane *see* Gümüşhane
171 V14 **Gumzai** Pulau Kola, E Indonesia
154 H9 **Guna** Madhya Pradesh, C India
Gunabad *see* Gonābād
Gunbad-i-Qawus *see* Gonbad-e Kāvūs
183 O9 **Gunbar** New South Wales, SE Australia
183 O9 **Gun Creek** *seasonal river* New South Wales, SE Australia
183 Q10 **Gundagai** New South Wales, SE Australia
79 K17 **Gundji** Equateur, N Dem. Rep. Congo (Zaire)
155 G20 **Gundlupet** Karnātaka, W India
136 G16 **Gündoğmuş** Antalya, S Turkey
137 O14 **Güney Doğu Toroslar** ⛰ SE Turkey
79 J21 **Gungu** Bandundu, SW Dem. Rep. Congo (Zaire)
129 P17 **Gunib** Respublika Dagestan, SW Russian Federation
112 J11 **Gunja** Vukovar-Srijem, E Croatia
31 P9 **Gun Lake** ◎ Michigan, N USA
165 N12 **Gunma** *off.* Gunma-ken, *var.* Gumma. ◈ *prefecture* Honshū, S Japan
197 P15 **Gunnbjørn Fjeld** *var.* Gunnbjørns Bjerge. ▲ C Greenland
183 S6 **Gunnedah** New South Wales, SE Australia
173 Y15 **Gunner's Quoin** *var.* Coin de Mire. *island* N Mauritius
37 R6 **Gunnison** Colorado, C USA
36 L5 **Gunnison** Utah, W USA
37 P5 **Gunnison River** ≈ Colorado, C USA
21 X2 **Gunpowder River** ≈ Maryland, NE USA
Güns *see* Kőszeg
Gunsan *see* Kunsan
Gunt *see* Ghund
109 S4 **Gunskirchen** Oberösterreich, N Austria
155 H17 **Guntakal** Andhra Pradesh, C India
23 Q2 **Guntersville** Alabama, S USA
23 Q2 **Guntersville Lake** ▣ Alabama, S USA
109 X4 **Guntramsdorf** Niederösterreich, E Austria
155 J16 **Guntūr** *var.* Guntur. Andhra Pradesh, SE India
168 H10 **Gunungsitoli** Pulau Nias, W Indonesia
155 M14 **Gunupur** Orissa, E India
101 J23 **Günz** ≈ S Germany
Gunzan *see* Kunsan
101 J22 **Günzburg** Bayern, S Germany
101 K21 **Gunzenhausen** Bayern, S Germany
161 P7 **Guoyang** Anhui, E China
116 G11 **Gurahonț** *Hung.* Honctő. Arad, W Romania
Gurahumora *see* Gura Humorului
116 K9 **Gura Humorului** *Ger.* Gurahumora. Suceava, NE Romania
158 K4 **Gurbantünggüt Shamo** *desert* W China
152 H7 **Gurdāspur** Punjab, N India
27 T13 **Gurdon** Arkansas, C USA
Gurdzhaani *see* Gurjaani
Gurgan *see* Gorgān
152 I10 **Gurgaon** Haryāna, N India
59 M15 **Gurguéia, Rio** ≈ NE Brazil
55 Q7 **Guri, Embalse de** ▣ E Venezuela
137 V10 **Gurjaani** *Rus.* Gurdzhaani. E Georgia
109 T8 **Gurk** Kärnten, S Austria
109 T9 **Gurk** *Slvn.* Krka. ≈ S Austria
Gurkfeld *see* Krško
114 K9 **Gurkovo** *prev.* Kolupchii. Stara Zagora, C Bulgaria
109 S9 **Gurktaler Alpen** ⛰ S Austria
146 H8 **Gurlan** *Rus.* Gurlen. Khorazm Wiloyati, W Uzbekistan
Gurlen *see* Gurlan
83 M16 **Guro** Manica, C Mozambique
136 M14 **Gürün** Sivas, C Turkey
59 K16 **Gurupi** Tocantins, C Brazil
58 L12 **Gurupi, Rio** ≈ NE Brazil
152 E14 **Guru Sikhar** ▲ NW India
Gur'yev/Gur'yevskaya Oblast' *see* Atyrau
77 U13 **Gusau** Zamfara, NW Nigeria
128 C3 **Gusev** *Ger.* Gumbinnen. Kaliningradskaya Oblast', W Russian Federation
146 J17 **Gushgy** *prev.* Kushka. Maryyskiy Velayat, S Turkmenistan
Gushiago *see* Gushiegu
77 Q14 **Gushiegu** *var.* Gushiago. NE Ghana
165 S17 **Gushikawa** Okinawa, Okinawa, SW Japan
113 L16 **Gusinje** Montenegro, SW Yugoslavia
128 M4 **Gus'-Khrustal'nyy** Vladimirskaya Oblast', W Russian Federation
107 B19 **Guspini** Sardegna, Italy, C Mediterranean Sea
109 X8 **Güssing** Burgenland, SE Austria
109 V6 **Gusswerk** Steiermark, E Austria
92 O2 **Gustav Adolf Land** *physical region* NE Svalbard
195 X5 **Gustav Bull Mountains** ⛰ Antarctica
39 W13 **Gustavus** Alaska, USA
92 O1 **Gustav V Land** *physical region* NE Svalbard
35 P9 **Gustine** California, W USA
25 R8 **Gustine** Texas, SW USA
100 M9 **Güstrow** Mecklenburg-Vorpommern, NE Germany
95 N18 **Gusum** Östergötland, S Sweden
Guta/Gúta *see* Kolárovo
Gutenstein *see* Ravne na Koroškem
101 G14 **Gütersloh** Nordrhein-Westfalen, W Germany
27 N10 **Guthrie** Oklahoma, C USA
25 P5 **Guthrie** Texas, SW USA
29 U14 **Guthrie Center** Iowa, C USA
41 Q13 **Gutiérrez Zamora** Veracruz-Llave, E Mexico
Gutta *see* Kolárovo
29 Y12 **Guttenberg** Iowa, C USA
Guttentag *see* Dobrodzień
Guttstadt *see* Dobre Miasto
162 G8 **Guulin** Govĭ-Altay, C Mongolia
153 V12 **Guwāhāti** *prev.* Gauhāti. Assam, NE India
139 R3 **Guwēr** *var.* Al Kuwayr, Al Quwayr, Quwair. N Iraq
Guwlumayak *see* Kuuli-Mayak
55 R9 **Guyana** *off.* Cooperative Republic of Guyana; *prev.* British Guiana. ◆ *republic* N South America
21 P5 **Guyandotte River** ≈ West Virginia, NE USA
Guyane *see* French Guiana
Guyi *see* Sanjiang
26 H8 **Guymon** Oklahoma, C USA
146 K12 **Guynuk** Lebapskiy Velayat, NE Turkmenistan
21 O9 **Guyot, Mount** ▲ North Carolina/Tennessee, SE USA
183 U5 **Guyra** New South Wales, SE Australia
159 W10 **Guyuan** Ningxia, N China
Guzar *see* Ghuzor
121 P2 **Güzelyurt** *Gk.* Mórfou, Morphou. W Cyprus
121 N2 **Güzelyurt Körfezi** *var.* Morfou Bay, Morphou Bay, *Gk.* Kólpos Mórfou. *bay* W Cyprus
40 I3 **Guzmán** Chihuahua, N Mexico
119 B14 **Gvardeysk** *Ger.* Tapaiu. Kaliningradskaya Oblast', W Russian Federation
Gvardeyskoye *see* Hvardiys'ke
183 R5 **Gwabegar** New South Wales, SE Australia
148 J16 **Gwādar** *var.* Gwadur. Baluchistān, SW Pakistan
148 J16 **Gwādar East Bay** *bay* SW Pakistan
148 J16 **Gwādar West Bay** *bay* SW Pakistan
Gwadur *see* Gwādar
83 J17 **Gwai** Matabeleland North, W Zimbabwe
154 I7 **Gwalior** Madhya Pradesh, C India
83 J18 **Gwanda** Matabeleland South, SW Zimbabwe
79 N15 **Gwane** Orientale, N Dem. Rep. Congo (Zaire)
83 I17 **Gwayi** ≈ W Zimbabwe
110 G8 **Gwda** *var.* Głda, *Ger.* Küddow. ≈ NW Poland
97 C14 **Gweebarra Bay** *Ir.* Béal an Bheara. *inlet* W Ireland
97 D14 **Gweedore** *Ir.* Gaoth Dobhair. NW Ireland
Gwelo *see* Gweru
97 K21 **Gwent** *cultural region* S Wales, UK
83 K17 **Gweru** *prev.* Gwelo. Midlands, C Zimbabwe
29 Q7 **Gwinner** North Dakota, N USA
77 Y13 **Gwoza** Borno, NE Nigeria
Gwy *see* Wye
183 R4 **Gwydir River** ≈ New South Wales, SE Australia
97 I19 **Gwynedd** *var.* Gwyneth. *cultural region* NW Wales, UK
Gwyneth *see* Gwynedd
159 O16 **Gyaca** Xizang Zizhiqu, W China
Gya'gya *see* Saga
115 M22 **Gyalí** *var.* Yialí. *island* Dodekánisos, Greece, Aegean Sea
Gyandzha *see* Gäncä
158 M16 **Gyangzê** Xizang Zizhiqu, W China
158 L14 **Gyaring Co** ◎ W China
159 Q12 **Gyaring Hu** ◎ C China
115 I20 **Gyáros** *var.* Yioúra. *island* Kykládes, Greece, Aegean Sea
122 J7 **Gyda** Yamalo-Nenetskiy Avtonomnyy Okrug, N Russian Federation
122 J7 **Gydanskiy Poluostrov** *Eng.* Gyda Peninsula. *peninsula* N Russian Federation
Gyda Peninsula *see* Gydanskiy Poluostrov
Gyéres *see* Câmpia Turzii
Gyergyószentmiklós *see* Gheorgheni
Gyergyótölgyes *see* Tulgheș
Gyertyámos *see* Cărpiniș
Gyeva *see* Detva
Gyigang *see* Zayü
95 I23 **Gyldenløves Høy** *hill range* C Denmark
181 Z10 **Gympie** Queensland, E Australia
166 L7 **Gyobingauk** Pegu, SW Myanmar
111 M23 **Gyomaendrőd** Békés, SE Hungary
Gyömbér *see* Ďumbier
111 L22 **Gyöngyös** Heves, NE Hungary
111 H22 **Győr** *Ger.* Raab; *Lat.* Arrabona. Győr-Moson-Sopron, NW Hungary
111 G22 **Győr-Moson-Sopron** *off.* Győr-Moson-Sopron Megye. ◈ *county* NW Hungary
11 X15 **Gypsumville** Manitoba, S Canada
12 M4 **Gyrfalcon Islands** *island group* Nunavut, NE Canada
95 N14 **Gysinge** Gävleborg, C Sweden
115 F22 **Gýtheio** *var.* Githio; *prev.* Yíthion. Pelopónnisos, S Greece
146 L13 **Gyuichbirleshik** Lebapskiy Velayat, E Turkmenistan
111 N24 **Gyula** *Rom.* Jula. Békés, SE Hungary
Gyulafehérvár *see* Alba Iulia
Gyulovo *see* Roza

◆ Country ● Country Capital ◇ Dependent Territory ○ Dependent Territory Capital ◈ Administrative Region × International Airport ▲ Mountain ⛰ Mountain Range Volcano ≈ River ◎ Lake ▣ Reservoir

137 T11 **Gyumri** var. Giumri, Rus. Kumayri; prev. Aleksandropol', Leninakan. W Armenia
146 D13 **Gyunuzyndag, Gora** ▲ W Turkmenistan
146 D12 **Gyzylarbat** prev. Kizyl-Arvat. Balkanskiy Velayat, W Turkmenistan
Gyzylbaydak see Krasnoye Znamya
Gyzyletrek see Kizyl-Atrek
Gyzylgaya see Kizyl-Kaya
Gyzylsu see Kizyl-Su

H

159 T12 **Ha** W Bhutan
Haabai see Ha'apai Group
99 H17 **Haacht** Vlaams Brabant, C Belgium
109 T4 **Haag** Niederösterreich, NE Austria
194 L8 **Haag Nunataks** ▲▲ Antarctica
92 N2 **Haakon VII Land** physical region NW Svalbard
98 O11 **Haaksbergen** Overijssel, E Netherlands
99 E14 **Haamstede** Zeeland, SW Netherlands
193 Y15 **Ha'ano** island Ha'apai Group, C Tonga
193 Y15 **Ha'apai Group** var. Haabai. island group C Tonga
93 L15 **Haapajärvi** Oulu, C Finland
93 L17 **Haapamäki** Länsi-Suomi, W Finland
93 L15 **Haapavesi** Oulu, C Finland
191 N7 **Haapiti** Moorea, W French Polynesia
118 F4 **Haapsalu** Ger. Hapsal. Läänemaa, W Estonia
Ha'Arava see 'Arabah, Wādī al
Haarby see Hårby
98 H10 **Haarlem** prev. Harlem. Noord-Holland, W Netherlands
185 D19 **Haast** West Coast, South Island, NZ
185 C20 **Haast** ≈ South Island, NZ
185 D20 **Haast Pass** pass South Island, NZ
193 W16 **Ha'atua** 'Eau, E Tonga
149 P15 **Hab** ≈ SW Pakistan
141 W7 **Haba** var. Al Haba. Dubayy, NE UAE
158 K2 **Habahe** var. Kaba. Xinjiang Uygur Zizhiqu, NW China
141 U13 **Ḩabarūt** var. Habrut. SW Oman
81 J18 **Habaswein** North Eastern, NE Kenya
99 L24 **Habay-la-Neuve** Luxembourg, SE Belgium
139 S8 **Ḩabbānīyah, Buḩayrat** ◎ C Iraq
Habelschwerdt see Bystrzyca Kłodzka
153 V14 **Habiganj** Chittagong, NE Bangladesh
163 Q12 **Habirag** Nei Mongol Zizhiqu, N China
95 L19 **Habo** Västra Götaland, S Sweden
123 V14 **Habomai Islands** island group Kuril'skiye Ostrova, SE Russian Federation
165 S2 **Haboro** Hokkaidō, NE Japan
153 S16 **Habra** West Bengal, NE India
Habrut see Ḩabarūt
143 P17 **Ḩabshān** Abū Ẓaby, C UAE
54 E14 **Hacha** Putumayo, S Colombia
165 X13 **Hachijō** Tōkyō, Hachijō-jima, SE Japan
165 X13 **Hachijō-jima** var. Hatizyô Zima. island Izu-shotō, SE Japan
164 L12 **Hachiman** Gifu, Honshū, SW Japan
165 P7 **Hachimori** Akita, Honshū, C Japan
165 R7 **Hachinohe** Aomori, Honshū, C Japan
93 G17 **Hackås** Jämtland, C Sweden
18 K14 **Hackensack** New Jersey, NE USA
Hadama see Nazrēt
141 W13 **Ḩadbaram** S Oman
139 U13 **Ḩaddānīyah** well S Iraq
96 K12 **Haddington** SE Scotland, UK
141 Z8 **Ḩadd, Ra's al** headland NE Oman
Haded see Xadeed
77 W12 **Hadejia** Jigawa, N Nigeria
77 W12 **Hadejia** ≈ N Nigeria
138 F9 **Hadera** var. Khadera. Haifa, C Israel
Hadersleben see Haderslev
95 G24 **Haderslev** Ger. Hadersleben. Sønderjylland, SW Denmark
151 J21 **Hadhdhunmathi Atoll** var. Haddummati Atoll, Laamu Atoll. atoll S Maldives
Hadhramaut see Ḩaḑramawt
141 W17 **Hadīboh** Suquṭrā, SE Yemen
158 K9 **Hadilik** Xinjiang Uygur Zizhiqu, W China
136 H16 **Hadım** Konya, S Turkey
140 K7 **Hadīyah** Al Madīnah, W Saudi Arabia
8 L5 **Hadley Bay** bay Victoria Island, Nunavut, N Canada
167 S6 **Ha Đông** var. Hadong. Ha Tây, N Vietnam
141 R15 **Ḩaḑramawt** Eng. Hadhramaut. ▲▲ S Yemen
Hadria see Adria
Hadrianopolis see Edirne
Hadria Picena see Apricena
95 G22 **Hadsten** Århus, C Denmark
95 G21 **Hadsund** Nordjylland, N Denmark
117 S4 **Hadyach** Rus. Gadyach. Poltavs'ka Oblast', NE Ukraine
112 I13 **Hadžići** Federacija Bosna I Hercegovina, SE Bosnia and Herzegovina
163 W14 **Haeju** S North Korea
Haerbin/Haerhpin/Ha-erh-pin see Harbin
141 P5 **Ḩafar al Bāṭin** Ash Sharqīyah, N Saudi Arabia
11 T15 **Hafford** Saskatchewan, S Canada
136 M13 **Hafik** Sivas, N Turkey
149 V8 **Hāfizābād** Punjab, E Pakistan
92 H4 **Hafnarfjördhur** Reykjanes, W Iceland
Hafnia see København, Denmark
Hafnia see Denmark
Hafren see Severn
Hafun see Xaafuun
Hafun, Ras see Xaafuun, Raas
80 G10 **Hag 'Abdullah** Sinnar, E Sudan
81 K18 **Hagadera** North Eastern, E Kenya
138 G8 **HaGalil** Eng. Galilee. ▲▲ N Israel
14 G10 **Hagar** Ontario, S Canada
155 G18 **Hagari** var. Vedāvati. ≈ W India
188 B16 **Hagåtña** var. Agana, Agaña. ○ (Guam) NW Guam
100 M13 **Hagelberg** hill NE Germany
39 N14 **Hagemeister Island** island Alaska, USA
101 F15 **Hagen** Nordrhein-Westfalen, W Germany
100 K10 **Hagenow** Mecklenburg-Vorpommern, N Germany
10 K15 **Hagensborg** British Columbia, SW Canada
80 I13 **Hägere Hiywet** var. Agere Hiywet, Ambo. Oromo, C Ethiopia
33 O15 **Hagerman** Idaho, NW USA
37 U14 **Hagerman** New Mexico, SW USA
21 V2 **Hagerstown** Maryland, NE USA
14 G16 **Hagersville** Ontario, S Canada
102 J15 **Hagetmau** Landes, SW France
95 K14 **Hagfors** Värmland, C Sweden
93 G16 **Häggenås** Jämtland, C Sweden
164 E12 **Hagi** Yamaguchi, Honshū, SW Japan
167 S5 **Ha Giang** Ha Giang, N Vietnam
Hagios Evstrátios see Ágios Efstrátios
HaGolan see Golan Heights
103 T4 **Hagondange** Moselle, NE France
97 B18 **Hag's Head** Ir. Ceann Caillí. headland W Ireland
102 I3 **Hague, Cap de la** headland N France
103 V5 **Haguenau** Bas-Rhin, NE France
165 X16 **Hahajima-rettō** island group SE Japan
15 R8 **Há Há , Lac** ◎ Quebec, SE Canada
172 H13 **Hahaya** × (Moroni) Grande Comore, NW Comoros
22 K9 **Hahnville** Louisiana, S USA
83 E22 **Haib** Karas, S Namibia
Haibak see Āybak
149 N15 **Haibo** ≈ SW Pakistan
163 U12 **Haicheng** Liaoning, NE China
Haida see Nový Bor
Haidarabad see Hyderābād
Haidenschaft see Ajdovščina
167 T6 **Hai Dương** Hai Hưng, N Vietnam
138 F9 **Haifa** ◈ district NW Israel
Haifa see Hefa
Haifa, Bay of see Hefa, Mifraz
161 P14 **Haifeng** Guangdong, S China
Haifong see Hai Phong
161 P3 **Hai He** ≈ E China
Haikang see Leizhou
160 L17 **Haikou** var. Hai-k'ou, Hoihow, Fr. Hoï-Hao. Hainan, S China
140 M6 **Ḩā'il** Ḩā'il, NW Saudi Arabia
141 N5 **Ḩā'il** off. Minṭaqah Ḩā'il. ◈ province N Saudi Arabia
Hai-la-erh see Hailar
163 S6 **Hailar** var. Hai-la-erh; prev. Hulun. Nei Mongol Zizhiqu, N China
163 S6 **Hailar He** ≈ NE China
33 P14 **Hailey** Idaho, NW USA
14 H9 **Haileybury** Ontario, S Canada
163 X9 **Hailin** Heilongjiang, NE China
Ḩā'il, Minṭaqah see Ḩā'il
Hailong see Meihekou
93 K14 **Hailuoto** Swe. Karlö. island W Finland
Haima see Haymā'
Haimen see Taizhou
160 M17 **Hainan** var. Hainan Sheng, Qiong. ◈ province S China
160 K17 **Hainan Dao** island S China
Hainan Sheng see Hainan
Hainan Strait see Qiongzhou Haixia
Hainasch see Ainaži
Hainau see Chojnów
99 E20 **Hainaut** ◈ province SW Belgium
Hainburg see Hainburg an der Donau
109 Z4 **Hainburg an der Donau** var. Hainburg. Niederösterreich, NE Austria
39 W12 **Haines** Alaska, USA
32 L12 **Haines** Oregon, NW USA
23 W12 **Haines City** Florida, SE USA
10 H8 **Haines Junction** Yukon Territory, W Canada
109 W4 **Hainfeld** Niederösterreich, NE Austria
101 N16 **Hainichen** Sachsen, E Germany
167 T6 **Hai Phong** var. Haifong, Haiphong. N Vietnam
161 S12 **Haitan Dao** island SE China
44 K8 **Haiti** off. Republic of Haiti. ◆ republic C West Indies
35 T11 **Haiwee Reservoir** ⊞ California, W USA
80 I7 **Haiya** Red Sea, NE Sudan
159 T10 **Haiyan** Qinghai, W China
160 M13 **Haiyang Shan** ▲▲ S China
159 V10 **Haiyuan** Ningxia, N China
Hajda see Nový Bor
111 M22 **Hajdú-Bihar** off. Hajdú-Bihar Megye. ◈ county E Hungary
111 N22 **Hajdúböszörmény** Hajdú-Bihar, E Hungary
111 N22 **Hajdúhadház** Hajdú-Bihar, E Hungary
111 N21 **Hajdúnánás** Hajdú-Bihar, E Hungary
111 N22 **Hajdúszoboszló** Hajdú-Bihar, E Hungary
142 I3 **Ḩājī Ebrāhīm, Kūh-e** ▲ Iran/Iraq
165 O9 **Hajiki-zaki** headland Sado, C Japan
Hajine see Abū Ḩardān
153 P13 **Hājīpur** Bihār, N India
141 N14 **Ḩajjah** W Yemen
139 U11 **Ḩajjama** S Iraq
143 R12 **Ḩājjīābād** Hormozgān, C Iran
139 U14 **Ḩājj, Thaqb al** well S Iraq
113 L16 **Hajla** ▲▲ SW Yugoslavia
110 P10 **Hajnówka** Ger. Hermhausen. Podlaskie, NE Poland
166 K4 **Haka** Chin State, W Myanmar
Hakapehi see Punaauia
Hakâri see Hakkâri
137 T16 **Hakkâri** var. Çölemerik, Hakâri. Hakkâri, SE Turkey
137 T16 **Hakkâri** var. Hakkari. ◈ province SE Turkey
92 J12 **Hakkas** Norrbotten, N Sweden
164 J14 **Hakken-zan** ▲ Honshū, SW Japan
165 R7 **Hakkōda-san** ▲ Honshū, C Japan
165 T2 **Hako-dake** ▲ Hokkaidō, NE Japan
165 R5 **Hakodate** Hokkaidō, NE Japan
164 L11 **Hakui** Ishikawa, Honshū, SW Japan
190 B16 **Hakupu** SE Niue
164 L12 **Haku-san** ▲ Honshū, SW Japan
Hal see Halle
149 Q15 **Hāla** Sind, SE Pakistan
138 J3 **Ḩalab** Eng. Aleppo, Fr. Alep; anc. Beroea. Ḩalab, NW Syria
138 J3 **Ḩalab** off. Muḩāfaẓat Ḩalab, var. Aleppo, Halab. ◈ governorate NW Syria
138 J3 **Ḩalab** × Ḩalab, NW Syria
141 O8 **Halabān** var. Halibān. Ar Riyāḑ, C Saudi Arabia
139 V4 **Ḩalabja** NE Iraq
190 A16 **Halagigie Point** headland W Niue
75 Z11 **Halaib** SE Egypt
190 G12 **Halalo** Île Uvea, N Wallis and Futuna
Halandri see Chalándri
141 X13 **Ḩalānīyāt, Juzur al** var. Jazā'ir Bin Ghalfān, Eng. Kuria Muria Islands. island group S Oman
141 W13 **Ḩalānīyāt, Khalīj al** Eng. Kuria Muria Bay. bay S Oman
Halas see Kiskunhalas
38 G11 **Halawa** Haw. Hālawa. Hawaii, USA, C Pacific Ocean
38 F9 **Halawa, Cape** headland Molokai, Hawaii, USA, C Pacific Ocean
162 H6 **Halban** Hövsgöl, N Mongolia
101 K14 **Halberstadt** Sachsen-Anhalt, C Germany
184 M12 **Halcombe** Manawatu-Wanganui, North Island, NZ
95 I16 **Halden** prev. Fredrikshald. Østfold, S Norway
100 L13 **Haldensleben** Sachsen-Anhalt, C Germany
Háldi see Halti
153 S17 **Haldia** West Bengal, NE India
152 K10 **Haldwāni** Uttar Pradesh, N India
38 F10 **Haleakala** crater Maui, Hawaii, USA, C Pacific Ocean
25 N4 **Hale Center** Texas, SW USA
99 J18 **Halen** Limburg, NE Belgium
23 O2 **Haleyville** Alabama, S USA
77 O17 **Half Assini** SW Ghana
35 R8 **Half Dome** ▲ California, W USA
185 C25 **Halfmoon Bay** var. Oban. Stewart Island, Southland, NZ
182 E5 **Half Moon Lake** salt lake South Australia
163 R7 **Halhgol** Dornod, E Mongolia
Haliacmon see Aliákmonas
Halibān see Ḩalabān
14 I13 **Haliburton** Ontario, SE Canada
14 I12 **Haliburton Highlands** var. Madawaska Highlands. hill range Ontario, SE Canada
13 Q15 **Halifax** Nova Scotia, SE Canada
97 L17 **Halifax** N England, UK
21 W8 **Halifax** North Carolina, SE USA
21 U7 **Halifax** Virginia, NE USA
13 Q15 **Halifax** × Nova Scotia, SE Canada
143 T13 **Halīl Rūd** seasonal river SE Iran
138 I6 **Ḩalīmah** ▲ Lebanon/Syria
162 G8 **Haliun** Govĭ-Altay, W Mongolia
118 I3 **Haljala** Ger. Halljal. Lääne-Virumaa, N Estonia
39 Q4 **Halkett, Cape** headland Alaska, USA
Halkida see Chalkída
96 J6 **Halkirk** N Scotland, UK
15 X7 **Hall** ≈ Quebec, SE Canada
Hall see Schwäbisch Hall
93 H15 **Hälla** Västerbotten, N Sweden
96 J6 **Halladale** ≈ N Scotland, UK
95 J21 **Halland** ◈ county S Sweden
23 Z15 **Hallandale** Florida, SE USA
95 K22 **Hallandsås** physical region S Sweden
9 P6 **Hall Beach** Nunavut, N Canada
99 G19 **Halle** Fr. Hal. Vlaams Brabant, C Belgium
101 M15 **Halle** var. Halle an der Saale. Sachsen-Anhalt, C Germany
Halle an der Saale see Halle
35 W3 **Halleck** Nevada, W USA
95 L15 **Hällefors** Örebro, C Sweden
95 N16 **Hälleforsnäs** Södermanland, C Sweden
109 Q6 **Hallein** Salzburg, N Austria
101 L15 **Halle-Neustadt** Sachsen-Anhalt, C Germany
25 U12 **Hallettsville** Texas, SW USA
195 N4 **Halley** UK research station Antarctica
28 L4 **Halliday** North Dakota, N USA
37 S2 **Halligan Reservoir** ⊞ Colorado, C USA
100 G7 **Halligen** island group N Germany
94 G13 **Hallingdal** valley S Norway
38 J12 **Hall Island** island Alaska, USA
Hall Island see Maiana
189 P15 **Hall Islands** island group C Micronesia
118 H6 **Halliste** ≈ S Estonia
Halljal see Haljala
93 I15 **Hällnäs** Västerbotten, N Sweden
29 R2 **Hallock** Minnesota, N USA
9 S6 **Hall Peninsula** peninsula Baffin Island, Nunavut, NE Canada
20 F9 **Halls** Tennessee, S USA
95 M16 **Hallsberg** Örebro, C Sweden
181 N5 **Halls Creek** Western Australia
182 L12 **Halls Gap** Victoria, SE Australia
95 N15 **Hallstahammar** Västmanland, C Sweden
109 R6 **Hallstatt** Salzburg, W Austria
109 R6 **Hallstatter See** ◎ C Austria
95 P14 **Hallstavik** Stockholm, C Sweden
24 X7 **Hallsville** Texas, SW USA
103 P1 **Halluin** Nord, N France
Halmahera, Laut see Halmahera Sea
171 R11 **Halmahera, Pulau** prev. Djailolo, Gilolo, Jailolo. island E Indonesia
171 S12 **Halmahera Sea** Ind. Laut Halmahera. sea E Indonesia
95 J21 **Halmstad** Halland, S Sweden
119 N15 **Halowchyn** Rus. Golovchin. Mahilyowskaya Voblasts', E Belarus
95 H20 **Hals** Nordjylland, N Denmark
94 F8 **Halsa** Møre og Romsdal, S Norway
119 I15 **Hal'shany** Rus. Gol'shany. Hrodzyenskaya Voblasts', W Belarus
Hälsingborg see Helsingborg
29 R5 **Halstad** Minnesota, N USA
27 N6 **Halstead** Kansas, C USA
99 G15 **Halsteren** Noord-Brabant, S Netherlands
93 L16 **Halsua** Länsi-Suomi, W Finland
101 E14 **Haltern** Nordrhein-Westfalen, W Germany
92 J9 **Halti** var. Haltiatunturi, Lapp. Háldi. ▲ Finland/Norway
Haltiatunturi see Halti
116 J6 **Halych** Ivano-Frankivs'ka Oblast', W Ukraine
Halycus see Platani
103 P3 **Ham** Somme, N France
Hama see Ḩamāh
164 F12 **Hamada** Shimane, Honshū, SW Japan
142 L6 **Hamadān** anc. Ecbatana. Hamadān, W Iran
142 L6 **Hamadān** off. Ostān-e Hamadān. ◈ province W Iran
138 I5 **Ḩamāh** var. Hama; anc. Epiphania, Bibl. Hamath. Ḩamāh, W Syria
138 I5 **Ḩamāh** off. Muḩāfaẓat Ḩamāh, var. Hama. ◈ governorate C Syria
165 S3 **Hamamasu** Hokkaidō, NE Japan
164 L14 **Hamamatsu** var. Hamamatu. Shizuoka, Honshū, S Japan
Hamamatu see Hamamatsu
165 W14 **Hamanaka** Hokkaidō, NE Japan
164 L14 **Hamana-ko** ◎ Honshū, S Japan
94 I13 **Hamar** prev. Storhammer. Hedmark, S Norway
141 U10 **Ḩamārir al Kidan, Qalamat** well E Saudi Arabia
164 I12 **Hamasaka** Hyōgo, Honshū, SW Japan
Hamath see Ḩamāh
165 T1 **Hamatonbetsu** Hokkaidō, NE Japan
155 K26 **Hambantota** Southern Province, SE Sri Lanka
Hambourg see Hamburg
100 J9 **Hamburg** Hamburg, N Germany
27 V14 **Hamburg** Arkansas, C USA
29 S16 **Hamburg** Iowa, C USA
18 D10 **Hamburg** New York, NE USA
100 I10 **Hamburg** Fr. Hambourg. ◈ state N Germany
148 K5 **Hamdam Āb, Dasht-e** Pash. Dasht-i Hamdamab. ▲▲ W Afghanistan
Hamdamab, Dasht-i see Hamdam Āb, Dasht-e
18 M13 **Hamden** Connecticut, NE USA
140 K6 **Ḩamḑ, Wādī al** dry watercourse W Saudi Arabia
93 K18 **Hämeenkyrö** Länsi-Suomi, W Finland
93 L19 **Hämeenlinna** Swe. Tavastehus. Etelä-Suomi, S Finland
HaMelaḥ, Yam see Dead Sea
Hamelin see Hameln
100 I13 **Hameln** Eng. Hamelin. Niedersachsen, N Germany
180 I8 **Hamersley Range** ▲▲ Western Australia
163 Y12 **Hamgyŏng-sanmaek** ▲▲ N North Korea
163 X13 **Hamhŭng** C North Korea
159 O6 **Hami** var. Ha-mi, Uigh. Kumul, Qomul. Xinjiang Uygur Zizhiqu, NW China
139 X10 **Ḩāmid Amīn** E Iraq
141 W11 **Ḩamīdān, Khawr** oasis SE Saudi Arabia
138 H5 **Ḩamīdīyah** var. Hamīdīyé. Ṭarṭūs, W Syria
114 L12 **Hamidiye** Edirne, NW Turkey
Hamīdīyé see Ḩamīdīyah
182 L12 **Hamilton** Victoria, SE Australia
64 B12 **Hamilton** ○ (Bermuda) C Bermuda
14 G16 **Hamilton** Ontario, S Canada
184 M7 **Hamilton** Waikato, North Island, NZ
96 I12 **Hamilton** S Scotland, UK
23 N3 **Hamilton** Alabama, S USA
38 M10 **Hamilton** Alaska, USA
30 J13 **Hamilton** Illinois, N USA
27 S3 **Hamilton** Missouri, C USA
33 P10 **Hamilton** Montana, NW USA
25 S8 **Hamilton** Texas, SW USA
14 G16 **Hamilton** × Ontario, SE Canada
64 I6 **Hamilton Bank** undersea feature SE Labrador Sea
182 E1 **Hamilton Creek** seasonal river South Australia
13 R8 **Hamilton Inlet** inlet Newfoundland, E Canada
27 T12 **Hamilton, Lake** ⊞ Arkansas, C USA
35 W6 **Hamilton, Mount** ▲ Nevada, W USA
75 S8 **Ḩamīm, Wādī al** ≈ NE Libya
93 N19 **Hamina** Swe. Fredrikshamn. Etelä-Suomi, S Finland
11 W16 **Hamiota** Manitoba, S Canada
152 L13 **Hamīrpur** Uttar Pradesh, N India
Hamis Musait see Khamīs Mushayt
21 T11 **Hamlet** North Carolina, SE USA
25 P6 **Hamlin** Texas, SW USA
21 P5 **Hamlin** West Virginia, NE USA
31 O7 **Hamlin Lake** ◎ Michigan, N USA
101 F14 **Hamm** var. Hamm in Westfalen. Nordrhein-Westfalen, W Germany
Ḩammāmāt, Khalīj al see Hammamet, Golfe de
75 N5 **Hammamet, Golfe de** Ar. Khalīj al Ḩammāmāt. gulf NE Tunisia
139 R3 **Ḩammām al 'Alīl** N Iraq
139 X12 **Ḩammār, Hawr al** ◎ SE Iraq
93 J20 **Hammarland** Åland, SW Finland
93 H16 **Hammarstrand** Jämtland, C Sweden
93 O17 **Hammaslahti** Itä-Suomi, E Finland
99 F17 **Hamme** Oost-Vlaanderen, NW Belgium
100 H10 **Hamme** ≈ NW Germany
95 G22 **Hammel** Århus, C Denmark
101 I18 **Hammelburg** Bayern, C Germany
99 H18 **Hamme-Mille** Wallon Brabant, C Belgium
100 H10 **Hamme-Oste-Kanal** canal NW Germany
93 G16 **Hammerdal** Jämtland, C Sweden
92 K8 **Hammerfest** Finnmark, N Norway
101 D14 **Hamminkeln** Nordrhein-Westfalen, W Germany
Hamm in Westfalen see Hamm
26 K10 **Hammon** Oklahoma, C USA
31 N11 **Hammond** Indiana, N USA
22 K8 **Hammond** Louisiana, S USA
99 K20 **Hamoir** Liège, E Belgium
99 J21 **Hamois** Namur, SE Belgium
99 K16 **Hamont** Limburg, NE Belgium
185 F22 **Hampden** Otago, South Island, NZ
19 R6 **Hampden** Maine, NE USA
97 M23 **Hampshire** cultural region S England, UK
13 O15 **Hampton** New Brunswick, SE Canada
27 U14 **Hampton** Arkansas, C USA
29 V12 **Hampton** Iowa, C USA
19 P10 **Hampton** New Hampshire, NE USA
21 R14 **Hampton** South Carolina, SE USA
21 P8 **Hampton** Tennessee, S USA
21 X7 **Hampton** Virginia, NE USA
94 L11 **Hamra** Gävleborg, C Sweden
80 D10 **Hamrat esh Sheikh** Northern Kordofan, C Sudan
139 S5 **Ḩamrīn, Jabal** ▲ N Iraq
121 P16 **Ħamrun** C Malta
167 U14 **Ham Thuận Nam** Bình Thuận, S Vietnam
Hāmūn, Daryācheh-ye see Şāberī, Hāmūn-e/Sīstān, Daryācheh-ye
Hamwih see Southampton
38 G10 **Hana** Haw. Hāna. Maui, Hawaii, USA, C Pacific Ocean
21 S14 **Hanahan** South Carolina, SE USA
38 B8 **Hanalei** Kauai, Hawaii, USA, C Pacific Ocean
167 U10 **Ha Nam** Quang Nam-Đa Nẵng, C Vietnam
165 Q9 **Hanamaki** Iwate, Honshū, C Japan
38 F10 **Hanamanioa, Cape** headland Maui, Hawaii, USA, C Pacific Ocean
190 B16 **Hanan** × (Alofi) SW Niue
101 H18 **Hanau** Hessen, W Germany
8 L9 **Hanbury** ≈ Northwest Territories, NW Canada
Hâncești see Hîncești
10 M15 **Hanceville** British Columbia, SW Canada
23 P3 **Hanceville** Alabama, S USA
Hancewicze see Hantsavichy
160 L6 **Hancheng** Shaanxi, C China
21 V2 **Hancock** Maryland, NE USA
30 M3 **Hancock** Michigan, N USA
29 S8 **Hancock** Minnesota, N USA
18 I12 **Hancock** New York, NE USA
80 Q12 **Handa** Bari, NE Somalia
161 O5 **Handan** var. Han-tan. Hebei, E China
95 P16 **Handen** Stockholm, C Sweden
81 J22 **Handeni** Tanga, E Tanzania
37 Q7 **Handies Peak** ▲ Colorado, C USA
111 J19 **Handlová** Ger. Krickerhäu, Hung. Nyitrabánya; prev. Ger. Kriegerhaj. Trenčiansky Kraj, W Slovakia
165 O13 **Haneda** × (Tōkyō) Tōkyō, Honshū, S Japan
138 F13 **HaNegev** Eng. Negev. desert S Israel
35 Q11 **Hanford** California, W USA
191 V16 **Hanga Roa** Easter Island, Chile, E Pacific Ocean
162 H7 **Hangayn Nuruu** ▲▲ C Mongolia
Hang-chou/Hangchow see Hangzhou
95 K20 **Hånger** Jönköping, S Sweden
Hangö see Hanko
161 R9 **Hangzhou** var. Hang-chou, Hangchow. Zhejiang, SE China
162 F5 **Hanhöhiy Uul** ▲▲ NW Mongolia
Hanhowuz see Khauz-Khan
137 P15 **Hani** Dıyarbakır, SE Turkey
Hania see Chaniá
141 R11 **Ḩanīsh al Kabīr, Jazīrat al** island SW Yemen
Hanka, Lake see Khanka, Lake
93 M17 **Hankasalmi** Länsi-Suomi, W Finland
29 R7 **Hankinson** North Dakota, N USA
93 K20 **Hanko** Swe. Hangö. Etelä-Suomi, SW Finland
Han-kou/Han-k'ou/Hankow see Wuhan
36 M6 **Hanksville** Utah, W USA
152 K6 **Hanle** Jammu and Kashmir, NW India
185 I17 **Hanmer Springs** Canterbury, South Island, NZ
11 R16 **Hanna** Alberta, SW Canada
27 V3 **Hannibal** Missouri, C USA
180 M3 **Hann, Mount** ▲ Western Australia
100 I12 **Hannover** Eng. Hanover. Niedersachsen, NW Germany
99 J19 **Hannut** Liège, C Belgium
95 L22 **Hanöbukten** bay S Sweden
167 T6 **Ha Nôi** Eng. Hanoi, Fr. Ha noï. ● (Vietnam) N Vietnam
14 F14 **Hanover** Ontario, S Canada
31 P15 **Hanover** Indiana, N USA
18 G16 **Hanover** Pennsylvania, NE USA
21 W6 **Hanover** Virginia, NE USA
Hanover see Hannover
63 G23 **Hanover, Isla** island S Chile
Hanselbeck see Érd
195 X5 **Hansen Mountains** ▲▲ Antarctica
160 M8 **Han Shui** ≈ C China
152 H10 **Hānsi** Haryāna, NW India
95 F20 **Hanstholm** Viborg, NW Denmark
Han-tan see Handan
158 H6 **Hantengri Feng** var. Pik Khan-Tengri. ▲ China/Kazakhstan see also Khan-Tengri, Pik
119 I18 **Hantsavichy** Pol. Hancewicze, Rus. Gantsevichi. Brestskaya Voblasts', SW Belarus
9 Q6 **Hantzsch** ≈ Baffin Island, Nunavut, NE Canada
152 G9 **Hanumāngarh** Rājasthān, NW India
183 O9 **Hanwood** New South Wales, SE Australia
Hanyang see Caidian
Hanyang see Wuhan
160 H10 **Hanyuan** var. Fulin. Sichuan, C China
160 J7 **Hanzhong** Shaanxi, C China
191 W11 **Hao** atoll Îles Tuamotu, C French Polynesia
153 S16 **Hāora** prev. Howrah. West Bengal, NE India
78 K8 **Haouach, Ouadi** dry watercourse E Chad
92 K13 **Haparanda** Norrbotten, N Sweden
25 N3 **Happy** Texas, SW USA
34 M1 **Happy Camp** California, W USA
13 Q9 **Happy Valley-Goose Bay** prev. Goose Bay. Newfoundland, E Canada
Hapsal see Haapsalu
152 J10 **Hāpur** Uttar Pradesh, N India
138 F12 **HaQatan, HaMakhtesh** ▲ S Israel
140 I4 **Ḩaql** Tabūk, NW Saudi Arabia
171 U14 **Har** Pulau Kai Besar, E Indonesia
162 M8 **Haraat** Dundgovĭ, C Mongolia
141 R8 **Ḩaraḑ** var. Haradh. Ash Sharqīyah, E Saudi Arabia
Haradh see Ḩaraḑ
118 N12 **Haradok** Rus. Gorodok. Vitsyebskaya Voblasts', N Belarus
92 J13 **Harads** Norrbotten, N Sweden
119 G19 **Haradzyets** Rus. Gorodets. Brestskaya Voblasts', SW Belarus
119 J17 **Haradzyeya** Rus. Gorodeya. Minskaya Voblasts', C Belarus
191 V10 **Haraiki** atoll Îles Tuamotu, C French Polynesia
165 Q11 **Haramachi** Fukushima, Honshū, E Japan
118 M12 **Harany** Rus. Gorany. Vitsyebskaya Voblasts', N Belarus
83 L16 **Harare** prev. Salisbury. ● (Zimbabwe) Mashonaland East, NE Zimbabwe
83 L16 **Harare** × Mashonaland East, NE Zimbabwe
78 J10 **Haraz-Djombo** Batha, C Chad
119 O16 **Harbavichy** Rus. Gorbovichi. Mahilyowskaya Voblasts', E Belarus

◆ Country ● Country Capital ◇ Dependent Territory ○ Dependent Territory Capital ◈ Administrative Region × International Airport ▲ Mountain ▲▲ Mountain Range ⩕ Volcano ≈ River ◎ Lake ⊞ Reservoir

76 *J16* **Harbel** W Liberia
163 *W8* **Harbin** *var.* Haerbin, Ha-erh-pin, Kharbin; *prev.* Haerhpin, Pingkiang, Pinkiang. Heilongjiang, NE China
31 *S7* **Harbor Beach** Michigan, N USA
13 *T13* **Harbour Breton** Newfoundland, E Canada
65 *D25* **Harbours, Bay of** *bay* East Falkland, Falkland Islands
95 *G24* **Hårby** *var.* Haarby. Fyn, C Denmark
36 *I13* **Harcuvar Mountains** ▲ Arizona, SW USA
108 *I7* **Hard** Vorarlberg, NW Austria
154 *H11* **Harda Khās** Madhya Pradesh, C India
95 *D14* **Hardanger** *physical region* S Norway
95 *D14* **Hardangerfjorden** *fjord* S Norway
94 *E13* **Hardangerjøkulen** *glacier* S Norway
95 *E14* **Hardangervidda** *plateau* S Norway
83 *D20* **Hardap** ◈ *district* S Namibia
21 *R15* **Hardeeville** South Carolina, SE USA
98 *L5* **Hardegarijp** *Fris.* Hurdegaryp. Friesland, N Netherlands
98 *O9* **Hardenberg** Overijssel, E Netherlands
183 *Q9* **Harden-Murrumburrah** New South Wales, SE Australia
98 *K10* **Harderwijk** Gelderland, C Netherlands
30 *J14* **Hardin** Illinois, N USA
33 *V11* **Hardin** Montana, NW USA
23 *R5* **Harding, Lake** ⊟ Alabama/Georgia, SE USA
20 *J6* **Hardinsburg** Kentucky, S USA
98 *I13* **Hardinxveld-Giessendam** Zuid-Holland, C Netherlands
11 *R15* **Hardisty** Alberta, SW Canada
152 *L12* **Hardoi** Uttar Pradesh, N India
23 *U4* **Hardwick** Georgia, SE USA
27 *W9* **Hardy** Arkansas, C USA
94 *D10* **Hareid** Møre og Romsdal, S Norway
8 *H7* **Hare Indian** ≈ Northwest Territories, NW Canada
99 *D18* **Harelbeke** *var.* Harlebeke. West-Vlaanderen, W Belgium
Harem *see* Ḩārim
100 *E11* **Haren** Niedersachsen, NW Germany
98 *N6* **Haren** Groningen, NE Netherlands
80 *L13* **Hārer** Hārer, E Ethiopia
95 *P14* **Harg** Uppsala, C Sweden
Hargeisa *see* Hargeysa
80 *M13* **Hargeysa** *var.* Hargeisa. Woqooyi Galbeed, NW Somalia
116 *J10* **Harghita** ◈ *county* NE Romania
25 *S17* **Hargill** Texas, SW USA
162 *J8* **Harhorin** Övörhangay, C Mongolia
159 *Q9* **Har Hu** ◎ C China
Hariana *see* Haryāna
141 *P15* **Ḩarīb** W Yemen
192 *M12* **Hari, Batang** *prev.* Djambi. ≈ Sumatera, W Indonesia
152 *J9* **Haridwār** *prev.* Hardwar. Uttar Pradesh, N India
155 *F18* **Harihar** Karnātaka, W India
185 *F18* **Harihari** West Coast, South Island, NZ
138 *I3* **Ḩārim** *var.* Harem. Idlib, W Syria
98 *F13* **Haringvliet** *channel* SW Netherlands
98 *F13* **Haringvlietdam** *dam* SW Netherlands
149 *U5* **Harīpur** North-West Frontier Province, NW Pakistan
148 *J4* **Harīrūd** *var.* Tedzhen, *Turkm.* Tejen. ≈ Afghanistan/Iran *see also* Tedzhen
94 *J11* **Härjåhågnen** *Swe.* Härjahågnen, Härjehågna. ▲ Norway/Sweden
93 *K18* **Harjavalta** Länsi-Suomi, W Finland
Härjehågna *see* Härjåhågnen
118 *G4* **Harjumaa** *off.* Harju Maakond. ◈ *province* NW Estonia
21 *X11* **Harkers Island** North Carolina, SE USA
139 *S1* **Harki** N Iraq
29 *T14* **Harlan** Iowa, C USA
21 *O7* **Harlan** Kentucky, S USA
29 *N17* **Harlan County Lake** ⊟ Nebraska, C USA
116 *L9* **Hârlău** *var.* Hîrlău. Iaşi, NE Romania
Harlebeke *see* Harelbeke
33 *U7* **Harlem** Montana, NW USA
Harlem *see* Haarlem
95 *G22* **Harlev** Århus, C Denmark
98 *K6* **Harlingen** *Fris.* Harns. Friesland, N Netherlands
25 *T17* **Harlingen** Texas, SW USA
97 *O21* **Harlow** E England, UK
33 *T10* **Harlowton** Montana, NW USA
94 *N11* **Harmånger** Gävleborg, C Sweden
98 *I11* **Harmelen** Utrecht, C Netherlands
29 *X11* **Harmony** Minnesota, N USA
32 *J14* **Harney Basin** *basin* Oregon, NW USA
(0) *F9* **Harney Basin** ▲ Oregon, NW USA
32 *J14* **Harney Lake** ◎ Oregon, NW USA
28 *J10* **Harney Peak** ▲ South Dakota, N USA
93 *H17* **Härnösand** *var.* Hernösand. Västernorrland, C Sweden
Harns *see* Harlingen
162 *F6* **Har Nuur** ◎ NW Mongolia
105 *P4* **Haro** La Rioja, N Spain
40 *F6* **Haro, Cabo** *headland* NW Mexico
94 *D9* **Harøy** *island* S Norway
97 *N21* **Harpenden** E England, UK
76 *L18* **Harper** *var.* Cape Palmas. NE Liberia
26 *M7* **Harper** Kansas, C USA
32 *L13* **Harper** Oregon, NW USA
25 *Q10* **Harper** Texas, SW USA
35 *U13* **Harper Lake** *salt flat* California, W USA
39 *T9* **Harper, Mount** ▲ Alaska, USA
95 *J21* **Harplinge** Halland, S Sweden
36 *J13* **Harquahala Mountains** ▲ Arizona, SW USA
141 *T15* **Ḩarrah** SE Yemen
12 *H11* **Harricana** ≈ Quebec, SE Canada
20 *M9* **Harriman** Tennessee, S USA
13 *R11* **Harrington Harbour** Quebec, E Canada
64 *B12* **Harrington Sound** *bay* Bermuda, NW Atlantic Ocean
96 *F8* **Harris** *physical region* NW Scotland, UK
27 *X10* **Harrisburg** Arkansas, C USA
30 *M17* **Harrisburg** Illinois, N USA
28 *I14* **Harrisburg** Nebraska, C USA
32 *F12* **Harrisburg** Oregon, NW USA
18 *G15* **Harrisburg** *state capital* Pennsylvania, NE USA
182 *F6* **Harris, Lake** ◎ South Australia
23 *W11* **Harris, Lake** ◎ Florida, SE USA
83 *J22* **Harrismith** Free State, E South Africa
27 *T9* **Harrison** Arkansas, C USA
31 *Q7* **Harrison** Michigan, N USA
28 *I12* **Harrison** Nebraska, C USA
39 *Q5* **Harrison Bay** *inlet* Alaska, USA
22 *I6* **Harrisonburg** Louisiana, S USA
21 *U4* **Harrisonburg** Virginia, NE USA
13 *R7* **Harrison, Cape** *headland* Newfoundland, E Canada
27 *R5* **Harrisonville** Missouri, C USA
Harris Ridge *see* Lomonosov Ridge
192 *M3* **Harris Seamount** *undersea feature* N Pacific Ocean
96 *F8* **Harris, Sound of** *strait* NW Scotland, UK
31 *R6* **Harrisville** Michigan, N USA
21 *R3* **Harrisville** West Virginia, NE USA
20 *M6* **Harrodsburg** Kentucky, S USA
97 *M16* **Harrogate** N England, UK
25 *Q4* **Harrold** Texas, SW USA
27 *S5* **Harry S.Truman Reservoir** ⊟ Missouri, C USA
100 *G13* **Harsewinkel** Nordrhein-Westfalen, W Germany
116 *M14* **Hârşova** *prev.* Hirşova. Constanţa, SE Romania
92 *H10* **Harstad** Troms, N Norway
31 *O8* **Hart** Michigan, N USA
24 *M4* **Hart** Texas, SW USA
10 *I5* **Hart** ≈ Yukon Territory, NW Canada
83 *F23* **Hartbees** ≈ C South Africa
109 *X7* **Hartberg** Steiermark, SE Austria
182 *I10* **Hart, Cape** *headland* South Australia
95 *E14* **Hårteigen** ▲ S Norway
23 *Q2* **Hartford** Alabama, S USA
27 *R11* **Hartford** Arkansas, C USA
18 *M12* **Hartford** *state capital* Connecticut, NE USA
20 *J6* **Hartford** Kentucky, S USA
31 *P10* **Hartford** Michigan, N USA
29 *R11* **Hartford** South Dakota, N USA
30 *M8* **Hartford** Wisconsin, N USA
31 *P13* **Hartford City** Indiana, N USA
29 *Q13* **Hartington** Nebraska, C USA
13 *N14* **Hartland** New Brunswick, SE Canada
97 *H23* **Hartland Point** *headland* SW England, UK
97 *M15* **Hartlepool** N England, UK
29 *T12* **Hartley** Iowa, C USA
24 *M1* **Hartley** Texas, SW USA
32 *J15* **Hart Mountain** ▲ Oregon, NW USA
173 *U10* **Hartog Ridge** *undersea feature* W Indian Ocean
93 *M18* **Hartola** Etelä-Suomi, S Finland
67 *U14* **Harts** *var.* Hartz. ≈ N South Africa
23 *P2* **Hartselle** Alabama, S USA
23 *S3* **Hartsfield Atlanta** ✕ Georgia, SE USA
27 *Q11* **Hartshorne** Oklahoma, C USA
21 *S12* **Hartsville** South Carolina, SE USA
20 *K8* **Hartsville** Tennessee, S USA
27 *U7* **Hartville** Missouri, C USA
23 *U2* **Hartwell** Georgia, SE USA
21 *O11* **Hartwell Lake** ⊟ Georgia/South Carolina, SE USA
Hartz *see* Harts
Harunabad *see* Eslāmābād
162 *E6* **Har-Us** Hovd, W Mongolia
162 *E6* **Har Us Nuur** ◎ NW Mongolia
30 *M10* **Harvard** Illinois, N USA
29 *P16* **Harvard** Nebraska, C USA
37 *R5* **Harvard, Mount** ▲ Colorado, C USA
31 *N11* **Harvey** Illinois, N USA
29 *N4* **Harvey** North Dakota, N USA
97 *Q21* **Harwich** E England, UK
152 *H10* **Haryāna** *var.* Hariana. ◈ *state* N India
141 *Y9* **Ḩaryān, Ţawī al** *spring/well* NE Oman
101 *J14* **Harz** ▲ C Germany
Hasakah *see* Al Ḩasakah
165 *Q9* **Hasama** Miyagi, Honshū, C Japan
136 *J15* **Hasan Dağı** ▲ C Turkey
139 *T9* **Ḩasan Ibn Ḩassūn** C Iraq
149 *R6* **Ḩasan Khēl** *var.* Ahmad Khel. Paktīā, SE Afghanistan
100 *F12* **Hase** ≈ NW Germany
Haselberg *see* Krasnoznamensk
100 *F12* **Haselünne** Niedersachsen, NW Germany
162 *K9* **Hashaat** Dundgovĭ, C Mongolia
Hashemite Kingdom of Jordan *see* Jordan
139 *V8* **Hāshimah** E Iraq
141 *W13* **Ḩāsik** S Oman
149 *U10* **Hāsilpur** Punjab, E Pakistan
Hasimoto *see* Hashimoto
27 *Q10* **Haskell** Oklahoma, C USA
25 *Q6* **Haskell** Texas, SW USA
114 *M11* **Hasköy** Edirne, NW Turkey
95 *L24* **Hasle** Bornholm, E Denmark
97 *N23* **Haslemere** SE England, UK
102 *I16* **Hasparren** Pyrénées-Atlantiques, SW France
Hassakeh *see* Al Ḩasakah
155 *G19* **Hassan** Karnātaka, W India
36 *J13* **Hassayampa River** ≈ Arizona, SW USA
101 *J18* **Hassberge** *hill range* C Germany
94 *N10* **Hassela** Gävleborg, C Sweden
99 *J18* **Hasselt** Limburg, NE Belgium
98 *M9* **Hasselt** Overijssel, E Netherlands
Hassetché *see* Al Ḩasakah
101 *J18* **Hassfurt** Bayern, C Germany
74 *L9* **Hassi Bel Guebbour** E Algeria
74 *L8* **Hassi Messaoud** E Algeria
95 *K22* **Hässleholm** Skåne, S Sweden
Hasta Colonia/Hasta Pompeia *see* Asti
183 *O13* **Hastings** Victoria, SE Australia
184 *O11* **Hastings** Hawke's Bay, North Island, NZ
97 *P23* **Hastings** SE England, UK
31 *P9* **Hastings** Michigan, N USA
29 *W9* **Hastings** Minnesota, N USA
29 *P16* **Hastings** Nebraska, C USA
95 *K22* **Hästveda** Skåne, S Sweden
92 *J8* **Hasvik** Finnmark, N Norway
37 *V6* **Haswell** Colorado, C USA
162 *I10* **Hatansuudal** Bayanhongor, C Mongolia
163 *P9* **Hatavch** Sühbaatar, E Mongolia
136 *K17* **Hatay** ◈ *province* S Turkey
37 *R15* **Hatch** New Mexico, SW USA
36 *K7* **Hatch** Utah, W USA
20 *F10* **Hatchie River** ≈ Tennessee, S USA
116 *G12* **Haţeg** *Ger.* Wallenthal, *Hung.* Hátszeg; *prev.* Hatzeg, Hötzing. Hunedoara, SW Romania
165 *O17* **Hateruma-jima** *island* Yaeyama-shotō, SW Japan
183 *N8* **Hatfield** New South Wales, SE Australia
162 *I5* **Hatgal** Hövsgöl, N Mongolia
153 *V16* **Hathazari** Chittagong, SE Bangladesh
141 *T13* **Hathūt, Hişā'** *oasis* NE Yemen
167 *R14* **Ha Tiên** Kiên Giang, S Vietnam
167 *T8* **Ha Tinh** Ha Tinh, N Vietnam
Hatiôzi *see* Hachiōji
138 *F12* **Ḩatira, Haré** *hill range* S Israel
167 *R6* **Hat Lot** Son La, N Vietnam
45 *P16* **Hato Airport** ✕ (Willemstad) Curaçao, SW Netherlands Antilles
54 *H9* **Hato Corozal** Casanare, C Colombia
Hato del Volcán *see* Volcán
45 *P9* **Hato Mayor** E Dominican Republic
Hatra *see* Al Ḩaḑr
Hatria *see* Adria
Hátszeg *see* Haţeg
143 *R16* **Ḩattá** Dubayy, NE UAE
182 *L9* **Hattah** Victoria, SE Australia
98 *M9* **Hattem** Gelderland, E Netherlands
21 *Z10* **Hatteras** Hatteras Island, North Carolina, SE USA
21 *Rr10* **Hatteras, Cape** *headland* North Carolina, SE USA
21 *Z9* **Hatteras Island** *island* North Carolina, SE USA
64 *F10* **Hatteras Plain** *undersea feature* W Atlantic Ocean
93 *G14* **Hattfjelldal** Troms, N Norway
22 *M7* **Hattiesburg** Mississippi, S USA
29 *Q4* **Hatton** North Dakota, N USA
Hatton Bank *see* Hatton Ridge
64 *L6* **Hatton Ridge** *var.* Hatton Bank. *undersea feature* N Atlantic Ocean
191 *W6* **Hatutu** *island* Îles Marquises, NE French Polynesia
111 *K22* **Hatvan** Heves, NE Hungary
167 *O16* **Hat Yai** *var.* Ban Hat Yai. Songkhla, SW Thailand
Hatzeg *see* Haţeg
Hatzfeld *see* Jimbolia
80 *N13* **Haud** *plateau* Ethiopia/Somalia
95 *D18* **Hauge** Rogaland, S Norway
95 *C15* **Haugesund** Rogaland, S Norway
109 *X2* **Haugsdorf** Niederösterreich, NE Austria
184 *M9* **Hauhungaroa Range** ▲ North Island, NZ
95 *E15* **Haukeligrend** Telemark, S Norway
93 *L14* **Haukipudas** Oulu, C Finland
93 *M17* **Haukivesi** ◎ SE Finland
93 *M17* **Haukivuori** Isä-Suomi, E Finland
Hauptkanal *see* Havelländ Grosse
187 *N10* **Hauraha** San Cristobal, SE Solomon Islands
184 *L5* **Hauraki Gulf** *gulf* North Island, NZ
185 *B24* **Hauroko, Lake** ◎ South Island, NZ
167 *S14* **Hâu, Sông** ≈ S Vietnam
92 *N12* **Hautajärvi** Lappi, NE Finland
74 *F7* **Haut Atlas** *Eng.* High Atlas. ▲ C Morocco
79 *M17* **Haut-Congo** *off.* Région du Haut-Congo; *prev.* Haut-Zaïre. ◈ *region* NE Dem. Rep. Congo (Zaire)
103 *Y14* **Haute-Corse** ◈ *department* Corse, France, C Mediterranean Sea
102 *L16* **Haute-Garonne** ◈ *department* S France
76 *J13* **Haute-Guinée** ◈ *state* NE Guinea
79 *K14* **Haute-Kotto** ◈ *prefecture* E Central African Republic
103 *P12* **Haute-Loire** ◈ *department* C France
103 *R6* **Haute-Marne** ◈ *department* N France
102 *M3* **Haute-Normandie** ◈ *region* N France
15 *U6* **Hauterive** Quebec, SE Canada
103 *T13* **Hautes-Alpes** ◈ *department* SE France
103 *S7* **Haute-Saône** ◈ *department* E France
103 *T10* **Haute-Savoie** ◈ *department* E France
99 *M20* **Hautes Fagnes** *Ger.* Hohes Venn. ▲ E Belgium
102 *K16* **Hautes-Pyrénées** ◈ *department* S France
99 *L23* **Haute Sûre, Lac de la** ⊟ NW Luxembourg
102 *M11* **Haute-Vienne** ◈ *department* C France
19 *S8* **Haut, Isle au** *island* Maine, NE USA
79 *M14* **Haut-Mbomou** ◈ *préfecture* SE Central African Republic
103 *Q2* **Hautmont** Nord, N France
79 *F19* **Haut-Ogooué** *off.* Province du Haut-Ogooué, *var.* Le Haut-Ogooué. ◈ *province* SE Gabon
Haut-Ogooué, Le *see* Haut-Ogooué
103 *U7* **Haut-Rhin** ◈ *department* NE France
74 *I6* **Hauts Plateaux** *plateau* Algeria/Morocco
38 *D9* **Hauula** *Haw.* Hau'ula. Oahu, Hawaii, USA, C Pacific Ocean
101 *O22* **Hauzenberg** Bayern, SE Germany
30 *K13* **Havana** Illinois, N USA
Havana *see* La Habana
97 *N23* **Havant** S England, UK
35 *Y14* **Havasu, Lake** ⊟ Arizona/California, W USA
95 *J23* **Havdrup** Roskilde, E Denmark
100 *N10* **Havel** ≈ NE Germany
99 *J21* **Havelange** Namur, SE Belgium
100 *M11* **Havelberg** Sachsen-Anhalt, NE Germany
149 *U5* **Haveliān** North-West Frontier Province, NW Pakistan
100 *N12* **Havelländ Grosse** *var.* Hauptkanal. *canal* NE Germany
14 *J14* **Havelock** Ontario, SE Canada
185 *J14* **Havelock** Marlborough, South Island, NZ
21 *X11* **Havelock** North Carolina, SE USA
184 *O11* **Havelock North** Hawke's Bay, North Island, NZ
98 *M8* **Havelte** Drenthe, NE Netherlands
27 *N6* **Haven** Kansas, C USA
97 *H21* **Haverfordwest** SW Wales, UK
97 *P20* **Haverhill** E England, UK
19 *O10* **Haverhill** Massachusetts, NE USA
93 *G17* **Haverö** Västernorrland, C Sweden
111 *I17* **Havířov** Ostravský Kraj, E Czech Republic
111 *E17* **Havlíčkův Brod** *Ger.* Deutsch-Brod; *prev.* Německý Brod. Jihlavský Kraj, C Czech Republic
92 *K7* **Havøysund** Finnmark, N Norway
33 *T7* **Havre** Montana, NW USA
Havre *see* le Havre
99 *F20* **Havré** Hainaut, S Belgium
13 *P11* **Havre-St-Pierre** Quebec, E Canada
136 *B10* **Havsa** Edirne, NW Turkey
38 *D8* **Hawaii** *off.* State of Hawaii; also known as Aloha State, Paradise of the Pacific. ◈ *state* USA, C Pacific Ocean
38 *G12* **Hawaii** *Haw.* Hawai'i. *island* Hawaiian Islands, USA, C Pacific Ocean
192 *M5* **Hawaiian Islands** *prev.* Sandwich Islands. *island group* Hawaii, USA, C Pacific Ocean
192 *L5* **Hawaiian Ridge** *undersea feature* N Pacific Ocean
193 *N6* **Hawaiian Trough** *undersea feature* N Pacific Ocean
29 *R12* **Hawarden** Iowa, C USA
Hawash *see* Āwash
139 *P6* **Hawbayn al Gharbīyah** C Iraq
185 *D21* **Hawea, Lake** ◎ South Island, NZ
184 *K11* **Hawera** Taranaki, North Island, NZ
20 *J5* **Hawesville** Kentucky, S USA
38 *G11* **Hawi** *Haw.* Hāwī. Hawaii, USA, C Pacific Ocean
96 *K13* **Hawick** SE Scotland, UK
139 *S4* **Ḩawījah** C Iraq
139 *Y10* **Ḩawīzah, Hawr al** ◎ S Iraq
185 *E21* **Hawkdun Range** ▲ South Island, NZ
184 *P10* **Hawke Bay** *bay* North Island, NZ
182 *I6* **Hawker** South Australia
184 *N11* **Hawke's Bay** *off.* Hawkes Bay Region. ◈ *region* North Island, NZ
149 *O16* **Hawkes Bay** *bay* SE Pakistan
15 *N12* **Hawkesbury** Ontario, SE Canada
Hawkeye State *see* Iowa
23 *T5* **Hawkinsville** Georgia, SE USA
14 *B7* **Hawk Junction** Ontario, S Canada
21 *N10* **Haw Knob** ▲ North Carolina/Tennessee, SE USA
21 *Q9* **Hawksbill Mountain** ▲ North Carolina, SE USA
33 *Z16* **Hawk Springs** Wyoming, C USA
Hawlēr *see* Arbīl
29 *S5* **Hawley** Minnesota, N USA
25 *P7* **Hawley** Texas, SW USA
141 *R14* **Ḩawrā'** C Yemen
139 *P7* **Ḩawrān, Wadi** *dry watercourse* W Iraq
21 *T9* **Haw River** ≈ North Carolina, SE USA
139 *U5* **Hawshqūrah** E Iraq
35 *S7* **Hawthorne** Nevada, W USA
37 *W3* **Haxtun** Colorado, C USA
183 *N9* **Hay** New South Wales, SE Australia
11 *O10* **Hay** ≈ W Canada
171 *S13* **Haya** Pulau Seram, E Indonesia
165 *R9* **Hayachine-san** ▲ Honshū, C Japan
103 *S4* **Hayange** Moselle, NE France
HaYarden *see* Jordan
Hayastani Hanrapetut'yun *see* Armenia
Hayasui-seto *see* Hōyo-kaikyō
39 *N9* **Haycock** Alaska, USA
36 *M14* **Hayden** Arizona, SW USA
37 *Q3* **Hayden** Colorado, C USA
28 *M10* **Hayes** South Dakota, N USA
11 *X13* **Hayes** ≈ Manitoba, C Canada
9 *P12* **Hayes** ≈ Nunavut, NE Canada
28 *M16* **Hayes Center** Nebraska, C USA
39 *S10* **Hayes, Mount** ▲ Alaska, USA
21 *N11* **Hayesville** North Carolina, SE USA
35 *X10* **Hayford Peak** ▲ Nevada, W USA
34 *M3* **Hayfork** California, W USA
Hayir, Qasr al *see* Ḩayr al Gharbī, Qaşr al
163 *P8* **Haylaastay** Sühbaatar, E Mongolia
14 *I12* **Hay Lake** ◎ Ontario, SE Canada
141 *X11* **Haymā'** *var.* Haima. C Oman
136 *H13* **Haymana** Ankara, C Turkey
138 *J7* **Ḩaymūr, Jabal** ▲ W Syria
Haynau *see* Chojnów
22 *G4* **Haynesville** Louisiana, S USA
23 *P6* **Hayneville** Alabama, S USA
114 *M12* **Hayrabolu** Tekirdağ, NW Turkey
136 *C10* **Hayrabolu Deresi** ≈ NW Turkey
138 *J6* **Ḩayr al Gharbī, Qaşr al** *var.* Qasr al Hayir, Qasr al Hir al Gharbi. *ruins* Ḩimş, C Syria
138 *L5* **Ḩayr ash Sharqī, Qaşr al** *var.* Qasr al Hir Ash Sharqī. *ruins* Ḩimş, C Syria
8 *J10* **Hay River** Northwest Territories, W Canada
26 *K4* **Hays** Kansas, C USA
28 *K12* **Hay Springs** Nebraska, C USA
65 *H25* **Haystack, The** ▲ NE Saint Helena
27 *N7* **Haysville** Kansas, C USA
117 *O7* **Haysyn** *Rus.* Gaysin. Vinnyts'ka Oblast', C Ukraine
27 *Y9* **Hayti** Missouri, C USA
29 *Q9* **Hayti** South Dakota, N USA
117 *O8* **Hayvoron** *Rus.* Gayvorno. Kirovohrads'ka Oblast', C Ukraine
35 *N9* **Hayward** California, W USA
30 *J4* **Hayward** Wisconsin, N USA
97 *O23* **Haywards Heath** SE England, UK
143 *S11* **Hazārān, Kūh-e** *var.* Kūh-e ā Hazr. ▲ SE Iran
Hazarat Imam *see* Emām Şāḩeb
21 *O7* **Hazard** Kentucky, S USA
137 *O15* **Hazar Gölü** ◎ C Turkey
153 *P15* **Hazārībāg** *var.* Hazāribāgh. Bihār, N India
Hazārībāgh *see* Hazārībāg
103 *O1* **Hazebrouck** Nord, N France
30 *K9* **Hazel Green** Wisconsin, N USA
192 *K9* **Hazel Holme Bank** *undersea feature* S Pacific Ocean
10 *K13* **Hazelton** British Columbia, SW Canada
29 *N6* **Hazelton** North Dakota, N USA
35 *R5* **Hazen** Nevada, W USA
28 *L5* **Hazen** North Dakota, N USA
38 *L12* **Hazen Bay** *bay* E Bering Sea
9 *N1* **Hazen, Lake** ◎ Nunavut, N Canada
139 *S5* **Hazīm, Bi'r** *well* C Iraq
23 *V6* **Hazlehurst** Georgia, SE USA
22 *K6* **Hazlehurst** Mississippi, S USA
18 *K15* **Hazlet** New Jersey, NE USA
146 *I9* **Hazorasp** *Rus.* Khazarosp. Khorazm Wiloyati, W Uzbekistan
147 *R13* **Hazratishoh, Qatorkŭhi** *var.* Khrebet Khazretishi, *Rus.* Khrebet Khozretishi. ▲ S Tajikistan
Hazr, Kūh-e ā *see* Hazārān, Kūh-e
149 *U6* **Hazro** Punjab, E Pakistan
23 *R7* **Headland** Alabama, S USA
182 *C6* **Head of Bight** *headland* South Australia
33 *N10* **Headquarters** Idaho, NW USA
34 *M7* **Healdsburg** California, W USA
27 *N13* **Healdton** Oklahoma, C USA
183 *O12* **Healesville** Victoria, SE Australia
39 *R10* **Healy** Alaska, USA
173 *R13* **Heard and McDonald Islands** ◇ *Australian external territory* S Indian Ocean
173 *R13* **Heard Island** *island* Heard and McDonald Islands, S Indian Ocean
25 *U9* **Hearne** Texas, SW USA
12 *F12* **Hearst** Ontario, S Canada
194 *J5* **Hearst Island** *island* Antarctica
Heart of Dixie *see* Alabama
28 *L5* **Heart River** ≈ North Dakota, N USA
31 *T13* **Heath** Ohio, N USA
183 *N11* **Heathcote** Victoria, SE Australia
97 *N22* **Heathrow** ✕ (London)SE England, UK
21 *X5* **Heathsville** Virginia, NE USA
27 *R11* **Heavener** Oklahoma, C USA
25 *R15* **Hebbronville** Texas, SW USA
163 *Q13* **Hebei** *var.* Hebei Sheng, Hopeh, Hopei, Ji; *prev.* Chihli. ◈ *province* E China
Hebei Sheng *see* Hebei
36 *M3* **Heber City** Utah, W USA
27 *V10* **Heber Springs** Arkansas, C USA
161 *N5* **Hebi** Henan, C China
32 *F11* **Hebo** Oregon, NW USA
96 *F9* **Hebrides, Sea of the** *sea* NW Scotland, UK
13 *P5* **Hebron** Newfoundland, E Canada
31 *N11* **Hebron** Indiana, N USA
29 *Q17* **Hebron** Nebraska, C USA
28 *L5* **Hebron** North Dakota, N USA
138 *F11* **Hebron** *var.* Al Khalīl, El Khalil, *Heb.* Hevron; *anc.* Kiriath-Arba. S West Bank
Hebrus *see* Évros/Maritsa/Meriç
95 *N14* **Heby** Västmanland, C Sweden
10 *I14* **Hecate Strait** *strait* British Columbia, W Canada
41 *W12* **Hecelchakán** Campeche, SE Mexico
160 *K13* **Hechi** *var.* Jinchengjiang. Guangxi Zhuangzu Zizhiqu, S China
101 *H23* **Hechingen** Baden-Württemberg, S Germany
99 *K17* **Hechtel** Limburg, NE Belgium
160 *J9* **Hechuan** Chongqing Shi, C China
29 *P7* **Hecla** South Dakota, N USA
9 *N1* **Hecla, Cape** *headland* Nunavut, N Canada
29 *T9* **Hector** Minnesota, N USA
93 *F17* **Hede** Jämtland, C Sweden
95 *M14* **Hedemora** Dalarna, C Sweden
92 *K13* **Hedenäset** Norrbotten, N Sweden
95 *G23* **Hedensted** Vejle, C Denmark
95 *N14* **Hedesunda** Gävleborg, C Sweden
95 *N14* **Hedesundafjord** ◎ C Sweden
25 *O3* **Hedley** Texas, SW USA
94 *I12* **Hedmark** ◈ *county* S Norway
165 *T16* **Hedo-misaki** *headland* Okinawa, SW Japan
29 *X15* **Hedrick** Iowa, C USA
99 *L16* **Heel** Limburg, SE Netherlands
189 *Y12* **Heel Point** *point* Wake Island
98 *H9* **Heemskerk** Noord-Holland, W Netherlands
98 *M10* **Heerde** Gelderland, E Netherlands
98 *L7* **Heerenveen** *Fris.* It Hearrenfean. Friesland, N Netherlands
98 *I8* **Heerhugowaard** Noord-Holland, NW Netherlands
92 *O3* **Heer Land** *physical region* C Svalbard
99 *M18* **Heerlen** Limburg, SE Netherlands
99 *J19* **Heers** Limburg, NE Belgium
Heerwegen *see* Polkowice
98 *K13* **Heesch** Noord-Brabant, S Netherlands
99 *K15* **Heeze** Noord-Brabant, SE Netherlands
138 *F8* **Ḩefa** *var.* Haifa; *hist.* Caiffa, Caiphas; *anc.* Sycaminum. Haifa, N Israel
138 *F8* **Ḩefa, Mifraz** *Eng.* Bay of Haifa. *bay* N Israel
161 *Q8* **Hefei** *var.* Hofei; *hist.* Luchow. Anhui, E China
23 *R3* **Heflin** Alabama, S USA
163 *X7* **Hegang** Heilongjiang, NE China
164 *L10* **Hegura-jima** *island* SW Japan
Heguri-jima *see* Heigun-tō
Hei *see* Heilongjiang
100 *H8* **Heide** Schleswig-Holstein, N Germany
101 *G20* **Heidelberg** Baden-Württemberg, SW Germany
83 *J21* **Heidelberg** Gauteng, NE South Africa
22 *M6* **Heidelberg** Mississippi, S USA
Heidenheim *see* Heidenheim an der Brenz
101 *J22* **Heidenheim an der Brenz** *var.* Heidenheim. Baden-Württemberg, S Germany
109 *U2* **Heidenreichstein** Niederösterreich, N Austria
164 *F14* **Heigun-tō** *var.* Heguri-jima. *island* SW Japan
163 *W5* **Heihe** *prev.* Ai-hun. Heilongjiang, NE China
Hei-ho *see* Nagqu
83 *J22* **Heilbron** Free State, N South Africa
101 *H21* **Heilbronn** Baden-Württemberg, SW Germany
Heiligenbeil *see* Mamonovo
109 *Q8* **Heiligenblut** Tirol, W Austria
100 *K7* **Heiligenhafen** Schleswig-Holstein, N Germany
Heiligenkreuz *see* Žiar nad Hronom
101 *J15* **Heiligenstadt** Thüringen, C Germany
Heilong Jiang *see* Amur

◆ Country ● Country Capital ◇ Dependent Territory ○ Dependent Territory Capital ◈ Administrative Region ✕ International Airport ▲ Mountain ▲ Mountain Range Volcano ≈ River ◎ Lake ⊟ Reservoir

163 W8 **Heilongjiang** var. Hei, Heilongjiang Sheng, Hei-lung-chiang, Heilungkiang. ◈ province NE China
Heilongjiang Sheng see Heilongjiang
98 H9 **Heiloo** Noord-Holland, NW Netherlands
Heilsberg see Lidzbark Warmiński
Hei-lung-chiang/Heilungkiang see Heilongjiang
92 I4 **Heimaey** var. Heimaæy. island S Iceland
94 H8 **Heimdal** Sør-Trøndelag, S Norway
Heinaste see Ainaži
93 N17 **Heinävesi** Itä-Suomi, E Finland
99 M22 **Heinerscheid** Diekirch, N Luxembourg
98 M10 **Heino** Overijssel, E Netherlands
93 M18 **Heinola** Etelä-Suomi, S Finland
101 C16 **Heinsberg** Nordrhein-Westfalen, W Germany
163 U12 **Heishan** Liaoning, NE China
160 H8 **Heishui** Sichuan, C China
99 H17 **Heist-op-den-Berg** Antwerpen, C Belgium
Heitō see P'ingtung
171 X15 **Heitske** Irian Jaya, E Indonesia
Hejanah see Al Hījānah
Hejaz see Al Ḥijāz
160 M14 **He Jiang** ~ S China
158 K6 **Hejing** Xinjiang Uygur Zizhiqu, NW China
Héjjasfalva see Vânători
159 S11 **Heka** Qinghai, W China
137 N14 **Hekimhan** Malatya, C Turkey
92 J4 **Hekla** ▲ S Iceland
110 J6 **Hel** Ger. Hela. Pomorskie, N Poland
Hela see Hel
93 F17 **Helagsfjället** ▲ C Sweden
159 W8 **Helan** var. Xigang. Ningxia, N China
162 K14 **Helan Shan** ▲▲ N China
99 M16 **Helden** Limburg, SE Netherlands
27 X12 **Helena** Arkansas, C USA
33 R10 **Helena** state capital Montana, NW USA
96 H12 **Helensburgh** W Scotland, UK
184 K5 **Helensville** Auckland, North Island, NZ
95 L20 **Helgasjön** ◎ S Sweden
100 G8 **Helgoland** Eng. Heligoland. island NW Germany
Helgoland Bay see Helgoländer Bucht
100 G8 **Helgoländer Bucht** var. Helgoland Bay, Heligoland Bight. bay NW Germany
Heligoland see Helgoland
Heligoland Bight see Helgoländer Bucht
Heliopolis see Baalbek
92 I4 **Hella** Sudhurland, SW Iceland
Hellas see Greece
143 N11 **Ḥelleh, Rūd-e** ~ S Iran
98 N10 **Hellendoorn** Overijssel, E Netherlands
Hellenic Republic see Greece
121 Q10 **Hellenic Trough** undersea feature Aegean Sea, C Mediterranean Sea
94 E10 **Hellesylt** Møre og Romsdal, S Norway
98 F13 **Hellevoetsluis** Zuid-Holland, SW Netherlands
105 Q12 **Hellín** Castilla-La Mancha, C Spain
115 H19 **Hellinikon** ✕ (Athína) Attikí, C Greece
32 M12 **Hells Canyon** valley Idaho/Oregon, NW USA
148 L9 **Helmand** ◈ province S Afghanistan
148 K10 **Helmand, Daryā-ye** var. Rūd-e Hīrmand. ~ Afghanistan/Iran see also Hīrmand, Rūd-e
Helmantica see Salamanca
101 K15 **Helme** ~ C Germany
99 L15 **Helmond** Noord-Brabant, S Netherlands
96 J7 **Helmsdale** N Scotland, UK
100 K13 **Helmstedt** Niedersachsen, N Germany
163 Y10 **Helong** Jilin, NE China
36 M4 **Helper** Utah, W USA
100 O10 **Helpter Berge** hill NE Germany
95 J22 **Helsingborg** prev. Hälsingborg. Skåne, S Sweden
Helsingfors see Helsinki
95 J22 **Helsingør** Eng. Elsinore. Frederiksborg, E Denmark
93 M20 **Helsinki** Swe. Helsingfors. ● (Finland) Etelä-Suomi, S Finland
97 H25 **Helston** SW England, UK
Heltau see Cisnădie
61 C17 **Helvecia** Santa Fe, C Argentina
97 K15 **Helvellyn** ▲ NW England, UK
Helvetia see Switzerland
75 W8 **Helwân** var. Hilwân, Hulwan, Hulwān. N Egypt
97 N21 **Hemel Hempstead** E England, UK
35 U16 **Hemet** California, W USA
28 J13 **Hemingford** Nebraska, C USA
21 T13 **Hemingway** South Carolina, SE USA
92 G13 **Hemnesberget** Nordland, C Norway
25 Y8 **Hemphill** Texas, SW USA
25 V11 **Hempstead** Texas, SW USA
95 P20 **Hemse** Gotland, SE Sweden
94 F13 **Hemsedal** valley S Norway
159 T11 **Henan** var. Henan Mongolzu Zizhixian, Yêgainnyin. Qinghai, C China
161 N6 **Henan** var. Henan Sheng, Honan, Yu. ◈ province C China
184 L4 **Hen and Chickens** island group N NZ
Henan Mongolzu Zizhixian/Henan Sheng see Henan
105 O7 **Henares** ~ C Spain
165 P7 **Henashi-zaki** headland Honshū, C Japan
102 I16 **Hendaye** Pyrénées-Atlantiques, SW France
136 F11 **Hendek** Sakarya, NW Turkey
61 B21 **Henderson** Buenos Aires, E Argentina
20 I5 **Henderson** Kentucky, S USA
35 X11 **Henderson** Nevada, W USA
21 V8 **Henderson** North Carolina, SE USA
20 G10 **Henderson** Tennessee, S USA
25 W7 **Henderson** Texas, SW USA
30 J12 **Henderson Creek** ~ Illinois, N USA
186 M9 **Henderson Field** ✕ (Honiara) Guadalcanal, C Solomon Islands
191 O17 **Henderson Island** atoll N Pitcairn Islands
21 O10 **Hendersonville** North Carolina, SE USA
20 J8 **Hendersonville** Tennessee, S USA
143 O14 **Hendorābī, Jazīreh-ye** island S Iran
55 V10 **Hendrik Top** var. Hendriktop. elevation C Surinam
Hendū Kosh see Hindu Kush
14 L12 **Heney, Lac** ◎ Quebec, SE Canada
Hengchow see Hengyang
161 S15 **Hengchun** S Taiwan
159 R16 **Hengduan Shan** ▲▲ SW China
98 N12 **Hengelo** Gelderland, E Netherlands
98 O10 **Hengelo** Overijssel, E Netherlands
Hengnan see Hengyang
161 N11 **Hengshan** Hunan, S China
160 L4 **Hengshan** Shaanxi, C China
161 O4 **Hengshui** Hebei, E China
161 N12 **Hengyang** var. Hengnan, Heng-yang; prev. Hengchow. Hunan, S China
117 U11 **Heniches'k** Rus. Genichesk. Khersons'ka Oblast', S Ukraine
21 Z4 **Henlopen, Cape** headland Delaware, NE USA
Henna see Enna
94 M10 **Hennan** Gävleborg, C Sweden
102 G7 **Hennebont** Morbihan, NW France
30 L11 **Hennepin** Illinois, N USA
26 M9 **Hennessey** Oklahoma, C USA
100 N12 **Hennigsdorf** var. Hennigsdorf bei Berlin. Brandenburg, NE Germany
Hennigsdorf bei Berlin see Hennigsdorf
19 N9 **Henniker** New Hampshire, NE USA
25 S5 **Henrietta** Texas, SW USA
Henrique de Carvalho see Saurimo
30 L12 **Henry** Illinois, N USA
21 Y7 **Henry, Cape** headland Virginia, NE USA
27 P10 **Henryetta** Oklahoma, C USA
194 M7 **Henry Ice Rise** ice cap Antarctica
9 Q5 **Henry Kater, Cape** headland Baffin Island, Nunavut, NE Canada
33 R13 **Henrys Fork** ~ Idaho, NW USA
14 E15 **Hensall** Ontario, S Canada
100 J9 **Henstedt-Ulzburg** Schleswig-Holstein, N Germany
163 N7 **Hentiy** ◈ province N Mongolia
162 M7 **Hentiyn Nuruu** ▲▲ N Mongolia
183 P10 **Henty** New South Wales, SE Australia
166 L8 **Henzada** Irrawaddy, SW Myanmar
101 G19 **Heppenheim** Hessen, W Germany
32 J11 **Heppner** Oregon, NW USA
160 L15 **Hepu** prev. Lianzhou. Guangxi Zhuangzu Zizhiqu, S China
92 J2 **Heradhsvötn** ~ C Iceland
Herakleion see Irákleio
148 K5 **Herat** var. Herat; anc. Aria. Herāt, W Afghanistan
148 J5 **Herāt** ◈ province W Afghanistan
103 P14 **Hérault** ◈ department S France
103 P15 **Hérault** ~ S France
11 T16 **Herbert** Saskatchewan, S Canada
185 F22 **Herbert** Otago, South Island, NZ
38 J17 **Herbert Island** island Aleutian Islands, Alaska, USA
Herbertshöhe see Kokopo
15 Q7 **Hérbertville** Quebec, SE Canada
101 G17 **Herborn** Hessen, W Germany
113 I17 **Herceg-Novi** It. Castelnuovo; prev. Ercegnovi. Montenegro, SW Yugoslavia
11 X10 **Herchmer** Manitoba, C Canada
186 E8 **Hercules Bay** bay E PNG
92 K2 **Herdhubreidh** ▲ C Iceland
42 M13 **Heredia** Heredia, C Costa Rica
42 M12 **Heredia** off. Provincia de Heredia. ◈ province N Costa Rica
97 K21 **Hereford** W England, UK
24 M3 **Hereford** Texas, SW USA
15 Q13 **Hereford, Mont** ▲ Quebec, SE Canada
97 K21 **Herefordshire** cultural region W England, UK
191 U11 **Hereheretue** atoll Îles Tuamotu, C French Polynesia
105 N10 **Herencia** Castilla-La Mancha, C Spain
99 H18 **Herent** Vlaams Brabant, C Belgium
99 I16 **Herentals** var. Herenthals. Antwerpen, N Belgium
Herenthals see Herentals
99 H17 **Herenthout** Antwerpen, N Belgium
95 J23 **Herfølge** Roskilde, E Denmark
100 G13 **Herford** Nordrhein-Westfalen, NW Germany
27 O5 **Herington** Kansas, C USA
108 H7 **Herisau** Fr. Hérisau. Appenzell Ausser Rhoden, NE Switzerland
Héristal see Herstal
99 J18 **Herk-de-Stad** Limburg, NE Belgium
Herkulesbad/Herkulesfürdő see Băile Herculane
Herlen Gol/Herlen He see Kerulen
35 Q4 **Herlong** California, W USA
97 L26 **Herm** island Channel Islands
109 R9 **Hermagor** Slvn. Šmohor. Kärnten, S Austria
29 S7 **Herman** Minnesota, N USA
96 L1 **Herma Ness** headland NE Scotland, UK
27 V4 **Hermann** Missouri, C USA
181 Q8 **Hermannsburg** Northern Territory, N Australia
Hermannstadt see Sibiu
94 E12 **Hermansverk** Sogn og Fjordane, S Norway
138 H6 **Hermel** var. Hirmil. NE Lebanon
Hermhausen see Hajnówka
183 P6 **Hermidale** New South Wales, SE Australia
55 X9 **Herminadorp** Sipaliwini, NE Surinam
32 K11 **Hermiston** Oregon, NW USA
27 T6 **Hermitage** Missouri, C USA
186 D4 **Hermit Islands** island group N PNG
25 O7 **Hermleigh** Texas, SW USA
138 G7 **Hermon, Mount** Ar. Jabal ash Shaykh. ▲ S Syria
Hermopolis Parva see Damanhûr
28 J10 **Hermosa** South Dakota, N USA
40 F5 **Hermosillo** Sonora, NW Mexico
Hermoupolis see Ermoúpoli
111 N20 **Hernád** var. Hornád, Ger. Kundert. ~ Hungary/Slovakia
61 C18 **Hernández** Entre Ríos, E Argentina
23 V11 **Hernando** Florida, SE USA
22 L1 **Hernando** Mississippi, S USA
105 Q2 **Hernani** País Vasco, N Spain
99 F19 **Herne** Vlaams Brabant, C Belgium
101 E14 **Herne** Nordrhein-Westfalen, W Germany
95 F22 **Herning** Ringkøbing, W Denmark
Hernösand see Härnösand
121 U11 **Herodotus Basin** undersea feature E Mediterranean Sea
121 Q12 **Herodotus Trough** undersea feature C Mediterranean Sea
29 T11 **Heron Lake** Minnesota, N USA
Herowābād see Khalkhāl
95 G16 **Herre** Telemark, S Norway
29 N7 **Herreid** South Dakota, N USA
101 H22 **Herrenberg** Baden-Württemberg, S Germany
104 L14 **Herrera** Andalucía, S Spain
43 R17 **Herrera** off. Provincia de Herrera. ◈ province S Panama
104 L10 **Herrera del Duque** Extremadura, W Spain
104 M4 **Herrera de Pisuerga** Castilla-León, N Spain
41 Z13 **Herrero, Punta** headland SE Mexico
183 P16 **Herrick** Tasmania, SE Australia
30 L17 **Herrin** Illinois, N USA
20 M6 **Herrington Lake** ▣ Kentucky, S USA
95 K18 **Herrljunga** Västra Götaland, S Sweden
103 N16 **Hers** ~ S France
10 I1 **Herschel Island** island Yukon Territory, NW Canada
99 I17 **Herselt** Antwerpen, C Belgium
18 G15 **Hershey** Pennsylvania, NE USA
99 K19 **Herstal** Fr. Héristal. Liège, E Belgium
97 O21 **Hertford** E England, UK
21 X8 **Hertford** North Carolina, SE USA
97 O21 **Hertfordshire** cultural region E England, UK
181 Z9 **Hervey Bay** Queensland, E Australia
101 O14 **Herzberg** Brandenburg, E Germany
99 E18 **Herzele** Oost-Vlaanderen, NW Belgium
101 K20 **Herzogenaurach** Bayern, SE Germany
109 W4 **Herzogenburg** Niederösterreich, NE Austria
Herzogenbusch see 's-Hertogenbosch
103 N2 **Hesdin** Pas-de-Calais, N France
160 K14 **Heshan** Guangxi Zhuangzu Zizhiqu, S China
159 X10 **Heshui** var. Xihuachi. Gansu, C China
99 M25 **Hespérange** Luxembourg, SE Luxembourg
35 U14 **Hesperia** California, W USA
37 P7 **Hesperus Mountain** ▲ Colorado, C USA
10 J6 **Hess** ~ Yukon Territory, NW Canada
Hesse see Hessen
101 J21 **Hesselberg** ▲ S Germany
95 I22 **Hesselø** island E Denmark
101 H17 **Hessen** Eng./Fr. Hesse. ◈ state C Germany
192 L6 **Hess Tablemount** undersea feature C Pacific Ocean
27 N6 **Hesston** Kansas, C USA
93 G15 **Hestskjølen** ▲ C Norway
97 K18 **Heswall** NW England, UK
153 P12 **Hetauda** Central, C Nepal
Hétfalu see Săcele
28 K7 **Hettinger** North Dakota, N USA
101 L14 **Hettstedt** Sachsen-Anhalt, C Germany
92 P3 **Heuglin, Kapp** headland SE Svalbard
187 N10 **Heuru** San Cristobal, SE Solomon Islands
99 J17 **Heusden** Limburg, NE Belgium
98 J13 **Heusden** Noord-Brabant, S Netherlands
102 K3 **Hève, Cap de la** headland N France
99 H18 **Heverlee** Vlaams Brabant, C Belgium
111 L22 **Heves** Heves, NE Hungary
111 L22 **Heves** off. Heves Megye. ◈ county NE Hungary
Hevron see Hebron
45 Y13 **Hewanorra** ✕ (Saint Lucia) S Saint Lucia
160 M13 **Hexian** var. Babu, He Xian. Guangxi Zhuangzu Zizhiqu, S China
160 L6 **Heyang** Shaanxi, C China
Heydebrech see Kędzierzyn-Koźle
Heydekrug see Šilutė
97 K16 **Heysham** NW England, UK
161 O14 **Heyuan** Guangdong, S China
182 L12 **Heywood** Victoria, SE Australia
180 K3 **Heywood Islands** island group Western Australia
161 O6 **Heze** var. Caozhou. Shandong, E China
159 U11 **Hezheng** Gansu, C China
159 U11 **Hezuozhen** Gansu, C China
23 Z16 **Hialeah** Florida, SE USA
27 Q3 **Hiawatha** Kansas, C USA
36 M4 **Hiawatha** Utah, W USA
29 V4 **Hibbing** Minnesota, N USA
183 N17 **Hibbs, Point** headland Tasmania, SE Australia
Hibernia see Ireland
20 F8 **Hickman** Kentucky, S USA
21 Q9 **Hickory** North Carolina, SE USA
21 Q9 **Hickory, Lake** ◎ North Carolina, SE USA
184 Q7 **Hicks Bay** Gisborne, North Island, NZ
25 S8 **Hico** Texas, SW USA
165 T4 **Hidaka** Hokkaidō, NE Japan
164 I12 **Hidaka** Hyōgo, Honshū, SW Japan
165 T5 **Hidaka-sanmyaku** ▲▲ Hokkaidō, NE Japan
41 O6 **Hidalgo** var. Villa Hidalgo. Coahuila de Zaragoza, NE Mexico
41 N8 **Hidalgo** Nuevo León, NE Mexico
41 O10 **Hidalgo** Tamaulipas, C Mexico
41 O13 **Hidalgo** ◈ state C Mexico
40 J7 **Hidalgo del Parral** var. Parral. Chihuahua, N Mexico
100 N7 **Hiddensee** island NE Germany
80 G6 **Hidiglib, Wadi** ~ NE Sudan
109 U6 **Hieflau** Salzburg, E Austria
187 P16 **Hienghène** Province Nord, C New Caledonia
Hierosolyma see Jerusalem
64 N12 **Hierro** var. Ferro. island Islas Canarias, Spain, NE Atlantic Ocean
164 G13 **Higashi-Hiroshima** var. Higasihirosima. Hiroshima, Honshū, SW Japan
164 C12 **Higashi-suidō** strait SW Japan
Higasihirosima see Higashi-Hiroshima
Higasine see Higashine
25 P1 **Higgins** Texas, SW USA
31 P7 **Higgins Lake** ◎ Michigan, N USA
27 S4 **Higginsville** Missouri, C USA
High Atlas see Haut Atlas
30 M5 **High Falls Reservoir** ▣ Wisconsin, N USA
44 K12 **Highgate** C Jamaica
25 X11 **High Island** Texas, SW USA
31 O5 **High Island** island Michigan, N USA
30 K15 **Highland** Illinois, N USA
31 N10 **Highland Park** Illinois, N USA
21 O10 **Highlands** North Carolina, SE USA
11 O11 **High Level** Alberta, W Canada
29 O9 **Highmore** South Dakota, N USA
171 N3 **High Peak** ▲ Luzon, N Philippines
High Plains see Great Plains
21 S9 **High Point** North Carolina, SE USA
18 J13 **High Point** hill New Jersey, NE USA
11 P13 **High Prairie** Alberta, W Canada
11 Q16 **High River** Alberta, SW Canada
21 S9 **High Rock Lake** ▣ North Carolina, SE USA
23 V9 **High Springs** Florida, SE USA
High Veld see Great Karoo
97 J24 **High Willhays** ▲ SW England, UK
97 N22 **High Wycombe** prev. Chepping Wycombe, Chipping Wycombe. SE England, UK
41 P12 **Higos** var. El Higo. Veracruz-Llave, E Mexico
102 I16 **Higuer, Cap** headland NE Spain
45 R5 **Higüero, Punta** headland W Puerto Rico
45 P9 **Higüey** var. Salvaleón de Higüey. E Dominican Republic
190 G11 **Hihifo** ✕ (Matā'utu) Île Uvea, N Wallis and Futuna
81 N16 **Hiiraan** off. Gobolka Hiiraan. ◈ region C Somalia
118 E4 **Hiiumaa** off. Hiiumaa Maakond. ◈ province W Estonia
118 D4 **Hiiumaa** Ger. Dagden, Swe. Dagö. island W Estonia
Hijanah see Al Hījānah
105 S6 **Híjar** Aragón, NE Spain
191 V10 **Hikueru** atoll Îles Tuamotu, C French Polynesia
184 K3 **Hikurangi** Northland, North Island, NZ
184 Q8 **Hikurangi** ▲ North Island, NZ
192 L11 **Hikurangi Trench** var. Hikurangi Trough. undersea feature SW Pacific Ocean
Hikurangi Trough see Hikurangi Trench
190 B15 **Hikutavake** NW Niue
121 Q12 **Hilāl, Ra's al** headland N Libya
61 A24 **Hilario Ascasubi** Buenos Aires, E Argentina
101 K17 **Hildburghausen** Thüringen, C Germany
101 E15 **Hilden** Nordrhein-Westfalen, W Germany
100 I13 **Hildesheim** Niedersachsen, N Germany
33 T9 **Hilger** Montana, NW USA
Hili see Hilli
Hilla see Al Ḥillah
45 O14 **Hillaby, Mount** ▲ N Barbados
95 K19 **Hillared** Västra Götaland, S Sweden
195 R12 **Hillary Coast** physical region Antarctica
42 G2 **Hill Bank** Orange Walk, N Belize
33 O14 **Hill City** Idaho, NW USA
26 K3 **Hill City** Kansas, C USA
29 V5 **Hill City** Minnesota, N USA
28 J10 **Hill City** South Dakota, N USA
65 C24 **Hill Cove Settlement** West Falkland, Falkland Islands
98 H10 **Hillegom** Zuid-Holland, W Netherlands
95 J22 **Hillerød** Frederiksborg, E Denmark
36 M7 **Hillers, Mount** ▲ Utah, W USA
153 S13 **Hilli** var. Hili. Rajshahi, NW Bangladesh
29 R11 **Hills** Minnesota, N USA
30 L14 **Hillsboro** Illinois, N USA
27 N5 **Hillsboro** Kansas, C USA
27 X5 **Hillsboro** Missouri, C USA
19 N10 **Hillsboro** New Hampshire, NE USA
37 Q14 **Hillsboro** New Mexico, SW USA
29 R4 **Hillsboro** North Dakota, N USA
31 R14 **Hillsboro** Ohio, N USA
32 G11 **Hillsboro** Oregon, NW USA
25 T8 **Hillsboro** Texas, SW USA
30 K8 **Hillsboro** Wisconsin, N USA
23 Y14 **Hillsboro Canal** canal Florida, SE USA
45 Y15 **Hillsborough** Carriacou, N Grenada
97 G15 **Hillsborough** E Northern Ireland, UK
21 U9 **Hillsborough** North Carolina, SE USA
31 Q10 **Hillsdale** Michigan, N USA
183 O8 **Hillston** New South Wales, SE Australia
21 R7 **Hillsville** Virginia, NE USA
96 L2 **Hillswick** NE Scotland, UK
Hill Tippera see Tripura
38 H11 **Hilo** Hawaii, USA, C Pacific Ocean
18 F9 **Hilton** New York, NE USA
14 C10 **Hilton Beach** Ontario, S Canada
21 R16 **Hilton Head Island** South Carolina, SE USA
21 R16 **Hilton Head Island** island South Carolina, SE USA
99 J15 **Hilvarenbeek** Noord-Brabant, S Netherlands
98 J11 **Hilversum** Noord-Holland, C Netherlands
Hilwân see Helwân
152 J7 **Himāchal Pradesh** ◈ state NW India
Himalaya/Himalaya Shan see Himalayas
152 M9 **Himalayas** var. Himalaya, Chin. Himalaya Shan. ▲▲ S Asia
171 P6 **Himamaylan** Negros, C Philippines
93 K15 **Himanka** Länsi-Suomi, W Finland
Himara see Himarë
113 L23 **Himarë** var. Himara. Vlorë, S Albania
138 M2 **Ḥimār, Wādī al** dry watercourse N Syria
154 D9 **Himatnagar** Gujarāt, W India
109 Y4 **Himberg** Niederösterreich, E Austria
164 I13 **Himeji** var. Himezi. Hyōgo, Honshū, SW Japan
164 E14 **Hime-jima** island SW Japan
Himezi see Himeji
164 L13 **Himi** Toyama, Honshū, SW Japan
109 S9 **Himmelberg** Kärnten, S Austria
138 I5 **Ḥimṣ** var. Homs; anc. Emesa. Ḥimṣ, C Syria
138 K6 **Ḥimṣ** off. Muḥāfaẓat Ḥimṣ, var. Homs. ◈ governorate C Syria
138 I5 **Ḥimṣ, Buḥayrat** var. Buḥayrat Qaṭṭīnah. ◎ W Syria
171 R7 **Hinatuan** Mindanao, S Philippines
117 N10 **Hînceşti** var. Hânceşti; prev. Kotovsk. C Moldova
44 M9 **Hinche** C Haiti
181 X5 **Hinchinbrook Island** island Queensland, NE Australia
39 S12 **Hinchinbrook Island** island Alaska, USA
97 M19 **Hinckley** C England, UK
29 V7 **Hinckley** Minnesota, N USA
36 K5 **Hinckley** Utah, W USA
18 J9 **Hinckley Reservoir** ▣ New York, NE USA
152 I12 **Hindaun** Rājasthān, N India
Hindenburg/Hindenburg in Oberschlesien see Zabrze
Hindiya see Al Hindīyah
21 O6 **Hindman** Kentucky, S USA
182 L10 **Hindmarsh, Lake** ◎ Victoria, SE Australia
185 G19 **Hinds** Canterbury, South Island, NZ
185 G19 **Hinds** ~ South Island, NZ
95 H23 **Hindsholm** island C Denmark
149 S4 **Hindu Kush** Per. Hendū Kosh. ▲▲ Afghanistan/Pakistan
155 H19 **Hindupur** Andhra Pradesh, E India
11 O12 **Hines Creek** Alberta, W Canada
23 W6 **Hinesville** Georgia, SE USA
154 I12 **Hinganghāt** Mahārāshtra, C India
149 N15 **Hingol** ~ SW Pakistan
154 H13 **Hingoli** Mahārāshtra, C India
137 R13 **Hınıs** Erzurum, E Turkey
92 O2 **Hinlopenstretet** strait N Svalbard
92 G10 **Hinnøya** island C Norway
108 H10 **Hinterrhein** ~ SW Switzerland
11 O14 **Hinton** Alberta, SW Canada
26 M10 **Hinton** Oklahoma, C USA
21 R6 **Hinton** West Virginia, NE USA
Hios see Chíos
41 N8 **Hipolito** Coahuila de Zaragoza, NE Mexico
Hipponium see Vibo Valentia
164 B13 **Hirado** Nagasaki, Hirado-shima, SW Japan
164 B13 **Hirado-shima** island SW Japan
165 P16 **Hirakubo-saki** headland Ishigaki-jima, SW Japan
154 M11 **Hīrākud Reservoir** ▣ E India
Hir al Gharbi, Qasr al see Ḥayr al Gharbī, Qaṣr al
165 Q16 **Hirara** Okinawa, Miyako-jima, SW Japan
Qasr al Hir Ash Sharqī see Ḥayr ash Sharqī, Qaṣr al
164 G12 **Hirata** Shimane, Honshū, SW Japan
Hiratuka see Hiratsuka
136 I13 **Hirfanlı Barajı** ▣ C Turkey
155 G18 **Hiriyūr** Karnātaka, W India
Hîrlău see Hârlău
148 K10 **Hīrmand, Rūd-e** var. Daryā-ye Helmand. ~ Afghanistan/Iran see also Helmand, Daryā-ye
Hirmil see Hermel
165 T5 **Hiroo** Hokkaidō, NE Japan
165 Q7 **Hirosaki** Aomori, Honshū, C Japan
164 F13 **Hiroshima** var. Hirosima. Hiroshima, Honshū, SW Japan
164 G13 **Hiroshima** off. Hiroshima-ken, var. Hirosima. ◈ prefecture Honshū, SW Japan
Hirosima see Hiroshima
Hirschberg/Hirschberg im Riesengebirge/Hirschberg in Schlesien see Jelenia Góra
103 Q3 **Hirson** Aisne, N France
Hîrşova see Hârşova
95 G19 **Hirtshals** Nordjylland, N Denmark
152 H10 **Hisār** Haryāna, NW India
186 E9 **Hisiu** Central, SW PNG
147 P13 **Hisor** Rus. Gissar. W Tajikistan
Hispalis see Sevilla
Hispana/Hispania see Spain
44 M7 **Hispaniola** island Dominion Republic/Haiti
64 F11 **Hispaniola Basin** var. Hispaniola Trough. undersea feature SW Atlantic Ocean
Hispaniola Trough see Hispaniola Basin
Histonium see Vasto
139 R7 **Hīt** SW Iraq
165 P14 **Hita** Ōita, Kyūshū, SW Japan
165 P12 **Hitachi** var. Hitati. Ibaraki, Honshū, S Japan
165 P12 **Hitachi-Ōta** var. Hitatiôta. Ibaraki, Honshū, S Japan
Hitati see Hitachi
Hitatiôta see Hitachi-Ōta
97 O21 **Hitchin** E England, UK
191 Q7 **Hitiaa** Tahiti, W French Polynesia
164 D15 **Hitoyoshi** var. Hitoyosi. Kumamoto, Kyūshū, SW Japan
Hitoyosi see Hitoyoshi
94 F7 **Hitra** prev. Hitteren. island S Norway
Hitteren see Hitra
187 Q11 **Hiu** island Torres Islands, N Vanuatu
165 O11 **Hiuchiga-take** ▲ Honshū, C Japan
191 X7 **Hiva Oa** island Îles Marquises, N French Polynesia
20 M10 **Hiwassee Lake** ▣ North Carolina, SE USA
20 M10 **Hiwassee River** ~ SE USA
95 H20 **Hjallerup** Nordjylland, N Denmark
95 M16 **Hjälmaren** Eng. Lake Hjalmar. ◎ C Sweden
Hjalmar, Lake see Hjälmaren
95 C14 **Hjellestad** Hordaland, S Norway
95 D16 **Hjelmeland** Rogaland, S Norway
94 G10 **Hjerkinn** Oppland, S Norway
95 L18 **Hjo** Västra Götaland, S Sweden
95 G19 **Hjørring** Nordjylland, N Denmark
167 O1 **Hkakabo Razi** ▲ Myanmar/China
167 N1 **Hkring Bum** ▲ N Myanmar
83 L21 **Hlathikulu** var. Hlatikulu. S Swaziland
Hlatikulu see Hlathikulu
Hliboka see Hlyboka
111 F17 **Hlinsko** var. Hlinsko v Čechách. Pardubický Kraj, C Czech Republic
Hlinsko v Čechách see Hlinsko
117 S6 **Hlobyne** Rus. Globino. Poltavs'ka Oblast', NE Ukraine
111 H20 **Hlohovec** Ger. Freistadtl, Hung. Galgóc; prev. Frakštát. Trnavský Kraj, W Slovakia
83 J23 **Hlotse** var. Leribe. NW Lesotho

◆ Country ● Country Capital ◇ Dependent Territory ○ Dependent Territory Capital ◈ Administrative Region ✕ International Airport ▲ Mountain ▲▲ Mountain Range Volcano ~ River ◎ Lake ▣ Reservoir

111 I17 **Hlučín** *Ger.* Hultschin, *Pol.* Hulczyn. Ostravský Kraj, E Czech Republic
117 S2 **Hlukhiv** *Rus.* Glukhov. Sums'ka Oblast', NE Ukraine
119 K21 **Hlushkavichy** *Rus.* Glushkevichi. Homyel'skaya Voblasts', SE Belarus
119 L18 **Hlusk** *Rus.* Glusk, Glussk. Mahilyowskaya Voblasts', E Belarus
116 K8 **Hlyboka** *Ger.* Hliboka, *Rus.* Glybokaya. Chernivets'ka Oblast', W Ukraine
118 K13 **Hlybokaye** *Rus.* Glubokoye. Vitsyebskaya Voblasts', N Belarus
77 Q16 **Ho** SE Ghana
167 S6 **Hoa Binh** Hoa Binh, N Vietnam
83 E20 **Hoachanas** Hardap, C Namibia
Hoai Nhơn *see* Bông Sơn
167 T8 **Hoa Lac** Quang Binh, C Vietnam
167 S5 **Hoang Liên Sơn** ▲ N Vietnam
83 B17 **Hoanib** ≈ NW Namibia
33 S15 **Hoback Peak** ▲ Wyoming, C USA
183 P17 **Hobart** *prev.* Hobarton, Hobart Town. *state capital* Tasmania, SE Australia
26 L11 **Hobart** Oklahoma, C USA
183 P17 **Hobart** × Tasmania, SE Australia
Hobarton/Hobart Town *see* Hobart
37 W14 **Hobbs** New Mexico, SW USA
194 L12 **Hobbs Coast** *physical region* Antarctica
23 Z14 **Hobe Sound** Florida, SE USA
Hobicaurikány *see* Uricani
54 E12 **Hobo** Huila, S Colombia
99 G16 **Hoboken** Antwerpen, N Belgium
158 K3 **Hoboksar** *var.* Hoboksar Mongol Zizhixian. Xinjiang Uygur Zizhiqu, NW China
Hoboksar Mongol Zizhixian *see* Hoboksar
95 G21 **Hobro** Nordjylland, N Denmark
21 X10 **Hobucken** North Carolina, SE USA
95 O20 **Hoburgen** *headland* SE Sweden
81 P15 **Hobyo** *It.* Obbia. Mudug, E Somalia
109 R8 **Hochalmspitze** ▲ SW Austria
109 Q4 **Hochburg** Oberösterreich, N Austria
108 F8 **Hochdorf** Luzern, N Switzerland
109 N8 **Hochfeiler** *It.* Gran Pilastro. ▲ Austria/Italy
167 T14 **Hô Chi Minh** *var.* Ho Chi Minhl City; *prev.* Saigon. S Vietnam
Ho Chi Minh City *see* Hô Chi Minh
108 I7 **Höchst** Vorarlberg, NW Austria
Höchstadt *see* Höchstadt an der Aisch
101 K19 **Höchstadt an der Aisch** *var.* Höchstadt. Bayern, C Germany
108 L9 **Hochwilde** *It.* L'Altissima. ▲ Austria/Italy
109 S7 **Hochwildstelle** ▲ C Austria
31 T14 **Hocking River** ≈ Ohio, N USA
Hoctúm *see* Hoctún
41 X12 **Hoctún** *var.* Hoctúm. Yucatán, E Mexico
Hodeida *see* Al Ḩudaydah
20 K6 **Hodgenville** Kentucky, S USA
11 T17 **Hodgeville** Saskatchewan, S Canada
76 L9 **Hodh ech Chargui** ◈ *region* E Mauritania
Hodh el Garbi *see* Hodh el Gharbi
76 J10 **Hodh el Gharbi** *var.* Hodh el Garbi. ◈ *region* S Mauritania
111 L25 **Hódmezővásárhely** Csongrád, SE Hungary
74 J6 **Hodna, Chott El** *var.* Chott el-Hodna, *Ar.* Shatt al-Hodna. *salt lake* N Algeria
Hodna, Shatt al- *see* Hodna, Chott El
111 G19 **Hodonín** *Ger.* Göding. Brněnský Kraj, SE Czech Republic
162 G6 **Hödrögö** Dzavhan, N Mongolia
Hodság/Hodschag *see* Odžaci
39 R7 **Hodzana River** ≈ Alaska, USA
Hoei *see* Huy
99 H19 **Hoeilaart** Vlaams Brabant, C Belgium
Hoë Karoo *see* Great Karoo
98 F12 **Hoek van Holland** *Eng.* Hook of Holland. Zuid-Holland, W Netherlands
98 L11 **Hoenderloo** Gelderland, E Netherlands
99 L18 **Hoensbroek** Limburg, SE Netherlands
163 Y11 **Hoeryŏng** NE North Korea
99 K18 **Hoeselt** Limburg, NE Belgium
98 K11 **Hoevelaken** Gelderland, C Netherlands
Hoey *see* Huy
101 M18 **Hof** Bayern, SE Germany
Höfdhakaupstadhur *see* Skagaströnd
Hofei *see* Hefei
101 G18 **Hofheim am Taunus** Hessen, W Germany
Hofmarkt *see* Odorheiu Secuiesc
92 L3 **Höfn** Austurland, SE Iceland
94 N13 **Hofors** Gävleborg, C Sweden
92 J6 **Hofsjökull** *glacier* C Iceland
92 J1 **Hofsós** Nordhurland Vestra, N Iceland
164 E13 **Hōfu** Yamaguchi, Honshū, SW Japan
Hofuf *see* Al Hufūf
95 J22 **Höganäs** Skåne, S Sweden
183 P14 **Hogan Group** *island group* Tasmania, SE Australia
23 R4 **Hogansville** Georgia, SE USA
39 P8 **Hogatza River** ≈ Alaska, USA
28 I14 **Hogback Mountain** ▲ Nebraska, C USA
95 G14 **Høgevarde** ▲ S Norway
Högfors *see* Karkkila
31 P5 **Hog Island** *island* Michigan, N USA
21 Y6 **Hog Island** *island* Virginia, NE USA
Hogoley Islands *see* Chuuk Islands
95 N20 **Högsby** Kalmar, S Sweden
36 K1 **Hogup Mountains** ▲ Utah, W USA
101 E17 **Hohe Acht** ▲ W Germany
Hohenelbe *see* Vrchlabí
108 I7 **Hohenems** Vorarlberg, W Austria
Hohenmauth *see* Vysoké Mýto
Hohensalza *see* Inowrocław
Hohenstadt *see* Zábřeh
Hohenstein in Ostpreussen *see* Olsztynek
20 I9 **Hohenwald** Tennessee, S USA
101 L17 **Hohenwarte-Stausee** ▣ C Germany
Hohes Venn *see* Hautes Fagnes
109 Q8 **Hohe Tauern** ▲ W Austria
163 O13 **Hohhot** *var.* Huhehot, Huhuohaote, *Mong.* Kukukhoto; *prev.* Kweisui, Kwesui. Nei Mongol Zizhiqu, N China
103 U6 **Hohneck** ▲ NE France
77 Q16 **Hohoe** E Ghana
164 E12 **Hōhoku** Yamaguchi, Honshū, SW Japan
159 O11 **Hoh Sai Hu** ◎ C China
159 N11 **Hoh Xil Hu** ◎ C China
158 L11 **Hoh Xil Shan** ▲ W China
167 U10 **Hôi An** *prev.* Faifo. Quang Nam-Đa Nẵng, C Vietnam
Hoï-Hao/Hoihow *see* Haikou
81 F17 **Hoima** W Uganda
26 L5 **Hoisington** Kansas, C USA
Hojagala *see* Khodzhakala
Hojambaz *see* Khodzhambas
95 H23 **Højby** Fyn, C Denmark
95 F24 **Højer** Sønderjylland, SW Denmark
164 E14 **Hōjō** *var.* Hôzyô. Ehime, Shikoku, SW Japan
184 J3 **Hokianga Harbour** *inlet* SE Tasman Sea
185 F17 **Hokitika** West Coast, South Island, NZ
165 U4 **Hokkai-dō** ◈ *territory* Hokkaidō, NE Japan
165 T3 **Hokkaidō** *prev.* Ezo, Yeso, Yezo. *island* NE Japan
95 G15 **Hokksund** Buskerud, S Norway
143 S4 **Hokmābād** Khorāsān, N Iran
Hokō *see* P'ohang
Hoko-guntō/Hoko-shotō *see* P'enghu Liehtao
137 T12 **Hoktemberyan** *Rus.* Oktemberyan. SW Armenia
94 F13 **Hol** Buskerud, S Norway
117 R11 **Hola Prystan'** *Rus.* Golaya Pristan. Khersons'ka Oblast', S Ukraine
95 I23 **Holbæk** Vestsjælland, E Denmark
162 G6 **Holboo** Dzavhan, W Mongolia
183 P10 **Holbrook** New South Wales, SE Australia
37 N11 **Holbrook** Arizona, SW USA
27 S5 **Holden** Missouri, C USA
36 K5 **Holden** Utah, W USA
27 O11 **Holdenville** Oklahoma, C USA
29 O16 **Holdrege** Nebraska, C USA
35 X3 **Hole in the Mountain Peak** ▲ Nevada, W USA
155 G20 **Hole Narsipur** Karnātaka, W India
111 H18 **Holešov** *Ger.* Holleschau. Zlínský Kraj, E Czech Republic
45 N14 **Holetown** *prev.* Jamestown. W Barbados
31 Q12 **Holgate** Ohio, N USA
44 I7 **Holguín** Holguín, SE Cuba
23 V12 **Holiday** Florida, SE USA
39 O12 **Holitna River** ≈ Alaska, USA
94 J13 **Höljes** Värmland, C Sweden
109 X3 **Hollabrunn** Niederösterreich, NE Austria
36 L3 **Holladay** Utah, W USA
11 X16 **Holland** Manitoba, S Canada
31 O9 **Holland** Michigan, N USA
25 T9 **Holland** Texas, SW USA
Holland *see* Netherlands
22 K4 **Hollandale** Mississippi, S USA
Hollandia *see* Jayapura
Hollandsch Diep *see* Hollands Diep
99 H14 **Hollands Diep** *var.* Hollandsch Diep. *channel* SW Netherlands
Holleschau *see* Holešov
25 R5 **Holliday** Texas, SW USA
18 E15 **Hollidaysburg** Pennsylvania, NE USA
21 S6 **Hollins** Virginia, NE USA
26 J12 **Hollis** Oklahoma, C USA
35 O10 **Hollister** California, W USA
27 T8 **Hollister** Missouri, C USA
93 M19 **Hollola** Etelä-Suomi, S Finland
98 K4 **Hollum** Friesland, N Netherlands
95 J23 **Höllviksnäs** Skåne, S Sweden
37 W6 **Holly** Colorado, C USA
31 R9 **Holly** Michigan, N USA
21 S14 **Holly Hill** South Carolina, SE USA
21 W11 **Holly Ridge** North Carolina, SE USA
22 L1 **Holly Springs** Mississippi, S USA
23 Z15 **Hollywood** Florida, SE USA
8 J6 **Holman** Victoria Island, Northwest Territories, N Canada
92 I2 **Hólmavík** Vestfirdhir, NW Iceland
30 J7 **Holmen** Wisconsin, N USA
23 R8 **Holmes Creek** ≈ Alabama/Florida, SE USA
95 H16 **Holmestrand** Vestfold, S Norway
93 J16 **Holmön** *island* N Sweden
95 E22 **Holmsland Klit** *beach* W Denmark
93 J16 **Holmsund** Västerbotten, N Sweden
95 Q18 **Holmudden** *headland* SE Sweden
138 F10 **Holon** *var.* Kholon. Tel Aviv, C Israel
117 P8 **Holovanivs'k** *Rus.* Golovanevsk. Kirovohrads'ka Oblast', C Ukraine
95 F21 **Holstebro** Ringkøbing, W Denmark
95 F23 **Holsted** Ribe, W Denmark
29 T13 **Holstein** Iowa, C USA
Holsteinborg/Holsteinsborg/Holstenborg/Holstensborg *see* Sisimiut
21 O8 **Holston River** ≈ Tennessee, S USA
31 Q9 **Holt** Michigan, N USA
98 N10 **Holten** Overijssel, E Netherlands
27 P3 **Holton** Kansas, C USA
27 U5 **Holts Summit** Missouri, C USA
35 X17 **Holtville** Califo rnia, W USA
98 L5 **Holwerd** *Fris.* Holwert. Friesland, N Netherlands
Holwert *see* Holwerd
39 O11 **Holy Cross** Alaska, USA
37 R4 **Holy Cross, Mount Of The** ▲ Colorado, C USA
97 I18 **Holyhead** *Wel.* Caer Gybi. NW Wales, UK
97 H18 **Holy Island** *island* NW Wales, UK
96 L12 **Holy Island** *island* NE England, UK
37 W3 **Holyoke** Colorado, C USA
18 M11 **Holyoke** Massachusetts, NE USA
101 I14 **Holzminden** Niedersachsen, C Germany
81 G19 **Homa Bay** Nyanza, W Kenya
Homāyūnshahr *see* Khomeynīshahr
77 P11 **Hombori** Mopti, S Mali
101 E20 **Homburg** Saarland, SW Germany
9 Q5 **Home Bay** *bay* Baffin Bay, Nunavut, NE Canada
Homenau *see* Humenné
39 Q13 **Homer** Alaska, USA
22 H4 **Homer** Louisiana, S USA
18 H10 **Homer** New York, NE USA
23 V7 **Homerville** Georgia, SE USA
23 Y16 **Homestead** Florida, SE USA
27 O9 **Hominy** Oklahoma, C USA
94 H8 **Hommelvik** Sør-Trøndelag, S Norway
95 C16 **Hommersåk** Rogaland, S Norway
155 H15 **Homnābād** Karnātaka, C India
22 J7 **Homochitto River** ≈ Mississippi, S USA
83 N20 **Homoine** Inhambane, SE Mozambique
112 O12 **Homoljske Planine** ▲ E Yugoslavia
Homonna *see* Humenné
Homs *see* Al Khums, Libya
Homs *see* Ḩimş, Syria
119 P19 **Homyel'** *Rus.* Gomel'. Homyel'skaya Voblasts', SE Belarus
118 L12 **Homyel'** Vitsyebskaya Voblasts', N Belarus
119 L19 **Homyel'skaya Voblasts'** *prev. Rus.* Gomel'skaya Oblast'. ◈ *province* SE Belarus
Honan *see* Henan, China
Honan *see* Luoyang, China
165 U4 **Honbetsu** Hokkaidō, NE Japan
Honctő *see* Gurahonţ
54 E9 **Honda** Tolima, C Colombia
83 D24 **Hondeklip** *Afr.* Hondeklipbaai. Northern Cape, W South Africa
Hondeklipbaai *see* Hondeklip
11 Q13 **Hondo** Alberta, W Canada
164 C15 **Hondo** Kumamoto, Shimo-jima, SW Japan
25 Q12 **Hondo** Texas, SW USA
42 G1 **Hondo** ≈ Central America
Hondo *see* Honshū
42 G6 **Honduras** *off.* Republic of Honduras. ◆ *republic* Central America
Honduras, Golfo de *see* Honduras, Gulf of
42 H4 **Honduras, Gulf of** *Sp.* Golfo de Honduras. *gulf* W Caribbean Sea
11 V12 **Hone** Manitoba, C Canada
21 P12 **Honea Path** South Carolina, SE USA
95 H14 **Hønefoss** Buskerud, S Norway
31 S12 **Honey Creek** ≈ Ohio, N USA
25 V5 **Honey Grove** Texas, SW USA
35 Q4 **Honey Lake** ◎ California, W USA
102 L4 **Honfleur** Calvados, N France
Hon Gai *see* Hông Gai
161 O8 **Hong'an** *prev.* Huang'an. Hubei, C China
Hongay *see* Hông Gai
167 T6 **Hông Gai** *var.* Hon Gai, Hongay. Quang Ninh, N Vietnam
161 O15 **Honghai Wan** *bay* N South China Sea
Hông Hà, Sông *see* Red River
161 O7 **Hong He** ≈ C China
161 N9 **Hong Hu** ◎ C China
160 L11 **Hongjiang** Hunan, S China
161 O15 **Hong Kong** *Chin.* Xianggang. S China
159 P7 **Hongliuyuan** Gansu, N China
163 O9 **Hongor** Dornogovĭ, SE Mongolia
161 S8 **Hongqiao** × (Shanghai) Shanghai Shi, E China
160 K14 **Hongshui He** ≈ S China
160 M5 **Hongtong** Shanxi, C China
164 J15 **Hongū** Wakayama, Honshū, SW Japan
Honguedo, Détroit d' *see* Honguedo Passage
15 Y5 **Honguedo Passage** *var.* Honguedo Strait, *Fr.* Détroit d'Honguedo. *strait* Quebec, E Canada
Honguedo Strait *see* Honguedo Passage
Hongwan *see* Sunan
163 X13 **Hongwŏn** E North Korea
160 H7 **Hongyuan** *prev.* Hurama. Sichuan, C China
161 Q7 **Hongze Hu** *var.* Hung-tse Hu. ◎ E China
186 L9 **Honiara** ● (Solomon Islands) Guadalcanal, C Solomon Islands
165 P8 **Honjō** *var.* Honzyô. Akita, Honshū, C Japan
93 K18 **Honkajoki** Länsi-Suomi, W Finland
92 K7 **Honningsvåg** Finnmark, N Norway
95 I19 **Hönö** Västra Götaland, S Sweden
38 G11 **Honokaa** *Haw.* Honoka'a. Hawaii, USA, C Pacific Ocean
38 G11 **Honokohau** *Haw.* Honokōhau. Hawaii, USA, C Pacific Ocean
38 D9 **Honolulu** ● Oahu, Hawaii, USA, C Pacific Ocean
38 H11 **Honomu** *Haw.* Honomū. Hawaii, USA, C Pacific Ocean
105 P10 **Honrubia** Castilla-La Mancha, C Spain
164 M12 **Honshū** *var.* Hondo, Honsyû. *island* SW Japan
Honsyû *see* Honshū
Honte *see* Westerschelde
Honzyô *see* Honjō
8 K8 **Hood** ≈ Nunavut, NW Canada
Hood Island *see* Española, Isla
32 H11 **Hood, Mount** ▲ Oregon, NW USA
32 H11 **Hood River** Oregon, NW USA
98 H10 **Hoofddorp** Noord-Holland, W Netherlands
99 G15 **Hoogerheide** Noord-Brabant, S Netherlands
98 N8 **Hoogeveen** Drenthe, NE Netherlands
98 O6 **Hoogezand-Sappemeer** Groningen, NE Netherlands
98 J8 **Hoogkarspel** Noord-Holland, NW Netherlands
98 N5 **Hoogkerk** Groningen, NE Netherlands
98 G13 **Hoogvliet** Zuid-Holland, SW Netherlands
26 I8 **Hooker** Oklahoma, C USA
97 E21 **Hook Head** *Ir.* Rinn Duáin. *headland* SE Ireland
Hook of Holland *see* Hoek van Holland
162 J9 **Hoolt** Övörhangay, C Mongolia
39 W13 **Hoonah** Chichagof Island, Alaska, USA
38 L11 **Hooper Bay** Alaska, USA
31 N13 **Hoopeston** Illinois, N USA
95 K22 **Höör** Skåne, S Sweden
98 I9 **Hoorn** Noord-Holland, NW Netherlands
18 L10 **Hoosic River** ≈ New York, NE USA
Hoosier State *see* Indiana
35 Y11 **Hoover Dam** *dam* Arizona/Nevada, W USA
162 I9 **Höövör** Övörhangay, C Mongolia
137 Q11 **Hopa** Artvin, NE Turkey
18 J14 **Hopatcong** New Jersey, NE USA
10 M17 **Hope** British Columbia, SW Canada
39 R12 **Hope** Alaska, USA
27 T14 **Hope** Arkansas, C USA
31 P14 **Hope** Indiana, N USA
29 Q5 **Hope** North Dakota, N USA
13 Q7 **Hopedale** Newfoundland, NE Canada
Hopeh/Hopei *see* Hebei
180 K13 **Hope, Lake** *salt lake* Western Australia
41 X13 **Hopelchén** Campeche, SE Mexico
21 U11 **Hope Mills** North Carolina, SE USA
183 O7 **Hope, Mount** New South Wales, SE Australia
92 P4 **Hopen** *island* SE Svalbard
197 Q4 **Hope, Point** *headland* Alaska, USA
12 M3 **Hopes Advance, Cap** *headland* Quebec, NE Canada
182 L10 **Hopetoun** Victoria, SE Australia
83 H23 **Hopetown** Northern Cape, W South Africa
21 W6 **Hopewell** Virginia, NE USA
109 O7 **Hopfgarten-im-Brixental** Tirol, W Austria
181 N8 **Hopkins Lake** *salt lake* Western Australia
182 M12 **Hopkins River** ≈ Victoria, SE Australia
20 I7 **Hopkinsville** Kentucky, S USA
34 M6 **Hopland** California, W USA
95 G24 **Hoptrup** Sønderjylland, SW Denmark
32 F9 **Hoquiam** Washington, NW USA
29 R6 **Horace** North Dakota, N USA
137 R12 **Horasan** Erzurum, NE Turkey
101 G22 **Horb am Neckar** Baden-Württemberg, S Germany
95 K23 **Hörby** Skåne, S Sweden
43 P16 **Horconcitos** Chiriquí, W Panama
95 C14 **Hordaland** ◈ *county* S Norway
116 H13 **Horezu** Vâlcea, SW Romania
108 G7 **Horgen** Zürich, N Switzerland
162 I7 **Horgo** Arhangay, C Mongolia
Hörin *see* Fenglin
163 O13 **Horinger** Nei Mongol Zizhiqu, N China
162 I9 **Horiult** Bayanhongor, C Mongolia
11 U17 **Horizon** Saskatchewan, S Canada
192 K9 **Horizon Bank** *undersea feature* S Pacific Ocean
192 L10 **Horizon Deep** *undersea feature* W Pacific Ocean
95 L14 **Hörken** Örebro, S Sweden
119 O15 **Horki** *Rus.* Gorki. Mahilyowskaya Voblasts', E Belarus
195 O10 **Horlick Mountains** ▲ Antarctica
117 X7 **Horlivka** *Rom.* Adâncata, *Rus.* Gorlovka. Donets'ka Oblast', E Ukraine
143 V11 **Ḩormak** Sīstān va Balūchestān, SE Iran
143 R13 **Hormozgān** *off.* Ostān-e Hormozgān. ◈ *province* S Iran
Hormoz, Tangeh-ye *see* Hormuz, Strait of
141 W6 **Hormuz, Strait of** *var.* Strait of Ormuz, *Per.* Tangeh-ye Hormoz. *strait* Iran/Oman
109 W2 **Horn** Niederösterreich, NE Austria
95 M18 **Horn** Östergötland, S Sweden
8 I9 **Horn** ≈ Northwest Territories, NW Canada
Hornád *see* Hernád
8 I6 **Hornaday** ≈ Northwest Territories, NW Canada
92 H13 **Hornavan** ◎ N Sweden
65 C24 **Hornby Mountains** *hill range* West Falkland, Falkland Islands
Horn, Cape *see* Hornos, Cabo de
97 O18 **Horncastle** E England, UK
95 N14 **Horndal** Dalarna, C Sweden
93 I16 **Hörnefors** Västerbotten, N Sweden
18 F11 **Hornell** New York, NE USA
Horné Nové Mesto *see* Kysucké Nové Mesto
12 F12 **Hornepayne** Ontario, S Canada
94 D10 **Hornindalsvatnet** ◎ S Norway
101 G22 **Hornisgrinde** ▲ SW Germany
22 M9 **Horn Island** *island* Mississippi, S USA
63 J26 **Hornos, Cabo de** *Eng.* Cape Horn. *headland* S Chile
117 S10 **Hornostayivka** Khersons'ka Oblast', S Ukraine
183 T9 **Hornsby** New South Wales, SE Australia
97 O16 **Hornsea** E England, UK
94 O11 **Hornslandet** *peninsula* C Sweden
95 H22 **Hornslet** Århus, C Denmark
92 O4 **Hornsundtind** ▲ S Svalbard
Horochów *see* Horokhiv
116 J7 **Horodenka** *Rus.* Gorodenka. Ivano-Frankivs'ka Oblast', W Ukraine
117 Q2 **Horodnya** *Rus.* Gorodnya. Chernihivs'ka Oblast', NE Ukraine
116 K6 **Horodok** Khmel'nyts'ka Oblast', W Ukraine
116 H5 **Horodok** *Pol.* Gródek Jagielloński, *Rus.* Gorodok, Gorodok Yagellonski. L'vivs'ka Oblast', NW Ukraine
117 Q6 **Horodyshche** *Rus.* Gorodishche. Cherkas'ka Oblast', C Ukraine
165 T3 **Horokanai** Hokkaidō, NE Japan
116 J4 **Horokhiv** *Pol.* Horochów, *Rus.* Gorokhov. Volyns'ka Oblast', NW Ukraine
165 T4 **Horoshiri-dake** *var.* Horosiri Dake. ▲ Hokkaidō, N Japan
Horosiri Dake *see* Horoshiri-dake
111 C17 **Hořovice** *Ger.* Horowitz. Středočeský Kraj, W Czech Republic
Horowitz *see* Hořovice
163 T9 **Horqin Youyi Zhongqi** Nei Mongol Zizhiqu, NE China
163 U11 **Horqin Zuoyi Houqi** Nei Mongol Zizhiqu, N China
163 T9 **Horqin Zuoyi Zhongqi** Nei Mongol Zizhiqu, N China
62 O5 **Horqueta** Concepción, C Paraguay
55 O12 **Horqueta Minas** Amazonas, S Venezuela
95 J20 **Horred** Västra Götaland, S Sweden
151 J19 **Horsburgh Atoll** *atoll* N Maldives
20 K7 **Horse Cave** Kentucky, S USA
37 V6 **Horse Creek** ≈ Colorado, C USA
27 S6 **Horse Creek** ≈ Missouri, C USA
18 G11 **Horseheads** New York, NE USA
37 P13 **Horse Mount** ▲ New Mexico, SW USA
95 G22 **Horsens** Vejle, C Denmark
65 F25 **Horse Pasture Point** *headland* W Saint Helena
33 N13 **Horseshoe Bend** Idaho, NW USA
36 L13 **Horseshoe Reservoir** ▣ Arizona, SW USA
64 M9 **Horseshoe Seamounts** *undersea feature* E Atlantic Ocean
182 L11 **Horsham** Victoria, SE Australia
97 O23 **Horsham** SE England, UK
99 M15 **Horst** Limburg, SE Netherlands
64 N2 **Horta** Faial, Azores, Portugal, NE Atlantic Ocean
95 H16 **Horten** Vestfold, S Norway
111 M23 **Hortobágy-Berettyó** ≈ E Hungary
27 Q3 **Horton** Kansas, C USA
8 I7 **Horton** ≈ Northwest Territories, NW Canada
95 I23 **Hørve** Vestsjælland, E Denmark
95 L22 **Hörvik** Blekinge, S Sweden
138 E11 **Horvot Haluza** *var.* Khorvot Khalutsa. *ruins* Southern, S Israel
14 E7 **Horwood Lake** ◎ Ontario, S Canada
116 K4 **Horyn'** *Rus.* Goryn. ≈ NW Ukraine
81 I14 **Hosa'ina** *var.* Hosseina, *It.* Hosanna. Southern, S Ethiopia
Hosanna *see* Hosa'ina
101 H18 **Hösbach** Bayern, C Germany
Hose Mountains *see* Hose, Pegunungan
169 T9 **Hose, Pegunungan** *var.* Hose Mountains. ▲ East Malaysia
148 L15 **Hoshāb** Baluchistān, SW Pakistan
154 H10 **Hoshangābād** Madhya Pradesh, C India
116 L4 **Hoshcha** Rivnens'ka Oblast', NW Ukraine
152 I7 **Hoshiārpur** Punjab, NW India
162 J7 **Höshööt** Arhangay, C Mongolia
99 M23 **Hosingen** Diekirch, NE Luxembourg
186 G7 **Hoskins** New Britain, E PNG
155 G17 **Hospet** Karnātaka, C India
104 K4 **Hospital de Orbigo** Castilla-León, N Spain
Hospitalet *see* L'Hospitalet de Llobregat
92 N13 **Hossa** Oulu, E Finland
Hosseina *see* Hosa'ina
Hosszúmezjő *see* Câmpulung Moldovenesc
63 I25 **Hoste, Isla** *island* S Chile
117 O4 **Hostomel'** *Rus.* Gostomel'. Kyyivs'ka Oblast', N Ukraine
155 H20 **Hosūr** Tamil Nādu, SE India
167 N8 **Hot** Chiang Mai, NW Thailand
158 G10 **Hotan** *var.* Khotan, *Chin.* Ho-t'ien. Xinjiang Uygur Zizhiqu, NW China
158 H9 **Hotan He** ≈ NW China
83 G22 **Hotazel** Northern Cape, N South Africa
37 Q5 **Hotchkiss** Colorado, C USA
35 V7 **Hot Creek Range** ▲ Nevada, W USA
Hote *see* Hoti
171 T13 **Hoti** *var.* Hote. Pulau Seram, E Indonesia
Ho-t'ien *see* Hotan
Hotin *see* Khotyn
93 H15 **Hoting** Jämtland, C Sweden
162 L14 **Hotong Qagan Nur** ◎ N China
162 J8 **Hotont** Arhangay, C Mongolia
27 T12 **Hot Springs** Arkansas, C USA
28 J11 **Hot Springs** South Dakota, N USA
21 S5 **Hot Springs** Virginia, NE USA
35 Q4 **Hot Springs Peak** ▲ California, W USA
27 T12 **Hot Springs Village** Arkansas, C USA
Hotspur Bank *see* Hotspur Seamount
65 J16 **Hotspur Seamount** *var.* Hotspur Bank. *undersea feature* C Atlantic Ocean
8 J8 **Hottah Lake** ◎ Northwest Territories, NW Canada
44 K9 **Hotte, Massif de la** ▲ SW Haiti
99 K21 **Hotton** Luxembourg, SE Belgium
Hötzing *see* Haţeg
187 P17 **Houaïlou** Province Nord, C New Caledonia
74 K5 **Houari Boumediène** × (Alger) N Algeria
167 P6 **Houayxay** *var.* Ban Houayxay, Ban Houei Sai. Bokèo, N Laos
103 N5 **Houdan** Yvelines, N France
99 F20 **Houdeng-Goegnies** *var.* Houdeng-Gœgnies. Hainaut, S Belgium
102 K14 **Houeillès** Lot-et-Garonne, SW France
99 L22 **Houffalize** Luxembourg, SE Belgium
30 M3 **Houghton** Michigan, N USA
31 Q7 **Houghton Lake** Michigan, N USA
31 Q7 **Houghton Lake** ◎ Michigan, N USA
19 T3 **Houlton** Maine, NE USA
160 M5 **Houma** Shanxi, C China
193 U15 **Houma** 'Eua, C Tonga
193 U16 **Houma** Tongatapu, S Tonga
22 J10 **Houma** Louisiana, S USA
196 V16 **Houma Taloa** *headland* Tongatapu, S Tonga
77 O13 **Houndé** SW Burkina
102 J12 **Hourtin-Carcans, Lac d'** ◎ SW France
36 J5 **House Range** ▲ Utah, W USA
10 K13 **Houston** British Columbia, SW Canada
39 R11 **Houston** Alaska, USA
29 X10 **Houston** Minnesota, N USA
22 M3 **Houston** Mississippi, S USA
27 V7 **Houston** Missouri, C USA
25 W11 **Houston** Texas, SW USA
25 W11 **Houston** × Texas, SW USA
98 J12 **Houten** Utrecht, C Netherlands
99 K17 **Houthalen** Limburg, NE Belgium
99 I22 **Houyet** Namur, SE Belgium
95 H22 **Hov** Århus, C Denmark
95 L17 **Hova** Västra Götaland, S Sweden
162 E6 **Hovd** *var.* Khovd. Hovd, W Mongolia
162 J10 **Hovd** Övörhangay, C Mongolia
162 E7 **Hovd** ◈ *province* W Mongolia
162 C5 **Hovd Gol** ≈ NW Mongolia
97 O23 **Hove** SE England, UK
29 N8 **Hoven** South Dakota, N USA
116 I8 **Hoverla, Hora** *Rus.* Gora Goverla. ▲ W Ukraine
162 H8 **Höviyn Am** Bayanhongor, C Mongolia
95 M21 **Hovmantorp** Kronoberg, S Sweden
163 N11 **Hövsgöl** Dornogovĭ, SE Mongolia
162 I5 **Hövsgöl** ◈ *province* N Mongolia
Hovsgol, Lake *see* Hövsgöl Nuur

162 J5 **Hövsgöl Nuur** *var.* Lake Hövsgöl. ◎ N Mongolia
78 L9 **Howa, Ouadi** *var.* Wādi Howar. ≈ Chad/Sudan *see also* Howar, Wādi
27 P7 **Howard** Kansas, C USA
29 Q10 **Howard** South Dakota, N USA
25 N10 **Howard Draw** *valley* Texas, SW USA
29 U8 **Howard Lake** Minnesota, N USA
80 B8 **Howar, Wādi** *var.* Ouadi Howa. ≈ Chad/Sudan *see also* Howa, Ouadi
25 U5 **Howe** Texas, SW USA
183 R12 **Howe, Cape** *headland* New South Wales/Victoria, SE Australia
31 R9 **Howell** Michigan, N USA
28 L9 **Howes** South Dakota, N USA
83 K23 **Howick** KwaZulu/Natal, E South Africa
Howrah *see* Hāora
27 W9 **Hoxie** Arkansas, C USA
26 J3 **Hoxie** Kansas, C USA
101 I14 **Höxter** Nordrhein-Westfalen, W Germany
158 K6 **Hoxud** Xinjiang Uygur Zizhiqu, NW China
96 J5 **Hoy** *island* N Scotland, UK
43 S17 **Hoya, Cerro** ▲ S Panama
94 D12 **Høyanger** Sogn og Fjordane, S Norway
101 P15 **Hoyerswerda** Sachsen, E Germany
164 E14 **Hōyo-kaikyō** *var.* Hayasui-seto. *strait* SW Japan
104 J8 **Hoyos** Extremadura, W Spain
29 W4 **Hoyt Lakes** Minnesota, N USA
87 V2 **Hoyvík** Streymoy, N Faeroe Islands
137 O14 **Hozat** Tunceli, E Turkey
Hôzyô *see* Hōjō
111 F16 **Hradec Králové** *Ger.* Königgrätz. Hradecký Kraj, N Czech Republic
111 E16 **Hradecký Kraj** ◈ *region* N Czech Republic
111 B16 **Hradiště** *Ger.* Burgstadlberg. ▲ NW Czech Republic
117 R6 **Hradyz'k** *Rus.* Gradizhsk. Poltavs'ka Oblast', NE Ukraine
119 M16 **Hradzyanka** *Rus.* Grodzyanka. Mahilyowskaya Voblasts', E Belarus
119 F16 **Hrandzichy** *Rus.* Grandichi. Hrodzyenskaya Voblasts', W Belarus
111 H18 **Hranice** *Ger.* Mährisch-Weisskirchen. Olomoucký Kraj, E Czech Republic
112 I13 **Hrasnica** Federacija Bosna I Hercegovina, SE Bosnia and Herzegovina
109 V11 **Hrastnik** C Slovenia
137 U12 **Hrazdan** *Rus.* Razdan. C Armenia
137 T12 **Hrazdan** *var.* Zanga, *Rus.* Razdan. ≈ C Armenia
117 R5 **Hrebinka** *Rus.* Grebenka. Poltavs'ka Oblast', NE Ukraine
119 K17 **Hresk** *Rus.* Gresk. Minskaya Voblasts', C Belarus
Hrisoupoli *see* Chrysoúpoli
119 F16 **Hrodna** *Pol.* Grodno. Hrodzyenskaya Voblasts', W Belarus
119 F16 **Hrodzyenskaya Voblasts'** *prev. Rus.* Grodnenskaya Oblast'. ◈ *province* W Belarus
111 J21 **Hron** *Ger.* Gran, *Hung.* Garam. ≈ C Slovakia
111 Q14 **Hrubieszów** *Rus.* Grubeshov. Lubelskie, E Poland
112 F13 **Hrvace** Split-Dalmacija, SE Croatia
Hrvatska *see* Croatia
112 F10 **Hrvatska Kostajnica** *var.* Kostajnica. Sisak-Moslavina, C Croatia
Hrvatsko Grahovo *see* Bosansko Grahovo
116 K6 **Hrymayliv** *Pol.* Gizymałów, *Rus.* Grimaylov. Ternopil's'ka Oblast', W Ukraine
167 N4 **Hsenwi** Shan State, E Myanmar
Hsia-men *see* Xiamen
Hsiang-t'an *see* Xiangtan
Hsi Chiang *see* Xi Jiang
167 N6 **Hsihseng** Shan State, C Myanmar
161 S13 **Hsinchu** *municipality* N Taiwan
Hsing-k'ai Hu *see* Khanka, Lake
Hsi-ning/Hsining *see* Xining
Hsinking *see* Changchun
Hsin-yang *see* Xinyang
161 S14 **Hsinying** *var.* Sinying, *Jap.* Shinei. C Taiwan
167 N4 **Hsipaw** Shan State, C Myanmar
Hsu-chou *see* Xuzhou
161 S13 **Hsüeh Shan** ▲ N Taiwan
Hu *see* Shanghai Shi
83 B18 **Huab** ≈ W Namibia
57 M21 **Huacaya** Chuquisaca, S Bolivia
57 J19 **Huachacalla** Oruro, SW Bolivia
159 X9 **Huachi** *var.* Rouyuanchengzi. Gansu, C China
57 N16 **Huachi, Laguna** ◎ N Bolivia
57 D14 **Huacho** Lima, W Peru
163 Y8 **Huachuan** Heilongjiang, NE China
163 P12 **Huade** Nei Mongol Zizhiqu, N China
163 W10 **Huadian** Jilin, NE China
56 E13 **Huagaruncho, Cordillera** ▲ C Peru
Hua Hin *see* Ban Hua Hin
191 S10 **Huahine** *island* Îles Sous le Vent, W French Polynesia
Huahua, Rio *see* Wawa, Río
167 R8 **Huai** ≈ E Thailand
161 P6 **Huaibei** Anhui, E China
Huaide *see* Gongzhuling
157 T10 **Huai He** ≈ C China
160 L11 **Huaihua** Hunan, S China
161 N14 **Huaiji** Guangdong, S China
161 O2 **Huailai** *prev.* Shacheng. Hebei, E China
161 P7 **Huainan** *var.* Huai-nan, Hwainan. Anhui, E China
161 N2 **Huairen** Shanxi, C China
161 O7 **Huaiyang** Henan, C China
161 Q7 **Huaiyin** *var.* Qingjiang. Jiangsu, E China
167 N16 **Huai Yot** Trang, SW Thailand
41 Q15 **Huajuapan** *var.* Huajuapan de León. Oaxaca, SE Mexico
Huajuapan de León *see* Huajuapan
41 O9 **Hualahuises** Nuevo León, NE Mexico
36 I11 **Hualapai Mountains** ▲ Arizona, SW USA
36 I11 **Hualapai Peak** ▲ Arizona, SW USA
62 J7 **Hualfín** Catamarca, N Argentina
161 T13 **Hualien** *var.* Hwalien, *Jap.* Karen. C Taiwan
56 E10 **Huallaga, Río** ≈ N Peru
56 C11 **Huamachuco** La Libertad, C Peru
41 Q14 **Huamantla** Tlaxcala, S Mexico
82 C13 **Huambo** *Port.* Nova Lisboa. Huambo, C Angola
82 B13 **Huambo** ◈ *province* C Angola
41 P15 **Huamuxtitlán** Guerrero, S Mexico
63 H17 **Huancache, Sierra** ▲ SW Argentina
57 I17 **Huancané** Puno, SE Peru
57 F16 **Huancapi** Ayacucho, C Peru
57 E15 **Huancavelica** Huancavelica, SW Peru
57 E15 **Huancavelica** *off.* Departamento de Huancavelica. ◈ *department* W Peru
57 E14 **Huancayo** Junín, C Peru
57 K20 **Huanchaca, Cerro** ▲ S Bolivia
56 C12 **Huandoy, Nevado** ▲ W Peru
161 O8 **Huangchuan** Henan, C China
Huang Hai *see* Yellow Sea
157 Q8 **Huang He** *var.* Yellow River. ≈ C China
161 Q4 **Huanghe Kou** *delta* E China
160 L5 **Huangling** Shaanxi, C China
161 O9 **Huangpi** Hubei, C China
163 P13 **Huangqi Hai** ◎ N China
161 Q9 **Huang Shan** ▲ Anhui, E China
161 Q9 **Huangshan** *var.* Tunxi. Anhui, E China
161 O9 **Huangshi** *var.* Huang-shih, Hwangshih. Hubei, C China
Huang-shih *see* Huangshi
160 L5 **Huangtu Gaoyuan** *plateau* C China
61 B22 **Huanguelén** Buenos Aires, E Argentina
161 S10 **Huangyan** Zhejiang, SE China
159 T10 **Huangyuan** Qinghai, C China
159 T10 **Huangzhong** Qinghai, C China
163 W12 **Huanren** Liaoning, NE China
57 F15 **Huanta** Ayacucho, C Peru
56 E13 **Huánuco** Huánuco, C Peru
56 D13 **Huánuco** *off.* Departamento de Huánuco. ◈ *department* C Peru
57 K19 **Huanuni** Oruro, W Bolivia
159 X9 **Huan Xian** Gansu, C China
161 S12 **Huap'ing Yu** *island* N Taiwan
62 H3 **Huara** Tarapacá, N Chile
57 D14 **Huaral** Lima, W Peru
Huarás *see* Huaraz
56 D13 **Huaraz** *var.* Huarás. Ancash, W Peru
57 I16 **Huari Huari, Río** ≈ S Peru
56 C13 **Huarmey** Ancash, W Peru
40 H4 **Huásabas** Sonora, NW Mexico
56 D8 **Huasaga, Río** ≈ Ecuador/Peru
167 O15 **Hua Sai** Nakhon Si Thammarat, SW Thailand
56 D12 **Huascarán, Nevado** ▲ W Peru
62 G8 **Huasco** Atacama, N Chile
62 G8 **Huasco, Río** ≈ C Chile
159 S11 **Huashikia** Qinghai, W China
40 G7 **Huatabampo** Sonora, NW Mexico
159 W10 **Huating** Gansu, C China
167 S7 **Huatt, Phou** ▲ N Vietnam
41 Q14 **Huatusco** *var.* Huatusco de Chicuellar. Veracruz-Llave, C Mexico
Huatusco de Chicuellar *see* Huatusco
41 P13 **Huauchinango** Puebla, S Mexico
Huaunta *see* Wounta
41 R15 **Huautla** *var.* Huautla de Jiménez. Oaxaca, SE Mexico
Huautla de Jiménez *see* Huautla
161 O5 **Huaxian** *var.* Daokou, Hua Xian. Henan, C China
29 V13 **Hubbard** Iowa, C USA
25 U8 **Hubbard** Texas, SW USA
25 Q6 **Hubbard Creek Lake** ▣ Texas, SW USA
31 R6 **Hubbard Lake** ◎ Michigan, N USA
160 M9 **Hubei** *var.* E, Hubei Sheng, Hupeh, Hupei. ◈ *province* C China
Hubei Sheng *see* Hubei
109 P8 **Huben** Tirol, W Austria
31 R13 **Huber Heights** Ohio, N USA
155 F17 **Hubli** Karnātaka, SW India
163 X12 **Huch'ang** N North Korea
97 M18 **Hucknall** C England, UK
97 L17 **Huddersfield** N England, UK
95 O16 **Huddinge** Stockholm, C Sweden
94 N11 **Hudiksvall** Gävleborg, C Sweden
29 W13 **Hudson** Iowa, C USA
19 O11 **Hudson** Massachusetts, NE USA
31 Q11 **Hudson** Michigan, N USA
30 H6 **Hudson** Wisconsin, N USA
11 V14 **Hudson Bay** Saskatchewan, S Canada
12 G6 **Hudson Bay** *bay* NE Canada
195 T16 **Hudson, Cape** *headland* Antarctica
Hudson, Détroit d' *see* Hudson Strait
27 Q9 **Hudson, Lake** ▣ Oklahoma, C USA
18 K9 **Hudson River** ≈ New Jersey/New York, NE USA
10 M12 **Hudson's Hope** British Columbia, W Canada
12 L2 **Hudson Strait** *Fr.* Détroit d'Hudson. *strait* Nunavut/Quebec, NE Canada
Hudūd ash Shamālīyah, Minṭaqat al *see* Al Ḥudūd ash Shamālīyah
Hudur *see* Xuddur
167 U9 **Huê** Thua Thiên-Huê, C Vietnam
104 J7 **Huebra** ≈ W Spain
24 H8 **Hueco Mountains** ▲ Texas, SW USA
116 G10 **Huedin** *Hung.* Bánffyhunyad. Cluj, NW Romania
40 J10 **Huehuento, Cerro** ▲ C Mexico
42 B5 **Huehuetenango** Huehuetenango, W Guatemala
42 B4 **Huehuetenango** *off.* Departamento de Huehuetenango. ◈ *department* W Guatemala
40 L11 **Huejuquilla** Jalisco, SW Mexico
41 P12 **Huejutla** *var.* Huejutla de Reyes. Hidalgo, C Mexico
Huejutla de Reyes *see* Huejutla
102 G6 **Huelgoat** Finistère, NW France
105 O13 **Huelma** Andalucía, S Spain
104 I14 **Huelva** *anc.* Onuba. Andalucía, SW Spain
104 I13 **Huelva** ◈ *province* Andalucía, SW Spain
104 J13 **Huelva** ≈ SW Spain
105 Q14 **Huercal-Overa** Andalucía, S Spain
37 Q9 **Huerfano Mountain** ▲ New Mexico, SW USA
37 T7 **Huerfano River** ≈ Colorado, C USA
105 S12 **Huertas, Cabo** *headland* SE Spain
105 R6 **Huerva** ≈ N Spain
105 S4 **Huesca** *anc.* Osca. Aragón, NE Spain
105 T4 **Huesca** ◈ *province* Aragón, NE Spain
105 P13 **Huéscar** Andalucía, S Spain
41 N15 **Huetamo** *var.* Huetamo de Núñez. Michoacán de Ocampo, SW Mexico
Huetamo de Núñez *see* Huetamo
105 P8 **Huete** Castilla-La Mancha, C Spain
23 P4 **Hueytown** Alabama, S USA
28 L16 **Hugh Butler Lake** ▣ Nebraska, C USA
181 V6 **Hughenden** Queensland, NE Australia
182 A6 **Hughes** South Australia
39 P8 **Hughes** Alaska, USA
27 X11 **Hughes** Arkansas, C USA
25 W6 **Hughes Springs** Texas, SW USA
37 V5 **Hugo** Colorado, C USA
27 Q13 **Hugo** Oklahoma, C USA
27 Q13 **Hugo Lake** ▣ Oklahoma, C USA
26 H7 **Hugoton** Kansas, C USA
Huhehot/Huhuohaote *see* Hohhot
161 R13 **Hui'an** Fujian, SE China
184 O9 **Huiarau Range** ▲ North Island, NZ
83 D22 **Huib-Hoch Plateau** *plateau* S Namibia
41 O13 **Huichapán** Hidalgo, C Mexico
Huicheng *see* Shexian
163 W13 **Hŭich'ŏn** C North Korea
54 E12 **Huila** *off.* Departmento del Huila. ◈ *province* S Colombia
83 B15 **Huíla** ◈ *province* SW Angola
54 D11 **Huila, Nevado del** *elevation* C Colombia
83 B15 **Huíla Plateau** *plateau* S Angola
160 G12 **Huili** Sichuan, C China
161 P4 **Huimin** Shandong, E China
163 W11 **Huinan** *var.* Chaoyang. Jilin, NE China
62 K12 **Huinca Renancó** Córdoba, C Argentina
159 V10 **Huining** Gansu, C China
160 J12 **Huishui** Guizhou, S China
102 L6 **Huisne** ≈ NW France
98 L12 **Huissen** Gelderland, SE Netherlands
159 N11 **Huiten Nur** ◎ C China
93 K19 **Huittinen** Länsi-Suomi, W Finland
41 O15 **Huitzuco** *var.* Huitzuco de los Figueroa. Guerrero, S Mexico
Huitzuco de los Figueroa *see* Huitzuco
159 W11 **Huixian** *var.* Hui Xian. Gansu, C China
41 V17 **Huixtla** Chiapas, SE Mexico
160 H12 **Huize** Yunnan, SW China
98 J10 **Huizen** Noord-Holland, C Netherlands
161 O14 **Huizhou** Guangdong, S China
162 J6 **Hujirt** Arhangay, C Mongolia
162 J8 **Hujirt** Övörhangay, C Mongolia
162 K8 **Hujrt** Töv, C Mongolia
Hukagawa *see* Fukagawa
Hŭksan-chedo *see* Hŭksan-gundo
163 W17 **Hŭksan-gundo** *var.* Hŭksan-chedo. *island group* SW South Korea
Hukue *see* Fukue
Hukui *see* Fukui
83 G20 **Hukuntsi** Kgalagadi, SW Botswana
Hukuoka *see* Fukuoka
Hukusima *see* Fukushima
Hukutiyama *see* Fukuchiyama
Hukuyama *see* Fukuyama
163 W8 **Hulan** Heilongjiang, NE China
163 W8 **Hulan He** ≈ NE China
31 Q4 **Hulbert Lake** ◎ Michigan, N USA
Hulczyn *see* Hlučín
163 Z8 **Hulin** Heilongjiang, NE China
163 S9 **Hulingol** *prev.* Huolin Gol. Nei Mongol Zizhiqu, N China
14 L12 **Hull** Quebec, SE Canada
29 S12 **Hull** Iowa, C USA
Hull *see* Kingston upon Hull
Hull Island *see* Orona
99 F16 **Hulst** Zeeland, SW Netherlands
163 Q7 **Hulstay** Dornod, NE Mongolia
Hultschin *see* Hlučín
95 M19 **Hultsfred** Kalmar, S Sweden
Hulun *see* Hailar
Hu-lun Ch'ih *see* Hulun Nur
163 Q6 **Hulun Nur** *var.* Hu-lun Ch'ih; *prev.* Dalai Nor. ◎ NE China
Hulwan/Hulwān *see* Helwān
117 V8 **Hulyaypole** *Rus.* Gulyaypole. Zaporiz'ka Oblast', SE Ukraine
163 V4 **Huma** Heilongjiang, NE China
45 V6 **Humacao** E Puerto Rico
163 U4 **Huma He** ≈ NE China
62 J5 **Humahuaca** Jujuy, N Argentina
59 E14 **Humaitá** Amazonas, N Brazil
62 N7 **Humaitá** Ñeembucú, S Paraguay
83 H26 **Humansdorp** Eastern Cape, S South Africa
27 S6 **Humansville** Missouri, C USA
40 I8 **Humaya, Río** ≈ C Mexico
83 C16 **Humbe** Cunene, SW Angola
97 N17 **Humber** *estuary* E England, UK
97 N17 **Humberside** *cultural region* E England, UK
Humberto *see* Umberto
25 W11 **Humble** Texas, SW USA
11 U15 **Humboldt** Saskatchewan, S Canada
29 U12 **Humboldt** Iowa, C USA
27 Q6 **Humboldt** Kansas, C USA
29 S17 **Humboldt** Nebraska, C USA
35 S3 **Humboldt** Nevada, W USA
20 G9 **Humboldt** Tennessee, S USA
34 K3 **Humboldt Bay** *bay* California, W USA
35 S4 **Humboldt Lake** ◎ Nevada, W USA
35 S4 **Humboldt River** ≈ Nevada, W USA
35 T5 **Humboldt Salt Marsh** *wetland* Nevada, W USA
183 P11 **Hume, Lake** ◎ New South Wales/Victoria, SE Australia
111 N19 **Humenné** *Ger.* Homenau, *Hung.* Homonna. Prešovský Kraj, E Slovakia
29 V15 **Humeston** Iowa, C USA
54 J5 **Humocaro Bajo** Lara, N Venezuela
29 Q14 **Humphrey** Nebraska, C USA
35 S9 **Humphreys, Mount** ▲ California, W USA
36 L11 **Humphreys Peak** ▲ Arizona, SW USA
111 E17 **Humpolec** *Ger.* Gumpolds, Humpoletz. Jihlavský Kraj, C Czech Republic
Humpoletz *see* Humpolec
93 K19 **Humppila** Etelä-Suomi, S Finland
32 F8 **Humptulips** Washington, NW USA
42 H7 **Humuya, Río** ≈ W Honduras
75 P9 **Hūn** N Libya
Hunabasi *see* Funabashi
92 I1 **Húnaflói** *bay* NW Iceland
160 M11 **Hunan** *var.* Hunan Sheng, Xiang. ◈ *province* S China
Hunan Sheng *see* Hunan
163 Y10 **Hunchun** Jilin, NE China
95 I22 **Hundested** Frederiksborg, E Denmark
Hundred Mile House *see* 100 Mile House
116 G12 **Hunedoara** *Ger.* Eisenmarkt, *Hung.* Vajdahunyad. Hunedoara, SW Romania
116 G12 **Hunedoara** ◈ *county* W Romania
101 I17 **Hünfeld** Hessen, C Germany
111 H23 **Hungary** *off.* Republic of Hungary, *Ger.* Ungarn, *Hung.* Magyarország, *Rom.* Ungaria, *SCr.* Mađarska, *Ukr.* Uhorshchyna; *prev.* Hungarian People's Republic. ◆ *republic* C Europe
Hungary, Plain of *see* Great Hungarian Plain
162 F6 **Hungiy** Dzavhan, W Mongolia
163 X13 **Hŭngnam** E North Korea
33 P8 **Hungry Horse Reservoir** ▣ Montana, NW USA
Hungt'ou *see* Lan Yü
Hung-tse Hu *see* Hongze Hu
167 T6 **Hưng Yên** Hai Hưng, N Vietnam
Hunjiang *see* Baishan
95 I18 **Hunnebostrand** Västra Götaland, S Sweden
101 E19 **Hunsrück** ▲ W Germany
97 P18 **Hunstanton** E England, UK
155 G20 **Hunsūr** Karnātaka, E India
162 I7 **Hunt** Arhangay, C Mongolia
100 G12 **Hunte** ≈ NW Germany
29 Q5 **Hunter** North Dakota, N USA
25 S11 **Hunter** Texas, SW USA
185 D20 **Hunter** ≈ South Island, NZ
183 N15 **Hunter Island** *island* Tasmania, SE Australia
18 K11 **Hunter Mountain** ▲ New York, NE USA
185 B23 **Hunter Mountains** ▲ South Island, NZ
183 S7 **Hunter River** ≈ New South Wales, SE Australia
32 L7 **Hunters** Washington, NW USA
185 F20 **Hunters Hills, The** *hill range* South Island, NZ
184 M12 **Hunterville** Manawatu-Wanganui, North Island, NZ
31 N16 **Huntingburg** Indiana, N USA
97 O20 **Huntingdon** E England, UK
18 E15 **Huntingdon** Pennsylvania, NE USA
20 G9 **Huntingdon** Tennessee, S USA
97 O20 **Huntingdonshire** *cultural region* C England, UK
31 P12 **Huntington** Indiana, N USA
32 L13 **Huntington** Oregon, NW USA
25 X9 **Huntington** Texas, SW USA
36 M5 **Huntington** Utah, W USA
21 P5 **Huntington** West Virginia, NE USA
35 T16 **Huntington Beach** California, W USA
35 W4 **Huntington Creek** ≈ Nevada, W USA
184 L7 **Huntly** Waikato, North Island, NZ
96 K8 **Huntly** NE Scotland, UK
10 K8 **Hunt, Mount** ▲ Yukon Territory, NW Canada
14 H12 **Huntsville** Ontario, S Canada
23 P2 **Huntsville** Alabama, S USA
27 S9 **Huntsville** Arkansas, C USA
27 U3 **Huntsville** Missouri, C USA
20 M8 **Huntsville** Tennessee, S USA
25 V10 **Huntsville** Texas, SW USA
36 L2 **Huntsville** Utah, W USA
41 W12 **Hunucmá** Yucatán, SE Mexico
149 W3 **Hunza** *var.* Karīmābād. Jammu and Kashmir, NE Pakistan
149 W3 **Hunza** ≈ NE Pakistan
Hunze *see* Oostermoers Vaart
158 H4 **Huocheng** *var.* Shuiding. Xinjiang Uygur Zizhiqu, NW China
161 N6 **Huojia** Henan, C China
Huolin Gol *see* Hulingol
186 N14 **Huon** *reef* N New Caledonia
186 E7 **Huon Peninsula** *headland* C PNG
Huoshao Dao *see* Lü Tao
Huoshao Tao *see* Lan Yü
Hupeh/Hupei *see* Hubei
Hurano *see* Furano
95 H14 **Hurdalssjøen** ◎ S Norway
14 E13 **Hurd, Cape** *headland* Ontario, S Canada
Hurdegaryp *see* Hardegarijp
29 N4 **Hurdsfield** North Dakota, N USA
162 J7 **Hüremt** Bulgan, C Mongolia
162 J8 **Hüremt** Övörhangay, C Mongolia
75 X9 **Hurghada** *var.* Al Ghurdaqah, Ghurdaqah. E Egypt
67 V9 **Huri Hills** ▲ NW Kenya
37 P15 **Hurley** New Mexico, SW USA
30 K4 **Hurley** Wisconsin, N USA
21 Y4 **Hurlock** Maryland, NE USA
29 P10 **Huron** South Dakota, N USA
31 S6 **Huron, Lake** ◎ Canada/USA
31 N3 **Huron Mountains** *hill range* Michigan, N USA
36 J8 **Hurricane** Utah, W USA
21 P5 **Hurricane** West Virginia, NE USA
36 J8 **Hurricane Cliffs** *cliff* Arizona, SW USA
23 V6 **Hurricane Creek** ≈ Georgia, SE USA
94 E12 **Hurrungane** ▲ S Norway
101 E16 **Hürth** Nordrhein-Westfalen, W Germany
Hurukawa *see* Furukawa
185 I17 **Hurunui** ≈ South Island, NZ
95 F21 **Hurup** Viborg, NW Denmark
117 T14 **Hurzuf** Respublika Krym, S Ukraine
Huş *see* Huşi
95 B19 **Húsavík** *Dan.* Husevig Faeroe Islands
92 K1 **Húsavík** Nordhurland Eystra, NE Iceland
116 M10 **Huşi** *var.* Huş. Vaslui, E Romania
95 L19 **Huskvarna** Jönköping, S Sweden
39 P8 **Huslia** Alaska, USA
Husn *see* Al Ḥuṣn
95 C15 **Husnes** Hordaland, S Norway
94 D8 **Hustadvika** *sea area* S Norway
Husté *see* Khust
100 H7 **Husum** Schleswig-Holstein, N Germany
93 I16 **Husum** Västernorrland, C Sweden
116 K6 **Husyatyn** Ternopil's'ka Oblast', W Ukraine
Huszt *see* Khust
162 K6 **Hutag** Bulgan, N Mongolia
26 M6 **Hutchinson** Kansas, C USA
29 U9 **Hutchinson** Minnesota, N USA
23 Y13 **Hutchinson Island** *island* Florida, SE USA
36 L11 **Hutch Mountain** ▲ Arizona, SW USA
141 O14 **Ḩūth** NW Yemen
186 I7 **Hutjena** Buka Island, NE PNG
109 T8 **Hüttenberg** Kärnten, S Austria
25 T10 **Hutto** Texas, SW USA
Huttu *see* Futtsu
108 E8 **Huttwil** Bern, W Switzerland
158 K5 **Hutubi** Xinjiang Uygur Zizhiqu, NW China
161 N4 **Hutuo He** ≈ C China
Hutyû *see* Fuchū
185 E20 **Huxley, Mount** ▲ South Island, NZ
99 J20 **Huy** *Dut.* Hoei, Hoey. Liège, E Belgium
161 R8 **Huzhou** *var.* Wuxing. Zhejiang, SE China
Huzi *see* Fuji
Huzieda *see* Fujieda
Huzinomiya *see* Fujinomiya
Huzisawa *see* Fujisawa
Huziyosida *see* Fuji-Yoshida
92 I2 **Hvammstangi** Nordhurland Vestra, N Iceland
92 K4 **Hvannadalshnúkur** ▲ S Iceland
113 E15 **Hvar** *It.* Lesina. Split-Dalmacija, S Croatia
113 F15 **Hvar** *It.* Lesina; *anc.* Pharus. *island* S Croatia
117 T13 **Hvardiys'ke** *Rus.* Gvardeyskoye. Respublika Krym, S Ukraine
92 I4 **Hveragerdhi** Sudhurland, SW Iceland
95 E22 **Hvide Sande** Ringkøbing, W Denmark
92 I3 **Hvítá** ≈ C Iceland
95 G15 **Hvittingfoss** Buskerud, S Norway
92 I4 **Hvolsvöllur** Sudhurland, SW Iceland
Hwach'ŏn-chŏsuji *see* P'aro-ho
Hwainan *see* Huainan
Hwalien *see* Hualien
83 I16 **Hwange** *prev.* Wankie. Matabeleland North, W Zimbabwe
Hwang-Hae *see* Yellow Sea
Hwangshih *see* Huangshi
83 L17 **Hwedza** Mashonaland East, E Zimbabwe
63 G20 **Hyades, Cerro** ▲ S Chile
19 Q12 **Hyannis** Massachusetts, NE USA
28 L13 **Hyannis** Nebraska, C USA
162 F6 **Hyargas Nuur** ◎ NW Mongolia
Hybla/Hybla Major *see* Paternò
39 Y14 **Hydaburg** Prince of Wales Island, Alaska, USA
185 F22 **Hyde** Otago, South Island, NZ
21 O7 **Hyden** Kentucky, S USA
18 K12 **Hyde Park** New York, NE USA
39 Z14 **Hyder** Alaska, USA
155 I15 **Hyderābād** *var.* Haidarabad. Andhra Pradesh, C India
149 Q16 **Hyderābād** *var.* Haidarabad. Sind, SE Pakistan
103 T16 **Hyères** Var, SE France
103 T16 **Hyères, Îles d'** *island group* S France
118 K12 **Hyermanavichy** *Rus.* Germanovichi. Vitsyebskaya Voblasts', N Belarus
163 X12 **Hyesan** NE North Korea
10 K8 **Hyland** ≈ Yukon Territory, NW Canada
95 K20 **Hyltebruk** Halland, S Sweden
18 D16 **Hyndman** Pennsylvania, NE USA
33 P14 **Hyndman Peak** ▲ Idaho, NW USA
164 I13 **Hyōgo** *off.* Hyōgo-ken. ◈ *prefecture* Honshū, SW Japan
Hypanis *see* Kuban'
Hypsas *see* Belice
Hyrcania *see* Gorgān
36 L1 **Hyrum** Utah, W USA
93 N14 **Hyrynsalmi** Oulu, C Finland
33 V10 **Hysham** Montana, NW USA
11 N13 **Hythe** Alberta, W Canada
97 Q23 **Hythe** SE England, UK
164 D15 **Hyūga** Miyazaki, Kyūshū, SW Japan
Hyvinge *see* Hyvinkää
93 L19 **Hyvinkää** *Swe.* Hyvinge. Etelä-Suomi, S Finland

I

118 J9 **Iacobeni** *Ger.* Jakobeny. Suceava, NE Romania
Iader *see* Zadar
172 I7 **Iakora** Fianarantsoa, SE Madagascar
116 K14 **Ialomiţa** *var.* Jalomitsa. ◈ *county* SE Romania
116 K14 **Ialomiţa** ≈ SE Romania
117 N10 **Ialoveni** *Rus.* Yaloveny. C Moldova
117 N11 **Ialpug** *var.* Ialpugul Mare, *Rus.* Yalpug. ≈ Moldova/Ukraine
Ialpugul Mare *see* Ialpug
23 T8 **Iamonia, Lake** ◎ Florida, SE USA
116 L13 **Ianca** Brăila, SE Romania
116 M10 **Iaşi** *Ger.* Jassy. Iaşi, NE Romania
116 L9 **Iaşi** *Ger.* Jassy, Yassy. ◈ *county* NE Romania
114 J13 **Íasmos** Anatolikí Makedonía kai Thrákí, NE Greece
22 H6 **Iatt, Lake** ▣ Louisiana, S USA
58 B11 **Iauaretê** Amazonas, NW Brazil
171 N3 **Iba** Luzon, N Philippines
77 S16 **Ibadan** Oyo, SW Nigeria
54 E10 **Ibagué** Tolima, C Colombia
60 J10 **Ibaiti** Paraná, S Brazil
36 J4 **Ibapah Peak** ▲ Utah, W USA
113 M15 **Ibar** *Alb.* Ibër. ≈ C Yugoslavia
165 P13 **Ibaraki** *off.* Ibaraki-ken. ◈ *prefecture* Honshū, S Japan
56 C5 **Ibarra** *var.* San Miguel de Ibarra. Imbabura, N Ecuador
Ibaşfalău *see* Dumbrăveni
141 O16 **Ibb** W Yemen
100 F13 **Ibbenbüren** Nordrhein-Westfalen, NW Germany
79 H16 **Ibenga** ≈ N Congo
Ibër *see* Ibar
57 I14 **Iberia** Madre de Dios, E Peru
Iberia *see* Spain
66 M1 **Iberian Basin** *undersea feature* E Atlantic Ocean
Iberian Mountains *see* Ibérico, Sistema
84 D12 **Iberian Peninsula** *physical region* Portugal/Spain

◆ Country ◇ Dependent Territory ◈ Administrative Region ▲ Mountain ⅹ Volcano ◎ Lake
● Country Capital ○ Dependent Territory Capital ✕ International Airport ▲ Mountain Range ≈ River ▣ Reservoir

64 M8 **Iberian Plain** undersea feature E Atlantic Ocean
Ibérica, Cordillera see Ibérico, Sistema
105 P6 **Ibérico, Sistema** var. Cordillera Ibérica, Eng. Iberian Mountains. ▲ NE Spain
12 K7 **Iberville Lac d'** ◎ Quebec, NE Canada
77 T14 **Ibeto** Niger, W Nigeria
77 W15 **Ibi** Taraba, C Nigeria
105 S11 **Ibi** País Valenciano, E Spain
59 L20 **Ibiá** Minas Gerais, SE Brazil
61 F15 **Ibicuí, Rio** ~ S Brazil
61 C19 **Ibicuy** Entre Ríos, E Argentina
61 F16 **Ibirapuitã** ~ S Brazil
Ibiza see Eivissa
138 J4 **Ibn Wardān, Qaṣr** ruins Ḩamāh, C Syria
Ibo see Sassandra
188 E9 **Ibobang** Babeldaob, N Palau
171 V13 **Ibonma** Irian Jaya, E Indonesia
59 N17 **Ibotirama** Bahia, E Brazil
141 Y8 **Ibrā** NE Oman
129 Q4 **Ibresi** Chuvashskaya Respublika, W Russian Federation
141 X8 **'Ibrī** NW Oman
164 C16 **Ibusuki** Kagoshima, Kyūshū, SW Japan
57 E16 **Ica** Ica, SW Peru
57 E16 **Ica** off. Departamento de Ica. ◈ department SW Peru
58 C11 **Içana** Amazonas, NW Brazil
Icaria see Ikaria
58 B13 **Içá, Rio** var. Río Putumayo. ~ NW South America see also Putumayo, Río
136 I17 **İçel** var. Ichili. ◈ province S Turkey
92 I3 **Iceland** off. Republic of Iceland, Dan. Island, Icel. Ísland. ◆ republic N Atlantic Ocean
86 B7 **Iceland** island N Atlantic Ocean
64 L5 **Iceland Basin** undersea feature N Atlantic Ocean
Icelandic Plateau see Iceland Plateau
197 Q15 **Iceland Plateau** var. Icelandic Plateau. undersea feature S Greenland Sea
155 E16 **Ichalkaranji** Mahārāshtra, W India
164 D15 **Ichifusa-yama** ▲ Kyūshū, SW Japan
Ichili see İçel
164 K13 **Ichinomiya** var. Itinomiya. Aichi, Honshū, SW Japan
165 Q9 **Ichinoseki** var. Itinoseki. Iwate, Honshū, C Japan
117 R3 **Ichnya** Chernihivs'ka Oblast', NE Ukraine
57 L17 **Ichoa, Río** ~ C Bolivia
I-ch'un see Yichun
Iconium see Konya
Iculisma see Angoulême
39 U12 **Icy Bay** inlet Alaska, USA
39 N5 **Icy Cape** headland Alaska, USA
39 W13 **Icy Strait** strait Alaska, USA
27 R13 **Idabel** Oklahoma, C USA
29 T13 **Ida Grove** Iowa, C USA
77 U16 **Idah** Kogi, S Nigeria
33 N13 **Idaho** off. State of Idaho; also known as Gem of the Mountains, Gem State. ◈ state NW USA
33 N14 **Idaho City** Idaho, NW USA
33 R14 **Idaho Falls** Idaho, NW USA
121 P2 **Idálion** var. Dali, Dhali. C Cyprus
25 N5 **Idalou** Texas, SW USA
104 I9 **Idanha-a-Nova** Castelo Branco, C Portugal
101 E19 **Idar-Oberstein** Rheinland-Pfalz, SW Germany
118 J3 **Ida-Virumaa** off. Ida-Viru Maakond. ◈ province NE Estonia
126 J8 **Idel'** Respublika Kareliya, NW Russian Federation
79 C15 **Idenao** Sud-Ouest, SW Cameroon
Idenburg-rivier see Taritatu, Sungai
Idensalmi see Iisalmi
162 I6 **Ider** Hövsgöl, C Mongolia
75 X10 **Idfu** var. Edfu. SE Egypt
Ídhi Óros see Ídi
Ídhra see Ýdra
168 H7 **Idi** Sumatera, W Indonesia
115 I25 **Ídi** var. Ídhi Óros. ▲ Kríti, Greece, E Mediterranean Sea
Idi Amin, Lac see Edward, Lake
106 G10 **Idice** ~ N Italy
76 G9 **Idîni** Trarza, W Mauritania
79 J21 **Idiofa** Bandundu, SW Dem. Rep. Congo (Zaire)
39 O10 **Iditarod River** ~ Alaska, USA
95 M14 **Idkerberget** Dalarna, C Sweden
138 I3 **Idlib** Idlib, NW Syria
138 I4 **Idlib** off. Muḩāfaẓat Idlib. ◈ governorate NW Syria
Idra see Ýdra
94 J11 **Idre** Dalarna, C Sweden
Idria see Idrija
109 S11 **Idrija** It. Idria. W Slovenia
101 G18 **Idstein** Hessen, W Germany
83 J25 **Idutywa** Eastern Cape, SE South Africa
Idzhevan see Ijevan
118 G9 **Iecava** Bauska, S Latvia
165 T16 **Ie-jima** var. Ii-shima. island Nansei-shotō, SW Japan
99 B18 **Ieper** Fr. Ypres. West-Vlaanderen, W Belgium
115 K25 **Ierápetra** Kríti, Greece, E Mediterranean Sea
115 G22 **Iérax, Akrotírio** headland S Greece
Ierisós see Ierissós
115 H14 **Ierissós** var. Ierisós. Kentrikí Makedonía, N Greece
116 I11 **Iernut** Hung. Radnót. Mureş, C Romania
106 J12 **Iesi** var. Jesi. Marche, C Italy
92 K9 **Iešjávri** var. Jiesjavrre. ◎ N Norway
Iesolo see Jesolo
188 K16 **Ifalik Atoll** atoll Caroline Islands, C Micronesia
172 I6 **Ifanadiana** Fianarantsoa, SE Madagascar
77 T16 **Ife** Osun, SW Nigeria
77 V8 **Iferouâne** Agadez, N Niger
Iferten see Yverdon
92 L8 **Ifjord** Finnmark, N Norway
77 R8 **Ifôghas, Adrar des** var. Adrar des Iforas. ▲ NE Mali
Iforas, Adrar des see Ifôghas, Adrar des
182 D6 **Ifould lake** salt lake South Australia
74 G6 **Ifrane** C Morocco
171 S11 **Iga** Pulau Halmahera, E Indonesia
81 G18 **Iganga** SE Uganda
60 L7 **Igarapava** São Paulo, S Brazil
122 K9 **Igarka** Krasnoyarskiy Kray, N Russian Federation
Igaunija see Estonia
I.G.Duca see General Toshevo
Igel see Jihlava
137 T12 **Iğdır** ◈ province E Turkey
94 N11 **Iggesund** Gävleborg, C Sweden
39 P7 **Igikpak, Mount** ▲ Alaska, USA
39 P13 **Igiugig** Alaska, USA
Iglau/Iglawa/Igława see Jihlava
107 B20 **Iglesias** Sardegna, Italy, C Mediterranean Sea
129 V4 **Iglino** Respublika Bashkortostan, W Russian Federation
Igló see Spišská Nová Ves
9 O6 **Igloolik** Nunavut, N Canada
12 B11 **Ignace** Ontario, S Canada
118 I12 **Ignalina** Ignalina, E Lithuania
129 Q5 **Ignatovka** Ul'yanovskaya Oblast', W Russian Federation
126 K12 **Ignatovo** Vologodskaya Oblast', NW Russian Federation
114 N11 **İğneada** Kırklareli, NW Turkey
121 S7 **İğneada Burnu** headland NW Turkey
Igombe see Gombe
115 B16 **Igoumenítsa** Ípeiros, W Greece
129 T2 **Igra** Udmurtskaya Respublika, NW Russian Federation
122 H9 **Igrim** Khanty-Mansiyskiy Avtonomnyy Okrug, N Russian Federation
60 G12 **Iguaçu, Rio** Sp. Río Iguazú. ~ Argentina/Brazil see also Iguazú, Río
59 I22 **Iguaçu, Salto do** Sp. Cataratas del Iguazú; prev. Victoria Falls. waterfall Argentina/Brazil see also Iguazú, Cataratas del
41 O15 **Iguala** var. Iguala de la Independencia. Guerrero, S Mexico
105 V5 **Igualada** Cataluña, NE Spain
Iguala de la Independencia see Iguala
60 G12 **Iguazú, Cataratas del** Port. Salto do Iguaçu, prev. Victoria Falls. waterfall Argentina/Brazil see also Iguaçu, Salto do
62 Q6 **Iguazú, Río** Port. Rio Iguaçu. ~ Argentina/Brazil see also Iguaçu, Rio
79 D19 **Iguéla** Ogooué-Maritime, SW Gabon
Iguid, Erg see Iguîdi, 'Erg
67 M5 **Iguîdi, 'Erg** var. Erg Iguid. desert Algeria/Mauritania
172 K2 **Iharaña** prev. Vohémar. Antsirañana, NE Madagascar
151 K18 **Ihavandippolhu Atoll** var. Ihavandiffulu Atoll. atoll N Maldives
162 M11 **Ih Bulag** Ömnögovĭ, S Mongolia
165 T16 **Iheya-jima** island Nansei-shotō, SW Japan
162 L8 **Ihhayrhan** Töv, C Mongolia
172 I6 **Ihosy** Fianarantsoa, S Madagascar
162 L7 **Ihsüüj** Töv, C Mongolia
93 L14 **Ii** Oulu, C Finland
164 M13 **Iida** Nagano, Honshū, S Japan
93 M14 **Iijoki** ~ C Finland
118 J4 **Iisaku** Ger. Isaak. Ida-Virumaa, NE Estonia
93 M16 **Iisalmi** var. Idensalmi. Itä-Suomi, C Finland
165 N11 **Iiyama** Nagano, Honshū, S Japan
77 S16 **Ijebu-Ode** Ogun, SW Nigeria
137 U11 **Ijevan** Rus. Idzhevan. N Armenia
98 H9 **IJmuiden** Noord-Holland, W Netherlands
98 M12 **IJssel** var. Yssel. ~ Netherlands/Germany
98 J8 **IJsselmeer** prev. Zuider Zee. ◎ N Netherlands
98 L9 **IJsselmuiden** Overijssel, E Netherlands
98 I12 **IJsselstein** Utrecht, C Netherlands
61 G14 **Ijuí** Rio Grande do Sul, S Brazil
61 G14 **Ijuí, Rio** ~ S Brazil
189 R8 **Ijuw** NE Nauru
99 E16 **IJzendijke** Zeeland, SW Netherlands
99 A18 **Ijzer** ~ W Belgium
93 K18 **Ikaalinen** Länsi-Suomi, W Finland
172 I6 **Ikalamavony** Fianarantsoa, SE Madagascar
185 G16 **Ikamatua** West Coast, South Island, NZ
77 U16 **Ikare** Ondo, SW Nigeria
115 L20 **Ikaría** var. Kariot, Nicaria, Nikaria; anc. Icaria. island Dodekánisos, Greece, Aegean Sea
95 F22 **Ikast** Ringkøbing, W Denmark
184 O9 **Ikawhenua Range** ▲ North Island, NZ
165 U4 **Ikeda** Hokkaidō, NE Japan
164 H14 **Ikeda** Tokushima, Shikoku, SW Japan
77 S16 **Ikeja** Lagos, SW Nigeria
79 L19 **Ikela** Equateur, C Dem. Rep. Congo (Zaire)
114 H10 **Ikhtiman** Sofiya, W Bulgaria
164 C13 **Iki** island SW Japan
129 O13 **Iki Burul** Respublika Kalmykiya, SW Russian Federation
137 P11 **İkizdere** Rize, NE Turkey
39 P14 **Ikolik, Cape** headland Kodiak Island, Alaska, USA
77 V17 **Ikom** Cross River, SE Nigeria
172 I6 **Ikongo** prev. Fort-Carnot. Fianarantsoa, SE Madagascar
39 P5 **Ikpikpuk River** ~ Alaska, USA
190 H1 **Iku** prev. Lone Tree Islet. atoll Tungaru, W Kiribati
164 I12 **Ikuno** Hyōgo, Honshū, SW Japan
190 H16 **Ikurangi** ▲ Rarotonga, S Cook Islands
171 X14 **Ilaga** Irian Jaya, E Indonesia
171 O2 **Ilagan** Luzon, N Philippines
153 R12 **Ilam** Eastern, E Nepal
142 J7 **Īlām** var. Elam. Īlām, W Iran
142 J8 **Īlām** off. Ostān-e Īlām. ◈ province W Iran
161 T13 **Ilan** Jap. Giran. N Taiwan
146 G9 **Ilanly Obvodnitel'nyy Kanal** canal N Turkmenistan
122 L12 **Ilanskiy** Krasnoyarskiy Kray, S Russian Federation
108 H9 **Ilanz** Graubünden, S Switzerland
77 S16 **Ilaro** Ogun, SW Nigeria
57 I17 **Ilave** Puno, S Peru
110 K8 **Iława** Ger. Deutsch-Eylau. Warmińsko-Mazurskie, NE Poland,
123 P10 **Il'benge** Respublika Sakha (Yakutiya), NE Russian Federation
Ile see Ili
11 S13 **Ile-à-la-Crosse** Saskatchewan, C Canada
79 J21 **Ilebo** prev. Port-Francqui. Kasai Occidental, W Dem. Rep. Congo (Zaire)
103 N5 **Île-de-France** ◈ region N France
144 I9 **Ilek** Kaz. Elek. ~ Kazakhstan/Russian Federation
Ilerda see Lleida
77 T16 **Ilesha** Osun, SW Nigeria
187 Q16 **Îles Loyauté, Province des** ◈ province E New Caledonia
11 X12 **Ilford** Manitoba, C Canada
97 I23 **Ilfracombe** SW England, UK
136 I11 **Ilgaz Dağları** ▲ N Turkey
136 G15 **Ilgın** Konya, W Turkey
60 I7 **Ilha Solteira** São Paulo, S Brazil
104 G7 **Ílhavo** Aveiro, N Portugal
59 O18 **Ilhéus** Bahia, E Brazil
131 R7 **Ili** Kaz. Ile, Rus. Reka Ili. ~ China/Kazakhstan
Ili see Ili He
116 G11 **Ilia** Hung. Marosillye. Hunedoara, SW Romania
39 P13 **Iliamna** Alaska, USA
39 P13 **Iliamna Lake** ◎ Alaska, USA
137 N13 **Iliç** Erzincan, C Turkey
Il'ichevsk see Şärur, Azerbaijan
Il'ichevsk see Illichivs'k, Ukraine
Ilici see Elche
37 V2 **Iliff** Colorado, C USA
171 Q7 **Iligan** off. Iligan City. Mindanao, S Philippines
171 Q7 **Iligan Bay** bay S Philippines
158 I5 **Ili He** Rus. Ili. ~ China/Kazakhstan
56 C6 **Iliniza** ▲ N Ecuador
Ilinski see Il'inskiy
127 U14 **Il'inskiy** var. Ilinski. Permskaya Oblast', NW Russian Federation
123 T13 **Il'inskiy** Ostrov Sakhalin, Sakhalinskaya Oblast', SE Russian Federation
18 I10 **Ilion** New York, NE USA
38 E9 **Ilio Point** headland Molokai, Hawaii, USA, C Pacific Ocean
109 T13 **Ilirska Bistrica** prev. Bistrica, Ger. Feistritz, Illyrisch-Feistritz, It. Villa del Nevoso. SW Slovenia
137 Q16 **Ilısu Barajı** ▣ SE Turkey
155 G17 **Ilkal** Karnātaka, C India
97 M19 **Ilkeston** C England, UK
121 O16 **Il-Kullana** headland SW Malta
108 J8 **Ill** ~ W Austria
103 U6 **Ill** ~ NE France
62 G10 **Illapel** Coquimbo, C Chile
Illaue Fartak Trench see Alula-Fartak Trench
182 C2 **Illbillee, Mount** ▲ South Australia
102 I6 **Ille-et-Vilaine** ◈ department NW France
77 T11 **Illéla** Tahoua, SW Niger
101 J24 **Iller** ~ S Germany
101 J23 **Illertissen** Bayern, S Germany
105 N8 **Illescas** Castilla-La Mancha, C Spain
Ille-sur-la-Têt see Ille-sur-Têt
103 O17 **Ille-sur-Têt** var. Ille-sur-la-Têt. Pyrénées-Orientales, S France
Illiberis see Elne
117 P11 **Illichivs'k** Rus. Il'ichevsk. Odes'ka Oblast', SW Ukraine
Illicis see Elche
102 M6 **Illiers-Combray** Eure-et-Loir, C France
30 K12 **Illinois** off. State of Illinois; also known as Prairie State, Sucker State. ◈ state C USA
30 J13 **Illinois River** ~ Illinois, N USA
117 N6 **Illintsi** Vinnyts'ka Oblast', C Ukraine
Illiturgis see Andújar
74 M10 **Illizi** SE Algeria
27 Y7 **Illmo** Missouri, C USA
Illur co see Lorca
Illuro see Mataró
Illyrisch-Feistritz see Ilirska Bistrica
101 K16 **Ilm** ~ C Germany
101 K17 **Ilmenau** Thüringen, C Germany
126 H14 **Il'men', Ozero** ◎ NW Russian Federation
57 H18 **Ilo** Moquegua, SW Peru
171 O6 **Iloilo** off. Iloilo City. Panay Island, C Philippines
112 K10 **Ilok** Hung. Újlak. Serbia, NW Yugoslavia
93 O16 **Ilomantsi** Itä-Suomi, E Finland
42 F8 **Ilopango, Lago de** volcanic lake C El Salvador
77 T15 **Ilorin** Kwara, W Nigeria
117 X8 **Ilovays'k** Rus. Ilovaysk. Donets'ka Oblast', SE Ukraine
129 O10 **Ilovlya** Volgogradskaya Oblast', SW Russian Federation
129 O10 **Ilovlya** ~ SW Russian Federation
123 V8 **Il'pyrskiy** Koryakskiy Avtonomnyy Okrug, E Russian Federation
128 K14 **Il'skiy** Krasnodarskiy Kray, SW Russian Federation
182 B2 **Iltur** South Australia
171 Y13 **Ilugwa** Irian Jaya, E Indonesia
Iluh see Batman
118 I11 **Ilūkste** Daugvapils, SE Latvia
171 U14 **Ilur** Pulau Gorong, E Indonesia
32 F10 **Ilwaco** Washington, NW USA
146 H8 **Il'yaly** var. Yylanly. Dashkhovuzskiy Velayat, N Turkmenistan
İlyasbaba Burnu see Tekke Burnu
127 U9 **Ilych** ~ NW Russian Federation
101 O21 **Ilz** ~ SE Germany
111 M14 **Iłża** Radom, SE Poland
164 G13 **Imabari** var. Imaharu. Ehime, Shikoku, SW Japan
Imaharu see Imabari
165 O12 **Imaichi** var. Imaiti. Tochigi, Honshū, S Japan
Imaiti see Imaichi
164 K12 **Imajō** Fukui, Honshū, SW Japan
139 R9 **Imām Ibn Hāshim** C Iraq
139 T11 **Imām 'Abd Allāh** S Iraq
126 J4 **Imandra, Ozero** ◎ NW Russian Federation
164 F15 **Imano-yama** ▲ Shikoku, SW Japan
164 C13 **Imari** Saga, Kyūshū, SW Japan
Imarssuak Mid-Ocean Seachannel see Imarssuak Seachannel
64 J6 **Imarssuak Seachannel** var. Imarssuak Mid-Ocean Seachannel. channel N Atlantic Ocean
93 N18 **Imatra** Etelä-Suomi, S Finland
164 K13 **Imazu** Shiga, Honshū, SW Japan
56 C6 **Imbabura** ◈ province N Ecuador
55 R9 **Imbaimadai** W Guyana
61 K14 **Imbituba** Santa Catarina, S Brazil
27 W9 **Imboden** Arkansas, C USA
Imbros see Gökçeada
146 B11 **Imeni 26 Bakinskikh Komissarov** Turkm. 26 Baku Komissarlary Adyndaky. Balkanskiy Velayat, W Turkmenistan
Imeni 26 Bakinskikh Komissarov see 26 Bakı Komissarı
127 N13 **Imeni Babushkina** Vologodskaya Oblast', NW Russian Federation
128 J7 **Imeni Karla Libknekhta** Kurskaya Oblast', W Russian Federation
146 I14 **Imeni Mollanepesa** Maryyskiy Velayat, S Turkmenistan
146 J15 **Imeni S.A.Niyazova** Maryyskiy Velayat, S Turkmenistan
Imeni Sverdlova Rudnik see Sverdlovs'k
188 E9 **Imeong** Babeldaob, N Palau
81 L14 **Īmī** Somali, E Ethiopia
115 M21 **Imia** Turk. Kardak. island Dodekánisos, Greece, Aegean Sea
Imishli see İmişli
137 X12 **İmişli** Rus. Imishli. C Azerbaijan
163 X14 **Imjin-gang** ~ North Korea/South Korea
35 S3 **Imlay** Nevada, W USA
31 S9 **Imlay City** Michigan, N USA
23 X15 **Immokalee** Florida, SE USA
77 U17 **Imo** ◈ state SE Nigeria
106 G10 **Imola** Emilia-Romagna, N Italy
186 A5 **Imonda** Sandaun, NW PNG
Imoschi see Imotski
113 G14 **Imotski** It. Imoschi. Split-Dalmacija, SE Croatia
59 L14 **Imperatriz** Maranhão, NE Brazil
106 B10 **Imperia** Liguria, NW Italy
57 E15 **Imperial** Lima, W Peru
35 X17 **Imperial** California, W USA
28 L16 **Imperial** Nebraska, C USA
24 M9 **Imperial** Texas, SW USA
35 Y17 **Imperial Dam** dam California, W USA
79 I17 **Impfondo** La Likouala, NE Congo
153 X14 **Imphāl** Manipur, NE India
103 P9 **Imphy** Nièvre, C France
106 G11 **Impruneta** Toscana, C Italy
115 K15 **İmroz** var. Gökçeada. Çanakkale, NW Turkey
İmroz Adası see Gökçeada
108 L7 **Imst** Tirol, W Austria
40 F3 **Imuris** Sonora, NW Mexico
164 M13 **Ina** Nagano, Honshū, S Japan
65 M18 **Inaccessible Island** island W Tristan da Cunha
115 F20 **Ínachos** ~ S Greece
188 H6 **I Naftan, Puntan** headland Saipan, S Northern Mariana Islands
Inagua Islands see Great Inagua/Little Inagua
185 H15 **Inangahua** West Coast, South Island, NZ
57 I14 **Iñapari** Madre de Dios, E Peru
188 B17 **Inarajan** SE Guam
92 L10 **Inari** Lapp. Anár, Aanaar. Lappi, N Finland
92 L10 **Inarijärvi** Lapp. Aanaarjävri, Swe. Enareträsk. ◎ N Finland
92 L9 **Inarijoki** Lapp. Anárjohka. ~ Finland/Norway
Inău see Ineu
165 P11 **Inawashiro-ko** var. Inawasiro Ko. ◎ Honshū, C Japan
Inawasiro Ko see Inawashiro-ko
62 H7 **Inca de Oro** Atacama, N Chile
115 J15 **İnce Burnu** headland NW Turkey
136 K9 **İnce Burnu** headland N Turkey
136 I17 **İncekum Burnu** headland S Turkey
76 G7 **Inchiri** ◈ region NW Mauritania
163 X15 **Inch'ŏn** off. Inch'ŏn-gwangyŏksi, Jap. Jinsen; prev. Chemulpo. NW South Korea
83 M17 **Inchope** Manica, C Mozambique
Incoronata see Kornat
103 Y15 **Incudine, Monte** ▲ Corse, France, C Mediterranean Sea
60 M10 **Indaiatuba** São Paulo, S Brazil
93 H17 **Indal** Västernorrland, C Sweden
93 H17 **Indalsälven** ~ C Sweden
40 K8 **Inde** Durango, C Mexico
Indefatigable Island see Santa Cruz, Isla
35 S10 **Independence** California, W USA
29 X13 **Independence** Iowa, C USA
27 P7 **Independence** Kansas, C USA
20 M4 **Independence** Kentucky, S USA
27 R4 **Independence** Missouri, C USA
21 R8 **Independence** Virginia, NE USA
30 J7 **Independence** Wisconsin, N USA
197 R12 **Independence Fjord** fjord N Greenland
Independence Island see Malden Island
35 W2 **Independence Mountains** ▲ Nevada, W USA
57 K18 **Independencia** Cochabamba, C Bolivia
57 E16 **Independencia, Bahía de la** bay W Peru
Independencia, Monte see Adam, Mount
116 M12 **Independenţa** Galaţi, SE Romania
Inderagiri see Indragiri, Sungai
Inderbor see Inderborskiy
144 F11 **Inderborskiy** Kaz. Inderbor. Atyrau, W Kazakhstan
151 I14 **India** off. Republic of India, var. Indian Union, Union of India, Hind. Bhārat. ◆ republic S Asia
India see Inđija
18 D14 **Indiana** Pennsylvania, NE USA
31 N13 **Indiana** off. State of Indiana; also known as The Hoosier State. ◈ state N USA
31 O14 **Indianapolis** state capital Indiana, N USA
11 O10 **Indian Cabins** Alberta, W Canada
42 G1 **Indian Church** Orange Walk, N Belize
Indian Desert see Thar Desert
11 U16 **Indian Head** Saskatchewan, S Canada
31 O4 **Indian Lake** ◎ Michigan, N USA
18 K9 **Indian Lake** ◎ New York, NE USA
31 R13 **Indian Lake** ▣ Ohio, N USA
180-181 **Indian Ocean** ocean
29 V15 **Indianola** Iowa, C USA
22 K4 **Indianola** Mississippi, S USA
36 J6 **Indian Peak** ▲ Utah, W USA
23 Y14 **Indian River** lagoon Florida, SE USA
35 W10 **Indian Springs** Nevada, W USA
23 Y14 **Indiantown** Florida, SE USA
59 K19 **Indiara** Goiás, S Brazil
127 Q4 **Indiga** Nenetskiy Avtonomnyy Okrug, NW Russian Federation
123 R9 **Indigirka** ~ NE Russian Federation
112 L10 **Inđija** Hung. India; prev. Indjija. Serbia, N Yugoslavia
35 V16 **Indio** California, W USA
42 M12 **Indio, Río** ~ SE Nicaragua
152 I10 **Indira Gandhi International** × (Delhi) Delhi, N India
151 Q23 **Indira Point** headland Andaman and Nicobar Islands, India, NE Indian Ocean
Indjija see Inđija
131 Q13 **Indo-Australian Plate** tectonic feature
173 N11 **Indomed Fracture Zone** tectonic feature SW Indian Ocean
170 L12 **Indonesia** off. Republic of Indonesia, Ind. Republik Indonesia; prev. Dutch East Indies, Netherlands East Indies, United States of Indonesia. ◆ republic SE Asia
Indonesian Borneo see Kalimantan
154 G10 **Indore** Madhya Pradesh, C India
168 L11 **Indragiri, Sungai** var. Batang Kuantan, Inderagiri. ~ Sumatera, W Indonesia
Indramajoe/Indramaju see Indramayu
169 P15 **Indramayu** prev. Indramajoe, Indramaju. Jawa, C Indonesia
155 K14 **Indrāvati** ~ S India
103 N9 **Indre** ◈ department C France
102 M8 **Indre** ~ C France
102 L8 **Indre-et-Loire** ◈ department C France
Indreville see Châteauroux
152 G3 **Indus** Chin. Yindu He; prev. Yin-tu Ho. ~ S Asia
Indus Cone see Indus Fan
173 P3 **Indus Fan** var. Indus Cone. undersea feature N Arabian Sea
149 P17 **Indus, Mouths of the** delta S Pakistan
83 I24 **Indwe** Eastern Cape, SE South Africa
136 I10 **İnebolu** Kastamonu, N Turkey
77 P8 **I-n-Échaï** oasis C Mali
114 M13 **İnecik** Tekirdağ, NW Turkey
136 E12 **İnegöl** Bursa, NW Turkey
Inessa see Biancavilla
116 F10 **Ineu** Hung. Borosjenő; prev. Inău. Arad, W Romania
Ineul/Ineu, Vîrful see Ineu, Vârful
116 J9 **Ineu, Vârful** var. Ineul; prev. Vîrful Ineu. ▲ N Romania
21 P6 **Inez** Kentucky, S USA
74 E8 **Inezgane** × (Agadir) W Morocco
41 T17 **Inferior, Laguna** lagoon S Mexico
40 M15 **Infiernillo, Presa del** ▣ S Mexico
104 L2 **Infiesto** Asturias, N Spain
93 L20 **Ingå** Fin. Inkoo. Etelä-Suomi, S Finland
77 U10 **Ingal** var. I-n-Gall. Agadez, C Niger
I-n-Gall see Ingal
99 C18 **Ingelmunster** West-Vlaanderen, W Belgium
79 I18 **Ingende** Equateur, W Dem. Rep. Congo (Zaire)
62 L5 **Ingeniero Guillermo Nueva Juárez** Formosa, N Argentina
63 H16 **Ingeniero Jacobacci** Río Negro, C Argentina
14 F16 **Ingersoll** Ontario, S Canada
162 K6 **Ingettolgoy** Bulgan, N Mongolia
181 W5 **Ingham** Queensland, NE Australia
146 M11 **Ingichka** Samarqand Wiloyati, C Uzbekistan
97 L16 **Ingleborough** ▲ N England, UK
25 T14 **Ingleside** Texas, SW USA
184 K10 **Inglewood** Taranaki, North Island, NZ
35 S15 **Inglewood** California, W USA
101 L21 **Ingolstadt** Bayern, S Germany
33 V9 **Ingomar** Montana, NW USA
13 R14 **Ingonish Beach** Cape Breton Island, Nova Scotia, SE Canada
153 S14 **Ingrāj Bāzār** prev. English Bazar. West Bengal, NE India
25 Q11 **Ingram** Texas, SW USA
195 X7 **Ingrid Christensen Coast** physical region Antarctica
74 K14 **I-n-Guezzam** S Algeria
Ingulets see Inhulets'
Inguri see Enguri
Ingushetia/Ingushetiya, Respublika see Ingushskaya Respublika
129 O15 **Ingushskaya Respublika** var. Respublika Ingushetiya, Eng. Ingushetia. ◈ autonomous republic SW Russian Federation
83 N20 **Inhambane** Inhambane, SE Mozambique
83 M20 **Inhambane** off. Província de Inhambane. ◈ province S Mozambique
83 N17 **Inhaminga** Sofala, C Mozambique
83 N20 **Inharrime** Inhambane, SE Mozambique
83 M18 **Inhassoro** Inhambane, E Mozambique
117 S9 **Inhulets'** Rus. Ingulets. Dnipropetrovs'ka Oblast', E Ukraine
117 R10 **Inhulets'** Rus. Ingulets. ~ S Ukraine
105 Q10 **Iniesta** Castilla-La Mancha, C Spain
I-ning see Yining
54 K11 **Inírida, Río** ~ E Colombia
Inis see Ennis
Inis Ceithleann see Enniskillen
Inis Córthaidh see Enniscorthy
Inis Díomáin see Ennistimon
97 A17 **Inishbofin** Ir. Inis Bó Finne. island W Ireland
97 B18 **Inisheer** var. Inishere, Ir. Inis Oírr. island W Ireland
Inishere see Inisheer
97 B18 **Inishmaan** Ir. Inis Meáin. island W Ireland
97 A18 **Inishmore** Ir. Árainn. island W Ireland
96 E13 **Inishtrahull** Ir. Inis Trá Tholl. island NW Ireland
97 A17 **Inishturk** Ir. Inis Toirc. island W Ireland
Inkoo see Ingå
185 J16 **Inland Kaikoura Range** ▲ South Island, NZ
Inland Sea see Seto-naikai
21 P11 **Inman** South Carolina, SE USA
108 L7 **Inn** ~ C Europe
197 O11 **Innaanganeq** var. Kap York. headland NW Greenland
182 K2 **Innamincka** South Australia
94 I12 **Innbygda** ~ Hedmark, S Norway
92 G12 **Inndyr** Nordland, C Norway
42 G3 **Inner Channel** inlet SE Belize
96 F11 **Inner Hebrides** island group W Scotland, UK
172 H15 **Inner Islands** var. Central Group. island group NE Seychelles
Inner Mongolia/Inner Mongolian Autonomous Region see Nei Mongol Zizhiqu
96 G8 **Inner Sound** strait NW Scotland, UK
100 J13 **Innerste** ~ C Germany
181 W5 **Innisfail** Queensland, NE Australia
11 Q15 **Innisfail** Alberta, SW Canada
Inniskilling see Enniskillen

◆ Country ● Country Capital ◇ Dependent Territory ○ Dependent Territory Capital ◈ Administrative Region × International Airport ▲ Mountain ▲ Mountain Range Volcano ~ River ◎ Lake ▣ Reservoir

39 O11 **Innoko River** ⁓ Alaska, USA
Innosima *see* Innoshima
Innsbruch *see* Innsbruck
108 M7 **Innsbruck** *var.* Innsbruch. Tirol, W Austria
79 I19 **Inongo** Bandundu, W Dem. Rep. Congo (Zaire)
Inoucdjouac *see* Inukjuak
Inowrazlaw *see* Inowrocław
110 I10 **Inowrocław** *Ger.* Hohensalza; *prev.* Inowrazlaw. Kujawski-pomorskie, C Poland
57 K18 **Inquisivi** La Paz, W Bolivia
Inrin *see* Yüanlin
77 O8 **I-n-Sâkâne, 'Erg** *desert* N Mali
74 J10 **I-n-Salah** *var.* In Salah. C Algeria
129 O5 **Insar** Respublika Mordoviya, W Russian Federation
189 X15 **Insiaf** Kosrae, E Micronesia
94 L13 **Insjön** Dalarna, C Sweden
Insterburg *see* Chernyakhovsk
Insula *see* Lille
116 L13 **Însurăței** Brăila, SE Romania
127 V6 **Inta** Respublika Komi, NW Russian Federation
77 R9 **I-n-Tebezas** Kidal, E Mali
Interamna *see* Teramo
Interamna Nahars *see* Terni
28 L11 **Interior** South Dakota, N USA
108 E9 **Interlaken** Bern, SW Switzerland
29 V2 **International Falls** Minnesota, N USA
167 O7 **Inthanon, Doi** ▲ NW Thailand
42 G7 **Intibucá** ⬖ *department* SW Honduras
42 G8 **Intipucá** La Unión, SE El Salvador
61 B15 **Intiyaco** Santa Fe, C Argentina
116 K12 **Întorsura Buzăului** *Ger.* Bozau, *Hung.* Bodzafordulő. Covasna, E Romania
22 H9 **Intracoastal Waterway** *inland waterway system* Louisiana, S USA
25 V13 **Intracoastal Waterway** *inland waterway system* Texas, SW USA
108 G11 **Intragna** Ticino, S Switzerland
165 P14 **Inubō-zaki** *headland* Honshū, S Japan
164 E14 **Inukai** Ōita, Kyūshū, SW Japan
12 I5 **Inukjuak** *var.* Inoucdjouac; *prev.* Port Harrison. Quebec, NE Canada
63 I24 **Inútil, Bahía** *bay* S Chile
Inuuvik *see* Inuvik
9 R8 **Inuvik** *var.* Inuuvik. Northwest Territories, NW Canada
164 L13 **Inuyama** Aichi, Honshū, SW Japan
56 G13 **Inuya, Río** ⁓ E Peru
127 U13 **In'va** ⁓ NW Russian Federation
96 H11 **Inveraray** W Scotland, UK
185 C24 **Invercargill** Southland, South Island, NZ
183 T5 **Inverell** New South Wales, SE Australia
96 I8 **Invergordon** N Scotland, UK
11 P16 **Invermere** British Columbia, SW Canada
13 R14 **Inverness** Cape Breton Island, Nova Scotia, SE Canada
96 I8 **Inverness** N Scotland, UK
23 V11 **Inverness** Florida, SE USA
96 I9 **Inverness** *cultural region* NW Scotland, UK
96 K9 **Inverurie** NE Scotland, UK
182 F8 **Investigator Group** *island group* South Australia
173 T7 **Investigator Ridge** *undersea feature* E Indian Ocean
182 H10 **Investigator Strait** *strait* South Australia
29 R11 **Inwood** Iowa, C USA
123 S10 **Inya** ⁓ E Russian Federation
Inyanga *see* Nyanga
83 M16 **Inyangani** ▲ NE Zimbabwe
83 J17 **Inyathi** Matabeleland North, SW Zimbabwe
35 T12 **Inyokern** California, W USA
35 T10 **Inyo Mountains** ▲ California, W USA
129 P6 **Inza** Ul'yanovskaya Oblast', W Russian Federation
129 W5 **Inzer** Respublika Bashkortostan, W Russian Federation
129 N7 **Inzhavino** Tambovskaya Oblast', W Russian Federation
115 C16 **Ioánnina** *var.* Janina, Yannina. Ípeiros, W Greece
164 B17 **Iō-jima** *var.* Iwojima. *island* Nansei-shotō, SW Japan
126 L4 **Iokan'ga** ⁓ NW Russian Federation
27 Q6 **Iola** Kansas, C USA
Iolcus *see* Iolkós
115 G16 **Iolkós** *anc.* Iolcus. *site of ancient city* Thessalía, C Greece
Iolotan' *see* Yëloten
83 A16 **Iona** Namibe, SW Angola
96 F11 **Iona** *island* W Scotland, UK
116 M15 **Ion Corvin** Constanța, SE Romania
35 P7 **Ione** California, W USA
116 I13 **Ionești** Vâlcea, SW Romania
31 Q9 **Ionia** Michigan, N USA
Ionia Basin *see* Ionian Basin
121 O10 **Ionian Basin** *var.* Ionia Basin. *undersea feature* Ionian Sea, C Mediterranean Sea
Ionian Islands *see* Iónioi Nísoi
121 O10 **Ionian Sea** *Gk.* Iónio Pélagos, *It.* Mar Ionio. *sea* C Mediterranean Sea
115 B17 **Iónioi Nísoi** *Eng.* Ionian Islands. ⬖ *region* W Greece
115 B17 **Iónioi Nísoi** *Eng.* Ionian Islands. *island group* W Greece
Ionio, Mar/Iónio Pélagos *see* Ionian Sea
Iordan *see* Jordan
137 U10 **Iori** *var.* Qabırrı. ⁓ Azerbaijan/Georgia
Iorrais, Ceann *see* Erris Head
115 J22 **Íos** Íos, Kykládes, Greece, Aegean Sea
115 J22 **Íos** *var.* Nio. *island* Kykládes, Greece, Aegean Sea
22 G9 **Iowa** Louisiana, S USA
29 V13 **Iowa** *off.* State of Iowa; also known as The Hawkeye State. ⬖ *state* C USA
29 Y14 **Iowa City** Iowa, C USA
29 V13 **Iowa Falls** Iowa, C USA
25 R4 **Iowa Park** Texas, SW USA
29 Y14 **Iowa River** ⁓ Iowa, C USA
119 M19 **Ipa** *Rus.* Ipa. ⁓ SE Belarus
59 N20 **Ipatinga** Minas Gerais, SE Brazil
129 N13 **Ipatovo** Stavropol'skiy Kray, SW Russian Federation
115 C16 **Ípeiros** *Eng.* Epirus. ⬖ *region* W Greece
Ipek *see* Peć
111 J21 **Ipel'** *var.* Ipoly, *Ger.* Eipel. ⁓ Hungary/Slovakia
54 C13 **Ipiales** Nariño, SW Colombia
189 V14 **Ipis** *atoll* Chuuk Islands, C Micronesia
59 A14 **Ipixuna** Amazonas, W Brazil
168 J8 **Ipoh** Perak, Peninsular Malaysia
Ipoly *see* Ipel'
187 S15 **Ipota** Erromango, S Vanuatu
79 K14 **Ippy** Ouaka, C Central African Republic
114 L13 **İpsala** Edirne, NW Turkey
Ipsario *see* Ypsário
183 V3 **Ipswich** Queensland, E Australia
97 Q20 **Ipswich** *hist.* Gipeswic. E England, UK
29 O8 **Ipswich** South Dakota, N USA
Iput' *see* Iputs'
119 P18 **Iputs'** *Rus.* Iput'. ⁓ Belarus/Russian Federation
9 R7 **Iqaluit** *prev.* Frobisher Bay. Baffin Island, Nunavut, NE Canada
159 P9 **Iqe** Qinghai, W China
159 P9 **Iqe He** ⁓ C China
Iqlid *see* Eqlīd
62 G3 **Iquique** Tarapacá, N Chile
56 G8 **Iquitos** Loreto, N Peru
25 N9 **Iraan** Texas, SW USA
79 K14 **Ira Banda** Haute-Kotto, E Central African Republic
165 P16 **Irabu-jima** *island* Miyako-shotō, SW Japan
55 Y9 **Iracoubo** N French Guiana
60 H13 **Iraí** Rio Grande do Sul, S Brazil
114 G12 **Irákleia** Kentrikí Makedonía, N Greece
115 J21 **Irákleia** *island* Kykládes, Greece, Aegean Sea
115 J25 **Irákleio** *var.* Herakleion, *Eng.* Candia; *prev.* Iráklion. Kríti, Greece, E Mediterranean Sea
115 J25 **Irákleio** ✕ Kríti, Greece, E Mediterranean Sea
115 F15 **Irákleio** *anc.* Heracleum. *castle* Kentrikí Makedonía, N Greece
Iráklion *see* Irákleio
143 O7 **Iran** *off.* Islamic Republic of Iran; *prev.* Persia. ◆ *republic* SW Asia
58 F13 **Iranduba** Amazonas, NW Brazil
85 P13 **Iranian Plate** *tectonic feature*
143 Q9 **Iranian Plateau** *var.* Plateau of Iran. *plateau* N Iran
169 U9 **Iran, Pegunungan** *var.* Iran Mountains. ▲ Indonesia/Malaysia
Iran, Plateau of *see* Iranian Plateau
143 W13 **Īrānshahr** Sīstān va Balūchestān, SE Iran
55 P5 **Irapa** Sucre, NE Venezuela
41 N13 **Irapuato** Guanajuato, C Mexico
139 R7 **Iraq** *off.* Republic of Iraq, *Ar.* 'Irāq. ◆ *republic* SW Asia
60 J12 **Irati** Paraná, S Brazil
105 R3 **Irati** ⁓ N Spain
127 T8 **Irayël'** Respublika Komi, NW Russian Federation
43 N13 **Irazú, Volcán** ✱ C Costa Rica
Irbenskiy Zaliv/Irbes Šaurums *see* Irbe Strait
118 D7 **Irbe Strait** *Est.* Kura Kurk, *Latv.* Irbes Šaurums, *Rus.* Irbenskiy Zaliv; *prev. Est.* Irbe Väin. *strait* Estonia/Latvia
Irbe Väin *see* Irbe Strait
138 G9 **Irbid** Irbid, N Jordan
138 G9 **Irbid** *off.* Muḥāfaẓat Irbid. ⬖ *governorate* N Jordan
Irbīl *see* Arbīl
109 S6 **Irdning** Steiermark, SE Austria
79 I18 **Irebu** Equateur, W Dem. Rep. Congo (Zaire)
84 C9 **Ireland** *Lat.* Hibernia. *island* Ireland/UK
Ireland *see* Ireland, Republic of
64 A12 **Ireland Island North** *island* W Bermuda
64 A12 **Ireland Island South** *island* W Bermuda
97 D17 **Ireland, Republic of** *off.* Republic of Ireland, *var.* Ireland, *Ir.* Éire. ◆ *republic* NW Europe
127 V15 **Iren'** ⁓ NW Russian Federation
185 A22 **Irene, Mount** ▲ South Island, NZ
Irgalem *see* Yirga 'Alem
144 L11 **Irgiz** Aktyubinsk, C Kazakhstan
Irian *see* New Guinea
Irian Barat *see* Irian Jaya
171 X13 **Irian Jaya** *var.* Irian Barat, West Irian, West New Guinea, West Papua ; *prev.* Dutch New Guinea, Netherlands New Guinea. ⬖ *province* E Indonesia
Irian, Teluk *see* Cenderawasih, Teluk
78 K9 **Iriba** Biltine, NE Chad
129 X7 **Iriklinskoye Vodokhranilishche** ▣ W Russian Federation
81 H23 **Iringa** Iringa, C Tanzania
81 H23 **Iringa** ⬖ *region* S Tanzania
165 O16 **Iriomote-jima** *island* Sakishima-shotō, SW Japan
42 L4 **Iriona** Colón, NE Honduras
47 U7 **Iriri** ⁓ N Brazil
58 I13 **Iriri, Rio** ⁓ C Brazil
Iris *see* Yeşilırmak
35 W9 **Irish, Mount** ▲ Nevada, W USA
97 H17 **Irish Sea** *Ir.* Muir Éireann. *sea* C British Isles
139 U12 **Irjal ash Shaykhīyah** S Iraq
147 U11 **Irkeshtam** Oshskaya Oblast', SW Kyrgyzstan
122 M13 **Irkutsk** Irkutskaya Oblast', S Russian Federation
122 M12 **Irkutskaya Oblast'** ⬖ *province* S Russian Federation
Irlir, Gora *see* Irlir Toghi
146 K8 **Irlir Toghi** *var.* Gora Irlir. ▲ N Uzbekistan
Irminger Basin *see* Reykjanes Basin
21 R12 **Irmo** South Carolina, SE USA
102 E6 **Iroise** *sea* NW France
189 X2 **Iroj** *var.* Eroj. *island* Ratak Chain, SE Marshall Islands
182 H7 **Iron Baron** South Australia
14 C10 **Iron Bridge** Ontario, S Canada
20 H10 **Iron City** Tennessee, S USA
14 I13 **Irondale** ⁓ Ontario, SE Canada
182 H7 **Iron Knob** South Australia
30 M5 **Iron Mountain** Michigan, N USA
30 M4 **Iron River** Michigan, N USA
30 J3 **Iron River** Wisconsin, N USA
27 X6 **Ironton** Missouri, C USA
31 S15 **Ironton** Ohio, N USA
30 K4 **Ironwood** Michigan, N USA
12 H12 **Iroquois Falls** Ontario, S Canada
31 N12 **Iroquois River** ⁓ Illinois/Indiana, N USA
164 M15 **Irō-zaki** *headland* Honshū, S Japan
Irpen' *see* Irpin'
117 O4 **Irpin'** *Rus.* Irpen'. Kyyivs'ka Oblast', N Ukraine
117 O4 **Irpin'** *Rus.* Irpen'. ⁓ N Ukraine
141 Q16 **'Irqah** SW Yemen
166 K8 **Irrawaddy** *var.* Ayeyarwady. ⬖ *division* SW Myanmar
166 L6 **Irrawaddy** *var.* Ayeyarwady. ⁓ W Myanmar
166 K8 **Irrawaddy, Mouths of the** *delta* SW Myanmar
117 N4 **Irsha** ⁓ N Ukraine
116 H7 **Irshava** Zakarpats'ka Oblast', W Ukraine
107 N18 **Irsina** Basilicata, S Italy
Irtish *see* Irtysh
131 R5 **Irtysh** *var.* Irtish, *Kaz.* Ertis. ⁓ C Asia
145 S7 **Irtyshsk** *Kaz.* Ertis. Pavlodar, NE Kazakhstan
79 P17 **Irumu** Orientale, E Dem. Rep. Congo (Zaire)
105 Q2 **Irún** País Vasco, N Spain
Iruña *see* Pamplona
105 Q3 **Irurtzun** Navarra, N Spain
96 I13 **Irvine** W Scotland, UK
21 N6 **Irvine** Kentucky, S USA
25 T6 **Irving** Texas, SW USA
20 K5 **Irvington** Kentucky, S USA
Isa *see* Isaku
28 L8 **Isabel** South Dakota, N USA
186 L8 **Isabel** *off.* Isabel Province. ⬖ *province* N Solomon Islands
171 O8 **Isabela** Basilan Island, SW Philippines
45 S5 **Isabela** W Puerto Rico
45 N8 **Isabela, Cabo** *headland* NW Dominican Republic
57 A18 **Isabela, Isla** *var.* Albemarle Island. *island* Galapagos Islands, Ecuador, E Pacific Ocean
40 I12 **Isabela, Isla** *island* C Mexico
42 K9 **Isabella, Cordillera** ▲ NW Nicaragua
35 S12 **Isabella Lake** ▣ California, W USA
31 N2 **Isabelle, Point** *headland* Michigan, N USA
Isabel Segunda *see* Vieques
116 M13 **Isaccea** Tulcea, E Romania
92 H1 **Ísafjardardjúp** *inlet* NW Iceland
92 H1 **Ísafjördhur** Vestfirdhir, NW Iceland
164 C14 **Isahaya** Nagasaki, Kyūshū, SW Japan
149 S7 **Īsa Khel** Punjab, E Pakistan
172 H7 **Isalo** *var.* Massif de L'Isalo. ▲ SW Madagascar
Isalo, Massif de L' *see* Isalo
79 K20 **Isandja** Kasai Occidental, C Dem. Rep. Congo (Zaire)
187 R15 **Isangel** Tanna, S Vanuatu
79 M18 **Isangi** Orientale, C Dem. Rep. Congo (Zaire)
101 L24 **Isar** ⁓ Austria/Germany
101 M23 **Isar-Kanal** *canal* SE Germany
Isbarta *see* Isparta
Isca Damnoniorum *see* Exeter
107 K18 **Ischia** *var.* Isola d'Ischia; *anc.* Aenaria. Campania, S Italy
107 J18 **Ischia, Isola d'** *island* S Italy
54 B12 **Iscuandé** *var.* Santa Bárbara. Nariño, SW Colombia
164 K14 **Ise** Mie, Honshū, SW Japan
100 J12 **Ise** ⁓ N Germany
95 I23 **Isefjord** *fjord* E Denmark
Iseghem *see* Izegem
192 M14 **Iselin Seamount** *undersea feature* S Pacific Ocean
Isenhof *see* Püssi
106 E7 **Iseo** Lombardia, N Italy
103 U12 **Iseran, Col de l'** *pass* E France
103 S11 **Isère** ⬖ *department* E France
103 S12 **Isère** ⁓ E France
101 F15 **Iserlohn** Nordrhein-Westfalen, W Germany
107 K16 **Isernia** *var.* Æsernia. Molise, C Italy
165 N12 **Isesaki** Gunma, Honshū, S Japan
131 Q5 **Iset'** ⁓ C Russian Federation
77 S15 **Iseyin** Oyo, W Nigeria
Isfahan *see* Eşfahān
147 Q11 **Isfana** Oshskaya Oblast', SW Kyrgyzstan
147 R11 **Isfara** N Tajikistan
149 O4 **Isfi Maidān** Ghowr, N Afghanistan
92 O3 **Isfjorden** *fjord* W Svalbard
Isha Baydhabo *see* Baydhabo
127 V11 **Isherim, Gora** ▲ NW Russian Federation
129 Q5 **Isheyevka** Ul'yanovskaya Oblast', W Russian Federation
165 P16 **Ishigaki** Okinawa, Ishigaki-jima, SW Japan
165 P16 **Ishigaki-jima** *var.* Isigaki Zima. *island* Sakishima-shotō, SW Japan
165 R3 **Ishikari-wan** *bay* Hokkaidō, NE Japan
165 S16 **Ishikawa** *var.* Isikawa. Okinawa, Okinawa, SW Japan
164 K11 **Ishikawa** *off.* Ishikawa-ken, *var.* Isikawa. ⬖ *prefecture* Honshū, SW Japan
122 H11 **Ishim** Tyumenskaya Oblast', C Russian Federation
131 R6 **Ishim** *Kaz.* Esil. ⁓ Kazakhstan/Russian Federation
129 V6 **Ishimbay** Respublika Bashkortostan, W Russian Federation
145 O9 **Ishimskoye** Akmola, C Kazakhstan
165 Q10 **Ishinomaki** *var.* Isinomaki. Miyagi, Honshū, C Japan
165 P13 **Ishioka** *var.* Isioka. Ibaraki, Honshū, S Japan
Ishkashim *see* Ishkoshim
Ishkashimskiy Khrebet *see* Ishkoshim, Qatorkŭhi
147 S15 **Ishkoshim** *Rus.* Ishkashim. S Tajikistan
147 S15 **Ishkoshim, Qatorkŭhi** *Rus.* Ishkashimskiy Khrebet. ▲ SE Tajikistan
31 N4 **Ishpeming** Michigan, N USA
147 N11 **Ishtikhon** *Rus.* Ishtykhan. Samarqand Wiloyati, C Uzbekistan
Ishtykhan *see* Ishtikhon
153 T15 **Ishurdi** *var.* Iswardi. Rajshahi, W Bangladesh
61 G17 **Isidoro Noblia** Cerro Largo, NE Uruguay
102 J4 **Isigny-sur-Mer** Calvados, N France
Isikari Gawa *see* Ishikari-gawa
Isikawa *see* Ishikawa
136 C11 **Işıklar Dağı** ▲ NW Turkey
107 C19 **Isili** Sardegna, Italy, C Mediterranean Sea
122 H12 **Isil'kul'** Omskaya Oblast', C Russian Federation
Isinomaki *see* Ishinomaki
Isioka *see* Ishioka
81 I18 **Isiolo** Eastern, C Kenya
79 O16 **Isiro** Orientale, NE Dem. Rep. Congo (Zaire)
92 P2 **Isispynten** *headland* NE Svalbard
123 P11 **Isit** Respublika Sakha (Yakutiya), NE Russian Federation
149 O2 **Iskabad Canal** *canal* N Afghanistan
147 Q9 **Iskandar** *Rus.* Iskander. Toshkent Wiloyati, E Uzbekistan
Iskander *see* Iskandar
Iskăr *see* Iskŭr
121 Q2 **İskele** *var.* Trikomo, *Gk.* Tríkomon. E Cyprus
136 K17 **İskenderun** *Eng.* Alexandretta. Hatay, S Turkey
138 H2 **İskenderun Körfezi** *Eng.* Gulf of Alexandretta. *gulf* S Turkey
136 J11 **İskilip** Çorum, N Turkey
Iski-Nauket *see* Eski-Nookat
114 J11 **Iskra** *prev.* Popovo. Kŭrdzhali, S Bulgaria
114 G10 **Iskŭr** *var.* Iskăr. ⁓ NW Bulgaria
114 H10 **Iskŭr, Yazovir** *prev.* Yazovir Stalin. ▣ W Bulgaria
41 S15 **Isla** Veracruz-Llave, SE Mexico
119 J15 **Islach** *Rus.* Isloch'. ⁓ C Belarus
104 H14 **Isla Cristina** Andalucía, S Spain
Isla de León *see* San Fernando
149 U6 **Islāmābād** ● (Pakistan) Federal Capital Territory Islāmābād, NE Pakistan
149 V6 **Islāmābād** ✕ Federal Capital Territory Islāmābād, NE Pakistan
Islamabad *see* Anantnāg
149 R17 **Islāmkot** Sind, SE Pakistan
23 Y17 **Islamorada** Florida Keys, Florida, SE USA
153 P14 **Islāmpur** Bihār, N India
Islam Qala *see* Eslām Qal'eh
Island/Ísland *see* Iceland
18 K16 **Island Beach** *spit* New Jersey, NE USA
19 S4 **Island Falls** Maine, NE USA
182 H6 **Island Lagoon** ◎ South Australia
11 Y13 **Island Lake** ◎ Manitoba, C Canada
29 W5 **Island Lake Reservoir** ▣ Minnesota, N USA
33 R13 **Island Park** Idaho, NW USA
19 N6 **Island Pond** Vermont, NE USA
184 K2 **Islands, Bay of** *inlet* North Island, NZ
103 R7 **Is-sur-Tille** Côte d'Or, C France
42 J3 **Islas de la Bahía** ⬖ *department* N Honduras
65 L20 **Islas Orcadas Rise** *undersea feature* S Atlantic Ocean
96 F12 **Islay** *island* SW Scotland, UK
116 I15 **Islaz** Teleorman, S Romania
29 V7 **Isle** Minnesota, N USA
102 M12 **Isle** ⁓ W France
97 I16 **Isle of Man** ◇ *UK crown dependency* NW Europe
21 X7 **Isle of Wight** Virginia, NE USA
97 M24 **Isle of Wight** *cultural region* S England, UK
191 Y3 **Isles Lagoon** ◎ Kiritimati, E Kiribati
37 R11 **Isleta Pueblo** New Mexico, SW USA
Isloch' *see* Islach
61 E19 **Ismael Cortinas** Flores, S Uruguay
Ismailia *see* Ismâ'ilîya
75 W7 **Ismâ'ilîya** *var.* Ismailia. N Egypt
Ismid *see* İzmit
75 X10 **Isna** *var.* Esna. SE Egypt
93 K18 **Isojoki** Länsi-Suomi, W Finland
82 M12 **Isoka** Northern, NE Zambia
Isola d'Ischia *see* Ischia
Isola d'Istria *see* Izola
Isonzo *see* Soča
15 U4 **Isoukustouc** ⁓ Quebec, SE Canada
136 F15 **Isparta** *var.* Isbarta. Isparta, SW Turkey
136 F15 **Isparta** *var.* Isbarta. ⬖ *province* SW Turkey
114 M7 **Isperikh** *prev.* Kemanlar. Razgrad, N Bulgaria
107 L26 **Ispica** Sicilia, Italy, C Mediterranean Sea
148 J14 **Ispikān** Balūchistān, SW Pakistan
137 Q12 **İspir** Erzurum, NE Turkey
138 E12 **Israel** *off.* State of Israel, *var.* Medinat Israel, *Heb.* Yisrael, Yisra'el. ◆ *republic* SW Asia
Issa *see* Vis
55 S9 **Issano** C Guyana
76 M16 **Issia** SW Ivory Coast
Issiq Köl *see* Issyk-Kul', Ozero
103 P11 **Issoire** Puy-de-Dôme, C France
103 N9 **Issoudun** *anc.* Uxellodunum. Indre, C France
81 H22 **Issuna** Singida, C Tanzania
Issyk *see* Yesik
Issyk-Kul' *see* Balykchy
147 X7 **Issyk-Kul', Ozero** *var.* Issiq Köl, *Kir.* Ysyk-Köl. ◎ E Kyrgyzstan
147 X7 **Issyk-Kul'skaya Oblast'** *Kir.* Ysyk-Köl Oblasty. ⬖ *province* E Kyrgyzstan
149 Q7 **Istādeh-ye Moqor, Āb-e-** *var.* Āb-i-Istāda. ◎ SE Afghanistan
136 D11 **İstanbul** *Bul.* Tsarigrad, *Eng.* Istanbul; *prev.* Constantinople, *anc.* Byzantium. İstanbul, NW Turkey
114 P12 **İstanbul** ⬖ *province* NW Turkey
114 P12 **İstanbul Boğazı** *var.* Bosporus Thracius, *Eng.* Bosphorus, Bosporus, *Turk.* Karadeniz Boğazı. *strait* NW Turkey
Istarska Županija *see* Istra
115 G19 **Isthmía** Pelopónnisos, S Greece
115 G17 **Istiaía** Évvoia, C Greece
54 D9 **Istmina** Chocó, W Colombia
23 W13 **Istokpoga, Lake** ◎ Florida, SE USA
112 A9 **Istra** *off.* Istarska županija. ⬖ *province* NW Croatia
112 I10 **Istra** *Eng.* Istria, *Ger.* Istrien. *cultural region* NW Croatia
103 R15 **Istres** Bouches-du-Rhône, SE France
Istria/Istrien *see* Istra
Iswardi *see* Ishurdi
129 V7 **Isyangulovo** Respublika Bashkortostan, W Russian Federation
62 O6 **Itá** Central, S Paraguay
59 O17 **Itaberaba** Bahia, E Brazil
59 M20 **Itabira** *prev.* Presidente Vargas. Minas Gerais, SE Brazil
59 O18 **Itabuna** Bahia, E Brazil
59 J18 **Itacaiu** Mato Grosso, S Brazil
58 G12 **Itacoatiara** Amazonas, N Brazil
54 D9 **Itagüí** Antioquia, W Colombia
60 D13 **Itá Ibaté** Corrientes, NE Argentina
60 G11 **Itaipú, Represa de** ▣ Brazil/Paraguay
58 H13 **Itaituba** Pará, NE Brazil
60 K13 **Itajaí** Santa Catarina, S Brazil
Italia/Italiana, Republica/Italian Republic, The *see* Italy
Italian Somaliland *see* Somalia
25 T7 **Italy** Texas, SW USA
106 G12 **Italy** *off.* The Italian Republic, *It.* Italia, Republica Italiana. ◆ *republic* S Europe
59 O19 **Itamaraju** Bahia, E Brazil
59 C14 **Itamarati** Amazonas, W Brazil
59 M19 **Itambé, Pico de** ▲ SE Brazil
164 J13 **Itami** ✕ (Ōsaka) Ōsaka, Honshū, SW Japan
115 H15 **Ítamos** ▲ N Greece
153 W11 **Itānagar** Arunāchal Pradesh, NE India
Itany *see* Litani
59 N19 **Itaobim** Minas Gerais, SE Brazil
59 P15 **Itaparica, Represa de** ▣ E Brazil
58 M13 **Itapecuru-Mirim** Maranhão, E Brazil
60 Q8 **Itaperuna** Rio de Janeiro, SE Brazil
59 O18 **Itapetinga** Bahia, E Brazil
60 L10 **Itapetininga** São Paulo, S Brazil
60 K10 **Itapeva** São Paulo, S Brazil
47 W6 **Itapicuru, Rio** ⁓ NE Brazil
58 O13 **Itapipoca** Ceará, E Brazil
60 M9 **Itapira** São Paulo, S Brazil
60 K8 **Itápolis** São Paulo, S Brazil
60 K10 **Itaporanga** São Paulo, S Brazil
62 P7 **Itapúa** *off.* Departamento de Itapúa. ⬖ *department* SE Paraguay
59 E15 **Itapuã do Oeste** Rondônia, W Brazil
61 E15 **Itaqui** Rio Grande do Sul, S Brazil
60 K10 **Itararé** São Paulo, S Brazil
60 K10 **Itararé, Rio** ⁓ S Brazil
154 H11 **Itārsi** Madhya Pradesh, C India
25 T7 **Itasca** Texas, SW USA
Itassi *see* Vieille Case
93 N17 **Itä-Suomi** ⬖ *province* E Finland
60 D13 **Itatí** Corrientes, NE Argentina
60 K10 **Itatinga** São Paulo, S Brazil
115 F18 **Itéas, Kólpos** *gulf* C Greece
57 N15 **Iténez, Río** *var.* Rio Guaporé. ⁓ Bolivia/Brazil *see also* Guaporé, Rio
54 H11 **Iteviate, Río** ⁓ C Colombia
100 I13 **Ith** *hill range* C Germany
31 Q8 **Ithaca** Michigan, N USA
18 H11 **Ithaca** New York, NE USA
115 C18 **Itháki** Itháki, Iónioi Nísoi, Greece, C Mediterranean Sea
115 C18 **Itháki** *island* Iónioi Nísoi, Greece, C Mediterranean Sea
It Hearrenfean *see* Heerenveen
79 L17 **Itimbiri** ⁓ N Dem. Rep. Congo (Zaire)
Itinomiya *see* Ichinomiya
Itinoseki *see* Ichinoseki
39 Q5 **Itkilik River** ⁓ Alaska, USA
164 M11 **Itoigawa** Niigata, Honshū, C Japan
15 R6 **Itomamo, Lac** ◎ Quebec, SE Canada
165 S17 **Itoman** Okinawa, SW Japan
102 M5 **Iton** ⁓ N France
57 M16 **Itonamas Río** ⁓ NE Bolivia
Itoupé, Mont *see* Sommet Tabulaire
Itseqqortoormiit *see* Ittoqqortoormiit
22 K4 **Itta Bena** Mississippi, S USA
107 B17 **Ittiri** Sardegna, Italy, C Mediterranean Sea
197 Q14 **Ittoqqortoormiit** *var.* Itseqqortoormiit, *Dan.* Scoresbysund, *Eng.* Scoresby Sound. Tunu, C Greenland
60 M10 **Itu** São Paulo, S Brazil
54 D8 **Ituango** Antioquia, NW Colombia
59 A14 **Ituí, Rio** ⁓ NW Brazil
79 O20 **Itula** Sud Kivu, E Dem. Rep. Congo (Zaire)
59 K19 **Itumbiara** Goiás, C Brazil
55 T9 **Ituni** E Guyana
41 X13 **Iturbide** Campeche, SE Mexico
Ituri *see* Aruwimi
123 V13 **Iturup, Ostrov** *island* Kuril'skiye Ostrova, SE Russian Federation
60 L7 **Ituverava** São Paulo, S Brazil
59 C15 **Ituxi, Rio** ⁓ W Brazil
61 E14 **Ituzaingó** Corrientes, NE Argentina
101 K18 **Itz** ⁓ C Germany
100 I9 **Itzehoe** Schleswig-Holstein, N Germany
23 N2 **Iuka** Mississippi, S USA
60 I11 **Ivaiporã** Paraná, S Brazil
60 I11 **Ivaí, Rio** ⁓ S Brazil
92 L10 **Ivalo** *Lapp.* Avveel, Avvil. Lappi, N Finland
92 L10 **Ivalojoki** *Lapp.* Avreel. ⁓ N Finland
119 H20 **Ivanava** *Pol.* Janów, Janów Poleski, *Rus.* Ivanovo. Brestskaya Voblasts', SW Belarus
Ivangorod *see* Dęblin
Ivangrad *see* Berane
183 N7 **Ivanhoe** New South Wales, SE Australia
29 S9 **Ivanhoe** Minnesota, N USA
14 D8 **Ivanhoe** ⁓ Ontario, S Canada
112 E8 **Ivanić-Grad** Sisak-Moslavina, N Croatia
117 T10 **Ivanivka** Khersons'ka Oblast', S Ukraine
117 P10 **Ivanivka** Odes'ka Oblast', SW Ukraine
113 L14 **Ivanjica** Serbia, C Yugoslavia
112 G11 **Ivanjska** *var.* Potkozarje. Republika Srpska, NW Bosnia & Herzegovina
111 H21 **Ivanka** ✕ (Bratislava) Bratislavský Kraj, W Slovakia
117 O3 **Ivankiv** *Rus.* Ivankov. Kyyivs'ka Oblast', N Ukraine
Ivankov *see* Ivankiv
39 O15 **Ivanof Bay** Alaska, USA
116 J7 **Ivano-Frankivs'k** *Ger.* Stanislau, *Pol.* Stanisławów, *Rus.* Ivano-Frankovsk; *prev.* Stanislav. Ivano-Frankivs'ka Oblast', W Ukraine
Ivano-Frankivs'k *see* Ivano-Frankivs'ka Oblast'
116 I7 **Ivano-Frankivs'ka Oblast'** *var.* Ivano-Frankivs'k, *Rus.* Ivano-Frankovskaya Oblast'; *prev.* Stanislavskaya Oblast'. ⬖ *province* W Ukraine
Ivano-Frankovsk *see* Ivano-Frankivs'k
Ivano-Frankovskaya Oblast' *see* Ivano-Frankivs'ka Oblast'
126 M16 **Ivanovo** Ivanovskaya Oblast', W Russian Federation
Ivanovo *see* Ivanava
126 M16 **Ivanovskaya Oblast'** ⬖ *province* W Russian Federation
35 X12 **Ivanpah Lake** ◎ California, W USA
112 E7 **Ivanšćica** ▲ NE Croatia
114 M8 **Ivanski** Shumen, NE Bulgaria
129 R7 **Ivanteyevka** Saratovskaya Oblast', W Russian Federation
Ivantsevichi/Ivatsevichi *see* Ivatsevichy
116 I4 **Ivanychi** Volyns'ka Oblast', NW Ukraine
119 H18 **Ivatsevichy** *Pol.* Iwacewicze, *Rus.* Ivantsevichi, Ivatsevichi. Brestskaya Voblasts', SW Belarus
114 L12 **Ivaylovgrad** Khaskovo, S Bulgaria

◆ Country ● Country Capital ◇ Dependent Territory ○ Dependent Territory Capital ⬖ Administrative Region ✕ International Airport ▲ Mountain ▲ Mountain Range ✱ Volcano ⁓ River ◎ Lake ▣ Reservoir

114 K11 **Ivaylovgrad, Yazovir** ⊠ S Bulgaria
122 G9 **Ivdel'** Sverdlovskaya Oblast', C Russian Federation
Ivenets see Ivyanyets
116 L12 **Iveşti** Galaţi, E Romania
Ivigtut see Ivittuut
79 F18 **Ivindo** ≈ Congo/Gabon
59 I21 **Ivinheima** Mato Grosso do Sul, SW Brazil
196 M15 **Ivittuut** var. Ivigtut. Kitaa, S Greenland
Iviza see Eivissa
172 I6 **Ivohibe** Fianarantsoa, SE Madagascar
Ivoire, Côte d' see Ivory Coast
76 L15 **Ivory Coast** off. Republic of the Ivory Coast, Fr. Côte d'Ivoire, République de la Côte d'Ivoire. ◆ republic W Africa
68 C11 **Ivory Coast** Fr. Côte d'Ivoire. coastal region S Ivory Coast
95 L22 **Ivösjön** ◎ S Sweden
106 B7 **Ivrea** anc. Eporedia. Piemonte, NW Italy
12 J2 **Ivujivik** Quebec, NE Canada
119 J16 **Ivyanyets** Rus. Ivenets. Minskaya Voblasts', C Belarus
Iv'ye see Iwye
Iwacewicze see Ivatsevichy
165 R8 **Iwaizumi** Iwate, Honshū, NE Japan
165 P12 **Iwaki** Fukushima, Honshū, N Japan
164 F13 **Iwakuni** Yamaguchi, Honshū, SW Japan
165 S4 **Iwamizawa** Hokkaidō, NE Japan
165 R4 **Iwanai** Hokkaidō, NE Japan
165 Q10 **Iwanuma** Miyagi, Honshū, C Japan
164 L14 **Iwata** Shizuoka, Honshū, S Japan
165 R8 **Iwate** Iwate, Honshū, N Japan
165 R8 **Iwate** off. Iwate-ken. ◈ prefecture Honshū, C Japan
Iwje see Iwye
77 S16 **Iwo** Oyo, SW Nigeria
Iwojima see Iō-jima
119 I16 **Iwye** Pol. Iwje, Rus. Iv'ye. Hrodzyenskaya Voblasts', W Belarus
42 C4 **Ixcán, Río** ≈ Guatemala/Mexico
99 G18 **Ixelles** Dut. Elsene. Brussels, C Belgium
57 J16 **Ixiamas** La Paz, NW Bolivia
41 O13 **Ixmiquilpan** var. Ixmiquilpán. Hidalgo, C Mexico
83 K23 **Ixopo** KwaZulu/Natal, E South Africa
Ixtaccíhuatal, Volcán see Iztaccíhuatl, Volcán
40 M16 **Ixtapa** Guerrero, S Mexico
41 S16 **Ixtepec** Oaxaca, SE Mexico
40 K12 **Ixtlán** var. Ixtlán del Río. Nayarit, C Mexico
Ixtlán del Río see Ixtlán
122 H11 **Iyevlevo** Tyumenskaya Oblast', C Russian Federation
164 F14 **Iyo** Ehime, Shikoku, SW Japan
Iyomisima see Iyomishima
164 E14 **Iyo-nada** sea S Japan
42 E4 **Izabal** off. Departamento de Izabal. ◈ department E Guatemala
42 F5 **Izabal, Lago de** prev. Golfo Dulce. ◎ E Guatemala
143 O9 **Īzad Khvāst** Fārs, C Iran
41 X12 **Izamal** Yucatán, SE Mexico
129 Q16 **Izberbash** Respublika Dagestan, SW Russian Federation
99 C18 **Izegem** prev. Iseghem. West-Vlaanderen, W Belgium
142 M9 **Īzeh** Khūzestān, SW Iran
165 T16 **Izena-jima** island Nansei-shotō, SW Japan
114 N10 **Izgrev** Burgas, E Bulgaria
129 T2 **Izhevsk** prev. Ustinov. Udmurtskaya Respublika, NW Russian Federation
127 S7 **Izhma** Respublika Komi, NW Russian Federation
127 S7 **Izhma** ≈ NW Russian Federation
141 X8 **Izkī** NE Oman
Izmail see Izmayil
117 N13 **Izmayil** Rus. Izmail. Odes'ka Oblast', SW Ukraine
136 B14 **İzmir** prev. Smyrna. İzmir, W Turkey
136 C14 **İzmir** prev. Smyrna. ◈ province W Turkey
136 E11 **İzmit** var. Ismid; anc. Astacus. Kocaeli, NW Turkey
104 M14 **Iznájar** Andalucía, S Spain
104 M14 **Iznajar, Embalse de** ⊠ S Spain
105 N14 **Iznalloz** Andalucía, S Spain
136 E11 **İznik** Bursa, NW Turkey
136 E12 **İznik Gölü** ◎ NW Turkey
128 M14 **Izobil'nyy** Stavropol'skiy Kray, SW Russian Federation
109 S13 **Izola** It. Isola d'Istria. SW Slovenia
138 H9 **Izra'** var. Ezra, Ezraa. Dar'ā, S Syria
41 P14 **Iztaccíhuatl, Volcán** var. Volcán Ixtaccíhuatal. ⛰ S Mexico
42 C7 **Iztapa** Escuintla, SE Guatemala
Izúcar de Matamoros see Matamoros
165 N14 **Izu-hantō** peninsula Honshū, S Japan
164 C12 **Izuhara** Nagasaki, Tsushima, SW Japan
164 J14 **Izumiōtsu** Ōsaka, Honshū, SW Japan
164 I14 **Izumi-Sano** Ōsaka, Honshū, SW Japan
164 G12 **Izumo** Shimane, Honshū, SW Japan
Izu Shichito see Izu-shotō
192 H5 **Izu Trench** undersea feature NW Pacific Ocean
122 K6 **Izvestiy TsIK, Ostrova** island N Russian Federation
114 G10 **Izvor** Pernik, W Bulgaria
116 L5 **Izyaslav** Khmel'nyts'ka Oblast', W Ukraine
117 W6 **Izyum** Kharkivs'ka Oblast', E Ukraine

J

95 M18 **Jaala** Etelä-Suomi, S Finland
140 J5 **Jabal ash Shifā** desert NW Saudi Arabia
141 U8 **Jabal az̧ Z̧annah** var. Jebel Dhanna. Abū Z̧aby, W UAE
138 E11 **Jabalīya** var. Jabāliyah. NE Gaza Strip
Jabāliyah see Jabalīya
105 N11 **Jabalón** ≈ C Spain
154 J10 **Jabalpur** prev. Jubbulpore. Madhya Pradesh, C India
141 N15 **Jabal Zuuqar, Jazīrat** var. Az Zuqur. island SW Yemen
Jabat see Jabwot
138 J3 **Jabbūl, Sabkhat al** salt flat NW Syria
181 P1 **Jabiru** Northern Territory, N Australia
138 H4 **Jablah** var. Jeble, Fr. Djéblé. Al Lādhiqīyah, W Syria
112 C11 **Jablanac** Lika-Senj, W Croatia
113 H14 **Jablanica** Federacija Bosna I Hercegovina, SW Bosnia and Herzegovina
113 M20 **Jablanica** Alb. Mali i Jabllanicës, var. Malet e Jabllanicës. ▲▲ Albania/FYR Macedonia **see also** Jabllanicës, Mali i
Jabllanicës, Malet e see Jablanica/Jabllanicës, Mali i
113 M20 **Jabllanicës, Mali i** var. Malet e Jabllanicës, Mac. Jablanica. ▲▲ Albania/FYR Macedonia **see also** Jablanica
111 E15 **Jablonec nad Nisou** Ger. Gablonz an der Neisse. Liberecký Kraj, N Czech Republic
Jabłonków/Jablunkau see Jablunkov
110 J9 **Jabłonowo Pomorskie** Kujawski-pomorskie, C Poland
111 J17 **Jablunkov** Ger. Jablunkau, Pol. Jabłonków. Ostravský Kraj, E Czech Republic
59 Q15 **Jaboatão** Pernambuco, E Brazil
60 L8 **Jaboticabal** São Paulo, S Brazil
189 U7 **Jabwot** var. Jabat, Jebat, Jōwat. island Ralik Chain, S Marshall Islands
105 S4 **Jaca** Aragón, NE Spain
42 B4 **Jacaltenango** Huehuetenango, W Guatemala
59 G14 **Jacaré-a-Canga** Pará, NE Brazil
60 N10 **Jacareí** São Paulo, S Brazil
59 I18 **Jaciara** Mato Grosso, W Brazil
59 E15 **Jaciparaná** Rondônia, W Brazil
19 P5 **Jackman** Maine, NE USA
35 X1 **Jackpot** Nevada, W USA
20 M8 **Jacksboro** Tennessee, S USA
25 S6 **Jacksboro** Texas, SW USA
23 N7 **Jackson** Alabama, S USA
35 P7 **Jackson** California, W USA
23 T4 **Jackson** Georgia, SE USA
21 O6 **Jackson** Kentucky, S USA
22 J8 **Jackson** Louisiana, S USA
31 Q10 **Jackson** Michigan, N USA
29 T11 **Jackson** Minnesota, N USA
22 K5 **Jackson** state capital Mississippi, S USA
27 Y7 **Jackson** Missouri, C USA
21 W8 **Jackson** North Carolina, SE USA
31 T15 **Jackson** Ohio, NE USA
20 G9 **Jackson** Tennessee, S USA
33 S14 **Jackson** Wyoming, C USA
185 C19 **Jackson Bay** bay South Island, NZ
186 E9 **Jackson Field** ✕ (Port Moresby) Central/National Capital District, S PNG
185 C20 **Jackson Head** headland South Island, NZ
23 S8 **Jackson, Lake** ◎ Florida, SE USA
33 S13 **Jackson Lake** ◎ Wyoming, C USA
194 J6 **Jackson, Mount** ▲ Antarctica
37 U3 **Jackson Reservoir** ◎ Colorado, C USA
23 Q3 **Jacksonville** Alabama, S USA
27 V11 **Jacksonville** Arkansas, C USA
23 W8 **Jacksonville** Florida, SE USA
30 K14 **Jacksonville** Illinois, N USA
21 W11 **Jacksonville** North Carolina, SE USA
25 W7 **Jacksonville** Texas, SW USA
23 X9 **Jacksonville Beach** Florida, SE USA
44 L9 **Jacmel** var. Jaquemel. S Haiti
Jacob see Nkayi
149 Q12 **Jacobābād** Sind, SE Pakistan
55 T11 **Jacobs Ladder Falls** waterfall S Guyana
45 O11 **Jaco, Pointe** headland N Dominica
15 Q9 **Jacques-Cartier** ≈ Quebec, SE Canada
13 P11 **Jacques-Cartier, Détroit de** var. Jacques-Cartier Passage. strait Gulf of St. Lawrence/St. Lawrence River
15 W6 **Jacques-Cartier, Mont** ▲ Quebec, SE Canada
Jacques-Cartier Passage see Jacques-Cartier, Détroit de
61 H16 **Jacuí, Rio** ≈ S Brazil
60 L11 **Jacupiranga** São Paulo, S Brazil
100 G10 **Jade** ≈ NW Germany
100 G10 **Jadebusen** bay NW Germany
Jadotville see Likasi
Jadransko More/Jadransko Morje see Adriatic Sea
105 O7 **Jadraque** Castilla-La Mancha, C Spain
56 C10 **Jaén** Cajamarca, N Peru
105 N13 **Jaén** Andalucía, SW Spain
105 N13 **Jaén** ◈ province Andalucía, S Spain
155 J23 **Jaffna** Northern Province, N Sri Lanka
155 K23 **Jaffna Lagoon** lagoon N Sri Lanka
19 N10 **Jaffrey** New Hampshire, NE USA
138 H13 **Jafr, Qā' al** var. El Jafr. salt pan S Jordan
152 J9 **Jagādhri** Haryāna, N India
118 H4 **Jägala** var. Jägala Jõgi, Ger. Jaggowal. ≈ NW Estonia
Jägala Jõgi see Jägala
Jagannath see Puri
155 L14 **Jagdalpur** Madhya Pradesh, C India
163 U5 **Jagdaqi** Nei Mongol Zizhiqu, N China
Jägerndorf see Krnov
Jaggowal see Jägala
139 O2 **Jaghjaghah, Nahr** ≈ N Syria
112 N13 **Jagodina** prev. Svetozarevo. Serbia, C Yugoslavia
112 K12 **Jagodnja** ▲ W Yugoslavia
101 I20 **Jagst** ≈ SW Germany
155 I14 **Jagtiāl** Andhra Pradesh, C India
61 H18 **Jaguarão** Rio Grande do Sul, S Brazil
61 H18 **Jaguarão, Rio** var. Río Yaguarón. ≈ Brazil/Uruguay
60 K11 **Jaguariaíva** Paraná, S Brazil
44 D5 **Jagüey Grande** Matanzas, W Cuba
153 P14 **Jahānābād** Bihār, N India
Jahra see Al Jahrā'
143 P12 **Jahrom** var. Jahrum. Fārs, S Iran
Jahrum see Jahrom
Jailolo see Halmahera, Pulau
Jainat see Chai Nat
Jainti see Jayanti
152 H12 **Jaipur** prev. Jeypore. Rājasthān, N India
153 T14 **Jaipur Hat** Rajshahi, NW Bangladesh
152 D11 **Jaisalmer** Rājasthān, NW India
154 O12 **Jājapur** Orissa, E India
143 R4 **Jājarm** Khorāsān, NE Iran
112 G12 **Jajce** Federacija Bosna I Hercegovina, W Bosnia and Herzegovina
Jajı see 'Alī Kheyl
83 D17 **Jakalsberg** Otjozondjupa, N Namibia
169 O15 **Jakarta** prev. Djakarta, Dut. Batavia. ● (Indonesia) Jawa, C Indonesia
10 I8 **Jakes Corner** Yukon Territory, W Canada
152 H9 **Jākhal** Haryāna, NW India
Jakobeny see Iacobeni
93 K16 **Jakobstad** Fin. Pietarsaari. Länsi-Suomi, W Finland
Jakobstadt see Jēkabpils
113 O18 **Jakupica** ▲ C FYR Macedonia
37 W15 **Jal** New Mexico, SW USA
141 P7 **Jalājil** var. Ĝalāğil. Ar Riyāḑ, C Saudi Arabia
Jalal-Abad see Dzhalal-Abad, Dzhalal-Abadskaya Oblast', W Kyrgyzstan
149 S5 **Jalālābād** var. Jalalabad, Jelalabad. Nangarhār, E Afghanistan
Jalal-Abad Oblasty see Dzhalal-Abadskaya Oblast'
149 V7 **Jalālpur** Punjab, E Pakistan
149 T11 **Jalālpur Pīrwāla** Punjab, E Pakistan
152 H8 **Jalandhar** prev. Jullundur. Punjab, N India
42 J7 **Jalán, Río** ≈ S Honduras
42 E6 **Jalapa** Jalapa, C Guatemala
42 J7 **Jalapa** Nueva Segovia, NW Nicaragua
42 A3 **Jalapa** off. Departamento de Jalapa. ◈ department SE Guatemala
42 E6 **Jalapa, Río** ≈ SE Guatemala
143 X13 **Jālaq** Sīstān va Balūchestān, SE Iran
93 K17 **Jalasjärvi** Länsi-Suomi, W Finland
149 O8 **Jaldak** Zābul, SE Afghanistan
60 J7 **Jales** São Paulo, S Brazil
154 P11 **Jaleshwar** var. Jaleswar. Orissa, NE India
Jaleswar see Jaleshwar
154 F12 **Jalgaon** Mahārāshtra, C India
139 W12 **Jalībah** S Iraq
139 W13 **Jalīb Shahāb** S Iraq
77 X15 **Jalingo** Taraba, E Nigeria
40 K13 **Jalisco** ◈ state SW Mexico
154 G13 **Jālna** Mahārāshtra, W India
Jalomitsa see Ialomiţa
105 R5 **Jalón** ≈ N Spain
152 E13 **Jālor** Rājasthān, N India
112 K11 **Jalovik** Serbia, W Yugoslavia
40 L12 **Jalpa** Zacatecas, C Mexico
153 S12 **Jalpāiguri** West Bengal, NE India
41 O12 **Jalpán** var. Jalpan. Querétaro de Arteaga, C Mexico
67 P2 **Jalta** island N Tunisia
75 S9 **Jālū** var. Jūlā. NE Libya
189 U8 **Jaluit Atoll** var. Jālwōj. atoll Ralik Chain, S Marshall Islands
Jālwōj see Jaluit Atoll
81 L18 **Jamaame** It. Giamame; prev. Margherita. Jubbada Hoose, S Somalia
77 W13 **Jamaare** ≈ NE Nigeria
44 G9 **Jamaica** ◆ commonwealth republic W West Indies
47 P3 **Jamaica** island W West Indies
44 I9 **Jamaica Channel** channel Haiti/Jamaica
153 T14 **Jamalpur** Dhaka, N Bangladesh
153 Q14 **Jamālpur** Bihār, NE India
168 L9 **Jamaluang** var. Jemaluang. Johor, Peninsular Malaysia
59 I14 **Jamanxim, Rio** ≈ C Brazil
56 B8 **Jambeli, Canal de** channel S Ecuador
99 I20 **Jambes** Namur, SE Belgium
168 Hh9 **Jambi** var. Telanaipura; prev. Djambi. Sumatera, W Indonesia
GG H9 **Jambi** off. Propinsi Jambi, var. Djambi. ◈ province W Indonesia
Jamdena see Yamdena, Pulau
12 H8 **James Bay** bay Ontario/Quebec, E Canada
63 F19 **James, Isla** island Archipiélago de los Chonos, S Chile
181 Q8 **James Ranges** ▲▲ Northern Territory, C Australia
29 P8 **James River** ≈ North Dakota/South Dakota, N USA
21 X7 **James River** ≈ Virginia, NE USA
194 H4 **James Ross Island** island Antarctica
182 I8 **Jamestown** South Australia
65 G25 **Jamestown** ○ (Saint Helena) NW Saint Helena
35 P8 **Jamestown** California, W USA
20 L7 **Jamestown** Kentucky, S USA
18 D11 **Jamestown** New York, NE USA
29 P5 **Jamestown** North Dakota, N USA
20 L8 **Jamestown** Tennessee, S USA
Jamestown see Holetown
15 N10 **Jamet** ≈ Quebec, SE Canada
41 Q17 **Jamiltepec** var. Santiago Jamiltepec. Oaxaca, SE Mexico
95 F20 **Jammerbugten** bay Skagerrak, E North Sea
152 H6 **Jammu** prev. Jummoo. Jammu and Kashmir, NW India
152 I5 **Jammu and Kashmir** var. Jammu-Kashmir, Kashmir. ◈ state NW India
149 V4 **Jammu and Kashmir** disputed region India/Pakistan
154 B10 **Jāmnagar** prev. Navanagar. Gujarāt, W India
149 S11 **Jāmpur** Punjab, E Pakistan
93 L18 **Jämsä** Länsi-Suomi, W Finland
93 L18 **Jämsänkoski** Länsi-Suomi, W Finland
153 Q16 **Jamshedpur** Bihār, NE India
94 K9 **Jämtland** ◈ county C Sweden
153 Q14 **Jamūi** Bihār, NE India
153 T14 **Jamuna** ≈ N Bangladesh
Jamuna see Brahmaputra
Jamundá see Nhamundá, Rio
54 D11 **Jamundí** Valle del Cauca, SW Colombia
153 Q12 **Janakpur** Central, C Nepal
59 N18 **Janaúba** Minas Gerais, SE Brazil
58 K11 **Janaucu, Ilha** island NE Brazil
143 Q7 **Jandaq** Eşfahān, C Iran
64 Q11 **Jandia, Punta de** headland Fuerteventura, Islas Canarias, Spain, NE Atlantic Ocean
59 B14 **Jandiatuba, Rio** ≈ NW Brazil
105 N12 **Jándula** ≈ S Spain
29 V10 **Janesville** Minnesota, N USA
30 L9 **Janesville** Wisconsin, N USA
149 N13 **Jangal** Baluchistān, SW Pakistan
83 N20 **Jangamo** Inhambane, SE Mozambique
155 J14 **Jangaon** Andhra Pradesh, C India
146 K10 **Jangeldi** Rus. Dzhankel'dy. Bukhoro Wiloyati, C Uzbekistan
153 S14 **Jangīpur** West Bengal, NE India
Janina see Ioánnina
Janischken see Joniškis
112 J11 **Janja** Republika Srpska, NE Bosnia and Herzegovina
Jankovac see Jánoshalma
197 Q15 **Jan Mayen** ◇ Norwegian dependency N Atlantic Ocean
84 D5 **Jan Mayen** island N Atlantic Ocean
197 R15 **Jan Mayen Fracture Zone** tectonic feature Greenland Sea/Norwegian Sea
197 R15 **Jan Mayen Ridge** undersea feature Greenland Sea/ Norwegian Sea
40 H3 **Janos** Chihuahua, N Mexico
111 K25 **Jánoshalma** SCr. Jankovac. Bács-Kiskun, S Hungary
Janow/Janów see Jonava, Lithuania
Janów see Ivanava, Belarus
110 H10 **Janowiec Wielkopolski** Ger. Janowitz. Kujawski-pomorskie, C Poland
Janowitz see Janowiec Wielkopolski
111 O15 **Janów Lubelski** Lubelskie, E Poland
Janów Poleski see Ivanava
83 H25 **Jansenville** Eastern Cape, S South Africa
59 M18 **Januária** Minas Gerais, SE Brazil
Janūbīyah, Al Bādiyah al see Ash Shāmīyah
102 I7 **Janzé** Ille-et-Vilaine, NW France
154 F10 **Jaora** Madhya Pradesh, C India
164 K11 **Japan** var. Nippon, Jap. Nihon. ◆ monarchy E Asia
131 Y9 **Japan** island group E Asia
192 H4 **Japan Basin** undersea feature N Sea of Japan
131 Y8 **Japan, Sea of** var. East Sea, Rus. Yapanskoye More. sea NW Pacific Ocean
192 H4 **Japan Trench** undersea feature NW Pacific Ocean
Japen see Yapen, Pulau
59 A15 **Japiim** var. Máncio Lima. Acre, W Brazil
58 D12 **Japurá** Amazonas, N Brazil
58 C12 **Japurá, Rio** var. Río Caquetá, Yapurá. ≈ Brazil/Colombia **see also** Caquetá, Río
43 W17 **Jaqué** Darién, SE Panama
Jaquemel see Jacmel
Jarablos see Jarābulus
138 K2 **Jarābulus** var. Jarablos, Jerablus, Fr. Djérablous. Ḩalab, N Syria
60 K13 **Jaraguá do Sul** Santa Catarina, S Brazil
104 K9 **Jaraicejo** Extremadura, W Spain
104 K9 **Jaráiz de la Vera** Extremadura, W Spain
105 O7 **Jarama** ≈ C Spain
63 J20 **Jaramillo** Santa Cruz, SE Argentina
Jarandilla de la Vega see Jarandilla de la Vera
104 K8 **Jarandilla de la Vera** var. Jarandilla de la Vega. Extremadura, W Spain
149 V9 **Jarānwāla** Punjab, E Pakistan
138 G9 **Jarash** var. Jerash; anc. Gerasa. Irbid, NW Jordan
Jarbah, Jazīrat see Jerba, Île de
94 N13 **Järbo** Gävleborg, C Sweden
Jardan see Jordan
44 F7 **Jardines de la Reina, Archipiélago de los** island group C Cuba
162 J7 **Jargalant** Arhangay, C Mongolia
162 I8 **Jargalant** Bayanhongor, C Mongolia
162 D7 **Jargalant** Bayan-Ölgiy, W Mongolia
162 K6 **Jargalant** Bulgan, N Mongolia
162 G9 **Jargalant** Govĭ-Altay, W Mongolia
Jarīd, Shaţţ al see Jerid, Chott el
58 I11 **Jari, Rio** var. Jary. ≈ N Brazil
141 N7 **Jarīr, Wādī al** dry watercourse C Saudi Arabia
Jarja see Yur'ya
94 L13 **Järna** var. Dala-Järna. Dalarna, C Sweden
95 O16 **Järna** Stockholm, C Sweden
102 K11 **Jarnac** Charente, W France
110 H12 **Jarocin** Wielkopolskie, C Poland
111 F16 **Jaroměř** Ger. Jermer. Hradecký Kraj, N Czech Republic
Jaroslau see Jarosław
111 O16 **Jarosław** Ger. Jaroslau, Rus. Yaroslav. Podkarpackie, SE Poland
93 F16 **Järpen** Jämtland, C Sweden
147 O14 **Jarqŭrghon** Rus. Dzharkurgan. Surkhondaryo Wiloyati, S Uzbekistan
139 P2 **Jarrāh, Wadi** dry watercourse NE Syria
Jars, Plain of see Xiangkhoang, Plateau de
162 K14 **Jartai Yanchi** ◎ N China
59 E16 **Jaru** Rondônia, W Brazil
163 T10 **Jarud Qi** Nei Mongol Zizhiqu, N China
118 I4 **Järva-Jaani** Ger. Sankt-Johannis. Järvamaa, N Estonia
118 G5 **Järvakandi** Ger. Jerwakant. Raplamaa, NW Estonia
118 H4 **Järvamaa** off. Järva Maakond. ◈ province N Estonia
93 L19 **Järvenpää** Etelä-Suomi, S Finland
14 G17 **Jarvis** Ontario, S Canada
177 R8 **Jarvis Island** ◇ US unincorporated territory C Pacific Ocean
94 M11 **Järvsö** Gävleborg, C Sweden
Jary see Jari, Rio
112 M9 **Jaša Tomić** Serbia, NE Yugoslavia
112 D12 **Jasenice** Zadar, SW Croatia
138 I11 **Jashshat al 'Adlah, Wādī al** dry watercourse C Jordan
77 Q16 **Jasikan** E Ghana
143 T15 **Jāsk** Hormozgān, SE Iran
146 F6 **Jasliq** Rus. Zhaslyk. Qoraqalpoghiston Respublikasi, NW Uzbekistan
111 N17 **Jasło** Podkarpackie, SE Poland
11 U16 **Jasmin** Saskatchewan, S Canada
65 A23 **Jason Islands** island group NW Falkland Islands
194 I4 **Jason Peninsula** peninsula Antarctica
31 N15 **Jasonville** Indiana, N USA
11 O15 **Jasper** Alberta, SW Canada
14 L13 **Jasper** Ontario, SE Canada
23 O3 **Jasper** Alabama, S USA
27 T9 **Jasper** Arkansas, C USA
23 U8 **Jasper** Florida, SE USA
31 N16 **Jasper** Indiana, N USA
29 R11 **Jasper** Minnesota, N USA
27 S7 **Jasper** Missouri, C USA
20 K10 **Jasper** Tennessee, S USA
25 Y9 **Jasper** Texas, SW USA
11 O15 **Jasper National Park** national park Alberta/British Columbia, SW Canada
Jassy see Iaşi
113 N14 **Jastrebac** ▲▲ SE Yugoslavia
112 D9 **Jastrebarsko** Zagreb, N Croatia
Jastrow see Jastrowie
110 G9 **Jastrowie** Ger. Jastrow. Wielkopolskie, C Poland
111 J17 **Jastrzębie-Zdrój** Śląskie, S Poland
111 L22 **Jászapáti** Jász-Nagykun-Szolnok, E Hungary
111 L22 **Jászberény** Jász-Nagykun-Szolnok, E Hungary
111 L23 **Jász-Nagykun-Szolnok** off. Jász-Nagykun-Szolnok Megye. ◈ county E Hungary
59 J19 **Jataí** Goiás, C Brazil
58 G12 **Jatapu, Serra do** ▲ N Brazil
41 W16 **Jatate, Río** ≈ SE Mexico
149 P17 **Jāti** Sind, SE Pakistan
44 F6 **Jatibonico** Sancti Spíritus, C Cuba
169 O16 **Jatiluhur, Danau** ◎ Jawa, S Indonesia
Jativa see Xátiva
149 S11 **Jattoi** Punjab, E Pakistan
60 L9 **Jaú** São Paulo, S Brazil
58 F11 **Jauaperi, Rio** ≈ N Brazil
99 I19 **Jauche** Wallon Brabant, C Belgium
Jauer see Jawor
Jauf see Al Jawf
149 U7 **Jauharābād** Punjab, E Pakistan
57 E14 **Jauja** Junín, C Peru
41 O10 **Jaumave** Tamaulipas, C Mexico
118 H10 **Jaunjelgava** Ger. Friedrichstadt. Aizkraukle, S Latvia
Jaunlatgale see Pytalovo
118 I8 **Jaunpiebalga** Gulbene, NE Latvia
118 E9 **Jaunpils** Tukums, C Latvia
153 N13 **Jaunpur** Uttar Pradesh, N India
29 N8 **Java** South Dakota, N USA
Java see Jawa
105 R9 **Javalambre** ▲ E Spain
173 V7 **Java Ridge** undersea feature E Indian Ocean
59 A14 **Javari, Rio** var. Yavarí. ≈ Brazil/Peru
163 O7 **Javarthushuu** Dornod, NE Mongolia
169 Q15 **Java Sea** Ind. Laut Jawa. sea W Indonesia
173 U7 **Java Trench** var. Sunda Trench. undersea feature E Indian Ocean
105 T11 **Jávea** var. Xàbia. País Valenciano, E Spain
163 O7 **Javhlant** Hentiy, E Mongolia
63 G20 **Javier, Isla** island S Chile
113 L14 **Javor** ▲▲ Bosnia and Herzegovina/Yugoslavia
111 K20 **Javorie** Hung. Jávoros. ▲ S Slovakia
Jávoros see Javorie
93 J14 **Jävre** Norrbotten, N Sweden
192 E8 **Jawa** Eng. Java; prev. Djawa. island C Indonesia
169 O16 **Jawa Barat** off. Propinsi Jawa Barat, Eng. West Java. ◈ province S Indonesia
Jawa, Laut see Java Sea
139 R3 **Jawān** NW Iraq
169 P16 **Jawa Tengah** off. Propinsi Jawa Tengah, Eng. Central Java. ◈ province S Indonesia
169 R16 **Jawa Timur** off. Propinsi Jawa Timur, Eng. East Java. ◈ province S Indonesia
81 N17 **Jawhar** var. Jowhar, It. Giohar. Shabeellaha Dhexe, S Somalia
111 F14 **Jawor** Ger. Jauer. Dolnośląskie, SW Poland
Jaworów see Yavoriv
111 J16 **Jaworzno** Śląskie, S Poland
Jaxartes see Syr Darya
27 R9 **Jay** Oklahoma, C USA
Jayabum see Chaiyaphum
Jayanath see Chai Nat
153 T12 **Jayanti** prev. Jainti. West Bengal, NE India
171 X14 **Jaya, Puncak** prev. Puntjak Carstensz, Puntjak Sukarno. ▲ Irian Jaya, E Indonesia
171 Z13 **Jayapura** var. Djajapura, Dut. Hollandia; prev. Kotabaru, Sukarnapura. Irian Jaya, E Indonesia
Jay Dairen see Dalian
Jayhawker State see Kansas
147 S12 **Jayilgan** Rus. Dzhailgan, Dzhayilgan. C Tajikistan
155 L14 **Jaypur** var. Jeypore, Jeypur. Orissa, E India
25 O6 **Jayton** Texas, SW USA
143 U13 **Jaz Murian, Hāmūn-e** ◎ SE Iran
138 M4 **Jazrah** Ar Raqqah, C Syria
138 G6 **Jbaïl** var. Jebeil, Jubayl, Jubeil; anc. Biblical Gebal, Bybles. W Lebanon
25 O7 **J.B.Thomas, Lake** ⊠ Texas, SW USA
Jdaïdé see Judaydah
35 X12 **Jean** Nevada, W USA
22 I9 **Jeanerette** Louisiana, S USA
44 L8 **Jean-Rabel** NW Haiti
143 T12 **Jebāl Bārez, Kūh-e** ▲▲ SE Iran
Jebat see Jabwot
77 T15 **Jebba** Kwara, W Nigeria
Jebeil see Jbaïl
116 E12 **Jebel** Hung. Széphely; prev. Hung. Zsebely. Timiş, W Romania
Jebel see Dzhebel
Jebel, Bahr el see White Nile
Jebel Dhanna see Jabal az̧ Z̧annah
Jeble see Jablah
96 K13 **Jedburgh** SE Scotland, UK
Jedda see Jiddah
111 L15 **Jędrzejów** Ger. Endersdorf. Świętokrzyskie, C Poland
100 K12 **Jeetze** var. Jeetzel. ≈ C Germany
Jeetzel see Jeetze
29 U14 **Jefferson** Iowa, C USA
21 Q8 **Jefferson** North Carolina, SE USA
25 X6 **Jefferson** Texas, SW USA
30 M9 **Jefferson** Wisconsin, N USA
27 U5 **Jefferson City** state capital Missouri, C USA
33 R10 **Jefferson City** Montana, NW USA
21 N9 **Jefferson City** Tennessee, S USA
35 U7 **Jefferson, Mount** ▲ Nevada, W USA
32 H12 **Jefferson, Mount** ▲ Oregon, NW USA
20 L5 **Jeffersontown** Kentucky, S USA
31 P16 **Jeffersonville** Indiana, N USA
33 V15 **Jeffrey City** Wyoming, C USA
77 T13 **Jega** Kebbi, NW Nigeria
Jehol see Chengde
62 P5 **Jejui-Guazú, Río** ≈ E Paraguay
118 I10 **Jēkabpils** Ger. Jakobstadt. Jēkabpils, S Latvia
23 W7 **Jekyll Island** island Georgia, SE USA
169 R13 **Jelai, Sungai** ≈ Borneo, N Indonesia
Jelalabad see Jalālābād
111 H14 **Jelcz-Laskowice** Dolnośląskie, SW Poland
111 E14 **Jelenia Góra** Ger. Hirschberg, Hirschberg im Riesengebirge, Hirschberg in Riesengebirge, Hirschberg in Schlesien. Dolnośląskie, SW Poland
153 S11 **Jelep La** pass N India
118 F9 **Jelgava** Ger. Mitau. Jelgava, C Latvia
112 L13 **Jelica** ▲▲ C Yugoslavia
20 M8 **Jellico** Tennessee, S USA
95 G23 **Jelling** Vejle, C Denmark
169 N9 **Jemaja, Pulau** island W Indonesia
Jemaluang see Jamaluang
99 E20 **Jemappes** Hainaut, S Belgium
169 S17 **Jember** prev. Djember. Jawa, C Indonesia

◆ Country ● Country Capital ◇ Dependent Territory ○ Dependent Territory Capital ◈ Administrative Region ✕ International Airport ▲ Mountain ▲▲ Mountain Range ⛰ Volcano ≈ River ◎ Lake ⊠ Reservoir

99 I20 **Jemeppe-sur-Sambre** Namur, S Belgium
37 R10 **Jemez Pueblo** New Mexico, SW USA
158 K2 **Jeminay** Xinjiang Uygur Zizhiqu, NW China
189 U5 **Jemo Island** *atoll* Ratak Chain, C Marshall Islands
169 U11 **Jempang, Danau** ◎ Borneo, N Indonesia
101 L16 **Jena** Thüringen, C Germany
22 I6 **Jena** Louisiana, S USA
108 I8 **Jenaz** Graubünden, SE Switzerland
109 N7 **Jenbach** Tirol, W Austria
171 N15 **Jeneponto** *prev.* Djeneponto. Sulawesi, C Indonesia
138 F9 **Jenīn** N West Bank
21 P7 **Jenkins** Kentucky, S USA
27 P9 **Jenks** Oklahoma, C USA
Jenné *see* Djenné
109 X8 **Jennersdorf** Burgenland, SE Austria
22 H9 **Jennings** Louisiana, S USA
9 N7 **Jenny Lind Island** *island* Nunavut, N Canada
23 Y13 **Jensen Beach** Florida, SE USA
9 P6 **Jens Munk Island** *island* Nunavut, NE Canada
59 O17 **Jequié** Bahia, E Brazil
59 O18 **Jequitinhonha, Rio** ≈ E Brazil
Jerablus *see* Jarābulus
74 H6 **Jerada** NE Morocco
Jerash *see* Jarash
75 N7 **Jerba, Île de** *var.* Djerba, Jazīrat Jarbah. *island* E Tunisia
44 K9 **Jérémie** SW Haiti
Jerez *see* Jeréz de la Frontera, Spain
Jeréz *see* Jerez de García Salinas, Mexico
40 L11 **Jerez de García Salinas** *var.* Jeréz. Zacatecas, C Mexico
104 J15 **Jeréz de la Frontera** *var.* Jerez; *prev.* Xeres. Andalucía, SW Spain
104 I12 **Jeréz de los Caballeros** Extremadura, W Spain
Jergucati *see* Jorgucat
138 G10 **Jericho** *Ar.* Arīḥā, *Heb.* Yeriḥo. E West Bank
74 M7 **Jerid, Chott el** *var.* Shaṭṭ al Jarīd. *salt lake* SW Tunisia
183 O10 **Jerilderie** New South Wales, SE Australia
Jerischmarkt *see* Câmpia Turzii
92 K11 **Jerisjärvi** ◎ NW Finland
Jermentau *see* Yereymentau
Jermer *see* Jaroměř
36 K11 **Jerome** Arizona, SW USA
33 O15 **Jerome** Idaho, NW USA
97 L26 **Jersey** *island* Channel Islands, NW Europe
18 K14 **Jersey City** New Jersey, NE USA
18 F13 **Jersey Shore** Pennsylvania, NE USA
30 K14 **Jerseyville** Illinois, N USA
104 K8 **Jerte** ≈ W Spain
138 F10 **Jerusalem** *Ar.* Al Quds, Al Quds ash Sharīf, *Heb.* Yerushalayim; *anc.* Hierosolyma. ● (Israel) Jerusalem, NE Israel
138 G10 **Jerusalem** ⬖ *district* E Israel
183 S10 **Jervis Bay** New South Wales, SE Australia
183 S10 **Jervis Bay Territory** ⬖ *territory* SE Australia
Jerwakant *see* Järvakandi
109 S10 **Jesenice** *Ger.* Assling. NW Slovenia
111 H16 **Jeseník** *Ger.* Freiwaldau. Olomoucký Kraj, E Czech Republic
Jesi *see* Iesi
106 I8 **Jesolo** *var.* Iesolo. Veneto, NE Italy
Jesselton *see* Kota Kinabalu
95 I14 **Jessheim** Akershus, S Norway
153 T15 **Jessore** Khulna, W Bangladesh
23 W6 **Jesup** Georgia, SE USA
41 S15 **Jesús Carranza** Veracruz-Llave, SE Mexico
62 K10 **Jesús María** Córdoba, C Argentina
26 K6 **Jetmore** Kansas, C USA
103 Q2 **Jeumont** Nord, N France
95 H14 **Jevnaker** Oppland, S Norway
Jewe *see* Jõhvi
25 V9 **Jewett** Texas, SW USA
19 N12 **Jewett City** Connecticut, NE USA
Jewish Autonomous Oblast *see* Yevreyskaya Avtonomnaya Oblast'
Jeypore/Jeypur *see* Jaypur, Orissa, India
Jeypore *see* Jaipur, Rājasthān, India
113 L17 **Jezercës, Maja e** ▲ N Albania
111 B18 **Jezerní Hora** ▲ SW Czech Republic
154 F10 **Jhābua** Madhya Pradesh, C India
152 H14 **Jhālāwār** Rājasthān, N India
Jhang/Jhang Sadar *see* Jhang Sadr
149 U9 **Jhang Sadr** *var.* Jhang, Jhang Sadar. Punjab, NE Pakistan
152 J13 **Jhānsi** Uttar Pradesh, N India
154 M11 **Jhārsuguda** Orissa, E India
149 V7 **Jhelum** Punjab, NE Pakistan
131 P9 **Jhelum** ≈ E Pakistan
Jhenaidaha *see* Jhenida
153 T15 **Jhenida** *var.* Jhenaidaha. Dhaka, W Bangladesh
149 P16 **Jhimpīr** Sind, SE Pakistan
Jhind *see* Jīnd
149 R16 **Jhudo** Sind, SE Pakistan
Jhumra *see* Chak Jhumra
152 H11 **Jhunjhunūn** Rājasthān, N India
Ji *see* Hebei, China
Ji *see* Jilin, China
153 S14 **Jiāganj** West Bengal, NE India
160 J7 **Jialing Jiang** ≈ C China
163 Y7 **Jiamusi** *var.* Chia-mu-ssu, Kiamusze. Heilongjiang, NE China
161 O11 **Ji'an** Jiangxi, S China
163 W12 **Ji'an** Jilin, NE China
163 T13 **Jianchang** Liaoning, NE China
160 F11 **Jianchuan** Yunnan, SW China
158 M4 **Jiangjunmiao** Xinjiang Uygur Zizhiqu, W China
160 K11 **Jiangkou** Guizhou, S China
161 Q12 **Jiangle** Fujian, SE China
161 N15 **Jiangmen** Guangdong, S China
161 Q10 **Jiangshan** Zhejiang, SE China
161 Q7 **Jiangsu** *var.* Chiang-su, Jiangsu Sheng, Kiangsu, Su. ⬖ *province* E China
Jiangsu Sheng *see* Jiangsu
161 O11 **Jiangxi** *var.* Chiang-hsi, Gan, Jiangxi Sheng, Kiangsi. ⬖ *province* S China
Jiangxi Sheng *see* Jiangxi
160 I8 **Jiangyou** *prev.* Zhongba. Sichuan, C China
161 N9 **Jianli** Hubei, C China
161 Q11 **Jian'ou** Fujian, SE China
163 S12 **Jianping** Liaoning, NE China
160 L9 **Jianshi** Hubei, C China
131 V11 **Jian Xi** ≈ SE China
161 Q11 **Jianyang** Fujian, SE China
160 I9 **Jianyang** Sichuan, C China
163 X10 **Jiaohe** Jilin, NE China
Jiaojiang *see* Taizhou
161 N6 **Jiaozuo** Henan, C China
Jiashan *see* Mingguang
158 F8 **Jiashi** *var.* Payzawat. Xinjiang Uygur Zizhiqu, NW China
154 L9 **Jiāwān** Madhya Pradesh, C India
161 S9 **Jiaxing** Zhejiang, SE China
Jiayi *see* Chiai
163 X6 **Jiayin** *var.* Chaoyang. Heilongjiang, NE China
159 R8 **Jiayuguan** Gansu, N China
138 M4 **Jibli** Ar Raqqah, C Syria
116 H9 **Jibou** *Hung.* Zsibó. Sălaj, NW Romania
141 Z9 **Jibsh, Ra's al** *headland* E Oman
Jibuti *see* Djibouti
111 E15 **Jičín** *Ger.* Jitschin. Hradecký Kraj, N Czech Republic
140 K10 **Jiddah** *Eng.* Jedda. Makkah, W Saudi Arabia
141 W11 **Jiddat al Ḥarāsīs** *desert* C Oman
Jiesjavrre *see* Iešjávri
160 M4 **Jiexiu** Shanxi, C China
161 P14 **Jieyang** Guangdong, S China
119 F14 **Jieznas** Prienai, S Lithuania
Jifa', Bi'r *see* Jif'īyah, Bi'r
141 P15 **Jif'īyah, Bi'r** *var.* Bi'r Jifa'. *well* C Yemen
77 W13 **Jigawa** ⬖ *state* N Nigeria
Jigerbent *see* Dzhigirbent
44 I7 **Jiguaní** Granma, E Cuba
159 T12 **Jigzhi** Qinghai, C China
Jih-k'a-tse *see* Xigazê
111 E18 **Jihlava** *Ger.* Iglau, *Pol.* Igława. Jihlavský Kraj, C Czech Republic
111 E18 **Jihlava** *var.* Igel, *Ger.* Iglawa. ≈ S Czech Republic
111 E18 **Jihlavský kraj** ⬖ *region* C Czech Republic
74 L5 **Jijel** *var.* Djidjel; *prev.* Djidjelli. NE Algeria
116 L9 **Jijia** ≈ N Romania
80 L13 **Jijiga** *It.* Giggiga. Somali, E Ethiopia
105 S12 **Jijona** *var.* Xixona. País Valenciano, E Spain
Jilf al Kabīr, Haḍabat al *see* Gilf Kebir Plateau
81 L18 **Jilib** *It.* Gelib. Jubbada Dhexe, S Somalia
163 W10 **Jilin** *var.* Chi-lin, Girin, Kirin; *prev.* Yungki, Yunki. Jilin, NE China
163 W10 **Jilin** *var.* Chi-lin, Girin, Ji, Jilin Sheng, Kirin. ⬖ *province* NE China
163 W11 **Jilin Hada Ling** ▲ NE China
Jilin Sheng *see* Jilin
163 S4 **Jiliu He** ≈ NE China
105 Q6 **Jiloca** ≈ N Spain
81 I14 **Jīma** *var.* Jimma, *It.* Gimma. Oromo, C Ethiopia
44 M9 **Jimaní** W Dominican Republic
116 E11 **Jimbolia** *Ger.* Hatzfeld, *Hung.* Zsombolya. Timiş, W Romania
104 K16 **Jimena de la Frontera** Andalucía, S Spain
40 K7 **Jiménez** Chihuahua, N Mexico
41 N5 **Jiménez** Coahuila de Zaragoza, NE Mexico
41 P9 **Jiménez** *var.* Santander Jiménez. Tamaulipas, C Mexico
40 L10 **Jiménez del Teul** Zacatecas, C Mexico
77 Y14 **Jimeta** Adamawa, E Nigeria
Jimma *see* Jīma
158 M5 **Jimsar** Xinjiang Uygur Zizhiqu, NW China
18 I14 **Jim Thorpe** Pennsylvania, NE USA
Jin *see* Shanxi, China
Jin *see* Tianjin Shi, China
161 P5 **Jinan** *var.* Chinan, Chi-nan, Tsinan. Shandong, E China
159 T8 **Jinchang** Gansu, N China
161 N5 **Jincheng** Shanxi, C China
Jinchengjiang *see* Hechi
152 I9 **Jīnd** *prev.* Jhind. Haryāna, NW India
183 Q11 **Jindabyne** New South Wales, SE Australia
111 O18 **Jindřichův Hradec** *Ger.* Neuhaus. Budějovický Kraj, S Czech Republic
Jing *see* Beijing Shi, China
Jing *see* Jinghe, China
159 X10 **Jingchuan** Gansu, C China
161 Q10 **Jingdezhen** Jiangxi, S China
161 O12 **Jinggangshan** Jiangxi, S China
161 P3 **Jinghai** Tianjin Shi, E China
160 K6 **Jing He** ≈ C China
158 I4 **Jinghe** *var.* Jing. Xinjiang Uygur Zizhiqu, NW China
160 F15 **Jinghong** *var.* Yunjinghong. Yunnan, SW China
160 M9 **Jingmen** Hubei, C China
163 X10 **Jingpo Hu** ◎ NE China
160 M8 **Jing Shan** ▲ C China
159 V9 **Jingtai** *var.* Yitiaoshan. Gansu, C China
160 J14 **Jingxi** Guangxi Zhuangzu Zizhiqu, S China
Jing Xian *see* Jingzhou
163 W11 **Jingyu** Jilin, NE China
159 V10 **Jingyuan** Gansu, C China
160 L12 **Jingzhou** *var.* Jing Xian. Hunan, S China
160 M9 **Jingzhou** *prev.* Shahi, Shashih, Shasi. Hubei, C China
161 R10 **Jinhua** Zhejiang, SE China
163 P13 **Jining** Nei Mongol Zizhiqu, N China
161 P5 **Jining** Shandong, E China
81 G18 **Jinja** S Uganda
161 O11 **Jin Jiang** ≈ S China
161 R13 **Jinjiang** *var.* Qingyang. Fujian, SE China
171 V15 **Jin, Kepulauan** *island group* E Indonesia
Jinmen Dao *see* Chinmen Tao
42 J9 **Jinotega** Jinotega, NW Nicaragua
42 K7 **Jinotega** ⬖ *department* N Nicaragua
42 J11 **Jinotepe** Carazo, SW Nicaragua
160 L13 **Jinping** *prev.* Sanjiang. Guizhou, S China
160 H14 **Jinping** Yunnan, SW China
Jinsen *see* Inch'ŏn
160 J11 **Jinsha** Guizhou, S China
157 N12 **Jinsha Jiang** ≈ SW China
160 M10 **Jinshi** Hunan, S China
159 R7 **Jinta** Gansu, N China
161 Q12 **Jin Xi** ≈ SE China
Jinxi *see* Lianshan
Jinxian *see* Jinzhou
161 P6 **Jinxiang** Shandong, E China
161 P8 **Jinzhai** *prev.* Meishan. Anhui, E China
163 U14 **Jinzhou** *prev.* Jinxian. Liaoning, NE China
163 T12 **Jinzhou** *var.* Chin-chou, Chinchow; *prev.* Chinhsien. Liaoning, NE China
138 H12 **Jinz, Qā' al** ◎ C Jordan
47 S8 **Jiparaná, Rio** ≈ W Brazil
56 A7 **Jipijapa** Manabí, W Ecuador
42 F8 **Jiquilisco** Usulután, S El Salvador
147 S12 **Jirgatol** *Rus.* Dzhirgatal'. C Tajikistan
Jirjā *see* Girga
111 B15 **Jirkov** *Ger.* Görkau. Ústecký Kraj, NW Czech Republic
Jiroft *see* Sabzvārān
160 L11 **Jishou** Hunan, S China
Jisr ash Shadadi *see* Ash Shadādah
116 I14 **Jitaru** Olt, S Romania
Jitschin *see* Jičín
116 H14 **Jiu** *Ger.* Schil, Schyl, *Hung.* Zsil, Zsily. ≈ S Romania
161 R11 **Jiufeng Shan** ▲ SE China
161 P9 **Jiujiang** Jiangxi, S China
161 O10 **Jiuling Shan** ▲ S China
160 G10 **Jiulong** Sichuan, C China
161 Q13 **Jiulong Jiang** ≈ SE China
161 Q12 **Jiulong Xi** ≈ SE China
159 R8 **Jiuquan** Gansu, N China
160 K17 **Jiusuo** Hainan, S China
163 W10 **Jiutai** Jilin, NE China
160 K13 **Jiuwan Dashan** ▲ S China
148 I16 **Jīwani** Baluchistān, SW Pakistan
163 Y8 **Jixi** Heilongjiang, NE China
163 Y7 **Jixian** Heilongjiang, NE China
160 M5 **Jixian** *var.* Ji Xian. Shanxi, C China
Jīzān *see* Al Jīzah
141 N13 **Jīzān** *var.* Qīzān. Jīzān, SW Saudi Arabia
141 N13 **Jīzān** *var.* Minṭaqat Jīzān. ⬖ *province* SW Saudi Arabia
140 K6 **Jizl, Wādī al** *dry watercourse* W Saudi Arabia
164 H12 **Jizō-zaki** *headland* Honshū, SW Japan
141 U14 **Jiz', Wādī al** *dry watercourse* E Yemen
147 O11 **Jizzakh** *Rus.* Dzhizak. Jizzakh Wiloyati, C Uzbekistan
147 N10 **Jizzakh Wiloyati** *Rus.* Dzhizakskaya Oblast'. ⬖ *province* C Uzbekistan
60 I13 **Joaçaba** Santa Catarina, S Brazil
Joal *see* Joal-Fadiout
76 F11 **Joal-Fadiout** *prev.* Joal. W Senegal
76 E10 **João Barrosa** Boa Vista, E Cape Verde
João Belo *see* Xai-Xai
João de Almeida *see* Chibia
59 Q15 **João Pessoa** *prev.* Paraíba. *state capital* Paraíba, E Brazil
25 X7 **Joaquin** Texas, SW USA
62 K6 **Joaquín V.González** Salta, N Argentina
Joazeiro *see* Juazeiro
Jo'burg *see* Johannesburg
109 O7 **Jochberger Ache** ≈ W Austria
Jo-ch'iang *see* Ruoqiang
92 K12 **Jock** Norrbotten, N Sweden
42 I5 **Jocón** Yoro, N Honduras
105 O13 **Jódar** Andalucía, S Spain
152 F12 **Jodhpur** Rājasthān, NW India
99 I19 **Jodoigne** Wallon Brabant, C Belgium
95 I22 **Jægerspris** Frederiksborg, E Denmark
93 O16 **Joensuu** Itä-Suomi, E Finland
95 C17 **Jæren** *physical region* S Norway
37 W4 **Joes** Colorado, C USA
191 Z3 **Joe's Hill** *hill* Kiritimati, NE Kiribati
165 N11 **Jōetsu** *var.* Zyôetu. Niigata, Honshū, C Japan
83 M18 **Jofane** Inhambane, S Mozambique
153 R12 **Jogbani** Bihār, NE India
118 I5 **Jõgeva** *Ger.* Laisholm. Jõgevamaa, E Estonia
118 I4 **Jõgevamaa** *off.* Jõgeva Maakond. ⬖ *province* E Estonia
155 E18 **Jog Falls** *waterfall* Karnātaka, W India
143 S4 **Joghatāy** Khorāsān, NE Iran
153 U12 **Jogīghopa** Assam, NE India
152 I7 **Jogindarnagar** Himāchal Pradesh, N India
Jogjakarta *see* Yogyakarta
164 L11 **Jōhana** Toyama, Honshū, SW Japan
83 J21 **Johannesburg** *var.* Egoli, Erautini, Gauteng, *abbrev.* Jo'burg. Gauteng, NE South Africa
35 T13 **Johannesburg** California, W USA
83 I21 **Johannesburg** ✕ Gauteng, NE South Africa
Johannisburg *see* Pisz
149 P14 **Johi** Sind, SE Pakistan
55 T13 **Johi Village** S Guyana
32 K13 **John Day** Oregon, NW USA
32 I11 **John Day River** ≈ Oregon, NW USA
18 L14 **John F Kennedy** ✕ (New York) Long Island, New York, NE USA
21 V8 **John H.Kerr Reservoir** *var.* Buggs Island Lake, Kerr Lake. ⊞ North Carolina/Virginia, SE USA
37 V6 **John Martin Reservoir** ⊞ Colorado, C USA
96 K6 **John o'Groats** N Scotland, UK
27 P5 **John Redmond Reservoir** ⊞ Kansas, C USA
39 Q7 **John River** ≈ Alaska, USA
26 H6 **Johnson** Kansas, C USA
18 M7 **Johnson** Vermont, NE USA
18 D13 **Johnsonburg** Pennsylvania, NE USA
18 H11 **Johnson City** New York, NE USA
21 P8 **Johnson City** Tennessee, S USA
25 R10 **Johnson City** Texas, SW USA
35 S12 **Johnsondale** California, W USA
10 I8 **Johnsons Crossing** Yukon Territory, W Canada
21 T13 **Johnsonville** South Carolina, SE USA
21 Q13 **Johnston** South Carolina, SE USA
192 M6 **Johnston Atoll** ◇ *US unincorporated territory* C Pacific Ocean
175 Q3 **Johnston Atoll** *atoll* C Pacific Ocean
30 L17 **Johnston City** Illinois, N USA
180 K12 **Johnston, Lake** *salt lake* Western Australia
31 S13 **Johnstown** Ohio, N USA
18 D15 **Johnstown** Pennsylvania, NE USA
168 L10 **Johor** *var.* Johore. ⬖ *state* Peninsular Malaysia
Johor Baharu *see* Johor Bahru
168 K10 **Johor Bahru** *var.* Johor Baharu, Johore Bahru. Johor, Peninsular Malaysia
Johore *see* Johor
Johore Bahru *see* Johor Bahru
118 K3 **Jõhvi** *Ger.* Jewe. Ida-Virumaa, NE Estonia
103 P7 **Joigny** Yonne, C France
Joinvile *see* Joinville
60 K12 **Joinville** *var.* Joinvile. Santa Catarina, S Brazil
103 R6 **Joinville** Haute-Marne, N France
194 H3 **Joinville Island** *island* Antarctica
41 O15 **Jojutla** *var.* Jojutla de Juárez. Morelos, S Mexico
Jojutla de Juárez *see* Jojutla
92 I12 **Jokkmokk** Norrbotten, N Sweden
92 L2 **Jökulsá á Dal** ≈ E Iceland
92 K2 **Jökulsá á Fjöllum** ≈ NE Iceland
Jokyakarta *see* Yogyakarta
30 M11 **Joliet** Illinois, N USA
15 O11 **Joliette** Quebec, SE Canada
171 O8 **Jolo** Jolo Island, SW Philippines
94 D11 **Jølstervatnet** ◎ S Norway
169 S16 **Jombang** *prev.* Djombang. Jawa, S Indonesia
159 R14 **Jomda** Xizang Zizhiqu, W China
56 A6 **Jome, Punta de** *headland* W Ecuador
118 G13 **Jonava** *Ger.* Janow, *Pol.* Janów. Jonava, C Lithuania
146 L11 **Jondor** *Rus.* Zhondor. Bukhoro Wiloyati, C Uzbekistan
159 V11 **Jonê** Gansu, C China
27 X9 **Jonesboro** Arkansas, C USA
23 S4 **Jonesboro** Georgia, SE USA
30 L17 **Jonesboro** Illinois, N USA
22 H5 **Jonesboro** Louisiana, S USA
21 P8 **Jonesboro** Tennessee, S USA
19 T6 **Jonesport** Maine, NE USA
9 N4 **Jones Sound** *channel* Nunavut, N Canada
22 I6 **Jonesville** Louisiana, S USA
31 Q10 **Jonesville** Michigan, N USA
21 Q11 **Jonesville** South Carolina, SE USA
81 F14 **Jonglei** Jonglei, SE Sudan
81 F14 **Jonglei** *var.* Gongoleh State. ⬖ *state* SE Sudan
81 F14 **Jonglei Canal** *canal* S Sudan
118 F11 **Joniškėlis** Pasvalys, N Lithuania
118 F10 **Joniškis** *Ger.* Janischken. Joniškis, N Lithuania
95 L19 **Jönköping** Jönköping, S Sweden
95 K20 **Jönköping** ⬖ *county* S Sweden
15 Q7 **Jonquière** Quebec, SE Canada
41 V15 **Jonuta** Tabasco, SE Mexico
102 K12 **Jonzac** Charente-Maritime, W France
27 R7 **Joplin** Missouri, C USA
33 W8 **Jordan** Montana, NW USA
147 S11 **Jordan** *var.* Iordan, *Rus.* Jardan. Farghona Wiloyati, E Uzbekistan
138 H12 **Jordan** *off.* Hashemite Kingdom of Jordan, *Ar.* Al Mamlakah al Urdunīyah al Hāshimīyah, Al Urdunn; *prev.* Transjordan. ◆ *monarchy* SW Asia
138 G9 **Jordan** *Ar.* Urdunn, *Heb.* HaYarden. ≈ SW Asia
Jordan Lake *see* B.Everett Jordan Reservoir
111 K17 **Jordanów** Małopolskie, S Poland
32 M15 **Jordan Valley** Oregon, NW USA
138 G9 **Jordan Valley** *valley* N Israel
57 D15 **Jorge Chávez International** *var.* Lima. ✕ (Lima) Lima, W Peru
113 L23 **Jorgucat** *var.* Jergucati, Jorgucati. Gjirokastër, S Albania
Jorgucati *see* Jorgucat
153 X12 **Jorhāt** Assam, NE India
93 J14 **Jörn** Västerbotten, N Sweden
37 R14 **Jornada Del Muerto** *valley* New Mexico, SW USA
93 N17 **Joroinen** Isä-Suomi, E Finland
95 C16 **Jørpeland** Rogaland, S Norway
77 W14 **Jos** Plateau, C Nigeria
171 Q8 **Jose Abad Santos** *var.* Trinidad. Mindanao, S Philippines
61 F19 **José Batlle y Ordóñez** *var.* Batlle y Ordóñez. Florida, C Uruguay
63 H18 **José de San Martín** Chubut, S Argentina
61 E19 **José Enrique Rodó** *var.* Rodó, José E.Rodo; *prev.* Drabble, Drable. Soriano, SW Uruguay
José E.Rodo *see* José Enrique Rodó
Josefsdorf *see* Žabalj
44 C4 **José Martí** ✕ (La Habana) Cuidad de La Habana, N Cuba
61 F19 **José Pedro Varela** *var.* José P.Varela. Lavalleja, S Uruguay
181 N2 **Joseph Bonaparte Gulf** *gulf* N Australia
37 N11 **Joseph City** Arizona, SW USA
13 O9 **Joseph, Lake** ◎ Newfoundland, E Canada
14 G13 **Joseph, Lake** ◎ Ontario, S Canada
186 C6 **Josephstaal** Madang, N PNG
José P.Varela *see* José Pedro Varela
59 J14 **José Rodrigues** Pará, N Brazil
152 K9 **Joshīmath** Uttar Pradesh, N India
25 T7 **Joshua** Texas, SW USA
35 V15 **Joshua Tree** California, W USA
77 V14 **Jos Plateau** *plateau* C Nigeria
102 H6 **Josselin** Morbihan, NW France
Jos Sudarso *see* Yos Sudarso, Pulau
94 E11 **Jostedalsbreen** *glacier* S Norway
94 F12 **Jotunheimen** ▲ S Norway
138 G7 **Joûnié** *var.* Junīyah. W Lebanon
25 R13 **Jourdanton** Texas, SW USA
98 L7 **Joure** *Fris.* De Jouwer. Friesland, N Netherlands
93 M18 **Joutsa** Länsi-Suomi, W Finland
93 N18 **Joutseno** Etelä-Suomi, S Finland
92 M12 **Joutsijärvi** Lappi, NE Finland
108 A9 **Joux, Lac de** ◎ W Switzerland
44 D5 **Jovellanos** Matanzas, W Cuba
153 V13 **Jowai** Meghālaya, NE India
Jowat *see* Jabwot
Jowhar *see* Jawhar
143 O12 **Jowkān** Fārs, S Iran
143 O10 **Jowzam** Kermān, C Iran
149 N2 **Jowzjān** ⬖ *province* N Afghanistan
Józseffalva *see* Žabalj
J.Storm Thurmond Reservoir *see* Clark Hill Lake
45 T6 **Juana Díaz** C Puerto Rico
40 L9 **Juan Aldama** Zacatecas, C Mexico
(0) E9 **Juan de Fuca Plate** *tectonic feature*
32 F7 **Juan de Fuca, Strait of** *strait* Canada/USA
Juan Fernandez Islands *see* Juan Fernández, Islas
193 S11 **Juan Fernández, Islas** *Eng.* Juan Fernandez Islands. *island group* W Chile
55 O4 **Juangriego** Nueva Esparta, NE Venezuela
56 D11 **Juanjuí** *var.* Juanjuy. San Martín, N Peru
Juanjuy *see* Juanjuí
93 N16 **Juankoski** Itä-Suomi, C Finland
Juan Lacaze *see* Juan L.Lacaze
61 E20 **Juan L.Lacaze** *var.* Juan Lacaze, Puerto Sauce; *prev.* Sauce. Colonia, SW Uruguay
62 L5 **Juan Solá** Salta, N Argentina
63 F21 **Juan Stuven, Isla** *island* S Chile
59 H16 **Juará** Mato Grosso, W Brazil
41 N7 **Juárez** *var.* Villa Juárez. Coahuila de Zaragoza, NE Mexico
40 C2 **Juárez, Sierra de** ▲ NW Mexico
59 O15 **Juazeiro** *prev.* Joazeiro. Bahia, E Brazil
59 P14 **Juazeiro do Norte** Ceará, E Brazil
81 F15 **Juba** *var.* Jūbā. Bahr el Gabel, S Sudan
81 L17 **Juba** *Amh.* Genalē Wenz, *It.* Guiba, *Som.* Ganaane, Webi Jubba. ≈ Ethiopia/Somalia
194 H2 **Jubany** *Argentinian research station* Antarctica
Jubayl *see* Jbaïl
81 L18 **Jubbada Dhexe** *off.* Gobolka Jubbada Dhexe. ⬖ *region* SW Somalia
81 K18 **Jubbada Hoose** ⬖ *region* SW Somalia
Jubba, Webi *see* Juba
Jubbulpore *see* Jabalpur
Jubeil *see* Jbaïl
74 B9 **Juby, Cap** *headland* SW Morocco
105 R10 **Júcar** *var.* Jucar. ≈ C Spain
40 L12 **Juchipila** Zacatecas, C Mexico
41 S16 **Juchitán** *var.* Juchitán de Zaragosa. Oaxaca, SE Mexico
Juchitán de Zaragosa *see* Juchitán
138 G11 **Judaea** *cultural region* Israel/West Bank
138 F11 **Judaean Hills** *Heb.* Haré Yehuda. *hill range* E Israel
138 H8 **Judaydah** *Fr.* Jdaïdé. Dimashq, W Syria
139 P11 **Judayyidat Hāmir** S Iraq
109 U8 **Judenburg** Steiermark, C Austria
33 T8 **Judith River** ≈ Montana, NW USA
27 V11 **Judsonia** Arkansas, C USA
141 P14 **Jufrah, Wādī al** *dry watercourse* NW Yemen
Jugoslavija/Jugoslavija, Savezna Republika *see* Yugoslavia
42 K10 **Juigalpa** Chontales, S Nicaragua
161 T13 **Juishui** C Taiwan
100 E9 **Juist** *island* NW Germany
59 M21 **Juiz de Fora** Minas Gerais, SE Brazil
62 J5 **Jujuy** *off.* Provincia de Jujuy. ⬖ *province* N Argentina
Jujuy *see* San Salvador de Jujuy
92 J11 **Jukkasjärvi** Norrbotten, N Sweden
Jula *see* Gyula, Hungary
Jūlā *see* Jālū, Libya
37 W2 **Julesburg** Colorado, C USA
Julia Beterrae *see* Béziers
57 I17 **Juliaca** Puno, SE Peru
181 U6 **Julia Creek** Queensland, C Australia
35 V17 **Julian** California, W USA
98 H7 **Julianadorp** Noord-Holland, NW Netherlands
109 S11 **Julian Alps** *Ger.* Julische Alpen, *It.* Alpi Giulie, *Slvn.* Julijske Alpe. ▲ Italy/Slovenia
55 V11 **Juliana Top** ▲ C Surinam
Julianehåb *see* Qaqortoq
Julijske Alpe *see* Julian Alps
40 J6 **Julimes** Chihuahua, N Mexico
Julio Briga *see* Bragança, Portugal
Juliobriga *see* Logroño, Spain
61 G15 **Júlio de Castilhos** Rio Grande do Sul, S Brazil
Juliomagus *see* Angers
Julische Alpen *see* Julian Alps
Jullundur *see* Jalandhar
147 N11 **Juma** *Rus.* Dzhuma. Samarqand Wiloyati, C Uzbekistan
161 O3 **Juma He** ≈ E China
81 L18 **Jumboo** Jubbada Hoose, S Somalia
35 Y11 **Jumbo Peak** ▲ Nevada, W USA
105 R12 **Jumilla** Murcia, SE Spain
153 N10 **Jumla** Mid Western, NW Nepal
Jummoo *see* Jammu
Jumna *see* Yamuna
Jumporn *see* Chumphon
30 K5 **Jump River** ≈ Wisconsin, N USA
154 B11 **Jūnāgadh** *var.* Junagarh. Gujarāt, W India
Junagarh *see* Jūnāgadh
161 Q6 **Junan** *prev.* Shizilu. Shandong, E China
62 G11 **Juncal, Cerro** ▲ C Chile
25 Q10 **Junction** Texas, SW USA
36 K6 **Junction** Utah, W USA
27 O4 **Junction City** Kansas, C USA
32 F13 **Junction City** Oregon, NW USA
60 M10 **Jundiaí** São Paulo, S Brazil
39 X12 **Juneau** *state capital* Alaska, USA
30 M8 **Juneau** Wisconsin, N USA
105 U6 **Juneda** Cataluña, NE Spain
183 Q9 **Junee** New South Wales, SE Australia
35 R8 **June Lake** California, W USA
Jungbunzlau *see* Mladá Boleslav
158 L4 **Junggar Pendi** *Eng.* Dzungarian Basin. *basin* NW China
99 N24 **Junglinster** Grevenmacher, C Luxembourg
18 F14 **Juniata River** ≈ Pennsylvania, NE USA
61 B20 **Junín** Buenos Aires, E Argentina
57 E14 **Junín** Junín, C Peru
57 F14 **Junín** *off.* Departamento de Junín. ⬖ *department* C Peru
63 H15 **Junín de los Andes** Neuquén, W Argentina
57 D14 **Junín, Lago de** ◎ C Peru
Junīyah *see* Joûnié
Junkseylon *see* Phuket
160 I11 **Junlian** Sichuan, C China
25 O11 **Juno** Texas, SW USA
92 J11 **Junosuando** Norrbotten, N Sweden
93 H16 **Junsele** Västernorrland, C Sweden
Junten *see* Sunch'ŏn
32 L14 **Juntura** Oregon, NW USA
93 N14 **Juntusranta** Oulu, E Finland
118 H11 **Juodupė** Rokiškis, NE Lithuania
119 H14 **Juozapinės Kalnas** ▲ SE Lithuania
99 K19 **Juprelle** Liège, E Belgium
80 D13 **Jur** ≈ C Sudan
103 S9 **Jura** ⬖ *department* E France
108 C7 **Jura** ⬖ *canton* NW Switzerland
108 B8 **Jura** *var.* Jura Mountains. ▲ France/Switzerland
96 G12 **Jura** *island* SW Scotland, UK
Juraciszki *see* Yuratsishki
54 C8 **Juradó** Chocó, NW Colombia
Jura Mountains *see* Jura
96 G12 **Jura, Sound of** *strait* W Scotland, UK
139 V15 **Jurayībīyāt, Bi'r** *well* S Iraq
118 E13 **Jurbarkas** *Ger.* Georgenburg, Jurburg. Jurbarkas, W Lithuania
99 F20 **Jurbise** Hainaut, SW Belgium
Jurburg *see* Jurbarkas
118 F9 **Jūrmala** Riga, C Latvia
58 D13 **Juruá** Amazonas, NW Brazil

◆ Country ● Country Capital ◇ Dependent Territory ○ Dependent Territory Capital ⬖ Administrative Region ✕ International Airport ▲ Mountain ▲ Mountain Range Volcano ≈ River ◎ Lake ⊞ Reservoir

48 F7 **Juruá, Rio** var. Río Yuruá. ≈ Brazil/Peru
59 G16 **Juruena** Mato Grosso, W Brazil
59 G16 **Juruena** ≈ W Brazil
165 Q6 **Jūsan-ko** ◎ Honshū, C Japan
25 O6 **Justiceburg** Texas, SW USA
Justinianopolis see Kirşehir
62 K11 **Justo Daract** San Luis, C Argentina
59 C14 **Jutaí** Amazonas, W Brazil
58 C13 **Jutaí, Rio** ≈ NW Brazil
100 N13 **Jüterbog** Brandenburg, E Germany
42 E6 **Jutiapa** Jutiapa, S Guatemala
42 A3 **Jutiapa** off. Departamento de Jutiapa. ⬖ department SE Guatemala
42 J6 **Juticalpa** Olancho, C Honduras
82 I13 **Jutila** North Western, NW Zambia
Jutland see Jylland
84 F8 **Jutland Bank** undersea feature SE North Sea
93 N16 **Juuka** Itä-Suomi, E Finland
93 N17 **Juva** Isä-Suomi, SE Finland
Juvavum see Salzburg
44 A6 **Juventud, Isla de la** var. Isla de Pinos, Eng. Isle of Youth; prev. The Isle of the Pines. island W Cuba
Ju Xian see Juxian
161 Q5 **Juxian** var. Ju Xian. Shandong, E China
161 P6 **Juye** Shandong, E China
113 O15 **Južna Morava** Ger. Südliche Morava. ≈ SE Yugoslavia
95 I23 **Jyderup** Vestsjælland, E Denmark
95 F22 **Jylland** Eng. Jutland. peninsula W Denmark
Jyrgalan see Dzhergalan
93 M17 **Jyväskylä** Länsi-Suomi, W Finland

K

155 X3 **K2** Chin. Qogir Feng, Eng. Mount Godwin Austen. ▲ China/Pakistan
38 D9 **Kaaawa** Haw. Ka'a'wa. Oahu, Hawaii, USA, C Pacific Ocean
81 G16 **Kaabong** NE Uganda
Kaaden see Kadaň
55 V9 **Kaaimanston** Sipaliwini, N Surinam
146 G14 **Kaakhka** var. Kaka. Akhalskiy Velayat, S Turkmenistan
Kaala see Caála
187 O16 **Kaala-Gomen** Province Nord, W New Caledonia
92 L9 **Kaamanen** Lapp. Gámas. Lappi, N Finland
Kaapstad see Cape Town
Kaarasjoki see Karasjok
Kaaresuanto see Karesuando
92 J10 **Kaaresuvanto** Lapp. Gárassavon. Lappi, N Finland
93 K19 **Kaarina** Länsi-Suomi, W Finland
99 I14 **Kaatsheuvel** Noord-Brabant, S Netherlands
93 N16 **Kaavi** Itä-Suomi, C Finland
Ka'a'wa see Kaaawa
Kaba see Habahe
171 O14 **Kabaena, Pulau** island C Indonesia
146 J11 **Kabakly** Turkm. Gabakly. Lebapskiy Velayat, NE Turkmenistan
76 J14 **Kabala** N Sierra Leone
81 E19 **Kabale** SW Uganda
55 U10 **Kabalebo Rivier** ≈ W Surinam
79 N22 **Kabalo** Katanga, SE Dem. Rep. Congo (Zaire)
145 W13 **Kabanbay** Kaz. Qabanbay prev. Andreyevka, Kaz. Andreevka. Almaty, SE Kazakhstan
79 O21 **Kabambare** Maniema, E Dem. Rep. Congo (Zaire)
187 Y15 **Kabara** prev. Kambara. island Lau Group, E Fiji
Kabardino-Balkaria see Kabardino-Balkarskaya Respublika
128 M15 **Kabardino-Balkarskaya Respublika** Eng. Kabardino-Balkaria. ⬖ autonomous republic SW Russian Federation
79 O19 **Kabare** Sud Kivu, E Dem. Rep. Congo (Zaire)
171 T11 **Kabarei** Irian Jaya, E Indonesia
171 P7 **Kabasalan** Mindanao, S Philippines
77 U15 **Kabba** Kogi, S Nigeria
92 I13 **Kåbdalis** Norrbotten, N Sweden
138 M6 **Kabd aş Şārim** hill range E Syria
14 B7 **Kabenung Lake** ◎ Ontario, S Canada
29 W3 **Kabetogama Lake** ◎ Minnesota, N USA
Kabia, Pulau see Kabin, Pulau
79 M22 **Kabinda** Kasai Oriental, SE Dem. Rep. Congo (Zaire)
Kabinda see Cabinda
171 O15 **Kabin, Pulau** var. Pulau Kabia. island W Indonesia
171 P16 **Kabir** Pulau Pantar, S Indonesia
149 T10 **Kabīrwāla** Punjab, E Pakistan
78 I13 **Kabo** Ouham, NW Central African Republic
Kābol see Kābul
83 H14 **Kabompo** North Western, W Zambia
83 H14 **Kabompo** ≈ W Zambia
79 M22 **Kabongo** Katanga, SE Dem. Rep. Congo (Zaire)
120 K11 **Kaboudia, Rass** headland E Tunisia
126 J14 **Kabozha** Novgorodskaya Oblast', W Russian Federation
143 U4 **Kabūd Gonbad** Khorāsān, NE Iran
142 L5 **Kabūd Rāhang** Hamadān, W Iran
82 L12 **Kabuko** Northern, NE Zambia
149 Q5 **Kābul** var. Kabul, Per. Kābol. ● (Afghanistan) Kābul, E Afghanistan
149 Q5 **Kābul** Eng. Kabul, Per. Kābol. ⬖ province E Afghanistan
149 Q5 **Kābul** ✕ Kābul, E Afghanistan
149 R5 **Kabul** var. Daryā-ye Kābul. ≈ Afghanistan/Pakistan see also Kābul, Daryā-ye
149 S5 **Kābul, Daryā-ye** var. Kabul. ≈ Afghanistan/Pakistan see also Kabul
79 O25 **Kabunda** Katanga, SE Dem. Rep. Congo (Zaire)
171 R9 **Kaburuang, Pulau** island Kepulauan Talaud, N Indonesia
80 G8 **Kabushiya** River Nile, NE Sudan
83 J14 **Kabwe** Central, C Zambia
186 E7 **Kabwum** Morobe, C PNG
113 N17 **Kačanik** Serbia, S Yugoslavia
118 F13 **Kačerginė** Kaunas, C Lithuania
117 S13 **Kacha** Respublika Krym, S Ukraine
154 A10 **Kachchh, Gulf of** var. Gulf of Cutch, Gulf of Kutch. gulf W India
154 I11 **Kachchhīdhāna** Madhya Pradesh, C India
149 Q11 **Kachchh, Rann of** var. Rann of Kachh, Rann of Kutch. salt marsh India/Pakistan
39 Q13 **Kachemak Bay** bay Alaska, USA
Kachh, Rann of see Kachchh, Rann of
77 V14 **Kachia** Kaduna, C Nigeria
167 N2 **Kachin State** ⬖ state N Myanmar
145 T7 **Kachiry** Pavlodar, NE Kazakhstan
137 Q11 **Kaçkar Dağları** ▲▲ NE Turkey
155 C21 **Kadamatt Island** island Lakshadweep, India, N Indian Ocean
111 B15 **Kadaň** Ger. Kaaden. Ústecký Kraj, NW Czech Republic
167 N11 **Kadan Kyun** prev. King Island. island Mergui Archipelago, S Myanmar
187 X15 **Kadavu** prev. Kandavu. island S Fiji
187 X15 **Kadavu Passage** channel S Fiji
79 G16 **Kadéï** ≈ Cameroon/Central African Republic
Kadhimain see Al Kāẓimīyah
Kadijica see Kadiytsa
114 M13 **Kadıköy Barajı** ▣ NW Turkey
182 I8 **Kadina** South Australia
136 H15 **Kadınhanı** Konya, C Turkey
76 M14 **Kadiolo** Sikasso, S Mali
136 L16 **Kadirli** Osmaniye, S Turkey
114 G11 **Kadiytsa** | Mac. Kadijica. ▲ Bulgaria/FYR Macedonia
28 L10 **Kadoka** South Dakota, N USA
129 N5 **Kadom** Ryazanskaya Oblast', W Russian Federation
83 K16 **Kadoma** prev. Gatooma. Mashonaland West, C Zimbabwe
80 E12 **Kadugli** Southern Kordofan, S Sudan
77 V14 **Kaduna** Kaduna, C Nigeria
77 V14 **Kaduna** ⬖ state C Nigeria
77 V15 **Kaduna** ≈ N Nigeria
126 K14 **Kaduy** Vologodskaya Oblast', NW Russian Federation
154 E13 **Kadwa** ≈ W India
123 S9 **Kadykchan** Magadanskaya Oblast', E Russian Federation
Kadzharan see K'ajaran
127 T7 **Kadzherom** Respublika Komi, NW Russian Federation
147 X8 **Kadzhi-Say** Kir. Kajisay. Issyk-Kul'skaya Oblast', NE Kyrgyzstan
76 I10 **Kaédi** Gorgol, S Mauritania
78 G12 **Kaélé** Extrême-Nord, N Cameroon
38 C9 **Kaena Point** headland Oahu, Hawaii, USA, C Pacific Ocean
184 J2 **Kaeo** Northland, North Island, NZ
163 X14 **Kaesŏng** var. Kaesŏng-si. S North Korea
Kaesŏng-si see Kaesŏng
Kaewieng see Kavieng
79 L24 **Kafakumba** Katanga, S Dem. Rep. Congo (Zaire)
Kafan see Kapan
77 V14 **Kafanchan** Kaduna, C Nigeria
Kaffa see Feodosiya
76 G11 **Kaffrine** C Senegal
Kafiau see Kofiau, Pulau
115 I19 **Kafiréas, Akrotírio** headland Évvoia, C Greece
115 I19 **Kafiréos, Stenó** strait Évvoia/Kykládes, Greece, Aegean Sea
Kafirnigan see Kofarnihon
Kafo see Kafu
Kafr ash Shaykh/Kafrel Sheik see Kafr el Sheikh
75 W7 **Kafr el Sheikh** var. Kafr ash Shaykh, Kafrel Sheik. N Egypt
81 F17 **Kafu** var. Kafo. ≈ W Uganda
83 J15 **Kafue** Lusaka, SE Zambia
83 I14 **Kafue** ≈ C Zambia
67 T13 **Kafue Flats** plain C Zambia
164 K12 **Kaga** Ishikawa, Honshū, SW Japan
79 J14 **Kaga Bandoro** prev. Fort-Crampel. Nana-Grébizi, C Central African Republic
81 E18 **Kagadi** W Uganda
38 H17 **Kagalaska Island** island Aleutian Islands, Alaska, USA
Kagan see Kogon
Kaganovichabad see Kolkhozobod
Kagarlyk see Kaharlyk
164 H14 **Kagawa** off. Kagawa-ken. ⬖ prefecture Shikoku, SW Japan
154 J13 **Kagaznagar** Andhra Pradesh, C India
93 J14 **Kåge** Västerbotten, N Sweden
81 E19 **Kagera** var. Ziwa Magharibi, Eng. West Lake. ⬖ region NW Tanzania
81 E19 **Kagera** var. Akagera. ≈ Rwanda/Tanzania see also Akagera
76 L5 **Kâgheț** var. Karet. physical region N Mauritania
Kagi see Chiai
137 S12 **Kağızman** Kars, NE Turkey
188 I6 **Kagman Point** headland Saipan, S Northern Mariana Islands
164 C16 **Kagoshima** var. Kagosima. Kagoshima, Kyūshū, SW Japan
164 C16 **Kagoshima** off. Kagoshima-ken, var. Kagosima. ⬖ prefecture Kyūshū, SW Japan
Kagosima see Kagoshima
Kagul see Cahul
Kagul, Ozero see Kahul, Ozero
38 B8 **Kahala Point** headland Kauai, Hawaii, USA, C Pacific Ocean
38 G12 **Kahaluu** Haw. Kahalu'u. Hawaii, USA, C Pacific Ocean
81 F21 **Kahama** Shinyanga, NW Tanzania
117 P5 **Kaharlyk** Rus. Kagarlyk. Kyyivs'ka Oblast', N Ukraine
169 T13 **Kahayan, Sungai** ≈ Borneo, C Indonesia
79 I22 **Kahemba** Bandundu, SW Dem. Rep. Congo (Zaire)
185 A23 **Kaherekoau Mountains** ▲▲ South Island, NZ
143 W14 **Kahīrī** var. Kūhīrī. Sīstān va Balūchestān, SE Iran
101 L16 **Kahla** Thüringen, C Germany
101 G15 **Kahler Asten** ▲ W Germany
149 Q4 **Kahmard, Daryā-ye** prev. Darya-i-Surkhab. ≈ NE Afghanistan
143 T13 **Kahnūj** Kermān, SE Iran
27 V1 **Kahoka** Missouri, C USA
38 E10 **Kahoolawe** island Hawaii, USA, C Pacific Ocean
136 M16 **Kahramanmaraş** var. Kahraman Maraş, Maraş, Marash. Kahramanmaraş, S Turkey
136 L15 **Kahramanmaraş** var. Kahraman Maraş, Maraş, Marash. ⬖ province C Turkey
Kahror/Kahror Pakka see Karor Pacca
137 N15 **Kâhta** Adıyaman, S Turkey
38 D8 **Kahuku** Oahu, Hawaii, USA, C Pacific Ocean
38 D8 **Kahuku Point** headland Oahu, Hawaii, USA, C Pacific Ocean
116 M12 **Kahul, Ozero** var. Lacul Cahul, Rus. Ozero Kagul. ◎ Moldova/Ukraine
143 V11 **Kahūrak** Sīstān va Balūchestān, SE Iran
184 G13 **Kahurangi Point** headland South Island, NZ
149 V6 **Kahūta** Punjab, E Pakistan
77 S14 **Kaiama** Kwara, W Nigeria
186 D7 **Kaiapit** Morobe, C PNG
185 I18 **Kaiapoi** Canterbury, South Island, NZ
36 K9 **Kaibab Plateau** plain Arizona, SW USA
171 U14 **Kai Besar, Pulau** island Kepulauan Kai, E Indonesia
36 L9 **Kaibito Plateau** plain Arizona, SW USA
158 K6 **Kaidu He** var. Karaxahar. ≈ NW China
55 S10 **Kaieteur Falls** waterfall C Guyana
161 O6 **Kaifeng** Henan, C China
184 J3 **Kaihu** Northland, North Island, NZ
171 U14 **Kai Kecil, Pulau** island Kepulauan Kai, E Indonesia
169 U16 **Kai, Kepulauan** prev. Kei Islands. island group Maluku, SE Indonesia
184 J3 **Kaikohe** Northland, North Island, NZ
185 J16 **Kaikoura** Canterbury, South Island, NZ
185 J16 **Kaikoura Peninsula** peninsula South Island, NZ
Kailas Range see Gangdisê Shan
160 K12 **Kaili** Guizhou, S China
38 F10 **Kailua** Maui, Hawaii, USA, C Pacific Ocean
38 G11 **Kailua** var. Kailua-Kona, Kona. Hawaii, USA, C Pacific Ocean
Kailua-Kona see Kailua
186 B7 **Kaim** ≈ W PNG
171 X14 **Kaima** Irian Jaya, E Indonesia
184 M7 **Kaimai Range** ▲▲ North Island, NZ
114 E13 **Kaïmaktsalán** ▲ Greece/FYR Macedonia
185 C20 **Kaimanawa Mountains** ▲▲ North Island, NZ
118 E4 **Käina** Ger. Keinis; prev. Keina. Hiiumaa, W Estonia
109 V7 **Kainach** ≈ SE Austria
164 I14 **Kainan** Tokushima, Shikoku, SW Japan
164 H15 **Kainan** Wakayama, Honshū, SW Japan
147 U7 **Kaindy** Kir. Kayyngdy. Chuyskaya Oblast', N Kyrgyzstan
77 T14 **Kainji Dam** dam W Nigeria
Kainji Lake see Kainji Reservoir
77 T14 **Kainji Reservoir** var. Kainji Lake. ▣ W Nigeria
186 D8 **Kaintiba** var. Kamina. Gulf, S PNG
92 K13 **Kainulaisjärvi** Norrbotten, N Sweden
184 K5 **Kaipara Harbour** harbour North Island, NZ
152 I10 **Kairāna** Uttar Pradesh, N India
74 M6 **Kairouan** var. Al Qayrawān. E Tunisia
Kaisaria see Kayseri
101 F20 **Kaiserslautern** Rheinland-Pfalz, SW Germany
118 G13 **Kaišiadorys** Kaišiadorys, S Lithuania
184 I2 **Kaitaia** Northland, North Island, NZ
185 E24 **Kaitangata** Otago, South Island, NZ
152 I9 **Kaithal** Haryāna, NW India
169 N13 **Kait, Tanjung** headland Sumatera, W Indonesia
38 E9 **Kaiwi Channel** channel Hawaii, USA, C Pacific Ocean
160 K9 **Kaixian** var. Kai Xian. Sichuan, C China
163 V11 **Kaiyuan** var. K'ai-yüan. Liaoning, NE China
160 H14 **Kaiyuan** Yunnan, SW China
39 O9 **Kaiyuh Mountains** ▲▲ Alaska, USA
93 M15 **Kajaani** Swe. Kajana. Oulu, C Finland
149 N7 **Kajakī, Band-e** ◎ C Afghanistan
Kajan see Kayan, Sungai
Kajana see Kajaani
137 V13 **K'ajaran** Rus. Kadzharan. SE Armenia
Kajisay see Kadzhi-Say
113 O20 **Kajmakčalan** ▲ S FYR Macedonia
Kajnar see Kaynar
149 N6 **Kajrān** Urūzgān, C Afghanistan
149 N5 **Kaj Rūd** ≈ C Afghanistan
Kaka see Kaakhka
12 C12 **Kakabeka Falls** Ontario, S Canada
83 F23 **Kakamas** Northern Cape, W South Africa
81 H18 **Kakamega** Western, W Kenya
112 H13 **Kakanj** Federacija Bosna I Hercegovina, Bosnia and Herzegovina
185 F22 **Kakanui Mountains** ▲▲ South Island, NZ
184 K11 **Kakaramea** Taranaki, North Island, NZ
76 J16 **Kakata** C Liberia
184 M11 **Kakatahi** Manawatu-Wanganui, North Island, NZ
113 M23 **Kakavi** Gjirokastër, S Albania
147 O14 **Kakaydi** Surkhondaryo Wiloyati, S Uzbekistan
164 F13 **Kake** Hiroshima, Honshū, SW Japan
39 X13 **Kake** Kupreanof Island, Alaska, USA
171 P14 **Kakea** Pulau Wowoni, C Indonesia
164 M14 **Kakegawa** Shizuoka, Honshū, S Japan
165 V16 **Kakeromajima** Kagoshima, SW Japan
143 T6 **Kākhak** var. Kākhk. Khorāsān, E Iran
118 L11 **Kakhanavichy** Rus. Kokhanovichi. Vitsyebskaya Voblasts', N Belarus
39 P13 **Kakhonak** Alaska, USA
117 S10 **Kakhovka** Khersons'ka Oblast', S Ukraine
117 U9 **Kakhovs'ka Vodoskhovyshche** Rus. Kakhovskoye Vodokhranilishche. ▣ SE Ukraine
Kakhovskoye Vodokhranilishche see Kakhovs'ka Vodoskhovyshche
117 T11 **Kakhovs'kyy Kanal** canal S Ukraine
Kakia see Khakhea
155 L16 **Kākināda** prev. Cocanada. Andhra Pradesh, E India
Käkisalmi see Priozersk
164 I13 **Kakogawa** Hyōgo, Honshū, SW Japan
81 F18 **Kakoge** C Uganda
145 O7 **Kak, Ozero** ◎ N Kazakhstan
Ka-Krem see Malyy Yenisey
Kakshaal-Too, Khrebet see Kokshaal-Tau
39 S5 **Kaktovik** Alaska, USA
165 Q11 **Kakuda** Miyagi, Honshū, C Japan
165 Q8 **Kakunodate** Akita, Honshū, C Japan
Kalaallit Nunaat see Greenland
149 T7 **Kālābāgh** Punjab, E Pakistan
171 Q16 **Kalabahi** Pulau Alor, S Indonesia
188 I5 **Kalabera** Saipan, S Northern Mariana Islands
83 G14 **Kalabo** Western, W Zambia
128 M9 **Kalach** Voronezhskaya Oblast', W Russian Federation
129 N10 **Kalach-na-Donu** Volgogradskaya Oblast', SW Russian Federation
166 K5 **Kaladan** ≈ W Myanmar
14 K14 **Kaladar** Ontario, SE Canada
38 G13 **Ka Lae** var. South Cape, South Point. headland Hawaii, USA, C Pacific Ocean
83 G19 **Kalahari Desert** desert Southern Africa
38 B8 **Kalaheo** Haw. Kalāheo. Kauai, Hawaii, USA, C Pacific Ocean
Kalaikhum see Qal'aikhum
146 J16 **Kala-i-Mor** Turkm. Galaymor. Maryyskiy Velayat, S Turkmenistan
93 K15 **Kalajoki** Oulu, W Finland
Kalak see Eski Kaļak
Kal al Sraghna see El Kelâa Srarhna
32 G10 **Kalama** Washington, NW USA
Kalámai see Kalámata
115 G14 **Kalamariá** Kentrikí Makedonía, N Greece
115 E21 **Kalámata** prev. Kalámai. Pelopónnisos, S Greece
31 P10 **Kalamazoo** Michigan, N USA
31 P9 **Kalamazoo River** ≈ Michigan, N USA
Kalambaka see Kalampáka
117 S13 **Kalamits'ka Zatoka** Rus. Kalamitskiy Zaliv. gulf S Ukraine
Kalamitskiy Zaliv see Kalamits'ka Zatoka
115 H18 **Kálamos** Attikí, C Greece
115 C18 **Kálamos** island Iónioi Nísoi, Greece, C Mediterranean Sea
115 D15 **Kalampáka** var. Kalambaka. Thessalía, C Greece
Kalan see Călan, Romania
Kalan see Tunceli, Turkey
117 S11 **Kalanchak** Khersons'ka Oblast', S Ukraine
171 O15 **Kalaotoa, Pulau** island W Indonesia
155 J24 **Kala Oya** ≈ NW Sri Lanka
Kalarash see Călăraşi
93 H17 **Kälarne** Jämtland, C Sweden
143 V15 **Kalar Rūd** ≈ SE Iran
167 R9 **Kalasin** var. Muang Kalasin. Kalasin, E Thailand
149 O8 **Kalāt** Per. Qalāt. Zābul, S Afghanistan
149 O11 **Kālat** var. Kelat, Khelat. Baluchistān, SW Pakistan
115 J14 **Kalathriá, Akrotírio** headland Samothráki, NE Greece
193 W17 **Kalau** island Tongatapu Group, SE Tonga
38 E9 **Kalaupapa** Molokai, Hawaii, USA, C Pacific Ocean
129 N13 **Kalaus** ≈ SW Russian Federation
Kalávrita see Kalávryta
115 E19 **Kalávryta** var. Kalávrita. Dytikí Ellás, S Greece
141 Y10 **Kalbān** W Oman
180 H11 **Kalbarri** Western Australia
145 X10 **Kalbinskiy Khrebet** Kaz. Qalba Zhotasy. ▲▲ E Kazakhstan
144 G10 **Kaldygayty** ≈ W Kazakhstan
136 I12 **Kalecik** Ankara, N Turkey
79 O19 **Kalehe** Sud Kivu, E Dem. Rep. Congo (Zaire)
79 P22 **Kalemie** prev. Albertville. Katanga, SE Dem. Rep. Congo (Zaire)
166 L4 **Kalemyo** Sagaing, W Myanmar
82 H12 **Kalene Hill** North Western, NW Zambia
Kale Sultanie see Çanakkale
126 I7 **Kalevala** Respublika Kareliya, NW Russian Federation
166 L4 **Kalewa** Sagaing, C Myanmar
Kalgan see Zhangjiakou
39 Q12 **Kalgin Island** island Alaska, USA
180 L12 **Kalgoorlie** Western Australia
Kali see Sārda
115 E17 **Kaliakoúda** ▲ C Greece
114 O8 **Kaliakra, Nos** headland NE Bulgaria
115 F19 **Kaliánoi** Pelopónnisos, S Greece
115 N24 **Kalí Límni** ▲ Kárpathos, SE Greece
79 N20 **Kalima** Maniema, E Dem. Rep. Congo (Zaire)
169 S11 **Kalimantan** Eng. Indonesian Borneo. geopolitical region Borneo, C Indonesia
169 Q11 **Kalimantan Barat** off. Propinsi Kalimantan Barat, Eng. West Borneo, West Kalimantan. ⬖ province N Indonesia
169 T13 **Kalimantan Selatan** off. Propinsi Kalimantan Selatan, Eng. South Borneo, South Kalimantan. ⬖ province N Indonesia
169 R12 **Kalimantan Tengah** off. Propinsi Kalimantan Tengah, Eng. Central Borneo, Central Kalimantan. ⬖ province N Indonesia
169 U10 **Kalimantan Timur** off. Propinsi Kalimantan Timur, Eng. East Borneo, East Kalimantan. ⬖ province N Indonesia
Kálimnos see Kálymnos
153 S12 **Kālimpang** West Bengal, NE India
Kalinin see Tver', Russian Federation
Kalinin see Boldumsaz, Turkmenistan
Kalininabad see Kalininobod
128 B3 **Kaliningrad** Kaliningradskaya Oblast', W Russian Federation
Kaliningrad see Kaliningradskaya Oblast'
128 A3 **Kaliningradskaya Oblast'** var. Kaliningrad. ⬖ province and enclave W Russian Federation
Kalinino see Tashir
147 P14 **Kalininobod** Rus. Kalininabad. SW Tajikistan
129 O8 **Kalininsk** Saratovskaya Oblast', W Russian Federation
Kalininsk see Boldumsaz
Kalinisk see Cupcina
119 M19 **Kalinkavichy** Rus. Kalinkovichi. Homyel'skaya Voblasts', SE Belarus
Kalinkovichi see Kalinkavichy
81 G18 **Kaliro** SE Uganda
Kalisch/Kalish see Kalisz
33 O7 **Kalispell** Montana, NW USA
110 I13 **Kalisz** Ger. Kalisch, Rus. Kalish; anc. Calisia. Wielkopolskie, C Poland
110 F9 **Kalisz Pomorski** Ger. Kallies. Zachodniopomorskie, NW Poland
128 M10 **Kalitva** ≈ SW Russian Federation
81 F21 **Kaliua** Tabora, C Tanzania
92 K13 **Kalix** Norrbotten, N Sweden
92 K12 **Kalixälven** ≈ N Sweden
92 J11 **Kalixfors** Norrbotten, N Sweden
145 T8 **Kalkaman** Pavlodar, NE Kazakhstan
Kalkandelen see Tetovo
181 O4 **Kalkarindji** Northern Territory, N Australia
31 P6 **Kalkaska** Michigan, N USA
93 F16 **Kall** Jämtland, C Sweden
189 X2 **Kallalen** var. Calalen. island Ratak Chain, SE Marshall Islands
118 J5 **Kallaste** Ger. Krasnogor. Tartumaa, SE Estonia
93 N16 **Kallavesi** ◎ SE Finland
115 F17 **Kallídromo** ▲▲ C Greece
Kallies see Kalisz Pomorski
95 M22 **Kallinge** Blekinge, S Sweden
115 L16 **Kalloní** Lésvos, E Greece
93 F16 **Kallsjön** ◎ C Sweden
95 N21 **Kalmar** var. Calmar. Kalmar, S Sweden
95 M19 **Kalmar** var. Calmar. ⬖ county S Sweden
95 N20 **Kalmarsund** strait S Sweden
148 L16 **Kalmat, Khor** Eng. Kalmat Lagoon. lagoon SW Pakistan
Kalmat Lagoon see Kalmat, Khor
117 X9 **Kal'mius** ≈ E Ukraine
99 H15 **Kalmthout** Antwerpen, N Belgium
Kalmykia/Kalmykiya-Khal'mg Tangch, Respublika see Kalmykiya, Respublika
129 O12 **Kalmykiya, Respublika** var. Respublika Kalmykiya-Khal'mg Tangch, Eng. Kalmykia; prev. Kalmytskaya ASSR. ⬖ autonomous republic SW Russian Federation
Kalmytskaya ASSR see Kalmykiya, Respublika
118 F9 **Kalnciems** Jelgava, C Latvia
114 L10 **Kalnitsa** ≈ SE Bulgaria
111 J24 **Kalocsa** Bács-Kiskun, S Hungary
114 J9 **Kalofer** Plovdiv, C Bulgaria
38 E10 **Kalohi Channel** channel C Pacific Ocean
83 I16 **Kalomo** Southern, S Zambia
29 X14 **Kalona** Iowa, C USA
115 K22 **Kalotási, Akrotírio** headland Amorgós, Kykládes, Greece, Aegean Sea
152 J8 **Kalpa** Himāchal Pradesh, N India
115 C15 **Kalpáki** Ípeiros, W Greece
155 C22 **Kalpeni Island** island Lakshadweep, India, N Indian Ocean
152 K13 **Kālpi** Uttar Pradesh, N India
158 G7 **Kalpin** Xinjiang Uygur Zizhiqu, NW China
146 K8 **Kalquduq** Rus. Kulkuduk. Nawoiy Wiloyati, N Uzbekistan
149 P16 **Kalri Lake** ◎ SE Pakistan
143 R5 **Kāl Shūr** N Iran
39 N11 **Kalskag** Alaska, USA
95 B18 **Kalsoy** Dan. Kalsø Island Faeroe Islands
39 O9 **Kaltag** Alaska, USA
108 H7 **Kaltbrunn** Sankt Gallen, NE Switzerland
Kaltdorf see Pruszków
77 X14 **Kaltungo** Gombe, E Nigeria
128 K4 **Kaluga** Kaluzhskaya Oblast', W Russian Federation
155 J26 **Kalu Ganga** ≈ S Sri Lanka
82 J13 **Kalulushi** Copperbelt, C Zambia
180 M2 **Kalumburu** Western Australia
95 H23 **Kalundborg** Vestsjælland, E Denmark
82 K11 **Kalungwishi** ≈ N Zambia
149 T8 **Kalūr Kot** Punjab, E Pakistan
116 I6 **Kalush** Pol. Kałusz. Ivano-Frankivs'ka Oblast', W Ukraine
Kałusz see Kalush
110 N11 **Kałuszyn** Mazowieckie, C Poland
155 J26 **Kalutara** Western Province, SW Sri Lanka
Kaluwawa see Fergusson Island
128 I5 **Kaluzhskaya Oblast'** ⬖ province W Russian Federation
119 E14 **Kalvarija** Pol. Kalwaria. Marijampolė, S Lithuania
93 K15 **Kälviä** Länsi-Suomi, W Finland
109 U6 **Kalwang** Steiermark, E Austria
Kalwaria see Kalvarija
154 D13 **Kalyān** Mahārāshtra, W India
126 K16 **Kalyazin** Tverskaya Oblast', W Russian Federation
115 D18 **Kalydón** anc. Calydon. site of ancient city Dytikí Ellás, C Greece
115 M21 **Kálymnos** var. Kálimnos. Kálymnos, Dodekánisos, Greece, Aegean Sea
115 M21 **Kálymnos** var. Kálimnos. island Dodekánisos, Greece, Aegean Sea
117 O5 **Kalynivka** Kyyivs'ka Oblast', N Ukraine
117 N6 **Kalynivka** Vinnyts'ka Oblast', C Ukraine
42 M10 **Kama** var. Cama. Región Autónoma Atlántico Sur, SE Nicaragua
165 R9 **Kamaishi** var. Kamaisi. Iwate, Honshū, C Japan
Kamaisi see Kamaishi
118 H13 **Kamajai** Molėtai, E Lithuania
118 H11 **Kamajai** Rokiškis, NE Lithuania
149 U9 **Kamālia** Punjab, NE Pakistan
83 I14 **Kamalondo** North Western, NW Zambia
136 I13 **Kaman** Kirşehir, C Turkey
79 O20 **Kamanyola** Sud Kivu, E Dem. Rep. Congo (Zaire)
141 N14 **Kamarān** island W Yemen
55 R9 **Kamarang** W Guyana
Kāmāreddi/Kamareddy see Rāmāreddi
Kama Reservoir see Kamskoye Vodokhranilishche
148 K13 **Kamarod** Baluchistān, SW Pakistan
171 P14 **Kamaru** Pulau Buton, C Indonesia
147 N12 **Kamashi** Qashqadaryo Wiloyati, S Uzbekistan
77 S13 **Kamba** Kebbi, NW Nigeria
Kambaeng Petch see Kamphaeng Phet
180 L12 **Kambalda** Western Australia

◆ Country ● Country Capital ◇ Dependent Territory ○ Dependent Territory Capital ⬖ Administrative Region ✕ International Airport ▲ Mountain ▲▲ Mountain Range ☗ Volcano ≈ River ◎ Lake ▣ Reservoir

149 *P13* **Kambar** *var.* Qambar. Sind, SE Pakistan
Kambara *see* Kabara
76 *I14* **Kambia** W Sierra Leone
Kambos *see* Kámpos
79 *N25* **Kambove** Katanga, SE Dem. Rep. Congo (Zaire)
Kambryk *see* Cambrai
123 *V10* **Kamchatka** ≈ E Russian Federation
Kamchatka *see* Kamchatka, Poluostrov
Kamchatka Basin *see* Komandorskaya Basin
123 *U10* **Kamchatka, Poluostrov** *Eng.* Kamchatka. *peninsula* E Russian Federation
123 *V10* **Kamchatskaya Oblast'** ◆ *province* E Russian Federation
123 *V10* **Kamchatskiy Zaliv** *gulf* E Russian Federation
114 *N9* **Kamchiya** ≈ E Bulgaria
114 *L9* **Kamchiya, Yazovir** ⊞ E Bulgaria
Kamdesh *see* Kāmdeysh
149 *T4* **Kāmdeysh** *var.* Kamdesh. Kunar, E Afghanistan
118 *M13* **Kamen'** *Rus.* Kamen'. Vitsyebskaya Voblasts', N Belarus
Kamenets *see* Kamyanyets
Kamenets-Podol'skaya Oblast' *see* Khmel'nyts'ka Oblast'
Kamenets-Podol'skiy *see* Kam"yanets'-Podil's'kyy
113 *Q18* **Kamenica** NE FYR Macedonia
112 *A11* **Kamenjak, Rt** *headland* NW Croatia
144 *F8* **Kamenka** Zapadnyy Kazakhstan, NW Kazakhstan
127 *O6* **Kamenka** Arkhangel'skaya Oblast', NW Russian Federation
128 *O6* **Kamenka** Penzenskaya Oblast', W Russian Federation
129 *L8* **Kamenka** Voronezhskaya Oblast', W Russian Federation
Kamenka *see* Camenca, Moldova
Kamenka *see* Kam"yanka, Ukraine
Kamenka-Bugskaya *see* Kam"yanka-Buz'ka
Kamenka Dneprovskaya *see* Kam"yanka-Dniprovs'ka
Kamen Kashirskiy *see* Kamin'-Kashyrs'kyy
1028*L15* **Kamennomostskiy** Respublika Adygeya, SW Russian Federation
128 *L11* **Kamenolomni** Rostovskaya Oblast', SW Russian Federation
129 *P8* **Kamenskiy** Saratovskaya Oblast', W Russian Federation
Kamenskoye *see* Dniprodzerzhyns'k
128 *L11* **Kamensk-Shakhtinskiy** Rostovskaya Oblast', SW Russian Federation
101 *P15* **Kamenz** Sachsen, E Germany
164 *J13* **Kameoka** Kyōto, Honshū, SW Japan
128 *M3* **Kameshkovo** Vladimirskaya Oblast', W Russian Federation
164 *C11* **Kami-Agata** Nagasaki, Tsushima, SW Japan
33 *N10* **Kamiah** Idaho, NW USA
Kamień Koszyrski *see* Kamin'-Kashyrs'kyy
110 *H9* **Kamień Krajeński** *Ger.* Kamin in Westpreussen. Kujawsko-pomorskie, C Poland
111 *F15* **Kamienna Góra** *Ger.* Landeshut, Landeshut in Schlesien. Dolnośląskie, SW Poland
110 *D8* **Kamień Pomorski** *Ger.* Cummin in Pommern. Zachodniopomorskie, NW Poland
165 *R5* **Kamiiso** Hokkaidō, NE Japan
79 *L22* **Kamiji** Kasai Oriental, S Dem. Rep. Congo (Zaire)
165 *T3* **Kamikawa** Hokkaidō, NE Japan
164 *B15* **Kami-Koshiki-jima** *island* SW Japan
79 *M23* **Kamina** Katanga, S Dem. Rep. Congo (Zaire)
Kamina *see* Kaintiba
42 *C6* **Kaminaljuyú** *ruins* Guatemala, C Guatemala
Kamin in Westpreussen *see* Kamień Krajeński
116 *J2* **Kamin'-Kashyrs'kyy** *Pol.* Kamień Koszyrski, *Rus.* Kamen Kashirskiy. Volyns'ka Oblast', NW Ukraine
165 *Q5* **Kaminokuni** Hokkaidō, NE Japan
165 *P10* **Kaminoyama** Yamagata, Honshū, C Japan
39 *Q13* **Kamishak Bay** *bay* Alaska, USA
165 *U4* **Kami-Shihoro** Hokkaidō, NE Japan
Kamishli *see* Al Qāmishlī
Kamissar *see* Kamsar
164 *C11* **Kami-Tsushima** Nagasaki, Tsushima, SW Japan
79 *O20* **Kamituga** Sud Kivu, E Dem. Rep. Congo (Zaire)
164 *B17* **Kamiyaku** Kagoshima, Yaku-shima, SW Japan
11 *N16* **Kamloops** British Columbia, SW Canada
107 *G25* **Kamma** Sicilia, Italy, C Mediterranean Sea
192 *K4* **Kammu Seamount** *undersea feature* N Pacific Ocean
109 *U11* **Kamnik** *Ger.* Stein. C Slovenia
Kamniške Alpe *see* Kamniško-Savinjske Alpe
109 *T10* **Kamniško-Savinjske Alpe** *var.* Kamniške Alpe, Sanntaler Alpen, *Ger.* Steiner Alpen. ▲ N Slovenia
165 *O14* **Kamogawa** Chiba, Honshū, S Japan
149 *W8* **Kāmoke** Punjab, E Pakistan
82 *L13* **Kamoto** Eastern, E Zambia
109 *V3* **Kamp** ≈ N Austria
81 *F18* **Kampala** ● (Uganda) S Uganda
168 *K11* **Kampar, Sungai** ≈ Sumatera, W Indonesia
98 *L9* **Kampen** Overijssel, E Netherlands
79 *N20* **Kampene** Maniema, E Dem. Rep. Congo (Zaire)
29 *Q9* **Kampeska, Lake** ◎ South Dakota, N USA
167 *O9* **Kamphaeng Phet** *var.* Kambaeng Petch. Kamphaeng Phet, W Thailand
Kampo *see* Campo, Cameroon
Kampo *see* Ntem, Cameroon/Equatorial Guinea
167 *S12* **Kâmpóng Cham** *prev.* Kompong Cham. Kâmpóng Cham, C Cambodia
167 *R12* **Kâmpóng Chhnăng** *prev.* Kompong. Kâmpóng Chhnăng, C Cambodia
167 *R12* **Kâmpóng Khleăng** *prev.* Kompong Kleang. Siĕmréab, NW Cambodia
167 *Q14* **Kâmpóng Saôm** *prev.* Kompong Som, Sihanoukville. Kâmpóng Saôm, SW Cambodia
167 *R13* **Kâmpóng Spoe** *prev.* Kompong Speu. Kâmpóng Spœ, S Cambodia
121 *O2* **Kámpos** *var.* Kambos. NW Cyprus
167 *R14* **Kâmpôt** Kâmpôt, SW Cambodia
Kamptee *see* Kāmthi
77 *O14* **Kampti** SW Burkina
Kampuchea *see* Cambodia
169 *Q9* **Kampung Sirik** Sarawak, East Malaysia
11 *V15* **Kamsack** Saskatchewan, S Canada
76 *H13* **Kamsar** *var.* Kamissar. Guinée-Maritime, W Guinea
129 *R4* **Kamskoye Ust'ye** Respublika Tatarstan, W Russian Federation
127 *U14* **Kamskoye Vodokhranilishche** *var.* Kama Reservoir. ⊞ NW Russian Federation
154 *I12* **Kāmthi** *prev.* Kamptee. Mahārāshtra, C India
Kamuela *see* Waimea
165 *R3* **Kamuenai** Hokkaidō, NE Japan
165 *T5* **Kamui-dake** ※ Hokkaidō, NE Japan
165 *R3* **Kamui-misaki** *headland* Hokkaidō, NE Japan
43 *O15* **Kámuk, Cerro** ▲ SE Costa Rica
116 *K7* **Kam"yanets'-Podil's'kyy** *Rus.* Kamenets-Podol'skiy. Khmel'nyts'ka Oblast', W Ukraine
117 *Q6* **Kam"yanka** *Rus.* Kamenka. Cherkas'ka Oblast', C Ukraine
116 *I5* **Kam"yanka-Buz'ka** *Rus.* Kamenka-Bugskaya. L'vivs'ka Oblast', NW Ukraine
117 *T9* **Kam"yanka-Dniprovs'ka** *Rus.* Kamenka Dneprovskaya. Zaporiz'ka Oblast', SE Ukraine
119 *F19* **Kamyanyets** *Rus.* Kamenets. Brestskaya Voblasts', SW Belarus
129 *P9* **Kamyshin** Volgogradskaya Oblast', SW Russian Federation
129 *Q13* **Kamyzyak** Astrakhanskaya Oblast', SW Russian Federation
12 *K8* **Kanaaupscow** ≈ Quebec, C Canada
36 *K8* **Kanab** Utah, W USA
36 *K9* **Kanab Creek** ≈ Arizona/Utah, SW USA
187 *Y14* **Kanacea** *prev.* Kanathea. Taveuni, N Fiji
38 *G17* **Kanaga Island** *island* Aleutian Islands, Alaska, USA
38 *G17* **Kanaga Volcano** ▲ Kanaga Island, Alaska, USA
165 *N14* **Kanagawa** *off.* Kanagawa-ken. ◆ *prefecture* Honshū, S Japan
13 *Q8* **Kanairiktok** ≈ Newfoundland, E Canada
Kanaky *see* New Caledonia
79 *K22* **Kananga** *prev.* Luluabourg. Kasai Occidental, S Dem. Rep. Congo (Zaire)
Kananur *see* Cannanore
Kanara *see* Karnātaka
36 *J7* **Kanarraville** Utah, W USA
129 *Q4* **Kanash** Chuvashskaya Respublika, W Russian Federation
Kanathea *see* Kanacea
21 *Q4* **Kanawha River** ≈ West Virginia, NE USA
164 *L13* **Kanayama** Gifu, Honshū, SW Japan
164 *L11* **Kanazawa** Ishikawa, Honshū, SW Japan
166 *M4* **Kanbalu** Sagaing, C Myanmar
166 *L8* **Kanbe** Yangon, SW Myanmar
167 *O11* **Kanchanaburi** Kanchanaburi, W Thailand
Känchenjunga *see* Kangchenjunga
145 *V11* **Kanchingiz, Khrebet** ▲ E Kazakhstan
155 *J19* **Kānchīpuram** *prev.* Conjeeveram. Tamil Nādu, SE India
149 *N8* **Kandahār** *Per.* Qandahār. Kandahār, S Afghanistan
149 *N9* **Kandahār** *Per.* Qandahār. ◆ *province* SE Afghanistan
Kandalakša *see* Kandalaksha
126 *I5* **Kandalaksha** *var.* Kandalakša, *Fin.* Kantalahti. Murmanskaya Oblast', NW Russian Federation
Kandalaksha Gulf/Kandalakshskaya Guba *see* Kandalakshskiy Zaliv
126 *K6* **Kandalakshskiy Zaliv** *var.* Kandalakshskaya Guba, *Eng.* Kandalaksha Gulf. *bay* NW Russian Federation
Kandalangodi *see* Kandalengoti
83 *G17* **Kandalengoti** *var.* Kandalangodi. Ngamiland, NW Botswana
169 *U13* **Kandangan** Borneo, C Indonesia
Kandau *see* Kandava
118 *E8* **Kandava** *Ger.* Kandau. Tukums, W Latvia
Kandavu *see* Kadavu
77 *R14* **Kandé** *var.* Kanté. NE Togo
101 *F23* **Kandel** ▲ SW Germany
186 *C7* **Kandep** Enga, W PNG
149 *R12* **Kandh Kot** Sind, SE Pakistan
77 *S13* **Kandi** N Benin
149 *P14* **Kandiāro** Sind, SE Pakistan
136 *F11* **Kandıra** Kocaeli, NW Turkey
183 *S8* **Kandos** New South Wales, SE Australia
148 *M16* **Kandrāch** *var.* Kanrach. Baluchistān, SW Pakistan
172 *I4* **Kandreho** Mahajanga, C Madagascar
186 *F7* **Kandrian** New Britain, E PNG
Kandukur *see* Kondukūr
155 *K25* **Kandy** Central Province, C Sri Lanka
144 *I10* **Kandyagash** *Kaz.* Qandyaghash; *prev.* Oktyabr'sk. Aktyubinsk, W Kazakhstan
18 *D12* **Kane** Pennsylvania, NE USA
64 *I11* **Kane Fracture Zone** *tectonic feature* NW Atlantic Ocean
Kanëka *see* Kanëvka
78 *G9* **Kanem** *off.* Préfecture du Kanem. ◆ *prefecture* W Chad
38 *D9* **Kaneohe** *Haw.* Kāne'ohe. Oahu, Hawaii, USA, C Pacific Ocean
Kanestron, Akrotírio *see* Palioúri, Akrotírio
Kanëv *see* Kaniv
126 *M5* **Kanëvka** *var.* Kanëka. Murmanskaya Oblast', NW Russian Federation
128 *K13* **Kanevskaya** Krasnodarskiy Kray, SW Russian Federation
Kanevskoye Vodokhranilishche *see* Kanivs'ke Vodoskhovyshche
165 *P9* **Kaneyama** Yamagata, Honshū, C Japan
83 *G20* **Kang** Kgalagadi, C Botswana
76 *L13* **Kangaba** Koulikoro, SW Mali
136 *M13* **Kangal** Sivas, C Turkey
143 *O13* **Kangān** Būshehr, S Iran
143 *S15* **Kangān** Hormozgān, SE Iran
168 *J6* **Kangar** Perlis, Peninsular Malaysia
76 *L13* **Kangaré** Sikasso, S Mali
182 *F10* **Kangaroo Island** *island* South Australia
93 *M17* **Kangasniemi** Itä-Suomi, E Finland
142 *K6* **Kangāvar** *var.* Kangāwar. Kermānshāh, W Iran
Kangāwar *see* Kangāvar
153 *S11* **Kangchenjunga** *var.* Känchenjunga. ▲ NE India
160 *G9* **Kangding** Sichuan, C China
169 *U16* **Kangean, Kepulauan** *island group* S Indonesia
169 *T16* **Kangean, Pulau** *island* Kepulauan Kangean, S Indonesia
67 *U8* **Kangen** *var.* Kengen. ≈ SE Sudan
197 *N14* **Kangerlussuaq** *Dan.* Sondre Strømfjord ✕ Kitaa, W Greenland
197 *Q15* **Kangertittivaq** *Dan.* Scoresby Sund. *fjord* E Greenland
167 *O2* **Kangfang** Kachin State, N Myanmar
163 *X12* **Kanggye** N North Korea
197 *P15* **Kangikajik** *var.* Kap Brewster. *headland* E Greenland
13 *N5* **Kangiqsualujjuaq** *prev.* George River, Port-Nouveau-Québec. Quebec, E Canada
12 *L2* **Kangiqsujuaq** *prev.* Maricourt, Wakeham Bay. Quebec, NE Canada
12 *M4* **Kangirsuk** *prev.* Bellin, Payne. Quebec, E Canada
158 *J15* **Kangmar** Xizang Zizhiqu, W China
158 *M16* **Kangmar** Xizang Zizhiqu, W China
163 *Y14* **Kangnŭng** *Jap.* Kōryō. NE South Korea
79 *D18* **Kango** Estuaire, NW Gabon
152 *I7* **Kāngra** Himāchal Pradesh, NW India
153 *Q16* **Kangsabati Reservoir** ⊞ N India
159 *O17* **Kangto** ▲ China/India
159 *W12* **Kangxian** *var.* Kang Xian, Zuitaizi. Gansu, C China
166 *L4* **Kani** Sagaing, C Myanmar
76 *M15* **Kani** NW Ivory Coast
79 *M23* **Kaniama** Katanga, S Dem. Rep. Congo (Zaire)
Kanibadam *see* Konibodom
169 *V6* **Kanibongan** Sabah, East Malaysia
185 *F17* **Kaniere** West Coast, South Island, NZ
185 *G17* **Kaniere, Lake** ◎ South Island, NZ
188 *E17* **Kanifaay** Yap, W Micronesia
127 *O4* **Kanin Kamen'** ▲ NW Russian Federation
127 *N3* **Kanin Nos** Nenetskiy Avtonomnyy Okrug, NW Russian Federation
127 *N3* **Kanin Nos, Mys** *headland* NW Russian Federation
127 *O5* **Kanin, Poluostrov** *peninsula* NW Russian Federation
139 *V8* **Kānī Sakht** E Iraq
139 *T3* **Kānī Sulaymān** N Iraq
165 *Q6* **Kanita** Aomori, Honshū, C Japan
117 *Q5* **Kaniv** *Rus.* Kanëv. Cherkas'ka Oblast', C Ukraine
182 *K11* **Kaniva** Victoria, SE Australia
117 *Q5* **Kanivs'ke Vodoskhovyshche** *Rus.* Kanevskoye Vodokhranilishche. ⊞ C Ukraine
112 *L8* **Kanjiža** *Ger.* Altkanischa, *Hung.* Magyarkanizsa, Ókanizsa; *prev.* Stara Kanjiža. Serbia, N Yugoslavia
93 *K18* **Kankaanpää** Länsi-Suomi, W Finland
30 *M12* **Kankakee** Illinois, N USA
31 *O11* **Kankakee River** ≈ Illinois/Indiana, N USA
76 *K14* **Kankan** Haute-Guinée, E Guinea
154 *K13* **Kānker** Madhya Pradesh, C India
76 *J10* **Kankossa** Assaba, S Mauritania
167 *N12* **Kanmaw Kyun** *var.* Kisseraing, Kithareng. *island* Mergui Archipelago, S Myanmar
164 *F12* **Kanmuri-yama** ▲ Kyūshū, SW Japan
21 *R10* **Kannapolis** North Carolina, SE USA
93 *L16* **Kannonkoski** Länsi-Suomi, W Finland
Kannur *see* Cannanore
93 *K15* **Kannus** Länsi-Suomi, W Finland
77 *V13* **Kano** Kano, N Nigeria
77 *V13* **Kano** ◆ *state* N Nigeria
77 *V13* **Kano** ✕ Kano, N Nigeria
164 *G14* **Kan'onji** *var.* Kanonzi. Kagawa, Shikoku, SW Japan
Kanonzi *see* Kan'onji
26 *M5* **Kanopolis Lake** ⊞ Kansas, C USA
36 *K5* **Kanosh** Utah, W USA
169 *R9* **Kanowit** Sarawak, East Malaysia
164 *C16* **Kanoya** Kagoshima, Kyūshū, SW Japan
152 *L13* **Kānpur** *Eng.* Cawnpore. Uttar Pradesh, N India
Kanrach *see* Kandrāch
164 *I14* **Kansai** ✕ (Ōsaka) Ōsaka, Honshū, SW Japan
27 *R9* **Kansas** Oklahoma, C USA
26 *L5* **Kansas** *off.* State of Kansas; also known as Jayhawker State, Sunflower State. ◆ *state* C USA
27 *R4* **Kansas City** Kansas, C USA
27 *R4* **Kansas City** Missouri, C USA
27 *R3* **Kansas City** ✕ Missouri, C USA
27 *P4* **Kansas River** ≈ Kansas, C USA
122 *L14* **Kansk** Krasnoyarskiy Kray, S Russian Federation
Kansu *see* Gansu
147 *V7* **Kant** Chuyskaya Oblast', N Kyrgyzstan
Kantalahti *see* Kandalaksha
167 *N16* **Kantang** *var.* Ban Kantang. Trang, SW Thailand
115 *H25* **Kántanos** Kríti, Greece, E Mediterranean Sea
77 *R12* **Kantchari** E Burkina
Kanté *see* Kandé
Kantemir *see* Cantemir
128 *L9* **Kantemirovka** Voronezhskaya Oblast', W Russian Federation
167 *R11* **Kantharalak** Si Sa Ket, E Thailand
Kantipur *see* Kathmandu
39 *Q9* **Kantishna River** ≈ Alaska, USA
191 *S3* **Kanton** *var.* Abariringa, Canton Island; *prev.* Mary Island. *atoll* Phoenix Islands, C Kiribati
97 *C20* **Kanturk** *Ir.* Ceann Toirc. SW Ireland
55 *T11* **Kanuku Mountains** ▲ S Guyana
165 *O12* **Kanuma** Tochigi, Honshū, S Japan
83 *H20* **Kanye** Southern, SE Botswana
83 *H17* **Kanyu** Ngamiland, C Botswana
166 *M7* **Kanyutkwin** Pegu, C Myanmar
79 *M24* **Kanzenze** Katanga, SE Dem. Rep. Congo (Zaire)
193 *Y15* **Kao** *island* Kotu Group, W Tonga
161 *S14* **Kaohsiung** *var.* Gaoxiong, *Jap.* Takao, Takow. S Taiwan
161 *S14* **Kaohsiung** ✕ S Taiwan
Kaokaona *see* Kirakira
83 *B17* **Kaoko Veld** ▲ N Namibia
76 *G11* **Kaolack** *var.* Kaolak. W Senegal
Kaolak *see* Kaolack
Kaolan *see* Lanzhou
186 *M8* **Kaolo** San Jorge, N Solomon Islands
83 *H14* **Kaoma** Western, W Zambia
38 *B8* **Kapaa** *Haw.* Kapa'a. Kauai, Hawaii, USA, C Pacific Ocean
113 *J16* **Kapa Moračka** ▲ SW Yugoslavia
137 *V13* **Kapan** *Rus.* Kafan; *prev.* Ghap'an. SE Armenia
82 *L13* **Kapandashila** Northern, NE Zambia
79 *L23* **Kapanga** Katanga, S Dem. Rep. Congo (Zaire)
145 *U15* **Kapchagay** *Kaz.* Kapshaghay. Almaty, SE Kazakhstan
145 *V15* **Kapchagayskoye Vodokhranilishche** *Kaz.* Qapshagay Böyeni. ⊞ SE Kazakhstan
99 *F15* **Kapelle** Zeeland, SW Netherlands
99 *G16* **Kapellen** Antwerpen, N Belgium
95 *P15* **Kapellskär** Stockholm, C Sweden
81 *H18* **Kapenguria** Rift Valley, W Kenya
109 *V6* **Kapfenberg** Steiermark, C Austria
83 *J14* **Kapiri Mposhi** Central, C Zambia
149 *R4* **Kāpīsā** ◆ *province* E Afghanistan
12 *G10* **Kapiskau** ≈ Ontario, C Canada
184 *K13* **Kapiti Island** *island* C NZ
78 *K9* **Kapka, Massif du** ▲ E Chad
Kaplamada *see* Kaubalatmada, Gunung
22 *H9* **Kaplan** Louisiana, S USA
146 *E9* **Kaplangky, Plato** *ridge* Turkmenistan/Uzbekistan
111 *D19* **Kaplice** *Ger.* Kaplitz. Budějovický Kraj, S Czech Republic
Kaplitz *see* Kaplice
Kapoche *see* Capoche
171 *T12* **Kapocol** Irian Jaya, E Indonesia
167 *N14* **Kapoe** Ranong, SW Thailand
Kapoeas *see* Kapuas, Sungai
81 *G15* **Kapoeta** Eastern Equatoria, SE Sudan
111 *I25* **Kapos** ≈ S Hungary
111 *H25* **Kaposvár** Somogy, SW Hungary
94 *H13* **Kapp** Oppland, S Norway
100 *I7* **Kappeln** Schleswig-Holstein, N Germany
Kaproncza *see* Koprivnica
109 *P7* **Kaprun** Salzburg, C Austria
Kapshaghay *see* Kapchagay
Kapstad *see* Cape Town
Kapsukas *see* Marijampolė
171 *Y13* **Kaptiau** Irian Jaya, E Indonesia
119 *L19* **Kaptsevichy** *Rus.* Koptsevichi. Homyel'skaya Voblasts', SE Belarus
Kapuas Hulu, Banjaran/Kapuas Hulu, Pegunungan *see* Kapuas Mountains
169 *S10* **Kapuas Mountains** *Ind.* Banjaran Kapuas Hulu, Pegunungan Kapuas Hulu. ▲ Indonesia/Malaysia
169 *P11* **Kapuas, Sungai** ≈ Borneo, N Indonesia
169 *T13* **Kapuas, Sungai** *prev.* Kapoeas. ≈ Borneo, C Indonesia
182 *J9* **Kapunda** South Australia
152 *H8* **Kapūrthala** Punjab, N India
12 *G12* **Kapuskasing** Ontario, S Canada
14 *D6* **Kapuskasing** ≈ Ontario, S Canada
129 *P11* **Kapustin Yar** Astrakhanskaya Oblast', SW Russian Federation
82 *K11* **Kaputa** Northern, NE Zambia
111 *G22* **Kapuvár** Győr-Moson-Sopron, NW Hungary
Kapydzhik, Gora *see* Qapıciğ Dağı
119 *J17* **Kapyl'** *Rus.* Kopyl'. Minskaya Voblasts', C Belarus
43 *N9* **Kara** *var.* Cara. Región Autónoma Atlántico Sur, E Nicaragua
77 *R14* **Kara** *var.* Lama-Kara. NE Togo
77 *Q14* **Kara** ≈ N Togo
147 *U7* **Kara-Balta** Chuyskaya Oblast', N Kyrgyzstan
144 *G11* **Karabau** Atyrau, W Kazakhstan
146 *E7* **Karabaur', Uval** *Kaz.* Korabavur Pastligi, *Uzb.* Qorabowur Kirlari. *physical region* Kazakhstan/Uzbekistan
146 *L13* **Karabekaul** *var.* Garabekevyul, *Turkm.* Garabekewül. Lebapskiy Velayat, E Turkmenistan
146 *K15* **Karabil', Vozvyshennost'** ▲ S Turkmenistan
146 *A9* **Kara-Bogaz-Gol** *Turkm.* Garabogazköl. Balkanskiy Velayat, NW Turkmenistan
146 *B9* **Kara-Bogaz-Gol, Zaliv** *bay* NW Turkmenistan
145 *R15* **Karaboget** *Kaz.* Qaraböget. Zhambyl, S Kazakhstan
136 *H11* **Karabük** Karabük, NW Turkey
136 *H11* **Karabük** ◆ *province* NW Turkey
122 *L12* **Karabula** Krasnoyarskiy Kray, C Russian Federation
145 *V14* **Karabulak** *Kaz.* Qarabulaq. Almaty, SE Kazakhstan
145 *Y11* **Karabulak** *Kaz.* Qarabulaq. Vostochnyy Kazakhstan, E Kazakhstan
145 *Q17* **Karabulak** *Kaz.* Qarabulaq. Yuzhnyy Kazakhstan, S Kazakhstan
136 *C17* **Kara Burnu** *headland* SW Turkey
144 *K10* **Karabutak** *Kaz.* Qarabutaq. Aktyubinsk, W Kazakhstan
136 *D12* **Karacabey** Bursa, NW Turkey
114 *O12* **Karacaköy** İstanbul, NW Turkey
114 *M12* **Karacaoğlan** Kırklareli, NW Turkey
Karachay-Cherkessia *see* Karachayevo-Cherkesskaya Respublika
128 *L15* **Karachayevo-Cherkesskaya Respublika** *Eng.* Karachay-Cherkessia. ◆ *autonomous republic* SW Russian Federation
128 *M15* **Karachayevsk** Karachayevo-Cherkesskaya Respublika, SW Russian Federation
128 *J6* **Karachev** Bryanskaya Oblast', W Russian Federation
149 *O16* **Karāchi** Sind, SE Pakistan
149 *O16* **Karāchi** ✕ Sind, S Pakistan
Karácsonkő *see* Piatra-Neamț
155 *E15* **Karād** Mahārāshtra, W India
136 *H16* **Karadağ** ▲ S Turkey
147 *T10* **Karadar'ya** *Uzb.* Qoradaryo. ≈ Kyrgyzstan/Uzbekistan
Karadeniz *see* Black Sea
Karadeniz Boğazı *see* İstanbul Boğazı
146 *B13* **Karadepe** Balkanskiy Velayat, W Turkmenistan
Karadzhar *see* Qorajar
Karaferiye *see* Véroia
146 *E13* **Karagan** *Turkm.* Garagan. Akhalskiy Velayat, C Turkmenistan
145 *R10* **Karaganda** *Kaz.* Qaraghandy. Karaganda, C Kazakhstan
145 *R10* **Karaganda** *off.* Karagandinskaya Oblast', *Kaz.* Qaraghandy Oblysy. ◆ *province* C Kazakhstan
Karagandinskaya Oblast' *see* Karaganda
145 *T10* **Karagayly** *Kaz.* Qaraghayly. Karaganda, C Kazakhstan
146 *A11* **Karagel'** *Turkm.* Garagöl. Balkanskiy Velayat, W Turkmenistan
123 *U9* **Karaginskiy, Ostrov** *island* E Russian Federation
197 *T1* **Karaginskiy Zaliv** *bay* E Russian Federation
137 *P13* **Karagöl Dağları** ▲ NE Turkey
114 *L13* **Karahisar** Edirne, NW Turkey
129 *V3* **Karaidel'** Respublika Bashkortostan, W Russian Federation
129 *V3* **Karaidel'skiy** Respublika Bashkortostan, W Russian Federation
114 *L13* **Karaidemir Barajı** ⊞ NW Turkey
155 *J21* **Kāraikāl** Pondicherry, SE India
155 *I22* **Kāraikkudi** Tamil Nādu, SE India
145 *Y11* **Kara Irtysh** *Rus.* Chërnyy Irtysh. ≈ NE Kazakhstan
143 *N5* **Karaj** Tehrān, N Iran
168 *K8* **Karak** Pahang, Peninsular Malaysia
Karak *see* Al Karak
147 *T11* **Kara-Kabak** Oshskaya Oblast', SW Kyrgyzstan
146 *D12* **Kara-Kala** *var.* Garrygala. Balkanskiy Velayat, W Turkmenistan
Karakala *see* Oqqal'a
Karakalpakstan, Respublika *see* Qoraqalpog'iston Respublikasi
Karakalpakya *see* Qoraqalpog'iston
Karakax *see* Moyu
158 *G10* **Karakax He** ≈ NW China
121 *X8* **Karakaya Barajı** ⊞ C Turkey
171 *Q9* **Karakelang, Pulau** *island* N Indonesia
Karakılısse *see* Ağrı
Karak, Muḥāfaẓat al *see* Al Karak
Kara-Köl *see* Kara-Kul'
147 *Y7* **Karakol** *prev.* Przheval'sk. Issyk-Kul'skaya Oblast', NE Kyrgyzstan
147 *X8* **Karakol** *var.* Karakolka. Issyk-Kul'skaya Oblast', NE Kyrgyzstan
Karakolka *see* Karakol
149 *W2* **Karakoram Highway** *road* China/Pakistan
149 *Z3* **Karakoram Pass** *Chin.* Karakoram Shankou. *pass* C Asia
152 *I3* **Karakoram Range** ▲ C Asia
Karakoram Shankou *see* Karakoram Pass
Karaköse *see* Ağrı
145 *P14* **Karakoyyn, Ozero** *Kaz.* Qaraqoyyn. ◎ C Kazakhstan
83 *F19* **Karakubis** Ghanzi, W Botswana
147 *T9* **Kara-Kul'** *Kir.* Kara-Köl. Dzhalal-Abadskaya Oblast', W Kyrgyzstan
Karakul' *see* Qorakŭl, Tajikistan
Karakul' *see* Qorakŭl, Uzbekistan
147 *U10* **Kara-Kul'dzha** Oshskaya Oblast', SW Kyrgyzstan
129 *T3* **Karakulino** Udmurtskaya Respublika, NW Russian Federation
Karakul', Ozero *see* Qorakŭl
Kara Kum *see* Garagumy
Kara Kum Canal/Karakumskiy Kanal *see* Garagumskiy Kanal
Karakumy, Peski *see* Garagumy
83 *E17* **Karakuwisa** Okavango, NE Namibia
122 *M13* **Karam** Irkutskaya Oblast', S Russian Federation
Karamai *see* Karamay
169 *T14* **Karamain, Pulau** *island* N Indonesia
136 *I16* **Karaman** Karaman, S Turkey
136 *H16* **Karaman** ◆ *province* S Turkey
114 *M8* **Karamandere** ≈ NE Bulgaria
158 *J4* **Karamay** *var.* Karamai, Kelamayi, *prev. Chin.* K'o-la-ma-i. Xinjiang Uygur Zizhiqu, NW China
169 *U14* **Karambu** Borneo, N Indonesia
185 *H14* **Karamea** West Coast, South Island, NZ
185 *H14* **Karamea** ≈ South Island, NZ
185 *G15* **Karamea Bight** *gulf* South Island, NZ
146 *L14* **Karamet-Niyaz** *Turkm.* Garamätnyýaz. Lebapskiy Velayat, E Turkmenistan
158 *K10* **Karamiran He** ≈ NW China
147 *S11* **Karamyk** Oshskaya Oblast', SW Kyrgyzstan
169 *U17* **Karangasem** Bali, S Indonesia
154 *H12* **Kāranja** Mahārāshtra, C India
Karanpur *see* Karanpura
152 *F9* **Karanpura** *var.* Karanpur. Rājasthān, NW India
Karánsebes/Karansebesch *see* Caransebeș
145 *T14* **Karaoy** *Kaz.* Qaraoy. Almaty, SE Kazakhstan
114 *N7* **Karapelit** *Rom.* Stejarul. Dobrich, NE Bulgaria
136 *I15* **Karapınar** Konya, C Turkey
83 *D22* **Karas** ◆ *district* S Namibia
147 *Y8* **Kara-Say** Issyk-Kul'skaya Oblast', NE Kyrgyzstan
83 *E22* **Karasburg** Karas, S Namibia
Kara Sea *see* Karskoye More
92 *K9* **Kárášjohka** *var.* Karašjokka. ≈ N Norway
92 *L9* **Karasjok** *Fin.* Kaarasjoki. Finnmark, N Norway
Karašjokka *see* Kárášjohka
Kara Strait *see* Karskiye Vorota, Proliv
Kara Su *see* Mesta/Néstos
145 *N8* **Karasu** *Kaz.* Qarasū. Kostanay, N Kazakhstan

◆ COUNTRY ● COUNTRY CAPITAL ◇ DEPENDENT TERRITORY ○ DEPENDENT TERRITORY CAPITAL ◆ ADMINISTRATIVE REGION ✕ INTERNATIONAL AIRPORT ▲ MOUNTAIN ▲ MOUNTAIN RANGE ※ VOLCANO ≈ RIVER ◎ LAKE ⊞ RESERVOIR

136 F11 **Karasu** Sakarya, NW Turkey
Karasubazar see Bilohirs'k
122 I12 **Karasuk** Novosibirskaya Oblast', C Russian Federation
145 U13 **Karatal** Kaz. Qaratal. ≈ SE Kazakhstan
136 K17 **Karataş** Adana, S Turkey
145 Q16 **Karatau** Kaz. Qarataū. Zhambyl, S Kazakhstan
Karatau see Karatau, Khrebet
145 P16 **Karatau, Khrebet** var. Karatau, Kaz. Qarataū. ▲ S Kazakhstan
144 G13 **Karaton** Kaz. Qaraton. Atyrau, W Kazakhstan
164 C13 **Karatsu** var. Karatu. Saga, Kyūshū, SW Japan
Karatu see Karatsu
122 K8 **Karaul** Taymyrskiy (Dolgano-Nenetskiy) Avtonomnyy Okrug, N Russian Federation
Karaulbazar see Qorowulbozor
Karauzyak see Qoraŭzak
115 D16 **Karáva** ▲ C Greece
Karavanke see Karawanken
115 F22 **Karavás** Kýthira, S Greece
113 J20 **Karavastasë, Laguna e** var. Kënet' e Karavastas, Kravasta Lagoon. lagoon W Albania
Karavastas, Kënet' e see Karavastasë, Laguna e
118 I5 **Karavere** Tartumaa, E Estonia
115 L23 **Karavonísia** island Kykládes, Greece, Aegean Sea
169 O15 **Karawang** prev. Krawang. Jawa, C Indonesia
109 T10 **Karawanken** Slvn. Karavanke. ▲ Austria/Yugoslavia
Karaxahar see Kaidu He
137 R13 **Karayazı** Erzurum, NE Turkey
145 Q12 **Karazhal** Zhezkazgan, C Kazakhstan
139 S9 **Karbalā'** var. Kerbala, Kerbela. S Iraq
94 L11 **Kårböle** Gävleborg, C Sweden
111 M23 **Karcag** Jász-Nagykun-Szolnok, E Hungary
Kardak see Imia
114 N7 **Kardam** Dobrich, NE Bulgaria
115 M22 **Kardámaina** Kos, Dodekánisos, Greece, Aegean Sea
Kardamila see Kardámyla
115 L18 **Kardámyla** var. Kardamila, Kardhámila. Chíos, E Greece
Kardeljevo see Ploče
Kardh see Qardho
Kardhámila see Kardámyla
Kardhítsa see Kardítsa
115 E16 **Kardítsa** var. Kardhítsa. Thessalía, C Greece
118 E4 **Kärdla** Ger. Kertel. Hiiumaa, W Estonia
Karelia see Kareliya, Respublika
119 I16 **Karelichy** Pol. Korelicze, Rus. Korelichi. Hrodzyenskaya Voblasts', W Belarus
126 I10 **Kareliya, Respublika** prev. Karel'skaya ASSR, Eng. Karelia. ◈ autonomous republic NW Russian Federation
Karel'skaya ASSR see Kareliya, Respublika
81 E22 **Karema** Rukwa, W Tanzania
Karen see Hualien
83 I14 **Karenda** Central, C Zambia
167 N8 **Karen State** var. Kawthule State, Kayin State. ◈ state S Myanmar
92 J10 **Karesuando** Lapp. Kaaresuanto. Norrbotten, N Sweden
Karet see Kâghet
Kareyz-e-Elyās/Kārez Iliās see Kārīz-e Elyās
122 J11 **Kargasok** Tomskaya Oblast', C Russian Federation
122 I12 **Kargat** Novosibirskaya Oblast', C Russian Federation
136 J11 **Kargı** Çorum, N Turkey
152 I5 **Kargil** Jammu and Kashmir, NW India
Kargilik see Yecheng
126 L11 **Kargopol'** Arkhangel'skaya Oblast', NW Russian Federation
110 F12 **Kargowa** Ger. Unruhstadt. Lubuskie, W Poland
77 X13 **Kari** Bauchi, E Nigeria
83 J15 **Kariba** Mashonaland West, N Zimbabwe
83 J16 **Kariba, Lake** ▣ Zambia/Zimbabwe
165 Q4 **Kariba-yama** ▲ Hokkaidō, NE Japan
83 C19 **Karibib** Erongo, C Namibia
Karies see Karyés
92 L9 **Karigasniemi** Lapp. Garegegasnjárga. Lappi, N Finland
184 J2 **Karikari, Cape** headland North Island, NZ
Karīmābād see Hunza
169 P12 **Karimata, Kepulauan** island group N Indonesia
169 P12 **Karimata, Pulau** island Kepulauan Karimata, N Indonesia
169 O11 **Karimata, Selat** strait W Indonesia
155 I14 **Karīmnagar** Andhra Pradesh, C India
186 C7 **Karimui** Chimbu, C PNG
169 Q15 **Karimunjawa, Pulau** island S Indonesia
80 N12 **Karin** Woqooyi Galbeed, N Somalia
Kariot see Ikaría
93 L20 **Karis** Fin. Karjaa. Etelä-Suomi, SW Finland
Káristos see Kárystos
148 J4 **Kārīz-e Elyās** var. Kareyz-e-Elyās, Kārez Iliās. Herāt, NW Afghanistan
Karjaa see Karis
145 T10 **Karkaralinsk** Kaz. Qarqaraly. Karaganda, E Kazakhstan
186 D6 **Karkar Island** island N PNG
143 N7 **Karkas, Kūh-e** ▲ C Iran
142 K8 **Karkheh, Rūd-e** ≈ SW Iran
115 L20 **Karkinágrio** Ikaría, Dodekánisos, Greece, Aegean Sea
117 R12 **Karkinits'ka Zatoka** Rus. Karkinitskiy Zaliv. gulf S Ukraine
Karkinitskiy Zaliv see Karkinits'ka Zatoka
93 L19 **Karkkila** Swe. Högfors. Etelä-Suomi, S Finland
93 M19 **Kärkölä** Etelä-Suomi, S Finland
182 G9 **Karkoo** South Australia
Karkūk see Kirkūk
118 D5 **Kärla** Ger. Kergel. Saaremaa, W Estonia
Karleby see Kokkola
110 F7 **Karlino** Ger. Körlin an der Persante. Zachodniopomorskie, NW Poland
137 Q13 **Karlıova** Bingöl, E Turkey
117 U6 **Karlivka** Poltavs'ka Oblast', C Ukraine
Karl-Marx-Stadt see Chemnitz
Karlö see Hailuoto
112 C11 **Karlobag** It. Carlopago. Lika-Senj, W Croatia
112 D9 **Karlovac** Ger. Karlstadt, Hung. Károlyváros. Karlovac, C Croatia
112 C10 **Karlovac** off. Karlovačka Županija. ◈ province C Croatia
Karlovačka Županija see Karlovac
111 A16 **Karlovarský Kraj** ◈ W Czech Republic
114 J9 **Karlovo** prev. Levskigrad. Plovdiv, C Bulgaria
111 A16 **Karlovy Vary** Ger. Karlsbad; prev. Eng. Carlsbad. Karlovarský Kraj, W Czech Republic
Karlsbad see Karlovy Vary
95 L17 **Karlsborg** Västra Götaland, S Sweden
Karlsburg see Alba Iulia
95 L22 **Karlshamn** Blekinge, S Sweden
95 L16 **Karlskoga** Örebro, C Sweden
95 M22 **Karlskrona** Blekinge, S Sweden
101 G21 **Karlsruhe** var. Carlsruhe. Baden-Württemberg, SW Germany
95 K16 **Karlstad** Värmland, C Sweden
29 R3 **Karlstad** Minnesota, N USA
101 I18 **Karlstadt** Bayern, C Germany
Karlstadt see Karlovac
39 Q14 **Karluk** Kodiak Island, Alaska, USA
Karluk see Qarluq
119 O17 **Karma** Rus. Korma. Homyel'skaya Voblasts', SE Belarus
155 F14 **Karmāla** Mahārāshtra, W India
146 M11 **Karmana** Nawoiy Wiloyati, C Uzbekistan
138 G8 **Karmi'él** var. Carmiel. Northern, N Israel
95 B16 **Karmøy** island S Norway
152 I9 **Karnāl** Haryāna, N India
153 W15 **Karnaphuli Reservoir** ▣ NE India
155 F17 **Karnātaka** var. Kanara; prev. Maisur, Mysore. ◈ state W India
25 S13 **Karnes City** Texas, SW USA
109 P9 **Karnische Alpen** It. Alpi Carniche. ▲ Austria/Italy
114 M9 **Karnobat** Burgas, E Bulgaria
109 Q9 **Kärnten** off. Land Kärnten, Eng. Carinthi, Slvn. Koroška. ◈ state S Austria
Karnul see Kurnool
83 K16 **Karoi** Mashonaland West, N Zimbabwe
Karol see Carei
Károly-Fehérvár see Alba Iulia
Károlyváros see Karlovac
82 M12 **Karonga** Northern, N Malawi
147 W10 **Karool-Tëbë** Narynskaya Oblast', C Kyrgyzstan
182 J9 **Karoonda** South Australia
149 S9 **Karor Lāl Esan** Punjab, E Pakistan
149 T11 **Karor Pacca** var. Kahror, Kahror Pakka. Punjab, E Pakistan
171 N12 **Karosa** Sulawesi, C Indonesia
Karpaten see Carpathian Mountains
115 L22 **Karpáthio Pélagos** sea Dodekánisos, Greece, Aegean Sea
115 N24 **Kárpathos** Kárpathos, SE Greece
115 N24 **Kárpathos** It. Scarpanto; anc. Carpathos, Carpathus. island SE Greece
Karpathos Strait see Karpathou, Stenó
115 N24 **Karpathou, Stenó** var. Karpathos Strait, Scarpanto Strait. strait Dodekánisos, Greece, Aegean Sea
Karpaty see Carpathian Mountains
115 E17 **Karpenísi** prev. Karpenísion. Stereá Ellás, C Greece
Karpenísion see Karpenísi
Karpilovka see Aktsyabrski
127 O8 **Karpogory** Arkhangel'skaya Oblast', NW Russian Federation
180 I7 **Karratha** Western Australia
137 S12 **Kars** var. Qars. Kars, NE Turkey
137 S12 **Kars** var. Qars. ◈ province NE Turkey
145 O12 **Karsakpay** Kaz. Qarsaqbay. Zhezkazgan, C Kazakhstan
93 L15 **Kärsämäki** Oulu, C Finland
Karsau see Kārsava
118 K9 **Kārsava** Ger. Karsau; prev. Rus. Korsovka. Ludza, E Latvia
146 A9 **Karshi** Turkm. Garshy. Balkanskiy Velayat, NW Turkmenistan
Karshi see Qarshi
Karshinskaya Step see Qarshi Chŭli
Karshinskiy Kanal see Qarshi Kanali
84 I5 **Karskiye Vorota, Proliv** Eng. Kara Strait. strait N Russian Federation
122 J6 **Karskoye More** Eng. Kara Sea. sea Arctic Ocean
93 L17 **Karstula** Länsi-Suomi, W Finland
129 Q5 **Karsun** Ul'yanovskaya Oblast', W Russian Federation
122 F11 **Kartaly** Chelyabinskaya Oblast', C Russian Federation
18 E13 **Karthaus** Pennsylvania, NE USA
110 I7 **Kartuzy** Pomorskie, NW Poland
165 R8 **Karumai** Iwate, Honshū, C Japan
181 U4 **Karumba** Queensland, NE Australia
142 L10 **Kārūn** var. Rūd-e Kārūn. ≈ SW Iran
92 K13 **Karungi** Norrbotten, N Sweden
92 K13 **Karunki** Lappi, N Finland
Kārūn, Rūd-e see Kārūn
155 H21 **Karūr** Tamil Nādu, SE India
93 K17 **Karvia** Länsi-Suomi, W Finland
111 J17 **Karviná** Ger. Karwin, Pol. Karwina; prev. Nová Karvinná. Ostravský Kraj, E Czech Republic
155 E17 **Kārwār** Karnātaka, W India
108 M7 **Karwendelgebirge** ▲ Austria/Germany
Karwin/Karwina see Karviná
115 I14 **Karyés** var. Karies. Ágion Óros, N Greece
115 I19 **Kárystos** var. Káristos. Évvoia, C Greece
136 E17 **Kaş** Antalya, SW Turkey
39 Y14 **Kasaan** Prince of Wales Island, Alaska, USA
164 I13 **Kasai** Hyōgo, Honshū, SW Japan
79 K21 **Kasai** var. Cassai, Kassai. ≈ Angola/Dem. Rep. Congo (Zaire)
79 K22 **Kasai Occidental** off. Région Kasai Occidental. ◈ region S Dem. Rep. Congo (Zaire)
79 L21 **Kasai Oriental** off. Région Kasai Oriental. ◈ region C Dem. Rep. Congo (Zaire)
79 L24 **Kasaji** Katanga, S Dem. Rep. Congo (Zaire)
82 L12 **Kasama** Northern, N Zambia
Kasan see Koson
83 H16 **Kasane** Chobe, NE Botswana
81 E23 **Kasanga** Rukwa, W Tanzania
79 G21 **Kasangulu** Bas-Congo, W Dem. Rep. Congo (Zaire)
Kasansay see Kosonsoy
Kasargen see Kasari
155 E20 **Kāsaragod** Kerala, SW India
118 P13 **Kasari** var. Kasari Jõgi, Ger. Kasargen. ≈ W Estonia
Kasari Jõgi see Kasari
8 L11 **Kasba Lake** ◎ Northwest Territories/Nunavut, N Canada
Kaschau see Košice
164 B16 **Kaseda** Kagoshima, Kyūshū, SW Japan
83 I14 **Kasempa** North Western, NW Zambia
79 O24 **Kasenga** Katanga, SE Dem. Rep. Congo (Zaire)
79 P17 **Kasenye** var. Kasenyi. Orientale, NE Dem. Rep. Congo (Zaire)
Kasenyi see Kasenye
81 E18 **Kasese** SW Uganda
79 O19 **Kasese** Maniema, E Dem. Rep. Congo (Zaire)
152 J11 **Kāsganj** Uttar Pradesh, N India
143 U4 **Kashaf Rūd** ≈ NE Iran
143 N7 **Kāshān** Eşfahān, C Iran
128 M10 **Kashary** Rostovskaya Oblast', SW Russian Federation
39 O12 **Kashegelok** Alaska, USA
Kashgar see Kashi
158 E7 **Kashi** Chin. Kaxgar, K'o-shih, Uigh. Kashgar. Xinjiang Uygur Zizhiqu, NW China
164 J14 **Kashihara** var. Kasihara. Nara, Honshū, SW Japan
165 P13 **Kashima-nada** gulf S Japan
126 K15 **Kashin** Tverskaya Oblast', W Russian Federation
152 K10 **Kāshīpur** Uttar Pradesh, N India
128 L4 **Kashira** Moskovskaya Oblast', W Russian Federation
165 N11 **Kashiwazaki** var. Kasiwazaki. Niigata, Honshū, C Japan
Kashkadar'inskaya Oblast' see Qashqadaryo Wiloyati
143 T5 **Kāshmar** var. Turshiz; prev. Solṭānābād, Torshiz. Khorāsān, NE Iran
Kashmir see Jammu and Kashmir
149 R12 **Kashmor** Sind, SE Pakistan
149 S5 **Kashmūnd Ghar** Eng. Kashmund Range. ▲ E Afghanistan
Kashmund Range see Kashmūnd Ghar
Kasi see Vārānasi
153 O12 **Kasia** Uttar Pradesh, N India
39 N12 **Kasigluk** Alaska, USA
Kasihara see Kashihara
39 R12 **Kasilof** Alaska, USA
Kasima see Kashima
Kasimköj see General Toshevo
128 M4 **Kasimov** Ryazanskaya Oblast', W Russian Federation
79 P18 **Kasindi** Nord Kivu, E Dem. Rep. Congo (Zaire)
82 M12 **Kasitu** ≈ N Malawi
Kasiwa see Kashiwa
Kasiwazaki see Kashiwazaki
30 L14 **Kaskaskia River** ≈ Illinois, N USA
93 J17 **Kaskinen** Swe. Kaskö. Länsi-Suomi, W Finland
Kaskö see Kaskinen
Kas Kong see Kŏng, Kaôh
11 O17 **Kaslo** British Columbia, SW Canada
Käsmark see Kežmarok
169 T12 **Kasongan** Borneo, C Indonesia
79 N21 **Kasongo** Maniema, E Dem. Rep. Congo (Zaire)
79 H22 **Kasongo-Lunda** Bandundu, SW Dem. Rep. Congo (Zaire)
115 M24 **Kásos** island S Greece
Kasos Strait see Kasou, Stenó
115 M25 **Kasou, Stenó** var. Kasos Strait. strait Dodekánisos/Kríti, Greece, Aegean Sea
137 T10 **Kaspi** C Georgia
114 M8 **Kaspichan** Shumen, NE Bulgaria
Kaspīy Mangy Oypaty see Caspian Depression
129 Q16 **Kaspiysk** Respublika Dagestan, SW Russian Federation
Kaspiyskiy see Lagan'
Kaspiyskoye More/Kaspiy Tengizi see Caspian Sea
Kassa see Košice
Kassai see Kasai
80 I9 **Kassala** Kassala, E Sudan
80 H9 **Kassala** ◈ state NE Sudan
115 G15 **Kassándra** prev. Pallíni; anc. Pallene. peninsula NE Greece
115 G15 **Kassándras, Akrotírio** headland N Greece
115 H15 **Kassándras, Kólpos** var. Kólpos Toronaíos. gulf N Greece
139 Y11 **Kassārah** E Iraq
101 I15 **Kassel** prev. Cassel. Hessen, C Germany
74 M6 **Kasserine** var. Al Qaşrayn. W Tunisia
14 J14 **Kasshabog Lake** ◎ Ontario, SE Canada
139 O5 **Kassīr, Sabkhat al** ◎ E Syria
29 W10 **Kasson** Minnesota, N USA
115 C17 **Kassópi** site of ancient city Ípeiros, W Greece
115 N24 **Kastállou, Akrotírio** headland Kárpathos, SE Greece
136 I11 **Kastamonu** var. Castamoni, Kastamuni. Kastamonu, N Turkey
136 I10 **Kastamonu** var. Kastamuni. ◈ province N Turkey
Kastamuni see Kastamonu
115 E14 **Kastaneá** Kentrikí Makedonía, N Greece
115 H24 **Kastélli** Kríti, Greece, E Mediterranean Sea
Kastellórizon see Megísti
95 N21 **Kastlösa** Kalmar, S Sweden
115 D14 **Kastoría** Dytikí Makedonía, N Greece
128 K7 **Kastornoye** Kurskaya Oblast', W Russian Federation
115 I21 **Kástro** Sífnos, Kykládes, Greece, Aegean Sea
95 J23 **Kastrup** ✕ (København) København, E Denmark
119 Q17 **Kastsyukovichy** Rus. Kostyukovichi. Mahilyowskaya Voblasts', E Belarus
119 O18 **Kastsyukowka** Rus. Kostyukovka. Homyel'skaya Voblasts', SE Belarus
164 D13 **Kasuga** Fukuoka, Kyūshū, SW Japan
164 L13 **Kasugai** Aichi, Honshū, SW Japan
81 E21 **Kasulu** Kigoma, W Tanzania
164 I12 **Kasumi** Hyōgo, Honshū, SW Japan
129 R17 **Kasumkent** Respublika Dagestan, SW Russian Federation
82 M13 **Kasungu** Central, C Malawi
149 W9 **Kasūr** Punjab, E Pakistan
83 G15 **Kataba** Western, W Zambia
19 R4 **Katahdin, Mount** ▲ Maine, NE USA
79 M20 **Katako-Kombe** Kasai Oriental, C Dem. Rep. Congo (Zaire)
39 T12 **Katalla** Alaska, USA
Katana see Qaṭanā
79 L24 **Katanga** off. Région du Katanga; prev. Shaba. ◈ region SE Dem. Rep. Congo (Zaire)
122 M11 **Katanga** ≈ C Russian Federation
154 J11 **Katangi** Madhya Pradesh, C India
180 J13 **Katanning** Western Australia
189 P8 **Kata Tjuta** var. Mount Olga ▲ Northern Territory, C Australia
Katawaz see Zarghūn Shahr
151 Q22 **Katchall Island** island Nicobar Islands, India, NE Indian Ocean
115 F14 **Kateríni** Kentrikí Makedonía, N Greece
117 P7 **Katerynopil'** Cherkas'ka Oblast', C Ukraine
166 M3 **Katha** Sagaing, N Myanmar
181 P2 **Katherine** Northern Territory, N Australia
154 B11 **Kāthiāwār Peninsula** peninsula W India
153 P11 **Kathmandu** prev. Kantipur. ● (Nepal) Central, C Nepal
152 H7 **Kathua** Jammu and Kashmir, NW India
76 L12 **Kati** Koulikoro, SW Mali
153 R13 **Katihār** Bihār, NE India
184 N7 **Katikati** Bay of Plenty, North Island, NZ
83 H16 **Katima Mulilo** Caprivi, NE Namibia
77 N15 **Katiola** C Ivory Coast
191 V10 **Katiu** atoll Îles Tuamotu, C French Polynesia
117 N12 **Katlabukh, Ozero** ◎ SW Ukraine
39 P14 **Katmai, Mount** ▲ Alaska, USA
154 J9 **Katni** Madhya Pradesh, C India
115 D19 **Káto Achaïa** var. Kato Ahaia, Káto Akhaía. Dytikí Ellás, S Greece
Kato Ahaia/Káto Akhaía see Káto Achaïa
121 P2 **Kato Lakatámeia** var. Kato Lakatamia. C Cyprus
Kato Lakatamia see Kato Lakatámeia
79 N22 **Katompi** Katanga, SE Dem. Rep. Congo (Zaire)
83 K14 **Katondwe** Lusaka, C Zambia
114 H12 **Káto Nevrokópi** prev. Káto Nevrokópion. Anatolikí Makedonía kai Thráki, NE Greece
Káto Nevrokópion see Káto Nevrokópi
81 E18 **Katonga** ≈ S Uganda
115 F15 **Káto Ólympos** ▲ C Greece
115 D17 **Katoúna** Dytikí Ellás, C Greece
115 E19 **Káto Vlasiá** Dytikí Makedonía, S Greece
111 J16 **Katowice** Ger. Kattowitz. Śląskie, S Poland
153 S15 **Kātoya** West Bengal, NE India
136 E16 **Katrançık Dağı** ▲ SW Turkey
95 N16 **Katrineholm** Södermanland, C Sweden
96 I11 **Katrine, Loch** ◎ C Scotland, UK
77 V12 **Katsina** Katsina, N Nigeria
77 U12 **Katsina** ◈ state N Nigeria
67 P8 **Katsina Ala** ≈ S Nigeria
164 C13 **Katsumoto** Nagasaki, Iki, SW Japan
165 P13 **Katsuta** var. Katuta. Ibaraki, Honshū, S Japan
165 O14 **Katsuura** var. Katuura. Chiba, Honshū, S Japan
164 K12 **Katsuyama** var. Katuyama. Fukui, Honshū, SW Japan
164 H12 **Katsuyama** Okayama, Honshū, SW Japan
Kattakurgan see Kattaqŭrghon
147 N11 **Kattaqŭrghon** Rus. Kattakurgan. Samarqand Wiloyati, C Uzbekistan
115 O23 **Kattavía** Ródos, Dodekánisos, Greece, Aegean Sea
95 I21 **Kattegat** Dan. Kattegatt. strait N Europe
Kattegatt see Kattegat
95 P19 **Katthammarsvik** Gotland, SE Sweden
Kattowitz see Katowice
122 J13 **Katun'** ≈ S Russian Federation
Katuta see Katsuta
Katuura see Katsuura
Katuyama see Katsuyama
Katwijk see Katwijk aan Zee
98 G11 **Katwijk aan Zee** var. Katwijk. Zuid-Holland, W Netherlands
38 B8 **Kauai** Haw. Kaua'i. island Hawaiian Islands, Hawaii, USA, C Pacific Ocean
38 C8 **Kauai Channel** channel Hawaii, USA, C Pacific Ocean
171 R13 **Kaubalatmada, Gunung** var. Kaplamada. ▲ Pulau Buru, E Indonesia
191 U10 **Kauehi** atoll Îles Tuamotu, C French Polynesia
Kauen see Kaunas
101 K24 **Kaufbeuren** Bayern, S Germany
25 U7 **Kaufman** Texas, SW USA
101 I15 **Kaufungen** Hessen, C Germany
93 K17 **Kauhajoki** Länsi-Suomi, W Finland
93 K16 **Kauhava** Länsi-Suomi, W Finland
30 M7 **Kaukauna** Wisconsin, N USA
92 L11 **Kaukonen** Lappi, N Finland
38 A8 **Kaulakahi Channel** channel Hawaii, USA, C Pacific Ocean
38 E9 **Kaunakakai** Molokai, Hawaii, USA, C Pacific Ocean
38 F12 **Kauna Point** headland Hawaii, USA, C Pacific Ocean
118 F13 **Kaunas** Ger. Kauen, Pol. Kowno; prev. Rus. Kovno. Kaunas, C Lithuania
186 C6 **Kaup** East Sepik, NW PNG
77 U12 **Kaura Namoda** Zamfara, NW Nigeria
Kaushany see Căuşeni
93 K16 **Kaustinen** Länsi-Suomi, W Finland
99 M23 **Kautenbach** Diekirch, NE Luxembourg
92 K10 **Kautokeino** Finnmark, N Norway
Kavadar see Kavadarci
113 P19 **Kavadarci** Turk. Kavadar. C FYR Macedonia
Kavaja see Kavajë
113 K20 **Kavajë** It. Cavaia, Kavaja. Tiranë, W Albania
114 M13 **Kavak Çayı** ≈ NW Turkey
Kavakli see Topolovgrad
114 I13 **Kavála** prev. Kaválla. Anatolikí Makedonía kai Thráki, NE Greece
114 I13 **Kaválas, Kólpos** gulf Aegean Sea, NE Mediterranean Sea
155 J17 **Kāvali** Andhra Pradesh, E India
Kaválla see Kavála
Kavango see Cubango/Okavango
155 C21 **Kavaratti** Lakshadweep, SW India
114 O8 **Kavarna** Dobrich, NE Bulgaria
118 G12 **Kavarskas** Anykščiai, E Lithuania
76 I13 **Kavendou** ▲ C Guinea
Kavengo see Cubango/Okavango
155 F20 **Kāveri** var. Cauvery. ≈ S India
186 G5 **Kavieng** var. Kaewieng. NE PNG
83 H16 **Kavimba** Chobe, NE Botswana
83 I15 **Kavingu** Southern, S Zambia
143 Q6 **Kavīr, Dasht-e** var. Great Salt Desert. salt pan N Iran
Kavirondo Gulf see Winam Gulf
Kavkaz see Caucasus
95 K23 **Kävlinge** Skåne, S Sweden
82 G12 **Kavungo** Moxico, E Angola
165 Q8 **Kawabe** Akita, Honshū, C Japan
165 R9 **Kawai** Iwate, Honshū, C Japan
38 A8 **Kawaihoa Point** headland Niihau, Hawaii, USA, C Pacific Ocean
184 K3 **Kawakawa** Northland, North Island, NZ
82 I13 **Kawama** North Western, NW Zambia
82 K11 **Kawambwa** Luapula, N Zambia
154 K11 **Kawardha** Madhya Pradesh, C India
14 I14 **Kawartha Lakes** ◎ Ontario, SE Canada
165 O13 **Kawasaki** Kanagawa, Honshū, S Japan
171 R12 **Kawassi** Pulau Obi, E Indonesia
165 R6 **Kawauchi** Aomori, Honshū, C Japan
184 L5 **Kawau Island** island N NZ
184 N10 **Kaweka Range** ▲ North Island, NZ
Kawelecht see Puhja
184 O8 **Kawerau** Bay of Plenty, North Island, NZ
184 L8 **Kawhia** Waikato, North Island, NZ
184 K8 **Kawhia Harbour** inlet North Island, NZ
35 V8 **Kawich Peak** ▲ Nevada, W USA
35 V9 **Kawich Range** ▲ Nevada, W USA
14 G12 **Kawigamog Lake** ◎ Ontario, S Canada
171 P9 **Kawio, Kepulauan** island group N Indonesia
167 N9 **Kawkareik** Karen State, S Myanmar
27 O8 **Kaw Lake** ▣ Oklahoma, C USA
166 M3 **Kawlin** Sagaing, N Myanmar
Kawm Umbū see Kôm Ombo
Kawthule State see Karen State
Kaxgar see Kashi
158 D7 **Kaxgar He** ≈ NW China
158 J5 **Kax He** ≈ NW China
77 P12 **Kaya** C Burkina
167 N6 **Kayah State** ◈ state C Myanmar
39 T12 **Kayak Island** island Alaska, USA
114 M11 **Kayalıköy Barajı** ▣ NW Turkey
155 G23 **Kāyamkulam** Kerala, SW India
166 M8 **Kayan** Yangon, SW Myanmar
169 V9 **Kayan, Sungai** prev. Kajan. ≈ Borneo, C Indonesia
144 F14 **Kaydak, Sor** salt flat SW Kazakhstan
Kaydanovo see Dzyarzhynsk
37 N9 **Kayenta** Arizona, SW USA
76 J11 **Kayes** Kayes, W Mali
76 J11 **Kayes** ◈ region SW Mali
Kayin State see Karen State
145 U10 **Kaynar** var. Kajnar. Vostochnyy Kazakhstan, E Kazakhstan
Kaynary see Căinari
83 H15 **Kayoya** Western, W Zambia
Kayrakkum see Qayroqqum
Kayrakkumskoye Vodokhranilishche see Qayroqqum, Obanbori
136 K14 **Kayseri** var. Kaisaria; anc. Caesarea Mazaca, Mazaca. Kayseri, C Turkey
136 K14 **Kayseri** var. Kaisaria. ◈ province C Turkey
36 L2 **Kaysville** Utah, W USA
Kayyngdy see Kaindy
14 L11 **Kazabazua** Quebec, SE Canada
14 L12 **Kazabazua** ≈ Quebec, SE Canada
123 Q7 **Kazach'ye** Respublika Sakha (Yakutiya), NE Russian Federation
Kazakdar'ya see Qozoqdaryo
146 E9 **Kazakhlyshor, Solonchak** var. Solonchak Shorkazakhly. salt marsh NW Turkmenistan
Kazakhskaya SSR/Kazakh Soviet Socialist Republic see Kazakhstan
145 R9 **Kazakhskiy Melkosopochnik** Eng. Kazakh Uplands, Kirghiz Steppe, Kaz. Saryarqa. uplands C Kazakhstan
144 L12 **Kazakhstan** off. Republic of Kazakhstan, var. Kazakstan, Kaz. Qazaqstan, Qazaqstan Respublikasy; prev. Kazakh Soviet Socialist Republic, Rus. Kazakhskaya SSR. ◆ republic C Asia
Kazakh Uplands see Kazakhskiy Melkosopochnik
Kazakstan see Kazakhstan
144 L14 **Kazalinsk** Kzylorda, S Kazakhstan
129 R4 **Kazan'** Respublika Tatarstan, W Russian Federation
129 R4 **Kazan'** ✕ Respublika Tatarstan, W Russian Federation
8 M10 **Kazan** ≈ Nunavut, NW Canada
Kazandzhik see Gazandzhyk
117 R8 **Kazanka** Mykolayivs'ka Oblast', S Ukraine
Kazanketken see Qizqetkan
Kazanlik see Kazanlŭk
114 J9 **Kazanlŭk** prev. Kazanlik. Stara Zagora, C Bulgaria
165 Y16 **Kazan-rettō** Eng. Volcano Islands. island group SE Japan
117 V12 **Kazantip, Mys** headland S Ukraine
147 U9 **Kazarman** Narynskaya Oblast', C Kyrgyzstan
Kazatin see Kozyatyn
Kazbegi see Kazbek
Kazbegi see Qazbegi

◆ Country ● Country Capital ◇ Dependent Territory ○ Dependent Territory Capital ◈ Administrative Region ✕ International Airport ▲ Mountain ▲ Mountain Range ℝ Volcano ≈ River ◎ Lake ▣ Reservoir

137 T9 **Kazbek** var. Kazbegi, Geor. Mqinvartsveri. ▲ N Georgia
82 M13 **Kazembe** Eastern, NE Zambia
143 N11 **Kāzerūn** Fārs, S Iran
127 R12 **Kazhym** Respublika Komi, NW Russian Federation
Kazi Ahmad see Qāzi Ahmad
Kazi Magomed see Qazimämmäd
136 H16 **Kazımkarabekir** Karaman, S Turkey
111 M20 **Kazincbarcika** Borsod-Abaúj-Zemplén, NE Hungary
119 H17 **Kazlowshchyna** Pol. Kozlowszczyzna, Rus. Kozlovshchina. Hrodzyenskaya Voblasts', W Belarus
119 E14 **Kazlų Rūda** Marijampolė, S Lithuania
144 E9 **Kaztalovka** Zapadnyy Kazakhstan, W Kazakhstan
79 K22 **Kazumba** Kasai Occidental, S Dem. Rep. Congo (Zaire)
165 Q8 **Kazuno** Akita, Honshū, C Japan
Kazvin see Qazvīn
118 J12 **Kaz'yany** Rus. Koz'yany. Vitsyebskaya Voblasts', NW Belarus
122 H9 **Kazym** ≈ N Russian Federation
110 H10 **Kcynia** Ger. Exin. Kujawsko-pomorskie, C Poland
115 I20 **Kéa** Kéa, Kykládes, Greece, Aegean Sea
115 I20 **Kéa** prev. Kéos, anc. Ceos. island Kykládes, Greece, Aegean Sea
38 H11 **Keaau** Haw. Kea'au. Hawaii, USA, C Pacific Ocean
38 F11 **Keahole Point** headland Hawaii, USA, C Pacific Ocean
38 G12 **Kealakekua** Hawaii, USA, C Pacific Ocean
38 H11 **Kea, Mauna** ▲ Hawaii, USA, C Pacific Ocean
37 N10 **Keams** Arizona, SW USA
Kéamu see Aneityum
29 O16 **Kearney** Nebraska, C USA
36 L3 **Kearns** Utah, W USA
115 H20 **Kéas, Stenó** strait SE Greece
137 O14 **Keban Barajı** dam C Turkey
137 O14 **Keban Barajı** ⊠ C Turkey
77 S13 **Kebbi** ◈ state NW Nigeria
76 G10 **Kébémèr** NW Senegal
74 M7 **Kebili** var. Qibilī. C Tunisia
138 H4 **Kebir, Nahr el** ≈ NW Syria
80 A10 **Kebkabiya** Northern Darfur, W Sudan
92 I11 **Kebnekaise** ▲ N Sweden
81 M14 **K'ebrī Dehar** Somali, E Ethiopia
148 K15 **Kech** ≈ SW Pakistan
10 K10 **Kechika** ≈ British Columbia, W Canada
111 K23 **Kecskemét** Bács-Kiskun, C Hungary
168 J6 **Kedah** ◈ state Peninsular Malaysia
118 F12 **Kėdainiai** Kėdainiai, C Lithuania
Kedder see Kehra
13 N13 **Kedgwick** New Brunswick, SE Canada
169 R16 **Kediri** Jawa, C Indonesia
171 Y13 **Kedir Sarmi** Irian Jaya, E Indonesia
163 V7 **Kedong** Heilongjiang, NE China
76 I12 **Kédougou** SE Senegal
122 I11 **Kedrovyy** Tomskaya Oblast', C Russian Federation
111 H16 **Kędzierzyn-Kozle** Ger. Heydebrecht. Opolskie, S Poland
8 H8 **Keele** ≈ Northwest Territories, NW Canada
10 K6 **Keele Peak** ▲ Yukon Territory, NW Canada
Keelung see Chilung
19 N10 **Keene** New Hampshire, NE USA
99 H17 **Keerbergen** Vlaams Brabant, C Belgium
83 E21 **Keetmanshoop** Karas, S Namibia
12 A11 **Keewatin** Ontario, S Canada
29 V4 **Keewatin** Minnesota, N USA
115 B18 **Kefallinía** var. Kefallonía. island Iónioi Nísoi, Greece, C Mediterranean Sea
Kefallonía see Kefallinía
115 M22 **Kéfalos** Kos, Dodekánisos, Greece, Aegean Sea
171 Q17 **Kefamenanu** Timor, C Indonesia
138 F10 **Kefar Sava** var. Kfar Saba. Central, C Israel
Kefe see Feodosiya
77 V15 **Keffi** Nassarawa, C Nigeria
92 H4 **Keflavík** ✕ (Reykjavík) Reykjanes, W Iceland
92 H4 **Keflavík** Reykjanes, W Iceland
Kegalee see Kegalla
155 J25 **Kegalla** var. Kegalee, Kegalle. Sabaragamuwa Province, C Sri Lanka
Kegalle see Kegalla
146 H7 **Kegayli** Rus. Kegeyli. Qoraqalpogiston Respublikasi, W Uzbekistan
Kegel see Keila
145 W16 **Kegen** Almaty, SE Kazakhstan
Kegeyli see Kegayli
101 F22 **Kehl** Baden-Württemberg, SW Germany
118 H3 **Kehra** Ger. Kedder. Harjumaa, NW Estonia
117 U6 **Kehychivka** Kharkivs'ka Oblast', E Ukraine
97 L17 **Keighley** N England, UK
Kei Islands see Kai, Kepulauan
Keijō see Sŏul
118 G3 **Keila** Ger. Kegel. Harjumaa, NW Estonia
Keilberg see Klínovec
83 F23 **Keimoes** Northern Cape, W South Africa
Keina/Keinis see Käina
Keishū see Kyŏngju
77 T11 **Keïta** Tahoua, C Niger
78 J12 **Kéita, Bahr** var. Doka. ≈ S Chad
93 M16 **Keitele** ◎ C Finland
182 K10 **Keith** South Australia
96 K8 **Keith** NE Scotland, UK
26 K3 **Keith Sebelius Lake** ⊠ Kansas, C USA
32 G11 **Keizer** Oregon, NW USA
38 A8 **Kekaha** Kauai, Hawaii, USA, C Pacific Ocean
147 U10 **Këk-Art** prev. Alaykel', Alay-Kuu. Oshskaya Oblast', SW Kyrgyzstan
147 W10 **Këk-Aygyr** var. Keyaygyr. Narynskaya Oblast', C Kyrgyzstan
147 V9 **Këk-Dzhar** Narynskaya Oblast', C Kyrgyzstan
14 L8 **Kekek** ≈ Quebec, SE Canada
185 K15 **Kekerengu** Canterbury, South Island, NZ
111 L21 **Kékes** ▲ N Hungary
171 P17 **Kekneno, Gunung** ▲ Timor, S Indonesia
147 S9 **Këk-Tash** Kir. Kök-Tash. Dzhalal-Abadskaya Oblast', W Kyrgyzstan
81 M15 **K'elafo** Somali, E Ethiopia
169 U10 **Kelai, Sungai** ≈ Borneo, N Indonesia
Kelamayi see Karamay
Kelang see Klang
168 K7 **Kelantan** ◈ state Peninsular Malaysia
Kelantan see Kelantan, Sungai
168 K7 **Kelantan, Sungai** var. Kelantan. ≈ Peninsular Malaysia
Kelat see Kālat
Këlcyra see Këlcyrë
113 L22 **Këlcyrë** var. Këlcyra. Gjirokastër, S Albania
146 L14 **Kelifskiy Uzboy** salt marsh E Turkmenistan
137 O12 **Kelkit** Gümüşhane, NE Turkey
136 M12 **Kelkit Çayı** ≈ N Turkey
77 W11 **Kellé** Zinder, S Niger
79 G18 **Kéllé** Cuvette, W Congo
145 P7 **Kellerovka** Severnyy Kazakhstan, N Kazakhstan
8 I5 **Kellett, Cape** headland Banks Island, Northwest Territories, NW Canada
31 S11 **Kelleys Island** island Ohio, N USA
33 N8 **Kellogg** Idaho, NW USA
92 M12 **Kelloselkä** Lappi, N Finland
97 F17 **Kells** Ir. Ceanannas. E Ireland
118 E12 **Kelmė** Kelmė, C Lithuania
99 M19 **Kelmis** var. La Calamine. Liège, E Belgium
78 H12 **Kélo** Tandjilé, SW Chad
83 I14 **Kelongwa** North Western, NW Zambia
11 N17 **Kelowna** British Columbia, SW Canada
11 X12 **Kelsey** Manitoba, C Canada
34 M6 **Kelseyville** California, W USA
96 K13 **Kelso** SE Scotland, UK
32 G10 **Kelso** Washington, NW USA
195 W15 **Keltie, Cape** headland Antarctica
Keltsy see Kielce
168 L9 **Keluang** var. Kluang. Johor, Peninsular Malaysia
168 M11 **Kelume** Pulau Lingga, W Indonesia
11 U15 **Kelvington** Saskatchewan, S Canada
126 J7 **Kem'** Respublika Kareliya, NW Russian Federation
126 I7 **Kem'** ≈ NW Russian Federation
137 O13 **Kemah** Erzincan, E Turkey
137 N13 **Kemaliye** Erzincan, C Turkey
Kemaman see Cukai
Kemanlar see Isperikh
10 K14 **Kemano** British Columbia, SW Canada
Kemarat see Khemmarat
171 P12 **Kembani** Pulau Peleng, N Indonesia
136 F17 **Kemer** Antalya, SW Turkey
122 J12 **Kemerovo** prev. Shcheglovsk. Kemerovskaya Oblast', C Russian Federation
122 K12 **Kemerovskaya Oblast'** ◈ province S Russian Federation
92 L13 **Kemi** Lappi, NW Finland
92 M12 **Kemijärvi** Swe. Kemiträsk. Lappi, N Finland
92 M12 **Kemijärvi** ◎ N Finland
92 L13 **Kemijoki** ≈ NW Finland
147 V7 **Kemin** prev. Bystrovka. Chuyskaya Oblast', N Kyrgyzstan
92 L13 **Keminmaa** Lappi, NW Finland
Kemins Island see Nikumaroro
Kemiö see Kimito
Kemiträsk see Kemijärvi
129 P5 **Kemlya** Respublika Mordoviya, W Russian Federation
99 B18 **Kemmel** West-Vlaanderen, W Belgium
33 S16 **Kemmerer** Wyoming, C USA
Kemmuna see Comino
79 I14 **Kémo** ◈ prefecture S Central African Republic
25 U7 **Kemp** Texas, SW USA
93 L14 **Kempele** Oulu, C Finland
101 D15 **Kempen** Nordrhein-Westfalen, W Germany
25 Q5 **Kemp, Lake** ◎ Texas, SW USA
195 W5 **Kemp Land** physical region Antarctica
25 S9 **Kempner** Texas, SW USA
44 H3 **Kemp's Bay** Andros Island, W Bahamas
183 U6 **Kempsey** New South Wales, SE Australia
101 J24 **Kempten** Bayern, S Germany
15 N9 **Kempt, Lac** ◎ Quebec, SE Canada
183 P17 **Kempton** Tasmania, SE Australia
154 J9 **Ken** ≈ C India
39 R12 **Kenai** Alaska, USA
(0) D5 **Kenai Mountains** ⛰ Alaska, USA
39 R12 **Kenai Peninsula** peninsula Alaska, USA
21 V11 **Kenansville** North Carolina, SE USA
121 U13 **Kenâyis, Râs el-** headland N Egypt
97 K16 **Kendal** NW England, UK
23 Y16 **Kendall** Florida, SE USA
9 O8 **Kendall, Cape** headland Nunavut, E Canada
18 J15 **Kendall Park** New Jersey, NE USA
31 Q11 **Kendallville** Indiana, N USA
171 P14 **Kendari** Sulawesi, C Indonesia
169 Q13 **Kendawangan** Borneo, C Indonesia
154 O12 **Kendrāpāra** var. Kendrāparha. Orissa, E India
Kendrāparha see Kendrāpāra
154 O11 **Kendujhargarh** prev. Keonjhargarh. Orissa, E India
25 S13 **Kenedy** Texas, SW USA
146 E13 **Kënekesir** Turkm. Könekesir. Balkanskiy Velayat, W Turkmenistan
76 J15 **Kenema** SE Sierra Leone
29 P16 **Kenesaw** Nebraska, C USA
146 G8 **Këneurgench** Turkm. Köneürgench; prev. Kunya-Urgench. Dashkhovuzskiy Velayat, N Turkmenistan
79 H21 **Kenge** Bandundu, SW Dem. Rep. Congo (Zaire)
Kengen see Kangen
167 O5 **Keng Tung** var. Kentung. Shan State, E Myanmar
83 F23 **Kenhardt** Northern Cape, W South Africa
76 J12 **Kéniéba** Kayes, W Mali
Kenimekh see Konimekh
169 U7 **Keningau** Sabah, East Malaysia
74 F6 **Kénitra** prev. Port-Lyautey. NW Morocco
21 V9 **Kenly** North Carolina, SE USA
97 B21 **Kenmare** Ir. Neidín. S Ireland
28 L2 **Kenmare** North Dakota, N USA
97 A21 **Kenmare River** Ir. An Ribhéar. inlet NE Atlantic Ocean
18 D10 **Kenmore** New York, NE USA
25 W8 **Kennard** Texas, SW USA
29 N10 **Kennebec** South Dakota, N USA
19 Q7 **Kennebec River** ≈ Maine, NE USA
19 P9 **Kennebunk** Maine, NE USA
39 R13 **Kennedy Entrance** strait Alaska, USA
166 L3 **Kennedy Peak** ▲ W Myanmar
22 K9 **Kenner** Louisiana, S USA
180 I8 **Kenneth Range** ⛰ Western Australia
27 Y9 **Kennett** Missouri, C USA
18 I16 **Kennett Square** Pennsylvania, NE USA
32 K10 **Kennewick** Washington, NW USA
12 E11 **Kenogami** ≈ Ontario, S Canada
15 Q7 **Kénogami, Lac** ◎ Quebec, SE Canada
14 G8 **Kenogami Lake** Ontario, S Canada
14 F7 **Kenogamissi Lake** ◎ Ontario, S Canada
10 I6 **Keno Hill** Yukon Territory, NW Canada
12 A11 **Kenora** Ontario, S Canada
31 N9 **Kenosha** Wisconsin, N USA
13 P14 **Kensington** Prince Edward Island, SE Canada
26 L3 **Kensington** Kansas, C USA
32 I11 **Kent** Oregon, NW USA
24 J9 **Kent** Texas, SW USA
32 H8 **Kent** Washington, NW USA
97 P22 **Kent** cultural region SE England, UK
145 P16 **Kentau** Yuzhnyy Kazakhstan, S Kazakhstan
183 P14 **Kent Group** island group Tasmania, SE Australia
31 N12 **Kentland** Indiana, N USA
31 R12 **Kenton** Ohio, N USA
8 K7 **Kent Peninsula** peninsula Nunavut, N Canada
115 F14 **Kentrikí Makedonía** Eng. Macedonia Central. ◈ region N Greece
20 J6 **Kentucky** off. Commonwealth of Kentucky; also known as The Bluegrass State. ◈ state C USA
20 H8 **Kentucky Lake** ⊠ Kentucky/Tennessee, S USA
Kentung see Keng Tung
13 P15 **Kentville** Nova Scotia, SE Canada
22 K8 **Kentwood** Louisiana, S USA
31 P9 **Kentwood** Michigan, N USA
81 H17 **Kenya** off. Republic of Kenya. ◆ republic E Africa
Kenya, Mount see Kirinyaga
168 L7 **Kenyir, Tasik** var. Tasek Kenyir. ◎ Peninsular Malaysia
29 W10 **Kenyon** Minnesota, N USA
29 Y16 **Keokuk** Iowa, C USA
Keonjhargarh see Kendujhargarh
Kéos see Kéa
29 X16 **Keosauqua** Iowa, C USA
29 X15 **Keota** Iowa, C USA
21 O11 **Keowee, Lake** ⊠ South Carolina, SE USA
126 I7 **Kepa** var. Kepe. Respublika Kareliya, NW Russian Federation
Kepe see Kepa
189 O13 **Kepirohi Falls** waterfall Pohnpei, E Micronesia
185 B22 **Kepler Mountains** ⛰ South Island, NZ
111 I14 **Kępno** Wielkopolskie, C Poland
65 C24 **Keppel Island** island N Falkland Islands
Keppel Island see Niuatoputapu
65 C23 **Keppel Sound** sound N Falkland Islands
136 D12 **Kepsut** Balıkesir, NW Turkey
171 V13 **Kerai** Irian Jaya, E Indonesia
Kerak see Al Karak
155 F22 **Kerala** ◈ state S India
165 R16 **Kerama-rettō** island group SW Japan
183 N10 **Kerang** Victoria, SE Australia
Kerasunt see Giresun
115 H19 **Keratéa** var. Keratea. Attikí, C Greece
93 M19 **Kerava** Swe. Kervo. Etelä-Suomi, S Finland
Kerbala/Kerbela see Karbalā'
32 F15 **Kerby** Oregon, NW USA
117 W12 **Kerch** Rus. Kerch'. Respublika Krym, SE Ukraine
Kerchens'ka Protska/Kerchenskiy Proliv see Kerch Strait
117 V13 **Kerchens'kyy Pivostriv** peninsula S Ukraine
121 V4 **Kerch Strait** var. Bosporus Cimmerius, Enikale Strait, Rus. Kerchenskiy Proliv, Ukr. Kerchens'ka Protska. strait Black Sea/Sea of Azov
152 K8 **Kerdārnāth** Uttar Pradesh, N India
Kerdilio see Kerdýlio
114 H13 **Kerdýlio** var. Kerdilio. ▲ N Greece
186 D8 **Kerema** Gulf, S PNG
Keremitlik see Lyulyakovo
136 I9 **Kerempe Burnu** headland N Turkey
80 J9 **Keren** var. Cheren. C Eritrea
25 U7 **Kerens** Texas, SW USA
184 M6 **Kerepehi** Waikato, North Island, NZ
145 P10 **Kerey, Ozero** ◎ C Kazakhstan
Kergel see Kärla
173 Q12 **Kerguelen** island C French Southern and Antarctic Territories
173 Q13 **Kerguelen Plateau** undersea feature S Indian Ocean
115 C20 **Kerí** Zákynthos, Iónioi Nísoi, Greece, C Mediterranean Sea
81 H19 **Kericho** Rift Valley, W Kenya
184 K2 **Kerikeri** Northland, North Island, NZ
93 O17 **Kerimäki** Isä-Suomi, E Finland
168 K12 **Kerinci, Gunung** ▲ Sumatera, W Indonesia
Keriya see Yutian
158 H9 **Keriya He** ≈ NW China
98 J9 **Kerkbuurt** Noord-Holland, C Netherlands
98 J13 **Kerkdriel** Gelderland, C Netherlands
75 N6 **Kerkenah, Îles de** var. Kerkenna Islands, Ar. Juzur Qarqannah. island group E Tunisia
Kerkenna Islands see Kerkenah, Îles de
115 M20 **Kerketévs** ▲ Sámos, Dodekánisos, Greece, Aegean Sea
29 T8 **Kerkhoven** Minnesota, N USA
146 M14 **Kerki** Lebapskiy Velayat, E Turkmenistan
146 M14 **Kerkichi** Lebapskiy Velayat, E Turkmenistan
115 F16 **Kerkíneo** prehistoric site Thessalía, C Greece
114 G12 **Kerkinitis, Límni** ◎ N Greece
Kérkira see Kérkyra
99 M18 **Kerkrade** Limburg, SE Netherlands
Kerkuk see Kirkūk
115 B16 **Kerkyra** ✕ Kérkyra, Iónioi Nísoi, Greece, C Mediterranean Sea
115 B16 **Kérkyra** var. Kérkira, Eng. Corfu. Kérkyra, Iónioi Nísoi, Greece, C Mediterranean Sea
115 A16 **Kérkyra** var. Kérkira, Eng. Corfu. island Iónioi Nísoi, Greece, C Mediterranean Sea
192 K10 **Kermadec Islands** island group NZ, SW Pacific Ocean
175 R10 **Kermadec Ridge** undersea feature SW Pacific Ocean
175 R11 **Kermadec Trench** undersea feature SW Pacific Ocean
143 S10 **Kermān** var. Kirman; anc. Carmana. Kermān, C Iran
143 R11 **Kermān** off. Ostān-e Kermān, var. Kirman; anc. Carmania. ◈ province SE Iran
143 U12 **Kermān, Bīābān-e** var. Kerman Desert. desert SE Iran
Kerman Desert see Kermān, Bīābān-e
143 Q9 **Kermānshāh** Yazd, C Iran
142 J6 **Kermānshāh** off. Ostān-e Kermānshāh; prev. Bākhtarān, Kermānshāhān. ◈ province W Iran
Kermānshāhān see Kermānshāh
114 L10 **Kermen** Sliven, C Bulgaria
24 L8 **Kermit** Texas, SW USA
21 P6 **Kermit** West Virginia, NE USA
21 S9 **Kernersville** North Carolina, SE USA
35 S12 **Kern River** ≈ California, W USA
35 S12 **Kernville** California, W USA
115 K21 **Kéros** island Kykládes, Greece, Aegean Sea
76 K14 **Kérouané** Haute-Guinée, SE Guinea
101 D16 **Kerpen** Nordrhein-Westfalen, W Germany
146 I11 **Kerpichli** Lebapskiy Velayat, NE Turkmenistan
24 M1 **Kerrick** Texas, SW USA
Kerr Lake see John H.Kerr Reservoir
11 S15 **Kerrobert** Saskatchewan, S Canada
25 Q11 **Kerrville** Texas, SW USA
97 B20 **Kerry** Ir. Ciarraí. cultural region SW Ireland
21 S11 **Kershaw** South Carolina, SE USA
Kertel see Kärdla
95 H23 **Kerteminde** Fyn, C Denmark
163 Q7 **Kerulen** Chin. Herlen He, Mong. Herlen Gol. ≈ China/Mongolia
Kervo see Kerava
Kerýneia see Girne
12 H11 **Kesagami Lake** ◎ Ontario, SE Canada
93 O17 **Kesälahti** Itä-Suomi, E Finland
136 B11 **Keşan** Edirne, NW Turkey
165 R9 **Kesennuma** Miyagi, Honshū, C Japan
163 V7 **Keshan** Heilongjiang, NE China
30 M6 **Keshena** Wisconsin, N USA
136 I13 **Keskin** Kırıkkale, C Turkey
Késmárk see Kežmarok
126 I6 **Kesten'ga** var. Kest Enga. Respublika Kareliya, NW Russian Federation
98 K12 **Kesteren** Gelderland, C Netherlands
14 H14 **Keswick** Ontario, S Canada
97 K15 **Keswick** NW England, UK
111 H24 **Keszthely** Zala, SW Hungary
122 K11 **Ket'** ≈ C Russian Federation
77 R17 **Keta** SE Ghana
169 Q12 **Ketapang** Borneo, C Indonesia
129 O12 **Ketchenery** prev. Sovetskoye. Respublika Kalmykiya, SW Russian Federation
39 Y14 **Ketchikan** Revillagigedo Island, Alaska, USA
33 O14 **Ketchum** Idaho, NW USA
Kete/Kete Krakye see Kete-Krachi
77 Q15 **Kete-Krachi** var. Kete, Kete Krakye. E Ghana
98 L9 **Ketelmeer** channel E Netherlands
149 P17 **Keti Bandar** Sind, SE Pakistan
145 W16 **Ketmen', Khrebet** ⛰ SE Kazakhstan
77 S16 **Kétou** SE Benin
110 M7 **Kętrzyn** Ger. Rastenburg. Warmińsko-Mazurskie, NE Poland,
97 N20 **Kettering** C England, UK
31 R14 **Kettering** Ohio, N USA
18 F13 **Kettle Creek** ≈ Pennsylvania, NE USA
32 L7 **Kettle Falls** Washington, NW USA
14 D16 **Kettle Point** headland Ontario, S Canada
29 V6 **Kettle River** ≈ Minnesota, N USA
186 B7 **Ketu** ≈ W PNG
18 G10 **Keuka Lake** ◎ New York, NE USA
Keupriya see Primorsko
93 L17 **Keuruu** Länsi-Suomi, W Finland
Kevevára see Kovin
92 L9 **Kevo** Lapp. Geavvú. Lappi, N Finland
44 M6 **Kew** North Caicos, N Turks and Caicos Islands
30 K11 **Kewanee** Illinois, N USA
31 N7 **Kewaunee** Wisconsin, N USA
30 M3 **Keweenaw Bay** ◎ Michigan, N USA
31 N2 **Keweenaw Peninsula** peninsula Michigan, N USA
31 N2 **Keweenaw Point** headland Michigan, N USA
29 N12 **Keya Paha River** ≈ Nebraska/South Dakota, N USA
Keyaygyr see Këk-Aygyr
23 Z16 **Key Biscayne** Florida, SE USA
26 G8 **Keyes** Oklahoma, C USA
23 Y17 **Key Largo** Key Largo, Florida, SE USA
21 U3 **Keyser** West Virginia, NE USA
27 O9 **Keystone Lake** ⊠ Oklahoma, C USA
36 L16 **Keystone Peak** ▲ Arizona, SW USA
Keystone State see Pennsylvania
21 U7 **Keysville** Virginia, NE USA
27 T3 **Keytesville** Missouri, C USA
23 W17 **Key West** Florida Keys, Florida, SE USA
129 T1 **Kez** Udmurtskaya Respublika, NW Russian Federation
Kezdivásárhely see Târgu Secuiesc
122 M12 **Kezhma** Krasnoyarskiy Kray, C Russian Federation
111 L18 **Kežmarok** Ger. Käsmark, Hung. Késmárk. Prešovský Kraj, E Slovakia
Kfar Saba see Kefar Sava
83 F20 **Kgalagadi** ◈ district SW Botswana
83 I20 **Kgatleng** ◈ district SE Botswana
188 F8 **Kgkeklau** Babeldaob, N Palau
127 R6 **Khabarikha** var. Chabaricha. Respublika Komi, NW Russian Federation
123 S14 **Khabarovsk** Khabarovskiy Kray, SE Russian Federation
123 R11 **Khabarovskiy Kray** ◈ territory E Russian Federation
141 W7 **Khabb** Abū Ẓaby, E UAE
Khabour, Nahr al see Khābūr, Nahr al
Khabura see Al Khābūrah
139 N2 **Khābūr, Nahr al** var. Nahr al Khabour. ≈ Syria/Turkey
Khachmas see Xaçmaz
80 B12 **Khadari** ≈ W Sudan
Khadera see Hadera
141 X12 **Khādhil** var. Khudal. SE Oman
155 E14 **Khadki** prev. Kirkee. Mahārāshtra, W India
128 L14 **Khadyzhensk** Krasnodarskiy Kray, SW Russian Federation
114 N9 **Khadzhiyska Reka** ≈ E Bulgaria
117 P10 **Khadzhybeys'kyy Lyman** ◎ SW Ukraine
138 K3 **Khafsah** Ḩalab, N Syria
152 M13 **Khāga** Uttar Pradesh, N India
153 Q13 **Khagaria** Bihār, NE India
149 Q13 **Khairpur** Sind, SE Pakistan
122 K13 **Khakasiya, Respublika** prev. Khakasskaya Avtonomnaya Oblast', Eng. Khakassia. ◈ autonomous republic C Russian Federation
Khakassia/Khakasskaya Avtonomnaya Oblast' see Khakasiya, Respublika
167 N9 **Kha Khaeng, Khao** ▲ W Thailand
83 G20 **Khakhea** var. Kakia. Southern, S Botswana
146 L13 **Khalach** Lebapskiy Velayat, E Turkmenistan
Khalándrion see Chalándri
129 W7 **Khalilovo** Orenburgskaya Oblast', W Russian Federation
Khalkabad see Khalqobod
142 L3 **Khalkhāl** prev. Herowābād. Ardabīl, NW Iran
Khalkidhikí see Chalkidikí
Khalkís see Chalkída
127 W3 **Khal'mer-Yu** Respublika Komi, NW Russian Federation
119 M14 **Khalopyenichy** Rus. Kholopenichi. Minskaya Voblasts', NE Belarus
146 H7 **Khalqobod** Rus. Khalkabad. Qoraqalpogiston Respublikasi, W Uzbekistan
Khalturin see Orlov
141 Y10 **Khalūf** var. Al Khaluf. E Oman
154 K10 **Khamaria** Madhya Pradesh, C India
154 D11 **Khambhāt** Gujarāt, W India
154 C12 **Khambhāt, Gulf of** Eng. Gulf of Cambay. gulf W India
167 U10 **Khâm Đuc** Quang Nam-Đa Nẵng, C Vietnam
154 G12 **Khāmgaon** Mahārāshtra, C India
141 O14 **Khamir** var. Khamr. W Yemen
141 N12 **Khamīs Mushayt** var. Hamīs Musait. 'Asīr, SW Saudi Arabia
123 P10 **Khampa** Respublika Sakha (Yakutiya), NE Russian Federation
Khamr see Khamir
83 C19 **Khan** ≈ W Namibia
149 Q2 **Khānābād** Kunduz, NE Afghanistan
Khân Abou Châmâte/Khan Abou Ech Cham see Khān Abū Shāmāt
138 I7 **Khān Abū Shāmāt** var. Khân Abou Châmâte, Khan Abou Ech Cham. Dimashq, W Syria
Khān al Baghdādī see Al Baghdādī
Khān al Maḩāwīl see Al Maḩāwīl
139 T7 **Khān al Mashāhidah** C Iraq
139 T10 **Khān al Muşallá** S Iraq
139 U6 **Khānaqīn** E Iraq
139 T11 **Khān ar Ruḩbah** S Iraq
139 P2 **Khān as Sūr** N Iraq
139 T8 **Khān Āzād** C Iraq
154 N13 **Khandaparha** prev. Khandpara. Orissa, E India
Khandpara see Khandaparha
149 T2 **Khandūd** var. Khandud, Wakhan. Badakhshān, NE Afghanistan
154 G11 **Khandwa** Madhya Pradesh, C India
123 R10 **Khandyga** Respublika Sakha (Yakutiya), NE Russian Federation
149 T10 **Khānewāl** Punjab, NE Pakistan
149 S10 **Khāngarh** Punjab, E Pakistan
Khanh Hung see Soc Trăng
Khaniá see Chaniá
Khanka see Khonqa
163 Z8 **Khanka, Lake** var. Hsing-k'ai Hu, Lake Hanka, Chin. Xingkai Hu, Rus. Ozero Khanka. ◎ China/Russian Federation
Khanka, Ozero see Khanka, Lake
Khankendi see Xankändi
Khanlar see Xanlar
123 O9 **Khannya** ≈ NE Russian Federation
149 S12 **Khānpur** Punjab, SE Pakistan
149 S12 **Khānpur** Punjab, E Pakistan
138 I4 **Khān Shaykhūn** var. Khan Sheikhun. Idlib, NW Syria
Khan Sheikhun see Khān Shaykhūn
145 S15 **Khantau** Zhambyl, S Kazakhstan
145 W16 **Khan Tengri, Pik** ▲ SE Kazakhstan
167 S9 **Khanthabouli** prev. Savannakhét. Savannakhét, S Laos
127 V8 **Khanty-Mansiyskiy Avtonomnyy Okrug** ◈ autonomous district C Russian Federation
139 R4 **Khānūqah** C Iraq
138 E11 **Khān Yūnis** var. Khān Yūnus. S Gaza Strip
Khān Yūnus see Khān Yūnis
Khanzi see Ghanzi
139 U5 **Khān Zūr** E Iraq
167 N10 **Khao Laem Reservoir** ⊠ W Thailand
123 O14 **Khapcheranga** Chitinskaya Oblast', S Russian Federation
129 Q12 **Kharabali** Astrakhanskaya Oblast', SW Russian Federation
153 R16 **Kharagpur** West Bengal, NE India
139 V11 **Kharā'ib 'Abd al Karīm** S Iraq
143 Q8 **Kharānaq** Yazd, C Iran
Kharbin see Harbin
146 H13 **Khardzhagaz** Akhalskiy Velayat, C Turkmenistan
Khārga Oasis see Great Oasis, The
154 F11 **Khargon** Madhya Pradesh, C India
149 V7 **Khāriān** Punjab, NE Pakistan
117 X8 **Kharisyz'k** Donets'ka Oblast', E Ukraine
117 V5 **Kharkiv** Rus. Khar'kov. Kharkivs'ka Oblast', NE Ukraine
117 V5 **Kharkiv** ✕ Kharkivs'ka Oblast', E Ukraine
Kharkiv see Kharkivs'ka Oblast'

◆ Country ● Country Capital ◇ Dependent Territory ○ Dependent Territory Capital ◈ Administrative Region ✕ International Airport ▲ Mountain ⛰ Mountain Range Volcano ≈ River ◎ Lake ⊠ Reservoir

117 U5 **Kharkivs'ka Oblast'** var. Kharkiv, Rus. Khar'kovskaya Oblast'. ◆ province E Ukraine
Khar'kov see Kharkiv
Khar'kovskaya Oblast' see Kharkivs'ka Oblast'
126 L3 **Kharlovka** Murmanskaya Oblast', NW Russian Federation
114 K11 **Kharmanli** Khaskovo, S Bulgaria
114 K11 **Kharmanliyska Reka** ≈ S Bulgaria
126 M13 **Kharovsk** Vologodskaya Oblast', NW Russian Federation
80 F9 **Khartoum** var. El Khartûm, Khartum. ● (Sudan) Khartoum, C Sudan
80 F9 **Khartoum** ◆ state NE Sudan
80 F9 **Khartoum** × Khartoum, C Sudan
80 F9 **Khartoum North** Khartoum, C Sudan
117 X8 **Khartsyz'k** Rus. Khartsyzsk. Donets'ka Oblast', SE Ukraine
Khartsyzsk see Khartsyz'k
Khartum see Khartoum
Khasab see Al Khaşab
123 S15 **Khasan** Primorskiy Kray, SE Russian Federation
129 P16 **Khasavyurt** Respublika Dagestan, SW Russian Federation
143 W12 **Khāsh** prev. Vāsht. Sīstān va Balūchestān, SE Iran
148 K8 **Khāsh, Dasht-e** Eng. Khash Desert. desert SW Afghanistan
Khash Desert see Khāsh, Dasht-e
Khashim Al Qirba/Khashm al Qirbah see Khashm el Girba
80 H9 **Khashm el Girba** var. Khashim Al Qirba, Khashm al Qirbah. Kassala, E Sudan
138 G14 **Khashsh, Jabal al** ▲ S Jordan
137 S10 **Khashuri** C Georgia
153 V13 **Khāsi Hills** hill range NE India
114 K11 **Khaskovo** Khaskovo, S Bulgaria
114 K11 **Khaskovo** ◆ province S Bulgaria
122 M7 **Khatanga** ≈ N Russian Federation
Khatanga, Gulf of see Khatangskiy Zaliv
123 N7 **Khatangskiy Zaliv** var. Gulf of Khatanga. bay N Russian Federation
141 W7 **Khatmat al Malāḩah** N Oman
143 S16 **Khaţmat al Malāḩah** Ash Shāriqah, E UAE
123 V7 **Khatyrka** Chukotskiy Avtonomnyy Okrug, NE Russian Federation
146 I14 **Khauz-Khan** Turkm. Hanhowuz. Akhalskiy Velayat, S Turkmenistan
146 I14 **Khauzkhanskoye Vodokhranilishche** ⊠ S Turkmenistan
Khavaling see Khovaling
Khavast see Khowos
139 W10 **Khawrah, Nahr al** ≈ S Iraq
Khawr Barakah see Baraka
141 W7 **Khawr Fakkān** var. Khor Fakkan. Ash Shāriqah, NE UAE
140 L6 **Khaybar** Al Madīnah, NW Saudi Arabia
Khaybar, Kowtal-e see Khyber Pass
147 S11 **Khaydarkan** var. Khaydarken. Oshskaya Oblast', SW Kyrgyzstan
Khaydarken see Khaydarkan
127 U2 **Khaypudyrskaya Guba** bay NW Russian Federation
139 S1 **Khayrūzuk** E Iraq
Khazar, Baḩr-e/Khazar, Daryā-ye see Caspian Sea
Khazarosp see Hazorasp
Khazretishi, Khrebet see Hazratishoh, Qatorkŭhi
Khelat see Kālat
74 F6 **Khemisset** NW Morocco
167 R10 **Khemmarat** var. Kemarat. Ubon Ratchathani, E Thailand
74 L6 **Khenchela** var. Khenchla. NE Algeria
Khenchla see Khenchela
74 G7 **Khénifra** C Morocco
Khersān, Rūd-e see Garm, Āb-e
117 R10 **Kherson** Khersons'ka Oblast', S Ukraine
Kherson see Khersons'ka Oblast'
117 S14 **Khersones, Mys** Rus. Mys Khersonesskiy. headland S Ukraine
Khersonesskiy, Mys see Khersones, Mys
117 R10 **Khersons'ka Oblast'** var. Kherson, Rus. Khersonskaya Oblast'. ◆ province S Ukraine
Khersonskaya Oblast' see Khersons'ka Oblast'
122 L8 **Kheta** ≈ N Russian Federation
167 S8 **Khe Ve** Quang Binh, C Vietnam
149 U7 **Khewra** Punjab, E Pakistan
Khiam see El Khiyam
126 J4 **Khibiny** ▲ NW Russian Federation
128 K3 **Khimki** Moskovskaya Oblast', W Russian Federation
147 S12 **Khingov** Rus. Obi-Khingou. ≈ C Tajikistan
Khíos see Chíos
149 R15 **Khipro** Sind, SE Pakistan
139 S10 **Khirr, Wādī al** dry watercourse S Iraq
114 I10 **Khisarya** Plovdiv, C Bulgaria
Khiva see Khiwa
146 H9 **Khiwa** Rus. Khiva. Khorazm Wiloyati, W Uzbekistan
167 N9 **Khlong Khlung** Kamphaeng Phet, W Thailand
167 N15 **Khlong Thom** Krabi, SW Thailand
167 P12 **Khlung** Chantaburi, S Thailand
Khmel'nik see Khmil'nyk
Khmel'nitskaya Oblast' see Khmel'nyts'ka Oblast'
Khmel'nitskiy see Khmel 'nyts'kyy
116 K5 **Khmel'nyts'ka Oblast'** var. Khmel'nyts'kyy, Rus. Khmel'nitskaya Oblast'; prev. Kamenets-Podol'skaya Oblast'. ◆ province NW Ukraine
116 L6 **Khmel 'nyts'kyy** Rus. Khmel'nitskiy; prev. Proskurov. Khmel'nyts'ka Oblast', W Ukraine
Khmel'nyts'kyy see Khmel'nyts'ka Oblast'
116 M6 **Khmil'nyk** Rus. Khmel'nik. Vinnyts'ka Oblast', C Ukraine
137 R9 **Khobi** W Georgia
119 P15 **Khodasy** Rus. Khodosy. Mahilyowskaya Voblasts', E Belarus
116 I6 **Khodoriv** Pol. Chodorów, Rus. Khodorov. L'vivs'ka Oblast', NW Ukraine
Khodorov see Khodoriv
Khodosy see Khodasy
146 D12 **Khodzhakala** Turkm. Hojagala. Balkanskiy Velayat, W Turkmenistan
146 M13 **Khodzhambas** Turkm. Hojambaz. Lebapskiy Velayat, E Turkmenistan
Khodzhent see Khŭjand
Khodzheyli see Khŭjayli
Khoi see Khvoy
Khojend see Khŭjand
Khokand see Qŭqon
128 L8 **Khokhol'skiy** Voronezhskaya Oblast', W Russian Federation
167 P10 **Khok Samrong** Lop Buri, C Thailand
149 P2 **Kholm** var. Tashqurghan, Pash. Khulm. Balkh, N Afghanistan
126 H15 **Kholm** Novgorodskaya Oblast', W Russian Federation
Kholm see Chełm
Kholmech' see Kholmyech
123 T13 **Kholmsk** Ostrov Sakhalin, Sakhalinskaya Oblast', SE Russian Federation
119 O19 **Kholmyech** Rus. Kholmech'. Homyel'skaya Voblasts', SE Belarus
Kholon see Holon
Kholopenichi see Khalopenichy
83 D19 **Khomas** ◆ district C Namibia
83 D19 **Khomas Hochland** var. Khomasplato. plateau C Namibia
Khomasplato see Khomas Hochland
Khomein see Khomeyn
142 M7 **Khomeyn** var. Khomein, Khumain. Markazī, W Iran
143 N8 **Khomeynīshahr** prev. Homāyūnshahr. Eşfahān, C Iran
Khoms see Al Khums
Khong Sedone see Muang Khôngxédôn
167 Q9 **Khon Kaen** var. Muang Khon Kaen. Khon Kaen, E Thailand
146 I9 **Khonqa** Rus. Khanka. Khorazm Wiloyati, W Uzbekistan
167 Q9 **Khon San** Khon Kaen, E Thailand
123 R8 **Khonuu** Respublika Sakha (Yakutiya), NE Russian Federation
129 N8 **Khopër** var. Khoper. ≈ SW Russian Federation
123 S14 **Khor** Khabarovskiy Kray, SE Russian Federation
143 S6 **Khorāsān** off. Ostān-e Khorāsān, var. Khorassan, Khurasan. ◆ province NE Iran
Khorassan see Khorāsān
Khorat see Nakhon Ratchasima
146 H9 **Khorazm Wiloyati** Rus. Khorezmskaya Oblast'. ◆ province W Uzbekistan
154 O13 **Khordha** prev. Khurda. Orissa, E India
127 U4 **Khorey-Ver** Nenetskiy Avtonomnyy Okrug, NW Russian Federation
Khorezmskaya Oblast' see Khorazm Wiloyati
Khor Fakkan see Khawr Fakkān
145 W15 **Khorgos** Almaty, SE Kazakhstan
123 N13 **Khorinsk** Respublika Buryatiya, S Russian Federation
83 C18 **Khorixas** Kunene, NW Namibia
141 O17 **Khormaksar** var. Aden. × ('Adan) SW Yemen
Khormal see Khurmāl
Khormuj see Khvormūj
Khorog see Khorugh
117 S5 **Khorol** Poltavs'ka Oblast', NE Ukraine
142 L7 **Khorramābād** var. Khurramabad. Lorestān, W Iran
142 K10 **Khorramshahr** var. Khurramshahr, Muhammerah; prev. Mohammerah. Khūzestān, SW Iran
147 S14 **Khorugh** Rus. Khorog. S Tajikistan
129 Q12 **Khosheutovo** Astrakhanskaya Oblast', SW Russian Federation
Khotan see Hotan
Khorvot Khalutsa see Horvot Haluza
Khotimsk see Khotsimsk
Khotin see Khotyn
119 R16 **Khotsimsk** Rus. Khotimsk. Mahilyowskaya Voblasts', E Belarus
116 K7 **Khotyn** Rom. Hotin, Rus. Khotin. Chernivets'ka Oblast', W Ukraine
74 F7 **Khouribga** C Morocco
147 Q13 **Khovaling** Rus. Khavaling. SW Tajikistan
Khovd see Hovd
147 P11 **Khowos** var. Ursat'yevskaya, Rus. Khavast. Sirdaryo Wiloyati, E Uzbekistan
149 R6 **Khowst** Paktīā, E Afghanistan
Khoy see Khvoy
119 N20 **Khoyniki** Rus. Khoyniki. Homyel'skaya Voblasts', SE Belarus
Khozretishi, Khrebet see Hazratishoh, Qatorkŭhi
Khrisoúpolis see Chrysoúpoli
144 J10 **Khromtau** Kaz. Khromtaū. Aktyubinsk, W Kazakhstan
Khrysokhou Bay see Chrysochoú, Kólpos
117 O7 **Khrystynivka** Cherkas'ka Oblast', C Ukraine
167 R10 **Khuang Nai** Ubon Ratchathani, E Thailand
Khudal see Khādhil
Khudat see Xudat
149 W9 **Khudiān** Punjab, E Pakistan
Khudzhand see Khŭjand
147 O13 **Khufar** Surkhondaryo Wiloyati, S Uzbekistan
83 G21 **Khuis** Kgalagadi, SW Botswana
147 Q11 **Khŭjand** var. Khodzhent, Khojend, Rus. Khudzhand; prev. Leninabad, Taj. Leninobod. N Tajikistan
146 H8 **Khŭjayli** Rus. Khodzheyli. Qoraqalpoghiston Respublikasi, W Uzbekistan
167 R11 **Khukhan** Si Sa Ket, E Thailand
Khulm see Kholm
153 T16 **Khulna** Khulna, SW Bangladesh
153 T16 **Khulna** ◆ division SW Bangladesh
Khumain see Khomeyn
Khums see Al Khums
149 W2 **Khunjerāb Pass** Chin. Kunjirap Daban. pass China/Pakistan see also Kunjirap Daban
153 P16 **Khunti** Bihār, N India
167 N7 **Khun Yuam** Mae Hong Son, NW Thailand
Khurais see Khurayş
Khurasan see Khorāsān
141 R7 **Khurayş** var. Khurais. Ash Sharqīyah, C Saudi Arabia
Khurda see Khordha
152 J11 **Khurja** Uttar Pradesh, N India
139 V4 **Khurmāl** var. Khormal. NE Iraq
Khurramabad see Khorramābād
Khurramshahr see Khorramshahr
149 U7 **Khushāb** Punjab, NE Pakistan
116 H8 **Khust** Cz. Chust, Husté, Hung. Huszt. Zakarpats'ka Oblast', W Ukraine
80 D11 **Khuwei** Western Kordofan, C Sudan
149 O13 **Khuzdār** Baluchistān, SW Pakistan
142 L9 **Khūzestān** off. Ostān-e Khūzestān, var. Khuzistan; prev. Arabistan, anc. Susiana. ◆ province SW Iran
Khuzistan see Khūzestān
149 R2 **Khvājeh Ghār** var. Khwajaghar, Khwaja-i-Ghar. Takhār, NE Afghanistan
129 Q7 **Khvalynsk** Saratovskaya Oblast', W Russian Federation
143 N12 **Khvormūj** var. Khormuj. Būshehr, S Iran
142 I2 **Khvoy** var. Khoi, Khoy. Āzarbāyjān-e Bākhtarī, NW Iran
Khwajaghar/Khwaja-i-Ghar see Khvājeh Ghār
149 S5 **Khyber Pass** var. Kowtal-e Khaybar. pass Afghanistan/Pakistan
186 L8 **Kia** Santa Isabel, N Solomon Islands
183 S10 **Kiama** New South Wales, SE Australia
79 O22 **Kiambi** Katanga, SE Dem. Rep. Congo (Zaire)
27 Q12 **Kiamichi Mountains** ▲ Oklahoma, C USA
27 Q12 **Kiamichi River** ≈ Oklahoma, C USA
14 M10 **Kiamika, Réservoir** ⊠ Quebec, SE Canada
Kiamusze see Jiamusi
39 N7 **Kiana** Alaska, USA
Kiangmai see Chiang Mai
Kiang-ning see Nanjing
Kiangsi see Jiangxi
Kiangsu see Jiangsu
93 M14 **Kiantajärvi** ⊚ E Finland
115 F19 **Kiáto** prev. Kiáton. Pelopónnisos, S Greece
Kiáton see Kiáto
Kiayi see Chiai
67 T9 **Kibali** var. Uele (upper course). ≈ NE Dem. Rep. Congo (Zaire)
79 E20 **Kibangou** Le Niari, SW Congo
Kibarty see Kybartai
92 M8 **Kiberg** Finnmark, N Norway
95 F22 **Kibæk** Ringkøbing, W Denmark
79 N20 **Kibombo** Maniema, E Dem. Rep. Congo (Zaire)
81 E20 **Kibondo** Kigoma, NW Tanzania
81 J15 **Kibre Mengist** var. Adola. Oromo, C Ethiopia
Kıbrıs/Kıbrıs Cumhuriyeti see Cyprus
81 E20 **Kibungo** var. Kibungu. SE Rwanda
Kibungu see Kibungo
113 N19 **Kičevo** SW FYR Macedonia
127 P13 **Kichmengskiy Gorodok** Vologodskaya Oblast', NW Russian Federation
30 J8 **Kickapoo River** ≈ Wisconsin, N USA
11 P16 **Kicking Horse Pass** pass Alberta/British Columbia, SW Canada
77 R9 **Kidal** Kidal, C Mali
77 Q8 **Kidal** ◆ region NE Mali
171 Q7 **Kidapawan** Mindanao, S Philippines
97 L20 **Kidderminster** C England, UK
76 I11 **Kidira** E Senegal
184 O11 **Kidnappers, Cape** headland North Island, NZ
100 J8 **Kiel** Schleswig-Holstein, N Germany
111 L15 **Kielce** Rus. Keltsy. Świętokrzyskie, C Poland
100 K7 **Kieler Bucht** bay N Germany
100 J7 **Kieler Förde** inlet N Germany
167 U13 **Kiên Đức** var. Đak Lap. Đắc Lắc, S Vietnam
79 N24 **Kienge** Katanga, SE Dem. Rep. Congo (Zaire)
100 Q12 **Kietz** Brandenburg, NE Germany
Kiev see Kyyiv
Kiev Reservoir see Kyyivs'ke Vodoskhovyshche
76 J10 **Kiffa** Assaba, S Mauritania
115 H19 **Kifisiá** Attikí, C Greece
115 F18 **Kifisós** ≈ C Greece
139 U5 **Kifrī** N Iraq
81 D20 **Kigali** ● (Rwanda) C Rwanda
81 E20 **Kigali** × C Rwanda
137 P13 **Kiğı** Bingöl, E Turkey
81 E21 **Kigoma** Kigoma, W Tanzania
81 E21 **Kigoma** ◆ region W Tanzania
38 F10 **Kihei** Haw. Kīhei. Maui, Hawaii, USA, C Pacific Ocean
93 K17 **Kihniö** Länsi-Suomi, W Finland
118 F6 **Kihnu** var. Kihnu Saar, Ger. Kühnö. island SW Estonia
Kihnu Saar see Kihnu
38 A8 **Kii Landing** Niihau, Hawaii, USA, C Pacific Ocean
93 L14 **Kiiminki** Oulu, C Finland
164 J14 **Kii-Nagashima** var. Nagashima. Mie, Honshū, SW Japan
164 J14 **Kii-sanchi** ▲ Honshū, SW Japan
92 L11 **Kiistala** Lappi, N Finland
164 I15 **Kii-suidō** strait S Japan
165 V16 **Kikai-shima** var. Kikaiga-shima. island Nansei-shotō, SW Japan
112 M8 **Kikinda** Ger. Grosskikinda, Hung. Nagykikinda; prev. Velika Kikinda. Serbia, N Yugoslavia
Kikládhes see Kykládes
165 Q5 **Kikonai** Hokkaidō, NE Japan
186 C8 **Kikori** Gulf, S PNG
186 C8 **Kikori** ≈ W PNG
165 O14 **Kikuchi** var. Kikuti. Kumamoto, Kyūshū, SW Japan
Kikuti see Kikuchi
129 N8 **Kikvidze** Volgogradskaya Oblast', SW Russian Federation
14 I10 **Kikwissi, Lac** ⊚ Quebec, SE Canada
79 I21 **Kikwit** Bandundu, W Dem. Rep. Congo (Zaire)
95 K15 **Kil** Värmland, C Sweden
94 N12 **Kilafors** Gävleborg, C Sweden
38 B8 **Kilauea** Haw. Kīlauea. Kauai, Hawaii, USA, C Pacific Ocean
38 H12 **Kilauea Caldera** crater Hawaii, USA, C Pacific Ocean
109 V4 **Kilb** Niederösterreich, C Austria
39 O12 **Kilbuck Mountains** ▲ Alaska, USA
163 Y12 **Kilchu** NE North Korea
97 F18 **Kilcock** Ir. Cill Choca. E Ireland
183 V2 **Kilcoy** Queensland, E Australia
97 F18 **Kildare** Ir. Cill Dara. E Ireland
97 F18 **Kildare** Ir. Cill Dara. cultural region E Ireland
126 K2 **Kil'din, Ostrov** island NW Russian Federation
25 W7 **Kilgore** Texas, SW USA
Kilien Mountains see Qilian Shan
114 K9 **Kilifarevo** Veliko Tŭrnovo, N Bulgaria
81 K20 **Kilifi** Coast, SE Kenya
189 U9 **Kili Island** var. Kōle. island Ralik Chain, S Marshall Islands
149 V2 **Kilik Pass** pass Afghanistan/China
Kilimane see Quelimane
81 I21 **Kilimanjaro** ◆ region E Tanzania
81 I20 **Kilimanjaro** var. Uhuru Peak. ▲ NE Tanzania
Kilimbangara see Kolombangara
Kilinailau Islands see Tulun Islands
81 K23 **Kilindoni** Pwani, E Tanzania
118 H6 **Kilingi-Nõmme** Ger. Kurkund. Pärnumaa, SW Estonia
136 M17 **Kilis** Kilis, S Turkey
136 M16 **Kilis** ◆ province S Turkey
117 N12 **Kiliya** Rom. Chilia-Nouă. Odes'ka Oblast', SW Ukraine
97 B19 **Kilkee** Ir. Cill Chaoi. W Ireland
97 E19 **Kilkenny** Ir. Cill Chainnigh. S Ireland
97 E19 **Kilkenny** Ir. Cill Chainnigh. cultural region S Ireland
97 B18 **Kilkieran Bay** Ir. Cuan Chill Chiaráin. bay W Ireland
114 G13 **Kilkís** Kentrikí Makedonía, N Greece
97 C15 **Killala Bay** Ir. Cuan Chill Ala. inlet NW Ireland
11 R15 **Killam** Alberta, SW Canada
183 U3 **Killarney** Queensland, E Australia
11 W17 **Killarney** Manitoba, S Canada
14 E11 **Killarney** Ontario, S Canada
97 B20 **Killarney** Ir. Cill Airne. SW Ireland
28 K4 **Killdeer** North Dakota, N USA
28 J4 **Killdeer Mountains** ▲ North Dakota, N USA
45 V15 **Killdeer River** ≈ Trinidad, Trinidad and Tobago
25 S9 **Killeen** Texas, SW USA
39 P6 **Killik River** ≈ Alaska, USA
9 T7 **Killinek Island** island Nunavut, NE Canada
Killini see Kyllíni
115 C19 **Killínis, Akrotírio** headland S Greece
97 D15 **Killybegs** Ir. Na Cealla Beaga. NW Ireland
Kilmain see Quelimane
96 I13 **Kilmarnock** W Scotland, UK
21 X6 **Kilmarnock** Virginia, NE USA
127 S16 **Kil'mez'** Kirovskaya Oblast', NW Russian Federation
129 S2 **Kil'mez'** Udmurtskaya Respublika, NW Russian Federation
127 R16 **Kil'mez'** ≈ NW Russian Federation
67 V11 **Kilombero** ≈ S Tanzania
92 J10 **Kilpisjarvi** Lappi, N Finland
97 B19 **Kilrush** Ir. Cill Rois. W Ireland
79 O24 **Kilwa** Katanga, SE Dem. Rep. Congo (Zaire)
Kilwa see Kilwa Kivinje
81 J24 **Kilwa Kivinje** var. Kilwa. Lindi, SE Tanzania
81 J24 **Kilwa Masoko** Lindi, SE Tanzania
171 T13 **Kilwo** Pulau Seram, E Indonesia
114 P12 **Kilyos** Istanbul, NW Turkey
37 V8 **Kim** Colorado, C USA
169 U7 **Kimanis, Teluk** bay Sabah, East Malaysia
182 H8 **Kimba** South Australia
28 I15 **Kimball** Nebraska, C USA
29 O11 **Kimball** South Dakota, N USA
79 I21 **Kimbao** Bandundu, SW Dem. Rep. Congo (Zaire)
186 F7 **Kimbe** New Britain, E PNG
186 G7 **Kimbe Bay** inlet New Britain, E PNG
11 P17 **Kimberley** British Columbia, SW Canada
83 H23 **Kimberley** Northern Cape, C South Africa
180 M4 **Kimberley Plateau** plateau Western Australia
33 P15 **Kimberly** Idaho, NW USA
163 Y12 **Kimch'aek** prev. Sŏngjin. E North Korea
163 Y15 **Kimch'ŏn** C South Korea
163 Z16 **Kim Hae** var. Pusan. × (Pusan) SE South Korea
Kími see Kými
93 K20 **Kimito** Swe. Kemiö. Länsi-Suomi, W Finland
165 R4 **Kimobetsu** Hokkaidō, NE Japan
115 I21 **Kímolos** island Kykládes, Greece, Aegean Sea
115 I21 **Kímolou Sífnou, Stenó** strait Kykládes, Greece, Aegean Sea
128 L5 **Kimovsk** Tul'skaya Oblast', W Russian Federation
163 X15 **Kimpo** × (Sŏul) NW South Korea
Kimpolung see Câmpulung Moldovenesc
126 K16 **Kimry** Tverskaya Oblast', W Russian Federation
79 H21 **Kimvula** Bas-Congo, SW Dem. Rep. Congo (Zaire)
169 U6 **Kinabalu, Gunung** ▲ East Malaysia
Kinabatangan see Kinabatangan, Sungai
169 V7 **Kinabatangan, Sungai** var. Kinabatangan. ≈ East Malaysia
115 L21 **Kínaros** island Kykládes, Greece, Aegean Sea
11 O15 **Kinbasket Lake** ⊠ British Columbia, SW Canada
96 I7 **Kinbrace** N Scotland, UK
14 E14 **Kincardine** Ontario, S Canada
96 K10 **Kincardine** cultural region E Scotland, UK
79 K21 **Kinda** Kasai Occidental, SE Dem. Rep. Congo (Zaire)
79 M24 **Kinda** Katanga, SE Dem. Rep. Congo (Zaire)
166 L3 **Kindat** Sagaing, N Myanmar
109 V6 **Kindberg** Steiermark, C Austria
22 H8 **Kinder** Louisiana, S USA
98 H13 **Kinderdijk** Zuid-Holland, SW Netherlands
97 M17 **Kinder Scout** ▲ C England, UK
11 S16 **Kindersley** Saskatchewan, S Canada
76 I14 **Kindia** Guinée-Maritime, SW Guinea
64 B11 **Kindley Field** air base E Bermuda
29 R6 **Kindred** North Dakota, N USA
79 N20 **Kindu** prev. Kindu-Port-Empain. Maniema, C Dem. Rep. Congo (Zaire)
Kindu-Port-Empain see Kindu
129 S6 **Kinel'** Samarskaya Oblast', W Russian Federation
127 N15 **Kineshma** Ivanovskaya Oblast', W Russian Federation
King see King William's Town
140 K10 **King Abdul Aziz** × (Makkah) Makkah, W Saudi Arabia
21 X6 **King and Queen Court House** Virginia, NE USA
King Charles Islands see Kong Karls Land
King Christian IX Land see Kong Christian IX Land
King Christian X Land see Kong Christian X Land
35 O11 **King City** California, W USA
27 R2 **King City** Missouri, C USA
38 M16 **King Cove** Alaska, USA
26 M10 **Kingfisher** Oklahoma, C USA
King Frederik VI Coast see Kong Frederik VI Kyst
King Frederik VIII Land see Kong Frederik VIII Land
65 B24 **King George Bay** bay West Falkland, Falkland Islands
194 G3 **King George Island** var. King George Land. island South Shetland Islands, Antarctica
12 I6 **King George Islands** island group Nunavut, C Canada
King George Land see King George Island
126 G13 **Kingisepp** Leningradskaya Oblast', NW Russian Federation
183 N14 **King Island** island Tasmania, SE Australia
10 J15 **King Island** island British Columbia, SW Canada
King Island see Kadan Kyun
Kingissepp see Kuressaare
141 Q7 **King Khalid** × (Ar Riyāḍ) Ar Riyāḍ, C Saudi Arabia
35 S2 **King Lear Peak** ▲ Nevada, W USA
195 Y8 **King Leopold and Queen Astrid Land** physical region Antarctica
180 M4 **King Leopold Ranges** ▲ Western Australia
36 I11 **Kingman** Arizona, SW USA
26 M6 **Kingman** Kansas, C USA
192 L7 **Kingman Reef** ◇ US territory C Pacific Ocean
79 N20 **Kingombe** Maniema, E Dem. Rep. Congo (Zaire)
182 F5 **Kingoonya** South Australia
194 J10 **King Peninsula** peninsula Antarctica
39 P13 **King Salmon** Alaska, USA
35 Q6 **Kings Beach** California, W USA
35 R11 **Kingsburg** California, W USA
182 I10 **Kingscote** South Australia
King's County see Offaly
194 H2 **King Sejong** South Korean research station Antarctica
183 T9 **Kingsford Smith** × (Sydney) New South Wales, SE Australia
11 P17 **Kingsgate** British Columbia, SW Canada
23 W8 **Kingsland** Georgia, SE USA
29 S13 **Kingsley** Iowa, C USA
97 O19 **King's Lynn** var. Bishop's Lynn, Kings Lynn, Lynn, Lynn Regis. E England, UK
21 Q10 **Kings Mountain** North Carolina, SE USA
180 K4 **King Sound** sound Western Australia
37 N2 **Kings Peak** ▲ Utah, W USA
21 O8 **Kingsport** Tennessee, S USA
35 R11 **Kings River** ≈ California, W USA
183 P17 **Kingston** Tasmania, SE Australia
14 K14 **Kingston** Ontario, SE Canada
44 K13 **Kingston** ● (Jamaica) E Jamaica
185 C22 **Kingston** Otago, South Island, NZ
19 P12 **Kingston** Massachusetts, NE USA
27 S3 **Kingston** Missouri, C USA
18 K12 **Kingston** New York, NE USA
31 S14 **Kingston** Ohio, N USA
19 O13 **Kingston** Rhode Island, NE USA
20 M9 **Kingston** Tennessee, S USA
35 W12 **Kingston Peak** ▲ California, W USA
182 J11 **Kingston Southeast** South Australia
97 N17 **Kingston upon Hull** var. Hull. E England, UK
97 N22 **Kingston upon Thames** SE England, UK
45 P14 **Kingstown** ● (Saint Vincent and the Grenadines) Saint Vincent, Saint Vincent and the Grenadines
Kingstown see Dún Laoghaire
21 T13 **Kingstree** South Carolina, SE USA
64 L8 **Kings Trough** undersea feature E Atlantic Ocean
14 C18 **Kingsville** Ontario, S Canada
25 S15 **Kingsville** Texas, SW USA
21 W6 **King William** Virginia, NE USA
8 M7 **King William Island** island Nunavut, N Canada Arctic Ocean
83 I25 **King William's Town** var. King, Kingwilliamstown. Eastern Cape, S South Africa
21 T3 **Kingwood** West Virginia, NE USA
136 C13 **Kınık** İzmir, W Turkey
79 G21 **Kinkala** Le Pool, S Congo
165 R10 **Kinka-san** headland Honshū, C Japan
184 M8 **Kinleith** Waikato, North Island, NZ
95 J19 **Kinna** Västra Götaland, S Sweden
96 L8 **Kinnaird Head** var. Kinnairds Head. headland NE Scotland, UK
95 K20 **Kinnared** Halland, S Sweden
Kinneret, Yam see Tiberias, Lake
155 K24 **Kinniyai** Eastern Province, NE Sri Lanka
93 L16 **Kinnula** Länsi-Suomi, W Finland
14 I8 **Kinojévis** ≈ Quebec, SE Canada
164 I14 **Kino-kawa** ≈ Honshū, SW Japan
11 U11 **Kinoosao** Saskatchewan, C Canada
99 L17 **Kinrooi** Limburg, NE Belgium
96 J11 **Kinross** C Scotland, UK
96 J11 **Kinross** cultural region C Scotland, UK
97 C21 **Kinsale** Ir. Cionn tSáile. SW Ireland
95 D14 **Kinsarvik** Hordaland, S Norway
79 G21 **Kinshasa** prev. Léopoldville. ● (Zaire) Kinshasa, W Dem. Rep. Congo (Zaire)
79 G21 **Kinshasa** off. Ville de Kinshasa, var. Kinshasa City. ◆ region SW Dem. Rep. Congo (Zaire)

◆ Country ● Country Capital ◇ Dependent Territory ○ Dependent Territory Capital ◆ Administrative Region × International Airport ▲ Mountain ▲ Mountain Range Volcano ≈ River ⊚ Lake ⊠ Reservoir

79 G21 **Kinshasa** ✕ Kinshasa, SW Dem. Rep. Congo (Zaire)
Kinshasa City *see* Kinshasa
117 U9 **Kins'ka** ∽ SE Ukraine
26 K6 **Kinsley** Kansas, C USA
21 W10 **Kinston** North Carolina, SE USA
77 P15 **Kintampo** W Ghana
182 B1 **Kintore, Mount** ▲ South Australia
96 G13 **Kintyre** *peninsula* W Scotland, UK
96 G13 **Kintyre, Mull of** *headland* W Scotland, UK
166 M4 **Kin-u** Sagaing, C Myanmar
12 G8 **Kinushseo** ∽ Ontario, C Canada
11 P13 **Kinuso** Alberta, W Canada
154 I13 **Kinwat** Mahārāshtra, C India
81 F16 **Kinyeti** ▲ S Sudan
101 I17 **Kinzig** ∽ SW Germany
Kioga, Lake *see* Kyoga, Lake
26 M8 **Kiowa** Kansas, C USA
27 P12 **Kiowa** Oklahoma, C USA
Kiparissía *see* Kyparissía
14 H10 **Kipawa, Lac** ◎ Quebec, SE Canada
81 G24 **Kipengere Range** ⛰ SW Tanzania
81 E23 **Kipili** Rukwa, W Tanzania
81 K20 **Kipini** Coast, SE Kenya
11 V16 **Kipling** Saskatchewan, S Canada
38 M13 **Kipnuk** Alaska, USA
97 F18 **Kippure** *Ir.* Cipiúr. ▲ E Ireland
79 N25 **Kipushi** Katanga, SE Dem. Rep. Congo (Zaire)
187 N10 **Kirakira** *var.* Kaokaona. San Cristobal, SE Solomon Islands
155 K14 **Kirandul** *var.* Bailādila. Madhya Pradesh, C India
155 I21 **Kīranūr** Tamil Nādu, SE India
119 N21 **Kiraw** *Rus.* Kirovo. Homyel'skaya Voblasts', SE Belarus
119 M17 **Kirawsk** *Rus.* Kirovsk; *prev.* Startsy. Mahilyowskaya Voblasts', E Belarus
118 F5 **Kirbla** Läänemaa, W Estonia
25 Y9 **Kirbyville** Texas, SW USA
114 M12 **Kırcasalih** Edirne, NW Turkey
109 W8 **Kirchbach** *var.* Kirchbach in Steiermark. Steiermark, SE Austria
Kirchbach in Steiermark *see* Kirchbach
108 H7 **Kirchberg** Sankt Gallen, NE Switzerland
109 S5 **Kirchdorf an der Krems** Oberösterreich, N Austria
Kirchheim *see* Kirchheim unter Teck
101 I22 **Kirchheim unter Teck** *var.* Kirchheim. Baden-Württemberg, SW Germany
Kirdzhali *see* Kŭrdzhali
123 N13 **Kirenga** ∽ S Russian Federation
123 N12 **Kirensk** Irkutskaya Oblast', C Russian Federation
Kirghizia *see* Kyrgyzstan
145 S16 **Kirghiz Range** *Rus.* Kirgizskiy Khrebet; *prev.* Alexander Range. ⛰ Kazakhstan/Kyrgyzstan
Kirghiz SSR *see* Kyrgyzstan
Kirghiz Steppe *see* Kazakhskiy Melkosopochnik
Kirgizskaya SSR *see* Kyrgyzstan
Kirgizskiy Khrebet *see* Kirghiz Range
79 I19 **Kiri** Bandundu, W Dem. Rep. Congo (Zaire)
Kiriath-Arba *see* Hebron
191 R3 **Kiribati** *off.* Republic of Kiribati. ◆ *republic* C Pacific Ocean
136 L17 **Kırıkhan** Hatay, S Turkey
136 I13 **Kırıkkale** Kırıkkale, C Turkey
136 C10 **Kırıkkale** ◈ *province* C Turkey
126 L13 **Kirillov** Vologodskaya Oblast', NW Russian Federation
Kirin *see* Jilin
81 I18 **Kirinyaga** *prev.* Mount Kenya. ☒ C Kenya
126 H13 **Kirishi** *var.* Kirisi. Leningradskaya Oblast', NW Russian Federation
164 C16 **Kirishima-yama** ▲ Kyūshū, SW Japan
Kirisi *see* Kirishi
191 Y2 **Kiritimati** ✕ Kiritimati, E Kiribati
191 Y2 **Kiritimati** *prev.* Christmas Island. *atoll* Line Islands, E Kiribati
186 G9 **Kiriwina Island** *Eng.* Trobriand Island. *island* SE PNG
186 G9 **Kiriwina Islands** *var.* Trobriand Islands. *island group* S PNG
96 K12 **Kirkcaldy** E Scotland, UK
97 I14 **Kirkcudbright** S Scotland, UK
97 I14 **Kirkcudbright** *cultural region* S Scotland, UK
Kirkee *see* Khadki
92 M8 **Kirkenes** *var.* Kirkkoniemi. Finnmark, N Norway
95 I14 **Kirkenær** Hedmark, S Norway
92 J4 **Kirkjubæjarklaustur** Sudhurland, S Iceland
Kirk-Kilissa *see* Kırklareli
Kirkkoniemi *see* Kirkenes
93 L20 **Kirkkonummi** *Swe.* Kyrkslätt. Etelä-Suomi, S Finland
14 G7 **Kirkland Lake** Ontario, S Canada
136 C9 **Kırklareli** *prev.* Kirk-Kilissa. Kırklareli, NW Turkey
136 I13 **Kırklareli** ◈ *province* NW Turkey
185 F20 **Kirkliston Range** ⛰ South Island, NZ
14 D10 **Kirkpatrick Lake** ◎ Ontario, S Canada
195 Q11 **Kirkpatrick, Mount** ▲ Antarctica
27 U2 **Kirksville** Missouri, C USA
139 T4 **Kirkūk** *var.* Karkūk, Kerkuk. N Iraq
139 U7 **Kir Kush** E Iraq
96 K5 **Kirkwall** NE Scotland, UK
83 H25 **Kirkwood** Eastern Cape, S South Africa
27 X5 **Kirkwood** Missouri, C USA
Kirman *see* Kermān
Kir Moab/Kir of Moab *see* Al Karak
128 I5 **Kirov** Kaluzhskaya Oblast', W Russian Federation
127 R14 **Kirov** *prev.* Vyatka. Kirovskaya Oblast', NW Russian Federation
Kīrov *see* Balpyk Bi, Kazakhstan
Kīrov *see* Kirova, Almaty, Kazakhstan
145 U13 **Kirova** *Kaz.* Kīrov. Almaty, SE Kazakhstan
Kirovabad *see* Gäncä, Azerbaijan
Kirovabad *see* Panj, Tajikistan
Kirovakan *see* Vanadzor
Kirovo *see* Kiraw, Belarus
Kirovo/Kirovograd *see* Kirovohrad, Ukraine
Kirovo *see* Beshariq, Uzbekistan
127 R14 **Kirovo-Chepetsk** Kirovskaya Oblast', NW Russian Federation
Kirovogradskaya Oblast'/Kirovohrad *see* Kirovohrads'ka Oblast'
117 R7 **Kirovohrad** *Rus.* Kirovograd; *prev.* Kirovo, Yelizavetgrad, Zinov'yevsk. Kirovohrads'ka Oblast', C Ukraine
117 P7 **Kirovohrads'ka Oblast'** *var.* Kirovohrad, *Rus.* Kirovogradskaya Oblast'. ◈ *province* C Ukraine
126 J4 **Kirovsk** Murmanskaya Oblast', NW Russian Federation
Kirovsk *see* Babadaykhan, Turkmenistan
Kirovsk *see* Kirawsk, Belarus
117 X7 **Kirovs'k** Luhans'ka Oblast', E Ukraine
122 E9 **Kirovskaya Oblast'** ◈ *province* NW Russian Federation
117 X8 **Kirov'ske** Donets'ka Oblast', E Ukraine
117 U13 **Kirovs'ke** *Rus.* Kirovskoye. Respublika Krym, S Ukraine
123 V10 **Kirovskiy** Kamchatskaya Oblast', E Russian Federation
Kirovskiy *see* Balpyk Bi
Kirovskoye *see* Kyzyl-Adyr
Kirovskoye *see* Kirovs'ke
146 E11 **Kirpili** Akhalskiy Velayat, C Turkmenistan
96 K10 **Kirriemuir** E Scotland, UK
127 S13 **Kirs** Kirovskaya Oblast', NW Russian Federation
129 N7 **Kirsanov** Tambovskaya Oblast', W Russian Federation
136 J14 **Kırşehir** *anc.* Justinianopolis. Kirşehir, C Turkey
136 I13 **Kirşehir** ◈ *province* C Turkey
149 P4 **Kīrthar Range** ⛰ S Pakistan
37 P9 **Kirtland** New Mexico, SW USA
Kirun/Kirun' *see* Chilung
92 J11 **Kiruna** Norrbotten, N Sweden
79 M18 **Kirundu** Orientale, NE Dem. Rep. Congo (Zaire)
26 L3 **Kirwin Reservoir** ⊞ Kansas, C USA
129 Q4 **Kirya** Chuvashskaya Respublika, W Russian Federation
Kiryat Gat *see* Qiryat Gat
95 M18 **Kisa** Östergötland, S Sweden
165 P9 **Kisakata** Akita, Honshū, C Japan
Kisalföld *see* Little Alföld
79 L18 **Kisangani** *prev.* Stanleyville. Orientale, NE Dem. Rep. Congo (Zaire)
39 N12 **Kisaralik River** ∽ Alaska, USA
165 O14 **Kisarazu** Chiba, Honshū, S Japan
111 I22 **Kisbér** Komárom-Esztergom, NW Hungary
11 V17 **Kisbey** Saskatchewan, S Canada
122 J13 **Kiselevsk** Kemerovskaya Oblast', S Russian Federation
153 R13 **Kishanganj** Bihār, NE India
152 G12 **Kishangarh** Rājasthān, N India
Kishegyes *see* Mali Iđoš
77 S15 **Kishi** Oyo, W Nigeria
Kishinev *see* Chişinău
Kishiözen *see* Malyy Uzen'
164 I14 **Kishiwada** *var.* Kisiwada. Ōsaka, Honshū, SW Japan
143 P14 **Kīsh, Jazīreh-ye** *var.* Qeys. *island* S Iran
145 R7 **Kishkenekol'** *prev.* Kzyltu. *Kaz.* Qyzyltu; Severnyy Kazakhstan, N Kazakhstan
152 I6 **Kishtwār** Jammu and Kashmir, NW India
81 H19 **Kisii** Nyanza, SW Kenya
81 J23 **Kisiju** Pwani, E Tanzania
Kisiwada *see* Kishiwada
Kisjenő *see* Chişineu-Criş
38 E17 **Kiska Island** *island* Aleutian Islands, Alaska, USA
Kiskapus *see* Copşa Mică
111 M22 **Kiskörei-víztároló** ⊞ E Hungary
Kis-Küküllo *see* Târnava Mică
111 L24 **Kiskunfélegyháza** *var.* Félegyháza. Bács-Kiskun, C Hungary
111 K25 **Kiskunhalas** *var.* Halas. Bács-Kiskun, S Hungary
111 K24 **Kiskunmajsa** Bács-Kiskun, S Hungary
129 N15 **Kislovodsk** Stavropol'skiy Kray, SW Russian Federation
81 L18 **Kismaayo** *var.* Chisimayu, Kismayu, *It.* Chisimaio. Jubbada Hoose, S Somalia
Kismayu *see* Kismaayo
164 M13 **Kiso-sanmyaku** ⛰ Honshū, S Japan
Kisseraing *see* Kanmaw Kyun
76 K14 **Kissidougou** Guinée-Forestière, S Guinea
23 X12 **Kissimmee** Florida, SE USA
23 X12 **Kissimmee, Lake** ◎ Florida, SE USA
23 X13 **Kissimmee River** ∽ Florida, SE USA
11 V13 **Kississing Lake** ◎ Manitoba, C Canada
111 L24 **Kistelek** Csongrád, SE Hungary
Kistna *see* Krishna
111 M23 **Kisújszállás** Jász-Nagykun-Szolnok, E Hungary
164 G12 **Kisuki** Shimane, Honshū, SW Japan
81 H18 **Kisumu** *prev.* Port Florence. Nyanza, W Kenya
Kisutzaneustadtl *see* Kysucké Nové Mesto
111 O20 **Kisvárda** *Ger.* Kleinwardein. Szabolcs-Szatmár-Bereg, E Hungary
81 J24 **Kiswere** Lindi, SE Tanzania
Kiszucaújhely *see* Kysucké Nové Mesto
76 K12 **Kita** Kayes, W Mali
207 N14 **Kitaa** ◈ *province* W Greenland
Kitab *see* Kitob
165 Q4 **Kitahiyama** Hokkaidō, NE Japan
165 P12 **Kita-Ibaraki** Ibaraki, Honshū, S Japan
165 X16 **Kita-Iō-jima** *Eng.* San Alessandro. *island* SE Japan
165 Q9 **Kitakami** Iwate, Honshū, C Japan
165 P11 **Kitakata** Fukushima, Honshū, C Japan
164 D13 **Kitakyūshū** *var.* Kitakyûsyû. Fukuoka, Kyūshū, SW Japan
Kitakyûsyû *see* Kitakyūshū
81 H18 **Kitale** Rift Valley, W Kenya
165 U3 **Kitami** Hokkaidō, NE Japan
165 T2 **Kitami-sanchi** ⛰ Hokkaidō, NE Japan
37 W5 **Kit Carson** Colorado, C USA
180 M12 **Kitchener** Western Australia
14 F16 **Kitchener** Ontario, S Canada
93 O17 **Kitee** Itä-Suomi, E Finland
81 G16 **Kitgum** N Uganda
Kithareng *see* Kanmaw Kyun
Kíthira *see* Kýthira
Kíthnos *see* Kýthnos
10 J13 **Kitimat** British Columbia, SW Canada
92 L11 **Kitinen** ∽ N Finland
147 N12 **Kitob** *Rus.* Kitab. Qashqadaryo Wiloyati, S Uzbekistan
116 K7 **Kitsman'** *Ger.* Kotzman, *Rom.* Cozmeni, *Rus.* Kitsman. Chernivets'ka Oblast', W Ukraine
164 E14 **Kitsuki** *var.* Kituki. Ōita, Kyūshū, SW Japan
18 C14 **Kittanning** Pennsylvania, NE USA
19 P10 **Kittery** Maine, NE USA
92 L11 **Kittilä** Lappi, N Finland
109 Z4 **Kittsee** Burgenland, E Austria
81 J19 **Kitui** Eastern, S Kenya
Kituki *see* Kitsuki
81 G22 **Kitunda** Tabora, C Tanzania
10 K13 **Kitwanga** British Columbia, SW Canada
82 J13 **Kitwe** *var.* Kitwe-Nkana. Copperbelt, C Zambia
Kitwe-Nkana *see* Kitwe
109 O7 **Kitzbühel** Tirol, W Austria
109 O7 **Kitzbüheler Alpen** ⛰ W Austria
101 J19 **Kitzingen** Bayern, SE Germany
153 Q14 **Kiul** Bihār, NE India
186 A7 **Kiunga** Western, SW PNG
93 M16 **Kiuruvesi** Itä-Suomi, C Finland
38 M7 **Kivalina** Alaska, USA
92 L13 **Kivalo** *ridge* C Finland
116 J3 **Kivertsi** *Pol.* Kiwerce, *Rus.* Kivertsy. Volyns'ka Oblast', NW Ukraine
Kivertsy *see* Kivertsi
93 L16 **Kivijärvi** Länsi-Suomi, W Finland
95 L23 **Kivik** Skåne, S Sweden
118 J3 **Kiviõli** Ida-Virumaa, NE Estonia
Kivu, Lac *see* Kivu, Lake
67 U10 **Kivu, Lake** *Fr.* Lac Kivu. ◎ Rwanda/Dem. Rep. Congo (Zaire)
186 C9 **Kiwai Island** *island* SW PNG
39 N8 **Kiwalik** Alaska, USA
Kiwerce *see* Kivertsi
Kiyev *see* Kyyiv
145 R10 **Kiyevka** Karaganda, C Kazakhstan
Kiyevskaya Oblast' *see* Kyyivs'ka Oblast'
Kiyevskoye Vodokhranilishche *see* Kyyivs'ke Vodoskhovyshche
136 D10 **Kıyıköy** Kırklareli, NW Turkey
145 O9 **Kiyma** Akmola, C Kazakhstan
127 V13 **Kizel** Permskaya Oblast', NW Russian Federation
127 O12 **Kizema** *var.* Kizëma. Arkhangel'skaya Oblast', NW Russian Federation
Kizilagach *see* Elkhovo
136 H12 **Kızılcahamam** Ankara, N Turkey
136 J10 **Kızıl Irmak** ∽ C Turkey
Kızılkoca *see* Şefaatli
Kizil Kum *see* Kyzyl Kum
137 P16 **Kızıltepe** Mardin, SE Turkey
Ki Zil Uzen *see* Qezel Owzan
129 Q16 **Kizilyurt** Respublika Dagestan, SW Russian Federation
129 Q15 **Kizlyar** Respublika Dagestan, SW Russian Federation
129 S3 **Kizner** Udmurtskaya Respublika, NW Russian Federation
Kizyl-Arvat *see* Gyzylarbat
146 B13 **Kizyl-Atrek** *Turkm.* Gyzyletrek. Balkanskiy Velayat, W Turkmenistan
146 D10 **Kizyl-Kaya** *Turkm.* Gyzylgaya. Balkanskiy Velayat, NW Turkmenistan
146 A10 **Kizyl-Su** *Turkm.* Gyzylsu. Balkanskiy Velayat, W Turkmenistan
95 H16 **Kjerkøy** *island* S Norway
Kjølen *see* Kölen
92 L7 **Kjøllefjord** Finnmark, N Norway
92 H11 **Kjøpsvik** Nordland, C Norway
169 N12 **Klabat, Teluk** *bay* Pulau Bangka, W Indonesia
112 I12 **Kladanj** Federacija Bosan I Hercegovina, C Bosnia and Herzegovina
171 X16 **Kladar** Irian Jaya, E Indonesia
111 C16 **Kladno** Středočeský Kraj, NW Czech Republic
112 P11 **Kladovo** Serbia, E Yugoslavia
167 P12 **Klaeng** Rayong, S Thailand
109 T9 **Klagenfurt** *Slvn.* Celovec. Kärnten, S Austria
118 B11 **Klaipėda** *Ger.* Memel. Klaipėda, NW Lithuania
95 B18 **Klaksvík** *Dan.* Klaksvig Faeroe Islands
34 L2 **Klamath** California, W USA
32 H16 **Klamath Falls** Oregon, NW USA
34 M1 **Klamath Mountains** ⛰ California/Oregon, W USA
34 L2 **Klamath River** ∽ California/Oregon, W USA
168 K9 **Klang** *var.* Kelang; *prev.* Port Swettenham. Selangor, Peninsular Malaysia
94 J13 **Klarälven** ∽ Norway/Sweden
111 B15 **Klášterec nad Ohří** *Ger.* Klösterle an der Eger. Ústecký Kraj, NW Czech Republic
111 B18 **Klatovy** *Ger.* Klattau. Plzeňský Kraj, W Czech Republic
Klattau *see* Klatovy
Klausenburg *see* Cluj-Napoca
39 Y14 **Klawock** Prince of Wales Island, Alaska, USA
98 P8 **Klazienaveen** Drenthe, NE Netherlands
Kleck *see* Klyetsk
110 H11 **Kłecko** Wielkolpolskie, C Poland
110 I11 **Kleczew** Wielkopolskie, C Poland
10 L15 **Kleena Kleene** British Columbia, SW Canada
83 D20 **Klein Aub** Hardap, C Namibia
Kleine Donau *see* Mosoni-Duna
101 O14 **Kleine Elster** ∽ E Germany
Kleine Kokel *see* Târnava Mică
99 I16 **Kleine Nete** ∽ N Belgium
Kleines Ungarisches Tiefland *see* Little Alföld
83 E22 **Klein Karas** Karas, S Namibia
Kleinkopisch *see* Copşa Mică
Klein-Marien *see* Väike-Maarja
Kleinschlatten *see* Zlatna
83 D23 **Kleinsee** Northern Cape, W South Africa
Kleinwardein *see* Kisvárda
115 C16 **Kleisoúra** Ípeiros, W Greece
95 C17 **Klepp** Rogaland, S Norway
83 I22 **Klerksdorp** North-West, N South Africa
128 I5 **Kletnya** Bryanskaya Oblast', W Russian Federation
Kletsk *see* Klyetsk
101 D14 **Kleve** *Eng.* Cleves, *Fr.* Clèves; *prev.* Cleve. Nordrhein-Westfalen, W Germany
113 J16 **Kličevo** Montenegro, SW Yugoslavia
119 M16 **Klichaw** *Rus.* Klichev. Mahilyowskaya Voblasts', E Belarus
Klichev *see* Klichaw
119 Q16 **Klimavichy** *Rus.* Klimovichi. Mahilyowskaya Voblasts', E Belarus
114 M7 **Kliment** Shumen, NE Bulgaria
Klimovichi *see* Klimavichy
93 G14 **Klimpfjäll** Västerbotten, N Sweden
128 K3 **Klin** Moskovskaya Oblast', W Russian Federation
113 M16 **Klina** Serbia, S Yugoslavia
111 B15 **Klínovec** *Ger.* Keilberg. ▲ NW Czech Republic
95 P19 **Klintehamn** Gotland, SE Sweden
129 R8 **Klintsovka** Saratovskaya Oblast', W Russian Federation
128 H6 **Klintsy** Bryanskaya Oblast', W Russian Federation
95 K22 **Klippan** Skåne, S Sweden
92 G13 **Klippen** Västerbotten, N Sweden
121 P2 **Klírou** W Cyprus
114 I9 **Klisura** Plovdiv, C Bulgaria
95 F20 **Klitmøller** Viborg, NW Denmark
112 F11 **Ključ** Federacija Bosna I Hercegovina, NW Bosnia and Herzegovina
111 J14 **Kłobuck** Śląskie, S Poland
110 J11 **Kłodawa** Wielkopolskie, C Poland
111 G16 **Kłodzko** *Ger.* Glatz. Dolnośląskie, SW Poland
95 I14 **Kløfta** Akershus, S Norway
112 P12 **Klokočevac** Serbia, E Yugoslavia
118 G3 **Klooga** *Ger.* Lodensee. Harjumaa, NW Estonia
99 F15 **Kloosterzande** Zeeland, SW Netherlands
113 L19 **Klos** *var.* Klosi. Dibër, C Albania
Klosi *see* Klos
Klösterle an der Eger *see* Klášterec nad Ohří
109 X3 **Klosterneuburg** Niederösterreich, NE Austria
108 J9 **Klosters** Graubünden, SE Switzerland
108 G7 **Kloten** Zürich, N Switzerland
108 G7 **Kloten** ✕ (Zürich) Zürich, N Switzerland
100 K12 **Klötze** Sachsen-Anhalt, C Germany
12 K3 **Klotz, Lac** ◎ Quebec, NE Canada
101 O15 **Klotzsche** ✕ (Dresden) Sachsen, E Germany
10 H7 **Kluane Lake** ◎ Yukon Territory, W Canada
Kluang *see* Keluang
111 I14 **Kluczbork** *Ger.* Kreuzburg, Kreuzburg in Oberschlesien. Opolskie, S Poland
39 W12 **Klukwan** Alaska, USA
Klyastitsy *see* Klyastsitsy
118 L11 **Klyastsitsy** *Rus.* Klyastitsy. Vitsyebskaya Voblasts', N Belarus
129 T5 **Klyavlino** Samarskaya Oblast', W Russian Federation
84 K9 **Klyaz'in** ∽ W Russian Federation
129 N3 **Klyaz'ma** ∽ W Russian Federation
119 J17 **Klyetsk** *Pol.* Kleck, *Rus.* Kletsk. Minskaya Voblasts', SW Belarus
147 S8 **Klyuchevka** Talasskaya Oblast', NW Kyrgyzstan
123 V10 **Klyuchevskaya Sopka, Vulkan** ☒ E Russian Federation
95 D17 **Knaben** Vest-Agder, S Norway
Knanzi *see* Ghanzi
95 K21 **Knäred** Halland, S Sweden
97 M16 **Knaresborough** N England, UK
114 H8 **Knezha** Vratsa , NW Bulgaria
25 O9 **Knickerbocker** Texas, SW USA
28 K5 **Knife River** ∽ North Dakota, N USA
10 K16 **Knight Inlet** *inlet* British Columbia, W Canada
39 S12 **Knight Island** *island* Alaska, USA
97 K20 **Knighton** E Wales, UK
35 O7 **Knights Landing** California, W USA
112 E13 **Knin** Šibenik-Knin, S Croatia
25 Q12 **Knippal** Texas, SW USA
109 U7 **Knittelfeld** Steiermark, C Austria
95 O15 **Knivsta** Uppsala, C Sweden
113 P14 **Knjaževac** Serbia, E Yugoslavia
27 S4 **Knob Noster** Missouri, C USA
99 D15 **Knokke-Heist** West-Vlaanderen, NW Belgium
95 H20 **Knøsen** *hill* N Denmark
Knosós *see* Knossos
115 J25 **Knossos** *Gk.* Knosós. *prehistoric site* Kríti, Greece, E Mediterranean Sea
25 N7 **Knott** Texas, SW USA
194 K5 **Knowles, Cape** *headland* Antarctica
31 O11 **Knox** Indiana, N USA
29 O3 **Knox** North Dakota, N USA
18 C13 **Knox** Pennsylvania, NE USA
189 X8 **Knox Atoll** *var.* Ņadikdik, Narikrik. *atoll* Ratak Chain, SE Marshall Islands
10 H13 **Knox, Cape** *headland* Graham Island, British Columbia, SW Canada
25 P5 **Knox City** Texas, SW USA
195 Y11 **Knox Coast** *physical region* Antarctica
31 T12 **Knox Lake** ⊞ Ohio, N USA
23 T5 **Knoxville** Georgia, SE USA
30 K12 **Knoxville** Illinois, N USA
29 W15 **Knoxville** Iowa, C USA
21 N9 **Knoxville** Tennessee, S USA
197 P11 **Knud Rasmussen Land** *physical region* N Greenland
Knüll *see* Knüllgebirge
101 I16 **Knüllgebirge** *var.* Knüll. ⛰ C Germany
Knyazhevo *see* Sredishte
Knyazhitsy *see* Knyazhytsy
119 O15 **Knyazhytsy** *Rus.* Knyazhitsy. Mahilyowskaya Voblasts', E Belarus
83 G26 **Knysna** Western Cape, SW South Africa
Koartac *see* Quaqtaq
169 N13 **Koba** Pulau Bangka, W Indonesia
164 D16 **Kobayashi** *var.* Kobayasi. Miyazaki, Kyūshū, SW Japan
Kobayasi *see* Kobayashi
164 I13 **Kōbe** Hyōgo, Honshū, SW Japan
Kobelyaki *see* Kobelyaky
117 T6 **Kobelyaky** *Rus.* Kobelyaki. Poltavs'ka Oblast', NE Ukraine
95 J22 **København** *Eng.* Copenhagen; *anc.* Hafnia. ● (Denmark) Sjælland, København, E Denmark
95 J23 **København** *off.* Københavns Amt. ◈ *county* E Denmark
76 K10 **Kobenni** Hodh el Gharbi, S Mauritania
171 T13 **Kobi** Pulau Seram, E Indonesia
101 F17 **Koblenz** *prev.* Coblenz, *Fr.* Coblence, *anc.* Confluentes. Rheinland-Pfalz, W Germany
108 F6 **Koblenz** Aargau, N Switzerland
Kobrin *see* Kobryn
171 V15 **Kobroor, Pulau** *island* Kepulauan Aru, E Indonesia
119 G19 **Kobryn** *Pol.* Kobryn, *Rus.* Kobrin. Brestskaya Voblasts', SW Belarus
39 O7 **Kobuk** Alaska, USA
39 O7 **Kobuk River** ∽ Alaska, USA
137 Q10 **K'obulet'i** W Georgia
123 P10 **Kobyay** Respublika Sakha (Yakutiya), NE Russian Federation
136 E11 **Kocaeli** ◈ *province* NW Turkey
113 P18 **Kočani** NE FYR Macedonia
112 K12 **Koceljevo** Serbia, W Yugoslavia
109 U12 **Kočevje** *Ger.* Gottschee. S Slovenia
153 T12 **Koch Bihār** West Bengal, NE India
122 M9 **Kochechum** ∽ N Russian Federation
101 I20 **Kocher** ∽ SW Germany
127 T13 **Kochevo** Komi-Permyatskiy Avtonomnyy Okrug, NW Russian Federation
164 G14 **Kōchi** *var.* Kôti. Kōchi, Shikoku, SW Japan
164 G14 **Kōchi** *off.* Kōchi-ken, *var.* Kôti. ◈ *prefecture* Shikoku, SW Japan
Kochi *see* Cochin
Kochiu *see* Gejiu
Kochkor *see* Kochkorka
147 V8 **Kochkorka** *Kir.* Kochkor. Narynskaya Oblast', C Kyrgyzstan
127 V5 **Kochmes** Respublika Komi, NW Russian Federation
129 P15 **Kochubey** Respublika Dagestan, SW Russian Federation
115 I17 **Kochýlas** ▲ Skýros, Vóreioi Sporádes, Greece, Aegean Sea
110 O13 **Kock** Lubelskie, E Poland
81 J19 **Kodacho** *spring/well* S Kenya
155 K24 **Koddiyar Bay** *bay* NE Sri Lanka
39 Q14 **Kodiak** Kodiak Island, Alaska, USA
39 Q14 **Kodiak Island** *island* Alaska, USA
154 B12 **Kodīnār** Gujarāt, W India
126 M9 **Kodino** Arkhangel'skaya Oblast', NW Russian Federation
122 M12 **Kodinsk** Krasnoyarskiy Kray, C Russian Federation
80 F12 **Kodok** Upper Nile, SE Sudan
117 N8 **Kodyma** Odes'ka Oblast', SW Ukraine
99 B17 **Koekelare** West-Vlaanderen, W Belgium
Koeln *see* Köln
Koepang *see* Kupang
Ko-erh-mu *see* Golmud
99 J17 **Koersel** Limburg, NE Belgium
83 E21 **Koës** Karas, SE Namibia
Koetai *see* Mahakam, Sungai
Koetaradja *see* Bandaaceh
36 I14 **Kofa Mountains** ⛰ Arizona, SW USA
171 Y15 **Kofarau** Irian Jaya, E Indonesia
147 P13 **Kofarnihon** *Rus.* Kofarnikhon; *prev.* Ordzhonikidzeabad, *Taj.* Orjonikidzeobod, Yangi-Bazar. W Tajikistan
147 P14 **Kofarnihon** *Rus.* Kafirnigan. ∽ SW Tajikistan
Kofarnikhon *see* Kofarnihon
114 M11 **Kofçaz** Kırklareli, NW Turkey
115 J25 **Kófinas** ▲ Kríti, Greece, E Mediterranean Sea
121 P3 **Kofínou** *var.* Kophinou. S Cyprus
109 V8 **Köflach** Steiermark, SE Austria
77 Q17 **Koforidua** SE Ghana
164 H12 **Kōfu** Tottori, Honshū, SW Japan
164 M13 **Kōfu** *var.* Kôhu. Yamanashi, Honshū, S Japan
81 F22 **Koga** Tabora, C Tanzania
Kogălniceanu *see* Mihail Kogălniceanu
13 P6 **Kogaluk** ∽ Newfoundland, E Canada
12 J4 **Kogaluk** ∽ Quebec, NE Canada
122 I10 **Kogalym** Khanty-Mansiyskiy Avtonomnyy Okrug, C Russian Federation
95 J23 **Køge** Roskilde, E Denmark
95 J23 **Køge Bugt** *bay* E Denmark
77 U16 **Kogi** ◈ *state* C Nigeria
146 L11 **Kogon** *Rus.* Kagan. Bukhoro Wiloyati, C Uzbekistan
163 Y17 **Kŏgŭm-do** *island* S South Korea
Kőhalom *see* Rupea
149 T6 **Kohāt** North-West Frontier Province, NW Pakistan
118 G4 **Kohila** *Ger.* Koil. Raplamaa, NW Estonia
153 X13 **Kohīma** Nāgāland, E India
Koh I Noh *see* Büyükağrı Dağı
142 L10 **Kohkīlūyeh va Būyer Aḩmadī** *off.* Ostān-e Kohklūyeh va Būyer Aḩmadi, *var.* Boyer Ahmadī va Kohkīlūyeh. ◈ *province* SW Iran
Kohsān *see* Kūhestān
118 J3 **Kohtla-Järve** Ida-Virumaa, NE Estonia
Kôhu *see* Kōfu
117 N10 **Kohyl'nyk** *Rom.* Cogîlnic. ∽ Moldova/Ukraine
165 N11 **Koide** Niigata, Honshū, C Japan
10 G7 **Koidern** Yukon Territory, W Canada
76 J15 **Koidu** E Sierra Leone
118 I4 **Koigi** Järvamaa, C Estonia
Koil *see* Kohila
172 H13 **Koimbani** Grande Comore, NW Comoros
139 T3 **Koi Sanjaq** *var.* Koysanjaq, Kūysanjaq. N Iraq
93 O16 **Koitere** ◎ E Finland
Koivisto *see* Primorsk
163 Z16 **Kŏje-do** *Jap.* Kyōsai-tō. *island* S South Korea
80 J13 **K'ok'a Hāyk'** ◎ C Ethiopia
Kokand *see* Qŭqon
182 F6 **Kokatha** South Australia
Kokcha *see* Kŭkcha
Kokchetav *see* Kokshetau
93 K18 **Kokemäenjoki** ∽ SW Finland
171 W14 **Kokenau** *var.* Kokonau. Irian Jaya, E Indonesia
83 E22 **Kokerboom** Karas, SE Namibia
119 N14 **Kokhanava** *Rus.* Kokhanovo. Vitsyebskaya Voblasts', NE Belarus
Kokhanovichi *see* Kakhanavichy
Kokhanovo *see* Kokhanava

◆ Country
● Country Capital
◇ Dependent Territory
○ Dependent Territory Capital
◈ Administrative Region
✕ International Airport
▲ Mountain
⛰ Mountain Range
☒ Volcano
∽ River
◎ Lake
⊞ Reservoir

Kök-Janggak *see* Kok-Yangak
93 *K16* **Kokkola** *Swe.* Karleby; *prev. Swe.* Gamlakarleby. Länsi-Suomi, W Finland
158 *L3* **Kok Kuduk** *well* N China
118 *H9* **Koknese** Aizkraukle, C Latvia
77 *T13* **Koko** Kebbi, W Nigeria
186 *E9* **Kokoda** Northern, S PNG
76 *K12* **Kokofata** Kayes, W Mali
39 *N6* **Kokolik River** ≈ Alaska, USA
31 *O13* **Kokomo** Indiana, N USA
Kokonau *see* Kokenau
Koko Nor *see* Qinghai Hu, China
Koko Nor *see* Qinghai, China
186 *H6* **Kokopo** *var.* Kopopo; *prev.* Herbertshöhe. New Britain, E PNG
145 *X10* **Kokpekti** *Kaz.* Kökpekti. Vostochnyy Kazakhstan, E Kazakhstan
145 *X11* **Kokpekti** ≈ E Kazakhstan
39 *P9* **Kokrines** Alaska, USA
39 *P9* **Kokrines Hills** ▲▲ Alaska, USA
145 *P17* **Koksaray** Yuzhnyy Kazakhstan, S Kazakhstan
147 *X9* **Kokshaal-Tau** *Rus.* Khrebet Kakshaal-Too. ▲▲ China/Kyrgyzstan
145 *P7* **Kokshetau** *Kaz.* Kökshetaū; *prev.* Kokchetav. Severnyy Kazakhstan, N Kazakhstan
99 *A17* **Koksijde** West-Vlaanderen, W Belgium
12 *M5* **Koksoak** ≈ Quebec, E Canada
83 *K24* **Kokstad** KwaZulu/Natal, E South Africa
145 *W15* **Koktal** *Kaz.* Köktal. Almaty, SE Kazakhstan
145 *Q12* **Koktas** ≈ C Kazakhstan
Kök-Tash *see* Këk-Tash
Koktokay *see* Fuyun
147 *T9* **Kok-Yangak** *Kir.* Kök-Janggak. Dzhalal-Abadskaya Oblast', W Kyrgyzstan
158 *F9* **Kokyar** Xinjiang Uygur Zizhiqu, W China
149 *O13* **Kolāchi** *var.* Kulachi. ≈ SW Pakistan
76 *J15* **Kolahun** N Liberia
171 *O14* **Kolaka** Sulawesi, C Indonesia
Kolam *see* Quilon
K'o-la-ma-i *see* Karamay
Kola Peninsula *see* Kol'skiy Poluostrov
155 *H19* **Kolār** Karnātaka, E India
155 *H19* **Kolār Gold Fields** Karnātaka, E India
92 *K11* **Kolari** Lappi, NW Finland
111 *I21* **Kolárovo** *Ger.* Gutta; *prev.* Guta, *Hung.* Gúta. Nitriansky Kraj, SW Slovakia
113 *K16* **Kolašin** Montenegro, SW Yugoslavia
152 *F11* **Kolāyat** Rājasthān, NW India
95 *N15* **Kolbäck** Västmanland, C Sweden
Kolbcha *see* Kowbcha
197 *Q15* **Kolbeinsey Ridge** *undersea feature* Denmark Strait/Norwegian Sea
Kolberg *see* Kołobrzeg
95 *H15* **Kolbotn** Akershus, S Norway
111 *N16* **Kolbuszowa** Podkarpackie, SE Poland
128 *L3* **Kol'chugino** Vladimirskaya Oblast', W Russian Federation
76 *H12* **Kolda** S Senegal
95 *G23* **Kolding** Vejle, C Denmark
79 *M17* **Kole** Orientale, N Dem. Rep. Congo (Zaire)
79 *K20* **Kole** Kasai Oriental, SW Dem. Rep. Congo (Zaire)
Kōle *see* Kili Island
84 *F6* **Kölen** *Nor.* Kjølen. ▲▲ Norway/Sweden
Kolepom, Pulau *see* Yos Sudarso, Pulau
118 *H3* **Kolga Laht** *Ger.* Kolko-Wiek. *bay* N Estonia
127 *Q3* **Kolguyev, Ostrov** *island* NW Russian Federation
155 *E16* **Kolhāpur** Mahārāshtra, SW India
151 *K21* **Kolhumadulu Atoll** *var.* Kolumadulu Atoll, Thaa Atoll. *atoll* S Maldives
93 *O16* **Koli** *var.* Kolinkylä. Itä-Suomi, E Finland
39 *O13* **Koliganek** Alaska, USA
111 *E16* **Kolín** *Ger.* Kolin. Středočeský Kraj, C Czech Republic
Kolinkylä *see* Koli
190 *E12* **Koliu** Île Futuna, W Wallis and Futuna
118 *E7* **Kolka** Talsi, NW Latvia
118 *E7* **Kolkasrags** *prev. Eng.* Cape Domesnes. *headland* NW Latvia
Kolkhozabad *see* Kolkhozobod
147 *P14* **Kolkhozobod** *Rus.* Kolkhozabad; *prev.* Kaganovichabad, Tugalan. SW Tajikistan
Kolki/Kołki *see* Kolky
Kolko-Wiek *see* Kolga Laht
116 *K3* **Kolky** *Pol.* Kołki, *Rus.* Kolki. Volyns'ka Oblast', NW Ukraine
Kollam *see* Quilon
155 *G20* **Kollegāl** Karnātaka, W India
98 *M5* **Kollum** Friesland, N Netherlands
Kolmar *see* Colmar
101 *E16* **Köln** *var.* Koeln, *Eng./Fr.* Cologne; *prev.* Cöln, *anc.* Colonia Agrippina, Oppidum Ubiorum. Nordrhein-Westfalen, W Germany
110 *N9* **Kolno** Podlaskie, NE Poland
110 *J12* **Koło** Wielkopolskie, C Poland
38 *B8* **Koloa** *Haw.* Kōloa. Kauai, Hawaii, USA, C Pacific Ocean
110 *E7* **Kołobrzeg** *Ger.* Kolberg. Zachodniopomorskie, NW Poland
128 *H4* **Kolodnya** Smolenskaya Oblast', W Russian Federation
190 *E13* **Kolofau, Mont** Ж Île Alofi, S Wallis and Futuna
127 *O14* **Kologriv** Kostromskaya Oblast', NW Russian Federation
76 *L12* **Kolokani** Koulikoro, W Mali
77 *N13* **Koloko** W Burkina
186 *K8* **Kolombangara** *var.* Kilimbangara, Nduke. *island* New Georgia Islands, NW Solomon Islands
Kolomea *see* Kolomyya
128 *L4* **Kolomna** Moskovskaya Oblast', W Russian Federation
116 *J7* **Kolomyya** *Ger.* Kolomea. Ivano-Frankivs'ka Oblast', W Ukraine
76 *M13* **Kolondiéba** Sikasso, SW Mali
193 *V15* **Kolonga** Tongatapu, S Tonga
189 *U16* **Kolonia** *var.* Colonia. Pohnpei, E Micronesia
Kolonja *see* Kolonjë
113 *K21* **Kolonjë** *var.* Kolonja. Fier, C Albania
Kolonjë *see* Ersekë
Kolotambu *see* Avuavu
193 *U15* **Kolovai** Tongatapu, S Tonga
Kolozsvár *see* Cluj-Napoca
112 *C9* **Kolpa** *Ger.* Kulpa, *SCr.* Kupa. ≈ Croatia/Slovenia
122 *J11* **Kolpashevo** Tomskaya Oblast', C Russian Federation
126 *H13* **Kolpino** Leningradskaya Oblast', NW Russian Federation
100 *M10* **Kölpinsee** ⊚ NE Germany
126 *K5* **Kol'skiy Poluostrov** *Eng.* Kola Peninsula. *peninsula* NW Russian Federation
129 *T6* **Koltubanovskiy** Orenburgskaya Oblast', W Russian Federation
112 *L11* **Kolubara** ≈ C Yugoslavia
Kolupchii *see* Gurkovo
110 *K13* **Koluszki** Łódzkie, C Poland
127 *T6* **Kolva** ≈ NW Russian Federation
93 *E14* **Kolvereid** Nord-Trøndelag, W Norway
148 *L15* **Kolwa** Baluchistān, SW Pakistan
79 *M24* **Kolwezi** Katanga, S Dem. Rep. Congo (Zaire)
123 *S7* **Kolyma** ≈ NE Russian Federation
Kolyma Lowland *see* Kolymskaya Nizmennost'
Kolyma Range/Kolymskiy, Khrebet *see* Kolymskoye Nagor'ye
123 *S7* **Kolymskaya Nizmennost'** *Eng.* Kolyma Lowland. *lowlands* NE Russian Federation
123 *S7* **Kolymskoye** Respublika Sakha (Yakutiya), NE Russian Federation
123 *U8* **Kolymskoye Nagor'ye** *var.* Khrebet Kolymskiy, *Eng.* Kolyma Range. ▲▲ E Russian Federation
123 *V5* **Kolyuchinskaya Guba** *bay* NE Russian Federation
145 *W15* **Kol'zhat** Almaty, SE Kazakhstan
114 *G8* **Kom** ▲ NW Bulgaria
80 *I13* **Koma** Oromo, C Ethiopia
77 *X12* **Komadugu Gana** ≈ NE Nigeria
164 *M13* **Komagane** Nagano, Honshū, S Japan
79 *P17* **Komanda** Orientale, NE Dem. Rep. Congo (Zaire)
197 *U1* **Komandorskaya Basin** *var.* Kamchatka Basin. *undersea feature* SW Bering Sea
127 *Pp9* **Komandorskiye Ostrova** *Eng.* Commander Islands. *island group* E Russian Federation
Kománfalva *see* Comănești
111 *I22* **Komárno** *Ger.* Komorn, *Hung.* Komárom. Nitriansky Kraj, SW Slovakia
111 *I22* **Komárom** Komárom-Esztergom, NW Hungary
Komárom *see* Komárno
111 *I22* **Komárom-Esztergom** *off.* Komárom-Esztergom Megye. ◈ *county* N Hungary
164 *K11* **Komatsu** *var.* Komatu. Ishikawa, Honshū, SW Japan
Komatu *see* Komatsu
83 *D17* **Kombat** Otjozondjupa, N Namibia
Kombissiguiri *see* Kombissiri
77 *P13* **Kombissiri** *var.* Kombissiguiri. C Burkina
188 *E10* **Komebail Lagoon** *lagoon* N Palau
81 *F20* **Kome Island** *island* N Tanzania
Komeyo *see* Wandai
117 *P10* **Kominternivs'ke** Odes'ka Oblast', SW Ukraine
127 *R12* **Komi-Permyatskiy Avtonomnyy Okrug** ◈ *autonomous district* W Russian Federation
127 *R8* **Komi, Respublika** ◈ *autonomous republic* NW Russian Federation
111 *I25* **Komló** Baranya, SW Hungary
Kommunarsk *see* Alchevs'k
147 *S12* **Kommunizm, Qullai** ▲ E Tajikistan
186 *B7* **Komo** Southern Highlands, W PNG
170 *M16* **Komodo, Pulau** *island* Nusa Tenggara, S Indonesia
77 *N15* **Komoé** *var.* Komoé Fleuve. ≈ E Ivory Coast
Komoé Fleuve *see* Komoé
75 *X11* **Kôm Ombo** *var.* Kawm Umbū. SE Egypt
79 *F20* **Komono** La Lékoumou, SW Congo
171 *Y16* **Komoran** Irian Jaya, E Indonesia
171 *Y16* **Komoran, Pulau** *island* E Indonesia
Komorn *see* Komárno
Komornok *see* Comorâște
Komosolabad *see* Komsomolobod
Komotau *see* Chomutov
114 *K13* **Komotiní** *var.* Gümüljina, *Turk.* Gümülcine. Anatolikí Makedonía kai Thráki, NE Greece
113 *K16* **Komovi** ▲▲ SW Yugoslavia
117 *R8* **Kompaniyivka** Kirovohrads'ka Oblast', C Ukraine
Kompong *see* Kâmpóng Chhnăng
Kompong Cham *see* Kâmpóng Cham
Kompong Kleang *see* Kâmpóng Khleăng
Kompong Som *see* Kâmpóng Saôm
Kompong Speu *see* Kâmpóng Spoe
Komrat *see* Comrat
Komsomol *see* Komsomol'skiy, Atyrau, Kazakhstan
Komsomol *see* Komsomolets, Kostanay, Kazakhstan
144 *L7* **Komsomolets** *Kaz.* Komsomol. Kostanay, N Kazakhstan
122 *K14* **Komsomolets, Ostrov** *island* Severnaya Zemlya, N Russian Federation
144 *F13* **Komsomolets, Zaliv** *lake gulf* SW Kazakhstan
147 *Q12* **Komsomolobod** *Rus.* Komosolabad. C Tajikistan
126 *M16* **Komsomol'sk** Ivanovskaya Oblast', W Russian Federation
117 *S6* **Komsomol's'k** Poltavs'ka Oblast', C Ukraine
146 *M11* **Komsomol'sk** Nawoiy Wiloyati, N Uzbekistan
144 *G12* **Komsomol'skiy** *Kaz.* Komsomol. Atyrau, W Kazakhstan
127 *W4* **Komsomol'skiy** Respublika Komi, NW Russian Federation
123 *S13* **Komsomol'sk-na-Amure** Khabarovskiy Kray, SE Russian Federation
Komsomol'sk-na-Ustyurte *see* Komsomol'sk-Ustyurt
144 *K10* **Komsomol'skoye** Aktyubinsk, NW Kazakhstan
129 *Q8* **Komsomol'skoye** Saratovskaya Oblast', W Russian Federation
146 *G6* **Komsomol'sk-Ustyurt** *Rus.* Komsomol'sk-na-Ustyurte. Qoraqalpoghiston Respublikasi, NW Uzbekistan
145 *P10* **Kon** ≈ C Kazakhstan
Kona *see* Kailua
126 *K16* **Konakovo** Tverskaya Oblast', W Russian Federation
143 *V15* **Konārak** Sīstān va Balūchestān, SE Iran
Konarhā *see* Kunar
27 *O11* **Konawa** Oklahoma, C USA
122 *H10* **Konda** ≈ C Russian Federation
154 *L13* **Kondagaon** Madhya Pradesh, C India
14 *K10* **Kondiaronk, Lac** ⊚ Quebec, SE Canada
180 *J13* **Kondinin** Western Australia
81 *H21* **Kondoa** Dodoma, C Tanzania
129 *P6* **Kondol'** Penzenskaya Oblast', W Russian Federation
114 *N10* **Kondolovo** Burgas, E Bulgaria
171 *Z16* **Kondomirat** Irian Jaya, E Indonesia
126 *J10* **Kondopoga** Respublika Kareliya, NW Russian Federation
Kondoz *see* Kunduz
155 *J17* **Kondukūr** *var.* Kandukur. Andhra Pradesh, E India
Kondūz *see* Kunduz
187 *P16* **Koné** Province Nord, W New Caledonia
Könekesir *see* Kënekesir
Köneürgench *see* Këneurgench
77 *N15* **Kong** N Ivory Coast
39 *S5* **Kongakut River** ≈ Alaska, USA
197 *O14* **Kong Christian IX Land** *Eng.* King Christian IX Land. *physical region* SE Greenland
197 *P13* **Kong Christian X Land** *Eng.* King Christian X Land. *physical region* E Greenland
197 *N13* **Kong Frederik IX Land** *Eng.* King Frederik IX Land. *physical region* SW Greenland
197 *Q12* **Kong Frederik VIII Land** *Eng.* King Frederik VIII Land. *physical region* NE Greenland
197 *N15* **Kong Frederik VI Kyst** *Eng.* King Frederik VI Coast. *physical region* SE Greenland
167 *P13* **Kông, Kaôh** *prev.* Kas Kong. *island* SW Cambodia
92 *P2* **Kong Karls Land** *Eng.* King Charles Islands. *island group* SE Svalbard
81 *G14* **Kong Kong** ≈ SE Sudan
Kongo *see* Congo (river)
83 *G16* **Kongola** Caprivi, NE Namibia
79 *N21* **Kongolo** Katanga, E Dem. Rep. Congo (Zaire)
81 *F14* **Kongor** Jonglei, SE Sudan
197 *Q14* **Kong Oscar Fjord** *fjord* E Greenland
77 *P12* **Kongoussi** N Burkina
95 *G15* **Kongsberg** Buskerud, S Norway
92 *Q2* **Kongsøya** *island* Kong Karls Land, E Svalbard
95 *I14* **Kongsvinger** Hedmark, S Norway
167 *T11* **Kông, Tônle** *Lao.* Xê Kong. ≈ Cambodia/Laos
158 *E8* **Kongur Shan** ▲ NW China
81 *I22* **Kongwa** Dodoma, C Tanzania
Kong, Xê *see* Kông, Tônle
Konia *see* Konya
147 *R11* **Konibodom** *Rus.* Kanibadam. N Tajikistan
111 *K15* **Koniecpol** Śląskie, S Poland
Konieh *see* Konya
Königgrätz *see* Hradec Králové
Königinhof an der Elbe *see* Dvůr Králové nad Labem
101 *K23* **Königsbrunn** Bayern, S Germany
Königshütte *see* Chorzów
101 *O24* **Königssee** ⊚ SE Germany
109 *S8* **Königstuhl** ▲ S Austria
109 *U3* **Königswiesen** Oberösterreich, N Austria
101 *E17* **Königswinter** Nordrhein-Westfalen, W Germany
146 *M11* **Konimekh** *Rus.* Kenimekh. Nawoiy Wiloyati, N Uzbekistan
110 *I12* **Konin** *Ger.* Kuhnau. Wielkopolskie, C Poland
Koninkrijk der Nederlanden *see* Netherlands
113 *L24* **Konispol** *var.* Konispoli. Vlorë, S Albania
Konispoli *see* Konispol
115 *C15* **Kónitsa** Ípeiros, W Greece
Konitz *see* Chojnice
108 *D8* **Köniz** Bern, W Switzerland
113 *H14* **Konjic** Federacija Bosna I Hercegovina, C Bosnia and Herzegovina
92 *J10* **Könkämäälven** ≈ Finland/Sweden
155 *D14* **Konkan** W India
83 *D22* **Konkiep** ≈ S Namibia
76 *I14* **Konkouré** ≈ W Guinea
77 *O11* **Konna** Mopti, S Mali
186 *H6* **Konogaiang, Mount** ▲ New Ireland, NE PNG
186 *H5* **Konogogo** New Ireland, NE PNG
108 *E9* **Konolfingen** Bern, W Switzerland
77 *P16* **Konongo** C Ghana
186 *H5* **Konos** New Ireland, NE PNG
126 *M12* **Konosha** Arkhangel'skaya Oblast', NW Russian Federation
117 *R3* **Konotop** Sums'ka Oblast', NE Ukraine
158 *L7* **Konqi He** ≈ NW China
111 *L14* **Końskie** Świętokrzyskie, C Poland
Konstantinovka *see* Kostyantynivka
128 *M11* **Konstantinovsk** Rostovskaya Oblast', SW Russian Federation
101 *H24* **Konstanz** *var.* Constanz, *Eng.* Constance; *hist.* Kostnitz, *anc.* Constantia. Baden-Württemberg, S Germany
Konstanza *see* Constanța
77 *T14* **Kontagora** Niger, W Nigeria
78 *E13* **Kontcha** Nord, N Cameroon
99 *G17* **Kontich** Antwerpen, N Belgium
93 *O16* **Kontiolahti** Itä-Suomi, E Finland
93 *M15* **Kontiomäki** Oulu, C Finland
167 *U11* **Kon Tum** *var.* Kontum. Kon Tum, C Vietnam
Konur *see* Sulakyurt
136 *H15* **Konya** *var.* Konieh; *prev.* Konia, *anc.* Iconium. Konya, C Turkey
136 *H15* **Konya** *var.* Konia, Konieh. ◈ *province* C Turkey
145 *T13* **Konyrat** *var.* Kounradskiy, *Kaz.* Qongyrat. Karaganda, C Kazakhstan
145 *W15* **Konyrolen** Almaty, SE Kazakhstan
81 *I19* **Konza** Eastern, S Kenya
98 *I9* **Koog aan den Zaan** Noord-Holland, C Netherlands
182 *E7* **Koonibba** South Australia
31 *O11* **Koontz Lake** Indiana, N USA
171 *U12* **Koor** Irian Jaya, E Indonesia
183 *R9* **Koorawatha** New South Wales, SE Australia
118 *J5* **Koosa** Tartumaa, E Estonia
33 *N7* **Kootenai** *var.* Kootenay. ≈ Canada/USA *see also* Kootenay
11 *P17* **Kootenay** *var.* Kootenai. ≈ Canada/USA *see also* Kootenai
83 *F24* **Kootjieskolk** Northern Cape, W South Africa
113 *M15* **Kopaonik** ▲▲ S Yugoslavia
Kopar *see* Koper
92 *K1* **Kópasker** Nordhurland Eystra, N Iceland
92 *H4* **Kópavogur** Reykjanes, W Iceland
109 *S13* **Koper** *It.* Capodistria; *prev.* Kopar. SW Slovenia
95 *C16* **Kopervik** Rogaland, S Norway
Kopetdag, Khrebet *see* Koppeh Dāgh
Kophinou *see* Kofínou
182 *G8* **Kopi** South Australia
Kopiago *see* Lake Copiago
153 *W12* **Kopili** ≈ NE India
95 *M15* **Köping** Västmanland, C Sweden
113 *K17* **Koplik** *var.* Kopliku. Shkodër, NW Albania
Kopliku *see* Koplik
Kopopo *see* Kokopo
94 *I11* **Koppang** Hedmark, S Norway
Kopparberg *see* Dalarna
143 *S3* **Koppeh Dāgh** *var.* Khrebet Kopetdag. ▲▲ Iran/Turkmenistan
Koppename *see* Coppename Rivier
95 *J15* **Koppom** Värmland, C Sweden
Kopreinitz *see* Koprivnica
114 *K9* **Koprinka, Yazovir** *prev.* Yazovir Georgi Dimitrov. ⊞ C Bulgaria
112 *F7* **Koprivnica** *Ger.* Kopreinitz, *Hung.* Kaproncza. Koprivnica-Križevci, N Croatia
112 *F8* **Koprivnica-Križevci** *off.* Koprivničko-Križevačka Županija. ◈ *province* N Croatia
111 *I17* **Kopřivnice** *Ger.* Nesselsdorf. Ostravský Kraj, E Czech Republic
Köprülü *see* Veles
Koptsevichi *see* Kaptsevichy
Kopyl' *see* Kapyl'
119 *O14* **Kopys'** *Rus.* Kopys'. Vitsyebskaya Voblasts', NE Belarus
113 *M18* **Korab** ▲ Albania/FYR Macedonia
Korabavur Pastligi *see* Karabaur', Uval
81 *M14* **K'orahē** Somali, E Ethiopia
115 *L16* **Kórakas, Akrotírio** *headland* Lésvos, E Greece
112 *D9* **Korana** ≈ C Croatia
155 *L14* **Korāput** Orissa, E India
Korat *see* Nakhon Ratchasima
167 *Q9* **Korat Plateau** *plateau* E Thailand
139 *T1* **Korāwa, Sar-i** ▲ NE Iraq
154 *L11* **Korba** Madhya Pradesh, C India
101 *H15* **Korbach** Hessen, C Germany
Korça *see* Korçë
113 *M21* **Korçë** *var.* Korça, *Gk.* Korytsa, *It.* Corriza; *prev.* Koritsa. Korçë, SE Albania
113 *M21* **Korçë** ◈ *district* SE Albania
113 *G15* **Korčula** *It.* Curzola. Dubrovnik-Neretva, S Croatia
113 *F15* **Korčula** *It.* Curzola; *anc.* Corcyra Nigra. *island* S Croatia
113 *F15* **Korčulanski Kanal** *channel* S Croatia
145 *T6* **Korday** *prev.* Georgiyevka. Zhambyl, SE Kazakhstan
142 *J5* **Kordestān** *off.* Ostān-e Kordestān, *var.* Kurdestan. ◈ *province* W Iran
143 *P4* **Kord Kūy** *var.* Kurd Kui. Golestān, N Iran
163 *V13* **Korea Bay** *bay* China/North Korea
Korea, Democratic People's Republic of *see* North Korea
171 *T15* **Koreare** Pulau Yamdena, E Indonesia
Korea, Republic of *see* South Korea
163 *Z17* **Korea Strait** *Jap.* Chōsen-kaikyō, *Kor.* Taehan-haehyŏp. *channel* Japan/South Korea
Korelichi/Korelicze *see* Karelichy
80 *J11* **Korem** Tigray, N Ethiopia
77 *U11* **Korén Adoua** ≈ C Niger
128 *I7* **Korenevo** Kurskaya Oblast', W Russian Federation
128 *L13* **Korenovsk** Krasnodarskiy Kray, SW Russian Federation
116 *L4* **Korets'** *Pol.* Korzec, *Rus.* Korets. Rivnens'ka Oblast', NW Ukraine
194 *L7* **Korff Ice Rise** *ice cap* Antarctica
92 *G13* **Korgen** Troms, N Norway
147 *R9* **Korgon-Dëbë** Dzhalal-Abadskaya Oblast', W Kyrgyzstan
76 *M14* **Korhogo** N Ivory Coast
115 *F19* **Korinthiakós Kólpos** *Eng.* Gulf of Corinth; *anc.* Corinthiacus Sinus. *gulf* C Greece
115 *F19* **Kórinthos** *Eng.* Corinth; *anc.* Corinthus. Pelopónnisos, S Greece
113 *M18* **Koritnik** ▲ S Yugoslavia
Koritsa *see* Korçë
165 *P11* **Kōriyama** Fukushima, Honshū, C Japan
136 *E16* **Korkuteli** Antalya, SW Turkey
158 *K6* **Korla** *Chin.* K'u-erh-lo. Xinjiang Uygur Zizhiqu, NW China
122 *J10* **Korliki** Khanty-Mansiyskiy Avtonomnyy Okrug, C Russian Federation
Körlin an der Persante *see* Karlino
Korma *see* Karma
14 *D8* **Kormak** Ontario, S Canada
Kormakíti, Akrotíri/Kormakíti, Cape/Kormakítis *see* Koruçam Burnu
111 *G23* **Körmend** Vas, W Hungary
139 *T5* **Kōrmōr** E Iraq
112 *C13* **Kornat** *It.* Incoronata. *island* W Croatia
Korneshty *see* Cornești
109 *X3* **Korneuburg** Niederösterreich, NE Austria
145 *P7* **Korneyevka** Severnyy Kazakhstan, N Kazakhstan
95 *I17* **Kornsjø** Østfold, S Norway
77 *O11* **Koro** Mopti, S Mali
187 *Y14* **Koro** *island* C Fiji
186 *B7* **Koroba** Southern Highlands, W PNG
128 *K8* **Korocha** Belgorodskaya Oblast', W Russian Federation
136 *H12* **Köroğlu Dağları** ▲▲ C Turkey
183 *V6* **Korogoro Point** *headland* New South Wales, SE Australia
81 *J21* **Korogwe** Tanga, E Tanzania
182 *L13* **Koroit** Victoria, SE Australia
187 *X15* **Korolevu** Viti Levu, W Fiji
190 *I17* **Koromiri** *island* S Cook Islands
171 *Q8* **Koronadal** Mindanao, S Philippines
115 *E22* **Koróni** Pelopónnisos, S Greece
114 *G13* **Korónia, Límni** ⊚ N Greece
110 *I9* **Koronowo** *Ger.* Krone an der Brahe. Kujawski-pomorskie, C Poland
117 *R2* **Korop** Chernihivs'ka Oblast', N Ukraine
115 *H19* **Koropí** Attikí, C Greece
Koror *see* Oreor
Körös *see* Križevci
111 *L23* **Körös** ≈ E Hungary
Körösbánya *see* Baia de Criș
187 *Y14* **Koro Sea** *sea* C Fiji
Koroška *see* Kärnten
117 *N3* **Korosten'** Zhytomyrs'ka Oblast', NW Ukraine
Korostyshev *see* Korostyshiv
117 *N4* **Korostyshiv** *Rus.* Korostyshev. Zhytomyrs'ka Oblast', N Ukraine
127 *V3* **Korotaikha** ≈ NW Russian Federation
122 *J9* **Korotchayevo** Yamalo-Nenetskiy Avtonomnyy Okrug, N Russian Federation
78 *I8* **Koro Toro** Borkou-Ennedi-Tibesti, N Chad
39 *N16* **Korovin Island** *island* Shumagin Islands, Alaska, USA
187 *X14* **Korovou** Viti Levu, W Fiji
93 *M17* **Korpilahti** Länsi-Suomi, W Finland
92 *K12* **Korpilombolo** Norrbotten, N Sweden
123 *T13* **Korsakov** Ostrov Sakhalin, Sakhalinskaya Oblast', SE Russian Federation
93 *J16* **Korsholm** *Fin.* Mustasaari. Länsi-Suomi, W Finland
95 *I23* **Korsør** Vestsjælland, E Denmark
Korsovka *see* Kārsava
117 *P6* **Korsun'-Shevchenkivs'kyy** *Rus.* Korsun'-Shevchenkovskiy. Cherkas'ka Oblast', C Ukraine
Korsun'-Shevchenkovskiy *see* Korsun'-Shevchenkivs'kyy
99 *C17* **Kortemark** West-Vlaanderen, W Belgium
99 *H18* **Kortenberg** Vlaams Brabant, C Belgium
99 *K18* **Kortessem** Limburg, NE Belgium
99 *E14* **Kortgene** Zeeland, SW Netherlands
80 *F8* **Korti** Northern, N Sudan
99 *C18* **Kortrijk** *Fr.* Courtrai. West-Vlaanderen, W Belgium
121 *O2* **Koruçam Burnu** *var.* Cape Kormakiti, Kormakítis, *Gk.* Akrotíri Kormakíti. *headland* N Cyprus
183 *O13* **Korumburra** Victoria, SE Australia
Koryak Range *see* Koryakskoye Nagor'ye
123 *V8* **Koryakskiy Avtonomnyy Okrug** ◈ *autonomous district* E Russian Federation
Koryakskiy Khrebet *see* Koryakskoye Nagor'ye
123 *V7* **Koryakskoye Nagor'ye** *var.* Koryakskiy Khrebet, *Eng.* Koryak Range. ▲▲ NE Russian Federation
127 *P11* **Koryazhma** Arkhangel'skaya Oblast', NW Russian Federation
Koryŏ *see* Kangnŭng
Korytsa *see* Korçë
117 *Q2* **Koryukivka** Chernihivs'ka Oblast', N Ukraine
Korzec *see* Korets'
115 *N21* **Kos** Kos, Dodekánisos, Greece, Aegean Sea
115 *M21* **Kos** *It.* Coo; *anc.* Cos. *island* Dodekánisos, Greece, Aegean Sea
127 *T12* **Kosa** Komi-Permyatskiy Avtonomnyy Okrug, NW Russian Federation
127 *T13* **Kosa** ≈ NW Russian Federation
164 *B12* **Kō-saki** *headland* Nagasaki, Tsushima, SW Japan
163 *X13* **Kosan** SE North Korea
119 *H18* **Kosava** *Rus.* Kosovo. Brestskaya Voblasts', SW Belarus
Kosch *see* Kose
144 *G12* **Koschagyl** *Kaz.* Qosshaghyl. Atyrau, W Kazakhstan
110 *G12* **Kościan** *Ger.* Kosten. Wielkopolskie, C Poland
110 *I7* **Kościerzyna** Pomorskie, NW Poland
22 *L4* **Kosciusko** Mississippi, S USA
Kosciusko, Mount *see* Kosciuszko, Mount
183 *R11* **Kosciuszko, Mount** *prev.* Mount Kosciusko ▲ New South Wales, SE Australia
118 *H4* **Kose** *Ger.* Kosch. Harjumaa, NW Estonia
114 *G6* **Koshava** Vidin, NW Bulgaria
147 *U9* **Kosh-Dëbë** *var.* Koshtebë. Narynskaya Oblast', C Kyrgyzstan
K'o-shih *see* Kashi
164 *B16* **Koshikijima-rettō** *var.* Kosikizima Rettô. *island group* SW Japan
145 *W13* **Koshkarkol', Ozero** ⊚ SE Kazakhstan
30 *L9* **Koshkonong, Lake** ⊚ Wisconsin, N USA
146 *B10* **Koshoba** *Turkm.* Goshoba. Balkanskiy Velayat, NW Turkmenistan
164 *M12* **Kōshoku** *var.* Kôsyoku. Nagano, Honshū, S Japan
Koshtebë *see* Kosh-Dëbë
Kōshū *see* Kwangju
111 *N19* **Košice** *Ger.* Kaschau, *Hung.* Kassa. Košický Kraj, E Slovakia
111 *M20* **Košický Kraj** ◈ *region* E Slovakia
Kosigaya *see* Koshigaya
Kosikizima Rettô *see* Koshikijima-retto
153 *R12* **Kosi Reservoir** ⊞ E Nepal
116 *J8* **Kosiv** Ivano-Frankivs'ka Oblast', W Ukraine
145 *O11* **Koskol'** Zhezkazgan, C Kazakhstan
127 *Q9* **Koslan** Respublika Komi, NW Russian Federation
Köslin *see* Koszalin
146 *M12* **Koson** *Rus.* Kasan. Qashqadaryo Wiloyati, S Uzbekistan
163 *Y13* **Kosŏng** SE North Korea
147 *S9* **Kosonsoy** *Rus.* Kasansay. Namangan Wiloyati, E Uzbekistan
113 *M16* **Kosovo** *prev.* Autonomous Province of Kosovo and Metohija. *region* S Yugoslavia
Kosovo *see* Kosava
Kosovo and Metohija, Autonomous Province of *see* Kosovo
113 *N16* **Kosovo Polje** Serbia, S Yugoslavia
113 *O16* **Kosovska Kamenica** Serbia, SE Yugoslavia
113 *M16* **Kosovska Mitrovica** *Alb.* Mitrovicë; *prev.* Mitrovica, Titova Mitrovica. Serbia, S Yugoslavia

◆ Country ◇ Dependent Territory ◈ Administrative Region ▲ Mountain Ж Volcano ⊚ Lake
● Country Capital ○ Dependent Territory Capital ✈ International Airport ▲▲ Mountain Range ≈ River ⊞ Reservoir

189 X17 **Kosrae** ◆ *state* E Micronesia
189 Y14 **Kosrae** *prev.* Kusaie. *island* Caroline Islands, E Micronesia
25 U9 **Kosse** Texas, SW USA
109 P6 **Kössen** Tirol, W Austria
76 M16 **Kossou, Lac de** ◎ C Ivory Coast
Kossukavak *see* Krumovgrad
Kostajnica *see* Hrvatska Kostajnica
150 M7 **Kostanay** *var.* Kustanay, *Kaz.* Qostanay. N Kazakhstan
150 L8 **Kostanay** *var.* Kostanayskaya Oblast, *Kaz.* Qostanay Oblysy. ◆ *province* N Kazakhstan
Kostanayskaya Oblast *see* Kostanay
Kostamus *see* Kostomuksha
Kosten *see* Kościan
114 H10 **Kostenets** *prev.* Georgi Dimitrov. Sofiya, W Bulgaria
80 F10 **Kosti** White Nile, C Sudan
Kostnitz *see* Konstanz
126 H7 **Kostomuksha** *Fin.* Kostamus. Respublika Kareliya, NW Russian Federation
116 K3 **Kostopil'** *Rus.* Kostopol'. Rivnens'ka Oblast', NW Ukraine
Kostopol' *see* Kostopil'
126 M15 **Kostroma** Kostromskaya Oblast', NW Russian Federation
127 N14 **Kostroma** ∾ NW Russian Federation
127 N14 **Kostromskaya Oblast'** ◆ *province* NW Russian Federation
110 D11 **Kostrzyn** *Ger.* Cüstrin, Küstrin. Lubuskie, W Poland
110 H11 **Kostrzyn** Wielkolpolskie, C Poland
117 X7 **Kostyantynivka** *Rus.* Konstantinovka. Donets'ka Oblast', SE Ukraine
Kostyukovichi *see* Kastsyukovichy
Kostyukovka *see* Kastsyukowka
Kôsyoku *see* Kôshoku
127 U6 **Kos'yu** Respublika Komi, NW Russian Federation
127 U6 **Kos'yu** ∾ NW Russian Federation
110 F7 **Koszalin** *Ger.* Köslin. Koszalin, NW Poland
111 F22 **Kőszeg** *Ger.* Güns. Vas, W Hungary
152 H13 **Kota** *prev.* Kotah. Rājasthān, N India
168 K12 **Kota Baru** Sumatera, W Indonesia
169 U13 **Kotabaru** Pulau Laut, C Indonesia
Kotabaru *see* Jayapura
168 K6 **Kota Bharu** *var.* Kota Baharu, Kota Bahru. Kelantan, Peninsular Malaysia
Kotaboemi *see* Kotabumi
168 M14 **Kotabumi** *prev.* Kotaboemi. Sumatera, W Indonesia
149 S10 **Kot Addu** Punjab, E Pakistan
Kotah *see* Kota
169 U7 **Kota Kinabalu** *prev.* Jesselton. Sabah, East Malaysia
169 U7 **Kota Kinabalu** ✕ Sabah, East Malaysia
92 M12 **Kotala** Lappi, N Finland
Kotamobagoe *see* Kotamobagu
171 Q11 **Kotamobagu** *prev.* Kotamobagoe. Sulawesi, C Indonesia
155 L14 **Kotapad** *var.* Kotapārh. Orissa, E India
Kotapārh *see* Kotapad
166 N17 **Ko Ta Ru Tao** *island* SW Thailand
169 R13 **Kotawaringin, Teluk** *bay* Borneo, C Indonesia
149 Q13 **Kot Dīji** Sind, SE Pakistan
152 K9 **Kotdwāra** Uttar Pradesh, N India
127 Q14 **Kotel'nich** Kirovskaya Oblast', NW Russian Federation
129 N12 **Kotel'nikovo** Volgogradskaya Oblast', SW Russian Federation
123 Q6 **Kotel'nyy, Ostrov** *island* Novosibirskiye Ostrova, N Russian Federation
117 T5 **Kotel'va** Poltavs'ka Oblast', C Ukraine
101 M14 **Köthen** *var.* Cöthen. Sachsen-Anhalt, C Germany
Kôti *see* Kôchi
81 G17 **Kotido** NE Uganda
93 N19 **Kotka** Etelä-Suomi, S Finland
127 P11 **Kotlas** Arkhangel'skaya Oblast', NW Russian Federation
38 M10 **Kotlik** Alaska, USA
77 Q17 **Kotoka** ✕ (Accra) S Ghana
Kotonu *see* Cotonou
113 J17 **Kotor** *It.* Cattaro. Montenegro, SW Yugoslavia
Kotor *see* Kotoriba
112 F7 **Kotoriba** *Hung.* Kotor. Medimurje, N Croatia
113 I17 **Kotorska, Boka** *It.* Bocche di Cattaro. *bay* Montenegro, SW Yugoslavia
112 H11 **Kotorsko** Republika Srpska, N Bosnia and Herzegovina
112 G11 **Kotor Varoš** Republika Srpska, N Bosnia and Herzegovina
Koto Sho/Kotosho *see* Lan Yü
128 M7 **Kotovsk** Tambovskaya Oblast', W Russian Federation
117 O9 **Kotovs'k** *Rus.* Kotovsk. Odes'ka Oblast', SW Ukraine
Kotovsk *see* Hînceşti
119 G16 **Kotra** *Rus.* Kotra. ∾ W Belarus
149 P16 **Kotri** Sind, SE Pakistan
109 Q9 **Kötschach** Kärnten, S Austria
155 K15 **Kottagūdem** Andhra Pradesh, E India
155 F21 **Kottappadi** Kerala, SW India
155 G23 **Kottayam** Kerala, SW India
Kottbus *see* Cottbus
Kotte *see* Sri Jayawardanapura
79 K15 **Kotto** ∾ Central African Republic/Dem. Rep. Congo (Zaire)
193 X15 **Kotu Group** *island group* W Tonga
146 B11 **Koturdepe** *Turkm.* Goturdepe. Balkanskiy Velayat, W Turkmenistan
122 M9 **Kotuy** ∾ N Russian Federation
83 M16 **Kotwa** Mashonaland East, NE Zimbabwe
39 N7 **Kotzebue** Alaska, USA
38 M7 **Kotzebue Sound** *inlet* Alaska, USA
Kotzenan *see* Chocianów
Kotzman *see* Kitsman'
77 R14 **Kouandé** NW Benin
79 J15 **Kouango** Ouaka, S Central African Republic
77 O13 **Koudougou** C Burkina
98 K7 **Koudum** Friesland, N Netherlands
115 L25 **Koufonísi** *island* SE Greece
115 K21 **Koufonísi** *island* Kykládes, Greece, Aegean Sea
38 M8 **Kougarok Mountain** ▲ Alaska, USA
79 E20 **Kouilou** ∾ S Congo
121 O3 **Koúklia** SW Cyprus
79 E19 **Koulamoutou** Ogooué-Lolo, C Gabon
76 L12 **Koulikoro** Koulikoro, SW Mali
76 L11 **Koulikoro** ◆ *region* SW Mali
187 P16 **Koumac** Province Nord, W New Caledonia
165 N12 **Koumi** Nagano, Honshū, S Japan
78 I13 **Koumra** Moyen-Chari, S Chad
Kounadougou *see* Koundougou
76 M15 **Kounahiri** C Ivory Coast
76 I12 **Koundâra** Moyenne-Guinée, NW Guinea
77 N13 **Koundougou** *var.* Kounadougou. C Burkina
76 H11 **Koungheul** C Senegal
Kounradskiy *see* Konyrat
25 X10 **Kountze** Texas, SW USA
77 Q13 **Koupéla** C Burkina
77 N13 **Kouri** Sikasso, SW Mali
55 Y9 **Kourou** N French Guiana
114 J12 **Kouroú** ∾ NE Greece
76 K14 **Kouroussa** Haute-Guinée, C Guinea
Kousseir *see* Al Quşayr
78 G11 **Kousséri** *prev.* Fort-Foureau. Extrême-Nord, NE Cameroon
Kouteifé *see* Al Quţayfah
76 M13 **Koutiala** Sikasso, S Mali
76 M14 **Kouto** NW Ivory Coast
93 M19 **Kouvola** Etelä-Suomi, S Finland
79 G18 **Kouyou** ∾ C Congo
112 M10 **Kovačica** *Hung.* Antafalva; *prev.* Kovacsicza. Serbia, N Yugoslavia
Kovacsicza *see* Kovačica
Kővárhosszúfalu *see* Satulung
Kovászna *see* Covasna
126 I4 **Kovdor** Murmanskaya Oblast', NW Russian Federation
126 I5 **Kovdozero, Ozero** ◎ NW Russian Federation
116 J3 **Kovel'** *Pol.* Kowel. Volyns'ka Oblast', NW Ukraine
112 M11 **Kovin** *Hung.* Keveváre; *prev.* Temes-Kubin. Serbia, NE Yugoslavia
Kovno *see* Kaunas
129 N3 **Kovrov** Vladimirskaya Oblast', W Russian Federation
129 O5 **Kovylkino** Respublika Mordoviya, W Russian Federation
110 J11 **Kowal** Kujawsko-pomorskie, C Poland
110 J9 **Kowalewo Pomorskie** *Ger.* Schönsee. Kujawsko-pomorskie, C Poland
Kowasna *see* Covasna
119 M16 **Kowbcha** *Rus.* Kolbcha. Mahilyowskaya Voblasts', E Belarus
Koweit *see* Kuwait
Kowel *see* Kovel'
185 F17 **Kowhitirangi** West Coast, South Island, NZ
161 O15 **Kowloon** *Chin.* Jiulong. Hong Kong, S China
Kowno *see* Kaunas
159 N7 **Kox Kuduk** *well* NW China
136 D16 **Köyceğiz** Muğla, SW Turkey
127 N6 **Koyda** Arkhangel'skaya Oblast', NW Russian Federation
146 D10 **Koymat** *Turkm.* Goymat. Balkanskiy Velayat, NW Turkmenistan
146 D10 **Koymatdag, Gory** *Turkm.* Goymatdag. *hill range* NW Turkmenistan
Koyna Reservoir *see* Shivāji Sāgar
165 P9 **Koyoshi-gawa** ∾ Honshū, C Japan
Koysanjaq *see* Koi Sanjaq
Koytash *see* Qŭytosh
39 N9 **Koyuk** Alaska, USA
39 N9 **Koyuk River** ∾ Alaska, USA
39 O9 **Koyukuk** Alaska, USA
39 O9 **Koyukuk River** ∾ Alaska, USA
136 J13 **Kozaklı** Nevşehir, C Turkey
136 K16 **Kozan** Adana, S Turkey
115 E14 **Kozáni** Dytikí Makedonía, N Greece
112 F10 **Kozara** ▲ NW Bosnia and Herzegovina
Kozarska Dubica *see* Bosanska Dubica
117 P3 **Kozelets'** *Rus.* Kozelets. Chernihivs'ka Oblast', NE Ukraine
117 S6 **Kozel'shchyna** Poltavs'ka Oblast', C Ukraine
128 J5 **Kozel'sk** Kaluzhskaya Oblast', W Russian Federation
Kozhikode *see* Calicut
127 V9 **Kozhimiz, Gora** ▲ NW Russian Federation
126 L9 **Kozhozero, Ozero** ◎ NW Russian Federation
127 T7 **Kozhva** *var.* Kozya. Respublika Komi, NW Russian Federation
127 T7 **Kozhva** ∾ NW Russian Federation
127 U6 **Kozhym** Respublika Komi, NW Russian Federation
110 N13 **Kozienice** Mazowieckie, C Poland
109 S13 **Kozina** SW Slovenia
114 H7 **Kozloduy** Vratsa, NW Bulgaria
129 Q3 **Kozlovka** Chuvashskaya Respublika, W Russian Federation
Kozlovshchina/ Kozlowszczyzna *see* Kazlowshchyna
129 P3 **Koz'modem'yansk** Respublika Mariy El, W Russian Federation
116 J6 **Kozova** Ternopil's'ka Oblast', W Ukraine
113 P20 **Kožuf** ▲ S FYR Macedonia
165 N15 **Kōzu-shima** *island* E Japan
Kozya *see* Kozhva
Koz'yany *see* Kaz'yany
117 N5 **Kozyatyn** *Rus.* Kazatin. Vinnyts'ka Oblast', C Ukraine
77 Q16 **Kpalimé** *var.* Palimé. SW Togo
77 Q16 **Kpandu** E Ghana
99 F15 **Krabbendijke** Zeeland, SW Netherlands
167 N15 **Krabi** *var.* Muang Krabi. Krabi, SW Thailand
167 N13 **Kra Buri** Ranong, SW Thailand
167 S12 **Krâchéh** *prev.* Kratie. Krâchéh, E Cambodia
95 G17 **Kragerø** Telemark, S Norway
112 M13 **Kragujevac** Serbia, C Yugoslavia
Krainburg *see* Kranj
166 N13 **Kra, Isthmus of** *isthmus* Malaysia/Thailand
112 D12 **Krajina** *cultural region* SW Croatia
Krakatau, Pulau *see* Rakata, Pulau
Krakau *see* Małopolskie
111 L16 **Kraków** *Eng.* Cracow, *Ger.* Krakau; *anc.* Cracovia. Małopolskie, S Poland
100 L9 **Krakower See** ◎ NE Germany
167 Q11 **Krâlănh** Siĕmréab, NW Cambodia
45 Q16 **Kralendijk** Bonaire, E Netherlands Antilles
112 B10 **Kraljevica** *It.* Porto Re. Primorje-Gorski Kotar, NW Croatia
112 M13 **Kraljevo** *prev.* Rankovićevo. Serbia, C Yugoslavia
Kralup an der Moldau *see* Kralupy nad Vltavou
111 C16 **Kralupy nad Vltavou** *Ger.* Kralup an der Moldau. Středočeský Kraj, NW Czech Republic
117 W7 **Kramators'k** *Rus.* Kramatorsk. Donets'ka Oblast', SE Ukraine
93 H17 **Kramfors** Västernorrland, C Sweden
115 D15 **Kranéa** Dytikí Makedonía, N Greece
108 M7 **Kranebitten** ✕ (Innsbruck) Tirol, W Austria
115 G20 **Kranídi** Pelopónnisos, S Greece
109 T11 **Kranj** *Ger.* Krainburg. NW Slovenia
115 F16 **Krannón** *battleground* Thessalía, C Greece
Kranz *see* Zelenogradsk
112 D7 **Krapina** Krapina-Zagorje, N Croatia
112 E8 **Krapina** ∾ N Croatia
112 D8 **Krapina-Zagorje** *off.* Krapinsko-Zagorska Županija. ◆ *province* N Croatia
114 L7 **Krapinets** ∾ NE Bulgaria
111 I15 **Krapkowice** *Ger.* Krappitz. Opolskie, S Poland
Krappitz *see* Krapkowice
127 O12 **Krasavino** Vologodskaya Oblast', NW Russian Federation
122 H6 **Krasino** Novaya Zemlya, Arkhangel'skaya Oblast', N Russian Federation
123 S15 **Kraskino** Primorskiy Kray, SE Russian Federation
118 J11 **Krāslava** Krāslava, SE Latvia
119 M14 **Krasnaluki** *Rus.* Krasnoluki. Vitsyebskaya Voblasts', N Belarus
119 P17 **Krasnapollye** *Rus.* Krasnopol'ye. Mahilyowskaya Voblasts', E Belarus
128 L15 **Krasnaya Polyana** Krasnodarskiy Kray, SW Russian Federation
119 J18 **Krasnaya Slabada** *var.* Chyrvonaya Slabada, *Rus.* Krasnaya Sloboda. Minskaya Voblasts', S Belarus
Krasnaya Sloboda *see* Krasnaya Slabada
119 J15 **Krasnaye** *Rus.* Krasnoye. Minskaya Voblasts', C Belarus
111 O14 **Kraśnik** *Ger.* Kratznick. Lubelskie, E Poland
111 O14 **Kraśnik Fabryczny** Lubelskie, SE Poland
117 O9 **Krasni Okny** Odes'ka Oblast', SW Ukraine
145 P7 **Krasnoarmeysk** Severnyy Kazakhstan, N Kazakhstan
129 P8 **Krasnoarmeysk** Saratovskaya Oblast', W Russian Federation
Krasnoarmeysk *see* Krasnoarmiys'k/Tayynsha
123 T6 **Krasnoarmeyskiy** Chukotskiy Avtonomnyy Okrug, NE Russian Federation
117 W7 **Krasnoarmiys'k** *Rus.* Krasnoarmeysk. Donets'ka Oblast', SE Ukraine
127 P11 **Krasnoborsk** Arkhangel'skaya Oblast', NW Russian Federation
128 K14 **Krasnodar** *prev.* Ekaterinodar, Yekaterinodar. Krasnodarskiy Kray, SW Russian Federation
128 K13 **Krasnodarskiy Kray** ◆ *territory* SW Russian Federation
117 Z7 **Krasnodon** Luhans'ka Oblast', E Ukraine
Krasnogor *see* Kallaste
129 T2 **Krasnogorskoye** *Latv.* Sarkaņi. Udmurtskaya Respublika, NW Russian Federation
Krasnograd *see* Krasnohrad
Krasnogvardeysk *see* Bulunghur
128 M13 **Krasnogvardeyskoye** Stavropol'skiy Kray, SW Russian Federation
Krasnogvardeyskoye *see* Krasnohvardiys'ke
117 U6 **Krasnohrad** *Rus.* Krasnograd. Kharkivs'ka Oblast', E Ukraine
117 S12 **Krasnohvardiys'ke** *Rus.* Krasnogvardeyskoye. Respublika Krym, S Ukraine
123 P14 **Krasnokamensk** Chitinskaya Oblast', S Russian Federation
127 U14 **Krasnokamsk** Permskaya Oblast', W Russian Federation
129 U8 **Krasnokholm** Orenburgskaya Oblast', W Russian Federation
117 U5 **Krasnokuts'k** *Rus.* Krasnokutsk. Kharkivs'ka Oblast', E Ukraine
128 L7 **Krasnolesnyy** Voronezhskaya Oblast', W Russian Federation
Krasnoluki *see* Krasnaluki
Krasnoosol'skoye Vodokhranilishche *see* Chervonooskil's'ke Vodoskhovyshche
117 S11 **Krasnoperekops'k** *Rus.* Krasnoperekopsk. Respublika Krym, S Ukraine
117 U4 **Krasnopillya** Sums'ka Oblast', NE Ukraine
Krasnopol'ye *see* Krasnapollye
126 L5 **Krasnoshchel'ye** Murmanskaya Oblast', NW Russian Federation
129 O5 **Krasnoslobodsk** Respublika Mordoviya, W Russian Federation
129 T2 **Krasnoslobodsk** Volgogradskaya Oblast', SW Russian Federation
Krasnostav *see* Krasnystaw
129 V5 **Krasnousol'skiy** Respublika Bashkortostan, W Russian Federation
127 U12 **Krasnovishersk** Permskaya Oblast', NW Russian Federation
Krasnovodsk *see* Turkmenbashi
146 A10 **Krasnovodskiy Zaliv** *Turkm.* Krasnowodsk Aylagy. *lake gulf* W Turkmenistan
146 B10 **Krasnovodskoye Plato** *Turkm.* Krasnowodsk Platosy. *plateau* NW Turkmenistan
Krasnowodsk Aylagy *see* Krasnovodskiy Zaliv
Krasnowodsk Platosy *see* Krasnovodskoye Plato
122 K12 **Krasnoyarsk** Krasnoyarskiy Kray, S Russian Federation
129 X7 **Krasnoyarskiy** Orenburgskaya Oblast', W Russian Federation
122 K11 **Krasnoyarskiy Kray** ◆ *territory* C Russian Federation
Krasnoye *see* Krasnaye
146 J15 **Krasnoye Znamya** *Turkm.* Gyzylbaydak. Maryyskiy Velayat, S Turkmenistan
127 R11 **Krasnozatonskiy** Respublika Komi, NW Russian Federation
118 D13 **Krasnoznamensk** *prev.* Lasdehnen, *Ger.* Haselberg. Kaliningradskaya Oblast', W Russian Federation
117 R11 **Krasnoznam"yans'kyy Kanal** *canal* S Ukraine
111 P14 **Krasnystaw** *Rus.* Krasnostav. Lubelskie, SE Poland
128 H4 **Krasnyy** Smolenskaya Oblast', W Russian Federation
129 P2 **Krasnyye Baki** Nizhegorodskaya Oblast', W Russian Federation
129 Q13 **Krasnyye Barrikady** Astrakhanskaya Oblast', SW Russian Federation
126 K15 **Krasnyy Kholm** Tverskaya Oblast', W Russian Federation
129 Q8 **Krasnyy Kut** Saratovskaya Oblast', W Russian Federation
Krasnyy Liman *see* Krasnyy Lyman
117 Y7 **Krasnyy Luch** *prev.* Krindachevka. Luhans'ka Oblast', E Ukraine
117 X6 **Krasnyy Lyman** *Rus.* Krasnyy Liman. Donets'ka Oblast', SE Ukraine
129 R3 **Krasnyy Steklovar** Respublika Mariy El, W Russian Federation
129 P8 **Krasnyy Tekstil'shchik** Saratovskaya Oblast', W Russian Federation
129 R13 **Krasnyy Yar** Astrakhanskaya Oblast', SW Russian Federation
Krassóvár *see* Caraşova
116 L5 **Krasyliv** Khmel'nyts'ka Oblast', W Ukraine
111 O21 **Kraszna** *Rom.* Crasna. ∾ Hungary/Romania
Kratie *see* Krâchéh
113 P17 **Kratovo** NE FYR Macedonia
Kratznick *see* Kraśnik
171 Y13 **Krau** Irian Jaya, E Indonesia
167 Q13 **Krâvanh, Chuŏr Phnum** *Eng.* Cardamom Mountains, *Fr.* Chaîne des Cardamomes. ▲ W Cambodia
Kravasta Lagoon *see* Karavastasë, Laguna e
Krawang *see* Karawang
Kraxatau *see* Rakata, Pulau
129 Q15 **Kraynovka** Respublika Dagestan, SW Russian Federation
118 D12 **Kražiai** Kelmė, C Lithuania
27 P11 **Krebs** Oklahoma, C USA
101 D15 **Krefeld** Nordrhein-Westfalen, W Germany
Kreisstadt *see* Krosno Odrzańskie
115 D17 **Kremastón, Technití Límni** ⊞ C Greece
Kremenchug *see* Kremenchuk
Kremenchugskoye Vodokhranilishche/Kremenchuk Reservoir *see* Kremenchuts'ke Vodoskhovyshche
117 S6 **Kremenchuk** *Rus.* Kremenchug. Poltavs'ka Oblast', NE Ukraine
117 R6 **Kremenchuts'ke Vodoskhovyshche** *Eng.* Kremenchuk Reservoir, *Rus.* Kremenchugskoye Vodokhranilishche. ⊞ C Ukraine
116 K5 **Kremenets'** *Pol.* Krzemieniec, *Rus.* Kremenets. Ternopil's'ka Oblast', W Ukraine
Kremennaya *see* Kreminna
117 X6 **Kreminna** *Rus.* Kremennaya. Luhans'ka Oblast', E Ukraine
37 R4 **Kremmling** Colorado, C USA
109 V3 **Krems** ∾ NE Austria
Krems *see* Krems an der Donau
109 W3 **Krems an der Donau** *var.* Krems. Niederösterreich, N Austria
Kremsier *see* Kroměříž
109 S4 **Kremsmünster** Oberösterreich, N Austria
38 M17 **Krenitzin Islands** *island* Aleutian Islands, Alaska, USA
Kresena *see* Kresna
114 G11 **Kresna** *var.* Kresena. Blagoevgrad, SW Bulgaria
112 O12 **Krespoljin** Serbia, E Yugoslavia
25 N4 **Kress** Texas, SW USA
123 V6 **Kresta, Zaliv** *bay* E Russian Federation
115 D20 **Kréstena** *prev.* Selinoús. Dytikí Ellás, S Greece
126 H14 **Kresttsy** Novgorodskaya Oblast', W Russian Federation
Kretikon Delagos *see* Kritikó Pélagos
118 C11 **Kretinga** *Ger.* Krottingen. Kretinga, NW Lithuania
Kreutz *see* Cristuru Secuiesc
Kreuz *see* Križevci, Croatia
Kreuz *see* Risti, Estonia
Kreuzburg/Kreuzburg in Oberschlesien *see* Kluczbork
Kreuzingen *see* Bol'shakovo
108 H6 **Kreuzlingen** Thurgau, NE Switzerland
101 K25 **Kreuzspitze** ▲ S Germany
101 F16 **Kreuztal** Nordrhein-Westfalen, W Germany
119 I15 **Kreva** *Rus.* Krevo. Hrodzyenskaya Voblasts', W Belarus
Krevo *see* Kreva
Kría Vrísi *see* Krýa Vrýsi
79 D16 **Kribi** Sud, SW Cameroon
Krichëv *see* Krychaw
Krickerhäu/Kriegerhaj *see* Handlová
109 W6 **Krieglach** Steiermark, E Austria
108 F8 **Kriens** Luzern, W Switzerland
Krimmitschau *see* Crimmitschau
98 H12 **Krimpen aan den IJssel** Zuid-Holland, SW Netherlands
Krindachevka *see* Krasnyy Luch
115 G25 **Kríos, Akrotírio** *headland* Kríti, Greece, E Mediterranean Sea
155 J16 **Krishna** *prev.* Kistna. ∾ C India
155 H20 **Krishnagiri** Tamil Nādu, SE India
155 K17 **Krishna, Mouths of the** *delta* SE India
153 S15 **Krishnanagar** West Bengal, N India
155 G20 **Krishnarājāsāgara Reservoir** ⊞ W India
95 N19 **Kristdala** Kalmar, S Sweden
Kristiania *see* Oslo
95 E18 **Kristiansand** *var.* Christiansand. Vest-Agder, S Norway
95 L22 **Kristianstad** Skåne, S Sweden
94 F8 **Kristiansund** *var.* Christiansund. Møre og Romsdal, S Norway
Kristiinankaupunki *see* Kristinestad
93 I14 **Kristineberg** Västerbotten, N Sweden
95 L16 **Kristinehamn** Värmland, C Sweden
93 J17 **Kristinestad** *Fin.* Kristiinankaupunki. Länsi-Suomi, W Finland
Kristyor *see* Crişcior
115 J25 **Kríti** *Eng.* Crete. ◆ *region* Greece, Aegean Sea
115 J24 **Kríti** *Eng.* Crete. *island* Greece, Aegean Sea
115 J23 **Kritikó Pélagos** *var.* Kretikon Delagos, *Eng.* Sea of Crete; *anc.* Mare Creticum. *sea* Greece, Aegean Sea
Kriulyany *see* Criuleni
112 I12 **Krivaja** ∾ NE Bosnia and Herzegovina
Krivaja *see* Mali Idoš
113 P17 **Kriva Palanka** *Turk.* Eğri Palanka. NE FYR Macedonia
Krivichi *see* Kryvychy
114 H8 **Krivodol** Vratsa, NW Bulgaria
128 M10 **Krivorozh'ye** Rostovskaya Oblast', SW Russian Federation
Krivoshin *see* Kryvoshyn
Krivoy Rog *see* Kryvyy Rih
112 F7 **Križevci** *Ger.* Kreuz, *Hung.* Kőrös. Varaždin, NE Croatia
112 B10 **Krk** *It.* Veglia. Primorje-Gorski Kotar, NW Croatia
112 B10 **Krk** *It.* Veglia; *anc.* Curieta. *island* NW Croatia
109 V12 **Krka** ∾ SE Slovenia
Krka *see* Gurk
109 R11 **Krn** ▲ NW Slovenia
111 H16 **Krnov** *Ger.* Jägerndorf. Ostravský Kraj, E Czech Republic
Kroatien *see* Croatia
95 G14 **Krøderen** Buskerud, S Norway
95 G14 **Krøderen** ◎ S Norway
Kroi *see* Krui
95 N17 **Krokek** Östergötland, S Sweden
Krokodil *see* Crocodile
93 G16 **Krokom** Jämtland, C Sweden
117 S2 **Krolevets'** *Rus.* Krolevets. Sums'ka Oblast', NE Ukraine
Królewska Huta *see* Chorzów
111 H18 **Kroměříž** *Ger.* Kremsier. Zlínský Kraj, E Czech Republic
98 I9 **Krommenie** Noord-Holland, C Netherlands
128 J6 **Kromy** Orlovskaya Oblast', W Russian Federation
101 L18 **Kronach** Bayern, E Germany
Krone an der Brahe *see* Koronowo
167 Q13 **Kröng Kaôh Kŏng** Kaôh Kŏng, SW Cambodia
95 K21 **Kronoberg** ◆ *county* S Sweden
123 V10 **Kronotskiy Zaliv** *bay* E Russian Federation
195 O2 **Kronprinsesse Märtha Kyst** *physical region* Antarctica
195 V3 **Kronprins Olav Kyst** *physical region* Antarctica
126 G12 **Kronshtadt** Leningradskaya Oblast', NW Russian Federation
Kronstadt *see* Braşov
83 I22 **Kroonstad** Free State, C South Africa
123 O12 **Kropotkin** Irkutskaya Oblast', C Russian Federation
128 L14 **Kropotkin** Krasnodarskiy Kray, SW Russian Federation
110 J11 **Krośniewice** Łódzkie, C Poland
111 N17 **Krosno** *Ger.* Krossen. Podkarpackie, SE Poland
110 E12 **Krosno Odrzańskie** *Ger.* Crossen, Kreisstadt. Lubuskie, W Poland
Krossen *see* Krosno
Krotoschin *see* Krotoszyn
110 H13 **Krotoszyn** *Ger.* Krotoschin. Wielkopolskie, C Poland
Krottingen *see* Kretinga
Krousón *see* Krousónas
115 J25 **Krousónas** *prev.* Krousón, Kroussón. Kríti, Greece, E Mediterranean Sea
Kroussón *see* Krousónas
Krraba *see* Krrabë
113 L20 **Krrabë** *var.* Krraba. Tiranë, C Albania
113 L17 **Krrabit, Mali i** ▲ N Albania
109 W12 **Krško** *Ger.* Gurkfeld; *prev.* Videm-Krško. E Slovenia
83 K19 **Kruger National Park** *national park* Northern, N South Africa
83 J21 **Krugersdorp** Gauteng, NE South Africa
38 D16 **Krugloi Point** *headland* Agattu Island, Alaska, USA
Krugloye *see* Kruhlaye
119 N15 **Kruhlaye** *Rus.* Krugloye. Mahilyowskaya Voblasts', E Belarus
168 L15 **Krui** *var.* Kroi. Sumatera, SW Indonesia
99 G16 **Kruibeke** Oost-Vlaanderen, N Belgium
83 G25 **Kruidfontein** Western Cape, SW South Africa
99 F15 **Kruiningen** Zeeland, SW Netherlands
Kruja *see* Krujë
113 L19 **Krujë** *var.* Kruja, *It.* Croia. Durrës, C Albania
Krulevshchina *see* Krulewshchyna
118 K13 **Krulewshchyna** *Rus.* Krulevshchina. Vitsyebskaya Voblasts', N Belarus
25 T6 **Krum** Texas, SW USA
101 J23 **Krumbach** Bayern, S Germany
113 M17 **Krumë** Kukës, NE Albania
Krummau *see* Český Krumlov
114 K12 **Krumovgrad** *prev.* Kossukavak. Kŭrdzhali, S Bulgaria
114 K12 **Krumovitsa** ∾ S Bulgaria
114 L10 **Krumovo** Yambol, E Bulgaria
167 O11 **Krung Thep** *var.* Krung Thep Mahanakhon, *Eng.* Bangkok. ● (Thailand) Bangkok, C Thailand
167 O11 **Krung Thep, Ao** *var.* Bight of Bangkok. *bay* S Thailand
Krung Thep Mahanakhon *see* Krung Thep
Krupa/Krupa na Uni *see* Bosanska Krupa
119 M15 **Krupki** *Rus.* Krupki. Minskaya Voblasts', C Belarus
95 G24 **Kruså** *var.* Krusaa. Sønderjylland, SW Denmark
Krusaa *see* Kruså
113 N14 **Kruševac** Serbia, C Yugoslavia
113 N19 **Kruševo** SW FYR Macedonia
111 A15 **Krušné Hory** *Eng.* Ore Mountains, *Ger.* Erzgebirge. ▲ Czech Republic/Germany *see also* Erzgebirge
39 W13 **Kruzof Island** *island* Alexander Archipelago, Alaska, USA
114 F13 **Krýa Vrýsi** *var.* Kría Vrísi. Kentrikí Makedonía, N Greece
119 P16 **Krychaw** *Rus.* Krichëv. Mahilyowskaya Voblasts', E Belarus
64 K11 **Krylov Seamount** *undersea feature* E Atlantic Ocean
Krym *see* Krym, Respublika
117 S13 **Krym, Respublika** *var.* Krym, *Eng.* Crimea, Crimean Oblast; *prev. Rus.* Krymskaya ASSR, Krymskaya Oblast'. ◆ *province* SE Ukraine
128 K14 **Krymsk** Krasnodarskiy Kray, SW Russian Federation

◆ Country ● Country Capital ◇ Dependent Territory ○ Dependent Territory Capital ◆ Administrative Region ✕ International Airport ▲ Mountain ▲ Mountain Range ⛰ Volcano ∾ River ◎ Lake ⊞ Reservoir

Krymskaya ASSR/Krymskaya Oblast' see Krym, Respublika
117 T13 **Kryms'ki Hory** ▲ S Ukraine
117 T13 **Kryms'kyy Pivostriv** peninsula S Ukraine
111 M18 **Krynica** Ger. Tannenhof. Małopolskie, S Poland
117 P8 **Kryve Ozero** Odes'ka Oblast', SW Ukraine
119 I18 **Kryvoshyn** Rus. Krivoshin. Brestskaya Voblasts', SW Belarus
119 K14 **Kryvychy** Rus. Krivichi. Minskaya Voblasts', C Belarus
117 S8 **Kryvyy Rih** Rus. Krivoy Rog. Dnipropetrovs'ka Oblast', SE Ukraine
117 N8 **Kryzhopil'** Vinnyts'ka Oblast', C Ukraine
Krzemieniec see Kremenets'
111 J14 **Krzepice** Śląskie, S Poland
110 F10 **Krzyż Wielkopolski** Wielkopolskie, C Poland
Ksar al Kabir see Ksar-el-Kebir
Ksar al Soule see Er-Rachidia
74 J5 **Ksar El Boukhari** N Algeria
74 G5 **Ksar-el-Kebir** var. Alcázar, Ksar al Kabir, Ksar-el-Kébir, Ar. Al-Kasr al-Kebir, Al-Qsar al-Kbir, Sp. Alcazarquivir. NW Morocco
110 H12 **Książ Wielkopolski** Ger. Xions. Wielkolpolskie, C Poland
129 O3 **Kstovo** Nizhegorodskaya Oblast', W Russian Federation
169 T8 **Kuala Belait** W Brunei
Kuala Dungun see Dungun
169 S10 **Kualakerian** Borneo, C Indonesia
169 S12 **Kualakuayan** Borneo, C Indonesia
168 K8 **Kuala Lipis** Pahang, Peninsular Malaysia
168 K9 **Kuala Lumpur** ● (Malaysia) Kuala Lumpur, Peninsular Malaysia
Kuala Pelabohan Kelang see Pelabuhan Klang
169 U7 **Kuala Penyu** Sabah, East Malaysia
38 E9 **Kualapuu** Haw. Kualapu'u. Molokai, Hawaii, USA, C Pacific Ocean
168 L7 **Kuala Terengganu** var. Kuala Trengganu. Terengganu, Peninsular Malaysia
168 L11 **Kualatungkal** Sumatera, W Indonesia
171 P11 **Kuandang** Sulawesi, N Indonesia
163 V12 **Kuandian** Liaoning, NE China
Kuando-Kubango see Cuando Cubango
Kuang-chou see Guangzhou
Kuang-hsi see Guangxi Zhuangzu Zizhiqu
Kuang-tung see Guangdong
Kuang-yuan see Guangyuan
Kuantan, Batang see Indragiri, Sungai
Kuanza Norte see Cuanza Norte
Kuanza Sul see Cuanza Sul
Kuba see Quba
Kubango see Cubango/Okavango
141 X8 **Kubārah** NW Oman
93 H16 **Kubbe** Västernorrland, C Sweden
80 A11 **Kubbum** Southern Darfur, W Sudan
126 L13 **Kubenskoye, Ozero** ◎ NW Russian Federation
164 G15 **Kubokawa** Kōchi, Shikoku, SW Japan
114 L7 **Kubrat** prev. Balbunar. Razgrad, N Bulgaria
112 O13 **Kučajske Planine** ▲▲ E Yugoslavia
165 T1 **Kuccharo-ko** ◎ Hokkaidō, N Japan
112 O11 **Kučevo** Serbia, NE Yugoslavia
Kuchan see Qūchān
169 Q10 **Kuching** prev. Sarawak. Sarawak, East Malaysia
169 Q10 **Kuching** ✕ Sarawak, East Malaysia
164 B17 **Kuchinoerabu-jima** island Nansei-shotō, SW Japan
164 C14 **Kuchinotsu** Nagasaki, Kyūshū, SW Japan
109 Q6 **Kuchl** Salzburg, NW Austria
148 L9 **Kūchnay Darweyshān** Helmand, S Afghanistan
Kuchurgan see Kuchurhan
117 O9 **Kuchurhan** Rus. Kuchurgan. ≈ NE Ukraine
Kuçova see Kuçovë
113 L21 **Kuçovë** var. Kuçova; prev. Qyteti Stalin. Berat, C Albania
136 D11 **Küçük Çekmece** İstanbul, NW Turkey
164 F14 **Kudamatsu** var. Kudamatu. Yamaguchi, Honshū, SW Japan
Kudamatu see Kudamatsu
Kudara see Ghŭdara
169 V6 **Kudat** Sabah, East Malaysia
Küddow see Gwda
155 G17 **Kūdligi** Karnātaka, W India
Kudowa see Kudowa-Zdrój
111 F16 **Kudowa-Zdrój** Ger. Kudowa. Wałbrzych, SW Poland
117 P9 **Kudryavtsivka** Mykolayivs'ka Oblast', S Ukraine
169 R16 **Kudus** prev. Koedoes. Jawa, C Indonesia
127 T13 **Kudymkar** Komi-Permyatskiy Avtonomnyy Okrug, NW Russian Federation
Kudzsir see Cugir
Kuei-chou see Guizhou
Kuei-lin see Guilin
Kuei-yang see Guiyang
K'u-erh-lo see Korla
Kueyang see Guiyang
Kufa see Al Kūfah
136 E14 **Küfiçayı** ≈ C Turkey
109 O6 **Kufstein** Tirol, W Austria
145 V14 **Kugaly** Kaz. Qoghaly. Almaty, SE Kazakhstan
8 K8 **Kugluktuk** var. Qurlurtuuq prev. Coppermine. Nunavut, NW Canada
143 Y13 **Kūhak** Sīstān va Balūchestān, SE Iran
143 R9 **Kūhbonān** Kermān, C Iran
148 J5 **Kūhestān** var. Kohsān. Herāt, W Afghanistan
93 N15 **Kuhmo** Oulu, E Finland
93 L18 **Kuhmoinen** Länsi-Suomi, W Finland
Kuhnau see Konin
Kūhnö see Kihnu
143 O8 **Kūhpāyeh** Eşfahān, C Iran
167 O12 **Kui Buri** var. Ban Kui Nua. Prachuap Khiri Khan, SW Thailand
Kuibyshev see Kuybyshevskoye Vodokhranilishche
82 D13 **Kuito** Port. Silva Porto. Bié, C Angola
39 X14 **Kuiu Island** island Alexander Archipelago, Alaska, USA
92 L13 **Kuivaniemi** Oulu, C Finland
77 V14 **Kujama** Kaduna, C Nigeria
110 I10 **Kujawsko-pomorskie** ✦ province, C Poland
165 R8 **Kuji** var. Kuzi. Iwate, Honshū, C Japan
Kujto, Ozero see Kuyto, Ozero
Kujū-renzan see Kujū-san
164 D14 **Kujū-san** var. Kujū-renzan. ▲ Kyūshū, SW Japan
43 N7 **Kukalaya, Rio** var. Rio Cuculaya, Rio Kukulaya. ≈ NE Nicaragua
113 O16 **Kukavica** var. Vlajna. ▲ SE Yugoslavia
146 M10 **Kŭkcha** Rus. Kokcha. Bukhoro Wiloyati, C Uzbekistan
113 M18 **Kukës** var. Kukësi. Kukës, NE Albania
113 L18 **Kukës** ✦ district NE Albania
Kukësi see Kukës
186 D8 **Kukipi** Gulf, S PNG
129 S3 **Kukmor** Respublika Tatarstan, W Russian Federation
Kukong see Shaoguan
39 N6 **Kukpowruk River** ≈ Alaska, USA
38 M6 **Kukpuk River** ≈ Alaska, USA
Kukukhoto see Hohhot
Kukulaya, Rio see Kukalaya, Rio
189 W12 **Kuku Point** headland NW Wake Island
146 G11 **Kukurtli** Akhalskiy Velayat, C Turkmenistan
Kül see Kül, Rūd-e
114 F7 **Kula** Vidin, NW Bulgaria
136 D14 **Kula** Manisa, W Turkey
112 K9 **Kula** Serbia, NW Yugoslavia
149 S8 **Kulāchi** North-West Frontier Province, NW Pakistan
Kulachi see Kolāchi
144 F11 **Kulagino** Kaz. Külagīno. Atyrau, W Kazakhstan
168 L10 **Kulai** Johor, Peninsular Malaysia
114 M7 **Kulak** ≈ NE Bulgaria
153 T11 **Kula Kangri** var. Kulhakangri. ▲ Bhutan/China
144 E13 **Kulaly, Ostrov** island SW Kazakhstan
147 V9 **Kulanak** Narynskaya Oblast', C Kyrgyzstan
146 B8 **Kulandag** ▲▲ W Turkmenistan
145 S16 **Kulan** Kaz. Qulan; prev. Lugovoy, Lugovoye. Zhambyl, S Kazakhstan
153 V14 **Kulaura** Chittagong, NE Bangladesh
118 D9 **Kuldīga** Ger. Goldingen. Kuldīga, W Latvia
Kuldja see Yining
Kul'dzhuktau, Gory see Quljuqtov-Toghi
129 N4 **Kulebaki** Nizhegorodskaya Oblast', W Russian Federation
112 E11 **Kulen Vakuf** var. Spasovo. Federacija Bosna I Hercegovina, NW Bosnia and Herzegovina
181 Q9 **Kulgera Roadhouse** Northern Territory, N Australia
Kulhakangri see Kula Kangri
129 T1 **Kuliga** Udmurtskaya Respublika, NW Russian Federation
Kulkuduk see Kalquduq
118 G4 **Kullamaa** Läänemaa, W Estonia
197 O12 **Kullorsuaq** var. Kuvdlorssuak. Kitaa, C Greenland
29 O6 **Kulm** North Dakota, N USA
Kulm see Chełmno
146 D12 **Kul'mach** Balkanskiy Velayat, W Turkmenistan
101 L18 **Kulmbach** Bayern, SE Germany
Kulmsee see Chełmża
147 Q14 **Kŭlob** Rus. Kulyab. SW Tajikistan
92 M13 **Kuloharju** Lappi, N Finland
127 N7 **Kuloy** Arkhangel'skaya Oblast', NW Russian Federation
127 N7 **Kuloy** ≈ NW Russian Federation
137 Q14 **Kulp** Dıyarbakır, SE Turkey
Kulpa see Kolpa
77 P14 **Kulpawn** ≈ N Ghana
143 R13 **Kül, Rūd-e** var. Kül. ≈ S Iran
144 G12 **Kul'sary** Kaz. Qulsary. Atyrau, W Kazakhstan
153 R15 **Kulti** West Bengal, NE India
93 G14 **Kultsjön** ◎ N Sweden
136 I14 **Kulu** Konya, W Turkey
123 S9 **Kulu** ≈ E Russian Federation
122 I13 **Kulunda** Altayskiy Kray, S Russian Federation
145 T7 **Kulunda Steppe** Kaz. Qulyndy Zhazyghy, Rus. Kulundinskaya Ravnina. grassland Kazakhstan/Russian Federation
Kulundinskaya Ravnina see Kulunda Steppe
182 M9 **Kulwin** Victoria, SE Australia
Kulyab see Kŭlob
117 Q3 **Kulykivka** Chernihivs'ka Oblast', N Ukraine
Kum see Qom
164 F14 **Kuma** Ehime, Shikoku, SW Japan
129 P14 **Kuma** ≈ SW Russian Federation
165 O12 **Kumagaya** Saitama, Honshū, S Japan
165 Q5 **Kumaishi** Hokkaidō, NE Japan
169 R13 **Kumai, Teluk** bay Borneo, C Indonesia
129 Y7 **Kumak** Orenburgskaya Oblast', W Russian Federation
164 C14 **Kumamoto** Kumamoto, Kyūshū, SW Japan
164 D15 **Kumamoto** off. Kumamoto-ken. ✦ prefecture Kyūshū, SW Japan
164 J15 **Kumano** Mie, Honshū, SW Japan
Kumanova see Kumanovo
113 O17 **Kumanovo** Turk. Kumanova. N FYR Macedonia
185 G17 **Kumara** West Coast, South Island, NZ
180 J8 **Kumarina Roadhouse** Western Australia
153 T15 **Kumarkhali** Khulna, W Bangladesh
77 P16 **Kumasi** prev. Coomassie. C Ghana
Kumayri see Gyumri
79 D15 **Kumba** Sud-Ouest, W Cameroon
114 N13 **Kumbağ** Tekirdağ, NW Turkey
155 J21 **Kumbakonam** Tamil Nādu, SE India
Kum-Dag see Gumdag
165 R16 **Kume-jima** island Nansei-shotō, SW Japan
129 V6 **Kumertau** Respublika Bashkortostan, W Russian Federation
35 R4 **Kumiva Peak** ▲ Nevada, W USA
159 N8 **Kum Kuduk** well NW China
159 N7 **Kumkuduk** Xinjiang Uygur Zizhiqu, W China
Kumkurgan see Qumqurghon
95 M16 **Kumla** Örebro, C Sweden
136 E17 **Kumluca** Antalya, SW Turkey
100 N9 **Kummerower See** ◎ NE Germany
77 X14 **Kumo** Gombe, E Nigeria
145 O13 **Kumola** ≈ C Kazakhstan
167 N1 **Kumon Range** ▲▲ N Myanmar
83 F22 **Kums** Karas, SE Namibia
155 E18 **Kumta** Karnātaka, W India
158 L6 **Kümük** Xinjiang Uygur Zizhiqu, W China
38 H12 **Kumukahi, Cape** headland Hawaii, USA, C Pacific Ocean
129 Q17 **Kumukh** Respublika Dagestan, SW Russian Federation
Kumul see Hami
129 N9 **Kumylzhenskaya** Volgogradskaya Oblast', SW Russian Federation
141 W6 **Kumzār** N Oman
149 S4 **Kunar** Per. Konarhā. ✦ province E Afghanistan
Kunashiri see Kunashir, Ostrov
123 U14 **Kunashir, Ostrov** var. Kunashiri. island Kuril'skiye Ostrova, SE Russian Federation
118 I3 **Kunda** Lääne-Virumaa, NE Estonia
152 M13 **Kunda** Uttar Pradesh, N India
155 E19 **Kundāpura** var. Coondapoor. Karnātaka, W India
79 O24 **Kundelungu, Monts** ▲ S Dem. Rep. Congo (Zaire)
Kundert see Hernád
186 D7 **Kundiawa** Chimbu, W PNG
Kundla see Sāvarkundla
168 L10 **Kundur, Pulau** island W Indonesia
149 Q2 **Kunduz** var. Kondoz, Kundūz, Qondūz, Per. Kondūz. Kunduz, NE Afghanistan
149 Q2 **Kunduz** Per. Kondūz. ✦ province NE Afghanistan
Kuneitra see Al Qunayţirah
83 B18 **Kunene** ✦ district NE Namibia
83 A16 **Kunene** var. Cunene. ≈ Angola/Namibia see also Cunene
Künes see Xinyuan
158 J5 **Künes He** ≈ NW China
95 I19 **Kungälv** Västra Götaland, S Sweden
147 W7 **Kungei Ala-Tau** Rus. Khrebet Kyungëy Ala-Too, Kir. Küngöy Ala-Too. ▲▲ Kazakhstan/Kyrgyzstan
Küngöy Ala-Too see Kungei Ala-Tau
Kungrad see Qŭnghirot
95 J19 **Kungsbacka** Halland, S Sweden
95 I18 **Kungshamn** Västra Götaland, S Sweden
95 M16 **Kungsör** Västmanland, C Sweden
79 J16 **Kungu** Equateur, NW Dem. Rep. Congo (Zaire)
127 V15 **Kungur** Permskaya Oblast', NW Russian Federation
166 L9 **Kungyangon** Yangon, SW Myanmar
111 M22 **Kunhegyes** Jász-Nagykun-Szolnok, E Hungary
167 O5 **Kunhing** Shan State, E Myanmar
158 D9 **Kunjirap Daban** var. Khūnjerāb Pass. pass China/Pakistan see also Khūnjerāb Pass
Kunlun Mountains see Kunlun Shan
158 H10 **Kunlun Shan** Eng. Kunlun Mountains. ▲▲ NW China
159 P11 **Kunlun Shankou** pass C China
160 G13 **Kunming** var. K'un-ming; prev. Yunnan. Yunnan, SW China
165 R4 **Kunnui** Hokkaidō, NE Japan
95 B18 **Kunoy** Dan. Kunø Island Faeroe Islands
163 X16 **Kunsan** var. Gunsan, Jap. Gunzan. W South Korea
111 L24 **Kunszentmárton** Jász-Nagykun-Szolnok, E Hungary
111 J23 **Kunszentmiklós** Bács-Kiskun, C Hungary
181 N3 **Kununurra** Western Australia
Kunya-Urgench see Këneurgench
Kunyé see Pins, Île des
169 T11 **Kunyi** Borneo, C Indonesia
101 I20 **Künzelsau** Baden-Württemberg, S Germany
161 S10 **Kuocang Shan** ▲ SE China
126 H5 **Kuoloyarvi** var. Luolajarvi. Murmanskaya Oblast', NW Russian Federation
93 N16 **Kuopio** Itä-Suomi, C Finland
93 K17 **Kuortane** Länsi-Suomi, W Finland
93 M18 **Kuortti** Itä-Suomi, E Finland
Kupa see Kolpa
171 P17 **Kupang** prev. Koepang. Timor, C Indonesia
39 Q5 **Kuparuk River** ≈ Alaska, USA
Kupchino see Cupcina
186 E9 **Kupiano** Central, S PNG
180 M4 **Kupingarri** Western Australia
122 I12 **Kupino** Novosibirskaya Oblast', C Russian Federation
118 H11 **Kupiškis** Kupiškis, NE Lithuania
114 L13 **Küplü** Edirne, NW Turkey
39 X13 **Kupreanof Island** island Alexander Archipelago, Alaska, USA
39 O16 **Kupreanof Point** headland Alaska, USA
112 G13 **Kupres** Federacija Bosna I Hercegovina, SW Bosnia and Herzegovina
117 W5 **Kup"yans'k** Rus. Kupyansk. Kharkivs'ka Oblast', E Ukraine
117 W5 **Kup"yans'k-Vuzlovyy** Kharkivs'ka Oblast', E Ukraine
158 I6 **Kuqa** Xinjiang Uygur Zizhiqu, NW China
Kür see Kura
137 W11 **Kura** Az. Kür, Geor. Mtkvari, Turk. Kura Nehri. ≈ SW Asia
55 R8 **Kuracki** NW Guyana
Kura Kurk see Irbe Strait
147 Q10 **Kurama Range** Rus. Kuraminskiy Khrebet. ▲▲ Tajikistan/Uzbekistan
Kuraminskiy Khrebet see Kurama Range
Kura Nehri see Kura
119 J14 **Kuranyets** Rus. Kurenets. Minskaya Voblasts', C Belarus
164 H13 **Kurashiki** var. Kurasiki. Okayama, Honshū, SW Japan
154 L10 **Kurasia** Madhya Pradesh, C India
Kurasiki see Kurashiki
164 H12 **Kurayoshi** var. Kurayosi. Tottori, Honshū, SW Japan
Kurayosi see Kurayoshi
163 X6 **Kurbin He** ≈ NE China
145 X10 **Kurchum** Kaz. Kürshim. Vostochnyy Kazakhstan, E Kazakhstan
145 Y10 **Kurchum** ≈ E Kazakhstan
137 X11 **Kürdämir** Rus. Kyurdamir. C Azerbaijan
Kurdestan see Kordestān
139 S1 **Kurdistan** cultural region SW Asia
Kurd Kui see Kord Küy
155 F15 **Kurduvādi** Mahārāshtra, W India
114 J11 **Kŭrdzhali** var. Kirdzhali. Kŭrdzhali, S Bulgaria
114 K11 **Kŭrdzhali** ✦ province S Bulgaria
114 J11 **Kŭrdzhali, Yazovir** ⊠ S Bulgaria
164 F13 **Kure** Hiroshima, Honshū, SW Japan
192 K5 **Kure Atoll** var. Ocean Island. atoll Hawaiian Islands, Hawaii, USA, C Pacific Ocean
136 J10 **Küre Dağları** ▲▲ N Turkey
Kurenets see Kuranyets
118 E6 **Kuressaare** Ger. Arensburg; prev. Kingissepp. Saaremaa, W Estonia
122 K9 **Kureyka** Krasnoyarskiy Kray, N Russian Federation
122 K9 **Kureyka** ≈ N Russian Federation
145 P10 **Kurgal'dzhin, Ozero** ◎ C Kazakhstan
145 Q10 **Kurgal'dzhinskiy** see Kurgal'dzhino
145 Q10 **Kurgal'dzhino** var. Kurgal'dzhinskiy, Kaz. Qorgazhyn. Akmola, C Kazakhstan
122 G11 **Kurgan** Kurganskaya Oblast', C Russian Federation
128 L14 **Kurganinsk** Krasnodarskiy Kray, SW Russian Federation
122 G11 **Kurganskaya Oblast'** ✦ province C Russian Federation
Kurgan-Tyube see Qŭrghonteppa
191 O2 **Kuria** prev. Woodle Island. island Tungaru, W Kiribati
Kuria Muria Bay see Ḩalāniyāt, Khalīj al
Kuria Muria Islands see Ḩalāniyāt, Juzur al
153 T13 **Kurigram** Rajshahi, N Bangladesh
93 K17 **Kurikka** Länsi-Suomi, W Finland
192 I3 **Kurile Basin** undersea feature NW Pacific Ocean
Kurile Islands see Kuril'skiye Ostrova
Kurile-Kamchatka Depression see Kurile Trench
192 J3 **Kurile Trench** var. Kurile-Kamchatka Depression. undersea feature NW Pacific Ocean
129 Q9 **Kurilovka** Saratovskaya Oblast', W Russian Federation
123 U13 **Kuril'sk** Kuril'skiye Ostrova, Sakhalinskaya Oblats', SE Russian Federation
122 G11 **Kuril'skiye Ostrova** Eng. Kurile Islands. island group SE Russian Federation
42 M9 **Kurinwas, Río** ≈ E Nicaragua
Kurisches Haff see Courland Lagoon
Kurkund see Kilingi-Nõmme
128 M4 **Kurlovskiy** Vladimirskaya Oblast', W Russian Federation
80 G12 **Kurmuk** Blue Nile, SE Sudan
Kurna see Al Qurnah
155 H17 **Kurnool** var. Karnul. Andhra Pradesh, S India
164 M11 **Kurobe** Toyama, Honshū, SW Japan
165 Q7 **Kuroishi** var. Kuroisi. Aomori, Honshū, C Japan
Kuroisi see Kuroishi
165 O12 **Kuroiso** Tochigi, Honshū, S Japan
165 Q4 **Kuromatsunai** Hokkaidō, NE Japan
164 B17 **Kuro-shima** island SW Japan
185 F21 **Kurow** Canterbury, South Island, NZ
129 N15 **Kursavka** Stavropol'skiy Kray, SW Russian Federation
118 E11 **Kuršėnai** Šiauliai, N Lithuania
Kürshim see Kurchum
Kurshskaya Kosa/Kuršių Nerija see Courland Spit
128 J7 **Kursk** Kurskaya Oblast', W Russian Federation
128 I7 **Kurskaya Oblast'** ✦ province W Russian Federation
Kurskiy Zaliv see Courland Lagoon
113 N15 **Kuršumlija** Serbia, S Yugoslavia
137 R15 **Kurtalan** Siirt, SE Turkey
Kurtbunar see Tervel
Kurt-Dere see Vŭlchidol
Kurtitsch/Kürtös see Curtici
145 U15 **Kurtty** ≈ SE Kazakhstan
93 L18 **Kuru** Länsi-Suomi, W Finland
80 C13 **Kuru** ≈ W Sudan
114 M13 **Kuru Dağı** ▲ NW Turkey
158 L7 **Kuruktag** ▲ NW China
83 G22 **Kuruman** Northern Cape, N South Africa
67 T14 **Kuruman** ≈ W South Africa
164 D14 **Kurume** Fukuoka, Kyūshū, SW Japan
123 N13 **Kurumkan** Respublika Buryatiya, S Russian Federation
155 J25 **Kurunegala** North Western Province, C Sri Lanka
55 T10 **Kurupukari** C Guyana
127 U10 **Kur"ya** Respublika Komi, NW Russian Federation
144 E15 **Kuryk** prev. Yeraliyev. Mangistau, SW Kazakhstan
136 B15 **Kuşadası** Aydın, SW Turkey
115 M19 **Kuşadası Körfezi** gulf SW Turkey
164 A17 **Kusagaki-guntō** island SW Japan
Kusaie see Kosrae
145 T12 **Kusak** ≈ C Kazakhstan
Kusary see Qusar
167 P7 **Ku Sathan, Doi** ▲ NW Thailand
164 J13 **Kusatsu** var. Kusatu. Shiga, Honshū, SW Japan
Kusatu see Kusatsu
138 F11 **Kuseifa** Southern, C Israel
136 C12 **Kuş Gölü** ◎ NW Turkey
128 L12 **Kushchevskaya** Krasnodarskiy Kray, SW Russian Federation
164 D16 **Kushima** var. Kusima. Miyazaki, Kyūshū, SW Japan
164 I15 **Kushimoto** Wakayama, Honshū, SW Japan
165 V4 **Kushiro** var. Kusiro. Hokkaidō, NE Japan
148 K4 **Kūshk** Herāt, W Afghanistan
146 J17 **Kushka** ≈ S Turkmenistan
Kushka see Gushgy
145 N8 **Kushmurun** Kaz. Qusmuryn. Kostanay, N Kazakhstan
145 N8 **Kushmurun, Ozero** Kaz. Qusmuryn. ◎ N Kazakhstan
129 U4 **Kushnarenkovo** Respublika Bashkortostan, W Russian Federation
Kushrabat see Qŭshrabot
153 T15 **Kushtia** var. Kustia. Khulna, W Bangladesh
Kusikino see Kushikino
Kusima see Kushima
Kusiro see Kushiro
38 M13 **Kuskokwim Bay** bay Alaska, USA
39 P11 **Kuskokwim Mountains** ▲▲ Alaska, USA
39 N12 **Kuskokwim River** ≈ Alaska, USA
108 G7 **Küsnacht** Zürich, N Switzerland
165 V4 **Kussharo-ko** var. Kussyaro. ◎ Hokkaidō, NE Japan
Küssnacht see Küssnacht am Rigi
108 F8 **Küssnacht am Rigi** var. Küssnacht. Schwyz, C Switzerland
Kussyaro see Kussharo-ko
Kustanay see Kostanay
Küstence/Küstendje see Constanța
100 F11 **Küstenkanal** var. Ems-Hunte Canal. canal NW Germany
Küstrin see Kostrzyn
Kustia see Kushtia
171 R11 **Kusu** Pulau Halmahera, E Indonesia
170 L16 **Kuta** Pulau Lombok, S Indonesia
139 T4 **Kutabān** N Iraq
136 E13 **Kütahya** prev. Kutaia. Kütahya, W Turkey
136 E13 **Kütahya** var. Kutaia. ✦ province W Turkey
Kutai see Mahakam, Sungai
Kutaia see Kütahya
137 R9 **K'ut'aisi** W Georgia
Kūt al 'Amārah see Al Kūt
Kut al Hai/Kūt al Ḩayy see Al Ḩayy
Kut al Imara see Al Kūt
123 Q11 **Kutana** Respublika Sakha (Yakutiya), NE Russian Federation
Kutaradja/Kutaraja see Bandaaceh
165 R4 **Kutchan** Hokkaidō, NE Japan
Kutch, Gulf of see Kachchh, Gulf of
Kutch, Rann of see Kachchh, Rann of
112 F9 **Kutina** Sisak-Moslavina, NE Croatia
112 H9 **Kutjevo** Požega-Slavonija, NE Croatia
111 E17 **Kutná Hora** Ger. Kuttenberg. Středočeský Kraj, C Czech Republic
110 K12 **Kutno** Łódzkie, C Poland
Kuttenberg see Kutná Hora
79 I20 **Kutu** Bandundu, W Dem. Rep. Congo (Zaire)
153 V17 **Kutubdia Island** island SE Bangladesh
80 B10 **Kutum** Northern Darfur, W Sudan
147 Y7 **Kuturgu** Issyk-Kul'skaya Oblast', E Kyrgyzstan
12 M5 **Kuujjuaq** prev. Fort-Chimo. Quebec, E Canada
12 I7 **Kuujjuarapik** Quebec, C Canada
146 A10 **Kuuli-Mayak** Turkm. Guwlumayak. Balkanskiy Velayat, NW Turkmenistan
118 I6 **Kuulse magi** ▲ S Estonia
92 N13 **Kuusamo** Oulu, E Finland
93 M19 **Kuusankoski** Etelä-Suomi, S Finland
129 W7 **Kuvandyk** Orenburgskaya Oblast', W Russian Federation
Kuvango see Cubango
Kuvasay see Quwasoy
Kuvdlorssuak see Kullorsuaq
126 I16 **Kuvshinovo** Tverskaya Oblast', W Russian Federation
141 Q4 **Kuwait** off. State of Kuwait, var. Dawlat al Kuwait, Koweit, Kuweit. ◆ monarchy SW Asia
Kuwait see Al Kuwayt
Kuwait Bay see Kuwayt, Jūn al
Kuwait City see Al Kuwayt
Kuwait, Dawlat al see Kuwait
Kuwajleen see Kwajalein Atoll
164 K13 **Kuwana** Mie, Honshū, SW Japan
139 X9 **Kuwayt** E Iraq
142 K11 **Kuwayt, Jūn al** var. Kuwait Bay. bay E Kuwait
Kuweit see Kuwait
117 P10 **Kuyal'nyts'kyy Lyman** ◎ SW Ukraine
122 I12 **Kuybyshev** Novosibirskaya Oblast', C Russian Federation
Kuybyshev see Bolgar, Respublika Tatarstan, Russian Federation
Kuybyshev see Samara
117 W9 **Kuybysheve** Rus. Kuybyshevo. Zaporiz'ka Oblast', SE Ukraine
Kuybyshevo see Kuybysheve
Kuybyshev Reservoir see Kuybyshevskoye Vodokhranilishche
Kuybyshevskaya Oblast' see Samarskaya Oblast'
145 O7 **Kuybyshevskiy** Severnyy Kazakhstan, N Kazakhstan
129 R4 **Kuybyshevskoye Vodokhranilishche** var. Kuibyshev, Eng. Kuybyshev Reservoir. ⊠ W Russian Federation
123 S9 **Kuydusun** Respublika Sakha (Yakutiya), NE Russian Federation
127 U16 **Kuyeda** Permskaya Oblast', NW Russian Federation
Kŭysanjaq see Koi Sanjaq
126 I7 **Kuyto, Ozero** var. Ozero Kujto. ◎ NW Russian Federation
158 J4 **Kuytun** Xinjiang Uygur Zizhiqu, NW China
122 M13 **Kuytun** Irkutskaya Oblast', S Russian Federation
55 S12 **Kuyuwini Landing** S Guyana
Kuzi see Kuji
38 M9 **Kuzitrin River** ≈ Alaska, USA
129 P6 **Kuznetsk** Penzenskaya Oblast', W Russian Federation
116 K3 **Kuznetsovs'k** Rivnens'ka Oblast', NW Ukraine
126 K6 **Kuzomen'** Murmanskaya Oblast', NW Russian Federation
165 R8 **Kuzumaki** Iwate, Honshū, C Japan
92 H9 **Kvaløya** island N Norway
92 K8 **Kvalsund** Finnmark, N Norway
94 G11 **Kvam** Oppland, S Norway
129 X7 **Kvarkeno** Orenburgskaya Oblast', W Russian Federation
93 G15 **Kvarnbergsvattnet** var. Frostviken. ◎ N Sweden
112 A11 **Kvarner** var. Carnaro, It. Quarnero. gulf W Croatia
112 B11 **Kvarnerić** channel W Croatia
39 O14 **Kvichak Bay** bay Alaska, USA
92 H12 **Kvikkjokk** Norrbotten, N Sweden
95 D17 **Kvina** ≈ S Norway
92 Q1 **Kvitøya** island NE Svalbard
95 F16 **Kvitseid** Telemark, S Norway
95 H24 **Kværndrup** Fyn, C Denmark
79 H20 **Kwa** ≈ W Dem. Rep. Congo (Zaire)
77 Q15 **Kwadwokurom** C Ghana

◆ Country ● Country Capital ◇ Dependent Territory ○ Dependent Territory Capital ✦ Administrative Region ✕ International Airport ▲ Mountain ▲▲ Mountain Range ⛰ Volcano ≈ River ◎ Lake ⊠ Reservoir

186 M8 **Kwailibesi** Malaita, N Solomon Islands
189 S6 **Kwajalein Atoll** *var.* Kuwajleen. *atoll* Ralik Chain, C Marshall Islands
55 W9 **Kwakoegron** Brokopondo, N Surinam
81 J21 **Kwale** Coast, S Kenya
77 U17 **Kwale** Delta, S Nigeria
79 H20 **Kwamouth** Bandundu, W Dem. Rep. Congo (Zaire)
Kwando *see* Cuando
Kwangchow *see* Guangzhou
Kwangchu *see* Kwangju
163 X16 **Kwangju** *off.* Kwangju-gwangyŏksi, *var.* Guangju, Kwangchu, *Jap.* Kōshū. SW South Korea
79 H20 **Kwango** *Port.* Cuango. ∼ Angola/Dem. Rep. Congo (Zaire) *see also* Cuango
Kwangsi/Kwangsi Chuang Autonomous Region *see* Guangxi Zhuangzu Zizhiqu
Kwangtung *see* Guangdong
Kwangyuan *see* Guangyuan
81 F17 **Kwania, Lake** ⊚ C Uganda
Kwanza *see* Cuanza
77 S15 **Kwara** ◈ *state* SW Nigeria
83 K22 **KwaZulu/Natal** *off.* KwaZulu/Natal Province; *prev.* Natal. ◈ *province* E South Africa
Kweichow *see* Guizhou
Kweichu *see* Guiyang
Kweilin *see* Guilin
Kweisui *see* Hohhot
Kweiyang *see* Guiyang
83 K17 **Kwekwe** *prev.* Que Que. Midlands, C Zimbabwe
83 G20 **Kweneng** ◈ *district* S Botswana
Kwesui *see* Hohhot
39 N12 **Kwethluk** Alaska, USA
39 N12 **Kwethluk River** ∼ Alaska, USA
110 J8 **Kwidzyń** *Ger.* Marienwerder. Pomorskie, N Poland
38 M13 **Kwigillingok** Alaska, USA
186 E9 **Kwikila** Central, S PNG
79 I20 **Kwilu** ∼ W Dem. Rep. Congo (Zaire)
Kwito *see* Cuito
171 U12 **Kwoka, Gunung** ▲ Irian Jaya, E Indonesia
78 I12 **Kyabé** Moyen-Chari, S Chad
183 O11 **Kyabram** Victoria, SE Australia
166 M9 **Kyaikkami** *prev.* Amherst. Mon State, S Myanmar
166 L9 **Kyaiklat** Irrawaddy, SW Myanmar
166 M8 **Kyaikto** Mon State, S Myanmar
123 N14 **Kyakhta** Respublika Buryatiya, S Russian Federation
182 G8 **Kyancutta** South Australia
167 T8 **Ky Anh** Ha Tinh, N Vietnam
166 L5 **Kyaukpadaung** Mandalay, C Myanmar
166 J6 **Kyaukpyu** Arakan State, W Myanmar
166 M5 **Kyaukse** Mandalay, C Myanmar
166 L8 **Kyaunggon** Irrawaddy, SW Myanmar
119 E14 **Kybartai** *Pol.* Kibarty. Vilkaviškis, S Lithuania
152 I7 **Kyelang** Himāchal Pradesh, NW India
111 G19 **Kyjov** *Ger.* Gaya. Brněnský Kraj, SE Czech Republic
115 J21 **Kykládes** *var.* Kikládhes, *Eng.* Cyclades. *island group* SE Greece
25 S11 **Kyle** Texas, SW USA
96 G9 **Kyle of Lochalsh** N Scotland, UK
101 D18 **Kyll** ∼ W Germany
115 F19 **Kyllíni** *var.* Killini. ▲ S Greece
93 M19 **Kymijoki** ∼ S Finland
115 H18 **Kými, Akrotírio** *headland* Évvoia, C Greece
127 W14 **Kyn** Permskaya Oblast', NW Russian Federation
183 N12 **Kyneton** Victoria, SE Australia
81 G17 **Kyoga, Lake** *var.* Lake Kioga. ⊚ C Uganda
164 J12 **Kyōga-misaki** *headland* Honshū, SW Japan
183 V4 **Kyogle** New South Wales, SE Australia
163 W15 **Kyŏnggi-man** *bay* NW South Korea
163 Z16 **Kyŏngju** *Jap.* Keishū. SE South Korea
Kyŏngsŏng *see* Sŏul
Kyōsai-tō *see* Kŏje-do
81 F19 **Kyotera** S Uganda
164 J13 **Kyōto** Kyōto, Honshū, SW Japan
164 J13 **Kyōto** *off.* Kyōto-fu, *var.* Kyōto Hu. ◈ *urban prefecture* Honshū, SW Japan
Kyōto-fu/Kyōto Hu *see* Kyōto
115 D21 **Kyparissía** *var.* Kiparissía. Pelopónnisos, S Greece
115 D20 **Kyparissiakós Kólpos** *gulf* S Greece
Kyperounda *see* Kyperoúnta
121 P3 **Kyperoúnta** *var.* Kyperounda. C Cyprus
Kypros *see* Cyprus
115 H16 **Kyrá Panagía** *island* Vóreioi Sporádes, Greece, Aegean Sea
Kyrenia *see* Girne
Kyrenia Mountains *see* Beşparmak Dağları
Kyrgyz Republic *see* Kyrgyzstan
147 U9 **Kyrgyzstan** *off.* Kyrgyz Republic, *var.* Kirghizia; *prev.* Kirgizskaya SSR, Kirghiz SSR, Republic of Kyrgyzstan. ◆ *republic* C Asia
100 M11 **Kyritz** Brandenburg, NE Germany
Kyrkslätt *see* Kirkkonummi
94 G8 **Kyrksæterøra** Sør-Trøndelag, S Norway
127 U8 **Kyrta** Respublika Komi, NW Russian Federation
111 J18 **Kysucké Nové Mesto** *prev.* Horné Nové Mesto, *Ger.* Kisutzaneustadtl, Oberneustadtl, *Hung.* Kiszucaújhely. Žilinnský Kraj, N Slovakia
117 N12 **Kytay, Ozero** ⊚ SW Ukraine
115 F23 **Kýthira** *var.* Kíthira, *It.* Cerigo; *Lat.* Cythera. Kýthira, S Greece
115 F23 **Kýthira** *var.* Kíthira, *It.* Cerigo; *Lat.* Cythera. *island* S Greece
115 I20 **Kýthnos** Kýthnos, Kykládes, Greece, Aegean Sea
115 I20 **Kýthnos** *var.* Kíthnos, Thermiá, *It.* Termia; *anc.* Cythnos. *island* Kykládes, Greece, Aegean Sea
115 I20 **Kýthnou, Stenó** *strait* Kykládes, Greece, Aegean Sea
Kyungëy Ala-Too, Khrebet *see* Kungei Ala-Tau
Kyurdamir *see* Kürdämir
146 C11 **Kyuren, Gora** ▲ W Turkmenistan
164 D15 **Kyūshū** *var.* Kyūsyū. *island* SW Japan
192 H6 **Kyushu-Palau Ridge** *var.* Kyusyu-Palau Ridge. *undersea feature* W Pacific Ocean
114 F10 **Kyustendil** *anc.* Pautalia. Kyustendil, W Bulgaria
114 G11 **Kyustendil** ◈ *province* W Bulgaria
Kyūsyū *see* Kyūshū
Kyusyu-Palau Ridge *see* Kyushu-Palau Ridge
123 P8 **Kyusyur** Respublika Sakha (Yakutiya), NE Russian Federation
183 P10 **Kywong** New South Wales, SE Australia
117 P4 **Kyyiv** *Eng.* Kiev, *Rus.* Kiyev. ● (Ukraine) Kyyivs'ka Oblast', N Ukraine
Kyyiv *see* Kyyivs'ka Oblast'
117 O4 **Kyyivs'ka Oblast'** *var.* Kyyiv, *Rus.* Kiyevskaya Oblast'. ◈ *province* N Ukraine
117 P3 **Kyyivs'ke Vodoskhovyshche** *Eng.* Kiev Reservoir, *Rus.* Kiyevskoye Vodokhranilishche. ⊠ N Ukraine
93 L16 **Kyyjärvi** Länsi-Suomi, W Finland
122 K14 **Kyzyl** Respublika Tyva, C Russian Federation
147 S8 **Kyzyl-Adyr** *prev.* Kirovskoye. Talasskaya Oblast', NW Kyrgyzstan
145 V14 **Kyzylagash** Almaty, SE Kazakhstan
146 C13 **Kyzylbair** Balkanskiy Velayat, W Turkmenistan
Kyzyl-Dzhiik, Pereval *see* Uzbel Shankou
145 S7 **Kyzylkak, Ozero** ⊚ NE Kazakhstan
145 X11 **Kyzylkesek** Vostochnyy Kazakhstan, E Kazakhstan
147 S10 **Kyzyl-Kiya** *Kir.* Kyzyl-Kyya. Oshskaya Oblast', SW Kyrgyzstan
144 L11 **Kyzylkol', Ozero** ⊚ C Kazakhstan
151 N15 **Kyzylorda** *var.* Kzyl-Orda, Qizil Orda *Kaz.* Qyzylorda; *prev.* Perovsk. Kyzylorda, S Kazakhstan
150 L14 **Kyzylorda** *off.* Kyzylordinskaya Oblast' *Kaz.* Qyzylorda Oblysy. ◈ *province* S Kazakhstan
122 K14 **Kyzyl Kum** *var.* Kizil Kum, Qizil Qum, *Uzb.* Qizilqum. *desert* Kazakhstan/Uzbekistan
Kyzyl-Kyya *see* Kyzyl-Kiya
Kyzylrabat *see* Qizilrawbe
Kyzylrabot *see* Qizilrabot
Kyzylsu *see* Kyzyl-Suu
147 X7 **Kyzyl-Suu** *prev.* Pokrovka. Issyk-Kul'skaya Oblast', NE Kyrgyzstan
147 S12 **Kyzyl-Suu** *var.* Kyzylsu. ∼ Kyrgyzstan/Tajikistan
147 X8 **Kyzyl-Tuu** Issyk-Kul'skaya Oblast', E Kyrgyzstan
145 Q12 **Kyzylzhar** *Kaz.* Qyzylzhar. Zhezkazgan, C Kazakhstan
Kzyl-Orda *see* Kyzylorda
Kzylordinskaya Oblast' *see* Kyzylorda
Kzyltu *see* Kishkenekol'

L

109 X2 **Laa an der Thaya** Niederösterreich, NE Austria
63 K15 **La Adela** La Pampa, SE Argentina
Laagen *see* Numedalslågen
109 S5 **Laakirchen** Oberösterreich, N Austria
Laaland *see* Lolland
104 I11 **La Albuera** Extremadura, W Spain
105 O7 **La Alcarria** *physical region* C Spain
104 K14 **La Algaba** Andalucía, S Spain
105 P9 **La Almarcha** Castilla-La Mancha, C Spain
105 R6 **La Almunia de Doña Godina** Aragón, NE Spain
41 N5 **La Amistad, Presa** ⊠ NW Mexico
118 F4 **Läänemaa** *off.* Lääne Maakond. ◈ *province* NW Estonia
118 I3 **Lääne-Virumaa** *off.* Lääne-Viru Maakond. ◈ *province* NE Estonia
62 J9 **La Antigua, Salina** *salt lake* W Argentina
99 E17 **Laarne** Oost-Vlaanderen, NW Belgium
80 O13 **Laas Caanood** Nugaal, N Somalia
41 O9 **La Ascensión** Nuevo León, NE Mexico
80 N12 **Laas Dhaareed** Woqooyi Galbeed, N Somalia
55 O4 **La Asunción** Nueva Esparta, NE Venezuela
Laatokka *see* Ladozhskoye Ozero
100 I13 **Laatzen** Niedersachsen, NW Germany
38 E9 **Laau Point** *headland* Molokai, Hawaii, USA, C Pacific Ocean
42 D6 **La Aurora** ✕ (Ciudad de Guatemala) Guatemala, C Guatemala
74 C9 **Laâyoune** *var.* Aaiún. ○ (Western Sahara) NW Western Sahara
128 L14 **Laba** ∼ SW Russian Federation
40 M6 **La Babia** Coahuila de Zaragoza, NE Mexico
15 R7 **La Baie** Quebec, SE Canada
171 P16 **Labala** Pulau Lomblen, S Indonesia
62 K8 **La Banda** Santiago del Estero, N Argentina
La Banda Oriental *see* Uruguay
104 K4 **La Bañeza** Castilla-León, N Spain
40 M13 **La Barca** Jalisco, SW Mexico
40 K14 **La Barra de Navidad** Jalisco, C Mexico
171 P16 **Labasa** *prev.* Lambasa. Vanua Levu, N Fiji
102 H8 **la Baule-Escoublac** Loire-Atlantique, NW France
Labe *see* Elbe
76 I13 **Labé** Moyenne-Guinée, NW Guinea
23 X14 **La Belle** Florida, SE USA
15 N11 **Labelle** Quebec, SE Canada
10 H7 **Laberge, Lake** ⊚ Yukon Territory, W Canada
Labes *see* Łobez
Labiau *see* Polessk
112 A10 **Labin** *It.* Albona. Istra, NW Croatia
128 L14 **Labinsk** Krasnodarskiy Kray, SW Russian Federation
105 X5 **La Bisbal d'Empordà** Cataluña, NE Spain
119 P16 **Labkovichy** *Rus.* Lobkovichi. Mahilyowskaya Voblasts', E Belarus
15 S4 **La Blache, Lac de** ⊚ Quebec, SE Canada
171 P4 **Labo** Luzon, N Philippines
Laboehanbadjo *see* Labuhanbajo
Laborca *see* Laborec
111 N18 **Laborec** *Hung.* Laborca. ∼ E Slovakia
108 D11 **La Borgne** ∼ S Switzerland
45 T12 **Laborie** SW Saint Lucia
79 F21 **La Bouenza** ◈ *province* S Congo
102 J14 **Labouheyre** Landes, SW France
62 L12 **Laboulaye** Córdoba, C Argentina
13 Q7 **Labrador** *cultural region* Newfoundland, SW Canada
64 I6 **Labrador Basin** *var.* Labrador Sea Basin. *undersea feature* Labrador Sea
13 N9 **Labrador City** Newfoundland, E Canada
13 Q5 **Labrador Sea** *sea* NW Atlantic Ocean
Labrador Sea Basin *see* Labrador Basin
Labrang *see* Xiahe
54 G9 **Labranzagrande** Boyacá, C Colombia
45 U15 **La Brea** Trinidad, Trinidad and Tobago
59 D14 **Lábrea** Amazonas, N Brazil
15 S6 **Labrieville** Quebec, SE Canada
102 K14 **Labrit** Landes, SW France
108 C9 **La Broye** ∼ SW Switzerland
103 N15 **Labruguière** Tarn, S France
168 M11 **Labu** Pulau Singkep, W Indonesia
169 T7 **Labuan** *var.* Victoria. Labuan, East Malaysia
169 T7 **Labuan** ◈ *federal territory* East Malaysia
Labuan *see* Labuan, Pulau
169 T7 **Labuan, Pulau** *var.* Labuan. *island* East Malaysia
171 N16 **Labuhanbajo** *prev.* Laboehanbadjo. Flores, S Indonesia
168 J9 **Labuhanbilik** Sumatera, N Indonesia
168 G8 **Labuhanhaji** Sumatera, W Indonesia
Labuk *see* Labuk, Sungai
Labuk Bay *see* Labuk, Teluk
169 V7 **Labuk, Sungai** *var.* Labuk. ∼ East Malaysia
169 W6 **Labuk, Teluk** *var.* Labuk Bay, Telukan Labuk. *bay* S Sulu Sea
Labuk, Telukan *see* Labuk, Teluk
166 K9 **Labutta** Irrawaddy, SW Myanmar
122 I8 **Labytnangi** Yamalo-Nenetskiy Avtonomnyy Okrug, N Russian Federation
78 F10 **Lac** *off.* Préfecture du Lac. ◈ *prefecture* W Chad
113 K19 **Laç** *var.* Laci. Lezhë, C Albania
57 K19 **Lacajahuira, Rio** ∼ W Bolivia
La Calamine *see* Kelmis
62 G11 **La Calera** Valparaíso, C Chile
13 P11 **Lac-Allard** Quebec, E Canada
104 L13 **La Campana** Andalucía, S Spain
102 J12 **Lacanau** Gironde, SW France
42 C2 **Lacandón, Sierra del** ▲ Guatemala/Mexico
La Cañiza *see* A Cañiza
41 W16 **Lacantún, Río** ∼ SE Mexico
103 Q3 **la Capelle** Aisne, N France
112 K10 **Laćarak** Serbia, NW Yugoslavia
62 L11 **La Carlota** Córdoba, C Argentina
104 L13 **La Carlota** Andalucía, S Spain
105 N12 **La Carolina** Andalucía, S Spain
103 O15 **Lacaune** Tarn, S France
15 P7 **Lac-Bouchette** Quebec, SE Canada
Laccadive Islands/Laccadive Minicoy and Amindivi Islands, the *see* Lakshadweep
11 Y16 **Lac du Bonnet** Manitoba, S Canada
30 L4 **Lac du Flambeau** Wisconsin, N USA
15 P8 **Lac-Édouard** Quebec, SE Canada
42 I4 **La Ceiba** Atlántida, N Honduras
54 E9 **La Ceja** Antioquia, W Colombia
182 J11 **Lacepede Bay** *bay* South Australia
32 G9 **Lacey** Washington, NW USA
103 P12 **la Chaise-Dieu** Haute-Loire, C France
114 G13 **Lachanás** Kentrikí Makedonía, N Greece
126 L11 **Lacha, Ozero** ⊚ NW Russian Federation
103 O8 **la Charité-sur-Loire** Nièvre, C France
103 N9 **la Châtre** Indre, C France
108 C8 **La Chaux-de-Fonds** Neuchâtel, W Switzerland
Lach Dera *see* Dheere Laaq
108 G8 **Lachen** Schwyz, C Switzerland
183 Q8 **Lachlan River** ∼ New South Wales, SE Australia
43 T15 **La Chorrera** Panamá, C Panama
15 V7 **Lac-Humqui** Quebec, SE Canada
15 N12 **Lachute** Quebec, SE Canada
Lachyn *see* Laçın
Laci *see* Laç
137 W13 **Laçın** *Rus.* Lachyn. SW Azerbaijan
103 S16 **la Ciotat** *anc.* Citharista. Bouches-du-Rhône, SE France
18 D10 **Lackawanna** New York, NE USA
11 Q13 **Lac La Biche** Alberta, SW Canada
Lac La Martre *see* Wha Ti
15 R12 **Lac-Mégantic** *var.* Mégantic. Quebec, SE Canada
Lacobriga *see* Lagos
40 G5 **La Colorada** Sonora, NW Mexico
11 Q15 **Lacombe** Alberta, SW Canada
30 L12 **Lacon** Illinois, N USA
43 P16 **La Concepción** *var.* Concepción. Chiriquí, W Panama
54 H5 **La Concepción** Zulia, NW Venezuela
54 H5 **La Concepción** Zulia, NW Venezuela
107 C19 **Laconi** Sardegna, Italy, C Mediterranean Sea
19 O9 **Laconia** New Hampshire, NE USA
61 H19 **La Coronilla** Rocha, E Uruguay
La Coruña *see* A Coruña
103 O11 **la Courtine** Creuse, C France
102 J16 **Lacq** Pyrénées-Atlantiques, SW France
15 P9 **La Croche** Quebec, SE Canada
29 X3 **la Croix, Lac** ⊚ Canada/USA
26 K5 **La Crosse** Kansas, C USA
21 V7 **La Crosse** Virginia, NE USA
32 L9 **La Crosse** Washington, NW USA
30 J7 **La Crosse** Wisconsin, N USA
54 C13 **La Cruz** Nariño, SW Colombia
42 K12 **La Cruz** Guanacaste, NW Costa Rica
40 I10 **La Cruz** Sinaloa, W Mexico
61 F19 **La Cruz** Florida, S Uruguay
42 M9 **La Cruz de Río Grande** Región Autónoma Atlántico Sur, E Nicaragua
54 J4 **La Cruz de Taratara** Falcón, N Venezuela
15 Q10 **Lac-St-Charles** Quebec, SE Canada
40 M6 **La Cuesta** Coahuila de Zaragoza, NE Mexico
57 A17 **La Cumbra, Volcán** ✱ Galapagos Islands, Ecuador, E Pacific Ocean
152 J5 **Ladākh Range** ▲ NE India
26 I5 **Ladder Creek** ∼ Kansas, C USA
45 X10 **la Désirade** *atoll* E Guadeloupe
Lādhiqīyah, Muḥāfaẓat al *see* Al Lādhiqīyah
83 F25 **Ladismith** Western Cape, SW South Africa
152 G11 **Lādnūn** Rājasthān, NW India
Ladoga, Lake *see* Ladozhskoye Ozero
115 E19 **Ládon** ∼ S Greece
54 E9 **La Dorada** Caldas, C Colombia
126 H11 **Ladozhskoye Ozero** *Eng.* Lake Ladoga, *Fin.* Laatokka. ⊚ NW Russian Federation
37 R12 **Ladron Peak** ▲ New Mexico, SW USA
126 J11 **Ladva-Vetka** Respublika Kareliya, NW Russian Federation
183 Q15 **Lady Barron** Tasmania, SE Australia
14 G9 **Lady Evelyn Lake** ⊚ Ontario, S Canada
23 W11 **Lady Lake** Florida, SE USA
10 L17 **Ladysmith** Vancouver Island, British Columbia, SW Canada
83 J22 **Ladysmith** KwaZulu/Natal, E South Africa
30 J5 **Ladysmith** Wisconsin, N USA
145 P9 **Ladyzhenka** Akmola, C Kazakhstan
186 E7 **Lae** Morobe, W PNG
189 R6 **Lae Atoll** *atoll* Ralik Chain, W Marshall Islands
40 C3 **La Encantada, Cerro de** ▲ NW Mexico
94 E12 **Lærdalsøyri** Sogn og Fjordane, S Norway
55 N11 **La Esmeralda** Amazonas, S Venezuela
42 G7 **La Esperanza** Intibucá, SW Honduras
30 K8 **La Farge** Wisconsin, N USA
23 R5 **Lafayette** Alabama, S USA
37 T4 **Lafayette** Colorado, C USA
23 R2 **La Fayette** Georgia, SE USA
31 O13 **Lafayette** Indiana, N USA
22 I9 **Lafayette** Louisiana, S USA
20 K8 **Lafayette** Tennessee, S USA
19 N7 **Lafayette, Mount** ▲ New Hampshire, NE USA
La Fe *see* Santa Fé
103 P3 **la Fère** Aisne, N France
102 L6 **la Ferté-Bernard** Sarthe, NW France
102 K5 **la Ferté-Macé** Orne, N France
103 N7 **la Ferté-St-Aubin** Loiret, C France
103 P5 **la Ferté-sous-Jouarre** Seine-et-Marne, N France
77 V15 **Lafia** Nassarawa, C Nigeria
77 T15 **Lafiagi** Kwara, W Nigeria
11 T17 **Lafleche** Saskatchewan, S Canada
102 K7 **la Flèche** Sarthe, NW France
109 X7 **Lafnitz** *Hung.* Lapines. ∼ Austria/Hungary
187 P17 **La Foa** Province Sud, S New Caledonia
20 M8 **La Follette** Tennessee, S USA
15 N12 **Lafontaine** Quebec, SE Canada
22 K10 **Lafourche, Bayou** ∼ Louisiana, S USA
62 K6 **La Fragua** Santiago del Estero, N Argentina
54 H7 **La Fría** Táchira, NW Venezuela
104 J7 **La Fuente de San Esteban** Castilla-León, N Spain
186 C7 **Lagaip** ∼ W PNG
61 B15 **La Gallareta** Santa Fe, C Argentina
129 Q14 **Lagan'** *prev.* Kaspiyskiy. Respublika Kalmykiya, SW Russian Federation
95 L20 **Lagan** Kronoberg, S Sweden
95 K21 **Lågan** ∼ S Sweden
92 L2 **Lagarfljót** *var.* Lögurinn. ⊚ E Iceland
37 R7 **La Garita Mountains** ▲ Colorado, C USA
171 O2 **Lagawe** Luzon, N Philippines
78 F13 **Lagdo** Nord, N Cameroon
78 F13 **Lagdo, Lac de** ⊚ N Cameroon
100 H13 **Lage** Nordrhein-Westfalen, W Germany
94 H12 **Lågen** ∼ S Norway
61 J14 **Lages** Santa Catarina, S Brazil
149 R4 **Laghmān** ◈ *province* E Afghanistan
74 J6 **Laghouat** N Algeria
105 Q10 **La Gineta** Castilla-La Mancha, C Spain
115 E21 **Lagkáda** *var.* Langada. Pelopónnisos, S Greece
114 G13 **Lagkadás** *var.* Langades, Langadhás. Kentrikí Makedonía, N Greece
115 E20 **Lagkádia** *var.* Langádhia, Langadia. Pelopónnisos, S Greece
54 F6 **La Gloria** Cesar, N Colombia
41 O7 **La Gloria** Nuevo León, NE Mexico
92 N3 **Lågneset** *headland* W Svalbard
104 G14 **Lagoa** Faro, S Portugal
La Goagira *see* La Guajira
61 I14 **Lagoa Vermelha** Rio Grande do Sul, S Brazil
137 V10 **Lagodekhi** SE Georgia
42 C7 **La Gomera** Escuintla, S Guatemala
Lagone *see* Logone
107 M19 **Lagonegro** Basilicata, S Italy
63 G16 **Lago Ranco** Los Lagos, S Chile
77 S16 **Lagos** Lagos, SW Nigeria
104 F14 **Lagos** *anc.* Lacobriga. Faro, S Portugal
77 S16 **Lagos** ◈ *state* SW Nigeria
40 M12 **Lagos de Moreno** Jalisco, SW Mexico
Lagosta *see* Lastovo
74 A12 **Lagouira** SW Western Sahara
92 O1 **Lågøya** *island* N Svalbard
32 L11 **La Grande** Oregon, NW USA
103 Q14 **la Grande-Combe** Gard, S France
12 K9 **La Grande Rivière** *var.* Fort George. ∼ Quebec, SE Canada
23 R4 **La Grange** Georgia, SE USA
31 P11 **Lagrange** Indiana, N USA
20 L5 **La Grange** Kentucky, S USA
27 V2 **La Grange** Missouri, C USA
21 V10 **La Grange** North Carolina, SE USA
25 U11 **La Grange** Texas, SW USA
105 N7 **La Granja** Castilla-León, N Spain
55 Q9 **La Gran Sabana** *grassland* E Venezuela
54 H7 **La Grita** Táchira, NW Venezuela
La Grulla *see* Grulla
15 R11 **La Guadeloupe** Quebec, SE Canada
64 F12 **La Guaira** Distrito Federal, N Venezuela
54 G4 **La Guajira** *off.* Departamento de La Guajira, *var.* Guajira, La Goagira. ◈ *province* NE Colombia
188 I4 **Lagua Lichan, Punta** *headland* Saipan, S Northern Mariana Islands
18 K14 **La Guardia** ✕ (New York) Long Island, New York, NE USA
La Guardia/Laguardia *see* A Guardia
105 P4 **Laguardia** País Vasco, N Spain
La Gudiña *see* A Gudiña
103 O9 **la Guerche-sur-l'Aubois** Cher, C France
103 O13 **Laguiole** Aveyron, S France
83 F26 **L'Agulhas** *var.* Agulhas. W Cape, SW South Africa
61 K14 **Laguna** Santa Catarina, S Brazil
37 Q11 **Laguna** New Mexico, SW USA
35 T16 **Laguna Beach** California, W USA
35 Y17 **Laguna Dam** *dam* Arizona/California, W USA
40 L7 **Laguna El Rey** Coahuila de Zaragoza, N Mexico
35 V17 **Laguna Mountains** ▲ California, W USA
61 B17 **Laguna Paiva** Santa Fe, C Argentina
62 H3 **Lagunas** Tarapacá, N Chile
56 E9 **Lagunas** Loreto, N Peru
57 M20 **Lagunillas** Santa Cruz, SE Bolivia
54 H6 **Lagunillas** Mérida, NW Venezuela
44 C4 **La Habana** *var.* Havana. ● (Cuba) Ciudad de La Habana, W Cuba
169 W7 **Lahad Datu** Sabah, East Malaysia
169 W7 **Lahad Datu, Teluk** *var.* Telukan Lahad Datu, Teluk Darvel, Teluk Datu; *prev.* Darvel Bay. *bay* Sabah, East Malaysia
38 F10 **Lahaina** Maui, Hawaii, USA, C Pacific Ocean
168 L14 **Lahat** Sumatera, W Indonesia
La Haye *see* 's-Gravenhage
Lahej *see* Laḥij
62 G9 **La Higuera** Coquimbo, N Chile
141 S13 **Lahī, Ḥisā' al** *spring/well* NE Yemen
141 O16 **Laḥij** *var.* Laḥj, *Eng.* Lahej. SW Yemen
142 M3 **Lāhījān** Gīlān, NW Iran
119 I19 **Lahishyn** *Pol.* Lohiszyn, *Rus.* Logishin. Brestskaya Voblasts', SW Belarus
Laḥj *see* Laḥij
101 F18 **Lahn** ∼ W Germany
Lähn *see* Wleń
95 J21 **Laholm** Halland, S Sweden
95 J21 **Laholmsbukten** *bay* S Sweden
35 R6 **Lahontan Reservoir** ⊠ Nevada, W USA
149 W8 **Lahore** Punjab, NE Pakistan
149 W8 **Lahore** ✕ Punjab, E Pakistan
55 Q6 **La Horqueta** Delta Amacuro, NE Venezuela
119 K15 **Lahoysk** *Rus.* Logoysk. Minskaya Voblasts', C Belarus
101 F22 **Lahr** Baden-Württemberg, S Germany
93 M19 **Lahti** *Swe.* Lahtis. Etelä-Suomi, S Finland
Lahtis *see* Lahti
40 M14 **La Huacana** Michoacán de Ocampo, SW Mexico
40 K14 **La Huerta** Jalisco, SW Mexico
78 H12 **Laï** *prev.* Behagle, De Behagle. Tandjilé, S Chad
Laibach *see* Ljubljana
167 Q5 **Lai Châu** Lai Châu, N Vietnam
38 D9 **Laie** *Haw.* Lā'ie. Oahu, Hawaii, USA, C Pacific Ocean
102 L5 **l'Aigle** Orne, N France
103 Q7 **Laignes** Côte d'Or, C France
93 K17 **Laihia** Länsi-Suomi, W Finland
Laila *see* Laylā
83 F25 **Laingsburg** Western Cape, SW South Africa
109 U2 **Lainsitz** *Cz.* Lužnice. ∼ Austria/Czech Republic
96 I7 **Lairg** N Scotland, UK
81 I17 **Laisamis** Eastern, N Kenya
Laisberg *see* Leisi
129 R4 **Laishevo** Respublika Tatarstan, W Russian Federation
Laisholm *see* Jõgeva
92 H13 **Laisvall** Norrbotten, N Sweden
93 K19 **Laitila** Länsi-Suomi, W Finland
161 P5 **Laiwu** Shandong, E China
161 R4 **Laixi** *var.* Shuiji. Shandong, E China
161 R4 **Laiyang** Shandong, E China
161 O3 **Laiyuan** Hebei, E China
161 R4 **Laizhou** *var.* Ye Xian. Shandong, E China
161 Q4 **Laizhou Wan** *var.* Laichow Bay. *bay* E China
37 S8 **La Jara** Colorado, C USA
61 I15 **Lajeado** Rio Grande do Sul, S Brazil
112 L12 **Lajkovac** Serbia, C Yugoslavia
111 K23 **Lajosmizse** Bács-Kiskun, C Hungary
Lajta *see* Leitha
40 I6 **La Junta** Chihuahua, N Mexico
37 V7 **La Junta** Colorado, C USA
92 J13 **Lakaträsk** Norrbotten, N Sweden
Lak Dera *see* Dheere Laaq
Lakeamu *see* Lakekamu
29 P12 **Lake Andes** South Dakota, N USA
22 H9 **Lake Arthur** Louisiana, S USA
187 Z15 **Lakeba** *prev.* Lakemba. *island* Lau Group, E Fiji
187 Z14 **Lakeba Passage** *channel* E Fiji
29 S10 **Lake Benton** Minnesota, N USA
23 V9 **Lake Butler** Florida, SE USA
183 P8 **Lake Cargelligo** New South Wales, SE Australia
22 G9 **Lake Charles** Louisiana, S USA
27 X9 **Lake City** Arkansas, C USA
37 Q7 **Lake City** Colorado, C USA
23 V9 **Lake City** Florida, SE USA
29 U13 **Lake City** Iowa, C USA
31 P7 **Lake City** Michigan, N USA
29 W9 **Lake City** Minnesota, N USA
21 T13 **Lake City** South Carolina, SE USA
29 Q7 **Lake City** South Dakota, N USA
20 M8 **Lake City** Tennessee, S USA
10 L17 **Lake Cowichan** Vancouver Island, British Columbia, SW Canada
29 U10 **Lake Crystal** Minnesota, N USA
25 T6 **Lake Dallas** Texas, SW USA
97 K15 **Lake District** *physical region* NW England, UK
18 D10 **Lake Erie Beach** New York, NE USA
29 T11 **Lakefield** Minnesota, N USA
25 V6 **Lake Fork Reservoir** ⊠ Texas, SW USA
30 M9 **Lake Geneva** Wisconsin, N USA
18 L9 **Lake George** New York, NE USA

◆ Country ● Country Capital ◇ Dependent Territory ○ Dependent Territory Capital ◈ Administrative Region ✕ International Airport ▲ Mountain ▲ Mountain Range ✱ Volcano ∼ River ⊚ Lake ⊠ Reservoir

9 R7 **Lake Harbour** Baffin Island, Nunavut, NE Canada
36 I12 **Lake Havasu City** Arizona, SW USA
25 W12 **Lake Jackson** Texas, SW USA
186 D8 **Lakeamu** *var.* Lakeamu. ≈ S PNG
180 K13 **Lake King** Western Australia
23 V12 **Lakeland** Florida, SE USA
23 U7 **Lakeland** Georgia, SE USA
181 W4 **Lakeland Downs** Queensland, NE Australia
11 P16 **Lake Louise** Alberta, SW Canada
Lakemba *see* Lakeba
29 V11 **Lake Mills** Iowa, C USA
39 Q10 **Lake Minchumina** Alaska, USA
Lakemti *see* Nek'emtē
186 A7 **Lake Murray** Western, SW PNG
80 F5 **Lake Nasser** *var.* Buhayrat Nasir, Buḩayrat Nāşir, Buḩeiret Nâşir. ◎ Egypt/Sudan
31 R9 **Lake Orion** Michigan, N USA
190 B16 **Lakepa** NE Niue
29 T11 **Lake Park** Iowa, C USA
18 K7 **Lake Placid** New York, NE USA
18 K9 **Lake Pleasant** New York, NE USA
34 M6 **Lakeport** California, W USA
29 Q10 **Lake Preston** South Dakota, N USA
22 J5 **Lake Providence** Louisiana, S USA
185 E20 **Lake Pukaki** Canterbury, South Island, NZ
183 Q12 **Lakes Entrance** Victoria, SE Australia
37 N12 **Lakeside** Arizona, SW USA
35 V17 **Lakeside** California, W USA
23 S9 **Lakeside** Florida, SE USA
28 K13 **Lakeside** Nebraska, C USA
32 E13 **Lakeside** Oregon, NW USA
21 W6 **Lakeside** Virginia, NE USA
Lakes State *see* El Buhayrat
Lake State *see* Michigan
185 F20 **Lake Tekapo** Canterbury, South Island, NZ
21 O10 **Lake Toxaway** North Carolina, SE USA
29 T13 **Lake View** Iowa, C USA
32 I16 **Lakeview** Oregon, NW USA
25 O3 **Lakeview** Texas, SW USA
27 W14 **Lake Village** Arkansas, C USA
23 W12 **Lake Wales** Florida, SE USA
37 T4 **Lakewood** Colorado, C USA
18 K15 **Lakewood** New Jersey, NE USA
18 C11 **Lakewood** New York, NE USA
31 T11 **Lakewood** Ohio, N USA
23 Y13 **Lakewood Park** Florida, SE USA
23 Z14 **Lake Worth** Florida, SE USA
152 H4 **Lake Wular** ◎ NE India
126 H11 **Lakhdenpokh'ya** Respublika Kareliya, NW Russian Federation
152 L11 **Lakhīmpur** Uttar Pradesh, N India
154 J11 **Lakhnādon** Madhya Pradesh, C India
Lakhnau *see* Lucknow
154 A9 **Lakhpat** Gujarāt, W India
119 K19 **Lakhva** *Rus.* Lakhva. Brestskaya Voblasts', SW Belarus
26 I6 **Lakin** Kansas, C USA
149 S7 **Lakki Marwat** North-West Frontier Province, NW Pakistan
115 F21 **Lakonía** *historical region* S Greece
115 F22 **Lakonikós Kólpos** *gulf* S Greece
76 M17 **Lakota** S Ivory Coast
29 U11 **Lakota** Iowa, C USA
29 P3 **Lakota** North Dakota, N USA
Lak Sao *see* Ban Lakxao
92 L8 **Laksefjorden** *fjord* N Norway
92 K8 **Lakselv** Finnmark, N Norway
155 B21 **Lakshadweep** *prev.* the Laccadive, Minicoy and Amindivi Islands. ◈ *union territory* India, N Indian Ocean
155 C22 **Lakshadweep** *Eng.* Laccadive Islands. *island group* India, N Indian Ocean
153 S17 **Lakshmikāntapur** West Bengal, NE India
112 G11 **Laktaši** Republika Srpska, N Bosnia and Herzegovina
149 V7 **Lāla Mūsa** Punjab, NE Pakistan
la Laon *see* Laon
114 M11 **Lalapaşa** Edirne, NW Turkey
83 P14 **Lalaua** Nampula, N Mozambique
105 S10 **L'Alcúdia** *var.* L'Alcudia. País Valenciano, E Spain
80 J11 **Lalibela** Amhara, N Ethiopia
153 T12 **Lalmanirhat** Rajshahi, N Bangladesh
79 F20 **La Lékoumou** ◈ *province* SW Congo
42 E8 **La Libertad** La Libertad, SW El Salvador
42 E3 **La Libertad** Petén, N Guatemala
42 H6 **La Libertad** Comayagua, SW Honduras
40 E4 **La Libertad** *var.* Puerto Libertad. Sonora, NW Mexico
42 K10 **La Libertad** Chontales, S Nicaragua
42 A9 **La Libertad** ◈ *department* SW El Salvador
56 B11 **La Libertad** *off.* Departamento de La Libertad. ◈ *department* W Peru
62 G11 **La Ligua** Valparaíso, C Chile
139 U5 **La'lī Khān** E Iraq
79 H16 **La Likouala** ◈ *province* NE Congo
104 H3 **Lalín** Galicia, NW Spain
102 L13 **Lalinde** Dordogne, SW France
104 K16 **La Línea** *var.* La Línea de la Concepción. Andalucía, S Spain
La Línea de la Concepción *see* La Línea
152 J14 **Lalitpur** Uttar Pradesh, N India
153 P11 **Lalitpur** Central, C Nepal
152 K10 **Lālkua** Uttar Pradesh, N India
11 R12 **La Loche** Saskatchewan, C Canada
102 M6 **la Loupe** Eure-et-Loir, C France
99 G20 **La Louvière** Hainaut, S Belgium
L'Altissima *see* Hochwilde
104 L14 **La Luisiana** Andalucía, S Spain
37 S14 **La Luz** New Mexico, SW USA
107 D16 **la Maddalena** Sardegna, Italy, C Mediterranean Sea
62 J7 **La Madrid** Tucumán, N Argentina
Lama-Kara *see* Kara
15 S8 **La Malbaie** Quebec, SE Canada
167 T10 **Lamam** Xékong, S Laos
105 P10 **La Mancha** *physical region* C Spain
la Manche *see* English Channel
187 R13 **Lamap** Malekula, C Vanuatu
37 W6 **Lamar** Colorado, C USA
27 S7 **Lamar** Missouri, C USA
21 S12 **Lamar** South Carolina, SE USA
107 C19 **La Marmora, Punta** ▲ Sardegna, Italy, C Mediterranean Sea
8 I9 **La Martre, Lac** ◎ Northwest Territories, NW Canada
56 D10 **Lamas** San Martín, N Peru
42 I5 **La Masica** Atlántida, NW Honduras
103 R12 **Lamastre** Ardèche, E France
La Matepec *see* Santa Ana, Volcán de
44 I7 **La Maya** Santiago de Cuba, E Cuba
109 S5 **Lambach** Oberösterreich, N Austria
168 I11 **Lambak** Pulau Pini, W Indonesia
102 H5 **Lamballe** Côtes d'Armor, NW France
79 D18 **Lambaréné** Moyen-Ogooué, W Gabon
Lambasa *see* Labasa
56 B11 **Lambayeque** Lambayeque, W Peru
56 A10 **Lambayeque** *off.* Departamento de Lambayeque. ◈ *department* NW Peru
97 G17 **Lambay Island** *Ir.* Reachrainn. *island* E Ireland
186 G6 **Lambert, Cape** *headland* New Britain, E PNG
195 W6 **Lambert Glacier** *glacier* Antarctica
29 T10 **Lamberton** Minnesota, N USA
27 X4 **Lambert-Saint Louis** ✕ Missouri, C USA
31 R11 **Lambertville** Michigan, N USA
18 J15 **Lambertville** New Jersey, NE USA
171 N12 **Lambogo** Sulawesi, N Indonesia
106 D8 **Lambro** ≈ N Italy
33 W11 **Lame Deer** Montana, NW USA
104 H6 **Lamego** Viseu, N Portugal
187 Q14 **Lamen Bay** Épi, C Vanuatu
45 X6 **Lamentin** Basse Terre, N Guadeloupe
Lamentin *see* le Lamentin
182 K10 **Lameroo** South Australia
54 F10 **La Mesa** Cundinamarca, C Colombia
35 U17 **La Mesa** California, W USA
37 R16 **La Mesa** New Mexico, SW USA
25 N6 **Lamesa** Texas, SW USA
115 F17 **Lamía** Stereá Ellás, C Greece
171 O8 **Lamitan** Basilan Island, SW Philippines
187 Y14 **Lamiti** Gau, C Fiji
171 T11 **Lamlam** Irian Jaya, E Indonesia
188 B16 **Lamlam, Mount** ▲ SW Guam
109 Q6 **Lammer** ≈ E Austria
185 E23 **Lammerlaw Range** ▲ South Island, NZ
95 L20 **Lammhult** Kronoberg, S Sweden
93 L18 **Lammi** Etelä-Suomi, S Finland
189 U11 **Lamoil** *island* Chuuk, C Micronesia
35 W3 **Lamoille** Nevada, W USA
18 M7 **Lamoille River** ≈ Vermont, NE USA
30 J13 **La Moine River** ≈ Illinois, N USA
171 P4 **Lamon Bay** *bay* Luzon, N Philippines
29 V16 **Lamoni** Iowa, C USA
35 R13 **Lamont** California, W USA
27 N8 **Lamont** Oklahoma, C USA
54 E13 **La Montañita** *var.* Montañita. Caquetá, S Colombia
43 N8 **La Mosquitia** *var.* Miskito Coast, *Eng.* Mosquito Coast. *coastal region* E Nicaragua
102 I9 **la Mothe-Achard** Vendée, NW France
188 L15 **Lamotrek Atoll** *atoll* Caroline Islands, C Micronesia
29 P6 **La Moure** North Dakota, N USA
167 O8 **Lampang** *var.* Muang Lampang. Lampang, NW Thailand
167 R9 **Lam Pao Reservoir** ▣ E Thailand
25 S9 **Lampasas** Texas, SW USA
25 S9 **Lampasas River** ≈ Texas, SW USA
41 N7 **Lampazos** *var.* Lampazos de Naranjo. Nuevo León, NE Mexico
Lampazos de Naranjo *see* Lampazos
115 E19 **Lámpeia** Dytikí Ellás, S Greece
101 G19 **Lampertheim** Hessen, W Germany
97 I20 **Lampeter** SW Wales, UK
167 O7 **Lamphun** *var.* Lampun, Muang Lamphun. Lamphun, NW Thailand
11 X10 **Lamprey** Manitoba, C Canada
Lampun *see* Lamphun
168 M15 **Lampung** *off.* Propinsi Lampung. ◈ *province* SW Indonesia
128 K6 **Lamskoye** Lipetskaya Oblast', W Russian Federation
81 K20 **Lamu** Coast, SE Kenya
43 N14 **La Muerte, Cerro** ▲ C Costa Rica
103 S13 **la Mure** Isère, E France
37 S10 **Lamy** New Mexico, SW USA
119 J18 **Lan'** *Rus.* Lan'. ≈ C Belarus
38 E10 **Lanai** *Haw.* Lāna'i. *island* Hawaii, USA, C Pacific Ocean
38 E10 **Lanai City** Lanai, Hawaii, USA, C Pacific Ocean
99 L18 **Lanaken** Limburg, NE Belgium
171 Q7 **Lanao, Lake** *var.* Lake Sultan Alonto. ◎ Mindanao, S Philippines
96 J12 **Lanark** S Scotland, UK
96 I13 **Lanark** *cultural region* C Scotland, UK
104 L9 **La Nava de Ricomalillo** Castilla-La Mancha, C Spain
166 M13 **Lanbi Kyun** *prev.* Sullivan Island. *island* Mergui Archipelago, S Myanmar
Lancang Jiang *see* Mekong
97 K17 **Lancashire** *cultural region* NW England, UK
15 N13 **Lancaster** Ontario, SE Canada
97 K16 **Lancaster** NW England, UK
35 T14 **Lancaster** California, W USA
20 M6 **Lancaster** Kentucky, S USA
27 U1 **Lancaster** Missouri, C USA
19 O7 **Lancaster** New Hampshire, NE USA
18 D10 **Lancaster** New York, NE USA
31 T14 **Lancaster** Ohio, N USA
18 H16 **Lancaster** Pennsylvania, NE USA
21 R11 **Lancaster** South Carolina, SE USA
25 U7 **Lancaster** Texas, SW USA
21 X5 **Lancaster** Virginia, NE USA
30 J9 **Lancaster** Wisconsin, N USA
9 O4 **Lancaster Sound** *sound* Nunavut, N Canada
Lan-chou/Lan-chow/Lanchow *see* Lanzhou
107 K14 **Lanciano** Abruzzo, C Italy
111 O16 **Łańcut** Podkarpackie, SE Poland
169 Q11 **Landak, Sungai** ≈ Borneo, N Indonesia
Landao *see* Lantau Island
Landau *see* Landau an der Isar, Bayern, Germany
Landau *see* Landau in der Pfalz, Rheinland-Pfalz, Germany
101 N22 **Landau an der Isar** *var.* Landau. Bayern, SE Germany
101 F20 **Landau in der Pfalz** *var.* Landau. Rheinland-Pfalz, SW Germany
Land Burgenland *see* Burgenland
108 K8 **Landeck** Tirol, W Austria
99 J19 **Landen** Vlaams Brabant, C Belgium
33 U15 **Lander** Wyoming, C USA
102 F5 **Landerneau** Finistère, NW France
95 K20 **Landeryd** Halland, S Sweden
102 J15 **Landes** ◈ *department* SW France
Landeshut/Landeshut in Schlesien *see* Kamienna Góra
105 R9 **Landete** Castilla-La Mancha, C Spain
99 M18 **Landgraaf** Limburg, SE Netherlands
102 F5 **Landivisiau** Finistère, NW France
Land of Enchantment *see* New Mexico
Land of Opportunity *see* Arkansas
Land of Steady Habits *see* Connecticut
Land of the Midnight Sun *see* Alaska
108 I8 **Landquart** Graubünden, SE Switzerland
108 J9 **Landquart** ≈ Austria/Switzerland
21 P10 **Landrum** South Carolina, SE USA
Landsberg *see* Gorowo Iławeckie, Warmińsko-Mazurskie, NE Poland
Landsberg *see* Gorzów Wielkopolski, Gorzów, Poland
101 K23 **Landsberg am Lech** Bayern, S Germany
Landsberg an der Warthe *see* Gorzów Wielkopolski
8 J4 **Lands End** *headland* Northwest Territories, NW Canada
97 G25 **Land's End** *headland* SW England, UK
101 M22 **Landshut** Bayern, SE Germany
Landskron *see* Lanškroun
95 J22 **Landskrona** Skåne, S Sweden
98 I10 **Landsmeer** Noord-Holland, C Netherlands
95 J19 **Landvetter** ✕ (Göteborg) Västra Götaland, S Sweden
Landwarów *see* Lentvaris
23 R5 **Lanett** Alabama, S USA
108 C8 **La Neuveville** *var.* Neuveville, *Ger.* Neuenstadt. Neuchâtel, W Switzerland
95 G21 **Langå** *var.* Langaa. Århus, C Denmark
Langaa *see* Langå
158 G14 **La'nga Co** ◎ W China
Langada *see* Lagkáda
Langades/Langadhás *see* Lagkadás
Langádhia/Langadia *see* Lagkádia
147 T14 **Langar** *Rus.* Lyangar. SE Tajikistan
146 M10 **Langar** *Rus.* Lyangar. Nawoiy Wiloyati, C Uzbekistan
142 M3 **Langarūd** Gīlān, NW Iran
11 V16 **Langbank** Saskatchewan, S Canada
29 P2 **Langdon** North Dakota, N USA
103 P12 **Langeac** Haute-Loire, C France
102 L8 **Langeais** Indre-et-Loire, C France
80 I8 **Langeb, Wadi** ≈ NE Sudan
Långed *see* Dals Långed
95 G25 **Langeland** *island* S Denmark
99 B18 **Langemark** West-Vlaanderen, W Belgium
101 G18 **Langen** Hessen, W Germany
101 J22 **Langenau** Baden-Württemberg, S Germany
11 V16 **Langenburg** Saskatchewan, S Canada
101 E16 **Langenfeld** Nordrhein-Westfalen, W Germany
108 L8 **Längenfeld** Tirol, W Austria
100 I12 **Langenhagen** Niedersachsen, N Germany
100 I12 **Langenhagen** ✕ (Hannover) Niedersachsen, NW Germany
109 W3 **Langenlois** Niederösterreich, NE Austria
108 E7 **Langenthal** Bern, NW Switzerland
109 W6 **Langenwang** Steiermark, E Austria
109 X3 **Langenzersdorf** Niederösterreich, E Austria
100 F9 **Langeoog** *island* NW Germany
95 H23 **Langeskov** Fyn, C Denmark
95 G16 **Langesund** Telemark, S Norway
95 G17 **Langesundsfjorden** *fjord* S Norway
94 D10 **Langevågen** Møre og Romsdal, S Norway
161 P3 **Langfang** Hebei, E China
94 E9 **Langfjorden** *fjord* S Norway
29 Q8 **Langford** South Dakota, N USA
168 I10 **Langgapayung** Sumatera, W Indonesia
106 E9 **Langhirano** Emilia-Romagna, C Italy
97 K14 **Langholm** S Scotland, UK
92 I3 **Langjökull** *glacier* C Iceland
168 I6 **Langkawi, Pulau** *island* Peninsular Malaysia
166 M14 **Langkha Tuk, Khao** ▲ SW Thailand
14 L8 **Langlade** Quebec, SE Canada
10 M17 **Langley** British Columbia, SW Canada
167 S7 **Lang Mô** Thanh Hoa, N Vietnam
Langnau *see* Langnau im Emmental
108 E8 **Langnau im Emmental** *var.* Langnau. Bern, W Switzerland
103 Q13 **Langogne** Lozère, S France
158 K16 **Langoi Kangri** ▲ W China
102 K13 **Langon** Gironde, SW France
La Ngounié *see* Ngounié
92 G10 **Langøya** *island* C Norway
158 G14 **Langqên Zangbo** ≈ China/India
104 K2 **Langreo** *var.* Sama de Langreo. Asturias, N Spain
103 S7 **Langres** Haute-Marne, N France
103 R8 **Langres, Plateau de** *plateau* C France
168 H8 **Langsa** Sumatera, W Indonesia
93 H16 **Långsele** Västernorrland, C Sweden
162 L12 **Lang Shan** ▲ N China
95 M14 **Långshyttan** Dalarna, C Sweden
167 T5 **Lang Son** *var.* Langson. Lang Sơn, N Vietnam
167 N14 **Lang Suan** Chumphon, SW Thailand
93 J14 **Långträsk** Norrbotten, N Sweden
25 N11 **Langtry** Texas, SW USA
103 P16 **Languedoc** *cultural region* S France
103 P15 **Languedoc-Roussillon** ◈ *region* S France
27 X10 **L'Anguille River** ≈ Arkansas, C USA
93 I16 **Långviksmon** Västernorrland, N Sweden
101 K22 **Langweid** Bayern, S Germany
160 J8 **Langzhong** Sichuan, C China
Lan Hsü *see* Lan Yü
11 U15 **Lanigan** Saskatchewan, S Canada
116 K5 **Lanivtsi** Ternopil's'ka Oblast', W Ukraine
137 Y13 **Länkäran** *Rus.* Lenkoran'. S Azerbaijan
102 L16 **Lannemezan** Hautes-Pyrénées, S France
102 G5 **Lannion** Côtes d'Armor, NW France
14 M11 **L'Annonciation** Quebec, SE Canada
105 V5 **L'Anoia** ≈ NE Spain
18 I15 **Lansdale** Pennsylvania, NE USA
14 L14 **Lansdowne** Ontario, SE Canada
152 K9 **Lansdowne** Uttar Pradesh, N India
30 M3 **L'Anse** Michigan, N USA
15 S7 **L'Anse-St-Jean** Quebec, SE Canada
93 K18 **Länsi-Suomi** ◈ *province* W Finland
29 Y11 **Lansing** Iowa, C USA
27 R4 **Lansing** Kansas, C USA
31 Q9 **Lansing** *state capital* Michigan, N USA
92 J12 **Lansjärv** Norrbotten, N Sweden
111 G17 **Lanškroun** *Ger.* Landskron. Pardubický Kraj, C Czech Republic
167 N16 **Lanta, Ko** *island* S Thailand
161 O15 **Lantau Island** *Cant.* Tai Yue Shan, *Chin.* Landao. *island* Hong Kong, S China
Lan-ts'ang Chiang *see* Mekong
171 O11 **Lanu** Sulawesi, N Indonesia
107 D19 **Lanusei** Sardegna, Italy, C Mediterranean Sea
102 H7 **Lanvaux, Landes de** *physical region* NW France
163 W8 **Lanxi** Heilongjiang, NE China
161 R10 **Lanxi** Zhejiang, SE China
La Nyanga *see* Nyanga
161 T15 **Lan Yü** *var.* Huoshao Tao, *var.* Hungt'ou, Lan Hsü, Lanyü, *Eng.* Orchid Island; *prev.* Kotosho, Koto Sho. *island* SE Taiwan
64 P11 **Lanzarote** *island* Islas Canarias, Spain, NE Atlantic Ocean
159 V10 **Lanzhou** *var.* Lan-chou, Lanchow, Lan-chow; *prev.* Kaolan. Gansu, C China
106 B8 **Lanzo Torinese** Piemonte, NE Italy
171 O1 **Laoag** Luzon, N Philippines
171 Q5 **Laoang** Samar, C Philippines
167 R5 **Lao Cai** Lao Cai, N Vietnam
Laodicea/Laodicea ad Mare *see* Al Lādhiqīyah
Laoet *see* Laut, Pulau
163 T11 **Laoha He** ≈ NE China
160 M8 **Laohekou** *prev.* Guanghua. Hubei, C China
Laoi, An *see* Lee
97 E19 **Laois** *prev.* Leix, Queen's County. *cultural region* C Ireland
Laojunmiao *see* Yumen
163 W12 **Lao Ling** ▲ N China
64 Q11 **La Oliva** *var.* Oliva. Fuerteventura, Islas Canarias, Spain, NE Atlantic Ocean
Lao, Loch *see* Belfast Lough
Lao Mangnai *see* Mangnai
103 P3 **Laon** *var.* la Laon; *anc.* Laudunum. Aisne, N France
Lao People's Democratic Republic *see* Laos
54 M3 **La Orchila, Isla** *island* N Venezuela
64 O11 **La Orotava** Tenerife, Islas Canarias, Spain, NE Atlantic Ocean
57 E14 **La Oroya** Junín, C Peru
167 Q7 **Laos** *off.* Lao People's Democratic Republic. ◆ *republic* SE Asia
161 R5 **Laoshan Wan** *bay* E China
163 Y10 **Laoye Ling** ▲ NE China
60 J12 **Lapa** Paraná, S Brazil
103 P10 **Lapalisse** Allier, C France
54 F9 **La Palma** Cundinamarca, C Colombia
42 F7 **La Palma** Chalatenango, N El Salvador
43 W16 **La Palma** Darién, SE Panama
64 N11 **La Palma** *island* Islas Canarias, Spain, NE Atlantic Ocean
104 J14 **La Palma del Condado** Andalucía, S Spain
61 F18 **La Paloma** Durazno, C Uruguay
61 G20 **La Paloma** Rocha, E Uruguay
61 A21 **La Pampa** *off.* Provincia de La Pampa. ◈ *province* C Argentina
55 P8 **La Paragua** Bolívar, E Venezuela
119 O16 **Lapatsichy** *Rus.* Lopatichi. Mahilyowskaya Voblasts', E Belarus
61 C16 **La Paz** Entre Ríos, E Argentina
62 I11 **La Paz** Mendoza, C Argentina
57 J18 **La Paz** *var.* La Paz de Ayacucho. ● (Bolivia-legislative and administrative capital) La Paz, W Bolivia
42 H6 **La Paz** La Paz, SW Honduras
40 F9 **La Paz** Baja California Sur, NW Mexico
61 F20 **La Paz** Canelones, S Uruguay
57 J16 **La Paz** ◈ *department* W Bolivia
42 B9 **La Paz** ◈ *department* S El Salvador
42 G7 **La Paz** ◈ *department* SW Honduras
La Paz *see* El Alto, Bolivia
La Paz *see* Robles, Colombia
La Paz *see* La Paz Centro, Nicaragua
40 F9 **La Paz, Bahía de** *bay* W Mexico
42 I10 **La Paz Centro** *var.* La Paz. León, W Nicaragua
La Paz de Ayacucho *see* La Paz
54 J15 **La Pedrera** Amazonas, SE Colombia
31 S9 **Lapeer** Michigan, N USA
40 K6 **La Perla** Chihuahua, N Mexico
165 T1 **La Perouse Strait** *Jap.* Sōya-kaikyō, *Rus.* Proliv Laperuza. *strait* Japan/Russian Federation
63 I14 **La Perra, Salitral de** *salt lake* C Argentina
Laperuza, Proliv *see* La Perouse Strait
41 Q10 **La Pesca** Tamaulipas, C Mexico
40 M13 **La Piedad Cavadas** Michoacán de Ocampo, C Mexico
Lapines *see* Lafnitz
93 M16 **Lapinlahti** Itä-Suomi, C Finland
Lápithos *see* Lapta
22 K9 **Laplace** Louisiana, S USA
45 X12 **La Plaine** SE Dominica
173 P16 **la Plaine-des-Palmistes** C Réunion
92 K11 **Lapland** *Fin.* Lappi, *Swe.* Lappland. *cultural region* N Europe
28 M8 **La Plant** South Dakota, N USA
61 D20 **La Plata** Buenos Aires, E Argentina
54 D12 **La Plata** Huila, SW Colombia
21 W4 **La Plata** Maryland, NE USA
La Plata *see* Sucre
45 U6 **la Plata, Río de** ≈ C Puerto Rico
105 W4 **La Pobla de Lillet** Cataluña, NE Spain
105 U4 **La Pobla de Segur** Cataluña, NE Spain
15 S9 **La Pocatière** Quebec, SE Canada
104 L3 **La Pola de Gordón** Castilla-León, N Spain
31 O11 **La Porte** Indiana, N USA
18 H13 **Laporte** Pennsylvania, NE USA
29 X13 **La Porte City** Iowa, C USA
62 J8 **La Posta** Catamarca, C Argentina
40 E8 **La Poza Grande** Baja California Sur, W Mexico
93 K16 **Lappajärvi** Länsi-Suomi, W Finland
93 L16 **Lappajärvi** ◎ W Finland
93 N18 **Lappeenranta** *Swe.* Villmanstrand. Etelä-Suomi, S Finland
93 J17 **Lappfjärd** *Fin.* Lapväärtti. Länsi-Suomi, W Finland
92 L12 **Lappi** *Swe.* Lappland. ◈ *province* N Finland
Lappi *see* Lapland
Lappland *see* Lappi
Lappland *see* Lapland, N Europe
Lappo *see* Lapua
61 C23 **Laprida** Buenos Aires, E Argentina
25 P13 **La Pryor** Texas, SW USA
136 B11 **Lâpseki** Çanakkale, NW Turkey
121 P2 **Lapta** *Gk.* Lápithos. NW Cyprus
Laptev Sea *see* Laptevykh, More
122 N6 **Laptevykh, More** *Eng.* Laptev Sea. *sea* Arctic Ocean
93 K16 **Lapua** *Swe.* Lappo. Länsi-Suomi, W Finland
105 P3 **La Puebla de Arganzón** País Vasco, N Spain
104 L14 **La Puebla de Cazalla** Andalucía, S Spain
104 M9 **La Puebla de Montalbán** Castilla-La Mancha, C Spain
54 I6 **La Puerta** Trujillo, NW Venezuela
Lapurdum *see* Bayonne
40 E7 **La Purísima** Baja California Sur, W Mexico
Lapväärtti *see* Lappfjärd
110 O10 **Łapy** Podlaskie, NE Poland
80 D6 **Laqiya Arba'in** Northern, NW Sudan
62 J4 **La Quiaca** Jujuy, N Argentina
107 J14 **L'Aquila** *var.* Aquila, Aquila degli Abruzzo. Abruzzo, C Italy
143 Q13 **Lār** Fārs, S Iran
54 J5 **Lara** *off.* Estado Lara. ◈ *state* NW Venezuela
104 G2 **Laracha** Galicia, NW Spain
74 G5 **Larache** *var.* al Araïch, El Araïch, El Araïche, *anc.* Lixus. NW Morocco
103 T14 **Laragne-Montéglin** Hautes-Alpes, SE France
104 M13 **La Rambla** Andalucía, S Spain
33 Y17 **Laramie** Wyoming, C USA
33 X15 **Laramie Mountains** ▲ Wyoming, C USA
33 Y16 **Laramie River** ≈ Wyoming, C USA
60 H12 **Laranjeiras do Sul** Paraná, S Brazil
Larantoeka *see* Larantuka
171 P16 **Larantuka** *prev.* Larantoeka. Flores, C Indonesia
171 U15 **Larat** Pulau Larat, E Indonesia
171 U15 **Larat, Pulau** *island* Kepulauan Tanimbar, E Indonesia
95 P19 **Lärbro** Gotland, SE Sweden
106 A9 **Larche, Col de** *pass* France/Italy
14 H8 **Larder Lake** Ontario, S Canada
105 O2 **Laredo** Cantabria, N Spain
25 Q15 **Laredo** Texas, SW USA
40 H9 **La Reforma** Sinaloa, W Mexico
98 N11 **Laren** Gelderland, E Netherlands
98 J11 **Laren** Noord-Holland, C Netherlands
102 K13 **la Réole** Gironde, SW France
La Réunion *see* Réunion
Largeau *see* Faya
103 U13 **l'Argentière-la-Bessée** Hautes-Alpes, SE France
149 O4 **Lar Gerd** *var.* Largird. Balkh, N Afghanistan
Largird *see* Lar Gerd
23 V12 **Largo** Florida, SE USA
37 Q9 **Largo, Canon** *valley* New Mexico, SW USA
44 D6 **Largo, Cayo** *island* W Cuba
23 Z17 **Largo, Key** *island* Florida Keys, Florida, SE USA
96 H12 **Largs** W Scotland, UK
102 I16 **la Rhune** *var.* Larrún. ▲ France/Spain *see also* Larrún
la Riege *see* Ariège
29 Q4 **Larimore** North Dakota, N USA
107 L15 **Larino** Molise, C Italy
Lario *see* Como, Lago di
62 J9 **La Rioja** La Rioja, NW Argentina
62 I9 **La Rioja** *off.* Provincia de La Rioja. ◈ *province* NW Argentina
105 O4 **La Rioja** ◈ *autonomous community* N Spain
115 F16 **Lárisa** *var.* Larissa. Thessalía, C Greece
Larissa *see* Lárisa
149 Q13 **Lärkāna** *var.* Larkhana. Sind, SE Pakistan
Larkhana *see* Lärkāna
Larnaca *see* Lárnaka
121 Q3 **Lárnaka** *var.* Larnaca, Larnax. SE Cyprus
121 Q3 **Lárnaka** ✕ SE Cyprus
Larnax *see* Lárnaka
97 G14 **Larne** *Ir.* Latharna. E Northern Ireland, UK
26 L5 **Larned** Kansas, C USA
104 L3 **La Robla** Castilla-León, N Spain

◆ Country ● Country Capital ◇ Dependent Territory ○ Dependent Territory Capital ◈ Administrative Region ✕ International Airport ▲ Mountain ▲ Mountain Range ▲ Volcano ≈ River ◎ Lake ▣ Reservoir

104 J10 **La Roca de la Sierra** Extremadura, W Spain
99 K22 **La Roche-en-Ardenne** Luxembourg, SE Belgium
102 L11 **la Rochefoucauld** Charente, W France
102 J10 **la Rochelle** *anc.* Rupella. Charente-Maritime, W France
102 I9 **la Roche-sur-Yon** *prev.* Bourbon Vendée, Napoléon-Vendée. Vendée, NW France
105 Q10 **La Roda** Castilla-La Mancha, C Spain
104 L14 **La Roda de Andalucía** Andalucía, S Spain
45 P9 **La Romana** E Dominican Republic
11 T13 **La Ronge** Saskatchewan, C Canada
11 U13 **La Ronge, Lac** ⊚ Saskatchewan, C Canada
22 K10 **Larose** Louisiana, S USA
42 M7 **La Rosita** Región Autónoma Atlántico Norte, NE Nicaragua
181 Q3 **Larrimah** Northern Territory, N Australia
62 N11 **Larroque** Entre Ríos, E Argentina
105 Q2 **Larrún** *Fr.* la Rhune. ▲ France/Spain *see also* la Rhune
195 X6 **Lars Christensen Coast** *physical region* Antarctica
39 Q14 **Larsen Bay** Kodiak Island, Alaska, USA
194 I5 **Larsen Ice Shelf** *ice shelf* Antarctica
8 M6 **Larsen Sound** *sound* Nunavut, N Canada
La Rúa *see* A Rúa
102 K16 **Laruns** Pyrénées-Atlantiques, SW France
95 G16 **Larvik** Vestfold, S Norway
La-sa *see* Lhasa
171 S13 **Lasahata** Pulau Seram, E Indonesia
Lasahau *see* Lasihao
37 O6 **La Sal** Utah, W USA
14 C17 **La Salle** Ontario, S Canada
30 L11 **La Salle** Illinois, N USA
45 O9 **Las Americas** ✕ (Santo Domingo) S Dominican Republic
79 G17 **La Sangha** ⬖ *province* N Congo
37 V6 **Las Animas** Colorado, C USA
108 D10 **La Sarine** *var.* Sarine. ≈ SW Switzerland
108 B9 **La Sarraz** Vaud, W Switzerland
12 H12 **La Sarre** Quebec, SE Canada
54 L3 **Las Aves, Islas** *var.* Islas de Aves. *island group* N Venezuela
55 N7 **Las Bonitas** Bolívar, C Venezuela
104 K15 **Las Cabezas de San Juan** Andalucía, S Spain
61 G19 **Lascano** Rocha, E Uruguay
62 I5 **Lascar, Volcán** ▲ N Chile
41 T15 **Las Choapas** *var.* Choapas. Veracruz-Llave, SE Mexico
37 R15 **Las Cruces** New Mexico, SW USA
Lasdehnen *see* Krasnoznamensk
105 V4 **La Seu d'Urgel** *var.* La Seu d'Urgell, Seo de Urgel. Cataluña, NE Spain
La Selle *see* Selle, Pic de la
62 G9 **La Serena** Coquimbo, C Chile
104 K11 **La Serena** *physical region* W Spain
La Seu d'Urgell *see* La Seu d'Urgel
103 T16 **la Seyne-sur-Mer** Var, SE France
61 D21 **Las Flores** Buenos Aires, E Argentina
62 H9 **Las Flores** San Juan, W Argentina
11 S14 **Lashburn** Saskatchewan, S Canada
62 I11 **Las Heras** Mendoza, W Argentina
167 N4 **Lashio** Shan State, E Myanmar
148 M8 **Lashkar Gāh** *var.* Lash-Kar-Gar'. Helmand, S Afghanistan
Lash-Kar-Gar' *see* Lashkar Gāh
171 P14 **Lasihao** *var.* Lasahau. Pulau Muna, C Indonesia
107 N21 **La Sila** ⛰ SW Italy
63 H23 **La Silueta, Cerro** ▲ S Chile
42 L9 **La Sirena** Región Autónoma Atlántico Sur, E Nicaragua
110 J13 **Łask** Łódzkie, C Poland
109 V11 **Laško** *Ger.* Tüffer. C Slovenia
63 H14 **Las Lajas** Neuquén, W Argentina
63 H15 **Las Lajas, Cerro** ▲ W Argentina
62 M6 **Las Lomitas** Formosa, N Argentina
41 V16 **Las Margaritas** Chiapas, SE Mexico
Las Marismas *see* Guadalquivir, Marismas del
54 M6 **Las Mercedes** Guárico, N Venezuela
42 F6 **Las Minas, Cerro** ▲ W Honduras
105 O11 **La Solana** Castilla-La Mancha, C Spain
45 Q14 **La Soufrière** ※ Saint Vincent, Saint Vincent and the Grenadines
102 M10 **la Souterraine** Creuse, C France
62 N7 **Las Palmas** Chaco, N Argentina
43 Q16 **Las Palmas** Veraguas, W Panama
64 P12 **Las Palmas** *var.* Las Palmas de Gran Canaria. Gran Canaria, Islas Canarias, Spain, NE Atlantic Ocean
64 P12 **Las Palmas** ⬖ *province* Islas Canarias, Spain, NE Atlantic Ocean
64 Q12 **Las Palmas** ✕ Gran Canaria, Islas Canarias, Spain, NE Atlantic Ocean
Las Palmas de Gran Canaria *see* Las Palmas
40 D6 **Las Palomas** Baja California Sur, W Mexico
105 P10 **Las Pedroñeras** Castilla-La Mancha, C Spain
106 E10 **La Spezia** Liguria, NW Italy
61 F20 **Las Piedras** Canelones, S Uruguay
63 J18 **Las Plumas** Chubut, S Argentina
61 B18 **Las Rosas** Santa Fe, C Argentina
Lassa *see* Lhasa
35 O4 **Lassen Peak** ▲ California, W USA
194 K6 **Lassiter Coast** *physical region* Antarctica
109 V9 **Lassnitz** ≈ SE Austria
15 O12 **L'Assomption** Quebec, SE Canada
15 N11 **L'Assomption** ≈ Quebec, SE Canada
43 S17 **Las Tablas** Los Santos, S Panama
Lastarria, Volcán *see* Azufre, Volcán
37 V4 **Last Chance** Colorado, C USA
Last Frontier, The *see* Alaska
11 U16 **Last Mountain Lake** ⊚ Saskatchewan, S Canada
62 H9 **Las Tórtolas, Cerro** ▲ W Argentina
61 C14 **Las Toscas** Santa Fe, C Argentina
79 F19 **Lastoursville** Ogooué-Lolo, E Gabon
113 F16 **Lastovo** *It.* Lagosta. *island* SW Croatia
113 F16 **Lastovski Kanal** *channel* SW Croatia
40 E6 **Las Tres Vírgenes, Volcán** ※ W Mexico
40 F4 **Las Trincheras** Sonora, NW Mexico
55 N8 **Las Trincheras** Bolívar, E Venezuela
44 H7 **Las Tunas** *var.* Victoria de las Tunas. Las Tunas, E Cuba
La Suisse *see* Switzerland
40 I5 **Las Varas** Chihuahua, N Mexico
40 J12 **Las Varas** Nayarit, C Mexico
62 L10 **Las Varillas** Córdoba, E Argentina
35 X11 **Las Vegas** Nevada, W USA
37 T10 **Las Vegas** New Mexico, SW USA
187 P10 **Lata** Nendö, Solomon Islands
13 R10 **La Tabatière** Quebec, E Canada
56 C6 **Latacunga** Cotopaxi, C Ecuador
194 I7 **Latady Island** *island* Antarctica
54 E14 **La Tagua** Putumayo, S Colombia
Latakia *see* Al Lādhiqīyah
92 J10 **Lätäseno** ≈ NW Finland
14 H9 **Latchford** Ontario, S Canada
14 J13 **Latchford Bridge** Ontario, SE Canada
193 Y14 **Late** *island* Vava'u Group, N Tonga
153 P15 **Lātehār** Bihār, N India
15 R7 **Laterrière** Quebec, SE Canada
102 J13 **la Teste** Gironde, SW France
25 V8 **Latexo** Texas, SW USA
18 L10 **Latham** New York, NE USA
Latharna *see* Larne
108 B9 **La Thielle** *var.* Thièle. ≈ W Switzerland
27 R3 **Lathrop** Missouri, C USA
107 I16 **Latina** *prev.* Littoria. Lazio, C Italy
41 R14 **La Tinaja** Veracruz-Llave, S Mexico
106 J7 **Latisana** Friuli-Venezia Giulia, NE Italy
Latium *see* Lazio
115 K25 **Lató** *site of ancient city* Kríti, Greece, E Mediterranean Sea
187 Q17 **La Tontouta** ✕ (Noumea) Province Sud, S New Caledonia
55 N4 **La Tortuga, Isla** *var.* Isla Tortuga. *island* N Venezuela
108 C10 **La Tour-de-Peilz** *var.* La Tour de Peilz. Vaud, SW Switzerland
103 S11 **la Tour-du-Pin** Isère, E France
102 J11 **la Tremblade** Charente-Maritime, W France
102 L10 **la Trimouille** Vienne, W France
42 J9 **La Trinidad** Estelí, NW Nicaragua
41 V16 **La Trinitaria** Chiapas, SE Mexico
45 Q11 **la Trinité** E Martinique
15 U7 **La Trinité-des-Monts** Quebec, SE Canada
18 C15 **Latrobe** Pennsylvania, NE USA
183 P13 **La Trobe River** ≈ Victoria, SE Australia
Lattakia/Lattaquié *see* Al Lādhiqīyah
171 S13 **Latu** Pulau Seram, E Indonesia
15 P9 **La Tuque** Quebec, SE Canada
155 G14 **Lātūr** Mahārāshtra, C India
118 G8 **Latvia** *off.* Republic of Latvia, *Ger.* Lettland, *Latv.* Latvija, Latvijas Republika; *prev.* Latvian SSR, *Rus.* Latviyskaya SSR. ◆ *republic* NE Europe
Latvian SSR/Latvija/Latvijas Republika/Latviyskaya SSR *see* Latvia
186 H7 **Lau** New Britain, E PNG
175 R9 **Lau Basin** *undersea feature* S Pacific Ocean
101 O15 **Lauchhammer** Brandenburg, E Germany
Laudunum *see* Laon
Laudus *see* St-Lô
Lauenburg/Lauenburg in Pommern *see* Lębork
101 L20 **Lauf an der Pegnitz** Bayern, SE Germany
108 D7 **Laufen** Basel, NW Switzerland
109 P5 **Lauffen** Salzburg, NW Austria
92 I2 **Laugarbakki** Nordhurland Vestra, N Iceland
92 I4 **Laugarvatn** Sudhurland, SW Iceland
31 O3 **Laughing Fish Point** *headland* Michigan, N USA
187 Z14 **Lau Group** *island group* E Fiji
Lauis *see* Lugano
93 M17 **Laukaa** Länsi-Suomi, W Finland
118 D12 **Laukuva** Šilalė, W Lithuania
Laun *see* Louny
183 P16 **Launceston** Tasmania, SE Australia
97 I24 **Launceston** *anc.* Dunheved. SW England, UK
54 C13 **La Unión** Nariño, SW Colombia
42 H8 **La Unión** La Unión, SE El Salvador
42 I6 **La Unión** Olancho, C Honduras
40 M15 **La Unión** Guerrero, S Mexico
41 Y14 **La Unión** Quintana Roo, E Mexico
105 S13 **La Unión** Murcia, SE Spain
54 L7 **La Unión** Barinas, C Venezuela
42 B10 **La Unión** ⬖ *department* E El Salvador
38 H11 **Laupahoehoe** *Haw.* Laupāhoehoe. Hawaii, USA, C Pacific Ocean
101 I23 **Laupheim** Baden-Württemberg, S Germany
181 W3 **Laura** Queensland, NE Australia
189 X2 **Laura** *atoll* Majuro Atoll, SE Marshall Islands
Laurana *see* Lovran
54 L8 **La Urbana** Bolívar, C Venezuela
21 Y4 **Laurel** Delaware, NE USA
23 V14 **Laurel** Florida, SE USA
21 W3 **Laurel** Maryland, NE USA
22 M6 **Laurel** Mississippi, S USA
33 U11 **Laurel** Montana, NW USA
29 R13 **Laurel** Nebraska, C USA
18 H15 **Laureldale** Pennsylvania, NE USA
18 C16 **Laurel Hill** *ridge* Pennsylvania, NE USA
29 T12 **Laurens** Iowa, C USA
21 P11 **Laurens** South Carolina, SE USA
Laurentian Highlands *see* Laurentian Mountains
15 P10 **Laurentian Mountains** *var.* Laurentian Highlands, *Fr.* Les Laurentides. *plateau* Newfoundland/Quebec, Canada
15 O12 **Laurentides** Quebec, SE Canada
Laurentides, Les *see* Laurentian Mountains
107 M19 **Lauria** Basilicata, S Italy
194 I1 **Laurie Island** *island* Antarctica
21 T11 **Laurinburg** North Carolina, SE USA
30 M2 **Laurium** Michigan, N USA
Lauru *see* Choiseul
108 B9 **Lausanne** *It.* Losanna. Vaud, SW Switzerland
101 Q16 **Lausche** *Cz.* Luže. ▲ Czech Republic/Germany *see also* Luže
101 Q16 **Lausitzer Bergland** *var.* Lausitzer Gebirge, *Cz.* Gory Lužycke, Lužické Hory, *Eng.* Lusatian Mountains. ⛰ E Germany
Lausitzer Gebirge *see* Lausitzer Bergland
Lausitzer Neisse *see* Neisse
103 T12 **Lautaret, Col du** *pass* SE France
63 G15 **Lautaro** Araucanía, C Chile
101 F21 **Lauter** ≈ W Germany
108 I7 **Lauterach** Vorarlberg, NW Austria
101 I17 **Lauterbach** Hessen, C Germany
108 E9 **Lauterbrunnen** Bern, C Switzerland
169 U14 **Laut Kecil, Kepulauan** *island group* N Indonesia
187 X14 **Lautoka** Viti Levu, W Fiji
169 O8 **Laut, Pulau** *prev.* Laoet. *island* Borneo, C Indonesia
169 V14 **Laut, Pulau** *island* Kepulauan Natuna, W Indonesia
169 U13 **Laut, Selat** *strait* Borneo, C Indonesia
168 H8 **Laut Tawar, Danau** ⊚ Sumatera, NW Indonesia
189 V14 **Lauvergne Island** *island* Chuuk, C Micronesia
98 M5 **Lauwers Meer** ⊚ N Netherlands
98 M4 **Lauwersoog** Groningen, NE Netherlands
102 M14 **Lauzerte** Tarn-et-Garonne, S France
25 U13 **Lavaca Bay** *bay* Texas, SW USA
25 U12 **Lavaca River** ≈ Texas, SW USA
15 O12 **Laval** Quebec, SE Canada
102 J6 **Laval** Mayenne, NW France
15 T6 **Laval** ≈ Quebec, SE Canada
61 F19 **Lavalleja** ⬖ *department* S Uruguay
15 O12 **Lavaltrie** Quebec, SE Canada
186 M10 **Lavanggu** Rennell, S Solomon Islands
143 O14 **Lāvān, Jazīreh-ye** *island* S Iran
109 U8 **Lavant** ≈ S Austria
118 G5 **Lavassaare** *Ger.* Lawassaar. Pärnumaa, SW Estonia
104 L3 **La Vecilla de Curueño** Castilla-León, N Spain
45 N8 **La Vega** *var.* Concepción de la Vega. C Dominican Republic
La Vela *see* La Vela de Coro
54 J4 **La Vela de Coro** *var.* La Vela. Falcón, N Venezuela
103 N17 **Lavelanet** Ariège, S France
107 M17 **Lavello** Basilicata, S Italy
36 J8 **La Verkin** Utah, W USA
26 J8 **Laverne** Oklahoma, C USA
25 S12 **La Vernia** Texas, SW USA
93 K18 **Lavia** Länsi-Suomi, W Finland
14 I12 **Lavieille, Lake** ⊚ Ontario, SE Canada
94 C12 **Lavik** Sogn og Fjordane, S Norway
La Vila Jojosa *see* Villajoyosa
33 U10 **Lavina** Montana, NW USA
194 H5 **Lavoisier Island** *island* Antarctica
23 U2 **Lavonia** Georgia, SE USA
103 R13 **la Voulte-sur-Rhône** Ardèche, E France
123 W5 **Lavrentiya** Chukotskiy Avtonomnyy Okrug, NE Russian Federation
115 H20 **Lávrio** *prev.* Lávrion. Attikí, C Greece
Lávrion *see* Lávrio
83 L22 **Lavumisa** *prev.* Gollel. SE Swaziland
149 T4 **Lawarai Pass** *pass* N Pakistan
Lawassaar *see* Lavassaare
141 P16 **Lawdar** SW Yemen
25 Q7 **Lawn** Texas, SW USA
195 Y4 **Law Promontory** *headland* Antarctica
77 O14 **Lawra** NW Ghana
185 E23 **Lawrence** Otago, South Island, NZ
31 P14 **Lawrence** Indiana, N USA
27 Q4 **Lawrence** Kansas, C USA
19 O10 **Lawrence** Massachusetts, NE USA
20 L5 **Lawrenceburg** Kentucky, S USA
20 I10 **Lawrenceburg** Tennessee, S USA
23 T3 **Lawrenceville** Georgia, SE USA
31 N15 **Lawrenceville** Illinois, N USA
21 V7 **Lawrenceville** Virginia, NE USA
27 S3 **Lawson** Missouri, C USA
26 L12 **Lawton** Oklahoma, C USA
140 I4 **Lawz, Jabal al** ▲ NW Saudi Arabia
95 L16 **Laxå** Örebro, C Sweden
127 T5 **Laya** ≈ NW Russian Federation
57 I19 **La Yarada** Tacna, SW Peru
141 S15 **Layjūn** C Yemen
141 Q9 **Laylā** *var.* Laila. Ar Riyāḍ, C Saudi Arabia
23 P4 **Lay Lake** ⊡ Alabama, S USA
45 P14 **Layou** Saint Vincent, Saint Vincent and the Grenadines
La Youne *see* El Ayoun
192 L5 **Laysan Island** *island* Hawaiian Islands, Hawaii, USA, C Pacific Ocean
36 L2 **Layton** Utah, W USA
34 L5 **Laytonville** California, W USA
172 H17 **Lazare, Pointe** *headland* Mahé, NE Seychelles
123 T12 **Lazarev** Khabarovskiy Kray, SE Russian Federation
112 L12 **Lazarevac** Serbia, C Yugoslavia
65 N22 **Lazarev Sea** *sea* Antarctica
40 M15 **Lázaro Cárdenas** Michoacán de Ocampo, SW Mexico
119 F15 **Lazdijai** Lazdijai, S Lithuania
107 H15 **Lazio** *anc.* Latium. ⬖ *region* C Italy
111 A16 **Lázně Kynžvart** *Ger.* Bad Königswart. Karlovarský Kraj, W Czech Republic
Lazovsk *see* Sîngerei
167 R12 **Leach** Poŭthĭsăt, W Cambodia
27 X9 **Leachville** Arkansas, C USA
28 I9 **Lead** South Dakota, N USA
11 S16 **Leader** Saskatchewan, S Canada
19 S6 **Lead Mountain** ▲ Maine, NE USA
37 R5 **Leadville** Colorado, C USA
11 V12 **Leaf Rapids** Manitoba, C Canada
22 M7 **Leaf River** ≈ Mississippi, S USA
25 W11 **League City** Texas, SW USA
23 N7 **Leakesville** Mississippi, S USA
25 Q11 **Leakey** Texas, SW USA
Leal *see* Lihula
83 G15 **Lealui** Western, W Zambia
Leamhcán *see* Lucan
14 C18 **Leamington** Ontario, S Canada
Leamington/Leamington Spa *see* Royal Leamington Spa
Leammi *see* Lemmenjoki
25 S10 **Leander** Texas, SW USA
60 F13 **Leandro N.Alem** Misiones, NE Argentina
97 A20 **Leane, Lough** *Ir.* Loch Léin. ⊚ SW Ireland
180 G8 **Learmouth** Western Australia
Leau *see* Zoutleeuw
L'Eau d'Heure *see* Plate Taille, Lac de la
190 D12 **Leava** Île Futuna, S Wallis and Futuna
27 R3 **Leavenworth** Kansas, C USA
32 I8 **Leavenworth** Washington, NW USA
92 L8 **Leavvajohka** *var.* Levajok, Lœvvajok. Finnmark, N Norway
27 R4 **Leawood** Kansas, C USA
110 H6 **Łeba** *Ger.* Leba. Pomorskie, N Poland
110 I6 **Łeba** *Ger.* Leba. ≈ N Poland
101 D20 **Lebach** Saarland, SW Germany
Łeba, Jezioro *see* Łebsko, Jezioro
171 P8 **Lebak** Mindanao, S Philippines
31 O13 **Lebanon** Indiana, N USA
20 L6 **Lebanon** Kentucky, S USA
27 U6 **Lebanon** Missouri, C USA
19 N9 **Lebanon** New Hampshire, NE USA
32 G12 **Lebanon** Oregon, NW USA
18 H15 **Lebanon** Pennsylvania, NE USA
20 J8 **Lebanon** Tennessee, S USA
21 P7 **Lebanon** Virginia, NE USA
138 G6 **Lebanon** *off.* Republic of Lebanon, *Ar.* Al Lubnān, *Fr.* Liban. ◆ *republic* SW Asia
20 K6 **Lebanon Junction** Kentucky, S USA
Lebanon, Mount *see* Liban, Jebel
146 J10 **Lebap** Lebapskiy Velayat, NE Turkmenistan
146 H11 **Lebapskiy Velayat** *Turkm.* Lebap Welaýaty; *prev. Rus.* Chardzhevskaya Oblast', *Turkm.* Chärjew Oblasty. ⬖ *province* E Turkmenistan
Lebap Welaýaty *see* Lebapskiy Velayat
Lebasee *see* Łebsko, Jezioro
99 F17 **Lebbeke** Oost-Vlaanderen, NW Belgium
35 S14 **Lebec** California, W USA
Lebedin *see* Lebedyn
123 Q11 **Lebedinyy** Respublika Sakha (Yakutiya), NE Russian Federation
128 L6 **Lebedyan'** Lipetskaya Oblast', W Russian Federation
117 T4 **Lebedyn** *Rus.* Lebedin. Sums'ka Oblast', NE Ukraine
12 I12 **Lebel-sur-Quévillon** Quebec, SE Canada
92 L8 **Lebesby** Finnmark, N Norway
102 M9 **le Blanc** Indre, C France
27 P5 **Lebo** Kansas, C USA
79 L15 **Lebo** Orientale, N Dem. Rep. Congo (Zaire)
110 H6 **Lębork** *var.* Lębórk, *Ger.* Lauenburg, Lauenburg in Pommern. Pomorskie, N Poland
103 O17 **le Boulou** Pyrénées-Orientales, S France
108 A9 **Le Brassus** Vaud, W Switzerland
104 J15 **Lebrija** Andalucía, S Spain
110 G6 **Łebsko, Jezioro** *Ger.* Lebasee; *prev.* Jezioro Łeba. ⊚ N Poland
63 F14 **Lebu** Bío Bío, C Chile
Lebyazh'ye *see* Akku
104 F6 **Leça da Palmeira** Porto, N Portugal
103 U15 **le Cannet** Alpes-Maritimes, SE France
Le Cap *see* Cap-Haïtien
103 P2 **le Cateau-Cambrésis** Nord, N France
107 Q18 **Lecce** Puglia, SE Italy
106 D7 **Lecco** Lombardia, N Italy
29 V10 **Le Center** Minnesota, N USA
108 J7 **Lech** Vorarlberg, W Austria
101 K22 **Lech** ≈ Austria/Germany
115 D19 **Lechainá** *var.* Lehena, Lekhainá. Dytikí Ellás, S Greece
102 J11 **le Château d'Oléron** Charente-Maritime, W France
103 R3 **le Chesne** Ardennes, N France
103 R13 **le Cheylard** Ardèche, E France
108 K7 **Lechtaler Alpen** ⛰ W Austria
100 H6 **Leck** Schleswig-Holstein, N Germany
14 L9 **Lecointre, Lac** ⊚ Quebec, SE Canada
22 H7 **Lecompte** Louisiana, S USA
103 Q9 **le Creusot** Saône-et-Loire, C France
Lecumberri *see* Lekunberri
110 P13 **Łęczna** Lubelskie, E Poland
110 J12 **Łęczyca** *Ger.* Lentschiza, *Rus.* Lenchitsa. Łódzkie, C Poland
100 F10 **Leda** ≈ NW Germany
99 F17 **Lede** Oost-Vlaanderen, NW Belgium
104 K6 **Ledesma** Castilla-León, N Spain
45 Q12 **le Diamant** SW Martinique
172 J16 **Le Digue** *island* Inner Islands, NE Seychelles
103 Q10 **le Donjon** Allier, C France
102 M10 **le Dorat** Haute-Vienne, C France
Ledo Salinarius *see* Lons-le-Saunier
11 Q14 **Leduc** Alberta, SW Canada
123 V7 **Ledyanaya, Gora** ▲ E Russian Federation
97 C21 **Lee** *Ir.* An Laoi. ≈ SW Ireland
29 U5 **Leech Lake** ⊚ Minnesota, N USA
26 K10 **Leedey** Oklahoma, C USA
97 M17 **Leeds** N England, UK
23 P4 **Leeds** Alabama, S USA
29 O3 **Leeds** North Dakota, N USA
98 N6 **Leek** Groningen, NE Netherlands
99 K15 **Leende** Noord-Brabant, SE Netherlands
100 F10 **Leer** Niedersachsen, NW Germany
98 J13 **Leerdam** Zuid-Holland, C Netherlands
98 K12 **Leersum** Utrecht, C Netherlands
23 W11 **Leesburg** Florida, SE USA
21 V3 **Leesburg** Virginia, NE USA
27 R4 **Lees Summit** Missouri, C USA
22 G7 **Leesville** Louisiana, S USA
25 S12 **Leesville** Texas, SW USA
31 U13 **Leesville Lake** ⊡ Ohio, N USA
Leesville Lake *see* Smith Mountain Lake
183 P9 **Leeton** New South Wales, SE Australia
98 L6 **Leeuwarden** *Fris.* Ljouwert. Friesland, N Netherlands
180 I14 **Leeuwin, Cape** *headland* Western Australia
35 R8 **Lee Vining** California, W USA
45 V8 **Leeward Islands** *island group* E West Indies
Leeward Islands *see* Vent, Îles Sous le, W French Polynesia
Leeward Islands *see* Sotavento, Ilhas de, Cape Verde
79 G20 **Léfini** ≈ SE Congo
Léfka *see* Lefke
115 C17 **Lefkáda** *prev.* Levkás. Lefkáda, Iónioi Nísoi, Greece, C Mediterranean Sea
115 B17 **Lefkáda** *It.* Santa Maura; *prev.* Levkás, *anc.* Leucas. *island* Iónioi Nísoi, Greece, C Mediterranean Sea
115 H25 **Lefká Óri** ⛰ Kríti, Greece, E Mediterranean Sea
115 B16 **Lefkímmi** *var.* Levkímmi. Kérkyra, Iónioi Nísoi, Greece, C Mediterranean Sea
Lefkoşa/Lefkosía *see* Nicosia
25 O2 **Lefors** Texas, SW USA
45 R12 **le François** E Martinique
180 L12 **Lefroy, Lake** *salt lake* Western Australia
Legaceaster *see* Chester
105 N8 **Leganés** Madrid, C Spain
171 P4 **Legaspi** *off.* Legaspi City. Luzon, N Philippines
Leghorn *see* Livorno
110 M11 **Legionowo** Mazowieckie, C Poland
99 K24 **Léglise** Luxembourg, SE Belgium
106 G8 **Legnago** Lombardia, NE Italy
106 D7 **Legnano** Veneto, NE Italy
111 F14 **Legnica** *Ger.* Liegnitz. Dolnośląskie, SW Poland
35 Q9 **Le Grand** California, W USA
103 Q15 **le Grau-du-Roi** Gard, S France
183 U3 **Legume** New South Wales, SE Australia
102 L4 **le Havre** *Eng.* Havre; *prev.* le Havre-de-Grâce. Seine-Maritime, N France
le Havre-de-Grâce *see* le Havre
Lehena *see* Lechainá
36 L3 **Lehi** Utah, W USA
18 I14 **Lehighton** Pennsylvania, NE USA
29 O6 **Lehr** North Dakota, N USA
38 A8 **Lehua Island** *island* Hawaiian Islands, Hawaii, USA, C Pacific Ocean
149 S9 **Leiāh** Punjab, NE Pakistan
109 W9 **Leibnitz** Steiermark, SE Austria
97 M19 **Leicester** *Lat.* Batae Coritanorum. C England, UK
97 M19 **Leicestershire** *cultural region* C England, UK
98 H11 **Leiden** *prev.* Leyden, *anc.* Lugdunum Batavorum. Zuid-Holland, W Netherlands
98 H11 **Leiderdorp** Zuid-Holland, W Netherlands
98 G11 **Leidschendam** Zuid-Holland, W Netherlands
99 D18 **Leie** *Fr.* Lys. ≈ Belgium/France
Leifear *see* Lifford
184 L4 **Leigh** Auckland, North Island, NZ
97 K17 **Leigh** NW England, UK
182 I5 **Leigh Creek** South Australia
23 O2 **Leighton** Alabama, S USA
97 M21 **Leighton Buzzard** E England, UK
Léim an Bhradáin *see* Leixlip
Léim an Mhadaidh *see* Limavady
Léime, Ceann *see* Loop Head, Ireland
Léime, Ceann *see* Slyne Head, Ireland
101 G20 **Leimen** Baden-Württemberg, SW Germany
100 I13 **Leine** ≈ NW Germany
101 J15 **Leinefelde** Thüringen, C Germany
Léin, Loch *see* Leane, Lough
97 D19 **Leinster** *Ir.* Cúige Laighean. *cultural region* E Ireland
97 F19 **Leinster, Mount** *Ir.* Stua Laighean. ▲ SE Ireland
119 F15 **Leipalingis** Lazdijai, S Lithuania
92 J12 **Leipojärvi** Norrbotten, N Sweden
31 R12 **Leipsic** Ohio, N USA
Leipsic *see* Leipzig
115 M20 **Leipsoí** *island* Dodekánisos, Greece, Aegean Sea
101 M15 **Leipzig** *Pol.* Lipsk; *hist.* Leipsic, *anc.* Lipsia. Sachsen, E Germany
101 M15 **Leipzig Halle** ✕ Sachsen, E Germany
104 G9 **Leiria** *anc.* Collipo. Leiria, C Portugal
104 F9 **Leiria** ⬖ *district* C Portugal
95 C15 **Leirvik** Hordaland, S Norway
118 E5 **Leisi** *Ger.* Laisberg. Saaremaa, W Estonia
104 J3 **Leitariegos, Puerto de** *pass* NW Spain
20 J6 **Leitchfield** Kentucky, S USA
109 Y5 **Leitha** *Hung.* Lajta. ≈ Austria/Hungary
Leitir Ceanainn *see* Letterkenny
Leitmeritz *see* Litoměřice
Leitomischl *see* Litomyšl
97 D16 **Leitrim** *Ir.* Liatroim. *cultural region* NW Ireland
115 F18 **Leivádia** *prev.* Levádhia. Stereá Ellás, C Greece
Leix *see* Laois
97 F18 **Leixlip** *Eng.* Salmon Leap, *Ir.* Léim an Bhradáin. E Ireland
64 N8 **Leixões** Porto, N Portugal
161 N12 **Leiyang** Hunan, S China
160 L16 **Leizhou** *var.* Haikang. Guangdong, S China
160 L16 **Leizhou Bandao** *var.* Luichow Peninsula. *peninsula* S China
98 H13 **Lek** ≈ SW Netherlands
114 I13 **Lekánis** ⛰ NE Greece
172 H13 **Le Kartala** ▲ Grande Comore, NW Comoros
Le Kef *see* El Kef
79 G20 **Lékéti, Monts de la** ⛰ S Congo
Lekhainá *see* Lechainá
114 H8 **Lekhchevo** Montana, NW Bulgaria
92 G11 **Leknes** Nordland, C Norway
79 E21 **Le Kouilou** ⬖ *province* SW Congo
94 L13 **Leksand** Dalarna, C Sweden
126 H8 **Leksozero, Ozero** ⊚ NW Russian Federation
105 Q3 **Lekunberri** *var.* Lecumberri. Navarra, N Spain
171 S11 **Lelai, Tanjung** *headland* Pulau Halmahera, N Indonesia
45 Q12 **le Lamentin** *var.* Lamentin. C Martinique
45 Q12 **le Lamentin** ✕ (Fort-de-France) C Martinique
31 P6 **Leland** Michigan, N USA
22 J4 **Leland** Mississippi, S USA
95 J16 **Lelång** *var.* Lelången. ⊚ S Sweden

◆ Country ● Country Capital ◇ Dependent Territory ○ Dependent Territory Capital ⬖ Administrative Region ✕ International Airport ▲ Mountain ⛰ Mountain Range ※ Volcano ≈ River ⊚ Lake ⊡ Reservoir

Lelången see Lelång
Lel'chytsy see Lyel'chytsy
le Léman see Geneva, Lake
25 O3 **Lelia Lake** Texas, SW USA
113 I14 **Lelija** ▲ SE Bosnia and Herzegovina
108 C8 **Le Locle** Neuchâtel, W Switzerland
189 Y14 **Lelu** Kosrae, E Micronesia
Lelu see Lelu Island
189 Y14 **Lelu Island** var. Lelu. island Kosrae, E Micronesia
55 W9 **Lelydorp** Wanica, N Surinam
98 K9 **Lelystad** Flevoland, C Netherlands
63 K25 **Le Maire, Estrecho de** strait S Argentina
168 L10 **Lemang** Pulau Rangsang, W Indonesia
186 I7 **Lemankoa** Buka Island, NE PNG
Léman, Lac see Geneva, Lake
102 L6 **le Mans** Sarthe, NW France
29 S12 **Le Mars** Iowa, C USA
109 S3 **Lembach im Mühlkreis** Oberösterreich, N Austria
101 G23 **Lemberg** ▲ SW Germany
Lemberg see L'viv
Lemdiyya see Médéa
121 P3 **Lemesós** var. Limassol. SW Cyprus
100 H13 **Lemgo** Nordrhein-Westfalen, W Germany
33 P13 **Lemhi Range** ▲ Idaho, NW USA
9 S6 **Lemieux Islands** island group Nunavut, NE Canada
171 O11 **Lemito** Sulawesi, N Indonesia
92 L10 **Lemmenjoki** Lapp. Leammi. ≈ NE Finland
98 L7 **Lemmer** Fris. De Lemmer. Friesland, N Netherlands
28 L7 **Lemmon** South Dakota, N USA
36 M15 **Lemmon, Mount** ▲ Arizona, SW USA
Lemnos see Límnos
31 O14 **Lemon, Lake** ◎ Indiana, N USA
102 J5 **le Mont St-Michel** castle Manche, N France
35 Q11 **Lemoore** California, W USA
189 T13 **Lemotol Bay** bay Chuuk Islands, C Micronesia
45 Y5 **le Moule** var. Moule. Grande Terre, NE Guadeloupe
Lemovices see Limoges
Le Moyen-Ogooué see Moyen-Ogooué
12 M6 **le Moyne, Lac** ◎ Quebec, E Canada
93 L18 **Lempäälä** Länsi-Suomi, W Finland
42 E7 **Lempa, Río** ≈ Central America
42 F7 **Lempira** prev. Gracias. ◆ department SW Honduras
Lemsalu see Limbaži
107 N17 **Le Murge** ▲ SE Italy
127 V6 **Lemva** ≈ NW Russian Federation
95 F21 **Lemvig** Ringkøbing, W Denmark
166 K8 **Lemyethna** Irrawaddy, SW Myanmar
30 K10 **Lena** Illinois, N USA
131 V4 **Lena** ≈ NE Russian Federation
173 N13 **Lena Tablemount** undersea feature S Indian Ocean
Lenchitsa see Łęczyca
59 N17 **Lençóis** Bahia, E Brazil
60 K9 **Lençóis Paulista** São Paulo, S Brazil
109 Y9 **Lendava** Hung. Lendva, Ger. Unterlimbach; prev. Dolnja Lendava. NE Slovenia
83 F20 **Lendepas** Hardap, SE Namibia
126 H9 **Lendery** Respublika Kareliya, NW Russian Federation
Lendum see Lens
Lendva see Lendava
27 R4 **Lenexa** Kansas, C USA
109 Q5 **Lengau** Oberösterreich, N Austria
145 Q17 **Lenger** Yuzhnyy Kazakhstan, S Kazakhstan
159 O9 **Lenghu** Qinghai, C China
159 T9 **Lenglong Ling** ▲ N China
108 D7 **Lengnau** Bern, W Switzerland
160 M12 **Lengshuitan** Hunan, S China
95 M20 **Lenhovda** Kronoberg, S Sweden
79 E20 **Le Niari** ◆ province SW Congo
Lenin see Leninskoye, Kazakhstan
Lenin see Akdepe, Turkmenistan
Leninabad see Khŭjand
Leninakan see Gyumri
Lenina, Pik see Lenin Peak
117 V12 **Lenine** Rus. Lenino. Respublika Krym, S Ukraine
Leningor see Leninogorsk
147 Q13 **Leningrad** Rus. Leningradskiy; prev. Mŭ'minobod, Rus. Muminabad. SW Tajikistan
Leningrad see Sankt-Peterburg
128 L13 **Leningradskaya** Krasnodarskiy Kray, SW Russian Federation
195 S16 **Leningradskaya** Russian research station Antarctica
126 H12 **Leningradskaya Oblast'** ◆ province NW Russian Federation
Leningradskiy see Leningrad
Lenino see Lenine, Ukraine
Lenino see Lyenina, Belarus
Leninobod see Khŭjand
145 X9 **Leninogorsk** Kaz. Leningor. Vostochnyy Kazakhstan, E Kazakhstan
129 T5 **Leninogorsk** Respublika Tatarstan, W Russian Federation
147 T12 **Lenin Peak** Rus. Pik Lenina, Taj. Qullai Lenin. ▲ Kyrgyzstan/Tajikistan
147 S8 **Leninpol'** Talasskaya Oblast', NW Kyrgyzstan
Lenin, Qullai see Lenin Peak
129 P11 **Leninsk** Volgogradskaya Oblast', SW Russian Federation
Leninsk see Akdepe, Turkmenistan
Leninsk see Asaka, Uzbekistan
Leninsk see Baykonyr, Kazakhstan
145 T8 **Leninskiy** Pavlodar, E Kazakhstan
122 I13 **Leninsk-Kuznetskiy** Kemerovskaya Oblast', S Russian Federation
145 N7 **Leninskoye** Kaz. Lenin. Kostanay, N Kazakhstan
127 P15 **Leninskoye** Kirovskaya Oblast', NW Russian Federation
Leninsk-Turkmenski see Chardzhev
Leninváros see Tiszaújváros
Lenkoran' see Länkäran
101 F15 **Lenne** ≈ W Germany
101 G16 **Lennestadt** Nordrhein-Westfalen, W Germany
29 R11 **Lennox** South Dakota, N USA
63 J25 **Lennox, Isla** Eng. Lennox Island. island S Chile
Lennox Island see Lennox, Isla
21 Q9 **Lenoir** North Carolina, SE USA
20 M9 **Lenoir City** Tennessee, S USA
108 C7 **Le Noirmont** Jura, NW Switzerland
14 L9 **Lenôtre, Lac** ◎ Quebec, SE Canada
29 U15 **Lenox** Iowa, C USA
103 O2 **Lens** anc. Lendum, Lentium. Pas-de-Calais, N France
123 O11 **Lensk** Respublika Sakha (Yakutiya), NE Russian Federation
111 F24 **Lenti** Zala, SW Hungary
Lentia see Linz
93 N14 **Lentiira** Oulu, E Finland
107 L25 **Lentini** anc. Leontini. Sicilia, Italy, C Mediterranean Sea
Lentium see Lens
Lentschiza see Łęczyca
93 N15 **Lentua** ◎ E Finland
119 H14 **Lentvaris** Pol. Landwarów. Trakai, SE Lithuania
108 F7 **Lenzburg** Aargau, N Switzerland
109 R5 **Lenzing** Oberösterreich, N Austria
77 P13 **Léo** SW Burkina
109 V7 **Leoben** Steiermark, C Austria
Leobschütz see Głubczyce
44 L9 **Léogâne** S Haiti
171 O11 **Leok** Sulawesi, N Indonesia
29 O7 **Leola** South Dakota, N USA
97 K20 **Leominster** W England, UK
19 N11 **Leominster** Massachusetts, NE USA
29 V16 **Leon** Iowa, C USA
40 M12 **León** var. León de los Aldamas. Guanajuato, C Mexico
42 I10 **León** León, NW Nicaragua
104 L4 **León** Castilla-León, NW Spain
42 I9 **León** ◆ department W Nicaragua
104 K4 **León** ◆ province Castilla-León, NW Spain
León see Cotopaxi
102 I15 **Léon** Landes, SW France
25 V9 **Leona** Texas, SW USA
180 K11 **Leonara** Western Australia
25 U5 **Leonard** Texas, SW USA
107 H15 **Leonardo da Vinci** prev. Fiumicino. ✕ (Roma) Lazio, C Italy
21 X5 **Leonardtown** Maryland, NE USA
25 Q13 **Leona River** ≈ Texas, SW USA
41 Z11 **Leona Vicario** Quintana Roo, SE Mexico
101 H21 **Leonberg** Baden-Württemberg, SW Germany
62 M3 **León, Cerro** ▲ NW Paraguay
León de los Aldamas see León
109 T4 **Leonding** Oberösterreich, N Austria
107 I14 **Leonessa** Lazio, C Italy
107 K24 **Leonforte** Sicilia, Italy, C Mediterranean Sea
183 O13 **Leongatha** Victoria, SE Australia
115 F21 **Leonídi** Pelopónnisos, S Greece
104 J4 **León, Montes de** ▲ NW Spain
25 S8 **Leon River** ≈ Texas, SW USA
Leontini see Lentini
Léopold II, Lac see Mai-Ndombe, Lac
99 J17 **Leopoldsburg** Limburg, NE Belgium
Léopoldville see Kinshasa
26 I5 **Leoti** Kansas, C USA
116 M11 **Leova** Rus. Leovo. SW Moldova
Leovo see Leova
102 G8 **le Palais** Morbihan, NW France
27 X10 **Lepanto** Arkansas, C USA
169 N13 **Lepar, Pulau** island W Indonesia
104 I14 **Lepe** Andalucía, S Spain
Lepel' see Lyepyel'
83 I19 **Lephepe** Kweneng, SE Botswana
161 Q10 **Leping** Jiangxi, S China
Lépontiennes, Alpes/Lepontine, Alpi see Lepontine Alps
108 G10 **Lepontine Alps** Fr. Alpes Lépontiennes, It. Alpi Lepontine. ▲ Italy/Switzerland
79 G20 **Le Pool** ◆ province S Congo
173 O16 **le Port** NW Réunion
103 N1 **le Portel** Pas-de-Calais, N France
93 N17 **Leppävirta** Itä-Suomi, C Finland
45 Q11 **le Prêcheur** NW Martinique
Lepsi see Lepsy
145 V13 **Lepsy** Kaz. Lepsi. Almaty, SE Kazakhstan
145 V13 **Lepsy** Kaz. Lepsi. ≈ SE Kazakhstan
Le Puglie see Puglia
103 Q12 **le Puy** prev. le Puy-en-Velay, hist. Anicium, Podium Anicensis. Haute-Loire, C France
le Puy-en-Velay see le Puy
Le Raizet see le Raizet
45 X11 **le Raizet** var. Le Raizet. ✕ (Pointe-à-Pitre) Grande Terre, C Guadeloupe
107 J24 **Lercara Friddi** Sicilia, Italy, C Mediterranean Sea
78 G12 **Léré** Mayo-Kébbi, SW Chad
Leribe see Hlotse
106 E10 **Lerici** Liguria, NW Italy
54 I14 **Lérida** Vaupés, SE Colombia
Lérida see Lleida
105 N5 **Lerma** Castilla-León, N Spain
40 M13 **Lerma, Río** ≈ C Mexico
115 F20 **Lérna** prehistoric site Pelopónnisos, S Greece
45 R11 **le Robert** E Martinique
115 M21 **Léros** island Dodekánisos, Greece, Aegean Sea
30 L13 **Le Roy** Illinois, N USA
27 Q6 **Le Roy** Kansas, C USA
29 W11 **Le Roy** Minnesota, N USA
18 E10 **Le Roy** New York, NE USA
Lerrnayin Gharabakh see Nagornyy Karabakh
95 J19 **Lerum** Västra Götaland, S Sweden
96 M2 **Lerwick** NE Scotland, UK
45 Y6 **les Abymes** var. Abymes. Grande Terre, C Guadeloupe
les Albères see Albères, Chaîne des
102 M4 **les Andelys** Eure, N France
45 Q12 **les Anses-d'Arlets** SW Martinique
105 U6 **Les Borges Blanques** var. Borjas Blancas. Cataluña, NE Spain
Lesbos see Lésvos
Les Cayes see Cayes
31 Q4 **Les Cheneaux Islands** island Michigan, N USA
103 T12 **les Écrins** ▲ E France
108 C10 **Le Sépey** Vaud, W Switzerland
15 T7 **Les Escoumins** Quebec, SE Canada
Les Gonaïves see Gonaïves
Lesh/Leshi see Lezhë
160 H9 **Leshan** Sichuan, C China
108 D11 **Les Haudères** Valais, SW Switzerland
102 J9 **les Herbiers** Vendée, NW France
127 O8 **Leshukonskoye** Arkhangel'skaya Oblast', NW Russian Federation
Lesina see Hvar
107 M15 **Lesina, Lago di** ◎ SE Italy
114 K13 **Lesítse** ▲ NE Greece
94 G10 **Lesja** Oppland, S Norway
95 L15 **Lesjöfors** Värmland, C Sweden
111 O18 **Lesko** Podkarpackie, SE Poland
113 O15 **Leskovac** Serbia, SE Yugoslavia
113 M22 **Leskovik** var. Leskoviku. Korçë, S Albania
Leskoviku see Leskovik
33 P14 **Leslie** Idaho, NW USA
31 Q10 **Leslie** Michigan, N USA
Leśna/Lesnaya see Lyasnaya
102 F5 **Lesneven** Finistère, NW France
112 J11 **Lešnica** Serbia, W Yugoslavia
127 S13 **Lesnoy** Kirovskaya Oblast', NW Russian Federation
122 K12 **Lesosibirsk** Krasnoyarskiy Kray, C Russian Federation
83 J23 **Lesotho** off. Kingdom of Lesotho; prev. Basutoland. ◆ monarchy S Africa
102 J12 **Lesparre-Médoc** Gironde, SW France
108 C8 **Les Ponts-de-Martel** Neuchâtel, W Switzerland
102 I9 **les Sables-d'Olonne** Vendée, NW France
103 P1 **Lesquin** ✕ Nord, N France
109 S7 **Lessach** var. Lessachbach. ≈ E Austria
Lessachbach see Lessach
45 W11 **les Saintes** var. Îles des Saintes. island group S Guadeloupe
74 L5 **Les Salines** ✕ (Annaba) NE Algeria
99 J22 **Lesse** ≈ SE Belgium
95 M21 **Lessebo** Kronoberg, S Sweden
194 M10 **Lesser Antarctica** var. West Antarctica. physical region Antarctica
45 P15 **Lesser Antilles** island group E West Indies
137 T10 **Lesser Caucasus** Rus. Malyy Kavkaz. ▲ SW Asia
Lesser Khingan Range see Xiao Hinggan Ling
11 P13 **Lesser Slave Lake** ◎ Alberta, W Canada
Lesser Sunda Islands see Nusa Tenggara
99 E19 **Lessines** Hainaut, SW Belgium
103 R16 **les Stes-Maries-de-la-Mer** Bouches-du-Rhône, SE France
14 G15 **Lester B.Pearson** var. Toronto. ✕ (Toronto) Ontario, S Canada
29 U9 **Lester Prairie** Minnesota, N USA
93 L16 **Lestijärvi** Länsi-Suomi, W Finland
L'Estuaire see Estuaire
29 U9 **Le Sueur** Minnesota, N USA
108 B8 **Les Verrières** Neuchâtel, W Switzerland
115 L17 **Lésvos** anc. Lesbos. island E Greece
110 G12 **Leszno** Ger. Lissa. Wielkopolskie, C Poland
83 L20 **Letaba** Northern, NE South Africa
173 P17 **le Tampon** SW Réunion
97 O21 **Letchworth** E England, UK
111 G25 **Letenye** Zala, SW Hungary
11 Q17 **Lethbridge** Alberta, SW Canada
55 S11 **Lethem** S Guyana
83 H18 **Letiahau** ≈ W Botswana
54 J18 **Leticia** Amazonas, S Colombia
171 S16 **Leti, Kepulauan** island group E Indonesia
83 I18 **Letlhakane** Central, C Botswana
83 H20 **Letlhakeng** Kweneng, SE Botswana
114 J8 **Letnitsa** Lovech, N Bulgaria
103 N1 **le Touquet-Paris-Plage** Pas-de-Calais, N France
166 L8 **Letpadan** Pegu, SW Myanmar
166 K6 **Letpan** Arakan State, W Myanmar
102 M2 **le Tréport** Seine-Maritime, N France
166 M12 **Letsôk-aw Kyun** var. Letsutan Island; prev. Domel Island. island Mergui Archipelago, S Myanmar
Letsutan Island see Letsôk-aw Kyun
97 E14 **Letterkenny** Ir. Leitir Ceanainn. NW Ireland
Lettland see Latvia
116 M6 **Letychiv** Khmel'nyts'ka Oblast', W Ukraine
Lëtzebuerg see Luxembourg
116 H14 **Leu** Dolj, SW Romania
Leucas see Lefkáda
103 P17 **Leucate** Aude, S France
103 P17 **Leucate, Étang de** ◎ S France
108 E10 **Leuk** Valais, SW Switzerland
108 E10 **Leukerbad** Valais, SW Switzerland
Leusden see Leusden-Centrum
98 K11 **Leusden-Centrum** var. Leusden. Utrecht, C Netherlands
Leutensdorf see Litvínov
Leutschau see Levoča
99 H18 **Leuven** Fr. Louvain, Ger. Löwen. Vlaams Brabant, C Belgium
99 I20 **Leuze** Namur, C Belgium
Leuze see Leuze-en-Hainaut
99 E19 **Leuze-en-Hainaut** var. Leuze. Hainaut, SW Belgium
Léva see Levice
Levádhia see Leivádia
Levajok see Leavvajohka
36 L4 **Levan** Utah, W USA
93 E16 **Levanger** Nord-Trøndelag, C Norway
121 S12 **Levantine Basin** undersea feature E Mediterranean Sea
106 D10 **Levanto** Liguria, W Italy
107 H23 **Levanzo, Isola di** island Isole Egadi, S Italy
129 Q17 **Levashi** Respublika Dagestan, SW Russian Federation
24 M5 **Levelland** Texas, SW USA
39 P13 **Levelock** Alaska, USA
101 E16 **Leverkusen** Nordrhein-Westfalen, W Germany
111 J21 **Levice** Ger. Lewentz, Hung. Léva. Nitriansky Kraj, SW Slovakia
106 G6 **Levico Terme** Trentino-Alto Adige, N Italy
115 E20 **Levídi** Pelopónnisos, S Greece
103 P14 **le Vigan** Gard, S France
184 L13 **Levin** Manawatu-Wanganui, North Island, NZ
15 R10 **Lévis** var. Levis. Quebec, SE Canada
21 P6 **Levisa Fork** ≈ Kentucky/Virginia, S USA
115 L21 **Levítha** island Kykládes, Greece, Aegean Sea
18 L14 **Levittown** Long Island, New York, NE USA
18 J15 **Levittown** Pennsylvania, NE USA
Levkás see Lefkáda
Levkímmi see Lefkímmi
111 L19 **Levoča** Ger. Leutschau, Hung. Locse. Prešovský Kraj, E Slovakia
Lévrier, Baie du see Nouâdhibou, Dakhlet
103 N9 **Levroux** Indre, C France
114 J8 **Levski** Pleven, N Bulgaria
Levskigrad see Karlovo
128 L6 **Lev Tolstoy** Lipetskaya Oblast', W Russian Federation
187 X14 **Levuka** Ovalau, C Fiji
166 L6 **Lewe** Mandalay, C Myanmar
Lewentz/Lewenz see Levice
97 O23 **Lewes** SE England, UK
21 Z4 **Lewes** Delaware, NE USA
29 Q12 **Lewis and Clark Lake** ▣ Nebraska/South Dakota, N USA
18 G14 **Lewisburg** Pennsylvania, NE USA
20 J10 **Lewisburg** Tennessee, S USA
21 S6 **Lewisburg** West Virginia, NE USA
96 F6 **Lewis, Butt of** headland NW Scotland, UK
96 F7 **Lewis, Isle of** island NW Scotland, UK
35 U4 **Lewis, Mount** ▲ Nevada, W USA
185 H16 **Lewis Pass** pass South Island, NZ
33 P7 **Lewis Range** ▲ Montana, NW USA
23 O3 **Lewis Smith Lake** ▣ Alabama, S USA
32 M10 **Lewiston** Idaho, NW USA
19 P7 **Lewiston** Maine, NE USA
29 X10 **Lewiston** Minnesota, N USA
18 D9 **Lewiston** New York, NE USA
36 L1 **Lewiston** Utah, W USA
30 K13 **Lewistown** Illinois, N USA
33 T9 **Lewistown** Montana, NW USA
27 T14 **Lewisville** Arkansas, C USA
25 T6 **Lewisville** Texas, SW USA
25 T6 **Lewisville, Lake** ▣ Texas, SW USA
Le Woleu-Ntem see Woleu-Ntem
23 U3 **Lexington** Georgia, SE USA
20 M5 **Lexington** Kentucky, S USA
22 L4 **Lexington** Mississippi, S USA
27 S4 **Lexington** Missouri, C USA
29 N16 **Lexington** Nebraska, C USA
20 S9 **Lexington** North Carolina, SE USA
27 N11 **Lexington** Oklahoma, C USA
21 R12 **Lexington** South Carolina, SE USA
20 G9 **Lexington** Tennessee, S USA
25 T10 **Lexington** Texas, SW USA
21 T6 **Lexington** Virginia, NE USA
21 X5 **Lexington Park** Maryland, NE USA
Leyden see Leiden
102 J14 **Leyre** ≈ SW France
171 Q5 **Leyte** island C Philippines
171 Q6 **Leyte Gulf** gulf E Philippines
111 O16 **Leżajsk** Podkarpackie, SE Poland
Lezha see Lezhë
113 K18 **Lezhë** var. Lezha; prev. Lesh, Leshi. Lezhë, NW Albania
113 K18 **Lezhë** ◆ district NW Albania
103 O16 **Lézignan-Corbières** Aude, S France
128 J7 **L'gov** Kurskaya Oblast', W Russian Federation
159 P15 **Lhari** Xizang Zizhiqu, W China
159 N16 **Lhasa** var. La-sa, Lassa. Xizang Zizhiqu, W China
159 O15 **Lhasa He** ≈ W China
158 K16 **Lhazê** Xizang Zizhiqu, W China
158 K14 **Lhazhong** Xizang Zizhiqu, W China
168 H7 **Lhoksukon** Sumatera, W Indonesia
159 Q15 **Lhorong** Xizang Zizhiqu, W China
105 W6 **L'Hospitalet de Llobregat** var. Hospitalet. Cataluña, NE Spain
153 R11 **Lhotse** ▲ China/Nepal
159 N17 **Lhozhag** Xizang Zizhiqu, W China
159 O16 **Lhünzê** Xizang Zizhiqu, W China
159 N15 **Lhünzhub** var. Poindo. Xizang Zizhiqu, W China
167 N8 **Li** Lamphun, NW Thailand
Liancheng see Qinglong
161 P12 **Liangcheng** Fujian, SE China
160 K9 **Liangping** Chongqing Shi, C China
Liangzhou see Wuwei
161 O9 **Liangzi Hu** ◎ C China
161 R12 **Lianjiang** Fujian, SE China
160 L15 **Lianjiang** Guangdong, S China
161 O13 **Lianping** Guangdong, S China
163 T13 **Lianshan** prev. Jinxi. Liaoning, NE China
Lian Xian see Lianzhou
160 M11 **Lianyuan** prev. Lantian. Hunan, S China
161 Q6 **Lianyungang** var. Xinpu. Jiangsu, E China
161 N13 **Lianzhou** var. Linxian; prev. Lian Xian. Guangdong, S China
Liao see Liaoning
161 P5 **Liaocheng** Shandong, E China
163 U13 **Liaodong Bandao** var. Liaotung Peninsula. peninsula NE China
163 T13 **Liaodong Wan** Eng. Gulf of Lantung, Gulf of Liaotung. gulf NE China
163 U11 **Liao He** ≈ NE China
163 W12 **Liao Ling** ▲ NE China
163 U12 **Liaoning** var. Liao, Liaoning Sheng, Shengking; hist. Fengtien, Shenking. ◆ province NE China
Liaoning Sheng see Liaoning
Liaotung, Gulf of see Liaodong Wan
Liaotung Peninsula see Liaodong Bandao
163 V12 **Liaoyang** var. Liao-yang. Liaoning, NE China
163 V11 **Liaoyuan** var. Dongliao, Shuang-liao, Jap. Chengchiatun. Jilin, NE China
163 U12 **Liaozhong** Liaoning, NE China
Liaqatabad see Piplān
10 M10 **Liard** ≈ W Canada
Liard see Fort Liard
10 L10 **Liard River** British Columbia, W Canada
149 O15 **Liāri** Baluchistān, SW Pakistan
Liatroim see Leitrim
189 S6 **Lib** var. Ellep. island Ralik Chain, C Marshall Islands
Liban see Lebanon
138 H6 **Liban, Jebel** Ar. Jabal al Gharbt, Jabal Lubnān, Eng. Mount Lebanon. ▲ C Lebanon
Libau see Liepāja
33 N7 **Libby** Montana, NW USA
79 I16 **Libenge** Equateur, NW Dem. Rep. Congo (Zaire)
26 I7 **Liberal** Kansas, C USA
27 R7 **Liberal** Missouri, C USA
Liberalitas Julia see Évora
111 D15 **Liberec** Ger. Reichenberg. Liberecký Kraj, N Czech Republic
111 D15 **Liberecký Kraj** ◆ region N Czech Republic
42 K12 **Liberia** Guanacaste, NW Costa Rica
76 K17 **Liberia** off. Republic of Liberia. ◆ republic W Africa
61 D16 **Libertad** Corrientes, NE Argentina
61 E20 **Libertad** San José, S Uruguay
54 I7 **Libertad** Barinas, NW Venezuela
54 K6 **Libertad** Cojedes, N Venezuela
62 G12 **Libertador** off. Región del Libertador General Bernardo O'Higgins. ◆ region C Chile
Libertador General San Martín see Ciudad de Libertador General San Martín
20 L6 **Liberty** Kentucky, S USA
22 J7 **Liberty** Mississippi, S USA
27 R4 **Liberty** Missouri, C USA
18 J12 **Liberty** New York, NE USA
21 T9 **Liberty** North Carolina, SE USA
Libian Desert see Libyan Desert
99 J23 **Libin** Luxembourg, SE Belgium
160 K13 **Libo** Guizhou, S China
Libohova see Libohovë
113 L23 **Libohovë** var. Libohova. Gjirokastër, S Albania
81 K18 **Liboi** North Eastern, E Kenya
102 K13 **Libourne** Gironde, SW France
99 K23 **Libramont** Luxembourg, SE Belgium
113 M20 **Librazhd** var. Librazhdi. Elbasan, E Albania
Librazhdi see Librazhd
79 C18 **Libreville** ● (Gabon) Estuaire, NW Gabon
75 P10 **Libya** off. Socialist People's Libyan Arab Jamahiriya, Ar. Al Jamāhīrīyah al 'Arabīyah al Lībīyah ash Sha'bīyah al Ishtirākīyah; prev. Libyan Arab Republic. ◆ Islamic state N Africa
75 T11 **Libyan Desert** var. Libian Desert, Ar. Aş Şahrā' al Lībīyah. desert N Africa
75 T8 **Libyan Plateau** var. Aḍ Ḍiffah. plateau Egypt/Libya
Lībīyah, Aş Şahrā' al see Libyan Desert
62 G12 **Licantén** Maule, C Chile
107 J25 **Licata** anc. Phintias. Sicilia, Italy, C Mediterranean Sea
137 P14 **Lice** Diyarbakır, SE Turkey
97 L19 **Lichfield** C England, UK
83 N14 **Lichinga** Niassa, N Mozambique
109 V3 **Lichtenau** Niederösterreich, N Austria
83 I21 **Lichtenburg** North-West, N South Africa
101 K18 **Lichtenfels** Bayern, SE Germany
98 O12 **Lichtenvoorde** Gelderland, E Netherlands
Lichtenwald see Sevnica
99 C17 **Lichtervelde** West-Vlaanderen, W Belgium
160 L9 **Lichuan** Hubei, C China
27 V7 **Licking** Missouri, C USA
20 M4 **Licking River** ≈ Kentucky, S USA
112 C11 **Lički Osik** Lika-Senj, C Croatia
Ličko-Senjska Županija see Lika-Senj
107 K19 **Licosa, Punta** headland S Italy
119 H16 **Lida** Rus. Lida. Hrodzyenskaya Voblasts', W Belarus
93 H17 **Liden** Västernorrland, C Sweden
29 R7 **Lidgerwood** North Dakota, N USA
Lidhorikíon see Lidoríki
95 K21 **Lidhult** Kronoberg, S Sweden
95 P16 **Lidingö** Stockholm, C Sweden
95 K17 **Lidköping** Västra Götaland, S Sweden
Lido di Iesolo see Lido di Jesolo
106 I8 **Lido di Jesolo** var. Lido di Iesolo. Veneto, NE Italy
107 H15 **Lido di Ostia** Lazio, C Italy
Lidokhorikion see Lidoríki
115 E18 **Lidoríki** prev. Lidhorikíon, Lidokhorikion. Stereá Ellás, C Greece
110 K9 **Lidzbark** Warmińsko-Mazurskie, NE Poland
110 L7 **Lidzbark Warmiński** Ger. Heilsberg. Warmińsko-Mazurskie, NE Poland
109 U3 **Liebenau** Oberösterreich, N Austria
181 P7 **Liebig, Mount** ▲ Northern Territory, C Australia
109 V8 **Lieboch** Steiermark, SE Austria
108 I8 **Liechtenstein** off. Principality of Liechtenstein. ◆ principality C Europe
99 F18 **Liedekerke** Vlaams Brabant, C Belgium
99 K19 **Liège** Dut. Luik, Ger. Lüttich. Liège, E Belgium
99 K20 **Liège** Dut. Luik. ◆ province E Belgium
Liegnitz see Legnica
93 O16 **Lieksa** Itä-Suomi, E Finland
118 F10 **Lielupe** ≈ Latvia/Lithuania
118 G9 **Lielvārde** Ogre, C Latvia
167 U13 **Liên Hương** var. Tuy Phong. Bình Thuận, S Vietnam
Liên Nghia see Đức Trong
109 P9 **Lienz** Tirol, W Austria
118 B10 **Liepāja** Ger. Libau. Liepāja, W Latvia
99 H17 **Lier** Fr. Lierre. Antwerpen, N Belgium
95 H15 **Lierbyen** Buskerud, S Norway
99 L21 **Lierneux** Liège, E Belgium
Lierre see Lier
101 D18 **Lieser** ≈ W Germany
109 U7 **Liesing** ≈ E Austria
108 E6 **Liestal** Basel-Land, N Switzerland
Lietuva see Lithuania
Lievenhof see Līvāni
103 O2 **Liévin** Pas-de-Calais, N France
14 M9 **Lièvre, Rivière du** ≈ Quebec, SE Canada
109 T6 **Liezen** Steiermark, C Austria
97 E14 **Lifford** Ir. Leifear. NW Ireland
187 Q16 **Lifou** island Îles Loyauté, E New Caledonia
193 Y15 **Lifuka** island Ha'apai Group, C Tonga
171 P4 **Ligao** Luzon, N Philippines
Liger see Loire
42 H2 **Lighthouse Reef** reef E Belize
183 Q4 **Lightning Ridge** New South Wales, SE Australia
103 N9 **Lignières** Cher, C France
103 S5 **Ligny-en-Barrois** Meuse, NE France
83 P15 **Ligonha** ≈ NE Mozambique
31 P11 **Ligonier** Indiana, N USA
81 I25 **Ligunga** Ruvuma, S Tanzania
106 D9 **Ligure, Appennino** Eng. Ligurian Mountains. ▲ NW Italy
Ligure, Mar see Ligurian Sea
106 C9 **Liguria** ◆ region NW Italy
Ligurian Mountains see Ligure, Appennino
120 K6 **Ligurian Sea** Fr. Mer Ligurienne, It. Mar Ligure. sea N Mediterranean Sea

Ligurienne, Mer *see* Ligurian Sea
186 H5 **Lihir Group** *island group* NE PNG
38 B8 **Līhue** *Haw.* Lihu'e. Kauai, Hawaii, USA, C Pacific Ocean
118 F5 **Lihula** *Ger.* Leal. Läänemaa, W Estonia
126 I2 **Liinakhamari** *var.* Linacmamari. Murmanskaya Oblast', NW Russian Federation
Liivi Laht *see* Riga, Gulf of
160 F11 **Lijiang** *var.* Dayan, Lijiang Naxizu Zizhixian. Yunnan, SW China
112 C11 **Lika-Senj** *off.* Ličko-Senjska Županija. ◈ *province* W Croatia
79 N25 **Likasi** *prev.* Jadotville. Katanga, SE Dem. Rep. Congo (Zaire)
79 L16 **Likati** Orientale, N Dem. Rep. Congo (Zaire)
10 M15 **Likely** British Columbia, SW Canada
153 Y11 **Likhapāni** Assam, NE India
126 J16 **Likhoslavl'** Tverskaya Oblast', W Russian Federation
189 U5 **Likiep Atoll** *atoll* Ratak Chain, C Marshall Islands
95 D18 **Liknes** Vest-Agder, S Norway
79 H18 **Likouala** ≈ N Congo
79 H18 **Likouala aux Herbes** ≈ E Congo
190 B16 **Liku** E Niue
Likupang, Selat *see* Bangka, Selat
27 Y8 **Lilbourn** Missouri, C USA
103 X14 **l'Île-Rousse** Corse, France, C Mediterranean Sea
109 W5 **Lilienfeld** Niederösterreich, NE Austria
161 N11 **Liling** Hunan, S China
95 J18 **Lilla Edet** Västra Götaland, S Sweden
103 P1 **Lille** *var.* l'Isle, *Dut.* Rijssel, *Flem.* Ryssel; *prev.* Lisle, *anc.* Insula. Nord, N France
95 G24 **Lillebælt** *var.* Lille Bælt, *Eng.* Little Belt. *strait* S Denmark
102 L3 **Lillebonne** Seine-Maritime, N France
94 H12 **Lillehammer** Oppland, S Norway
103 O1 **Lillers** Pas-de-Calais, N France
95 F18 **Lillesand** Aust-Agder, S Norway
95 I15 **Lillestrøm** Akershus, S Norway
93 F18 **Lillhärdal** Jämtland, C Sweden
21 U10 **Lillington** North Carolina, SE USA
105 O9 **Lillo** Castilla-La Mancha, C Spain
10 M16 **Lillooet** British Columbia, SW Canada
83 M14 **Lilongwe** ● (Malawi) Central, W Malawi
83 M14 **Lilongwe** × Central, W Malawi
83 M14 **Lilongwe** ≈ W Malawi
171 P7 **Liloy** Mindanao, S Philippines
Lilybaeum *see* Marsala
182 J7 **Lilydale** South Australia
183 P16 **Lilydale** Tasmania, SE Australia
113 J14 **Lim** ≈ Bosnia and Herzegovina/Yugoslavia
57 D15 **Lima** ● (Peru) Lima, W Peru
94 K13 **Lima** Dalarna, C Sweden
31 R12 **Lima** Ohio, NE USA
57 D14 **Lima** ◈ *department* W Peru
Lima *see* Jorge Chávez International
104 G5 **Lima, Rio** *Sp.* Limia ≈ Portugal/Spain *see also* Limia
111 L17 **Limanowa** Małopolskie, S Poland
168 M11 **Limas** Pulau Sebangka, W Indonesia
Limassol *see* Lemesós
97 F14 **Limavady** *Ir.* Léim an Mhadaidh. NW Northern Ireland, UK
63 J14 **Limay Mahuida** La Pampa, C Argentina
63 H15 **Limay, Río** ≈ W Argentina
101 N16 **Limbach-Oberfrohna** Sachsen, E Germany
81 F22 **Limba Limba** ≈ C Tanzania
107 C17 **Limbara, Monte** ▲ Sardegna, Italy, C Mediterranean Sea
118 G7 **Limbaži** *Est.* Lemsalu. Limbaži, N Latvia
44 M8 **Limbé** N Haiti
99 L19 **Limbourg** Liège, E Belgium
99 K17 **Limburg** ◈ *province* NE Belgium
99 L16 **Limburg** ◈ *province* SE Netherlands
101 F17 **Limburg an der Lahn** Hessen, W Germany
94 K13 **Limedsforsen** Dalarna, C Sweden
60 L9 **Limeira** São Paulo, S Brazil
97 C19 **Limerick** *Ir.* Luimneach. SW Ireland
97 C20 **Limerick** *Ir.* Luimneach. *cultural region* SW Ireland
19 S2 **Limestone** Maine, NE USA
25 U9 **Limestone, Lake** ◎ Texas, SW USA
39 P12 **Lime Village** Alaska, USA
95 F20 **Limfjorden** *fjord* N Denmark
95 J23 **Limhamn** Skåne, S Sweden
104 H5 **Limia** *Port.* Rio Lima ≈ Portugal/ Spain *see also* Lima, Rio
93 L14 **Liminka** Oulu, C Finland
Limín Vathéos *see* Sámos
115 G17 **Límni** Évvoia, C Greece
115 J15 **Límnos** *anc.* Lemnos. *island* E Greece
102 M11 **Limoges** *anc.* Augustoritum Lemovicensium, Lemovices. Haute-Vienne, C France
37 U5 **Limon** Colorado, C USA
43 O13 **Limón** *var.* Puerto Limón. Limón, E Costa Rica
42 K4 **Limón** Colón, NE Honduras
43 N13 **Limón** *off.* Provincia de Limón. ◈ *province* E Costa Rica
106 A10 **Limone Piemonte** Piemonte, NE Italy
Limones *see* Valdéz
Limonum *see* Poitiers
103 N11 **Limousin** ◈ *region* C France
103 N16 **Limoux** Aude, S France
83 L19 **Limpopo** *var.* Crocodile. ≈ S Africa
160 K17 **Limu Ling** ▲ S China
113 M20 **Lin** *var.* Lini. Elbasan, E Albania
Linacmamari *see* Liinakhamari
62 G13 **Linares** Maule, C Chile
54 C13 **Linares** Nariño, SW Colombia
41 O9 **Linares** Nuevo León, NE Mexico
105 N12 **Linares** Andalucía, S Spain
107 G15 **Linaro, Capo** *headland* C Italy
106 D8 **Linate** × (Milano) Lombardia, N Italy
160 F13 **Lincang** Yunnan, SW China
161 P11 **Linchuan** *var.* Fuzhou. Jiangxi, S China
61 B20 **Lincoln** Buenos Aires, E Argentina
185 H19 **Lincoln** Canterbury, South Island, NZ
97 N18 **Lincoln** *anc.* Lindum, Lindum Colonia. E England, UK
35 O6 **Lincoln** California, W USA
30 L13 **Lincoln** Illinois, N USA
26 M4 **Lincoln** Kansas, C USA
19 S5 **Lincoln** Maine, NE USA
27 T5 **Lincoln** Missouri, C USA
29 R16 **Lincoln** *state capital* Nebraska, C USA
32 F11 **Lincoln City** Oregon, NW USA
167 X10 **Lincoln Island** *island* E Paracel Islands
197 Q11 **Lincoln Sea** *sea* Arctic Ocean
97 N18 **Lincolnshire** *cultural region* E England, UK
21 R10 **Lincolnton** North Carolina, SE USA
25 V7 **Lindale** Texas, SW USA
101 I25 **Lindau** *var.* Lindau am Bodensee. Bayern, S Germany
Lindau am Bodensee *see* Lindau
123 P9 **Linde** ≈ NE Russian Federation
55 T9 **Linden** E Guyana
23 O6 **Linden** Alabama, S USA
20 H9 **Linden** Tennessee, S USA
25 X6 **Linden** Texas, SW USA
18 J16 **Lindenwold** New Jersey, NE USA
95 M15 **Lindesberg** Örebro, C Sweden
95 D18 **Lindesnes** *headland* S Norway
Líndhos *see* Líndos
81 K24 **Lindi** Lindi, SE Tanzania
81 J24 **Lindi** ◈ *region* SE Tanzania
79 N17 **Lindi** ≈ NE Dem. Rep. Congo (Zaire)
163 V7 **Lindian** Heilongjiang, NE China
185 E21 **Lindis Pass** *pass* South Island, NZ
83 J22 **Lindley** Free State, C South Africa
95 J19 **Lindome** Västra Götaland, S Sweden
Lindong *see* Bairin Zuoqi
115 O23 **Líndos** *var.* Líndhos. Ródos, Dodekánisos, Greece, Aegean Sea
14 I14 **Lindsay** Ontario, SE Canada
35 R11 **Lindsay** California, W USA
33 X8 **Lindsay** Montana, NW USA
27 N11 **Lindsay** Oklahoma, C USA
27 N5 **Lindsborg** Kansas, C USA
95 N21 **Lindsdal** Kalmar, S Sweden
Lindum/Lindum Colonia *see* Lincoln
191 W3 **Line Islands** *island group* E Kiribati
Linëvo *see* Linova
160 M5 **Linfen** *var.* Lin-fen. Shanxi, C China
155 F18 **Linganamakki Reservoir** ⊡ SW India
160 L17 **Lingao** Hainan, S China
171 N3 **Lingayen** Luzon, N Philippines
160 M6 **Lingbao** *var.* Guolüezhen. Henan, C China
94 N12 **Lingbo** Gävleborg, C Sweden
Lingeh *see* Bandar-e Langeh
100 E12 **Lingen** *var.* Lingen an der Ems. Niedersachsen, NW Germany
Lingen an der Ems *see* Lingen
168 M11 **Lingga, Kepulauan** *island group* W Indonesia
168 L11 **Lingga, Pulau** *island* Kepulauan Lingga, W Indonesia
14 J14 **Lingham Lake** ◎ Ontario, SE Canada
94 M13 **Linghed** Dalarna, C Sweden
33 Z15 **Lingle** Wyoming, C USA
18 G15 **Linglestown** Pennsylvania, NE USA
79 K18 **Lingomo II** Equateur, NW Dem. Rep. Congo (Zaire)
160 L15 **Lingshan** Guangxi Zhuangzu Zizhiqu, S China
160 L17 **Lingshui** Hainan, S China
155 G16 **Lingsugūr** Karnātaka, C India
107 L23 **Linguaglossa** Sicilia, Italy, C Mediterranean Sea
76 H10 **Linguère** N Senegal
159 W8 **Lingwu** Ningxia, N China
Lingxi *see* Yongshun
161 O12 **Lingxian** *var.* Ling Xian. Hunan, S China
163 S12 **Lingyuan** Liaoning, NE China
163 U4 **Linhai** Heilongjiang, NE China
161 S10 **Linhai** *var.* Taizhou. Zhejiang, SE China
59 O20 **Linhares** Espírito Santo, SE Brazil
162 M13 **Linhe** Nei Mongol Zizhiqu, N China
Lini *see* Lin
139 S1 **Līnik, Chiyā-ē** ▲ N Iraq
95 M18 **Linköping** Östergötland, S Sweden
163 Y8 **Linkou** Heilongjiang, NE China
118 F11 **Linkuva** Pakruojis, N Lithuania
27 V5 **Linn** Missouri, C USA
25 S16 **Linn** Texas, SW USA
27 T2 **Linneus** Missouri, C USA
96 H10 **Linnhe, Loch** *inlet* W Scotland, UK
119 G19 **Linova** *Rus.* Linëvo. Brestskaya Voblasts', SW Belarus
161 O5 **Linqing** Shandong, E China
161 N6 **Linruzhen** Henan, C China
60 K8 **Lins** São Paulo, S Brazil
93 F17 **Linsell** Jämtland, C Sweden
160 J9 **Linshui** Sichuan, C China
44 K12 **Linstead** C Jamaica
159 U11 **Lintan** Gansu, N China
159 V11 **Lintao** Gansu, C China
15 S12 **Lintère** ≈ Quebec, SE Canada
108 H8 **Linth** ≈ NW Switzerland
108 H8 **Linthal** Glarus, NE Switzerland
31 N15 **Linton** Indiana, N USA
29 N6 **Linton** North Dakota, N USA
163 R11 **Linxi** Nei Mongol Zizhiqu, N China
159 U11 **Linxia** *var.* Linxia Huizu Zizhizhou. Gansu, C China
Linxia Huizu Zizhizhou *see* Linxia
Linxian *see* Lianzhou
161 Q6 **Linyi** Shandong, S China
161 P4 **Linyi** Shandong, E China
160 M6 **Linyi** Shanxi, C China
109 T4 **Linz** *anc.* Lentia. Oberösterreich, N Austria
159 S8 **Linze** *var.* Shahepu. Gansu, N China
44 J13 **Lionel Town** C Jamaica
103 Q16 **Lion, Golfe du** *Eng.* Gulf of Lion, Gulf of Lions; *anc.* Sinus Gallicus. *gulf* S France
Lion, Gulf of/Lions, Gulf of *see* Lion, Golfe du
83 K16 **Lions Den** Mashonaland West, N Zimbabwe
14 F13 **Lion's Head** Ontario, S Canada
Lios Ceannúir, Bá *see* Liscannor Bay
Lios Mór *see* Lismore
Lios na gCearrbhach *see* Lisburn
Lios Tuathail *see* Listowel
79 G17 **Liouesso** La Sangha, N Congo
Liozno *see* Lyozna
171 O4 **Lipa** *off.* Lipa City. Luzon, N Philippines
25 S7 **Lipan** Texas, SW USA
Lipari Islands/Lipari, Isole *see* Eolie, Isole
107 L22 **Lipari, Isola** *island* Isole Eolie, S Italy
116 L8 **Lipcani** *Rus.* Lipkany. N Moldova
93 N17 **Liperi** Itä-Suomi, E Finland
128 L7 **Lipetsk** Lipetskaya Oblast', W Russian Federation
128 K6 **Lipetskaya Oblast'** ◈ *province* W Russian Federation
57 K22 **Lipez, Cordillera de** ▲ SW Bolivia
110 E10 **Lipiany** *Ger.* Lippehne. Zachodniopomorskie, W Poland
112 G9 **Lipik** Požega-Slavonija, NE Croatia
126 L12 **Lipin Bor** Vologodskaya Oblast', NW Russian Federation
160 L12 **Liping** Guizhou, S China
Lipkany *see* Lipcani
119 H15 **Lipnishki** *Rus.* Lipnishki. Hrodzyenskaya Voblasts', W Belarus
110 J10 **Lipno** Kujawsko-pomorskie, C Poland
116 F11 **Lipova** *Hung.* Lippa. Arad, W Romania
Lipovets *see* Lypovets'
Lippa *see* Lipova
101 E14 **Lippe** ≈ W Germany
Lippehne *see* Lipiany
101 G14 **Lippstadt** Nordrhein-Westfalen, W Germany
25 P1 **Lipscomb** Texas, SW USA
Lipsia/Lipsk *see* Leipzig
Liptau-Sankt-Nikolaus/Liptószentmiklós *see* Liptovský Mikuláš
111 K19 **Liptovský Mikuláš** *Ger.* Liptau-Sankt-Nikolaus, *Hung.* Liptószentmiklós. Žilinský Kraj, N Slovakia
183 O13 **Liptrap, Cape** *headland* Victoria, SE Australia
160 L13 **Lipu** Guangxi Zhuangzu Zizhiqu, S China
141 X12 **Liqbi** S Oman
81 G17 **Lira** N Uganda
57 F15 **Lircay** Huancavelica, C Peru
107 J15 **Liri** ≈ C Italy
144 M8 **Lisakovsk** Kostanay, NW Kazakhstan
79 K17 **Lisala** Equateur, N Dem. Rep. Congo (Zaire)
104 F11 **Lisboa** *Eng.* Lisbon; *anc.* Felicitas Julia, Olisipo. ● (Portugal) Lisboa, W Portugal
104 F10 **Lisboa** ◈ *Eng.* Lisbon. *district* C Portugal
19 N7 **Lisbon** New Hampshire, NE USA
29 Q6 **Lisbon** North Dakota, N USA
Lisbon *see* Lisboa
19 Q8 **Lisbon Falls** Maine, NE USA
97 G15 **Lisburn** *Ir.* Lios na gCearrbhach. E Northern Ireland, UK
38 L6 **Lisburne, Cape** *headland* Alaska, USA
97 B19 **Liscannor Bay** *Ir.* Bá Lios Ceannúir. *inlet* W Ireland
113 Q18 **Lisec** ▲ E FYR Macedonia
161 R13 **Lishe Jiang** ≈ SW China
160 M4 **Lishi** Shanxi, C China
163 V10 **Lishu** Jilin, NE China
161 R10 **Lishui** Zhejiang, SE China
192 L5 **Lisianski Island** *island* Hawaiian Islands, Hawaii, USA, C Pacific Ocean
Lisichansk *see* Lysychans'k
102 L4 **Lisieux** *anc.* Noviomagus. Calvados, N France
128 L8 **Liski** *prev.* Georgiu-Dezh. Voronezhskaya Oblast', W Russian Federation
Lisle/l'Isle *see* Lille
103 N4 **l'Isle-Adam** Val-d'Oise, N France
103 R15 **l'Isle-sur-la-Sorgue** Vaucluse, SE France
15 S9 **L'Islet** Quebec, SE Canada
182 M12 **Lismore** Victoria, SE Australia
97 D20 **Lismore** *Ir.* Lios Mór. S Ireland
Lissa *see* Vis, Croatia
Lissa *see* Leszno, Poland
98 H11 **Lisse** Zuid-Holland, W Netherlands
95 D18 **Lista** *peninsula* S Norway
95 D18 **Listafjorden** *fjord* S Norway
195 R13 **Lister, Mount** ▲ Antarctica
128 M8 **Listopadovka** Voronezhskaya Oblast', W Russian Federation
14 F15 **Listowel** Ontario, S Canada
97 B20 **Listowel** *Ir.* Lios Tuathail. SW Ireland
160 L14 **Litang** Guangxi Zhuangzu Zizhiqu, S China
160 F9 **Litang** Sichuan, C China
160 F10 **Litang Qu** ≈ C China
55 X12 **Litani** *var.* Itany. ≈ French Guiana/Surinam
138 G8 **Līṭāni, Nahr el** *var.* Nahr al Litant. ≈ C Lebanon
Litant, Nahr al *see* Līṭāni, Nahr el
Litauen *see* Lithuania
30 K14 **Litchfield** Illinois, N USA
29 U8 **Litchfield** Minnesota, N USA
36 K13 **Litchfield Park** Arizona, SW USA
183 S8 **Lithgow** New South Wales, SE Australia
115 I26 **Líthino, Akrotírio** *headland* Kríti, Greece, E Mediterranean Sea
118 D12 **Lithuania** *off.* Republic of Lithuania, *Ger.* Litauen, *Lith.* Lietuva, *Pol.* Litwa, *Rus.* Litva; *prev.* Lithuanian SSR, *Rus.* Litovskaya SSR. ◆ *republic* NE Europe
Lithuanian SSR *see* Lithuania
109 U11 **Litija** *Ger.* Littai. C Slovenia
18 H15 **Lititz** Pennsylvania, NE USA
115 F15 **Litóchoro** *var.* Litohoro, Litókhoron. Kentrikí Makedonía, N Greece
Litohoro/Litókhoron *see* Litóchoro
111 C15 **Litoměřice** *Ger.* Leitmeritz. Ústecký Kraj, NW Czech Republic
111 F17 **Litomyšl** *Ger.* Leitomischl. Pardubický Kraj, C Czech Republic
111 G17 **Litovel** *Ger.* Littau. Olomoucký Kraj, E Czech Republic
123 S13 **Litovko** Khabarovskiy Kray, SE Russian Federation
Litovskaya SSR *see* Lithuania
Littai *see* Litija
Littau *see* Litovel
44 G1 **Little Abaco** *var.* Abaco Island. *island* N Bahamas
111 I21 **Little Alföld** *Ger.* Kleines Ungarisches Tiefland, *Hung.* Kisalföld, *Slvk.* Podunajská Rovina. *plain* Hungary/Slovakia
151 Q20 **Little Andaman** *island* Andaman Islands, India, NE Indian Ocean
26 M5 **Little Arkansas River** ≈ Kansas, C USA
184 L4 **Little Barrier Island** *island* N NZ
Little Belt *see* Lillebælt
38 M11 **Little Black River** ≈ Alaska, USA
27 O2 **Little Blue River** ≈ Kansas/Nebraska, C USA
44 D8 **Little Cayman** *island* E Cayman Islands
11 X11 **Little Churchill** ≈ Manitoba, C Canada
166 J10 **Little Coco Island** *island* SW Myanmar
36 L10 **Little Colorado River** ≈ Arizona, SW USA
14 E11 **Little Current** Manitoulin Island, Ontario, S Canada
12 E11 **Little Current** ≈ Ontario, S Canada
38 L8 **Little Diomede Island** *island* Alaska, USA
44 I4 **Little Exuma** *island* C Bahamas
29 U7 **Little Falls** Minnesota, N USA
18 J10 **Little Falls** New York, NE USA
24 M5 **Littlefield** Texas, SW USA
29 V3 **Littlefork** Minnesota, N USA
29 V3 **Little Fork River** ≈ Minnesota, N USA
11 N16 **Little Fort** British Columbia, SW Canada
11 Y14 **Little Grand Rapids** Manitoba, C Canada
97 N23 **Littlehampton** SE England, UK
35 T2 **Little Humboldt River** ≈ Nevada, W USA
44 K6 **Little Inagua** *var.* Inagua Islands. *island* S Bahamas
21 Q4 **Little Kanawha River** ≈ West Virginia, NE USA
83 F25 **Little Karoo** *plateau* S South Africa
39 O16 **Little Koniuji Island** *island* Shumagin Islands, Alaska, USA
44 H12 **Little London** W Jamaica
13 R10 **Little Mecatina** *Fr.* Rivière du Petit Mécatina. ≈ Newfoundland/Quebec, E Canada
96 F8 **Little Minch, The** *strait* NW Scotland, UK
27 T13 **Little Missouri River** ≈ Arkansas, USA
28 J7 **Little Missouri River** ≈ NW USA
28 J3 **Little Muddy River** ≈ North Dakota, N USA
151 Q22 **Little Nicobar** *island* Nicobar Islands, India, NE Indian Ocean
27 R6 **Little Osage River** ≈ Missouri, C USA
97 P20 **Little Ouse** ≈ E England, UK
149 V2 **Little Pamir** *Pash.* Pāmīr-e Khord, *Rus.* Malyy Pamir. ▲ Afghanistan/Tajikistan
21 U12 **Little Pee Dee River** ≈ North Carolina/South Carolina, SE USA
27 V10 **Little Red River** ≈ Arkansas, C USA
Little Rhody *see* Rhode Island
185 I19 **Little River** Canterbury, South Island, NZ
21 U12 **Little River** South Carolina, SE USA
27 Y9 **Little River** ≈ Arkansas/Missouri, C USA
27 R13 **Little River** ≈ Arkansas/Oklahoma, USA
23 T7 **Little River** ≈ Georgia, SE USA
22 H6 **Little River** ≈ Louisiana, S USA
25 T10 **Little River** ≈ Texas, SW USA
27 V12 **Little Rock** *state capital* Arkansas, C USA
31 N8 **Little Sable Point** *headland* Michigan, N USA
103 U11 **Little Saint Bernard Pass** *Fr.* Col du Petit St-Bernard, *It.* Colle di Piccolo San Bernardo. *pass* France/Italy
36 K7 **Little Salt Lake** ◎ Utah, W USA
180 K8 **Little Sandy Desert** *desert* Western Australia
29 S13 **Little Sioux River** ≈ Iowa, C USA
38 E17 **Little Sitkin Island** *island* Aleutian Islands, Alaska, USA
11 O13 **Little Smoky** Alberta, W Canada
11 O14 **Little Smoky** ≈ Alberta, W Canada
37 P3 **Little Snake River** ≈ Colorado, C USA
64 A12 **Little Sound** *bay* Bermuda, NW Atlantic Ocean
37 T4 **Littleton** Colorado, C USA
19 N7 **Littleton** New Hampshire, NE USA
18 D11 **Little Valley** New York, NE USA
30 M15 **Little Wabash River** ≈ Illinois, N USA
14 D10 **Little White River** ≈ Ontario, S Canada
28 M12 **Little White River** ≈ South Dakota, N USA
25 R5 **Little Wichita River** ≈ Texas, SW USA
142 I4 **Little Zab** *Ar.* Nahraz Zāb aş Şaghīr, *Kurd.* Zē-i Kōya, *Per.* Rūdkhāneh-ye Zāb-e Kūchek. ≈ Iran/Iraq
79 D15 **Littoral** ◈ *province* W Cameroon
Littoria *see* Latina
Litva/Litwa *see* Lithuania
111 B15 **Litvínov** *Ger.* Ústecký Kraj, NW Czech Republic
116 M6 **Lityn** Vinnyts'ka Oblast', C Ukraine
Liu-chou/Liuchow *see* Liuzhou
163 W11 **Liuhe** Jilin, NE China
83 Q15 **Liúpo** Nampula, NE Mozambique
83 G14 **Liuwa Plain** *plain* W Zambia
160 L13 **Liuzhou** *var.* Liu-chou, Liuchow. Guangxi Zhuangzu Zizhiqu, S China
116 H8 **Livada** *Hung.* Sárköz. Satu Mare, NW Romania
115 J20 **Liváda, Akrotírio** *headland* Tínos, Kykládes, Greece, Aegean Sea
115 L21 **Livádi** *island* Kykládes, Greece, Aegean Sea
Livanátai *see* Livanátes
115 G18 **Livanátes** *prev.* Livanátai. Stereá Ellás, C Greece
118 I10 **Līvāni** *Ger.* Lievenhof. Preiļi, SE Latvia
65 E25 **Lively Island** *island* SE Falkland Islands
65 D25 **Lively Sound** *sound* SE Falkland Islands
39 R8 **Livengood** Alaska, USA
106 I7 **Livenza** ≈ NE Italy
35 O6 **Live Oak** California, W USA
23 U9 **Live Oak** Florida, SE USA
35 O9 **Livermore** California, W USA
20 I6 **Livermore** Kentucky, S USA
19 Q7 **Livermore Falls** Maine, NE USA
24 J10 **Livermore, Mount** ▲ Texas, SW USA
97 K17 **Liverpool** NW England, UK
183 S7 **Liverpool Range** ▲ New South Wales, SE Australia
96 J12 **Livingston** C Scotland, UK
23 N5 **Livingston** Alabama, S USA
35 P9 **Livingston** California, W USA
22 J8 **Livingston** Louisiana, S USA
33 S11 **Livingston** Montana, NW USA
20 L8 **Livingston** Tennessee, S USA
25 W9 **Livingston** Texas, SW USA
42 F4 **Livingston** Izabal, E Guatemala
83 I16 **Livingstone** *var.* Maramba. Southern, S Zambia
185 B22 **Livingstone Mountains** ▲ South Island, NZ
80 K13 **Livingstone Mountains** ▲ S Tanzania
82 N12 **Livingstonia** Northern, N Malawi
194 G4 **Livingston Island** *island* Antarctica
25 W9 **Livingston, Lake** ⊡ Texas, SW USA
112 F13 **Livno** Federacija Bosna I Hercegovina, SW Bosnia and Herzegovina
128 K7 **Livny** Orlovskaya Oblast', W Russian Federation
93 M14 **Livojoki** ≈ C Finland
31 R10 **Livonia** Michigan, N USA
106 E11 **Livorno** *Eng.* Leghorn. Toscana, C Italy
Livramento *see* Santana do Livramento
141 U8 **Liwā** *var.* Al Liwā'. *oasis region* S UAE
81 I24 **Liwale** Lindi, SE Tanzania
159 W9 **Liwangbu** Ningxia, N China
83 N15 **Liwonde** Southern, S Malawi
159 V11 **Lixian** *var.* Li Xian, Gansu, C China
160 H8 **Lixian** *var.* Li Xian; *prev.* Zagunao. Sichuan, C China
Lixian Jiang *see* Black River
115 B18 **Lixoúri** *prev.* Lixoúrion. Kefallinía, Iónioi Nísoi, Greece, C Mediterranean Sea
Lixoúrion *see* Lixoúri
Lixus *see* Larache
Lizarra *see* Estella-Lizarra
33 U15 **Lizard Head Peak** ▲ Wyoming, C USA
97 H25 **Lizard Point** *headland* SW England, UK
112 L12 **Ljig** Serbia, C Yugoslavia
Ljouwert *see* Leeuwarden
Ljubelj *see* Loibl Pass
109 U11 **Ljubljana** *Ger.* Laibach, *It.* Lubiana; *anc.* Aemona, Emona. ● (Slovenia) C Slovenia
109 T11 **Ljubljana** × C Slovenia
113 N17 **Ljuboten** ▲ S Yugoslavia
95 P19 **Ljugarn** Gotland, SE Sweden
84 G7 **Ljungan** ≈ N Sweden
93 F17 **Ljungan** ≈ C Sweden
95 K21 **Ljungby** Kronoberg, S Sweden
95 M17 **Ljungsbro** Östergötland, S Sweden
95 I18 **Ljungskile** Västra Götaland, S Sweden
94 M11 **Ljusdal** Gävleborg, C Sweden
94 M11 **Ljusnan** ≈ C Sweden
94 N12 **Ljusne** Gävleborg, C Sweden
95 P15 **Ljusterö** Stockholm, C Sweden
109 X9 **Ljutomer** *Ger.* Luttenberg. NE Slovenia
63 G15 **Llaima, Volcán** ▲ S Chile
105 X4 **Llançà** *var.* Llansá. Cataluña, NE Spain
97 J21 **Llandovery** C Wales, UK
97 J20 **Llandrindod Wells** E Wales, UK
97 J18 **Llandudno** N Wales, UK
97 I21 **Llanelli** *prev.* Llanelly. SW Wales, UK
Llanelly *see* Llanelli
104 M2 **Llanes** Asturias, N Spain
97 K19 **Llangollen** NE Wales, UK
25 R10 **Llano** Texas, SW USA
25 Q10 **Llano River** ≈ Texas, SW USA
54 I9 **Llanos** *physical region* Colombia/Venezuela
63 G16 **Llanquihue, Lago** ◎ S Chile
Llansá *see* Llançà
105 U5 **Lleida** *Cast.* Lérida; *anc.* Ilerda. Cataluña, NE Spain
105 U5 **Lleida** *Cast.* Lérida ◈ *province* Cataluña, NE Spain
104 K12 **Llerena** Extremadura, W Spain
105 S9 **Lliria** País Valenciano, E Spain
105 W4 **Llivia** Cataluña, NE Spain
105 O3 **Llodio** País Vasco, N Spain
105 X5 **Lloret de Mar** Cataluña, NE Spain
Llorri *see* Tossal de l'Orri
10 L11 **Lloyd George, Mount** ▲ British Columbia, W Canada
11 R14 **Lloydminster** Alberta/Saskatchewan, SW Canada
36 L6 **Loa** Utah, W USA
169 S8 **Loagan Bunut** ◎ East Malaysia
38 G12 **Loa, Mauna** ▲ Hawaii, USA, C Pacific Ocean
Loanda *see* Luanda
79 J22 **Loange** ≈ S Dem. Rep. Congo (Zaire)
79 E21 **Loango** Le Kouilou, S Congo
106 B10 **Loano** Liguria, NW Italy
62 H4 **Loa, Río** ≈ N Chile
83 I20 **Lobatse** *var.* Lobatsi. Kgatleng, SE Botswana
Lobatsi *see* Lobatse
101 Q15 **Löbau** Sachsen, E Germany
79 H16 **Lobaye** ◈ *prefecture* SW Central African Republic
79 I16 **Lobaye** ≈ SW Central African Republic
99 G21 **Lobbes** Hainaut, S Belgium
61 D23 **Lobería** Buenos Aires, E Argentina
110 F8 **Łobez** *Ger.* Labes. Zachodniopomorskie, NW Poland
82 A13 **Lobito** Benguela, W Angola
Lobkovichi *see* Labkovichy
Lob Nor *see* Lop Nur
171 V13 **Lobo** Irian Jaya, E Indonesia
104 J11 **Lobón** Extremadura, W Spain
61 D20 **Lobos** Buenos Aires, E Argentina
40 E4 **Lobos, Cabo** *headland* NW Mexico
40 F6 **Lobos, Isla** *island* NW Mexico
Lobositz *see* Lovosice
Lobsens *see* Łobżenica
Loburi *see* Lop Buri
110 H9 **Łobżenica** *Ger.* Lobsens. Wielkopolskie, C Poland
108 G11 **Locarno** *Ger.* Luggarus. Ticino, S Switzerland
96 E9 **Lochboisdale** NW Scotland, UK
98 N11 **Lochem** Gelderland, E Netherlands
102 M8 **Loches** Indre-et-Loire, C France
Loch Garman *see* Wexford
96 H12 **Lochgilphead** W Scotland, UK
96 H7 **Lochinver** N Scotland, UK
96 F8 **Lochmaddy** NW Scotland, UK
96 J10 **Lochnagar** ▲ C Scotland, UK
99 E17 **Lochristi** Oost-Vlaanderen, NW Belgium
96 H9 **Lochy, Loch** ◎ N Scotland, UK
182 G8 **Lock** South Australia
97 J14 **Lockerbie** S Scotland, UK
27 S13 **Lockesburg** Arkansas, C USA
183 P10 **Lockhart** New South Wales, SE Australia
25 S11 **Lockhart** Texas, SW USA

◆ Country ● Country Capital ◇ Dependent Territory ○ Dependent Territory Capital ◈ Administrative Region × International Airport ▲ Mountain ▲ Mountain Range Volcano ≈ River ◎ Lake ⊡ Reservoir

18 F13 **Lock Haven** Pennsylvania, NE USA
25 N4 **Lockney** Texas, SW USA
100 O12 **Löcknitz** ≈ NE Germany
18 E9 **Lockport** New York, NE USA
167 T13 **Lôc Ninh** Sông Be, S Vietnam
107 N23 **Locri** Calabria, SW Italy
Locse see Levoča
27 T2 **Locust Creek** ≈ Missouri, C USA
23 P3 **Locust Fork** ≈ Alabama, S USA
27 Q9 **Locust Grove** Oklahoma, C USA
94 E11 **Lodalskåpa** ▲ S Norway
183 N10 **Loddon River** ≈ Victoria, SE Australia
Lodensee see Klooga
103 P15 **Lodève** anc. Luteva. Hérault, S France
126 I12 **Lodeynoye Pole** Leningradskaya Oblast', NW Russian Federation
33 V11 **Lodge Grass** Montana, NW USA
28 J15 **Lodgepole Creek** ≈ Nebraska/Wyoming, C USA
149 T11 **Lodhrān** Punjab, E Pakistan
106 D8 **Lodi** Lombardia, NW Italy
35 O8 **Lodi** California, W USA
31 T12 **Lodi** Ohio, N USA
92 H10 **Lødingen** Nordland, C Norway
79 L20 **Lodja** Kasai Oriental, C Dem. Rep. Congo (Zaire)
37 O3 **Lodore, Canyon of** canyon Colorado, C USA
105 Q4 **Lodosa** Navarra, N Spain
81 H16 **Lodwar** Rift Valley, NW Kenya
110 K13 **Łódź** Rus. Lodz. Łódź, C Poland
110 J13 **Łódzkie** ◆ province C Poland
167 P8 **Loei** var. Loey, Muang Loei. Loei, C Thailand
98 I11 **Loenen** Utrecht, C Netherlands
167 R9 **Loeng Nok Tha** Yasothon, E Thailand
83 F24 **Loeriesfontein** Northern Cape, W South Africa
95 H20 **Læsø** island N Denmark
Loewoek see Luwuk
Loey see Loei
76 J16 **Lofa** ≈ N Liberia
109 P6 **Lofer** Salzburg, C Austria
92 F11 **Lofoten** var. Lofoten Islands. island group C Norway
Lofoten Islands see Lofoten
95 N18 **Loftahammar** Kalmar, S Sweden
129 O10 **Log** Volgogradskaya Oblast', SW Russian Federation
77 S12 **Loga** Dosso, SW Niger
29 S14 **Logan** Iowa, C USA
26 K3 **Logan** Kansas, C USA
31 T14 **Logan** Ohio, N USA
36 L1 **Logan** Utah, W USA
21 P6 **Logan** West Virginia, NE USA
35 Y10 **Logandale** Nevada, W USA
19 O11 **Logan International** ✕ (Boston) Massachusetts, NE USA
11 N16 **Logan Lake** British Columbia, SW Canada
23 Q4 **Logan Martin Lake** ▣ Alabama, S USA
10 G8 **Logan, Mount** ▲ Yukon Territory, W Canada
32 I7 **Logan, Mount** ▲ Washington, NW USA
33 P7 **Logan Pass** pass Montana, NW USA
31 O12 **Logansport** Indiana, N USA
22 F6 **Logansport** Louisiana, S USA
Logar see Lowgar
67 R11 **Loge** ≈ NW Angola
Logishin see Lahishyn
Log na Coille see Lugnaquillia Mountain
78 G11 **Logone** var. Logone. ≈ Cameroon/Chad
78 G13 **Logone-Occidental** off. Préfecture du Logone-Occidental. ◆ prefecture SW Chad
78 H13 **Logone Occidental** ≈ SW Chad
78 G13 **Logone-Oriental** off. Préfecture du Logone-Oriental. ◆ prefecture SW Chad
78 H13 **Logone Oriental** ≈ SW Chad
Logone Oriental see Pendé
L'Ogooué-Ivindo see Ogooué-Ivindo
L'Ogooué-Lolo see Ogooué-Lolo
L'Ogooué-Maritime see Ogooué-Maritime
Logoysk see Lahoysk
105 P4 **Logroño** anc. Vareia, Lat. Juliobriga. La Rioja, N Spain
104 L10 **Logrosán** Extremadura, W Spain
95 G20 **Løgstør** Nordjylland, N Denmark
95 H22 **Løgten** Århus, C Denmark
95 F24 **Løgumkloster** Sønderjylland, SW Denmark
Lögurinn see Lagarfljót
153 P15 **Lohārdaga** Bihār, N India
152 H10 **Lohāru** Haryāna, N India
101 D15 **Lohausen** ✕ (Düsseldorf) Nordrhein-Westfalen, W Germany
189 O14 **Lohd** Pohnpei, E Micronesia
92 L12 **Lohiniva** Lappi, N Finland
Lohiszyn see Lahishyn
93 L20 **Lohja** var. Lojo. Etelä-Suomi, S Finland
169 V11 **Lohjanan** Borneo, C Indonesia
25 Q9 **Lohn** Texas, SW USA
100 G12 **Lohne** Niedersachsen, NW Germany
Lohr see Lohr am Main
101 I18 **Lohr am Main** var. Lohr. Bayern, C Germany
109 T10 **Loibl Pass** Ger. Loiblpass, Slvn. Ljubelj. pass Austria/Slovenia
167 N6 **Loi-Kaw** Kayah State, C Myanmar
93 K19 **Loimaa** Länsi-Suomi, W Finland
103 O6 **Loing** ≈ C France
167 R6 **Loi, Phou** ▲ N Laos
102 L7 **Loir** ≈ C France
103 Q11 **Loire** ◆ department E France
102 M7 **Loire** var. Liger. ≈ C France
102 I7 **Loire-Atlantique** ◆ department NW France
103 O7 **Loiret** ◆ department C France
102 M8 **Loir-et-Cher** ◆ department C France
101 L24 **Loisach** ≈ SE Germany
56 B9 **Loja** Loja, S Ecuador
104 M14 **Loja** Andalucía, S Spain
56 B9 **Loja** ◆ province S Ecuador
Lojo see Lohja
116 J4 **Lokachi** Volyns'ka Oblast', NW Ukraine
79 M20 **Lokandu** Maniema, C Dem. Rep. Congo (Zaire)
92 M11 **Lokan Tekojärvi** ◎ NE Finland
137 Z11 **Lökbatan** Rus. Lokbatan. E Azerbaijan
99 F17 **Lokeren** Oost-Vlaanderen, NW Belgium
Lokhvitsa see Lokhvytsya
117 S4 **Lokhvytsya** Rus. Lokhvitsa. Poltavs'ka Oblast', NE Ukraine
81 H17 **Lokichar** Rift Valley, NW Kenya
81 G16 **Lokichokio** Rift Valley, NW Kenya
81 H16 **Lokitaung** Rift Valley, NW Kenya
92 M11 **Lokka** Lappi, N Finland
94 G8 **Løkken Verk** Sør-Trøndelag, S Norway
126 G16 **Loknya** Pskovskaya Oblast', W Russian Federation
77 V15 **Loko** Nassarawa, C Nigeria
77 U15 **Lokoja** Kogi, C Nigeria
81 H17 **Lokori** Rift Valley, W Kenya
77 R16 **Lokossa** S Benin
118 I3 **Loksa** Ger. Loxa. Harjumaa, NW Estonia
9 T7 **Loks Land** island Nunavut, NE Canada
80 C13 **Lol** ≈ S Sudan
76 K15 **Lola** Guinée-Forestière, SE Guinea
35 Q5 **Lola, Mount** ▲ California, W USA
81 H20 **Loliondo** Arusha, NE Tanzania
95 H25 **Lolland** prev. Laaland. island S Denmark
186 G6 **Lolobau Island** island E PNG
79 E16 **Lolodorf** Sud, SW Cameroon
114 G7 **Lom** prev. Lom-Palanka. Oblast Montana, NW Bulgaria
114 G7 **Lom** ≈ Montana, NW Bulgaria
79 M19 **Lomami** ≈ C Dem. Rep. Congo (Zaire)
57 F17 **Lomas** Arequipa, SW Peru
63 I23 **Lomas, Bahía** bay S Chile
61 D20 **Lomas de Zamora** Buenos Aires, E Argentina
61 D20 **Loma Verde** Buenos Aires, E Argentina
180 K4 **Lombadina** Western Australia
106 E6 **Lombardia** Eng. Lombardy. ◆ region N Italy
Lombardy see Lombardia
102 M15 **Lombez** Gers, S France
171 Q16 **Lomblen, Pulau** island Nusa Tenggara, S Indonesia
173 W7 **Lombok Basin** undersea feature E Indian Ocean
170 L16 **Lombok, Pulau** island Nusa Tenggara, C Indonesia
77 Q16 **Lomé** ● (Togo) S Togo
77 Q16 **Lomé** ✕ S Togo
79 L19 **Lomela** Kasai Oriental, C Dem. Rep. Congo (Zaire)
25 R9 **Lometa** Texas, SW USA
79 F16 **Lomié** Est, SE Cameroon
30 M8 **Lomira** Wisconsin, N USA
95 K23 **Lomma** Skåne, S Sweden
99 J16 **Lommel** Limburg, N Belgium
96 I11 **Lomond, Loch** ◎ C Scotland, UK
197 R9 **Lomonosov Ridge** var. Harris Ridge, Rus. Khrebet Lomonsova. undersea feature Arctic Ocean
Lomonsova, Khrebet see Lomonosov Ridge
Lom-Palanka see Lom
Lomphat see Lumphăt
35 P14 **Lompoc** California, W USA
167 P9 **Lom Sak** var. Muang Lom Sak. Phetchabun, C Thailand
110 N9 **Łomża** Rus. Lomzha. Podlaskie, NE Poland
Lomzha see Łomża
155 D14 **Lonāvale** prev. Lonauli. Mahārāshtra, W India
63 G15 **Loncoche** Araucanía, C Chile
63 H14 **Loncopue** Neuquén, W Argentina
99 G17 **Londerzeel** Vlaams Brabant, C Belgium
Londinium see London
14 E16 **London** Ontario, S Canada
191 Y2 **London** Kiritimati, E Kiribati
97 O22 **London** anc. Augusta, Lat. Londinium. ● (UK) SE England, UK
21 N7 **London** Kentucky, S USA
31 S13 **London** Ohio, NE USA
25 Q10 **London** Texas, SW USA
97 O22 **London City** ✕ SE England, UK
97 E14 **Londonderry** var. Derry, Ir. Doire. NW Northern Ireland, UK
97 F14 **Londonderry** cultural region NW Northern Ireland, UK
180 M2 **Londonderry, Cape** headland Western Australia
63 H25 **Londonderry, Isla** island S Chile
43 O7 **Londres, Cayos** reef NE Nicaragua
60 I10 **Londrina** Paraná, S Brazil
27 N13 **Lone Grove** Oklahoma, C USA
14 E12 **Lonely Island** island Ontario, S Canada
35 T8 **Lone Mountain** ▲ Nevada, W USA
25 V6 **Lone Oak** Texas, SW USA
35 T11 **Lone Pine** California, W USA
Lone Star State see Texas
83 D14 **Longa** Cuando Cubango, C Angola
82 B12 **Longa** ≈ W Angola
83 E15 **Longa** ≈ SE Angola
163 W11 **Longang Shan** ▲ NE China
197 S4 **Longa, Proliv** Eng. Long Strait. strait NE Russian Federation
44 J13 **Long Bay** bay W Jamaica
21 V13 **Long Bay** bay North Carolina/South Carolina, E USA
35 T16 **Long Beach** California, W USA
22 M9 **Long Beach** Mississippi, S USA
18 L14 **Long Beach** Long Island, New York, NE USA
32 F9 **Long Beach** Washington, NW USA
18 K16 **Long Beach Island** island New Jersey, NE USA
65 M25 **Longbluff** headland SW Tristan da Cunha
23 U13 **Longboat Key** island Florida, SE USA
18 K15 **Long Branch** New Jersey, NE USA
44 J5 **Long Cay** island SE Bahamas
161 P14 **Longchuan** prev. Laolong. Guangdong, S China
Longchuan Jiang see Shweli
32 K12 **Long Creek** Oregon, NW USA
159 W10 **Longde** Ningxia, N China
183 P16 **Longford** Tasmania, SE Australia
97 D17 **Longford** Ir. An Longfort. C Ireland
97 E17 **Longford** Ir. An Longfort. cultural region C Ireland
161 P1 **Longhua** Hebei, E China
169 U11 **Longiram** Borneo, C Indonesia
44 J4 **Long Island** island C Bahamas
12 H8 **Long Island** island Nunavut, C Canada
186 D7 **Long Island** var. Arop Island. island N PNG
18 L14 **Long Island** island New York, NE USA
Long Island see Bermuda
18 M14 **Long Island Sound** sound NE USA
160 K13 **Long Jiang** ≈ S China
163 U7 **Longjiang** Heilongjiang, NE China
163 Y10 **Longjing** var. Yanji. Jilin, NE China
161 R4 **Longkou** Shandong, E China
12 E11 **Longlac** Ontario, S Canada
19 S1 **Long Lake** ◎ Maine, NE USA
31 O6 **Long Lake** ◎ Michigan, N USA
31 R5 **Long Lake** ◎ Michigan, N USA
29 N6 **Long Lake** ◎ North Dakota, N USA
30 J4 **Long Lake** ▣ Wisconsin, N USA
99 K23 **Longlier** Luxembourg, SE Belgium
160 I13 **Longlin** var. Longlin Gezu Zizhixian. Guangxi Zhuangzu Zizhiqu, S China
37 T3 **Longmont** Colorado, C USA
29 N13 **Long Pine** Nebraska, C USA
Longping see Luodian
14 F17 **Long Point** headland Ontario, S Canada
14 K15 **Long Point** headland Ontario, SE Canada
184 P10 **Long Point** headland North Island, NZ
30 L2 **Long Point** headland Michigan, N USA
14 G17 **Long Point Bay** lake bay Ontario, S Canada
29 T7 **Long Prairie** Minnesota, N USA
13 S11 **Long Range Mountains** hill range Newfoundland, E Canada
65 H25 **Long Range Point** headland SE Saint Helena
181 V8 **Longreach** Queensland, E Australia
160 H7 **Longriba** Sichuan, C China
160 L10 **Longshan** Hunan, S China
37 S3 **Longs Peak** ▲ Colorado, C USA
Long Strait see Longa, Proliv
102 K8 **Longué** Maine-et-Loire, NW France
13 P11 **Longue-Pointe** Quebec, E Canada
103 S4 **Longuyon** Meurthe-et-Moselle, NE France
25 W7 **Longview** Texas, SW USA
32 G10 **Longview** Washington, NW USA
65 H25 **Longwood** C Saint Helena
25 P7 **Longworth** Texas, SW USA
103 S3 **Longwy** Meurthe-et-Moselle, NE France
159 V11 **Longxi** Gansu, C China
167 S14 **Long Xuyên** var. Longxuyen. An Giang, S Vietnam
161 Q13 **Longyan** Fujian, SE China
92 O3 **Longyearbyen** ○ (Svalbard) Spitsbergen, W Svalbard
160 J15 **Longzhou** Guangxi Zhuangzu Zizhiqu, S China
100 F12 **Löningen** Niedersachsen, NW Germany
27 V11 **Lonoke** Arkansas, C USA
95 L21 **Lönsboda** Skåne, S Sweden
103 S9 **Lons-le-Saunier** anc. Ledo Salinarius. Jura, E France
31 O15 **Loogootee** Indiana, N USA
31 Q9 **Looking Glass River** ≈ Michigan, N USA
21 X11 **Lookout, Cape** headland North Carolina, SE USA
39 O6 **Lookout Ridge** ridge Alaska, USA
181 N11 **Loongana** Western Australia
99 I14 **Loon op Zand** Noord-Brabant, S Netherlands
97 A19 **Loop Head** Ir. Ceann Léime. headland W Ireland
109 V4 **Loosdorf** Niederösterreich, NE Austria
158 G10 **Lop** Xinjiang Uygur Zizhiqu, NW China
112 J11 **Lopare** Republika Srpska, NE Bosnia and Herzegovina
Lopatichi see Lapatsichy
129 Q15 **Lopatin** Respublika Dagestan, SW Russian Federation
129 P7 **Lopatino** Penzenskaya Oblast', W Russian Federation
167 P10 **Lop Buri** var. Loburi. Lop Buri, C Thailand
25 R16 **Lopeno** Texas, SW USA
79 C18 **Lopez, Cap** headland W Gabon
98 I12 **Lopik** Utrecht, C Netherlands
Lop Nor see Lop Nur
158 M7 **Lop Nur** var. Lob Nor, Lop Nor, Lo-pu Po. seasonal lake NW China
Lopnur see Yuli
79 K17 **Lopori** ≈ NW Dem. Rep. Congo (Zaire)
98 O5 **Loppersum** Groningen, NE Netherlands
92 I8 **Lopphavet** sound N Norway
Lo-pu Po see Lop Nur
Lora see Lowrah
182 F3 **Lora Creek** seasonal river South Australia
104 K13 **Lora del Río** Andalucía, S Spain
148 M11 **Lora, Hāmūn-i** wetland SW Pakistan
31 T11 **Lorain** Ohio, N USA
25 O7 **Loraine** Texas, SW USA
31 R13 **Loramie, Lake** ▣ Ohio, N USA
105 Q13 **Lorca** Ar. Lurka; anc. Eliocroca, Lat. Illur co. Murcia, S Spain
192 I10 **Lord Howe Island** island E Australia
Lord Howe Island see Ontong Java Atoll
175 O10 **Lord Howe Rise** undersea feature SW Pacific Ocean
192 J10 **Lord Howe Seamounts** undersea feature W Pacific Ocean
37 P15 **Lordsburg** New Mexico, SW USA
186 E5 **Lorengau** var. Lorungau. Manus Island, N PNG
25 N5 **Lorenzo** Texas, SW USA
142 K7 **Lorestān** off. Ostān-e Lorestān, var. Luristan. ◆ province W Iran
57 M17 **Loreto** Beni, N Bolivia
106 J12 **Loreto** Marche, C Italy
40 F8 **Loreto** Baja California Sur, W Mexico
40 M11 **Loreto** Zacatecas, C Mexico
56 E9 **Loreto** off. Departamento de Loreto. ◆ department NE Peru
81 K18 **Lorian Swamp** swamp E Kenya
54 E6 **Lorica** Córdoba, NW Colombia
102 G7 **Lorient** prev. l'Orient. Morbihan, NW France
111 K22 **Lőrinci** Heves, NE Hungary
14 G11 **Loring** Ontario, S Canada
33 V6 **Loring** Montana, NW USA
103 R13 **Loriol-sur-Drôme** Drôme, E France
21 U12 **Loris** South Carolina, SE USA
57 I18 **Loriscota, Laguna** ◎ S Peru
183 N13 **Lorne** Victoria, SE Australia
96 G11 **Lorn, Firth of** inlet W Scotland, UK
Loro Sae see East Timor
101 F24 **Lörrach** Baden-Württemberg, S Germany
103 T5 **Lorraine** ◆ region NE France
Lorungau see Lorengau
94 L11 **Los** Gävleborg, C Sweden
35 P14 **Los Alamos** California, W USA
37 S10 **Los Alamos** New Mexico, SW USA
42 F5 **Los Amates** Izabal, E Guatemala
35 S15 **Los Angeles** California, W USA
35 S15 **Los Angeles** ✕ California, W USA
63 G14 **Los Ángeles** Bío Bío, C Chile
35 T13 **Los Angeles Aqueduct** aqueduct California, W USA
Losanna see Lausanne
63 H20 **Los Antiguos** Santa Cruz, SW Argentina
189 Q16 **Losap Atoll** atoll C Micronesia
35 P10 **Los Banos** California, W USA
104 K16 **Los Barrios** Andalucía, S Spain
62 L5 **Los Blancos** Salta, N Argentina
42 L12 **Los Chiles** Alajuela, NW Costa Rica
105 O2 **Los Corrales de Buelna** Cantabria, N Spain
25 T17 **Los Fresnos** Texas, SW USA
35 N9 **Los Gatos** California, W USA
110 O11 **Łosice** Mazowieckie, E Poland
112 B11 **Lošinj** Ger. Lussin, It. Lussino. island W Croatia
Los Jardines see Ngetik Atoll
63 G15 **Los Lagos** Los Lagos, C Chile
63 F17 **Los Lagos** off. Región de los Lagos. ◆ region C Chile
Loslau see Wodzisław Śląski
64 N11 **Los Llanos** var. Los Llanos de Aridane. La Palma, Islas Canarias, Spain, NE Atlantic Ocean
Los Llanos de Aridane see Los Llanos
37 R11 **Los Lunas** New Mexico, SW USA
63 I16 **Los Menucos** Río Negro, C Argentina
40 H8 **Los Mochis** Sinaloa, C Mexico
35 N4 **Los Molinos** California, W USA
104 M9 **Los Navalmorales** Castilla-La Mancha, C Spain
25 S15 **Los Olmos Creek** ≈ Texas, SW USA
Losonc/Losontz see Lučenec
167 S5 **Lô, Sông** Chin. Panlong Jiang. ≈ China/Vietnam
44 B5 **Los Palacios** Pinar del Río, W Cuba
104 K14 **Los Palacios y Villafranca** Andalucía, S Spain
171 R16 **Lospalos** E East Timor
37 R12 **Los Pinos Mountains** ▲ New Mexico, SW USA
37 R11 **Los Ranchos De Albuquerque** New Mexico, SW USA
40 M14 **Los Reyes** Michoacán de Ocampo, SW Mexico
56 B7 **Los Ríos** ◆ province C Ecuador
64 O11 **Los Rodeos** ✕ (Santa Cruz de Tenerife) Tenerife, Islas Canarias, Spain, NE Atlantic Ocean
54 L4 **Los Roques, Islas** island group N Venezuela
43 S17 **Los Santos** Los Santos, S Panama
43 S17 **Los Santos** off. Provincia de Los Santos. ◆ province S Panama
Los Santos see Los Santos de Maimona
104 J12 **Los Santos de Maimona** var. Los Santos. Extremadura, W Spain
98 P10 **Losser** Overijssel, E Netherlands
96 J8 **Lossiemouth** NE Scotland, UK
61 B14 **Los Tábanos** Santa Fe, C Argentina
54 J4 **Los Taques** Falcón, N Venezuela
14 G11 **Lost Channel** Ontario, S Canada
54 L5 **Los Teques** Miranda, N Venezuela
35 Q12 **Lost Hills** California, W USA
36 I7 **Lost Peak** ▲ Utah, W USA
33 P11 **Lost Trail Pass** pass Montana, NW USA
186 G9 **Losuia** Kiriwina Island, SE PNG
62 G10 **Los Vilos** Coquimbo, C Chile
105 N10 **Los Yébenes** Castilla-La Mancha, C Spain
103 N13 **Lot** ◆ department S France
103 N13 **Lot** ≈ S France
63 F14 **Lota** Bío Bío, C Chile
81 G15 **Lotagipi Swamp** wetland Kenya/Sudan
102 K14 **Lot-et-Garonne** ◆ department SW France
83 K21 **Lothair** Mpumalanga, NE South Africa
33 R7 **Lothair** Montana, NW USA
79 L20 **Loto** Kasai Oriental, C Dem. Rep. Congo (Zaire)
192 H16 **Lotofagā** Upolu, SE Samoa
108 E10 **Lötschbergtunnel** tunnel Valais, SW Switzerland
25 T9 **Lott** Texas, SW USA
126 H3 **Lotta** var. Lutto. ≈ Finland/Russian Federation
184 Q7 **Lottin Point** headland North Island, NZ
Lötzen see Giżycko
Loualaba see Lualaba
167 P6 **Louangnamtha** var. Luong Nam Tha. Louang Namtha, N Laos
167 Q7 **Louangphabang** var. Louangphrabang, Luang Prabang. Louangphabang, N Laos
Louangphrabang see Louangphabang
194 H5 **Loubet Coast** physical region Antarctica
Loubomo see Dolisie
Louch see Loukhi
102 H6 **Loudéac** Côtes d'Armor, NW France
160 M11 **Loudi** Hunan, S China
79 F21 **Loudima** La Bouenza, S Congo
20 M9 **Loudon** Tennessee, S USA
31 T12 **Loudonville** Ohio, N USA
102 L8 **Loudun** Vienne, W France
102 K7 **Loué** Sarthe, NW France
76 G10 **Louga** NW Senegal
97 M19 **Loughborough** C England, UK
8 L4 **Lougheed Island** island Nunavut, N Canada
97 C18 **Loughrea** Ir. Baile Locha Riach. W Ireland
103 S9 **Louhans** Saône-et-Loire, C France
21 P5 **Louisa** Kentucky, S USA
21 V5 **Louisa** Virginia, NE USA
21 V9 **Louisburg** North Carolina, SE USA
25 U12 **Louise** Texas, SW USA
15 P11 **Louiseville** Quebec, SE Canada
27 W3 **Louisiana** Missouri, C USA
22 G8 **Louisiana** off. State of Louisiana; also known as Creole State, Pelican State. ◆ state S USA
186 E5 **Lou Island** island N PNG
83 K19 **Louis Trichardt** Northern, NE South Africa
23 V4 **Louisville** Georgia, SE USA
30 M15 **Louisville** Illinois, N USA
20 K5 **Louisville** Kentucky, S USA
22 M4 **Louisville** Mississippi, S USA
29 S15 **Louisville** Nebraska, C USA
192 L11 **Louisville Ridge** undersea feature S Pacific Ocean
126 J6 **Loukhi** var. Louch. Respublika Kareliya, NW Russian Federation
79 H19 **Loukoléla** Cuvette, E Congo
104 G14 **Loulé** Faro, S Portugal
111 C16 **Louny** Ger. Laun. Ústecký kraj NW Czech Republic
29 O15 **Loup City** Nebraska, C USA
29 P15 **Loup River** ≈ Nebraska, C USA
15 S9 **Loup, Rivière du** ≈ Quebec, SE Canada
12 K7 **Loups Marins, Lacs des** lakes Quebec, NE Canada
102 K16 **Lourdes** Hautes-Pyrénées, S France
Lourenço Marques see Maputo
104 F11 **Loures** Lisboa, C Portugal
104 F10 **Lourinhã** Lisboa, C Portugal
115 C16 **Loúros** ≈ W Greece
104 G8 **Lousã** Coimbra, N Portugal
160 M10 **Lou Shui** ≈ C China
183 O5 **Louth** New South Wales, SE Australia
97 O18 **Louth** E England, UK
97 F17 **Louth** Ir. Lú. cultural region NE Ireland
115 H15 **Loutrá** Kentrikí Makedonía, N Greece
115 G19 **Loutráki** Pelopónnisos, S Greece
Louvain see Leuven
99 H19 **Louvain-la Neuve** Wallon Brabant, C Belgium
14 J8 **Louvicourt** Quebec, SE Canada
102 M4 **Louviers** Eure, N France
30 K14 **Lou Yaeger, Lake** ▣ Illinois, N USA
93 J15 **Lövånger** Västerbotten, N Sweden
126 J14 **Lovat'** ≈ NW Russian Federation
113 J17 **Lovćen** ▲ S Yugoslavia
114 I8 **Lovech** Lovech, N Bulgaria
114 I9 **Lovech** ◆ province N Bulgaria
25 V9 **Lovelady** Texas, SW USA
37 T3 **Loveland** Colorado, C USA
33 U12 **Lovell** Wyoming, C USA
Lovello, Monte see Grosser Löffler
35 S4 **Lovelock** Nevada, W USA
106 E7 **Lovere** Lombardia, N Italy
30 L10 **Loves Park** Illinois, N USA
26 M2 **Lovewell Reservoir** ▣ Kansas, C USA
93 M19 **Loviisa** Swe. Lovisa. Etelä-Suomi, S Finland
37 V15 **Loving** New Mexico, SW USA
21 U6 **Lovingston** Virginia, NE USA
37 V14 **Lovington** New Mexico, SW USA
Lovisa see Loviisa
111 C15 **Lovosice** Ger. Lobositz. Ústecký Kraj, NW Czech Republic
126 K4 **Lovozero** Murmanskaya Oblast', NW Russian Federation
126 K4 **Lovozero, Ozero** ◎ NW Russian Federation
112 B9 **Lovran** It. Laurana. Primorje-Gorski Kotar, NW Croatia
116 E11 **Lovrin** Ger. Lowrin. Timiş, W Romania
82 E10 **Lóvua** Lunda Norte, NE Angola
82 G12 **Lóvua** Moxico, E Angola
65 D25 **Low Bay** bay East Falkland, Falkland Islands
9 P9 **Low, Cape** headland Nunavut, E Canada
33 N10 **Lowell** Idaho, NW USA
19 O10 **Lowell** Massachusetts, NE USA
Löwen see Leuven
Löwenberg in Schlesien see Lwówek Śląski
Lower Austria see Niederösterreich
Lower Bann see Bann
Lower California see Baja California
Lower Danube see Niederösterreich
185 L14 **Lower Hutt** Wellington, North Island, NZ
39 N11 **Lower Kalskag** Alaska, USA
35 O1 **Lower Klamath Lake** ◎ California, W USA
35 Q2 **Lower Lake** ◎ California/Nevada, W USA
97 E15 **Lower Lough Erne** ◎ SW Northern Ireland, UK
Lower Lusatia see Niederlausitz
Lower Normandy see Basse-Normandie, France
10 K9 **Lower Post** British Columbia, W Canada
29 T4 **Lower Red Lake** ◎ Minnesota, N USA
Lower Rhine see Neder Rijn
Lower Saxony see Niedersachsen
Lower Tunguska see Nizhnyaya Tunguska
97 Q19 **Lowestoft** E England, UK
149 Q5 **Lowgar** var. Logar. ◆ province E Afghanistan
182 H7 **Low Hill** South Australia
110 K12 **Łowicz** Łódzkie, C Poland
33 N13 **Lowman** Idaho, NW USA
149 P8 **Lowrah** var. Lora. ≈ SE Afghanistan
Lowrin see Lovrin
183 N17 **Low Rocky Point** headland Tasmania, SE Australia
18 I8 **Lowville** New York, NE USA
Loxa see Loksa
182 K9 **Loxton** South Australia
81 G22 **Loya** Tabora, C Tanzania
30 K6 **Loyal** Wisconsin, N USA
18 G13 **Loyalsock Creek** ≈ Pennsylvania, NE USA
35 Q5 **Loyalton** California, W USA
Lo-yang see Luoyang
187 Q16 **Loyauté, Îles** island group S New Caledonia
Loyev see Loyew
119 O20 **Loyew** Rus. Loyev. Homyel'skaya Voblasts', SE Belarus
127 S13 **Loyno** Kirovskaya Oblast', NW Russian Federation
103 P13 **Lozère** ◆ department S France
103 Q14 **Lozère, Mont** ▲ S France
112 J11 **Loznica** Serbia, W Yugoslavia
117 V7 **Lozova** Rus. Lozovaya. Kharkivs'ka Oblast', E Ukraine
Lozovaya see Lozova
105 N7 **Lozoyuela** Madrid, C Spain
Lœvvajok see Leavvajohka
Lu see Shandong, China
Lú see Louth, Ireland
82 F12 **Luacano** Moxico, E Angola
79 N21 **Lualaba** Fr. Loualaba. ≈ SE Dem. Rep. Congo (Zaire)
83 H14 **Luampa** Western, NW Zambia
83 H15 **Luampa Kuta** Western, W Zambia
161 P8 **Lu'an** Anhui, E China
104 K2 **Luanco** Asturias, N Spain
82 A11 **Luanda** var. Loanda, Port. São Paulo de Loanda. ● (Angola) Luanda, NW Angola
82 A11 **Luanda** ◆ province NW Angola

◆ Country ● Country Capital ◇ Dependent Territory ○ Dependent Territory Capital ◆ Administrative Region ✕ International Airport ▲ Mountain ▲ Mountain Range ▲ Volcano ≈ River ◎ Lake ▣ Reservoir

82 A11 **Luanda** × Luanda, NW Angola
82 D12 **Luando** ≈ C Angola
Luang see Tapi, Mae Nam
83 G14 **Luanginga** var. Luanguinga. ≈ Angola/Zambia
167 N15 **Luang, Khao** ▲ SW Thailand
Luang Prabang see Louangphabang
167 P8 **Luang Prabang Range** Th. Thiukhaoluang Phrahang. ▲ Laos/Thailand
167 N16 **Luang, Thale** lagoon S Thailand
Luangua, Rio see Luangwa
82 E11 **Luangue** ≈ NE Angola
Luanguinga see Luanginga
83 K15 **Luangwa** var. Aruângua. Lusaka, C Zambia
83 K14 **Luangwa** var. Aruângua, Rio Luangua. ≈ Mozambique/Zambia
161 Q2 **Luan He** ≈ E China
190 G11 **Luaniva, Île** island E Wallis and Futuna
161 P2 **Luanping** var. Anjiangying. Hebei, E China
82 J13 **Luanshya** Copperbelt, C Zambia
62 K13 **Luan Toro** La Pampa, C Argentina
161 Q2 **Luanxian** var. Luan Xian. Hebei, E China
82 J12 **Luapula** ◈ province N Zambia
79 O25 **Luapula** ≈ Dem. Rep. Congo (Zaire)/Zambia
104 J2 **Luarca** Asturias, N Spain
169 R10 **Luar, Danau** ◎ Borneo, N Indonesia
79 L25 **Luashi** Katanga, S Dem. Rep. Congo (Zaire)
82 G12 **Luau** Port. Vila Teixeira de Sousa. Moxico, NE Angola
79 C16 **Luba** prev. San Carlos. Isla de Bioco, NW Equatorial Guinea
42 F4 **Lubaantun** ruins Toledo, S Belize
111 P16 **Lubaczów** var. Lúbaczów. Podkarpackie, SE Poland
Lubale see Lubalo
82 E11 **Lubalo** Lunda Norte, NE Angola
82 E11 **Lubalo** var. Lubale. ≈ Angola/Zaire
118 J9 **Lubāna** Madona, E Latvia
Lubānas Ezers see Lubāns
171 N4 **Lubang Island** island N Philippines
83 B15 **Lubango** Port. Sá da Bandeira. Huíla, SW Angola
118 J9 **Lubāns** var. Lubānas Ezers. ◎ E Latvia
79 M21 **Lubao** Kasai Oriental, C Dem. Rep. Congo (Zaire)
110 O13 **Lubartów** Ger. Qumälisch. Lubelskie, E Poland
100 G13 **Lübbecke** Nordrhein-Westfalen, NW Germany
100 O13 **Lübben** Brandenburg, E Germany
101 P14 **Lübbenau** Brandenburg, E Germany
25 N5 **Lubbock** Texas, SW USA
Lubcz see Lyubcha
19 U6 **Lubec** Maine, NE USA
100 K9 **Lübeck** Schleswig-Holstein, N Germany
100 K8 **Lübecker Bucht** bay N Germany
79 M21 **Lubefu** Kasai Oriental, C Dem. Rep. Congo (Zaire)
111 O14 **Lubelska, Wyżyna** plateau SE Poland
111 O14 **Lubelskie** ◈ province E Poland
Lubembe see Luembe
Lüben see Lubin
144 H9 **Lubenka** Zapadnyy Kazakhstan, W Kazakhstan
79 P18 **Lubero** Nord Kivu, E Dem. Rep. Congo (Zaire)
79 L22 **Lubi** ≈ S Dem. Rep. Congo (Zaire)
Lubiana see Ljubljana
110 J11 **Lubień Kujawski** Kujawskio-pomorskie, C Poland
67 T11 **Lubilandji** ≈ S Dem. Rep. Congo (Zaire)
110 F13 **Lubin** Ger. Lüben. Dolnośląskie, SW Poland
111 O14 **Lublin** Rus. Lyublin. Lubelskie, E Poland
111 J15 **Lubliniec** Śląskie, S Poland
Lubnān, Jabal see Liban, Jebel
117 R5 **Lubny** Poltavs'ka Oblast', NE Ukraine
Luboml see Lyuboml'
110 G11 **Luboń** Ger. Peterhof. Wielkolpolskie, C Poland
110 D12 **Lubsko** Ger. Sommerfeld. Lubuskie, W Poland
79 N24 **Lubudi** Katanga, SE Dem. Rep. Congo (Zaire)
168 L13 **Lubuklinggau** Sumatera, W Indonesia
79 N25 **Lubumbashi** prev. Élisabethville. Katanga, SE Dem. Rep. Congo (Zaire)
83 I14 **Lubungu** Central, C Zambia
110 E12 **Lubuskie** ◈ province W Poland
79 N18 **Lubutu** Maniema, E Dem. Rep. Congo (Zaire)
Luca see Lucca
82 C11 **Lucala** ≈ W Angola
14 E16 **Lucan** Ontario, S Canada
97 F18 **Lucan** Ir. Leamhcán. E Ireland
Lucanian Mountains see Lucano, Appennino
107 M18 **Lucano, Appennino** Eng. Lucanian Mountains. ▲ S Italy
82 F11 **Lucapa** var. Lukapa. Lunda Norte, NE Angola
29 V15 **Lucas** Iowa, C USA
61 C18 **Lucas González** Entre Ríos, E Argentina
65 C25 **Lucas Point** headland West Falkland, Falkland Islands
31 S15 **Lucasville** Ohio, N USA
106 F11 **Lucca** anc. Luca. Toscana, C Italy
44 H12 **Lucea** W Jamaica
97 H15 **Luce Bay** inlet SW Scotland, UK
22 M8 **Lucedale** Mississippi, S USA
171 O4 **Lucena** off. Lucena City. Luzon, N Philippines
104 M14 **Lucena** Andalucía, S Spain
105 S8 **Lucena del Cid** País Valenciano, E Spain
111 D15 **Lučenec** Ger. Losontz, Hung. Losonc. Banskobystrický Kraj, C Slovakia
Lucentum see Alicante
107 M16 **Lucera** Puglia, SE Italy
Lucerna/Lucerne see Luzern
Lucerne, Lake of see Vierwaldstätter See
40 J4 **Lucero** Chihuahua, N Mexico
123 S14 **Luchegorsk** Primorskiy Kray, SE Russian Federation
105 Q13 **Luchena** ≈ SE Spain
82 N13 **Lucheringo** var. Luchulingo. ≈ N Mozambique
Luchesa see Luchosa
Luchin see Luchyn
118 N13 **Luchosa** Rus. Luchesa. ≈ N Belarus
Luchow see Hefei
100 K11 **Lüchow** Mecklenburg-Vorpommern, N Germany
Luchulingo see Lucheringo
119 N17 **Luchyn** Rus. Luchin. Homyel'skaya Voblasts', SE Belarus
55 U11 **Lucie Rivier** ≈ W Surinam
182 K11 **Lucindale** South Australia
83 A14 **Lucira** Namibe, SW Angola
Łuck see Luts'k
101 O14 **Luckau** Brandenburg, E Germany
100 N13 **Luckenwalde** Brandenburg, E Germany
14 E15 **Lucknow** Ontario, S Canada
152 L12 **Lucknow** var. Lakhnau. Uttar Pradesh, N India
102 J10 **Luçon** Vendée, NW France
44 I7 **Lucrecia, Cabo** headland E Cuba
82 F13 **Lucusse** Moxico, E Angola
Lüda see Dalian
114 M9 **Luda Kamchiya** ≈ E Bulgaria
Ludasch see Luduş
114 I10 **Luda Yana** ≈ C Bulgaria
112 F7 **Ludbreg** Varaždin, N Croatia
29 P7 **Ludden** North Dakota, N USA
101 F15 **Lüdenscheid** Nordrhein-Westfalen, W Germany
83 C21 **Lüderitz** prev. Angra Pequena. Karas, SW Namibia
152 H8 **Ludhiāna** Punjab, N India
31 O7 **Ludington** Michigan, N USA
97 K20 **Ludlow** W England, UK
35 W14 **Ludlow** California, W USA
28 J7 **Ludlow** South Dakota, N USA
18 M9 **Ludlow** Vermont, NE USA
114 L7 **Ludogorie** physical region NE Bulgaria
23 W6 **Ludowici** Georgia, SE USA
Ludsan see Ludza
116 I10 **Luduş** Ger. Ludasch, Hung. Marosludas. Mureş, C Romania
95 M14 **Ludvika** Dalarna, C Sweden
101 H21 **Ludwigsburg** Baden-Württemberg, SW Germany
100 O13 **Ludwigsfelde** Brandenburg, NE Germany
101 G20 **Ludwigshafen** var. Ludwigshafen am Rhein. Rheinland-Pfalz, W Germany
Ludwigshafen am Rhein see Ludwigshafen
101 L20 **Ludwigskanal** canal SE Germany
100 L10 **Ludwigslust** Mecklenburg-Vorpommern, N Germany
118 K10 **Ludza** Ger. Ludsan. Ludza, E Latvia
79 K21 **Luebo** Kasai Occidental, SW Dem. Rep. Congo (Zaire)
25 Q6 **Lueders** Texas, SW USA
79 N20 **Lueki** Maniema, C Dem. Rep. Congo (Zaire)
82 F10 **Luembe** var. Lubembe. ≈ Angola/Dem. Rep. Congo (Zaire)
82 E13 **Luena** var. Lwena, Port. Luso. Moxico, E Angola
79 M24 **Luena** Katanga, SE Dem. Rep. Congo (Zaire)
82 K12 **Luena** Northern, NE Zambia
82 F13 **Luena** ≈ E Angola
83 F16 **Luengue** ≈ SE Angola
67 V13 **Luenha** ≈ W Mozambique
83 G15 **Lueti** ≈ Angola/Zambia
160 J7 **Lüeyang** Shaanxi, C China
161 P14 **Lufeng** Guangdong, S China
79 N24 **Lufira** ≈ SE Dem. Rep. Congo (Zaire)
79 N25 **Lufira, Lac de Retenue de la** var. Lac Tshangalele. ◎ SE Dem. Rep. Congo (Zaire)
25 W8 **Lufkin** Texas, SW USA
82 L11 **Lufubu** ≈ N Zambia
126 G14 **Luga** Leningradskaya Oblast', NW Russian Federation
126 G13 **Luga** ≈ NW Russian Federation
Luganer See see Lugano, Lago di
108 H11 **Lugano** Ger. Lauis. Ticino, S Switzerland
108 H12 **Lugano, Lago di** var. Ceresio, Ger. Luganer See. ◎ S Switzerland
Lugansk see Luhans'k
187 Q13 **Luganville** Espiritu Santo, C Vanuatu
Lugdunum see Lyon
Lugdunum Batavorum see Leiden
83 O15 **Lugela** Zambézia, NE Mozambique
83 O16 **Lugela** ≈ C Mozambique
82 P13 **Lugenda, Rio** ≈ N Mozambique
Luggarus see Locarno
Lugh Ganana see Luuq
97 G19 **Lugnaquillia Mountain** Ir. Log na Coille. ▲ E Ireland
106 H10 **Lugo** Emilia-Romagna, N Italy
104 I3 **Lugo** anc. Lugus Augusti. Galicia, NW Spain
104 I3 **Lugo** ◈ province Galicia, NW Spain
21 R12 **Lugoff** South Carolina, SE USA
116 F12 **Lugoj** Ger. Lugosch, Hung. Lugos. Timiş, W Romania
Lugos/Lugosch see Lugoj
Lugovoy/Lugovoye see Kulan
158 I13 **Lugu** Xizang Zizhiqu, W China
Lugus Augusti see Lugo
Luguvallium/Luguvallum see Carlisle
117 Y7 **Luhans'k** Rus. Lugansk; prev. Voroshilovgrad. Luhans'ka Oblast', E Ukraine
117 Y7 **Luhans'k** × Luhans'ka Oblast', E Ukraine
117 X6 **Luhans'ka Oblast'** var. Luhans'k; prev. Voroshilovgrad, Rus. Voroshilovgradskaya Oblast'. ◈ province E Ukraine
161 Q7 **Luhe** Jiangsu, E China
171 S13 **Luhu** Pulau Seram, E Indonesia
160 G8 **Luhuo** var. Zhaggo. Sichuan, C China
116 M3 **Luhyny** Zhytomyrs'ka Oblast', N Ukraine
83 G15 **Lui** ≈ W Zambia
83 G16 **Luiana** ≈ SE Angola
83 L15 **Luia, Rio** var. Ruya. ≈ Mozambique/Zimbabwe
Luichow Peninsula see Leizhou Bandao
Luik see Liège
82 C13 **Luimbale** Huambo, C Angola
Luimneach see Limerick
106 D6 **Luino** Lombardia, N Italy
82 E13 **Luio** ≈ E Angola
92 L11 **Luiro** ≈ NE Finland
79 N25 **Luishia** Katanga, SE Dem. Rep. Congo (Zaire)
59 M19 **Luislândia do Oeste** Minas Gerais, SE Brazil
40 K5 **Luis L.León, Presa** ▣ N Mexico
Luis Muñoz Marin see San Juan
195 N5 **Luitpold Coast** physical region Antarctica
79 K22 **Luiza** Kasai Occidental, S Dem. Rep. Congo (Zaire)
61 D20 **Luján** Buenos Aires, E Argentina
79 N24 **Lukafu** Katanga, SE Dem. Rep. Congo (Zaire)
Lukapa see Lucapa
112 I11 **Lukavac** Federacija Bosna I Hercegovina, NE Bosnia and Herzegovina
79 I20 **Lukenie** ≈ C Dem. Rep. Congo (Zaire)
79 H19 **Lukolela** Equateur, W Dem. Rep. Congo (Zaire)
119 M14 **Lukoml'skaye, Vozyera** Rus. Ozero Lukoml'skoye. ◎ N Belarus
Lukoml'skoye, Ozero see Lukoml'skaye, Vozyera
114 I8 **Lukovit** Lovech, N Bulgaria
110 O12 **Łuków** Ger. Bogendorf. Lubelskie, E Poland
129 O4 **Lukoyanov** Nizhegorodskaya Oblast', W Russian Federation
79 N22 **Lukuga** ≈ SE Dem. Rep. Congo (Zaire)
79 F21 **Lukula** Bas-Congo, SW Dem. Rep. Congo (Zaire)
83 G14 **Lukulu** Western, NW Zambia
189 R17 **Lukunor Atoll** atoll Mortlock Islands, C Micronesia
82 J12 **Lukwesa** Luapula, NE Zambia
93 K14 **Luleå** Norrbotten, N Sweden
92 J13 **Luleälven** ≈ N Sweden
136 C10 **Lüleburgaz** Kırklareli, NW Turkey
160 M4 **Lüliang Shan** ▲ C China
79 O21 **Lulimba** Maniema, E Dem. Rep. Congo (Zaire)
22 K9 **Luling** Louisiana, S USA
25 T11 **Luling** Texas, SW USA
79 I18 **Lulonga** ≈ NW Dem. Rep. Congo (Zaire)
79 K22 **Lulua** ≈ S Dem. Rep. Congo (Zaire)
Luluabourg see Kananga
192 L17 **Luma** Ta'ū, E American Samoa
169 S17 **Lumajang** Jawa, C Indonesia
158 G12 **Lumajangdong Co** ◎ W China
82 G13 **Lumbala Kaquengue** Moxico, E Angola
83 F14 **Lumbala N'Guimbo** var. Nguimbo, Port. Gago Coutinho, Vila Gago Coutinho. Moxico, SE Angola
21 T11 **Lumber River** ≈ North Carolina/South Carolina, SE USA
Lumber State see Maine
22 L8 **Lumberton** Mississippi, S USA
21 U11 **Lumberton** North Carolina, SE USA
105 R4 **Lumbier** Navarra, N Spain
83 Q15 **Lumbo** Nampula, NE Mozambique
126 M4 **Lumbovka** Murmanskaya Oblast', NW Russian Federation
104 J7 **Lumbrales** Castilla-León, N Spain
153 W13 **Lumding** Assam, NE India
82 F12 **Lumege** var. Lumeje. Moxico, E Angola
Lumeje see Lumege
99 J17 **Lummen** Limburg, NE Belgium
93 J20 **Lumparland** Åland, SW Finland
167 T11 **Lumphăt** prev. Lomphat. Rôtânôkiri, NE Cambodia
11 U16 **Lumsden** Saskatchewan, S Canada
185 C23 **Lumsden** Southland, South Island, NZ
169 N14 **Lumut, Tanjung** headland Sumatera, W Indonesia
157 P4 **Lün** Töv, C Mongolia
160 H13 **Lunan** var. Lunan Yizu Zizhixian. Yunnan, SW China
Lunan Yizu Zizhixian see Lunan
116 I13 **Lunca Corbului** Argeş, S Romania
95 K23 **Lund** Skåne, S Sweden
35 X6 **Lund** Nevada, W USA
82 D11 **Lunda Norte** ◈ province NE Angola
82 E12 **Lunda Sul** ◈ province NE Angola
82 M13 **Lundazi** Eastern, NE Zambia
95 G16 **Lunde** Telemark, S Norway
Lundenburg see Břeclav
95 C17 **Lundevatnet** ◎ S Norway
Lundi see Runde
97 I23 **Lundy** island SW England, UK
100 J10 **Lüneburg** Niedersachsen, N Germany
100 J11 **Lüneburger Heide** heathland NW Germany
103 Q15 **Lunel** Hérault, S France
101 F14 **Lünen** Nordrhein-Westfalen, W Germany
13 P16 **Lunenburg** Nova Scotia, SE Canada
21 V7 **Lunenburg** Virginia, NE USA
103 T5 **Lunéville** Meurthe-et-Moselle, NE France
83 I14 **Lunga** ≈ C Zambia
Lunga, Isola see Dugi Otok
158 H12 **Lungdo** Xizang Zizhiqu, W China
158 I14 **Lunggar** Xizang Zizhiqu, W China
76 I15 **Lungi** × (Freetown) W Sierra Leone
Lungkiang see Qiqihar
Lungleh see Lunglei
153 W15 **Lunglei** prev. Lungleh. Mizoram, NE India
158 L15 **Lungsang** Xizang Zizhiqu, W China
82 E13 **Lungué-Bungo** var. Lungwebungu. ≈ Angola/Zambia see also Lungwebungu
83 G14 **Lungwebungu** var. Lungué-Bungo. ≈ Angola/Zambia see also Lungué-Bungo
152 F12 **Lūni** Rājasthān, N India
152 F12 **Lūni** ≈ N India
Luninets see Luninyets
35 S7 **Luning** Nevada, W USA
Łuniniec see Luninyets
129 P6 **Lunino** Penzenskaya Oblast', W Russian Federation
119 J19 **Luninyets** Pol. Łuniniec, Rus. Luninets. Brestskaya Voblasts', SW Belarus
152 F10 **Lūnkaransar** Rājasthān, NW India
119 G17 **Lunna** Pol. Łunna, Rus. Lunna. Hrodzyenskaya Voblasts', W Belarus
76 I15 **Lunsar** W Sierra Leone
83 K14 **Lunsemfwa** ≈ C Zambia
158 J6 **Luntai** var. Bügür. Xinjiang Uygur Zizhiqu, NW China
98 K11 **Lunteren** Gelderland, C Netherlands
109 U5 **Lunz am See** Niederösterreich, C Austria
163 Y7 **Luobei** var. Fengxiang. Heilongjiang, NE China
160 J13 **Luodian** var. Longping. Guizhou, S China
160 M15 **Luoding** Guangdong, S China
160 M6 **Luo He** ≈ C China
160 L5 **Luo He** ≈ C China
161 N7 **Luohe** Henan, C China
Luolajarvi see Kuoloyarvi
Luong Nam Tha see Louangnamtha
160 L13 **Luoqing Jiang** ≈ S China
161 O8 **Luoshan** Henan, C China
161 O12 **Luoxiao Shan** ▲ S China
161 N6 **Luoyang** var. Honan, Lo-yang. Henan, C China
161 R12 **Luoyuan** Fujian, SE China
79 F21 **Luozi** Bas-Congo, W Dem. Rep. Congo (Zaire)
83 J17 **Lupane** Matabeleland North, W Zimbabwe
160 I12 **Lupanshui** prev. Shuicheng. Guizhou, S China
169 R10 **Lupar, Batang** ≈ East Malaysia
Lupatia see Altamura
116 G12 **Lupeni** Hung. Lupény. Hunedoara, SW Romania
Lupény see Lupeni
82 N13 **Lupiliche** Niassa, N Mozambique
83 E14 **Lupire** Cuando Cubango, E Angola
79 L22 **Luputa** Kasai Oriental, S Dem. Rep. Congo (Zaire)
121 P16 **Luqa** × (Valletta) S Malta
159 U11 **Luqu** Gansu, C China
45 U5 **Luquillo, Sierra de** ▲ E Puerto Rico
26 L4 **Luray** Kansas, C USA
21 U4 **Luray** Virginia, NE USA
103 T7 **Lure** Haute-Saône, E France
82 D11 **Luremo** Lunda Norte, NE Angola
97 F15 **Lurgan** Ir. An Lorgain. S Northern Ireland, UK
57 K18 **Luribay** La Paz, W Bolivia
83 Q14 **Lúrio** Nampula, NE Mozambique
83 P14 **Lúrio, Rio** ≈ NE Mozambique
Luristan see Lorestān
Lurka see Lorca
83 J15 **Lusaka** ● (Zambia) Lusaka, SE Zambia
83 J15 **Lusaka** ◈ province C Zambia
83 J15 **Lusaka** × Lusaka, C Zambia
79 L21 **Lusambo** Kasai Oriental, C Dem. Rep. Congo (Zaire)
186 F8 **Lusancay Islands and Reefs** island group SE PNG
79 I21 **Lusanga** Bandundu, SW Dem. Rep. Congo (Zaire)
79 N21 **Lusangi** Maniema, E Dem. Rep. Congo (Zaire)
Lusatian Mountains see Lausitzer Bergland
Lushnja see Lushnjë
113 K21 **Lushnjë** var. Lushnja. Fier, C Albania
81 J21 **Lushoto** Tanga, E Tanzania
102 L10 **Lusignan** Vienne, W France
33 Z15 **Lusk** Wyoming, C USA
Luso see Luena
102 L10 **Lussac-les-Châteaux** Vienne, W France
Lussin/Lussino see Lošinj
Lussinpiccolo see Mali Lošinj
108 I7 **Lustenau** Vorarlberg, W Austria
161 T14 **Lü Tao** var. Huoshao Dao, Lütao, Eng. Green Island. island SE Taiwan
Lūt, Baḩrat/Lut, Bahret see Dead Sea
22 K9 **Lutcher** Louisiana, S USA
143 T9 **Lūt, Dasht-e** var. Kavīr-e Lūt. desert E Iran
83 F14 **Lutembo** Moxico, E Angola
Lutetia/Lutetia Parisiorum see Paris
Luteva see Lodève
14 G15 **Luther Lake** ◎ Ontario, S Canada
186 K8 **Luti** Choiseul Island, NW Solomon Islands
Lūt, Kavīr-e see Lūt, Dasht-e
97 N21 **Luton** SE England, UK
97 N21 **Luton** × (London) SE England, UK
108 B10 **Lutry** Vaud, SW Switzerland
8 K10 **Łutselk'e** prev. Snowdrift. Northwest Territories, W Canada
29 Y4 **Lutsen** Minnesota, N USA
116 J4 **Luts'k** Pol. Łuck, Rus. Lutsk. Volyns'ka Oblast', NW Ukraine
Luttenberg see Ljutomer
Lüttich see Liège
83 G25 **Luttig** Western Cape, SW South Africa
Lutto see Lotta
82 E13 **Lutuai** Moxico, E Angola
117 Y7 **Lutuhyne** Luhans'ka Oblast', E Ukraine
171 V14 **Lutur, Pulau** island Kepulauan Aru, E Indonesia
23 V12 **Lutz** Florida, SE USA
Lutzow-Holm Bay see Lützow Holmbukta
195 V2 **Lützow Holmbukta** var. Lutzow-Holm Bay. bay Antarctica
81 L16 **Luuq** It. Lugh Ganana. Gedo, SW Somalia
92 M12 **Luusua** Lappi, NE Finland
23 Q6 **Luverne** Alabama, S USA
29 S11 **Luverne** Minnesota, N USA
79 O22 **Luvua** ≈ SE Dem. Rep. Congo (Zaire)
82 F13 **Luvuei** Moxico, E Angola
81 H24 **Luwego** ≈ S Tanzania
82 K12 **Luwingu** Northern, NE Zambia
171 P12 **Luwuk** prev. Loewoek. Sulawesi, C Indonesia
23 N3 **Luxapallila Creek** ≈ Alabama/Mississippi, S USA
99 M25 **Luxembourg** ● (Luxembourg) Luxembourg, S Luxembourg
99 M25 **Luxembourg** off. Grand Duchy of Luxembourg, var. Lëtzebuerg, Luxemburg. ◆ monarchy NW Europe
99 J23 **Luxembourg** ◈ province SE Belgium
99 L24 **Luxembourg** ◈ district S Luxembourg
31 N6 **Luxemburg** Wisconsin, N USA
Luxemburg see Luxembourg
103 U7 **Luxeuil-les-Bains** Haute-Saône, E France
160 E13 **Luxi** prev. Mangshi. Yunnan, SW China
82 E10 **Luxico** ≈ Angola/Dem. Rep. Congo (Zaire)
75 X10 **Luxor** Ar. Al Uqşur. E Egypt
75 X10 **Luxor** × C Egypt
160 M4 **Luya Shan** ▲ C China
102 J15 **Luy de Béarn** ≈ SW France
102 J15 **Luy de France** ≈ SW France
127 P12 **Luza** Kirovskaya Oblast', NW Russian Federation
127 Q12 **Luza** ≈ NW Russian Federation
104 I16 **Luz, Costa de la** coastal region SW Spain
111 K20 **Luže** var. Lausche. ▲ Czech Republic/Germany see also Lausche
108 F8 **Luzern** Fr. Lucerne, It. Lucerna. Luzern, C Switzerland
108 E8 **Luzern** Fr. Lucerne. ◈ canton C Switzerland
160 L13 **Luzhai** Guangxi Zhuangzu Zizhiqu, S China
118 K12 **Luzhki** Rus. Luzhki. Vitsyebskaya Voblasts', N Belarus
160 I10 **Luzhou** Sichuan, C China
Lužická Nisa see Neisse
Lužické Hory see Lausitzer Bergland
Lužnice see Lainsitz
171 O2 **Luzon** island N Philippines
171 N1 **Luzon Strait** strait Philippines/Taiwan
116 I5 **L'viv** Ger. Lemberg, Pol. Lwów, Rus. L'vov. L'vivs'ka Oblast', W Ukraine
L'viv see L'vivs'ka Oblast'
116 I4 **L'vivs'ka Oblast'** var. L'viv, Rus. L'vovskaya Oblast'. ◈ province NW Ukraine
L'vov see L'viv
L'vovskaya Oblast' see L'vivs'ka Oblast'
Lwena see Luena
Lwów see L'viv
110 F11 **Lwówek** Ger. Neustadt bei Pinne. Wielkolpolskie, C Poland
111 E14 **Lwówek Śląski** Ger. Löwenberg in Schlesien. Dolnośląskie, SW Poland
119 I18 **Lyakhavichy** Rus. Lyakhovichi. Brestskaya Voblasts', SW Belarus
Lyakhovichi see Lyakhavichy
185 B22 **Lyall, Mount** ▲ South Island, NZ
Lyallpur see Faisalābād
Lyangar see Langar
126 H11 **Lyaskelya** Respublika Kareliya, NW Russian Federation
119 I18 **Lyasnaya** Rus. Lesnaya. Brestskaya Voblasts', SW Belarus
119 F19 **Lyasnaya** Pol. Leśna, Rus. Lesnaya. ≈ SW Belarus
126 H15 **Lychkovo** Novgorodskaya Oblast', W Russian Federation
Lyck see Ełk
93 I15 **Lycksele** Västerbotten, N Sweden
18 G13 **Lycoming Creek** ≈ Pennsylvania, NE USA
Lycopolis see Asyūt
195 N3 **Lyddan Island** island Antarctica
83 K20 **Lydenburg** Mpumalanga, NE South Africa
119 L20 **Lyel'chytsy** Rus. Lel'chitsy. Homyel'skaya Voblasts', SE Belarus
119 P14 **Lyenina** Rus. Lenino. Mahilyowskaya Voblasts', E Belarus
118 L13 **Lyepyel'** Rus. Lepel'. Vitsyebskaya Voblasts', N Belarus
25 S17 **Lyford** Texas, SW USA
95 E17 **Lygna** ≈ S Norway
18 G14 **Lykens** Pennsylvania, NE USA
115 E21 **Lykódimo** ▲ S Greece
97 K24 **Lyme Bay** bay S England, UK
97 K24 **Lyme Regis** S England, UK
110 L7 **Łyna** Ger. Alle. ≈ N Poland
29 P12 **Lynch** Nebraska, C USA
20 J10 **Lynchburg** Tennessee, S USA
21 T6 **Lynchburg** Virginia, NE USA
21 T12 **Lynches River** ≈ South Carolina, SE USA
32 H6 **Lynden** Washington, NW USA
182 I5 **Lyndhurst** South Australia
27 Q5 **Lyndon** Kansas, C USA
19 N7 **Lyndonville** Vermont, NE USA
95 D18 **Lyngdal** Vest-Agder, S Norway
92 I9 **Lyngen** inlet Arctic Ocean
95 G17 **Lyngør** Aust-Agder, S Norway
92 I9 **Lyngseidet** Troms, N Norway
19 P11 **Lynn** Massachusetts, NE USA
Lynn see King's Lynn
23 R9 **Lynn Haven** Florida, SE USA
11 V11 **Lynn Lake** Manitoba, C Canada
Lynn Regis see King's Lynn
118 I13 **Lyntupy** Rus. Lyntupy. Vitsyebskaya Voblasts', NW Belarus
103 R11 **Lyon** Eng. Lyons; anc. Lugdunum. Rhône, E France
8 I6 **Lyon, Cape** headland Northwest Territories, NW Canada
18 K6 **Lyon Mountain** ▲ New York, NE USA
103 Q11 **Lyonnais, Monts du** ▲ C France
65 N25 **Lyon Point** headland SE Tristan da Cunha
182 E5 **Lyons** South Australia
37 T3 **Lyons** Colorado, C USA
23 V6 **Lyons** Georgia, SE USA
26 M5 **Lyons** Kansas, C USA
29 R14 **Lyons** Nebraska, C USA
18 G10 **Lyons** New York, NE USA
Lyons see Lyon
118 O13 **Lyozna** Rus. Liozno. Vitsyebskaya Voblasts', NE Belarus
117 S4 **Lypova Dolyna** Sums'ka Oblast', NE Ukraine
117 N6 **Lypovets'** Rus. Lipovets. Vinnyts'ka Oblast', C Ukraine
Lys see Leie
111 I17 **Lysá Hora** ▲ E Czech Republic
95 D16 **Lysefjorden** fjord S Norway
95 I18 **Lysekil** Västra Götaland, S Sweden
Lýsi see Akdoğan
33 V14 **Lysite** Wyoming, C USA
129 P3 **Lyskovo** Nizhegorodskaya Oblast', W Russian Federation
108 D8 **Lyss** Bern, W Switzerland
95 H22 **Lystrup** Århus, C Denmark
127 V14 **Lys'va** Permskaya Oblast', NW Russian Federation
117 P6 **Lysyanka** Cherkas'ka Oblast', C Ukraine
117 X6 **Lysychans'k** Rus. Lisichansk. Luhans'ka Oblast', E Ukraine
97 K17 **Lytham St Anne's** NW England, UK
185 I19 **Lyttelton** Canterbury, South Island, NZ
10 M17 **Lytton** British Columbia, SW Canada
119 L18 **Lyuban'** Rus. Lyuban'. Minskaya Voblasts', S Belarus
119 L18 **Lyubanskaye Vodaskhovishcha** ▣ C Belarus
116 M5 **Lyubar** Zhytomyrs'ka Oblast', N Ukraine
Lyubashëvka see Lyubashivka
117 O8 **Lyubashivka** Rus. Lyubashëvka. Odes'ka Oblast', SW Ukraine
119 I16 **Lyubcha** Pol. Lubcz, Rus. Lyubcha. Hrodzyenskaya Voblasts', W Belarus
128 L4 **Lyubertsy** Moskovskaya Oblast', W Russian Federation
116 K2 **Lyubeshiv** Volyns'ka Oblast', NW Ukraine
126 M14 **Lyubim** Yaroslavskaya Oblast', NW Russian Federation
114 K11 **Lyubimets** Khaskovo, S Bulgaria
Lyublin see Lublin
116 I3 **Lyuboml'** Pol. Luboml. Volyns'ka Oblast', NW Ukraine
Lyubotin see Lyubotyn
117 U5 **Lyubotyn** Rus. Lyubotin. Kharkivs'ka Oblast', E Ukraine
128 I5 **Lyudinovo** Kaluzhskaya Oblast', W Russian Federation
129 T2 **Lyuk** Udmurtskaya Respublika, NW Russian Federation
114 M9 **Lyulyakovo** prev. Keremitlik. Burgas, E Bulgaria
119 I18 **Lyusina** Rus. Lyusino. Brestskaya Voblasts', SW Belarus
Lyusino see Lyusina

M

138 G9 **Ma'ād** Irbid, N Jordan
Maalahti see Malax
Maale see Male'

◆ Country ● Country Capital ◇ Dependent Territory ○ Dependent Territory Capital ◈ Administrative Region × International Airport ▲ Mountain ▲ Mountain Range ⩓ Volcano ≈ River ◎ Lake ▣ Reservoir

138 G13 **Ma'ān** Ma'ān, SW Jordan
138 H13 **Ma'ān** off. Muḩāfaẓat Ma'ān, var. Ma'an, Ma'ān. ◆ governorate S Jordan
93 M16 **Maaninka** Itä-Suomi, C Finland
162 K7 **Maanĭt** Bulgan, C Mongolia
162 M8 **Maanĭt** Töv, C Mongolia
93 N15 **Maanselkä** Oulu, C Finland
161 Q8 **Ma'anshan** Anhui, E China
188 F16 **Maap** island Caroline Islands, W Micronesia
118 H3 **Maardu** Ger. Maart. Harjumaa, NW Estonia
Ma'aret-en-Nu'man see Ma'arrat an Nu'mān
99 K16 **Maarheeze** Noord-Brabant, SE Netherlands
Maarianhamina see Mariehamn
138 I4 **Ma'arrat an Nu'mān** var. Ma'aret-en-Nu'man, Fr. Maarret enn Naamâne. Idlib, NW Syria
Maarret enn Naamâne see Ma'arrat an Nu'mān
98 I11 **Maarssen** Utrecht, C Netherlands
Maart see Maardu
99 L17 **Maas** Fr. Meuse. ≈ W Europe see also Meuse
99 M15 **Maasbree** Limburg, SE Netherlands
99 L17 **Maaseik** prev. Maeseyck. Limburg, NE Belgium
171 Q6 **Maasin** Leyte, C Philippines
99 L17 **Maasmechelen** Limburg, NE Belgium
98 G12 **Maassluis** Zuid-Holland, SW Netherlands
99 L18 **Maastricht** var. Maestricht; anc. Traietum ad Mosam, Traiectum Tungorum. Limburg, SE Netherlands
183 N18 **Maatsuyker Group** island group Tasmania, SE Australia
Maba see Qujiang
83 L20 **Mabalane** Gaza, S Mozambique
25 V7 **Mabank** Texas, SW USA
97 O18 **Mablethorpe** E England, UK
171 V12 **Maboi** Irian Jaya, E Indonesia
83 M19 **Mabote** Inhambane, S Mozambique
32 J10 **Mabton** Washington, NW USA
Mabuchi-gawa see Mabechi-gawa
83 H20 **Mabutsane** Southern, S Botswana
63 G19 **Macá, Cerro** ▲ S Chile
60 Q9 **Macaé** Rio de Janeiro, SE Brazil
82 N13 **Macaloge** Niassa, N Mozambique
Macan see Bonerate, Kepulauan
161 N15 **Macao** Chin. Aomen, Port. Macau. S China
104 H9 **Mação** Santarém, C Portugal
58 J11 **Macapá** state capital Amapá, N Brazil
43 S17 **Macaracas** Los Santos, S Panama
55 P6 **Macare, Caño** ≈ NE Venezuela
55 Q6 **Macareo, Caño** ≈ NE Venezuela
Macarsca see Makarska
MacArthur see Ormoc
182 L12 **Macarthur** Victoria, SE Australia
56 C7 **Macas** Morona Santiago, SE Ecuador
Macassar see Ujungpandang
59 Q14 **Macau** Rio Grande do Norte, E Brazil
Macau see Macao
Macău see Makó, Hungary
65 E24 **Macbride Head** headland East Falkland, Falkland Islands
23 V9 **Macclenny** Florida, SE USA
97 L18 **Macclesfield** C England, UK
192 F6 **Macclesfield Bank** undersea feature N South China Sea
MacCluer Gulf see Berau, Teluk
181 N7 **Macdonald, Lake** salt lake Western Australia
181 Q7 **Macdonnell Ranges** ▲ Northern Territory, C Australia
96 K8 **Macduff** NE Scotland, UK
104 I6 **Macedo de Cavaleiros** Bragança, N Portugal
Macedonia Central see Kentrikí Makedonía
Macedonia East and Thrace see Anatolikí Makedonía kai Thráki
113 O19 **Macedonia, FYR** off. the Former Yugoslav Republic of Macedonia, var. Macedonia, Mac. Makedonija, abbrev. FYR Macedonia, FYROM. ◆ republic SE Europe
Macedonia West see Dytikí Makedonía
59 Q16 **Maceió** state capital Alagoas, E Brazil
76 K15 **Macenta** Guinée-Forestière, SE Guinea
106 J12 **Macerata** Marche, C Italy
11 S11 **MacFarlane** ≈ Saskatchewan, C Canada
182 H7 **Macfarlane, Lake** var. Lake Mcfarlane. ◎ South Australia
Macgillicuddy's Reeks Mountains see Macgillycuddy's Reeks
97 B21 **Macgillycuddy's Reeks** var. Macgillicuddy's Reeks Mountains, Ir. Na Cruacha Dubha. ▲ SW Ireland
11 X16 **MacGregor** Manitoba, S Canada
149 O10 **Mach** Baluchistān, SW Pakistan
56 C6 **Machachi** Pichincha, C Ecuador
83 M19 **Machaila** Gaza, S Mozambique
Machaire Fíolta see Magherafelt
Machaire Rátha see Maghera
81 I19 **Machakos** Eastern, S Kenya
56 B8 **Machala** El Oro, SW Ecuador
83 J19 **Machaneng** Central, SE Botswana
83 M18 **Machanga** Sofala, E Mozambique
80 G13 **Machar Marshes** wetland SE Sudan
102 I8 **Machecoul** Loire-Atlantique, NW France
161 O8 **Macheng** Hubei, C China
155 J16 **Mācherla** Andhra Pradesh, C India
153 O11 **Machhapuchhre** ▲ C Nepal
19 T6 **Machias** Maine, NE USA
19 R3 **Machias River** ≈ Maine, NE USA
19 T6 **Machias River** ≈ Maine, NE USA
64 P5 **Machico** Madeira, Portugal, NE Atlantic Ocean
155 K16 **Machilīpatnam** var. Bandar Masulipatnam. Andhra Pradesh, E India
54 G5 **Machiques** Zulia, NW Venezuela
57 G15 **Machupicchu** Cusco, C Peru
83 M20 **Macia** var. Vila de Macia. Gaza, S Mozambique
Macías Nguema Biyogo see Bioco, Isla de
116 M13 **Măcin** Tulcea, SE Romania
183 T4 **Macintyre River** ≈ New South Wales/Queensland, SE Australia
181 Y7 **Mackay** Queensland, NE Australia
181 O7 **Mackay, Lake** salt lake Northern Territory/Western Australia
10 M13 **Mackenzie** British Columbia, W Canada
8 I9 **Mackenzie** ≈ Northwest Territories, NW Canada
195 Y6 **Mackenzie Bay** bay Antarctica
10 J1 **Mackenzie Bay** bay NW Canada
2 D9 **Mackenzie Delta** delta Northwest Territories, NW Canada
8 K3 **Mackenzie King Island** island Queen Elizabeth Islands, Northwest Territories, N Canada
8 H8 **Mackenzie Mountains** ▲ Northwest Territories, NW Canada
31 Q5 **Mackinac, Straits of** ◎ Michigan, N USA
194 K5 **Mackintosh, Cape** headland Antarctica
11 R15 **Macklin** Saskatchewan, S Canada
183 V6 **Macksville** New South Wales, SE Australia
183 V5 **Maclean** New South Wales, SE Australia
83 J24 **Maclear** Eastern Cape, SE South Africa
183 U6 **Macleay River** ≈ New South Wales, SE Australia
MacLeod see Fort Macleod
180 G9 **Macleod, Lake** ◎ Western Australia
10 I6 **Macmillan** ≈ Yukon Territory, NW Canada
30 J12 **Macomb** Illinois, N USA
107 B18 **Macomer** Sardegna, Italy, C Mediterranean Sea
82 Q13 **Macomia** Cabo Delgado, NE Mozambique
23 T5 **Macon** Georgia, SE USA
23 N4 **Macon** Mississippi, S USA
27 U3 **Macon** Missouri, C USA
103 R10 **Mâcon** anc. Matisco, Matisco Ædourum. Saône-et-Loire, C France
22 J6 **Macon, Bayou** ≈ Arkansas/Louisiana, S USA
82 G13 **Macondo** Moxico, E Angola
83 M16 **Macossa** Manica, C Mozambique
11 T12 **Macoun Lake** ◎ Saskatchewan, C Canada
30 K14 **Macoupin Creek** ≈ Illinois, N USA
Macouria see Tonate
83 N18 **Macovane** Inhambane, SE Mozambique
183 N17 **Macquarie Harbour** inlet Tasmania, SE Australia
192 J13 **Macquarie Island** island NZ, SW Pacific Ocean
183 T8 **Macquarie, Lake** lagoon New South Wales, SE Australia
183 Q6 **Macquarie Marshes** wetland New South Wales, SE Australia
175 O13 **Macquarie Ridge** undersea feature SW Pacific Ocean
183 Q6 **Macquarie River** ≈ New South Wales, SE Australia
183 P17 **Macquarie River** ≈ Tasmania, SE Australia
195 V5 **Mac. Robertson Land** physical region Antarctica
97 C21 **Macroom** Ir. Maigh Chromtha. SW Ireland
42 G5 **Macuelizo** Santa Bárbara, NW Honduras
182 G2 **Macumba River** ≈ South Australia
57 I16 **Macusani** Puno, S Peru
56 E8 **Macusari, Río** ≈ N Peru
41 U15 **Macuspana** Tabasco, SE Mexico
138 G10 **Ma'dabā** var. Mādabā, Madeba; anc. Medeba. 'Ammān, NW Jordan
172 G2 **Madagascar** off. Democratic Republic of Madagascar, Malg. Madagasikara; prev. Malagasy Republic. ◆ republic W Indian Ocean
172 I5 **Madagascar** island W Indian Ocean
130 L17 **Madagascar Basin** undersea feature W Indian Ocean
130 L16 **Madagascar Plain** undersea feature W Indian Ocean
67 Y14 **Madagascar Plateau** var. Madagascar Ridge, Madagascar Rise, Rus. Madagaskarskiy Khrebet. undersea feature W Indian Ocean
Madagascar Ridge/Madagascar Rise see Madagascar Plateau
Madagasikara see Madagascar
Madagaskarskiy Khrebet see Madagascar Plateau
64 N2 **Madalena** Pico, Azores, Portugal, NE Atlantic Ocean
77 Y6 **Madama** Agadez, NE Niger
114 J12 **Madan** Smolyan, S Bulgaria
155 I19 **Madanapalle** Andhra Pradesh, E India
186 D7 **Madang** Madang, N PNG
186 C6 **Madang** ◆ province N PNG
146 G7 **Madaniyat** Rus. Madeniyet. Qoraqalpoghiston Respublikasi, W Uzbekistan
Madanīyīn see Médenine
77 U11 **Madaoua** Tahoua, SW Niger
Madaras see Vtáčnik
153 U15 **Madaripur** Dhaka, C Bangladesh
77 U12 **Madarounfa** Maradi, S Niger
Mađarska see Hungary
146 B13 **Madau** Turkm. Madaw. Balkanskiy Velayat, W Turkmenistan
186 H9 **Madau Island** island SE PNG
Madaw see Madau
19 S1 **Madawaska** Maine, NE USA
14 J13 **Madawaska** ≈ Ontario, SE Canada
Madawaska Highlands see Haliburton Highlands
166 M4 **Madaya** Mandalay, C Myanmar
107 K17 **Maddaloni** Campania, S Italy
29 O3 **Maddock** North Dakota, N USA
99 I14 **Made** Noord-Brabant, S Netherlands
Madeba see Ma'dabā
64 L9 **Madeira** var. Ilha de Madeira. island Madeira, Portugal, NE Atlantic Ocean
Madeira, Ilha de see Madeira
64 O5 **Madeira Islands** Port. Região Autoónoma da Madeira. ◆ autonomous region Madeira, Portugal, NE Atlantic Ocean
64 L9 **Madeira Plain** undersea feature E Atlantic Ocean
64 L9 **Madeira Ridge** undersea feature E Atlantic Ocean
59 F14 **Madeira, Rio** Sp. Río Madera. ≈ Bolivia/Brazil see also Madera, Río
101 J25 **Mädelegabel** ▲ Austria/Germany
15 X6 **Madeleine** ≈ Quebec, SE Canada
15 X5 **Madeleine, Cap de la** headland Quebec, SE Canada
13 Q13 **Madeleine, Îles de la** Eng. Magdalen Islands. island group Quebec, E Canada
29 U10 **Madelia** Minnesota, N USA
35 P3 **Madeline** California, W USA
30 K3 **Madeline Island** island Apostle Islands, Wisconsin, N USA
137 O15 **Maden** Elâzığ, SE Turkey
145 V12 **Madeniyet** Vostochnyy Kazakhstan, E Kazakhstan
Madeniyet see Madaniyat
40 H5 **Madera** Chihuahua, N Mexico
35 Q10 **Madera** California, W USA
56 L13 **Madera, Río** Port. Rio Madeira. ≈ Bolivia/Brazil see also Madeira, Rio
106 D6 **Madesimo** Lombardia, N Italy
141 O14 **Madhāb, Wādī** dry watercourse NW Yemen
153 R13 **Madhepura** prev. Madhipure. Bihār, NE India
Madhipure see Madhepura
153 Q13 **Madhubani** Bihār, N India
153 Q15 **Madhupur** Bihār, NE India
152 K15 **Madhya Pradesh** prev. Central Provinces and Berar. ◆ state C India
57 K15 **Madidi, Río** ≈ W Bolivia
155 F20 **Madikeri** prev. Mercara. Karnātaka, W India
27 O13 **Madill** Oklahoma, C USA
79 G21 **Madimba** Bas-Congo, SW Dem. Rep. Congo (Zaire)
138 M4 **Ma'din** Ar Raqqah, C Syria
Madīnah, Minṭaqat al see Al Madīnah
76 M14 **Madinani** NW Ivory Coast
141 O17 **Madīnat ash Sha'b** prev. Al Ittiḩād. SW Yemen
138 K3 **Madīnat ath Thawrah** var. Ath Thawrah. Ar Raqqah, N Syria Asia
173 O6 **Madingley Rise** undersea feature W Indian Ocean
79 E21 **Madingo-Kayes** Le Kouilou, S Congo
79 F21 **Madingou** La Bouenza, S Congo
Madioen see Madiun
23 U8 **Madison** Florida, SE USA
23 T3 **Madison** Georgia, SE USA
31 P15 **Madison** Indiana, N USA
27 P6 **Madison** Kansas, C USA
19 Q6 **Madison** Maine, NE USA
29 S9 **Madison** Minnesota, N USA
22 K5 **Madison** Mississippi, S USA
29 Q14 **Madison** Nebraska, C USA
29 R10 **Madison** South Dakota, N USA
21 V5 **Madison** Virginia, NE USA
21 Q5 **Madison** West Virginia, NE USA
30 L9 **Madison** state capital Wisconsin, N USA
21 T6 **Madison Heights** Virginia, NE USA
20 I6 **Madisonville** Kentucky, S USA
20 M10 **Madisonville** Tennessee, S USA
25 V9 **Madisonville** Texas, SW USA
169 R16 **Madiun** prev. Madioen. Jawa, C Indonesia
Madjene see Majene
14 J14 **Madoc** Ontario, SE Canada
Madoera see Madura, Pulau
81 J18 **Mado Gashi** North Eastern, E Kenya
159 R11 **Madoi** Qinghai, C China
189 O13 **Madolenihmw** Pohnpei, E Micronesia
118 I9 **Madona** Ger. Modohn. Madona, E Latvia
107 J23 **Madonie** ▲ Sicilia, Italy, C Mediterranean Sea
141 Y11 **Madrakah, Ra's** headland E Oman
32 I12 **Madras** Oregon, NW USA
Madras see Chennai
57 H14 **Madre de Dios** off. Departamento de Madre de Dios. ◆ department E Peru
63 F22 **Madre de Dios, Isla** island S Chile
57 J14 **Madre de Dios, Río** ≈ Bolivia/Peru
25 T16 **Madre, Laguna** ◎ Texas, SW USA
41 Q9 **Madre, Laguna** lagoon NE Mexico
37 Q12 **Madre Mount** ▲ New Mexico, SW USA
105 N8 **Madrid** ● (Spain) Madrid, C Spain
29 V14 **Madrid** Iowa, C USA
105 N7 **Madrid** ◆ autonomous community C Spain
105 N10 **Madridejos** Castilla-La Mancha, C Spain
104 L7 **Madrigal de las Altas Torres** Castilla-León, N Spain
104 K10 **Madrigalejo** Extremadura, W Spain
34 L3 **Mad River** ≈ California, W USA
42 J8 **Madriz** ◆ department NW Nicaragua
104 K10 **Madroñera** Extremadura, W Spain
181 N12 **Madura** Western Australia
Madura see Madurai
155 H22 **Madurai** prev. Madura, Mathurai. Tamil Nādu, S India
169 S16 **Madura, Pulau** prev. Madoera. island C Indonesia
169 S16 **Madura, Selat** strait C Indonesia
129 Q17 **Madzhalis** Respublika Dagestan, SW Russian Federation
114 K12 **Madzharovo** Khaskovo, S Bulgaria
83 M14 **Madzimoyo** Eastern, E Zambia
165 O12 **Maebashi** var. Maebasi, Mayebashi. Gunma, Honshū, S Japan
Maebasi see Maebashi
167 O6 **Mae Chan** Chiang Rai, NW Thailand
167 N7 **Mae Hong Son** var. Maehongson, Muai To. Mae Hong Son, NW Thailand
Mae Nam Khong see Mekong
167 Q7 **Mae Nam Nan** ≈ NW Thailand
167 O10 **Mae Nam Tha Chin** ≈ W Thailand
167 P7 **Mae Nam Yom** ≈ W Thailand
37 O3 **Maeser** Utah, W USA
Maeseyck see Maaseik
167 N9 **Mae Sot** var. Ban Mae Sot. Tak, W Thailand
Maestricht see Maastricht
167 O7 **Mae Suai** var. Ban Mae Suai. Chiang Rai, NW Thailand
167 O7 **Mae Tho, Doi** ▲ NW Thailand
172 I4 **Maevatanana** Mahajanga, C Madagascar
187 R13 **Maéwo** prev. Aurora. island C Vanuatu
171 S11 **Mafa** Pulau Halmahera, E Indonesia
83 I23 **Mafeteng** W Lesotho
99 J21 **Maffe** Namur, SE Belgium
183 P12 **Maffra** Victoria, SE Australia
81 K23 **Mafia** island E Tanzania
81 J23 **Mafia Channel** sea waterway E Tanzania
83 I21 **Mafikeng** North-West, N South Africa
60 J12 **Mafra** Santa Catarina, S Brazil
104 F10 **Mafra** Lisboa, C Portugal
143 Q17 **Mafraq** Abū Ẓaby, C UAE
Mafraq/Mafraq, Muḩāfaẓat al see Al Mafraq
123 T10 **Magadan** Magadanskaya Oblast', E Russian Federation
123 T9 **Magadanskaya Oblast'** ◆ province E Russian Federation
108 G11 **Magadino** Ticino, S Switzerland
63 G23 **Magallanes** off. Región de Magallanes y de la Antártica Chilena. ◆ region S Chile
Magallanes see Punta Arenas
Magallanes, Estrecho de see Magellan, Strait of
14 I10 **Maganasipi, Lac** ◎ Quebec, SE Canada
54 F6 **Magangué** Bolívar, N Colombia
Magareva see Mangareva
77 V12 **Magaria** Zinder, S Niger
186 F10 **Magarida** Central, SW PNG
171 O2 **Magat** ≈ Luzon, N Philippines
27 T11 **Magazine Mountain** ▲ Arkansas, C USA
76 I15 **Magburaka** C Sierra Leone
123 Q13 **Magdagachi** Amurskaya Oblast', SE Russian Federation
62 O12 **Magdalena** Buenos Aires, E Argentina
57 M15 **Magdalena** Beni, N Bolivia
40 F4 **Magdalena** Sonora, NW Mexico
37 Q13 **Magdalena** New Mexico, SW USA
54 F5 **Magdalena** off. Departamento del Magdalena. ◆ province N Colombia
40 E9 **Magdalena, Bahía** bay W Mexico
63 G19 **Magdalena, Isla** island Archipiélago de los Chonos, S Chile
40 D8 **Magdalena, Isla** island W Mexico
47 P6 **Magdalena, Río** ≈ C Colombia
40 F4 **Magdalena, Río** ≈ NW Mexico
Magdalen Islands see Madeleine, Îles de la
100 L13 **Magdeburg** Sachsen-Anhalt, C Germany
22 L6 **Magee** Mississippi, S USA
169 Q16 **Magelang** Jawa, C Indonesia
192 K7 **Magellan Rise** undersea feature C Pacific Ocean
63 H24 **Magellan, Strait of** Sp. Estrecho de Magallanes. strait Argentina/Chile
106 D7 **Magenta** Lombardia, NW Italy
Magerøy see Magerøya
92 K7 **Magerøya** var. Magerøy. island N Norway
164 C17 **Mage-shima** island Nansei-shotō, SW Japan
108 G11 **Maggia** Ticino, S Switzerland
108 G10 **Maggia** ≈ SW Switzerland
Maggiore, Lago see Maggiore, Lake
106 C6 **Maggiore, Lake** It. Lago Maggiore. ◎ Italy/Switzerland
44 I12 **Maggotty** W Jamaica
76 I10 **Maghama** Gorgol, S Mauritania
97 F14 **Maghera** Ir. Machaire Rátha. C Northern Ireland, UK
97 F15 **Magherafelt** Ir. Machaire Fíolta. C Northern Ireland, UK
188 H6 **Magicienne Bay** bay Saipan, S Northern Mariana Islands
105 O13 **Magina** ▲ S Spain
81 H24 **Magingo** Ruvuma, S Tanzania
112 H11 **Maglaj** Federacija Bosna I Hercegovina, N Bosnia and Herzegovina
107 Q19 **Maglie** Puglia, SE Italy
36 L2 **Magna** Utah, W USA
Magnesia see Manisa
14 G12 **Magnetawan** ≈ Ontario, S Canada
27 T14 **Magnolia** Arkansas, C USA
22 K7 **Magnolia** Mississippi, S USA
25 V10 **Magnolia** Texas, SW USA
Magnolia State see Mississippi
95 J15 **Magnor** Hedmark, S Norway
187 Y14 **Mago** prev. Mango. island Lau Group, E Fiji
83 L15 **Màgoé** Tete, NW Mozambique
15 Q13 **Magog** Quebec, SE Canada
83 J15 **Magoye** Southern, S Zambia
41 Q12 **Magozal** Veracruz-Llave, C Mexico
14 B7 **Magpie** ≈ Ontario, S Canada
11 Q17 **Magrath** Alberta, SW Canada
105 R10 **Magro** ≈ E Spain
76 I9 **Magta' Lahjar** var. Magta Lahjar, Magta' Lahjar, Magtá Lahjar. Brakna, SW Mauritania
83 L20 **Magude** Maputo, S Mozambique
77 Y12 **Magumeri** Borno, NE Nigeria
189 O14 **Magur Islands** island group Caroline Islands, C Micronesia
Magway see Magwe
166 L6 **Magwe** var. Magway. Magwe, W Myanmar
166 L6 **Magwe** var. Magway. ◆ division C Myanmar
Magyar-Becse see Bečej
Magyarkanizsa see Kanjiža
Magyarország see Hungary
Magyarzsombor see Zimbor
142 J4 **Mahābād** var. Mehabad; prev. Sāūjbulāgh. Āzarbāyjān-e Bākhtarī, NW Iran
172 H5 **Mahabo** Toliara, W Madagascar
Maha Chai see Samut Sakhon
155 D14 **Mahād** Mahārāshtra, W India
81 N17 **Mahadday Weyne** Shabeellaha Dhexe, C Somalia
79 Q17 **Mahagi** Orientale, NE Dem. Rep. Congo (Zaire)
Mahāil see Muḩāyil
172 I4 **Mahajamba** seasonal river NW Madagascar
152 G10 **Mahājan** Rājasthān, NW India
172 I3 **Mahajanga** var. Majunga. Mahajanga, NW Madagascar
172 I3 **Mahajanga** ◆ province W Madagascar
172 I3 **Mahajanga** ✕ Mahajanga, NW Madagascar
169 U10 **Mahakam, Sungai** var. Koetai, Kutai. ≈ Borneo, C Indonesia
83 I19 **Mahalapye** var. Mahalatswe. Central, SE Botswana
Mahalatswe see Mahalapye
Mahalla el Kubra see El Maḩalla el Kubra
171 O13 **Mahalona** Sulawesi, C Indonesia
Mahameru see Semeru, Gunung
143 S11 **Mahān** Kermān, E Iran
154 N12 **Mahānadi** ≈ E India
172 J5 **Mahanoro** Toamasina, E Madagascar
153 P13 **Mahārājganj** Bihār, N India
154 G13 **Mahārāshtra** ◆ state W India
172 I4 **Mahavavy** seasonal river N Madagascar
155 K24 **Mahaweli Ganga** ≈ C Sri Lanka
Mahbés see El Mahbas
155 J15 **Mahbūbābād** Andhra Pradesh, E India
155 H16 **Mahbūbnagar** Andhra Pradesh, C India
140 M8 **Mahd adh Dhahab** Al Madīnah, W Saudi Arabia
55 S9 **Mahdia** C Guyana
75 N6 **Mahdia** var. Al Mahdīyah, Mehdia. NE Tunisia
155 F20 **Mahe** Fr. Mahé; prev. Mayyali. Pondicherry, SW India
172 I16 **Mahé** ✕ Mahé, NE Seychelles
172 H16 **Mahé** island Inner Islands, NE Seychelles
173 Y17 **Mahebourg** SE Mauritius
152 L10 **Mahendranagar** Far Western, W Nepal
81 I23 **Mahenge** Morogoro, SE Tanzania
185 F22 **Maheno** Otago, South Island, NZ
154 D9 **Mahesāna** Gujarāt, W India
154 F11 **Maheshwar** Madhya Pradesh, C India
151 F14 **Mahi** ≈ N India
184 Q10 **Mahia Peninsula** peninsula North Island, NZ
119 O16 **Mahilyow** Rus. Mogilëv. Mahilyowskaya Voblasts', E Belarus
119 M16 **Mahilyowskaya Voblasts'** prev. Rus. Mogilëvskaya Oblast'. ◆ province E Belarus
191 P7 **Mahina** Tahiti, W French Polynesia
185 E23 **Mahinerangi, Lake** ◎ South Island, NZ
83 L22 **Mahlabatini** KwaZulu/Natal, E South Africa
166 L5 **Mahlaing** Mandalay, C Myanmar
109 X8 **Mahldorf** Steiermark, SE Austria
Maḩmūd-e 'Erāqī see Maḩmūd-e Rāqī
149 R4 **Maḩmūd-e Rāqī** var. Mahmūd-e 'Erāqī. Kāpīsā, NE Afghanistan
Mahmudiya see Al Maḩmūdīyah
29 S5 **Mahnomen** Minnesota, N USA
152 K14 **Mahoba** Uttar Pradesh, N India
105 Z9 **Mahón** Cat. Maó, Eng. Port Mahon; anc. Portus Magonis. Menorca, Spain, W Mediterranean Sea
18 D14 **Mahoning Creek Lake** ⊠ Pennsylvania, NE USA
105 Q10 **Mahora** Castilla-La Mancha, C Spain
Mähren see Moravia
Mährisch-Budwitz see Moravské Budějovice
Mährisch-Kromau see Moravský Krumlov
Mährisch-Neustadt see Uničov
Mährisch-Schönberg see Šumperk
Mährisch-Trübau see Moravská Třebová
Mährisch-Weisskirchen see Hranice
Māh-Shahr see Bandar-e Māhshahr
79 N19 **Mahulu** Maniema, E Dem. Rep. Congo (Zaire)
154 C12 **Mahuva** Gujarāt, W India
114 N11 **Mahya Dağı** ▲ NW Turkey
105 T6 **Maials** var. Mayals. Cataluña, NE Spain
191 O2 **Maiana** prev. Hall Island. atoll Tungaru, W Kiribati
191 S11 **Maiao** var. Tapuaemanu, Tubuai-Manu. island Îles du Vent, W French Polynesia
54 H4 **Maicao** La Guajira, N Colombia
Mai Ceu/Mai Chio see Maych'ew
103 U8 **Maîche** Doubs, E France
97 N22 **Maidenhead** S England, UK
11 S15 **Maidstone** Saskatchewan, S Canada
97 P22 **Maidstone** SE England, UK
77 Y13 **Maiduguri** Borno, NE Nigeria
108 I8 **Maienfeld** Sankt Gallen, NE Switzerland
116 J12 **Măieruş** Hung. Szászmagyarós. Braşov, C Romania
Maigh Chromtha see Macroom
Maigh Eo see Mayo
55 N9 **Maigualida, Sierra** ▲ S Venezuela
154 K9 **Maihar** Madhya Pradesh, C India
154 K11 **Maikala Range** ▲ C India
67 T10 **Maiko** ≈ W Dem. Rep. Congo (Zaire)
Mailand see Milano
152 L11 **Mailāni** Uttar Pradesh, N India
149 U10 **Māilsi** Punjab, E Pakistan
147 R8 **Maimak** Talasskaya Oblast', NW Kyrgyzstan
Maimāna see Meymaneh
Maimansingh see Mymensingh
171 V13 **Maimawa** Irian Jaya, E Indonesia
Maimuna see Al Maymūnah
101 G18 **Main** ≈ C Germany
115 F22 **Maïna** ancient monument Pelopónnisos, S Greece
115 E20 **Maïnalo** ▲ S Greece
101 L22 **Mainburg** Bayern, SE Germany
Main Camp see Banana
14 E12 **Main Channel** lake channel Ontario, S Canada
79 I20 **Mai-Ndombe, Lac** prev. Lac Léopold II. ◎ W Dem. Rep. Congo (Zaire)
101 K20 **Main-Donau-Kanal** canal SE Germany
19 R6 **Maine** off. State of Maine; also known as Lumber State, Pine Tree State. ◆ state NE USA
102 K6 **Maine** cultural region NW France
102 J7 **Maine-et-Loire** ◆ department NW France
19 Q9 **Maine, Gulf of** gulf NE USA
77 X12 **Mainé-Soroa** Diffa, SE Niger
167 N2 **Maingkwan** var. Mungkawn. Kachin State, N Myanmar
Main Island see Bermuda
Mainistir Fhear Maí see Fermoy
Mainistirna Búille see Boyle
Mainistir na Corann see Midleton
Mainistir na Féile see Abbeyfeale
96 J5 **Mainland** island Orkney, N Scotland, UK
96 L2 **Mainland** island Shetland, NE Scotland, UK
159 P16 **Mainling** Xizang Zizhiqu, W China

◆ Country ◇ Dependent Territory ◆ Administrative Region ▲ Mountain ⩓ Volcano ◎ Lake
● Country Capital ○ Dependent Territory Capital ✕ International Airport ▲ Mountain Range ≈ River ⊠ Reservoir

152 K12 **Mainpuri** Uttar Pradesh, N India
103 N5 **Maintenon** Eure-et-Loir, C France
172 H4 **Maintirano** Mahajanga, W Madagascar
93 M15 **Mainua** Oulu, C Finland
101 G18 **Mainz** Fr. Mayence. Rheinland-Pfalz, SW Germany
76 I9 **Maio** var. Vila do Maio. Maio, S Cape Verde
76 E10 **Maio** var. Mayo. island Ilhas de Sotavento, SE Cape Verde
62 G12 **Maipo, Río** ≈ C Chile
62 H12 **Maipo, Volcán** ▲ W Argentina
61 E22 **Maipú** Buenos Aires, E Argentina
62 I11 **Maipú** Mendoza, E Argentina
62 H11 **Maipú** Santiago, C Chile
54 L5 **Maiquetía** Distrito Federal, N Venezuela
108 I10 **Maira** It. Mera. ≈ Italy/Switzerland
106 A9 **Maira** ≈ NW Italy
153 V12 **Mairābari** Assam, NE India
44 K7 **Maisí** Guantánamo, E Cuba
118 H13 **Maišiagala** Vilnius, SE Lithuania
153 V17 **Maiskhal Island** island SE Bangladesh
167 N13 **Mai Sombun** Chumphon, SW Thailand
Maisur see Karnātaka, India
Maisur see Mysore, India
183 T8 **Maitland** New South Wales, SE Australia
182 I9 **Maitland** South Australia
14 F15 **Maitland** ≈ Ontario, S Canada
195 R1 **Maitri** Indian research station Antarctica
159 N15 **Maizhokunggar** Xizang Zizhiqu, W China
43 O10 **Maíz, Islas del** var. Corn Islands. island group SE Nicaragua
164 J12 **Maizuru** Kyōto, Honshū, SW Japan
54 F6 **Majagual** Sucre, N Colombia
41 Z13 **Majahual** Quintana Roo, E Mexico
Majardah, Wādī see Medjerda, Oued/Mejerda
Mājeej see Mejit Island
171 N13 **Majene** prev. Madjene. Sulawesi, C Indonesia
43 V15 **Majé, Serranía de** ▲▲ E Panama
112 I11 **Majevica** ▲▲ NE Bosnia and Herzegovina
81 H15 **Majī** Southern, S Ethiopia
141 X7 **Majīs** NW Oman
Majorca see Mallorca
Mājro see Majuro Atoll
Majunga see Mahajanga
189 Y3 **Majuro** × Majuro Atoll, SE Marshall Islands
189 Y2 **Majuro Atoll** var. Mājro. atoll Ratak Chain, SE Marshall Islands
189 X2 **Majuro Lagoon** lagoon Majuro Atoll, SE Marshall Islands
76 H11 **Maka** C Senegal
79 F20 **Makabana** Le Niari, SW Congo
38 D9 **Makaha** Haw. Mākaha. Oahu, Hawaii, USA, C Pacific Ocean
38 B8 **Makahuena Point** headland Kauai, Hawaii, USA, C Pacific Ocean
38 D9 **Makakilo City** Oahu, Hawaii, USA, C Pacific Ocean
83 H18 **Makalamabedi** Central, C Botswana
Makale see Mek'elē
158 K17 **Makalu** Chin. Makaru Shan. ▲ China/Nepal
81 G23 **Makampi** Mbeya, S Tanzania
145 X12 **Makanchi** Kaz. Maqanshy. Vostochnyy Kazakhstan, E Kazakhstan
42 M8 **Makantaka** Región Autónoma Atlántico Norte, NE Nicaragua
190 B16 **Makapu Point** headland W Niue
185 C24 **Makarewa** Southland, South Island, NZ
117 O4 **Makariv** Kyyivs'ka Oblast', N Ukraine
185 D20 **Makarora** ≈ South Island, NZ
123 T13 **Makarov** Ostrov Sakhalin, Sakhalinskaya Oblast', SE Russian Federation
197 R9 **Makarov Basin** undersea feature Arctic Ocean
192 I5 **Makarov Seamount** undersea feature W Pacific Ocean
113 F15 **Makarska** It. Macarsca. Split-Dalmacija, SE Croatia
Makaru Shan see Makalu
127 O15 **Makar'yev** Kostromskaya Oblast', NW Russian Federation
82 L11 **Makasa** Northern, NE Zambia
Makasar see Ujungpandang
Makasar, Selat see Makassar Straits
Makassar see Ujungpandang
192 F7 **Makassar Straits** Ind. Selat Makasar. strait C Indonesia
144 G12 **Makat** Kaz. Maqat. Atyrau, SW Kazakhstan
191 T10 **Makatea** island Îles Tuamotu, C French Polynesia
139 U7 **Makātū** E Iraq
172 H6 **Makay** var. Massif du Makay. ▲▲ SW Madagascar
114 J12 **Makaza** pass Bulgaria/Greece
Makedonija see Macedonia, FYR
190 B16 **Makefu** W Niue
191 V10 **Makemo** atoll Îles Tuamotu, C French Polynesia
76 I15 **Makeni** C Sierra Leone
Makenzen see Orlyak
Makeyevka see Makiyivka
129 Q16 **Makhachkala** prev. Petrovsk-Port. Respublika Dagestan, SW Russian Federation
144 F11 **Makhambet** Atyrau, W Kazakhstan
Makharadze see Ozurget'i
139 W13 **Makhfar Al Buşayyah** S Iraq
139 R4 **Makhmūr** N Iraq
138 I11 **Makhrūq, Wadi al** dry watercourse E Jordan
139 R4 **Makḩūl, Jabal** ▲▲ C Iraq
141 R13 **Makhyah, Wādī** dry watercourse N Yemen
171 V13 **Maki** Irian Jaya, E Indonesia
185 G21 **Makikihi** Canterbury, South Island, NZ
191 O2 **Makin** prev. Pitt Island. atoll Tungaru, W Kiribati
81 I20 **Makindu** Eastern, S Kenya
145 Q8 **Makinsk** Akmola, N Kazakhstan
187 N10 **Makira** off. Makira Province. ◈ province SE Solomon Islands
Makira see San Cristobal
117 X8 **Makiyivka** Rus. Makeyevka; prev. Dmitriyevsk. Donets'ka Oblast', E Ukraine
140 L10 **Makkah** Eng. Mecca. Makkah, W Saudi Arabia
140 M10 **Makkah** var. Minṭaqat Makkah. ◈ province W Saudi Arabia
13 R7 **Makkovik** Newfoundland, NE Canada
98 K6 **Makkum** Friesland, N Netherlands
Mako see Makung
111 M25 **Makó** Rom. Macău. Csongrád, SE Hungary
14 G9 **Makobe Lake** ◎ Ontario, S Canada
79 F18 **Makokou** Ogooué-Ivindo, NE Gabon
81 G23 **Makongolosi** Mbeya, S Tanzania
81 E19 **Makota** SW Uganda
79 G18 **Makoua** Cuvette, C Congo
110 M10 **Maków Mazowiecki** Mazowieckie, C Poland
111 K17 **Maków Podhalański** Małopolskie, S Poland
143 V14 **Makran** cultural region Iran/Pakistan
152 G12 **Makrāna** Rājasthān, N India
143 U15 **Makran Coast** coastal region SE Iran
119 F20 **Makrany** Rus. Mokrany. Brestskaya Voblasts', SW Belarus
Makrinoros see Makrynóros
115 H20 **Makrónisosi** island Kykládes, Greece, Aegean Sea
115 D17 **Makrynóros** var. Makrinoros. ▲▲ C Greece
115 G19 **Makryplági** ▲ C Greece
Maksamaa see Maxmo
126 J15 **Maksatikha** var. Maksatha, Maksaticha. Tverskaya Oblast', W Russian Federation
154 G10 **Maksi** Madhya Pradesh, C India
142 I1 **Mākū** Āžarbāyjān-e Bākhtarī, NW Iran
153 Y11 **Mākum** Assam, NE India
Makun see Makung
161 R14 **Makung** prev. Mako, Makun. W Taiwan
164 B16 **Makurazaki** Kagoshima, Kyūshū, SW Japan
77 V15 **Makurdi** Benue, C Nigeria
38 L17 **Makushin Volcano** ▲ Unalaska Island, Alaska, USA
83 K16 **Makwiro** Mashonaland West, N Zimbabwe
57 D15 **Mala** Lima, W Peru
Mala see Mallow, Ireland
Mala see Malaita, Solomon Islands
93 I14 **Malå** Västerbotten, N Sweden
190 G12 **Mala'atoli** Île Uvea, E Wallis and Futuna
171 P8 **Malabang** E Mindanao, S Philippines
155 E21 **Malabār Coast** coast SW India
79 C16 **Malabo** prev. Santa Isabel. ● (Equatorial Guinea) Isla de Bioco, NW Equatorial Guinea
79 C16 **Malabo** × Isla de Bioco, N Equatorial Guinea
Malaca see Málaga
Malacca see Melaka
168 I7 **Malacca, Strait of** Ind. Selat Malaka. strait Indonesia/Malaysia
Malacka see Malacky
111 G20 **Malacky** Hung. Malacka. Bratislavský Kraj, W Slovakia
33 R16 **Malad City** Idaho, NW USA
117 Q4 **Mala Divytsya** Chernihivs'ka Oblast', N Ukraine
119 J15 **Maladzyechna** Pol. Molodeczno, Rus. Molodechno. Minskaya Voblasts', C Belarus
190 D12 **Malaee** Île Futuna, N Wallis and Futuna
37 V15 **Malaga** New Mexico, SW USA
54 G8 **Málaga** Santander, C Colombia
104 M15 **Málaga** anc. Malaca. Andalucía, S Spain
104 L15 **Málaga** ◈ province Andalucía, S Spain
104 M15 **Málaga** × Andalucía, S Spain
Malagasy Republic see Madagascar
105 N10 **Malagón** Castilla-La Mancha, C Spain
97 G18 **Malahide** Ir. Mullach Íde. E Ireland
187 N9 **Malaita** off. Malaita Province. ◈ province N Solomon Islands
187 N8 **Malaita** var. Mala. island N Solomon Islands
80 F13 **Malakal** Upper Nile, S Sudan
112 C10 **Mala Kapela** ▲▲ NW Croatia
25 V7 **Malakoff** Texas, SW USA
Malakula see Malekula
149 V7 **Malakwāl** var. Mālikwāla. Punjab, E Pakistan
186 E7 **Malalamai** Madang, W PNG
GG Q11 **Malamala** Sulawesi, C Indonesia
169 S17 **Malang** Jawa, C Indonesia
83 O14 **Malanga** Niassa, N Mozambique
Malange see Malanje
92 I9 **Malangen** sound N Norway
82 C11 **Malanje** var. Malange. Malanje, NW Angola
82 C11 **Malanje** var. Malange. ◈ province N Angola
148 M16 **Malān, Rās** headland SW Pakistan
77 S13 **Malanville** NE Benin
Malapane see Ozimek
155 F21 **Malappuram** Kerala, SW India
43 T17 **Mala, Punta** headland S Panama
95 N16 **Mälaren** ◎ C Sweden
62 H13 **Malargüe** Mendoza, W Argentina
14 J8 **Malartic** Quebec, SE Canada
119 F20 **Malaryta** Pol. Maloryta, Rus. Malorita. Brestskaya Voblasts', SW Belarus
63 J19 **Malaspina** Chubut, SE Argentina
39 U12 **Malaspina Glacier** glacier Alaska, USA
137 N15 **Malatya** anc. Melitene. Malatya, SE Turkey
136 M14 **Malatya** ◈ province C Turkey
117 Q7 **Mala Vyska** Rus. Malaya Viska. Kirovohrads'ka Oblast', S Ukraine
83 M14 **Malawi** off. Republic of Malaŵi; prev. Nyasaland, Nyasaland Protectorate. ◆ republic S Africa
Malawi, Lake see Nyasa, Lake
93 J17 **Malax** Fin. Maalahti. Länsi-Suomi, W Finland
126 H14 **Malaya Vishera** Novgorodskaya Oblast', W Russian Federation
Malaya Viska see Mala Vyska
171 Q7 **Malaybalay** Mindanao, S Philippines
142 L6 **Malāyer** prev. Daulatabad. Hamadān, W Iran
168 L7 **Malay Peninsula** peninsula Malaysia/Thailand
192 D7 **Malaysia** var. Federation of Malaysia; prev. the separate territories of Federation of Malaya, Sarawak and Sabah (North Borneo) and Singapore. ◆ monarchy SE Asia
137 R14 **Malazgirt** Muş, E Turkey
15 R8 **Malbaie** ≈ Quebec, SE Canada
77 T12 **Malbaza** Tahoua, S Niger
110 J7 **Malbork** Ger. Marienburg, Marienburg in Westpreussen. Pomorskie, N Poland
100 N9 **Malchin** Mecklenburg-Vorpommern, N Germany
100 M9 **Malchiner See** ◎ NE Germany
99 D16 **Maldegem** Oost-Vlaanderen, NW Belgium
98 L13 **Malden** Gelderland, SE Netherlands
19 O11 **Malden** Massachusetts, NE USA
27 Y8 **Malden** Missouri, C USA
191 X4 **Malden Island** prev. Independence Island. atoll E Kiribati
173 Q6 **Maldives** off. Maldivian Divehi, Republic of Maldives. ◆ republic N Indian Ocean
Maldivian Divehi see Maldives
97 P21 **Maldon** E England, UK
61 G20 **Maldonado** Maldonado, S Uruguay
61 G20 **Maldonado** ◈ department S Uruguay
41 P17 **Maldonado, Punta** headland S Mexico
151 K19 **Male'** Div. Maale. ● (Maldives) Male' Atoll, C Maldives
106 G6 **Malè** Trentino-Alto Adige, N Italy
76 K13 **Maléa** var. Maléya. Haute-Guinée, NE Guinea
115 G22 **Maléas, Akrotírio** headland S Greece
115 L17 **Maléas, Akrotírio** headland Lésvos, E Greece
151 K19 **Male' Atoll** var. Kaafu Atoll. atoll C Maldives
Malebo, Pool see Stanley Pool
154 E12 **Mālegaon** Mahārāshtra, W India
81 F15 **Malek** Jonglei, S Sudan
187 Q13 **Malekula** var. Malakula; prev. Mallicolo. island W Vanuatu
189 Y15 **Malem** Kosrae, E Micronesia
83 O15 **Malema** Nampula, N Mozambique
79 N23 **Malemba-Nkulu** Katanga, SE Dem. Rep. Congo (Zaire)
126 K9 **Malen'ga** Respublika Kareliya, NW Russian Federation
95 M20 **Målerås** Kalmar, S Sweden
103 O6 **Malesherbes** Loiret, C France
115 G18 **Malesína** Stereá Ellás, E Greece
Maléya see Maléa
129 O15 **Malgobek** Chechenskaya Respublika, SW Russian Federation
105 X5 **Malgrat de Mar** Cataluña, NE Spain
80 C9 **Malha** Northern Darfur, W Sudan
139 Q5 **Malḩāt** C Iraq
32 K14 **Malheur Lake** ◎ Oregon, NW USA
32 L14 **Malheur River** ≈ Oregon, NW USA
76 I13 **Mali** Moyenne-Guinée, NW Guinea
77 O9 **Mali** off. Republic of Mali, Fr. République du Mali; prev. French Sudan, Sudanese Republic. ◆ republic W Africa
171 Q16 **Maliana** W East Timor
167 O2 **Mali Hka** ≈ N Myanmar
Mali Idjoš see Mali Iđoš
112 K8 **Mali Iđoš** var. Mali Idjoš, Hung. Kishegyes; prev. Krivaja. Serbia, N Yugoslavia
112 K9 **Mali Kanal** canal N Yugoslavia
171 P12 **Maliku** Sulawesi, N Indonesia
Malik, Wadi al see Milk, Wadi el
Mālikwāla see Malakwāl
167 N11 **Mali Kyun** var. Tavoy Island. island Mergui Archipelago, S Myanmar
95 M19 **Målilla** Kalmar, S Sweden
112 B11 **Mali Lošinj** It. Lussinpiccolo. Primorje-Gorski Kotar, W Croatia
Malin see Malyn
171 P7 **Malindang, Mount** ▲ Mindanao, S Philippines
81 K20 **Malindi** Coast, SE Kenya
Malines see Mechelen
96 E13 **Malin Head** Ir. Cionn Mhálanna. headland NW Ireland
171 O11 **Malino, Gunung** ▲ Sulawesi, N Indonesia
113 M21 **Maliq** var. Maliqi. Korçë, SE Albania
Maliqi see Maliq
171 Q8 **Malita** Mindanao, S Philippines
154 G12 **Malkāpur** Mahārāshtra, C India
136 B10 **Malkara** Tekirdağ, NW Turkey
119 J19 **Mal'kavichy** Rus. Mal'kovichi. Brestskaya Voblasts', SW Belarus
Malkiye see Al Mālikīyah
114 L11 **Malko Sharkovo, Yazovir** ▣ SE Bulgaria
114 N11 **Malko Tŭrnovo** Burgas, E Bulgaria
Mal'kovichi see Mal'kavichy
183 R12 **Mallacoota** Victoria, SE Australia
96 G10 **Mallaig** N Scotland, UK
182 I9 **Mallala** South Australia
75 W9 **Mallawi** C Egypt
105 R5 **Mallén** Aragón, NE Spain
106 F5 **Malles Venosta** Trentino-Alto Adige, N Italy
Mallicolo see Malekula
109 Q8 **Mallnitz** Salzburg, S Austria
105 W9 **Mallorca** Eng. Majorca; anc. Baleares Major. island Islas Baleares, Spain, W Mediterranean Sea
97 C20 **Mallow** Ir. Mala. SW Ireland
93 E15 **Malm** Nord-Trøndelag, C Norway
95 L19 **Malmbäck** Jönköping, S Sweden
92 J12 **Malmberget** Norrbotten, N Sweden
99 M20 **Malmédy** Liège, E Belgium
83 E25 **Malmesbury** Western Cape, SW South Africa
95 N16 **Malmköping** Södermanland, C Sweden
95 K23 **Malmö** Skåne, S Sweden
95 K23 **Malmo** × Skåne, S Sweden
45 Q16 **Malmok** headland Bonaire, S Netherlands Antilles
95 M18 **Malmslätt** Östergötland, S Sweden
127 R16 **Malmyzh** Kirovskaya Oblast', NW Russian Federation
187 Q13 **Malo** island W Vanuatu
128 J7 **Maloarkhangel'sk** Orlovskaya Oblast', W Russian Federation
Maloeļap see Maloelap Atoll
189 V6 **Maloelap Atoll** var. Maloeļap. atoll E Marshall Islands
Maloenda see Malunda
108 I10 **Maloja** Graubünden, S Switzerland
82 L12 **Malole** Northern, NE Zambia
171 O3 **Malolos** Luzon, N Philippines
18 K6 **Malone** New York, NE USA
79 K25 **Malonga** Katanga, S Dem. Rep. Congo (Zaire)
111 L15 **Małopolska** plateau S Poland
111 K17 **Małopolskie** ◈ province S Poland
Malorita/Maloryta see Malaryta
126 K9 **Maloshuyka** Arkhangel'skaya Oblast', NW Russian Federation
114 G10 **Mal'ovitsa** ▲ W Bulgaria
145 V15 **Malovodnoye** Almaty, SE Kazakhstan
94 C10 **Måløy** Sogn og Fjordane, S Norway
128 K4 **Maloyaroslavets** Kaluzhskaya Oblast', W Russian Federation
122 G7 **Malozemel'skaya Tundra** physical region NW Russian Federation
104 J10 **Malpartida de Cáceres** Extremadura, W Spain
104 K9 **Malpartida de Plasencia** Extremadura, W Spain
106 C7 **Malpensa** × (Milano) Lombardia, N Italy
76 J6 **Malqteïr** desert N Mauritania
118 J10 **Malta** Rēzekne, SE Latvia
33 V7 **Malta** Montana, NW USA
120 M11 **Malta** off. Republic of Malta. ◆ republic C Mediterranean Sea
109 R8 **Malta** var. Maltabach. ≈ S Austria
120 M11 **Malta** island Malta, C Mediterranean Sea
Maltabach see Malta
Malta, Canale di see Malta Channel
120 M11 **Malta Channel** It. Canale di Malta. strait Italy/Malta
83 D20 **Maltahöhe** Hardap, SW Namibia
97 N16 **Malton** N England, UK
171 R13 **Maluku** off. Propinsi Maluku, Dut. Molukken, Eng. Moluccas. ◈ province E Indonesia
171 R13 **Maluku** Dut. Molukken, Eng. Moluccas; prev. Spice Islands. island group E Indonesia
Maluku, Laut see Molucca Sea
77 V13 **Malumfashi** Katsina, N Nigeria
171 N13 **Malunda** prev. Maloenda. Sulawesi, C Indonesia
94 K13 **Malung** Dalarna, C Sweden
94 K13 **Malungsfors** Dalarna, C Sweden
186 M8 **Maluu** var. Malu'u. Malaita, N Solomon Islands
155 D16 **Mālvan** Mahārāshtra, W India
Malventum see Benevento
27 U12 **Malvern** Arkansas, C USA
29 S15 **Malvern** Iowa, C USA
44 I13 **Malvern** ▲ W Jamaica
Malvinas, Islas see Falkland Islands
117 N4 **Malyn** Rus. Malin. Zhytomyrs'ka Oblast', N Ukraine
129 O11 **Malyye Derbety** Respublika Kalmykiya, SW Russian Federation
Malyy Kavkaz see Lesser Caucasus
123 Q6 **Malyy Lyakhovskiy, Ostrov** island NE Russian Federation
Malyy Pamir see Little Pamir
122 N5 **Malyy Taymyr, Ostrov** island Severnaya Zemlya, N Russian Federation
144 E10 **Malyy Uzen'** Kaz. Kishiözen. ≈ Kazakhstan/Russian Federation
122 L14 **Malyy Yenisey** var. Ka-Krem. ≈ S Russian Federation
129 S3 **Mamadysh** Respublika Tatarstan, W Russian Federation
117 N14 **Mamaia** Constanța, E Romania
187 W14 **Mamanuca Group** island group Yasawa Group, W Fiji
146 L13 **Mamash** Lebapskiy Velayat, E Turkmenistan
79 O17 **Mambasa** Orientale, NE Dem. Rep. Congo (Zaire)
171 X13 **Mamberamo, Sungai** ≈ Irian Jaya, E Indonesia
79 G15 **Mambéré** ≈ SW Central African Republic
79 G15 **Mambéré-Kadéï** ◈ prefecture SW Central African Republic
Mambij see Manbij
79 H18 **Mambili** ≈ W Congo
83 N18 **Mambone** var. Nova Mambone. Inhambane, E Mozambique
171 O4 **Mamburao** Mindoro, N Philippines
172 I16 **Mamelles** island Inner Islands, NE Seychelles
99 M25 **Mamer** Luxembourg, SW Luxembourg
102 L6 **Mamers** Sarthe, NW France
79 D15 **Mamfe** Sud-Ouest, W Cameroon
145 P6 **Mamlyutka** Severnyy Kazakhstan, N Kazakhstan
36 M15 **Mammoth** Arizona, SW USA
33 S12 **Mammoth Hot Springs** Wyoming, C USA
Mamoedjoe see Mamuju
119 A14 **Mamonovo** Ger. Heiligenbeil. Kaliningradskaya Oblast', W Russian Federation
57 L14 **Mamoré, Río** ≈ Bolivia/Brazil
76 I14 **Mamou** Moyenne-Guinée, W Guinea
22 H8 **Mamou** Louisiana, S USA
172 I14 **Mamoudzou** ○ (Mayotte) C Mayotte
172 I3 **Mampikony** Mahajanga, N Madagascar
77 P16 **Mampong** C Ghana
110 M7 **Mamry, Jezioro** Ger. Mauersee. ◎ NE Poland
171 N13 **Mamuju** prev. Mamoedjoe. Sulawesi, S Indonesia
83 F19 **Mamuno** Ghanzi, W Botswana
113 K19 **Mamuras** var. Mamurasi, Mamurras. Lezhë, C Albania
Mamurasi/Mamurras see Mamuras
76 L16 **Man** W Ivory Coast
55 X9 **Mana** NW French Guiana
56 A6 **Manabí** ◈ province W Ecuador
42 G4 **Manabique, Punta** var. Cabo Tres Puntas. headland E Guatemala
54 G11 **Manacacías, Río** ≈ C Colombia
58 F13 **Manacapuru** Amazonas, N Brazil
171 Q11 **Manado** prev. Menado. Sulawesi, C Indonesia
188 H5 **Managaha** island S Northern Mariana Islands
99 G20 **Manage** Hainaut, S Belgium
42 J10 **Managua** ● (Nicaragua) Managua, W Nicaragua
42 J10 **Managua** ◈ department W Nicaragua
42 J10 **Managua** × Managua, W Nicaragua
42 J10 **Managua, Lago de** var. Xolotlán. ◎ W Nicaragua
Manah see Bilād Manaḩ
18 K16 **Manahawkin** New Jersey, NE USA
184 K11 **Manaia** Taranaki, North Island, NZ
172 J6 **Manakara** Fianarantsoa, SE Madagascar
152 J7 **Manāli** Himāchal Pradesh, NW India
131 U12 **Ma, Nam** Vtn. Sông Mã. ≈ Laos/Vietnam
Manama see Al Manāmah
186 D6 **Manam Island** island N PNG
67 Y13 **Mananara** ≈ SE Madagascar
182 M9 **Manangatang** Victoria, SE Australia
172 J6 **Mananjary** Fianarantsoa, SE Madagascar
76 L14 **Manankoro** Sikasso, SW Mali
76 J12 **Manantali, Lac de** ▣ W Mali
Manáos see Manaus
185 B23 **Manapouri** Southland, South Island, NZ
185 B23 **Manapouri, Lake** ◎ South Island, NZ
58 F13 **Manaquiri** Amazonas, NW Brazil
Manar see Mannar
158 K5 **Manas** Xinjiang Uygur Zizhiqu, NW China
153 U12 **Manās** var. Dangme Chu. ≈ Bhutan/India
147 R8 **Manas, Gora** ▲ Kyrgyzstan/Uzbekistan
158 K3 **Manas Hu** ◎ NW China
153 P10 **Manaslu** ▲ C Nepal
37 S8 **Manassa** Colorado, C USA
21 W4 **Manassas** Virginia, NE USA
45 T5 **Manatí** C Puerto Rico
171 R16 **Manatuto** N East Timor
186 E8 **Manau** Northern, S PNG
54 H4 **Manaure** La Guajira, N Colombia
58 F12 **Manaus** prev. Manáos. state capital Amazonas, NW Brazil
136 G17 **Manavgat** Antalya, SW Turkey
184 M13 **Manawatu** ≈ North Island, NZ
184 L11 **Manawatu-Wanganui** off. Manawatu-Wanganui Region. ◈ region North Island, NZ
171 R7 **Manay** Mindanao, S Philippines
138 K2 **Manbij** var. Mambij, Fr. Membidj. Ḩalab, N Syria
105 N13 **Mancha Real** Andalucía, S Spain
102 I4 **Manche** ◈ department N France
97 L17 **Manchester** Lat. Mancunium. NW England, UK
23 S5 **Manchester** Georgia, SE USA
29 Y13 **Manchester** Iowa, C USA
21 N7 **Manchester** Kentucky, S USA
19 O10 **Manchester** New Hampshire, NE USA
20 K10 **Manchester** Tennessee, S USA
18 M9 **Manchester** Vermont, NE USA
97 L18 **Manchester** × NW England, UK
149 P15 **Manchhar Lake** ◎ SE Pakistan
Man-chou-li see Manzhouli
131 X7 **Manchurian Plain** plain NE China
Máncio Lima see Japiim
Mancunium see Manchester
148 J15 **Mand** Baluchistān, SW Pakistan
Mand see Mand, Rūd-e
81 H25 **Manda** Iringa, SW Tanzania
172 H6 **Mandabe** Toliara, W Madagascar
162 I5 **Mandal** Hövsgöl, N Mongolia
162 L7 **Mandal** Töv, C Mongolia
95 E18 **Mandal** Vest-Agder, S Norway
166 L5 **Mandalay** Mandalay, C Myanmar
166 M6 **Mandalay** ◈ division C Myanmar
162 L9 **Mandalgovĭ** Dundgovĭ, C Mongolia
139 V7 **Mandalī** E Iraq
95 E18 **Mandalselva** ≈ S Norway
28 M5 **Mandan** North Dakota, N USA
Mandargiri Hill see Mandār Hill
153 R14 **Mandār Hill** prev. Mandargiri Hill. Bihār, NE India
170 M13 **Mandar, Teluk** bay Sulawesi, C Indonesia
107 C19 **Mandas** Sardegna, Italy, C Mediterranean Sea
Mandasor see Mandsaur
81 L16 **Mandera** North Eastern, NE Kenya
33 V13 **Manderson** Wyoming, C USA
44 J12 **Mandeville** C Jamaica
22 K9 **Mandeville** Louisiana, S USA
152 I7 **Mandi** Himāchal Pradesh, NW India
76 K14 **Mandiana** Haute-Guinée, E Guinea
149 U10 **Mandi Būrewāla** var. Būrewāla. Punjab, E Pakistan
152 G9 **Mandi Dabwāli** Haryāna, NW India
Mandidzudzure see Chimanimani
83 M15 **Mandié** Manica, NW Mozambique
83 N14 **Mandimba** Niassa, N Mozambique
57 Q19 **Mandioré, Laguna** ◎ E Bolivia
154 J10 **Mandla** Madhya Pradesh, C India
83 M20 **Mandlakazi** var. Manjacaze. Gaza, S Mozambique
95 E24 **Mandø** var. Manø. island W Denmark
Mandoúdhion/Mandoudi see Mantoúdi
115 G19 **Mándra** Attikí, C Greece
172 I7 **Mandrare** ≈ S Madagascar
114 M10 **Mandra, Yazovir** salt lake SE Bulgaria
107 L23 **Mandrazzi, Portella** pass Sicilia, Italy, C Mediterranean Sea
172 J3 **Mandritsara** Mahajanga, N Madagascar
143 O13 **Mand, Rūd-e** var. Mand. ≈ S Iran
154 F9 **Mandsaur** prev. Mandasor. Madhya Pradesh, C India
154 F11 **Māndu** Madhya Pradesh, C India
169 W8 **Mandul, Pulau** island N Indonesia
83 G15 **Mandundu** Western, W Zambia
180 I13 **Mandurah** Western Australia
107 P18 **Manduria** Puglia, SE Italy
155 G20 **Mandya** Karnātaka, C India
77 P12 **Mané** C Burkina
106 E8 **Manerbio** Lombardia, NW Italy
Manevichi see Manevychi
116 K3 **Manevychi** Pol. Maniewicze, Rus. Manevichi. Volyns'ka Oblast', NW Ukraine
107 N16 **Manfredonia** Puglia, SE Italy
107 N16 **Manfredonia, Golfo di** gulf Adriatic Sea, N Mediterranean Sea
77 P13 **Manga** C Burkina
59 L16 **Mangabeiras, Chapada das** ▲▲ E Brazil

◆ Country ● Country Capital ◇ Dependent Territory ○ Dependent Territory Capital ◈ Administrative Region × International Airport ▲ Mountain ▲▲ Mountain Range ⛰ Volcano ≈ River ◎ Lake ▣ Reservoir

79 J20 **Mangai** Bandundu, W Dem. Rep. Congo (Zaire)
190 L17 **Mangaia** island group S Cook Islands
184 M9 **Mangakino** Waikato, North Island, NZ
116 M15 **Mangalia** anc. Callatis. Constanța, SE Romania
78 J11 **Mangalmé** Guéra, SE Chad
155 E19 **Mangalore** Karnātaka, W India
191 Y13 **Mangareva** var. Magareva. island Îles Tuamotu, SE French Polynesia
83 I23 **Mangaung** Free State, C South Africa
Mangaung see Bloemfontein
154 K9 **Mangawān** Madhya Pradesh, C India
184 M11 **Mangaweka** Manawatu-Wanganui, North Island, NZ
184 N11 **Mangaweka** ▲ North Island, NZ
79 P17 **Mangbwalu** Orientale, NE Dem. Rep. Congo (Zaire)
101 L24 **Mangfall** ≈ SE Germany
169 P13 **Manggar** Pulau Belitung, W Indonesia
146 H8 **Manghit** Rus. Mangit. Qoraqalpoghiston Respublikasi, W Uzbekistan
166 M2 **Mangin Range** ▲▲ N Myanmar
139 R1 **Mangish** N Iraq
144 F15 **Mangistau** Kaz. Mangqystaū Oblysy; prev. Mangyshlaskaya. ◈ province SW Kazakhstan
Mangit see Manghit
54 A13 **Manglares, Cabo** headland SW Colombia
149 V6 **Mangla Reservoir** ▣ NE Pakistan
159 N9 **Mangnai** var. Lao Mangnai. Qinghai, C China
Mango see Mago, Fiji
Mango see Sansanné-Mango, Togo
Mangoche see Mangochi
83 N14 **Mangochi** var. Mangoche; prev. Fort Johnston. Southern, SE Malawi
77 N14 **Mangodara** SW Burkina
172 H6 **Mangoky** ≈ W Madagascar
171 Q12 **Mangole, Pulau** island Kepulauan Sula, E Indonesia
184 J2 **Mangonui** Northland, North Island, NZ
Mangqystaū Oblysy see Mangistau
Mangqystaū Shyghanaghy see Mangyshlakskiy Zaliv
104 H7 **Mangualde** Viseu, N Portugal
61 H18 **Mangueira, Lagoa** ◎ S Brazil
77 X6 **Manguéni, Plateau du** ▲▲ NE Niger
26 K11 **Mangum** Oklahoma, C USA
79 O18 **Manguredjipa** Nord Kivu, E Dem. Rep. Congo (Zaire)
83 L16 **Mangwendi** Mashonaland East, E Zimbabwe
144 F15 **Mangyshlak, Plato** plateau SW Kazakhstan
144 E14 **Mangyshlakskiy Zaliv** Kaz. Mangqystaū Shyghanaghy. gulf SW Kazakhstan
Mangyshlaskaya see Mangistau
162 I5 **Manhan** Hövsgöl, N Mongolia
27 O4 **Manhattan** Kansas, C USA
99 L21 **Manhay** Luxembourg, SE Belgium
83 L21 **Manhiça** prev. Vila de Manhiça. Maputo, S Mozambique
83 L21 **Manhoca** Maputo, S Mozambique
59 N20 **Manhuaçu** Minas Gerais, SE Brazil
143 R11 **Mānī** Kermān, C Iran
54 H10 **Maní** Casanare, C Colombia
56 A6 **Manía, Bahía de** bay W Ecuador
83 M17 **Manica** var. Vila de Manica. Manica, W Mozambique
83 M17 **Manica** off. Província de Manica. ◈ province W Mozambique
83 L17 **Manicaland** ◈ province E Zimbabwe
15 U5 **Manic Deux, Réservoir** ▣ Quebec, SE Canada
Manich see Manych
59 F14 **Manicoré** Amazonas, N Brazil
13 N11 **Manicouagan** Quebec, SE Canada
13 N11 **Manicouagan** ≈ Quebec, SE Canada
15 U6 **Manicouagan, Péninsule de** peninsula Quebec, SE Canada
13 N11 **Manicouagan, Réservoir** ◎ Quebec, E Canada
15 T4 **Manic Trois, Réservoir** ▣ Quebec, SE Canada
79 M20 **Maniema** off. Région du Maniema. ◈ region E Dem. Rep. Congo (Zaire)
Maniewicze see Manevychi
160 F8 **Maniganggo** Sichuan, C China
11 Y15 **Manigotagan** Manitoba, S Canada
153 R13 **Manihāri** Bihār, N India
191 U9 **Manihi** island Îles Tuamotu, C French Polynesia
190 L13 **Manihiki** atoll N Cook Islands
175 U8 **Manihiki Plateau** undersea feature C Pacific Ocean
196 M14 **Maniitsoq** var. Manītsoq, Dan. Sukkertoppen. Kita, S Greenland
153 T15 **Manikganj** Dhaka, C Bangladesh
152 M14 **Mānikpur** Uttar Pradesh, N India
171 N4 **Manila** off. City of Manila. ● (Philippines) Luzon, N Philippines
27 Y9 **Manila** Arkansas, C USA
189 N16 **Manila Reef** reef W Micronesia
183 T6 **Manilla** New South Wales, SE Australia
192 F6 **Maniloa** island Tongatapu Group, S Tonga
123 U8 **Manily** Koryakskiy Avtonomnyy Okrug, E Russian Federation
171 V12 **Manim, Pulau** island E Indonesia
168 I11 **Maninjau, Danau** ◎ Sumatera, W Indonesia
153 W13 **Manipur** ◈ state NE India
153 X14 **Manipur Hills** hill range E India
136 C14 **Manisa** var. Manissa; prev. Saruhan, anc. Magnesia. Manisa, W Turkey
136 C13 **Manisa** var. Manissa. ◈ province W Turkey
Manissa see Manisa
31 O7 **Manistee** Michigan, N USA
31 P7 **Manistee River** ≈ Michigan, N USA
31 O4 **Manistique** Michigan, N USA
31 P4 **Manistique Lake** ◎ Michigan, N USA
11 W13 **Manitoba** ◈ province S Canada
11 X16 **Manitoba, Lake** ◎ Manitoba, S Canada
11 X17 **Manitou** Manitoba, S Canada
31 N2 **Manitou Island** island Michigan, N USA
14 H11 **Manitou Lake** ◎ Ontario, SE Canada
12 G15 **Manitoulin Island** island Ontario, S Canada
37 T5 **Manitou Springs** Colorado, C USA
14 G12 **Manitouwabing Lake** ◎ Ontario, S Canada
12 E12 **Manitouwadge** Ontario, S Canada
12 G15 **Manitowaning** Manitoulin Island, Ontario, S Canada
14 B7 **Manitowik Lake** ◎ Ontario, S Canada
31 N7 **Manitowoc** Wisconsin, N USA
Manītsoq see Maniitsoq
139 O7 **Mānī', Wādī al** dry watercourse W Iraq
12 J14 **Maniwaki** Quebec, SE Canada
171 W13 **Maniwori** Irian Jaya, E Indonesia
54 E10 **Manizales** Caldas, W Colombia
112 F11 **Manjača** ▲▲ NW Bosnia and Herzegovina
Manjacaze see Mandlakazi
180 J14 **Manjimup** Western Australia
109 V4 **Mank** Niederösterreich, C Austria
79 I17 **Mankanza** Equateur, NW Dem. Rep. Congo (Zaire)
153 N12 **Mankāpur** Uttar Pradesh, N India
26 M3 **Mankato** Kansas, C USA
29 U10 **Mankato** Minnesota, N USA
117 O7 **Man'kivka** Cherkas'ka Oblast', C Ukraine
76 M15 **Mankono** C Ivory Coast
11 T17 **Mankota** Saskatchewan, S Canada
155 K23 **Mankulam** Northern Province, N Sri Lanka
39 Q9 **Manley Hot Springs** Alaska, USA
18 H10 **Manlius** New York, NE USA
105 W5 **Manlleu** Cataluña, NE Spain
29 V11 **Manly** Iowa, C USA
154 E13 **Manmād** Mahārāshtra, W India
182 J7 **Mannahill** South Australia
155 J23 **Mannar** var. Manar. Northern Province, NW Sri Lanka
155 I24 **Mannar, Gulf of** gulf India/Sri Lanka
155 J23 **Mannar Island** island N Sri Lanka
Mannersdorf see Mannersdorf am Leithagebirge
109 Y5 **Mannersdorf am Leithagebirge** var. Mannersdorf. Niederösterreich, E Austria
109 Y6 **Mannersdorf an der Rabnitz** Burgenland, E Austria
101 G20 **Mannheim** Baden-Württemberg, SW Germany
11 O12 **Manning** Alberta, W Canada
29 T14 **Manning** Iowa, C USA
28 K5 **Manning** North Dakota, N USA
21 S13 **Manning** South Carolina, SE USA
191 Y2 **Manning, Cape** headland Kiritimati, NE Kiribati
21 S3 **Mannington** West Virginia, NE USA
182 A1 **Mann Ranges** ▲▲ South Australia
107 C19 **Mannu** ≈ Sardegna, Italy, C Mediterranean Sea
11 R14 **Mannville** Alberta, SW Canada
76 J15 **Mano** ≈ Liberia/Sierra Leone
Manø see Mandø
39 O13 **Manokotak** Alaska, USA
171 V12 **Manokwari** Irian Jaya, E Indonesia
79 N22 **Manono** Shabo, SE Dem. Rep. Congo (Zaire)
25 T10 **Manor** Texas, SW USA
97 D16 **Manorhamilton** Ir. Cluainín. NW Ireland
103 S15 **Manosque** Alpes-de-Haute-Provence, SE France
12 L11 **Manouane, Lac** ◎ Quebec, SE Canada
163 W12 **Manp'o** var. Manp'ojin. NW North Korea
Manp'ojin see Manp'o
191 T4 **Manra** prev. Sydney Island. atoll Phoenix Islands, C Kiribati
105 V5 **Manresa** Cataluña, NE Spain
152 H9 **Mānsa** Punjab, NW India
82 J12 **Mansa** prev. Fort Rosebery. Luapula, N Zambia
76 G12 **Mansa Konko** C Gambia
15 Q11 **Manseau** Quebec, SE Canada
149 U5 **Mānsehra** North-West Frontier Province, NW Pakistan
9 Q9 **Mansel Island** island Nunavut, NE Canada
183 O12 **Mansfield** Victoria, SE Australia
97 M18 **Mansfield** C England, UK
27 S11 **Mansfield** Arkansas, C USA
22 G6 **Mansfield** Louisiana, S USA
19 O12 **Mansfield** Massachusetts, NE USA
31 T12 **Mansfield** Ohio, N USA
18 G12 **Mansfield** Pennsylvania, NE USA
18 M7 **Mansfield, Mount** ▲ Vermont, NE USA
59 M16 **Mansidão** Bahia, E Brazil
102 L11 **Mansle** Charente, W France
76 G12 **Mansôa** C Guinea-Bissau
47 V8 **Manso, Rio** ≈ C Brazil
Manşûra see El Manşûra
Mansurabad see Mehrān, Rūd-e
56 A6 **Manta** Manabí, W Ecuador
57 F14 **Mantaro, Río** ≈ C Peru
35 O8 **Manteca** California, W USA
54 J7 **Mantecal** Apure, C Venezuela
31 N11 **Manteno** Illinois, N USA
21 Y9 **Manteo** Roanoke Island, North Carolina, SE USA
Mantes-Gassicourt see Mantes-la-Jolie
103 N5 **Mantes-la-Jolie** prev. Mantes-Gassicourt, Mantes-sur-Seine, anc. Medunta. Yvelines, N France
Mantes-sur-Seine see Mantes-la-Jolie
36 L5 **Manti** Utah, W USA
Mantinea see Mantíneia
115 F20 **Mantíneia** anc. Mantinea. site of ancient city Pelopónnisos, S Greece
59 M21 **Mantiqueira, Serra da** ▲▲ S Brazil
29 W10 **Mantorville** Minnesota, N USA
115 G17 **Mantoúdi** var. Mandoudi; prev. Mandoúdhion. Évvoia, C Greece
Mantoue see Mantova
106 F8 **Mantova** Eng. Mantua, Fr. Mantoue. Lombardia, NW Italy
93 M19 **Mäntsälä** Etelä-Suomi, S Finland
93 L17 **Mänttä** Länsi-Suomi, W Finland
Mantua see Mantova
127 O14 **Manturovo** Kostromskaya Oblast', NW Russian Federation
93 M18 **Mäntyharju** Itä-Suomi, SE Finland
92 M13 **Mäntyjärvi** Lappi, N Finland
190 L16 **Manuae** island S Cook Islands
191 Q10 **Manuae** atoll Îles Sous le Vent, W French Polynesia
192 L16 **Manua Islands** island group E American Samoa
40 L5 **Manuel Benavides** Chihuahua, N Mexico
61 D21 **Manuel J.Cobo** Buenos Aires, E Argentina
58 M12 **Manuel Luís, Recife** reef E Brazil
61 F15 **Manuel Viana** Rio Grande do Sul, S Brazil
59 I14 **Manuel Zinho** Pará, N Brazil
191 V11 **Manuhangi** atoll Îles Tuamotu, C French Polynesia
185 E22 **Manuherikia** ≈ South Island, NZ
171 P13 **Manui, Pulau** island N Indonesia
Manukau see Manurewa
184 L6 **Manukau Harbour** harbor North Island, NZ
191 Z2 **Manulu Lagoon** ◎ Kiritimati, E Kiribati
182 J7 **Manunda Creek** seasonal river South Australia
57 K15 **Manupari, Río** ≈ N Bolivia
184 L6 **Manurewa** var. Manukau. Auckland, North Island, NZ
57 K15 **Manurimi, Río** ≈ NW Bolivia
186 D5 **Manus** ◈ province N PNG
186 D5 **Manus Island** var. Great Admiralty Island. island N PNG
171 T16 **Manuwui** Pulau Babar, E Indonesia
29 Q3 **Manvel** North Dakota, N USA
33 Z14 **Manville** Wyoming, C USA
22 G6 **Many** Louisiana, S USA
81 H21 **Manyara, Lake** ◎ NE Tanzania
128 L12 **Manych** var. Manich. ≈ SW Russian Federation
129 N13 **Manych-Gudilo, Ozero** salt lake SW Russian Federation
83 H14 **Manyinga** North Western, NW Zambia
105 O11 **Manzanares** Castilla-La Mancha, C Spain
44 H7 **Manzanillo** Granma, E Cuba
40 K14 **Manzanillo** Colima, SW Mexico
40 K14 **Manzanillo, Bahía** bay SW Mexico
37 S11 **Manzano Mountains** ▲▲ New Mexico, SW USA
37 R12 **Manzano Peak** ▲ New Mexico, SW USA
163 R6 **Manzhouli** var. Man-chou-li. Nei Mongol Zizhiqu, N China
Manzil Bū Ruqaybah see Menzel Bourguiba
139 X9 **Manzilīyah** E Iraq
83 L21 **Manzini** prev. Bremersdorp. C Swaziland
83 L21 **Manzini** ✕ (Mbabane) C Swaziland
78 G10 **Mao** Kanem, W Chad
45 N8 **Mao** NW Dominican Republic
Maó see Mahón
Maoemere see Maumere
159 W9 **Maojing** Gansu, N China
171 Y14 **Maoke, Pegunungan** Dut. Sneeuw-gebergte, Eng. Snow Mountains. ▲▲ Irian Jaya, E Indonesia
Maol Réidh, Caoc see Mweelrea
160 M15 **Maoming** Guangdong, S China
160 H8 **Maoxian** var. Mao Xian; prev. Fengyizhen. Sichuan, C China
83 L19 **Mapai** Gaza, SW Mozambique
158 H15 **Mapam Yumco** ◎ W China
83 I15 **Mapanza** Southern, S Zambia
54 J4 **Maparari** Falcón, N Venezuela
41 U17 **Mapastepec** Chiapas, SE Mexico
169 V9 **Mapat, Pulau** island N Indonesia
171 Y15 **Mapi** Irian Jaya, E Indonesia
171 V11 **Mapia, Kepulauan** island group E Indonesia
40 L8 **Mapimí** Durango, C Mexico
83 N19 **Mapinhane** Inhambane, SE Mozambique
55 N7 **Mapire** Monagas, NE Venezuela
11 S17 **Maple Creek** Saskatchewan, S Canada
31 Q9 **Maple River** ≈ Michigan, N USA
29 P7 **Maple River** ≈ North Dakota/South Dakota, N USA
29 S13 **Mapleton** Iowa, C USA
29 U10 **Mapleton** Minnesota, N USA
29 R5 **Mapleton** North Dakota, N USA
32 F13 **Mapleton** Oregon, NW USA
36 L3 **Mapleton** Utah, W USA
192 K5 **Mapmaker Seamounts** undersea feature N Pacific Ocean
186 B6 **Maprik** East Sepik, NW PNG
83 L21 **Maputo** prev. Lourenço Marques. ● (Mozambique) Maputo, S Mozambique
83 L21 **Maputo** ◈ province S Mozambique
83 L21 **Maputo** ✕ Maputo, S Mozambique
67 V14 **Maputo** ≈ S Mozambique
Maqanshy see Makanchi
Maqat see Makat
113 K19 **Maqë** ≈ NW Albania
113 M19 **Maqellarë** Dibër, C Albania
159 S12 **Maqên** var. Dawu. Qinghai, C China
159 S11 **Maqên Gangri** ▲ C China
159 U12 **Maqu** Gansu, C China
104 M9 **Maqueda** Castilla-La Mancha, C Spain
82 B9 **Maquela do Zombo** Uíge, NW Angola
63 I16 **Maquinchao** Río Negro, C Argentina
29 Z13 **Maquoketa** Iowa, C USA
29 Y13 **Maquoketa River** ≈ Iowa, C USA
14 F13 **Mar** Ontario, S Canada
95 F14 **Mår** ◎ S Norway
81 G19 **Mara** ◈ region N Tanzania
191 P8 **Maraa** Tahiti, W French Polynesia
58 D12 **Maraã** Amazonas, NW Brazil
191 O8 **Maraa, Pointe** headland Tahiti, W French Polynesia
59 K14 **Marabá** Pará, NE Brazil
54 H5 **Maracaibo** Zulia, NW Venezuela
Maracaibo, Gulf of see Venezuela, Golfo de
54 H5 **Maracaibo, Lago de** var. Lake Maracaibo. inlet NW Venezuela
Maracaibo, Lake see Maracaibo, Lago de
58 K10 **Maracá, Ilha de** island NE Brazil
59 H20 **Maracaju, Serra de** ▲▲ S Brazil
58 I11 **Maracanaquará, Planalto** ▲▲ NE Brazil
54 L5 **Maracay** Aragua, N Venezuela
Marada see Marādah
75 R9 **Marādah** var. Marada. N Libya
77 U12 **Maradi** Maradi, S Niger
77 U11 **Maradi** ◈ department S Niger
81 E21 **Maragarazi** var. Muragarazi. ≈ Burundi/Tanzania
Maragha see Marāgheh
142 J3 **Marāgheh** var. Maragha. Āžarbāyjān-e Khāvarī, NW Iran
141 P7 **Marāh** var. Marrāt. Ar Riyāḑ, C Saudi Arabia
55 N11 **Marahuaca, Cerro** ▲ S Venezuela
27 R5 **Marais des Cygnes River** ≈ Kansas/Missouri, C USA
58 L11 **Marajó, Baía de** bay N Brazil
59 K12 **Marajó, Ilha de** island N Brazil
191 O2 **Marakei** atoll Tungaru, W Kiribati
Marakesh see Marrakech
81 I18 **Maralal** Rift Valley, C Kenya
83 G21 **Maralaleng** Kgalagadi, S Botswana
145 U8 **Maraldy, Ozero** ◎ NE Kazakhstan
182 C5 **Maralinga** South Australia
Máramarossziget see Sighetu Marmației
187 N9 **Maramasike** var. Small Malaita. island N Solomon Islands
Maramba see Livingstone
194 H3 **Marambio** Argentinian research station Antarctica
116 H9 **Maramureș** ◈ county NW Romania
36 L15 **Marana** Arizona, SW USA
105 P7 **Maranchón** Castilla-La Mancha, C Spain
142 J2 **Marand** var. Merend. Āžarbāyjān-e Khāvarī, NW Iran
Marandellas see Marondera
58 L13 **Maranhão** off. Estado do Maranhão. ◈ state E Brazil
104 H10 **Maranhão, Barragem do** ▣ C Portugal
149 O11 **Mārān, Koh-i** ▲ SW Pakistan
106 J7 **Marano, Laguna di** lagoon NE Italy
56 E9 **Marañón, Río** ≈ N Peru
102 J10 **Marans** Charente-Maritime, W France
83 M20 **Marão** Inhambane, S Mozambique
185 B23 **Mararoa** ≈ South Island, NZ
Maraş/Marash see Kahramanmaraş
107 M19 **Maratea** Basilicata, S Italy
104 G11 **Marateca** Setúbal, S Portugal
115 B20 **Marathiá, Akrotírio** headland Zákynthos, Iónioi Nísoi, Greece, C Mediterranean Sea
12 E12 **Marathon** Ontario, S Canada
23 Y17 **Marathon** Florida Keys, Florida, SE USA
24 L10 **Marathon** Texas, SW USA
Marathón see Marathónas
115 H19 **Marathónas** prev. Marathón. Attikí, C Greece
169 W9 **Maratua, Pulau** island N Indonesia
59 O18 **Maraú** Bahia, SE Brazil
143 R3 **Marāveh Tappeh** Golestān, N Iran
24 L11 **Maravillas Creek** ≈ Texas, SW USA
186 D8 **Marawaka** Eastern Highlands, C PNG
171 Q7 **Marawi** Mindanao, S Philippines
Marbat see Mirbāţ
104 L16 **Marbella** Andalucía, S Spain
180 J7 **Marble Bar** Western Australia
36 L9 **Marble Canyon** canyon Arizona, SW USA
25 S10 **Marble Falls** Texas, SW USA
27 Y7 **Marble Hill** Missouri, C USA
33 T15 **Marbleton** Wyoming, C USA
Marburg see Maribor
Marburg see Marburg an der Lahn, Germany
101 H16 **Marburg an der Lahn** hist. Marburg. Hessen, W Germany
111 H23 **Marcal** ≈ W Hungary
42 G7 **Marcala** La Paz, SW Honduras
111 H24 **Marcali** Somogy, SW Hungary
83 A16 **Marca, Ponta da** headland SW Angola
59 I16 **Marcelândia** Mato Grosso, W Brazil
27 T3 **Marceline** Missouri, C USA
60 I13 **Marcelino Ramos** Rio Grande do Sul, S Brazil
55 Y12 **Marcel, Mont** ▲ S French Guiana
97 O19 **March** E England, UK
109 Z3 **March** var. Morava. ≈ C Europe see also Morava
106 I12 **Marche** Eng. Marches. ◈ region C Italy
103 N11 **Marche** cultural region C France
99 J21 **Marche-en-Famenne** Luxembourg, SE Belgium
104 K14 **Marchena** Andalucía, S Spain
57 B17 **Marchena, Isla** var. Bindloe Island. island Galapagos Islands, Ecuador, E Pacific Ocean
Marches see Marche
99 J20 **Marchin** Liège, E Belgium
181 S1 **Marchinbar Island** island Wessel Islands, Northern Territory, N Australia
62 L9 **Mar Chiquita, Laguna** ◎ C Argentina
103 Q10 **Marcigny** Saône-et-Loire, C France
23 W16 **Marco** Florida, SE USA
Marcodurum see Düren
59 O15 **Marcolândia** Pernambuco, E Brazil
106 I8 **Marco Polo** ✕ (Venezia) Veneto, NE Italy
Marcq see Mark
116 M8 **Mărculeşti** Rus. Markuleshty. N Moldova
29 S12 **Marcus** Iowa, C USA
39 S11 **Marcus Baker, Mount** ▲ Alaska, USA
192 I5 **Marcus Island** var. Minami Tori Shima. island E Japan
18 K8 **Marcy, Mount** ▲ New York, NE USA
149 T5 **Mardān** North-West Frontier Province, N Pakistan
63 N14 **Mar del Plata** Buenos Aires, E Argentina
137 Q16 **Mardin** Mardin, SE Turkey
137 Q16 **Mardin** ◈ province SE Turkey
137 Q16 **Mardin Dağları** ▲▲ SE Turkey
162 J9 **Mardzad** Övörhangay, C Mongolia
187 R17 **Maré** island Îles Loyauté, E New Caledonia
Marea Neagră see Black Sea
105 Z8 **Mare de Déu del Toro** ▲ Menorca, Spain, W Mediterranean Sea
181 W4 **Mareeba** Queensland, NE Australia
96 G8 **Maree, Loch** ◎ N Scotland, UK
Mareeq see Mereeg
Marek see Dupnitsa
76 J11 **Maréna** Kayes, W Mali
190 I2 **Marenanuka** atoll Tungaru, W Kiribati
29 X14 **Marengo** Iowa, C USA
102 J11 **Marennes** Charente-Maritime, W France
107 G23 **Marettimo, Isola** island Isole Egadi, S Italy
24 K10 **Marfa** Texas, SW USA
57 P17 **Marfil, Laguna** ◎ E Bolivia
Marganets see Marhanets'
25 Q4 **Margaret** Texas, SW USA
180 I14 **Margaret River** Western Australia
186 C7 **Margarima** Southern Highlands, W PNG
55 N4 **Margarita, Isla de** island N Venezuela
115 I25 **Margarítes** Kríti, Greece, E Mediterranean Sea
97 Q22 **Margate** prev. Mergate. SE England, UK
23 Z15 **Margate** Florida, SE USA
Margelan see Marghilon
103 P13 **Margeride, Montagnes de la** ▲▲ C France
Margherita see Jamaame
107 N16 **Margherita di Savoia** Puglia, SE Italy
Margherita, Lake see Ābaya Hāyk'
81 E18 **Margherita Peak** Fr. Pic Marguerite. ▲ Uganda/Dem. Rep. Congo (Zaire)
149 O4 **Marghī** Bāmīān, N Afghanistan
147 S10 **Marghilon** var. Margelan, Rus. Margilan. Farghona Wiloyati, E Uzbekistan
116 G9 **Marghita** Hung. Margitta. Bihor, NW Romania
Margilan see Marghilon
116 K8 **Marginea** Suceava, NE Romania
Margitta see Marghita
148 K9 **Mārgow, Dasht-e** desert SW Afghanistan
99 L18 **Margraten** Limburg, SE Netherlands
10 M15 **Marguerite** British Columbia, SW Canada
194 I6 **Marguerite Bay** bay Antarctica
Marguerite, Pic see Margherita Peak
117 T9 **Marhanets'** Rus. Marganets. Dnipropetrovs'ka Oblast', E Ukraine
186 B9 **Mari** Western, SW PNG
191 R12 **Maria** island Îles Australes, SW French Polynesia
191 Y12 **Maria** atoll Groupe Actéon, SE French Polynesia
40 I12 **María Cleofas, Isla** island C Mexico
62 H4 **María Elena** var. Oficina María Elena. Antofagasta, N Chile
95 G21 **Mariager** Århus, C Denmark
61 C22 **María Ignacia** Buenos Aires, E Argentina
183 P17 **Maria Island** island Tasmania, SE Australia
40 H12 **María Madre, Isla** island C Mexico
40 I12 **María Magdalena, Isla** island C Mexico
192 H6 **Mariana Islands** island group Guam/Northern Mariana Islands
175 N3 **Mariana Trench** var. Challenger Deep. undersea feature W Pacific Ocean
153 X12 **Mariāni** Assam, NE India
27 X11 **Marianna** Arkansas, C USA
23 R8 **Marianna** Florida, SE USA
172 J16 **Marianne** island Inner Islands, NE Seychelles
95 M19 **Mariannelund** Jönköping, S Sweden
61 D15 **Mariano I.Loza** Corrientes, NE Argentina
Mariano Machado see Ganda
111 A16 **Mariánské Lázně** Ger. Marienbad. Karlovarský Kraj, W Czech Republic
Máriaradna see Radna
33 S7 **Marias River** ≈ Montana, NW USA
Maria-Theresiopel see Subotica
Máriatölgyes see Dubnica nad Váhom
184 H1 **Maria van Diemen, Cape** headland North Island, NZ
109 V5 **Mariazell** Steiermark, E Austria
141 P15 **Mar'ib** W Yemen
95 I25 **Maribo** Storstrøm, S Denmark
109 W9 **Maribor** Ger. Marburg. NE Slovenia
Marica see Maritsa
35 R13 **Maricopa** California, W USA
Maricourt see Kangiqsujuaq
81 D15 **Maridi** Western Equatoria, SW Sudan
194 M11 **Marie Byrd Land** physical region Antarctica
193 P14 **Marie Byrd Seamount** undersea feature N Amundsen Sea
45 X11 **Marie-Galante** var. Ceyre to the Caribs. island SE Guadeloupe
45 Y6 **Marie-Galante, Canal de** channel S Guadeloupe
93 J20 **Mariehamn** Fin. Maarianhamina. Åland, SW Finland
44 C4 **Mariel** La Habana, W Cuba
99 H22 **Mariembourg** Namur, S Belgium
Marienbad see Mariánské Lázně
Marienburg see Alūksne, Latvia
Marienburg see Malbork, Poland
Marienburg see Feldioara, Romania
Marienburg in Westpreussen see Malbork
Marienhausen see Viļaka
83 D20 **Mariental** Hardap, SW Namibia
18 D13 **Marienville** Pennsylvania, NE USA
Marienwerder see Kwidzyń
58 C12 **Marié, Rio** ≈ NW Brazil
95 K17 **Mariestad** Västra Götaland, S Sweden
23 S3 **Marietta** Georgia, SE USA
31 U14 **Marietta** Ohio, N USA
27 N13 **Marietta** Oklahoma, C USA
81 H18 **Marigat** Rift Valley, W Kenya
103 S16 **Marignane** Bouches-du-Rhône, SE France
Marignano see Melegnano
45 O11 **Marigot** NE Dominica
122 K12 **Mariinsk** Kemerovskaya Oblast', S Russian Federation
129 Q3 **Mariinskiy Posad** Respublika Mariy El, W Russian Federation
119 E14 **Marijampolė** prev. Kapsukas. Marijampolė, S Lithuania
114 G12 **Marikostenovo** Blagoevgrad, SW Bulgaria
60 J9 **Marília** São Paulo, S Brazil
82 D11 **Marimba** Malanje, NW Angola
139 T1 **Marī Mīlā** E Iraq
104 G4 **Marín** Galicia, NW Spain
35 N10 **Marina** California, W USA
Marina di Catanzaro see Catanzaro Marina
Mar'ina Gorka see Mar"ina Horka
119 L17 **Mar"ina Horka** Rus. Mar'ina Gorka. Minskaya Voblasts', C Belarus
171 O4 **Marinduque** island C Philippines
31 S9 **Marine City** Michigan, N USA
31 N6 **Marinette** Wisconsin, N USA

◆ Country ● Country Capital ◇ Dependent Territory ○ Dependent Territory Capital ◈ Administrative Region ✕ International Airport ▲ Mountain ▲▲ Mountain Range Volcano ≈ River ◎ Lake ▣ Reservoir

60 I10 **Maringá** Paraná, S Brazil
83 N16 **Maringuè** Sofala, C Mozambique
104 F9 **Marinha Grande** Leiria, C Portugal
107 I15 **Marino** Lazio, C Italy
59 A15 **Mário Lobão** Acre, W Brazil
23 O5 **Marion** Alabama, S USA
27 Y11 **Marion** Arkansas, C USA
30 L17 **Marion** Illinois, N USA
31 P13 **Marion** Indiana, N USA
29 X13 **Marion** Iowa, C USA
27 O5 **Marion** Kansas, C USA
20 H6 **Marion** Kentucky, S USA
21 P9 **Marion** North Carolina, SE USA
31 S12 **Marion** Ohio, N USA
21 T12 **Marion** South Carolina, SE USA
21 Q7 **Marion** Virginia, NE USA
27 O5 **Marion Lake** ⊞ Kansas, C USA
21 S13 **Marion, Lake** ⊞ South Carolina, SE USA
27 S8 **Marionville** Missouri, C USA
55 N7 **Maripa** Bolívar, E Venezuela
55 X11 **Maripasoula** W French Guiana
35 Q9 **Mariposa** California, W USA
61 G19 **Mariscala** Lavalleja, S Uruguay
62 M4 **Mariscal Estigarribia** Boquerón, NW Paraguay
56 C6 **Mariscal Sucre** var. Quito. × (Quito) Pichincha, C Ecuador
30 K16 **Marissa** Illinois, N USA
103 U14 **Maritime Alps** Fr. Alpes Maritimes, It. Alpi Marittime. ▲ France/Italy
Maritimes, Alpes see Maritime Alps
Maritime Territory see Primorskiy Kray
114 K11 **Maritsa** var. Marica, Gk. Évros, Turk. Meriç; anc. Hebrus. ≈ SW Europe see also Évros/Meriç
Maritsa see Simeonovgrad
Marittime, Alpi see Maritime Alps
Maritzburg see Pietermaritzburg
117 X9 **Mariupol'** prev. Zhdanov. Donets'ka Oblast', SE Ukraine
55 Q6 **Mariusa, Caño** ≈ NE Venezuela
142 J5 **Marīvān** prev. Dezh Shāhpūr. Kordestān, W Iran
129 R3 **Mariyets** Respublika Mariy El, W Russian Federation
Mariyskaya ASSR see Mariy El, Respublika
118 G4 **Märjamaa** Ger. Merjama. Raplamaa, NW Estonia
99 I15 **Mark** Fr. Marcq. ≈ Belgium/Netherlands
81 N17 **Marka** var. Merca. Shabeellaha Hoose, S Somalia
145 Z10 **Markakol', Ozero** Kaz. Marqaköl. ◎ E Kazakhstan
76 M12 **Markala** Ségou, W Mali
159 S15 **Markam** var. Gartog. Xizang Zizhiqu, W China
95 K21 **Markaryd** Kronoberg, S Sweden
142 L7 **Markazī** off. Ostān-e Markazī. ◈ province W Iran
14 F14 **Markdale** Ontario, S Canada
27 X10 **Marked Tree** Arkansas, C USA
98 N11 **Markelo** Overijssel, E Netherlands
98 J9 **Markermeer** ◎ C Netherlands
97 N20 **Market Harborough** C England, UK
97 N18 **Market Rasen** E England, UK
123 O10 **Markha** ≈ NE Russian Federation
12 H16 **Markham** Ontario, S Canada
25 V12 **Markham** Texas, SW USA
186 E7 **Markham** ≈ C PNG
195 Q11 **Markham, Mount** ▲ Antarctica
110 M11 **Marki** Mazowieckie, C Poland
158 F8 **Markit** Xinjiang Uygur Zizhiqu, NW China
117 Y5 **Markivka** Rus. Markovka. Luhans'ka Oblast', E Ukraine
35 Q7 **Markleeville** California, W USA
98 L8 **Marknesse** Flevoland, N Netherlands
79 H14 **Markounda** var. Marcounda. Ouham, NW Central African Republic
Markovka see Markivka
123 U7 **Markovo** Chukotskiy Avtonomnyy Okrug, NE Russian Federation
129 P8 **Marks** Saratovskaya Oblast', W Russian Federation
22 K2 **Marks** Mississippi, S USA
22 I7 **Marksville** Louisiana, S USA
101 I19 **Marktheidenfeld** Bayern, C Germany
101 J24 **Marktoberdorf** Bayern, S Germany
101 M18 **Marktredwitz** Bayern, E Germany
Markt-Übelbach see Übelbach
27 V3 **Mark Twain Lake** ⊞ Missouri, C USA
Markuleshty see Mărculeşti
101 E14 **Marl** Nordrhein-Westfalen, W Germany
182 E2 **Marla** South Australia
181 Y8 **Marlborough** Queensland, E Australia
97 M22 **Marlborough** S England, UK
185 I15 **Marlborough** off. Marlborough District. ◈ unitary authority South Island, NZ
103 P3 **Marle** Aisne, N France
31 S8 **Marlette** Michigan, N USA
25 T9 **Marlin** Texas, SW USA
21 S5 **Marlinton** West Virginia, NE USA
26 M12 **Marlow** Oklahoma, C USA
155 E17 **Marmagao** Goa, W India
Marmanda see Marmande
102 L13 **Marmande** anc. Marmanda. Lot-et-Garonne, SW France
136 C11 **Marmara** Balıkesir, NW Turkey
136 D11 **Marmara Denizi** Eng. Sea of Marmara. sea NW Turkey
114 N13 **Marmaraereğlisi** Tekirdağ, NW Turkey
Marmara, Sea of see Marmara Denizi
136 C16 **Marmaris** Muğla, SW Turkey
28 J6 **Marmarth** North Dakota, N USA
21 Q5 **Marmet** West Virginia, NE USA
106 H5 **Marmolada, Monte** ▲ N Italy
104 M13 **Marmolejo** Andalucía, S Spain
14 J14 **Marmora** Ontario, SE Canada
39 Q14 **Marmot Bay** bay Alaska, USA
103 Q4 **Marne** ◈ department N France
103 Q4 **Marne** ≈ N France
137 U10 **Marneuli** prev. Borchalo, Sarvani. S Georgia
78 I13 **Maro** Moyen-Chari, S Chad
54 L12 **Maroa** Amazonas, S Venezuela
172 J3 **Maroantsetra** Toamasina, NE Madagascar
191 W11 **Marokau** atoll Îles Tuamotu, C French Polynesia
172 J5 **Marolambo** Toamasina, E Madagascar
172 J2 **Maromokotro** ▲ N Madagascar
83 L16 **Marondera** prev. Marandellas. Mashonaland East, NE Zimbabwe
55 X9 **Maroni** Dut. Marowijne. ≈ French Guiana/Surinam
183 V2 **Maroochydore-Mooloolaba** Queensland, E Australia
171 N14 **Maros** Sulawesi, C Indonesia
116 H11 **Maros** var. Mureş, Mureşul, Ger. Marosch, Mieresch. ≈ Hungary/Romania see also Mureş
Marosch see Maros/Mureş
Maroshévíz see Toplița
Marosillye see Ilia
Marosludas see Luduş
Marosújvár/Marosújvárakna see Ocna Mureş
Marosvásárhely see Târgu Mureş
191 V14 **Marotiri** var. Îlots de Bass, Morotiri. island group Îles Australes, SW French Polynesia
78 G12 **Maroua** Extrême-Nord, N Cameroon
55 X12 **Marouini Rivier** ≈ SE Surinam
172 I3 **Marovoay** Mahajanga, NW Madagascar
55 W9 **Marowijne** ◈ district NE Surinam
Marowijne see Maroni
Marqaköl see Markakol', Ozero
193 P8 **Marquesas Fracture Zone** tectonic feature E Pacific Ocean
Marquesas Islands see Marquises, Îles
23 W17 **Marquesas Keys** island group Florida, SE USA
29 Y12 **Marquette** Iowa, C USA
31 N3 **Marquette** Michigan, N USA
103 N1 **Marquise** Pas-de-Calais, N France
191 X7 **Marquises, Îles** Eng. Marquesas Islands. island group N French Polynesia
183 Q6 **Marra Creek** ≈ New South Wales, SE Australia
80 B10 **Marra Hills** plateau W Sudan
80 B11 **Marra, Jebel** ▲ W Sudan
74 E7 **Marrakech** var. Marakesh, Eng. Marrakesh; prev. Morocco. W Morocco
Marrakesh see Marrakech
Marrāt see Marāh
183 N15 **Marrawah** Tasmania, SE Australia
182 I4 **Marree** South Australia
81 L17 **Marrehan** ▲ SW Somalia
83 N17 **Marromeu** Sofala, C Mozambique
104 J17 **Marroquí, Punta** headland SW Spain
183 N8 **Marrowie Creek** seasonal river New South Wales, SE Australia
83 O14 **Marrupa** Niassa, N Mozambique
182 D1 **Marryat** South Australia
75 Y10 **Marsa 'Alam** SE Egypt
75 R8 **Marsá al Burayqah** var. Al Burayqah. N Libya
81 J17 **Marsabit** Eastern, N Kenya
107 H23 **Marsala** anc. Lilybaeum. Sicilia, Italy, C Mediterranean Sea
121 P16 **Marsaxlokk Bay** bay SE Malta
65 G15 **Mars Bay** bay Ascension Island, C Atlantic Ocean
101 H15 **Marsberg** Nordrhein-Westfalen, W Germany
11 R15 **Marsden** Saskatchewan, S Canada
98 H7 **Marsdiep** strait NW Netherlands
103 R16 **Marseille** Eng. Marseilles; anc. Massilia. Bouches-du-Rhône, SE France
Marseille-Marignane see Provence
30 M11 **Marseilles** Illinois, N USA
Marseilles see Marseille
76 J16 **Marshall** W Liberia
39 N11 **Marshall** Alaska, USA
27 U9 **Marshall** Arkansas, C USA
31 N14 **Marshall** Illinois, N USA
31 Q10 **Marshall** Michigan, N USA
29 S9 **Marshall** Minnesota, N USA
27 T4 **Marshall** Missouri, C USA
21 O9 **Marshall** North Carolina, SE USA
25 X6 **Marshall** Texas, SW USA
189 S4 **Marshall Islands** off. Republic of the Marshall Islands. ◆ republic W Pacific Ocean
175 Q3 **Marshall Islands** island group W Pacific Ocean
192 K6 **Marshall Seamounts** undersea feature SW Pacific Ocean
29 W13 **Marshalltown** Iowa, C USA
19 P12 **Marshfield** Massachusetts, NE USA
27 T7 **Marshfield** Missouri, C USA
30 K6 **Marshfield** Wisconsin, N USA
44 H1 **Marsh Harbour** Great Abaco, W Bahamas
19 S3 **Mars Hill** Maine, NE USA
21 P9 **Mars Hill** North Carolina, SE USA
22 H10 **Marsh Island** island Louisiana, S USA
21 S11 **Marshville** North Carolina, SE USA
15 W5 **Marsoui** Quebec, SE Canada
15 R8 **Mars, Rivière à** ≈ Quebec, SE Canada
95 O15 **Märsta** Stockholm, C Sweden
95 H24 **Marstal** Fyn, C Denmark
95 I19 **Marstrand** Västra Götaland, S Sweden
25 U8 **Mart** Texas, SW USA
166 M9 **Martaban** var. Moktama. Mon State, S Myanmar
166 L9 **Martaban, Gulf of** gulf S Myanmar
107 Q19 **Martano** Puglia, SE Italy
Martapoera see Martapura
169 T13 **Martapura** prev. Martapoera. Borneo, C Indonesia
99 L23 **Martelange** Luxembourg, SE Belgium
114 L7 **Marten** Ruse, N Bulgaria
14 H10 **Marten River** Ontario, S Canada
11 T15 **Martensville** Saskatchewan, S Canada
Marteskirch see Târnăveni
Martes Tolosane see Martres-Tolosane
115 K25 **Mártha** Kríti, Greece, E Mediterranean Sea
183 Q6 **Marthaguy Creek** ≈ New South Wales, SE Australia
19 P13 **Martha's Vineyard** island Massachusetts, NE USA
108 C11 **Martigny** Valais, SW Switzerland
103 R16 **Martigues** Bouches-du-Rhône, SE France
111 J19 **Martin** Ger. Sankt Martin, Hung. Turócszentmárton; prev. Turčianský Svätý Martin. Žilinský Kraj, N Slovakia
28 L11 **Martin** South Dakota, N USA
20 G8 **Martin** Tennessee, S USA
105 S7 **Martín** ≈ E Spain
107 P18 **Martina Franca** Puglia, SE Italy
185 M14 **Martinborough** Wellington, North Island, NZ
25 S11 **Martindale** Texas, SW USA
35 N8 **Martinez** California, W USA
23 V3 **Martinez** Georgia, SE USA
41 Q13 **Martínez de La Torre** Veracruz-Llave, E Mexico
45 Y12 **Martinique** ◇ French overseas department E West Indies
1 O15 **Martinique** island E West Indies
Martinique Channel see Martinique Passage
45 X12 **Martinique Passage** var. Dominica Channel, Martinique Channel. channel Dominica/Martinique
23 Q5 **Martin Lake** ⊞ Alabama, S USA
115 G18 **Martíno** prev. Martínon. Stereá Ellás, C Greece
Martínon see Martíno
194 J11 **Martin Peninsula** peninsula Antarctica
39 S5 **Martin Point** headland Alaska, USA
109 V3 **Martinsberg** Niederösterreich, NE Austria
21 V3 **Martinsburg** West Virginia, NE USA
31 V13 **Martins Ferry** Ohio, N USA
Martinskirch see Târnăveni
31 O14 **Martinsville** Indiana, N USA
21 S8 **Martinsville** Virginia, NE USA
65 K16 **Martin Vaz, Ilhas** island group E Brazil
Martök see Martuk
184 M12 **Marton** Manawatu-Wanganui, North Island, NZ
105 N13 **Martos** Andalucía, S Spain
102 M16 **Martres-Tolosane** var. Martes Tolosane. Haute-Garonne, S France
92 M11 **Martti** Lappi, NE Finland
144 I9 **Martuk** Kaz. Martök. Aktyubinsk, NW Kazakhstan
137 U12 **Martuni** E Armenia
58 L11 **Marudá** Pará, E Brazil
169 V6 **Marudu, Teluk** bay East Malaysia
149 O8 **Ma'rūf** Kandahār, SE Afghanistan
164 H13 **Marugame** Kagawa, Shikoku, SW Japan
185 H16 **Maruia** ≈ South Island, NZ
98 M6 **Marum** Groningen, NE Netherlands
187 R13 **Marum, Mount** ▲ Ambrym, C Vanuatu
79 P23 **Marungu** ▲ SE Dem. Rep. Congo (Zaire)
191 Y12 **Marutea** atoll Groupe Actéon, C French Polynesia
143 O11 **Marv Dasht** var. Mervdasht. Fārs, S Iran
103 P13 **Marvejols** Lozère, S France
27 X12 **Marvell** Arkansas, C USA
36 L6 **Marvine, Mount** ▲ Utah, W USA
139 Q7 **Marwānīyah** C Iraq
152 F13 **Mārwār** var. Marwar Junction. Rājasthān, N India
Marwar Junction see Mārwār
11 R14 **Marwayne** Alberta, SW Canada
146 I14 **Mary** prev. Merv. Maryyskiy Velayat, S Turkmenistan
Mary see Maryyskiy Velayat
181 Z9 **Maryborough** Queensland, E Australia
182 M11 **Maryborough** Victoria, SE Australia
Maryborough see Port Laoise
83 G23 **Marydale** Northern Cape, W South Africa
117 W8 **Mar"yinka** Donets'ka Oblast', E Ukraine
Mary Island see Kanton
21 W4 **Maryland** off. State of Maryland; also known as America in Miniature, Cockade State, Free State, Old Line State. ◈ state NE USA
25 P7 **Maryneal** Texas, SW USA
97 J15 **Maryport** NW England, UK
13 U13 **Marystown** Newfoundland, SE Canada
36 K6 **Marysvale** Utah, W USA
35 O6 **Marysville** California, W USA
27 O3 **Marysville** Kansas, C USA
31 S13 **Marysville** Michigan, N USA
31 S9 **Marysville** Ohio, NE USA
32 H7 **Marysville** Washington, NW USA
27 R2 **Maryville** Missouri, C USA
21 N9 **Maryville** Tennessee, S USA
Mary Welayaty see Maryyskiy Velayat
146 I15 **Maryyskiy Velayat** var. Mary, Turkm. Mary Welaýaty. ◈ province S Turkmenistan
Marzūq see Murzuq
42 J11 **Masachapa** var. Puerto Masachapa. Managua, W Nicaragua
81 G19 **Masai Mara National Reserve** reserve C Kenya
81 I21 **Masai Steppe** grassland NW Tanzania
81 F19 **Masaka** SW Uganda
169 T15 **Masalembo Besar, Pulau** island S Indonesia
137 Y13 **Masallı** Rus. Masally. S Azerbaijan
Masally see Masallı
171 N13 **Masamba** Sulawesi, C Indonesia
Masampo see Masan
163 Y16 **Masan** prev. Masampo. S South Korea
Masandam Peninsula see Musandam Peninsula
81 J25 **Masasi** Mtwara, SE Tanzania
Masawa see Massawa
42 J10 **Masaya** Masaya, W Nicaragua
42 J10 **Masaya** ◈ department W Nicaragua
171 P5 **Masbate** Masbate, N Philippines
171 P5 **Masbate** island C Philippines
74 I6 **Mascara** var. Mouaskar. NW Algeria
173 O7 **Mascarene Basin** undersea feature W Indian Ocean
173 O9 **Mascarene Islands** island group W Indian Ocean
173 N9 **Mascarene Plain** undersea feature W Indian Ocean
173 O7 **Mascarene Plateau** undersea feature W Indian Ocean
194 H5 **Mascart, Cape** headland Adelaide Island, Antarctica
62 J10 **Mascasín, Salinas de** salt lake C Argentina
40 K13 **Mascota** Jalisco, C Mexico
15 O12 **Mascouche** Quebec, SE Canada
126 J9 **Masel'gskaya** Respublika Kareliya, NW Russian Federation
83 J23 **Maseru** ● (Lesotho) W Lesotho
83 J23 **Maseru** × W Lesotho
Mashaba see Mashava
160 K14 **Mashan** Guangxi Zhuangzu Zizhiqu, S China
83 K17 **Mashava** prev. Mashaba. Masvingo, SE Zimbabwe
143 U4 **Mashhad** var. Meshed. Khorāsān, NE Iran
165 S3 **Mashike** Hokkaidō, NE Japan
Mashīz see Bardsīr
149 N14 **Mashkai** ≈ SW Pakistan
143 X13 **Māshkel** var. Rūd-i Māshkel, Rūd-e Māshkīd. ≈ Iran/Pakistan
148 K12 **Māshkel, Hāmūn-i** salt marsh SW Pakistan
Māshkel, Rūd-i/Māshkīd, Rūd-e see Māshkel
83 K15 **Mashonaland Central** ◈ province N Zimbabwe
83 K16 **Mashonaland East** ◈ province NE Zimbabwe
83 J16 **Mashonaland West** ◈ province NW Zimbabwe
Mashtagi see Maştağa
141 S14 **Masīlah, Wādī al** dry watercourse SE Yemen
79 I21 **Masi-Manimba** Bandundu, SW Dem. Rep. Congo (Zaire)
81 F17 **Masindi** W Uganda
81 I19 **Masinga Reservoir** ⊞ S Kenya
Masīra see Maşīrah, Jazīrat
Masira, Gulf of see Maşīrah, Khalīj
141 Y10 **Maşīrah, Jazīrat** var. Masīra. island E Oman
141 Y10 **Maşīrah, Khalīj** var. Gulf of Masira. bay E Oman
Masis see Büyükağrı Dağı
79 O19 **Masisi** Nord Kivu, E Dem. Rep. Congo (Zaire)
Masjed-e Soleymān see Masjed Soleymān
142 L9 **Masjed Soleymān** var. Masjed-e Soleymān, Masjid-i Sulaiman. Khūzestān, SW Iran
Masjid-i Sulaiman see Masjed Soleymān
Maskat see Masqaṭ
139 Q7 **Maskhān** C Iraq
141 X8 **Maskin** var. Miskin. NW Oman
97 B17 **Mask, Lough** Ir. Loch Measca. ◎ W Ireland
114 N10 **Maslen Nos** headland E Bulgaria
172 K3 **Masoala, Tanjona** headland NE Madagascar
Masohi see Amahai
31 Q9 **Mason** Michigan, N USA
31 R14 **Mason** Ohio, N USA
25 Q10 **Mason** Texas, SW USA
21 P4 **Mason** West Virginia, NE USA
185 B25 **Mason Bay** bay Stewart Island, NZ
30 K13 **Mason City** Illinois, N USA
29 V12 **Mason City** Iowa, C USA
Mā, Sông see Ma, Nam
18 B16 **Masontown** Pennsylvania, NE USA
141 Y8 **Masqaṭ** var. Maskat, Eng. Muscat. ● (Oman) NE Oman
106 E10 **Massa** Toscana, C Italy
18 M11 **Massachusetts** off. Commonwealth of Massachusetts; also known as Bay State, Old Bay State, Old Colony State. ◈ state NE USA
19 P11 **Massachusetts Bay** bay Massachusetts, NE USA
35 R2 **Massacre Lake** ◎ Nevada, W USA
107 O18 **Massafra** Puglia, SE Italy
108 G11 **Massagno** Ticino, S Switzerland
78 G11 **Massaguet** Chari-Baguirmi, W Chad
Massakori see Massakory
78 G10 **Massakory** var. Massakori; prev. Dagana. Chari-Baguirmi, W Chad
78 H11 **Massalassef** Chari-Baguirmi, SW Chad
106 F13 **Massa Marittima** Toscana, C Italy
82 B11 **Massangano** Cuanza Norte, NW Angola
83 M18 **Massangena** Gaza, S Mozambique
80 J9 **Massawa** var. Masawa, Amh. Mits'iwa. E Eritrea
80 K9 **Massawa Channel** channel E Eritrea
18 J6 **Massena** New York, NE USA
78 H11 **Massenya** Chari-Baguirmi, SW Chad
10 I13 **Masset** Graham Island, British Columbia, SW Canada
102 L16 **Masseube** Gers, S France
14 E11 **Massey** Ontario, S Canada
103 P12 **Massiac** Cantal, C France
103 P12 **Massif Central** plateau C France
Massilia see Marseille
31 U12 **Massillon** Ohio, N USA
77 N12 **Massina** Ségou, W Mali
83 N19 **Massinga** Inhambane, SE Mozambique
83 L20 **Massingir** Gaza, SW Mozambique
195 Z10 **Masson Island** island Antarctica
Massoukou see Franceville
137 Z11 **Maştağa** Rus. Mashtagi, Mastaga. E Azerbaijan
Mastanli see Momchilgrad
184 M13 **Masterton** Wellington, North Island, NZ
18 M14 **Mastic** Long Island, New York, NE USA
149 O10 **Mastung** Baluchistān, SW Pakistan
119 J20 **Mastva** Rus. Mostva. ≈ SW Belarus
119 G17 **Masty** Rus. Mosty. Hrodzyenskaya Voblasts', W Belarus
164 F12 **Masuda** Shimane, Honshū, SW Japan
92 J11 **Masugnsbyn** Norrbotten, N Sweden
Masuku see Franceville
83 K17 **Masvingo** prev. Fort Victoria, Nyanda, Victoria. Masvingo, SE Zimbabwe
83 K18 **Masvingo** prev. Victoria. ◈ province SE Zimbabwe
138 H5 **Maşyāf** Fr. Misiaf. Ḩamāh, C Syria
Masyû Ko see Mashū-ko
110 E9 **Maszewo** Zachodniopomorskie, NW Poland
83 I17 **Matabeleland North** ◈ province W Zimbabwe
83 J18 **Matabeleland South** ◈ province S Zimbabwe
82 O13 **Mataca** Niassa, N Mozambique
14 G8 **Matachewan** Ontario, S Canada
79 F22 **Matadi** Bas-Congo, W Dem. Rep. Congo (Zaire)
25 O4 **Matador** Texas, SW USA
42 J9 **Matagalpa** Matagalpa, C Nicaragua
42 K9 **Matagalpa** ◈ department W Nicaragua
12 I12 **Matagami** Quebec, S Canada
25 U13 **Matagorda** Texas, SW USA
25 U13 **Matagorda Bay** inlet Texas, SW USA
25 U14 **Matagorda Island** island Texas, SW USA
25 V13 **Matagorda Peninsula** headland Texas, SW USA
191 Q8 **Mataiea** Tahiti, W French Polynesia
191 T9 **Mataiva** atoll Îles Tuamotu, C French Polynesia
183 O7 **Matakana** New South Wales, SE Australia
184 N7 **Matakana Island** island NE NZ
83 C15 **Matala** Huíla, SW Angola
190 G12 **Matala'a Pointe** headland Île Uvea, N Wallis and Futuna
155 K25 **Matale** Central Province, C Sri Lanka
190 E12 **Matalelesina, Pointe** headland Île Alofi, W Wallis and Futuna
76 I10 **Matam** NE Senegal
184 M8 **Matamata** Waikato, North Island, NZ
77 V12 **Matamey** Zinder, S Niger
40 L8 **Matamoros** Coahuila de Zaragoza, NE Mexico
41 P15 **Matamoros** var. Izúcar de Matamoros. Puebla, S Mexico
41 Q8 **Matamoros** Tamaulipas, C Mexico
75 S13 **Ma'ṭan as Sārah** SE Libya
82 J12 **Matanda** Luapula, N Zambia
81 J24 **Matandu** ≈ S Tanzania
15 V6 **Matane** Quebec, SE Canada
15 V6 **Matane** ≈ Quebec, SE Canada
77 S12 **Matankari** Dosso, SW Niger
39 R11 **Matanuska River** ≈ Alaska, USA
54 G7 **Matanza** Santander, N Colombia
44 D4 **Matanzas** Matanzas, NW Cuba
15 V7 **Matapédia** ≈ Quebec, SE Canada
15 V6 **Matapédia, Lac** ◎ Quebec, SE Canada
190 B17 **Mata Point** headland SE Niue
190 D12 **Matapu, Pointe** headland Île Futuna, W Wallis and Futuna
62 G12 **Mataquito, Río** ≈ C Chile
155 K26 **Matara** Southern Province, S Sri Lanka
115 D18 **Matarágka** var. Mataránga. Dytikí Ellás, C Greece
170 K16 **Mataram** Pulau Lombok, C Indonesia
Mataránga see Matarágka
181 Q3 **Mataranka** Northern Territory, N Australia
105 W6 **Mataró** anc. Illuro. Cataluña, E Spain
184 O8 **Matata** Bay of Plenty, North Island, NZ
192 K16 **Matātula, Cape** headland Tutuila, W American Samoa
185 D24 **Mataura** Southland, South Island, NZ
185 D24 **Mataura** ≈ South Island, NZ
Mata Uta see Matā'utu
190 G11 **Matā'utu** var. Mata Uta. ○ (Wallis and Futuna) Île Uvea, Wallis and Futuna
192 H16 **Matāutu** Upolu, C Samoa
190 G12 **Matā'utu, Baie de** bay Île Uvea, Wallis and Futuna
191 P7 **Matavai, Baie de** bay Tahiti, W French Polynesia
190 I16 **Matavera** Rarotonga, S Cook Islands
191 V16 **Mataveri** Easter Island, Chile, E Pacific Ocean
191 V17 **Mataveri** × (Easter Island) Easter Island, Chile, E Pacific Ocean
184 P9 **Matawai** Gisborne, North Island, NZ
15 O10 **Matawin** ≈ Quebec, SE Canada
145 V13 **Matay** Almaty, SE Kazakhstan
14 K8 **Matchi-Manitou, Lac** ◎ Quebec, SE Canada
41 O10 **Matehuala** San Luis Potosí, C Mexico
45 V13 **Matelot** Trinidad, Trinidad and Tobago
83 M15 **Matenge** Tete, NW Mozambique
107 O18 **Matera** Basilicata, S Italy
111 O21 **Mátészalka** Szabolcs-Szatmár-Bereg, E Hungary
93 H17 **Matfors** Västernorrland, C Sweden
102 K11 **Matha** Charente-Maritime, W France
(0) F15 **Mathematicians Seamounts** undersea feature E Pacific Ocean
21 X6 **Mathews** Virginia, NE USA
25 S14 **Mathis** Texas, SW USA
152 J11 **Mathura** prev. Muttra. Uttar Pradesh, N India
Mathurai see Madurai
171 R7 **Mati** Mindanao, S Philippines
Matianus see Orūmīyeh, Daryācheh-ye
Matiara see Matiāri
149 Q15 **Matiāri** var. Matiara. Sind, SE Pakistan
41 S16 **Matías Romero** Oaxaca, SE Mexico
43 O13 **Matina** Limón, E Costa Rica
14 D10 **Matinenda Lake** ◎ Ontario, S Canada
19 R8 **Matinicus Island** island Maine, NE USA
Matisco/Matisco Ædourum see Mâcon
149 Q16 **Mātli** Sind, SE Pakistan
97 M18 **Matlock** C England, UK
59 F18 **Mato Grosso** prev. Vila Bela da Santissima Trindade. Mato Grosso, W Brazil
59 G17 **Mato Grosso** off. Estado de Mato Grosso; prev. Matto Grosso. ◈ state W Brazil
60 H8 **Mato Grosso do Sul** off. Estado de Mato Grosso do Sul. ◈ state S Brazil
59 I18 **Mato Grosso, Planalto de** plateau C Brazil
104 G6 **Matosinhos** prev. Matozinhos. Porto, NW Portugal
55 Z10 **Matoury** NE French Guiana
Matozinhos see Matosinhos
111 L21 **Mátra** ▲ N Hungary
141 Y8 **Maṭraḩ** var. Mutrah. NE Oman
116 L12 **Mătrașești** Vrancea, E Romania
108 M8 **Matrei Am Brenner** Tirol, W Austria
109 P8 **Matrei in Osttirol** Tirol, W Austria
76 I15 **Matru** SW Sierra Leone
75 U7 **Maṭrūḩ** var. Mersa Maṭrûḩ; anc. Paraetonium. NW Egypt
165 U16 **Matsubara** var. Matubara. Kagoshima, Tokuno-shima, SW Japan
164 G12 **Matsue** var. Matsuye, Matue. Shimane, Honshū, SW Japan
165 Q6 **Matsumae** Hokkaidō, NE Japan
164 M12 **Matsumoto** var. Matumoto. Nagano, Honshū, S Japan
164 K14 **Matsusaka** var. Matsuzaka, Matusaka. Mie, Honshū, SW Japan
161 S12 **Matsu Tao** Chin. Mazu Dao. island NW Taiwan
Matsutō see Mattō
164 F14 **Matsuyama** var. Matuyama. Ehime, Shikoku, SW Japan
Matsuye see Matsue
Matsuzaka see Matsusaka
164 M14 **Matsuzaki** Shizuoka, Honshū, S Japan
14 F8 **Mattagami** ≈ Ontario, S Canada
14 F8 **Mattagami Lake** ◎ Ontario, S Canada
62 K12 **Mattaldi** Córdoba, C Argentina
21 Y9 **Mattamuskeet, Lake** ◎ North Carolina, SE USA
21 W6 **Mattaponi River** ≈ Virginia, NE USA
14 I11 **Mattawa** Ontario, SE Canada
14 I11 **Mattawa** ≈ Ontario, SE Canada
19 S5 **Mattawamkeag** Maine, NE USA
19 S4 **Mattawamkeag Lake** ◎ Maine, NE USA

◆ Country ● Country Capital ◇ Dependent Territory ○ Dependent Territory Capital ◈ Administrative Region × International Airport ▲ Mountain ▲ Mountain Range Volcano ≈ River ◎ Lake ⊞ Reservoir

108 D11 Matterhorn It. Monte Cervino. ▲ Italy/Switzerland see also Cervino, Monte
35 W1 Matterhorn ▲ Nevada, W USA
32 L12 Matterhorn var. Sacajawea Peak. ▲ Oregon, NW USA
35 R8 Matterhorn Peak ▲ California, W USA
109 Y5 Mattersburg Burgenland, E Austria
108 E11 Matter Vispa ≈ S Switzerland
55 R7 Matthews Ridge N Guyana
44 K7 Matthew Town Great Inagua, S Bahamas
109 Q4 Mattighofen Oberösterreich, NW Austria
107 N16 Mattinata Puglia, SE Italy
141 T9 Maṭṭī, Sabkhat salt flat Saudi Arabia/UAE
18 M14 Mattituck Long Island, New York, NE USA
164 L11 Mattō var. Matsutō. Ishikawa, Honshū, SW Japan
Matto Grosso see Mato Grosso
30 M14 Mattoon Illinois, N USA
57 L16 Mattos, Río ≈ C Bolivia
Mattu see Metu
169 R9 Matu Sarawak, East Malaysia
57 E14 Matucana Lima, W Peru
Matudo see Matsudo
Matue see Matsue
187 Y15 Matuku island S Fiji
112 B9 Matulji Primorje-Gorski Kotar, NW Croatia
Matumoto see Matsumoto
55 P5 Maturín Monagas, NE Venezuela
Matusaka see Matsusaka
Matuura see Matsuura
Matuyama see Matsuyama
128 K11 Matveyev Kurgan Rostovskaya Oblast', SW Russian Federation
129 O8 Matyshevo Volgogradskaya Oblast', SW Russian Federation
153 O13 Mau var. Maunāth Bhanjan. Uttar Pradesh, N India
83 O14 Maúa Niassa, N Mozambique
102 M17 Maubermé, Pic de var. Tuc de Moubermé, Sp. Pico Mauberme; prev. Tuc de Maubermé. ▲ France/Spain see also Moubermé, Tuc de
Mauberme, Pico see Maubermé, Pic de/Moubermé, Tuc de
Maubermé, Tuc de see Maubermé, Pic de/Moubermé, Tuc de
103 Q2 Maubeuge Nord, N France
166 L8 Maubin Irrawaddy, SW Myanmar
152 L13 Maudaha Uttar Pradesh, N India
183 N9 Maude New South Wales, SE Australia
195 P3 Maudheimvidda physical region Antarctica
65 N22 Maud Rise undersea feature S Atlantic Ocean
109 Q4 Mauerkirchen Oberösterreich, NW Austria
Mauersee see Mamry, Jezioro
188 K2 Maug Islands island group N Northern Mariana Islands
103 Q15 Mauguio Hérault, S France
193 N5 Maui island Hawaii, USA, C Pacific Ocean
190 M16 Mauke atoll S Cook Islands
62 G13 Maule off. Región del Maule. ◐ region C Chile
102 J9 Mauléon Deux-Sèvres, W France
102 J16 Mauléon-Licharre Pyrénées-Atlantiques, SW France
62 G13 Maule, Río ≈ C Chile
63 G17 Maullín Los Lagos, S Chile
Maulmain see Moulmein
31 R11 Maumee Ohio, N USA
31 Q12 Maumee River ≈ Indiana/Ohio, N USA
27 U11 Maumelle Arkansas, C USA
27 T11 Maumelle, Lake ▣ Arkansas, C USA
171 O16 Maumere prev. Maoemere. Flores, S Indonesia
83 G17 Maun Ngamiland, C Botswana
Maunāth Bhanjan see Mau
Maunawai see Waimea
190 H16 Maungaroa ▲ Rarotonga, S Cook Islands
184 K3 Maungatapere Northland, North Island, NZ
184 K4 Maungaturoto Northland, North Island, NZ
191 R10 Maupiti var. Maurua. island Îles Sous le Vent, W French Polynesia
152 K14 Mau Rānīpur Uttar Pradesh, N India
22 K9 Maurepas, Lake ◎ Louisiana, S USA
103 T16 Maures ▲▲ SE France
103 O12 Mauriac Cantal, C France
Maurice see Mauritius
65 J20 Maurice Ewing Bank undersea feature SW Atlantic Ocean
182 C4 Maurice, Lake salt lake South Australia
18 I17 Maurice River ≈ New Jersey, NE USA
25 Y10 Mauriceville Texas, SW USA
98 K12 Maurik Gelderland, C Netherlands
76 H8 Mauritania off. Islamic Republic of Mauritania, Ar. Mūrītānīyah. ◆ republic W Africa
173 W15 Mauritius off. Republic of Mauritius, Fr. Maurice. ◆ republic W Indian Ocean
130 M17 Mauritius island W Indian Ocean
173 N9 Mauritius Trench undersea feature W Indian Ocean
102 H6 Mauron Morbihan, NW France
103 N13 Maurs Cantal, C France
Maurua see Maupiti
Maury Mid-Ocean Channel see Maury Seachannel
64 L6 Maury Seachannel var. Maury Mid-Ocean Channel. undersea feature N Atlantic Ocean
30 K8 Mauston Wisconsin, N USA
109 R8 Mauterndorf Salzburg, NW Austria
109 T4 Mauthausen Oberösterreich, N Austria
109 Q9 Mauthen Kärnten, S Austria
83 F15 Mavinga Cuando Cubango, SE Angola
83 M17 Mavita Manica, W Mozambique
115 K22 Mavrópetra, Akrotírio headland Thíra, Kykládes, Greece, Aegean Sea
115 F16 Mavrovoúni ▲ C Greece
184 Q8 Mawhai Point headland North Island, NZ
166 L3 Mawlaik Sagaing, C Myanmar
Mawlamyine see Moulmein
141 N14 Mawr, Wādī dry watercourse NW Yemen
195 X5 Mawson Australian research station Antarctica
195 X5 Mawson Coast physical region Antarctica
28 M4 Max North Dakota, N USA
41 W12 Maxcanú Yucatán, SE Mexico
Maxesibebi see Mount Ayliff
109 Q5 Maxglan × (Salzburg) Salzburg, W Austria
93 K16 Maxmo Fin. Maksamaa. Länsi-Suomi, W Finland
21 T11 Maxton North Carolina, SE USA
25 R8 May Texas, SW USA
186 B6 May ≈ NW PNG
123 R10 Maya ≈ E Russian Federation
151 Q19 Māyābandar Andaman and Nicobar Islands, India, E Indian Ocean
Mayadin see Al Mayādīn
44 L5 Mayaguana island SE Bahamas
44 L5 Mayaguana Passage passage SE Bahamas
45 S6 Mayagüez W Puerto Rico
45 R6 Mayagüez, Bahía de bay W Puerto Rico
Mayals see Maials
79 G20 Mayama Le Pool, SE Congo
37 V8 Maya, Mesa De ▲ Colorado, C USA
143 R4 Mayamey Semnān, N Iran
42 F3 Maya Mountains Sp. Montañas Mayas. ▲▲ Belize/Guatemala
44 I7 Mayarí Holguín, E Cuba
Mayas, Montañas see Maya Mountains
18 I17 May, Cape headland New Jersey, NE USA
80 J11 Maych'ew var. Mai Chio, It. Mai Ceu. Tigray, N Ethiopia
138 I2 Maydān Ikbiz Ḩalab, N Syria
149 Q5 Maydān Shahr Wardag, E Afghanistan
80 O12 Maydh Sanaag, N Somalia
Maydī see Midī
Mayebashi see Maebashi
Mayence see Mainz
102 K6 Mayenne Mayenne, NW France
102 J6 Mayenne ◐ department NW France
102 J7 Mayenne ≈ N France
36 K12 Mayer Arizona, SW USA
22 J4 Mayersville Mississippi, S USA
11 P14 Mayerthorpe Alberta, SW Canada
21 S12 Mayesville South Carolina, SE USA
185 G19 Mayfield Canterbury, South Island, NZ
33 N14 Mayfield Idaho, NW USA
20 G7 Mayfield Kentucky, S USA
36 L5 Mayfield Utah, W USA
162 K9 Mayhan Övörhangay, C Mongolia
37 T14 Mayhill New Mexico, SW USA
145 T9 Maykain Kaz. Mayqayyng. Pavlodar, NE Kazakhstan
128 L14 Maykop Respublika Adygeya, SW Russian Federation
Maylibash see Maylybas
Mayli-Say see Mayluu-Suu
147 T9 Mayluu-Suu prev. Mayli-Say, Kir. Mayly-Say. Dzhalal-Abadskaya Oblast', W Kyrgyzstan
144 L14 Maylybas prev. Maylibash. Kzylorda, S Kazakhstan
Mayly-Say see Mayluu-Suu
Maymana see Meymaneh
166 M5 Maymyo Mandalay, C Myanmar
123 V7 Mayn ≈ NE Russian Federation
129 Q5 Mayna Ul'yanovskaya Oblast', W Russian Federation
21 N8 Maynardville Tennessee, S USA
14 J13 Maynooth Ontario, SE Canada
10 I6 Mayo Yukon Territory, NW Canada
23 U9 Mayo Florida, SE USA
97 B16 Mayo Ir. Maigh Eo. cultural region W Ireland
Mayo see Maio
78 G12 Mayo-Kébbi off. Préfecture du Mayo-Kébbu, var. Mayo-Kébi. ◐ prefecture SW Chad
Mayo-Kébi see Mayo-Kébbi
79 F19 Mayoko Le Niari, SW Congo
171 P4 Mayon Volcano ※ Luzon, N Philippines
61 A24 Mayor Buratovich Buenos Aires, E Argentina
104 L4 Mayorga Castilla-León, N Spain
184 N6 Mayor Island island NE NZ
Mayor Pablo Lagerenza see Capitán Pablo Lagerenza
173 I14 Mayotte ◇ French territorial collectivity E Africa
Mayoumba see Mayumba
44 J13 May Pen C Jamaica
Mayqayyng see Maykain
171 O1 Mayraira Point headland Luzon, N Philippines
109 N8 Mayrhofen Tirol, W Austria
186 A6 May River East Sepik, NW PNG
123 R13 Mayskiy Amurskaya Oblast', SE Russian Federation
129 O15 Mayskiy Kabardino-Balkarskaya Respublika, SW Russian Federation
145 U9 Mayskoye Pavlodar, NE Kazakhstan
18 J17 Mays Landing New Jersey, NE USA
21 N4 Maysville Kentucky, S USA
27 R2 Maysville Missouri, C USA
79 D20 Mayumba var. Mayoumba. Nyanga, S Gabon
31 S8 Mayville Michigan, N USA
18 C11 Mayville New York, NE USA
29 Q4 Mayville North Dakota, N USA
Mayyali see Mahe
Mayyit, Al Baḩr al see Dead Sea
83 J15 Mazabuka Southern, S Zambia
Mazaca see Kayseri
Mazagan see El-Jadida
32 J7 Mazama Washington, NW USA
103 O15 Mazamet Tarn, S France
143 O4 Māzandarān off. Ostān-e Māzandarān. ◐ province N Iran
156 F7 Mazar Xinjiang Uygur Zizhiqu, NW China
107 H24 Mazara del Vallo Sicilia, Italy, C Mediterranean Sea
149 O2 Mazār-e Sharīf var. Mazār-i Sharif. Balkh, N Afghanistan
Mazār-i Sharif see Mazār-e Sharīf
105 R13 Mazarrón Murcia, SE Spain
105 R14 Mazarrón, Golfo de gulf SE Spain
55 S9 Mazaruni River ≈ N Guyana
42 B6 Mazatenango Suchitepéquez, SW Guatemala
40 I10 Mazatlán Sinaloa, C Mexico
36 L12 Mazatzal Mountains ▲▲ Arizona, SW USA
118 D10 Mažeikiai Mažeikiai, NW Lithuania
118 D7 Mazirbe Talsi, NW Latvia
40 G5 Mazocahui Sonora, NW Mexico
57 I18 Mazocruz Puno, S Peru
Mazoe, Rio see Mazowe
79 N21 Mazomeno Maniema, E Dem. Rep. Congo (Zaire)
159 Q6 Mazong Shan ▲ N China
83 L16 Mazowe var. Rio Mazoe. ≈ Mozambique/Zimbabwe
110 L11 Mazowieckie ◐ province C Poland
Mazra'a see Al Mazra'ah
138 G6 Mazraat Kfar Debiâne C Lebanon
118 H7 Mazsalaca Est. Väike-Salatsi, Ger. Salisburg. Valmiera, N Latvia
110 L9 Mazury physical region NE Poland
119 M20 Mazyr Rus. Mozyr'. Homyel'skaya Voblasts', SE Belarus
107 K25 Mazzarino Sicilia, Italy, C Mediterranean Sea
Mba see Ba
83 L21 Mbabane ● (Swaziland) NW Swaziland
Mbacké see Mbaké
77 N16 Mbahiakro E Ivory Coast
79 I16 Mbaïki var. M'Baiki. Lobaye, SW Central African Republic
79 F14 Mbakaou, Lac de ◎ C Cameroon
76 G11 Mbaké var. Mbacké. W Senegal
82 L11 Mbala prev. Abercorn. Northern, NE Zambia
83 J18 Mbalabala prev. Balla Balla. Matabeleland South, SW Zimbabwe
81 G18 Mbale E Uganda
79 E16 Mbalmayo var. M'Balmayo. Centre, S Cameroon
81 H25 Mbamba Bay Ruvuma, S Tanzania
79 I18 Mbandaka prev. Coquilhatville. Equateur, NW Dem. Rep. Congo (Zaire)
82 B9 M'Banza Congo var. Mbanza Congo; prev. São Salvador, São Salvador do Congo. Zaire, NW Angola
79 G21 Mbanza-Ngungu Bas-Congo, W Dem. Rep. Congo (Zaire)
67 V11 Mbarangandu ≈ E Tanzania
81 E19 Mbarara SW Uganda
79 L15 Mbari ≈ SE Central African Republic
81 I24 Mbarika Mountains ▲▲ S Tanzania
83 J24 Mbashe ≈ S South Africa
Mbatiki see Batiki
78 F13 Mbé Nord, N Cameroon
81 J24 Mbemkuru var. Mbwemkuru. ≈ S Tanzania
Mbengga see Beqa
172 H13 Mbéni Grande Comore, NW Comoros
83 K18 Mberengwa Midlands, S Zimbabwe
81 G24 Mbeya Mbeya, SW Tanzania
81 G23 Mbeya ◐ region S Tanzania
79 E19 Mbigou Ngounié, C Gabon
Mbilua see Vella Lavella
79 F19 Mbinda Le Niari, SW Congo
79 D17 Mbini W Equatorial Guinea
Mbini see Uolo, Río
83 L18 Mbizi Masvingo, SE Zimbabwe
81 G23 Mbogo Mbeya, W Tanzania
79 N15 Mboki Haut-Mbomou, SE Central African Republic
79 G18 Mbomo Cuvette, NW Congo
79 L15 Mbomou ◐ prefecture SE Central African Republic
Mbomou/M'Bomu/Mbomu see Bomu
76 F11 Mbour W Senegal
76 I10 Mbout Gorgol, S Mauritania
79 J14 Mbrès var. Mbrés. Nana-Grébizi, C Central African Republic
79 L22 Mbuji-Mayi prev. Bakwanga. Kasai Oriental, S Dem. Rep. Congo (Zaire)
81 H21 Mbulu Arusha, N Tanzania
186 E5 M'bunai var. Bunai. Manus Island, N PNG
62 N8 Mburucuyá Corrientes, NE Argentina
Mbutha see Buca
Mbwemkuru see Mbemkuru
81 G21 Mbwikwe Singida, C Tanzania
13 O15 McAdam New Brunswick, SE Canada
25 O5 McAdoo Texas, SW USA
35 V2 McAfee Peak ▲ Nevada, W USA
27 P11 McAlester Oklahoma, C USA
25 S17 McAllen Texas, SW USA
21 S11 McBee South Carolina, SE USA
11 N14 McBride British Columbia, SW Canada
24 M9 McCamey Texas, SW USA
33 R15 McCammon Idaho, NW USA
35 X11 McCarran × (Las Vegas) Nevada, W USA
39 T11 McCarthy Alaska, USA
30 M5 McCaslin Mountain hill Wisconsin, N USA
25 O2 McClellan Creek ≈ Texas, SW USA
21 T14 McClellanville South Carolina, SE USA
8 L6 McClintock Channel channel Nunavut, N Canada
195 R12 McClintock, Mount ▲ Antarctica
35 N2 McCloud California, W USA
35 N3 McCloud River ≈ California, W USA
35 Q9 McClure, Lake ▣ California, W USA
197 O8 McClure Strait strait Northwest Territories, N Canada
29 N4 McClusky North Dakota, N USA
21 T11 McColl South Carolina, SE USA
22 K7 McComb Mississippi, S USA
18 E16 McConnellsburg Pennsylvania, NE USA
31 T14 McConnelsville Ohio, N USA
28 M17 McCook Nebraska, C USA
21 P13 McCormick South Carolina, SE USA
11 W16 McCreary Manitoba, S Canada
27 W11 McCrory Arkansas, C USA
25 T10 McDade Texas, SW USA
23 O8 McDavid Florida, SE USA
35 T1 McDermitt Nevada, W USA
23 S4 McDonough Georgia, SE USA
36 L12 McDowell Mountains ▲▲ Arizona, SW USA
20 H8 McEwen Tennessee, S USA
35 R12 McFarland California, W USA
Mcfarlane, Lake see Macfarlane, Lake
27 P12 McGee Creek Lake ▣ Oklahoma, C USA
27 W13 McGehee Arkansas, C USA
35 X5 Mcgill Nevada, W USA
14 K11 McGillivray, Lac ◎ Quebec, SE Canada
39 P10 Mcgrath Alaska, USA
25 T8 McGregor Texas, SW USA
33 O12 McGuire, Mount ▲ Idaho, NW USA
83 M14 Mchinji prev. Fort Manning. Central, W Malawi
28 M7 McIntosh South Dakota, N USA
9 S7 McKeand ≈ Baffin Island, Nunavut, NE Canada
191 R4 McKean Island island Phoenix Islands, C Kiribati
30 J13 McKee Creek ≈ Illinois, N USA
18 C15 Mckeesport Pennsylvania, NE USA
21 V7 McKenney Virginia, NE USA
20 G8 McKenzie Tennessee, S USA
185 B20 McKerrow, Lake ◎ South Island, NZ
39 Q10 McKinley, Mount var. Denali. ▲ Alaska, USA
39 R10 McKinley Park Alaska, USA
34 K3 McKinleyville California, W USA
25 U6 McKinney Texas, SW USA
26 I5 McKinney, Lake ◎ Kansas, C USA
28 M7 McLaughlin South Dakota, N USA
25 O2 McLean Texas, SW USA
30 M16 Mcleansboro Illinois, N USA
11 O13 McLennan Alberta, W Canada
14 L9 McLennan, Lac ◎ Quebec, SE Canada
10 M13 McLeod Lake British Columbia, W Canada
27 N10 McLoud Oklahoma, C USA
32 G15 McLoughlin, Mount ▲ Oregon, NW USA
8 J4 M'Clure Strait strait NW Canada
37 U15 McMillan, Lake ▣ New Mexico, SW USA
32 G11 McMinnville Oregon, NW USA
20 K9 McMinnville Tennessee, S USA
195 R13 McMurdo US research station Antarctica
24 H9 McNary Texas, SW USA
37 N13 Mcnary Arizona, SW USA
27 N5 McPherson Kansas, C USA
McPherson see Fort McPherson
23 U6 McRae Georgia, SE USA
29 P4 McVille North Dakota, N USA
83 J25 Mdantsane Eastern Cape, SE South Africa
167 T6 Me Ninh Binh, N Vietnam
26 J7 Meade Kansas, C USA
39 O5 Meade River ≈ Alaska, USA
35 Y11 Mead, Lake ▣ Arizona/Nevada, W USA
24 M5 Meadow Texas, SW USA
11 S14 Meadow Lake Saskatchewan, C Canada
35 Y10 Meadow Valley Wash ≈ Nevada, W USA
22 J7 Meadville Mississippi, S USA
18 B12 Meadville Pennsylvania, NE USA
14 F14 Meaford Ontario, S Canada
Meáin, Inis see Inishmaan
104 G8 Mealhada Aveiro, N Portugal
13 R8 Mealy Mountains ▲▲ Newfoundland, E Canada
11 O10 Meander River Alberta, W Canada
32 E11 Meares, Cape headland Oregon, NW USA
47 V6 Mearim, Rio ≈ NE Brazil
Measca, Loch see Mask, Lough
97 F17 Meath Ir. An Mhí. cultural region E Ireland
11 T14 Meath Park Saskatchewan, S Canada
103 O5 Meaux Seine-et-Marne, N France
21 T9 Mebane North Carolina, SE USA
171 U12 Mebo, Gunung ▲ Irian Jaya, E Indonesia
94 I8 Mebonden Sør-Trøndelag, S Norway
82 A10 Mebridege ≈ NW Angola
35 W16 Mecca California, W USA
Mecca see Makkah
29 Y14 Mechanicsville Iowa, C USA
18 L10 Mechanicville New York, NE USA
99 H17 Mechelen Eng. Mechlin, Fr. Malines. Antwerpen, C Belgium
188 C8 Mecherchar var. Eil Malk. island Palau Islands, Palau
101 D17 Mechernich Nordrhein-Westfalen, W Germany
128 L12 Mechetinskaya Rostovskaya Oblast', SW Russian Federation
114 J11 Mechka ≈ S Bulgaria
Mechlin see Mechelen
61 D23 Mechongué Buenos Aires, E Argentina
115 L14 Mecidiye Edirne, NW Turkey
101 I24 Meckenbeuren Baden-Württemberg, S Germany
100 L8 Mecklenburger Bucht bay N Germany
100 M10 Mecklenburgische Seenplatte wetland NE Germany
100 L9 Mecklenburg-Vorpommern ◐ state NE Germany
83 Q15 Meconta Nampula, NE Mozambique
111 I25 Mecsek ▲▲ SW Hungary
83 P14 Mecubúri ≈ N Mozambique
83 Q14 Mecúfi Cabo Delgado, NE Mozambique
82 O13 Mecula Niassa, N Mozambique
168 I8 Medan Sumatera, E Indonesia
61 A24 Médanos var. Medanos. Buenos Aires, E Argentina
61 C19 Médanos Entre Ríos, E Argentina
155 K24 Medawachchiya North Central Province, N Sri Lanka
106 C8 Mede Lombardia, N Italy
74 J5 Médéa var. El Mediyya, Lemdiyya. N Algeria
Medeba see Ma'dabā
54 E8 Medellín Antioquia, NW Colombia
100 H9 Medem ≈ NW Germany
98 J8 Medemblik Noord-Holland, NW Netherlands
75 N7 Médenine var. Madanīyīn. SE Tunisia
76 G9 Mederdra Trarza, SW Mauritania
Medeshamstede see Peterborough
42 F4 Medesto Mendez Izabal, NE Guatemala
19 O11 Medford Massachusetts, NE USA
27 N8 Medford Oklahoma, C USA
32 G15 Medford Oregon, NW USA
30 K6 Medford Wisconsin, N USA
39 P10 Medfra Alaska, USA
116 M14 Medgidia Constanța, SE Romania
Medgyes see Mediaş
43 O5 Media Luna, Arrecifes de la reef E Honduras
60 G11 Medianeira Paraná, S Brazil
29 Y15 Mediapolis Iowa, C USA
116 I11 Mediaş Ger. Mediasch, Hung. Medgyes. Sibiu, C Romania
41 S15 Medias Aguas Veracruz-Llave, SE Mexico
Mediasch see Mediaş
106 G10 Medicina Emilia-Romagna, C Italy
33 X16 Medicine Bow Wyoming, C USA
37 S2 Medicine Bow Mountains ▲▲ Colorado/Wyoming, C USA
33 X16 Medicine Bow River ≈ Wyoming, C USA
11 R17 Medicine Hat Alberta, SW Canada
26 L7 Medicine Lodge Kansas, C USA
26 L7 Medicine Lodge River ≈ Kansas/Oklahoma, C USA
112 E7 Međimurje off. Međimurska Županija. ◐ province N Croatia
Međimurska Županija see Međimurje
54 G10 Medina Cundinamarca, C Colombia
18 E9 Medina New York, NE USA
29 O5 Medina North Dakota, N USA
31 T11 Medina Ohio, N USA
25 Q11 Medina Texas, SW USA
Medina see Al Madīnah
105 P6 Medinaceli Castilla-León, N Spain
104 L6 Medina del Campo Castilla-León, N Spain
104 L5 Medina de Ríoseco Castilla-León, N Spain
Médina Gonassé see Médina Gounas
76 H12 Médina Gounas var. Médina Gonassé. S Senegal
25 S12 Medina River ≈ Texas, SW USA
104 K16 Medina Sidonia Andalucía, S Spain
Medinat Israel see Israel
119 H14 Medininkai Vilnius, SE Lithuania
153 R16 Medinīpur West Bengal, NE India
Mediolanum see Saintes, France
Mediolanum see Milano, Italy
Mediomatrica see Metz
121 Q11 Mediterranean Ridge undersea feature C Mediterranean Sea
121 O16 Mediterranean Sea Fr. Mer Méditerranée. sea Africa/Asia/Europe
Méditerranée, Mer see Mediterranean Sea
79 N17 Medje Orientale, NE Dem. Rep. Congo (Zaire)
114 G7 Medkovets Montana, NW Bulgaria
93 J15 Medle Västerbotten, N Sweden
129 W7 Mednogorsk Orenburgskaya Oblast', W Russian Federation
123 W9 Mednyy, Ostrov island E Russian Federation
102 J12 Médoc cultural region SW France
159 Q16 Mêdog Xizang Zizhiqu, W China
28 J5 Medora North Dakota, N USA
79 E17 Médouneu Woleu-Ntem, N Gabon
106 I7 Meduna ≈ NE Italy
Medunta see Mantes-la-Jolie
Medvedica see Medveditsa
126 J16 Medveditsa var. Medvedica. ≈ W Russian Federation
129 O9 Medveditsa ≈ SW Russian Federation
112 E8 Medvednica ▲▲ NE Croatia
127 R15 Medvedok Kirovskaya Oblast', NW Russian Federation
123 S6 Medvezh'i, Ostrova island group NE Russian Federation
126 J9 Medvezh'yegorsk Respublika Kareliya, NW Russian Federation
109 T11 Medvode Ger. Zwischenwässern. NW Slovenia
128 J4 Medyn' Kaluzhskaya Oblast', W Russian Federation
180 J10 Meekatharra Western Australia
37 Q4 Meeker Colorado, C USA
13 T12 Meelpaeg Lake ◎ Newfoundland, E Canada
Meenen see Menen
101 M16 Meerane Sachsen, E Germany
101 D15 Meerbusch Nordrhein-Westfalen, W Germany
98 I12 Meerkerk Zuid-Holland, C Netherlands
99 L18 Meerssen var. Mersen. Limburg, SE Netherlands
152 J10 Meerut Uttar Pradesh, N India
33 U13 Meeteetse Wyoming, C USA
99 K17 Meeuwen Limburg, NE Belgium
81 J16 Mēga Oromo, C Ethiopia
81 J16 Mēga Escarpment escarpment S Ethiopia
Megála Kalívia see Megála Kalývia
115 E16 Megála Kalývia var. Megála Kalívia. Thessalía, C Greece
115 H14 Megáli Panagiá var. Megáli Panayía. Kentrikí Makedonía, N Greece
Megáli Panayía see Megáli Panagiá
Megáli Préspa, Límni see Prespa, Lake
114 K12 Megálo Livádi ▲ Bulgaria/Greece
115 E20 Megalópoli prev. Megalópolis. Pelopónnisos, S Greece
Megalópolis see Megalópoli
171 U12 Megamo Irian Jaya, E Indonesia
115 C18 Meganísi island Iónioi Nísoi, Greece, C Mediterranean Sea
Meganom, Mys see Mehanom, Mys
Mégantic see Lac-Mégantic
15 R12 Mégantic, Mont ▲ Quebec, SE Canada
115 G19 Mégara Attikí, C Greece
25 R5 Megargel Texas, SW USA
98 K13 Megen Noord-Brabant, S Netherlands
153 U13 Meghālaya ◐ state NE India
153 U16 Meghna ≈ S Bangladesh
137 V14 Meghri Rus. Megri. SE Armenia
115 Q23 Megísti var. Kastellórizon. island SE Greece
Megri see Meghri
Mehabad see Mahābād
116 F13 Mehadia Hung. Mehádia. Caraş-Severin, SW Romania
92 L7 Mehamn Finnmark, N Norway
117 U13 Mehanom, Mys Rus. Mys Meganom. headland S Ukraine
149 P14 Mehar Sind, SE Pakistan
180 J8 Meharry, Mount ▲ Western Australia
Mehdia see Mahdia
116 G14 Mehedinți ◐ county SW Romania
153 S15 Meherpur Khulna, W Bangladesh
21 W8 Meherrin River ≈ North Carolina/Virginia, SE USA
Meheso see Mī'ēso
191 T11 Mehetia island Îles du Vent, W French Polynesia
118 K6 Mehikoorma Tartumaa, E Estonia
Me Hka see Nmai Hka
143 N5 Mehrabad × (Tehrān) Tehrān, N Iran
142 J7 Mehrān Īlām, W Iran
143 Q14 Mehrān, Rūd-e prev. Mansurabad. ≈ W Iran
143 Q9 Mehrīz Yazd, C Iran
149 R5 Mehtarlām var. Mehtar Lām, Meterlam, Methariam, Metharlam. Laghmān, E Afghanistan
103 N8 Mehun-sur-Yèvre Cher, C France
79 G14 Meiganga Adamaoua, NE Cameroon
160 H10 Meigu Sichuan, C China
163 W11 Meihekou var. Hailong. Jilin, NE China
99 L15 Meijel Limburg, SE Netherlands

◆ Country ● Country Capital ◇ Dependent Territory ○ Dependent Territory Capital ◐ Administrative Region × International Airport ▲ Mountain ▲▲ Mountain Range ※ Volcano ≈ River ◎ Lake ▣ Reservoir

166 M5 **Meiktila** Mandalay, C Myanmar
Meilbhe, Loch see Melvin, Lough
108 G7 **Meilen** Zürich, N Switzerland
Meilu see Wuchuan
161 T12 **Meinhua Yu** island N Taiwan
101 J17 **Meiningen** Thüringen, C Germany
108 F9 **Meiringen** Bern, S Switzerland
101 O15 **Meissen** var. Meißen. Sachsen, E Germany
101 I15 **Meissner** ▲ C Germany
99 K25 **Meix-devant-Virton** Luxembourg, SE Belgium
Mei Xian see Meizhou
161 P13 **Meizhou** var. Meixian, Mei Xian. Guangdong, S China
67 P2 **Mejerda** var. Oued Medjerda, Wādī Majardah. ≈ Algeria/Tunisia see also Medjerda, Oued
42 F7 **Mejicanos** San Salvador, C El Salvador
Méjico see Mexico
62 G5 **Mejillones** Antofagasta, N Chile
189 V5 **Mejit Island** var. Mājeej. island Ratak Chain, NE Marshall Islands
79 F17 **Mékambo** Ogooué-Ivindo, NE Gabon
80 J10 **Mek'elē** var. Makale. Tigray, N Ethiopia
74 I10 **Mekerrhane, Sebkha** var. Sebkha Meqerghane, Sebkra Mekerrhane. salt flat C Algeria
Mekerrhane, Sebkra see Mekerrhane, Sebkha
76 G10 **Mékhé** NW Senegal
146 G14 **Mekhinli** Akhalskiy Velayat, C Turkmenistan
15 P9 **Mékinac, Lac** ◎ Quebec, SE Canada
Meklong see Samut Songhram
74 G6 **Meknès** N Morocco
131 U12 **Mekong** var. Lan-ts'ang Chiang, Cam. Mékôngk, Chin. Lancang Jiang, Lao. Mènam Khong, Th. Mae Nam Khong, Tib. Dza Chu, Vtn. Sông Tiên Giang. ≈ SE Asia
Mékôngk see Mekong
167 T15 **Mekong, Mouths of the** delta S Vietnam
38 L12 **Mekoryuk** Nunivak Island, Alaska, USA
77 R14 **Mékrou** ≈ N Benin
168 K9 **Melaka** var. Malacca. Melaka, Peninsular Malaysia
168 L9 **Melaka** var. Malacca. ◆ state Peninsular Malaysia
Melaka, Selat see Malacca, Strait of
175 O6 **Melanesia** island group W Pacific Ocean
175 P5 **Melanesian Basin** undersea feature W Pacific Ocean
171 R9 **Melanguane** Pulau Karakelang, N Indonesia
169 R11 **Melawi, Sungai** ≈ Borneo, N Indonesia
183 N12 **Melbourne** state capital Victoria, SE Australia
27 V9 **Melbourne** Arkansas, C USA
23 Y12 **Melbourne** Florida, SE USA
29 W14 **Melbourne** Iowa, C USA
92 G10 **Melbu** Nordland, C Norway
Melchor de Mencos see Ciudad Melchor de Mencos
63 F19 **Melchor, Isla** island Archipiélago de los Chonos, S Chile
40 M9 **Melchor Ocampo** Zacatecas, C Mexico
14 C11 **Meldrum Bay** Manitoulin Island, Ontario, S Canada
Meleda see Mljet
106 D8 **Melegnano** prev. Marignano. Lombardia, N Italy
188 F9 **Melekeok** var. Melekeiok. Babeldaob, N Palau
112 L9 **Melenci** Hung. Melencze. Serbia, N Yugoslavia
Melencze see Melenci
129 N4 **Melenki** Vladimirskaya Oblast', W Russian Federation
129 V6 **Meleuz** Respublika Bashkortostan, W Russian Federation
12 L6 **Mélèzes, Rivière aux** ≈ Quebec, C Canada
78 I11 **Melfi** Guéra, S Chad
107 M17 **Melfi** Basilicata, S Italy
11 U14 **Melfort** Saskatchewan, S Canada
104 H4 **Melgaço** Viana do Castelo, N Portugal
105 N4 **Melgar de Fernamental** Castilla-León, N Spain
74 L6 **Melghir, Chott** var. Chott Melrhir. salt lake E Algeria
94 H8 **Melhus** Sør-Trøndelag, S Norway
104 H3 **Melide** Galicia, NW Spain
Meligalá see Meligalás
115 E21 **Meligalás** prev. Meligalá. Pelopónnisos, S Greece
60 L12 **Mel, Ilha do** island S Brazil
120 E10 **Melilla** anc. Rusaddir, Russadir. Melilla, Spain, N Africa
71 N1 **Melilla** enclave Spain, N Africa
63 G18 **Melimoyu, Monte** ▲ S Chile
169 V11 **Melintang, Danau** ◎ Borneo, N Indonesia
117 U7 **Melioratyvne** Dnipropetrovs'ka Oblast', E Ukraine
62 G11 **Melipilla** Santiago, C Chile
115 I25 **Mélissa, Akrotírio** headland Kríti, Greece, E Mediterranean Sea
9 N15 **Melita** Manitoba, S Canada
Melita see Mljet
Melitene see Malatya
107 M23 **Melito di Porto Salvo** Calabria, SW Italy
117 U10 **Melitopol'** Zaporiz'ka Oblast', SE Ukraine
109 V4 **Melk** Niederösterreich, NE Austria
95 K15 **Mellan-Fryken** ◎ C Sweden
99 E17 **Melle** Oost-Vlaanderen, NW Belgium
100 G13 **Melle** Niedersachsen, NW Germany
95 J17 **Mellerud** Västra Götaland, S Sweden
102 K10 **Melle-sur-Bretonne** Deux-Sèvres, W France
29 P8 **Mellette** South Dakota, N USA
121 O15 **Mellieha** E Malta
80 B10 **Mellit** Northern Darfur, W Sudan
75 N7 **Mellita** × SE Tunisia
63 G21 **Mellizo Sur, Cerro** ▲ S Chile
100 G9 **Mellum** island NW Germany
83 L22 **Melmoth** KwaZulu/Natal, E South Africa
111 D16 **Mělník** Ger. Melnik. Středočeský Kraj, NW Czech Republic
122 J12 **Mel'nikovo** Tomskaya Oblast', C Russian Federation
61 G18 **Melo** Cerro Largo, NE Uruguay
Melodunum see Melun
Melrhir, Chott see Melghir, Chott
183 P7 **Melrose** New South Wales, SE Australia
182 I7 **Melrose** South Australia
29 T7 **Melrose** Minnesota, N USA
33 Q11 **Melrose** Montana, NW USA
37 V12 **Melrose** New Mexico, SW USA
108 I8 **Mels** Sankt Gallen, NE Switzerland
Melsetter see Chimanimani
33 V9 **Melstone** Montana, NW USA
101 I16 **Melsungen** Hessen, C Germany
92 L12 **Meltaus** Lappi, NW Finland
97 N19 **Melton Mowbray** C England, UK
82 Q13 **Meluco** Cabo Delgado, NE Mozambique
103 O5 **Melun** anc. Melodunum. Seine-et-Marne, N France
80 F12 **Melut** Upper Nile, SE Sudan
27 P5 **Melvern Lake** ⊞ Kansas, C USA
11 V16 **Melville** Saskatchewan, S Canada
Melville Bay/Melville Bugt see Qimusseriarsuaq
45 O11 **Melville Hall** × (Dominica) NE Dominica
181 O1 **Melville Island** island Northern Territory, N Australia
8 K5 **Melville Island** island Parry Islands, Northwest Territories, NW Canada
9 W9 **Melville, Lake** ◎ Newfoundland, E Canada
9 O7 **Melville Peninsula** peninsula Nunavut, NE Canada
Melville Sound see Viscount Melville Sound
25 Q9 **Melvin** Texas, SW USA
97 D15 **Melvin, Lough** Ir. Loch Meilbhe. ◎ S Northern Ireland, UK/Ireland
169 S12 **Memala** Borneo, C Indonesia
113 L22 **Memaliaj** Gjirokastër, S Albania
83 Q14 **Memba** Nampula, NE Mozambique
83 Q14 **Memba, Baia de** inlet NE Mozambique
Membidj see Manbij
Memel see Neman, NE Europe
Memel see Klaipėda, Lithuania
101 J23 **Memmingen** Bayern, S Germany
27 U1 **Memphis** Missouri, C USA
20 E10 **Memphis** Tennessee, S USA
25 P3 **Memphis** Texas, SW USA
20 E10 **Memphis** × Tennessee, S USA
15 Q13 **Memphrémagog, Lac** var. Lake Memphremagog. ◎ Canada/USA see also Memphremagog, Lake
19 N6 **Memphremagog, Lake** var. Lac Memphrémagog. ◎ Canada/USA see also Memphrémagog, Lac
117 Q2 **Mena** Chernihivs'ka Oblast', NE Ukraine
27 S12 **Mena** Arkansas, C USA
Menaam see Menaldum
Menado see Manado
106 D6 **Menaggio** Lombardia, N Italy
29 T6 **Menahga** Minnesota, N USA
77 R10 **Ménaka** Goa, E Mali
98 K5 **Menaldum** Fris. Menaam. Friesland, N Netherlands
Mènam Khong see Mekong
74 E7 **Menara** × (Marrakech) C Morocco
25 Q9 **Menard** Texas, SW USA
193 Q12 **Menard Fracture Zone** tectonic feature E Pacific Ocean
30 M7 **Menasha** Wisconsin, N USA
Mencezi Garagum see Tsentral'nyye Nizmennye Garagumy
193 U9 **Mendaña Fracture Zone** tectonic feature E Pacific Ocean
169 S13 **Mendawai, Sungai** ≈ Borneo, C Indonesia
103 P13 **Mende** anc. Mimatum. Lozère, S France
81 J14 **Mendebo** ▲ C Ethiopia
80 J9 **Mendefera** prev. Adi Ugri. S Eritrea
197 S7 **Mendeleyev Ridge** undersea feature Arctic Ocean
129 T3 **Mendeleyevsk** Respublika Tatarstan, W Russian Federation
101 F15 **Menden** Nordrhein-Westfalen, W Germany
22 L6 **Mendenhall** Mississippi, S USA
38 L13 **Mendenhall, Cape** headland Nunivak Island, Alaska, USA
41 P9 **Méndez** var. Villa de Méndez. Tamaulipas, C Mexico
80 H13 **Mendī** Oromo, C Ethiopia
186 C7 **Mendi** Southern Highlands, W PNG
97 K22 **Mendip Hills** var. Mendips. hill range S England, UK
Mendips see Mendip Hills
34 L6 **Mendocino** California, W USA
34 J3 **Mendocino, Cape** headland California, W USA
(0) B8 **Mendocino Fracture Zone** tectonic feature NE Pacific Ocean
35 P10 **Mendota** California, W USA
30 L11 **Mendota** Illinois, N USA
30 K8 **Mendota, Lake** ◎ Wisconsin, N USA
62 I11 **Mendoza** Mendoza, W Argentina
62 I12 **Mendoza** off. Provincia de Mendoza. ◆ province W Argentina
108 H12 **Mendrisio** Ticino, S Switzerland
168 L10 **Mendung** Pulau Mendol, W Indonesia
54 I5 **Mene de Mauroa** Falcón, NW Venezuela
54 I5 **Mene Grande** Zulia, NW Venezuela
136 B14 **Menemen** İzmir, W Turkey
99 C18 **Menen** var. Meenen, Fr. Menin. West-Vlaanderen, W Belgium
163 Q8 **Menengiyn Tal** plain E Mongolia
189 R9 **Meneng Point** headland SW Nauru
92 L10 **Menesjärvi** Lapp. Menešjávri. Lappi, N Finland
Menešjávri see Menesjärvi
107 I24 **Menfi** Sicilia, Italy, C Mediterranean Sea
161 P7 **Mengcheng** Anhui, E China
160 F15 **Menghai** Yunnan, SW China
160 F15 **Mengla** Yunnan, SW China
65 F24 **Menguera Point** headland East Falkland, Falkland Islands
160 M13 **Mengzhu Ling** ▲ S China
160 H14 **Mengzi** Yunnan, SW China
Menin see Menen
182 L7 **Menindee** New South Wales, SE Australia
182 L7 **Menindee Lake** ◎ New South Wales, SE Australia
182 J10 **Meningie** South Australia
103 O5 **Mennecy** Essonne, N France
29 Q12 **Menno** South Dakota, N USA
114 H13 **Menoíkio** ▲ NE Greece
31 N5 **Menominee** Michigan, N USA
30 M5 **Menominee River** ≈ Michigan/Wisconsin, N USA
30 M8 **Menomonee Falls** Wisconsin, N USA
30 I6 **Menomonie** Wisconsin, N USA
83 D14 **Menongue** var. Vila Serpa Pinto, Port. Serpa Pinto. Cuando Cubango, C Angola
120 H8 **Menorca** Eng. Minorca; anc. Balearis Minor. island Islas Baleares, Spain, W Mediterranean Sea
105 S13 **Menor, Mar** lagoon SE Spain
39 S10 **Mentasta Lake** ◎ Alaska, USA
39 S10 **Mentasta Mountains** ▲ Alaska, USA
168 I13 **Mentawai, Kepulauan** island group W Indonesia
168 I12 **Mentawai, Selat** strait W Indonesia
168 M12 **Mentok** Pulau Bangka, W Indonesia
103 V15 **Menton** It. Mentone. Alpes-Maritimes, SE France
24 K8 **Mentone** Texas, SW USA
Mentone see Menton
31 U11 **Mentor** Ohio, N USA
169 U10 **Menyapa, Gunung** ▲ Borneo, N Indonesia
159 T9 **Menyuan** var. Menyuan Huizu Zizhixian. Qinghai, C China
Menyuan Huizu Zizhixian see Menyuan
74 M5 **Menzel Bourguiba** var. Manzil Bū Ruqaybah; prev. Ferryville. N Tunisia
136 M15 **Menzelet Barajı** ⊞ C Turkey
129 T4 **Menzelinsk** Respublika Tatarstan, W Russian Federation
180 K11 **Menzies** Western Australia
195 V6 **Menzies, Mount** ▲ Antarctica
40 J6 **Meoqui** Chihuahua, N Mexico
83 N14 **Meponda** Niassa, NE Mozambique
98 M8 **Meppel** Drenthe, NE Netherlands
100 E12 **Meppen** Niedersachsen, NW Germany
Meqerghane, Sebkha see Mekerrhane, Sebkha
105 T6 **Mequinenza, Embalse de** ⊞ NE Spain
30 M8 **Mequon** Wisconsin, N USA
Mera see Maira
182 D3 **Meramangye, Lake** salt lake South Australia
27 W5 **Meramec River** ≈ Missouri, C USA
Meran see Merano
168 K13 **Merangin** ≈ Sumatera, W Indonesia
106 G5 **Merano** Ger. Meran. Trentino-Alto Adige, N Italy
168 K8 **Merapuh Lama** Pahang, Peninsular Malaysia
106 D7 **Merate** Lombardia, N Italy
169 U13 **Meratus, Pegunungan** ▲ Borneo, N Indonesia
171 Y16 **Merauke, Sungai** ≈ Irian Jaya, E Indonesia
182 L9 **Merbein** Victoria, SE Australia
99 F21 **Merbes-le-Château** Hainaut, S Belgium
Merca see Marka
54 C13 **Mercaderes** Cauca, SW Colombia
Mercara see Madikeri
35 P9 **Merced** California, W USA
61 C20 **Mercedes** Buenos Aires, E Argentina
61 D15 **Mercedes** Corrientes, NE Argentina
62 J11 **Mercedes** prev. Villa Mercedes. San Luis, C Argentina
61 D19 **Mercedes** Soriano, SW Uruguay
25 S17 **Mercedes** Texas, SW USA
35 R9 **Merced Peak** ▲ California, W USA
35 P9 **Merced River** ≈ California, W USA
18 B13 **Mercer** Pennsylvania, NE USA
99 G18 **Merchtem** Vlaams Brabant, C Belgium
15 O13 **Mercier** Quebec, SE Canada
25 Q9 **Mercury** Texas, SW USA
184 M5 **Mercury Islands** island group N NZ
19 O9 **Meredith** New Hampshire, NE USA
65 B25 **Meredith, Cape** var. Cabo Belgrano. headland West Falkland, Falkland Islands
37 V6 **Meredith, Lake** ◎ Colorado, C USA
25 N2 **Meredith, Lake** ⊞ Texas, SW USA
81 O16 **Mereeg** var. Mareeq, It. Meregh. Galguduud, E Somalia
117 V5 **Merefa** Kharkivs'ka Oblast', E Ukraine
Meregh see Mereeg
99 E17 **Merelbeke** Oost-Vlaanderen, NW Belgium
Merend see Marand
167 T12 **Mereuch** Môndól Kiri, E Cambodia
Mergate see Margate
144 F9 **Mergenevo** Zapadnyy Kazakhstan, NW Kazakhstan
167 N12 **Mergui** Tenasserim, S Myanmar
166 M12 **Mergui Archipelago** island group S Myanmar
114 L12 **Meriç** Edirne, NW Turkey
114 L12 **Meriç** Bul. Maritsa, Gk. Évros; anc. Hebrus. ≈ SE Europe see also Évros/Maritsa
41 X12 **Mérida** Yucatán, SW Mexico
104 J11 **Mérida** anc. Augusta Emerita. Extremadura, W Spain
54 I6 **Mérida** Mérida, W Venezuela
54 H7 **Mérida** off. Estado Mérida. ◆ state W Venezuela
18 M13 **Meriden** Connecticut, NE USA
22 M5 **Meridian** Mississippi, S USA
25 S8 **Meridian** Texas, SW USA
102 J13 **Mérignac** Gironde, SW France
102 J13 **Mérignac** × (Bordeaux) Gironde, SW France
93 J18 **Merikarvia** Länsi-Suomi, W Finland
183 R12 **Merimbula** New South Wales, SE Australia
182 L9 **Meringur** Victoria, SE Australia
Merín, Laguna see Mirim Lagoon
97 I19 **Merioneth** cultural region W Wales, UK
188 A11 **Merir** island Palau Islands, N Palau
188 B17 **Merizo** SW Guam
Merjama see Märjamaa
145 S16 **Merke** Zhambyl, S Kazakhstan
25 P7 **Merkel** Texas, SW USA
119 F15 **Merkinė** Varėna, S Lithuania
99 G16 **Merksem** Antwerpen, N Belgium
99 I15 **Merksplas** Antwerpen, N Belgium
Merkulovichi see Myerkulavichy
119 G15 **Merkys** ≈ S Lithuania
32 F15 **Merlin** Oregon, NW USA
61 C20 **Merlo** Buenos Aires, E Argentina
138 G8 **Meron, Haré** ▲ N Israel
74 K6 **Merouane, Chott** salt lake NE Algeria
80 F7 **Merowe** Northern, N Sudan
180 J12 **Merredin** Western Australia
97 I14 **Merrick** ▲ S Scotland, UK
32 H16 **Merrill** Oregon, NW USA
30 L5 **Merrill** Wisconsin, N USA
31 N11 **Merrillville** Indiana, N USA
19 O10 **Merrimack River** ≈ Massachusetts/New Hampshire, NE USA
28 L12 **Merriman** Nebraska, C USA
11 N17 **Merritt** British Columbia, SW Canada
23 Y12 **Merritt Island** Florida, SE USA
23 Y11 **Merritt Island** island Florida, SE USA
28 M12 **Merritt Reservoir** ⊞ Nebraska, C USA
183 S7 **Merriwa** New South Wales, SE Australia
183 O8 **Merriwagga** New South Wales, SE Australia
22 G8 **Merryville** Louisiana, S USA
80 K9 **Mersa Fatma** E Eritrea
102 M7 **Mer St-Aubin** Loir-et-Cher, C France
Mersa Maṭrûḥ see Maṭrûḥ
99 M24 **Mersch** Luxembourg, C Luxembourg
101 M15 **Merseburg** Sachsen-Anhalt, C Germany
Mersen see Meerssen
97 K18 **Mersey** ≈ NW England, UK
136 J17 **Mersin** İçel, S Turkey
168 L9 **Mersing** Johor, Peninsular Malaysia
118 E8 **Mērsrags** Talsi, NW Latvia
152 G12 **Merta** var. Merta City. Rājasthān, N India
Merta City see Merta
152 F12 **Merta Road** Rājasthān, N India
97 J21 **Merthyr Tydfil** S Wales, UK
104 H13 **Mértola** Beja, S Portugal
195 V16 **Mertz Glacier** glacier Antarctica
99 M24 **Mertzig** Diekirch, C Luxembourg
25 O9 **Mertzon** Texas, SW USA
81 J18 **Meru** Eastern, C Kenya
103 N4 **Méru** Oise, N France
81 I20 **Meru, Mount** ▲ NE Tanzania
Merv see Mary
Mervdasht see Marv Dasht
136 K11 **Merzifon** Amasya, N Turkey
101 D20 **Merzig** Saarland, SW Germany
36 L14 **Mesa** Arizona, SW USA
29 V4 **Mesabi Range** ▲ Minnesota, N USA
54 H6 **Mesa Bolívar** Mérida, NW Venezuela
107 Q18 **Mesagne** Puglia, SE Italy
39 P12 **Mesa Mountain** ▲ Alaska, USA
115 J25 **Mesará** lowland Kríti, Greece, E Mediterranean Sea
37 S14 **Mescalero** New Mexico, SW USA
101 G15 **Meschede** Nordrhein-Westfalen, W Germany
137 Q12 **Mescit Dağları** ▲ NE Turkey
189 V13 **Mesegon** island Chuuk, C Micronesia
Meseritz see Międzyrzecz
54 F11 **Mesetas** Meta, C Colombia
Meshchera Lowland see Meshcherskaya Nizina
128 M4 **Meshcherskaya Nizina** Eng. Meshchera Lowland. basin W Russian Federation
128 J5 **Meshchovsk** Kaluzhskaya Oblast', W Russian Federation
127 R9 **Meshchura** Respublika Komi, NW Russian Federation
Meshed see Mashhad
Meshed-i-Sar see Bābolsar
80 E13 **Meshra'er Req** Warab, S Sudan
37 R15 **Mesilla** New Mexico, SW USA
108 H10 **Mesocco** Ger. Misox. Ticino, S Switzerland
115 D18 **Mesolóngi** prev. Mesolóngion. Dytikí Ellás, W Greece
Mesolóngion see Mesolóngi
14 E8 **Mesomikenda Lake** ◎ Ontario, S Canada
61 D15 **Mesopotamia** var. Mesopotamia Argentina. physical region NE Argentina
Mesopotamia Argentina see Mesopotamia
35 Y10 **Mesquite** Nevada, W USA
82 Q13 **Messalo, Rio** var. Mualo. ≈ NE Mozambique
Messana/Messene see Messina
99 L25 **Messancy** Luxembourg, SE Belgium
107 M23 **Messina** var. Messana, Messene; anc. Zancle. Sicilia, Italy, C Mediterranean Sea
83 K19 **Messina** Northern, NE South Africa
Messina, Strait of see Messina, Stretto di
107 M23 **Messina, Stretto di** Eng. Strait of Messina. strait SW Italy
115 E21 **Messíni** Pelopónnisos, S Greece
115 E21 **Messinía** peninsula S Greece
115 E22 **Messiniakós Kólpos** gulf S Greece
122 J8 **Messoyakha** ≈ N Russian Federation
114 H11 **Mesta** Gk. Néstos, Turk. Kara Su. ≈ Bulgaria/Greece see also Néstos
Mestghanem see Mostaganem
137 R8 **Mestia** var. Mestiya. N Georgia
Mestiya see Mestia
115 K18 **Mestón, Akrotírio** headland Chíos, E Greece
106 H8 **Mestre** Veneto, NE Italy
59 M16 **Mestre, Espigão** ▲ E Brazil
169 N14 **Mesuji** ≈ Sumatera, W Indonesia
Mesule see Grosser Möseler
10 J10 **Meszah Peak** ▲ British Columbia, W Canada
54 G11 **Meta** off. Departamento del Meta. ◆ province C Colombia
15 Q8 **Metabetchouane** ≈ Quebec, SE Canada
9 S7 **Meta Incognita Peninsula** peninsula Baffin Island, Nunavut, NE Canada
22 K9 **Metairie** Louisiana, S USA
32 M6 **Metaline Falls** Washington, NW USA
62 K6 **Metán** Salta, N Argentina
82 N13 **Metangula** Niassa, N Mozambique
42 E7 **Metapán** Santa Ana, NW El Salvador
54 K9 **Meta, Río** ≈ Colombia/Venezuela
106 I11 **Metauro** ≈ C Italy
80 H11 **Metema** Amhara, N Ethiopia
115 D15 **Metéora** religious building Thessalía, C Greece
65 O20 **Meteor Rise** undersea feature SW Indian Ocean
186 G5 **Meteran** New Hanover, NE PNG
Meterlam/Methariam/Metharlam see Mehtarlām
115 G20 **Methanon** peninsula S Greece
32 J6 **Methow River** ≈ Washington, NW USA
19 O10 **Methuen** Massachusetts, NE USA
185 G19 **Methven** Canterbury, South Island, NZ
Metis see Metz
113 G15 **Metković** Dubrovnik-Neretva, SE Croatia
39 Y14 **Metlakatla** Annette Island, Alaska, USA
109 V13 **Metlika** Ger. Möttling. SE Slovenia
109 T8 **Metnitz** Kärnten, S Austria
27 W12 **Meto, Bayou** ≈ Arkansas, C USA
168 M15 **Metro** Sumatera, W Indonesia
30 M17 **Metropolis** Illinois, N USA
Metropolitan see Santiago
35 N8 **Metropolitan Oakland** × California, W USA
115 D15 **Métsovo** prev. Métsovon. Ípeiros, C Greece
Métsovon see Métsovo
23 V5 **Metter** Georgia, SE USA
99 H21 **Mettet** Namur, S Belgium
101 D20 **Mettlach** Saarland, SW Germany
Mettu see Metu
80 H13 **Metu** var. Mattu, Mettu. Oromo, C Ethiopia
169 T10 **Metulang** Borneo, N Indonesia
138 G8 **Metulla** Northern, N Israel
144 G14 **Metvyy Kultuk, Sor** salt flat SW Kazakhstan
103 T4 **Metz** anc. Divodurum Mediomatricum, Mediomatrica, Metis. Moselle, NE France
101 H22 **Metzingen** Baden-Württemberg, S Germany
168 G8 **Meulaboh** Sumatera, W Indonesia
99 D18 **Meulebeke** West-Vlaanderen, W Belgium
103 U6 **Meurthe** ≈ NE France
103 S5 **Meurthe-et-Moselle** ◆ department NE France
103 S4 **Meuse** ◆ department NE France
84 F10 **Meuse** Dut. Maas. ≈ W Europe see also Maas
Mexcala, Río see Balsas, Río
25 U8 **Mexia** Texas, SW USA
58 K11 **Mexiana, Ilha** island NE Brazil
40 C1 **Mexicali** Baja California, NW Mexico
27 V4 **Mexico** Missouri, C USA
18 H9 **Mexico** New York, NE USA
40 L7 **Mexico** off. United Mexican States, var. Méjico, México, Sp. Estados Unidos Mexicanos. ◆ federal republic N Central America
41 O14 **México** var. Ciudad de México, Eng. Mexico City. ● (Mexico) México, C Mexico
41 O13 **México** ◆ state S Mexico
(0) J13 **Mexico Basin** var. Sigsbee Deep. undersea feature C Gulf of Mexico
Mexico City see México
México, Golfo de see Mexico, Gulf of
44 B4 **Mexico, Gulf of** Sp. Golfo de México. gulf W Atlantic Ocean
Meyadine see Al Mayādīn
39 Y14 **Meyers Chuck** Etolin Island, Alaska, USA
148 M3 **Meymaneh** var. Maimāna, Maymana. Fāryāb, NW Afghanistan
143 N7 **Meymeh** Eşfahān, C Iran
123 V7 **Meynypil'gyno** Chukotskiy Avtonomnyy Okrug, NE Russian Federation
108 A10 **Meyrin** Genève, SW Switzerland
166 L7 **Mezaligon** Irrawaddy, SW Myanmar
41 O15 **Mezcala** Guerrero, S Mexico
114 H8 **Mezdra** Vratsa, NW Bulgaria
103 P16 **Mèze** Hérault, S France
127 O6 **Mezen'** Arkhangel'skaya Oblast', NW Russian Federation
127 P8 **Mezen'** ≈ NW Russian Federation
Mezen, Bay of see Mezenskaya Guba
103 Q13 **Mézenc, Mont** ▲ C France
127 O8 **Mezenskaya Guba** var. Bay of Mezen. bay NW Russian Federation
Mezha see Myazha
122 H6 **Mezhdusharskiy, Ostrov** island Novaya Zemlya, N Russian Federation
Mezhëvo see Myezhava
Mezhgor'ye see Mizhhir"ya
117 V8 **Mezhova** Dnipropetrovs'ka Oblast', E Ukraine
10 J12 **Meziadin Junction** British Columbia, W Canada
111 G16 **Mezileské Sedlo** var. Przełęcz Międzyleska. pass Czech Republic/Poland
102 L14 **Mézin** Lot-et-Garonne, SW France
111 M24 **Mezőberény** Békés, SE Hungary
111 M25 **Mezőhegyes** Békés, SE Hungary
111 M25 **Mezőkovácsháza** Békés, SE Hungary
111 M21 **Mezőkövesd** Borsod-Abaúj-Zemplén, NE Hungary
Mezőtelegd see Tileagd
111 M23 **Mezőtúr** Jász-Nagykun-Szolnok, E Hungary
40 K10 **Mezquital** Durango, C Mexico
106 G6 **Mezzolombardo** Trentino-Alto Adige, N Italy
82 L13 **Mfuwe** Northern, N Zambia
121 O15 **Mgarr** Gozo, N Malta
128 H6 **Mglin** Bryanskaya Oblast', W Russian Federation
Mhálanna, Cionn see Malin Head
154 G10 **Mhow** Madhya Pradesh, C India
Miadzioł Nowy see Myadzyel
171 O6 **Miagao** Panay Island, C Philippines
41 R17 **Miahuatlán** var. Miahuatlán de Porfirio Díaz. Oaxaca, SE Mexico
Miahuatlán de Porfirio Díaz see Miahuatlán
104 K10 **Miajadas** Extremadura, W Spain
Miajlar see Myājlār
36 M14 **Miami** Arizona, SW USA
23 Z16 **Miami** Florida, SE USA
27 R8 **Miami** Oklahoma, C USA
25 O2 **Miami** Texas, SW USA
23 Z16 **Miami** × Florida, SE USA
23 Z16 **Miami Beach** Florida, SE USA
23 Y15 **Miami Canal** canal Florida, SE USA
31 R14 **Miamisburg** Ohio, N USA
149 U10 **Miān Channūn** Punjab, E Pakistan
142 J4 **Miāndowāb** var. Miandowāb, Miyāndoāb. Āzarbāyjān-e Bākhtarī, NW Iran
172 H5 **Miandrivazo** Toliara, C Madagascar
Mianduab see Miāndowāb
142 K3 **Mīāneh** var. Miyāneh. Āzarbāyjān-e Khāvarī, NW Iran
149 O16 **Miāni Hōr** lagoon S Pakistan
160 G10 **Mianning** Sichuan, C China
149 T7 **Miānwāli** Punjab, NE Pakistan
160 J7 **Mianxian** var. Mian Xian. Shaanxi, C China
160 I8 **Mianyang** Sichuan, C China
Mianyang see Xiantao
161 R3 **Miaodao Qundao** island group E China
161 S13 **Miaoli** N Taiwan
122 F11 **Miass** Chelyabinskaya Oblast', C Russian Federation
110 G8 **Miastko** Ger. Rummelsburg in Pommern. Pomorskie, N Poland

◆ Country ● Country Capital ◇ Dependent Territory ○ Dependent Territory Capital ◆ Administrative Region × International Airport ▲ Mountain ▲ Mountain Range Volcano ≈ River ◎ Lake ⊞ Reservoir

Miava *see* Myjava
11 *O15* **Mica Creek** British Columbia, SW Canada
160 *J7* **Micang Shan** ▲ C China
Mi Chai *see* Nong Khai
111 *O19* **Michalovce** *Ger.* Grossmichel, *Hung.* Nagymihály. Košický Kraj, E Slovakia
99 *M20* **Michel, Baraque** *hill* E Belgium
39 *S5* **Michelson, Mount** ▲ Alaska, USA
45 *P9* **Miches** E Dominican Republic
30 *M4* **Michigamme, Lake** ◎ Michigan, N USA
30 *M4* **Michigamme Reservoir** ⊡ Michigan, N USA
31 *N4* **Michigamme River** ⇝ Michigan, N USA
31 *O7* **Michigan** *off.* State of Michigan; also known as Great Lakes State, Lake State, Wolverine State. ◆ *state* N USA
31 *O11* **Michigan City** Indiana, N USA
31 *O8* **Michigan, Lake** ◎ N USA
31 *P2* **Michipicoten Bay** *lake bay* Ontario, N Canada
14 *A8* **Michipicoten Island** *island* Ontario, S Canada
14 *B7* **Michipicoten River** Ontario, S Canada
Michurin *see* Tsarevo
128 *M6* **Michurinsk** Tambovskaya Oblast', W Russian Federation
Mico, Punta/Mico, Punto *see* Monkey Point
42 *L10* **Mico, Río** ⇝ SE Nicaragua
45 *T12* **Micoud** SE Saint Lucia
189 *N16* **Micronesia** *off.* Federated States of Micronesia. ◆ *federation* W Pacific Ocean
175 *P4* **Micronesia** *island group* W Pacific Ocean
169 O9 **Midai, Pulau** *island* Kepulauan Natuna, W Indonesia
Mid-Atlantic Cordillera *see* Mid-Atlantic Ridge
65 *M17* **Mid-Atlantic Ridge** *var.* Mid-Atlantic Cordillera, Mid-Atlantic Rise, Mid-Atlantic Swell. *undersea feature* Atlantic Ocean
Mid-Atlantic Rise/Mid-Atlantic Swell *see* Mid-Atlantic Ridge
99 *E15* **Middelburg** Zeeland, SW Netherlands
83 *H24* **Middelburg** Eastern Cape, S South Africa
83 *K21* **Middelburg** Mpumalanga, NE South Africa
95 *G23* **Middelfart** Fyn, C Denmark
98 *G13* **Middelharnis** Zuid-Holland, SW Netherlands
99 *B16* **Middelkerke** West-Vlaanderen, W Belgium
98 *I9* **Middenbeemster** Noord-Holland, C Netherlands
98 *I8* **Middenmeer** Noord-Holland, NW Netherlands
35 *Q2* **Middle Alkali Lake** ◎ California, W USA
193 S6 **Middle America Trench** *undersea feature* E Pacific Ocean
151 *P19* **Middle Andaman** *island* Andaman Islands, India, NE Indian Ocean
Middle Atlas *see* Moyen Atlas
21 *R3* **Middlebourne** West Virginia, NE USA
23 *W9* **Middleburg** Florida, SE USA
Middleburg Island *see* 'Eua
Middle Caicos *see* Grand Caicos
25 *N8* **Middle Concho River** ⇝ Texas, SW USA
Middle Congo *see* Congo (Republic of)
39 *R6* **Middle Fork Chandalar River** ⇝ Alaska, USA
39 *Q7* **Middle Fork Koyukuk River** ⇝ Alaska, USA
33 *O12* **Middle Fork Salmon River** ⇝ Idaho, NW USA
11 *T15* **Middle Lake** Saskatchewan, S Canada
28 *L13* **Middle Loup River** ⇝ Nebraska, C USA
185 *E22* **Middlemarch** Otago, South Island, NZ
31 *T15* **Middleport** Ohio, N USA
29 *U14* **Middle Raccoon River** ⇝ Iowa, C USA
29 *R3* **Middle River** ⇝ Minnesota, N USA
21 *N8* **Middlesboro** Kentucky, S USA
97 *M15* **Middlesbrough** N England, UK
42 *G3* **Middlesex** Stann Creek, C Belize
97 *N22* **Middlesex** *cultural region* SE England, UK
13 *P15* **Middleton** Nova Scotia, SE Canada
20 *F10* **Middleton** Tennessee, S USA
30 *L9* **Middleton** Wisconsin, N USA
39 *S13* **Middleton Island** *island* Alaska, USA
34 *M7* **Middletown** California, W USA
21 *Y2* **Middletown** Delaware, NE USA
18 *K15* **Middletown** New Jersey, NE USA
18 *K13* **Middletown** New York, NE USA
31 *R14* **Middletown** Ohio, N USA
18 *G15* **Middletown** Pennsylvania, NE USA
141 *N14* **Mīdī** *var.* Maydī. NW Yemen
103 *O16* **Midi, Canal du** *canal* S France
102 *K17* **Midi de Bigorre, Pic du** ▲ S France
102 *K17* **Midi d'Ossau, Pic du** ▲ SW France
173 *R7* **Mid-Indian Basin** *undersea feature* N Indian Ocean
173 *P7* **Mid-Indian Ridge** *var.* Central Indian Ridge. *undersea feature* C Indian Ocean
103 *N14* **Midi-Pyrénées** ◆ *region* S France
25 *N8* **Midkiff** Texas, SW USA
14 *G13* **Midland** Ontario, S Canada
31 *R8* **Midland** Michigan, N USA
28 *M10* **Midland** South Dakota, N USA
24 *M8* **Midland** Texas, SW USA
83 *K17* **Midlands** ◆ *province* C Zimbabwe
97 *D21* **Midleton** *Ir.* Mainistir na Corann. SW Ireland
25 *T7* **Midlothian** Texas, SW USA
96 *K12* **Midlothian** *cultural region* S Scotland, UK
172 *I7* **Midongy** Fianarantsoa, S Madagascar
102 *K15* **Midou** ⇝ SW France
192 J6 **Mid-Pacific Mountains** *var.* Mid-Pacific Seamounts. *undersea feature* NW Pacific Ocean
Mid-Pacific Seamounts *see* Mid-Pacific Mountains
171 Q7 **Midsayap** Mindanao, S Philippines
36 *L3* **Midway** Utah, W USA
192 L5 **Midway Islands** ◇ *US territory* C Pacific Ocean
33 *X14* **Midwest** Wyoming, C USA
27 *N10* **Midwest City** Oklahoma, C USA
152 *M10* **Mid Western** ◆ *zone* W Nepal
98 *P5* **Midwolda** Groningen, NE Netherlands
137 *Q16* **Midyat** Mardin, SE Turkey
114 *F8* **Midzhur** *SCr.* Midžor. ▲ Bulgaria/Yugoslavia *see also* Midžor
113 *Q14* **Midžor** *Bul.* Midzhur. ▲ Bulgaria/Yugoslavia *see also* Midzhur
164 K14 **Mie** *off.* Mie-ken. ◆ *prefecture* Honshū, SW Japan
111 *L16* **Miechów** Małopolskie, S Poland
110 *F11* **Międzychód** *Ger.* Mitteldorf. Wielkopolskie, C Poland
Międzyleska, Przełęcz *see* Mezileské Sedlo
110 *O12* **Międzyrzec Podlaski** Lubelskie, E Poland
110 *E11* **Międzyrzecz** *Ger.* Meseritz. Lubelskie, W Poland
Mie-ken *see* Mie
102 *L16* **Miélan** Gers, S France
111 *N16* **Mielec** Podkarpackie, SE Poland
95 *L21* **Mien** ◎ S Sweden
41 *O8* **Mier** Tamaulipas, C Mexico
116 *J11* **Miercurea-Ciuc** *Ger.* Szeklerburg, *Hung.* Csíkszereda. Harghita, C Romania
Mieresch *see* Maros/Mureş
Mieres del Camín *see* Mieres del Camino
104 *K2* **Mieres del Camino** *var.* Mieres del Camín. Asturias, NW Spain
99 *K15* **Mierlo** Noord-Brabant, SE Netherlands
41 *O10* **Mier y Noriega** Nuevo León, NE Mexico
Mies *see* Stříbro
80 *K13* **Mī'ēso** *var.* Meheso, Oromo. C Ethiopia
Miesso *see* Mī'ēso
110 *D10* **Mieszkowice** *Ger.* Bärwalde Neumark. Zachodniopomorskie, W Poland
18 *G14* **Mifflinburg** Pennsylvania, NE USA
18 *F14* **Mifflintown** Pennsylvania, NE USA
41 *R15* **Miguel Alemán, Presa** ⊡ SE Mexico
40 *L9* **Miguel Asua** *var.* Miguel Auza. Zacatecas, C Mexico
Miguel Auza *see* Miguel Asua
43 *S15* **Miguel de la Borda** *var.* Donoso. Colón, C Panama
41 *N13* **Miguel Hidalgo** ✕ (Guadalajara) Jalisco, SW Mexico
40 *H7* **Miguel Hidalgo, Presa** ⊡ W Mexico
116 *J14* **Mihăileşti** Giurgiu, S Romania
116 *M14* **Mihail Kogălniceanu** *var.* Kogălniceanu; *prev.* Caramurat, Ferdinand. Constanţa, SE Romania
117 *N14* **Mihai Viteazu** Constanţa, SE Romania
136 *G12* **Mihalıççık** Eskişehir, NW Turkey
164 G13 **Mihara** Hiroshima, Honshū, SW Japan
165 N14 **Mihara-yama** Ѫ Miyako-jima, SE Japan
105 *S8* **Mijares** ⇝ E Spain
98 *I11* **Mijdrecht** Utrecht, C Netherlands
165 S4 **Mikasa** Hokkaidō, NE Japan
Mikashevichi *see* Mikashevichy
119 *K19* **Mikashevichy** *Pol.* Mikaszewicze, *Rus.* Mikashevichi. Brestskaya Voblasts', SW Belarus
Mikaszewicze *see* Mikashevichy
128 *L5* **Mikhaylov** Ryazanskaya Oblast', W Russian Federation
Mikhaylovgrad *see* Montana
195 *Z8* **Mikhaylov Island** *island* Antarctica
145 *T6* **Mikhaylovka** Pavlodar, N Kazakhstan
129 *N9* **Mikhaylovka** Volgogradskaya Oblast', SW Russian Federation
Mikhaylovka *see* Mykhaylivka
81 *K24* **Mikindani** Mtwara, SE Tanzania
93 *N18* **Mikkeli** *Swe.* Sankt Michel. Itä-Suomi, E Finland
110 *M8* **Mikołajki** *Ger.* Nikolaiken. Warmińsko-Mazurskie, NE Poland
Míkonos *see* Mýkonos
114 *I9* **Mikre** Lovech, N Bulgaria
114 *C13* **Mikrí Préspa, Límni** ◎ N Greece
127 *P4* **Mikulkin, Mys** *headland* NW Russian Federation
81 *I23* **Mikumi** Morogoro, SE Tanzania
127 *R10* **Mikun'** Respublika Komi, NW Russian Federation
164 K13 **Mikuni** Fukui, Honshū, SW Japan
165 X13 **Mikura-jima** *island* E Japan
29 *V7* **Milaca** Minnesota, N USA
62 *J10* **Milagro** La Rioja, C Argentina
56 *B7* **Milagro** Guayas, SW Ecuador
31 *P4* **Milakokia Lake** ◎ Michigan, N USA
30 *J1* **Milan** Illinois, N USA
31 *R10* **Milan** Michigan, N USA
27 *T2* **Milan** Missouri, C USA
37 *Q11* **Milan** New Mexico, SW USA
20 *G9* **Milan** Tennessee, S USA
Milan *see* Milano
95 *F15* **Miland** Telemark, S Norway
83 *N15* **Milange** Zambézia, NE Mozambique
106 *D8* **Milano** *Eng.* Milan, *Ger.* Mailand; *anc.* Mediolanum. Lombardia, N Italy
25 *U10* **Milano** Texas, SW USA
136 *C15* **Milas** Muğla, SW Turkey
119 *K21* **Milashavichy** *Rus.* Milashevichi. Homyel'skaya Voblasts', SE Belarus
Milashevichi *see* Milashavichy
119 *I18* **Milavidy** *Rus.* Milovidy. Brestskaya Voblasts', SW Belarus
107 *L23* **Milazzo** *anc.* Mylae. Sicilia, Italy, C Mediterranean Sea
29 *R8* **Milbank** South Dakota, N USA
19 *T7* **Milbridge** Maine, NE USA
100 *L11* **Milde** ⇝ C Germany
14 *F14* **Mildmay** Ontario, S Canada
182 *L9* **Mildura** Victoria, SE Australia
137 *X12* **Mil Düzü** *Rus.* Mil'skaya Ravnina, Mil'skaya Step'. *physical region* C Azerbaijan
160 *H13* **Mile** Yunnan, SW China
Mile *see* Mili Atoll
181 *Y10* **Miles** Queensland, E Australia
25 *P8* **Miles** Texas, SW USA
33 *X9* **Miles City** Montana, NW USA
11 *U17* **Milestone** Saskatchewan, S Canada
107 *N22* **Mileto** Calabria, SW Italy
107 *K16* **Miletto, Monte** ▲ C Italy
18 *M13* **Milford** Connecticut, NE USA
21 *Y3* **Milford** *var.* Milford City. Delaware, NE USA
29 *T11* **Milford** Iowa, C USA
19 *S6* **Milford** Maine, NE USA
29 *R16* **Milford** Nebraska, C USA
19 *O10* **Milford** New Hampshire, NE USA
18 *J13* **Milford** Pennsylvania, NE USA
25 *T7* **Milford** Texas, SW USA
36 *K6* **Milford** Utah, W USA
Milford *see* Milford Haven
Milford City *see* Milford
97 *H21* **Milford Haven** *prev.* Milford. SW Wales, UK
27 *O4* **Milford Lake** ⊡ Kansas, C USA
185 *B21* **Milford Sound** Southland, South Island, NZ
185 *B21* **Milford Sound** *inlet* South Island, NZ
Milhau *see* Millau
Milḩ, Baḩr al *see* Razāzah, Buḩayrat ar
139 *T10* **Milḩ, Wādī al** *dry watercourse* S Iraq
189 *W8* **Mili Atoll** *var.* Mile. *atoll* Ratak Chain, SE Marshall Islands
110 *H13* **Milicz** Dolnośląskie, SW Poland
107 *L25* **Militello in Val di Catania** Sicilia, Italy, C Mediterranean Sea
123 V10 **Mil'kovo** Kamchatskaya Oblast', E Russian Federation
11 *R17* **Milk River** Alberta, SW Canada
44 *J13* **Milk River** ⇝ C Jamaica
33 *W7* **Milk River** ⇝ Montana, NW USA
80 *D9* **Milk, Wadi el** *var.* Wadi al Malik. ⇝ C Sudan
99 *L14* **Mill** Noord-Brabant, SE Netherlands
103 *P14* **Millau** *var.* Milhau; *anc.* Æmilianum. Aveyron, S France
14 *I14* **Millbrook** Ontario, SE Canada
23 *U4* **Milledgeville** Georgia, SE USA
12 *C12* **Mille Lacs, Lac des** ◎ Ontario, S Canada
29 *V6* **Mille Lacs Lake** ◎ Minnesota, N USA
23 *V4* **Millen** Georgia, SE USA
191 *Y5* **Millennium Island** *prev.* Caroline Island, Thornton Island. *atoll* Line Islands, E Kiribati
29 *O9* **Miller** South Dakota, N USA
30 *K5* **Miller Dam Flowage** ◎ Wisconsin, N USA
39 *U12* **Miller, Mount** ▲ Alaska, USA
128 *L10* **Millerovo** Rostovskaya Oblast', SW Russian Federation
37 *N17* **Miller Peak** ▲ Arizona, SW USA
31 *T12* **Millersburg** Ohio, N USA
18 *G15* **Millersburg** Pennsylvania, NE USA
185 *D23* **Millers Flat** Otago, South Island, NZ
25 *Q8* **Millersview** Texas, SW USA
106 *B10* **Millesimo** Piemonte, NE Italy
17 N6 **Milles Lacs, Lac des** ◎ Ontario, SW Canada
25 *Q13* **Millett** Texas, SW USA
103 *N11* **Millevaches, Plateau de** *plateau* C France
182 *K12* **Millicent** South Australia
98 *M13* **Millingen aan den Rijn** Gelderland, SE Netherlands
20 *E10* **Millington** Tennessee, S USA
19 *R4* **Millinocket** Maine, NE USA
19 *R4* **Millinocket Lake** ◎ Maine, NE USA
195 *Z11* **Mill Island** *island* Antarctica
183 *T3* **Millmerran** Queensland, E Australia
109 *R9* **Millstatt** Kärnten, S Austria
97 *B19* **Milltown Malbay** *Ir.* Sráid na Cathrach. W Ireland
18 *J17* **Millville** New Jersey, NE USA
27 *S13* **Millwood Lake** ⊡ Arkansas, C USA
Milne Bank *see* Milne Seamounts
186 G10 **Milne Bay** ◆ *province* SE PNG
64 *J8* **Milne Seamounts** *var.* Milne Bank. *undersea feature* N Atlantic Ocean
29 *Q6* **Milnor** North Dakota, N USA
19 *R5* **Milo** Maine, NE USA
115 *I22* **Mílos** Mílos, Kykládes, Greece, Aegean Sea
115 *I22* **Mílos** *island* Kykládes, Greece, Aegean Sea
110 *H11* **Miłosław** Wielkopolskie, C Poland
113 *K19* **Milot** *var.* Miloti. Lezhë, C Albania
Miloti *see* Milot
117 *Z5* **Milove** Luhans'ka Oblast', E Ukraine
Milovidy *see* Milavidy
182 *L4* **Milparinka** New South Wales, SE Australia
35 *N9* **Milpitas** California, W USA
Mil'skaya Ravnina/Mil'skaya Step' *see* Mil Düzü
14 *G15* **Milton** Ontario, S Canada
185 *E24* **Milton** Otago, South Island, NZ
21 *Y4* **Milton** Delaware, NE USA
23 *P8* **Milton** Florida, SE USA
18 *G14* **Milton** Pennsylvania, NE USA
18 *L7* **Milton** Vermont, NE USA
32 *K11* **Milton-Freewater** Oregon, NW USA
97 *N21* **Milton Keynes** SE England, UK
27 *N3* **Miltonvale** Kansas, C USA
161 *N10* **Miluo** Hunan, S China
30 *M9* **Milwaukee** Wisconsin, N USA
Milyang *see* Miryang
Mimatum *see* Mende
37 *Q15* **Mimbres Mountains** ▲ New Mexico, SW USA
182 *D2* **Mimili** South Australia
102 *J14* **Mimizan** Landes, SW France
Mimmaya *see* Minmaya
79 *E19* **Mimongo** Ngounié, C Gabon
Min *see* Fujian
35 *T7* **Mina** Nevada, W USA
143 *S14* **Mīnāb** Hormozgān, SE Iran
Mīnā Baranīs *see* Berenice
149 *R9* **Mīna Bāzār** Baluchistān, SW Pakistan
165 X17 **Minami-Iō-jima** *Eng.* San Augustine. *island* SE Japan
165 R5 **Minami-Kayabe** Hokkaidō, NE Japan
164 C17 **Minamitane** Kagoshima, Tanega-shima, SW Japan
Minami Tori Shima *see* Marcus Island
62 *J4* **Mina Pirquitas** Jujuy, NW Argentina
173 *O3* **Mīnā' Qābūs** NE Oman
61 *F19* **Minas** Lavalleja, S Uruguay
13 *P15* **Minas Basin** *bay* Nova Scotia, SE Canada
61 *F17* **Minas de Corrales** Rivera, NE Uruguay
44 *A5* **Minas de Matahambre** Pinar del Río, W Cuba
104 *J13* **Minas de Ríotinto** Andalucía, S Spain
60 *K7* **Minas Gerais** *off.* Estado de Minas Gerais. ◆ *state* E Brazil
42 *E5* **Minas, Sierra de las** ▲ E Guatemala
41 *T15* **Minatitlán** Veracruz-Llave, E Mexico
166 L6 **Minbu** Magwe, W Myanmar
149 *V10* **Minchinābād** Punjab, E Pakistan
63 *G17* **Minchinmávida, Volcán** ▲ S Chile
96 *G7* **Minch, The** *var.* North Minch. *strait* NW Scotland, UK
106 *F8* **Mincio** *anc.* Mincius. ⇝ N Italy
Mincius *see* Mincio
26 *M11* **Minco** Oklahoma, C USA
171 Q7 **Mindanao** *island* S Philippines
Mindanao Sea *see* Bohol Sea
101 *J23* **Mindel** ⇝ S Germany
101 *J23* **Mindelheim** Bayern, S Germany
Mindello *see* Mindelo
76 *C9* **Mindelo** *var.* Mindello; *prev.* Porto Grande. São Vicente, N Cape Verde
14 *I13* **Minden** Ontario, SE Canada
100 *H13* **Minden** *anc.* Minthun. Nordrhein-Westfalen, NW Germany
22 *G5* **Minden** Louisiana, S USA
29 *O16* **Minden** Nebraska, C USA
35 *Q6* **Minden** Nevada, W USA
182 *L8* **Mindona Lake** *seasonal lake* New South Wales, SE Australia
171 O4 **Mindoro** *island* N Philippines
171 N5 **Mindoro Strait** *strait* W Philippines
159 *S9* **Mine** Gansu, N China
97 *E21* **Mine Head** *Ir.* Mionn Ard. *headland* S Ireland
97 *J23* **Minehead** SW England, UK
59 *J19* **Mineiros** Goiás, C Brazil
25 *V6* **Mineola** Texas, SW USA
25 *S13* **Mineral** Texas, SW USA
129 *N15* **Mineral'nyye Vody** Stavropol'skiy Kray, SW Russian Federation
30 *K9* **Mineral Point** Wisconsin, N USA
25 *S6* **Mineral Wells** Texas, SW USA
36 *K6* **Minersville** Utah, W USA
31 *U12* **Minerva** Ohio, N USA
107 *N17* **Minervino Murge** Puglia, SE Italy
103 *O16* **Minervois** *physical region* S France
158 *I10* **Minfeng** *var.* Niya. Xinjiang Uygur Zizhiqu, NW China
79 *O25* **Minga** Katanga, SE Dem. Rep. Congo (Zaire)
137 *W11* **Mingäçevir** *Rus.* Mingechaur, Mingechevir. C Azerbaijan
137 *W11* **Mingäçevir Su Anbarı** *Rus.* Mingechaurskoye Vodokhranilishche, Mingechevirskoye Vodokhranilishche. ⊡ NW Azerbaijan
166 L8 **Mingaladon** ✕ (Yangon) Yangon, SW Myanmar
13 *P11* **Mingan** Quebec, E Canada
149 *U5* **Mingāora** *var.* Mingora, Mongora. North-West Frontier Province, N Pakistan
146 *K8* **Mingbuloq** *Rus.* Mynbulak. Nawoiy Wiloyati, N Uzbekistan
146 *K9* **Mingbuloq Botighi** *Rus.* Vpadina Mynbulak. *depression* N Uzbekistan
Mingechaur/Mingechevir *see* Mingäçevir
Mingechaurskoye Vodokhranilishche/Mingechevirskoye Vodokhranilishche *see* Mingäçevir Su Anbarı
161 Q7 **Mingguang** *prev.* Jiashan. Anhui, S China
166 L4 **Mingin** Sagaing, C Myanmar
105 *Q10* **Minglanilla** Castilla-La Mancha, C Spain
31 *V13* **Mingo Junction** Ohio, N USA
Mingora *see* Mingāora
163 *V7* **Mingshui** Heilongjiang, NE China
Mingteke Daban *see* Mintaka Pass
83 *Q14* **Minguri** Nampula, NE Mozambique
159 *U10* **Minhe** *var.* Shangchuankou. Qinghai, C China
166 L6 **Minhla** Magwe, W Myanmar
167 S14 **Minh Lương** Kiên Giang, S Vietnam
104 *G5* **Minho, Rio** *Sp.* Miño. ⇝ Portugal/Spain *see also* Miño
104 *G5* **Minho** *former province* N Portugal
155 *C24* **Minicoy Island** *island* SW India
33 *P15* **Minidoka** Idaho, NW USA
118 *C11* **Minija** ⇝ W Lithuania
180 *G9* **Minilya** Western Australia
14 *E8* **Minisinakwa Lake** ◎ Ontario, S Canada
45 *T12* **Ministre Point** *headland* S Saint Lucia
11 *V15* **Minitonas** Manitoba, S Canada
Minius *see* Miño
161 *R12* **Min Jiang** ⇝ SE China
160 *H10* **Min Jiang** ⇝ C China
182 *H9* **Minlaton** South Australia
165 Q6 **Minmaya** *var.* Mimmaya. Aomori, Honshū, C Japan
77 *U14* **Minna** Niger, C Nigeria
165 P16 **Minna-jima** *island* Sakishima-shotō, SW Japan
27 *N4* **Minneapolis** Kansas, C USA
29 *U9* **Minneapolis** Minnesota, N USA
29 *V8* **Minneapolis-Saint Paul** ✕ Minnesota, N USA
9 N15 **Minnedosa** Manitoba, S Canada
26 *J7* **Minneola** Kansas, C USA
29 *S7* **Minnesota** *off.* State of Minnesota; also known as Gopher State, New England of the West, North Star State. ◆ *state* N USA
29 *S9* **Minnesota River** ⇝ Minnesota/South Dakota, N USA
29 *V9* **Minnetonka** Minnesota, N USA
29 *O3* **Minnewaukan** North Dakota, N USA
182 *F7* **Minnipa** South Australia
104 *H2* **Miño** Galicia, NW Spain
104 *G5* **Miño** *var.* Mino, Minius, *Port.* Rio Minho. ⇝ Portugal/Spain *see also* Minho, Rio
30 *L4* **Minocqua** Wisconsin, N USA
30 *L12* **Minonk** Illinois, N USA
Minorca *see* Menorca
28 *M3* **Minot** North Dakota, N USA
159 *U8* **Minqin** Gansu, N China
119 *J16* **Minsk** ● (Belarus) Minskaya Voblasts', C Belarus
119 *L16* **Minsk** ✕ Minskaya Voblasts', C Belarus
Minskaya Oblast' *see* Minskaya Voblasts'
119 *K16* **Minskaya Voblasts'** *prev. Rus.* Minskaya Oblast'. ◆ *province* C Belarus
119 *J16* **Minskaya Wzvyshsha** ▲ C Belarus
110 *N12* **Mińsk Mazowiecki** *var.* Nowo-Minsk. Mazowieckie, C Poland
31 *Q13* **Minster** Ohio, N USA
79 *F15* **Minta** Centre, C Cameroon
149 *W2* **Mintaka Pass** *Chin.* Mingteke Daban. *pass* China/Pakistan
115 *D20* **Mínthi** ▲ S Greece
Minthun *see* Minden
13 *O14* **Minto** New Brunswick, SE Canada
10 *H6* **Minto** Yukon Territory, W Canada
39 *R9* **Minto** Alaska, USA
29 *Q3* **Minto** North Dakota, N USA
12 *K6* **Minto, Lac** ◎ Quebec, C Canada
195 *R16* **Minto, Mount** ▲ Antarctica
11 *U17* **Minton** Saskatchewan, S Canada
189 *R15* **Minto Reef** *atoll* Caroline Islands, C Micronesia
37 *R4* **Minturn** Colorado, C USA
107 *J16* **Minturno** Lazio, C Italy
122 K13 **Minusinsk** Krasnoyarskiy Kray, S Russian Federation
108 *G11* **Minusio** Ticino, S Switzerland
79 *E17* **Minvoul** Woleu-Ntem, N Gabon
141 *R13* **Minwakh** N Yemen
159 *V11* **Minxian** *var.* Min Xian. Gansu, C China
Minya *see* El Minya
31 *R6* **Mio** Michigan, N USA
Mionn Ard *see* Mine Head
158 *L5* **Miquan** Xinjiang Uygur Zizhiqu, NW China
119 *I17* **Mir** Hrodzyenskaya Voblasts', W Belarus
106 *H8* **Mira** Veneto, NE Italy
104 *G13* **Mira, Rio** ⇝ S Portugal
12 *K15* **Mirabel** *var.* Montreal. ✕ (Montréal) Quebec, SE Canada
60 *Q8* **Miracema** Rio de Janeiro, SE Brazil
54 *G9* **Miraflores** Boyacá, C Colombia
40 *G10* **Miraflores** Baja California Sur, W Mexico
44 *L9* **Miragoâne** S Haiti
155 *E16* **Miraj** Mahārāshtra, W India
61 *E23* **Miramar** Buenos Aires, E Argentina
103 *R15* **Miramas** Bouches-du-Rhône, SE France
102 *K12* **Mirambeau** Charente-Maritime, W France
102 *L13* **Miramont-de-Guyenne** Lot-et-Garonne, SW France
115 *L25* **Mirampéllou Kólpos** *gulf* Kríti, Greece, E Mediterranean Sea
158 *L8* **Miran** Xinjiang Uygur Zizhiqu, NW China
54 *M5* **Miranda** *off.* Estado Miranda. ◆ *state* N Venezuela
Miranda de Corvo *see* Miranda do Corvo
105 *O3* **Miranda de Ebro** La Rioja, N Spain
104 *G8* **Miranda do Corvo** *var.* Miranda de Corvo. Coimbra, N Portugal
104 *J6* **Miranda do Douro** Bragança, N Portugal
102 *L15* **Mirande** Gers, S France
104 *I6* **Mirandela** Bragança, N Portugal
25 *R15* **Mirando City** Texas, SW USA
106 *G9* **Mirandola** Emilia-Romagna, N Italy
60 *I8* **Mirandópolis** São Paulo, S Brazil
60 *K8* **Mirassol** São Paulo, S Brazil
104 *J3* **Miravalles** ▲ NW Spain
42 *L12* **Miravalles, Volcán** Ѫ NW Costa Rica
141 *W13* **Mirbāṭ** *var.* Marbat. S Oman
44 *M9* **Mirebalais** C Haiti
103 *T6* **Mirecourt** Vosges, NE France
103 *N16* **Mirepoix** Ariège, S France
Mirgorod *see* Myrhorod
139 *W10* **Mīr Ḩājī Khalīl** E Iraq
169 T8 **Miri** Sarawak, East Malaysia
77 *W12* **Miria** Zinder, S Niger
182 *F5* **Mirikata** South Australia
54 *K4* **Mirimire** Falcón, N Venezuela
61 *H18* **Mirim Lagoon** *var.* Lake Mirim, *Sp.* Laguna Merín. *lagoon* Brazil/Uruguay
Mirim, Lake *see* Mirim Lagoon
Mírina *see* Mýrina
172 *H14* **Miringoni** Mohéli, S Comoros
143 *W11* **Mīrjāveh** Sīstān va Balūchestān, SE Iran
195 *Z9* **Mirny** *Russian research station* Antarctica
123 O10 **Mirnyy** Respublika Sakha (Yakutiya), NE Russian Federation
Mironovka *see* Myronivka
110 *F9* **Mirosławiec** Zachodniopomorskie, NW Poland
Mirovo *see* Vrattsa
100 *N10* **Mirow** Mecklenburg-Vorpommern, N Germany
152 *G6* **Mīrpur** Jammu and Kashmir, NW India
Mīrpur *see* New Mirpur
149 *P17* **Mīrpur Batoro** Sind, SE Pakistan
149 *Q16* **Mīrpur Khās** Sind, SE Pakistan
149 *P17* **Mīrpur Sakro** Sind, SE Pakistan
143 *T14* **Mīr Shahdād** Hormozgān, S Iran
Mirtoan Sea *see* Mirtóo Pélagos
115 *G21* **Mirtóo Pélagos** *Eng.* Mirtoan Sea; *anc.* Myrtoum Mare. *sea* S Greece
163 *Z16* **Miryang** *var.* Milyang, *Jap.* Mitsuō. SE South Korea
Mirzachirla *see* Murzechirla
164 E14 **Misaki** Ehime, Shikoku, SW Japan
41 *Q13* **Misantla** Veracruz-Llave, E Mexico
165 R7 **Misawa** Aomori, Honshū, C Japan
57 *G14* **Mishagua, Río** ⇝ C Peru
163 *Z8* **Mishan** Heilongjiang, NE China
31 *O11* **Mishawaka** Indiana, N USA
39 *N6* **Misheguk Mountain** ▲ Alaska, USA
165 N14 **Mishima** *var.* Misima. Shizuoka, Honshū, S Japan
164 E12 **Mi-shima** *island* SW Japan
129 *V4* **Mishkino** Respublika Bashkortostan, W Russian Federation
153 *Y10* **Mishmi Hills** *hill range* NE India
161 *N11* **Mi Shui** ⇝ S China
Misiaf *see* Maşyāf
107 *J23* **Misilmeri** Sicilia, Italy, C Mediterranean Sea
Misima *see* Mishima
Misión de Guana *see* Guana
60 *F13* **Misiones** *off.* Provincia de Misiones. ◆ *province* NE Argentina
62 *P8* **Misiones** *off.* Departamento de las Misiones. ◆ *department* S Paraguay
Misión San Fernando *see* San Fernando
Miskin *see* Maskin
Miskito Coast *see* La Mosquitia
43 *O7* **Miskitos, Cayos** *island group* NE Nicaragua
111 *M21* **Miskolc** Borsod-Abaúj-Zemplén, NE Hungary
171 T12 **Misool, Pulau** *island* Maluku, E Indonesia
Misox *see* Mesocco
29 *Y3* **Misquah Hills** *hill range* Minnesota, N USA
75 *P7* **Mişrātah** *var.* Misurata. NW Libya
14 *C7* **Missanabie** Ontario, S Canada

◆ Country ● Country Capital ◇ Dependent Territory ○ Dependent Territory Capital ◆ Administrative Region ✕ International Airport ▲ Mountain ▲ Mountain Range Ѫ Volcano ⇝ River ◎ Lake ⊡ Reservoir

58 *E10* **Missão Catrimani** Roraima, N Brazil
14 *D6* **Missinaibi** ≈ Ontario, S Canada
14 *C7* **Missinaibi Lake** ◎ Ontario, S Canada
11 *T13* **Missinipe** Saskatchewan, C Canada
28 *M11* **Mission** South Dakota, N USA
25 *S17* **Mission** Texas, SW USA
12 *F10* **Missisa Lake** ◎ Ontario, C Canada
18 *M6* **Missisquoi Bay** *lake bay* Canada/USA
14 *C10* **Mississagi** ≈ Ontario, S Canada
14 *G15* **Mississauga** Ontario, S Canada
31 *P12* **Mississinewa Lake** ⊟ Indiana, N USA
31 *P12* **Mississinewa River** ≈ Indiana/Ohio, N USA
22 *K4* **Mississippi** *off.* State of Mississippi; also known as Bayou State, Magnolia State. ◈ *state* SE USA
14 *K13* **Mississippi** ≈ Ontario, SE Canada
22 *M10* **Mississippi Delta** *delta* Louisiana, S USA
47 *N1* **Mississippi Fan** *undersea feature* N Gulf of Mexico
14 *L13* **Mississippi Lake** ◎ Ontario, SE Canada
(0) *J11* **Mississippi River** ≈ C USA
22 *M9* **Mississippi Sound** *sound* Alabama/Mississippi, S USA
33 *P9* **Missoula** Montana, NW USA
27 *T5* **Missouri** *off.* State of Missouri; also known as Bullion State, Show Me State. ◈ *state* C USA
25 *V11* **Missouri City** Texas, SW USA
(0) *J10* **Missouri River** ≈ C USA
15 *Q6* **Mistassibi** ≈ Quebec, SE Canada
15 *P6* **Mistassini** Quebec, SE Canada
15 *P6* **Mistassini** ≈ Quebec, SE Canada
12 *J11* **Mistassini, Lac** ◎ Quebec, SE Canada
109 *Y3* **Mistelbach an der Zaya** Niederösterreich, NE Austria
107 *L24* **Misterbianco** Sicilia, Italy, C Mediterranean Sea
95 *N19* **Misterhult** Kalmar, S Sweden
57 *H17* **Misti, Volcán** ▲ S Peru
Mistras *see* Mystrás
107 *K23* **Mistretta** *anc.* Amestratus. Sicilia, Italy, C Mediterranean Sea
164 F12 **Misumi** Shimane, Honshū, SW Japan
Misurata *see* Mişrātah
83 *O14* **Mitande** Niassa, N Mozambique
40 *J13* **Mita, Punta de** *headland* C Mexico
55 *W12* **Mitaraka, Massif du** ▲ NE South America
Mitau *see* Jelgava
181 *X9* **Mitchell** Queensland, E Australia
14 *E15* **Mitchell** Ontario, S Canada
28 *I13* **Mitchell** Nebraska, C USA
32 *J12* **Mitchell** Oregon, NW USA
29 *P11* **Mitchell** South Dakota, N USA
23 *P5* **Mitchell Lake** ⊟ Alabama, S USA
31 *P7* **Mitchell, Lake** ◎ Michigan, N USA
21 *P9* **Mitchell, Mount** ▲ North Carolina, SE USA
181 *V3* **Mitchell River** ≈ Queensland, NE Australia
97 *D20* **Mitchelstown** *Ir.* Baile Mhistéala. SW Ireland
14 *M9* **Mitchinamécus, Lac** ◎ Quebec, SE Canada
Mitèmboni *see* Mitemele, Río
79 *D17* **Mitemele, Río** *var.* Mitèmboni, Temboni, Utamboni. ≈ S Equatorial Guinea
149 *S12* **Mithānkot** Punjab, E Pakistan
149 *T7* **Mitha Tiwāna** Punjab, E Pakistan
149 *R17* **Mithi** Sind, SE Pakistan
Míthimna *see* Míthymna
Mi Tho *see* My Tho
115 *L16* **Míthymna** *var.* Míthimna. Lésvos, E Greece
190 *L16* **Mitiaro** *island* S Cook Islands
Mitilíni *see* Mytilíni
15 *U7* **Mitis** ≈ Quebec, SE Canada
41 *R16* **Mitla** Oaxaca, SE Mexico
165 P13 **Mito** Ibaraki, Honshū, S Japan
92 *N2* **Mitra, Kapp** *headland* W Svalbard
184 *M13* **Mitre** ▲ North Island, NZ
185 *B21* **Mitre Peak** ▲ South Island, NZ
39 *O15* **Mitrofania Island** *island* Alaska, USA
Mitrovica/Mitrowitz *see* Sremska Mitrovica, Serbia, Yugoslavia
Mitrovica/Mitrovicë *see* Kosovska Mitrovica, Serbia, Yugoslavia
172 *H12* **Mitsamiouli** Grande Comore, NW Comoros
172 *I3* **Mitsinjo** Mahajanga, NW Madagascar
Mits'iwa *see* Massawa
172 *H13* **Mitsoudjé** Grande Comore, NW Comoros
Mitspe Ramon *see* Mizpé Ramon
165 T5 **Mitsuishi** Hokkaidō, NE Japan
165 O11 **Mitsuke** *var.* Mituke. Niigata, Honshū, C Japan
Mitsuō *see* Miryang
164 C12 **Mitsushima** Nagasaki, Tsushima, SW Japan
100 *G12* **Mittelandkanal** *canal* NW Germany
108 *J7* **Mittelberg** Vorarlberg, NW Austria
Mitteldorf *see* Międzychód
Mittelstadt *see* Baia Sprie
Mitterburg *see* Pazin
109 *P7* **Mittersill** Salzburg, NW Austria
101 *N16* **Mittweida** Sachsen, E Germany
54 *J13* **Mitú** Vaupés, SE Colombia
Mituke *see* Mitsuke
Mitumba, Chaîne des/Mitumba Range *see* Mitumba, Monts
79 *O22* **Mitumba, Monts** *var.* Chaîne des Mitumba, Mitumba Range. ▲ E Dem. Rep. Congo (Zaire)
79 *N23* **Mitwaba** Katanga, SE Dem. Rep. Congo (Zaire)
79 *E18* **Mitzic** Woleu-Ntem, N Gabon
82 *K11* **Miueru Wantipa, Lake** ◎ N Zambia
165 N14 **Miura** Kanagawa, Honshū, S Japan
165 *Q10* **Miyagi** *off.* Miyagi-ken. ◈ *prefecture* Honshū, C Japan
138 *M7* **Miyāh, Wādī al** *dry watercourse* E Syria
165 X13 **Miyake** Tōkyō, Miyako-jima, SE Japan
165 R8 **Miyako** Iwate, Honshū, C Japan
165 Q16 **Miyako-jima** *island* Sakishima-shotō, SW Japan
164 D16 **Miyakonojō** *var.* Miyakonzyô. Miyazaki, Kyūshū, SW Japan
Miyakonzyô *see* Miyakonojō
165 Q16 **Miyako-shotō** *island group* SW Japan
144 *G11* **Miyaly** Atyrau, W Kazakhstan
Miyāndoāb *see* Miāndowāb
Miyāneh *see* Miāneh
164 D16 **Miyazaki** Miyazaki, Kyūshū, SW Japan
164 D16 **Miyazaki** *off.* Miyazaki-ken. ◈ *prefecture* Kyūshū, SW Japan
164 J12 **Miyazu** Kyōto, Honshū, SW Japan
Miyory *see* Myory
164 G12 **Miyoshi** *var.* Miyosi. Hiroshima, Honshū, SW Japan
Miyosi *see* Miyoshi
Miza *see* Mizë
81 *H14* **Mīzan Teferī** Southern, S Ethiopia
Mizda *see* Mizdah
75 *O8* **Mizdah** *var.* Mizda. NW Libya
113 *K20* **Mizë** *var.* Miza. Fier, W Albania
97 *A22* **Mizen Head** *Ir.* Carn Uí Néid. *headland* SW Ireland
116 *H7* **Mizhhir"ya** *Rus.* Mezhgor'ye. Zakarpats'ka Oblast', W Ukraine
160 *L4* **Mizhi** Shaanxi, C China
116 *K13* **Mizil** Prahova, SE Romania
114 *H7* **Miziya** Vratsa, NW Bulgaria
153 *W15* **Mizo Hills** *hill range* E India
153 *W15* **Mizoram** ◈ *state* NE India
138 *F12* **Mizpé Ramon** *var.* Mitspe Ramon. Southern, S Israel
57 *L19* **Mizque** Cochabamba, C Bolivia
57 *M19* **Mizque, Río** ≈ C Bolivia
165 *Q9* **Mizusawa** Iwate, Honshū, C Japan
95 *M18* **Mjölby** Östergötland, S Sweden
95 *G15* **Mjøndalen** Buskerud, S Norway
95 *J19* **Mjörn** ◎ S Sweden
94 *I13* **Mjøsa** *var.* Mjøsen. ◎ S Norway
Mjøsen *see* Mjøsa
81 *G21* **Mkalama** Singida, C Tanzania
80 *K13* **Mkata** ≈ C Tanzania
83 *K14* **Mkushi** Central, C Zambia
83 *L22* **Mkuze** KwaZulu/Natal, E South Africa
81 *J22* **Mkwaja** Tanga, E Tanzania
111 *D16* **Mladá Boleslav** *Ger.* Jungbunzlau. Středočeský Kraj, N Czech Republic
112 *M12* **Mladenovac** Serbia, C Yugoslavia
114 *L11* **Mladinovo** Khaskovo, S Bulgaria
113 *O17* **Mlado Nagoričane** N FYR Macedonia
Mlanje *see* Mulanje
112 *N12* **Mlava** ≈ E Yugoslavia
110 *L9* **Mława** Mazowieckie, C Poland
113 *G16* **Mljet** *It.* Meleda; *anc.* Melita. *island* S Croatia
116 *K4* **Mlyniv** Rivnens'ka Oblast', NW Ukraine
83 *I21* **Mmabatho** North-West, N South Africa
83 *I19* **Mmashoro** Central, E Botswana
44 *J7* **Moa** Holguín, E Cuba
76 *J15* **Moa** ≈ Guinea/Sierra Leone
37 *O6* **Moab** Utah, W USA
181 *V1* **Moa Island** *island* Queensland, NE Australia
187 Y15 **Moala** *island* S Fiji
83 *L21* **Moamba** Maputo, SW Mozambique
79 *F19* **Moanda** *var.* Mouanda. Haut-Ogooué, SE Gabon
83 *M15* **Moatize** Tete, NW Mozambique
79 *P22* **Moba** Katanga, E Dem. Rep. Congo (Zaire)
Mobay *see* Montego Bay
79 *K15* **Mobaye** Basse-Kotto, S Central African Republic
79 *K15* **Mobayi-Mbongo** Equateur, NW Dem. Rep. Congo (Zaire)
25 *P2* **Mobeetie** Texas, SW USA
27 *U3* **Moberly** Missouri, C USA
23 *N8* **Mobile** Alabama, S USA
23 *N9* **Mobile Bay** *bay* Alabama, S USA
23 *N8* **Mobile River** ≈ Alabama, S USA
29 *N8* **Mobridge** South Dakota, N USA
Mobutu Sese Seko, Lac *see* Albert, Lake
45 *N8* **Moca** N Dominican Republic
Moçâmedes *see* Namibe
167 *S6* **Môc Châu** Sơn La, N Vietnam
187 Z15 **Moce** *island* Lau Group, E Fiji
83 *Q15* **Moçambique** Nampula, NE Mozambique
Mocha *see* Al Mukhā
193 T11 **Mocha Fracture Zone** *tectonic feature* SE Pacific Ocean
63 *F14* **Mocha, Isla** *island* C Chile
56 *C12* **Moche, Río** ≈ W Peru
167 S14 **Môc Hoa** Long An, S Vietnam
83 *I20* **Mochudi** Kgatleng, SE Botswana
82 *Q13* **Mocímboa da Praia** *var.* Vila de Mocímboa da Praia. Cabo Delgado, N Mozambique
94 *L13* **Mockfjärd** Dalarna, C Sweden
21 *R9* **Mocksville** North Carolina, SE USA
32 *F8* **Moclips** Washington, NW USA
82 *C13* **Môco** *var.* Morro de Môco. ▲ W Angola
54 *D13* **Mocoa** Putumayo, SW Colombia
60 *M8* **Mococa** São Paulo, S Brazil
Môco, Morro de *see* Môco
40 *H8* **Mocorito** Sinaloa, C Mexico
40 *J4* **Moctezuma** Chihuahua, N Mexico
41 *N11* **Moctezuma** San Luis Potosí, C Mexico
40 *G4* **Moctezuma** Sonora, NW Mexico
41 *P12* **Moctezuma, Río** ≈ C Mexico
Mó, Cuan *see* Clew Bay
83 *O16* **Mocuba** Zambézia, NE Mozambique
103 *U12* **Modane** Savoie, E France
106 *F9* **Modena** *anc.* Mutina. Emilia-Romagna, N Italy
36 *I7* **Modena** Utah, W USA
35 *O9* **Modesto** California, W USA
107 *L25* **Modica** *anc.* Motyca. Sicilia, Italy, C Mediterranean Sea
79 *K17* **Modjamboli** Equateur, N Dem. Rep. Congo (Zaire)
109 *X4* **Mödling** Niederösterreich, NE Austria
Modohn *see* Madona
163 *N8* **Modot** Hentiy, C Mongolia
171 *V14* **Modowi** Irian Jaya, E Indonesia
112 *I12* **Modračko Jezero** ⊟ NE Bosnia and Herzegovina
112 *I10* **Modriča** Republika Srpska, N Bosnia and Herzegovina
183 *O13* **Moe** Victoria, SE Australia
Moearatewe *see* Muaratewe
Moei, Mae Nam *see* Thaungyin
94 *H13* **Moelv** Hedmark, S Norway
92 *I10* **Moen** Troms, N Norway
Moen *see* Weno, Micronesia
Möen *see* Møn, Denmark
Moena *see* Muna, Pulau
36 *M10* **Moenkopi Wash** ≈ Arizona, SW USA
185 *F22* **Moeraki Point** *headland* South Island, NZ
99 *F16* **Moerbeke** Oost-Vlaanderen, NW Belgium
99 *H14* **Moerdijk** Noord-Brabant, S Netherlands
Moero, Lac *see* Mweru, Lake
101 *D15* **Moers** *var.* Mörs. Nordrhein-Westfalen, W Germany
Moesi *see* Musi, Air
Moeskroen *see* Mouscron
96 *J13* **Moffat** S Scotland, UK
185 *C22* **Moffat Peak** ▲ South Island, NZ
152 *H8* **Moga** Punjab, N India
79 *N19* **Moga** Sud Kivu, E Dem. Rep. Congo (Zaire)
Mogadiscio/Mogadishu *see* Muqdisho
Mogador *see* Essaouira
104 *J6* **Mogadouro** Bragança, N Portugal
167 *N2* **Mogaung** Kachin State, N Myanmar
110 *L13* **Mogielnica** Mazowieckie, C Poland
Mogilëv *see* Mahilyow
Mogilev-Podol'skiy *see* Mohyliv-Podil's'kyy
Mogilëvskaya Oblast' *see* Mahilyowskaya Voblasts'
110 *I11* **Mogilno** Kujawsko-pomorskie, C Poland
60 *L9* **Mogi-Mirim** *var.* Moji-Mirim. São Paulo, S Brazil
83 *Q15* **Mogincual** Nampula, NE Mozambique
114 *E13* **Moglenítsas** ≈ N Greece
106 *H8* **Mogliano Veneto** Veneto, NE Italy
113 *M21* **Moglicë** Korçë, SE Albania
123 O13 **Mogocha** Chitinskaya Oblast', S Russian Federation
122 J11 **Mogochin** Tomskaya Oblast', C Russian Federation
80 *F13* **Mogogh** Jonglei, SE Sudan
171 U12 **Mogoi** Irian Jaya, E Indonesia
166 M4 **Mogok** Mandalay, C Myanmar
37 *P14* **Mogollon Mountains** ▲ New Mexico, SW USA
36 *M12* **Mogollon Rim** *cliff* Arizona, SW USA
61 *E23* **Mogotes, Punta** *headland* E Argentina
42 *J8* **Mogotón** ▲ NW Nicaragua
104 *I14* **Moguer** Andalucía, S Spain
111 *J26* **Mohács** Baranya, SW Hungary
185 *C20* **Mohaka** ≈ North Island, NZ
28 *M2* **Mohall** North Dakota, N USA
Moḩammadābād *see* Dargaz
74 *F6* **Mohammedia** *prev.* Fédala. NW Morocco
74 *F6* **Mohammed V** × (Casablanca) W Morocco
Mohammerah *see* Khorramshahr
36 *H10* **Mohave, Lake** ⊟ Arizona/Nevada, W USA
36 *I12* **Mohave Mountains** ▲ Arizona, SW USA
36 *I15* **Mohawk Mountains** ▲ Arizona, SW USA
18 *J10* **Mohawk River** ≈ New York, NE USA
163 *T3* **Mohe** Heilongjiang, NE China
95 *L20* **Moheda** Kronoberg, S Sweden
172 *H13* **Mohéli** *var.* Mwali, Mohilla, Mohila, *Fr.* Moili. *island* S Comoros
152 *I11* **Mohendergarh** Haryāna, N India
38 *K12* **Mohican, Cape** *headland* Nunivak Island, Alaska, USA
Mohn *see* Muhu
101 *G15* **Möhne** ≈ W Germany
101 *G15* **Möhne-Stausee** ⊟ W Germany
92 *P2* **Mohn, Kapp** *headland* NW Svalbard
197 *S14* **Mohns Ridge** *undersea feature* Greenland Sea/Norwegian Sea
57 *I17* **Moho** Puno, SW Peru
Mohokare *see* Caledon
95 *L17* **Moholm** Västra Götaland, S Sweden
36 *J11* **Mohon Peak** ▲ Arizona, SW USA
81 *J23* **Mohoro** Pwani, E Tanzania
Mohra *see* Moravice
Mohrungen *see* Morąg
116 *M7* **Mohyliv-Podil's'kyy** *Rus.* Mogilev-Podol'skiy. Vinnyts'ka Oblast', C Ukraine
95 *D17* **Moi** Rogaland, S Norway
116 *K11* **Moinești** *Hung.* Mojnest. Bacău, E Romania
Móinteach Mílic *see* Mountmellick
14 *J14* **Moira** ≈ Ontario, SE Canada
92 *G13* **Mo i Rana** Nordland, C Norway
153 *X14* **Moirāng** Manipur, NE India
115 *J25* **Moíres** Kríti, Greece, E Mediterranean Sea
118 *H6* **Mõisaküla** *Ger.* Moiseküll. Viljandimaa, S Estonia
Moiseküll *see* Mõisaküla
15 *W4* **Moisie** Quebec, E Canada
15 *W3* **Moisie** ≈ Quebec, SE Canada
102 *M14* **Moissac** Tarn-et-Garonne, S France
78 *I13* **Moïssala** Moyen-Chari, S Chad
55 *O7* **Moitaco** Bolívar, E Venezuela
95 *P15* **Möja** Stockholm, C Sweden
105 *Q14* **Mojácar** Andalucía, S Spain
35 *T13* **Mojave** California, W USA
35 *V13* **Mojave Desert** *plain* California, W USA
35 *V13* **Mojave River** ≈ California, W USA
Moji-Mirim *see* Mogi-Mirim
113 *K15* **Mojkovac** Montenegro, SW Yugoslavia
Mojnest *see* Moinești
Mōka *see* Mooka
153 *Q13* **Mokāma** *prev.* Mokameh, Mukama. Bihār, N India
79 *O25* **Mokambo** Katanga, SE Dem. Rep. Congo (Zaire)
Mokameh *see* Mokāma
38 *D9* **Mokapu Point** *headland* Oahu, Hawaii, USA, C Pacific Ocean
184 *L9* **Mokau** Waikato, North Island, NZ
184 *L9* **Mokau** ≈ North Island, NZ
35 *P7* **Mokelumne River** ≈ California, W USA
83 *J23* **Mokhotlong** NE Lesotho
Mokil Atoll *see* Mwokil Atoll
95 *N14* **Möklinta** Västmanland, C Sweden
184 *L4* **Mokohinau Islands** *island group* N NZ
153 *X12* **Mokokchūng** Nāgāland, NE India
78 *F12* **Mokolo** Extrême-Nord, N Cameroon
185 *D24* **Mokoreta** ≈ South Island, NZ
163 *X17* **Mokp'o** *Jap.* Moppo. SW South Korea
113 *L16* **Mokra Gora** ▲ S Yugoslavia
Mokrany *see* Makrany
129 *O5* **Moksha** ≈ W Russian Federation
Moktama *see* Martaban
77 *T14* **Mokwa** Niger, W Nigeria
99 *J16* **Mol** *prev.* Moll. Antwerpen, N Belgium
107 *O17* **Mola di Bari** Puglia, SE Italy
Molai *see* Moláoi
41 *P13* **Molango** Hidalgo, C Mexico
115 *F22* **Moláoi** *var.* Molai. Pelopónnisos, S Greece
41 *Z12* **Molas del Norte, Punta** *var.* Punta Molas. *headland* SE Mexico
Molas, Punta *see* Molas del Norte, Punta
105 *R11* **Molatón** ▲ C Spain
97 *K18* **Mold** NE Wales, UK
Moldau *see* Moldova
Moldau *see* Vltava, Czech Republic
Moldavia *see* Moldova
Moldavian SSR/Moldavskaya SSR *see* Moldova
94 *E9* **Molde** Møre og Romsdal, S Norway
Moldotau, Khrebet *see* Moldo-Too, Khrebet
147 *V9* **Moldo-Too, Khrebet** *prev.* Khrebet Moldotau. ▲ C Kyrgyzstan
116 *K9* **Moldova** ≈ N Romania
116 *K9* **Moldova** *Eng.* Moldavia, *Ger.* Moldau. *former province* NE Romania
116 *L9* **Moldova** *off.* Republic of Moldova, *var.* Moldavia; *prev.* Moldavian SSR, *Rus.* Moldavskaya SSR. ◆ *republic* SE Europe
116 *F13* **Moldova Nouă** *Ger.* Neumoldowa, *Hung.* Újmoldova. Caraș-Severin, SW Romania
116 *F13* **Moldova Veche** *Ger.* Altmoldowa, *Hung.* Ómoldova. Caraș-Severin, SW Romania
Moldoveanul *see* Vârful Moldoveanu
83 *I20* **Molepolole** Kweneng, SE Botswana
44 *L8* **Môle-St-Nicolas** NW Haiti
118 *H13* **Molėtai** Molėtai, E Lithuania
107 *O17* **Molfetta** Puglia, SE Italy
171 P11 **Molibagu** Sulawesi, N Indonesia
62 *G12* **Molina** Maule, C Chile
105 *Q7* **Molina de Aragón** Castilla-La Mancha, C Spain
105 *R13* **Molina de Segura** Murcia, SE Spain
30 *J11* **Moline** Illinois, N USA
27 *P7* **Moline** Kansas, C USA
79 *P23* **Moliro** Katanga, SE Dem. Rep. Congo (Zaire)
107 *K16* **Molise** ◈ *region* S Italy
95 *K15* **Molkom** Värmland, C Sweden
Moll *see* Mol
109 *Q9* **Möll** ≈ S Austria
95 *J22* **Mölle** Skåne, S Sweden
57 *H18* **Mollendo** Arequipa, SW Peru
105 *U5* **Mollerussa** Cataluña, NE Spain
108 *H8* **Mollis** Glarus, NE Switzerland
95 *J19* **Mölndal** Västra Götaland, S Sweden
95 *J19* **Mölnlycke** Västra Götaland, S Sweden
117 *U9* **Molochans'k** *Rus.* Molochansk. Zaporiz'ka Oblast', SE Ukraine
117 *U10* **Molochna** *Rus.* Molochnaya. ≈ S Ukraine
Molochnaya *see* Molochna
117 *U10* **Molochnyy Lyman** *bay* N Black Sea
Molodechno/Molodeczno *see* Maladzyechna
195 *V3* **Molodezhnaya** *Russian research station* Antarctica
126 *J14* **Mologa** ≈ NW Russian Federation
38 *E9* **Molokai** *Haw.* Moloka'i. *island* Hawaii, USA, C Pacific Ocean
175 *X3* **Molokai Fracture Zone** *tectonic feature* NE Pacific Ocean
126 *K15* **Molokovo** Tverskaya Oblast', W Russian Federation
127 *Q14* **Moloma** ≈ NW Russian Federation
183 *R8* **Molong** New South Wales, SE Australia
83 *H21* **Molopo** *seasonal river* Botswana/South Africa
115 *F17* **Mólos** Stereá Ellás, C Greece
171 O11 **Molosipat** Sulawesi, N Indonesia
Molotov *see* Severodvinsk, Arkhangel'skaya Oblast', Russian Federation
Molotov *see* Perm', Permskaya Oblast', Russian Federation
79 *G17* **Moloundou** Est, SE Cameroon
103 *U5* **Molsheim** Bas-Rhin, NE France
9 *O13* **Molson Lake** ◎ Manitoba, C Canada
Moluccas *see* Maluku
171 Q12 **Molucca Sea** *Ind.* Laut Maluku. *sea* E Indonesia
Molukken *see* Maluku
83 *O15* **Molumbo** Zambézia, N Mozambique
171 T15 **Molu, Pulau** *island* Maluku, E Indonesia
83 *P16* **Moma** Nampula, NE Mozambique
171 X14 **Momats** ≈ Irian Jaya, E Indonesia
42 *J11* **Mombacho, Volcán** ☒ SW Nicaragua
81 *K21* **Mombasa** Coast, SE Kenya
81 *J21* **Mombasa** × Coast, SE Kenya
Mombetsu *see* Monbetsu
114 *J12* **Momchilgrad** *prev.* Mastanli. Kŭrdzhali, S Bulgaria
99 *F23* **Momignies** Hainaut, S Belgium
54 *E6* **Momil** Córdoba, NW Colombia
42 *I10* **Momotombo, Volcán** ☒ W Nicaragua
56 *B5* **Mompiche, Ensenada de** *bay* NW Ecuador
79 *K18* **Mompono** Equateur, NW Dem. Rep. Congo (Zaire)
54 *F6* **Mompós** Bolívar, NW Colombia
95 *J24* **Møn** *prev.* Möen. *island* SE Denmark
36 *L4* **Mona** Utah, W USA
Mona, Canal de la *see* Mona Passage
96 *E8* **Monach Islands** *island group* NW Scotland, UK
103 *V14* **Monaco** *var.* Monaco-Ville; *anc.* Monoecus. ● (Monaco) S Monaco
103 *V14* **Monaco** *off.* Principality of Monaco. ◆ *monarchy* W Europe
Monaco *see* München
Monaco Basin *see* Canary Basin
Monaco-Ville *see* Monaco
96 *I9* **Monadhliath Mountains** ▲ N Scotland, UK
55 *O6* **Monagas** *off.* Estado Monagas. ◈ *state* NE Venezuela
97 *F16* **Monaghan** *Ir.* Muineachán. N Ireland
97 *E16* **Monaghan** *Ir.* Muineachán. *cultural region* N Ireland
43 *S16* **Monagrillo** Herrera, S Panama
24 *L8* **Monahans** Texas, SW USA
45 *Q9* **Mona, Isla** *island* W Puerto Rico
45 *Q9* **Mona Passage** *Sp.* Canal de la Mona. *channel* Dominican Republic/Puerto Rico
43 *O14* **Mona, Punta** *headland* E Costa Rica
155 *K25* **Monaragala** Uva Province, SE Sri Lanka
33 *S9* **Monarch** Montana, NW USA
8 H14 **Monarch Mountain** ▲ British Columbia, SW Canada
Monasterio *see* Monesterio
Monasterzyska *see* Monastyrys'ka
Monastir *see* Bitola
Monastyriska *see* Monastyrys'ka
117 *O7* **Monastyrshche** Cherkas'ka Oblast', C Ukraine
116 *J6* **Monastyrys'ka** *Pol.* Monasterzyska, *Rus.* Monastyriska. Ternopil's'ka Oblast', W Ukraine
79 *E15* **Monatélé** Centre, SW Cameroon
165 U2 **Monbetsu** *var.* Mombetsu, Monbetu. Hokkaidō, NE Japan
Monbetu *see* Monbetsu
106 *B8* **Moncalieri** Piemonte, NW Italy
104 *G4* **Monção** Viana do Castelo, N Portugal
105 *Q5* **Moncayo** ▲ N Spain
105 *Q5* **Moncayo, Sierra del** ▲ N Spain
126 *J4* **Monchegorsk** Murmanskaya Oblast', NW Russian Federation
101 *D15* **Mönchengladbach** *prev.* München-Gladbach. Nordrhein-Westfalen, W Germany
104 *F14* **Monchique** Faro, S Portugal
104 *G14* **Monchique, Serra de** ▲ S Portugal
21 *S14* **Moncks Corner** South Carolina, SE USA
41 *N7* **Monclova** Coahuila de Zaragoza, NE Mexico
Moncorvo *see* Torre de Moncorvo
13 *P14* **Moncton** New Brunswick, SE Canada
104 *F8* **Mondego, Cabo** *headland* N Portugal
104 *G8* **Mondego, Rio** ≈ N Portugal
104 *I2* **Mondoñedo** Galicia, NW Spain
99 *N25* **Mondorf-les-Bains** Grevenmacher, SE Luxembourg
102 *M7* **Mondoubleau** Loir-et-Cher, C France
30 *J6* **Mondovi** Wisconsin, N USA
106 *B9* **Mondovì** Piemonte, NW Italy
105 *P3* **Mondragón** *var.* Arrasate. País Vasco, N Spain
107 *J17* **Mondragone** Campania, S Italy
109 *R5* **Mondsee** ◎ N Austria
115 *G22* **Monemvasía** Pelopónnisos, S Greece
18 *B15* **Monessen** Pennsylvania, NE USA
104 *J12* **Monesterio** *var.* Monasterio. Extremadura, W Spain
14 *L8* **Monet** Quebec, SE Canada
27 *S8* **Monett** Missouri, C USA
27 *X9* **Monette** Arkansas, C USA
14 *G11* **Monetville** Ontario, S Canada
106 *J7* **Monfalcone** Friuli-Venezia Giulia, NE Italy
104 *H10* **Monforte** Portalegre, C Portugal
104 *I4* **Monforte** Galicia, NW Spain
81 *I24* **Monga** Lindi, SE Tanzania
79 *L16* **Monga** Orientale, N Dem. Rep. Congo (Zaire)
81 *F15* **Mongalla** Bahr el Gabel, S Sudan
153 *U11* **Mongar** E Bhutan
167 U6 **Mong Cai** Quang Ninh, N Vietnam
180 *I11* **Mongers Lake** *salt lake* Western Australia
186 K8 **Mongga** Kolombangara, NW Solomon Islands
167 O6 **Möng Hpayak** Shan State, E Myanmar
Monghyr *see* Munger
106 *B10* **Mongioie** ▲ NW Italy
167 N5 **Möng Küng** Shan State, E Myanmar
Mongla *see* Mungla
188 *C15* **Mongmong** C Guam
167 N6 **Möng Nai** Shan State, E Myanmar
78 *I11* **Mongo** Guéra, C Chad
76 *I14* **Mongo** ≈ N Sierra Leone
163 *I8* **Mongolia** *Mong.* Mongol Uls. ◆ *republic* E Asia
131 *V8* **Mongolia, Plateau of** *plateau* E Mongolia
Mongolküre *see* Zhaosu
Mongol Uls *see* Mongolia
79 *E17* **Mongomo** E Equatorial Guinea
77 *Y12* **Mongonu** *var.* Monguno. Borno, NE Nigeria
Mongora *see* Mingãora
78 *K11* **Mongororo** Ouaddaï, SE Chad
Mongos, Chaîne des *see* Bongo, Massif des
79 *I16* **Mongoumba** Lobaye, SW Central African Republic
Mongrove, Punta *see* Cayacal, Punta
83 *G15* **Mongu** Western, W Zambia
76 *I10* **Monguel** Gorgol, SW Mauritania
Monguno *see* Mongonu
167 *N4* **Möng Yai** Shan State, E Myanmar
167 *O5* **Möng Yang** Shan State, E Myanmar
167 *N3* **Möng Yu** Shan State, E Myanmar
162 *K8* **Mönhbulag** Övörhangay, C Mongolia
Mönh Sarīdag *see* Munku-Sardyk, Gora
186 F9 **Moni** ≈ S Papau New Guinea
115 *I15* **Moní Megístis Lávras** *monastery* Kentrikí Makedonía, N Greece
115 *F18* **Moní Osíou Loúkas** *monastery* Stereá Ellás, C Greece
54 *F9* **Moniquirá** Boyacá, C Colombia
103 *Q12* **Monistrol-sur-Loire** Haute-Loire, C France
35 *V7* **Monitor Range** ▲ Nevada, W USA
115 *I14* **Moní Vatopedíou** *monastery* Kentrikí Makedonía, N Greece
Monkchester *see* Newcastle upon Tyne
83 *N14* **Monkey Bay** Southern, SE Malawi
43 *N11* **Monkey Point** *var.* Punta Mico, Punte Mono, Punto Mico. *headland* SE Nicaragua
Monkey River *see* Monkey River Town
42 *G3* **Monkey River Town** *var.* Monkey River. Toledo, SE Belize
14 *M13* **Monkland** Ontario, SE Canada
79 *J19* **Monkoto** Equateur, NW Dem. Rep. Congo (Zaire)
97 *K21* **Monmouth** *Wel.* Trefynwy. SE Wales, UK
30 *J12* **Monmouth** Illinois, N USA
32 *F12* **Monmouth** Oregon, NW USA

◆ COUNTRY ● COUNTRY CAPITAL ◇ DEPENDENT TERRITORY ○ DEPENDENT TERRITORY CAPITAL ◈ ADMINISTRATIVE REGION × INTERNATIONAL AIRPORT ▲ MOUNTAIN ▲ MOUNTAIN RANGE ☒ VOLCANO ≈ RIVER ◎ LAKE ⊟ RESERVOIR

97 K21 **Monmouth** *cultural region* SE Wales, UK
98 I10 **Monnickendam** Noord-Holland, C Netherlands
77 R15 **Mono** ≈ C Togo
Monoecus *see* Monaco
35 R8 **Mono Lake** ◎ California, W USA
115 O23 **Monólithos** Ródos, Dodekánisos, Greece, Aegean Sea
19 Q12 **Monomoy Island** *island* Massachusetts, NE USA
31 O12 **Monon** Indiana, N USA
29 Y12 **Monona** Iowa, C USA
30 L9 **Monona** Wisconsin, N USA
18 B15 **Monongahela** Pennsylvania, NE USA
18 B16 **Monongahela River** ≈ NE USA
107 P17 **Monopoli** Puglia, SE Italy
Mono, Punte *see* Monkey Point
111 K23 **Monor** Pest, C Hungary
Monostor *see* Beli Manastir
78 K8 **Monou** Borkou-Ennedi-Tibesti, NE Chad
105 S12 **Monóvar** País Valenciano, E Spain
105 R7 **Monreal del Campo** Aragón, NE Spain
107 I23 **Monreale** Sicilia, Italy, C Mediterranean Sea
23 T3 **Monroe** Georgia, SE USA
29 W14 **Monroe** Iowa, C USA
22 I5 **Monroe** Louisiana, S USA
31 S10 **Monroe** Michigan, N USA
18 K13 **Monroe** New York, NE USA
21 S11 **Monroe** North Carolina, SE USA
36 L6 **Monroe** Utah, W USA
32 H7 **Monroe** Washington, NW USA
30 L9 **Monroe** Wisconsin, N USA
27 V3 **Monroe City** Missouri, C USA
31 O15 **Monroe Lake** ▣ Indiana, N USA
23 O7 **Monroeville** Alabama, S USA
18 C15 **Monroeville** Pennsylvania, NE USA
76 J16 **Monrovia** ● (Liberia) W Liberia
76 J16 **Monrovia** ✈ W Liberia
105 T7 **Monroyo** Aragón, NE Spain
99 F20 **Mons** *Dut.* Bergen. Hainaut, S Belgium
104 I8 **Monsanto** Castelo Branco, C Portugal
106 H8 **Monselice** Veneto, NE Italy
166 M9 **Mon State** ◈ *state* S Myanmar
98 G12 **Monster** Zuid-Holland, W Netherlands
95 N20 **Mönsterås** Kalmar, S Sweden
101 F17 **Montabaur** Rheinland-Pfalz, W Germany
106 G8 **Montagnana** Veneto, NE Italy
35 N1 **Montague** California, W USA
25 S5 **Montague** Texas, SW USA
183 S11 **Montague Island** *island* New South Wales, SE Australia
39 S12 **Montague Island** *island* Alaska, USA
39 S13 **Montague Strait** *strait* N Gulf of Alaska
102 J8 **Montaigu** Vendée, NW France
Montaigu *see* Scherpenheuvel
105 S7 **Montalbán** Aragón, NE Spain
106 G13 **Montalcino** Toscana, C Italy
104 H5 **Montalegre** Vila Real, N Portugal
114 G8 **Montana** *prev.* Ferdinand, Mikhaylovgrad. Montana, NW Bulgaria
108 D10 **Montana** Valais, SW Switzerland
39 R11 **Montana** Alaska, USA
114 G8 **Montana** ◈ *province* NW Bulgaria
33 T9 **Montana** *off.* State of Montana; also known as Mountain State, Treasure State. ◈ *state* NW USA
104 J10 **Montánchez** Extremadura, W Spain
Montañita *see* La Montañita
15 Q8 **Mont-Apica** Quebec, SE Canada
104 G10 **Montargil** Portalegre, C Portugal
104 G10 **Montargil, Barragem de** ▣ C Portugal
103 O7 **Montargis** Loiret, C France
103 O4 **Montataire** Oise, N France
102 M14 **Montauban** Tarn-et-Garonne, S France
19 N14 **Montauk** Long Island, New York, NE USA
19 N14 **Montauk Point** *headland* Long Island, New York, NE USA
103 Q7 **Montbard** Côte d'Or, C France
103 U7 **Montbéliard** Doubs, E France
25 W11 **Mont Belvieu** Texas, SW USA
105 U6 **Montblanc** *var.* Montblanch. Cataluña, NE Spain
Montblanch *see* Montblanc
103 Q11 **Montbrison** Loire, E France
Montcalm, Lake *see* Dogai Coring
103 Q9 **Montceau-les-Mines** Saône-et-Loire, C France
103 U12 **Mont Cenis, Col du** *pass* E France
102 K15 **Mont-de-Marsan** Landes, SW France
103 O3 **Montdidier** Somme, N France
187 Q17 **Mont-Dore** Province Sud, S New Caledonia
20 K10 **Monteagle** Tennessee, S USA
57 M20 **Monteagudo** Chuquisaca, S Bolivia
41 R16 **Monte Albán** *ruins* Oaxaca, S Mexico
105 R11 **Montealegre del Castillo** Castilla-La Mancha, C Spain
59 N18 **Monte Azul** Minas Gerais, SE Brazil
14 M12 **Montebello** Quebec, SE Canada
106 H7 **Montebelluna** Veneto, NE Italy
60 G13 **Montecarlo** Misiones, NE Argentina
61 D16 **Monte Caseros** Corrientes, NE Argentina
60 J13 **Monte Castelo** Santa Catarina, S Brazil
106 F11 **Montecatini Terme** Toscana, C Italy
42 H7 **Montecillos, Cordillera de** ▲▲ W Honduras
62 I12 **Monte Comén** Mendoza, W Argentina
44 M8 **Monte Cristi** *var.* San Fernando de Monte Cristi. NW Dominican Republic
58 C13 **Monte Cristo** Amazonas, W Brazil
107 E14 **Montecristo, Isola di** *island* Archipelago Toscano, C Italy
Monte Croce Carnico, Passo di *see* Plöcken Pass
58 J12 **Monte Dourado** Pará, NE Brazil
40 L11 **Monte Escobedo** Zacatecas, C Mexico
106 I13 **Montefalco** Umbria, C Italy
107 H14 **Montefiascone** Lazio, C Italy
105 N14 **Montefrío** Andalucía, S Spain
44 I11 **Montego Bay** *var.* Mobay. W Jamaica
Montego Bay *see* Sangster
104 J8 **Montehermoso** Extremadura, W Spain
104 F10 **Montejunto, Serra de** ▲ C Portugal
Monteleone di Calabria *see* Vibo Valentia
54 E7 **Montelíbano** Córdoba, NW Colombia
103 R13 **Montélimar** *anc.* Acunum Acusio, Montilium Adhemari. Drôme, E France
104 K15 **Montellano** Andalucía, S Spain
35 Y2 **Montello** Nevada, W USA
30 L8 **Montello** Wisconsin, N USA
63 J18 **Montemayor, Meseta de** *plain* SE Argentina
41 O9 **Montemorelos** Nuevo León, NE Mexico
104 G11 **Montemor-o-Novo** Évora, S Portugal
104 G8 **Montemor-o-Velho** *var.* Montemor-o-Vélho. Coimbra, N Portugal
104 H7 **Montemuro, Serra de** ▲ N Portugal
102 K12 **Montendre** Charente-Maritime, W France
61 I15 **Montenegro** Rio Grande do Sul, S Brazil
113 J16 **Montenegro** *Serb.* Crna Gora. ◈ *republic* SW Yugoslavia
62 G10 **Monte Patria** Coquimbo, N Chile
45 O9 **Monte Plata** E Dominican Republic
83 P14 **Montepuez** Cabo Delgado, N Mozambique
83 P14 **Montepuez** ≈ N Mozambique
106 G13 **Montepulciano** Toscana, C Italy
62 L6 **Monte Quemado** Santiago del Estero, N Argentina
103 O6 **Montereau-Faut-Yonne** *anc.* Condate. Seine-St-Denis, N France
35 N11 **Monterey** California, W USA
20 L9 **Monterey** Tennessee, S USA
21 T5 **Monterey** Virginia, NE USA
Monterey *see* Monterrey
35 N10 **Monterey Bay** *bay* California, W USA
54 D6 **Montería** Córdoba, NW Colombia
57 N18 **Montero** Santa Cruz, C Bolivia
62 J7 **Monteros** Tucumán, C Argentina
104 I5 **Monterrei** Galicia, NW Spain
41 O8 **Monterrey** *var.* Monterey. Nuevo León, NE Mexico
32 F9 **Montesano** Washington, NW USA
107 M19 **Montesano sulla Marcellana** Campania, S Italy
107 N16 **Monte Sant' Angelo** Puglia, SE Italy
59 O16 **Monte Santo** Bahia, E Brazil
107 D18 **Monte Santu, Capo di** *headland* Sardegna, Italy, C Mediterranean Sea
59 M19 **Montes Claros** Minas Gerais, SE Brazil
107 K14 **Montesilvano Marina** Abruzzo, C Italy
23 P4 **Montevallo** Alabama, S USA
106 G12 **Montevarchi** Toscana, C Italy
29 S9 **Montevideo** Minnesota, N USA
61 F20 **Montevideo** ● (Uruguay) Montevideo, S Uruguay
37 S7 **Monte Vista** Colorado, C USA
23 T5 **Montezuma** Georgia, SE USA
29 W14 **Montezuma** Iowa, C USA
26 J6 **Montezuma** Kansas, C USA
103 U12 **Montgenèvre, Col de** *pass* France/Italy
97 K20 **Montgomery** E Wales, UK
23 Q5 **Montgomery** *state capital* Alabama, S USA
29 V9 **Montgomery** Minnesota, N USA
18 G13 **Montgomery** Pennsylvania, NE USA
21 Q5 **Montgomery** West Virginia, NE USA
97 K19 **Montgomery** *cultural region* E Wales, UK
Montgomery *see* Sāhīwāl
27 V4 **Montgomery City** Missouri, C USA
35 S8 **Montgomery Pass** *pass* Nevada, W USA
102 K12 **Montguyon** Charente-Maritime, W France
108 C10 **Monthey** Valais, SW Switzerland
27 V13 **Monticello** Arkansas, C USA
23 T4 **Monticello** Florida, SE USA
23 T8 **Monticello** Georgia, SE USA
30 M13 **Monticello** Illinois, N USA
31 O12 **Monticello** Indiana, N USA
29 Y13 **Monticello** Iowa, C USA
20 L7 **Monticello** Kentucky, S USA
29 V8 **Monticello** Minnesota, N USA
22 K7 **Monticello** Mississippi, S USA
27 V2 **Monticello** Missouri, C USA
18 J12 **Monticello** New York, NE USA
37 O7 **Monticello** Utah, W USA
106 F8 **Montichiari** Lombardia, N Italy
102 M12 **Montignac** Dordogne, SW France
99 G21 **Montignies-le-Tilleul** *var.* Montigny-le-Tilleul. Hainaut, S Belgium
14 J8 **Montigny, Lac de** ◎ Quebec, SE Canada
103 S6 **Montigny-le-Roi** Haute-Marne, N France
Montigny-le-Tilleul *see* Montignies-le-Tilleul
43 R16 **Montijo** Veraguas, S Panama
104 F11 **Montijo** Setúbal, W Portugal
104 J11 **Montijo** Extremadura, W Spain
Montilium Adhemari *see* Montélimar
104 M13 **Montilla** Andalucía, S Spain
102 L3 **Montivilliers** Seine-Maritime, N France
15 U7 **Mont-Joli** Quebec, SE Canada
14 M10 **Mont-Laurier** Quebec, SE Canada
15 X5 **Mont-Louis** Quebec, SE Canada
103 N17 **Mont-Louis** *var.* Mont Louis. Pyrénées-Orientales, S France
103 O10 **Montluçon** Allier, C France
15 R10 **Montmagny** Quebec, SE Canada
103 S3 **Montmédy** Meuse, NE France
103 P5 **Montmirail** Marne, N France
15 R9 **Montmorency** ≈ Quebec, SE Canada
102 M10 **Montmorillon** Vienne, W France
107 J14 **Montorio al Vomano** Abruzzo, C Italy
104 M13 **Montoro** Andalucía, S Spain
33 S16 **Montpelier** Idaho, NW USA
29 P6 **Montpelier** North Dakota, N USA
18 M7 **Montpelier** *state capital* Vermont, NE USA
103 Q15 **Montpellier** Hérault, S France
102 L12 **Montpon-Ménestérol** Dordogne, SW France
14 G8 **Montreal** ≈ Ontario, S Canada
14 C8 **Montreal** ≈ Ontario, S Canada
Montreal *see* Mirabel
12 K15 **Montréal** *Eng.* Montreal. Quebec, SE Canada
11 T14 **Montreal Lake** ◎ Saskatchewan, C Canada
14 B9 **Montreal River** Ontario, S Canada
103 N2 **Montreuil** Pas-de-Calais, N France
102 K8 **Montreuil-Bellay** Maine-et-Loire, NW France
108 C10 **Montreux** Vaud, SW Switzerland
108 B9 **Montricher** Vaud, W Switzerland
96 K10 **Montrose** E Scotland, UK
27 W14 **Montrose** Arkansas, C USA
37 Q6 **Montrose** Colorado, C USA
29 Y16 **Montrose** Iowa, C USA
18 H12 **Montrose** Pennsylvania, NE USA
21 X5 **Montross** Virginia, NE USA
15 O12 **Mont-St-Hilaire** Quebec, SE Canada
103 S3 **Mont-St-Martin** Meurthe-et-Moselle, NE France
45 V10 **Montserrat** *var.* Emerald Isle. ◇ *UK dependent territory* E West Indies
105 V5 **Montserrat** ▲ NE Spain
104 M7 **Montuenga** Castilla-León, N Spain
99 M19 **Montzen** Liège, E Belgium
37 N8 **Monument Valley** *valley* Arizona/Utah, SW USA
166 L4 **Monywa** Sagaing, C Myanmar
106 D7 **Monza** Lombardia, N Italy
83 J15 **Monze** Southern, S Zambia
105 T5 **Monzón** Aragón, NE Spain
25 T9 **Moody** Texas, SW USA
98 L13 **Mook** Limburg, SE Netherlands
165 O12 **Mooka** *var.* Mōka. Tochigi, Honshū, S Japan
182 K3 **Moomba** South Australia
14 G13 **Moon** ≈ Ontario, S Canada
Moon *see* Muhu
181 Y10 **Moonie** Queensland, E Australia
193 O5 **Moonless Mountains** *undersea feature* E Pacific Ocean
182 L13 **Moonlight Head** *headland* Victoria, SE Australia
Moon-Sund *see* Väinameri
182 H8 **Moonta** South Australia
Moor *see* Mór
180 I12 **Moora** Western Australia
98 H12 **Moordrecht** Zuid-Holland, C Netherlands
33 T9 **Moore** Montana, NW USA
27 N11 **Moore** Oklahoma, C USA
25 R12 **Moore** Texas, SW USA
191 S10 **Moorea** *island* Îles du Vent, W French Polynesia
21 U3 **Moorefield** West Virginia, NE USA
23 X14 **Moore Haven** Florida, SE USA
180 J11 **Moore, Lake** ◎ Western Australia
19 N7 **Moore Reservoir** ▣ New Hampshire/Vermont, NE USA
44 G1 **Moores Island** *island* N Bahamas
21 R10 **Mooresville** North Carolina, SE USA
29 R5 **Moorhead** Minnesota, N USA
22 K4 **Moorhead** Mississippi, S USA
99 F18 **Moorsel** Oost-Vlaanderen, C Belgium
99 C18 **Moorslede** West-Vlaanderen, W Belgium
18 L8 **Moosalamoo, Mount** ▲ Vermont, NE USA
101 M22 **Moosburg** Bayern, SE Germany
33 S14 **Moose** Wyoming, C USA
12 H11 **Moose** ≈ Ontario, S Canada
12 H10 **Moose Factory** Ontario, S Canada
19 Q4 **Moosehead Lake** ◎ Maine, NE USA
11 U16 **Moose Jaw** Saskatchewan, S Canada
11 V14 **Moose Lake** Manitoba, C Canada
29 W6 **Moose Lake** Minnesota, N USA
19 P6 **Mooselookmeguntic Lake** ◎ Maine, NE USA
39 R12 **Moose Pass** Alaska, USA
19 P5 **Moose River** ≈ Maine, NE USA
18 J9 **Moose River** ≈ New York, NE USA
11 V16 **Moosomin** Saskatchewan, S Canada
12 H10 **Moosonee** Ontario, SE Canada
19 N12 **Moosup** Connecticut, NE USA
83 N16 **Mopeia** Zambézia, NE Mozambique
83 H18 **Mopipi** Central, C Botswana
Moppo *see* Mokp'o
77 N11 **Mopti** Mopti, C Mali
77 O11 **Mopti** ◈ *region* S Mali
57 H18 **Moquegua** Moquegua, SE Peru
57 H18 **Moquegua** *off.* Departamento de Moquegua. ◈ *department* S Peru
111 I23 **Mór** *Ger.* Moor. Fejér, C Hungary
78 G11 **Mora** Extrême-Nord, N Cameroon
104 G11 **Mora** Évora, S Portugal
105 N9 **Mora** Castilla-La Mancha, C Spain
94 L12 **Mora** Dalarna, C Sweden
29 V7 **Mora** Minnesota, N USA
37 T10 **Mora** New Mexico, SW USA
113 J17 **Morača** ≈ SW Yugoslavia
152 K10 **Morādābād** Uttar Pradesh, N India
105 U6 **Móra d'Ebre** *var.* Mora de Ebro. Cataluña, NE Spain
Mora de Ebro *see* Móra d'Ebre
105 S8 **Mora de Rubielos** Aragón, NE Spain
172 H4 **Morafenobe** Mahajanga, W Madagascar
110 K8 **Morąg** *Ger.* Mohrungen. Warmińsko-Mazurskie, NE Poland,
111 L25 **Mórahalom** Csongrád, S Hungary
105 N11 **Moral de Calatrava** Castilla-La Mancha, C Spain
63 G19 **Moraleda, Canal** *strait* SE Pacific Ocean
54 J3 **Morales** Bolívar, N Colombia
54 D12 **Morales** Cauca, SW Colombia
42 F5 **Morales** Izabal, E Guatemala
172 J5 **Moramanga** Toamasina, E Madagascar
27 Q6 **Moran** Kansas, C USA
25 Q7 **Moran** Texas, SW USA
181 X7 **Moranbah** Queensland, NE Australia
44 L13 **Morant Bay** E Jamaica
96 G10 **Morar, Loch** ◎ N Scotland, UK
Morata *see* Goodenough Island
105 Q12 **Moratalla** Murcia, SE Spain
108 C8 **Morat, Lac de** *Ger.* Murtensee. ◎ W Switzerland
84 I11 **Morava** *var.* March. ≈ C Europe *see also* March
Morava *see* Moravia, Czech Republic
Morava *see* Velika Morava, Yugoslavia
29 W15 **Moravia** Iowa, C USA
111 F18 **Moravia** *Cz.* Morava, *Ger.* Mähren. *cultural region* E Czech Republic
111 H17 **Moravice** *Ger.* Mohra. ≈ NE Czech Republic
118 E12 **Moravița** Timiș, SW Romania
111 G17 **Moravská Třebová** *Ger.* Mährisch-Trübau. Pardubický Kraj, C Czech Republic
111 E19 **Moravské Budějovice** *Ger.* Mährisch-Budwitz. Jihlavský Kraj, C Czech Republic
111 F19 **Moravský Krumlov** *Ger.* Mährisch-Kromau. Brněnský Kraj, SE Czech Republic
96 J8 **Moray** *cultural region* N Scotland, UK
96 J8 **Moray Firth** *inlet* N Scotland, UK
42 B10 **Morazán** ◈ *department* NE El Salvador
154 C10 **Morbi** Gujarāt, W India
102 G7 **Morbihan** ◈ *department* NW France
Mörbisch *see* Mörbisch am See
109 Y5 **Mörbisch am See** *var.* Mörbisch. Burgenland, E Austria
95 N21 **Mörbylånga** Kalmar, S Sweden
102 J14 **Morcenx** Landes, SW France
Morcheh Khort *see* Mūrcheh Khvort
11 X17 **Morden** Manitoba, S Canada
Mordovskaya ASSR/Mordvinia *see* Mordoviya, Respublika
129 N5 **Mordoviya, Respublika** *prev.* Mordovskaya ASSR, *Eng.* Mordovia, Mordvinia. ◈ *autonomous republic* W Russian Federation
128 M7 **Mordovo** Tambovskaya Oblast', W Russian Federation
Morea *see* Pelopónnisos
28 K8 **Moreau River** ≈ South Dakota, N USA
97 K16 **Morecambe** NW England, UK
97 K16 **Morecambe Bay** *inlet* NW England, UK
183 S4 **Moree** New South Wales, SE Australia
21 N5 **Morehead** Kentucky, S USA
21 X11 **Morehead City** North Carolina, SE USA
27 Y8 **Morehouse** Missouri, C USA
108 E10 **Mörel** Valais, SW Switzerland
54 D13 **Morelia** Caquetá, S Colombia
41 N14 **Morelia** Michoacán de Ocampo, S Mexico
105 T7 **Morella** País Valenciano, E Spain
40 I7 **Morelos** Chihuahua, N Mexico
41 O15 **Morelos** ◈ *state* S Mexico
154 H7 **Morena** Madhya Pradesh, C India
104 L12 **Morena, Sierra** ▲▲ S Spain
37 O14 **Morenci** Arizona, SW USA
31 R11 **Morenci** Michigan, N USA
116 J13 **Moreni** Dâmbovița, S Romania
94 D9 **Møre og Romsdal** ◈ *county* S Norway
8 E13 **Moresby Island** *island* Queen Charlotte Islands, British Columbia, SW Canada
183 W2 **Moreton Island** *island* Queensland, E Australia
103 O3 **Moreuil** Somme, N France
35 V7 **Morey Peak** ▲ Nevada, W USA
127 U4 **More-Yu** ≈ NW Russian Federation
103 T9 **Morez** Jura, E France
Mórfou *see* Güzelyurt
Morfou Bay/Mórfou, Kólpos *see* Güzelyurt Körfezi
182 J8 **Morgan** South Australia
23 S7 **Morgan** Georgia, SE USA
25 S8 **Morgan** Texas, SW USA
22 J10 **Morgan City** Louisiana, S USA
20 H6 **Morganfield** Kentucky, S USA
35 O10 **Morgan Hill** California, W USA
21 Q9 **Morganton** North Carolina, SE USA
20 J7 **Morgantown** Kentucky, S USA
21 S2 **Morgantown** West Virginia, NE USA
108 B10 **Morges** Vaud, SW Switzerland
148 M4 **Morghāb, Daryā-ye** *var.* Murgab, Murghab, *Turkm.* Murgap Deryasy. ≈ Afghanistan/ Turkmenistan *see also* Murgab
Morghāb, Daryā-ye *see* Murgab
96 I9 **Mor, Glen** *var.* Glen Albyn, Great Glen. *valley* N Scotland, UK
103 T5 **Morhange** Moselle, NE France
158 M5 **Mori** *var.* Mori Kazak Zizhixian. Xinjiang Uygur Zizhiqu, NW China
165 R5 **Mori** Hokkaidō, NE Japan
35 Y6 **Moriah, Mount** ▲ Nevada, W USA
37 S11 **Moriarty** New Mexico, SW USA
54 J12 **Morichal** Guainía, E Colombia
Mori Kazak Zizhixian *see* Mori
163 U7 **Morin Dawa** *var.* Morin Dawa Daurzu Zizhiqi. Nei Mongol Zizhiqu, N China
Morin Dawa Daurzu Zizhiqi *see* Morin Dawa
8 J13 **Morinville** Alberta, SW Canada
165 R8 **Morioka** Iwate, Honshū, C Japan
183 T8 **Morisset** New South Wales, SE Australia
165 Q8 **Moriyoshi-yama** ▲ Honshū, C Japan
92 K13 **Morjärv** Norrbotten, N Sweden
129 R3 **Morki** Respublika Mariy El, W Russian Federation
123 N10 **Morkoka** ≈ NE Russian Federation
102 F5 **Morlaix** Finistère, NW France
95 M20 **Mörlunda** Kalmar, S Sweden
107 N19 **Mormanno** Calabria, SW Italy
36 L11 **Mormon Lake** ◎ Arizona, SW USA
35 Y10 **Mormon Peak** ▲ Nevada, W USA
Mormon State *see* Utah
45 Y5 **Morne-à-l'Eau** Grande Terre, N Guadeloupe
29 Y15 **Morning Sun** Iowa, C USA
193 S12 **Mornington Abyssal Plain** *undersea feature* SE Pacific Ocean
63 F22 **Mornington, Isla** *island* S Chile
181 T4 **Mornington Island** *island* Wellesley Islands, Queensland, N Australia
115 E18 **Mórnos** ≈ C Greece
149 P14 **Moro** Sind, SE Pakistan
32 I11 **Moro** Oregon, NW USA
186 E8 **Morobe** Morobe, C PNG
186 E8 **Morobe** ◈ *province* C PNG
31 N12 **Morocco** Indiana, N USA
74 E8 **Morocco** *off.* Kingdom of Morocco, *Ar.* Al Mamlakah. ◆ *monarchy* N Africa
Morocco *see* Marrakech
81 I22 **Morogoro** Morogoro, E Tanzania
81 H24 **Morogoro** ◈ *region* SE Tanzania
171 Q7 **Moro Gulf** *gulf* S Philippines
41 N13 **Moroleón** Guanajuato, C Mexico
172 H6 **Morombe** Toliara, W Madagascar
44 G5 **Morón** Ciego de Ávila, C Cuba
54 K5 **Morón** Carabobo, N Venezuela
Morón *see* Morón de la Frontera
163 N8 **Mörön** Hentiy, C Mongolia
162 I6 **Mörön** Hövsgöl, N Mongolia
56 D8 **Morona, Río** ≈ N Peru
56 C8 **Morona Santiago** ◈ *province* E Ecuador
172 H5 **Morondava** Toliara, W Madagascar
104 K14 **Morón de la Frontera** *var.* Morón. Andalucía, S Spain
172 G13 **Moroni** ● (Comoros) Grande Comore, NW Comoros
171 S10 **Morotai, Pulau** *island* Maluku, E Indonesia
Morotiri *see* Marotiri
81 H17 **Moroto** NE Uganda
Morozov *see* Bratan
128 M11 **Morozovsk** Rostovskaya Oblast', SW Russian Federation
97 L14 **Morpeth** N England, UK
Morphou *see* Güzelyurt
Morphou Bay *see* Güzelyurt Körfezi
28 I13 **Morrill** Nebraska, C USA
27 U11 **Morrilton** Arkansas, C USA
11 Q16 **Morrin** Alberta, SW Canada
184 M7 **Morrinsville** Waikato, North Island, NZ
11 X16 **Morris** Manitoba, S Canada
30 M11 **Morris** Illinois, N USA
29 S8 **Morris** Minnesota, N USA
14 M13 **Morrisburg** Ontario, SE Canada
197 R11 **Morris Jesup, Kap** *headland* N Greenland
182 B1 **Morris, Mount** ▲ South Australia
30 K10 **Morrison** Illinois, N USA
36 K13 **Morristown** Arizona, SW USA
18 J14 **Morristown** New Jersey, NE USA
21 O8 **Morristown** Tennessee, S USA
42 L11 **Morrito** Río San Juan, SW Nicaragua
35 P13 **Morro Bay** California, W USA
95 L22 **Mörrum** Blekinge, S Sweden
83 N16 **Morrumbala** Zambézia, NE Mozambique
83 N20 **Morrumbene** Inhambane, SE Mozambique
95 F21 **Mors** *island* NW Denmark
Mörs *see* Moers
25 N1 **Morse** Texas, SW USA
129 N6 **Morshansk** Tambovskaya Oblast', W Russian Federation
102 L5 **Mortagne-au-Perche** Orne, N France
102 J8 **Mortagne-sur-Sèvre** Vendée, NW France
104 G8 **Mortágua** Viseu, N Portugal
102 J5 **Mortain** Manche, N France
106 C8 **Mortara** Lombardia, N Italy
59 J17 **Mortes, Rio das** ≈ C Brazil
182 M12 **Mortlake** Victoria, SE Australia
Mortlock Group *see* Takuu Islands
189 Q17 **Mortlock Islands** *prev.* Nomoi Islands. *island group* C Micronesia
29 T9 **Morton** Minnesota, N USA
22 L5 **Morton** Mississippi, S USA
24 M5 **Morton** Texas, SW USA
32 H9 **Morton** Washington, NW USA
(0) D7 **Morton Seamount** *undersea feature* NE Pacific Ocean
45 U15 **Moruga** Trinidad, Trinidad and Tobago
183 P9 **Morundah** New South Wales, SE Australia
Moruroa *see* Mururoa
183 S11 **Moruya** New South Wales, SE Australia
103 Q8 **Morvan** *physical region* C France
185 G21 **Morven** Canterbury, South Island, NZ
183 O13 **Morwell** Victoria, SE Australia
127 N6 **Morzhovets, Ostrov** *island* NW Russian Federation
104 G4 **Mos** Galicia, NW Spain
128 J4 **Mosal'sk** Kaluzhskaya Oblast', W Russian Federation
101 H20 **Mosbach** Baden-Württemberg, SW Germany
95 E18 **Mosby** Vest-Agder, S Norway
33 V9 **Mosby** Montana, NW USA
32 M9 **Moscow** Idaho, NW USA
20 F10 **Moscow** Tennessee, S USA
Moscow *see* Moskva
101 D19 **Mosel** *Fr.* Moselle. ≈ W Europe *see also* Moselle
103 T4 **Moselle** ◈ *department* NE France
103 T6 **Moselle** *Ger.* Mosel. ≈ W Europe *see also* Mosel
32 K9 **Moses Lake** ◎ Washington, NW USA
83 I18 **Mosetse** Central, E Botswana
92 H4 **Mosfellsbær** Sudhurland, SW Iceland
185 F23 **Mosgiel** Otago, South Island, NZ
126 M11 **Mosha** ≈ NW Russian Federation
81 I20 **Moshi** Kilimanjaro, NE Tanzania
110 G12 **Mosina** Wielkolpolskie, C Poland
30 L6 **Mosinee** Wisconsin, N USA
92 F13 **Mosjøen** Nordland, C Norway
123 S12 **Moskal'vo** Ostrov Sakhalin, Sakhalinskaya Oblast', SE Russian Federation
92 I13 **Moskosel** Norrbotten, N Sweden
128 K4 **Moskovskaya Oblast'** ◈ *province* W Russian Federation
Moskovskiy *see* Moskva
128 J3 **Moskva** *Eng.* Moscow. ● (Russian Federation) Gorod Moskva, W Russian Federation
147 Q14 **Moskva** *Rus.* Moskovskiy; *prev.* Chubek. SW Tajikistan
128 L4 **Moskva** ≈ W Russian Federation
83 I20 **Mosomane** Kgatleng, SE Botswana
Moson and Magyaróvár *see* Mosonmagyaróvár
111 H21 **Mosoni-Duna** *Ger.* Kleine Donau. ≈ NW Hungary
111 H21 **Mosonmagyaróvár** *Ger.* Wieselburg-Ungarisch-Altenburg; *prev.* Moson and Magyaróvár, *Ger.* Wieselburg and Ungarisch-Altenburg. Győr-Moson-Sopron, NW Hungary

◆ COUNTRY ● COUNTRY CAPITAL ◇ DEPENDENT TERRITORY ○ DEPENDENT TERRITORY CAPITAL ◈ ADMINISTRATIVE REGION ✈ INTERNATIONAL AIRPORT ▲ MOUNTAIN ▲▲ MOUNTAIN RANGE VOLCANO ≈ RIVER ◎ LAKE ▣ RESERVOIR

Mospino see Mospyne
117 X8 Mospyne Rus. Mospino. Donets'ka Oblast', E Ukraine
54 B12 Mosquera Nariño, SW Colombia
37 U10 Mosquero New Mexico, SW USA
Mosquito Coast see La Mosquitia
31 U11 Mosquito Creek Lake ▣ Ohio, N USA
Mosquito Gulf see Mosquitos, Golfo de los
23 X11 Mosquito Lagoon wetland Florida, SE USA
43 N10 Mosquito, Punta headland E Nicaragua
43 W14 Mosquito, Punta headland NE Panama
43 Q15 Mosquitos, Golfo de los Eng. Mosquito Gulf. gulf N Panama
95 H16 Moss Østfold, S Norway
Mossâmedes see Namibe
22 G8 Moss Bluff Louisiana, S USA
185 C23 Mossburn Southland, South Island, NZ
83 G26 Mosselbaai var. Mosselbai, Eng. Mossel Bay. Western Cape, SW South Africa
Mosselbai/Mossel Bay see Mosselbaai
79 F20 Mossendjo Le Niari, SW Congo
183 N8 Mossgiel New South Wales, SE Australia
101 H22 Mössingen Baden-Württemberg, S Germany
181 W4 Mossman Queensland, NE Australia
59 P14 Mossoró Rio Grande do Norte, NE Brazil
23 N9 Moss Point Mississippi, S USA
183 S9 Moss Vale New South Wales, SE Australia
32 G9 Mossyrock Washington, NW USA
111 B15 Most Ger. Brüx. Ústecký Kraj, NW Czech Republic
121 P16 Mosta var. Musta. C Malta
74 I5 Mostaganem var. Mestghanem. NW Algeria
113 H14 Mostar Federacija Bosna I Hercegovina, S Bosnia and Herzegovina
61 J17 Mostardas Rio Grande do Sul, S Brazil
116 K14 Mostiștea ≈ S Romania
Mostva see Mastva
Mosty see Masty
116 H5 Mostys'ka L'vivs'ka Oblast', W Ukraine
Mosul see Al Mawșil
95 F15 Møsvatnet ◎ S Norway
80 J12 Mot'a Amhara, N Ethiopia
79 H16 Motaba ≈ N Congo
105 O10 Mota del Cuervo Castilla-La Mancha, C Spain
104 L5 Mota del Marqués Castilla-León, N Spain
42 F5 Motagua, Río ≈ Guatemala/Honduras
119 H19 Motal' Brestskaya Voblasts', SW Belarus
95 L17 Motala Östergötland, S Sweden
191 X7 Motane var. Mohotani. island Îles Marquises, NE French Polynesia
152 K13 Moth Uttar Pradesh, N India
Mother of Presidents/Mother of States see Virginia
96 I12 Motherwell C Scotland, UK
153 P12 Motīhāri Bihār, N India
105 Q10 Motilla del Palancar Castilla-La Mancha, C Spain
184 N7 Motiti Island island NE NZ
65 E25 Motley Island island SE Falkland Islands
83 J19 Motloutse ≈ E Botswana
41 V17 Motozintla de Mendoza Chiapas, SE Mexico
105 N15 Motril Andalucía, S Spain
116 G13 Motru Gorj, SW Romania
165 Q4 Motsuta-misaki headland Hokkaidō, NE Japan
28 L6 Mott North Dakota, N USA
Möttling see Metlika
107 O18 Mottola Puglia, SE Italy
184 P8 Motu ≈ North Island, NZ
185 I14 Motueka Tasman, South Island, NZ
185 I14 Motueka ≈ South Island, NZ
Motu Iti see Tupai
41 X12 Motul var. Motul de Felipe Carrillo Puerto. Yucatán, SE Mexico
Motul de Felipe Carrillo Puerto see Motul
191 U17 Motu Nui island Easter Island, Chile, E Pacific Ocean
191 Q10 Motu One var. Bellingshausen. atoll Îles Sous le Vent, W French Polynesia
190 I16 Motutapu island E Cook Islands
193 V15 Motu Tapu island Tongatapu Group, S Tonga
184 L5 Motutapu Island island N NZ
Motyca see Modica
Mouanda see Moanda
Mouaskar see Mascara
105 U3 Moubermé, Tuc de Fr. Pic de Maubermé, Sp. Pico Mauberme; prev. Tuc de Maubermé. ▲ France/Spain see also Maubermé, Pic de
45 N7 Mouchoir Passage passage SE Turks and Caicos Islands
76 I9 Moudjéria Tagant, SW Mauritania
108 C9 Moudon Vaud, W Switzerland
Mouhoun see Black Volta
79 E19 Mouila Ngounié, C Gabon
79 K14 Mouka Haute-Kotto, C Central African Republic
Moukden see Shenyang
183 N10 Moulamein New South Wales, SE Australia
Moulamein Creek see Billabong Creek
74 F6 Moulay-Bousselham NW Morocco
Moule see le Moule
80 M11 Moulhoulé N Djibouti
103 P9 Moulins Allier, C France
166 M9 Moulmein var. Maulmain, Mawlamyine. Mon State, S Myanmar
166 L8 Moulmeingyun Irrawaddy, SW Myanmar
74 G6 Moulouya var. Mulucha, Muluya, Mulwiya. seasonal river NE Morocco
23 O2 Moulton Alabama, S USA
29 W16 Moulton Iowa, C USA
25 T11 Moulton Texas, SW USA
23 T7 Moultrie Georgia, SE USA
21 S14 Moultrie, Lake ▣ South Carolina, SE USA
22 K3 Mound Bayou Mississippi, S USA
30 L17 Mound City Illinois, N USA
27 R6 Mound City Kansas, C USA
27 Q2 Mound City Missouri, C USA
29 N7 Mound City South Dakota, N USA
78 H13 Moundou Logone-Occidental, SW Chad
27 P10 Mounds Oklahoma, C USA
21 R2 Moundsville West Virginia, NE USA
167 Q12 Moŭng Roessei Bătdâmbâng, W Cambodia
Moun Hou see Black Volta
8 H8 Mountain ≈ Northwest Territories, NW Canada
37 S12 Mountainair New Mexico, SW USA
35 V1 Mountain City Nevada, W USA
21 Q8 Mountain City Tennessee, S USA
27 U7 Mountain Grove Missouri, C USA
27 U9 Mountain Home Arkansas, C USA
33 N15 Mountain Home Idaho, NW USA
25 Q11 Mountain Home Texas, SW USA
29 W4 Mountain Iron Minnesota, N USA
29 T10 Mountain Lake Minnesota, N USA
23 S3 Mountain Park Georgia, SE USA
35 W12 Mountain Pass pass California, W USA
27 T12 Mountain Pine Arkansas, C USA
39 Y14 Mountain Point Annette Island, Alaska, USA
Mountain State see Montana, USA
Mountain State see West Virginia, USA
27 V7 Mountain View Arkansas, C USA
38 H12 Mountain View Hawaii, USA, C Pacific Ocean
27 V10 Mountain View Missouri, C USA
38 M11 Mountain Village Alaska, USA
21 R8 Mount Airy North Carolina, SE USA
83 K24 Mount Ayliff Xh. Maxesibebi. Eastern Cape, SE South Africa
29 U16 Mount Ayr Iowa, C USA
182 J9 Mount Barker South Australia
180 J14 Mount Barker Western Australia
183 P11 Mount Beauty Victoria, SE Australia
14 E16 Mount Brydges Ontario, S Canada
31 N16 Mount Carmel Illinois, N USA
30 K10 Mount Carroll Illinois, N USA
31 S9 Mount Clemens Michigan, N USA
185 E19 Mount Cook Canterbury, South Island, NZ
83 L16 Mount Darwin Mashonaland Central, NE Zimbabwe
19 S7 Mount Desert Island island Maine, NE USA
23 W11 Mount Dora Florida, SE USA
182 G5 Mount Eba South Australia
25 W8 Mount Enterprise Texas, SW USA
182 J4 Mount Fitton South Australia
83 J24 Mount Fletcher Eastern Cape, SE South Africa
14 F15 Mount Forest Ontario, S Canada
182 K12 Mount Gambier South Australia
181 W5 Mount Garnet Queensland, NE Australia
21 P6 Mount Gay West Virginia, NE USA
31 S12 Mount Gilead Ohio, N USA
186 C7 Mount Hagen Western Highlands, C PNG
18 J16 Mount Holly New Jersey, NE USA
21 R10 Mount Holly North Carolina, SE USA
27 T12 Mount Ida Arkansas, C USA
181 T6 Mount Isa Queensland, C Australia
21 U4 Mount Jackson Virginia, NE USA
18 D12 Mount Jewett Pennsylvania, NE USA
18 L13 Mount Kisco New York, NE USA
18 B15 Mount Lebanon Pennsylvania, NE USA
182 J8 Mount Lofty Ranges ▲ South Australia
180 J10 Mount Magnet Western Australia
184 N7 Mount Maunganui Bay of Plenty, North Island, NZ
97 E18 Mountmellick Ir. Móinteach Mílic. C Ireland
30 L10 Mount Morris Illinois, N USA
31 R9 Mount Morris Michigan, N USA
18 F10 Mount Morris New York, NE USA
18 B16 Mount Morris Pennsylvania, NE USA
30 K15 Mount Olive Illinois, N USA
21 V10 Mount Olive North Carolina, SE USA
21 N4 Mount Olivet Kentucky, S USA
29 Y15 Mount Pleasant Iowa, C USA
31 Q8 Mount Pleasant Michigan, N USA
18 C15 Mount Pleasant Pennsylvania, NE USA
21 T14 Mount Pleasant South Carolina, SE USA
20 I9 Mount Pleasant Tennessee, S USA
25 W6 Mount Pleasant Texas, SW USA
36 L4 Mount Pleasant Utah, W USA
63 N23 Mount Pleasant × (Stanley) East Falkland, Falkland Islands
97 G25 Mount's Bay inlet SW England, UK
35 N2 Mount Shasta California, W USA
30 J13 Mount Sterling Illinois, N USA
21 N5 Mount Sterling Kentucky, S USA
18 E15 Mount Union Pennsylvania, NE USA
23 V6 Mount Vernon Georgia, SE USA
30 L16 Mount Vernon Illinois, N USA
20 M6 Mount Vernon Kentucky, S USA
27 S7 Mount Vernon Missouri, C USA
31 T13 Mount Vernon Ohio, N USA
32 K13 Mount Vernon Oregon, NW USA
25 W6 Mount Vernon Texas, SW USA
32 H7 Mount Vernon Washington, NW USA
20 L5 Mount Washington Kentucky, S USA
182 F8 Mount Wedge South Australia
30 L14 Mount Zion Illinois, N USA
181 Y9 Moura Queensland, NE Australia
58 F12 Moura Amazonas, NW Brazil
104 H12 Moura Beja, S Portugal
104 I12 Mourão Évora, S Portugal
76 L11 Mourdiah Koulikoro, W Mali
78 K7 Mourdi, Dépression du desert lowland Chad/Sudan
102 J16 Mourenx Pyrénées-Atlantiques, SW France
Mourgana see Mourgkána
115 C15 Mourgkána var. Mourgana. ▲ Albania/Greece
97 G16 Mourne Mountains Ir. Beanna Boirche. ▲ SE Northern Ireland, UK
115 J15 Moúrtzeflos, Akrotírio headland Límnos, E Greece
99 C19 Mouscron Dut. Moeskroen. Hainaut, W Belgium
Mouse River see Souris River
78 H10 Moussoro Kanem, W Chad
103 T11 Moûtiers Savoie, E France
172 J14 Moutsamoudou var. Mutsamudu. Anjouan, SE Comoros
74 K11 Mouydir, Monts de ▲ S Algeria
79 F20 Mouyondzi La Bouenza, S Congo
115 E16 Mouzáki prev. Mouzákion. Thessalía, C Greece
Mouzákion see Mouzáki
29 S13 Moville Iowa, C USA
82 E13 Moxico ◈ province E Angola
172 J14 Moya Anjouan, SE Comoros
40 L12 Moyahua Zacatecas, C Mexico
81 J16 Moyalē Oromo, C Ethiopia
76 I15 Moyamba W Sierra Leone
74 G7 Moyen Atlas Eng. Middle Atlas. ▲ N Morocco
78 H13 Moyen-Chari off. Préfecture du Moyen-Chari. ◈ prefecture S Chad
Moyen-Congo see Congo (Republic of)
83 J24 Moyeni var. Quthing. SW Lesotho
76 H13 Moyenne-Guinée ◈ state NW Guinea
79 D18 Moyen-Ogooué off. Province du Moyen-Ogooué, var. Le Moyen-Ogooué. ◈ province C Gabon
103 S4 Moyeuvre-Grande Moselle, NE France
33 N7 Moyie Springs Idaho, NW USA
145 S15 Moynnkum prev. Fumanovka, Kaz. Fürmanov. Zhambyl, S Kazakhstan
81 F16 Moyo NW Uganda
56 D10 Moyobamba San Martín, NW Peru
78 H10 Moyto Chari-Baguirmi, W Chad
158 G9 Moyu var. Karakax. Xinjiang Uygur Zizhiqu, NW China
122 M9 Moyyero ≈ N Russian Federation
145 Q15 Moyynkum, Peski Kaz. Moyynqum. desert S Kazakhstan
Moyynqum see Moyynkum, Peski
145 S12 Moyynty Zhezkazgan, C Kazakhstan
145 S12 Moyynty ≈ C Kazakhstan
Mozambika, Lakandranon' i see Mozambique Channel
83 M18 Mozambique off. Republic of Mozambique; prev. People's Republic of Mozambique, Portuguese East Africa. ◆ republic S Africa
Mozambique Basin see Natal Basin
Mozambique, Canal de see Mozambique Channel
83 P17 Mozambique Channel Fr. Canal de Mozambique, Mal. Lakandranon' i Mozambika. strait W Indian Ocean
172 L11 Mozambique Escarpment var. Mozambique Scarp. undersea feature SW Indian Ocean
172 L10 Mozambique Plateau var. Mozambique Rise. undersea feature SW Indian Ocean
Mozambique Rise see Mozambique Plateau
Mozambique Scarp see Mozambique Escarpment
129 O15 Mozdok Respublika Severnaya Osetiya, SW Russian Federation
57 K17 Mozetenes, Serranías de ▲ C Bolivia
128 J4 Mozhaysk Moskovskaya Oblast', W Russian Federation
129 T3 Mozhga Udmurtskaya Respublika, NW Russian Federation
Mozyr' see Mazyr
79 P22 Mpala Katanga, E Dem. Rep. Congo (Zaire)
79 G19 Mpama ≈ C Congo
81 E22 Mpanda Rukwa, W Tanzania
82 L11 Mpande Northern, NE Zambia
83 J18 Mphoengs Matabeleland South, SW Zimbabwe
81 F18 Mpigi S Uganda
82 L13 Mpika Northern, NE Zambia
83 J14 Mpima Central, C Zambia
82 J13 Mpongwe Copperbelt, C Zambia
82 K11 Mporokoso Northern, N Zambia
79 H20 Mpouya Plateaux, SE Congo
77 P16 Mpraeso C Ghana
82 L11 Mpulungu Northern, N Zambia
83 K21 Mpumalanga prev. Eastern Transvaal, Afr. Oos-Transvaal. ◈ province NE South Africa
83 D16 Mpungu Okavango, N Namibia
81 I22 Mpwapwa Dodoma, C Tanzania
Mqinvartsveri see Kazbek
110 M8 Mrągowo Ger. Sensburg. Warmińsko-Mazurskie, NE Poland
129 V6 Mrakovo Respublika Bashkortostan, W Russian Federation
172 I13 Mramani Anjouan, E Comoros
112 F12 Mrkonjić Grad Republika Srpska, W Bosnia and Herzegovina
110 H9 Mrocza Kujawsko-pomorskie, NW Poland
126 I14 Msta ≈ NW Russian Federation
Mtkvari see Kura
Mtoko see Mutoko
128 K6 Mtsensk Orlovskaya Oblast', W Russian Federation
81 K24 Mtwara Mtwara, SE Tanzania
81 J25 Mtwara ◈ region SE Tanzania
104 G14 Mu ▲ S Portugal
193 V15 Mu'a Tongatapu, S Tonga
Muai To see Mae Hong Son
83 P16 Mualama Zambézia, NE Mozambique
Mualo see Messalo, Rio
79 E22 Muanda Bas-Congo, SW Dem. Rep. Congo (Zaire)
Muang Chiang Rai see Chiang Rai
167 R6 Muang Ham Houaphan, N Laos
167 S8 Muang Hinboun Khammouan, C Laos
Muang Kalasin see Kalasin
Muang Khammouan see Thakhèk
167 S11 Muang Không Champasak, S Laos
167 S10 Muang Khôngxédôn var. Khong Sedone. Salavan, S Laos
Muang Khon Kaen see Khon Kaen
167 Q6 Muang Khoua Phôngsali, N Laos
Muang Krabi see Krabi
Muang Lampang see Lampang
Muang Lamphun see Lamphun
Muang Loei see Loei
Muang Lom Sak see Lom Sak
Muang Nakhon Sawan see Nakhon Sawan
167 Q6 Muang Namo Oudômxai, N Laos
Muang Nan see Nan
167 Q6 Muang Ngoy Louangphabang, N Laos
167 Q5 Muang Ou Tai Phôngsali, N Laos
Muang Pak Lay see Pak Lay
Muang Pakxan see Pakxan
167 T10 Muang Pakxong Champasak, S Laos
167 S9 Muang Phalan var. Muang Phalane. Savannakhét, S Laos
Muang Phalane see Muang Phalan
Muang Phan see Phan
Muang Phayao see Phayao
Muang Phichit see Phichit
167 T9 Muang Phin Savannakhét, S Laos
Muang Phitsanulok see Phitsanulok
Muang Phrae see Phrae
Muang Roi Et see Roi Et
Muang Sakon Nakhon see Sakon Nakhon
Muang Samut Prakan see Samut Prakan
167 P6 Muang Sing Louang Namtha, N Laos
Muang Ubon see Ubon Ratchathani
Muang Uthai Thani see Uthai Thani
167 P7 Muang Vangviang Viangchan, C Laos
Muang Xaignabouri see Xaignabouli
Muang Xay see Xai
167 S9 Muang Xépôn var. Sepone. Savannakhét, S Laos
168 K10 Muar var. Bandar Maharani. Johor, Peninsular Malaysia
168 I9 Muara Sumatera, W Indonesia
168 L13 Muarabeliti Sumatera, W Indonesia
168 K12 Muarabungo Sumatera, W Indonesia
168 L13 Muaraenim Sumatera, W Indonesia
169 T11 Muarajuloi Borneo, C Indonesia
169 U12 Muarakaman Borneo, C Indonesia
168 H12 Muarasigep Pulau Siberut, W Indonesia
168 L12 Muaratembesi Sumatera, W Indonesia
169 T12 Muaratewe var. Muarateweh; prev. Moearatewe. Borneo, C Indonesia
Muarateweh see Muaratewe
169 U10 Muarawahau Borneo, N Indonesia
138 G13 Mubārak, Jabal ▲ S Jordan
153 N13 Mubārakpur Uttar Pradesh, N India
Mubarek see Muborak
81 F18 Mubende SW Uganda
77 Y14 Mubi Adamawa, NE Nigeria
146 M12 Muborak Rus. Mubarek. Qashqadaryo Wiloyati, S Uzbekistan
171 U12 Mubrani Irian Jaya, E Indonesia
67 U12 Muchinga Escarpment escarpment NE Zambia
129 N7 Muchkapskiy Tambovskaya Oblast', W Russian Federation
96 G10 Muck island W Scotland, UK
82 Q13 Mucojo Cabo Delgado, N Mozambique
82 F12 Muconda Lunda Sul, NE Angola
54 I10 Muco, Río ≈ E Colombia
83 O16 Mucubela Zambézia, NE Mozambique
42 J5 Mucupina, Monte ▲ N Honduras
136 J14 Mucur Kirşehir, C Turkey
143 U8 Mūd Khorāsān, E Iran
163 Y9 Mudanjiang var. Mu-tan-chiang. Heilongjiang, NE China
163 Y9 Mudan Jiang ≈ NE China
136 D11 Mudanya Bursa, NW Turkey
28 K8 Mud Butte South Dakota, N USA
155 G16 Muddebihāl Karnātaka, C India
27 P12 Muddy Boggy Creek ≈ Oklahoma, C USA
36 M6 Muddy Creek ≈ Utah, W USA
37 V7 Muddy Creek Reservoir ▣ Colorado, C USA
33 W15 Muddy Gap Wyoming, C USA
35 Y11 Muddy Peak ▲ Nevada, W USA
183 R7 Mudgee New South Wales, SE Australia
29 S3 Mud Lake ◎ Minnesota, N USA
29 P7 Mud Lake Reservoir ▣ South Dakota, N USA
167 N9 Mudon Mon State, S Myanmar
81 O14 Mudug off. Gobolka Mudug. ◈ region NE Somalia
81 O14 Mudug var. Mudugh. plain N Somalia
Mudugh see Mudug
83 Q15 Muecate Nampula, NE Mozambique
82 Q13 Mueda Cabo Delgado, NE Mozambique
42 L10 Muelle de los Bueyes Región Autónoma Atlántico Sur, SE Nicaragua
Muenchen see München
83 M14 Muende Tete, NW Mozambique
25 T5 Muenster Texas, SW USA
Muenster see Münster
43 O6 Muerto, Cayo reef NE Nicaragua
41 T17 Muerto, Mar lagoon SE Mexico
64 F11 Muertos Trough undersea feature N Caribbean Sea
83 H14 Mufaya Kuta Western, NW Zambia
82 J13 Mufulira Copperbelt, C Zambia
161 O10 Mufu Shan ▲ C China
Mugalzhar Taŭlary see Mugodzhary, Gory
137 Y12 Muğan Düzü Rus. Muganskaya Ravnina, Muganskaya Step'. physical region S Azerbaijan
Muganskaya Ravnina/Muganskaya Step' see Muğan Düzü
106 K8 Múggia Friuli-Venezia Giulia, NE Italy
153 N14 Mughal Sarāi Uttar Pradesh, N India
Mughla see Muğla
141 W11 Mughshin var. Muqshin. S Oman
147 S12 Mughsu Rus. Muksu. ≈ C Tajikistan
164 H14 Mugi Tokushima, Shikoku, SW Japan
136 C16 Muğla var. Mughla. Muğla, SW Turkey
136 C16 Muğla var. Mughla. ◈ province SW Turkey
144 J11 Mugodzhary, Gory Kaz. Mugalzhar Taŭlary. ▲ W Kazakhstan
83 O15 Mugulama Zambézia, NE Mozambique
139 U9 Muḩammad E Iraq
139 R8 Muḩammadīyah C Iraq
80 I6 Muhammad Qol Red Sea, NE Sudan
75 Y9 Muhammad, Râs headland E Egypt
Muhammerah see Khorramshahr
140 M12 Muhāyil var. Mahāil. 'Asīr, SW Saudi Arabia
139 O7 Muḩaywīr W Iraq
101 H21 Mühlacker Baden-Württemberg, SW Germany
Mühlbach see Sebeș
Mühldorf see Mühldorf am Inn
101 N23 Mühldorf am Inn var. Mühldorf. Bayern, SE Germany
101 J15 Mühlhausen var. Mühlhausen in Thüringen. Thüringen, C Germany
Mühlhausen in Thüringen see Mühlhausen
195 Q2 Mühlig-Hofmann Mountains ▲ Antarctica
93 L14 Muhos Oulu, C Finland
138 K6 Muḩ, Sabkhat al ◎ C Syria
118 E5 Muhu Ger. Mohn, Moon. island W Estonia
81 F19 Muhutwe Kagera, NW Tanzania
Muhu Väin see Väinameri
98 J10 Muiden Noord-Holland, C Netherlands
193 W15 Mui Hopohoponga headland Tongatapu, S Tonga
Muikamachi see Muika
Muinchille see Cootehill
Muineachán see Monaghan
97 F19 Muine Bheag Eng. Bagenalstown. SE Ireland
56 B5 Muisne Esmeraldas, NW Ecuador
83 P14 Muite Nampula, NE Mozambique
41 Z11 Mujeres, Isla island E Mexico
116 G7 Mukacheve Hung. Munkács, Rus. Mukachevo. Zakarpats'ka Oblast', W Ukraine
Mukachevo see Mukacheve
169 R9 Mukah Sarawak, East Malaysia
Mukalla see Al Mukallā
Mukama see Mokāma
Mukāshafa/Mukashshafah see Mukayshīfah
139 S6 Mukayshīfah var. Mukāshafa, Mukashshafah. N Iraq
167 R9 Mukdahan Mukdahan, E Thailand
Mukden see Shenyang
165 Y15 Mukojima-rettō Eng. Parry group. island group SE Japan
146 M14 Mukry Lebapskiy Velayat, E Turkmenistan
Muksu see Mughsu
153 U14 Muktagacha var. Muktagachha Dhaka, N Bangladesh
Muktagachha see Muktagacha
82 K13 Mukuku Central, C Zambia
82 K11 Mukupa Kaoma Northern, NE Zambia
81 I18 Mukutan Rift Valley, W Kenya
83 F16 Mukwe Caprivi, NE Namibia
105 R13 Mula Murcia, SE Spain
151 K20 Mulaku Atoll var. Meemu Atoll. atoll C Maldives
83 J15 Mulalika Lusaka, C Zambia
163 X8 Mulan Heilongjiang, NE China
83 N15 Mulanje var. Mlanje. Southern, S Malawi
40 H5 Mulatos Sonora, NW Mexico
23 P3 Mulberry Fork ≈ Alabama, S USA
39 P12 Mulchatna River ≈ Alaska, USA
127 W4 Mul'da Respublika Komi, NW Russian Federation
101 M14 Mulde ≈ E Germany
27 R10 Muldrow Oklahoma, C USA
40 E7 Mulegé Baja California Sur, W Mexico
108 I10 Mulegns Graubünden, S Switzerland
79 M21 Mulenda Kasai Oriental, C Dem. Rep. Congo (Zaire)
24 M4 Muleshoe Texas, SW USA
83 O15 Mulevala Zambézia, NE Mozambique
183 P5 Mulgoa Creek seasonal river New South Wales, SE Australia
105 O15 Mulhacén var. Cerro de Mulhacén. ▲ S Spain
Mulhacén, Cerro de see Mulhacén
Mülhausen see Mulhouse
101 E24 Müllheim Baden-Württemberg, SW Germany
101 E15 Mülheim var. Mulheim an der Ruhr. Nordrhein-Westfalen, W Germany
Mülheim an der Ruhr see Mülheim
103 U7 Mulhouse Ger. Mülhausen. Haut-Rhin, NE France
160 G11 Muli var. Bowa, Muli Zangzu Zizhixian. Sichuan, C China
171 X15 Muli channel Irian Jaya, E Indonesia
163 Y9 Muling Heilongjiang, NE China
Mullach Íde see Malahide
Mullaitivu see Mullaittivu
155 K23 Mullaittivu var. Mullaitivu. Northern Province, N Sri Lanka
33 N8 Mullan Idaho, NW USA
28 M13 Mullen Nebraska, C USA
183 Q6 Mullengudgery New South Wales, SE Australia
21 Q6 Mullens West Virginia, NE USA
Müller-gerbergte see Muller, Pegunungan
169 T10 Muller, Pegunungan Dut. Müller-gerbergte. ▲ Borneo, C Indonesia
31 Q5 Mullett Lake ◎ Michigan, N USA
18 J16 Mullica River ≈ New Jersey, NE USA
25 R8 Mullin Texas, SW USA
97 E17 Mullingar Ir. An Muileann gCearr. C Ireland
21 T12 Mullins South Carolina, SE USA
96 G11 Mull, Isle of island W Scotland, UK
129 R5 Mullovka Ul'yanovskaya Oblast', W Russian Federation
95 K19 Mullsjö Västra Götaland, S Sweden
183 V4 Mullumbimby New South Wales, SE Australia
83 H15 Mulobezi Western, SW Zambia
83 C15 Mulondo Huíla, SW Angola
83 G15 Mulonga Plain plain W Zambia
79 N23 Mulongo Katanga, SE Dem. Rep. Congo (Zaire)
149 T10 Multān Punjab, E Pakistan
93 L17 Multia Länsi-Suomi, W Finland
Mulucha see Moulouya
83 J14 Mulungushi Central, C Zambia
83 K14 Mulungwe Central, C Zambia
Muluya see Moulouya
27 N7 Mulvane Kansas, C USA
183 O10 Mulwala New South Wales, SE Australia
Mulwiya see Moulouya
182 K6 Mulyungarie South Australia
154 D13 Mumbai prev. Bombay. Mahārāshtra, W India
154 D13 Mumbai × Mahārāshtra, W India

◆ Country ● Country Capital ◇ Dependent Territory ○ Dependent Territory Capital ◈ Administrative Region × International Airport ▲ Mountain ▲ Mountain Range ☒ Volcano ≈ River ◎ Lake ▣ Reservoir

83 D14 **Mumbué** Bié, C Angola
186 E8 **Mumeng** Morobe, C PNG
171 V12 **Mumi** Irian Jaya, E Indonesia
Muminabad/Mŭ'minobod see Leningrad
129 Q13 **Mumra** Astrakhanskaya Oblast', SW Russian Federation
41 X12 **Muna** Yucatán, SE Mexico
123 O9 **Muna** ⁓ NE Russian Federation
152 C12 **Munābāo** Rājasthān, NW India
Munamägi see Suur Munamägi
171 O14 **Muna, Pulau** prev. Moena. island C Indonesia
101 L18 **Münchberg** Bayern, E Germany
101 L23 **München** var. Muenchen, Eng. Munich, It. Monaco. Bayern, SE Germany
München-Gladbach see Mönchengladbach
108 E6 **Münchenstein** Basel-Land, NW Switzerland
10 L10 **Muncho Lake** British Columbia, W Canada
31 P13 **Muncie** Indiana, N USA
18 G13 **Muncy** Pennsylvania, NE USA
11 Q14 **Mundare** Alberta, SW Canada
25 Q5 **Munday** Texas, SW USA
31 N10 **Mundelein** Illinois, N USA
101 I15 **Münden** Niedersachsen, C Germany
105 Q12 **Mundo** ⁓ S Spain
82 B12 **Munenga** Cuanza Sul, NW Angola
105 P11 **Munera** Castilla-La Mancha, C Spain
20 E9 **Munford** Tennessee, S USA
20 K7 **Munfordville** Kentucky, S USA
182 D5 **Mungala** South Australia
83 M16 **Mungári** Manica, C Mozambique
79 O16 **Mungbere** Orientale, NE Dem. Rep. Congo (Zaire)
153 Q13 **Munger** prev. Monghyr. Bihār, NE India
182 I2 **Mungeranie** South Australia
Mu Nggava see Rennell
169 O10 **Mungguresak, Tanjung** headland Borneo, N Indonesia
Mungiki see Bellona
183 R4 **Mungindi** New South Wales, SE Australia
Mungkawn see Maingkwan
153 T16 **Mungla** var. Mongla. Khulna, S Bangladesh
82 C13 **Mungo** Huambo, W Angola
188 F16 **Munguuy Bay** bay Yap, W Micronesia
82 E13 **Munhango** Bié, C Angola
Munich see München
105 S7 **Muniesa** Aragón, NE Spain
31 O4 **Munising** Michigan, N USA
Munkács see Mukacheve
95 I17 **Munkedal** Västra Götaland, S Sweden
95 K15 **Munkfors** Värmland, C Sweden
122 M14 **Munku-Sardyk, Gora** var. Mönh Sarĭdag. ▲ Mongolia/Russian Federation
99 E18 **Munkzwalm** Oost-Vlaanderen, NW Belgium
167 R10 **Mun, Mae Nam** ⁓ E Thailand
153 U15 **Munshiganj** Dhaka, C Bangladesh
108 D8 **Münsingen** Bern, W Switzerland
103 U6 **Munster** Haut-Rhin, NE France
100 J11 **Munster** Niedersachsen, NW Germany
97 B20 **Munster** Ir. Cúige Mumhan. cultural region S Ireland
100 F13 **Münster** var. Muenster, Münster in Westfalen. Nordrhein-Westfalen, W Germany
108 F10 **Münster** Valais, S Switzerland
Münsterberg in Schlesien see Ziębice
Münster in Westfalen see Münster
100 E13 **Münsterland** cultural region NW Germany
100 F13 **Münster-Osnabruck** ✕ Nordrhein-Westfalen, NW Germany
31 R4 **Munuscong Lake** ◎ Michigan, N USA
83 K17 **Munyati** ⁓ C Zimbabwe
109 R3 **Münzkirchen** Oberösterreich, N Austria
92 K11 **Muodoslompolo** Norrbotten, N Sweden
92 M13 **Muojärvi** ◎ NE Finland
167 S6 **Mương Khến** Hoa Binh, N Vietnam
Muong Sai see Xai
167 Q7 **Muong Xiang Ngeun** var. Xieng Ngeun. Louangphabang, N Laos
92 K11 **Muonio** Lappi, N Finland
Muonioälv/Muoniojoki see Muonionjoki
92 K11 **Muonionjoki** var. Muoniojoki, Swe. Muonioälv. ⁓ Finland/Sweden
83 N17 **Mupa** ⁓ C Mozambique
83 E16 **Mupini** Okavango, NE Namibia
80 F8 **Muqaddam, Wadi** ⁓ N Sudan
138 K9 **Muqāṭ** Al Mafraq, E Jordan
141 X7 **Muqaz** N Oman
81 N17 **Muqdisho** Eng. Mogadishu, It. Mogadiscio. ● (Somalia) Banaadir, S Somalia
81 N17 **Muqdisho** ✕ Banaadir, E Somalia
Muqshin see Mughshin
109 T8 **Mur** SCr. Mura. ⁓ C Europe
Mura see Mur
137 T14 **Muradiye** Van, E Turkey
Muragarazi see Maragarazi
165 O10 **Murakami** Niigata, Honshū, C Japan
63 G22 **Murallón, Cerro** ▲ S Argentina
81 E20 **Muramvya** C Burundi
81 I19 **Murang'a** prev. Fort Hall. Central, SW Kenya
81 H16 **Murangering** Rift Valley, NW Kenya
Murapara see Murupara
140 M5 **Murār, Bi'r al** well NW Saudi Arabia
127 Q13 **Murashi** Kirovskaya Oblast', NW Russian Federation
103 O12 **Murat** Cantal, C France
114 N12 **Muratlı** Tekirdağ, NW Turkey
137 R14 **Murat Nehri** var. Eastern Euphrates; anc. Arsanias. ⁓ NE Turkey
107 D20 **Muravera** Sardegna, Italy, C Mediterranean Sea
165 P10 **Murayama** Yamagata, Honshū, C Japan
121 R13 **Muraysah, Ra's al** headland N Libya
104 I6 **Murça** Vila Real, N Portugal
80 Q11 **Murcanyo** Bari, NE Somalia
143 N8 **Mūrcheh Khvort** var. Morcheh Khort. Eşfahān, C Iran
185 H15 **Murchison** Tasman, South Island, NZ
185 B22 **Murchison Mountains** ▲▲ South Island, NZ
180 I10 **Murchison River** ⁓ Western Australia
105 R13 **Murcia** Murcia, SE Spain
105 Q13 **Murcia** ❖ autonomous community SE Spain
103 O13 **Mur-de-Barrez** Aveyron, S France
182 G8 **Murdinga** South Australia
28 M10 **Murdo** South Dakota, N USA
15 X6 **Murdochville** Quebec, SE Canada
109 W9 **Mureck** Steiermark, SE Austria
114 M13 **Mürefte** Tekirdağ, NW Turkey
116 I10 **Mureş** ❖ county N Romania
84 J11 **Mureş** var. Maros, Mureşul, Ger. Marosch, Mieresch. ⁓ Hungary/Romania see also Maros
Mureşul see Maros/Mureş
102 M16 **Muret** Haute-Garonne, S France
27 T13 **Murfreesboro** Arkansas, C USA
21 W8 **Murfreesboro** North Carolina, SE USA
20 J9 **Murfreesboro** Tennessee, S USA
146 I14 **Murgab** prev. Murgap see also Morghāb, Daryā-ye. Maryyskiy Velayat, S Turkmenistan
146 J16 **Murgab** var. Murghab, Pash. Daryā-ye Morghāb, Turkm. Murgap Deryasy. ⁓ Afghanistan/Turkmenistan see also Morghāb, Daryā-ye
Murgab see Murghob
Murgap see Murgab
Murgap Deryasy see Morghāb, Daryā-ye/Murgab
114 H9 **Murgash** ▲ W Bulgaria
Murghab see Morghāb, Daryā-ye/Murgab
147 U13 **Murghob** Rus. Murgab. SE Tajikistan
147 U13 **Murghob** Rus. Murgab. ⁓ SE Tajikistan
181 Z10 **Murgon** Queensland, E Australia
190 I16 **Muri** Rarotonga, S Cook Islands
108 F7 **Muri** Aargau, W Switzerland
108 D8 **Muri** var. Muri bei Bern. Bern, W Switzerland
104 K3 **Murias de Paredes** Castilla-León, N Spain
Muri bei Bern see Muri
82 F11 **Muriege** Lunda Sul, NE Angola
189 P14 **Murilo Atoll** atoll Hall Islands, C Micronesia
Mūrītānīyah see Mauritania
100 N10 **Müritz** var. Müritzee. ◎ NE Germany
Müritzee see Müritz
100 L10 **Müritz-Elde-Kanal** canal N Germany
184 K6 **Muriwai Beach** Auckland, North Island, NZ
92 J13 **Murjek** Norrbotten, N Sweden
126 J3 **Murmansk** Murmanskaya Oblast', NW Russian Federation
126 J4 **Murmanskaya Oblast'** ❖ province NW Russian Federation
197 V14 **Murmansk Rise** undersea feature SW Barents Sea
126 J3 **Murmashi** Murmanskaya Oblast', NW Russian Federation
128 M5 **Murmino** Ryazanskaya Oblast', W Russian Federation
101 K24 **Murnau** Bayern, SE Germany
103 X16 **Muro, Capo di** headland Corse, France, C Mediterranean Sea
107 M18 **Muro Lucano** Basilicata, S Italy
129 N4 **Murom** Vladimirskaya Oblast', W Russian Federation
122 I11 **Muromtsevo** Omskaya Oblast', C Russian Federation
165 R5 **Muroran** Hokkaidō, NE Japan
104 G3 **Muros** Galicia, NW Spain
104 F3 **Muros e Noia, Ría de** estuary NW Spain
164 H15 **Muroto** Kōchi, Shikoku, SW Japan
164 H15 **Muroto-zaki** headland Shikoku, SW Japan
116 L7 **Murovani Kurylivtsi** Vinnyts'ka Oblast', C Ukraine
110 G11 **Murowana Goślina** Wielkolpolskie, C Poland
32 M14 **Murphy** Idaho, NW USA
21 N10 **Murphy** North Carolina, SE USA
35 P8 **Murphys** California, W USA
30 L17 **Murphysboro** Illinois, N USA
29 V15 **Murray** Iowa, C USA
20 H8 **Murray** Kentucky, S USA
182 J10 **Murray Bridge** South Australia
175 X2 **Murray Fracture Zone** tectonic feature NE Pacific Ocean
192 H11 **Murray, Lake** ◎ SW PNG
21 P12 **Murray, Lake** ⊡ South Carolina, SE USA
10 K8 **Murray, Mount** ▲ Yukon Territory, NW Canada
Murray Range see Murray Ridge
173 O3 **Murray Ridge** var. Murray Range. undersea feature N Arabian Sea
183 N10 **Murray River** ⁓ SE Australia
182 K10 **Murrayville** Victoria, SE Australia
149 U5 **Murree** Punjab, E Pakistan
101 I21 **Murrhardt** Baden-Württemberg, S Germany
183 O9 **Murrumbidgee River** ⁓ New South Wales, SE Australia
83 P15 **Murrupula** Nampula, NE Mozambique
183 T7 **Murrurundi** New South Wales, SE Australia
109 X9 **Murska Sobota** Ger. Olsnitz. NE Slovenia
154 G12 **Murtajāpur** prev. Murtazapur. Mahārāshtra, C India
77 S16 **Murtala Muhammed** ✕ (Lagos) Ogun, SW Nigeria
Murtazapur see Murtajāpur
108 C8 **Murten** Neuchâtel, W Switzerland
Murtensee see Morat, Lac de
182 L11 **Murtoa** Victoria, SE Australia
92 N13 **Murtovaara** Oulu, E Finland
Murua Island see Woodlark Island
155 D14 **Murud** Mahārāshtra, W India
184 O9 **Murupara** var. Murapara. Bay of Plenty, North Island, NZ
191 X12 **Mururoa** var. Moruroa. atoll Îles Tuamotu, SE French Polynesia
Murviedro see Sagunto
154 J9 **Murwāra** Madhya Pradesh, N India
183 V4 **Murwillumbah** New South Wales, SE Australia
146 H11 **Murzechirla** prev. Mirzachirla. Akhalskiy Velayat, C Turkmenistan
Murzuk see Murzuq
75 O11 **Murzuq** var. Marzūq, Murzuk. SW Libya
Murzuq, Edeyin see Murzuq, Idhān
75 N11 **Murzuq, Ḩamādat** plateau W Libya
75 O11 **Murzuq, Idhān** var. Edeyin Murzuq. desert SW Libya
109 W6 **Mürzzuschlag** Steiermark, E Austria
137 Q14 **Muş** var. Mush. Muş, E Turkey
137 Q14 **Muş** var. Mush. ❖ province E Turkey
186 F9 **Musa** ⁓ S PNG
118 G11 **Mūša** ⁓ Latvia/Lithuania
75 X8 **Mûsa, Gebel** ▲ NE Egypt
Musaiyib see Al Musayyib
Musa Khel see Mūsā Khel Bāzār
149 R9 **Mūsā Khel Bāzār** var. Musa Khel. Baluchistān, SW Pakistan
114 H10 **Musala** ▲ W Bulgaria
168 H10 **Musala, Pulau** island W Indonesia
83 L15 **Musale** Southern, S Zambia
141 Y9 **Muşalla** NE Oman
141 W6 **Musandam Peninsula** Ar. Masandam Peninsula. peninsula N Oman
Musay'īd see Umm Sa'īd
Muscat see Masqaṭ
Muscat and Oman see Oman
29 Y14 **Muscatine** Iowa, C USA
Muscat Sīb Airport see Seeb
31 O15 **Muscatuck River** ⁓ Indiana, N USA
30 K8 **Muscoda** Wisconsin, N USA
185 F19 **Musgrave, Mount** ▲ South Island, NZ
181 P9 **Musgrave Ranges** ▲▲ South Australia
Mush see Muş
138 H12 **Mushayyish, Qaşr al** castle Ma'ān, C Jordan
79 H20 **Mushie** Bandundu, W Dem. Rep. Congo (Zaire)
168 M13 **Musi, Air** prev. Moesi. ⁓ Sumatera, W Indonesia
192 M4 **Musicians Seamounts** undersea feature N Pacific Ocean
54 D8 **Musinga, Alto** ▲ NW Colombia
29 T2 **Muskeg Bay** lake bay Minnesota, N USA
31 O8 **Muskegon** Michigan, N USA
31 O8 **Muskegon Heights** Michigan, N USA
31 P8 **Muskegon River** ⁓ Michigan, N USA
31 T14 **Muskingum River** ⁓ Ohio, N USA
95 P16 **Muskö** Stockholm, C Sweden
Muskogean see Tallahassee
27 Q10 **Muskogee** Oklahoma, C USA
14 H13 **Muskoka, Lake** ◎ Ontario, S Canada
80 H8 **Musmar** Red Sea, NE Sudan
83 K14 **Musofu** Central, C Zambia
81 G19 **Musoma** Mara, N Tanzania
82 L13 **Musoro** Central, C Zambia
186 F4 **Mussau Island** island NE PNG
98 P7 **Musselkanaal** Groningen, NE Netherlands
33 V9 **Musselshell River** ⁓ Montana, NW USA
82 C12 **Mussende** Cuanza Sul, NW Angola
102 L12 **Mussidan** Dordogne, SW France
99 L25 **Musson** Luxembourg, SE Belgium
152 J9 **Mussoorie** Uttar Pradesh, N India
Musta see Mosta
152 M13 **Mustafābād** Uttar Pradesh, N India
136 D12 **Mustafakemalpaşa** Bursa, NW Turkey
Mustafa-Pasha see Svilengrad
81 M15 **Mustahīl** Somali, E Ethiopia
24 M7 **Mustang Draw** valley Texas, SW USA
25 T14 **Mustang Island** island Texas, SW USA
Mustasaari see Korsholm
Mustér see Disentis
63 I19 **Musters, Lago** ◎ S Argentina
45 Y14 **Mustique** island C Saint Vincent and the Grenadines
118 I6 **Mustla** Viljandimaa, S Estonia
118 J4 **Mustvee** Ger. Tschorna. Jõgevamaa, E Estonia
42 L9 **Musún, Cerro** ▲ NE Nicaragua
183 T7 **Muswellbrook** New South Wales, SE Australia
111 M18 **Muszyna** Małopolskie, SE Poland
136 I17 **Mut** İçel, S Turkey
75 V10 **Mūt** var. Mut. C Egypt
109 V9 **Muta** N Slovenia
190 B15 **Mutalau** N Niue
Mu-tan-chiang see Mudanjiang
82 I13 **Mutanda** North Western, NW Zambia
59 O17 **Mutá, Ponta do** headland E Brazil
83 L17 **Mutare** var. Mutari; prev. Umtali. Manicaland, E Zimbabwe
Mutari see Mutare
54 D8 **Mutatá** Antioquia, NW Colombia
Mutina see Modena
83 L16 **Mutoko** prev. Mtoko. Mashonaland East, NE Zimbabwe
81 J20 **Mutomo** Eastern, S Kenya
Mutrah see Maţraḩ
79 M24 **Mutshatsha** Katanga, S Dem. Rep. Congo (Zaire)
165 R6 **Mutsu** var. Mutu. Aomori, Honshū, N Japan
165 R6 **Mutsu-wan** bay N Japan
108 E6 **Muttenz** Basel-Land, NW Switzerland
185 A26 **Muttonbird Islands** island group SW NZ
Mutu see Mutsu
83 O15 **Mutuáli** Nampula, N Mozambique
82 D13 **Mutumbo** Bié, C Angola
189 Y14 **Mutunte, Mount** var. Mount Buache. ▲ Kosrae, E Micronesia
155 K24 **Mutur** Eastern Province, E Sri Lanka
92 L13 **Muurola** Lappi, NW Finland
162 M14 **Mu Us Shamo** var. Ordos Desert. desert N China
82 B11 **Muxima** Bengo, NW Angola
126 I8 **Muyezerskiy** Respublika Kareliya, NW Russian Federation
81 E20 **Muyinga** NE Burundi
42 K9 **Muy Muy** Matagalpa, C Nicaragua
Muynak see Mŭynoq
146 G6 **Mŭynoq** Rus. Muynak. Qoraqalpogiston Respublikasi, NW Uzbekistan
79 N22 **Muyumba** Katanga, SE Dem. Rep. Congo (Zaire)
149 V5 **Muzaffarābād** Jammu and Kashmir, NE Pakistan
149 S10 **Muzaffargarh** Punjab, E Pakistan
152 J9 **Muzaffarnagar** Uttar Pradesh, N India
153 P13 **Muzaffarpur** Bihār, N India
158 H6 **Muzat He** ⁓ W China
83 L15 **Muze** Tete, NW Mozambique
122 H8 **Muzhi** Yamalo-Nenetskiy Avtonomnyy Okrug, N Russian Federation
102 H7 **Muzillac** Morbihan, NW France
Muzkol, Khrebet see Muzqūl, Qatorkŭhi
112 L9 **Mužlja** Hung. Felsőmuzslya; prev. Gornja Mužlja. Serbia, N Yugoslavia
54 F9 **Muzo** Boyacá, C Colombia
83 J15 **Muzoka** Southern, S Zambia
39 Y15 **Muzon, Cape** headland Dall Island, Alaska, USA
40 M6 **Múzquiz** Coahuila de Zaragoza, NE Mexico
147 U13 **Muzqŭl, Qatorkŭhi** Rus. Khrebet Muzkol. ▲▲ SE Tajikistan
158 G10 **Muztag** ▲ NW China
158 D8 **Muztagata** ▲ NW China
158 K10 **Muztag Feng** var. Ulugh Muztag. ▲ W China
83 K17 **Mvuma** prev. Umvuma. Midlands, C Zimbabwe
82 L13 **Mwanya** Eastern, E Zambia
81 G20 **Mwanza** Mwanza, NW Tanzania
79 N23 **Mwanza** Katanga, SE Dem. Rep. Congo (Zaire)
81 F20 **Mwanza** ❖ region N Tanzania
82 M13 **Mwase Lundazi** Eastern, E Zambia
97 B17 **Mweelrea** Ir. Caoc Maol Réidh. ▲ W Ireland
79 K21 **Mweka** Kasai Occidental, C Dem. Rep. Congo (Zaire)
82 K12 **Mwenda** Luapula, N Zambia
79 L22 **Mwene-Ditu** Kasai Oriental, S Dem. Rep. Congo (Zaire)
83 L18 **Mwenezi** ⁓ S Zimbabwe
79 O20 **Mwenga** Sud Kivu, E Dem. Rep. Congo (Zaire)
82 K11 **Mweru, Lake** var. Lac Moero. ◎ Dem. Rep. Congo (Zaire)/Zambia
82 H13 **Mwinilunga** North Western, NW Zambia
189 V16 **Mwokil Atoll** var. Mokil Atoll. atoll Caroline Islands, E Micronesia
Myadel' see Myadzyel
118 J13 **Myadzyel** Pol. Miadzioł Nowy, Rus. Myadel'. Minskaya Voblasts', N Belarus
152 C12 **Myājlār** var. Miajlar. Rājasthān, NW India
123 T9 **Myakit** Magadanskaya Oblast', E Russian Federation
23 W13 **Myakka River** ⁓ Florida, SE USA
126 L14 **Myaksa** Vologodskaya Oblast', NW Russian Federation
183 U8 **Myall Lake** ◎ New South Wales, SE Australia
166 L7 **Myanaung** Irrawaddy, SW Myanmar
166 M4 **Myanmar** off. Union of Myanmar, var. Burma ◆ military dictatorship SE Asia
166 K8 **Myaungmya** Irrawaddy, SW Myanmar
118 N11 **Myazha** Rus. Mezha. Vitsyebskaya Voblasts', NE Belarus
119 O18 **Myerkulavichy** Rus. Merkulovichi. Homyel'skaya Voblasts', SE Belarus
119 N14 **Myezhava** Rus. Mezhëvo. Vitsyebskaya Voblasts', NE Belarus
166 L5 **Myingyan** Mandalay, C Myanmar
167 N2 **Myitkyina** Kachin State, N Myanmar
166 M5 **Myittha** Mandalay, C Myanmar
111 H19 **Myjava** Hung. Miava. Trenčiansky Kraj, W Slovakia
Myjeldino see Myyëldino
117 U9 **Mykhaylivka** Rus. Mikhaylovka. Zaporiz'ka Oblast', SE Ukraine
95 A18 **Mykines** Dan. Myggenaes Island Faeroe Islands
116 I5 **Mykolayiv** L'vivs'ka Oblast', W Ukraine
117 Q10 **Mykolayiv** Rus. Nikolayev. Mykolayivs'ka Oblast', S Ukraine
117 Q10 **Mykolayiv** ✕ Mykolayivs'ka Oblast', S Ukraine
Mykolayiv see Mykolayivs'ka Oblast'
117 P9 **Mykolayivka** Odes'ka Oblast', SW Ukraine
117 S13 **Mykolayivka** Respublika Krym, S Ukraine
117 P9 **Mykolayivs'ka Oblast'** var. Mykolayiv, Rus. Nikolayevskaya Oblast'. ❖ province S Ukraine
115 J20 **Mýkonos** Mýkonos, Kykládes, Greece, Aegean Sea
115 K20 **Mýkonos** var. Míkonos. island Kykládes, Greece, Aegean Sea
127 R7 **Myla** Respublika Komi, NW Russian Federation
Mylae see Milazzo
93 M19 **Myllykoski** Etelä-Suomi, S Finland
Mymensing see Mymensingh
153 U14 **Mymensingh** var. Maimansingh, Mymensing; prev. Nasirābād. Dhaka, N Bangladesh
93 K19 **Mynämäki** Länsi-Suomi, W Finland
145 S14 **Mynaral** Kaz. Myngaral. Zhambyl, S Kazakhstan
Mynbulak see Mingbuloq
Mynbulak, Vpadina see Mingbuloq Botighi
Myngaral see Mynaral
166 K5 **Myohaung** Arakan State, W Myanmar
163 W13 **Myohyang-sanmaek** ▲▲ C North Korea
164 M11 **Myōkō-san** ▲ Honshū, S Japan
83 J15 **Myooye** Central, C Zambia
118 K12 **Myory** prev. Miyory. Vitsyebskaya Voblasts', N Belarus
92 J4 **Mýrdalsjökull** glacier S Iceland
92 G10 **Myre** Nordland, C Norway
117 S5 **Myrhorod** Rus. Mirgorod. Poltavs'ka Oblast', NE Ukraine
115 J15 **Mýrina** var. Mírina. Límnos, SE Greece
117 P5 **Myronivka** Rus. Mironovka. Kyyivs'ka Oblast', N Ukraine
21 U13 **Myrtle Beach** South Carolina, SE USA
32 F14 **Myrtle Creek** Oregon, NW USA
183 P11 **Myrtleford** Victoria, SE Australia
32 E14 **Myrtle Point** Oregon, NW USA
115 K25 **Mýrtos** Kríti, Greece, E Mediterranean Sea
Myrtoum Mare see Mirtóo Pélagos
93 G17 **Myrviken** Jämtland, C Sweden
95 I15 **Mysen** Østfold, S Norway
126 L15 **Myshkin** Yaroslavskaya Oblast', NW Russian Federation
111 K17 **Myślenice** Małopolskie, S Poland
110 D10 **Myślibórz** Zachodniopomorskie, NW Poland
155 G20 **Mysore** var. Maisur. Karnātaka, W India
Mysore see Karnātaka
115 F21 **Mystrás** var. Mistras. Pelopónnisos, S Greece
127 T12 **Mysy** Komi-Permyatskiy Avtonomnyy Okrug, NW Russian Federation
111 K15 **Myszków** Śląskie, S Poland
167 T14 **My Tho** var. Mi Tho. Tiền Giang, S Vietnam
Mytilene see Mytilíni
115 L17 **Mytilíni** var. Mitilíni; anc. Mytilene. Lésvos, E Greece
128 K3 **Mytishchi** Moskovskaya Oblast', W Russian Federation
37 N3 **Myton** Utah, W USA
92 K2 **Mývatn** ◎ C Iceland
127 T11 **Myyëldino** var. Myjeldino. Respublika Komi, NW Russian Federation
82 M13 **Mzimba** Northern, NW Malawi
82 M12 **Mzuzu** Northern, N Malawi

N

101 M19 **Naab** ⁓ SE Germany
98 G12 **Naaldwijk** Zuid-Holland, W Netherlands
38 G12 **Naalehu** var. Nā'ālehu. Hawaii, USA, C Pacific Ocean
93 K19 **Naantali** Swe. Nådendal. Länsi-Suomi, W Finland
98 J10 **Naarden** Noord-Holland, C Netherlands
109 U4 **Naarn** ⁓ N Austria
97 F18 **Naas** Ir. An Nás, Nás na Ríogh. C Ireland
92 M9 **Näätämöjoki** Lapp. Njávdám. ⁓ NE Finland
83 E23 **Nababeep** var. Nababiep. Northern Cape, W South Africa
Nababiep see Nababeep
Nabadwip see Navadwip
164 J14 **Nabari** Mie, Honshū, SW Japan
Nabatié see Nabatīyé
138 G8 **Nabatīyé** var. An Nabatīyah at Taḩtā, Nabatié, Nabatiyet et Tahta. SW Lebanon
Nabatiyet et Tahta see Nabatīyé
187 X14 **Nabavatu** Vanua Levu, N Fiji
190 I2 **Nabeina** island Tungaru, W Kiribati
129 T4 **Naberezhnyye Chelny** prev. Brezhnev. Respublika Tatarstan, W Russian Federation
39 T10 **Nabesna** Alaska, USA
39 T10 **Nabesna River** ⁓ Alaska, USA
75 N5 **Nabeul** var. Nābul. NE Tunisia
152 I9 **Nābha** Punjab, NW India
171 W13 **Nabire** Irian Jaya, E Indonesia
141 O15 **Nabī Shu'ayb, Jabal an** ▲ W Yemen
138 F10 **Nablus** var. Nābulus, Heb. Shekhem; anc. Neapolis, Bibl. Shechem. N West Bank
187 X14 **Nabouwalu** Vanua Levu, N Fiji
Nābul see Nabeul
Nābulus see Nablus
187 Y13 **Nabuna** Vanua Levu, N Fiji
83 Q14 **Nacala** Nampula, NE Mozambique
42 H8 **Nacaome** Valle, S Honduras
Na Cealla Beaga see Killybegs
Na-ch'ii see Nagqu
164 J15 **Nachikatsuura** var. Nachi-Katsuura. Wakayama, Honshū, SE Japan
81 J24 **Nachingwea** Lindi, SE Tanzania
111 F16 **Náchod** Hradecký Kraj, N Czech Republic
Na Clocha Liatha see Greystones
40 G3 **Naco** Sonora, NW Mexico
25 X8 **Nacogdoches** Texas, SW USA
40 G4 **Nacozari de García** Sonora, NW Mexico
Nada see Danzhou
77 O14 **Nadawli** NW Ghana
104 I3 **Nadela** Galicia, NW Spain
Nådendal see Naantali
144 M7 **Nadezhdinka** prev. Nadezhdinskiy. Kostanay, N Kazakhstan
Nadezhdinskiy see Nadezhdinka
Nadgan see Nadqān, Qalamat
187 W14 **Nadi** prev. Nandi. Viti Levu, W Fiji
187 X14 **Nadi** prev. Nandi. ✕ Viti Levu, W Fiji
154 D10 **Nadiād** Gujarāt, W India
Nadikdik see Knox Atoll
116 E11 **Nădlac** Ger. Nadlak, Hung. Nagylak. Arad, W Romania
Nadlak see Nădlac
74 H6 **Nador** prev. Villa Nador. NE Morocco
141 S9 **Nadqān, Qalamat** var. Nadgan. well E Saudi Arabia
111 N22 **Nádudvar** Hajdú-Bihar, E Hungary
121 O15 **Nadur** Gozo, N Malta
187 X13 **Naduri** prev. Nanduri. Vanua Levu, N Fiji
116 I7 **Nadvirna** Pol. Nadwórna, Rus. Nadvornaya. Ivano-Frankivs'ka Oblast', W Ukraine
126 J8 **Nadvoitsy** Respublika Kareliya, NW Russian Federation
Nadvornaya/Nadwórna see Nadvirna
122 I9 **Nadym** Yamalo-Nenetskiy Avtonomnyy Okrug, N Russian Federation
122 I9 **Nadym** ⁓ C Russian Federation
186 E7 **Nadzab** Morobe, C PNG
77 X13 **Nafada** Gombe, E Nigeria
108 H8 **Näfels** Glarus, NE Switzerland
115 E18 **Náfpaktos** var. Návpaktos. Dytikí Ellás, C Greece
115 F20 **Náfplio** prev. Návplion. Pelopónnisos, S Greece
139 U6 **Naft Khāneh** E Iraq
149 N13 **Nāg** Baluchistān, SW Pakistan
171 P4 **Naga** off. Naga City; prev. Nueva Caceres. Luzon, N Philippines
Nagaarzê see Nagarzê
12 F11 **Nagagami** ⁓ Ontario, S Canada
164 F14 **Nagahama** Ehime, Shikoku, SW Japan
153 X12 **Nāga Hills** ▲▲ NE India
165 P10 **Nagai** Yamagata, Honshū, C Japan
Na Gaibhlte see Galty Mountains
39 N16 **Nagai Island** island Shumagin Islands, Alaska, USA
153 X12 **Nāgāland** ❖ state NE India
164 M11 **Nagano** Nagano, Honshū, S Japan
164 M12 **Nagano** off. Nagano-ken. ❖ prefecture Honshū, S Japan
165 N11 **Nagaoka** Niigata, Honshū, C Japan
153 W12 **Nagaon** prev. Nowgong. Assam, NE India
155 J21 **Nāgappattinam** var. Negapatam, Negapattinam. Tamil Nādu, SE India
Nagara Nayok see Nakhon Nayok
Nagara Panom see Nakhon Phanom
Nagara Pathom see Nakhon Pathom
Nagara Sridharmaraj see Nakhon Si Thammarat
Nagara Svarga see Nakhon Sawan
155 H16 **Nāgārjuna Sāgar** ⊡ E India
42 I10 **Nagarote** León, SW Nicaragua

◆ Country ● Country Capital ◇ Dependent Territory ○ Dependent Territory Capital ❖ Administrative Region ✕ International Airport ▲ Mountain ▲▲ Mountain Range Volcano ⁓ River ◎ Lake ⊡ Reservoir

158 M16 **Nagarzê** *var.* Nagaarzê. Xizang Zizhiqu, W China
164 C14 **Nagasaki** Nagasaki, Kyūshū, SW Japan
164 C14 **Nagasaki** *off.* Nagasaki-ken. ◆ *prefecture* Kyūshū, SW Japan
Nagashima *see* Kii-Nagashima
164 E12 **Nagato** Yamaguchi, Honshū, SW Japan
152 F11 **Nāgaur** Rājasthān, NW India
154 F10 **Nāgda** Madhya Pradesh, C India
98 L8 **Nagele** Flevoland, N Netherlands
155 H24 **Nāgercoil** Tamil Nādu, SE India
153 X12 **Nāginimāra** Nāgāland, NE India
Na Gleannta *see* Glenties
165 T16 **Nago** Okinawa, Okinawa, SW Japan
154 K9 **Nāgod** Madhya Pradesh, C India
155 J26 **Nagoda** Southern Province, S Sri Lanka
101 G22 **Nagold** Baden-Württemberg, SW Germany
Nagorno-Karabakhskaya Avtonomnaya Oblast *see* Nagornyy Karabakh
123 Q12 **Nagornyy** Respublika Sakha (Yakutiya), NE Russian Federation
137 V12 **Nagornyy Karabakh** *var.* Nagorno-Karabakhskaya Avtonomnaya Oblast , *Arm.* Lerrnayin Gharabakh, *Az.* Dağliq Qarabağ. *former autonomous region* SW Azerbaijan
127 R13 **Nagorsk** Kirovskaya Oblast', NW Russian Federation
164 K13 **Nagoya** Aichi, Honshū, SW Japan
154 I12 **Nāgpur** Mahārāshtra, C India
156 K10 **Nagqu** *Chin.* Na-ch'ü; *prev.* Hei-ho. Xizang Zizhiqu, W China
152 J8 **Nāg Tibba Range** ▲ N India
45 O8 **Nagua** NE Dominican Republic
111 H25 **Nagyatád** Somogy, SW Hungary
Nagybánya *see* Baia Mare
Nagybecskerek *see* Zrenjanin
Nagydisznód *see* Cisnădie
Nagyenyed *see* Aiud
111 N21 **Nagykálló** Szabolcs-Szatmár-Bereg, E Hungary
111 G25 **Nagykanizsa** *Ger.* Grosskanizsa. Zala, SW Hungary
Nagykároly *see* Carei
111 K22 **Nagykáta** Pest, C Hungary
Nagykikinda *see* Kikinda
111 K23 **Nagykőrös** Pest, C Hungary
Nagy-Küküllő *see* Târnava Mare
Nagylak *see* Nădlac
Nagymihály *see* Michalovce
Nagyrőce *see* Revúca
Nagysomkút *see* Şomcuta Mare
Nagysurány *see* Šurany
Nagyszalonta *see* Salonta
Nagyszeben *see* Sibiu
Nagyszentmiklós *see* Sânnicolau Mare
Nagyszőllős *see* Vynohradiv
Nagyszombat *see* Trnava
Nagytapolcsány *see* Topoľčany
Nagyvárad *see* Oradea
165 S17 **Naha** Okinawa, Okinawa, SW Japan
152 J8 **Nāhan** Himāchal Pradesh, NW India
Nahang, Rūd-e *see* Nihing
Nahariya *see* Nahariyya
138 F8 **Nahariyya** *var.* Nahariya. Northern, N Israel
142 L6 **Nahāvand** *var.* Nehavend. Hamadān, W Iran
101 F19 **Nahe** ⛰ SW Germany
Na h-Iarmhidhe *see* Westmeath
189 O13 **Nahnalaud** ▲ Pohnpei, E Micronesia
Nahoi, Cape *see* Cumberland, Cape
63 H16 **Nahuel Huapi, Lago** ◎ W Argentina
23 W7 **Nahunta** Georgia, SE USA
40 J6 **Naica** Chihuahua, N Mexico
11 U15 **Naicam** Saskatchewan, S Canada
163 T11 **Naiman Qi** Nei Mongol Zizhiqu, N China
158 M4 **Naimin Bulak** *spring* NW China
13 P6 **Nain** Newfoundland, NE Canada
143 P8 **Nā'īn** Eşfahān, C Iran
152 K10 **Naini Tāl** Uttar Pradesh, N India
154 J11 **Nainpur** Madhya Pradesh, C India
96 J8 **Nairn** N Scotland, UK
96 I8 **Nairn** *cultural region* NE Scotland, UK
81 I19 **Nairobi** ● (Kenya) Nairobi Area, S Kenya
81 I19 **Nairobi** ✕ Nairobi Area, S Kenya
82 P13 **Nairoto** Cabo Delgado, NE Mozambique
118 G3 **Naissaar** *island* N Estonia
Naissus *see* Niš
187 Z14 **Naitaba** *var.* Naitauba; *prev.* Naitamba. *island* Lau Group, E Fiji
Naitamba/Naitauba *see* Naitaba
81 I19 **Naivasha** Rift Valley, SW Kenya
81 H19 **Naivasha, Lake** ◎ SW Kenya
Najaf *see* An Najaf
143 N8 **Najafābād** *var.* Nejafabad. Eşfahān, C Iran
141 N7 **Najd** *var.* Nejd. *cultural region* C Saudi Arabia
105 O4 **Nájera** La Rioja, N Spain
105 P4 **Najerilla** ⛰ N Spain
152 J9 **Najībābād** Uttar Pradesh, N India
Najima *see* Fukuoka
163 Y11 **Najin** NE North Korea
139 T9 **Najm al Ḩassūn** C Iraq
141 O13 **Najrān** *var.* Abā as Su'ūd. Najrān, S Saudi Arabia
141 P12 **Najrān** *off.* Minţaqat al Najrān. ◆ *province* S Saudi Arabia
165 T2 **Nakagawa** Hokkaidō, NE Japan
38 F9 **Nakalele Pont** *headland* Maui, Hawaii, USA, C Pacific Ocean
164 D13 **Nakama** Fukuoka, Kyūshū, SW Japan
Nakambé *see* White Volta
Nakamti *see* Nek'emtē
164 F15 **Nakamura** Kōchi, Shikoku, SW Japan
186 H7 **Nakanai Mountains** ▲ New Britain, E PNG
164 H11 **Nakano-shima** *island* Oki-shotō, SW Japan
165 Q6 **Nakasato** Aomori, Honshū, C Japan
165 T5 **Nakasatsunai** Hokkaidō, NE Japan
165 W4 **Nakashibetsu** Hokkaidō, NE Japan
81 F18 **Nakasongola** C Uganda
165 T1 **Nakatonbetsu** Hokkaidō, NE Japan
164 L13 **Nakatsugawa** *var.* Nakatugawa. Gifu, Honshū, SW Japan
Nakatsu *see* Nakatsu
Nakatugawa *see* Nakatsugawa
Naka-umi *see* Nakano-umi
Nakdong *see* Naktong-gang
Nakel *see* Nakło nad Notecią
80 J8 **Nakfa** N Eritrea
Nakhichevan' *see* Naxçıvan
123 S15 **Nakhodka** Primorskiy Kray, SE Russian Federation
122 J8 **Nakhodka** Yamalo-Nenetskiy Avtonomnyy Okrug, N Russian Federation
Nakhon Navok *see* Nakhon Nayok
167 P11 **Nakhon Nayok** *var.* Nagara Nayok, Nakhon Navok. Nakhon Nayok, C Thailand
167 O11 **Nakhon Pathom** *var.* Nagara Pathom, Nakorn Pathom. Nakhon Pathom, W Thailand
167 R8 **Nakhon Phanom** *var.* Nagara Panom. Nakhon Phanom, E Thailand
167 Q10 **Nakhon Ratchasima** *var.* Khorat, Korat. Nakhon Ratchasima, E Thailand
167 O9 **Nakhon Sawan** *var.* Muang Nakhon Sawan, Nagara Svarga. Nakhon Sawan, W Thailand
167 N15 **Nakhon Si Thammarat** *var.* Nagara Sridharmaraj, Nakhon Sithammaraj. Nakhon Si Thammarat, SW Thailand
Nakhon Sithamnaraj *see* Nakhon Si Thammarat
139 Y11 **Nakhrash** SE Iraq
10 I9 **Nakina** British Columbia, W Canada
110 H9 **Nakło nad Notecią** *Ger.* Nakel. Kujawsko-pomorskie, C Poland
39 P13 **Naknek** Alaska, USA
152 H8 **Nakodar** Punjab, NW India
82 M11 **Nakonde** Northern, NE Zambia
Nakorn Pathom *see* Nakhon Pathom
95 H24 **Nakskov** Storstrøm, SE Denmark
163 Y15 **Naktong-gang** *var.* Nakdong, *Jap.* Rakutō-kō. ⛰ C South Korea
83 H18 **Nakuru** Rift Valley, SW Kenya
81 H19 **Nakuru, Lake** ◎ Rift Valley, C Kenya
11 O17 **Nakusp** British Columbia, SW Canada
149 N15 **Nāl** ⛰ W Pakistan
162 M7 **Nalayh** Töv, C Mongolia
153 V12 **Nalbāri** Assam, NE India
63 G19 **Nalcayec, Isla** *island* Archipiélago de los Chonos, S Chile
129 N15 **Nal'chik** Kabardino-Balkarskaya Respublika, SW Russian Federation
155 I16 **Nalgonda** Andhra Pradesh, C India
153 S14 **Nalhāti** West Bengal, NE India
153 U14 **Nalitabari** Dhaka, N Bangladesh
155 I17 **Nallamala Hills** ▲ E India
136 G12 **Nallıhan** Ankara, NW Turkey
104 K2 **Nalón** ⛰ NW Spain
167 N3 **Nalong** Kachin State, N Myanmar
75 N8 **Nālūt** NW Libya
171 T14 **Nama** Pulau Manawoka, E Indonesia
189 Q16 **Nama** *island* C Micronesia
83 O16 **Namacurra** Zambézia, NE Mozambique
188 F9 **Namai Bay** *bay* Babeldaob, N Palau
29 W2 **Namakan Lake** ◎ Canada/USA
143 O6 **Namak, Daryācheh-ye** *marsh* N Iran
143 T6 **Namak, Kavīr-e** *salt pan* NE Iran
167 O6 **Namaklwe** Shan State, E Myanmar
Namaksār, Kowl-e/Namakzār, Daryācheh-ye *see* Namakzar
148 I5 **Namakzar** *Pash.* Daryācheh-ye Namakzār, Kowl-e Namaksār. *marsh* Afghanistan/Iran
171 V15 **Namalau** Pulau Jursian, E Indonesia
81 I20 **Namanga** Rift Valley, S Kenya
147 S10 **Namangan** Namangan Wiloyati, E Uzbekistan
Namanganskaya Oblast' *see* Namangan Wiloyati
147 R10 **Namangan Wiloyati** *Rus.* Namanganskaya Oblast'. ◆ *province* E Uzbekistan
83 Q14 **Namapa** Nampula, NE Mozambique
83 C21 **Namaqualand** *physical region* S Namibia
81 G18 **Namasagali** C Uganda
186 H6 **Namatanai** New Ireland, NE PNG
83 I14 **Nambala** Central, C Zambia
81 J23 **Nambanje** Lindi, SE Tanzania
83 G16 **Nambiya** Ngamiland, N Botswana
183 V2 **Nambour** Queensland, E Australia
183 V6 **Nambucca Heads** New South Wales, SE Australia
159 N15 **Nam Co** ◎ W China
167 R5 **Nậm Cum** Lai Châu, N Vietnam
Namdik *see* Namorik Atoll
167 T6 **Nam Đinh** Nam Ha, N Vietnam
99 I20 **Namêche** Namur, SE Belgium
30 J4 **Namekagon Lake** ◎ Wisconsin, N USA
188 F10 **Namekakl Passage** *passage* Babeldaob, N Palau
Namen *see* Namur
83 P15 **Nametil** Nampula, NE Mozambique
163 X14 **Nam-gang** ⛰ C North Korea
163 Y16 **Nam-gang** ⛰ S South Korea
163 Y17 **Namhae-do** *Jap.* Nankai-tō. *island* S South Korea
Namhoi *see* Foshan
83 C19 **Namib Desert** *desert* W Namibia
83 A15 **Namibe** *Port.* Moçâmedes, Mossâmedes. Namibe, SW Angola
83 A15 **Namibe** ◆ *province* SE Angola
83 C18 **Namibia** *off.* Republic of Namibia, *var.* South West Africa, *Afr.* Suidwes-Afrika, *Ger.* Deutsch-Südwestafrika; *prev.* German Southwest Africa, South-West Africa. ◆ *republic* S Africa
65 O17 **Namibia Plain** *undersea feature* S Atlantic Ocean
165 Q11 **Namie** Fukushima, Honshū, C Japan
165 Q7 **Namioka** Aomori, Honshū, C Japan
40 I5 **Namiquipa** Chihuahua, N Mexico
159 P15 **Namjagbarwa Feng** ▲ W China
171 R13 **Namlea** Pulau Buru, E Indonesia
158 L16 **Namling** Xizang Zizhiqu, W China
Namnetes *see* Nantes
167 R8 **Nam Ngum** ⛰ C Laos
Namo *see* Namu Atoll
183 R5 **Namoi River** ⛰ New South Wales, SE Australia
189 Q17 **Namoluk Atoll** *atoll* Mortlock Islands, C Micronesia
189 O15 **Namonuito Atoll** *atoll* Caroline Islands, C Micronesia
189 T9 **Namorik Atoll** *var.* Namdik. *atoll* Ralik Chain, S Marshall Islands
167 Q6 **Nam Ou** ⛰ N Laos
32 M14 **Nampa** Idaho, NW USA
76 M11 **Nampala** Ségou, W Mali
163 W14 **Namp'o** SW North Korea
83 P15 **Nampula** Nampula, NE Mozambique
83 P15 **Nampula** *off.* Província de Nampula. ◆ *province* NE Mozambique
163 W13 **Namsan-ni** NW North Korea
Namslau *see* Namysłów
93 E15 **Namsos** Nord-Trøndelag, C Norway
93 F14 **Namsskogan** Nord-Trøndelag, C Norway
123 Q10 **Namsty** Respublika Sakha (Yakutiya), NE Russian Federation
167 O6 **Nam Teng** ⛰ E Myanmar
167 P6 **Nam Tha** ⛰ N Laos
167 N4 **Namtu** Shan State, E Myanmar
10 J15 **Namu** British Columbia, SW Canada
189 T7 **Namu Atoll** *var.* Namo. *atoll* Ralik Chain, C Marshall Islands
187 Y15 **Namuka-i-lau** *island* Lau Group, E Fiji
83 O15 **Namuli, Mont** ▲ NE Mozambique
83 P14 **Namuno** Cabo Delgado, N Mozambique
99 I20 **Namur** *Dut.* Namen. Namur, SE Belgium
99 H21 **Namur** *Dut.* Namen. ◆ *province* S Belgium
83 D17 **Namutoni** Kunene, N Namibia
163 Y16 **Namwŏn** *Jap.* Nangen. S South Korea
111 H14 **Namysłów** *Ger.* Namslau. Opolskie, S Poland
167 P7 **Nan** *var.* Muang Nan. Nan, NW Thailand
79 G15 **Nana** ⛰ W Central African Republic
165 R5 **Nanae** Hokkaidō, NE Japan
79 I14 **Nana-Grébizi** ◆ *prefecture* N Central African Republic
10 L17 **Nanaimo** Vancouver Island, British Columbia, SW Canada
38 C9 **Nanakuli** *Haw.* Nānākuli. Oahu, Hawaii, USA, C Pacific Ocean
79 G15 **Nana-Mambéré** ◆ *prefecture* W Central African Republic
161 R13 **Nan'an** Fujian, SE China
183 U2 **Nanango** Queensland, E Australia
164 L11 **Nanao** Ishikawa, Honshū, SW Japan
161 Q14 **Nan'ao Dao** *island* S China
164 L10 **Nanatsu-shima** *island* SW Japan
56 F8 **Nanay, Río** ⛰ NE Peru
160 J8 **Nanbu** Sichuan, C China
163 X7 **Nancha** Heilongjiang, NE China
161 P10 **Nanchang** *var.* Nan-ch'ang, Nanch'ang-hsien. Jiangxi, S China
Nanch'ang-hsien *see* Nanchang
161 P11 **Nancheng** Jiangxi, S China
Nan-ching *see* Nanjing
160 J9 **Nanchong** Sichuan, C China
160 J10 **Nanchuan** Chongqing Shi, C China
103 T5 **Nancy** Meurthe-et-Moselle, NE France
185 A22 **Nancy Sound** *sound* South Island, NZ
152 L9 **Nanda Devi** ▲ NW India
42 J11 **Nandaime** Granada, SW Nicaragua
160 K13 **Nandan** Guangxi Zhuangzu Zizhiqu, S China
155 H14 **Nānded** Mahārāshtra, C India
183 S5 **Nandewar Range** ▲ New South Wales, SE Australia
Nandi *see* Nadi
160 E13 **Nanding He** ⛰ China/Vietnam
Nándorhgy *see* Oţelu Roşu
154 E11 **Nandurbār** Mahārāshtra, W India
Nanduri *see* Naduri
155 I17 **Nandyāl** Andhra Pradesh, E India
161 P11 **Nanfeng** Jiangxi, S China
Nang *see* Nang Xian
79 E15 **Nanga Eboko** Centre, C Cameroon
149 W4 **Nanga Parbat** ▲ India/Pakistan
169 R11 **Nangapinoh** Borneo, C Indonesia
149 R5 **Nangarhār** ◆ *province* E Afghanistan
169 S11 **Nangaserawai** *var.* Nangah Serawai. Borneo, C Indonesia
169 Q12 **Nangatayap** Borneo, C Indonesia
Nangen *see* Namwŏn
103 P5 **Nangis** Seine-et-Marne, N France
163 X13 **Nangnim-sanmaek** ▲ C North Korea
161 O4 **Nangong** Hebei, E China
159 Q14 **Nangqên** Qinghai, C China
167 Q10 **Nang Rong** Buri Ram, E Thailand
159 O16 **Nang Xian** *var.* Nang. Xizang Zizhiqu, W China
Nan Hai *see* South China Sea
160 L8 **Nan He** ⛰ C China
160 F12 **Nanhua** Yunnan, SW China
Naniwa *see* Ōsaka
155 G20 **Nanjangūd** Karnātaka, W India
161 Q8 **Nanjing** *var.* Nan-ching, Nanking; *prev.* Chianning, Chian-ning, Kiang-ning. Jiangsu, E China
Nankai-tō *see* Namhae-do
161 O12 **Nankang** Jiangxi, S China
Nanking *see* Nanjing
161 N13 **Nan Ling** ▲ S China
160 L15 **Nanliu Jiang** ⛰ S China
189 P13 **Nan Madol** *ruins* Temwen Island, E Micronesia
160 K15 **Nanning** *var.* Nan-ning; *prev.* Yung-ning. Guangxi Zhuangzu Zizhiqu, S China
196 M15 **Nanortalik** Kitaa, S Greenland
Nanouki *see* Aranuka
160 H13 **Nanpan Jiang** ⛰ S China
152 M11 **Nānpāra** Uttar Pradesh, N India
161 Q12 **Nanping** *var.* Nan-p'ing; *prev.* Yenping. Fujian, SE China
160 I7 **Nanping** Sichuan, C China
161 R12 **Nanri Dao** *island* SE China
165 S16 **Nansei-shotō** *Eng.* Ryukyu Islands. *island group* SW Japan
Nansei Syotō Trench *see* Ryukyu Trench
197 T10 **Nansen Basin** *undersea feature* Arctic Ocean
197 T10 **Nansen Cordillera** *var.* Arctic-Mid Oceanic Ridge, Nansen Ridge. *undersea feature* Arctic Ocean
Nansen Ridge *see* Nansen Cordillera
131 T9 **Nan Shan** ▲ C China
Nansha Qundao *see* Spratly Islands
12 K3 **Nantais, Lac** ◎ Quebec, NE Canada
103 N5 **Nanterre** Hauts-de-Seine, N France
102 I8 **Nantes** *Bret.* Naoned; *anc.* Condivincum, Namnetes. Loire-Atlantique, NW France
14 G17 **Nanticoke** Ontario, S Canada
18 H13 **Nanticoke** Pennsylvania, NE USA
21 Y4 **Nanticoke River** ⛰ Delaware/Maryland, NE USA
11 Q17 **Nanton** Alberta, SW Canada
161 S8 **Nantong** Jiangsu, E China
161 S13 **Nant'ou** W Taiwan
103 S10 **Nantua** Ain, E France
19 Q13 **Nantucket** Nantucket Island, Massachusetts, NE USA
19 Q13 **Nantucket Island** *island* Massachusetts, NE USA
19 Q13 **Nantucket Sound** *sound* Massachusetts, NE USA
82 P13 **Nantulo** Cabo Delgado, N Mozambique
189 O12 **Nanuh** Pohnpei, E Micronesia
190 D6 **Nanumaga** *var.* Nanumanga. *atoll* NW Tuvalu
Nanumanga *see* Nanumaga
190 D5 **Nanumea Atoll** *atoll* NW Tuvalu
59 O19 **Nanuque** Minas Gerais, SE Brazil
171 R10 **Nanusa, Kepulauan** *island group* N Indonesia
163 U4 **Nanweng He** ⛰ NE China
160 I10 **Nanxi** Sichuan, C China
161 N10 **Nanxian** *var.* Nan Xian. Hunan, S China
161 N7 **Nanyang** *var.* Nan-yang. Henan, C China
161 P6 **Nanyang Hu** ◎ E China
165 P10 **Nan'yō** Yamagata, Honshū, C Japan
81 I18 **Nanyuki** Central, C Kenya
160 M8 **Nanzhang** Hubei, C China
105 T11 **Nao, Cabo de La** *headland* E Spain
12 M9 **Naococane, Lac** ◎ Quebec, E Canada
153 S14 **Naogaon** Rajshahi, NW Bangladesh
Naokot *see* Naukot
187 R13 **Naone** Maewo, C Vanuatu
Naoned *see* Nantes
115 E14 **Náousa** Kentrikí Makedonía, N Greece
35 N8 **Napa** California, W USA
39 O11 **Napaimiut** Alaska, USA
39 N12 **Napakiak** Alaska, USA
122 J7 **Napalkovo** Yamalo-Nenetskiy Avtonomnyy Okrug, N Russian Federation
12 I16 **Napanee** Ontario, SE Canada
39 N12 **Napaskiak** Alaska, USA
167 S5 **Na Phac** Cao Bằng, N Vietnam
184 O11 **Napier** Hawke's Bay, North Island, NZ
195 X3 **Napier Mountains** ▲ Antarctica
15 O13 **Napierville** Quebec, SE Canada
23 W15 **Naples** Florida, SE USA
25 W5 **Naples** Texas, SW USA
Naples *see* Napoli
160 I14 **Napo** Guangxi Zhuangzu Zizhiqu, S China
56 D6 **Napo** ◆ *province* NE Ecuador
29 O6 **Napoleon** North Dakota, N USA
31 R11 **Napoleon** Ohio, N USA
Napoléon-Vendée *see* la Roche-sur-Yon
22 J9 **Napoleonville** Louisiana, S USA
107 K17 **Napoli** *Eng.* Naples, *Ger.* Neapel; *anc.* Neapolis. Campania, S Italy
107 J18 **Napoli, Golfo di** *gulf* S Italy
57 F7 **Napo, Río** ⛰ Ecuador/Peru
191 W9 **Napuka** *island* Îles Tuamotu, C French Polynesia
142 J3 **Naqadeh** Āžarbāyjān-e Bākhtarī, NW Iran
139 U6 **Naqnah** E Iraq
Nar *see* Nera
164 J14 **Nara** Nara, Honshū, SW Japan
76 L11 **Nara** Koulikoro, W Mali
164 J14 **Nara** *off.* Nara-ken. ◆ *prefecture* Honshū, SW Japan
149 R14 **Nāra Canal** *irrigation canal* S Pakistan
182 K11 **Naracoorte** South Australia
183 P8 **Naradhan** New South Wales, SE Australia
Naradhivas *see* Narathiwat
56 B8 **Naranjal** Guayas, W Ecuador
57 Q19 **Naranjos** Santa Cruz, E Bolivia
41 Q12 **Naranjos** Veracruz-Llave, E Mexico
159 Q6 **Naran Sebstein Bulag** *spring* NW China
143 X12 **Narānū** Sīstān va Balūchestān, SE Iran
164 B14 **Narao** Nagasaki, Nakadōri-jima, SW Japan
155 J16 **Narasaraopet** Andhra Pradesh, E India
158 J5 **Narat** Xinjiang Uygur Zizhiqu, W China
167 P17 **Narathiwat** *var.* Naradhivas. Narathiwat, SW Thailand
37 V10 **Nara Visa** New Mexico, SW USA
Nārāyāni *see* Gandak
Narbada *see* Narmada
Narbo Martius *see* Narbonne
103 P16 **Narbonne** *anc.* Narbo Martius. Aude, S France
Narborough Island *see* Fernandina, Isla
104 J2 **Narcea** ⛰ NW Spain
152 J9 **Narendranagar** Uttar Pradesh, N India
Nares Abyssal Plain *see* Nares Plain
64 G11 **Nares Plain** *var.* Nares Abyssal Plain. *undersea feature* NW Atlantic Ocean
197 P10 **Nares Strait** *Dan.* Nares Stræde. *strait* Canada/Greenland
Nares Stræde *see* Nares Strait
110 O9 **Narew** ⛰ E Poland
155 F17 **Nargund** Karnātaka, W India
83 D20 **Narib** Hardap, S Namibia
Narikrik *see* Knox Atoll
54 B13 **Nariño** *off.* Departamento de Nariño. ◆ *province* SW Colombia
165 P13 **Narita** Chiba, Honshū, S Japan
165 P13 **Narita** ✕ (Tōkyō) Chiba, Honshū, S Japan
Nariya *see* An Nu'ayriyah
152 J8 **Nārkanda** Himāchal Pradesh, NW India
92 L13 **Narkaus** Lappi, NW Finland
154 E11 **Narmada** *var.* Narbada. ⛰ C India
152 H11 **Narnaul** *var.* Nārnaul. Haryāna, N India
107 I14 **Narni** Umbria, C Italy
107 J24 **Naro** Sicilia, Italy, C Mediterranean Sea
Narodichi *see* Narodychi
127 V7 **Narodnaya, Gora** ▲ NW Russian Federation
117 N3 **Narodychi** *Rus.* Narodichi. Zhytomyrs'ka Oblast', N Ukraine
128 J4 **Naro-Fominsk** Moskovskaya Oblast', W Russian Federation
81 H19 **Narok** Rift Valley, SW Kenya
104 H2 **Narón** Galicia, NW Spain
183 S11 **Narooma** New South Wales, SE Australia
Narova *see* Narva
Narovlya *see* Narowlya
149 W8 **Nārowāl** Punjab, E Pakistan
119 N20 **Narowlya** *Rus.* Narovlya. Homyel'skaya Voblasts', SE Belarus
93 J17 **Närpes** *Fin.* Närpiö. Länsi-Suomi, W Finland
Närpiö *see* Närpes
183 S5 **Narrabri** New South Wales, SE Australia
183 P9 **Narrandera** New South Wales, SE Australia
183 Q4 **Narran Lake** ◎ New South Wales, SE Australia
183 Q4 **Narran River** ⛰ New South Wales/Queensland, SE Australia
180 J13 **Narrogin** Western Australia
183 Q7 **Narromine** New South Wales, SE Australia
21 R6 **Narrows** Virginia, NE USA
196 M15 **Narsarsuaq** ✕ Kitaa, S Greenland
154 I10 **Narsimhapur** Madhya Pradesh, C India
Narsingdi *see* Narsinghdi
153 U15 **Narsinghdi** *var.* Narsingdi. Dhaka, C Bangladesh
154 H9 **Narsinghgarh** Madhya Pradesh, C India
163 Q11 **Nart** Nei Mongol Zizhiqu, N China
Nartës, Gjol i/Nartës, Laguna e *see* Nartës, Liqeni i
113 J22 **Nartës, Liqeni i** *var.* Gjol i Nartës, Laguna e Nartës. ◎ SW Albania
115 F17 **Narthăki** ▲ C Greece
129 O15 **Nartkala** Kabardino-Balkarskaya Respublika, SW Russian Federation
118 K3 **Narva** Ida-Virumaa, NE Estonia
118 K4 **Narva** *prev.* Narova. ⛰ Estonia/Russian Federation
118 J3 **Narva Bay** *Est.* Narva Laht, *Ger.* Narwa-Bucht, *Rus.* Narvskiy Zaliv. *bay* Estonia/Russian Federation
Narva Laht *see* Narva Bay
126 F13 **Narva Reservoir** *Est.* Narva Veehoidla, *Rus.* Narvskoye Vodokhranilishche. ▣ Estonia/Russian Federation
Narva Veehoidla *see* Narva Reservoir
92 H10 **Narvik** Nordland, C Norway
Narvskiy Zaliv *see* Narva Bay
Narvskoye Vodokhranilishche *see* Narva Reservoir
Narwa-Bucht *see* Narva Bay
152 I9 **Narwāna** Haryāna, NW India
127 R4 **Nar'yan-Mar** *prev.* Beloshchel'ye, Dzerzhinskiy. Nenetskiy Avtonomnyy Okrug, NW Russian Federation
122 J12 **Narym** Tomskaya Oblast', C Russian Federation
145 Y10 **Narymskiy Khrebet** *Kaz.* Naryn Zhotasy. ▲ E Kazakhstan
147 W9 **Naryn** Narynskaya Oblast', C Kyrgyzstan
147 U8 **Naryn** ⛰ Kyrgyzstan/Uzbekistan
145 W16 **Narynkol** *Kaz.* Naryngol. Almaty, SE Kazakhstan
Naryn Oblasty *see* Narynskaya Oblast'
Narynqol *see* Narynkol
147 V9 **Narynskaya Oblast'** *Kir.* Naryn Oblasty. ◆ *province* C Kyrgyzstan
Naryn Zhotasy *see* Narymskiy Khrebet
128 J6 **Naryshkino** Orlovskaya Oblast', W Russian Federation
95 L14 **Nås** Dalarna, C Sweden
92 G13 **Nasa** ▲ C Norway
93 H16 **Nasåker** Västernorrland, C Sweden
187 Y14 **Nasau** Koro, C Fiji
116 I9 **Năsăud** *Ger.* Nussdorf, *Hung.* Naszód. Bistriţa-Năsăud, N Romania
103 P13 **Nasbinals** Lozère, S France
Na Sceirí *see* Skerries
Nase *see* Naze
185 E22 **Naseby** Otago, South Island, NZ
143 R10 **Nāşerīyeh** Kermān, C Iran
25 X5 **Nash** Texas, SW USA
154 E13 **Nāshik** *prev.* Nāsik. Mahārāshtra, W India
56 E7 **Nashiño, Río** ⛰ Ecuador/Peru
29 W12 **Nashua** Iowa, C USA
33 W7 **Nashua** Montana, NW USA
19 O10 **Nashua** New Hampshire, NE USA
27 S13 **Nashville** Arkansas, C USA
23 U7 **Nashville** Georgia, SE USA
30 L16 **Nashville** Illinois, N USA
31 O14 **Nashville** Indiana, N USA
21 V9 **Nashville** North Carolina, SE USA
20 J8 **Nashville** *state capital* Tennessee, S USA
20 J9 **Nashville** ✕ Tennessee, S USA
64 H10 **Nashville Seamount** *undersea feature* NW Atlantic Ocean
112 H9 **Našice** Osijek-Baranja, E Croatia
110 M11 **Nasielsk** Mazowieckie, C Poland
93 K18 **Näsijärvi** ◎ SW Finland
Nāsik *see* Nāshik
80 G13 **Nasir** Upper Nile, SE Sudan
149 Q12 **Nasīrābād** Baluchistān, SW Pakistan
148 K15 **Nasīrābād** Baluchistān, SW Pakistan
Nasīrābād *see* Mymensingh
Nasir, Buhayrat/Nâşir, Buheiret *see* Nasser, Lake
Nāsiri *see* Ahvāz
Nasiriya *see* An Nāşirīyah
Nás na Ríogh *see* Naas
107 L23 **Naso** Sicilia, Italy, C Mediterranean Sea
Nasratabad *see* Zābol
10 J11 **Nass** ⛰ British Columbia, SW Canada
77 V15 **Nassarawa** Nassarawa, C Nigeria
44 H2 **Nassau** ● (Bahamas) New Providence, N Bahamas
44 H2 **Nassau** ✕ New Providence, C Bahamas
190 J13 **Nassau** *island* N Cook Islands
23 W8 **Nassau Sound** *sound* Florida, SE USA
108 L7 **Nassereith** Tirol, W Austria
95 L19 **Nässjö** Jönköping, S Sweden
99 K22 **Nassogne** Luxembourg, SE Belgium
12 J6 **Nastapoka Islands** *island group* Nunavut, C Canada
93 M19 **Nastola** Etelä-Suomi, S Finland
171 O4 **Nasugbu** Luzon, N Philippines
94 N11 **Näsviken** Gävleborg, C Sweden
Naszód *see* Năsăud
83 I17 **Nata** Central, NE Botswana
54 E11 **Natagaima** Tolima, C Colombia
59 Q14 **Natal** Rio Grande do Norte, E Brazil
168 I11 **Natal** Sumatera, N Indonesia
Natal *see* KwaZulu/Natal
173 L10 **Natal Basin** *var.* Mozambique Basin. *undersea feature* W Indian Ocean
25 R12 **Natalia** Texas, SW USA
67 W15 **Natal Valley** *undersea feature* SW Indian Ocean
Natanya *see* Netanya
143 O7 **Naţanz** Eşfahān, C Iran
13 Q11 **Natashquan** Quebec, E Canada

◆ Country ● Country Capital ◇ Dependent Territory ○ Dependent Territory Capital ◆ Administrative Region ✕ International Airport ▲ Mountain ▲ Mountain Range ⛰ Volcano ⛰ River ◎ Lake ▣ Reservoir

13 Q10 **Natashquan** ≈ Newfoundland/Quebec, E Canada
22 J7 **Natchez** Mississippi, S USA
22 G6 **Natchitoches** Louisiana, S USA
108 E10 **Naters** Valais, S Switzerland
Nathanya see Netanya
92 O3 **Nathorst Land** physical region W Svalbard
Nathula see Nacula
186 E9 **National Capital District** ◈ province S PNG
35 U17 **National City** California, W USA
184 M10 **National Park** Manawatu-Wanganui, North Island, NZ
77 R14 **Natitingou** NW Benin
40 B5 **Natividad, Isla** island W Mexico
165 Q10 **Natori** Miyagi, Honshū, C Japan
18 C14 **Natrona Heights** Pennsylvania, NE USA
81 H20 **Natron, Lake** ◎ Kenya/Tanzania
Natsrat see Nazerat
166 L7 **Nattalin** Pegu, C Myanmar
92 J12 **Nattavaara** Norrbotten, N Sweden
109 S3 **Natternbach** Oberösterreich, N Austria
95 M22 **Nättraby** Blekinge, S Sweden
169 P10 **Natuna Besar, Pulau** island Kepulauan Natuna, W Indonesia
169 O9 **Natuna Islands** see Natuna, Kepulauan
169 O9 **Natuna, Kepulauan** var. Natuna Islands. island group W Indonesia
169 N9 **Natuna, Laut** sea W Indonesia
21 N6 **Natural Bridge** tourist site Kentucky, C USA
173 V11 **Naturaliste Fracture Zone** tectonic feature E Indian Ocean
174 J10 **Naturaliste Plateau** undersea feature E Indian Ocean
Nau see Nov
103 O14 **Naucelle** Aveyron, S France
83 D20 **Nauchas** Hardap, C Namibia
108 K9 **Nauders** Tirol, W Austria
Naugard see Nowogard
118 F12 **Naujamiestis** Panevėžys, C Lithuania
118 E10 **Naujoji Akmenė** Akmenė, NW Lithuania
149 R16 **Naukot** var. Naokot. Sind, SE Pakistan
101 L16 **Naumburg** var. Naumburg an der Saale. Sachsen-Anhalt, C Germany
Naumburg am Queis see Nowogrodziec
Naumburg an der Saale see Naumburg
191 W15 **Naunau** ancient monument Easter Island, Chile, E Pacific Ocean
138 G10 **Nā'ūr** 'Ammān, W Jordan
189 Q8 **Nauru** off. Republic of Nauru; prev. Pleasant Island. ◆ republic W Pacific Ocean
175 P5 **Nauru** island W Pacific Ocean
189 Q9 **Nauru International** × S Nauru
Nausari see Navsāri
19 Q12 **Nauset Beach** beach Massachusetts, NE USA
Naushahra see Nowshera
149 P14 **Naushahro Fīroz** Sind, SE Pakistan
Naushara see Nowshera
187 X14 **Nausori** Viti Levu, W Fiji
56 F9 **Nauta** Loreto, N Peru
153 O12 **Nautanwa** Uttar Pradesh, N India
41 R13 **Nautla** Veracruz-Llave, E Mexico
Nauzad see Now Zād
41 N6 **Nava** Coahuila de Zaragoza, NE Mexico
Navabad see Navobod
104 L6 **Nava del Rey** Castilla-León, N Spain
153 S15 **Navadwīp** prev. Nabadwip. West Bengal, NE India
104 M9 **Navahermosa** Castilla-La Mancha, C Spain
119 I16 **Navahrudak** Pol. Nowogródek, Rus. Novogrudok. Hrodzyenskaya Voblasts', W Belarus
119 I16 **Navahrudskaye Wzvyshsha** ▲▲ W Belarus
36 M8 **Navajo Mount** ▲ Utah, W USA
37 Q9 **Navajo Reservoir** ▣ New Mexico, SW USA
104 K9 **Navalmoral de la Mata** Extremadura, W Spain
104 K10 **Navalvillar de Pelea** Extremadura, W Spain
97 F17 **Navan** Ir. An Uaimh. E Ireland
Navanagar see Jāmnagar
118 L12 **Navapolatsk** Rus. Novopolotsk. Vitsyebskaya Voblasts', N Belarus
149 P6 **Nāvar, Dasht-e** Pash. Dasht-i-Nawar. desert C Afghanistan
123 W6 **Navarin, Mys** headland NE Russian Federation
63 I25 **Navarino, Isla** island S Chile
105 Q4 **Navarra** Eng./Fr. Navarre. ◈ autonomous community N Spain
Navarre see Navarra
105 P4 **Navarrete** La Rioja, N Spain
61 C20 **Navarro** Buenos Aires, E Argentina
105 O12 **Navas de San Juan** Andalucía, S Spain
25 V10 **Navasota** Texas, SW USA
25 U9 **Navasota River** ≈ Texas, SW USA
44 I9 **Navassa Island** ◇ US unincorporated territory C West Indies
119 L19 **Navasyolki** Rus. Novosëlki. Homyel'skaya Voblasts', SE Belarus
119 H17 **Navayel'nya** Pol. Nowojelnia, Rus. Novoyel'nya. Hrodzyenskaya Voblasts', W Belarus
171 Y13 **Naver** Irian Jaya, E Indonesia
118 H5 **Navesti** ≈ C Estonia
104 J2 **Navia** Asturias, N Spain
104 J2 **Navia** ≈ NW Spain
59 I21 **Naviraí** Mato Grosso do Sul, SW Brazil
128 I6 **Navlya** Bryanskaya Oblast', W Russian Federation
187 X13 **Navoalevu** Vanua Levu, N Fiji
147 R12 **Navobod** Rus. Navabad, Novabad. C Tajikistan
147 P13 **Navobod** Rus. Navabad. W Tajikistan
Navoi see Nawoiy
Navoiyskaya Oblast' see Nawoiy Wiloyati
40 G7 **Navojoa** Sonora, NW Mexico
Navolat see Navolato
42 H9 **Navolato** var. Navolat. Sinaloa, C Mexico
187 Q13 **Navonda** Ambae, C Vanuatu
Návpaktos see Náfpaktos
Návplion see Náfplio
77 P14 **Navrongo** N Ghana
154 D12 **Navsāri** var. Nausari. Gujarāt, W India
187 X15 **Navua** Viti Levu, W Fiji
138 H8 **Nawá** Dar'ā, S Syria
Nawabashah see Nawābshāh
153 S14 **Nawabganj** Rajshahi, NW Bangladesh
153 S14 **Nawābganj** Uttar Pradesh, N India
149 Q15 **Nawābshāh** var. Nawabashah. Sind, S Pakistan
153 P14 **Nawāda** Bihār, N India
152 H11 **Nawalgarh** Rājasthān, N India
Nawāl, Sabkhat an see Noual, Sebkhet en
Nawar, Dasht-i- see Nāvar, Dasht-e
167 N4 **Nawnghkio** var. Nawngkio. Shan State, C Myanmar
Nawngkio see Nawnghkio
146 M11 **Nawoiy** Rus. Navoi. Nawoiy Wiloyati, C Uzbekistan
146 K8 **Nawoiy Wiloyati** Rus. Navoiyskaya Oblast'. ◈ province N Uzbekistan
137 U13 **Naxçıvan** Rus. Nakhichevan'. SW Azerbaijan
160 I10 **Naxi** Sichuan, C China
115 K21 **Náxos** var. Naxos. Náxos, Kykládes, Greece, Aegean Sea
115 K21 **Náxos** island Kykládes, Greece, Aegean Sea
40 J11 **Nayarit** ◈ state C Mexico
187 Y14 **Nayau** island Lau Group, E Fiji
143 S8 **Nāy Band** Khorāsān, E Iran
165 T2 **Nayoro** Hokkaidō, NE Japan
104 F9 **Nazaré** var. Nazare. Leiria, C Portugal
24 M4 **Nazareth** Texas, SW USA
Nazareth see Nazerat
173 O8 **Nazareth Bank** undersea feature W Indian Ocean
40 K9 **Nazas** Durango, C Mexico
57 F16 **Nazca** Ica, S Peru
(0) L17 **Nazca Plate** tectonic feature
193 U9 **Nazca Ridge** undersea feature E Pacific Ocean
165 V15 **Naze** var. Nase. Kagoshima, Amami-ōshima, SW Japan
138 G9 **Nazerat** var. Natsrat, Ar. En Nazira, Eng. Nazareth. Northern, N Israel
137 R14 **Nazik Gölü** ◎ E Turkey
136 C15 **Nazilli** Aydın, SW Turkey
137 P14 **Nazimiye** Tunceli, E Turkey
Nazinon see Red Volta
10 L15 **Nazko** British Columbia, SW Canada
129 O16 **Nazran'** Ingushskaya Respublika, SW Russian Federation
80 J13 **Nazrēt** var. Adama, Hadama. Oromo, C Ethiopia
Nazwāh see Nizwá
82 J13 **Nchanga** Copperbelt, C Zambia
82 J11 **Nchelenge** Luapula, N Zambia
Ncheu see Ntcheu
Ndaghamcha, Sebkra de see Te-n-Dghâmcha, Sebkhet
81 G21 **Ndala** Tabora, C Tanzania
82 B11 **N'Dalatando** Port. Salazar, Vila Salazar. Cuanza Norte, NW Angola
77 S14 **Ndali** C Benin
81 E18 **Ndeke** SW Uganda
78 J13 **Ndélé** Bamingui-Bangoran, N Central African Republic
79 E19 **Ndendé** Ngounié, S Gabon
79 E20 **Ndindi** Nyanga, S Gabon
78 G11 **Ndjamena** var. N'Djamena; prev. Fort-Lamy. ● (Chad) Chari-Baguirmi, W Chad
78 G11 **Ndjamena** × Chari-Baguirmi, W Chad
79 D18 **Ndjolé** Moyen-Ogooué, W Gabon
82 J13 **Ndola** Copperbelt, C Zambia
Ndrhamcha, Sebkha de see Te-n-Dghâmcha, Sebkhet
79 L15 **Ndu** Orientale, N Dem. Rep. Congo (Zaire)
81 H21 **Nduguti** Singida, C Tanzania
186 M9 **Nduindui** Guadalcanal, C Solomon Islands
Nduke see Kolombangara
115 F16 **Néa Anchíalos** var. Nea Anhialos, Néa Ankhíalos. Thessalía, C Greece
Nea Anhialos/Néa Ankhíalos see Néa Anchíalos
115 H18 **Néa Artáki** Évvoia, C Greece
97 F15 **Neagh, Lough** ◎ E Northern Ireland, UK
32 F7 **Neah Bay** Washington, NW USA
115 J22 **Nea Kaméni** island Kykládes, Greece, Aegean Sea
181 O8 **Neale, Lake** ◎ Northern Territory, C Australia
182 G2 **Neales River** seasonal river South Australia
115 G14 **Néa Moudanía** var. Néa Moudhaniá. Kentrikí Makedonía, N Greece
Néa Moudhaniá see Néa Moudanía
116 K10 **Neamţ** ◈ county NE Romania
Neapel see Napoli
115 D14 **Neápoli** prev. Neápolis. Dytikí Makedonía, N Greece
115 K25 **Neápoli** Kríti, Greece, E Mediterranean Sea
115 G22 **Neápoli** Pelopónnisos, S Greece
Neapolis see Napoli, Italy
Neapolis see Nablus, West Bank
Neápolis see Neápoli, Greece
38 D16 **Near Islands** island group Aleutian Islands, Alaska, USA
97 J21 **Neath** S Wales, UK
114 H13 **Néa Zíchni** var. Néa Zíkhni; prev. Néa Zíkhna. Kentrikí Makedonía, NE Greece
Néa Zíkhna/Néa Zíkhni see Néa Zíchni
42 C5 **Nebaj** Quiché, W Guatemala
77 P13 **Nebbou** S Burkina
146 B11 **Nebitdag** Balkanskiy Velayat, W Turkmenistan
54 M13 **Neblina, Pico da** ▲ NW Brazil
126 I13 **Nebolchi** Novgorodskaya Oblast', W Russian Federation
36 L4 **Nebo, Mount** ▲ Utah, W USA
28 L14 **Nebraska** off. State of Nebraska; also known as Blackwater State, Cornhusker State, Tree Planters State. ◈ state C USA
29 S16 **Nebraska City** Nebraska, C USA
107 K23 **Nebrodi, Monti** var. Monti Caronie. ▲▲ Sicilia, Italy, C Mediterranean Sea
10 L14 **Nechako** ≈ British Columbia, SW Canada
29 Q2 **Neche** North Dakota, N USA
25 V8 **Neches** Texas, SW USA
25 W8 **Neches River** ≈ Texas, SW USA
101 H20 **Neckar** ≈ SW Germany
101 H20 **Neckarsulm** Baden-Württemberg, SW Germany
192 L5 **Necker Island** island C British Virgin Islands
175 U3 **Necker Ridge** undersea feature N Pacific Ocean
61 D23 **Necochea** Buenos Aires, E Argentina
104 H2 **Neda** Galicia, NW Spain
115 E20 **Nédas** ≈ S Greece
25 Y11 **Nederland** Texas, SW USA
Nederland see Netherlands
98 K12 **Neder Rijn** Eng. Lower Rhine. ≈ C Netherlands
99 L16 **Nederweert** Limburg, SE Netherlands
95 G16 **Nedre Tokke** ◎ S Norway
Nedrigaylov see Nedryhayliv
117 S3 **Nedryhayliv** Rus. Nedrigaylov. Sums'ka Oblast', NE Ukraine
98 O11 **Neede** Gelderland, E Netherlands
33 T13 **Needle Mountain** ▲ Wyoming, C USA
35 Y14 **Needles** California, W USA
97 M24 **Needles, The** rocks Isle of Wight, S England, UK
62 O7 **Ñeembucú** off. Departamento de Ñeembucú. ◈ department SW Paraguay
30 M7 **Neenah** Wisconsin, N USA
11 W16 **Neepawa** Manitoba, S Canada
99 K16 **Neerpelt** Limburg, NE Belgium
74 M6 **Nefta** × W Tunisia
128 L15 **Neftegorsk** Krasnodarskiy Kray, SW Russian Federation
129 U3 **Neftekamsk** Respublika Bashkortostan, W Russian Federation
129 O14 **Neftekumsk** Stavropol'skiy Kray, SW Russian Federation
Neftezavodsk see Seydi
82 C10 **Negage** var. N'Gage. Uíge, NW Angola
Negapatam/Negapattinam see Nāgappattinam
169 T17 **Negara** Bali, Indonesia
169 T13 **Negara** Borneo, C Indonesia
Negara Brunei Darussalam see Brunei
31 N4 **Negaunee** Michigan, N USA
81 J15 **Negēlē** var. Negelli, It. Neghelli. Oromo, C Ethiopia
Negelli see Negēlē
Negeri Pahang Darul Makmur see Pahang
Negeri Selangor Darul Ehsan see Selangor
168 K9 **Negeri Sembilan** var. Negri Sembilan. ◈ state Peninsular Malaysia
92 P3 **Negerpynten** headland S Svalbard
Negev see HaNegev
Neghelli see Negēlē
116 I12 **Negoiu** var. Negoiul. ▲ S Romania
Negoiul see Negoiu
82 P13 **Negomane** var. Negomano. Cabo Delgado, N Mozambique
Negomano see Negomane
155 J25 **Negombo** Western Province, SW Sri Lanka
Negoreloye see Nyeharelaye
112 P12 **Negotin** Serbia, E Yugoslavia
113 P19 **Negotino** C FYR Macedonia
56 A10 **Negra, Punta** headland NW Peru
104 G3 **Negreira** Galicia, NW Spain
116 L10 **Negreşti** Vaslui, E Romania
Negreşti see Negreşti-Oaş
116 H8 **Negreşti-Oaş** Hung. Avasfelsőfalu; prev. Negreşti. Satu Mare, NE Romania
44 H12 **Negril** W Jamaica
Negri Sembilan see Negeri Sembilan
63 K15 **Negro, Río** ≈ E Argentina
62 N7 **Negro, Río** ≈ NE Argentina
57 N17 **Negro, Río** ≈ E Bolivia
62 O5 **Negro, Río** ≈ C Paraguay
48 F6 **Negro, Río** ≈ N South America
61 E18 **Negro, Río** ≈ Brazil/Uruguay
Negro, Río see Sico Tinto, Río, Honduras
Negro, Río see Chixoy, Río, Guatemala/Mexico
171 P6 **Negros** island C Philippines
116 M15 **Negru Vodă** Constanţa, SE Romania
13 P13 **Neguac** New Brunswick, SE Canada
14 B7 **Negwazu, Lake** ◎ Ontario, S Canada
Négyfalu see Săcele
32 F10 **Nehalem** Oregon, NW USA
32 F10 **Nehalem River** ≈ Oregon, NW USA
Nehavend see Nahāvand
143 V9 **Nehbandān** Khorāsān, E Iran
163 V6 **Nehe** Heilongjiang, NE China
193 Y14 **Neiafu** 'Uta Vava'u, N Tonga
45 N9 **Neiba** var. Neyba. SW Dominican Republic
Néid, Carn Uí see Mizen Head
92 M9 **Neiden** Finnmark, N Norway
Neidín see Kenmare
Néifinn see Nephin
103 S10 **Neige, Crêt de la** ▲ E France
173 O16 **Neiges, Piton des** ▲ C Réunion
15 R9 **Neiges, Rivière des** ≈ Quebec, SE Canada
160 I10 **Neijiang** Sichuan, C China
30 K6 **Neillsville** Wisconsin, N USA
Nei Monggol Zizhiqu/Nei Mongol see Nei Mongol Zizhiqu
163 Q10 **Nei Mongol Gaoyuan** plateau NE China
163 O12 **Nei Mongol Zizhiqu** var. Nei Mongol, Eng. Inner Mongolia, Inner Mongolian Autonomous Region; prev. Nei Monggol Zizhiqu. ◈ autonomous region N China
161 O4 **Neiqiu** Hebei, E China
Neiriz see Neyrīz
101 Q16 **Neisse** Cz. Lužická Nisa, Ger. Lausitzer Neisse, Pol. Nisa, Nysa Łużycka. ≈ C Europe
Neisse see Nysa
54 E11 **Neiva** Huila, S Colombia
160 M7 **Neixiang** Henan, C China
Nejafabad see Najafābād
11 V9 **Nejanilini Lake** ◎ Manitoba, C Canada
Nejd see Najd
80 I13 **Nek'emtē** var. Lakemti, Nakamti. Oromo, C Ethiopia
128 M9 **Nekhayevskiy** Volgogradskaya Oblast', SW Russian Federation
30 K7 **Nekoosa** Wisconsin, N USA
95 M24 **Neksø** Bornholm, E Denmark
115 C16 **Nekyomanteío** ancient monument Ípeiros, W Greece
104 H7 **Nelas** Viseu, N Portugal
126 H16 **Nelidovo** Tverskaya Oblast', W Russian Federation
29 P13 **Neligh** Nebraska, C USA
123 R11 **Nel'kan** Khabarovskiy Kray, E Russian Federation
92 M10 **Nellim** var. Nellimö, Lapp. Njellim. Lappi, N Finland
Nellimö see Nellim
155 J18 **Nellore** Andhra Pradesh, E India
123 T14 **Nel'ma** Khabarovskiy Kray, SE Russian Federation
61 B17 **Nelson** Santa Fe, C Argentina
11 O17 **Nelson** British Columbia, SW Canada
185 I14 **Nelson** Nelson, South Island, NZ
97 L17 **Nelson** NW England, UK
29 P17 **Nelson** Nebraska, C USA
185 J14 **Nelson** ◈ unitary authority South Island, NZ
11 X12 **Nelson** ≈ Manitoba, C Canada
183 U8 **Nelson Bay** New South Wales, SE Australia
182 K13 **Nelson, Cape** headland Victoria, SE Australia
63 G23 **Nelson, Estrecho** strait SE Pacific Ocean
11 W12 **Nelson House** Manitoba, C Canada
30 J4 **Nelson Lake** ◎ Wisconsin, N USA
31 T14 **Nelsonville** Ohio, N USA
27 S2 **Nelsoon River** ≈ Iowa/Missouri, C USA
83 K21 **Nelspruit** Mpumalanga, NE South Africa
76 L10 **Néma** Hodh ech Chargui, SE Mauritania
118 D13 **Neman** Ger. Ragnit. Kaliningradskaya Oblast', W Russian Federation
84 I9 **Neman** Bel. Nyoman, Ger. Memel, Lith. Nemunas, Pol. Niemen, Rus. Neman. ≈ NE Europe
Nemausus see Nîmes
115 F19 **Neméa** Pelopónnisos, S Greece
Německý Brod see Havlíčkův Brod
14 D7 **Nemegosenda** ≈ Ontario, S Canada
14 D8 **Nemegosenda Lake** ◎ Ontario, S Canada
119 H14 **Nemenčinė** Vilnius, SE Lithuania
Nemetocenna see Arras
Nemirov see Nemyriv
103 O6 **Nemours** Seine-et-Marne, N France
Nemunas see Neman
165 W4 **Nemuro** Hokkaidō, NE Japan
165 W4 **Nemuro-hantō** peninsula Hokkaidō, NE Japan
165 W3 **Nemuro-kaikyō** strait Japan/Russian Federation
165 W4 **Nemuro-wan** bay N Japan
116 H5 **Nemyriv** Rus. Nemirov. L'vivs'ka Oblast', NW Ukraine
117 N7 **Nemyriv** Rus. Nemirov. Vinnyts'ka Oblast', C Ukraine
97 D19 **Nenagh** Ir. An tAonach. C Ireland
39 R9 **Nenana** Alaska, USA
39 R9 **Nenana River** ≈ Alaska, USA
187 P10 **Nendö** var. Swallow Island. island Santa Cruz Islands, E Solomon Islands
97 O19 **Nene** ≈ E England, UK
127 R4 **Nenetskiy Avtonomnyy Okrug** ◈ autonomous district NW Russian Federation
191 W11 **Nengonengo** atoll Îles Tuamotu, C French Polynesia
163 U6 **Nen Jiang** var. Nonni. ≈ NE China
163 V6 **Nenjiang** Heilongjiang, NE China
189 P16 **Neoch** atoll Caroline Islands, C Micronesia
115 D18 **Neochóri** Dytikí Ellás, C Greece
27 Q7 **Neodesha** Kansas, C USA
29 S14 **Neola** Iowa, C USA
115 M19 **Néon Karlovási** var. Néon Karlovásion. Sámos, Dodekánisos, Greece, Aegean Sea
Néon Karlovásion see Néon Karlovási
115 E16 **Néon Monastíri** Thessalía, C Greece
27 R8 **Neosho** Missouri, C USA
27 Q7 **Neosho River** ≈ Kansas/Oklahoma, C USA
123 N12 **Nepa** ≈ C Russian Federation
153 N10 **Nepal** off. Kingdom of Nepal. ◆ monarchy S Asia
152 M11 **Nepalganj** Mid Western, SW Nepal
14 L13 **Nepean** Ontario, SE Canada
36 L4 **Nephi** Utah, W USA
97 B16 **Nephin** Ir. Néifinn. ▲ W Ireland
67 T9 **Nepoko** ≈ NE Dem. Rep. Congo (Zaire)
18 K15 **Neptune** New Jersey, NE USA
182 G10 **Neptune Islands** island group South Australia
107 I14 **Nera** anc. Nar. ≈ C Italy
102 L14 **Nérac** Lot-et-Garonne, SW France
111 D16 **Neratovice** Ger. Neratowitz. Středočeský Kraj, C Czech Republic
Neratowitz see Neratovice
123 O13 **Nercha** ≈ S Russian Federation
123 O13 **Nerchinsk** Chitinskaya Oblast', S Russian Federation
123 P14 **Nerchinskiy Zavod** Chitinskaya Oblast', S Russian Federation
126 M15 **Nerekhta** Kostromskaya Oblast', NW Russian Federation
118 H10 **Nereta** Aizkraukle, S Latvia
106 K13 **Nereto** Abruzzo, C Italy
113 H15 **Neretva** ≈ Bosnia and Herzegovina/Croatia
115 C17 **Nerikós** ruins Lefkáda, Iónioi Nísoi, Greece, C Mediterranean Sea
118 B12 **Neringa** Ger. Nidden; prev. Nida. Neringa, SW Lithuania
83 F15 **Neriquinha** Cuando Cubango, SE Angola
118 I13 **Neris** Bel. Viliya, Pol. Wilia; prev. Pol. Wilja. ≈ Belarus/Lithuania
Neris see Viliya
105 N15 **Nerja** Andalucía, S Spain
126 L16 **Nerl'** ≈ W Russian Federation
105 P12 **Nerpio** Castilla-La Mancha, C Spain
104 J13 **Nerva** Andalucía, S Spain
98 L4 **Nes** Friesland, N Netherlands
94 G13 **Nesbyen** Buskerud, S Norway
92 L2 **Neskaupstadhur** Austurland, E Iceland
92 F13 **Nesna** Nordland, C Norway
26 K5 **Ness City** Kansas, C USA
Nesselsdorf see Kopřivnice
108 H7 **Nesslau** Sankt Gallen, NE Switzerland
96 I9 **Ness, Loch** ◎ N Scotland, UK
Nesterov see Zhovkva
114 I12 **Néstos** Bul. Mesta, Turk. Kara Su. ≈ Bulgaria/Greece see also Mesta
95 C14 **Nesttun** Hordaland, S Norway
Nesvizh see Nyasvizh
138 F9 **Netanya** var. Natanya, Nathanya. Central, C Israel
98 I9 **Netherlands** off. Kingdom of the Netherlands, var. Holland, Dut. Koninkrijk der Nederlanden, Nederland. ◆ monarchy NW Europe
45 S9 **Netherlands Antilles** prev. Dutch West Indies. ◇ Dutch autonomous region S Caribbean Sea
Netherlands East Indies see Indonesia
Netherlands Guiana see Surinam
Netherlands New Guinea see Irian Jaya
116 L4 **Netishyn** Khmel'nyts'ka Oblast', W Ukraine
138 E11 **Netivot** Southern, S Israel
107 O21 **Neto** ≈ S Italy
9 Q6 **Nettilling Lake** ◎ Baffin Island, Nunavut, N Canada
29 V3 **Nett Lake** ◎ Minnesota, N USA
107 I16 **Nettuno** Lazio, C Italy
Netum see Noto
41 U16 **Netzahualcóyotl, Presa** ▣ SE Mexico
Netze see Noteć
Neu Amerika see Puławy
Neubetsche see Novi Bečej
Neubidschow see Nový Bydžov
Neubistritz see Nová Bystřice
100 N9 **Neubrandenburg** Mecklenburg-Vorpommern, NE Germany
101 K22 **Neuburg an der Donau** Bayern, S Germany
108 C8 **Neuchâtel** Ger. Neuenburg. Neuchâtel, W Switzerland
108 C8 **Neuchâtel** Ger. Neuenburg. ◈ canton W Switzerland
108 C8 **Neuchâtel, Lac de** Ger. Neuenburger See. ◎ W Switzerland
Neudorf see Spišská Nová Ves
100 L10 **Neue Elde** canal N Germany
Neuenburg see Neuchâtel
Neuenburg an der Elbe see Nymburk
Neuenburger See see Neuchâtel, Lac de
108 F7 **Neuenhof** Aargau, N Switzerland
100 H11 **Neuenland** × (Bremen) Bremen, NW Germany
Neuenstadt see La Neuveville
101 C18 **Neuerburg** Rheinland-Pfalz, W Germany
99 K24 **Neufchâteau** Luxembourg, SE Belgium
103 S6 **Neufchâteau** Vosges, NE France
102 M3 **Neufchâtel-en-Bray** Seine-Maritime, N France
109 S3 **Neufelden** Oberösterreich, N Austria
Neugradisk see Nova Gradiška
Neuhaus see Jindřichův Hradec
Neuhäusel see Nové Zámky
108 G6 **Neuhausen** var. Neuhausen am Rheinfall. Schaffhausen, N Switzerland
Neuhausen am Rheinfall see Neuhausen
101 I17 **Neuhof** Hessen, C Germany
Neuhof see Zgierz
Neukuhren see Pionerskiy
Neu-Langenburg see Tukuyu
109 W4 **Neulengbach** Niederösterreich, NE Austria
113 G15 **Neum** Federacija Bosna I Hercegovina, S Bosnia and Herzegovina
Neumark see Nowy Targ, Nowy Sącz, Poland
Neumark see Nowe Miasto Lubawskie, Toruń, Poland
Neumarkt see Neumarkt im Hausruckkreis, Oberösterreich, Austria
Neumarkt see Neumarkt am Wallersee, Salzburg, Austria
Neumarkt see Środa Śląska, Wrocław, Poland
Neumarkt see Târgu Secuiesc, Covasna, Romania
Neumarkt see Târgu Mureş, Mureş, Romania
109 Q5 **Neumarkt am Wallersee** var. Neumarkt. Salzburg, NW Austria
109 R4 **Neumarkt im Hausruckkreis** var. Neumarkt. Oberösterreich, N Austria
101 L20 **Neumarkt in der Oberpfalz** Bayern, SE Germany
Neumarktl see Tržič
Neumoldowa see Moldova Nouă
100 J8 **Neumünster** Schleswig-Holstein, N Germany
109 X5 **Neunkirchen** var. Neunkirchen am Steinfeld. Niederösterreich, E Austria
101 E20 **Neunkirchen** Saarland, SW Germany
Neunkirchen am Steinfeld see Neunkirchen
Neuoderberg see Bohumín
63 I15 **Neuquén** Neuquén, SE Argentina
63 H14 **Neuquén** off. Provincia de Neuquén. ◈ province W Argentina
63 H14 **Neuquén, Río** ≈ W Argentina
Neurode see Nowa Ruda
100 N11 **Neuruppin** Brandenburg, NE Germany
Neusalz an der Oder see Nowa Sól
Neu Sandec/Neusandez see Małopolskie
101 K22 **Neusäss** Bayern, S Germany
Neusatz see Novi Sad
Neuschliss see Gherla
21 N8 **Neuse River** ≈ North Carolina, SE USA
109 Z5 **Neusiedl am See** Burgenland, E Austria
111 G22 **Neusiedler See** Hung. Fertő. ◎ Austria/Hungary
Neusohl see Banská Bystrica
101 D15 **Neuss** anc. Novaesium, Novesium. Nordrhein-Westfalen, W Germany
Neuss see Nyon
Neustadt see Neustadt an der Aisch, Bayern, Germany
Neustadt see Neustadt bei Coburg, Bayern, Germany
Neustadt see Prudnik, Opole, Poland
Neustadt see Baia Mare, Maramureş, Romania
100 I12 **Neustadt am Rübenberge** Niedersachsen, N Germany
101 J19 **Neustadt an der Aisch** var. Neustadt. Bayern, C Germany
Neustadt an der Haardt see Neustadt an der Weinstrasse
101 F20 **Neustadt an der Weinstrasse** prev. Neustadt an der Haardt, hist. Niewenstat, anc. Nova Civitas. Rheinland-Pfalz, SW Germany
101 K18 **Neustadt bei Coburg** var. Neustadt. Bayern, C Germany
Neustadt bei Pinne see Lwówek
Neustadt in Oberschlesien see Prudnik
Neustadtl see Novo mesto
Neustadtl in Mähren see Nové Město na Moravě
Neustettin see Szczecinek
108 M8 **Neustift im Stubaital** var. Stubaital. Tirol, W Austria
100 N10 **Neustrelitz** Mecklenburg-Vorpommern, NE Germany
Neutitschein see Nový Jičín
Neutra see Nitra
101 J22 **Neu-Ulm** Bayern, S Germany
Neuveville see La Neuveville
103 N12 **Neuvic** Corrèze, C France
Neuwarp see Nowe Warpno
100 G9 **Neuwerk** island NW Germany
101 E17 **Neuwied** Rheinland-Pfalz, W Germany
Neuzen see Terneuzen
126 H12 **Neva** ≈ NW Russian Federation
29 V14 **Nevada** Iowa, C USA
27 R6 **Nevada** Missouri, C USA
35 R5 **Nevada** off. State of Nevada; also known as Battle Born State, Sagebrush State, Silver State. ◈ state W USA
35 P6 **Nevada City** California, W USA
126 G16 **Nevel'** Pskovskaya Oblast', W Russian Federation
123 T14 **Nevel'sk** Ostrov Sakhalin, Sakhalinskaya Oblast', SE Russian Federation

◆ Country ● Country Capital ◇ Dependent Territory ○ Dependent Territory Capital ◈ Administrative Region × International Airport ▲ Mountain ▲▲ Mountain Range ⨯ Volcano ≈ River ◎ Lake ▣ Reservoir

123 Q13 **Never** Amurskaya Oblast', SE Russian Federation
129 Q6 **Neverkino** Penzenskaya Oblast', W Russian Federation
103 P9 **Nevers** *anc.* Noviodunum. Nièvre, C France
18 J12 **Neversink River** ≈ New York, NE USA
183 Q6 **Nevertire** New South Wales, SE Australia
113 H15 **Nevesinje** Republika Srpska, S Bosnia and Herzegovina
118 G12 **Nevėžis** ≈ C Lithuania
128 M14 **Nevinnomyssk** Stavropol'skiy Kray, SW Russian Federation
45 W10 **Nevis** *island* Saint Kitts and Nevis
Nevoso, Monte *see* Veliki Snežnik
Nevrokop *see* Gotse Delchev
136 J14 **Nevşehir** *var.* Nevshehr. Nevşehir, C Turkey
136 J14 **Nevşehir** *var.* Nevshehr. ⬖ *province* C Turkey
Nevshehr *see* Nevşehir
122 G10 **Nev'yansk** Sverdlovskaya Oblast', C Russian Federation
81 J25 **Newala** Mtwara, SE Tanzania
31 P16 **New Albany** Indiana, N USA
22 M2 **New Albany** Mississippi, S USA
29 Y11 **New Albin** Iowa, C USA
55 U8 **New Amsterdam** E Guyana
183 Q4 **New Angledool** New South Wales, SE Australia
21 Y2 **Newark** Delaware, NE USA
18 K14 **Newark** New Jersey, NE USA
18 G10 **Newark** New York, NE USA
31 T13 **Newark** Ohio, N USA
Newark *see* Newark-on-Trent
35 W5 **Newark Lake** ◎ Nevada, W USA
97 N18 **Newark-on-Trent** *var.* Newark. C England, UK
22 M7 **New Augusta** Mississippi, S USA
19 P12 **New Bedford** Massachusetts, NE USA
32 G11 **Newberg** Oregon, NW USA
21 X10 **New Bern** North Carolina, SE USA
20 F8 **Newbern** Tennessee, S USA
31 P4 **Newberry** Michigan, N USA
21 Q12 **Newberry** South Carolina, SE USA
18 F15 **New Bloomfield** Pennsylvania, NE USA
25 X5 **New Boston** Texas, SW USA
25 S11 **New Braunfels** Texas, SW USA
31 Q13 **New Bremen** Ohio, N USA
97 F18 **Newbridge** *Ir.* An Droichead Nua. C Ireland
18 B14 **New Brighton** Pennsylvania, NE USA
18 M12 **New Britain** Connecticut, NE USA
186 G7 **New Britain** *island* E PNG
192 I8 **New Britain Trench** *undersea feature* W Pacific Ocean
18 J15 **New Brunswick** New Jersey, NE USA
15 V8 **New Brunswick** *Fr.* Nouveau-Brunswick. ⬖ *province* SE Canada
18 K13 **Newburgh** New York, NE USA
97 M22 **Newbury** S England, UK
19 P10 **Newburyport** Massachusetts, NE USA
77 T14 **New Bussa** Niger, W Nigeria
187 O17 **New Caledonia** *var.* Kanaky, *Fr.* Nouvelle-Calédonie. ◇ *French overseas territory* SW Pacific Ocean
187 O15 **New Caledonia** *island* SW Pacific Ocean
175 O10 **New Caledonia Basin** *undersea feature* W Pacific Ocean
183 T8 **Newcastle** New South Wales, SE Australia
13 O14 **Newcastle** New Brunswick, SE Canada
14 I15 **Newcastle** Ontario, SE Canada
97 C20 **Newcastle** *Ir.* An Caisleán Nua. SW Ireland
83 K22 **Newcastle** KwaZulu/Natal, E South Africa
97 G16 **Newcastle** *Ir.* An Caisleán Nua. SE Northern Ireland, UK
31 P13 **New Castle** Indiana, N USA
20 L5 **New Castle** Kentucky, S USA
27 N11 **Newcastle** Oklahoma, C USA
18 B13 **New Castle** Pennsylvania, NE USA
26 R6 **Newcastle** Texas, SW USA
36 J7 **Newcastle** Utah, W USA
21 S6 **New Castle** Virginia, NE USA
33 Z13 **Newcastle** Wyoming, C USA
45 W10 **Newcastle** ✕ Nevis, Saint Kitts and Nevis
97 L14 **Newcastle** ✕ NE England, UK
Newcastle *see* Newcastle upon Tyne
97 L18 **Newcastle-under-Lyme** C England, UK
97 M14 **Newcastle upon Tyne** *var.* Newcastle; *hist.* Monkchester, *Lat.* Pons Aelii. NE England, UK
181 Q4 **Newcastle Waters** Northern Territory, N Australia
Newchwang *see* Yingkou
18 K13 **New City** New York, NE USA
31 U13 **Newcomerstown** Ohio, N USA
18 G15 **New Cumberland** Pennsylvania, NE USA
21 R1 **New Cumberland** West Virginia, NE USA
152 I10 **New Delhi** ● (India) Delhi, N India
11 O17 **New Denver** British Columbia, SW Canada
28 J9 **Newell** South Dakota, N USA
21 Q13 **New Ellenton** South Carolina, SE USA
22 J6 **Newellton** Louisiana, S USA
28 K6 **New England** North Dakota, N USA
19 P8 **New England** *cultural region* NE USA
New England of the West *see* Minnesota
183 U5 **New England Range** ▲ New South Wales, SE Australia
64 G9 **New England Seamounts** *var.* Bermuda-New England Seamount Arc. *undersea feature* W Atlantic Ocean
38 M14 **Newenham, Cape** *headland* Alaska, USA
138 F11 **Newé Zohar** Southern, E Israel
18 D9 **Newfane** New York, NE USA
97 M23 **New Forest** *physical region* S England, UK
9 W10 **Newfoundland** *Fr.* Terre-Neuve. *island* Newfoundland, SE Canada
13 R9 **Newfoundland** *Fr.* Terre Neuve. ⬖ *province* E Canada
65 J8 **Newfoundland Basin** *undersea feature* NW Atlantic Ocean
64 I8 **Newfoundland Ridge** *undersea feature* NW Atlantic Ocean
64 J8 **Newfoundland Seamounts** *undersea feature* N Sargasso Sea
18 G16 **New Freedom** Pennsylvania, NE USA
186 K9 **New Georgia** *island* New Georgia Islands, NW Solomon Islands
186 K8 **New Georgia Islands** *island group* NW Solomon Islands
186 L8 **New Georgia Sound** *var.* The Slot. *sound* E Solomon Sea
30 L9 **New Glarus** Wisconsin, N USA
13 Q15 **New Glasgow** Nova Scotia, SE Canada
New Goa *see* Panaji
186 A6 **New Guinea** *Dut.* Nieuw Guinea, *Ind.* Irian. *island* Indonesia/PNG
192 H8 **New Guinea Trench** *undersea feature* SW Pacific Ocean
32 I6 **Newhalem** Washington, NW USA
39 P13 **Newhalen** Alaska, USA
29 X13 **Newhall** Iowa, C USA
14 F16 **New Hamburg** Ontario, S Canada
19 N9 **New Hampshire** *off.* State of New Hampshire; also known as The Granite State. ⬖ *state* NE USA
29 W12 **New Hampton** Iowa, C USA
186 G5 **New Hanover** *island* NE PNG
18 M13 **New Haven** Connecticut, NE USA
31 Q12 **New Haven** Indiana, N USA
27 W5 **New Haven** Missouri, C USA
97 P23 **Newhaven** SE England, UK
10 K13 **New Hazelton** British Columbia, SW Canada
New Hebrides *see* Vanuatu
175 P9 **New Hebrides Trench** *undersea feature* N Coral Sea
18 H15 **New Holland** Pennsylvania, NE USA
22 I9 **New Iberia** Louisiana, S USA
186 G5 **New Ireland** ⬖ *province* NE PNG
186 G5 **New Ireland** *island* NE PNG
65 A24 **New Island** *island* W Falkland Islands
18 J15 **New Jersey** *off.* State of New Jersey; also known as The Garden State. ⬖ *state* NE USA
18 C14 **New Kensington** Pennsylvania, NE USA
21 W6 **New Kent** Virginia, NE USA
27 O8 **Newkirk** Oklahoma, C USA
21 Q9 **Newland** North Carolina, SE USA
28 L6 **New Leipzig** North Dakota, N USA
14 H9 **New Liskeard** Ontario, S Canada
22 G7 **Newllano** Louisiana, S USA
19 N13 **New London** Connecticut, NE USA
29 Y15 **New London** Iowa, C USA
29 T8 **New London** Minnesota, N USA
27 V3 **New London** Missouri, C USA
30 M7 **New London** Wisconsin, N USA
27 Y8 **New Madrid** Missouri, C USA
180 J8 **Newman** Western Australia
194 M13 **Newman Island** *island* Antarctica
14 H15 **Newmarket** Ontario, S Canada
97 P20 **Newmarket** E England, UK
19 P10 **Newmarket** New Hampshire, NE USA
21 U4 **New Market** Virginia, NE USA
21 R2 **New Martinsville** West Virginia, NE USA
31 U14 **New Matamoras** Ohio, N USA
32 M12 **New Meadows** Idaho, NW USA
26 R12 **New Mexico** *off.* State of New Mexico; also known as Land of Enchantment, Sunshine State. ⬖ *state* SW USA
149 V6 **New Mīrpur** *var.* Mīrpur. Sind, SE Pakistan
151 T17 **New Moore Island** *island* E India
23 S4 **Newnan** Georgia, SE USA
183 P17 **New Norfolk** Tasmania, SE Australia
22 K9 **New Orleans** Louisiana, S USA
22 K9 **New Orleans** ✕ Louisiana, S USA
18 K12 **New Paltz** New York, NE USA
31 U12 **New Philadelphia** Ohio, N USA
184 K10 **New Plymouth** Taranaki, North Island, NZ
97 M24 **Newport** S England, UK
97 K22 **Newport** SE Wales, UK
27 W10 **Newport** Arkansas, C USA
31 N13 **Newport** Indiana, N USA
22 M3 **Newport** Kentucky, S USA
31 W9 **Newport** Minnesota, N USA
34 F12 **Newport** Oregon, NW USA
21 O13 **Newport** Rhode Island, NE USA
23 O9 **Newport** Tennessee, S USA
21 N6 **Newport** Vermont, NE USA
34 M7 **Newport** Washington, NW USA
23 X7 **Newport News** Virginia, NE USA
99 N20 **Newport Pagnell** SE England, UK
25 U12 **New Port Richey** Florida, SE USA
31 V9 **New Prague** Minnesota, N USA
46 H3 **New Providence** *island* N Bahamas
99 H24 **Newquay** SW England, UK
99 I20 **New Quay** SW Wales, UK
31 V10 **New Richland** Minnesota, N USA
13 X7 **New-Richmond** Quebec, SE Canada
31 R15 **New Richmond** Ohio, N USA
32 I5 **New Richmond** Wisconsin, N USA
44 G1 **New River** ≈ N Belize
57 T12 **New River** ≈ SE Guyana
23 R6 **New River** ≈ West Virginia, NE USA
44 G1 **New River Lagoon** ◎ N Belize
24 J8 **New Roads** Louisiana, S USA
20 L14 **New Rochelle** New York, NE USA
31 O4 **New Rockford** North Dakota, N USA
97 P23 **New Romney** SE England, UK
97 F20 **New Ross** *Ir.* Ros Mhic Thriúin. SE Ireland
97 F16 **Newry** *Ir.* An tIúr. SE Northern Ireland, UK
28 M5 **New Salem** North Dakota, N USA
New Sarum *see* Salisbury
29 W14 **New Sharon** Iowa, C USA
New Siberian Islands *see* Novosibirskiye Ostrova
23 X11 **New Smyrna Beach** Florida, SE USA
183 O7 **New South Wales** ⬖ *state* SE Australia
39 O13 **New Stuyahok** Alaska, USA
21 N8 **New Tazewell** Tennessee, S USA
38 M12 **Newtok** Alaska, USA
23 S7 **Newton** Georgia, SE USA
29 W14 **Newton** Iowa, C USA
27 N6 **Newton** Kansas, C USA
19 O11 **Newton** Massachusetts, NE USA
22 M5 **Newton** Mississippi, S USA
18 J14 **Newton** New Jersey, NE USA
21 R9 **Newton** North Carolina, SE USA
25 Y9 **Newton** Texas, SW USA
97 J24 **Newton Abbot** SW England, UK
96 K13 **Newton St Boswells** SE Scotland, UK
97 I14 **Newton Stewart** S Scotland, UK
92 O2 **Newtontoppen** ▲ C Svalbard
28 K3 **New Town** North Dakota, N USA
97 J20 **Newtown** E Wales, UK
97 G15 **Newtownabbey** *Ir.* Baile na Mainistreach. E Northern Ireland, UK
97 G15 **Newtownards** *Ir.* Baile Nua na hArda. SE Northern Ireland, UK
29 U10 **New Ulm** Minnesota, N USA
28 K10 **New Underwood** South Dakota, N USA
25 V10 **New Waverly** Texas, SW USA
18 K14 **New York** New York, NE USA
18 G10 **New York** ⬖ *state* NE USA
35 X13 **New York Mountains** ▲ California, W USA
184 K12 **New Zealand** *abbrev.* NZ. ◆ *commonwealth republic* SW Pacific Ocean
127 O15 **Neya** Kostromskaya Oblast', NW Russian Federation
Neyba *see* Neiba
143 Q12 **Neyrīz** *var.* Neiriz, Niriz. Fārs, S Iran
143 T4 **Neyshābūr** *var.* Nishapur. Khorāsān, NE Iran
155 J21 **Neyveli** Tamil Nādu, SE India
Nezhin *see* Nizhyn
33 N10 **Nezperce** Idaho, NW USA
22 H8 **Nezpique, Bayou** ≈ Louisiana, S USA
77 Y13 **Ngadda** ≈ NE Nigeria
N'Gage *see* Negage
185 G16 **Ngahere** West Coast, South Island, NZ
77 Z12 **Ngala** Borno, NE Nigeria
83 G17 **Ngamiland** ⬖ *district* N Botswana
158 K16 **Ngamring** Xizang Zizhiqu, W China
81 K19 **Ngangerabeli Plain** *plain* SE Kenya
158 I14 **Ngangla Ringco** ◎ W China
158 G13 **Nganglong Kangri** ▲ W China
158 K15 **Ngangzê Co** ◎ W China
79 F14 **Ngaoundéré** *var.* N'Gaoundéré. Adamaoua, N Cameroon
81 E20 **Ngara** Kagera, NW Tanzania
188 F8 **Ngardmau Bay** *bay* Babeldaob, N Palau
188 F7 **Ngaregur** *island* Palau Islands, N Palau
184 L7 **Ngaruawahia** Waikato, North Island, NZ
184 N11 **Ngaruroro** ≈ North Island, NZ
190 I16 **Ngatangiia** Rarotonga, S Cook Islands
184 M6 **Ngatea** Waikato, North Island, NZ
166 L8 **Ngathainggyaung** Irrawaddy, SW Myanmar
Ngatik *see* Ngetik Atoll
Ngau *see* Gau
188 C7 **Ngcheangel** *var.* Kayangel Islands. *island* Palau Islands, N Palau
188 E10 **Ngchemiangel** Babeldaob, N Palau
188 C8 **Ngeaur** *var.* Angaur. *island* Palau Islands, S Palau
188 E10 **Ngerkeai** Babeldaob, N Palau
188 F9 **Ngermechau** Babeldaob, N Palau
188 C8 **Ngeruktabel** *prev.* Urukthapel. *island* Palau Islands, S Palau
188 F8 **Ngetbong** Babeldaob, N Palau
189 T17 **Ngetik Atoll** *var.* Ngatik; *prev.* Los Jardines. *atoll* Caroline Islands, E Micronesia
188 E10 **Ngetkip** Babeldaob, N Palau
Nggamea *see* Qamea
83 C16 **N'Giva** *var.* Ondjiva, *Port.* Vila Pereira de Eça. Cunene, S Angola
79 G20 **Ngo** Plateaux, SE Congo
167 S7 **Ngoc Lac** Thanh Hoa, N Vietnam
79 G17 **Ngoko** ≈ Cameroon/Congo
81 H19 **Ngorengore** Rift Valley, SW Kenya
159 Q11 **Ngoring Hu** ◎ C China
Ngorolaka *see* Banifing
81 H20 **Ngorongoro Crater** *crater* N Tanzania
79 D19 **Ngounié** *off.* Province de la Ngounié, *var.* La Ngounié. ⬖ *province* S Gabon
79 D19 **Ngounié** ≈ Congo/Gabon
78 H10 **Ngoura** *var.* NGoura. Chari-Baguirmi, W Chad
78 G10 **Ngouri** *var.* NGouri; *prev.* Fort-Millot. Lac, W Chad
77 Y10 **Ngourti** Diffa, E Niger
77 Y11 **Nguigmi** *var.* N'Guigmi. Diffa, SE Niger
Nguimbo *see* Lumbala N'Guimbo
188 F15 **Ngulu Atoll** *atoll* Caroline Islands, W Micronesia
187 R14 **Nguna** *island* C Vanuatu
N'Gunza *see* Sumbe
169 U17 **Ngurah Rai** ✕ (Bali) Bali, S Indonesia
77 W12 **Nguru** Yobe, NE Nigeria
Ngwaketse *see* Southern
83 I16 **Ngweze** ≈ S Zambia
83 M17 **Nhamatanda** Sofala, C Mozambique
58 G12 **Nhamundá, Rio** *var.* Jamundá, Yamundá. ≈ N Brazil
60 J7 **Nhandeara** São Paulo, S Brazil
N'Harea *see* Nharêa
82 D12 **Nharêa** *var.* N'Harea, Nhareia. Bié, W Angola
Nhareia *see* Nharêa
167 V12 **Nha Trang** Khanh Hoa, S Vietnam
182 L11 **Nhill** Victoria, SE Australia
83 L22 **Nhlangano** *prev.* Goedgegun. SW Swaziland
181 S1 **Nhulunbuy** Northern Territory, N Australia
77 N10 **Niafounké** Tombouctou, W Mali
31 N5 **Niagara** Wisconsin, N USA
14 H16 **Niagara** ≈ Ontario, S Canada
14 G15 **Niagara Escarpment** *hill range* Ontario, S Canada
14 H16 **Niagara Falls** Ontario, S Canada
18 D9 **Niagara Falls** New York, NE USA
17 S7 **Niagara Falls** *waterfall* Canada/USA
76 K12 **Niagassola** *var.* Nyagassola. Haute-Guinée, NE Guinea
77 R12 **Niamey** ● (Niger) Niamey, SW Niger
77 R12 **Niamey** ✕ Niamey, SW Niger
77 R14 **Niamtougou** N Togo
79 O16 **Niangara** Orientale, NE Dem. Rep. Congo (Zaire)
77 O10 **Niangay, Lac** ◎ E Mali
77 N14 **Niangoloko** SW Burkina
27 U6 **Niangua River** ≈ Missouri, C USA
79 O17 **Nia-Nia** Orientale, NE Dem. Rep. Congo (Zaire)
19 N13 **Niantic** Connecticut, NE USA
163 U7 **Nianzishan** Heilongjiang, NE China
168 H10 **Nias, Pulau** *island* W Indonesia
82 O13 **Niassa** *off.* Província do Niassa. ⬖ *province* N Mozambique
191 U10 **Niau** *island* Îles Tuamotu, C French Polynesia
95 G20 **Nibe** Nordjylland, N Denmark
189 Q8 **Nibok** N Nauru
118 C10 **Nīca** Liepāja, W Latvia
Nicaea *see* Nice
42 J9 **Nicaragua** *off.* Republic of Nicaragua. ◆ *republic* Central America
42 K11 **Nicaragua, Lago de** *var.* Cocibolca, Gran Lago, *Eng.* Lake Nicaragua. ◎ S Nicaragua
Nicaragua, Lake *see* Nicaragua, Lago de
64 D11 **Nicaraguan Rise** *undersea feature* NW Caribbean Sea
Nicaria *see* Ikaría
107 N21 **Nicastro** Calabria, SW Italy
103 V15 **Nice** *It.* Nizza; *anc.* Nicaea. Alpes-Maritimes, SE France
Nice *see* Côte d'Azur
Nicephorium *see* Ar Raqqah
12 M9 **Nichicun, Lac** ◎ Quebec, E Canada
164 D16 **Nichinan** *var.* Nitinan. Miyazaki, Kyūshū, SW Japan
44 E4 **Nicholas Channel** *channel* N Cuba
Nicholas II Land *see* Severnaya Zemlya
149 U2 **Nicholas Range** *Pash.* Selseleh-ye Kūh-e Vākhān, *Taj.* Qatorkŭhi Vakhon. ▲ Afghanistan/Tajikistan
20 M6 **Nicholasville** Kentucky, S USA
44 G2 **Nicholls Town** Andros Island, NW Bahamas
21 U12 **Nichols** South Carolina, SE USA
55 U9 **Nickerie** ⬖ *district* NW Surinam
55 V9 **Nickerie Rivier** ≈ NW Surinam
151 P22 **Nicobar Islands** *island group* India, E Indian Ocean
116 L9 **Nicolae Bălcescu** Botoşani, NE Romania
15 P11 **Nicolet** Quebec, SE Canada
15 Q12 **Nicolet** ≈ Quebec, SE Canada
31 Q4 **Nicolet, Lake** ◎ Michigan, N USA
29 U10 **Nicollet** Minnesota, N USA
61 F19 **Nico Pérez** Florida, S Uruguay
Nicopolis *see* Nikopol, Bulgaria
Nicopolis *see* Nikópoli, Greece
121 P2 **Nicosia** *Gk.* Lefkosía, *Turk.* Lefkoşa. ● (Cyprus) C Cyprus
107 K24 **Nicosia** Sicilia, Italy, C Mediterranean Sea
107 N22 **Nicotera** Calabria, SW Italy
42 K13 **Nicoya** Guanacaste, W Costa Rica
42 L14 **Nicoya, Golfo de** *gulf* W Costa Rica
42 L14 **Nicoya, Península de** *peninsula* NW Costa Rica
Nictheroy *see* Niterói
111 L15 **Nida** ≈ S Poland
Nida *see* Neringa
Nidaros *see* Trondheim
108 D8 **Nidau** Bern, W Switzerland
101 H17 **Nidda** ≈ W Germany
Nidden *see* Neringa
95 F17 **Nidelva** ≈ S Norway
110 L9 **Nidzica** *Ger.* Niedenburg. Warmińsko-Mazurskie, NE Poland,
100 H6 **Niebüll** Schleswig-Holstein, N Germany
Niedenburg *see* Nidzica
99 N25 **Niederanven** Luxembourg, C Luxembourg
103 V4 **Niederbronn-les-Bains** Bas-Rhin, NE France
Niederdonau *see* Niederösterreich
109 S7 **Niedere Tauern** ▲ C Austria
101 P14 **Niederlausitz** *Eng.* Lower Lusatia. *physical region* E Germany
109 U5 **Niederösterreich** *off.* Land Niederösterreich, *Eng.* Lower Austria, *Ger.* Niederdonau; *prev.* Lower Danube. ⬖ *state* NE Austria
100 G12 **Niedersachsen** *Eng.* Lower Saxony, *Fr.* Basse-Saxe. ⬖ *state* NW Germany
79 D17 **Niefang** *var.* Sevilla de Niefang. NW Equatorial Guinea
83 G23 **Niekerkshoop** Northern Cape, W South Africa
99 G17 **Niel** Antwerpen, N Belgium
Niélé *see* Niellé
76 M14 **Niellé** *var.* Niélé. N Ivory Coast
79 O22 **Niemba** Katanga, E Dem. Rep. Congo (Zaire)
111 G15 **Niemcza** *Ger.* Nimptsch. Dolnośląskie, SW Poland
Niemen *see* Neman
92 J13 **Niemisel** Norrbotten, N Sweden
111 H15 **Niemodlin** *Ger.* Falkenberg. Opolskie, S Poland
76 M13 **Niéna** Sikasso, SW Mali
100 H12 **Nienburg** Niedersachsen, N Germany
100 N13 **Nieplitz** ≈ NE Germany
111 L16 **Niepołomice** Małopolskie, S Poland
101 D14 **Niers** ≈ Germany/Netherlands
101 Q15 **Niesky** *Lus.* Niska. Sachsen, E Germany
Nieśwież *see* Nyasvizh
Nieuport *see* Nieuwpoort
98 O8 **Nieuw-Amsterdam** Drenthe, NE Netherlands
55 W9 **Nieuw Amsterdam** Commewijne, NE Surinam
99 M14 **Nieuw-Bergen** Limburg, SE Netherlands
98 O7 **Nieuw-Buinen** Drenthe, NE Netherlands
98 J12 **Nieuwegein** Utrecht, C Netherlands
98 P6 **Nieuwe Pekela** Groningen, NE Netherlands
98 P5 **Nieuweschans** Groningen, NE Netherlands
Nieuw Guinea *see* New Guinea
98 I11 **Nieuwkoop** Zuid-Holland, C Netherlands
98 M9 **Nieuwleusen** Overijssel, S Netherlands
98 J11 **Nieuw-Loosdrecht** Utrecht, C Netherlands
55 U9 **Nieuw Nickerie** Nickerie, NW Surinam
98 P5 **Nieuwolda** Groningen, NE Netherlands
99 B17 **Nieuwpoort** *var.* Nieuport. West-Vlaanderen, W Belgium
99 G14 **Nieuw-Vossemeer** Noord-Brabant, S Netherlands
98 P7 **Nieuw-Weerdinge** Drenthe, NE Netherlands
40 L10 **Nieves** Zacatecas, C Mexico
64 O11 **Nieves, Pico de las** ▲ Gran Canaria, Islas Canarias, Spain, NE Atlantic Ocean
103 P8 **Nièvre** ⬖ *department* C France
Niewenstat *see* Neustadt an der Weinstrasse
136 J15 **Niğde** Niğde, C Turkey
136 J15 **Niğde** ⬖ *province* C Turkey
83 J21 **Nigel** Gauteng, NE South Africa
77 V10 **Niger** *off.* Republic of Niger. ◆ *republic* W Africa
77 T14 **Niger** ⬖ *state* C Nigeria
67 P8 **Niger** ≈ W Africa
Niger Cone *see* Niger Fan
67 P9 **Niger Delta** *delta* S Nigeria
67 P9 **Niger Fan** *var.* Niger Cone. *undersea feature* E Atlantic Ocean
77 T13 **Nigeria** *off.* Federal Republic of Nigeria. ◆ *federal republic* W Africa
77 T17 **Niger, Mouths of the** *delta* S Nigeria
185 C24 **Nightcaps** Southland, South Island, NZ
14 F7 **Night Hawk Lake** ◎ Ontario, S Canada
65 M19 **Nightingale Island** *island* S Tristan da Cunha, S Atlantic Ocean
38 M12 **Nightmute** Alaska, USA
114 G13 **Nigrita** Kentrikí Makedonía, NE Greece
148 J15 **Nihing** *Per.* Rūd-e Nahang. ≈ Iran/Pakistan
191 V10 **Nihiru** *atoll* Îles Tuamotu, C French Polynesia
Nihommatsu *see* Nihonmatsu
Nihon *see* Japan
165 P11 **Nihonmatsu** *var.* Nihommatsu, Nihonmatu. Fukushima, Honshū, C Japan
Nihonmatu *see* Nihonmatsu
62 I12 **Nihuil, Embalse del** ◎ W Argentina
165 O10 **Niigata** Niigata, Honshū, C Japan
165 O11 **Niigata** *off.* Niigata-ken. ⬖ *prefecture* Honshū, C Japan
165 G14 **Niihama** Ehime, Shikoku, SW Japan
38 A8 **Niihau** *island* Hawaii, USA, C Pacific Ocean
165 X12 **Nii-jima** *island* E Japan
165 H12 **Niimi** Okayama, Honshū, SW Japan
165 O10 **Niitsu** *var.* Niitu. Niigata, Honshū, C Japan
Niitu *see* Niitsu
105 P15 **Nijar** Andalucía, S Spain
98 K11 **Nijkerk** Gelderland, C Netherlands
99 H16 **Nijlen** Antwerpen, N Belgium
98 L13 **Nijmegen** *Ger.* Nimwegen; *anc.* Noviomagus. Gelderland, SE Netherlands
98 N10 **Nijverdal** Overijssel, E Netherlands
190 G16 **Nikao** Rarotonga, S Cook Islands
Nikaria *see* Ikaría
126 I2 **Nikel'** Murmanskaya Oblast', NW Russian Federation
171 Q17 **Nikiniki** Timor, S Indonesia
131 Q15 **Nikitin Seamount** *undersea feature* E Indian Ocean
77 S14 **Nikki** E Benin
Niklasmarkt *see* Gheorgheni
39 P10 **Nikolai** Alaska, USA
Nikolaiken *see* Mikołajki
Nikolainkaupunki *see* Länsi-Suomi
Nikolayev *see* Mykolayiv
145 U15 **Nikolayevka** Almaty, SE Kazakhstan
145 O6 **Nikolayevka** Severnyy Kazakhstan, N Kazakhstan
129 P9 **Nikolayevsk** Volgogradskaya Oblast', SW Russian Federation
Nikolayevskaya Oblast' *see* Mykolayivs'ka Oblast'
123 S12 **Nikolayevsk-na-Amure** Khabarovskiy Kray, SE Russian Federation
129 P6 **Nikol'sk** Penzenskaya Oblast', W Russian Federation
127 O13 **Nikol'sk** Vologodskaya Oblast', NW Russian Federation
Nikol'sk *see* Ussuriysk
38 K17 **Nikolski** Umnak Island, Alaska, USA
Nikol'skiy *see* Satpayev
129 V7 **Nikol'skoye** Orenburgskaya Oblast', W Russian Federation
Nikol'sk-Ussuriyskiy *see* Ussuriysk
114 J7 **Nikopol** *anc.* Nicopolis. Pleven, N Bulgaria
117 S9 **Nikopol'** Dnipropetrovs'ka Oblast', SE Ukraine
115 C17 **Nikópoli** *anc.* Nicopolis. *site of ancient city* Ípeiros, W Greece
136 M12 **Niksar** Tokat, N Turkey
143 V14 **Nīkshahr** Sīstān va Balūchestān, SE Iran
113 J16 **Nikšić** Montenegro, SW Yugoslavia
191 R4 **Nikumaroro** *prev.* Gardner Island, Kemins Island. *atoll* Phoenix Islands, C Kiribati
191 P3 **Nikunau** *var.* Nukunau; *prev.* Byron Island. *atoll* Tungaru, W Kiribati
155 G21 **Nīlambūr** Kerala, SW India
35 X16 **Niland** California, W USA
67 T3 **Nile** *Ar.* Nahr an Nīl. ≈ N Africa
80 G8 **Nile** *former province* NW Uganda
75 W7 **Nile Delta** *delta* N Egypt
67 T3 **Nile Fan** *undersea feature* E Mediterranean Sea
31 O11 **Niles** Michigan, N USA
31 V11 **Niles** Ohio, N USA
155 F20 **Nīleswaram** Kerala, SW India
14 K10 **Nilgaut, Lac** ◎ Quebec, SE Canada
158 I5 **Nilka** Xinjiang Uygur Zizhiqu, NW China
Nīl, Nahr an *see* Nile
93 N16 **Nilsiä** Itä-Suomi, C Finland
154 F9 **Nīmach** Madhya Pradesh, C India
152 G14 **Nīmbāhera** Rājasthān, N India
76 L15 **Nimba, Monts** *var.* Nimba Mountains. ▲ W Africa
Nimba Mountains *see* Nimba, Monts
Nimburg *see* Nymburk
103 Q15 **Nîmes** *anc.* Nemausus, Nismes. Gard, S France
152 H11 **Nīm ka Thāna** Rājasthān, N India
183 R11 **Nimmitabel** New South Wales, SE Australia
Nimptsch *see* Niemcza
195 R11 **Nimrod Glacier** *glacier* Antarctica
Nimroze *see* Nīmrūz
148 K8 **Nīmrūz** *var.* Nimroze; *prev.* Chakhānsūr. ⬖ *province* SW Afghanistan
81 F16 **Nimule** Eastern Equatoria, S Sudan
Nimwegen *see* Nijmegen
155 C23 **Nine Degree Channel** *channel* India/Maldives
18 G9 **Ninemile Point** *headland* New York, NE USA
173 S8 **Ninetyeast Ridge** *undersea feature* E Indian Ocean

◆ Country ● Country Capital ◇ Dependent Territory ○ Dependent Territory Capital ⬖ Administrative Region ✕ International Airport ▲ Mountain ▲ Mountain Range Volcano ≈ River ◎ Lake Reservoir

183 P13 **Ninety Mile Beach** *beach* Victoria, SE Australia
184 I2 **Ninety Mile Beach** *beach* North Island, NZ
21 P12 **Ninety Six** South Carolina, SE USA
163 Y9 **Ning'an** Heilongjiang, NE China
161 S9 **Ningbo** *var.* Ning-po, Yin-hsien; *prev.* Ninghsien. Zhejiang, SE China
161 U12 **Ningde** Fujian, SE China
161 P12 **Ningdu** Jiangxi, S China
186 A7 **Ningerum** Western, SW PNG
161 R9 **Ningguo** Anhui, E China
161 S9 **Ninghai** Zhejiang, SE China
Ning-hsia *see* Ningxia
Ninghsien *see* Ningbo
160 J15 **Ningming** Guangxi Zhuangzu Zizhiqu, S China
160 H11 **Ningnan** Sichuan, C China
Ning-po *see* Ningbo
Ningsia/Ningsia Hui/Ningsia Hui Autonomous Region *see* Ningxia
160 J5 **Ningxia** *off.* Ningxia Huizu Zizhiqu, *var.* Ning-hsia, Ningsia, *Eng.* Ningsia Hui, Ningsia Hui Autonomous Region. ◆ *autonomous region* N China
159 X10 **Ningxian** Gansu, N China
167 T7 **Ninh Binh** Ninh Binh, N Vietnam
167 V12 **Ninh Hoa** Khanh Hoa, S Vietnam
186 C4 **Ninigo Group** *island group* N PNG
39 Q12 **Ninilchik** Alaska, USA
27 N7 **Ninnescah River** ≈ Kansas, C USA
195 U16 **Ninnis Glacier** *glacier* Antarctica
165 R8 **Ninohe** Iwate, Honshū, C Japan
99 F18 **Ninove** Oost-Vlaanderen, C Belgium
171 O4 **Ninoy Aquino** ✕ (Manila) Luzon, N Philippines
Nio *see* Íos
29 P12 **Niobrara** Nebraska, C USA
28 M12 **Niobrara River** ≈ Nebraska/Wyoming, C USA
79 I20 **Nioki** Bandundu, W Dem. Rep. Congo (Zaire)
76 M11 **Niono** Ségou, C Mali
76 K11 **Nioro** *var.* Nioro du Sahel. Kayes, W Mali
76 G11 **Nioro du Rip** SW Senegal
Nioro du Sahel *see* Nioro
102 K10 **Niort** Deux-Sèvres, W France
172 H14 **Nioumachoua** Mohéli, S Comoros
186 C7 **Nipa** Southern Highlands, W PNG
11 U14 **Nipawin** Saskatchewan, S Canada
12 D12 **Nipigon** Ontario, S Canada
12 D11 **Nipigon, Lake** ⊚ Ontario, S Canada
11 S13 **Nipin** ≈ Saskatchewan, C Canada
14 G11 **Nipissing, Lake** ⊚ Ontario, S Canada
35 P13 **Nipomo** California, W USA
Nippon *see* Japan
138 K6 **Niqniqiyah, Jabal an** ▲ C Syria
62 I9 **Niquivil** San Juan, W Argentina
171 Y13 **Nirabotong** Irian Jaya, E Indonesia
Niriz *see* Neyrīz
155 I14 **Nirmal** Andhra Pradesh, C India
153 Q13 **Nirmāli** Bihār, NE India
113 O14 **Niš** *Eng.* Nish, *Ger.* Nisch; *anc.* Naissus. Serbia, SE Yugoslavia
104 H9 **Nisa** Portalegre, C Portugal
Nisa *see* Neisse
141 P4 **Niṣāb** Al Ḥudūd ash Shamālīyah, N Saudi Arabia
141 Q15 **Niṣāb** *var.* Anṣāb. SW Yemen
113 P14 **Nišava** *Bul.* Nishava. ≈ Bulgaria/Yugoslavia *see also* Nishava
107 K25 **Niscemi** Sicilia, Italy, C Mediterranean Sea
Nisch/Nish *see* Niš
165 R4 **Niseko** Hokkaidō, NE Japan
Nishapur *see* Neyshābūr
114 G9 **Nishava** *var.* Nišava. ≈ Bulgaria/Yugoslavia *see also* Nišava
118 L11 **Nishcha** *Rus.* Nishcha. ≈ N Belarus
165 C17 **Nishinoomote** Kagoshima, Tanega-shima, SW Japan
165 X15 **Nishino-shima** *Eng.* Rosario. *island* Ogasawara-shotō, SE Japan
165 I13 **Nishiwaki** *var.* Nisiwaki. Hyōgo, Honshū, SW Japan
141 U14 **Nishtūn** SE Yemen
Nisiros *see* Nísyros
Nisiwaki *see* Nishiwaki
Niska *see* Niesky
113 O14 **Niška Banja** Serbia, SE Yugoslavia
12 D6 **Niskibi** ≈ Ontario, C Canada
111 O15 **Nisko** Podkarpackie, SE Poland
10 H7 **Nisling** ≈ Yukon Territory, W Canada
99 H22 **Nismes** Namur, S Belgium
Nismes *see* Nîmes
116 M10 **Nisporeni** *Rus.* Nisporeny. W Moldova
Nisporeny *see* Nisporeni
95 K20 **Nissan** ≈ S Sweden
Nissan Islands *see* Green Islands
95 F16 **Nisser** ⊚ S Norway
95 E21 **Nissum Bredning** *inlet* NW Denmark
29 U6 **Nisswa** Minnesota, N USA
Nistru *see* Dniester
115 M22 **Nísyros** *var.* Nisiros. *island* Dodekánisos, Greece, Aegean Sea
118 H8 **Nītaure** Cēsis, C Latvia
60 P10 **Niterói** *prev.* Nictheroy. Rio de Janeiro, SE Brazil
14 F16 **Nith** ≈ Ontario, S Canada
96 J13 **Nith** ≈ S Scotland, UK
Nitinan *see* Nichinan
111 I21 **Nitra** *Ger.* Neutra, *Hung.* Nyitra. Nitriansky Kraj, SW Slovakia
111 I20 **Nitra** *Ger.* Neutra, *Hung.* Nyitra. ≈ W Slovakia
111 I21 **Nitriansky Kraj** ◈ *region* SW Slovakia
21 Q5 **Nitro** West Virginia, NE USA
95 H14 **Nittedal** Akershus, S Norway
Niuatobutabu *see* Niuatoputapu
193 X13 **Niuatoputapu** *var.* Niuatobutabu; *prev.* Keppel Island. *island* N Tonga
193 U15 **Niu'Aunofa** *headland* Tongatapu, S Tonga
Niuchwang *see* Yingkou
190 B16 **Niue** ◇ *self-governing territory in free association with NZ* S Pacific Ocean
190 F10 **Niulakita** *var.* Nurakita. *atoll* S Tuvalu
190 E6 **Niutao** *atoll* NW Tuvalu
93 L15 **Nivala** Oulu, C Finland
102 I15 **Nive** ≈ SW France
99 G19 **Nivelles** Wallon Brabant, C Belgium
103 P8 **Nivernais** *cultural region* C France
15 N8 **Niverville, Lac** ⊚ Quebec, SE Canada
27 T7 **Nixa** Missouri, C USA
35 R5 **Nixon** Nevada, W USA
25 S12 **Nixon** Texas, SW USA
146 K12 **Niyazov** Lebapskiy Velayat, NE Turkmenistan
155 H14 **Nizāmābād** Andhra Pradesh, C India
155 H15 **Nizām Sāgar** ⊚ C India
127 N16 **Nizhegorodskaya Oblast'** ◈ *province* W Russian Federation
Nizhnegorskiy *see* Nyzhn'ohirs'kyy
129 S4 **Nizhnekamsk** Respublika Tatarstan, W Russian Federation
129 U3 **Nizhnekamskoye Vodokhranilishche** ⊡ W Russian Federation
123 S14 **Nizhne Leninskoye** Yevreyskaya Avtonomnaya Oblast', SE Russian Federation
122 L13 **Nizhneudinsk** Irkutskaya Oblast', S Russian Federation
122 I10 **Nizhnevartovsk** Khanty-Mansiyskiy Avtonomnyy Okrug, C Russian Federation
123 Q7 **Nizhneyansk** Respublika Sakha (Yakutiya), NE Russian Federation
129 Q11 **Nizhniy Baskunchak** Astrakhanskaya Oblast', SW Russian Federation
129 O6 **Nizhniy Lomov** Penzenskaya Oblast', W Russian Federation
129 P3 **Nizhniy Novgorod** *prev.* Gor'kiy. Nizhegorodskaya Oblast', W Russian Federation
127 T8 **Nizhniy Odes** Respublika Komi, NW Russian Federation
Nizhniy Pyandzh *see* Panji Poyon
122 G10 **Nizhniy Tagil** Sverdlovskaya Oblast', C Russian Federation
127 T9 **Nizhnyaya-Omra** Respublika Komi, NW Russian Federation
127 P5 **Nizhnyaya Pesha** Nenetskiy Avtonomnyy Okrug, NW Russian Federation
117 Q3 **Nizhyn** *Rus.* Nezhin. Chernihivs'ka Oblast', NE Ukraine
136 M17 **Nizip** Gaziantep, S Turkey
141 X8 **Nizwá** *var.* Nazwāh. NE Oman
Nizza *see* Nice
106 C9 **Nizza Monferrato** Piemonte, NE Italy
Njávdám *see* Näätämöjoki
Njellim *see* Nellim
81 H24 **Njombe** Iringa, S Tanzania
81 G23 **Njombe** ≈ C Tanzania
92 I10 **Njunis** ▲ N Norway
93 H17 **Njurunda** Västernorrland, C Sweden
94 N11 **Njutånger** Gävleborg, C Sweden
79 D14 **Nkambe** Nord-Ouest, NW Cameroon
Nkata Bay *see* Nkhata Bay
79 F21 **Nkayi** *prev.* Jacob. La Bouenza, S Congo
83 J17 **Nkayi** Matabeleland North, W Zimbabwe
82 N13 **Nkhata Bay** *var.* Nkata Bay. Northern, N Malawi
81 E22 **Nkonde** Kigoma, N Tanzania
79 D15 **Nkongsamba** *var.* N'Kongsamba. Littoral, W Cameroon
83 E16 **Nkurenkuru** Okavango, N Namibia
77 Q15 **Nkwanta** E Ghana
167 O2 **Nmai Hka** *var.* Me Hka. ≈ N Myanmar
Noardwâlde *see* Noordwolde
39 N7 **Noatak** Alaska, USA
39 N7 **Noatak River** ≈ Alaska, USA
Nobeji *see* Noheji
164 E15 **Nobeoka** Miyazaki, Kyūshū, SW Japan
27 N11 **Noble** Oklahoma, C USA
31 P13 **Noblesville** Indiana, N USA
165 R5 **Noboribetsu** *var.* Noboribetu. Hokkaidō, NE Japan
Noboribetu *see* Noboribetsu
59 H18 **Nobres** Mato Grosso, W Brazil
107 N21 **Nocera Terinese** Calabria, S Italy
41 Q16 **Nochixtlán** *var.* Asunción Nochixtlán. Oaxaca, SE Mexico
25 S5 **Nocona** Texas, SW USA
63 K21 **Nodales, Bahía de los** *bay* S Argentina
27 Q2 **Nodaway River** ≈ Iowa/Missouri, C USA
27 R8 **Noel** Missouri, C USA
95 C17 **Nærbø** Rogaland, S Norway
95 I24 **Næstved** Storstrøm, SE Denmark
40 H3 **Nogales** Chihuahua, NW Mexico
40 F3 **Nogales** Sonora, NW Mexico
36 M17 **Nogales** Arizona, SW USA
Nogal Valley *see* Dooxo Nugaaleed
102 K15 **Nogaro** Gers, S France
110 J7 **Nogat** ≈ N Poland
164 D12 **Nōgata** Fukuoka, Kyūshū, SW Japan
129 P15 **Nogayskaya Step'** *steppe* SW Russian Federation
102 M6 **Nogent-le-Rotrou** Eure-et-Loir, C France
103 O4 **Nogent-sur-Oise** Oise, N France
103 P6 **Nogent-sur-Seine** Aube, N France
122 L10 **Noginsk** Evenkiyskiy Avtonomnyy Okrug, N Russian Federation
128 L3 **Noginsk** Moskovskaya Oblast', W Russian Federation
123 T12 **Nogliki** Ostrov Sakhalin, Sakhalinskaya Oblast', SE Russian Federation
164 K12 **Nōgōhaku-san** ▲ Honshū, SW Japan
162 D5 **Nogoonnuur** Bayan-Ölgiy, NW Mongolia
61 C18 **Nogoyá** Entre Ríos, E Argentina
111 K21 **Nógrád** *off.* Nógrád Megye. ◈ *county* N Hungary
105 U5 **Noguera Pallaresa** ≈ NE Spain
105 U4 **Noguera Ribagorçana** ≈ NE Spain
101 E19 **Nohfelden** Saarland, SW Germany
38 A8 **Nohili Point** *headland* Kauai, Hawaii, USA, C Pacific Ocean
104 G3 **Noia** Galicia, NW Spain
103 N16 **Noire, Montagne** ▲ S France
15 P12 **Noire, Rivière** ≈ Quebec, SE Canada
14 J10 **Noire, Rivière** ≈ Quebec, SE Canada
Noire, Rivière *see* Black River
102 G6 **Noires, Montagnes** ▲ NW France
102 H8 **Noirmoutier-en-l'Île** Vendée, NW France
102 H8 **Noirmoutier, Île de** *island* NW France
187 Q10 **Noka** Nendö, E Solomon Islands
83 G17 **Nokaneng** Ngamiland, NW Botswana
93 L18 **Nokia** Länsi-Suomi, W Finland
148 K11 **Nok Kundi** Baluchistān, SW Pakistan
30 L14 **Nokomis** Illinois, N USA
30 K5 **Nokomis, Lake** ⊡ Wisconsin, N USA
78 G9 **Nokou** Kanem, W Chad
187 Q12 **Nokuku** Espiritu Santo, W Vanuatu
95 J18 **Nol** Västra Götaland, S Sweden
79 H16 **Nola** Sangha-Mbaéré, SW Central African Republic
25 P7 **Nolan** Texas, SW USA
127 R15 **Nolinsk** Kirovskaya Oblast', NW Russian Federation
95 B19 **Nólsoy** *Dan.* Nolsø *Island* Faeroe Islands
186 B7 **Nomad** Western, SW Papau New Guinea
164 B16 **Noma-zaki** *headland* Kyūshū, SW Japan
40 K10 **Nombre de Dios** Durango, C Mexico
42 I5 **Nombre de Dios, Cordillera** ▲ N Honduras
38 M9 **Nome** Alaska, USA
29 Q6 **Nome** North Dakota, N USA
38 M9 **Nome, Cape** *headland* Alaska, USA
Nōmi-jima *see* Nishi-Nōmi-jima
14 M11 **Nominingue, Lac** ⊚ Quebec, SE Canada
Nomoi Islands *see* Mortlock Islands
164 B16 **Nomo-zaki** *headland* Kyūshū, SW Japan
193 X15 **Nomuka** *island* Nomuka Group, C Tonga
193 X15 **Nomuka Group** *island group* W Tonga
189 Q15 **Nomwin Atoll** *atoll* Hall Islands, C Micronesia
8 L10 **Nonacho Lake** ⊚ Northwest Territories, NW Canada
Nondaburi *see* Nonthaburi
39 P12 **Nondalton** Alaska, USA
163 V10 **Nong'an** Jilin, NE China
167 P10 **Nong Bua Khok** Nakhon Ratchasima, C Thailand
167 Q9 **Nong Bua Lamphu** Udon Thani, E Thailand
167 R7 **Nông Hèt** Xiangkhoang, N Laos
Nongkaya *see* Nong Khai
167 Q8 **Nong Khai** *var.* Mi Chai, Nongkaya. Nong Khai, E Thailand
167 N14 **Nong Met** Surat Thani, SW Thailand
83 L22 **Nongoma** KwaZulu/Natal, E South Africa
167 P9 **Nong Phai** Phetchabun, C Thailand
153 U13 **Nongstoin** Meghālaya, NE India
83 C19 **Nonidas** Erongo, N Namibia
Nonni *see* Nen Jiang
40 I7 **Nonoava** Chihuahua, N Mexico
191 O3 **Nonouti** *prev.* Sydenham Island. *atoll* Tungaru, W Kiribati
167 O11 **Nonthaburi** *var.* Nondaburi, Nontha Buri. Nonthaburi, C Thailand
102 L11 **Nontron** Dordogne, SW France
181 P1 **Noonamah** Northern Territory, N Australia
28 K2 **Noonan** North Dakota, N USA
99 E14 **Noord-Beveland** *var.* North Beveland. *island* SW Netherlands
99 J14 **Noord-Brabant** *Eng.* North Brabant. ◈ *province* S Netherlands
98 H7 **Noorder Haaks** *spit* NW Netherlands
98 H9 **Noord-Holland** *Eng.* North Holland. ◈ *province* NW Netherlands
Noordhollandsch Kanaal *see* Noordhollands Kanaal
98 H8 **Noordhollands Kanaal** *var.* Noordhollandsch Kanaal. *canal* NW Netherlands
Noord-Kaap *see* Northern Cape
98 L8 **Noordoostpolder** *island* N Netherlands
45 P16 **Noordpunt** *headland* Curaçao, C Netherlands Antilles
98 I8 **Noord-Scharwoude** Noord-Holland, NW Netherlands
Noordwes *see* North-West
98 G11 **Noordwijk aan Zee** Zuid-Holland, W Netherlands
98 H11 **Noordwijkerhout** Zuid-Holland, W Netherlands
98 M7 **Noordwolde** *Fris.* Noardwâlde. Friesland, N Netherlands
Noordzee *see* North Sea
98 H10 **Noordzee-Kanaal** *canal* NW Netherlands
93 K18 **Noormarkku** *Swe.* Norrmark. Länsi-Suomi, W Finland
39 N8 **Noorvik** Alaska, USA
10 J17 **Nootka Sound** *inlet* British Columbia, W Canada
82 A9 **Nóqui** Zaire, NW Angola
95 L15 **Nora** Örebro, C Sweden
147 Q13 **Norak** *Rus.* Nurek. W Tajikistan
9 T14 **Noranda** Quebec, SE Canada
29 W12 **Nora Springs** Iowa, C USA
95 M14 **Norberg** Västmanland, C Sweden
14 K13 **Norcan Lake** ⊚ Ontario, SE Canada
197 R12 **Nord** Avannaarsua, N Greenland
78 F13 **Nord** *Eng.* North. ◈ *province* N Cameroon
103 P2 **Nord** ◈ *department* N France
92 P1 **Nordaustlandet** *island* NE Svalbard
95 G24 **Nordborg** *Ger.* Nordburg. Sønderjylland, SW Denmark
Nordburg *see* Nordborg
95 F23 **Nordby** Ribe, W Denmark
11 P15 **Nordegg** Alberta, SW Canada
100 E9 **Norden** Niedersachsen, NW Germany
100 G10 **Nordenham** Niedersachsen, NW Germany
122 M6 **Nordenshel'da, Arkhipelag** *island group* N Russian Federation
92 O3 **Nordenskiold Land** *physical region* W Svalbard
100 E9 **Norderney** *island* NW Germany
100 J9 **Norderstedt** Schleswig-Holstein, N Germany
94 C11 **Nordfjord** *physical region* S Norway
94 D11 **Nordfjord** *fjord* S Norway
94 D11 **Nordfjordeid** Sogn og Fjordane, S Norway
92 G11 **Nordfold** Nordland, C Norway
Nordfriesische Inseln *see* North Frisian Islands
100 H7 **Nordfriesland** *cultural region* N Germany
101 K15 **Nordhausen** Thüringen, C Germany
25 T13 **Nordheim** Texas, SW USA
94 C13 **Nordhordland** *physical region* S Norway
100 E12 **Nordhorn** Niedersachsen, NW Germany
92 I1 **Nordhurfjördhur** Vestfirdhir, NW Iceland
92 J1 **Nordhurland Eystra** ◈ *region* N Iceland
92 I2 **Nordhurland Vestra** ◈ *region* N Iceland
172 H16 **Nord, Île du** *island* Inner Islands, NE Seychelles
95 F20 **Nordjylland** *off.* Nordjyllands Amt. ◈ *county* N Denmark
92 K7 **Nordkapp** *Eng.* North Cape. *headland* N Norway
92 O1 **Nordkapp** *headland* N Svalbard
92 L7 **Nordkinn** *headland* N Norway
79 N19 **Nord Kivu** *off.* Région du Nord Kivu. ◈ *region* E Dem. Rep. Congo (Zaire)
92 G12 **Nordland** ◈ *county* C Norway
101 J21 **Nördlingen** Bayern, S Germany
93 I16 **Nordmaling** Västerbotten, N Sweden
95 K15 **Nordmark** Värmland, C Sweden
Nord, Mer du *see* North Sea
94 F8 **Nordmøre** *physical region* S Norway
100 I8 **Nord-Ostee-Kanal** *canal* N Germany
(0) J3 **Nordostrundingen** *headland* NE Greenland
79 D14 **Nord-Ouest** *Eng.* North-West. ◈ *province* NW Cameroon
Nord-Ouest, Territoires du *see* Northwest Territories
103 N2 **Nord-Pas-de-Calais** ◈ *region* N France
101 F19 **Nordpfälzer Bergland** ⛰ W Germany
Nord, Pointe *see* Fatua, Pointe
187 P16 **Nord, Province** ◈ *province* C New Caledonia
101 D14 **Nordrhein-Westfalen** *Eng.* North Rhine-Westphalia, *Fr.* Rhénanie du Nord-Westphalie. ◈ *state* W Germany
Nordsee/Nordsjøen/Nordsøen *see* North Sea
100 H7 **Nordstrand** *island* N Germany
93 E15 **Nord-Trøndelag** ◈ *county* C Norway
97 E19 **Nore** *Ir.* An Fheoir. ≈ S Ireland
29 Q14 **Norfolk** Nebraska, C USA
21 X7 **Norfolk** Virginia, NE USA
97 P19 **Norfolk** *cultural region* E England, UK
192 K10 **Norfolk Island** ◇ *Australian external territory* SW Pacific Ocean
175 P9 **Norfolk Ridge** *undersea feature* W Pacific Ocean
27 U8 **Norfork Lake** ⊡ Arkansas/Missouri, C USA
98 N6 **Norg** Drenthe, NE Netherlands
Norge *see* Norway
95 D14 **Norheimsund** Hordaland, S Norway
25 S16 **Norias** Texas, SW USA
164 L12 **Norikura-dake** ▲ Honshū, S Japan
122 K8 **Noril'sk** Taymyrskiy (Dolgano-Nenetskiy) Avtonomnyy Okrug, N Russian Federation
14 I13 **Norland** Ontario, SE Canada
21 V8 **Norlina** North Carolina, SE USA
30 L13 **Normal** Illinois, N USA
27 N11 **Norman** Oklahoma, C USA
Norman *see* Tulita
186 G9 **Normanby Island** *island* SE PNG
Normandes, Îles *see* Channel Islands
58 G9 **Normandia** Roraima, N Brazil
102 L5 **Normandie** *Eng.* Normandy. *cultural region* N France
102 J5 **Normandie, Collines de** *hill range* NW France
Normandy *see* Normandie
25 V9 **Normangee** Texas, SW USA
21 Q10 **Norman, Lake** ⊡ North Carolina, SE USA
44 K13 **Norman Manley** ✕ (Kingston) E Jamaica
181 U5 **Norman River** ≈ Queensland, NE Australia
181 U4 **Normanton** Queensland, NE Australia
16 L12 **Norman Wells** Northwest Territories, NW Canada
12 H12 **Normétal** Quebec, S Canada
11 V15 **Norquay** Saskatchewan, S Canada
94 N11 **Norra Dellen** ⊚ C Sweden
93 G15 **Norråker** Jämtland, C Sweden
94 N12 **Norrala** Gävleborg, C Sweden
Norra Ny *see* Stöllet
92 G13 **Norra Storfjället** ▲ N Sweden
92 I13 **Norrbotten** ◈ *county* N Sweden
Nørre Aaby *see* Nørre Åby
95 G23 **Nørre Åby** *var.* Nørre Aaby. Fyn, C Denmark
95 I24 **Nørre Alslev** Storstrøm, SE Denmark
95 E23 **Nørre Nebel** Ribe, W Denmark
95 G20 **Nørresundby** Nordjylland, N Denmark
21 N8 **Norris Lake** ⊡ Tennessee, S USA
18 I15 **Norristown** Pennsylvania, NE USA
95 N17 **Norrköping** Östergötland, S Sweden
Norrmark *see* Noormarkku
94 N13 **Norrsundet** Gävleborg, C Sweden
95 P15 **Norrtälje** Stockholm, C Sweden
180 L12 **Norseman** Western Australia
93 I14 **Norsjö** Västerbotten, N Sweden
95 G16 **Norsjø** ⊚ S Norway
123 R13 **Norsk** Amurskaya Oblast', SE Russian Federation
Norske Havet *see* Norwegian Sea
187 Q13 **Norsup** Malekula, C Vanuatu
191 V15 **Norte, Cabo** *headland* Easter Island, Chile, E Pacific Ocean
54 F7 **Norte de Santander** *off.* Departamento de Norte de Santander. ◈ *province* N Colombia
61 E21 **Norte, Punta** *headland* E Argentina
21 R13 **North** South Carolina, SE USA
North *see* Nord
18 L10 **North Adams** Massachusetts, NE USA
113 L17 **North Albanian Alps** *Alb.* Bjeshkët e Namuna, *SCr.* Prokletije. ⛰ Albania/Yugoslavia
97 M15 **Northallerton** N England, UK
180 J12 **Northam** Western Australia
83 J20 **Northam** Northern, N South Africa
1 **North America** *continent*
1 N12 **North American Basin** *undersea feature* W Sargasso Sea
(0) C5 **North American Plate** *tectonic feature*
18 M11 **North Amherst** Massachusetts, NE USA
97 N20 **Northampton** C England, UK
97 M20 **Northamptonshire** *cultural region* C England, UK
151 P18 **North Andaman** *island* Andaman Islands, India, NE Indian Ocean
65 D25 **North Arm** East Falkland, Falkland Islands
21 Q13 **North Augusta** South Carolina, SE USA
173 W8 **North Australian Basin** *Fr.* Bassin Nord de l' Australie. *undersea feature* E Indian Ocean
31 R11 **North Baltimore** Ohio, N USA
11 T15 **North Battleford** Saskatchewan, S Canada
14 H11 **North Bay** Ontario, S Canada
12 H6 **North Belcher Islands** *island group* Belcher Islands, Nunavut, C Canada
29 R15 **North Bend** Nebraska, C USA
32 E14 **North Bend** Oregon, NW USA
96 K12 **North Berwick** SE Scotland, UK
North Beveland *see* Noord-Beveland
North Borneo *see* Sabah
183 P5 **North Bourke** New South Wales, SE Australia
North Brabant *see* Noord-Brabant
182 F2 **North Branch Neales** *seasonal river* South Australia
44 M6 **North Caicos** *island* NW Turks and Caicos Islands
26 L10 **North Canadian River** ≈ Oklahoma, C USA
31 U12 **North Canton** Ohio, N USA
13 R13 **North, Cape** *headland* Cape Breton Island, Nova Scotia, SE Canada
184 I1 **North Cape** *headland* North Island, NZ
186 G5 **North Cape** *headland* New Ireland, NE PNG
North Cape *see* Nordkapp
18 J17 **North Cape May** New Jersey, NE USA
12 C9 **North Caribou Lake** ⊚ Ontario, C Canada
21 U10 **North Carolina** *off.* State of North Carolina; also known as Old North State, Tar Heel State, Turpentine State. ◈ *state* SE USA
North Celebes *see* Sulawesi Utara
155 J24 **North Central Province** ◈ *province* N Sri Lanka
31 S4 **North Channel** *lake channel* Canada/USA
97 G14 **North Channel** *strait* Northern Ireland/Scotland, UK
21 S14 **North Charleston** South Carolina, SE USA
31 N10 **North Chicago** Illinois, N USA
195 Y10 **Northcliffe Glacier** *glacier* Antarctica
31 Q14 **North College Hill** Ohio, N USA
25 O8 **North Concho River** ≈ Texas, SW USA
19 O8 **North Conway** New Hampshire, NE USA
27 V14 **North Crossett** Arkansas, C USA
28 L4 **North Dakota** *off.* State of North Dakota; also known as Flickertail State, Peace Garden State, Sioux State. ◈ *state* N USA
North Devon Island *see* Devon Island
97 O22 **North Downs** *hill range* SE England, UK
18 C11 **North East** Pennsylvania, NE USA
83 I18 **North East** ◈ *district* NE Botswana
65 G15 **North East Bay** *bay* Ascension Island, C Atlantic Ocean
38 L10 **Northeast Cape** *headland* Saint Lawrence Island, Alaska, USA
81 J17 **North Eastern** ◈ *province* Kenya
North East Frontier Agency/North East Frontier Agency of Assam *see* Arunāchal Pradesh
65 E25 **North East Island** *island* E Falkland Islands
189 V11 **Northeast Island** *island* Chuuk, C Micronesia
44 L12 **North East Point** *headland* E Jamaica
44 L6 **Northeast Point** *headland* Great Inagua, S Bahamas
44 K5 **Northeast Point** *headland* Acklins Island, SE Bahamas
191 Z2 **Northeast Point** *headland* Kiritimati, E Kiribati
44 H2 **Northeast Providence Channel** *channel* N Bahamas
101 J14 **Northeim** Niedersachsen, C Germany
29 X14 **North English** Iowa, C USA
138 G8 **Northern** ◈ *district* N Israel
82 M12 **Northern** ◈ *region* N Malawi
186 F8 **Northern** ◈ *province* S PNG
83 J20 **Northern** *off.* Northern Province; *prev.* Northern Transvaal. ◈ *province* NE South Africa
80 D7 **Northern** ◈ *state* N Sudan
82 K12 **Northern** ◈ *province* NE Zambia
80 B13 **Northern Bahr el Ghazal** ◈ *state* SW Sudan
Northern Border Region *see* Al Ḥudūd ash Shamālīyah
83 F24 **Northern Cape** *off.* Northern Cape Province, *Afr.* Noord-Kaap. ◈ *province* W South Africa
190 K14 **Northern Cook Islands** *island group* N Cook Islands
80 B8 **Northern Darfur** ◈ *state* NW Sudan
Northern Dvina *see* Severnaya Dvina
97 F14 **Northern Ireland** *var.* The Six Counties. *political division* UK
80 D9 **Northern Kordofan** ◈ *state* C Sudan
187 Z14 **Northern Lau Group** *island group* Lau Group, NE Fiji
188 K3 **Northern Mariana Islands** ◇ *US commonwealth territory* W Pacific Ocean
155 J23 **Northern Province** ◈ *province* N Sri Lanka
Northern Rhodesia *see* Zambia
Northern Sporades *see* Vóreioi Sporádes
182 D1 **Northern Territory** ◈ *territory* N Australia
Northern Transvaal *see* Northern
Northern Ural Hills *see* Severnyye Uvaly
84 I9 **North European Plain** *plain* N Europe
27 V2 **North Fabius River** ≈ Missouri, C USA
65 D24 **North Falkland Sound** *sound* N Falkland Islands
29 V9 **Northfield** Minnesota, N USA
19 O9 **Northfield** New Hampshire, NE USA
175 Q8 **North Fiji Basin** *undersea feature* N Coral Sea
97 Q22 **North Foreland** *headland* SE England, UK
35 P6 **North Fork American River** ≈ California, W USA

◆ Country ● Country Capital ◇ Dependent Territory ○ Dependent Territory Capital ◈ Administrative Region ✕ International Airport ▲ Mountain ⛰ Mountain Range ⚲ Volcano ≈ River ⊚ Lake ⊡ Reservoir

39 R7 **North Fork Chandalar River** ≈ Alaska, USA
28 K7 **North Fork Grand River** ≈ North Dakota/South Dakota, N USA
21 O6 **North Fork Kentucky River** ≈ Kentucky, S USA
39 Q7 **North Fork Koyukuk River** ≈ Alaska, USA
39 Q10 **North Fork Kuskokwim River** ≈ Alaska, USA
26 K11 **North Fork Red River** ≈ Oklahoma/Texas, SW USA
26 K3 **North Fork Solomon River** ≈ Kansas, C USA
23 W14 **North Fort Myers** Florida, SE USA
31 P5 **North Fox Island** *island* Michigan, N USA
100 G6 **North Frisian Islands** *var.* Nordfriesische Inseln. *island group* N Germany
197 N9 **North Geomagnetic Pole** *pole* Arctic Ocean
18 M13 **North Haven** Connecticut, NE USA
184 J5 **North Head** *headland* North Island, NZ
18 L6 **North Hero** Vermont, NE USA
35 O7 **North Highlands** California, W USA
North Holland *see* Noord-Holland
81 I16 **North Horr** Eastern, N Kenya
151 K21 **North Huvadhu Atoll** *var.* Gaafu Alifu Atoll. *atoll* S Maldives
65 A24 **North Island** *island* W Falkland Islands
184 N9 **North Island** *island* N NZ
21 U14 **North Island** *island* South Carolina, SE USA
31 O11 **North Judson** Indiana, N USA
North Kazakhstan *see* Severnyy Kazakhstan
31 V10 **North Kingsville** Ohio, N USA
163 Y13 **North Korea** *off.* Democratic People's Republic of Korea, *Kor.* Chosŏn-minjujuŭi-inmin-kanghwaguk. ◆ *republic* E Asia
153 X11 **North Lakhimpur** Assam, NE India
184 J3 **Northland** *off.* Northland Region. ◆ *region* North Island, NZ
192 K11 **Northland Plateau** *undersea feature* S Pacific Ocean
35 X11 **North Las Vegas** Nevada, W USA
31 O11 **North Liberty** Indiana, N USA
29 X14 **North Liberty** Iowa, C USA
27 V12 **North Little Rock** Arkansas, C USA
28 M13 **North Loup River** ≈ Nebraska, C USA
151 K18 **North Maalhosmadulu Atoll** *var.* North Malosmadulu Atoll, Raa Atoll. *atoll* N Maldives
31 U10 **North Madison** Ohio, N USA
31 P12 **North Manchester** Indiana, N USA
31 P6 **North Manitou Island** *island* Michigan, N USA
29 U10 **North Mankato** Minnesota, N USA
23 Z15 **North Miami** Florida, SE USA
151 K18 **North Miladummadulu Atoll** *atoll* N Maldives
North Minch *see* Minch, The
23 W15 **North Naples** Florida, SE USA
175 P8 **North New Hebrides Trench** *undersea feature* N Coral Sea
23 Y15 **North New River Canal** ≈ Florida, SE USA
151 K20 **North Nilandhe Atoll** *var.* Faafu Atoll. *atoll* C Maldives
36 L2 **North Ogden** Utah, W USA
North Ossetia *see* Severnaya Osetiya-Alaniya, Respublika
35 S10 **North Palisade** ▲ California, W USA
189 U11 **North Pass** *passage* Chuuk Islands, C Micronesia
28 M15 **North Platte** Nebraska, C USA
33 X17 **North Platte River** ≈ C USA
65 G14 **North Point** *headland* Ascension Island, C Atlantic Ocean
172 I16 **North Point** *headland* Mahé, NE Seychelles
31 S6 **North Point** *headland* Michigan, N USA
31 R5 **North Point** *headland* Michigan, N USA
39 S9 **North Pole** Alaska, USA
197 R9 **North Pole** *pole* Arctic Ocean
23 O4 **Northport** Alabama, S USA
23 W14 **North Port** Florida, SE USA
32 L6 **Northport** Washington, NW USA
32 L12 **North Powder** Oregon, NW USA
29 U13 **North Raccoon River** ≈ Iowa, C USA
North Rhine-Westphalia *see* Nordrhein-Westfalen
97 M16 **North Riding** *cultural region* N England, UK
96 G5 **North Rona** *island* NW Scotland, UK
96 K4 **North Ronaldsay** *island* NE Scotland, UK
36 L2 **North Salt Lake** Utah, W USA
11 P15 **North Saskatchewan** ≈ Alberta/Saskatchewan, S Canada
35 X5 **North Schell Peak** ▲ Nevada, W USA
North Scotia Ridge *see* South Georgia Ridge
86 D10 **North Sea** *Dan.* Nordsøen, *Dut.* Noordzee, *Fr.* Mer du Nord, *Ger.* Nordsee, *Nor.* Nordsjøen; *prev.* German Ocean, *Lat.* Mare Germanicum. *sea* NW Europe
35 T6 **North Shoshone Peak** ▲ Nevada, W USA
North Siberian Lowland/North Siberian Plain *see* Severo-Sibirskaya Nizmennost'
29 R13 **North Sioux City** South Dakota, N USA
96 K4 **North Sound, The** *sound* N Scotland, UK
183 T4 **North Star** New South Wales, SE Australia
North Star State *see* Minnesota
183 V3 **North Stradbroke Island** *island* Queensland, E Australia
North Sulawesi *see* Sulawesi Utara
North Sumatra *see* Sumatera Utara
14 D17 **North Sydenham** ≈ Ontario, S Canada
18 H9 **North Syracuse** New York, NE USA
184 K9 **North Taranaki Bight** *gulf* North Island, NZ
12 H9 **North Twin Island** *island* Nunavut, C Canada
96 E8 **North Uist** *island* NW Scotland, UK
97 L14 **Northumberland** *cultural region* N England, UK
181 Y7 **Northumberland Isles** *island group* Queensland, NE Australia
13 Q14 **Northumberland Strait** *strait* SE Canada
32 G14 **North Umpqua River** ≈ Oregon, NW USA
45 Q13 **North Union** Saint Vincent, Saint Vincent and the Grenadines
10 L17 **North Vancouver** British Columbia, SW Canada
18 K9 **Northville** New York, NE USA
97 Q19 **North Walsham** E England, UK
39 T10 **Northway** Alaska, USA
83 G21 **North-West** *off.* North-West Province, *Afr.* Noordwes. ◆ *province* N South Africa
North-West *see* Nord-Ouest
64 I6 **Northwest Atlantic Mid-Ocean Canyon** *undersea feature* N Atlantic Ocean
180 G8 **North West Cape** *headland* Western Australia
38 J9 **Northwest Cape** *headland* Saint Lawrence Island, Alaska, USA
82 H13 **North Western** ◆ *province* W Zambia
155 J24 **North Western Province** ◆ *province* W Sri Lanka
149 U4 **North-West Frontier Province** ◆ *province* NW Pakistan
96 H8 **North West Highlands** ▲ N Scotland, UK
192 J4 **Northwest Pacific Basin** *undersea feature* NW Pacific Ocean
191 Y2 **Northwest Point** *headland* Kiritimati, E Kiribati
44 G1 **Northwest Providence Channel** *channel* N Bahamas
13 Q8 **North West River** Newfoundland, E Canada
8 J9 **Northwest Territories** *Fr.* Territoires du Nord-Ouest. ◆ *territory* NW Canada
97 K18 **Northwich** C England, UK
25 Q5 **North Wichita River** ≈ Texas, SW USA
18 J17 **North Wildwood** New Jersey, NE USA
21 R9 **North Wilkesboro** North Carolina, SE USA
19 P8 **North Windham** Maine, NE USA
197 Q6 **Northwind Plain** *undersea feature* Arctic Ocean
29 V11 **Northwood** Iowa, C USA
29 Q4 **Northwood** North Dakota, N USA
97 M15 **North York Moors** *moorland* N England, UK
25 V9 **North Zulch** Texas, SW USA
26 K2 **Norton** Kansas, C USA
31 S13 **Norton** Ohio, N USA
21 P7 **Norton** Virginia, NE USA
39 N9 **Norton Bay** *bay* Alaska, USA
Norton de Matos *see* Balombo
31 O9 **Norton Shores** Michigan, N USA
38 M10 **Norton Sound** *inlet* Alaska, USA
27 Q3 **Nortonville** Kansas, C USA
102 I8 **Nort-sur-Erdre** Loire-Atlantique, NW France
195 N2 **Norvegia, Cape** *headland* Antarctica
18 L13 **Norwalk** Connecticut, NE USA
29 V14 **Norwalk** Iowa, C USA
31 S11 **Norwalk** Ohio, N USA
19 P7 **Norway** Maine, NE USA
31 N5 **Norway** Michigan, N USA
93 E17 **Norway** *off.* Kingdom of Norway, *Nor.* Norge. ◆ *monarchy* N Europe
11 X13 **Norway House** Manitoba, C Canada
197 R16 **Norwegian Basin** *undersea feature* NW Norwegian Sea
84 D6 **Norwegian Sea** *Nor.* Norske Havet. *sea* NE Atlantic Ocean
197 S17 **Norwegian Trench** *undersea feature* NE North Sea
14 F16 **Norwich** Ontario, S Canada
97 Q19 **Norwich** E England, UK
19 N13 **Norwich** Connecticut, NE USA
18 I11 **Norwich** New York, NE USA
29 U9 **Norwood** Minnesota, N USA
31 Q15 **Norwood** Ohio, N USA
14 H11 **Nosbonsing, Lake** ◎ Ontario, S Canada
Nösen *see* Bistrița
165 T1 **Nosappu-misaki** *headland* Hokkaidō, NE Japan
165 P7 **Noshiro** *var.* Nosiro; *prev.* Noshirominato. Akita, Honshū, C Japan
Noshirominato/Nosiro *see* Noshiro
117 Q3 **Nosivka** *Rus.* Nosovka. Chernihivs'ka Oblast', NE Ukraine
67 T14 **Nosop** *var.* Nossob, Nossop. ≈ Botswana/Namibia
127 S4 **Nosovaya** Nenetskiy Avtonomnyy Okrug, NW Russian Federation
Nosovka *see* Nosivka
143 V11 **Noșratābād** Sīstān va Balūchestān, E Iran
95 J18 **Nossebro** Västra Götaland, S Sweden
96 K6 **Noss Head** *headland* N Scotland, UK
Nossi-Bé *see* Be, Nosy
83 E20 **Nossob** ≈ E Namibia
Nossob/Nossop *see* Nosop
172 J2 **Nosy Be** ✕ Antsiraňana, N Madagascar
172 J6 **Nosy Varika** Fianarantsoa, SE Madagascar
14 L10 **Notawassi** ≈ Quebec, SE Canada
14 M9 **Notawassi, Lac** ◎ Quebec, SE Canada
36 J5 **Notch Peak** ▲ Utah, W USA
110 G10 **Noteć** *Ger.* Netze. ≈ NW Poland
Nótiès Sporádes *see* Dodekánisos
115 J22 **Nótion Aigaíon** *Eng.* Aegean South. ◆ *region* E Greece
115 H18 **Nótios Evvoïkós Kólpos** *gulf* E Greece
115 B16 **Nótio Stenó Kérkyras** *strait* W Greece
107 L25 **Noto** *anc.* Netum. Sicilia, Italy, C Mediterranean Sea
164 M10 **Noto** Ishikawa, Honshū, SW Japan
95 G15 **Notodden** Telemark, S Norway
107 L25 **Noto, Golfo di** *gulf* Sicilia, Italy, C Mediterranean Sea
164 L10 **Noto-hantō** *peninsula* Honshū, SW Japan
164 L11 **Noto-jima** *island* SW Japan
13 T11 **Notre Dame Bay** *bay* Newfoundland, E Canada
15 P6 **Notre-Dame-de-Lorette** Quebec, SE Canada
14 L11 **Notre-Dame-de-Pontmain** Quebec, SE Canada
15 T8 **Notre-Dame-du-Lac** Quebec, SE Canada
15 Q6 **Notre-Dame-du-Rosaire** Quebec, SE Canada
15 U8 **Notre-Dame, Monts** ▲ Quebec, S Canada
77 R16 **Notsé** S Togo
14 G14 **Nottawasaga** ≈ Ontario, S Canada
14 G14 **Nottawasaga Bay** *lake bay* Ontario, S Canada
12 I11 **Nottaway** ≈ Quebec, SE Canada
23 S1 **Nottely Lake** ▣ Georgia, SE USA
95 H16 **Nøtterøy** *island* S Norway
97 M19 **Nottingham** C England, UK
9 P8 **Nottingham Island** *island* Nunavut, NE Canada
97 N18 **Nottinghamshire** *cultural region* C England, UK
21 V7 **Nottoway** Virginia, NE USA
21 V7 **Nottoway River** ≈ Virginia, NE USA
76 G7 **Nouâdhibou** *prev.* Port-Étienne. Dakhlet Nouâdhibou, W Mauritania
76 G7 **Nouâdhibou** ✕ Dakhlet Nouâdhibou, W Mauritania
76 F7 **Nouâdhibou, Dakhlet** *prev.* Baie du Lévrier. *bay* W Mauritania
76 F7 **Nouâdhibou, Râs** *prev.* Cap Blanc. *headland* NW Mauritania
76 G9 **Nouakchott** ● (Mauritania) Nouakchott District, SW Mauritania
76 G9 **Nouakchott** ✕ Trarza, SW Mauritania
120 J11 **Noual, Sebkhet en** *var.* Sabkhat an Nawāl. *salt flat* C Tunisia
76 G8 **Nouâmghâr** *var.* Nouamrhar. Dakhlet Nouâdhibou, W Mauritania
Nouamrhar *see* Nouâmghâr
Nouă Sulița *see* Novoselytsya
187 Q17 **Nouméa** ○ (New Caledonia) Province Sud, S New Caledonia
79 E15 **Noun** ≈ C Cameroon
77 N12 **Nouna** W Burkina
83 H24 **Noupoort** Northern Cape, C South Africa
Nouveau-Brunswick *see* New Brunswick
Nouveau-Comptoir *see* Wemindji
15 T4 **Nouvel, Lacs** ◎ Quebec, SE Canada
15 W7 **Nouvelle** Quebec, SE Canada
15 W7 **Nouvelle** ≈ Quebec, SE Canada
Nouvelle-Calédonie *see* New Caledonia
Nouvelle Écosse *see* Nova Scotia
103 R3 **Nouzonville** Ardennes, N France
147 Q11 **Nov** *Rus.* Nau. NW Tajikistan
59 I21 **Nova Alvorada** Mato Grosso do Sul, SW Brazil
Novabad *see* Navobod
111 D19 **Nová Bystřice** *Ger.* Neubistritz. Budějovický Kraj, S Czech Republic
116 H13 **Novaci** Gorj, SW Romania
Nova Civitas *see* Neustadt an der Weinstrasse
Novaesium *see* Neuss
60 H10 **Nova Esperança** Paraná, S Brazil
106 H11 **Novafeltria** Marche, C Italy
60 Q9 **Nova Friburgo** Rio de Janeiro, SE Brazil
82 D12 **Nova Gaia** *var.* Cambundi-Catembo. Malanje, NE Angola
109 S12 **Nova Gorica** W Slovenia
112 G10 **Nova Gradiška** *Ger.* Neugradisk, *Hung.* Újgradiska. Brod-Posavina, NE Croatia
60 K7 **Nova Granada** São Paulo, S Brazil
60 O10 **Nova Iguaçu** Rio de Janeiro, SE Brazil
117 S10 **Nova Kakhovka** *Rus.* Novaya Kakhovka. Khersons'ka Oblast', SE Ukraine
Nová Karvinná *see* Karviná
Nova Lamego *see* Gabú
Nova Lisboa *see* Huambo
112 C11 **Novalja** Lika-Senj, W Croatia
119 M14 **Navalukoml'** *Rus.* Novolukoml'. Vitsyebskaya Voblasts', N Belarus
Nova Mambone *see* Mambone
83 P16 **Nova Nabúri** Zambézia, NE Mozambique
117 Q9 **Nova Odesa** *var.* Novaya Odessa. Mykolayivs'ka Oblast', S Ukraine
60 H10 **Nova Olímpia** Paraná, S Brazil
61 I15 **Nova Prata** Rio Grande do Sul, S Brazil
14 H12 **Novar** Ontario, S Canada
106 C7 **Novara** *anc.* Novaria. Piemonte, NW Italy
Novaria *see* Novara
117 P7 **Novarkanels'k** Kirovohrads'ka Oblast', C Ukraine
13 P15 **Nova Scotia** *Fr.* Nouvelle Écosse. ◆ *province* SE Canada
(0) M9 **Nova Scotia** *physical region* SE Canada
34 M8 **Novato** California, W USA
192 M7 **Nova Trough** *undersea feature* W Pacific Ocean
116 L7 **Nova Ushtsya** Khmel'nyts'ka Oblast', W Ukraine
83 M17 **Nova Vanduzi** Manica, C Mozambique
117 U5 **Nova Vodolaha** *Rus.* Novaya Vodolaga. Kharkivs'ka Oblast', E Ukraine
123 O12 **Novaya Chara** Chitinskaya Oblast', S Russian Federation
122 M12 **Novaya Igirma** Irkutskaya Oblast', C Russian Federation
Novaya Kakhovka *see* Nova Kakhovka
144 E10 **Novaya Kazanka** Zapadnyy Kazakhstan, W Kazakhstan
126 I12 **Novaya Ladoga** Leningradskaya Oblast', NW Russian Federation
129 R5 **Novaya Malykla** Ul'yanovskaya Oblast', W Russian Federation
Novaya Odessa *see* Nova Odesa
123 Q5 **Novaya Sibir', Ostrov** *island* Novosibirskiye Ostrova, NE Russian Federation
Novaya Vodolaga *see* Nova Vodolaha
119 P17 **Novaya Yel'nya** *Rus.* Novaya Yel'nya. Mahilyowskaya Voblasts', E Belarus
122 I6 **Novaya Zemlya** *island group* N Russian Federation
Novaya Zemlya Trough *see* East Novaya Zemlya Trough
114 K10 **Nova Zagora** Sliven, C Bulgaria
105 S12 **Novelda** País Valenciano, E Spain
111 H19 **Nové Mesto nad Váhom** *Ger.* Waagneustadtl, *Hung.* Vágújhely. Trenčiansky Kraj, W Slovakia
111 F17 **Nové Město na Moravě** *Ger.* Neustadtl in Mähren. Jihlavský Kraj, C Czech Republic
Novesium *see* Neuss
111 I21 **Nové Zámky** *Ger.* Neuhäusel, *Hung.* Érsekújvár. Nitriansky Kraj, SW Slovakia
122 C7 **Novgorod** Novgorodskaya Oblast', W Russian Federation
Novgorod-Severskiy *see* Novhorod-Sivers'kyy
122 C7 **Novgorodskaya Oblast'** ◆ *province* W Russian Federation
117 R8 **Novhorodka** Kirovohrads'ka Oblast', C Ukraine
117 R2 **Novhorod-Sivers'kyy** *Rus.* Novgorod-Severskiy. Chernihivs'ka Oblast', NE Ukraine
31 R10 **Novi** Michigan, N USA
Novi *see* Novi Vinodolski
112 L9 **Novi Bečej** *prev.* Új-Becse, Vološinovo, *Ger.* Neubetsche, *Hung.* Törökbecse. Serbia, N Yugoslavia
25 Q8 **Novice** Texas, SW USA
112 A9 **Novigrad** Istra, NW Croatia
Novi Grad *see* Bosanski Novi
114 G9 **Novi Iskŭr** Sofiya-Grad, W Bulgaria
106 C9 **Novi Ligure** Piemonte, NW Italy
99 L22 **Noville** Luxembourg, SE Belgium
194 I10 **Noville Peninsula** *peninsula* Thurston Island, Antarctica
Noviodunum *see* Soissons, Aisne, France
Noviodunum *see* Nevers, Nièvre, France
Noviodunum *see* Nyon, Vaud, Switzerland
Noviomagus *see* Lisieux, France
Noviomagus *see* Nijmegen, Netherlands
114 M8 **Novi Pazar** Shumen, NE Bulgaria
113 M15 **Novi Pazar** *Turk.* Yenipazar. Serbia, S Yugoslavia
112 K10 **Novi Sad** *Ger.* Neusatz, *Hung.* Újvidék. Serbia, N Yugoslavia
117 T6 **Novi Sanzhary** Poltavs'ka Oblast', C Ukraine
112 H12 **Novi Travnik** *prev.* Pučarevo. Federacija Bosna I Hercegovina, C Bosnia and Herzegovina
112 B10 **Novi Vinodolski** *var.* Novi. Primorje-Gorski Kotar, NW Croatia
58 F12 **Novo Airão** Amazonas, N Brazil
129 N14 **Novoaleksandrovsk** Stavropol'skiy Kray, SW Russian Federation
Novoalekseyevka *see* Zhobda
129 N9 **Novoanninskiy** Volgogradskaya Oblast', SW Russian Federation
58 F13 **Novo Aripuanã** Amazonas, N Brazil
117 Y6 **Novoaydar** Luhans'ka Oblast', E Ukraine
117 X9 **Novoazovs'k** *Rus.* Novoazovsk. Donets'ka Oblast', E Ukraine
123 R14 **Novobureyskiy** Amurskaya Oblast', SE Russian Federation
129 Q3 **Novocheboksarsk** Chuvashskaya Respublika, W Russian Federation
129 R5 **Novocheremshansk** Ul'yanovskaya Oblast', W Russian Federation
128 L12 **Novocherkassk** Rostovskaya Oblast', SW Russian Federation
129 R6 **Novodevich'ye** Samarskaya Oblast', W Russian Federation
126 M8 **Novodvinsk** Arkhangel'skaya Oblast', NW Russian Federation
Novograd-Volynskiy *see* Novohrad-Volyns'kyy
Novogrudok *see* Navahrudak
61 I15 **Novo Hamburgo** Rio Grande do Sul, S Brazil
59 H16 **Novo Horizonte** Mato Grosso, W Brazil
60 K8 **Novo Horizonte** São Paulo, S Brazil
116 M4 **Novohrad-Volyns'kyy** *Rus.* Novograd-Volynskiy. Zhytomyrs'ka Oblast', N Ukraine
144 L14 **Novokazalinsk** *see* Ayteke Bi
128 M8 **Novokhopersk** Voronezhskaya Oblast', W Russian Federation
129 R6 **Novokuybyshevsk** Samarskaya Oblast', W Russian Federation
122 J13 **Novokuznetsk** *prev.* Stalinsk. Kemerovskaya Oblast', S Russian Federation
195 R1 **Novolazarevskaya** *Russian research station* Antarctica
Novolukoml' *see* Navalukoml'
109 V12 **Novo mesto** *Ger.* Rudolfswert; *prev. Ger.* Neustadtl. SE Slovenia
128 K15 **Novomikhaylovskiy** Krasnodarskiy Kray, SW Russian Federation
112 L8 **Novo Miloševo** Serbia, N Yugoslavia
Novomirgorod *see* Novomyrhorod
128 L5 **Novomoskovsk** Tul'skaya Oblast', W Russian Federation
117 U7 **Novomoskovs'k** *Rus.* Novomoskovsk. Dnipropetrovs'ka Oblast', E Ukraine
117 V8 **Novomykolayivka** Zaporiz'ka Oblast', SE Ukraine
117 Q7 **Novomyrhorod** *Rus.* Novomirgorod. Kirovohrads'ka Oblast', S Ukraine
129 N8 **Novonikolayevskiy** Volgogradskaya Oblast', SW Russian Federation
129 P10 **Novonikol'skoye** Volgogradskaya Oblast', SW Russian Federation
129 X7 **Novoorsk** Orenburgskaya Oblast', W Russian Federation
128 M13 **Novopokrovskaya** Krasnodarskiy Kray, SW Russian Federation
Novopolotsk *see* Navapolatsk
117 Y5 **Novopskov** Luhans'ka Oblast', E Ukraine
Novoradomsk *see* Radomsko
Novo Redondo *see* Sumbe
129 R8 **Novorepnoye** Saratovskaya Oblast', W Russian Federation
128 K14 **Novorossiysk** Krasnodarskiy Kray, SW Russian Federation
Novorossiyskiy *see* Novorossiyskoye
144 J10 **Novorossiyskoye** *prev.* Novorossiyskiy. Aktyubinsk, NW Kazakhstan
126 F15 **Novorzhev** Pskovskaya Oblast', W Russian Federation
Novoselitsa *see* Novoselytsya
117 S12 **Novoselivs'ke** Respublika Krym, S Ukraine
Novosëlki *see* Navasyolki
114 G6 **Novo Selo** Vidin, NW Bulgaria
113 M14 **Novo Selo** Serbia, C Yugoslavia
116 K8 **Novoselytsya** *Rom.* Nouă Sulița, *Rus.* Novoselitsa. Chernivets'ka Oblast', W Ukraine
129 U7 **Novosergiyevka** Orenburgskaya Oblast', W Russian Federation
128 L11 **Novoshakhtinsk** Rostovskaya Oblast', SW Russian Federation
122 J12 **Novosibirsk** Novosibirskaya Oblast', C Russian Federation
122 J12 **Novosibirskaya Oblast'** ◆ *province* C Russian Federation
122 M4 **Novosibirskiye Ostrova** *Eng.* New Siberian Islands. *island group* N Russian Federation
128 K6 **Novosil'** Orlovskaya Oblast', W Russian Federation
126 G16 **Novosokol'niki** Pskovskaya Oblast', W Russian Federation
129 Q6 **Novospasskoye** Ul'yanovskaya Oblast', W Russian Federation
129 X8 **Novotroitsk** Orenburgskaya Oblast', W Russian Federation
Novotroitskoye *see* Brlik, Kazakhstan
Novotroitskoye *see* Novotroyits'ke, Ukraine
117 T11 **Novotroyits'ke** *Rus.* Novotroitskoye. Khersons'ka Oblast', S Ukraine
Novoukrainka *see* Novoukrayinka
117 Q8 **Novoukrayinka** *Rus.* Novoukrainka. Kirovohrads'ka Oblast', C Ukraine
129 Q5 **Novoul'yanovsk** Ul'yanovskaya Oblast', W Russian Federation
129 W8 **Novouralets** Orenburgskaya Oblast', W Russian Federation
Novo-Urgench *see* Urganch
116 I4 **Novovolyns'k** *Rus.* Novovolynsk. Volyns'ka Oblast', NW Ukraine
117 S9 **Novovorontsovka** Khersons'ka Oblast', S Ukraine
147 Y7 **Novovoznesenovka** Issyk-Kul'skaya Oblast', E Kyrgyzstan
127 R14 **Novovyatsk** Kirovskaya Oblast', NW Russian Federation
Novoyel'nya *see* Navayel'nya
117 O6 **Novozhyvotiv** Vinnyts'ka Oblast', C Ukraine
128 H6 **Novozybkov** Bryanskaya Oblast', W Russian Federation
112 F9 **Novska** Sisak-Moslavina, NE Croatia
Nový Bohumín *see* Bohumín
111 D15 **Nový Bor** *Ger.* Haida; *prev.* Bor u České Lípy, Hajda. Liberecký Kraj, N Czech Republic
111 E16 **Nový Bydžov** *Ger.* Neubidschow. Hradecký Kraj, N Czech Republic
119 G18 **Novy Dvor** *Rus.* Novyy Dvor. Hrodzyenskaya Voblasts', W Belarus
111 I17 **Nový Jičín** *Ger.* Neutitschein. Ostravský Kraj, E Czech Republic
118 K12 **Novy Pahost** *Rus.* Novyy Pogost. Vitsyebskaya Voblasts', NW Belarus
Novyy Bug *see* Novyy Buh
117 R9 **Novyy Buh** *Rus.* Novyy Bug. Mykolayivs'ka Oblast', S Ukraine
117 Q4 **Novyy Bykiv** Chernihivs'ka Oblast', N Ukraine
Novyy Dvor *see* Novy Dvor
Novyye Aneny *see* Anenii Noi
129 P7 **Novyye Burasy** Saratovskaya Oblast', W Russian Federation
Novyy Margilan *see* Farghona
128 K8 **Novyy Oskol** Belgorodskaya Oblast', W Russian Federation
Novyy Pogost *see* Novy Pahost
129 R2 **Novyy Tor"yal** Respublika Mariy El, W Russian Federation
123 N12 **Novyy Uoyan** Respublika Buryatiya, S Russian Federation
122 J9 **Novyy Urengoy** Yamalo-Nenetskiy Avtonomnyy Okrug, N Russian Federation
Novyy Uzen' *see* Zhanaozen
111 N16 **Nowa Dęba** Podkarpackie, SE Poland
111 G15 **Nowa Ruda** *Ger.* Neurode. Dolnośląskie, SW Poland
110 F12 **Nowa Sól** *var.* Nowasól, *Ger.* Neusalz an der Oder. Lubuskie, W Poland
27 Q8 **Nowata** Oklahoma, C USA
142 M6 **Nowbarān** Markazī, W Iran
110 J8 **Nowe** Kujawski-pomorskie, C Poland
110 K9 **Nowe Miasto Lubawskie** *Ger.* Neumark. Warmińsko-Mazurskie, NE Poland
110 L13 **Nowe Miasto nad Pilicą** Mazowieckie, C Poland
110 D8 **Nowe Warpno** *Ger.* Neuwarp. Zachodniopomorskie, NW Poland
Nowgong *see* Nagaon
110 E8 **Nowogard** *var.* Nowógard, *Ger.* Naugard. Zachodniopomorskie, NW Poland
110 N9 **Nowogród** Podlaskie, NE Poland
Nowogródek *see* Navahrudak
111 E14 **Nowogrodziec** *Ger.* Naumburg am Queis. Dolnośląskie, SW Poland
Nowojelnia *see* Navayel'nya
Nowo-Minsk *see* Mińsk Mazowiecki
33 V13 **Nowood River** ≈ Wyoming, C USA
Nowo-Święciany *see* Švenčioneliai
183 S10 **Nowra-Bomaderry** New South Wales, SE Australia
149 T5 **Nowshera** *var.* Naushahra, Naushara. North-West Frontier Province, NE Pakistan
110 J7 **Nowy Dwór Gdański** *Ger.* Tiegenhof. Pomorskie, N Poland
110 L11 **Nowy Dwór Mazowiecki** Mazowieckie, C Poland
111 M17 **Nowy Sącz** *Ger.* Neu Sandec. Małopolskie, S Poland
111 L18 **Nowy Targ** *Ger.* Neumark. Małopolskie, S Poland
110 F11 **Nowy Tomyśl** *var.* Nowy Tomysl. Wielkolpolskie, C Poland
148 M7 **Now Zād** *var.* Nauzad. Helmand, S Afghanistan
23 N4 **Noxubee River** ≈ Alabama/Mississippi, S USA
122 I10 **Noyabr'sk** Yamalo-Nenetskiy Avtonomnyy Okrug, N Russian Federation
102 L8 **Noyant** Maine-et-Loire, NW France
39 X14 **Noyes Island** *island* Alexander Archipelago, Alaska, USA
103 O3 **Noyon** Oise, N France
102 I7 **Nozay** Loire-Atlantique, NW France

◆ Country ● Country Capital ◇ Dependent Territory ○ Dependent Territory Capital ◆ Administrative Region ✕ International Airport ▲ Mountain ▲ Mountain Range ⛰ Volcano ≈ River ◎ Lake ▣ Reservoir

82 L12 Nsando Northern, NE Zambia
83 N16 Nsanje Southern, S Malawi
77 Q17 Nsawam SE Ghana
79 E16 Nsimalen ✕ Centre, C Cameroon
82 K12 Nsombo Northern, NE Zambia
82 H13 Ntambu North Western, NW Zambia
83 N14 Ntcheu var. Ncheu. Central, S Malawi
79 D17 Ntem prev. Campo, Kampo. ≈ Cameroon/Equatorial Guinea
83 I14 Ntemwa North Western, NW Zambia
Ntlenyana, Mount see Thabana Ntlenyana
79 I19 Ntomba, Lac var. Lac Tumba. ◎ NW Dem. Rep. Congo (Zaire)
81 E19 Ntungamo SW Uganda
81 E18 Ntusi SW Uganda
83 H18 Ntwetwe Pan salt lake NE Botswana
93 M15 Nuasjärvi ◎ C Finland
80 F11 Nuba Mountains ▲ C Sudan
68 I9 Nubian Desert desert NE Sudan
116 G10 Nucet Hung. Diófás. Bihor, W Romania
Nu Chiang see Salween
145 U9 Nuclear Testing Ground nuclear site Pavlodar, E Kazakhstan
56 E9 Nucuray, Río ≈ N Peru
25 R14 Nueces River ≈ Texas, SW USA
11 V9 Nueltin Lake ◎ Manitoba/Nunavut, C Canada
99 K15 Nuenen Noord-Brabant, S Netherlands
62 G6 Nuestra Señora, Bahía bay N Chile
61 D14 Nuestra Señora Rosario de Caa Catí Corrientes, NE Argentina
54 J9 Nueva Antioquia Vichada, E Colombia
Nueva Caceres see Naga
41 O7 Nueva Ciudad Guerrera Tamaulipas, C Mexico
55 N4 Nueva Esparta off. Estado Nueva Esparta. ◈ state NE Venezuela
44 C5 Nueva Gerona Isla de la Juventud, S Cuba
42 H8 Nueva Guadalupe San Miguel, E El Salvador
42 M11 Nueva Guinea Región Autónoma Atlántico Sur, SE Nicaragua
61 D19 Nueva Helvecia Colonia, SW Uruguay
63 J25 Nueva, Isla island S Chile
40 M14 Nueva Italia Michoacán de Ocampo, SW Mexico
56 D6 Nueva Loja var. Lago Agrio. Sucumbíos, NE Ecuador
42 F6 Nueva Ocotepeque prev. Ocotepeque. Ocotepeque, W Honduras
61 D19 Nueva Palmira Colonia, SW Uruguay
41 N6 Nueva Rosita Coahuila de Zaragoza, NE Mexico
42 E7 Nueva San Salvador prev. Santa Tecla. La Libertad, SW El Salvador
42 J8 Nueva Segovia ◈ department NW Nicaragua
Nueva Tabarca see Plana, Isla
Nueva Villa de Padilla see Nuevo Padilla
61 B21 Nueve de Julio Buenos Aires, E Argentina
44 H6 Nuevitas Camagüey, E Cuba
61 D18 Nuevo Berlín Río Negro, W Uruguay
40 I4 Nuevo Casas Grandes Chihuahua, N Mexico
43 T14 Nuevo Chagres Colón, C Panama
41 W15 Nuevo Coahuila Campeche, E Mexico
63 K17 Nuevo, Golfo gulf S Argentina
41 O7 Nuevo Laredo Tamaulipas, NE Mexico
41 N8 Nuevo León ◈ state NE Mexico
41 P10 Nuevo Padilla var. Nueva Villa de Padilla. Tamaulipas, C Mexico
56 E6 Nuevo Rocafuerte Napo, E Ecuador
162 G6 Nuga Dzavhan, W Mongolia
80 O13 Nugaal off. Gobolka Nugaal. ◈ region N Somalia
185 E24 Nugget Point headland South Island, NZ
186 J5 Nuguria Islands island group E PNG
184 P10 Nuhaka Hawke's Bay, North Island, NZ
138 M10 Nuhaydayn, Wādī an dry watercourse W Iraq
190 E7 Nui Atoll atoll W Tuvalu
Nu Jiang see Salween
Nûk see Nuuk
182 G7 Nukey Bluff hill South Australia
Nukha see Şäki
123 T9 Nukh Yablonevyy, Gora ▲ E Russian Federation
186 K7 Nukiki Choiseul Island, NW Solomon Islands
186 B6 Nuku Sandaun, NW PNG
193 W15 Nuku island Tongatapu Group, NE Tonga
193 U15 Nuku'alofa Tongatapu, S Tonga
193 Y16 Nuku'alofa ● (Tonga) Tongatapu, S Tonga
190 G12 Nukuatea island N Wallis and Futuna
190 F7 Nukufetau Atoll atoll C Tuvalu
190 G12 Nukuhifala island E Wallis and Futuna
191 W7 Nuku Hiva island Îles Marquises, NE French Polynesia
193 O8 Nuku Hiva Island island Îles Marquises, N French Polynesia
190 F9 Nukulaelae Atoll var. Nukulailai. atoll E Tuvalu
Nukulailai see Nukulaelae Atoll
190 G11 Nukuloa island N Wallis and Futuna
186 L6 Nukumanu Islands prev. Tasman Group. island group NE PNG
Nukunau see Nikunau
190 J9 Nukunonu Atoll island C Tokelau
190 J9 Nukunonu Village Nukunonu Atoll, C Tokelau
189 S18 Nukuoro Atoll atoll Caroline Islands, S Micronesia
146 H8 Nukus Qoraqalpoghiston Respublikasi, W Uzbekistan
190 G11 Nukutapu island N Wallis and Futuna
39 O9 Nulato Alaska, USA
39 O10 Nulato Hills ▲ Alaska, USA
105 T9 Nules País Valenciano, E Spain
Nuling see Sultan Kudarat
182 C6 Nullarbor South Australia
180 M11 Nullarbor Plain plateau South Australia/Western Australia
163 S12 Nulu'erhu Shan ▲ N China
77 X14 Numan Adamawa, E Nigeria
165 S3 Numata Hokkaidō, NE Japan
81 C15 Numatinna ≈ W Sudan
95 F14 Numedalen valley S Norway
95 G14 Numedalslågen var. Laagen. ≈ S Norway
93 L19 Nummela Etelä-Suomi, S Finland
183 O11 Numurkah Victoria, SE Australia
196 L16 Nunap Isua var. Uummannarsuaq, Dan. Kap Farvel, Eng. Cape Farewell. headland S Greenland
9 N8 Nunavut ◈ Territory N Canada
54 H9 Nunchia Casanare, C Colombia
97 M20 Nuneaton C England, UK
153 W14 Nungba Manipur, NE India
38 L12 Nunivak Island island Alaska, USA
152 I5 Nun Kun ▲ NW India
98 L10 Nunspeet Gelderland, E Netherlands
107 C18 Nuoro Sardegna, Italy, C Mediterranean Sea
75 R12 Nuqayy, Jabal hill range S Libya
54 C9 Nuquí Chocó, W Colombia
143 O4 Nūr Māzandarān, N Iran
145 Q9 Nura ≈ N Kazakhstan
143 N11 Nūrābād Fārs, C Iran
Nurakita see Niulakita
Nurata see Nurota
Nuratau, Khrebet see Nurota Tizmasi
136 L17 Nur Dağları ▲ S Turkey
Nurek see Norak
Nuremberg see Nürnberg
136 M15 Nurhak Kahramanmaraş, S Turkey
182 J9 Nuriootpa South Australia
129 S5 Nurlat Respublika Tatarstan, W Russian Federation
93 N15 Nurmes Itä-Suomi, E Finland
101 K20 Nürnberg Eng. Nuremberg. Bayern, S Germany
101 K20 Nürnberg ✕ Bayern, SE Germany
146 M10 Nurota Rus. Nurata. Nawoiy Wiloyati, C Uzbekistan
147 N10 Nurota Tizmasi Rus. Khrebet Nuratau. ▲ C Uzbekistan
149 T8 Nūrpur Punjab, E Pakistan
183 P6 Nurri, Mount hill New South Wales, SE Australia
25 T13 Nursery Texas, SW USA
171 O16 Nusa Tenggara Eng. Lesser Sunda Islands. island group East Timor/ Indonesia
169 V17 Nusa Tenggara Barat off. Propinsi Nusa Tenggara Barat, Eng. West Nusa Tenggara. ◈ province S Indonesia
171 O16 Nusa Tenggara Timur off. Propinsi Nusa Tenggara Timur, Eng. East Nusa Tenggara. ◈ province S Indonesia
171 U14 Nusawulan Irian Jaya, E Indonesia
137 Q16 Nusaybin var. Nisibin. Manisa, SE Turkey
39 O14 Nushagak Bay bay Alaska, USA
39 O13 Nushagak Peninsula headland Alaska, USA
39 O13 Nushagak River ≈ Alaska, USA
160 E11 Nu Shan ▲ SW China
149 N11 Nushki Baluchistān, SW Pakistan
Nussdorf see Năsăud
112 J9 Nuštar Vukovar-Srijem, E Croatia
99 L18 Nuth Limburg, SE Netherlands
100 N13 Nuthe ≈ NE Germany
Nutmeg State see Connecticut
39 T10 Nutzotin Mountains ▲ Alaska, USA
64 I5 Nuuk var. Nûk, Dan. Godthaab, Godthåb. ○ (Greenland). Kitaa, SW Greenland
92 L13 Nuupas Lappi, NW Finland
191 O7 Nuupere, Pointe headland Moorea, W French Polynesia
191 O7 Nuuroa, Pointe headland Tahiti, W French Polynesia
162 M8 Nüürst Töv, C Mongolia
Nuwara see Nuwara Eliya
155 K25 Nuwara Eliya var. Nuwara. Central Province, S Sri Lanka
182 E7 Nuyts Archipelago island group South Australia
83 F17 Nxaunxau Ngamiland, NW Botswana
39 N12 Nyac Alaska, USA
122 H9 Nyagan' Khanty-Mansiyskiy Avtonomnyy Okrug, N Russian Federation
Nyagassola see Niagassola
81 I18 Nyahururu Central, W Kenya
182 M10 Nyah West Victoria, SE Australia
158 M15 Nyainqêntanglha Feng ▲ W China
159 N15 Nyainqêntanglha Shan ▲ W China
80 B11 Nyala Southern Darfur, W Sudan
83 M16 Nyamapanda Mashonaland East, NE Zimbabwe
81 H25 Nyamtumbo Ruvuma, S Tanzania
Nyanda see Masvingo
126 M11 Nyandoma Arkhangel'skaya Oblast', NW Russian Federation
83 M16 Nyanga prev. Inyanga. Manicaland, E Zimbabwe
79 D20 Nyanga off. Province de la Nyanga, var. La Nyanga. ◈ province SW Gabon
79 E20 Nyanga ≈ Congo/Gabon
81 F20 Nyantakara Kagera, NW Tanzania
81 G19 Nyanza ◈ province W Kenya
81 E21 Nyanza-Lac S Burundi
68 J14 Nyasa, Lake var. Lake Malawi; prev. Lago Nyassa. ◎ E Africa
Nyasaland/Nyasaland Protectorate see Malawi
Nyassa, Lago see Nyasa, Lake
119 J17 Nyasvizh Pol. Nieśwież, Rus. Nesvizh. Minskaya Voblasts', C Belarus
166 M8 Nyaunglebin Pegu, SW Myanmar
166 M5 Nyaung-u Magwe, C Myanmar
95 H24 Nyborg Fyn, C Denmark
95 N21 Nybro Kalmar, S Sweden
119 J16 Nyeharelaye Rus. Negoreloye. Minskaya Voblasts', C Belarus
195 W3 Nye Mountains ▲ Antarctica
81 I19 Nyeri Central, C Kenya
118 M11 Nyeshcharda, Vozyera ◎ N Belarus
92 O2 Ny-Friesland physical region N Svalbard
95 L14 Nyhammar Dalarna, C Sweden
160 F7 Nyikog Qu ≈ C China
158 L14 Nyima Xizang Zizhiqu, W China
83 L14 Nyimba Eastern, E Zambia
159 P16 Nyingchi Xizang Zizhiqu, W China
111 O21 Nyírbátor Szabolcs-Szatmár-Bereg, E Hungary
111 N21 Nyíregyháza Szabolcs-Szatmár-Bereg, NE Hungary
Nyiro see Ewaso Ng'iro
Nyitra see Nitra
Nyitrabánya see Handlová
93 K16 Nykarleby Fin. Uusikaarlepyy. Länsi-Suomi, W Finland
95 I25 Nykøbing Storstrøm, SE Denmark
95 I22 Nykøbing Vestsjælland, C Denmark
95 F21 Nykøbing Viborg, NW Denmark
95 N17 Nyköping Södermanland, S Sweden
95 L15 Nykroppa Värmland, C Sweden
83 J20 Nylstroom Northern, NE South Africa
183 P7 Nymagee New South Wales, SE Australia
183 V5 Nymboida New South Wales, SE Australia
183 U5 Nymboida River ≈ New South Wales, SE Australia
111 D16 Nymburk var. Neuenburg an der Elbe, Ger. Nimburg. Středočeský Kraj, C Czech Republic
95 O16 Nynäshamn Stockholm, C Sweden
183 Q6 Nyngan New South Wales, SE Australia
Nyoman see Neman
108 A10 Nyon Ger. Neuss; anc. Noviodunum. Vaud, SW Switzerland
79 D16 Nyong ≈ SW Cameroon
103 S14 Nyons Drôme, E France
79 D14 Nyos, Lac Eng. Lake Nyos. ◎ NW Cameroon
Nyos, Lake see Nyos, Lac
127 U11 Nyrob var. Nyrov. Permskaya Oblast', NW Russian Federation
Nyrov see Nyrob
111 H15 Nysa Ger. Neisse. Opolskie, S Poland
Nysa Łużycka see Neisse
Nyslott see Savonlinna
32 M13 Nyssa Oregon, NW USA
Nystad see Uusikaupunki
95 I25 Nysted Storstrøm, SE Denmark
127 U14 Nytva Permskaya Oblast', NW Russian Federation
165 P8 Nyūdō-zaki headland Honshū, C Japan
127 P9 Nyukhcha Arkhangel'skaya Oblast', NW Russian Federation
126 H8 Nyuk, Ozero var. Ozero Njuk. ◎ NW Russian Federation
127 O12 Nyuksenitsa var. Njuksenica. Vologodskaya Oblast', NW Russian Federation
79 O22 Nyunzu Katanga, SE Dem. Rep. Congo (Zaire)
123 O10 Nyurba Respublika Sakha (Yakutiya), NE Russian Federation
123 O11 Nyuya Respublika Sakha (Yakutiya), NE Russian Federation
117 T10 Nyzhni Sirohozy Khersons'ka Oblast', S Ukraine
117 U12 Nyzhn'ohirs'kyy Rus. Nizhnegorskiy. Respublika Krym, S Ukraine
81 G21 Nzega Tabora, C Tanzania
76 K15 Nzérékoré Guinée-Forestière, SE Guinea
82 A10 N'Zeto prev. Ambrizete. Zaire, NW Angola
79 M24 Nzilo, Lac prev. Lac Delcommune. ◎ SE Dem. Rep. Congo (Zaire)

O

29 O11 Oacoma South Dakota, N USA
29 N9 Oahe Dam dam South Dakota, N USA
28 M9 Oahe, Lake ▣ North Dakota/ South Dakota, N USA
38 C9 Oahu Haw. O'ahu. island Hawaii, USA, C Pacific Ocean
165 V4 O-Akan-dake ▲ Hokkaidō, NE Japan
182 K8 Oakbank South Australia
19 P13 Oak Bluffs Martha's Vineyard, New York, NE USA
36 K4 Oak City Utah, W USA
37 R3 Oak Creek Colorado, C USA
35 P8 Oakdale California, W USA
22 H8 Oakdale Louisiana, S USA
29 P7 Oakes North Dakota, N USA
22 J4 Oak Grove Louisiana, S USA
97 N19 Oakham C England, UK
32 H7 Oak Harbor Washington, NW USA
21 R5 Oak Hill West Virginia, NE USA
35 N8 Oakland California, W USA
29 T15 Oakland Iowa, C USA
19 Q7 Oakland Maine, NE USA
21 T3 Oakland Maryland, NE USA
29 R14 Oakland Nebraska, C USA
31 N11 Oak Lawn Illinois, N USA
33 P16 Oakley Idaho, NW USA
26 I4 Oakley Kansas, C USA
31 N10 Oak Park Illinois, N USA
11 X16 Oak Point Manitoba, S Canada
32 G13 Oakridge Oregon, NW USA
20 M9 Oak Ridge Tennessee, S USA
184 K10 Oakura Taranaki, North Island, NZ
22 L7 Oak Vale Mississippi, S USA
14 G16 Oakville Ontario, S Canada
25 V8 Oakwood Texas, SW USA
185 F22 Oamaru Otago, South Island, NZ
96 F13 Oa, Mull of headland W Scotland, UK
171 O11 Oan Sulawesi, N Indonesia
185 J17 Oaro Canterbury, South Island, NZ
35 X2 Oasis Nevada, W USA
195 S15 Oates Land physical region Antarctica
183 P17 Oatlands Tasmania, SE Australia
36 I11 Oatman Arizona, SW USA
41 R16 Oaxaca var. Oaxaca de Juárez; prev. Antequera. Oaxaca, SE Mexico
41 Q16 Oaxaca ◈ state SE Mexico
Oaxaca de Juárez see Oaxaca
122 H9 Ob' ≈ C Russian Federation
14 G9 Obabika Lake ◎ Ontario, S Canada
Obagan see Ubagan
118 M12 Obal' Rus. Obol'. Vitsyebskaya Voblasts', N Belarus
79 E16 Obala Centre, SW Cameroon
14 C6 Oba Lake ◎ Ontario, S Canada
164 J12 Obama Fukui, Honshū, SW Japan
96 H11 Oban W Scotland, UK
Oban see Halfmoon Bay
Obando see Puerto Inírida
104 I4 O Barco var. El Barco, El Barco de Valdeorras, O Barco de Valdeorras. Galicia, NW Spain
O Barco de Valdeorras see O Barco
Obbia see Hobyo
93 J16 Obbola Västerbotten, N Sweden
Obbrovazzo see Obrovac
Obchuga see Abchuha
Obdorsk see Salekhard
Óbecse see Bečej
118 I11 Obeliai Rokiškis, NE Lithuania
60 F13 Oberá Misiones, NE Argentina
108 E8 Oberburg Bern, W Switzerland
109 Q9 Oberdrauburg Salzburg, S Austria
Oberglogau see Głogówek
109 W4 Ober Grafendorf Niederösterreich, NE Austria
101 E15 Oberhausen Nordrhein-Westfalen, W Germany
Oberhollabrunn see Tulln
Oberlaibach see Vrhnika
101 Q15 Oberlausitz physical region E Germany
26 J2 Oberlin Kansas, C USA
22 H8 Oberlin Louisiana, S USA
31 T11 Oberlin Ohio, N USA
103 U5 Obernai Bas-Rhin, NE France
109 R4 Obernberg-am-Inn Oberösterreich, N Austria
Oberndorf see Oberndorf am Neckar
101 G23 Oberndorf am Neckar var. Oberndorf. Baden-Württemberg, SW Germany
109 Q5 Oberndorf bei Salzburg Salzburg, W Austria
Oberneustadtl see Kysucké Nové Mesto
183 S8 Oberon New South Wales, SE Australia
109 Q4 Oberösterreich off. Land Oberösterreich, Eng. Upper Austria. ◈ state NW Austria
Oberpahlen see Põltsamaa
101 M19 Oberpfälzer Wald ▲ SE Germany
109 Y6 Oberpullendorf Burgenland, E Austria
Oberradkersburg see Gornja Radgona
101 G18 Oberursel Hessen, W Germany
109 Q8 Obervellach Salzburg, S Austria
109 X7 Oberwart Burgenland, SE Austria
Oberwischau see Vişeu de Sus
109 T7 Oberwölz var. Oberwölz-Stadt. Steiermark, SE Austria
Oberwölz-Stadt see Oberwölz
31 S13 Obetz Ohio, N USA
Ob', Gulf of see Obskaya Guba
54 G8 Obia Santander, C Colombia
58 H12 Óbidos Pará, NE Brazil
104 F10 Óbidos Leiria, C Portugal
Obidovichi see Abidavichy
147 Q13 Obigarm W Tajikistan
165 T2 Obihiro Hokkaidō, NE Japan
Obi-Khingou see Khingov
147 P13 Obikiik SW Tajikistan
113 N16 Obilić Serbia, S Yugoslavia
129 O12 Obil'noye Respublika Kalmykiya, SW Russian Federation
20 F8 Obion Tennessee, S USA
20 F8 Obion River ≈ Tennessee, S USA
171 S12 Obi, Pulau island Maluku, E Indonesia
165 S2 Obira Hokkaidō, NE Japan
129 N11 Oblivskaya Rostovskaya Oblast', SW Russian Federation
123 R14 Obluch'ye Yevreyskaya Avtonomnaya Oblast', SE Russian Federation
128 K4 Obninsk Kaluzhskaya Oblast', W Russian Federation
114 J8 Obnova Pleven, N Bulgaria
79 N15 Obo Haut-Mbomou, E Central African Republic
80 M11 Obock E Djibouti
Obol' see Obal'
Obolyanka see Abalyanka
171 V13 Obome Irian Jaya, E Indonesia
110 G11 Oborniki Wielkolpolskie, C Poland
79 G19 Obouya Cuvette, C Congo
128 J8 Oboyan' Kurskaya Oblast', W Russian Federation
126 M9 Obozerskiy Arkhangel'skaya Oblast', NW Russian Federation
112 L11 Obrenovac Serbia, N Yugoslavia
112 D12 Obrovac It. Obbrovazzo. Zadar, SW Croatia
Obrovo see Abrova
35 Q3 Observation Peak ▲ California, W USA
122 J8 Obskaya Guba Eng. Gulf of Ob'. gulf N Russian Federation
173 N13 Ob' Tablemount undersea feature S Indian Ocean
173 T10 Ob' Trench undersea feature E Indian Ocean
77 P16 Obuasi S Ghana
117 P5 Obukhiv Rus. Obukhov. Kyyivs'ka Oblast', N Ukraine
Obukhov see Obukhiv
127 U14 Obva ≈ NW Russian Federation
117 V10 Obytichna Kosa spit SE Ukraine
117 V10 Obytichna Zatoka gulf SE Ukraine
105 O3 Oca ≈ N Spain
23 W10 Ocala Florida, SE USA
40 M7 Ocampo Coahuila de Zaragoza, NE Mexico
54 G7 Ocaña Norte de Santander, N Colombia
105 N9 Ocaña Castilla-La Mancha, C Spain
106 H4 O Carballiño Cast. Carballiño Galicia, NW Spain
37 T9 Ocate New Mexico, SW USA
Ocavango see Okavango
54 D14 Occidental, Cordillera ▲ W Colombia
57 D14 Occidental, Cordillera ▲ W S America
21 Q6 Oceana West Virginia, NE USA
21 Z4 Ocean City Maryland, NE USA
18 J17 Ocean City New Jersey, NE USA
10 K15 Ocean Falls British Columbia, SW Canada
Ocean Island see Kure Atoll
Ocean Island see Banaba
64 J9 Oceanographer Fracture Zone tectonic feature NW Atlantic Ocean
35 U17 Oceanside California, W USA
22 M9 Ocean Springs Mississippi, S USA
Ocean State see Rhode Island
25 O9 O C Fisher Lake ▣ Texas, SW USA
117 Q10 Ochakiv Rus. Ochakov. Mykolayivs'ka Oblast', S Ukraine
Ochakov see Ochakiv
Ochamchira see Och'amch'ire
137 Q9 Och'amch'ire Rus. Ochamchira. W Georgia
Ochansk see Okhansk
127 T15 Ocher Permskaya Oblast', NW Russian Federation
115 I19 Óchi ▲ Évvoia, C Greece
165 W4 Ochiishi-misaki headland Hokkaidō, NE Japan
23 S9 Ochlockonee River ≈ Florida/Georgia, SE USA
44 K12 Ocho Rios C Jamaica
Ochrida see Ohrid
Ochrida, Lake see Ohrid, Lake
101 J19 Ochsenfurt Bayern, C Germany
23 U7 Ocilla Georgia, SE USA
94 N13 Ockelbo Gävleborg, C Sweden
Ocker see Oker
95 I19 Öckerö Västra Götaland, S Sweden
23 U6 Ocmulgee River ≈ Georgia, SE USA
116 H11 Ocna Mureş Hung. Marosújvár; prev. Ocna Mureşului; prev. Hung. Marosújvárakna. Alba, C Romania
Ocna Mureşului see Ocna Mureş
116 H11 Ocna Sibiului Ger. Salzburg, Hung. Vizakna. Sibiu, C Romania
116 H13 Ocnele Mari prev. Vioara. Vâlcea, S Romania
116 L7 Ocniţa Rus. Oknitsa. N Moldova
23 U4 Oconee, Lake ▣ Georgia, SE USA
23 U5 Oconee River ≈ Georgia, SE USA
30 M9 Oconomowoc Wisconsin, N USA
30 M6 Oconto Wisconsin, N USA
30 M6 Oconto Falls Wisconsin, N USA
30 M6 Oconto River ≈ Wisconsin, N USA
104 I3 O Corgo Galicia, NW Spain
41 V16 Ocosingo Chiapas, SE Mexico
42 J8 Ocotal Nueva Segovia, NW Nicaragua
42 F6 Ocotepeque ◈ department W Honduras
Ocotepeque see Nueva Ocotepeque
40 L13 Ocotlán Jalisco, SW Mexico
41 R16 Ocotlán var. Ocotlán de Morelos. Oaxaca, SE Mexico
Ocotlán de Morelos see Ocotlán
41 U16 Ocozocuautla Chiapas, SE Mexico
21 Y10 Ocracoke Island island North Carolina, SE USA
102 I3 Octeville Manche, N France
October Revolution Island see Oktyabr'skoy Revolyutsii, Ostrov
43 R17 Ocú Herrera, S Panama
83 Q14 Ocua Cabo Delgado, NE Mozambique
Ocumare see Ocumare del Tuy
54 M5 Ocumare del Tuy var. Ocumare. Miranda, N Venezuela
77 P17 Oda SE Ghana
165 G12 Ōda var. Oda. Shimane, Honshū, SW Japan
92 K3 Ódáðahraun lava flow C Iceland
165 Q7 Ōdate Akita, Honshū, C Japan
165 N14 Odawara Kanagawa, Honshū, S Japan
95 D14 Odda Hordaland, S Norway
95 G22 Odder Århus, C Denmark
Oddur see Xuddur
29 T13 Odebolt Iowa, C USA
104 H14 Odeleite Faro, S Portugal
25 Q4 Odell Texas, SW USA
25 T14 Odem Texas, SW USA
104 F13 Odemira Beja, S Portugal
136 C14 Ödemiş İzmir, SW Turkey
Ödenburg see Sopron
83 I22 Odendaalsrus Free State, C South Africa
Odenpäh see Otepää
95 H23 Odense Fyn, C Denmark
101 H19 Odenwald ▲ W Germany
84 H10 Oder Cz./Pol. Odra. ≈ C Europe
Oderberg see Bohumín
100 P11 Oderbruch wetland Germany/Poland
Oderhaff see Szczeciński, Zalew
100 O11 Oder-Havel-Kanal canal NE Germany
Oderhellen see Odorheiu Secuiesc
100 P13 Oder-Spree-Kanal canal NE Germany
Odertal see Zdzieszowice
106 I7 Oderzo Veneto, NE Italy
16 J14 Odesa Rus. Odessa. Odes'ka Oblast', SW Ukraine
Odesa see Odes'ka Oblast'
95 L18 Ödeshög Östergötland, S Sweden
117 O9 Odes'ka Oblast' var. Odesa, Rus. Odesskaya Oblast'. ◈ province SW Ukraine
24 M8 Odessa Texas, SW USA
32 K8 Odessa Washington, NW USA
Odessa see Odesa
Odesskaya Oblast' see Odes'ka Oblast'
122 H12 Odesskoye Omskaya Oblast', C Russian Federation
Odessus see Varna
102 F6 Odet ≈ NW France
104 I14 Odiel ≈ SW Spain
76 L14 Odienné NW Ivory Coast
171 O4 Odiongan Tablas Island, C Philippines
116 L12 Odobeşti Vrancea, E Romania
110 H13 Odolanów Ger. Adelnau. Wielkopolskie, C Poland
167 R13 Ŏdôngk Kâmpóng Spoe, S Cambodia
25 N6 O'donnell Texas, SW USA
98 O7 Odoorn Drenthe, NE Netherlands
Odorhei see Odorheiu Secuiesc
116 J11 Odorheiu Secuiesc Ger. Oderhellen, Hung. Vámosudvarhely; prev. Odorhei; Ger. Hofmarkt. Harghita, C Romania
Odra see Oder
112 J9 Odžaci Ger. Hodschag, Hung. Hodság. Serbia, NW Yugoslavia
59 N14 Oeiras Piauí, E Brazil
104 F11 Oeiras Lisboa, C Portugal
101 G14 Oelde Nordrhein-Westfalen, W Germany
28 J11 Oelrichs South Dakota, N USA
Oels/Oels in Schlesien see Oleśnica
101 M17 Oelsnitz Sachsen, E Germany
29 X12 Oelwein Iowa, C USA
Oeniadae see Oiniádes
191 N17 Oeno Island atoll Pitcairn Islands, C Pacific Ocean
Oesel see Saaremaa
108 L7 Oetz var. Ötz. Tirol, W Austria
137 P11 Of Trabzon, NE Turkey
30 K15 O'Fallon Illinois, N USA
27 W4 O'Fallon Missouri, C USA
107 N16 Ofanto ≈ S Italy
97 D18 Offaly Ir. Ua Uíbh Fhailí; prev. King's County. cultural region C Ireland
101 H18 Offenbach var. Offenbach am Main. Hessen, W Germany
Offenbach am Main see Offenbach
101 F22 Offenburg Baden-Württemberg, SW Germany
182 C2 Officer Creek seasonal river South Australia
Oficina María Elena see María Elena
Oficina Pedro de Valdivia see Pedro de Valdivia
115 K22 Ofidoússa island Kykládes, Greece, Aegean Sea
Ofiral see Sharm el Sheikh
92 H10 Ofotfjorden fjord N Norway
192 L16 Ofu island Manua Islands, E American Samoa
165 R9 Ōfunato Iwate, Honshū, C Japan
165 P8 Oga Akita, Honshū, C Japan
Ogaadeen see Ogadēn
165 Q9 Ogachi Akita, Honshū, C Japan

◆ Country ● Country Capital ◇ Dependent Territory ○ Dependent Territory Capital ◈ Administrative Region ✕ International Airport ▲ Mountain ▲ Mountain Range Volcano ≈ River ◎ Lake ▣ Reservoir

165 P9 **Ogachi-tōge** pass Honshū, C Japan
81 N14 **Ogadēn** Som. Ogaadeen. plateau Ethiopia/Somalia
165 P8 **Oga-hantō** peninsula Honshū, C Japan
165 K13 **Ōgaki** Gifu, Honshū, SW Japan
28 L15 **Ogallala** Nebraska, C USA
168 M14 **Ogan, Air** ≈ Sumatera, W Indonesia
165 Y15 **Ogasawara-shotō** Eng. Bonin Islands. island group SE Japan
14 I9 **Ogascanane, Lac** ◎ Quebec, SE Canada
165 R7 **Ogawara-ko** ◎ Honshū, C Japan
77 T15 **Ogbomosho** Oyo, W Nigeria
29 U13 **Ogden** Iowa, C USA
36 L2 **Ogden** Utah, W USA
18 I6 **Ogdensburg** New York, NE USA
23 W5 **Ogeechee River** ≈ Georgia, SE USA
Oger see Ogre
146 F6 **Oghiyon Shūrkhogi** wetland NW Uzbekistan
165 N10 **Ogi** Niigata, Sado, C Japan
10 H5 **Ogilvie** Yukon Territory, NW Canada
10 H4 **Ogilvie** ≈ Yukon Territory, NW Canada
10 H5 **Ogilvie Mountains** ▲ Yukon Territory, NW Canada
Oginskiy Kanal see Ahinski Kanal
146 B10 **Oglanly** Balkanskiy Velayat, W Turkmenistan
23 T5 **Oglethorpe** Georgia, SE USA
23 T2 **Oglethorpe, Mount** ▲ Georgia, SE USA
106 F7 **Oglio** anc. Ollius. ≈ N Italy
103 T8 **Ognon** ≈ E France
123 R13 **Ogodzha** Amurskaya Oblast', S Russian Federation
77 W16 **Ogoja** Cross River, S Nigeria
12 C10 **Ogoki** ≈ Ontario, S Canada
12 D11 **Ogoki Lake** ◎ Ontario, C Canada
162 K10 **Ögöömör** Ömnögovĭ, S Mongolia
79 F19 **Ogooué** ≈ Congo/Gabon
79 E18 **Ogooué-Ivindo** off. Province de l'Ogooué-Ivindo, var. L'Ogooué-Ivindo. ◆ province N Gabon
79 E19 **Ogooué-Lolo** off. Province de l'Ogooué-Lolo, var. L'Ogooué-Lolo. ◆ province C Gabon
79 C19 **Ogooué-Maritime** off. Province de l'Ogooué-Maritime, var. L'Ogooué-Maritime. ◆ province W Gabon
165 D14 **Ogōri** Fukuoka, Kyūshū, SW Japan
114 H7 **Ogosta** ≈ NW Bulgaria
112 Q9 **Ogražden** Bul. Ograzhden. ▲ Bulgaria/FYR Macedonia see also Ograzhden
114 G12 **Ograzhden** | Mac. Ogražden. ▲ Bulgaria/FYR Macedonia see also Ogražden
118 G9 **Ogre** Ger. Oger. Ogre, C Latvia
118 H9 **Ogre** ≈ C Latvia
112 C10 **Ogulin** Karlovac, NW Croatia
77 S16 **Ogun** ◆ state SW Nigeria
146 A12 **Ogurdzhaly, Ostrov** Turkm. Ogurjaly Adasy. island W Turkmenistan
Ogurjaly Adasy see Ogurdzhaly, Ostrov
77 U16 **Ogwashi-Uku** Delta, S Nigeria
185 B23 **Ohai** Southland, South Island, NZ
147 Q10 **Ohangaron** Rus. Akhangaran. Toshkent Wiloyati, E Uzbekistan
147 Q10 **Ohangaron** Rus. Akhangaran. ≈ E Uzbekistan
83 C16 **Ohangwena** ◆ district N Namibia
30 M10 **O'Hare** × (Chicago) Illinois, N USA
165 R6 **Ōhata** Aomori, Honshū, C Japan
184 L13 **Ohau** Manawatu-Wanganui, North Island, NZ
185 E20 **Ohau, Lake** ◎ South Island, NZ
Ohcejohka see Utsjoki
99 J20 **Ohey** Namur, SE Belgium
191 X15 **O'Higgins, Cabo** headland Easter Island, Chile, E Pacific Ocean
O'Higgins, Lago see San Martín, Lago
31 S12 **Ohio** off. State of Ohio; also known as The Buckeye State. ◆ state N USA
(0) L10 **Ohio River** ≈ N USA
Ohlau see Oława
101 H16 **Ohm** ≈ C Germany
193 W16 **Ohonua** 'Eua, E Tonga
23 V5 **Ohoopee River** ≈ Georgia, SE USA
100 L12 **Ohre** Ger. Eger. ≈ Czech Republic/Germany
Ohri see Ohrid
113 M20 **Ohrid** Turk. Ochrida, Ohri. SW FYR Macedonia
113 M20 **Ohrid, Lake** var. Lake Ochrida, Alb. Liqeni i Ohrit, Mac. Ohridsko Ezero. ◎ Albania/FYR Macedonia
Ohridsko Ezero/Ohrit, Liqeni i see Ohrid, Lake
184 L9 **Ohura** Manawatu-Wanganui, North Island, NZ
58 J9 **Oiapoque** Amapá, E Brazil
58 J10 **Oiapoque, Rio** var. Fleuve l'Oyapok, Oyapock. ≈ Brazil/French Guiana see also Oyapok, Fleuve l'
15 O9 **Oies, Île aux** island Quebec, SE Canada
92 L13 **Oijärvi** Oulu, C Finland
92 L12 **Oikarainen** Lappi, N Finland
188 F10 **Oikuul** Babeldaob, N Palau
18 C13 **Oil City** Pennsylvania, NE USA
18 C12 **Oil Creek** ≈ Pennsylvania, NE USA
35 R13 **Oildale** California, W USA
Oileán Ciarral see Castleisland
Oil Islands see Chagos Archipelago
115 D18 **Oiniádes** anc. Oeniadae. site of ancient city Dytikí Ellás, W Greece
115 L18 **Oinoússes** island E Greece
Oírr, Inis see Inisheer
99 J15 **Oirschot** Noord-Brabant, S Netherlands
103 N4 **Oise** ◆ department N France
103 P3 **Oise** ≈ N France
99 J14 **Oisterwijk** Noord-Brabant, S Netherlands
45 O14 **Oistins** S Barbados
165 E4 **Ōita** Ōita, Kyūshū, SW Japan
165 D14 **Ōita** off. Ōita-ken. ◆ prefecture Kyūshū, SW Japan
115 E17 **Oíti** ▲ C Greece
165 S4 **Oiwake** Hokkaidō, NE Japan
35 R14 **Ojai** California, W USA
94 K13 **Öje** Dalarna, C Sweden
93 J14 **Öjebyn** Norrbotten, N Sweden
165 B13 **Ojika-jima** island SW Japan
40 K5 **Ojinaga** Chihuahua, N Mexico
40 M11 **Ojo Caliente** var. Ojocaliente. Zacatecas, C Mexico
40 D6 **Ojo de Liebre, Laguna** var. Laguna Scammon, Scammon Lagoon. lagoon W Mexico
62 I7 **Ojos del Salado, Cerro** ▲ W Argentina
105 R7 **Ojos Negros** Aragón, NE Spain
40 M12 **Ojuelos de Jalisco** Aguascalientes, C Mexico
129 N4 **Oka** ≈ W Russian Federation
83 D19 **Okahandja** Otjozondjupa, C Namibia
184 L9 **Okahukura** Manawatu-Wanganui, North Island, NZ
184 J3 **Okaihau** Northland, North Island, NZ
83 D18 **Okakarara** Otjozondjupa, N Namibia
13 P5 **Okak Islands** island group Newfoundland, E Canada
10 M17 **Okanagan** ≈ British Columbia, SW Canada
11 N17 **Okanagan Lake** ◎ British Columbia, SW Canada
Ókanizsa see Kanjiža
83 C16 **Okankolo** Otjikoto, N Namibia
32 K6 **Okanogan River** ≈ Washington, NW USA
83 D18 **Okaputa** Otjozondjupa, N Namibia
149 V9 **Okāra** Punjab, E Pakistan
26 M10 **Okarche** Oklahoma, C USA
146 B13 **Okarem** Turkm. Ekerem. Balkanskiy Velayat, W Turkmenistan
189 X14 **Okat Harbor** harbor Kosrae, E Micronesia
22 M5 **Okatibbee Creek** ≈ Mississippi, S USA
83 C17 **Okaukuejo** Kunene, N Namibia
Okavanggo see Cubango/Okavango
83 E17 **Okavango** ◆ district NW Namibia
83 G17 **Okavango** var. Cubango, Kavango, Kavengo, Kubango, Okavanggo, Port. Ocavango. ≈ S Africa see also Cubango
83 G17 **Okavango Delta** wetland N Botswana
164 M12 **Okaya** Nagano, Honshū, S Japan
164 H13 **Okayama** Okayama, Honshū, SW Japan
164 H13 **Okayama** off. Okayama-ken. ◆ prefecture Honshū, SW Japan
164 L14 **Okazaki** Aichi, Honshū, C Japan
110 M12 **Okęcie** × (Warszawa) Mazowieckie, C Poland
23 Y13 **Okeechobee** Florida, SE USA
23 Y14 **Okeechobee, Lake** ◎ Florida, SE USA
26 M9 **Okeene** Oklahoma, C USA
23 V8 **Okefenokee Swamp** wetland Georgia, SE USA
97 J24 **Okehampton** SW England, UK
27 P10 **Okemah** Oklahoma, C USA
77 U16 **Okene** Kogi, S Nigeria
100 K13 **Oker** var. Ocker. ≈ NW Germany
101 J14 **Oker-Stausee** ◎ C Germany
123 T12 **Okha** Ostrov Sakhalin, Sakhalinskaya Oblast', SE Russian Federation
127 U15 **Okhansk** var. Ochansk. Permskaya Oblast', NW Russian Federation
123 S10 **Okhotsk** Khabarovskiy Kray, E Russian Federation
192 J2 **Okhotsk, Sea of** sea NW Pacific Ocean
117 T4 **Okhtyrka** Rus. Akhtyrka. Sums'ka Oblast', NE Ukraine
83 E23 **Okiep** Northern Cape, W South Africa
Oki-guntō see Oki-shotō
164 H11 **Oki-kaikyō** strait SW Japan
165 P16 **Okinawa** Okinawa, SW Japan
165 S16 **Okinawa** off. Okinawa-ken. ◆ prefecture Okinawa, SW Japan
165 S16 **Okinawa** island SW Japan
165 U16 **Okinoerabu-jima** island Nansei-shotō, SW Japan
164 F15 **Okino-shima** island SW Japan
164 H11 **Oki-shotō** var. Oki-guntō. island group SW Japan
77 T16 **Okitipupa** Ondo, SW Nigeria
166 L8 **Okkan** Pegu, SW Myanmar
27 N10 **Oklahoma** off. State of Oklahoma; also known as The Sooner State. ◆ state C USA
27 N11 **Oklahoma City** state capital Oklahoma, C USA
25 Q4 **Oklaunion** Texas, SW USA
23 W10 **Oklawaha River** ≈ Florida, SE USA
27 P10 **Okmulgee** Oklahoma, C USA
Oknitsa see Ocniţa
22 M3 **Okolona** Mississippi, S USA
165 U2 **Okoppe** Hokkaidō, NE Japan
11 Q16 **Okotoks** Alberta, SW Canada
80 H6 **Oko, Wadi** ≈ NE Sudan
79 G19 **Okoyo** Cuvette, W Congo
77 S15 **Okpara** ≈ Benin/Nigeria
92 J8 **Øksfjord** Finnmark, N Norway
127 R4 **Oksino** Nenetskiy Avtonomnyy Okrug, NW Russian Federation
92 G13 **Oksskolten** ▲ C Norway
Oksu see Oqsu
144 M8 **Oktaybr'skiy** Kostanay, N Kazakhstan
186 B7 **Ok Tedi** Western, W PNG
Oktemberyan see Hoktemberyan
166 M7 **Oktwin** Pegu, C Myanmar
129 R6 **Oktyabr'sk** Samarskaya Oblast', W Russian Federation
Oktyabr'sk see Kandyagash
127 N12 **Oktyabr'skiy** Arkhangel'skaya Oblast', NW Russian Federation
122 E10 **Oktyabr'skiy** Kamchatskaya Oblast', E Russian Federation
129 T5 **Oktyabr'skiy** Respublika Bashkortostan, W Russian Federation
129 O11 **Oktyabr'skiy** Volgogradskaya Oblast', SW Russian Federation
Oktyabr'skiy see Aktsyabrski
129 V7 **Oktyabr'skoye** Orenburgskaya Oblast', W Russian Federation
122 M5 **Oktyabr'skoy Revolyutsii, Ostrov** Eng. October Revolution Island. island Severnaya Zemlya, N Russian Federation
164 C15 **Ōkuchi** var. Ōkuti. Kagoshima, Kyūshū, SW Japan
Okulovka see Uglovka
165 Q4 **Okushiri-tō** var. Okusiri Tô. island NE Japan
Okusiri Tô see Okushiri-tō
77 S15 **Okuta** Kwara, W Nigeria
Ōkuti see Ōkuchi
83 F19 **Okwa** var. Chapman's. ≈ Botswana/Namibia
123 T10 **Ola** Magadanskaya Oblast', E Russian Federation
27 T11 **Ola** Arkansas, C USA
Ola see Ala
35 T11 **Olacha Peak** ▲ California, W USA
92 J1 **Ólafsfjördhur** Nordhurland Eystra, N Iceland
92 H3 **Ólafsvík** Vesturland, W Iceland
Oláhbrettye see Bretea-Română
Oláhszentgyörgy see Sângeorz-Băi
Oláh-Toplicza see Toplița
35 T11 **Olancha** California, W USA
42 J5 **Olanchito** Yoro, C Honduras
42 J6 **Olancho** ◆ department E Honduras
95 O20 **Öland** island S Sweden
95 O19 **Ölands norra udde** headland S Sweden
95 N22 **Ölands södra udde** headland S Sweden
182 K7 **Olary** South Australia
27 R4 **Olathe** Kansas, C USA
61 C22 **Olavarría** Buenos Aires, E Argentina
92 O2 **Olav V Land** physical region C Svalbard
111 H14 **Oława** Ger. Ohlau. Dolnośląskie, SW Poland
107 D17 **Olbia** prev. Terranova Pausania. Sardegna, Italy, C Mediterranean Sea
44 G5 **Old Bahama Channel** channel Bahamas/Cuba
Old Bay State/Old Colony State see Massachusetts
10 H2 **Old Crow** Yukon Territory, NW Canada
Old Dominion see Virginia
Oldeberkeap see Oldeberkoop
98 M7 **Oldeberkoop** Fris. Oldeberkeap. Friesland, N Netherlands
98 L10 **Oldebroek** Gelderland, E Netherlands
98 L8 **Oldemarkt** Overijssel, N Netherlands
94 E11 **Olden** Sogn og Fjordane, C Norway
100 G10 **Oldenburg** Niedersachsen, NW Germany
100 K8 **Oldenburg** Schleswig-Holstein, N Germany
98 P10 **Oldenzaal** Overijssel, E Netherlands
18 J8 **Old Forge** New York, NE USA
Old Goa see Goa
97 L17 **Oldham** NW England, UK
39 Q14 **Old Harbor** Kodiak Island, Alaska, USA
44 J13 **Old Harbour** C Jamaica
97 C22 **Old Head of Kinsale** Ir. An Seancheann. headland SW Ireland
20 J8 **Old Hickory Lake** ▣ Tennessee, S USA
Old Line State see Maryland
Old North State see North Carolina
81 I17 **Ol Doinyo Lengeyo** ▲ C Kenya
11 Q16 **Olds** Alberta, SW Canada
19 O7 **Old Speck Mountain** ▲ Maine, NE USA
19 S6 **Old Town** Maine, NE USA
11 T17 **Old Wives Lake** ◎ Saskatchewan, S Canada
162 J7 **Öldziyt** Arhangay, C Mongolia
163 N10 **Öldziyt** Dornogovĭ, SE Mongolia
188 H6 **Oleai** var. San Jose. Saipan, S Northern Mariana Islands
18 E11 **Olean** New York, NE USA
110 O7 **Olecko** Ger. Treuburg. Warmińsko-Mazurskie, NE Poland
106 C7 **Oleggio** Piemonte, NE Italy
123 P11 **Olëkma** Amurskaya Oblast', SE Russian Federation
123 P12 **Olëkma** ≈ C Russian Federation
123 P11 **Olëkminsk** Respublika Sakha (Yakutiya), NE Russian Federation
117 W7 **Oleksandrivka** Donets'ka Oblast', E Ukraine
117 R7 **Oleksandrivka** Rus. Aleksandrovka. Kirovohrads'ka Oblast', C Ukraine
117 Q9 **Oleksandrivka** Mykolayivs'ka Oblast', S Ukraine
117 S7 **Oleksandriya** Rus. Aleksandriya. Kirovohrads'ka Oblast', C Ukraine
93 B20 **Ølen** Hordaland, S Norway
126 J4 **Olenegorsk** Murmanskaya Oblast', NW Russian Federation
123 N9 **Olenëk** Respublika Sakha (Yakutiya), NE Russian Federation
123 N9 **Olenëk** ≈ NE Russian Federation
123 O7 **Olenëkskiy Zaliv** bay N Russian Federation
126 K6 **Olenitsa** Murmanskaya Oblast', NW Russian Federation
102 I11 **Oléron, Île d'** island W France
111 H14 **Oleśnica** Ger. Oels, Oels in Schlesien. Dolnośląskie, SW Poland
111 I15 **Olesno** Ger. Rosenberg. Opolskie, S Poland
116 M3 **Olevs'k** Rus. Olevsk. Zhytomyrs'ka Oblast', N Ukraine
123 S15 **Ol'ga** Primorskiy Kray, SE Russian Federation
Olga, Mount see Kata Tjuta
92 P2 **Olgastretet** strait E Svalbard
162 D5 **Ölgiy** Bayan-Ölgiy, W Mongolia
95 F23 **Ølgod** Ribe, W Denmark
104 H14 **Olhão** Faro, S Portugal
93 L14 **Olhava** Oulu, C Finland
112 B12 **Olib** It. Ulbo. island W Croatia
83 B16 **Olifa** Kunene, NW Namibia
83 E20 **Olifants** var. Elephant River. ≈ E Namibia
83 E25 **Olifants** var. Elefantes. ≈ SW South Africa
83 G22 **Olifantshoek** Northern Cape, N South Africa
188 L15 **Olimarao Atoll** atoll Caroline Islands, C Micronesia
Ólimbos see Ólympos
Olimpo see Fuerte Olimpo
59 Q15 **Olinda** Pernambuco, E Brazil
Olinthos see Ólynthos
83 I20 **Oliphants Drift** Kgatleng, SE Botswana
Olisipo see Lisboa
Olita see Alytus
105 Q4 **Olite** Navarra, N Spain
62 K10 **Oliva** Córdoba, C Argentina
105 T11 **Oliva** País Valenciano, E Spain
104 I12 **Oliva de la Frontera** Extremadura, W Spain
Olivares see Olivares de Júcar
62 H9 **Olivares, Cerro de** ▲ N Chile
105 P9 **Olivares de Júcar** var. Olivares. Castilla-La Mancha, C Spain
22 L1 **Olive Branch** Mississippi, S USA
21 O5 **Olive Hill** Kentucky, S USA
35 O6 **Olivehurst** California, W USA
104 G7 **Oliveira de Azeméis** Aveiro, N Portugal
104 I11 **Olivenza** Extremadura, W Spain
11 N17 **Oliver** British Columbia, SW Canada
103 N7 **Olivet** Loiret, C France
29 Q12 **Olivet** South Dakota, N USA
29 T9 **Olivia** Minnesota, N USA
185 C20 **Olivine Range** ▲ South Island, NZ
108 H10 **Olivone** Ticino, S Switzerland
Ölkeyek see Ul'kayak
129 O9 **Ol'khovka** Volgogradskaya Oblast', SW Russian Federation
111 K16 **Olkusz** Małopolskie, S Poland
22 I6 **Olla** Louisiana, S USA
62 I4 **Ollagüe, Volcán** var. Oyahue, Volcán Oyahue. ▲ N Chile
189 U13 **Ollan** island Chuuk, C Micronesia
188 F7 **Ollei** Babeldaob, N Palau
Ollius see Oglio
108 C10 **Ollon** Vaud, W Switzerland
147 Q10 **Olmaliq** Rus. Almalyk. Toshkent Wiloyati, E Uzbekistan
104 M6 **Olmedo** Castilla-León, N Spain
56 B10 **Olmos** Lambayeque, W Peru
Olmütz see Olomouc
30 M15 **Olney** Illinois, N USA
25 R5 **Olney** Texas, SW USA
95 L22 **Olofström** Blekinge, S Sweden
187 N9 **Olomburi** Malaita, N Solomon Islands
111 H17 **Olomouc** Ger. Olmütz, Pol. Ołomuniec. Olomoucký Kraj, E Czech Republic
111 H18 **Olomoucký Kraj** ◆ region E Czech Republic
Ołomuniec see Olomouc
122 D7 **Olonets** Respublika Kareliya, NW Russian Federation
171 N3 **Olongapo** off. Olongapo City. Luzon, N Philippines
102 J16 **Oloron-Ste-Marie** Pyrénées-Atlantiques, SW France
192 L16 **Olosega** island Manua Islands, E American Samoa
105 W4 **Olot** Cataluña, NE Spain
146 K12 **Olot** Rus. Alat. Bukhoro Wiloyati, C Uzbekistan
112 I12 **Olovo** Federacija Bosna I Hercegovina, E Bosnia and Herzegovina
123 O14 **Olovyannaya** Chitinskaya Oblast', S Russian Federation
123 T7 **Oloy** ≈ NE Russian Federation
101 F16 **Olpe** Nordrhein-Westfalen, W Germany
109 N8 **Olperer** ▲ SW Austria
Olshanka see Vil'shanka
Ol'shany see Al'shany
Olsnitz see Murska Sobota
98 M10 **Olst** Overijssel, E Netherlands
110 L8 **Olsztyn** Ger. Allenstein. Warmińsko-Mazurskie, NE Poland,
110 L8 **Olsztynek** Ger. Hohenstein in Ostpreussen. Warmińsko-Mazurskie, NE Poland,
116 I14 **Olt** ◆ county SW Romania
116 I14 **Olt** var. Oltul, Ger. Alt. ≈ S Romania
108 E7 **Olten** Solothurn, NW Switzerland
116 K14 **Oltenița** prev. Eng. Oltenitsa, anc. Constantiola. Călărași, SE Romania
Oltenitsa see Oltenița
116 H14 **Olteț** ≈ S Romania
24 M4 **Olton** Texas, SW USA
137 R12 **Oltu** Erzurum, NE Turkey
Oltul see Olt
146 G7 **Oltynkŭl** Qoraqalpoghiston Respublikasi, NW Uzbekistan
161 S15 **Oluan Pi** Eng. Cape Olwanpi. headland S Taiwan
Ólubló see Stará Ľubovňa
137 R11 **Olur** Erzurum, NE Turkey
104 L15 **Olvera** Andalucía, S Spain
Ol'viopol' see Pervomays'k
Olwanpi, Cape see Oluan Pi
16 D5 **Olympia** state capital Washington, NW USA
115 D20 **Olympía** Dytikí Ellás, S Greece
182 H5 **Olympic Dam** South Australia
32 F7 **Olympic Mountains** ▲ Washington, NW USA
121 O3 **Ólympos** var. Troodos, Eng. Mount Olympus. ▲ C Cyprus
115 F15 **Ólympos** var. Ólimbos, Eng. Mount Olympus. ▲ N Greece
115 L17 **Ólympos** ▲ Lésvos, E Greece
16 C5 **Olympus, Mount** ▲ Washington, NW USA
Olympus, Mount see Ólympos
115 G14 **Ólynthos** var. Olinthos; anc. Olynthus. site of ancient city Kentrikí Makedonía, N Greece
Olynthus see Ólynthos
117 Q3 **Olyshivka** Chernihivs'ka Oblast', N Ukraine
123 W8 **Olyutorskiy, Mys** headland E Russian Federation
123 V8 **Olyutorskiy Zaliv** bay E Russian Federation
186 M10 **Om** ≈ W PNG
131 S6 **Om'** ≈ N Russian Federation
158 I13 **Oma** Xizang Zizhiqu, W China
165 R6 **Ōma** Aomori, Honshū, C Japan
127 P6 **Oma** ≈ NW Russian Federation
164 M12 **Ōmachi** var. Ōmati. Nagano,Honshū, S Japan
165 Q8 **Ōmagari** Akita, Honshū, C Japan
97 E15 **Omagh** Ir. An Ómaigh. W Northern Ireland, UK
29 S15 **Omaha** Nebraska, C USA
83 E19 **Omaheke** ◆ district W Namibia
141 W10 **Oman** off. Sultanate of Oman, Ar. Salṭanat 'Umān; prev. Muscat and Oman. ◆ monarchy SW Asia
131 O10 **Oman Basin** var. Bassin d'Oman. undersea feature N Indian Ocean
Oman, Bassin d' see Oman Basin
131 N10 **Oman, Gulf of** Ar. Khalīj 'Umān. gulf N Arabian Sea
184 J3 **Omapere** Northland, North Island, NZ
185 E20 **Omarama** Canterbury, South Island, NZ
112 F11 **Omarska** Republika Srpska, NW Bosnia and Herzegovina
83 C18 **Omaruru** Erongo, NW Namibia
83 C19 **Omaruru** ≈ W Namibia
83 E17 **Omatako** ≈ NE Namibia
Ōmati see Ōmachi
83 E18 **Omawewozonyanda** Omaheke, E Namibia
165 R6 **Oma-zaki** headland Honshū, C Japan
Ombai see Alor, Pulau
83 C16 **Ombalantu** Omusati, N Namibia
79 H15 **Ombella-Mpoko** ◆ prefecture S Central African Republic
Ombetsu see Onbetsu
83 B17 **Ombombo** Kunene, NW Namibia
79 D19 **Omboué** Ogooué-Maritime, W Gabon
106 G13 **Ombrone** ≈ C Italy
80 F9 **Omdurman** var. Umm Durmān. Khartoum, C Sudan
165 N13 **Ōme** Tōkyō, Honshū, S Japan
106 C6 **Omegna** Piemonte, NE Italy
183 P12 **Omeo** Victoria, SE Australia
138 F11 **'Omer** Southern, C Israel
41 P16 **Ometepec** Guerrero, S Mexico
42 K11 **Ometepe, Isla de** island S Nicaragua
Om Hager see Om Hajer
80 I10 **Om Hajer** var. Om Hager. SW Eritrea
165 J13 **Ōmi-Hachiman** var. Ōmihachiman. Shiga, Honshū, SW Japan
10 L12 **Omineca Mountains** ▲ British Columbia, W Canada
113 F14 **Omiš** It. Almissa. Split-Dalmacija, S Croatia
112 B10 **Omišalj** Primorje-Gorski Kotar, NW Croatia
83 D19 **Omitara** Khomas, C Namibia
41 O16 **Omitlán, Río** ≈ S Mexico
39 X14 **Ommaney, Cape** headland Baranof Island, Alaska, USA
98 N9 **Ommen** Overijssel, E Netherlands
162 K11 **Ömnögovĭ** ◆ province S Mongolia
191 X7 **Omoa** Fatu Hira, NE French Polynesia
Omo Botego see Omo Wenz
Ómoldova see Moldova Veche
123 T7 **Omolon** Chukotskiy Avtonomnyy Okrug, NE Russian Federation
123 T7 **Omolon** ≈ NE Russian Federation
123 Q8 **Omoloy** ≈ NE Russian Federation
165 P8 **Omono-gawa** ≈ Honshū, C Japan
81 I14 **Omo Wenz** var. Omo Botego. ≈ Ethiopia/Kenya
122 H12 **Omsk** Omskaya Oblast', C Russian Federation
122 H11 **Omskaya Oblast'** ◆ province C Russian Federation
165 U2 **Ōmu** Hokkaidō, NE Japan
110 M9 **Omulew** ≈ NE Poland
116 J12 **Omul, Vârful** prev. Vîrful Omu. ▲ C Romania
83 D16 **Omundaungilo** Ohangwena, N Namibia
164 C14 **Ōmura** Nagasaki, Kyūshū, SW Japan
83 B17 **Omusati** ◆ district N Namibia
164 C14 **Ōmuta** Fukuoka, Kyūshū, SW Japan
127 S14 **Omutninsk** Kirovskaya Oblast', NW Russian Federation
Omu, Vîrful see Omul, Vârful
29 V7 **Onamia** Minnesota, N USA
21 Y5 **Onancock** Virginia, NE USA
14 E10 **Onaping Lake** ◎ Ontario, S Canada
30 M12 **Onarga** Illinois, N USA
15 R6 **Onatchiway, Lac** ◎ Quebec, SE Canada
29 S14 **Onawa** Iowa, C USA
165 U5 **Onbetsu** var. Ombetsu. Hokkaidō, NE Japan
83 B16 **Oncócua** Cunene, SW Angola
105 S9 **Onda** País Valenciano, E Spain
111 N18 **Ondava** ≈ NE Slovakia
Ondjiva see N'Giva
77 T16 **Ondo** Ondo, SW Nigeria
77 T16 **Ondo** ◆ state SW Nigeria
163 N8 **Öndörhaan** Hentiy, E Mongolia
83 D18 **Ondundazongonda** Otjozondjupa, N Namibia
151 K21 **One and Half Degree Channel** channel S Maldives
187 Z15 **Oneata** island Lau Group, E Fiji
126 L9 **Onega** Arkhangel'skaya Oblast', NW Russian Federation
122 E7 **Onega** ≈ NW Russian Federation
Onega Bay see Onezhskaya Guba
Onega, Lake see Onezhskoye Ozero
18 I10 **Oneida** New York, NE USA
20 M8 **Oneida** Tennessee, S USA
18 H9 **Oneida Lake** ◎ New York, NE USA
29 P13 **O'Neill** Nebraska, C USA
123 V12 **Onekotan, Ostrov** island Kuril'skiye Ostrova, SE Russian Federation
23 P3 **Oneonta** Alabama, S USA
18 J11 **Oneonta** New York, NE USA
190 I16 **Oneroa** island S Cook Islands
116 K11 **Onești** Hung. Onyest; prev. Gheorghe Gheorghiu-Dej. Bacău, E Romania
193 V15 **Onevai** island Tongatapu Group, S Tonga
108 A11 **Onex** Genève, SW Switzerland
126 K8 **Onezhskaya Guba** Eng. Onega Bay. bay NW Russian Federation
122 D7 **Onezhskoye Ozero** Eng. Lake Onega. ◎ NW Russian Federation
83 C16 **Ongandjera** Omusati, N Namibia
184 N12 **Ongaonga** Hawke's Bay, North Island, NZ
162 K9 **Ongi** Dundgovĭ, C Mongolia
162 J8 **Ongi** Övörhangay, C Mongolia
163 W14 **Ongjin** SW North Korea
155 J17 **Ongole** Andhra Pradesh, E India
162 K8 **Ongon** Övörhangay, C Mongolia
Ongtüstik Qazaqstan Oblysy see Yuzhnyy Kazakhstan
99 I21 **Onhaye** Namur, S Belgium
166 M8 **Onhne** Pegu, SW Myanmar
137 S9 **Oni** N Georgia
29 N9 **Onida** South Dakota, N USA
164 F15 **Onigajō-yama** ▲ Shikoku, SW Japan
172 H7 **Onilahy** ≈ S Madagascar
77 U16 **Onitsha** Anambra, S Nigeria
164 I13 **Ono** Hyōgo, Honshū, SW Japan
187 X15 **Ono** island SW Fiji
164 K12 **Ōno** Fukui, Honshū, SW Japan
164 E13 **Onoda** Yamaguchi, Honshū, SW Japan
187 Z16 **Ono-i-lau** island SE Fiji
164 D13 **Ōnojō** var. Ōnoyô. Fukuoka, Kyūshū, SW Japan
Onomiti see Onomichi
163 O7 **Onon Gol** ≈ N Mongolia
Ononte see Orontes
55 N6 **Onoto** Anzoátegui, NE Venezuela
191 O3 **Onotoa** prev. Clerk Island. atoll Tungaru, W Kiribati
Ōnoyô see Ōnojō
95 I19 **Onsala** Halland, S Sweden
83 E23 **Onseepkans** Northern Cape, W South Africa
104 F4 **Ons, Illa de** island NW Spain
180 H7 **Onslow** Western Australia
21 W11 **Onslow Bay** bay North Carolina, E USA
98 P6 **Onstwedde** Groningen, NE Netherlands
164 C16 **On-take** ▲ Kyūshū, SW Japan
35 T15 **Ontario** California, W USA
32 M13 **Ontario** Oregon, NW USA
12 D10 **Ontario** ◆ province S Canada
9 P14 **Ontario, Lake** ◎ Canada/USA
(0) L9 **Ontario Peninsula** peninsula Canada/USA
Onteniente see Ontinyent
105 S11 **Ontinyent** var. Onteniente. País Valenciano, E Spain
93 N15 **Ontojärvi** ◎ E Finland
30 L3 **Ontonagon** Michigan, N USA

◆ Country ● Country Capital ◇ Dependent Territory ○ Dependent Territory Capital ◆ Administrative Region × International Airport ▲ Mountain ▲ Mountain Range Volcano ≈ River ◎ Lake ▣ Reservoir

30 L3 **Ontonagon River** ≈ Michigan, N USA
186 M7 **Ontong Java Atoll** *prev.* Lord Howe Island. *atoll* N Solomon Islands
175 N5 **Ontong Java Rise** *undersea feature* W Pacific Ocean
Onuba *see* Huelva
55 W9 **Onverwacht** Para, N Surinam
Onyest *see* Onești
182 J7 **Oodla Wirra** South Australia
182 F2 **Oodnadatta** South Australia
182 C5 **Ooldea** South Australia
27 Q8 **Oologah Lake** ⊡ Oklahoma, C USA
Oos-Kaap *see* Eastern Cape
Oos-Londen *see* East London
99 E17 **Oostakker** Oost-Vlaanderen, NW Belgium
99 D15 **Oostburg** Zeeland, SW Netherlands
98 K9 **Oostelijk-Flevoland** *polder* C Netherlands
99 B16 **Oostende** *Eng.* Ostend, *Fr.* Ostende. West-Vlaanderen, NW Belgium
99 B16 **Oostende** ✕ West-Vlaanderen, NW Belgium
98 L12 **Oosterbeek** Gelderland, SE Netherlands
99 I14 **Oosterhout** Noord-Brabant, S Netherlands
98 O6 **Oostermoers Vaart** *var.* Hunze. ≈ NE Netherlands
99 F14 **Oosterschelde** *Eng.* Eastern Scheldt. *inlet* SW Netherlands
99 E14 **Oosterscheldedam** *dam* SW Netherlands
98 M7 **Oosterwolde** *Fris.* Easterwâlde. Friesland, N Netherlands
98 I9 **Oosthuizen** Noord-Holland, NW Netherlands
99 H16 **Oostmalle** Antwerpen, N Belgium
Oos-Transvaal *see* Mpumalanga
99 E15 **Oost-Souburg** Zeeland, SW Netherlands
99 E17 **Oost-Vlaanderen** *Eng.* East Flanders. ◐ *province* NW Belgium
98 J5 **Oost-Vlieland** Friesland, N Netherlands
98 F12 **Oostvoorne** Zuid-Holland, SW Netherlands
Ootacamund *see* Udagamandalam
98 O10 **Ootmarsum** Overijssel, E Netherlands
10 K14 **Ootsa Lake** ⊡ British Columbia, SW Canada
114 L8 **Opaka** Tŭrgovishte, N Bulgaria
79 M18 **Opala** Orientale, C Dem. Rep. Congo (Zaire)
127 Q13 **Oparino** Kirovskaya Oblast', NW Russian Federation
14 H8 **Opasatica, Lac** ⊚ Quebec, SE Canada
112 B9 **Opatija** *It.* Abbazia. Primorje-Gorski Kotar, NW Croatia
111 N15 **Opatów** Świętokrzyskie, C Poland
111 I17 **Opava** *Ger.* Troppau. Ostravský Kraj, E Czech Republic
111 H16 **Opava** *Ger.* Oppa. ≈ NE Czech Republic
Ópazova *see* Stara Pazova
Ópécska *see* Pecica
14 E8 **Opeepeesway Lake** ⊚ Ontario, S Canada
23 R5 **Opelika** Alabama, S USA
22 I8 **Opelousas** Louisiana, S USA
186 G6 **Open Bay** *bay* New Britain, E PNG
14 I12 **Opeongo Lake** ⊚ Ontario, SE Canada
99 K17 **Opglabbeek** Limburg, NE Belgium
33 W6 **Opheim** Montana, NW USA
39 P10 **Ophir** Alaska, USA
Ophiusa *see* Formentera
79 N18 **Opienge** Orientale, E Dem. Rep. Congo (Zaire)
185 G20 **Opihi** ≈ South Island, NZ
12 J9 **Opinaca** ≈ Quebec, C Canada
12 J10 **Opinaca, Réservoir** ⊡ Quebec, E Canada
117 T5 **Opishnya** *Rus.* Oposhnya. Poltavs'ka Oblast', NE Ukraine
98 I8 **Opmeer** Noord-Holland, NW Netherlands
77 V17 **Opobo** Akwa Ibom, S Nigeria
126 F16 **Opochka** Pskovskaya Oblast', W Russian Federation
110 L13 **Opoczno** Łodzkie, C Poland
111 I15 **Opole** *Ger.* Oppeln. Opolskie, S Poland
111 H15 **Opolskie** ◐ *province* S Poland
144 G13 **Opornyy** Mangistau, SW Kazakhstan
Oporto *see* Porto
Oposhnya *see* Opishnya
184 P8 **Opotiki** Bay of Plenty, North Island, NZ
23 Q7 **Opp** Alabama, S USA
Oppa *see* Opava
94 G9 **Oppdal** Sør-Trøndelag, S Norway
Oppeln *see* Opole
107 N23 **Oppido Mamertina** Calabria, SW Italy
Oppidum Ubiorum *see* Köln
94 F12 **Oppland** ◐ *county* S Norway
118 J12 **Opsa** *Rus.* Opsa. Vitsyebskaya Voblasts', NW Belarus
26 I8 **Optima Lake** ⊡ Oklahoma, C USA
184 J11 **Opunake** Taranaki, North Island, NZ
191 N6 **Opunohu, Baie d'** *bay* Moorea, W French Polynesia
83 B17 **Opuwo** Kunene, NW Namibia
146 H6 **Oqqal'a** *var.* Akkala, *Rus.* Karakala. Qoraqalpoghiston Respublikasi, NW Uzbekistan
147 V13 **Oqsu** *Rus.* Oksu. ≈ SE Tajikistan
147 P14 **Oqtogh, Qatorkŭhi** *Rus.* Khrebet Aktau. ⛰ SW Tajikistan
146 M11 **Oqtosh** *Rus.* Aktash. Samarqand Wiloyati, C Uzbekistan
147 N11 **Oqtow Tizmasi** *Rus.* Khrebet Aktau. ⛰ C Uzbekistan
30 J12 **Oquawka** Illinois, N USA
144 J10 **Or'** *Kaz.* Or. ≈ Kazakhstan/Russian Federation
36 M15 **Oracle** Arizona, SW USA
116 F9 **Oradea** *prev.* Oradea Mare, *Ger.* Grosswardein, *Hung.* Nagyvárad. Bihor, NW Romania
Oradea Mare *see* Oradea
113 M17 **Orahovac** *Alb.* Rahovec. Serbia, S Yugoslavia
112 H9 **Orahovica** Virovitica-Podravina, NE Croatia
152 K13 **Orai** Uttar Pradesh, N India
92 K12 **Orajärvi** Lappi, NW Finland
Or Akiva *see* Or 'Aqiva
Oral *see* Ural'sk
74 I5 **Oran** *var.* Ouahran, Wahran. NW Algeria
183 R8 **Orange** New South Wales, SE Australia
103 R14 **Orange** *anc.* Arausio. Vaucluse, SE France
25 Y10 **Orange** Texas, SW USA
21 V5 **Orange** Virginia, NE USA
21 R13 **Orangeburg** South Carolina, SE USA
58 J9 **Orange, Cabo** *headland* NE Brazil
29 S12 **Orange City** Iowa, C USA
Orange Cone *see* Orange Fan
172 J10 **Orange Fan** *var.* Orange Cone. *undersea feature* SW Indian Ocean
Orange Free State *see* Free State
25 S14 **Orange Grove** Texas, SW USA
18 K13 **Orange Lake** New York, NE USA
23 V10 **Orange Lake** ⊚ Florida, SE USA
Orange Mouth/Orangemund *see* Oranjemund
23 W9 **Orange Park** Florida, SE USA
83 E23 **Orange River** *Afr.* Oranjerivier. ≈ S Africa
14 G15 **Orangeville** Ontario, S Canada
36 M5 **Orangeville** Utah, W USA
42 G1 **Orange Walk** Orange Walk, N Belize
42 F1 **Orange Walk** ◐ *district* NW Belize
100 N11 **Oranienburg** Brandenburg, NE Germany
98 O7 **Oranjekanaal** *canal* NE Netherlands
83 D23 **Oranjemund** *var.* Orangemund; *prev.* Orange Mouth. Karas, SW Namibia
Oranjerivier *see* Orange River
45 N16 **Oranjestad** ○ (Aruba) W Aruba
Oranje Vrystaat *see* Free State
Orany *see* Varėna
83 H18 **Orapa** Central, C Botswana
138 F9 **Or 'Aqiva** *var.* Or Akiva. Haifa, W Israel
112 I10 **Orašje** Federacija Bosna I Hercegovina, N Bosnia and Herzegovina
116 G11 **Orăştie** *Ger.* Broos, *Hung.* Szászváros. Hunedoara, W Romania
Orașul Stalin *see* Brașov
111 K18 **Orava** *Hung.* Árva, *Pol.* Orawa. ≈ N Slovakia
Oravainen *see* Oravais
93 K16 **Oravais** *Fin.* Oravainen. Länsi-Suomi, W Finland
Oravicabánya *see* Oravița
116 F13 **Oravița** *Ger.* Orawitza, *Hung.* Oravicabánya. Caraș-Severin, SW Romania
Orawa *see* Orava
185 B24 **Orawia** Southland, South Island, NZ
Orawitza *see* Oravița
103 P16 **Orb** ≈ S France
106 C9 **Orba** ≈ NW Italy
158 H12 **Orba Co** ⊚ W China
108 B9 **Orbe** Vaud, W Switzerland
107 G14 **Orbetello** Toscana, C Italy
104 K3 **Orbigo** ≈ NW Spain
183 Q12 **Orbost** Victoria, SE Australia
95 O14 **Örbyhus** Uppsala, C Sweden
194 I1 **Orcadas** *Argentinian research station* South Orkney Islands, Antarctica
105 P12 **Orcera** Andalucía, S Spain
33 P9 **Orchard Homes** Montana, NW USA
37 P5 **Orchard Mesa** Colorado, C USA
18 D10 **Orchard Park** New York, NE USA
Orchid Island *see* Lan Yü
115 G18 **Orchómenos** *var.* Orhomenos, Orkhómenos; *prev.* Skripón, *anc.* Orchomenus. Stereá Ellás, C Greece
Orchomenus *see* Orchómenos
106 B7 **Orco** ≈ NW Italy
103 R8 **Or, Côte d'** *physical region* C France
29 O14 **Ord** Nebraska, C USA
Ordat' *see* Ordats'
119 O15 **Ordats'** *Rus.* Ordat'. Mahilyowskaya Voblasts', E Belarus
36 K8 **Orderville** Utah, W USA
104 H2 **Ordes** Galicia, NW Spain
35 V14 **Ord Mountain** ▲ California, W USA
Ordos Desert *see* Mu Us Shamo
188 B16 **Ordot** C Guam
137 N11 **Ordu** *anc.* Cotyora. Ordu, N Turkey
136 M11 **Ordu** ◐ *province* N Turkey
137 V14 **Ordubad** SW Azerbaijan
105 O3 **Orduña** País Vasco, N Spain
37 U6 **Ordway** Colorado, C USA
144 L8 **Ordzhonikidze** Kostanay, N Kazakhstan
117 T9 **Ordzhonikidze** Dnipropetrovs'ka Oblast', E Ukraine
Ordzhonikidze *see* Vladikavkaz, Russian Federation
Ordzhonikidze *see* Yenakiyeve, Ukraine
Ordzhonikidzeabad *see* Kofarnihon
55 U9 **Orealla** E Guyana
113 G15 **Orebić** *It.* Sabbioncello. Dubrovnik-Neretva, S Croatia
95 M16 **Örebro** Örebro, C Sweden
95 L16 **Örebro** ◐ *county* C Sweden
25 W6 **Ore City** Texas, SW USA
30 L10 **Oregon** Illinois, N USA
27 Q2 **Oregon** Missouri, C USA
31 R11 **Oregon** Ohio, N USA
32 H13 **Oregon** *off.* State of Oregon; also known as Beaver State, Sunset State, Valentine State, Webfoot State. ◐ *state* NW USA
32 G11 **Oregon City** Oregon, NW USA
95 P14 **Öregrund** Uppsala, C Sweden
Orekhov *see* Orikhiv
128 L3 **Orekhovo-Zuyevo** Moskovskaya Oblast', W Russian Federation
Orekhovsk *see* Arekhawsk
Orel *see* Oril'
128 J6 **Orël** Orlovskaya Oblast', W Russian Federation
56 E11 **Orellana** Loreto, N Peru
104 L11 **Orellana, Embalse de** ⊡ W Spain
36 L3 **Orem** Utah, W USA
Ore Mountains *see* Erzgebirge/Krušné Hory
129 V7 **Orenburg** *prev.* Chkalov. Orenburgskaya Oblast', W Russian Federation
129 V7 **Orenburg** ✕ Orenburgskaya Oblast', W Russian Federation
129 T7 **Orenburgskaya Oblast'** ◐ *province* W Russian Federation
Orense *see* Ourense
188 C8 **Oreor** *var.* Koror. ● (Palau) Oreor, N Palau
188 C8 **Oreor** *var.* Koror. *island* N Palau
185 B24 **Orepuki** Southland, South Island, NZ
114 L12 **Orestiáda** *prev.* Orestiás. Anatolikí Makedonía kai Thráki, NE Greece
Orestiás *see* Orestiáda
Öresund/Øresund *see* Sound, The
185 C23 **Oreti** ≈ South Island, NZ
184 L5 **Orewa** Auckland, North Island, NZ
65 A25 **Orford, Cape** *headland* West Falkland, Falkland Islands
44 B5 **Órganos, Sierra de los** ⛰ W Cuba
37 R15 **Organ Peak** ▲ New Mexico, SW USA
105 N9 **Orgaz** Castilla-La Mancha, C Spain
Orgeyev *see* Orhei
162 I6 **Orgil** Hövsgöl, C Mongolia
105 O15 **Orgiva** *var.* Orjiva. Andalucía, S Spain
162 I9 **Örgön** Bayanhongor, C Mongolia
117 N9 **Orhei** *var.* Orheiu, *Rus.* Orgeyev. N Moldova
Orheiu *see* Orhei
105 R3 **Orhi** *var.* Orhy, Pico de Orhy, Pic d'Orhy. ▲ France/Spain *see also* Orhy
Orhomenos *see* Orchómenos
162 L6 **Orhon Gol** ≈ N Mongolia
102 J16 **Orhy** *var.* Orhi, Pico de Orhy, Pic d'Orhy. ▲ France/Spain *see also* Orhi
Orhy, Pic d'/Orhy, Pico de *see* Orhi/Orhy
34 L2 **Orick** California, W USA
32 L6 **Orient** Washington, NW USA
48 D6 **Oriental, Cordillera** ⛰ Bolivia/Peru
48 D6 **Oriental, Cordillera** ⛰ C Colombia
57 H16 **Oriental, Cordillera** ⛰ C Peru
63 M15 **Oriente** Buenos Aires, E Argentina
105 R12 **Orihuela** País Valenciano, E Spain
117 V9 **Orikhiv** *Rus.* Orekhov. Zaporiz'ka Oblast', SE Ukraine
113 K22 **Orikum** *var.* Orikumi. Vlorë, SW Albania
Orikumi *see* Orikum
117 V6 **Oril'** *Rus.* Orel. ≈ E Ukraine
14 H14 **Orillia** Ontario, S Canada
93 M19 **Orimattila** Etelä-Suomi, S Finland
33 Y15 **Orin** Wyoming, C USA
47 R4 **Orinoco, Río** ≈ Colombia/Venezuela
186 C9 **Oriomo** Western, SW PNG
30 K11 **Orion** Illinois, N USA
29 Q5 **Oriska** North Dakota, N USA
153 P17 **Orissa** ◐ *state* NE India
Orissaar *see* Orissaare
118 E5 **Orissaare** *Ger.* Orissaar. Saaremaa, W Estonia
107 B19 **Oristano** Sardegna, Italy, C Mediterranean Sea
107 A19 **Oristano, Golfo di** *gulf* Sardegna, Italy, C Mediterranean Sea
54 D13 **Orito** Putumayo, SW Colombia
93 L18 **Orivesi** Häme, SW Finland
93 N17 **Orivesi** ⊚ Länsi-Suomi, SE Finland
58 H12 **Oriximiná** Pará, NE Brazil
41 Q14 **Orizaba** Veracruz-Llave, E Mexico
41 Q14 **Orizaba, Volcán Pico de** *var.* Citlaltépetl. ▲ S Mexico
95 I16 **Ørje** Østfold, S Norway
113 I16 **Orjen** ⛰ Bosnia and Herzegovina/Yugoslavia
Orjiva *see* Orgiva
94 G8 **Orkanger** Sør-Trøndelag, S Norway
94 G8 **Orkdalen** *valley* S Norway
95 K22 **Örkelljunga** Skåne, S Sweden
Orkhaniye *see* Botevgrad
Orkhómenos *see* Orchómenos
94 H9 **Orkla** ≈ S Norway
Orkney *see* Orkney Islands
65 J22 **Orkney Deep** *undersea feature* Scotia Sea/Weddell Sea
96 J4 **Orkney Islands** *var.* Orkney, Orkneys. *island group* N Scotland, UK
Orkneys *see* Orkney Islands
24 K8 **Orla** Texas, SW USA
35 N5 **Orland** California, W USA
23 X11 **Orlando** Florida, SE USA
23 X12 **Orlando** ✕ Florida, SE USA
107 K23 **Orlando, Capo d'** *headland* Sicilia, Italy, C Mediterranean Sea
Orlau *see* Orlová
103 N6 **Orléanais** *cultural region* C France
34 L2 **Orleans** California, W USA
19 Q12 **Orleans** Massachusetts, NE USA
103 N7 **Orléans** *anc.* Aurelianum. Loiret, C France
15 R10 **Orléans, Île d'** *island* Quebec, SE Canada
Orléansville *see* Chlef
111 F16 **Orlice** *Ger.* Adler. ≈ NE Czech Republic
122 L13 **Orlik** Respublika Buryatiya, S Russian Federation
127 Q14 **Orlov** *prev.* Khalturin. Kirovskaya Oblast', NW Russian Federation
111 I17 **Orlová** *Ger.* Orlau, *Pol.* Orłowa. Ostravský Kraj, E Czech Republic
Orlov, Mys *see* Orlovskiy, Mys
128 J6 **Orlovskaya Oblast'** ◐ *province* W Russian Federation
126 M5 **Orlovskiy, Mys** *var.* Mys Orlov. *headland* NW Russian Federation
Orłowa *see* Orlová
103 O5 **Orly** ✕ (Paris) Essonne, N France
119 G16 **Orlya** *Rus.* Orlya. Hrodzyenskaya Voblasts', W Belarus
114 M7 **Orlyak** *prev.* Makenzen, Trubchular, *Rom.* Trupcilar. Dobrich, NE Bulgaria
148 L16 **Ormāra** Baluchistān, SW Pakistan
171 P5 **Ormoc** *off.* Ormoc City, *var.* MacArthur. Leyte, C Philippines
23 X10 **Ormond Beach** Florida, SE USA
109 X10 **Ormož** *Ger.* Friedau. NE Slovenia
14 J13 **Ormsby** Ontario, SE Canada
97 K17 **Ormskirk** NW England, UK
Ormsö *see* Vormsi
15 N13 **Ormstown** Quebec, SE Canada
Ormuz, Strait of *see* Hormuz, Strait of
103 T8 **Ornans** Doubs, E France
102 K5 **Orne** ◐ *department* N France
102 K5 **Orne** ≈ N France
92 G12 **Ørnes** Nordland, C Norway
110 L7 **Orneta** Warmińsko-Mazurskie, NE Poland
95 P16 **Ornö** Stockholm, C Sweden
37 Q3 **Orno Peak** ▲ Colorado, C USA
93 I16 **Örnsköldsvik** Västernorrland, C Sweden
163 X13 **Oro** E North Korea
45 T6 **Orocovis** C Puerto Rico
54 H10 **Orocué** Casanare, E Colombia
77 N13 **Orodara** SW Burkina
105 S4 **Oroel, Peña de** ▲ N Spain
33 N10 **Orofino** Idaho, NW USA
162 I9 **Orog Nuur** ⊚ S Mongolia
35 U14 **Oro Grande** California, W USA
37 S15 **Orogrande** New Mexico, SW USA
191 Q7 **Orohena, Mont** ⩕ Tahiti, W French Polynesia
Orolaunum *see* Arlon
Orol Dengizi *see* Aral Sea
189 S15 **Oroluk Atoll** *atoll* Caroline Islands, C Micronesia
80 J13 **Oromo** ◐ *region* C Ethiopia
13 O15 **Oromocto** New Brunswick, SE Canada
191 S4 **Orona** *prev.* Hull Island. *atoll* Phoenix Islands, C Kiribati
191 V17 **Orongo** *ancient monument* Easter Island, Chile, E Pacific Ocean
138 I3 **Orontes** *var.* Ononte, *Ar.* Nahr el Aassi, Nahr al 'Āṣī. ≈ SW Asia
104 L9 **Oropesa** Castilla-La Mancha, C Spain
105 T8 **Oropesa** País Valenciano, E Spain
Oropeza *see* Cochabamba
163 U5 **Oroqen Zizhiqi** Nei Mongol Zizhiqu, N China
171 P7 **Oroquieta** *var.* Oroquieta City. Mindanao, S Philippines
40 J8 **Oro, Río del** ≈ C Mexico
59 O14 **Orós, Açude** ⊡ E Brazil
107 D18 **Orosei, Golfo di** *gulf* Tyrrhenian Sea, C Mediterranean Sea
111 M24 **Orosháza** Békés, SE Hungary
Orosirá Rodhópis *see* Rhodope Mountains
111 I22 **Oroszlány** Komárom-Esztergom. W Hungary
188 B16 **Orote Peninsula** *peninsula* W Guam
123 T9 **Orotukan** Magadanskaya Oblast', E Russian Federation
35 O5 **Oroville** California, W USA
32 K6 **Oroville** Washington, NW USA
35 O5 **Oroville, Lake** ⊡ California, W USA
(0) G15 **Orozco Fracture Zone** *tectonic feature* E Pacific Ocean
64 I7 **Orphan Knoll** *undersea feature* NW Atlantic Ocean
29 V3 **Orr** Minnesota, N USA
95 M21 **Orrefors** Kalmar, S Sweden
182 I7 **Orroroo** South Australia
31 T12 **Orrville** Ohio, N USA
94 L12 **Orsa** Dalarna, C Sweden
Orschowa *see* Orşova
Orschütz *see* Orzyc
119 O14 **Orsha** *Rus.* Orsha. Vitsyebskaya Voblasts', NE Belarus
129 Q2 **Orshanka** Respublika Mariy El, W Russian Federation
108 C11 **Orsières** Valais, SW Switzerland
122 E12 **Orsk** Orenburgskaya Oblast', W Russian Federation
116 F13 **Orşova** *Ger.* Orschowa, *Hung.* Orsova. Mehedinţi, SW Romania
94 D10 **Ørsta** Møre og Romsdal, S Norway
95 O15 **Örsundsbro** Uppsala, C Sweden
136 D16 **Ortaca** Muğla, SW Turkey
107 M16 **Orta Nova** Puglia, SE Italy
136 I17 **Orta Toroslar** ⛰ S Turkey
54 E11 **Ortega** Tolima, W Colombia
104 H1 **Ortegal, Cabo** *headland* NW Spain
Ortelsburg *see* Szczytno
102 J15 **Orthez** Pyrénées-Atlantiques, SW France
57 K14 **Orthon, Río** ≈ N Bolivia
60 I10 **Ortigueira** Paraná, S Brazil
104 H1 **Ortigueira** Galicia, NW Spain
106 H5 **Ortisei** *Ger.* Sankt-Ulrich. Trentino-Alto Adige, N Italy
40 F6 **Ortiz** Sonora, NW Mexico
54 L5 **Ortiz** Guárico, N Venezuela
Ortler *see* Ortles
106 F5 **Ortles** *Ger.* Ortler. ▲ N Italy
107 K14 **Ortona** Abruzzo, C Italy
29 R8 **Ortonville** Minnesota, N USA
147 W8 **Orto-Tokoy** Issyk-Kul'skaya Oblast', NE Kyrgyzstan
93 I15 **Örträsk** Västerbotten, N Sweden
100 J12 **Örtze** ≈ NW Germany
Oruba *see* Aruba
142 I3 **Orūmīyeh** *var.* Rizaiyeh, Urmia, Urmiyeh; *prev.* Reẓā'īyeh. Āžarbāyjān-e Bākhtarī, NW Iran
142 J3 **Orūmīyeh, Daryācheh-ye** *var.* Matianus, Sha Hi, Urumi Yeh, *Eng.* Lake Urmia; *prev.* Daryācheh-ye Reẓā'īyeh. ⊚ NW Iran
57 K19 **Oruro** Oruro, W Bolivia
57 J19 **Oruro** ◐ *department* W Bolivia
95 I18 **Orust** *island* S Sweden
Oruzgān/Orūzgān *see* Ūrūzgān
106 H13 **Orvieto** *anc.* Velsuna. Umbria, C Italy
194 K7 **Orville Coast** *physical region* Antarctica
114 H7 **Oryakhovo** Vratsa, NW Bulgaria
Oryokko *see* Yalu
117 R5 **Orzhytsya** Poltavs'ka Oblast', C Ukraine
110 M9 **Orzyc** *Ger.* Orschütz. ≈ NE Poland
110 N8 **Orzysz** *Ger.* Arys. Warmińsko-Mazurskie, NE Poland
94 I10 **Os** Hedmark, S Norway
95 C14 **Os** Hordaland, S Norway
127 U15 **Osa** Permskaya Oblast', NW Russian Federation
29 W11 **Osage** Iowa, C USA
27 U5 **Osage Beach** Missouri, C USA
27 P5 **Osage City** Kansas, C USA
27 U7 **Osage Fork River** ≈ Missouri, C USA
27 U5 **Osage River** ≈ Missouri, C USA
164 J13 **Ōsaka** *hist.* Naniwa. Ōsaka, Honshū, SW Japan
164 I13 **Ōsaka** *off.* Ōsaka-fu, *var.* Ōsaka Hu. ◐ *urban prefecture* Honshū, SW Japan
Ōsaka-fu/Ōsaka Hu *see* Ōsaka
145 R10 **Osakarovka** Karaganda, C Kazakhstan
29 T7 **Osakis** Minnesota, N USA
43 N16 **Osa, Península de** *peninsula* S Costa Rica
60 M10 **Osasco** São Paulo, S Brazil
27 R5 **Osawatomie** Kansas, C USA
26 L3 **Osborne** Kansas, C USA
173 S8 **Osborn Plateau** *undersea feature* E Indian Ocean
95 L21 **Osby** Skåne, S Sweden
Osca *see* Huesca
92 N2 **Oscar II Land** *physical region* W Svalbard
27 Y10 **Osceola** Arkansas, C USA
29 V15 **Osceola** Iowa, C USA
27 S6 **Osceola** Missouri, C USA
29 Q15 **Osceola** Nebraska, C USA
101 N15 **Oschatz** Sachsen, E Germany
100 K13 **Oschersleben** Sachsen-Anhalt, C Germany
31 R7 **Oscoda** Michigan, N USA
Ösel *see* Saaremaa
94 H6 **Osen** Sør-Trøndelag, S Norway
164 A14 **Ōse-zaki** *headland* Fukue-jima, SW Japan
147 T10 **Osh** Oshskaya Oblast', SW Kyrgyzstan
83 C16 **Oshakati** Oshana, N Namibia
83 C16 **Oshana** ◐ *district* N Namibia
14 H15 **Oshawa** Ontario, SE Canada
165 R10 **Oshika-hantō** *peninsula* Honshū, C Japan
83 C16 **Oshikango** Ohangwena, N Namibia
Oshikoto *see* Otjikoto
165 P5 **Ō-shima** *island* NE Japan
165 N14 **Ō-shima** *island* S Japan
165 Q5 **Oshima-hantō** ⛰ Hokkaidō, NE Japan
83 D17 **Oshivelo** Otjikoto, N Namibia
28 K14 **Oshkosh** Nebraska, C USA
30 M7 **Oshkosh** Wisconsin, N USA
Oshmyany *see* Ashmyany
Osh Oblasty *see* Oshskaya Oblast'
77 T16 **Oshogbo** Osun, W Nigeria
147 S11 **Oshskaya Oblast'** *Kir.* Osh Oblasty. ◐ *province* SW Kyrgyzstan
79 J20 **Oshwe** Bandundu, C Dem. Rep. Congo (Zaire)
Osiek *see* Osijek
112 I9 **Osijek** *prev.* Osiek, Osjek, *Ger.* Esseg, *Hung.* Eszék. Osijek-Baranja, E Croatia
112 I9 **Osijek-Baranja** *off.* Osječko-Baranjska Županija. ◐ *province* E Croatia
106 J12 **Osimo** Marche, C Italy
122 M12 **Osinovka** Irkutskaya Oblast', C Russian Federation
Osintorf *see* Asintorf
112 N11 **Osipaonica** Serbia, NE Yugoslavia
Osipenko *see* Berdyans'k
Osipovichi *see* Asipovichy
Osječko-Baranjska Županija *see* Osijek-Baranja
Osjek *see* Osijek
29 W15 **Oskaloosa** Iowa, C USA
27 Q4 **Oskaloosa** Kansas, C USA
95 N20 **Oskarshamn** Kalmar, S Sweden
95 J21 **Oskarström** Halland, S Sweden
14 M8 **Oskélanéo** Quebec, SE Canada
Öskemen *see* Ust'-Kamenogorsk
Oskil *see* Oskol
117 W5 **Oskol** *Ukr.* Oskil. ≈ Russian Federation/Ukraine
93 D20 **Oslo** *prev.* Christiania, Kristiania. ● (Norway) Oslo, S Norway
93 D20 **Oslo** ◐ *county* S Norway
93 D21 **Oslofjorden** *fjord* S Norway
155 G15 **Osmānābād** Mahārāshtra, C India
136 J11 **Osmancık** Çorum, N Turkey
136 L16 **Osmaniye** Osmaniye, S Turkey
136 L16 **Osmaniye** ◐ *province* S Turkey
95 O16 **Ösmo** Stockholm, C Sweden
118 E3 **Osmussaar** *island* W Estonia
100 G13 **Osnabrück** Niedersachsen, NW Germany
110 D11 **Ośno Lubuskie** *Ger.* Drossen. Lubuskie, W Poland
113 P19 **Osogov Mountains** *var.* Osogovske Planine, Osogovski Planina, *Mac.* Osogovski Planini. ⛰ Bulgaria/FYR Macedonia
Osogovske Planine/Osogovski Planina/Osogovski Planini *see* Osogov Mountains
165 R6 **Osore-yama** ▲ Honshū, C Japan
Oşorhei *see* Târgu Mureş
61 J16 **Osório** Rio Grande do Sul, S Brazil
63 G16 **Osorno** Los Lagos, C Chile
104 M4 **Osorno** Castilla-León, N Spain
11 N17 **Osoyoos** British Columbia, SW Canada
54 J6 **Ospino** Portuguesa, N Venezuela
98 K13 **Oss** Noord-Brabant, S Netherlands
104 H11 **Ossa** ▲ S Portugal
115 F15 **Óssa** ⛰ C Greece
23 X6 **Ossabaw Island** *island* Georgia, SE USA
23 X6 **Ossabaw Sound** *sound* Georgia, SE USA
183 O16 **Ossa, Mount** ▲ Tasmania, SE Australia
104 H11 **Ossa, Serra d'** ⛰ SE Portugal
77 U16 **Osse** ≈ S Nigeria
30 J6 **Osseo** Wisconsin, N USA
109 S9 **Ossiacher See** ⊚ S Austria
18 K13 **Ossining** New York, NE USA
94 I12 **Ossjøen** ⊚ S Norway
123 V9 **Ossora** Koryakskiy Avtonomnyy Okrug, E Russian Federation
126 I15 **Ostashkov** Tverskaya Oblast', W Russian Federation
100 H9 **Oste** ≈ NW Germany
Ostee *see* Baltic Sea
Ostend/Ostende *see* Oostende
117 P3 **Oster** Chernihivs'ka Oblast', N Ukraine
95 O14 **Österbybruk** Uppsala, C Sweden
95 M19 **Österbymo** Östergotland, S Sweden
94 K12 **Österdalälven** ≈ C Sweden
94 I12 **Østerdalen** *valley* S Norway
95 L18 **Östergötland** ◐ *county* S Sweden
100 H10 **Osterholz-Scharmbeck** Niedersachsen, NW Germany
Östermark *see* Teuva
Östermyra *see* Seinäjoki
Osterode/Osterode in Ostpreussen *see* Ostróda
101 J14 **Osterode am Harz** Niedersachsen, C Germany
94 C13 **Osterøy** *island* S Norway
Österreich *see* Austria
93 G16 **Östersund** Jämtland, C Sweden
95 N14 **Östervåla** Västmanland, C Sweden
101 H22 **Ostfildern** Baden-Württemberg, SW Germany
95 H16 **Østfold** ◐ *county* S Norway
100 E9 **Ostfriesische Inseln** *Eng.* East Frisian Islands. *island group* NW Germany
100 F10 **Ostfriesland** *historical region* NW Germany
95 P14 **Östhammar** Uppsala, C Sweden
Ostia Aterni *see* Pescara
106 G8 **Ostiglia** Lombardia, N Italy
95 J14 **Östmark** Värmland, C Sweden
95 K22 **Östra Ringsjön** ⊚ S Sweden
111 I17 **Ostrava** Ostravský Kraj, E Czech Republic
111 H17 **Ostravský Kraj** ◐ *region* E Czech Republic
110 K8 **Ostróda** *Ger.* Osterode, Osterode in Ostpreussen. Warmińsko-Mazurskie, NE Poland
Ostrog/Ostróg *see* Ostroh
128 L8 **Ostrogozhsk** Voronezhskaya Oblast', W Russian Federation
116 L4 **Ostroh** *Pol.* Ostróg, *Rus.* Ostrog. Rivnens'ka Oblast', NW Ukraine
110 N9 **Ostrołęka** *Ger.* Wiesenhof, *Rus.* Ostrolenka. Mazowieckie, C Poland
111 A16 **Ostrov** *Ger.* Schlackenwerth. Karlovarský Kraj, W Czech Republic
126 F15 **Ostrov** *Latv.* Austrava. Pskovskaya Oblast', W Russian Federation
Ostrovets *see* Ostrowiec Świętokrzyski
113 M21 **Ostrovicës, Mali i** ▲ SE Albania
165 Z2 **Ostrov Iturup** *island* NE Russian Federation
114 L7 **Ostrovo** *prev.* Golema Ada. Razgrad, N Bulgaria
127 N15 **Ostrovskoye** Kostromskaya Oblast', NW Russian Federation

◆ Country ● Country Capital ◇ Dependent Territory ○ Dependent Territory Capital ◐ Administrative Region ✕ International Airport ▲ Mountain ⛰ Mountain Range ⩕ Volcano ≈ River ⊚ Lake ⊡ Reservoir

Ostrów see Ostrów Wielkopolski
Ostrowiec see Ostrowiec Świętokrzyski
111 M14 **Ostrowiec Świętokrzyski** var. Ostrowiec, Rus. Ostrovets. Świętokrzyskie, C Poland
110 P13 **Ostrów Lubelski** Lubelskie, E Poland
110 N10 **Ostrów Mazowiecka** var. Ostrów Mazowiecki. Mazowieckie, C Poland
Ostrów Mazowiecki see Ostrów Mazowiecka
Ostrowo see Ostrów Wielkopolski
110 H13 **Ostrów Wielkopolski** var. Ostrów, Ger. Ostrowo. Wielkopolskie, C Poland
Ostryna see Astryna
110 I13 **Ostrzeszów** Wielkopolskie, C Poland
107 P18 **Ostuni** Puglia, SE Italy
Ostyako-Voguls'k see Khanty-Mansiysk
Osum see Osumit, Lumi i
114 I9 **Osŭm** ≈ N Bulgaria
164 C17 **Ōsumi-hantō** ▲ Kyūshū, SW Japan
164 C17 **Ōsumi-kaikyō** strait SW Japan
113 L22 **Osumit, Lumi i** var. Osum. ≈ SE Albania
77 T16 **Osun** ◈ state SW Nigeria
104 L14 **Osuna** Andalucía, S Spain
60 J8 **Osvaldo Cruz** São Paulo, S Brazil
Osveya see Asvyeya
18 J7 **Oswegatchie River** ≈ New York, NE USA
27 Q7 **Oswego** Kansas, C USA
18 H9 **Oswego** New York, NE USA
97 K19 **Oswestry** W England, UK
111 J16 **Oświęcim** Ger. Auschwitz. Małopolskie, S Poland
185 E22 **Otago** off. Otago Region. ◈ region South Island, NZ
185 F23 **Otago Peninsula** peninsula South Island, NZ
165 F13 **Ōtake** Hiroshima, Honshū, SW Japan
184 L13 **Otaki** Wellington, North Island, NZ
93 M15 **Otanmäki** Oulu, C Finland
145 T15 **Otar** Zhambyl, SE Kazakhstan
165 R4 **Otaru** Hokkaidō, NE Japan
185 C24 **Otatara** Southland, South Island, NZ
185 C24 **Otautau** Southland, South Island, NZ
93 M18 **Otava** Isä-Suomi, E Finland
111 B18 **Otava** Ger. Wottawa. ≈ SW Czech Republic
56 C6 **Otavalo** Imbabura, N Ecuador
83 D17 **Otavi** Otjozondjupa, N Namibia
165 P12 **Ōtawara** Tochigi, Honshū, S Japan
83 B16 **Otchinjau** Cunene, SW Angola
116 F12 **Oţelu Roşu** Ger. Ferdinandsberg, Hung. Nándorhgy. Caras-Severin, SW Romania
185 E21 **Otematata** Canterbury, South Island, NZ
118 I6 **Otepää** Ger. Odenpäh. Valgamaa, SE Estonia
32 K9 **Othello** Washington, NW USA
115 A15 **Othonoí** island Iónioi Nísoi, Greece, C Mediterranean Sea
Othris see Óthrys
115 F17 **Óthrys** var. Othris. ▲ C Greece
77 Q14 **Oti** ≈ N Togo
40 K10 **Otinapa** Durango, C Mexico
185 G17 **Otira** West Coast, South Island, NZ
37 V3 **Otis** Colorado, C USA
12 L10 **Otish, Monts** ▲ Quebec, E Canada
83 C17 **Otjikondo** Kunene, N Namibia
83 C17 **Otjikoto** var. Oshikoto. ◈ district N Namibia
83 E18 **Otjinene** Omaheke, NE Namibia
83 D18 **Otjiwarongo** Otjozondjupa, N Namibia
83 D18 **Otjosondu** var. Otjosundu. Otjozondjupa, C Namibia
Otjosundu see Otjosondu
83 D18 **Otjozondjupa** ◈ district C Namibia
112 C11 **Otočac** Lika-Senj, W Croatia
162 M14 **Otog Qi** Nei Mongol Zizhiqu, N China
112 J10 **Otok** Vukovar-Srijem, E Croatia
116 K14 **Otopeni** ✕ (Bucureşti) Bucureşti, S Romania
184 L8 **Otorohanga** Waikato, North Island, NZ
12 D9 **Otoskwin** ≈ Ontario, C Canada
165 G14 **Ōtoyo** Kōchi, Shikoku, SW Japan
95 E16 **Otra** ≈ S Norway
107 R19 **Otranto** Puglia, SE Italy
Otranto, Canale d' see Otranto, Strait of
107 Q18 **Otranto, Strait of** It. Canale d'Otranto. strait Albania/Italy
111 H18 **Otrokovice** Ger. Otrokowitz. Zlínský Kraj, E Czech Republic
Otrokowitz see Otrokovice
31 P10 **Otsego** Michigan, N USA
31 Q6 **Otsego Lake** ◎ Michigan, N USA
18 I11 **Otselic River** ≈ New York, NE USA
164 J13 **Ōtsu** var. Ōtu. Shiga, Honshū, SW Japan
94 G11 **Otta** Oppland, S Norway
189 U13 **Otta** island Chuuk, C Micronesia
94 F11 **Otta** ≈ S Norway
189 U13 **Otta Pass** passage Chuuk Islands, C Micronesia
95 J22 **Ottarp** Skåne, S Sweden
14 L12 **Ottawa** ● (Canada) Ontario, SE Canada
30 L11 **Ottawa** Illinois, N USA
27 Q5 **Ottawa** Kansas, C USA
31 R12 **Ottawa** Ohio, N USA
14 L12 **Ottawa** var. Uplands. ✕ Ontario, SE Canada
14 M12 **Ottawa** Fr. Outaouais. ≈ Ontario/Quebec, SE Canada
12 I4 **Ottawa Islands** island group Nunavut, C Canada
18 L8 **Otter Creek** ≈ Vermont, NE USA
36 L6 **Otter Creek Reservoir** ⊞ Utah, W USA
98 L11 **Otterlo** Gelderland, E Netherlands
94 D9 **Otterøya** island S Norway
29 S6 **Otter Tail Lake** ◎ Minnesota, N USA
29 R7 **Otter Tail River** ≈ Minnesota, C USA
95 H23 **Otterup** Fyn, C Denmark
99 H19 **Ottignies** Wallon Brabant, C Belgium
101 L23 **Ottobrunn** Bayern, SE Germany
29 X15 **Ottumwa** Iowa, C USA
Ōtu see Ōtsu
83 B16 **Otuazuma** Kunene, NW Namibia
Otuki see Ōtsuki
77 V16 **Oturkpo** Benue, S Nigeria
193 Y15 **Otu Tolu Group** island group SE Tonga
182 M13 **Otway, Cape** headland Victoria, SE Australia
63 H24 **Otway, Seno** inlet S Chile
Ötz see Oetz
108 L8 **Ötztaler Ache** ≈ W Austria
108 L9 **Ötztaler Alpen** It. Alpi Venoste. ▲ SW Austria
27 T12 **Ouachita, Lake** ⊞ Arkansas, C USA
27 R11 **Ouachita Mountains** ▲ Arkansas/Oklahoma, C USA
27 U13 **Ouachita River** ≈ Arkansas/Louisiana, C USA
Ouadaï see Ouaddaï
76 J7 **Ouadâne** var. Ouadane. Adrar, C Mauritania
78 K13 **Ouadda** Haute-Kotto, N Central African Republic
78 J10 **Ouaddaï** off. Préfecture du Ouaddaï, var. Ouadaï, Wadai. ◈ prefecture SE Chad
77 P13 **Ouagadougou** var. Wagadugu. ● (Burkina) C Burkina
77 P13 **Ouagadougou** ✕ C Burkina
77 O12 **Ouahigouya** NW Burkina
Ouahran see Oran
79 J14 **Ouaka** ◈ prefecture C Central African Republic
79 J15 **Ouaka** ≈ S Central African Republic
Oualam see Ouallam
76 M9 **Oualâta** var. Oualata. Hodh ech Chargui, SE Mauritania
77 R11 **Ouallam** var. Oualam. Tillabéri, W Niger
172 H14 **Ouanani** Mohéli, S Comoros
55 Z10 **Ouanary** E French Guiana
78 L13 **Ouanda Djallé** Vakaga, NE Central African Republic
79 N14 **Ouando** Haut-Mbomou, SE Central African Republic
79 L15 **Ouango** Mbomou, S Central African Republic
77 N14 **Ouangolodougou** var. Wangolodougou. N Ivory Coast
172 I13 **Ouani** Anjouan, SE Comoros
79 M15 **Ouara** ≈ E Central African Republic
76 K7 **Ouarâne** desert C Mauritania
15 O11 **Ouareau** ≈ Quebec, SE Canada
74 K7 **Ouargla** var. Wargla. NE Algeria
74 F8 **Ouarzazate** S Morocco
77 Q11 **Ouatagouna** Gao, E Mali
74 G6 **Ouazzane** var. Ouezzane, Ar. Wazan, Wazzan. N Morocco
Oubangui see Ubangi
Oubangui-Chari see Central African Republic
Oubari, Edeyen d' see Awbāri, Idhān
98 G13 **Oud-Beijerland** Zuid-Holland, SW Netherlands
98 F13 **Ouddorp** Zuid-Holland, SW Netherlands
77 P9 **Oudeïka** oasis C Mali
98 G13 **Oude Maas** ≈ SW Netherlands
99 E18 **Oudenaarde** Fr. Audenarde. Oost-Vlaanderen, SW Belgium
99 H14 **Oudenbosch** Noord-Brabant, S Netherlands
98 P6 **Oude Pekela** Groningen, NE Netherlands
Ouderkerk see Ouderkerk aan den Amstel
98 I10 **Ouderkerk aan den Amstel** var. Ouderkerk. Noord-Holland, C Netherlands
98 I6 **Oudeschild** Noord-Holland, NW Netherlands
99 G14 **Oude-Tonge** Zuid-Holland, SW Netherlands
98 I12 **Oudewater** Utrecht, C Netherlands
Oudjda see Oujda
98 L5 **Oudkerk** Friesland, N Netherlands
102 J7 **Oudon** ≈ NW France
98 I9 **Oudorp** Noord-Holland, NW Netherlands
83 G25 **Oudtshoorn** Western Cape, SW South Africa
99 I16 **Oud-Turnhout** Antwerpen, N Belgium
74 F7 **Oued-Zem** C Morocco
187 P16 **Ouégoa** Province Nord, C New Caledonia
76 L13 **Ouéléssébougou** var. Ouolossébougou. Koulikoro, SW Mali
77 N16 **Ouellé** E Ivory Coast
77 R16 **Ouémé** ≈ C Benin
77 O13 **Ouessa** S Burkina
102 D5 **Ouessant, Île d'** Eng. Ushant. island NW France
79 H17 **Ouésso** La Sangha, NW Congo
79 D15 **Ouest** Eng. West. ◈ province W Cameroon
190 G11 **Ouest, Baie de l'** bay Îles Wallis, Wallis and Futuna
15 Y7 **Ouest, Pointe de l'** headland Quebec, SE Canada
Ouezzane see Ouazzane
99 K20 **Ouffet** Liège, E Belgium
79 H14 **Ouham** ◈ prefecture NW Central African Republic
78 I13 **Ouham** ≈ Central African Republic/Chad
79 G14 **Ouham-Pendé** ◈ prefecture W Central African Republic
77 R16 **Ouidah** Eng. Whydah, Wida. S Benin
74 H6 **Oujda** Ar. Oudjda, Ujda. NE Morocco
76 I7 **Oujeft** Adrar, C Mauritania
93 L15 **Oulainen** Oulu, C Finland
Ould Yanja see Ould Yenjé
76 J10 **Ould Yenjé** var. Ould Yanja. Guidimaka, S Mauritania
93 L14 **Oulu** Swe. Uleåborg. Oulu, C Finland
93 M14 **Oulu** Swe. Uleåborg. ◈ province N Finland
93 L15 **Oulujärvi** Swe. Uleträsk. ◎ C Finland
93 M14 **Oulujoki** Swe. Uleälv. ≈ C Finland
93 L14 **Oulunsalo** Oulu, C Finland
106 A8 **Oulx** Piemonte, NE Italy
78 J9 **Oum-Chalouba** Borkou-Ennedi-Tibesti, NE Chad
76 M16 **Oumé** C Ivory Coast
74 F7 **Oum er Rbia** ≈ C Morocco
78 J10 **Oum-Hadjer** Batha, E Chad
92 K10 **Ounasjoki** ≈ N Finland
78 J7 **Ounianga Kébir** Borkou-Ennedi-Tibesti, N Chad
Ouolossébougou see Ouéléssébougou
Oup see Auob
99 K19 **Oupeye** Liège, E Belgium
99 N21 **Our** ≈ NW Europe
37 Q7 **Ouray** Colorado, C USA
103 R7 **Ource** ≈ C France
104 G9 **Ourém** Santarém, C Portugal
104 H4 **Ourense** Cast. Orense; Lat. Aurium. Galicia, NW Spain
104 I4 **Ourense** Cast. Orense ◈ province Galicia, NW Spain
59 O15 **Ouricuri** Pernambuco, E Brazil
60 J9 **Ourinhos** São Paulo, S Brazil
104 G13 **Ourique** Beja, S Portugal
59 M20 **Ouro Preto** Minas Gerais, NE Brazil
Ours, Grand Lac de l' see Great Bear Lake
99 K20 **Ourthe** ≈ E Belgium
165 Q9 **Ōu-sanmyaku** ▲ Honshū, C Japan
97 M17 **Ouse** ≈ N England, UK
Ouse see Great Ouse
102 H7 **Oust** ≈ NW France
Outaouais see Ottawa
15 T4 **Outardes Quatre, Réservoir** ⊞ Quebec, SE Canada
15 T5 **Outardes, Rivière aux** ≈ Quebec, SE Canada
96 E8 **Outer Hebrides** var. Western Isles. island group NW Scotland, UK
30 K3 **Outer Island** island Apostle Islands, Wisconsin, N USA
35 S16 **Outer Santa Barbara Passage** passage California, SW USA
104 G3 **Outes** Galicia, NW Spain
83 C18 **Outjo** Kunene, N Namibia
11 T16 **Outlook** Saskatchewan, S Canada
93 N16 **Outokumpu** Itä-Suomi, E Finland
96 M2 **Out Skerries** island group NE Scotland, UK
187 Q16 **Ouvéa** island Îles Loyauté, NE New Caledonia
103 S14 **Ouvèze** ≈ SE France
182 L9 **Ouyen** Victoria, SE Australia
39 Q14 **Ouzinkie** Kodiak Island, Alaska, USA
137 O13 **Ovacık** Tunceli, E Turkey
106 C9 **Ovada** Piemonte, NE Italy
187 X14 **Ovalau** island C Fiji
62 G9 **Ovalle** Coquimbo, N Chile
83 C17 **Ovamboland** physical region N Namibia
54 L10 **Ovana, Cerro** ▲ S Venezuela
104 G7 **Ovar** Aveiro, N Portugal
114 L10 **Ovcharitsa, Yazovir** ⊞ SE Bulgaria
54 E6 **Ovejas** Sucre, NW Colombia
101 E16 **Overath** Nordrhein-Westfalen, W Germany
98 F13 **Overflakkee** island SW Netherlands
99 H19 **Overijse** Vlaams Brabant, C Belgium
98 N10 **Overijssel** ◈ province E Netherlands
98 M9 **Overijssels Kanaal** canal E Netherlands
92 K13 **Överkalix** Norrbotten, N Sweden
27 R4 **Overland Park** Kansas, C USA
99 L14 **Overloon** Noord-Brabant, SE Netherlands
99 K16 **Overpelt** Limburg, NE Belgium
35 Y10 **Overton** Nevada, W USA
25 W7 **Overton** Texas, SW USA
92 K13 **Övertorneå** Norrbotten, N Sweden
95 N18 **Överum** Kalmar, S Sweden
92 G13 **Överuman** ◎ N Sweden
162 H6 **Övgödiy** Dzavhan, C Mongolia
117 P11 **Ovidiopol'** Odes'ka Oblast', SW Ukraine
116 M14 **Ovidiu** Constanţa, SE Romania
45 N10 **Oviedo** SW Dominican Republic
104 K2 **Oviedo** anc. Asturias. Asturias, NW Spain
104 K2 **Oviedo** ✕ Asturias, N Spain
Ovilava see Wels
118 D7 **Oviši** Ventspils, W Latvia
163 P10 **Ovoot** Sühbaatar, SE Mongolia
157 O4 **Övörhangay** ◈ province C Mongolia
94 E12 **Øvre Årdal** Sogn og Fjordane, S Norway
95 J14 **Övre Fryken** ◎ C Sweden
92 J11 **Övre Soppero** Norrbotten, N Sweden
117 N3 **Ovruch** Zhytomyrs'ka Oblast', N Ukraine
162 J8 **Övt** Övörhangay, C Mongolia
185 E24 **Owaka** Otago, South Island, NZ
79 H18 **Owando** prev. Fort-Rousset. Cuvette, C Congo
164 J14 **Owase** Mie, Honshū, SW Japan
27 P9 **Owasso** Oklahoma, C USA
29 V10 **Owatonna** Minnesota, N USA
173 O4 **Owen Fracture Zone** tectonic feature W Arabian Sea
185 H15 **Owen, Mount** ▲ South Island, NZ
185 H15 **Owen River** Tasman, South Island, NZ
44 D8 **Owen Roberts** ✕ Grand Cayman, Cayman Islands
20 I6 **Owensboro** Kentucky, S USA
35 T11 **Owens Lake** salt flat California, W USA
14 F14 **Owen Sound** Ontario, S Canada
14 F13 **Owen Sound** ◎ Ontario, S Canada
35 T10 **Owens River** ≈ California, W USA
186 F9 **Owen Stanley Range** ▲ S PNG
27 V5 **Owensville** Missouri, C USA
20 M4 **Owenton** Kentucky, S USA
77 U17 **Owerri** Imo, S Nigeria
184 M10 **Owhango** Manawatu-Wanganui, North Island, NZ
21 N5 **Owingsville** Kentucky, S USA
146 K10 **Owminzatovo-Toshi** Rus. Gory Auminzatau. ▲ N Uzbekistan
77 T16 **Owo** Ondo, SW Nigeria
31 R9 **Owosso** Michigan, N USA
35 V1 **Owyhee** Nevada, W USA
32 L14 **Owyhee, Lake** ◎ Oregon, NW USA
32 L15 **Owyhee River** ≈ Idaho/Oregon, NW USA
92 K1 **Öxarfjördhur** var. Axarfjördhur. fjord N Iceland
94 K12 **Oxberg** Dalarna, C Sweden
11 V17 **Oxbow** Saskatchewan, S Canada
95 O17 **Oxelösund** Södermanland, S Sweden
185 H18 **Oxford** Canterbury, South Island, NZ
97 M21 **Oxford** Lat. Oxonia. S England, UK
23 Q3 **Oxford** Alabama, S USA
22 L2 **Oxford** Mississippi, S USA
29 N16 **Oxford** Nebraska, C USA
18 I11 **Oxford** New York, NE USA
21 U8 **Oxford** North Carolina, SE USA
31 Q14 **Oxford** Ohio, N USA
18 H16 **Oxford** Pennsylvania, NE USA
11 X12 **Oxford House** Manitoba, C Canada
29 Y13 **Oxford Junction** Iowa, C USA
11 X12 **Oxford Lake** ◎ Manitoba, C Canada
97 M21 **Oxfordshire** cultural region S England, UK
Oxia see Oxyá
41 X12 **Oxkutzcab** Yucatán, SE Mexico
35 R15 **Oxnard** California, W USA
Oxonia see Oxford
14 I12 **Oxtongue** ≈ Ontario, SE Canada
Oxus see Amu Darya
115 E15 **Oxyá** var. Oxia. ▲ C Greece
164 L11 **Oyabe** Toyama, Honshū, SW Japan
Oyahue/Oyahue, Volcán see Ollagüe, Volcán
165 O12 **Oyama** Tochigi, Honshū, S Japan
47 U5 **Oyapock** ≈ E French Guiana
Oyapock see Oiapoque, Rio
55 Z10 **Oyapok, Baie de L'** bay Brazil/French Guiana
55 Z11 **Oyapok, Fleuve l'** var. Oyapock, Rio Oiapoque. ≈ Brazil/French Guiana see also Oiapoque, Rio
79 E17 **Oyem** Woleu-Ntem, N Gabon
11 R16 **Oyen** Alberta, SW Canada
95 I15 **Øyeren** ◎ S Norway
162 G6 **Oygon** Dzavhan, N Mongolia
96 I7 **Oykel** ≈ N Scotland, UK
123 R9 **Oymyakon** Respublika Sakha (Yakutiya), NE Russian Federation
79 H19 **Oyo** Cuvette, C Congo
77 S15 **Oyo** Oyo, W Nigeria
77 S15 **Oyo** ◈ state SW Nigeria
56 D13 **Oyón** Lima, C Peru
103 S10 **Oyonnax** Ain, E France
146 L10 **Oyoqighitma** Rus. Ayakagytma. Bukhoro Wiloyati, C Uzbekistan
146 M9 **Oyoqquduq** Rus. Ayakkuduk. Nawoiy Wiloyati, N Uzbekistan
32 F9 **Oysterville** Washington, NW USA
95 D14 **Øystese** Hordaland, S Norway
147 U10 **Oy-Tal** Oshskaya Oblast', SW Kyrgyzstan
147 T10 **Oy-Tal** ≈ SW Kyrgyzstan
145 S16 **Oytal** Zhambyl, S Kazakhstan
Oyyl see Uil
Ozarichi see Azarychy
23 R7 **Ozark** Alabama, S USA
27 S10 **Ozark** Arkansas, C USA
27 T8 **Ozark** Missouri, C USA
27 T8 **Ozark Plateau** plain Arkansas/Missouri, C USA
27 T6 **Ozarks, Lake of the** ⊞ Missouri, C USA
192 L10 **Ozbourn Seamount** undersea feature W Pacific Ocean
111 L20 **Ózd** Borsod-Abaúj-Zemplén, NE Hungary
112 D11 **Ozeblin** ▲ C Croatia
123 V11 **Ozernovskiy** Kamchatskaya Oblast', E Russian Federation
144 M7 **Ozërnoye** var. Ozërnyy. Kostanay, N Kazakhstan
Ozërnyy see Ozërnoye
115 D18 **Ozerós, Límni** ◎ W Greece
119 D14 **Ozersk** prev. Darkehnen, Ger. Angerapp. Kaliningradskaya Oblast', W Russian Federation
128 L4 **Ozery** Moskovskaya Oblast', W Russian Federation
Özgön see Uzgen
107 C17 **Ozieri** Sardegna, Italy, C Mediterranean Sea
111 I15 **Ozimek** Ger. Malapane. Opolskie, S Poland
129 R8 **Ozinki** Saratovskaya Oblast', W Russian Federation
Oziya see Ojiya
25 O10 **Ozona** Texas, SW USA
Ozorkow see Ozorków
110 J12 **Ozorków** Rus. Ozorkov. Łódź, C Poland
164 F14 **Ōzu** Ehime, Shikoku, SW Japan
137 R10 **Ozurget'i** prev. Makharadze. W Georgia

P

99 J17 **Paal** Limburg, NE Belgium
196 M14 **Paamiut** var. Pâmiut, Dan. Frederikshåb. Kitaa, S Greenland
167 N8 **Pa-an** Karen State, S Myanmar
101 L22 **Paar** ≈ SE Germany
83 E26 **Paarl** Western Cape, SW South Africa
93 L15 **Paavola** Oulu, C Finland
96 E8 **Pabbay** island NW Scotland, UK
153 T15 **Pabna** Rajshahi, W Bangladesh
109 U4 **Pabneukirchen** Oberösterreich, N Austria
118 H13 **Pabradė** Pol. Podbrodzie. Švenčionys, SE Lithuania
56 L13 **Pacahuaras, Río** ≈ N Bolivia
Pacaraima, Sierra/Pacaraim, Serra see Pakaraima Mountains
56 B11 **Pacasmayo** La Libertad, W Peru
42 D6 **Pacaya, Volcán de** ⛰ S Guatemala
115 K23 **Pachía** island Kykládes, Greece, Aegean Sea
107 L26 **Pachino** Sicilia, Italy, C Mediterranean Sea
56 F12 **Pachitea, Río** ≈ C Peru
154 I11 **Pachmarhi** Madhya Pradesh, C India
121 P3 **Páchna** var. Pakhna. SW Cyprus
115 H25 **Páchnes** ▲ Kríti, Greece, E Mediterranean Sea
54 F9 **Pacho** Cundinamarca, C Colombia
154 F12 **Pāchora** Mahārāshtra, C India
41 P13 **Pachuca** var. Pachuca de Soto. Hidalgo, C Mexico
Pachuca de Soto see Pachuca
27 W5 **Pacific** Missouri, C USA
192 L14 **Pacific-Antarctic Ridge** undersea feature S Pacific Ocean
32 F8 **Pacific Beach** Washington, NW USA
35 N10 **Pacific Grove** California, W USA
29 S15 **Pacific Junction** Iowa, C USA
198-199 **Pacific Ocean** ocean
131 Z10 **Pacific Plate** tectonic feature
113 J15 **Pačir** ▲ SW Yugoslavia
182 L5 **Packsaddle** New South Wales, SE Australia
32 H9 **Packwood** Washington, NW USA
Padalung see Phatthalung
168 J12 **Padang** Sumatera, W Indonesia
168 L9 **Padang Endau** Pahang, Peninsular Malaysia
Padangpandjang see Padangpanjang
168 I11 **Padangpanjang** prev. Padangpandjang. Sumatera, W Indonesia
168 I10 **Padangsidempuan** prev. Padangsidimpoean. Sumatera, W Indonesia
Padangsidimpoean see Padangsidempuan
126 I9 **Padany** Respublika Kareliya, NW Russian Federation
93 M18 **Padasjoki** Etelä-Suomi, S Finland
57 M22 **Padcaya** Tarija, S Bolivia
101 H14 **Paderborn** Nordrhein-Westfalen, NW Germany
Padeşul/Padeş, Vîrful see Padeş, Vârful
116 F12 **Padeş, Vârful** var. Padeşul; prev. Vîrful Padeş. ▲ W Romania
112 L10 **Padinska Skela** Serbia, N Yugoslavia
Padma see Brahmaputra
153 S14 **Padma** var. Ganges. ≈ Bangladesh/India see also Ganges
106 H8 **Padova** Eng. Padua; anc. Patavium. Veneto, NE Italy
82 A10 **Padrão, Ponta do** headland NW Angola
25 T16 **Padre Island** island Texas, SW USA
104 G3 **Padrón** Galicia, NW Spain
118 K13 **Padsvillye** Rus. Podsvil'ye. Vitsyebskaya Voblasts', N Belarus
182 K11 **Padthaway** South Australia
Padua see Padova
20 G7 **Paducah** Kentucky, S USA
25 P4 **Paducah** Texas, SW USA
105 N15 **Padul** Andalucía, S Spain
191 P8 **Paea** Tahiti, W French Polynesia
185 L14 **Paekakariki** Wellington, North Island, NZ
163 X11 **Paektu-san** var. Baitou Shan. ▲ China/North Korea
163 V15 **Paengnyŏng-do** island NW South Korea
184 M7 **Paeroa** Waikato, North Island, NZ
54 D12 **Páez** Cauca, SW Colombia
121 O3 **Páfos** var. Paphos. W Cyprus
121 O3 **Páfos** ✕ SW Cyprus
83 L19 **Pafúri** Gaza, SW Mozambique
112 C12 **Pag** It. Pago. Lika-Senj, W Croatia
112 B11 **Pag** It. Pago. island Zadar, SW Croatia
171 P7 **Pagadian** Mindanao, S Philippines
168 J13 **Pagai Selatan, Pulau** island Kepulauan Mentawai, W Indonesia
168 J13 **Pagai Utara, Pulau** island Kepulauan Mentawai, W Indonesia
188 K4 **Pagan** island C Northern Mariana Islands
115 G16 **Pagasitikós Kólpos** gulf E Greece
36 L8 **Page** Arizona, SW USA
29 Q5 **Page** North Dakota, N USA
118 D13 **Pagėgiai** Ger. Pogegen. Šilutė, SW Lithuania
21 S11 **Pageland** South Carolina, SE USA
81 G16 **Pager** ≈ NE Uganda
149 Q5 **Paghmān** Kābul, E Afghanistan
Pago see Pag
188 C16 **Pago Bay** bay E Guam, W Pacific Ocean
115 M20 **Pagóndas** var. Pagóndhas. Sámos, Dodekánisos, Greece, Aegean Sea
Pagóndhas see Pagóndas
192 J16 **Pago Pago** ○ (American Samoa) Tutuila, W American Samoa
37 R8 **Pagosa Springs** Colorado, C USA
38 H12 **Pahala** var. Pāhala. Hawaii, USA, C Pacific Ocean
168 K8 **Pahang** off. Negeri Pahang Darul Makmur. ◈ state Peninsular Malaysia
Pahang see Pahang, Sungai
168 L8 **Pahang, Sungai** var. Pahang, Sungei Pahang. ≈ Peninsular Malaysia
149 S8 **Pahārpur** North-West Frontier Province, NW Pakistan
185 B24 **Pahia Point** headland South Island, NZ
184 M13 **Pahiatua** Manawatu-Wanganui, North Island, NZ
38 H12 **Pahoa** Haw. Pāhoa. Hawaii, USA, C Pacific Ocean
23 Y14 **Pahokee** Florida, SE USA
35 X9 **Pahranagat Range** ▲ Nevada, W USA
35 W11 **Pahrump** Nevada, W USA
Pahsien see Chongqing
35 V9 **Pahute Mesa** ▲ Nevada, W USA
167 N7 **Pai** Mae Hong Son, NW Thailand
38 F10 **Paia** Haw. Pā'ia. Maui, Hawaii, USA, C Pacific Ocean
Pai-ch'eng see Baicheng
118 H4 **Paide** Ger. Weissenstein. Järvamaa, N Estonia
97 J24 **Paignton** SW England, UK
184 K3 **Paihia** Northland, North Island, NZ
93 M18 **Päijänne** ◎ S Finland
114 F13 **Päiko** ▲ N Greece
57 M17 **Paila, Río** ≈ C Bolivia
167 Q12 **Pailin** Bătdâmbâng, W Cambodia
54 F6 **Pailitas** Cesar, N Colombia
38 F9 **Pailolo Channel** channel Hawaii, USA, C Pacific Ocean
93 K19 **Paimio** Swe. Pemar. Länsi-Suomi, W Finland
165 O16 **Paimi-saki** var. Yaeme-saki. headland Iriomote-jima, SW Japan
102 G5 **Paimpol** Côtes d'Armor, NW France
168 J12 **Painan** Sumatera, W Indonesia
63 G23 **Paine, Cerro** ▲ S Chile
31 U11 **Painesville** Ohio, N USA
31 S14 **Paint Creek** ≈ Ohio, N USA
36 L10 **Painted Desert** desert Arizona, SW USA
Paint Hills see Wemindji
30 M4 **Paint River** ≈ Michigan, N USA
25 P8 **Paint Rock** Texas, SW USA
21 O6 **Paintsville** Kentucky, S USA
Paisance see Piacenza
96 I12 **Paisley** W Scotland, UK
32 I15 **Paisley** Oregon, NW USA
105 R10 **País Valenciano** var. Valencia, Cat. València; anc. Valentia. ◈ autonomous community NE Spain
105 O3 **País Vasco** Basq. Euskadi, Eng. The Basque Country, Sp. Provincias Vascongadas. ◈ autonomous community N Spain
56 A9 **Paita** Piura, NW Peru
169 V6 **Paitan, Teluk** bay Sabah, East Malaysia
104 H7 **Paiva, Rio** ≈ N Portugal
92 K12 **Pajala** Norrbotten, N Sweden
104 K3 **Pajares, Puerto de** pass NW Spain
54 G9 **Pajárito** Boyacá, C Colombia
54 G4 **Pajaro** La Guajira, S Colombia
Pakanbaru see Pekanbaru
55 Q10 **Pakaraima Mountains** var. Serra Pacaraim, Sierra Pacaraima. ▲ N South America
167 P10 **Pak Chong** Nakhon Ratchasima, C Thailand
123 V8 **Pakhachi** Koryakskiy Avtonomnyy Okrug, E Russian Federation
Pakhna see Páchna
147 O11 **Pakhtakor** Jizzakh Wiloyati, C Uzbekistan
189 U16 **Pakin Atoll** atoll Caroline Islands, E Micronesia
149 Q12 **Pakistan** off. Islamic Republic of Pakistan, var. Islami Jamhuriya e Pakistan. ◆ republic S Asia
Pakistan, Islami Jamhuriya e see Pakistan
167 P8 **Pak Lay** var. Muang Pak Lay. Xaignabouli, C Laos
Paknam see Samut Prakan
166 L5 **Pakokku** Magwe, C Myanmar
110 I10 **Pakość** Ger. Pakosch. Kujawski-pomorskie, C Poland
Pakosch see Pakość
149 V10 **Pākpattan** Punjab, E Pakistan
167 O15 **Pak Phanang** var. Ban Pak Phanang. Nakhon Si Thammarat, SW Thailand
112 G9 **Pakrac** Hung. Pakrácz. Požega-Slavonija, NE Croatia
Pakrácz see Pakrac
118 F11 **Pakruojis** Pakruojis, N Lithuania
111 J24 **Paks** Tolna, S Hungary
Pak Sane see Pakxan
Paksé see Pakxé
167 Q10 **Pak Thong Chai** Nakhon Ratchasima, C Thailand
149 R6 **Paktīā** ◈ province SE Afghanistan

◆ Country ● Country Capital ◇ Dependent Territory ○ Dependent Territory Capital ◈ Administrative Region ✕ International Airport ▲ Mountain ▲ Mountain Range ⛰ Volcano ≈ River ◎ Lake ⊞ Reservoir

149 Q7 **Paktīkā** ◈ *province* SE Afghanistan
171 N12 **Pakuli** Sulawesi, C Indonesia
81 F17 **Pakwach** NW Uganda
167 R8 **Pakxan** *var.* Muang Pakxan, Pak Sane. Bolikhamxai, C Laos
167 S10 **Pakxé** *var.* Paksé. Champasak, S Laos
78 G12 **Pala** Mayo-Kébbi, SW Chad
61 A17 **Palacios** Santa Fe, C Argentina
25 V13 **Palacios** Texas, SW USA
105 X5 **Palafrugell** Cataluña, NE Spain
107 L24 **Palagonia** Sicilia, Italy, C Mediterranean Sea
113 E17 **Palagruža** *It.* Pelagosa. *island* SW Croatia
115 G20 **Palaiá Epídavros** Pelopónnisos, S Greece
121 P3 **Palaichóri** *var.* Palekhori. C Cyprus
115 H25 **Palaiochóra** Kríti, Greece, E Mediterranean Sea
115 A15 **Palaiolastrítsa** *religious building* Kérkyra, Iónioi Nísoi, Greece, C Mediterranean Sea
115 J19 **Palaiópoli** Ándros, Kykládes, Greece, Aegean Sea
103 N5 **Palaiseau** Essonne, N France
Palakkad *see* Pālghāt
154 N11 **Pāla Laharha** Orissa, E India
83 G19 **Palamakoloi** Ghanzi, C Botswana
115 E16 **Palamás** Thessalía, C Greece
105 X5 **Palamós** Cataluña, NE Spain
118 J5 **Palamuse** *Ger.* Sankt-Bartholomäi. Jõgevamaa, E Estonia
183 Q14 **Palana** Tasmania, SE Australia
123 U9 **Palana** Koryakskiy Avtonomnyy Okrug, E Russian Federation
118 C11 **Palanga** *Ger.* Polangen. Palanga, NW Lithuania
143 V10 **Palangān, Kūh-e** ▲ E Iran
Palangkaraja *see* Palangkaraya
169 T12 **Palangkaraya** *prev.* Palangkaraja. Borneo, C Indonesia
155 H22 **Palani** Tamil Nādu, SE India
Palanka *see* Bačka Palanka
154 D9 **Pālanpur** Gujarāt, W India
Palantia *see* Palencia
83 I19 **Palapye** Central, SE Botswana
155 J19 **Pālār** ≈ SE India
104 H3 **Palas de Rei** Galicia, NW Spain
123 T9 **Palatka** Magadanskaya Oblast', E Russian Federation
23 W10 **Palatka** Florida, SE USA
188 B9 **Palau** *var.* Belau. ◆ *republic* W Pacific Ocean
131 Y14 **Palau Islands** *var.* Palau. *island group* N Palau
192 G16 **Palauli Bay** *bay* Savai'i, Samoa, C Pacific Ocean
167 N11 **Palaw** Tenasserim, S Myanmar
170 M6 **Palawan** *island* W Philippines
171 N6 **Palawan Passage** *passage* W Philippines
192 E7 **Palawan Trough** *undersea feature* S South China Sea
155 H23 **Pālayankottai** Tamil Nādu, SE India
107 L25 **Palazzola Acreide** *anc.* Acrae. Sicilia, Italy, C Mediterranean Sea
118 G3 **Paldiski** *prev.* Baltiski, *Eng.* Baltic Port, *Ger.* Baltischport. Harjumaa, NW Estonia
112 I13 **Pale** Republika Srpska, E Bosnia and Herzegovina
Palekhori *see* Palaichóri
168 L13 **Palembang** Sumatera, W Indonesia
63 G18 **Palena** Los Lagos, S Chile
63 G18 **Palena, Río** ≈ S Chile
104 M5 **Palencia** *anc.* Palantia, Pallantia. Castilla-León, NW Spain
104 M3 **Palencia** ◈ *province* Castilla-León, N Spain
35 X15 **Palen Dry Lake** ◎ California, W USA
41 V15 **Palenque** Chiapas, SE Mexico
41 V15 **Palenque** *var.* Ruinas de Palenque. *ruins* Chiapas, SE Mexico
45 O9 **Palenque, Punta** *headland* S Dominican Republic
Palenque, Ruinas de *see* Palenque
Palerme *see* Palermo
107 I23 **Palermo** *Fr.* Palerme; *anc.* Panhormus, Panormus. Sicilia, Italy, C Mediterranean Sea
25 V8 **Palestine** Texas, SW USA
25 V7 **Palestine, Lake** ⊟ Texas, SW USA
107 I15 **Palestrina** Lazio, C Italy
166 K5 **Paletwa** Chin State, W Myanmar
155 G21 **Pālghāt** *var.* Palakkad; *prev.* Pulicat. Kerala, SW India
152 F13 **Pāli** Rājasthān, N India
167 N16 **Palian** Trang, SW Thailand
189 O12 **Palikir** ● (Micronesia) Pohnpei, E Micronesia
Palimé *see* Kpalimé
107 L19 **Palinuro, Capo** *headland* S Italy
115 H15 **Palioúri, Akrotírio** *var.* Akra Kanestron. *headland* N Greece
33 R14 **Palisades Reservoir** ⊟ Idaho, NW USA
99 J23 **Paliseul** Luxembourg, SE Belgium
154 C11 **Pālitāna** Gujarāt, W India
118 F4 **Palivere** Läänemaa, W Estonia
41 V14 **Palizada** Campeche, SE Mexico
93 L18 **Pälkäne** Länsi-Suomi, W Finland
155 J22 **Palk Strait** *strait* India/Sri Lanka
155 J23 **Pallai** Northern Province, NW Sri Lanka
Pallantia *see* Palencia
106 C6 **Pallanza** Piemonte, NE Italy
129 Q9 **Pallasovka** Volgogradskaya Oblast', SW Russian Federation
Pallene/Pallíni *see* Kassándra
185 L15 **Palliser Bay** *bay* North Island, NZ
185 L15 **Palliser, Cape** *headland* North Island, NZ
191 U9 **Palliser, Îles** *island group* Îles Tuamotu, C French Polynesia
105 X9 **Palma** *var.* Palma de Mallorca. Mallorca, Spain, W Mediterranean Sea
105 X9 **Palma** × Mallorca, Spain, W Mediterranean Sea
82 Q12 **Palma** Cabo Delgado, N Mozambique
105 X10 **Palma, Badia de** *bay* Mallorca, Spain, W Mediterranean Sea
104 L13 **Palma del Río** Andalucía, S Spain
Palma de Mallorca *see* Palma
107 J25 **Palma di Montechiaro** Sicilia, Italy, C Mediterranean Sea
106 J7 **Palmanova** Friuli-Venezia Giulia, NE Italy
54 J7 **Palmarito** Apure, C Venezuela
43 N15 **Palmar Sur** Puntarenas, SE Costa Rica
60 I12 **Palmas** Paraná, S Brazil
59 K16 **Palmas** *var.* Palmas do Tocantins. Tocantins, C Brazil
Palmas do Tocantins *see* Palmas
54 D11 **Palmaseca** × (Cali) Valle del Cauca, SW Colombia
107 B21 **Palmas, Golfo di** *gulf* Sardegna, Italy, C Mediterranean Sea
44 I7 **Palma Soriano** Santiago de Cuba, E Cuba
23 Y12 **Palm Bay** Florida, SE USA
35 T14 **Palmdale** California, W USA
61 H14 **Palmeira das Missões** Rio Grande do Sul, S Brazil
82 A11 **Palmeirinhas, Ponta das** *headland* NW Angola
39 R11 **Palmer** Alaska, USA
19 N11 **Palmer** Massachusetts, NE USA
25 U7 **Palmer** Texas, SW USA
194 H4 **Palmer** *US research station* Antarctica
15 R11 **Palmer** ≈ Quebec, SE Canada
37 T5 **Palmer Lake** Colorado, C USA
194 J6 **Palmer Land** *physical region* Antarctica
14 F15 **Palmerston** Ontario, SE Canada
185 F22 **Palmerston** Otago, South Island, NZ
190 K15 **Palmerston** *island* S Cook Islands
Palmerston *see* Darwin
184 M12 **Palmerston North** Manawatu-Wanganui, North Island, NZ
76 L18 **Palmés, Cap des** *headland* SW Ivory Coast
23 V13 **Palmetto** Florida, SE USA
Palmetto State *see* South Carolina
107 M22 **Palmi** Calabria, SW Italy
54 D11 **Palmira** Valle del Cauca, W Colombia
56 F8 **Palmira, Río** ≈ N Peru
61 D19 **Palmitas** Soriano, SW Uruguay
Palmnicken *see* Yantarnyy
35 V15 **Palm Springs** California, W USA
27 V2 **Palmyra** Missouri, C USA
18 G10 **Palmyra** New York, NE USA
18 G15 **Palmyra** Pennsylvania, NE USA
21 V5 **Palmyra** Virginia, NE USA
Palmyra *see* Tudmur
192 L7 **Palmyra Atoll** ◇ *US privately owned unincorporated territory* C Pacific Ocean
154 P12 **Palmyras Point** *headland* E India
35 N9 **Palo Alto** California, W USA
25 O1 **Palo Duro Creek** ≈ Texas, SW USA
Paloe *see* Palu
Paloe *see* Denpasar, Bali, C Indonesia
168 L9 **Paloh** Johor, Peninsular Malaysia
80 F12 **Paloich** Upper Nile, SE Sudan
40 I3 **Palomas** Chihuahua, N Mexico
107 I15 **Palombara Sabina** Lazio, C Italy
105 S13 **Palos, Cabo de** *headland* SE Spain
104 I14 **Palos de la Frontera** Andalucía, S Spain
60 G11 **Palotina** Paraná, S Brazil
32 M9 **Palouse** Washington, NW USA
32 L9 **Palouse River** ≈ Washington, NW USA
35 Y16 **Palo Verde** California, W USA
57 E16 **Palpa** Ica, W Peru
95 M16 **Pålsboda** Örebro, C Sweden
93 M15 **Paltamo** Oulu, C Finland
171 N12 **Palu** *prev.* Paloe. Sulawesi, C Indonesia
137 P14 **Palu** Elâzığ, E Turkey
152 I11 **Palwal** Haryāna, N India
123 U6 **Palyavaam** ≈ NE Russian Federation
77 Q13 **Pama** SE Burkina
172 J14 **Pamandzi** × (Mamoudzou) Petite-Terre, E Mayotte
Pamangkat *see* Pemangkat
143 R11 **Pā Mazār** Kermān, C Iran
83 N19 **Pambarra** Inhambane, SE Mozambique
171 X12 **Pamdai** Irian Jaya, E Indonesia
103 N16 **Pamiers** Ariège, S France
147 T14 **Pamir** *var.* Daryā-ye Pāmīr, *Taj.* Dar"yoi Pomir. ≈ Afghanistan/Tajikistan *see also* Pāmīr, Daryā-ye
Pamir/Pāmīr, Daryā-ye *see* Pamirs
149 U1 **Pāmīr, Daryā-ye** *var.* Pamir, *Taj.* Dar"yoi Pomir. ≈ Afghanistan/Tajikistan *see also* Pamir
Pāmīr-e Khord *see* Little Pamir
131 Q8 **Pamirs** *Pash.* Daryā-ye Pāmīr, *Rus.* Pamir. ▲▲ C Asia
Pāmiut *see* Paamiut
21 X10 **Pamlico River** ≈ North Carolina, SE USA
21 Y10 **Pamlico Sound** *sound* North Carolina, SE USA
25 O2 **Pampa** Texas, SW USA
Pampa Aullagas, Lago *see* Poopó, Lago
61 B21 **Pampa Húmeda** *grassland* E Argentina
56 A10 **Pampa las Salinas** *salt lake* NW Peru
57 F15 **Pampas** Huancavelica, C Peru
62 K13 **Pampas** *plain* C Argentina
55 O4 **Pampatar** Nueva Esparta, NE Venezuela
Pampeluna *see* Pamplona
104 H8 **Pampilhosa da Serra** *var.* Pampilhosa de Serra. Coimbra, N Portugal
173 Y15 **Pamplemousses** N Mauritius
54 G7 **Pamplona** Norte de Santander, N Colombia
105 Q3 **Pamplona** *Basq.* Iruña; *prev.* Pampeluna, *anc.* Pompaelo. Navarra, N Spain
114 I11 **Pamporovo** *prev.* Vasil Kolarov. Smolyan, S Bulgaria
136 D15 **Pamukkale** Denizli, W Turkey
21 W5 **Pamunkey River** ≈ Virginia, NE USA
152 K5 **Pamzal** Jammu and Kashmir, NW India
30 L14 **Pana** Illinois, N USA
41 Y11 **Panabá** Yucatán, SE Mexico
35 Y8 **Panaca** Nevada, W USA
115 E19 **Panachaikó** ▲▲ S Greece
14 F11 **Panache Lake** ◎ Ontario, S Canada
114 I10 **Panagyurishte** Pazardzhik, C Bulgaria
168 M16 **Panaitan, Pulau** *island* S Indonesia
115 D18 **Panaitolikó** ▲▲ C Greece
155 E17 **Panaji** *var.* Pangim, Panjim, New Goa. Goa, W India
43 T14 **Panama** *off.* Republic of Panama. ◆ *republic* Central America
43 T15 **Panamá** *var.* Ciudad de Panamá, *Eng.* Panama City. ● (Panama) Panamá, C Panama
43 U14 **Panamá** *off.* Provincia de Panamá. ◈ *province* E Panama
43 U15 **Panamá, Bahía de** *bay* N Gulf of Panama
193 T7 **Panama Basin** *undersea feature* E Pacific Ocean
43 T15 **Panama Canal** *canal* E Panama
23 R9 **Panama City** Florida, SE USA
43 T14 **Panama City** × Panamá, C Panama
Panama City *see* Panamá
23 Q9 **Panama City Beach** Florida, SE USA
43 T17 **Panamá, Golfo de** *var.* Gulf of Panama. *gulf* S Panama
Panama, Gulf of *see* Panamá, Golfo de
Panama, Isthmus of *see* Panamá, Istmo de
43 T15 **Panamá, Istmo de** *Eng.* Isthmus of Panama; *prev.* Isthmus of Darien. *isthmus* E Panama
35 U11 **Panamint Range** ▲▲ California, W USA
107 L22 **Panarea, Isola** *island* Isole Eolie, S Italy
106 G9 **Panaro** ≈ N Italy
171 P6 **Panay Gulf** *gulf* C Philippines
171 P5 **Panay Island** *island* C Philippines
35 W7 **Pancake Range** ▲▲ Nevada, W USA
112 M11 **Pančevo** *Ger.* Pantschowa, *Hung.* Pancsova. Serbia, N Yugoslavia
113 M15 **Pančićev Vrh** ▲ SW Yugoslavia
116 L12 **Panciu** Vrancea, E Romania
116 F10 **Pâncota** *Hung.* Pankota; *prev.* Pincota. Arad, W Romania
Pancsova *see* Pančevo
83 N20 **Panda** Inhambane, SE Mozambique
171 X12 **Pandaidori, Kepulauan** *island group* E Indonesia
25 N11 **Pandale** Texas, SW USA
169 P12 **Pandang Tikar, Pulau** *island* N Indonesia
61 F20 **Pan de Azúcar** Maldonado, S Uruguay
118 H11 **Pandėlys** Rokiškis, NE Lithuania
155 F15 **Pandharpur** Mahārāshtra, W India
182 J1 **Pandie Pandie** South Australia
171 O12 **Pandiri** Sulawesi, C Indonesia
61 F20 **Pando** Canelones, S Uruguay
57 J14 **Pando** ◈ *department* N Bolivia
192 K9 **Pandora Bank** *undersea feature* W Pacific Ocean
95 G20 **Pandrup** Nordjylland, N Denmark
153 V12 **Pandu** Assam, NE India
79 J15 **Pandu** Equateur, NW Dem. Rep. Congo (Zaire)
Paneas *see* Bāniyās
59 F15 **Panelas** Mato Grosso, W Brazil
118 G12 **Panevėžys** Panevėžys, C Lithuania
Panfilov *see* Zharkent
129 N9 **Panfilovo** Volgogradskaya Oblast', SW Russian Federation
79 N17 **Panga** Orientale, N Dem. Rep. Congo (Zaire)
193 Y15 **Pangai** Lifuka, C Tonga
114 H13 **Pangaío** ▲▲ N Greece
79 G20 **Pangala** Le Pool, S Congo
81 J22 **Pangani** Tanga, E Tanzania
81 I21 **Pangani** ≈ NE Tanzania
186 K8 **Panggoe** Choiseul Island, NW Solomon Islands
79 N20 **Pangi** Maniema, E Dem. Rep. Congo (Zaire)
Pangim *see* Panaji
168 H8 **Pangkalanbrandan** Sumatera, W Indonesia
Pangkalanbuun *see* Pangkalanbun
169 R13 **Pangkalanbun** *var.* Pangkalanbuun. Borneo, C Indonesia
169 N12 **Pangkalpinang** Pulau Bangka, W Indonesia
11 U17 **Pangman** Saskatchewan, S Canada
Pang-Nga *see* Phang-Nga
9 S6 **Pangnirtung** Baffin Island, Nunavut, NE Canada
152 K6 **Pangong Tso** *var.* Bangong Co. ◎ China/India *see also* Bangong Co
36 K7 **Panguitch** Utah, W USA
186 J7 **Panguna** Bougainville Island, NE PNG
171 N8 **Pangutaran Group** *island group* Sulu Archipelago, SW Philippines
25 N2 **Panhandle** Texas, SW USA
Panhormus *see* Palermo
171 W14 **Paniai, Danau** ◎ Irian Jaya, E Indonesia
79 L21 **Pania-Mutombo** Kasai Oriental, C Dem. Rep. Congo (Zaire)
Panicherevo *see* Dolno Panicherevo
187 P16 **Panié, Mont** ▲ C New Caledonia
152 I10 **Pānīpat** Haryāna, N India
147 Q14 **Panj** *Rus.* Pyandzh; *prev.* Kirovabad. SW Tajikistan
147 P15 **Panj** *Rus.* Pyandzh. ≈ Afghanistan/Tajikistan
149 O5 **Panjāb** Bāmīān, C Afghanistan
147 O12 **Panjakent** *Rus.* Pendzhikent. W Tajikistan
148 L14 **Panjgūr** Baluchistān, SW Pakistan
Panjim *see* Panaji
163 U12 **Panjin** Liaoning, NE China
147 P14 **Panji Poyon** *Rus.* Nizhniy Pyandzh. SW Tajikistan
149 Q4 **Panjshīr** ≈ E Afghanistan
Pankota *see* Pâncota
77 W14 **Pankshin** Plateau, C Nigeria
163 Y10 **Pan Ling** ▲▲ N China
Panlong Jiang *see* Lô, Sông
154 J9 **Panna** Madhya Pradesh, C India
99 M16 **Panningen** Limburg, SE Netherlands
149 R13 **Pāno Āqil** Sind, SE Pakistan
121 P3 **Páno Léfkara** S Cyprus
121 O3 **Páno Panagiá** *var.* Pano Panayia. W Cyprus
Pano Panayia *see* Páno Panagiá
Panopolis *see* Akhmīm
29 U14 **Panora** Iowa, C USA
60 I8 **Panorama** São Paulo, S Brazil
115 I24 **Pánormos** Kríti, Greece, E Mediterranean Sea
Panormus *see* Palermo
163 W11 **Panshi** Jilin, NE China
59 H19 **Pantanal** *var.* Pantanalmato-Grossense. *swamp* SW Brazil
Pantanalmato-Grossense *see* Pantanal
61 H16 **Pântano Grande** Rio Grande do Sul, S Brazil
171 Q16 **Pantar, Pulau** *island* Kepulauan Alor, S Indonesia
21 X9 **Pantego** North Carolina, SE USA
107 G25 **Pantelleria** *anc.* Cossyra, Cosyra. Sicilia, Italy, C Mediterranean Sea
107 G25 **Pantelleria, Isola di** *island* SW Italy
Pante Macassar/Pante Makassar *see* Pante Makasar
171 Q16 **Pante Makasar** *var.* Pante Macassar, Pante Makassar. W East Timor
152 K10 **Pantnagar** Uttar Pradesh, N India
115 A15 **Pantokrátoras** ▲ Kérkyra, Iónioi Nísoi, Greece, C Mediterranean Sea
Pantschowa *see* Pančevo
41 P11 **Pánuco** Veracruz-Llave, E Mexico
41 P11 **Pánuco, Río** ≈ C Mexico
160 I12 **Panxian** Guizhou, S China
168 I10 **Panyabungan** Sumatera, N Indonesia
77 W14 **Panyam** Plateau, C Nigeria
157 N13 **Panzhihua** *prev.* Dukou, Tu-k'ou. Sichuan, C China
79 I22 **Panzi** Bandundu, SW Dem. Rep. Congo (Zaire)
42 E5 **Panzós** Alta Verapaz, E Guatemala
Pao-chi/Paoki *see* Baoji
Pao-king *see* Shaoyang
107 N20 **Paola** Calabria, SW Italy
121 P16 **Paola** E Malta
27 R5 **Paola** Kansas, C USA
31 O15 **Paoli** Indiana, N USA
187 R14 **Paonangisu** Éfaté, C Vanuatu
171 S13 **Paoni** *var.* Pauni. Pulau Seram, E Indonesia
37 Q5 **Paonia** Colorado, C USA
191 O7 **Paopao** Moorea, W French Polynesia
Pao-shan *see* Baoshan
Pao-ting *see* Baoding
Pao-t'ou/Paotow *see* Baotou
79 H14 **Paoua** Ouham-Pendé, W Central African Republic
Pap *see* Pop
111 H23 **Pápa** Veszprém, W Hungary
42 J12 **Papagayo, Golfo de** *gulf* NW Costa Rica
38 H11 **Papaikou** *var.* Pāpa'ikou. Hawaii, USA, C Pacific Ocean
41 R15 **Papaloapan, Río** ≈ S Mexico
184 L6 **Papakura** Auckland, North Island, NZ
41 Q13 **Papantla** *var.* Papantla de Olarte. Veracruz-Llave, E Mexico
Papantla de Olarte *see* Papantla
191 P8 **Papara** Tahiti, W French Polynesia
184 K4 **Paparoa** Northland, North Island, NZ
185 G16 **Paparoa Range** ▲▲ South Island, NZ
115 K20 **Pápas, Akrotírio** *headland* Ikaría, Dodekánisos, Greece, Aegean Sea
96 L2 **Papa Stour** *island* NE Scotland, UK
184 L6 **Papatoetoe** Auckland, North Island, NZ
185 E25 **Papatowai** Otago, South Island, NZ
96 K4 **Papa Westray** *island* NE Scotland, UK
191 T10 **Papeete** ○ (French Polynesia) Tahiti, W French Polynesia
100 F11 **Papenburg** Niedersachsen, NW Germany
98 H13 **Papendrecht** Zuid-Holland, SW Netherlands
191 Q7 **Papenoo** Tahiti, W French Polynesia
191 Q7 **Papenoo Rivière** ≈ Tahiti, W French Polynesia
191 N7 **Papetoai** Moorea, W French Polynesia
92 L3 **Papey** *island* E Iceland
Paphos *see* Páfos
40 H5 **Papigochic, Río** ≈ NW Mexico
118 E10 **Papilė** Akmenė, NW Lithuania
29 S15 **Papillion** Nebraska, C USA
15 T5 **Papinachois** ≈ Quebec, SE Canada
186 C9 **Papua, Gulf of** *gulf* S PNG
192 H8 **Papua New Guinea** *off.* Independent State of Papua New Guinea; *prev.* Territory of Papua and New Guinea, *abbrev.* PNG. ◆ *commonwealth republic* NW Melanesia
192 H8 **Papua Plateau** *undersea feature* N Coral Sea
112 G9 **Papuk** ▲▲ NE Croatia
167 N8 **Papun** Karen State, S Myanmar
42 L14 **Paquera** Puntarenas, W Costa Rica
55 V9 **Para** ◈ *district* N Surinam
58 I13 **Pará** *off.* Estado do Pará. ◈ *state* NE Brazil
Pará *see* Belém
180 I8 **Paraburdoo** Western Australia
57 E16 **Paracas, Península de** *peninsula* W Peru
59 L19 **Paracatu** Minas Gerais, NE Brazil
192 E6 **Paracel Islands** ◇ *disputed territory* SE Asia
182 I6 **Parachilna** South Australia
149 R6 **Pārachinār** North-West Frontier Province, NW Pakistan
112 N13 **Paraćin** Serbia, C Yugoslavia
14 K8 **Paradis** Quebec, SE Canada
39 N11 **Paradise** *var.* Paradise Hill. Alaska, USA
35 O5 **Paradise** California, W USA
35 X11 **Paradise** Nevada, W USA
Paradise Hill *see* Paradise
37 R11 **Paradise Hills** New Mexico, SW USA
Paradise of the Pacific *see* Hawaii
36 L13 **Paradise Valley** Arizona, SW USA
35 T2 **Paradise Valley** Nevada, W USA
115 O22 **Paradísi** × (Ródos) Ródos, Dodekánisos, Greece, Aegean Sea
154 P12 **Pārādwīp** Orissa, E India
Paraetonium *see* Maṭrūḥ
117 R4 **Parafiyivka** Chernihivs'ka Oblast', N Ukraine
36 K7 **Paragonah** Utah, W USA
27 X9 **Paragould** Arkansas, C USA
47 X8 **Paraguaçu** *var.* Paraguassú. ≈ E Brazil
60 J9 **Paraguaçu Paulista** São Paulo, S Brazil
54 H4 **Paraguaipoa** Zulia, NW Venezuela
62 O6 **Paraguarí** Paraguarí, S Paraguay
62 O7 **Paraguarí** *off.* Departamento de Paraguarí. ◈ *department* S Paraguay
55 O8 **Paragua, Río** ≈ SE Venezuela
57 O16 **Paraguá, Río** ≈ NE Bolivia
Paraguassú *see* Paraguaçu
62 N5 **Paraguay** ◆ *republic* C South America
47 U10 **Paraguay** *var.* Río Paraguay. ≈ C South America
Parahiba/Parahyba *see* Paraíba
59 P15 **Paraíba** *off.* Estado da Paraíba; *prev.* Parahiba, Parahyba. ◈ *state* E Brazil
Paraíba *see* João Pessoa
60 P9 **Paraíba do Sul, Rio** ≈ SE Brazil
Parainen *see* Pargas
43 N14 **Paraíso** Cartago, C Costa Rica
41 U14 **Paraíso** Tabasco, SE Mexico
57 O17 **Paraiso, Río** ≈ E Bolivia
Parajd *see* Praid
77 S14 **Parakou** C Benin
121 Q2 **Paralímni** E Cyprus
115 G18 **Paralímni, Límni** ◎ C Greece
55 W8 **Paramaribo** ● (Surinam) Paramaribo, N Surinam
55 W9 **Paramaribo** ◈ *district* N Surinam
55 W9 **Paramaribo** × Paramaribo, N Surinam
Paramithiá *see* Paramythiá
56 C13 **Paramonga** Lima, W Peru
123 V12 **Paramushir, Ostrov** *island* SE Russian Federation
115 C16 **Paramythiá** *var.* Paramithiá. Ípeiros, W Greece
62 M10 **Paraná** Entre Ríos, E Argentina
60 H11 **Paraná** *off.* Estado do Paraná. ◈ *state* S Brazil
47 U11 **Paraná** *var.* Alto Paraná. ≈ C South America
60 K12 **Paranaguá** Paraná, S Brazil
59 J20 **Paranaíba, Rio** ≈ E Brazil
61 C19 **Paraná Ibicuy, Río** ≈ E Argentina
59 H15 **Paranaíta** Mato Grosso, W Brazil
60 H9 **Paranapanema, Rio** ≈ S Brazil
60 K11 **Paranapiacaba, Serra do** ▲▲ S Brazil
60 H9 **Paranavaí** Paraná, S Brazil
143 N5 **Parandak** Markazi, W Iran
114 I12 **Paranéstio** Anatolikí Makedonía kai Thráki, NE Greece
191 W11 **Paraoa** *atoll* Îles Tuamotu, C French Polynesia
184 L13 **Paraparaumu** Wellington, North Island, NZ
57 N20 **Parapeti, Río** ≈ SE Bolivia
54 L10 **Paraque, Cerro** ▲ W Venezuela
154 I11 **Parasiya** Madhya Pradesh, C India
115 M23 **Paraspóri, Akrotírio** *headland* Kárpathos, SE Greece
60 O10 **Parati** Rio de Janeiro, SE Brazil
59 K14 **Parauapebas** Pará, N Brazil
103 Q10 **Paray-le-Monial** Saône-et-Loire, C France
Parbatsar *see* Parvatsar
154 G13 **Parbhani** Mahārāshtra, C India
100 L10 **Parchim** Mecklenburg-Vorpommern, N Germany
Parchwitz *see* Prochowice
110 P13 **Parczew** Lubelskie, E Poland
60 L8 **Pardo, Rio** ≈ S Brazil
111 E16 **Pardubice** *Ger.* Pardubitz. Pardubický Kraj, C Czech Republic
111 E17 **Pardubický Kraj** ◈ region C Czech Republic
Pardubitz *see* Pardubice
119 F16 **Parechcha** *Pol.* Porzecze, *Rus.* Porech'ye. Hrodzyenskaya Voblasts', W Belarus
59 F17 **Parecis, Chapada dos** *var.* Serra dos Parecis. ▲▲ W Brazil
Parecis, Serra dos *see* Parecis, Chapada dos
104 M4 **Paredes de Nava** Castilla-León, N Spain
189 U12 **Parem** *island* Chuuk, C Micronesia
189 O12 **Parem Island** *island* E Micronesia
184 I1 **Parengarenga Harbour** *inlet* North Island, NZ
15 N8 **Parent** Quebec, SE Canada
102 J14 **Parentis-en-Born** Landes, SW France
Parenzo *see* Poreč
185 G20 **Pareora** Canterbury, South Island, NZ
171 N14 **Parepare** Sulawesi, C Indonesia
115 B16 **Párga** Ípeiros, W Greece
93 K20 **Pargas** *Swe.* Parainen. Länsi-Suomi, W Finland
64 O5 **Pargo, Ponta do** *headland* Madeira, Portugal, NE Atlantic Ocean
Paria, Golfo de *see* Paria, Gulf of
55 N6 **Pariaguán** Anzoátegui, NE Venezuela
45 X17 **Paria, Gulf of** *var.* Golfo de Paria. *gulf* Trinidad and Tobago/Venezuela
57 I15 **Pariamanu, Río** ≈ E Peru
36 L8 **Paria River** ≈ Utah, W USA
Parichi *see* Parychy
40 M14 **Paricutín, Volcán** ※ C Mexico
43 P16 **Parida, Isla** *island* SW Panama
55 T8 **Parika** NE Guyana
93 O18 **Parikkala** Etelä-Suomi, S Finland
58 E10 **Parima, Serra** *var.* Sierra Parima. ▲▲ Brazil/Venezuela *see also* Parima, Sierra
55 N11 **Parima, Sierra** *var.* Serra Parima. ▲▲ Brazil/Venezuela *see also* Parima, Serra
57 F17 **Parinacochas, Laguna** ◎ SW Peru
56 A9 **Pariñas, Punta** *headland* NW Peru
58 H12 **Parintins** Amazonas, N Brazil
103 O5 **Paris** *anc.* Lutetia, Lutetia Parisiorum, Parisii. ● (France) Paris, N France
191 Y2 **Paris** Kiritimati, E Kiribati
27 S11 **Paris** Arkansas, C USA
33 S16 **Paris** Idaho, NW USA
31 N14 **Paris** Illinois, N USA
20 M5 **Paris** Kentucky, S USA
27 V3 **Paris** Missouri, C USA
20 H8 **Paris** Tennessee, S USA
25 V5 **Paris** Texas, SW USA
Parisii *see* Paris
43 S16 **Parita** Herrera, S Panama
43 S16 **Parita, Bahía de** *bay* S Panama
Parkan/Párkány *see* Štúrovo
93 K18 **Parkano** Länsi-Suomi, W Finland
27 N6 **Park City** Kansas, C USA
36 L3 **Park City** Utah, W USA
36 I12 **Parker** Arizona, SW USA
23 R9 **Parker** Florida, SE USA
29 R11 **Parker** South Dakota, N USA
35 Z14 **Parker Dam** California, W USA
29 W13 **Parkersburg** Iowa, C USA
21 Q3 **Parkersburg** West Virginia, NE USA
29 T7 **Parkers Prairie** Minnesota, N USA
171 P8 **Parker Volcano** ※ Mindanao, S Philippines
181 W13 **Parkes** New South Wales, SE Australia
30 K4 **Park Falls** Wisconsin, N USA
Parkhar *see* Farkhor
14 E16 **Parkhill** Ontario, S Canada
29 T5 **Park Rapids** Minnesota, N USA
29 Q3 **Park River** North Dakota, N USA
29 Q11 **Parkston** South Dakota, N USA
10 L17 **Parksville** Vancouver Island, British Columbia, SW Canada
37 S3 **Parkview Mountain** ▲ Colorado, C USA
105 N8 **Parla** Madrid, C Spain
29 S8 **Parle, Lac qui** ⊟ Minnesota, N USA
115 F20 **Parlía Tyroú** Pelopónnisos, S Greece
155 G14 **Parli Vaijnāth** Mahārāshtra, C India
106 F9 **Parma** Emilia-Romagna, N Italy
31 T11 **Parma** Ohio, N USA
Parnahyba *see* Parnaíba

58 N13 **Parnaíba** *var.* Parnahyba. Piauí, E Brazil
65 J14 **Parnaíba Ridge** *undersea feature* C Atlantic Ocean
58 N13 **Parnaíba, Rio** ≈ NE Brazil
115 F18 **Parnassós** ▲ C Greece
185 J17 **Parnassus** Canterbury, South Island, NZ
182 H10 **Parndana** South Australia
115 H19 **Párnitha** ▲▲ C Greece
115 F21 **Párnon** ▲▲ S Greece
118 G5 **Pärnu** *Ger.* Pernau, *Latv.* Pērnava; *prev. Rus.* Pernov. Pärnumaa, SW Estonia
118 G6 **Pärnu** *var.* Parnu Jõgi, *Ger.* Pernau. ≈ SW Estonia
118 G5 **Pärnu-Jaagupi** *Ger.* Sankt-Jakobi. Pärnumaa, SW Estonia
Parnu Jõgi *see* Pärnu
118 G5 **Pärnu Laht** *Ger.* Pernauer Bucht. *bay* SW Estonia
118 F5 **Pärnumaa** *off.* Pärnu Maakond. ◆ *province* SW Estonia
153 T11 **Paro** W Bhutan
153 T11 **Paro** × (Thimphu) W Bhutan
185 G17 **Paroa** West Coast, South Island, NZ
163 X14 **P'aro-ho** *var.* Hwach'ŏn-chŏsuji. ⊡ N South Korea
183 N6 **Paroo River** *seasonal river* New South Wales/Queensland, SE Australia
Paropamisus Range *see* Sefīdkūh, Selseleh-ye
115 J21 **Páros** Páros, Kykládes, Greece, Aegean Sea
115 J21 **Páros** *island* Kykládes, Greece, Aegean Sea
36 K7 **Parowan** Utah, W USA
103 U13 **Parpaillon** ▲▲ SE France
108 I9 **Parpan** Graubünden, S Switzerland
62 G13 **Parral** Maule, C Chile
Parral *see* Hidalgo del Parral
183 T9 **Parramatta** New South Wales, SE Australia
21 Y6 **Parramore Island** *island* Virginia, NE USA
40 M8 **Parras** *var.* Parras de la Fuente. Coahuila de Zaragoza, NE Mexico
Parras de la Fuente *see* Parras
42 M14 **Parrita** Puntarenas, S Costa Rica
8 L5 **Parry Channel** *channel* N Canada
14 G13 **Parry Island** *island* Ontario, S Canada
8 M4 **Parry Islands** *island group* Nunavut, NW Canada
14 G12 **Parry Sound** Ontario, S Canada
110 F7 **Parsęta** *Ger.* Persante. ≈ NW Poland
28 L3 **Parshall** North Dakota, N USA
27 Q7 **Parsons** Kansas, C USA
20 H9 **Parsons** Tennessee, S USA
21 T3 **Parsons** West Virginia, NE USA
Parsonstown *see* Birr
100 P11 **Parsteiner See** ◎ NE Germany
107 I24 **Partanna** Sicilia, Italy, C Mediterranean Sea
108 J8 **Partenen** Graubünden, E Switzerland
102 K9 **Parthenay** Deux-Sèvres, W France
95 J19 **Partille** Västra Götaland, S Sweden
107 I23 **Partinico** Sicilia, Italy, C Mediterranean Sea
111 I20 **Partizánske** *prev.* Šimonovany; *Hung.* Simony. Trenčiansky Kraj, W Slovakia
58 H11 **Paru de Oeste, Rio** ≈ N Brazil
182 K9 **Paruna** South Australia
58 I11 **Paru, Rio** ≈ N Brazil
Parvān *see* Parwān
155 M14 **Pārvatipuram** Andhra Pradesh, E India
152 G12 **Parvatsar** *prev.* Parbatsar. Rājasthān, N India
149 Q5 **Parwān** *Per.* Parvān. ◆ *province* E Afghanistan
158 I15 **Paryang** Xizang Zizhiqu, W China
119 M18 **Parychy** *Rus.* Parichi. Homyel'skaya Voblasts', SE Belarus
83 J21 **Parys** Free State, C South Africa
35 T15 **Pasadena** California, W USA
25 W11 **Pasadena** Texas, SW USA
56 B8 **Pasaje** El Oro, SW Ecuador
137 T9 **P'asanauri** N Georgia
168 I13 **Pasapuat** Pulau Pagai Utara, W Indonesia
167 N7 **Pasawng** Kayah State, C Myanmar
114 L13 **Paşayiğit** Edirne, NW Turkey
23 N9 **Pascagoula** Mississippi, S USA
22 M8 **Pascagoula River** ≈ Mississippi, S USA
116 F12 **Paşcani** *Hung.* Páskán. Iaşi, NE Romania
109 T4 **Pasching** Oberösterreich, N Austria
32 K10 **Pasco** Washington, NW USA
56 E13 **Pasco** *off.* Departamento de Pasco. ◆ *department* C Peru
191 N11 **Pascua, Isla de** *var.* Rapa Nui, *Eng.* Easter Island. *island* E Pacific Ocean
63 G21 **Pascua, Río** ≈ S Chile
103 N1 **Pas-de-Calais** ◆ *department* N France
100 P10 **Pasewalk** Mecklenburg-Vorpommern, NE Germany
11 T10 **Pasfield Lake** ◎ Saskatchewan, C Canada
Pa-shih Hai-hsia *see* Bashi Channel
Pashkeni *see* Bolyarovo
Pashmakli *see* Smolyan
153 X10 **Pāsighāt** Arunāchel Pradesh, NE India
137 Q12 **Pasinler** Erzurum, NE Turkey
Pasi Oloy, Qatorkŭhi *see* Zaalayskiy Khrebet
42 E3 **Pasión, Río de la** ≈ N Guatemala
168 J12 **Pasirganting** Sumatera, W Indonesia
Pasirpangarayan *see* Bagansiapiapi
168 K6 **Pasir Puteh** *var.* Pasir Putih. Kelantan, Peninsular Malaysia
169 R9 **Pasir, Tanjung** *headland* East Malaysia
95 N20 **Påskallavik** Kalmar, S Sweden
Páskán *see* Paşcani
110 K7 **Pasłęk** *Ger.* Preußisch Holland. Warmińsko-Mazurskie, NE Poland
110 K7 **Pasłęka** *Ger.* Passarge. ≈ N Poland
148 K16 **Pasni** Baluchistān, SW Pakistan
63 I18 **Paso de Indios** Chubut, S Argentina
54 L7 **Paso del Caballo** Guárico, N Venezuela
61 E15 **Paso de los Libres** Corrientes, NE Argentina
61 E18 **Paso de los Toros** Tacuarembó, C Uruguay
35 P12 **Paso Robles** California, W USA
15 Y7 **Paspébiac** Quebec, SE Canada
11 U14 **Pasquia Hills** ▲▲ Saskatchewan, S Canada
149 W7 **Pasrūr** Punjab, E Pakistan
30 M1 **Passage Island** *island* Michigan, N USA
65 B24 **Passage Islands** *island group* W Falkland Islands
8 K5 **Passage Point** *headland* Banks Island, Northwest Territories, NW Canada
Passarge *see* Pasłęka
115 C15 **Passarón** *ancient monument* Ípeiros, W Greece
Passarowitz *see* Požarevac
101 O22 **Passau** Bayern, SE Germany
22 M9 **Pass Christian** Mississippi, S USA
107 L26 **Passero, Capo** *headland* Sicilia, Italy, C Mediterranean Sea
171 P5 **Passi** Panay Island, C Philippines
61 H14 **Passo Fundo** Rio Grande do Sul, S Brazil
60 H13 **Passo Fundo, Barragem de** ⊡ S Brazil
61 H15 **Passo Real, Barragem de** ⊡ S Brazil
59 L20 **Passos** Minas Gerais, NE Brazil
167 X10 **Passu Keah** *island* S Paracel Islands
118 J13 **Pastavy** *Pol.* Postawy, *Rus.* Postavy. Vitsyebskaya Voblasts', NW Belarus
56 D7 **Pastaza** ◆ *province* E Ecuador
56 D9 **Pastaza, Río** ≈ Ecuador/Peru
61 A21 **Pasteur** Buenos Aires, E Argentina
15 V3 **Pasteur** ≈ Quebec, SE Canada
147 Q12 **Pastigav** *Rus.* Pastigov. W Tajikistan
Pastigov *see* Pastigav
54 C13 **Pasto** Nariño, SW Colombia
38 M10 **Pastol Bay** *bay* Alaska, USA
37 O8 **Pastora Peak** ▲ Arizona, SW USA
105 O8 **Pastrana** Castilla-La Mancha, C Spain
169 S16 **Pasuruan** *prev.* Pasoeroean. Jawa, C Indonesia
118 F11 **Pasvalys** Pasvalys, N Lithuania
111 K21 **Pásztó** Nógrád, N Hungary
189 U12 **Pata** *var.* Patta. *atoll* Chuuk Islands, C Micronesia
36 M16 **Patagonia** Arizona, SW USA
63 H20 **Patagonia** *physical region* Argentina/Chile
Patalung *see* Phatthalung
154 D9 **Pātan** Gujarāt, W India
154 J10 **Pātan** Madhya Pradesh, C India
171 S11 **Patani** Pulau Halmahera, E Indonesia
Patani *see* Pattani
15 V7 **Patapédia Est** ≈ Quebec, SE Canada
116 K13 **Pătâriagele** *prev.* Pătîriagele. Buzău, SE Romania
Patavium *see* Padova
182 I5 **Patawarta Hill** ▲ South Australia
182 L10 **Patchewollock** Victoria, SE Australia
184 K11 **Patea** Taranaki, North Island, NZ
184 K11 **Patea** ≈ North Island, NZ
77 U15 **Pategi** Kwara, C Nigeria
81 K20 **Pate Island** *var.* Patta Island. *island* SE Kenya
105 S10 **Paterna** País Valenciano, E Spain
109 R9 **Paternion** *Slvn.* Špatrjan. Kärnten, S Austria
107 L24 **Paternò** *anc.* Hybla, Hybla Major. Sicilia, Italy, C Mediterranean Sea
32 J7 **Pateros** Washington, NW USA
18 J14 **Paterson** New Jersey, NE USA
32 J10 **Paterson** Washington, NW USA
185 C25 **Paterson Inlet** *inlet* Stewart Island, NZ
98 N6 **Paterswolde** Drenthe, NE Netherlands
152 H7 **Pathānkot** Himāchal Pradesh, N India
Pathein *see* Bassein
33 W15 **Pathfinder Reservoir** ⊡ Wyoming, C USA
167 O11 **Pathum Thani** *var.* Patumdhani, Prathum Thani. Pathum Thani, C Thailand
54 C12 **Patía** *var.* El Bordo. Cauca, SW Colombia
152 I9 **Patiāla** *var.* Puttiala. Punjab, NW India
54 B12 **Patía, Río** ≈ SW Colombia
188 D15 **Pati Point** *headland* NE Guam
Pătîriagele *see* Pătâriagele
56 C13 **Pativilca** Lima, W Peru
166 M1 **Pātkai Bum** *var.* Patkai Range. ▲▲ Myanmar/India
Patkai Range *see* Pātkai Bum
115 L20 **Pátmos** Pátmos, Dodekánisos, Greece, Aegean Sea
115 L20 **Pátmos** *island* Dodekánisos, Greece, Aegean Sea
153 P13 **Patna** *var.* Azimabad. Bihār, N India
154 M12 **Patnāgarh** Orissa, E India
171 O5 **Patnongon** Panay Island, C Philippines
137 S13 **Patnos** Ağrı, E Turkey
60 H12 **Pato Branco** Paraná, S Brazil
31 O16 **Patoka Lake** ◎ Indiana, N USA
92 L9 **Patoniva** *Lapp.* Buoddobohki. Lappi, N Finland
113 K21 **Patos** *var.* Patosi. Fier, SW Albania
Patos *see* Patos de Minas
59 K19 **Patos de Minas** *var.* Patos. Minas Gerais, NE Brazil
Patosi *see* Patos
61 I17 **Patos, Lagoa dos** *lagoon* S Brazil
62 J9 **Patquía** La Rioja, C Argentina
115 E19 **Pátra** *Eng.* Patras; *prev.* Pátrai. Dytikí Ellás, S Greece
Pátrai/Patras *see* Pátra
115 D18 **Patraïkós Kólpos** *gulf* S Greece
92 G2 **Patreksfjördhur** Vestfirdhir, W Iceland
24 M7 **Patricia** Texas, SW USA
63 F21 **Patricio Lynch, Isla** *island* S Chile
Patta *see* Pata
Patta Island *see* Pate Island
167 O16 **Pattani** *var.* Patani. Pattani, SW Thailand
167 P12 **Pattaya** Chon Buri, S Thailand
19 S4 **Patten** Maine, NE USA
35 O9 **Patterson** California, W USA
22 J10 **Patterson** Louisiana, S USA
35 R7 **Patterson, Mount** ▲ California, W USA
31 P4 **Patterson, Point** *headland* Michigan, N USA
107 L23 **Patti** Sicilia, Italy, C Mediterranean Sea
107 L23 **Patti, Golfo di** *gulf* Sicilia, Italy, C Mediterranean Sea
93 L14 **Pattijoki** Oulu, W Finland
193 Q4 **Patton Escarpment** *undersea feature* E Pacific Ocean
27 S2 **Pattonsburg** Missouri, C USA
(0) D6 **Patton Seamount** *undersea feature* NE Pacific Ocean
10 J12 **Pattullo, Mount** ▲ British Columbia, W Canada
Patuakhali *see* Patukhali
42 M5 **Patuca, Río** ≈ E Honduras
153 U16 **Patukhali** *var.* Patuakhali. Khulna, S Bangladesh
Patumdhani *see* Pathum Thani
40 M14 **Pátzcuaro** Michoacán de Ocampo, SW Mexico
42 C6 **Patzicía** Chimaltenango, S Guatemala
102 K16 **Pau** Pyrénées-Atlantiques, SW France
102 J12 **Pauillac** Gironde, SW France
166 L5 **Pauk** Magwe, W Myanmar
8 I6 **Paulatuk** Northwest Territories, NW Canada
42 K5 **Paulayá, Río** ≈ NE Honduras
22 M6 **Paulding** Mississippi, S USA
31 Q12 **Paulding** Ohio, N USA
29 S12 **Paullina** Iowa, C USA
59 P15 **Paulo Afonso** Bahia, E Brazil
38 M16 **Pauloff Harbor** *var.* Pavlor Harbour. Sanak Island, Alaska, USA
27 N12 **Pauls Valley** Oklahoma, C USA
166 L7 **Paungde** Pegu, C Myanmar
Pauni *see* Paoni
152 K9 **Pauri** Uttar Pradesh, N India
Pautalia *see* Kyustendil
142 J5 **Pāveh** Kermānshāh, NW Iran
128 L5 **Pavelets** Ryazanskaya Oblast', W Russian Federation
106 D8 **Pavia** *anc.* Ticinum. Lombardia, N Italy
118 C9 **Pāvilosta** Liepāja, W Latvia
127 P14 **Pavino** Kostromskaya Oblast', NW Russian Federation
114 J8 **Pavlikeni** Veliko Tŭrnovo, N Bulgaria
145 T8 **Pavlodar** Pavlodar, NE Kazakhstan
145 S9 **Pavlodar** *off.* Pavlodarskaya Oblast', *Kaz.* Pavlodar Oblysy. ◆ *province* NE Kazakhstan
Pavlodar Oblysy/Pavlodarskaya Oblast' *see* Pavlodar
Pavlograd *see* Pavlohrad
117 U7 **Pavlohrad** *Rus.* Pavlograd. Dnipropetrovs'ka Oblast', E Ukraine
Pavlor Harbour *see* Pauloff Harbor
145 R9 **Pavlovka** Akmola, C Kazakhstan
129 V4 **Pavlovka** Respublika Bashkortostan, W Russian Federation
129 Q7 **Pavlovka** Ul'yanovskaya Oblast', W Russian Federation
129 N3 **Pavlovo** Nizhegorodskaya Oblast', W Russian Federation
128 L9 **Pavlovsk** Voronezhskaya Oblast', W Russian Federation
128 L13 **Pavlovskaya** Krasnodarskiy Kray, SW Russian Federation
117 S7 **Pavlysh** Kirovohrads'ka Oblast', C Ukraine
106 F10 **Pavullo nel Frignano** Emilia-Romagna, C Italy
27 P8 **Pawhuska** Oklahoma, C USA
21 U13 **Pawleys Island** South Carolina, SE USA
167 N6 **Pawn** ≈ C Myanmar
30 K14 **Pawnee** Illinois, N USA
27 O9 **Pawnee** Oklahoma, C USA
37 U2 **Pawnee Buttes** ▲ Colorado, C USA
29 S17 **Pawnee City** Nebraska, C USA
26 K5 **Pawnee River** ≈ Kansas, C USA
31 O10 **Paw Paw** Michigan, N USA
31 O10 **Paw Paw Lake** Michigan, N USA
19 O12 **Pawtucket** Rhode Island, NE USA
Pax Augusta *see* Badajoz
115 I25 **Paximádia** *island* SE Greece
Pax Julia *see* Beja
115 B16 **Paxoí** *island* Iónioi Nísoi, Greece, C Mediterranean Sea
39 S10 **Paxson** Alaska, USA
30 M13 **Paxton** Illinois, N USA
126 J11 **Pay** Respublika Kareliya, NW Russian Federation
166 M8 **Payagyi** Pegu, SW Myanmar
108 C9 **Payerne** *Ger.* Peterlingen. Vaud, W Switzerland
32 M13 **Payette** Idaho, NW USA
32 M13 **Payette River** ≈ Idaho, NW USA
127 V2 **Pay-Khoy, Khrebet** ▲▲ NW Russian Federation
Payne *see* Kangirsuk
12 K4 **Payne, Lac** ◎ Quebec, NE Canada
29 T8 **Paynesville** Minnesota, N USA
169 S8 **Payong, Tanjung** *headland* East Malaysia
Payo Obispo *see* Chetumal
61 D18 **Paysandú** Paysandú, W Uruguay
61 D17 **Paysandú** ◆ *department* W Uruguay
102 I7 **Pays de la Loire** ◆ *region* NW France
36 L12 **Payson** Arizona, SW USA
36 L4 **Payson** Utah, W USA
127 W4 **Payyer, Gora** ▲ NW Russian Federation
Payzawat *see* Jiashi
137 Q11 **Pazar** Rize, NE Turkey
136 F10 **Pazarbaşı Burnu** *headland* NW Turkey
136 M16 **Pazarcık** Kahramanmaraş, S Turkey
114 I10 **Pazardzhik** *prev.* Tatar Pazardzhik. Pazardzhik, C Bulgaria
114 H11 **Pazardzhik** ◆ *province* C Bulgaria
54 H9 **Paz de Ariporo** Casanare, E Colombia
112 A10 **Pazin** *Ger.* Mitterburg, *It.* Pisino. Istra, NW Croatia
42 D7 **Paz, Río** ≈ El Salvador/Guatemala
113 O18 **Pčinja** ≈ N FYR Macedonia
193 V15 **Pea** Tongatapu, S Tonga
27 O6 **Peabody** Kansas, C USA
11 O12 **Peace** ≈ Alberta/British Columbia, W Canada
Peace Garden State *see* North Dakota
11 Q10 **Peace Point** Alberta, C Canada
11 O12 **Peace River** Alberta, W Canada
23 W13 **Peace River** ≈ Florida, SE USA
11 N17 **Peachland** British Columbia, SW Canada
36 J10 **Peach Springs** Arizona, SW USA
Peach State *see* Georgia
23 S4 **Peachtree City** Georgia, SE USA
189 Y13 **Peacock Point** *point* SE Wake Island
97 M18 **Peak District** *physical region* C England, UK
183 Q7 **Peak Hill** New South Wales, SE Australia
65 G15 **Peak, The** ▲ C Ascension Island
105 O13 **Peal de Becerro** Andalucía, S Spain
189 X11 **Peale Island** *island* N Wake Island
37 O6 **Peale, Mount** ▲ Utah, W USA
39 O4 **Peard Bay** *bay* Alaska, USA
23 Q7 **Pea River** ≈ Alabama/Florida, S USA
25 W11 **Pearland** Texas, SW USA
38 D9 **Pearl City** Oahu, Hawaii, USA, C Pacific Ocean
38 D9 **Pearl Harbor** *inlet* Oahu, Hawaii, USA, C Pacific Ocean
Pearl Islands *see* Perlas, Archipiélago de las
Pearl Lagoon *see* Perlas, Laguna de
22 M5 **Pearl River** ≈ Louisiana/Mississippi, S USA
25 Q13 **Pearsall** Texas, SW USA
23 U7 **Pearson** Georgia, SE USA
25 P4 **Pease River** ≈ Texas, SW USA
12 F7 **Peawanuk** Ontario, C Canada
83 P16 **Pebane** Zambézia, NE Mozambique
65 C23 **Pebble Island** *island* N Falkland Islands
65 C23 **Pebble Island Settlement** Pebble Island, N Falkland Islands
113 L16 **Peć** *Alb.* Pejë, *Turk.* Ipek. Serbia, S Yugoslavia
25 R8 **Pecan Bayou** ≈ Texas, SW USA
22 H10 **Pecan Island** Louisiana, S USA
60 L12 **Peças, Ilha das** *island* S Brazil
30 L10 **Pecatonica River** ≈ Illinois/Wisconsin, N USA
108 G10 **Peccia** Ticino, S Switzerland
Pechenegi *see* Pechenihy
Pechenezhskoye Vodokhranilishche *see* Pecheniz'ke Vodoskhovyshche
126 I2 **Pechenga** *Fin.* Petsamo. Murmanskaya Oblast', NW Russian Federation
117 V5 **Pechenihy** *Rus.* Pechenegi. Kharkivs'ka Oblast', E Ukraine
117 V5 **Pecheniz'ke Vodoskhovyshche** *Rus.* Pechenezhskoye Vodokhranilishche. ⊡ E Ukraine
127 U7 **Pechora** Respublika Komi, NW Russian Federation
127 R6 **Pechora** ≈ NW Russian Federation
Pechora Bay *see* Pechorskaya Guba
Pechora Sea *see* Pechorskoye More
127 S3 **Pechorskaya Guba** *Eng.* Pechora Bay. *bay* NW Russian Federation
122 H7 **Pechorskoye More** *Eng.* Pechora Sea. *sea* NW Russian Federation
116 E11 **Pecica** *Ger.* Petschka, *Hung.* Ópécska. Arad, W Romania
24 K8 **Pecos** Texas, SW USA
25 N11 **Pecos River** ≈ New Mexico/Texas, SW USA
111 I25 **Pécs** *Ger.* Fünfkirchen; *Lat.* Sopianae. Baranya, SW Hungary
43 T17 **Pedasí** Los Santos, S Panama
Pedde *see* Pedja
183 O17 **Pedder, Lake** ◎ Tasmania, SE Australia
44 M10 **Pedernales** SW Dominican Republic
55 Q5 **Pedernales** Delta Amacuro, NE Venezuela
25 R10 **Pedernales River** ≈ Texas, SW USA
62 H6 **Pedernales, Salar de** *salt lake* N Chile
Pedhoulas *see* Pedoulás
55 X11 **Pédima** *var.* Malavate. SW French Guiana
182 F1 **Pedirka** South Australia
171 S11 **Pedjiwang** Pulau Halmahera, E Indonesia
118 I5 **Pedja** *var.* Pedja Jõgi, *Ger.* Pedde. ≈ E Estonia
Pedja Jõgi *see* Pedja
121 O3 **Pedoulás** *var.* Pedhoulas. W Cyprus
59 N18 **Pedra Azul** Minas Gerais, NE Brazil
104 I3 **Pedrafita, Porto de** *var.* Puerto de Piedrafita. *pass* NW Spain
76 E9 **Pedra Lume** Sal, NE Cape Verde
43 P16 **Pedregal** Chiriquí, W Panama
54 J4 **Pedregal** Falcón, N Venezuela
40 L9 **Pedriceña** Durango, C Mexico
60 L11 **Pedro Barros** São Paulo, S Brazil
39 Q13 **Pedro Bay** Alaska, USA
62 H4 **Pedro de Valdivia** *var.* Oficina Pedro de Valdivia. Antofagasta, N Chile
62 P4 **Pedro Juan Caballero** Amambay, E Paraguay
63 L15 **Pedro Luro** Buenos Aires, E Argentina
105 O10 **Pedro Muñoz** Castilla-La Mancha, C Spain
155 J22 **Pedro, Point** *headland* NW Sri Lanka
182 K9 **Peebinga** South Australia
96 J13 **Peebles** SE Scotland, UK
31 S15 **Peebles** Ohio, N USA
96 J12 **Peebles** *cultural region* SE Scotland, UK
18 K13 **Peekskill** New York, NE USA
97 I16 **Peel** W Isle of Man
8 G7 **Peel** ≈ Northwest Territories/Yukon Territory, NW Canada
8 K5 **Peel Point** *headland* Victoria Island, Northwest Territories, NW Canada
8 M5 **Peel Sound** *passage* Nunavut, N Canada
100 N9 **Peene** ≈ NE Germany
99 K17 **Peer** Limburg, NE Belgium
14 H14 **Pefferlaw** Ontario, S Canada
185 I18 **Pegasus Bay** *bay* South Island, NZ
121 O3 **Pégeia** *var.* Peyia. SW Cyprus
109 V7 **Peggau** Steiermark, SE Austria
101 L19 **Pegnitz** Bayern, SE Germany
101 L19 **Pegnitz** ≈ SE Germany
105 T11 **Pego** País Valenciano, E Spain
166 L8 **Pegu** *var.* Bago. Pegu, SW Myanmar
166 L7 **Pegu** ◆ *division* S Myanmar
189 N13 **Pehleng** Pohnpei, E Micronesia
114 M12 **Pehlivanköy** Kırklareli, NW Turkey
77 R14 **Péhonko** C Benin
61 B21 **Pehuajó** Buenos Aires, E Argentina
Pei-ching *see* Beijing/Beijing Shi
100 J13 **Peine** Niedersachsen, C Germany
Pei-p'ing *see* Beijing/Beijing Shi
Peipsi Järv/Peipus-See *see* Peipus, Lake
118 J5 **Peipus, Lake** *Est.* Peipsi Järv, *Ger.* Peipus-See, *Rus.* Chudskoye Ozero. ◎ Estonia/Russian Federation
115 H19 **Peiraías** *prev.* Piraiévs, *Eng.* Piraeus. Attikí, C Greece
Peisern *see* Pyzdry
60 I8 **Peixe, Rio do** ≈ S Brazil
59 I16 **Peixoto de Azevedo** Mato Grosso, W Brazil
168 O11 **Pejantan, Pulau** *island* W Indonesia
Pejë *see* Peć
112 N11 **Pek** ≈ E Yugoslavia
167 R7 **Pèk** *var.* Xieng Khouang; *prev.* Xiangkhoang. Xiangkhoang, N Laos
169 Q16 **Pekalongan** Jawa, C Indonesia
168 K11 **Pekanbaru** *var.* Pakanbaru. Sumatera, W Indonesia
30 L12 **Pekin** Illinois, N USA
Peking *see* Beijing/Beijing Shi
Pelabohan Kelang/Pelabuhan Kelang *see* Pelabuhan Klang
168 J9 **Pelabuhan Klang** *var.* Kuala Pelabohan Kelang, Pelabohan Kelang, Pelabuhan Kelang, Port Klang, Port Swettenham. Selangor, Peninsular Malaysia
120 L11 **Pelagie, Isole** *island group* SW Italy
Pelagosa *see* Palagruža
22 L5 **Pelahatchie** Mississippi, S USA
169 T14 **Pelaihari** *var.* Pleihari. Borneo, C Indonesia
103 U14 **Pelat, Mont** ▲ SE France
116 F12 **Peleaga, Vârful** *prev.* Vîrful Peleaga. ▲ W Romania
Peleaga, Vîrful *see* Peleaga, Vârful
123 O11 **Peleduy** Respublika Sakha (Yakutiya), NE Russian Federation
14 C18 **Pelee Island** *island* Ontario, S Canada
45 Q11 **Pelée, Montagne** ⚹ N Martinique
14 D18 **Pelee, Point** *headland* Ontario, S Canada
171 P12 **Pelei** Pulau Peleng, N Indonesia
Peleliu *see* Beliliou
171 P12 **Peleng, Pulau** *island* Kepulauan Banggai, N Indonesia
23 T7 **Pelham** Georgia, SE USA
111 E18 **Pelhřimov** *Ger.* Pilgram. Jihlavský Kraj, C Czech Republic
39 W13 **Pelican** Chichagof Island, Alaska, USA
191 Z3 **Pelican Lagoon** ◎ Kiritimati, E Kiribati
29 U6 **Pelican Lake** ◎ Minnesota, N USA
29 V3 **Pelican Lake** ◎ Minnesota, N USA
30 L5 **Pelican Lake** ◎ Wisconsin, N USA
44 G1 **Pelican Point** Grand Bahama Island, N Bahamas
83 B19 **Pelican Point** *headland* W Namibia
29 S6 **Pelican Rapids** Minnesota, N USA
Pelican State *see* Louisiana
11 U13 **Pelikan Narrows** Saskatchewan, C Canada
115 L18 **Pelinaío** ▲ Chíos, E Greece
Pelinnaeum *see* Pelinnaío
115 E16 **Pelinnaío** *anc.* Pelinnaeum. *ruins* Thessalía, C Greece
113 N20 **Pelister** ▲ SW FYR Macedonia
113 G15 **Pelješac** *peninsula* S Croatia
92 M12 **Pelkosenniemi** Lappi, NE Finland
29 W15 **Pella** Iowa, C USA
114 F13 **Pélla** *site of ancient city* Kentrikí Makedonía, N Greece
23 Q3 **Pell City** Alabama, S USA
61 A22 **Pellegrini** Buenos Aires, E Argentina
92 K12 **Pello** Lappi, NW Finland
100 G7 **Pellworm** *island* N Germany
10 H6 **Pelly** ≈ Yukon Territory, NW Canada
9 N7 **Pelly Bay** Nunavut, N Canada
10 I8 **Pelly Mountains** ▲▲ Yukon Territory, W Canada
Pélmonostor *see* Beli Manastir
37 P13 **Pelona Mountain** ▲ New Mexico, SW USA
Peloponnese/Peloponnesus *see* Pelopónnisos
115 E20 **Pelopónnisos** *Eng.* Peloponnese. ◆ *region* S Greece
115 E20 **Pelopónnisos** *var.* Morea, *Eng.* Peloponnese; *anc.* Peloponnesus. *peninsula* S Greece
107 L23 **Peloritani, Monti** *anc.* Pelorus and Neptunius. ▲▲ Sicilia, Italy, C Mediterranean Sea
107 M22 **Peloro, Capo** *var.* Punta del Faro. *headland* S Italy
Pelorus and Neptunius *see* Peloritani, Monti
61 H17 **Pelotas** Rio Grande do Sul, S Brazil
61 I14 **Pelotas, Rio** ≈ S Brazil
92 K10 **Peltovuoma** *Lapp.* Bealdovuopmi. Lappi, N Finland
19 R4 **Pemadumcook Lake** ◎ Maine, NE USA
169 Q16 **Pemalang** Jawa, C Indonesia
169 P10 **Pemangkat** *var.* Pamangkat. Borneo, C Indonesia
Pemar *see* Paimio
168 I9 **Pematangsiantar** Sumatera, W Indonesia
83 Q14 **Pemba** *prev.* Port Amelia, Porto Amélia. Cabo Delgado, NE Mozambique
81 J22 **Pemba** ◆ *region* E Tanzania
81 K21 **Pemba** *island* E Tanzania
83 Q14 **Pemba, Baia de** *inlet* NE Mozambique
81 J21 **Pemba Channel** *channel* E Tanzania
180 J14 **Pemberton** Western Australia
10 M16 **Pemberton** British Columbia, SW Canada
29 Q2 **Pembina** North Dakota, N USA
29 Q2 **Pembina** ≈ Canada/USA
11 P15 **Pembina** ≈ Alberta, SW Canada
171 X16 **Pembre** Irian Jaya, E Indonesia
14 K12 **Pembroke** Ontario, SE Canada
97 H21 **Pembroke** SW Wales, UK
23 W6 **Pembroke** Georgia, SE USA
21 U11 **Pembroke** North Carolina, SE USA
21 R7 **Pembroke** Virginia, NE USA
97 H21 **Pembroke** *cultural region* SW Wales, UK
Pembuang, Sungai *see* Seruyan, Sungai
43 S15 **Peña Blanca, Cerro** ▲ C Panama
104 K8 **Peña de Francia, Sierra de la** ▲▲ W Spain
104 G6 **Penafiel** *var.* Peñafiel. Porto, N Portugal
105 N6 **Peñafiel** Castilla-León, N Spain
105 S8 **Peñagolosa** ▲ E Spain
105 N7 **Peñalara, Pico de** ▲ C Spain

◆ Country ● Country Capital ◇ Dependent Territory ○ Dependent Territory Capital ◆ Administrative Region × International Airport ▲ Mountain ▲▲ Mountain Range ⚹ Volcano ≈ River ◎ Lake ⊡ Reservoir

171 X16 **Penambo, Banjaran** var. Banjaran Tama Abu, Penambo Range. ▲ Indonesia/Malaysia
Penambo Range see Penambo, Banjaran
41 O10 **Peña Nevada, Cerro** ▲ C Mexico
Penang see Pinang, Pulau, Peninsular Malaysia
Penang see Pinang
Penang see George Town
60 J8 **Penápolis** São Paulo, S Brazil
104 L7 **Peñaranda de Bracamonte** Castilla-León, N Spain
105 S8 **Peñarroya** ▲ E Spain
104 L12 **Peñarroya-Pueblonuevo** Andalucía, S Spain
97 K22 **Penarth** S Wales, UK
104 K1 **Peñas, Cabo de** headland N Spain
63 F20 **Penas, Golfo de** gulf S Chile
Pen-ch'i see Benxi
79 H14 **Pendé** var. Logone Oriental. ~ Central African Republic/Chad
76 I14 **Pendembu** E Sierra Leone
29 R13 **Pender** Nebraska, C USA
Penderma see Bandırma
32 K11 **Pendleton** Oregon, NW USA
32 M7 **Pend Oreille, Lake** ◎ Idaho, NW USA
32 M7 **Pend Oreille River** ~ Idaho/Washington, NW USA
Pendzhikent see Panjakent
Peneius see Pineiós
104 G8 **Penela** Coimbra, N Portugal
14 G13 **Penetanguishene** Ontario, S Canada
151 H15 **Penganga** ~ C India
161 T12 **P'engchia Yu** island N Taiwan
79 M21 **Penge** Kasai Oriental, C Dem. Rep. Congo (Zaire)
Penghu Archipelago/P'enghu Ch'üntao/Penghu Islands see P'enghu Liehtao
161 R14 **P'enghu Liehtao** var. P'enghu Ch'üntao, Penghu Islands, Eng. Penghu Archipelago, Pescadores, Jap. Hoko-guntō, Hoko-shotō. island group W Taiwan
Penghu Shuidao/P'enghu Shuitao see Pescadores Channel
161 R4 **Penglai** var. Dengzhou. Shandong, E China
Peng-pu see Bengbu
Penhsihu see Benxi
Penibético, Sistema see Béticos, Sistemas
104 F10 **Peniche** Leiria, W Portugal
169 U17 **Penida, Nusa** island S Indonesia
Peninsular State see Florida
105 T8 **Peñíscola** País Valenciano, E Spain
40 M13 **Pénjamo** Guanajuato, C Mexico
Penki see Benxi
102 F7 **Penmarch, Pointe de** headland NW France
107 L15 **Penna, Punta della** headland C Italy
107 K14 **Penne** Abruzzo, C Italy
Penner see Penneru
155 J18 **Penneru** var. Penner. ~ C India
182 I10 **Penneshaw** South Australia
18 C14 **Penn Hills** Pennsylvania, NE USA
Penninae, Alpes/Pennine, Alpi see Pennine Alps
108 D11 **Pennine Alps** Fr. Alpes Pennines, It. Alpi Pennine; Lat. Alpes Penninae. ▲ Italy/Switzerland
Pennine Chain see Pennines
97 L15 **Pennines** var. Pennine Chain. ▲ N England, UK
Pennines, Alpes see Pennine Alps
21 O8 **Pennington Gap** Virginia, NE USA
18 I16 **Penns Grove** New Jersey, NE USA
18 I16 **Pennsville** New Jersey, NE USA
18 E14 **Pennsylvania** off. Commonwealth of Pennsylvania; also known as The Keystone State. ◈ state NE USA
18 G10 **Penn Yan** New York, NE USA
126 H16 **Peno** Tverskaya Oblast', W Russian Federation
19 R7 **Penobscot Bay** bay Maine, NE USA
19 S5 **Penobscot River** ~ Maine, NE USA
182 K12 **Penola** South Australia
40 K9 **Peñón Blanco** Durango, C Mexico
182 E7 **Penong** South Australia
43 S16 **Penonomé** Coclé, C Panama
190 L13 **Penrhyn** atoll N Cook Islands
192 M9 **Penrhyn Basin** undersea feature C Pacific Ocean
183 S9 **Penrith** New South Wales, SE Australia
97 K15 **Penrith** NW England, UK
23 O9 **Pensacola** Florida, SE USA
23 O9 **Pensacola Bay** bay Florida, SE USA
195 N7 **Pensacola Mountains** ▲ Antarctica
182 L12 **Penshurst** Victoria, SE Australia
187 R13 **Pentecost** Fr. Pentecôte. island C Vanuatu
15 V4 **Pentecôte** ~ Quebec, SE Canada
Pentecôte see Pentecost
15 V4 **Pentecôte, Lac** ◎ Quebec, SE Canada
8 H15 **Penticton** British Columbia, SW Canada
96 J6 **Pentland Firth** strait N Scotland, UK
96 J12 **Pentland Hills** hill range S Scotland, UK
171 Q12 **Penu** Pulau Taliabu, E Indonesia
155 H18 **Penukonda** Andhra Pradesh, E India
166 L7 **Penwegon** Pegu, C Myanmar
24 M8 **Penwell** Texas, SW USA
97 J21 **Pen y Fan** ▲ SE Wales, UK
97 L16 **Pen-y-ghent** ▲ N England, UK
129 O6 **Penza** Penzenskaya Oblast', W Russian Federation
97 G25 **Penzance** SW England, UK
129 N6 **Penzenskaya Oblast'** ◈ province W Russian Federation
123 U7 **Penzhina** ~ E Russian Federation
123 U9 **Penzhinskaya Guba** bay E Russian Federation
Penzig see Pieńsk
36 K13 **Peoria** Arizona, SW USA
30 L12 **Peoria** Illinois, N USA
30 L12 **Peoria Heights** Illinois, N USA
31 N11 **Peotone** Illinois, N USA
18 J11 **Pepacton Reservoir** ⊟ New York, NE USA
76 I15 **Pepel** W Sierra Leone
30 I6 **Pepin, Lake** ⊟ Minnesota/Wisconsin, N USA
99 L20 **Pepinster** Liège, E Belgium
113 L20 **Peqin** var. Peqini. Elbasan, C Albania
Peqini see Peqin
40 D7 **Pequeña, Punta** headland W Mexico
168 J8 **Perak** ◈ state Peninsular Malaysia
105 R7 **Perales del Alfambra** Aragón, NE Spain
115 C15 **Pérama** var. Perama. Ípeiros, W Greece
92 M13 **Perä-Posio** Lappi, NE Finland
15 Z6 **Percé** Quebec, SE Canada
15 Z6 **Percé, Rocher** island Quebec, S Canada
102 L5 **Perche, Collines de** ▲ N France
109 X4 **Perchtoldsdorf** Niederösterreich, NE Austria
180 L6 **Percival Lakes** lakes Western Australia
105 T3 **Perdido, Monte** ▲ NE Spain
23 O8 **Perdido River** ~ Alabama/Florida, S USA
Perece Vela Basin see West Mariana Basin
116 G7 **Perechyn** Zakarpats'ka Oblast', W Ukraine
54 E10 **Pereira** Risaralda, W Colombia
60 I7 **Pereira Barreto** São Paulo, S Brazil
59 G15 **Pereirinha** Pará, N Brazil
129 N10 **Perelazovskiy** Volgogradskaya Oblast', SW Russian Federation
129 S7 **Perelyub** Saratovskaya Oblast', W Russian Federation
31 P7 **Pere Marquette River** ~ Michigan, N USA
Peremyshl see Podkarpackie
116 I5 **Peremyshlyany** L'vivs'ka Oblast', W Ukraine
Pereshchepino see Pereshchepyne
116 L9 **Pereshchepyne** Rus. Pereshchepino. Dnipropetrovs'ka Oblast', E Ukraine
126 L16 **Pereslavl'-Zalesskiy** Yaroslavskaya Oblast', W Russian Federation
117 Y7 **Pereval's'k** Luhans'ka Oblast', E Ukraine
129 U7 **Perevolotskiy** Orenburgskaya Oblast', W Russian Federation
Pereyaslav-Khmel'nitskiy see Pereyaslav-Khmel'nyts'kyy
117 Q5 **Pereyaslav-Khmel'nyts'kyy** Rus. Pereyaslav-Khmel'nitskiy. Kyyivs'ka Oblast', N Ukraine
109 U4 **Perg** Oberösterreich, N Austria
61 B19 **Pergamino** Buenos Aires, E Argentina
106 G6 **Pergine Valsugana** Ger. Persen. Trentino-Alto Adige, N Italy
29 S6 **Perham** Minnesota, N USA
93 L16 **Perho** Länsi-Suomi, W Finland
116 E11 **Periam** Ger. Perjamosch, Hung. Perjámos. Timiş, W Romania
15 Q6 **Péribonca** ~ Quebec, SE Canada
12 L11 **Péribonca, Lac** ◎ Quebec, SE Canada
15 Q6 **Péribonca, Petite Rivière** ~ Quebec, SE Canada
15 Q7 **Péribonka** Quebec, SE Canada
40 I9 **Pericos** Sinaloa, C Mexico
169 Q10 **Perigi** Borneo, C Indonesia
102 L12 **Périgueux** anc. Vesuna. Dordogne, SW France
54 G5 **Perijá, Serranía de** ▲ Columbia/Venezuela
115 H17 **Peristéra** island Vóreioi Sporádes, Greece, Aegean Sea
63 H20 **Perito Moreno** Santa Cruz, S Argentina
155 G22 **Periyāl** var. Periyār. ~ SW India
Periyār see Periyāl
155 G23 **Periyār Lake** ◎ S India
Perjámos/Perjamosch see Periam
27 O9 **Perkins** Oklahoma, C USA
116 L7 **Perkivtsi** Chernivets'ka Oblast', W Ukraine
43 U15 **Perlas, Archipiélago de las** Eng. Pearl Islands. island group SE Panama
43 O10 **Perlas, Cayos de** reef SE Nicaragua
43 N9 **Perlas, Laguna de** Eng. Pearl Lagoon. lagoon E Nicaragua
43 N10 **Perlas, Punta de** headland E Nicaragua
100 L11 **Perleberg** Brandenburg, N Germany
Perlepe see Prilep
168 I6 **Perlis** ◈ state Peninsular Malaysia
127 U14 **Perm'** prev. Molotov. Permskaya Oblast', NW Russian Federation
113 M22 **Përmet** var. Përmeti, Prëmet. Gjirokastër, S Albania
Përmeti see Përmet
127 U15 **Permskaya Oblast'** ◈ province NW Russian Federation
59 P15 **Pernambuco** off. Estado de Pernambuco. ◈ state E Brazil
Pernambuco see Recife
Pernambuco Abyssal Plain see Pernambuco Plain
47 Y6 **Pernambuco Plain** var. Pernambuco Abyssal Plain. undersea feature E Atlantic Ocean
65 K15 **Pernambuco Seamounts** undersea feature C Atlantic Ocean
182 H6 **Pernatty Lagoon** salt lake South Australia
Pernau see Pärnu
Pernauer Bucht see Pärnu Laht
Pērnava see Pärnu
114 G9 **Pernik** prev. Dimitrovo. Pernik, W Bulgaria
114 G10 **Pernik** ◈ province W Bulgaria
93 K20 **Perniö** Swe. Bjärnå. Länsi-Suomi, W Finland
109 X5 **Pernitz** Niederösterreich, E Austria
Pernov see Pärnu
103 O3 **Péronne** Somme, N France
14 L8 **Péronne, Lac** ◎ Quebec, SE Canada
106 A8 **Perosa Argentina** Piemonte, NE Italy
41 Q14 **Perote** Veracruz-Llave, E Mexico
Pérouse see Perugia
191 W15 **Pérouse, Bahía de la** bay Easter Island, Chile, E Pacific Ocean
Perovsk see Kyzylorda
103 O17 **Perpignan** Pyrénées-Orientales, S France
113 M20 **Përrenjas** var. Përrenjasi, Prenjas, Prenjasi. Elbasan, E Albania
Përrenjasi see Përrenjas
92 O2 **Perriertoppen** ▲ C Svalbard
25 S6 **Perrin** Texas, SW USA
23 Y16 **Perrine** Florida, SE USA
37 S12 **Perro, Laguna del** ◎ New Mexico, SW USA
102 G5 **Perros-Guirec** Côtes d'Armor, NW France
23 T9 **Perry** Florida, SE USA
23 T5 **Perry** Georgia, SE USA
29 U14 **Perry** Iowa, C USA
18 E10 **Perry** New York, NE USA
27 N9 **Perry** Oklahoma, C USA
27 Q3 **Perry Lake** ⊟ Kansas, C USA
31 R11 **Perrysburg** Ohio, N USA
25 O1 **Perryton** Texas, SW USA
39 O15 **Perryville** Alaska, USA
27 U11 **Perryville** Arkansas, C USA
27 Y6 **Perryville** Missouri, C USA
Persante see Parsęta
Persen see Pergine Valsugana
Pershay see Pyarshai
117 V7 **Pershotravens'k** Dnipropetrovs'ka Oblast', E Ukraine
117 W9 **Pershotravneve** Donets'ka Oblast', E Ukraine
Persia see Iran
Persian Gulf see The Gulf
Persis see Fārs
95 K22 **Perstorp** Skåne, S Sweden
137 O14 **Pertek** Tunceli, C Turkey
183 P16 **Perth** Tasmania, SE Australia
180 I13 **Perth** state capital Western Australia
14 L13 **Perth** Ontario, SE Canada
96 J11 **Perth** C Scotland, UK
180 I12 **Perth** ✈ Western Australia
96 J10 **Perth** cultural region C Scotland, UK
173 V10 **Perth Basin** undersea feature SE Indian Ocean
103 S15 **Pertuis** Vaucluse, SE France
103 Y16 **Pertusato, Capo** headland Corse, France, C Mediterranean Sea
30 L11 **Peru** Illinois, N USA
31 P12 **Peru** Indiana, N USA
57 E13 **Peru** off. Republic of Peru. ◆ republic W South America
Peru see Beru
193 T9 **Peru Basin** undersea feature E Pacific Ocean
193 U8 **Peru-Chile Trench** undersea feature E Pacific Ocean
112 F13 **Perućko Jezero** ◎ S Croatia
106 H13 **Perugia** Fr. Pérouse; anc. Perusia. Umbria, C Italy
Perugia, Lake of see Trasimeno, Lago
61 D15 **Perugorría** Corrientes, NE Argentina
60 M11 **Peruíbe** São Paulo, S Brazil
155 B21 **Perumalpār** reef India, N Indian Ocean
Perusia see Perugia
99 D20 **Péruwelz** Hainaut, SW Belgium
137 R15 **Pervari** Siirt, SE Turkey
129 O4 **Pervomaysk** Nizhegorodskaya Oblast', W Russian Federation
117 X7 **Pervomays'k** Luhans'ka Oblast', E Ukraine
117 P8 **Pervomays'k** prev. Ol'viopol'. Mykolayivs'ka Oblast', S Ukraine
117 S12 **Pervomays'ke** Respublika Krym, S Ukraine
129 V7 **Pervomayskiy** Orenburgskaya Oblast', W Russian Federation
128 M6 **Pervomayskiy** Tambovskaya Oblast', W Russian Federation
117 V6 **Pervomays'kyy** Kharkivs'ka Oblast', E Ukraine
122 F10 **Pervoural'sk** Sverdlovskaya Oblast', C Russian Federation
123 V11 **Pervyy Kuril'skiy Proliv** strait E Russian Federation
99 I19 **Perwez** Wallon Brabant, C Belgium
106 I11 **Pesaro** anc. Pisaurum. Marche, C Italy
35 N9 **Pescadero** California, W USA
Pescadores see P'enghu Liehtao
161 S14 **Pescadores Channel** var. Penghu Shuidao, P'enghu Shuitao. channel W Taiwan
107 K14 **Pescara** anc. Aternum, Ostia Aterni. Abruzzo, C Italy
107 K15 **Pescara** ~ C Italy
106 F11 **Pescia** Toscana, C Italy
108 C8 **Peseux** Neuchâtel, W Switzerland
127 P6 **Pesha** ~ NW Russian Federation
149 T5 **Peshāwar** North-West Frontier Province, N Pakistan
149 T6 **Peshāwar** ✈ North-West Frontier Province, N Pakistan
113 M19 **Peshkopi** var. Peshkopia, Peshkopija. Dibër, NE Albania
Peshkopia/Peshkopija see Peshkopi
114 I11 **Peshtera** Pazardzhik, C Bulgaria
31 N6 **Peshtigo** Wisconsin, N USA
31 N6 **Peshtigo River** ~ Wisconsin, N USA
Peski see Pyeski
127 S13 **Peskovka** Kirovskaya Oblast', NW Russian Federation
103 S8 **Pesmes** Haute-Saône, E France
104 H6 **Peso da Régua** var. Pêso da Regua. Vila Real, N Portugal
40 F5 **Pesqueira** Sonora, NW Mexico
102 J13 **Pessac** Gironde, SW France
111 J23 **Pest** off. Pest Megye. ◈ county C Hungary
126 J14 **Pestovo** Novgorodskaya Oblast', W Russian Federation
40 M15 **Petacalco, Bahía** bay W Mexico
Petach-Tikva/Petah Tiqva see Petah Tiqwa
138 F10 **Petah Tiqwa** var. Petach-Tikva, Petah Tiqva, Petakh Tikva.Tel Aviv, C Israel
Petakh Tikva see Petah Tiqwa
93 L17 **Petäjävesi** Länsi-Suomi, W Finland
22 M7 **Petal** Mississippi, S USA
115 I19 **Petalioí** island C Greece
115 H19 **Petalión, Kólpos** gulf E Greece
115 J19 **Pétalo** ▲ Ándros, Kykládes, Greece, Aegean Sea
34 M8 **Petaluma** California, W USA
99 L25 **Pétange** Luxembourg, SW Luxembourg
54 M5 **Petare** Miranda, N Venezuela
41 N16 **Petatlán** Guerrero, S Mexico
83 L14 **Petauke** Eastern, E Zambia
14 J12 **Petawawa** Ontario, SE Canada
14 J11 **Petawawa** ~ Ontario, SE Canada
Petchaburi see Phetchaburi
42 D2 **Petén** off. Departamento del Petén. ◈ department N Guatemala
42 D2 **Petén Itzá, Lago** var. Lago de Flores. ◎ N Guatemala
30 K7 **Petenwell Lake** ⊟ Wisconsin, N USA
14 D6 **Peterbell** Ontario, S Canada
182 I7 **Peterborough** South Australia
14 I14 **Peterborough** Ontario, SE Canada
97 N20 **Peterborough** prev. Medeshamstede. E England, UK
19 N10 **Peterborough** New Hampshire, NE USA
96 L8 **Peterhead** NE Scotland, UK
Peterhof see Luboń
193 Q14 **Peter I Island** ◇ Norwegian dependency Antarctica
194 H9 **Peter I Island** var. Peter I øy. island Antarctica
Peter I øy see Peter I Island
97 M14 **Peterlee** N England, UK
Peterlingen see Payerne
197 P14 **Petermann Bjerg** ▲ C Greenland
11 S12 **Peter Pond Lake** ◎ Saskatchewan, C Canada
39 X13 **Petersburg** Mytkof Island, Alaska, USA
30 K13 **Petersburg** Illinois, N USA
31 N16 **Petersburg** Indiana, N USA
29 Q3 **Petersburg** North Dakota, N USA
25 N5 **Petersburg** Texas, SW USA
21 V7 **Petersburg** Virginia, NE USA
21 T4 **Petersburg** West Virginia, NE USA
100 H12 **Petershagen** Nordrhein-Westfalen, NW Germany
55 S9 **Peters Mine** var. Peter's Mine. N Guyana
107 O21 **Petilia Policastro** Calabria, SW Italy
44 M9 **Pétionville** S Haiti
45 X6 **Petit-Bourg** Basse Terre, C Guadeloupe
15 Y5 **Petit-Cap** Quebec, SE Canada
45 Y6 **Petit Cul-de-Sac Marin** bay C Guadeloupe
12 K7 **Petite Rivière de la Baleine** ~ Quebec, NE Canada
44 M9 **Petite-Rivière-de-l'Artibonite** C Haiti
173 X16 **Petite Rivière Noire, Piton de la** ▲ C Mauritius
15 R9 **Petite-Rivière-St-François** Quebec, SE Canada
44 L9 **Petit-Goâve** S Haiti
Petitjean see Sidi-Kacem
13 N10 **Petit Lac Manicouagan** ◎ Quebec, E Canada
19 T7 **Petit Manan Point** headland Maine, NE USA
Petit Mécatina, Rivière du see Little Mecatina
11 N10 **Petitot** ~ Alberta/British Columbia, W Canada
45 S12 **Petit Piton** ▲ SW Saint Lucia
Petit-Popo see Aného
Petit St-Bernard, Col du see Little Saint Bernard Pass
13 O8 **Petitsikapau Lake** ◎ Newfoundland, E Canada
92 L11 **Petkula** Lappi, N Finland
41 X12 **Peto** Yucatán, SE Mexico
62 G10 **Petorca** Valparaíso, C Chile
31 Q5 **Petoskey** Michigan, N USA
138 G14 **Petra** archaeological site Ma'ān, W Jordan
Petra see Wādī Mūsā
115 F14 **Pétras, Sténa** pass N Greece
123 S16 **Petra Velikogo, Zaliv** bay SE Russian Federation
Petrel see Petrer
14 K15 **Petre, Point** headland Ontario, SE Canada
105 S12 **Petrer** var. Petrel. País Valenciano, E Spain
127 U11 **Petretsovo** Permskaya Oblast', NW Russian Federation
114 G12 **Petrich** Blagoevgrad, SW Bulgaria
187 P15 **Petrie, Récif** reef N New Caledonia
37 N11 **Petrified Forest** prehistoric site Arizona, SW USA
Petrikau see Piotrków Trybunalski
Petrikov see Pyetrykaw
116 H12 **Petrila** Hung. Petrilla. Hunedoara, W Romania
Petrilla see Petrila
112 E9 **Petrinja** Sisak-Moslavina, C Croatia
Petroaleksandrovsk see Türtkül
Petrőcz see Bački Petrovac
126 G12 **Petrodvorets** Fin. Pietarhovi. Leningradskaya Oblast', NW Russian Federation
Petrograd see Sankt-Peterburg
Petrokov see Piotrków Trybunalski
54 G6 **Petrólea** Norte de Santander, NE Colombia
14 D16 **Petrolia** Ontario, S Canada
25 S4 **Petrolia** Texas, SW USA
59 O15 **Petrolina** Pernambuco, E Brazil
45 T6 **Petrona, Punta** headland C Puerto Rico
Petropavl see Petropavlovsk
117 V7 **Petropavlivka** Dnipropetrovs'ka Oblast', E Ukraine
145 P6 **Petropavlovsk** Kaz. Petropavl. Severnyy Kazakhstan, N Kazakhstan
123 V11 **Petropavlovsk-Kamchatskiy** Kamchatskaya Oblast', E Russian Federation
60 P9 **Petrópolis** Rio de Janeiro, SE Brazil
116 H12 **Petroşani** var. Petroşeni, Ger. Petroschen, Hung. Petrozsény. Hunedoara, W Romania
Petroschen/Petroşeni see Petroşani
Petroskoi see Petrozavodsk
Petrovac/Petrovácz see Bački Petrovac
113 J17 **Petrovac na Moru** Montenegro, SW Yugoslavia
117 S8 **Petrove** Kirovohrads'ka Oblast', C Ukraine
113 O18 **Petrovec** C FYR Macedonia
Petrovgrad see Zrenjanin
129 P7 **Petrovsk** Saratovskaya Oblast', W Russian Federation
126 J9 **Petrovskiy Yam** Respublika Kareliya, NW Russian Federation
Petrovsk-Port see Makhachkala
129 P9 **Petrov Val** Volgogradskaya Oblast', SW Russian Federation
126 J11 **Petrozavodsk** Fin. Petroskoi. Respublika Kareliya, NW Russian Federation
Petrozsény see Petroşani
83 D20 **Petrusdal** Hardap, C Namibia
117 T7 **Petrykivka** Dnipropetrovs'ka Oblast', E Ukraine
Petsamo see Pechenga
Petschka see Pecica
Pettau see Ptuj
109 S5 **Pettenbach** Oberösterreich, C Austria
25 S13 **Pettus** Texas, SW USA
122 G11 **Petukhovo** Kurganskaya Oblast', C Russian Federation
Petuna see Songyuan
109 R4 **Peuerbach** Oberösterreich, N Austria
62 G12 **Peumo** Libertador, C Chile
123 T6 **Pevek** Chukotskiy Avtonomnyy Okrug, NE Russian Federation
27 X5 **Pevely** Missouri, C USA
Peyia see Pégeia
102 J15 **Peyrehorade** Landes, SW France
126 J14 **Peza** ~ NW Russian Federation
103 P16 **Pézenas** Hérault, S France
111 H20 **Pezinok** Ger. Bösing, Hung. Bazin. Bratislavský Kraj, W Slovakia
101 L22 **Pfaffenhofen an der Ilm** Bayern, SE Germany
108 G7 **Pfäffikon** Schwyz, C Switzerland
101 F20 **Pfälzer Wald** hill range W Germany
101 N22 **Pfarrkirchen** Bayern, SE Germany
101 G21 **Pforzheim** Baden-Württemberg, SW Germany
101 H24 **Pfullendorf** Baden-Württemberg, S Germany
108 K8 **Pfunds** Tirol, W Austria
101 G19 **Pfungstadt** Hessen, W Germany
83 L20 **Phalaborwa** Northern, NE South Africa
152 E11 **Phalodi** Rājasthān, NW India
152 E12 **Phalsund** Rājasthān, NW India
155 E15 **Phaltan** Mahārāshtra, W India
167 O7 **Phan** var. Muang Phan. Chiang Rai, NW Thailand
167 O14 **Phangan, Ko** island SW Thailand
166 M15 **Phang-Nga** var. Pang-Nga, Phangnga. Phangnga, SW Thailand
Phan Rang/Phanrang see Phan Rang-Thap Cham
167 V13 **Phan Rang-Thap Cham** var. Phanrang, Phan Rang, Phan Rang Thap Cham. Ninh Thuân, S Vietnam
167 U13 **Phan Ri** Binh Thuân, S Vietnam
167 U13 **Phan Thiêt** Binh Thuân, S Vietnam
Pharnacia see Giresun
25 S17 **Pharr** Texas, SW USA
Pharus see Hvar
167 N16 **Phatthalung** var. Padalung, Patalung. Phatthalung, SW Thailand
167 O7 **Phayao** var. Muang Phayao. Phayao, NW Thailand
11 U10 **Phelps Lake** ◎ Saskatchewan, C Canada
21 X9 **Phelps Lake** ◎ North Carolina, SE USA
23 R5 **Phenix City** Alabama, S USA
167 T8 **Pheo** Quang Binh, C Vietnam
Phet Buri see Phetchaburi
167 O11 **Phetchaburi** var. Bejraburi, Petchaburi, Phet Buri. Phetchaburi, SW Thailand
167 O9 **Phichit** var. Bichitra, Muang Phichit, Pichit. Phichit, C Thailand
22 M5 **Philadelphia** Mississippi, S USA
18 I7 **Philadelphia** New York, NE USA
18 I16 **Philadelphia** Pennsylvania, NE USA
18 I16 **Philadelphia** ✈ Pennsylvania, NE USA
Philadelphia see 'Ammān
28 L10 **Philip** South Dakota, N USA
99 H22 **Philippeville** Namur, S Belgium
Philippeville see Skikda
21 S3 **Philippi** West Virginia, NE USA
Philippi see Fílippoi
195 Y9 **Philippi Glacier** glacier Antarctica
192 G6 **Philippine Basin** undersea feature W Pacific Ocean
131 X12 **Philippine Plate** tectonic feature
169 W6 **Philippines** off. Republic of the Philippines. ◆ republic SE Asia
131 X13 **Philippines** island group W Pacific Ocean
171 P3 **Philippine Sea** sea W Pacific Ocean
192 F6 **Philippine Trench** undersea feature W Philippine Sea
83 H23 **Philippolis** Free State, C South Africa
Philippopolis see Plovdiv, Bulgaria
Philippopolis see Shahbā', Syria
45 V9 **Philipsburg** Sint Maarten, N Netherlands Antilles
33 P10 **Philipsburg** Montana, NW USA
39 R6 **Philip Smith Mountains** ▲ Alaska, USA
152 H8 **Phillaur** Punjab, N India
183 N13 **Phillip Island** island Victoria, SE Australia
25 N2 **Phillips** Texas, SW USA
30 K5 **Phillips** Wisconsin, N USA
26 K3 **Phillipsburg** Kansas, C USA
18 I14 **Phillipsburg** New Jersey, NE USA
21 S7 **Philpott Lake** ⊟ Virginia, NE USA
Phintias see Licata
167 P9 **Phitsanulok** var. Bisnulok, Muang Phitsanulok, Pitsanulok. Phitsanulok, C Thailand
Phlórina see Flórina
Phnom Penh see Phnum Penh
167 S13 **Phnum Penh** var. Phnom Penh. ● (Cambodia) Phnum Penh, S Cambodia
167 S11 **Phnum Tbêng Meanchey** Preăh Vihéar, N Cambodia
36 K13 **Phoenix** state capital Arizona, SW USA
Phoenix Island see Rawaki
191 R3 **Phoenix Islands** island group C Kiribati
18 I15 **Phoenixville** Pennsylvania, NE USA
83 K22 **Phofung** var. Mont-aux-Sources. ▲ N Lesotho
167 Q10 **Phon** Khon Kaen, E Thailand
167 Q5 **Phôngsali** var. Phong Saly. Phôngsali, N Laos
Phong Saly see Phôngsali
167 Q8 **Phônhông** C Laos
167 R5 **Phô Rang** Lao Cai, N Vietnam
Phort Láirge, Cuan see Waterford Harbour
167 N10 **Phra Chedi Sam Ong** Kanchanaburi, W Thailand
167 O8 **Phrae** var. Muang Phrae, Prae. Phrae, NW Thailand
Phra Nakhon Si Ayutthaya see Ayutthaya
167 M14 **Phra Thong, Ko** island SW Thailand
Phu Cương see Thu Dâu Môt
166 M15 **Phuket** var. Bhuket, Puket, Mal. Ujung Salang; prev. Junkseylon, Salang. Phuket, SW Thailand
166 M15 **Phuket** ✈ Phuket, SW Thailand
166 M15 **Phuket, Ko** island SW Thailand
154 N12 **Phulabāni** prev. Phulbani. Orissa, E India
Phulbani see Phulabāni
167 U9 **Phu Lôc** Th,a Thiên-Huê, C Vietnam
167 S13 **Phumĭ Banam** Prey Vêng, S Cambodia

◆ COUNTRY ● COUNTRY CAPITAL ◇ DEPENDENT TERRITORY ○ DEPENDENT TERRITORY CAPITAL ◈ ADMINISTRATIVE REGION ✈ INTERNATIONAL AIRPORT ▲ MOUNTAIN ▲ MOUNTAIN RANGE VOLCANO ~ RIVER ◎ LAKE ⊟ RESERVOIR

167 R13 **Phumĭ Chŏâm** Kâmpóng Spœ, SW Cambodia
167 T11 **Phumĭ Kalêng** Stœ̆ng Trêng, NE Cambodia
167 S12 **Phumĭ Kâmpóng Trâbêk** *prev.* Phum Kompong Trabek. Kâmpóng Thum, C Cambodia
167 Q11 **Phumĭ Koŭk Kduŏch** Bătdâmbâng, NW Cambodia
167 T11 **Phumĭ Labăng** Rôtânôkiri, NE Cambodia
167 S11 **Phumĭ Mlu Prey** Preăh Vihéar, N Cambodia
167 R11 **Phumĭ Moŭng** Siĕmréab, NW Cambodia
167 Q12 **Phumĭ Prâmaôy** Poŭthĭsăt, W Cambodia
167 Q13 **Phumĭ Samĭt** Kaôh Kông, SW Cambodia
167 R11 **Phumĭ Sâmraông** *prev.* Phum Samrong. Siĕmréab, NW Cambodia
167 S12 **Phumĭ Siĕmbok** Stœ̆ng Trêng, N Cambodia
167 S11 **Phumĭ Thalabârĭvăt** Stœ̆ng Trêng, N Cambodia
167 R13 **Phumĭ Veal Renh** Kâmpôt, SW Cambodia
167 P13 **Phumĭ Yeay Sên** Kaôh Kông, SW Cambodia
Phum Kompong Trabek *see* Phumĭ Kâmpóng Trâbêk
Phum Samrong *see* Phumĭ Sâmraông
167 V11 **Phu My** Binh Đinh, C Vietnam
167 S14 **Phung Hiêp** Cân Thơ, S Vietnam
153 T12 **Phuntsholing** SW Bhutan
167 R15 **Phươc Long** Minh Hai, S Vietnam
167 R14 **Phu Quôc, Đao** *var.* Phu Quoc Island. *island* S Vietnam
Phu Quoc Island *see* Phu Quôc, Đao
167 S6 **Phu Tho** Vinh Phu, N Vietnam
Phu Vinh *see* Tra Vinh
189 T13 **Piaanu Pass** *passage* Chuuk Islands, C Micronesia
106 E8 **Piacenza** *Fr.* Paisance; *anc.* Placentia. Emilia-Romagna, N Italy
107 K14 **Pianella** Abruzzo, C Italy
107 M15 **Pianosa, Isola** *island* Archipelago Toscano, C Italy
171 U13 **Piar** Irian Jaya, E Indonesia
45 U14 **Piarco** *var.* Port of Spain. ✕ (Port-of-Spain) Trinidad, Trinidad and Tobago
110 M12 **Piaseczno** Mazowieckie, C Poland
116 I15 **Piatra** Teleorman, S Romania
116 L10 **Piatra-Neamț** *Hung.* Karácsonkő. Neamț, NE Romania
Piauhy *see* Piauí
59 N15 **Piauí** *off.* Estado do Piauí; *prev.* Piauhy. ◈ *state* E Brazil
106 I7 **Piave** ≈ NE Italy
107 K24 **Piazza Armerina** *var.* Chiazza. Sicilia, Italy, C Mediterranean Sea
81 G14 **Pibor** *Amh.* Pībor Wenz. ≈ Ethiopia/Sudan
81 G14 **Pibor Post** Jonglei, SE Sudan
Pībor Wenz *see* Pibor
Pibrans *see* Příbram
36 K11 **Picacho Butte** ▲ Arizona, SW USA
40 D4 **Picachos, Cerro** ▲ NW Mexico
103 O4 **Picardie** *Eng.* Picardy. ◈ *region* N France
Picardy *see* Picardie
22 L8 **Picayune** Mississippi, S USA
Piccolo San Bernardo, Colle di *see* Little Saint Bernard Pass
62 K5 **Pichanal** Salta, N Argentina
147 P12 **Pichandar** W Tajikistan
27 R8 **Picher** Oklahoma, C USA
62 G12 **Pichilemu** Libertador, C Chile
40 F9 **Pichilingue** Baja California Sur, W Mexico
56 B6 **Pichincha** ◈ *province* N Ecuador
56 C6 **Pichincha** ▲ N Ecuador
Pichit *see* Phichit
41 U15 **Pichucalco** Chiapas, SE Mexico
22 L5 **Pickens** Mississippi, S USA
21 O11 **Pickens** South Carolina, SE USA
14 G11 **Pickerel** ≈ Ontario, S Canada
14 H15 **Pickering** Ontario, S Canada
97 N16 **Pickering** N England, UK
31 S13 **Pickerington** Ohio, N USA
12 C10 **Pickle Lake** Ontario, C Canada
29 P12 **Pickstown** South Dakota, N USA
25 V6 **Pickton** Texas, SW USA
23 N1 **Pickwick Lake** ▣ S USA
64 N2 **Pico** *var.* Ilha do Pico. *island* Azores, Portugal, NE Atlantic Ocean
63 J19 **Pico de Salamanca** Chubut, SE Argentina
1 P9 **Pico Fracture Zone** *tectonic feature* NW Atlantic Ocean
Pico, Ilha do *see* Pico
59 O14 **Picos** Piauí, E Brazil
63 I20 **Pico Truncado** Santa Cruz, SE Argentina
183 S9 **Picton** New South Wales, SE Australia
14 K15 **Picton** Ontario, SE Canada
185 K14 **Picton** Marlborough, South Island, NZ
63 H15 **Pićun Leufú, Arroyo** ≈ SW Argentina
Pidálion *see* Gkréko, Akrotíri
155 K25 **Pidurutalagala** ▲ S Sri Lanka
116 K6 **Pidvolochys'k** Ternopil's'ka Oblast', W Ukraine
107 K16 **Piedimonte Matese** Campania, S Italy
27 X7 **Piedmont** Missouri, C USA
21 P11 **Piedmont** South Carolina, SE USA
17 S12 **Piedmont** *escarpment* E USA
Piedmont *see* Piemonte
31 U13 **Piedmont Lake** ▣ Ohio, N USA
104 M11 **Piedrabuena** Castilla-La Mancha, C Spain
Piedrafita, Puerto de *see* Pedrafita, Porto de
104 L8 **Piedrahita** Castilla-León, N Spain
41 N6 **Piedras Negras** *var.* Ciudad Porfirio Díaz. Coahuila de Zaragoza, NE Mexico
61 E21 **Piedras, Punta** *headland* E Argentina
57 I14 **Piedras, Río de las** ≈ E Peru
111 J16 **Piekary Śląskie** Śląskie, S Poland
93 M17 **Pieksämäki** Isä-Suomi, E Finland
109 V5 **Pielach** ≈ NE Austria
93 M16 **Pielavesi** Itä-Suomi, C Finland
93 N16 **Pielinen** *var.* Pielisjärvi. ◎ E Finland
Pielisjärvi *see* Pielinen
106 A8 **Piemonte** *Eng.* Piedmont. ◈ *region* NW Italy
111 L18 **Pieniny** ▲ Poland/Slovakia
111 E14 **Pieńsk** *Ger.* Penzig. Dolnośląskie, SW Poland
29 Q13 **Pierce** Nebraska, C USA
11 R14 **Pierceland** Saskatchewan, C Canada
115 E14 **Piéria** ▲ N Greece
29 N10 **Pierre** *state capital* South Dakota, N USA
102 K16 **Pierrefitte-Nestalas** Hautes-Pyrénées, S France
103 R14 **Pierrelatte** Drôme, E France
15 P11 **Pierreville** Quebec, SE Canada
15 O7 **Pierriche** ≈ Quebec, SE Canada
111 H20 **Piešt'any** *Ger.* Pistyan, *Hung.* Pöstyén. Trnavský, W Slovakia
109 X5 **Piesting** ≈ E Austria
Pietarhovi *see* Petrodvorets
Pietari *see* Sankt-Peterburg
Pietarsaari *see* Jakobstad
83 K23 **Pietermaritzburg** *var.* Maritzburg. KwaZulu/Natal, E South Africa
83 K20 **Pietersburg** Northern, NE South Africa
107 K24 **Pietraperzia** Sicilia, Italy, C Mediterranean Sea
107 N22 **Pietra Spada, Passo della** *pass* SW Italy
83 K22 **Piet Retief** Mpumalanga, E South Africa
116 I9 **Pietrosul, Vârful** *prev.* Vîrful Pietrosu. ▲ N Romania
116 J10 **Pietrosul, Vârful** *prev.* Vîrful Pietrosu. ▲ N Romania
Pietrosu, Vîrful *see* Pietrosul, Vârful
106 I6 **Pieve di Cadore** Veneto, NE Italy
14 C18 **Pigeon Bay** *lake bay* Ontario, S Canada
27 X8 **Piggott** Arkansas, C USA
83 L21 **Piggs Peak** NW Swaziland
Pigs, Bay of *see* Cochinos, Bahía de
61 A23 **Pigüé** Buenos Aires, E Argentina
41 O12 **Piguícas** ▲ C Mexico
193 W15 **Piha Passage** *passage* S Tonga
Pihkva Järv *see* Pskov, Lake
93 N18 **Pihlajavesi** ◎ SE Finland
93 J18 **Pihlava** Länsi-Suomi, W Finland
93 L16 **Pihtipudas** Länsi-Suomi, W Finland
40 L14 **Pihuamo** Jalisco, SW Mexico
189 U11 **Piis Moen** *var.* Pis. *atoll* Chuuk Islands, C Micronesia
41 U17 **Pijijiapán** Chiapas, SE Mexico
98 G12 **Pijnacker** Zuid-Holland, W Netherlands
42 H5 **Pijol, Pico** ▲ NW Honduras
Pikaar *see* Bikar Atoll
126 I13 **Pikalevo** Leningradskaya Oblast', NW Russian Federation
188 M15 **Pikelot** *island* Caroline Islands, C Micronesia
30 M5 **Pike River** ≈ Wisconsin, N USA
37 T5 **Pikes Peak** ▲ Colorado, C USA
21 P6 **Pikeville** Kentucky, S USA
20 L9 **Pikeville** Tennessee, S USA
Pikinni *see* Bikini Atoll
79 H18 **Pikounda** La Sangha, C Congo
110 G9 **Piła** *Ger.* Schneidemühl. Wielkopolskie, C Poland
62 N6 **Pilagá, Riacho** ≈ NE Argentina
61 D20 **Pilar** Buenos Aires, E Argentina
62 N7 **Pilar** *var.* Villa del Pilar. Ñeembucú, S Paraguay
62 N6 **Pilcomayo, Río** ≈ C South America
147 R12 **Pildon** *Rus.* Pil'don. C Tajikistan
Piles *see* Pylés
Pilgram *see* Pelhřimov
152 L10 **Pīlībhīt** Uttar Pradesh, N India
110 M13 **Pilica** ≈ C Poland
115 G16 **Pílio** ▲ C Greece
111 J22 **Pilisvörösvár** Pest, N Hungary
65 G15 **Pillar Bay** *bay* Ascension Island, C Atlantic Ocean
183 P17 **Pillar, Cape** *headland* Tasmania, SE Australia
Pillau *see* Baltiysk
183 R5 **Pilliga** New South Wales, SE Australia
44 H8 **Pilón** Granma, E Cuba
Pilos *see* Pýlos
11 W17 **Pilot Mound** Manitoba, S Canada
21 S8 **Pilot Mountain** North Carolina, SE USA
39 O14 **Pilot Point** Alaska, USA
25 T5 **Pilot Point** Texas, SW USA
32 K11 **Pilot Rock** Oregon, NW USA
38 M11 **Pilot Station** Alaska, USA
Pilsen *see* Plzeň
111 K18 **Pilsko** ▲ N Slovakia
Pilten *see* Piltene
118 D8 **Piltene** *Ger.* Pilten. Ventspils, W Latvia
111 M16 **Pilzno** Podkarpackie, SE Poland
Pilzno *see* Plzeň
37 N14 **Pima** Arizona, SW USA
58 H13 **Pimenta** Pará, N Brazil
59 F16 **Pimenta Bueno** Rondônia, W Brazil
56 B11 **Pimentel** Lambayeque, W Peru
105 S6 **Pina** Aragón, NE Spain
119 I20 **Pina** *Rus.* Pina. ≈ SW Belarus
40 E2 **Pinacate, Sierra del** ▲ NW Mexico
63 H22 **Pináculo, Cerro** ▲ S Argentina
191 X11 **Pinaki** *atoll* Îles Tuamotu, E French Polynesia
37 N15 **Pinaleno Mountains** ▲ Arizona, SW USA
171 P4 **Pinamalayan** Mindoro, N Philippines
169 Q10 **Pinang** Borneo, C Indonesia
168 J7 **Pinang** *var.* Penang. ◈ *state* Peninsular Malaysia
Pinang *see* Pinang, Pulau, Peninsular Malaysia
Pinang *see* George Town
168 J7 **Pinang, Pulau** *var.* Penang, Pinang; *prev.* Prince of Wales Island. *island* Peninsular Malaysia
44 B5 **Pinar del Río** Pinar del Río, W Cuba
114 N11 **Pınarhisar** Kırklareli, NW Turkey
171 O3 **Pinatubo, Mount** ▲ Luzon, N Philippines
11 Y16 **Pinawa** Manitoba, S Canada
11 Q17 **Pincher Creek** Alberta, SW Canada
30 L16 **Pinckneyville** Illinois, N USA
Pîncota *see* Pâncota
111 L15 **Pińczów** Świętokrzyskie, C Poland
149 U7 **Pind Dādan Khān** Punjab, E Pakistan
Píndhos/Píndhos Óros *see* Píndos
149 V8 **Pindi Bhattiān** Punjab, E Pakistan
149 U6 **Pindi Gheb** Punjab, E Pakistan
115 D15 **Píndos** *var.* Píndhos Óros, *Eng.* Pindus Mountains; *prev.* Píndhos. ▲ C Greece
Pindus Mountains *see* Píndos
18 J16 **Pine Barrens** *physical region* New Jersey, NE USA
27 V12 **Pine Bluff** Arkansas, C USA
23 X11 **Pine Castle** Florida, SE USA
29 V7 **Pine City** Minnesota, N USA
181 P2 **Pine Creek** Northern Territory, N Australia
35 V4 **Pine Creek** ≈ Nevada, W USA
18 F13 **Pine Creek** ≈ Pennsylvania, NE USA
27 Q13 **Pine Creek Lake** ▣ Oklahoma, C USA
33 T15 **Pinedale** Wyoming, C USA
11 X15 **Pine Dock** Manitoba, S Canada
11 Y16 **Pine Falls** Manitoba, S Canada
35 R10 **Pine Flat Lake** ▣ California, W USA
127 N8 **Pinega** Arkhangel'skaya Oblast', NW Russian Federation
127 N8 **Pinega** ≈ NW Russian Federation
15 N12 **Pine Hill** Quebec, SE Canada
11 T12 **Pinehouse Lake** ◎ Saskatchewan, C Canada
21 T10 **Pinehurst** North Carolina, SE USA
115 D19 **Pineiós** ≈ S Greece
115 E16 **Pineiós** *var.* Piniós; *anc.* Peneius. ≈ C Greece
29 W10 **Pine Island** Minnesota, N USA
23 V15 **Pine Island** *island* Florida, SE USA
194 K10 **Pine Island Glacier** *glacier* Antarctica
25 X9 **Pineland** Texas, SW USA
23 V13 **Pinellas Park** Florida, SE USA
10 M13 **Pine Pass** *pass* British Columbia, W Canada
8 J10 **Pine Point** Northwest Territories, W Canada
28 K12 **Pine Ridge** South Dakota, N USA
29 U6 **Pine River** Minnesota, N USA
31 Q8 **Pine River** ≈ Michigan, N USA
30 M4 **Pine River** ≈ Wisconsin, N USA
106 A8 **Pinerolo** Piemonte, NE Italy
25 W6 **Pines, Lake O' the** ▣ Texas, SW USA
Pines, The Isle of the *see* Juventud, Isla de la
Pine Tree State *see* Maine
21 N7 **Pineville** Kentucky, S USA
22 H7 **Pineville** Louisiana, S USA
27 R8 **Pineville** Missouri, C USA
21 R10 **Pineville** North Carolina, SE USA
21 Q6 **Pineville** West Virginia, NE USA
33 V8 **Piney Buttes** *physical region* Montana, NW USA
163 W9 **Ping'an** Jilin, NE China
160 H14 **Pingbian** *var.* Pingbian Miaozu Zizhixian. Yunnan, SW China
157 S9 **Pingdingshan** Henan, C China
161 R4 **Pingdu** Shandong, E China
189 W16 **Pingelap Atoll** *atoll* Caroline Islands, E Micronesia
160 K14 **Pingguo** Guangxi Zhuangzu Zizhiqu, S China
161 Q13 **Pinghe** Fujian, SE China
P'ing-hsiang *see* Pingxiang
161 N10 **Pingjiang** Hunan, S China
Pingkiang *see* Harbin
160 L8 **Pingli** Shaanxi, C China
159 W10 **Pingliang** *var.* P'ing-liang. Gansu, C China
159 W8 **Pingluo** Ningxia, N China
Pingma *see* Tiandong
167 O7 **Ping, Mae Nam** ≈ W Thailand
161 Q1 **Pingquan** Hebei, E China
29 P5 **Pingree** North Dakota, N USA
Pingsiang *see* Pingxiang
161 S14 **P'ingtung** *Jap.* Heitō. S Taiwan
160 I8 **Pingwu** Sichuan, C China
160 J15 **Pingxiang** Guangxi Zhuangzu Zizhiqu, S China
161 O11 **Pingxiang** *var.* P'ing-hsiang; *prev.* Pingsiang. Jiangxi, S China
161 S11 **Pingyang** Zhejiang, SE China
161 P5 **Pingyi** Shandong, E China
161 P5 **Pingyin** Shandong, E China
60 H13 **Pinhalzinho** Santa Catarina, S Brazil
60 I12 **Pinhão** Paraná, S Brazil
61 H17 **Pinheiro Machado** Rio Grande do Sul, S Brazil
104 I7 **Pinhel** Guarda, N Portugal
Piniós *see* Pineiós
168 I11 **Pini, Pulau** *island* Kepulauan Batu, W Indonesia
109 Y7 **Pinka** ≈ SE Austria
109 X7 **Pinkafeld** Burgenland, SE Austria
Pinkiang *see* Harbin
10 M12 **Pink Mountain** British Columbia, W Canada
166 M3 **Pinlebu** Sagaing, N Myanmar
38 J12 **Pinnacle Island** *island* Alaska, USA
180 I12 **Pinnacles, The** *tourist site* Western Australia
182 K10 **Pinnaroo** South Australia
Pinne *see* Pniewy
100 I9 **Pinneberg** Schleswig-Holstein, N Germany
115 I15 **Pínnes, Akrotírio** *headland* N Greece
Pinos, Isla de *see* Juventud, Isla de la
35 R14 **Pinos, Mount** ▲ California, W USA
105 R12 **Pinoso** País Valenciano, E Spain
105 N14 **Pinos-Puente** Andalucía, S Spain
41 Q17 **Pinotepa Nacional** *var.* Santiago Pinotepa Nacional. Oaxaca, SE Mexico
114 F13 **Pínovo** ▲ N Greece
187 R17 **Pins, Île des** *var.* Kunyé. *island* E New Caledonia
119 I20 **Pinsk** *Pol.* Pińsk. Brestskaya Voblasts', SW Belarus
14 D18 **Pins, Pointe aux** *headland* Ontario, S Canada
57 B16 **Pinta, Isla** *var.* Abingdon. *island* Galapagos Islands, Ecuador, E Pacific Ocean
127 Q12 **Pinyug** Kirovskaya Oblast', NW Russian Federation
57 B17 **Pinzón, Isla** *var.* Duncan Island. *island* Galapagos Islands, Ecuador, E Pacific Ocean
35 Y8 **Pioche** Nevada, W USA
106 F13 **Piombino** Toscana, C Italy
(0) C9 **Pioneer Fracture Zone** *tectonic feature* NE Pacific Ocean
122 L5 **Pioner, Ostrov** *island* Severnaya Zemlya, N Russian Federation
118 A13 **Pionerskiy** *Ger.* Neukuhren. Kaliningradskaya Oblast', W Russian Federation
110 N13 **Pionki** Mazowieckie, C Poland
184 L9 **Piopio** Waikato, North Island, NZ
110 K13 **Piotrków Trybunalski** *Ger.* Petrikau, *Rus.* Petrokov. Łodzkie, C Poland
152 F12 **Pīpār Road** Rājasthān, N India
115 I16 **Pipéri** *island* Vóreioi Sporádes, Greece, Aegean Sea
29 S10 **Pipestone** Minnesota, N USA
12 C9 **Pipestone** ≈ Ontario, C Canada
61 E21 **Pipinas** Buenos Aires, E Argentina
149 T7 **Piplān** *prev.* Liaqatabad. Punjab, E Pakistan
15 R5 **Pipmuacan, Réservoir** ▣ Quebec, SE Canada
Piqan *see* Shanshan
31 R13 **Piqua** Ohio, N USA
105 P5 **Piqueras, Puerto de** *pass* N Spain
60 H11 **Piquiri, Rio** ≈ S Brazil
60 L9 **Piracicaba** São Paulo, S Brazil
Piraeus/Piraiévs *see* Peiraías
60 K10 **Piraju** São Paulo, S Brazil
60 K9 **Pirajuí** São Paulo, S Brazil
63 G21 **Pirámide, Cerro** ▲ S Chile
Piramiva *see* Pyramíva
109 R13 **Piran** *It.* Pirano. SW Slovenia
62 N6 **Pirané** Formosa, N Argentina
59 J18 **Piranhas** Goiás, S Brazil
Pirano *see* Piran
142 I4 **Pīrānshahr** Āzarbāyjān-e Bākhtarī, NW Iran
59 M19 **Pirapora** Minas Gerais, NE Brazil
60 I9 **Pirapòzinho** São Paulo, S Brazil
61 G19 **Piraraja** Lavalleja, S Uruguay
60 L9 **Pirassununga** São Paulo, S Brazil
45 V6 **Pirata, Monte** ▲ E Puerto Rico
60 I13 **Piratuba** Santa Catarina, S Brazil
114 I9 **Pirdop** *prev.* Srednogorie. Sofiya, W Bulgaria
191 P7 **Pirea** Tahiti, W French Polynesia
59 K18 **Pirenópolis** Goiás, S Brazil
153 S13 **Pirganj** Rajshahi, NW Bangladesh
Pirgi *see* Pyrgí
Pírgos *see* Pýrgos
61 F20 **Piriápolis** Maldonado, S Uruguay
114 G11 **Pirin** ▲ SW Bulgaria
Pirineos *see* Pyrenees
58 N13 **Piripiri** Piauí, E Brazil
118 H4 **Pirita** *var.* Pirita Jõgi. ≈ NW Estonia
Pirita Jõgi *see* Pirita
54 J6 **Píritu** Portuguesa, N Venezuela
93 L18 **Pirkkala** Länsi-Suomi, W Finland
101 F20 **Pirmasens** Rheinland-Pfalz, SW Germany
101 P16 **Pirna** Sachsen, E Germany
Piroe *see* Piru
113 Q15 **Pirot** Serbia, SE Yugoslavia
152 H6 **Pīr Panjāl Range** ▲ NE India
43 W16 **Pirre, Cerro** ▲ SE Panama
137 Y11 **Pirsaat** *Rus.* Pirsagat. ≈ E Azerbaijan
Pirsagat *see* Pirsaat
143 V11 **Pīr Shūrān, Selseleh-ye** ▲ SE Iran
92 M12 **Pirttikoski** Lappi, N Finland
Pirttikylä *see* Pörtom
171 R13 **Piru** *prev.* Piroe. Pulau Seram, E Indonesia
Piryatin *see* Pyryatyn
Pis *see* Piis Moen
106 F11 **Pisa** *var.* Pisae. Toscana, C Italy
Pisae *see* Pisa
189 V12 **Pisar** *atoll* Chuuk Islands, C Micronesia
Pisaurum *see* Pesaro
14 M10 **Piscatosine, Lac** ◎ Quebec, SE Canada
109 W7 **Pischeldorf** Steiermark, SE Austria
Pischk *see* Simeria
107 L19 **Pisciotta** Campania, S Italy
57 E16 **Pisco** Ica, SW Peru
116 G9 **Pişcolt** *Hung.* Piskolt. Satu Mare, NW Romania
57 E16 **Pisco, Río** ≈ E Peru
111 C18 **Písek** Budějovický Kraj, S Czech Republic
31 R14 **Pisgah** Ohio, N USA
158 F9 **Pishan** *var.* Guma. Xinjiang Uygur Zizhiqu, NW China
117 N8 **Pishchanka** Vinnyts'ka Oblast', C Ukraine
113 K21 **Pishë** Fier, SW Albania
143 X14 **Pīshīn** Sīstān va Balūchestān, SE Iran
149 O9 **Pishīn** North-West Frontier Province, NW Pakistan
149 N11 **Pishin Lora** *var.* Psein Lora, *Pash.* Pseyn Bowr. ≈ SW Pakistan
Pishma *see* Pizhma
Pishpek *see* Bishkek
171 O14 **Pising** Pulau Kabaena, C Indonesia
Pisino *see* Pazin
Piski *see* Simeria
Piskolt *see* Pişcolt
147 Q9 **Piskom** *Rus.* Pskem. ≈ E Uzbekistan
Piskom Tizmasi *see* Pskemskiy Khrebet
35 P13 **Pismo Beach** California, W USA
77 P12 **Pissila** C Burkina
62 H8 **Pissis, Monte** ▲ N Argentina
41 X12 **Piste** Yucatán, E Mexico
107 O18 **Pisticci** Basilicata, S Italy
106 F11 **Pistoia** *anc.* Pistoria, Pistoriæ. Toscana, C Italy
32 E15 **Pistol River** Oregon, NW USA
Pistoria/Pistoriæ *see* Pistoia
15 U5 **Pistuacanis** ≈ Quebec, SE Canada
Pistyan *see* Piešt'any
104 M5 **Pisuerga** ≈ N Spain
110 N8 **Pisz** *Ger.* Johannisburg. Warmińsko-Mazurskie, NE Poland
76 I13 **Pita** Moyenne-Guinée, NW Guinea
54 D12 **Pitalito** Huila, S Colombia
60 I11 **Pitanga** Paraná, S Brazil
182 M9 **Pitarpunga Lake** *salt lake* New South Wales, SE Australia
193 P10 **Pitcairn Island** *island* S Pitcairn Islands
193 P10 **Pitcairn Islands** ◇ *UK dependent territory* C Pacific Ocean
93 J14 **Piteå** Norrbotten, N Sweden
92 I13 **Piteälven** ≈ N Sweden
116 I13 **Pitești** Argeș, S Romania
Pithagorio *see* Pythagóreio
180 I12 **Pithara** Western Australia
103 N6 **Pithiviers** Loiret, C France
152 L9 **Pithorāgarh** Uttar Pradesh, N India
188 B16 **Piti** W Guam
106 G13 **Pitigliano** Toscana, C Italy
40 F3 **Pitiquito** Sonora, NW Mexico
Pitkäranta *see* Pitkyaranta
38 M11 **Pitkas Point** Alaska, USA
126 H11 **Pitkyaranta** *Fin.* Pitkäranta. Respublika Kareliya, NW Russian Federation
96 J10 **Pitlochry** C Scotland, UK
18 I16 **Pitman** New Jersey, NE USA
112 G8 **Pitomača** Virovitica-Podravina, NE Croatia
35 O2 **Pit River** ≈ California, W USA
63 G15 **Pitrufquén** Araucanía, S Chile
Pitsanulok *see* Phitsanulok
Pitschen *see* Byczyna
Pitsunda *see* Bichvint'a
109 X6 **Pitten** ≈ E Austria
10 J14 **Pitt Island** *island* British Columbia, W Canada
Pitt Island *see* Makin
22 M3 **Pittsboro** Mississippi, S USA
21 T9 **Pittsboro** North Carolina, SE USA
27 R7 **Pittsburg** Kansas, C USA
25 W6 **Pittsburg** Texas, SW USA
18 B14 **Pittsburgh** Pennsylvania, NE USA
30 J14 **Pittsfield** Illinois, N USA
19 R6 **Pittsfield** Maine, NE USA
18 L11 **Pittsfield** Massachusetts, NE USA
183 U3 **Pittsworth** Queensland, E Australia
62 I8 **Pituil** La Rioja, NW Argentina
56 A10 **Piura** Piura, NW Peru
56 A9 **Piura** *off.* Departamento de Piura. ◈ *department* NW Peru
35 S13 **Piute Peak** ▲ California, W USA
113 J15 **Piva** ≈ SW Yugoslavia
117 V5 **Pivdenne** Kharkivs'ka Oblast', E Ukraine
117 P8 **Pivdennyy Buh** *Rus.* Yuzhnyy Bug. ≈ S Ukraine
54 F5 **Pivijay** Magdalena, N Colombia
109 T13 **Pivka** *prev.* Šent Peter, *Ger.* Sankt Peter, *It.* San Pietro del Carso. SW Slovenia
117 U13 **Pivnichno-Kryms'kyy Kanal** *canal* S Ukraine
113 J15 **Pivsko Jezero** ◎ SW Yugoslavia
111 M18 **Piwniczna** Małopolskie, S Poland
35 R12 **Pixley** California, W USA
127 Q15 **Pizhma** *var.* Pishma. ≈ NW Russian Federation
13 U13 **Placentia** Newfoundland, SE Canada
Placentia *see* Piacenza
13 U13 **Placentia Bay** *inlet* Newfoundland, SE Canada
171 P5 **Placer** Masbate, N Philippines
35 P7 **Placerville** California, W USA
44 F5 **Placetas** Villa Clara, C Cuba
113 Q18 **Plačkovica** ▲ E FYR Macedonia
36 L2 **Plain City** Utah, W USA
22 G4 **Plain Dealing** Louisiana, S USA
31 O14 **Plainfield** Indiana, N USA
18 K14 **Plainfield** New Jersey, NE USA
33 O8 **Plains** Montana, NW USA
24 L6 **Plains** Texas, SW USA
29 X10 **Plainview** Minnesota, N USA
29 Q13 **Plainview** Nebraska, C USA
25 N4 **Plainview** Texas, SW USA
26 K4 **Plainville** Kansas, C USA
115 L25 **Pláka, Akrotírio** *headland* Kríti, Greece, E Mediterranean Sea
115 J15 **Pláka, Akrotírio** *headland* Límnos, E Greece
113 N19 **Plakenska Planina** ▲ SW FYR Macedonia
44 K5 **Plana Cays** *islets* SE Bahamas
105 S12 **Plana, Isla** *var.* Nueva Tabarca. *island* E Spain
59 L18 **Planaltina** Goiás, S Brazil
83 O14 **Planalto Moçambicano** *plateau* N Mozambique
112 N10 **Plandište** Serbia, NE Yugoslavia
100 N13 **Plane** ≈ NE Germany
54 E6 **Planeta Rica** Córdoba, NW Colombia
29 P11 **Plankinton** South Dakota, N USA
30 M11 **Plano** Illinois, N USA
25 U6 **Plano** Texas, SW USA
23 W12 **Plant City** Florida, SE USA
22 J9 **Plaquemine** Louisiana, S USA
104 K9 **Plasencia** Extremadura, W Spain
112 P7 **Plaska** Podlaskie, NE Poland
114 C10 **Plaški** Karlovac, C Croatia
113 N19 **Plasnica** SW FYR Macedonia
13 N14 **Plaster Rock** New Brunswick, SE Canada
107 J24 **Platani** *anc.* Halycus. ≈ Sicilia, Italy, C Mediterranean Sea
115 G17 **Plataniá** Thessalía, C Greece
115 G24 **Plátanos** Kríti, Greece, E Mediterranean Sea
65 H18 **Plata, Río de la** *var.* River Plate. *estuary* Argentina/Uruguay
77 V15 **Plateau** ◈ *state* C Nigeria
79 G19 **Plateaux** *var.* Région des Plateaux. ◈ *province* C Congo
92 P1 **Platen, Kapp** *headland* NE Svalbard
Plate, River *see* Plata, Río de la
99 G22 **Plate Taille, Lac de la** *var.* L'Eau d'Heure. ◎ SE Belgium
Plathe *see* Płoty
39 N13 **Platinum** Alaska, USA
54 F5 **Plato** Magdalena, N Colombia
29 O11 **Platte** South Dakota, N USA
27 R3 **Platte City** Missouri, C USA
Plattensee *see* Balaton
27 R3 **Platte River** ≈ Iowa/Missouri, USA
29 Q15 **Platte River** ≈ Nebraska, C USA
37 T3 **Platteville** Colorado, C USA
30 K9 **Platteville** Wisconsin, N USA
101 N21 **Plattling** Bayern, SE Germany
27 R3 **Plattsburg** Missouri, C USA
18 L6 **Plattsburgh** New York, NE USA
29 S15 **Plattsmouth** Nebraska, C USA
101 M17 **Plauen** *var.* Plauen im Vogtland. Sachsen, E Germany
Plauen im Vogtland *see* Plauen
100 M10 **Plauer See** ◎ NE Germany
113 L16 **Plav** Montenegro, SW Yugoslavia
118 I10 **Pļaviņas** *Ger.* Stockmannshof. Aizkraukle, S Latvia
128 K5 **Plavsk** Tul'skaya Oblast', W Russian Federation
41 Z12 **Playa del Carmen** Quintana Roo, E Mexico
40 J12 **Playa Los Corchos** Nayarit, SW Mexico
37 P16 **Playas Lake** ◎ New Mexico, SW USA
41 S15 **Playa Vicenté** Veracruz-Llave, SE Mexico
167 U11 **Plây Cu** *var.* Pleiku. Gia Lai, C Vietnam
28 L3 **Plaza** North Dakota, N USA
63 I15 **Plaza Huincul** Neuquén, C Argentina
36 L3 **Pleasant Grove** Utah, W USA
29 V14 **Pleasant Hill** Iowa, C USA
27 R4 **Pleasant Hill** Missouri, C USA
Pleasant Island *see* Nauru
36 K13 **Pleasant, Lake** ▣ Arizona, SW USA
19 P8 **Pleasant Mountain** ▲ Maine, NE USA
27 R5 **Pleasanton** Kansas, C USA

◆ Country ● Country Capital ◇ Dependent Territory ○ Dependent Territory Capital ◈ Administrative Region ✕ International Airport ▲ Mountain ▲ Mountain Range ▲ Volcano ≈ River ◎ Lake ▣ Reservoir

25 R12 **Pleasanton** Texas, SW USA
185 G20 **Pleasant Point** Canterbury, South Island, NZ
19 R5 **Pleasant River** ≈ Maine, NE USA
18 J17 **Pleasantville** New Jersey, NE USA
103 N12 **Pléaux** Cantal, C France
111 B19 **Plechý** *Ger.* Plöckenstein. ▲ Austria/Czech Republic
Pleebo *see* Plibo
Pleihari *see* Pelaihari
Pleiku *see* Plây Cu
101 M16 **Pleisse** ≈ E Germany
Plencia *see* Plentzia
184 O7 **Plenty, Bay of** *bay* North Island, NZ
33 Y6 **Plentywood** Montana, NW USA
105 O2 **Plentzia** *var.* Plencia. País Vasco, N Spain
102 H5 **Plérin** Côtes d'Armor, NW France
126 M10 **Plesetsk** Arkhangel'skaya Oblast', NW Russian Federation
Pleshchenitsy *see* Plyeshchanitsy
Pleskau *see* Pskov
Pleskauer See *see* Pskov, Lake
Pleskava *see* Pskov
112 E8 **Pleso International** × (Zagreb) Zagreb, NW Croatia
Pless *see* Pszczyna
15 Q11 **Plessisville** Quebec, SE Canada
110 H12 **Pleszew** Wielkopolskie, C Poland
12 L10 **Plétipi, Lac** ◎ Quebec, SE Canada
101 F15 **Plettenberg** Nordrhein-Westfalen, W Germany
114 I8 **Pleven** *prev.* Plevna. Pleven, N Bulgaria
114 I8 **Pleven** ◈ *province* N Bulgaria
Plevlja/Plevlje *see* Pljevlja
Plevna *see* Pleven
Plezzo *see* Bovec
Pliberk *see* Bleiburg
76 L17 **Plibo** *var.* Pleebo. SE Liberia
121 R11 **Pliny Trench** *undersea feature* C Mediterranean Sea
118 K13 **Plisa** *Rus.* Plissa. Vitsyebskaya Voblasts', N Belarus
Plissa *see* Plisa
112 D11 **Plitvica Selo** Lika-Senj, W Croatia
112 D11 **Plješevica** ▲ C Croatia
113 K14 **Pljevlja** *prev.* Plevlja, Plevlje. Montenegro, N Yugoslavia
Ploça *see* Ploçë
Plocce *see* Ploče
113 G15 **Ploče** *It.* Plocce; *prev.* Kardeljevo. Dubrovnik-Neretva, SE Croatia
113 K22 **Ploçë** *var.* Ploça. Vlorë, SW Albania
110 K11 **Płock** *Ger.* Plozk. Mazowieckie, C Poland
109 Q10 **Plöcken Pass** *Ger.* Plöckenpass, *It.* Passo di Monte Croce Carnico. *pass* SW Austria
Plöckenstein *see* Plechý
99 B19 **Ploegsteert** Hainaut, W Belgium
102 H6 **Ploërmel** Morbihan, NW France
Ploești *see* Ploiești
116 K13 **Ploiești** *prev.* Ploești. Prahova, SE Romania
115 L17 **Plomári** *prev.* Plomárion. Lésvos, E Greece
Plomárion *see* Plomári
103 O12 **Plomb du Cantal** ▲ C France
183 V6 **Plomer, Point** *headland* New South Wales, SE Australia
100 J8 **Plön** Schleswig-Holstein, N Germany
110 L11 **Płońsk** Mazowieckie, C Poland
119 J20 **Plotnitsa** *Rus.* Plotnitsa. Brestskaya Voblasts', SW Belarus
110 E8 **Płoty** *Ger.* Plathe. Zachodniopomorskie, NW Poland
102 G7 **Plouay** Morbihan, NW France
111 D15 **Ploučnice** *Ger.* Polzen. ≈ NE Czech Republic
114 I10 **Plovdiv** *prev.* Eumolpias, *anc.* Evmolpia, Philippopolis, *Lat.* Trimontium. Plovdiv, C Bulgaria 24.47
116 J11 **Plovdiv** ◈ *province* C Bulgaria
30 L6 **Plover** Wisconsin, N USA
Plozk *see* Płock
27 U11 **Plumerville** Arkansas, C USA
19 P10 **Plum Island** *island* Massachusetts, NE USA
32 M9 **Plummer** Idaho, NW USA
83 J18 **Plumtree** Matabeleland South, SW Zimbabwe
118 D11 **Plungė** Plungė, W Lithuania
113 J15 **Plužine** Montenegro, SW Yugoslavia
119 K14 **Plyeshchanitsy** *Rus.* Pleshchenitsy. Minskaya Voblasts', N Belarus
45 V10 **Plymouth** ○ (Montserrat) SW Montserrat
97 I24 **Plymouth** SW England, UK
31 O11 **Plymouth** Indiana, N USA
19 P12 **Plymouth** Massachusetts, NE USA
19 N8 **Plymouth** New Hampshire, NE USA
21 X9 **Plymouth** North Carolina, SE USA
30 M8 **Plymouth** Wisconsin, N USA
97 J20 **Plynlimon** ▲ C Wales, UK
126 G14 **Plyussa** Pskovskaya Oblast', W Russian Federation
111 B17 **Plzeň** *Ger.* Pilsen, *Pol.* Pilzno. Plzeňský Kraj, W Czech Republic
111 B17 **Plzeňský Kraj** ◈ *region* W Czech Republic
110 F11 **Pniewy** *Ger.* Pinne. Wielkolpolskie, C Poland
106 D8 **Po** ≈ N Italy
77 P13 **Pô** S Burkina
42 M13 **Poás, Volcán** ※ NW Costa Rica
77 S16 **Pobè** S Benin
123 S8 **Pobeda, Gora** ▲ NE Russian Federation
Pobeda Peak *see* Pobedy, Pik/Tomur Feng
147 Z7 **Pobedy, Pik** *var.* Pobeda Peak, *Chin.* Tomur Feng. ▲ China/Kyrgyzstan *see also* Tomur Feng
110 H11 **Pobiedziska** *Ger.* Pudewitz. Wielkolpolskie, C Poland
Po, Bocche del *see* Po, Foci del
27 W9 **Pocahontas** Arkansas, C USA
29 U12 **Pocahontas** Iowa, C USA
33 Q15 **Pocatello** Idaho, NW USA
167 S13 **Pochentong** × (Phnum Penh) Phnum Penh, S Cambodia
128 I6 **Pochep** Bryanskaya Oblast', W Russian Federation
128 H4 **Pochinok** Smolenskaya Oblast', W Russian Federation
41 R17 **Pochutla** *var.* San Pedro Pochutla. Oaxaca, SE Mexico
62 I6 **Pocitos, Salar** *var.* Salar Quiróm. *salt lake* NW Argentina
101 O22 **Pocking** Bayern, SE Germany
186 I10 **Pocklington Reef** *reef* SE PNG
27 R11 **Pocola** Oklahoma, C USA
21 Y5 **Pocomoke City** Maryland, NE USA
59 L21 **Poços de Caldas** Minas Gerais, NE Brazil
126 H14 **Podberez'ye** Novgorodskaya Oblast', NW Russian Federation
Podbrodzie *see* Pabradė
127 U8 **Podcher'ye** Respublika Komi, NW Russian Federation
111 E16 **Poděbrady** *Ger.* Podiebrad. Středočeský Kraj, C Czech Republic
128 L9 **Podgorenskiy** Voronezhskaya Oblast', W Russian Federation
113 J17 **Podgorica** *prev.* Titograd. Montenegro, SW Yugoslavia
113 K17 **Podgorica** × Montenegro, SW Yugoslavia
109 T13 **Podgrad** SW Slovenia
Podiebrad *see* Poděbrady
116 M5 **Podil's'ka Vysochina** *plateau* W Ukraine
Podium Anicensis *see* le Puy
122 L11 **Podkamennaya Tunguska** *Eng.* Stony Tunguska. ≈ C Russian Federation
113 N17 **Podkarpackie** ◈ *province* SE Poland
Pod Klošter *see* Arnoldstein
110 O9 **Podlaskie** ◈ *province* NE Poland
129 Q8 **Podlesnoye** Saratovskaya Oblast', W Russian Federation
128 K4 **Podol'sk** Moskovskaya Oblast', W Russian Federation
76 H10 **Podor** N Senegal
127 P12 **Podosinovets** Kirovskaya Oblast', NW Russian Federation
126 I12 **Podporozh'ye** Leningradskaya Oblast', NW Russian Federation
Podravska Slatina *see* Slatina, Croatia
112 J13 **Podromanlja** Republika Srpska, SE Bosnia & Herzegovina
Podsvil'ye *see* Padsvillye
116 L9 **Podu Iloaiei** *prev.* Podul Iloaiei. Iaşi, NE Romania
113 N15 **Podujevo** Serbia, S Yugoslavia
Podul Iloaiei *see* Podu Iloaiei
Podunajská Rovina *see* Little Alföld
126 M12 **Podyuga** Arkhangel'skaya Oblast', NW Russian Federation
56 A9 **Poechos, Embalse** ◎ NW Peru
55 W10 **Poeketi** Sipaliwini, E Surinam
100 L8 **Poel** *island* N Germany
83 M20 **Poelela, Lagoa** ◎ S Mozambique
Poerwodadi *see* Purwodadi
Poetovio *see* Ptuj
83 E23 **Pofadder** Northern Cape, W South Africa
106 I9 **Po, Foci del** *var.* Bocche del Po. ≈ NE Italy
116 E12 **Pogăniş** ≈ W Romania
Pogegen *see* Pagėgiai
106 G12 **Poggibonsi** Toscana, C Italy
107 I14 **Poggio Mirteto** Lazio, C Italy
109 V4 **Pöggstall** Niederösterreich, N Austria
116 L13 **Pogoanele** Buzău, SE Romania
Pogónion *see* Delvináki
113 M21 **Pogradec** *var.* Pogradeci. Korçë, SE Albania
Pogradeci *see* Pogradec
123 S15 **Pogranichnyy** Primorskiy Kray, SE Russian Federation
38 M16 **Pogromni Volcano** ▲ Unimak Island, Alaska, USA
163 Z15 **P'ohang** *Jap.* Hokō. E South Korea
15 T9 **Pohénégamook, Lac** ◎ Quebec, SE Canada
93 L20 **Pohja** *Swe.* Pojo. Etelä-Suomi, SW Finland
Pohjanlahti *see* Bothnia, Gulf of
189 U16 **Pohnpei** ◆ *state* E Micronesia
189 O12 **Pohnpei** × Pohnpei, E Micronesia
189 O12 **Pohnpei** *prev.* Ponape Ascension Island. *island* E Micronesia
111 F19 **Pohořelice** *Ger.* Pohrlitz. Brněnský Kraj, SE Czech Republic
109 V10 **Pohorje** *Ger.* Bacher. ▲ N Slovenia
117 N6 **Pohrebyshche** Vinnyts'ka Oblast', C Ukraine
Pohrlitz *see* Pohořelice
161 P9 **Po Hu** ⊟ E China
116 G15 **Poiana Mare** Dolj, S Romania
Poictiers *see* Poitiers
129 N6 **Poim** Penzenskaya Oblast', W Russian Federation
Poindo *see* Lhünzhub
195 Y13 **Poinsett, Cape** *headland* Antarctica
29 R9 **Poinsett, Lake** ◎ South Dakota, N USA
22 I10 **Point Au Fer Island** *island* Louisiana, S USA
39 X14 **Point Baker** Prince of Wales Island, Alaska, USA
25 U13 **Point Comfort** Texas, SW USA
Point de Galle *see* Galle
44 K10 **Pointe à Gravois** *headland* SW Haiti
22 L10 **Pointe a la Hache** Louisiana, S USA
45 Y6 **Pointe-à-Pitre** Grande Terre, C Guadeloupe
15 U7 **Pointe-au-Père** Quebec, SE Canada
15 V5 **Pointe-aux-Anglais** Quebec, SE Canada
45 T10 **Pointe du Cap** *headland* N Saint Lucia
79 E21 **Pointe-Noire** Le Kouilou, S Congo
45 X6 **Pointe Noire** Basse Terre, W Guadeloupe
79 E21 **Pointe-Noire** × Le Kouilou, S Congo
45 U15 **Point Fortin** Trinidad, Trinidad and Tobago
38 M6 **Point Hope** Alaska, USA
39 N5 **Point Lay** Alaska, USA
18 B16 **Point Marion** Pennsylvania, NE USA
18 K16 **Point Pleasant** New Jersey, NE USA
21 P4 **Point Pleasant** West Virginia, NE USA
45 R14 **Point Salines** × (St.George's) SW Grenada
102 L9 **Poitiers** *prev.* Poictiers, *anc.* Limonum. Vienne, W France
102 K9 **Poitou** *cultural region* W France
102 K10 **Poitou-Charentes** ◈ *region* W France
103 N3 **Poix-de-Picardie** Somme, N France
Pojo *see* Pohja
37 S10 **Pojoaque** New Mexico, SW USA
152 E11 **Pokaran** Rājasthān, NW India
183 R4 **Pokataroo** New South Wales, SE Australia
119 P18 **Pokats'** *Rus.* Pokot'. ≈ SE Belarus
29 V5 **Pokegama Lake** ◎ Minnesota, N USA
184 L6 **Pokeno** Waikato, North Island, NZ
153 O11 **Pokhara** Western, C Nepal
129 T6 **Pokhvistnevo** Samarskaya Oblast', W Russian Federation
55 W10 **Pokigron** Sipaliwini, C Surinam
92 L10 **Pokka** *Lapp.* Bohkká. Lappi, N Finland
79 N16 **Poko** Orientale, NE Dem. Rep. Congo (Zaire)
Pokot' *see* Pokats'
Po-ko-to Shan *see* Bogda Shan
147 S7 **Pokrovka** Talasskaya Oblast', NW Kyrgyzstan
Pokrovka *see* Kyzyl-Suu
117 V8 **Pokrovs'ke** *Rus.* Pokrovskoye. Dnipropetrovs'ka Oblast', E Ukraine
Pokrovskoye *see* Pokrovs'ke
Pola *see* Pula
37 N10 **Polacca** Arizona, SW USA
104 L2 **Pola de Laviana** Asturias, N Spain
104 K2 **Pola de Lena** Asturias, N Spain
104 L2 **Pola de Siero** Asturias, N Spain
191 Y3 **Poland** Kiritimati, E Kiribati
110 H12 **Poland** *off.* Republic of Poland, *var.* Polish Republic, *Pol.* Polska, Rzeczpospolita Polska; *prev. Pol.* Polska Rzeczpospolita Ludowa, Polish People's Republic. ◆ *republic* C Europe
Polangen *see* Palanga
110 G7 **Polanów** *Ger.* Pollnow. Zachodniopomorskie, NW Poland
136 H13 **Polatlı** Ankara, C Turkey
118 L12 **Polatsk** *Rus.* Polotsk. Vitsyebskaya Voblasts', N Belarus
110 F8 **Połczyn-Zdrój** *Ger.* Bad Polzin. Zachodniopomorskie, NW Poland
146 I16 **Polekhatum** *prev.* Pul'-I-Khatum. Akhalskiy Velayat, S Turkmenistan
149 Q3 **Pol-e Khomrī** *var.* Pul-i-Khumri. Baghlān, NE Afghanistan
197 S10 **Pole Plain** *undersea feature* Arctic Ocean
143 P5 **Pol-e Safīd** *var.* Pol-e-Sefid, Pul-i-Sefid. Māzandarān, N Iran
Pol-e-Sefid *see* Pol-e Safid
118 B13 **Polessk** *Ger.* Labiau. Kaliningradskaya Oblast', W Russian Federation
Polesskoye *see* Polis'ke
171 N13 **Polewali** Sulawesi, C Indonesia
114 G11 **Polezhan** ▲ SW Bulgaria
78 F13 **Poli** Nord, N Cameroon
Poli *see* Pólis
107 M19 **Policastro, Golfo di** *gulf* S Italy
110 D8 **Police** *Ger.* Politz. Zachodniopomorskie, NW Poland
172 I17 **Police, Pointe** *headland* Mahé, NE Seychelles
115 L17 **Polichnítos** *var.* Polihnitos, Políkhnitos. Lésvos, E Greece
Poligiros *see* Polýgyros
107 P17 **Polignano a Mare** Puglia, SE Italy
103 S9 **Poligny** Jura, E France
Polihnitos *see* Polichnítos
Polikastro/Políkastron *see* Polýkastro
Políkhnitos *see* Polichnítos
114 K8 **Polikrayshte** Veliko Tŭrnovo, N Bulgaria
171 O3 **Polillo Islands** *island group* N Philippines
109 Q9 **Polinik** ▲ SW Austria
121 O2 **Pólis** *var.* Poli. W Cyprus
Polish People's Republic *see* Poland
Polish Republic *see* Poland
117 O3 **Polis'ke** *Rus.* Polesskoye. Kyyivs'ka Oblast', N Ukraine
107 N22 **Polistena** Calabria, SW Italy
Politz *see* Police
Políyiros *see* Polýgyros
29 V14 **Polk City** Iowa, C USA
110 F13 **Polkowice** *Ger.* Heerwegen. Dolnośląskie, SW Poland
155 G22 **Pollāchi** Tamil Nādu, SE India
109 W7 **Pöllau** Steiermark, SE Austria
189 T13 **Polle** *atoll* Chuuk Islands, C Micronesia
Pollnow *see* Polanów
29 N7 **Pollock** South Dakota, N USA
92 L8 **Polmak** Finnmark, N Norway
30 L10 **Polo** Illinois, N USA
193 V15 **Poloa** *island* Tongatapu Group, N Tonga
42 E5 **Polochic, Río** ≈ C Guatemala
Pologi *see* Polohy
117 V9 **Polohy** *Rus.* Pologi. Zaporiz'ka Oblast', SE Ukraine
14 M10 **Polonais, Lac des** ◎ Quebec, SE Canada
61 G20 **Polonio, Cabo** *headland* E Uruguay
155 K24 **Polonnaruwa** North Central Province, C Sri Lanka
116 L5 **Polonne** *Rus.* Polonnoye. Khmel'nyts'ka Oblast', NW Ukraine
Polonnoye *see* Polonne
Polotsk *see* Polatsk
109 T7 **Pöls** *var.* Pölsbach. ≈ E Austria
Pölsbach *see* Pöls
Polska/Polska, Rzeczpospolita/Polska Rzeczpospolita Ludowa *see* Poland
114 L10 **Polski Gradets** Stara Zagora, C Bulgaria
114 K8 **Polsko Kosovo** Ruse, N Bulgaria
33 P8 **Polson** Montana, NW USA
117 T6 **Poltava** Poltavs'ka Oblast', NE Ukraine
Poltava *see* Poltavs'ka Oblast'
117 R5 **Poltavs'ka Oblast'** *var.* Poltava, *Rus.* Poltavskaya Oblast'. ◈ *province* NE Ukraine
Poltavskaya Oblast' *see* Poltavs'ka Oblast'
Poltoratsk *see* Ashgabat
118 I5 **Põltsamaa** *Ger.* Oberpahlen. Jõgevamaa, E Estonia
118 I4 **Põltsamaa** *var.* Põltsamaa Jõgi. ≈ C Estonia
Põltsamaa Jõgi *see* Põltsamaa
122 I8 **Poluy** ≈ N Russian Federation
118 J6 **Põlva** *Ger.* Pölwe. Põlvamaa, SE Estonia
93 N16 **Polvijärvi** Itä-Suomi, E Finland
Pölwe *see* Põlva
115 I22 **Polýaigos** *island* Kykládes, Greece, Aegean Sea
115 I22 **Polyaígou Folégandrou, Stenó** *strait* Kykládes, Greece, Aegean Sea
126 J3 **Polyarnyy** Murmanskaya Oblast', NW Russian Federation
127 W5 **Polyarnyy Ural** ▲ NW Russian Federation
115 G14 **Polýgyros** *var.* Poligiros, Políyiros. Kentrikí Makedonía, N Greece
114 F13 **Polýkastro** *var.* Polikastro; *prev.* Políkastron. Kentrikí Makedonía, N Greece
193 O9 **Polynesia** *island group* C Pacific Ocean
115 J15 **Polýochni** *site of ancient city* Límnos, E Greece
41 Y13 **Polyuc** Quintana Roo, E Mexico
109 V10 **Polzela** C Slovenia
Polzen *see* Ploučnice
56 D12 **Pomabamba** Ancash, C Peru
185 D23 **Pomahaka** ≈ South Island, NZ
106 F12 **Pomarance** Toscana, C Italy
104 G9 **Pombal** Leiria, C Portugal
76 D9 **Pombas** Santo Antão, NW Cape Verde
83 N19 **Pomene** Inhambane, SE Mozambique
110 G8 **Pomerania** *cultural region* Germany/Poland
110 D7 **Pomeranian Bay** *Ger.* Pommersche Bucht, *Pol.* Zatoka Pomorska. *bay* Germany/Poland
31 T15 **Pomeroy** Ohio, N USA
32 L10 **Pomeroy** Washington, NW USA
117 Q8 **Pomichna** Kirovohrads'ka Oblast', C Ukraine
186 H7 **Pomio** New Britain, E PNG
Pomir, Dar"yoi *see* Pamir/Pāmīr, Daryā-ye
27 T6 **Pomme de Terre Lake** ⊟ Missouri, C USA
29 S8 **Pomme de Terre River** ≈ Minnesota, N USA
Pommersche Bucht *see* Pomeranian Bay
35 T15 **Pomona** California, W USA
114 N9 **Pomorie** Burgas, E Bulgaria
Pomorska, Zatoka *see* Pomeranian Bay
110 H8 **Pomorskie** ◈ *province* N Poland
127 Q4 **Pomorskiy Proliv** *strait* NW Russian Federation
127 T10 **Pomozdino** Respublika Komi, NW Russian Federation
Pompaelo *see* Pamplona
23 Z15 **Pompano Beach** Florida, SE USA
107 K18 **Pompei** Campania, S Italy
33 V10 **Pompeys Pillar** Montana, NW USA
Ponape Ascension Island *see* Pohnpei
29 R13 **Ponca** Nebraska, C USA
27 O8 **Ponca City** Oklahoma, C USA
45 T6 **Ponce** C Puerto Rico
23 X10 **Ponce de Leon Inlet** *inlet* Florida, SE USA
22 K8 **Ponchatoula** Louisiana, S USA
26 M8 **Pond Creek** Oklahoma, C USA
155 J20 **Pondicherry** *var.* Puduchcheri, *Fr.* Pondichéry. Pondicherry, SE India
151 I20 **Pondicherry** *var.* Puduchcheri, *Fr.* Pondichéry. ◈ *union territory* India
Pondichéry *see* Pondicherry
197 N11 **Pond Inlet** Baffin Island, Nunavut, NE Canada
187 P16 **Ponérihouen** Province Nord, C New Caledonia
104 J4 **Ponferrada** Castilla-León, NW Spain
184 N13 **Pongaroa** Manawatu-Wanganui, North Island, NZ
167 Q12 **Pong Nam Ron** Chantaburi, S Thailand
81 C14 **Pongo** ≈ S Sudan
152 I7 **Pong Reservoir** ⊟ N India
111 N14 **Poniatowa** Lubelskie, E Poland
167 R12 **Pônley** Kâmpóng Chhnăng, C Cambodia
155 I20 **Ponnaiyār** ≈ SE India
11 Q15 **Ponoka** Alberta, SW Canada
129 U6 **Ponomarevka** Orenburgskaya Oblast', W Russian Federation
169 Q17 **Ponorogo** Jawa, C Indonesia
126 M5 **Ponoy** Murmanskaya Oblast', NW Russian Federation
122 F6 **Ponoy** ≈ NW Russian Federation
102 K11 **Pons** Charente-Maritime, W France
Pons *see* Ponts
Pons Aelii *see* Newcastle upon Tyne
Pons Vetus *see* Pontevedra
99 G20 **Pont-à-Celles** Hainaut, S Belgium
102 K16 **Pontacq** Pyrénées-Atlantiques, SW France
64 P3 **Ponta Delgada** São Miguel, Azores, Portugal, NE Atlantic Ocean
64 P3 **Ponta Delgado** × São Miguel, Azores, Portugal, NE Atlantic Ocean
64 N2 **Ponta do Pico** ▲ Pico, Azores, Portugal, NE Atlantic Ocean
60 J11 **Ponta Grossa** Paraná, S Brazil
103 S5 **Pont-à-Mousson** Meurthe-et-Moselle, NE France
103 T9 **Pontarlier** Doubs, E France
106 G11 **Pontassieve** Toscana, C Italy
102 L4 **Pont-Audemer** Eure, N France
22 K9 **Pontchartrain, Lake** ◎ Louisiana, S USA
102 I8 **Pontchâteau** Loire-Atlantique, NW France
103 R10 **Pont-de-Vaux** Ain, E France
104 G4 **Ponteareas** Galicia, NW Spain
106 J6 **Pontebba** Friuli-Venezia Giulia, NE Italy
104 G4 **Ponte Caldelas** Galicia, NW Spain
107 J16 **Pontecorvo** Lazio, C Italy
104 G5 **Ponte da Barca** Viana do Castelo, N Portugal
104 G5 **Ponte de Lima** Viana do Castelo, N Portugal
106 F11 **Pontedera** Toscana, C Italy
104 H10 **Ponte de Sor** Portalegre, C Portugal
104 H2 **Pontedeume** Galicia, NW Spain
106 F6 **Ponte di Legno** Lombardia, N Italy
11 T17 **Ponteix** Saskatchewan, S Canada
59 N20 **Ponte Nova** Minas Gerais, NE Brazil
59 G18 **Pontes e Lacerda** Mato Grosso, W Brazil
104 G4 **Pontevedra** *anc.* Pons Vetus. Galicia, NW Spain
104 G3 **Pontevedra** ◈ *province* Galicia, NW Spain
104 G4 **Pontevedra, Ría de** *estuary* NW Spain
30 M12 **Pontiac** Illinois, N USA
31 R9 **Pontiac** Michigan, N USA
169 P11 **Pontianak** Borneo, C Indonesia
107 I16 **Pontino, Agro** *plain* C Italy
Pontisarae *see* Pontoise
102 H6 **Pontivy** Morbihan, NW France
102 F6 **Pont-l'Abbé** Finistère, NW France
103 N4 **Pontoise** *anc.* Briva Isarae, Cergy-Pontoise, Pontisarae. Val-d'Oise, N France
11 W13 **Ponton** Manitoba, C Canada
102 J5 **Pontorson** Manche, N France
22 M2 **Pontotoc** Mississippi, S USA
25 R9 **Pontotoc** Texas, SW USA
106 E10 **Pontremoli** Toscana, C Italy
108 J10 **Pontresina** Graubünden, S Switzerland
105 U5 **Ponts** *var.* Pons. Cataluña, NE Spain
103 R14 **Pont-St-Esprit** Gard, S France
97 K21 **Pontypool** *Wel.* Pontypŵl. SE Wales, UK
97 J22 **Pontypridd** S Wales, UK
Pontypŵl *see* Pontypool
43 R17 **Ponuga** Veraguas, SE Panama
184 L5 **Ponui Island** *island* N NZ
119 K14 **Ponya** *Rus.* Ponya. ≈ N Belarus
107 I17 **Ponziane, Isole** *island* C Italy
182 F7 **Poochera** South Australia
97 L24 **Poole** S England, UK
25 S6 **Poolville** Texas, SW USA
Poona *see* Pune
182 M8 **Pooncarie** New South Wales, SE Australia
183 N6 **Poopelloe Lake** *seasonal lake* New South Wales, SE Australia
57 K19 **Poopó** Oruro, C Bolivia
57 K19 **Poopó, Lago** *var.* Lago Pampa Aullagas. ◎ W Bolivia
184 L3 **Poor Knights Islands** *island* N NZ
39 P10 **Poorman** Alaska, USA
182 E3 **Pootnoura** South Australia
147 R10 **Pop** *Rus.* Pap. Namangan Wiloyati, E Uzbekistan
117 X7 **Popasna** *Rus.* Popasnaya. Luhans'ka Oblast', E Ukraine
Popasnaya *see* Popasna
54 D12 **Popayán** Cauca, SW Colombia
99 B18 **Poperinge** West-Vlaanderen, W Belgium
123 N7 **Popigay** Taymyrskiy (Dolgano-Nenetskiy) Avtonomnyy Okrug, N Russian Federation
123 N7 **Popigay** ≈ N Russian Federation
117 O5 **Popil'nya** Zhytomyrs'ka Oblast', N Ukraine
182 K8 **Popiltah Lake** *seasonal lake* New South Wales, SE Australia
33 X7 **Poplar** Montana, NW USA
11 Y14 **Poplar** ≈ Manitoba, C Canada
27 X8 **Poplar Bluff** Missouri, C USA
33 X6 **Poplar River** ≈ Montana, NW USA
41 P14 **Popocatépetl** ※ S Mexico
79 H21 **Popokabaka** Bandundu, SW Dem. Rep. Congo (Zaire)
107 J15 **Popoli** Abruzzo, C Italy
186 F9 **Popondetta** Northern, S PNG
112 F9 **Popovača** Sisak-Moslavina, NE Croatia
114 J10 **Popovitsa** Tŭrgovishte, C Bulgaria
114 L8 **Popovo** Tŭrgovishte, N Bulgaria
Popovo *see* Iskra
Popper *see* Poprad
30 M5 **Popple River** ≈ Wisconsin, N USA
111 L19 **Poprad** *Ger.* Deutschendorf, *Hung.* Poprád. Prešovský Kraj, E Slovakia
111 L18 **Poprad** *Ger.* Popper, *Hung.* Poprád. ≈ Poland/Slovakia
111 L19 **Poprad-Tatry** × (Poprad) Prešovský Kraj, E Slovakia
21 X7 **Poquoson** Virginia, NE USA
149 O15 **Porāli** ≈ SW Pakistan
184 N12 **Porangahau** Hawke's Bay, North Island, NZ
59 K17 **Porangatu** Goiás, C Brazil
119 G18 **Porazava** *Pol.* Porozow, *Rus.* Porozovo. Hrodzyenskaya Voblasts', W Belarus
154 A11 **Porbandar** Gujarāt, W India
10 I13 **Porcher Island** *island* British Columbia, SW Canada
104 M13 **Porcuna** Andalucía, S Spain
14 F7 **Porcupine** Ontario, S Canada
64 M6 **Porcupine Bank** *undersea feature* N Atlantic Ocean
11 V15 **Porcupine Hills** ▲ Manitoba/Saskatchewan, S Canada
30 L3 **Porcupine Mountains** *hill range* Michigan, N USA
64 M7 **Porcupine Plain** *undersea feature* E Atlantic Ocean
8 G7 **Porcupine River** ≈ Canada/USA
106 I7 **Pordenone** *anc.* Portenau. Friuli-Venezia Giulia, NE Italy
54 H9 **Pore** Casanare, E Colombia
112 A9 **Poreč** *It.* Parenzo. Istra, NW Croatia
60 I9 **Porecatu** Paraná, S Brazil
Porech'ye *see* Parechcha
129 P4 **Poretskoye** Chuvashskaya Respublika, W Russian Federation
77 Q13 **Porga** N Benin
186 B7 **Porgera** Enga, W PNG
93 K18 **Pori** *Swe.* Björneborg. Länsi-Suomi, W Finland
185 L14 **Porirua** Wellington, North Island, NZ
92 I12 **Porjus** Norrbotten, N Sweden
126 G14 **Porkhov** Pskovskaya Oblast', W Russian Federation
55 O4 **Porlamar** Nueva Esparta, NE Venezuela
102 I8 **Pornic** Loire-Atlantique, NW France
186 B7 **Poroma** Southern Highlands, W PNG
123 T13 **Poronaysk** Ostrov Sakhalin, Sakhalinskaya Oblast', SE Russian Federation
115 G20 **Póros** Póros, S Greece
115 C19 **Póros** Kefallinía, Iónioi Nísoi, Greece, C Mediterranean Sea
115 G20 **Póros** *island* S Greece
81 G24 **Poroto Mountains** ▲ SW Tanzania
112 B10 **Porozina** Primorje-Gorski Kotar, NW Croatia
Porozovo/Porozow *see* Porazava
195 X15 **Porpoise Bay** *bay* Antarctica
65 G15 **Porpoise Point** *headland* NE Ascension Island
65 C25 **Porpoise Point** *headland* East Falkland, Falkland Islands
108 C6 **Porrentruy** Jura, NW Switzerland
106 F10 **Porretta Terme** Emilia-Romagna, C Italy
104 G4 **Porriño** Galicia, NW Spain
92 L7 **Porsangen** *fjord* N Norway

◆ Country ● Country Capital ◇ Dependent Territory ○ Dependent Territory Capital ◈ Administrative Region × International Airport ▲ Mountain ▲ Mountain Range ※ Volcano ≈ River ◎ Lake ⊟ Reservoir

92 K8 **Porsangerhalvøya** *peninsula* N Norway
95 G16 **Porsgrunn** Telemark, S Norway
136 E13 **Porsuk Çayı** ≈ C Turkey
Porsy *see* Boldumsaz
57 N18 **Portachuelo** Santa Cruz, C Bolivia
182 I9 **Port Adelaide** South Australia
97 F15 **Portadown** *Ir.* Port An Dúnáin. S Northern Ireland, UK
31 P10 **Portage** Michigan, N USA
18 D15 **Portage** Pennsylvania, NE USA
30 K8 **Portage** Wisconsin, N USA
30 M3 **Portage Lake** ◎ Michigan, N USA
11 X16 **Portage la Prairie** Manitoba, S Canada
31 R11 **Portage River** ≈ Ohio, N USA
27 Y8 **Portageville** Missouri, C USA
28 L2 **Portal** North Dakota, N USA
10 L17 **Port Alberni** Vancouver Island, British Columbia, SW Canada
14 E15 **Port Albert** Ontario, S Canada
104 I10 **Portalegre** *anc.* Ammaia, Amoea. Portalegre, E Portugal
104 H10 **Portalegre** ◈ *district* C Portugal
37 V12 **Portales** New Mexico, SW USA
39 X14 **Port Alexander** Baranof Island, Alaska, USA
83 I25 **Port Alfred** Eastern Cape, S South Africa
10 J16 **Port Alice** Vancouver Island, British Columbia, SW Canada
22 J8 **Port Allen** Louisiana, S USA
Port Amelia *see* Pemba
Port An Dúnáin *see* Portadown
32 G7 **Port Angeles** Washington, NW USA
44 L12 **Port Antonio** NE Jamaica
115 D16 **Pórta Panagiá** *religious building* Thessalía, C Greece
25 T14 **Port Aransas** Texas, SW USA
97 E18 **Portarlington** *Ir.* Cúil an tSúdaire. C Ireland
183 P17 **Port Arthur** Tasmania, SE Australia
25 Y11 **Port Arthur** Texas, SW USA
96 G12 **Port Askaig** W Scotland, UK
182 I7 **Port Augusta** South Australia
44 M9 **Port-au-Prince** ● (Haiti) C Haiti
44 M9 **Port-au-Prince** × E Haiti
22 I8 **Port Barre** Louisiana, S USA
151 Q19 **Port Blair** Andaman and Nicobar Islands, SE India
25 X12 **Port Bolivar** Texas, SW USA
105 X4 **Portbou** Cataluña, NE Spain
77 N17 **Port Bouet** × (Abidjan) SE Ivory Coast
182 I8 **Port Broughton** South Australia
14 F17 **Port Burwell** Ontario, S Canada
12 G17 **Port Burwell** Quebec, NE Canada
182 M13 **Port Campbell** Victoria, SE Australia
15 V4 **Port-Cartier** Quebec, SE Canada
185 F23 **Port Chalmers** Otago, South Island, NZ
23 W14 **Port Charlotte** Florida, SE USA
38 L9 **Port Clarence** Alaska, USA
10 I13 **Port Clements** Graham Island, British Columbia, SW Canada
31 S11 **Port Clinton** Ohio, N USA
14 H17 **Port Colborne** Ontario, S Canada
15 Y7 **Port-Daniel** Quebec, SE Canada
Port Darwin *see* Darwin
183 O17 **Port Davey** *headland* Tasmania, SE Australia
44 K8 **Port-de-Paix** NW Haiti
181 W4 **Port Douglas** Queensland, NE Australia
10 J13 **Port Edward** British Columbia, SW Canada
83 K24 **Port Edward** KwaZulu/Natal, SE South Africa
58 J12 **Portel** Pará, NE Brazil
104 H12 **Portel** Évora, S Portugal
14 E14 **Port Elgin** Ontario, S Canada
45 Y14 **Port Elizabeth** Bequia, Saint Vincent and the Grenadines
83 I26 **Port Elizabeth** Eastern Cape, S South Africa
96 G13 **Port Ellen** W Scotland, UK
Portenau *see* Pordenone
97 H16 **Port Erin** SW Isle of Man
45 Q13 **Porter Point** *headland* Saint Vincent, Saint Vincent and the Grenadines
185 G18 **Porters Pass** *pass* South Island, NZ
83 E25 **Porterville** Western Cape, SW South Africa
35 R12 **Porterville** California, W USA
Port-Étienne *see* Nouâdhibou
182 L13 **Port Fairy** Victoria, SE Australia
184 M4 **Port Fitzroy** Great Barrier Island, Auckland, NE NZ
Port Florence *see* Kisumu
Port-Francqui *see* Ilebo
79 C18 **Port-Gentil** Ogooué-Maritime, W Gabon
182 I7 **Port Germein** South Australia
22 J6 **Port Gibson** Mississippi, S USA
39 Q13 **Port Graham** Alaska, USA
77 U17 **Port Harcourt** Rivers, S Nigeria
10 J16 **Port Hardy** Vancouver Island, British Columbia, SW Canada
Port Harrison *see* Inukjuak
13 R14 **Port Hawkesbury** Cape Breton Island, Nova Scotia, SE Canada
180 I6 **Port Hedland** Western Australia
39 O15 **Port Heiden** Alaska, USA
97 I19 **Porthmadog** *var.* Portmadoc. NW Wales, UK
14 I15 **Port Hope** Ontario, SE Canada
13 S9 **Port Hope Simpson** Newfoundland, E Canada
65 C24 **Port Howard Settlement** West Falkland, Falkland Islands
31 T9 **Port Huron** Michigan, N USA
107 K17 **Portici** Campania, S Italy
137 Y13 **Port-Iliç** *Rus.* Port Il'ich. SE Azerbaijan
Port Il'ich *see* Port-Iliç
104 G14 **Portimão** *var.* Vila Nova de Portimão. Faro, S Portugal
25 T17 **Port Isabel** Texas, SW USA
18 J13 **Port Jervis** New York, NE USA
55 S7 **Port Kaituma** NW Guyana
128 K12 **Port Katon** Rostovskaya Oblast', SW Russian Federation
183 S9 **Port Kembla** New South Wales, SE Australia
182 F8 **Port Kenny** South Australia
Port Klang *see* Pelabuhan Klang
Port Láirge *see* Waterford
183 S8 **Portland** New South Wales, SE Australia
182 L13 **Portland** Victoria, SE Australia
184 K4 **Portland** Northland, North Island, NZ
31 Q13 **Portland** Indiana, N USA
19 P8 **Portland** Maine, NE USA
31 Q9 **Portland** Michigan, N USA
29 Q4 **Portland** North Dakota, N USA
32 G11 **Portland** Oregon, NW USA
20 J8 **Portland** Tennessee, S USA
25 T14 **Portland** Texas, SW USA
32 G11 **Portland** × Oregon, NW USA
182 L13 **Portland Bay** *bay* Victoria, SE Australia
44 K13 **Portland Bight** *bay* S Jamaica
97 L24 **Portland Bill** *var.* Bill of Portland. *headland* S England, UK
Portland, Bill of *see* Portland Bill
183 P15 **Portland, Cape** *headland* Tasmania, SE Australia
10 J12 **Portland Inlet** *inlet* British Columbia, W Canada
184 P11 **Portland Island** *island* E NZ
65 F15 **Portland Point** *headland* SW Ascension Island
44 J13 **Portland Point** *headland* C Jamaica
103 P16 **Port-la-Nouvelle** Aude, S France
Portlaoighise *see* Port Laoise
97 E18 **Port Laoise** *var.* Portlaoise, *Ir.* Portlaoighise; *prev.* Maryborough. C Ireland
25 U13 **Port Lavaca** Texas, SW USA
182 G9 **Port Lincoln** South Australia
39 Q14 **Port Lions** Kodiak Island, Alaska, USA
76 I15 **Port Loko** W Sierra Leone
65 E24 **Port Louis** East Falkland, Falkland Islands
45 Y5 **Port-Louis** Grande Terre, N Guadeloupe
173 X16 **Port Louis** ● (Mauritius) NW Mauritius
Port Louis *see* Scarborough
Port-Lyautey *see* Kénitra
182 K12 **Port MacDonnell** South Australia
183 U7 **Port Macquarie** New South Wales, SE Australia
Portmadoc *see* Porthmadog
Port Mahon *see* Mahón
44 K12 **Port Maria** C Jamaica
10 K16 **Port McNeill** Vancouver Island, British Columbia, SW Canada
13 P11 **Port-Menier** Île d'Anticosti, Quebec, E Canada
39 N15 **Port Moller** Alaska, USA
44 L13 **Port Morant** E Jamaica
44 K13 **Portmore** C Jamaica
186 D9 **Port Moresby** ● (PNG) Central/National Capital District, SW PNG
Port Natal *see* Durban
25 Y11 **Port Neches** Texas, SW USA
182 G9 **Port Neill** South Australia
15 S6 **Portneuf** ≈ Quebec, SE Canada
15 R6 **Portneuf, Lac** ◎ Quebec, SE Canada
83 D23 **Port Nolloth** Northern Cape, W South Africa
18 J17 **Port Norris** New Jersey, NE USA
Port-Nouveau-Québec *see* Kangiqsualujjuaq
104 G6 **Porto** *Eng.* Oporto; *anc.* Portus Cale. Porto, NW Portugal
104 G6 **Porto** *var.* Pôrto. ◈ *district* N Portugal
104 G6 **Porto** × Porto, W Portugal
61 I16 **Porto Alegre** *var.* Pôrto Alegre. *state capital* Rio Grande do Sul, S Brazil
Porto Alexandre *see* Tombua
82 B12 **Porto Amboim** Cuanza Sul, NW Angola
Porto Amélia *see* Pemba
Porto Bello *see* Portobelo
43 T14 **Portobelo** *var.* Porto Bello, Puerto Bello. Colón, N Panama
60 G10 **Pôrto Camargo** Paraná, S Brazil
25 U13 **Port O'Connor** Texas, SW USA
Pôrto de Mós *see* Porto de Moz
58 J12 **Porto de Moz** *var.* Pôrto de Mós. Pará, NE Brazil
64 O5 **Porto do Moniz** Madeira, Portugal, NE Atlantic Ocean
59 H16 **Porto dos Gaúchos** Mato Grosso, W Brazil
Porto Edda *see* Sarandë
107 J24 **Porto Empedocle** Sicilia, Italy, C Mediterranean Sea
59 H20 **Porto Esperança** Mato Grosso do Sul, SW Brazil
106 E13 **Portoferraio** Toscana, C Italy
96 G6 **Port of Ness** NW Scotland, UK
45 U14 **Port-of-Spain** ● (Trinidad and Tobago) Trinidad, Trinidad and Tobago
Port of Spain *see* Piarco
103 X15 **Porto, Golfe de** *gulf* Corse, France, C Mediterranean Sea
Porto Grande *see* Mindelo
106 I7 **Portogruaro** Veneto, NE Italy
35 P5 **Portola** California, W USA
187 Q13 **Port-Olry** Espiritu Santo, C Vanuatu
93 J17 **Pörtom** *Fin.* Pirttikylä. Länsi-Suomi, W Finland
Port Omna *see* Portumna
59 G21 **Porto Murtinho** Mato Grosso do Sul, SW Brazil
59 K16 **Porto Nacional** Tocantins, C Brazil
77 S16 **Porto-Novo** ● (Benin) S Benin
23 X10 **Port Orange** Florida, SE USA
32 G8 **Port Orchard** Washington, NW USA
Porto Re *see* Kraljevica
32 E15 **Port Orford** Oregon, NW USA
Porto Rico *see* Puerto Rico
106 J13 **Porto San Giorgio** Marche, C Italy
107 F14 **Porto San Stefano** Toscana, C Italy
64 P5 **Porto Santo** *var.* Vila Baleira. Porto Santo, Madeira, Portugal, NE Atlantic Ocean
64 Q5 **Porto Santo** × Porto Santo, Madeira, Portugal, NE Atlantic Ocean
64 P5 **Porto Santo** *var.* Ilha do Porto Santo. *island* Madeira, Portugal, NE Atlantic Ocean
60 H9 **Porto São José** Paraná, S Brazil
59 O19 **Porto Seguro** Bahia, E Brazil
107 B17 **Porto Torres** Sardegna, Italy, C Mediterranean Sea
59 J23 **Porto União** Santa Catarina, S Brazil
103 Y16 **Porto-Vecchio** Corse, France, C Mediterranean Sea
59 E15 **Porto Velho** *var.* Velho. *state capital* Rondônia, W Brazil
56 A6 **Portoviejo** *var.* Puertoviejo. Manabí, W Ecuador
185 B26 **Port Pegasus** *bay* Stewart Island, NZ
14 H15 **Port Perry** Ontario, SE Canada
183 N12 **Port Phillip Bay** *harbour* Victoria, SE Australia
182 I8 **Port Pirie** South Australia
96 G9 **Portree** N Scotland, UK
Port Rex *see* East London
Port Rois *see* Portrush
44 K13 **Port Royal** E Jamaica
21 R15 **Port Royal** South Carolina, SE USA
21 R15 **Port Royal Sound** *inlet* South Carolina, SE USA
97 F14 **Portrush** *Ir.* Port Rois. N Northern Ireland, UK
75 W7 **Port Said** *Ar.* Būr Sa'īd. N Egypt
23 R9 **Port Saint Joe** Florida, SE USA
23 Y11 **Port Saint John** Florida, SE USA
83 K24 **Port St.Johns** Eastern Cape, SE South Africa
103 R16 **Port-St-Louis-du-Rhône** Bouches-du-Rhône, SE France
44 K10 **Port Salut** SW Haiti
65 E24 **Port Salvador** *inlet* East Falkland, Falkland Islands
65 D24 **Port San Carlos** East Falkland, Falkland Islands
13 S10 **Port Saunders** Newfoundland, SE Canada
83 K24 **Port Shepstone** KwaZulu/Natal, E South Africa
45 O11 **Portsmouth** *var.* Grand-Anse. NW Dominica
97 N24 **Portsmouth** S England, UK
19 P10 **Portsmouth** New Hampshire, NE USA
31 S15 **Portsmouth** Ohio, N USA
21 X7 **Portsmouth** Virginia, NE USA
14 E17 **Port Stanley** Ontario, S Canada
65 B25 **Port Stephens** *inlet* West Falkland, Falkland Islands
65 B25 **Port Stephens Settlement** West Falkland, Falkland Islands
97 F14 **Portstewart** *Ir.* Port Stíobhaird. N Northern Ireland, UK
Port Stíobhaird *see* Portstewart
80 I7 **Port Sudan** Red Sea, NE Sudan
22 L10 **Port Sulphur** Louisiana, S USA
Port Swettenham *see* Klang/Pelabuhan Klang
97 J22 **Port Talbot** S Wales, UK
92 L11 **Porttipahdan Tekojärvi** ⊞ N Finland
32 G7 **Port Townsend** Washington, NW USA
104 H9 **Portugal** *off.* Republic of Portugal. ◆ *republic* SW Europe
105 O2 **Portugalete** País Vasco, N Spain
54 J6 **Portuguesa** *off.* Estado Portuguesa. ◈ *state* N Venezuela
Portuguese East Africa *see* Mozambique
Portuguese Guinea *see* Guinea-Bissau
Portuguese Timor *see* East Timor
Portuguese West Africa *see* Angola
97 D18 **Portumna** *Ir.* Port Omna. W Ireland
Portus Cale *see* Porto
Portus Magnus *see* Almería
Portus Magonis *see* Mahón
103 P17 **Port-Vendres** *var.* Port Vendres. Pyrénées-Orientales, S France
182 H9 **Port Victoria** South Australia
187 Q14 **Port-Vila** *var.* Vila. ● (Vanuatu) Éfaté, C Vanuatu
182 I9 **Port Wakefield** South Australia
31 N8 **Port Washington** Wisconsin, N USA
57 J14 **Porvenir** Pando, NW Bolivia
63 I24 **Porvenir** Magallanes, S Chile
61 D18 **Porvenir** Paysandú, W Uruguay
93 M19 **Porvoo** *Swe.* Borgå. Etelä-Suomi, S Finland
Porzecze *see* Parechcha
104 M10 **Porzuna** Castilla-La Mancha, C Spain
61 E14 **Posadas** Misiones, NE Argentina
104 L13 **Posadas** Andalucía, S Spain
Poschega *see* Požega
108 J11 **Poschiavino** ≈ Italy/Switzerland
108 J10 **Poschiavo** *Ger.* Puschlav. Graubünden, S Switzerland
112 D12 **Posedarje** Zadar, SW Croatia
Posen *see* Poznań
126 L14 **Poshekhon'ye** Yaroslavskaya Oblast', W Russian Federation
92 M13 **Posio** Lappi, NE Finland
Poskam *see* Zepu
Posnania *see* Poznań
171 O12 **Poso** Sulawesi, C Indonesia
59 P15 **Poço da Cruz, Açude** ⊞ E Brazil
171 O12 **Poso, Danau** ◎ Sulawesi, C Indonesia
137 R10 **Posof** Ardahan, NE Turkey
25 R6 **Possum Kingdom Lake** ⊞ Texas, SW USA
25 N6 **Post** Texas, SW USA
Postavy/Postawy *see* Pastavy
12 I7 **Poste-de-la-Baleine** Quebec, NE Canada
99 M17 **Posterholt** Limburg, SE Netherlands
83 G22 **Postmasburg** Northern Cape, N South Africa
Pôsto Diauarum *see* Campo de Diauarum
59 I16 **Pôsto Jacaré** Mato Grosso, W Brazil
109 T12 **Postojna** *Ger.* Adelsberg, *It.* Postumia. SW Slovenia
Postumia *see* Postojna
29 X12 **Postville** Iowa, C USA
Pöstyén *see* Piešt'any
113 G14 **Posušje** Federacija Bosna I Hercegovina, SE Bosnia & Herzegovina
171 O16 **Pota** Flores, C Indonesia
115 G23 **Potamós** Antikýthira, S Greece
55 S9 **Potaru River** ≈ C Guyana
83 I21 **Potchefstroom** North-West, N South Africa
27 R11 **Poteau** Oklahoma, C USA
25 R12 **Poteet** Texas, SW USA
115 G14 **Poteídaia** *site of ancient city* Kentrikí Makedonía, N Greece
Potentia *see* Potenza
107 M18 **Potenza** *anc.* Potentia. Basilicata, S Italy
185 A24 **Poteriteri, Lake** ◎ South Island, NZ
104 M2 **Potes** Cantabria, N Spain
83 J20 **Potgietersrus** Northern, NE South Africa
25 S12 **Poth** Texas, SW USA
32 J9 **Potholes Reservoir** ⊞ Washington, NW USA
137 Q9 **P'ot'i** W Georgia
77 X13 **Potiskum** Yobe, NE Nigeria
Potkozarje *see* Ivanjska
32 M9 **Potlatch** Idaho, NW USA
33 N9 **Pot Mountain** ▲ Idaho, NW USA
113 H14 **Potoci** Federacija Bosna I Hercegovina, SE Bosnia & Herzegovina
21 V3 **Potomac River** ≈ NE USA
27 W6 **Potosi** Missouri, C USA
57 L20 **Potosí** Potosí, S Bolivia
42 H9 **Potosí** Chinandega, NW Nicaragua
57 K21 **Potosí** ◈ *department* SW Bolivia
62 H7 **Potrerillos** Atacama, N Chile
42 H5 **Potrerillos** Cortés, NW Honduras
62 H8 **Potro, Cerro del** ▲ N Chile
100 N12 **Potsdam** Brandenburg, NE Germany
18 J7 **Potsdam** New York, NE USA
109 X5 **Pottendorf** Niederösterreich, E Austria
109 X5 **Pottenstein** Niederösterreich, E Austria
18 I15 **Pottstown** Pennsylvania, NE USA
18 H14 **Pottsville** Pennsylvania, NE USA
155 L25 **Pottuvil** Eastern Province, SE Sri Lanka
149 U6 **Potwar Plateau** *plateau* NE Pakistan
102 J7 **Pouancé** Maine-et-Loire, W France
15 R6 **Poulin de Courval, Lac** ◎ Quebec, SE Canada
18 L9 **Poultney** Vermont, NE USA
187 O16 **Poum** Province Nord, W New Caledonia
59 L21 **Pouso Alegre** Minas Gerais, NE Brazil
192 I16 **Poutasi** Upolu, SE Samoa
167 R12 **Poŭthĭsăt** *prev.* Pursat. Poŭthĭsăt, W Cambodia
167 R12 **Poŭthĭsăt, Stœng** *prev.* Pursat. ≈ W Cambodia
102 J9 **Pouzauges** Vendée, NW France
Po, Valle del *see* Po Valley
106 F8 **Po Valley** *It.* Valle del Po. *valley* N Italy
111 I19 **Považská Bystrica** *Ger.* Waagbistritz, *Hung.* Vágbeszterce. Trenčiansky Kraj, W Slovakia
126 J10 **Povenets** Respublika Kareliya, NW Russian Federation
184 Q9 **Poverty Bay** *inlet* North Island, NZ
112 K12 **Povlen** ▲ W Yugoslavia
104 G6 **Póvoa de Varzim** Porto, NW Portugal
129 N8 **Povorino** Voronezhskaya Oblast', W Russian Federation
Povungnituk *see* Puvirnituq
12 J3 **Povungnituk, Rivière de** ≈ Quebec, NE Canada
14 H11 **Powassan** Ontario, S Canada
35 U17 **Poway** California, W USA
33 W14 **Powder River** Wyoming, C USA
33 Y10 **Powder River** ≈ Montana/Wyoming, NW USA
32 L12 **Powder River** ≈ Oregon, NW USA
33 W13 **Powder River Pass** *pass* Wyoming, C USA
33 U12 **Powell** Wyoming, C USA
65 I22 **Powell Basin** *undersea feature* NW Weddell Sea
36 M8 **Powell, Lake** ◎ Utah, W USA
37 R4 **Powell, Mount** ▲ Colorado, C USA
10 L17 **Powell River** British Columbia, SW Canada
31 N5 **Powers** Michigan, N USA
28 K2 **Powers Lake** North Dakota, N USA
21 V6 **Powhatan** Virginia, NE USA
31 V13 **Powhatan Point** Ohio, N USA
97 J20 **Powys** *cultural region* E Wales, UK
187 P17 **Poya** Province Nord, C New Caledonia
161 P10 **Poyang Hu** ◎ S China
30 L7 **Poygan, Lake** ◎ Wisconsin, N USA
109 Y2 **Poysdorf** Niederösterreich, NE Austria
112 N11 **Požarevac** *Ger.* Passarowitz. Serbia, NE Yugoslavia
41 Q13 **Poza Rica** *var.* Poza Rica de Hidalgo. Veracruz-Llave, E Mexico
Poza Rica de Hidalgo *see* Poza Rica
112 L13 **Požega** *Prev.* Slavonska Požega; *Ger.* Poschega, *Hung.* Pozsega. Požega-Slavonija, NE Croatia
112 H9 **Požega-Slavonija** *off.* Požeško-Slavonska Županija. ◈ *province* NE Croatia
127 U13 **Pozhva** Komi-Permyatskiy Avtonomnyy Okrug, NW Russian Federation
110 G11 **Poznań** *Ger.* Posen, Posnania. Wielkolpolskie, C Poland
105 O13 **Pozo Alcón** Andalucía, S Spain
62 H3 **Pozo Almonte** Tarapacá, N Chile
104 L12 **Pozoblanco** Andalucía, S Spain
105 Q11 **Pozo Cañada** Castilla-La Mancha, C Spain
62 N5 **Pozo Colorado** Presidente Hayes, C Paraguay
63 J20 **Pozos, Punta** *headland* S Argentina
Pozsega *see* Požega
Pozsony *see* Bratislava
55 N5 **Pozuelos** Anzoátegui, NE Venezuela
107 L26 **Pozzallo** Sicilia, Italy, C Mediterranean Sea
107 K17 **Pozzuoli** *anc.* Puteoli. Campania, S Italy
77 P17 **Pra** ≈ S Ghana
111 C19 **Prachatice** *Ger.* Prachatitz. Budějovický Kraj, S Czech Republic
Prachatitz *see* Prachatice
167 P11 **Prachin Buri** *var.* Prachinburi. Prachin Buri, C Thailand
Prachuab Girikhand *see* Prachuap Khiri Khan
167 O12 **Prachuap Khiri Khan** *var.* Prachuab Girikhand. Prachuap Khiri Khan, SW Thailand
111 H16 **Praděd** *Ger.* Altvater. ▲ NE Czech Republic
54 D11 **Pradera** Valle del Cauca, SW Colombia
103 O17 **Prades** Pyrénées-Orientales, S France
59 O19 **Prado** Bahia, SE Brazil
54 E11 **Prado** Tolima, C Colombia
Prado del Ganso *see* Goose Green
Prae *see* Phrae
Prag/Praga/Prague *see* Praha
27 O10 **Prague** Oklahoma, C USA
111 D16 **Praha** *Eng.* Prague, *Ger.* Prag, *Pol.* Praga. ● (Czech Republic) Středočeský Kraj, NW Czech Republic
116 J13 **Prahova** ◈ *county* SE Romania
116 J13 **Prahova** ≈ S Romania
76 E10 **Praia** ● (Cape Verde) Santiago, S Cape Verde
83 M21 **Praia do Bilene** Gaza, S Mozambique
83 M20 **Praia do Xai-Xai** Gaza, S Mozambique
116 J10 **Praid** *Hung.* Parajd. Harghita, C Romania
26 J3 **Prairie Dog Creek** ≈ Kansas/Nebraska, C USA
30 J9 **Prairie du Chien** Wisconsin, N USA
27 S9 **Prairie Grove** Arkansas, C USA
31 P10 **Prairie River** ≈ Michigan, N USA
Prairie State *see* Illinois
25 V11 **Prairie View** Texas, SW USA
167 Q10 **Prakhon Chai** Buri Ram, E Thailand
109 R4 **Pram** ≈ N Austria
109 S4 **Prambachkirchen** Oberösterreich, N Austria
118 H2 **Prangli** *island* N Estonia
154 J13 **Prānhita** ≈ C India
172 I15 **Praslin** *island* Inner Islands, NE Seychelles
115 O23 **Prasonísi, Akrotírio** *headland* Ródos, Dodekánisos, Greece, Aegean Sea
111 I14 **Praszka** Opolskie, S Poland
119 M18 **Pratasy** *Rus.* Protasy. Homyel'skaya Voblasts', SE Belarus
167 Q10 **Prathai** Nakhon Ratchasima, E Thailand
Prathet Thai *see* Thailand
Prathum Thani *see* Pathum Thani
63 F21 **Prat, Isla** *island* S Chile
106 G11 **Prato** Toscana, C Italy
103 O17 **Prats-de-Mollo-la-Preste** Pyrénées-Orientales, S France
26 L6 **Pratt** Kansas, C USA
108 E6 **Pratteln** Basel-Land, NW Switzerland
193 O2 **Pratt Seamount** *undersea feature* N Pacific Ocean
23 P5 **Prattville** Alabama, S USA
Praust *see* Pruszcz Gdański
114 M7 **Pravda** *prev.* Dogrular. Silistra, NE Bulgaria
119 B14 **Pravdinsk** *Ger.* Friedland. Kaliningradskaya Oblast', W Russian Federation
104 K2 **Pravia** Asturias, N Spain
118 L12 **Prazaroki** *Rus.* Prozoroki. Vitsyebskaya Voblasts', N Belarus
Prázsmár *see* Prejmer
167 S11 **Preăh Vihéar** Preăh Vihéar, N Cambodia
116 J12 **Predeal** *Hung.* Predeál. Braşov, C Romania
109 S8 **Predlitz** Steiermark, SE Austria
11 V15 **Preeceville** Saskatchewan, S Canada
Preenkuln *see* Priekule
102 K6 **Pré-en-Pail** Mayenne, NW France
109 T4 **Pregarten** Oberösterreich, N Austria
54 H7 **Pregonero** Táchira, NW Venezuela
118 J10 **Preiļi** *Ger.* Preli. Preiļi, SE Latvia
116 J12 **Prejmer** *Ger.* Tartlau, *Hung.* Prázsmár. Braşov, S Romania
113 J16 **Prekornica** ▲ SW Yugoslavia
Preli *see* Preiļi
Prëmet *see* Përmet
100 M12 **Premnitz** Brandenburg, NE Germany
25 S15 **Premont** Texas, SW USA
113 H14 **Prenj** ▲ S Bosnia and Herzegovina
Prenjas/Prenjasi *see* Përrenjas
22 L7 **Prentiss** Mississippi, S USA
Preny *see* Prienai
100 O10 **Prenzlau** Brandenburg, NE Germany
123 N11 **Preobrazhenka** Irkutskaya Oblast', C Russian Federation
166 J9 **Preparis Island** *island* SW Myanmar
Prerau *see* Přerov
111 H18 **Přerov** *Ger.* Prerau. Olomoucký Kraj, E Czech Republic
Preschau *see* Prešov
14 M14 **Prescott** Ontario, SE Canada
36 K12 **Prescott** Arizona, SW USA
27 T13 **Prescott** Arkansas, C USA
32 L10 **Prescott** Washington, NW USA
30 H6 **Prescott** Wisconsin, N USA
185 A24 **Preservation Inlet** *inlet* South Island, NZ
112 O7 **Preševo** Serbia, SE Yugoslavia
29 N10 **Presho** South Dakota, N USA
58 M13 **Presidente Dutra** Maranhão, E Brazil
60 I8 **Presidente Epitácio** São Paulo, S Brazil
62 N5 **Presidente Hayes** *off.* Departamento de Presidente Hayes. ◈ *department* C Paraguay
60 I9 **Presidente Prudente** São Paulo, S Brazil
Presidente Stroessner *see* Ciudad del Este
Presidente Vargas *see* Itabira
60 I8 **Presidente Venceslau** São Paulo, S Brazil
193 O10 **President Thiers Seamount** *undersea feature* C Pacific Ocean
24 J11 **Presidio** Texas, SW USA
Preslav *see* Veliki Preslav
111 M19 **Prešov** *var.* Preschau, *Ger.* Eperies, *Hung.* Eperjes. Prešovský Kraj, E Slovakia
111 M19 **Prešovský Kraj** ◈ *region* E Slovakia
113 N20 **Prespa, Lake** *Alb.* Liqen i Prespës, *Gk.* Límni Megáli Préspa, Limni Prespa, *Mac.* Prespansko Ezero, *Serb.* Prespansko Jezero. ◎ SE Europe
Prespa, Limni/Prespansko Ezero/Prespansko Jezero/Prespës, Liqen i *see* Prespa, Lake
19 S2 **Presque Isle** Maine, NE USA
18 B11 **Presque Isle** *headland* Pennsylvania, NE USA
Pressburg *see* Bratislava
77 P17 **Prestea** SW Ghana
111 B17 **Přeštice** *Ger.* Pschestitz. Plzeňský Kraj, W Czech Republic
97 K17 **Preston** NW England, UK
23 S6 **Preston** Georgia, SE USA
33 R16 **Preston** Idaho, NW USA
29 Z13 **Preston** Iowa, C USA
29 X11 **Preston** Minnesota, N USA
21 O6 **Prestonsburg** Kentucky, S USA
96 I13 **Prestwick** W Scotland, UK
83 J21 **Pretoria** *var.* Epitoli, Tshwane. ● (South Africa-administrative capital) Gauteng, NE South Africa
Pretoria-Witwatersrand-Vereeniging *see* Gauteng
Pretusha *see* Pretushë
113 M21 **Pretushë** *var.* Pretusha. Korçë, SE Albania

Preussisch Eylau see Bagrationovsk
Preussisch-Stargard see Starogard Gdański
Preußisch Holland see Pasłęk
115 C17 **Préveza** Ípeiros, W Greece
37 V3 **Prewitt Reservoir** ⊠ Colorado, C USA
167 S13 **Prey Vêng** Prey Vêng, S Cambodia
144 M12 **Priaral'skiye Karakumy, Peski** desert SW Kazakhstan
123 P14 **Priargunsk** Chitinskaya Oblast', S Russian Federation
38 K14 **Pribilof Islands** island group Alaska, USA
113 K14 **Priboj** Serbia, W Yugoslavia
111 C17 **Příbram** Ger. Pibrans. Středočeský Kraj, W Czech Republic
36 M4 **Price** Utah, W USA
37 N5 **Price River** ∽ Utah, W USA
23 N8 **Prichard** Alabama, S USA
25 R8 **Priddy** Texas, SW USA
105 P8 **Priego** Castilla-La Mancha, C Spain
104 M14 **Priego de Córdoba** Andalucía, S Spain
118 C10 **Priekule** Ger. Preenkuln. Liepāja, SW Latvia
118 C12 **Priekulė** Ger. Prökuls. Gargždai, W Lithuania
119 F14 **Prienai** Pol. Preny. Prienai, S Lithuania
83 G23 **Prieska** Northern Cape, C South Africa
32 M7 **Priest Lake** ⊠ Idaho, NW USA
32 M7 **Priest River** Idaho, NW USA
104 M3 **Prieta, Peña** ▲ N Spain
40 J10 **Prieto, Cerro** ▲ C Mexico
111 J19 **Prievidza** var. Priewitz, Ger. Priwitz, Hung. Privigye. Trenčiansky Kraj, C Slovakia
Priewitz see Prievidza
112 F10 **Prijedor** Republika Srpska, NW Bosnia & Herzegovina
113 K14 **Prijepolje** Serbia, W Yugoslavia
Prikaspiyskaya Nizmennost' see Caspian Depression
113 O19 **Prilep** Turk. Perlepe. S FYR Macedonia
108 B9 **Prilly** Vaud, SW Switzerland
Priluki see Pryluky
62 L10 **Primero, Río** ∽ C Argentina
29 S12 **Primghar** Iowa, C USA
112 B9 **Primorje-Gorski Kotar** off. Primorsko-Goranska Županija. ◆ province NW Croatia
118 A13 **Primorsk** Ger. Fischhausen. Kaliningradskaya Oblast', W Russian Federation
126 G12 **Primorsk** Fin. Koivisto. Leningradskaya Oblast', NW Russian Federation
Primorsk/Primorskoye see Prymors'k
123 S14 **Primorskiy Kray** prev. Eng. Maritime Territory. ◆ territory SE Russian Federation
114 N10 **Primorsko** prev. Keupriya. Burgas, E Bulgaria
128 K13 **Primorsko-Akhtarsk** Krasnodarskiy Kray, SW Russian Federation
117 U13 **Primors'kyy** Respublika Krym, S Ukraine
113 D14 **Primošten** Šibenik-Knin, S Croatia
11 R13 **Primrose Lake** ◎ Saskatchewan, C Canada
11 T14 **Prince Albert** Saskatchewan, S Canada
83 G25 **Prince Albert** Western Cape, SW South Africa
8 J5 **Prince Albert Peninsula** peninsula Victoria Island, Northwest Territories, NW Canada
8 J6 **Prince Albert Sound** inlet Northwest Territories, N Canada
8 J5 **Prince Alfred, Cape** headland Northwest Territories, NW Canada
9 P6 **Prince Charles Island** island Nunavut, NE Canada
195 W6 **Prince Charles Mountains** ▲ Antarctica
Prince-Édouard, Île-du see Prince Edward Island
172 M13 **Prince Edward Fracture Zone** tectonic feature SW Indian Ocean
13 P14 **Prince Edward Island** Fr. Île-du Prince-Édouard. ◆ province SE Canada
13 Q14 **Prince Edward Island** Fr. Île-du Prince-Édouard. island SE Canada
173 M12 **Prince Edward Islands** island group S South Africa
21 X4 **Prince Frederick** Maryland, NE USA
10 M14 **Prince George** British Columbia, SW Canada
21 W6 **Prince George** Virginia, NE USA
8 L3 **Prince Gustaf Adolf Sea** sea Nunavut, N Canada
197 Q3 **Prince of Wales, Cape** headland Alaska, USA
9 N3 **Prince of Wales Icefield** ice feature Nunavut, N Canada
181 V1 **Prince of Wales Island** island Queensland, E Australia
8 L5 **Prince of Wales Island** island Queen Elizabeth Islands, Nunavut, NW Canada
39 Y14 **Prince of Wales Island** island Alexander Archipelago, Alaska, USA
Prince of Wales Island see Pinang, Pulau
8 J5 **Prince of Wales Strait** strait Northwest Territories, N Canada
8 K4 **Prince Patrick Island** island Parry Islands, Northwest Territories, NW Canada
9 N5 **Prince Regent Inlet** channel Nunavut, N Canada
10 J13 **Prince Rupert** British Columbia, SW Canada
Prince's Island see Príncipe
21 Y5 **Princess Anne** Maryland, NE USA
195 R1 **Princess Astrid Kyst** physical region Antarctica
181 W2 **Princess Charlotte Bay** bay Queensland, NE Australia
195 W7 **Princess Elizabeth Land** physical region Antarctica
10 J14 **Princess Royal Island** island British Columbia, SW Canada
45 U15 **Princes Town** Trinidad, Trinidad and Tobago
11 N17 **Princeton** British Columbia, SW Canada
30 L11 **Princeton** Illinois, N USA
31 N16 **Princeton** Indiana, N USA
29 Z14 **Princeton** Iowa, C USA
20 H7 **Princeton** Kentucky, S USA
29 V8 **Princeton** Minnesota, N USA
27 S1 **Princeton** Missouri, C USA
18 J15 **Princeton** New Jersey, NE USA
21 R6 **Princeton** West Virginia, NE USA
39 S12 **Prince William Sound** inlet Alaska, USA
67 P9 **Príncipe** var. Príncipe Island, Eng. Prince's Island. island N Sao Tome and Principe
Príncipe Island see Príncipe
32 I13 **Prineville** Oregon, NW USA
28 J11 **Pringle** South Dakota, N USA
25 N1 **Pringle** Texas, SW USA
99 H14 **Prinsenbeek** Noord-Brabant, S Netherlands
98 L6 **Prinses Margriet Kanaal** canal N Netherlands
195 T2 **Prinsesse Ragnhild Kyst** physical region Antarctica
195 U2 **Prins Harald Kyst** physical region Antarctica
92 N2 **Prins Karls Forland** island W Svalbard
43 N8 **Prinzapolka** Región Autónoma Atlántico Norte, NE Nicaragua
42 L8 **Prinzapolka, Río** ∽ NE Nicaragua
122 H9 **Priob'ye** Khanty-Mansiyskiy Avtonomnyy Okrug, N Russian Federation
104 H1 **Prior, Cabo** headland NW Spain
29 V9 **Prior Lake** Minnesota, N USA
126 H11 **Priozersk** Fin. Käkisalmi. Leningradskaya Oblast', NW Russian Federation
119 J20 **Pripet** Bel. Prypyats', Ukr. Pryp"yat'. ∽ Belarus/Ukraine
119 J20 **Pripet Marshes** wetland Belarus/Ukraine
Prishtinë see Priština
128 J8 **Pristen'** Kurskaya Oblast', W Russian Federation
113 N16 **Priština** Alb. Prishtinë. Serbia, S Yugoslavia
100 M10 **Pritzwalk** Brandenburg, NE Germany
103 R13 **Privas** Ardèche, E France
107 I16 **Priverno** Lazio, C Italy
Privigye see Prievidza
112 C12 **Privlaka** Zadar, SW Croatia
126 M15 **Privolzhsk** Ivanovskaya Oblast', NW Russian Federation
129 P7 **Privolzhskaya Vozvyshennost'** var. Volga Uplands. ▲ W Russian Federation
129 P8 **Privolzhskoye** Saratovskaya Oblast', W Russian Federation
Priwitz see Prievidza
129 N13 **Priyutnoye** Respublika Kalmykiya, SW Russian Federation
113 M17 **Prizren** Alb. Prizreni. Serbia, S Yugoslavia
Prizreni see Prizren
107 I24 **Prizzi** Sicilia, Italy, C Mediterranean Sea
113 P18 **Probištip** NE FYR Macedonia
169 S16 **Probolinggo** Jawa, C Indonesia
Probstberg see Wyszków
111 F14 **Prochowice** Ger. Parchwitz. Dolnośląskie, SW Poland
29 W5 **Proctor** Minnesota, N USA
25 R8 **Proctor** Texas, SW USA
25 R8 **Proctor Lake** ⊠ Texas, SW USA
155 I18 **Proddatūr** Andhra Pradesh, E India
104 H9 **Proença-a-Nova** Castelo Branco, C Portugal
95 I24 **Præstø** Storstrøm, SE Denmark
99 I21 **Profondeville** Namur, SE Belgium
41 W11 **Progreso** Yucatán, SE Mexico
123 R14 **Progress** Amurskaya Oblast', SE Russian Federation
129 O15 **Prokhladnyy** Kabardino-Balkarskaya Respublika, SW Russian Federation
Prokletije see North Albanian Alps
Prökuls see Priekulė
113 O15 **Prokuplje** Serbia, SE Yugoslavia
126 H14 **Proletariy** Novgorodskaya Oblast', W Russian Federation
128 M12 **Proletarsk** Rostovskaya Oblast', SW Russian Federation
128 J8 **Proletarskiy** Belgorodskaya Oblast', W Russian Federation
166 L7 **Prome** var. Pyè. Pegu, C Myanmar
60 J8 **Promissão** São Paulo, S Brazil
60 J8 **Promissão, Represa de** ⊠ S Brazil
127 V4 **Promyshlennyy** Respublika Komi, NW Russian Federation
119 O16 **Pronya** Rus. Pronya. ∽ E Belarus
10 M11 **Prophet River** British Columbia, W Canada
30 K11 **Prophetstown** Illinois, N USA
59 P16 **Propriá** Sergipe, E Brazil
103 X16 **Propriano** Corse, France, C Mediterranean Sea
Prościejów see Prostějov
Proskurov see Khmel 'nyts'kyy
114 H12 **Prosotsáni** Anatolikí Makedonía kai Thráki, NE Greece
171 Q7 **Prosperidad** Mindanao, S Philippines
32 J10 **Prosser** Washington, NW USA
Prossnitz see Prostějov
111 G18 **Prostějov** Ger. Prossnitz, Pol. Prościejów. Olomoucký Kraj, E Czech Republic
117 V8 **Prosyana** Dnipropetrovs'ka Oblast', E Ukraine
111 L16 **Proszowice** Małopolskie, S Poland
Protasy see Pratasy
172 J11 **Protea Seamount** undersea feature SW Indian Ocean
115 D21 **Próti** island S Greece
114 N8 **Provadiya** Varna, E Bulgaria
103 S15 **Provence** prev. Marseille-Marignane. ✕ (Marseille) Bouches-du-Rhône, SE France
103 T14 **Provence** cultural region SE France
103 T14 **Provence-Alpes-Côte d'Azur** ◆ region SE France
20 H6 **Providence** Kentucky, S USA
19 N12 **Providence** state capital Rhode Island, NE USA
36 L1 **Providence** Utah, W USA
Providence see Fort Providence
67 X10 **Providence Atoll** var. Providence. atoll S Seychelles
14 D12 **Providence Bay** Manitoulin Island, Ontario, S Canada
23 R6 **Providence Canyon** valley Alabama/Georgia, S USA
22 I5 **Providence, Lake** ◎ Louisiana, S USA
35 X13 **Providence Mountains** ▲ California, W USA
44 L6 **Providenciales** island W Turks and Caicos Islands
19 Q12 **Provincetown** Massachusetts, NE USA
103 P5 **Provins** Seine-et-Marne, N France
36 L3 **Provo** Utah, W USA
11 R15 **Provost** Alberta, SW Canada
112 G13 **Prozor** Federacija Bosna I Hercegovina, SW Bosnia & Herzegovina
Prozoroki see Prazaroki
60 I11 **Prudentópolis** Paraná, S Brazil
39 R5 **Prudhoe Bay** Alaska, USA
39 R4 **Prudhoe Bay** bay Alaska, USA
111 H16 **Prudnik** Ger. Neustadt, Neustadt in Oberschlesien. Opolskie, S Poland
119 J16 **Prudy** Rus. Prudy. Minskaya Voblasts', C Belarus
101 D18 **Prüm** Rheinland-Pfalz, W Germany
101 D18 **Prüm** ∽ W Germany
Prusa see Bursa
110 J7 **Pruszcz Gdański** Ger. Praust. Pomorskie, N Poland
110 M12 **Pruszków** Ger. Kaltdorf. Mazowieckie, C Poland
116 K8 **Prut** Ger. Pruth. ∽ E Europe
Pruth see Prut
108 L8 **Prutz** Tirol, W Austria
Prużana see Pruzhany
119 G19 **Pruzhany** Pol. Prużana. Brestskaya Voblasts', SW Belarus
126 I11 **Pryazha** Respublika Kareliya, NW Russian Federation
117 U10 **Pryazovs'ke** Zaporiz'ka Oblast', SE Ukraine
Prychornomors'ka Nyzovyna see Black Sea Lowland
Prydniprovs'ka Nyzovyna/Prydnyaprows kaya Nizina see Dnieper Lowland
195 Y7 **Prydz Bay** bay Antarctica
117 R4 **Pryluky** Rus. Priluki. Chernihivs'ka Oblast', NE Ukraine
117 V10 **Prymors'k** Rus. Primorsk; prev. Primorskoye. Zaporiz'ka Oblast', SE Ukraine
27 Q9 **Pryor** Oklahoma, C USA
33 U11 **Pryor Creek** ∽ Montana, NW USA
Pryp"yat'/Prypyats' see Pripet
110 M10 **Przasnysz** Mazowieckie, C Poland
111 K14 **Przedbórz** Łodzkie, S Poland
111 P17 **Przemyśl** Rus. Peremyshl. Podkarpackie, SE Poland
111 O16 **Przeworsk** Podkarpackie, SE Poland
Przheval'sk see Karakol
110 L13 **Przysucha** Mazowieckie, SE Poland
115 H18 **Psachná** var. Psahna, Psakhná. Évvoia, C Greece
Psahna/Psakhná see Psachná
115 K18 **Psará** island E Greece
115 I16 **Psathoúra** island Vóreioi Sporádes, Greece, Aegean Sea
Pschestitz see Přeštice
Psein Lora see Pishin Lora
117 S5 **Psël** ∽ Russian Federation/Ukraine
115 M21 **Psérimos** island Dodekánisos, Greece, Aegean Sea
Pseyn Bowr see Pishin Lora
Pskem see Piskom
147 R8 **Pskemskiy Khrebet** Uzb. Piskom Tizmasi. ▲ Kyrgyzstan/Uzbekistan
126 F14 **Pskov** Ger. Pleskau, Latv. Pleskava. Pskovskaya Oblast', W Russian Federation
118 K6 **Pskov, Lake** Est. Pihkva Järv, Ger. Pleskauer See, Rus. Pskovskoye Ozero. ◎ Estonia/Russian Federation
126 F15 **Pskovskaya Oblast'** ◆ province W Russian Federation
Pskovskoye Ozero see Pskov, Lake
112 G9 **Psunj** ▲ NE Croatia
111 J17 **Pszczyna** Ger. Pless. Śląskie, S Poland
Ptačnik/Ptacsnik see Vtáčnik
115 D17 **Ptéri** ▲ C Greece
Ptich' see Ptsich
115 E14 **Ptolemaïda** prev. Ptolemaïs. Dytikí Makedonía, N Greece
Ptolemaïs see Ptolemaïda, Greece
Ptolemaïs see 'Akko, Israel
119 M19 **Ptsich** Rus. Ptich'. Homyel'skaya Voblasts', SE Belarus
119 M18 **Ptsich** Rus. Ptich'. ∽ SE Belarus
109 X10 **Ptuj** Ger. Pettau; anc. Poetovio. NE Slovenia
61 A23 **Puán** Buenos Aires, E Argentina
192 H15 **Pu'apu'a** Savai'i, C Samoa
192 G15 **Puava, Cape** headland Savai'i, NW Samoa
56 F12 **Pucallpa** Ucayali, C Peru
57 J17 **Pucarani** La Paz, NW Bolivia
Pučarevo see Novi Travnik
157 U12 **Pucheng** Fujian, SE China
160 L6 **Pucheng** Shaanxi, C China
127 N16 **Puchezh** Ivanovskaya Oblast', W Russian Federation
111 I19 **Púchov** Hung. Puhó. Trenčiansky Kraj, W Slovakia
116 J13 **Pucioasa** Dâmbovița, S Romania
110 I6 **Puck** Pomorskie, N Poland
30 L8 **Puckaway Lake** ◎ Wisconsin, N USA
63 G15 **Pucón** Araucanía, S Chile
93 M14 **Pudasjärvi** Oulu, C Finland
148 L8 **Pūdeh Tal, Shelleh-ye** ∽ SW Afghanistan
129 S1 **Pudem** Udmurtskaya Respublika, NW Russian Federation
Pudewitz see Pobiedziska
126 K11 **Pudozh** Respublika Kareliya, NW Russian Federation
97 M17 **Pudsey** N England, UK
Puduchcheri see Pondicherry
151 H21 **Pudukkottai** Tamil Nādu, SE India
171 Z13 **Pue** Irian Jaya, E Indonesia
41 P14 **Puebla** var. Puebla de Zaragoza. Puebla, S Mexico
41 P15 **Puebla** ◆ state S Mexico
104 L11 **Puebla de Alcocer** Extremadura, W Spain
Puebla de Don Fabrique see Puebla de Don Fadrique
105 P13 **Puebla de Don Fadrique** var. Puebla de Don Fabrique. Andalucía, S Spain
104 J11 **Puebla de la Calzada** Extremadura, W Spain
104 J5 **Puebla de Sanabria** Castilla-León, N Spain
104 I4 **Puebla de Trives** see A Pobla de Trives
Puebla de Zaragoza see Puebla
37 T6 **Pueblo** Colorado, C USA
37 N10 **Pueblo Colorado Wash** valley Arizona, SW USA
61 C16 **Pueblo Libertador** Corrientes, NE Argentina
40 J10 **Pueblo Nuevo** Durango, C Mexico
42 J8 **Pueblo Nuevo** Estelí, NW Nicaragua
54 J3 **Pueblo Nuevo** Falcón, N Venezuela
42 B6 **Pueblo Nuevo Tiquisate** var. Tiquisate. Escuintla, SW Guatemala
41 Q11 **Pueblo Viejo, Laguna de** lagoon E Mexico
63 J14 **Puelches** La Pampa, C Argentina
104 L14 **Puente-Genil** Andalucía, S Spain
105 Q3 **Puente la Reina** Navarra, N Spain
104 L12 **Puente Nuevo, Embalse de** ⊠ S Spain
57 D14 **Puente Piedra** Lima, W Peru
160 F14 **Pu'er** Yunnan, SW China
45 V6 **Puerca, Punta** headland E Puerto Rico
37 R12 **Puerco, Rio** ∽ New Mexico, SW USA
57 J17 **Puerto Acosta** La Paz, W Bolivia
63 G19 **Puerto Aisén** Aisén, S Chile
41 R17 **Puerto Ángel** Oaxaca, SE Mexico
Puerto Argentino see Stanley
41 T17 **Puerto Arista** Chiapas, SE Mexico
43 O16 **Puerto Armuelles** Chiriquí, SW Panama
Puerto Arrecife see Arrecife
54 D14 **Puerto Asís** Putumayo, SW Colombia
54 L9 **Puerto Ayacucho** Amazonas, SW Venezuela
57 C18 **Puerto Ayora** Galapagos Islands, Ecuador, E Pacific Ocean
57 C18 **Puerto Baquerizo Moreno** var. Baquerizo Moreno. Galapagos Islands, Ecuador, E Pacific Ocean
42 G4 **Puerto Barrios** Izabal, E Guatemala
Puerto Bello see Portobelo
54 F8 **Puerto Berrío** Antioquia, C Colombia
54 F9 **Puerto Boyaca** Boyacá, C Colombia
54 K4 **Puerto Cabello** Carabobo, N Venezuela
43 N7 **Puerto Cabezas** var. Bilwi. Región Autónoma Atlántico Norte, NE Nicaragua
54 L9 **Puerto Carreño** Vichada, E Colombia
54 E4 **Puerto Colombia** Atlántico, N Colombia
42 H4 **Puerto Cortés** Cortés, NW Honduras
54 J4 **Puerto Cumarebo** Falcón, N Venezuela
Puerto de Cabras see Puerto del Rosario
55 Q5 **Puerto de Hierro** Sucre, NE Venezuela
64 O11 **Puerto de la Cruz** Tenerife, Islas Canarias, Spain, NE Atlantic Ocean
64 Q11 **Puerto del Rosario** var. Puerto de Cabras. Fuerteventura, Islas Canarias, Spain, NE Atlantic Ocean
63 J20 **Puerto Deseado** Santa Cruz, SE Argentina
40 F8 **Puerto Escondido** Baja California Sur, W Mexico
41 R17 **Puerto Escondido** Oaxaca, SE Mexico
60 G12 **Puerto Esperanza** Misiones, NE Argentina
56 D6 **Puerto Francisco de Orellana** var. Coca. Napo, N Ecuador
54 H10 **Puerto Gaitán** Meta, C Colombia
Puerto Gallegos see Río Gallegos
60 G12 **Puerto Iguazú** Misiones, NE Argentina
56 F12 **Puerto Inca** Huánuco, N Peru
54 L11 **Puerto Inírida** var. Obando. Guainía, E Colombia
42 K13 **Puerto Jesús** Guanacaste, NW Costa Rica
41 Z11 **Puerto Juárez** Quintana Roo, SE Mexico
55 N5 **Puerto La Cruz** Anzoátegui, NE Venezuela
54 E14 **Puerto Leguízamo** Putumayo, S Colombia
43 N5 **Puerto Lempira** Gracias a Dios, E Honduras
Puerto Libertad see La Libertad
54 I11 **Puerto Limón** Meta, E Colombia
54 D13 **Puerto Limón** Putumayo, SW Colombia
Puerto Limón see Limón
105 N11 **Puertollano** Castilla-La Mancha, C Spain
63 K17 **Puerto Lobos** Chubut, SE Argentina
54 I3 **Puerto López** La Guajira, N Colombia
105 Q14 **Puerto Lumbreras** Murcia, SE Spain
41 V17 **Puerto Madero** Chiapas, SE Mexico
63 K17 **Puerto Madryn** Chubut, S Argentina
Puerto Magdalena see Bahía Magdalena
57 J15 **Puerto Maldonado** Madre de Dios, E Peru
Puerto Masachapa see Masachapa
Puerto México see Coatzacoalcos
63 G17 **Puerto Montt** Los Lagos, C Chile
41 Z12 **Puerto Morelos** Quintana Roo, SE Mexico
54 L10 **Puerto Nariño** Vichada, E Colombia
63 H23 **Puerto Natales** Magallanes, S Chile
43 X15 **Puerto Obaldía** San Blas, NE Panama
44 H6 **Puerto Padre** Las Tunas, E Cuba
54 L9 **Puerto Páez** Apure, C Venezuela
40 E3 **Puerto Peñasco** Sonora, NW Mexico
55 N5 **Puerto Píritu** Anzoátegui, NE Venezuela
45 N8 **Puerto Plata** var. San Felipe de Puerto Plata. N Dominican Republic
45 N8 **Puerto Plata** ✕ N Dominican Republic
Puerto Presidente Stroessner see Ciudad del Este
171 N6 **Puerto Princesa** off. Puerto Princesa City. Palawan, W Philippines
Puerto Princesa City see Puerto Princesa
Puerto Príncipe see Camagüey
Puerto Quellón see Quellón
60 F13 **Puerto Rico** Misiones, NE Argentina
57 K14 **Puerto Rico** Pando, N Bolivia
54 E12 **Puerto Rico** Caquetá, S Colombia
45 U5 **Puerto Rico** off. Commonwealth of Puerto Rico; prev. Porto Rico. ◇ US commonwealth territory C West Indies
64 F11 **Puerto Rico** island C West Indies
64 G11 **Puerto Rico Trench** undersea feature NE Caribbean Sea
54 I8 **Puerto Rondón** Arauca, E Colombia
Puerto San José see San José
63 J21 **Puerto San Julián** var. San Julián. Santa Cruz, SE Argentina
63 I22 **Puerto Santa Cruz** var. Santa Cruz. Santa Cruz, SE Argentina
Puerto Sauce see Juan L.Lacaze
57 Q20 **Puerto Suárez** Santa Cruz, E Bolivia
54 D13 **Puerto Umbría** Putumayo, SW Colombia
40 J13 **Puerto Vallarta** Jalisco, SW Mexico
63 G16 **Puerto Varas** Los Lagos, C Chile
42 M13 **Puerto Viejo** Heredia, NE Costa Rica
Puertoviejo see Portoviejo
57 B18 **Puerto Villamil** var. Villamil. Galapagos Islands, Ecuador, E Pacific Ocean
54 F8 **Puerto Wilches** Santander, N Colombia
63 H20 **Pueyrredón, Lago** var. Lago Cochrane. ◎ S Argentina
129 R7 **Pugachëv** Saratovskaya Oblast', W Russian Federation
129 T3 **Pugachëvo** Udmurtskaya Respublika, NW Russian Federation
32 H8 **Puget Sound** sound Washington, NW USA
107 O17 **Puglia** var. Le Puglie, Eng. Apulia. ◆ region SE Italy
107 N17 **Puglia, Canosa di** anc. Canusium. Puglia, SE Italy
118 I6 **Puhja** Ger. Kawelecht. Tartumaa, SE Estonia
Puhó see Púchov
105 V4 **Puigcerdà** Cataluña, NE Spain
Puigmal see Puigmal d'Err
103 N17 **Puigmal d'Err** var. Puigmal. ▲ S France
76 I16 **Pujehun** S Sierra Leone
Puka see Pukë
185 E20 **Pukaki, Lake** ◎ South Island, NZ
38 F10 **Pukalani** Maui, Hawaii, USA, C Pacific Ocean
190 J13 **Pukapuka** atoll N Cook Islands
191 X9 **Pukapuka** atoll Îles Tuamotu, E French Polynesia
Pukari Neem see Purekkari Neem
191 X11 **Pukarua** var. Pukaruha. atoll Îles Tuamotu, E French Polynesia
Pukaruha see Pukarua
14 A7 **Pukaskwa** ∽ Ontario, S Canada
11 V12 **Pukatawagan** Manitoba, C Canada
191 X16 **Pukatikei, Maunga** (volcano) Easter Island, Chile, E Pacific Ocean
182 C1 **Pukatja** var. Ernabella. South Australia
163 Y12 **Pukch'ŏng** E North Korea
113 L18 **Pukë** var. Puka. Shkodër, N Albania
184 L6 **Pukekohe** Auckland, North Island, NZ
184 L7 **Pukemiro** Waikato, North Island, NZ
190 D12 **Puke, Mont** ▲ Île Futuna, W Wallis and Futuna
Puket see Phuket
185 C20 **Puketeraki Range** ▲ South Island, NZ
184 N13 **Puketoi Range** ▲ North Island, NZ
185 F21 **Pukeuri Junction** Otago, South Island, NZ
119 L16 **Pukhavichy** Rus. Pukhovichi. Minskaya Voblasts', C Belarus
Pukhovichi see Pukhavichy
126 M10 **Puksoozero** Arkhangel'skaya Oblast', NW Russian Federation
112 A10 **Pula** It. Pola; prev. Pulj. Istra, NW Croatia
163 U14 **Pulandian** var. Xinjin. Liaoning, NE China
163 T14 **Pulandian Wan** bay NE China
189 O15 **Pulap Atoll** atoll Caroline Islands, C Micronesia
18 H9 **Pulaski** New York, NE USA
20 I10 **Pulaski** Tennessee, S USA
21 R7 **Pulaski** Virginia, NE USA
171 Y14 **Pulau, Sungai** ∽ Irian Jaya, E Indonesia
110 N13 **Puławy** Ger. Neu Amerika. Lubelskie, E Poland
101 E16 **Pulheim** Nordrhein-Westfalen, W Germany
Pulicat see Pālghāt
155 J19 **Pulicat Lake** lagoon SE India
Pul'-I-Khatum see Polekhatum
Pul-i-Khumri see Pol-e Khomrī
Pul-i-Sefid see Pol-e Safīd
Pulj see Pula
109 W2 **Pulkau** ∽ NE Austria
93 L15 **Pulkkila** Oulu, C Finland
122 C7 **Pul'kovo** ✕ (Sankt-Peterburg) Leningradskaya Oblast', NW Russian Federation
32 M9 **Pullman** Washington, NW USA
108 B10 **Pully** Vaud, SW Switzerland
40 F7 **Púlpita, Punta** headland W Mexico
110 M10 **Pułtusk** Mazowieckie, C Poland
158 H10 **Pulu** Xinjiang Uygur Zizhiqu, W China
137 P13 **Pülümür** Tunceli, E Turkey
189 N16 **Pulusuk** island Caroline Islands, C Micronesia
189 N16 **Puluwat Atoll** atoll Caroline Islands, C Micronesia
25 N11 **Pumpville** Texas, SW USA
191 P7 **Punaauia** var. Hakapehi. Tahiti, W French Polynesia
56 B8 **Puná, Isla** island SW Ecuador
185 G16 **Punakaiki** West Coast, South Island, NZ
153 T11 **Punakha** C Bhutan
57 L18 **Punata** Cochabamba, C Bolivia
155 E14 **Pune** prev. Poona. Mahārāshtra, W India
83 M17 **Pungoè, Rio** var. Púnguè, Pungwe. ∽ C Mozambique
21 X10 **Pungo River** ∽ North Carolina, SE USA
Púnguè/Pungwe see Pungoè, Rio
79 N19 **Punia** Maniema, E Dem. Rep. Congo (Zaire)
62 H8 **Punilla, Sierra de la** ▲ W Argentina
161 P14 **Puning** Guangdong, S China
62 G10 **Punitaqui** Coquimbo, C Chile
152 H8 **Punjab** ◆ state NW India
149 T9 **Punjab** prev. West Punjab, Western Punjab. ◆ province E Pakistan
131 Q9 **Punjab Plains** plain N India
93 O17 **Punkaharju** var. Punkasalmi. Isä-Suomi, E Finland

◆ Country ● Country Capital ◇ Dependent Territory ○ Dependent Territory Capital ◆ Administrative Region ✕ International Airport ▲ Mountain ▲ Mountain Range Volcano ∽ River ◎ Lake ⊠ Reservoir

Punkasalmi see Punkaharju
57 I17 **Puno** Puno, SE Peru
57 H17 **Puno** off. Departamento de Puno. ◈ department S Peru
61 B24 **Punta Alta** Buenos Aires, E Argentina
63 H24 **Punta Arenas** prev. Magallanes. Magallanes, S Chile
45 T6 **Punta, Cerro de** ▲ C Puerto Rico
43 T15 **Punta Chame** Panamá, C Panama
57 G17 **Punta Colorada** Arequipa, SW Peru
40 F9 **Punta Coyote** Baja California Sur, W Mexico
62 G8 **Punta de Díaz** Atacama, N Chile
61 G20 **Punta del Este** Maldonado, S Uruguay
63 K17 **Punta Delgada** Chubut, SE Argentina
55 O5 **Punta de Mata** Monagas, NE Venezuela
55 O4 **Punta de Piedras** Nueva Esparta, NE Venezuela
42 F4 **Punta Gorda** Toledo, SE Belize
43 N11 **Punta Gorda** Región Autónoma Atlántico Sur, SE Nicaragua
23 W14 **Punta Gorda** Florida, SE USA
42 M11 **Punta Gorda, Río** ≈ SE Nicaragua
62 H6 **Punta Negra, Salar de** salt lake N Chile
40 D5 **Punta Prieta** Baja California, NW Mexico
42 L13 **Puntarenas** Puntarenas, W Costa Rica
42 L13 **Puntarenas** off. Provincia de Puntarenas. ◈ province W Costa Rica
54 J4 **Punto Fijo** Falcón, N Venezuela
105 S4 **Puntón de Guara** ▲ N Spain
18 D14 **Punxsutawney** Pennsylvania, NE USA
93 M14 **Puolanka** Oulu, C Finland
57 J17 **Pupuya, Nevado** ▲ W Bolivia
161 O10 **Puqi** Hubei, C China
57 F16 **Puquio** Ayacucho, S Peru
122 J9 **Pur** ≈ N Russian Federation
186 D7 **Purari** ≈ S PNG
27 N11 **Purcell** Oklahoma, C USA
11 O16 **Purcell Mountains** ▲ British Columbia, SW Canada
105 P14 **Purchena** Andalucía, S Spain
27 S8 **Purdy** Missouri, C USA
118 I2 **Purekkari Neem** prev. Pukari Neem. headland N Estonia
37 U7 **Purgatoire River** ≈ Colorado, C USA
Purgstall see Purgstall an der Erlauf
109 V5 **Purgstall an der Erlauf** var. Purgstall. Niederösterreich, NE Austria
154 O13 **Puri** var. Jagannath. Orissa, E India
Puriramya see Buriram
109 X4 **Purkersdorf** Niederösterreich, NE Austria
98 I9 **Purmerend** Noord-Holland, C Netherlands
151 G16 **Pūrna** ≈ C India
Purnea see Pūrnia
153 R13 **Pūrnia** prev. Purnea. Bihār, NE India
Pursat see Poŭthĭsăt, Poŭthĭsăt, W Cambodia
Pursat see Poŭthĭsăt, Stœng, W Cambodia
Purulia see Puruliya
150 L13 **Puruliya** prev. Purulia. West Bengal, NE India
47 G7 **Purus, Rio** Sp. Río Purús. ≈ Brazil/Peru
186 C9 **Purutu Island** island SW PNG
93 N17 **Puruvesi** ◎ SE Finland
22 L7 **Purvis** Mississippi, S USA
114 J11 **Pŭrvomay** prev. Borisovgrad. Plovdiv, C Bulgaria
169 R16 **Purwodadi** prev. Poerwodadi. Jawa, C Indonesia
169 P16 **Purwokerto** prev. Poerwokerto. Jawa, C Indonesia
169 P16 **Purworejo** prev. Poerworedjo. Jawa, C Indonesia
20 H8 **Puryear** Tennessee, S USA
154 H13 **Pusad** Mahārāshtra, C India
163 Z16 **Pusan** off. Pusan-gwangyŏksi, var. Busan, Jap. Fusan. SE South Korea
168 H7 **Pusatgajo, Pegunungan** ▲ Sumatera, NW Indonesia
Puschlav see Poschiavo
Pushkin see Tsarskoye Selo
129 Q8 **Pushkino** Saratovskaya Oblast', W Russian Federation
Pushkino see Biläsuvar
111 M22 **Püspökladány** Hajdú-Bihar, E Hungary
118 J3 **Püssi** Ger. Isenhof. Ida-Virumaa, NE Estonia
116 I5 **Pustomyty** L'vivs'ka Oblast', W Ukraine
126 F16 **Pustoshka** Pskovskaya Oblast', W Russian Federation
Pusztakalán see Călan
167 N1 **Putao** prev. Fort Hertz. Kachin State, N Myanmar
184 M8 **Putaruru** Waikato, North Island, NZ
Puteoli see Pozzuoli
161 R12 **Putian** Fujian, SE China
107 O17 **Putignano** Puglia, SE Italy
Putivl' see Putyvl'
41 Q16 **Putla** var. Putla de Guerrero. Oaxaca, SE Mexico
Putla de Guerrero see Putla
19 N12 **Putnam** Connecticut, NE USA
25 Q7 **Putnam** Texas, SW USA
18 M10 **Putney** Vermont, NE USA
111 L20 **Putnok** Borsod-Abaúj-Zemplén, NE Hungary
Putorana, Gory/Putorana Mountains see Putorana, Plato
122 L8 **Putorana, Plato** var. Gory Putorana, Eng. Putorana Mountains. ▲ N Russian Federation
62 H2 **Putre** Tarapacá, N Chile
155 J24 **Puttalam** North Western Province, W Sri Lanka
155 J24 **Puttalam Lagoon** lagoon W Sri Lanka
99 H17 **Putte** Antwerpen, C Belgium
98 K11 **Putten** Gelderland, C Netherlands
100 K7 **Puttgarden** Schleswig-Holstein, N Germany
Puttiala see Patiāla
101 D20 **Püttlingen** Saarland, SW Germany
54 D14 **Putumayo** off. Intendencia del Putumayo. ◈ province S Colombia
48 E7 **Putumayo, Río** var. Rio Içá. ≈ NW South America see also Içá, Rio
169 P11 **Putus, Tanjung** headland Borneo, N Indonesia
116 J8 **Putyla** Chernivets'ka Oblast', W Ukraine
117 S3 **Putyvl'** Rus. Putivl'. Sums'ka Oblast', NE Ukraine
93 M18 **Puula** ◎ SE Finland
93 N18 **Puumala** Isä-Suomi, E Finland
118 I5 **Puurmani** Ger. Talkhof. Jõgevamaa, E Estonia
99 G17 **Puurs** Antwerpen, N Belgium
Pu'uUla'ula see Red Hill
38 A8 **Puuwai** Niihau, Hawaii, USA, C Pacific Ocean
12 J4 **Puvirnituq** prev. Povungnituk. Quebec, NE Canada
32 H8 **Puyallup** Washington, NW USA
161 O5 **Puyang** Henan, C China
161 R9 **Puyang Jiang** var. Tsien Tang. ≈ SE China
103 O11 **Puy-de-Dôme** ◈ department C France
103 N15 **Puylaurens** Tarn, S France
102 M13 **Puy-l'Evêque** Lot, S France
103 N17 **Puymorens, Col de** pass S France
56 C7 **Puyo** Pastaza, C Ecuador
185 A24 **Puysegur Point** headland South Island, NZ
148 J8 **Pūzak, Hāmūn-e** Pash. Hāmūn-i-Puzak. ◎ SW Afghanistan
Puzak, Hāmūn-i- see Pūzak, Hāmūn-e
81 J23 **Pwani** Eng. Coast. ◈ region E Tanzania
79 O23 **Pweto** Katanga, SE Dem. Rep. Congo (Zaire)
97 I19 **Pwllheli** NW Wales, UK
189 O14 **Pwok** Pohnpei, E Micronesia
122 I9 **Pyakupur** ≈ N Russian Federation
126 M6 **Pyalitsa** Murmanskaya Oblast', NW Russian Federation
126 K10 **Pyal'ma** Respublika Kareliya, NW Russian Federation
Pyandzh see Panj
126 I6 **Pyaozero, Ozero** ◎ NW Russian Federation
166 L9 **Pyapon** Irrawaddy, SW Myanmar
119 J15 **Pyarshai** Rus. Pershay. Minskaya Voblasts', C Belarus
122 K8 **Pyasina** ≈ N Russian Federation
114 I10 **Pyasŭchnik, Yazovir** ⊟ C Bulgaria
Pyatikhatki see P"yatykhatky
117 S7 **P"yatykhatky** Rus. Pyatikhatki. Dnipropetrovs'ka Oblast', E Ukraine
166 M6 **Pyawbwe** Mandalay, C Myanmar
129 T3 **Pychas** Udmurtskaya Respublika, NW Russian Federation
Pyè see Prome
166 K6 **Pyechin** Chin State, W Myanmar
119 G17 **Pyeski** Rus. Peski. Hrodzyenskaya Voblasts', W Belarus
119 L19 **Pyetrykaw** Rus. Petrikov. Homyel'skaya Voblasts', SE Belarus
93 M16 **Pyhäjärvi** ◎ C Finland
93 O17 **Pyhäjärvi** ◎ SE Finland
93 L15 **Pyhäjoki** Oulu, W Finland
93 L15 **Pyhäjoki** ≈ W Finland
93 M15 **Pyhäntä** Oulu, C Finland
93 M16 **Pyhäsalmi** Oulu, C Finland
93 O17 **Pyhäselkä** ◎ SE Finland
93 M19 **Pyhtää** Swe. Pyttis. Etelä-Suomi, S Finland
166 M6 **Pyinmana** Mandalay, C Myanmar
115 N24 **Pylés** var. Piles. Kárpathos, SE Greece
115 D21 **Pýlos** var. Pilos. Pelopónnisos, S Greece
18 B12 **Pymatuning Reservoir** ⊟ Ohio/Pennsylvania, NE USA
163 X15 **P'yŏngt'aek** NW South Korea
163 V14 **P'yŏngyang** var. P'yŏngyang-si, Eng. Pyongyang. ● (North Korea) SW North Korea
P'yŏngyang-si see P'yŏngyang
35 Q4 **Pyramid Lake** ◎ Nevada, W USA
37 P15 **Pyramid Mountains** ▲ New Mexico, SW USA
37 R5 **Pyramid Peak** ▲ Colorado, C USA
115 D17 **Pyramíva** var. Piramiva. ▲ C Greece
Pyrenaei Montes see Pyrenees
86 B12 **Pyrenees** Fr. Pyrénées, Sp. Pirineos; anc. Pyrenaei Montes. ▲ SW Europe
102 J16 **Pyrénées-Atlantiques** ◈ department SW France
103 N17 **Pyrénées-Orientales** ◈ department S France
115 L19 **Pyrgí** var. Pirgi. Chíos, E Greece
115 D20 **Pýrgos** var. Pírgos. Dytikí Elláda, S Greece
Pyritz see Pyrzyce
115 E19 **Pýrros** ≈ S Greece
117 R4 **Pyryatyn** Rus. Piryatin. Poltavs'ka Oblast', NE Ukraine
110 D9 **Pyrzyce** Ger. Pyritz. Zachodniopomorskie, NW Poland
126 F15 **Pytalovo** Latv. Abrene; prev. Jaunlatgale. Pskovskaya Oblast', W Russian Federation
115 M20 **Pythagóreio** var. Pithagorio. Sámos, Dodekánisos, Greece, Aegean Sea
14 L11 **Pythonga, Lac** ◎ Quebec, SE Canada
94 E10 **Pyttegga** ▲ S Norway
Pyttis see Pyhtää
166 M7 **Pyu** Pegu, C Myanmar
166 M8 **Pyuntaza** Pegu, SW Myanmar
153 N11 **Pyuthan** Mid Western, W Nepal
110 H12 **Pyzdry** Ger. Peisern. Wielkopolskie, C Poland

Q

138 H13 **Qā' al Jafr** ◎ S Jordan
197 O11 **Qaanaaq** var. Qânâq, Dan. Thule. Avannaarsua, N Greenland
138 G7 **Qabb Eliâs** E Lebanon
Qabil see Al Qābil
Qabırrı see Iori
Qābis see Gabès
Qābis, Khalīj see Gabès, Golfe de
141 S14 **Qabr Hūd** C Yemen
Qacentina see Constantine
148 L4 **Qādes** Bādghīs, NW Afghanistan
139 T11 **Qādisīyah** S Iraq
143 O4 **Qā'emshahr** prev. 'Alīābad, Shāhī. Māzandarān, N Iran
143 U7 **Qā'en** var. Qain, Qāyen. Khorāsān, E Iran
141 U13 **Qafa** spring/well SW Oman
Qafṣah see Gafsa
163 V9 **Qagan Nur** ◎ NE China
162 Q11 **Qagan Nur** ◎ N China
Qagan Us see Dulan
158 H13 **Qagcaka** Xizang Zizhiqu, W China
Qahremānshahr see Bākhtarān
159 Q10 **Qaidam He** ≈ C China
156 L8 **Qaidam Pendi** basin C China
Qain see Qā'en
Qala Āhangarān see Chaghcharān
139 U3 **Qalā Diza** var. Qal 'at Dīzah. NE Iraq
Qal'ah Sālih see Qal'at Ṣāliḥ
147 R13 **Qal'aikhum** Rus. Kalaikhum. S Tajikistan
Qala Nau see Qal'eh-ye Now
141 V17 **Qalansīyah** Suquṭrā, W Yemen
Qala Panja see Qal'eh-ye Panjeh
Qala Shāhar see Qal'eh Shahr
Qalāt see Kalāt
139 W9 **Qal'at Aḥmad** E Iraq
141 N11 **Qal'at Bīshah** 'Asīr, SW Saudi Arabia
138 H4 **Qal'at Burzay** Ḥamāh, W Syria
Qal 'at Dīzah see Qalā Diza
139 W9 **Qal'at Ḥusayh** E Iraq
139 V10 **Qal'at Majnūnah** S Iraq
139 X11 **Qal'at Ṣāliḥ** var. Qal'ah Sālih. E Iraq
139 V10 **Qal'at Sukkar** SE Iraq
Qalba Zhotasy see Kalbinskiy Khrebet
143 Q12 **Qal'eh Biābān** Fārs, S Iran
149 N4 **Qal'eh Shahr** Pash. Qala Shāhar. Sar-e Pol, N Afghanistan
148 L4 **Qal'eh-ye Now** var. Qala Nau. Bādghīs, NW Afghanistan
149 T2 **Qal'eh-ye Panjeh** var. Qala Panja. Badakhshān, NE Afghanistan
Qamar Bay see Qamar, Ghubbat al
141 U14 **Qamar, Ghubbat al** Eng. Qamar Bay. bay Oman/Yemen
141 V13 **Qamar, Jabal al** ▲ SW Oman
Qambar see Kambar
159 R14 **Qamdo** Xizang Zizhiqu, W China
75 R7 **Qaminis** NE Libya
Qamishly see Al Qāmishlī
Qânâq see Qaanaaq
Qandahār see Kandahār
80 Q11 **Qandala** Bari, NE Somalia
Qandyaghash see Kandyagash
138 L2 **Qanṭārī** Ar Raqqah, N Syria
137 V13 **Qapiciğ Dağı** Rus. Gora Kapydzhik. ▲ SW Azerbaijan
158 H5 **Qapqal** var. Qapqal Xibe Zizhixian. Xinjiang Uygur Zizhiqu, NW China
Qapqal Xibe Zizhixian see Qapqal
Qapshagay Böyeni see Kapchagayskoye Vodokhranilishche
196 M15 **Qaqortoq** Dan. Julianehåb. Kitaa, S Greenland
75 U8 **Qâra** var. Qārah. NW Egypt
139 T4 **Qara Anjīr** N Iraq
Qarabāgh see Qarah Bāgh
Qaraböget see Karaboget
Qarabulaq see Karabulak
Qarabutaq see Karabutak
Qaraghandy/Qaraghandy Oblysy see Karaganda
Qaraghayly see Karagayly
139 U4 **Qara Gol** NE Iraq
Qārah see Qâra
148 J4 **Qarah Bāgh** var. Qarabāgh. Herāt, NW Afghanistan
138 G7 **Qaraoun, Lac de** var. Buḥayrat al Qir'awn. ◎ S Lebanon
Qaraoy see Karaoy
Qaraqoyyn see Karakoyyn, Ozero
Qara Qum see Garagumy
Qarasū see Karasu
Qaratal see Karatal
Qarataū see Karatau, Khrebet, Kazakhstan
Qarataū see Karatau, Zhambyl, Kazakhstan
Qaraton see Karaton
80 P13 **Qardho** var. Kardh, It. Gardo. Bari, N Somalia
142 M6 **Qareh Chāy** ≈ N Iran
142 K2 **Qareh Sū** ≈ NW Iran
Qariateïne see Al Qaryatayn
Qarkilik see Ruoqiang
147 O13 **Qarluq** Rus. Karluk. Surkhondaryo Wiloyati, S Uzbekistan
147 U12 **Qarokŭl** Rus. Karakul'. E Tajikistan
147 T12 **Qarokŭl** Rus. Ozero Karakul'. ◎ E Tajikistan
Qarqan see Qiemo
158 K9 **Qarqan He** ≈ NW China
Qarqannah, Juzur see Kerkenah, Îles de
Qarqaraly see Karkaralinsk
149 O1 **Qarqīn** Jowzjān, N Afghanistan
Qars see Kars
Qarsaqbay see Karsakpay
146 M12 **Qarshi** Rus. Karshi; prev. Bek-Budi. Qashqadaryo Wiloyati, S Uzbekistan
146 L12 **Qarshi Chŭli** Rus. Karshinskaya Step. grassland S Uzbekistan
146 M13 **Qarshi Kanali** Rus. Karshinskiy Kanal. canal Turkmenistan/Uzbekistan
Qaryatayn see Al Qaryatayn
146 M12 **Qashqadaryo Wiloyati** Rus. Kashkadar'inskaya Oblast'. ◈ province S Uzbekistan
Qasigianguit see Qasigiannguit
197 N13 **Qasigiannguit** var. Qasigianguit, Dan. Christianshåb. Kitaa, C Greenland
Qaşim, Minṭaqat see Al Qaşīm
139 P8 **Qaṣr 'Amīj** C Iraq
139 R9 **Qaṣr Darwīshāh** C Iraq
142 J6 **Qaṣr-e Shīrīn** Kermānshāh, W Iran
75 V10 **Qasr Farâfra** W Egypt
Qassim see Al Qaşīm
141 O16 **Qa'ṭabah** SW Yemen
138 H7 **Qaṭanā** var. Katana. Dimashq, S Syria
143 N15 **Qatar** off. State of Qatar, Ar. Dawlat Qaṭar. ◆ monarchy SW Asia
Qatrana see Al Qaṭrānah
143 Q12 **Qaṭrūyeh** Fārs, S Iran
Qattara Depression/Qaṭṭārah, Munkhafaḍ al see Qaṭṭâra, Monkhafad el
75 U8 **Qaṭṭâra, Monkhafad el** var. Munkhafaḍ al Qaṭṭārah, Eng. Qattara Depression. desert NW Egypt
Qaṭṭīnah, Buḥayrat see Ḥimṣ, Buḥayrat
Qaydār see Qeydār
Qāyen see Qā'en
147 Q11 **Qayroqqum** Rus. Kayrakkum. NW Tajikistan
147 Q10 **Qayroqqum, Obanbori** Rus. Kayrakkumskoye Vodokhranilishche. ⊟ NW Tajikistan
139 U7 **Qazānīyah** var. Dhū Shaykh. E Iraq
Qazaqstan/Qazaqstan Respublikasy see Kazakhstan
137 T9 **Qazbegi** Rus. Kazbegi. NE Georgia
149 P15 **Qāzi Ahmad** var. Kazi Ahmad. Sind, SE Pakistan
137 Y12 **Qazimämmäd** Rus. Kazi Magomed. SE Azerbaijan
Qazris see Cáceres
142 M4 **Qazvīn** var. Kazvin. Qazvīn, N Iran
142 M5 **Qazvīn** ◈ province N Iran
187 Z13 **Qelelevu Lagoon** lagoon NE Fiji
75 X10 **Qena** var. Qinā; anc. Caene, Caenepolis. E Egypt
113 L23 **Qeparo** Vlorë, S Albania
Qeqertarssuaq see Qeqertarsuaq
197 N13 **Qeqertarsuaq** var. Qeqertarssuaq, Dan. Godhavn. Kitaa, Greenland
196 M13 **Qeqertarsuaq** island W Greenland
197 N13 **Qeqertarsuup Tunua** Dan. Disko Bugt. inlet W Greenland
Qerveh see Qorveh
143 S14 **Qeshm** Hormozgān, S Iran
143 R14 **Qeshm** var. Jazīreh-ye Qeshm, Qeshm Island. island S Iran
Qeshm Island/Qeshm, Jazīreh-ye see Qeshm
142 L4 **Qeydār** var. Qaydār. Zanjān, NW Iran
142 K5 **Qezel Owzan** var. Ki Zil Uzen, Qi Zil Uzun. ≈ NW Iran
142 L5 **Qezel Owzan, Rūd-e** ≈ NW Iran
Qian see Guizhou
Qian Gorlo see Qian Gorlos
163 V9 **Qian Gorlos** var. Qian Gorlo, Qian Gorlos Mongolzu Zizhixian, Qianguozhen. Jilin, NE China
Qian Gorlos Mongolzu Zizhixian/Qianguozhen see Qian Gorlos
161 N9 **Qianjiang** Hubei, C China
160 K10 **Qianjiang** Sichuan, C China
160 L14 **Qian Jiang** ≈ S China
160 G9 **Qianning** var. Gartar. Sichuan, C China
163 U13 **Qian Shan** ▲ NE China
160 H10 **Qianwei** Sichuan, C China
160 J11 **Qianxi** Guizhou, S China
159 Q7 **Qiaowan** Gansu, N China
Qibilī see Kebili
158 K9 **Qiemo** var. Qarqan. Xinjiang Uygur Zizhiqu, NW China
160 J10 **Qijiang** Chongqing Shi, C China
159 N5 **Qijiaojing** Xinjiang Uygur Zizhiqu, NW China
149 P9 **Qila Saifullāh** Baluchistān, SW Pakistan
159 S9 **Qilian** Qinghai, C China
159 N8 **Qilian Shan** var. Kilien Mountains. ▲ N China
197 O11 **Qimusseriarsuaq** Dan. Melville Bugt, Eng. Melville Bay. bay NW Greenland
Qinā see Qena
159 W11 **Qin'an** Gansu, C China
Qing see Qinghai
163 W7 **Qing'an** Heilongjiang, NE China
161 R5 **Qingdao** var. Ching-Tao, Ch'ing-tao, Tsingtao, Tsintao, Ger. Tsingtau. Shandong, E China
163 V8 **Qinggang** Heilongjiang, NE China
Qinggil see Qinghe
159 P11 **Qinghai** var. Chinghai, Koko Nor, Qing, Qinghai Sheng, Tsinghai. ◈ province C China
159 S10 **Qinghai Hu** var. Ch'ing Hai, Tsing Hai, Mong. Koko Nor. ◎ C China
Qinghai Sheng see Qinghai
158 M3 **Qinghe** var. Qinggil. Xinjiang Uygur Zizhiqu, NW China
160 L4 **Qingjian** Shaanxi, C China
160 L9 **Qing Jiang** ≈ C China
Qingjiang see Huaiyin
Qingkou see Ganyu
160 I12 **Qinglong** var. Liancheng. Guizhou, S China
161 Q2 **Qinglong** Hebei, E China
Qingshan see Dedu
159 R12 **Qingshuihe** Qinghai, C China
Qingyang see Jinjiang
163 V11 **Qingyuan** Liaoning, NE China
158 L13 **Qingzang Gaoyuan** var. Xizang Gaoyuan, Eng. Plateau of Tibet. plateau W China
161 Q4 **Qingzhou** prev. Yidu. Shandong, E China
157 R9 **Qin He** ≈ C China
161 Q2 **Qinhuangdao** Hebei, E China
160 K7 **Qin Ling** ▲ C China
Qin Xian see Qinxian
161 N5 **Qinxian** var. Qin Xian. Shanxi, C China
161 N6 **Qinyang** Henan, C China
160 K15 **Qinzhou** Guangxi Zhuangzu Zizhiqu, S China
Qiong see Hainan
160 L17 **Qionghai** prev. Jiaji. Hainan, S China
160 H9 **Qionglai** Sichuan, C China
160 H8 **Qionglai Shan** ▲ C China
160 L17 **Qiongzhou Haixia** var. Hainan Strait. strait S China
163 U7 **Qiqihar** var. Ch'i-ch'i-ha-erh, Tsitsihar; prev. Lungkiang. Heilongjiang, NE China
143 P12 **Qīr** Fārs, S Iran
158 H10 **Qira** Xinjiang Uygur Zizhiqu, NW China
Qir'awn, Buḥayrat al see Qaraoun, Lac de
138 F11 **Qiryat Gat** var. Kiryat Gat. Southern, C Israel
138 G8 **Qiryat Shemona** Northern, N Israel
Qishlaq see Garmsār
141 U14 **Qishn** SE Yemen
138 G9 **Qishon, Naḥal** ≈ N Israel
Qita Ghazzah see Gaza Strip
156 K5 **Qitai** Xinjiang Uygur Zizhiqu, NW China
163 Y8 **Qitaihe** Heilongjiang, NE China
141 W12 **Qitbit, Wādī** dry watercourse S Oman
161 O5 **Qixian** var. Qi Xian, Zhaoge. Henan, C China
Qīzān see Jīzān
Qizil Orda see Kyzylorda
Qizil Qum/Qizilqum see Kyzyl Kum
147 V14 **Qizilrabot** Rus. Kyzylrabot. SE Tajikistan
146 J10 **Qizilrawbe** Rus. Kyzylrabat. Bukhoro Wiloyati, C Uzbekistan
Qi Zil Uzun see Qezel Owzan
139 S4 **Qīzil Yār** N Iraq
146 G7 **Qizqetkan** Rus. Kazanketken. Qoraqalpoghiston Respublikasi, W Uzbekistan
Qoghaly see Kugaly
Qogir Feng see K2
143 N6 **Qom** var. Kum, Qum. Qom, N Iran
143 N6 **Qom** ◈ province N Iran
Qomisheh see Shahreẓā
Qomolangma Feng see Everest, Mount
142 M7 **Qom, Rūd-e** ≈ C Iran
Qomsheh see Shahreẓā
Qomul see Hami
Qondūz see Kunduz
Qongyrat see Konyrat
Qoqek see Tacheng
Qorabowur Kirlari see Karabaur', Uval
Qoradaryo see Karadar'ya
146 G6 **Qorajar** Rus. Karadzhar. Qoraqalpoghiston Respublikasi, NW Uzbekistan
146 K12 **Qorakŭl** Rus. Karakul'. Bukhoro Wiloyati, C Uzbekistan
146 E5 **Qoraqalpoghiston** Rus. Karakalpakya. Qoraqalpoghiston Respublikasi, NW Uzbekistan
146 G7 **Qoraqalpoghiston Respublikasi** Rus. Respublika Karakalpakstan. ◈ autonomous republic NW Uzbekistan
146 H7 **Qoraŭzak** Rus. Karauzyak. Qoraqalpoghiston Respublikasi, NW Uzbekistan
Qorghazhyn see Kurgal'dzhino
138 H6 **Qornet es Saouda** ▲ NE Lebanon
146 L12 **Qorowulbozor** Rus. Karaulbazar. Bukhoro Wiloyati, C Uzbekistan
142 K5 **Qorveh** var. Qerveh, Qurveh. Kordestān, W Iran
Qosshaghyl see Koschagyl
Qostanay/Qostanay Oblysy see Kostanay
143 P12 **Qoṭbābād** Fārs, S Iran
143 R13 **Qoṭbābād** Hormozgān, S Iran
138 H6 **Qoubaïyât** var. Al Qubayyāt. N Lebanon
Qoussantîna see Constantine
158 K16 **Qowowuyag** see Cho Oyu
146 H6 **Qozoqdaryo** Rus. Kazakdar'ya. Qoraqalpoghiston Respublikasi, NW Uzbekistan
19 N11 **Quabbin Reservoir** ⊟ Massachusetts, NE USA
100 F12 **Quakenbrück** Niedersachsen, NW Germany
18 I15 **Quakertown** Pennsylvania, NE USA
182 M10 **Quambatook** Victoria, SE Australia
25 Q4 **Quanah** Texas, SW USA
167 V10 **Quang Ngai** var. Quangngai, Quang Nghia. Quang Ngai, C Vietnam
Quang Nghia see Quang Ngai
167 T9 **Quang Tri** Quang Tri, C Vietnam
Quan Long see Ca Mau
152 L4 **Quanshuigou** China/India
161 R13 **Quanzhou** var. Ch'uan-chou, Tsinkiang; prev. Chin-chiang. Fujian, SE China
160 M12 **Quanzhou** Guangxi Zhuangzu Zizhiqu, S China
11 V16 **Qu'Appelle** ≈ Saskatchewan, S Canada
12 M3 **Quaqtaq** prev. Koartac. Quebec, NE Canada
61 E16 **Quaraí** Rio Grande do Sul, S Brazil
59 H24 **Quaraí, Rio** Sp. Río Cuareim. ≈ Brazil/Uruguay see also Cuareim, Río
171 N13 **Quarles, Pegunungan** ▲ Sulawesi, C Indonesia
Quarnero see Kvarner
107 C20 **Quartu Sant' Elena** Sardegna, Italy, C Mediterranean Sea
29 X13 **Quasqueton** Iowa, C USA
173 X16 **Quatre Bornes** W Mauritius
172 I17 **Quatre Bornes** Mahé, NE Seychelles
137 X10 **Quba** Rus. Kuba. N Azerbaijan
Qubba see Ba'qūbah
143 T3 **Qūchān** var. Kuchan. Khorāsān, NE Iran
183 R10 **Queanbeyan** New South Wales, SE Australia
15 Q10 **Québec** var. Quebec. Quebec, SE Canada
14 K10 **Quebec** var. Quebec. ◈ province SE Canada
61 D17 **Quebracho** Paysandú, W Uruguay
101 K14 **Quedlinburg** Sachsen-Anhalt, C Germany
138 H10 **Queen Alia** ✕ ('Ammān) 'Ammān, C Jordan
10 L16 **Queen Bess, Mount** ▲ British Columbia, SW Canada
10 I14 **Queen Charlotte** British Columbia, SW Canada
65 B24 **Queen Charlotte Bay** bay West Falkland, Falkland Islands
10 H14 **Queen Charlotte Islands** Fr. Îles de la Reine-Charlotte. island group British Columbia, SW Canada
10 I15 **Queen Charlotte Sound** sea area British Columbia, W Canada
10 J16 **Queen Charlotte Strait** strait British Columbia, W Canada
27 U1 **Queen City** Missouri, C USA
25 X5 **Queen City** Texas, SW USA
8 L3 **Queen Elizabeth Islands** Fr. Îles de la Reine-Élisabeth. island group Nunavut, N Canada
195 Y10 **Queen Mary Coast** physical region Antarctica
65 N24 **Queen Mary's Peak** ▲ C Tristan da Cunha
196 M8 **Queen Maud Gulf** gulf Arctic Ocean
195 P11 **Queen Maud Mountains** ▲ Antarctica
Queen's County see Laois
181 U7 **Queensland** ◈ state N Australia
192 I9 **Queensland Plateau** undersea feature N Coral Sea
183 O16 **Queenstown** Tasmania, SE Australia
185 C22 **Queenstown** Otago, South Island, NZ
83 I24 **Queenstown** Eastern Cape, S South Africa
Queenstown see Cobh
32 F8 **Queets** Washington, NW USA
61 D18 **Queguay Grande, Río** ≈ W Uruguay
59 O16 **Queimadas** Bahia, E Brazil
82 D11 **Quela** Malanje, NW Angola
83 O16 **Quelimane** var. Kilimane, Kilmain, Quilimane. Zambézia, NE Mozambique
63 G18 **Quellón** var. Puerto Quellón. Los Lagos, S Chile
Quelpart see Cheju-do
37 P12 **Quemado** New Mexico, SW USA
25 O12 **Quemado** Texas, SW USA
44 K7 **Quemado, Punta de** headland E Cuba
Quemoy see Chinmen Tao
62 K13 **Quemú Quemú** La Pampa, E Argentina
155 E17 **Quepem** Goa, W India
42 M14 **Quepos** Puntarenas, S Costa Rica
Que Que see Kwekwe
61 D23 **Quequén** Buenos Aires, E Argentina
61 D23 **Quequén Grande, Río** ≈ E Argentina
61 C23 **Quequén Salado, Río** ≈ E Argentina

◆ Country ● Country Capital ◇ Dependent Territory ○ Dependent Territory Capital ◈ Administrative Region ✕ International Airport ▲ Mountain ▲ Mountain Range ⊼ Volcano ≈ River ◎ Lake ⊟ Reservoir

Quera see Chur
41 N13 **Querétaro** Querétaro de Arteaga, C Mexico
40 F4 **Querobabi** Sonora, NW Mexico
42 M13 **Quesada** var. Ciudad Quesada, San Carlos. Alajuela, N Costa Rica
105 O13 **Quesada** Andalucía, S Spain
161 O7 **Queshan** Henan, C China
10 M15 **Quesnel** British Columbia, SW Canada
37 S9 **Questa** New Mexico, SW USA
102 H7 **Questembert** Morbihan, NW France
57 K22 **Quetena, Río** ~ SW Bolivia
149 O10 **Quetta** Baluchistān, SW Pakistan
Quetzalcoalco see Coatzacoalcos
Quetzaltenango see Quezaltenango
56 B6 **Quevedo** Los Ríos, C Ecuador
42 B6 **Quezaltenango** var. Quetzaltenango. Quezaltenango, W Guatemala
42 A2 **Quezaltenango** off. Departamento de Quezaltenango, var. Quetzaltenango. ⬖ department SW Guatemala
42 E6 **Quezaltepeque** Chiquimula, SE Guatemala
170 M6 **Quezon** Palawan, W Philippines
161 P5 **Qufu** Shandong, E China
82 B12 **Quibala** Cuanza Sul, NW Angola
82 B11 **Quibaxe** var. Quibaxi. Cuanza Norte, NW Angola
Quibaxi see Quibaxe
54 D9 **Quibdó** Chocó, W Colombia
102 G7 **Quiberon** Morbihan, NW France
102 G7 **Quiberon, Baie de** bay NW France
54 J5 **Quíbor** Lara, N Venezuela
42 C4 **Quiché** off. Departamento del Quiché. ⬖ department W Guatemala
99 E21 **Quiévrain** Hainaut, S Belgium
40 I9 **Quila** Sinaloa, C Mexico
83 B14 **Quilengues** Huíla, SW Angola
Quilimane see Quelimane
57 G15 **Quillabamba** Cusco, C Peru
57 L18 **Quillacollo** Cochabamba, C Bolivia
62 H4 **Quillagua** Antofagasta, N Chile
103 N17 **Quillan** Aude, S France
11 U15 **Quill Lakes** ◎ Saskatchewan, S Canada
62 G11 **Quillota** Valparaíso, C Chile
155 G23 **Quilon** var. Kolam, Kollam. Kerala, SW India
181 V9 **Quilpie** Queensland, C Australia
149 O4 **Quil-Qala** Bāmīān, N Afghanistan
62 L7 **Quimilí** Santiago del Estero, C Argentina
57 O19 **Quimome** Santa Cruz, E Bolivia
102 F6 **Quimper** anc. Quimper Corentin. Finistère, NW France
Quimper Corentin see Quimper
102 G7 **Quimperlé** Finistère, NW France
32 F8 **Quinault** Washington, NW USA
32 F8 **Quinault River** ~ Washington, NW USA
35 P5 **Quincy** California, W USA
23 S8 **Quincy** Florida, SE USA
30 I13 **Quincy** Illinois, N USA
19 O11 **Quincy** Massachusetts, NE USA
32 J9 **Quincy** Washington, NW USA
54 E10 **Quindío** off. Departamento del Quindío. ⬖ province C Colombia
54 E10 **Quindío, Nevado del** ▲ C Colombia
62 J10 **Quines** San Luis, C Argentina
39 N13 **Quinhagak** Alaska, USA
76 G13 **Quinhámel** W Guinea-Bissau
Qui Nhon/Quinhon see Quy Nhơn
Quinindé see Rosa Zárate
25 U6 **Quinlan** Texas, SW USA
61 H17 **Quinta** Rio Grande do Sul, S Brazil
105 O10 **Quintanar de la Orden** Castilla-La Mancha, C Spain
41 X13 **Quintana Roo** ⬖ state SE Mexico
105 S6 **Quinto** Aragón, NE Spain
108 G10 **Quinto** Ticino, S Switzerland
27 Q11 **Quinton** Oklahoma, C USA
62 K12 **Quinto, Río** ~ C Argentina
82 A10 **Quinzau** Zaire, NW Angola
14 H8 **Quinze, Lac des** ◎ Quebec, SE Canada
83 B15 **Quipungo** Huíla, C Angola
62 G13 **Quirihue** Bío Bío, C Chile
82 D12 **Quirima** Malanje, NW Angola
183 T6 **Quirindi** New South Wales, SE Australia
55 P5 **Quiriquire** Monagas, NE Venezuela
14 D10 **Quirke Lake** ◎ Ontario, S Canada
61 B21 **Quiroga** Buenos Aires, E Argentina
104 I4 **Quiroga** Galicia, NW Spain
Quiróm, Salar see Pocitos, Salar
56 B9 **Quiroz, Río** ~ NW Peru
82 Q13 **Quissanga** Cabo Delgado, NE Mozambique
83 M20 **Quissico** Inhambane, S Mozambique
25 O4 **Quitaque** Texas, SW USA
82 Q13 **Quiterajo** Cabo Delgado, NE Mozambique
23 T6 **Quitman** Georgia, SE USA
22 M6 **Quitman** Mississippi, S USA
25 V6 **Quitman** Texas, SW USA
56 C6 **Quito** ● (Ecuador) Pichincha, N Ecuador
Quito see Mariscal Sucre
58 P13 **Quixadá** Ceará, E Brazil
83 Q15 **Quixaxe** Nampula, NE Mozambique
160 J9 **Qu Jiang** ~ C China
161 R10 **Qu Jiang** ~ SE China
161 N13 **Qujiang** prev. Maba. Guangdong, S China
160 H12 **Qujing** Yunnan, SW China
Qulan see Kulan
146 L10 **Quljuqtov-Toghi** Rus. Gory Kul'dzhuktau. ▲ C Uzbekistan
Qulsary see Kul'sary
Qulyndy Zhazyghy see Kulunda Steppe
Qum see Qom
Qumälisch see Lubartów
159 P11 **Qumar He** ~ C China
159 Q12 **Qumarlêb** Qinghai, C China
Qumisheh see Shahreẓā
147 O14 **Qumqurghon** Rus. Kumkurgan. Surkhondaryo Wiloyati, S Uzbekistan
Qunaytirah/Qunayṭirah, Muḥāfaẓat al/Qunaytra see Al Qunayṭirah
146 G7 **Qŭnghirot** Rus. Kungrad. Qoraqalpoghiston Respublikasi, NW Uzbekistan
189 V12 **Quoi** island Chuuk, C Micronesia
9 N8 **Quoich** ~ Nunavut, NE Canada
83 E26 **Quoin Point** headland SW South Africa
182 I7 **Quorn** South Australia
147 R10 **Qŭqon** var. Khokand, Rus. Kokand. Farghona Wiloyati, E Uzbekistan
Qurein see Al Kuwayt
147 P14 **Qŭrghonteppa** Rus. Kurgan-Tyube. SW Tajikistan
Qurlurtuuq see Kugluktuk
Qurveh see Qorveh
Qusair see Quseir
137 X10 **Qusar** Rus. Kusary. NE Azerbaijan
Quşayr see Al Quşayr
75 Y10 **Quseir** var. Al Quşayr, Qusair. E Egypt
142 I2 **Qūshchī** Āzarbāyjān-e Bākhtarī, N Iran
147 N11 **Qŭshrabot** Rus. Kushrabat. Samarqand Wiloyati, C Uzbekistan
Qusmuryn see Kushmurun, Kostanay, Kazakhstan
Qusmuryn see Kushmurun, Ozero, Kazakhstan
Quṭayfah/Qutayfe/Quteife see Al Quṭayfah
Quthing see Moyeni
Quwair see Guwēr
147 S10 **Quwasoy** Rus. Kuvasay. Farghona Wiloyati, E Uzbekistan
Qu Xian see Quzhou
159 N16 **Qüxü** Xizang Zizhiqu, W China
167 V13 **Quy Chanh** Ninh Thuận, S Vietnam
167 V11 **Quy Nhơn** var. Quinhon, Qui Nhon. Bình Định, C Vietnam
147 O11 **Qŭytosh** Rus. Koytash. Jizzakh Wiloyati, C Uzbekistan
161 R10 **Quzhou** var. Qu Xian. Zhejiang, SE China
Qyteti Stalin see Kuçovë
Qyzylorda/Qyzylorda Oblysy see Kyzylorda
Qyzyltū see Kishkenekol'
Qyzylzhar see Kyzylzhar

R

109 R4 **Raab** Oberösterreich, N Austria
109 X8 **Raab** Hung. Rába. ~ Austria/Hungary **see also** Rába
Raab see Győr
109 V2 **Raabs an der Thaya** Niederösterreich, E Austria
93 L14 **Raahe** Swe. Brahestad. Oulu, W Finland
98 M10 **Raalte** Overijssel, E Netherlands
99 I14 **Raamsdonksveer** Noord-Brabant, S Netherlands
92 L12 **Raanujärvi** Lappi, NW Finland
96 G9 **Raasay** island NW Scotland, UK
118 H3 **Raasiku** Ger. Rasik. Harjumaa, NW Estonia
112 B11 **Rab** It. Arbe. Primorje-Gorski Kotar, NW Croatia
112 B11 **Rab** It. Arbe. island NW Croatia
171 N16 **Raba** Sumbawa, S Indonesia
111 G22 **Rába** Ger. Raab. ~ Austria/Hungary **see also** Raab
112 A10 **Rabac** Istra, NW Croatia
104 I2 **Rábade** Galicia, NW Spain
80 F10 **Rabak** White Nile, C Sudan
186 G9 **Rabaraba** Milne Bay, SE PNG
102 K16 **Rabastens-de-Bigorre** Hautes-Pyrénées, S France
121 O16 **Rabat** W Malta
74 F6 **Rabat** var. al Dar al Baida. ● (Morocco) NW Morocco
Rabat see Victoria
186 H6 **Rabaul** New Britain, E PNG
Rabbah Ammon/Rabbath Ammon see 'Ammān
28 K8 **Rabbit Creek** ~ South Dakota, N USA
14 H10 **Rabbit Lake** ◎ Ontario, S Canada
187 Y14 **Rabi** prev. Rambi. island N Fiji
140 K9 **Rābigh** Makkah, W Saudi Arabia
42 D5 **Rabinal** Baja Verapaz, C Guatemala
168 G9 **Rabi, Pulau** island NW Indonesia, East Indies
111 L17 **Rabka** Małopolskie, S Poland
155 F16 **Rabkavi** Karnātaka, W India
Râbniţa see Rîbniţa
109 Y6 **Rabnitz** ~ E Austria
126 J7 **Rabocheostrovsk** Respublika Kareliya, NW Russian Federation
23 U1 **Rabun Bald** ▲ Georgia, SE USA
75 S11 **Rabyānah** SE Libya
75 S11 **Rabyānah, Ramlat** var. Rebiana Sand Sea, Şahrā' Rabyānah. desert SE Libya
Rabyānah, Şahrā' see Rabyānah, Ramlat
116 L11 **Răcăciuni** Bacău, E Romania
107 J24 **Racalmuto** Sicilia, Italy, C Mediterranean Sea
116 J14 **Răcari** Dâmboviţa, SE Romania
Răcari see Durankulak
116 F13 **Răcăşdia** Hung. Rakasd. Caraş-Severin, SW Romania
106 B9 **Racconigi** Piemonte, NE Italy
31 T15 **Raccoon Creek** ~ Ohio, N USA
13 V13 **Race, Cape** headland Newfoundland, E Canada
22 K10 **Raceland** Louisiana, S USA
19 Q12 **Race Point** headland Massachusetts, NE USA
167 S14 **Rach Gia** Kiên Giang, S Vietnam
167 S14 **Rach Gia, Vinh** bay S Vietnam
76 J8 **Rachid** Tagant, C Mauritania
110 L10 **Raciąż** Mazowieckie, C Poland
111 I16 **Racibórz** Ger. Ratibor. Śląskie, S Poland
31 N9 **Racine** Wisconsin, N USA
14 D7 **Racine Lake** ◎ Ontario, S Canada
111 J23 **Ráckeve** Pest, C Hungary
Rácz-Becse see Bečej
141 O15 **Radā'** var. Ridā'. W Yemen
113 O15 **Radan** ▲ SE Yugoslavia
63 J19 **Rada Tilly** Chubut, SE Argentina
116 K8 **Rădăuţi** Ger. Radautz, Hung. Rádóc. Suceava, N Romania
116 L8 **Rădăuţi-Prut** Botoşani, NE Romania
Radautz see Rădăuţi
Radbusa see Radbuza
111 A17 **Radbuza** Ger. Radbusa. ~ SE Czech Republic
20 K6 **Radcliff** Kentucky, S USA
139 O2 **Radd, Wādī ar** dry watercourse N Syria
95 H16 **Råde** Østfold, S Norway
109 V11 **Radeče** Ger. Ratschach. C Slovenia
Radein see Radenci
116 J4 **Radekhiv** Pol. Radziechów, Rus. Radekhov. L'vivs'ka Oblast', W Ukraine
Radekhov see Radekhiv
109 X9 **Radenci** Ger. Radein; prev. Radinci. NE Slovenia
109 S9 **Radenthein** Kärnten, S Austria
21 R7 **Radford** Virginia, NE USA
154 C9 **Rādhanpur** Gujarāt, W India
Radinci see Radenci
129 Q6 **Radishchevo** Ul'yanovskaya Oblast', W Russian Federation
12 I9 **Radisson** Quebec, E Canada
11 P16 **Radium Hot Springs** British Columbia, SW Canada
116 F11 **Radna** Hung. Máriaradna. Arad, W Romania
114 K10 **Radnevo** Stara Zagora, C Bulgaria
97 J20 **Radnor** cultural region E Wales, UK
Radnót see Iernut
Rádóc see Rădăuţi
101 H24 **Radolfzell am Bodensee** Baden-Württemberg, S Germany
110 M13 **Radom** Mazowieckie, C Poland
116 I14 **Radomireşti** Olt, S Romania
111 K14 **Radomsko** Rus. Novoradomsk. Łodzkie, C Poland
117 N4 **Radomyshl'** Zhytomyrs'ka Oblast', N Ukraine
113 P19 **Radoviš** prev. Radovište. E FYR Macedonia
Radovište see Radoviš
94 B13 **Radøy** island S Norway
109 R7 **Radstadt** Salzburg, NW Austria
182 E8 **Radstock, Cape** headland South Australia
119 G15 **Radun'** Rus. Radun'. Hrodzyenskaya Voblasts', W Belarus
118 F11 **Radviliškis** Radviliškis, N Lithuania
11 U17 **Radville** Saskatchewan, S Canada
140 K7 **Raḍwā, Jabal** ▲ W Saudi Arabia
111 P16 **Radymno** Podkarpackie, SE Poland
116 J5 **Radyvyliv** Rivnens'ka Oblast', NW Ukraine
Radziechów see Radekhiv
110 I11 **Radziejów** Kujawskio-pomorskie, C Poland
110 O12 **Radzyń Podlaski** Lubelskie, E Poland
8 J7 **Rae** ~ Nunavut, NW Canada
152 M13 **Rāe Bareli** Uttar Pradesh, N India
Rae-Edzo see Edzo
21 T11 **Raeford** North Carolina, SE USA
99 M19 **Raeren** Liège, E Belgium
9 N7 **Rae Strait** strait Nunavut, N Canada
184 L11 **Raetihi** Manawatu-Wanganui, North Island, NZ
191 U13 **Raevavae** var. Raivavae. island Îles Australes, SW French Polynesia
Rafa see Rafah
62 M10 **Rafaela** Santa Fe, E Argentina
138 E11 **Rafah** var. Rafa, Rafaḥ, Heb. Rafiaḥ, Raphiah. SW Gaza Strip
79 L15 **Rafaï** Mbomou, SE Central African Republic
141 O4 **Rafḥah** Al Ḥudūd ash Shamālīyah, N Saudi Arabia
Rafiaḥ see Rafah
143 R10 **Rafsanjān** Kermān, C Iran
80 B13 **Raga** Western Bahr el Ghazal, SW Sudan
19 S8 **Ragged Island** island Maine, NE USA
44 I5 **Ragged Island Range** island group S Bahamas
184 L7 **Raglan** Waikato, North Island, NZ
22 G8 **Ragley** Louisiana, S USA
Ragnit see Neman
107 K25 **Ragusa** Sicilia, Italy, C Mediterranean Sea
Ragusa see Dubrovnik
Ragusavecchia see Cavtat
171 P14 **Raha** Pulau Muna, C Indonesia
119 N17 **Rahachow** Rus. Rogachëv. Homyel'skaya Voblasts', SE Belarus
67 U6 **Rahad** var. Nahr ar Rahad. ~ W Sudan
Rahad, Nahr ar see Rahad
Rahaeng see Tak
138 F11 **Rahat** Southern, C Israel
140 L8 **Rahaṭ, Ḥarrat** lavaflow W Saudi Arabia
149 S12 **Rahīmyār Khān** Punjab, SE Pakistan
95 I14 **Råholt** Akershus, S Norway
Rahovec see Orahovac
191 S10 **Raiatea** island Îles Sous le Vent, W French Polynesia
155 H16 **Rāichūr** Karnātaka, C India
Raidestos see Tekirdağ
153 S13 **Rāiganj** West Bengal, NE India
154 M11 **Raigarh** Madhya Pradesh, C India
183 O16 **Railton** Tasmania, SE Australia
36 L8 **Rainbow Bridge** natural arch Utah, W USA
23 Q3 **Rainbow City** Alabama, S USA
11 N11 **Rainbow Lake** Alberta, W Canada
21 R5 **Rainelle** West Virginia, NE USA
32 G10 **Rainier** Oregon, NW USA
32 H9 **Rainier, Mount** ⛰ Washington, NW USA
23 Q2 **Rainsville** Alabama, S USA
12 B11 **Rainy Lake** ◎ Canada/USA
12 A11 **Rainy River** Ontario, C Canada
Raippaluoto see Replot
154 K12 **Raipur** Madhya Pradesh, C India
154 H10 **Raisen** Madhya Pradesh, C India
15 N13 **Raisin** ~ Ontario, SE Canada
31 R11 **Raisin, River** ~ Michigan, N USA
Raivavae see Raevavae
149 W9 **Rāiwind** Punjab, E Pakistan
171 T12 **Raja Ampat, Kepulauan** island group E Indonesia
155 L16 **Rājahmundry** Andhra Pradesh, E India
155 I18 **Rājampet** Andhra Pradesh, E India
Rajang see Rajang, Batang
169 S9 **Rajang, Batang** var. Rajang. ~ East Malaysia
149 S11 **Rājanpur** Punjab, E Pakistan
155 H23 **Rājapālaiyam** Tamil Nādu, SE India
152 E12 **Rājasthān** ⬖ state NW India
153 T15 **Rajbari** Dhaka, C Bangladesh
153 R12 **Rajbiraj** Eastern, E Nepal
154 G9 **Rājgarh** Madhya Pradesh, C India
152 H10 **Rājgarh** Rājasthān, NW India
153 P14 **Rājgīr** Bihār, N India
110 O8 **Rajgród** Podlaskie, NE Poland
154 L12 **Rājim** Madhya Pradesh, C India
112 C11 **Rajinac, Mali** ▲ W Croatia
154 B10 **Rājkot** Gujarāt, W India
153 R14 **Rājmahal** Bihār, NE India
153 Q14 **Rājmahāl Hills** hill range N India
154 K12 **Rāj Nāndgaon** Madhya Pradesh, C India
152 I8 **Rājpura** Punjab, NW India
153 S14 **Rajshahi** prev. Rampur Boalia. Rajshahi, W Bangladesh
153 S13 **Rajshahi** ⬖ division NW Bangladesh
190 K13 **Rakahanga** atoll N Cook Islands
185 H19 **Rakaia** Canterbury, South Island, NZ
185 G19 **Rakaia** ~ South Island, NZ
152 H3 **Rakaposhi** ▲ N India
Rakasd see Răcăşdia
169 N15 **Rakata, Pulau** var. Pulau Krakatau. island S Indonesia
158 K16 **Raka Zangbo** ~ W China
141 U10 **Rakbah, Qalamat ar** well SE Saudi Arabia
Rakhine State see Arakan State
116 I8 **Rakhiv** Zakarpats'ka Oblast', W Ukraine
141 Y11 **Rakhyūt** SW Oman
192 K9 **Rakiraki** Viti Levu, W Fiji
Rakka see Ar Raqqah
118 I4 **Rakke** Lääne-Virumaa, NE Estonia
95 I16 **Rakkestad** Østfold, S Norway
110 F12 **Rakoniewice** Ger. Rakwitz. Wielkolpolskie, C Poland
Rakonitz see Rakovník
83 H18 **Rakops** Central, C Botswana
111 C16 **Rakovník** Ger. Rakonitz. Středočeský Kraj, W Czech Republic
114 J10 **Rakovski** Plovdiv, C Bulgaria
Rakutō-kō see Naktong-gang
118 I3 **Rakvere** Ger. Wesenberg. Lääne-Virumaa, N Estonia
Rakwitz see Rakoniewice
22 L6 **Raleigh** Mississippi, S USA
21 U9 **Raleigh** state capital North Carolina, SE USA
21 Y11 **Raleigh Bay** bay North Carolina, SE USA
21 U9 **Raleigh-Durham** × North Carolina, SE USA
189 S6 **Ralik Chain** island group Ralik Chain, W Marshall Islands
25 N5 **Ralls** Texas, SW USA
18 G13 **Ralston** Pennsylvania, NE USA
141 O16 **Ramādah** W Yemen
Ramadi see Ar Ramādī
105 N2 **Ramales de la Victoria** Cantabria, N Spain
138 F10 **Ramallah** C West Bank
61 C19 **Ramallo** Buenos Aires, E Argentina
155 H20 **Rāmanagaram** Karnātaka, E India
155 I23 **Rāmanāthapuram** Tamil Nādu, SE India
154 N12 **Rāmapur** Orissa, E India
155 I14 **Rāmāreddi** var. Kāmāreddi, Kamareddy. Andhra Pradesh, C India
138 F10 **Ramat Gan** Tel Aviv, W Israel
103 T6 **Rambervillers** Vosges, NE France
Rambi see Rabi
103 N5 **Rambouillet** Yvelines, N France
186 E5 **Rambutyo Island** island N PNG
153 Q12 **Ramechhap** Central, C Nepal
183 R12 **Rame Head** headland Victoria, SE Australia
128 L4 **Ramenskoye** Moskovskaya Oblast', W Russian Federation
126 J15 **Rameshki** Tverskaya Oblast', W Russian Federation
153 P14 **Rāmgarh** Bihār, N India
152 D11 **Rāmgarh** Rājasthān, NW India
142 M9 **Rāmhormoz** var. Ram Hormuz, Ramuz. Khūzestān, SW Iran
Ram Hormuz see Rāmhormoz
Ram, Jebel see Ramm, Jabal
138 F10 **Ramla** var. Ramle, Ramleh, Ar. Er Ramle. Central, C Israel
Ramle/Ramleh see Ramla
138 F14 **Ramm, Jabal** var. Jebel Ram. ▲ SW Jordan
152 K10 **Rāmnagar** Uttar Pradesh, N India
95 N15 **Ramnäs** Västmanland, C Sweden
Râmnicul-Sărat see Râmnicu Sărat
116 L12 **Râmnicu Sărat** prev. Râmnicul-Sărat, Rîmnicu-Sărat. Buzău, E Romania
116 I13 **Râmnicu Vâlcea** prev. Rîmnicu Vîlcea. Vâlcea, C Romania
Ramokgwebana see Ramokgwebane
83 J18 **Ramokgwebane** var. Ramokgwebana. Central, NE Botswana
128 L7 **Ramon'** Voronezhskaya Oblast', W Russian Federation
35 V17 **Ramona** California, W USA
56 A10 **Ramón, Laguna** ◎ NW Peru
14 G7 **Ramore** Ontario, S Canada
40 M11 **Ramos** San Luis Potosí, C Mexico
41 N8 **Ramos Arizpe** Coahuila de Zaragoza, NE Mexico
40 J9 **Ramos, Río de** ~ C Mexico
39 R8 **Rampart** Alaska, USA
8 H8 **Ramparts** ~ Northwest Territories, NW Canada
152 K10 **Rāmpur** Uttar Pradesh, N India
154 F9 **Rāmpura** Madhya Pradesh, C India
Rampur Boalia see Rajshahi
166 K6 **Ramree Island** island W Myanmar
141 W6 **Rams** var. Ar Rams. Ra's al Khaymah, NE UAE
143 N4 **Rāmsar** prev. Sakhtsar. Māzandarān, N Iran
93 H16 **Ramsele** Västernorrland, N Sweden
21 T9 **Ramseur** North Carolina, SE USA
97 I16 **Ramsey** NE Isle of Man
97 I16 **Ramsey Bay** bay NE Isle of Man
14 E9 **Ramsey Lake** ◎ Ontario, S Canada
97 Q22 **Ramsgate** SE England, UK
94 M10 **Ramsjö** Gävleborg, C Sweden
154 I12 **Rāmtek** Mahārāshtra, C India
Ramtha see Ar Ramthā
Ramuz see Rāmhormoz
118 G12 **Ramygala** Panevėžys, C Lithuania
92 G12 **Rana** ~ C Norway
152 H14 **Rāna Pratāp Sāgar** ◎ N India
169 V7 **Ranau** Sabah, East Malaysia
168 L14 **Ranau, Danau** ◎ Sumatera, W Indonesia
62 H12 **Rancagua** Libertador, C Chile
99 G22 **Rance** Hainaut, S Belgium
102 H6 **Rance** ~ NW France
60 J9 **Rancharia** São Paulo, S Brazil
153 P15 **Rānchi** Bihār, N India
61 D21 **Ranchos** Buenos Aires, E Argentina
37 S9 **Ranchos De Taos** New Mexico, SW USA
63 G16 **Ranco, Lago** ◎ C Chile
95 C16 **Randaberg** Rogaland, S Norway
29 U7 **Randall** Minnesota, N USA
107 L23 **Randazzo** Sicilia, Italy, C Mediterranean Sea
95 G21 **Randers** Århus, C Denmark
92 I12 **Randijaure** ◎ N Sweden
21 T9 **Randleman** North Carolina, SE USA
19 O11 **Randolph** Massachusetts, NE USA
29 Q13 **Randolph** Nebraska, C USA
36 M1 **Randolph** Utah, W USA
100 P9 **Randow** ~ NE Germany
95 H14 **Randsfjorden** ◎ S Norway
92 K13 **Råneå** Norrbotten, N Sweden
93 F15 **Rånemsletta** Nord-Trøndelag, C Norway
76 H10 **Ranérou** C Senegal
185 E22 **Ranfurly** Otago, South Island, NZ
167 P17 **Rangae** Narathiwat, SW Thailand
153 V16 **Rangamati** Chittagong, SE Bangladesh
184 I2 **Rangaunu Bay** bay North Island, NZ
19 P6 **Rangeley** Maine, NE USA
37 O4 **Rangely** Colorado, C USA
25 R7 **Ranger** Texas, SW USA
14 C9 **Ranger Lake** Ontario, S Canada
14 C9 **Ranger Lake** ◎ Ontario, S Canada
153 V12 **Rangia** Assam, NE India
185 I18 **Rangiora** Canterbury, South Island, NZ
191 T9 **Rangiroa** atoll Îles Tuamotu, W French Polynesia
184 N9 **Rangitaiki** ~ North Island, NZ
185 F19 **Rangitata** ~ South Island, NZ
184 M12 **Rangitikei** ~ North Island, NZ
184 L6 **Rangitoto Island** island N NZ
Rangkasbitoeng see Rangkasbitung
169 N16 **Rangkasbitung** prev. Rangkasbitoeng. Jawa, SW Indonesia
167 P9 **Rang, Khao** ▲ C Thailand
147 V13 **Rangkŭl** Rus. Rangkul'. SE Tajikistan
Rangkul' see Rangkŭl
Rangoon see Yangon
153 T13 **Rangpur** Rajshahi, N Bangladesh
155 F18 **Rānibennur** Karnātaka, W India
153 R15 **Rāniganj** West Bengal, NE India
149 Q13 **Rānīpur** Sind, SE Pakistan
Rāniyah see Rānya
25 N9 **Rankin** Texas, SW USA
9 O9 **Rankin Inlet** Nunavut, C Canada
183 P8 **Rankins Springs** New South Wales, SE Australia
Rankovićevo see Kraljevo
108 I7 **Rankweil** Vorarlberg, W Austria
Rann see Brežice
129 T8 **Ranneye** Orenburgskaya Oblast', W Russian Federation
96 I10 **Rannoch, Loch** ◎ C Scotland, UK
191 U17 **Rano Kau** var. Rano Kao. crater Easter Island, Chile, E Pacific Ocean
167 N14 **Ranong** Ranong, SW Thailand
186 J8 **Ranongga** var. Ghanongga. island NW Solomon Islands
191 W16 **Rano Raraku** ancient monument Easter Island, Chile, E Pacific Ocean
171 V12 **Ransiki** Irian Jaya, E Indonesia
92 K12 **Rantajärvi** Norrbotten, N Sweden
93 N17 **Rantasalmi** Isä-Suomi, SE Finland
169 U13 **Rantau** Borneo, C Indonesia
168 L10 **Rantau, Pulau** var. Pulau Tebingtinggi. island W Indonesia
171 N13 **Rantepao** Sulawesi, C Indonesia
30 M13 **Rantoul** Illinois, N USA
93 L15 **Rantsila** Oulu, C Finland
92 L13 **Ranua** Lappi, NW Finland
139 T3 **Rānya** var. Rāniyah. NE Iraq
157 X3 **Raohe** Heilongjiang, NE China
74 H9 **Raoui, Erg er** desert W Algeria
193 O10 **Rapa** island Îles Australes, S French Polynesia
191 V14 **Rapa Iti** island Îles Australes, SW French Polynesia
106 D10 **Rapallo** Liguria, NW Italy
Rapa Nui see Pascua, Isla de
Raphiah see Rafah
21 V5 **Rapidan River** ~ Virginia, NE USA
28 J10 **Rapid City** South Dakota, N USA
15 P8 **Rapide-Blanc** Quebec, SE Canada
14 I8 **Rapide-Deux** Quebec, SE Canada
118 K6 **Räpina** Ger. Rappin. Põlvamaa, SE Estonia
118 G4 **Rapla** Ger. Rappel. Raplamaa, NW Estonia
118 G4 **Raplamaa** off. Rapla Maakond. ⬖ province NW Estonia
21 X6 **Rappahannock River** ~ Virginia, NE USA
Rappel see Rapla
108 G7 **Rapperswil** Sankt Gallen, NE Switzerland
Rappin see Räpina
153 N12 **Rāpti** ~ N India
57 K16 **Rapulo, Río** ~ E Bolivia
Raqqah/Raqqah, Muḥāfaẓat al see Ar Raqqah
18 J8 **Raquette Lake** ◎ New York, NE USA
18 J6 **Raquette River** ~ New York, NE USA
191 V10 **Raraka** atoll Îles Tuamotu, C French Polynesia
191 V10 **Raroia** atoll Îles Tuamotu, C French Polynesia
190 H15 **Rarotonga** × Rarotonga, S Cook Islands, C Pacific Ocean
190 H16 **Rarotonga** island S Cook Islands, C Pacific Ocean
147 P12 **Rarz** W Tajikistan
Ras al 'Ain see Ra's al 'Ayn
139 N2 **Ra's al 'Ayn** var. Ras al 'Ain. Al Ḥasakah, N Syria
138 H3 **Ra's al Basīṭ** Al Lādhiqīyah, W Syria
Ra's al-Hafgī see Ra's al Khafjī
141 R5 **Ra's al Khafjī** var. Ra's al-Hafgī. Ash Sharqīyah, NE Saudi Arabia
Ras al-Khaimah/Ras al Khaimah see Ra's al Khaymah
143 R15 **Ra's al Khaymah** var. Ras al Khaimah. Ra's al Khaymah, NE UAE
143 R15 **Ra's al Khaymah** var. Ras al-Khaimah. × Ra's al Khaymah, NE UAE

◆ Country ● Country Capital ◇ Dependent Territory ○ Dependent Territory Capital ⬖ Administrative Region × International Airport ▲ Mountain ▲ Mountain Range ⛰ Volcano ~ River ◎ Lake ▣ Reservoir

138 G13 **Ra's an Naqb** Ma'ān, S Jordan
61 B26 **Rasa, Punta** headland E Argentina
171 V12 **Rasawi** Irian Jaya, E Indonesia
Râşcani see Rîşcani
80 J10 **Ras Dashen Terara** ▲ N Ethiopia
151 K19 **Rasdu Atoll** atoll C Maldives
118 E12 **Raseiniai** Raseiniai, C Lithuania
75 X8 **Râs Ghârib** E Egypt
162 D6 **Rashaant** Bayan-Ölgiy, W Mongolia
162 L10 **Rashaant** Dundgovĭ, C Mongolia
162 J6 **Rashaant** Hövsgöl, N Mongolia
139 Y11 **Rashīd** E Iraq
75 V7 **Rashîd** Eng. Rosetta. N Egypt
142 M3 **Rasht** var. Resht. Gīlān, NW Iran
139 S2 **Rashwān** N Iraq
Rasik see Raasiku
113 M15 **Raška** Serbia, C Yugoslavia
119 P15 **Rasna** Rus. Ryasna. Mahilyowskaya Voblasts', E Belarus
116 J12 **Râşnov** prev. Rişno, Rozsnyó, Hung. Barcarozsnyó. Braşov, C Romania
118 L11 **Rasony** Rus. Rossony. Vitsyebskaya Voblasts', N Belarus
Ra's Shamrah see Ugarit
129 N7 **Rasskazovo** Tambovskaya Oblast', W Russian Federation
119 O16 **Rasta** ≈ E Belarus
Rastadt see Rastatt
Rastâne see Ar Rastān
141 S6 **Ra's Tannūrah** Eng. Ras Tanura. Ash Sharqīyah, NE Saudi Arabia
Ras Tanura see Ra's Tannūrah
101 G21 **Rastatt** var. Rastadt. Baden-Württemberg, SW Germany
Rastenburg see Kętrzyn
149 V7 **Rasūlnagar** Punjab, E Pakistan
189 U6 **Ratak Chain** island group Ratak Chain, E Marshall Islands
119 K15 **Ratamka** Rus. Ratomka. Minskaya Voblasts', C Belarus
93 G17 **Ratan** Jämtland, C Sweden
152 G11 **Ratangarh** Rājasthān, NW India
Rat Buri see Ratchaburi
167 O11 **Ratchaburi** var. Rat Buri. Ratchaburi, W Thailand
29 W15 **Rathbun Lake** ⊠ Iowa, C USA
Ráth Caola see Rathkeale
166 K5 **Rathedaung** Arakan State, W Myanmar
100 M12 **Rathenow** Brandenburg, NE Germany
97 C19 **Rathkeale** Ir. Ráth Caola. SW Ireland
96 F13 **Rathlin Island** Ir. Reachlainn. island N Northern Ireland, UK
97 C20 **Ráthluirc** Ir. An Ráth. SW Ireland
Ratibor see Racibórz
Ratisbon/Ratisbona/Ratisbonne see Regensburg
Rätische Alpen see Rhaetian Alps
38 E17 **Rat Island** island Aleutian Islands, Alaska, USA
38 E17 **Rat Islands** island group Aleutian Islands, Alaska, USA
154 F10 **Ratlām** prev. Rutlam. Madhya Pradesh, C India
155 D15 **Ratnāgiri** Mahārāshtra, W India
155 K26 **Ratnapura** Sabaragamuwa Province, S Sri Lanka
116 J2 **Ratne** Rus. Ratno. Volyns'ka Oblast', NW Ukraine
Ratno see Ratne
Ratomka see Ratamka
37 U8 **Raton** New Mexico, SW USA
139 O7 **Ratqah, Wādī ar** dry watercourse W Iraq
Ratschach see Radeče
167 O16 **Rattaphum** Songkhla, SW Thailand
26 L6 **Rattlesnake Creek** ≈ Kansas, C USA
94 L13 **Rättvik** Dalarna, C Sweden
100 K9 **Ratzeburg** Mecklenburg-Vorpommern, N Germany
100 K9 **Ratzeburger See** ⊚ N Germany
10 J10 **Ratz, Mount** ▲ British Columbia, SW Canada
61 D22 **Rauch** Buenos Aires, E Argentina
41 U16 **Raudales** Chiapas, SE Mexico
Raudhatain see Ar Rawḍatayn
Raudnitz an der Elbe see Roudnice nad Labem
92 K1 **Raufarhöfn** Nordhurland Eystra, NE Iceland
94 H13 **Raufoss** Oppland, S Norway
Raukawa see Cook Strait
184 Q8 **Raukumara** ▲ North Island, NZ
192 K11 **Raukumara Plain** undersea feature N Coral Sea
184 P8 **Raukumara Range** ▲ North Island, NZ
154 N11 **Rāulakela** var. Raurkela; prev. Rourkela. Orissa, E. India
95 F15 **Rauland** Telemark, S Norway
93 J19 **Rauma** Swe. Raumo. Länsi-Suomi, W Finland
94 F10 **Rauma** ≈ S Norway
Raumo see Rauma
118 H8 **Rauna** Cēsis, C Latvia
169 T17 **Raung, Gunung** ▲ Jawa, S Indonesia
Raurkela see Rāulakela
95 J22 **Raus** Skåne, S Sweden
165 W3 **Rausu** Hokkaidō, NE Japan
165 W3 **Rausu-dake** ▲ Hokkaidō, NE Japan
93 M17 **Rautalampi** Itä-Suomi, C Finland
93 N16 **Rautavaara** Itä-Suomi, C Finland
116 M9 **Răutel** ≈ C Moldova
93 O18 **Rautjärvi** Etelä-Suomi, S Finland
Rautu see Sosnovo
191 V11 **Ravahere** atoll Îles Tuamotu, C French Polynesia
107 J25 **Ravanusa** Sicilia, Italy, C Mediterranean Sea
143 S9 **Rāvar** Kermān, C Iran
147 Q11 **Ravat** Oshskaya Oblast', SW Kyrgyzstan
18 K11 **Ravena** New York, NE USA
106 H10 **Ravenna** Emilia-Romagna, N Italy
29 O15 **Ravenna** Nebraska, C USA
31 U11 **Ravenna** Ohio, N USA
101 I24 **Ravensburg** Baden-Württemberg, S Germany
181 W4 **Ravenshoe** Queensland, NE Australia
180 K13 **Ravensthorpe** Western Australia
21 Q4 **Ravenswood** West Virginia, NE USA
149 U9 **Rāvi** ≈ India/Pakistan
112 C9 **Ravna Gora** Primorje-Gorski Kotar, NW Croatia
109 U10 **Ravne na Koroškem** Ger. Gutenstein. N Slovenia
139 P6 **Rāwah** W Iraq
191 T4 **Rawaki** prev. Phoenix Island. atoll Phoenix Islands, C Kiribati
149 U6 **Rāwalpindi** Punjab, NE Pakistan
110 L13 **Rawa Mazowiecka** Łódzkie, C Poland
139 T2 **Ṛawāndiz** var. Rawandoz, Rawāndūz. N Iraq
Rawandoz/Rawāndūz see Ṛawāndiz
171 U12 **Rawas** Irian Jaya, E Indonesia
139 O4 **Rawḍah** ⊚ E Syria
110 G13 **Rawicz** Ger. Rawitsch. Wielkopolskie, C Poland
Rawitsch see Rawicz
180 M11 **Rawlinna** Western Australia
33 W16 **Rawlins** Wyoming, C USA
63 K17 **Rawson** Chubut, SE Argentina
159 R16 **Rawu** Xizang Zizhiqu, W China
153 P12 **Raxaul** Bihār, N India
28 K3 **Ray** North Dakota, N USA
169 S11 **Raya, Bukit** ▲ Borneo, C Indonesia
155 I18 **Rāyachoti** Andhra Pradesh, E India
Rāyagada see Rāyagarha
155 M14 **Rāyagarha** prev. Rāyadrug. Orissa, E India
138 H7 **Rayak** var. Rayaq, Riyāq. E Lebanon
Rayaq see Rayak
139 T2 **Rāyat** E Iraq
169 N12 **Raya, Tanjung** headland Pulau Bangka, W Indonesia
13 R13 **Ray, Cape** headland Newfoundland, E Canada
123 Q13 **Raychikhinsk** Amurskaya Oblast', SE Russian Federation
129 U5 **Rayevskiy** Respublika Bashkortostan, W Russian Federation
11 Q17 **Raymond** Alberta, SW Canada
22 K6 **Raymond** Mississippi, S USA
32 F9 **Raymond** Washington, NW USA
183 T8 **Raymond Terrace** New South Wales, SE Australia
25 T17 **Raymondville** Texas, SW USA
11 U16 **Raymore** Saskatchewan, S Canada
39 Q8 **Ray Mountains** ▲ Alaska, USA
22 H9 **Rayne** Louisiana, S USA
41 O12 **Rayón** San Luis Potosí, C Mexico
40 G4 **Rayón** Sonora, NW Mexico
167 P12 **Rayong** Rayong, S Thailand
25 T5 **Ray Roberts, Lake** ⊚ Texas, SW USA
18 E15 **Raystown Lake** ⊠ Pennsylvania, NE USA
141 V13 **Raysūt** SW Oman
27 R4 **Raytown** Missouri, C USA
22 I5 **Rayville** Louisiana, S USA
142 L5 **Razan** Hamadān, W Iran
139 S9 **Razāzah, Buḥayrat ar** var. Baḥr al Milḥ. ⊚ C Iraq
114 L9 **Razboyna** ▲ E Bulgaria
Razdan see Hrazdan
Razdolnoye see Rozdol'ne
Razelm, Lacul see Razim, Lacul
139 U2 **Razga** E Iraq
114 L8 **Razgrad** Razgrad, N Bulgaria
114 L8 **Razgrad** ◈ province N Bulgaria
117 N13 **Razim, Lacul** prev. Lacul Razelm. lagoon NW Black Sea
114 G11 **Razlog** Blagoevgrad, SW Bulgaria
118 K10 **Rāznas Ezers** ⊚ SE Latvia
102 E6 **Raz, Pointe du** headland NW France
Reachlainn see Rathlin Island
Reachrainn see Lambay Island
97 N22 **Reading** S England, UK
18 H15 **Reading** Pennsylvania, NE USA
48 C7 **Real, Cordillera** ▲ C Ecuador
62 K12 **Realicó** La Pampa, C Argentina
25 R15 **Realitos** Texas, SW USA
108 G9 **Realp** Uri, C Switzerland
167 Q12 **Reăng Kesei** Bătdâmbâng, W Cambodia
191 Y11 **Reao** atoll Îles Tuamotu, E French Polynesia
Reate see Rieti
180 L11 **Rebecca, Lake** ⊚ Western Australia
Rebiana Sand Sea see Rabyānah, Ramlat
126 H8 **Reboly** Respublika Kareliya, NW Russian Federation
165 S1 **Rebun** Rebun-tō, NE Japan
165 S1 **Rebun-tō** island NE Japan
106 J12 **Recanati** Marche, C Italy
Rechitsa see Rechytsa
109 Y7 **Rechnitz** Burgenland, SE Austria
119 J20 **Rechytsa** Rus. Rechitsa. Brestskaya Voblasts', SW Belarus
119 O19 **Rechytsa** Rus. Rechitsa. Homyel'skaya Voblasts', SE Belarus
59 Q15 **Recife** prev. Pernambuco. state capital Pernambuco, E Brazil
83 I26 **Recife, Cape** Afr. Kaap Recife. headland S South Africa
Recife, Kaap see Recife, Cape
172 I16 **Récifs, Îles aux** island Inner Islands, NE Seychelles
101 E14 **Recklinghausen** Nordrhein-Westfalen, W Germany
100 M8 **Recknitz** ≈ NE Germany
99 K23 **Recogne** Luxembourg, SE Belgium
61 C15 **Reconquista** Santa Fe, C Argentina
195 O6 **Recovery Glacier** glacier Antarctica
59 G15 **Recreio** Mato Grosso, W Brazil
27 X9 **Rector** Arkansas, C USA
110 E9 **Recz** Ger. Reetz Neumark. Zachodniopomorskie, NW Poland
99 L24 **Redange** var. Redange-sur-Attert. Diekirch, W Luxembourg
Redange-sur-Attert see Redange
18 C13 **Redbank Creek** ≈ Pennsylvania, NE USA
13 S9 **Red Bay** Quebec, E Canada
23 N2 **Red Bay** Alabama, S USA
35 N4 **Red Bluff** California, W USA
24 J8 **Red Bluff Reservoir** ⊠ New Mexico/Texas, SW USA
30 K16 **Red Bud** Illinois, N USA
30 J5 **Red Cedar River** ≈ Wisconsin, N USA
11 R17 **Redcliff** Alberta, SW Canada
83 K17 **Redcliff** Midlands, C Zimbabwe
182 L9 **Red Cliffs** Victoria, SE Australia
29 P17 **Red Cloud** Nebraska, C USA
22 L8 **Red Creek** ≈ Mississippi, S USA
11 P15 **Red Deer** Alberta, SW Canada
11 Q16 **Red Deer** ≈ Alberta, SW Canada
39 O11 **Red Devil** Alaska, USA
35 N3 **Redding** California, W USA
97 L20 **Redditch** W England, UK
29 P9 **Redfield** South Dakota, N USA
24 J12 **Redford** Texas, SW USA
45 V13 **Redhead** Trinidad, Trinidad and Tobago
182 I8 **Red Hill** South Australia
38 F10 **Red Hill** Haw. Pu'uUla'ula. ▲ Maui, Hawaii, USA, C Pacific Ocean
26 K7 **Red Hills** hill range Kansas, C USA
13 T12 **Red Indian Lake** ⊚ Newfoundland, E Canada
126 J16 **Redkino** Tverskaya Oblast', W Russian Federation
12 A10 **Red Lake** Ontario, C Canada
36 I10 **Red Lake** salt flat Arizona, SW USA
29 S4 **Red Lake Falls** Minnesota, N USA
29 R4 **Red Lake River** ≈ Minnesota, N USA
35 U15 **Redlands** California, W USA
18 G16 **Red Lion** Pennsylvania, NE USA
33 U11 **Red Lodge** Montana, NW USA
32 H13 **Redmond** Oregon, NW USA
36 L5 **Redmond** Utah, W USA
32 H8 **Redmond** Washington, NW USA
Rednitz see Regnitz
29 T15 **Red Oak** Iowa, C USA
18 K12 **Red Oaks Mill** New York, NE USA
102 I7 **Redon** Ille-et-Vilaine, NW France
45 W10 **Redonda** island SW Antigua and Barbuda
104 G4 **Redondela** Galicia, NW Spain
104 H11 **Redondo** Évora, S Portugal
39 Q12 **Redoubt Volcano** ▲ Alaska, USA
11 Y16 **Red River** ≈ Canada/USA
131 U12 **Red River** var. Yuan, Chin. Yuan Jiang, Vtn. Sông Hông Hà. ≈ China/Vietnam
25 W4 **Red River** ≈ S USA
22 H7 **Red River** ≈ Louisiana, S USA
30 M6 **Red River** ≈ Wisconsin, N USA
Red Rock, Lake see Red Rock Reservoir
29 W14 **Red Rock Reservoir** var. Lake Red Rock. ⊠ Iowa, C USA
80 H7 **Red Sea** ◈ state NE Sudan
75 Y9 **Red Sea** anc. Sinus Arabicus. sea Africa/Asia
21 T11 **Red Springs** North Carolina, SE USA
8 I9 **Redstone** ≈ Northwest Territories, NW Canada
11 V17 **Redvers** Saskatchewan, S Canada
77 P13 **Red Volta** var. Nazinon, Fr. Volta Rouge. ≈ Burkina/Ghana
11 Q14 **Redwater** Alberta, SW Canada
28 M16 **Red Willow Creek** ≈ Nebraska, C USA
29 W9 **Red Wing** Minnesota, N USA
35 N9 **Redwood City** California, W USA
29 T9 **Redwood Falls** Minnesota, N USA
31 P7 **Reed City** Michigan, N USA
28 K6 **Reeder** North Dakota, N USA
35 R11 **Reedley** California, W USA
33 T11 **Reedpoint** Montana, NW USA
30 K8 **Reedsburg** Wisconsin, N USA
32 E13 **Reedsport** Oregon, NW USA
187 Q9 **Reef Islands** island group Santa Cruz Islands, E Solomon Islands
185 H16 **Reefton** West Coast, South Island, NZ
20 F8 **Reelfoot Lake** ⊚ Tennessee, S USA
97 D17 **Ree, Lough** Ir. Loch Rí. ⊚ C Ireland
Reengus see Rīngas
35 U4 **Reese River** ≈ Nevada, W USA
98 M8 **Reest** ≈ E Netherlands
Reetz Neumark see Recz
137 N13 **Refahiye** Erzincan, C Turkey
23 N4 **Reform** Alabama, S USA
95 K20 **Refteleb** Jönköping, S Sweden
25 T14 **Refugio** Texas, SW USA
110 E8 **Rega** ≈ NW Poland
Regar see Tursunzoda
101 O21 **Regen** Bayern, SE Germany
101 M20 **Regen** ≈ SE Germany
101 M21 **Regensburg** Eng. Ratisbon, Fr. Ratisbonne; hist. Ratisbona, anc. Castra Regina, Reginum. Bayern, SE Germany
101 M21 **Regenstauf** Bayern, SE Germany
74 I10 **Reggane** C Algeria
98 N9 **Regge** ≈ E Netherlands
Reggio see Reggio nell' Emilia
Reggio Calabria see Reggio di Calabria
107 M23 **Reggio di Calabria** var. Reggio Calabria, Gk. Rhegion; anc. Regium, Rhegium. Calabria, SW Italy
Reggio Emilia see Reggio nell' Emilia
106 F9 **Reggio nell' Emilia** var. Reggio Emilia, abbrev. Reggio; anc. Regium Lepidum. Emilia-Romagna, N Italy
116 I10 **Reghin** Ger. Sächsisch-Reen, Hung. Szászrégen; prev. Reghinul Săsesc, Ger. Sächsisch-Regen. Mureş, C Romania
Reghinul Săsesc see Reghin
11 U16 **Regina** Saskatchewan, S Canada
11 U16 **Regina** × Saskatchewan, S Canada
55 Z10 **Régina** E French Guiana
11 U16 **Regina Beach** Saskatchewan, S Canada
Reginum see Regensburg
Registan see Rīgestān
60 L11 **Registro** São Paulo, S Brazil
Regium see Reggio di Calabria
Regium Lepidum see Reggio nell' Emilia
101 K19 **Regnitz** var. Rednitz. ≈ SE Germany
40 K10 **Regocijo** Durango, W Mexico
104 H12 **Reguengos de Monsaraz** Évora, S Portugal
101 M18 **Rehau** Bayern, E Germany
83 D19 **Rehoboth** Hardap, C Namibia
Rehoboth/Rehovoth see Reḥovot
21 Z4 **Rehoboth Beach** Delaware, NE USA
138 F10 **Reḥovot** var. Rehoboth, Rekhovot, Rehovoth. Central, C Israel
81 J20 **Rei** spring/well S Kenya
Reichenau see Rychnov nad Kněžnou, Czech Republic
Reichenau see Bogatynia, Poland
101 M17 **Reichenbach** var. Reichenbach im Vogtland. Sachsen, E Germany
Reichenbach see Dzierżoniów
Reichenbach im Vogtland see Reichenbach
Reichenberg see Liberec
181 O11 **Reid** Western Australia
23 V6 **Reidsville** Georgia, SE USA
21 T8 **Reidsville** North Carolina, SE USA
Reifnitz see Ribnica
97 O22 **Reigate** SE England, UK
Reikjavik see Reykjavík
102 I10 **Ré, Île de** island W France
37 N15 **Reiley Peak** ▲ Arizona, SW USA
103 Q4 **Reims** Eng. Rheims; anc. Durocortorum, Remi. Marne, N France
63 G23 **Reina Adelaida, Archipiélago** island group S Chile
45 O16 **Reina Beatrix** × (Oranjestad) C Aruba
108 F7 **Reinach** Aargau, W Switzerland
108 E6 **Reinach** Basel-Land, NW Switzerland
64 O11 **Reina Sofía** × (Tenerife) Tenerife, Islas Canarias, Spain, NE Atlantic Ocean
29 W13 **Reinbeck** Iowa, C USA
100 J10 **Reinbek** Schleswig-Holstein, N Germany
11 U12 **Reindeer** ≈ Saskatchewan, C Canada
11 U11 **Reindeer Lake** ⊚ Manitoba/Saskatchewan, C Canada
Reine-Charlotte, Îles de la see Queen Charlotte Islands
Reine-Élisabeth, Îles de la see Queen Elizabeth Islands
94 F13 **Reineskarvet** ▲ S Norway
184 H1 **Reinga, Cape** headland North Island, NZ
105 N3 **Reinosa** Cantabria, N Spain
109 R8 **Reisseck** ▲ S Austria
21 W3 **Reisterstown** Maryland, NE USA
Reisui see Yŏsu
98 N5 **Reitdiep** ≈ NE Netherlands
191 V10 **Reitoru** atoll Îles Tuamotu, C French Polynesia
95 M17 **Rejmyre** Östergötland, S Sweden
Reka see Rijeka
Reka Ili see Ili
95 N16 **Rekarne** Västmanland, C Sweden 16.04
Rekhovot see Reḥovot
8 K9 **Reliance** Northwest Territories, C Canada
33 U16 **Reliance** Wyoming, C USA
74 I5 **Relizane** var. Ghelîzâne, Ghilizane. NW Algeria
182 I7 **Remarkable, Mount** ▲ South Australia
54 E8 **Remedios** Antioquia, N Colombia
43 Q16 **Remedios** Veraguas, W Panama
42 D8 **Remedios, Punta** headland SW El Salvador
Remi see Reims
99 N25 **Remich** Grevenmacher, SE Luxembourg
99 J19 **Remicourt** Liège, E Belgium
14 H8 **Rémigny, Lac** ⊚ Quebec, SE Canada
55 Z10 **Rémire** NE French Guiana
129 N13 **Remontnoye** Rostovskaya Oblast', SW Russian Federation
171 U14 **Remoon** Pulau Kur, E Indonesia
99 L20 **Remouchamps** Liège, E Belgium
103 R15 **Remoulins** Gard, S France
173 X16 **Rempart, Mont du** var. Mount Rempart. hill W Mauritius
101 E15 **Remscheid** Nordrhein-Westfalen, W Germany
29 S12 **Remsen** Iowa, C USA
94 I12 **Rena** Hedmark, S Norway
94 I11 **Rena** ≈ S Norway
Renaix see Ronse
118 H7 **Rencēni** Valmiera, N Latvia
118 D9 **Renda** Kuldīga, W Latvia
107 N20 **Rende** Calabria, SW Italy
99 K21 **Rendeux** Luxembourg, SE Belgium
Rendina see Rentína
30 L16 **Rend Lake** ⊠ Illinois, N USA
186 K9 **Rendova** island New Georgia Islands, NW Solomon Islands
100 I8 **Rendsburg** Schleswig-Holstein, N Germany
108 B9 **Renens** Vaud, SW Switzerland
14 K12 **Renfrew** Ontario, SE Canada
96 I12 **Renfrew** cultural region SW Scotland, UK
168 L11 **Rengat** Sumatera, W Indonesia
153 W12 **Rengma Hills** ▲ NE India
62 H12 **Rengo** Libertador, C Chile
116 M12 **Reni** Odes'ka Oblast', SW Ukraine
80 F11 **Renk** Upper Nile, E Sudan
93 L19 **Renko** Etelä-Suomi, S Finland
98 L12 **Renkum** Gelderland, SE Netherlands
182 K9 **Renmark** South Australia
186 L10 **Rennell** var. Mu Nggava. island S Solomon Islands
181 Q4 **Renner Springs Roadhouse** Northern Territory, N Australia
102 I6 **Rennes** Bret. Roazon; anc. Condate. Ille-et-Vilaine, NW France
195 S16 **Rennick Glacier** glacier Antarctica
11 Y16 **Rennie** Manitoba, S Canada
35 Q5 **Reno** Nevada, W USA
106 H10 **Reno** ≈ N Italy
35 Q5 **Reno-Cannon** × Nevada, W USA
83 F24 **Renoster** ≈ SW South Africa
15 T5 **Renouard, Lac** ⊚ Quebec, SE Canada
18 F13 **Renovo** Pennsylvania, NE USA
161 O3 **Renqiu** Hebei, E China
160 I9 **Renshou** Sichuan, C China
31 N12 **Rensselaer** Indiana, N USA
18 L11 **Rensselaer** New York, NE USA
105 Q2 **Rentería** Basq. Errenteria. País Vasco, N Spain
115 E17 **Rentína** var. Rendina. Thessalía, C Greece
29 T9 **Renville** Minnesota, N USA
77 O13 **Réo** W Burkina
15 O12 **Repentigny** Quebec, SE Canada
146 K13 **Repetek** Lebapskiy Velayat, E Turkmenistan
93 J16 **Replot** Fin. Raippaluoto. island W Finland
Reppen see Rzepin
Reps see Rupea
27 T7 **Republic** Missouri, C USA
32 K7 **Republic** Washington, NW USA
27 N3 **Republican River** ≈ Kansas/Nebraska, C USA
9 O7 **Repulse Bay** Northwest Territories, N Canada
56 F9 **Requena** Loreto, NE Peru
105 R10 **Requena** País Valenciano, E Spain
103 O14 **Réquista** Aveyron, S France
136 M12 **Reşadiye** Tokat, N Turkey
Reschenpass see Resia, Passo di
Reschitza see Reşiţa
113 N20 **Resen** Turk. Resne. SW FYR Macedonia
60 J11 **Reserva** Paraná, S Brazil
11 V15 **Reserve** Saskatchewan, S Canada
37 P13 **Reserve** New Mexico, SW USA
Reshetilovka see Reshetylivka
117 S6 **Reshetylivka** Rus. Reshetilovka. Poltavs'ka Oblast', NE Ukraine
Resht see Rasht
106 F5 **Resia, Passo di** Ger. Reschenpass. pass Austria/Italy
Resicabánya see Reşiţa
62 N7 **Resistencia** Chaco, NE Argentina
116 F12 **Reşiţa** Ger. Reschitza, Hung. Resicabánya. Caraş-Severin, W Romania
Resne see Resen
8 K4 **Resolute** var. Qausuittuq. Nunavut, N Canada
Resolution see Fort Resolution
9 T7 **Resolution Island** island Nunavut, NE Canada
185 A23 **Resolution Island** island SW NZ
15 W7 **Restigouche** Quebec, SE Canada
11 W17 **Reston** Manitoba, S Canada
14 H11 **Restoule Lake** ⊚ Ontario, S Canada
54 F10 **Restrepo** Meta, C Colombia
42 B6 **Retalhuleu** Retalhuleu, SW Guatemala
42 A1 **Retalhuleu** off. Departamento de Retalhuleu. ◈ department SW Guatemala
97 N18 **Retford** C England, UK
103 Q3 **Rethel** Ardennes, N France
Rethimno/Réthimnon see Réthymno
115 I25 **Réthymno** var. Rethimno; prev. Réthimnon. Kríti, Greece, E Mediterranean Sea
Retiche, Alpi see Rhaetian Alps
99 J16 **Retie** Antwerpen, N Belgium
111 J21 **Rétság** Nógrád, N Hungary
109 W2 **Retz** Niederösterreich, NE Austria
173 N15 **Réunion** off. La Réunion. ◇ French overseas department W Indian Ocean
130 L17 **Réunion** island W Indian Ocean
105 U6 **Reus** Cataluña, E Spain
99 J15 **Reusel** Noord-Brabant, S Netherlands
108 F7 **Reuss** ≈ NW Switzerland
Reuṭel see Ciuhuru
101 H22 **Reutlingen** Baden-Württemberg, S Germany
108 L7 **Reutte** Tirol, W Austria
99 M16 **Reuver** Limburg, SE Netherlands
28 K7 **Reva** South Dakota, N USA
Reval/Revel' see Tallinn
126 J4 **Revda** Murmanskaya Oblast', NW Russian Federation
122 F6 **Revda** Sverdlovskaya Oblast', C Russian Federation
103 N16 **Revel** Haute-Garonne, S France
11 O16 **Revelstoke** British Columbia, SW Canada
43 N13 **Reventazón, Río** ≈ E Costa Rica
106 G9 **Revere** Lombardia, N Italy
39 Y14 **Revillagigedo Island** island Alexander Archipelago, Alaska, USA
193 Y14 **Revillagigedo Islands** island group NW Mexico
103 R3 **Revin** Ardennes, N France
92 O3 **Revnosa** headland C Svalbard
Revolyutsii, Pik see Revolyutsiya, Qullai
147 T13 **Revolyutsiya, Qullai** Rus. Pik Revolyutsii. ▲ SE Tajikistan
111 L19 **Revúca** Ger. Grossrauschenbach, Hung. Nagyrőce. Banskobystrický Kraj, C Slovakia
154 K9 **Rewa** Madhya Pradesh, C India
152 I11 **Rewāri** Haryāna, N India
33 R14 **Rexburg** Idaho, NW USA
78 G13 **Rey Bouba** Nord, NE Cameroon
92 L3 **Reydharfjördhur** Austurland, E Iceland
57 K16 **Reyes** Beni, NW Bolivia
34 L8 **Reyes, Point** headland California, W USA
54 B12 **Reyes, Punta** headland SW Colombia
136 L17 **Reyhanlı** Hatay, S Turkey
43 U16 **Rey, Isla del** island Archipiélago de las Perlas, SE Panama
92 H2 **Reykhólar** Vestfirdhir, W Iceland
92 K2 **Reykjahlídh** Nordhurland Eystra, NE Iceland
92 I4 **Reykjanes** ◈ region SW Iceland
197 O16 **Reykjanes Basin** var. Irminger Basin. undersea feature N Atlantic Ocean
197 N17 **Reykjanes Ridge** undersea feature N Atlantic Ocean
92 H4 **Reykjavík** var. Reikjavik. ● (Iceland) Höfudhborgarsvaedhi, W Iceland
18 D13 **Reynoldsville** Pennsylvania, NE USA
41 P8 **Reynosa** Tamaulipas, C Mexico
Reẓā'īyeh see Orūmīyeh
Reẓā'īyeh, Daryācheh-ye see Orūmīyeh, Daryācheh-ye
102 I8 **Rezé** Loire-Atlantique, NW France
118 K10 **Rēzekne** Ger. Rositten; prev. Rus. Rezhitsa. Rēzekne, SE Latvia
Rezhitsa see Rēzekne
117 N9 **Rezina** NE Moldova
114 N11 **Rezovo** Turk. Rezve. Burgas, E Bulgaria
114 N11 **Rezovska Reka** Turk. Rezve Deresi. ≈ Bulgaria/Turkey see also Rezve Deresi
Rezve see Rezovo
114 N11 **Rezve Deresi** Bul. Rezovska Reka. ≈ Bulgaria/Turkey see also Rezovska Reka
Rhadames see Ghadāmis
Rhaedestus see Tekirdağ
108 J10 **Rhaetian Alps** Fr. Alpes Rhétiques, Ger. Rätische Alpen, It. Alpi Retiche. ▲ C Europe
108 I8 **Rhätikon** ▲ C Europe
101 G14 **Rheda-Wiedenbrück** Nordrhein-Westfalen, W Germany
98 M12 **Rheden** Gelderland, E Netherlands
Rhegion/Rhegium see Reggio di Calabria
Rheims see Reims
Rhein see Rhine
101 E17 **Rheinbach** Nordrhein-Westfalen, W Germany
100 F13 **Rheine** var. Rheine in Westfalen. Nordrhein-Westfalen, NW Germany
Rheine in Westfalen see Rheine
Rheinfeld see Rheinfelden
101 F24 **Rheinfelden** Baden-Württemberg, S Germany

◆ Country ● Country Capital ◇ Dependent Territory ○ Dependent Territory Capital ◈ Administrative Region × International Airport ▲ Mountain ▲ Mountain Range ▲ Volcano ≈ River ⊚ Lake ⊠ Reservoir

108 E6 **Rheinfelden** var. Rheinfeld. Aargau, N Switzerland
101 E17 **Rheinisches Schiefergebirge** var. Rhine State Uplands, Eng. Rhenish Slate Mountains. ▲ W Germany
101 D18 **Rheinland-Pfalz** Eng. Rhineland-Palatinate, Fr. Rhénanie-Palatinat. ◆ state W Germany
101 G18 **Rhein/Main** ✕ (Frankfurt am Main) Hessen, W Germany
Rhénanie du Nord-Westphalie see Nordrhein-Westfalen
Rhénanie-Palatinat see Rheinland-Pfalz
98 K12 **Rhenen** Utrecht, C Netherlands
Rhenish Slate Mountains see Rheinisches Schiefergebirge
Rhétiques, Alpes see Rhaetian Alps
100 N10 **Rhin** ≈ NE Germany
Rhin see Rhine
84 F10 **Rhine** Dut. Rijn, Fr. Rhin, Ger. Rhein. ≈ W Europe
30 L5 **Rhinelander** Wisconsin, N USA
Rhineland-Palatinate see Rheinland-Pfalz
Rhine State Uplands see Rheinisches Schiefergebirge
100 N11 **Rhinkanal** canal NE Germany
81 F17 **Rhino Camp** NW Uganda
74 D7 **Rhir, Cap** headland W Morocco
106 D7 **Rho** Lombardia, N Italy
19 N12 **Rhode Island** off. State of Rhode Island and Providence Plantations; also known as Little Rhody, Ocean State. ◆ state NE USA
19 O13 **Rhode Island** island Rhode Island, NE USA
19 O13 **Rhode Island Sound** sound Maine/Rhode Island, NE USA
Rhodes see Ródos
Rhode-Saint-Genèse see Sint-Genesius-Rode
84 L14 **Rhodes Basin** undersea feature E Mediterranean Sea
Rhodesia see Zimbabwe
114 I12 **Rhodope Mountains** var. Rodhópi Óri, Bul. Rhodope Planina, Rodopi, Gk. Orosirá Rodhópis, Turk. Dospad Dagh. ▲ Bulgaria/Greece
Rhodope Planina see Rhodope Mountains
Rhodos see Ródos
101 I18 **Rhön** ▲ C Germany
103 Q10 **Rhône** ◆ department E France
86 C12 **Rhône** ≈ France/Switzerland
103 R12 **Rhône-Alpes** ◆ region E France
98 G13 **Rhoon** Zuid-Holland, SW Netherlands
96 G9 **Rhum** var. Rum. island W Scotland, UK
Rhuthun see Ruthin
97 J18 **Rhyl** NE Wales, UK
59 K18 **Rialma** Goiás, S Brazil
104 L3 **Riaño** Castilla-León, N Spain
105 O9 **Riansáres** ≈ C Spain
152 H6 **Riāsi** Jammu and Kashmir, NW India
168 K10 **Riau** off. Propinsi Riau. ◆ province W Indonesia
Riau Archipelago see Riau, Kepulauan
168 M11 **Riau, Kepulauan** var. Riau Archipelago, Dut. Riouw-Archipel. island group W Indonesia
105 O6 **Riaza** Castilla-León, N Spain
105 N6 **Riaza** ≈ N Spain
81 K17 **Riba** spring/well NE Kenya
104 H4 **Ribadavia** Galicia, NW Spain
104 J2 **Ribadeo** Galicia, NW Spain
104 L2 **Ribadesella** Asturias, N Spain
104 G10 **Ribatejo** former province C Portugal
143 Q8 **Ribāṭ-e Rizāb** Yazd, C Iran
83 P15 **Ribáuè** Nampula, N Mozambique
97 K17 **Ribble** ≈ NW England, UK
95 F23 **Ribe** Ribe, W Denmark
95 F23 **Ribe** off. Ribe Amt, var. Ripen. ◆ county W Denmark
104 G3 **Ribeira** Galicia, NW Spain
64 O5 **Ribeira Brava** Madeira, Portugal, NE Atlantic Ocean
64 P3 **Ribeira Grande** São Miguel, Azores, Portugal, NE Atlantic Ocean
60 L8 **Ribeirão Preto** São Paulo, S Brazil
60 L11 **Ribeira, Rio** ≈ S Brazil
107 I24 **Ribera** Sicilia, Italy, C Mediterranean Sea
57 L14 **Riberalta** Beni, N Bolivia
105 W4 **Ribes de Freser** Cataluña, NE Spain
30 L6 **Rib Mountain** ▲ Wisconsin, N USA
109 U12 **Ribnica** Ger. Reifnitz. S Slovenia
117 N9 **Rîbniţa** var. Râbniţa, Rus. Rybnitsa. NE Moldova
100 M8 **Ribnitz-Damgarten** Mecklenburg-Vorpommern, NE Germany
111 D16 **Říčany** Ger. Ritschan. Středočeský Kraj, W Czech Republic
29 U7 **Rice** Minnesota, N USA
30 J5 **Rice Lake** Wisconsin, N USA
14 I15 **Rice Lake** ◎ Ontario, S Canada
14 E8 **Rice Lake** ◎ Ontario, S Canada
23 V3 **Richard B.Russell Lake** ⊠ Georgia, SE USA
25 U6 **Richardson** Texas, SW USA
11 R11 **Richardson** ≈ Alberta, C Canada
10 I3 **Richardson Mountains** ▲ Yukon Territory, NW Canada
185 C21 **Richardson Mountains** ▲ South Island, NZ
42 F3 **Richardson Peak** ▲ SE Belize
76 G10 **Richard Toll** N Senegal
28 L5 **Richardton** North Dakota, N USA
14 F13 **Rich, Cape** headland Ontario, S Canada
102 L8 **Richelieu** Indre-et-Loire, C France
33 P15 **Richfield** Idaho, NW USA
36 K5 **Richfield** Utah, W USA
18 J10 **Richfield Springs** New York, NE USA
18 M6 **Richford** Vermont, NE USA
27 R6 **Rich Hill** Missouri, C USA
13 P14 **Richibucto** New Brunswick, SE Canada
108 G8 **Richisau** Glarus, NE Switzerland
23 S6 **Richland** Georgia, SE USA
27 U6 **Richland** Missouri, C USA
25 U8 **Richland** Texas, SW USA
32 K10 **Richland** Washington, NW USA
30 K8 **Richland Center** Wisconsin, N USA
21 W11 **Richlands** North Carolina, SE USA
21 Q7 **Richlands** Virginia, NE USA
25 R9 **Richland Springs** Texas, SW USA
183 S8 **Richmond** New South Wales, SE Australia
10 L17 **Richmond** British Columbia, SW Canada
14 L13 **Richmond** Ontario, SE Canada
15 Q12 **Richmond** Quebec, SE Canada
185 I14 **Richmond** Tasman, South Island, NZ
35 N8 **Richmond** California, W USA
31 Q14 **Richmond** Indiana, N USA
20 M6 **Richmond** Kentucky, S USA
27 S4 **Richmond** Missouri, C USA
25 V11 **Richmond** Texas, SW USA
36 L1 **Richmond** Utah, W USA
21 W6 **Richmond** state capital Virginia, NE USA
14 H15 **Richmond Hill** Ontario, S Canada
185 J15 **Richmond Range** ▲ South Island, NZ
27 S12 **Rich Mountain** ▲ Arkansas, C USA
31 S13 **Richwood** Ohio, N USA
21 R5 **Richwood** West Virginia, NE USA
104 K5 **Ricobayo, Embalse de** ⊠ NW Spain
Ricomagus see Riom
Ridā' see Radā'
98 H13 **Ridderkerk** Zuid-Holland, SW Netherlands
33 N16 **Riddle** Idaho, NW USA
32 F14 **Riddle** Oregon, NW USA
14 L13 **Rideau** ≈ Ontario, SE Canada
35 T12 **Ridgecrest** California, W USA
18 L13 **Ridgefield** Connecticut, NE USA
22 K5 **Ridgeland** Mississippi, S USA
21 R15 **Ridgeland** South Carolina, SE USA
20 F8 **Ridgely** Tennessee, S USA
14 D17 **Ridgetown** Ontario, S Canada
Ridgeway see Ridgway
21 R12 **Ridgeway** South Carolina, SE USA
18 D13 **Ridgway** var. Ridgeway. Pennsylvania, NE USA
11 W16 **Riding Mountain** ▲ Manitoba, S Canada
Ried see Ried im Innkreis
109 R4 **Ried im Innkreis** var. Ried. Oberösterreich, NW Austria
109 X8 **Riegersburg** Steiermark, SE Austria
108 E6 **Riehen** Basel-Stadt, NW Switzerland
92 J9 **Riehppegáisá** var. Rieppe. ▲ N Norway
99 K18 **Riemst** Limburg, NE Belgium
Rieppe see Riehppegáisá
101 O15 **Riesa** Sachsen, E Germany
63 H24 **Riesco, Isla** island S Chile
107 K25 **Riesi** Sicilia, Italy, C Mediterranean Sea
83 F25 **Riet** ≈ SW South Africa
83 I23 **Riet** ≈ SW South Africa
118 D11 **Rietavas** Plungė, W Lithuania
83 F19 **Rietfontein** Omaheke, E Namibia
107 I14 **Rieti** anc. Reate. Lazio, C Italy
84 D14 **Rif** var. Er Rif, Er Riff, Riff. ▲ N Morocco
Riff see Rif
37 Q4 **Rifle** Colorado, C USA
31 R7 **Rifle River** ≈ Michigan, N USA
81 H18 **Rift Valley** ◆ province Kenya
Rift Valley see Great Rift Valley
118 F9 **Rīga** Eng. Riga. ● (Latvia) Riga, C Latvia
Rigaer Bucht see Riga, Gulf of
118 F6 **Riga, Gulf of** Est. Liivi Laht, Ger. Rigaer Bucht, Latv. Rigas Jūras Līcis, Rus. Rizhskiy Zaliv; prev. Est. Riia Laht. gulf Estonia/Latvia
143 U12 **Rīgān** Kermān, SE Iran
Rīgas Jūras Līcis see Riga, Gulf of
15 N12 **Rigaud** ≈ Ontario/Quebec, SE Canada
33 R14 **Rigby** Idaho, NW USA
148 M10 **Rīgestān** var. Registan. desert region S Afghanistan
32 M11 **Riggins** Idaho, NW USA
13 R8 **Rigolet** Newfoundland, NE Canada
78 G9 **Rig-Rig** Kanem, W Chad
118 F4 **Riguldi** Läänemaa, W Estonia
Riia Laht see Riga, Gulf of
93 L19 **Riihimäki** Etelä-Suomi, S Finland
195 O2 **Riiser-Larsen Ice Shelf** ice shelf Antarctica
195 U2 **Riiser-Larsen Peninsula** peninsula Antarctica
65 P22 **Riiser-Larsen Sea** sea Antarctica
40 D2 **Riíto** Sonora, NW Mexico
112 B9 **Rijeka** Ger. Sankt Veit am Flaum, It. Fiume, Slvn. Reka; anc. Tarsatica. Primorje-Gorski Kotar, NW Croatia
99 I14 **Rijen** Noord-Brabant, S Netherlands
99 H15 **Rijkevorsel** Antwerpen, N Belgium
Rijn see Rhine
98 G11 **Rijnsburg** Zuid-Holland, W Netherlands
Rijssel see Lille
98 N10 **Rijssen** Overijssel, E Netherlands
98 G12 **Rijswijk** Eng. Ryswick. Zuid-Holland, W Netherlands
92 I10 **Riksgränsen** Norrbotten, N Sweden
165 U4 **Rikubetsu** Hokkaidō, NE Japan
165 R9 **Rikuzen-Takata** Iwate, Honshū, C Japan
27 O4 **Riley** Kansas, C USA
99 I17 **Rillaar** Vlaams Brabant, C Belgium
Rí, Loch see Ree, Lough
114 G11 **Rilska Reka** ≈ W Bulgaria
77 T12 **Rima** ≈ N Nigeria
141 N7 **Rimah, Wādī ar** var. Wādī ar Rummah. dry watercourse C Saudi Arabia
Rimaszombat see Rimavská Sobota
191 R12 **Rimatara** island Îles Australes, SW French Polynesia
111 L20 **Rimavská Sobota** Ger. Gross-Steffelsdorf, Hung. Rimaszombat. Banskobystrický Kraj, C Slovakia
11 Q15 **Rimbey** Alberta, SW Canada
95 P15 **Rimbo** Stockholm, C Sweden
95 M18 **Rimforsa** Östergötland, S Sweden
106 I11 **Rimini** anc. Ariminum. Emilia-Romagna, N Italy
Rîmnicu-Sărat see Râmnicu Sărat
Rîmnicu Vîlcea see Râmnicu Vâlcea
149 Y3 **Rimo Muztāgh** ▲ India/Pakistan
15 U7 **Rimouski** Quebec, SE Canada
158 M16 **Rinbung** Xizang Zizhiqu, W China
162 I5 **Rinchinlhümbe** Hövsgöl, N Mongolia
62 I5 **Rincón, Cerro** ▲ N Chile
104 M15 **Rincón de la Victoria** Andalucía, S Spain
Rincón del Bonete, Lago Artificial de see Río Negro, Embalse del
105 Q4 **Rincón de Soto** La Rioja, N Spain
94 G8 **Rindal** Møre og Romsdal, S Norway
115 J20 **Rineia** island Kykládes, Greece, Aegean Sea
152 H11 **Rīngas** prev. Reengus, Ringus. Rājasthān, N India
95 H24 **Ringe** Fyn, C Denmark
94 H11 **Ringebu** Oppland, S Norway
Ringen see Rõngu
186 K8 **Ringgi** Kolombangara, NW Solomon Islands
23 R1 **Ringgold** Georgia, SE USA
22 G5 **Ringgold** Louisiana, S USA
25 S5 **Ringgold** Texas, SW USA
95 E22 **Ringkøbing** Ringkøbing, W Denmark
95 E21 **Ringkøbing** off. Ringkøbing Amt. ◆ county W Denmark
95 E22 **Ringkøbing Fjord** fjord W Denmark
33 S10 **Ringling** Montana, NW USA
27 N13 **Ringling** Oklahoma, C USA
94 H13 **Ringsaker** Hedmark, S Norway
95 I23 **Ringsted** Vestsjælland, E Denmark
Ringus see Rīngas
92 I9 **Ringvassøya** island N Norway
18 K13 **Ringwood** New Jersey, NE USA
Rinn Duáin see Hook Head
100 H13 **Rinteln** Niedersachsen, NW Germany
Rio see Rio de Janeiro
115 E18 **Río** Dytikí Ellás, S Greece
56 C7 **Riobamba** Chimborazo, C Ecuador
60 P9 **Rio Bonito** Rio de Janeiro, SE Brazil
59 C16 **Rio Branco** state capital Acre, W Brazil
61 H18 **Río Branco** Cerro Largo, NE Uruguay
Rio Branco, Território de see Roraima
41 P8 **Río Bravo** Tamaulipas, C Mexico
63 G16 **Río Bueno** Los Lagos, C Chile
55 P5 **Río Caribe** Sucre, NE Venezuela
54 M5 **Río Chico** Miranda, N Venezuela
63 H18 **Río Cisnes** Aisén, S Chile
60 L9 **Rio Claro** São Paulo, S Brazil
45 V14 **Rio Claro** Trinidad, Trinidad and Tobago
54 J5 **Río Claro** Lara, N Venezuela
63 K15 **Río Colorado** Río Negro, E Argentina
62 K11 **Río Cuarto** Córdoba, C Argentina
60 P10 **Rio de Janeiro** var. Rio. state capital Rio de Janeiro, SE Brazil
60 P9 **Rio de Janeiro** off. Estado do Rio de Janeiro. ◆ state SE Brazil
43 R17 **Río de Jesús** Veraguas, S Panama
34 K3 **Rio Dell** California, W USA
60 K13 **Rio do Sul** Santa Catarina, S Brazil
63 I23 **Río Gallegos** var. Gallegos, Puerto Gallegos. Santa Cruz, S Argentina
61 I18 **Rio Grande** var. São Pedro do Rio Grande do Sul. Rio Grande do Sul, S Brazil
24 I9 **Rio Grande** ≈ Texas, SW USA
63 J24 **Río Grande** Tierra del Fuego, S Argentina
40 L10 **Río Grande** Zacatecas, C Mexico
42 J9 **Río Grande** León, NW Nicaragua
45 V5 **Río Grande** E Puerto Rico
25 R17 **Rio Grande City** Texas, SW USA
59 P14 **Rio Grande do Norte** off. Estado do Rio Grande do Norte. ◆ state E Brazil
61 G15 **Rio Grande do Sul** off. Estado do Rio Grande do Sul. ◆ state S Brazil
65 M17 **Rio Grande Fracture Zone** tectonic feature C Atlantic Ocean
65 J18 **Rio Grande Gap** undersea feature S Atlantic Ocean
Rio Grande Plateau see Rio Grande Rise
65 J18 **Rio Grande Rise** var. Rio Grande Plateau. undersea feature SW Atlantic Ocean
54 G4 **Ríohacha** La Guajira, N Colombia
43 S16 **Río Hato** Coclé, C Panama
25 T17 **Rio Hondo** Texas, SW USA
56 D10 **Rioja** San Martín, N Peru
41 Y11 **Río Lagartos** Yucatán, SE Mexico
103 P11 **Riom** anc. Ricomagus. Puy-de-Dôme, C France
104 F10 **Rio Maior** Santarém, C Portugal
103 O12 **Riom-ès-Montagnes** Cantal, C France
60 J12 **Rio Negro** Paraná, S Brazil
63 I15 **Río Negro** off. Provincia de Río Negro. ◆ province C Argentina
61 D18 **Río Negro** ◆ department W Uruguay
47 V12 **Río Negro, Embalse del** var. Lago Artificial de Rincón del Bonete. ⊠ C Uruguay
107 M17 **Rionero in Vulture** Basilicata, S Italy
137 S9 **Rioni** ≈ W Georgia
105 P12 **Riópar** Castilla-La Mancha, C Spain
61 H16 **Rio Pardo** Rio Grande do Sul, S Brazil
37 R11 **Rio Rancho Estates** New Mexico, SW USA
42 L11 **Río San Juan** ◆ department S Nicaragua
54 E9 **Ríosucio** Caldas, W Colombia
54 C7 **Ríosucio** Chocó, NW Colombia
62 K10 **Río Tercero** Córdoba, C Argentina
54 J5 **Río Tocuyo** Lara, N Venezuela
Riouw-Archipel see Riau, Kepulauan
59 J19 **Rio Verde** Goiás, C Brazil
41 O12 **Río Verde** var. Rioverde. San Luis Potosí, C Mexico
35 O8 **Rio Vista** California, W USA
112 M11 **Ripanj** Serbia, N Yugoslavia
106 J13 **Ripatransone** Marche, C Italy
Ripen see Ribe
22 M2 **Ripley** Mississippi, S USA
31 R15 **Ripley** Ohio, N USA
20 F9 **Ripley** Tennessee, S USA
21 Q4 **Ripley** West Virginia, NE USA
105 W4 **Ripoll** Cataluña, NE Spain
97 M16 **Ripon** N England, UK
30 M7 **Ripon** Wisconsin, N USA
107 L24 **Riposto** Sicilia, Italy, C Mediterranean Sea
99 L14 **Rips** Noord-Brabant, SE Netherlands
54 D9 **Risaralda** off. Departamento de Risaralda. ◆ province C Colombia
116 L8 **Rîşcani** var. Râşcani, Rus. Ryshkany. NW Moldova
152 J9 **Rishikesh** Uttar Pradesh, N India
165 S1 **Rishiri-tō** var. Risiri Tô. island NE Japan
165 S1 **Rishiri-yama** ✶ Rishiri-tō, NE Japan
25 R7 **Rising Star** Texas, SW USA
31 Q15 **Rising Sun** Indiana, N USA
Risiri Tô see Rishiri-tō
102 L4 **Risle** ≈ N France
Rišno see Râşnov
27 V13 **Rison** Arkansas, C USA
95 G17 **Risør** Aust-Agder, S Norway
92 H10 **Risøyhamn** Nordland, C Norway
101 I23 **Riss** ≈ S Germany
118 G4 **Risti** Ger. Kreuz. Läänemaa, W Estonia
15 V8 **Ristigouche** ≈ Quebec, SE Canada
93 N18 **Ristiina** Isä-Suomi, E Finland
93 N14 **Ristijärvi** Oulu, C Finland
188 C14 **Ritidian Point** headland N Guam
Ritschan see Říčany
35 R9 **Ritter, Mount** ▲ California, W USA
31 T12 **Rittman** Ohio, N USA
32 L9 **Ritzville** Washington, NW USA
Riva see Riva del Garda
61 A21 **Rivadavia** Buenos Aires, E Argentina
108 F7 **Riva del Garda** var. Riva. Trentino-Alto Adige, N Italy
106 B8 **Rivarolo Canavese** Piemonte, W Italy
42 K11 **Rivas** Rivas, SW Nicaragua
42 J11 **Rivas** ◆ department SW Nicaragua
103 R11 **Rive-de-Gier** Loire, E France
61 A22 **Rivera** Buenos Aires, E Argentina
61 F16 **Rivera** Rivera, NE Uruguay
61 F17 **Rivera** ◆ department NE Uruguay
35 P9 **Riverbank** California, W USA
76 K17 **River Cess** SW Liberia
28 M4 **Riverdale** North Dakota, N USA
30 I6 **River Falls** Wisconsin, N USA
11 T16 **Riverhurst** Saskatchewan, S Canada
183 O10 **Riverina** physical region New South Wales, SE Australia
80 G8 **River Nile** ◆ state NE Sudan
63 F19 **Rivero, Isla** island Archipiélago de los Chonos, S Chile
11 W16 **Rivers** Manitoba, S Canada
77 U17 **Rivers** ◆ state S Nigeria
185 D23 **Riversdale** Southland, South Island, NZ
83 F26 **Riversdale** Western Cape, SW South Africa
35 U15 **Riverside** California, W USA
25 W9 **Riverside** Texas, SW USA
37 U3 **Riverside Reservoir** ⊠ Colorado, C USA
10 K15 **Rivers Inlet** British Columbia, SW Canada
10 K15 **Rivers Inlet** inlet British Columbia, SW Canada
11 X15 **Riverton** Manitoba, S Canada
185 C24 **Riverton** Southland, South Island, NZ
30 L13 **Riverton** Illinois, N USA
36 L3 **Riverton** Utah, W USA
33 V15 **Riverton** Wyoming, C USA
14 G10 **River Valley** Ontario, S Canada
13 P14 **Riverview** New Brunswick, SE Canada
103 O17 **Rivesaltes** Pyrénées-Orientales, S France
36 H11 **Riviera** Arizona, SW USA
25 S15 **Riviera** Texas, SW USA
23 Z14 **Riviera Beach** Florida, SE USA
15 Q10 **Rivière-à-Pierre** Quebec, SE Canada
15 T9 **Rivière-Bleue** Quebec, SE Canada
15 T8 **Rivière-du-Loup** Quebec, SE Canada
173 Y15 **Rivière du Rempart** NE Mauritius
45 R12 **Rivière-Pilote** S Martinique
173 O17 **Rivière St-Etienne, Point de la** headland SW Réunion
13 S10 **Rivière-St-Paul** Quebec, E Canada
Rivière Sèche see Bel Air
116 K4 **Rivne** Pol. Równe, Rus. Rovno. Rivnens'ka Oblast', NW Ukraine
Rivne see Rivnens'ka Oblast'
116 K3 **Rivnens'ka Oblast'** var. Rivne, Rus. Rovenskaya Oblast'. ◆ province NW Ukraine
106 B8 **Rivoli** Piemonte, NW Italy
159 Q14 **Riwoqê** Xizang Zizhiqu, W China
99 H19 **Rixensart** Wallon Brabant, C Belgium
Riyadh/Riyāḍ, Minṭaqat ar see Ar Riyāḍ
Riyāq see Rayak
Rizaiyeh see Orūmīyeh
137 P11 **Rize** Rize, NE Turkey
137 P11 **Rize** prev. Çoruh. ◆ province NE Turkey
161 R5 **Rizhao** Shandong, E China
Rizhskiy Zaliv see Riga, Gulf of
Rizokarpaso/Rizokárpason see Dipkarpaz
107 O21 **Rizzuto, Capo** headland S Italy
95 F15 **Rjukan** Telemark, S Norway
95 D16 **Rjuven** ▲ S Norway
76 H9 **Rkîz** Trarza, W Mauritania
95 H14 **Roa** Oppland, S Norway
105 N5 **Roa** Castilla-León, N Spain
45 T9 **Road Town** ○ (British Virgin Islands) Tortola, C British Virgin Islands
96 F6 **Roag, Loch** inlet NW Scotland, UK
37 O5 **Roan Cliffs** cliff Colorado/Utah, W USA
21 P9 **Roan High Knob** var. Roan Mountain. ▲ North Carolina/Tennessee, SE USA
Roan Mountain see Roan High Knob
103 Q10 **Roanne** anc. Rodunma. Loire, E France
23 R4 **Roanoke** Alabama, S USA
21 S7 **Roanoke** Virginia, NE USA
21 Z9 **Roanoke Island** island North Carolina, SE USA
21 W8 **Roanoke Rapids** North Carolina, SE USA
21 X9 **Roanoke River** ≈ North Carolina/Virginia, SE USA
37 O4 **Roan Plateau** plain Utah, W USA
37 R5 **Roaring Fork River** ≈ Colorado, C USA
25 O5 **Roaring Springs** Texas, SW USA
42 J4 **Roatán** var. Coxen Hole, Coxin Hole. Islas de la Bahía, N Honduras
42 I4 **Roatán, Isla de** island Islas de la Bahía, N Honduras
Roat Kampuchea see Cambodia
Roazon see Rennes
143 T7 **Robāṭ-e Chāh Gonbad** Khorāsān, E Iran
143 R7 **Robāṭ-e Khān** Khorāsān, C Iran
143 T7 **Robāṭ-e Khvosh Āb** Khorāsān, E Iran
143 R8 **Robāṭ-e Posht-e Bādām** Khorāsān, NE Iran
175 S8 **Robbie Ridge** undersea feature W Pacific Ocean
21 T10 **Robbins** North Carolina, SE USA
183 N15 **Robbins Island** island Tasmania, SE Australia
21 N10 **Robbinsville** North Carolina, SE USA
182 J12 **Robe** South Australia
21 W9 **Robersonville** North Carolina, SE USA
25 P8 **Robert Lee** Texas, SW USA
35 V5 **Roberts Creek Mountain** ▲ Nevada, W USA
93 J15 **Robertsfors** Västerbotten, N Sweden
27 R11 **Robert S.Kerr Reservoir** ⊠ Oklahoma, C USA
38 L12 **Roberts Mountain** ▲ Nunivak Island, Alaska, USA
83 F26 **Robertson** Western Cape, SW South Africa
194 H4 **Robertson Island** island Antarctica
76 J16 **Robertsport** W Liberia
182 J8 **Robertstown** South Australia
Robert Williams see Caála
15 P7 **Roberval** Quebec, SE Canada
31 N15 **Robinson** Illinois, N USA
193 U11 **Róbinson Crusoe, Isla** island Islas Juan Fernández, Chile, E Pacific Ocean
180 J9 **Robinson Range** ▲ Western Austral
182 M9 **Robinvale** Victoria, SE Australia
105 P11 **Robledo** Castilla-La Mancha, C Spain
54 G5 **Robles** var. La Paz, Robles La Paz. Cesar, N Colombia
Robles La Paz see Robles
11 V15 **Roblin** Manitoba, S Canada
11 S17 **Robsart** Saskatchewan, S Canada
11 N15 **Robson, Mount** ▲ British Columbia, SW Canada
25 T14 **Robstown** Texas, SW USA
25 P6 **Roby** Texas, SW USA
104 E11 **Roca, Cabo da** headland C Portugal
Rocadas see Xangongo
41 S14 **Roca Partida, Punta** headland C Mexico
47 X6 **Rocas, Atol das** island E Brazil
107 L18 **Roccadaspide** var. Rocca d'Aspide. Campania, S Italy
107 K15 **Roccaraso** Abruzzo, C Italy
106 H10 **Rocca San Casciano** Emilia-Romagna, C Italy
106 G13 **Roccastrada** Toscana, C Italy
61 G20 **Rocha** Rocha, E Uruguay
61 G19 **Rocha** ◆ department E Uruguay
97 L17 **Rochdale** NW England, UK
102 L11 **Rochechouart** Haute-Vienne, C France
99 J22 **Rochefort** Namur, SE Belgium
102 J11 **Rochefort** var. Rochefort sur Mer. Charente-Maritime, W France
Rochefort sur Mer see Rochefort
127 N10 **Rochegda** Arkhangel'skaya Oblast', NW Russian Federation
30 L10 **Rochelle** Illinois, N USA
25 Q9 **Rochelle** Texas, SW USA
13 P13 **Rocher Percé** island Rocher Percé, Quebec, E Canada
15 V3 **Rochers Ouest, Rivière aux** ≈ Quebec, SE Canada
97 O22 **Rochester** anc. Durobrivae. SE England, UK
31 O12 **Rochester** Indiana, N USA
29 W10 **Rochester** Minnesota, N USA
19 O9 **Rochester** New Hampshire, NE USA
18 F9 **Rochester** New York, NE USA
25 P5 **Rochester** Texas, SW USA
31 S9 **Rochester Hills** Michigan, N USA
Rocheuses, Montagnes/Rockies see Rocky Mountains
64 M6 **Rockall** island UK, N Atlantic Ocean
64 L6 **Rockall Bank** undersea feature N Atlantic Ocean
84 B8 **Rockall Rise** undersea feature N Atlantic Ocean
84 C9 **Rockall Trough** undersea feature N Atlantic Ocean
35 U2 **Rock Creek** ≈ Nevada, W USA
25 T10 **Rockdale** Texas, SW USA
195 N12 **Rockefeller Plateau** plateau Antarctica
30 K11 **Rock Falls** Illinois, N USA
23 Q5 **Rockford** Alabama, S USA
30 L10 **Rockford** Illinois, N USA
15 Q12 **Rock Forest** Quebec, SE Canada
11 T17 **Rockglen** Saskatchewan, S Canada
181 Y8 **Rockhampton** Queensland, E Australia
21 R11 **Rock Hill** South Carolina, SE USA
180 I13 **Rockingham** Western Australia
21 T11 **Rockingham** North Carolina, SE USA
30 J11 **Rock Island** Illinois, N USA
25 U12 **Rock Island** Texas, SW USA
14 C10 **Rock Lake** Ontario, S Canada
29 O2 **Rock Lake** North Dakota, N USA
14 I12 **Rock Lake** ◎ Ontario, SE Canada
14 M12 **Rockland** Ontario, SE Canada
19 R7 **Rockland** Maine, NE USA
182 L11 **Rocklands Reservoir** ⊠ Victoria, SE Australia
35 O7 **Rocklin** California, W USA
23 R3 **Rockmart** Georgia, SE USA
31 N16 **Rockport** Indiana, N USA
27 Q1 **Rock Port** Missouri, C USA
25 T14 **Rockport** Texas, SW USA
32 I7 **Rockport** Washington, NW USA
29 S11 **Rock Rapids** Iowa, C USA
30 K11 **Rock River** ≈ Illinois/Wisconsin, N USA
44 I3 **Rock Sound** Eleuthera Island, C Bahamas
33 U17 **Rock Springs** Wyoming, C USA
25 P11 **Rocksprings** Texas, SW USA
55 T9 **Rockstone** C Guyana
29 S12 **Rock Valley** Iowa, C USA
31 N14 **Rockville** Indiana, N USA
21 W3 **Rockville** Maryland, NE USA
25 U6 **Rockwall** Texas, SW USA
29 U13 **Rockwell City** Iowa, C USA
31 S10 **Rockwood** Michigan, N USA
20 M9 **Rockwood** Tennessee, S USA
25 Q8 **Rockwood** Texas, SW USA
37 U6 **Rocky Ford** Colorado, C USA
14 D9 **Rocky Island Lake** ◎ Ontario, S Canada
21 V9 **Rocky Mount** North Carolina, SE USA

◆ Country ● Country Capital ◇ Dependent Territory ○ Dependent Territory Capital ◆ Administrative Region ✕ International Airport ▲ Mountain ▲ Mountain Range ✶ Volcano ≈ River ◎ Lake ⊠ Reservoir

21 S7 **Rocky Mount** Virginia, NE USA
33 Q8 **Rocky Mountain** ▲ Montana, NW USA
11 P15 **Rocky Mountain House** Alberta, SW Canada
37 T3 **Rocky Mountain National Park** national park Colorado, C USA
2 E12 **Rocky Mountains** var. Rockies, Fr. Montagnes Rocheuses. ▲ Canada/USA
42 H1 **Rocky Point** headland NE Belize
83 A17 **Rocky Point** headland NW Namibia
95 F14 **Rødberg** Buskerud, S Norway
95 I25 **Rødby** Storstrøm, SE Denmark
95 I25 **Rødbyhavn** Storstrøm, SE Denmark
13 T10 **Roddickton** Newfoundland, SE Canada
95 F23 **Rødding** Sønderjylland, SW Denmark
95 M22 **Rödeby** Blekinge, S Sweden
98 N6 **Roden** Drenthe, NE Netherlands
62 H9 **Rodeo** San Juan, W Argentina
103 O14 **Rodez** anc. Segodunum. Aveyron, S France
Rodholívos see Rodolívos
Rodhópi Óri see Rhodope Mountains
Ródhos/Rodi see Ródos
107 N15 **Rodi Garganico** Puglia, SE Italy
101 N20 **Roding** Bayern, SE Germany
113 J19 **Rodinit, Kepi i** headland W Albania
116 I9 **Rodnei, Munţii** ▲ N Romania
184 L4 **Rodney, Cape** headland North Island, NZ
38 L9 **Rodney, Cape** headland Alaska, USA
126 M16 **Rodniki** Ivanovskaya Oblast', W Russian Federation
119 Q16 **Rodnya** Rus. Rodnya. Mahilyowskaya Voblasts', E Belarus
Rodó see José Enrique Rodó
114 H13 **Rodolívos** var. Rodholívos. Kentrikí Makedonía, NE Greece
Rodopi see Rhodope Mountains
115 O22 **Ródos** var. Ródhos, Eng. Rhodes, It. Rodi. Ródos, Dodekánisos, Greece, Aegean Sea
115 O22 **Ródos** var. Ródhos, Eng. Rhodes, It. Rodi; anc. Rhodos. island Dodekánisos, Greece, Aegean Sea
Rodosto see Tekirdağ
59 A14 **Rodrigues** Amazonas, W Brazil
173 P8 **Rodrigues** var. Rodriquez. island E Mauritius
Rodriquez see Rodrigues
Rodunma see Roanne
180 I7 **Roebourne** Western Australia
83 J20 **Roedtan** Northern, NE South Africa
98 H11 **Roelofarendsveen** Zuid-Holland, W Netherlands
Roepat see Rupat, Pulau
Roer see Rur
99 M16 **Roermond** Limburg, SE Netherlands
99 C18 **Roeselare** Fr. Roulers; prev. Rousselaere. West-Vlaanderen, W Belgium
9 P8 **Roes Welcome Sound** strait Nunavut, N Canada
Roeteng see Ruteng
Rofreit see Rovereto
Rogachëv see Rahachow
57 L15 **Rogagua, Laguna** ◎ NW Bolivia
95 C16 **Rogaland** ◆ county S Norway
25 Y9 **Roganville** Texas, SW USA
109 W11 **Rogaška Slatina** Ger. Rohitsch-Sauerbrunn; prev. Rogatec-Slatina. E Slovenia
Rogatec-Slatina see Rogaška Slatina
112 J13 **Rogatica** Republica Srpska, SE Bosnia & Herzegovina
Rogatin see Rohatyn
93 F17 **Rogen** ◎ C Sweden
27 S9 **Rogers** Arkansas, C USA
29 P5 **Rogers** North Dakota, N USA
25 T9 **Rogers** Texas, SW USA
31 R5 **Rogers City** Michigan, N USA
Roger Simpson Island see Abemama
35 T14 **Rogers Lake** salt flat California, W USA
21 Q8 **Rogers, Mount** ▲ Virginia, NE USA
33 O16 **Rogerson** Idaho, NW USA
11 O16 **Rogers Pass** pass British Columbia, SW Canada
21 O8 **Rogersville** Tennessee, S USA
99 L16 **Roggel** Limburg, SE Netherlands
Roggeveen see Roggewein, Cabo
193 R10 **Roggeveen Basin** undersea feature E Pacific Ocean
191 X16 **Roggewein, Cabo** var. Roggeveen. headland Easter Island, Chile, E Pacific Ocean
103 Y13 **Rogliano** Corse, France, C Mediterranean Sea
107 N21 **Rogliano** Calabria, SW Italy
92 G12 **Rognan** Nordland, C Norway
100 K10 **Rögnitz** ≈ N Germany
Rogozhina/Rogozhinë see Rrogozhinë
110 G10 **Rogoźno** Wielkopolskie, C Poland
32 E15 **Rogue River** ≈ Oregon, NW USA
116 I6 **Rohatyn** Rus. Rogatin. Ivano-Frankivs'ka Oblast', W Ukraine
189 O14 **Rohi** Pohnpei, E Micronesia
Rohitsch-Sauerbrunn see Rogaška Slatina
149 Q13 **Rohri** Sind, SE Pakistan
152 I10 **Rohtak** Haryāna, N India
Roi Ed see Roi Et
167 R9 **Roi Et** var. Muang Roi Et, Roi Ed. Roi Et, E Thailand
191 U9 **Roi Georges, Îles du** island group Îles Tuamotu, C French Polynesia
153 Y10 **Roing** Arunāchal Pradesh, NE India
118 E7 **Roja** Talsi, NW Latvia
61 B20 **Rojas** Buenos Aires, E Argentina
149 R12 **Rojhān** Punjab, E Pakistan
41 Q12 **Rojo, Cabo** headland C Mexico
45 Q10 **Rojo, Cabo** headland W Puerto Rico
168 K10 **Rokan Kiri, Sungai** ≈ Sumatera, W Indonesia
Rokha see Rokhah
149 R4 **Rokhah** var. Rokha. Kāpīsā, E Afghanistan
118 I11 **Rokiškis** Rokiškis, NE Lithuania
165 R7 **Rokkasho** Aomori, Honshū, C Japan
111 B17 **Rokycany** Ger. Rokytzan. Plzeňský Kraj, NW Czech Republic
117 P6 **Rokytne** Kyyivs'ka Oblast', N Ukraine
116 L3 **Rokytne** Rivnens'ka Oblast', NW Ukraine
Rokytzan see Rokycany
158 L11 **Rola Co** ◎ W China
29 V13 **Roland** Iowa, C USA
95 D15 **Røldal** Hordaland, S Norway
98 O7 **Rolde** Drenthe, NE Netherlands
29 O2 **Rolette** North Dakota, N USA
27 V6 **Rolla** Missouri, C USA
29 O2 **Rolla** North Dakota, N USA
108 A10 **Rolle** Vaud, W Switzerland
181 X8 **Rolleston** Queensland, E Australia
185 H19 **Rolleston** Canterbury, South Island, NZ
185 G18 **Rolleston Range** ▲ South Island, NZ
14 H8 **Rollet** Quebec, SE Canada
22 J4 **Rolling Fork** Mississippi, S USA
20 L6 **Rolling Fork** ≈ Kentucky, S USA
14 J11 **Rolphton** Ontario, SE Canada
Röm see Rømø
181 X10 **Roma** Queensland, E Australia
107 I15 **Roma** Eng. Rome. ● (Italy) Lazio, C Italy
95 P19 **Roma** Gotland, SE Sweden
21 T14 **Romain, Cape** headland South Carolina, SE USA
13 P11 **Romaine** ≈ Newfoundland/Quebec, E Canada
25 R17 **Roma Los Saenz** Texas, SW USA
114 H8 **Roman** Vratsa, NW Bulgaria
116 L10 **Roman** Hung. Románvásár. Neamţ, NE Romania
64 M13 **Romanche Fracture Zone** tectonic feature E Atlantic Ocean
61 C15 **Romang** Santa Fe, C Argentina
171 R15 **Romang, Pulau** var. Pulau Roma. island Kepulauan Damar, E Indonesia
171 R15 **Romang, Selat** strait Nusa Tenggara, S Indonesia
116 J11 **Romania** Bul. Rumŭniya, Ger. Rumänien, Hung. Románia, Rom. România, SCr. Rumunjska, Ukr. Rumuniya; prev. Republica Socialistă România, Roumania, Rumania, Socialist Republic of Romania, Rom. Romînia. ◆ republic SE Europe
117 T14 **Roman-Kash** ▲ S Ukraine
23 W16 **Romano, Cape** headland Florida, SE USA
44 G5 **Romano, Cayo** island C Cuba
123 O13 **Romanovka** Respublika Buryatiya, S Russian Federation
129 N8 **Romanovka** Saratovskaya Oblast', W Russian Federation
108 I6 **Romanshorn** Thurgau, NE Switzerland
103 R12 **Romans-sur-Isère** Drôme, E France
189 U12 **Romanum** island Chuuk, C Micronesia
Románvásár see Roman
39 S5 **Romanzof Mountains** ▲ Alaska, USA
Roma, Pulau see Romang, Pulau
23 S4 **Rombas** Moselle, NE France
23 R2 **Rome** Georgia, SE USA
18 I9 **Rome** New York, NE USA
Rome see Roma
31 S9 **Romeo** Michigan, N USA
Römerstadt see Rýmařov
Rometan see Romitan
103 P5 **Romilly-sur-Seine** Aube, N France
Romînia see Romania
146 L11 **Romitan** Rus. Rometan. Bukhoro Wiloyati, C Uzbekistan
21 U3 **Romney** West Virginia, NE USA
117 S4 **Romny** Sums'ka Oblast', NE Ukraine
95 E24 **Rømø** Ger. Röm. island SW Denmark
117 S5 **Romodan** Poltavs'ka Oblast', NE Ukraine
129 P5 **Romodanovo** Respublika Mordoviya, W Russian Federation
Romorantin see Romorantin-Lanthenay
103 N8 **Romorantin-Lanthenay** var. Romorantin. Loir-et-Cher, C France
94 F9 **Romsdal** physical region S Norway
94 F10 **Romsdalen** valley S Norway
94 E9 **Romsdalsfjorden** fjord S Norway
33 P8 **Ronan** Montana, NW USA
59 M14 **Roncador** Maranhão, E Brazil
186 M7 **Roncador Reef** reef N Solomon Islands
59 J17 **Roncador, Serra do** ▲ C Brazil
21 S6 **Ronceverte** West Virginia, NE USA
107 H14 **Ronciglione** Lazio, C Italy
104 L15 **Ronda** Andalucía, S Spain
94 G11 **Rondane** ▲ S Norway
104 L15 **Ronda, Serranía de** ▲ S Spain
95 H22 **Rønde** Århus, C Denmark
Rōndik see Rongrik Atoll
59 E16 **Rondônia** off. Estado de Rondônia; prev. Território de Rondônia. ◆ state W Brazil
59 I18 **Rondonópolis** Mato Grosso, W Brazil
94 G11 **Rondslottet** ▲ S Norway
95 P20 **Ronehamn** Gotland, SE Sweden
160 L13 **Rong'an** var. Chang'an, Rongan. Guangxi Zhuangzu Zizhiqu, S China
189 R4 **Rongelap Atoll** var. Rōnļap. atoll Ralik Chain, NW Marshall Islands
Rongerik see Rongrik Atoll
160 L13 **Rong Jiang** ≈ S China
160 K12 **Rongjiang** prev. Guzhou. Guizhou, S China
Rong, Kas see Rŭng, Kaôh
167 P8 **Rong Kwang** Phrae, NW Thailand
189 T4 **Rongrik Atoll** var. Rōndik, Rongerik. atoll Ralik Chain, N Marshall Islands
189 X2 **Rongrong** island SE Marshall Islands
160 L13 **Rongshui** var. Rongshui Miaozu Zizhixian. Guangxi Zhuangzu Zizhiqu, S China
Rongshui Miaozu Zizhixian see Rongshui
118 I6 **Rõngu** Ger. Ringen. Tartumaa, SE Estonia
160 L15 **Rongxian** var. Rong Xian. Guangxi Zhuangzu Zizhiqu, S China
Roniu see Ronui, Mont
189 N13 **Ronkiti** Pohnpei, E Micronesia
Rōnļap see Rongelap Atoll
95 L24 **Rønne** Bornholm, E Denmark
95 M22 **Ronneby** Blekinge, S Sweden
194 J7 **Ronne Entrance** inlet Antarctica
194 L6 **Ronne Ice Shelf** ice shelf Antarctica
99 E19 **Ronse** Fr. Renaix. Oost-Vlaanderen, SW Belgium
191 R8 **Ronui, Mont** var. Roniu. ⋇ Tahiti, W French Polynesia
30 K14 **Roodhouse** Illinois, N USA
83 C19 **Rooibank** Erongo, W Namibia
65 N24 **Rookery Point** headland NE Tristan da Cunha
171 V13 **Roon, Pulau** island E Indonesia
173 V7 **Roo Rise** undersea feature E Indian Ocean
152 J9 **Roorkee** Uttar Pradesh, N India
99 H15 **Roosendaal** Noord-Brabant, S Netherlands
25 P10 **Roosevelt** Texas, SW USA
37 N3 **Roosevelt** Utah, W USA
47 T8 **Roosevelt** ≈ W Brazil
195 O13 **Roosevelt Island** island Antarctica
10 L10 **Roosevelt, Mount** ▲ British Columbia, W Canada
11 P17 **Roosville** British Columbia, SW Canada
29 X10 **Root River** ≈ Minnesota, N USA
111 N16 **Ropczyce** Podkarpackie, SE Poland
181 Q3 **Roper Bar** Northern Territory, N Australia
24 M5 **Ropesville** Texas, SW USA
102 K14 **Roquefort** Landes, SW France
61 C21 **Roque Pérez** Buenos Aires, E Argentina
58 E10 **Roraima** off. Estado de Roraima; prev. Território de Rio Branco, Território de Roraima. ◆ state N Brazil
58 F9 **Roraima, Mount** ▲ N South America
Ro Ro Reef see Malolo Barrier Reef
94 I9 **Røros** Sør-Trøndelag, S Norway
108 I7 **Rorschach** Sankt Gallen, NE Switzerland
93 E14 **Rørvik** Nord-Trøndelag, C Norway
119 G17 **Ros'** Rus. Ross'. Hrodzyenskaya Voblasts', W Belarus
119 G17 **Ros'** Rus. Ross'. ≈ W Belarus
117 O6 **Ros'** ≈ N Ukraine
44 K7 **Rosa, Lake** ◎ Great Inagua, S Bahamas
32 M9 **Rosalia** Washington, NW USA
191 W15 **Rosalia, Punta** headland Easter Island, Chile, E Pacific Ocean
45 P12 **Rosalie** E Dominica
35 T14 **Rosamond** California, W USA
35 S14 **Rosamond Lake** salt flat California, W USA
61 B18 **Rosario** Santa Fe, C Argentina
40 J11 **Rosario** Sinaloa, C Mexico
40 G6 **Rosario** Sonora, NW Mexico
62 O6 **Rosario** San Pedro, C Paraguay
61 E20 **Rosario** Colonia, SW Uruguay
54 H5 **Rosario** Zulia, NW Venezuela
Rosario see Rosarito
40 B4 **Rosario, Bahía del** bay NW Mexico
62 K6 **Rosario de la Frontera** Salta, N Argentina
61 C18 **Rosario del Tala** Entre Ríos, E Argentina
61 F16 **Rosário do Sul** Rio Grande do Sul, S Brazil
59 H18 **Rosário Oeste** Mato Grosso, W Brazil
40 E7 **Rosarito** Baja California, NW Mexico
40 B1 **Rosarito** var. Rosario. Baja California, NW Mexico
40 E7 **Rosarito** Baja California Sur, W Mexico
104 L9 **Rosarito, Embalse del** ⊡ W Spain
107 N22 **Rosarno** Calabria, SW Italy
56 B5 **Rosa Zárate** var. Quinindé. Esmeraldas, SW Ecuador
Roscianum see Rossano
29 O8 **Roscoe** South Dakota, N USA
25 P7 **Roscoe** Texas, SW USA
102 F5 **Roscoff** Finistère, NW France
Ros Comáin see Roscommon
97 C17 **Roscommon** Ir. Ros Comáin. C Ireland
31 Q7 **Roscommon** Michigan, N USA
97 C17 **Roscommon** Ir. Ros Comáin. cultural region C Ireland
Ros. Cré see Roscrea
97 D19 **Roscrea** Ir. Ros. Cré. C Ireland
45 X12 **Roseau** prev. Charlotte Town. ● (Dominica) SW Dominica
29 S2 **Roseau** Minnesota, N USA
173 Y16 **Rose Belle** SE Mauritius
183 O16 **Rosebery** Tasmania, SE Australia
21 U11 **Roseboro** North Carolina, SE USA
25 T9 **Rosebud** Texas, SW USA
33 W10 **Rosebud Creek** ≈ Montana, NW USA
32 F14 **Roseburg** Oregon, NW USA
22 J3 **Rosedale** Mississippi, S USA
99 H21 **Rosée** Namur, S Belgium
55 U8 **Rose Hall** E Guyana
173 X16 **Rose Hill** W Mauritius
80 H12 **Roseires, Reservoir** var. Lake Rusayris. ⊡ E Sudan
Rosenau see Rožnov pod Radhoštěm, Czech Republic
Rosenau see Rožňava, Slovakia
25 V11 **Rosenberg** Texas, SW USA
Rosenberg see Olesno, Poland
Rosenberg see Ružomberok, Slovakia
100 I10 **Rosengarten** Niedersachsen, N Germany
101 M24 **Rosenheim** Bayern, S Germany
Rosenhof see Zilupe
105 X4 **Roses** Cataluña, NE Spain
105 X4 **Roses, Golfo de** gulf NE Spain
107 K14 **Roseto degli Abruzzi** Abruzzo, C Italy
11 S16 **Rosetown** Saskatchewan, S Canada
Rosetta see Rashīd
35 O7 **Roseville** California, W USA
30 J12 **Roseville** Illinois, N USA
29 V8 **Roseville** Minnesota, N USA
29 R7 **Rosholt** South Dakota, N USA
106 F12 **Rosignano Marittimo** Toscana, C Italy
116 I14 **Roşiori de Vede** Teleorman, S Romania
114 K8 **Rositsa** ≈ N Bulgaria
Rositten see Rēzekne
95 J23 **Roskilde** Roskilde, E Denmark
95 I23 **Roskilde** off. Roskilde Amt. ◆ county E Denmark
Ros Láir see Rosslare
128 H5 **Roslavl'** Smolenskaya Oblast', W Russian Federation
32 I8 **Roslyn** Washington, NW USA
99 K14 **Rosmalen** Noord-Brabant, S Netherlands
Ros Mhic Thriúin see New Ross
113 P19 **Rosoman** C FYR Macedonia
102 F6 **Rosporden** Finistère, NW France
185 F17 **Ross** West Coast, South Island, NZ
10 J7 **Ross** ≈ Yukon Territory, W Canada
Ross' see Ros'
96 H8 **Ross and Cromarty** cultural region N Scotland, UK
107 O20 **Rossano** anc. Roscianum. Calabria, SW Italy
22 L5 **Ross Barnett Reservoir** ⊡ Mississippi, S USA
11 W16 **Rossburn** Manitoba, S Canada
14 H13 **Rosseau** Ontario, S Canada
14 H13 **Rosseau, Lake** ◎ Ontario, S Canada
186 I10 **Rossel Island** prev. Yela Island. island SE PNG
195 P12 **Ross Ice Shelf** ice shelf Antarctica
13 P16 **Rossignol, Lake** ◎ Nova Scotia, SE Canada
83 C19 **Rössing** Erongo, W Namibia
195 Q14 **Ross Island** island Antarctica
Rossitten see Rybachiy
Rossiyskaya Federatsiya see Russian Federation
11 N17 **Rossland** British Columbia, SW Canada
97 F20 **Rosslare** Ir. Ros Láir. SE Ireland
97 F20 **Rosslare Harbour** Wexford, SE Ireland
101 M14 **Rosslau** Sachsen-Anhalt, E Germany
76 G10 **Rosso** Trarza, SW Mauritania
103 X14 **Rosso, Cap** headland Corse, France, C Mediterranean Sea
93 H16 **Rossön** Jämtland, C Sweden
97 K21 **Ross-on-Wye** W England, UK
Rossony see Rasony
128 L9 **Rossosh'** Voronezhskaya Oblast', W Russian Federation
181 Q7 **Ross River** Northern Territory, N Australia
10 J7 **Ross River** Yukon Territory, W Canada
205 O15 **Ross Sea** sea Antarctica
92 G13 **Røssvatnet** ◎ C Norway
23 R1 **Rossville** Georgia, SE USA
Rostak see Ar Rustāq
143 P14 **Rostāq** Hormozgān, S Iran
117 N5 **Rostavytsya** ≈ N Ukraine
11 T15 **Rosthern** Saskatchewan, S Canada
100 M8 **Rostock** Mecklenburg-Vorpommern, NE Germany
126 L16 **Rostov** Yaroslavskaya Oblast', W Russian Federation
Rostov see Rostov-na-Donu
128 L12 **Rostov-na-Donu** var. Rostov, Eng. Rostov-on-Don. Rostovskaya Oblast', SW Russian Federation
Rostov-on-Don see Rostov-na-Donu
128 L10 **Rostovskaya Oblast'** ◆ province SW Russian Federation
93 J14 **Rosvik** Norrbotten, N Sweden
23 S3 **Roswell** Georgia, SE USA
37 U14 **Roswell** New Mexico, SW USA
94 K12 **Rot** Dalarna, C Sweden
101 I23 **Rot** ≈ S Germany
104 J15 **Rota** Andalucía, S Spain
188 K9 **Rota** island S Northern Mariana Islands
25 P6 **Rotan** Texas, SW USA
Rotcher Island see Tamana
100 I11 **Rotenburg** Niedersachsen, NW Germany
Rotenburg see Rotenburg an der Fulda
101 I16 **Rotenburg an der Fulda** var. Rotenburg. Thüringen, C Germany
101 L18 **Roter Main** ≈ E Germany
101 K20 **Roth** Bayern, SE Germany
101 G16 **Rothaargebirge** ▲ W Germany
Rothenburg see Rothenburg ob der Tauber
101 J20 **Rothenburg ob der Tauber** var. Rothenburg. Bayern, S Germany
194 H6 **Rothera** UK research station Antarctica
185 I17 **Rotherham** Canterbury, South Island, NZ
97 M17 **Rotherham** N England, UK
96 H12 **Rothesay** W Scotland, UK
108 E7 **Rothrist** Aargau, N Switzerland
194 H6 **Rothschild Island** island Antarctica
171 P17 **Roti, Pulau** island S Indonesia
183 O8 **Roto** New South Wales, SE Australia
184 N8 **Rotoiti, Lake** ◎ North Island, NZ
Rotomagus see Rouen
107 N19 **Rotondella** Basilicata, S Italy
103 X15 **Rotondo, Monte** ▲ Corse, France, C Mediterranean Sea
185 I15 **Rotoroa, Lake** ◎ South Island, NZ
184 N8 **Rotorua** Bay of Plenty, North Island, NZ
184 N8 **Rotorua, Lake** ◎ North Island, NZ
101 N22 **Rott** ≈ SE Germany
108 F10 **Rotten** ≈ S Switzerland
109 T6 **Rottenmann** Steiermark, E Austria
98 H12 **Rotterdam** Zuid-Holland, SW Netherlands
18 K10 **Rotterdam** New York, NE USA
95 M21 **Rottnen** ◎ S Sweden
98 N4 **Rottumeroog** island Waddeneilanden, NE Netherlands
98 N4 **Rottumerplaat** island Waddeneilanden, NE Netherlands
101 G23 **Rottweil** Baden-Württemberg, S Germany
191 O7 **Rotui, Mont** ⋇ Moorea, W French Polynesia
103 P1 **Roubaix** Nord, N France
111 C15 **Roudnice nad Labem** Ger. Raudnitz an der Elbe. Ústecký Kraj, NW Czech Republic
102 M4 **Rouen** anc. Rotomagus. Seine-Maritime, N France
171 X13 **Rouffaer Reserves** reserve Irian Jaya, E Indonesia
15 N10 **Rouge, Rivière** ≈ Quebec, SE Canada
20 J6 **Rough River** ≈ Kentucky, S USA
20 J6 **Rough River Lake** ⊡ Kentucky, S USA
Rouhaïbé see Ar Ruḩaybah
102 K11 **Rouillac** Charente, W France
Roulers see Roeselare
Roumania see Romania
173 Y15 **Round Island** var. Île Ronde. island NE Mauritius
14 J12 **Round Lake** ◎ Ontario, SE Canada
35 U7 **Round Mountain** Nevada, W USA
25 R10 **Round Mountain** Texas, SW USA
183 U5 **Round Mountain** ▲ New South Wales, SE Australia
25 S10 **Round Rock** Texas, SW USA
33 U10 **Roundup** Montana, NW USA
55 Y10 **Roura** NE French Guiana
Rourkela see Rāulakela
96 J4 **Rousay** island N Scotland, UK
Rousselaere see Roeselare
103 O17 **Roussillon** cultural region S France
15 V7 **Routhierville** Quebec, SE Canada
99 K25 **Rouvroy** Luxembourg, SE Belgium
14 I7 **Rouyn-Noranda** Quebec, SE Canada
Rouyuanchengzi see Huachi
92 L12 **Rovaniemi** Lappi, N Finland
106 E7 **Rovato** Lombardia, N Italy
127 N11 **Rovdino** Arkhangel'skaya Oblast', NW Russian Federation
Roven'ki see Roven'ky
117 Y8 **Roven'ky** var. Roven'ki. Luhans'ka Oblast', E Ukraine
Rovenskaya Oblast' see Rivnens'ka Oblast'
Rovenskaya Sloboda see Rovyenskaya Slabada
106 G7 **Rovereto** Ger. Rofreit. Trentino-Alto Adige, N Italy
167 S12 **Rôviĕng Tbong** Preăh Vihéar, N Cambodia
Rovigno see Rovinj
106 H8 **Rovigo** Veneto, NE Italy
112 A10 **Rovinj** It. Rovigno. Istra, NW Croatia
54 E10 **Rovira** Tolima, C Colombia
Rovno see Rivne
129 P9 **Rovnoye** Saratovskaya Oblast', W Russian Federation
82 Q12 **Rovuma, Rio** var. Ruvuma. ≈ Mozambique/Tanzania see also Ruvuma
119 O19 **Rovyenskaya Slabada** Rus. Rovenskaya Sloboda. Homyel'skaya Voblasts', SE Belarus
183 R5 **Rowena** New South Wales, SE Australia
21 T11 **Rowland** North Carolina, SE USA
9 P5 **Rowley** ≈ Baffin Island, Nunavut, NE Canada
9 P6 **Rowley Island** island Nunavut, NE Canada
173 W8 **Rowley Shoals** reef NW Australia
171 O4 **Roxas** Mindoro, N Philippines
171 P5 **Roxas City** Panay Island, C Philippines
21 U8 **Roxboro** North Carolina, SE USA
185 D23 **Roxburgh** Otago, South Island, NZ
96 K13 **Roxburgh** cultural region SE Scotland, UK
182 H5 **Roxby Downs** South Australia
95 M17 **Roxen** ◎ S Sweden
25 V5 **Roxton** Texas, SW USA
15 P12 **Roxton-Sud** Quebec, SE Canada
33 U8 **Roy** Montana, NW USA
37 U10 **Roy** New Mexico, SW USA
97 E17 **Royal Canal** Ir. An Chanáil Ríoga. canal C Ireland
30 L1 **Royale, Isle** island Michigan, N USA
37 S6 **Royal Gorge** valley Colorado, C USA
97 M20 **Royal Leamington Spa** var. Leamington, Leamington Spa. C England, UK
97 O23 **Royal Tunbridge Wells** var. Tunbridge Wells. SE England, UK
24 L9 **Royalty** Texas, SW USA
102 J11 **Royan** Charente-Maritime, W France
65 B24 **Roy Cove Settlement** West Falkland, Falkland Islands
103 O3 **Roye** Somme, N France
95 H15 **Røyken** Buskerud, S Norway
93 F14 **Røyrvik** Nord-Trøndelag, C Norway
25 U6 **Royse City** Texas, SW USA
97 O21 **Royston** E England, UK
23 U2 **Royston** Georgia, SE USA
114 L10 **Roza** prev. Gyulovo. Yambol, E Bulgaria
113 L16 **Rožaje** Montenegro, SW Yugoslavia
110 M10 **Różan** Mazowieckie, C Poland
117 O10 **Rozdil'na** Odes'ka Oblast', SW Ukraine
117 S12 **Rozdol'ne** Rus. Razdolnoye. Respublika Krym, S Ukraine
145 Q9 **Rozhdestvenka** Akmola, C Kazakhstan
116 I6 **Rozhnyativ** Ivano-Frankivs'ka Oblast', W Ukraine
116 J3 **Rozhyshche** Volyns'ka Oblast', NW Ukraine
Roznau am Radhost see Rožnov pod Radhoštěm
111 L19 **Rožňava** Ger. Rosenau, Hung. Rozsnyó. Košický Kraj, E Slovakia
116 K10 **Roznov** Neamţ, NE Romania
111 I18 **Rožnov pod Radhoštěm** Ger. Rosenau, Roznau am Radhost. Zlínský Kraj, E Czech Republic
Rózsahegy see Ružomberok
Rozsnyó see Râşnov, Romania
Rozsnyó see Rožňava, Slovakia
113 K18 **Rranxë** Shkodër, NW Albania
113 L18 **Rrëshen** var. Rresheni, Rrshen. Lezhë, C Albania
Rresheni see Rrëshen
Rrogozhina see Rrogozhinë
113 K20 **Rrogozhinë** var. Rogozhina, Rogozhinë, Rrogozhina. Tiranë, W Albania
Rrshen see Rrëshen
112 O13 **Rtanj** ▲ E Yugoslavia
129 O7 **Rtishchevo** Saratovskaya Oblast', W Russian Federation
184 N12 **Ruahine Range** var. Ruarine. ▲ North Island, NZ
185 L14 **Ruamahanga** ≈ North Island, NZ
Ruanda see Rwanda
184 M10 **Ruapehu, Mount** ▲ North Island, NZ
185 C25 **Ruapuke Island** island SW NZ
Ruarine see Ruahine Range
184 O9 **Ruatahuna** Bay of Plenty, North Island, NZ
184 Q8 **Ruatoria** Gisborne, North Island, NZ
184 K4 **Ruawai** Northland, North Island, NZ
15 N8 **Ruban** ≈ Quebec, SE Canada
81 I22 **Rubeho Mountains** ▲ C Tanzania
165 U3 **Rubeshibe** Hokkaidō, NE Japan
Rubezhnoye see Rubizhne
113 L18 **Rubik** Lezhë, C Albania
54 H7 **Rubio** Táchira, W Venezuela
117 X6 **Rubizhne** Rus. Rubezhnoye. Luhans'ka Oblast', E Ukraine
81 F20 **Rubondo Island** island N Tanzania
122 I13 **Rubtsovsk** Altayskiy Kray, S Russian Federation
39 P9 **Ruby** Alaska, USA
35 W3 **Ruby Dome** ▲ Nevada, W USA
35 W4 **Ruby Lake** ◎ Nevada, W USA
35 W4 **Ruby Mountains** ▲ Nevada, W USA
33 Q12 **Ruby Range** ▲ Montana, NW USA

◆ Country ● Country Capital ◇ Dependent Territory ○ Dependent Territory Capital ◆ Administrative Region ✈ International Airport ▲ Mountain ▲ Mountain Range ⋇ Volcano ≈ River ◎ Lake ⊡ Reservoir

118 C10 **Rucava** Liepāja, SW Latvia
Rūdān *see* Dehbārez
Rudelstadt *see* Ciechanowiec
Rudensk *see* Rudzyensk
119 G14 **Rūdiškės** Trakai, S Lithuania
95 H24 **Rudkøbing** Fyn, C Denmark
145 V14 **Rudnichnyy** *Kaz.* Rūdnīchnyy. Almaty, SE Kazakhstan
127 S13 **Rudnichnyy** Kirovskaya Oblast', NW Russian Federation
114 N9 **Rudnik** Varna, E Bulgaria
Rudny *see* Rudnyy
128 H4 **Rudnya** Smolenskaya Oblast', W Russian Federation
129 O8 **Rudnya** Volgogradskaya Oblast', SW Russian Federation
144 M7 **Rudnyy** *var.* Rudny. Kostanay, N Kazakhstan
122 K3 **Rudol'fa, Ostrov** *island* Zemlya Frantsa-Iosifa, NW Russian Federation
81 H16 **Rudolf, Lake** *var.* Lake Turkana. ◎ N Kenya
Rudolfswert *see* Novo mesto
101 L17 **Rudolstadt** Thüringen, C Germany
31 Q4 **Rudyard** Michigan, N USA
33 S7 **Rudyard** Montana, NW USA
119 K16 **Rudzyensk** *Rus.* Rudensk. Minskaya Voblasts', C Belarus
104 L6 **Rueda** Castilla-León, N Spain
114 F10 **Ruen** ▲ Bulgaria/FYR Macedonia
80 G10 **Rufa'a** Gezira, C Sudan
102 L10 **Ruffec** Charente, W France
21 R14 **Ruffin** South Carolina, SE USA
81 J23 **Rufiji** ≈ E Tanzania
61 A20 **Rufino** Santa Fe, C Argentina
76 F11 **Rufisque** W Senegal
83 K14 **Rufunsa** Lusaka, C Zambia
118 J9 **Rugāji** Balvi, E Latvia
161 R7 **Rugao** Jiangsu, E China
97 M20 **Rugby** C England, UK
29 N3 **Rugby** North Dakota, N USA
100 N7 **Rügen** *headland* NE Germany
Ruhaybeh *see* Ar Ruḩaybah
161 N7 **Ru He** ≈ C China
81 E19 **Ruhengeri** NW Rwanda
Ruhja *see* Rūjiena
100 M10 **Ruhner Berg** *hill* N Germany
118 F7 **Ruhnu** *var.* Ruhnu Saar, *Swe.* Runö. *island* SW Estonia
Ruhnu Saar *see* Ruhnu
101 G15 **Ruhr** ≈ W Germany
91 W6 **Ruhr Valley** *industrial region* W Germany
161 S11 **Rui'an** *var.* Rui an. Zhejiang, SE China
161 P10 **Ruichang** Jiangxi, S China
24 J11 **Ruidosa** Texas, SW USA
37 S14 **Ruidoso** New Mexico, SW USA
161 P12 **Ruijin** Jiangxi, S China
160 D13 **Ruili** Yunnan, SW China
98 N8 **Ruinen** Drenthe, NE Netherlands
99 D17 **Ruiselede** West-Vlaanderen, W Belgium
64 P5 **Ruivo de Santana, Pico** ▲ Madeira, Portugal, NE Atlantic Ocean
40 J12 **Ruiz** Nayarit, SW Mexico
54 E10 **Ruiz, Nevado del** ※ W Colombia
138 J9 **Rujaylah, Ḩarrat ar** *salt lake* N Jordan
Rujen *see* Rūjiena
118 H7 **Rūjiena** *Est.* Ruhja, *Ger.* Rujen. Valmiera, N Latvia
79 I18 **Ruki** ≈ W Dem. Rep. Congo (Zaire)
81 E22 **Rukwa** ◈ *region* SW Tanzania
81 F23 **Rukwa, Lake** ◎ SE Tanzania
25 P6 **Rule** Texas, SW USA
22 K3 **Ruleville** Mississippi, S USA
Rum *see* Rhum
112 K10 **Ruma** Serbia, N Yugoslavia
Rumadiya *see* Ar Ramādī
141 Q7 **Rumāḩ** Ar Riyāḑ, C Saudi Arabia
Rumaitha *see* Ar Rumaythah
Rumania/Rumänien *see* Romania
Rumänisch-Sankt-Georgen *see* Sângeorz-Băi
139 Y13 **Rumaylah** SE Iraq
139 P2 **Rumaylah, Wādī** *dry watercourse* NE Syria
171 U13 **Rumbati** Irian Jaya, E Indonesia
81 E14 **Rumbek** El Buhayrat, S Sudan
Rumburg *see* Rumburk
111 D14 **Rumburk** *Ger.* Rumburg. Ústecký Kraj, NW Czech Republic
44 J4 **Rum Cay** *island* C Bahamas
99 M26 **Rumelange** Luxembourg, S Luxembourg
99 D20 **Rumes** Hainaut, SW Belgium
19 P7 **Rumford** Maine, NE USA
110 I6 **Rumia** Pomorskie, N Poland
113 J17 **Rumija** ▲▲ SW Yugoslavia
103 T11 **Rumilly** Haute-Savoie, E France
139 O6 **Rūmiyah** W Iraq
Rummah, Wādī ar *see* Rimah, Wādī ar
Rummelsburg in Pommern *see* Miastko
165 S3 **Rumoi** Hokkaidō, NE Japan
82 M12 **Rumphi** *var.* Rumpi. Northern, N Malawi
Rumpi *see* Rumphi
29 V7 **Rum River** ≈ Minnesota, N USA
188 F16 **Rumung** *island* Caroline Islands, W Micronesia
Rumuniya/Rumŭniya/Rumunjska *see* Romania
185 G16 **Runanga** West Coast, South Island, NZ
184 P7 **Runaway, Cape** *headland* North Island, NZ
97 K18 **Runcorn** C England, UK
118 K10 **Rundāni** Ludza, E Latvia
83 L18 **Runde** *var.* Lundi. ≈ SE Zimbabwe
83 E16 **Rundu** *var.* Runtu. Okavango, NE Namibia
93 I16 **Rundvik** Västerbotten, N Sweden
81 G20 **Runere** Mwanza, N Tanzania
25 S13 **Runge** Texas, SW USA
167 Q13 **Rŭng, Kaôh** *prev.* Kas Rong. *island* SW Cambodia
79 O16 **Rungu** Orientale, NE Dem. Rep. Congo (Zaire)
81 F23 **Rungwa** Rukwa, W Tanzania
81 G22 **Rungwa** Singida, C Tanzania
94 M13 **Runn** ◎ C Sweden
24 M4 **Running Water Draw** *valley* New Mexico/Texas, SW USA
Runö *see* Ruhnu
Runtu *see* Rundu
189 V12 **Ruo** *island* Caroline Islands, C Micronesia
158 L9 **Ruoqiang** *var.* Jo-ch'iang, *Uigh.* Charkhlik, Charkhliq, Qarkilik. Xinjiang Uygur Zizhiqu, NW China
159 S7 **Ruo Shui** ≈ N China
92 L8 **Ruostefjelbma** *var.* Rustefjelbma Finnmark, N Norway
93 L18 **Ruovesi** Länsi-Suomi, W Finland
112 B9 **Rupa** Primorje-Gorski Kotar, NW Croatia
182 M11 **Rupanyup** Victoria, SE Australia
168 K9 **Rupat, Pulau** *prev.* Roepat. *island* W Indonesia
168 K10 **Rupat, Selat** *strait* Sumatera, W Indonesia
116 J11 **Rupea** *Ger.* Reps, *Hung.* Kőhalom; *prev.* Cohalm. Braşov, C Romania
99 G17 **Rupel** ≈ N Belgium
Rupella *see* la Rochelle
33 P15 **Rupert** Idaho, NW USA
21 R5 **Rupert** West Virginia, NE USA
Rupert House *see* Fort Rupert
12 J10 **Rupert, Rivière de** ≈ Quebec, C Canada
194 M13 **Ruppert Coast** *physical region* Antarctica
100 N11 **Ruppiner Kanal** *canal* NE Germany
55 S11 **Rupununi River** ≈ S Guyana
101 D16 **Rur** *Dut.* Roer. ≈ Germany/Netherlands
58 H13 **Rurópolis Presidente Medici** Pará, N Brazil
191 S12 **Rurutu** *island* Îles Australes, SW French Polynesia
Rusaddir *see* Melilla
83 L17 **Rusape** Manicaland, E Zimbabwe
Rusayris, Lake *see* Roseires, Reservoir
Ruschuk/Rusçuk *see* Ruse
114 K7 **Ruse** *var.* Ruschuk, Rustchuk, *Turk.* Rusçuk. Ruse, N Bulgaria
114 L7 **Ruse** ◈ *province* N Bulgaria
109 W10 **Ruše** NE Slovenia
114 K7 **Rusenski Lom** ≈ N Bulgaria
97 G17 **Rush** *Ir.* An Ros. E Ireland
161 S4 **Rushan** *var.* Xiacun. Shandong, E China
Rushan *see* Rŭshon
Rushanskiy Khrebet *see* Rushon, Qatorkŭhi
29 V7 **Rush City** Minnesota, N USA
37 V5 **Rush Creek** ≈ Colorado, C USA
29 X10 **Rushford** Minnesota, N USA
154 N13 **Rushikulya** ≈ E India
14 D8 **Rush Lake** ◎ Ontario, S Canada
30 M7 **Rush Lake** ◎ Wisconsin, N USA
28 J10 **Rushmore, Mount** ▲ South Dakota, N USA
147 S13 **Rŭshon** *Rus.* Rushan. S Tajikistan
147 S14 **Rushon, Qatorkŭhi** *Rus.* Rushanskiy Khrebet. ▲▲ SE Tajikistan
26 M12 **Rush Springs** Oklahoma, C USA
45 V15 **Rushville** Trinidad, Trinidad and Tobago
30 J13 **Rushville** Illinois, N USA
28 K12 **Rushville** Nebraska, C USA
183 O11 **Rushworth** Victoria, SE Australia
25 W8 **Rusk** Texas, SW USA
93 I14 **Rusksele** Västerbotten, N Sweden
118 C12 **Rusnė** Šilutė, W Lithuania
114 M10 **Rusokastrenska Reka** ≈ E Bulgaria
Russadir *see* Melilla
109 X3 **Russbach** ≈ NE Austria
11 V16 **Russell** Manitoba, S Canada
184 K2 **Russell** Northland, North Island, NZ
26 L4 **Russell** Kansas, C USA
21 O4 **Russell** Kentucky, S USA
20 L7 **Russell Springs** Kentucky, S USA
23 O2 **Russellville** Alabama, S USA
27 T11 **Russellville** Arkansas, C USA
20 J7 **Russellville** Kentucky, S USA
101 G18 **Rüsselsheim** Hessen, W Germany
92 K8 **Russenes** Finnmark, N Norway
Russia *see* Russian Federation
Russian America *see* Alaska
122 J11 **Russian Federation** *off.* Russian Federation, *var.* Russia, *Latv.* Krievija, *Rus.* Rossiyskaya Federatsiya. ◆ *republic* Asia/Europe
39 N11 **Russian Mission** Alaska, USA
34 M7 **Russian River** ≈ California, W USA
194 L13 **Russkaya** *Russian research station* Antarctica
122 J5 **Russkaya Gavan'** Novaya Zemlya, Arkhangel'skaya Oblast', N Russian Federation
122 J5 **Russkiy, Ostrov** *island* N Russian Federation
109 Y5 **Rust** Burgenland, E Austria
Rustaq *see* Ar Rustāq
137 U10 **Rust'avi** SE Georgia
21 T7 **Rustburg** Virginia, NE USA
Rustchuk *see* Ruse
Rustefjelbma *see* Ruostefjelbma
83 I21 **Rustenburg** North-West, N South Africa
22 H5 **Ruston** Louisiana, S USA
81 E21 **Rutana** SE Burundi
62 I4 **Rutana, Volcán** ▲ N Chile
Rutanzige, Lake *see* Edward, Lake
Rutba *see* Ar Ruṭbah
104 M14 **Rute** Andalucía, S Spain
171 N16 **Ruteng** *prev.* Roeteng. Flores, C Indonesia
194 L8 **Rutford Ice Stream** *ice feature* Antarctica
35 X6 **Ruth** Nevada, W USA
101 G15 **Rüthen** Nordrhein-Westfalen, W Germany
14 D17 **Rutherford** Ontario, S Canada
21 Q10 **Rutherfordton** North Carolina, SE USA
97 J18 **Ruthin** *Wel.* Rhuthun. NE Wales, UK
108 G7 **Rüti** Zürich, N Switzerland
Rutlam *see* Ratlām
18 M9 **Rutland** Vermont, NE USA
97 N19 **Rutland** *cultural region* C England, UK
21 N8 **Rutledge** Tennessee, S USA
158 G12 **Rutog** *var.* Rutok. Xizang Zizhiqu, W China
Rutok *see* Rutog
79 P19 **Rutshuru** Nord Kivu, E Dem. Rep. Congo (Zaire)
98 L8 **Rutten** Flevoland, N Netherlands
129 Q17 **Rutul** Respublika Dagestan, SW Russian Federation
93 L14 **Ruukki** Oulu, C Finland
98 N11 **Ruurlo** Gelderland, E Netherlands
143 S15 **Ru'ūs al Jibāl** *headland* Oman/UAE
138 I7 **Ru'ūs aṭ Ṭiwāl, Jabal** ▲▲ W Syria
81 H23 **Ruvuma** ◈ *region* SE Tanzania
81 I25 **Ruvuma** *var.* Rio Rovuma. ≈ Mozambique/Tanzania *see also* Rovuma, Rio
Ruwais *see* Ar Ruways
138 L9 **Ruwayshid, Wadi ar** *dry watercourse* NE Jordan
141 Z10 **Ruways, Ra's ar** *headland* E Oman
79 P18 **Ruwenzori** ▲▲ Uganda/Dem. Rep. Congo (Zaire)
141 Y8 **Ruwī** NE Oman
114 F9 **Ruy** ▲ Bulgaria/Yugoslavia
Ruya *see* Luia, Rio
81 E20 **Ruyigi** E Burundi
129 P5 **Ruzayevka** Respublika Mordoviya, W Russian Federation
119 G18 **Ruzhany** *Rus.* Ruzhany. Brestskaya Voblasts', SW Belarus
114 I10 **Rŭzhevo Konare** *var.* Rŭzhevo Konare. Plovdiv, C Bulgaria
Ruzhin *see* Ruzhyn
114 G7 **Ruzhintsi** Vidin, NW Bulgaria
117 N5 **Ruzhyn** *Rus.* Ruzhin. Zhytomyrs'ka Oblast', N Ukraine
111 K19 **Ružomberok** *Ger.* Rosenberg, *Hung.* Rózsahegy. Žilinský Kraj, N Slovakia
111 C16 **Ruzyně** × (Praha) Praha, C Czech Republic
81 D19 **Rwanda** *off.* Rwandese Republic; *prev.* Ruanda. ◆ *republic* C Africa
Rwandese Republic *see* Rwanda
95 G22 **Ry** Århus, C Denmark
Ryasna *see* Rasna
128 L5 **Ryazan'** Ryazanskaya Oblast', W Russian Federation
128 L5 **Ryazanskaya Oblast'** ◈ *province* W Russian Federation
128 M6 **Ryazhsk** Ryazanskaya Oblast', W Russian Federation
118 B13 **Rybachiy** *Ger.* Rossitten. Kaliningradskaya Oblast', W Russian Federation
126 J2 **Rybachiy, Poluostrov** *peninsula* NW Russian Federation
Rybach'ye *see* Balykchy
126 L15 **Rybinsk** *prev.* Andropov. Yaroslavskaya Oblast', W Russian Federation
126 K14 **Rybinskoye Vodokhranilishche** *Eng.* Rybinsk Reservoir, Rybinsk Sea. ▣ W Russian Federation
Rybinsk Reservoir/Rybinsk Sea *see* Rybinskoye Vodokhranilishche
111 I16 **Rybnik** Śląskie, S Poland
Rybnitsa *see* Rîbniţa
111 F16 **Rychnov nad Kněžnou** *Ger.* Reichenau. Hradecký Kraj, N Czech Republic
110 I12 **Rychwał** Wielkolpolskie, C Poland
11 O13 **Rycroft** Alberta, W Canada
95 L21 **Ryd** Kronoberg, S Sweden
95 L20 **Rydaholm** Jönköping, S Sweden
194 I8 **Rydberg Peninsula** *peninsula* Antarctica
97 P23 **Rye** SE England, UK
33 T10 **Ryegate** Montana, NW USA
35 S3 **Rye Patch Reservoir** ▣ Nevada, W USA
95 D15 **Ryfylke** *physical region* S Norway
95 H16 **Rygge** Østfold, S Norway
110 N13 **Ryki** Lubelskie, E Poland
Rykovo *see* Yenakiyeve
128 I7 **Ryl'sk** Kurskaya Oblast', W Russian Federation
183 S8 **Rylstone** New South Wales, SE Australia
111 H17 **Rýmařov** *Ger.* Römerstadt. Ostravský Kraj, E Czech Republic
144 E11 **Ryn-Peski** *desert* W Kazakhstan
165 N10 **Ryōtsu** *var.* Ryôtu. Niigata, Sado, C Japan
Ryôtu *see* Ryōtsu
110 K10 **Rypin** Kujawsko-pomorskie, C Poland
Ryshkany *see* Rîşcani
Ryssel *see* Lille
Ryswick *see* Rijswijk
95 M24 **Rytterknægten** *hill* E Denmark
192 G5 **Ryukyu Trench** *var.* Nansei Syotō Trench. *undersea feature* S East China Sea
110 D11 **Rzepin** *Ger.* Reppen. Lubuskie, W Poland
111 N16 **Rzeszów** Podkarpackie, SE Poland
126 I16 **Rzhev** Tverskaya Oblast', W Russian Federation
Rzhishchev *see* Rzhyshchiv
117 P5 **Rzhyshchiv** *Rus.* Rzhishchev. Kyyivs'ka Oblast', N Ukraine

S

138 E11 **Sa'ad** Southern, W Israel
109 P7 **Saalach** ≈ W Austria
101 L14 **Saale** ≈ C Germany
101 L17 **Saalfeld** *var.* Saalfeld an der Saale. Thüringen, C Germany
Saalfeld *see* Zalewo
Saalfeld an der Saale *see* Saalfeld
108 C8 **Saane** ≈ W Switzerland
101 D19 **Saar** *Fr.* Sarre. ≈ France/Germany
101 E20 **Saarbrücken** *Fr.* Sarrebruck. Saarland, SW Germany
Saarburg *see* Sarrebourg
Saare *see* Saaremaa
118 D6 **Sääre** *var.* Sjar. Saaremaa, W Estonia
118 D5 **Saaremaa** *off.* Saare Maakond. ◈ *province* W Estonia
118 E6 **Saaremaa** *Ger.* Oesel, Ösel; *prev.* Saare. *island* W Estonia
92 L12 **Saarenkylä** Lappi, N Finland
Saargemund *see* Sarreguemines
93 L17 **Saarijärvi** Länsi-Suomi, W Finland
Saar in Mähren *see* Žďár nad Sázavou
92 M10 **Saariselkä** *Lapp.* Suoločielgi. Lappi, N Finland
92 L10 **Saariselkä** *hill range* NE Finland
101 D20 **Saarland** *Fr.* Sarre. ◈ *state* SW Germany
Saarlautern *see* Saarlouis
101 D20 **Saarlouis** *prev.* Saarlautern. Saarland, SW Germany
108 E11 **Saaser Vispa** ≈ S Switzerland
137 X12 **Saatlı** *Rus.* Saatly. C Azerbaijan
Saatly *see* Saatlı
Saaz *see* Žatec
45 V9 **Saba** *island* N Netherlands Antilles
138 J7 **Sab' Ābār** *var.* Sab'a Biyar, Sa'b Bi'ār. Ḩimş, C Syria
Sab'a Biyar *see* Sab' Ābār
112 K11 **Šabac** Serbia, W Yugoslavia
105 W5 **Sabadell** Cataluña, E Spain
164 K12 **Sabae** Fukui, Honshū, SW Japan
169 V7 **Sabah** *prev.* British North Borneo, North Borneo. ◈ *state* East Malaysia
168 J8 **Sabak** *var.* Sabak Bernam. Selangor, Peninsular Malaysia
Sabak Bernam *see* Sabak
38 D16 **Sabak, Cape** *headland* Agattu Island, Alaska, USA
81 J20 **Sabaki** ≈ S Kenya
142 L2 **Sabalān, Kuhhā-ye** ▲ NW Iran
154 H7 **Sabalgarh** Madhya Pradesh, C India
44 E4 **Sabana, Archipiélago de** *island group* C Cuba
42 H7 **Sabanagrande** *var.* Sabana Grande. Francisco Morazán, S Honduras
54 E5 **Sabanalarga** Atlántico, N Colombia
41 W14 **Sabancuy** Campeche, SE Mexico
45 N8 **Sabaneta** NW Dominican Republic
54 J4 **Sabaneta** Falcón, N Venezuela
188 H4 **Sabaneta, Puntan** *prev.* Ushi Point. *headland* Saipan, S Northern Mariana Islands
171 X14 **Sabang** Irian Jaya, E Indonesia
116 L10 **Săbăoani** Neamţ, NE Romania
155 J26 **Sabaragamuwa Province** ◈ *province* C Sri Lanka
Sabaria *see* Szombathely
154 D10 **Sābarmati** ≈ NW India
171 S10 **Sabatai** Pulau Morotai, E Indonesia
141 Q15 **Sab'atayn, Ramlat as** *desert* C Yemen
107 I16 **Sabaudia** Lazio, C Italy
57 J19 **Sabaya** Oruro, S Bolivia
Sa'b Bi'ār *see* Sab' Ābār
Sabbioncello *see* Orebić
148 I8 **Şāberī, Hāmūn-e** *var.* Daryācheh-ye Hāmūn, Daryācheh-ye Sīstān. ◎ Afghanistan/Iran *see also* Sīstān, Daryācheh-ye
27 P2 **Sabetha** Kansas, C USA
75 P10 **Sabhā** C Libya
67 V13 **Sabi** *var.* Rio Save. ≈ Mozambique/Zimbabwe *see also* Save, Rio
118 E8 **Sabile** *Ger.* Zabeln. Talsi, NW Latvia
31 R14 **Sabina** Ohio, N USA
40 I3 **Sabinal** Chihuahua, N Mexico
25 Q12 **Sabinal** Texas, SW USA
25 Q11 **Sabinal River** ≈ Texas, SW USA
105 S4 **Sabiñánigo** Aragón, NE Spain
41 N6 **Sabinas** Coahuila de Zaragoza, NE Mexico
41 O8 **Sabinas Hidalgo** Nuevo León, NE Mexico
41 N6 **Sabinas, Río** ≈ NE Mexico
22 F9 **Sabine Lake** ◎ Louisiana/Texas, S USA
92 O3 **Sabine Land** *physical region* C Svalbard
25 W7 **Sabine River** ≈ Louisiana/Texas, SW USA
137 X12 **Sabirabad** C Azerbaijan
Sabkha *see* As Sabkhah
171 O4 **Sablayan** Mindoro, N Philippines
13 P16 **Sable, Cape** *headland* Newfoundland, SE Canada
23 X17 **Sable, Cape** *headland* Florida, SE USA
13 R16 **Sable Island** *island* Nova Scotia, SE Canada
14 L11 **Sables, Lac des** ◎ Quebec, SE Canada
14 E10 **Sables, Rivière aux** ≈ Ontario, S Canada
102 K7 **Sable-sur-Sarthe** Sarthe, NW France
127 U7 **Sablya, Gora** ▲ NW Russian Federation
77 U14 **Sabon Birnin Gwari** Kaduna, C Nigeria
77 V11 **Sabon Kafi** Zinder, C Niger
104 I6 **Sabor, Rio** ≈ N Portugal
14 J8 **Sabourin, Lac** ◎ Quebec, SE Canada
102 J14 **Sabres** Landes, SW France
195 X13 **Sabrina Coast** *physical region* Antarctica
140 M11 **Sabt al Ulayā** 'Asīr, SW Saudi Arabia
104 I8 **Sabugal** Guarda, N Portugal
29 Z13 **Sabula** Iowa, C USA
141 N13 **Şabyā** Jīzān, SW Saudi Arabia
Sabzawar *see* Sabzevār
Sabzawaran *see* Sabzvārān
143 S4 **Sabzevār** *var.* Sabzawar. Khorāsān, NE Iran
143 T12 **Sabzvārān** *var.* Sabzawaran; *prev.* Jiroft. Kermān, SE Iran
Sacajawea Peak *see* Matterhorn
82 C9 **Sacandica** Uíge, NW Angola
42 A2 **Sacatepéquez** *off.* Departamento de Sacatepéquez. ◈ *department* S Guatemala
104 F11 **Sacavém** Lisboa, W Portugal
29 T13 **Sac City** Iowa, C USA
105 P8 **Sacedón** Castilla-La Mancha, C Spain
116 J12 **Săcele** *Ger.* Vierdörfer, *Hung.* Négyfalu; *prev. Ger.* Sieben Dörfer, *Hung.* Hétfalu. Braşov, C Romania
12 C8 **Sachigo** Ontario, C Canada
12 C7 **Sachigo** ≈ Ontario, C Canada
12 C8 **Sachigo Lake** ◎ Ontario, C Canada
163 Y16 **Sach'ŏn** *Jap.* Sansenhō; *prev.* Samch'ŏnpŏ. S South Korea
101 O15 **Sachsen** *Eng.* Saxony, *Fr.* Saxe. ◈ *state* E Germany
101 K14 **Sachsen-Anhalt** *Eng.* Saxony-Anhalt. ◈ *state* C Germany
109 R9 **Sachsenburg** Salzburg, S Austria
Sachsenfeld *see* Žalec
8 I5 **Sachs Harbour** Banks Island, Northwest Territories, N Canada
Sächsisch-Reen/Sächsisch-Regen *see* Reghin
18 H8 **Sackets Harbor** New York, NE USA
13 P14 **Sackville** New Brunswick, SE Canada
19 P9 **Saco** Maine, NE USA
19 P8 **Saco River** ≈ Maine/New Hampshire, NE USA
35 O7 **Sacramento** *state capital* California, W USA
37 T14 **Sacramento Mountains** ▲▲ New Mexico, SW USA
35 N6 **Sacramento River** ≈ California, W USA
35 N5 **Sacramento Valley** *valley* California, W USA
36 I10 **Sacramento Wash** *valley* Arizona, SW USA
105 N15 **Sacratif, Cabo** *headland* S Spain
116 F9 **Săcueni** *prev.* Săcuieni, *Hung.* Székelyhid. Bihor, W Romania
Săcuieni *see* Săcueni
105 R4 **Sádaba** Aragón, NE Spain
Sá da Bandeira *see* Lubango
138 I6 **Şadad** Ḩimş, W Syria
141 O13 **Şa'dah** NW Yemen
167 O16 **Sadao** Songkhla, SW Thailand
142 L8 **Sadd-e Dez, Daryācheh-ye** ◎ W Iran
19 S3 **Saddleback Mountain** *hill* Maine, NE USA
19 P6 **Saddleback Mountain** ▲ Maine, NE USA
167 S14 **Sa Đec** Đông Thap, S Vietnam
141 W13 **Sadḩ** S Oman
76 J11 **Sadiola** Kayes, W Mali
149 R12 **Sādiqābād** Punjab, E Pakistan
153 Y10 **Sadiya** Assam, NE India
139 W9 **Sa'dīyah, Hawr as** ◎ E Iraq
165 N9 **Sado** *var.* Sadoga-shima. *island* C Japan
Sadoga-shima *see* Sado
104 F12 **Sado, Rio** ≈ S Portugal
114 I8 **Sadovets** Pleven, N Bulgaria
129 O11 **Sadovoye** Respublika Kalmykiya, SW Russian Federation
105 W9 **Sa Dragonera** *var.* Isla Dragonera. *island* Islas Baleares, Spain, W Mediterranean Sea
95 H20 **Sæby** Nordjylland, N Denmark
105 P9 **Saelices** Castilla-La Mancha, C Spain
Saena Julia *see* Siena
Saetabicula *see* Alzira
114 O12 **Safaalan** Tekirdağ, NW Turkey
Safad *see* Ẕefat
Şafāqis *see* Sfax
192 I16 **Safata Bay** *bay* Upolo, Samoa, C Pacific Ocean
Safed *see* Ẕefat
Safed, Āb-i- *see* Sefid, Darya-ye
139 X11 **Şaffāf, Ḩawr aş** *wetland* S Iraq
95 J16 **Säffle** Värmland, C Sweden
37 N15 **Safford** Arizona, SW USA
74 E7 **Safi** W Morocco
143 V9 **Safidābeh** Khorāsān, E Iran
142 M4 **Safīd, Rūd-e** ≈ NW Iran
128 I4 **Safonovo** Smolenskaya Oblast', W Russian Federation
136 H11 **Safranbolu** Karabük, N Turkey
139 Y13 **Safwān** SE Iraq
158 J16 **Saga** *var.* Gya'gya. Xizang Zizhiqu, W China
164 C14 **Saga** Saga, Kyūshū, SW Japan
164 C13 **Saga** *off.* Saga-ken. ◈ *prefecture* Kyūshū, SW Japan
165 P10 **Sagae** Yamagata, Honshū, C Japan
166 L3 **Sagaing** Sagaing, C Myanmar
166 L5 **Sagaing** ◈ *division* N Myanmar
165 N13 **Sagamihara** Kanagawa, Honshū, S Japan
165 N14 **Sagami-nada** *inlet* SW Japan
Sagan *see* Żagań
29 Y3 **Saganaga Lake** ◎ Minnesota, N USA
155 F18 **Sāgar** Karnātaka, W India
154 I9 **Sāgar** *prev.* Saugor. Madhya Pradesh, C India
15 S8 **Sagard** Quebec, SE Canada
Sagarmatha *see* Everest, Mount
Sagebrush State *see* Nevada
143 V11 **Sāghand** Yazd, C Iran
19 N14 **Sag Harbor** Long Island, New York, NE USA
Saghez *see* Saqqez
31 R8 **Saginaw** Michigan, N USA
31 R8 **Saginaw Bay** *lake bay* Michigan, N USA
144 H11 **Sagiz** Atyrau, W Kazakhstan
64 H6 **Saglek Bank** *undersea feature* W Labrador Sea
13 P5 **Saglek Bay** *bay* SW Labrador Sea
Saglouc/Sagluk *see* Salluit
103 X15 **Sagonne, Golfe de** *gulf* Corse, France, C Mediterranean Sea
105 P13 **Sagra** ▲ S Spain
104 F14 **Sagres** Faro, S Portugal
37 S7 **Saguache** Colorado, C USA
44 J7 **Sagua de Tánamo** Holguín, E Cuba
44 E5 **Sagua la Grande** Villa Clara, C Cuba
15 R7 **Saguenay** ≈ Quebec, SE Canada
74 C9 **Saguia al Hamra** *var.* As Saqia al Hamra. ≈ N Western Sahara
Sagunt/Saguntum *see* Sagunto
105 S9 **Sagunto** *var.* Sagunt, *Ar.* Murviedro; *anc.* Saguntum. País Valenciano, E Spain
138 H10 **Saḩāb** 'Ammān, NW Jordan
54 E6 **Sahagún** Córdoba, NW Colombia
104 L4 **Sahagún** Castilla-León, N Spain
141 X8 **Saḩam** N Oman
68 F9 **Sahara** *desert* Libya/Algeria
75 U9 **Sahara el Gharbîya** *var.* Aş Şaḩrā' al Gharbīyah, *Eng.* Western Desert. *desert* C Egypt
75 X9 **Sahara el Sharqîya** *var.* Aş Şaḩrā' ash Sharqīyah, *Eng.* Arabian Desert, Eastern Desert. *desert* E Egypt
Saharan Atlas *see* Atlas Saharien
152 J9 **Sahāranpur** Uttar Pradesh, N India
64 L10 **Saharan Seamounts** *var.* Saharian Seamounts. *undersea feature* E Atlantic Ocean
153 Q13 **Saharsa** Bihār, NE India
67 O7 **Sahel** *physical region* C Africa
153 R14 **Sāhibganj** Bihār, NE India
139 Q7 **Sahīlīyah** C Iraq
138 H4 **Sāḩilīyah, Jibāl as** ▲▲ NW Syria
114 M13 **Şahin** Tekirdağ, NW Turkey
149 U8 **Sāhīwāl** Punjab, E Pakistan
149 U9 **Sāhīwāl** *prev.* Montgomery. Punjab, E Pakistan
141 W11 **Saḩmah, Ramlat as** *desert* C Oman
139 T13 **Şaḩrā' al Ḩijārah** *desert* S Iraq
40 H5 **Sahuaripa** Sonora, NW Mexico
36 M16 **Sahuarita** Arizona, SW USA
40 L13 **Sahuayo** *var.* Sahuayo de José Mariá Morelos; *prev.* Sahuayo de Díaz, Sahuayo de Porfirio Díaz. Michoacán de Ocampo, SW Mexico
Sahuayo de Díaz/Sahuayo de José Mariá Morelos/Sahuayo de Porfirio Díaz *see* Sahuayo
173 W8 **Sahul Shelf** *undersea feature* N Timor Sea
167 P17 **Sai Buri** Pattani, SW Thailand
74 I6 **Saïda** NW Algeria
138 G7 **Saïda** *var.* Şaydā, Sayida; *anc.* Sidon. W Lebanon
Sa'īdābād *see* Sīrjān
80 B13 **Sa'id Bundas** Western Bahr el Ghazal, SW Sudan
186 E7 **Saidor** Madang, N PNG
153 S13 **Saidpur** *var.* Syedpur. Rajshahi, NW Bangladesh
108 C7 **Saignelégier** Jura, NW Switzerland
164 H11 **Saigō** Shimane, Dōgo, SW Japan
Saigon *see* Hô Chi Minh
162 I12 **Saihan Toroi** Nei Mongol Zizhiqu, N China
Saihon Tal *see* Sonid Youqi
Sai Hun *see* Syr Darya
92 M11 **Saija** Lappi, NE Finland
164 G14 **Saijō** Ehime, Shikoku, SW Japan
164 E15 **Saiki** Ōita, Kyūshū, SW Japan
93 N18 **Saimaa** ◎ SE Finland
93 N18 **Saimaa Canal** *Fin.* Saimaan Kanava, *Rus.* Saymenskiy Kanal. *canal* Finland/Russian Federation
Saimaan Kanava *see* Saimaa Canal
40 L10 **Saín Alto** Zacatecas, C Mexico
96 L12 **St Abb's Head** *headland* SE Scotland, UK
11 Y16 **St.Adolphe** Manitoba, S Canada
103 O15 **St-Affrique** Aveyron, S France
15 Q10 **St-Agapit** Quebec, SE Canada
97 O21 **St Albans** *anc.* Verulamium. E England, UK
18 L6 **Saint Albans** Vermont, NE USA

◆ Country ● Country Capital ◇ Dependent Territory ○ Dependent Territory Capital ◈ Administrative Region × International Airport ▲ Mountain ▲▲ Mountain Range ※ Volcano ≈ River ◎ Lake ▣ Reservoir

21 Q5 **Saint Albans** West Virginia, NE USA
St Alban's Head *see* St.Aldhelm's Head
11 Q14 **St.Albert** Alberta, SW Canada
99 M24 **St. Aldhelm's Head** *var.* St.Alban's Head. *headland* S England, UK
15 S8 **St-Alexandre** Quebec, SE Canada
15 O11 **St-Alexis-des-Monts** Quebec, SE Canada
103 P2 **St-Amand-les-Eaux** Nord, N France
103 O9 **St-Amand-Montrond** *var.* St-Amand-Mont-Rond. Cher, C France
15 Q7 **St-Ambroise** Quebec, SE Canada
173 P16 **St-André** NE Réunion
14 M12 **St-André-Avellin** Quebec, SE Canada
102 K12 **St-André-de-Cubzac** Gironde, SW France
96 K11 **St Andrews** E Scotland, UK
23 Q9 **Saint Andrews Bay** *bay* Florida, SE USA
23 W7 **Saint Andrew Sound** *sound* Georgia, SE USA
Saint Anna Trough *see* Svyataya Anna Trough
44 J11 **St.Ann's Bay** C Jamaica
13 T10 **St.Anthony** Newfoundland, SE Canada
33 R13 **Saint Anthony** Idaho, NW USA
182 M11 **Saint Arnaud** Victoria, SE Australia
185 I15 **St.Arnaud Range** ▲▲ South Island, NZ
15 T8 **St-Arsène** Quebec, SE Canada
13 R10 **St-Augustin** Quebec, E Canada
23 X9 **Saint Augustine** Florida, SE USA
97 H24 **St Austell** SW England, UK
103 T4 **St-Avold** Moselle, NE France
103 N17 **St-Barthélemy** ▲▲ S France
102 L17 **St-Béat** Haute-Garonne, S France
97 I15 **St Bees Head** *headland* NW England, UK
173 P16 **St-Benoit** E Réunion
103 T13 **St-Bonnet** Hautes-Alpes, SE France
St.Botolph's Town *see* Boston
97 G21 **St Brides Bay** *inlet* SW Wales, UK
102 H5 **St-Brieuc** Côtes d'Armor, NW France
102 H5 **St-Brieuc, Baie de** *bay* NW France
102 L7 **St-Calais** Sarthe, NW France
15 Q10 **St-Casimir** Quebec, SE Canada
14 H16 **St.Catharines** Ontario, S Canada
45 S14 **St.Catherine, Mount** ▲ N Grenada
64 C11 **St Catherine Point** *headland* E Bermuda
23 X6 **Saint Catherines Island** *island* Georgia, SE USA
97 M24 **St Catherine's Point** *headland* S England, UK
103 N13 **St-Céré** Lot, S France
108 A10 **St.Cergue** Vaud, W Switzerland
103 R11 **St-Chamond** Loire, E France
33 S16 **Saint Charles** Idaho, NW USA
27 X4 **Saint Charles** Missouri, C USA
103 P13 **St-Chély-d'Apcher** Lozère, S France
Saint Christopher-Nevis *see* Saint Kitts and Nevis
31 S9 **Saint Clair** Michigan, N USA
14 D17 **St.Clair** ≈ Canada/USA
183 O17 **St.Clair, Lake** ◎ Tasmania, SE Australia
14 C17 **St.Clair, Lake** *var.* Lac à L'eau Claire. ◎ Canada/USA
31 S10 **Saint Clair Shores** Michigan, N USA
103 S10 **St-Claude** *anc.* Condate. Jura, E France
45 X6 **St-Claude** Basse Terre, SW Guadeloupe
23 X12 **Saint Cloud** Florida, SE USA
29 U8 **Saint Cloud** Minnesota, N USA
45 T9 **Saint Croix** *island* S Virgin Islands (US)
30 J4 **Saint Croix Flowage** ⊞ Wisconsin, N USA
19 T5 **Saint Croix River** ≈ Canada/USA
29 W7 **Saint Croix River** ≈ Minnesota/Wisconsin, N USA
45 S14 **St.David's** SE Grenada
97 H21 **St David's** SW Wales, UK
97 G21 **St David's Head** *headland* SW Wales, UK
64 C12 **St David's Island** *island* E Bermuda
173 O16 **St-Denis** ○ (Réunion) NW Réunion
103 U6 **St-Dié** Vosges, NE France
103 R5 **St-Dizier** *anc.* Desiderii Fanum. Haute-Marne, N France
15 N11 **St-Donat** Quebec, SE Canada
15 N11 **Ste-Adèle** Quebec, SE Canada
15 N11 **Ste-Agathe-des-Monts** Quebec, SE Canada
172 I16 **Sainte Anne** *island* Inner Islands, NE Seychelles
11 Y16 **Ste.Anne** Manitoba, S Canada
45 R12 **Ste-Anne** Grande Terre, E Guadeloupe
45 Y6 **Ste-Anne** SE Martinique
15 Q10 **Ste-Anne** ≈ Quebec, SE Canada
15 W6 **Ste-Anne-des-Monts** Quebec, SE Canada
14 M10 **Ste-Anne-du-Lac** Quebec, SE Canada
15 U4 **Ste-Anne, Lac** ◎ Quebec, SE Canada
15 S10 **Ste-Apolline** Quebec, SE Canada
15 U7 **Ste-Blandine** Quebec, SE Canada
15 R10 **Ste-Claire** Quebec, SE Canada
15 Q10 **Ste-Croix** Quebec, SE Canada
108 B8 **Ste.Croix** Vaud, SW Switzerland
103 P14 **Ste-Énimie** Lozère, S France
27 Y6 **Sainte Genevieve** Missouri, C USA
103 S12 **St-Egrève** Isère, E France
39 T12 **Saint Elias, Cape** *headland* Kayak Island, Alaska, USA
39 U11 **Saint Elias, Mount** ▲ Alaska, USA
10 G8 **Saint Elias Mountains** ▲▲ Canada/USA
55 Y10 **St-Élie** N French Guiana
103 O10 **St-Eloy-les-Mines** Puy-de-Dôme, C France
15 S7 **Ste-Maguerite Nord-Est** ≈ Quebec, SE Canada
15 R7 **Ste-Marguerite** ≈ Quebec, SE Canada
15 V4 **Ste-Marguerite, Pointe** *headland* Quebec, SE Canada
15 V3 **Ste-Marguesite** ≈ Quebec, SE Canada
15 R10 **Ste-Marie** Quebec, SE Canada
45 Q11 **Ste-Marie** NE Martinique
173 P16 **Ste-Marie** NE Réunion
103 U6 **Ste-Marie-aux-Mines** Haut-Rhin, NE France
12 J14 **Ste-Marie, Lac** ⊞ Quebec, S Canada
172 K4 **Sainte Marie, Nosy** *island* E Madagascar
102 L8 **Ste-Maure-de-Touraine** Indre-et-Loire, C France
103 R4 **Ste-Menehould** Marne, NE France
Ste-Perpétue *see* Ste-Perpétue-de-l'Islet
15 S9 **Ste-Perpétue-de-l'Islet** *var.* Ste-Perpétue. Quebec, SE Canada
45 X11 **Ste-Rose** Basse Terre, N Guadeloupe
173 P16 **Ste-Rose** E Réunion
11 W15 **Ste.Rose du Lac** Manitoba, S Canada
102 J11 **Saintes** *anc.* Mediolanum. Charente-Maritime, W France
45 X7 **Saintes, Canal des** *channel* SW Guadeloupe
Saintes, Îles des *see* les Saintes
173 P16 **Ste-Suzanne** N Réunion
15 P10 **Ste-Thècle** Quebec, SE Canada
103 Q12 **St-Étienne** Loire, E France
102 M4 **St-Étienne-du-Rouvray** Seine-Maritime, N France
Saint Eustatius *see* Sint Eustatius
14 M11 **Ste-Véronique** Quebec, SE Canada
15 T7 **St-Fabien** Quebec, SE Canada
15 P7 **St-Félicien** Quebec, SE Canada
15 O11 **St-Félix-de-Valois** Quebec, SE Canada
103 Y14 **St-Florent** Corse, France, C Mediterranean Sea
103 Y14 **St-Florent, Golfe de** *gulf* Corse, France, C Mediterranean Sea
103 P6 **St-Florentin** Yonne, C France
103 N9 **St-Florent-sur-Cher** Cher, C France
103 P12 **St-Flour** Cantal, C France
26 H2 **Saint Francis** Kansas, C USA
83 H26 **St.Francis, Cape** *headland* S South Africa
27 X10 **Saint Francis River** ≈ Arkansas/Missouri, C USA
22 J8 **Saint Francisville** Louisiana, S USA
15 Q12 **St-François** ≈ Quebec, SE Canada
45 Y6 **St-François** Grande Terre, E Guadeloupe
15 R11 **St-François, Lac** ◎ Quebec, SE Canada
27 X7 **Saint Francois Mountains** ▲▲ Missouri, C USA
St-Gall/Saint Gall/St.Gallen *see* Sankt Gallen
102 L16 **St-Gaudens** Haute-Garonne, S France
15 R12 **St-Gédéon** Quebec, SE Canada
181 X10 **Saint George** Queensland, E Australia
64 B12 **St George** N Bermuda
38 K15 **Saint George** Saint George Island, Alaska, USA
21 S14 **Saint George** South Carolina, SE USA
36 J8 **Saint George** Utah, W USA
13 R12 **St.George, Cape** *headland* Newfoundland, E Canada
9 W13 **St.George, Cape** *headland* New Ireland, NE PNG
38 J15 **Saint George Island** *island* Pribilof Islands, Alaska, USA
23 S10 **Saint George Island** *island* Florida, SE USA
99 J19 **Saint-Georges** Liège, E Belgium
15 R11 **St-Georges** Quebec, SE Canada
55 Z11 **St-Georges** E French Guiana
45 R14 **St.George's** ● (Grenada) SW Grenada
13 R12 **St.George's Bay** *inlet* Newfoundland, E Canada
97 G21 **Saint George's Channel** *channel* Ireland/Wales, UK
186 H6 **St.George's Channel** *channel* NE PNG
64 B11 **St George's Island** *island* E Bermuda
99 I21 **Saint-Gérard** Namur, S Belgium
Saint-Germain *see* St-Germain-en-Laye
15 P12 **St-Germain-de-Grantham** Quebec, SE Canada
103 N5 **St-Germain-en-Laye** *var.* St-Germain. Yvelines, N France
102 H8 **St-Gildas, Pointe du** *headland* NW France
103 R15 **St-Gilles** Gard, S France
102 I9 **St-Gilles-Croix-de-Vie** Vendée, NW France
173 O16 **St-Gilles-les-Bains** W Réunion
102 M16 **St-Girons** Ariège, S France
Saint Gotthard *see* Szentgotthárd
108 G9 **St.Gotthard Tunnel** *tunnel* Ticino, S Switzerland
97 H22 **St Govan's Head** *headland* SW Wales, UK
34 M7 **Saint Helena** California, W USA
65 F24 **Saint Helena** ◇ *UK dependent territory* C Atlantic Ocean
67 O12 **Saint Helena** *island* C Atlantic Ocean
83 E25 **St.Helena Bay** *bay* SW South Africa
65 M16 **Saint Helena Fracture Zone** *tectonic feature* C Atlantic Ocean
34 M7 **Saint Helena, Mount** ▲ California, W USA
21 S15 **Saint Helena Sound** *inlet* South Carolina, SE USA
31 Q7 **Saint Helen, Lake** ◎ Michigan, N USA
183 Q16 **Saint Helens** Tasmania, SE Australia
97 K18 **St Helens** NW England, UK
32 G10 **Saint Helens** Oregon, NW USA
32 H10 **Saint Helens, Mount** ⛰ Washington, NW USA
97 L26 **St Helier** ○ (Jersey) S Jersey, Channel Islands
15 S9 **St-Hilarion** Quebec, SE Canada
99 K22 **Saint-Hubert** Luxembourg, SE Belgium
15 T8 **St-Hubert** Quebec, SE Canada
15 P12 **St-Hyacinthe** Quebec, SE Canada
St.Iago de la Vega *see* Spanish Town
31 Q4 **Saint Ignace** Michigan, N USA
15 O10 **St-Ignace-du-Lac** Quebec, SE Canada
12 D12 **St.Ignace Island** *island* Ontario, S Canada
108 C7 **St.Imier** Bern, W Switzerland
97 G25 **St Ives** SW England, UK
29 U10 **Saint James** Minnesota, N USA
10 I15 **St.James, Cape** *headland* Graham Island, British Columbia, SW Canada
15 O13 **St-Jean** *var.* St-Jean-sur-Richelieu. Quebec, SE Canada
55 X9 **St-Jean** NW French Guiana
15 R8 **St-Jean** ≈ Quebec, SE Canada
Saint-Jean-d'Acre *see* 'Akko
102 K11 **St-Jean-d'Angély** Charente-Maritime, W France
103 N7 **St-Jean-de-Braye** Loiret, C France
102 I16 **St-Jean-de-Luz** Pyrénées-Atlantiques, SW France
103 T12 **St-Jean-de-Maurienne** Savoie, E France
102 I9 **St-Jean-de-Monts** Vendée, NW France
103 Q14 **St-Jean-du-Gard** Gard, S France
15 Q7 **St-Jean, Lac** ◎ Quebec, SE Canada
102 I16 **St-Jean-Pied-de-Port** Pyrénées-Atlantiques, SW France
15 S9 **St-Jean-Port-Joli** Quebec, SE Canada
St-Jean-sur-Richelieu *see* St-Jean
15 N12 **St-Jérôme** Quebec, SE Canada
25 T5 **Saint Jo** Texas, SW USA
13 O15 **St.John** New Brunswick, SE Canada
26 L6 **Saint John** Kansas, C USA
76 K16 **Saint John** ≈ C Liberia
45 T9 **Saint John** *island* C Virgin Islands (US)
22 I6 **Saint John, Lake** ◎ Louisiana, S USA
19 Q2 **Saint John** *Fr.* Saint-John. ≈ Canada/USA
45 W10 **St John's** ● (Antigua and Barbuda) Antigua, Antigua and Barbuda
13 V12 **St.John's** Newfoundland, E Canada
37 O12 **Saint Johns** Arizona, SW USA
31 Q9 **Saint Johns** Michigan, N USA
13 V12 **St.John's** ✈ Newfoundland, E Canada
23 X11 **Saint Johns River** ≈ Florida, SE USA
45 N12 **St.Joseph** W Dominica
173 P17 **St-Joseph** S Réunion
22 J6 **Saint Joseph** Louisiana, S USA
31 O10 **Saint Joseph** Michigan, N USA
27 R3 **Saint Joseph** Missouri, C USA
20 I10 **Saint Joseph** Tennessee, S USA
22 R9 **Saint Joseph Bay** *bay* Florida, SE USA
15 R11 **St-Joseph-de-Beauce** Quebec, SE Canada
12 C10 **St.Joseph, Lake** ◎ Ontario, C Canada
31 Q11 **Saint Joseph River** ≈ N USA
14 C11 **Saint Joseph's Island** *island* Ontario, S Canada
15 N11 **St-Jovite** Quebec, SE Canada
121 P16 **St Julian's** N Malta
St-Julien *see* St-Julien-en-Genevois
103 T10 **St-Julien-en-Genevois** *var.* St-Julien. Haute-Savoie, E France
102 M11 **St-Junien** Haute-Vienne, C France
103 Q11 **St-Just-St-Rambert** Loire, E France
96 D8 **St Kilda** *island* NW Scotland, UK
45 V10 **Saint Kitts** *island* Saint Kitts and Nevis
45 U10 **Saint Kitts and Nevis** *off.* Federation of Saint Christopher and Nevis, *var.* Saint Christopher-Nevis. ◆ *commonwealth republic* E West Indies
11 X16 **St.Laurent** Manitoba, S Canada
St-Laurent *see* St-Laurent-du-Maroni
55 X9 **St-Laurent-du-Maroni** *var.* St-Laurent. NW French Guiana
St-Laurent, Fleuve *see* St.Lawrence
102 J12 **St-Laurent-Médoc** Gironde, SW France
13 N12 **St.Lawrence** *Fr.* Fleuve St-Laurent. ≈ Canada/USA
13 Q12 **St.Lawrence, Gulf of** *gulf* NW Atlantic Ocean
38 K10 **Saint Lawrence Island** *island* Alaska, USA
14 M14 **Saint Lawrence River** ≈ Canada/USA
99 L25 **Saint-Léger** Luxembourg, SE Belgium
13 N14 **St.Léonard** New Brunswick, SE Canada
15 P11 **St-Léonard** Quebec, SE Canada
173 O17 **St-Leu** W Réunion
102 J4 **St-Lô** *anc.* Briovera, Laudus. Manche, N France
11 T15 **St.Louis** Saskatchewan, S Canada
103 V7 **St-Louis** Haut-Rhin, NE France
173 O17 **St-Louis** S Réunion
76 G10 **Saint Louis** NW Senegal
27 X4 **Saint Louis** Missouri, C USA
29 W5 **Saint Louis River** ≈ Minnesota, N USA
103 T7 **St-Loup-sur-Semouse** Haute-Saône, E France
15 O12 **St-Luc** Quebec, SE Canada
83 L22 **St.Lucia** KwaZulu/Natal, E South Africa
45 X13 **Saint Lucia** ◆ *commonwealth republic* SE West Indies
47 S3 **Saint Lucia** *island* SE West Indies
83 L22 **St.Lucia, Cape** *headland* E South Africa
45 Y13 **Saint Lucia Channel** *channel* Martinique/Saint Lucia
23 Y14 **Saint Lucie Canal** *canal* Florida, SE USA
23 Z13 **Saint Lucie Inlet** *inlet* Florida, SE USA
96 L2 **St Magnus Bay** *bay* N Scotland, UK
102 K10 **St-Maixent-l'École** Deux-Sèvres, W France
11 Y16 **St.Malo** Manitoba, S Canada
102 I5 **St-Malo** Ille-et-Vilaine, NW France
102 H4 **St-Malo, Golfe de** *gulf* NW France
44 L9 **St-Marc** C Haiti
44 L9 **St-Marc, Canal de** *channel* W Haiti
55 Y12 **Saint-Marcel, Mont** ▲ S French Guiana
103 S12 **St-Marcellin-le-Mollard** Isère, E France
96 K5 **St Margaret's Hope** NE Scotland, UK
32 M9 **Saint Maries** Idaho, NW USA
23 T9 **Saint Marks** Florida, SE USA
108 D11 **St.Martin** Valais, SW Switzerland
Saint Martin *see* Sint Maarten
31 O5 **Saint Martin Island** *island* Michigan, N USA
22 I9 **Saint Martinville** Louisiana, S USA
185 E20 **St.Mary, Mount** ▲ South Island, NZ
186 E8 **St.Mary, Mount** ▲ S PNG
182 I6 **Saint Mary Peak** ▲ South Australia
183 Q16 **Saint Marys** Tasmania, SE Australia
14 E16 **St.Marys** Ontario, S Canada
38 M11 **Saint Marys** Alaska, USA
23 W8 **Saint Marys** Georgia, SE USA
27 P4 **Saint Marys** Kansas, C USA
31 Q4 **Saint Marys** Ohio, N USA
21 R3 **Saint Marys** West Virginia, NE USA
23 W8 **Saint Marys River** ≈ Florida/Georgia, SE USA
31 Q4 **Saint Marys River** ≈ Michigan, N USA
102 D6 **St-Mathieu, Pointe** *headland* NW France
38 J12 **Saint Matthew Island** *island* Alaska, USA
21 R13 **Saint Matthews** South Carolina, SE USA
St.Matthew's Island *see* Zadetkyi Kyun
186 G4 **St.Matthias Group** *island group* NE PNG
108 C11 **St.Maurice** Valais, SW Switzerland
15 P9 **St-Maurice** ≈ Quebec, SE Canada
102 J13 **St-Médard-en-Jalles** Gironde, SW France
39 N10 **Saint Michael** Alaska, USA
St.Michel *see* Mikkeli
15 N10 **St-Michel-des-Saints** Quebec, SE Canada
103 S5 **St-Mihiel** Meuse, NE France
108 J10 **St.Moritz** *Ger.* Sankt Moritz, *Rmsch.* San Murezzan. Graubünden, SE Switzerland
102 H8 **St-Nazaire** Loire-Atlantique, NW France
Saint Nicholas *see* São Nicolau
Saint-Nicolas *see* Sint-Niklaas
103 N1 **St-Omer** Pas-de-Calais, N France
102 J11 **Saintonge** *cultural region* W France
15 S9 **St-Pacôme** Quebec, SE Canada
15 S10 **St-Pamphile** Quebec, SE Canada
15 S9 **St-Pascal** Quebec, SE Canada
14 J11 **St-Patrice, Lac** ◎ Quebec, SE Canada
11 R14 **St.Paul** Alberta, SW Canada
173 O16 **St-Paul** NW Réunion
38 K14 **Saint Paul** Saint Paul Island, Alaska, USA
29 V8 **Saint Paul** *state capital* Minnesota, N USA
29 P15 **Saint Paul** Nebraska, C USA
21 P7 **Saint Paul** Virginia, NE USA
77 Q17 **Saint Paul, Cape** *headland* S Ghana
103 O17 **St-Paul-de-Fenouillet** Pyrénées-Orientales, S France
65 K14 **Saint Paul Fracture Zone** *tectonic feature* E Atlantic Ocean
38 J14 **Saint Paul Island** *island* Pribilof Islands, Alaska, USA
102 J15 **St-Paul-les-Dax** Landes, SW France
21 U11 **Saint Pauls** North Carolina, SE USA
Saint Paul's Bay *see* San Pawl il-Bahar
191 R16 **St Paul's Point** *headland* Pitcairn Island, Pitcairn Islands
29 U10 **Saint Peter** Minnesota, N USA
97 L26 **St Peter Port** ○ (Guernsey) C Guernsey, Channel Islands
23 V13 **Saint Petersburg** Florida, SE USA
Saint Petersburg *see* Sankt-Peterburg
23 V13 **Saint Petersburg Beach** Florida, SE USA
173 P17 **St-Philippe** SE Réunion
45 Q11 **St-Pierre** NW Martinique
173 O17 **St-Pierre** SW Réunion
13 S13 **St-Pierre and Miquelon** *Fr.* Îles St-Pierre et Miquelon. ◇ *French territorial collectivity* NE North America
15 P11 **St-Pierre, Lac** ◎ Quebec, SE Canada
102 F5 **St-Pol-de-Léon** Finistère, NW France
103 O2 **St-Pol-sur-Ternoise** Pas-de-Calais, N France
St. Pons *see* St-Pons-de-Thomières
103 O16 **St-Pons-de-Thomières** *var.* St.Pons. Hérault, S France
103 P10 **St-Pourçain-sur-Sioule** Allier, C France
15 S11 **St-Prosper** Quebec, SE Canada
103 P3 **St-Quentin** Aisne, N France
15 R10 **St-Raphaël** Quebec, SE Canada
103 U15 **St-Raphaël** Var, SE France
15 Q10 **St-Raymond** Quebec, SE Canada
33 O9 **Saint Regis** Montana, NW USA
18 J7 **Saint Regis River** ≈ New York, NE USA
103 R15 **St-Rémy-de-Provence** Bouches-du-Rhône, SE France
15 V6 **St-René-de-Matane** Quebec, SE Canada
102 M9 **St-Savin** Vienne, W France
15 S8 **St-Siméon** Quebec, SE Canada
23 X7 **Saint Simons Island** *island* Georgia, SE USA
191 Y2 **Saint Stanislas Bay** *bay* Kiritimati, E Kiribati
13 O15 **St.Stephen** New Brunswick, SE Canada
39 X12 **Saint Terese** Alaska, USA
14 E17 **St.Thomas** Ontario, S Canada
29 Q2 **Saint Thomas** North Dakota, N USA
45 T9 **Saint Thomas** *island* W Virgin Islands (US)
Saint Thomas *see* São Tomé, Sao Tome and Principe
Saint Thomas *see* Charlotte Amalie, Virgin Islands (US)
15 P10 **St-Tite** Quebec, SE Canada
Saint-Trond *see* Sint-Truiden
103 U16 **St-Tropez** Var, SE France
Saint Ubes *see* Setúbal
102 L3 **St-Valéry-en-Caux** Seine-Maritime, N France
103 Q9 **St-Vallier** Saône-et-Loire, C France
106 B7 **St-Vincent** Valle d'Aosta, NW Italy
45 Q14 **Saint Vincent** *island* N Saint Vincent and the Grenadines
Saint Vincent *see* São Vicente
45 W14 **Saint Vincent and the Grenadines** ◆ *commonwealth republic* SE West Indies
Saint Vincent, Cape *see* São Vicente, Cabo de
102 I15 **St-Vincent-de-Tyrosse** Landes, SW France
182 I9 **Saint Vincent, Gulf** *gulf* South Australia
23 R10 **Saint Vincent Island** *island* Florida, SE USA
45 T12 **Saint Vincent Passage** *passage* Saint Lucia/Saint Vincent and the Grenadines
183 N18 **Saint Vincent, Point** *headland* Tasmania, SE Australia
Saint-Vith *see* Sankt-Vith
11 S14 **St.Walburg** Saskatchewan, S Canada
St Wolfgangsee *see* Wolfgangsee
102 M11 **St-Yrieix-la-Perche** Haute-Vienne, C France
Saint Yves *see* Setúbal
15 Y5 **St-Yvon** Quebec, SE Canada
188 H5 **Saipan** *island* ● (Northern Mariana Islands) S Northern Mariana Islands
188 H6 **Saipan Channel** *channel* S Northern Mariana Islands
188 H6 **Saipan International Airport** ✈ Saipan, S Northern Mariana Islands
74 G6 **Saïs** ✈ (Fès) C Morocco
Saishū *see* Cheju
Saishū *see* Cheju-do
102 J16 **Saison** ≈ SW France
169 R10 **Sai, Sungai** ≈ Borneo, N Indonesia
165 N13 **Saitama** *off.* Saitama-ken. ◈ *prefecture* Honshū, S Japan
Saiyid Abid *see* Sayyid 'Abīd
57 J19 **Sajama, Nevado** ▲ W Bolivia
141 V13 **Sājir, Ras** *headland* S Oman
111 M20 **Sajószentpéter** Borsod-Abaúj-Zemplén, NE Hungary
83 F24 **Sak** ≈ SW South Africa
81 J18 **Saka** Coast, E Kenya
167 P11 **Sa Kaeo** Prachin Buri, C Thailand
164 J14 **Sakai** Ōsaka, Honshū, SW Japan
164 H14 **Sakaide** Kagawa, Shikoku, SW Japan
164 H12 **Sakaiminato** Tottori, Honshū, SW Japan
140 M3 **Sakākah** Al Jawf, NW Saudi Arabia
28 L4 **Sakakawea, Lake** ◎ North Dakota, N USA
12 J9 **Sakami, Lac** ◎ Quebec, C Canada
79 O26 **Sakania** Katanga, SE Dem. Rep. Congo (Zaire)
146 K12 **Sakar** Lebapskiy Velayat, E Turkmenistan
172 H7 **Sakaraha** Toliara, SW Madagascar
146 I14 **Sakar-Chaga** *Turkm.* Sakarchäge. Maryyskiy Velayat, C Turkmenistan
Sakarchäge *see* Sakar-Chaga
Sak'art'velo *see* Georgia
136 F11 **Sakarya** ◈ *province* NW Turkey
136 F12 **Sakarya Nehri** ≈ NW Turkey
150 K13 **Sakasaul'skiy** *var.* Saksaul'skoye *Kaz.* Sekseūil. Kyzylorda, S Kazakhstan
Saksaul'skoye *see* Sakasaul'skiy
165 P9 **Sakata** Yamagata, Honshū, C Japan
123 P9 **Sakha (Yakutiya), Respublika** *var.* Respublika Yakutiya, Yakutiya, *Eng.* Yakutia. ◈ *autonomous republic* NE Russian Federation
Sakhalin *see* Sakhalin, Ostrov
192 I3 **Sakhalin, Ostrov** *var.* Sakhalin. *island* SE Russian Federation
123 U12 **Sakhalinskaya Oblast'** ◈ *province* SE Russian Federation
123 T12 **Sakhalinskiy Zaliv** *gulf* E Russian Federation
Sakhnovshchina *see* Sakhnovshchyna
117 U6 **Sakhnovshchyna** *Rus.* Sakhnovshchina. Kharkivs'ka Oblast', E Ukraine
Sakhon Nakhon *see* Sakon Nakhon
Sakhtsar *see* Rāmsar
Saki *see* Saky
137 W10 **Şäki** *Rus.* Sheki; *prev.* Nukha. NW Azerbaijan
118 E13 **Šakiai** *Ger.* Schaken. Šakiai, S Lithuania
165 O16 **Sakishima-shotō** *var.* Sakisima Syotô. *island group* SW Japan
Sakiz *see* Saqqez
Sakiz-Adasi *see* Chíos
155 F19 **Sakleshpur** Karnātaka, E India
167 S9 **Sakon Nakhon** *var.* Muang Sakon Nakhon, Sakhon Nakhon. Sakon Nakhon, E Thailand
149 P15 **Sakrand** Sind, SE Pakistan
83 F24 **Sak River** *Afr.* Sakrivier. Northern Cape, W South Africa
Sakrivier *see* Sak River
Saksaul'skiy *see* Saksaul'skoye
144 K13 **Saksaul'skoye** *prev.* Saksaul'skiy, *Kaz.* Sekseūil. Kzylorda, S Kazakhstan
95 I25 **Sakskøbing** Storstrøm, SE Denmark
165 N12 **Saku** Nagano, Honshū, S Japan
117 S13 **Saky** *Rus.* Saki. Respublika Krym, S Ukraine
76 E9 **Sal** *island* Ilhas de Barlavento, NE Cape Verde
129 N12 **Sal** ≈ SW Russian Federation
111 I21 **Sal'a** *Hung.* Sellye, Vágsellye. Nitriansky Kraj, SW Slovakia
95 N15 **Sala** Västmanland, C Sweden
15 N13 **Salaberry-de-Valleyfield** *var.* Valleyfield. Quebec, SE Canada
118 G7 **Salacgrīva** *Est.* Salatsi. Limbaži, N Latvia
107 M18 **Sala Consilina** Campania, S Italy
40 C2 **Salada, Laguna** ◎ NW Mexico
61 D14 **Saladas** Corrientes, NE Argentina
61 C21 **Saladillo** Buenos Aires, E Argentina
61 B16 **Saladillo, Río** ≈ C Argentina
25 T9 **Salado** Texas, SW USA
63 J16 **Salado, Arroyo** ≈ SE Argentina
37 Q12 **Salado, Rio** ≈ New Mexico, SW USA
61 D21 **Salado, Río** ≈ E Argentina
62 J12 **Salado, Río** ≈ C Argentina
41 N7 **Salado, Río** ≈ NE Mexico
143 N6 **Salafchegān** *var.* Sarafjagān. Qom, N Iran
77 Q15 **Salaga** C Ghana
192 G5 **Sala'ilua** Savai'i, W Samoa
116 G9 **Sălaj** ◈ *county* NW Romania
83 H20 **Salajwe** Kweneng, SE Botswana
78 H9 **Salal** Kanem, W Chad
80 I6 **Salala** Red Sea, NE Sudan
141 V13 **Şalālah** SW Oman
42 D5 **Salamá** Baja Verapaz, C Guatemala
42 J6 **Salamá** Olancho, C Honduras
62 G10 **Salamanca** Coquimbo, C Chile
41 N13 **Salamanca** Guanajuato, C Mexico
104 K7 **Salamanca** *anc.* Helmantica, Salmantica. Castilla-León, NW Spain
18 D11 **Salamanca** New York, NE USA
104 J7 **Salamanca** ◈ *province* Castilla-León, W Spain
63 J19 **Salamanca, Pampa de** *plain* S Argentina
78 J12 **Salamat** *off.* Préfecture du Salamat. ◈ *prefecture* SE Chad
78 I12 **Salamat, Bahr** ≈ S Chad
54 F5 **Salamina** Magdalena, N Colombia
115 G19 **Salamína** *var.* Salamís. Salamína, C Greece
115 G19 **Salamína** *island* C Greece
Salamís *see* Salamína

◆ Country ● Country Capital ◇ Dependent Territory ○ Dependent Territory Capital ◈ Administrative Region ✈ International Airport ▲ Mountain ▲▲ Mountain Range ⛰ Volcano ≈ River ◎ Lake ⊞ Reservoir

138 I5 Salamīyah var. As Salamīyah. Ḩamāh, W Syria
31 P12 Salamonie Lake ⊞ Indiana, N USA
31 P12 Salamonie River Indiana, N USA
Salang see Phuket
192 I16 Salani Upolu, SE Samoa
118 C11 Salantai Kretinga, NW Lithuania
104 K2 Salas Asturias, N Spain
105 O5 Salas de los Infantes Castilla-León, N Spain
102 M16 Salat S France
189 V13 Salat island Chuuk, C Micronesia
169 Q16 Salatiga Jawa, C Indonesia
189 V13 Salat Pass passage W Pacific Ocean
Salatsi see Salacgrīva
167 T10 Salavan var. Saravan, Saravane. Salavan, S Laos
129 V6 Salavat Respublika Bashkortostan, W Russian Federation
56 C12 Salaverry La Libertad, N Peru
171 T12 Salawati, Pulau island E Indonesia
193 R10 Sala y Gomez island Chile, E Pacific Ocean
Sala y Gomez Fracture Zone see Sala y Gomez Ridge
193 S10 Sala y Gomez Ridge var. Sala y Gomez Fracture Zone. tectonic feature SE Pacific Ocean
61 A22 Salazar Buenos Aires, E Argentina
54 G7 Salazar Norte de Santander, N Colombia
Salazar see N'Dalatando
173 P16 Salazie C Réunion
103 N8 Salbris Loir-et-Cher, C France
57 G15 Salcantay, Nevado ▲ C Peru
45 O8 Salcedo N Dominican Republic
39 S9 Salcha River Alaska, USA
119 H15 Šalčininkai Šalčininkai, SE Lithuania
Saldae see Béjaïa
54 E11 Saldaña Tolima, C Colombia
104 M4 Saldaña Castilla-León, N Spain
83 E25 Saldanha Western Cape, SW South Africa
Salduba see Zaragoza
61 B23 Saldungaray Buenos Aires, E Argentina
118 D9 Saldus Ger. Frauenburg. Saldus, W Latvia
183 P13 Sale Victoria, SE Australia
74 F6 Salé NW Morocco
74 F6 Salé × (Rabat) W Morocco
Salehābād see Andīmeshk
170 M16 Saleh, Teluk bay Nusa Tenggara, S Indonesia
122 H8 Salekhard prev. Obdorsk. Yamalo-Nenetskiy Avtonomnyy Okrug, N Russian Federation
192 H16 Sālelologa Savai'i, C Samoa
155 H21 Salem Tamil Nādu, SE India
27 V9 Salem Arkansas, C USA
30 L15 Salem Illinois, N USA
31 P15 Salem Indiana, N USA
19 P11 Salem Massachusetts, NE USA
27 V6 Salem Missouri, C USA
18 I16 Salem New Jersey, NE USA
31 U12 Salem Ohio, N USA
32 G12 Salem state capital Oregon, NW USA
29 Q11 Salem South Dakota, N USA
36 L4 Salem Utah, W USA
21 S7 Salem Virginia, NE USA
21 R3 Salem West Virginia, NE USA
107 H23 Salemi Sicilia, Italy, C Mediterranean Sea
Salemy see As Sālimī
94 K12 Sälen Dalarna, C Sweden
107 Q18 Salentina, Campi Puglia, SE Italy
107 Q18 Salentina, Penisola peninsula SE Italy
107 L18 Salerno anc. Salernum. Campania, S Italy
107 L18 Salerno, Golfo di Eng. Gulf of Salerno. gulf S Italy
Salerno, Gulf of see Salerno, Golfo di
Salernum see Salerno
97 K17 Salford NW England, UK
Salgir see Salhyr
111 K21 Salgótarján Nógrád, N Hungary
59 O15 Salgueiro Pernambuco, E Brazil
94 C13 Salhus Hordaland, S Norway
117 T12 Salhyr Rus. Salgir. S Ukraine
171 Q9 Salibabu, Pulau island N Indonesia
37 S6 Salida Colorado, C USA
102 J15 Salies-de-Béarn Pyrénées-Atlantiques, SW France
136 C14 Salihli Manisa, W Turkey
119 K18 Salihorsk Rus. Soligorsk. Minskaya Voblasts', S Belarus
119 K18 Salihorskaye Vodaskhovishcha ⊞ C Belarus
83 N14 Salima Central, C Malawi
166 L5 Salin Magwe, W Myanmar
27 N4 Salina Kansas, C USA
36 L5 Salina Utah, W USA
41 S17 Salina Cruz Oaxaca, SE Mexico
107 L22 Salina, Isola island Isole Eolie, S Italy
44 J5 Salina Point headland Acklins Island, SE Bahamas
56 A7 Salinas Guayas, W Ecuador
40 M11 Salinas var. Salinas de Hidalgo. San Luis Potosí, C Mexico
45 T6 Salinas C Puerto Rico
35 O10 Salinas California, W USA
Salinas, Cabo de see Salines, Cap de ses
Salinas de Hidalgo see Salinas
82 A13 Salinas, Ponta das headland W Angola
45 O10 Salinas, Punta headland S Dominican Republic
Salinas, Río see Chixoy, Río
35 O11 Salinas River California, W USA
22 H6 Saline Lake ⊙ Louisiana, S USA
25 R17 Salineno Texas, SW USA
27 V14 Saline River Arkansas, C USA
30 M17 Saline River Illinois, N USA
105 X10 Salines, Cap de ses var. Cabo de Salinas. headland Mallorca, Spain, W Mediterranean Sea
Salisburg see Mazsalaca
45 O12 Salisbury var. Baroui. W Dominica
97 M23 Salisbury var. New Sarum. S England, UK
21 Y4 Salisbury Maryland, NE USA
27 T3 Salisbury Missouri, C USA
21 S9 Salisbury North Carolina, SE USA
Salisbury see Harare
9 Q7 Salisbury Island island Nunavut, NE Canada
Salisbury, Lake see Bisina, Lake
97 L23 Salisbury Plain plain S England, UK
21 R14 Salkehatchie River South Carolina, SE USA
138 I9 Şalkhad As Suwaydā', SW Syria
92 M12 Salla Lappi, NE Finland
103 U11 Sallanches Haute-Savoie, E France
105 V5 Sallent Cataluña, NE Spain
61 A22 Salliqueló Buenos Aires, E Argentina
27 R10 Sallisaw Oklahoma, C USA
80 I7 Sallom Red Sea, NE Sudan
12 J2 Salluit prev. Saglouc, Sagluk. Quebec, NE Canada
Sallūm, Khalīj as see Salûm, Gulf of
13 S11 Sally's Cove Newfoundland, E Canada
139 W9 Salmān Bin 'Arāzah E Iraq
Salmantica see Salamanca
142 I2 Salmās prev. Dilman, Shāpūr. Āzarbāyjān-e Bākhtarī, NW Iran
126 I11 Salmi Respublika Kareliya, NW Russian Federation
33 P12 Salmon Idaho, NW USA
11 N16 Salmon Arm British Columbia, SW Canada
192 L5 Salmon Bank undersea feature N Pacific Ocean
Salmon Leap see Leixlip
34 L2 Salmon Mountains ▲ California, W USA
14 J15 Salmon Point headland Ontario, SE Canada
33 N11 Salmon River Idaho, NW USA
18 K6 Salmon River New York, NE USA
33 N12 Salmon River Mountains ▲ Idaho, NW USA
18 I9 Salmon River Reservoir ⊞ New York, NE USA
93 K19 Salo Länsi-Suomi, W Finland
106 F7 Salò Lombardia, N Italy
Salona/Salonae see Solin
103 S15 Salon-de-Provence Bouches-du-Rhône, SE France
Salonica/Salonika see Thessaloníki
115 I14 Salonikós, Akrotírio headland Thásos, E Greece
116 F10 Salonta Hung. Nagyszalonta. Bihor, W Romania
104 I9 Salor W Spain
105 U6 Salou Cataluña, NE Spain
76 H11 Saloum C Senegal
42 H4 Sal, Punta headland NW Honduras
92 N3 Salpynten headland W Svalbard
138 I3 Salqīn Idlib, W Syria
93 F14 Salsbruket Nord-Trøndelag, C Norway
128 M13 Sal'sk Rostovskaya Oblast', SW Russian Federation
107 K25 Salso Sicilia, Italy, C Mediterranean Sea
107 J25 Salso Sicilia, Italy, C Mediterranean Sea
106 E9 Salsomaggiore Terme Emilia-Romagna, N Italy
Salt see As Salṭ
62 J6 Salta Salta, NW Argentina
62 K6 Salta off. Provincia de Salta. ◆ province N Argentina
97 I24 Saltash SW England, UK
24 I8 Salt Basin basin Texas, SW USA
11 V16 Saltcoats Saskatchewan, S Canada
30 L13 Salt Creek Illinois, N USA
24 J9 Salt Draw Texas, SW USA
97 F21 Saltee Islands island group SE Ireland
92 G12 Saltfjorden inlet C Norway
24 I8 Salt Flat Texas, SW USA
27 N8 Salt Fork Arkansas River Oklahoma, C USA
31 T13 Salt Fork Lake ⊞ Ohio, N USA
26 J11 Salt Fork Red River Oklahoma/Texas, C USA
95 J23 Saltholm island E Denmark
41 N8 Saltillo Coahuila de Zaragoza, NE Mexico
182 L5 Salt Lake salt lake New South Wales, SE Australia
37 V15 Salt Lake ⊙ New Mexico, SW USA
36 K2 Salt Lake City state capital Utah, W USA
61 C20 Salto Buenos Aires, E Argentina
61 D17 Salto Salto, N Uruguay
61 E17 Salto ◆ department N Uruguay
107 I14 Salto C Italy
62 Q6 Salto del Guairá Canindeyú, E Paraguay
61 D17 Salto Grande, Embalse de var. Lago de Salto Grande. ⊞ Argentina/Uruguay
Salto Grande, Lago de see Salto Grande, Embalse de
35 W16 Salton Sea ⊙ California, W USA
60 I12 Salto Santiago, Represa de ⊞ S Brazil
149 U7 Salt Range ▲ E Pakistan
36 M13 Salt River Arizona, SW USA
20 L5 Salt River Kentucky, S USA
27 V3 Salt River Missouri, C USA
95 F17 Saltrød Aust-Agder, S Norway
95 P16 Saltsjöbaden Stockholm, C Sweden
92 G12 Saltstraumen Nordland, C Norway
21 Q7 Saltville Virginia, NE USA
Saluces/Saluciae see Saluzzo
21 Q12 Saluda South Carolina, SE USA
21 X6 Saluda Virginia, NE USA
21 Q12 Saluda River South Carolina, SE USA
75 T7 Salûm var. As Sallūm. NW Egypt
152 F14 Sālūmbar Rājasthān, N India
75 T7 Salûm, Gulf of Ar. Khalīj as Sallūm. gulf Egypt/Libya
171 O11 Salumpaga Sulawesi, N Indonesia
155 M14 Sālūr Andhra Pradesh, E India
55 Y9 Salut, Îles du island group N French Guiana
106 A9 Saluzzo Fr. Saluces; anc. Saluciae. Piemonte, NW Italy
63 F23 Salvación, Bahía bay S Chile
59 P17 Salvador prev. São Salvador. Bahia, E Brazil
65 E24 Salvador East Falkland, Falkland Islands
22 K10 Salvador, Lake ⊙ Louisiana, S USA
Salvaleón de Higüey see Higüey
104 F10 Salvaterra de Magos Santarém, C Portugal
41 N13 Salvatierra Guanajuato, C Mexico
105 P3 Salvatierra Basq. Agurain. País Vasco, N Spain
Salwa/Salwah see As Salwā
166 M7 Salween Bur. Thanlwin, Chin. Nu Chiang, Nu Jiang. SE Asia
137 Y12 Salyan Rus. Sal'yany. SE Azerbaijan
153 N11 Salyan var. Sallyana. Mid Western, W Nepal
Sal'yany see Salyan
21 O6 Salyersville Kentucky, S USA
109 V6 Salza E Austria
109 Q7 Salzach Austria/Germany
109 Q6 Salzburg anc. Juvavum. Salzburg, N Austria
109 O8 Salzburg off. Land Salzburg. ◆ state C Austria
Salzburg see Ocna Sibiului
Salzburg Alps see Salzburger Kalkalpen
109 Q7 Salzburger Kalkalpen Eng. Salzburg Alps. ▲ C Austria
100 J13 Salzgitter prev. Watenstedt-Salzgitter. Niedersachsen, C Germany
101 G14 Salzkotten Nordrhein-Westfalen, W Germany
100 K11 Salzwedel Sachsen-Anhalt, N Germany
152 D11 Sām Rājasthān, NW India
Samac see Bosanski Šamac
54 G9 Samacá Boyacá, C Colombia
40 I7 Samachique Chihuahua, N Mexico
141 Y8 Şamad NE Oman
Sama de Langreo see Sama
Samaden see Samedan
57 M19 Samaipata Santa Cruz, C Bolivia
167 T10 Samakhixai var. Attapu, Attopeu. Attapu, S Laos
Samakov see Samokov
42 B6 Samalá, Río SW Guatemala
40 J3 Samalayuca Chihuahua, N Mexico
155 L16 Sāmalkot Andhra Pradesh, E India
45 P8 Samaná var. Santa Bárbara de Samaná. E Dominican Republic
45 P8 Samaná, Bahía de bay E Dominican Republic
44 K4 Samana Cay island SE Bahamas
136 K17 Samandağı Hatay, S Turkey
149 P3 Samangān ◆ province N Afghanistan
Samangān see Āybak
165 T5 Samani Hokkaidō, NE Japan
54 C13 Samaniego Nariño, SW Colombia
171 Q5 Samar island C Philippines
129 S6 Samara prev. Kuybyshev. Samarskaya Oblast', W Russian Federation
129 S6 Samara × Samarskaya Oblast', W Russian Federation
129 T7 Samara W Russian Federation
117 V7 Samara E Ukraine
186 G10 Samarai Milne Bay, SE PNG
Samarang see Semarang
138 G9 Samarian Hills hill range N Israel
54 L9 Samariapo Amazonas, C Venezuela
169 V11 Samarinda Borneo, C Indonesia
Samarkand see Samarqand
Samarkandskaya Oblast' see Samarqand Wiloyati
Samarkandski/Samarkandskoye see Temirtau
Samarobriva see Amiens
147 N11 Samarqand Rus. Samarkand. Samarqand Wiloyati, C Uzbekistan
146 M11 Samarqand Wiloyati Rus. Samarkandskaya Oblast'. ◆ province C Uzbekistan
139 S6 Sāmarrā' C Iraq
129 R7 Samarskaya Oblast' prev. Kuybyshevskaya Oblast'. ◆ province W Russian Federation
153 Q13 Samastīpur Bihār, N India
76 L14 Samatiguila NW Ivory Coast
119 Q17 Samatsevichy Rus. Samotevichi. Mahilyowskaya Voblasts', E Belarus
Samawa see As Samāwah
137 Y11 Şamaxı Rus. Shemakha. C Azerbaijan
152 H6 Samba Jammu and Kashmir, NW India
79 K18 Samba Equateur, NW Dem. Rep. Congo (Zaire)
79 N21 Samba Maniema, E Dem. Rep. Congo (Zaire)
169 W10 Sambaliung, Pegunungan ▲ Borneo, N Indonesia
154 M11 Sambalpur Orissa, E India
67 X12 Sambao W Madagascar
170 Q10 Sambas, Sungai Borneo, N Indonesia
172 K2 Sambava Antsirañana, NE Madagascar
152 J10 Sambhal Uttar Pradesh, N India
152 H12 Sāmbhar Salt Lake ⊙ N India
107 N21 Sambiase Calabria, SW Italy
116 H5 Sambir Rus. Sambor. L'vivs'ka Oblast', NW Ukraine
82 C13 Sambo Huambo, C Angola
Sambor see Sambir
61 E21 Samborombón, Bahía bay NE Argentina
99 H20 Sambre Belgium/France
43 V16 Sambú, Río SE Panama
163 Z14 Samch'ŏk Jap. Sanchoku. NE South Korea
Samch'ŏnpŏ see Sach'ŏn
81 I21 Same Kilimanjaro, NE Tanzania
108 J10 Samedan Ger. Samaden. Graubünden, S Switzerland
82 K12 Samfya Luapula, N Zambia
141 W13 Samḩān, Jabal ▲ SW Oman
115 C18 Sámi Kefallinía, Iónioi Nísoi, Greece, C Mediterranean Sea
56 F10 Samiria, Río N Peru
Samirum see Semīrom
137 V11 Şämkir Rus. Shamkhor. NW Azerbaijan
167 S7 Sam, Nam Vtn. Sông Chu. Laos/Vietnam
Samnān see Semnān
Sam Neua see Xam Nua
75 P10 Samnū C Libya
192 H15 Samoa off. Independent State of Samoa, var. Sāmoa; prev. Western Samoa ◆ monarchy W Polynesia
192 L9 Sāmoa island group American /Samoa
175 T9 Samoa Basin undersea feature W Pacific Ocean
Sāmoa-i-Sisifo see Samoa
112 D8 Samobor Zagreb, N Croatia
114 H10 Samokov var. Samakov. Sofiya, W Bulgaria
111 H21 Šamorín Ger. Sommerein, Hung. Somorja. Trnavský Kraj, W Slovakia
115 M19 Sámos prev. Limín Vathéos. Sámos, Dodekánisos, Greece, Aegean Sea
115 M20 Sámos island Dodekánisos, Greece, Aegean Sea
Samosch see Szamos
168 I9 Samosir, Pulau island W Indonesia
Samotevichi see Samatsevichy
Samothrace see Samothráki
115 K14 Samothráki Samothráki, NE Greece
115 J14 Samothráki anc. Samothrace. island NE Greece
115 A15 Samothráki island Iónioi Nísoi, Greece, C Mediterranean Sea
Samotschin see Szamocin
169 S13 Sampit Borneo, C Indonesia
169 S12 Sampit, Sungai Borneo, N Indonesia
Sampoku see Sanpoku
186 H7 Sampun New Britain, E PNG
79 N24 Sampwe Katanga, SE Dem. Rep. Congo (Zaire)
25 X8 Sam Rayburn Reservoir ⊞ Texas, SW USA
167 Q6 Sam Sao, Phou ▲ Laos/Thailand
95 H22 Samsø island E Denmark
95 H23 Samsø Bælt channel E Denmark
167 T7 Sâm Sơn Thanh Hoa, N Vietnam
136 L11 Samsun anc. Amisus. Samsun, N Turkey
136 K11 Samsun ◆ province N Turkey
137 R9 Samtredia W Georgia
59 E15 Samuel, Represa de ⊞ W Brazil
167 O14 Samui, Ko island SW Thailand
Samundari see Samundri
149 U9 Samundri var. Samundari. Punjab, E Pakistan
137 X10 Samur Azerbaijan/Russian Federation
137 Y11 Samur-Abşeron Kanalı Rus. Samur-Apsheronskiy Kanal. canal E Azerbaijan
Samur-Apsheronskiy Kanal see Samur-Abşeron Kanalı
167 O11 Samut Prakan var. Muang Samut Prakan, Paknam. Samut Prakan, C Thailand
167 O11 Samut Sakhon var. Maha Chai, Samut Sakorn, Tha Chin. Samut Sakhon, C Thailand
Samut Sakorn see Samut Sakhon
167 O11 Samut Songhram prev. Meklong. Samut Songkhram, SW Thailand
77 N12 San Ségou, C Mali
111 O15 San SE Poland
141 O15 Şan'ā' Eng. Sana. ● (Yemen) W Yemen
112 F11 Sana NW Bosnia and Herzegovina
80 O12 Sanaag off. Gobolka Sanaag. ◆ region N Somalia
114 J8 Sanadinovo Pleven, N Bulgaria
195 P1 Sanae South African research station Antarctica
139 Y10 Sanāf, Hawr as ⊙ S Iraq
79 E15 Sanaga C Cameroon
54 D12 San Agustín Huila, SW Colombia
171 R8 San Agustin, Cape headland Mindanao, S Philippines
37 Q13 San Agustin, Plains of plain New Mexico, SW USA
38 M16 Sanak Islands island group Aleutian Islands, Alaska, USA
193 U10 San Ambrosio, Isla Eng. San Ambrosio Island. island W Chile
San Ambrosio Island see San Ambrosio, Isla
171 Q12 Sanana Pulau Sanana, E Indonesia
171 Q12 Sanana, Pulau island Maluku, E Indonesia
142 K5 Sanandaj prev. Sinneh. Kordestān, W Iran
35 P8 San Andreas California, W USA
2 C13 San Andreas Fault fault W USA
54 G8 San Andrés Santander, C Colombia
61 C20 San Andrés de Giles Buenos Aires, E Argentina
37 R14 San Andres Mountains ▲ New Mexico, SW USA
41 S15 San Andrés Tuxtla var. Tuxtla. Veracruz-Llave, E Mexico
25 P8 San Angelo Texas, SW USA
107 A20 San Antioco, Isola di island W Italy
42 F4 San Antonio Toledo, S Belize
62 G11 San Antonio Valparaíso, C Chile
188 H6 San Antonio Saipan, S Northern Mariana Islands
37 R13 San Antonio New Mexico, SW USA
25 R12 San Antonio Texas, SW USA
54 M11 San Antonio Amazonas, S Venezuela
54 I7 San Antonio Barinas, C Venezuela
55 O5 San Antonio Monagas, NE Venezuela
25 S12 San Antonio × Texas, SW USA
San Antonio see San Antonio del Táchira
105 V11 San Antonio Abad Eivissa, Spain, W Mediterranean Sea
25 U13 San Antonio Bay inlet Texas, SW USA
61 E22 San Antonio, Cabo headland E Argentina
44 A5 San Antonio, Cabo de headland W Cuba
105 T11 San Antonio, Cabo de headland E Spain
54 H7 San Antonio de Caparo Táchira, W Venezuela
62 J5 San Antonio de los Cobres Salta, NE Argentina
54 H7 San Antonio del Táchira var. San Antonio. Táchira, W Venezuela
35 T15 San Antonio, Mount ▲ California, W USA
63 K16 San Antonio Oeste Río Negro, E Argentina
25 T13 San Antonio River Texas, SW USA
54 J5 Sanare Lara, N Venezuela
103 T16 Sanary-sur-Mer Var, SE France
25 X8 San Augustine Texas, SW USA
141 T13 Sanāw var. Sanaw. NE Yemen
41 O11 San Bartolo San Luis Potosí, C Mexico
107 L16 San Bartolomeo in Galdo Campania, S Italy
106 K13 San Benedetto del Tronto Marche, C Italy
42 E3 San Benito Petén, N Guatemala
25 T17 San Benito Texas, SW USA
54 E6 San Benito Abad Sucre, N Colombia
35 P11 San Benito Mountain ▲ California, W USA
35 O10 San Benito River California, W USA
108 H10 San Bernardino Graubünden, S Switzerland
35 U15 San Bernardino California, W USA
62 H11 San Bernardo Santiago, C Chile
40 J8 San Bernardo Durango, C Mexico
164 G12 Sanbe-san ▲ Kyūshū, SW Japan
40 J12 San Blas Nayarit, C Mexico
40 H8 San Blas Sinaloa, C Mexico
43 V14 San Blas off. Comarca de San Blas. ◆ special territory NE Panama
43 U14 San Blas, Archipiélago de island group NE Panama
23 Q10 San Blas, Cape headland Florida, SE USA
43 V14 San Blas, Cordillera de ▲ NE Panama
62 J8 San Blas de los Sauces Catamarca, NW Argentina
106 G8 San Bonifacio Veneto, NE Italy
29 S12 Sanborn Iowa, C USA
40 M7 San Buenaventura Coahuila de Zaragoza, NE Mexico
105 S5 San Caprasio ▲ N Spain
62 G13 San Carlos Bío Bío, C Chile
40 E9 San Carlos Baja California Sur, W Mexico
41 N5 San Carlos Coahuila de Zaragoza, NE Mexico
San Carlos, Estrecho de see Falkland Sound
41 P9 San Carlos Tamaulipas, C Mexico
42 L12 San Carlos Río San Juan, S Nicaragua
43 T16 San Carlos Panamá, C Panama
171 N3 San Carlos off. San Carlos City. Luzon, N Philippines
36 M14 San Carlos Arizona, SW USA
61 G20 San Carlos Maldonado, S Uruguay
54 K5 San Carlos Cojedes, N Venezuela
San Carlos see Quesada, Costa Rica
San Carlos see Luba, Equatorial Guinea
61 B17 San Carlos Centro Santa Fe, C Argentina
171 P6 San Carlos City Negros, C Philippines
San Carlos de Ancud see Ancud
63 H16 San Carlos de Bariloche Río Negro, SW Argentina
61 B21 San Carlos de Bolívar Buenos Aires, E Argentina
54 H6 San Carlos del Zulia Zulia, W Venezuela
54 L12 San Carlos de Río Negro Amazonas, S Venezuela
San Carlos, Estrecho de see Falkland Sound
36 M14 San Carlos Reservoir ⊞ Arizona, SW USA
42 M12 San Carlos, Río N Costa Rica
65 D24 San Carlos Settlement East Falkland, Falkland Islands
61 C23 San Cayetano Buenos Aires, E Argentina
103 O8 Sancerre Cher, C France
158 G7 Sanchakou Xinjiang Uygur Zizhiqu, NW China
Sanchoku see Samch'ŏk
41 O12 San Ciro San Luis Potosí, C Mexico
105 P10 San Clemente Castilla-La Mancha, C Spain
35 T16 San Clemente California, W USA
61 E21 San Clemente del Tuyú Buenos Aires, E Argentina
35 S17 San Clemente Island island Channel Islands, California, W USA
103 O9 Sancoins Cher, C France
187 N10 San Cristobal var. Makira. island SE Solomon Islands
61 B16 San Cristóbal Santa Fe, C Argentina
44 B4 San Cristóbal Pinar del Río, W Cuba
45 O9 San Cristóbal var. Benemérita de San Cristóbal. S Dominican Republic
54 H7 San Cristóbal Táchira, W Venezuela
San Cristóbal see San Cristóbal de Las Casas
41 U16 San Cristóbal de Las Casas var. San Cristóbal. Chiapas, SE Mexico
187 N10 San Cristóbal, Isla var. Chatham Island. island Galapagos Islands, Ecuador, E Pacific Ocean
42 D5 San Cristóbal Verapaz Alta Verapaz, C Guatemala
44 F6 Sancti Spíritus Sancti Spíritus, C Cuba
103 O11 Sancy, Puy de ▲ C France
95 D15 Sand Rogaland, S Norway
169 W7 Sandakan Sabah, East Malaysia
182 K9 Sandalwood South Australia
Sandalwood Island see Sumba, Pulau
94 D11 Sandane Sogn og Fjordane, S Norway
114 G12 Sandanski prev. Sveti Vrach. Blagoevgrad, SW Bulgaria
76 J11 Sandaré Kayes, W Mali
95 J19 Sandared Västra Götaland, S Sweden
94 N12 Sandarne Gävleborg, C Sweden
186 B5 Sandaun prev. West Sepik. ◆ province NW PNG
96 K4 Sanday island NE Scotland, UK
31 P15 Sand Creek Indiana, N USA
95 H15 Sande Vestfold, S Norway
95 H16 Sandefjord Vestfold, S Norway
77 O15 Sandégué E Ivory Coast
77 P14 Sandema N Ghana
37 O11 Sanders Arizona, SW USA
24 M11 Sanderson Texas, SW USA
23 U4 Sandersville Georgia, SE USA
92 H4 Sandgerdhi Sudhurland, SW Iceland
28 K14 Sand Hills ▲ Nebraska, C USA
25 S14 Sandia Texas, SW USA
35 T17 San Diego California, W USA
25 S14 San Diego Texas, SW USA
136 F14 Sandıklı Afyon, W Turkey
152 L12 Sandīla Uttar Pradesh, N India
121 N15 San Dimitri, Ras var. San Dimitri Point. headland Gozo, NW Malta
168 J13 Sanding, Selat strait W Indonesia
30 J3 Sand Island island Apostle Islands, Wisconsin, N USA
95 C16 Sandnes Rogaland, S Norway
92 F13 Sandnessjøen Nordland, C Norway
79 L24 Sandoa Katanga, S Dem. Rep. Congo (Zaire)
111 N15 Sandomierz Rus. Sandomir. Świętokrzyskie, C Poland
Sandomir see Sandomierz
54 C13 Sandoná Nariño, SW Colombia
106 I7 San Donà di Piave Veneto, NE Italy
126 K14 Sandovo Tverskaya Oblast', W Russian Federation
166 K7 Sandoway Arakan State, W Myanmar
97 M24 Sandown S England, UK
95 B19 Sandoy Dan. Sandø Island Faeroe Islands
39 N16 Sand Point Popof Island, Alaska, USA
65 N24 Sand Point headland E Tristan da Cunha
31 R7 Sand Point headland Michigan, N USA
32 M7 Sandpoint Idaho, NW USA
93 H14 Sandsele Västerbotten, N Sweden
10 I14 Sandspit Moresby Island, British Columbia, SW Canada
27 P9 Sand Springs Oklahoma, C USA
29 W7 Sandstone Minnesota, N USA
36 K15 Sand Tank Mountains ▲ Arizona, SW USA
31 S8 Sandusky Michigan, N USA
31 S11 Sandusky Ohio, N USA
31 S12 Sandusky River Ohio, N USA
83 D22 Sandverhaar Karas, S Namibia
95 L24 Sandvig Bornholm, E Denmark
95 H15 Sandvika Akershus, S Norway
94 N13 Sandviken Gävleborg, C Sweden

◆ Country ● Country Capital ◇ Dependent Territory ○ Dependent Territory Capital ◆ Administrative Region × International Airport ▲ Mountain ▲ Mountain Range Volcano River ⊙ Lake ⊞ Reservoir

30 M11 **Sandwich** Illinois, N USA
Sandwich Island *see* Éfaté
Sandwich Islands *see* Hawaiian Islands
153 V16 **Sandwip Island** *island* SE Bangladesh
11 U12 **Sandy Bay** Saskatchewan, C Canada
183 N16 **Sandy Cape** *headland* Tasmania, SE Australia
36 L3 **Sandy City** Utah, W USA
31 U12 **Sandy Creek** ≈ Ohio, N USA
21 O5 **Sandy Hook** Kentucky, S USA
18 K15 **Sandy Hook** *headland* New Jersey, NE USA
146 J15 **Sandykachi** *Turkm.* Sandykgachy. Maryyskiy Velayat, S Turkmenistan
Sandykgachy *see* Sandykachi
146 L13 **Sandykly, Peski** *desert* E Turkmenistan
11 Q13 **Sandy Lake** Alberta, W Canada
12 B8 **Sandy Lake** Ontario, C Canada
12 B8 **Sandy Lake** ⊚ Ontario, C Canada
23 S3 **Sandy Springs** Georgia, SE USA
24 H8 **San Elizario** Texas, SW USA
99 L25 **Sanem** Luxembourg, SW Luxembourg
42 K5 **San Esteban** Olancho, C Honduras
105 O6 **San Esteban de Gormaz** Castilla-León, N Spain
40 E5 **San Esteban, Isla** *island* NW Mexico
San Eugenio/San Eugenio del Cuareim *see* Artigas
62 H11 **San Felipe** *var.* San Felipe de Aconcagua. Valparaíso, C Chile
40 D3 **San Felipe** Baja California, NW Mexico
40 N12 **San Felipe** Guanajuato, C Mexico
54 K5 **San Felipe** Yaracuy, NW Venezuela
44 B5 **San Felipe, Cayos de** *island group* W Cuba
San Felipe de Aconcagua *see* San Felipe
San Felipe de Puerto Plata *see* Puerto Plata
37 R11 **San Felipe Pueblo** New Mexico, SW USA
San Feliú de Guixols *see* Sant Feliu de Guíxols
193 T10 **San Félix, Isla** *Eng.* San Felix Island. *island* W Chile
San Felix Island *see* San Félix, Isla
54 L11 **San Fernanado de Atabapo** Amazonas, S Venezuela
40 C4 **San Fernando** *var.* Misión San Fernando. Baja California, NW Mexico
41 P9 **San Fernando** Tamaulipas, C Mexico
171 N2 **San Fernando** Luzon, N Philippines
171 O3 **San Fernando** Luzon, N Philippines
104 J16 **San Fernando** *prev.* Isla de León. Andalucía, S Spain
45 U14 **San Fernando** Trinidad, Trinidad and Tobago
35 S15 **San Fernando** California, W USA
54 L7 **San Fernando** *var.* San Fernando de Apure. Apure, C Venezuela
San Fernando de Apure *see* San Fernando
62 L8 **San Fernando del Valle de Catamarca** *var.* Catamarca. Catamarca, NW Argentina
San Fernando de Monte Cristi *see* Monte Cristi
41 P9 **San Fernando, Río** ≈ C Mexico
23 X11 **Sanford** Florida, SE USA
19 P9 **Sanford** Maine, NE USA
21 T10 **Sanford** North Carolina, SE USA
25 N2 **Sanford** Texas, SW USA
39 T10 **Sanford, Mount** ▲ Alaska, USA
42 G8 **San Francisco** *var.* Gotera, San Francisco Gotera. Morazán, E El Salvador
43 R16 **San Francisco** Veraguas, C Panama
171 N2 **San Francisco** *var.* Aurora. Luzon, N Philippines
35 L8 **San Francisco** California, W USA
54 H5 **San Francisco** Zulia, NW Venezuela
34 M8 **San Francisco** ✕ California, W USA
35 N9 **San Francisco Bay** *bay* California, W USA
61 C24 **San Francisco de Bellocq** Buenos Aires, E Argentina
40 I6 **San Francisco de Borja** Chihuahua, N Mexico
42 J6 **San Francisco de la Paz** Olancho, C Honduras
40 J7 **San Francisco del Oro** Chihuahua, N Mexico
40 M12 **San Francisco del Rincón** Jalisco, SW Mexico
45 O8 **San Francisco de Macorís** C Dominican Republic
San Francisco de Satipo *see* Satipo
San Francisco Gotera *see* San Francisco
San Francisco Telixtlahuaca *see* Telixtlahuaca
107 K23 **San Fratello** Sicilia, Italy, C Mediterranean Sea
San Fructuoso *see* Tacuarembó
82 C12 **Sanga** Cuanza Sul, NW Angola
56 C5 **San Gabriel** Carchi, N Ecuador
159 S15 **Sa'ngain** Xizang Zizhiqu, W China
154 E13 **Sangamner** Mahārāshtra, W India
152 H12 **Sāngāner** Rājasthān, N India
Sangan, Koh-i- *see* Sangān, Kūh-e
149 N6 **Sangān, Kūh-e** *Pash.* Koh-i-Sangan. ▲ C Afghanistan
123 P10 **Sangar** Respublika Sakha (Yakutiya), NE Russian Federation
169 V11 **Sangasanga** Borneo, C Indonesia
103 N1 **Sangatte** Pas-de-Calais, N France
107 B19 **San Gavino Monreale** Sardegna, Italy, C Mediterranean Sea
57 D16 **Sangayan, Isla** *island* W Peru
30 L14 **Sangchris Lake** ⊟ Illinois, N USA
171 N16 **Sangeang, Pulau** *island* S Indonesia
116 I10 **Sângeorgiu de Pădure** *prev.* Erdăt-Sângeorz, Sîngeorgiu de Pădure, *Hung.* Erdőszentgyörgy. Mureș, C Romania
116 I9 **Sângeorz-Băi** *var.* Singeroz Băi, *Ger.* Rumänisch-Sankt-Georgen, *Hung.* Oláhszentgyőrgy; *prev.* Sîngeorz-Băi. Bistrița-Năsăud, N Romania
35 R10 **Sanger** California, W USA
25 T5 **Sanger** Texas, SW USA
Sângerei *see* Sîngerei
101 L15 **Sangerhausen** Sachsen-Anhalt, C Germany
45 S6 **San Germán** W Puerto Rico
San Germano *see* Cassino
161 N2 **Sanggan He** ≈ E China
169 Q11 **Sanggau** Borneo, C Indonesia
79 H16 **Sangha** ≈ Central African Republic/Congo
79 G16 **Sangha-Mbaéré** ◈ *prefecture* SW Central African Republic
149 Q15 **Sānghar** Sind, SE Pakistan
115 F22 **Sangiás** ▲ S Greece
Sangihe, Kepulauan *see* Sangir, Kepulauan
171 Q9 **Sangihe, Pulau** *var.* Sangir. *island* N Indonesia
54 G8 **San Gil** Santander, C Colombia
106 F12 **San Gimignano** Toscana, C Italy
148 M8 **Sangīn** *var.* Sangin. Helmand, S Afghanistan
107 O21 **San Giovanni in Fiore** Calabria, SW Italy
107 M16 **San Giovanni Rotondo** Puglia, SE Italy
106 G12 **San Giovanni Valdarno** Toscana, C Italy
Sangir *see* Sangihe, Pulau
171 Q10 **Sangir, Kepulauan** *var.* Kepulauan Sangihe. *island group* N Indonesia
162 K9 **Sangiyn Dalay** Dundgovĭ, C Mongolia
162 H9 **Sangiyn Dalay** Govĭ-Altay, C Mongolia
162 K11 **Sangiyn Dalay** Ömnögovĭ, S Mongolia
162 K8 **Sangiyn Dalay** Övörhangay, C Mongolia
163 Y15 **Sangju** *Jap.* Shōshū. C South Korea
167 R11 **Sangkha** Surin, E Thailand
169 W10 **Sangkulirang** Borneo, N Indonesia
169 W10 **Sangkulirang, Teluk** *bay* Borneo, N Indonesia
155 E16 **Sāngli** Mahārāshtra, W India
79 E16 **Sangmélima** Sud, S Cameroon
35 V15 **San Gorgonio Mountain** ▲ California, W USA
37 T8 **Sangre de Cristo Mountains** ▲▲ Colorado/New Mexico, C USA
61 A20 **San Gregorio** Santa Fe, C Argentina
61 F18 **San Gregorio de Polanco** Tacuarembó, C Uruguay
45 V14 **Sangre Grande** Trinidad, Trinidad and Tobago
159 N16 **Sangri** Xizang Zizhiqu, W China
152 H9 **Sangrūr** Punjab, NW India
44 I11 **Sangster** *off.* Sir Donald Sangster International Airport, *var.* Montego Bay. ✕ (Montego Bay) W Jamaica
59 G17 **Sangue, Rio do** ≈ W Brazil
105 R4 **Sangüesa** Navarra, N Spain
61 C16 **San Gustavo** Entre Ríos, E Argentina
Sangyuan *see* Wuqiao
40 C6 **San Hipólito, Punta** *headland* W Mexico
23 W15 **Sanibel** Sanibel Island, Florida, SE USA
23 V15 **Sanibel Island** *island* Florida, SE USA
60 F13 **San Ignacio** Misiones, NE Argentina
42 F2 **San Ignacio** *prev.* Cayo, El Cayo. Cayo, W Belize
57 L16 **San Ignacio** Beni, N Bolivia
57 O18 **San Ignacio** Santa Cruz, E Bolivia
42 M14 **San Ignacio** *var.* San Ignacio de Acosta. San José, W Costa Rica
40 E6 **San Ignacio** Baja California Sur, W Mexico
40 J10 **San Ignacio** Sinaloa, W Mexico
56 B9 **San Ignacio** Cajamarca, N Peru
San Ignacio de Acosta *see* San Ignacio
40 D7 **San Ignacio, Laguna** *lagoon* W Mexico
12 I6 **Sanikiluaq** Belcher Islands, Nunavut, C Canada
171 O3 **San Ildefonso Peninsula** *peninsula* Luzon, N Philippines
Saniquillie *see* Sanniquellie
61 D20 **San Isidro** Buenos Aires, E Argentina
43 N14 **San Isidro** *var.* San Isidro de El General. San José, SE Costa Rica
San Isidro de El General *see* San Isidro
54 E5 **San Jacinto** Bolívar, N Colombia
35 U16 **San Jacinto** California, W USA
35 V15 **San Jacinto Peak** ▲ California, W USA
61 F14 **San Javier** Misiones, NE Argentina
61 C16 **San Javier** Santa Fe, C Argentina
105 S13 **San Javier** Murcia, SE Spain
61 D18 **San Javier** Río Negro, W Uruguay
61 C16 **San Javier, Río** ≈ C Argentina
Sanjiang *see* Jinping
160 L12 **Sanjiang** *var.* Guyi, Sanjiang Dongzu Zizhixian. Guangxi Zhuangzu Zizhiqu, S China
Sanjiang Dongzu Zizhixian *see* Sanjiang
165 N11 **Sanjō** *var.* Sanzyô. Niigata, Honshū, C Japan
57 M15 **San Joaquín** Beni, N Bolivia
55 O6 **San Joaquín** Anzoátegui, NE Venezuela
35 O9 **San Joaquin River** ≈ California, W USA
35 P10 **San Joaquin Valley** *valley* California, W USA
61 A18 **San Jorge** Santa Fe, C Argentina
40 D3 **San Jorge, Bahía de** *bay* NW Mexico
San Jorge, Isla de *see* Weddell Island
63 J19 **San Jorge, Golfo** *var.* Gulf of San Jorge. *gulf* S Argentina
San Jorge, Gulf of *see* San Jorge, Golfo
188 K8 **San Jose** Tinian, S Northern Mariana Islands
35 N9 **San Jose** California, W USA
61 F14 **San José** Misiones, NE Argentina
57 P19 **San José** *var.* San José de Chiquitos. Santa Cruz, E Bolivia
42 M14 **San José** ● (Costa Rica) San José, C Costa Rica
42 C7 **San José** *var.* Puerto San José. Escuintla, S Guatemala
40 G6 **San José** Sonora, NW Mexico
105 U11 **San José** Eivissa, Spain, W Mediterranean Sea
54 H5 **San José** Zulia, NW Venezuela
42 M14 **San José** *off.* Provincia de San José. ◈ *province* W Costa Rica
61 E19 **San José** ◈ *department* S Uruguay
42 M13 **San José** ✕ Alajuela, C Costa Rica
San José *see* San José del Guaviare, Colombia
San José *see* San José de Mayo, S Uruguay
171 O3 **San Jose City** Luzon, N Philippines
San José de Cúcuta *see* Cúcuta
61 D16 **San José de Feliciano** Entre Ríos, E Argentina
55 O6 **San José de Guanipa** *var.* El Tigrito. Anzoátegui, NE Venezuela
62 I9 **San José de Jáchal** San Juan, W Argentina
40 G10 **San José del Cabo** Baja California Sur, W Mexico
54 G12 **San José del Guaviare** *var.* San José. Guaviare, S Colombia
61 E20 **San José de Mayo** *var.* San José. San José, S Uruguay
54 I10 **San José de Ocuné** Vichada, E Colombia
41 O9 **San José de Raíces** Nuevo León, NE Mexico
63 K17 **San José, Golfo** *gulf* E Argentina
40 F9 **San José, Isla** *island* W Mexico
43 U16 **San José, Isla** *island* SE Panama
25 U14 **San Jose Island** *island* Texas, SW USA
62 I10 **San Juan** San Juan, W Argentina
45 N9 **San Juan** *var.* San Juan de la Maguana. C Dominican Republic
57 E17 **San Juan** Ica, S Peru
45 U5 **San Juan** ○ (Puerto Rico) NE Puerto Rico
62 H10 **San Juan** *off.* Provincia de San Juan. ◈ *province* W Argentina
45 U5 **San Juan** *var.* Luis Muñoz Marin. ✕ NE Puerto Rico
San Juan *see* San Juan de los Morros
62 O7 **San Juan Bautista** Misiones, S Paraguay
35 O10 **San Juan Bautista** California, W USA
San Juan Bautista *see* Villahermosa
San Juan Bautista Cuicatlán *see* Cuicatlán
San Juan Bautista Tuxtepec *see* Tuxtepec
79 C17 **San Juan, Cabo** *headland* S Equatorial Guinea
105 S12 **San Juan de Alicante** País Valenciano, E Spain
54 H7 **San Juan de Colón** Táchira, NW Venezuela
40 L9 **San Juan de Guadalupe** Durango, C Mexico
San Juan de la Maguana *see* San Juan
54 G4 **San Juan del Cesar** La Guajira, N Colombia
40 L15 **San Juan de Lima, Punta** *headland* SW Mexico
42 I8 **San Juan de Limay** Estelí, NW Nicaragua
43 N12 **San Juan del Norte** *var.* Greytown. Río San Juan, SE Nicaragua
54 K4 **San Juan de los Cayos** Falcón, N Venezuela
40 M12 **San Juan de los Lagos** Jalisco, C Mexico
54 L5 **San Juan de los Morros** *var.* San Juan. Guárico, N Venezuela
40 K9 **San Juan del Río** Durango, C Mexico
41 O13 **San Juan del Río** Querétaro de Arteaga, C Mexico
42 J11 **San Juan del Sur** Rivas, SW Nicaragua
54 M9 **San Juan de Manapiare** Amazonas, S Venezuela
40 E7 **San Juanico** Baja California Sur, W Mexico
40 D7 **San Juanico, Punta** *headland* W Mexico
32 G6 **San Juan Islands** *island group* Washington, NW USA
40 I6 **San Juanito** Chihuahua, N Mexico
40 I12 **San Juanito, Isla** *island* C Mexico
37 R8 **San Juan Mountains** ▲▲ Colorado, C USA
54 E5 **San Juan Nepomuceno** Bolívar, NW Colombia
44 E5 **San Juan, Pico** ▲ C Cuba
191 W15 **San Juan, Punta** *headland* Easter Island, Chile, E Pacific Ocean
42 M12 **San Juan, Río** ≈ Costa Rica/Nicaragua
41 S15 **San Juan, Río** ≈ SE Mexico
37 O8 **San Juan River** ≈ Colorado/Utah, W USA
San Julián *see* Puerto San Julián
61 B17 **San Justo** Santa Fe, C Argentina
109 W5 **Sankt Aegyd-am-Neuwalde** Niederösterreich, E Austria
109 U9 **Sankt Andrä** *Slvn.* Šent Andraž. Kärnten, S Austria
Sankt Andrä *see* Szentendre
Sankt Anna *see* Sântana
108 K8 **Sankt Anton-am-Arlberg** Vorarlberg, W Austria
101 E16 **Sankt Augustin** Nordrhein-Westfalen, W Germany
Sankt-Bartholomäi *see* Palamuse
101 F24 **Sankt Blasien** Baden-Württemberg, SW Germany
109 R3 **Sankt Florian am Inn** Oberösterreich, N Austria
108 I7 **Sankt Gallen** *var.* St.Gallen, *Eng.* Saint Gall, *Fr.* St-Gall. Sankt Gallen, NE Switzerland
108 H8 **Sankt Gallen** *var.* St.Gallen, Eng. Saint Gall, *Fr.* St-Gall. ◈ *canton* NE Switzerland
108 J8 **Sankt Gallenkirch** Vorarlberg, W Austria
109 Q5 **Sankt Georgen** Salzburg, N Austria
Sankt Georgen *see* Đurđevac, Croatia
Sankt-Georgen *see* Sfântu Gheorghe, Romania
109 R6 **Sankt Gilgen** Salzburg, NW Austria
Sankt Gotthard *see* Szentgotthárd
101 E20 **Sankt Ingbert** Saarland, SW Germany
Sankt-Jakobi *see* Viru-Jaagupi, Lääne-Virumaa, Estonia
Sankt-Jakobi *see* Pärnu-Jaagupi, Pärnumaa, Estonia
Sankt Johann *see* Sankt Johann in Tirol
109 T7 **Sankt Johann am Tauern** Steiermark, E Austria
109 Q7 **Sankt Johann im Pongau** Salzburg, NW Austria
109 P6 **Sankt Johann in Tirol** *var.* Sankt Johann. Tirol, W Austria
Sankt-Johannis *see* Järva-Jaani
108 L8 **Sankt Leonhard** Tirol, W Austria
Sankt Margarethen *see* Sankt Margarethen im Burgenland
109 Y5 **Sankt Margarethen im Burgenland** *var.* Sankt Margarethen. Burgenland, E Austria
Sankt Martin *see* Martin
109 X8 **Sankt Martin an der Raab** Burgenland, SE Austria
109 U7 **Sankt Michael in Obersteiermark** Steiermark, SE Austria
Sankt Michel *see* Mikkeli
Sankt Moritz *see* St.Moritz
108 E11 **Sankt Niklaus** Valais, S Switzerland
109 S7 **Sankt Nikolai** *var.* Sankt Nikolai im Sölktal. Steiermark, SE Austria
Sankt Nikolai im Sölktal *see* Sankt Nikolai
109 U9 **Sankt Paul** *var.* Sankt Paul im Lavanttal. Kärnten, S Austria
Sankt Paul im Lavanttal *see* Sankt Paul
Sankt Peter *see* Pivka
109 W9 **Sankt Peter am Ottersbach** Steiermark, SE Austria
126 J13 **Sankt-Peterburg** *prev.* Leningrad, Petrograd, *Eng.* Saint Petersburg, *Fin.* Pietari. Leningradskaya Oblast', NW Russian Federation
100 H8 **Sankt Peter-Ording** Schleswig-Holstein, N Germany
109 V4 **Sankt Pölten** Niederösterreich, N Austria
109 W7 **Sankt Ruprecht** *var.* Sankt Ruprecht an der Raab. Steiermark, SE Austria
Sankt Ruprecht an der Raab *see* Sankt Ruprecht
Sankt-Ulrich *see* Ortisei
109 T4 **Sankt Valentin** Niederösterreich, C Austria
Sankt Veit am Flaum *see* Rijeka
109 T9 **Sankt Veit an der Glan** *Slvn.* Šent Vid. Kärnten, S Austria
99 M21 **Sankt-Vith** *var.* Saint-Vith. Liège, E Belgium
101 E20 **Sankt Wendel** Saarland, SW Germany
109 R6 **Sankt Wolfgang** Salzburg, NW Austria
79 K21 **Sankuru** ≈ C Dem. Rep. Congo (Zaire)
40 D8 **San Lázaro, Cabo** *headland* W Mexico
137 O16 **Şanlıurfa** *prev.* Sanli Urfa, Urfa, *anc.* Edessa. Şanlıurfa, S Turkey
137 O16 **Şanlıurfa** *prev.* Urfa. ◈ *province* SE Turkey
137 O16 **Şanlıurfa Yaylası** *plateau* SE Turkey
61 B18 **San Lorenzo** Santa Fe, C Argentina
57 M21 **San Lorenzo** Tarija, S Bolivia
56 C5 **San Lorenzo** Esmeraldas, N Ecuador
42 H8 **San Lorenzo** Valle, S Honduras
105 N8 **San Lorenzo de El Escorial** *var.* El Escorial. Madrid, C Spain
40 E5 **San Lorenzo, Isla** *island* NW Mexico
57 C14 **San Lorenzo, Isla** *island* W Peru
63 G20 **San Lorenzo, Monte** ▲ S Argentina
40 I9 **San Lorenzo, Río** ≈ C Mexico
104 J15 **Sanlúcar de Barrameda** Andalucía, S Spain
104 J14 **Sanlúcar la Mayor** Andalucía, S Spain
40 F11 **San Lucas** Baja California Sur, NW Mexico
40 E6 **San Lucas** *var.* Cabo San Lucas. Baja California Sur, W Mexico
40 G11 **San Lucas, Cabo** *var.* San Lucas Cape. *headland* W Mexico
San Lucas Cape *see* San Lucas, Cabo
62 J11 **San Luis** San Luis, C Argentina
42 E4 **San Luis** Petén, NE Guatemala
40 D2 **San Luis** *var.* San Luis Río Colorado. Sonora, NW Mexico
42 M7 **San Luis** Región Autónoma Atlántico Norte, NE Nicaragua
36 H15 **San Luis** Arizona, SW USA
37 T8 **San Luis** Colorado, C USA
54 J4 **San Luis** Falcón, N Venezuela
62 J11 **San Luis** *off.* Provincia de San Luis. ◈ *province* C Argentina
41 N12 **San Luis de la Paz** Guanajuato, C Mexico
40 K8 **San Luis del Cordero** Durango, C Mexico
40 D4 **San Luis, Isla** *island* NW Mexico
42 E6 **San Luis Jilotepeque** Jalapa, SE Guatemala
57 M16 **San Luis, Laguna de** ⊚ NW Bolivia
35 P13 **San Luis Obispo** California, W USA
37 R7 **San Luis Peak** ▲ Colorado, C USA
41 N11 **San Luis Potosí** San Luis Potosí, C Mexico
41 N11 **San Luis Potosí** ◈ *state* C Mexico
35 O10 **San Luis Reservoir** ⊟ California, W USA
San Luis Río Colorado *see* San Luis
37 S8 **San Luis Valley** *basin* Colorado, C USA
107 C19 **Sanluri** Sardegna, Italy, C Mediterranean Sea
61 D23 **San Manuel** Buenos Aires, E Argentina
36 M15 **San Manuel** Arizona, SW USA
106 F11 **San Marcello Pistoiese** Toscana, C Italy
107 N20 **San Marco Argentano** Calabria, SW Italy
54 E6 **San Marcos** Sucre, N Colombia
42 M14 **San Marcos** San José, C Costa Rica
42 B5 **San Marcos** San Marcos, W Guatemala
42 F6 **San Marcos** Ocotepeque, SW Honduras
41 O16 **San Marcos** Guerrero, S Mexico
25 S11 **San Marcos** Texas, SW USA
42 A5 **San Marcos** *off.* Departamento de San Marcos. ◈ *department* W Guatemala
San Marcos de Arica *see* Arica
40 E6 **San Marcos, Isla** *island* W Mexico
106 H11 **San Marino** ● (San Marino) C San Marino
106 I11 **San Marino** *off.* Republic of San Marino. ◆ *republic* S Europe
62 I11 **San Martín** Mendoza, C Argentina
54 F11 **San Martín** Meta, C Colombia
56 D11 **San Martín** *off.* Departamento de San Martín. ◈ *department* C Peru
194 I5 **San Martín** *Argentinian research station* Antarctica
63 H16 **San Martín de los Andes** Neuquén, W Argentina
104 M8 **San Martín de Valdeiglesias** Madrid, C Spain
63 G21 **San Martín, Lago** *var.* Lago O'Higgins. ⊚ S Argentina
106 H6 **San Martino di Castrozza** Trentino-Alto Adige, N Italy
57 N16 **San Martín, Río** ≈ N Bolivia
San Martín Texmelucan *see* Texmelucan
35 N9 **San Mateo** California, W USA
55 O6 **San Mateo** Anzoátegui, NE Venezuela
42 B4 **San Mateo Ixtatán** Huehuetenango, W Guatemala
57 Q18 **San Matías** Santa Cruz, E Bolivia
63 K16 **San Matías, Golfo** *var.* Gulf of San Matías. *gulf* E Argentina
San Matías, Gulf of *see* San Matías
15 O8 **Sanmaur** Quebec, SE Canada
161 T10 **Sanmen Wan** *bay* E China
160 M6 **Sanmenxia** *var.* Shan Xian. Henan, C China
Sânmiclăuș Mare *see* Sânnicolau Mare
61 D14 **San Miguel** Corrientes, NE Argentina
57 L16 **San Miguel** Beni, N Bolivia
42 G8 **San Miguel** San Miguel, SE El Salvador
40 L6 **San Miguel** Coahuila de Zaragoza, N Mexico
40 J9 **San Miguel** *var.* San Miguel de Cruces. Durango, C Mexico
43 U16 **San Miguel** Panamá, SE Panama
35 P12 **San Miguel** California, W USA
42 B9 **San Miguel** ◈ *department* E El Salvador
41 N13 **San Miguel de Allende** Guanajuato, C Mexico
San Miguel de Cruces *see* San Miguel
San Miguel de Ibarra *see* Ibarra
61 D21 **San Miguel del Monte** Buenos Aires, E Argentina
62 J7 **San Miguel de Tucumán** *var.* Tucumán. Tucumán, N Argentina
43 V16 **San Miguel, Golfo de** *gulf* S Panama
35 P15 **San Miguel Island** *island* California, W USA
42 L11 **San Miguelito** Río San Juan, S Nicaragua
43 T15 **San Miguelito** Panamá, C Panama
57 N18 **San Miguel, Río** ≈ E Bolivia
56 D6 **San Miguel, Río** ≈ Colombia/Ecuador
40 I7 **San Miguel, Río** ≈ N Mexico
42 G8 **San Miguel, Volcán de** ⅄ SE El Salvador
161 Q12 **Sanming** Fujian, SE China
106 F11 **San Miniato** Toscana, C Italy
San Murezzan *see* St.Moritz
Sannār *see* Sennar
107 M15 **Sannicandro Garganico** Puglia, SE Italy
40 H6 **San Nicolás** Sonora, NW Mexico
61 C19 **San Nicolás de los Arroyos** Buenos Aires, E Argentina
35 R16 **San Nicolas Island** *island* Channel Islands, California, W USA
Sânnicolaul-Mare *see* Sânnicolau Mare
116 E11 **Sânnicolau Mare** *var.* Sânnicolaul-Mare, *Hung.* Nagyszentmiklós; *prev.* Sânmiclăuș Mare, Sînnicolau Mare. Timiș, W Romania
123 Q6 **Sannikova, Proliv** *strait* NE Russian Federation
76 K16 **Sanniquellie** *var.* Saniquillie. NE Liberia
165 R7 **Sannohe** Aomori, Honshū, C Japan
Sanntaler Alpen *see* Kamniško-Savinjske Alpe
111 O17 **Sanok** Podkarpackie, SE Poland
54 E5 **San Onofre** Sucre, NW Colombia
57 K21 **San Pablo** Potosí, S Bolivia
171 O4 **San Pablo** *off.* San Pablo City. Luzon, N Philippines
San Pablo Balleza *see* Balleza
35 N8 **San Pablo Bay** *bay* California, W USA
40 C6 **San Pablo, Punta** *headland* W Mexico
43 R16 **San Pablo, Río** ≈ C Panama
171 P4 **San Pascual** Burias Island, C Philippines
121 Q16 **San Pawl il-Bahar** *Eng.* Saint Paul's Bay. E Malta
61 C19 **San Pedro** Buenos Aires, E Argentina
62 K5 **San Pedro** Jujuy, N Argentina
60 G13 **San Pedro** Misiones, NE Argentina
42 H1 **San Pedro** Corozal, NE Belize
40 L8 **San Pedro** *var.* San Pedro de las Colonias. Coahuila de Zaragoza, NE Mexico
62 O5 **San Pedro** San Pedro, SE Paraguay
62 O6 **San Pedro** *off.* Departamento de San Pedro. ◈ *department* C Paraguay
77 N16 **San Pedro** ✕ (Yamoussoukro) C Ivory Coast
44 G6 **San Pedro** ≈ C Cuba
San Pedro *see* San Pedro del Pinatar
76 M17 **San-Pédro** S Ivory Coast
42 D5 **San Pedro Carchá** Alta Verapaz, C Guatemala
35 S16 **San Pedro Channel** *channel* California, W USA
62 I5 **San Pedro de Atacama** Antofagasta, N Chile
San Pedro de Durazno *see* Durazno
40 G5 **San Pedro de la Cueva** Sonora, NW Mexico
San Pedro de las Colonias *see* San Pedro
56 B11 **San Pedro de Lloc** La Libertad, NW Peru
105 S13 **San Pedro del Pinatar** *var.* San Pedro. Murcia, SE Spain
45 P9 **San Pedro de Macorís** SE Dominican Republic
40 C3 **San Pedro Mártir, Sierra** ▲▲ NW Mexico
San Pedro Pochutla *see* Pochutla
42 D2 **San Pedro, Río** ≈ Guatemala/Mexico
40 K10 **San Pedro, Río** ≈ C Mexico
104 J10 **San Pedro, Sierra de** ▲▲ W Spain
42 G5 **San Pedro Sula** Cortés, NW Honduras
San Pedro Tapanatepec *see* Tapanatepec
62 I4 **San Pedro, Volcán** ▲ N Chile
106 E7 **San Pellegrino Terme** Lombardia, N Italy
25 T16 **San Perlita** Texas, SW USA
San Pietro *see* Supetar
San Pietro del Carso *see* Pivka
107 A20 **San Pietro, Isola di** *island* W Italy
32 K7 **Sanpoil River** ≈ Washington, NW USA
165 O9 **Sanpoku** *var.* Sampoku. Niigata, Honshū, C Japan
40 C3 **San Quintín** Baja California, NW Mexico
40 B3 **San Quintín, Bahía de** *bay* NW Mexico
40 B3 **San Quintín, Cabo** *headland* NW Mexico
62 I12 **San Rafael** Mendoza, W Argentina
41 N9 **San Rafael** Nuevo León, NE Mexico
34 M8 **San Rafael** California, W USA

◆ Country ● Country Capital ◇ Dependent Territory ○ Dependent Territory Capital ◈ Administrative Region ✕ International Airport ▲ Mountain ▲▲ Mountain Range ⅄ Volcano ≈ River ⊚ Lake ⊟ Reservoir

37 Q11 **San Rafael** New Mexico, SW USA
54 H4 **San Rafael** *var.* El Moján. Zulia, NW Venezuela
42 J8 **San Rafael del Norte** Jinotega, NW Nicaragua
42 J10 **San Rafael del Sur** Managua, SW Nicaragua
36 M5 **San Rafael Knob** ▲ Utah, W USA
35 Q14 **San Rafael Mountains** ▲ California, W USA
42 M13 **San Ramón** Alajuela, C Costa Rica
57 E14 **San Ramón** Junín, C Peru
61 F19 **San Ramón** Canelones, S Uruguay
62 K5 **San Ramón de la Nueva Orán** Salta, N Argentina
57 O16 **San Ramón, Río** ≈ E Bolivia
106 B11 **San Remo** Liguria, NW Italy
54 J3 **San Román, Cabo** *headland* NW Venezuela
61 C15 **San Roque** Corrientes, NE Argentina
188 I4 **San Roque** Saipan, S Northern Mariana Islands
104 K16 **San Roque** Andalucía, S Spain
25 R9 **San Saba** Texas, SW USA
25 Q9 **San Saba River** ≈ Texas, SW USA
61 D17 **San Salvador** Entre Ríos, E Argentina
42 F7 **San Salvador** ● (El Salvador) San Salvador, SW El Salvador
42 A10 **San Salvador** ◈ *department* C El Salvador
42 F8 **San Salvador** ✈ La Paz, S El Salvador
44 K4 **San Salvador** *prev.* Watlings Island. *island* E Bahamas
62 J5 **San Salvador de Jujuy** *var.* Jujuy. Jujuy, N Argentina
42 F7 **San Salvador, Volcán de** ※ C El Salvador
77 Q14 **Sansanné-Mango** *var.* Mango. N Togo
45 S5 **San Sebastián** W Puerto Rico
63 J24 **San Sebastián, Bahía** *bay* S Argentina
Sansenhō *see* Sach'ŏn
106 H12 **Sansepolcro** Toscana, C Italy
107 M16 **San Severo** Puglia, SE Italy
112 F11 **Sanski Most** Federacija Bosna I Hercegovina, NW Bosnia & Herzegovina
171 W12 **Sansundi** Irian Jaya, E Indonesia
104 K11 **Santa Amalia** Extremadura, W Spain
60 F13 **Santa Ana** Misiones, NE Argentina
57 L16 **Santa Ana** Beni, N Bolivia
42 E7 **Santa Ana** Santa Ana, NW El Salvador
40 F4 **Santa Ana** Sonora, NW Mexico
35 T16 **Santa Ana** California, W USA
55 N6 **Santa Ana** Nueva Esparta, NE Venezuela
42 A9 **Santa Ana** ◈ *department* NW El Salvador
Santa Ana de Coro *see* Coro
42 E7 **Santa Ana, Volcán de** *var.* La Matepec. ※ W El Salvador
40 J7 **Santa Barbara** Chihuahua, N Mexico
35 Q14 **Santa Barbara** California, W USA
42 G6 **Santa Bárbara** Santa Bárbara, W Honduras
54 L11 **Santa Bárbara** Amazonas, S Venezuela
54 I7 **Santa Bárbara** Barinas, W Venezuela
42 F5 **Santa Bárbara** ◈ *department* NW Honduras
Santa Bárbara *see* Iscuandé
35 Q15 **Santa Barbara Channel** *channel* California, W USA
Santa Bárbara de Samaná *see* Samaná
35 R16 **Santa Barbara Island** *island* Channel Islands, California, W USA
54 E5 **Santa Catalina** Bolívar, N Colombia
43 R15 **Santa Catalina** Bocas del Toro, W Panama
35 T17 **Santa Catalina, Gulf of** *gulf* California, W USA
40 F8 **Santa Catalina, Isla** *island* W Mexico
35 S16 **Santa Catalina Island** *island* Channel Islands, California, W USA
41 N8 **Santa Catarina** Nuevo León, NE Mexico
60 H13 **Santa Catarina** *off.* Estado de Santa Catarina. ◈ *state* S Brazil
Santa Catarina de Tepehuanes *see* Tepehuanes
60 L13 **Santa Catarina, Ilha de** *island* S Brazil
45 Q16 **Santa Catherina** Curaçao, C Netherlands Antilles
44 E5 **Santa Clara** Villa Clara, C Cuba
35 N9 **Santa Clara** California, W USA
36 J8 **Santa Clara** Utah, W USA
Santa Clara *see* Santa Clara de Olimar
61 F18 **Santa Clara de Olimar** *var.* Santa Clara. Cerro Largo, NE Uruguay
61 A17 **Santa Clara de Saguier** Santa Fe, C Argentina
Santa Coloma *see* Santa Coloma de Gramanet
105 X5 **Santa Coloma de Farners** *var.* Santa Coloma de Farnés. Cataluña, NE Spain
Santa Coloma de Farnés *see* Santa Coloma de Farners
105 W6 **Santa Coloma de Gramanet** *var.* Santa Coloma. Cataluña, NE Spain
104 G2 **Santa Comba** Galicia, NW Spain
Santa Comba *see* Uaco Cungo
104 H8 **Santa Comba Dão** Viseu, N Portugal
82 C10 **Santa Cruz** Uíge, NW Angola
57 N19 **Santa Cruz** *var.* Santa Cruz de la Sierra. Santa Cruz, C Bolivia
62 G12 **Santa Cruz** Libertador, C Chile
42 K13 **Santa Cruz** Guanacaste, W Costa Rica
44 I12 **Santa Cruz** W Jamaica
64 P6 **Santa Cruz** Madeira, Portugal, NE Atlantic Ocean
35 N10 **Santa Cruz** California, W USA
63 H20 **Santa Cruz** *off.* Provincia de Santa Cruz. ◈ *province* S Argentina
57 O18 **Santa Cruz** ◈ *department* E Bolivia
Santa Cruz *see* Viru-Viru
Santa Cruz *see* Puerto Santa Cruz
Santa Cruz Barillas *see* Barillas
59 O18 **Santa Cruz Cabrália** Bahia, E Brazil
Santa Cruz de El Seibo *see* El Seibo
64 N11 **Santa Cruz de la Palma** La Palma, Islas Canarias, Spain, NE Atlantic Ocean
Santa Cruz de la Sierra *see* Santa Cruz
105 O9 **Santa Cruz de la Zarza** Castilla-La Mancha, C Spain
42 C5 **Santa Cruz del Quiché** Quiché, W Guatemala
105 N8 **Santa Cruz del Retamar** Castilla-La Mancha, C Spain
Santa Cruz del Seibo *see* El Seibo
44 G7 **Santa Cruz del Sur** Camagüey, C Cuba
105 O11 **Santa Cruz de Mudela** Castilla-La Mancha, C Spain
64 Q11 **Santa Cruz de Tenerife** Tenerife, Islas Canarias, Spain, NE Atlantic Ocean
64 P11 **Santa Cruz de Tenerife** ◈ *province* Islas Canarias, Spain, NE Atlantic Ocean
60 K9 **Santa Cruz do Rio Pardo** São Paulo, S Brazil
61 H15 **Santa Cruz do Sul** Rio Grande do Sul, S Brazil
57 C17 **Santa Cruz, Isla** *var.* Indefatigable Island, Isla Chávez. *island* Galapagos Islands, Ecuador, E Pacific Ocean
40 F8 **Santa Cruz, Isla** *island* W Mexico
35 Q15 **Santa Cruz Island** *island* California, W USA
187 Q10 **Santa Cruz Islands** *island group* E Solomon Islands
63 I22 **Santa Cruz, Río** ≈ S Argentina
36 L15 **Santa Cruz River** ≈ Arizona, SW USA
61 C17 **Santa Elena** Entre Ríos, E Argentina
42 F2 **Santa Elena** Cayo, W Belize
25 R16 **Santa Elena** Texas, SW USA
56 A7 **Santa Elena, Bahía de** *bay* W Ecuador
55 R10 **Santa Elena de Uairén** Bolívar, E Venezuela
42 K12 **Santa Elena, Península** *peninsula* NW Costa Rica
56 A7 **Santa Elena, Punta** *headland* W Ecuador
104 L11 **Santa Eufemia** Andalucía, S Spain
107 N21 **Santa Eufemia, Golfo di** *gulf* S Italy
107 N21 **Santa Eufemia Lamezia Terme** Calabria, SE Italy
105 S4 **Santa Eulalia de Gállego** Aragón, NE Spain
105 V11 **Santa Eulalia del Río** Eivissa, Spain, W Mediterranean Sea
61 B17 **Santa Fe** Santa Fe, C Argentina
105 N14 **Santa Fe** Andalucía, S Spain
37 S10 **Santa Fe** *state capital* New Mexico, SW USA
61 B15 **Santa Fe** *off.* Provincia de Santa Fe. ◈ *province* C Argentina
Santa Fe *see* Bogotá
44 C6 **Santa Fé** *var.* La Fe. Isla de la Juventud, W Cuba
43 R16 **Santa Fé** Veraguas, C Panama
Santa Fe de Bogotá *see* Bogotá
60 J7 **Santa Fé do Sul** São Paulo, S Brazil
57 B18 **Santa Fe, Isla** *var.* Barrington Island. *island* Galapagos Islands, Ecuador, E Pacific Ocean
23 V9 **Santa Fe River** ≈ Florida, SE USA
59 M15 **Santa Filomena** Piauí, E Brazil
40 G10 **Santa Genoveva** ▲ W Mexico
153 S14 **Santahar** Rajshahi, NW Bangladesh
60 G11 **Santa Helena** Paraná, S Brazil
54 J5 **Santa Inés** Lara, N Venezuela
63 G24 **Santa Inés, Isla** *island* S Chile
62 J13 **Santa Isabel** La Pampa, C Argentina
43 U14 **Santa Isabel** Colón, N Panama
186 L8 **Santa Isabel** *var.* Bughotu. *island* N Solomon Islands
Santa Isabel *see* Malabo
58 D11 **Santa Isabel do Rio Negro** Amazonas, NW Brazil
61 C15 **Santa Lucia** Corrientes, NE Argentina
57 I17 **Santa Lucía** Puno, S Peru
61 F20 **Santa Lucía** *var.* Santa Lucia. Canelones, S Uruguay
42 B6 **Santa Lucía Cotzumalguapa** Escuintla, SW Guatemala
107 L23 **Santa Lucia del Mela** Sicilia, Italy, C Mediterranean Sea
35 O11 **Santa Lucia Range** ▲ California, W USA
40 D9 **Santa Margarita, Isla** *island* W Mexico
61 G15 **Santa Maria** Rio Grande do Sul, S Brazil
35 P13 **Santa Maria** California, W USA
64 Q4 **Santa Maria** ✈ Santa Maria, Azores, Portugal, NE Atlantic Ocean
64 P3 **Santa Maria** *island* Azores, Portugal, NE Atlantic Ocean
Santa Maria *see* Gaua.
62 J7 **Santa María** Catamarca, N Argentina
Santa María Asunción Tlaxiaco *see* Tlaxiaco
40 G9 **Santa María, Bahía** *bay* W Mexico
83 L21 **Santa Maria, Cabo de** *headland* S Mozambique
104 G15 **Santa Maria, Cabo de** *headland* S Portugal
44 J4 **Santa Maria, Cape** *headland* Long Island, C Bahamas
107 J17 **Santa Maria Capua Vetere** Campania, S Italy
59 M17 **Santa Maria da Vitória** Bahia, E Brazil
55 N9 **Santa Maria de Erebato** Bolívar, SE Venezuela
104 G7 **Santa Maria da Feira** Aveiro, N Portugal
55 N6 **Santa María de Ipire** Guárico, C Venezuela
Santa María del Buen Aire *see* Buenos Aires
40 J8 **Santa María del Oro** Durango, C Mexico
41 N12 **Santa María del Río** San Luis Potosí, C Mexico
Santa Maria di Castellabate *see* Castellabate
107 Q20 **Santa Maria di Leuca, Capo** *headland* SE Italy
108 K10 **Santa Maria-im-Münstertal** Graubünden, SE Switzerland
57 B18 **Santa María, Isla** *var.* Isla Floreana, Charles Island. *island* Galapagos Islands, Ecuador, E Pacific Ocean
40 J3 **Santa María, Laguna de** ◎ N Mexico
61 G16 **Santa Maria, Rio** ≈ S Brazil
43 R16 **Santa María, Río** ≈ C Panama
36 J12 **Santa Maria River** ≈ Arizona, SW USA
107 G15 **Santa Marinella** Lazio, C Italy
54 F4 **Santa Marta** Magdalena, N Colombia
104 J11 **Santa Marta** Extremadura, W Spain
Santa Maura *see* Lefkáda
35 S15 **Santa Monica** California, W USA
116 F10 **Sântana** *Ger.* Sankt Anna, *Hung.* Újszentanna; *prev.* Sîntana. Arad, W Romania
61 F16 **Santana, Coxilha de** *hill range* S Brazil
61 H16 **Santana da Boa Vista** Rio Grande do Sul, S Brazil
61 F16 **Santana do Livramento** *prev.* Livramento. Rio Grande do Sul, S Brazil
105 N2 **Santander** Cantabria, N Spain
54 F8 **Santander** *off.* Departamento de Santander. ◈ *province* C Colombia
Santander Jiménez *see* Jiménez
Sant'Andrea *see* Svetac
107 B20 **Sant'Antioco** Sardegna, Italy, C Mediterranean Sea
104 J13 **Santa Olalla del Cala** Andalucía, S Spain
35 R15 **Santa Paula** California, W USA
36 L4 **Santaquin** Utah, W USA
58 I12 **Santarém** Pará, N Brazil
104 G10 **Santarém** *anc.* Scalabis. Santarém, W Portugal
104 G10 **Santarém** ◈ *district* C Portugal
44 F4 **Santaren Channel** *channel* W Bahamas
54 K10 **Santa Rita** Vichada, E Colombia
188 B16 **Santa Rita** SW Guam
42 H5 **Santa Rita** Cortés, NW Honduras
40 E9 **Santa Rita** Baja California Sur, W Mexico
54 H5 **Santa Rita** Zulia, NW Venezuela
59 I19 **Santa Rita de Araguaia** Goiás, S Brazil
Santa Rita de Cassia *see* Cássia
61 D14 **Santa Rosa** Corrientes, NE Argentina
62 K13 **Santa Rosa** La Pampa, C Argentina
61 G14 **Santa Rosa** Rio Grande do Sul, S Brazil
58 E10 **Santa Rosa** Roraima, N Brazil
56 B8 **Santa Rosa** El Oro, SW Ecuador
57 I16 **Santa Rosa** Puno, S Peru
34 M7 **Santa Rosa** California, W USA
37 U11 **Santa Rosa** New Mexico, SW USA
55 O6 **Santa Rosa** Anzoátegui, NE Venezuela
42 A3 **Santa Rosa** *off.* Departamento de Santa Rosa. ◈ *department* SE Guatemala
Santa Rosa *see* Santa Rosa de Copán
63 J15 **Santa Rosa, Bajo de** *basin* E Argentina
42 F6 **Santa Rosa de Copán** *var.* Santa Rosa. Copán, W Honduras
54 E8 **Santa Rosa de Osos** Antioquia, C Colombia
35 Q15 **Santa Rosa Island** *island* California, W USA
23 O9 **Santa Rosa Island** *island* Florida, SE USA
40 E6 **Santa Rosalía** Baja California Sur, W Mexico
54 K6 **Santa Rosalía** Portuguesa, NW Venezuela
188 C15 **Santa Rosa, Mount** ▲ NE Guam
35 V16 **Santa Rosa Mountains** ▲ California, W USA
35 T2 **Santa Rosa Range** ▲ Nevada, W USA
62 M8 **Santa Sylvina** Chaco, N Argentina
Santa Tecla *see* Nueva San Salvador
61 B19 **Santa Teresa** Santa Fe, C Argentina
59 O20 **Santa Teresa** Espírito Santo, SE Brazil
107 M23 **Santa Teresa di Riva** Sicilia, Italy, C Mediterranean Sea
61 E21 **Santa Teresita** Buenos Aires, E Argentina
61 H19 **Santa Vitória do Palmar** Rio Grande do Sul, S Brazil
35 Q14 **Santa Ynez River** ≈ California, W USA
Sant Carles de la Rápida *see* Sant Carles de la Ràpita
105 U7 **Sant Carles de la Ràpita** *var.* Sant Carles de la Rápida. Cataluña, NE Spain
105 W5 **Sant Celoni** Cataluña, NE Spain
35 U17 **Santee** California, W USA
21 T13 **Santee River** ≈ South Carolina, SE USA
40 K15 **San Telmo, Punta** *headland* SW Mexico
107 O17 **Santeramo in Colle** Puglia, SE Italy
105 X5 **Sant Feliu de Guíxols** *var.* San Feliú de Guixols. Cataluña, NE Spain
105 W6 **Sant Feliu de Llobregat** Cataluña, NE Spain
106 C7 **Santhià** Piemonte, NE Italy
61 F15 **Santiago** Rio Grande do Sul, S Brazil
62 H11 **Santiago** *var.* Gran Santiago. ● (Chile) Santiago, C Chile
45 N8 **Santiago** *var.* Santiago de los Caballeros. N Dominican Republic
40 G10 **Santiago** Baja California Sur, W Mexico
41 O8 **Santiago** Nuevo León, NE Mexico
43 R16 **Santiago** Veraguas, S Panama
57 E16 **Santiago** Ica, SW Peru
104 G3 **Santiago** *var.* Santiago de Compostela, *Eng.* Compostella; *anc.* Campus Stellae. Galicia, NW Spain
62 H11 **Santiago** *off.* Región Metropolitana de Santiago, *var.* Metropolitan. ◈ *region* C Chile
62 H11 **Santiago** ✈ Santiago, C Chile
104 G3 **Santiago** ✈ Galicia, NW Spain
76 D10 **Santiago** *var.* São Tiago. *island* Ilhas de Sotavento, S Cape Verde
Santiago *see* Santiago de Cuba, Cuba
Santiago *see* Grande de Santiago, Río, Mexico
42 B6 **Santiago Atitlán** Sololá, SW Guatemala
43 Q16 **Santiago, Cerro** ▲ W Panama
Santiago de Compostela *see* Santiago
44 I8 **Santiago de Cuba** *var.* Santiago. Santiago de Cuba, E Cuba
Santiago de Guayaquil *see* Guayaquil
62 K8 **Santiago del Estero** Santiago del Estero, C Argentina
61 A15 **Santiago del Estero** *off.* Provincia de Santiago del Estero. ◈ *province* N Argentina
40 I8 **Santiago de los Caballeros** Sinaloa, W Mexico
Santiago de los Caballeros *see* Santiago, Dominican Republic
Santiago de los Caballeros *see* Guatemala, Guatemala
42 F8 **Santiago de María** Usulután, SE El Salvador
104 F12 **Santiago do Cacém** Setúbal, S Portugal
40 J12 **Santiago Ixcuintla** Nayarit, C Mexico
Santiago Jamiltepec *see* Jamiltepec
24 L11 **Santiago Mountains** ▲ Texas, SW USA
40 J9 **Santiago Papasquiaro** Durango, C Mexico
Santiago Pinotepa Nacional *see* Pinotepa Nacional
56 C8 **Santiago, Río** ≈ N Peru
40 M10 **San Tiburcio** Zacatecas, C Mexico
105 N2 **Santillana** Cantabria, N Spain
54 I5 **San Timoteo** Zulia, NW Venezuela
Santi Quaranta *see* Sarandë
Santissima Trinidad *see* Chilung
105 O12 **Santisteban del Puerto** Andalucía, S Spain
105 U7 **Sant Jordi, Golf de** *gulf* NE Spain
105 T8 **Sant Mateu** País Valenciano, E Spain
25 S7 **Santo** Texas, SW USA
Santo *see* Espiritu Santo
60 M10 **Santo Amaro, Ilha de** *island* SE Brazil
61 G14 **Santo Ângelo** Rio Grande do Sul, S Brazil
76 C9 **Santo Antão** *island* Ilhas de Barlavento, N Cape Verde
60 J10 **Santo Antônio da Platina** Paraná, S Brazil
58 C13 **Santo Antônio do Içá** Amazonas, N Brazil
57 Q18 **Santo Corazón, Río** ≈ E Bolivia
44 E5 **Santo Domingo** Villa Clara, C Cuba
45 O9 **Santo Domingo** *prev.* Ciudad Trujillo. ● (Dominican Republic) SE Dominican Republic
40 E8 **Santo Domingo** Baja California Sur, W Mexico
40 M10 **Santo Domingo** San Luis Potosí, C Mexico
42 L10 **Santo Domingo** Chontales, S Nicaragua
105 P4 **Santo Domingo de la Calzada** La Rioja, N Spain
56 B6 **Santo Domingo de los Colorados** Pichincha, NW Ecuador
Santo Domingo Tehuantepec *see* Tehuantepec
55 O6 **San Tomé** Anzoátegui, NE Venezuela
San Tomé de Guayana *see* Ciudad Guayana
105 R13 **Santomera** Murcia, SE Spain
105 O2 **Santoña** Cantabria, N Spain
Santorin/Santoríni *see* Thíra
60 M10 **Santos** São Paulo, S Brazil
65 J17 **Santos Plateau** *undersea feature* SW Atlantic Ocean
104 G6 **Santo Tirso** Porto, N Portugal
40 B2 **Santo Tomás** Baja California, NW Mexico
42 L10 **Santo Tomás** Chontales, S Nicaragua
42 G5 **Santo Tomás de Castilla** Izabal, E Guatemala
40 B2 **Santo Tomás, Punta** *headland* NW Mexico
57 H16 **Santo Tomás, Río** ≈ C Peru
57 B18 **Santo Tomás, Volcán** ※ Galapagos Islands, Ecuador, E Pacific Ocean
61 F14 **Santo Tomé** Corrientes, NE Argentina
Santo Tomé de Guayana *see* Ciudad Guayana
98 H10 **Santpoort** Noord-Holland, W Netherlands
Santurce *see* Santurtzi
105 O2 **Santurtzi** *var.* Santurce, Santurzi. País Vasco, N Spain
Santurzi *see* Santurtzi
63 G20 **San Valentín, Cerro** ▲ S Chile
42 F8 **San Vicente** San Vicente, C El Salvador
40 C2 **San Vicente** Baja California, NW Mexico
188 H6 **San Vicente** Saipan, S Northern Mariana Islands
42 B9 **San Vicente** ◈ *department* E El Salvador
104 I10 **San Vicente de Alcántara** Extremadura, W Spain
105 N2 **San Vicente de Barakaldo** *var.* Baracaldo. País Vasco, N Spain
57 E15 **San Vicente de Cañete** *var.* Cañete. Lima, W Peru
104 M2 **San Vicente de la Barquera** Cantabria, N Spain
54 E12 **San Vicente del Caguán** Caquetá, S Colombia
42 F8 **San Vicente, Volcán de** ※ C El Salvador
43 O15 **San Vito** Puntarenas, SE Costa Rica
106 I7 **San Vito al Tagliamento** Friuli-Venezia Giulia, NE Italy
107 H23 **San Vito, Capo** *headland* Sicilia, Italy, C Mediterranean Sea
107 P18 **San Vito dei Normanni** Puglia, SE Italy
160 L17 **Sanya** *var.* Ya Xian. Hainan, S China
83 J16 **Sanyati** ≈ N Zimbabwe
25 Q16 **San Ygnacio** Texas, SW USA
160 L6 **Sanyuan** Shaanxi, C China
123 P11 **Sanyyakhtakh** Respublika Sakha (Yakutiya), NE Russian Federation
82 C10 **Sanza Pombo** Uíge, NW Angola
Sanzyô *see* Sanjō
104 G14 **São Bartolomeu de Messines** Faro, S Portugal
60 M10 **São Bernardo do Campo** São Paulo, S Brazil
61 F15 **São Borja** Rio Grande do Sul, S Brazil
104 H14 **São Brás de Alportel** Faro, S Portugal
60 M10 **São Caetano do Sul** São Paulo, S Brazil
60 L9 **São Carlos** São Paulo, S Brazil
59 P16 **São Cristóvão** Sergipe, E Brazil
61 F15 **São Francisco de Assis** Rio Grande do Sul, S Brazil
58 K13 **São Félix** Pará, NE Brazil
São Félix *see* São Félix do Araguaia
59 J16 **São Félix do Araguaia** *var.* São Félix. Mato Grosso, W Brazil
59 J14 **São Félix do Xingu** Pará, NE Brazil
60 Q9 **São Fidélis** Rio de Janeiro, SE Brazil
76 D10 **São Filipe** Fogo, S Cape Verde
60 K12 **São Francisco do Sul** Santa Catarina, S Brazil
60 K12 **São Francisco, Ilha de** *island* S Brazil
59 P16 **São Francisco, Rio** ≈ E Brazil
61 G16 **São Gabriel** Rio Grande do Sul, S Brazil
60 P10 **São Gonçalo** Rio de Janeiro, SE Brazil
81 H23 **Sao Hill** Iringa, S Tanzania
60 R9 **São João da Barra** Rio de Janeiro, SE Brazil
104 G7 **São João da Madeira** Aveiro, N Portugal
58 M12 **São João de Cortês** Maranhão, E Brazil
59 M21 **São João del Rei** Minas Gerais, NE Brazil
59 N15 **São João do Piauí** Piauí, E Brazil
59 N14 **São João dos Patos** Maranhão, E Brazil
58 C11 **São Joaquim** Amazonas, NW Brazil
61 J14 **São Joaquim** Santa Catarina, S Brazil
60 L7 **São Joaquim da Barra** São Paulo, S Brazil
64 N2 **São Jorge** *island* Azores, Portugal, NE Atlantic Ocean
61 K14 **São José** Santa Catarina, S Brazil
60 M8 **São José do Rio Pardo** São Paulo, S Brazil
60 K8 **São José do Rio Preto** São Paulo, S Brazil
60 N10 **São Jose dos Campos** São Paulo, S Brazil
61 I17 **São Lourenço do Sul** Rio Grande do Sul, S Brazil
58 F11 **São Luís** Roraima, N Brazil
58 M12 **São Luís** *state capital* Maranhão, NE Brazil
58 M12 **São Luís, Ilha de** *island* NE Brazil
61 F14 **São Luiz Gonzaga** Rio Grande do Sul, S Brazil
104 I10 **São Mamede** ▲ C Portugal
São Mandol *see* São Manuel, Rio
47 U8 **São Manuel** ≈ C Brazil
59 H15 **São Manuel, Rio** *var.* São Mandol, Teles Pirés. ≈ C Brazil
58 C11 **São Marcelino** Amazonas, NW Brazil
58 N12 **São Marcos, Baía de** *bay* N Brazil
59 O20 **São Mateus** Espírito Santo, SE Brazil
60 J12 **São Mateus do Sul** Paraná, S Brazil
64 P3 **São Miguel** *island* Azores, Portugal, NE Atlantic Ocean
60 G13 **São Miguel d'Oeste** Santa Catarina, S Brazil
45 P9 **Saona, Isla** *island* SE Dominican Republic
172 H12 **Saondzou** ▲ Grande Comore, NW Comoros
103 R10 **Saône** ≈ E France
103 Q9 **Saône-et-Loire** ◈ *department* C France
76 D9 **São Nicolau** *Eng.* Saint Nicholas. *island* Ilhas de Barlavento, N Cape Verde
60 M10 **São Paulo** *state capital* São Paulo, S Brazil
60 K9 **São Paulo** *off.* Estado de São Paulo. ◈ *state* S Brazil
São Paulo de Loanda *see* Luanda
São Pedro do Rio Grande do Sul *see* Rio Grande
104 H7 **São Pedro do Sul** Viseu, N Portugal
64 K13 **São Pedro e São Paulo** *undersea feature* C Atlantic Ocean
59 M14 **São Raimundo das Mangabeiras** Maranhão, E Brazil
59 Q14 **São Roque, Cabo de** *headland* E Brazil
São Salvador/São Salvador do Congo *see* M'Banza Congo, Angola
São Salvador *see* Salvador, Brazil
60 N10 **São Sebastião, Ilha de** *island* S Brazil
83 N19 **São Sebastião, Ponta** *headland* C Mozambique
104 F13 **São Teotónio** Beja, S Portugal
São Tiago *see* Santiago
79 B18 **São Tomé** ● (Sao Tome and Principe) São Tomé, S Sao Tome and Principe
79 B18 **São Tomé** ✈ São Tomé, S Sao Tome and Principe
79 B18 **São Tomé** *Eng.* Saint Thomas. *island* S Sao Tome and Principe
79 B17 **Sao Tome and Principe** *off.* Democratic Republic of Sao Tome and Principe. ◆ *republic* E Atlantic Ocean
74 H9 **Saoura, Oued** ≈ NW Algeria
60 M10 **São Vicente** *Eng.* Saint Vincent. São Paulo, S Brazil
64 O5 **São Vicente** Madeira, Portugal, NE Atlantic Ocean
76 C9 **São Vicente** *Eng.* Saint Vincent. *island* Ilhas de Barlavento, N Cape Verde
São Vicente, Cabo de *see* São Vicente, Cabo de
104 F14 **São Vicente, Cabo de** *Eng.* Cape Saint Vincent, *Port.* Cabo de São Vicente. *headland* S Portugal
Sápai *see* Sápes
Sapaleri, Cerro *see* Zapaleri, Cerro
Saparoea *see* Saparua
171 S13 **Saparua** *prev.* Saparoea. C Indonesia
168 L11 **Sapat** Sumatera, W Indonesia
77 U17 **Sapele** Delta, S Nigeria
23 X7 **Sapelo Island** *island* Georgia, SE USA
23 X7 **Sapelo Sound** *sound* Georgia, SE USA
114 K13 **Sápes** *var.* Sápai. Anatolikí Makedonía kai Thráki, NE Greece
115 D22 **Sapiéntza** *island* S Greece
Sapir *see* Sappir
61 I15 **Sapiranga** Rio Grande do Sul, S Brazil
114 K13 **Sápka** ▲ NE Greece
56 D11 **Saposoa** San Martín, N Peru
119 F16 **Sapotskino** *Pol.* Sopockinie, *Rus.* Sopotskin. Hrodzyenskaya Voblasts', W Belarus
77 P13 **Sapoui** *var.* Sapouy. S Burkina
Sapouy *see* Sapoui
138 F12 **Sappir** *var.* Sapir. Southern, S Israel
165 S4 **Sapporo** Hokkaidō, NE Japan
107 M19 **Sapri** Campania, S Italy
169 T16 **Sapudi, Pulau** *island* S Indonesia
27 P9 **Sapulpa** Oklahoma, C USA
142 J4 **Saqqez** *var.* Saghez, Sakiz, Saqqiz. Kordestān, NW Iran
Saqqiz *see* Saqqez
139 U8 **Sarābādī** E Iraq
167 P10 **Sara Buri** *var.* Saraburi. Saraburi, C Thailand
24 K9 **Saragosa** Texas, SW USA
Saragossa *see* Zaragoza
Saragt *see* Serakhs
56 B8 **Saraguro** Loja, S Ecuador
128 M6 **Sarai** Ryazanskaya Oblast', W Russian Federation
Sarāi *see* Saray
154 M12 **Saraipāli** Madhya Pradesh, C India
149 T9 **Sarāi Sidhu** Punjab, E Pakistan
93 M15 **Säräisniemi** Oulu, C Finland
113 I14 **Sarajevo** ● (Bosnia and Herzegovina) Federacija Bosna I Hercegovina, SE Bosnia and Herzegovina
112 I13 **Sarajevo** ✈ Federacija Bosna I Hercegovina, C Bosnia and Herzegovina
143 V4 **Sarakhs** Khorāsān, NE Iran
115 H17 **Sarakíniko, Akrotírio** *headland* Évvoia, C Greece
115 I18 **Sarakinó** *island* Vóreioi Sporádes, Greece, Aegean Sea

◆ Country ● Country Capital ◇ Dependent Territory ○ Dependent Territory Capital ◈ Administrative Region ✈ International Airport ▲ Mountain ▲ Mountain Range ※ Volcano ≈ River ◎ Lake ▣ Reservoir

129 V7 **Saraktash** Orenburgskaya Oblast', W Russian Federation
30 L15 **Sara, Lake** ◎ Illinois, N USA
23 N8 **Saraland** Alabama, S USA
55 V9 **Saramacca** ◈ *district* N Surinam
55 V10 **Saramacca Rivier** ≈ C Surinam
166 M2 **Saramati** ▲ N Myanmar
145 R10 **Saran'** *Kaz.* Saran. Karaganda, C Kazakhstan
18 K7 **Saranac Lake** New York, NE USA
18 K7 **Saranac River** ≈ New York, NE USA
Saranda *see* Sarandë
113 L23 **Sarandë** *var.* Saranda, *It.* Porto Edda; *prev.* Santi Quaranta. Vlorë, S Albania
61 H14 **Sarandi** Rio Grande do Sul, S Brazil
61 F19 **Sarandí del Yí** Durazno, C Uruguay
61 F19 **Sarandí Grande** Florida, S Uruguay
171 Q8 **Sarangani Islands** *island group* S Philippines
129 P5 **Saransk** Respublika Mordoviya, W Russian Federation
115 C14 **Sarantáporos** ≈ N Greece
114 H9 **Sarantsi** Sofiya, W Bulgaria
129 T3 **Sarapul** Udmurtskaya Respublika, NW Russian Federation
Sarâqeb *see* Sarāqib
138 I3 **Sarāqib** *Fr.* Sarâqeb. Idlib, N Syria
54 J5 **Sarare** Lara, N Venezuela
55 O10 **Sarariña** Amazonas, S Venezuela
143 S10 **Sar Ashk** Kermān, C Iran
23 V13 **Sarasota** Florida, SE USA
117 O11 **Sarata** Odes'ka Oblast', SW Ukraine
116 I10 **Sărățel** *Hung.* Szeretfalva. Bistrița-Năsăud, N Romania
25 X10 **Saratoga** Texas, SW USA
18 K10 **Saratoga Springs** New York, NE USA
129 P8 **Saratov** Saratovskaya Oblast', W Russian Federation
129 P8 **Saratovskaya Oblast'** ◈ *province* W Russian Federation
129 Q7 **Saratovskoye Vodokhranilishche** ⊟ W Russian Federation
Saravan/Saravane *see* Salavan
169 S9 **Sarawak** ◈ *state* East Malaysia
Sarawak *see* Kuching
139 U6 **Sarāy** *var.* Sarāi. E Iraq
136 D10 **Saray** Tekirdağ, NW Turkey
76 J12 **Saraya** SE Senegal
143 W14 **Sarbāz** Sīstān va Balūchestān, SE Iran
143 U8 **Sarbīsheh** Khorāsān, E Iran
111 J24 **Sárbogárd** Fejér, C Hungary
Şărcad *see* Sarkad
27 S7 **Sarcoxie** Missouri, C USA
152 L11 **Sārda** *Nep.* Kali. ≈ India/Nepal
152 G10 **Sardārshahr** Rājasthān, NW India
107 C18 **Sardegna** *Eng.* Sardinia. ◈ *region* Italy, C Mediterranean Sea
107 A18 **Sardegna** *Eng.* Sardinia. *island* Italy, C Mediterranean Sea
42 K13 **Sardinal** Guanacaste, NW Costa Rica
54 G7 **Sardinata** Norte de Santander, N Colombia
Sardinia *see* Sardegna
120 K8 **Sardinia-Corsica Trough** *undersea feature* Tyrrhenian Sea, C Mediterranean Sea
22 L2 **Sardis** Mississippi, S USA
22 L2 **Sardis Lake** ⊟ Mississippi, S USA
27 P12 **Sardis Lake** ⊟ Oklahoma, C USA
92 H12 **Sarek** ▲ N Sweden
149 N3 **Sar-e Pul** *var.* Sar-i-Pul. Sar-e Pul, N Afghanistan
149 O3 **Sar-e Pol** ◈ *province* N Afghanistan
Sar-e Pol *see* Sar-e Pol-e Żahāb
142 J6 **Sar-e Pol-e Żahāb** *var.* Sar-e Pol, Sar-i Pul. Kermānshāh, W Iran
147 T13 **Sarez, Kŭli** *Rus.* Sarezskoye Ozero. ◎ SE Tajikistan
Sarezskoye Ozero *see* Sarez, Kŭli
64 G10 **Sargasso Sea** *sea* W Atlantic Ocean
149 U8 **Sargodha** Punjab, NE Pakistan
78 I13 **Sarh** *prev.* Fort-Archambault. Moyen-Chari, S Chad
143 P4 **Sārī** *var.* Sari, Sāri. Māzandarān, N Iran
115 N23 **Saría** *island* SE Greece
Sariasiya *see* Sariosiyo
40 F3 **Saric** Sonora, NW Mexico
188 K6 **Sarigan** *island* C Northern Mariana Islands
136 D14 **Sarıgöl** Manisa, SW Turkey
139 T6 **Sārihah** E Iraq
137 R12 **Sarıkamış** Kars, NE Turkey
169 R9 **Sarikei** Sarawak, East Malaysia
147 U12 **Sarikol Range** *Rus.* Sarykol'skiy Khrebet. ▲ China/Tajikistan
181 Y7 **Sarina** Queensland, NE Australia
Sarine *see* La Sarine
105 S5 **Sariñena** Aragón, NE Spain
147 O13 **Sariosiyo** *Rus.* Sariasiya. Surkhondaryo Wiloyati, S Uzbekistan
Sar-i-Pul *see* Sar-e Pol, Afghanistan
Sar-i Pul *see* Sar-e Pol-e Żahāb, Iran
Sariqamish Kŭli *see* Sarykamyshkoye Ozero
149 V1 **Sarī Qūl** *Rus.* Ozero Zurkul', *Taj.* Zŭrkŭl. ◎ Afghanistan/Tajikistan *see also* Zŭrkŭl
75 Q12 **Sarīr Tībistī** *var.* Serir Tibesti. *desert* S Libya
25 S15 **Sarita** Texas, SW USA
163 W14 **Sariwŏn** SW North Korea
114 P12 **Sarıyer** İstanbul, NW Turkey
97 L26 **Sark** *Fr.* Sercq. *island* Channel Islands
111 N24 **Sarkad** *Rom.* Şărcad. Békés, SE Hungary
145 W14 **Sarkand** Almaty, SW Kazakhstan
Sarkaņi *see* Krasnogorskoye
152 D11 **Sarkāri Tala** Rājasthān, NW India
136 G15 **Şarkîkaraağaç** *var.* Şarki Karaağaç. Isparta, SW Turkey
136 L13 **Şarkışla** Sivas, C Turkey
136 C11 **Şarköy** Tekirdağ, NW Turkey
Sárköz *see* Livada
Sarlat *see* Sarlat-la-Canéda
102 M13 **Sarlat-la-Canéda** *var.* Sarlat. Dordogne, SW France
109 S3 **Sarleinsbach** Oberösterreich, N Austria
171 Y12 **Sarmi** Irian Jaya, E Indonesia
63 I19 **Sarmiento** Chubut, S Argentina
63 H25 **Sarmiento, Monte** ▲ S Chile
94 J11 **Särna** Dalarna, C Sweden
108 F8 **Sarnen** Obwalden, C Switzerland
108 F9 **Sarner See** ◎ C Switzerland
14 D16 **Sarnia** Ontario, S Canada
116 L3 **Sarny** Rivnens'ka Oblast', NW Ukraine
171 O13 **Saroako** Sulawesi, C Indonesia
118 L13 **Sarochyna** *Rus.* Sorochino. Vitsyebskaya Voblasts', N Belarus
168 L12 **Sarolangun** Sumatera, W Indonesia
165 U3 **Saroma** Hokkaidō, NE Japan
165 V3 **Saroma-ko** ◎ Hokkaidō, NE Japan
Saronic Gulf *see* Saronikós Kólpos
115 H20 **Saronikós Kólpos** *Eng.* Saronic Gulf. *gulf* S Greece
106 D7 **Saronno** Lombardia, N Italy
136 B11 **Saros Körfezi** *gulf* NW Turkey
111 N20 **Sárospatak** Borsod-Abaúj-Zemplén, NE Hungary
129 P12 **Sarpa** Respublika Kalmykiya, SW Russian Federation
129 P12 **Sarpa, Ozero** ◎ SW Russian Federation
113 M18 **Šar Planina** ▲ FYR Macedonia/Yugoslavia
95 I16 **Sarpsborg** Østfold, S Norway
139 U5 **Sarqaļā** N Iraq
103 U4 **Sarralbe** Moselle, NE France
Sarre *see* Saar, France/Germany
Sarre *see* Saarland, Germany
103 U5 **Sarrebourg** *Ger.* Saarburg. Moselle, NE France
Sarrebruck *see* Saarbrücken
103 U4 **Sarreguemines** *prev.* Saargemund. Moselle, NE France
104 I3 **Sarria** Galicia, NW Spain
105 S8 **Sarrión** Aragón, NE Spain
42 F4 **Sarstoon** *Sp.* Río Sarstún. ≈ Belize/Guatemala
Sarstún, Río *see* Sarstoon
123 Q9 **Sartang** ≈ NE Russian Federation
103 X16 **Sartène** Corse, France, C Mediterranean Sea
102 K7 **Sarthe** ◈ *department* NW France
102 K7 **Sarthe** ≈ N France
115 H15 **Sárti** Kentrikí Makedonía, N Greece
165 T1 **Sarufutsu** Hokkaidō, NE Japan
Saruhan *see* Manisa
152 G9 **Sarūpsar** Rājasthān, NW India
137 U13 **Şärur** *prev.* Il'ichevsk. SW Azerbaijan
Sarvani *see* Marneuli
111 G23 **Sárvár** Vas, W Hungary
143 P11 **Sarvestān** Fārs, S Iran
171 W12 **Sarwon** Irian Jaya, E Indonesia
145 P17 **Saryagach** *Kaz.* Saryaghash. Yuzhnyy Kazakhstan, S Kazakhstan
Saryaghash *see* Saryagach
Saryarqa *see* Kazakhskiy Melkosopochnik
147 W8 **Sary-Bulak** Narynskaya Oblast', C Kyrgyzstan
147 U10 **Sary-Bulak** Oshskaya Oblast', SW Kyrgyzstan
117 S14 **Sarych, Mys** *headland* S Ukraine
147 Z7 **Sary-Dzhaz** *var.* Aksu He. ≈ China/Kyrgyzstan *see also* Aksu He
145 T14 **Saryesik-Atyrau, Peski** *desert* E Kazakhstan
144 G13 **Sarykamys** *Kaz.* Saryqamys. Mangistau, SW Kazakhstan
146 F8 **Sarykamyshkoye Ozero** *Uzb.* Sariqamish Kŭli. *salt lake* Kazakhstan/Uzbekistan
Sarykol'skiy Khrebet *see* Sarikol Range
144 M10 **Sarykopa, Ozero** ◎ C Kazakhstan
145 V15 **Saryozek** *Kaz.* Saryözek. Almaty, SE Kazakhstan
Saryqamys *see* Sarykamys
145 S13 **Saryshagan** *Kaz.* Saryshahan. Zhezkazgan, SE Kazakhstan
Saryshahan *see* Saryshagan
145 O13 **Sarysu** ≈ S Kazakhstan
147 T11 **Sary-Tash** Oshskaya Oblast', SW Kyrgyzstan
146 J15 **Saryyazynskoye Vodokhranilishche** ⊟ S Turkmenistan
106 E10 **Sarzana** Liguria, NW Italy
188 B17 **Sasalaguan, Mount** ▲ S Guam
153 O14 **Sasarām** Bihār, N India
186 M8 **Sasari, Mount** ▲ Santa Isabel, N Solomon Islands
164 C13 **Sasebo** Nagasaki, Kyūshū, SW Japan
14 I9 **Saseginaga, Lac** ◎ Quebec, SE Canada
Saseno *see* Sazan
11 R13 **Saskatchewan** ◈ *province* SW Canada
11 U14 **Saskatchewan** ≈ Manitoba/Saskatchewan, C Canada
11 T15 **Saskatoon** Saskatchewan, S Canada
11 T15 **Saskatoon** ✕ Saskatchewan, S Canada
123 N7 **Saskylakh** Respublika Sakha (Yakutiya), NE Russian Federation
42 L7 **Saslaya, Cerro** ▲ N Nicaragua
38 G17 **Sasmik, Cape** *headland* Tanaga Island, Alaska, USA
119 N19 **Sasnovy Bor** *Rus.* Sosnovyy Bor. Homyel'skaya Voblasts', SE Belarus
129 N5 **Sasovo** Ryazanskaya Oblast', W Russian Federation
25 S12 **Saspamco** Texas, SW USA
109 W9 **Sass** *var.* Sassbach. ≈ SE Austria
76 M17 **Sassandra** S Ivory Coast
76 M17 **Sassandra** *var.* Ibo, Sassandra Fleuve. ≈ S Ivory Coast
Sassandra Fleuve *see* Sassandra
107 B17 **Sassari** Sardegna, Italy, C Mediterranean Sea
Sassbach *see* Sass
98 H11 **Sassenheim** Zuid-Holland, W Netherlands
Sassmacken *see* Valdemārpils
100 O7 **Sassnitz** Mecklenburg-Vorpommern, NE Germany
99 E16 **Sas van Gent** Zeeland, SW Netherlands
145 W12 **Sasykkol', Ozero** ◎ E Kazakhstan
117 O12 **Sasyk Kunduk, Ozero** ◎ SW Ukraine
76 J12 **Satadougou** Kayes, SW Mali
105 V11 **Sa Talaiassa** ▲ Eivissa, Spain, W Mediterranean Sea
164 C17 **Sata-misaki** *headland* Kyūshū, SW Japan
26 I7 **Satanta** Kansas, C USA
155 E15 **Sātāra** Mahārāshtra, W India
192 G15 **Sātaua** Savai'i, NW Samoa
188 M16 **Satawal** *island* Caroline Islands, C Micronesia
189 R17 **Satawan Atoll** *atoll* Mortlock Islands, C Micronesia
23 Y12 **Satellite Beach** Florida, SE USA
95 M14 **Säter** Dalarna, C Sweden
Sathmar *see* Satu Mare
23 V7 **Satilla River** ≈ Georgia, SE USA
57 F14 **Satipo** *var.* San Francisco de Satipo. Junín, C Peru
122 F11 **Satka** Chelyabinskaya Oblast', C Russian Federation
153 T16 **Satkhira** Khulna, SW Bangladesh
154 K9 **Satna** *prev.* Sutna. Madhya Pradesh, C India
103 R11 **Satolas** ✕ (Lyon) Rhône, E France
111 N20 **Sátoraljaújhely** Borsod-Abaúj-Zemplén, NE Hungary
145 O12 **Satpayev** *prev.* Nikol'skiy. Zhezkazgan, C Kazakhstan
154 G11 **Sātpura Range** ▲ C India
167 P12 **Sattahip** *var.* Ban Sattahip, Ban Sattahipp. Chon Buri, S Thailand
92 L11 **Sattanen** Lappi, NE Finland
Satul *see* Satun
116 H9 **Satulung** *Hung.* Kővárhosszúfalu. Maramureș, N Romania
Satul-Vechi *see* Staro Selo
116 G8 **Satu Mare** *Ger.* Sathmar, *Hung.* Szatmárnémeti. Satu Mare, NW Romania
116 G8 **Satu Mare** ◈ *county* NW Romania
167 N16 **Satun** *var.* Satul, Setul. Satun, SW Thailand
192 G16 **Satupaiteau** Savai'i, W Samoa
Sau *see* Sava
14 F14 **Sauble** ≈ Ontario, S Canada
14 F13 **Sauble Beach** Ontario, S Canada
61 C16 **Sauce** Corrientes, NE Argentina
Sauce *see* Juan L.Lacaze
36 K15 **Sauceda Mountains** ▲ Arizona, SW USA
61 C17 **Sauce de Luna** Entre Ríos, E Argentina
63 L15 **Sauce Grande, Río** ≈ E Argentina
40 K6 **Saucillo** Chihuahua, N Mexico
95 D15 **Sauda** Rogaland, S Norway
145 Q16 **Saudakent** *Kaz.* Saūdakent; *prev.* Baykadam *Kaz.* Bayqadam. Zhambyl, S Kazakhstan
92 J2 **Saudhárkrókur** Nordhurland Vestra, N Iceland
141 P9 **Saudi Arabia** *off.* Kingdom of Saudi Arabia, *Ar.* Al 'Arabīyah as Su'ūdīyah, Al Mamlakah al 'Arabīyah as Su'ūdīyah. ◆ *monarchy* SW Asia
101 D19 **Sauer** *var.* Sûre. ≈ NW Europe *see also* Sûre
101 F15 **Sauerland** *forest* W Germany
14 F14 **Saugeen** ≈ Ontario, S Canada
18 K12 **Saugerties** New York, NE USA
Saugor *see* Sāgar
10 K15 **Saugstad, Mount** ▲ British Columbia, SW Canada
Sāūjbulāgh *see* Mahābād
102 J11 **Saujon** Charente-Maritime, W France
29 T7 **Sauk Centre** Minnesota, N USA
30 L8 **Sauk City** Wisconsin, N USA
29 U7 **Sauk Rapids** Minnesota, N USA
55 Y11 **Saül** C French Guiana
103 O7 **Sauldre** ≈ C France
101 I23 **Saulgau** Baden-Württemberg, SW Germany
103 Q8 **Saulieu** Côte d'Or, C France
118 G8 **Saulkrasti** Rīga, C Latvia
15 S6 **Sault-aux-Cochons, Rivière du** ≈ Quebec, SE Canada
31 Q4 **Sault Sainte Marie** Michigan, N USA
12 F14 **Sault Ste.Marie** Ontario, S Canada
145 P7 **Saumalkol'** *prev.* Volodarskoye. Severnyy Kazakhstan, N Kazakhstan
190 E13 **Sauma, Pointe** *headland* Île Alofi, W Wallis and Futuna
171 T16 **Saumlaki** *var.* Saumlakki. Pulau Yamdena, E Indonesia
Saumlakki *see* Saumlaki
15 R12 **Saumon, Rivière au** ≈ Quebec, SE Canada
102 K8 **Saumur** Maine-et-Loire, NW France
185 F23 **Saunders, Cape** *headland* South Island, NZ
195 N13 **Saunders Coast** *physical region* Antarctica
65 B23 **Saunders Island** *island* NW Falkland Islands
65 C24 **Saunders Island Settlement** Saunders Island, NW Falkland Islands
82 F11 **Saurimo** *Port.* Henrique de Carvalho, Vila Henrique de Carvalho. Lunda Sul, NE Angola
55 S11 **Sauriwaunawa** S Guyana
82 D12 **Sautar** Malanje, NW Angola
42 J3 **Sauteurs** N Grenada
102 K13 **Sauveterre-de-Guyenne** Gironde, SW France
119 O14 **Sava** *Rus.* Sava. Mahilyowskaya Voblasts', E Belarus
84 H11 **Sava** *Eng.* Save, *Ger.* Sau, *Hung.* Száva. ≈ SE Europe
42 J5 **Savá** Colón, N Honduras
33 Y8 **Savage** Montana, NW USA
183 N16 **Savage River** Tasmania, SE Australia
77 R15 **Savalou** S Benin
30 K10 **Savanna** Illinois, N USA
23 X6 **Savannah** Georgia, SE USA
27 R2 **Savannah** Missouri, C USA
20 H10 **Savannah** Tennessee, S USA
21 O12 **Savannah River** ≈ Georgia/South Carolina, SE USA
Savannakhét *see* Khanthabouli
44 H12 **Savanna-La-Mar** W Jamaica
12 B10 **Savant Lake** ◎ Ontario, S Canada
155 F17 **Savanūr** Karnātaka, W India
93 J16 **Sävar** Västerbotten, N Sweden
Savaria *see* Szombathely
154 C11 **Sāvarkundla** *var.* Kundla. Gujarāt, W India
116 F11 **Săvârșin** *Hung.* Soborsin; *prev.* Săvîrșin. Arad, W Romania
136 C13 **Savaştepe** Balıkesir, W Turkey
Savat *see* Sawot
83 N18 **Save** Inhambane, E Mozambique
102 L16 **Save** ≈ S France
83 L17 **Save** *var.* Sabi. ≈ Mozambique/Zimbabwe *see also* Sabi
Save *see* Sava
77 R15 **Savè** SE Benin
142 M6 **Sāveh** Markazī, W Iran
116 L8 **Săveni** Botoșani, NE Romania
103 N16 **Saverdun** Ariège, S France
103 U5 **Saverne** *var.* Zabern; *anc.* Tres Tabernae. Bas-Rhin, NE France
Savichi *see* Savichy
119 O21 **Savichy** *Rus.* Savichi. Homyel'skaya Voblasts', SE Belarus
106 B9 **Savigliano** Piemonte, NW Italy
Savigsivik *see* Savissivik
Savinichi *see* Savinichy
119 Q16 **Savinichy** *Rus.* Savinichi. Mahilyowskaya Voblasts', E Belarus
Savinski *see* Savinskiy
106 H11 **Savio** ≈ C Italy
Săvîrșin *see* Săvârșin
197 O11 **Savissivik** *var.* Savigsivik. Avannaarsua, S Greenland
93 N18 **Savitaipale** Etelä-Suomi, S Finland
113 J15 **Šavnik** Montenegro, SW Yugoslavia
108 I9 **Savognin** Graubünden, S Switzerland
103 T12 **Savoie** ◈ *department* E France
106 C10 **Savona** Liguria, NW Italy
93 N17 **Savonlinna** *Swe.* Nyslott. Itä-Suomi, SE Finland
93 N17 **Savonranta** Itä-Suomi, SE Finland
38 K10 **Savoonga** Saint Lawrence Island, Alaska, USA
30 M13 **Savoy** Illinois, N USA
117 O8 **Savran'** Odes'ka Oblast', SW Ukraine
137 R11 **Şavşat** Artvin, NE Turkey
95 L19 **Sävsjö** Jönköping, S Sweden
Savu, Kepulauan *see* Sawu, Kepulauan
92 M11 **Savukoski** Lappi, NE Finland
Savu, Pulau *see* Sawu, Pulau
187 Y14 **Savusavu** Vanua Levu, N Fiji
171 O17 **Savu Sea** *Ind.* Laut Sawu. *sea* S Indonesia
83 H17 **Savute** Chobe, N Botswana
139 N7 **Şawāb 'Uqlat** *well* W Iraq
138 M7 **Şawāb, Wādī as** *dry watercourse* W Iraq
152 H13 **Sawāi Mādhopur** Rājasthān, N India**Sawakin** *see* Suakin
167 R8 **Sawang Daen Din** Sakon Nakhon, E Thailand
167 O8 **Sawankhalok** *var.* Swankalok. Sukhothai, NW Thailand
165 P13 **Sawara** Chiba, Honshū, S Japan
37 R5 **Sawatch Range** ▲ Colorado, C USA
141 N12 **Sawdā', Jabal** ▲ SW Saudi Arabia
75 P9 **Sawdā', Jabal as** ▲ C Libya
Sawdirī *see* Sodiri
97 F14 **Sawel Mountain** ▲ C Northern Ireland, UK
Sawhāj *see* Sohāg
77 O15 **Sawla** N Ghana
147 P11 **Sawot** *Rus.* Savat. Sirdaryo Wiloyati, E Uzbekistan
141 X12 **Şawqirah** *var.* Suqrah. S Oman
141 X12 **Şawqirah, Dawḩat** *var.* Ghubbat Sawqirah, Sukra Bay, Suqrah Bay. *bay* S Oman
Sawqirah, Ghubbat *see* Şawqirah, Dawḩat
183 V5 **Sawtell** New South Wales, SE Australia
138 K7 **Şawt, Wādī aş** *dry watercourse* S Syria
171 O17 **Sawu, Kepulauan** *var.* Kepulauan Savu. *island group* S Indonesia
Sawu, Laut *see* Savu Sea
171 O17 **Sawu, Pulau** *var.* Pulau Savu. *island* Kepulauan Sawu, S Indonesia
105 S12 **Sax** País Valenciano, E Spain
Saxe *see* Sachsen
108 C11 **Saxon** Valais, SW Switzerland
Saxony *see* Sachsen
Saxony-Anhalt *see* Sachsen-Anhalt
77 R12 **Say** Niamey, SW Niger
15 V7 **Sayabec** Quebec, SE Canada
Sayaboury *see* Xaignabouli
145 U12 **Sayak** *Kaz.* Sayaq. Zhezkazgan, E Kazakhstan
57 D14 **Sayán** Lima, W Peru
131 T6 **Sayanskiy Khrebet** ▲ S Russian Federation
Sayaq *see* Sayak
146 K13 **Sayat** Lebapskiy Velayat, E Turkmenistan
42 D3 **Sayaxché** Petén, N Guatemala
Şaydā/Sayida *see* Saïda
141 T15 **Sayḩūt** E Yemen
29 U14 **Saylorville Lake** ⊟ Iowa, C USA
Saymenskiy Kanal *see* Saimaa Canal
163 N10 **Saynshand** Dornogovĭ, SE Mongolia
162 J11 **Saynshand** Ömnögovĭ, S Mongolia
162 F7 **Sayn-Ust** Govĭ-Altay, W Mongolia
Say-Ötesh *see* Say-Utës
138 J7 **Şayqal, Baḩr** ◎ S Syria
Sayrab *see* Sayrob
158 H4 **Sayram Hu** ◎ NW China
26 K11 **Sayre** Oklahoma, C USA
18 H12 **Sayre** Pennsylvania, NE USA
18 K15 **Sayreville** New Jersey, NE USA
147 N13 **Sayrob** *Rus.* Sayrab. Surkhondaryo Wiloyati, S Uzbekistan
40 L13 **Sayula** Jalisco, SW Mexico
141 R14 **Say 'ūn** *var.* Saywūn. C Yemen
144 G14 **Say-Utës** *Kaz.* Say-Ötesh. Mangistau, SW Kazakhstan
10 K16 **Sayward** Vancouver Island, British Columbia, SW Canada
Saywūn *see* Say 'ūn
Sayyāl *see* As Sayyāl
139 U8 **Sayyid 'Abid** *var.* Saiyid Abid. E Iraq
113 J22 **Sazan** *var.* Ishulli i Sazanit, *It.* Saseno. *island* SW Albania
Sazanit, Ishulli i *see* Sazan
Sazau/Sazawa *see* Sázava
111 E17 **Sázava** *var.* Sazau, *Ger.* Sazawa. ≈ C Czech Republic
126 J14 **Sazonovo** Vologodskaya Oblast', NW Russian Federation
102 G6 **Scaër** Finistère, NW France
97 J15 **Scafell Pike** ▲ NW England, UK
Scalabis *see* Santarém
96 M2 **Scalloway** N Scotland, UK
38 M11 **Scammon Bay** Alaska, USA
Scammon Lagoon/Scammon, Laguna *see* Ojo de Liebre, Laguna
84 F7 **Scandinavia** *geophysical region* NW Europe
Scania *see* Skåne
96 K5 **Scapa Flow** *sea basin* N Scotland, UK
107 K26 **Scaramia, Capo** *headland* Sicilia, Italy, C Mediterranean Sea
14 H15 **Scarborough** Ontario, SE Canada
45 Z16 **Scarborough** *prev.* Port Louis. Tobago, Trinidad and Tobago
97 N16 **Scarborough** N England, UK
185 I17 **Scargill** Canterbury, South Island, NZ
96 E7 **Scarp** *island* NW Scotland, UK
Scarpanto *see* Kárpathos
Scarpanto Strait *see* Karpathou, Stenó
107 G25 **Scauri** Sicilia, Italy, C Mediterranean Sea
Scealg, Bá na *see* Ballinskelligs Bay
Scebeli *see* Shebeli
100 K10 **Schaale** ≈ N Germany
100 K9 **Schaalsee** ◎ N Germany
99 G18 **Schaerbeek** Brussels, C Belgium
108 G6 **Schaffhausen** *Fr.* Schaffhouse. Schaffhausen, N Switzerland
108 G6 **Schaffhausen** *Fr.* Schaffhouse. ◈ *canton* N Switzerland
Schaffhouse *see* Schaffhausen
98 I8 **Schagen** Noord-Holland, NW Netherlands
Schaken *see* Šakiai
98 M10 **Schalkhaar** Overijssel, E Netherlands
109 R3 **Schärding** Oberösterreich, N Austria
100 G9 **Scharhörn** *island* NW Germany
Schässburg *see* Sighișoara
Schaulen *see* Šiauliai
30 M10 **Schaumburg** Illinois, N USA
Schebschi Mountains *see* Shebshi Mountains
98 P6 **Scheemda** Groningen, NE Netherlands
100 I10 **Scheessel** Niedersachsen, NW Germany
13 N8 **Schefferville** Quebec, E Canada
Schelde *see* Scheldt
99 D18 **Scheldt** *Dut.* Schelde, *Fr.* Escaut. ≈ W Europe
35 X5 **Schell Creek Range** ▲ Nevada, W USA
18 K10 **Schenectady** New York, NE USA
99 I17 **Scherpenheuvel** *Fr.* Montaigu. Vlaams Brabant, C Belgium
98 K11 **Scherpenzeel** Gelderland, C Netherlands
25 S12 **Schertz** Texas, SW USA
98 G11 **Scheveningen** Zuid-Holland, W Netherlands
98 G12 **Schiedam** Zuid-Holland, SW Netherlands
99 M24 **Schieren** Diekirch, NE Luxembourg
98 M4 **Schiermonnikoog** *Fris.* Skiermûntseach. Friesland, N Netherlands
98 M4 **Schiermonnikoog** *Fris.* Skiermûntseach. *island* Waddeneilanden, N Netherlands
99 K14 **Schijndel** Noord-Brabant, S Netherlands
Schil *see* Jiu
99 H16 **Schilde** Antwerpen, N Belgium
Schillen *see* Zhilino
103 V5 **Schiltigheim** Bas-Rhin, NE France
106 G7 **Schio** Veneto, NE Italy
98 H10 **Schiphol** ✕ (Amsterdam) Noord-Holland, C Netherlands
Schippenbeil *see* Sępopol
Schiria *see* Şiria
Schivelbein *see* Świdwin
115 D22 **Schíza** *island* S Greece
175 U3 **Schjetman Reef** *reef* Antarctica
Schlackenwerth *see* Ostrov
109 R7 **Schladming** Steiermark, SE Austria
Schlan *see* Slaný
Schlanders *see* Silandro
100 I7 **Schlei** *inlet* N Germany
101 D17 **Schleiden** Nordrhein-Westfalen, W Germany
Schlelau *see* Szydłowiec
100 I7 **Schleswig** Schleswig-Holstein, N Germany
29 T13 **Schleswig** Iowa, C USA
100 H8 **Schleswig-Holstein** ◈ *state* N Germany
Schlettstadt *see* Sélestat
108 F7 **Schlieren** Zürich, N Switzerland
Schlochau *see* Człuchów
Schloppe *see* Człopa
101 I18 **Schlüchtern** Hessen, C Germany
101 J17 **Schmalkalden** Thüringen, C Germany
109 W2 **Schmida** ≈ NE Austria
65 P19 **Schmidt-Ott Seamount** *var.* Schmitt-Ott Seamount, Schmitt-Ott Tablemount. *undersea feature* SW Indian Ocean
Schmiegel *see* Śmigiel
Schmitt-Ott Seamount/Schmitt-Ott Tablemount *see* Schmidt-Ott Seamount
15 V3 **Schmon** ≈ Quebec, SE Canada
101 M18 **Schneeberg** ▲ W Germany
Schneeberg *see* Veliki Snežnik
Schnee-Eifel *see* Schneifel
Schneekoppe *see* Sněžka
Schneidemühl *see* Piła
101 D18 **Schneifel** *var.* Schnee-Eifel. *plateau* W Germany
Schnelle Körös/Schnelle Kreisch *see* Crişul Repede
100 I11 **Schneverdingen** *var.* Schneverdingen (Wümme). Niedersachsen, NW Germany
Schneverdingen (Wümme) *see* Schneverdingen
Schoden *see* Skuodas
18 K10 **Schoharie** New York, NE USA
18 K11 **Schoharie Creek** ≈ New York, NE USA
115 J21 **Schoinoússa** *island* Kykládes, Greece, Aegean Sea
100 L13 **Schönebeck** Sachsen-Anhalt, C Germany
Schöneck *see* Skarszewy
100 O12 **Schönefeld** ✕ (Berlin) Berlin, NE Germany
101 K24 **Schongau** Bayern, S Germany
100 K13 **Schöningen** Niedersachsen, C Germany
Schönlanke *see* Trzcianka
Schönsee *see* Kowalewo Pomorskie
31 P10 **Schoolcraft** Michigan, N USA
98 O8 **Schoonebeek** Drenthe, NE Netherlands
98 I12 **Schoonhoven** Zuid-Holland, C Netherlands
98 H8 **Schoorl** Noord-Holland, NW Netherlands
Schooten *see* Schoten
101 F24 **Schopfheim** Baden-Württemberg, SW Germany
101 I21 **Schorndorf** Baden-Württemberg, S Germany
100 F10 **Schortens** Niedersachsen, NW Germany
99 H16 **Schoten** *var.* Schooten. Antwerpen, N Belgium
183 Q17 **Schouten Island** *island* Tasmania, SE Australia
186 C5 **Schouten Islands** *island group* NW PNG
98 E13 **Schouwen** *island* SW Netherlands
45 Q12 **Schœlcher** W Martinique
Schreiberhau *see* Szklarska Poręba
109 U2 **Schrems** Niederösterreich, E Austria
101 L22 **Schrobenhausen** Bayern, SE Germany
18 L8 **Schroon Lake** ◎ New York, NE USA
108 J8 **Schruns** Vorarlberg, W Austria
Schubin *see* Szubin
25 U11 **Schulenburg** Texas, SW USA
Schuls *see* Scuol
108 E8 **Schüpfheim** Luzern, C Switzerland
35 S6 **Schurz** Nevada, W USA
101 I24 **Schussen** ≈ S Germany
Schüttenhofen *see* Sušice
29 R15 **Schuyler** Nebraska, C USA
18 L10 **Schuylerville** New York, NE USA

◆ Country ● Country Capital ◇ Dependent Territory ○ Dependent Territory Capital ◈ Administrative Region ✕ International Airport ▲ Mountain ▲ Mountain Range ⩘ Volcano ≈ River ◎ Lake ⊟ Reservoir

101 K20 **Schwabach** Bayern, SE Germany
Schwabenalb see Schwäbische Alb
101 I23 **Schwäbische Alb** var. Schwabenalb, Eng. Swabian Jura. ⛰ S Germany
101 I22 **Schwäbisch Gmünd** var. Gmünd. Baden-Württemberg, SW Germany
101 I21 **Schwäbisch Hall** var. Hall. Baden-Württemberg, SW Germany
101 H16 **Schwalm** ≈ C Germany
109 V9 **Schwanberg** Steiermark, SE Austria
108 H8 **Schwanden** Glarus, E Switzerland
101 M20 **Schwandorf** Bayern, SE Germany
109 S5 **Schwanenstadt** Oberösterreich, NW Austria
169 S11 **Schwaner, Pegunungan** ⛰ Borneo, N Indonesia
109 W5 **Schwarza** ≈ E Austria
109 P9 **Schwarzach** ≈ S Austria
101 M20 **Schwarzach** Cz. Černice. ≈ Czech Republic/Germany
Schwarzach see Schwarzach im Pongau, Austria
Schwarzach see Svratka, Czech Republic
109 Q7 **Schwarzach im Pongau** var. Schwarzach. Salzburg, NW Austria
Schwarzawa see Svratka
101 N14 **Schwarze Elster** ≈ E Germany
Schwarze Körös see Crişul Negru
108 D9 **Schwarzenburg** Bern, W Switzerland
83 D21 **Schwarzrand** ⛰ S Namibia
101 G23 **Schwarzwald** Eng. Black Forest. ⛰ SW Germany
Schwarzwasser see Wda
39 P7 **Schwatka Mountains** ⛰ Alaska, USA
109 N7 **Schwaz** Tirol, W Austria
109 Y4 **Schwechat** Niederösterreich, NE Austria
109 Y4 **Schwechat** ✕ (Wien) Wien, E Austria
100 P11 **Schwedt** Brandenburg, NE Germany
101 D19 **Schweich** Rheinland-Pfalz, SW Germany
Schweidnitz see Świdnica
101 J18 **Schweinfurt** Bayern, SE Germany
Schweiz see Switzerland
100 L9 **Schwerin** Mecklenburg-Vorpommern, N Germany
Schwerin see Skwierzyna
100 L9 **Schweriner See** ◎ N Germany
Schwertberg see Świecie
101 F15 **Schwerte** Nordrhein-Westfalen, W Germany
Schwiebus see Świebodzin
100 P13 **Schwielochsee** ◎ NE Germany
Schwihau see Švihov
Schwiz see Schwyz
108 G8 **Schwyz** var. Schwiz. Schwyz, C Switzerland
108 G8 **Schwyz** var. Schwiz. ◈ canton C Switzerland
14 J11 **Schyan** ≈ Quebec, SE Canada
Schyl see Jiu
107 I24 **Sciacca** Sicilia, Italy, C Mediterranean Sea
Sciasciamana see Shashemenē
107 L26 **Scicli** Sicilia, Italy, C Mediterranean Sea
97 F25 **Scilly, Isles of** island group SW England, UK
111 H17 **Ścinawa** Ger. Steinau an der Elbe. Dolnośląskie, SW Poland
Scio see Chíos
31 S14 **Scioto River** ≈ Ohio, N USA
36 L5 **Scipio** Utah, W USA
33 X6 **Scobey** Montana, NW USA
183 T7 **Scone** New South Wales, SE Australia
Scoresby Sound/Scoresbysund see Ittoqqortoormiit
Scoresby Sund see Kangertittivaq
Scorno, Punta dello see Caprara, Punta
34 K3 **Scotia** California, W USA
47 Y14 **Scotia Plate** tectonic feature
47 V15 **Scotia Ridge** undersea feature S Atlantic Ocean
194 H2 **Scotia Sea** sea SW Atlantic Ocean
29 Q12 **Scotland** South Dakota, N USA
25 R5 **Scotland** Texas, SW USA
96 H11 **Scotland** national region UK
21 W8 **Scotland Neck** North Carolina, SE USA
195 R13 **Scott Base** NZ research station Antarctica
10 J16 **Scott, Cape** headland Vancouver Island, British Columbia, SW Canada
26 I5 **Scott City** Kansas, C USA
27 Y7 **Scott City** Missouri, C USA
195 R14 **Scott Coast** physical region Antarctica
18 C15 **Scottdale** Pennsylvania, NE USA
195 Y11 **Scott Glacier** glacier Antarctica
195 Q17 **Scott Island** island Antarctica
26 L11 **Scott, Mount** ▲ Oklahoma, USA
32 G15 **Scott, Mount** ▲ Oregon, NW USA
34 M1 **Scott River** ≈ California, W USA
28 I13 **Scottsbluff** Nebraska, C USA
23 Q2 **Scottsboro** Alabama, S USA
31 P15 **Scottsburg** Indiana, N USA
183 P16 **Scottsdale** Tasmania, SE Australia
36 L13 **Scottsdale** Arizona, SW USA
45 O12 **Scotts Head Village** var. Cachacrou. S Dominica
192 L14 **Scott Shoal** undersea feature S Pacific Ocean
20 K7 **Scottsville** Kentucky, S USA
29 U14 **Scranton** Iowa, C USA
18 I13 **Scranton** Pennsylvania, NE USA
186 B6 **Screw** ≈ NW PNG
29 R14 **Scribner** Nebraska, C USA
Scrobesbyrig' see Shrewsbury
14 I14 **Scugog** ≈ Ontario, SE Canada
14 I14 **Scugog, Lake** ◎ Ontario, SE Canada
97 N17 **Scunthorpe** E England, UK
108 K9 **Scuol** Ger. Schuls. Graubünden, E Switzerland
Scupi see Skopje
Scutari see Shkodër
113 K17 **Scutari, Lake** Alb. Liqeni i Shkodrës, SCr. Skadarsko Jezero. ◎ Albania/Yugoslavia
Scyros see Skýros
Scythopolis see Bet She'an
25 U13 **Seadrift** Texas, SW USA
21 Y4 **Seaford** var. Seaford City. Delaware, NE USA
Seaford City see Seaford
14 E15 **Seaforth** Ontario, S Canada
24 M6 **Seagraves** Texas, SW USA
11 X9 **Seal** ≈ Manitoba, C Canada
182 M10 **Sea Lake** Victoria, SE Australia
83 G26 **Seal, Cape** headland S South Africa
65 D26 **Sea Lion Islands** island group SE Falkland Islands
19 S8 **Seal Island** island Maine, NE USA
25 V11 **Sealy** Texas, SW USA
35 X12 **Searchlight** Nevada, W USA
27 V11 **Searcy** Arkansas, C USA
19 R7 **Searsport** Maine, NE USA
35 N10 **Seaside** California, W USA
32 F10 **Seaside** Oregon, NW USA
18 K16 **Seaside Heights** New Jersey, NE USA
32 H8 **Seattle** Washington, NW USA
32 H9 **Seattle-Tacoma** ✕ Washington, NW USA
185 J16 **Seaward Kaikoura Range** ⛰ South Island, NZ
42 J9 **Sébaco** Matagalpa, W Nicaragua
19 P8 **Sebago Lake** ◎ Maine, NE USA
169 S13 **Sebangan, Teluk** bay Borneo, C Indonesia
169 S13 **Sebanganu, Teluk** bay Borneo, C Indonesia
Sebaste/Sebastia see Sivas
23 Y12 **Sebastian** Florida, SE USA
40 C5 **Sebastían Vizcaíno, Bahía** bay NW Mexico
19 R6 **Sebasticook Lake** ◎ Maine, NE USA
34 M7 **Sebastopol** California, W USA
Sebastopol see Sevastopol'
169 W8 **Sebatik, Pulau** island N Indonesia
19 R5 **Sebec Lake** ◎ Maine, NE USA
76 K12 **Sébékoro** Kayes, W Mali
Sebenico see Šibenik
40 G6 **Seberi, Cerro** ▲ NW Mexico
116 H11 **Sebeş** Ger. Mühlbach, Hung. Szászsebes; prev. Sebeşu Săsesc. Alba, W Romania
Sebes-Körös see Crişul Repede
Sebeşu Săsesc see Sebeş
31 R8 **Sebewaing** Michigan, N USA
126 F16 **Sebezh** Pskovskaya Oblast', W Russian Federation
137 N12 **Şebinkarahisar** Giresun, N Turkey
116 F11 **Sebiş** Hung. Borossebes. Arad, W Romania
Sebkra Azz el Matti see Azzel Matti, Sebkha
19 Q4 **Seboomook Lake** ◎ Maine, NE USA
74 G6 **Sebou** var. Sebu. ≈ N Morocco
20 I6 **Sebree** Kentucky, S USA
23 X13 **Sebring** Florida, SE USA
Sebta see Ceuta
Sebu see Sebou
169 U13 **Sebuku, Pulau** island N Indonesia
169 W8 **Sebuku, Teluk** bay Borneo, N Indonesia
106 F10 **Secchia** ≈ N Italy
10 L17 **Sechelt** British Columbia, SW Canada
56 C12 **Sechin, Río** ≈ W Peru
56 A10 **Sechura, Bahía de** bay NW Peru
185 A22 **Secretary Island** island SW NZ
155 I15 **Secunderābād** var. Sikandarabad. Andhra Pradesh, C India
57 L17 **Sécure, Río** ≈ C Bolivia
118 D10 **Seda** Mažeikiai, NW Lithuania
27 T5 **Sedalia** Missouri, C USA
103 R3 **Sedan** Ardennes, N France
27 P7 **Sedan** Kansas, C USA
105 N3 **Sedano** Castilla-León, N Spain
104 H10 **Seda, Ribeira de** stream C Portugal
185 K15 **Seddon** Marlborough, South Island, NZ
185 H15 **Seddonville** West Coast, South Island, NZ
143 U7 **Sedeh** Khorāsān, E Iran
138 E11 **Sederot** Southern, S Israel
65 B23 **Sedge Island** island NW Falkland Islands
76 G12 **Sédhiou** SW Senegal
11 U16 **Sedley** Saskatchewan, S Canada
Sedlez see Siedlce
122 I11 **Sednel'nikovo** Omskaya Oblast', C Russian Federation
117 Q2 **Sedniv** Chernihivs'ka Oblast', N Ukraine
36 L11 **Sedona** Arizona, SW USA
Sedunum see Sion
118 F12 **Šeduva** Radviliškis, N Lithuania
141 Y8 **Seeb** var. Muscat Sīb Airport. ✕ (Masqaṭ) NE Oman
Seeb see As Sīb
108 M7 **Seefeld-in-Tirol** Tirol, W Austria
83 E22 **Seeheim Noord** Karas, S Namibia
Seeland see Sjælland
195 N9 **Seelig, Mount** ▲ Antarctica
Seeonee see Seoni
162 E6 **Seer** Hovd, W Mongolia
102 L5 **Sées** Orne, N France
101 J14 **Seesen** Niedersachsen, C Germany
Seesker Höhe see Szeskie Wzgórza
100 J10 **Seevetal** Niedersachsen, N Germany
109 V6 **Seewiesen** Steiermark, E Austria
136 J13 **Şefaatli** var. Kızılkoca. Yozgat, C Turkey
149 N3 **Sefid, Darya-ye** Pash. Āb-i-Safed. ≈ N Afghanistan
148 K5 **Sefīd Kūh, Selseleh-ye** Eng. Paropamisus Range. ⛰ W Afghanistan
74 G6 **Sefrou** N Morocco
185 E19 **Sefton, Mount** ▲ South Island, NZ
171 S13 **Segaf, Kepulauan** island group E Indonesia
169 W7 **Segama, Sungai** ≈ East Malaysia
168 L9 **Segamat** Johor, Peninsular Malaysia
77 S13 **Ségbana** NE Benin
Segestica see Sisak
Segesvár see Sighişoara
171 T12 **Seget** Irian Jaya, E Indonesia
Segewold see Sigulda
126 J9 **Segezha** Respublika Kareliya, NW Russian Federation
Seghedin see Szeged
Segna see Senj
107 I16 **Segni** Lazio, C Italy
Segodunum see Rodez
105 S9 **Segorbe** País Valenciano, E Spain
76 M12 **Ségou** var. Segu. Ségou, C Mali
76 M12 **Ségou** ◈ region SW Mali
54 E8 **Segovia** Antioquia, N Colombia
105 N7 **Segovia** Castilla-León, C Spain
104 M6 **Segovia** ◈ province Castilla-León, N Spain
Segoviao Wangkí see Coco, Río
126 J9 **Segozero, Ozero** ◎ NW Russian Federation
105 U5 **Segre** ≈ NE Spain
102 J7 **Segré** Maine-et-Loire, NW France
Segu see Ségou
38 I17 **Seguam Island** island Aleutian Islands, Alaska, USA
38 I17 **Seguam Pass** strait Aleutian Islands, Alaska, USA
77 Y7 **Séguédine** Agadez, NE Niger
76 M15 **Séguéla** W Ivory Coast
25 S11 **Seguin** Texas, SW USA
38 E17 **Segula Island** island Aleutian Islands, Alaska, USA
62 K10 **Segundo, Río** ≈ C Argentina
105 Q12 **Segura** ≈ S Spain
105 P13 **Sierra de Segura** ⛰ S Spain
83 G18 **Sehithwa** Ngamiland, N Botswana
154 H10 **Sehore** Madhya Pradesh, C India
186 G9 **Sehulea** Normanby Island, S PNG
149 P15 **Sehwān** Sind, SE Pakistan
109 V8 **Seiersberg** Steiermark, SE Austria
26 L9 **Seiling** Oklahoma, C USA
103 S9 **Seille** ≈ E France
99 J20 **Seilles** Namur, SE Belgium
93 K17 **Seinäjoki** Swe. Östermyra. Länsi-Suomi, W Finland
12 B12 **Seine** ≈ Ontario, S Canada
102 M4 **Seine** ≈ N France
102 K4 **Seine, Baie de la** bay N France
Seine, Banc de la see Seine Seamount
103 O5 **Seine-et-Marne** ◈ department N France
102 L3 **Seine-Maritime** ◈ department N France
84 B14 **Seine Plain** undersea feature E Atlantic Ocean
84 B15 **Seine Seamount** var. Banc de la Seine. undersea feature E Atlantic Ocean
102 E6 **Sein, Île de** island NW France
171 Y14 **Seinma** Irian Jaya, E Indonesia
Seisbierrum see Sexbierum
109 U5 **Seitenstetten Markt** Niederösterreich, C Austria
Seiyu see Chŏnju
95 H22 **Sejerø** island E Denmark
110 P7 **Sejny** Podlaskie, NE Poland
81 G20 **Seke** Shinyanga, N Tanzania
164 L13 **Seki** Gifu, Honshū, SW Japan
161 U12 **Sekibi-sho** island China/Japan/Taiwan
165 U3 **Sekihoku-tōge** pass Hokkaidō, NE Japan
Sekondi see Sekondi-Takoradi
77 P17 **Sekondi-Takoradi** var. Sekondi. S Ghana
80 J11 **Sek'ot'a** Amhara, N Ethiopia
Sekseŭil see Saksaul'skiy
32 I9 **Selah** Washington, NW USA
168 J8 **Selangor** var. Negeri Selangor Darul Ehsan. ◈ state Peninsular Malaysia
Selânik see Thessaloníki
168 K10 **Selapanjang** Pulau Rantau, W Indonesia
167 R10 **Selaphum** Roi Et, E Thailand
171 T16 **Selaru, Pulau** island Kepulauan Tanimbar, E Indonesia
171 U13 **Selassi** Irian Jaya, E Indonesia
168 J7 **Selatan, Selat** strait Peninsular Malaysia
39 N8 **Selawik** Alaska, USA
39 N8 **Selawik Lake** ◎ Alaska, USA
171 N14 **Selayar, Selat** strait Sulawesi, C Indonesia
95 C14 **Selbjørnsfjorden** fjord S Norway
94 H8 **Selbusjøen** ◎ S Norway
97 M17 **Selby** N England, UK
29 N8 **Selby** South Dakota, N USA
21 Z4 **Selbyville** Delaware, NE USA
136 B15 **Selçuk** var. Akıncılar. İzmir, SW Turkey
39 Q13 **Seldovia** Alaska, USA
107 M18 **Sele** anc. Silarus. ≈ S Italy
42 B5 **Selegua, Río** ≈ W Guatemala
131 X7 **Selemdzha** ≈ SE Russian Federation
131 U7 **Selenga** Mong. Selenge Mörön. ≈ Mongolia/Russian Federation
162 K6 **Selenge** Bulgan, N Mongolia
162 J6 **Selenge** Hövsgöl, N Mongolia
79 I19 **Selenge** Bandundu, W Dem. Rep. Congo (Zaire)
162 L6 **Selenge** ◈ province N Mongolia
Selenge Mörön see Selenga
123 N14 **Selenginsk** Respublika Buryatiya, S Russian Federation
Selenica see Selenicë
113 K22 **Selenicë** var. Selenica. Vlorë, SW Albania
123 Q8 **Selennyakh** ≈ NE Russian Federation
100 J8 **Selenter See** ◎ N Germany
Sele Sound see Soela Väin
103 U6 **Sélestat** Ger. Schlettstadt. Bas-Rhin, NE France
Selety see Sileti
Seleucia see Silifke
92 I4 **Selfoss** Sudhurland, SW Iceland
28 M7 **Selfridge** North Dakota, N USA
76 I15 **Seli** ≈ N Sierra Leone
76 I11 **Sélibabi** var. Sélibaby. Guidimaka, S Mauritania
Sélibaby see Sélibabi
Selidovka/Selidovo see Selydove
126 I15 **Seliger, Ozero** ◎ W Russian Federation
36 J11 **Seligman** Arizona, SW USA
27 S8 **Seligman** Missouri, C USA
80 E6 **Selima Oasis** oasis N Sudan
76 L13 **Sélingué, Lac de** ⊡ S Mali
Selinoús see Kréstena
18 G14 **Selinsgrove** Pennsylvania, NE USA
Selishche see Syelishcha
126 I16 **Selizharovo** Tverskaya Oblast', W Russian Federation
94 C10 **Selje** Sogn og Fjordane, S Norway
11 X16 **Selkirk** Manitoba, S Canada
96 K13 **Selkirk** SE Scotland, UK
96 K13 **Selkirk** cultural region SE Scotland, UK
11 O16 **Selkirk Mountains** ⛰ British Columbia, SW Canada
9 O15 **Selkirk Rise** undersea feature SE Pacific Ocean
115 F21 **Sellasía** Pelopónnisos, S Greece
44 M9 **Selle, Pic de la** var. La Selle. ▲ SE Haiti
102 M8 **Selles-sur-Cher** Loir-et-Cher, C France
36 K16 **Sells** Arizona, SW USA
Sellye see Sal'a
23 P5 **Selma** Alabama, S USA
35 Q11 **Selma** California, W USA
20 G10 **Selmer** Tennessee, S USA
173 N17 **Sel, Pointe au** headland W Réunion
Selseleh-ye Kūh-e Vākhān see Nicholas Range
129 S2 **Selty** Udmurtskaya Respublika, NW Russian Federation
Selukwe see Shurugwi
62 L9 **Selva** Santiago del Estero, N Argentina
11 T9 **Selwyn Lake** ◎ Northwest Territories/Saskatchewan, C Canada
10 K6 **Selwyn Mountains** ⛰ Yukon Territory, NW Canada
181 T6 **Selwyn Range** ⛰ Queensland, C Australia
117 W8 **Selydove** var. Selidovka, Rus. Selidovo. Donets'ka Oblast', SE Ukraine
Selzaete see Zelzate
Seman see Semanit, Lumi i
168 M15 **Semangka, Teluk** bay Sumatera, SW Indonesia
113 D22 **Semanit, Lumi i** var. Seman. ≈ W Albania
169 Q16 **Semarang** var. Samarang. Jawa, C Indonesia
169 Q10 **Sematan** Sarawak, East Malaysia
171 P17 **Semau, Pulau** island S Indonesia
169 V8 **Sembakung, Sungai** ≈ Borneo, N Indonesia
79 G17 **Sembé** La Sangha, NW Congo
169 S13 **Sembulu, Danau** ◎ Borneo, N Indonesia
Semendria see Smederevo
117 R1 **Semenivka** Chernihivs'ka Oblast', N Ukraine
117 S6 **Semenivka** Rus. Semenovka. Poltavs'ka Oblast', NE Ukraine
129 O3 **Semenov** Nizhegorodskaya Oblast', W Russian Federation
Semenovka see Semenivka
169 S17 **Semeru, Gunung** var. Mahameru. ▲ Jawa, S Indonesia
Semey see Semipalatinsk
Semezhevo see Syemyezhava
128 L7 **Semiluki** Voronezhskaya Oblast', W Russian Federation
33 W16 **Seminoe Reservoir** ⊡ Wyoming, C USA
27 O11 **Seminole** Oklahoma, C USA
24 M6 **Seminole** Texas, SW USA
23 S8 **Seminole, Lake** ⊡ Florida/Georgia, SE USA
144 M8 **Semiozernoye** Kostanay, N Kazakhstan
145 V9 **Semipalatinsk** Kaz. Semey. Vostochnyy Kazakhstan, E Kazakhstan
143 O9 **Semīrom** var. Samirum. Eşfahān, C Iran
38 F17 **Semisopochnoi Island** island Aleutian Islands, Alaska, USA
169 R11 **Semitau** Borneo, C Indonesia
81 E18 **Semliki** ≈ Uganda/Dem. Rep. Congo (Zaire)
143 P5 **Semnān** var. Samnān. Semnān, N Iran
143 Q5 **Semnān** off. Ostān-e Semnān. ◈ province N Iran
99 K24 **Semois** ≈ SE Belgium
108 E8 **Sempacher See** ◎ C Switzerland
Sena see Vila de Sena
30 L12 **Senachwine Lake** ◎ Illinois, N USA
59 O14 **Senador Pompeu** Ceará, E Brazil
Sena Gallica see Senigallia
59 C15 **Sena Madureira** Acre, W Brazil
155 L25 **Senanayake Samudra** ◎ E Sri Lanka
83 G15 **Senanga** Western, SW Zambia
27 Y9 **Senath** Missouri, C USA
22 L2 **Senatobia** Mississippi, S USA
164 C16 **Sendai** Kagoshima, Kyūshū, SW Japan
165 Q10 **Sendai** Miyagi, Honshū, C Japan
165 Q11 **Sendai-wan** bay E Japan
101 J23 **Senden** Bayern, S Germany
154 F11 **Sendhwa** Madhya Pradesh, C India
111 H21 **Senec** Ger. Wartberg, Hung. Szenc; prev. Szempcz. Bratislavský Kraj, W Slovakia
27 P3 **Seneca** Kansas, C USA
27 R8 **Seneca** Missouri, C USA
32 K13 **Seneca** Oregon, NW USA
21 O11 **Seneca** South Carolina, SE USA
18 G11 **Seneca Lake** ◎ New York, NE USA
31 U13 **Senecaville Lake** ⊡ Ohio, N USA
76 G11 **Senegal** off. Republic of Senegal, Fr. Sénégal. ◆ republic W Africa
76 H9 **Senegal** Fr. Sénégal. ≈ W Africa
31 O4 **Seney Marsh** wetland Michigan, N USA
101 P14 **Senftenberg** Brandenburg, E Germany
82 L11 **Senga Hill** Northern, NE Zambia
158 G13 **Sênggê Zangbo** ≈ W China
171 Z13 **Senggi** Irian Jaya, E Indonesia
129 R5 **Sengiley** Ul'yanovskaya Oblast', W Russian Federation
63 I19 **Senguerr, Río** ≈ S Argentina
83 J16 **Sengwa** ≈ C Zimbabwe
Senia see Senj
111 H19 **Senica** Ger. Senitz, Hung. Szenice. Trnavský Kraj, W Slovakia
Seniça see Sjenica
106 J11 **Senigallia** anc. Sena Gallica. Marche, C Italy
136 F15 **Senirkent** Isparta, SW Turkey
Senitz see Senica
112 C10 **Senj** Ger. Zengg, It. Segna; anc. Senia. Lika-Senj, NW Croatia
163 O10 **Senj** Dornogovĭ, SE Mongolia
92 H9 **Senja** prev. Senjen. island N Norway
Senjen see Senja
161 U12 **Senkaku-shotō** island group SW Japan
137 R12 **Şenkaya** Erzurum, NE Turkey
83 I16 **Senkobo** Southern, S Zambia
103 O4 **Senlis** Oise, N France
167 T12 **Senmonorom** Môndól Kiri, E Cambodia
80 G10 **Sennar** var. Sannār. Sinnar, C Sudan
Senno see Syanno
Senones see Sens
109 W11 **Senovo** E Slovenia
103 P6 **Sens** anc. Agendicum, Senones. Yonne, C France
Sensburg see Mrągowo
167 S11 **Sên, Stœng** ≈ C Cambodia
42 F7 **Sensuntepeque** Cabañas, NE El Salvador
112 L8 **Senta** Hung. Zenta. Serbia, N Yugoslavia
Šent Andraž see Sankt Andrä
171 Y13 **Sentani, Danau** ◎ Irian Jaya, E Indonesia
28 J5 **Sentinel Butte** ▲ North Dakota, N USA
10 M13 **Sentinel Peak** ▲ British Columbia, W Canada
59 N16 **Sento Sé** Bahia, E Brazil
Šent Peter see Pivka
Šent Vid see Sankt Veit an der Glan
Seo de Urgel see La See d'Urgel
154 I7 **Seondha** Madhya Pradesh, C India
154 J11 **Seoni** prev. Seeonee. Madhya Pradesh, C India
Seoul see Sŏul
184 I13 **Separation Point** headland South Island, NZ
169 V10 **Sepasu** Borneo, N Indonesia
186 B6 **Sepik** ≈ Indonesia/PNG
Sepone see Muang Xépôn
110 M7 **Sępopol** Ger. Schippenbeil. Warmińsko-Mazurskie, NE Poland,
116 F10 **Şepreuş** Hung. Seprős. Arad, W Romania
Seprős see Şepreuş
Şepşi-Sângeorz/Sepsiszentgyőrgy see Sfântu Gheorghe
15 W4 **Sept-Îles** Quebec, SE Canada
105 N6 **Sepúlveda** Castilla-León, N Spain
104 K8 **Sequeros** Castilla-León, N Spain
104 L5 **Sequillo** ≈ NW Spain
32 G7 **Sequim** Washington, NW USA
35 S11 **Sequoia National Park** national park California, W USA
137 Q14 **Şerafettin Dağları** ⛰ E Turkey
129 N10 **Serafimovich** Volgogradskaya Oblast', SW Russian Federation
171 Q10 **Serai** Sulawesi, N Indonesia
99 K19 **Seraing** Liège, E Belgium
Sêraitang see Baima
Serajgonj see Shirajganj Ghat
146 I15 **Serakhs** var. Saragt. Akhalskiy Velayat, S Turkmenistan
171 W13 **Serami** Irian Jaya, E Indonesia
Seram, Laut see Ceram Sea
Serampore/Serampur see Shrīrāmpur
171 S13 **Seram, Pulau** var. Serang, Eng. Ceram. island Maluku, E Indonesia
169 N15 **Serang** Jawa, C Indonesia
Serang see Seram, Pulau
169 P9 **Serasan, Pulau** island Kepulauan Natuna, W Indonesia
169 P9 **Serasan, Selat** strait Indonesia/Malaysia
112 M12 **Serbia** Ger. Serbien, Serb. Srbija. ◈ republic Yugoslavia
Serbien see Serbia
Sercq see Sark
Serdica see Sofiya
129 O7 **Serdobsk** Penzenskaya Oblast', W Russian Federation
145 X9 **Serebryansk** Vostochnyy Kazakhstan, E Kazakhstan
123 Q12 **Serebryanyy Bor** Respublika Sakha (Yakutiya), NE Russian Federation
111 H20 **Sered'** Hung. Szered. Trnavský Kraj, SW Slovakia
117 S1 **Seredyna-Buda** Sums'ka Oblast', NE Ukraine
118 E13 **Seredžius** Jurbarkas, C Lithuania
136 I14 **Şereflikoçhisar** Ankara, C Turkey
106 D7 **Seregno** Lombardia, N Italy
103 P7 **Serein** ≈ C France
168 K9 **Seremban** Negeri Sembilan, Peninsular Malaysia
81 H20 **Serengeti Plain** plain N Tanzania
82 K13 **Serenje** Central, E Zambia
Seres see Sérres
116 J5 **Seret** ≈ W Ukraine
Seret/Sereth see Siret
115 I21 **Serfopoúla** island Kykládes, Greece, Aegean Sea
129 P4 **Sergach** Nizhegorodskaya Oblast', W Russian Federation
29 S13 **Sergeant Bluff** Iowa, C USA
163 P7 **Sergelen** Dornod, NE Mongolia
163 O9 **Sergelen** Sühbaatar, E Mongolia
168 H8 **Sergeulangit, Pegunungan** ⛰ Sumatera, NW Indonesia
122 L5 **Sergeya Kirova, Ostrova** island N Russian Federation
Sergeyevichi see Syarhyeyevichy
145 O7 **Sergeyevka** Severnyy Kazakhstan, N Kazakhstan
Sergiopol see Ayagoz
59 P16 **Sergipe** off. Estado de Sergipe. ◈ state E Brazil
128 L3 **Sergiyev Posad** Moskovskaya Oblast', W Russian Federation
126 K5 **Sergozero, Ozero** ◎ NW Russian Federation
169 Q10 **Serian** Sarawak, East Malaysia
169 O15 **Seribu, Kepulauan** island group S Indonesia
115 I21 **Sérifos** anc. Seriphos. island Kykládes, Greece, Aegean Sea
115 I21 **Sérifou, Stenó** strait SE Greece
136 F16 **Serik** Antalya, SW Turkey
106 E7 **Serio** ≈ N Italy
Seriphos see Sérifos
Serir Tibesti see Sarīr Tibistī
129 S5 **Sernovodsk** Samarskaya Oblast', W Russian Federation
129 R2 **Sernur** Respublika Mariy El, W Russian Federation
110 M11 **Serock** Mazowieckie, C Poland
61 B18 **Serodino** Santa Fe, C Argentina
Seroei see Serui
105 P14 **Serón** Andalucía, S Spain
99 E14 **Serooskerke** Zeeland, SW Netherlands
105 T5 **Seròs** Cataluña, NE Spain
122 G10 **Serov** Sverdlovskaya Oblast', C Russian Federation
83 I19 **Serowe** Central, SE Botswana
104 H13 **Serpa** Beja, S Portugal
Serpa Pinto see Menongue
182 A4 **Serpentine Lakes** salt lake South Australia
45 T15 **Serpent's Mouth, The** Sp. Boca de la Serpiente. strait Trinidad and Tobago/Venezuela
Serpiente, Boca de la see Serpent's Mouth, The
128 K4 **Serpukhov** Moskovskaya Oblast', W Russian Federation
60 K13 **Serra do Mar** ⛰ S Brazil
Sérrai see Sérres
107 N22 **Serra San Bruno** Calabria, SW Italy
103 S14 **Serres** Hautes-Alpes, SE France
114 H13 **Sérres** var. Seres; prev. Sérrai. Kentrikí Makedonía, NE Greece
62 J9 **Serrezuela** Córdoba, C Argentina
59 O16 **Serrinha** Bahia, E Brazil
59 M19 **Serro** var. Sêrro. Minas Gerais, NE Brazil
Sêrro see Serro
Sert see Siirt
Sertá see Sertã
104 H9 **Sertã** var. Sertá. Castelo Branco, C Portugal
60 L8 **Sertãozinho** São Paulo, S Brazil
160 F7 **Sêrtar** Sichuan, C China
171 W13 **Serui** prev. Seroei. Irian Jaya, E Indonesia
83 J19 **Serule** Central, E Botswana
169 S12 **Seruyan, Sungai** var. Sungai Pembuang. ≈ Borneo, N Indonesia
115 E14 **Sérvia** Dytikí Makedonía, N Greece
160 E7 **Sêrxü** Sichuan, C China
123 R13 **Seryshevo** Amurskaya Oblast', SE Russian Federation
Sesana see Sežana
169 V8 **Sesayap, Sungai** ≈ Borneo, N Indonesia
Sesdlets see Siedlce
79 N17 **Sese** Orientale, N Dem. Rep. Congo (Zaire)

81 F18 **Sese Islands** island group S Uganda
83 H16 **Sesheke** var. Sesheko. Western, SE Zambia
Sesheko see Sesheke
106 C8 **Sesia** anc. Sessites. ≈ NW Italy
104 F11 **Sesimbra** Setúbal, S Portugal
115 N22 **Sesklió** island Dodekánisos, Greece, Aegean Sea
30 L16 **Sesser** Illinois, N USA
Sessites see Sesia
106 G11 **Sesto Fiorentino** Toscana, C Italy
106 E7 **Sesto San Giovanni** Lombardia, N Italy
106 A8 **Sestriere** Piemonte, NE Italy
106 D10 **Sestri Levante** Liguria, NW Italy
107 C20 **Sestu** Sardegna, Italy, C Mediterranean Sea
112 E8 **Sesvete** Zagreb, N Croatia
118 G12 **Šeta** Kėdainiai, C Lithuania
Setabis see Xátiva
165 Q4 **Setana** Hokkaidō, NE Japan
103 Q16 **Sète** prev. Cette. Hérault, S France
58 J11 **Sete Ilhas** Amapá, NE Brazil
59 L20 **Sete Lagoas** Minas Gerais, NE Brazil
60 G10 **Sete Quedas, Ilha das** island S Brazil
92 I10 **Setermoen** Troms, N Norway
95 E17 **Setesdal** valley S Norway
43 W16 **Setetule, Cerro** ▲ SE Panama
21 Q5 **Seth** West Virginia, NE USA
Setia see Sezze
74 K5 **Sétif** var. Stif. N Algeria
164 L13 **Seto** Aichi, Honshū, SW Japan
164 G13 **Seto-naikai** Eng. Inland Sea. sea S Japan
165 V16 **Setouchi** var. Setoushi. Kagoshima, Amami-Ō-shima, SW Japan
74 F6 **Settat** W Morocco
79 D20 **Setté Cama** Ogooué-Maritime, SW Gabon
11 W13 **Setting Lake** ◎ Manitoba, C Canada
97 L16 **Settle** N England, UK
189 Y12 **Settlement** E Wake Island
104 F11 **Setúbal** Eng. Saint Ubes, Saint Yves. Setúbal, W Portugal
104 F11 **Setúbal** ◈ district S Portugal
104 F12 **Setúbal, Baía de** bay W Portugal
Setul see Satun
12 B10 **Seul, Lac** ◎ Ontario, S Canada
103 R8 **Seurre** Côte d'Or, C France
137 U11 **Sevan** C Armenia
137 V12 **Sevana Lich** Eng. Lake Sevan, Rus. Ozero Sevan. ◎ E Armenia
Sevan, Lake/Sevan, Ozero see Sevana Lich
77 N11 **Sévaré** Mopti, C Mali
117 S14 **Sevastopol'** Eng. Sebastopol. Respublika Krym, S Ukraine
25 R14 **Seven Sisters** Texas, SW USA
10 K13 **Seven Sisters Peaks** ▲ British Columbia, SW Canada
99 M15 **Sevenum** Limburg, SE Netherlands
103 P14 **Séverac-le-Château** Aveyron, S France
14 H13 **Severn** ≈ Ontario, S Canada
97 L21 **Severn** Wel. Hafren. ≈ England/Wales, UK
127 O11 **Severnaya Dvina** var. Northern Dvina. ≈ NW Russian Federation
129 N16 **Severnaya Osetiya-Alaniya, Respublika** Eng. North Ossetia; prev. Respublika Severnaya Osetiya, Severo-Osetinskaya SSR. ◈ autonomous republic SW Russian Federation
Severnaya Osetiya, Respublika see Severnaya Osetiya-Alaniya Respublika
122 M5 **Severnaya Zemlya** var. Nicholas II Land. island group N Russian Federation
129 T5 **Severnoye** Orenburgskaya Oblast', W Russian Federation
35 S3 **Severn Troughs Range** ▲▲ Nevada, W USA
127 W3 **Severnyy** Respublika Komi, NW Russian Federation
144 I13 **Severnyy Chink Ustyurta** ▲ W Kazakhstan
127 Q13 **Severnyye Uvaly** var. Northern Ural Hills. hill range NW Russian Federation
145 O6 **Severnyy Kazakhstan** off. Severo-Kazakhstanskaya Oblast', var. North Kazakhstan, Kaz. Soltüstik Qazaqstan Oblysy. ◈ province N Kazakhstan
127 V9 **Severnyy Ural** ▲▲ NW Russian Federation
Severo-Alichurskiy Khrebet see Alichuri Shimolí, Qatorkŭhi
123 N12 **Severobaykal'sk** Respublika Buryatiya, S Russian Federation
Severodonetsk see Syeverodonets'k
126 M8 **Severodvinsk** prev. Molotov, Sudostroy. Arkhangel'skaya Oblast', NW Russian Federation
Severo-Kazakhstanskaya Oblast' see Severnyy Kazakhstan
123 U11 **Severo-Kuril'sk** Sakhalinskaya Oblast', SE Russian Federation
126 J3 **Severomorsk** Murmanskaya Oblast', NW Russian Federation
Severo-Osetinskaya SSR see Severnaya Osetiya-Alaniya, Respublika
122 M7 **Severo-Sibirskaya Nizmennost'** var. North Siberian Plain, Eng. North Siberian Lowland. lowlands N Russian Federation
122 G10 **Severoural'sk** Sverdlovskaya Oblast', C Russian Federation
122 L11 **Severo-Yeniseyskiy** Krasnoyarskiy Kray, C Russian Federation
128 M11 **Severskiy Donets** Ukr. Sivers'kyy Donets'. ≈ Russian Federation/Ukraine see also Sivers'kyy Donets'
92 M9 **Sevettijärvi** Lappi, N Finland
36 M5 **Sevier Bridge Reservoir** ▣ Utah, W USA
36 J4 **Sevier Desert** plain Utah, W USA
36 J5 **Sevier Lake** ◎ Utah, W USA
21 N9 **Sevierville** Tennessee, S USA
104 J14 **Sevilla** Eng. Seville; anc. Hispalis. Andalucía, SW Spain
104 J13 **Sevilla** ◈ province Andalucía, SW Spain
Sevilla de Niefang see Niefang
43 O16 **Sevilla, Isla** island SW Panama
Seville see Sevilla
114 J9 **Sevlievo** Gabrovo, N Bulgaria
Sevluš/Sevlyush see Vynohradiv
109 V11 **Sevnica** Ger. Lichtenwald. E Slovenia
128 I7 **Sevsk** Bryanskaya Oblast', W Russian Federation
76 J15 **Sewa** ≈ E Sierra Leone
39 R12 **Seward** Alaska, USA
29 R15 **Seward** Nebraska, C USA
10 G8 **Seward Glacier** glacier Yukon Territory, W Canada
197 Q3 **Seward Peninsula** peninsula Alaska, USA
Seward's Folly see Alaska
62 H12 **Sewell** Libertador, C Chile
98 K5 **Sexbierum** Fris. Seisbierrum. Friesland, N Netherlands
11 O13 **Sexsmith** Alberta, W Canada
41 W13 **Seybaplaya** Campeche, SE Mexico
173 N6 **Seychelles** off. Republic of Seychelles. ◆ republic W Indian Ocean
67 Z9 **Seychelles** island group NE Seychelles
173 N6 **Seychelles Bank** var. Le Banc des Seychelles. undersea feature W Indian Ocean
Seychelles, Le Banc des see Seychelles Bank
172 H17 **Seychellois, Morne** ▲ Mahé, NE Seychelles
92 L2 **Seydhisfjördhur** Austurland, E Iceland
146 J12 **Seydi** prev. Neftezavodsk. Lebapskiy Velayat, E Turkmenistan
136 G16 **Seydişehir** Konya, SW Turkey
136 J13 **Seyfe Gölü** ◎ C Turkey
Seyhan see Adana
136 K16 **Seyhan Barajı** ▣ S Turkey
136 K17 **Seyhan Nehri** ≈ S Turkey
136 F13 **Seyitgazi** Eskişehir, W Turkey
128 J7 **Seym** ≈ W Russian Federation
117 S3 **Seym** ≈ N Ukraine
123 T9 **Seymchan** Magadanskaya Oblast', E Russian Federation
114 N12 **Seymen** Tekirdağ, NW Turkey
183 O11 **Seymour** Victoria, SE Australia
83 I25 **Seymour** Eastern Cape, S South Africa
29 W16 **Seymour** Iowa, C USA
27 U7 **Seymour** Missouri, C USA
25 Q5 **Seymour** Texas, SW USA
114 M12 **Şeytan Deresi** ≈ NW Turkey
109 S12 **Sežana** It. Sesana. SW Slovenia
103 P5 **Sézanne** Marne, N France
107 I16 **Sezze** anc. Setia. Lazio, C Italy
115 H25 **Sfákia** Kríti, Greece, E Mediterranean Sea
115 D21 **Sfaktiría** island S Greece
116 J11 **Sfântu Gheorghe** Ger. Sankt-Georgen, Hung. Sepsiszentgyörgy; prev. Şepşi-Sângeorz, Sfintu Gheorghe. Covasna, C Romania
117 N13 **Sfântu Gheorghe, Braţul** var. Gheorghe Braţul. ≈ E Romania
75 N6 **Sfax** Ar. Şafāqis. E Tunisia
75 N6 **Sfax** ✕ E Tunisia
Sfintu Gheorghe see Sfântu Gheorghe
98 H13 **'s-Gravendeel** Zuid-Holland, SW Netherlands
98 F11 **'s-Gravenhage** var. Den Haag, Eng. The Hague, Fr. La Haye. ● (Netherlands-seat of government) Zuid-Holland, W Netherlands
98 G12 **'s-Gravenzande** Zuid-Holland, W Netherlands
Shaan/Shaanxi Sheng see Shaanxi
159 X11 **Shaanxi** var. Shaan, Shaanxi Sheng, Shan-hsi, Shenshi, Shensi. ◈ province C China
Shaartuz see Shahrtuz
Shabani see Zvishavane
81 N17 **Shabeellaha Dhexe** off. Gobolka Shabeellaha Dhexe. ◈ region E Somalia
81 L17 **Shabeellaha Hoose** off. Gobolka Shabeellaha Hoose. ◈ region S Somalia
Shabeelle, Webi see Shebeli
114 O7 **Shabla** Dobrich, NE Bulgaria
114 O7 **Shabla, Nos** headland NE Bulgaria
13 N9 **Shabogama Lake** ◎ Newfoundland, E Canada
79 N20 **Shabunda** Sud Kivu, E Dem. Rep. Congo (Zaire)
141 Q15 **Shabwah** C Yemen
158 F8 **Shache** var. Yarkant. Xinjiang Uygur Zizhiqu, NW China
Shacheng see Huailai
195 R12 **Shackleton Coast** physical region Antarctica
195 Z10 **Shackleton Ice Shelf** ice shelf Antarctica
Shaddādī see Ash Shadādah
28 K7 **Shadehill Reservoir** ▣ South Dakota, N USA
122 G11 **Shadrinsk** Kurganskaya Oblast', C Russian Federation
31 O12 **Shafer, Lake** ▣ Indiana, N USA
35 R13 **Shafter** California, W USA
24 J11 **Shafter** Texas, SW USA
97 L23 **Shaftesbury** S England, UK
185 F22 **Shag** ≈ South Island, NZ
145 V9 **Shagan** ≈ E Kazakhstan
39 O11 **Shageluk** Alaska, USA
122 K14 **Shagonar** Respublika Tyva, S Russian Federation
185 F22 **Shag Point** headland South Island, NZ
144 J12 **Shagyray, Plato** plain SW Kazakhstan
Shāhābād see Eslāmābād
168 K9 **Shah Alam** Selangor, Peninsular Malaysia
117 O12 **Shahany, Ozero** ◎ SW Ukraine
138 H9 **Shahbā'** anc. Philippopolis. As Suwaydā', S Syria
Shahbān see Ad Dayr
149 P17 **Shāhbandar** Sind, SE Pakistan
149 P13 **Shāhdād Kot** Sind, SW Pakistan
143 T10 **Shahdād, Namakzār-e** salt pan E Iran
149 Q15 **Shāhdādpur** Sind, SE Pakistan
154 K10 **Shahdol** Madhya Pradesh, C India
161 N7 **Sha He** ≈ C China
Shahepu see Linze
153 N13 **Shāhganj** Uttar Pradesh, N India
152 C11 **Shāhgarh** Rājasthān, NW India
Sha Hi see Orūmīyeh, Daryācheh-ye, Iran
Shāhī see Qā'emshahr, Māzandarān, Iran
139 Q6 **Shāhimah** var. Shahma. C Iraq
Shahjahanabad see Delhi
152 L11 **Shāhjahānpur** Uttar Pradesh, N India
Shahma see Shāhimah
149 U7 **Shāhpur** Punjab, E Pakistan
Shāhpur see Shāhpur Chākar
152 G13 **Shāhpura** Rājasthān, N India
149 Q15 **Shāhpur Chākar** var. Shāhpur. Sind, SE Pakistan
148 M5 **Shahrak** Ghowr, C Afghanistan
143 Q11 **Shahr-e Bābak** Kermān, C Iran
143 N8 **Shahr-e Kord** var. Shahr Kord. Chahār Maḩall va Bakhtīārī, C Iran
143 O9 **Shahreẓā** var. Qomisheh, Qumisheh, Shahriza; prev. Qomsheh. Eşfahān, C Iran
147 S10 **Shahrikhon** Rus. Shakhrikhan. Andijon Wiloyati, E Uzbekistan
147 N12 **Shahrisabz** Rus. Shakhrisabz. Qashqadaryo Wiloyati, S Uzbekistan
147 P11 **Shahriston** Rus. Shakhristan. NW Tajikistan
Shahriza see Shahreẓā
Shahr-i-Zabul see Zābol
Shahr Kord see Shahr-e Kord
147 P14 **Shahrtuz** Rus. Shaartuz. SW Tajikistan
143 Q4 **Shāhrūd** prev. Emāmrūd, Emāmshahr. Semnān, N Iran
Shahsavār/Shahsawar see Tonekābon
Shaidara see Step' Nardara
Shaikh Ābid see Shaykh 'Ābid
Shaikh Fāris see Shaykh Fāris
Shaikh Najm see Shaykh Najm
138 K5 **Shā'ir, Jabal** ▲ C Syria
154 G10 **Shājāpur** Madhya Pradesh, C India
80 J8 **Shakal, Ras** headland NE Sudan
Shakhdarinskiy Khrebet see Shokhdara, Qatorkŭhi
Shakhrikhan see Shahrikhon
Shakhrisabz see Shahrisabz
Shakhristan see Shahriston
117 X8 **Shakhtars'k** Rus. Shakhtërsk. Donets'ka Oblast', SE Ukraine
Shakhtërsk see Shakhtars'k
145 R10 **Shakhtinsk** Karaganda, C Kazakhstan
128 L11 **Shakhty** Rostovskaya Oblast', SW Russian Federation
129 P2 **Shakhun'ya** Nizhegorodskaya Oblast', W Russian Federation
77 S15 **Shaki** Oyo, W Nigeria
81 J15 **Shakīso** Oromo, C Ethiopia
117 X8 **Shakmars'k** Donets'ka Oblast', E Ukraine
29 V9 **Shakopee** Minnesota, N USA
165 R3 **Shakotan-misaki** headland Hokkaidō, NE Japan
39 N9 **Shaktoolik** Alaska, USA
81 J14 **Shala Hāyk'** ◎ C Ethiopia
126 M10 **Shalakusha** Arkhangel'skaya Oblast', NW Russian Federation
145 U8 **Shalday** Pavlodar, NE Kazakhstan
129 P16 **Shali** Chechenskaya Respublika, SW Russian Federation
141 W12 **Shalīm** var. Shelim. S Oman
Shaliuhe see Gangca
144 F9 **Shalkar, Ozero** prev. Chelkar, Ozero. ◎ W Kazakhstan
21 V12 **Shallotte** North Carolina, SE USA
25 N5 **Shallowater** Texas, SW USA
126 K11 **Shal'skiy** Respublika Kareliya, NW Russian Federation
160 F9 **Shaluli Shan** ▲▲ C China
81 F22 **Shama** ≈ C Tanzania
11 Z11 **Shamattawa** Manitoba, C Canada
12 F8 **Shamattawa** ≈ Ontario, C Canada
Shām, Bādiyat ash see Syrian Desert
Shamiya see Ash Shāmīyah
141 X8 **Shām, Jabal ash** var. Jebel Sham. ▲ NW Oman
Sham, Jebel see Shām, Jabal ash
Shamkhor see Şämkir
18 G14 **Shamokin** Pennsylvania, NE USA
25 P2 **Shamrock** Texas, SW USA
Sha'nabi, Jabal ash see Chambi, Jebel
139 Y12 **Shanāwah** E Iraq
159 T8 **Shandan** Gansu, N China
Shandī see Shendi
161 Q5 **Shandong** var. Lu, Shandong Sheng, Shantung. ◈ province E China
161 R4 **Shandong Bandao** var. Shantung Peninsula. peninsula E China
Shandong Peninsula see Shandong Bandao
Shandong Sheng see Shandong
139 U8 **Shandrūkh** E Iraq
83 J17 **Shangani** ≈ W Zimbabwe
161 O15 **Shangchuan Dao** island S China
Shangchuankou see Minhe
163 P12 **Shangdu** Nei Mongol Zizhiqu, N China
161 O11 **Shanggao** Jiangxi, S China
161 S8 **Shanghai** var. Shang-hai. Shanghai Shi, E China
Shanghai see Shanghai Shi
161 S8 **Shanghai Shi** var. Hu, Shanghai. ◈ municipality E China
161 P13 **Shanghang** Fujian, SE China
160 K14 **Shanglin** Guangxi Zhuangzu Zizhiqu, S China
83 G15 **Shangombo** Western, W Zambia
161 O6 **Shangqiu** var. Zhuji. Henan, C China
161 Q10 **Shangrao** Jiangxi, S China
161 S9 **Shangyu** var. Baiguan. Zhejiang, SE China
163 X9 **Shangzhi** Heilongjiang, NE China
160 L7 **Shangzhou** var. Shang Xian. Shaanxi, C China
163 W9 **Shanhetun** Heilongjiang, NE China
Shan-hsi see Shaanxi, China
Shan-hsi see Shanxi, China
159 O6 **Shankou** Xinjiang Uygur Zizhiqu, W China
184 M13 **Shannon** Manawatu-Wanganui, North Island, NZ
97 B19 **Shannon** ✕ W Ireland
97 C17 **Shannon** Ir. An tSionainn. ≈ W Ireland
167 N6 **Shan Plateau** plateau E Myanmar
158 M6 **Shanshan** var. Piqan. Xinjiang Uygur Zizhiqu, NW China
Shansi see Shanxi
167 N5 **Shan State** ◈ state E Myanmar
Shantar Islands see Shantarskiye Ostrova
123 S12 **Shantarskiye Ostrova** Eng. Shantar Islands. island group E Russian Federation
161 Q14 **Shantou** var. Shan-t'ou, Swatow. Guangdong, S China
Shantung see Shandong
Shantung Peninsula see Shandong Bandao
163 O14 **Shanxi** var. Jin, Shan-hsi, Shansi, Shanxi Sheng. ◈ province C China
Shan Xian see Sanmenxia
161 P6 **Shanxian** var. Shan Xian. Shandong, E China
Shanxi Sheng see Shanxi
160 L7 **Shanyang** Shaanxi, C China
161 O13 **Shaoguan** var. Shao-kuan, Cant. Kukong; prev. Ch'u-chiang. Guangdong, S China
Shao-kuan see Shaoguan
161 Q11 **Shaowu** Fujian, SE China
161 S9 **Shaoxing** Zhejiang, SE China
160 M12 **Shaoyang** prev. Tangdukou. Hunan, S China
160 M11 **Shaoyang** var. Baoqing, Shao-yang; prev. Pao-king. Hunan, S China
96 K5 **Shapinsay** island NE Scotland, UK
127 S4 **Shapkina** ≈ NW Russian Federation
Shāpūr see Salmās
158 M4 **Shaqiuhe** Xinjiang Uygur Zizhiqu, W China
139 T2 **Shaqlāwa** var. Shaqlāwah. E Iraq
Shaqlāwah see Shaqlāwa
138 I8 **Shaqqā** As Suwaydā', S Syria
141 P7 **Shaqrā'** Ar Riyāḑ, C Saudi Arabia
Shaqrā see Shuqrah
145 W10 **Shar** var. Charsk. Vostochnyy Kazakhstan, E Kazakhstan
149 O6 **Sharan** Urūzgān, SE Afghanistan
Sharaqpur see Sharqpur
Sharbaqty see Shcherbakty
141 X12 **Sharbatāt** S Oman
141 X12 **Sharbithāt, Ras** var. Ra's Sharbatāt. headland S Oman
14 K14 **Sharbot Lake** Ontario, SE Canada
145 P17 **Shardara** var. Chardara. Yuznhyy Kazakhstan, S Kazakhstan
Shardara Dalasy see Step' Nardara
162 F8 **Sharga** Govĭ-Altay, W Mongolia
162 H6 **Sharga** Hövsgöl, N Mongolia
116 M7 **Sharhorod** Vinnyts'ka Oblast', C Ukraine
162 K10 **Sharhulsan** Ömnögovĭ, S Mongolia
165 V3 **Shari** Hokkaidō, NE Japan
Shari see Chari
139 T6 **Shārī, Buḩayrat** ◎ C Iraq
Sharjah see Ash Shāriqah
118 K12 **Sharkawshchyna** var. Sharkowshchyna, Pol. Szarkowszczyzna, Rus. Sharkovshchina. Vitsyebskaya Voblasts', NW Belarus
180 G9 **Shark Bay** bay Western Australia
141 Y9 **Sharkh** E Oman
Sharkovshchina/Sharkowshchyna see Sharkawshchyna
129 U6 **Sharlyk** Orenburgskaya Oblast', W Russian Federation
Sharm ash Shaykh see Sharm el Sheikh
75 Y9 **Sharm el Sheikh** var. Ofiral, Sharm ash Shaykh. E Egypt
18 B13 **Sharon** Pennsylvania, NE USA
26 H4 **Sharon Springs** Kansas, C USA
31 Q14 **Sharonville** Ohio, N USA
Sharourah see Sharūrah
29 O10 **Sharpe, Lake** ▣ South Dakota, N USA
Sharqī, Al Jabal ash/Sharqi, Jebel esh see Anti-Lebanon
Sharqīyah, Al Minṭaqah ash see Ash Sharqīyah
138 I6 **Sharqīyat an Nabk, Jabal** ▲ W Syria
149 W8 **Sharqpur** var. Sharaqpur. Punjab, E Pakistan
141 Q13 **Sharūrah** var. Sharourah. Najrān, S Saudi Arabia
127 O14 **Shar'ya** Kostromskaya Oblast', NW Russian Federation
145 V15 **Sharyn** var. Charyn. ≈ SE Kazakhstan
Sharyn see Charyn
83 J18 **Shashe** Central, NE Botswana
83 J18 **Shashe** var. Shashi. ≈ Botswana/Zimbabwe
81 J14 **Shashemenē** var. Shashemenne, Shashhamana, It. Sciasciamana. Oromo, C Ethiopia
Shashemenne/Shashhamana see Shashemenē
Shashi see Shashe
Shashi/Sha-shih/Shasi see Jingzhou
35 N3 **Shasta Lake** ▣ California, W USA
35 N2 **Shasta, Mount** ▲ California, W USA
129 O4 **Shatki** Nizhegorodskaya Oblast', W Russian Federation
146 J13 **Shatlyk** Maryyskiy Velayat, C Turkmenistan
Shatra see Ash Shaṭrah
119 K17 **Shatsk** Rus. Shatsk. Minskaya Voblasts', C Belarus
129 N5 **Shatsk** Ryazanskaya Oblast', W Russian Federation
26 J9 **Shattuck** Oklahoma, C USA
145 P16 **Shaul'der** Yuzhnyy Kazakhstan, S Kazakhstan
11 S17 **Shaunavon** Saskatchewan, S Canada
Shavat see Showot
158 K4 **Shawan** Xinjiang Uygur Zizhiqu, NW China
14 G12 **Shawanaga** Ontario, S Canada
30 M6 **Shawano** Wisconsin, N USA
30 M6 **Shawano Lake** ◎ Wisconsin, N USA
15 P10 **Shawinigan** prev. Shawinigan Falls. Quebec, SE Canada
Shawinigan Falls see Shawinigan
15 P10 **Shawinigan-Sud** Quebec, SE Canada
138 J5 **Shawmarīyah, Jabal ash** ▲ C Syria
27 O11 **Shawnee** Oklahoma, C USA
14 K12 **Shawville** Quebec, SE Canada
Shaykh see Ash Shakk
139 W9 **Shaykh 'Ābid** var. Shaikh Ābid. E Iraq
139 Y10 **Shaykh Fāris** var. Shaikh Fāris. E Iraq
139 T7 **Shaykh Ḩātim** E Iraq
Shaykh, Jabal ash see Hermon, Mount
139 X10 **Shaykh Najm** var. Shaikh Najm. E Iraq
139 W9 **Shaykh Sa'd** E Iraq
147 T14 **Shazud** SE Tajikistan
119 N18 **Shchadryn** Rus. Shchedrin. Homyel'skaya Voblasts', SE Belarus
119 H18 **Shchara** ≈ SW Belarus
Shchedrin see Shchadryn
Shcheglovsk see Kemerovo
128 K5 **Shchëkino** Tul'skaya Oblast', W Russian Federation
127 S7 **Shchel'yayur** Respublika Komi, NW Russian Federation
145 U8 **Shcherbakty** Kaz. Sharbaqty. Pavlodar, E Kazakhstan
128 K7 **Shchigry** Kurskaya Oblast', W Russian Federation
Shchitkovichi see Shchytkavichy
117 Q2 **Shchors** Chernihivs'ka Oblast', N Ukraine
117 T8 **Shchors'k** Dnipropetrovs'ka Oblast', E Ukraine
Shchuchin see Shchuchyn
145 Q7 **Shchuchinsk** prev. Shchuchye. Severnyy Kazakhstan, N Kazakhstan
Shchuchye see Shchuchinsk
119 G16 **Shchuchyn** Pol. Szczuczyn Nowogródzki, Rus. Shchuchin. Hrodzyenskaya Voblasts', W Belarus
119 K17 **Shchytkavichy** Rus. Shchitkovichi. Minskaya Voblasts', C Belarus
122 J13 **Shebalino** Respublika Altay, S Russian Federation
128 J9 **Shebekino** Belgorodskaya Oblast', W Russian Federation
Shebelē Wenz, Wabē see Shebeli
81 L14 **Shebeli** Amh. Wabē Shebelē Wenz, It. Scebeli, Som. Webi Shabeelle. ≈ Ethiopia/Somalia
113 M20 **Shebenikut, Maja e** ▲ E Albania
149 N2 **Sheberghān** var. Shibarghān, Shiberghan, Shiberghān. Jowzjān, N Afghanistan
144 F14 **Shebir** Mangistau, SW Kazakhstan
31 N8 **Sheboygan** Wisconsin, N USA
77 X15 **Shebshi Mountains** var. Schebschi Mountains. ▲ E Nigeria
Shechem see Nablus
Shedadi see Ash Shadādah
13 P14 **Shediac** New Brunswick, SE Canada
128 L15 **Shedok** Krasnodarskiy Kray, SW Russian Federation
80 N12 **Sheekh** Woqooyi Galbeed, N Somalia
38 M11 **Sheenjek River** ≈ Alaska, USA
96 D13 **Sheep Haven** Ir. Cuan na gCaorach. inlet N Ireland
35 X10 **Sheep Range** ▲▲ Nevada, W USA
98 M13 **'s-Heerenberg** Gelderland, E Netherlands
97 P22 **Sheerness** SE England, UK
13 Q15 **Sheet Harbour** Nova Scotia, SE Canada
185 H18 **Sheffield** Canterbury, South Island, NZ
97 M18 **Sheffield** N England, UK
23 O2 **Sheffield** Alabama, S USA
29 V12 **Sheffield** Iowa, C USA
25 N10 **Sheffield** Texas, SW USA
63 H22 **Shehuen, Río** ≈ S Argentina
Shekhem see Nablus
149 V8 **Shekhūpura** Punjab, NE Pakistan
Sheki see Şäki
126 L14 **Sheksna** Vologodskaya Oblast', NW Russian Federation
123 T5 **Shelagskiy, Mys** headland NE Russian Federation
27 V3 **Shelbina** Missouri, C USA
13 P16 **Shelburne** Nova Scotia, SE Canada
14 G14 **Shelburne** Ontario, S Canada
33 R7 **Shelby** Montana, NW USA
21 Q10 **Shelby** North Carolina, SE USA
31 S12 **Shelby** Ohio, N USA
30 L14 **Shelbyville** Illinois, N USA
31 P14 **Shelbyville** Indiana, N USA
20 L5 **Shelbyville** Kentucky, S USA
27 V2 **Shelbyville** Missouri, C USA
20 J10 **Shelbyville** Tennessee, S USA
25 X8 **Shelbyville** Texas, SW USA
30 L14 **Shelbyville, Lake** ▣ Illinois, N USA
29 S12 **Sheldon** Iowa, C USA
38 M11 **Sheldons Point** Alaska, USA
Shelekhov Gulf see Shelikhova, Zaliv
123 U9 **Shelikhova, Zaliv** Eng. Shelekhov Gulf. gulf E Russian Federation
39 P14 **Shelikof Strait** strait Alaska, USA
Shelim see Shalīm
11 T14 **Shellbrook** Saskatchewan, S Canada
28 L3 **Shell Creek** ≈ North Dakota, N USA
Shellif see Chelif, Oued
22 I10 **Shell Keys** island group Louisiana, S USA
30 I4 **Shell Lake** Wisconsin, N USA
29 W12 **Shell Rock** Iowa, C USA
185 C26 **Shelter Point** headland Stewart Island, NZ
18 L13 **Shelton** Connecticut, NE USA
32 G8 **Shelton** Washington, NW USA
Shemakha see Şamaxı
145 W9 **Shemonaikha** Vostochnyy Kazakhstan, E Kazakhstan
129 Q4 **Shemursha** Chuvashskaya Respublika, W Russian Federation
38 D16 **Shemya Island** island Aleutian Islands, Alaska, USA
29 T16 **Shenandoah** Iowa, C USA
21 U4 **Shenandoah** Virginia, NE USA
21 U4 **Shenandoah Mountains** ridge West Virginia, NE USA
21 V3 **Shenandoah River** ≈ West Virginia, NE USA
77 W15 **Shendam** Plateau, C Nigeria
80 G8 **Shendi** var. Shandī. River Nile, NE Sudan
76 I15 **Shenge** SW Sierra Leone
145 U15 **Shengel'dy** Almaty, SE Kazakhstan
113 K18 **Shëngjin** var. Shëngjini. Lezhë, NW Albania
Shëngjini see Shëngjin
Shengking see Liaoning
Sheng Xian/Shengxian see Shengzhou
161 S9 **Shengzhou** var. Shengxian, Sheng Xian. Zhejiang, SE China
Shenking see Liaoning
127 N11 **Shenkursk** Arkhangel'skaya Oblast', NW Russian Federation
160 L3 **Shenmu** Shaanxi, C China
113 L19 **Shën Noj i Madh** ▲ C Albania
Shenshi/Shensi see Shaanxi
163 V12 **Shenyang** Chin. Shen-yang, Eng. Moukden, Mukden; prev. Fengtien. Liaoning, NE China
161 O15 **Shenzhen** Guangdong, S China
154 G8 **Sheopur** Madhya Pradesh, C India
116 L5 **Shepetivka** Rus. Shepetovka. Khmel'nyts'ka Oblast', NW Ukraine
Shepetovka see Shepetivka
25 W10 **Shepherd** Texas, SW USA
187 R14 **Shepherd Islands** island group C Vanuatu
20 K5 **Shepherdsville** Kentucky, S USA
183 O11 **Shepparton** Victoria, SE Australia
97 P22 **Sheppey, Isle of** island SE England, UK
Sherabad see Sherobod
9 O4 **Sherard, Cape** headland Nunavut, N Canada
97 L23 **Sherborne** S England, UK
76 H16 **Sherbro Island** island SW Sierra Leone
15 Q12 **Sherbrooke** Quebec, SE Canada
29 T11 **Sherburn** Minnesota, N USA
78 H6 **Sherda** Borkou-Ennedi-Tibesti, N Chad
80 G7 **Shereik** River Nile, N Sudan

◆ Country ● Country Capital ◇ Dependent Territory ○ Dependent Territory Capital ◈ Administrative Region ✕ International Airport ▲ Mountain ▲▲ Mountain Range ⚠ Volcano ≈ River ◎ Lake ▣ Reservoir

128 K3 **Sheremet'yevo** ✈ (Moskva) Moskovskaya Oblast', W Russian Federation
153 P14 **Shergāti** Bihār, N India
27 U12 **Sheridan** Arkansas, C USA
33 W12 **Sheridan** Wyoming, C USA
182 G8 **Sheringa** South Australia
25 U5 **Sherman** Texas, SW USA
194 J10 **Sherman Island** *island* Antarctica
19 S4 **Sherman Mills** Maine, NE USA
29 O15 **Sherman Reservoir** ▣ Nebraska, C USA
147 N14 **Sherobod** *Rus.* Sherabad. Surkhondaryo Wiloyati, S Uzbekistan
147 O13 **Sherobod** *Rus.* Sherabad. ≈ S Uzbekistan
153 T14 **Sherpur** Dhaka, N Bangladesh
37 T4 **Sherrelwood** Colorado, C USA
99 J14 **'s-Hertogenbosch** *Fr.* Bois-le-Duc, *Ger.* Herzogenbusch. Noord-Brabant, S Netherlands
28 M2 **Sherwood** North Dakota, N USA
11 Q14 **Sherwood Park** Alberta, SW Canada
56 F13 **Sheshea, Río** ≈ E Peru
143 T5 **Sheshtamad** Khorāsān, NE Iran
29 S10 **Shetek, Lake** ◎ Minnesota, N USA
96 M2 **Shetland Islands** *island group* NE Scotland, UK
144 F14 **Shetpe** Mangistau, SW Kazakhstan
154 C11 **Shetrunji** ≈ W India
Shevchenko *see* Aktau
117 W5 **Shevchenkove** Kharkivs'ka Oblast', E Ukraine
81 H14 **Shewa Gimira** Southern, S Ethiopia
161 Q9 **Shexian** *var.* Huicheng, She Xian. Anhui, E China
161 R6 **Sheyang** *prev.* Hede. Jiangsu, E China
29 O4 **Sheyenne** North Dakota, N USA
29 P4 **Sheyenne River** ≈ North Dakota, N USA
96 G7 **Shiant Islands** *island group* NW Scotland, UK
123 U12 **Shiashkotan, Ostrov** *island* Kuril'skiye Ostrova, SE Russian Federation
31 R9 **Shiawassee River** ≈ Michigan, N USA
141 R14 **Shibām** C Yemen
Shibarghān *see* Sheberghān
165 O10 **Shibata** *var.* Sibata. Niigata, Honshū, C Japan
Shiberghan/Shiberghān *see* Sheberghān
Shibh Jazīrat Sīnā' *see* Sinai
Shibīn al Kawm *see* Shibîn el Kôm
75 W8 **Shibîn el Kôm** *var.* Shibīn al Kawm. N Egypt
143 O13 **Shīb, Kūh-e** ▲ S Iran
12 D8 **Shibogama Lake** ◎ Ontario, C Canada
Shibotsu-jima *see* Zelënyy, Ostrov
164 B16 **Shibushi** Kagoshima, Kyūshū, SW Japan
189 U13 **Shichiyo Islands** *island group* Chuuk, C Micronesia
Shickshock Mountains *see* Chic-Chocs, Monts
145 S9 **Shiderti** ≈ N Kazakhstan
145 S8 **Shiderty** Pavlodar, NE Kazakhstan
96 G10 **Shiel, Loch** ◎ N Scotland, UK
164 J13 **Shiga** *off.* Shiga-ken, *var.* Siga. ◈ *prefecture* Honshū, SW Japan
Shigatse *see* Xigazê
141 U13 **Shiḥan** *oasis* NE Yemen
Shih-chia-chuang/Shihmen *see* Shijiazhuang
158 K4 **Shihezi** Xinjiang Uygur Zizhiqu, NW China
Shiichi *see* Shyichy
113 K19 **Shijak** *var.* Shijaku. Durrës, W Albania
Shijaku *see* Shijak
161 O4 **Shijiazhuang** *var.* Shih-chia-chuang; *prev.* Shihmen. Hebei, E China
165 R5 **Shikabe** Hokkaidō, NE Japan
149 Q13 **Shikārpur** Sind, S Pakistan
189 V12 **Shiki Islands** *island group* Chuuk, C Micronesia
164 G14 **Shikoku** *var.* Sikoku. *island* SW Japan
192 H5 **Shikoku Basin** *var.* Sikoku Basin. *undersea feature* N Philippine Sea
164 G14 **Shikoku-sanchi** ▲ Shikoku, SW Japan
165 X4 **Shikotan, Ostrov** *Jap.* Shikotan-tō. *island* NE Russian Federation
Shikotan-tō *see* Shikotan, Ostrov
165 R4 **Shikotsu-ko** *var.* Sikotu Ko. ◎ Hokkaidō, NE Japan
81 N15 **Shilabo** Somali, E Ethiopia
129 X7 **Shil'da** Orenburgskaya Oblast', W Russian Federation
139 V3 **Shilēr, Āw-e** ≈ E Iraq
153 S12 **Shiliguri** *prev.* Siliguri. West Bengal, NE India
131 V7 **Shilka** ≈ S Russian Federation
18 H15 **Shillington** Pennsylvania, NE USA
153 V13 **Shillong** Meghālaya, NE India
128 M5 **Shilovo** Ryazanskaya Oblast', W Russian Federation
164 C14 **Shimabara** *var.* Simabara. Nagasaki, Kyūshū, SW Japan
164 C14 **Shimabara-wan** *bay* SW Japan
164 F12 **Shimane** *off.* Shimane-ken, *var.* Simane. ◈ *prefecture* Honshū, SW Japan
164 G11 **Shimane-hantō** *peninsula* Honshū, SW Japan
123 Q13 **Shimanovsk** Amurskaya Oblast', SE Russian Federation
Shimbir Berris *see* Shimbiris
80 O12 **Shimbiris** *var.* Shimbir Berris. ▲ N Somalia
165 T4 **Shimizu** Hokkaidō, NE Japan
164 M14 **Shimizu** *var.* Simizu. Shizuoka, Honshū, S Japan
152 I8 **Shimla** *prev.* Simla. Himāchal Pradesh, N India
Shimminato *see* Shinminato
165 N14 **Shimoda** *var.* Simoda. Shizuoka, Honshū, S Japan
165 O13 **Shimodate** *var.* Simodate. Ibaraki, Honshū, S Japan
155 F18 **Shimoga** Karnātaka, W India
164 C15 **Shimo-jima** *island* SW Japan
164 B15 **Shimo-Koshiki-jima** *island* SW Japan
81 J21 **Shimoni** Coast, S Kenya
164 D13 **Shimonoseki** *var.* Simonoseki; *hist.* Akamagaseki, Bakan. Yamaguchi, Honshū, SW Japan
126 G14 **Shimsk** Novgorodskaya Oblast', NW Russian Federation
141 W7 **Shināş** N Oman
148 J6 **Shīndand** Farāh, W Afghanistan
Shinei *see* Hsinying
25 T12 **Shiner** Texas, SW USA
167 N1 **Shingbwiyang** Kachin State, N Myanmar
145 W11 **Shingozha** Vostochnyy Kazakhstan, E Kazakhstan
164 J15 **Shingū** *var.* Singû. Wakayama, Honshū, SW Japan
14 F8 **Shining Tree** Ontario, S Canada
165 P9 **Shinjō** *var.* Sinzyô. Yamagata, Honshū, C Japan
96 I7 **Shin, Loch** ◎ N Scotland, UK
21 S3 **Shinnston** West Virginia, NE USA
138 I6 **Shinshār** *Fr.* Chinnchâr. Ḥimş, W Syria
Shinshū *see* Chinju
165 T4 **Shintoku** Hokkaidō, NE Japan
81 G20 **Shinyanga** Shinyanga, NW Tanzania
81 G20 **Shinyanga** ◈ *region* N Tanzania
165 Q10 **Shiogama** *var.* Siogama. Miyagi, Honshū, C Japan
164 M12 **Shiojiri** *var.* Sioziri. Nagano, Honshū, S Japan
164 I15 **Shiono-misaki** *headland* Honshū, SW Japan
165 Q12 **Shioya-zaki** *headland* Honshū, C Japan
114 J9 **Shipchenski Prokhod** *pass* C Bulgaria
160 G14 **Shiping** Yunnan, SW China
13 P13 **Shippagan** *var.* Shippegan. New Brunswick, SE Canada
Shippegan *see* Shippagan
18 F15 **Shippensburg** Pennsylvania, NE USA
37 O9 **Ship Rock** ▲ New Mexico, SW USA
37 P9 **Shiprock** New Mexico, SW USA
15 R6 **Shipshaw** ≈ Quebec, SE Canada
123 V10 **Shipunskiy, Mys** *headland* E Russian Federation
160 K7 **Shiquan** Shaanxi, C China
122 K13 **Shira** Respublika Khakasiya, S Russian Federation
153 T14 **Shirajganj Ghat** *var.* Serajgonj, Sirajganj. Rajshahi, C Bangladesh
165 P12 **Shirakawa** *var.* Sirakawa. Fukushima, Honshū, C Japan
164 M13 **Shirane-san** ▲ Honshū, S Japan
165 U14 **Shiranuka** Hokkaidō, NE Japan
195 N12 **Shirase Coast** *physical region* Antarctica
165 U3 **Shirataki** Hokkaidō, NE Japan
143 O11 **Shīrāz** *var.* Shīrāz. Fārs, S Iran
83 N15 **Shire** *var.* Chire. ≈ Malawi/Mozambique
162 G7 **Shiree** Dzavhan, W Mongolia
163 O9 **Shireet** Sühbaatar, SE Mongolia
165 W3 **Shiretoko-hantō** *headland* Hokkaidō, NE Japan
165 W3 **Shiretoko-misaki** *headland* Hokkaidō, NE Japan
129 N5 **Shiringushi** Respublika Mordoviya, W Russian Federation
148 M3 **Shīrīn Tagāb** Fāryāb, N Afghanistan
149 N2 **Shīrīn Tagāb** ≈ N Afghanistan
165 R6 **Shiriya-zaki** *headland* Honshū, C Japan
144 I12 **Shirkala, Gryada** *plain* W Kazakhstan
165 P10 **Shiroishi** *var.* Siroisi. Miyagi, Honshū, C Japan
Shirokoye *see* Shyroke
165 O10 **Shirone** *var.* Sirone. Niigata, Honshū, C Japan
164 L12 **Shirotori** Gifu, Honshū, SW Japan
197 T1 **Shirshov Ridge** *undersea feature* W Bering Sea
Shirshūtūr *see* Shirshyutyur, Peski
146 K12 **Shirshyutyur, Peski** *Turkm.* Shirshütür. *desert* E Turkmenistan
143 T3 **Shīrvān** *var.* Shirwān. Khorāsān, NE Iran
Shirwa, Lake *see* Chilwa, Lake
Shirwān *see* Shīrvān
159 N5 **Shisanjianfang** Xinjiang Uygur Zizhiqu, W China
38 M16 **Shishaldin Volcano** ▲ Unimak Island, Alaska, USA
Shishchitsy *see* Shyshchytsy
38 M8 **Shishmaref** Alaska, USA
Shisur *see* Ash Shişar
164 L13 **Shitara** Aichi, Honshū, SW Japan
152 D12 **Shiv** Rājasthān, NW India
151 E15 **Shivāji Sāgar** *prev.* Konya Reservoir ▣ W India
154 H8 **Shivpuri** Madhya Pradesh, C India
36 J9 **Shivwits Plateau** *plain* Arizona, SW USA
Shiwālik Range *see* Siwalik Range
160 M8 **Shiyan** Hubei, C China
160 H13 **Shizong** Yunnan, SW China
165 R10 **Shizugawa** Miyagi, Honshū, NE Japan
159 W8 **Shizuishan** *var.* Dawukou. Ningxia, N China
165 T5 **Shizunai** Hokkaidō, NE Japan
165 M14 **Shizuoka** *var.* Sizuoka. Shizuoka, Honshū, S Japan
164 M13 **Shizuoka** *off.* Shizuoka-ken, *var.* Sizuoka. ◈ *prefecture* Honshū, S Japan
Shklov *see* Shklow
119 N15 **Shklow** *Rus.* Shklov. Mahilyowskaya Voblasts', E Belarus
113 K18 **Shkodër** *var.* Shkodra, *It.* Scutari, *SCr.* Skadar. Shkodër, NW Albania
113 K17 **Shkodër** ◈ *district* NW Albania
Shkodra *see* Shkodër
Shkodrës, Liqeni i *see* Scutari, Lake
Shkumbi/Shkumbin *see* Shkumbinit, Lumi i
113 L20 **Shkumbinit, Lumi i** *var.* Shkumbi, Shkumbin. ≈ C Albania
Shligigh, Cuan *see* Sligo Bay
122 L4 **Shmidta, Ostrov** *island* Severnaya Zemlya, N Russian Federation
183 S10 **Shoalhaven River** ≈ New South Wales, SE Australia
11 W16 **Shoal Lake** Manitoba, S Canada
31 O15 **Shoals** Indiana, N USA
164 I13 **Shōdo-shima** *island* SW Japan
Shōka *see* Changhua
122 M5 **Shokal'skogo, Proliv** *strait* N Russian Federation
147 T14 **Shokhdara, Qatorkŭhi** *Rus.* Shakhdarinskiy Khrebet. ▲ SE Tajikistan
145 N9 **Sholaksay** Kostanay, N Kazakhstan
Sholāpur *see* Solāpur
Sholdaneshty *see* Şoldăneşti
145 P17 **Shollakorgan** *var.* Chulakkurgan. Yuznhyy Kazakhstan, S Kazakhstan
Shoqpar *see* Chokpar
155 G21 **Shorānūr** Kerala, SW India
155 G16 **Shorāpur** Karnātaka, C India
30 M11 **Shorewood** Illinois, N USA
Shorkazakhly, Solonchak *see* Kazakhlyshor, Solonchak
145 Q9 **Shortandy** Akmola, C Kazakhstan
Shortepa/Shor Tepe *see* Shūr Tappeh
186 J7 **Shortland Island** *var.* Alu. *island* Solomon Islands
Shosambetsu *see* Shosanbetsu
165 S2 **Shosanbetsu** *var.* Shosambetsu. Hokkaidō, NE Japan
33 O15 **Shoshone** Idaho, NW USA
35 T6 **Shoshone Mountains** ▲ Nevada, W USA
33 U12 **Shoshone River** ≈ Wyoming, C USA
83 I19 **Shoshong** Central, SE Botswana
33 V14 **Shoshoni** Wyoming, C USA
Shōshū *see* Sangju
117 S2 **Shostka** Sums'ka Oblast', NE Ukraine
185 C21 **Shotover** ≈ South Island, NZ
37 N12 **Show Low** Arizona, SW USA
Show Me State *see* Missouri
146 H9 **Showot** *Rus.* Shavat. Khorazm Wiloyati, W Uzbekistan
127 O4 **Shoyna** Nenetskiy Avtonomnyy Okrug, NW Russian Federation
126 M11 **Shozhma** Arkhangel'skaya Oblast', NW Russian Federation
117 Q7 **Shpola** Cherkas'ka Oblast', N Ukraine
Shqipëria/Shqipërisë, Republika e *see* Albania
22 G5 **Shreveport** Louisiana, S USA
97 K19 **Shrewsbury** *hist.* Scrobesbyrig'. W England, UK
152 D11 **Shri Mohangarh** *prev.* Sri Mohangorh. Rājasthān, NW India
153 S16 **Shrīrāmpur** *prev.* Serampore, Serampur. West Bengal, NE India
97 K19 **Shropshire** *cultural region* W England, UK
145 S16 **Shu** *Kaz.* Shū. Zhambyl, SE Kazakhstan
Shū *see* Chu
160 G13 **Shuangbai** Yunnan, SW China
163 W9 **Shuangcheng** Heilongjiang, NE China
160 E14 **Shuangjiang** Yunnan, SW China
163 U10 **Shuangliao** *var.* Zhengjiatun. Jilin, NE China
Shuang-liao *see* Liaoyuan
163 Y7 **Shuangyashan** *var.* Shuang-ya-shan. Heilongjiang, NE China
Shu'aymiah *see* Shu'aymīyah
141 W12 **Shu'aymīyah** *var.* Shu'aymiah. S Oman
144 I10 **Shubarkuduk** *Kaz.* Shubarqudyq. Aktyubinsk, W Kazakhstan
Shubarqudyq *see* Shubarkuduk
145 N12 **Shubar-Tengiz, Ozero** ◎ C Kazakhstan
39 S5 **Shublik Mountains** ▲ Alaska, USA
Shubrā al Khaymah *see* Shubrâ el Kheima
121 U13 **Shubrâ el Kheima** *var.* Shubrā al Khaymah. N Egypt
158 E8 **Shufu** Xinjiang Uygur Zizhiqu, NW China
147 S14 **Shughnon, Qatorkŭhi** *Rus.* Shugnanskiy Khrebet. ▲ SE Tajikistan
Shugnanskiy Khrebet *see* Shughnon, Qatorkŭhi
161 Q6 **Shu He** ≈ E China
Shuiding *see* Huocheng
Shuiji *see* Laixi
Shū-Ile Taūlary *see* Chu-Iliyskiye Gory
149 T10 **Shujāābād** Punjab, E Pakistan
163 W9 **Shulan** Jilin, NE China
158 E8 **Shule** Xinjiang Uygur Zizhiqu, NW China
Shuleh *see* Shule He
159 Q8 **Shule He** *var.* Shuleh, Sulo. ≈ C China
30 K9 **Shullsburg** Wisconsin, N USA
39 N16 **Shumagin Islands** *island group* Alaska, USA
146 G7 **Shumanay** Qoraqalpoghiston Respublikasi, W Uzbekistan
114 M8 **Shumen** Shumen, NE Bulgaria
114 M8 **Shumen** ◈ *province* NE Bulgaria
129 P4 **Shumerlya** Chuvashskaya Respublika, W Russian Federation
122 G11 **Shumikha** Kurganskaya Oblast', C Russian Federation
118 M12 **Shumilina** *Rus.* Shumilino. Vitsyebskaya Voblasts', NE Belarus
Shumilino *see* Shumilina
123 V11 **Shumshu, Ostrov** *island* SE Russian Federation
116 K5 **Shums'k** Ternopil's'ka Oblast', W Ukraine
39 O7 **Shungnak** Alaska, USA
Shunsen *see* Ch'unch'ŏn
160 M3 **Shuo Xian** Shanxi, NE China
Shuo Xian/Shuoxian *see* Shuozhou
161 N3 **Shuozhou** *var.* Shuoxian; *prev.* Shuo Xian. Shanxi, C China
141 P16 **Shuqrah** *var.* Shaqrā. SW Yemen
Shurab *see* Shūrob
147 O14 **Shŭrchi** *Rus.* Shurchi. Surkhondaryo Wiloyati, S Uzbekistan
147 R11 **Shūrob** *Rus.* Shurab. NW Tajikistan
143 T10 **Shūr, Rūd-e** ≈ E Iran
149 O2 **Shūr Tappeh** *var.* Shortepa, Shor Tepe. Balkh, N Afghanistan
83 K17 **Shurugwi** *prev.* Selukwe. Midlands, C Zimbabwe
142 L8 **Shūsh** *anc.* Susa, *Bibl.* Shushan. Khūzestān, SW Iran
Shushan *see* Shūsh
142 L9 **Shūshtar** *var.* Shustar, Shushter. Khūzestān, SW Iran
Shushter/Shustar *see* Shūshtar
141 T9 **Shuṭfah, Qalamat** *well* E Saudi Arabia
139 V9 **Shuwayjah, Hawr ash** *var.* Hawr as Suwayqiyah. ◎ E Iraq
126 M16 **Shuya** Ivanovskaya Oblast', W Russian Federation
39 Q14 **Shuyak Island** *island* Alaska, USA
166 M4 **Shwebo** Sagaing, C Myanmar
166 L7 **Shwedaung** Pegu, W Myanmar
166 M7 **Shwegyin** Pegu, SW Myanmar
167 N4 **Shweli** *Chin.* Longchuan Jiang. ≈ Myanmar/China
166 M6 **Shwemyo** Mandalay, C Myanmar
Shyghys Qazagastan Oblysy *see* Vostochnyy Kazakhstan
Shyghys Qongyrat *see* Shygys Konyrat
145 T12 **Shygys Konyrat** *var.* Vostochno-Kounradskiy, *Kaz.* Shyghys Qongyrat. Karaganda, C Kazakhstan
119 M19 **Shyichy** *Rus.* Shiichi. Homyel'skaya Voblasts', SE Belarus
145 Q17 **Shymkent** *prev.* Chimkent. Yuzhnyy Kazakhstan, S Kazakhstan
Shyngghyrlaū *see* Chingirlau
152 J5 **Shyok** Jammu and Kashmir, NW India
117 S9 **Shyroke** *Rus.* Shirokoye. Dnipropetrovs'ka Oblast', E Ukraine
117 O9 **Shyryayeve** Odes'ka Oblast', SW Ukraine
117 S5 **Shyshaky** Poltavs'ka Oblast', C Ukraine
119 K17 **Shyshchytsy** *Rus.* Shishchitsy. Minskaya Voblasts', C Belarus
149 Y3 **Siachen Muztāgh** ▲ NE Pakistan
Siadehan *see* Tākestān
148 M13 **Siāhān Range** ▲ W Pakistan
142 I1 **Siāh Chashmeh** Āzarbāyjān-e Bākhtarī, N Iran
149 W7 **Siālkot** Punjab, NE Pakistan
186 E7 **Sialum** Morobe, C PNG
Siam *see* Thailand
Siam, Gulf of *see* Thailand, Gulf of
Sian *see* Xi'an
Siang *see* Brahmaputra
Siangtan *see* Xiangtan
169 N8 **Siantan, Pulau** *island* Kepulauan Anambas, W Indonesia
54 H11 **Siare, Río** ≈ C Colombia
171 R6 **Siargao Island** *island* S Philippines
186 F72 **Siassi** Umboi Island, C PNG
115 D14 **Siátista** Dytikí Makedonía, N Greece
166 K4 **Siatlai** Chin State, W Myanmar
171 P6 **Siaton** Negros, C Philippines
171 P6 **Siaton Point** *headland* Negros, C Philippines
118 F11 **Šiauliai** *Ger.* Schaulen. Šiauliai, N Lithuania
171 Q10 **Siau, Pulau** *island* N Indonesia
83 J15 **Siavonga** Southern, SE Zambia
Siazan' *see* Siyäzän
Sibah *see* As Sībah
107 N20 **Sibari** Calabria, S Italy
Sibata *see* Shibata
129 X6 **Sibay** Respublika Bashkortostan, W Russian Federation
93 M19 **Sibbo** *Fin.* Sipoo. Etelä-Suomi, S Finland
112 D13 **Šibenik** *It.* Sebenico. Šibenik-Knin, S Croatia
Šibenik *see* Šibenik-Knin
112 E13 **Šibenik-Knin** *off.* Šibenska Županija. *var.* Šibenik. ◈ *province* S Croatia
Šibenska Županija *see* Šibenik-Knin
Siberia *see* Sibir'
Siberoet *see* Siberut, Pulau
168 H12 **Siberut, Pulau** *prev.* Siberoet. *island* Kepulauan Mentawai, W Indonesia
168 I12 **Siberut, Selat** *strait* W Indonesia
Sibetu *see* Shibetsu
149 P11 **Sibi** Baluchistān, SW Pakistan
186 B9 **Sibidiri** Western, SW PNG
123 N10 **Sibir'** *var.* Siberia. *physical region* NE Russian Federation
79 F20 **Sibiti** La Lékoumou, S Congo
81 G21 **Sibiti** ≈ C Tanzania
116 I12 **Sibiu** *Ger.* Hermannstadt, *Hung.* Nagyszeben. Sibiu, C Romania
116 I11 **Sibiu** ◈ *county* C Romania
29 S11 **Sibley** Iowa, C USA
169 R9 **Sibu** Sarawak, East Malaysia
Sibukawa *see* Shibukawa
42 G2 **Sibun** ≈ E Belize
79 I15 **Sibut** *prev.* Fort-Sibut. Kémo, S Central African Republic
171 P4 **Sibuyan Island** *island* C Philippines
171 P4 **Sibuyan Sea** *sea* C Philippines
189 U1 **Sibylla Island** *island* N Marshall Islands
11 N16 **Sicamous** British Columbia, SW Canada
Sichelburger Gebirge *see* Gorjanci/Žumberačko Gorje
167 N14 **Sichon** *var.* Ban Sichon, Si Chon. Nakhon Si Thammarat, SW Thailand
160 H9 **Sichuan** *var.* Chuan, Sichuan Sheng, Ssu-ch'uan, Szechuan, Szechwan. ◈ *province* C China
160 I9 **Sichuan Pendi** *basin* C China
Sichuan Sheng *see* Sichuan
103 S16 **Sicie, Cap** *headland* SE France
107 J24 **Sicilia** *Eng.* Sicily; *anc.* Trinacria. ◈ *region* Italy, C Mediterranean Sea
107 M24 **Sicilia** *Eng.* Sicily; *anc.* Trinacria. *island* Italy, C Mediterranean Sea
Sicilian Channel *see* Sicily, Strait of
Sicily *see* Sicilia
107 H24 **Sicily, Strait of** *var.* Sicilian Channel. *strait* C Mediterranean Sea
42 K5 **Sico Tinto, Río** *var.* Río Negro. ≈ NE Honduras
57 H16 **Sicuani** Cusco, S Peru
112 J10 **Šid** Serbia, NW Yugoslavia
115 A15 **Sidári** Kérkyra, Iónioi Nísoi, Greece, C Mediterranean Sea
169 Q11 **Sidas** Borneo, C Indonesia
98 O5 **Siddeburen** Groningen, NE Netherlands
154 D9 **Siddhapur** *prev.* Siddhpur, Sidhpur. Gujarāt, W India
Siddhpur *see* Siddhapur
155 I15 **Siddipet** Andhra Pradesh, C India
77 N14 **Sidéradougou** SW Burkina
107 N23 **Siderno** Calabria, SW Italy
Siders *see* Sierre
154 L9 **Sidhi** Madhya Pradesh, C India
Sidhirókastron *see* Sidirókastro
Sidhpur *see* Siddhapur
Sîdî al Hānī', Sabkhat *see* Sidi el Hani, Sebkhet de
75 U7 **Sîdî Barrânî** NW Egypt
74 I6 **Sidi Bel Abbès** *var.* Sidi bel Abbès, Sidi-Bel-Abbès. NW Algeria
74 E7 **Sidi-Bennour** W Morocco
74 M6 **Sidi Bouzid** *var.* Gammouda, Sīdī Bu Zayd. C Tunisia
74 D8 **Sidi-Ifni** SW Morocco
74 G6 **Sidi-Kacem** *prev.* Petitjean. N Morocco
114 G12 **Sidirókastro** *prev.* Sidhirókastron. Kentrikí Makedonía, NE Greece
194 L12 **Sidley, Mount** ▲ Antarctica
29 S16 **Sidney** Iowa, C USA
33 Y7 **Sidney** Montana, NW USA
28 J15 **Sidney** Nebraska, C USA
18 I11 **Sidney** New York, NE USA
31 R13 **Sidney** Ohio, N USA
23 T2 **Sidney Lanier, Lake** ◎ Georgia, SE USA
Sidon *see* Saïda
122 J9 **Sidorovsk** Yamalo-Nenetskiy Avtonomnyy Okrug, N Russian Federation
Sidra/Sidra, Gulf of *see* Surt, Khalīj, N Libya
Sidra *see* Surt, N Libya
Sīdī Bu Zayd *see* Sidi Bouzid
Siebenbürgen *see* Transylvania
Sieben Dörfer *see* Săcele
110 O12 **Siedlce** *Ger.* Sedlez, *Rus.* Sesdlets. Mazowieckie, C Poland
101 E16 **Sieg** ≈ W Germany
101 F16 **Siegen** Nordrhein-Westfalen, W Germany
109 X4 **Sieghartskirchen** Niederösterreich, E Austria
110 O11 **Siemiatycze** Podlaskie, NE Poland
167 T11 **Siĕmpang** Stœ̆ng Trĕng, NE Cambodia
167 R11 **Siĕmréab** *prev.* Siemreap. Siĕmréab, NW Cambodia
Siemreap *see* Siĕmréab
106 G12 **Siena** *Fr.* Sienne; *anc.* Saena Julia. Toscana, C Italy
Sienne *see* Siena
92 K12 **Sieppijärvi** Lappi, NW Finland
110 J13 **Sieradz** Sieradz, C Poland
110 K10 **Sierpc** Mazowieckie, C Poland
24 J9 **Sierra Blanca** Texas, SW USA
37 S14 **Sierra Blanca Peak** ▲ New Mexico, SW USA
35 P5 **Sierra City** California, W USA
63 I16 **Sierra Colorada** Río Negro, S Argentina
62 I13 **Sierra del Nevado** ▲ W Argentina
63 J16 **Sierra Grande** Río Negro, E Argentina
76 G15 **Sierra Leone** *off.* Republic of Sierra Leone. ◆ *republic* W Africa
64 M13 **Sierra Leone Basin** *undersea feature* E Atlantic Ocean
66 K8 **Sierra Leone Fracture Zone** *tectonic feature* E Atlantic Ocean
Sierra Leone Ridge *see* Sierra Leone Rise
64 L13 **Sierra Leone Rise** *var.* Sierra Leone Ridge, Sierra Leone Schwelle. *undersea feature* E Atlantic Ocean
Sierra Leone Schwelle *see* Sierra Leone Rise
41 U17 **Sierra Madre** *var.* Sierra de Soconusco. ▲ Guatemala/Mexico
37 R2 **Sierra Madre** ▲ Colorado/Wyoming, C USA
(0) H15 **Sierra Madre del Sur** ▲ S Mexico
(0) G13 **Sierra Madre Occidental** *var.* Western Sierra Madre. ▲ C Mexico
(0) H13 **Sierra Madre Oriental** *var.* Eastern Sierra Madre. ▲ C Mexico
44 H8 **Sierra Maestra** ▲ E Cuba
40 L7 **Sierra Mojada** Coahuila de Zaragoza, NE Mexico
105 O14 **Sierra Nevada** ▲ S Spain
35 P6 **Sierra Nevada** ▲ W USA
54 F4 **Sierra Nevada de Santa Marta** ▲ NE Colombia
42 K5 **Sierra Río Tinto** ▲ NE Honduras
24 J10 **Sierra Vieja** ▲ Texas, SW USA
37 N16 **Sierra Vista** Arizona, SW USA
108 D10 **Sierre** *Ger.* Siders. Valais, SW Switzerland
36 L16 **Sierrita Mountains** ▲ Arizona, SW USA
Siete Moai *see* Ahu Akivi
76 M15 **Sifié** W Ivory Coast
115 I21 **Sífnos** *anc.* Siphnos. *island* Kykládes, Greece, Aegean Sea
115 I21 **Sífnou, Stenó** *strait* SE Greece
Siga *see* Shiga
103 P16 **Sigean** Aude, S France
Sighet *see* Sighetu Marmaţiei
Sighetul Marmaţiei *see* Sighetu Marmaţiei
116 I8 **Sighetu Marmaţiei** *var.* Sighet, Sighetul Marmaţiei, *Hung.* Máramarossziget. Maramureş, N Romania
116 I11 **Sighişoara** *Ger.* Schässburg, *Hung.* Segesvár. Mureş, C Romania
168 G7 **Sigli** Sumatera, W Indonesia
92 J1 **Siglufjördhur** Nordhurland Vestra, N Iceland
101 H23 **Sigmaringen** Baden-Württemberg, S Germany
101 N20 **Signalberg** ▲ SE Germany
36 I13 **Signal Peak** ▲ Arizona, SW USA
Signan *see* Xi'an
194 H1 **Signy** *UK research station* South Orkney Islands, Antarctica
29 X15 **Sigourney** Iowa, C USA
115 K17 **Sígri, Akrotírio** *headland* Lésvos, E Greece
Sigsbee Deep *see* Mexico Basin
47 N2 **Sigsbee Escarpment** *undersea feature* N Gulf of Mexico
56 C8 **Sigsig** Azuay, S Ecuador
95 O15 **Sigtuna** Stockholm, C Sweden
42 H6 **Siguatepeque** Comayagua, W Honduras
105 P7 **Sigüenza** Castilla-La Mancha, C Spain
105 R4 **Sigües** Aragón, NE Spain
76 K13 **Siguiri** Haute-Guinée, NE Guinea
118 G8 **Sigulda** *Ger.* Segewold. Rīga, C Latvia
Sihanoukville *see* Kâmpóng Saôm
108 G8 **Sihlsee** ◎ NW Switzerland
93 K18 **Siikainen** Länsi-Suomi, W Finland
93 M16 **Siilinjärvi** Itä-Suomi, C Finland
137 R15 **Siirt** *var.* Sert; *anc.* Tigranocerta. Siirt, SE Turkey
137 R15 **Siirt** *var.* Sert. ◈ *province* SE Turkey
187 N8 **Sikaiana** *var.* Stewert Islands. *island group* W Solomon Islands
Sikandarabad *see* Secunderābād
152 J11 **Sikandra Rao** Uttar Pradesh, N India
10 M11 **Sikanni Chief** British Columbia, W Canada
10 M11 **Sikanni Chief** ≈ British Columbia, W Canada
152 H11 **Sīkar** Rājasthān, N India
76 M13 **Sikasso** Sikasso, S Mali
76 L13 **Sikasso** ◈ *region* SW Mali
167 N3 **Sikaw** Kachin State, C Myanmar
83 H14 **Sikelenge** Western, W Zambia
27 Y7 **Sikeston** Missouri, C USA
93 J14 **Sikfors** Norrbotten, N Sweden
123 T14 **Sikhote-Alin', Khrebet** ▲ SE Russian Federation
Siking *see* Xi'an
115 J22 **Síkinos** *island* Kykládes, Greece, Aegean Sea
153 S11 **Sikkim** *Tib.* Denjong. ◈ *state* N India
111 I26 **Siklós** Baranya, SW Hungary
Sikoku *see* Shikoku
Sikoku Basin *see* Shikoku Basin
83 G14 **Sikongo** Western, W Zambia
Sikotu Ko *see* Shikotsu-ko

◆ Country ◇ Dependent Territory ◈ Administrative Region ▲ Mountain ▲ Volcano ◎ Lake
● Country Capital ○ Dependent Territory Capital ✈ International Airport ▲ Mountain Range ≈ River ▣ Reservoir

Sikouri/Sikoúrion see Sykoúri
123 P8 **Siktyakh** Respublika Sakha (Yakutiya), NE Russian Federation
118 D12 **Šilalė** Šilalė, W Lithuania
106 G5 **Silandro** Ger. Schlanders. Trentino-Alto Adige, N Italy
41 N12 **Silao** Guanajuato, C Mexico
Silarius see Sele
153 W14 **Silchar** Assam, NE India
108 G9 **Silenen** Uri, C Switzerland
21 T9 **Siler City** North Carolina, SE USA
33 U11 **Silesia** Montana, NW USA
110 F13 **Silesia** physical region SW Poland
74 K12 **Silet** S Algeria
145 R8 **Sileti** var. Selety. ~ N Kazakhstan
Siletitengiz see Siletiteniz, Ozero
145 R7 **Siletiteniz, Ozero** Kaz. Siletitengiz. ◎ N Kazakhstan
172 H16 **Silhouette** island Inner Islands, SE Seychelles
136 I17 **Silifke** anc. Seleucia. İçel, S Turkey
Siliguri see Shiliguri
156 J10 **Siling Co** ◎ W China
Silinhot see Xilinhot
192 G15 **Silisili** ▲ Savai'i, C Samoa
114 M6 **Silistra** var. Silistria; anc. Durostorum. Silistra, NE Bulgaria
116 M7 **Silistra** ◈ province NE Bulgaria
Silistria see Silistra
136 D10 **Silivri** İstanbul, NW Turkey
94 L13 **Siljan** ◎ C Sweden
95 G22 **Silkeborg** Århus, C Denmark
108 M8 **Sill** ~ W Austria
105 S10 **Silla** País Valenciano, E Spain
62 H3 **Sillajguay, Cordillera** ▲ N Chile
118 K3 **Sillamäe** Ger. Sillamäggi. Ida-Virumaa, NE Estonia
Sillamäggi see Sillamäe
Sillein see Žilina
109 P9 **Sillian** Tirol, W Austria
112 B10 **Šilo** Primorje-Gorski Kotar, NW Croatia
27 R9 **Siloam Springs** Arkansas, C USA
25 X10 **Silsbee** Texas, SW USA
143 W15 **Sīlūp, Rūd-e** ~ SE Iran
118 C12 **Šilutė** Ger. Heydekrug. Šilutė, W Lithuania
137 Q15 **Silvan** Diyarbakır, SE Turkey
108 J10 **Silvaplana** Graubünden, S Switzerland
Silva Porto see Kuito
58 M12 **Silva, Recife do** reef E Brazil
154 D12 **Silvassa** Dādra and Nagar Haveli, W India
29 X4 **Silver Bay** Minnesota, N USA
37 P15 **Silver City** New Mexico, SW USA
18 D10 **Silver Creek** New York, NE USA
37 N12 **Silver Creek** ~ Arizona, SW USA
27 P4 **Silver Lake** Kansas, C USA
32 I14 **Silver Lake** Oregon, NW USA
35 T9 **Silver Peak Range** ▲ Nevada, W USA
21 W3 **Silver Spring** Maryland, NE USA
Silver State see Nevada
Silver State see Colorado
37 Q7 **Silverton** Colorado, C USA
18 K16 **Silverton** New Jersey, NE USA
32 G11 **Silverton** Oregon, NW USA
25 N4 **Silverton** Texas, SW USA
104 G14 **Silves** Faro, S Portugal
54 D12 **Silvia** Cauca, SW Colombia
108 J9 **Silvrettagruppe** ▲ Austria/Switzerland
Sily-Vajdej see Vulcan
108 L7 **Silz** Tirol, W Austria
172 I13 **Sima** Anjouan, SE Comoros
Simabara see Shimabara
Simada see Shimada
83 H15 **Simakando** Western, W Zambia
Simane see Shimane
119 L20 **Simanichy** Rus. Simonichi. Homyel'skaya Voblasts', SE Belarus
160 F14 **Simao** Yunnan, SW China
153 P12 **Simara** Central, C Nepal
14 I8 **Simard, Lac** ◎ Quebec, SE Canada
136 D13 **Simav** Kütahya, W Turkey
136 D13 **Simav Çayı** ~ NW Turkey
79 L18 **Simba** Orientale, N Dem. Rep. Congo (Zaire)
186 C7 **Simbai** Madang, N PNG
Simbirsk see Ul'yanovsk
14 F17 **Simcoe** Ontario, S Canada
14 H14 **Simcoe, Lake** ◎ Ontario, S Canada
80 J11 **Sīmēn** ▲ N Ethiopia
114 K11 **Simeonovgrad** prev. Maritsa. Khaskovo, S Bulgaria
116 G11 **Simeria** Ger. Pischk, Hung. Piski. Hunedoara, W Romania
107 L24 **Simeto** ~ Sicilia, Italy, C Mediterranean Sea
168 G9 **Simeulue, Pulau** island NW Indonesia
117 T13 **Simferopol'** Respublika Krym, S Ukraine
117 T13 **Simferopol'** × Respublika Krym, S Ukraine
Simi see Sými
152 M9 **Simikot** Far Western, NW Nepal
54 F7 **Simití** Bolívar, N Colombia
114 G11 **Simitla** Blagoevgrad, SW Bulgaria
35 S15 **Simi Valley** California, W USA
Simizu see Shimizu
Simla see Shimla
Şimlăul Silvaniei/Şimleul Silvaniei see Şimleu Silvaniei
116 G9 **Şimleu Silvaniei** Hung. Szilágysomlyó; prev. Şimlăul Silvaniei, Şimleul Silvaniei. Sălaj, NW Romania
Simmer see Simmerbach
101 E19 **Simmerbach** var. Simmer. ~ W Germany
101 F18 **Simmern** Rheinland-Pfalz, W Germany
22 I7 **Simmesport** Louisiana, S USA
119 F14 **Simnas** Alytus, S Lithuania
92 L13 **Simo** Lappi, NW Finland
Simoda see Shimoda
Simodate see Shimodate
92 M13 **Simojärvi** ◎ N Finland
92 L13 **Simojoki** ~ NW Finland
41 U15 **Simojovel** var. Simojovel de Allende. Chiapas, SE Mexico
Simojovel de Allende see Simojovel
56 B7 **Simon Bolivar** var. Guayaquil. × (Guayaquil) Guayas, W Ecuador
54 L5 **Simon Bolívar** × (Caracas) Distrito Federal, N Venezuela
Simonichi see Simanichy
14 M12 **Simon, Lac** ◎ Quebec, SE Canada
Simonoseki see Shimonoseki
Šimonovany see Partizánske
Simonstad see Simon's Town
83 E26 **Simon's Town** var. Simonstad. Western Cape, SW South Africa
Simony see Partizánske
Simotuma see Shimotsuma
Simpeln see Simplon
99 M18 **Simpelveld** Limburg, SE Netherlands
108 E11 **Simplon** var. Simpeln. Valais, SW Switzerland
108 E11 **Simplon Pass** pass S Switzerland
106 C6 **Simplon Tunnel** tunnel Italy/Switzerland
Simpson see Fort Simpson
182 G1 **Simpson Desert** desert Northern Territory/South Australia
10 J9 **Simpson Peak** ▲ British Columbia, W Canada
9 N7 **Simpson Peninsula** peninsula Nunavut, NE Canada
21 P11 **Simpsonville** South Carolina, SE USA
95 L23 **Simrishamn** Skåne, S Sweden
123 U13 **Simushir, Ostrov** island Kuril'skiye Ostrova, SE Russian Federation
Sīnā'/Sinai Peninsula see Sinai
168 G9 **Sinabang** Sumatera, W Indonesia
81 N15 **Sina Dhaqa** Galguduud, C Somalia
75 X8 **Sinai** var. Sinai Peninsula, Ar. Shibh Jazīrat Sīnā', Sīnā'. physical region NE Egypt
116 J12 **Sinaia** Prahova, SE Romania
188 B16 **Sinajana** C Guam
40 H8 **Sinaloa** ◈ state C Mexico
54 H4 **Sinamaica** Zulia, NW Venezuela
163 X14 **Sinan-ni** SE North Korea
Sinano Gawa see Shinano-gawa
Sināwan see Sīnāwin
75 N8 **Sīnāwin** var. Sīnāwan. NW Libya
83 J16 **Sinazongwe** Southern, S Zambia
166 L6 **Sinbaungwe** Magwe, W Myanmar
166 L5 **Sinbyugyun** Magwe, W Myanmar
54 E6 **Since** Sucre, NW Colombia
54 E6 **Sincelejo** Sucre, NW Colombia
166 J5 **Sinchaingbyin** var. Zullapara. Arakan State, W Myanmar
23 U4 **Sinclair, Lake** ▣ Georgia, SE USA
10 M14 **Sinclair Mills** British Columbia, SW Canada
149 Q14 **Sind** var. Sindh. ◈ province SE Pakistan
154 I8 **Sind** ~ N India
95 H19 **Sindal** Nordjylland, N Denmark
171 P7 **Sindañgan** Mindanao, S Philippines
79 D19 **Sindara** Ngounié, W Gabon
152 E13 **Sindari** prev. Sindri. Rājasthān, N India
114 N8 **Sindel** Varna, E Bulgaria
101 H22 **Sindelfingen** Baden-Württemberg, SW Germany
155 G16 **Sindgi** Karnātaka, C India
Sindh see Sind
118 G5 **Sindi** Ger. Zintenhof. Pärnumaa, SW Estonia
136 C13 **Sındırgı** Balıkesir, W Turkey
77 N14 **Sindou** SW Burkina
Sindri see Sindari
149 T9 **Sind Sāgar Doāb** desert E Pakistan
128 M11 **Sinegorskiy** Rostovskaya Oblast', SW Russian Federation
123 S9 **Sinegor'ye** Magadanskaya Oblast', E Russian Federation
114 O12 **Sinekli** İstanbul, NW Turkey
104 F12 **Sines** Setúbal, S Portugal
104 F12 **Sines, Cabo de** headland S Portugal
92 L12 **Sinettä** Lappi, NW Finland
186 H6 **Sinewit, Mount** ▲ New Britain, C PNG
80 G11 **Singa** var. Sinja, Sinjah. Sinnar, E Sudan
78 J12 **Singako** Moyen-Chari, S Chad
Singan see Xi'an
168 K10 **Singapore** ● (Singapore) S Singapore
168 L10 **Singapore** off. Republic of Singapore. ◆ republic SE Asia
168 L10 **Singapore Strait** var. Strait of Singapore, Mal. Selat Singapura. strait Indonesia/Singapore
Singapore, Strait of/Singapura, Selat see Singapore Strait
169 U17 **Singaraja** Bali, C Indonesia
Singatoka see Sigatoka
167 O10 **Sing Buri** var. Singhaburi. Sing Buri, C Thailand
101 H24 **Singen** Baden-Württemberg, S Germany
Singeorgiu de Pădure see Sângeorgiu de Pădure
Singeorz-Băi/Singeroz Băi see Sângeorz-Băi
116 M9 **Sîngerei** var. Sângerei; prev. Lazovsk. N Moldova
Singhaburi see Sing Buri
81 H21 **Singida** Singida, C Tanzania
81 G22 **Singida** ◈ region C Tanzania
Singidunum see Beograd
166 M2 **Singkaling Hkamti** Sagaing, N Myanmar
171 N14 **Singkang** Sulawesi, C Indonesia
168 J11 **Singkarak, Danau** ◎ Sumatera, W Indonesia
169 N10 **Singkawang** Borneo, C Indonesia
168 M11 **Singkep, Pulau** island Kepulauan Lingga, W Indonesia
168 H9 **Singkilbaru** Sumatera, W Indonesia
183 T7 **Singleton** New South Wales, SE Australia
Singora see Songkhla
Singû see Shingū
Sining see Xining
107 D17 **Siniscola** Sardegna, Italy, C Mediterranean Sea
113 F14 **Sinj** Split-Dalmacija, SE Croatia
Sinja/Sinjah see Singa
Sinjajevina see Sinjavina
139 P3 **Sinjār** NW Iraq
139 P2 **Sinjār, Jabal** ▲ N Iraq
113 K15 **Sinjavina** var. Sinjajevina. ▲ SW Yugoslavia
80 I7 **Sinkat** Red Sea, NE Sudan
Sinkiang/Sinkiang Uighur Autonomous Region see Xinjiang Uygur Zizhiqu
Sînmartin see Târnăveni
163 V13 **Sinmi-do** island NW North Korea
Sinminato see Shinminato
101 I18 **Sinn** ~ C Germany
Sinnamarie see Sinnamary
55 Y9 **Sinnamary** var. Sinnamarie. N French Guiana
Sinn'anyô see Shinnanyō
80 G11 **Sinnar** ◈ state E Sudan
Sinneh see Sanandaj
18 E13 **Sinnemahoning Creek** ~ Pennsylvania, NE USA
Sînnicolau Mare see Sânnicolau Mare
Sino/Sinoe see Greenville
Sinoe, Lacul see Sinoie, Lacul
Sinoia see Chinhoyi
117 N14 **Sinoie, Lacul** prev. Lacul Sinoe. lagoon SE Romania
59 H16 **Sinop** Mato Grosso, W Brazil
136 K10 **Sinop** anc. Sinope. Sinop, N Turkey
136 J10 **Sinop** ◈ province N Turkey
136 K10 **Sinop Burnu** headland N Turkey
Sinope see Sinop
163 Y12 **Sinp'o** E North Korea
101 H20 **Sinsheim** Baden-Württemberg, SW Germany
Sinsiro see Shinshiro
Sintana see Sântana
169 R11 **Sintang** Borneo, C Indonesia
99 F14 **Sint Annaland** Zeeland, SW Netherlands
98 L5 **Sint Annaparochie** Friesland, N Netherlands
45 V9 **Sint Eustatius** Eng. Saint Eustatius. island N Netherlands Antilles
99 G19 **Sint-Genesius-Rode** Fr. Rhode-Saint-Genèse. Vlaams Brabant, C Belgium
99 F16 **Sint-Gillis-Waas** Oost-Vlaanderen, N Belgium
99 H17 **Sint-Katelijne-Waver** Antwerpen, C Belgium
99 E18 **Sint-Lievens-Houtem** Oost-Vlaanderen, NW Belgium
45 V9 **Sint Maarten** Eng. Saint Martin. island N Netherlands Antilles
99 F14 **Sint Maartensdijk** Zeeland, SW Netherlands
99 L19 **Sint-Martens-Voeren** Fr. Fouron-Saint-Martin. Limburg, NE Belgium
99 J14 **Sint-Michielsgestel** Noord-Brabant, S Netherlands
Sînt-Miclăuş see Gheorgheni
45 O16 **Sint Nicholaas** S Aruba
99 F16 **Sint-Niklaas** Fr. Saint-Nicolas. Oost-Vlaanderen, N Belgium
99 K14 **Sint-Oedenrode** Noord-Brabant, S Netherlands
25 T14 **Sinton** Texas, SW USA
99 G14 **Sint Philipsland** Zeeland, SW Netherlands
99 G19 **Sint-Pieters-Leeuw** Vlaams Brabant, C Belgium
104 E11 **Sintra** prev. Cintra. Lisboa, W Portugal
99 J18 **Sint-Truiden** Fr. Saint-Trond. Limburg, NE Belgium
99 H14 **Sint Willebrord** Noord-Brabant, S Netherlands
163 V13 **Sinŭiju** W North Korea
80 P13 **Sinujiif** Nugaal, NE Somalia
Sinus Aelaniticus see Aqaba, Gulf of
Sinus Gallicus see Lion, Golfe du
Sinyang see Xinyang
Sinyavka see Sinyawka
119 I18 **Sinyawka** Rus. Sinyavka. Minskaya Voblasts', SW Belarus
Sinying see Hsinying
Sinyukha see Synyukha
Sinzi-ko see Shinji-ko
Sinzyô see Shinjō
111 I24 **Sió** ~ W Hungary
171 O7 **Siocon** Mindanao, S Philippines
111 I24 **Siófok** Somogy, C Hungary
Siogama see Shiogama
83 G15 **Sioma** Western, SW Zambia
108 D11 **Sion** Ger. Sitten; anc. Sedunum. Valais, SW Switzerland
103 O11 **Sioule** ~ C France
29 S12 **Sioux Center** Iowa, C USA
29 S13 **Sioux City** Iowa, C USA
29 R11 **Sioux Falls** South Dakota, N USA
12 B11 **Sioux Lookout** Ontario, S Canada
29 T12 **Sioux Rapids** Iowa, C USA
Sioux State see North Dakota
Sioziri see Shiojiri
171 P6 **Sipalay** Negros, C Philippines
55 V11 **Sipaliwini** ◈ district S Surinam
45 U15 **Siparia** Trinidad, Trinidad and Tobago
Siphnos see Sífnos
163 V11 **Siping** var. Ssu-p'ing, Szeping; prev. Ssu-p'ing-chieh. Jilin, NE China
11 X12 **Sipiwesk** Manitoba, C Canada
11 W13 **Sipiwesk Lake** ◎ Manitoba, C Canada
195 O11 **Siple Coast** physical region Antarctica
194 K12 **Siple Island** island Antarctica
194 K13 **Siple, Mount** ▲ Siple Island, Antarctica
Sipoo see Sibbo
112 G12 **Šipovo** Republika Srpska, W Bosnia and Herzegovina
23 O4 **Sipsey River** ~ Alabama, S USA
168 I13 **Sipura, Pulau** island W Indonesia
(0) G16 **Siqueiros Fracture Zone** tectonic feature E Pacific Ocean
42 L10 **Siquia, Río** ~ SE Nicaragua
43 N13 **Siquirres** Limón, E Costa Rica
54 J5 **Siquisique** Lara, N Venezuela
155 G19 **Sira** Karnātaka, W India
95 D16 **Sira** ~ S Norway
167 P12 **Siracha** var. Ban Si Racha, Si Racha. Chon Buri, S Thailand
107 L25 **Siracusa** Eng. Syracuse. Sicilia, Italy, C Mediterranean Sea
Sirajganj see Shirajganj Ghat
Sirakawa see Shirakawa
11 N14 **Sir Alexander, Mount** ▲ British Columbia, W Canada
137 O12 **Şiran** Gümüşhane, NE Turkey
77 Q12 **Sirba** ~ E Burkina
143 O17 **Şīr Banī Yās** island W UAE
95 D17 **Sirdalsvatnet** ◎ S Norway
Sir Darya/Sirdaryo see Syr Darya
147 O11 **Sirdaryo Wiloyati** Rus. Syrdar'inskaya Oblast'. ◈ province E Uzbekistan
Sir Donald Sangster International Airport see Sangster
181 S3 **Sir Edward Pellew Group** island group Northern Territory, NE Australia
116 K8 **Siret** Ger. Sereth, Hung. Szeret. Suceava, N Romania
116 K8 **Siret** var. Siretul, Ger. Sereth, Rus. Seret, Ukr. Siret. ~ Romania/Ukraine
Siretul see Siret
140 K3 **Sirhān, Wādī as** dry watercourse Jordan/Saudi Arabia
152 I8 **Sirhind** Punjab, N India
116 F11 **Şiria** Ger. Schiria. Arad, W Romania
Siria see Syria
143 S14 **Sīrīk** Hormozgān, SE Iran
167 P8 **Sirikit Reservoir** ▣ N Thailand
58 K12 **Sirituba, Ilha** island NE Brazil
143 R11 **Sīrjān** prev. Sa'īdābād. Kermān, S Iran
182 H9 **Sir Joseph Banks Group** island group South Australia
92 K11 **Sirkka** Lappi, N Finland
Sirna see Sýrna
137 R16 **Şırnak** Şırnak, SE Turkey
137 S16 **Şırnak** ◈ province SE Turkey
Siroisi see Shiroishi
155 J14 **Sironcha** Mahārāshtra, C India
Sirone see Shirone
Síros see Sýros
Sirotino see Sirotsina
118 M12 **Sirotsina** Rus. Sirotino. Vitsyebskaya Voblasts', N Belarus
152 H9 **Sirsa** Haryāna, NW India
173 Y17 **Sir Seewoosagur Ramgoolam** × (Port Louis) SE Mauritius
155 E18 **Sirsi** Karnātaka, W India
Sirte see Surt
182 A2 **Sir Thomas, Mount** ▲ South Australia
Sirti, Gulf of see Surt, Khalīj
142 J5 **Sīrvān, Rūdkhāneh-ye** var. Nahr Diyālá, Sirwan. ~ Iran/Iraq see also Diyālá, Nahr
118 H13 **Širvintos** Širvintos, SE Lithuania
Sirwan see Diyālá, Nahr/Sīrvān, Rūdkhāneh-ye
11 N15 **Sir Wilfrid Laurier, Mount** ▲ British Columbia, SW Canada
14 M10 **Sir-Wilfrid, Mont** ▲ Quebec, SE Canada
Sisačko-Moslavačka Županija see Sisak-Moslavina
112 E9 **Sisak** var. Siscia, Ger. Sissek, Hung. Sziszek; anc. Segestica. Sisak-Moslavina, C Croatia
167 R10 **Si Sa Ket** var. Sisaket, Sri Saket. Si Sa Ket, E Thailand
112 E9 **Sisak-Moslavina** off. Sisačko-Moslavačka Županija. ◈ province C Croatia
167 O8 **Si Satchanala** Sukhothai, NW Thailand
Siscia see Sisak
83 G22 **Sishen** Northern Cape, NW South Africa
137 V13 **Sisian** SE Armenia
197 N13 **Sisimiut** var. Holsteinborg, Holsteinsborg, Holstenborg, Holstensborg. Kitaa, S Greenland
30 M1 **Siskiwit Bay** lake bay Michigan, N USA
34 L1 **Siskiyou Mountains** ▲ California/Oregon, W USA
167 Q11 **Sisŏphŏn** Bătdâmbâng, NW Cambodia
108 E7 **Sissach** Basel-Land, NW Switzerland
186 B5 **Sissano** Sandaun, NW PNG
Sissek see Sisak
29 R7 **Sisseton** South Dakota, N USA
143 W9 **Sīstān, Daryācheh-ye** var. Daryācheh-ye Hāmūn, Hāmūn-e Şāberī. ◎ Afghanistan/Iran see also Şāberī, Hāmūn-e
143 V12 **Sīstān va Balūchestān** off. Ostān-e Sīstān va Balūchestān, var. Balūchestān va Sīstān. ◈ province SE Iran
103 T14 **Sisteron** Alpes-de-Haute-Provence, SE France
32 H13 **Sisters** Oregon, NW USA
65 G15 **Sisters Peak** ▲ N Ascension Island
21 R3 **Sistersville** West Virginia, NE USA
Sistova see Svishtov
Sitakund see Sitakunda
153 V16 **Sitakunda** var. Sitakund. Chittagong, SE Bangladesh
153 P12 **Sītāmarhi** Bihār, N India
152 L11 **Sītāpur** Uttar Pradesh, N India
Sitaş Cristuru see Cristuru Secuiesc
115 L25 **Siteía** var. Sitía. Kríti, Greece, E Mediterranean Sea
105 V6 **Sitges** Cataluña, NE Spain
115 H15 **Sithoniá** peninsula NE Greece
Sitía see Siteía
54 F4 **Sitionuevo** Magdalena, N Colombia
39 X13 **Sitka** Baranof Island, Alaska, USA
39 Q15 **Sitkinak Island** island Trinity Islands, Alaska, USA
166 M7 **Sittang** var. Sittoung. ~ S Myanmar
99 L17 **Sittard** Limburg, SE Netherlands
Sitten see Sion
108 H7 **Sitter** ~ NW Switzerland
109 U10 **Sittersdorf** Kärnten, S Austria
Sittoung see Sittang
166 K6 **Sittwe** var. Akyab. Arakan State, W Myanmar
42 L8 **Siuna** Región Autónoma Atlántico Norte, NE Nicaragua
153 R15 **Siuri** West Bengal, NE India
Siut see Asyūt
123 Q13 **Sivaki** Amurskaya Oblast', SE Russian Federation
136 M13 **Sivas** anc. Sebastia, Sebaste. Sivas, C Turkey
136 M13 **Sivas** ◈ province C Turkey
137 O15 **Siverek** Şanlıurfa, S Turkey
117 X6 **Sivers'k** Donets'ka Oblast', E Ukraine
126 G13 **Siverskiy** Leningradskaya Oblast', NW Russian Federation
117 X6 **Sivers'kyy Donets'** Rus. Severskiy Donets. ~ Russian Federation/Ukraine see also Severskiy Donets
127 W5 **Sivomaskinskiy** Respublika Komi, NW Russian Federation
136 G13 **Sivrihisar** Eskişehir, W Turkey
99 F22 **Sivry** Hainaut, S Belgium
123 V9 **Sivuchiy, Mys** headland E Russian Federation
75 U9 **Sīwa** var. Sīwah. NW Egypt
Sīwah see Sīwa
152 J9 **Siwalik Range** var. Shiwālik Range. ▲ India/Nepal
153 O13 **Siwān** Bihār, N India
43 O14 **Sixaola, Río** ~ Costa Rica/Panama
Six Counties, The see Northern Ireland
103 T16 **Six-Fours-les-Plages** Var, SE France
161 Q7 **Sixian** var. Si Xian. Anhui, E China
22 J9 **Six Mile Lake** ◎ Louisiana, S USA
139 V3 **Sīyāh Gūz** E Iraq
155 L25 **Siyambalanduwa** Uva Province, SE Sri Lanka
137 Y10 **Siyäzän** Rus. Siazan'. NE Azerbaijan
Sizebolu see Sozopol
Sizuoka see Shizuoka
Sjar see Sääre
113 L15 **Sjenica** Turk. Seniça. Serbia, SW Yugoslavia
94 G11 **Sjoa** ~ S Norway
95 K23 **Sjöbo** Skåne, S Sweden
95 I24 **Sjælland** Eng. Zealand, Ger. Seeland. island E Denmark
94 E9 **Sjøholt** Møre og Romsdal, S Norway
92 O1 **Sjuøyane** island group N Svalbard
Skadar see Shkodër
Skadarsko Jezero see Scutari, Lake
117 R11 **Skadovs'k** Khersons'ka Oblast', S Ukraine
92 I2 **Skagaströnd** prev. Höfdhakaupstadhur. Nordhurland Vestra, N Iceland
95 H19 **Skagen** Nordjylland, N Denmark
Skagerak see Skagerrak
95 L16 **Skagern** ◎ C Sweden
197 T17 **Skagerrak** var. Skagerak. channel N Europe
94 G12 **Skaget** ▲ S Norway
32 H7 **Skagit River** ~ Washington, NW USA
39 W12 **Skagway** Alaska, USA
92 K8 **Skaidi** Finnmark, N Norway
115 F21 **Skála** Pelopónnisos, S Greece
116 K6 **Skalat** Pol. Skałat. Ternopil's'ka Oblast', W Ukraine
95 J22 **Skälderviken** inlet Denmark/Sweden
92 I12 **Skalka** ◎ N Sweden
114 I12 **Skalotí** Anatolikí Makedonía kai Thráki, NE Greece
95 G22 **Skanderborg** Århus, C Denmark
95 K22 **Skåne** prev. Eng. Scania. ◈ county S Sweden
75 N6 **Skanès** × (Sousse) E Tunisia
95 C15 **Skånevik** Hordaland, S Norway
95 M18 **Skänninge** Östergötland, S Sweden
95 J23 **Skanör** Skåne, S Sweden
115 H17 **Skantzoúra** island Vóreioi Sporádes, Greece, Aegean Sea
95 K18 **Skara** Västra Götaland, S Sweden
95 M17 **Skärblacka** Östergötland, S Sweden
95 I18 **Skärhamn** Västra Götaland, S Sweden
95 I14 **Skarnes** Hedmark, S Norway
119 M21 **Skarodnaye** Rus. Skorodnoye. Homyel'skaya Voblasts', SE Belarus
110 I8 **Skarszewy** Ger. Schöneck. Pomorskie, NW Poland
111 M14 **Skarżysko-Kamienna** Świętokrzyskie, C Poland
95 K16 **Skattkärr** Värmland, C Sweden
118 D12 **Skaudvilė** Tauragė, SW Lithuania
92 J12 **Skaulo** Norrbotten, N Sweden
111 K17 **Skawina** Małopolskie, S Poland
10 K12 **Skeena** ~ British Columbia, SW Canada
10 J11 **Skeena Mountains** ▲ British Columbia, W Canada
97 O18 **Skegness** E England, UK
92 J4 **Skeidharársandur** coast S Iceland
93 J15 **Skellefteå** Västerbotten, N Sweden
93 I14 **Skellefteälven** ~ N Sweden
93 J15 **Skelleftehamn** Västerbotten, N Sweden
25 O2 **Skellytown** Texas, SW USA
95 J19 **Skene** Västra Götaland, S Sweden
97 G17 **Skerries** Ir. Na Sceirí. E Ireland
95 H15 **Ski** Akershus, S Norway
115 G17 **Skíathos** Skíathos, Vóreioi Sporádes, Greece, Aegean Sea
115 G17 **Skíathos** island Vóreioi Sporádes, Greece, Aegean Sea
27 P9 **Skiatook** Oklahoma, C USA
27 P9 **Skiatook Lake** ▣ Oklahoma, C USA
97 B22 **Skibbereen** Ir. An Sciobairín. SW Ireland
92 I9 **Skibotn** Troms, N Norway
119 F16 **Skidal'** Rus. Skidel'. Hrodzyenskaya Voblasts', W Belarus
97 K15 **Skiddaw** ▲ NW England, UK
Skidel' see Skidal'
25 T14 **Skidmore** Texas, SW USA
95 G16 **Skien** Telemark, S Norway
Skiermûntseach see Schiermonnikoog
110 L12 **Skierniewice** Łodzkie, C Poland
74 L5 **Skikda** prev. Philippeville. NE Algeria
30 M16 **Skillet Fork** ~ Illinois, N USA
95 L19 **Skillingaryd** Jönköping, S Sweden
115 B19 **Skinári, Akrotírio** headland Zákynthos, Iónioi Nísoi, Greece, C Mediterranean Sea
95 M15 **Skinnskatteberg** Västmanland, C Sweden
182 M12 **Skipton** Victoria, SE Australia
97 L16 **Skipton** N England, UK
Skiropoula see Skyropoúla
Skíros see Skýros
95 F21 **Skive** Viborg, NW Denmark
94 F11 **Skjåk** Oppland, S Norway
92 K2 **Skjálfandafljót** ~ C Iceland
95 F22 **Skjern** Ringkøbing, W Denmark
95 F22 **Skjern Å** var. Skjern Aa. ~ W Denmark
Skjern Aa see Skjern Å
92 G12 **Skjerstad** Nordland, C Norway
92 J8 **Skjervøy** Troms, N Norway
92 I10 **Skjold** Troms, N Norway
111 I17 **Skoczów** Śląskie, S Poland
95 I24 **Skælskør** Vestsjælland, E Denmark
109 T11 **Škofja Loka** Ger. Bischoflack. NW Slovenia
94 N12 **Skog** Gävleborg, C Sweden
95 K16 **Skoghall** Värmland, C Sweden
31 N10 **Skokie** Illinois, N USA
116 H6 **Skole** L'vivs'ka Oblast', W Ukraine
115 D19 **Skóllis** ▲ S Greece
167 S13 **Skon** Kâmpóng Cham, C Cambodia
115 H17 **Skópelos** Skópelos, Vóreioi Sporádes, Greece, Aegean Sea
115 H17 **Skópelos** island Vóreioi Sporádes, Greece, Aegean Sea
128 L5 **Skopin** Ryazanskaya Oblast', W Russian Federation
113 N18 **Skopje** var. Üsküb, Turk. Üsküp; prev. Skoplje, anc. Scupi. ● (FYR Macedonia) N FYR Macedonia
113 O18 **Skopje** × N FYR Macedonia
Skoplje see Skopje
110 I8 **Skórcz** Ger. Skurz. Pomorskie, N Poland
Skorodnoye see Skarodnaye
93 H16 **Skorped** Västernorrland, C Sweden
95 G21 **Skørping** Nordjylland, N Denmark
95 K18 **Skövde** Västra Götaland, S Sweden
123 Q13 **Skovorodino** Amurskaya Oblast', SE Russian Federation
19 Q6 **Skowhegan** Maine, NE USA
11 W15 **Skownan** Manitoba, S Canada
94 H13 **Skreia** Oppland, S Norway
Skripón see Orchómenos
118 H9 **Skriveri** Aizkraukle, S Latvia
118 J11 **Skrudaliena** Daugvapils, SE Latvia
118 D9 **Skrunda** Kuldīga, W Latvia
95 C16 **Skudeneshavn** Rogaland, S Norway
83 L20 **Skukuza** Mpumalanga, NE South Africa
97 B22 **Skull** Ir. An Scoil. SW Ireland
22 L3 **Skuna River** ~ Mississippi, S USA
29 X15 **Skunk River** ~ Iowa, C USA
118 C10 **Skuodas** Ger. Schoden, Pol. Szkudy. Skuodas, NW Lithuania
95 K23 **Skurup** Skåne, S Sweden
Skurz see Skórcz
114 H8 **Skŭt** ~ NW Bulgaria
94 O13 **Skutskär** Uppsala, C Sweden
95 B19 **Skúvoy** Dan. Skuø Island Faeroe Islands
Skvira see Skvyra
117 O5 **Skvyra** Rus. Skvira. Kyyivs'ka Oblast', N Ukraine
39 Q11 **Skwentna** Alaska, USA
110 E11 **Skwierzyna** Ger. Schwerin. Lubuskie, W Poland

◆ Country ● Country Capital ◇ Dependent Territory ○ Dependent Territory Capital ◈ Administrative Region × International Airport ▲ Mountain ▲ Mountain Range Volcano ~ River ◎ Lake ▣ Reservoir

36 K13 **Sky Harbour** ✕ (Phoenix) Arizona, SW USA
96 G9 **Skye, Isle of** *island* NW Scotland, UK
32 I8 **Skykomish** Washington, NW USA
Skylge *see* Terschelling
63 F19 **Skyring, Peninsula** *peninsula* S Chile
63 H24 **Skyring, Seno** *inlet* S Chile
115 H17 **Skyropoúla** *var.* Skiropoula. *island* Vóreioi Sporádes, Greece, Aegean Sea
115 I17 **Skýros** *var.* Skíros. Skýros, Vóreioi Sporádes, Greece, Aegean Sea
115 I17 **Skýros** *var.* Skíros; *anc.* Scyros. *island* Vóreioi Sporádes, Greece, Aegean Sea
118 J12 **Slabodka** *Rus.* Slobodka. Vitsyebskaya Voblasts', NW Belarus
95 I23 **Slagelse** Vestsjælland, E Denmark
93 I14 **Slagnäs** Norrbotten, N Sweden
39 T10 **Slana** Alaska, USA
97 F20 **Slaney** *Ir.* An tSláine. ≈ SE Ireland
116 J13 **Slănic** Prahova, SE Romania
116 K11 **Slănic Moldova** Bacău, E Romania
113 H16 **Slano** Dubrovnik-Neretva, SE Croatia
126 F13 **Slantsy** Leningradskaya Oblast', NW Russian Federation
111 C16 **Slaný** *Ger.* Schlan. Střední Čechy, NW Czech Republic
111 I16 **Śląskie** ◈ *province* S Poland
12 C10 **Slate Falls** Ontario, S Canada
27 T4 **Slater** Missouri, C USA
112 H9 **Slatina** *Hung.* Szlatina *prev.* Podravska Slatina. Virovitica-Podravina, NE Croatia
116 I14 **Slatina** Olt, S Romania
25 N5 **Slaton** Texas, SW USA
95 H14 **Slattum** Akershus, S Norway
11 R10 **Slave** ≈ Alberta/Northwest Territories, C Canada
68 E11 **Slave Coast** *coastal region* W Africa
11 P13 **Slave Lake** Alberta, SW Canada
122 I13 **Slavgorod** Altayskiy Kray, S Russian Federation
Slavgorod *see* Slawharad
Slavonia *see* Slavonija
112 G9 **Slavonija** *Eng.* Slavonia, *Ger.* Slawonien, *Hung.* Szlavonia, Szlavonország. *cultural region* NE Croatia
Slavonska Požega *see* Požega.
112 H10 **Slavonski Brod** *Ger.* Brod, *Hung.* Bród; *prev.* Brod, Brod na Savi. Brod-Posavina, NE Croatia
116 L4 **Slavuta** Khmel'nyts'ka Oblast', NW Ukraine
117 P2 **Slavutych** Chernihivs'ka Oblast', N Ukraine
123 R15 **Slavyanka** Primorskiy Kray, SE Russian Federation
114 J8 **Slavyanovo** Pleven, N Bulgaria
Slavyansk *see* Slov"yans'k
128 K14 **Slavyansk-na-Kubani** Krasnodarskiy Kray, SW Russian Federation
119 N20 **Slavyechna** *Rus.* Slovechna. ≈ Belarus/Ukraine
119 O16 **Slawharad** *Rus.* Slavgorod. Mahilyowskaya Voblasts', E Belarus
110 G7 **Sławno** Zachodniopomorskie, NW Poland
Slawonien *see* Slavonija
29 S10 **Slayton** Minnesota, N USA
97 N18 **Sleaford** E England, UK
97 A20 **Slea Head** *Ir.* Ceann Sléibhe. *headland* SW Ireland
96 G9 **Sleat, Sound of** *strait* NW Scotland, UK
Sledyuki *see* Slyedzyuki
12 I5 **Sleeper Islands** *island group* Nunavut, C Canada
31 O6 **Sleeping Bear Point** *headland* Michigan, N USA
29 T10 **Sleepy Eye** Minnesota, N USA
39 O11 **Sleetmute** Alaska, USA
Sléibhe, Ceann *see* Slea Head
Slēmānī *see* As Sulaymānīyah
195 O5 **Slessor Glacier** *glacier* Antarctica
22 L9 **Slidell** Louisiana, S USA
18 K12 **Slide Mountain** ▲ New York, NE USA
98 I13 **Sliedrecht** Zuid-Holland, C Netherlands
121 P16 **Sliema** N Malta
97 G16 **Slieve Donard** ▲ SE Northern Ireland, UK
Sligeach *see* Sligo
97 D16 **Sligo** *Ir.* Sligeach. NW Ireland
97 C16 **Sligo** *Ir.* Sligeach. *cultural region* NW Ireland
97 C15 **Sligo Bay** *Ir.* Cuan Shligigh. *inlet* NW Ireland
18 B13 **Slippery Rock** Pennsylvania, NE USA
95 P19 **Slite** Gotland, SE Sweden
114 L9 **Sliven** *var.* Slivno. Sliven, C Bulgaria
114 L10 **Sliven** ◈ *province* C Bulgaria
114 G9 **Slivnitsa** Sofiya, W Bulgaria
Slivno *see* Sliven
114 L7 **Slivo Pole** Ruse, N Bulgaria
29 S13 **Sloan** Iowa, C USA
35 X12 **Sloan** Nevada, W USA
Slobodka *see* Slabodka
127 R14 **Slobodskoy** Kirovskaya Oblast', NW Russian Federation
Slobodzeya *see* Slobozia
117 O10 **Slobozia** *Rus.* Slobodzeya. E Moldova
116 L14 **Slobozia** Ialomiţa, SE Romania
98 O5 **Slochteren** Groningen, NE Netherlands
119 H17 **Slonim** *Pol.* Słonim, *Rus.* Slonim. Hrodzyenskaya Voblasts', W Belarus
98 K7 **Sloter Meer** ◎ N Netherlands
Slot, The *see* New Georgia Sound
97 N22 **Slough** S England, UK
111 J20 **Slovakia** *off.* Slovenská Republika, *Ger.* Slowakei, *Hung.* Szlovákia, *Slvk.* Slovensko. ◆ *republic* C Europe
Slovak Ore Mountains *see* Slovenské rudohorie
Slovechna *see* Slavyechna
109 S12 **Slovenia** *off.* Republic of Slovenia, *Ger.* Slowenien, *Slvn.* Slovenija. ◆ *republic* SE Europe
Slovenija *see* Slovenia
109 V10 **Slovenj Gradec** *Ger.* Windischgraz. N Slovenia
109 W10 **Slovenska Bistrica** *Ger.* Windischfeistritz. NE Slovenia
Slovenská Republika *see* Slovakia
109 W10 **Slovenske Konjice** E Slovenia
111 K20 **Slovenské rudohorie** *Eng.* Slovak Ore Mountains, *Ger.* Slowakisches Erzgebirge, Ungarisches Erzgebirge. ⛰ C Slovakia
Slovensko *see* Slovakia
117 Y7 **Slov"yanoserbs'k** Luhans'ka Oblast', E Ukraine
117 W6 **Slov"yans'k** *Rus.* Slavyansk. Donets'ka Oblast', E Ukraine
Slowakei *see* Slovakia
Slowakisches Erzgebirge *see* Slovenské rudohorie
Slowenien *see* Slovenia
110 D11 **Słubice** *Ger.* Frankfurt. Lubuskie, W Poland
119 K19 **Sluch** *Rus.* Sluch'. ≈ C Belarus
116 L4 **Sluch** ≈ NW Ukraine
99 D16 **Sluis** Zeeland, SW Netherlands
112 D10 **Slunj** *Hung.* Szluin. Karlovac, C Croatia
110 I11 **Słupca** Wielkolpolskie, C Poland
110 G6 **Słupia** *Ger.* Stolpe. ≈ NW Poland
110 G6 **Słupsk** *Ger.* Stolp. Pomorskie, N Poland
119 K18 **Slutsk** *Rus.* Slutsk. Minskaya Voblasts', S Belarus
119 O16 **Slyedzyuki** *Rus.* Sledyuki. Mahilyowskaya Voblasts', E Belarus
97 A17 **Slyne Head** *Ir.* Ceann Léime. *headland* W Ireland
27 U14 **Smackover** Arkansas, C USA
95 L20 **Småland** *cultural region* S Sweden
95 K20 **Smålandsstenar** Jönköping, S Sweden
Small Malaita *see* Maramasike
13 O8 **Smallwood Reservoir** ◎ Newfoundland, S Canada
119 N14 **Smalyany** *Rus.* Smolyany. Vitsyebskaya Voblasts', NE Belarus
119 L15 **Smalyavichy** *Rus.* Smolevichi. Minskaya Voblasts', C Belarus
74 C9 **Smara** *var.* Es Semara. N Western Sahara
119 I14 **Smarhon'** *Pol.* Smorgonie, *Rus.* Smorgon'. Hrodzyenskaya Voblasts', W Belarus
112 M11 **Smederevo** *Ger.* Semendria. Serbia, N Yugoslavia
112 M12 **Smederevska Palanka** Serbia, C Yugoslavia
95 M14 **Smedjebacken** Dalarna, C Sweden
116 L13 **Smeeni** Buzău, SE Romania
Smela *see* Smila
107 D16 **Smeralda, Costa** *cultural region* Sardegna, Italy, C Mediterranean Sea
111 J22 **Šmigiel** *Ger.* Schmiegel. Wielkolpolskie, C Poland
117 Q6 **Smila** *Rus.* Smela. Cherkas'ka Oblast', C Ukraine
98 N7 **Smilde** Drenthe, NE Netherlands
11 S16 **Smiley** Saskatchewan, S Canada
25 T12 **Smiley** Texas, SW USA
Smilten *see* Smiltene
118 I8 **Smiltene** *Ger.* Smilten. Valka, N Latvia
123 T13 **Smirnykh** Ostrov Sakhalin, Sakhalinskaya Oblast', SE Russian Federation
11 Q13 **Smith** Alberta, W Canada
39 P4 **Smith Bay** *bay* Alaska, USA
12 I3 **Smith, Cape** *headland* Quebec, NE Canada
26 L3 **Smith Center** Kansas, C USA
10 K13 **Smithers** British Columbia, SW Canada
21 V10 **Smithfield** North Carolina, SE USA
36 L1 **Smithfield** Utah, W USA
21 X7 **Smithfield** Virginia, NE USA
12 I3 **Smith Island** *island* Nunavut, C Canada
Smith Island *see* Sumisu-jima
20 H7 **Smithland** Kentucky, S USA
21 T7 **Smith Mountain Lake** *var.* Leesville Lake. ⊞ Virginia, NE USA
34 L1 **Smith River** California, W USA
33 R9 **Smith River** ≈ Montana, NW USA
14 L13 **Smiths Falls** Ontario, SE Canada
33 N13 **Smiths Ferry** Idaho, NW USA
20 K7 **Smiths Grove** Kentucky, S USA
183 N15 **Smithton** Tasmania, SE Australia
18 L14 **Smithtown** Long Island, New York, NE USA
20 K9 **Smithville** Tennessee, S USA
25 T11 **Smithville** Texas, SW USA
Šmohor *see* Hermagor
35 Q4 **Smoke Creek Desert** *desert* Nevada, W USA
11 O14 **Smoky** ≈ Alberta, W Canada
182 E7 **Smoky Bay** South Australia
183 V6 **Smoky Cape** *headland* New South Wales, SE Australia
26 L4 **Smoky Hill River** ≈ Kansas, C USA
26 L4 **Smoky Hills** *hill range* Kansas, C USA
11 Q14 **Smoky Lake** Alberta, SW Canada
94 E8 **Smøla** *island* W Norway
128 H4 **Smolensk** Smolenskaya Oblast', W Russian Federation
128 H4 **Smolenskaya Oblast'** ◈ *province* W Russian Federation
Smolensk-Moscow Upland *see* Smolensko-Moskovskaya Vozvyshennost'
128 J3 **Smolensko-Moskovskaya Vozvyshennost'** *var.* Smolensk-Moscow Upland. ⛰ W Russian Federation
Smolevichi *see* Smalyavichy
115 C15 **Smolikás** ▲ W Greece
114 I12 **Smolyan** *prev.* Pashmakli. Smolyan, S Bulgaria
114 I12 **Smolyan** ◈ *province* S Bulgaria
Smolyany *see* Smalyany
33 S15 **Smoot** Wyoming, C USA
12 G12 **Smooth Rock Falls** Ontario, S Canada
Smorgon'/Smorgonie *see* Smarhon'
95 K23 **Smygehamn** Skåne, S Sweden
194 I7 **Smyley Island** *island* Antarctica
21 Y3 **Smyrna** Delaware, NE USA
23 S3 **Smyrna** Georgia, SE USA
20 J9 **Smyrna** Tennessee, S USA
Smyrna *see* İzmir
97 I16 **Snaefell** ▲ C Isle of Man
92 H3 **Snaefellsjökull** ▲ W Iceland
10 J4 **Snake** ≈ Yukon Territory, NW Canada
29 O8 **Snake Creek** ≈ South Dakota, N USA
183 P13 **Snake Island** *island* Victoria, SE Australia
35 Y6 **Snake Range** ⛰ Nevada, W USA
32 K10 **Snake River** ≈ NW USA
29 V6 **Snake River** ≈ Minnesota, N USA
28 L12 **Snake River** ≈ Nebraska, C USA
33 Q14 **Snake River Plain** *plain* Idaho, NW USA
93 F15 **Snåsa** Nord-Trøndelag, C Norway
21 O8 **Sneedville** Tennessee, S USA
98 K6 **Sneek** Friesland, N Netherlands
Sneeuw-gebergte *see* Maoke, Pegunungan
95 F22 **Snejbjerg** Ringkøbing, C Denmark
122 K9 **Snezhnogorsk** Taymyrskiy (Dolgano-Nenetskiy) Avtonomnyy Okrug, N Russian Federation
Snezhnoye *see* Snizhne
111 G15 **Sněžka** *Ger.* Schneekoppe. ▲ N Czech Republic
110 N8 **Śniardwy, Jezioro** *Ger.* Spirdingsee. ◎ NE Poland
Sniečkus *see* Visaginas
117 R10 **Snihurivka** Mykolayivs'ka Oblast', S Ukraine
116 I5 **Snilov** ✕ (L'viv) L'vivs'ka Oblast', W Ukraine
111 O19 **Snina** *Hung.* Szinna. Prešovský Kraj, E Slovakia
117 Y8 **Snizhne** *Rus.* Snezhnoye. Donets'ka Oblast', SE Ukraine
92 J3 **Snækollur** ▲ C Iceland
94 G10 **Snøhetta** *var.* Snohetta. ▲ S Norway
92 G12 **Snøtinden** ▲ C Norway
97 I18 **Snowdon** ▲ NW Wales, UK
97 I18 **Snowdonia** ⛰ NW Wales, UK
8 K10 **Snowdrift** ≈ Northwest Territories, NW Canada
Snowdrift *see* Łutselk'e
37 N12 **Snowflake** Arizona, SW USA
21 Y5 **Snow Hill** Maryland, NE USA
21 W10 **Snow Hill** North Carolina, SE USA
194 H3 **Snowhill Island** *island* Antarctica
11 V13 **Snow Lake** Manitoba, C Canada
37 R5 **Snowmass Mountain** ▲ Colorado, C USA
18 M10 **Snow, Mount** ▲ Vermont, NE USA
34 M5 **Snow Mountain** ▲ California, W USA
Snow Mountains *see* Maoke, Pegunungan
33 N7 **Snowshoe Peak** ▲ Montana, NW USA
182 I8 **Snowtown** South Australia
36 K1 **Snowville** Utah, W USA
35 X3 **Snow Water Lake** ◎ Nevada, W USA
183 Q11 **Snowy Mountains** ⛰ New South Wales/Victoria, SE Australia
183 Q12 **Snowy River** ≈ New South Wales/Victoria, SE Australia
44 K5 **Snug Corner** Acklins Island, SE Bahamas
167 T13 **Snuŏl** Krâchéh, E Cambodia
116 J7 **Snyatyn** *Rus.* Snyatyn. Ivano-Frankivs'ka Oblast', W Ukraine
26 L12 **Snyder** Oklahoma, C USA
25 O6 **Snyder** Texas, SW USA
172 H3 **Soalala** Mahajanga, W Madagascar
172 J4 **Soanierana-Ivongo** Toamasina, E Madagascar
171 R11 **Soasiu** *var.* Tidore. Pulau Tidore, E Indonesia
54 G8 **Soatá** Boyacá, C Colombia
172 I5 **Soavinandriana** Antananarivo, C Madagascar
77 V13 **Soba** Kaduna, C Nigeria
163 Y16 **Sobaek-sanmaek** ⛰ S South Korea
80 F13 **Sobat** ≈ E Sudan
171 Z14 **Sobger, Sungai** ≈ Irian Jaya, E Indonesia
171 V13 **Sobiei** Irian Jaya, E Indonesia
128 M3 **Sobinka** Vladimirskaya Oblast', W Russian Federation
129 S7 **Sobolevo** Orenburgskaya Oblast', W Russian Federation
Soborsin *see* Săvârşin
164 D15 **Sobo-san** ▲ Kyūshū, SW Japan
111 G14 **Sobótka** Dolnośląskie, SW Poland
59 O15 **Sobradinho** Bahia, E Brazil
Sobradinho, Barragem de *see* Sobradinho, Represa de
59 O16 **Sobradinho, Represa de** *var.* Barragem de Sobradinho. ⊞ E Brazil
58 O13 **Sobral** Ceará, E Brazil
105 T4 **Sobrarbe** *physical region* NE Spain
109 R10 **Soča** *It.* Isonzo. ≈ Italy/Slovenia
110 L11 **Sochaczew** Mazowieckie, C Poland
128 L15 **Sochi** Krasnodarskiy Kray, SW Russian Federation
114 G13 **Sochós** *var.* Sohos, Sokhós. Kentrikí Makedonía, N Greece
191 R11 **Société, Archipel de la** *var.* Archipel de Tahiti, Îles de la Société, *Eng.* Society Islands. *island group* W French Polynesia
Société, Îles de la/Society Islands *see* Société, Archipel de la
21 T11 **Society Hill** South Carolina, SE USA
175 W9 **Society Ridge** *undersea feature* C Pacific Ocean
62 I5 **Socompa, Volcán** ▲ N Chile
Soconusco, Sierra de *see* Sierra Madre
54 G8 **Socorro** Santander, C Colombia
37 R13 **Socorro** New Mexico, SW USA
Socotra *see* Suquṭrā
167 S14 **Soc Trăng** *var.* Khanh Hung. Soc Trăng, S Vietnam
105 P10 **Socuéllamos** Castilla-La Mancha, C Spain
35 W13 **Soda Lake** *salt flat* California, W USA
92 L11 **Sodankylä** Lappi, N Finland
Sodari *see* Sodiri
33 R15 **Soda Springs** Idaho, NW USA
Soddo/Soddu *see* Sodo
20 L10 **Soddy Daisy** Tennessee, S USA
95 N14 **Söderfors** Uppsala, C Sweden
94 N12 **Söderhamn** Gävleborg, C Sweden
95 N17 **Söderköping** Östergötland, S Sweden
95 N17 **Södermanland** ◈ *county* C Sweden
95 O16 **Södertälje** Stockholm, C Sweden
80 D10 **Sodiri** *var.* Sawdirī, Sodari. Northern Kordofan, C Sudan
81 I14 **Sodo** *var.* Soddo, Soddu. Southern, S Ethiopia
94 N11 **Södra Dellen** ◎ C Sweden
95 M19 **Södra Vi** Kalmar, S Sweden
18 G9 **Sodus Point** *headland* New York, NE USA
171 Q17 **Soe** *prev.* Soë. Timor, C Indonesia
169 N15 **Soekarno-Hatta** ✕ (Jakarta) Jawa, S Indonesia
Soëla-Sund *see* Soela Väin
118 E5 **Soela Väin** *prev. Eng.* Sele Sound, *Ger.* Dagden-Sund, Soëla-Sund. *strait* W Estonia
Soemba *see* Sumba, Pulau
Soembawa *see* Sumbawa
Soemenep *see* Sumenep
Soengaipenoeh *see* Sungaipenuh
Soerabaja *see* Surabaya
101 G14 **Soest** Nordrhein-Westfalen, W Germany
98 J11 **Soest** Utrecht, C Netherlands
100 F11 **Soeste** ≈ NW Germany
98 J11 **Soesterberg** Utrecht, C Netherlands
115 E16 **Sofádes** *var.* Sofádhes. Thessalía, C Greece
Sofádhes *see* Sofádes
83 N18 **Sofala** Sofala, C Mozambique
83 N17 **Sofala** ◈ *province* C Mozambique
83 N18 **Sofala, Baia de** *bay* E Mozambique
172 J3 **Sofia** *seasonal river* NW Madagascar
Sofia *see* Sofiya
115 G19 **Sofikó** Pelopónnisos, S Greece
Sofi-Kurgan *see* Sopu-Korgon
114 G10 **Sofiya** *var.* Sophia, *Eng.* Sofia; *Lat.* Serdica. ● (Bulgaria) Sofiya-Grad, W Bulgaria
114 G9 **Sofiya** ✕ Sofiya-Grad, W Bulgaria
114 H9 **Sofiya** ◈ *province* W Bulgaria
114 G9 **Sofiya-Grad** ◈ *municipality* W Bulgaria
Sofiyevka *see* Sofiyivka
117 S8 **Sofiyivka** *Rus.* Sofiyevka. Dnipropetrovs'ka Oblast', E Ukraine
123 R13 **Sofiysk** Khabarovskiy Kray, SE Russian Federation
123 S12 **Sofiysk** Khabarovskiy Kray, SE Russian Federation
126 I6 **Sofporog** Respublika Kareliya, NW Russian Federation
165 Y14 **Sōfu-gan** *island* Izu-shotō, SE Japan
Sog *see* Sog Xian
54 G9 **Sogamoso** Boyacá, C Colombia
136 I11 **Soğanlı Çayı** ≈ N Turkey
94 E12 **Sogn** *physical region* S Norway
94 E12 **Sogndal** *var.* Sogndalsfjøra. Sogn og Fjordane, S Norway
Sogndalsfjøra *see* Sogndal
95 E18 **Søgne** Vest-Agder, S Norway
94 D12 **Sognefjorden** *fjord* NE North Sea
94 C12 **Sogn Og Fjordane** ◈ *county* S Norway
162 I11 **Sogo Nur** ◎ N China
159 T12 **Sogruma** Qinghai, W China
163 X17 **Sŏgwip'o** S South Korea
156 K10 **Sog Xian** *var.* Sog. Xizang Zizhiqu, W China
75 X10 **Sohâg** *var.* Sawhāj, Suliag. C Egypt
Sohar *see* Ṣuḥār
64 H9 **Sohm Plain** *undersea feature* NW Atlantic Ocean
100 H7 **Soholmer Au** ≈ N Germany
Sohos *see* Sochós
Sohrau *see* Żory
99 F20 **Soignies** Hainaut, SW Belgium
159 R15 **Soila** Xizang Zizhiqu, W China
103 P4 **Soissons** *anc.* Augusta Suessionum, Noviodunum. Aisne, N France
164 H13 **Sōja** Okayama, Honshū, SW Japan
152 F13 **Sojat** Rājasthān, N India
163 W13 **Sŏjosŏn-man** *inlet* W North Korea
116 I4 **Sokal'** *Rus.* Sokal. L'vivs'ka Oblast', NW Ukraine
163 Y14 **Sokch'o** N South Korea
136 B15 **Söke** Aydın, SW Turkey
189 N12 **Sokehs Island** *island* E Micronesia
79 M24 **Sokele** Katanga, SE Dem. Rep. Congo (Zaire)
147 R11 **Sokh** *Uzb.* Sŭkh. ≈ Kyrgyzstan/Uzbekistan
Sokh *see* Sŭkh
Sokhós *see* Sochós
137 Q8 **Sokhumi** *Rus.* Sukhumi. NW Georgia
113 O14 **Sokobanja** Serbia, E Yugoslavia
77 R15 **Sokodé** C Togo
123 T10 **Sokol** Magadanskaya Oblast', E Russian Federation
126 M13 **Sokol** Vologodskaya Oblast', NW Russian Federation
110 P9 **Sokółka** Podlaskie, NE Poland
76 M11 **Sokolo** Ségou, W Mali
111 A16 **Sokolov** *Ger.* Falkenau an der Eger; *prev.* Falknov nad Ohří. Karlovarský Kraj, W Czech Republic
111 O16 **Sokołów Małopolski** Podkarpackie, SE Poland
110 O11 **Sokołów Podlaski** Mazowieckie, E Poland
76 G11 **Sokone** W Senegal
77 T12 **Sokoto** Sokoto, NW Nigeria
77 T12 **Sokoto** ◈ *state* NW Nigeria
77 S12 **Sokoto** ≈ NW Nigeria
Sokotra *see* Suquṭrā
147 U7 **Sokuluk** Chuyskaya Oblast', N Kyrgyzstan
116 L7 **Sokyryany** Chernivets'ka Oblast', W Ukraine
95 C16 **Sola** Rogaland, S Norway
187 R12 **Sola** Vanua Lava, N Vanuatu
95 C17 **Sola** ✕ (Stavanger) Rogaland, S Norway
81 H18 **Solai** Rift Valley, W Kenya
152 I8 **Solan** Himāchal Pradesh, N India
185 A25 **Solander Island** *island* SW NZ
Solano *see* Bahía Solano
155 F15 **Solāpur** *var.* Sholāpur. Mahārāshtra, W India
93 H16 **Solberg** Västernorrland, C Sweden
116 K9 **Solca** *Ger.* Solka. Suceava, N Romania
105 O16 **Sol, Costa del** *coastal region* S Spain
106 F5 **Solda** Trentino-Alto Adige, N Italy
117 N9 **Şoldăneşti** *Rus.* Sholdaneshty. N Moldova
Soldau *see* Wkra
108 L8 **Sölden** Tirol, W Austria
27 P3 **Soldier Creek** ≈ Kansas, C USA
39 R12 **Soldotna** Alaska, USA
110 I10 **Solec Kujawski** Kujawsko-pomorskie, C Poland
61 B16 **Soledad** Santa Fe, C Argentina
55 E4 **Soledad** Atlántico, N Colombia
35 O11 **Soledad** California, W USA
55 O7 **Soledad** Anzoátegui, NE Venezuela
Soledad *see* East Falkland
Soledad, Isla *see* East Falkland
61 H15 **Soledade** Rio Grande do Sul, S Brazil
103 Y15 **Solenzara** Corse, France, C Mediterranean Sea
Soleure *see* Solothurn
94 C12 **Solheim** Hordaland, S Norway
127 N14 **Soligalich** Kostromskaya Oblast', NW Russian Federation
Soligorsk *see* Salihorsk
97 L20 **Solihull** C England, UK
127 U13 **Solikamsk** Permskaya Oblast', NW Russian Federation
129 V8 **Sol'-Iletsk** Orenburgskaya Oblast', W Russian Federation
57 G17 **Solimana, Nevado** ▲ S Peru
58 E13 **Solimões, Rio** ≈ C Brazil
113 E14 **Solin** *It.* Salona; *anc.* Salonae. Split-Dalmacija, S Croatia
101 E15 **Solingen** Nordrhein-Westfalen, W Germany
Solka *see* Solca
93 H16 **Sollefteå** Västernorrland, C Sweden
95 O15 **Sollentuna** Stockholm, C Sweden
94 L13 **Sollerön** Dalarna, C Sweden
101 I14 **Solling** *hill range* C Germany
95 O16 **Solna** Stockholm, C Sweden
128 K3 **Solnechnogorsk** Moskovskaya Oblast', W Russian Federation
123 R10 **Solnechnyy** Khabarovskiy Kray, SE Russian Federation
123 S13 **Solnechnyy** Respublika Sakha (Yakutiya), NE Russian Federation
94 H11 **Sølnkletten** ▲ S Norway
107 L17 **Solofra** Campania, S Italy
168 J11 **Solok** Sumatera, W Indonesia
42 C6 **Sololá** Sololá, W Guatemala
42 A2 **Sololá** *off.* Departamento de Sololá. ◈ *department* SW Guatemala
81 J16 **Sololo** Eastern, N Kenya
42 C4 **Soloma** Huehuetenango, W Guatemala
38 M9 **Solomon** Alaska, USA
27 N4 **Solomon** Kansas, C USA
187 N9 **Solomon Islands** *prev.* British Solomon Islands Protectorate. ◆ *commonwealth republic* W Pacific Ocean
186 L7 **Solomon Islands** *island group* PNG/Solomon Islands
26 M3 **Solomon River** ≈ Kansas, C USA
186 H8 **Solomon Sea** *sea* W Pacific Ocean
31 U11 **Solon** Ohio, N USA
117 T8 **Solone** Dnipropetrovs'ka Oblast', E Ukraine
171 P16 **Solor, Kepulauan** *island group* S Indonesia
128 M4 **Solotcha** Ryazanskaya Oblast', W Russian Federation
108 D7 **Solothurn** *Fr.* Soleure. Solothurn, NW Switzerland
108 D7 **Solothurn** *Fr.* Soleure. ◈ *canton* NW Switzerland
126 J7 **Solovetskiye Ostrova** *island group* NW Russian Federation
105 V5 **Solsona** Cataluña, NE Spain
113 E14 **Šolta** *It.* Solta. *island* S Croatia
Solṭānābād *see* Kāshmar
142 L4 **Solṭānīyeh** Zanjān, NW Iran
100 I11 **Soltau** Niedersachsen, NW Germany
126 G14 **Sol'tsy** Novgorodskaya Oblast', W Russian Federation
Soltüstik Qazaqstan Oblysy *see* Severnyy Kazakhstan
Solun *see* Thessaloníki
113 O19 **Solunska Glava** ▲ C FYR Macedonia
95 L22 **Sölvesborg** Blekinge, S Sweden
97 J15 **Solway Firth** *inlet* England/Scotland, UK
82 I13 **Solwezi** North Western, NW Zambia
165 Q11 **Sōma** Fukushima, Honshū, C Japan
136 C13 **Soma** Manisa, W Turkey
81 M14 **Somali** ◈ *region* E Ethiopia
81 O15 **Somalia** *off.* Somali Democratic Republic, *Som.* Jamuuriyada Demuqraadiga Soomaaliyeed, Soomaaliya; *prev.* Italian Somaliland, Somaliland Protectorate. ◆ *republic* E Africa
173 N6 **Somali Basin** *undersea feature* W Indian Ocean
67 Y8 **Somali Plain** *undersea feature* W Indian Ocean
112 J8 **Sombor** *Hung.* Zombor. Serbia, NW Yugoslavia
99 H20 **Sombreffe** Namur, S Belgium
40 L10 **Sombrerete** Zacatecas, C Mexico
45 V8 **Sombrero** *island* N Anguilla
151 Q21 **Sombrero Channel** *channel* Nicobar Islands, India
116 H9 **Şomcuta Mare** *Hung.* Nagysomkút; *prev.* Somcuţa Mare. Maramureş, N Romania
167 R9 **Somdet** Kalasin, E Thailand
99 L15 **Someren** Noord-Brabant, SE Netherlands
93 L19 **Somero** Länsi-Suomi, W Finland
33 P7 **Somers** Montana, NW USA
64 A12 **Somerset** *var.* Somerset Village. W Bermuda
37 Q5 **Somerset** Colorado, C USA
20 M7 **Somerset** Kentucky, S USA
19 O12 **Somerset** Massachusetts, NE USA
97 K23 **Somerset** *cultural region* SW England, UK
Somerset East *see* Somerset-Oos
64 A12 **Somerset Island** *island* W Bermuda
197 N9 **Somerset Island** *island* Queen Elizabeth Islands, Nunavut, NW Canada
Somerset Nile *see* Victoria Nile
83 I25 **Somerset-Oos** *Eng.* Somerset East. Eastern Cape, S South Africa
83 E26 **Somerset-Wes** *Eng.* Somerset West. Western Cape, SW South Africa
Somerset West *see* Somerset-Wes
Somers Islands *see* Bermuda
18 J17 **Somers Point** New Jersey, NE USA
19 P9 **Somersworth** New Hampshire, NE USA
36 H15 **Somerton** Arizona, SW USA
18 J14 **Somerville** New Jersey, NE USA
20 F10 **Somerville** Tennessee, S USA
25 U10 **Somerville** Texas, SW USA
25 T10 **Somerville Lake** ⊞ Texas, SW USA
Someş/Somesch/Someşul *see* Szamos
103 N2 **Somme** ◈ *department* N France
103 N2 **Somme** ≈ N France
95 L18 **Sommen** Jönköping, S Sweden
95 M18 **Sommen** ◎ S Sweden
101 K16 **Sömmerda** Thüringen, C Germany
Sommerein *see* Šamorín
Sommerfeld *see* Lubsko
55 Y11 **Sommet Tabulaire** *var.* Mont Itoupé. ▲ S French Guiana
111 H25 **Somogy** *off.* Somogy Megye. ◈ *county* SW Hungary
Somorja *see* Šamorín
105 N7 **Somosierra, Puerto de** *pass* N Spain
187 Y14 **Somosomo** Taveuni, N Fiji
42 I9 **Somotillo** Chinandega, NW Nicaragua
42 I8 **Somoto** Madriz, NW Nicaragua
110 I11 **Sompolno** Wielkolpolskie, C Poland
105 S3 **Somport** *var.* Puerto de Somport, *Fr.* Col du Somport; *anc.* Summus Portus. *pass* France/Spain *see also* Somport, Col du
102 J17 **Somport, Col du** *var.* Puerto de Somport, *Sp.* Somport; *anc.* Summus Portus. *pass* France/Spain *see also* Somport
Somport, Puerto de *see* Somport/Somport, Col du
99 K15 **Son** Noord-Brabant, S Netherlands
95 H15 **Son** Akershus, S Norway

◆ Country
● Country Capital
◇ Dependent Territory
○ Dependent Territory Capital
◈ Administrative Region
✕ International Airport
▲ Mountain
⛰ Mountain Range
Volcano
≈ River
◎ Lake
⊞ Reservoir

154 *L9* **Son** *var.* Sone. ≈ C India
43 *R16* **Soná** Veraguas, W Panama
154 *M12* **Sonapur** *prev.* Sonepur. Orissa, E India
95 *G24* **Sønderborg** *Ger.* Sonderburg. Sønderjylland, SW Denmark
Sonderburg *see* Sønderborg
95 *F24* **Sønderjylland** *off.* Sønderjyllands Amt. ◆ *county* SW Denmark
101 *K15* **Sondershausen** Thüringen, C Germany
Søndre Strømfjord *see* Kangerlussuaq
106 *E6* **Sondrio** Lombardia, N Italy
Sone *see* Son
Sonepur *see* Sonapur
57 *K22* **Sonequera** ▲ S Bolivia
167 V12 **Sông Câu** Phu Yên, C Vietnam
167 R15 **Sông Đôc** Minh Hai, S Vietnam
81 *H25* **Songea** Ruvuma, S Tanzania
163 *X10* **Songhua Hu** ⊚ NE China
163 *Y7* **Songhua Jiang** *var.* Sungari. ≈ NE China
161 *S8* **Songjiang** Shanghai Shi, E China
Sŏngjin *see* Kimch'aek
167 O16 **Songkhla** *var.* Songkla, ***Mal.*** Singora. Songkhla, SW Thailand
Songkla *see* Songkhla
163 *T13* **Song Ling** ▲▲ NE China
163 *W14* **Songnim** SW North Korea
82 *B10* **Songo** Uíge, NW Angola
83 *M15* **Songo** Tete, NW Mozambique
79 *F21* **Songololo** Bas-Congo, SW Dem. Rep. Congo (Zaire)
160 *H7* **Songpan** *prev.* Sungpu. Sichuan, C China
163 *Y17* **Sŏngsan** S South Korea
161 *R11* **Songxi** Fujian, SE China
160 *M6* **Songxian** *var.* Song Xian. Henan, C China
161 *R10* **Songyin** Zhejiang, SE China
163 *V9* **Songyuan** *var.* Fu-yü, Petuna; *prev.* Fuyu. Jilin, NE China
163 *P11* **Sonid Youqi** *var.* Saihon Tal. Nei Mongol Zizhiqu, N China
163 *P11* **Sonid Zuoqi** Nei Mongol Zizhiqu, N China
152 *I10* **Sonīpat** Haryāna, N India
93 *M15* **Sonkajärvi** Itä-Suomi, C Finland
167 R6 **Sơn La** Sơn La, N Vietnam
149 *O16* **Sonmiāni** Baluchistān, S Pakistan
149 *O16* **Sonmiāni Bay** *bay* S Pakistan
101 *K18* **Sonneberg** Thüringen, C Germany
101 *N24* **Sonntagshorn** ▲ Austria/Germany
Sonoita *see* Sonoyta
40 *E3* **Sonoita, Rio** *var.* Río Sonoyta. ≈ Mexico/USA
35 *N7* **Sonoma** California, W USA
35 *T3* **Sonoma Peak** ▲ Nevada, W USA
35 *P8* **Sonora** California, W USA
25 *O10* **Sonora** Texas, SW USA
40 *F5* **Sonora** ◆ *state* NW Mexico
35 *X17* **Sonoran Desert** *var.* Desierto de Altar. *desert* Mexico/USA ***see also*** Altar, Desierto de
40 *G5* **Sonora, Río** ≈ NW Mexico
40 *E2* **Sonoyta** *var.* Sonoita. Sonora, NW Mexico
Sonoyta, Río *see* Sonoita, Rio
142 *K6* **Sonqor** *var.* Sunqur. Kermānshāh, W Iran
105 *N9* **Sonseca** *var.* Sonseca con Casalgordo. Castilla-La Mancha, C Spain
Sonseca con Casalgordo *see* Sonseca
54 *E9* **Sonsón** Antioquia, W Colombia
42 *E7* **Sonsonate** Sonsonate, W El Salvador
42 *A9* **Sonsonate** ◆ *department* SW El Salvador
188 *A10* **Sonsorol Islands** *island group* S Palau
112 *J9* **Sonta** ***Hung.*** Szond; ***prev.*** Szonta. Serbia, NW Yugoslavia
167 S6 **Sơn Tây** *var.* Sontay. Ha Tây, N Vietnam
101 *J25* **Sonthofen** Bayern, S Germany
Soochow *see* Suzhou
Soomaaliya/Soomaaliyeed, Jamuuriyada Demuqraadiga *see* Somalia
Soome Laht *see* Finland, Gulf of
Sooner State *see* Oklahoma
23 *V5* **Soperton** Georgia, SE USA
167 S6 **Sop Hao** Houaphan, N Laos
Sophia *see* Sofiya
171 S10 **Sopi** Pulau Morotai, E Indonesia
Sopianae *see* Pécs
171 U13 **Sopinusa** Irian Jaya, E Indonesia
81 *B14* **Sopo** ≈ W Sudan
Sopockinie/Sopotskin *see* Sapotskino
114 *I9* **Sopot** Plovdiv, C Bulgaria
110 *I7* **Sopot** ***Ger.*** Zoppot. Pomorskie, N Poland
167 O8 **Sop Prap** *var.* Ban Sop Prap. Lampang, NW Thailand
111 *G22* **Sopron** ***Ger.*** Ödenburg. Győr-Moson-Sopron, NW Hungary
147 *U11* **Sopu-Korgon** *var.* Sofi-Kurgan. Oshskaya Oblast', SW Kyrgyzstan
152 *H5* **Sopur** Jammu and Kashmir, NW India
107 *J15* **Sora** Lazio, C Italy
154 *N13* **Sorada** Orissa, E India
93 *H17* **Soråker** Västernorrland, C Sweden
57 *J17* **Sorata** La Paz, W Bolivia
Sorau/Sorau in der Niederlausitz *see* Żary
105 *Q14* **Sorbas** Andalucía, S Spain
Sord/Sórd Choluim Chille *see* Swords
15 *O11* **Sorel** Quebec, SE Canada
183 *P17* **Sorell** Tasmania, SE Australia
183 *O17* **Sorell, Lake** ⊚ Tasmania, SE Australia
106 *E8* **Soresina** Lombardia, N Italy
95 *D14* **Sørfjorden** *fjord* S Norway
94 *N11* **Sörforsa** Gävleborg, C Sweden
103 *R14* **Sorgues** Vaucluse, SE France
136 *K13* **Sorgun** Yozgat, C Turkey
105 *P5* **Soria** Castilla-León, N Spain
105 *P6* **Soria** ◆ *province* Castilla-León, N Spain
61 *D19* **Soriano** Soriano, SW Uruguay
61 *D19* **Soriano** ◆ *department* SW Uruguay
92 *O4* **Sørkapp** *headland* SW Svalbard
143 *T5* **Sorkh, Kūh-e** ▲▲ NE Iran
Soro *see* Ghazal, Bahr el
95 *I23* **Sorø** Vestsjælland, E Denmark
116 *M8* **Soroca** ***Rus.*** Soroki. N Moldova
60 *L10* **Sorocaba** São Paulo, S Brazil
Sorochino *see* Sarochyna
129 *T7* **Sorochinsk** Orenburgskaya Oblast', W Russian Federation
Soroki *see* Soroca
188 *H15* **Sorol** *atoll* Caroline Islands, W Micronesia
171 T12 **Sorong** Irian Jaya, E Indonesia
81 *G17* **Soroti** C Uganda
Sørøy *see* Sørøya
92 *J8* **Sørøya** *var.* Sørøy. *island* N Norway
104 *G11* **Sorraia, Rio** ≈ C Portugal
92 *I10* **Sørreisa** Troms, N Norway
107 *K18* **Sorrento** *anc.* Surrentum. Campania, S Italy
104 *H10* **Sor, Ribeira de** *stream* C Portugal
195 *T3* **Sør Rondane Mountains** ▲▲ Antarctica
93 *H14* **Sorsele** Västerbotten, N Sweden
107 *B17* **Sorso** Sardegna, Italy, C Mediterranean Sea
171 P4 **Sorsogon** Luzon, N Philippines
105 *U4* **Sort** Cataluña, NE Spain
126 *H11* **Sortavala** Respublika Kareliya, NW Russian Federation
107 *L25* **Sortino** Sicilia, Italy, C Mediterranean Sea
92 *G10* **Sortland** Nordland, C Norway
94 *G9* **Sør-Trøndelag** ◆ *county* S Norway
95 *I15* **Sørumsand** Akershus, S Norway
118 *D6* **Sõrve Säär** *headland* SW Estonia
95 *K22* **Sösdala** Skåne, S Sweden
105 *R4* **Sos del Rey Católico** Aragón, NE Spain
93 *F15* **Sösjöfjällen** ▲ C Sweden
128 *K7* **Sosna** ≈ W Russian Federation
62 *H12* **Sosneado, Cerro** ▲ W Argentina
127 *S9* **Sosnogorsk** Respublika Komi, NW Russian Federation
126 *J8* **Sosnovets** Respublika Kareliya, NW Russian Federation
Sosnovets *see* Sosnowiec
129 *Q3* **Sosnovka** Chuvashskaya Respublika, W Russian Federation
127 *S16* **Sosnovka** Kirovskaya Oblast', NW Russian Federation
126 *M6* **Sosnovka** Murmanskaya Oblast', NW Russian Federation
128 *M6* **Sosnovka** Tambovskaya Oblast', W Russian Federation
126 *H12* **Sosnovo** ***Fin.*** Rautu. Leningradskaya Oblast', NW Russian Federation
Sosnovyy Bor *see* Sasnovy Bor
111 *J16* **Sosnowiec** ***Ger.*** Sosnowitz, ***Rus.*** Sosnovets. Śląskie, S Poland
Sosnowitz *see* Sosnowiec
117 *R2* **Sosnytsya** Chernihivs'ka Oblast', N Ukraine
109 *V10* **Šoštanj** N Slovenia
122 *G10* **Sos'va** Sverdlovskaya Oblast', C Russian Federation
54 *D12* **Sotará, Volcán** ⛰ S Colombia
76 *D10* **Sotavento, Ilhas de** *var.* Leeward Islands. *island group* S Cape Verde
93 *N15* **Sotkamo** Oulu, C Finland
41 *P10* **Soto la Marina** Tamaulipas, C Mexico
41 *P10* **Soto la Marina, Río** ≈ C Mexico
41 *X12* **Sotuta** Yucatán, SE Mexico
79 *F17* **Souanké** La Sangha, NW Congo
76 *M17* **Soubré** S Ivory Coast
115 *H24* **Soúda** *var.* Soúdha, ***Eng.*** Suda. Kríti, Greece, E Mediterranean Sea
Soúdha *see* Soúda
Soueida *see* As Suwaydā'
114 *L12* **Souflí** *prev.* Souflíon. Anatolikí Makedonía kai Thráki, NE Greece
Souflíon *see* Souflí
45 *S11* **Soufrière** W Saint Lucia
45 *X6* **Soufrière** ⛰ Basse Terre, S Guadeloupe
102 *M13* **Souillac** Lot, S France
173 *Y17* **Souillac** S Mauritius
74 *M5* **Souk Ahras** NE Algeria
74 *E6* **Souk-el-Arba-Rharb** *var.* Souk el Arba du Rharb, Souk-el-Arba-du-Rharb, Souk-el-Arba-el-Rhab. NW Morocco
Soukhné *see* As Sukhnah
163 *X14* **Sŏul** *off.* Sŏul-t'ŭkpyŏlsi, ***Eng.*** Seoul, ***Jap.*** Keijō; ***prev.*** Kyŏngsŏng. • (South Korea) NW South Korea
102 *J11* **Soulac-sur-Mer** Gironde, SW France
99 *L19* **Soumagne** Liège, E Belgium
18 *M14* **Sound Beach** Long Island, New York, NE USA
95 *J22* **Sound, The** ***Dan.*** Øresund, ***Swe.*** Öresund. *strait* Denmark/Sweden
115 *H20* **Soúnio, Akrotírio** *headland* C Greece
138 *F8* **Soûr** *var.* Şūr; ***anc.*** Tyre. SW Lebanon
Sources, Mont-aux- *see* Phofung
104 *G8* **Soure** Coimbra, N Portugal
11 *W17* **Souris** Manitoba, S Canada
13 *Q14* **Souris** Prince Edward Island, SE Canada
28 *L2* **Souris River** *var.* Mouse River. ≈ Canada/USA
25 *X10* **Sour Lake** Texas, SW USA
115 *F17* **Sourpi** Thessalía, C Greece
104 *H11* **Sousel** Portalegre, C Portugal
75 *N6* **Sousse** *var.* Sūsah. NE Tunisia
14 *H11* **South** ≈ Ontario, S Canada
South *see* Sud
83 *G23* **South Africa** ***off.*** Republic of South Africa, ***Afr.*** Suid-Afrika. ◆ *republic* S Africa
48-49 **South America** *continent*
2 *J17* **South American Plate** *tectonic feature*
97 *M23* **Southampton** ***hist.*** Hamwih, ***Lat.*** Clausentum. S England, UK
19 *N14* **Southampton** Long Island, New York, NE USA
9 P8 **Southampton Island** *island* Nunavut, NE Canada
151 *P20* **South Andaman** *island* Andaman Islands, India, NE Indian Ocean
13 *Q6* **South Aulatsivik Island** *island* Newfoundland, E Canada
182 *E4* **South Australia** ◆ *state* S Australia
South Australian Abyssal Plain *see* South Australian Plain
192 G11 **South Australian Basin** *undersea feature* SW Indian Ocean
173 *X12* **South Australian Plain** *var.* South Australian Abyssal Plain. *undersea feature* SE Indian Ocean
37 *R13* **South Baldy** ▲ New Mexico, SW USA
23 *Y14* **South Bay** Florida, SE USA
14 *E12* **South Baymouth** Manitoulin Island, Ontario, S Canada
30 *L10* **South Beloit** Illinois, N USA
31 *O11* **South Bend** Indiana, N USA
25 *R6* **South Bend** Texas, SW USA
32 *F9* **South Bend** Washington, NW USA
South Beveland *see* Zuid-Beveland
South Borneo *see* Kalimantan Selatan
21 *U7* **South Boston** Virginia, NE USA
182 *F2* **South Branch Neales** *seasonal river* South Australia
21 *U3* **South Branch Potomac River** ≈ West Virginia, NE USA
185 *H19* **Southbridge** Canterbury, South Island, NZ
19 *N12* **Southbridge** Massachusetts, NE USA
183 *P17* **South Bruny Island** *island* Tasmania, SE Australia
18 *L7* **South Burlington** Vermont, NE USA
44 *M6* **South Caicos** *island* S Turks and Caicos Islands
South Cape *see* Ka Lae
23 *V3* **South Carolina** *off.* State of South Carolina; also known as The Palmetto State. ◆ *state* SE USA
South Carpathians *see* Carpaţii Meridionali
South Celebes *see* Sulawesi Selatan
21 *Q5* **South Charleston** West Virginia, NE USA
192 D7 **South China Basin** *undersea feature* SE South China Sea
169 R8 **South China Sea** ***Chin.*** Nan Hai, ***Ind.*** Laut Cina Selatan, ***Vtn.*** Biên Đông. *sea* SE Asia
33 *Z10* **South Dakota** *off.* State of South Dakota; also known as The Coyote State, Sunshine State. ◆ *state* N USA
23 *X10* **South Daytona** Florida, SE USA
37 *R10* **South Domingo Pueblo** New Mexico, SW USA
97 *N23* **South Downs** *hill range* SE England, UK
83 *I21* **South East** ◆ *district* SE Botswana
65 *H15* **South East Bay** *bay* Ascension Island, C Atlantic Ocean
183 *O17* **South East Cape** *headland* Tasmania, SE Australia
38 *K10* **Southeast Cape** *headland* Saint Lawrence Island, Alaska, USA
South-East Celebes *see* Sulawesi Tenggara
192 G12 **Southeast Indian Ridge** *undersea feature* Indian Ocean/Pacific Ocean
Southeast Island *see* Tagula Island
193 P13 **Southeast Pacific Basin** *var.* Belling Hausen Mulde. *undersea feature* SE Pacific Ocean
65 *H15* **South East Point** *headland* SE Ascension Island
183 *O14* **South East Point** *headland* Victoria, S Australia
191 *Z3* **South East Point** *headland* Kiritimati, NE Kiribati
44 *L5* **Southeast Point** *headland* Mayaguana, SE Bahamas
South-East Sulawesi *see* Sulawesi Tenggara
11 *U12* **Southend** Saskatchewan, C Canada
97 *P22* **Southend-on-Sea** E England, UK
83 *H20* **Southern** *var.* Bangwaketse, Ngwaketze. ◆ *district* SE Botswana
81 *I15* **Southern** ◆ *region* S Ethiopia
138 *E13* **Southern** ◆ *district* S Israel
83 *N15* **Southern** ◆ *region* S Malawi
83 *I15* **Southern** ◆ *province* S Zambia
185 *E19* **Southern Alps** ▲▲ South Island, NZ
190 *K15* **Southern Cook Islands** *island group* S Cook Islands
180 *K12* **Southern Cross** Western Australia
80 *A12* **Southern Darfur** ◆ *state* W Sudan
186 B7 **Southern Highlands** ◆ *province* W PNG
11 *V11* **Southern Indian Lake** ⊚ Manitoba, C Canada
80 *E11* **Southern Kordofan** ◆ *state* C Sudan
187 Z15 **Southern Lau Group** *island group* Lau Group, SE Fiji
173 *S13* **Southern Ocean** *ocean*
21 *T10* **Southern Pines** North Carolina, SE USA
155 *J26* **Southern Province** ◆ *province* S Sri Lanka
96 *I13* **Southern Uplands** ▲▲ S Scotland, UK
Southern Urals *see* Yuzhnyy Ural
183 *P16* **South Esk River** ≈ Tasmania, SE Australia
11 *U16* **Southey** Saskatchewan, S Canada
27 *V2* **South Fabius River** ≈ Missouri, C USA
31 *S10* **Southfield** Michigan, N USA
192 K10 **South Fiji Basin** *undersea feature* S Pacific Ocean
97 *Q22* **South Foreland** *headland* SE England, UK
35 *P7* **South Fork American River** ≈ California, W USA
28 *K7* **South Fork Grand River** ≈ South Dakota, N USA
35 *T12* **South Fork Kern River** ≈ California, W USA
39 *Q7* **South Fork Koyukuk River** ≈ Alaska, USA
39 *Q11* **South Fork Kuskokwim River** ≈ Alaska, USA
26 *H2* **South Fork Republican River** ≈ C USA
26 *L3* **South Fork Solomon River** ≈ Kansas, C USA
31 *P5* **South Fox Island** *island* Michigan, N USA
20 *G8* **South Fulton** Tennessee, S USA
195 *U10* **South Geomagnetic Pole** *pole* Antarctica
65 *J20* **South Georgia** *island* South Georgia and the South Sandwich Islands, SW Atlantic Ocean
65 *K21* **South Georgia and the South Sandwich Islands** ◇ *UK dependent territory* SW Atlantic Ocean
47 *Y14* **South Georgia Ridge** *var.* North Scotia Ridge. *undersea feature* SW Atlantic Ocean
181 *Q1* **South Goulburn Island** *island* Northern Territory, N Australia
153 U16 **South Hatia Island** *island* SE Bangladesh
31 *O10* **South Haven** Michigan, N USA
21 *V7* **South Hill** Virginia, NE USA
South Holland *see* Zuid-Holland
21 *P8* **South Holston Lake** ⊞ Tennessee/Virginia, S USA
175 *N1* **South Honshu Ridge** *undersea feature* W Pacific Ocean
26 *M6* **South Hutchinson** Kansas, C USA
151 *K21* **South Huvadhu Atoll** *var.* Gaafu Dhaalu Atoll. *atoll* S Maldives
173 *U14* **South Indian Basin** *undersea feature* Indian Ocean/Pacific Ocean
11 *W11* **South Indian Lake** Manitoba, C Canada
81 *I17* **South Island** *island* NW Kenya
185 *C20* **South Island** *island* S NZ
65 *B23* **South Jason** *island* Jason Islands, NW Falkland Islands
South Kalimantan *see* Kalimantan Selatan
South Kazakhstan *see* Yuzhnyy Kazakhstan
163 *X15* **South Korea** *off.* Republic of Korea, ***Kor.*** Taehan Min'guk. ◆ *republic* E Asia
35 *Q6* **South Lake Tahoe** California, W USA
25 *N6* **Southland** Texas, SW USA
185 *B23* **Southland** *off.* Southland Region. ◆ *region* South Island, NZ
29 *N15* **South Loup River** ≈ Nebraska, C USA
151 *K19* **South Maalhosmadulu Atoll** *var.* Baa Atoll. *atoll* N Maldives
14 *E15* **South Maitland** ≈ Ontario, S Canada
192 E8 **South Makassar Basin** *undersea feature* E Java Sea
31 *O6* **South Manitou Island** *island* Michigan, N USA
151 *K18* **South Miladummadulu Atoll** *atoll* N Maldives
21 *X8* **South Mills** North Carolina, SE USA
8 H9 **South Nahanni** ≈ Northwest Territories, NW Canada
39 *P13* **South Naknek** Alaska, USA
14 *M13* **South Nation** ≈ Ontario, SE Canada
44 *F9* **South Negril Point** *headland* W Jamaica
151 *K20* **South Nilandhe Atoll** *var.* Dhaalu Atoll. *atoll* C Maldives
36 *L2* **South Ogden** Utah, W USA
18 *M14* **Southold** Long Island, New York, NE USA
194 *H1* **South Orkney Islands** *island group* Antarctica
137 *S9* **South Ossetia** *former autonomous region* SW Georgia
South Pacific Basin *see* Southwest Pacific Basin
19 *P7* **South Paris** Maine, NE USA
33 *U15* **South Pass** *pass* Wyoming, C USA
189 *U13* **South Pass** *passage* Chuuk Islands, C Micronesia
20 *K10* **South Pittsburg** Tennessee, S USA
28 *K15* **South Platte River** ≈ Colorado/Nebraska, C USA
31 *T16* **South Point** Ohio, N USA
65 *G15* **South Point** *headland* S Ascension Island
31 *R6* **South Point** *headland* Michigan, N USA
South Point *see* Ka Lae
195 *P9* **South Pole** *pole* Antarctica
183 *P17* **Southport** Tasmania, SE Australia
97 *K17* **Southport** NW England, UK
21 *V12* **Southport** North Carolina, SE USA
19 *P8* **South Portland** Maine, NE USA
14 *H12* **South River** Ontario, S Canada
21 *U11* **South River** ≈ North Carolina, SE USA
96 *K5* **South Ronaldsay** *island* NE Scotland, UK
36 *L2* **South Salt Lake** Utah, W USA
65 *L21* **South Sandwich Islands** *island group* SE South Georgia and South Sandwich Islands
65 *K21* **South Sandwich Trench** *undersea feature* SW Atlantic Ocean
11 *S16* **South Saskatchewan** ≈ Alberta/Saskatchewan, S Canada
65 *I21* **South Scotia Ridge** *undersea feature* S Scotia Sea
11 *V10* **South Seal** ≈ Manitoba, C Canada
194 *G4* **South Shetland Islands** *island group* Antarctica
65 *H22* **South Shetland Trough** *undersea feature* Atlantic Ocean/Pacific Ocean
97 *M14* **South Shields** NE England, UK
29 *R13* **South Sioux City** Nebraska, C USA
192 J9 **South Solomon Trench** *undersea feature* W Pacific Ocean
183 *V3* **South Stradbroke Island** *island* Queensland, E Australia
South Sulawesi *see* Sulawesi Selatan
South Sumatra *see* Sumatera Selatan
184 *K11* **South Taranaki Bight** *bight* SE Tasman Sea
South Tasmania Plateau *see* Tasman Plateau
36 *M15* **South Tucson** Arizona, SW USA
12 *H9* **South Twin Island** *island* Nunavut, C Canada
96 *E9* **South Uist** *island* NW Scotland, UK
South-West *see* Sud-Ouest
South-West Africa/South West Africa *see* Namibia
65 *F15* **South West Bay** *bay* Ascension Island, C Atlantic Ocean
183 *N18* **South West Cape** *headland* Tasmania, SE Australia
185 *B26* **South West Cape** *headland* Stewart Island, NZ
38 *J10* **Southwest Cape** *headland* Saint Lawrence Island, Alaska, USA
Southwest Indian Ocean Ridge *see* Southwest Indian Ridge
173 *N11* **Southwest Indian Ridge** *var.* Southwest Indian Ocean Ridge. *undersea feature* SW Indian Ocean
192 L10 **Southwest Pacific Basin** *var.* South Pacific Basin. *undersea feature* SE Pacific Ocean
44 *H2* **Southwest Point** *headland* Great Abaco, N Bahamas
191 *X3* **South West Point** *headland* Kiritimati, NE Kiribati
65 *G25* **South West Point** *headland* SW Saint Helena
25 *P5* **South Wichita River** ≈ Texas, SW USA
97 *Q20* **Southwold** E England, UK
19 *Q12* **South Yarmouth** Massachusetts, NE USA
116 *J10* **Sovata** ***Hung.*** Szováta. Mureş, C Romania
107 *N22* **Soverato** Calabria, SW Italy
Sovetabad *see* Ghafurov
128 *C2* **Sovetsk** ***Ger.*** Tilsit. Kaliningradskaya Oblast', W Russian Federation
127 *Q15* **Sovetsk** Kirovskaya Oblast', NW Russian Federation
129 *N10* **Sovetskaya** Rostovskaya Oblast', SW Russian Federation
Sovetskoye *see* Ketchenery
146 *I15* **Sovet"yab** ***prev.*** Sovet"yap. Akhalskiy Velayat, S Turkmenistan
Sovet"yap *see* Sovet"yab
117 *U12* **Sovyets'kyy** Respublika Krym, S Ukraine
83 *I18* **Sowa** *var.* Sua. Central, NE Botswana
83 *I18* **Sowa Pan** *salt lake* NE Botswana
83 *J21* **Soweto** Gauteng, NE South Africa
Sōya-kaikyō *see* La Perouse Strait
165 T1 **Sōya-misaki** *headland* Hokkaidō, NE Japan
127 *N7* **Soyana** ≈ NW Russian Federation
146 *A8* **Soye, Mys** *var.* Mys Suz. *headland* NW Turkmenistan
82 *A10* **Soyo** Zaire, NW Angola
80 *J10* **Soyra** ▲ C Eritrea
Sozaq *see* Suzak
119 *P16* **Sozh** ***Rus.*** Sozh. ≈ NE Europe
114 *N10* **Sozopol** ***prev.*** Sizebolu ***anc.*** Apollonia. Burgas, E Bulgaria
172 *J15* **Sœurs, Les** *island group* Inner Islands, W Seychelles
99 *L20* **Spa** Liège, E Belgium
194 *I7* **Spaatz Island** *island* Antarctica
144 *M14* **Space Launching Centre** *space station* Kzylorda, S Kazakhstan
105 *O7* **Spain** *off.* Kingdom of Spain, ***Sp.*** España; ***anc.*** Hispania, Iberia, ***Lat.*** Hispana. ◆ *monarchy* SW Europe
Spalato *see* Split
97 *O19* **Spalding** E England, UK
14 *D11* **Spanish** Ontario, S Canada
36 *L3* **Spanish Fork** Utah, W USA
64 *B12* **Spanish Point** *headland* C Bermuda
14 *E9* **Spanish River** ≈ Ontario, S Canada
44 *K13* **Spanish Town** ***hist.*** St.Iago de la Vega. C Jamaica
115 *H24* **Spánta, Akrotírio** *headland* Kríti, Greece, E Mediterranean Sea
35 *Q5* **Sparks** Nevada, W USA
Sparnacum *see* Épernay
95 *N16* **Sparreholm** Södermanland, C Sweden
23 *U4* **Sparta** Georgia, SE USA
30 *K16* **Sparta** Illinois, N USA
31 *P9* **Sparta** Michigan, N USA
21 *R8* **Sparta** North Carolina, SE USA
20 *L9* **Sparta** Tennessee, S USA
30 *J7* **Sparta** Wisconsin, N USA
Sparta *see* Spárti
21 *Q11* **Spartanburg** South Carolina, SE USA
115 *F21* **Spárti** ***Eng.*** Sparta. Pelopónnisos, S Greece
107 *B21* **Spartivento, Capo** *headland* Sardegna, Italy, C Mediterranean Sea
11 *P17* **Sparwood** British Columbia, SW Canada
128 *I4* **Spas-Demensk** Kaluzhskaya Oblast', W Russian Federation
128 *M4* **Spas-Klepiki** Ryazanskaya Oblast', W Russian Federation
Spasovo *see* Kulen Vakuf
123 R15 **Spassk-Dal'niy** Primorskiy Kray, SE Russian Federation
128 *M5* **Spassk-Ryazanskiy** Ryazanskaya Oblast', 111 *N20* **Trebišov** ***Hung.*** Tőketerebes. Košický Kraj, E Slovakia
Trebitsch *see* Třebíč
Trebizond *see* Trabzon
ZaporizhzhyaŚląskie, S Poland
31 *P9* **Sparta** Michigan, N USA
21 *R8* **Sparta** North Carolina, SE USA
20 *L9* **Sparta** Tennessee, S USA
30 *I7* **Sparta** Wisconsin, N USA
Sparta *see* Spárti
21 *Q11* **Spartanburg** South Carolina, SE USA
115 *F21* **Spárti** ***Eng.*** Sparta. Pelopónnisos, S Greece
107 *B21* **Spartivento, Capo** *headland* Sardegna, Italy, C Mediterranean Sea
11 *P17* **Sparwood** British Columbia, SW Canada
128 *I4* **Spas-Demensk** Kaluzhskaya Oblast', W Russian Federation
128 *M4* **Spas-Klepiki** Ryazanskaya Oblast', W Russian Federation
Spasovo *see* Kulen Vakuf
123 R15 **Spassk-Dal'niy** Primorskiy Kray, SE Russian Federation
128 *M5* **Spassk-Ryazanskiy** Ryazanskaya Oblast', W Russian Federation
115 *H19* **Spáta** Attikí, C Greece
121 Q11 **Spátha, Akrotírio** *headland* Kríti, Greece, E Mediterranean Sea
Špatrjan *see* Paternion
28 *I9* **Spearfish** South Dakota, N USA
25 *O1* **Spearman** Texas, SW USA
65 *C25* **Speedwell Island** *island* S Falkland Islands
65 *C25* **Speedwell Island Settlement** S Falkland Islands
65 *G25* **Speery Island** *island* S Saint Helena
45 *N14* **Speightstown** NW Barbados
106 *I13* **Spello** Umbria, C Italy
39 *R12* **Spenard** Alaska, USA
Spence Bay *see* Taloyoak
31 *O14* **Spencer** Indiana, N USA
29 *T12* **Spencer** Iowa, C USA
29 *P12* **Spencer** Nebraska, C USA
21 *S9* **Spencer** North Carolina, SE USA
20 *L9* **Spencer** Tennessee, S USA
21 *Q4* **Spencer** West Virginia, NE USA
30 *K6* **Spencer** Wisconsin, N USA
182 *G10* **Spencer, Cape** *headland* South Australia
39 *V13* **Spencer, Cape** *headland* Alaska, USA
182 *H9* **Spencer Gulf** *gulf* South Australia
18 *F9* **Spencerport** New York, NE USA
31 *Q12* **Spencerville** Ohio, N USA
115 *E17* **Spercheiáda** *var.* Spercheiás, Sperkhiás. Stereá Ellás, C Greece
115 *E17* **Spercheiós** ≈ C Greece
Sperhiada *see* Spercheiáda
95 *G14* **Sperillen** ⊚ S Norway
Sperkhiás *see* Spercheiáda
101 *I18* **Spessart** *hill range* C Germany
Spétsai *see* Spétses
115 *G21* **Spétses** *prev.* Spétsai. Spétses, S Greece
115 *G21* **Spétses** *island* S Greece
96 *J8* **Spey** ≈ NE Scotland, UK
101 *G20* **Speyer** ***Eng.*** Spires; ***anc.*** Civitas Nemetum, Spira. Rheinland-Pfalz, SW Germany
101 *G20* **Speyerbach** ≈ W Germany
107 *N20* **Spezzano Albanese** Calabria, SW Italy
Spice Islands *see* Maluku
100 *F9* **Spiekeroog** *island* NW Germany
109 *W9* **Spielfeld** Steiermark, SE Austria
65 *N21* **Spiess Seamount** *undersea feature* S Atlantic Ocean
108 *E9* **Spiez** Bern, W Switzerland
98 *G13* **Spijkenisse** Zuid-Holland, SW Netherlands
39 *T6* **Spike Mountain** ▲ Alaska, USA
115 *I25* **Spíli** Kríti, Greece, E Mediterranean Sea
108 *D10* **Spillgerten** ▲ W Switzerland
118 *F9* **Spilva** ✖ (Rīga) Rīga, C Latvia
107 *N17* **Spinazzola** Puglia, SE Italy
149 *O9* **Spīn Būldak** Kandahār, S Afghanistan
Spira *see* Speyer
Spirdingsee *see* Śniardwy, Jezioro
Spires *see* Speyer
29 *T11* **Spirit Lake** Iowa, C USA
29 *T11* **Spirit Lake** ⊚ Iowa, C USA
11 *N13* **Spirit River** Alberta, W Canada

◆ Country • Country Capital ◇ Dependent Territory ○ Dependent Territory Capital ◆ Administrative Region ✖ International Airport ▲ Mountain ▲▲ Mountain Range ⛰ Volcano ≈ River ⊚ Lake ⊞ Reservoir

11 S14 **Spiritwood** Saskatchewan, S Canada
27 R11 **Spiro** Oklahoma, C USA
111 L19 **Spišská Nová Ves** *Ger.* Neudorf, Zipser Neudorf, *Hung.* Igló. Košický Kraj, E Slovakia
137 T11 **Spitak** NW Armenia
92 O2 **Spitsbergen** *island* NW Svalbard
Spittal *see* Spittal an der Drau
109 R9 **Spittal an der Drau** *var.* Spittal. Kärnten, S Austria
109 V3 **Spitz** Niederösterreich, NE Austria
94 D9 **Spjelkavik** Møre og Romsdal, S Norway
25 W10 **Splendora** Texas, SW USA
113 E14 **Split** *It.* Spalato. Split-Dalmacija, S Croatia
113 E14 **Split** ✕ Split-Dalmacija, S Croatia
113 E14 **Split-Dalmacija** *off.* Splitsko-Dalmatinska Županija. ◈ *province* S Croatia
11 X12 **Split Lake** ◎ Manitoba, C Canada
Splitsko-Dalmatinska Županija *see* Split-Dalmacija
108 H10 **Splügen** Graubünden, S Switzerland
Spodnji Dravograd *see* Dravograd
25 P12 **Spofford** Texas, SW USA
118 J11 **Špoģi** Daugvapils, SE Latvia
32 L8 **Spokane** Washington, NW USA
32 L8 **Spokane River** ≈ Washington, NW USA
106 I13 **Spoleto** Umbria, C Italy
30 I4 **Spooner** Wisconsin, N USA
30 K12 **Spoon River** ≈ Illinois, N USA
21 W5 **Spotsylvania** Virginia, NE USA
32 L8 **Sprague** Washington, NW USA
170 J5 **Spratly Island** *island* SW Spratly Islands
192 E6 **Spratly Islands** *Chin.* Nansha Qundao. ◇ *disputed territory* SE Asia
32 J12 **Spray** Oregon, NW USA
112 I11 **Spreča** ≈ N Bosnia and Herzegovina
100 P13 **Spree** ≈ E Germany
100 P13 **Spreewald** *wetland* NE Germany
101 P14 **Spremberg** Brandenburg, E Germany
25 W11 **Spring** Texas, SW USA
31 Q10 **Spring Arbor** Michigan, N USA
83 E23 **Springbok** Northern Cape, W South Africa
18 I15 **Spring City** Pennsylvania, NE USA
20 L9 **Spring City** Tennessee, S USA
36 L4 **Spring City** Utah, W USA
35 W3 **Spring Creek** Nevada, W USA
27 S9 **Springdale** Arkansas, C USA
31 Q14 **Springdale** Ohio, N USA
100 I13 **Springe** Niedersachsen, N Germany
37 U9 **Springer** New Mexico, SW USA
37 W7 **Springfield** Colorado, C USA
23 W5 **Springfield** Georgia, SE USA
30 K14 **Springfield** *state capital* Illinois, N USA
20 L6 **Springfield** Kentucky, S USA
18 M12 **Springfield** Massachusetts, NE USA
29 T10 **Springfield** Minnesota, N USA
27 T7 **Springfield** Missouri, C USA
31 R13 **Springfield** Ohio, N USA
32 G13 **Springfield** Oregon, NW USA
29 Q12 **Springfield** South Dakota, N USA
20 J8 **Springfield** Tennessee, S USA
18 M9 **Springfield** Vermont, NE USA
30 K14 **Springfield, Lake** ▣ Illinois, N USA
55 T8 **Spring Garden** NE Guyana
30 K8 **Spring Green** Wisconsin, N USA
29 X11 **Spring Grove** Minnesota, N USA
22 G4 **Springhill** Louisiana, S USA
23 V12 **Spring Hill** Florida, SE USA
27 R4 **Spring Hill** Kansas, C USA
13 P15 **Springhill** Nova Scotia, SE Canada
20 I9 **Spring Hill** Tennessee, S USA
21 U10 **Spring Lake** North Carolina, SE USA
24 M4 **Springlake** Texas, SW USA
35 W11 **Spring Mountains** ▲▲ Nevada, W USA
65 B24 **Spring Point** West Falkland, Falkland Islands
27 W9 **Spring River** ≈ Arkansas/Missouri, C USA
27 S7 **Spring River** ≈ Missouri/Oklahoma, C USA
83 J21 **Springs** Gauteng, NE South Africa
185 H16 **Springs Junction** West Coast, South Island, NZ
181 X8 **Springsure** Queensland, E Australia
29 W11 **Spring Valley** Minnesota, N USA
18 K13 **Spring Valley** New York, NE USA
29 N12 **Springview** Nebraska, C USA
18 D11 **Springville** New York, NE USA
36 L3 **Springville** Utah, W USA
Sprottau *see* Szprotawa
15 V4 **Sproule, Pointe** *headland* Quebec, SE Canada
11 Q14 **Spruce Grove** Alberta, SW Canada
21 T4 **Spruce Knob** ▲ West Virginia, NE USA
35 X3 **Spruce Mountain** ▲ Nevada, W USA
21 P9 **Spruce Pine** North Carolina, SE USA
98 G13 **Spui** ≈ SW Netherlands
107 O19 **Spulico, Capo** *headland* S Italy
25 O5 **Spur** Texas, SW USA
97 O17 **Spurn Head** *headland* E England, UK
99 H20 **Spy** Namur, S Belgium
95 I15 **Spydeberg** Østfold, S Norway
185 J17 **Spy Glass Point** *headland* South Island, NZ
10 L17 **Squamish** British Columbia, SW Canada
19 O8 **Squam Lake** ◎ New Hampshire, NE USA
19 S2 **Squa Pan Mountain** ▲ Maine, NE USA
39 N16 **Squaw Harbor** Unga Island, Alaska, USA
14 E11 **Squaw Island** *island* Ontario, S Canada
107 O22 **Squillace, Golfo di** *gulf* S Italy
107 Q18 **Squinzano** Puglia, SE Italy
Sráid na Cathrach *see* Milltown Malbay
167 S11 **Srâlau** Stœng Trêng, N Cambodia
Srath an Urláir *see* Stranorlar
112 G10 **Srbac** Republika Srpska, N Bosnia & Herzegovina
Srbinje *see* Foča
Srbija *see* Serbia
Srbobran *see* Donji Vakuf
112 K9 **Srbobran** *var.* Bácsszenttamás, *Hung.* Szenttamás. Serbia, N Yugoslavia
167 R13 **Srê Âmběl** Kaôh Kông, SW Cambodia
112 K13 **Srebrenica** Republika Srpska, E Bosnia & Herzegovina
112 I11 **Srebrenik** Federacija Bosna I Hercegovina, E Bosnia & Herzegovina
114 M10 **Sredets** *prev.* Grudovo. Burgas, E Bulgaria
114 K10 **Sredets** *prev.* Syulemeshlii. Stara Zagora, C Bulgaria
114 M10 **Sredetska Reka** ≈ SE Bulgaria
123 U9 **Sredinnyy Khrebet** ▲▲ E Russian Federation
114 N7 **Sredishte** *Rom.* Beibunar; *prev.* Knyazhevo. Dobrich, NE Bulgaria
114 I10 **Sredna Gora** ▲▲ C Bulgaria
123 R7 **Srednekolymsk** Respublika Sakha (Yakutiya), NE Russian Federation
128 K7 **Srednerusskaya Vozvyshennost'** *Eng.* Central Russian Upland. ▲▲ W Russian Federation
122 L9 **Srednesibirskoye Ploskogor'ye** *var.* Central Siberian Uplands, *Eng.* Central Siberian Plateau. ▲▲ N Russian Federation
127 V13 **Sredniy Ural** ▲▲ NW Russian Federation
167 T12 **Srê Khtŭm** Môndól Kiri, E Cambodia
111 G12 **Śrem** Wielkolpolskie, C Poland
112 K10 **Sremska Mitrovica** *prev.* Mitrovica, *Ger.* Mitrowitz. Serbia, NW Yugoslavia
167 R11 **Srêng, Stœng** ≈ NW Cambodia
167 R11 **Srê Noy** Siĕmréab, NW Cambodia
Srepok, Sông *see* Srêpôk, Tônle
167 T12 **Srêpôk, Tônle** *var.* Sông Srepok. ≈ Cambodia/Vietnam
123 P13 **Sretensk** Chitinskaya Oblast', S Russian Federation
169 R10 **Sri Aman** Sarawak, East Malaysia
117 R4 **Sribne** Chernihivs'ka Oblast', N Ukraine
155 I25 **Sri Jayawardanapura** *var.* Sri Jayawardenepura; *prev.* Kotte. Western Province, W Sri Lanka
155 M14 **Srikākulam** Andhra Pradesh, E India
155 I25 **Sri Lanka** *off.* Democratic Socialist Republic of Sri Lanka; *prev.* Ceylon. ◆ *republic* S Asia
130 F14 **Sri Lanka** *island* S Asia
153 V14 **Srimangal** Chittagong, E Bangladesh
Sri Mohangorh *see* Shri Mohangarh
152 H5 **Srinagar** Jammu and Kashmir, N India
167 N10 **Srinagarind Reservoir** ▣ W Thailand
155 F19 **Sringeri** Karnātaka, W India
155 K25 **Sri Pada** *Eng.* Adam's Peak. ▲ S Sri Lanka
Sri Saket *see* Si Sa Ket
111 G14 **Środa Śląska** *Ger.* Neumarkt. Dolnośląskie, SW Poland
110 H12 **Środa Wielkopolska** Wielkolpolskie, C Poland
Srpska Kostajnica *see* Bosanska Kostajnica
113 G14 **Srpska, Republika** ◈ *republic* Bosnia & Herzegovina
Srpski Brod *see* Bosanski Brod
Ssu-ch'uan *see* Sichuan
Ssu-p'ing/Ssu-p'ing-chieh *see* Siping
Stablo *see* Stavelot
99 G15 **Stabroek** Antwerpen, N Belgium
Stackeln *see* Strenči
96 I5 **Stack Skerry** *island* N Scotland, UK
94 C10 **Stad** *peninsula* S Norway
100 I9 **Stade** Niedersachsen, NW Germany
109 R5 **Stadl-Paura** Oberösterreich, NW Austria
119 L20 **Stadolichy** *Rus.* Stodolichi. Homyel'skaya Voblasts', SE Belarus
98 P7 **Stadskanaal** Groningen, NE Netherlands
101 H16 **Stadtallendorf** Hessen, C Germany
101 K23 **Stadtbergen** Bayern, S Germany
108 G7 **Stäfa** Zürich, NE Switzerland
95 K23 **Staffanstorp** Skåne, S Sweden
101 K18 **Staffelstein** Bayern, C Germany
97 L19 **Stafford** C England, UK
26 L6 **Stafford** Kansas, C USA
21 W4 **Stafford** Virginia, NE USA
97 L19 **Staffordshire** *cultural region* C England, UK
19 N12 **Stafford Springs** Connecticut, NE USA
115 H14 **Stágira** Kentrikí Makedonía, N Greece
118 G7 **Staicele** Limbaži, N Latvia
Staierdorf-Anina *see* Anina
109 V8 **Stainz** Steiermark, SE Austria
Stájerlakanina *see* Anina
117 Y7 **Stakhanov** Luhans'ka Oblast', E Ukraine
108 E11 **Stalden** Valais, SW Switzerland
Stalin *see* Varna
Stalinabad *see* Dushanbe
Stalingrad *see* Volgograd
Staliniri *see* Ts'khinvali
Stalino *see* Donets'k
Stalinobod *see* Dushanbe
Stalinov Štít *see* Gerlachovský štít
Stalinsk *see* Novokuznetsk
Stalinskaya Oblast' *see* Donets'ka Oblast'
Stalinski Zaliv *see* Varnenski Zaliv
Stalin, Yazovir *see* Iskŭr, Yazovir
8 K2 **Stallworthy, Cape** *headland* Nunavut, N Canada
111 N15 **Stalowa Wola** Podkarpackie, SE Poland
114 I11 **Stamboliyski** Plovdiv, C Bulgaria
114 J8 **Stamboliyski, Yazovir** ▣ N Bulgaria
97 N19 **Stamford** E England, UK
18 L14 **Stamford** Connecticut, NE USA
25 P6 **Stamford** Texas, SW USA
25 Q6 **Stamford, Lake** ▣ Texas, SW USA
108 I10 **Stampa** Graubünden, SE Switzerland
Stampalia *see* Astypálaia
27 T14 **Stamps** Arkansas, C USA
92 G11 **Stamsund** Nordland, C Norway
27 R2 **Stanberry** Missouri, C USA
195 O3 **Stancomb-Wills Glacier** *glacier* Antarctica
83 K21 **Standerton** Mpumalanga, E South Africa
31 R7 **Standish** Michigan, N USA
20 M6 **Stanford** Kentucky, S USA
33 S9 **Stanford** Montana, NW USA
95 P19 **Stånga** Gotland, SE Sweden
94 I13 **Stange** Hedmark, S Norway
83 L23 **Stanger** KwaZulu/Natal, E South Africa
Stanimaka *see* Asenovgrad
Stanislau *see* Ivano-Frankivs'k
35 P8 **Stanislaus River** ≈ California, W USA
Stanislav *see* Ivano-Frankivs'k
Stanislavskaya Oblast' *see* Ivano-Frankivs'ka Oblast'
Stanisławów *see* Ivano-Frankivs'k
Stanke Dimitrov *see* Dupnitsa
183 O15 **Stanley** Tasmania, SE Australia
65 E24 **Stanley** *var.* Port Stanley, Puerto Argentino ○ (Falkland Islands) East Falkland, Falkland Islands
33 O13 **Stanley** Idaho, NW USA
28 L3 **Stanley** North Dakota, N USA
21 U4 **Stanley** Virginia, NE USA
30 J6 **Stanley** Wisconsin, N USA
79 G21 **Stanley Pool** *var.* Pool Malebo. ◎ Congo/Dem. Rep. Congo (Zaire)
155 H20 **Stanley Reservoir** ▣ S India
Stanleyville *see* Kisangani
42 G3 **Stann Creek** ◈ *district* SE Belize
Stann Creek *see* Dangriga
123 Q12 **Stanovoy Khrebet** ▲▲ SE Russian Federation
108 F8 **Stans** Unterwalden, C Switzerland
97 O21 **Stansted** ✕ (London) Essex, E England, UK
183 U4 **Stanthorpe** Queensland, E Australia
21 N6 **Stanton** Kentucky, S USA
31 Q8 **Stanton** Michigan, N USA
29 Q14 **Stanton** Nebraska, C USA
28 L5 **Stanton** North Dakota, N USA
25 N7 **Stanton** Texas, SW USA
32 H7 **Stanwood** Washington, NW USA
117 Y7 **Stanychno-Luhans'ke** Luhans'ka Oblast', E Ukraine
108 K7 **Stanzach** Tirol, W Austria
98 M9 **Staphorst** Overijssel, E Netherlands
14 D18 **Staples** Ontario, S Canada
29 T6 **Staples** Minnesota, N USA
28 M14 **Stapleton** Nebraska, C USA
25 S8 **Star** Texas, SW USA
111 M14 **Starachowice** Świętokrzyskie, C Poland
Stara Kanjiža *see* Kanjiža
111 M18 **Stará L'ubovňa** *Ger.* Altlublau, *Hung.* Prešovský Kraj, E Slovakia
112 L10 **Stara Pazova** *Ger.* Altpasua, *Hung.* Ópazova. Serbia, N Yugoslavia
Stara Planina *see* Balkan Mountains
114 L9 **Stara Reka** ≈ C Bulgaria
116 M5 **Stara Synyava** Khmel'nyts'ka Oblast', W Ukraine
116 I2 **Stara Vyzhivka** Volyns'ka Oblast', NW Ukraine
Staraya Belitsa *see* Staraya Byelitsa
119 M14 **Staraya Byelitsa** *Rus.* Staraya Belitsa. Vitsyebskaya Voblasts', NE Belarus
129 R5 **Staraya Mayna** Ul'yanovskaya Oblast', W Russian Federation
119 O18 **Staraya Rudnya** *Rus.* Staraya Rudnya. Homyel'skaya Voblasts', SE Belarus
126 H14 **Staraya Russa** Novgorodskaya Oblast', W Russian Federation
114 K10 **Stara Zagora** *Lat.* Augusta Trajana. Stara Zagora, C Bulgaria
116 K10 **Stara Zagora** ◈ *province* C Bulgaria
29 S8 **Starbuck** Minnesota, N USA
191 W4 **Starbuck Island** *prev.* Volunteer Island. *island* E Kiribati
27 V13 **Star City** Arkansas, C USA
112 F13 **Staretina** ▲▲ W Bosnia and Herzegovina
Stargard in Pommern *see* Stargard Szczeciński
110 E9 **Stargard Szczeciński** *Ger.* Stargard in Pommern. Zachodniopomorskie, NW Poland
187 N10 **Star Harbour** *harbor* San Cristobal, SE Solomon Islands
Stari Bečej *see* Bečej
113 F15 **Stari Grad** *It.* Cittavecchia. Split-Dalmacija, S Croatia
126 J16 **Staritsa** Tverskaya Oblast', W Russian Federation
23 V9 **Starke** Florida, SE USA
22 M4 **Starkville** Mississippi, S USA
186 B7 **Star Mountains** *Ind.* Pegunungan Sterren. ▲▲ Indonesia/PNG
101 L23 **Starnberg** Bayern, SE Germany
101 L24 **Starnberger See** ◎ SE Germany
Starobel'sk *see* Starobil's'k
117 X8 **Starobesheve** Donets'ka Oblast', E Ukraine
117 Y6 **Starobil's'k** *Rus.* Starobel'sk. Luhans'ka Oblast', E Ukraine
Starobin *see* Starobyn
119 K18 **Starobyn** *Rus.* Starobin. Minskaya Voblasts', S Belarus
128 H6 **Starodub** Bryanskaya Oblast', W Russian Federation
110 I8 **Starogard Gdański** *Ger.* Preussisch-Stargard. Pomorskie, N Poland
145 P16 **Staroikan** Yuzhnyy Kazakhstan, S Kazakhstan
Starokonstantinov *see* Starokostyantyniv
116 L5 **Starokostyantyniv** *Rus.* Starokonstantinov. Khmel'nyts'ka Oblast', NW Ukraine
128 K12 **Starominskaya** Krasnodarskiy Kray, SW Russian Federation
114 L7 **Staro Selo** *Rom.* Satul-Vechi; *prev.* Star-Smil. Silistra, NE Bulgaria
128 K12 **Staroshcherbinovskaya** Krasnodarskiy Kray, SW Russian Federation
129 V6 **Starosubkhangulovo** Respublika Bashkortostan, W Russian Federation
35 S4 **Star Peak** ▲ Nevada, W USA
Star-Smil *see* Staro Selo
97 J25 **Start Point** *headland* SW England, UK
Startsy *see* Kirawsk
Starum *see* Stavoren
119 L18 **Staryya Darohi** *Rus.* Staryye Dorogi. Minskaya Voblasts', S Belarus
Staryye Dorogi *see* Staryya Darohi
129 T2 **Staryye Zyatsy** Udmurtskaya Respublika, NW Russian Federation
117 U13 **Staryy Krym** Respublika Krym, S Ukraine
128 K8 **Staryy Oskol** Belgorodskaya Oblast', W Russian Federation
116 H6 **Staryy Sambir** L'vivs'ka Oblast', W Ukraine
101 L14 **Stassfurt** *var.* Staßfurt. Sachsen-Anhalt, C Germany
111 M15 **Staszów** Świętokrzyskie, C Poland
29 W13 **State Center** Iowa, C USA
18 E14 **State College** Pennsylvania, NE USA
18 K15 **Staten Island** *island* New York, NE USA
Staten Island *see* Estados, Isla de los
23 U8 **Statenville** Georgia, SE USA
23 W5 **Statesboro** Georgia, SE USA
States, The *see* United States of America
21 R9 **Statesville** North Carolina, SE USA
95 G16 **Stathelle** Telemark, S Norway
30 K15 **Staunton** Illinois, N USA
21 T5 **Staunton** Virginia, NE USA
95 C16 **Stavanger** Rogaland, S Norway
99 L21 **Stavelot** *Dut.* Stablo. Liège, E Belgium
95 G16 **Stavern** Vestfold, S Norway
Stavers Island *see* Vostok Island
98 J7 **Stavoren** *Fris.* Starum. Friesland, N Netherlands
128 M14 **Stavropol'** *prev.* Voroshilovsk. Stavropol'skiy Kray, SW Russian Federation
Stavropol' *see* Tol'yatti
128 M14 **Stavropol'skaya Vozvyshennost'** ▲▲ SW Russian Federation
128 M14 **Stavropol'skiy Kray** ◈ *territory* SW Russian Federation
115 H14 **Stavrós** Kentrikí Makedonía, N Greece
115 J24 **Stavrós, Akrotírio** *headland* Kríti, Greece, E Mediterranean Sea
115 K21 **Stavrós, Akrotírio** *headland* Náxos, Kykládes, Greece, Aegean Sea
114 I12 **Stavroúpoli** *prev.* Stavroúpolis. Anatolikí Makedonía kai Thráki, NE Greece
Stavroúpolis *see* Stavroúpoli
117 O6 **Stavyshche** Kyyivs'ka Oblast', N Ukraine
182 M11 **Stawell** Victoria, SE Australia
110 N9 **Stawiski** Podlaskie, NE Poland
14 G14 **Stayner** Ontario, S Canada
37 R3 **Steamboat Springs** Colorado, C USA
20 M8 **Stearns** Kentucky, S USA
39 N10 **Stebbins** Alaska, USA
108 K7 **Steeg** Tirol, W Austria
27 Y9 **Steele** Missouri, C USA
29 N5 **Steele** North Dakota, N USA
194 J5 **Steele Island** *island* Antarctica
30 K16 **Steeleville** Illinois, N USA
27 W6 **Steelville** Missouri, C USA
99 G14 **Steenbergen** Noord-Brabant, S Netherlands
Steenkool *see* Bintuni
11 O10 **Steen River** Alberta, W Canada
98 M8 **Steenwijk** Overijssel, N Netherlands
65 A23 **Steeple Jason** *island* Jason Islands, NW Falkland Islands
174 J8 **Steep Point** *headland* Western Australia
116 L9 **Ştefăneşti** Botoşani, NE Romania
Stefanie, Lake *see* Ch'ew Bahir
8 L5 **Stefansson Island** *island* Nunavut, N Canada
117 O10 **Ştefan Vodă** *Rus.* Suvorovo. SE Moldova
63 H18 **Steffen, Cerro** ▲ S Chile
108 D9 **Steffisburg** Bern, C Switzerland
95 J24 **Stege** Storstrøm, SE Denmark
116 G10 **Ştei** *Hung.* Vaskohsziklás. Bihor, W Romania
Steier *see* Steyr
Steierdorf/Steierdorf-Anina *see* Anina
109 T7 **Steiermark** *off.* Land Steiermark, *Eng.* Styria. ◈ *state* C Austria
101 J19 **Steigerwald** *hill range* C Germany
99 L17 **Stein** Limburg, SE Netherlands
Stein *see* Stein an der Donau, Austria
Stein *see* Kamnik, Slovenia
108 M8 **Steinach** Tirol, W Austria
Steinamanger *see* Szombathely
109 W3 **Stein an der Donau** *var.* Stein. Niederösterreich, NE Austria
Steinau an der Elbe *see* Ścinawa
11 Y16 **Steinbach** Manitoba, S Canada
Steiner Alpen *see* Kamniško-Savinjske Alpe
99 L24 **Steinfort** Luxembourg, W Luxembourg
100 H12 **Steinhuder Meer** ◎ NW Germany
93 E15 **Steinkjer** Nord-Trøndelag, C Norway
Stejarul *see* Karapelit
99 F16 **Stekene** Oost-Vlaanderen, NW Belgium
83 E26 **Stellenbosch** Western Cape, SW South Africa
98 F13 **Stellendam** Zuid-Holland, SW Netherlands
39 T12 **Steller, Mount** ▲ Alaska, USA
103 Y14 **Stello, Monte** ▲ Corse, France, C Mediterranean Sea
106 F5 **Stelvio, Passo dello** *pass* Italy/Switzerland
103 R3 **Stenay** Meuse, NE France
100 L12 **Stendal** Sachsen-Anhalt, C Germany
118 E8 **Stende** Talsi, NW Latvia
182 H10 **Stenhouse Bay** South Australia
95 J23 **Stenløse** Frederiksborg, E Denmark
95 L19 **Stensjön** Jönköping, S Sweden
95 K18 **Stenstorp** Västra Götaland, S Sweden
95 I18 **Stenungsund** Västra Götaland, S Sweden
Stepanakert *see* Xankändi
137 T11 **Step'anavan** N Armenia
100 K9 **Stepenitz** ≈ N Germany
29 O10 **Stephan** South Dakota, N USA
29 R3 **Stephen** Minnesota, N USA
27 T14 **Stephens** Arkansas, C USA
184 J13 **Stephens, Cape** *headland* D'Urville Island, Marlborough, SW NZ
21 V3 **Stephens City** Virginia, NE USA
182 L6 **Stephens Creek** New South Wales, SE Australia
184 K13 **Stephens Island** *island* C NZ
31 N5 **Stephenson** Michigan, N USA
13 S12 **Stephenville** Newfoundland, SE Canada
25 S7 **Stephenville** Texas, SW USA
145 P17 **Step' Nardara** *Kaz.* Shardara Dalasy; *prev.* Shaidara. *grassland* S Kazakhstan
145 R8 **Stepnogorsk** Akmola, C Kazakhstan
129 O15 **Stepnoye** Stavropol'skiy Kray, SW Russian Federation
145 Q8 **Stepnyak** Severnyy Kazakhstan, N Kazakhstan
192 J17 **Steps Point** *headland* Tutuila, W American Samoa
115 F17 **Stereá Ellás** *Eng.* Greece Central. ◈ *region* C Greece
83 J24 **Sterkspruit** Eastern Cape, SE South Africa
129 U6 **Sterlibashevo** Respublika Bashkortostan, W Russian Federation
39 R12 **Sterling** Alaska, USA
37 V3 **Sterling** Colorado, C USA
30 K11 **Sterling** Illinois, N USA
26 M5 **Sterling** Kansas, C USA
25 O8 **Sterling City** Texas, SW USA
31 S9 **Sterling Heights** Michigan, N USA
21 W3 **Sterling Park** Virginia, NE USA
37 V2 **Sterling Reservoir** ▣ Colorado, C USA
22 I5 **Sterlington** Louisiana, S USA
129 U6 **Sterlitamak** Respublika Bashkortostan, W Russian Federation
Sternberg *see* Šternberk
111 H17 **Šternberk** *Ger.* Sternberg. Olomoucký Kraj, E Czech Republic
141 V17 **Stĕroh** Suquṭrā, S Yemen
110 G11 **Stęszew** Wielkolpolskie, C Poland
Stettin *see* Szczecin
Stettiner Haff *see* Szczeciński, Zalew
11 Q15 **Stettler** Alberta, SW Canada
31 V13 **Steubenville** Ohio, N USA
97 O21 **Stevenage** E England, UK
23 Q1 **Stevenson** Alabama, S USA
32 H11 **Stevenson** Washington, NW USA
182 E1 **Stevenson Creek** *seasonal river* South Australia
39 Q13 **Stevenson Entrance** *strait* Alaska, USA
30 L6 **Stevens Point** Wisconsin, N USA
39 R8 **Stevens Village** Alaska, USA
33 P10 **Stevensville** Montana, NW USA
93 E25 **Stevns Klint** *headland* E Denmark
10 J12 **Stewart** British Columbia, W Canada
10 J6 **Stewart** ≈ Yukon Territory, NW Canada
10 I6 **Stewart Crossing** Yukon Territory, NW Canada
63 H25 **Stewart, Isla** *island* S Chile
185 B25 **Stewart Island** *island* S NZ
181 W6 **Stewart, Mount** ▲ Queensland, E Australia
10 H6 **Stewart River** Yukon Territory, NW Canada
27 R3 **Stewartsville** Missouri, C USA
11 S16 **Stewart Valley** Saskatchewan, S Canada
29 W10 **Stewartville** Minnesota, N USA
Steyerlak-Anina *see* Anina
109 T5 **Steyr** *var.* Steier. Oberösterreich, N Austria
109 T5 **Steyr** ≈ NW Austria
29 P11 **Stickney** South Dakota, N USA
98 L5 **Stiens** Friesland, N Netherlands
Stif *see* Sétif
27 Q11 **Stigler** Oklahoma, C USA
107 N18 **Stigliano** Basilicata, S Italy
95 N17 **Stigtomta** Södermanland, C Sweden
10 I11 **Stikine** ≈ British Columbia, W Canada
Stilida/Stilís *see* Stylída
95 G22 **Stilling** Århus, C Denmark
29 W8 **Stillwater** Minnesota, N USA
27 O9 **Stillwater** Oklahoma, C USA
35 S5 **Stillwater Range** ▲▲ Nevada, W USA
18 I8 **Stillwater Reservoir** ▣ New York, NE USA
107 O22 **Stilo, Punta** *headland* S Italy
27 R10 **Stilwell** Oklahoma, C USA
113 N17 **Štimlje** Serbia, S Yugoslavia
25 N1 **Stinnett** Texas, SW USA
113 P18 **Štip** E FYR Macedonia
Stira *see* Stýra
96 J12 **Stirling** C Scotland, UK
96 I12 **Stirling** *cultural region* C Scotland, UK
180 J14 **Stirling Range** ▲▲ Western Australia
93 E16 **Stjørdal** Nord-Trøndelag, C Norway
Stochód *see* Stokhid
101 H24 **Stockach** Baden-Württemberg, S Germany
25 S12 **Stockdale** Texas, SW USA
109 X3 **Stockerau** Niederösterreich, NE Austria
93 H20 **Stockholm** ● (Sweden) Stockholm, C Sweden
95 O15 **Stockholm** ◈ *county* C Sweden
Stockmannshof *see* Pļaviņas
97 L18 **Stockport** NW England, UK
65 K15 **Stocks Seamount** *undersea feature* C Atlantic Ocean
35 O8 **Stockton** California, W USA
26 L3 **Stockton** Kansas, C USA
27 S6 **Stockton** Missouri, C USA
30 K3 **Stockton Island** *island* Apostle Islands, Wisconsin, N USA
27 S7 **Stockton Lake** ▣ Missouri, C USA
97 M15 **Stockton-on-Tees** *var.* Stockton on Tees. N England, UK
24 M10 **Stockton Plateau** *plain* Texas, SW USA
28 M16 **Stockville** Nebraska, C USA
93 H17 **Stöde** Västernorrland, C Sweden
Stodolichi *see* Stadolichy
167 S11 **Stœng Trêng** *prev.* Stung Treng. Stœng Trêng, NE Cambodia
113 M19 **Stogovo Karaorman** ▲▲ W FYR Macedonia
Stoke *see* Stoke-on-Trent
97 L19 **Stoke-on-Trent** *var.* Stoke. C England, UK
182 M15 **Stokes Point** *headland* Tasmania, SE Australia
116 J2 **Stokhid** *Pol.* Stochód, *Rus.* Stokhod. ≈ NW Ukraine
Stokhod *see* Stokhid
92 I4 **Stokkseyri** Sudhurland, SW Iceland
92 G10 **Stokmarknes** Nordland, C Norway
Stol *see* Veliki Krš
113 H15 **Stolac** Federacija Bosna I Hercegovina, S Bosnia and Herzegovina
Stolbce *see* Stowbtsy
101 D16 **Stolberg** *var.* Stolberg im Rheinland. Nordrhein-Westfalen, W Germany
Stolberg im Rheinland *see* Stolberg
123 P6 **Stolbovoy, Ostrov** *island* NE Russian Federation
Stolbtsy *see* Stowbtsy
119 J20 **Stolin** *Rus.* Stolin. Brestskaya Voblasts', SW Belarus
95 K14 **Stöllet** *var.* Norra Ny. Värmland, C Sweden
Stolp *see* Słupsk
Stolpe *see* Słupia
Stolpmünde *see* Ustka
115 F15 **Stómio** Thessalía, C Greece
14 J11 **Stonecliffe** Ontario, SE Canada
96 L10 **Stonehaven** NE Scotland, UK
97 M23 **Stonehenge** *ancient monument* Wiltshire, S England, UK

◆ Country ● Country Capital ◇ Dependent Territory ○ Dependent Territory Capital ◈ Administrative Region ✕ International Airport ▲ Mountain ▲▲ Mountain Range Volcano ≈ River ◎ Lake ▣ Reservoir

23 T3 **Stone Mountain** ▲ Georgia, SE USA
11 X16 **Stonewall** Manitoba, S Canada
21 S3 **Stonewood** West Virginia, NE USA
14 D17 **Stoney Point** Ontario, S Canada
92 H10 **Stonglandseidet** Troms, N Norway
65 N25 **Stonybeach Bay** *bay* Tristan da Cunha, SE Atlantic Ocean
35 N5 **Stony Creek** ≈ California, W USA
65 N25 **Stonyhill Point** *headland* S Tristan da Cunha
14 I14 **Stony Lake** ◎ Ontario, SE Canada
11 Q14 **Stony Plain** Alberta, SW Canada
21 R9 **Stony Point** North Carolina, SE USA
18 G8 **Stony Point** *headland* New York, NE USA
11 T10 **Stony Rapids** Saskatchewan, C Canada
39 P11 **Stony River** Alaska, USA
Stony Tunguska *see* Podkamennaya Tunguska
12 G10 **Stooping** ≈ Ontario, C Canada
100 I9 **Stör** ≈ N Germany
95 M15 **Storå** Örebro, S Sweden
95 J16 **Stora Gla** ◎ C Sweden
95 I16 **Stora Le** *Nor.* Store Le. ◎ Norway/Sweden
92 I12 **Stora Lulevatten** ◎ N Sweden
92 H13 **Storavan** ◎ N Sweden
93 I20 **Storby** Åland, SW Finland
94 E10 **Stordalen** Møre og Romsdal, S Norway
Storebelt *see* Storebælt
95 H23 **Storebælt** *var.* Store Bælt, *Eng.* Great Belt, Storebelt. *channel* Baltic Sea/Kattegat
95 M19 **Storebro** Kalmar, S Sweden
95 J24 **Store Heddinge** Storstrøm, SE Denmark
Store Le *see* Stora Le
93 E16 **Støren** Sør-Trøndelag, S Norway
95 B14 **Store Sotra** *island* S Norway
92 O4 **Storfjorden** *fjord* S Norway
95 L15 **Storfors** Värmland, C Sweden
92 G13 **Storforshei** Nordland, C Norway
Storhammer *see* Hamar
100 L10 **Störkanal** *canal* N Germany
93 F16 **Storlien** Jämtland, C Sweden
183 P17 **Storm Bay** *inlet* Tasmania, SE Australia
29 T12 **Storm Lake** Iowa, C USA
29 S13 **Storm Lake** ◎ Iowa, C USA
96 G7 **Stornoway** NW Scotland, UK
Storojineţ *see* Storozhynets'
92 P1 **Storøya** *island* NE Svalbard
127 S10 **Storozhevsk** Respublika Komi, NW Russian Federation
Storozhinets *see* Storozhynets'
116 K8 **Storozhynets'** *Ger.* Storozynetz, *Rom.* Storojineţ, *Rus.* Storozhinets. Chernivets'ka Oblast', W Ukraine
Storozynetz *see* Storozhynets'
92 H11 **Storriten** ▲ C Norway
19 N12 **Storrs** Connecticut, NE USA
94 I11 **Storsjøen** ◎ S Norway
94 N13 **Storsjön** ◎ C Sweden
93 F16 **Storsjön** ◎ C Sweden
92 J9 **Storslett** Troms, N Norway
92 I9 **Storsteinnes** Troms, N Norway
95 I24 **Storstrøm** *off.* Storstrøms Amt. ⬖ *county* SE Denmark
93 J14 **Storsund** Norrbotten, N Sweden
95 F16 **Storsylen** ▲ S Norway
92 H11 **Stortoppen** ▲ N Sweden
93 H14 **Storuman** Västerbotten, N Sweden
93 H14 **Storuman** ◎ N Sweden
94 N13 **Storvik** Gävleborg, C Sweden
95 O14 **Storvreta** Uppsala, C Sweden
29 V13 **Story City** Iowa, C USA
11 V17 **Stoughton** Saskatchewan, S Canada
19 O11 **Stoughton** Massachusetts, NE USA
30 L9 **Stoughton** Wisconsin, N USA
97 L23 **Stour** ≈ E England, UK
97 P21 **Stour** ≈ S England, UK
27 T5 **Stover** Missouri, C USA
95 G21 **Støvring** Nordjylland, N Denmark
119 J17 **Stowbtsy** *Pol.* Stołbce, *Rus.* Stolbtsy. Minskaya Voblasts', C Belarus
25 X11 **Stowell** Texas, SW USA
97 P20 **Stowmarket** E England, UK
114 N8 **Stozher** Dobrich, NE Bulgaria
97 E14 **Strabane** *Ir.* An Srath Bán. W Northern Ireland, UK
121 S11 **Strabo Trench** *undersea feature* C Mediterranean Sea
27 T7 **Strafford** Missouri, C USA
183 N17 **Strahan** Tasmania, SE Australia
111 C18 **Strakonice** *Ger.* Strakonitz. Budějovický Kraj, S Czech Republic
Strakonitz *see* Strakonice
100 N8 **Stralsund** Mecklenburg-Vorpommern, NE Germany
99 L16 **Stramproy** Limburg, SE Netherlands
83 E26 **Strand** Western Cape, SW South Africa
94 E10 **Stranda** Møre og Romsdal, S Norway
97 G15 **Strangford Lough** *Ir.* Loch Cuan. *inlet* E Northern Ireland, UK
95 N16 **Strängnäs** Södermanland, C Sweden
97 E14 **Stranorlar** *Ir.* Srath an Urláir. NW Ireland
97 H14 **Stranraer** S Scotland, UK
11 U16 **Strasbourg** Saskatchewan, S Canada
103 V5 **Strasbourg** *Ger.* Strassburg; *anc.* Argentoratum. Bas-Rhin, NE France
37 U4 **Strasburg** Colorado, C USA
29 N7 **Strasburg** North Dakota, N USA
31 U12 **Strasburg** Ohio, N USA
21 U3 **Strasburg** Virginia, NE USA
117 N10 **Strășeni** *var.* Strasheny. C Moldova
Strasheny *see* Strășeni
109 T8 **Strassburg** Kärnten, S Austria
Strassburg *see* Strasbourg, France
Strassburg *see* Aiud, Romania
99 M25 **Strassen** Luxembourg, S Luxembourg
109 R5 **Strasswalchen** Salzburg, C Austria
14 F16 **Stratford** Ontario, S Canada
184 K10 **Stratford** Taranaki, North Island, NZ
35 Q11 **Stratford** California, W USA
29 V13 **Stratford** Iowa, C USA
27 O12 **Stratford** Oklahoma, C USA
25 N1 **Stratford** Texas, SW USA
30 K6 **Stratford** Wisconsin, N USA
Stratford *see* Stratford-upon-Avon
97 M20 **Stratford-upon-Avon** *var.* Stratford. C England, UK
183 O17 **Strathgordon** Tasmania, SE Australia
11 Q16 **Strathmore** Alberta, SW Canada
35 R11 **Strathmore** California, W USA
14 E16 **Strathroy** Ontario, S Canada
96 I6 **Strathy Point** *headland* N Scotland, UK
37 W4 **Stratton** Colorado, C USA
19 P6 **Stratton** Maine, NE USA
18 M10 **Stratton Mountain** ▲ Vermont, NE USA
101 N21 **Straubing** Bayern, SE Germany
100 O12 **Strausberg** Brandenburg, E Germany
32 K13 **Strawberry Mountain** ▲ Oregon, NW USA
29 X12 **Strawberry Point** Iowa, C USA
36 M3 **Strawberry Reservoir** ▣ Utah, W USA
36 M4 **Strawberry River** ≈ Utah, W USA
25 R7 **Strawn** Texas, SW USA
113 P17 **Straža** ▲ Bulgaria/FYR Macedonia
111 I19 **Strážov** *Hung.* Sztrazsó. ▲ NW Slovakia
182 F7 **Streaky Bay** South Australia
182 E7 **Streaky Bay** *bay* South Australia
30 L12 **Streator** Illinois, N USA
Streckenbach *see* Świdnik
111 C17 **Středočeský kraj** ⬖ *region* C Czech Republic
Strednogorie *see* Pirdop
29 O6 **Streeter** North Dakota, N USA
25 U8 **Streetman** Texas, SW USA
116 G13 **Strehaia** Mehedinţi, SW Romania
Strehlen *see* Strzelin
114 I10 **Strelcha** Pazardzhik, C Bulgaria
122 L12 **Strelka** Krasnoyarskiy Kray, C Russian Federation
126 L6 **Strel'na** ≈ NW Russian Federation
118 H7 **Strenči** *Ger.* Stackeln. Valka, N Latvia
108 K8 **Strengen** Tirol, W Austria
106 C6 **Stresa** Piemonte, NE Italy
Streshin *see* Streshyn
119 N18 **Streshyn** *Rus.* Streshin. Homyel'skaya Voblasts', SE Belarus
95 B18 **Streymoy** *Dan.* Strømø *Island* Faeroe Islands
95 G23 **Strib** Fyn, C Denmark
111 A17 **Stříbro** *Ger.* Mies. Plzeňský Kraj, W Czech Republic
186 B7 **Strickland** ≈ SW PNG
Striegau *see* Strzegom
Strigonium *see* Esztergom
98 H13 **Strijen** Zuid-Holland, SW Netherlands
63 H21 **Strobel, Lago** ◎ S Argentina
61 B25 **Stroeder** Buenos Aires, E Argentina
115 C20 **Strofádes** *island* Iónioi Nísoi, Greece, C Mediterranean Sea
Strofilia *see* Strofyliá
115 G17 **Strofyliá** *var.* Strofilia. Évvoia, C Greece
100 O10 **Strom** ≈ NE Germany
107 L22 **Stromboli** ⛰ Isola Stromboli, SW Italy
107 L22 **Stromboli, Isola** *island* Isole Eolie, S Italy
96 H9 **Stromeferry** N Scotland, UK
96 J5 **Stromness** N Scotland, UK
94 N11 **Strömsbruk** Gävleborg, C Sweden
29 Q15 **Stromsburg** Nebraska, C USA
95 K21 **Strömsnäsbruk** Kronoberg, S Sweden
95 I17 **Strömstad** Västra Götaland, S Sweden
93 G16 **Strömsund** Jämtland, C Sweden
93 G15 **Ströms Vattudal** *valley* N Sweden
27 V14 **Strong** Arkansas, C USA
Strongilí *see* Strongylí
107 O21 **Strongoli** Calabria, SW Italy
31 T11 **Strongsville** Ohio, N USA
115 Q23 **Strongylí** *var.* Strongilí. *island* SE Greece
96 K5 **Stronsay** *island* NE Scotland, UK
97 L21 **Stroud** C England, UK
27 O10 **Stroud** Oklahoma, C USA
18 I14 **Stroudsburg** Pennsylvania, NE USA
95 F21 **Struer** Ringkøbing, W Denmark
113 M20 **Struga** SW FYR Macedonia
Strugi-Kranyse *see* Strugi-Krasnyye
126 G14 **Strugi-Krasnyye** *var.* Strugi-Kranyse. Pskovskaya Oblast', W Russian Federation
114 G11 **Struma** *Gk.* Strymónas. ≈ Bulgaria/Greece *see also* Strymónas
97 G21 **Strumble Head** *headland* SW Wales, UK
113 Q19 **Strumeshnitsa** *Mac.* Strumica. ≈ Bulgaria/FYR Macedonia
113 Q19 **Strumica** E FYR Macedonia
Strumica *see* Strumeshnitsa
114 G11 **Strumyani** Blagoevgrad, SW Bulgaria
31 V12 **Struthers** Ohio, N USA
114 I10 **Stryama** ≈ C Bulgaria
114 G13 **Strymónas** *Bul.* Struma. ≈ Bulgaria/Greece *see also* Struma
115 H14 **Strymonikós Kólpos** *gulf* N Greece
116 I6 **Stryy** L'vivs'ka Oblast', NW Ukraine
116 H6 **Stryy** ≈ W Ukraine
111 F14 **Strzegom** *Ger.* Striegau. Wałbrzych, SW Poland
110 E10 **Strzelce Krajeńskie** *Ger.* Friedeberg Neumark. Lubuskie, W Poland
111 I15 **Strzelce Opolskie** *Ger.* Gross Strehlitz. Opolskie, S Poland
182 K3 **Strzelecki Creek** *seasonal river* South Australia
182 J3 **Strzelecki Desert** *desert* South Australia
111 G15 **Strzelin** *Ger.* Strehlen. Dolnośląskie, SW Poland
110 I11 **Strzelno** Kujawsko-pomorskie, C Poland
111 N17 **Strzyżów** Podkarpackie, SE Poland
Stua Laighean *see* Leinster, Mount
23 Y13 **Stuart** Florida, SE USA
29 U14 **Stuart** Iowa, C USA
29 O13 **Stuart** Nebraska, C USA
21 S8 **Stuart** Virginia, NE USA
10 L13 **Stuart** ≈ British Columbia, SW Canada
39 N10 **Stuart Island** *island* Alaska, USA
10 L13 **Stuart Lake** ◎ British Columbia, SW Canada
185 B22 **Stuart Mountains** ▲ South Island, NZ
182 F3 **Stuart Range** *hill range* South Australia
Stubaital *see* Neustift im Stubaital
95 I24 **Stubbekøbing** Storstrøm, SE Denmark
45 P14 **Stubbs** Saint Vincent, Saint Vincent and the Grenadines
109 V6 **Stübming** ≈ E Austria
114 J11 **Studen Kladenets, Yazovir** ▣ S Bulgaria
185 G21 **Studholme** Canterbury, South Island, NZ
Stuhlweissenberg *see* Székesfehérvár
Stuhm *see* Sztum
12 C7 **Stull Lake** ◎ Ontario, C Canada
Stung Treng *see* Stœng Trêng
128 L4 **Stupino** Moskovskaya Oblast', W Russian Federation
27 U4 **Sturgeon** Missouri, C USA
14 G10 **Sturgeon** ≈ Ontario, S Canada
31 N6 **Sturgeon Bay** Wisconsin, N USA
14 G11 **Sturgeon Falls** Ontario, S Canada
12 C11 **Sturgeon Lake** ◎ Ontario, S Canada
30 M3 **Sturgeon River** ≈ Michigan, N USA
20 H6 **Sturgis** Kentucky, S USA
31 P11 **Sturgis** Michigan, N USA
28 J9 **Sturgis** South Dakota, N USA
112 D10 **Šturlić** Federacija Bosna I Hercegovina, NW Bosnia and Herzegovina
111 J22 **Štúrovo** *Hung.* Párkány; *prev.* Parkan. Nitriansky Kraj, W Slovakia
182 L4 **Sturt, Mount** *hill* New South Wales, SE Australia
181 P4 **Sturt Plain** *plain* Northern Territory, N Australia
181 T9 **Sturt Stony Desert** *desert* South Australia
83 J25 **Stutterheim** Eastern Cape, S South Africa
101 H21 **Stuttgart** Baden-Württemberg, SW Germany
27 W12 **Stuttgart** Arkansas, C USA
92 H2 **Stykkishólmur** Vesturland, W Iceland
115 F17 **Stylída** *var.* Stilida, Stilís. Stereá Ellás, C Greece
116 K2 **Styr** *Rus.* Styr'. ≈ Belarus/Ukraine
115 I19 **Stýra** *var.* Stira. Évvoia, C Greece
Styria *see* Steiermark
Su *see* Jiangsu
Sua *see* Sowa
171 Q17 **Suai** W East Timor
54 G9 **Suaita** Santander, C Colombia
80 I7 **Suakin** *var.* Sawakin. Red Sea, NE Sudan
161 T13 **Suao** *Jap.* Suō. N Taiwan
Suao *see* Suau
40 G6 **Suaqui Grande** Sonora, NW Mexico
61 A16 **Suardi** Santa Fe, C Argentina
54 D11 **Suárez** Cauca, SW Colombia
186 G10 **Suau** *var.* Suao. Suaul Island, SE PNG
118 G12 **Subačius** Kupiškis, NE Lithuania
168 K9 **Subang** *prev.* Soebang. Jawa, C Indonesia
169 O16 **Subang** ✕ (Kuala Lumpur) Pahang, Peninsular Malaysia
131 S10 **Subansiri** ≈ NE India
118 I11 **Subate** Daugvapils, SE Latvia
139 N5 **Subaykhān** Dayr az Zawr, E Syria
159 P8 **Subei** *var.* Dangchengwan, Subei Mongolzu Zizhixian. Gansu, N China
Subei Mongolzu Zizhixian *see* Subei
169 P9 **Subi Besar, Pulau** *island* Kepulauan Natuna, W Indonesia
Subiyah *see* Aş Şubayḩīyah
26 I7 **Sublette** Kansas, C USA
112 K8 **Subotica** *Ger.* Maria-Theresiopel, *Hung.* Szabadka. Serbia, N Yugoslavia
116 K9 **Suceava** *Ger.* Suczawa, *Hung.* Szucsava. Suceava, NE Romania
116 J9 **Suceava** ⬖ *county* NE Romania
116 K9 **Suceava** *Ger.* Suczawa. ≈ N Romania
112 E12 **Sučevići** Zadar, SW Croatia
111 K17 **Sucha Beskidzka** Małopolskie, S Poland
111 M14 **Suchedniów** Świętokrzyskie, C Poland
42 A2 **Suchitepéquez** *off.* Departamento de Suchitepéquez. ⬖ *department* SW Guatemala
Su-chou *see* Suzhou
Suchow *see* Suzhou, Jiangsu, China
Suchow *see* Xuzhou, Jiangsu, China
97 D17 **Suck** ≈ C Ireland
Sucker State *see* Illinois
186 F9 **Suckling, Mount** ▲ S PNG
57 L19 **Sucre** *hist.* Chuquisaca, La Plata. ● (Bolivia-legal capital) Chuquisaca, S Bolivia
54 E6 **Sucre** Santander, N Colombia
56 A7 **Sucre** Manabí, W Ecuador
54 E6 **Sucre** *off.* Departamento de Sucre. ⬖ *province* N Colombia
55 O5 **Sucre** *off.* Estado Sucre. ⬖ *state* NE Venezuela
56 D6 **Sucumbíos** ⬖ *province* NE Ecuador
113 G15 **Sućuraj** Split-Dalmacija, S Croatia
58 K10 **Sucuriju** Amapá, NE Brazil
Suczawa *see* Suceava
79 E16 **Sud** *Eng.* South. ⬖ *province* S Cameroon
126 K13 **Suda** ≈ NW Russian Federation
Suda *see* Soúda
117 U13 **Sudak** Respublika Krym, S Ukraine
24 M4 **Sudan** Texas, SW USA
80 C10 **Sudan** *off.* Republic of Sudan, *Ar.* Jumhuriyat as-Sudan; *prev.* Anglo-Egyptian Sudan. ◆ *republic* N Africa
Sudanese Republic *see* Mali
Sudan, Jumhuriyat as- *see* Sudan
14 F10 **Sudbury** Ontario, S Canada
97 P20 **Sudbury** E England, UK
Sud, Canal de *see* Gonâve, Canal de la
80 E13 **Sudd** *swamp region* S Sudan
100 K10 **Sude** ≈ N Germany
Sudest Island *see* Tagula Island
111 E15 **Sudeten** *var.* Sudetes, Sudetic Mountains, *Cz./Pol.* Sudety. ▲ Czech Republic/Poland
Sudetes/Sudetic Mountains/Sudety *see* Sudeten
92 G1 **Sudhureyri** Vestfirdhir, NW Iceland
92 J4 **Sudhurland** ⬖ *region* S Iceland
95 B19 **Sudhuroy** *Dan.* Suderø *Island* Faeroe Islands
126 M15 **Sudislavl'** Kostromskaya Oblast', NW Russian Federation
Südkarpaten *see* Carpaţii Meridionali
79 N20 **Sud Kivu** *off.* Région Sud Kivu. ⬖ *region* E Dem. Rep. Congo (Zaire)
Südliche Morava *see* Južna Morava
100 E12 **Süd-Nord-Kanal** *canal* NW Germany
128 M3 **Sudogda** Vladimirskaya Oblast', W Russian Federation
Sudostroy *see* Severodvinsk
79 C15 **Sud-Ouest** *Eng.* South-West. ⬖ *province* W Cameroon
173 X17 **Sud Ouest, Pointe** *headland* SW Mauritius
187 P17 **Sud, Province** ⬖ *province* S New Caledonia
128 J8 **Sudzha** Kurskaya Oblast', W Russian Federation
81 D15 **Sue** ≈ S Sudan
105 S10 **Sueca** País Valenciano, E Spain
114 I10 **Sŭedinenie** Plovdiv, C Bulgaria
Suero *see* Alzira
75 X8 **Suez** *Ar.* As Suways, El Suweis. NE Egypt
75 W7 **Suez Canal** *Ar.* Qanāt as Suways. *canal* NE Egypt
75 X8 **Suez, Gulf of** *Ar.* Khalīj as Suways. *gulf* NE Egypt
11 R17 **Suffield** Alberta, SW Canada
21 X7 **Suffolk** Virginia, NE USA
97 P20 **Suffolk** *cultural region* E England, UK
142 J2 **Şūfīān** Āzarbāyjān-e Khāvarī, N Iran
31 N12 **Sugar Creek** ≈ Illinois, N USA
30 L13 **Sugar Creek** ≈ Illinois, N USA
31 R3 **Sugar Island** *island* Michigan, N USA
25 V11 **Sugar Land** Texas, SW USA
19 P6 **Sugarloaf Mountain** ▲ Maine, NE USA
65 G24 **Sugar Loaf Point** *headland* N Saint Helena
136 G16 **Suğla Gölü** ◎ SW Turkey
123 T8 **Sugoy** ≈ E Russian Federation
158 F7 **Sugun** Xinjiang Uygur Zizhiqu, W China
147 U11 **Sugut, Gora** ▲ SW Kyrgyzstan
169 V6 **Sugut, Sungai** ≈ East Malaysia
159 O9 **Suhai Hu** ◎ C China
162 K14 **Suhait** Nei Mongol Zizhiqu, N China
141 X7 **Şuḩār** *var.* Sohar. N Oman
162 L6 **Sühbaatar** Selenge, N Mongolia
163 P9 **Sühbaatar** ⬖ *province* E Mongolia
101 K17 **Suhl** Thüringen, C Germany
108 F7 **Suhr** Aargau, N Switzerland
161 O12 **Suichuan** Jiangxi, S China
Suid-Afrika *see* South Africa
160 L4 **Suide** Shaanxi, C China
Suidwes-Afrika *see* Namibia
163 Y9 **Suifenhe** Heilongjiang, NE China
Suigen *see* Suwŏn
163 W8 **Suihua** Heilongjiang, NE China
Súilí, Loch *see* Swilly, Lough
161 Q6 **Suining** Jiangsu, E China
160 I9 **Suining** Sichuan, C China
103 Q4 **Suippes** Marne, N France
97 E20 **Suir** *Ir.* An tSiúir. ≈ S Ireland
165 J13 **Suita** Ōsaka, Honshū, SW Japan
160 L16 **Suixi** Guangdong, S China
Sui Xian *see* Suizhou
163 T13 **Suizhong** Liaoning, NE China
161 N8 **Suizhou** *prev.* Sui Xian. Hubei, C China
149 P17 **Sujāwal** Sind, SE Pakistan
169 O16 **Sukabumi** *prev.* Soekaboemi. Jawa, C Indonesia
169 Q12 **Sukadana, Teluk** *bay* Borneo, W Indonesia
165 P11 **Sukagawa** Fukushima, Honshū, C Japan
Sukarnapura *see* Jayapura
Sukarno, Puntjak *see* Jaya, Puncak
147 R11 **Sūkh** *Rus.* Sokh. Farghona Wiloyati, E Uzbekistan
Sūkh *see* Sokh
114 N8 **Sukha Reka** ≈ NE Bulgaria
128 J5 **Sukhinichi** Kaluzhskaya Oblast', W Russian Federation
Sukhne *see* As Sukhnah
131 Q4 **Sukhona** *var.* Tot'ma. ≈ NW Russian Federation
167 O8 **Sukhothai** *var.* Sukotai. Sukhothai, W Thailand
Sukhumi *see* Sokhumi
Sukkertoppen *see* Maniitsoq
149 Q13 **Sukkur** Sind, SE Pakistan
Sukotai *see* Sukhothai
Sukra Bay *see* Şawqirah, Dawḩat
127 V15 **Suksun** Permskaya Oblast', NW Russian Federation
165 F15 **Sukumo** Kōchi, Shikoku, SW Japan
94 B12 **Sula** *island* S Norway
127 Q5 **Sula** ≈ NW Russian Federation
117 R5 **Sula** ≈ N Ukraine
42 H6 **Sulaco, Río** ≈ NW Honduras
Sulaimaniya *see* As Sulaymānīyah
149 S10 **Sulaimān Range** ▲ C Pakistan
129 Q16 **Sulak** Respublika Dagestan, SW Russian Federation
129 Q16 **Sulak** ≈ SW Russian Federation
171 Q13 **Sula, Kepulauan** *island group* C Indonesia
136 I12 **Sulakyurt** *var.* Konur. Kırıkkale, N Turkey
171 P17 **Sulamu** Timor, S Indonesia
96 F5 **Sula Sgeir** *island* NW Scotland, UK
171 N13 **Sulawesi** *Eng.* Celebes. *island* C Indonesia
Sulawesi, Laut *see* Celebes Sea
171 N14 **Sulawesi Selatan** *off.* Propinsi Sulawesi Selatan, *Eng.* South Celebes, South Sulawesi. ⬖ *province* C Indonesia
171 P12 **Sulawesi Tengah** *off.* Propinsi Sulawesi Tengah, *Eng.* Central Celebes, Central Sulawesi. ⬖ *province* N Indonesia
171 O14 **Sulawesi Tenggara** *off.* Propinsi Sulawesi Tenggara, *Eng.* South-East Celebes, South-East Sulawesi. ⬖ *province* C Indonesia
171 P11 **Sulawesi Utara** *off.* Propinsi Sulawesi Utara, *Eng.* North Celebes, North Sulawesi. ⬖ *province* N Indonesia
139 T5 **Sulaymān Beg** N Iraq
95 D15 **Suldalsvatnet** ◎ S Norway
110 E12 **Sulechów** *Ger.* Züllichau. Lubuskie, W Poland
110 E11 **Sulęcin** Lubuskie, W Poland
77 U14 **Suleja** Niger, C Nigeria
111 K14 **Sulejów** Łodzkie, S Poland
96 I5 **Sule Skerry** *island* N Scotland, UK
Suliag *see* Sohâg
76 J16 **Sulima** S Sierra Leone
117 O13 **Sulina** Tulcea, SE Romania
117 N13 **Sulina Bratul** ≈ SE Romania
100 H12 **Sulingen** Niedersachsen, NW Germany
92 H12 **Suliskongen** ▲ C Norway
92 H12 **Sulitjelma** Nordland, C Norway
56 A9 **Sullana** Piura, NW Peru
23 N3 **Sulligent** Alabama, S USA
30 M14 **Sullivan** Illinois, N USA
31 N15 **Sullivan** Indiana, N USA
27 W5 **Sullivan** Missouri, C USA
Sullivan Island *see* Lanbi Kyun
96 M1 **Sullom Voe** NE Scotland, UK
103 O7 **Sully-sur-Loire** Loiret, C France
Sulmo *see* Sulmona
107 K15 **Sulmona** *anc.* Sulmo. Abruzzo, C Italy
Sulo *see* Shule He
114 M11 **Süloğlu** Edirne, NW Turkey
22 G9 **Sulphur** Louisiana, S USA
27 O12 **Sulphur** Oklahoma, C USA
28 K9 **Sulphur Creek** ≈ South Dakota, N USA
24 M5 **Sulphur Draw** ≈ Texas, SW USA
25 W5 **Sulphur River** ≈ Arkansas/Texas, SW USA
25 V6 **Sulphur Springs** Texas, SW USA
24 M6 **Sulphur Springs Draw** ≈ Texas, SW USA
14 D8 **Sultan** Ontario, S Canada
Sultānābād *see* Arāk
Sultan Alonto, Lake *see* Lanao, Lake
136 G15 **Sultan Dağları** ▲ C Turkey
114 N13 **Sultanköy** Tekirdağ, NW Turkey
171 Q7 **Sultan Kudarat** *var.* Nuling. Mindanao, S Philippines
152 M13 **Sultānpur** Uttar Pradesh, N India
171 O9 **Sulu Archipelago** *island group* SW Philippines
192 F7 **Sulu Basin** *undersea feature* SE South China Sea
Sülüktü *see* Sulyukta
Sulu, Laut *see* Sulu Sea
169 X6 **Sulu Sea** *Ind.* Laut Sulu. *sea* SW Philippines
145 O15 **Sulutobe** *Kaz.* Sulūtöbe. Kzylorda, S Kazakhstan
147 Q11 **Sulyukta** *Kir.* Sülüktü. Oshskaya Oblast', SW Kyrgyzstan
Sulz *see* Sulz am Neckar
101 G22 **Sulz am Neckar** *var.* Sulz. Baden-Württemberg, SW Germany
101 L20 **Sulzbach-Rosenberg** Bayern, SE Germany
195 N13 **Sulzberger Bay** *bay* Antarctica
Sumail *see* Summēl
113 F15 **Šumartin** Split-Dalmacija, S Croatia
32 H6 **Sumas** Washington, NW USA
168 J10 **Sumatera** *Eng.* Sumatra. *island* W Indonesia
168 J12 **Sumatera Barat** *off.* Propinsi Sumatera Barat, *Eng.* West Sumatra. ⬖ *province* W Indonesia
168 L13 **Sumatera Selatan** *off.* Propinsi Sumatera Selatan, *Eng.* South Sumatra. ⬖ *province* W Indonesia
168 H10 **Sumatera Utara** *off.* Propinsi Sumatera Utara, *Eng.* North Sumatra. ⬖ *province* W Indonesia
Sumatra *see* Sumatera
Šumava *see* Bohemian Forest
Sumayl *see* Summēl
139 U7 **Sumayr al Muḩammad** E Iraq
171 N17 **Sumba, Pulau** *Eng.* Sandalwood Island; *prev.* Soemba. *island* Nusa Tenggara, C Indonesia
146 D12 **Sumbar** ≈ W Turkmenistan
192 E9 **Sumbawa** *prev.* Soembawa. *island* Nusa Tenggara, C Indonesia
170 L16 **Sumbawabesar** Sumbawa, S Indonesia
81 F23 **Sumbawanga** Rukwa, W Tanzania
82 B12 **Sumbe** *prev.* N'Gunza, *Port.* Novo Redondo. Cuanza Sul, W Angola
96 M3 **Sumburgh Head** *headland* NE Scotland, UK
111 H23 **Sümeg** Veszprém, W Hungary
80 C12 **Sumeih** Southern Darfur, S Sudan
169 T16 **Sumenep** *prev.* Soemenep. Pulau Madura, C Indonesia
Sumgait *see* Sumqayıt, Azerbaijan
Sumgait *see* Sumqayıtçay, Azerbaijan
165 Y14 **Sumisu-jima** *Eng.* Smith Island. *island* SE Japan
139 Q2 **Summēl** *var.* Sumail, Sumayl. N Iraq
31 O5 **Summer Island** *island* Michigan, N USA
32 H15 **Summer Lake** ◎ Oregon, NW USA
11 N17 **Summerland** British Columbia, SW Canada
13 P14 **Summerside** Prince Edward Island, SE Canada
21 R5 **Summersville** West Virginia, NE USA
21 R5 **Summersville Lake** ▣ West Virginia, NE USA
21 S13 **Summerton** South Carolina, SE USA
23 R2 **Summerville** Georgia, SE USA
21 S14 **Summerville** South Carolina, SE USA
39 R10 **Summit** Alaska, USA
35 V6 **Summit Mountain** ▲ Nevada, W USA
37 R8 **Summit Peak** ▲ Colorado, C USA
Summus Portus *see* Somport, Col du
29 X12 **Sumner** Iowa, C USA
22 K3 **Sumner** Mississippi, S USA
185 H17 **Sumner, Lake** ◎ South Island, NZ
37 U12 **Sumner, Lake** ▣ New Mexico, SW USA
111 G17 **Šumperk** *Ger.* Mährisch-Schönberg. Olomoucký Kraj, E Czech Republic
42 F7 **Sumpul, Río** ≈ El Salvador/Honduras
137 Z11 **Sumqayıt** *Rus.* Sumgait. E Azerbaijan
137 Y11 **Sumqayıtçay** *Rus.* Sumgait. ≈ E Azerbaijan
147 R9 **Sumsar** Dzhalal-Abadskaya Oblast', W Kyrgyzstan
117 S3 **Sums'ka Oblast'** *var.* Sumy, *Rus.* Sumskaya Oblast'. ⬖ *province* NE Ukraine
Sumskaya Oblast' *see* Sums'ka Oblast'
126 J8 **Sumskiy Posad** Respublika Kareliya, NW Russian Federation
21 S12 **Sumter** South Carolina, SE USA
117 T3 **Sumy** Sums'ka Oblast', NE Ukraine
Sumy *see* Sums'ka Oblast'
159 Q15 **Sumzom** Xizang Zizhiqu, W China
127 R15 **Suna** Kirovskaya Oblast', NW Russian Federation
126 I10 **Suna** ≈ NW Russian Federation
165 S3 **Sunagawa** Hokkaidō, NE Japan
153 V13 **Sunamganj** Chittagong, NE Bangladesh
159 S8 **Sunan** *var.* Hongwan, Sunan Yugurzu Zizhixian. Gansu, N China
163 W14 **Sunan** ✕ (P'yŏngyang) SW North Korea
Sunan Yugurzu Zizhixian *see* Sunan
19 N9 **Sunapee Lake** ◎ New Hampshire, NE USA
139 P4 **Sunaysilah** *salt marsh* N Iraq
20 M8 **Sunbright** Tennessee, S USA
33 R6 **Sunburst** Montana, NW USA
183 N12 **Sunbury** Victoria, SE Australia
21 X8 **Sunbury** North Carolina, SE USA
18 G14 **Sunbury** Pennsylvania, NE USA
61 A17 **Sunchales** Santa Fe, C Argentina
163 W13 **Sunch'ŏn** SW North Korea
163 Y16 **Sunch'ŏn** *Jap.* Junten. S South Korea

◆ COUNTRY
● COUNTRY CAPITAL
◇ DEPENDENT TERRITORY
○ DEPENDENT TERRITORY CAPITAL
⬖ ADMINISTRATIVE REGION
✕ INTERNATIONAL AIRPORT
▲ MOUNTAIN
▲ MOUNTAIN RANGE
⛰ VOLCANO
≈ RIVER
◎ LAKE
▣ RESERVOIR

36 *K13* **Sun City** Arizona, SW USA
19 *O9* **Suncook** New Hampshire, NE USA
Sunda Islands *see* Greater Sunda Islands
33 *Z12* **Sundance** Wyoming, C USA
153 *T17* **Sundarbans** *wetland* Bangladesh/India
154 *M11* **Sundargarh** Orissa, E India
131 *U15* **Sunda Shelf** *undersea feature* S South China Sea
Sunda Trench *see* Java Trench
131 *U17* **Sunda Trough** *undersea feature* E Indian Ocean
95 *O16* **Sundbyberg** Stockholm, C Sweden
97 *M14* **Sunderland** *var.* Wearmouth. NE England, UK
101 *F15* **Sundern** Nordrhein-Westfalen, W Germany
136 *F12* **Sündiken Dağları** ▲ C Turkey
24 *M5* **Sundown** Texas, SW USA
11 *P16* **Sundre** Alberta, SW Canada
14 *H12* **Sundridge** Ontario, S Canada
93 *H17* **Sundsvall** Västernorrland, C Sweden
26 *H4* **Sunflower, Mount** ▲ Kansas, C USA
Sunflower State *see* Kansas
169 N14 **Sungaibuntu** Sumatera, SW Indonesia
168 K12 **Sungaidareh** Sumatera, W Indonesia
167 P17 **Sungai Kolok** *var.* Sungai Ko-Lok. Narathiwat, SW Thailand
168 K12 **Sungaipenuh** *prev.* Soengaipenoeh. Sumatera, W Indonesia
169 P11 **Sungaipinyuh** Borneo, C Indonesia
Sungari *see* Songhua Jiang
Sungaria *see* Dzungaria
Sungei Pahang *see* Pahang, Sungai
167 O8 **Sung Men** Phrae, NW Thailand
83 *M15* **Sungo** Tete, NW Mozambique
168 M13 **Sungsang** Sumatera, W Indonesia
114 *M9* **Sungurlare** Burgas, E Bulgaria
136 *J12* **Sungurlu** Çorum, N Turkey
112 *F9* **Sunja** Sisak-Moslavina, C Croatia
153 *Q12* **Sun Koshi** ⁓ E Nepal
94 *F9* **Sunndalen** *valley* S Norway
94 *F9* **Sunndalsøra** Møre og Romsdal, S Norway
95 *K15* **Sunne** Värmland, C Sweden
95 *O15* **Sunnersta** Uppsala, C Sweden
94 *C11* **Sunnfjord** *physical region* S Norway
95 *C15* **Sunnhordland** *physical region* S Norway
94 *D10* **Sunnmøre** *physical region* S Norway
37 *N4* **Sunnyside** Utah, W USA
32 *J10* **Sunnyside** Washington, NW USA
35 *N9* **Sunnyvale** California, W USA
30 *L8* **Sun Prairie** Wisconsin, N USA
Sunqur *see* Sonqor
25 *N1* **Sunray** Texas, SW USA
22 *I8* **Sunset** Louisiana, S USA
25 *S5* **Sunset** Texas, SW USA
Sunset State *see* Oregon
181 *Z10* **Sunshine Coast** *cultural region* Queensland, E Australia
Sunshine State *see* Florida, USA
Sunshine State *see* New Mexico, USA
Sunshine State *see* South Dakota, USA
123 O10 **Suntar** Respublika Sakha (Yakutiya), NE Russian Federation
39 *R10* **Suntrana** Alaska, USA
148 *J15* **Suntsar** Baluchistān, SW Pakistan
163 *W15* **Sunwi-do** *island* SW North Korea
163 *W6* **Sunwu** Heilongjiang, NE China
77 *O16* **Sunyani** W Ghana
Suō *see* Suao
93 *M17* **Suolahti** Länsi-Suomi, W Finland
Suoločielgi *see* Saariselkä
Suomenlahti *see* Finland, Gulf of
Suomen Tasavalta/Suomi *see* Finland
93 *N14* **Suomussalmi** Oulu, E Finland
165 E13 **Suō-nada** *sea* SW Japan
93 *M17* **Suonenjoki** Itä-Suomi, C Finland
167 S13 **Suŏng** Kâmpóng Cham, C Cambodia
126 *I10* **Suoyarvi** Respublika Kareliya, NW Russian Federation
Supanburi *see* Suphan Buri
57 *D14* **Supe** Lima, W Peru
15 *V7* **Supérieur, Lac** ◎ Quebec, SE Canada
Supérieur, Lac *see* Superior, Lake
36 *M14* **Superior** Arizona, SW USA
33 *O9* **Superior** Montana, NW USA
29 *P17* **Superior** Nebraska, C USA
30 *I3* **Superior** Wisconsin, N USA
41 *S17* **Superior, Laguna** *lagoon* S Mexico
31 *N2* **Superior, Lake** *Fr.* Lac Supérieur. ◎ Canada/USA
36 *L13* **Superstition Mountains** ▲ Arizona, SW USA
113 *F14* **Supetar** *It.* San Pietro. Split-Dalmacija, S Croatia
167 O10 **Suphan Buri** *var.* Supanburi. Suphan Buri, W Thailand
171 V12 **Supiori, Pulau** *island* E Indonesia
188 *K2* **Supply Reef** *reef* N Northern Mariana Islands
195 *O7* **Support Force Glacier** *glacier* Antarctica
137 *R10* **Sup'sa** *var.* Supsa. ⁓ W Georgia
Sūq 'Abs *see* 'Abs
139 *W12* **Sūq ash Shuyūkh** SE Iraq
138 *H4* **Şuqaylibīyah** Ḩamāh, W Syria
161 *Q6* **Suqian** Jiangsu, E China
Suqrah *see* Şawqirah
Suqrah Bay *see* Şawqirah, Dawḩat
141 *V16* **Suquṭrā** *var.* Sokotra, *Eng.* Socotra. *island* SE Yemen
141 *Z8* **Şūr** NE Oman
Şūr *see* Soûr
129 *P5* **Sura** Penzenskaya Oblast', W Russian Federation
129 *P4* **Sura** ⁓ W Russian Federation
149 *N12* **Sūrāb** Baluchistān, SW Pakistan
Surabaja *see* Surabaya
192 E8 **Surabaya** *prev.* Soerabaja, Surabaja. Jawa, C Indonesia
95 *N15* **Surahammar** Västmanland, C Sweden
169 Q16 **Surakarta** *Eng.* Solo; *prev.* Soerakarta. Jawa, S Indonesia
Surakhany *see* Suraxanı
137 *S10* **Surami** C Georgia
143 *X13* **Sūrān** Sīstān va Balūchestān, SE Iran
111 *I21* **Šurany** *Hung.* Nagysurány. Nitriansky Kraj, SW Slovakia
154 *D12* **Sūrat** Gujarāt, W India
Suratdhani *see* Surat Thani
152 *G9* **Sūratgarh** Rājasthān, NW India
167 N14 **Surat Thani** *var.* Suratdhani. Surat Thani, SW Thailand
119 *Q16* **Suraw** *Rus.* Surov. ⁓ E Belarus
137 *Z11* **Suraxanı** *Rus.* Surakhany. E Azerbaijan
141 *Y11* **Surayr** E Oman
138 *K2* **Suraysāt** Ḩalab, N Syria
118 *O12* **Surazh** *Rus.* Surazh. Vitsyebskaya Voblasts', NE Belarus
128 *H6* **Surazh** Bryanskaya Oblast', W Russian Federation
191 *V17* **Sur, Cabo** *headland* Easter Island, Chile, E Pacific Ocean
112 *L11* **Surčin** Serbia, N Yugoslavia
116 *H9* **Surduc** *Hung.* Szurduk. Sălaj, NW Romania
113 *P16* **Surdulica** Serbia, SE Yugoslavia
99 *L24* **Sûre** *var.* Sauer. ⁓ W Europe *see also* Sauer
154 *C10* **Surendranagar** Gujarāt, W India
18 *K16* **Surf City** New Jersey, NE USA
183 *V3* **Surfers Paradise** Queensland, E Australia
21 *U13* **Surfside Beach** South Carolina, SE USA
102 *J10* **Surgères** Charente-Maritime, W France
122 H10 **Surgut** Khanty-Mansiyskiy Avtonomnyy Okrug, C Russian Federation
122 K10 **Surgutikha** Krasnoyarskiy Kray, N Russian Federation
98 *M6* **Surhuisterveen** Friesland, N Netherlands
105 *V5* **Súria** Cataluña, NE Spain
143 P10 **Sūrīān** Fārs, S Iran
155 *J15* **Suriāpet** Andhra Pradesh, C India
171 Q6 **Surigao** Mindanao, S Philippines
167 R10 **Surin** Surin, E Thailand
55 *U11* **Suriname** *off.* Republic of Suriname, *var.* Surinam; *prev.* Dutch Guiana, Netherlands Guiana. ◆ *republic* N South America
Sūrīya/Sūrīyah, Al-Jumhūrīyah al-'Arabīyah as - *see* Syria
Surkhab, Darya-i- *see* Kahmard, Daryā-ye
Surkhandar'inskaya Oblast' *see* Surkhondaryo Wiloyati
Surkhandar'ya *see* Surkhondaryo
Surkhet *see* Birendranagar
147 *R12* **Surkhob** ⁓ C Tajikistan
147 *P13* **Surkhondaryo** *Rus.* Surkhandar'ya. ⁓ Tajikistan/Uzbekistan
147 *N13* **Surkhondaryo Wiloyati** *Rus.* Surkhandar'inskaya Oblast'. ◆ *province* S Uzbekistan
137 *P11* **Sürmene** Trabzon, NE Turkey
Surov *see* Suraw
129 *N11* **Surovikino** Volgogradskaya Oblast', SW Russian Federation
35 *N11* **Sur, Point** *headland* California, W USA
187 N15 **Surprise, Île** *island* N New Caledonia
61 *E22* **Sur, Punta** *headland* E Argentina
Surrentum *see* Sorrento
28 *M3* **Surrey** North Dakota, N USA
97 *O22* **Surrey** *cultural region* SE England, UK
21 *X7* **Surry** Virginia, NE USA
108 *F8* **Sursee** Luzern, W Switzerland
129 *P6* **Sursk** Penzenskaya Oblast', W Russian Federation
129 *P5* **Surskoye** Ul'yanovskaya Oblast', W Russian Federation
75 *P8* **Surt** *var.* Sidra, Sirte. N Libya
95 *I19* **Surte** Västra Götaland, S Sweden
75 *Q8* **Surt, Khalīj** *Eng.* Gulf of Sidra, Gulf of Sirti, Sidra. *gulf* N Libya
92 *I5* **Surtsey** *island* S Iceland
137 *N17* **Suruç** Şanlıurfa, S Turkey
168 L13 **Surulangun** Sumatera, W Indonesia
Süs *see* Susch
106 *A8* **Susa** Piemonte, NE Italy
165 E12 **Susa** Yamaguchi, Honshū, SW Japan
Susa *see* Shūsh
113 *E16* **Sušac** *It.* Cazza. *island* SW Croatia
Sūsah *see* Sousse
165 G14 **Susaki** Kōchi, Shikoku, SW Japan
165 I15 **Susami** Wakayama, Honshū, SW Japan
142 *K9* **Sūsangerd** *var.* Susangird. Khūzestān, SW Iran
Susangird *see* Sūsangerd
35 *P4* **Susanville** California, W USA
108 *J9* **Susch** *var.* Süs. Graubünden, SE Switzerland
137 *N12* **Suşehri** Sivas, N Turkey
Susiana *see* Khūzestān
111 *B18* **Sušice** *Ger.* Schüttenhofen. Plzeňský Kraj, W Czech Republic
39 *R11* **Susitna** Alaska, USA
39 *R11* **Susitna River** ⁓ Alaska, USA
129 Q3 **Suslonger** Respublika Mariy El, W Russian Federation
105 *N14* **Suspiro del Moro, Puerto del** *pass* S Spain
18 *H16* **Susquehanna River** ⁓ New York/Pennsylvania, NE USA
13 *O15* **Sussex** New Brunswick, SE Canada
18 *J13* **Sussex** New Jersey, NE USA
21 *W7* **Sussex** Virginia, NE USA
97 *O23* **Sussex** *cultural region* S England, UK
183 *S10* **Sussex Inlet** New South Wales, SE Australia
99 *L17* **Susteren** Limburg, SE Netherlands
10 *K12* **Sustut Peak** ▲ British Columbia, W Canada
123 S9 **Susuman** Magadanskaya Oblast', E Russian Federation
188 *H6* **Susupe** Saipan, S Northern Mariana Islands
136 *D12* **Susurluk** Balıkesir, NW Turkey
114 *M13* **Susuzmüsellim** Tekirdağ, NW Turkey
136 *F15* **Sütçüler** Isparta, SW Turkey
116 *L13* **Şuteşti** Brăila, SE Romania
83 *F25* **Sutherland** Western Cape, SW South Africa
28 *L15* **Sutherland** Nebraska, C USA
96 *I7* **Sutherland** *cultural region* N Scotland, UK
185 *B21* **Sutherland Falls** *waterfall* South Island, NZ
32 *F14* **Sutherlin** Oregon, NW USA
149 *V10* **Sutlej** ⁓ India/Pakistan
Sutna *see* Satna
35 *P7* **Sutter Creek** California, W USA
39 *R11* **Sutton** Alaska, USA
29 *Q16* **Sutton** Nebraska, C USA
21 *R4* **Sutton** West Virginia, NE USA
12 *F8* **Sutton** ⁓ Ontario, C Canada
97 *M19* **Sutton Coldfield** C England, UK
21 *R4* **Sutton Lake** ⊡ West Virginia, NE USA
15 *P13* **Sutton, Monts** *hill range* Quebec, SE Canada
12 *F8* **Sutton Ridges** ▲ Ontario, C Canada
165 Q4 **Suttsu** Hokkaidō, NE Japan
39 *P15* **Sutwik Island** *island* Alaska, USA
162 *K7* **Süüj** Bulgan, C Mongolia
118 *H5* **Suure-Jaani** *Ger.* Gross-Sankt-Johannis. Viljandimaa, S Estonia
118 *J7* **Suur Munamägi** *var.* Munamägi, *Ger.* Eier-Berg. ▲ SE Estonia
118 *F5* **Suur Väin** *Ger.* Grosser Sund. *strait* W Estonia
147 *U8* **Suusamyr** Chuyskaya Oblast', C Kyrgyzstan
187 X14 **Suva** ● (Fiji) Viti Levu, W Fiji
187 X15 **Suva** ✕ Viti Levu, C Fiji
113 *N18* **Suva Gora** ▲ W FYR Macedonia
118 *H11* **Suvainiškis** Rokiškis, NE Lithuania
Suvalkai/Suvalki *see* Suwałki
113 *P15* **Suva Planina** ▲ SE Yugoslavia
113 *M17* **Suva Reka** Serbia, S Yugoslavia
128 *K5* **Suvorov** Tul'skaya Oblast', W Russian Federation
117 *N12* **Suvorove** Odes'ka Oblast', SW Ukraine
Suvorovo *see* Ştefan Vodă
Suwaik *see* As Suwayq
Suwaira *see* Aş Şuwayrah
110 *O7* **Suwałki** *Lith.* Suvalkai, *Rus.* Suvalki. Podlaskie, NE Poland
167 R10 **Suwannaphum** Roi Et, E Thailand
23 *V8* **Suwannee River** ⁓ Florida/Georgia, SE USA
Şuwār *see* Aş Şuwār
190 *K14* **Suwarrow** *atoll* N Cook Islands
Suwaydá/Suwaydā', Muḩāfaẓat as *see* As Suwaydā'
143 *R16* **Suwaydān** *var.* Sweiham. Abū Ẓaby, E UAE
Suwayqiyah, Hawr as *see* Shuwayjah, Hawr ash
Suways, Khalīj as *see* Suez, Gulf of
Suways, Qanāt as *see* Suez Canal
Suweida *see* As Suwaydā'
Suweon *see* Suwŏn
163 *X15* **Suwŏn** *var.* Suweon, *Jap.* Suigen. NW South Korea
Su Xian *see* Suzhou
143 *R14* **Sūzā** Hormozgān, S Iran
145 *P15* **Suzak** *Kaz.* Sozaq. Yuzhnyy Kazakhstan, S Kazakhstan
Suzaka *see* Suzuka
128 *M3* **Suzdal'** Vladimirskaya Oblast', W Russian Federation
161 *P7* **Suzhou** *var.* Su Xian. Anhui, E China
161 *R8* **Suzhou** *var.* Soochow, Su-chou, Suchow; *prev.* Wuhsien. Jiangsu, E China
Suz, Mys *see* Soye, Mys
165 M10 **Suzu** Ishikawa, Honshū, SW Japan
165 K14 **Suzuka** Mie, Honshū, SW Japan
165 N12 **Suzuka** *var.* Suzaka. Nagano, Honshū, S Japan
165 M10 **Suzu-misaki** *headland* Honshū, SW Japan
Svågälv *see* Svågan
94 *M10* **Svågan** *var.* Svågälv. ⁓ C Sweden
Svalava/Svaljava *see* Svalyava
92 *O2* **Svalbard** ◇ *Norwegian dependency* Arctic Ocean
92 *J2* **Svalbardhseyri** Nordhurland Eystra, N Iceland
95 *K22* **Svalöv** Skåne, S Sweden
116 *H7* **Svalyava** *Cz.* Svalava, Svaljava, *Hung.* Szolyva. Zakarpats'ka Oblast', W Ukraine
92 *O2* **Svanbergfjellet** ▲ C Svalbard
95 *M24* **Svaneke** Bornholm, E Denmark
95 *L22* **Svängsta** Blekinge, S Sweden
95 *J16* **Svanskog** Värmland, C Sweden
95 *L16* **Svartå** Örebro, C Sweden
95 *L15* **Svartälven** ⁓ C Sweden
92 *G12* **Svartisen** *glacier* C Norway
117 *X6* **Svatove** *Rus.* Svatovo. Luhans'ka Oblast', E Ukraine
Svatovo *see* Svatove
Sväty Kríž nad Hronom *see* Žiar nad Hronom
167 Q11 **Svay Chék, Stœng** ⁓ Cambodia/Thailand
167 S13 **Svay Riĕng** Svay Riĕng, S Cambodia
92 *O3* **Sveagruva** Spitsbergen, W Svalbard
95 *K23* **Svedala** Skåne, S Sweden
118 *H12* **Svėdesai** Anykščiai, NE Lithuania
93 *G18* **Sveg** Jämtland, C Sweden
118 *C12* **Švėkšna** Šilutė, W Lithuania
94 *C11* **Svelgen** Sogn og Fjordane, S Norway
95 *H15* **Svelvik** Vestfold, S Norway
118 *I13* **Švenčionėliai** *Pol.* Nowo-Święciany. Švenčionys, SE Lithuania
118 *I13* **Švenčionys** *Pol.* Swięciany. Švenčionys, SE Lithuania
95 *H24* **Svendborg** Fyn, C Denmark
95 *K19* **Svenljunga** Västra Götaland, S Sweden
92 *P2* **Svenskøya** *island* E Svalbard
93 *G17* **Svenstavik** Jämtland, C Sweden
95 *G20* **Svenstrup** Nordjylland, N Denmark
118 *H12* **Šventoji** ⁓ C Lithuania
117 *Z8* **Sverdlovs'k** *Rus.* Sverdlovsk; *prev.* Imeni Sverdlova Rudnik. Luhans'ka Oblast', E Ukraine
Sverdlovsk *see* Yekaterinburg
129 *W2* **Sverdlovskaya Oblast'** ◆ *province* C Russian Federation
8 *M3* **Sverdrup Islands** *island group* Nunavut, N Canada
8 L3 **Sverdrup, Ostrov** *island* N Russian Federation
Sverige *see* Sweden
113 *D15* **Svetac** *prev.* Sveti Andrea, *It.* Sant'Andrea. *island* SW Croatia
Sveti Andrea *see* Svetac
Sveti Nikola *see* Sveti Nikole
113 *O18* **Sveti Nikole** *prev.* Sveti Nikola. C FYR Macedonia
Sveti Vrach *see* Sandanski
123 T14 **Svetlaya** Primorskiy Kray, SE Russian Federation
128 *B2* **Svetlogorsk** Kaliningradskaya Oblast', W Russian Federation
122 K9 **Svetlogorsk** Krasnoyarskiy Kray, N Russian Federation
Svetlogorsk *see* Svyetlahorsk
129 *N14* **Svetlograd** Stavropol'skiy Kray, SW Russian Federation
Svetlovodsk *see* Svitlovods'k
119 *A14* **Svetlyy** *Ger.* Zimmerbude. Kaliningradskaya Oblast', W Russian Federation
129 *Y8* **Svetlyy** Orenburgskaya Oblast', W Russian Federation
126 *G11* **Svetogorsk** *Fin.* Enso. Leningradskaya Oblast', NW Russian Federation
Svetozarevo *see* Jagodina
111 *B18* **Švihov** *Ger.* Schwihau. Plzeňský Kraj, W Czech Republic
112 *E13* **Svilaja** ▲ SE Croatia
112 *N12* **Svilajnac** Serbia, C Yugoslavia
114 *L11* **Svilengrad** *prev.* Mustafa-Pasha. Khaskovo, S Bulgaria
Svinecea Mare, Munte *see* Svinecea Mare, Vârful
116 *F13* **Svinecea Mare, Vârful** *var.* Munte Svinecea Mare. ▲ SW Romania
95 *B18* **Svínoy** *Dan.* Svinø *Island* Faeroe Islands
147 *N14* **Svintsovyy Rudnik** *Turkm.* Swintsowyy Rudnik. Lebapskiy Velayat, E Turkmenistan
118 *I13* **Svir** *Rus.* Svir'. Minskaya Voblasts', NW Belarus
126 *I12* **Svir'** *canal* NW Russian Federation
Svir', Ozero *see* Svir, Vozyera
119 *I14* **Svir, Vozyera** *Rus.* Ozero Svir'. ◎ C Belarus
114 *J7* **Svishtov** *prev.* Sistova. Veliko Tŭrnovo, N Bulgaria
119 *F18* **Svislach** *Pol.* Świsłocz, *Rus.* Svisloch'. Hrodzyenskaya Voblasts', W Belarus
119 *M17* **Svislach** *Rus.* Svisloch'. Mahilyowskaya Voblasts', E Belarus
119 *L17* **Svislach** *Rus.* Svisloch'. ⁓ E Belarus
Svisloch' *see* Svislach
111 *F17* **Svitavy** *Ger.* Zwittau. Pardubický Kraj, C Czech Republic
117 *S6* **Svitlovods'k** *Rus.* Svetlovodsk. Kirovohrads'ka Oblast', C Ukraine
Svizzera *see* Switzerland
123 Q13 **Svobodnyy** Amurskaya Oblast', SE Russian Federation
114 *G9* **Svoge** Sofiya, W Bulgaria
92 *G11* **Svolvær** Nordland, C Norway
111 *F18* **Svratka** *Ger.* Schwarzach, Schwarzawa. ⁓ SE Czech Republic
113 *P14* **Svrljig** Serbia, E Yugoslavia
197 *U10* **Svyataya Anna Trough** *var.* Saint Anna Trough. *undersea feature* N Kara Sea
126 *M4* **Svyatoy Nos, Mys** *headland* NW Russian Federation
119 *N18* **Svyetlahorsk** *Rus.* Svetlogorsk. Homyel'skaya Voblasts', SE Belarus
Swabian Jura *see* Schwäbische Alb
97 *P19* **Swaffham** E England, UK
23 *V5* **Swainsboro** Georgia, SE USA
83 *C19* **Swakop** ⁓ W Namibia
83 *C19* **Swakopmund** Erongo, W Namibia
97 *M15* **Swale** ⁓ N England, UK
Swallow Island *see* Nendö
99 *M16* **Swalmen** Limburg, SE Netherlands
12 *G8* **Swan** ⁓ Ontario, C Canada
97 *L24* **Swanage** S England, UK
182 *M10* **Swan Hill** Victoria, SE Australia
11 *P13* **Swan Hills** Alberta, W Canada
65 *D24* **Swan Island** *island* C Falkland Islands
Swankalok *see* Sawankhalok
29 *U10* **Swan Lake** ◎ Minnesota, N USA
21 *Y10* **Swanquarter** North Carolina, SE USA
182 *J9* **Swan Reach** South Australia
11 *V15* **Swan River** Manitoba, S Canada
183 *P17* **Swansea** Tasmania, SE Australia
97 *J22* **Swansea** *Wel.* Abertawe. S Wales, UK
21 *R13* **Swansea** South Carolina, SE USA
19 *S7* **Swans Island** *island* Maine, NE USA
28 *L17* **Swanson Lake** ⊡ Nebraska, C USA
31 *R11* **Swanton** Ohio, N USA
110 *G11* **Swarzędz** Poznań, C Poland
Swatow *see* Shantou
83 *L22* **Swaziland** *off.* Kingdom of Swaziland. ◆ *monarchy* S Africa
93 *G18* **Sweden** *off.* Kingdom of Sweden, *Swe.* Sverige. ◆ *monarchy* N Europe
Swedru *see* Agona Swedru
25 *V12* **Sweeny** Texas, SW USA
33 *R6* **Sweetgrass** Montana, NW USA
32 *G12* **Sweet Home** Oregon, NW USA
25 *T12* **Sweet Home** Texas, SW USA
27 *T4* **Sweet Springs** Missouri, C USA
20 *M10* **Sweetwater** Tennessee, S USA
25 *P7* **Sweetwater** Texas, SW USA
33 *V15* **Sweetwater River** ⁓ Wyoming, C USA
Sweiham *see* Suwaydān
83 *F26* **Swellendam** Western Cape, SW South Africa
111 *G15* **Świdnica** *Ger.* Schweidnitz. Wałbrzych, SW Poland
111 *O14* **Świdnik** *Ger.* Streckenbach. Lubelskie, E Poland
110 *F8* **Świdwin** *Ger.* Schivelbein. Zachodniopomorskie, NW Poland
111 *F15* **Świebodzice** *Ger.* Freiburg in Schlesien, Swiebodzice. Wałbrzych, SW Poland
110 *E11* **Świebodzin** *Ger.* Schwiebus. Lubuskie, W Poland
Święciany *see* Švenčionys
110 *I9* **Świecie** *Ger.* Schwertberg. Kujawsko-pomorskie, N Poland
111 *L15* **Świętokrzyskie** ◈ *province* C Poland
11 *T16* **Swift Current** Saskatchewan, S Canada
98 *K9* **Swifterbant** Flevoland, C Netherlands
183 *Q12* **Swifts Creek** Victoria, SE Australia
96 *E13* **Swilly, Lough** *Ir.* Loch Súilí. *inlet* N Ireland
97 *M22* **Swindon** S England, UK
Swinemünde *see* Świnoujście
110 *D8* **Świnoujście** *Ger.* Swinemünde. Zachodniopomorskie, NW Poland
Swintsowyy Rudnik *see* Svintsovyy Rudnik
Świsłocz *see* Svislach
Swiss Confederation *see* Switzerland
108 *E9* **Switzerland** *off.* Swiss Confederation, *Fr.* La Suisse, *Ger.* Schweiz, *It.* Svizzera; *anc.* Helvetia. ◆ *federal republic* C Europe
97 *F17* **Swords** *Ir.* Sord Choluim Chille. E Ireland
18 *H13* **Swoyersville** Pennsylvania, NE USA
126 *I10* **Syamozera, Ozero** ◎ NW Russian Federation
126 *M13* **Syamzha** Vologodskaya Oblast', NW Russian Federation
118 *N13* **Syanno** *Rus.* Senno. Vitsyebskaya Voblasts', NE Belarus
119 *K16* **Syarhyeyevichy** *Rus.* Sergeyevichi. Minskaya Voblasts', C Belarus
126 *I12* **Syas'stroy** Leningradskaya Oblast', NW Russian Federation
Sycaminum *see* Ḩefa
30 *M10* **Sycamore** Illinois, N USA
128 *J3* **Sychëvka** Smolenskaya Oblast', W Russian Federation
111 *H14* **Syców** *Ger.* Gross Wartenberg. Dolnośląskie, SW Poland
14 *E17* **Sydenham** ⁓ Ontario, S Canada
Sydenham Island *see* Nonouti
183 *T9* **Sydney** *state capital* New South Wales, SE Australia
13 *R14* **Sydney** Cape Breton Island, Nova Scotia, SE Canada
Sydney Island *see* Manra
13 *R14* **Sydney Mines** Cape Breton Island, Nova Scotia, SE Canada
Syedpur *see* Saidpur
119 *K18* **Syelishcha** *Rus.* Selishche. Minskaya Voblasts', C Belarus
119 *J18* **Syemyezhava** *Rus.* Semezhevo. Minskaya Voblasts', C Belarus
Syene *see* Aswân
117 *X6* **Syeverodonets'k** *Rus.* Severodonetsk. Luhans'ka Oblast', E Ukraine
161 *T6* **Syiao Shan** *island* SE China
100 *H11* **Syke** Niedersachsen, NW Germany
94 *D10* **Sykkylven** Møre og Romsdal, S Norway
115 *F15* **Sykoúri** *var.* Sikouri; *prev.* Sikoúrion. Thessalía, C Greece
127 *R11* **Syktyvkar** *prev.* Ust'-Sysol'sk. Respublika Komi, NW Russian Federation
23 *Q4* **Sylacauga** Alabama, S USA
Sylarna *see* Sylene
94 *I9* **Sylene** *Swe.* Sylarna. ▲ Norway/Sweden
153 *V14* **Sylhet** Chittagong, NE Bangladesh
100 *G6* **Sylt** *island* NW Germany
21 *O10* **Sylva** North Carolina, SE USA
127 *V15* **Sylva** ⁓ NW Russian Federation
23 *W5* **Sylvania** Georgia, SE USA
31 *R11* **Sylvania** Ohio, N USA
11 *Q15* **Sylvan Lake** Alberta, SW Canada
33 *T13* **Sylvan Pass** *pass* Wyoming, C USA
23 *T7* **Sylvester** Georgia, SE USA
25 *P6* **Sylvester** Texas, SW USA
10 *L11* **Sylvia, Mount** ▲ British Columbia, W Canada
122 K11 **Sym** ⁓ C Russian Federation
115 *N22* **Sými** *var.* Simi. *island* Dodekánisos, Greece, Aegean Sea
117 *U8* **Synel'nykove** Dnipropetrovs'ka Oblast', E Ukraine
127 *U6* **Synya** Respublika Komi, NW Russian Federation
117 *P7* **Synyukha** *Rus.* Sinyukha. ⁓ S Ukraine
Syôbara *see* Shōbara
195 *V2* **Syowa** *Japanese research station* Antarctica
26 *H6* **Syracuse** Kansas, C USA
29 *S16* **Syracuse** Nebraska, C USA
18 *H10* **Syracuse** New York, NE USA
Syracuse *see* Siracusa
Syrdar'inskaya Oblast' *see* Sirdaryo Wiloyati
Syrdariya *see* Syr Darya
144 *L14* **Syr Darya** *var.* Sai Hun, Sir Darya, Syrdarya, *Kaz.* Syrdariya, *Rus.* Syrdar'ya, *Uzb.* Sirdaryo; *anc.* Jaxartes. ⁓ C Asia
147 *P10* **Syrdar'ya** Sirdaryo Wiloyati, E Uzbekistan
138 *J6* **Syria** *off.* Syrian Arab Republic, *var.* Siria, Syrie, *Ar.* Al-Jumhūrīyah al-'Arabīyah as-Sūrīyah, Sūrīya. ◆ *republic* SW Asia
138 *L9* **Syrian Desert** *Ar.* Al Hamad, Bādiyat ash Shām. *desert* SW Asia
Syrie *see* Syria
115 *L22* **Sýrna** *var.* Sirna. *island* Kykládes, Greece, Aegean Sea
115 *I20* **Sýros** *var.* Síros. *island* Kykládes, Greece, Aegean Sea
93 *M18* **Sysmä** Etelä-Suomi, S Finland
127 *R12* **Sysola** ⁓ NW Russian Federation
Syulemeshlii *see* Sredets
129 *S2* **Syumsi** Udmurtskaya Respublika, NW Russian Federation
114 *K10* **Syuyutliyka** ⁓ C Bulgaria
Syvash, Zaliv *see* Syvash, Zatoka
117 *U12* **Syvash, Zatoka** *Rus.* Zaliv Syvash. *inlet* S Ukraine
129 *Q6* **Syzran'** Samarskaya Oblast', W Russian Federation
Szabadka *see* Subotica
111 *N21* **Szabolcs-Szatmár-Bereg** *off.* Szabolcs-Szatmár-Bereg Megye. ◈ *county* E Hungary
110 *G10* **Szamocin** *Ger.* Samotschin. Wielkolpolskie, C Poland
116 *H8* **Szamos** *var.* Someş, Someşul, *Ger.* Samosch, Somesch. ⁓ Hungary/Romania
Szamosújvár *see* Gherla
110 *G11* **Szamotuły** Poznań, C Poland
Szarkowszczyzna *see* Sharkawshchyna
111 *M24* **Szarvas** Békés, SE Hungary
Szászmagyarós *see* Măieruş
Szászrégen *see* Reghin
Szászsebes *see* Sebeş
Szászváros *see* Orăştie
Szatmárrnémeti *see* Satu Mare
Száva *see* Sava
111 *P15* **Szczebrzeszyn** Lubelskie, E Poland
110 *D9* **Szczecin** *Eng./Ger.* Stettin. Zachodniopomorskie, NW Poland
110 *G8* **Szczecinek** *Ger.* Neustettin. Zachodniopomorskie, NW Poland
110 *D8* **Szczeciński, Zalew** *var.* Stettiner Haff, *Ger.* Oderhaff. *bay* Germany/Poland
111 *K15* **Szczekociny** Śląskie, S Poland
110 *N8* **Szczuczyn** Podlaskie, NE Poland
Szczuczyn Nowogródzki *see* Shchuchyn
110 *M8* **Szczytno** *Ger.* Ortelsburg. Warmińsko-Mazurskie, NE Poland,
Szechuan/Szechwan *see* Sichuan
111 *K21* **Szécsény** Nógrád, N Hungary
111 *L25* **Szeged** *Ger.* Szegedin, *Rom.* Seghedin. Csongrád, SE Hungary
Szegedin *see* Szeged
111 *N23* **Szeghalom** Békés, SE Hungary
Székelyhid *see* Săcueni
Székelykeresztúr *see* Cristuru Secuiesc

◆ Country ◇ Dependent Territory ◈ Administrative Region ▲ Mountain ⛰ Volcano ◎ Lake
● Country Capital ○ Dependent Territory Capital ✕ International Airport ▲ Mountain Range ⁓ River ⊡ Reservoir

- 111 I23 **Székesfehérvár** Ger. Stuhlweissenberg; anc. Alba Regia. Fejér, W Hungary
- **Szeklerburg** see Miercurea-Ciuc
- **Szekler Neumarkt** see Târgu Secuiesc
- 111 J25 **Szekszárd** Tolna, S Hungary
- **Szempcz/Szenc** see Senec
- **Szenice** see Senica
- **Szentágota** see Agnita
- 111 J22 **Szentendre** Ger. Sankt Andrä. Pest, N Hungary
- 111 L24 **Szentes** Csongrád, SE Hungary
- 111 F23 **Szentgotthárd** Eng. Saint Gotthard, Ger. Sankt Gotthard. Vas, W Hungary
- **Szentgyörgy** see Ðurđevac
- **Szenttamás** see Srbobran
- **Széphely** see Jebel
- **Szeping** see Siping
- **Szered** see Sereď
- 111 N21 **Szerencs** Borsod-Abaúj-Zemplén, NE Hungary
- **Szeret** see Siret
- **Szeretfalva** see Sărăţel
- 110 N7 **Szeskie Wzgórza** Ger. Seesker Höhe. hill NE Poland
- 111 H25 **Szigetvár** Baranya, SW Hungary
- **Szilágysomlyó** see Şimleu Silvaniei
- **Szinna** see Snina
- **Sziszek** see Sisak
- **Szitás-Keresztúr** see Cristuru Secuiesc
- 111 E15 **Szklarska Poręba** Ger. Schreiberhau. Dolnośląskie, SW Poland
- **Szkudy** see Skuodas
- **Szlatina** see Slatina, Croatia
- **Szlavonia/Szlavonország** see Slavonija
- **Szlovákia** see Slovakia
- **Szluin** see Slunj
- 111 L23 **Szolnok** Jász-Nagykun-Szolnok, C Hungary
- **Szolyva** see Svalyava
- 111 G23 **Szombathely** Ger. Steinamanger; anc. Sabaria, Savaria. Vas, W Hungary
- **Szond/Szonta** see Sonta
- **Szováta** see Sovata
- 110 F13 **Szprotawa** Ger. Sprottau. Lubuskie, W Poland
- **Sztálinváros** see Dunaújváros
- **Sztrazsó** see Strážov
- 110 J8 **Sztum** Ger. Stuhm. Pomorskie, N Poland
- 110 H10 **Szubin** Ger. Schubin. Kujawsko-pomorskie, W Poland
- **Szucsava** see Suceava
- **Szurduk** see Surduc
- 111 M14 **Szydłowiec** Ger. Schlelau. Mazowieckie, C Poland

T

- **Taalintehdas** see Dalsbruk
- 171 O4 **Taal, Lake** ⊚ Luzon, NW Philippines
- **Taastrup** see Tåstrup
- 111 I24 **Tab** Somogy, W Hungary
- 171 P4 **Tabaco** Luzon, N Philippines
- 186 G4 **Tabalo** Mussau Island, NE PNG
- 104 K5 **Tábara** Castilla-León, N Spain
- 186 H5 **Tabar Islands** island group NE PNG
- **Tabariya, Bahrat** see Tiberias, Lake
- 143 S7 **Ţabas** var. Golshan. Khorāsān, C Iran
- 43 P15 **Tabasará, Serranía de** ▲ W Panama
- 41 U15 **Tabasco** ◆ state SE Mexico
- **Tabasco** see Grijalva, Río
- 129 Q2 **Tabashino** Respublika Mariy El, W Russian Federation
- 58 B13 **Tabatinga** Amazonas, N Brazil
- 74 G9 **Tabelbala** W Algeria
- 11 Q17 **Taber** Alberta, SW Canada
- 171 V15 **Taberfane** Pulau Trangan, E Indonesia
- 95 L19 **Taberg** Jönköping, S Sweden
- 191 O3 **Tabiteuea** prev. Drummond Island. atoll Tungaru, W Kiribati
- 171 O5 **Tablas Island** island C Philippines
- 184 Q10 **Table Cape** headland North Island, NZ
- 13 S13 **Table Mountain** ▲ Newfoundland, E Canada
- 173 P17 **Table, Pointe de la** headland SE Réunion
- 27 S8 **Table Rock Lake** ⊞ Arkansas/Missouri, C USA
- 36 K14 **Table Top** ▲ Arizona, SW USA
- 186 D8 **Tabletop, Mount** ▲ C PNG
- 123 R7 **Tabor** Respublika Sakha (Yakutiya), NE Russian Federation
- 29 S15 **Tabor** Iowa, C USA
- 111 D18 **Tábor** Budějovický Kraj, S Czech Republic
- 81 F21 **Tabora** Tabora, W Tanzania
- 81 F21 **Tabora** ◆ region C Tanzania
- 21 U12 **Tabor City** North Carolina, SE USA
- 147 Q10 **Taboshar** NW Tajikistan
- 76 L18 **Tabou** var. Tabu. S Ivory Coast
- 142 J2 **Tabrīz** var. Tebriz; anc. Tauris. Āžarbāyjān-e Khāvarī, NW Iran
- **Tabu** see Tabou
- 191 W1 **Tabuaeran** prev. Fanning Island. atoll Line Islands, E Kiribati
- 171 O2 **Tabuk** Luzon, N Philippines
- 140 J4 **Tabūk** Tabūk, NW Saudi Arabia
- 140 J5 **Tabūk** off. Minţaqat Tabūk. ◆ province NW Saudi Arabia
- 187 Q13 **Tabwemasana, Mount** ▲ Espiritu Santo, W Vanuatu
- 95 O15 **Täby** Stockholm, C Sweden
- 41 N14 **Tacámbaro** Michoacán de Ocampo, SW Mexico
- 42 A5 **Tacaná, Volcán** ▲ Guatemala/Mexico
- 43 X16 **Tacarcuna, Cerro** ▲ SE Panama
- **Tachau** see Tachov
- 158 J3 **Tacheng** var. Qoqek. Xinjiang Uygur Zizhiqu, NW China
- 54 H7 **Táchira** off. Estado Táchira. ◆ state W Venezuela
- 161 T13 **Tachoshui** N Taiwan
- 111 A17 **Tachov** Ger. Tachau. Plzeňský Kraj, W Czech Republic
- 171 Q5 **Tacloban** off. Tacloban City. Leyte, C Philippines
- 57 I19 **Tacna** Tacna, SE Peru
- 57 H18 **Tacna** off. Departamento de Tacna. ◆ department S Peru
- 32 H8 **Tacoma** Washington, NW USA
- 18 L11 **Taconic Range** ▲ NE USA
- 62 L6 **Taco Pozo** Formosa, N Argentina
- 57 M20 **Tacsara, Cordillera de** ▲ S Bolivia
- 61 F17 **Tacuarembó** prev. San Fructuoso. Tacuarembó, C Uruguay
- 61 E18 **Tacuarembó** ◆ department C Uruguay
- 61 F17 **Tacuarembó, Río** ≈ C Uruguay
- 83 I14 **Taculi** North Western, NW Zambia
- 171 Q8 **Tacurong** Mindanao, S Philippines
- 77 V8 **Tadek** ≈ NW Niger
- 74 J9 **Tademaït, Plateau du** plateau C Algeria
- 187 R17 **Tadine** Province des Îles Loyauté, E New Caledonia
- 80 L11 **Tadjoura** E Djibouti
- 80 M11 **Tadjoura, Golfe de** Eng. Gulf of Tajura. inlet E Djibouti
- **Tadmor/Tadmur** see Tudmur
- 11 W10 **Tadoule Lake** ⊚ Manitoba, C Canada
- 15 S8 **Tadoussac** Quebec, SE Canada
- 155 H18 **Tādpatri** Andhra Pradesh, E India
- **Tadzhikabad** see Tojikobod
- **Tadzhikistan** see Tajikistan
- 163 Y14 **T'aebaek-sanmaek** ▲ E South Korea
- 163 V15 **Taechŏng-do** island NW South Korea
- 163 X13 **Taedong-gang** ≈ C North Korea
- 163 Y16 **Taegu** off. Taegu-gwangyŏksi, var. Daegu, Jap. Taikyū. SE South Korea
- **Taehan-haehyŏp** see Korea Strait
- **Taehan Min'guk** see South Korea
- 163 Y15 **Taejŏn** off. Taejŏn-gwangyŏksi, Jap. Taiden. C South Korea
- 193 Z13 **Tafahi** island N Tonga
- 105 Q4 **Tafalla** Navarra, N Spain
- 75 M12 **Tafassâsset, Oued** ≈ SE Algeria
- 77 W7 **Tafassâsset, Ténéré du** desert N Niger
- 55 U11 **Tafelberg** ▲ S Suriname
- 97 J21 **Taff** ≈ SE Wales, UK
- **Tafila/Ţafīlah, Muḩāfaẓat aţ** see Aţ Ţafīlah
- 77 N15 **Tafiré** N Ivory Coast
- 142 M6 **Tafresh** Markazī, W Iran
- 143 Q9 **Taft** Yazd, C Iran
- 35 R13 **Taft** California, W USA
- 25 T14 **Taft** Texas, SW USA
- 143 W12 **Taftān, Kūh-e** ▲ SE Iran
- 35 R13 **Taft Heights** California, W USA
- 189 Y14 **Tafunsak** Kosrae, E Micronesia
- 192 G16 **Tāga** Savai'i, SW Samoa
- 149 Q5 **Tagāb** Kāpīsā, E Afghanistan
- 39 O8 **Tagagawik River** ≈ Alaska, USA
- 165 Q10 **Tagajō** var. Tagazyô. Miyagi, Honshū, C Japan
- 128 K12 **Taganrog** Rostovskaya Oblast', SW Russian Federation
- 128 K12 **Taganrog, Gulf of** Rus. Taganrogskiy Zaliv, Ukr. Tahanroz'ka Zatoka. gulf Russian Federation/Ukraine
- **Taganrogskiy Zaliv** see Taganrog, Gulf of
- 76 J8 **Tagant** ◆ region C Mauritania
- 148 M14 **Tagas** Baluchistān, SW Pakistan
- 171 O4 **Tagaytay** Luzon, N Philippines
- **Tagazyô** see Tagajō
- 171 P6 **Tagbilaran** var. Tagbilaran City. Bohol, C Philippines
- 106 B10 **Taggia** Liguria, NW Italy
- 77 V9 **Taghouaji, Massif de** ▲ C Niger
- 107 J15 **Tagliacozzo** Lazio, C Italy
- 106 J7 **Tagliamento** ≈ NE Italy
- 149 N3 **Tagow Bāy** var. Bai. Sar-e Pol, N Afghanistan
- **Tagtabazar** see Takhtabazar
- 59 L17 **Taguatinga** Tocantins, C Brazil
- 186 I10 **Tagula** Tagula Island, SE PNG
- 186 I11 **Tagula Island** prev. Southeast Island, Sudest Island. island SE PNG
- 171 Q7 **Tagum** Mindanao, S Philippines
- 54 C7 **Tagún, Cerro** elevation Colombia/Panama
- 105 P7 **Tagus** Port. Rio Tejo, Sp. Río Tajo. ≈ Portugal/Spain
- 64 M9 **Tagus Plain** undersea feature E Atlantic Ocean
- 191 S10 **Tahaa** island Îles Sous le Vent, W French Polynesia
- 191 U10 **Tahanea** atoll Îles Tuamotu, C French Polynesia
- **Tahanroz'ka Zatoka** see Taganrog, Gulf of
- 74 K12 **Tahat** ▲ SE Algeria
- 163 V12 **Ta He** ≈ NE China
- 163 U4 **Tahe** Heilongjiang, NE China
- 162 G9 **Tahilt** Govĭ-Altay, W Mongolia
- 191 T10 **Tahiti** island Îles du Vent, W French Polynesia
- **Tahiti, Archipel de** see Société, Archipel de la
- 118 E4 **Tahkuna nina** headland W Estonia
- 148 K12 **Tāhlāb** ≈ W Pakistan
- 148 K12 **Tāhlāb, Dasht-i** desert SW Pakistan
- 27 R10 **Tahlequah** Oklahoma, C USA
- 35 Q6 **Tahoe City** California, W USA
- 35 P6 **Tahoe, Lake** ⊚ California/Nevada, W USA
- **Tahoena** see Tahuna
- 25 N6 **Tahoka** Texas, SW USA
- 32 F8 **Taholah** Washington, NW USA
- 77 T11 **Tahoua** Tahoua, W Niger
- 77 T11 **Tahoua** ◆ department W Niger
- 31 P3 **Tahquamenon Falls** waterfall Michigan, N USA
- 31 P4 **Tahquamenon River** ≈ Michigan, N USA
- 139 V10 **Ţahrīr** S Iraq
- 10 K17 **Tahsis** Vancouver Island, British Columbia, SW Canada
- **Tahta** see Takhta
- 75 W9 **Ţahta** C Egypt
- 136 L15 **Tahtalı Dağları** ▲ C Turkey
- 57 I14 **Tahuamanu, Río** ≈ Bolivia/Peru
- 56 F13 **Tahuanía, Río** ≈ E Peru
- 191 X7 **Tahuata** island Îles Marquises, NE French Polynesia
- 171 Q10 **Tahuna** prev. Tahoena. Pulau Sangihe, N Indonesia
- 76 L17 **Taï** SW Ivory Coast
- 161 P5 **Tai'an** Shandong, E China
- 191 R8 **Taiarapu, Presqu'île de** peninsula Tahiti, W French Polynesia
- **Taibad** see Tāybād
- 160 K7 **Taibai Shan** ▲ C China
- 105 Q12 **Taibilla, Sierra de** ▲ S Spain
- 163 Q12 **Taibus Qi** var. Baochang. Nei Mongol Zizhiqu, N China
- **Taichū** see T'aichung
- 161 S13 **T'aichung** Jap. Taichū; prev. Taiwan. C Taiwan
- **Taiden** see Taejŏn
- 185 E23 **Taieri** ≈ South Island, NZ
- 115 E21 **Taïgetos** ▲ S Greece
- 163 N14 **Taihang Shan** ▲ C China
- 184 M11 **Taihape** Manawatu-Wanganui, North Island, NZ
- 161 O7 **Taihe** Anhui, E China
- 161 O12 **Taihe** Jiangxi, S China
- **Taihoku** see T'aipei
- 161 R8 **Tai Hu** ⊚ E China
- 161 P9 **Taihu** Anhui, E China
- 161 O6 **Taikang** Henan, C China
- 165 T5 **Taiki** Hokkaidō, NE Japan
- 166 L8 **Taikkyi** Yangon, SW Burma
- **Taikyū** see Taegu
- 163 U8 **Tailai** Heilongjiang, NE China
- 168 I12 **Taileleo** Pulau Siberut, W Indonesia
- 182 J10 **Tailem Bend** South Australia
- 96 I8 **Tain** N Scotland, UK
- 161 S14 **T'ainan** Jap. Tainan; prev. Dainan. S Taiwan
- 115 E22 **Taínaro, Akrotírio** headland S Greece
- 161 Q11 **Taining** Fujian, SE China
- 191 W7 **Taiohae** prev. Madisonville. Nuku Hiva, NE French Polynesia
- 161 T13 **T'aipei** Jap. Taihoku; prev. Daihoku. ● (Taiwan) N Taiwan
- 168 J7 **Taiping** Perak, Peninsular Malaysia
- 163 S8 **Taiping Ling** ▲ NE China
- 165 Q4 **Taisei** Hokkaidō, NE Japan
- 165 G12 **Taisha** Shimane, Honshū, SW Japan
- 109 R4 **Taiskirchen** Oberösterreich, NW Austria
- 63 F20 **Taitao, Peninsula de** peninsula S Chile
- **Taitō** see T'aitung
- 161 T14 **T'aitung** Jap. Taitō. S Taiwan
- 92 M13 **Taivalkoski** Oulu, E Finland
- 93 K19 **Taivassalo** Länsi-Suomi, W Finland
- 161 T14 **Taiwan** off. Republic of China, var. Formosa, Formo'sa. ◆ republic E Asia
- 192 F5 **Taiwan** var. Formosa. island E Asia
- **Taiwan** see T'aichung
- **T'aiwan Haihsia/Taiwan Haixia** see Taiwan Strait
- **Taiwan Shan** see Chungyang Shanmo
- 161 R13 **Taiwan Strait** var. Formosa Strait, Chin. T'aiwan Haihsia, Taiwan Haixia. strait China/Taiwan
- 161 N4 **Taiyuan** prev. T'ai-yuan, T'ai-yüan, Yangku. Shanxi, C China
- 161 R7 **Taizhou** Jiangsu, E China
- 161 S10 **Taizhou** prev. Haimen, Jiaojiang. Zhejiang, SE China
- **Taizhou** see Linhai
- 141 O16 **Ta'izz** SW Yemen
- 141 O16 **Ta'izz** ✕ SW Yemen
- 75 P12 **Tajarhī** SW Libya
- 147 P13 **Tajikistan** off. Republic of Tajikistan, Rus. Tadzhikistan, Taj. Jumhurii Tojikiston; prev. Tajik S.S.R. ◆ republic C Asia
- **Tajik S.S.R** see Tajikistan
- 165 O11 **Tajima** Fukushima, Honshū, C Japan
- **Tajoe** see Tayu
- **Tajo, Río** see Tagus
- 42 B5 **Tajumulco, Volcán** ▲ W Guatemala
- 105 P7 **Tajuña** ≈ C Spain
- **Tajura, Gulf of** see Tadjoura, Golfe de
- 167 O9 **Tak** var. Rahaeng. Tak, W Thailand
- 189 U4 **Taka Atoll** var. Tōke. atoll Ratak Chain, N Marshall Islands
- 165 P12 **Takahagi** Ibaraki, Honshū, S Japan
- 165 H13 **Takahashi** var. Takahasi. Okayama, Honshū, SW Japan
- **Takahasi** see Takahashi
- 189 P12 **Takaieu Island** island E Micronesia
- 184 I13 **Takaka** Tasman, South Island, NZ
- 170 M14 **Takalar** Sulawesi, C Indonesia
- 165 H13 **Takamatsu** var. Takamatu. Kagawa, Shikoku, SW Japan
- **Takamatu** see Takamatsu
- 165 D14 **Takamori** Kumamoto, Kyūshū, SW Japan
- 165 D16 **Takanabe** Miyazaki, Kyūshū, SW Japan
- 170 M16 **Takan, Gunung** ▲ Pulau Sumba, S Indonesia
- 165 Q7 **Takanosu** Akita, Honshū, C Japan
- **Takao** see Kaohsiung
- 165 L11 **Takaoka** Toyama, Honshū, SW Japan
- 184 N12 **Takapau** Hawke's Bay, North Island, NZ
- 191 U9 **Takapoto** atoll Îles Tuamotu, C French Polynesia
- 184 L5 **Takapuna** Auckland, North Island, NZ
- 165 J3 **Takarazuka** Hyōgo, Honshū, SW Japan
- 191 U9 **Takaroa** atoll Îles Tuamotu, C French Polynesia
- 165 N12 **Takasaki** Gunma, Honshū, S Japan
- 164 L12 **Takayama** Gifu, Honshū, SW Japan
- 164 K12 **Takefu** var. Takehu. Fukui, Honshū, SW Japan
- **Takehu** see Takefu
- 164 C14 **Takeo** Saga, Kyūshū, SW Japan
- **Takeo** see Takêv
- 164 C17 **Take-shima** island Nansei-shotō, SW Japan
- 142 M5 **Tākestān** var. Takistan; prev. Siadehan. Qazvīn, N Iran
- 164 D14 **Taketa** Ōita, Kyūshū, SW Japan
- 167 R13 **Takêv** prev. Takeo. Takêv, S Cambodia
- 167 O10 **Tak Fah** Nakhon Sawan, C Thailand
- 139 T13 **Takhādīd** well S Iraq
- 149 R3 **Takhār** ◆ province NE Afghanistan
- **Takhiatash** see Takhiatosh
- 146 H8 **Takhiatosh** Rus. Takhiatash. Qoraqalpoghiston Respublikasi, W Uzbekistan
- 167 S13 **Ta Khmau** Kândal, S Cambodia
- 146 H9 **Takhta** Turkm. Tahta. Dashkhovuzskiy Velayat, N Turkmenistan
- 146 J16 **Takhtabazar** var. Tagtabazar. Maryyskiy Velayat, S Turkmenistan
- 145 O8 **Takhtabrod** Severnyy Kazakhstan, N Kazakhstan
- 146 H7 **Takhtakŭpir** Rus. Takhtakupyr. Qoraqalpoghiston Respublikasi, NW Uzbekistan
- **Takhtakupyr** see Takhtakŭpir
- 142 M8 **Takht-e Shāh, Kūh-e** ▲ C Iran
- 77 V12 **Takiéta** Zinder, S Niger
- 8 J8 **Takijuq Lake** ⊚ Nunavut, NW Canada
- 165 S3 **Takikawa** Hokkaidō, NE Japan
- 165 U3 **Takinoue** Hokkaidō, NE Japan
- **Takistan** see Tākestān
- 185 B23 **Takitimu Mountains** ▲ South Island, NZ
- **Takkaze** see Tekezē
- 165 R7 **Takko** Aomori, Honshū, C Japan
- 10 L13 **Takla Lake** ⊚ British Columbia, SW Canada
- **Takla Makan Desert** see Taklimakan Shamo
- 158 H9 **Taklimakan Shamo** Eng. Takla Makan Desert. desert NW China
- 167 T12 **Takôk** Môndól Kiri, E Cambodia
- 39 P10 **Takotna** Alaska, USA
- **Takow** see Kaohsiung
- 123 O12 **Taksimo** Respublika Buryatiya, S Russian Federation
- 164 C13 **Taku** Saga, Kyūshū, SW Japan
- 10 I10 **Taku** ≈ British Columbia, W Canada
- 166 M15 **Takua Pa** var. Ban Takua Pa. Phangnga, SW Thailand
- 77 W16 **Takum** Taraba, E Nigeria
- 191 V10 **Takume** atoll Îles Tuamotu, C French Polynesia
- 190 L16 **Takutea** island S Cook Islands
- 186 K6 **Takuu Islands** prev. Mortlock Group. island group NE PNG
- 119 L18 **Tal'** Rus. Tal'. Minskaya Voblasts', S Belarus
- 40 L13 **Tala** Jalisco, C Mexico
- 61 F19 **Tala** Canelones, S Uruguay
- **Talabriga** see Aveiro, Portugal
- **Talabriga** see Talavera de la Reina, Spain
- 119 N14 **Talachyn** Rus. Tolochin. Vitsyebskaya Voblasts', NE Belarus
- 149 U7 **Talagang** Punjab, E Pakistan
- 155 J23 **Talaimannar** Northern Province, NW Sri Lanka
- 117 R3 **Talalayivka** Chernihivs'ka Oblast', N Ukraine
- 43 O15 **Talamanca, Cordillera de** ▲ S Costa Rica
- 56 A9 **Talara** Piura, NW Peru
- 104 L11 **Talarrubias** Extremadura, W Spain
- 147 S8 **Talas** Talasskaya Oblast', NW Kyrgyzstan
- 147 S8 **Talas** ≈ NW Kyrgyzstan
- 186 G7 **Talasea** New Britain, E PNG
- **Talas Oblasty** see Talasskaya Oblast'
- 147 S8 **Talasskaya Oblast'** Kir. Talas Oblasty. ◆ province NW Kyrgyzstan
- 147 S8 **Talasskiy Alatau, Khrebet** ▲ Kazakhstan/Kyrgyzstan
- 77 U12 **Talata Mafara** Zamfara, NW Nigeria
- 171 R9 **Talaud, Kepulauan** island group E Indonesia
- 104 M9 **Talavera de la Reina** anc. Caesarobriga, Talabriga. Castilla-La Mancha, C Spain
- 104 J11 **Talavera la Real** Extremadura, W Spain
- 186 F7 **Talawe, Mount** ▲ New Britain, C PNG
- 23 S5 **Talbotton** Georgia, SE USA
- 183 R7 **Talbragar River** ≈ New South Wales, SE Australia
- 62 G13 **Talca** Maule, C Chile
- 62 F13 **Talcahuano** Bío Bío, C Chile
- 154 N12 **Tālcher** Orissa, E India
- 25 W5 **Talco** Texas, SW USA
- 145 V14 **Taldykorgan** Kaz. Taldyqorghan; prev. Taldy-Kurgan. Almaty, SE Kazakhstan
- **Taldy-Kurgan/Taldyqorghan** see Taldykorgan
- 147 Y7 **Taldy-Suu** Issyk-Kul'skaya Oblast', E Kyrgyzstan
- 147 U10 **Taldy-Suu** Oshskaya Oblast', SW Kyrgyzstan
- **Tal-e Khosravī** see Yāsūj
- 193 Y15 **Taleki Tonga** island Otu Tolu Group, C Tonga
- 193 Y15 **Taleki Vavu'u** island Otu Tolu Group, C Tonga
- 102 J13 **Talence** Gironde, SW France
- 145 U16 **Talgar** Kaz. Talghar. Almaty, SE Kazakhstan
- **Talghar** see Talgar
- 171 Q12 **Taliabu, Pulau** island Kepulauan Sula, C Indonesia
- 115 L22 **Taliarós, Akrotírio** headland Astypálaia, Kykládes, Greece, Aegean Sea
- **Ta-lien** see Dalian
- 27 Q12 **Talihina** Oklahoma, C USA
- **Talimardzhan** see Tollimarjon
- **Talin** see T'alin
- 137 T12 **T'alin** Rus. Talin; prev. Verin T'alin. W Armenia
- 81 E15 **Tali Post** Bahr el Gabel, S Sudan
- **Taliq-an** see Tāloqān
- **Taliş Dağları** see Talish Mountains
- 142 L2 **Talish Mountains** Az. Taliş Dağları, Per. Kūhhā-ye Ţavālesh, Rus. Talyshskiye Gory. ▲ Azerbaijan/Iran
- 170 M16 **Taliwang** Sumbawa, C Indonesia
- 119 L17 **Tal'ka** Rus. Tal'ka. Minskaya Voblasts', C Belarus
- **Talkang** see Dorbod
- 39 R11 **Talkeetna** Alaska, USA
- 39 R11 **Talkeetna Mountains** ▲ Alaska, USA
- **Talkhof** see Puurmani
- 92 H2 **Tálknafjördhur** Vestfirdhir, W Iceland
- 139 Q3 **Tall 'Abţah** N Iraq
- 138 M2 **Tall Abyaḑ** var. Tell Abiad. Ar Raqqah, N Syria
- 23 Q4 **Talladega** Alabama, S USA
- 139 Q2 **Tall 'Afar** N Iraq
- 23 S8 **Tallahassee** prev. Muskogean. state capital Florida, SE USA
- 22 L2 **Tallahatchie River** ≈ Mississippi, S USA
- **Tall al Abyaḑ** see At Tall al Abyaḑ
- 139 W12 **Tall al Laḩm** S Iraq
- 183 P11 **Tallangatta** Victoria, SE Australia
- 23 R4 **Tallapoosa River** ≈ Alabama/Georgia, S USA
- 103 T13 **Tallard** Hautes-Alpes, SE France
- 139 Q3 **Tall ash Sha'īr** N Iraq
- 23 Q5 **Tallassee** Alabama, S USA
- 139 R4 **Tall 'Azbah** NW Iraq
- 138 I5 **Tall Bīsah** Ḩimş, W Syria
- 139 R3 **Tall Ḩassūnah** N Iraq
- 139 Q2 **Tall Ḩuqnah** var. Tell Huqnah. N Iraq
- **Tallin** see Tallinn
- 118 G3 **Tallinn** Ger. Reval, Rus. Tallin; prev. Revel. ● (Estonia) Harjumaa, NW Estonia
- 118 H3 **Tallinn** ✕ Harjumaa, NW Estonia
- 138 H5 **Tall Kalakh** var. Tell Kalakh. Ḩimş, C Syria
- 139 R2 **Tall Kayf** NW Iraq
- **Tall Kūchak** see Tall Kūshik
- 139 P2 **Tall Kūshik** var. Tall Kūchak. Al Ḩasakah, E Syria
- 31 U12 **Tallmadge** Ohio, N USA
- 22 J5 **Tallulah** Louisiana, S USA
- 139 Q2 **Tall 'Uwaynāt** NW Iraq
- 139 Q2 **Tall Zāhir** N Iraq
- 122 J13 **Tal'menka** Altayskiy Kray, S Russian Federation
- 122 K8 **Talnakh** Taymyrskiy (Dolgano-Nenetskiy) Avtonomnyy Okrug, N Russian Federation
- 117 P7 **Tal'ne** Rus. Tal'noye. Cherkas'ka Oblast', C Ukraine
- **Tal'noye** see Tal'ne
- 80 E12 **Talodi** Southern Kordofan, C Sudan
- 188 B16 **Talofofo** SE Guam
- 188 B16 **Talofofo Bay** bay SE Guam
- 26 L9 **Taloga** Oklahoma, C USA
- 123 T10 **Talon** Magadanskaya Oblast', E Russian Federation
- 14 H11 **Talon, Lake** ⊚ Ontario, S Canada
- 149 R2 **Tāloqān** var. Taliq-an. Takhār, NE Afghanistan
- 128 M8 **Talovaya** Voronezhskaya Oblast', W Russian Federation
- 9 N6 **Taloyoak** prev. Spence Bay. Nunavut, N Canada
- 25 Q8 **Talpa** Texas, SW USA
- 40 K13 **Talpa de Allende** Jalisco, C Mexico
- 23 S9 **Talquin, Lake** ⊞ Florida, SE USA
- **Talsen** see Talsi
- 162 H9 **Talshand** Govĭ-Altay, C Mongolia
- 118 E8 **Talsi** Ger. Talsen. Talsi, NW Latvia
- 143 V11 **Tal Sīāh** Sīstān va Balūchestān, SE Iran
- 62 G6 **Taltal** Antofagasta, N Chile
- 8 K10 **Taltson** ≈ Northwest Territories, NW Canada
- 168 K11 **Taluk** Sumatera, W Indonesia
- 92 J8 **Talvik** Finnmark, N Norway
- 182 M7 **Talyawalka Creek** ≈ New South Wales, SE Australia
- **Talyshskiye Gory** see Talish Mountains
- 29 W14 **Tama** Iowa, C USA
- **Tama Abu, Banjaran** see Penambo, Banjaran
- 169 U9 **Tamabo, Banjaran** ▲ East Malaysia
- 190 B16 **Tamakautoga** SW Niue
- 129 N7 **Tamala** Penzenskaya Oblast', W Russian Federation
- 77 P15 **Tamale** C Ghana
- 191 P3 **Tamana** prev. Rotcher Island. atoll Tungaru, W Kiribati
- 74 K12 **Tamanrasset** var. Tamenghest. S Algeria
- 74 J13 **Tamanrasset** wadi Algeria/Mali
- 166 M2 **Tamanthi** Sagaing, N Burma
- 97 I24 **Tamar** ≈ SW England, UK
- **Tamar** see Tudmur
- 54 H9 **Támara** Casanare, C Colombia
- 54 F7 **Tamar, Alto de** ▲ C Colombia
- 173 X16 **Tamarin** E Mauritius
- 105 T5 **Tamarite de Litera** var. Tararite de Llitera. Aragón, NE Spain
- 111 I24 **Tamási** Tolna, S Hungary
- **Tamatave** see Toamasina
- 41 O9 **Tamaulipas** ◆ state C Mexico
- 41 P10 **Tamaulipas, Sierra de** ▲ C Mexico
- 56 F12 **Tamaya, Río** ≈ E Peru
- 40 I9 **Tamazula** Durango, C Mexico
- 40 L14 **Tamazula** Jalisco, C Mexico
- **Tamazulápam** see Tamazulapán
- 41 Q15 **Tamazulapán** var. Tamazulápam. Oaxaca, SE Mexico
- 41 P12 **Tamazunchale** San Luis Potosí, C Mexico
- 76 H11 **Tambacounda** SE Senegal
- 83 M16 **Tambara** Manica, C Mozambique
- 77 T13 **Tambawel** Sokoto, NW Nigeria
- 186 M9 **Tambea** Guadalcanal, C Solomon Islands
- 169 N10 **Tambelan, Kepulauan** island group W Indonesia
- 57 E15 **Tambo de Mora** Ica, W Peru
- 170 L16 **Tambora, Gunung** ▲ Sumbawa, S Indonesia
- 61 E17 **Tambores** Paysandú, W Uruguay
- 57 F14 **Tambo, Río** ≈ C Peru
- 56 F7 **Tamboryacu, Río** ≈ N Peru
- 128 M7 **Tambov** Tambovskaya Oblast', W Russian Federation
- 128 L6 **Tambovskaya Oblast'** ◆ province W Russian Federation
- 104 H3 **Tambre** ≈ NW Spain
- 169 V7 **Tambunan** Sabah, East Malaysia
- 81 C15 **Tambura** Western Equatoria, SW Sudan
- **Tamchaket** see Tâmchekkeţ
- 76 J9 **Tâmchekkeţ** var. Tamchaket. Hodh el Gharbi, S Mauritania
- 167 T7 **Tam Điêp** Ninh Binh, N Vietnam
- **Tamdybulak** see Tomdibuloq
- 54 H8 **Tame** Arauca, C Colombia
- 104 H6 **Tâmega, Rio** Sp. Río Támega. ≈ Portugal/Spain
- 115 H20 **Tamélos, Akrotírio** headland Kéa, Kykládes, Greece, Aegean Sea
- **Tamenghest** see Tamanrasset
- 77 V8 **Tamgak, Adrar** ▲ C Niger
- 76 I13 **Tamgue** ▲ NW Guinea
- 41 Q12 **Tamiahua** Veracruz-Llave, E Mexico
- 41 Q12 **Tamiahua, Laguna de** lagoon E Mexico
- 23 Y16 **Tamiami Canal** canal Florida, SE USA
- 188 F17 **Tamil Harbor** harbor Yap, W Micronesia
- 155 H21 **Tamil Nādu** prev. Madras. ◆ state SE India
- 99 H20 **Tamines** Namur, S Belgium
- 116 E12 **Tamiš** Ger. Temesch, Hung. Temes, SCr. Tamiš. ≈ Romania/Yugoslavia
- 167 U10 **Tam Kỳ** Quang Nam-Đa Nẵng, C Vietnam
- **Tammerfors** see Tampere
- **Tammisaari** see Ekenäs
- 95 N14 **Tämnaren** ⊚ C Sweden
- 191 Q7 **Tamotoe, Passe** passage Tahiti, W French Polynesia
- 23 V12 **Tampa** Florida, SE USA
- 23 V12 **Tampa** ✕ Florida, SE USA
- 23 V13 **Tampa Bay** bay Florida, SE USA
- 93 L18 **Tampere** Swe. Tammerfors. Länsi-Suomi, W Finland
- 41 Q11 **Tampico** Tamaulipas, C Mexico
- 171 P14 **Tampo** Pulau Muna, C Indonesia
- 167 V11 **Tam Quan** Binh Đinh, C Vietnam
- 162 J13 **Tamsag Muchang** Nei Mongol Zizhiqu, N China
- **Tamsal** see Tamsalu
- 118 I4 **Tamsalu** Ger. Tamsal. Lääne-Virumaa, NE Estonia
- 109 S8 **Tamsweg** Salzburg, SW Austria
- 166 L3 **Tamu** Sagaing, N Burma
- 41 P12 **Tamuín** San Luis Potosí, C Mexico
- 188 C15 **Tamuning** NW Guam
- 183 T6 **Tamworth** New South Wales, SE Australia
- 97 M19 **Tamworth** C England, UK
- 92 L8 **Tana** Finnmark, N Norway
- 92 M8 **Tana** var. Tenojoki, Fin. Teno, Lapp. Dealnu. ≈ Finland/Norway see also Teno
- 81 K19 **Tana** ≈ SE Kenya
- 164 I15 **Tanabe** Wakayama, Honshū, SW Japan
- 39 T10 **Tanacross** Alaska, USA
- 92 L7 **Tanafjorden** fjord N Norway
- 38 G17 **Tanaga Island** island Aleutian Islands, Alaska, USA
- 38 G17 **Tanaga Volcano** ▲ Tanaga Island, Alaska, USA
- 107 M18 **Tanagro** ≈ S Italy
- 80 H11 **T'ana Hāyk'** Eng. Lake Tana. ⊚ NW Ethiopia
- 168 H11 **Tanahbela, Pulau** island Kepulauan Batu, W Indonesia
- 171 H15 **Tanahjampea, Pulau** island W Indonesia
- 168 H11 **Tanahmasa, Pulau** island Kepulauan Batu, W Indonesia
- **Tanais** see Don
- 152 L10 **Tanakpur** Uttar Pradesh, N India
- **Tana, Lake** see T'ana Hāyk'

◆ Country ● Country Capital ◇ Dependent Territory ○ Dependent Territory Capital ◆ Administrative Region ✕ International Airport ▲ Mountain ▲ Mountain Range ▲ Volcano ≈ River ⊚ Lake ⊞ Reservoir

181 P5 Tanami Desert desert Northern Territory, N Australia
167 T14 Tân An Long An, S Vietnam
39 Q9 Tanana Alaska, USA
Tananarive see Antananarivo
39 Q9 Tanana River ≈ Alaska, USA
95 C16 Tananger Rogaland, S Norway
188 H5 Tanapag Saipan, S Northern Mariana Islands
188 H5 Tanapag, Puetton bay Saipan, S Northern Mariana Islands
106 C9 Tanaro ≈ N Italy
163 Y12 Tanch'ŏn E North Korea
40 M14 Tancítaro, Cerro ✹ C Mexico
153 N12 Tānda Uttar Pradesh, N India
77 O15 Tanda E Ivory Coast
116 L14 Țăndărei Ialomița, SE Romania
63 N14 Tandil Buenos Aires, E Argentina
78 H12 Tandjilé off. Préfecture du Tandjilé. ⬖ prefecture SW Chad
Tandjoeng see Tanjung
Tandjoengpandan see Tanjungpandan
Tandjoengpinang see Tanjungpinang
Tandjoengredeb see Tanjungredeb
149 Q16 Tando Allāhyār Sind, SE Pakistan
149 Q17 Tando Bāgo Sind, SE Pakistan
149 Q16 Tando Muhammad Khān Sind, SE Pakistan
182 L7 Tandou Lake seasonal lake New South Wales, SE Australia
94 L11 Tandsjöborg Gävleborg, C Sweden
155 H15 Tāndūr Andhra Pradesh, C India
164 C17 Tanega-shima island Nansei-shotō, SW Japan
165 R7 Taneichi Iwate, Honshū, C Japan
Tanen Taunggyi see Tane Range
167 N8 Tane Range Bur. Tanen Taunggyi. ⛰ W Thailand
111 P15 Tanew ≈ SE Poland
21 W2 Taneytown Maryland, NE USA
74 H12 Tanezrouft desert Algeria/Mali
138 L7 Țanf, Jabal aț ▲ SE Syria
81 J21 Tanga Tanga, E Tanzania
81 I22 Tanga ⬖ region E Tanzania
153 T14 Tangail Dhaka, C Bangladesh
186 I5 Tanga Islands island group NE PNG
155 K26 Tangalla Southern Province, S Sri Lanka
Tanganyika and Zanzibar see Tanzania
68 I13 Tanganyika, Lake ◎ E Africa
56 E7 Tangarana, Río ≈ N Peru
191 V16 Tangaroa, Maunga ✹ Easter Island, Chile, E Pacific Ocean
74 G5 Tanger var. Tangiers, Tangier, Fr./Ger. Tangerk, Sp. Tánger; anc. Tingis. NW Morocco
169 N15 Tangerang Jawa, C Indonesia
Tangerk see Tanger
100 M12 Tangermünde Sachsen-Anhalt, C Germany
156 K10 Tanggula Shan var. Dangla, Tangla Range. ⛰ W China
159 N13 Tanggula Shan ▲ W China
Tanggulashan see Tuotuoheyan
156 K10 Tanggula Shankou pass W China
161 N7 Tanghe Henan, C China
149 T5 Tāngi North-West Frontier Province, NW Pakistan
Tangier see Tanger
21 Y5 Tangier Island island Virginia, NE USA
Tangiers see Tanger
22 K8 Tangipahoa River ≈ Louisiana, S USA
Tangla Range see Tanggula Shan
164 J12 Tango-hantō peninsula Honshū, SW Japan
156 I10 Tangra Yumco var. Tangro Tso. ◎ W China
Tangro Tso see Tangra Yumco
157 T7 Tangshan var. T'ang-shan. Hebei, E China
77 R14 Tanguiéta NW Benin
163 X7 Tangwang He ≈ NE China
163 X7 Tangyuan Heilongjiang, NE China
92 M11 Tanhua Lappi, N Finland
171 U16 Tanimbar, Kepulauan island group Maluku, E Indonesia
Tanintharyi see Tenasserim
139 U4 Tānjarō ≈ E Iraq
131 T15 Tanjong Piai headland Peninsular Malaysia
Tanjore see Thanjāvūr
169 U12 Tanjung prev. Tandjoeng. Borneo, C Indonesia
169 W9 Tanjungbatu Borneo, N Indonesia
Tanjungkarang see Bandarlampung
169 N13 Tanjungpandan prev. Tandjoengpandan. Pulau Belitung, W Indonesia
168 M10 Tanjungpinang prev. Tandjoengpinang. Pulau Bintan, W Indonesia
169 V9 Tanjungredeb var. Tanjungredep; prev. Tandjoengredeb. Borneo, C Indonesia
Tanjungredep see Tanjungredeb
149 S8 Tānk North-West Frontier Province, NW Pakistan
187 S15 Tanna island S Vanuatu
93 F17 Tännäs Jämtland, C Sweden
Tannenhof see Krynica
108 K7 Tannheim Tirol, W Austria
Tannu-Tuva see Tyva, Respublika
171 Q12 Tano Pulau Taliabu, E Indonesia
77 O17 Tano ≈ S Ghana
152 D10 Tanot Rājasthān, NW India
77 V11 Tanout Zinder, C Niger
41 P12 Tanquián San Luis Potosí, C Mexico
77 R13 Tansarga E Burkina
167 T13 Tan Son Nhat ✕ (Hô Chi Minh) Tây Ninh, S Vietnam
75 V8 Tanta var. Tantā, Tantâ. N Egypt
74 D9 Tan-Tan SW Morocco
41 P12 Tantoyuca Veracruz-Llave, E Mexico
152 J12 Tāntpur Uttar Pradesh, N India
Tan-tung see Dandong
38 M12 Tanunak Alaska, USA
166 L5 Ta-nyaung Magwe, W Burma
167 S5 Tân Yên Tuyên Quang, N Vietnam
81 F22 Tanzania off. United Republic of Tanzania, Swa. Jamhuri ya Muungano wa Tanzania; prev. German East Africa, Tanganyika and Zanzibar. ◆ republic E Africa
Tanzania, Jamhuri ya Muungano wa see Tanzania
163 U9 Tao'an var. Taoan, Taonan. Jilin, NE China
163 T8 Tao'er He ≈ NE China
159 U11 Tao He ≈ C China
T'aon-an see Baicheng
Taongi see Bokaak Atoll
107 M23 Taormina anc. Tauromenium. Sicilia, Italy, C Mediterranean Sea
37 S9 Taos New Mexico, SW USA
Taoudenit see Taoudenni
77 O6 Taoudenni var. Taoudenit. Tombouctou, N Mali
74 G6 Taounate N Morocco
161 S13 T'aoyüan Jap. Tōen. N Taiwan
118 I3 Tapa Ger. Taps. Lääne-Virumaa, NE Estonia
41 V17 Tapachula Chiapas, SE Mexico
Tapaiu see Gvardeysk
59 H14 Tapajós, Rio var. Tapajóz. ≈ NW Brazil
Tapajóz see Tapajós, Rio
61 C21 Tapalqué var. Tapalquén. Buenos Aires, E Argentina
Tapalquén see Tapalqué
Tapanahoni see Tapanahony Rivier
55 W11 Tapanahony Rivier var. Tapanahoni. ≈ E Suriname
41 T16 Tapanatepec var. San Pedro Tapanatepec. Oaxaca, SE Mexico
185 D23 Tapanui Otago, South Island, NZ
59 E14 Tapauá Amazonas, N Brazil
47 R7 Tapauá, Rio ≈ W Brazil
185 I14 Tapawera Tasman, South Island, NZ
61 I16 Tapes Rio Grande do Sul, S Brazil
76 K16 Tapeta C Liberia
154 H11 Tāpi prev. Tāpti. ≈ W India
104 J2 Tapia de Casariego Asturias, N Spain
56 F10 Tapiche, Río ≈ N Peru
167 N15 Tapi, Mae Nam var. Luang. ≈ SW Thailand
186 E8 Tapini Central, S PNG
Tapirapecó, Serra see Tapirapecó, Sierra
55 N13 Tapirapecó, Sierra Port. Serra Tapirapecó. ⛰ Brazil/Venezuela
77 R13 Tapoa ≈ Benin/Niger
188 H5 Tapochau, Mount ▲ Saipan, S Northern Mariana Islands
111 H24 Tapolca Veszprém, W Hungary
21 X5 Tappahannock Virginia, NE USA
31 U13 Tappan Lake ⊡ Ohio, N USA
165 Q6 Tappi-zaki headland Honshū, C Japan
Taps see Tapa
Tāpti see Tāpi
185 J16 Tapuaenuku ▲ South Island, NZ
171 N8 Tapul Group island group Sulu Archipelago, SW Philippines
58 E11 Tapurmcuará var. Tapuruquara. Amazonas, NW Brazil
Tapuruquara see Tapurmcuará
192 J17 Taputapu, Cape headland Tutuila, W American Samoa
141 W13 Țāqah S Oman
139 T3 Taqtaq N Iraq
61 J15 Taquara Rio Grande do Sul, S Brazil
59 H19 Taquari, Rio ≈ C Brazil
60 L8 Taquaritinga São Paulo, S Brazil
122 I11 Tara Omskaya Oblast', C Russian Federation
83 I16 Tara Southern, S Zambia
113 J15 Tara ≈ SW Yugoslavia
112 K13 Tara ⛰ W Yugoslavia
77 W15 Taraba ⬖ state E Nigeria
77 X15 Taraba ≈ E Nigeria
75 O7 Țarābulus var. Țarābulus al Gharb, Eng. Tripoli. ● (Libya) NW Libya
75 O7 Țarābulus ✕ NW Libya
Țarābulus/Țarābulus ash Shām see Tripoli
Țarābulus al Gharb see Țarābulus
105 O7 Taracena Castilla-La Mancha, C Spain
117 N12 Taraclia Rus. Tarakilya. S Moldova
139 V10 Tarād al Kahf SE Iraq
183 R10 Tarago New South Wales, SE Australia
169 V8 Tarakan Borneo, C Indonesia
169 V9 Tarakan, Pulau island N Indonesia
Tarakilya see Taraclia
165 P16 Tarama-jima island Sakishima-shotō, SW Japan
184 K10 Taranaki off. Taranaki Region. ⬖ region North Island, NZ
184 K10 Taranaki, Mount var. Egmont. ▲ North Island, NZ
105 O9 Tarancón Castilla-La Mancha, C Spain
188 M15 Tarang Reef reef C Micronesia
96 E7 Taransay island NW Scotland, UK
107 P18 Taranto var. Tarentum. Puglia, SE Italy
107 O19 Taranto, Golfo di Eng. Gulf of Taranto. gulf S Italy
Taranto, Gulf of see Taranto, Golfo di
62 G3 Tarapacá off. Región de Tarapacá. ⬖ region N Chile
187 N9 Tarapaina Maramasike Island, N Solomon Islands
56 D10 Tarapoto San Martín, N Peru
138 M6 Țaraq an Na'jah hill range E Syria
138 M6 Țaraq Sidāwī hill range E Syria
103 Q11 Tarare Rhône, E France
Tararite de Llitera see Tamarite de Litera
184 M13 Tararua Range ⛰ North Island, NZ
151 Q22 Tarāsa Dwīp island Nicobar Islands, India, NE Indian Ocean
103 Q15 Tarascon Bouches-du-Rhône, SE France
102 M17 Tarascon-sur-Ariège Ariège, S France
117 P6 Tarashcha Kyyivs'ka Oblast', N Ukraine
57 L18 Tarata Cochabamba, C Bolivia
57 I18 Tarata Tacna, SW Peru
190 H2 Taratai atoll Tungaru, W Kiribati
59 B15 Tarauacá Acre, W Brazil
59 B15 Tarauacá, Rio ≈ NW Brazil
191 Q8 Taravao Tahiti, W French Polynesia
191 R8 Taravao, Baie de bay Tahiti, W French Polynesia
191 Q8 Taravao, Isthme de isthmus Tahiti, W French Polynesia
103 X16 Taravo ≈ Corse, France, C Mediterranean Sea
190 J3 Tarawa ✕ Tarawa, W Kiribati
190 H2 Tarawa atoll Tungaru, W Kiribati
184 N10 Tarawera Hawke's Bay, North Island, NZ
184 N8 Tarawera, Lake ◎ North Island, NZ
184 N8 Tarawera, Mount ▲ North Island, NZ
105 S8 Tarayuela ▲ N Spain
151 R16 Taraz prev. Aulie Ata, Auliye-Ata, Dzhambul, Zhambyl. Zhambyl, S Kazakhstan.
105 Q5 Tarazona Aragón, NE Spain
105 Q10 Tarazona de la Mancha Castilla-La Mancha, C Spain
145 X12 Tarbagatay, Khrebet ⛰ China/Kazakhstan
96 J8 Tarbat Ness headland N Scotland, UK
149 U5 Tarbela Reservoir ⊡ N Pakistan
96 H12 Tarbert W Scotland, UK
96 F7 Tarbert Western Isles, NW Scotland, UK
102 K16 Tarbes anc. Bigorra. Hautes-Pyrénées, S France
21 W9 Tarboro North Carolina, SE USA
Tarca see Torysa
106 J6 Tarcento Friuli-Venezia Giulia, NE Italy
182 F5 Tarcoola South Australia
105 S5 Tardienta Aragón, NE Spain
102 L11 Tardoire ≈ W France
183 U7 Taree New South Wales, SE Australia
92 K12 Tärendö Norrbotten, N Sweden
Tarentum see Taranto
74 C9 Tarfaya SW Morocco
116 J13 Târgoviște prev. Tîrgoviște. Dâmbovița, S Romania
116 M12 Târgu Bujor prev. Tîrgu Bujor. Galați, E Romania
116 H13 Târgu Cărbunești prev. Tîrgu. Gorj, SW Romania
116 L9 Târgu Frumos prev. Tîrgu Frumos. Iași, NE Romania
116 H13 Târgu Jiu prev. Tîrgu Jiu. Gorj, W Romania
116 H9 Târgu Lăpuș prev. Tîrgu Lăpuș. Maramureș, N Romania
Târgul-Neamț see Târgu-Neamț
Târgul-Săcuiesc see Târgu Secuiesc
116 I10 Târgu Mureș prev. Oșorhei, Tîrgu Mures, Ger. Neumarkt, Hung. Marosvásárhely. Mureș, C Romania
116 K9 Târgu-Neamț var. Târgul-Neamț; prev. Tîrgu-Neamț. Neamț, NE Romania
116 K11 Târgu Ocna Hung. Aknavásár; prev. Tîrgu Ocna. Bacău, E Romania
116 K11 Târgu Secuiesc Ger. Neumarkt, Szekler Neumarkt, Hung. Kezdivásárhely; prev. Chezdi-Oșorheiu, Târgul-Săcuiesc, Tîrgu Secuiesc. Covasna, E Romania
145 X10 Targyn Vostochnyy Kazakhstan, E Kazakhstan
Tar Heel State see North Carolina
186 C7 Tari Southern Highlands, W PNG
143 P17 Țarīf Abū Ẓaby, C UAE
104 K16 Tarifa Andalucía, S Spain
84 C14 Tarifa, Punta de headland SW Spain
57 M21 Tarija Tarija, S Bolivia
57 M21 Tarija ⬖ department S Bolivia
141 R14 Tarīm C Yemen
Tarim Basin see Tarim Pendi
81 G19 Tarime Mara, N Tanzania
131 S8 Tarim He ≈ NW China
159 H8 Tarim Pendi Eng. Tarim Basin. basin NW China
149 N7 Tarīn Kowt var. Terinkot. Urūzgān, C Afghanistan
171 O12 Taripa Sulawesi, C Indonesia
117 Q12 Tarkhankut, Mys headland S Ukraine
27 Q1 Tarkio Missouri, C USA
122 J9 Tarko-Sale Yamalo-Nenetskiy Avtonomnyy Okrug, N Russian Federation
77 P17 Tarkwa S Ghana
171 O3 Tarlac Luzon, N Philippines
95 F22 Tarm Ringkøbing, W Denmark
57 E14 Tarma Junín, C Peru
103 N15 Tarn ⬖ department S France
102 M15 Tarn ≈ S France
111 L22 Tarna ≈ C Hungary
92 G13 Tärnaby Västerbotten, N Sweden
149 P8 Tarnak Rūd ≈ SE Afghanistan
116 J11 Târnava Mare Ger. Grosse Kokel, Hung. Nagy-Küküllő; prev. Tîrnava Mare. ≈ S Romania
116 I11 Târnava Mică Ger. Kleine Kokel, Hung. Kis-Küküllo; prev. Tîrnava Mică. ≈ C Romania
116 I11 Târnăveni Ger. Marteskirch, Martinskirch, Hung. Dicsőszentmárton; prev. Sînmartin, Tîrnăveni. Mureș, C Romania
102 L14 Tarn-et-Garonne ⬖ department S France
111 P18 Tarnica ▲ SE Poland
111 N15 Tarnobrzeg Podkarpackie, SE Poland
127 N12 Tarnogskiy Gorodok Vologodskaya Oblast', NW Russian Federation
Tarnopol see Ternopil'
111 M16 Tarnów Małopolskie, SE Poland
Tarnowice/Tarnowitz see Tarnowskie Góry
111 J16 Tarnowskie Góry var. Tarnowice, Tarnowskie Gory, Ger. Tarnowitz. Śląskie, S Poland
95 N14 Tärnsjö Västmanland, C Sweden
106 E9 Taro ≈ NW Italy
186 I6 Taron New Ireland, NE PNG
74 E8 Taroudannt var. Taroudant. SW Morocco
Taroudant see Taroudannt
23 V12 Tarpon, Lake ◎ Florida, SE USA
23 V12 Tarpon Springs Florida, SE USA
107 G14 Tarquinia anc. Tarquinii; hist. Corneto. Lazio, C Italy
Tarquinii see Tarquinia
Tarraco see Tarragona
76 D10 Tarrafal Santiago, S Cape Verde
105 V6 Tarragona anc. Tarraco. Cataluña, E Spain
105 T7 Tarragona ⬖ province Cataluña, NE Spain
183 O17 Tarraleah Tasmania, SE Australia
23 P3 Tarrant City Alabama, S USA
185 D21 Tarras Otago, South Island, NZ
Tarrasa see Terrassa
105 U5 Tàrrega var. Tarrega. Cataluña, NE Spain
21 W9 Tar River ≈ North Carolina, SE USA
Tarsatica see Rijeka
136 J17 Tarsus İçel, S Turkey
62 K4 Tartagal Salta, N Argentina
137 V12 Tärtär Rus. Terter. ≈ SW Azerbaijan
102 J15 Tartas Landes, SW France
139 Q6 Tārtasah C Iraq
Tartlau see Prejmer
Tartous/Tartouss see Țarțūs
118 J5 Tartu Ger. Dorpat; prev. Rus. Yurev, Yur'yev. Tartumaa, SE Estonia
118 I5 Tartumaa off. Tartu Maakond. ⬖ province E Estonia
138 H5 Țarțūs Fr. Tartouss; anc. Tortosa. Țarțūs, W Syria
138 H5 Țarțūs off. Muḩāfaẓat Țarțūs, var. Tartous, Tartus. ⬖ governorate W Syria
164 C16 Tarumizu Kagoshima, Kyūshū, SW Japan
128 K4 Tarusa Kaluzhskaya Oblast', W Russian Federation
117 N11 Tarutyne Odes'ka Oblast', SW Ukraine
162 I7 Tarvagatyn Nuruu ⛰ N Mongolia
106 J6 Tarvisio Friuli-Venezia Giulia, NE Italy
Tarvisium see Treviso
57 O16 Tarvo, Río ≈ E Bolivia
14 G8 Tarzwell Ontario, S Canada
40 K5 Tasajera, Sierra de la ⛰ N Mexico
145 S13 Tasaral Zhezkazgan, C Kazakhstan
Tasböget see Tasbuget
145 N15 Tasbuget Kaz. Tasböget. Kzylorda, S Kazakhstan
108 E11 Tasch Valais, SW Switzerland
Tasek Kenyir see Kenyir, Tasik
122 J14 Tashanta Respublika Altay, S Russian Federation
Tashauz see Dashkhovuz
Tashi Chho Dzong see Thimphu
153 U11 Tashigang E Bhutan
137 T11 Tashir prev. Kalinino. N Armenia
143 Q11 Țashk, Daryācheh-ye ◎ C Iran
Tashkent see Toshkent
Tashkentskaya Oblast' see Toshkent Wiloyati
146 J16 Tashkepri Turkm. Dashköpri. Maryyskiy Velayat, S Turkmenistan
Tash-Kömür see Tash-Kumyr
147 S9 Tash-Kumyr Kir. Tash-Kömür. Dzhalal-Abadskaya Oblast', W Kyrgyzstan
129 T7 Tashla Orenburgskaya Oblast', W Russian Federation
Tashqurghan see Kholm
122 J13 Tashtagol Kemerovskaya Oblast', S Russian Federation
95 H24 Tåsinge island C Denmark
12 M5 Tasiujaq Quebec, E Canada
77 W11 Tasker Zinder, C Niger
145 W12 Taskesken Vostochnyy Kazakhstan, E Kazakhstan
136 J10 Taşköprü Kastamonu, N Turkey
Taskuduk, Peski see Goshquduq Qum
186 G5 Taskul New Ireland, NE PNG
137 S13 Taşlıçay Ağrı, E Turkey
185 H14 Tasman off. Tasman District. ⬖ unitary authority South Island, NZ
192 J12 Tasman Basin var. East Australian Basin. undersea feature S Tasman Sea
185 I14 Tasman Bay inlet South Island, NZ
192 I13 Tasman Fracture Zone tectonic feature S Indian Ocean
185 E19 Tasman Glacier glacier South Island, NZ
Tasman Group see Nukumanu Islands
183 N15 Tasmania prev. Van Diemen's Land. ⬖ state SE Australia
183 Q16 Tasmania island SE Australia
185 H14 Tasman Mountains ⛰ South Island, NZ
183 P17 Tasman Peninsula peninsula Tasmania, SE Australia
192 I11 Tasman Plain undersea feature W Tasman Sea
192 I12 Tasman Plateau var. South Tasmania Plateau. undersea feature SW Tasman Sea
192 I11 Tasman Sea sea SW Pacific Ocean
116 G9 Tășnad Ger. Trestenberg, Trestendorf, Hung. Tasnád. Satu Mare, NW Romania
136 L11 Tașova Amasya, N Turkey
77 T10 Tassara Tahoua, W Niger
12 K4 Tassialouc, Lac ◎ Quebec, C Canada
Tassili du Hoggar see Tassili ta-n-Ahaggar
74 L11 Tassili-n-Ajjer plateau E Algeria
74 K14 Tassili ta-n-Ahaggar var. Tassili du Hoggar. plateau S Algeria
59 M15 Tasso Fragoso Maranhão, E Brazil
95 J23 Tåstrup var. Taastrup. København, E Denmark
145 O9 Tasty-Taldy Akmola, C Kazakhstan
143 W10 Tāsūkī Sīstān va Balūchestān, SE Iran
111 I22 Tata Ger. Totis. Komárom-Esztergom, NW Hungary
74 E8 Tata SW Morocco
Tataaihoa, Pointe see Vénus, Pointe
111 I22 Tatabánya Komárom-Esztergom, NW Hungary
191 X10 Tatakoto atoll Îles Tuamotu, E French Polynesia
75 N7 Tataouine var. Taṭāwīn. SE Tunisia
55 O5 Tataracual, Cerro ▲ NE Venezuela
117 O12 Tatarbunary Odes'ka Oblast', SW Ukraine
119 M17 Tatarka Rus. Tatarka. Mahilyowskaya Voblasts', E Belarus
Tatar Pazardzhik see Pazardzhik
122 I12 Tatarsk Novosibirskaya Oblast', C Russian Federation
Tatarskaya ASSR see Tatarstan, Respublika
123 T13 Tatarskiy Proliv Eng. Tatar Strait. strait SE Russian Federation
129 R4 Tatarstan, Respublika prev. Tatarskaya ASSR. ⬖ autonomous republic W Russian Federation
Tatar Strait see Tatarskiy Proliv
Taṭāwīn see Tataouine
171 N12 Tate Sulawesi, N Indonesia
141 N11 Tathlīth 'Asīr, S Saudi Arabia
141 O11 Tathlīth, Wādī dry watercourse S Saudi Arabia
183 R11 Tathra New South Wales, SE Australia
129 P8 Tatishchevo Saratovskaya Oblast', W Russian Federation
39 S12 Tatitlek Alaska, USA
10 L15 Tatla Lake British Columbia, SW Canada
121 Q2 Tatlısu Gk. Akanthoú. N Cyprus
11 Z10 Tatnam, Cape headland Manitoba, C Canada
Tatra/Tátra see Tatra Mountains
111 K18 Tatra Mountains Ger. Tatra, Hung. Tátra, Pol./Slvk. Tatry. ⛰ Poland/Slovakia
Tatry see Tatra Mountains
164 I13 Tatsuno var. Tatuno. Hyōgo, Honshū, SW Japan
145 S16 Tatti var. Tatty. Zhambyl, S Kazakhstan
Tatty see Tatti
60 L10 Tatuí São Paulo, S Brazil
37 V14 Tatum New Mexico, SW USA
25 X7 Tatum Texas, SW USA
Ta-t'ung/Tatung see Datong
Tatuno see Tatsuno
137 R14 Tatvan Bitlis, SE Turkey
95 C16 Tau Rogaland, S Norway
192 L17 Ta'ū var. Tau. island Manua Islands, E American Samoa
193 W15 Tau island Tongatapu Group, N Tonga
59 O14 Tauá Ceará, E Brazil
60 N10 Taubaté São Paulo, S Brazil
101 I19 Tauber ≈ SW Germany
101 I19 Tauberbischofsheim Baden-Württemberg, C Germany
144 E14 Tauchik Kaz. Taūshyq. Mangistau, SW Kazakhstan
191 W10 Tauere atoll Îles Tuamotu, C French Polynesia
101 H17 Taufstein ▲ C Germany
190 I17 Taukoka island SE Cook Islands
145 T15 Taukum, Peski desert SE Kazakhstan
184 L10 Taumarunui Manawatu-Wanganui, North Island, NZ
59 A15 Taumaturgo Acre, W Brazil
27 X6 Taum Sauk Mountain ▲ Missouri, C USA
83 H22 Taung North-West, N South Africa
166 L6 Taungdwingyi Magwe, C Burma
166 M6 Taunggyi Shan State, C Burma
166 L5 Taungtha Mandalay, C Burma
166 K7 Taungup Arakan State, W Burma
149 S9 Taunsa Punjab, E Pakistan
97 K23 Taunton SW England, UK
19 O12 Taunton Massachusetts, NE USA
101 F18 Taunus ⛰ W Germany
101 G18 Taunusstein Hessen, W Germany
184 N9 Taupo Waikato, North Island, NZ
184 M9 Taupo, Lake ◎ North Island, NZ
109 R8 Taurach var. Taurachbach. ≈ E Austria
Taurachbach see Taurach
118 D12 Tauragė Ger. Tauroggen. Tauragė, SW Lithuania
54 G10 Tauramena Casanare, C Colombia
184 N7 Tauranga Bay of Plenty, North Island, NZ
15 O10 Taureau, Réservoir ⊡ Quebec, SE Canada
107 N22 Taurianova Calabria, SW Italy
Tauris see Tabrīz
184 I2 Tauroa Point headland North Island, NZ
Tauroggen see Tauragė
Tauromenium see Taormina
Taurus Mountains see Toros Dağları
Taus see Domažlice
Taūshyq see Tauchik
105 R5 Tauste Aragón, NE Spain
191 V16 Tautara, Motu island Easter Island, Chile, E Pacific Ocean
191 R8 Tautira Tahiti, W French Polynesia
Tauz see Tovuz
Ṭavālesh, Kūhhā-ye see Talish Mountains
136 D15 Tavas Denizli, SW Turkey
Tavastehus see Hämeenlinna
Tavau see Davos
122 G10 Tavda Sverdlovskaya Oblast', C Russian Federation
122 G10 Tavda ≈ C Russian Federation
105 T11 Tavernes de la Valldigna País Valenciano, E Spain
81 I20 Taveta Coast, S Kenya
187 Y14 Taveuni island N Fiji
147 R13 Tavildara Rus. Tavil'dara, Tovil'-Dora. C Tajikistan
162 L8 Tavin Dundgovĭ, C Mongolia
104 H14 Tavira Faro, S Portugal
97 I24 Tavistock SW England, UK
167 N10 Tavoy var. Dawei. Tenasserim, S Burma
Tavoy Island see Mali Kyun
115 E16 Tavropoú, Techníti Límni ⊡ C Greece
136 E13 Tavşanlı Kütahya, NW Turkey
187 X14 Tavua Viti Levu, W Fiji
97 J23 Taw ≈ SW England, UK
185 L14 Tawa Wellington, North Island, NZ
25 V6 Tawakoni, Lake ⊡ Texas, SW USA
153 V11 Tawang Arunāchal Pradesh, NE India
169 R17 Tawang, Teluk bay Jawa, S Indonesia
31 R7 Tawas Bay ◎ Michigan, N USA
31 R7 Tawas City Michigan, N USA
169 V8 Tawau Sabah, East Malaysia
141 U10 Ṭawīl, Qalamat aṭ well SE Saudi Arabia
171 N9 Tawitawi island SW Philippines
Ṭawkar see Tokar
Tāwūq see Dāqūq
Tawzar see Tozeur
41 O15 Taxco var. Taxco de Alarcón. Guerrero, S Mexico
Taxco de Alarcón see Taxco
158 D9 Taxkorgan var. Taxkorgan Tajik Zizhixian. Xinjiang Uygur Zizhiqu, NW China
Taxkorgan Tajik Zizhixian see Taxkorgan
96 J10 Tay ≈ C Scotland, UK
143 V6 Tāybād var. Taibad, Tāyyebād, Tayyebāt. Khorāsān, NE Iran
Taybert at Turkz see Ṭayyibat at Turkī
126 J3 Taybola Murmanskaya Oblast', NW Russian Federation
81 M16 Tayeeglow Bakool, C Somalia
96 K11 Tay, Firth of inlet E Scotland, UK
122 J12 Tayga Kemerovskaya Oblast', S Russian Federation
162 G8 Taygan Govĭ-Altay, C Mongolia
123 T9 Taygonos, Mys headland E Russian Federation
96 I11 Tay, Loch ◎ C Scotland, UK
11 N12 Taylor British Columbia, W Canada
29 O14 Taylor Nebraska, C USA
18 I13 Taylor Pennsylvania, NE USA
25 T10 Taylor Texas, SW USA
37 Q11 Taylor, Mount ▲ New Mexico, SW USA
37 R5 Taylor Park Reservoir ⊡ Colorado, C USA
37 R6 Taylor River ≈ Colorado, C USA
21 P11 Taylors South Carolina, SE USA
20 L5 Taylorsville Kentucky, S USA
21 R6 Taylorsville North Carolina, SE USA
30 L14 Taylorville Illinois, N USA
140 K5 Taymā' Tabūk, NW Saudi Arabia
122 M10 Taymura ≈ C Russian Federation
123 O7 Taymylyr Respublika Sakha (Yakutiya), NE Russian Federation
122 L7 Taymyr, Ozero ◎ N Russian Federation
122 M6 Taymyr, Poluostrov peninsula N Russian Federation
122 L8 Taymyrskiy (Dolgano-Nenetskiy) Avtonomnyy Okrug var. Taymyrskiy Avtonomnyy Okrug. ⬖ autonomous district N Russian Federation
167 S13 Tây Ninh Tây Ninh, S Vietnam

◆ Country ● Country Capital ◇ Dependent Territory ○ Dependent Territory Capital ⬖ Administrative Region ✕ International Airport ▲ Mountain ⛰ Mountain Range ✹ Volcano ≈ River ◎ Lake ⊡ Reservoir

122 L12 **Tayshet** Irkutskaya Oblast', S Russian Federation
171 N5 **Taytay** Palawan, W Philippines
169 Q16 **Tayu** *prev.* Tajoe. Jawa, C Indonesia
Tāyybād/Tayyebāt *see* Tāybād
138 L5 **Ṭayyibah** *var.* At Taybé. Ḥimṣ, C Syria
138 I4 **Ṭayyibat at Turkī** *var.* Taybert at Turkz. Ḥamāh, W Syria
145 P7 **Tayynsha** *prev.* Krasnoarmeysk. Severnyy Kazakhstan, N Kazakhstan
122 J10 **Taz** ≈ N Russian Federation
74 G6 **Taza** NE Morocco
139 T4 **Tāza Khurmātū** E Iraq
165 Q8 **Tazawa-ko** ◎ Honshū, C Japan
Taz, Bay of *see* Tazovskaya Guba
21 N8 **Tazewell** Tennessee, S USA
21 Q7 **Tazewell** Virginia, NE USA
75 S11 **Tāzirbū** SE Libya
39 S11 **Tazlina Lake** ◎ Alaska, USA
122 J8 **Tazovskiy** Yamalo-Nenetskiy Avtonomnyy Okrug, N Russian Federation
137 U10 **T'bilisi** *Eng.* Tiflis. ● (Georgia) SE Georgia
137 T10 **T'bilisi** × S Georgia
79 E14 **Tchabal Mbabo** ▲ NW Cameroon
Tchad *see* Chad
Tchad, Lac *see* Chad, Lake
77 S15 **Tchaourou** E Benin
79 E20 **Tchibanga** Nyanga, S Gabon
Tchien *see* Zwedru
77 Z6 **Tchigaï, Plateau du** ▲ NE Niger
77 V9 **Tchighozérine** Agadez, C Niger
77 T10 **Tchin-Tabaradene** Tahoua, W Niger
78 G13 **Tcholliré** Nord, NE Cameroon
Tchongking *see* Chongqing
22 K4 **Tchula** Mississippi, S USA
110 I7 **Tczew** *Ger.* Dirschau. Pomorskie, N Poland
116 I10 **Teaca** *Ger.* Tekendorf, *Hung.* Teke; *prev. Ger.* Teckendorf. Bistriţa-Năsăud, N Romania
40 J11 **Teacapán** Sinaloa, C Mexico
190 A10 **Teafuafou** *island* Funafuti Atoll, C Tuvalu
25 U8 **Teague** Texas, SW USA
191 R9 **Teahupoo** Tahiti, W French Polynesia
190 H15 **Te Aiti Point** *headland* Rarotonga, S Cook Islands
65 D24 **Teal Inlet** East Falkland, Falkland Islands
185 B22 **Te Anau** Southland, South Island, NZ
185 B22 **Te Anau, Lake** ◎ South Island, NZ
41 U15 **Teapa** Tabasco, SE Mexico
184 Q7 **Te Araroa** Gisborne, North Island, NZ
184 M7 **Te Aroha** Waikato, North Island, NZ
Teate *see* Chieti
190 A9 **Te Ava Fuagea** *channel* Funafuti Atoll, SE Tuvalu
190 B8 **Te Ava I Te Lape** *channel* Funafuti Atoll, SE Tuvalu
190 B9 **Te Ava Pua Pua** *channel* Funafuti Atoll, SE Tuvalu
184 M8 **Te Awamutu** Waikato, North Island, NZ
171 X12 **Teba** Irian Jaya, E Indonesia
104 L15 **Teba** Andalucía, S Spain
128 M15 **Teberda** Karachayevo-Cherkesskaya Respublika, SW Russian Federation
74 M6 **Tébessa** NE Algeria
62 O7 **Tebicuary, Río** ≈ S Paraguay
168 L13 **Tebingtinggi** Sumatera, W Indonesia
168 I8 **Tebingtinggi** Sumatera, N Indonesia
Tebingtinggi, Pulau *see* Rantau, Pulau
Tebriz *see* Tabrīz
137 U9 **Tebulos Mt'a** *Rus.* Gora Tebulosmta. ▲ Georgia/Russian Federation
Tebulosmta, Gora *see* Tebulos Mt'a
41 Q14 **Tecamachalco** Puebla, S Mexico
40 B1 **Tecate** Baja California, NW Mexico
136 M13 **Tecer Dağları** ▲ C Turkey
103 O17 **Tech** ≈ S France
77 P16 **Techiman** W Ghana
117 N15 **Techirghiol** Constanţa, SE Romania
74 A12 **Techla** *var.* Techlé. SW Western Sahara
Techlé *see* Techla
63 H18 **Tecka, Sierra de** ▲ SW Argentina
Teckendorf *see* Teaca
40 K13 **Tecolotlán** Jalisco, SW Mexico
40 K14 **Tecomán** Colima, SW Mexico
35 V12 **Tecopa** California, W USA
40 G5 **Tecoripa** Sonora, NW Mexico
41 N16 **Tecpan** *var.* Tecpan de Galeana. Guerrero, S Mexico
Tecpan de Galeana *see* Tecpan
40 J11 **Tecuala** Nayarit, C Mexico
116 L12 **Tecuci** Galaţi, E Romania
31 R10 **Tecumseh** Michigan, N USA
29 S16 **Tecumseh** Nebraska, C USA
27 O11 **Tecumseh** Oklahoma, C USA
146 H14 **Tedzhen** *Turkm.* Tejen. Akhalskiy Velayat, S Turkmenistan
146 I15 **Tedzhen** *Per.* Harīrūd, *Turkm.* Tejen. ≈ Afghanistan/Iran *see also* Harīrūd
146 H15 **Tedzhenstroy** *Turkm.* Tejenstroy. Akhalskiy Velayat, S Turkmenistan
162 I7 **Teel** Arhangay, C Mongolia
97 L15 **Tees** ≈ N England, UK
14 E15 **Teeswater** Ontario, S Canada
190 A10 **Tefala** *island* Funafuti Atoll, C Tuvalu
58 D13 **Tefé** Amazonas, N Brazil
74 K11 **Tefedest** ▲ S Algeria
136 E16 **Tefenni** Burdur, SW Turkey
58 D13 **Tefé, Rio** ≈ NW Brazil
169 P16 **Tegal** Jawa, C Indonesia
100 O12 **Tegel** × (Berlin) Berlin, NE Germany
99 M15 **Tegelen** Limburg, SE Netherlands
101 L24 **Tegernsee** ◎ SE Germany
107 M18 **Teggiano** Campania, S Italy
77 U14 **Tegina** Niger, C Nigeria
42 I7 **Tegucigalpa** ● (Honduras) Francisco Morazán, SW Honduras
42 H7 **Tegucigalpa** × Central District, C Honduras
Tegucigalpa *see* Central District, Honduras
Tegucigalpa *see* Francisco Morazán, Honduras
77 U9 **Teguidda-n-Tessoumt** Agadez, C Niger
64 Q11 **Teguise** Lanzarote, Islas Canarias, Spain, NE Atlantic Ocean
122 K12 **Tegul'det** Tomskaya Oblast', C Russian Federation
35 S13 **Tehachapi** California, W USA
35 S13 **Tehachapi Mountains** ▲ California, W USA
Tehama *see* Tihāmah
Teheran *see* Tehrān
77 O14 **Téhini** NE Ivory Coast
143 N5 **Tehrān** *var.* Teheran. ● (Iran) Tehrān, N Iran
143 N6 **Tehrān** *off.* Ostān-e Tehrān, *var.* Tehran. ◈ *province* N Iran
152 K9 **Tehri** Uttar Pradesh, N India
Tehri *see* Tīkamgarh
41 Q15 **Tehuacán** Puebla, S Mexico
41 S17 **Tehuantepec** *var.* Santo Domingo Tehuantepec. Oaxaca, SE Mexico
41 S17 **Tehuantepec, Golfo de** *var.* Gulf of Tehuantepec. *gulf* S Mexico
Tehuantepec, Gulf of *see* Tehuantepec, Golfo de
Tehuantepec, Isthmus of *see* Tehuantepec, Istmo de
41 T16 **Tehuantepec, Istmo de** *var.* Isthmus of Tehuantepec. *isthmus* SE Mexico
(0) I16 **Tehuantepec Ridge** *undersea feature* E Pacific Ocean
41 S16 **Tehuantepec, Río** ≈ SE Mexico
191 W10 **Tehuata** *atoll* Îles Tuamotu, C French Polynesia
64 O11 **Teide, Pico de** ▲ Gran Canaria, Islas Canarias, Spain, NE Atlantic Ocean
97 I21 **Teifi** ≈ SW Wales, UK
80 B9 **Teiga Plateau** *plateau* W Sudan
97 J24 **Teignmouth** SW England, UK
Teisen *see* Chech'ŏn
116 H1 **Teiuş** *Ger.* Dreikirchen, *Hung.* Tövis. Alba, C Romania
169 U17 **Tejakula** Bali, C Indonesia
Tejen *see* Harīrūd/Tedzhen
Tejenstroy *see* Tedzhenstroy
35 S14 **Tejon Pass** *pass* California, W USA
Tejo, Rio *see* Tagus
41 O14 **Tejupilco** *var.* Tejupilco de Hidalgo. México, S Mexico
Tejupilco de Hidalgo *see* Tejupilco
184 P7 **Te Kaha** Bay of Plenty, North Island, NZ
29 S14 **Tekamah** Nebraska, C USA
184 I1 **Te Kao** Northland, North Island, NZ
185 F20 **Tekapo** ≈ South Island, NZ
185 F19 **Tekapo, Lake** ◎ South Island, NZ
184 P9 **Te Karaka** Gisborne, North Island, NZ
184 L7 **Te Kauwhata** Waikato, North Island, NZ
41 X12 **Tekax** *var.* Tekax de Álvaro Obregón. Yucatán, SE Mexico
Tekax de Álvaro Obregón *see* Tekax
Teke/Tekendorf *see* Teaca
136 A14 **Teke Burnu** *headland* W Turkey
114 M12 **Teke Deresi** ≈ NW Turkey
146 D10 **Tekedzhik, Gory** *hill range* NW Turkmenistan
145 V14 **Tekeli** Almaty, SE Kazakhstan
145 R7 **Teke, Ozero** ◎ N Kazakhstan
158 I5 **Tekes** Xinjiang Uygur Zizhiqu, NW China
145 W16 **Tekes** Almaty, SE Kazakhstan
Tekes *see* Tekes He
158 H5 **Tekes He** *Rus.* Tekes. ≈ China/Kazakhstan
80 I10 **Tekezē** *var.* Takkaze. ≈ Eritrea/Ethiopia
Tekhtin *see* Tsyakhtsin
136 C10 **Tekirdağ** *It.* Rodosto; *anc.* Bisanthe, Raidestos, Rhaedestus. Tekirdağ, NW Turkey
136 C10 **Tekirdağ** ◈ *province* NW Turkey
155 N14 **Tekkali** Andhra Pradesh, E India
115 K15 **Tekke Burnu** *Turk.* İlyasbaba Burnu. *headland* NW Turkey
137 Q13 **Tekman** Erzurum, NE Turkey
32 M9 **Tekoa** Washington, NW USA
190 H16 **Te Kou** ▲ Rarotonga, S Cook Islands
Tekrit *see* Tikrīt
171 P12 **Teku** Sulawesi, N Indonesia
184 L9 **Te Kuiti** Waikato, North Island, NZ
42 H4 **Tela** Atlántida, NW Honduras
138 F12 **Telalim** Southern, S Israel
Telanaipura *see* Jambi
137 U10 **T'elavi** E Georgia
138 F10 **Tel Aviv** ◈ *district* W Israel
Tel Aviv-Jaffa *see* Tel Aviv-Yafo
138 F10 **Tel Aviv-Yafo** *var.* Tel Aviv-Jaffa. Tel Aviv, C Israel
138 F10 **Tel Aviv-Yafo** × Tel Aviv, C Israel
111 E18 **Telč** *Ger.* Teltsch. Jihlavský Kraj, C Czech Republic
186 B6 **Telefomin** Sandaun, NW PNG
10 J10 **Telegraph Creek** British Columbia, W Canada
190 B10 **Telele** *island* Funafuti Atoll, C Tuvalu
60 J11 **Telêmaco Borba** Paraná, S Brazil
95 E15 **Telemark** ◈ *county* S Norway
62 J13 **Telén** La Pampa, C Argentina
Teleneshty *see* Teleneşti
116 M9 **Teleneşti** *Rus.* Teleneshty. C Moldova
104 J4 **Teleno, El** ▲ NW Spain
116 J15 **Teleorman** ◈ *county* S Romania
116 J14 **Teleorman** ≈ S Romania
25 V5 **Telephone** Texas, SW USA
35 U11 **Telescope Peak** ▲ California, W USA
Teles Pirés *see* São Manuel, Rio
97 L19 **Telford** C England, UK
108 L7 **Telfs** Tirol, W Austria
42 I9 **Telica** León, NW Nicaragua
42 J6 **Telica, Río** ≈ C Honduras
76 I13 **Télimélé** Guinée-Maritime, W Guinea
43 O14 **Telire, Río** ≈ Costa Rica/Panama
114 I8 **Telish** *prev.* Azizie. Pleven, N Bulgaria
41 R16 **Telixtlahuaca** *var.* San Francisco Telixtlahuaca. Oaxaca, SE Mexico
10 K13 **Telkwa** British Columbia, SW Canada
25 P4 **Tell** Texas, SW USA
Tell Abiad *see* Tall Abyaḍ
Tell Abiad/Tell Abyad *see* At Tall al Abyaḍ
31 O16 **Tell City** Indiana, N USA
38 M9 **Teller** Alaska, USA
Tell Huqnah *see* Tall Ḥuqnah
155 F20 **Tellicherry** *var.* Thalassery. Kerala, SW India
20 M10 **Tellico Plains** Tennessee, S USA
Tell Kalakh *see* Tall Kalakh
Tell Mardikh *see* Ebla
54 E11 **Tello** Huila, C Colombia
Tell Shedadi *see* Ash Shadādah
37 Q7 **Telluride** Colorado, C USA
Tel'man/Tel'mansk *see* Gubadag
117 X9 **Tel'manove** Donets'ka Oblast', E Ukraine
162 H6 **Telmen Nuur** ◎ NW Mongolia
Teloekbetoeng *see* Bandarlampung
41 O15 **Teloloapán** Guerrero, S Mexico
Telo Martius *see* Toulon
127 V8 **Telposiz, Gora** ▲ NW Russian Federation
Telschen *see* Telšiai
63 J17 **Telsen** Chubut, S Argentina
118 D11 **Telšiai** *Ger.* Telschen. Telšiai, NW Lithuania
Teltsch *see* Telč
Telukbetung *see* Bandarlampung
168 H10 **Telukdalam** Pulau Nias, W Indonesia
14 H9 **Temagami** Ontario, S Canada
14 G9 **Temagami, Lake** ◎ Ontario, S Canada
190 H16 **Te Manga** ▲ Rarotonga, S Cook Islands
191 W12 **Tematangi** *atoll* Îles Tuamotu, S French Polynesia
41 X11 **Temax** Yucatán, SE Mexico
171 W14 **Tembagapura** Irian Jaya, E Indonesia
131 U5 **Tembenchi** ≈ N Russian Federation
55 P6 **Temblador** Monagas, NE Venezuela
105 N9 **Tembleque** Castilla-La Mancha, C Spain
Temboni *see* Mitemele, Río
35 U16 **Temecula** California, W USA
168 K7 **Temengor, Tasik** ▣ Peninsular Malaysia
112 L9 **Temerin** Serbia, N Yugoslavia
Temes/Temesch *see* Tamiš
Temeschburg/Temeschwar *see* Timişoara
Temes-Kubin *see* Kovin
Temesvár/Temeswar *see* Timişoara
Teminaboean *see* Teminabuan
171 U12 **Teminabuan** *prev.* Teminaboean. Irian Jaya, E Indonesia
145 P17 **Temirlanovka** Yuzhnyy Kazakhstan, S Kazakhstan
145 R10 **Temirtau** *prev.* Samarkandskiy, Samarkandskoye. Karaganda, C Kazakhstan
14 H10 **Témiscaming** Quebec, SE Canada
Témiscamingue, Lac *see* Timiskaming, Lake
15 T8 **Témiscouata, Lac** ◎ Quebec, SE Canada
129 N5 **Temnikov** Respublika Mordoviya, W Russian Federation
191 Y13 **Temoe** *island* Îles Gambier, E French Polynesia
183 Q9 **Temora** New South Wales, SE Australia
40 H7 **Témoris** Chihuahua, W Mexico
40 I5 **Temósachic** Chihuahua, N Mexico
187 Q10 **Temotu** *off.* Temotu Province. ◈ *province* E Solomon Islands
36 L14 **Tempe** Arizona, SW USA
Tempelburg *see* Czaplinek
107 C17 **Tempio Pausania** Sardegna, Italy, C Mediterranean Sea
42 K12 **Tempisque, Río** ≈ NW Costa Rica
25 T9 **Temple** Texas, SW USA
100 O12 **Templehof** × (Berlin) Berlin, NE Germany
97 D19 **Templemore** *Ir.* An Teampall Mór. C Ireland
100 O11 **Templin** Brandenburg, NE Germany
41 P12 **Tempoal** *var.* Tempoal de Sánchez. Veracruz-Llave, E Mexico
Tempoal de Sánchez *see* Tempoal
41 P13 **Tempoal, Río** ≈ C Mexico
83 E14 **Tempué** Moxico, C Angola
128 J14 **Temryuk** Krasnodarskiy Kray, SW Russian Federation
99 G17 **Temse** Oost-Vlaanderen, N Belgium
63 F15 **Temuco** Araucanía, C Chile
185 G20 **Temuka** Canterbury, South Island, NZ
189 P13 **Temwen Island** *island* E Micronesia
56 C6 **Tena** Napo, C Ecuador
41 W13 **Tenabo** Campeche, E Mexico
Tenaghau *see* Aola
25 X7 **Tenaha** Texas, SW USA
39 X13 **Tenake** Chichagof Island, Alaska, USA
155 K16 **Tenāli** Andhra Pradesh, E India
Tenan *see* Ch'ŏnan
41 O14 **Tenancingo** *var.* Tenencingo de Degollado. México, S Mexico
191 X12 **Tenararo** *island* Groupe Actéon, SE French Polynesia
167 N12 **Tenasserim** Tenasserim, S Burma
167 N11 **Tenasserim** *var.* Tanintharyi. ◈ *division* S Burma
98 O5 **Ten Boer** Groningen, NE Netherlands
97 I21 **Tenby** SW Wales, UK
80 K11 **Tendaho** Afar, NE Ethiopia
103 V14 **Tende** Alpes Maritimes, SE France
151 Q20 **Ten Degree Channel** *strait* Andaman and Nicobar Islands, India, E Indian Ocean
80 F11 **Tendelti** White Nile, E Sudan
76 G8 **Te-n-Dghâmcha, Sebkhet** *var.* Sebkha de Ndrhamcha, Sebkra de Ndaghamcha. *salt lake* W Mauritania
165 P10 **Tendō** Yamagata, Honshū, C Japan
74 H7 **Tendrara** NE Morocco
117 Q11 **Tendrivs'ka Kosa** *spit* S Ukraine
117 Q11 **Tendrivs'ka Zatoka** *gulf* S Ukraine
Tenencingo de Degollado *see* Tenancingo
77 N11 **Ténenkou** Mopti, C Mali
77 W9 **Ténéré** *physical region* C Niger
77 W9 **Ténére, Erg du** *desert* C Niger
64 O11 **Tenerife** *island* Islas Canarias, Spain, NE Atlantic Ocean
74 J5 **Ténès** NW Algeria
170 M15 **Tengah, Kepulauan** *island group* C Indonesia
169 V11 **Tenggarong** Borneo, C Indonesia
162 J15 **Tengger Shamo** *desert* N China
168 L8 **Tenggul, Pulau** *island* Peninsular Malaysia
Tengiz Köl *see* Tengiz, Ozero
145 P9 **Tengiz, Ozero** *Kaz.* Tengiz Köl. *salt lake* C Kazakhstan
76 M14 **Tengréla** *var.* Tingréla. N Ivory Coast
160 M14 **Tengxian** *var.* Teng Xian. Guangxi Zhuangzu Zizhiqu, S China
194 H2 **Teniente Rodolfo Marsh** *Chilean research station* South Shetland Islands, Antarctica
32 G9 **Tenino** Washington, NW USA
112 I9 **Tenja** Osijek-Baranja, E Croatia
188 B16 **Tenjo, Mount** ▲ W Guam
155 H23 **Tenkāsi** Tamil Nādu, SE India
79 N24 **Tenke** Katanga, SE Dem. Rep. Congo (Zaire)
Tenke *see* Tinca
123 Q7 **Tenkeli** Respublika Sakha (Yakutiya), NE Russian Federation
27 R10 **Tenkiller Ferry Lake** ▣ Oklahoma, C USA
77 Q13 **Tenkodogo** S Burkina
181 Q5 **Tennant Creek** Northern Territory, C Australia
20 G9 **Tennessee** *off.* State of Tennessee; also known as The Volunteer State. ◈ *state* SE USA
37 R5 **Tennessee Pass** *pass* Colorado, C USA
20 H10 **Tennessee River** ≈ S USA
23 N2 **Tennessee Tombigbee Waterway** *canal* Alabama/Mississippi, S USA
99 K22 **Tenneville** Luxembourg, SE Belgium
92 M11 **Tenniöjoki** ≈ NE Finland
92 L9 **Teno** *var.* Tenojoki, *Lapp.* Dealnu, *Nor.* Tana. ≈ Finland/Norway *see also* Tana
Tenojoki *see* Tana/Teno
169 U7 **Tenom** Sabah, East Malaysia
Tenos *see* Tínos
41 V15 **Tenosique** *var.* Tenosique de Pino Suárez. Tabasco, SE Mexico
Tenosique de Pino Suárez *see* Tenosique
22 I6 **Tensas River** ≈ Louisiana, S USA
23 O8 **Tensaw River** ≈ Alabama, S USA
74 E7 **Tensift** *seasonal river* W Morocco
171 O12 **Tentena** *var.* Tenteno. Sulawesi, C Indonesia
Tenteno *see* Tentena
183 U4 **Tenterfield** New South Wales, SE Australia
23 X16 **Ten Thousand Islands** *island group* Florida, SE USA
60 H9 **Teodoro Sampaio** São Paulo, S Brazil
59 N19 **Teófilo Otoni** *var.* Theophilo Ottoni. Minas Gerais, NE Brazil
116 K5 **Teofipol'** Khmel'nyts'ka Oblast', W Ukraine
191 Q8 **Teohatu** Tahiti, W French Polynesia
41 P14 **Teotihuacán** *ruins* México, S Mexico
Teotitlán *see* Teotitlán del Camino
41 Q15 **Teotitlán del Camino** *var.* Teotitlán. Oaxaca, S Mexico
190 G12 **Tepa** Île Uvea, E Wallis and Futuna
191 P8 **Tepaee, Récif** *reef* Tahiti, W French Polynesia
40 L14 **Tepalcatepec** Michoacán de Ocampo, SW Mexico
190 A16 **Tepa Point** *headland* SW Niue
40 L13 **Tepatitlán** *var.* Tepatitlán de Morelos. Jalisco, SW Mexico
Tepatitlán de Morelos *see* Tepatitlán
40 J9 **Tepehuanes** *var.* Santa Catarina de Tepehuanes. Durango, C Mexico
Tepelena *see* Tepelenë
113 L22 **Tepelenë** *var.* Tepelena, *It.* Tepeleni. Gjirokastër, S Albania
Tepeleni *see* Tepelenë
40 K12 **Tepic** Nayarit, C Mexico
111 C15 **Teplice** *Ger.* Teplitz; *prev.* Teplice-Šanov, Teplitz-Schönau. Ústecký Kraj, NW Czech Republic
Teplice-Šanov/Teplitz/Teplitz-Schönau *see* Teplice
117 O7 **Teplyk** Vinnyts'ka Oblast', C Ukraine
123 R10 **Teplyy Klyuch** Respublika Sakha (Yakutiya), NE Russian Federation
40 E5 **Tepoca, Cabo** *headland* NW Mexico
191 W9 **Tepoto** *island* Îles du Désappointement, C French Polynesia
92 L11 **Tepsa** Lappi, N Finland
190 B8 **Tepuka** *atoll* Funafuti Atoll, C Tuvalu
184 N7 **Te Puke** Bay of Plenty, North Island, NZ
40 L13 **Tequila** Jalisco, SW Mexico
41 O13 **Tequisquiapan** Querétaro de Arteaga, C Mexico
104 J5 **Tera** ≈ NW Spain
77 Q12 **Téra** Tillabéri, W Niger
191 V1 **Teraina** *prev.* Washington Island. *atoll* Line Islands, E Kiribati
81 F15 **Terakeka** Bahr el Gabel, S Sudan
107 J14 **Teramo** *anc.* Interamna. Abruzzo, C Italy
98 P7 **Ter Apel** Groningen, NE Netherlands
104 H11 **Tera, Ribeira de** ≈ S Portugal
185 K14 **Terawhiti, Cape** *headland* North Island, NZ
98 N12 **Terborg** Gelderland, E Netherlands
137 P13 **Tercan** Erzincan, NE Turkey
64 O2 **Terceira** × Terceira, Azores, Portugal, NE Atlantic Ocean
64 O2 **Terceira** *var.* Ilha Terceira. *island* Azores, Portugal, NE Atlantic Ocean
Terceira, Ilha *see* Terceira
116 K6 **Terebovlya** Ternopil's'ka Oblast', W Ukraine
129 O15 **Terek** ≈ SW Russian Federation
Terekhovka *see* Tsyerakhowka
147 R9 **Terek-Say** Dzhalal-Abadskaya Oblast', W Kyrgyzstan
168 L7 **Terengganu** *var.* Trengganu. ◈ *state* Peninsular Malaysia
129 X7 **Terensay** Orenburgskaya Oblast', W Russian Federation
58 N13 **Teresina** *var.* Therezina. *state capital* Piauí, NE Brazil
60 P9 **Teresópolis** Rio de Janeiro, SE Brazil
110 P12 **Terespol** Lubelskie, E Poland
191 V16 **Terevaka, Maunga** ☒ Easter Island, Chile, E Pacific Ocean
103 P3 **Tergnier** Aisne, N France
43 O14 **Teribe, Río** ≈ NW Panama
126 K3 **Teriberka** Murmanskaya Oblast', NW Russian Federation
Terijoki *see* Zelenogorsk
Terinkot *see* Tarīn Kowt
Terisaqqan *see* Tersakkan
24 K12 **Terlingua** Texas, SW USA
24 K11 **Terlingua Creek** ≈ Texas, SW USA
62 K7 **Termas de Río Hondo** Santiago del Estero, N Argentina
136 M11 **Terme** Samsun, N Turkey
Termez *see* Termiz
Termia *see* Kýthnos
107 J23 **Termini Imerese** *anc.* Thermae Himerenses. Sicilia, Italy, C Mediterranean Sea
41 V14 **Términos, Laguna de** *lagoon* SE Mexico
77 X10 **Termit-Kaoboul** Zinder, C Niger
147 O14 **Termiz** *Rus.* Termez. Surkhondaryo Wiloyati, S Uzbekistan
107 L15 **Termoli** Molise, C Italy
Termonde *see* Dendermonde
98 P5 **Termunten** Groningen, NE Netherlands
171 R11 **Ternate** Pulau Ternate, E Indonesia
109 T5 **Ternberg** Oberösterreich, N Austria
99 E15 **Terneuzen** *var.* Neuzen. Zeeland, SW Netherlands
123 T14 **Terney** Primorskiy Kray, SE Russian Federation
107 I14 **Terni** *anc.* Interamna Nahars. Umbria, C Italy
109 X6 **Ternitz** Niederösterreich, E Austria
117 V7 **Ternivka** Dnipropetrovs'ka Oblast', E Ukraine
116 K6 **Ternopil'** *Pol.* Tarnopol, *Rus.* Ternopol'. Ternopil's'ka Oblast', W Ukraine
Ternopil' *see* Ternopil's'ka Oblast'
116 I6 **Ternopil's'ka Oblast'** *var.* Ternopil', *Rus.* Ternopol'skaya Oblast'. ◈ *province* NW Ukraine
Ternopol' *see* Ternopil'
Ternopol'skaya Oblast' *see* Ternopil's'ka Oblast'
123 U13 **Terpeniya, Mys** *headland* Ostrov Sakhalin, SE Russian Federation
Térraba, Río *see* Grande de Térraba, Río
10 J13 **Terrace** British Columbia, W Canada
12 D12 **Terrace Bay** Ontario, S Canada
107 I16 **Terracina** Lazio, C Italy
93 F14 **Terråk** Troms, N Norway
26 M13 **Terral** Oklahoma, C USA
107 B19 **Terralba** Sardegna, Italy, C Mediterranean Sea
Terranova di Sicilia *see* Gela
Terranova Pausania *see* Olbia
105 W5 **Terrassa** *Cast.* Tarrasa. Cataluña, E Spain
15 O12 **Terrebonne** Quebec, SE Canada
22 J11 **Terrebonne Bay** *bay* Louisiana, SE USA
31 N14 **Terre Haute** Indiana, N USA
25 U6 **Terrell** Texas, SW USA
Terre Neuve *see* Newfoundland
33 Q14 **Terreton** Idaho, NW USA
103 T7 **Territoire-de-Belfort** ◈ *department* E France
33 X9 **Terry** Montana, NW USA
28 I9 **Terry Peak** ▲ South Dakota, N USA
136 H14 **Tersakan Gölü** ◎ C Turkey
145 O10 **Tersakkan** *Kaz.* Terisaqqan. ≈ C Kazakhstan
98 J4 **Terschelling** *Fris.* Skylge. *island* Waddeneilanden, N Netherlands
78 H10 **Tersef** Chari-Baguirmi, C Chad
147 X8 **Terskey Ala-Too, Khrebet** ▲ Kazakhstan/Kyrgyzstan
Terter *see* Tärtär
105 R8 **Teruel** *anc.* Turba. Aragón, E Spain
105 R7 **Teruel** ◈ *province* Aragón, E Spain
114 M7 **Tervel** *prev.* Kurtbunar, *Rom.* Curtbunar. Dobrich, NE Bulgaria
93 M16 **Tervo** Itä-Suomi, C Finland
92 L13 **Tervola** Lappi, NW Finland
Tervueren *see* Tervuren
99 H18 **Tervuren** *var.* Tervueren. Vlaams Brabant, C Belgium
112 H11 **Tešanj** Federacija Bosna I Hercegovina, N Bosnia and Herzegovina
Teschen *see* Cieszyn
83 M19 **Tesenane** Inhambane, S Mozambique
80 I9 **Teseney** *var.* Tessenei. W Eritrea
39 P5 **Teshekpuk Lake** ◎ Alaska, USA
162 K6 **Teshig** Bulgan, N Mongolia
165 T2 **Teshio** Hokkaidō, NE Japan
165 T2 **Teshio-sanchi** ▲ Hokkaidō, NE Japan
Těšín *see* Cieszyn
Tesio Gawa *see* Teshio-gawa
162 F5 **Tesiyn Gol** *var.* Tes-Khem. ≈ Mongolia/Russian Federation *see also* Tes-Khem
131 T7 **Tes-Khem** *var.* Tesiyn Gol. ≈ Mongolia/Russian Federation *see also* Tesiyn Gol
112 H11 **Teslić** Republika Srpska, N Bosnia and Herzegovina
10 I9 **Teslin** Yukon Territory, W Canada
10 I8 **Teslin** ≈ British Columbia/Yukon Territory, W Canada
77 Q8 **Tessalit** Kidal, NE Mali
77 V12 **Tessaoua** Maradi, S Niger
99 J17 **Tessenderlo** Limburg, NE Belgium
Tessenei *see* Teseney
14 L7 **Tessier, Lac** ◎ Quebec, SE Canada
Tessin *see* Ticino
97 M23 **Test** ≈ S England, UK
Testama *see* Tõstamaa
55 P4 **Testigos, Islas los** *island group* N Venezuela
37 S10 **Tesuque** New Mexico, SW USA
103 O17 **Têt** *var.* Tet. ≈ S France
54 G5 **Tetas, Cerro de las** ▲ NW Venezuela
83 M15 **Tete** Tete, NW Mozambique
83 M15 **Tete** *off.* Província de Tete. ◈ *province* NW Mozambique
11 N15 **Tête Jaune Cache** British Columbia, SW Canada
184 O8 **Te Teko** Bay of Plenty, North Island, NZ
186 K9 **Tetepare** *island* New Georgia Islands, NW Solomon Islands
Teterev *see* Teteriv
116 M5 **Teteriv** *Rus.* Teterev. ≈ N Ukraine
100 M9 **Teterow** Mecklenburg-Vorpommern, NE Germany
114 I9 **Teteven** Lovech, N Bulgaria
191 T10 **Tetiaroa** *atoll* Îles du Vent, W French Polynesia
105 P14 **Tetica de Bacares** ▲ S Spain
Tetiyev *see* Tetiyiv
117 O6 **Tetiyiv** *Rus.* Tetiyev. Kyyivs'ka Oblast', N Ukraine
39 T10 **Tetlin** Alaska, USA
33 R8 **Teton River** ≈ Montana, NW USA
74 G5 **Tétouan** *var.* Tetouan, Tetuán. N Morocco
Tetova/Tetovë *see* Tetovo
114 L7 **Tetovo** Razgrad, N Bulgaria
113 N18 **Tetovo** *Alb.* Tetovë, Tetova, *Turk.* Kalkandelen. NW FYR Macedonia
115 E20 **Tetrázio** ▲ S Greece
Tetschen *see* Děčín
Tetuán *see* Tétouan
191 Q8 **Tetufera, Mont** ▲ Tahiti, W French Polynesia
129 R4 **Tetyushi** Respublika Tatarstan, W Russian Federation
108 I7 **Teufen** Sankt Gallen, NE Switzerland
40 L12 **Teul** *var.* Teul de Gonźáles Ortega. Zacatecas, C Mexico
107 B21 **Teulada** Sardegna, Italy, C Mediterranean Sea
Teul de Gonźáles Ortega *see* Teul
11 X16 **Teulon** Manitoba, S Canada
42 I7 **Teupasenti** El Paraíso, S Honduras
165 S2 **Teuri-tō** *island* NE Japan
100 G13 **Teutoburger Wald** *Eng.* Teutoburg Forest. *hill range* NW Germany

◆ Country ● Country Capital ◇ Dependent Territory ○ Dependent Territory Capital ◈ Administrative Region × International Airport ▲ Mountain ▲ Mountain Range ☒ Volcano ≈ River ◎ Lake ▣ Reservoir

Teutoburg Forest *see* Teutoburger Wald
93 K17 **Teuva** *Swe.* Östermark. Länsi-Suomi, W Finland
107 H15 **Tevere** *Eng.* Tiber. ≈ C Italy
138 G9 **Teverya** *var.* Tiberias, Tverya. Northern, N Israel
96 K13 **Teviot** ≈ SE Scotland, UK
Tevli *see* Tewli
122 H11 **Tevriz** Omskaya Oblast', C Russian Federation
185 B24 **Te Waewae Bay** *bay* South Island, NZ
97 L21 **Tewkesbury** C England, UK
119 F19 **Tewli** *Rus.* Tevli. Brestskaya Voblasts', SW Belarus
159 U12 **Têwo** *var.* Dêngkagoin. Gansu, C China
25 U12 **Texana, Lake** ⊚ Texas, SW USA
27 S14 **Texarkana** Arkansas, C USA
25 X5 **Texarkana** Texas, SW USA
25 N9 **Texas** *off.* State of Texas; also known as The Lone Star State. ◆ *state* S USA
25 W12 **Texas City** Texas, SW USA
41 P14 **Texcoco** México, C Mexico
98 I6 **Texel** *island* Waddeneilanden, NW Netherlands
26 H8 **Texhoma** Oklahoma, C USA
25 N1 **Texhoma** Texas, SW USA
37 W12 **Texico** New Mexico, SW USA
24 L1 **Texline** Texas, SW USA
41 P14 **Texmelucan** *var.* San Martín Texmelucan. Puebla, S Mexico
27 O13 **Texoma, Lake** ⊠ Oklahoma/Texas, C USA
25 N9 **Texon** Texas, SW USA
83 J23 **Teyateyaneng** NW Lesotho
126 M16 **Teykovo** Ivanovskaya Oblast', W Russian Federation
126 M16 **Teza** ≈ W Russian Federation
41 Q13 **Teziutlán** Puebla, S Mexico
153 W12 **Tezpur** Assam, NE India
9 N10 **Tha-Anne** ≈ Nunavut, NE Canada
83 K23 **Thabana Ntlenyana** *var.* Thabantshonyana, Mount Ntlenyana. ▲ E Lesotho
Thabantshonyana *see* Thabana Ntlenyana
83 J23 **Thaba Putsoa** ▲ C Lesotho
167 Q8 **Tha Bo** Nong Khai, E Thailand
103 T12 **Thabor, Pic du** ▲ E France
Tha Chin *see* Samut Sakhon
166 M7 **Thagaya** Pegu, C Burma
Thai, Ao *see* Thailand, Gulf of
167 T6 **Thai Binh** Thai Binh, N Vietnam
167 S7 **Thai Hoa** Nghê An, N Vietnam
167 P9 **Thailand** *off.* Kingdom of Thailand, *Th.* Prathet Thai; *prev.* Siam. ◆ *monarchy* SE Asia
167 P13 **Thailand, Gulf of** *var.* Gulf of Siam, *Th.* Ao Thai, *Vtn.* Vinh Thai Lan. *gulf* SE Asia
Thai Lan, Vinh *see* Thailand, Gulf of
167 T6 **Thai Nguyên** Băc Thai, N Vietnam
167 S8 **Thakhèk** *prev.* Muang Khammouan. Khammouan, C Laos
153 S13 **Thakurgaon** Rajshahi, NW Bangladesh
149 S6 **Thal** North-West Frontier Province, NW Pakistan
166 M15 **Thalang** Phuket, SW Thailand
Thalassery *see* Tellicherry
167 Q10 **Thalat Khae** Nakhon Ratchasima, C Thailand
109 Q5 **Thalgau** Salzburg, NW Austria
108 G7 **Thalwil** Zürich, NW Switzerland
83 I20 **Thamaga** Kweneng, SE Botswana
Thamarīd *see* Thamarīt
141 V13 **Thamarīt** *var.* Thamarīd, Thumrayt. SW Oman
141 P16 **Thamar, Jabal** ▲ SW Yemen
184 M6 **Thames** Waikato, North Island, NZ
14 D17 **Thames** ≈ Ontario, S Canada
97 O22 **Thames** ≈ S England, UK
184 M6 **Thames, Firth of** *gulf* North Island, NZ
14 D17 **Thamesville** Ontario, S Canada
141 S13 **Thamūd** N Yemen
167 N9 **Thanbyuzayat** Mon State, S Burma
152 I9 **Thānesar** Haryāna, NW India
167 T7 **Thanh Hoa** Thanh Hoa, N Vietnam
Thanintari Taungdan *see* Bilauktaung Range
155 I21 **Thanjāvūr** *prev.* Tanjore. Tamil Nādu, SE India
Thanlwin *see* Salween
103 U7 **Thann** Haut-Rhin, NE France
167 O16 **Tha Nong Phrom** Phatthalung, SW Thailand
167 N13 **Thap Sakae** *var.* Thap Sakau. Prachuap Khiri Khan, SW Thailand
Thap Sakau *see* Thap Sakae
98 L10 **'t Harde** Gelderland, E Netherlands
152 D11 **Thar Desert** *var.* Great Indian Desert, Indian Desert. *desert* India/Pakistan
181 V10 **Thargomindah** Queensland, C Australia
150 D11 **Thar Pārkar** *desert* SE Pakistan
139 S7 **Tharthār al Furāt, Qanāt ath** *canal* C Iraq
139 R7 **Tharthār, Buḩayrat ath** ⊚ C Iraq
139 R5 **Tharthār, Wādī ath** *dry watercourse* N Iraq
167 N13 **Tha Sae** Chumphon, SW Thailand
167 N15 **Tha Sala** Nakhon Si Thammarat, SW Thailand
114 I13 **Thásos** Thásos, E Greece
115 I14 **Thásos** *island* E Greece
37 N14 **Thatcher** Arizona, SW USA
167 T5 **Thât Khê** *var.* Trâng Dinh. Lang Sơn, N Vietnam
166 M8 **Thaton** Mon State, S Burma
167 S9 **That Phanom** Nakhon Phanom, E Thailand
167 R10 **Tha Tum** Surin, E Thailand
103 P16 **Thau, Bassin de** *var.* Étang de Thau. ⊚ S France
Thau, Étang de *see* Thau, Bassin de
166 L3 **Thaungdut** Sagaing, N Burma
167 O8 **Thaungyin** *Th.* Mae Nam Moei. ≈ Burma/Thailand
167 R8 **Tha Uthen** Nakhon Phanom, E Thailand
109 W2 **Thaya** *var.* Dyje. ≈ Austria/Czech Republic *see also* Dyje
27 V8 **Thayer** Missouri, C USA
166 L6 **Thayetmyo** Magwe, C Burma
33 S15 **Thayne** Wyoming, C USA
166 M5 **Thazi** Mandalay, C Burma
Thebes *see* Thíva
44 L5 **The Carlton** *var.* Abraham Bay. Mayaguana, SE Bahamas
45 O14 **The Crane** *var.* Crane. S Barbados
32 I11 **The Dalles** Oregon, NW USA
28 M14 **Thedford** Nebraska, C USA
The Hague *see* 's-Gravenhage
Theiss *see* Tisa/Tisza
8 M9 **Thelon** ≈ Northwest Territories/Nunavut, N Canada
11 V15 **Theodore** Saskatchewan, S Canada
23 N8 **Theodore** Alabama, S USA
36 L13 **Theodore Roosevelt Lake** ⊠ Arizona, SW USA
Theodosia *see* Feodosiya
Theophilo Ottoni *see* Teófilo Otoni
9 N13 **The Pas** Manitoba, C Canada
31 T14 **The Plains** Ohio, N USA
Thera *see* Thíra
172 H17 **Thérèse, Île** *island* Inner Islands, NE Seychelles
Therezina *see* Teresina
115 L20 **Thérma** Ikaría, Dodekánisos, Greece, Aegean Sea
Thermae Himerenses *see* Termini Imerese
Thermae Pannonicae *see* Baden
Thermaic Gulf/Thermaicus Sinus *see* Thermaïkós Kólpos
121 Q8 **Thermaïkós Kólpos** *Eng.* Thermaic Gulf; *anc.* Thermaicus Sinus. *gulf* N Greece
Thermiá *see* Kýthnos
115 L17 **Thermís** Lésvos, E Greece
115 E18 **Thérmo** Dytikí Ellás, C Greece
33 V14 **Thermopolis** Wyoming, C USA
183 P10 **The Rock** New South Wales, SE Australia
195 O5 **Theron Mountains** ▲ Antarctica
115 G18 **Thespiés** Stereá Ellás, C Greece
115 E16 **Thessalía** *Eng.* Thessaly. ◆ *region* C Greece
14 C10 **Thessalon** Ontario, S Canada
115 G14 **Thessaloníki** *Eng.* Salonica, Salonika, *SCr.* Solun, *Turk.* Selânik. Kentrikí Makedonía, N Greece
115 G14 **Thessaloníki** ✕ Kentrikí Makedonía, N Greece
Thessaly *see* Thessalía
84 B12 **Theta Gap** *undersea feature* E Atlantic Ocean
97 P20 **Thetford** E England, UK
15 R11 **Thetford-Mines** Quebec, SE Canada
113 K17 **Theth** *var.* Thethi. Shkodër, N Albania
Thethi *see* Theth
99 L20 **Theux** Liège, E Belgium
45 V9 **The Valley** ○ (Anguilla) E Anguilla
27 N10 **The Village** Oklahoma, C USA
25 W10 **The Woodlands** Texas, SW USA
Thiamis *see* Thýamis
Thian Shan *see* Tien Shan
22 J9 **Thibodaux** Louisiana, S USA
29 S3 **Thief Lake** ⊚ Minnesota, N USA
29 S3 **Thief River** ≈ Minnesota, C USA
29 S3 **Thief River Falls** Minnesota, N USA
Thièle *see* La Thielle
32 G14 **Thielsen, Mount** ▲ Oregon, NW USA
Thielt *see* Tielt
106 G7 **Thiene** Veneto, NE Italy
Thienen *see* Tienen
103 P11 **Thiers** Puy-de-Dôme, C France
76 F11 **Thiès** W Senegal
81 I19 **Thika** Central, S Kenya
Thikombia *see* Cikobia
151 K18 **Thiladhunmathi Atoll** *var.* Tiladummati Atoll. *atoll* N Maldives
Thimbu *see* Thimphu
153 T11 **Thimphu** *var.* Thimbu; *prev.* Tashi Chho Dzong. ● (Bhutan) W Bhutan
92 H2 **Thingeyri** Vestfirdhir, NW Iceland
92 I3 **Thingvellir** Sudhurland, SW Iceland
187 Q17 **Thio** Province Sud, C New Caledonia
103 T4 **Thionville** *Ger.* Diedenhofen. Moselle, NE France
115 K22 **Thíra** Thíra, Kykládes, Greece, Aegean Sea
115 K22 **Thíra** *prev.* Santorin, Santoríni, *anc.* Thera. *island* Kykládes, Greece, Aegean Sea
115 J22 **Thirasía** *island* Kykládes, Greece, Aegean Sea
97 M16 **Thirsk** N England, UK
14 F12 **Thirty Thousand Islands** *island group* Ontario, S Canada
Thiruvanathapuram *see* Trivandrum
95 F20 **Thisted** Viborg, NW Denmark
Thistil Fjord *see* Thistilfjördhur
92 L1 **Thistilfjördhur** *var.* Thistil Fjord. *fjord* NE Iceland
182 G9 **Thistle Island** *island* South Australia
Thithia *see* Cicia
Thiukhaoluang Phrahang *see* Luang Prabang Range
115 G18 **Thíva** *Eng.* Thebes; *prev.* Thívai. Stereá Ellás, C Greece
Thívai *see* Thíva
102 M12 **Thiviers** Dordogne, SW France
92 J4 **Thjórsá** ≈ C Iceland
9 N10 **Thlewiaza** ≈ Nunavut, NE Canada
8 L10 **Thoa** ≈ Northwest Territories, NW Canada
99 G14 **Tholen** Zeeland, SW Netherlands
99 F14 **Tholen** *island* SW Netherlands
26 L10 **Thomas** Oklahoma, C USA
21 T3 **Thomas** West Virginia, NE USA
27 U3 **Thomas Hill Reservoir** ⊠ Missouri, C USA
23 S5 **Thomaston** Georgia, SE USA
19 R7 **Thomaston** Maine, NE USA
25 T12 **Thomaston** Texas, SW USA
23 O6 **Thomasville** Alabama, S USA
23 T8 **Thomasville** Georgia, SE USA
21 S9 **Thomasville** North Carolina, SE USA
35 N5 **Thomes Creek** ≈ California, W USA
11 W12 **Thompson** Manitoba, C Canada
29 R4 **Thompson** North Dakota, N USA
(0) F8 **Thompson** ≈ Alberta/British Columbia, SW Canada
33 O8 **Thompson Falls** Montana, NW USA
29 Q10 **Thompson, Lake** ⊚ South Dakota, N USA
34 M3 **Thompson Peak** ▲ California, W USA
27 S2 **Thompson River** ≈ Missouri, C USA
185 A22 **Thompson Sound** *sound* South Island, NZ
8 J5 **Thomsen** ≈ Banks Island, Northwest Territories, NW Canada
23 V4 **Thomson** Georgia, SE USA
103 T10 **Thonon-les-Bains** Haute-Savoie, E France
103 O15 **Thoré** *var.* Thore. ≈ S France
37 P11 **Thoreau** New Mexico, SW USA
Thorenburg *see* Turda
92 J3 **Thórisvatn** ⊚ C Iceland
92 P4 **Thor, Kapp** *headland* S Svalbard
92 I4 **Thorlákshöfn** Sudhurland, SW Iceland
Thorn *see* Toruń
25 T10 **Thorndale** Texas, SW USA
14 H10 **Thorne** Ontario, S Canada
97 J14 **Thornhill** S Scotland, UK
25 U8 **Thornton** Texas, SW USA
Thornton Island *see* Millennium Island
14 H16 **Thorold** Ontario, S Canada
32 I9 **Thorp** Washington, NW USA
195 S3 **Thorshavnheiane** *physical region* Antarctica
92 L1 **Thórshöfn** Nordhurland Eystra, NE Iceland
Thospitis *see* Van Gölü
167 S14 **Thôt Nôt** Cân Thơ, S Vietnam
102 K8 **Thouars** Deux-Sèvres, W France
153 X14 **Thoubal** Manipur, NE India
102 K9 **Thouet** ≈ W France
Thoune *see* Thun
18 H7 **Thousand Islands** *island* Canada/USA
35 S15 **Thousand Oaks** California, W USA
114 L12 **Thrace** *cultural region* SE Europe
114 J13 **Thracian Sea** *Gk.* Thrakikó Pélagos; *anc.* Thracium Mare. *sea* Greece/Turkey
Thracium Mare/Thrakikó Pélagos *see* Thracian Sea
Thrá Lí, Bá *see* Tralee Bay
33 R11 **Three Forks** Montana, NW USA
11 Q16 **Three Hills** Alberta, SW Canada
183 N15 **Three Hummock Island** *island* Tasmania, SE Australia
184 H1 **Three Kings Islands** *island group* N NZ
175 P10 **Three Kings Rise** *undersea feature* W Pacific Ocean
77 O18 **Three Points, Cape** *headland* S Ghana
31 P10 **Three Rivers** Michigan, N USA
25 S13 **Three Rivers** Texas, SW USA
83 G24 **Three Sisters** Northern Cape, SW South Africa
32 H13 **Three Sisters** ▲ Oregon, NW USA
187 N10 **Three Sisters Islands** *island group* SE Solomon Islands
Thrissur *see* Trichūr
25 Q6 **Throckmorton** Texas, SW USA
180 M10 **Throssell, Lake** *salt lake* Western Australia
115 K25 **Thrýptis** ▲ Kríti, Greece, E Mediterranean Sea
167 T13 **Thu Dâu Môt** *var.* Phu Cương. Sông Be, S Vietnam
167 S6 **Thu Do** ✕ (Ha Nôi) Ha Nôi, N Vietnam
99 G21 **Thuin** Hainaut, S Belgium
149 Q12 **Thul** Sind, SE Pakistan
Thule *see* Qaanaaq
83 J18 **Thuli** *var.* Tuli. ≈ S Zimbabwe
Thumrayt *see* Thamarīt
108 D9 **Thun** *Fr.* Thoune. Bern, W Switzerland
12 C12 **Thunder Bay** Ontario, S Canada
30 M1 **Thunder Bay** *lake bay* S Canada
31 R6 **Thunder Bay** *lake bay* Michigan, N USA
31 R6 **Thunder Bay River** ≈ Michigan, N USA
27 N11 **Thunderbird, Lake** ⊠ Oklahoma, C USA
28 L8 **Thunder Butte Creek** ≈ South Dakota, N USA
108 E9 **Thuner See** ⊚ C Switzerland
167 N15 **Thung Song** *var.* Cha Mai. Nakhon Si Thammarat, SW Thailand
108 H7 **Thur** ≈ N Switzerland
108 G6 **Thurgau** *Fr.* Thurgovie. ◆ *canton* NE Switzerland
Thurgovie *see* Thurgau
Thuringe *see* Thüringen
108 J7 **Thüringen** Vorarlberg, W Austria
101 J17 **Thüringen** *Eng.* Thuringia, *Fr.* Thuringe. ◆ *state* C Germany
101 J17 **Thüringer Wald** *Eng.* Thuringian Forest. ▲ C Germany
Thuringia *see* Thüringen
Thuringian Forest *see* Thüringer Wald
97 D19 **Thurles** *Ir.* Durlas. S Ireland
21 W2 **Thurmont** Maryland, NE USA
Thurø *see* Thurø By
95 H24 **Thurø By** *var.* Thurø. Fyn, C Denmark
14 M12 **Thurso** Quebec, SE Canada
96 J6 **Thurso** N Scotland, UK
194 I10 **Thurston Island** *island* Antarctica
108 I9 **Thusis** Graubünden, S Switzerland
115 C15 **Thýamis** *var.* Thiamis. ≈ W Greece
95 E21 **Thyborøn** *var.* Tyborøn. Ringkøbing, W Denmark
195 U3 **Thyer Glacier** *glacier* Antarctica
115 L20 **Thýmaina** *island* Dodekánisos, Greece, Aegean Sea
83 N15 **Thyolo** *var.* Cholo. Southern, S Malawi
183 U6 **Tia** New South Wales, SE Australia
54 H5 **Tía Juana** Zulia, NW Venezuela
160 J14 **Tiandong** *var.* Pingma. Guangxi Zhuangzu Zizhiqu, S China
161 O3 **Tianjin** *var.* Tientsin. Tianjin Shi, E China
Tianjin *see* Tianjin Shi
161 P3 **Tianjin Shi** *var.* Jin, Tianjin, T'ien-ching, Tientsin. ◆ *municipality* E China
159 S10 **Tianjun** *var.* Xinyuan. Qinghai, C China
160 J13 **Tianlin** *prev.* Leli. Guangxi Zhuangzu Zizhiqu, S China
Tian Shan *see* Tien Shan
159 W11 **Tianshui** Gansu, C China
150 I7 **Tianshuihai** Xinjiang Uygur Zizhiqu, W China
161 S10 **Tiantai** Zhejiang, SE China
160 J14 **Tianyang** Guangxi Zhuangzu Zizhiqu, S China
159 U9 **Tianzhu** *var.* Tianzhu Zangzu Zizhixian. Gansu, C China
Tianzhu Zangzu Zizhixian *see* Tianzhu
191 Q7 **Tiarei** Tahiti, W French Polynesia
74 J6 **Tiaret** *var.* Tihert. NW Algeria
77 N17 **Tiassalé** S Ivory Coast
192 I16 **Ti'avea** Upolu, SE Samoa
Tiba *see* Chiba
60 J11 **Tibagi** *var.* Tibají. Paraná, S Brazil
60 J10 **Tibagi, Rio** *var.* Rio Tibají. ≈ S Brazil
Tibají *see* Tibagi
Tibají, Rio *see* Tibagi, Rio
139 Q9 **Tibal, Wādī** *dry watercourse* S Iraq
54 G9 **Tibaná** Boyacá, C Colombia
79 F14 **Tibati** Adamaoua, N Cameroon
76 K15 **Tibé, Pic de** ▲ SE Guinea
Tiber *see* Tivoli, Italy
Tiber *see* Tevere, Italy
Tiberias *see* Teverya
138 G8 **Tiberias, Lake** *var.* Chinnereth, Sea of Bahr Tabariya, Sea of Galilee, *Ar.* Bahrat Tabariya, *Heb.* Yam Kinneret. ⊚ N Israel
67 Q5 **Tibesti** *var.* Tibesti Massif, *Ar.* Tibistī. ▲ N Africa
Tibesti Massif *see* Tibesti
Tibetan Autonomous Region *see* Xizang Zizhiqu
Tibet, Plateau of *see* Qingzang Gaoyuan
Tibistī *see* Tibesti
14 K7 **Tiblemont, Lac** ⊚ Quebec, SE Canada
139 X9 **Ţīb, Nahr aţ** ≈ S Iraq
Tibnī *see* At Tibnī
182 L4 **Tibooburra** New South Wales, SE Australia
95 L18 **Tibro** Västra Götaland, S Sweden
40 E5 **Tiburón, Isla** *var.* Isla del Tiburón. *island* NW Mexico
Tiburón, Isla del *see* Tiburón, Isla
23 W14 **Tice** Florida, SE USA
Tichau *see* Tychy
114 L8 **Ticha, Yazovir** ⊚ NE Bulgaria
76 K9 **Tichît** *var.* Tichitt. Tagant, C Mauritania
Tichitt *see* Tichît
108 G11 **Ticino** *Fr./Ger.* Tessin. ◆ *canton* S Switzerland
106 D8 **Ticino** ≈ Italy/Switzerland
108 H11 **Ticino** *Ger.* Tessin. ≈ SW Switzerland
Ticinum *see* Pavia
41 X12 **Ticul** Yucatán, SE Mexico
95 K18 **Tidaholm** Västra Götaland, S Sweden
Tidjikdja *see* Tidjikja
76 J8 **Tidjikja** *var.* Tidjikdja; *prev.* Fort-Cappolani. Tagant, C Mauritania
Tidore *see* Soasiu
171 R11 **Tidore, Pulau** *island* E Indonesia
Tidra, Ile *see* Et Tîdra
77 N16 **Tiébissou** *var.* Tiebissou. C Ivory Coast
163 V11 **Tiefa** Liaoning, NE China
108 I9 **Tiefencastel** Graubünden, S Switzerland
Tiegenhof *see* Nowy Dwór Gdański
T'ieh-ling *see* Tieling
98 K13 **Tiel** Gelderland, C Netherlands
163 W7 **Tieli** Heilongjiang, NE China
163 V11 **Tieling** *var.* T'ieh-ling. Liaoning, NE China
152 L4 **Tielongtan** China/India
99 D17 **Tielt** *var.* Thielt. West-Vlaanderen, W Belgium
T'ien-ching *see* Tianjin Shi
99 I18 **Tienen** *var.* Thienen, *Fr.* Tirlemont. Vlaams Brabant, C Belgium
Tiên Giang, Sông *see* Mekong
147 X9 **Tien Shan** *Chin.* Thian Shan, Tian Shan, T'ien Shan, *Rus.* Tyan'-Shan'. ▲ C Asia
Tientsin *see* Tianjin
Tientsin *see* Tianjin Shi
167 U6 **Tiên Yên** Quang Ninh, N Vietnam
95 O14 **Tierp** Uppsala, C Sweden
62 H7 **Tierra Amarilla** Atacama, N Chile
37 R9 **Tierra Amarilla** New Mexico, SW USA
41 R15 **Tierra Blanca** Veracruz-Llave, E Mexico
41 O16 **Tierra Colorada** Guerrero, S Mexico
63 J17 **Tierra Colorada, Bajo de la** *basin* SE Argentina
63 I25 **Tierra del Fuego** *off.* Provincia de la Tierra del Fuego. ◆ *province* S Argentina
63 J24 **Tierra del Fuego** *island* Argentina/Chile
54 D7 **Tierralta** Córdoba, NW Colombia
104 K9 **Tiétar** ≈ W Spain
60 L10 **Tietê** São Paulo, S Brazil
60 J8 **Tietê, Rio** ≈ S Brazil
32 I9 **Tieton** Washington, NW USA
32 J6 **Tiffany Mountain** ▲ Washington, NW USA
31 S12 **Tiffin** Ohio, N USA
31 Q11 **Tiffin River** ≈ Ohio, N USA
Tiflis *see* T'bilisi
23 U7 **Tifton** Georgia, SE USA
171 R13 **Tifu** Pulau Buru, E Indonesia
38 L17 **Tigalda Island** *island* Aleutian Islands, Alaska, USA
115 I15 **Tigáni, Akrotírio** *headland* Límnos, E Greece
169 V6 **Tiga Tarok** Sabah, East Malaysia
117 O10 **Tighina** *Rus.* Bendery; *prev.* Bender. E Moldova
145 X9 **Tigiretskiy Khrebet** ▲ E Kazakhstan
79 F14 **Tignère** Adamaoua, N Cameroon
13 P14 **Tignish** Prince Edward Island, SE Canada
Tigranocerta *see* Siirt
80 I11 **Tigray** ◆ *province* N Ethiopia
41 O11 **Tigre, Cerro del** ▲ C Mexico
56 F8 **Tigre, Río** ≈ N Peru
139 X10 **Tigris** *Ar.* Dijlah, *Turk.* Dicle. ≈ Iraq/Turkey
76 G9 **Tiguent** Trarza, SW Mauritania
74 M10 **Tiguentourine** E Algeria
77 V10 **Tiguidit, Falaise de** *ridge* C Niger
141 N13 **Tihāmah** *var.* Tehama. *plain* Saudi Arabia/Yemen
Tihert *see* Tiaret
Ti-hua/Tihwa *see* Ürümqi
41 Q13 **Tihuatlán** Veracruz-Llave, E Mexico
40 B1 **Tijuana** Baja California, NW Mexico
42 E2 **Tikal** Petén, N Guatemala
154 I9 **Tikamgarh** *prev.* Tehri. Madhya Pradesh, C India
158 L7 **Tikanlik** Xinjiang Uygur Zizhiqu, NW China
77 P12 **Tikaré** N Burkina
39 O12 **Tikchik Lakes** *lakes* Alaska, USA
191 T9 **Tikehau** *atoll* Îles Tuamotu, C French Polynesia
191 V9 **Tikei** *island* Îles Tuamotu, C French Polynesia
122 B11 **Tikhoretsk** Krasnodarskiy Kray, SW Russian Federation
126 I13 **Tikhvin** Leningradskaya Oblast', NW Russian Federation
193 P9 **Tiki Basin** *undersea feature* S Pacific Ocean
76 K13 **Tikinsso** ≈ NE Guinea
184 Q8 **Tikitiki** Gisborne, North Island, NZ
79 D16 **Tiko** Sud-Ouest, SW Cameroon
187 R11 **Tikopia** *island*, E Solomon Islands
139 S6 **Tikrīt** *var.* Tekrit. N Iraq
126 I8 **Tiksha** Respublika Kareliya, NW Russian Federation
126 I6 **Tikshozero, Ozero** ⊚ NW Russian Federation
123 P7 **Tiksi** Respublika Sakha (Yakutiya), NE Russian Federation
42 A6 **Tilapa** San Marcos, SW Guatemala
42 L13 **Tilarán** Guanacaste, NW Costa Rica
99 J14 **Tilburg** Noord-Brabant, S Netherlands
14 D17 **Tilbury** Ontario, S Canada
182 K4 **Tilcha** South Australia
Tilcha Creek *see* Callabonna Creek
29 Q14 **Tilden** Nebraska, C USA
25 R13 **Tilden** Texas, SW USA
14 H10 **Tilden Lake** Ontario, S Canada
116 G9 **Tileagd** *Hung.* Mezőtelegd. Bihor, W Romania
77 Q8 **Tilemsi, Vallée de** ≈ C Mali
123 V8 **Tilichiki** Koryakskiy Avtonomnyy Okrug, E Russian Federation
Tiligul *see* Tilihul
Tiligul'skiy Liman *see* Tilihul's'kyy Lyman
117 P9 **Tilihul** *Rus.* Tiligul. ≈ SW Ukraine
117 P10 **Tilihul's'kyy Lyman** *Rus.* Tiligul'skiy Liman. ⊚ S Ukraine
Tilimsen *see* Tlemcen
Tilio Martius *see* Toulon
77 R11 **Tillabéri** *var.* Tillabéry. Tillabéri, W Niger
77 R11 **Tillabéri** ◆ *department* SW Niger
Tillabéry *see* Tillabéri
32 F11 **Tillamook** Oregon, NW USA
32 E11 **Tillamook Bay** *inlet* Oregon, NW USA
151 Q22 **Tillanchāng Dwīp** *island* Nicobar Islands, India, NE Indian Ocean
95 N15 **Tillberga** Västmanland, C Sweden
Tillenberg *see* Dyleň
21 S10 **Tillery, Lake** ⊠ North Carolina, SE USA
77 T10 **Tillia** Tahoua, W Niger
23 N8 **Tillmans Corner** Alabama, S USA
14 F17 **Tillsonburg** Ontario, S Canada
115 N22 **Tílos** *island* Dodekánisos, Greece, Aegean Sea
183 N5 **Tilpa** New South Wales, SE Australia
Tilsit *see* Sovetsk
31 N13 **Tilton** Illinois, N USA
128 K7 **Tim** Kurskaya Oblast', W Russian Federation
54 D12 **Timaná** Huila, S Colombia
Timan Ridge *see* Timanskiy Kryazh
127 Q6 **Timanskiy Kryazh** *Eng.* Timan Ridge. *ridge* NW Russian Federation
185 G20 **Timaru** Canterbury, South Island, NZ
129 S6 **Timashevo** Samarskaya Oblast', W Russian Federation
128 K13 **Timashevsk** Krasnodarskiy Kray, SW Russian Federation
Timbaki/Timbákion *see* Tympáki
22 K10 **Timbalier Bay** *bay* Louisiana, S USA
22 K11 **Timbalier Island** *island* Louisiana, S USA
76 L10 **Timbedgha** *var.* Timbédra. Hodh ech Chargui, SE Mauritania
Timbédra *see* Timbedgha
32 G10 **Timber** Oregon, NW USA
181 O3 **Timber Creek** Northern Territory, N Australia
28 M8 **Timber Lake** South Dakota, N USA
54 D12 **Timbío** Cauca, SW Colombia
54 C12 **Timbiquí** Cauca, SW Colombia
83 O17 **Timbue, Ponta** *headland* C Mozambique
Timbuktu *see* Tombouctou
169 W8 **Timbun Mata, Pulau** *island* E Malaysia
77 P8 **Timétrine** *var.* Ti-n-Kâr. *oasis* C Mali
Timfi *see* Týmfi
Timfristos *see* Tymfristós
77 V9 **Timia** Agadez, C Niger
171 X14 **Timika** Irian Jaya, E Indonesia
74 I9 **Timimoun** C Algeria
Timiris, Cap *see* Timirist, Râs
76 F8 **Timirist, Râs** *var.* Cap Timiris. *headland* NW Mauritania
145 O7 **Timiryazevo** Severnyy Kazakhstan, N Kazakhstan
116 E11 **Timiş** ◆ *county* SW Romania
14 H9 **Timiskaming, Lake** *Fr.* Lac Témiscamingue. ⊚ Ontario/Quebec, SE Canada
116 E11 **Timişoara** *Ger.* Temeschwar, Temeswar, *Hung.* Temesvár; *prev.* Temeschburg. Timiş, W Romania
116 E11 **Timişoara** ✕ Timiş, W Romania
Timkovichi *see* Tsimkavichy
77 U8 **Ti-m-Meghsoï** ≈ NW Niger
100 K8 **Timmerdorfer Strand** Schleswig-Holstein, N Germany
14 F7 **Timmins** Ontario, S Canada
21 S12 **Timmonsville** South Carolina, SE USA
30 K5 **Timms Hill** ▲ Wisconsin, N USA
112 P12 **Timok** ≈ E Yugoslavia
58 N13 **Timon** Maranhão, E Brazil
171 Q16 **Timor** *island* East Timor/Indonesia
171 Q17 **Timor Sea** *sea* E Indian Ocean
Timor Timur *see* East Timor
Timor Trench *see* Timor Trough
192 G8 **Timor Trough** *var.* Timor Trench. *undersea feature* NE Timor Sea
61 A21 **Timote** Buenos Aires, E Argentina
54 I6 **Timotes** Mérida, NW Venezuela
25 X8 **Timpson** Texas, SW USA
123 Q11 **Timpton** ≈ NE Russian Federation
93 H17 **Timrå** Västernorrland, C Sweden
20 J10 **Tims Ford Lake** ⊠ Tennessee, S USA
168 L7 **Timur, Banjaran** ▲ Peninsular Malaysia
171 Q8 **Tinaca Point** *headland* Mindanao, S Philippines
54 K5 **Tinaco** Cojedes, N Venezuela
64 Q11 **Tinajo** Lanzarote, Islas Canarias, Spain, NE Atlantic Ocean
187 P10 **Tinakula** *island* Santa Cruz Islands, E Solomon Islands
54 K5 **Tinaquillo** Cojedes, N Venezuela
116 F10 **Tinca** *Hung.* Tenke. Bihor, W Romania
155 J20 **Tindivanam** Tamil Nādu, SE India
74 E9 **Tindouf** W Algeria
74 E9 **Tindouf, Sebkha de** *salt lake* W Algeria
104 J2 **Tineo** Asturias, N Spain
77 R9 **Ti-n-Essako** Kidal, E Mali
183 T5 **Tingha** New South Wales, SE Australia
Tingis *see* Tanger
Tinglett *see* Tinglev
95 F24 **Tinglev** *Ger.* Tinglett. Sønderjylland, SW Denmark
56 E12 **Tingo María** Huánuco, C Peru

Tingréla see Tengréla
158 K16 **Tingri** var. Xêgar. Xizang Zizhiqu, W China
95 M21 **Tingsryd** Kronoberg, S Sweden
95 P19 **Tingstäde** Gotland, SE Sweden
62 H12 **Tinguiririca, Volcán** ▲ C Chile
94 F9 **Tingvoll** Møre og Romsdal, S Norway
188 K8 **Tinian** island S Northern Mariana Islands
Ti-n-Kâr see Timétrine
Tinnevelly see Tirunelveli
95 G15 **Tinnoset** Telemark, S Norway
95 F15 **Tinnsjø** ◎ S Norway
Tino see Chino
115 J20 **Tínos** Tínos, Kykládes, Greece, Aegean Sea
115 J20 **Tínos** anc. Tenos. island Kykládes, Greece, Aegean Sea
153 R14 **Tinpahar** Bihār, NE India
153 X11 **Tinsukia** Assam, NE India
76 K10 **Tintâne** Hodh el Gharbi, S Mauritania
62 L7 **Tintina** Santiago del Estero, N Argentina
182 K10 **Tintinara** South Australia
104 I14 **Tinto** ∽ SW Spain
77 S8 **Ti-n-Zaouâtene** Kidal, NE Mali
Tiobraid Árann see Tipperary
28 K3 **Tioga** North Dakota, N USA
18 G12 **Tioga** Pennsylvania, NE USA
25 T5 **Tioga** Texas, SW USA
35 Q8 **Tioga Pass** pass California, W USA
18 G12 **Tioga River** ∽ New York/Pennsylvania, NE USA
Tioman Island see Tioman, Pulau
168 M9 **Tioman, Pulau** var. Tioman Island. island Peninsular Malaysia
18 C12 **Tionesta** Pennsylvania, NE USA
18 D12 **Tionesta Creek** ∽ Pennsylvania, NE USA
168 J13 **Tiop** Pulau Pagai Selatan, W Indonesia
77 O12 **Tiou** NW Burkina
18 H11 **Tioughnioga River** ∽ New York, NE USA
74 J5 **Tipasa** var. Tipaza. N Algeria
Tipaza see Tipasa
42 J10 **Tipitapa** Managua, W Nicaragua
31 R13 **Tipp City** Ohio, N USA
31 O12 **Tippecanoe River** ∽ Indiana, N USA
97 D20 **Tipperary** Ir. Tiobraid Árann. S Ireland
97 D19 **Tipperary** Ir. Tiobraid Árann. cultural region S Ireland
35 R12 **Tipton** California, W USA
31 P13 **Tipton** Indiana, N USA
29 Y14 **Tipton** Iowa, C USA
27 U5 **Tipton** Missouri, C USA
36 I10 **Tipton, Mount** ▲ Arizona, SW USA
20 F8 **Tiptonville** Tennessee, S USA
12 E12 **Tip Top Mountain** ▲ Ontario, S Canada
155 G19 **Tiptūr** Karnātaka, W India
Tiquisate see Pueblo Nuevo Tiquisate
58 L13 **Tiracambu, Serra do** ⛰ E Brazil
Tirana see Tiranë
113 K19 **Tirana Rinas** ✕ Durrës, W Albania
113 L20 **Tiranë** var. Tirana. ● (Albania) Tiranë, C Albania
113 K20 **Tiranë** ◈ district W Albania
140 I5 **Tirān, Jazīrat** island Egypt/Saudi Arabia
106 F6 **Tirano** Lombardia, N Italy
182 I2 **Tirari Desert** desert South Australia
117 O10 **Tiraspol** Rus. Tiraspol'. E Moldova
184 M8 **Tirau** Waikato, North Island, NZ
136 C14 **Tire** İzmir, SW Turkey
137 O11 **Tirebolu** Giresun, N Turkey
96 F11 **Tiree** island W Scotland, UK
Tîrgovişte see Târgovişte
Tîrgu see Târgu Cărbuneşti
Tîrgu Bujor see Târgu Bujor
Tîrgu Frumos see Târgu Frumos
Tîrgu Jiu see Targu Jui
Tîrgu Lăpuş see Târgu Lăpuş
Tîrgu Mures see Târgu Mureş
Tîrgu-Neamţ see Târgu-Neamţ
Tîrgu Ocna see Târgu Ocna
Tîrgu Secuiesc see Târgu Secuiesc
149 T3 **Tirich Mīr** ▲ NW Pakistan
76 J5 **Tiris Zemmour** ◈ region N Mauritania
Tirlemont see Tienen
129 W5 **Tirlyanskiy** Respublika Bashkortostan, W Russian Federation
Tîrnava Mare see Târnava Mare
Tîrnava Mică see Târnava Mică
Tîrnăveni see Târnăveni
Tírnavos see Týrnavos
Tirnovo see Veliko Tŭrnovo
154 J11 **Tirodi** Madhya Pradesh, C India
108 K8 **Tirol** off. Land Tirol, var. Tyrol, It. Tirolo. ◈ state W Austria
Tirolo see Tirol
Tirreno, Mare see Tyrrhenian Sea
107 B19 **Tirso** ∽ Sardegna, Italy, C Mediterranean Sea
95 H22 **Tirstrup** ✕ (Århus) Århus, C Denmark
155 I21 **Tiruchchirāppalli** prev. Trichinopoly. Tamil Nādu, SE India
155 H23 **Tirunelveli** var. Tinnevelly. Tamil Nādu, SE India
155 J19 **Tirupati** Andhra Pradesh, E India
155 I20 **Tiruppattūr** Tamil Nādu, SE India
155 H21 **Tiruppūr** Tamil Nādu, SW India
155 I20 **Tiruvannāmalai** Tamil Nādu, SE India
112 L10 **Tisa** Ger. Theiss, Hung. Tisza, Rus. Tissa, Ukr. Tysa. ∽ SE Europe see also Tisza
Tischnowitz see Tišnov
11 U14 **Tisdale** Saskatchewan, S Canada
27 O13 **Tishomingo** Oklahoma, C USA
95 M17 **Tisnaren** ◎ S Sweden
111 F18 **Tišnov** Ger. Tischnowitz. Brnenský Kraj, SE Czech Republic
Tissa see Tisa/Tisza
74 J6 **Tissemsilt** N Algeria
153 S12 **Tista** ∽ NE India
112 L8 **Tisza** Ger. Theiss, Rom./Slvn./SCr. Tisa, Rus. Tissa, Ukr. Tysa. ∽ SE Europe see also Tisa
111 L23 **Tiszaföldvár** Jász-Nagykun-Szolnok, E Hungary
111 M22 **Tiszafüred** Jász-Nagykun-Szolnok, E Hungary
111 L23 **Tiszakécske** Bács-Kiskun, C Hungary
111 M21 **Tiszaújváros** prev. Leninváros. Borsod-Abaúj-Zemplén, NE Hungary
111 N21 **Tiszavasvári** Szabolcs-Szatmár-Bereg, NE Hungary
Titibu see Chichibu
57 I17 **Titicaca, Lake** ◎ Bolivia/Peru
190 H17 **Titikaveka** Rarotonga, S Cook Islands
154 M13 **Titilāgarh** Orissa, E India
168 K8 **Titiwangsa, Banjaran** ⛰ Peninsular Malaysia
Titograd see Podgorica
Titose see Chitose
Titova Mitrovica see Kosovska Mitrovica
Titovo Užice see Užice
113 M18 **Titov Vrv** ▲ NW FYR Macedonia
94 F7 **Titran** Sør-Trøndelag, S Norway
31 Q8 **Tittabawassee River** ∽ Michigan, N USA
116 J13 **Titu** Dâmboviţa, S Romania
79 M16 **Titule** Orientale, N Dem. Rep. Congo (Zaire)
23 X11 **Titusville** Florida, SE USA
18 C12 **Titusville** Pennsylvania, NE USA
76 G11 **Tivaouane** W Senegal
113 J17 **Tivat** Montenegro, SW Yugoslavia
14 E14 **Tiverton** Ontario, S Canada
97 J23 **Tiverton** SW England, UK
19 O12 **Tiverton** Rhode Island, NE USA
107 I15 **Tivoli** anc. Tiber. Lazio, C Italy
25 U13 **Tivoli** Texas, SW USA
141 Z8 **Ţīwī** NE Oman
Tiworo see Tioro, Selat
41 Y11 **Tizimín** Yucatán, SE Mexico
74 K5 **Tizi Ouzou** var. Tizi-Ouzou. N Algeria
74 D8 **Tiznit** SW Morocco
113 I14 **Tjentište** Republika Srpska, SE Bosnia and Herzegovina
Tjepoe/Tjepu see Cepu
98 L7 **Tjeukemeer** ◎ N Netherlands
Tjiamis see Ciamis
Tjiandjoer see Cianjur
Tjilatjap see Cilacap
Tjiledoeg see Ciledug
95 F23 **Tjæreborg** Ribe, W Denmark
95 I18 **Tjörn** island S Sweden
92 O3 **Tjuvfjorden** fjord S Svalbard
Tkvarcheli see Tqvarch'eli
40 L8 **Tlahualillo** Durango, N Mexico
41 P14 **Tlalnepantla** México, C Mexico
41 Q13 **Tlapacoyán** Veracruz-Llave, E Mexico
41 P16 **Tlapa de Comonfort** Guerrero, S Mexico
40 L13 **Tlaquepaque** Jalisco, C Mexico
Tlascala see Tlaxcala
41 P14 **Tlaxcala** var. Tlascala, Tlaxcala de Xicohténcatl. Tlaxcala, C Mexico
41 P14 **Tlaxcala** ◈ state S Mexico
Tlaxcala de Xicohténcatl see Tlaxcala
41 P14 **Tlaxco** var. Tlaxco de Morelos. Tlaxcala, S Mexico
Tlaxco de Morelos see Tlaxco
41 Q16 **Tlaxiaco** var. Santa María Asunción Tlaxiaco. Oaxaca, S Mexico
74 I6 **Tlemcen** var. Tilimsen, Tlemsen. NW Algeria
Tlemsen see Tlemcen
138 L4 **Tlété Ouâte Rharbi, Jebel** ▲ N Syria
116 J7 **Tlumach** Ivano-Frankivs'ka Oblast', W Ukraine
129 P17 **Tlyarata** Respublika Dagestan, SW Russian Federation
116 K10 **Toaca, Vârful** prev. Vîrful Toaca. ▲ NE Romania
Toaca, Vîrful see Toaca, Vârful
187 R13 **Toak** Ambrym, C Vanuatu
172 J4 **Toamasina** var. Tamatave. Toamasina, E Madagascar
172 J4 **Toamasina** ◈ province E Madagascar
172 J4 **Toamasina** ✕ Toamasina, E Madagascar
21 X6 **Toano** Virginia, NE USA
191 U10 **Toau** atoll Îles Tuamotu, C French Polynesia
45 T6 **Toa Vaca, Embalse** ▣ C Puerto Rico
62 K13 **Toay** La Pampa, C Argentina
159 R14 **Toba** Xizang Zizhiqu, W China
164 K14 **Toba** Mie, Honshū, SW Japan
168 I9 **Toba, Danau** ◎ Sumatera, W Indonesia
45 Y16 **Tobago** island NE Trinidad and Tobago
149 Q9 **Toba Kākar Range** ⛰ NW Pakistan
105 Q12 **Tobarra** Castilla-La Mancha, C Spain
149 U9 **Toba Tek Singh** Punjab, E Pakistan
171 R11 **Tobelo** Pulau Halmahera, E Indonesia
14 E12 **Tobermory** Ontario, S Canada
96 G10 **Tobermory** W Scotland, UK
165 S4 **Tōbetsu** Hokkaidō, NE Japan
180 M6 **Tobin Lake** ◎ Western Australia
11 U14 **Tobin Lake** ◎ Saskatchewan, C Canada
35 T4 **Tobin, Mount** ▲ Nevada, W USA
165 O9 **Tobi-shima** island C Japan
169 N13 **Toboali** Pulau Bangka, W Indonesia
144 M8 **Tobol** Kaz. Tobyl. Kostanay, N Kazakhstan
144 L8 **Tobol** Kaz. Tobyl. ∽ Kazakhstan/Russian Federation
122 H11 **Tobol'sk** Tyumenskaya Oblast', C Russian Federation
Tobruch/Tobruk see Ţubruq
127 R3 **Tobseda** Nenetskiy Avtonomnyy Okrug, NW Russian Federation
Tobyl see Tobol
127 Q6 **Tobysh** ∽ NW Russian Federation
54 F10 **Tocaima** Cundinamarca, C Colombia
59 K16 **Tocantins** off. Estado do Tocantins. ◈ state C Brazil
59 K15 **Tocantins, Rio** ∽ N Brazil
23 T2 **Toccoa** Georgia, SE USA
165 O12 **Tochigi** off. Tochigi-ken, var. Totigi. ◈ prefecture Honshū, S Japan
165 O11 **Tochio** var. Totio. Niigata, Honshū, C Japan
95 I15 **Töcksfors** Värmland, C Sweden
42 J5 **Tocoa** Colón, N Honduras
62 H4 **Tocopilla** Antofagasta, N Chile
62 I4 **Tocorpuri, Cerro de** ▲ Bolivia/Chile
183 O10 **Tocumwal** New South Wales, SE Australia
54 K4 **Tocuyo de La Costa** Falcón, NW Venezuela
152 H13 **Toda Rāisingh** Rājasthān, N India
106 H13 **Todi** Umbria, C Italy
108 G9 **Tödi** ▲ NE Switzerland
171 T12 **Todlo** Irian Jaya, E Indonesia
165 S9 **Todoga-saki** headland Honshū, C Japan
59 P17 **Todos os Santos, Baía de** bay E Brazil
40 F10 **Todos Santos** Baja California Sur, W Mexico
40 B2 **Todos Santos, Bahía de** bay NW Mexico
Toeban see Tuban
Toekang Besi Eilanden see Tukangbesi, Kepulauan
Tōen see T'aoyüan
185 D25 **Toetoes Bay** bay South Island, NZ
11 Q14 **Tofield** Alberta, SW Canada
10 K17 **Tofino** Vancouver Island, British Columbia, SW Canada
189 X17 **Tofol** Kosrae, E Micronesia
95 J20 **Tofta** Halland, S Sweden
95 H15 **Tofte** Buskerud, S Norway
95 F24 **Toftlund** Sønderjylland, SW Denmark
193 X15 **Tofua** island Ha'apai Group, C Tonga
187 Q12 **Toga** island Torres Islands, N Vanuatu
80 N13 **Togdheer** off. Gobolka Togdheer. ◈ region NW Somalia
Toghyzaq see Toguzak
164 L11 **Togi** Ishikawa, Honshū, SW Japan
39 N13 **Togiak** Alaska, USA
171 O11 **Togian, Kepulauan** island group C Indonesia
77 Q15 **Togo** off. Togolese Republic; prev. French Togoland. ◆ republic W Africa
162 F8 **Tögrög** Govĭ-Altay, SW Mongolia
162 E7 **Tögrög** Hovd, W Mongolia
Togton-heyan see Tuotuoheyan
144 L7 **Toguzak** Kaz. Toghyzaq. ∽ Kazakhstan/Russian Federation
37 P10 **Tohatchi** New Mexico, SW USA
191 O7 **Tohiea, Mont** Ӿ Moorea, W French Polynesia
93 O17 **Tohmajärvi** Itä-Suomi, E Finland
137 N14 **Tohma Çayı** ∽ C Turkey
93 L16 **Toholampi** Länsi-Suomi, W Finland
162 M10 **Töhöm** Dornogovĭ, SE Mongolia
23 X12 **Tohopekaliga, Lake** ◎ Florida, SE USA
164 M14 **Toi** Shizuoka, Honshū, S Japan
190 B15 **Toi** N Niue
93 L19 **Toijala** Länsi-Suomi, W Finland
171 P12 **Toima** Sulawesi, N Indonesia
164 D17 **Toi-misaki** headland Kyūshū, SW Japan
171 Q17 **Toineke** Timor, S Indonesia
Toirc, Inis see Inishturk
35 U6 **Toiyabe Range** ⛰ Nevada, W USA
Tojikiston, Jumhurii see Tajikistan
147 R12 **Tojikobod** Rus. Tadzhikabad. C Tajikistan
164 G12 **Tōjō** Hiroshima, Honshū, SW Japan
39 T10 **Tok** Alaska, USA
164 K13 **Tōkai** Aichi, Honshū, SW Japan
111 N21 **Tokaj** Borsod-Abaúj-Zemplén, NE Hungary
165 N11 **Tōkamachi** Niigata, Honshū, C Japan
185 D25 **Tokanui** Southland, South Island, NZ
80 I7 **Tokar** var. Ţawkar. Red Sea, NE Sudan
136 L12 **Tokat** Tokat, N Turkey
136 L12 **Tokat** ◈ province N Turkey
Tokati Gawa see Tokachi-gawa
163 X15 **Tŏkchŏk-gundo** island group NW South Korea
Tŏke see Taka Atoll
190 J9 **Tokelau** ◇ NZ overseas territory W Polynesia
Tőketerebes see Trebišov
Tokhtamyshbek see Tŭkhtamish
24 M6 **Tokio** Texas, SW USA
Tokio see Tōkyō
189 W11 **Toki Point** point NW Wake Island
Tokkuztara see Gongliu
147 V7 **Tokmak** Kir. Tokmok. Chuyskaya Oblast', N Kyrgyzstan
117 V9 **Tokmak** var. Velykyy Tokmak. Zaporiz'ka Oblast', SE Ukraine
Tokmok see Tokmak
184 Q8 **Tokomaru Bay** Gisborne, North Island, NZ
165 V3 **Tokoro** Hokkaidō, NE Japan
184 M8 **Tokoroa** Waikato, North Island, NZ
76 K14 **Tokounou** Haute-Guinée, C Guinea
38 M12 **Toksook Bay** Alaska, USA
Toksu see Xinhe
Toksum see Toksun
158 L6 **Toksun** var. Toksum. Xinjiang Uygur Zizhiqu, NW China
147 T8 **Toktogul** Talasskaya Oblast', NW Kyrgyzstan
147 T9 **Toktogul'skoye Vodokhranilishche** ▣ W Kyrgyzstan
Toktomush see Tŭkhtamish
193 Y14 **Toku** island Vava'u Group, N Tonga
165 U16 **Tokunoshima** Kagoshima, Tokuno-shima, SW Japan
165 U16 **Tokuno-shima** island Nansei-shotō, SW Japan
164 I14 **Tokushima** var. Tokusima. Tokushima, Shikoku, SW Japan
164 H14 **Tokushima** off. Tokushima-ken, var. Tokusima. ◈ prefecture Shikoku, SW Japan
Tokusima see Tokushima
164 E13 **Tokuyama** Yamaguchi, Honshū, SW Japan
165 N13 **Tōkyō** var. Tokio. ● (Japan) Tōkyō, Honshū, S Japan
165 O13 **Tōkyō** off. Tōkyō-to. ◈ capital district Honshū, S Japan
145 T12 **Tokyrau** ∽ C Kazakhstan
149 O3 **Tokzār** Pash. Tukzār. Sar-e Pol, N Afghanistan
189 U12 **Tol** atoll Chuuk Islands, C Micronesia
184 Q9 **Tolaga Bay** Gisborne, North Island, NZ
172 I7 **Tôlañaro** prev. Faradofay, Fort-Dauphin. Toliara, SE Madagascar
162 D6 **Tolbo** Bayan-Ölgiy, W Mongolia
Tolbukhin see Dobrich
60 G11 **Toledo** Paraná, S Brazil
54 G8 **Toledo** Norte de Santander, N Colombia
105 N9 **Toledo** anc. Toletum. Castilla-La Mancha, C Spain
30 M14 **Toledo** Illinois, N USA
29 W13 **Toledo** Iowa, C USA
31 R11 **Toledo** Ohio, N USA
32 F12 **Toledo** Oregon, NW USA
32 G9 **Toledo** Washington, NW USA
42 F3 **Toledo** ◈ district S Belize
104 M9 **Toledo** ◈ province Castilla-La Mancha, C Spain
25 Y7 **Toledo Bend Reservoir** ▣ Louisiana/Texas, SW USA
104 M10 **Toledo, Montes de** ⛰ C Spain
106 J12 **Tolentino** Marche, C Italy
Toletum see Toledo
94 H10 **Tolga** Hedmark, S Norway
158 J3 **Toli** Xinjiang Uygur Zizhiqu, NW China
172 H7 **Toliara** var. Toliary; prev. Tuléar. Toliara, SW Madagascar
172 H7 **Toliara** ◈ province SW Madagascar
Toliary see Toliara
54 D11 **Tolima** off. Departamento del Tolima. ◈ province C Colombia
171 N11 **Tolitoli** Sulawesi, C Indonesia
95 K22 **Tollarp** Skåne, S Sweden
100 N9 **Tollense** ∽ NE Germany
100 N10 **Tollensesee** ◎ NE Germany
36 K13 **Tolleson** Arizona, SW USA
146 M13 **Tollimarjon** Rus. Talimardzhan. Qashqadaryo Wiloyati, S Uzbekistan
Tolmein see Tolmin
106 J6 **Tolmezzo** Friuli-Venezia Giulia, NE Italy
109 S11 **Tolmin** Ger. Tolmein, It. Tolmino. W Slovenia
Tolmino see Tolmin
111 J25 **Tolna** Ger. Tolnau. Tolna, S Hungary
111 I24 **Tolna** off. Tolna Megye. ◈ county SW Hungary
Tolnau see Tolna
79 I20 **Tolo** Bandundu, W Dem. Rep. Congo (Zaire)
Tolochin see Talachyn
190 D12 **Toloke** Île Futuna, W Wallis and Futuna
30 M13 **Tolono** Illinois, N USA
105 Q3 **Tolosa** País Vasco, N Spain
Tolosa see Toulouse
171 O13 **Tolo, Teluk** bay Sulawesi, C Indonesia
39 R9 **Tolovana River** ∽ Alaska, USA
123 U10 **Tolstoy, Mys** headland E Russian Federation
63 G15 **Toltén** Araucanía, C Chile
63 G15 **Toltén, Río** ∽ S Chile
54 E6 **Tolú** Sucre, NW Colombia
41 O14 **Toluca** var. Toluca de Lerdo. México, S Mexico
Toluca de Lerdo see Toluca
41 O14 **Toluca, Nevado de** Ӿ C Mexico
129 R6 **Tol'yatti** prev. Stavropol'. Samarskaya Oblast', W Russian Federation
77 O12 **Toma** NW Burkina
30 K7 **Tomah** Wisconsin, N USA
30 L5 **Tomahawk** Wisconsin, N USA
117 T8 **Tomakivka** Dnipropetrovs'ka Oblast', E Ukraine
165 S4 **Tomakomai** Hokkaidō, NE Japan
165 S2 **Tomamae** Hokkaidō, NE Japan
104 G9 **Tomar** Santarém, W Portugal
123 T13 **Tomari** Ostrov Sakhalin, Sakhalinskaya Oblast', SE Russian Federation
115 C16 **Tómaros** ▲ W Greece
Tomaschow see Tomaszów Lubelski, Poland
Tomaschow see Tomaszów Mazowiecki, Poland
61 E16 **Tomás Gomensoro** Artigas, N Uruguay
117 N7 **Tomashpil'** Vinnyts'ka Oblast', C Ukraine
Tomaszów see Tomaszów Mazowiecki
111 P15 **Tomaszów Lubelski** Ger. Tomaschow. Lubelskie, E Poland
Tomaszów Mazowiecka see Tomaszów Mazowiecki
110 L13 **Tomaszów Mazowiecki** var. Tomaszów Mazowiecka; prev. Tomaszów, Ger. Tomaschow. Łodzkie, C Poland
40 J13 **Tomatlán** Jalisco, C Mexico
81 F15 **Tombe** Jonglei, S Sudan
23 N4 **Tombigbee River** ∽ Alabama/Mississippi, S USA
82 A10 **Tomboco** Zaire, NW Angola
77 O10 **Tombouctou** Eng. Timbuktu. Tombouctou, N Mali
77 N9 **Tombouctou** ◈ region W Mali
37 N16 **Tombstone** Arizona, SW USA
83 A15 **Tombua** Port. Porto Alexandre. Namibe, SW Angola
83 J19 **Tom Burke** Northern, NE South Africa
146 L9 **Tomdibuloq** Rus. Tamdybulak. Nawoiy Wiloyati, N Uzbekistan
146 L9 **Tomditow-Toghi** ⛰ N Uzbekistan
62 G13 **Tomé** Bío Bío, C Chile
58 L12 **Tomé-Açu** Pará, NE Brazil
95 L23 **Tomelilla** Skåne, S Sweden
105 O10 **Tomelloso** Castilla-La Mancha, C Spain
14 H10 **Tomiko Lake** ◎ Ontario, S Canada
77 N12 **Tominian** Ségou, C Mali
171 N12 **Tomini, Gulf of** var. Teluk Tomini; prev. Teluk Gorontalo. bay Sulawesi, C Indonesia
Tomini, Teluk see Tomini, Gulf of
165 Q11 **Tomioka** Fukushima, Honshū, C Japan
113 G14 **Tomislavgrad** Federacija Bosna I Hercegovina, SW Bosnia and Herzegovina
181 O9 **Tomkinson Ranges** ⛰ South Australia/Western Australia
123 Q11 **Tommot** Respublika Sakha (Yakutiya), NE Russian Federation
171 Q11 **Tomohon** Sulawesi, N Indonesia
54 K9 **Tomo, Río** ∽ E Colombia
113 L21 **Tomorrit, Mali i** ▲ S Albania
11 S17 **Tompkins** Saskatchewan, S Canada
20 K8 **Tompkinsville** Kentucky, S USA
171 N11 **Tompo** Sulawesi, N Indonesia
180 I8 **Tom Price** Western Australia
122 J12 **Tomsk** Tomskaya Oblast', C Russian Federation
122 I11 **Tomskaya Oblast'** ◈ province C Russian Federation
18 K16 **Toms River** New Jersey, NE USA
Tom Steed Lake see Tom Steed Reservoir
26 L12 **Tom Steed Reservoir** var. Tom Steed Lake. ▣ Oklahoma, C USA
171 U13 **Tomu** Irian Jaya, E Indonesia
158 H6 **Tomur Feng** var. Pik Pobedy, Pobeda Peak. ▲ China/Kyrgyzstan see also Pobedy, Pik
189 N13 **Tomworoahlang** Pohnpei, E Micronesia
41 U17 **Tonalá** Chiapas, SE Mexico
106 F6 **Tonale, Passo del** pass N Italy
164 I11 **Tonami** Toyama, Honshū, SW Japan
58 C12 **Tonantins** Amazonas, W Brazil
32 K6 **Tonasket** Washington, NW USA
55 Y9 **Tonate** var. Macouria. N French Guiana
18 D10 **Tonawanda** New York, NE USA
171 Q11 **Tondano** Sulawesi, C Indonesia
104 H7 **Tondela** Viseu, N Portugal
95 F24 **Tønder** Ger. Tondern. Sønderjylland, SW Denmark
Tondern see Tønder
143 N4 **Tonekābon** var. Shahsawar, Tonkābon; prev. Shahsavār. Māzandarān, N Iran
Tonezh see Tonyezh
193 Y14 **Tonga** off. Kingdom of Tonga, var. Friendly Islands. ◆ monarchy SW Pacific Ocean
175 R9 **Tonga** island group SW Pacific Ocean
83 K23 **Tongaat** KwaZulu/Natal, E South Africa
161 Q13 **Tong'an** var. Tong an. Fujian, SE China
27 Q4 **Tonganoxie** Kansas, C USA
39 Y13 **Tongass National Forest** reserve Alaska, USA
193 Y16 **Tongatapu** ✕ Tongatapu, S Tonga
193 Y16 **Tongatapu** island Tongatapu Group, S Tonga
193 Y16 **Tongatapu Group** island group S Tonga
175 S9 **Tonga Trench** undersea feature S Pacific Ocean
161 N8 **Tongbai Shan** ⛰ C China
161 P8 **Tongcheng** Anhui, E China
160 L6 **Tongchuan** Shaanxi, C China
160 L12 **Tongdao** var. Tongdao Dongzu Zizhixian; prev. Shuangjiang. Hunan, S China
159 T11 **Tongde** Qinghai, C China
99 K19 **Tongeren** Fr. Tongres. Limburg, NE Belgium
Tonggou see Tongyu
163 Y14 **Tonghae** NE South Korea
160 G13 **Tonghai** Yunnan, SW China
163 X8 **Tonghe** Heilongjiang, NE China
163 W11 **Tonghua** Jilin, NE China
163 Z6 **Tongjiang** Heilongjiang, NE China
163 Y13 **Tongjosŏn-man** prev. Broughton Bay. bay E North Korea
163 V7 **Tongken He** ∽ NE China
167 T7 **Tongking, Gulf of** Chin. Beibu Wan, Vtn. Vinh Bắc Bô. gulf China/Vietnam
163 U10 **Tongliao** Nei Mongol Zizhiqu, N China
161 Q9 **Tongling** Anhui, E China
161 R9 **Tonglu** Zhejiang, SE China
187 R14 **Tongoa** island Shepherd Islands, S Vanuatu
62 G9 **Tongoy** Coquimbo, C Chile
160 L11 **Tongren** Guizhou, S China
159 T11 **Tongren** Qinghai, C China
Tongres see Tongeren
153 U11 **Tongsa** var. Tongsa Dzong. C Bhutan
Tongsa Dzong see Tongsa
Tongshan see Xuzhou
160 L17 **Tongshi** Hainan, S China
159 P12 **Tongtian He** ∽ C China
96 I6 **Tongue** N Scotland, UK
44 H3 **Tongue of the Ocean** strait C Bahamas
33 X10 **Tongue River** ∽ Montana, NW USA
33 W11 **Tongue River Resevoir** ▣ Montana, NW USA
159 V11 **Tongwei** Gansu, C China
159 W9 **Tongxin** Ningxia, N China
163 U9 **Tongyu** var. Tonggou. Jilin, NE China
160 J11 **Tongzi** Guizhou, S China
40 G5 **Tónichi** Sonora, NW Mexico
81 D14 **Tonj** Warab, SW Sudan
152 H13 **Tonk** Rājasthān, N India
Tonkābon see Tonekābon
27 N8 **Tonkawa** Oklahoma, C USA
167 Q12 **Tônlé Sap** Eng. Great Lake. ◎ W Cambodia
102 L14 **Tonneins** Lot-et-Garonne, SW France
103 Q7 **Tonnerre** Yonne, C France
Tonoas see Dublon
35 U8 **Tonopah** Nevada, W USA
164 H13 **Tonoshō** Okayama, Shōdo-shima, SW Japan
43 S17 **Tonosí** Los Santos, S Panama
95 H16 **Tønsberg** Vestfold, S Norway
39 T11 **Tonsina** Alaska, USA
95 D17 **Tonstad** Vest-Agder, S Norway
193 X15 **Tonumea** island Nomuka Group, W Tonga
137 O11 **Tonya** Trabzon, NE Turkey
119 K20 **Tonyezh** Rus. Tonezh. Homyel'skaya Voblasts', SE Belarus
36 L3 **Tooele** Utah, W USA
122 L13 **Toora-Khem** Respublika Tyva, S Russian Federation
183 O5 **Toorale East** New South Wales, SE Australia
83 H25 **Toorberg** ▲ S South Africa
118 G5 **Tootsi** Pärnumaa, SW Estonia
183 U3 **Toowoomba** Queensland, E Australia
27 Q4 **Topeka** state capital Kansas, C USA
111 M18 **Topla** Hung. Toplya. ∽ NE Slovakia
122 J12 **Topki** Kemerovskaya Oblast', S Russian Federation
Toplicza see Toplița
116 J10 **Toplița** Ger. Töplitz, Hung. Maroshévíz; prev. Toplița Română, Hung. Oláh-Toplicza, Toplicza. Harghita, C Romania
Toplița Română/Töplitz see Toplița
Toplya see Topla
111 I20 **Topoľčany** Hung. Nagytapolcsány. Nitriansky Kraj, SW Slovakia
40 G8 **Topolobampo** Sinaloa, C Mexico
116 I13 **Topoloveni** Argeş, S Romania
114 L11 **Topolovgrad** prev. Kavakli. Khaskovo, S Bulgaria
Topolya see Bačka Topola
126 I6 **Topozero, Ozero** ◎ NW Russian Federation
32 J10 **Toppenish** Washington, NW USA
181 P4 **Top Springs Roadhouse** Northern Territory, N Australia
189 U11 **Tora** island Chuuk, C Micronesia
Toraigh see Tory Island
189 U11 **Tora Island Pass** passage Chuuk Islands, C Micronesia
143 U5 **Torbat-e Ḩeydarīyeh** var. Turbat-i-Haidari. Khorāsān, NE Iran
143 V5 **Torbat-e Jām** var. Turbat-i-Jam. Khorāsān, NE Iran
39 Q11 **Torbert, Mount** ▲ Alaska, USA
31 P6 **Torch Lake** ◎ Michigan, N USA
Törcsvár see Bran
Torda see Turda
104 L6 **Tordesillas** Castilla-León, N Spain
92 K13 **Töre** Norrbotten, N Sweden
95 L17 **Töreboda** Västra Götaland, S Sweden
95 J21 **Torekov** Skåne, S Sweden
92 O3 **Torell Land** physical region SW Svalbard
117 Y8 **Torez** Donets'ka Oblast', SE Ukraine
101 N14 **Torgau** Sachsen, E Germany
Torgay Üstirti see Turgayskaya Stolovaya Strana
Torghay see Turgay
95 N22 **Torhamn** Blekinge, S Sweden
99 C17 **Torhout** West-Vlaanderen, W Belgium
106 B8 **Torino** Eng. Turin. Piemonte, NW Italy

◆ Country ● Country Capital ◇ Dependent Territory ○ Dependent Territory Capital ◈ Administrative Region ✕ International Airport ▲ Mountain ⛰ Mountain Range Ӿ Volcano ∽ River ◎ Lake ▣ Reservoir

165 U15 **Tori-shima** island Izu-shotō, SE Japan
81 F16 **Torit** Eastern Equatoria, S Sudan
186 H6 **Toriu** New Britain, E PNG
148 M4 **Torkestān, Selseleh-ye Band-e** var. Bandi-i Turkistan. ▲ NW Afghanistan
104 L7 **Tormes** ≈ W Spain
Tornacum see Tournai
Torneå see Tornio
92 K12 **Torneälven** | var.Torniojoki, Fin. Tornionjoki. ≈ Finland/Sweden
92 I11 **Torneträsk** ◎ N Sweden
13 O4 **Torngat Mountains** ▲ Newfoundland, NE Canada
24 H8 **Tornillo** Texas, SW USA
92 K13 **Tornio** Swe. Torneå. Lappi, NW Finland
Torniojoki/Tornionjoki see Torneälven
61 B23 **Tornquist** Buenos Aires, E Argentina
104 L6 **Toro** Castilla-León, N Spain
62 H9 **Toro, Cerro del** ▲ N Chile
77 R12 **Torodi** Tillabéri, SW Niger
Törökbecse see Novi Bečej
186 J7 **Torokina** Bougainville Island, NE PNG
111 L23 **Törökszentmiklós** Jász-Nagykun-Szolnok, E Hungary
42 G7 **Torola, Río** ≈ El Salvador/Honduras
Toronaíos, Kólpos see Kassándras, Kólpos
14 H15 **Toronto** Ontario, S Canada
31 V12 **Toronto** Ohio, N USA
Toronto see Lester B.Pearson
27 P6 **Toronto Lake** ▣ Kansas, C USA
35 V16 **Toro Peak** ▲ California, W USA
126 H16 **Toropets** Tverskaya Oblast', W Russian Federation
81 G18 **Tororo** E Uganda
136 H16 **Toros Dağları** Eng. Taurus Mountains. ▲ S Turkey
183 N13 **Torquay** Victoria, SE Australia
97 J24 **Torquay** SW England, UK
104 M5 **Torquemada** Castilla-León, N Spain
35 S16 **Torrance** California, W USA
104 G12 **Torrão** Setúbal, S Portugal
104 H8 **Torre, Alto da** ▲ C Portugal
107 K18 **Torre Annunziata** Campania, S Italy
105 T8 **Torreblanca** País Valenciano, E Spain
104 L15 **Torrecilla** ▲ S Spain
105 P4 **Torrecilla en Cameros** La Rioja, N Spain
105 N13 **Torredelcampo** Andalucía, S Spain
107 K17 **Torre del Greco** Campania, S Italy
104 I6 **Torre de Moncorvo** var. Moncorvo, Tôrre de Moncorvo. Bragança, N Portugal
104 J9 **Torrejoncillo** Extremadura, W Spain
105 O8 **Torrejón de Ardoz** Madrid, C Spain
105 N7 **Torrelaguna** Madrid, C Spain
105 N2 **Torrelavega** Cantabria, N Spain
107 M16 **Torremaggiore** Puglia, SE Italy
104 M15 **Torremolinos** Andalucía, S Spain
182 I6 **Torrens, Lake** salt lake South Australia
Torrent/Torrent de l'Horta see Torrente
105 S10 **Torrente** var. Torrent, Torrent de l'Horta. País Valenciano, E Spain
40 L8 **Torreón** Coahuila de Zaragoza, NE Mexico
105 R13 **Torre Pacheco** Murcia, SE Spain
106 A8 **Torre Pellice** Piemonte, NE Italy
105 O13 **Torreperogil** Andalucía, S Spain
61 J15 **Torres** Rio Grande do Sul, S Brazil
Torrès, Îles see Torres Islands
187 Q11 **Torres Islands** Fr. Îles Torrès. island group N Vanuatu
104 G9 **Torres Novas** Santarém, C Portugal
181 V1 **Torres Strait** strait Australia/PNG
104 F10 **Torres Vedras** Lisboa, C Portugal
105 S13 **Torrevieja** País Valenciano, E Spain
186 B6 **Torricelli Mountains** ▲ NW PNG
96 G8 **Torridon, Loch** inlet NW Scotland, UK
106 D9 **Torriglia** Liguria, NW Italy
104 M9 **Torrijos** Castilla-La Mancha, C Spain
18 L12 **Torrington** Connecticut, NE USA
33 Z15 **Torrington** Wyoming, C USA
93 F16 **Torröjen** var. Torrön. ◎ C Sweden
Torrön see Torröjen
105 N15 **Torrox** Andalucía, S Spain
94 N13 **Torsåker** Gävleborg, C Sweden
95 N21 **Torsås** Kalmar, S Sweden
95 J14 **Torsby** Värmland, C Sweden
95 N16 **Torshälla** Södermanland, C Sweden
95 B19 **Tórshavn** Dan. Thorshavn Dependent territory capital Faeroe Islands
Torshiz see Kāshmar
45 T9 **Tortola** island C British Virgin Islands
106 D9 **Tortona** anc. Dertona. Piemonte, NW Italy
107 L23 **Tortorici** Sicilia, Italy, C Mediterranean Sea
105 U7 **Tortosa** anc. Dertosa. Cataluña, E Spain
Tortosa see Ţarţūs
105 U7 **Tortosa, Cap** headland E Spain
44 L8 **Tortue, Île de la** var. Tortuga Island. island N Haiti
55 Y10 **Tortue, Montagne** ▲ C French Guiana
Tortuga, Isla see La Tortuga, Isla
Tortuga Island see Tortue, Île de la
54 C11 **Tortugas, Golfo** gulf W Colombia
45 T5 **Tortuguero, Laguna** lagoon N Puerto Rico
137 Q12 **Tortum** Erzurum, NE Turkey
Torugart, Pereval see Turugart Shankou
137 O12 **Torul** Gümüşhane, NE Turkey
110 J10 **Toruń** Ger. Thorn. Toruń, Kujawsko-pomorskie, C Poland
95 K20 **Torup** Halland, S Sweden
118 I6 **Tõrva** Ger. Törwa. Valgamaa, S Estonia
Törwa see Tõrva
96 D13 **Tory Island** Ir. Toraigh. island NW Ireland
111 N19 **Torysa** Hung. Tarca. ≈ NE Slovakia
Törzburg see Bran
126 J16 **Torzhok** Tverskaya Oblast', W Russian Federation
164 F15 **Tosa-Shimizu** var. Tosasimizu. Kōchi, Shikoku, SW Japan
Tosasimizu see Tosa-Shimizu
164 G15 **Tosa-wan** bay SW Japan
83 H21 **Tosca** North-West, N South Africa
106 F12 **Toscana** Eng. Tuscany. ◐ region C Italy
107 E14 **Toscano, Archipelago** Eng. Tuscan Archipelago. island group C Italy
106 G10 **Tosco-Emiliano, Appennino** Eng. Tuscan-Emilian Mountains. ▲ C Italy
Tōsei see Tungshih
165 N15 **To-shima** island Izu-shotō, SE Japan
147 Q9 **Toshkent** Eng./Rus. Tashkent. ● (Uzbekistan) Toshkent Wiloyati, E Uzbekistan
147 Q9 **Toshkent** ✕ Toshkent Wiloyati, E Uzbekistan
147 P9 **Toshkent Wiloyati** Rus. Tashkentskaya Oblast'. ◐ province E Uzbekistan
126 H13 **Tosno** Leningradskaya Oblast', NW Russian Federation
159 Q10 **Toson Hu** ◎ C China
162 H6 **Tosontsengel** Dzavhan, NW Mongolia
Tosquduq Qumlari see Goshquduq Qum
105 U4 **Tossal de l'Orri** var. Llorri. ▲ NE Spain
61 A15 **Tostado** Santa Fe, C Argentina
118 F6 **Tõstamaa** Ger. Testama. Pärnumaa, SW Estonia
100 I10 **Tostedt** Niedersachsen, NW Germany
136 J11 **Tosya** Kastamonu, N Turkey
95 F15 **Totak** ◎ S Norway
105 R13 **Totana** Murcia, SE Spain
94 H13 **Toten** physical region S Norway
83 G18 **Toteng** Ngamiland, C Botswana
102 M3 **Tôtes** Seine-Maritime, N France
Totigi see Tochigi
Totio see Tochio
Totis see Tata
189 U13 **Totiw** island Chuuk, C Micronesia
127 N13 **Tot'ma** var. Totma. Vologodskaya Oblast', NW Russian Federation
Tot'ma see Sukhona
55 V9 **Totness** Coronie, N Suriname
42 C5 **Totonicapán** Totonicapán, W Guatemala
42 A2 **Totonicapán** off. Departamento de Totonicapán. ◐ department W Guatemala
61 B18 **Totoras** Santa Fe, C Argentina
187 Y15 **Totoya** island S Fiji
183 Q7 **Tottenham** New South Wales, SE Australia
164 I12 **Tottori** Tottori, Honshū, SW Japan
164 H12 **Tottori** off. Tottori-ken. ◐ prefecture Honshū, SW Japan
76 I6 **Touâjil** Tiris Zemmour, N Mauritania
76 L15 **Touba** W Ivory Coast
76 G11 **Touba** W Senegal
74 E7 **Toubkal, Jbel** ▲ W Morocco
32 K10 **Touchet** Washington, NW USA
103 P7 **Toucy** Yonne, C France
77 O12 **Tougan** W Burkina
74 L7 **Touggourt** NE Algeria
77 Q12 **Tougouri** N Burkina
76 J13 **Tougué** Moyenne-Guinée, NW Guinea
76 K12 **Toukoto** Kayes, W Mali
103 S5 **Toul** Meurthe-et-Moselle, NE France
76 L16 **Toulépleu** var. Toulobli. W Ivory Coast
161 S14 **Touliu** C Taiwan
15 U3 **Toulnustouc** ≈ Quebec, SE Canada
Toulobli see Toulépleu
103 T16 **Toulon** anc. Telo Martius, Tilio Martius. Var, SE France
30 K12 **Toulon** Illinois, N USA
102 M15 **Toulouse** anc. Tolosa. Haute-Garonne, S France
102 M15 **Toulouse** ✕ Haute-Garonne, S France
77 N16 **Toumodi** C Ivory Coast
74 G9 **Tounassine, Hamada** hill range W Algeria
166 M7 **Toungoo** Pegu, C Burma
102 L8 **Touraine** cultural region C France
Tourane see Đà Nẵng
103 P1 **Tourcoing** Nord, N France
104 F2 **Touriñán, Cabo** headland NW Spain
76 J6 **Tourine** Tiris Zemmour, N Mauritania
102 J3 **Tourlaville** Manche, N France
99 D19 **Tournai** var. Tournay, Dut. Doornik; anc. Tornacum. Hainaut, SW Belgium
102 L16 **Tournay** Hautes-Pyrénées, S France
Tournay see Tournai
103 R12 **Tournon** Ardèche, E France
103 R9 **Tournus** Saône-et-Loire, C France
59 Q14 **Touros** Rio Grande do Norte, E Brazil
102 L8 **Tours** anc. Caesarodunum, Turoni. Indre-et-Loire, C France
183 Q17 **Tourville, Cape** headland Tasmania, SE Australia
162 I8 **Töv** ◐ province C Mongolia
54 H7 **Tovar** Mérida, NW Venezuela
128 L5 **Tovarkovskiy** Tul'skaya Oblast', W Russian Federation
Tovil'-Dora see Tavildara
Tövis see Teiuş
137 V11 **Tovuz** Rus. Tauz. W Azerbaijan
165 R7 **Towada** Aomori, Honshū, C Japan
184 K3 **Towai** Northland, North Island, NZ
18 H12 **Towanda** Pennsylvania, NE USA
29 W4 **Tower** Minnesota, N USA
171 N12 **Towera** Sulawesi, N Indonesia
Tower Island see Genovesa, Isla
180 M13 **Tower Peak** ▲ Western Australia
35 U11 **Towne Pass** pass California, W USA
29 N3 **Towner** North Dakota, N USA
33 R10 **Townsend** Montana, NW USA
181 X6 **Townsville** Queensland, NE Australia
Towoeti Meer see Towuti, Danau
148 K4 **Towraghoudī** Herāt, NW Afghanistan
21 X3 **Towson** Maryland, NE USA
171 O13 **Towuti, Danau** Dut. Towoeti Meer. ◎ Sulawesi, C Indonesia
Toxkan He see Ak-say
24 K9 **Toyah** Texas, SW USA
165 R4 **Tōya-ko** ◎ Hokkaidō, NE Japan
164 L11 **Toyama** Toyama, Honshū, SW Japan
164 L11 **Toyama** off. Toyama-ken. ◐ prefecture Honshū, SW Japan
164 L11 **Toyama-wan** bay W Japan
164 H15 **Tōyo** Kōchi, Shikoku, SW Japan
Toyohara see Yuzhno-Sakhalinsk
164 L14 **Toyohashi** var. Toyohasi. Aichi, Honshū, SW Japan
Toyohasi see Toyohashi
164 L14 **Toyokawa** Aichi, Honshū, SW Japan
164 I14 **Toyooka** Hyōgo, Honshū, SW Japan
164 L13 **Toyota** Aichi, Honshū, SW Japan
165 T1 **Toyotomi** Hokkaidō, NE Japan
Toytepa see Tuytepa
74 M6 **Tozeur** var. Tawzar. W Tunisia
39 Q8 **Tozi, Mount** ▲ Alaska, USA
137 Q9 **Tqvarch'eli** Rus. Tkvarcheli. NW Georgia
Trâblous see Tripoli
137 O11 **Trabzon** Eng. Trebizond; anc. Trapezus. Trabzon, NE Turkey
137 O11 **Trabzon** Eng. Trebizond. ◐ province NE Turkey
13 P13 **Tracadie** New Brunswick, SE Canada
Trachenberg see Żmigród
15 O11 **Tracy** Quebec, SE Canada
35 O8 **Tracy** California, W USA
29 S10 **Tracy** Minnesota, N USA
20 K10 **Tracy City** Tennessee, S USA
106 D7 **Tradate** Lombardia, N Italy
84 F6 **Traena Bank** undersea feature E Norwegian Sea
29 W13 **Traer** Iowa, C USA
104 J16 **Trafalgar, Cabo de** headland SW Spain
Traiectum ad Mosam/Traiectum Tungorum see Maastricht
Tráigh Mhór see Tramore
11 O17 **Trail** British Columbia, SW Canada
58 B11 **Traíra, Serra do** ▲ NW Brazil
109 V5 **Traisen** Niederösterreich, NE Austria
109 W4 **Traisen** ≈ NE Austria
109 X4 **Traiskirchen** Niederösterreich, NE Austria
Trajani Portus see Civitavecchia
Trajectum ad Rhenum see Utrecht
119 H14 **Trakai** Ger. Traken, Pol. Troki. Trakai, SE Lithuania
Traken see Trakai
97 B20 **Tralee** Ir. Trá Lí. SW Ireland
97 A20 **Tralee Bay** Ir. Bá Thrá Lí. bay SW Ireland
Trá Lí see Tralee
Trälleborg see Trelleborg
Tralles see Aydın
61 J16 **Tramandaí** Rio Grande do Sul, S Brazil
108 C7 **Tramelan** Bern, W Switzerland
Trá Mhór see Tramore
97 E20 **Tramore** Ir. Tráigh Mhór, Trá Mhór. S Ireland
95 L18 **Tranås** Jönköping, S Sweden
62 J7 **Trancas** Tucumán, N Argentina
104 I7 **Trancoso** Guarda, N Portugal
95 H22 **Tranebjerg** Århus, C Denmark
95 K19 **Tranemo** Västra Götaland, S Sweden
167 N16 **Trang** Trang, S Thailand
171 V15 **Trangan, Pulau** island Kepulauan Aru, E Indonesia
Trâng Dinh see Thât Khê
183 Q7 **Trangie** New South Wales, SE Australia
94 K12 **Trängslet** Dalarna, C Sweden
107 N16 **Trani** Puglia, SE Italy
61 F17 **Tranqueras** Rivera, NE Uruguay
63 G17 **Tranqui, Isla** island S Chile
39 V6 **Trans-Alaska pipeline** oil pipeline Alaska, USA
195 Q10 **Transantarctic Mountains** ▲ Antarctica
Transcarpathian Oblast see Zakarpats'ka Oblast'
Transilvania see Transylvania
Transilvaniei, Alpi see Carpaţii Meridionali
Transjordan see Jordan
172 L11 **Transkei Basin** undersea feature SW Indian Ocean
122 E9 **Trans-Siberian Railway** Railroad Russian Federation
Transsylvanische Alpen/Transylvanian Alps see Carpaţii Meridionali
94 K12 **Transtrand** Dalarna, C Sweden
116 G10 **Transylvania** Eng. Ardeal, Transilvania, Ger. Siebenbürgen, Hung. Erdély. cultural region NW Romania
167 S14 **Tra Ôn** Vinh Long, S Vietnam
107 H23 **Trapani** anc. Drepanum. Sicilia, Italy, C Mediterranean Sea
167 S12 **Trâpeăng Vêng** Kâmpóng Thum, C Cambodia
Trapezus see Trabzon
114 L9 **Trapoklovo** Sliven, C Bulgaria
183 P13 **Traralgon** Victoria, SE Australia
76 H9 **Trarza** ◐ region SW Mauritania
Trasimenischersee see Trasimeno, Lago
106 H12 **Trasimeno, Lago** Eng. Lake of Perugia, Ger. Trasimenischersee. ◎ C Italy
95 J20 **Träslövsläge** Halland, S Sweden
Trás-os-Montes see Cucumbi
104 I6 **Trás-os-Montes e Alto Douro** former province N Portugal
167 Q12 **Trat** var. Bang Phra. Trat, S Thailand
Trá Tholl, Inis see Inishtrahull
Traù see Trogir
109 T4 **Traun** Oberösterreich, N Austria
109 S5 **Traun** ≈ N Austria
Traun, Lake see Traunsee
101 N23 **Traunreut** Bayern, SE Germany
109 S5 **Traunsee** var. Gmundner See, Eng. Lake Traun. ◎ N Austria
Trautenau see Trutnov
21 P11 **Travelers Rest** South Carolina, SE USA
182 L8 **Travellers Lake** seasonal lake New South Wales, SE Australia
31 P6 **Traverse City** Michigan, N USA
29 R7 **Traverse, Lake** ◎ Minnesota/South Dakota, N USA
185 I16 **Travers, Mount** ▲ South Island, NZ
11 P17 **Travers Reservoir** ▣ Alberta, SW Canada
167 T14 **Tra Vinh** var. Phu Vinh. Tra Vinh, S Vietnam
25 S10 **Travis, Lake** ▣ Texas, SW USA
112 H12 **Travnik** Federacija Bosna I Hercegovina, C Bosnia and Herzegovina
109 V11 **Trbovlje** Ger. Trifail. C Slovenia
23 V13 **Treasure Island** Florida, SE USA
Treasure State see Montana
186 I8 **Treasury Islands** island group NW Solomon Islands
106 D9 **Trebbia** anc. Trebia. ≈ NW Italy
100 N8 **Trebel** ≈ NE Germany
103 O16 **Trèbes** Aude, S France
Trebia see Trebbia
111 F18 **Třebíč** Ger. Trebitsch. Jihlavský Kraj, S Czech Republic
113 I16 **Trebinje** Republika Srpska, S Bosnia and Herzegovina
Trebišnica see Trebišnjica
113 H16 **Trebišnjica** var. Trebišnica. ≈ S Bosnia and Herzegovina
111 N20 **Trebišov** Hung. Tőketerebes. Košický Kraj, E Slovakia
Trebitsch see Třebíč
Trebizond see Trabzon
Trebnitz see Trzebnica
109 V12 **Trebnje** SE Slovenia
111 D19 **Třeboň** Ger. Wittingau. Budějovický Kraj, S Czech Republic
104 J15 **Trebujena** Andalucía, S Spain
100 I7 **Treene** ≈ N Germany
Tree Planters State see Nebraska
109 S9 **Treffen** Kärnten, S Austria
Trefynwy see Monmouth
102 G5 **Tréguier** Côtes d'Armor, NW France
61 G18 **Treinta y Tres** Treinta y Tres, E Uruguay
61 F18 **Treinta y Tres** ◐ department E Uruguay
114 F9 **Treklyanska Reka** ≈ W Bulgaria
102 K8 **Trélazé** Maine-et-Loire, NW France
63 K17 **Trelew** Chubut, SE Argentina
95 K23 **Trelleborg** var. Trälleborg. Skåne, S Sweden
113 P15 **Trem** ▲ SE Yugoslavia
15 N11 **Tremblant, Mont** ▲ Quebec, SE Canada
99 H17 **Tremelo** Vlaams Brabant, C Belgium
107 M15 **Tremiti, Isole** island group SE Italy
30 K12 **Tremont** Illinois, N USA
36 L1 **Tremonton** Utah, W USA
105 U4 **Tremp** Cataluña, NE Spain
30 J7 **Trempealeau** Wisconsin, N USA
15 P8 **Trenche** ≈ Quebec, SE Canada
15 O7 **Trenche, Lac** ◎ Quebec, SE Canada
111 I20 **Trenčiansky Kraj** ◐ region W Slovakia
111 I19 **Trenčín** Ger. Trentschin, Hung. Trencsén. Trenčiansky Kraj, W Slovakia
Trencsén see Trenčín
Trengganu see Terengganu
61 A21 **Trenque Lauquen** Buenos Aires, E Argentina
14 J14 **Trent** ≈ Ontario, SE Canada
97 N18 **Trent** ≈ C England, UK
Trent see Trento
106 F5 **Trentino-Alto Adige** prev. Venezia Tridentina. ◐ region N Italy
106 G6 **Trento** Eng. Trent, Ger. Trient; anc. Tridentum. Trentino-Alto Adige, N Italy
14 J15 **Trenton** Ontario, SE Canada
23 V10 **Trenton** Florida, SE USA
23 R1 **Trenton** Georgia, SE USA
31 S10 **Trenton** Michigan, N USA
27 S2 **Trenton** Missouri, C USA
28 M17 **Trenton** Nebraska, C USA
18 J15 **Trenton** state capital New Jersey, NE USA
21 W10 **Trenton** North Carolina, SE USA
20 G9 **Trenton** Tennessee, S USA
36 L1 **Trenton** Utah, W USA
Trentschin see Trenčín
Treptow an der Rega see Trzebiatów
61 C23 **Tres Arroyos** Buenos Aires, E Argentina
61 J15 **Três Cachoeiras** Rio Grande do Sul, S Brazil
106 E7 **Trescore Balneario** Lombardia, N Italy
41 V17 **Tres Cruces, Cerro** ▲ SE Mexico
57 K18 **Tres Cruces, Cordillera** ▲ W Bolivia
113 N18 **Treska** ≈ NW FYR Macedonia
113 I14 **Treskavica** ▲ SE Bosnia and Herzegovina
59 J20 **Três Lagoas** Mato Grosso do Sul, SW Brazil
40 H12 **Tres Marías, Islas** island group C Mexico
59 M19 **Três Marias, Represa** ▣ SE Brazil
63 F20 **Tres Montes, Península** headland S Chile
105 O3 **Trespaderne** Castilla-León, N Spain
60 G13 **Três Passos** Rio Grande do Sul, S Brazil
61 A23 **Tres Picos, Cerro** ▲ E Argentina
63 G17 **Tres Picos, Cerro** ▲ SW Argentina
60 I12 **Três Pinheiros** Paraná, S Brazil
59 M21 **Três Pontas** Minas Gerais, SE Brazil
Tres Puntas, Cabo see Manabique, Punta
60 P9 **Três Rios** Rio de Janeiro, SE Brazil
Tres Tabernae see Saverne
Trestenberg/Trestendorf see Tăşnad
41 R15 **Tres Valles** Veracruz-Llave, SE Mexico
94 H12 **Tretten** Oppland, S Norway
Treuburg see Olecko
101 K21 **Treuchtlingen** Bayern, S Germany
100 N13 **Treuenbrietzen** Brandenburg, E Germany
95 F16 **Treungen** Telemark, S Norway
63 H17 **Trevelín** Chubut, SW Argentina
Treves/Trèves see Trier
106 I13 **Trevi** Umbria, C Italy
106 E7 **Treviglio** Lombardia, N Italy
104 J4 **Trevinca, Peña** ▲ NW Spain
105 P3 **Treviño** Castilla-León, N Spain
106 I7 **Treviso** anc. Tarvisium. Veneto, NE Italy
97 G24 **Trevose Head** headland SW England, UK
Trg see Feldkirchen in Kärnten
183 P17 **Triabunna** Tasmania, SE Australia
21 W4 **Triangle** Virginia, NE USA
83 L18 **Triangle** Masvingo, SE Zimbabwe
115 L23 **Tría Nisía** island Kykládes, Greece, Aegean Sea
Triberg see Triberg im Schwarzwald
101 G23 **Triberg im Schwarzwald** var. Triberg. Baden-Württemberg, SW Germany
153 P11 **Tribhuvan** ✕ (Kathmandu) Central, C Nepal
54 C9 **Tribugá, Golfo de** gulf W Colombia
181 W4 **Tribulation, Cape** headland Queensland, NE Australia
108 M8 **Tribulaun** ▲ SW Austria
11 U17 **Tribune** Saskatchewan, S Canada
26 H5 **Tribune** Kansas, C USA
107 N18 **Tricarico** Basilicata, S Italy
107 Q19 **Tricase** Puglia, SE Italy
Trichinopoly see Tiruchchirāppalli
115 D18 **Trichonída, Límni** ◎ C Greece
155 G22 **Trichūr** var. Thrissur. Kerala, SW India
Tricorno see Triglav
183 O8 **Trida** New South Wales, SE Australia
35 S1 **Trident Peak** ▲ Nevada, W USA
Tridentum/Trient see Trento
109 T6 **Trieben** Steiermark, SE Austria
101 D19 **Trier** Eng. Treves, Fr. Trèves; anc. Augusta Treverorum. Rheinland-Pfalz, SW Germany
106 K7 **Trieste** Slvn. Trst. Friuli-Venezia Giulia, NE Italy
Trieste, Golfo di/Triest, Golf von see Trieste, Gulf of
106 J8 **Trieste, Gulf of** Cro. Tršćanski Zaljev, Ger. Golf von Triest, It. Golfo di Trieste, Slvn. Tržaški Zaliv. gulf S Europe
109 W4 **Triesting** ≈ W Austria
Trifail see Trbovlje
116 L9 **Trifeşti** Iaşi, NE Romania
109 S10 **Triglav** It. Tricorno. ▲ NW Slovenia
104 I14 **Trigueros** Andalucía, S Spain
115 E16 **Tríkala** prev. Trikkala. Thessalía, C Greece
115 E17 **Trikeriótis** ≈ C Greece
Trikkala see Tríkala
Trikomo/Tríkomon see Iskele
97 F17 **Trim** Ir. Baile Átha Troim. E Ireland
108 E7 **Trimbach** Solothurn, NW Switzerland
109 Q5 **Trimmelkam** Oberösterreich, N Austria
29 U11 **Trimont** Minnesota, N USA
Trimontium see Plovdiv
Trinacria see Sicilia
155 K24 **Trincomalee** var. Trinkomali. Eastern Province, NE Sri Lanka
65 K16 **Trindade, Ilha da** island Brazil, W Atlantic Ocean
47 Y9 **Trindade Spur** undersea feature SW Atlantic Ocean
111 J17 **Třinec** Ger. Trzynietz. Ostravský Kraj, E Czech Republic
57 M16 **Trinidad** Beni, N Bolivia
54 H9 **Trinidad** Casanare, E Colombia
44 E6 **Trinidad** Sancti Spíritus, C Cuba
37 U8 **Trinidad** Colorado, C USA
61 E19 **Trinidad** Flores, S Uruguay
45 Y17 **Trinidad** island C Trinidad and Tobago
Trinidad see Jose Abad Santos
45 Y16 **Trinidad and Tobago** off. Republic of Trinidad and Tobago. ◆ republic SE West Indies
63 F22 **Trinidad, Golfo** gulf S Chile
61 B24 **Trinidad, Isla** island E Argentina
107 N16 **Trinitapoli** Puglia, SE Italy
55 X10 **Trinité, Montagnes de la** ▲ C French Guiana
25 W9 **Trinity** Texas, SW USA
13 U12 **Trinity Bay** inlet Newfoundland, E Canada
39 P15 **Trinity Islands** island group Alaska, USA
35 N2 **Trinity Mountains** ▲ California, W USA
35 S4 **Trinity Peak** ▲ Nevada, W USA
35 S5 **Trinity Range** ▲ Nevada, W USA
35 N2 **Trinity River** ≈ California, W USA
25 V8 **Trinity River** ≈ Texas, SW USA
Trinkomali see Trincomalee
173 Y15 **Triolet** NW Mauritius
107 O20 **Trionto, Capo** headland S Italy
115 J16 **Tripití, Akrotírio** headland Ágios Efstrátios, E Greece
138 G6 **Tripoli** var. Tarābulus, Ţarābulus ash Shām, Trâblous; anc. Tripolis. N Lebanon
29 X12 **Tripoli** Iowa, C USA
Tripoli see Ţarābulus
115 F20 **Trípoli** prev. Trípolis. Pelopónnisos, S Greece
Tripolis see Tripoli, Lebanon
Tripolis see Trípoli, Greece
29 Q12 **Tripp** South Dakota, N USA
153 V15 **Tripura** var. Hill Tippera. ◐ state NE India
108 K8 **Trisanna** ≈ W Austria
100 H8 **Trischen** island NW Germany
65 M24 **Tristan da Cunha** ◇ dependency of Saint Helena SE Atlantic Ocean
67 P15 **Tristan da Cunha** island SE Atlantic Ocean
65 L18 **Tristan da Cunha Fracture Zone** tectonic feature S Atlantic Ocean
167 S14 **Tri Tôn** An Giang, S Vietnam
167 W10 **Triton Island** island S Paracel Islands
155 G24 **Trivandrum** var. Thiruvanathapuram. Kerala, SW India
111 H20 **Trnava** Ger. Tyrnau, Hung. Nagyszombat. Trnavský Kraj, W Slovakia
111 H20 **Trnavský Kraj** ◐ region W Slovakia
Trnovo see Veliko Tŭrnovo
Trobriand Island see Kiriwina Island
Trobriand Islands see Kiriwina Islands
11 Q16 **Trochu** Alberta, SW Canada
109 U7 **Trofaiach** Steiermark, SE Austria
93 F14 **Trofors** Troms, N Norway
113 E14 **Trogir** It. Traù. Split-Dalmacija, S Croatia
112 F13 **Troglav** ▲ Bosnia and Herzegovina/Croatia
107 M16 **Troia** Puglia, SE Italy
107 K24 **Troina** Sicilia, Italy, C Mediterranean Sea
173 O16 **Trois-Bassins** W Réunion
101 E17 **Troisdorf** Nordrhein-Westfalen, W Germany
74 H5 **Trois Fourches, Cap des** headland NE Morocco
15 T8 **Trois-Pistoles** Quebec, SE Canada
99 L21 **Trois-Ponts** Liège, E Belgium
15 P11 **Trois-Rivières** Quebec, SE Canada
55 Y12 **Trois Sauts** S French Guiana
99 M22 **Troisvierges** Diekirch, N Luxembourg
122 F11 **Troitsk** Chelyabinskaya Oblast', S Russian Federation
127 T9 **Troitsko-Pechorsk** Respublika Komi, NW Russian Federation
129 V7 **Troitskoye** Orenburgskaya Oblast', W Russian Federation
Troki see Trakai
94 F9 **Trolla** ▲ S Norway
95 J18 **Trollhättan** Västra Götaland, S Sweden
94 G9 **Trollheimen** ▲ S Norway
94 E9 **Trolltindane** ▲ S Norway
58 H11 **Trombetas, Rio** ≈ NE Brazil
130 L16 **Tromelin, Île** island N Réunion
92 I9 **Troms** ◐ county N Norway
92 I9 **Tromsø** Fin. Tromssa. Troms, N Norway
84 F5 **Tromsøflaket** undersea feature W Barents Sea

◆ Country ● Country Capital ◇ Dependent Territory ○ Dependent Territory Capital ◐ Administrative Region ✕ International Airport ▲ Mountain ▲ Mountain Range Volcano ≈ River ◎ Lake ▣ Reservoir

Tromssa see Tromsø
94 H10 **Tron** ▲ S Norway
35 U12 **Trona** California, W USA
63 G16 **Tronador, Cerro** ▲ S Chile
94 H8 **Trondheim** Ger. Drontheim; prev. Nidaros, Trondhjem. Sør-Trøndelag, S Norway
94 H7 **Trondheimsfjorden** fjord S Norway
Trondhjem see Trondheim
107 J14 **Tronto** ≈ C Italy
Troodos see Ólympos
121 P3 **Troódos** var. Troodos Mountains. ▲ C Cyprus
Troodos Mountains see Troódos
96 I13 **Troon** W Scotland, UK
107 M22 **Tropea** Calabria, SW Italy
36 L7 **Tropic** Utah, W USA
64 L10 **Tropic Seamount** var. Banc du Tropique. undersea feature E Atlantic Ocean
Tropique, Banc du see Tropic Seamount
Tropoja see Tropojë
113 L17 **Tropojë** var. Tropoja. Kukës, N Albania
Troppau see Opava
95 O16 **Trosa** Södermanland, C Sweden
118 H12 **Troškūnai** Anykščiai, E Lithuania
101 G23 **Trossingen** Baden-Württemberg, SW Germany
117 T4 **Trostyanets'** Rus. Trostyanets. Sums'ka Oblast', NE Ukraine
117 N7 **Trostyanets'** Rus. Trostyanets. Vinnyts'ka Oblast', C Ukraine
116 L11 **Trotuş** ≈ E Romania
44 M8 **Trou-du-Nord** N Haiti
25 W7 **Troup** Texas, SW USA
8 I10 **Trout** ≈ Northwest Territories, NW Canada
33 N8 **Trout Creek** Montana, NW USA
32 H10 **Trout Lake** Washington, NW USA
12 B9 **Trout Lake** ◎ Ontario, S Canada
33 T12 **Trout Peak** ▲ Wyoming, C USA
102 L4 **Trouville** Calvados, N France
97 L22 **Trowbridge** S England, UK
23 Q6 **Troy** Alabama, S USA
27 Q3 **Troy** Kansas, C USA
27 W4 **Troy** Missouri, C USA
18 L10 **Troy** New York, NE USA
21 S10 **Troy** North Carolina, SE USA
31 R13 **Troy** Ohio, N USA
25 T9 **Troy** Texas, SW USA
114 I9 **Troyan** Lovech, N Bulgaria
114 I9 **Troyanski Prokhod** pass N Bulgaria
145 N6 **Troyebratskiy** Severnyy Kazakhstan, N Kazakhstan
103 Q6 **Troyes** anc. Augustobona Tricassium. Aube, N France
117 X5 **Troyits'ke** Luhans'ka Oblast', E Ukraine
35 W7 **Troy Peak** ▲ Nevada, W USA
113 G15 **Trpanj** Dubrovnik-Neretva, S Croatia
Trščanski Zaljev see Trieste, Gulf of
Trst see Trieste
113 N14 **Trstenik** Serbia, C Yugoslavia
128 I6 **Trubchevsk** Bryanskaya Oblast', W Russian Federation
Trubchular see Orlyak
37 S10 **Truchas Peak** ▲ New Mexico, SW USA
143 P16 **Trucial Coast** physical region C UAE
Trucial States see United Arab Emirates
35 Q6 **Truckee** California, W USA
35 R5 **Truckee River** ≈ Nevada, W USA
129 Q13 **Trudfront** Astrakhanskaya Oblast', SW Russian Federation
14 I9 **Truite, Lac à la** ◎ Quebec, SE Canada
42 K4 **Trujillo** Colón, NE Honduras
56 C12 **Trujillo** La Libertad, NW Peru
104 K10 **Trujillo** Extremadura, W Spain
54 I6 **Trujillo** Trujillo, NW Venezuela
54 I6 **Trujillo** off. Estado Trujillo. ◈ state W Venezuela
Truk see Chuuk
Truk Islands see Chuuk Islands
29 U10 **Truman** Minnesota, N USA
27 X10 **Trumann** Arkansas, C USA
36 J9 **Trumbull, Mount** ▲ Arizona, SW USA
114 F9 **Trŭn** Pernik, W Bulgaria
183 Q8 **Trundle** New South Wales, SE Australia
131 U13 **Trung Phân** physical region S Vietnam
Trupcilar see Orlyak
13 Q15 **Truro** Nova Scotia, SE Canada
97 H25 **Truro** SW England, UK
25 P5 **Truscott** Texas, SW USA
116 K9 **Truşeşti** Botoşani, NE Romania
116 H6 **Truskavets'** L'vivs'ka Oblast', W Ukraine
95 H22 **Trustrup** Århus, C Denmark
10 M11 **Trutch** British Columbia, W Canada
37 Q14 **Truth Or Consequences** New Mexico, SW USA
111 F15 **Trutnov** Ger. Trautenau. Hradecký Kraj, NE Czech Republic
103 P13 **Truyère** ≈ C France
114 K9 **Tryavna** Lovech, N Bulgaria
28 M14 **Tryon** Nebraska, C USA
94 I11 **Trysilelva** ≈ S Norway
112 D10 **Tržac** Federacija Bosna I Hercegovina, NW Bosnia and Herzegovina
Tržaški Zaliv see Trieste, Gulf of
110 G10 **Trzcianka** Ger. Schönlanke. Piła, Wielkopolskie, C Poland
110 E7 **Trzebiatów** Ger. Treptow an der Rega. Zachodniopomorskie, NW Poland
111 G14 **Trzebnica** Ger. Trebnitz. Dolnośląskie, SW Poland
109 T10 **Tržič** Ger. Neumarktl. NW Slovenia
Trzynietz see Třinec
Tsabong see Tshabong
162 G7 **Tsagaanchuluut** Dzavhan, C Mongolia
163 P7 **Tsagaanders** Dornod, NE Mongolia
163 S8 **Tsagaannuur** Dornod, E Mongolia
162 G8 **Tsagaan-Olom** Govĭ-Altay, C Mongolia
162 J8 **Tsagaan-Ovoo** Övörhangay, C Mongolia
162 D5 **Tsagaantüngi** Bayan-Ölgiy, NW Mongolia
129 P12 **Tsagan Aman** Respublika Kalmykiya, SW Russian Federation
23 V11 **Tsala Apopka Lake** ◎ Florida, SE USA
Tsamkong see Zhanjiang
Tsangpo see Brahmaputra
162 L9 **Tsant** Dundgovĭ, C Mongolia
83 G17 **Tsao** Ngamiland, NW Botswana
172 I4 **Tsaratanana** Mahajanga, C Madagascar
114 N10 **Tsarevo** prev. Michurin. Burgas, E Bulgaria
Tsarigrad see Istanbul
Tsaritsyn see Volgograd
126 G13 **Tsarskoye Selo** prev. Pushkin. Leningradskaya Oblast', NW Russian Federation
117 T7 **Tsarychanka** Dnipropetrovs'ka Oblast', E Ukraine
83 H21 **Tsatsu** Southern, S Botswana
81 J20 **Tsavo** Coast, S Kenya
83 E21 **Tsawisis** Karas, S Namibia
Tschakathurn see Čakovec
Tschaslau see Čáslav
Tschenstochau see Częstochowa
Tschernembl see Črnomelj
28 K6 **Tschida, Lake** ◎ North Dakota, N USA
Tschorna see Mustvee
83 I17 **Tsebanana** Central, NE Botswana
Tsefat see Ẕefat
162 G8 **Tseel** Govĭ-Altay, SW Mongolia
128 M13 **Tselina** Rostovskaya Oblast', SW Russian Federation
Tselinograd see Astana
Tselinogradskaya Oblast' see Akmola
162 J6 **Tsengel** Hövsgöl, N Mongolia
162 E7 **Tsenher** Hovd, W Mongolia
146 E12 **Tsentral'nyye Garagumy** Turkm. Merkezi Garagum. desert C Turkmenistan
83 E21 **Tses** Karas, S Namibia
Tseshevlya see Tsyeshawlya
162 E7 **Tsetsegnuur** Hovd, W Mongolia
162 J7 **Tsetserleg** Arhangay, C Mongolia
77 R16 **Tsévié** S Togo
83 G21 **Tshabong** var. Tsabong. Kgalagadi, SW Botswana
83 G20 **Tshane** Kgalagadi, SW Botswana
Tshangalele, Lac see Lufira, Lac de Retenue de la
83 H17 **Tshauxaba** Central, C Botswana
79 F21 **Tshela** Bas-Congo, W Dem. Rep. Congo (Zaire)
79 K22 **Tshibala** Kasai Occidental, S Dem. Rep. Congo (Zaire)
79 J22 **Tshikapa** Kasai Occidental, SW Dem. Rep. Congo (Zaire)
79 L22 **Tshilenge** Kasai Oriental, S Dem. Rep. Congo (Zaire)
79 L24 **Tshimbalanga** Katanga, S Dem. Rep. Congo (Zaire)
79 L22 **Tshimbulu** Kasai Occidental, S Dem. Rep. Congo (Zaire)
Tshiumbe see Chiumbe
79 M21 **Tshofa** Kasai Oriental, C Dem. Rep. Congo (Zaire)
79 K18 **Tshuapa** ≈ C Dem. Rep. Congo (Zaire)
Tshwane see Pretoria
114 G7 **Tsibritsa** ≈ NW Bulgaria
Tsien Tang see Puyang Jiang
114 I12 **Tsigansko Gradishte** ▲ Bulgaria/Greece
8 H7 **Tsiigehtchic** prev. Arctic Red River. Northwest Territories, NW Canada
127 Q7 **Tsil'ma** ≈ NW Russian Federation
119 J17 **Tsimkavichy** Rus. Timkovichi. Minskaya Voblasts', C Belarus
128 M11 **Tsimlyansk** Rostovskaya Oblast', SW Russian Federation
129 N11 **Tsimlyanskoye Vodokhranilishche** var. Tsimlyansk Vodoskhovshche, Eng. Tsimlyansk Reservoir ⊡ SW Russian Federation
Tsimlyansk Reservoir see Tsimlyanskoye Vodokhranilishche
Tsimlyansk Vodoskhovshche see Tsimlyanskoye Vodokhranilishche
Tsinan see Jinan
Tsing Hai see Qinghai Hu, China
Tsinghai see Qinghai, China
Tsingtao/Tsingtau see Qingdao
Tsingyuan see Baoding
Tsinkiang see Quanzhou
Tsintao see Qingdao
83 D17 **Tsintsabis** Otjikoto, N Namibia
172 H8 **Tsiombe** var. Tsihombe. Toliara, S Madagascar
123 O13 **Tsipa** ≈ S Russian Federation
172 H5 **Tsiribihina** ≈ W Madagascar
172 I5 **Tsiroanomandidy** Antananarivo, C Madagascar
189 U13 **Tsis** island Chuuk, C Micronesia
Tsitsihar see Qiqihar
129 Q3 **Tsivil'sk** Chuvashskaya Respublika, W Russian Federation
137 T9 **Ts'khinvali** prev. Staliniri. C Georgia
119 J19 **Tsna** ≈ SW Belarus
126 I15 **Tsna** var. Zna. ≈ W Russian Federation
162 K11 **Tsoohor** Ömnögovĭ, S Mongolia
164 K14 **Tsu** var. Tu. Mie, Honshū, SW Japan
165 O10 **Tsubame** var. Tubame. Niigata, Honshū, C Japan
165 V3 **Tsubetsu** Hokkaidō, NE Japan
165 O13 **Tsuchiura** var. Tutiura. Ibaraki, Honshū, S Japan
165 Q6 **Tsugaru-kaikyō** strait N Japan
164 E14 **Tsukumi** var. Tukumi. Ōita, Kyūshū, SW Japan
162 E5 **Tsul-Ulaan** Bayan-Ölgiy, W Mongolia
83 D17 **Tsumeb** Otjikoto, N Namibia
83 F17 **Tsumkwe** Otjozondjupa, NE Namibia
164 D15 **Tsuno** Miyazaki, Kyūshū, SW Japan
164 D12 **Tsuno-shima** island SW Japan
164 K12 **Tsuruga** var. Turuga. Fukui, Honshū, SW Japan
164 H12 **Tsurugi-san** ▲ Shikoku, SW Japan
165 P9 **Tsuruoka** var. Turuoka. Yamagata, Honshū, C Japan
164 C12 **Tsushima** var. Tsushima-tō, Tusima. island group SW Japan
Tsushima-tō see Tsushima
164 H12 **Tsuyama** var. Tuyama. Okayama, Honshū, SW Japan
83 G19 **Tswaane** Ghanzi, W Botswana
119 N16 **Tsyakhtsin** Rus. Tekhtin. Mahilyowskaya Voblasts', E Belarus
119 P19 **Tsyerakhowka** Rus. Terekhovka. Homyel'skaya Voblasts', SE Belarus
119 I17 **Tsyeshawlya** Rus. Cheshevlya, Tseshevlya. Brestskaya Voblasts', SW Belarus
Tsyurupinsk see Tsyurupyns'k
117 R10 **Tsyurupyns'k** Rus. Tsyurupinsk. Khersons'ka Oblast', S Ukraine
Tu see Tsu
186 C7 **Tua** ≈ C PNG
Tuaim see Tuam
184 L6 **Tuakau** Waikato, North Island, NZ
97 C17 **Tuam** Ir. Tuaim. W Ireland
185 K14 **Tuamarina** Marlborough, South Island, NZ
Tuamotu, Archipel des see Tuamotu, Îles
193 Q9 **Tuamotu Fracture Zone** tectonic feature E Pacific Ocean
191 W9 **Tuamotu, Îles** var. Archipel des Tuamotu, Dangerous Archipelago, Tuamotu Islands. island group N French Polynesia
Tuamotu Islands see Tuamotu, Îles
175 X10 **Tuamotu Ridge** undersea feature C Pacific Ocean
167 R5 **Tuân Giao** Lai Châu, N Vietnam
171 O2 **Tuao** Luzon, N Philippines
190 B15 **Tuapa** NW Niue
43 N7 **Tuapi** Región Autónoma Atlántico Norte, NE Nicaragua
128 K15 **Tuapse** Krasnodarskiy Kray, SW Russian Federation
169 U6 **Tuaran** Sabah, East Malaysia
104 I6 **Tua, Rio** ≈ N Portugal
192 H15 **Tuasivi** Savai'i, C Samoa
185 B24 **Tuatapere** Southland, South Island, NZ
36 M9 **Tuba City** Arizona, SW USA
138 H11 **Ţūbah, Qaşr aţ** castle Ma'ān, C Jordan
Tubame see Tsubame
169 R16 **Tuban** prev. Toeban. Jawa, C Indonesia
141 O16 **Tuban, Wādī** dry watercourse SW Yemen
61 K14 **Tubarão** Santa Catarina, S Brazil
98 O10 **Tubbergen** Overijssel, E Netherlands
Tubeke see Tubize
101 H22 **Tübingen** var. Tuebingen. Baden-Württemberg, SW Germany
129 W6 **Tubinskiy** Respublika Bashkortostan, W Russian Federation
99 G19 **Tubize** Dut. Tubeke. Wallon Brabant, C Belgium
76 J16 **Tubmanburg** NW Liberia
75 T7 **Ţubruq** Eng. Tobruk, It. Tobruch. NE Libya
191 T13 **Tubuai** island Îles Australes, SW French Polynesia
Tubuai, Îles/Tubuai Islands see Australes, Îles
40 F3 **Tubutama** Sonora, NW Mexico
54 K4 **Tucacas** Falcón, N Venezuela
59 P16 **Tucano** Bahia, E Brazil
57 P19 **Tucavaca, Río** ≈ E Bolivia
110 H8 **Tuchola** Kujawsko-pomorskie, C Poland
111 M17 **Tuchów** Małopolskie, SE Poland
23 S3 **Tucker** Georgia, SE USA
27 W10 **Tuckerman** Arkansas, C USA
64 B12 **Tucker's Town** E Bermuda
Tuckum see Tukums
36 M15 **Tucson** Arizona, SW USA
62 J7 **Tucumán** off. Provincia de Tucumán. ◈ province N Argentina
Tucumán see San Miguel de Tucumán
37 V11 **Tucumcari** New Mexico, SW USA
58 H13 **Tucunaré** Pará, N Brazil
55 Q6 **Tucupita** Delta Amacuro, NE Venezuela
58 K13 **Tucuruí, Represa de** ⊡ NE Brazil
110 F9 **Tuczno** Zachodniopomorskie, NW Poland
Tuddo see Tudu
105 Q5 **Tudela** Basq. Tutera; anc. Tutela. Navarra, N Spain
104 M6 **Tudela de Duero** Castilla-León, N Spain
138 K6 **Tudmur** var. Tadmur, Tamar, Gk. Palmyra; Bibl. Tadmor. Ḩimş, C Syria
118 J4 **Tudu** Ger. Tuddo. Lääne-Virumaa, NE Estonia
Tuebingen see Tübingen
122 J14 **Tuekta** Respublika Altay, S Russian Federation
104 I5 **Tuela, Rio** ≈ N Portugal
153 X12 **Tuensang** Nāgāland, NE India
136 L15 **Tufanbeyli** Adana, C Turkey
Tüffer see Laško
186 F9 **Tufi** Northern, S PNG
193 O3 **Tufts Plain** undersea feature N Pacific Ocean
Tugalan see Kolkhozobod
67 V14 **Tugela** ≈ SE South Africa
21 P6 **Tug Fork** ≈ S USA
39 P15 **Tugidak Island** island Trinity Islands, Alaska, USA
171 O2 **Tuguegarao** Luzon, N Philippines
123 S12 **Tugur** Khabarovskiy Kray, SE Russian Federation
161 P4 **Tuhai He** ≈ E China
104 G4 **Tui** Galicia, NW Spain
77 O13 **Tui** var. Grand Balé. ≈ W Burkina
57 J16 **Tuichi, Río** ≈ W Bolivia
64 Q11 **Tuineje** Fuerteventura, Islas Canarias, Spain, NE Atlantic Ocean
43 X16 **Tuira, Río** ≈ SE Panama
Tuisarkan see Tūysarkān
Tujiabu see Yongxiu
129 W5 **Tukan** Respublika Bashkortostan, W Russian Federation
171 P14 **Tukangbesi, Kepulauan** Dut. Toekang Besi Eilanden. island group C Indonesia
147 V13 **Tŭkhtamish** Rus. Toktomush, prev. Tokhtamyshbek. SE Tajikistan
184 O12 **Tukituki** ≈ North Island, NZ
Tu-k'ou see Panzhihua
121 P12 **Tūkrah** NE Libya
8 H6 **Tuktoyaktuk** Northwest Territories, NW Canada
168 I9 **Tuktuk** Pulau Samosir, W Indonesia
Tukumi see Tsukumi
118 E9 **Tukums** Ger. Tuckum. Tukums, W Latvia
81 G24 **Tukuyu** prev. Neu-Langenburg. Mbeya, S Tanzania
Tukzār see Tokzār
41 O13 **Tula** var. Tula de Allende. Hidalgo, C Mexico
41 O11 **Tula** Tamaulipas, C Mexico
128 K5 **Tula** Tul'skaya Oblast', W Russian Federation
Tulach Mhór see Tullamore
Tula de Allende see Tula
159 N10 **Tulage Ar Gol** ≈ W China
186 M9 **Tulaghi** var. Tulagi. Florida Islands, C Solomon Islands
Tulagi see Tulaghi
41 P13 **Tulancingo** Hidalgo, C Mexico
35 R11 **Tulare** California, W USA
29 P9 **Tulare** South Dakota, N USA
35 Q12 **Tulare Lake Bed** salt flat California, W USA
37 S14 **Tularosa** New Mexico, SW USA
37 P13 **Tularosa Mountains** ▲ New Mexico, SW USA
37 S15 **Tularosa Valley** basin New Mexico, SW USA
83 E25 **Tulbagh** Western Cape, SW South Africa
56 C5 **Tulcán** Carchi, N Ecuador
117 N13 **Tulcea** Tulcea, E Romania
117 N13 **Tulcea** ◈ county SE Romania
Tul'chin see Tul'chyn
117 N7 **Tul'chyn** Rus. Tul'chin. Vinnyts'ka Oblast', C Ukraine
Tuléar see Toliara
35 O1 **Tulelake** California, W USA
116 J10 **Tulgheş** Hung. Gyergyótölgyes. Harghita, C Romania
Tul'govichi see Tul'havichy
119 N20 **Tul'havichy** Rus. Tul'govichi. Homyel'skaya Voblasts', SE Belarus
Tuli see Thuli
25 N4 **Tulia** Texas, SW USA
8 I9 **Tulita** prev. Fort Norman, Norman. Northwest Territories, NW Canada
20 J10 **Tullahoma** Tennessee, S USA
183 N12 **Tullamarine** ✕ (Melbourne) Victoria, SE Australia
183 Q7 **Tullamore** New South Wales, SE Australia
97 E18 **Tullamore** Ir. Tulach Mhór. C Ireland
103 N12 **Tulle** anc. Tutela. Corrèze, C France
109 X3 **Tulln** var. Oberhollabrunn. Niederösterreich, NE Austria
109 W4 **Tulln** ≈ NE Austria
22 H6 **Tullos** Louisiana, S USA
97 F19 **Tullow** Ir. An Tullach. SE Ireland
181 W5 **Tully** Queensland, NE Australia
126 J3 **Tuloma** ≈ NW Russian Federation
114 K10 **Tulovo** Stara Zagora, C Bulgaria
27 P9 **Tulsa** Oklahoma, C USA
153 N11 **Tulsipur** Mid Western, W Nepal
128 K6 **Tul'skaya Oblast'** ◈ province W Russian Federation
128 L14 **Tul'skiy** Respublika Adygeya, SW Russian Federation
186 E5 **Tulu** Manus Island, N PNG
54 D10 **Tuluá** Valle del Cauca, W Colombia
116 M12 **Tulucești** Galați, E Romania
39 N12 **Tuluksak** Alaska, USA
41 Z12 **Tulum, Ruinas de** ruins Quintana Roo, SE Mexico
122 M13 **Tulun** Irkutskaya Oblast', S Russian Federation
169 R17 **Tulungagung** prev. Toeloengagoeng. Jawa, C Indonesia
186 J6 **Tulun Islands** var. Kilinailau Islands; prev. Carteret Islands. island group NE PNG
128 M4 **Tuma** Ryazanskaya Oblast', W Russian Federation
54 B12 **Tumaco** Nariño, SW Colombia
54 B12 **Tumaco, Bahía de** bay SW Colombia
Tuman-gang see Tumen
42 L8 **Tuma, Río** ≈ N Nicaragua
95 O16 **Tumba** Stockholm, C Sweden
Tumba, Lac see Ntomba, Lac
169 S12 **Tumbangsenamang** Borneo, C Indonesia
183 Q10 **Tumbarumba** New South Wales, SE Australia
56 A8 **Tumbes** Tumbes, NW Peru
56 A9 **Tumbes** off. Departamento de Tumbes. ◈ department NW Peru
19 P5 **Tumbledown Mountain** ▲ Maine, NE USA
11 N13 **Tumbler Ridge** British Columbia, W Canada
167 Q12 **Tumbŏt, Phnum** ▲ W Cambodia
182 G9 **Tumby Bay** South Australia
163 Y10 **Tumen** Jilin, NE China
163 Y11 **Tumen** Chin. Tumen Jiang, Kor. Tuman-gang, Rus. Tumyn'tszyan. ≈ E Asia
Tumen Jiang see Tumen
55 Q8 **Tumeremo** Bolívar, E Venezuela
155 G19 **Tumkūr** Karnātaka, W India
96 I10 **Tummel** ≈ C Scotland, UK
188 B15 **Tumon Bay** bay W Guam
77 P14 **Tumu** NW Ghana
58 I10 **Tumuc Humac Mountains** var. Serra Tumucumaque. ▲ N South America
Tumucumaque, Serra see Tumuc Humac Mountains
183 Q10 **Tumut** New South Wales, SE Australia
Tumyn'tszyan see Tumen
Tün see Ferdows
45 U14 **Tunapuna** Trinidad, Trinidad and Tobago
60 K11 **Tunas** Paraná, S Brazil
Tunbridge Wells see Royal Tunbridge Wells
114 L11 **Tunca Nehri** Bul. Tundzha. ≈ Bulgaria/Turkey **see also** Tundzha
137 O14 **Tunceli** var. Kalan. Tunceli, E Turkey
137 O14 **Tunceli** ◈ province C Turkey
152 J12 **Tūndla** Uttar Pradesh, N India
81 I25 **Tunduru** Ruvuma, S Tanzania
114 L10 **Tundzha** Turk. Tunca Nehri. ≈ Bulgaria/Turkey **see also** Tunca Nehri
155 H17 **Tungabhadra** ≈ S India
155 F17 **Tungabhadra Reservoir** ◎ S India
191 P2 **Tungaru** prev. Gilbert Islands. island group W Kiribati
171 P7 **Tungawan** Mindanao, S Philippines
T'ung-shan see Xuzhou
161 Q16 **Tungsha Tao** Chin. Dongsha Qundao, Eng. Pratas Island. island S Taiwan
161 S13 **Tungshih** Jap. Tōsei. N Taiwan
8 H9 **Tungsten** Northwest Territories, W Canada
Tung-t'ing Hu see Dongting Hu
56 A13 **Tungurahua** ◈ province C Ecuador
95 F14 **Tunhovdfjorden** ◎ S Norway
22 K2 **Tunica** Mississippi, S USA
75 N5 **Tunis** var. Tūnis. ● (Tunisia) NE Tunisia
75 N5 **Tunis, Golfe de** Ar. Khalīj Tūnis. gulf NE Tunisia
75 N6 **Tunisia** off. Republic of Tunisia, Ar. Al Jumhūrīyah at Tūnisīyah, Fr. République Tunisienne. ◆ republic N Africa
Tūnisīyah, Al Jumhūrīyah at see Tunisia
Tūnis, Khalīj see Tunis, Golfe de
54 G9 **Tunja** Boyacá, C Colombia
93 F14 **Tunnsjøen** ◎ C Norway
39 N12 **Tuntutuliak** Alaska, USA
147 U8 **Tunuk** Chuyskaya Oblast', C Kyrgyzstan
13 Q6 **Tunungayualok Island** island Newfoundland, E Canada
62 H11 **Tunuyán** Mendoza, W Argentina
197 P14 **Tunu** ◈ province E Greenland
62 I11 **Tunuyán, Río** ≈ W Argentina
Tunxi see Huangshan
35 P9 **Tuolumne River** ≈ California, W USA
Tuong Buong see Tương Đương
167 R7 **Tương Đương** var. Tuong Buong. Nghê An, N Vietnam
160 I13 **Tuoniang Jiang** ≈ S China
159 N12 **Tuotuo He** ≈ C China
159 O12 **Tuotuoheyan** var. Tanggulashan, Togton-heyan. Qinghai, C China
Tüp see Tyup
60 J9 **Tupã** São Paulo, S Brazil
191 S10 **Tupai** var. Motu Iti. atoll Îles Sous le Vent, W French Polynesia
61 G15 **Tupanciretã** Rio Grande do Sul, S Brazil
22 M2 **Tupelo** Mississippi, S USA
59 K18 **Tupiraçaba** Goiás, S Brazil
57 L21 **Tupiza** Potosí, S Bolivia
11 N13 **Tupper** British Columbia, W Canada
18 J8 **Tupper Lake** ◎ New York, NE USA
62 H11 **Tupungato, Volcán** ▲ W Argentina
163 T9 **Tuquan** Nei Mongol Zizhiqu, N China
54 C13 **Túquerres** Nariño, SW Colombia
153 U13 **Tura** Meghālaya, NE India
122 M10 **Tura** Evenkiyskiy Avtonomnyy Okrug, N Russian Federation
122 G10 **Tura** ≈ C Russian Federation
140 M10 **Turabah** Makkah, W Saudi Arabia
55 O8 **Turagua, Cerro** ▲ C Venezuela
184 L12 **Turakina** Manawatu-Wanganui, North Island, NZ
185 K15 **Turakirae Head** headland North Island, NZ
186 B8 **Turama** ≈ S PNG
122 K13 **Turan** Respublika Tyva, S Russian Federation
184 M10 **Turangi** Waikato, North Island, NZ
146 F11 **Turan Lowland** var. Turan Plain, Kaz. Turan Oypaty, Rus. Turanskaya Nizmennost', Turk. Turan Pesligi, Uzb. Turon Pasttekisligi. plain C Asia
Turan Oypaty/Turan Pesligi/Turan Plain/Turanskaya Nizmennost' see Turan Lowland
138 K7 **Ţurāq al 'Ilab** hill range S Syria
119 K20 **Turaw** Rus. Turov. Homyel'skaya Voblasts', SE Belarus
140 L2 **Ţurayf** Al Ḩudūd ash Shamālīyah, NW Saudi Arabia
Turba see Teruel
54 E5 **Turbaco** Bolívar, N Colombia
148 K15 **Turbat** Baluchistān, SW Pakistan
Turbat-i-Haidari see Torbat-e Ḩeydarīyeh
Turbat-i-Jam see Torbat-e Jām
54 D7 **Turbo** Antioquia, NW Colombia
Turčianský Svätý Martin see Martin
116 H10 **Turda** Ger. Thorenburg, Hung. Torda. Cluj, NW Romania
142 M7 **Ţūreh** Markazī, W Iran
191 X12 **Tureia** atoll Îles Tuamotu, SE French Polynesia
110 I12 **Turek** Wielkopolskie, C Poland
93 L19 **Turenki** Etelä-Suomi, S Finland
Turfan see Turpan
145 R8 **Turgay** Kaz. Torghay. Akmola, W Kazakhstan
145 N10 **Turgay** Kaz. Torgay. ≈ C Kazakhstan
144 M8 **Turgayskaya Stolovaya Strana** Kaz. Torgay Üstirti. plateau Kazakhstan/Russian Federation
Turgel see Türi
114 L8 **Tŭrgovishte** prev. Eski Dzhumaya. Tŭrgovishte, N Bulgaria
114 L8 **Tŭrgovishte** ◈ province N Bulgaria
136 C14 **Turgutlu** Manisa, W Turkey
136 L12 **Turhal** Tokat, N Turkey
118 H4 **Türi** Ger. Turgel. Järvamaa, N Estonia
105 S9 **Turia** ≈ E Spain
58 M12 **Turiaçu** Maranhão, E Brazil
Turin see Torino
116 I3 **Turiys'k** Volyns'ka Oblast', NW Ukraine
Turja see Tur"ya
116 H6 **Turka** L'vivs'ka Oblast', W Ukraine
Turkana, Lake see Rudolf, Lake
145 P16 **Turkestan** Kaz. Türkistan. Yuzhnyy Kazakhstan, S Kazakhstan
147 Q12 **Turkestan Range** Rus. Turkestanskiy Khrebet. ▲ C Asia
Turkestanskiy Khrebet see Turkestan Range
111 M23 **Túrkeve** Jász-Nagykun-Szolnok, E Hungary
25 O4 **Turkey** Texas, SW USA
136 H14 **Turkey** off. Republic of Turkey, Turk. Türkiye Cumhuriyeti. ◆ republic SW Asia
181 N4 **Turkey Creek** Western Australia
26 M9 **Turkey Creek** ≈ Oklahoma, C USA
37 T9 **Turkey Mountains** ▲ New Mexico, SW USA
29 X11 **Turkey River** ≈ Iowa, C USA
129 N7 **Turki** Saratovskaya Oblast', W Russian Federation
121 O1 **Turkish Republic of Northern Cyprus** ◇ disputed territory Cyprus
Türkistan see Turkestan
Turkistan, Bandi-i see Torkestān, Selseleh-ye Band-e
Türkiye Cumhuriyeti see Turkey
Türkmen Aylagy see Turkmenskiy Zaliv
146 A10 **Turkmenbashi** prev. Krasnovodsk. Balkanskiy Velayat, W Turkmenistan
Türkmengala see Turkmen-kala
146 G13 **Turkmenistan** off. Turkmenistan; prev. Turkmenskaya Soviet Socialist Republic. ◆ republic C Asia
146 J14 **Turkmen-kala** Turkm. Türkmengala; prev. Turkmen-Kala. Maryyskiy Velayat, S Turkmenistan
Turkmenskaya Soviet Socialist Republic see Turkmenistan
146 A11 **Turkmenskiy Zaliv** Turkm. Türkmen Aylagy. lake gulf W Turkmenistan
136 L16 **Türkoğlu** Kahramanmaraş, S Turkey
44 L6 **Turks and Caicos Islands** ◇ UK dependent territory N West Indies
64 G10 **Turks and Caicos Islands** island group N West Indies
45 N6 **Turks Islands** island group SE Turks and Caicos Islands
93 K19 **Turku** Swe. Åbo. Länsi-Suomi, W Finland
81 H17 **Turkwel** seasonal river NW Kenya
27 P9 **Turley** Oklahoma, C USA
35 P9 **Turlock** California, W USA
118 I12 **Turmantas** Zarasai, NE Lithuania
54 L5 **Turmero** Aragua, N Venezuela
Turmberg see Wieżyca

◆ Country ● Country Capital ◇ Dependent Territory ○ Dependent Territory Capital ◈ Administrative Region ✕ International Airport ▲ Mountain ▲ Mountain Range ※ Volcano ≈ River ◎ Lake ⊡ Reservoir

184 N13 **Turnagain, Cape** headland North Island, NZ
Turnau see Turnov
42 H2 **Turneffe Islands** island group E Belize
18 M11 **Turners Falls** Massachusetts, NE USA
11 P16 **Turner Valley** Alberta, SW Canada
99 I16 **Turnhout** Antwerpen, N Belgium
109 V5 **Turnitz** Niederösterreich, E Austria
11 S12 **Turnor Lake** ◎ Saskatchewan, C Canada
111 E15 **Turnov** Ger. Turnau. Liberecký Kraj, N Czech Republic
Tŭrnovo see Veliko Tŭrnovo
116 I15 **Turnu Măgurele** var. Turnu-Măgurele. Teleorman, S Romania
Turnu Severin see Drobeta-Turnu Severin
Turócszentmárton see Martin
Turoni see Tours
Turan Pasttekisligi see Turan Lowland
Turov see Turaw
Turpakkla see Turpoqqal'a
158 M6 **Turpan** var. Turfan. Xinjiang Uygur Zizhiqu, NW China
Turpan Depression see Turpan Pendi
158 M6 **Turpan Pendi** Eng. Turpan Depression. depression NW China
158 M5 **Turpan Zhan** Xinjiang Uygur Zizhiqu, W China
Turpentine State see North Carolina
146 J10 **Turpoqqal'a** Rus. Turpakkla. Khorazm Wiloyati, W Uzbekistan
44 H8 **Turquino, Pico** ▲ E Cuba
27 Y10 **Turrell** Arkansas, C USA
43 N14 **Turrialba** Cartago, E Costa Rica
96 K8 **Turriff** NE Scotland, UK
139 V7 **Tursāq** E Iraq
Turshiz see Kāshmar
Tursunzade see Tursunzoda
147 P13 **Tursunzoda** Rus. Tursunzade; prev. Regar. W Tajikistan
162 J4 **Turt** Hövsgöl, N Mongolia
146 I9 **Tŭrtkŭl** Rus. Turtkul'; prev. Petroaleksandrovsk. Qoraqalpoghiston Respublikasi, W Uzbekistan
29 O9 **Turtle Creek** ≈ South Dakota, N USA
30 K4 **Turtle Flambeau Flowage** ▣ Wisconsin, N USA
11 S14 **Turtleford** Saskatchewan, S Canada
28 M4 **Turtle Lake** North Dakota, N USA
92 K12 **Turtola** Lappi, NW Finland
122 M10 **Turu** ≈ N Russian Federation
Turuga see Tsuruga
147 V10 **Turugart Pass** pass China/Kyrgyzstan
158 E7 **Turugart Shankou** var. Pereval Torugart. pass China/Kyrgyzstan
122 K9 **Turukhan** ≈ N Russian Federation
122 K9 **Turukhansk** Krasnoyarskiy Kray, N Russian Federation
139 N3 **Ţurumbah** well NE Syria
Turuoka see Tsuruoka
144 H14 **Turush** Mangistau, SW Kazakhstan
60 K7 **Turvo, Rio** ≈ S Brazil
116 J2 **Tur"ya** Pol. Turja, Rus. Tur'ya. ≈ NW Ukraine
23 O4 **Tuscaloosa** Alabama, S USA
23 O4 **Tuscaloosa, Lake** ◎ Alabama, S USA
Tuscan Archipelago see Toscano, Archipelago
Tuscan-Emilian Mountains see Tosco-Emiliano, Appennino
Tuscany see Toscana
35 V2 **Tuscarora** Nevada, W USA
18 F15 **Tuscarora Mountain** ridge Pennsylvania, NE USA
30 M14 **Tuscola** Illinois, N USA
25 P7 **Tuscola** Texas, SW USA
23 O2 **Tuscumbia** Alabama, S USA
92 O4 **Tusenøyane** island group S Svalbard
144 K13 **Tushybas, Zaliv** prev. Zaliv Paskevicha. lake gulf SW Kazakhstan
171 Y15 **Tusirah** Irian Jaya, E Indonesia
23 Q5 **Tuskegee** Alabama, S USA
94 E8 **Tustna** island S Norway
39 R12 **Tustumena Lake** ◎ Alaska, USA
110 K13 **Tuszyn** Łodzkie, C Poland
137 S13 **Tutak** Ağrı, E Turkey
185 C20 **Tutamoe Range** ▲ North Island, NZ
Tutasev see Tutayev
126 L15 **Tutayev** var. Tutasev. Yaroslavskaya Oblast', W Russian Federation
Tutela see Tulle, France
Tutela see Tudela, Spain
Tutera see Tudela
155 H23 **Tuticorin** Tamil Nādu, SE India
113 L15 **Tutin** Serbia, S Yugoslavia
184 O10 **Tutira** Hawke's Bay, North Island, NZ
Tutiura see Tsuchiura
122 K10 **Tutonchany** Evenkiyskiy Avtonomnyy Okrug, N Russian Federation
114 L6 **Tutrakan** Silistra, NE Bulgaria
29 N5 **Tuttle** North Dakota, N USA
26 M11 **Tuttle** Oklahoma, C USA
27 O3 **Tuttle Creek Lake** ▣ Kansas, C USA
101 H23 **Tuttlingen** Baden-Württemberg, S Germany
171 R16 **Tutuala** W East Timor
192 K17 **Tutuila** island W American Samoa
83 I18 **Tutume** Central, E Botswana
39 N7 **Tututalak Mountain** ▲ Alaska, USA
22 K3 **Tutwiler** Mississippi, S USA
162 L8 **Tuul Gol** ≈ N Mongolia
93 O16 **Tuupovaara** Itä-Suomi, E Finland
Tuva see Tyva, Respublika
190 E7 **Tuvalu** prev. Ellice Islands. ◆ commonwealth republic SW Pacific Ocean
Tuvana-i-Tholo see Tuvana-i-Colo
Tuvinskaya ASSR see Tyva, Respublika
Tuvutha see Tuvuca
141 P9 **Ţuwayq, Jabal** ▲ C Saudi Arabia
138 H13 **Ţuwayyil ash Shihāq** desert S Jordan
11 U16 **Tuxford** Saskatchewan, S Canada
167 U12 **Tu Xoay** Đắc Lắc, S Vietnam
40 L14 **Tuxpan** Jalisco, C Mexico
40 J12 **Tuxpan** Nayarit, C Mexico
41 Q12 **Tuxpán** var. Tuxpán de Rodríguez Cano. Veracruz-Llave, E Mexico
Tuxpán de Rodríguez Cano see Tuxpán
41 R15 **Tuxtepec** var. San Juan Bautista Tuxtepec. Oaxaca, S Mexico
41 U16 **Tuxtla** var. Tuxtla Gutiérrez. Chiapas, SE Mexico
Tuxtla see San Andrés Tuxtla
Tuxtla Gutiérrez see Tuxtla
Tuyama see Tsuyama
167 T5 **Tuyên Quang** Tuyên Quang, N Vietnam
167 U13 **Tuy Hoa** Binh Thuân, S Vietnam
167 V12 **Tuy Hoa** Phu Yên, S Vietnam
129 U5 **Tuymazy** Respublika Bashkortostan, W Russian Federation
142 L6 **Tūysarkān** var. Tuisarkan, Tuyserkān. Hamadān, W Iran
Tuyserkān see Tūysarkān
147 Q10 **Tuytepa** Rus. Toytepa. Toshkent Wiloyati, E Uzbekistan
145 W16 **Tuyuk** Kaz. Tuyyq. Almaty, SE Kazakhstan
Tuyyq see Tuyuk
136 I14 **Tuz Gölü** ◎ C Turkey
127 Q15 **Tuzha** Kirovskaya Oblast', NW Russian Federation
113 K17 **Tuzi** Montenegro, SW Yugoslavia
139 T5 **Ţuz Khurmātū** N Iraq
112 I11 **Tuzla** Federacija Bosna I Hercegovina, NE Bosnia and Herzegovina
117 N15 **Tuzla** Constanţa, SE Romania
137 T12 **Tuzluca** Iğdır, NE Turkey
95 J20 **Tvååker** Halland, S Sweden
95 F17 **Tvedestrand** Aust-Agder, S Norway
126 J16 **Tver'** prev. Kalinin. Tverskaya Oblast', W Russian Federation
Tverya see Teverya
128 I15 **Tverskaya Oblast'** ◈ province W Russian Federation
126 I15 **Tvertsa** ≈ W Russian Federation
110 H13 **Twardogóra** Ger. Festenberg. Dolnośląskie, SW Poland
14 J14 **Tweed** Ontario, SE Canada
96 K13 **Tweed** ≈ England/Scotland, UK
98 O7 **Tweede-Exloërmond** Drenthe, NE Netherlands
183 V3 **Tweed Heads** New South Wales, SE Australia
98 M11 **Twello** Gelderland, E Netherlands
35 W15 **Twentynine Palms** California, W USA
25 P9 **Twin Buttes Reservoir** ▣ Texas, SW USA
33 O15 **Twin Falls** Idaho, NW USA
39 N13 **Twin Hills** Alaska, USA
11 O11 **Twin Lakes** Alberta, W Canada
33 O12 **Twin Peaks** ▲ Idaho, NW USA
185 I14 **Twins, The** ▲ South Island, NZ
29 S5 **Twin Valley** Minnesota, N USA
100 G11 **Twistringen** Niedersachsen, NW Germany
185 E20 **Twizel** Canterbury, South Island, NZ
29 X5 **Two Harbors** Minnesota, N USA
11 R14 **Two Hills** Alberta, SW Canada
31 N7 **Two Rivers** Wisconsin, N USA
116 H8 **Tyachiv** Zakarpats'ka Oblast', W Ukraine
Tyan'-Shan' see Tien Shan
166 L3 **Tyao** ≈ Burma/India
117 R6 **Tyas'myn** ≈ N Ukraine
23 X6 **Tybee Island** Georgia, SE USA
Tyborøn see Thyborøn
111 J16 **Tychy** Ger. Tichau. Śląskie, S Poland
111 O16 **Tyczyn** Podkarpackie, SE Poland
94 I8 **Tydal** Sør-Trøndelag, S Norway
115 H24 **Tyflós** ≈ Kríti, Greece, E Mediterranean Sea
21 S3 **Tygart Lake** ▣ West Virginia, NE USA
123 Q13 **Tygda** Amurskaya Oblast', SE Russian Federation
21 Q11 **Tyger River** ≈ South Carolina, SE USA
32 I11 **Tygh Valley** Oregon, NW USA
94 F12 **Tyin** ◎ S Norway
29 S10 **Tyler** Minnesota, N USA
25 W7 **Tyler** Texas, SW USA
25 W7 **Tyler, Lake** ▣ Texas, SW USA
22 K7 **Tylertown** Mississippi, S USA
22 K7 **Tylihuls'kyy Lyman** ◎ SW Ukraine
Tylos see Bahrain
115 C15 **Týmfi** var. Timfi. ▲ W Greece
115 E17 **Tymfristós** var. Timfristos. ▲ C Greece
115 J25 **Tympáki** var. Timbaki; prev. Timbákion. Kríti, Greece, E Mediterranean Sea
123 Q12 **Tynda** Amurskaya Oblast', SE Russian Federation
29 Q12 **Tyndall** South Dakota, N USA
97 L14 **Tyne** ≈ N England, UK
97 M14 **Tynemouth** NE England, UK
97 L14 **Tyneside** cultural region NE England, UK
94 H10 **Tynset** Hedmark, S Norway
39 Q12 **Tyonek** Alaska, USA
Tyôsi see Chōshi
Tyras see Dniester, Moldova/Ukraine
Tyras see Bilhorod-Dnistrovs'kyy, Ukraine
Tyre see Soûr
95 G14 **Tyrifjorden** ◎ S Norway
95 K22 **Tyringe** Skåne, S Sweden
123 R13 **Tyrma** Khabarovskiy Kray, SE Russian Federation
Tyrnau see Trnava
115 F15 **Týrnavos** var. Tírnavos. Thessalía, C Greece
129 N16 **Tyrnyauz** Kabardino-Balkarskaya Respublika, SW Russian Federation
Tyrol see Tirol
18 E14 **Tyrone** Pennsylvania, NE USA
97 E15 **Tyrone** cultural region W Northern Ireland, UK
182 M10 **Tyrrell, Lake** salt lake Victoria, SE Australia
84 H14 **Tyrrhenian Basin** undersea feature Tyrrhenian Sea, C Mediterranean Sea
120 L8 **Tyrrhenian Sea** It. Mare Tirreno. sea N Mediterranean Sea
Tysa see Tisa/Tisza
116 J7 **Tysmenytsya** Ivano-Frankivs'ka Oblast', W Ukraine
95 C14 **Tysnesøya** island S Norway
95 C14 **Tysse** Hordaland, S Norway
95 D14 **Tyssedal** Hordaland, S Norway
95 O17 **Tystberga** Södermanland, C Sweden
118 E12 **Tytuvėnai** Kelmė, C Lithuania
144 D14 **Tyub-Karagan, Mys** headland SW Kazakhstan
147 V8 **Tyugel'-Say** Narynskaya Oblast', C Kyrgyzstan
122 H11 **Tyukalinsk** Omskaya Oblast', C Russian Federation
129 V7 **Tyul'gan** Orenburgskaya Oblast', W Russian Federation
122 G11 **Tyumen'** Tyumenskaya Oblast', C Russian Federation
122 H11 **Tyumenskaya Oblast'** ◈ province C Russian Federation
147 Y7 **Tyup** Kir. Tüp. Issyk-Kul'skaya Oblast', NE Kyrgyzstan
122 L14 **Tyva, Respublika** prev. Tannu-Tuva, Tuva, Tuvinskaya ASSR. ◈ autonomous republic C Russian Federation
117 N7 **Tyvriv** Vinnyts'ka Oblast', C Ukraine
97 J21 **Tywi** ≈ S Wales, UK
97 I19 **Tywyn** W Wales, UK
83 K20 **Tzaneen** Northern, NE South Africa
Tzekung see Zigong
41 X12 **Tzucacab** Yucatán, SE Mexico

U

82 B12 **Uaco Cungo** var. Waku Kungo, Port. Santa Comba. Cuanza Sul, C Angola
UAE see United Arab Emirates
191 X7 **Ua Huka** island Îles Marquises, NE French Polynesia
58 E10 **Uaiacás** Roraima, N Brazil
Uamba see Wamba
Uanle Uen see Wanlaweyn
191 W7 **Ua Pu** island Îles Marquises, NE French Polynesia
81 L17 **Uar Garas** spring/well SW Somalia
58 G12 **Uatumã, Rio** ≈ C Brazil
Ua Uíbh Fhailí see Offaly
58 C11 **Uaupés, Rio** var. Río Vaupés. ≈ Brazil/Colombia see also Vaupés, Río
145 X9 **Uba** ≈ E Kazakhstan
145 N6 **Ubagan** Kaz. Obagan. ≈ Kazakhstan/Russian Federation
186 G7 **Ubai** New Britain, E PNG
79 J15 **Ubangi** Fr. Oubangui. ≈ C Africa
Ubangi-Shari see Central African Republic
116 M3 **Ubarts'** Ukr. Ubort'. ≈ Belarus/Ukraine see also Ubort'
54 F9 **Ubaté** Cundinamarca, C Colombia
60 N10 **Ubatuba** São Paulo, S Brazil
149 R12 **Ubauro** Sind, SE Pakistan
171 Q6 **Ubay** Bohol, C Philippines
103 U14 **Ubaye** ≈ SE France
Ubayid, Wadi al see Ubayyiḑ, Wādī al
139 N8 **Ubaylah** W Iraq
139 O10 **Ubayyiḑ, Wādī al** var. Wadi al Ubayid. dry watercourse SW Iraq
98 L13 **Ubbergen** Gelderland, E Netherlands
164 E13 **Ube** Yamaguchi, Honshū, SW Japan
105 O13 **Ubeda** Andalucía, S Spain
109 V7 **Übelbach** var. Markt-Übelbach. Steiermark, SE Austria
59 L20 **Uberaba** Minas Gerais, SE Brazil
57 Q19 **Uberaba, Laguna** ◎ E Bolivia
59 K19 **Uberlândia** Minas Gerais, SE Brazil
101 H24 **Überlingen** Baden-Württemberg, S Germany
77 U16 **Ubiaja** Edo, S Nigeria
104 K3 **Ubiña, Peña** ▲ NW Spain
57 H17 **Ubinas, Volcán** 🌋 S Peru
Ubol Rajadhani/Ubol Ratchathani see Ubon Ratchathani
167 P9 **Ubolratna Reservoir** ▣ C Thailand
167 S10 **Ubon Ratchathani** var. Muang Ubon, Ubol Rajadhani, Ubol Ratchathani, Udon Ratchathani. Ubon Ratchathani, E Thailand
119 L20 **Ubort'** Bel. Ubarts'. ≈ Belarus/Ukraine see also Ubarts'
104 K15 **Ubrique** Andalucía, S Spain
Ubsu-Nur, Ozero see Uvs Nuur
79 M18 **Ubundu** Orientale, C Dem. Rep. Congo (Zaire)
137 X11 **Ucar** Rus. Udzhary. C Azerbaijan
56 G13 **Ucayali** off. Departamento de Ucayali. ◈ department E Peru
56 F10 **Ucayali, Río** ≈ C Peru
Uccle see Ukkel
146 J13 **Uch-Adzhi** Turkm. Üchajy. Maryyskiy Velayat, C Turkmenistan
Üchajy see Uch-Adzhi
129 X4 **Uchaly** Respublika Bashkortostan, W Russian Federation
145 W13 **Ucharal** Kaz. Üsharal. Almaty, E Kazakhstan
164 C17 **Uchinoura** Kagoshima, Kyūshū, SW Japan
165 R5 **Uchiura-wan** bay NW Pacific Ocean
Uchkuduk see Uchquduq
Uchkurghan see Uchqŭrghon
146 K8 **Uchquduq** Rus. Uchkuduk. Nawoiy Wiloyati, N Uzbekistan
147 S9 **Uchqŭrghon** Rus. Uchkurghan. Namangan Wiloyati, E Uzbekistan
Uchsay see Uchsoy
146 G6 **Uchsoy** Rus. Uchsay. Qoraqalpoghiston Respublikasi, NW Uzbekistan
Uchtagan Gumy see Uchtagan, Peski
146 D10 **Uchtagan, Peski** Turkm. Uchtagan Gumy. desert NW Turkmenistan
123 R11 **Uchur** ≈ E Russian Federation
100 O10 **Uckermark** cultural region E Germany
10 K17 **Ucluelet** Vancouver Island, British Columbia, SW Canada
122 M13 **Uda** ≈ S Russian Federation
123 R12 **Uda** ≈ E Russian Federation
123 N6 **Udachnyy** Respublika Sakha (Yakutiya), NE Russian Federation
155 G21 **Udagamandalam** var. Udhagamandalam; prev. Ootacamund. Tamil Nādu, SW India
152 F14 **Udaipur** prev. Oodeypore. Rājasthān, N India
Udayadhani see Uthai Thani
143 N16 **'Udayd, Khawr al** var. Khor al Udeid. inlet Qatar/Saudi Arabia
112 D11 **Udbina** Lika-Senj, W Croatia
95 I18 **Uddevalla** Västra Götaland, S Sweden
Uddjaur see Uddjaure
92 H13 **Uddjaure** var. Uddjaur. ◎ N Sweden
Udeid, Khor al see 'Udayd, Khawr al
99 K14 **Uden** Noord-Brabant, SE Netherlands
Uden see Udenhout
99 J14 **Udenhout** var. Uden. Noord-Brabant, S Netherlands
155 H14 **Udgīr** Mahārāshtra, C India
Udhagamandalam see Udagamandalam
152 H6 **Udhampur** Jammu and Kashmir, NW India
139 X14 **'Udhaybah, 'Uqlat al** well S Iraq
106 J7 **Udine** anc. Utina. Friuli-Venezia Giulia, NE Italy
175 T14 **Udintsev Fracture Zone** tectonic feature S Pacific Ocean
Udipi see Udupi
Udmurtia see Udmurtskaya Respublika
129 S2 **Udmurtskaya Respublika** Eng. Udmurtia. ◈ autonomous republic NW Russian Federation
126 J15 **Udomlya** Tverskaya Oblast', W Russian Federation
Udon Ratchathani see Ubon Ratchathani
167 Q8 **Udon Thani** var. Ban Mak Khaeng, Udorndhani. Udon Thani, N Thailand
Udorndhani see Udon Thani
189 U12 **Udot** atoll Chuuk Islands, C Micronesia
123 S12 **Udskaya Guba** bay E Russian Federation
155 E19 **Udupi** var. Udipi. Karnātaka, SW India
Udzhary see Ucar
100 O9 **Uecker** ≈ NE Germany
100 P9 **Ueckermünde** Mecklenburg-Vorpommern, NE Germany
164 M12 **Ueda** var. Uyeda. Nagano, Honshū, S Japan
79 L16 **Uele** var. Welle. ≈ NE Dem. Rep. Congo (Zaire)
Uele (upper course) see Uolo, Río, Equatorial Guinea/Gabon
Uele (upper course) see Kibali, Dem. Rep. Congo (Zaire)
123 W5 **Uelen** Chukotskiy Avtonomnyy Okrug, NE Russian Federation
100 J11 **Uelzen** Niedersachsen, N Germany
164 J14 **Ueno** Mie, Honshū, SW Japan
129 V4 **Ufa** Respublika Bashkortostan, W Russian Federation
129 V4 **Ufa** ≈ W Russian Federation
146 A10 **Ufra** Balkanskiy Velayat, NW Turkmenistan
83 C18 **Ugab** ≈ C Namibia
118 D8 **Ugāle** Ventspils, NW Latvia
81 F17 **Uganda** off. Republic of Uganda. ◆ republic E Africa
138 G4 **Ugarit** Ar. Ra's Shamrah. site of ancient city Al Lādhiqīyah, NW Syria
39 O14 **Ugashik** Alaska, USA
107 Q19 **Ugento** Puglia, SE Italy
105 O15 **Ugíjar** Andalucía, S Spain
103 T11 **Ugine** Savoie, E France
127 V13 **Ugleural'skiy** Permskaya Oblast', NW Russian Federation
126 L15 **Uglich** Yaroslavskaya Oblast', W Russian Federation
126 I14 **Uglovka** var. Okulovka. Novgorodskaya Oblast', W Russian Federation
128 I4 **Ugra** ≈ W Russian Federation
147 V9 **Ugyut** Narynskaya Oblast', C Kyrgyzstan
111 H19 **Uherské Hradiště** Ger. Ungarisch-Hradisch. Zlínský kraj, E Czech Republic
111 H19 **Uherský Brod** Ger. Ungarisch-Brod. Zlínský kraj, E Czech Republic
111 B17 **Úhlava** Ger. Angel. ≈ W Czech Republic
Uhorshchyna see Hungary
31 T13 **Uhrichsville** Ohio, N USA
Uhuru Peak see Kilimanjaro
96 G8 **Uig** N Scotland, UK
82 B10 **Uíge** Port. Carmona, Vila Marechal Carmona. Uíge, NW Angola
82 B10 **Uíge** ◈ province N Angola
193 Y15 **Uiha** island Ha'apai Group, C Tonga
189 U13 **Uijec** island Chuuk, C Micronesia
163 X14 **Ŭijŏngbu** Jap. Giseifu. NW South Korea
144 H10 **Uil** Kaz. Oyyl. Aktyubinsk, W Kazakhstan
144 H10 **Uil** Kaz. Oyyl. ≈ W Kazakhstan
36 M3 **Uinta Mountains** ▲ Utah, W USA
83 C18 **Uis** Erongo, NW Namibia
83 I25 **Uitenhage** Eastern Cape, S South Africa
98 H9 **Uitgeest** Noord-Holland, W Netherlands
98 I11 **Uithoorn** Noord-Holland, C Netherlands
98 O4 **Uithuizen** Groningen, NE Netherlands
98 O4 **Uithuizermeeden** Groningen, NE Netherlands
189 R6 **Ujae Atoll** var. Wūjae. atoll Ralik Chain, W Marshall Islands
Ujain see Ujjain
111 I16 **Ujazd** Opolskie, S Poland
Új-Becse see Novi Bečej
Ujda see Oujda
189 N5 **Ujelang Atoll** var. Wujlān. atoll Ralik Chain, W Marshall Islands
111 N21 **Újfehértó** Szabolcs-Szatmár-Bereg, E Hungary
Újgradiska see Nova Gradiška
164 J13 **Uji** var. Uzi. Kyōto, Honshū, SW Japan
81 E21 **Ujiji** Kigoma, W Tanzania
154 G10 **Ujjain** prev. Ujain. Madhya Pradesh, C India
Újlak see Ilok
'Ujmān see 'Ajmān
Újmoldova see Moldova Nouă
Újszentanna see Sântana
170 M14 **Ujungpandang** var. Macassar, Makassar; prev. Makasar. Sulawesi, C Indonesia
Ujung Salang see Phuket
Újvidék see Novi Sad
154 E11 **Ukāi Reservoir** ▣ W India
81 G19 **Ukara Island** island N Tanzania
'Ukash, Wādī see 'Akāsh, Wādī
81 F19 **Ukerewe Island** island N Tanzania
139 S9 **Ukhayḑhir** C Iraq
153 X13 **Ukhrul** Manipur, NE India
127 S9 **Ukhta** Respublika Komi, NW Russian Federation
34 L6 **Ukiah** California, W USA
32 K12 **Ukiah** Oregon, NW USA
99 G18 **Ukkel** Fr. Uccle. Brussels, C Belgium
118 G13 **Ukmergė** Pol. Wiłkomierz. Ukmergė, C Lithuania
Ukraina see Ukraine
116 L6 **Ukraine** off. Ukraine, Rus. Ukraina, Ukr. Ukrayina; prev. Ukrainian Soviet Socialist Republic, Ukrainskaya S.S.R. ◆ republic SE Europe
Ukrainskay S.S.R/Ukrayina see Ukraine
82 B13 **Uku** Cuanza Sul, NW Angola
164 B13 **Uku-jima** island Gotō-rettō, SW Japan
83 F20 **Ukwi** Kgalagadi, SW Botswana
118 M13 **Ula** Rus. Ulla. Vitsyebskaya Voblasts', N Belarus
136 C16 **Ula** Muğla, SW Turkey
118 M13 **Ula** Rus. Ulla. ≈ N Belarus
162 L7 **Ulaanbaatar** Eng. Ulan Bator. ● (Mongolia) Töv, C Mongolia
163 N8 **Ulaan-Ereg** Hentiy, E Mongolia
162 E5 **Ulaangom** Uvs, NW Mongolia
162 E7 **Ulaantolgoy** Hovd, W Mongolia
162 I8 **Ulaan-Uul** Bayanhongor, C Mongolia
163 O10 **Ulaan-Uul** Dornogovĭ, SE Mongolia
159 R10 **Ulan** Qinghai, C China
Ulan Bator see Ulaanbaatar
162 L13 **Ulan Buh Shamo** desert N China
Ulanhad see Chifeng
163 T8 **Ulanhot** Nei Mongol Zizhiqu, N China
129 Q14 **Ulan Khol** Respublika Kalmykiya, SW Russian Federation
162 M13 **Ulansuhai Nur** ◎ N China
123 N14 **Ulan-Ude** prev. Verkhneudinsk. Respublika Buryatiya, S Russian Federation
159 N12 **Ulan Ul Hu** ◎ C China
187 N9 **Ulawa Island** island SE Solomon Islands
138 J7 **'Ulayyānīyah, Bi'r al** var. Al Hilbeh. well S Syria
123 S12 **Ul'banskiy Zaliv** strait E Russian Federation
Ulbo see Olib
113 J18 **Ulcinj** Montenegro, SW Yugoslavia
163 O7 **Uldz** Hentiy, NE Mongolia
Uleåborg see Oulu
Uleälv see Oulujoki
95 G16 **Ulefoss** Telemark, S Norway
Uleträsk see Oulujärvi
113 L19 **Ulëz** var. Ulëza. Dibër, C Albania
Ulëza see Ulëz
95 F22 **Ulfborg** Ringkøbing, W Denmark
98 N13 **Ulft** Gelderland, E Netherlands
162 G7 **Uliastay** Dzavhan, W Mongolia
188 F8 **Ulimang** Babeldaob, N Palau
67 T10 **Ulindi** ≈ W Dem. Rep. Congo (Zaire)
188 H14 **Ulithi Atoll** atoll Caroline Islands, W Micronesia
112 N10 **Uljma** Serbia, NE Yugoslavia
144 L11 **Ul'kayak** Kaz. Ölkeyek. ≈ C Kazakhstan
145 Q7 **Ul'ken-Karoy, Ozero** ◎ N Kazakhstan
Ülkenözen see Bol'shoy Uzen'
Ülkenqobda see Bol'shaya Khobda
104 G3 **Ulla** ≈ NW Spain
Ulla see Ula
183 S10 **Ulladulla** New South Wales, SE Australia
153 T14 **Ullapara** Rajshahi, W Bangladesh
96 H7 **Ullapool** N Scotland, UK
95 J20 **Ullared** Halland, S Sweden
105 T7 **Ulldecona** Cataluña, NE Spain
92 I9 **Ullsfjorden** fjord N Norway
97 K15 **Ullswater** ◎ NW England, UK
101 I22 **Ulm** Baden-Württemberg, S Germany
33 R8 **Ulm** Montana, NW USA
183 V5 **Ulmarra** New South Wales, SE Australia
116 K13 **Ulmeni** Buzău, C Romania
116 K14 **Ulmeni** Călăraşi, S Romania
42 L7 **Ulmukhuás** Región Autónoma Atlántico Norte, NE Nicaragua
188 C8 **Ulong** var. Aulong. island Palau Islands, N Palau
83 N14 **Ulonguè** var. Ulongwé. Tete, NW Mozambique
Ulongwé see Ulonguè
95 K19 **Ulricehamn** Västra Götaland, S Sweden
98 N5 **Ulrum** Groningen, NE Netherlands
163 Z16 **Ulsan** Jap. Urusan. SE South Korea
94 D10 **Ulsteinvik** Møre og Romsdal, S Norway
97 D15 **Ulster** ◈ province Northern Ireland, UK/Ireland
171 Q10 **Ulu** Pulau Siau, N Indonesia
123 Q11 **Ulu** Respublika Sakha (Yakutiya), NE Russian Federation
42 H5 **Ulúa, Río** ≈ NW Honduras
136 D12 **Ulubat Gölü** ◎ NW Turkey
136 E12 **Uludağ** ▲ NW Turkey
Ulugh Muztag see Muztag Feng
158 D7 **Ulugqat** Xinjiang Uygur Zizhiqu, W China
136 J16 **Ulukışla** Niğde, S Turkey
189 O15 **Ulul** island Caroline Islands, C Micronesia
83 L22 **Ulundi** KwaZulu/Natal, E South Africa
158 M3 **Ulungur He** ≈ NW China
158 K2 **Ulungur Hu** ◎ NW China
181 P8 **Uluru** var. Ayers Rock. rocky outcrop Northern Territory, C Australia
97 K16 **Ulverston** NW England, UK
183 O16 **Ulverstone** Tasmania, SE Australia
94 D13 **Ulvik** Hordaland, S Norway
93 J18 **Ulvila** Länsi-Suomi, W Finland
117 O8 **Ulyanivka** Rus. Ul'yanovka. Kirovohrads'ka Oblast', C Ukraine
Ul'yanovka see Ulyanivka
129 Q5 **Ul'yanovsk** prev. Simbirsk. Ul'yanovskaya Oblast', W Russian Federation
129 Q5 **Ul'yanovskaya Oblast'** ◈ province W Russian Federation
145 S10 **Ul'yanovskiy** Karaganda, C Kazakhstan
Ul'yanovskiy Kanal see Ul'yanow Kanali
146 M13 **Ul'yanow Kanali** Rus. Ul'yanovskiy Kanal. canal Turkmenistan/Uzbekistan
Ulyshylanshyq see Uly-Zhylanshyk
26 H6 **Ulysses** Kansas, C USA
145 O12 **Ulytau, Gory** ▲ C Kazakhstan
145 N11 **Uly-Zhylanshyk** Kaz. Ulyshylanshyq. ≈ C Kazakhstan
112 A9 **Umag** It. Umago. Istra, NW Croatia
Umago see Umag
189 V13 **Uman** atoll Chuuk Islands, C Micronesia
117 O7 **Uman'** Rus. Uman. Cherkas'ka Oblast', C Ukraine
41 W12 **Umán** Yucatán, SE Mexico
Umanak/Umanaq see Uummannaq
'Umān, Khalīj see Oman, Gulf of
'Umān, Salţanat see Oman
154 K10 **Umaria** Madhya Pradesh, C India
149 R16 **Umar Kot** Sind, SE Pakistan
188 B17 **Umatac** SW Guam
188 A17 **Umatac Bay** bay SW Guam
139 S6 **Umayqah** C Iraq
126 J5 **Umba** Murmanskaya Oblast', NW Russian Federation
138 I8 **Umbāshī, Khirbat al** ruins As Suwaydā', S Syria
80 A12 **Umbelasha** ≈ W Sudan
106 H12 **Umbertide** Umbria, C Italy
61 B17 **Umberto** var. Humberto. Santa Fe, C Argentina
186 E7 **Umboi Island** var. Rooke Island. island C PNG
126 J4 **Umbozero, Ozero** ◎ NW Russian Federation
106 H13 **Umbria** ◈ region C Italy
Umbrian-Machigian Mountains see Umbro-Marchigiano, Appennino

106 I12 **Umbro-Marchigiano, Appennino** *Eng.* Umbrian-Machigian Mountains. ▲ C Italy
93 J16 **Umeå** Västerbotten, N Sweden
93 H14 **Umeälven** ≈ N Sweden
39 Q5 **Umiat** Alaska, USA
83 K23 **Umlazi** KwaZulu/Natal, E South Africa
139 X10 **Umm al Baqar, Hawr** *var.* Birkat ad Dawaymah. *spring* S Iraq
141 U12 **Umm al Ḥayt, Wādī** *var.* Wādī Amilḥayt. *seasonal river* SW Oman
Umm al Qaiwain *see* Umm al Qaywayn
143 R15 **Umm al Qaywayn** *var.* Umm al Qaiwain. Umm al Qaywayn, NE UAE
139 Q5 **Umm al Tūz** C Iraq
138 J3 **Umm 'Āmūd** Ḥalab, N Syria
141 Y10 **Umm ar Ruṣāṣ** *var.* Umm Ruṣayṣ. W Oman
141 X9 **Ummas Samīn** *salt flat* C Oman
141 V9 **Umm az Zumūl** *oasis* E Saudi Arabia
80 A9 **Umm Buru** Western Darfur, W Sudan
80 A12 **Umm Dafag** Southern Darfur, W Sudan
Umm Durmān *see* Omdurman
138 F9 **Umm el Fahm** Haifa, N Israel
80 F9 **Umm Inderab** Northern Kordofan, C Sudan
80 C10 **Umm Keddada** Northern Darfur, W Sudan
140 J7 **Umm Lajj** Tabūk, W Saudi Arabia
138 L10 **Umm Maḥfur** ≈ N Jordan
139 Y13 **Umm Qaṣr** SE Iraq
Umm Ruṣayṣ *see* Umm ar Ruṣāṣ
80 F11 **Umm Ruwaba** *var.* Umm Ruwābah, Um Ruwāba. Northern Kordofan, C Sudan
Umm Ruwābah *see* Umm Ruwaba
143 N16 **Umm Sa'īd** *var.* Musay'īd. S Qatar
138 K10 **Umm Ṭuways, Wādī** *dry watercourse* N Jordan
38 J17 **Umnak Island** *island* Aleutian Islands, Alaska, USA
32 F13 **Umpqua River** ≈ Oregon, NW USA
82 D13 **Umpulo** Bié, C Angola
154 I12 **Umred** Mahārāshtra, C India
139 Y10 **Umr Sawān, Hawr** ◎ S Iraq
Um Ruwāba *see* Umm Ruwaba
Umtali *see* Mutare
83 J24 **Umtata** Eastern Cape, SE South Africa
77 V17 **Umuahia** Abia, SW Nigeria
60 H10 **Umuarama** Paraná, S Brazil
Umvuma *see* Mvuma
83 K18 **Umzingwani** ≈ S Zimbabwe
112 D11 **Una** ≈ Bosnia and Herzegovina/Croatia
112 E12 **Unac** ≈ W Bosnia and Herzegovina
23 T6 **Unadilla** Georgia, SE USA
18 I10 **Unadilla River** ≈ New York, NE USA
59 L18 **Unaí** Minas Gerais, SE Brazil
39 N10 **Unalakleet** Alaska, USA
38 K17 **Unalaska Island** *island* Aleutian Islands, Alaska, USA
185 I16 **Una, Mount** ▲ South Island, NZ
82 N13 **Unango** Niassa, N Mozambique
Unao *see* Unnão
92 L12 **Unari** Lappi, N Finland
141 O6 **'Unayzah** *var.* Anaiza. Al Qaṣīm, C Saudi Arabia
138 L10 **'Unayzah, Jabal** ▲ Jordan/Saudi Arabia
Unci *see* Almería
57 K19 **Uncía** Potosí, C Bolivia
37 Q7 **Uncompahgre Peak** ▲ Colorado, C USA
37 P6 **Uncompahgre Plateau** *plain* Colorado, C USA
95 L17 **Unden** ◎ S Sweden
28 M4 **Underwood** North Dakota, N USA
171 T13 **Undur** Pulau Seram, E Indonesia
128 H6 **Unecha** Bryanskaya Oblast', W Russian Federation
39 N16 **Unga** Unga Island, Alaska, USA
Ungaria *see* Hungary
183 P8 **Ungarie** New South Wales, SE Australia
Ungarisch-Brod *see* Uherský Brod
Ungarisches Erzgebirge *see* Slovenské rudohorie
Ungarisch-Hradisch *see* Uherské Hradiště
Ungarn *see* Hungary
12 M4 **Ungava Bay** *bay* Quebec, E Canada
12 J2 **Ungava, Péninsule d'** *peninsula* Quebec, SE Canada
Ungeny *see* Ungheni
116 M9 **Ungheni** *Rus.* Ungeny. W Moldova
Unguja *see* Zanzibar
Üngüz Angyrsyndaky Garagum *see* Zaungukskiye Garagumy
146 H11 **Unguz, Solonchakovyye Vpadiny** *salt marsh* C Turkmenistan
Ungvár *see* Uzhhorod
60 I12 **União da Vitória** Paraná, S Brazil
111 G17 **Uničov** *Ger.* Mährisch-Neustadt. Olomoucký Kraj, E Czech Republic
110 J12 **Uniejów** Łódzkie, C Poland
112 A11 **Unije** *island* W Croatia
38 L16 **Unimak Island** *island* Aleutian Islands, Alaska, USA
38 L16 **Unimak Pass** *strait* Aleutian Islands, Alaska, USA
27 W5 **Union** Missouri, C USA
32 L12 **Union** Oregon, NW USA
21 Q11 **Union** South Carolina, SE USA
21 R6 **Union** West Virginia, NE USA
62 J12 **Unión** San Luis, C Argentina
61 B25 **Unión, Bahía** *bay* E Argentina
31 Q13 **Union City** Indiana, N USA
31 Q10 **Union City** Michigan, N USA
18 C12 **Union City** Pennsylvania, NE USA
20 G8 **Union City** Tennessee, S USA
32 G14 **Union Creek** Oregon, NW USA
83 G25 **Uniondale** Western Cape, SW South Africa
40 K13 **Unión de Tula** Jalisco, SW Mexico
30 M9 **Union Grove** Wisconsin, N USA
45 Y15 **Union Island** *island* S Saint Vincent and the Grenadines
46 K5 **Union Reefs** *reef* SW Mexico
(0) D7 **Union Seamount** *undersea feature* NE Pacific Ocean
23 Q6 **Union Springs** Alabama, S USA
20 H6 **Uniontown** Kentucky, S USA
18 C16 **Uniontown** Pennsylvania, NE USA
27 T1 **Unionville** Missouri, C USA
141 V8 **United Arab Emirates** *Ar.* Al Imārāt al 'Arabīyah al Muttaḥidah, *abbrev.* UAE; *prev.* Trucial States. ◆ *federation* SW Asia
United Arab Republic *see* Egypt
97 H14 **United Kingdom** *off.* UK of Great Britain and Northern Ireland, *abbrev.* UK. ◆ *monarchy* NW Europe
United Mexican States *see* Mexico
United Provinces *see* Uttar Pradesh
16 L10 **United States of America** *off.* United States of America, *var.* America, The States, *abbrev.* U.S., USA. ◆ *federal republic*
126 J10 **Unitsa** Respublika Kareliya, NW Russian Federation
11 S15 **Unity** Saskatchewan, S Canada
Unity State *see* Wahda
105 Q8 **Universales, Montes** ▲ C Spain
27 X4 **University City** Missouri, C USA
187 Q13 **Unmet** Malekula, C Vanuatu
101 F15 **Unna** Nordrhein-Westfalen, W Germany
152 L12 **Unnão** *prev.* Unao. Uttar Pradesh, N India
187 R15 **Unpongkor** Erromango, S Vanuatu
Unruhstadt *see* Kargowa
96 M1 **Unst** *island* NE Scotland, UK
101 K16 **Unstrut** ≈ C Germany
Unterdrauburg *see* Dravograd
Unterlimbach *see* Lendava
101 L23 **Unterschleissheim** Bayern, SE Germany
101 H24 **Untersee** ◎ Germany/Switzerland
100 O10 **Unterueckersee** ◎ NE Germany
108 F9 **Unterwalden** ◈ *canton* C Switzerland
55 N12 **Unturán, Sierra de** ▲ Brazil/Venezuela
159 N11 **Unuli Horog** Qinghai, W China
136 M11 **Ünye** Ordu, W Turkey
Unza *see* Unzha
127 O14 **Unzha** *var.* Unza. ≈ NW Russian Federation
79 E17 **Uolo, Río** *var.* Eyo (lower course), Mbini, Uele (upper course), Woleu; *prev.* Benito. ≈ Equatorial Guinea/Gabon
55 Q10 **Uonán** Bolívar, SE Venezuela
161 T12 **Uotsuri-shima** *island* China/Japan/Taiwan
165 M11 **Uozu** Toyama, Honshū, SW Japan
42 L12 **Upala** Alajuela, NW Costa Rica
55 P7 **Upata** Bolívar, E Venezuela
79 M23 **Upemba, Lac** ◎ SE Dem. Rep. Congo (Zaire)
197 O12 **Upernavik** *var.* Upernivik. Kitaa, C Greenland
Upernivik *see* Upernavik
83 F22 **Upington** Northern Cape, W South Africa
Uplands *see* Ottawa
192 I16 **Upolu** *island* SE Samoa
38 G11 **Upolu Point** *headland* Hawaii, USA, C Pacific Ocean
Upper Austria *see* Oberösterreich
Upper Bann *see* Bann
14 M13 **Upper Canada Village** *tourist site* Ontario, SE Canada
18 I16 **Upper Darby** Pennsylvania, NE USA
28 L2 **Upper Des Lacs Lake** ⊠ North Dakota, N USA
185 L14 **Upper Hutt** Wellington, North Island, NZ
29 X11 **Upper Iowa River** ≈ Iowa, C USA
32 H15 **Upper Klamath Lake** ◎ Oregon, NW USA
34 M6 **Upper Lake** California, W USA
35 Q1 **Upper Lake** ◎ California, W USA
10 K9 **Upper Liard** Yukon Territory, W Canada
97 E16 **Upper Lough Erne** ◎ SW Northern Ireland, UK
80 F12 **Upper Nile** ◈ *state* E Sudan
29 T3 **Upper Red Lake** ◎ Minnesota, N USA
31 S12 **Upper Sandusky** Ohio, N USA
Upper Volta *see* Burkina
95 O15 **Upplandsväsby** *var.* Upplands Väsby. Stockholm, C Sweden
95 O15 **Uppsala** Uppsala, C Sweden
95 O14 **Uppsala** ◈ *county* C Sweden
38 J12 **Upright Cape** *headland* Saint Matthew Island, Alaska, USA
20 K6 **Upton** Kentucky, S USA
33 Y13 **Upton** Wyoming, C USA
141 N7 **'Uqlat aṣ Ṣuqūr** Al Qaṣīm, W Saudi Arabia
Uqturpan *see* Wushi
54 C7 **Urabá, Golfo de** *gulf* NW Colombia
Uracas *see* Farallon de Pajaros
Uradar'ya *see* Ŭradaryo
147 N13 **Ŭradaryo** *Rus.* Uradar'ya. ≈ S Uzbekistan
162 M13 **Urad Qianqi** *var.* Xishanzui. Nei Mongol Zizhiqu, N China
165 U5 **Urahoro** Hokkaidō, NE Japan
165 T5 **Urakawa** Hokkaidō, NE Japan
129 X6 **Ural** *Kaz.* Zayyq. ≈ Kazakhstan/Russian Federation
183 T6 **Uralla** New South Wales, SE Australia
Ural Mountains *see* Ural'skiye Gory
144 F8 **Ural'sk** *Kaz.* Oral. Zapadnyy Kazakhstan, NW Kazakhstan
Ural'skaya Oblast' *see* Zapadnyy Kazakhstan
129 W5 **Ural'skiye Gory** *var.* Ural'skiy Khrebet, *Eng.* Ural Mountains. ▲ Kazakhstan/Russian Federation
Ural'skiy Khrebet *see* Ural'skiye Gory
138 I3 **Urām aṣ Ṣughrá** Ḥalab, N Syria
183 P10 **Urana** New South Wales, SE Australia
11 S10 **Uranium City** Saskatchewan, C Canada
58 F10 **Uraricoera** Roraima, N Brazil
47 S5 **Uraricoera, Rio** ≈ N Brazil
Ura-Tyube *see* Ŭroteppa
165 O13 **Urawa** Saitama, Honshū, S Japan
122 H10 **Uray** Khanty-Mansiyskiy Avtonomnyy Okrug, C Russian Federation
141 R7 **'Uray'irah** Ash Sharqīyah, E Saudi Arabia
30 M13 **Urbana** Illinois, N USA
31 R13 **Urbana** Ohio, N USA
29 V14 **Urbandale** Iowa, C USA
106 I11 **Urbania** Marche, C Italy
106 I11 **Urbino** Marche, C Italy
57 H16 **Urcos** Cusco, S Peru
144 D10 **Urda** Zapadnyy Kazakhstan, W Kazakhstan
105 N10 **Urda** Castilla-La Mancha, C Spain
162 E7 **Urdgol** Hovd, W Mongolia
Urdunn *see* Jordan
145 X12 **Urdzhar** *Kaz.* Ürzhar. Vostochnyy Kazakhstan, E Kazakhstan
97 L16 **Ure** ≈ N England, UK
119 K18 **Urechcha** *Rus.* Urech'ye. Minskaya Voblasts', S Belarus
Urech'ye *see* Urechcha
129 P2 **Uren'** Nizhegorodskaya Oblast', W Russian Federation
122 J9 **Urengoy** Yamalo-Nenetskiy Avtonomnyy Okrug, N Russian Federation
184 K10 **Urenui** Taranaki, North Island, NZ
187 Q12 **Ureparapara** *island* Banks Islands, N Vanuatu
40 G5 **Ures** Sonora, NW Mexico
Urfa *see* Şanlıurfa
146 H9 **Urganch** *Rus.* Urgench; *prev.* Novo-Urgench. Khorazm Wiloyati, W Uzbekistan
Urgench *see* Urganch
136 J14 **Ürgüp** Nevşehir, C Turkey
147 O12 **Urgut** Samarqand Wiloyati, C Uzbekistan
158 K3 **Urho** Xinjiang Uygur Zizhiqu, W China
152 G5 **Uri** Jammu and Kashmir, NW India
108 G9 **Uri** ◈ *canton* C Switzerland
54 F11 **Uribe** Meta, C Colombia
54 H4 **Uribia** La Guajira, N Colombia
116 G12 **Uricani** *Hung.* Hobicaurikány. Hunedoara, SW Romania
57 M21 **Uriondo** Tarija, S Bolivia
40 I7 **Urique** Chihuahua, N Mexico
40 I7 **Urique, Río** ≈ N Mexico
56 E9 **Uritiyacu, Río** ≈ N Peru
145 N7 **Uritskoy** Kostanay, N Kazakhstan
98 K8 **Urk** Flevoland, N Netherlands
136 B14 **Urla** İzmir, W Turkey
116 K13 **Urlaţi** Prahova, SE Romania
129 V4 **Urman** Respublika Bashkortostan, W Russian Federation
147 P12 **Urmetan** W Tajikistan
Urmia *see* Orūmīyeh
Urmia, Lake *see* Orūmīyeh, Daryācheh-ye
Urmiyeh *see* Orūmīyeh
113 N17 **Uroševac** *Alb.* Ferizaj. Serbia, S Yugoslavia
147 P11 **Ŭroteppa** *Rus.* Ura-Tyube. NW Tajikistan
54 D8 **Urrao** Antioquia, W Colombia
Ursat'yevskaya *see* Khowos
162 I11 **Urt** Ömnögovĭ, S Mongolia
129 X7 **Urtazym** Orenburgskaya Oblast', W Russian Federation
59 K18 **Uruaçu** Goiás, C Brazil
40 M14 **Uruapan** *var.* Uruapan del Progreso. Michoacán de Ocampo, SW Mexico
Uruapan del Progreso *see* Uruapan
57 G15 **Urubamba, Cordillera** ▲ C Peru
57 G14 **Urubamba, Río** ≈ C Peru
58 G12 **Urucará** Amazonas, N Brazil
61 E16 **Uruguaiana** Rio Grande do Sul, S Brazil
Uruguai, Rio *see* Uruguay
61 E18 **Uruguay** *off.* Oriental Republic of Uruguay; *prev.* La Banda Oriental. ◆ *republic* E South America
61 E15 **Uruguay** *var.* Rio Uruguai, Río Uruguay. ≈ E South America
Uruguay, Río *see* Uruguay
Urumchi *see* Ürümqi
158 L5 **Ürümqi** *var.* Tihwa, Urumchi, Urumqi, Urumtsi, Wu-lu-k'o-mu-shi, Wu-lu-mu-ch'i; *prev.* Ti-hua. *autonomous region capital* Xinjiang Uygur Zizhiqu, NW China
Urumtsi *see* Ürümqi
Urundi *see* Burundi
183 V6 **Urunga** New South Wales, SE Australia
188 C15 **Uruno Point** *headland* NW Guam
123 U13 **Urup, Ostrov** *island* Kuril'skiye Ostrova, SE Russian Federation
141 P11 **'Uruq al Mawārid** *desert* S Saudi Arabia
Urusan *see* Ulsan
129 T5 **Urussu** Respublika Tatarstan, W Russian Federation
184 K10 **Uruti** Taranaki, North Island, NZ
57 K19 **Uru Uru, Lago** ◎ W Bolivia
55 P9 **Uruyén** Bolívar, SE Venezuela
149 O7 **Ūrūzgān** *var.* Oruzgān, Orūzgān. Urūzgān, C Afghanistan
149 N6 **Ūrūzgān** *Per.* Orūzgān. ◈ *province* C Afghanistan
165 T3 **Uryū-gawa** ≈ Hokkaidō, NE Japan
165 T2 **Uryū-ko** ◎ Hokkaidō, NE Japan
129 N8 **Uryupinsk** Volgogradskaya Oblast', SW Russian Federation
Ürzhar *see* Urdzhar
127 R16 **Urzhum** Kirovskaya Oblast', NW Russian Federation
116 K13 **Urziceni** Ialomiţa, SE Romania
U.S./USA *see* United States of America
164 E14 **Usa** Ōita, Kyūshū, SW Japan
119 L16 **Usa** *Rus.* Usa. ≈ C Belarus
127 T6 **Usa** ≈ NW Russian Federation
136 E14 **Uşak** *prev.* Ushak. Uşak, W Turkey
136 D14 **Uşak** *var.* Ushak. ◈ *province* W Turkey
83 C19 **Usakos** Erongo, W Namibia
81 J21 **Usambara Mountains** ▲ NE Tanzania
81 G23 **Usangu Flats** *wetland* SW Tanzania
65 D24 **Usborne, Mount** ▲ East Falkland, Falkland Islands
100 O8 **Usedom** *island* NE Germany
99 M24 **Useldange** Diekirch, C Luxembourg
118 L12 **Ushacha** *Rus.* Ushacha. Vitsyebskaya Voblasts', N Belarus
Ushachi *see* Ushachy
118 L13 **Ushachy** *Rus.* Ushachi. Vitsyebskaya Voblasts', N Belarus
Ushak *see* Uşak
122 L4 **Ushakova, Ostrov** *island* Severnaya Zemlya, N Russian Federation
Ushant *see* Ouessant, Île d'
Ūsharal *see* Ucharal
164 B15 **Ushibuka** *var.* Usibuka. Kumamoto, Shimo-jima, SW Japan
Ushi Point *see* Sabaneta, Puntan
145 V14 **Ushtobe** *Kaz.* Üshtöbe. Almaty, SE Kazakhstan
63 I25 **Ushuaia** Tierra del Fuego, S Argentina
39 R10 **Usibelli** Alaska, USA
Usibuka *see* Ushibuka
186 D7 **Usino** Madang, N PNG
127 U6 **Usinsk** Respublika Komi, NW Russian Federation
97 K22 **Usk** *Wel.* Wysg. ≈ SE Wales, UK
Uskočke Planine/Uskokengebirge *see* Gorjanci/Žumberačko Gorje
Uskoplje *see* Gornji Vakuf
Üsküb *see* Skopje
114 M11 **Üsküpdere** Kırklareli, NW Turkey
128 L7 **Usman'** Lipetskaya Oblast', W Russian Federation
118 D8 **Usmas Ezers** ◎ NW Latvia
127 U13 **Usol'ye** Permskaya Oblast', NW Russian Federation
41 T16 **Uspanapa, Río** ≈ SE Mexico
145 R11 **Uspenskiy** Zhezkazgan, C Kazakhstan
103 O11 **Ussel** Corrèze, C France
163 Z6 **Ussuri** *var.* Usuri, Wusuri, *Chin.* Wusuli Jiang. ≈ China/Russian Federation
123 S15 **Ussuriysk** *prev.* Nikol'sk, Nikol'sk-Ussuriyskiy, Voroshilov. Primorskiy Kray, SE Russian Federation
136 J10 **Usta Burnu** *headland* N Turkey
149 P13 **Usta Muhammad** Baluchistān, SW Pakistan
123 V11 **Ust'-Bol'sheretsk** Kamchatskaya Oblast', E Russian Federation
129 N9 **Ust'-Buzulukskaya** Volgogradskaya Oblast', SW Russian Federation
111 C16 **Ústecký Kraj** ◈ *region* NW Czech Republic
108 G7 **Uster** Zürich, NE Switzerland
107 I22 **Ustica, Isola d'** *island* S Italy
122 M12 **Ust'-Ilimsk** Irkutskaya Oblast', C Russian Federation
111 C15 **Ústí nad Labem** *Ger.* Aussig. Ústecký Kraj, NW Czech Republic
111 F17 **Ústí nad Orlicí** *Ger.* Wildenschwert. Pardubický Kraj, E Czech Republic
Ustinov *see* Izhevsk
113 J14 **Ustiprača** Republika Srpska, SE Bosnia and Herzegovina
122 H11 **Ust'-Ishim** Omskaya Oblast', C Russian Federation
110 G6 **Ustka** *Ger.* Stolpmünde. Pomorskie, N Poland
123 V9 **Ust'-Kamchatsk** Kamchatskaya Oblast', E Russian Federation
145 X9 **Ust'-Kamenogorsk** *Kaz.* Öskemen. Vostochnyy Kazakhstan, E Kazakhstan
123 T10 **Ust'-Khayryuzovo** Koryakskiy Avtonomnyy Okrug, E Russian Federation
122 I14 **Ust'-Koksa** Respublika Altay, S Russian Federation
127 S11 **Ust'-Kulom** Respublika Komi, NW Russian Federation
123 Q8 **Ust'-Kuyga** Respublika Sakha (Yakutiya), NE Russian Federation
128 L14 **Ust'-Labinsk** Krasnodarskiy Kray, SW Russian Federation
123 R10 **Ust'-Maya** Respublika Sakha (Yakutiya), NE Russian Federation
123 R9 **Ust'-Nera** Respublika Sakha (Yakutiya), NE Russian Federation
123 P12 **Ust'-Nyukzha** Amurskaya Oblast', S Russian Federation
123 O7 **Ust'-Olenëk** Respublika Sakha (Yakutiya), NE Russian Federation
123 T9 **Ust'-Omchug** Magadanskaya Oblast', E Russian Federation
122 M13 **Ust'-Ordynskiy** Ust'-Ordynskiy Buryatskiy Avtonomnyy Okrug, S Russian Federation
122 M13 **Ust'-Ordynskiy Buryatskiy Avtonomnyy Okrug** ◈ *autonomous district* S Russian Federation
127 N8 **Ust'-Pinega** Arkhangel'skaya Oblast', NW Russian Federation
122 K8 **Ust'-Port** Taymyrskiy (Dolgano-Nenetskiy) Avtonomnyy Okrug, N Russian Federation
114 L11 **Ustrem** *prev.* Vakav. Yambol, E Bulgaria
111 O18 **Ustrzyki Dolne** Podkarpackie, SE Poland
Ust'-Sysol'sk *see* Syktyvkar
127 R7 **Ust'-Tsil'ma** Respublika Komi, NW Russian Federation
Ust Urt *see* Ustyurt Plateau
127 O11 **Ust'ya** ≈ NW Russian Federation
117 R8 **Ustynivka** Kirovohrads'ka Oblast', C Ukraine
144 H15 **Ustyurt Plateau** *var.* Ust Urt, *Uzb.* Ustyurt Platosi. *plateau* Kazakhstan/Uzbekistan
Ustyurt Platosi *see* Ustyurt Plateau
126 K14 **Ustyuzhna** Vologodskaya Oblast', NW Russian Federation
158 J4 **Usu** Xinjiang Uygur Zizhiqu, NW China
171 O13 **Usu** Sulawesi, C Indonesia
164 E14 **Usuki** Ōita, Kyūshū, SW Japan
42 G8 **Usulután** Usulután, SE El Salvador
42 B9 **Usulután** ◈ *department* SE El Salvador
41 W16 **Usumacinta, Río** ≈ Guatemala/Mexico
Usumbura *see* Bujumbura
Usuri *see* Ussuri
171 W14 **Uta** Irian Jaya, E Indonesia
36 K5 **Utah** *off.* State of Utah; also known as Beehive State, Mormon State. ◈ *state* W USA
36 L3 **Utah Lake** ◎ Utah, W USA
Utaidhani *see* Uthai Thani
93 M14 **Utajärvi** Oulu, C Finland
Utamboni *see* Mitemele, Río
Utaradit *see* Uttaradit
165 T3 **Utashinai** *var.* Utasinai. Hokkaidō, NE Japan
Utasinai *see* Utashinai
193 Y14 **'Uta Vava'u** *island* Vava'u Group, N Tonga
37 V9 **Ute Creek** ≈ New Mexico, SW USA
118 H12 **Utena** Utena, E Lithuania
37 V10 **Ute Reservoir** ⊠ New Mexico, SW USA
167 O10 **Uthai Thani** *var.* Muang Uthai Thani, Udayadhani, Utaidhani. Uthai Thani, W Thailand
149 O15 **Uthal** Baluchistān, SW Pakistan
18 I10 **Utica** New York, NE USA
105 R10 **Utiel** País Valenciano, E Spain
11 O13 **Utikuma Lake** ◎ Alberta, W Canada
42 I4 **Utila, Isla de** *island* Islas de la Bahía, N Honduras
Utina *see* Udine
59 O17 **Utinga** Bahia, E Brazil
Utirik *see* Utrik Atoll
95 M22 **Utlängan** *island* S Sweden
117 U11 **Utlyuts'kyy Lyman** *bay* S Ukraine
95 P16 **Utö** Stockholm, C Sweden
25 Q12 **Utopia** Texas, SW USA
98 J11 **Utrecht** *Lat.* Trajectum ad Rhenum. Utrecht, C Netherlands
83 K22 **Utrecht** KwaZulu/Natal, E South Africa
98 I11 **Utrecht** ◈ *province* C Netherlands
104 K14 **Utrera** Andalucía, S Spain
189 V4 **Utrik Atoll** *var.* Utirik, Utrōk, Utrönk. *atoll* Ratak Chain, N Marshall Islands
Utrōk/Utrönk *see* Utrik Atoll
95 B16 **Utsira** *island* SW Norway
92 L8 **Utsjoki** *var.* Ohcejohka. Lappi, N Finland
165 O12 **Utsunomiya** *var.* Utunomiya. Tochigi, Honshū, S Japan
129 P13 **Utta** Respublika Kalmykiya, SW Russian Federation
167 O8 **Uttaradit** *var.* Utaradit. Uttaradit, N Thailand
152 J8 **Uttarkāshi** Uttar Pradesh, N India
152 K11 **Uttar Pradesh** *prev.* United Provinces, United Provinces of Agra and Oudh. ◈ *state* N India
45 T5 **Utuado** C Puerto Rico
158 K3 **Utubulak** Xinjiang Uygur Zizhiqu, W China
39 N5 **Utukok River** ≈ Alaska, USA
Utunomiya *see* Utsunomiya
187 P10 **Utupua** *island* Santa Cruz Islands, E Soloman Islands
144 G9 **Utva** ≈ NW Kazakhstan
189 Y15 **Utwe** Kosrae, E Micronesia
189 X15 **Utwe Harbor** *harbor* Kosrae, E Micronesia
162 J7 **Uubulan** Arhangay, C Mongolia
118 G6 **Uulu** Pärnumaa, SW Estonia
197 N13 **Uummannaq** *var.* Umanak, Umanaq. Kitaa, C Greenland
Uummannarsuaq *see* Nunap Isua
162 E4 **Üüreg Nuur** ◎ NW Mongolia
Uusikaarlepyy *see* Nykarleby
93 J19 **Uusikaupunki** *Swe.* Nystad. Länsi-Suomi, W Finland
129 S2 **Uva** Udmurtskaya Respublika, NW Russian Federation
113 L14 **Uvac** ≈ W Yugoslavia
25 Q12 **Uvalde** Texas, SW USA
155 K25 **Uva Province** ◈ *province* SE Sri Lanka
119 O18 **Uvaravichy** *Rus.* Uvarovichi. Homyel'skaya Voblasts', SE Belarus
54 J11 **Uvá, Río** ≈ E Colombia
Uvarovichi *see* Uvaravichy
129 N7 **Uvarovo** Tambovskaya Oblast', W Russian Federation
122 H10 **Uvat** Tyumenskaya Oblast', C Russian Federation
190 G12 **Uvea, Île** *island* N Wallis and Futuna
81 E21 **Uvinza** Kigoma, W Tanzania
79 O20 **Uvira** Sud Kivu, E Dem. Rep. Congo (Zaire)
162 E5 **Uvs** ◈ *province* NW Mongolia
162 F5 **Uvs Nuur** *var.* Ozero Ubsu-Nur. ◎ Mongolia/Russian Federation
164 F14 **Uwa** Ehime, Shikoku, SW Japan
164 F14 **Uwajima** *var.* Uwazima. Ehime, Shikoku, SW Japan
80 B5 **'Uwaynāt, Jabal al** *var.* Jebel Uweinat. ▲ Libya/Sudan
Uwazima *see* Uwajima
Uweinat, Jebel *see* 'Uwaynāt, Jabal al
14 H14 **Uxbridge** Ontario, S Canada
Uxellodunum *see* Issoudun
162 M15 **Uxin Qi** Nei Mongol Zizhiqu, N China
41 X12 **Uxmal, Ruinas** *ruins* Yucatán, SE Mexico
131 Q5 **Uy** ≈ Kazakhstan/Russian Federation
144 K15 **Uyaly** Kzylorda, S Kazakhstan
123 R8 **Uyandina** ≈ NE Russian Federation
122 L12 **Uyar** Krasnoyarskiy Kray, S Russian Federation
162 L10 **Üydzen** Ömnögovĭ, S Mongolia
Uyeda *see* Ueda
122 K5 **Uyedineniya, Ostrov** *island* N Russian Federation
77 V17 **Uyo** Akwa Ibom, S Nigeria
162 D8 **Üyönch** Hovd, W Mongolia
145 Q15 **Uyuk** Zhambyl, S Kazakhstan
141 V13 **'Uyūn** SW Oman
57 K20 **Uyuni** Potosí, W Bolivia
57 J20 **Uyuni, Salar de** *wetland* SW Bolivia
146 I9 **Uzbekistan** *off.* Republic of Uzbekistan. ◆ *republic* C Asia
158 D8 **Uzbel Shankou** *Rus.* Pereval Kyzyl-Dzhiik. *pass* China/Tajikistan
119 J17 **Uzda** *Rus.* Uzda. Minskaya Voblasts', C Belarus
103 N12 **Uzerche** Corrèze, C France
103 R14 **Uzès** Gard, S France
147 T10 **Uzgen** *Kir.* Özgön. Oshskaya Oblast', SW Kyrgyzstan
117 O3 **Uzh** ≈ N Ukraine
Uzhgorod *see* Uzhhorod
116 G7 **Uzhhorod** *Rus.* Uzhgorod; *prev.* Ungvár. Zakarpats'ka Oblast', W Ukraine
Uzi *see* Uji
112 K13 **Užice** *prev.* Titovo Užice. Serbia, W Yugoslavia
Uzin *see* Uzyn
128 L5 **Uzlovaya** Tul'skaya Oblast', W Russian Federation
108 H7 **Uznach** Sankt Gallen, NE Switzerland
145 U16 **Uzunagach** Almaty, SE Kazakhstan
136 B10 **Uzunköprü** Edirne, NW Turkey
118 D11 **Užventis** Kelmė, C Lithuania
117 P5 **Uzyn** *Rus.* Uzin. Kyyivs'ka Oblast', N Ukraine

V

Vääksy *see* Asikkala
83 H23 **Vaal** ≈ C South Africa
93 M14 **Vaala** Oulu, C Finland
93 N19 **Vaalimaa** Etelä-Suomi, SE Finland
99 M19 **Vaals** Limburg, SE Netherlands
93 J16 **Vaasa** *Swe.* Vasa; *prev.* Nikolainkaupunki. Vaasa, W Finland
98 L10 **Vaassen** Gelderland, E Netherlands
118 G11 **Vabalninkas** Biržai, NE Lithuania
Vabkent *see* Wobkent
111 J22 **Vác** *Ger.* Waitzen. Pest, N Hungary
61 I14 **Vacaria** Rio Grande do Sul, S Brazil
35 N7 **Vacaville** California, W USA
103 R15 **Vaccarès, Étang de** ◎ SE France
44 L10 **Vache, Île à** *island* SW Haiti
173 Y16 **Vacoas** W Mauritius
32 G10 **Vader** Washington, NW USA
94 D12 **Vadheim** Sogn og Fjordane, S Norway
154 D11 **Vadodara** *prev.* Baroda. Gujarāt, W India
92 M8 **Vadsø** *Fin.* Vesisaari. Finnmark, N Norway
95 L17 **Vadstena** Östergötland, S Sweden
108 I8 **Vaduz** ● (Liechtenstein) W Liechtenstein
Vág *see* Váh
127 N12 **Vaga** ≈ NW Russian Federation
94 G11 **Vågåmo** Oppland, S Norway
112 D12 **Vaganski Vrh** ▲ W Croatia

◆ Country ● Country Capital ◇ Dependent Territory ○ Dependent Territory Capital ◈ Administrative Region ✕ International Airport ▲ Mountain ▲ Mountain Range Volcano ≈ River ◎ Lake ⊠ Reservoir

95 A19 Vágar Dan. Vågø Island Faeroe Islands
Vágbeszterce see Považská Bystrica
95 L19 Vaggeryd Jönköping, S Sweden
95 O16 Vagnhärad Södermanland, C Sweden
104 G7 Vagos Aveiro, N Portugal
Vágsellye see Sal'a
92 H10 Vågsfjorden fjord N Norway
94 C10 Vågsøy island S Norway
Vágújhely see Nové Mesto nad Váhom
111 I21 Váh Ger. Waag, Hung. Vág. ≈ W Slovakia
93 K16 Vähäkyrö Länsi-Suomi, W Finland
191 X11 Vahitahi atoll Îles Tuamotu, E French Polynesia
Vaidei see Vulcan
22 L4 Vaiden Mississippi, S USA
155 I23 Vaigai ≈ SE India
191 V16 Vaihu Easter Island, Chile, E Pacific Ocean
118 I6 Väike Emajõgi ≈ S Estonia
118 I4 Väike-Maarja Ger. Klein-Marien. Lääne-Virumaa, NE Estonia
Väike-Salatsi see Mazsalaca
37 R4 Vail Colorado, C USA
193 V15 Vaina Tongatapu, S Tonga
118 E5 Väinameri prev. Muhu Väin, Ger. Moon-Sund. sea E Baltic Sea
93 N18 Vainikkala Etelä-Suomi, SE Finland
118 D10 Vaiņode Liepāja, SW Latvia
155 H23 Vaippār ≈ SE India
191 W11 Vairaatea atoll Îles Tuamotu, C French Polynesia
191 R8 Vairao Tahiti, W French Polynesia
103 R14 Vaison-la-Romaine Vaucluse, SE France
190 G11 Vaitupu Île Uvea, E Wallis and Futuna
190 F7 Vaitupu atoll C Tuvalu
Vajdahunyad see Hunedoara
Vajdej see Vulcan
78 K12 Vakaga ◆ prefecture NE Central African Republic
114 H10 Vakarel Sofiya, W Bulgaria
Vakav see Ustrem
137 O11 Vakfıkebir Trabzon, NE Turkey
122 J10 Vakh ≈ C Russian Federation
Vakhon, Qatorkŭhi see Nicholas Range
147 P14 Vakhsh SW Tajikistan
147 Q12 Vakhsh ≈ SW Tajikistan
129 P1 Vakhtan Nizhegorodskaya Oblast', W Russian Federation
94 C13 Vaksdal Hordaland, S Norway
127 O8 Vashka ≈ NW Russian Federation
Valachia see Wallachia
108 D11 Valais Ger. Wallis. ◆ canton SW Switzerland
113 M21 Valamarës, Mali i ▲ SE Albania
129 S2 Valamaz Udmurtskaya Respublika, NW Russian Federation
113 Q19 Valandovo SE FYR Macedonia
111 I18 Valašské Meziříčí Ger. Wallachisch-Meseritsch, Pol. Wałeckie Międzyrzecze. Zlínský Kraj, E Czech Republic
115 I17 Valáxa island Vóreioi Sporádes, Greece, Aegean Sea
95 K16 Vålberg Värmland, C Sweden
116 H12 Vâlcea prev. Vîlcea. ◆ county SW Romania
63 J16 Valcheta Río Negro, E Argentina
15 P12 Valcourt Quebec, SE Canada
Valdai Hills see Valdayskaya Vozvyshennost'
104 M3 Valdavia ≈ N Spain
126 I15 Valday Novgorodskaya Oblast', W Russian Federation
126 I15 Valdayskaya Vozvyshennost' var. Valdai Hills. hill range W Russian Federation
104 L9 Valdecañas, Embalse de ⊟ W Spain
118 E8 Valdemārpils Ger. Sassmacken. Talsi, NW Latvia
95 N18 Valdemarsvik Östergötland, S Sweden
105 N8 Valdemoro Madrid, C Spain
105 O11 Valdepeñas Castilla-La Mancha, C Spain
104 L5 Valderaduey ≈ NE Spain
104 L5 Valderas Castilla-León, N Spain
105 T7 Valderrobres var. Vall-de-roures. Aragón, NE Spain
63 K17 Valdés, Península peninsula SE Argentina
39 S11 Valdez Alaska, USA
56 C5 Valdéz var. Limones. Esmeraldas, NW Ecuador
Valdia see Weldiya
103 U11 Val d'Isère Savoie, E France
63 G15 Valdivia Los Lagos, C Chile
Valdivia Bank see Valdivia Seamount
65 P17 Valdivia Seamount var. Valdivia Bank. undersea feature E Atlantic Ocean
103 N4 Val-d'Oise ◆ department N France
14 J8 Val-d'Or Quebec, SE Canada
23 U8 Valdosta Georgia, SE USA
94 G13 Valdres physical region S Norway
32 L13 Vale Oregon, NW USA
116 F9 Valea lui Mihai Hung. Érmihályfalva. Bihor, NW Romania
11 N15 Valemount British Columbia, SW Canada
59 O17 Valença Bahia, E Brazil
104 F4 Valença do Minho Viana do Castelo, N Portugal
59 N14 Valença do Piauí Piauí, E Brazil
103 N8 Valençay Indre, C France
103 R13 Valence anc. Valentia, Valentia Julia, Ventia. Drôme, E France
105 S10 Valencia País Valenciano, E Spain
54 K5 Valencia Carabobo, N Venezuela
105 R10 Valencia Cat. València. ◆ province País Valenciano, E Spain
105 S10 Valencia × Valencia, E Spain
València/Valencia see País Valenciano
104 I10 Valencia de Alcántara Extremadura, W Spain
104 L4 Valencia de Don Juan Castilla-León, N Spain
105 U9 Valencia, Golfo de var. Gulf of Valencia. gulf E Spain
Valencia, Gulf of see Valencia, Golfo de
97 A21 Valencia Island Ir. Dairbhre. island SW Ireland
103 P2 Valenciennes Nord, N France
116 K13 Vălenii de Munte Prahova, SE Romania
Valentia see Valence, France
Valentia see País Valenciano
Valentia Julia see Valence
103 T8 Valentigney Doubs, E France
28 M12 Valentine Nebraska, C USA
24 J10 Valentine Texas, SW USA
Valentine State see Oregon
106 C8 Valenza Piemonte, NW Italy
94 I13 Våler Hedmark, S Norway
54 I6 Valera Trujillo, NW Venezuela
192 M11 Valerie Guyot undersea feature S Pacific Ocean
Valetta see Valletta
118 I7 Valga Ger. Walk, Latv. Valka. Valgamaa, S Estonia
118 I7 Valgamaa off. Valga Maakond. ◆ province S Estonia
43 Q15 Valiente, Península peninsula NW Panama
103 X16 Valinco, Golfe de gulf Corse, France, C Mediterranean Sea
112 L12 Valjevo Serbia, W Yugoslavia
Valjok see Válljohka
118 I7 Valka Ger. Walk. Valka, N Latvia
Valka see Valga
93 L18 Valkeakoski Länsi-Suomi, W Finland
93 M19 Valkeala Etelä-Suomi, S Finland
99 L18 Valkenburg Limburg, SE Netherlands
99 K15 Valkenswaard Noord-Brabant, S Netherlands
119 G15 Valkininkai Varėna, S Lithuania
117 U5 Valky Kharkivs'ka Oblast', E Ukraine
41 Y12 Valladolid Yucatán, SE Mexico
104 M5 Valladolid Castilla-León, NW Spain
104 L5 Valladolid ◆ province Castilla-León, N Spain
103 U15 Vallauris Alpes-Maritimes, SE France
Vall-de-roures see Valderrobres
105 S9 Vall d'Uxó País Valenciano, E Spain
95 E16 Valle Aust-Agder, S Norway
105 N2 Valle Cantabria, N Spain
42 H8 Valle ◆ department S Honduras
105 N8 Vallecas Madrid, C Spain
37 Q8 Vallecito Reservoir ⊟ Colorado, C USA
106 A7 Valle d'Aosta ◆ region NW Italy
41 O14 Valle de Bravo México, S Mexico
55 N5 Valle de Guanape Anzoátegui, N Venezuela
54 M6 Valle de La Pascua Guárico, N Venezuela
54 B11 Valle del Cauca off. Departamento del Valle del Cauca. ◆ province W Colombia
41 N13 Valle de Santiago Guanajuato, C Mexico
40 J7 Valle de Zaragoza Chihuahua, N Mexico
54 G5 Valledupar Cesar, N Colombia
76 G10 Vallée de Ferlo ≈ NW Senegal
57 M19 Vallegrande Santa Cruz, C Bolivia
41 P8 Valle Hermoso Tamaulipas, C Mexico
35 N8 Vallejo California, W USA
62 G8 Vallenar Atacama, N Chile
95 O15 Vallentuna Stockholm, C Sweden
121 P16 Valletta prev. Valetta. ● (Malta) E Malta
27 N6 Valley Center Kansas, C USA
29 Q5 Valley City North Dakota, N USA
32 I15 Valley Falls Oregon, NW USA
Valleyfield see Salaberry-de-Valleyfield
21 S4 Valley Head West Virginia, NE USA
25 T8 Valley Mills Texas, SW USA
75 W10 Valley of the Kings ancient monument E Egypt
29 R11 Valley Springs South Dakota, N USA
20 K5 Valley Station Kentucky, S USA
11 O13 Valleyview Alberta, W Canada
25 T5 Valley View Texas, SW USA
61 C21 Vallimanca, Arroyo ≈ E Argentina
92 L9 Válljohka var. Valjok Finnmark, N Norway
107 M19 Vallo della Lucania Campania, S Italy
108 B9 Vallorbe Vaud, W Switzerland
105 V6 Valls Cataluña, NE Spain
94 N11 Vallsta Gävleborg, C Sweden
94 N12 Vallvik Gävleborg, C Sweden
11 T17 Val Marie Saskatchewan, S Canada
118 H7 Valmiera Est. Volmari, Ger. Wolmar. Valmiera, N Latvia
105 N3 Valnera ▲ N Spain
102 J3 Valognes Manche, N France
Valona see Vlorë
Valona Bay see Vlorës, Gjiri i
104 G6 Valongo var. Valongo de Gaia. Porto, N Portugal
Valongo de Gaia see Valongo
104 M5 Valoria la Buena Castilla-León, N Spain
119 J15 Valozhyn Pol. Wołożyn, Rus. Volozhin. Minskaya Voblasts', C Belarus
104 I5 Valpaços Vila Real, N Portugal
23 P8 Valparaiso Florida, SE USA
31 N11 Valparaiso Indiana, N USA
62 G11 Valparaíso Valparaíso, C Chile
40 L11 Valparaíso Zacatecas, C Mexico
62 G11 Valparaíso off. Región de Valparaíso. ◆ region C Chile
Valpo see Valpovo
112 I9 Valpovo Hung. Valpó. Osijek-Baranja, E Croatia
103 R14 Valréas Vaucluse, SE France
Vals see Vals-Platz
154 D12 Valsād prev. Bulsar. Gujarāt, W India
Valsbaai see False Bay
171 T12 Valse Pisang, Kepulauan island group E Indonesia
108 H9 Vals-Platz var. Vals. Graubünden, S Switzerland
171 X16 Vals, Tanjung headland Irian Jaya, SE Indonesia
93 N15 Valtimo Itä-Suomi, E Finland
115 D17 Váltou ▲ C Greece
129 O12 Valuyevka Rostovskaya Oblast', SW Russian Federation
128 K9 Valuyki Belgorodskaya Oblast', W Russian Federation
36 L2 Val Verda Utah, W USA
64 N12 Valverde Hierro, Islas Canarias, Spain, NE Atlantic Ocean
104 I13 Valverde del Camino Andalucía, S Spain
95 G23 Vamdrup Vejle, C Denmark
94 L12 Våmhus Dalarna, C Sweden
93 K18 Vammala Länsi-Suomi, W Finland
Vámosudvarhely see Odorheiu Secuiesc
137 S14 Van Van, E Turkey
25 V7 Van Texas, SW USA
137 T14 Van ◆ province E Turkey
137 T11 Vanadzor prev. Kirovakan. N Armenia
25 U5 Van Alstyne Texas, SW USA
33 W10 Vananda Montana, NW USA
116 I11 Vânători Hung. Héjjasfalva; prev. Vînători. Mureș, C Romania
191 W12 Vanavana atoll Îles Tuamotu, SE French Polynesia
Vana-Vändra see Vändra
122 M11 Vanavara Evenkiyskiy Avtonomnyy Okrug, C Russian Federation
15 Q8 Van Bruyssel Quebec, SE Canada
27 R10 Van Buren Arkansas, C USA
19 S1 Van Buren Maine, NE USA
27 W7 Van Buren Missouri, C USA
19 T5 Vanceboro Maine, NE USA
21 W10 Vanceboro North Carolina, SE USA
21 O4 Vanceburg Kentucky, S USA
Vanch see Vanj
10 L17 Vancouver British Columbia, SW Canada
32 G11 Vancouver Washington, NW USA
10 L17 Vancouver × British Columbia, SW Canada
10 K16 Vancouver Island island British Columbia, SW Canada
Vanda see Vantaa
171 X13 Van Daalen ≈ Irian Jaya, E Indonesia
30 L15 Vandalia Illinois, N USA
27 V3 Vandalia Missouri, C USA
31 R13 Vandalia Ohio, N USA
25 U13 Vanderbilt Texas, SW USA
31 Q10 Vandercook Lake Michigan, N USA
10 L14 Vanderhoof British Columbia, SW Canada
18 K8 Vanderwhacker Mountain ▲ New York, NE USA
181 P1 Van Diemen Gulf gulf Northern Territory, N Australia
Van Diemen's Land see Tasmania
118 H5 Vändra Ger. Fennern; prev. Vana-Vändra. Pärnumaa, SW Estonia
Vandsburg see Więcbork
34 L4 Van Duzen River ≈ California, W USA
118 F13 Vandžiogala Kaunas, C Lithuania
41 N10 Vanegas San Luis Potosí, C Mexico
Vaner, Lake see Vänern
95 K17 Vänern Eng. Lake Vaner; prev. Lake Vener. ◎ S Sweden
95 J18 Vänersborg Västra Götaland, S Sweden
94 F12 Vang Oppland, S Norway
172 I7 Vangaindrano Fianarantsoa, SE Madagascar
137 S14 Van Gölü Eng. Lake Van; anc. Thospitis. salt lake E Turkey
186 L9 Vangunu island New Georgia Islands, NW Solomon Islands
24 J9 Van Horn Texas, SW USA
187 Q11 Vanikolo var. Vanikoro. island Santa Cruz Islands, E Solomon Islands
Vanikoro see Vanikolo
186 A5 Vanimo Sandaun, NW PNG
123 T13 Vanino Khabarovskiy Kray, SE Russian Federation
155 G19 Vānīvilāsa Sāgara ◎ SW India
147 S13 Vanj Rus. Vanch. S Tajikistan
116 G14 Vânju Mare prev. Vînju Mare. Mehedinți, SW Romania
15 N12 Vankleek Hill Ontario, SE Canada
Van, Lake see Van Gölü
93 I16 Vännäs Västerbotten, N Sweden
93 I15 Vännäsby Västerbotten, N Sweden
102 H7 Vannes anc. Dariorigum. Morbihan, NW France
92 I8 Vannøya island N Norway
103 T12 Vanoise, Massif de la ▲ E France
83 E24 Vanrhynsdorp Western Cape, SW South Africa
21 P7 Vansant Virginia, NE USA
94 L13 Vansbro Dalarna, C Sweden
95 D18 Vanse Vest-Agder, S Norway
9 P7 Vansittart Island island Nunavut, NE Canada
93 M20 Vantaa Swe. Vanda. Etelä-Suomi, S Finland
93 L19 Vantaa × (Helsinki) Etelä-Suomi, S Finland
32 J9 Vantage Washington, NW USA
187 Z14 Vanua Balavu prev. Vanua Mbalavu. island Lau Group, E Fiji
187 R12 Vanua Lava island Banks Islands, N Vanuatu
187 Y13 Vanua Levu island N Fiji
Vanua Mbalavu see Vanua Balavu
187 R12 Vanuatu off. Republic of Vanuatu; prev. New Hebrides. ◆ republic SW Pacific Ocean
175 P8 Vanuatu island group SW Pacific Ocean
31 Q12 Van Wert Ohio, N USA
187 Q17 Vao Province Sud, S New Caledonia
Vapincum see Gap
117 N7 Vapnyarka Vinnyts'ka Oblast', C Ukraine
103 T15 Var ◆ department SE France
103 U14 Var ≈ SE France
95 J18 Vara Västra Götaland, S Sweden
Varadinska Županija see Varaždin
118 J10 Varakļani Madona, C Latvia
106 C7 Varallo Piemonte, NE Italy
143 O5 Varāmīn var. Veramin. Tehrān, N Iran
153 N14 Vārānasi prev. Banaras, Benares, hist. Kasi. Uttar Pradesh, N India
127 T3 Varandey Nenetskiy Avtonomnyy Okrug, NW Russian Federation
92 M8 Varangerbotn Finnmark, N Norway
92 M8 Varangerfjorden fjord N Norway
92 M8 Varangerhalvøya peninsula N Norway
Varannó see Vranov nad Topl'ou
107 M15 Varano, Lago di ◎ SE Italy
118 J13 Varapayeva Rus. Voropayevo. Vitsyebskaya Voblasts', NW Belarus
Varasd see Varaždin
112 E7 Varaždin Ger. Warasdin, Hung. Varasd. Varaždin, N Croatia
112 E7 Varaždin off. Varadinska Županija. ◆ province N Croatia
106 C10 Varazze Liguria, NW Italy
95 J20 Varberg Halland, S Sweden
Vardak see Wardag
113 Q19 Vardar Gk. Axiós. ≈ FYR Macedonia/Greece see also Axiós
95 F23 Varde Ribe, W Denmark
137 V12 Vardenis E Armenia
92 N8 Vardø Fin. Vuoreija. Finnmark, N Norway
115 E18 Vardoúsia ▲ C Greece
Vareia see Logroño
100 G10 Varel Niedersachsen, NW Germany
119 G15 Varėna Pol. Orany. Varėna, S Lithuania
15 O12 Varennes Quebec, SE Canada
103 P10 Varennes-sur-Allier Allier, C France
112 I12 Vareš Federacija Bosna I Hercegovina, E Bosnia and Herzegovina
106 D7 Varese Lombardia, N Italy
116 J12 Vârful Moldoveanu var. Moldoveanul; prev. Vîrful Moldoveanu. ▲ C Romania
Varganzi see Warganza
95 J18 Vårgårda Västra Götaland, S Sweden
95 J18 Vargön Västra Götaland, S Sweden
95 C17 Varhaug Rogaland, S Norway
93 N17 Varkaus Itä-Suomi, C Finland
92 J2 Varmahlidh Nordhurland Vestra, N Iceland
95 J15 Värmland ◆ county C Sweden
95 K16 Värmlandsnäs peninsula S Sweden
114 N8 Varna prev. Stalin, anc. Odessus. Varna, E Bulgaria
114 N8 Varna × Varna, E Bulgaria
114 N8 Varna ◆ province E Bulgaria
95 L20 Värnamo Jönköping, S Sweden
114 N8 Varnenski Zaliv prev. Stalinski Zaliv. bay E Bulgaria
114 N8 Varnensko Ezero estuary E Bulgaria
118 D11 Varniai Telšiai, W Lithuania
Varnoús see Baba
111 D14 Varnsdorf Ger. Warnsdorf. Ústecký Kraj, N Czech Republic
111 I23 Várpalota Veszprém, W Hungary
Varshava see Warszawa
118 K6 Värska Põlvamaa, SE Estonia
98 N12 Varsseveld Gelderland, E Netherlands
115 D19 Vartholomió prev. Vartholomión. Dytikí Ellás, S Greece
Vartholomión see Vartholomió
137 Q14 Varto Muş, E Turkey
95 K18 Vartofta Västra Götaland, S Sweden
93 O17 Värtsilä Itä-Suomi, E Finland
Värtsilä see Vyartsilya
117 R4 Varva Chernihivs'ka Oblast', NE Ukraine
59 H18 Várzea Grande Mato Grosso, SW Brazil
106 D9 Varzi Lombardia, N Italy
Varzimanor Ayni see Ayní
126 K5 Varzuga ≈ NW Russian Federation
103 P8 Varzy Nièvre, C France
111 G23 Vas off. Vas Megye. ◆ county W Hungary
Vasa see Vaasa
190 A9 Vasafua island Funafuti Atoll, C Tuvalu
111 O21 Vásárosnamény Szabolcs-Szatmár-Bereg, E Hungary
104 H13 Vascão, Ribeira de ≈ S Portugal
116 G10 Vașcău Hung. Vaskoh. Bihor, NE Romania
Vascongadas, Provincias see País Vasco
Vashess Bay see Vaskess Bay
Vāsht see Khāsh
Vasilevichi see Vasilyevichy
115 G14 Vasilikà Kentrikí Makedonía, NE Greece
115 C18 Vasilikí Lefkáda, Iónioi Nísoi, Greece, C Mediterranean Sea
115 K25 Vasilikí Kríti, Greece, E Mediterranean Sea
119 G16 Vasilishki Pol. Wasiliszki, Rus. Vasilishki. Hrodzyenskaya Voblasts', W Belarus
Vasil Kolarov see Pamporovo
Vasil'kov see Vasyl'kiv
119 N19 Vasilyevichy Rus. Vasilevichi. Homyel'skaya Voblasts', SE Belarus
191 Y3 Vaskess Bay var. Vashess Bay. bay Kiritimati, E Kiribati
Vaskoh see Vașcău
Vaskohsziklás see Ștei
116 M10 Vaslui Vaslui, C Romania
116 L11 Vaslui ◆ county NE Romania
31 R8 Vassar Michigan, N USA
95 E15 Vassdalseggi ▲ S Norway
60 P9 Vassouras Rio de Janeiro, SE Brazil
92 H11 Vastenjaure ◎ N Sweden
95 N15 Västerås Västmanland, C Sweden
93 G15 Västerbotten ◆ county N Sweden
94 K12 Västerdalälven ≈ C Sweden
95 O16 Västerhaninge Stockholm, C Sweden
94 M10 Västernorrland ◆ county C Sweden
95 N19 Västervik Kalmar, S Sweden
95 M15 Västmanand ◆ county C Sweden
107 L15 Vasto anc. Histonium. Abruzzo, C Italy
95 J19 Västra Götaland ◆ county S Sweden
95 J16 Västra Silen ◎ S Sweden
111 G23 Vasvár Ger. Eisenburg. Vas, W Hungary
117 U9 Vasylivka Zaporiz'ka Oblast', SE Ukraine
117 O5 Vasyl'kiv Rus. Vasil'kov. Kyyivs'ka Oblast', N Ukraine
122 I11 Vasyugan ≈ C Russian Federation
103 N8 Vatan Indre, C France
Vaté see Efate
107 G15 Vatican City off. Vatican City State. ◆ papal state S Europe
107 M22 Vaticano, Capo headland S Italy
92 K3 Vatnajökull glacier SE Iceland
95 P15 Vätö Stockholm, C Sweden
187 Z16 Vatoa island Lau Group, SE Fiji
172 J5 Vatomandry Toamasina, E Madagascar
116 J9 Vatra Dornei Ger. Dorna Watra. Suceava, NE Romania
116 J9 Vatra Moldoviței Suceava, NE Romania
Vatter, Lake see Vättern
95 L18 Vättern Eng. Lake Vatter; prev. Lake Vetter. ◎ S Sweden
187 X5 Vatulele island SW Fiji
117 P7 Vatutine Cherkas'ka Oblast', C Ukraine
187 W15 Vatu Vara island Lau Group, E Fiji
103 R14 Vaucluse ◆ department SE France
103 S5 Vaucouleurs Meuse, NE France
108 B9 Vaud Ger. Waadt. ◆ canton SW Switzerland
15 N12 Vaudreuil Quebec, SE Canada
37 T12 Vaughn New Mexico, SW USA
54 I14 Vaupés off. Comisaría del Vaupés. ◆ province SE Colombia
54 J13 Vaupés, Río var. Rio Uaupés. ≈ Brazil/Colombia see also Uaupés, Rio
103 Q15 Vauvert Gard, S France
11 R17 Vauxhall Alberta, SW Canada
99 K23 Vaux-sur-Sûre Luxembourg, SE Belgium
172 J4 Vavatenina Toamasina, E Madagascar
193 Y14 Vava'u Group island group N Tonga
76 M16 Vavoua W Ivory Coast
129 S2 Vavozh Udmurtskaya Respublika, NW Russian Federation
155 K23 Vavuniya Northern Province, N Sri Lanka
119 G17 Vawkavysk Pol. Wołkowysk, Rus. Volkovysk. Hrodzyenskaya Voblasts', W Belarus
119 F17 Vawkavyskaye Wzvyshsha Rus. Volkovyskiye Vysoty. hill range W Belarus
95 P15 Vaxholm Stockholm, C Sweden
95 L21 Växjö var. Vexiö. Kronoberg, S Sweden
127 T1 Vaygach, Ostrov island NW Russian Federation
137 V13 Vayk' prev. Azizbekov. SE Armenia
127 P8 Vazhgort prev. Chasovo. Respublika Komi, NW Russian Federation
45 V10 V.C.Bird × (St John's) Antigua, Antigua and Barbuda
95 C16 Veavågen Rogaland, S Norway
29 Q7 Veblen South Dakota, N USA
98 N9 Vecht Ger. Vechte. ≈ Germany/Netherlands see also Vechte
100 G12 Vechta Niedersachsen, NW Germany
100 E12 Vechte Dut. Vecht. ≈ Germany/Netherlands see also Vecht
118 I8 Vecpiebalga Cēsis, C Latvia
118 G9 Vecumnieki Bauska, C Latvia
Vedāvati see Hagari
95 J20 Veddige Halland, S Sweden
116 J15 Vedea ≈ S Romania
129 P16 Vedeno Chechenskaya Respublika, SW Russian Federation
98 O6 Veendam Groningen, NE Netherlands
98 K12 Veenendaal Utrecht, C Netherlands
99 E14 Veere Zeeland, SW Netherlands
24 M2 Vega Texas, SW USA
92 E13 Vega island C Norway
45 T5 Vega Baja C Puerto Rico
38 D17 Vega Point headland Kiska Island, Alaska, USA
95 F17 Vegår ◎ S Norway
99 K14 Veghel Noord-Brabant, S Netherlands
Veglia see Krk
114 E13 Vegorítis, Límni ◎ N Greece
11 Q14 Vegreville Alberta, SW Canada
95 K21 Veinge Halland, S Sweden
61 B21 Veinticinco de Mayo var. 25 de Mayo. Buenos Aires, E Argentina
63 I14 Veinticinco de Mayo La Pampa, C Argentina
119 F15 Veisiejai Lazdijai, S Lithuania
95 F23 Vejen Ribe, W Denmark
104 K16 Vejer de la Frontera Andalucía, S Spain
95 G23 Vejle Vejle, C Denmark
95 F23 Vejle off. Vejle Amt. ◆ county C Denmark
114 M7 Vekilski Shumen, NE Bulgaria
54 G3 Vela, Cabo de la headland NE Colombia
Vela Goa see Goa
113 F15 Vela Luka Dubrovnik-Neretva, S Croatia
61 G19 Velázquez Rocha, E Uruguay
101 E15 Velbert Nordrhein-Westfalen, W Germany
109 S9 Velden Kärnten, S Austria
Veldes see Bled
99 K15 Veldhoven Noord-Brabant, S Netherlands
112 C11 Velebit ▲ C Croatia
114 N11 Veleka ≈ SE Bulgaria
109 V10 Velenje Ger. Wöllan. N Slovenia
190 E12 Vele, Pointe headland Île Futuna, S Wallis and Futuna
113 O18 Veles Turk. Köprülü. C FYR Macedonia
113 M20 Velešta SW FYR Macedonia
115 F16 Velestíno prev. Velestínon. Thessalía, C Greece
Velestínon see Velestíno
Velevshchina see Vyelyewshchyna
54 F9 Vélez Santander, C Colombia
105 Q13 Vélez Blanco Andalucía, S Spain
104 M17 Vélez de la Gomera, Peñon de island group S Spain
105 N15 Vélez-Málaga Andalucía, S Spain
105 Q13 Vélez Rubio Andalucía, S Spain
Velha Goa see Goa
Velho see Porto Velho
112 E8 Velika Gorica Zagreb, N Croatia
112 C9 Velika Kapela ▲ NW Croatia
Velika Kikinda see Kikinda
112 D10 Velika Kladuša Federacija Bosna I Hercegovina, NW Bosnia and Herzegovina
112 N11 Velika Morava var. Glavn'a Morava, Morava, Ger. Grosse Morava. ≈ C Yugoslavia
112 N12 Velika Plana Serbia, C Yugoslavia
109 U10 Velika Raduha ▲ N Slovenia
123 V7 Velikaya ≈ NE Russian Federation
126 F15 Velikaya ≈ W Russian Federation
Velikaya Berestovitsa see Vyalikaya Byerastavitsa
Velikaya Lepetikha see Velyka Lepetykha
Veliki Bečkerek see Zrenjanin
112 P12 Veliki Krš var. Stol. ▲ E Yugoslavia
114 L8 Veliki Preslav prev. Preslav. Shumen, NE Bulgaria
112 B9 Veliki Risnjak ▲ NW Croatia
109 T13 Veliki Snežnik Ger. Schneeberg, It. Monte Nevoso. ▲ SW Slovenia
112 J13 Veliki Stolac ▲ E Bosnia and Herzegovina
Velikiy Bor see Vyaliki Bor
126 G16 Velikiye Luki Pskovskaya Oblast', W Russian Federation
127 P12 Velikiy Ustyug Vologodskaya Oblast', NW Russian Federation
112 N11 Veliko Gradište Serbia, NE Yugoslavia
155 I18 Velikonda Range ▲ SE India
114 K9 Veliko Tŭrnovo prev. Tirnovo, Trnovo, Tŭrnovo. Veliko Tŭrnovo, N Bulgaria
114 K8 Veliko Tŭrnovo ◆ province N Bulgaria
Velikovec see Völkermarkt
127 R5 Velikovisochnoye Nenetskiy Avtonomnyy Okrug, NW Russian Federation
76 H12 Vélingara C Senegal
76 H11 Vélingara S Senegal
114 H11 Velingrad Pazardzhik, C Bulgaria
128 H3 Velizh Smolenskaya Oblast', W Russian Federation
111 F16 Velká Deštná var. Deštná, Grosskoppe, Ger. Deschnaer Koppe. ▲ NE Czech Republic

◆ Country ● Country Capital ◇ Dependent Territory ○ Dependent Territory Capital ◆ Administrative Region × International Airport ▲ Mountain ▲ Mountain Range Volcano ≈ River ◎ Lake ⊟ Reservoir

111 F18 **Velké Meziříčí** *Ger.* Grossmeseritsch. Jihlavský Kraj, C Czech Republic
92 N1 **Velkomstpynten** *headland* NW Svalbard
111 K21 **Veľký Krtíš** Banskobystrický Kraj, C Slovakia
186 J8 **Vella Lavella** *var.* Mbilua. *island* New Georgia Islands, NW Solomon Islands
107 I15 **Velletri** Lazio, C Italy
95 K23 **Vellinge** Skåne, S Sweden
155 I19 **Vellore** Tamil Nādu, SE India
Velobriga *see* Viana do Castelo
115 G21 **Velopoúla** *island* S Greece
98 M12 **Velp** Gelderland, SE Netherlands
Velsen *see* Velsen-Noord
98 H9 **Velsen-Noord** *var.* Velsen. Noord-Holland, W Netherlands
127 N12 **Vel'sk** *var.* Velsk. Arkhangel'skaya Oblast', NW Russian Federation
Velsuna *see* Orvieto
98 K10 **Veluwemeer** *lake channel* C Netherlands
28 M3 **Velva** North Dakota, N USA
115 E14 **Velvendós** *var.* Velvendos. Dytikí Makedonía, N Greece
117 S5 **Velyka Bahachka** Poltavs'ka Oblast', C Ukraine
117 S9 **Velyka Lepetykha** *Rus.* Velikaya Lepetikha. Khersons'ka Oblast', S Ukraine
117 O10 **Velyka Mykhaylivka** Odes'ka Oblast', SW Ukraine
117 W8 **Velyka Novosilka** Donets'ka Oblast', E Ukraine
117 S9 **Velyka Oleksandrivka** Khersons'ka Oblast', S Ukraine
117 T4 **Velyka Pysanivka** Sums'ka Oblast', NE Ukraine
116 G6 **Velykyy Bereznyy** Zakarpats'ka Oblast', W Ukraine
117 W4 **Velykyy Burluk** Kharkivs'ka Oblast', E Ukraine
Velykyy Tokmak *see* Tokmak
173 P7 **Vema Fracture Zone** *tectonic feature* W Indian Ocean
65 P18 **Vema Seamount** *undersea feature* SW Indian Ocean
93 F17 **Vemdalen** Jämtland, C Sweden
95 N19 **Vena** Kalmar, S Sweden
41 N11 **Venado** San Luis Potosí, C Mexico
62 L11 **Venado Tuerto** Entre Ríos, E Argentina
61 A19 **Venado Tuerto** Santa Fe, C Argentina
107 K16 **Venafro** Molise, C Italy
55 Q5 **Venamo, Cerro** ▲ E Venezuela
106 B8 **Venaria** Piemonte, NW Italy
103 U15 **Vence** Alpes-Maritimes, SE France
104 H5 **Venda Nova** Vila Real, N Portugal
104 G11 **Vendas Novas** Évora, S Portugal
102 J9 **Vendée** ◆ *department* NW France
103 Q6 **Vendeuvre-sur-Barse** Aube, NE France
102 M7 **Vendôme** Loir-et-Cher, C France
Venedig *see* Venezia
Vener, Lake *see* Vänern
106 I8 **Veneta, Laguna** *lagoon* NE Italy
Venetia *see* Venezia
39 S7 **Venetie** Alaska, USA
106 H8 **Veneto** *var.* Venezia Euganea. ◆ *region* NE Italy
114 M7 **Venets** Shumen, NE Bulgaria
128 L5 **Venev** Tul'skaya Oblast', W Russian Federation
106 I8 **Venezia** *Eng.* Venice, *Fr.* Venise, *Ger.* Venedig; *anc.* Venetia. Veneto, NE Italy
Venezia Euganea *see* Veneto
Venezia, Golfo di *see* Venice, Gulf of
Venezia Tridentina *see* Trentino-Alto Adige
54 K8 **Venezuela** *off.* Republic of Venezuela; *prev.* Estados Unidos de Venezuela, United States of Venezuela. ◆ *republic* N South America
Venezuela, Cordillera de *see* Costa, Cordillera de la
54 I4 **Venezuela, Golfo de** *Eng.* Gulf of Maracaibo, Gulf of Venezuela. *gulf* NW Venezuela
Venezuela, Gulf of *see* Venezuela, Golfo de
64 F11 **Venezuelan Basin** *undersea feature* E Caribbean Sea
155 D16 **Vengurla** Mahārāshtra, W India
39 O15 **Veniaminof, Mount** ▲ Alaska, USA
23 V14 **Venice** Florida, SE USA
22 L10 **Venice** Louisiana, S USA
Venice *see* Venezia
106 J8 **Venice, Gulf of** *It.* Golfo di Venezia, *Slvn.* Beneški Zaliv. *gulf* N Adriatic Sea
Venise *see* Venezia
94 K13 **Venjan** Dalarna, C Sweden
94 K13 **Venjansjön** ◎ C Sweden
155 J18 **Venkatagiri** Andhra Pradesh, E India
99 M15 **Venlo** *prev.* Venloo. Limburg, SE Netherlands
Venloo *see* Venlo
95 E18 **Vennesla** Vest-Agder, S Norway
107 M17 **Venosa** *anc.* Venusia. Basilicata, S Italy
Venoste, Alpi *see* Ötztaler Alpen
Venraij *see* Venray
99 M14 **Venray** *var.* Venraij. Limburg, SE Netherlands
118 C8 **Venta** *Ger.* Windau. ≈ Latvia/Lithuania
Venta Belgarum *see* Winchester
40 G9 **Ventana, Punta Arena de la** *var.* Punta de la Ventana. *headland* W Mexico
Ventana, Punta de la *see* Ventana, Punta Arena de la
61 B23 **Ventana, Sierra de la** *hill range* E Argentina
Ventia *see* Valence
191 S11 **Vent, Îles du** *var.* Windward Islands. *island group* Archipel de la Société, W French Polynesia
191 R10 **Vent, Îles Sous le** *var.* Leeward Islands. *island group* Archipel de la Société, W French Polynesia
106 B11 **Ventimiglia** Liguria, NW Italy
97 M24 **Ventnor** S England, UK
18 J17 **Ventnor City** New Jersey, NE USA
103 S14 **Ventoux, Mont** ▲ SE France
118 C8 **Ventspils** *Ger.* Windau. Ventspils, NW Latvia
54 M10 **Ventuari, Río** ≈ S Venezuela
35 R15 **Ventura** California, W USA
182 F8 **Venus Bay** South Australia
Venusia *see* Venosa
191 P7 **Vénus, Pointe** *var.* Pointe Tataaihoa. *headland* Tahiti, W French Polynesia
41 V16 **Venustiano Carranza** Chiapas, SE Mexico
41 N7 **Venustiano Carranza, Presa** ⊞ NE Mexico
61 B15 **Vera** Santa Fe, C Argentina
105 Q14 **Vera** Andalucía, S Spain
63 K18 **Vera, Bahía** *bay* E Argentina
41 R14 **Veracruz** *var.* Veracruz Llave. Veracruz-Llave, E Mexico
41 Q13 **Veracruz-Llave** *var.* Veracruz. ◆ *state* E Mexico
43 Q16 **Veraguas** *off.* Provincia de Veraguas. ◆ *province* W Panama
Veramin *see* Varāmīn
154 B12 **Verāval** Gujarāt, W India
106 C6 **Verbania** Piemonte, NW Italy
107 N20 **Verbicaro** Calabria, SW Italy
108 D11 **Verbier** Valais, SW Switzerland
Vercellae *see* Vercelli
106 C8 **Vercelli** *anc.* Vercellae. Piemonte, NW Italy
103 S13 **Vercors** *physical region* E France
93 E16 **Verdalsøra** Nord-Trøndelag, C Norway
Verde, Cabo *see* Cape Verde
44 J5 **Verde, Cape** *headland* Long Island, C Bahamas
104 M2 **Verde, Costa** *coastal region* N Spain
Verde Grande, Río/Verde Grande y de Belem, Río *see* Verde, Río
100 H11 **Verden** Niedersachsen, NW Germany
59 J19 **Verde, Rio** ≈ SE Brazil
57 P16 **Verde, Río** ≈ Bolivia/Brazil
40 M12 **Verde, Río** *var.* Río Verde Grande, Río Verde Grande y de Belem. ≈ C Mexico
41 Q16 **Verde, Río** ≈ SE Mexico
36 L13 **Verde River** ≈ Arizona, SW USA
Verdhikoúsa/Verdhikoússa *see* Verdikoússa
27 Q8 **Verdigris River** ≈ Kansas/Oklahoma, C USA
115 E15 **Verdikoússa** *var.* Verdhikoúsa, Verdhikoússa. Thessalía, C Greece
103 S15 **Verdon** ≈ SE France
15 O12 **Verdun** Quebec, SE Canada
103 S4 **Verdun** *var.* Verdun-sur-Meuse; *anc.* Verodunum. Meuse, NE France
Verdun-sur-Meuse *see* Verdun
83 J21 **Vereeniging** Gauteng, NE South Africa
Veremeyki *see* Vyeramyeyki
127 T14 **Vereshchagino** Permskaya Oblast', NW Russian Federation
76 G14 **Verga, Cap** *headland* W Guinea
61 G18 **Vergara** Treinta y Tres, E Uruguay
108 G11 **Vergeletto** Ticino, S Switzerland
18 L8 **Vergennes** Vermont, NE USA
Veria *see* Véroia
104 I5 **Verín** Galicia, NW Spain
Verin T'alin *see* T'alin
118 K6 **Veriora** Põlvamaa, SE Estonia
117 T7 **Verkhivtseve** Dnipropetrovs'ka Oblast', E Ukraine
129 W3 **Verkhiye Kigi** Respublika Bashkortostan, W Russian Federation
Verkhnedvinsk *see* Vyerkhnyadzvinsk
122 L10 **Verkhneimbatsk** Krasnoyarskiy Kray, N Russian Federation
126 I3 **Verkhnetulomskiy** Murmanskaya Oblast', NW Russian Federation
126 I3 **Verkhnetulomskoye Vodokhranilishche** ⊞ NW Russian Federation
Verkhneudinsk *see* Ulan-Ude
123 P10 **Verkhnevilyuysk** Respublika Sakha (Yakutiya), NE Russian Federation
129 W5 **Verkhniy Avzyan** Respublika Bashkortostan, W Russian Federation
129 Q11 **Verkhniy Baskunchak** Astrakhanskaya Oblast', SW Russian Federation
117 T9 **Verkhniy Rohachyk** Khersons'ka Oblast', S Ukraine
123 Q11 **Verkhnyaya Amga** Respublika Sakha (Yakutiya), NE Russian Federation
127 V6 **Verkhnyaya Inta** Respublika Komi, NW Russian Federation
127 O10 **Verkhnyaya Toyma** Arkhangel'skaya Oblast', NW Russian Federation
128 K6 **Verkhov'ye** Orlovskaya Oblast', W Russian Federation
116 I8 **Verkhovyna** Ivano-Frankivs'ka Oblast', W Ukraine
123 P8 **Verkhoyanskiy Khrebet** ▲ NE Russian Federation
117 T7 **Verkhn'odniprovs'k** Dnipropetrovs'ka Oblast', E Ukraine
101 G14 **Verl** Nordrhein-Westfalen, NW Germany
92 N1 **Verlegenhuken** *headland* N Svalbard
82 A9 **Vermelha, Ponta** *headland* NW Angola
103 P7 **Vermenton** Yonne, C France
11 R14 **Vermilion** Alberta, SW Canada
31 T11 **Vermilion** Ohio, N USA
22 I10 **Vermilion Bay** *bay* Louisiana, S USA
29 V4 **Vermilion Lake** ◎ Minnesota, N USA
14 F9 **Vermilion River** ≈ Ontario, S Canada
30 L12 **Vermilion River** ≈ Illinois, N USA
29 R12 **Vermillion** South Dakota, N USA
29 R12 **Vermillion River** ≈ South Dakota, N USA
15 O9 **Vermillon, Rivière** ≈ Quebec, SE Canada
115 E14 **Vérmio** ▲ N Greece
18 L8 **Vermont** *off.* State of Vermont; *also known as* The Green Mountain State. ◆ *state* NE USA
113 K16 **Vermosh** *var.* Vermoshi. Shkodër, N Albania
Vermoshi *see* Vermosh
37 O3 **Vernal** Utah, W USA
14 G11 **Verner** Ontario, S Canada
102 M5 **Verneuil-sur-Avre** Eure, N France
114 D13 **Vérno** ▲ N Greece
11 N17 **Vernon** British Columbia, SW Canada
102 M4 **Vernon** Eure, N France
23 N3 **Vernon** Alabama, S USA
31 P15 **Vernon** Indiana, N USA
25 Q4 **Vernon** Texas, SW USA
32 G10 **Vernonia** Oregon, NW USA
14 H12 **Vernon, Lake** ◎ Ontario, S Canada
22 G7 **Vernon Lake** ⊞ Louisiana, S USA
23 Y13 **Vero Beach** Florida, SE USA
Verőcze *see* Virovitica
Verodunum *see* Verdun
115 E14 **Véroia** *var.* Veria, Vérroia, *Turk.* Karaferiye. Kentrikí Makedonía, N Greece
106 E8 **Verolanuova** Lombardia, N Italy
14 K14 **Verona** Ontario, SE Canada
106 G8 **Verona** Veneto, NE Italy
29 P6 **Verona** North Dakota, N USA
30 L9 **Verona** Wisconsin, N USA
61 E20 **Verónica** Buenos Aires, E Argentina
22 J9 **Verret, Lake** ◎ Louisiana, S USA
Vérroia *see* Véroia
103 N5 **Versailles** Yvelines, N France
31 P15 **Versailles** Indiana, N USA
20 M5 **Versailles** Kentucky, S USA
27 U5 **Versailles** Missouri, C USA
31 Q13 **Versailles** Ohio, N USA
Versecz *see* Vršac
108 A10 **Versoix** Genève, SW Switzerland
15 Z6 **Verte, Pointe** *headland* Quebec, SE Canada
111 I22 **Vértes** ▲ NW Hungary
44 G6 **Vertientes** Camagüey, C Cuba
114 G13 **Vertískos** ▲ N Greece
102 I8 **Vertou** Loire-Atlantique, NW France
Verulamium *see* St Albans
99 L19 **Verviers** Liège, E Belgium
103 Y14 **Vescovato** Corse, France, C Mediterranean Sea
99 L20 **Vesdre** ≈ E Belgium
117 U10 **Vesele** *Rus.* Veseloye. Zaporiz'ka Oblast', S Ukraine
111 D18 **Veselí nad Lužnicí** *var.* Weseli an der Lainsitz, *Ger.* Frohenbruck. Budějovický Kraj, S Czech Republic
114 M9 **Veselinovo** Shumen, E Bulgaria
128 L12 **Veselovskoye Vodokhranilishche** ⊞ SW Russian Federation
Veseloye *see* Vesele
117 Q9 **Veselynove** Mykolayivs'ka Oblast', S Ukraine
Veseya *see* Vyaseyya
128 M10 **Veshenskaya** Rostovskaya Oblast', SW Russian Federation
129 Q5 **Veshkayma** Ul'yanovskaya Oblast', W Russian Federation
Vesisaari *see* Vadsø
Vesontio *see* Besançon
103 T7 **Vesoul** *anc.* Vesulium, Vesulum. Haute-Saône, E France
95 J20 **Vessigebro** Halland, S Sweden
95 D17 **Vest-Agder** ◆ *county* S Norway
23 P4 **Vestavia Hills** Alabama, S USA
84 F6 **Vesterålen** *island* NW Norway
92 G10 **Vesterålen** *island group* N Norway
87 V3 **Vestervig** Viborg, NW Denmark
92 H2 **Vestfirdhir** ◆ *region* NW Iceland
92 G11 **Vestfjorden** *fjord* C Norway
95 G16 **Vestfold** ◆ *county* S Norway
95 B18 **Vestmanna** *Dan.* Vestmanhavn Faeroe Islands
92 I4 **Vestmannaeyjar** Sudhurland, S Iceland
94 E9 **Vestnes** Møre og Romsdal, S Norway
95 I23 **Vestsjælland** *off.* Vestsjællands Amt. ◆ *county* E Denmark
92 H3 **Vesturland** ◆ *region* W Iceland
92 G11 **Vestvågøya** *island* C Norway
Vesulium/Vesulum *see* Vesoul
Vesuna *see* Périgueux
107 K17 **Vesuvio** *Eng.* Vesuvius. ☒ S Italy
Vesuvius *see* Vesuvio
126 K14 **Ves'yegonsk** Tverskaya Oblast', W Russian Federation
111 I23 **Veszprém** *Ger.* Veszprim. Veszprém, W Hungary
111 H23 **Veszprém** *off.* Veszprém Megye. ◆ *county* W Hungary
Veszprim *see* Veszprém
Vetka *see* Vyetka
95 M19 **Vetlanda** Jönköping, S Sweden
129 P1 **Vetluga** Nizhegorodskaya Oblast', W Russian Federation
127 P14 **Vetluga** ≈ NW Russian Federation
127 O14 **Vetluzhskiy** Kostromskaya Oblast', NW Russian Federation
129 P2 **Vetluzhskiy** Nizhegorodskaya Oblast', W Russian Federation
107 H14 **Vetralla** Lazio, C Italy
114 M9 **Vetren** *prev.* Zhitarovo. Burgas, E Bulgaria
114 M8 **Vetrino** Varna, E Bulgaria
Vetrino *see* Vyetryna
122 L7 **Vetrovaya, Gora** ▲ N Russian Federation
Vetter, Lake *see* Vättern
106 J13 **Vettore, Monte** ▲ C Italy
99 A17 **Veurne** *var.* Furnes. West-Vlaanderen, W Belgium
31 Q15 **Vevay** Indiana, N USA
108 C10 **Vevey** *Ger.* Vivis; *anc.* Vibiscum. Vaud, SW Switzerland
Vexiö *see* Växjö
103 S13 **Veynes** Hautes-Alpes, SE France
103 N11 **Vézère** ≈ W France
114 I9 **Vezhen** ▲ C Bulgaria
136 K11 **Vezirköprü** Samsun, N Turkey
57 J18 **Viacha** La Paz, W Bolivia
27 R10 **Vian** Oklahoma, C USA
104 H12 **Viana de Castelo** *see* Viana do Castelo
104 H12 **Viana do Alentejo** Évora, S Portugal
104 I4 **Viana do Bolo** Galicia, NW Spain
104 G5 **Viana do Castelo** *var.* Viana de Castelo; *anc.* Velobriga. Viana do Castelo, NW Portugal
104 G5 **Viana do Castelo** *var.* Viana de Castelo. ◆ *district* N Portugal
98 J12 **Vianen** Zuid-Holland, C Netherlands
167 Q8 **Viangchan** *Eng./Fr.* Vientiane. ● (Laos) C Laos
167 P6 **Viangphoukha** *var.* Vieng Pou Kha. Louang Namtha, N Laos
104 K13 **Viar** ≈ SW Spain
106 E11 **Viareggio** Toscana, C Italy
103 O14 **Viaur** ≈ S France
Vibiscum *see* Vevey
95 G21 **Viborg** Viborg, NW Denmark
29 R12 **Viborg** South Dakota, N USA
95 F21 **Viborg** *off.* Viborg Amt. ◆ *county* NW Denmark
107 N22 **Vibo Valentia** *prev.* Monteleone di Calabria; *anc.* Hipponium. Calabria, SW Italy
105 W5 **Vic** *var.* Vich; *anc.* Ausa, Vicus Ausonensis. Cataluña, NE Spain
102 K16 **Vic-en-Bigorre** Hautes-Pyrénées, S France
40 K10 **Vicente Guerrero** Durango, C Mexico
41 P10 **Vicente Guerrero, Presa** *var.* Presa de las Adjuntas. ⊞ NE Mexico
Vicentia *see* Vicenza
106 G8 **Vicenza** *anc.* Vicentia. Veneto, NE Italy
Vich *see* Vic
54 J10 **Vichada** *off.* Comisaría del Vichada. ◆ *province* E Colombia
54 K10 **Vichada, Río** ≈ E Colombia
61 G17 **Vichadero** Rivera, NE Uruguay
Vichegda *see* Vychegda
126 M16 **Vichuga** Ivanovskaya Oblast', W Russian Federation
103 P10 **Vichy** Allier, C France
26 K9 **Vici** Oklahoma, C USA
31 P10 **Vicksburg** Michigan, N USA
22 J5 **Vicksburg** Mississippi, S USA
103 O12 **Vic-sur-Cère** Cantal, C France
29 X14 **Victor** Iowa, C USA
59 I21 **Victor** Mato Grosso do Sul, SW Brazil
182 I10 **Victor Harbor** South Australia
61 C18 **Victoria** Entre Ríos, E Argentina
10 L17 **Victoria** Vancouver Island, British Columbia, SW Canada
45 R14 **Victoria** NW Grenada
42 H6 **Victoria** Yoro, NW Honduras
121 O15 **Victoria** *var.* Rabat. Gozo, NW Malta
116 I12 **Victoria** *Ger.* Viktoriastadt. Brașov, C Romania
172 H17 **Victoria** ● (Seychelles) Mahé, SW Seychelles
25 U13 **Victoria** Texas, SW USA
183 N12 **Victoria** ◆ *state* SE Australia
174 K7 **Victoria** ≈ Western Australia
Victoria *see* Labuan, East Malaysia
Victoria *see* Masvingo, Zimbabwe
Victoria Bank *see* Vitória Seamount
11 Y15 **Victoria Beach** Manitoba, S Canada
Victoria de Durango *see* Durango
Victoria de las Tunas *see* Las Tunas
83 I16 **Victoria Falls** Matabeleland North, W Zimbabwe
83 I16 **Victoria Falls** ✕ Matabeleland North, W Zimbabwe
83 I16 **Victoria Falls** *waterfall* Zambia/Zimbabwe
Victoria Falls *see* Iguaçu, Salto do
63 F19 **Victoria, Isla** *island* Archipiélago de los Chonos, S Chile
8 K6 **Victoria Island** *island* Northwest Territories/Nunavut, NW Canada
182 L8 **Victoria, Lake** ◎ New South Wales, SE Australia
68 I12 **Victoria, Lake** *var.* Victoria Nyanza. ◎ E Africa
195 S13 **Victoria Land** *physical region* Antarctica
166 L5 **Victoria, Mount** ▲ W Burma
187 X14 **Victoria, Mount** ▲ Viti Levu, W Fiji
186 E9 **Victoria, Mount** ▲ S PNG
81 F17 **Victoria Nile** *var.* Somerset Nile. ≈ C Uganda
Victoria Nyanza *see* Victoria, Lake
42 G3 **Victoria Peak** ▲ SE Belize
185 H16 **Victoria Range** ▲ South Island, NZ
181 O3 **Victoria River** ≈ Northern Territory, N Australia
181 P3 **Victoria River Roadhouse** Northern Territory, N Australia
15 Q11 **Victoriaville** Quebec, SE Canada
Victoria-Wes *see* Victoria West
83 G24 **Victoria West** *Afr.* Victoria-Wes. Northern Cape, W South Africa
62 J13 **Victorica** La Pampa, C Argentina
195 T3 **Victor, Mount** ▲ Antarctica
35 U14 **Victorville** California, W USA
62 G9 **Vicuña** Coquimbo, N Chile
62 K11 **Vicuña Mackenna** Córdoba, C Argentina
Vicus Ausonensis *see* Vic
Vicus Elbii *see* Viterbo
33 X7 **Vida** Montana, NW USA
23 V6 **Vidalia** Georgia, SE USA
22 J7 **Vidalia** Louisiana, S USA
95 F22 **Videbæk** Ringkøbing, C Denmark
60 I13 **Videira** Santa Catarina, S Brazil
116 J14 **Videle** Teleorman, S Romania
Videm-Krško *see* Krško
Víden *see* Wien
104 H12 **Vidigueira** Beja, S Portugal
114 J9 **Vidima** ≈ N Bulgaria
114 G7 **Vidin** *anc.* Bononia. Vidin, NW Bulgaria
114 F8 **Vidin** ◆ *province* NW Bulgaria
154 H10 **Vidisha** Madhya Pradesh, C India
25 Y10 **Vidor** Texas, SW USA
95 L20 **Vidöstern** ◎ S Sweden
92 J13 **Vidsel** Norrbotten, N Sweden
118 H9 **Vidzemes Augstiene** ▲ C Latvia
118 J12 **Vidzy** *Rus.* Vidzy. Vitsyebskaya Voblasts', NW Belarus
63 L16 **Viedma** Río Negro, E Argentina
63 H22 **Viedma, Lago** ◎ S Argentina
45 O11 **Vieille Case** *var.* Itassi. N Dominica
104 M2 **Vieja, Peña** ▲ N Spain
40 E4 **Viejo, Cerro** ▲ NW Mexico
56 B9 **Viejo, Cerro** ▲ N Peru
118 E10 **Viekšniai** Akmenė, NW Lithuania
105 U3 **Vielha** *var.* Viella. Cataluña, NE Spain
Viella *see* Vielha
99 L21 **Vielsalm** Luxembourg, E Belgium
Vieng Pou Kha *see* Viangphoukha
23 T6 **Vienna** Georgia, SE USA
30 L17 **Vienna** Illinois, N USA
27 V5 **Vienna** Missouri, C USA
21 Q3 **Vienna** West Virginia, NE USA
Vienna *see* Wien, Austria
Vienna *see* Vienne, France
103 R11 **Vienne** *anc.* Vienna. Isère, E France
102 L10 **Vienne** ◆ *department* W France
102 L9 **Vienne** ≈ W France
Vientiane *see* Viangchan
Vientos, Paso de los *see* Windward Passage
45 V6 **Vieques** *var.* Isabel Segunda. E Puerto Rico
45 V6 **Vieques, Isla de** *island* E Puerto Rico
45 V6 **Vieques, Pasaje de** *passage* E Puerto Rico
45 V5 **Vieques, Sonda de** *sound* E Puerto Rico
Vierdörfer *see* Săcele
93 M15 **Vieremä** Itä-Suomi, C Finland
99 M14 **Vierlingsbeek** Noord-Brabant, SE Netherlands
101 G20 **Viernheim** Hessen, W Germany
101 D15 **Viersen** Nordrhein-Westfalen, W Germany
108 G8 **Vierwaldstätter See** *Eng.* Lake of Lucerne. ◎ C Switzerland
103 N8 **Vierzon** Cher, C France
40 L8 **Viesca** Coahuila de Zaragoza, NE Mexico
118 H10 **Viesīte** *Ger.* Eckengraf. Jēkabpils, S Latvia
107 N15 **Vieste** Puglia, SE Italy
167 T8 **Vietnam** *off.* Socialist Republic of Vietnam, *Vtn.* Công Hoa Xã Hôi Chu Nghia Viêt Nam. ◆ *republic* SE Asia
167 S5 **Viêt Quang** Ha Giang, N Vietnam
Vietri *see* Viêt Tri
167 S6 **Viêt Tri** *var.* Vietri. Vinh Phu, N Vietnam
30 L4 **Vieux Desert, Lac** ◎ Michigan/Wisconsin, N USA
45 Y13 **Vieux Fort** S Saint Lucia
45 X6 **Vieux-Habitants** Basse Terre, SW Guadeloupe
119 G14 **Vievis** Kaišiadorys, S Lithuania
171 N2 **Vigan** Luzon, N Philippines
106 D8 **Vigevano** Lombardia, N Italy
107 N18 **Viggiano** Basilicata, S Italy
58 L12 **Vigia** Pará, NE Brazil
41 Y12 **Vigía Chico** Quintana Roo, SE Mexico
45 T11 **Vigie** ✕ (Castries) NE Saint Lucia
102 K17 **Vignemale** *var.* Pic de Vignemale. ▲ France/Spain
Vignemale, Pic de *see* Vignemale
106 G10 **Vignola** Emilia-Romagna, C Italy
104 G4 **Vigo** Galicia, NW Spain
104 G4 **Vigo, Ría de** *estuary* NW Spain
94 D9 **Vigra** *island* S Norway
95 C17 **Vigrestad** Rogaland, S Norway
93 L15 **Vihanti** Oulu, C Finland
149 U10 **Vihāri** Punjab, E Pakistan
102 K8 **Vihiers** Maine-et-Loire, NW France
111 O19 **Vihorlat** ▲ E Slovakia
93 L19 **Vihti** Etelä-Suomi, S Finland
Viipuri *see* Vyborg
93 M16 **Viitasaari** Länsi-Suomi, W Finland
118 K3 **Viivikonna** Ida-Virumaa, NE Estonia
155 K16 **Vijayawāda** *prev.* Bezwada. Andhra Pradesh, SE India
Vijosa/Vijosë *see* Aóos, Albania/Greece
Vijosa/Vijosë *see* Vjosës, Lumi i, Albania/Greece
Vik *see* Vikøyri
92 J4 **Vík** Sudhurland, S Iceland
94 L13 **Vika** Dalarna, C Sweden
92 L12 **Vikajärvi** Lappi, N Finland
94 L13 **Vikarbyn** Dalarna, C Sweden
95 J22 **Viken** Skåne, S Sweden
95 L17 **Viken** ◎ C Sweden
95 G15 **Vikersund** Buskerud, S Norway
114 G11 **Vikhren** ▲ SW Bulgaria
11 R15 **Viking** Alberta, SW Canada
84 E7 **Viking Bank** *undersea feature* N North Sea
95 M14 **Vikmanshyttan** Dalarna, C Sweden
94 D12 **Vikøyri** *var.* Vik. Sogn og Fjordane, S Norway
93 H17 **Viksjö** Västernorrland, C Sweden
Viktoriastadt *see* Victoria
Vila *see* Port-Vila
Vila Arriaga *see* Bibala
Vila Artur de Paiva *see* Cubango
Vila Bela da Santissima Trindade *see* Mato Grosso
58 B12 **Vila Bittencourt** Amazonas, NW Brazil
Vila da Ponte *see* Cubango
64 O2 **Vila da Praia da Vitória** Terceira, Azores, Portugal, NE Atlantic Ocean
Vila de Aljustrel *see* Cangamba
Vila de Almoster *see* Chiange
Vila de João Belo *see* Xai-Xai
Vila de Macia *see* Macia
Vila de Manhiça *see* Manhiça
Vila de Manica *see* Manica
Vila de Mocímboa da Praia *see* Mocímboa da Praia
83 N16 **Vila de Sena** *var.* Sena. Sofala, C Mozambique
104 F14 **Vila do Bispo** Faro, S Portugal
104 G6 **Vila do Conde** Porto, NW Portugal
Vila do Maio *see* Maio
64 P3 **Vila do Porto** Santa Maria, Azores, Portugal, NE Atlantic Ocean
83 K15 **Vila do Zumbo** *prev.* Vila do Zumbu, Zumbo. Tete, NW Mozambique
Vila do Zumbu *see* Vila do Zumbo
104 I6 **Vila Flor** *var.* Vila Flôr. Bragança, N Portugal
105 V6 **Vilafranca del Penedès** *var.* Villafranca del Panadés. Cataluña, NE Spain
104 F10 **Vila Franca de Xira** *var.* Vilafranca de Xira. Lisboa, C Portugal
Vila Gago Coutinho *see* Lumbala N'Guimbo
104 G3 **Vilagarcía de Arousa** *var.* Villagarcía de Arosa. Galicia, NW Spain
Vila General Machado *see* Camacupa
Vila Henrique de Carvalho *see* Saurimo
102 I7 **Vilaine** ≈ NW France
Vila João de Almeida *see* Chibia
118 K8 **Viļaka** *Ger.* Marienhausen. Balvi, NE Latvia
104 I2 **Vilalba** Galicia, NW Spain
Vila Marechal Carmona *see* Uíge
Vila Mariano Machado *see* Ganda
172 G3 **Vilanandro, Tanjona** *headland* W Madagascar
Vilanculos *see* Vilankulo
118 J10 **Viļāni** Rēzekne, E Latvia
83 N19 **Vilankulo** *var.* Vilanculos. Inhambane, E Mozambique
Vila Norton de Matos *see* Balombo
104 G6 **Vila Nova de Famalicão** *var.* Vila Nova de Famalicao. Braga, N Portugal
104 I6 **Vila Nova de Foz Côa** *var.* Vila Nova de Fozcôa. Guarda, N Portugal
104 F6 **Vila Nova de Gaia** Porto, NW Portugal
Vila Nova de Portimão *see* Portimão
105 V6 **Vilanova i La Geltrú** Cataluña, NE Spain
Vila Pereira de Eça *see* N'Giva
104 H6 **Vila Pouca de Aguiar** Vila Real, N Portugal
104 H6 **Vila Real** *var.* Vila Rial. Vila Real, N Portugal
104 H6 **Vila Real** ◆ *district* N Portugal
105 T9 **Vila-real de los Infantes** *var.* Villarreal. País Valenciano, E Spain
104 H14 **Vila Real de Santo António** Faro, S Portugal
104 J7 **Vilar Formoso** Guarda, N Portugal
Vila Rial *see* Vila Real
59 J15 **Vila Rica** Mato Grosso, W Brazil

◆ Country ● Country Capital ◇ Dependent Territory ○ Dependent Territory Capital ◆ Administrative Region ✕ International Airport ▲ Mountain ▲ Mountain Range ☒ Volcano ≈ River ◎ Lake ⊞ Reservoir

Vila Robert Williams see Caála
Vila Salazar see N'Dalatando
Vila Serpa Pinto see Menongue
Vila Teixeira da Silva see Bailundo
Vila Teixeira de Sousa see Luau
104 H9 **Vila Velha de Ródão** Castelo Branco, C Portugal
104 G5 **Vila Verde** Braga, N Portugal
104 H11 **Vila Viçosa** Évora, S Portugal
57 G15 **Vilcabamba, Cordillera de** ▲ C Peru
Vîlcea see Vâlcea
122 J4 **Vil'cheka, Zemlya** *Eng.* Wilczek Land. *island* Zemlya Frantsa-Iosifa, NW Russian Federation
95 F22 **Vildbjerg** Ringkøbing, C Denmark
Vileyka see Vilyeyka
93 H15 **Vilhelmina** Västerbotten, N Sweden
59 F17 **Vilhena** Rondônia, W Brazil
115 G19 **Vília** Attikí, C Greece
Viliya see Viliya
119 I14 **Viliya** *Lith.* Neris, *Rus.* Viliya. ~ W Belarus
Viliya see Neris
118 H5 **Viljandi** *Ger.* Fellin. Viljandimaa, S Estonia
118 H5 **Viljandimaa** *off.* Viljandi Maakond. ◆ *province* SW Estonia
119 E14 **Vilkaviškis** *Pol.* Wyłkowyszki. Vilkaviškis, SW Lithuania
118 F13 **Vilkija** Kaunas, C Lithuania
197 V9 **Vil'kitskogo, Proliv** *strait* N Russian Federation
Vilkovo see Vylkove
57 L21 **Villa Abecia** Chuquisaca, S Bolivia
41 N5 **Villa Acuña** *var.* Ciudad Acuña. Coahuila de Zaragoza, NE Mexico
40 J4 **Villa Ahumada** Chihuahua, N Mexico
45 O9 **Villa Altagracia** C Dominican Republic
56 L13 **Villa Bella** Beni, N Bolivia
104 J3 **Villablino** Castilla-León, N Spain
54 K6 **Villa Bruzual** Portuguesa, N Venezuela
105 O9 **Villacañas** Castilla-La Mancha, C Spain
105 O12 **Villacarrillo** Andalucía, S Spain
104 M7 **Villacastín** Castilla-León, N Spain
Villa Cecilia see Ciudad Madero
109 S9 **Villach** *Slvn.* Beljak. Kärnten, S Austria
107 B20 **Villacidro** Sardegna, Italy, C Mediterranean Sea
Villa Concepción see Concepción
104 L4 **Villada** Castilla-León, N Spain
40 M10 **Villa de Cos** Zacatecas, C Mexico
54 L5 **Villa de Cura** *var.* Cura. Aragua, N Venezuela
Villa del Nevoso see Ilirska Bistrica
Villa del Pilar see Pilar
104 M13 **Villa del Río** Andalucía, S Spain
Villa de Méndez see Méndez
42 H6 **Villa de San Antonio** Comayagua, W Honduras
105 N4 **Villadiego** Castilla-León, N Spain
105 T8 **Villafames** País Valenciano, E Spain
41 U16 **Villa Flores** Chiapas, SE Mexico
104 J3 **Villafranca del Bierzo** Castilla-León, N Spain
105 S8 **Villafranca del Cid** País Valenciano, E Spain
104 J11 **Villafranca de los Barros** Extremadura, W Spain
105 N10 **Villafranca de los Caballeros** Castilla-La Mancha, C Spain
Villafranca del Panadés see Vilafranca del Penedès
106 F8 **Villafranca di Verona** Veneto, NE Italy
107 J23 **Villafrati** Sicilia, Italy, C Mediterranean Sea
Villagarcía de Arosa see Vilagarcía de Arousa
41 O9 **Villagrán** Tamaulipas, C Mexico
61 C17 **Villaguay** Entre Ríos, E Argentina
62 O6 **Villa Hayes** Presidente Hayes, S Paraguay
41 U15 **Villahermosa** *prev.* San Juan Bautista. Tabasco, SE Mexico
105 O11 **Villahermosa** Castilla-La Mancha, C Spain
64 O11 **Villahermoso** Gomera, Islas Canarias, Spain, NE Atlantic Ocean
Villa Hidalgo see Hidalgo
105 T12 **Villajoyosa** *var.* La Vila Jojosa. País Valenciano, E Spain
Villa Juárez see Juárez
Villalba see Collado Villalba
41 N8 **Villaldama** Nuevo León, NE Mexico
104 L5 **Villalón de Campos** Castilla-León, N Spain
61 A25 **Villalonga** Buenos Aires, E Argentina
104 L5 **Villalpando** Castilla-León, N Spain
40 K9 **Villa Madero** *var.* Francisco I.Madero. Durango, C Mexico
41 O9 **Villa Mainero** Tamaulipas, C Mexico
Villamaña see Villamañán
104 L4 **Villamañán** *var.* Villamaña. Castilla-León, N Spain
62 L10 **Villa María** Córdoba, C Argentina
61 C17 **Villa María Grande** Entre Ríos, E Argentina
57 K21 **Villa Martín** Potosí, SW Bolivia
104 K15 **Villamartín** Andalucía, S Spain
62 J8 **Villa Mazán** La Rioja, NW Argentina
Villa Mercedes see Mercedes
Villamil see Puerto Villamil
Villa Nador see Nador
54 G5 **Villanueva** La Guajira, N Colombia
42 H5 **Villanueva** Cortés, NW Honduras
40 L11 **Villanueva** Zacatecas, C Mexico
42 I9 **Villa Nueva** Chinandega, NW Nicaragua
37 T11 **Villanueva** New Mexico, SW USA
104 M12 **Villanueva de Córdoba** Andalucía, S Spain
105 O12 **Villanueva del Arzobispo** Andalucía, S Spain
104 K11 **Villanueva de la Serena** Extremadura, W Spain
104 L5 **Villanueva del Campo** Castilla-León, N Spain
105 O11 **Villanueva de los Infantes** Castilla-La Mancha, C Spain
61 C14 **Villa Ocampo** Santa Fe, C Argentina
40 J8 **Villa Ocampo** Durango, C Mexico
40 J7 **Villa Orestes Pereyra** Durango, C Mexico
105 N3 **Villarcayo** Castilla-León, N Spain
104 L5 **Villardefrades** Castilla-León, N Spain
105 S9 **Villar del Arzobispo** País Valenciano, E Spain
105 Q6 **Villaroya de la Sierra** Aragón, NE Spain
Villarreal see Vila-real de los Infantes
62 P6 **Villarrica** Guairá, SE Paraguay
63 G15 **Villarrica, Volcán** ☒ S Chile
105 P10 **Villarrobledo** Castilla-La Mancha, C Spain
105 N10 **Villarrubia de los Ojos** Castilla-La Mancha, C Spain
18 J17 **Villas** New Jersey, NE USA
105 O3 **Villasana de Mena** Castilla-León, N Spain
107 M23 **Villa San Giovanni** Calabria, S Italy
61 D18 **Villa San José** Entre Ríos, E Argentina
Villa Sanjurjo see Al-Hoceïma
105 P6 **Villasayas** Castilla-León, N Spain
107 C20 **Villasimius** Sardegna, Italy, C Mediterranean Sea
41 N6 **Villa Unión** Coahuila de Zaragoza, NE Mexico
40 K10 **Villa Unión** Durango, C Mexico
40 J10 **Villa Unión** Sinaloa, C Mexico
62 K12 **Villa Valeria** Córdoba, C Argentina
105 N8 **Villaverde** Madrid, C Spain
54 F10 **Villavicencio** Meta, C Colombia
104 L2 **Villaviciosa** Asturias, N Spain
104 L12 **Villaviciosa de Córdoba** Andalucía, S Spain
57 L22 **Villazón** Potosí, S Bolivia
14 J8 **Villebon, Lac** ◎ Quebec, SE Canada
Ville de Kinshasa see Kinshasa
102 J5 **Villedieu-les-Poêles** Manche, N France
Villefranche see Villefranche-sur-Saône
103 N16 **Villefranche-de-Lauragais** Haute-Garonne, S France
103 N14 **Villefranche-de-Rouergue** Aveyron, S France
103 R10 **Villefranche-sur-Saône** *var.* Villefranche. Rhône, E France
14 H9 **Ville-Marie** Quebec, SE Canada
102 M15 **Villemur-sur-Tarn** Haute-Garonne, S France
105 S11 **Villena** País Valenciano, E Spain
Villeneuve-d'Agen see Villeneuve-sur-Lot
102 L13 **Villeneuve-sur-Lot** *var.* Villeneuve-d'Agen; *hist.* Gajac. Lot-et-Garonne, SW France
103 P6 **Villeneuve-sur-Yonne** Yonne, C France
22 H8 **Ville Platte** Louisiana, S USA
103 R11 **Villeurbanne** Rhône, E France
101 G23 **Villingen-Schwenningen** Baden-Württemberg, S Germany
29 T15 **Villisca** Iowa, C USA
Villmanstrand see Lappeenranta
Vilna see Vilnius
119 H14 **Vilnius** *Pol.* Wilno, *Ger.* Wilna; *prev. Rus.* Vilna. ● (Lithuania) Vilnius, SE Lithuania
119 H14 **Vilnius** ✕ Vilnius, SE Lithuania
117 S7 **Vil'nohirs'k** Dnipropetrovs'ka Oblast', E Ukraine
117 U8 **Vil'nyans'k** Zaporiz'ka Oblast', SE Ukraine
93 L17 **Vilppula** Länsi-Suomi, W Finland
101 M20 **Vils** ~ SE Germany
118 C5 **Vilsandi Saar** *island* W Estonia
117 P8 **Vil'shanka** *Rus.* Olshanka. Kirovohrads'ka Oblast', C Ukraine
101 O22 **Vilshofen** Bayern, SE Germany
155 J20 **Viluppuram** Tamil Nādu, SE India
113 I16 **Vilusi** Montenegro, SW Yugoslavia
99 G18 **Vilvoorde** *Fr.* Vilvorde. Vlaams Brabant, C Belgium
Vilvorde see Vilvoorde
119 J14 **Vilyeyka** *Pol.* Wilejka, *Rus.* Vileyka. Minskaya Voblasts', NW Belarus
123 P10 **Vilyuy** ~ NE Russian Federation
123 P10 **Vilyuysk** Respublika Sakha (Yakutiya), NE Russian Federation
123 N10 **Vilyuyskoye Vodokhranilishche** ⊠ NE Russian Federation
104 G2 **Vimianzo** Galicia, NW Spain
95 M19 **Vimmerby** Kalmar, S Sweden
102 L5 **Vimoutiers** Orne, N France
93 L16 **Vimpeli** Länsi-Suomi, W Finland
79 G14 **Vina** ~ Cameroon/Chad
62 G11 **Viña del Mar** Valparaíso, C Chile
19 R8 **Vinalhaven Island** *island* Maine, NE USA
105 T8 **Vinaròs** País Valenciano, E Spain
Vînători see Vânători
31 N15 **Vincennes** Indiana, N USA
195 Y12 **Vincennes Bay** *bay* Antarctica
25 O7 **Vincent** Texas, SW USA
95 H24 **Vindeby** Fyn, C Denmark
93 I15 **Vindeln** Västerbotten, N Sweden
95 F21 **Vinderup** Ringkøbing, C Denmark
Vindhya Mountains see Vindhya Range
153 N14 **Vindhya Range** *var.* Vindhya Mountains. ▲ N India
Vindobona see Wien
20 K6 **Vine Grove** Kentucky, S USA
18 J17 **Vineland** New Jersey, NE USA
116 E11 **Vinga** Arad, W Romania
95 M16 **Vingåker** Södermanland, C Sweden
167 S8 **Vinh** Nghê An, N Vietnam
104 I5 **Vinhais** Bragança, N Portugal
167 T9 **Vinh Linh** Quang Tri, C Vietnam
Vinh Loi see Bac Liêu
167 S14 **Vinh Long** *var.* Vinhlong. Vinh Long, S Vietnam
113 Q18 **Vinica** NE FYR Macedonia
109 V13 **Vinica** SE Slovenia
114 G8 **Vinishte** Montana, NW Bulgaria
27 Q8 **Vinita** Oklahoma, C USA
Vinju Mare see Vânju Mare
98 I11 **Vinkeveen** Utrecht, C Netherlands
116 L6 **Vin'kivtsi** Khmel'nyts'ka Oblast', W Ukraine
112 I10 **Vinkovci** *Ger.* Winkowitz, *Hung.* Vinkovcze. Vukovar-Srijem, E Croatia
Vinkovcze see Vinkovci
Vinnitsa see Vinnytsya
Vinnitskaya Oblast'/Vinnytsya see Vinnyts'ka Oblast'
116 M7 **Vinnyts'ka Oblast'** *var.* Vinnytsya, *Rus.* Vinnitskaya Oblast'. ◆ *province* C Ukraine
117 N6 **Vinnytsya** *Rus.* Vinnitsa. Vinnyts'ka Oblast', C Ukraine
117 N6 **Vinnytsya** ✕ Vinnyts'ka Oblast', N Ukraine
Vinogradov see Vynohradiv
194 L8 **Vinson Massif** ▲ Antarctica
94 G11 **Vinstra** Oppland, S Norway
116 K12 **Vintilă Vodă** Buzău, SE Romania
29 X13 **Vinton** Iowa, C USA
22 F9 **Vinton** Louisiana, S USA
155 J17 **Vinukonda** Andhra Pradesh, E India
Vioara see Ocnele Mari
83 E23 **Vioolsdrif** Northern Cape, SW South Africa
82 M13 **Viphya Mountains** ▲ C Malawi
171 Q4 **Virac** Catanduanes Island, N Philippines
126 K8 **Virandozero** Respublika Kareliya, NW Russian Federation
137 P16 **Viranşehir** Şanlıurfa, SE Turkey
154 D13 **Virār** Mahārāshtra, W India
11 W16 **Virden** Manitoba, S Canada
30 K14 **Virden** Illinois, N USA
Virdois see Virrat
102 J5 **Vire** Calvados, N France
102 J4 **Vire** ~ N France
83 A15 **Virei** Namibe, SW Angola
Vîrful Moldoveanu see Vârful Moldoveanu
35 R5 **Virgina Peak** ▲ Nevada, W USA
45 U9 **Virgin Gorda** *island* C British Virgin Islands
83 I22 **Virginia** Free State, C South Africa
30 K13 **Virginia** Illinois, N USA
29 W4 **Virginia** Minnesota, N USA
21 T6 **Virginia** *off.* Commonwealth of Virginia; also known as Mother of Presidents, Mother of States, Old Dominion. ◆ *state* NE USA
21 Y7 **Virginia Beach** Virginia, NE USA
33 R11 **Virginia City** Montana, NW USA
35 Q6 **Virginia City** Nevada, W USA
14 H8 **Virginiatown** Ontario, S Canada
Virgin Islands see British Virgin Islands
45 T9 **Virgin Islands (US)** *var.* Virgin Islands of the United States; *prev.* Danish West Indies. ◇ *US unincorporated territory* E West Indies
45 T9 **Virgin Passage** *passage* Puerto Rico/Virgin Islands (US)
35 Y10 **Virgin River** ~ Nevada/Utah, W USA
Virihaur see Virihaure
92 H12 **Virihaure** *var.* Virihaur. ◎ N Sweden
167 T11 **Virôchey** Rôtânôkiri, NE Cambodia
93 N19 **Virolahti** Etelä-Suomi, S Finland
30 J8 **Viroqua** Wisconsin, N USA
112 G8 **Virovitica** *Ger.* Virovititz, *Hung.* Verőcze; *prev. Ger.* Werowitz. Virovitica-Podravina, NE Croatia
112 G8 **Virovitica-Podravina** *off.* Virovitičko-Podravska Županija. ◆ *province* NE Croatia
Virovititz see Virovitica
113 J17 **Virpazar** Montenegro, SW Yugoslavia
93 L17 **Virrat** *Swe.* Virdois. Länsi-Suomi, SW Finland
95 M20 **Virserum** Kalmar, S Sweden
99 K25 **Virton** Luxembourg, SE Belgium
118 F5 **Virtsu** *Ger.* Werder. Läänemaa, W Estonia
56 C12 **Virú** La Libertad, C Peru
Virudhungar see Virudunagar
155 H23 **Virudunagar** *var.* Virudhungar. Tamil Nādu, SE India
118 I3 **Viru-Jaagupi** *Ger.* Sankt-Jakobi. Lääne-Virumaa, NE Estonia
57 N19 **Viru-Viru** *var.* Santa Cruz. ✕ (Santa Cruz) Santa Cruz, C Bolivia
113 E15 **Vis** *It.* Lissa; *anc.* Issa. *island* S Croatia
Vis see Fish
118 I12 **Visaginas** *prev.* Sniečkus. Ignalina, E Lithuania
155 M15 **Visākhapatnam** Andhra Pradesh, SE India
35 R11 **Visalia** California, W USA
Višău see Vişeu
95 P19 **Visby** *Ger.* Wisby. Gotland, SE Sweden
197 N9 **Viscount Melville Sound** *prev.* Melville Sound. *sound* Northwest Territories/Nunavut, N Canada
99 L19 **Visé** Liège, E Belgium
112 K13 **Višegrad** Republika Srpska, E Bosnia and Herzegovina
58 L12 **Viseu** Pará, NE Brazil
104 H7 **Viseu** *prev.* Vizeu. Viseu, N Portugal
104 H7 **Viseu** *var.* Vizeu. ◆ *district* N Portugal
116 I8 **Vişeu** *Hung.* Visó; *prev.* Vişău. ~ NW Romania
116 I8 **Vişeu de Sus** *var.* Vişeul de Sus, *Ger.* Oberwischau, *Hung.* Felsővisó. Maramureş, N Romania
Vişeul de Sus see Vişeu de Sus
127 R10 **Vishera** ~ NW Russian Federation
95 J19 **Viskafors** Västra Götaland, S Sweden
95 J20 **Viskan** ~ S Sweden
95 L21 **Vislanda** Kronoberg, S Sweden
Vislinskiy Zaliv see Vistula Lagoon
Visó see Vişeu
112 H13 **Visoko** Federacija Bosna I Hercegovina, C Bosnia and Herzegovina
106 A9 **Viso, Monte** ▲ NW Italy
108 E10 **Visp** Valais, SW Switzerland
108 E10 **Vispa** ~ S Switzerland
95 M21 **Vissefjärda** Kalmar, S Sweden
100 I11 **Visselhövede** Niedersachsen, NW Germany
95 G23 **Vissenbjerg** Fyn, C Denmark
35 U17 **Vista** California, W USA
58 C11 **Vista Alegre** Amazonas, NW Brazil
114 J13 **Vistonída, Límni** ◎ NE Greece
Vistula see Wisła
119 A14 **Vistula Lagoon** *Ger.* Frisches Haff, *Pol.* Zalew Wiślany, *Rus.* Vislinskiy Zaliv. *lagoon* Poland/Russian Federation
114 I8 **Vit** ~ NW Bulgaria
Vitebsk see Vitsyebsk
Vitebskaya Oblast' see Vitsyebskaya Voblasts'
107 H14 **Viterbo** *anc.* Vicus Elbii. Lazio, C Italy
112 H12 **Vitez** Federacija Bosna I Hercegovina, C Bosnia and Herzegovina
167 S14 **Vi Thanh** Cân Thơ, S Vietnam
Viti see Fiji
186 E7 **Vitiaz Strait** *strait* NE PNG
104 J7 **Vitigudino** Castilla-León, N Spain
187 W15 **Viti Levu** *island* W Fiji
123 O11 **Vitim** ~ C Russian Federation
123 O12 **Vitimskiy** Irkutskaya Oblast', C Russian Federation
109 V2 **Vitis** Niederösterreich, N Austria
Vitoria see Vitoria-Gasteiz
59 O20 **Vitória** Espírito Santo, SE Brazil
Vitoria Bank see Vitória Seamount
59 N18 **Vitória da Conquista** Bahia, E Brazil
105 P3 **Vitoria-Gasteiz** *var.* Vitoria, *Eng.* Vittoria. País Vasco, N Spain
65 J16 **Vitória Seamount** *var.* Victoria Bank, Vitoria Bank. *undersea feature* C Atlantic Ocean
112 F13 **Vitorog** ▲ SW Bosnia and Herzegovina
102 J6 **Vitré** Ille-et-Vilaine, NW France
103 R5 **Vitry-le-François** Marne, N France
114 D13 **Vítsoi** ▲ N Greece
118 N13 **Vitsyebsk** *Rus.* Vitebsk. Vitsyebskaya Voblasts', NE Belarus
118 K13 **Vitsyebskaya Voblasts'** *prev. Rus.* Vitebskaya Oblast'. ◆ *province* N Belarus
92 J11 **Vittangi** Norrbotten, N Sweden
103 R8 **Vitteaux** Côte d'Or, C France
103 S6 **Vittel** Vosges, NE France
95 N15 **Vittinge** Västmanland, C Sweden
107 K25 **Vittoria** Sicilia, Italy, C Mediterranean Sea
Vittoria see Vitoria-Gasteiz
106 I7 **Vittorio Veneto** Veneto, NE Italy
175 Q9 **Vitu Levu** *island* W Fiji
192 L6 **Vityaz Seamount** *undersea feature* C Pacific Ocean
175 Q7 **Vityaz Trench** *undersea feature* W Pacific Ocean
108 G8 **Vitznau** Luzern, W Switzerland
104 I1 **Viveiro** Galicia, NW Spain
105 S9 **Viver** País Valenciano, E Spain
103 Q13 **Viverais, Monts du** ▲ C France
122 L9 **Vivi** ~ N Russian Federation
22 F4 **Vivian** Louisiana, S USA
29 N10 **Vivian** South Dakota, N USA
103 R13 **Viviers** Ardèche, E France
Vivis see Vevey
83 K19 **Vivo** Northern, NE South Africa
102 L10 **Vivonne** Vienne, W France
Vizakna see Ocna Sibiului
105 O2 **Vizcaya** *Basq.* Bizkaia. ◆ *province* País Vasco, N Spain
Vizcaya, Golfo de see Biscay, Bay of
136 C10 **Vize** Kırklareli, NW Turkey
122 K4 **Vize, Ostrov** *island* Severnaya Zemlya, N Russian Federation
Vizeu see Viseu
155 M15 **Vizianagaram** *var.* Vizianagram. Andhra Pradesh, E India
Vizianagram see Vizianagaram
103 S12 **Vizille** Isère, E France
127 R11 **Vizinga** Respublika Komi, NW Russian Federation
116 M13 **Viziru** Brăila, SE Romania
113 K21 **Vjosës, Lumi i** *var.* Vijosa, Vijosë, *Gk.* Aóos. ~ Albania/Greece *see also* Aóos
99 H18 **Vlaams Brabant** ◆ *province* C Belgium
Vlaanderen see Flanders
98 G12 **Vlaardingen** Zuid-Holland, SW Netherlands
116 F10 **Vlădeasa, Vârful** *prev.* Vîrful Vlădeasa. ▲ NW Romania
Vlădeasa, Vîrful see Vlădeasa, Vârful
113 P16 **Vladičin Han** Serbia, SE Yugoslavia
129 O16 **Vladikavkaz** *prev.* Dzaudzhikau, Ordzhonikidze. Respublika Severnaya Osetiya, SW Russian Federation
128 M3 **Vladimir** Vladimirskaya Oblast', W Russian Federation
144 M7 **Vladimirovka** Kostanay, N Kazakhstan
Vladimirovka see Yuzhno-Sakhalinsk
128 L3 **Vladimirskaya Oblast'** ◆ *province* W Russian Federation
128 I3 **Vladimirskiy Tupik** Smolenskaya Oblast', W Russian Federation
Vladimir-Volynskiy see Volodymyr-Volyns'kyy
123 Q7 **Vladivostok** Primorskiy Kray, SE Russian Federation
117 U13 **Vladyslavivka** Respublika Krym, S Ukraine
98 P6 **Vlagtwedde** Groningen, NE Netherlands
Vlajna see Kukavica
112 J12 **Vlasenica** Republika Srpska, E Bosnia and Herzegovina
112 G12 **Vlašić** ▲ C Bosnia and Herzegovina
111 D17 **Vlašim** *Ger.* Wlaschim. Středočeský Kraj, C Czech Republic
113 P15 **Vlasotince** Serbia, SE Yugoslavia
123 Q7 **Vlasovo** Respublika Sakha (Yakutiya), NE Russian Federation
98 I11 **Vleuten** Utrecht, C Netherlands
98 I5 **Vlieland** *Fris.* Flylân. *island* Waddeneilanden, N Netherlands
98 I5 **Vliestroom** *strait* NW Netherlands
99 J14 **Vlijmen** Noord-Brabant, S Netherlands
99 E15 **Vlissingen** *Eng.* Flushing, *Fr.* Flessingue. Zeeland, SW Netherlands
Vlodava see Włodawa
Vlonë/Vlora see Vlorë
113 K22 **Vlorë** *prev.* Vlonë, *It.* Valona, Vlora. Vlorë, SW Albania
113 K22 **Vlorë** ◆ *district* SW Albania
113 K22 **Vlorës, Gjiri i** *var.* Valona Bay. *bay* SW Albania
Vlotslavsk see Włocławek
111 C16 **Vltava** *Ger.* Moldau. ~ W Czech Republic
128 K3 **Vnukovo** ✕ (Moskva) Gorod Moskva, W Russian Federation
25 Q9 **Voca** Texas, SW USA
109 R5 **Vöcklabruck** Oberösterreich, NW Austria
112 D13 **Vodice** Šibenik-Knin, S Croatia
126 K10 **Vodlozero, Ozero** ◎ NW Russian Federation
112 A10 **Vodnjan** *It.* Dignano d'Istria. Istra, NW Croatia
127 S9 **Vodnyy** Respublika Komi, NW Russian Federation
95 G20 **Vodskov** Nordjylland, N Denmark
92 H4 **Vogar** Sudhurland, SW Iceland
Vogelkop see Doberai, Jazirah
77 X15 **Vogel Peak** *prev.* Dim lang. ▲ E Nigeria
101 H17 **Vogelsberg** ▲ C Germany
106 D8 **Voghera** Lombardia, N Italy
112 I13 **Vogošća** Federacija Bosna I Hercegovina, SE Bosnia and Herzegovina
101 M17 **Vogtland** *historical region* E Germany
127 V12 **Vogul'skiy Kamen', Gora** ▲ NW Russian Federation
187 P16 **Voh** Province Nord, C New Caledonia
Vohémar see Iharaña
172 H8 **Vohimena, Tanjona** *Fr.* Cap Sainte Marie. *headland* S Madagascar
172 J6 **Vohipeno** Fianarantsoa, SE Madagascar
118 H5 **Võhma** *Ger.* Wöchma. Viljandimaa, S Estonia
81 J20 **Voi** Coast, S Kenya
76 K15 **Voinjama** N Liberia
103 S12 **Voiron** Isère, E France
109 V8 **Voitsberg** Steiermark, SE Austria
95 F24 **Vojens** *Ger.* Woyens. Sønderjylland, SW Denmark
112 K9 **Vojvodina** *Ger.* Wojwodina. *Region* N Yugoslavia
15 S6 **Volant** ~ Quebec, SE Canada
Volaterrae see Volterra
43 P15 **Volcán** *var.* Hato del Volcán. Chiriquí, W Panama
Volchansk see Vovchans'k
Volchya see Vovcha
94 D10 **Volda** Møre og Romsdal, S Norway
98 J9 **Volendam** Noord-Holland, C Netherlands
126 L15 **Volga** Yaroslavskaya Oblast', W Russian Federation
29 R10 **Volga** South Dakota, N USA
122 C11 **Volga** ~ NW Russian Federation
Volga-Baltic Waterway see Volgo-Baltiyskiy Kanal
Volga Hills/Volga Uplands see Privolzhskaya Vozvyshennost'
126 L13 **Volgo-Baltiyskiy Kanal** *Eng.* Volga-Baltic Waterway. *canal* NW Russian Federation
128 M12 **Volgodonsk** Rostovskaya Oblast', SW Russian Federation
129 O10 **Volgograd** *prev.* Stalingrad, Tsaritsyn. Volgogradskaya Oblast', SW Russian Federation
129 N9 **Volgogradskaya Oblast'** ◆ *province* SW Russian Federation
129 P10 **Volgogradskoye Vodokhranilishche** ⊠ SW Russian Federation
101 J19 **Volkach** Bayern, C Germany
109 U9 **Völkermarkt** *Slvn.* Velikovec. Kärnten, S Austria
126 I12 **Volkhov** Leningradskaya Oblast', NW Russian Federation
101 D20 **Völklingen** Saarland, SW Germany
Volkovysk see Vawkavysk
Volkovyskiye Vysoty see Vawkavyskaye Wzvyshsha
83 K22 **Volksrust** Mpumalanga, E South Africa
98 L8 **Vollenhove** Overijssel, N Netherlands
119 L16 **Volma** *Rus.* Volma. ~ C Belarus
Volmari see Valmiera
117 W9 **Volnovakha** Donets'ka Oblast', SE Ukraine
116 K6 **Volochys'k** Khmel'nyts'ka Oblast', W Ukraine
117 O6 **Volodarka** Kyyivs'ka Oblast', N Ukraine
117 W9 **Volodars'ke** Donets'ka Oblast', E Ukraine
129 R13 **Volodarskiy** Astrakhanskaya Oblast', SW Russian Federation
Volodarskoye see Saumalkol'
117 N8 **Volodars'k-Volyns'kyy** Zhytomyrs'ka Oblast', N Ukraine
116 K3 **Volodymerets'** Rivnens'ka Oblast', NW Ukraine
116 I3 **Volodymyr-Volyns'kyy** *Pol.* Włodzimierz, *Rus.* Vladimir-Volynskiy. Volyns'ka Oblast', NW Ukraine
126 L14 **Vologda** Vologodskaya Oblast', W Russian Federation
126 L12 **Vologodskaya Oblast'** ◆ *province* NW Russian Federation
128 K3 **Volokolamsk** Moskovskaya Oblast', W Russian Federation
128 K9 **Volokonovka** Belgorodskaya Oblast', W Russian Federation
115 G16 **Vólos** Thessalía, C Greece
126 M11 **Voloshka** Arkhangel'skaya Oblast', NW Russian Federation
Vološinovo see Novi Bečej
116 H7 **Volovets'** Zakarpats'ka Oblast', W Ukraine
114 K7 **Volovo** Ruse, N Bulgaria
Volozhin see Valozhyn
129 Q7 **Vol'sk** Saratovskaya Oblast', W Russian Federation
77 Q17 **Volta** ~ SE Ghana
Volta Blanche see White Volta
77 P16 **Volta, Lake** ⊠ SE Ghana
Volta Noire see Black Volta
60 O9 **Volta Redonda** Rio de Janeiro, SE Brazil
Volta Rouge see Red Volta
106 F12 **Volterra** *anc.* Volaterrae. Toscana, C Italy
107 K17 **Volturno** ~ S Italy
113 I15 **Volujak** ▲ SW Yugoslavia
Volunteer Island see Starbuck Island
65 F24 **Volunteer Point** *headland* East Falkland, Falkland Islands
Volunteer State see Tennessee
114 H13 **Vólvi, Límni** ◎ N Greece
Volyn see Volyns'ka Oblast'
116 I3 **Volyns'ka Oblast'** *var.* Volyn, *Rus.* Volynskaya Oblast'. ◆ *province* NW Ukraine
Volynskaya Oblast' see Volyns'ka Oblast'
129 Q3 **Volzhsk** Respublika Mariy El, W Russian Federation
129 O10 **Volzhskiy** Volgogradskaya Oblast', SW Russian Federation
172 I7 **Vondrozo** Fianarantsoa, SE Madagascar
114 K9 **Voneshta Voda** Veliko Tŭrnovo, N Bulgaria
39 P10 **Von Frank Mountain** ▲ Alaska, USA
115 C17 **Vónitsa** Dytikí Ellás, W Greece
118 J6 **Võnnu** *Ger.* Wendau. Tartumaa, SE Estonia
98 G12 **Voorburg** Zuid-Holland, W Netherlands
98 H11 **Voorschoten** Zuid-Holland, W Netherlands
98 M11 **Voorst** Gelderland, E Netherlands
98 K11 **Voorthuizen** Gelderland, C Netherlands

◆ Country ● Country Capital ◇ Dependent Territory ○ Dependent Territory Capital ◆ Administrative Region ✕ International Airport ▲ Mountain ▲ Mountain Range ☒ Volcano ~ River ◎ Lake ⊠ Reservoir

92 L2 **Vopnafjördhur** Austurland, E Iceland
92 L2 **Vopnafjördhur** *bay* E Iceland
Vora *see* Vorë
119 H15 **Voranava** *Pol.* Werenów, *Rus.* Voronovo. Hrodzyenskaya Voblasts', W Belarus
108 I8 **Vorarlberg** *off.* Land Vorarlberg. ◈ *state* W Austria
109 X7 **Vorau** Steiermark, E Austria
98 N11 **Vorden** Gelderland, E Netherlands
108 H9 **Vorderrhein** ≈ SE Switzerland
92 J2 **Vordhufell** ▲ N Iceland
95 I24 **Vordingborg** Storstrøm, SE Denmark
113 K19 **Vorë** *var.* Vora. Tiranë, W Albania
115 H17 **Vóreioi Sporádes** *var.* Vórioi Sporádhes, *Eng.* Northern Sporades. *island group* E Greece
115 J17 **Vóreion Aigaíon** *Eng.* Aegean North. ◈ *region* SE Greece
115 G18 **Voreiós Evvoïkós Kólpos** *gulf* E Greece
197 S16 **Voring Plateau** *undersea feature* N Norwegian Sea
Vórioi Sporádhes *see* Vóreioi Sporádes
127 W4 **Vorkuta** Respublika Komi, NW Russian Federation
95 I14 **Vorma** ≈ S Norway
118 E4 **Vormsi** *var.* Vormsi Saar, *Ger.* Worms, Swed. Ormsö. *island* W Estonia
Vormsi Saar *see* Vormsi
129 N7 **Vorona** ≈ W Russian Federation
128 L7 **Voronezh** Voronezhskaya Oblast', W Russian Federation
128 L7 **Voronezh** ≈ W Russian Federation
128 K8 **Voronezhskaya Oblast'** ◈ *province* W Russian Federation
Voronovitsya *see* Voronovytsya
Voronovo *see* Voranava
117 N6 **Voronovytsya** *Rus.* Voronovitsya. Vinnyts'ka Oblast', C Ukraine
122 K7 **Vorontsovo** Taymyrskiy (Dolgano-Nenetskiy) Avtonomnyy Okrug, N Russian Federation
126 K3 **Voron'ya** ≈ NW Russian Federation
Voropayevo *see* Varapayeva
Voroshilov *see* Ussuriysk
Voroshilovgrad *see* Luhans'k, Ukraine
Voroshilovgrad *see* Luhans'ka Oblast', Ukraine
Voroshilovgradskaya Oblast' *see* Luhans'ka Oblast'
Voroshilovsk *see* Stavropol', Russian Federation
Voroshilovsk *see* Alchevs'k, Ukraine
137 V13 **Vorotan** *Az.* Bärguşad. ≈ Armenia/Azerbaijan
129 P3 **Vorotynets** Nizhegorodskaya Oblast', W Russian Federation
117 S3 **Vorozhba** Sums'ka Oblast', NE Ukraine
117 T5 **Vorskla** ≈ Russian Federation/Ukraine
99 I17 **Vorst** Antwerpen, N Belgium
83 G21 **Vorstershoop** North-West, N South Africa
118 H6 **Võrtsjärv** *Ger.* Wirz-See. ◎ SE Estonia
118 J7 **Võru** *Ger.* Werro. Võrumaa, SE Estonia
147 R11 **Vorukh** N Tajikistan
118 I7 **Võrumaa** *off.* Võru Maakond. ◈ *province* SE Estonia
83 G24 **Vosburg** Northern Cape, W South Africa
147 Q14 **Vose'** *Rus.* Vose; *prev.* Aral. SW Tajikistan
103 S6 **Vosges** ◈ *department* NE France
103 U6 **Vosges** ▲▲ NE France
126 K13 **Voskresenkoye** Vologodskaya Oblast', NW Russian Federation
128 L4 **Voskresensk** Moskovskaya Oblast', W Russian Federation
129 P2 **Voskresenskoye** Nizhegorodskaya Oblast', W Russian Federation
129 V6 **Voskresenskoye** Respublika Bashkortostan, W Russian Federation
94 D13 **Voss** Hordaland, S Norway
94 D13 **Voss** *physical region* S Norway
99 I16 **Vosselaar** Antwerpen, N Belgium
94 D13 **Vosso** ≈ S Norway
Vostochno-Kazakhstanskaya Oblast' *see* Shygys Konyrat
145 T12 **Vostochno-Kounradskiy** *Kaz.* Shyghys Qongyrat. Zhezkazgan, C Kazakhstan
123 S5 **Vostochno-Sibirskoye More** *Eng.* East Siberian Sea. *sea* Arctic Ocean
145 X10 **Vostochnyy Kazakhstan** *off.* Vostochno-Kazakhstanskaya Oblast', *var.* East Kazakhstan, *Kaz.* Shyghys Qazaqastan Oblysy. ◈ *province* E Kazakhstan
Vostochnyy Sayan *see* Eastern Sayans
Vostock Island *see* Vostok Island
195 U10 **Vostok** *Russian research station* Antarctica
191 X5 **Vostok Island** *var.* Vostock Island; *prev.* Stavers Island. *island* Line Islands, SE Kiribati
129 T2 **Votkinsk** Udmurtskaya Respublika, NW Russian Federation
127 U15 **Votkinskoye Vodokhranilishche** *var.* Votkinsk Reservoir. ▣ NW Russian Federation
Votkinsk Reservoir *see* Votkinskoye Vodokhranilishche
60 J7 **Votuporanga** São Paulo, S Brazil
104 H7 **Vouga, Rio** ≈ N Portugal
115 E14 **Voúrinos** ▲ N Greece
115 G24 **Voúxa, Akrotírio** *headland* Kríti, Greece, E Mediterranean Sea
103 R4 **Vouziers** Ardennes, N France
117 V7 **Vovcha** *Rus.* Volchya. ≈ E Ukraine
117 V4 **Vovchans'k** *Rus.* Volchansk. Kharkivs'ka Oblast', E Ukraine
103 N6 **Voves** Eure-et-Loir, C France
79 M14 **Vovodo** ≈ S Central African Republic
94 M12 **Voxna** Gävleborg, C Sweden
94 L11 **Voxnan** ≈ C Sweden
114 F7 **Voynishka Reka** ≈ NW Bulgaria
127 T9 **Voyvozh** Respublika Komi, NW Russian Federation
126 M12 **Vozhega** Vologodskaya Oblast', NW Russian Federation
126 L12 **Vozhe, Ozero** ◎ NW Russian Federation
117 Q9 **Voznesens'k** *Rus.* Voznesensk. Mykolayivs'ka Oblast', S Ukraine
126 J12 **Voznesen'ye** Leningradskaya Oblast', NW Russian Federation
144 J14 **Vozrozhdeniya, Ostrov** *Uzb.* Wozrojdeniye Oroli. *island* Kazakhstan/Uzbekistan
95 G20 **Vrå** *var.* Vraa. Nordjylland, N Denmark
Vraa *see* Vrå
114 H9 **Vrachesh** Sofiya, NW Bulgaria
115 C19 **Vrachíonas** ▲ Zákynthos, Iónioi Nísoi, Greece, C Mediterranean Sea
117 P8 **Vradiyivka** Mykolayivs'ka Oblast', S Ukraine
113 G14 **Vran** ▲ SW Bosnia and Herzegovina
116 K12 **Vrancea** ◈ *county* E Romania
147 T14 **Vrang** SE Tajikistan
123 T4 **Vrangelya, Ostrov** *Eng.* Wrangel Island. *island* NE Russian Federation
112 H13 **Vranica** ▲ C Bosnia and Herzegovina
113 O16 **Vranje** Serbia, SE Yugoslavia
Vranov *see* Vranov nad Topl'ou
111 N19 **Vranov nad Topl'ou** *var.* Vranov, *Hung.* Varannó. Prešovský Kraj, E Slovakia
114 H8 **Vratsa** Vratsa, NW Bulgaria
114 H8 **Vratsa** ◈ *province* NW Bulgaria
114 F10 **Vrattsa** *prev.* Mirovo. Kyustendil, W Bulgaria
112 G11 **Vrbanja** ≈ NW Bosnia and Herzegovina
112 K9 **Vrbas** Serbia, NW Yugoslavia
112 G13 **Vrbas** ≈ N Bosnia and Herzegovina
112 E8 **Vrbovec** Zagreb, N Croatia
112 C9 **Vrbovsko** Primorje-Gorski Kotar, NW Croatia
111 E15 **Vrchlabí** *Ger.* Hohenelbe. Hradecký Kraj, NE Czech Republic
83 J22 **Vrede** Free State, E South Africa
100 E13 **Vreden** Nordrhein-Westfalen, NW Germany
83 E25 **Vredenburg** Western Cape, SW South Africa
99 I23 **Vresse-sur-Semois** Namur, SE Belgium
95 L16 **Vretstorp** Örebro, C Sweden
113 G15 **Vrgorac** *prev.* Vrhgorac. Split-Dalmacija, SE Croatia
Vrhgorac *see* Vrgorac
109 T12 **Vrhnika** *Ger.* Oberlaibach. W Slovenia
155 I21 **Vriddhāchalam** Tamil Nādu, SE India
98 N6 **Vries** Drenthe, NE Netherlands
98 O10 **Vriezenveen** Overijssel, E Netherlands
95 L20 **Vrigstad** Jönköping, S Sweden
108 H9 **Vrin** Graubünden, S Switzerland
112 E13 **Vrlika** Split-Dalmacija, S Croatia
113 M14 **Vrnjačka Banja** Serbia, C Yugoslavia
Vrondádhes/Vrondados *see* Vrontádos
115 L18 **Vrontádos** *var.* Vrondados; *prev.* Vrondádhes. Chíos, E Greece
98 N9 **Vroomshoop** Overijssel, E Netherlands
112 N10 **Vršac** *Ger.* Werschetz, *Hung.* Versecz. Serbia, NE Yugoslavia
112 M10 **Vršački Kanal** *canal* N Yugoslavia
83 H21 **Vryburg** North-West, N South Africa
83 K22 **Vryheid** KwaZulu/Natal, E South Africa
111 I18 **Vsetín** *Ger.* Wsetin. Zlínský Kraj, E Czech Republic
111 J20 **Vtáčnik** *Hung.* Madaras, Ptacsnik; *prev.* Ptačnik. ▲ W Slovakia
Vuadil' *see* Wodil
Vuanggava *see* Vuaqava
114 I11 **Vŭcha** ≈ SW Bulgaria
113 N16 **Vučitrn** Serbia, S Yugoslavia
99 J14 **Vught** Noord-Brabant, S Netherlands
117 W8 **Vuhledar** Donets'ka Oblast', E Ukraine
112 I9 **Vuka** ≈ E Croatia
113 K17 **Vukël** *var.* Vukli. Shkodër, N Albania
Vukli *see* Vukël
112 J9 **Vukovar** *Hung.* Vukovár. Vukovar-Srijem, E Croatia
112 I10 **Vukovar-Srijem** *off.* Vukovarsko-Srijemska Županija. ◈ *province* E Croatia
127 U8 **Vuktyl** Respublika Komi, NW Russian Federation
11 Q17 **Vulcan** Alberta, SW Canada
116 G12 **Vulcan** *Ger.* Wulkan, *Hung.* Zsilyvajdevulkán; *prev.* Crivadia Vulcanului, Vaidei, *Hung.* Sily-Vajdej, Vajdej. Hunedoara, W Romania
116 M12 **Vulcăneşti** *Rus.* Vulkaneshty. S Moldova
107 L22 **Vulcano, Isola** *island* Isole Eolie, S Italy
114 G7 **Vŭlchedrŭm** Montana, NW Bulgaria
114 N8 **Vŭlchidol** *prev.* Kurt-Dere. Varna, NE Bulgaria
Vulkaneshty *see* Vulcăneşti
36 J13 **Vulture Mountains** ▲▲ Arizona, SW USA
167 T14 **Vung Tau** *prev. Fr.* Cape Saint Jacques, Cap Saint-Jacques. Ba Ria-Vung Tau, S Vietnam
187 X15 **Vunisea** Kadavu, SE Fiji
Vuohčču *see* Vuotso
93 N15 **Vuokatti** Oulu, C Finland
93 M15 **Vuolijoki** Oulu, C Finland
92 J13 **Vuollerim** Norrbotten, N Sweden
Vuoreija *see* Vardø
92 L10 **Vuotso** *Lapp.* Vuohčču. Lappi, N Finland
114 J11 **Vŭrbitsa** *prev.* Filevo. Khaskovo, S Bulgaria
114 J12 **Vŭrbitsa** ≈ S Bulgaria
129 Q4 **Vurnary** Chuvashskaya Respublika, W Russian Federation
114 G8 **Vŭrshets** Montana, NW Bulgaria
119 F17 **Vyalikaya Byerastavitsa** *Pol.* Brzostowica Wielka, *Rus.* Bol'shaya Berëstovitsa; *prev.* Velikaya Berestovitsa. Hrodzyenskaya Voblasts', SW Belarus
119 N20 **Vyaliki Bor** *Rus.* Velikiy Bor. Homyel'skaya Voblasts', SE Belarus
119 J18 **Vyaliki Rozhan** *Rus.* Bol'shoy Rozhan. Minskaya Voblasts', S Belarus
126 H10 **Vyartsilya** *Fin.* Värtsilä. Respublika Kareliya, NW Russian Federation
119 K17 **Vyasyeya** *Rus.* Veseya. Minskaya Voblasts', C Belarus
127 R15 **Vyatka** ≈ NW Russian Federation
Vyatka *see* Kirov
127 S16 **Vyatskiye Polyany** Kirovskaya Oblast', NW Russian Federation
123 S14 **Vyazemskiy** Khabarovskiy Kray, SE Russian Federation
128 I4 **Vyaz'ma** Smolenskaya Oblast', W Russian Federation
129 N3 **Vyazniki** Vladimirskaya Oblast', W Russian Federation
129 O8 **Vyazovka** Volgogradskaya Oblast', SW Russian Federation
119 J14 **Vyazyn'** *Rus.* Vyazyn'. Minskaya Voblasts', NW Belarus
126 G11 **Vyborg** *Fin.* Viipuri. Leningradskaya Oblast', NW Russian Federation
127 P11 **Vychegda** *var.* Vichegda. ≈ NW Russian Federation
119 L14 **Vyelyewshchyna** *Rus.* Velevshchina. Vitsyebskaya Voblasts', N Belarus
119 P16 **Vyeramyeyki** *Rus.* Veremeyki. Mahilyowskaya Voblasts', E Belarus
118 K11 **Vyerkhnyadzvinsk** *Rus.* Verkhnedvinsk. Vitsyebskaya Voblasts', N Belarus
119 P18 **Vyetka** *Rus.* Vetka. Homyel'skaya Voblasts', SE Belarus
118 L12 **Vyetryna** *Rus.* Vetrino. Vitsyebskaya Voblasts', N Belarus
Vygonovskoye, Ozero *see* Vyhanawskaye, Vozyera
126 J9 **Vygozero, Ozero** ◎ NW Russian Federation
Vyhanashchanskaye Vozyera *see* Vyhanawskaye, Vozyera
119 I18 **Vyhanawskaye, Vozyera** *var.* Vyhanashchanskaye Vozyera, *Rus.* Ozero Vygonovskoye. ◎ SW Belarus
129 N4 **Vyksa** Nizhegorodskaya Oblast', W Russian Federation
117 O12 **Vylkove** *Rus.* Vilkovo. Odes'ka Oblast', SW Ukraine
127 R9 **Vym'** ≈ NW Russian Federation
116 H8 **Vynohradiv** *Cz.* Sevluš, *Hung.* Nagyszöllös, *Rus.* Vinogradov; *prev.* Sevlyush. Zakarpats'ka Oblast', W Ukraine
126 G13 **Vyritsa** Leningradskaya Oblast', NW Russian Federation
97 J19 **Vyrnwy** *Wel.* Afon Efyrnwy. ≈ E Wales, UK
145 X9 **Vyshe Ivanovskiy Belak, Gora** ▲ E Kazakhstan
117 P4 **Vyshhorod** Kyyivs'ka Oblast', N Ukraine
126 I15 **Vyshniy Volochek** Tverskaya Oblast', W Russian Federation
111 G18 **Vyškov** *Ger.* Wischau. Brněnský Kraz, SE Czech Republic
111 F17 **Vysoké Mýto** *Ger.* Hohenmauth. Pardubický Kraj, C Czech Republic
117 S9 **Vysokopillya** Khersons'ka Oblast', S Ukraine
128 K3 **Vysokovsk** Moskovskaya Oblast', W Russian Federation
126 K12 **Vytegra** Vologodskaya Oblast', NW Russian Federation
116 J8 **Vyzhnytsya** Chernivets'ka Oblast', W Ukraine

W

77 O14 **Wa** NW Ghana
Waadt *see* Vaud
Waag *see* Váh
Waagbistritz *see* Považská Bystrica
Waagneustadtl *see* Nové Mesto nad Váhom
81 M16 **Waajid** Gedo, SW Somalia
98 L13 **Waal** ≈ S Netherlands
187 O16 **Waala** Province Nord, W New Caledonia
99 I14 **Waalwijk** Noord-Brabant, S Netherlands
99 E16 **Waarschoot** Oost-Vlaanderen, NW Belgium
186 C7 **Wabag** Enga, W PNG
15 N7 **Wabano** ≈ Quebec, SE Canada
11 P11 **Wabasca** ≈ Alberta, SW Canada
31 P12 **Wabash** Indiana, N USA
29 X9 **Wabasha** Minnesota, N USA
31 N13 **Wabash River** ≈ N USA
14 C7 **Wabatongushi Lake** ◎ Ontario, S Canada
81 L15 **Wabē Gestro Wenz** ≈ SE Ethiopia
14 B9 **Wabos** Ontario, S Canada
11 W13 **Wabowden** Manitoba, C Canada
110 J9 **Wąbrzeźno** Kujawsko-pomorskie, N Poland
21 U12 **Waccamaw River** ≈ South Carolina, SE USA
23 U11 **Waccasassa Bay** *bay* Florida, SE USA
99 F16 **Wachtebeke** Oost-Vlaanderen, NW Belgium
25 T8 **Waco** Texas, SW USA
26 M3 **Waconda Lake** *var.* Great Elder Reservoir. ▣ Kansas, C USA
Wadai *see* Ouaddaï
Wad Al-Hajarah *see* Guadalajara
164 I12 **Wadayama** Hyōgo, Honshū, SW Japan
80 D10 **Wad Banda** Western Kordofan, C Sudan
75 P9 **Waddān** NW Libya
98 J4 **Waddeneilanden** *Eng.* West Frisian Islands. *island group* N Netherlands
98 J6 **Waddenzee** *var.* Wadden Zee. *sea* SE North Sea
10 L16 **Waddington, Mount** ▲ British Columbia, SW Canada
98 H12 **Waddinxveen** Zuid-Holland, C Netherlands
11 U15 **Wadena** Saskatchewan, S Canada
29 T6 **Wadena** Minnesota, N USA
108 G7 **Wädenswil** Zürich, N Switzerland
21 S11 **Wadesboro** North Carolina, SE USA
155 G16 **Wādi** Karnātaka, C India
138 G10 **Wādī as Sīr** *var.* Wadi es Sir. 'Ammān, NW Jordan
Wadi es Sir *see* Wādī as Sīr
80 F5 **Wadi Halfa** *var.* Wādī Ḥalfā'. Northern, N Sudan
138 G13 **Wādī Mūsā** *var.* Petra. Ma'ān, S Jordan
23 V4 **Wadley** Georgia, SE USA
Wad Madanī *see* Wad Medani
80 G10 **Wad Medani** *var.* Wad Madanī. Gezira, C Sudan
80 F10 **Wad Nimr** White Nile, C Sudan
165 U16 **Wadomari** Kagoshima, Okinoerabu-jima, SW Japan
111 K17 **Wadowice** Małopolskie, S Poland
35 R5 **Wadsworth** Nevada, W USA
31 T12 **Wadsworth** Ohio, N USA
25 T11 **Waelder** Texas, SW USA
Waereghem *see* Waregem
163 U13 **Wafangdian** *var.* Fuxian, Fu Xian. Liaoning, NE China
171 R13 **Waflia** Pulau Buru, E Indonesia
Wagadugu *see* Ouagadougou
98 K12 **Wageningen** Gelderland, SE Netherlands
55 V9 **Wageningen** Nickerie, NW Suriname
9 O8 **Wager Bay** *inlet* Nunavut, N Canada
183 P10 **Wagga Wagga** New South Wales, SE Australia
180 J13 **Wagin** Western Australia
108 H8 **Wägitaler See** ◎ SW Switzerland
29 P12 **Wagner** South Dakota, N USA
27 Q9 **Wagoner** Oklahoma, C USA
37 U10 **Wagon Mound** New Mexico, SW USA
32 J14 **Wagontire** Oregon, NW USA
110 H10 **Wągrowiec** Wielkopolskie, NW Poland
149 U6 **Wāh** Punjab, NE Pakistan
171 S13 **Wahai** Pulau Seram, E Indonesia
169 V10 **Wahau, Sungai** ≈ Borneo, C Indonesia
Wahaybah, Ramlat Al *see* Wahībah, Ramlat Āl
80 D13 **Wahda** *var.* Unity State. ◈ *state* S Sudan
38 D9 **Wahiawa** *Haw.* Wahiawā. Oahu, Hawaii, USA, C Pacific Ocean
Wahībah, Ramlat Ahl *see* Wahībah, Ramlat Āl
141 Y9 **Wahībah, Ramlat Āl** *var.* Ramlat Ahl Wahībah, Ramlat Al Wahaybah, *Eng.* Wahibah Sands. *desert* N Oman
Wahibah Sands *see* Wahībah, Ramlat Āl
101 E16 **Wahn** × (Köln) Nordrhein-Westfalen, W Germany
29 R15 **Wahoo** Nebraska, C USA
29 R6 **Wahpeton** North Dakota, N USA
Wahran *see* Oran
36 J6 **Wah Wah Mountains** ▲▲ Utah, W USA
38 D9 **Waialua** Oahu, Hawaii, USA, C Pacific Ocean
38 D9 **Waianae** *Haw.* Wai'anae. Oahu, Hawaii, USA, C Pacific Ocean
184 Q8 **Waiapu** ≈ North Island, NZ
185 I17 **Waiau** Canterbury, South Island, NZ
185 I17 **Waiau** ≈ South Island, NZ
185 B23 **Waiau** ≈ South Island, NZ
101 H21 **Waiblingen** Baden-Württemberg, S Germany
Waidhofen *see* Waidhofen an der Ybbs, Niederösterreich, Austria
Waidhofen *see* Waidhofen an der Thaya, Niederösterreich, Austria
109 V2 **Waidhofen an der Thaya** *var.* Waidhofen. Niederösterreich, NE Austria
109 U5 **Waidhofen an der Ybbs** *var.* Waidhofen. Niederösterreich, E Austria
171 T11 **Waigeo, Pulau** *island* Maluku, E Indonesia
184 L5 **Waiheke Island** *island* N NZ
184 M7 **Waihi** Waikato, North Island, NZ
185 C20 **Waihou** ≈ North Island, NZ
Waikaboebak *see* Waikabubak
170 M17 **Waikabubak** *prev.* Waikaboebak. Pulau Sumba, C Indonesia
185 D23 **Waikaia** ≈ South Island, NZ
185 D23 **Waikaka** Southland, South Island, NZ
184 L13 **Waikanae** Wellington, North Island, NZ
184 M7 **Waikare, Lake** ◎ North Island, NZ
184 O9 **Waikaremoana, Lake** ◎ North Island, NZ
185 I17 **Waikari** Canterbury, South Island, NZ
184 L8 **Waikato** *off.* Waikato Region. ◈ *region* North Island, NZ
184 M8 **Waikato** ≈ North Island, NZ
182 J9 **Waikerie** South Australia
185 F23 **Waikouaiti** Otago, South Island, NZ
38 H11 **Wailea** Hawaii, USA, C Pacific Ocean
38 F10 **Wailuku** Maui, Hawaii, USA, C Pacific Ocean
185 H18 **Waimakariri** ≈ South Island, NZ
38 D9 **Waimanalo Beach** Oahu, Hawaii, USA, C Pacific Ocean
185 G15 **Waimangaroa** West Coast, South Island, NZ
185 G21 **Waimate** Canterbury, South Island, NZ
38 G11 **Waimea** *var.* Kamuela. Hawaii, USA, C Pacific Ocean
38 D9 **Waimea** *var.* Maunawai. Oahu, Hawaii, USA, C Pacific Ocean
38 B8 **Waimea** Kauai, Hawaii, USA, C Pacific Ocean
99 M20 **Waimes** Liège, E Belgium
154 J11 **Wainganga** *var.* Wain River. ≈ C India
Waingapoe *see* Waingapu
171 N17 **Waingapu** *prev.* Waingapoe. Pulau Sumba, C Indonesia
55 S7 **Waini** ≈ N Guyana
55 S7 **Waini Point** *headland* NW Guyana
Wain River *see* Wainganga
11 R15 **Wainwright** Alberta, SW Canada
39 O5 **Wainwright** Alaska, USA
184 K4 **Waiotira** Northland, North Island, NZ
184 M11 **Waiouru** Manawatu-Wanganui, North Island, NZ
171 W14 **Waipa** Irian Jaya, E Indonesia
184 L8 **Waipa** ≈ North Island, NZ
184 P9 **Waipaoa** ≈ North Island, NZ
185 D25 **Waipapa Point** *headland* South Island, NZ
185 I18 **Waipara** Canterbury, South Island, NZ
184 N12 **Waipawa** Hawke's Bay, North Island, NZ
184 K4 **Waipu** Northland, North Island, NZ
184 N12 **Waipukurau** Hawke's Bay, North Island, NZ
171 U14 **Wair** Pulau Kai Besar, E Indonesia
Wairakai *see* Wairakei
184 N9 **Wairakei** *var.* Wairakai. Waikato, North Island, NZ
185 M14 **Wairarapa, Lake** ◎ North Island, NZ
185 J15 **Wairau** ≈ South Island, NZ
184 P10 **Wairoa** Hawke's Bay, North Island, NZ
184 P10 **Wairoa** ≈ North Island, NZ
184 J4 **Wairoa** ≈ North Island, NZ
184 N9 **Waitahanui** Waikato, North Island, NZ
184 M6 **Waitakaruru** Waikato, North Island, NZ
185 F21 **Waitaki** ≈ South Island, NZ
184 K10 **Waitara** Taranaki, North Island, NZ
184 M7 **Waitoa** Waikato, North Island, NZ
184 L8 **Waitomo Caves** Waikato, North Island, NZ
184 L11 **Waitotara** Taranaki, North Island, NZ
184 L11 **Waitotara** ≈ North Island, NZ
32 L10 **Waitsburg** Washington, NW USA
Waitzen *see* Vác
184 L6 **Waiuku** Auckland, North Island, NZ
164 L10 **Wajima** *var.* Wazima. Ishikawa, Honshū, SW Japan
81 K17 **Wajir** North Eastern, NE Kenya
81 I14 **Waka** Southern, SW Ethiopia
79 J17 **Waka** Equateur, NW Dem. Rep. Congo (Zaire)
14 D9 **Wakami Lake** ◎ Ontario, S Canada
164 I12 **Wakasa** Tottori, Honshū, SW Japan
164 J12 **Wakasa-wan** *bay* C Japan
185 C22 **Wakatipu, Lake** ◎ South Island, NZ
11 T15 **Wakaw** Saskatchewan, S Canada
164 I14 **Wakayama** Wakayama, Honshū, SW Japan
164 I15 **Wakayama** *off.* Wakayama-ken. ◈ *prefecture* Honshū, SW Japan
26 K4 **Wa Keeney** Kansas, C USA
185 I14 **Wakefield** Tasman, South Island, NZ
97 M17 **Wakefield** N England, UK
27 O4 **Wakefield** Kansas, C USA
30 L4 **Wakefield** Michigan, N USA
21 U9 **Wake Forest** North Carolina, SE USA
Wakeham Bay *see* Kangiqsujuaq
189 Y11 **Wake Island** ◇ *US unincorporated territory* NW Pacific Ocean
189 Y12 **Wake Island** × NW Pacific Ocean
189 Y12 **Wake Island** *atoll* NW Pacific Ocean
189 X12 **Wake Lagoon** *lagoon* Wake Island, NW Pacific Ocean
166 L8 **Wakema** Irrawaddy, SW Burma
Wakhan *see* Khandūd
164 H14 **Waki** Tokushima, Shikoku, SW Japan
165 T1 **Wakkanai** Hokkaidō, NE Japan
83 K22 **Wakkerstroom** Mpumalanga, E South Africa
14 C10 **Wakomata Lake** ◎ Ontario, S Canada
183 N10 **Wakool** New South Wales, SE Australia
Wakra *see* Al Wakrah
Waku Kungo *see* Uaco Cungo
186 J7 **Wakunai** Bougainville Island, NE PNG
Walachei/Walachia *see* Wallachia
155 K26 **Walawe Ganga** ≈ S Sri Lanka
111 F15 **Wałbrzych** *Ger.* Waldenburg, Waldenburg in Schlesien. Dolnośląskie, SW Poland
183 T6 **Walcha** New South Wales, SE Australia
101 K24 **Walchensee** ◎ SE Germany
99 D14 **Walcheren** *island* SW Netherlands
29 Z14 **Walcott** Iowa, C USA
33 W16 **Walcott** Wyoming, C USA
99 G21 **Walcourt** Namur, S Belgium
110 G9 **Wałcz** *Ger.* Deutsch Krone. Zachodniopomorskie, NW Poland
108 H7 **Wald** Zürich, N Switzerland
109 U3 **Waldaist** ≈ N Austria
180 I9 **Waldburg Range** ▲▲ Western Australia
37 R3 **Walden** Colorado, C USA
18 K13 **Walden** New York, NE USA
Waldenburg/Waldenburg in Schlesien *see* Wałbrzych
11 T15 **Waldheim** Saskatchewan, S Canada
Waldia *see* Weldiya
101 M23 **Waldkraiburg** Bayern, SE Germany
27 T14 **Waldo** Arkansas, C USA
23 V9 **Waldo** Florida, SE USA
19 R7 **Waldoboro** Maine, NE USA
21 W4 **Waldorf** Maryland, NE USA
32 F12 **Waldport** Oregon, NW USA
27 S11 **Waldron** Arkansas, C USA
195 Y13 **Waldron, Cape** *headland* Antarctica
101 F24 **Waldshut-Tiengen** Baden-Württemberg, S Germany
171 P12 **Walea, Selat** *strait* Sulawesi, C Indonesia
Wałeckie Międzyrzecze *see* Valašské Meziříčí
108 H8 **Walensee** ◎ NW Switzerland
38 L8 **Wales** Alaska, USA
97 J20 **Wales** *Wel.* Cymru. *national region* UK
9 O7 **Wales Island** *island* Nunavut, NE Canada
77 P14 **Walewale** N Ghana
99 M24 **Walferdange** Luxembourg, C Luxembourg
183 Q5 **Walgett** New South Wales, SE Australia
194 K10 **Walgreen Coast** *physical region* Antarctica
29 Q2 **Walhalla** North Dakota, N USA
21 O11 **Walhalla** South Carolina, SE USA
79 O19 **Walikale** Nord Kivu, E Dem. Rep. Congo (Zaire)
Walk *see* Valga, Estonia
Walk *see* Valka, Latvia
29 U5 **Walker** Minnesota, N USA
15 V4 **Walker, Lac** ◎ Quebec, SE Canada
35 S7 **Walker Lake** ◎ Nevada, W USA
35 R6 **Walker River** ≈ Nevada, W USA
28 K10 **Wall** South Dakota, N USA
173 U9 **Wallaby Plateau** *undersea feature* E Indian Ocean
33 N8 **Wallace** Idaho, NW USA
21 V11 **Wallace** North Carolina, SE USA
14 D17 **Wallaceburg** Ontario, S Canada
22 F5 **Wallace Lake** ▣ Louisiana, S USA
11 P13 **Wallace Mountain** ▲ Alberta, W Canada
116 J14 **Wallachia** *var.* Walachia, *Ger.* Walachei, *Rom.* Valachia. *cultural region* S Romania
Wallachisch-Meseritsch *see* Valašské Meziříčí
183 U4 **Wallangarra** New South Wales, SE Australia
182 I8 **Wallaroo** South Australia
32 L10 **Walla Walla** Washington, NW USA
45 V9 **Wallblake** × (The Valley) C Anguilla
101 H19 **Walldürn** Baden-Württemberg, SW Germany
100 F12 **Wallenhorst** Niedersachsen, NW Germany
Wallenthal *see* Haţeg
109 S4 **Wallern** Oberösterreich, N Austria
Wallern *see* Wallern im Burgenland
109 Z5 **Wallern im Burgenland** *var.* Wallern. Burgenland, E Austria
18 M9 **Wallingford** Vermont, NE USA
25 V11 **Wallis** Texas, SW USA
Wallis *see* Valais
192 K9 **Wallis and Futuna** *Fr.* Territoire de Wallis et Futuna. ◇ *French overseas territory* C Pacific Ocean
108 G7 **Wallisellen** Zürich, N Switzerland

◆ Country
● Country Capital
◇ Dependent Territory
○ Dependent Territory Capital
◈ Administrative Region
× International Airport
▲ Mountain
▲▲ Mountain Range
Volcano
≈ River
◎ Lake
▣ Reservoir

190 H11 **Wallis, Îles** *island group* N Wallis and Futuna
99 H19 **Wallon Brabant** ◈ *province* C Belgium
31 Q5 **Walloon Lake** ⊚ Michigan, N USA
32 K10 **Wallula** Washington, NW USA
32 K10 **Wallula, Lake** ⊚ Washington, NW USA
21 S8 **Walnut Cove** North Carolina, SE USA
35 N8 **Walnut Creek** California, W USA
26 K5 **Walnut Creek** ≈ Kansas, C USA
27 W9 **Walnut Ridge** Arkansas, C USA
25 S7 **Walnut Springs** Texas, SW USA
182 L10 **Walpeup** Victoria, SE Australia
187 R17 **Walpole, Île** *island* SE New Caledonia
39 N13 **Walrus Islands** *island group* Alaska, USA
97 L19 **Walsall** C England, UK
37 T7 **Walsenburg** Colorado, C USA
11 S17 **Walsh** Alberta, SW Canada
37 W7 **Walsh** Colorado, C USA
100 I11 **Walsrode** Niedersachsen, NW Germany
Waltenberg *see* Zalău
21 R14 **Walterboro** South Carolina, SE USA
Walter F. George Lake *see* Walter F. George Reservoir
23 R6 **Walter F. George Reservoir** *var.* Walter F. George Lake. ⊡ Alabama/Georgia, SE USA
26 M12 **Walters** Oklahoma, C USA
101 J16 **Waltershausen** Thüringen, C Germany
173 N10 **Walters Shoal** *var.* Walters Shoals. *reef* S Madagascar
Walters Shoals *see* Walters Shoal
22 M3 **Walthall** Mississippi, S USA
20 M4 **Walton** Kentucky, S USA
18 J11 **Walton** New York, NE USA
79 O20 **Walungu** Sud Kivu, E Dem. Rep. Congo (Zaire)
Walvisbaai *see* Walvis Bay
83 C19 **Walvis Bay** *Afr.* Walvisbaai. Erongo, NW Namibia
83 B19 **Walvis Bay** *bay* NW Namibia
Walvish Ridge *see* Walvis Ridge
65 O17 **Walvis Ridge** *var.* Walvish Ridge. *undersea feature* E Atlantic Ocean
171 X16 **Wamal** Irian Jaya, E Indonesia
171 U15 **Wamar, Pulau** *island* Kepulauan Aru, E Indonesia
77 V15 **Wamba** Nassarawa, C Nigeria
79 O17 **Wamba** Orientale, NE Dem. Rep. Congo (Zaire)
79 H22 **Wamba** *var.* Uamba. ≈ Angola/Dem. Rep. Congo (Zaire)
27 P4 **Wamego** Kansas, C USA
18 I10 **Wampsville** New York, NE USA
42 K6 **Wampú, Río** ≈ E Honduras
171 X16 **Wan** Irian Jaya, E Indonesia
Wan *see* Anhui
183 N4 **Wanaaring** New South Wales, SE Australia
185 D21 **Wanaka** Otago, South Island, NZ
185 D20 **Wanaka, Lake** ⊚ South Island, NZ
171 W14 **Wanapiri** Irian Jaya, E Indonesia
14 F9 **Wanapitei** ≈ Ontario, S Canada
14 F10 **Wanapitei Lake** ⊚ Ontario, S Canada
18 K14 **Wanaque** New Jersey, NE USA
171 U12 **Wanau** Irian Jaya, E Indonesia
185 F22 **Wanbrow, Cape** *headland* South Island, NZ
Wanchuan *see* Zhangjiakou
171 W13 **Wandai** *var.* Komeyo. Irian Jaya, E Indonesia
163 Z8 **Wanda Shan** ▲ NE China
197 R11 **Wandel Sea** *sea* Arctic Ocean
160 D13 **Wanding** *var.* Wandingzhen. Yunnan, SW China
Wandingzhen *see* Wanding
99 H20 **Wanfercée-Baulet** Hainaut, S Belgium
184 L12 **Wanganui** Manawatu-Wanganui, North Island, NZ
184 L11 **Wanganui** ≈ North Island, NZ
183 P11 **Wangaratta** Victoria, SE Australia
160 J8 **Wangcang** *prev.* Fengjiaba. Sichuan, C China
Wangda *see* Zogang
101 I24 **Wangen im Allgäu** Baden-Württemberg, S Germany
Wangerin *see* Węgorzyno
100 F9 **Wangerooge** *island* NW Germany
171 W13 **Wanggar** Irian Jaya, E Indonesia
160 J13 **Wangmo** *var.* Fuxing. Guizhou, S China
Wangolodougou *see* Ouangolodougou
161 S9 **Wangpan Yang** *sea* E China
163 Y10 **Wangqing** Jilin, NE China
167 P8 **Wang Saphung** Loei, C Thailand
167 O6 **Wan Hsa-la** Shan State, E Burma
55 W9 **Wanica** ◈ *district* N Suriname
79 M18 **Wanie-Rukula** Orientale, C Dem. Rep. Congo (Zaire)
Wankie *see* Hwange
Wanki, Río *see* Coco, Río
81 N17 **Wanlaweyn** *var.* Wanle Weyn, *It.* Uanle Uen. Shabeellaha Hoose, SW Somalia
Wanle Weyn *see* Wanlaweyn
180 I12 **Wanneroo** Western Australia
160 L17 **Wanning** Hainan, S China
167 Q8 **Wanon Niwat** Sakon Nakhon, E Thailand
155 H16 **Wanparti** Andhra Pradesh, C India
Wansen *see* Wiązów
160 L11 **Wanshan** Guizhou, S China
99 M14 **Wanssum** Limburg, SE Netherlands
184 N12 **Wanstead** Hawke's Bay, North Island, NZ
160 K9 **Wanxian** Chongqing Shi, C China
188 F16 **Wanyaan** Yap, Micronesia
160 K8 **Wanyuan** Sichuan, C China
161 O11 **Wanzai** Jiangxi, S China
99 J20 **Wanze** Liège, E Belgium
31 R12 **Wapakoneta** Ohio, N USA
12 D7 **Wapaseese** ≈ Ontario, C Canada
32 I10 **Wapato** Washington, NW USA
29 Y15 **Wapello** Iowa, C USA
11 N13 **Wapiti** ≈ Alberta/British Columbia, SW Canada
27 X7 **Wappapello Lake** ⊡ Missouri, C USA
18 K13 **Wappingers Falls** New York, NE USA
29 X13 **Wapsipinicon River** ≈ Iowa, C USA
14 L9 **Wapus** ≈ Quebec, SE Canada
160 H7 **Waqên** Sichuan, C China
21 Q7 **War** West Virginia, NE USA
80 D13 **Warab** Warab, SW Sudan
81 D14 **Warab** ◈ *state* SW Sudan
155 J15 **Warangal** Andhra Pradesh, C India
Warasdin *see* Varaždin
183 O16 **Waratah** Tasmania, SE Australia
183 O14 **Waratah Bay** *bay* Victoria, SE Australia
101 H15 **Warburg** Nordrhein-Westfalen, W Germany
182 I1 **Warburton Creek** *seasonal river* South Australia
180 M9 **Warburton** Western Australia
99 M20 **Warche** ≈ E Belgium
149 P5 **Wardag** *var.* Wardak, *Per.* Vardak. ◈ *province* E Afghanistan
Wardak *see* Wardag
32 K9 **Warden** Washington, NW USA
154 I12 **Wardha** Mahārāshtra, W India
121 N15 **Wardija, Ras il-** *var.* Wardija Point. *headland* Gozo, NW Malta
139 P3 **Wardīyah** N Iraq
185 E19 **Ward, Mount** ▲ South Island, NZ
10 L11 **Ware** British Columbia, W Canada
99 D18 **Waregem** *var.* Waereghem. West-Vlaanderen, W Belgium
99 J19 **Waremme** Liège, E Belgium
100 N10 **Waren** Mecklenburg-Vorpommern, NE Germany
171 W13 **Waren** Irian Jaya, E Indonesia
101 F14 **Warendorf** Nordrhein-Westfalen, W Germany
21 P12 **Ware Shoals** South Carolina, SE USA
98 N4 **Warffum** Groningen, NE Netherlands
81 O15 **Wargalo** Mudug, E Somalia
146 M12 **Warganza** *Rus.* Varganzi. Qashqadaryo Wiloyati, S Uzbekistan
Wargla *see* Ouargla
183 T4 **Warialda** New South Wales, SE Australia
154 F13 **Wāri Godri** Mahārāshtra, C India
167 R10 **Warin Chamrap** Ubon Ratchathani, E Thailand
25 R11 **Waring** Texas, SW USA
39 O8 **Waring Mountains** ▲▲ Alaska, USA
110 M12 **Warka** Mazowieckie, E Poland
184 L5 **Warkworth** Auckland, North Island, NZ
171 U12 **Warmandi** Irian Jaya, E Indonesia
83 E22 **Warmbad** Karas, S Namibia
98 H8 **Warmenhuizen** Noord-Holland, NW Netherlands
110 L8 **Warmińsko-Mazurskie** ◈ *province* NW Poland
97 L22 **Warminster** S England, UK
18 I15 **Warminster** Pennsylvania, NE USA
35 V8 **Warm Springs** Nevada, W USA
32 H12 **Warm Springs** Oregon, NW USA
21 S5 **Warm Springs** Virginia, NE USA
100 M8 **Warnemünde** Mecklenburg-Vorpommern, NE Germany
27 Q10 **Warner** Oklahoma, C USA
35 Q2 **Warner Mountains** ▲▲ California, W USA
23 T5 **Warner Robins** Georgia, SE USA
57 N18 **Warnes** Santa Cruz, C Bolivia
100 M9 **Warnow** ≈ NE Germany
Warnsdorf *see* Varnsdorf
98 M11 **Warnsveld** Gelderland, E Netherlands
154 I13 **Warora** Mahārāshtra, C India
182 L11 **Warracknabeal** Victoria, SE Australia
183 O13 **Warragul** Victoria, SE Australia
183 O4 **Warrego River** *seasonal river* New South Wales/Queensland, E Australia
183 Q6 **Warren** New South Wales, SE Australia
11 X16 **Warren** Manitoba, S Canada
27 V14 **Warren** Arkansas, C USA
31 S10 **Warren** Michigan, N USA
29 R3 **Warren** Minnesota, N USA
31 U11 **Warren** Ohio, N USA
18 D12 **Warren** Pennsylvania, NE USA
25 X10 **Warren** Texas, SW USA
97 G16 **Warrenpoint** *Ir.* An Pointe. SE Northern Ireland, UK
27 S4 **Warrensburg** Missouri, C USA
83 H22 **Warrenton** Northern Cape, N South Africa
23 U4 **Warrenton** Georgia, SE USA
27 W4 **Warrenton** Missouri, C USA
21 V8 **Warrenton** North Carolina, SE USA
21 V4 **Warrenton** Virginia, NE USA
77 U17 **Warri** Delta, S Nigeria
97 L18 **Warrington** C England, UK
23 O9 **Warrington** Florida, SE USA
23 P3 **Warrior** Alabama, S USA
182 L13 **Warrnambool** Victoria, SE Australia
29 T2 **Warroad** Minnesota, N USA
183 S6 **Warrumbungle Range** ▲▲ New South Wales, SE Australia
154 J12 **Wārsa** Mahārāshtra, C India
31 P11 **Warsaw** Indiana, N USA
20 L4 **Warsaw** Kentucky, S USA
27 T5 **Warsaw** Missouri, C USA
18 E10 **Warsaw** New York, NE USA
21 V10 **Warsaw** North Carolina, SE USA
21 X5 **Warsaw** Virginia, NE USA
Warsaw/Warschau *see* Warszawa
81 N17 **Warshiikh** Shabeellaha Dhexe, C Somalia
101 G15 **Warstein** Nordrhein-Westfalen, W Germany
110 M11 **Warszawa** *Eng.* Warsaw, *Ger.* Warschau, *Rus.* Varshava. ● (Poland) Mazowieckie, C Poland
110 J13 **Warta** Sieradz, C Poland
110 D11 **Warta** *Ger.* Warthe. ≈ W Poland
Wartberg *see* Senec
20 M9 **Wartburg** Tennessee, S USA
108 J7 **Warth** Vorarlberg, NW Austria
Warthe *see* Warta
169 U12 **Waru** Borneo, C Indonesia
171 T13 **Waru** Pulau Seram, E Indonesia
139 N6 **Wa'r, Wādī al** *dry watercourse* E Syria
183 U3 **Warwick** Queensland, E Australia
15 Q11 **Warwick** Quebec, SE Canada
97 M20 **Warwick** C England, UK
18 K13 **Warwick** New York, NE USA
29 P4 **Warwick** North Dakota, N USA
19 O12 **Warwick** Rhode Island, NE USA
97 L20 **Warwickshire** *cultural region* C England, UK
14 G14 **Wasaga Beach** Ontario, S Canada
77 U13 **Wasagu** Kebbi, NW Nigeria
36 M2 **Wasatch Range** ▲▲ W USA
35 R12 **Wasco** California, W USA
29 V10 **Waseca** Minnesota, N USA
14 H13 **Washago** Ontario, S Canada
19 S2 **Washburn** Maine, NE USA
28 M5 **Washburn** North Dakota, N USA
30 K3 **Washburn** Wisconsin, N USA
31 S14 **Washburn Hill** *hill* Ohio, N USA
154 H13 **Wāshīm** Mahārāshtra, C India
97 M14 **Washington** NE England, UK
23 U3 **Washington** Georgia, SE USA
30 L12 **Washington** Illinois, N USA
31 N15 **Washington** Indiana, N USA
29 X15 **Washington** Iowa, C USA
27 O3 **Washington** Kansas, C USA
27 W5 **Washington** Missouri, C USA
21 X9 **Washington** North Carolina, SE USA
18 B15 **Washington** Pennsylvania, NE USA
25 V10 **Washington** Texas, SW USA
36 J8 **Washington** Utah, W USA
21 V4 **Washington** Virginia, NE USA
32 I9 **Washington** *off.* State of Washington; also known as Chinook State, Evergreen State. ◈ *state* NW USA
Washington *see* Washington Court House
31 S14 **Washington Court House** *var.* Washington. Ohio, NE USA
21 W4 **Washington DC** ● (USA) District of Columbia, NE USA
31 O5 **Washington Island** *island* Wisconsin, N USA
Washington Island *see* Teraina
19 O7 **Washington, Mount** ▲ New Hampshire, NE USA
26 M11 **Washita River** ≈ Oklahoma/Texas, C USA
97 O18 **Wash, The** *inlet* E England, UK
32 L9 **Washtucna** Washington, NW USA
Wasiliszki *see* Vasilishki
110 P9 **Wasilków** Podlaskie, NE Poland
39 R11 **Wasilla** Alaska, USA
55 U9 **Wasjabo** Sipaliwini, NW Suriname
11 X11 **Waskaiowaka Lake** ⊚ Manitoba, C Canada
11 T14 **Waskesiu Lake** Saskatchewan, C Canada
25 X7 **Waskom** Texas, SW USA
110 G13 **Wąsosz** Dolnośląskie, SW Poland
42 M6 **Waspam** *var.* Waspán. Región Autónoma Atlántico Norte, NE Nicaragua
Waspán *see* Waspam
165 T3 **Wassamu** Hokkaidō, NE Japan
108 G9 **Wassen** Uri, C Switzerland
98 G11 **Wassenaar** Zuid-Holland, W Netherlands
99 N24 **Wasserbillig** Grevenmacher, E Luxembourg
Wasserburg *see* Wasserburg am Inn
101 M23 **Wasserburg am Inn** *var.* Wasserburg. Bayern, SE Germany
101 I17 **Wasserkuppe** ▲ C Germany
103 R5 **Wassy** Haute-Marne, N France
171 N14 **Watampone** *var.* Bone. Sulawesi, C Indonesia
171 R13 **Watawa** Pulau Buru, E Indonesia
Watenstedt-Salzgitter *see* Salzgitter
18 M13 **Waterbury** Connecticut, NE USA
21 R11 **Wateree Lake** ⊡ South Carolina, SE USA
21 R12 **Wateree River** ≈ South Carolina, SE USA
97 E20 **Waterford** *Ir.* Port Láirge. S Ireland
31 S9 **Waterford** Michigan, N USA
97 E20 **Waterford** *Ir.* Port Láirge. *cultural region* S Ireland
97 E21 **Waterford Harbour** *Ir.* Cuan Phort Láirge. *inlet* S Ireland
98 G12 **Wateringen** Zuid-Holland, W Netherlands
99 G19 **Waterloo** Wallon Brabant, C Belgium
14 F16 **Waterloo** Ontario, S Canada
15 P12 **Waterloo** Quebec, SE Canada
30 K16 **Waterloo** Illinois, N USA
29 X13 **Waterloo** Iowa, C USA
18 G10 **Waterloo** New York, NE USA
30 L4 **Watersmeet** Michigan, N USA
23 V9 **Watertown** Florida, SE USA
18 I8 **Watertown** New York, NE USA
29 R9 **Watertown** South Dakota, N USA
30 M8 **Watertown** Wisconsin, N USA
22 L3 **Water Valley** Mississippi, S USA
27 O3 **Waterville** Kansas, C USA
17 V6 **Waterville** Maine, NE USA
29 V10 **Waterville** Minnesota, N USA
18 I10 **Waterville** New York, NE USA
14 E16 **Watford** Ontario, S Canada
97 N21 **Watford** SE England, UK
28 K4 **Watford City** North Dakota, N USA
141 X12 **Wāṭif** S Oman
18 G11 **Watkins Glen** New York, NE USA
Watlings Island *see* San Salvador
171 U15 **Watnil** Pulau Kai Kecil, E Indonesia
26 M10 **Watonga** Oklahoma, C USA
11 T16 **Watrous** Saskatchewan, S Canada
37 T10 **Watrous** New Mexico, SW USA
79 P16 **Watsa** Orientale, NE Dem. Rep. Congo (Zaire)
31 N12 **Watseka** Illinois, N USA
79 J19 **Watsikengo** Equateur, C Dem. Rep. Congo (Zaire)
182 C5 **Watson** South Australia
11 U15 **Watson** Saskatchewan, S Canada
195 O10 **Watson Escarpment** ▲ Antarctica
10 K9 **Watson Lake** Yukon Territory, W Canada
35 N10 **Watsonville** California, W USA
167 Q8 **Wattay** ✕ (Viangchan) Viangchan, C Laos
109 N7 **Wattens** Tirol, W Austria
20 M9 **Watts Bar Lake** ⊡ Tennessee, S USA
108 H7 **Wattwil** Sankt Gallen, NE Switzerland
171 T14 **Watubela, Kepulauan** *island group* E Indonesia
101 N24 **Watzmann** ▲ SE Germany
186 E8 **Wau** Morobe, C PNG
81 D14 **Wau** *var.* Wāw. Western Bahr el Ghazal, S Sudan
29 Q8 **Waubay** South Dakota, N USA
29 Q8 **Waubay Lake** ⊚ South Dakota, N USA
183 U7 **Wauchope** New South Wales, SE Australia
23 W13 **Wauchula** Florida, SE USA
30 M10 **Wauconda** Illinois, N USA
182 J7 **Waukaringa** South Australia
31 N10 **Waukegan** Illinois, N USA
30 M9 **Waukesha** Wisconsin, N USA
29 X11 **Waukon** Iowa, C USA
30 L8 **Waunakee** Wisconsin, N USA
30 L7 **Waupaca** Wisconsin, N USA
30 M8 **Waupun** Wisconsin, N USA
26 M13 **Waurika** Oklahoma, C USA
26 M12 **Waurika Lake** ⊡ Oklahoma, C USA
30 L6 **Wausau** Wisconsin, N USA
31 R11 **Wauseon** Ohio, N USA
30 L7 **Wautoma** Wisconsin, N USA
30 M9 **Wauwatosa** Wisconsin, N USA
22 L9 **Waveland** Mississippi, S USA
97 Q20 **Waveney** ≈ E England, UK
184 L11 **Waverley** Taranaki, North Island, NZ
29 W12 **Waverly** Iowa, C USA
27 T4 **Waverly** Missouri, C USA
29 R15 **Waverly** Nebraska, C USA
18 G12 **Waverly** New York, NE USA
20 H8 **Waverly** Tennessee, S USA
21 W7 **Waverly** Virginia, NE USA
99 H19 **Wavre** Wallon Brabant, C Belgium
166 M8 **Waw** Pegu, SW Burma
Wāw *see* Wau
14 B7 **Wawa** Ontario, S Canada
77 T14 **Wawa** Niger, W Nigeria
75 Q11 **Wāw al Kabīr** S Libya
43 N7 **Wawa, Río** *var.* Rio Huahua. ≈ NE Nicaragua
186 B8 **Wawoi** ≈ SW PNG
25 T7 **Waxahachie** Texas, SW USA
158 L9 **Waxxari** Xinjiang Uygur Zizhiqu, NW China
23 V7 **Waycross** Georgia, SE USA
180 K10 **Way, Lake** ⊚ Western Australia
31 P9 **Wayland** Michigan, N USA
29 R13 **Wayne** Nebraska, C USA
18 K14 **Wayne** New Jersey, NE USA
21 P5 **Wayne** West Virginia, NE USA
23 V4 **Waynesboro** Georgia, SE USA
22 M7 **Waynesboro** Mississippi, S USA
20 H10 **Waynesboro** Tennessee, S USA
21 U5 **Waynesboro** Virginia, NE USA
18 B16 **Waynesburg** Pennsylvania, NE USA
27 U6 **Waynesville** Missouri, C USA
21 O10 **Waynesville** North Carolina, SE USA
26 L8 **Waynoka** Oklahoma, C USA
Wazan *see* Ouazzane
Wazima *see* Wajima
149 V7 **Wazīrābād** Punjab, NE Pakistan
Wazzan *see* Ouazzane
110 I8 **Wda** *var.* Czarna Woda, *Ger.* Schwarzwasser. ≈ N Poland
187 Q16 **Wé** Province des Îles Loyauté, E New Caledonia
97 O23 **Weald, The** *lowlands* SE England, UK
186 A9 **Weam** Western, SW PNG
97 L15 **Wear** ≈ N England, UK
Wearmouth *see* Sunderland
26 L10 **Weatherford** Oklahoma, C USA
25 S6 **Weatherford** Texas, SW USA
34 M3 **Weaverville** California, W USA
27 R7 **Webb City** Missouri, C USA
192 G8 **Weber Basin** *undersea feature* S Ceram Sea
Webfoot State *see* Oregon
18 F9 **Webster** New York, NE USA
29 Q8 **Webster** South Dakota, N USA
29 V13 **Webster City** Iowa, C USA
27 X5 **Webster Groves** Missouri, C USA
21 S4 **Webster Springs** *var.* Addison. West Virginia, NE USA
171 S11 **Weda, Teluk** *bay* Pulau Halmahera, E Indonesia
65 B25 **Weddell Island** *var.* Isla San Jose. *Island* W Falkland Islands
65 K22 **Weddell Plain** *undersea feature* SW Atlantic Ocean
65 K23 **Weddell Sea** *sea* SW Atlantic Ocean
65 B25 **Weddell Settlement** Weddell Island, W Falkland Islands
182 M11 **Wedderburn** Victoria, SE Australia
100 I9 **Wedel** Schleswig-Holstein, N Germany
92 N3 **Wedel Jarlsberg Land** *physical region* SW Svalbard
100 I12 **Wedemark** Niedersachsen, NW Germany
10 M17 **Wedge Mountain** ▲ British Columbia, SW Canada
23 R4 **Wedowee** Alabama, S USA
171 U15 **Weduar** Pulau Kai Besar, E Indonesia
35 N2 **Weed** California, W USA
15 Q12 **Weedon Centre** Quebec, SE Canada
18 E13 **Weedville** Pennsylvania, NE USA
100 F10 **Weener** Niedersachsen, NW Germany
29 S16 **Weeping Water** Nebraska, C USA
99 L16 **Weert** Limburg, SE Netherlands
98 I10 **Weesp** Noord-Holland, C Netherlands
183 S5 **Wee Waa** New South Wales, SE Australia
110 N7 **Węgorzewo** *Ger.* Angerburg. Warmińsko-Mazurskie, NE Poland
110 E9 **Węgorzyno** *Ger.* Wangerin. Zachodniopomorskie, NW Poland
110 N11 **Węgrów** *Ger.* Bingerau. Mazowieckie, E Poland
98 N5 **Wehe-Den Hoorn** Groningen, NE Netherlands
98 M12 **Wehl** Gelderland, E Netherlands
Wehlau *see* Znamensk
168 F7 **Weh, Pulau** *island* NW Indonesia
Wei *see* Weifang
161 P1 **Weichang** *prev.* Zhuizishan. Hebei, E China
Weichsel *see* Wisła
101 M16 **Weida** Thüringen, C Germany
Weiden *see* Weiden in der Oberpfalz
101 M19 **Weiden in der Oberpfalz** *var.* Weiden. Bayern, SE Germany
161 Q4 **Weifang** *var.* Wei, Wei-fang; *prev.* Weihsien. Shandong, E China
161 S4 **Weihai** Shandong, E China
160 K6 **Wei He** ≈ C China
Weihsien *see* Weifang
101 G17 **Weilburg** Hessen, W Germany
101 K24 **Weilheim** Bayern, SE Germany
183 P4 **Weilmoringle** New South Wales, SE Australia
101 L16 **Weimar** Thüringen, C Germany
25 U11 **Weimar** Texas, SW USA
160 L6 **Weinan** Shaanxi, C China
108 H6 **Weinfelden** Thurgau, NE Switzerland
101 I24 **Weingarten** Baden-Württemberg, S Germany
101 G20 **Weinheim** Baden-Württemberg, SW Germany
160 H11 **Weining** *var.* Weining Yizu Huizu Miaozu Zizhixian. Guizhou, S China
Weining Yizu Huizu Miaozu Zizhixian *see* Weining
181 V2 **Weipa** Queensland, NE Australia
11 Y11 **Weir River** Manitoba, C Canada
21 R1 **Weirton** West Virginia, NE USA
32 M13 **Weiser** Idaho, NW USA
160 F12 **Weishan** Yunnan, SW China
161 P6 **Weishan Hu** ⊚ E China
101 M15 **Weisse Elster** *Eng.* White Elster. ≈ Czech Republic/Germany
Weisse Körös/Weisse Kreisch *see* Crişul Alb
108 L7 **Weissenbach am Lech** Tirol, W Austria
101 K21 **Weissenburg** Bayern, SE Germany
Weissenburg *see* Wissembourg, France
Weissenburg *see* Alba Iulia, Romania
101 M15 **Weissenfels** *var.* Weißenfels. Sachsen-Anhalt, C Germany
109 R9 **Weissensee** ⊚ S Austria
Weissenstein *see* Paide
108 E11 **Weisshorn** *var.* Flüela Wisshorn. ▲ SW Switzerland
Weisskirchen *see* Bela Crkva
23 R3 **Weiss Lake** ⊡ Alabama, S USA
101 Q14 **Weisswasser** *Lus.* Běla Woda. Sachsen, E Germany
99 M22 **Weiswampach** Diekirch, N Luxembourg
109 U2 **Weitra** Niederösterreich, N Austria
161 O4 **Weixian** *var.* Wei Xian. Hebei, E China
159 V11 **Weiyuan** Gansu, C China
160 F14 **Weiyuan Jiang** ≈ SW China
109 W7 **Weiz** Steiermark, SE Austria
160 K16 **Weizhou Dao** *island* S China
110 I6 **Wejherowo** Pomorskie, NW Poland
27 Q8 **Welch** Oklahoma, C USA
24 M6 **Welch** Texas, SW USA
21 Q6 **Welch** West Virginia, NE USA
45 O14 **Welchman Hall** C Barbados
80 J11 **Weldiya** *var.* Waldia, *It.* Valdia. Amhara, N Ethiopia
21 W8 **Weldon** North Carolina, SE USA
25 V9 **Weldon** Texas, SW USA
99 M19 **Welkenraedt** Liège, E Belgium
193 O2 **Welker Seamount** *undersea feature* N Pacific Ocean
83 I22 **Welkom** Free State, C South Africa
14 H16 **Welland** Ontario, S Canada
14 G16 **Welland** ≈ Ontario, S Canada
97 O19 **Welland** ≈ C England, UK
14 H17 **Welland Canal** *canal* Ontario, S Canada
155 K25 **Wellawaya** Uva Province, SE Sri Lanka
Welle *see* Uele
181 T4 **Wellesley Islands** *island group* Queensland, N Australia
99 J22 **Wellin** Luxembourg, SE Belgium
97 N20 **Wellingborough** C England, UK
183 R7 **Wellington** New South Wales, SE Australia
14 J15 **Wellington** Ontario, SE Canada
185 L14 **Wellington** ● (NZ) Wellington, North Island, NZ
83 E26 **Wellington** Western Cape, SW South Africa
37 T2 **Wellington** Colorado, C USA
27 N7 **Wellington** Kansas, C USA
35 R7 **Wellington** Nevada, W USA
31 T11 **Wellington** Ohio, N USA
25 P3 **Wellington** Texas, SW USA
36 M4 **Wellington** Utah, W USA
185 M14 **Wellington** *off.* Wellington Region. ◈ *region* North Island, NZ
185 L14 **Wellington** ✕ Wellington, North Island, NZ
Wellington *see* Wellington, Isla
63 F22 **Wellington, Isla** *var.* Wellington. *island* S Chile
183 P12 **Wellington, Lake** ⊚ Victoria, SE Australia
29 X14 **Wellman** Iowa, C USA
24 M6 **Wellman** Texas, SW USA
97 K22 **Wells** SW England, UK
29 V11 **Wells** Minnesota, N USA
35 X2 **Wells** Nevada, W USA
25 W8 **Wells** Texas, SW USA
18 F12 **Wellsboro** Pennsylvania, NE USA
21 R1 **Wellsburg** West Virginia, NE USA
184 K4 **Wellsford** Auckland, North Island, NZ
180 L9 **Wells, Lake** ⊚ Western Australia
181 N4 **Wells, Mount** ▲ Western Australia
97 P18 **Wells-next-the-Sea** E England, UK
31 T15 **Wellston** Ohio, N USA
27 O10 **Wellston** Oklahoma, C USA
18 E11 **Wellsville** New York, NE USA
31 V12 **Wellsville** Ohio, N USA
36 L1 **Wellsville** Utah, W USA
36 I14 **Wellton** Arizona, SW USA
109 S4 **Wels** *anc.* Ovilava. Oberösterreich, N Austria
99 K15 **Welschap** ✕ (Eindhoven) Noord-Brabant, S Netherlands
100 P10 **Welse** ≈ NE Germany
22 H9 **Welsh** Louisiana, S USA
97 K19 **Welshpool** *Wel.* Y Trallwng. E Wales, UK
97 O21 **Welwyn Garden City** SE England, UK
79 K18 **Wema** Equateur, NW Dem. Rep. Congo (Zaire)
81 G21 **Wembere** ≈ C Tanzania
11 N13 **Wembley** Alberta, W Canada
12 I9 **Wemindji** *prev.* Nouveau-Comptoir, Paint Hills. Quebec, C Canada
99 G18 **Wemmel** Vlaams Brabant, C Belgium
32 J8 **Wenatchee** Washington, NW USA
160 M17 **Wenchang** Hainan, S China
161 R11 **Wencheng** *prev.* Daxue. Zhejiang, SE China
77 P16 **Wenchi** W Ghana
Wen-chou/Wenchow *see* Wenzhou
160 H8 **Wenchuan** *prev.* Weizhou. Sichuan, C China
Wendau *see* Võnnu
Wenden *see* Cēsis
161 S4 **Wendeng** Shandong, E China
81 J14 **Wendo** Southern, S Ethiopia
36 J2 **Wendover** Utah, W USA
14 D9 **Wenebegon** ≈ Ontario, S Canada
14 D8 **Wenebegon Lake** ⊚ Ontario, S Canada
108 E9 **Wengen** Bern, W Switzerland

◆ Country ● Country Capital ◇ Dependent Territory ○ Dependent Territory Capital ◈ Administrative Region ✕ International Airport ▲ Mountain ▲▲ Mountain Range ⩘ Volcano ≈ River ⊚ Lake ⊡ Reservoir

161 O13 **Wengyuan** *prev.* Longxian. Guangdong, S China
189 P15 **Weno** *prev.* Moen. Chuuk, C Micronesia
189 V12 **Weno** *prev.* Moen. *atoll* Chuuk Islands, C Micronesia
158 N13 **Wenquan** Qinghai, C China
159 H4 **Wenquan** *var.* Arixang. Xinjiang Uygur Zizhiqu, NW China
160 H14 **Wenshan** Yunnan, SW China
158 H6 **Wensu** Xinjiang Uygur Zizhiqu, W China
182 L8 **Wentworth** New South Wales, SE Australia
27 W4 **Wentzville** Missouri, C USA
159 V12 **Wenxian** *var.* Wen Xian. Gansu, C China
161 S10 **Wenzhou** *var.* Wen-chou, Wenchow. Zhejiang, SE China
34 L4 **Weott** California, W USA
99 I20 **Wépion** Namur, SE Belgium
100 O11 **Werbellinsee** ◎ NE Germany
99 L21 **Werbomont** Liège, E Belgium
83 G20 **Werda** Kgalagadi, S Botswana
Werder *see* Virtsu
81 N14 **Werdër** Somalil, E Ethiopia
Werenów *see* Voranava
171 U13 **Weri** Irian Jaya, E Indonesia
98 I13 **Werkendam** Noord-Brabant, S Netherlands
101 M20 **Wernberg-Köblitz** Bayern, SE Germany
101 J18 **Werneck** Bayern, C Germany
101 K14 **Wernigerode** Sachsen-Anhalt, C Germany
Werowitz *see* Virovitica
101 J16 **Werra** ≈ C Germany
183 N12 **Werribee** Victoria, SE Australia
183 T6 **Werris Creek** New South Wales, SE Australia
Werro *see* Võru
Werschetz *see* Vršac
101 K23 **Wertach** ≈ S Germany
101 I19 **Wertheim** Baden-Württemberg, SW Germany
98 J8 **Wervershoof** Noord-Holland, NW Netherlands
Wervicq *see* Wervik
99 C18 **Wervik** *var.* Wervicq, Werwick. West-Vlaanderen, W Belgium
Werwick *see* Wervik
101 D14 **Wesel** Nordrhein-Westfalen, W Germany
Weseli an der Lainsitz *see* Veselí nad Lužnicí
Wesenberg *see* Rakvere
100 H12 **Weser** ≈ NW Germany
Wes-Kaap *see* Western Cape
25 S17 **Weslaco** Texas, SW USA
14 J13 **Weslemkoon Lake** ◎ Ontario, SE Canada
181 R1 **Wessel Islands** *island group* Northern Territory, N Australia
29 P9 **Wessington** South Dakota, N USA
29 P10 **Wessington Springs** South Dakota, N USA
25 T8 **West** Texas, SW USA
West *see* Ouest
30 M9 **West Allis** Wisconsin, N USA
182 E8 **Westall, Point** *headland* South Australia
West Antarctica *see* Lesser Antarctica
14 G11 **West Arm** Ontario, S Canada
West Azerbaijan *see* Āzarbāyjān-e Gharbī
138 F10 **West Bank** *disputed region* SW Asia
11 N17 **Westbank** British Columbia, SW Canada
14 E11 **West Bay** Manitoulin Island, Ontario, S Canada
22 L11 **West Bay** *bay* Louisiana, S USA
30 M8 **West Bend** Wisconsin, N USA
153 R16 **West Bengal** ◈ *state* NE India
West Borneo *see* Kalimantan Barat
29 Y14 **West Branch** Iowa, C USA
31 R7 **West Branch** Michigan, N USA
18 F13 **West Branch Susquehanna River** ≈ Pennsylvania, NE USA
97 L20 **West Bromwich** C England, UK
19 P8 **Westbrook** Maine, NE USA
29 T10 **Westbrook** Minnesota, N USA
29 Y15 **West Burlington** Iowa, C USA
96 L2 **West Burra** *island* NE Scotland, UK
30 J8 **Westby** Wisconsin, N USA
44 L6 **West Caicos** *island* W Turks and Caicos Islands
185 A24 **West Cape** *headland* South Island, NZ
174 L4 **West Caroline Basin** *undersea feature* SW Pacific Ocean
18 I16 **West Chester** Pennsylvania, NE USA
185 E18 **West Coast** *off.* West Coast Region. ◈ *region* South Island, NZ
25 V12 **West Columbia** Texas, SW USA
29 W10 **West Concord** Minnesota, N USA
29 V14 **West Des Moines** Iowa, C USA
37 Q6 **West Elk Peak** ▲ Colorado, C USA
44 F1 **West End** Grand Bahama Island, N Bahamas
44 F1 **West End Point** *headland* Grand Bahama Island, N Bahamas
98 O7 **Westerbork** Drenthe, NE Netherlands
98 N3 **Westereems** *strait* Germany/Netherlands
98 O9 **Westerhaar-Vriezenveensewijk** Overijssel, E Netherlands
100 G6 **Westerland** Schleswig-Holstein, N Germany
99 I17 **Westerlo** Antwerpen, N Belgium
19 N13 **Westerly** Rhode Island, NE USA
81 G18 **Western** ◈ *province* W Kenya
153 N11 **Western** ◈ *zone* C Nepal
186 A8 **Western** ◈ *province* SW PNG
186 J8 **Western** *off.* Western Province. ◈ *province* NW Solomon Islands
83 G15 **Western** ◈ *province* SW Zambia
180 K8 **Western Australia** ◈ *state* W Australia
80 A13 **Western Bahr el Ghazal** ◈ *state* SW Sudan
Western Bug *see* Bug
83 F25 **Western Cape** *off.* Western Cape Province, *Afr.* Wes-Kaap. ◈ *province* SW South Africa
80 A11 **Western Darfur** ◈ *state* W Sudan
Western Desert *see* Sahara el Gharbîya
118 G9 **Western Dvina** *Bel.* Dzvina, *Ger.* Düna, *Latv.* Daugava, *Rus.* Zapadnaya Dvina. ≈ W Europe
81 D15 **Western Equatoria** ◈ *state* SW Sudan
155 E16 **Western Ghats** ▲▲ SW India
186 C7 **Western Highlands** ◈ *province* C PNG
Western Isles *see* Outer Hebrides
80 C12 **Western Kordofan** ◈ *state* C Sudan
21 T3 **Westernport** Maryland, NE USA
155 J26 **Western Province** ◈ *province* SW Sri Lanka
74 B10 **Western Sahara** ◇ *disputed territory* N Africa
Western Samoa *see* Samoa
Western Sayans *see* Zapadnyy Sayan
Western Scheldt *see* Westerschelde
Western Sierra Madre *see* Madre Occidental, Sierra
99 E15 **Westerschelde** *Eng.* Western Scheldt; *prev.* Honte. *inlet* S North Sea
31 S13 **Westerville** Ohio, N USA
101 F17 **Westerwald** ▲▲ W Germany
65 C25 **West Falkland** *var.* Gran Malvina, Isla Gran Malvina. *island* W Falkland Islands
29 R5 **West Fargo** North Dakota, N USA
188 M15 **West Fayu Atoll** *atoll* Caroline Islands, C Micronesia
18 C11 **Westfield** New York, NE USA
30 L7 **Westfield** Wisconsin, N USA
West Flanders *see* West-Vlaanderen
27 S10 **West Fork** Arkansas, C USA
29 P16 **West Fork Big Blue River** ≈ Nebraska, C USA
29 U12 **West Fork Des Moines River** ≈ Iowa/Minnesota, C USA
25 S5 **West Fork Trinity River** ≈ Texas, SW USA
30 L16 **West Frankfort** Illinois, N USA
98 I8 **West-Friesland** *physical region* NW Netherlands
West Frisian Islands *see* Waddeneilanden
19 T5 **West Grand Lake** ◎ Maine, NE USA
18 M12 **West Hartford** Connecticut, NE USA
18 M13 **West Haven** Connecticut, NE USA
27 X12 **West Helena** Arkansas, C USA
28 M2 **Westhope** North Dakota, N USA
195 Y8 **West Ice Shelf** *ice shelf* Antarctica
47 R2 **West Indies** *island group* SE North America
West Irian *see* Irian Jaya
West Java *see* Jawa Barat
36 L3 **West Jordan** Utah, W USA
West Kalimantan *see* Kalimantan Barat
99 D14 **Westkapelle** Zeeland, SW Netherlands
31 O13 **West Lafayette** Indiana, N USA
31 T13 **West Lafayette** Ohio, N USA
West Lake *see* Kagera
29 Y14 **West Liberty** Iowa, C USA
21 O5 **West Liberty** Kentucky, S USA
Westliche Morava *see* Zapadna Morava
8 J13 **Westlock** Alberta, SW Canada
14 E17 **West Lorne** Ontario, S Canada
96 J12 **West Lothian** *cultural region* S Scotland, UK
99 H16 **Westmalle** Antwerpen, N Belgium
192 G6 **West Mariana Basin** *var.* Perece Vela Basin. *undersea feature* W Pacific Ocean
97 E17 **Westmeath** *Ir.* An Iarmhí, Na h-Iarmhidhe. *cultural region* C Ireland
27 Y11 **West Memphis** Arkansas, C USA
21 W2 **Westminster** Maryland, NE USA
21 O11 **Westminster** South Carolina, SE USA
22 I5 **West Monroe** Louisiana, S USA
18 D15 **Westmont** Pennsylvania, NE USA
27 O3 **Westmoreland** Kansas, C USA
35 W17 **Westmorland** California, W USA
186 E6 **West New Britain** ◈ *province* E PNG
West New Guinea *see* Irian Jaya
83 K18 **West Nicholson** Matabeleland South, S Zimbabwe
29 T14 **West Nishnabotna River** ≈ Iowa, C USA
175 P11 **West Norfolk Ridge** *undersea feature* W Pacific Ocean
25 P12 **West Nueces River** ≈ Texas, SW USA
West Nusa Tenggara *see* Nusa Tenggara Barat
29 T11 **West Okoboji Lake** ◎ Iowa, C USA
33 R16 **Weston** Idaho, NW USA
21 R4 **Weston** West Virginia, NE USA
97 J22 **Weston-super-Mare** SW England, UK
23 Z14 **West Palm Beach** Florida, SE USA
West Papua *see* Irian Jaya
188 E9 **West Passage** *passage* Babeldaob, N Palau
23 O9 **West Pensacola** Florida, SE USA
27 V8 **West Plains** Missouri, C USA
35 P7 **West Point** California, W USA
23 R5 **West Point** Georgia, SE USA
22 M3 **West Point** Mississippi, S USA
29 R14 **West Point** Nebraska, C USA
21 X6 **West Point** Virginia, NE USA
182 G10 **West Point** *headland* South Australia
65 B24 **Westpoint Island Settlement** Westpoint Island, NW Falkland Islands
23 R4 **West Point Lake** ⊞ Alabama/Georgia, SE USA
97 B16 **Westport** *Ir.* Cathair na Mart. W Ireland
185 G15 **Westport** West Coast, South Island, NZ
32 F10 **Westport** Oregon, NW USA
32 F9 **Westport** Washington, NW USA
31 S15 **West Portsmouth** Ohio, N USA
West Punjab *see* Punjab
11 V14 **Westray** Manitoba, C Canada
96 J4 **Westray** *island* NE Scotland, UK
14 F9 **Westree** Ontario, S Canada
97 L16 **West Riding** *cultural region* N England, UK
West River *see* Xi Jiang
30 J7 **West Salem** Wisconsin, N USA
65 H21 **West Scotia Ridge** *undersea feature* W Scotia Sea
West Sepik *see* Sandaun
173 N4 **West Sheba Ridge** *undersea feature* W Indian Ocean
West Siberian Plain *see* Zapadno-Sibirskaya Ravnina
31 S11 **West Sister Island** *island* Ohio, N USA
West-Skylge *see* West-Terschelling
West Sumatra *see* Sumatera Barat
98 J5 **West-Terschelling** *Fris.* West-Skylge. Friesland, N Netherlands
64 J7 **West Thulean Rise** *undersea feature* N Atlantic Ocean
29 X12 **West Union** Iowa, C USA
31 R15 **West Union** Ohio, N USA
21 R3 **West Union** West Virginia, NE USA
31 N13 **Westville** Illinois, N USA
21 R3 **West Virginia** *off.* State of West Virginia; also known as The Mountain State. ◈ *state* NE USA
99 A17 **West-Vlaanderen** *Eng.* West Flanders. ◈ *province* W Belgium
35 R7 **West Walker River** ≈ California/Nevada, W USA
35 P4 **Westwood** California, W USA
183 P9 **West Wyalong** New South Wales, SE Australia
171 Q16 **Wetar, Pulau** *island* Kepulauan Damar, E Indonesia
171 R16 **Wetar, Selat** *var.* Wetar Strait. *strait* Nusa Tenggara, S Indonesia
Wetar Strait *see* Wetar, Selat
11 Q15 **Wetaskiwin** Alberta, SW Canada
81 K21 **Wete** Pemba, E Tanzania
166 M4 **Wetlet** Sagaing, C Burma
37 T6 **Wet Mountains** ▲▲ Colorado, C USA
101 E15 **Wetter** Nordrhein-Westfalen, W Germany
101 H17 **Wetter** ≈ W Germany
99 F17 **Wetteren** Oost-Vlaanderen, NW Belgium
108 F7 **Wettingen** Aargau, N Switzerland
27 P11 **Wetumka** Oklahoma, C USA
23 Q5 **Wetumpka** Alabama, S USA
108 G7 **Wetzikon** Zürich, N Switzerland
101 G17 **Wetzlar** Hessen, W Germany
99 C18 **Wevelgem** West-Vlaanderen, W Belgium
38 M6 **Wevok** *var.* Wewuk. Alaska, USA
23 R9 **Wewahitchka** Florida, SE USA
186 C6 **Wewak** East Sepik, NW PNG
27 O11 **Wewoka** Oklahoma, C USA
Wewuk *see* Wevok
97 F20 **Wexford** *Ir.* Loch Garman. SE Ireland
97 F20 **Wexford** *Ir.* Loch Garman. *cultural region* SE Ireland
30 L7 **Weyauwega** Wisconsin, N USA
11 U17 **Weyburn** Saskatchewan, S Canada
Weyer *see* Weyer Markt
109 U5 **Weyer Markt** *var.* Weyer. Oberösterreich, N Austria
100 H11 **Weyhe** Niedersachsen, NW Germany
97 L24 **Weymouth** S England, UK
19 P11 **Weymouth** Massachusetts, NE USA
99 H18 **Wezembeek-Oppem** Vlaams Brabant, C Belgium
98 M9 **Wezep** Gelderland, E Netherlands
184 M9 **Whakamaru** Waikato, North Island, NZ
184 O8 **Whakatane** Bay of Plenty, North Island, NZ
184 O8 **Whakatane** ≈ North Island, NZ
9 O9 **Whale Cove** Nunavut, C Canada
96 M2 **Whalsay** *island* NE Scotland, UK
184 L11 **Whangaehu** ≈ North Island, NZ
184 M6 **Whangamata** Waikato, North Island, NZ
184 Q9 **Whangara** Gisborne, North Island, NZ
184 K3 **Whangarei** Northland, North Island, NZ
184 K3 **Whangaruru Harbour** *inlet* North Island, NZ
25 V12 **Wharton** Texas, SW USA
173 U8 **Wharton Basin** *var.* West Australian Basin. *undersea feature* E Indian Ocean
185 E18 **Whataroa** West Coast, South Island, NZ
8 K10 **Wha Ti** *prev.* Lac La Martre. Northwest Territories, W Canada
184 K6 **Whatipu** Auckland, North Island, NZ
33 Y16 **Wheatland** Wyoming, C USA
14 D18 **Wheatley** Ontario, S Canada
30 M10 **Wheaton** Illinois, N USA
29 R7 **Wheaton** Minnesota, N USA
37 T4 **Wheat Ridge** Colorado, C USA
25 P2 **Wheeler** Texas, SW USA
23 O2 **Wheeler Lake** ⊞ Alabama, S USA
35 Y6 **Wheeler Peak** ▲ Nevada, W USA
37 T9 **Wheeler Peak** ▲ New Mexico, SW USA
31 S15 **Wheelersburg** Ohio, N USA
21 R2 **Wheeling** West Virginia, NE USA
97 L16 **Whernside** ▲ N England, UK
182 F9 **Whidbey, Point** *headland* South Australia
180 I7 **Whim Creek** Western Australia
10 L17 **Whistler** British Columbia, SW Canada
21 W8 **Whitakers** North Carolina, SE USA
14 H15 **Whitby** Ontario, S Canada
97 N15 **Whitby** N England, UK
10 G6 **White** ≈ Yukon Territory, W Canada
13 T11 **White Bay** *bay* Newfoundland, E Canada
20 I8 **White Bluff** Tennessee, S USA
28 J6 **White Butte** ▲ North Dakota, N USA
19 R5 **White Cap Mountain** ▲ Maine, NE USA
22 J9 **White Castle** Louisiana, S USA
182 M5 **White Cliffs** New South Wales, SE Australia
31 P8 **White Cloud** Michigan, N USA
11 P14 **Whitecourt** Alberta, SW Canada
25 O2 **White Deer** Texas, SW USA
White Elster *see* Weisse Elster
24 M5 **Whiteface** Texas, SW USA
18 K7 **Whiteface Mountain** ▲ New York, NE USA
29 W5 **Whiteface Reservoir** ⊞ Minnesota, N USA
33 O7 **Whitefish** Montana, NW USA
31 N9 **Whitefish Bay** Wisconsin, N USA
31 Q3 **Whitefish Bay** *lake bay* Canada/USA
14 E11 **Whitefish Falls** Ontario, S Canada
14 B7 **Whitefish Lake** ◎ Ontario, S Canada
29 U6 **Whitefish Lake** ◎ Minnesota, C USA
31 Q3 **Whitefish Point** *headland* Michigan, N USA
31 O4 **Whitefish River** ≈ Michigan, N USA
25 O4 **Whiteflat** Texas, SW USA
27 V12 **White Hall** Arkansas, C USA
30 K14 **White Hall** Illinois, N USA
31 O8 **Whitehall** Michigan, N USA
18 L9 **Whitehall** New York, NE USA
31 S13 **Whitehall** Ohio, N USA
30 J7 **Whitehall** Wisconsin, N USA
97 J15 **Whitehaven** NW England, UK
10 I8 **Whitehorse** *territory capital* Yukon Territory, W Canada
184 O7 **White Island** *island* NE NZ
14 K13 **White Lake** ◎ Ontario, SE Canada
22 H10 **White Lake** ◎ Louisiana, S USA
186 G7 **Whiteman Range** ▲▲ New Britain, E PNG
183 Q15 **Whitemark** Tasmania, SE Australia
35 S9 **White Mountains** ▲▲ California/Nevada, W USA
19 N7 **White Mountains** ▲▲ Maine/New Hampshire, NE USA
80 F11 **White Nile** ◈ *state* C Sudan
67 U7 **White Nile** *var.* Bahr el Jebel. ≈ S Sudan
81 E14 **White Nile** *Ar.* Al Baḩr al Abyaḑ, An Nīl al Abyaḑ, Bahr el Jebel. ≈ SE Sudan
25 W5 **White Oak Creek** ≈ Texas, SW USA
10 H9 **White Pass** *pass* Canada/USA
32 I9 **White Pass** *pass* Washington, NW USA
21 O9 **White Pine** Tennessee, S USA
18 K14 **White Plains** New York, NE USA
25 O5 **White River** ≈ Texas, SW USA
28 M11 **White River** South Dakota, N USA
27 W12 **White River** ≈ Arkansas, SE USA
37 P3 **White River** ≈ Colorado/Utah, C USA
31 N15 **White River** ≈ Indiana, N USA
31 O8 **White River** ≈ Michigan, N USA
28 K11 **White River** ≈ South Dakota, N USA
18 M8 **White River** ≈ Vermont, NE USA
37 N13 **Whiteriver** Arizona, SW USA
25 O5 **White River Lake** ⊞ Texas, SW USA
32 H11 **White Salmon** Washington, NW USA
18 I10 **Whitesboro** New York, NE USA
25 T5 **Whitesboro** Texas, SW USA
21 O7 **Whitesburg** Kentucky, S USA
White Sea *see* Beloye More
White Sea-Baltic Canal/White Sea Canal *see* Belomorsko-Baltiyskiy Kanal
63 I25 **Whiteside, Canal** *channel* S Chile
33 S10 **White Sulphur Springs** Montana, NW USA
21 R6 **White Sulphur Springs** West Virginia, NE USA
20 J6 **Whitesville** Kentucky, S USA
32 I10 **White Swan** Washington, NW USA
21 U12 **Whiteville** North Carolina, SE USA
20 F10 **Whiteville** Tennessee, S USA
77 Q13 **White Volta** *var.* Nakambé, *Fr.* Volta Blanche. ≈ Burkina/Ghana
30 M9 **Whitewater** Wisconsin, N USA
37 P14 **Whitewater Baldy** ▲ New Mexico, SW USA
23 X17 **Whitewater Bay** *bay* Florida, SE USA
31 Q14 **Whitewater River** ≈ Indiana/Ohio, N USA
11 V16 **Whitewood** Saskatchewan, S Canada
28 J9 **Whitewood** South Dakota, N USA
25 U5 **Whitewright** Texas, SW USA
97 I15 **Whithorn** S Scotland, UK
184 M6 **Whitianga** Waikato, North Island, NZ
19 N11 **Whitinsville** Massachusetts, NE USA
20 M8 **Whitley City** Kentucky, S USA
21 Q11 **Whitmire** South Carolina, SE USA
31 R10 **Whitmore Lake** Michigan, N USA
195 N9 **Whitmore Mountains** ▲▲ Antarctica
14 I12 **Whitney** Ontario, SE Canada
25 T8 **Whitney** Texas, SW USA
25 S8 **Whitney, Lake** ⊞ Texas, SW USA
35 S11 **Whitney, Mount** ▲ California, W USA
181 Y6 **Whitsunday Group** *island group* Queensland, E Australia
25 S6 **Whitt** Texas, SW USA
29 U12 **Whittemore** Iowa, C USA
39 R12 **Whittier** Alaska, USA
35 T15 **Whittier** California, W USA
83 I25 **Whittlesea** Eastern Cape, S South Africa
20 K10 **Whitwell** Tennessee, S USA
8 L10 **Wholdaia Lake** ◎ Northwest Territories, NW Canada
182 H7 **Whyalla** South Australia
Whydah *see* Ouidah
14 F13 **Wiarton** Ontario, S Canada
171 O13 **Wiau** Sulawesi, C Indonesia
111 H15 **Wiązów** *Ger.* Wansen. Dolnośląskie, SW Poland
33 Y8 **Wibaux** Montana, NW USA
27 N6 **Wichita** Kansas, C USA
25 R5 **Wichita Falls** Texas, SW USA
26 L11 **Wichita Mountains** ▲▲ Oklahoma, C USA
25 R5 **Wichita River** ≈ Texas, SW USA
96 K6 **Wick** N Scotland, UK
36 K13 **Wickenburg** Arizona, SW USA
24 L8 **Wickett** Texas, SW USA
180 I7 **Wickham** Western Australia
182 M14 **Wickham, Cape** *headland* Tasmania, SE Australia
20 G7 **Wickliffe** Kentucky, S USA
97 G19 **Wicklow** *Ir.* Cill Mhantáin. E Ireland
97 F19 **Wicklow** *Ir.* Cill Mhantáin. *cultural region* E Ireland
97 G19 **Wicklow Head** *Ir.* Ceann Chill Mhantáin. *headland* E Ireland
97 F18 **Wicklow Mountains** *Ir.* Sléibhte Chill Mhantáin. ▲▲ E Ireland
14 H10 **Wicksteed Lake** ◎ Ontario, S Canada
Wida *see* Ouidah
65 G15 **Wideawake Airfield** ✕ (Georgetown) SW Ascension Island
97 K18 **Widnes** C England, UK
110 H9 **Więcbork** *Ger.* Vandsburg. Kujawsko-pomorskie, C Poland
101 E17 **Wied** ≈ W Germany
101 F16 **Wiehl** Nordrhein-Westfalen, W Germany
111 L17 **Wieliczka** Małopolskie, S Poland
110 G12 **Wielkopolskie** ◈ *province* C Poland
111 J14 **Wieluń** Sieradz, C Poland
109 X4 **Wien** *Eng.* Vienna, *Hung.* Bécs, *Slvk.* Vídeň, *Slvn.* Dunaj; *anc.* Vindobona. ● (Austria) Wien, NE Austria
109 X4 **Wien** *off.* Land Wien, *Eng.* Vienna. ◈ *state* NE Austria
109 X5 **Wiener Neustadt** Niederösterreich, E Austria
110 G7 **Wieprza** *Ger.* Wipper. ≈ NW Poland
98 O10 **Wierden** Overijssel, E Netherlands
98 I7 **Wieringerwerf** Noord-Holland, NW Netherlands
Wieruschow *see* Wieruszów
111 I14 **Wieruszów** *Ger.* Wieruschow. Łódzkie, C Poland
109 V9 **Wies** Steiermark, SE Austria
Wiesbachhorn *see* Grosses Wiesbachhorn
101 G18 **Wiesbaden** Hessen, W Germany
Wieselburg and Ungarisch-Altenburg/Wieselburg-Ungarisch-Altenburg *see* Mosonmagyaróvár
Wiesenhof *see* Ostrołęka
101 G20 **Wiesloch** Baden-Württemberg, SW Germany
100 F10 **Wiesmoor** Niedersachsen, NW Germany
110 I7 **Wieżyca** *Ger.* Turmberg. *hill* Pomorskie, N Poland
97 L17 **Wigan** NW England, UK
37 U3 **Wiggins** Colorado, C USA
22 M8 **Wiggins** Mississippi, S USA
Wigorna Ceaster *see* Worcester
97 I14 **Wigtown** S Scotland, UK
97 H14 **Wigtown** *cultural region* SW Scotland, UK
97 I15 **Wigtown Bay** *bay* SW Scotland, UK
98 L13 **Wijchen** Gelderland, SE Netherlands
92 N1 **Wijdefjorden** *fjord* NW Svalbard
98 M10 **Wijhe** Overijssel, E Netherlands
98 J12 **Wijk bij Duurstede** Utrecht, C Netherlands
98 J13 **Wijk en Aalburg** Noord-Brabant, S Netherlands
99 H16 **Wijnegem** Antwerpen, N Belgium
14 E11 **Wikwemikong** Manitoulin Island, Ontario, S Canada
108 H7 **Wil** Sankt Gallen, NE Switzerland
29 R16 **Wilber** Nebraska, C USA
32 K8 **Wilbur** Washington, NW USA
27 Q11 **Wilburton** Oklahoma, C USA
182 M6 **Wilcannia** New South Wales, SE Australia
18 D12 **Wilcox** Pennsylvania, NE USA
Wilczek Land *see* Vil'cheka, Zemlya
109 U6 **Wildalpen** Steiermark, E Austria
31 O13 **Wildcat Creek** ≈ Indiana, N USA
108 L9 **Wilde Kreuzspitze** *It.* Picco di Croce. ▲ Austria/Italy
Wildenschwert *see* Ústí nad Orlicí
98 O6 **Wildervank** Groningen, NE Netherlands
100 G11 **Wildeshausen** Niedersachsen, NW Germany
108 D10 **Wildhorn** ▲ SW Switzerland
11 R17 **Wild Horse** Alberta, SW Canada
27 N12 **Wildhorse Creek** ≈ Oklahoma, C USA
28 L14 **Wild Horse Hill** ▲ Nebraska, C USA
109 W8 **Wildon** Steiermark, SE Austria
24 M2 **Wildorado** Texas, SW USA
29 R6 **Wild Rice River** ≈ Minnesota/North Dakota, N USA
Wilejka *see* Vilyeyka
195 Y9 **Wilhelm II Coast** *physical region* Antarctica
195 X9 **Wilhelm II Land** *physical region* Antarctica
55 U11 **Wilhelmina Gebergte** ▲▲ C Suriname
18 B13 **Wilhelm, Lake** ⊞ Pennsylvania, NE USA
92 O2 **Wilhelmøya** *island* C Svalbard
Wilhelm-Pieck-Stadt *see* Guben
109 W4 **Wilhelmsburg** Niederösterreich, E Austria
100 G10 **Wilhelmshaven** Niedersachsen, NW Germany
Wilia/Wilja *see* Neris
18 H13 **Wilkes Barre** Pennsylvania, NE USA
21 R9 **Wilkesboro** North Carolina, SE USA
195 W15 **Wilkes Coast** *physical region* Antarctica
189 W12 **Wilkes Island** *island* N Wake Island
195 X12 **Wilkes Land** *physical region* Antarctica
11 S15 **Wilkie** Saskatchewan, S Canada
194 I6 **Wilkins Ice Shelf** *ice shelf* Antarctica
182 D4 **Wilkinson Lakes** *salt lake* South Australia
Wilkomierz *see* Ukmergė
182 K11 **Willalooka** South Australia
32 G11 **Willamette River** ≈ Oregon, NW USA
183 O8 **Willandra Billabong Creek** *seasonal river* New South Wales, SE Australia
32 F9 **Willapa Bay** *inlet* Washington, NW USA
27 T7 **Willard** Missouri, C USA
37 S12 **Willard** New Mexico, SW USA
31 S12 **Willard** Ohio, N USA
36 L1 **Willard** Utah, W USA
186 G6 **Willaumez Peninsula** *headland* New Britain, E PNG
37 N15 **Willcox** Arizona, SW USA
37 N16 **Willcox Playa** *salt flat* Arizona, SW USA
99 G17 **Willebroek** Antwerpen, C Belgium
45 P16 **Willemstad** ○ (Netherlands Antilles) Curaçao, Netherlands Antilles
99 G14 **Willemstad** Noord-Brabant, S Netherlands
11 S11 **William** ≈ Saskatchewan, C Canada
23 O6 **William "Bill" Dannelly Reservoir** ⊞ Alabama, S USA
182 G3 **William Creek** South Australia
181 T15 **William, Mount** ▲ South Australia
36 K11 **Williams** Arizona, SW USA
29 X14 **Williamsburg** Iowa, C USA
20 M8 **Williamsburg** Kentucky, S USA

31 R15 **Williamsburg** Ohio, N USA
21 X6 **Williamsburg** Virginia, NE USA
10 M15 **Williams Lake** British Columbia, SW Canada
21 P6 **Williamson** West Virginia, NE USA
31 N13 **Williamsport** Indiana, N USA
18 G13 **Williamsport** Pennsylvania, NE USA
21 W9 **Williamston** North Carolina, SE USA
21 P11 **Williamston** South Carolina, SE USA
20 M4 **Williamstown** Kentucky, S USA
18 L10 **Williamstown** Massachusetts, NE USA
18 J16 **Willingboro** New Jersey, NE USA
11 Q14 **Willingdon** Alberta, SW Canada
25 W10 **Willis** Texas, SW USA
108 F8 **Willisau** Luzern, W Switzerland
83 F24 **Williston** Northern Cape, W South Africa
23 V10 **Williston** Florida, SE USA
28 J3 **Williston** North Dakota, N USA
21 Q13 **Williston** South Carolina, SE USA
10 L12 **Williston Lake** ⊠ British Columbia, W Canada
34 L5 **Willits** California, W USA
29 T8 **Willmar** Minnesota, N USA
10 K11 **Will, Mount** ▲ British Columbia, W Canada
31 T11 **Willoughby** Ohio, N USA
11 U17 **Willow Bunch** Saskatchewan, S Canada
32 J11 **Willow Creek** ≈ Oregon, NW USA
39 R11 **Willow Lake** Alaska, USA
8 I9 **Willowlake** ≈ Northwest Territories, NW Canada
83 H25 **Willowmore** Eastern Cape, S South Africa
30 L5 **Willow Reservoir** ⊠ Wisconsin, N USA
35 N5 **Willows** California, W USA
27 V7 **Willow Springs** Missouri, C USA
182 I7 **Wilmington** South Australia
21 Y2 **Wilmington** Delaware, NE USA
21 V12 **Wilmington** North Carolina, SE USA
31 R14 **Wilmington** Ohio, N USA
20 M6 **Wilmore** Kentucky, S USA
29 R8 **Wilmot** South Dakota, N USA
Wilna/Wilno *see* Vilnius
101 G16 **Wilnsdorf** Nordrhein-Westfalen, W Germany
99 G16 **Wilrijk** Antwerpen, N Belgium
100 I10 **Wilseder Berg** *hill* NW Germany
67 Z12 **Wilshaw Ridge** *undersea feature* W Indian Ocean
21 V9 **Wilson** North Carolina, SE USA
25 N5 **Wilson** Texas, SW USA
182 A7 **Wilson Bluff** *headland* South Australia/Western Australia
35 Y7 **Wilson Creek Range** ▲▲ Nevada, W USA
23 O1 **Wilson Lake** ⊠ Alabama, S USA
26 M4 **Wilson Lake** ⊠ Kansas, SE USA
37 P7 **Wilson, Mount** ▲ Colorado, C USA
183 P13 **Wilsons Promontory** *peninsula* Victoria, SE Australia
29 Y14 **Wilton** Iowa, C USA
19 P7 **Wilton** Maine, NE USA
28 M5 **Wilton** North Dakota, N USA
97 L22 **Wiltshire** *cultural region* S England, UK
99 M23 **Wiltz** Diekirch, NW Luxembourg
180 K9 **Wiluna** Western Australia
99 M23 **Wilwerwiltz** Diekirch, NE Luxembourg
29 P5 **Wimbledon** North Dakota, N USA
42 K7 **Wina** *var.* Güina. Jinotega, N Nicaragua
31 O12 **Winamac** Indiana, N USA
81 G19 **Winam Gulf** *var.* Kavirondo Gulf. *gulf* SW Kenya
83 I22 **Winburg** Free State, C South Africa
19 N10 **Winchendon** Massachusetts, NE USA
14 M13 **Winchester** Ontario, SE Canada
97 M23 **Winchester** *hist.* Wintanceaster, *Lat.* Venta Belgarum. S England, UK
32 M10 **Winchester** Idaho, NW USA
30 J14 **Winchester** Illinois, N USA
31 Q13 **Winchester** Indiana, N USA
20 M5 **Winchester** Kentucky, S USA
18 M10 **Winchester** New Hampshire, NE USA
20 K10 **Winchester** Tennessee, S USA
21 V3 **Winchester** Virginia, NE USA
99 L22 **Wincrange** Diekirch, NW Luxembourg
10 I5 **Wind** ≈ Yukon Territory, NW Canada
183 S8 **Windamere, Lake** ◎ New South Wales, SE Australia
Windau *see* Ventspils, Latvia
Windau *see* Venta, Latvia/Lithuania
18 D15 **Windber** Pennsylvania, NE USA
23 T3 **Winder** Georgia, SE USA
97 K15 **Windermere** NW England, UK
14 C7 **Windermere Lake** ◎ Ontario, S Canada
31 U11 **Windham** Ohio, N USA
83 D19 **Windhoek** *Ger.* Windhuk. ● (Namibia) Khomas, C Namibia
83 D20 **Windhoek** ✕ Khomas, C Namibia
Windhuk *see* Windhoek
15 O8 **Windigo** Quebec, SE Canada
15 O8 **Windigo** ≈ Quebec, SE Canada
Windischfeistritz *see* Slovenska Bistrica
109 T6 **Windischgarsten** Oberösterreich, W Austria
Windischgraz *see* Slovenj Gradec
37 T16 **Wind Mountain** ▲ New Mexico, SW USA
29 T10 **Windom** Minnesota, N USA
37 Q7 **Windom Peak** ▲ Colorado, C USA
181 U9 **Windorah** Queensland, C Australia
37 O10 **Window Rock** Arizona, SW USA
31 N9 **Wind Point** *headland* Wisconsin, N USA
33 U14 **Wind River** ≈ Wyoming, C USA
13 P15 **Windsor** Nova Scotia, SE Canada
14 C17 **Windsor** Ontario, S Canada
15 Q12 **Windsor** Quebec, SE Canada
97 N22 **Windsor** S England, UK
37 T3 **Windsor** Colorado, C USA
18 M12 **Windsor** Connecticut, NE USA
27 T5 **Windsor** Missouri, C USA
21 X9 **Windsor** North Carolina, SE USA
18 M12 **Windsor Locks** Connecticut, NE USA
25 R5 **Windthorst** Texas, SW USA
45 Z14 **Windward Islands** *island group* E West Indies
Windward Islands *see* Vent, Îles du, Archipel de la Société, French Polynesia
Windward Islands *see* Barlavento, Ilhas de, Cape Verde
44 K8 **Windward Passage** *Sp.* Paso de los Vientos. *channel* Cuba/Haiti
55 T9 **Wineperu** C Guyana
23 O3 **Winfield** Alabama, S USA
29 Y15 **Winfield** Iowa, C USA
27 O7 **Winfield** Kansas, C USA
25 W6 **Winfield** Texas, SW USA
21 Q4 **Winfield** West Virginia, NE USA
29 N5 **Wing** North Dakota, N USA
183 U7 **Wingham** New South Wales, SE Australia
12 G16 **Wingham** Ontario, S Canada
33 T8 **Winifred** Montana, NW USA
12 E8 **Winisk** ≈ Ontario, S Canada
12 E9 **Winisk Lake** ◎ Ontario, C Canada
24 L8 **Wink** Texas, SW USA
36 M14 **Winkelman** Arizona, SW USA
11 X17 **Winkler** Manitoba, S Canada
109 Q9 **Winklern** Tirol, W Austria
Winkowitz *see* Vinkovci
32 G9 **Winlock** Washington, NW USA
77 P17 **Winneba** SE Ghana
29 U11 **Winnebago** Minnesota, N USA
29 R13 **Winnebago** Nebraska, C USA
30 M7 **Winnebago, Lake** ◎ Wisconsin, N USA
30 M7 **Winneconne** Wisconsin, N USA
35 T3 **Winnemucca** Nevada, W USA
35 R4 **Winnemucca Lake** ◎ Nevada, W USA
101 H21 **Winnenden** Baden-Württemberg, SW Germany
29 N11 **Winner** South Dakota, N USA
33 U9 **Winnett** Montana, NW USA
14 I9 **Winneway** Quebec, SE Canada
22 H6 **Winnfield** Louisiana, S USA
29 U4 **Winnibigoshish, Lake** ◎ Minnesota, N USA
25 X11 **Winnie** Texas, SW USA
11 Y16 **Winnipeg** Manitoba, S Canada
11 X16 **Winnipeg** ✕ Manitoba, S Canada
(0) J8 **Winnipeg** ≈ Manitoba, S Canada
11 X16 **Winnipeg Beach** Manitoba, S Canada
11 W14 **Winnipeg, Lake** ◎ Manitoba, C Canada
11 W15 **Winnipegosis** Manitoba, S Canada
11 W15 **Winnipegosis, Lake** ◎ Manitoba, C Canada
19 O8 **Winnipesaukee, Lake** ◎ New Hampshire, NE USA
22 I6 **Winnsboro** Louisiana, S USA
21 R12 **Winnsboro** South Carolina, SE USA
25 W6 **Winnsboro** Texas, SW USA
29 X10 **Winona** Minnesota, N USA
22 L4 **Winona** Mississippi, S USA
27 W7 **Winona** Missouri, C USA
25 W7 **Winona** Texas, SW USA
18 M7 **Winooski River** ≈ Vermont, NE USA
98 P6 **Winschoten** Groningen, NE Netherlands
100 J10 **Winsen** Niedersachsen, N Germany
36 M11 **Winslow** Arizona, SW USA
19 Q7 **Winslow** Maine, NE USA
18 M12 **Winsted** Connecticut, NE USA
32 F14 **Winston** Oregon, NW USA
21 S9 **Winston Salem** North Carolina, SE USA
98 N5 **Winsum** Groningen, NE Netherlands
Wintanceaster *see* Winchester
23 W11 **Winter Garden** Florida, SE USA
10 J16 **Winter Harbour** Vancouver Island, British Columbia, SW Canada
23 W12 **Winter Haven** Florida, SE USA
23 X11 **Winter Park** Florida, SE USA
25 P8 **Winters** Texas, SW USA
29 U15 **Winterset** Iowa, C USA
98 O12 **Winterswijk** Gelderland, E Netherlands
108 G6 **Winterthur** Zürich, NE Switzerland
29 U9 **Winthrop** Minnesota, N USA
32 J7 **Winthrop** Washington, NW USA
181 V7 **Winton** Queensland, E Australia
185 C24 **Winton** Southland, South Island, NZ
21 X8 **Winton** North Carolina, SE USA
101 K15 **Wipper** ≈ C Germany
101 K14 **Wipper** ≈ C Germany
Wipper *see* Wieprza
182 G6 **Wirraminna** South Australia
182 F4 **Wirrida** South Australia
182 F7 **Wirrulla** South Australia
Wirsitz *see* Wyrzysk
Wirz-See *see* Võrtsjärv
97 O19 **Wisbech** E England, UK
Wisby *see* Visby
19 Q8 **Wiscasset** Maine, NE USA
Wischau *see* Vyškov
30 J5 **Wisconsin** *off.* State of Wisconsin; also known as The Badger State. ◈ *state* N USA
30 L8 **Wisconsin Dells** Wisconsin, N USA
30 L8 **Wisconsin, Lake** ⊠ Wisconsin, N USA
30 L7 **Wisconsin Rapids** Wisconsin, N USA
30 L7 **Wisconsin River** ≈ Wisconsin, N USA
33 P11 **Wisdom** Montana, NW USA
21 P7 **Wise** Virginia, NE USA
39 Q7 **Wiseman** Alaska, USA
96 J12 **Wishaw** W Scotland, UK
29 O6 **Wishek** North Dakota, N USA
32 I11 **Wishram** Washington, NW USA
111 J17 **Wisła** Śląskie, S Poland
110 K11 **Wisła** *Eng.* Vistula, *Ger.* Weichsel. ≈ C Poland
Wiślany, Zalew *see* Vistula Lagoon
111 M16 **Wisłoka** ≈ SE Poland
100 L9 **Wismar** Mecklenburg-Vorpommern, N Germany
29 R14 **Wisner** Nebraska, C USA
103 V4 **Wissembourg** *var.* Weissenburg. Bas-Rhin, NE France
30 J6 **Wissota, Lake** ⊠ Wisconsin, N USA
97 O18 **Witham** ≈ E England, UK
97 O17 **Withernsea** E England, UK
37 Q13 **Withington, Mount** ▲ New Mexico, SW USA
23 U8 **Withlacoochee River** ≈ Florida/Georgia, SE USA
110 H11 **Witkowo** Wielkopolskie, C Poland
97 M21 **Witney** S England, UK
101 E15 **Witten** Nordrhein-Westfalen, W Germany
101 N14 **Wittenberg** Sachsen-Anhalt, E Germany
30 L6 **Wittenberg** Wisconsin, N USA
100 L11 **Wittenberge** Brandenburg, N Germany
103 U7 **Wittenheim** Haut-Rhin, NE France
180 I7 **Wittenoom** Western Australia
Wittingau *see* Třeboň
100 K12 **Wittingen** Niedersachsen, C Germany
101 E18 **Wittlich** Rheinland-Pfalz, SW Germany
100 F9 **Wittmund** Niedersachsen, NW Germany
100 M10 **Wittstock** Brandenburg, NE Germany
186 F6 **Witu Islands** *island group* E PNG
110 O7 **Wiżajny** Podlaskie, NE Poland
55 W10 **W.J. van Blommesteinmeer** ⊠ E Suriname
110 L11 **Wkra** *Ger.* Soldau. ≈ C Poland
110 I6 **Władysławowo** Pomorskie, N Poland
Wlaschim *see* Vlašim
111 E14 **Wleń** *Ger.* Lähn. Dolnośląskie, SW Poland
110 J11 **Włocławek** *Ger./Rus.* Vlotslavsk. Kujawsko-pomorskie, C Poland
110 P13 **Włodawa** *Rus.* Vlodava. Lubelskie, SE Poland
Włodzimierz *see* Volodymyr-Volyns'kyy
111 K15 **Włoszczowa** Świętokrzyskie, C Poland
83 C19 **Wlotzkasbaken** Erongo, W Namibia
146 L11 **Wobkent** *Rus.* Vabkent. Bukhoro Wiloyati, C Uzbekistan
15 R12 **Woburn** Quebec, SE Canada
19 O11 **Woburn** Massachusetts, NE USA
Wocheiner Feistritz *see* Bohinjska Bistrica
Wöchma *see* Võhma
147 S11 **Wodil** *var.* Vuadil'. Farghona Wiloyati, E Uzbekistan
181 V14 **Wodonga** Victoria, SE Australia
111 I17 **Wodzisław Śląski** *Ger.* Loslau. Śląskie, S Poland
98 I11 **Woerden** Zuid-Holland, C Netherlands
98 I8 **Wognum** Noord-Holland, NW Netherlands
Wohlau *see* Wołów
108 F7 **Wohlen** Aargau, NW Switzerland
195 R2 **Wohlthat Mountains** ▲▲ Antarctica
Wōjjā *see* Wotje Atoll
Wojwodina *see* Vojvodina
171 V15 **Wokam, Pulau** *island* Kepulauan Aru, E Indonesia
97 N22 **Woking** SE England, UK
Woldenberg Neumark *see* Dobiegniew
188 K15 **Woleai Atoll** *atoll* Caroline Islands, W Micronesia
Woleu *see* Uolo, Río
79 E17 **Woleu-Ntem** *off.* Province du Woleu-Ntem, *var.* Le Woleu-Ntem. ◈ *province* W Gabon
32 F15 **Wolf Creek** Oregon, NW USA
26 K9 **Wolf Creek** ≈ Oklahoma/Texas, SW USA
37 R7 **Wolf Creek Pass** *pass* Colorado, C USA
19 O9 **Wolfeboro** New Hampshire, NE USA
25 U5 **Wolfe City** Texas, SW USA
14 L15 **Wolfe Island** *island* Ontario, SE Canada
101 M14 **Wolfen** Sachsen-Anhalt, E Germany
100 J13 **Wolfenbüttel** Niedersachsen, C Germany
109 T4 **Wolfern** Oberösterreich, N Austria
109 Q6 **Wolfgangsee** *var.* Abersee, St Wolfgangsee. ◎ N Austria
39 P9 **Wolf Mountain** ▲ Alaska, USA
33 X7 **Wolf Point** Montana, NW USA
22 L8 **Wolf River** ≈ Mississippi, S USA
30 M7 **Wolf River** ≈ Wisconsin, N USA
109 U9 **Wolfsberg** Kärnten, SE Austria
100 K12 **Wolfsburg** Niedersachsen, N Germany
57 B17 **Wolf, Volcán** ☒ Galapagos Islands, Ecuador, E Pacific Ocean
100 O8 **Wolgast** Mecklenburg-Vorpommern, NE Germany
108 F8 **Wolhusen** Luzern, W Switzerland
110 D8 **Wolin** *Ger.* Wollin. Zachodniopomorskie, NW Poland
109 Y3 **Wolkersdorf** Niederösterreich, NE Austria
Wołkowysk *see* Vawkavysk
Wöllan *see* Velenje
8 J6 **Wollaston, Cape** *headland* Victoria Island, Northwest Territories, NW Canada
63 J25 **Wollaston, Isla** *island* S Chile
11 U11 **Wollaston Lake** Saskatchewan, C Canada
11 T10 **Wollaston Lake** ◎ Saskatchewan, C Canada
8 J6 **Wollaston Peninsula** *peninsula* Victoria Island, Northwest Territories/Nunavut, NW Canada
Wollin *see* Wolin
183 S9 **Wollongong** New South Wales, SE Australia
Wolmar *see* Valmiera
100 L13 **Wolmirstedt** Sachsen-Anhalt, C Germany
110 M11 **Wołomin** Mazowieckie, C Poland
110 G3 **Wołów** *Ger.* Wohlau. Dolnośląskie, SW Poland
Wołożyn *see* Valozhyn
14 G11 **Wolseley Bay** Ontario, S Canada
29 P10 **Wolsey** South Dakota, N USA
110 F12 **Wolsztyn** Wielkopolskie, W Poland
98 M7 **Wolvega** *Fris.* Wolvegea. Friesland, N Netherlands
Wolvegea *see* Wolvega
97 K19 **Wolverhampton** C England, UK
Wolverine State *see* Michigan
99 G18 **Wolvertem** Vlaams Brabant, C Belgium
99 H16 **Wommelgem** Antwerpen, N Belgium
186 D7 **Wonenara** *var.* Wonerara. Eastern Highlands, C PNG
Wonerara *see* Wonenara
Wongalara Lake *see* Wongalarroo Lake
183 N6 **Wongalarroo Lake** *var.* Wongalara Lake. *seasonal lake* New South Wales, SE Australia
163 Y15 **Wŏnju** *Jap.* Genshū. N South Korea
10 M12 **Wonowon** British Columbia, W Canada
163 X13 **Wŏnsan** SE North Korea
183 O13 **Wonthaggi** Victoria, SE Australia
23 N2 **Woodall Mountain** ▲ Mississippi, S USA
23 W7 **Woodbine** Georgia, SE USA
29 S14 **Woodbine** Iowa, C USA
18 J17 **Woodbine** New Jersey, NE USA
21 W4 **Woodbridge** Virginia, NE USA
183 V4 **Woodburn** New South Wales, SE Australia
32 G11 **Woodburn** Oregon, NW USA
20 K9 **Woodbury** Tennessee, S USA
183 V5 **Wooded Bluff** *headland* New South Wales, SE Australia
183 V3 **Woodenbong** New South Wales, SE Australia
35 R11 **Woodlake** California, W USA
35 N7 **Woodland** California, W USA
19 T5 **Woodland** Maine, NE USA
32 G10 **Woodland** Washington, NW USA
37 T5 **Woodland Park** Colorado, C USA
186 I9 **Woodlark Island** *var.* Murua Island. *island* SE PNG
Woodle Island *see* Kuria
11 T17 **Wood Mountain** ▲ Saskatchewan, S Canada
30 K15 **Wood River** Illinois, N USA
29 P16 **Wood River** Nebraska, C USA
39 R9 **Wood River** ≈ Alaska, USA
39 O13 **Wood River Lakes** *lakes* Alaska, USA
182 C1 **Woodroffe, Mount** ▲ South Australia
21 P11 **Woodruff** South Carolina, SE USA
30 K4 **Woodruff** Wisconsin, N USA
25 T14 **Woodsboro** Texas, SW USA
31 U13 **Woodsfield** Ohio, N USA
181 P4 **Woods, Lake** ◎ Northern Territory, N Australia
11 Z16 **Woods, Lake of the** *Fr.* Lac des Bois. ◎ Canada/USA
25 Q6 **Woodson** Texas, SW USA
13 N14 **Woodstock** New Brunswick, SE Canada
14 F16 **Woodstock** Ontario, S Canada
30 M10 **Woodstock** Illinois, N USA
18 M9 **Woodstock** Vermont, NE USA
21 U4 **Woodstock** Virginia, NE USA
19 N8 **Woodsville** New Hampshire, NE USA
184 M12 **Woodville** Manawatu-Wanganui, North Island, NZ
22 J7 **Woodville** Mississippi, S USA
25 X9 **Woodville** Texas, SW USA
26 K9 **Woodward** Oklahoma, C USA
29 O5 **Woodworth** North Dakota, N USA
171 W12 **Wool** Irian Jaya, E Indonesia
183 V5 **Woolgoolga** New South Wales, E Australia
182 H6 **Woomera** South Australia
19 O12 **Woonsocket** Rhode Island, NE USA
29 P10 **Woonsocket** South Dakota, N USA
31 T12 **Wooster** Ohio, N USA
80 L12 **Woqooyi Galbeed** *off.* Gobolka Woqooyi Galbeed. ◈ *region* NW Somalia
108 E8 **Worb** Bern, C Switzerland
83 F26 **Worcester** Western Cape, SW South Africa
97 L20 **Worcester** *hist.* Wigorna Ceaster. W England, UK
19 N11 **Worcester** Massachusetts, NE USA
97 L20 **Worcestershire** *cultural region* C England, UK
32 H16 **Worden** Oregon, NW USA
109 O6 **Wörgl** Tirol, W Austria
171 V15 **Workai, Pulau** *island* Kepulauan Aru, E Indonesia
97 J15 **Workington** NW England, UK
98 K7 **Workum** Friesland, N Netherlands
33 V13 **Worland** Wyoming, C USA
Wormatia *see* Worms
99 N25 **Wormeldange** Grevenmacher, E Luxembourg
98 I9 **Wormer** Noord-Holland, C Netherlands
101 G19 **Worms** *anc.* Augusta Vangionum, Borbetomagus, Wormatia. Rheinland-Pfalz, SW Germany
Worms *see* Vormsi
101 K21 **Wörnitz** ≈ S Germany
101 G21 **Wörth** Rheinland-Pfalz, SW Germany
25 U8 **Wortham** Texas, SW USA
109 S9 **Worther See** ◎ S Austria
97 O23 **Worthing** SE England, UK
29 S11 **Worthington** Minnesota, N USA
31 S13 **Worthington** Ohio, N USA
35 W8 **Worthington Peak** ▲ Nevada, W USA
171 Y13 **Wosi** Irian Jaya, E Indonesia
171 V13 **Wosimi** Irian Jaya, E Indonesia
189 R5 **Wotho Atoll** *var.* Wōtto. *atoll* Ralik Chain, W Marshall Islands
189 V5 **Wotje Atoll** *var.* Wōjjā. *atoll* Ratak Chain, E Marshall Islands
Wotoe *see* Wotu
Wottawa *see* Otava
Wōtto *see* Wotho Atoll
171 O13 **Wotu** *prev.* Wotoe. Sulawesi, C Indonesia
98 K11 **Woudenberg** Utrecht, C Netherlands
98 I13 **Woudrichem** Noord-Brabant, S Netherlands
43 N8 **Wounta** *var.* Huaunta. Región Autónoma Atlántico Norte, NE Nicaragua
171 P14 **Wowoni, Pulau** *island* C Indonesia
81 J17 **Woyamdero Plain** *plain* E Kenya
Woyens *see* Vojens
Wozrojdeniye Oroli *see* Vozrozhdeniya, Ostrov
Wrangel Island *see* Vrangelya, Ostrov
39 Y13 **Wrangell** Wrangell Island, Alaska, USA
38 C15 **Wrangell, Cape** *headland* Attu Island, Alaska, USA
39 S11 **Wrangell, Mount** ▲ Alaska, USA
39 T11 **Wrangell Mountains** ▲▲ Alaska, USA
197 S7 **Wrangel Plain** *undersea feature* Arctic Ocean
96 H6 **Wrath, Cape** *headland* N Scotland, UK
37 W3 **Wray** Colorado, C USA
44 K13 **Wreck Point** *headland* C Jamaica
83 C23 **Wreck Point** *headland* W South Africa
23 V4 **Wrens** Georgia, SE USA
97 K18 **Wrexham** NE Wales, UK
27 R13 **Wright City** Oklahoma, C USA
194 J12 **Wright Island** *island* Antarctica
13 N9 **Wright, Mont** ▲ Quebec, E Canada
25 X5 **Wright Patman Lake** ⊠ Texas, SW USA
36 M16 **Wrightson, Mount** ▲ Arizona, SW USA
23 U5 **Wrightsville** Georgia, SE USA
21 W12 **Wrightsville Beach** North Carolina, SE USA
35 T15 **Wrightwood** California, W USA
8 H9 **Wrigley** Northwest Territories, W Canada
111 G14 **Wrocław** *Eng./Ger.* Breslau. Dolnośląskie, SW Poland
110 F10 **Wronki** *Ger.* Fronicken. Wielkopolskie, NW Poland
110 H11 **Września** Wielkopolskie, C Poland
110 F12 **Wschowa** Lubuskie, W Poland
Wsetin *see* Vsetín
180 I12 **Wubin** Western Australia
163 W9 **Wuchang** Heilongjiang, NE China
Wuchang *see* Wuhan
Wu-chou/Wuchow *see* Wuzhou
160 M16 **Wuchuan** *var.* Meilu. Guangdong, S China
160 K10 **Wuchuan** *prev.* Duru. Guizhou, S China
163 O13 **Wuchuan** Nei Mongol Zizhiqu, N China
163 V6 **Wudalianchi** Heilongjiang, NE China
159 O11 **Wudaoliang** Qinghai, C China
141 Q13 **Wuday'ah** *spring/well* S Saudi Arabia
77 V13 **Wudil** Kano, N Nigeria
160 G12 **Wuding** Yunnan, SW China
160 L4 **Wuding He** ≈ C China
182 G8 **Wudinna** South Australia
157 P10 **Wudu** Gansu, C China
160 L9 **Wufeng** Hubei, C China
161 O11 **Wugong Shan** ▲▲ S China
157 P7 **Wuhai** Nei Mongol Zizhiqu, N China
161 O9 **Wuhan** *var.* Han-kou, Han-k'ou, Hanyang, Wuchang, Wu-han; *prev.* Hankow. Hubei, C China
161 Q7 **Wuhe** Anhui, E China
Wuhsi/Wu-hsi *see* Wuxi
Wuhsien *see* Suzhou
161 Q8 **Wuhu** *var.* Wu-na-mu. Anhui, E China
Wūjae *see* Ujae Atoll
160 K11 **Wu Jiang** ≈ C China
Wujlān *see* Ujelang Atoll
77 W15 **Wukari** Taraba, E Nigeria
160 H11 **Wulian Feng** ▲▲ SW China
160 F13 **Wuliang Shan** ▲▲ SW China
160 K11 **Wuling Shan** ▲▲ S China
109 Y5 **Wulka** ≈ E Austria
Wulkan *see* Vulcan
109 T3 **Wullowitz** Oberösterreich, N Austria
Wu-lu-k'o-mu-shi/Wu-lu-mu-ch'i *see* Ürümqi
79 D14 **Wum** Nord-Ouest, NE Cameroon
160 H12 **Wumeng Shan** ▲▲ SW China
160 K14 **Wuming** Guangxi Zhuangzu Zizhiqu, S China
100 I10 **Wümme** ≈ NW Germany
Wu-na-mu *see* Wuhu
171 X13 **Wunen** Irian Jaya, E Indonesia
12 D9 **Wunnummin Lake** ◎ Ontario, C Canada
80 D13 **Wun Rog** Warab, S Sudan
101 M18 **Wunsiedel** Bayern, E Germany
100 I12 **Wunstorf** Niedersachsen, NW Germany
166 M3 **Wuntho** Sagaing, N Burma
101 F15 **Wupper** ≈ W Germany
101 E15 **Wuppertal** *prev.* Barmen-Elberfeld. Nordrhein-Westfalen, W Germany
160 K5 **Wuqi** Shaanxi, C China
161 P4 **Wuqiao** *var.* Sangyuan. Hebei, E China
101 L23 **Würm** ≈ SE Germany
77 T12 **Wurno** Sokoto, NW Nigeria
101 I19 **Würzburg** Bayern, SW Germany
101 N15 **Wurzen** Sachsen, E Germany
160 L9 **Wu Shan** ▲▲ C China
158 G7 **Wushi** *var.* Uqturpan. Xinjiang Uygur Zizhiqu, NW China
Wusih *see* Wuxi
65 N18 **Wüst Seamount** *undersea feature* S Atlantic Ocean
Wusuli Jiang/Wusuri *see* Ussuri
161 N3 **Wutai Shan** ▲ C China
160 H10 **Wutongqiao** Sichuan, C China
159 P6 **Wutongwozi Quan** *spring* NW China
99 H15 **Wuustwezel** Antwerpen, N Belgium
186 B4 **Wuvulu Island** *island* NW PNG
159 U9 **Wuwei** *var.* Liangzhou. Gansu, C China
161 R8 **Wuxi** *var.* Wuhsi, Wu-hsi, Wusih. Jiangsu, E China
Wuxing *see* Huzhou
160 L14 **Wuxuan** Guangxi Zhuangzu Zizhiqu, S China
160 K11 **Wuyang He** ≈ S China
163 X6 **Wuyiling** Heilongjiang, NE China
157 T12 **Wuyi Shan** ▲▲ SE China
161 Q11 **Wuyishan** *prev.* Chong'an. Fujian, SE China
162 M13 **Wuyuan** Nei Mongol Zizhiqu, N China
160 L17 **Wuzhi Shan** ▲ S China
159 W8 **Wuzhong** Ningxia, N China
160 M14 **Wuzhou** *var.* Wu-chou, Wuchow. Guangxi Zhuangzu Zizhiqu, S China
18 H12 **Wyalusing** Pennsylvania, NE USA
182 M10 **Wycheproof** Victoria, SE Australia
97 K21 **Wye** *Wel.* Gwy. ≈ England/Wales, UK
Wyłkowyszki *see* Vilkaviškis
97 P19 **Wymondham** E England, UK
29 R17 **Wymore** Nebraska, C USA
182 E5 **Wynbring** South Australia
181 N3 **Wyndham** Western Australia
29 R6 **Wyndmere** North Dakota, N USA
27 X11 **Wynne** Arkansas, C USA
27 N12 **Wynnewood** Oklahoma, C USA
183 O15 **Wynyard** Tasmania, SE Australia
11 U15 **Wynyard** Saskatchewan, S Canada
33 V11 **Wyola** Montana, NW USA
182 A4 **Wyola Lake** *salt lake* South Australia
31 P9 **Wyoming** Michigan, N USA
33 V14 **Wyoming** *off.* State of Wyoming; also known as The Equality State. ◈ *state* C USA
33 S15 **Wyoming Range** ▲▲ Wyoming, C USA
183 T8 **Wyong** New South Wales, SE Australia
110 G9 **Wyrzysk** *Ger.* Wirsitz. Wielkopolskie, C Poland
Wysg *see* Usk
110 O10 **Wysokie Mazowieckie** Łomża, E Poland
110 M11 **Wyszków** *Ger.* Probstberg. Mazowieckie, C Poland

110 L11 **Wyszogród** Mazowieckie, C Poland
21 R7 **Wytheville** Virginia, NE USA

X

80 Q12 **Xaafuun** *It.* Hafun. Bari, NE Somalia
80 Q12 **Xaafuun, Raas** *var.* Ras Hafun. *headland* NE Somalia
Xábia *see* Jávea
42 C4 **Xacbal, Río** *var.* Xalbal. ≈ Guatemala/Mexico
137 Y10 **Xaçmaz** *Rus.* Khachmas. N Azerbaijan
80 O12 **Xadeed** *var.* Haded. *physical region* N Somalia
159 O14 **Xagquka** Xizang Zizhiqu, W China
167 Q6 **Xai** *var.* Muang Xay, Muong Sai. Oudômxai, N Laos
158 F10 **Xaidulla** Xinjiang Uygur Zizhiqu, W China
167 Q7 **Xaignabouli** *prev.* Muang Xaignabouri, *Fr.* Sayaboury. Xaignabouli, N Laos
167 R7 **Xai Lai Leng, Phou** ▲ Laos/Vietnam
158 L15 **Xainza** Xizang Zizhiqu, W China
158 L16 **Xaitongmoin** Xizang Zizhiqu, W China
83 M20 **Xai-Xai** *prev.* João Belo, Vila de João *Bel.* Gaza, S Mozambique
Xalbal *see* Xacbal, Río
80 P13 **Xalin** Nugaal, N Somalia
167 R6 **Xam Nua** *var.* Sam Neua. Houaphan, N Laos
82 D11 **Xá-Muteba** *Port.* Cinco de Outubro. Lunda Norte, NE Angola
83 C16 **Xangongo** *Port.* Rocadas. Cunene, SW Angola
137 W12 **Xankändi** *Rus.* Khankendi; *prev.* Stepanakert. SW Azerbaijan
137 V11 **Xanlar** *Rus.* Khanlar. NW Azerbaijan
114 J13 **Xánthi** Anatolikí Makedonía kai Thráki, NE Greece
60 H13 **Xanxerê** Santa Catarina, S Brazil
81 O15 **Xarardheere** Mudug, E Somalia
131 W8 **Xar Moron** ≈ NE China
Xarra *see* Xarrë
113 L23 **Xarrë** *var.* Xarra. Vlorë, S Albania
82 D12 **Xassengue** Lunda Sul, NW Angola
105 S11 **Xátiva** *var.* Jativa; *anc.* Setabis. País Valenciano, E Spain
Xauen *see* Chefchaouen
60 K10 **Xavantes, Represa de** *var.* Represa de Chavantes. ⊞ S Brazil
158 I7 **Xayar** Xinjiang Uygur Zizhiqu, W China
Xäzär Dänizi *see* Caspian Sea
167 S8 **Xé Bangfai** ≈ C Laos
167 T9 **Xé Banghiang** *var.* Bang Hieng. ≈ S Laos
Xégar *see* Tingri
31 R14 **Xenia** Ohio, N USA
Xeres *see* Jeréz de la Frontera
115 E15 **Xeriás** ≈ C Greece
115 G17 **Xeró** ▲ Évvoia, C Greece
83 H18 **Xhumo** Central, C Botswana
161 N15 **Xiachuan Dao** *island* S China
Xiacun *see* Rushan
Xiaguan *see* Dali
159 U11 **Xiahe** *var.* Labrang. Gansu, C China
161 Q13 **Xiamen** *var.* Hsia-men; *prev.* Amoy. Fujian, SE China
160 L6 **Xi'an** *var.* Changan, Sian, Signan, Siking, Singan, Xian. Shaanxi, C China
160 L10 **Xianfeng** Hubei, C China
Xiang *see* Hunan
161 N7 **Xiangcheng** Henan, C China
160 F10 **Xiangcheng** *prev.* Qagchêng. Sichuan, C China
160 M8 **Xiangfan** *var.* Xiangyang. Hubei, C China
161 N10 **Xiang Jiang** ≈ S China
Xiangkhoang *see* Pèk
167 Q7 **Xiangkhoang, Plateau de** *var.* Plain of Jars. *plateau* N Laos
161 N11 **Xiangtan** *var.* Hsiang-t'an, Siangtan. Hunan, S China
161 N11 **Xiangxiang** Hunan, S China
Xiangyang *see* Xiangfan
161 S10 **Xianju** Zhejiang, SE China
160 F8 **Xianshui He** ≈ C China
161 N9 **Xiantao** *var.* Mianyang. Hubei, C China
161 R10 **Xianxia Ling** ▲ SE China
160 K6 **Xianyang** Shaanxi, C China
158 L5 **Xiaocaohu** Xinjiang Uygur Zizhiqu, W China
163 W6 **Xiao Hinggan Ling** *Eng.* Lesser Khingan Range. ▲ NE China
160 M6 **Xiao Shan** ▲ C China
160 M12 **Xiao Shui** ≈ S China
161 P6 **Xiaoxian** *var.* Xiao Xian. Anhui, E China
160 G11 **Xichang** Sichuan, C China
41 P11 **Xicoténcatl** Tamaulipas, C Mexico
Xieng Khouang *see* Pèk
Xieng Ngeun *see* Muong Xiang Ngeun
159 X10 **Xifeng** Gansu, C China
160 J11 **Xifeng** Guizhou, S China
Xigang *see* Helan
158 L16 **Xigazê** *var.* Jih-k'a-tse, Shigatse, Xigaze. Xizang Zizhiqu, W China
160 I8 **Xi He** ≈ C China
159 W11 **Xihe** Gansu, C China
Xihuachi *see* Heshui
159 Q7 **Xijian Quan** *spring* NW China
159 W10 **Xiji** Ningxia, N China
160 M14 **Xi Jiang** *var.* Hsi Chiang, *Eng.* West River. ≈ S China
160 K15 **Xijin Shuiku** ⊞ S China
Xilaganí *see* Xylaganí
160 I13 **Xilin** *prev.* Bada. Guangxi Zhuangzu Zizhiqu, S China
163 Q10 **Xilinhot** *var.* Silinhot. Nei Mongol Zizhiqu, N China
Xilokastro *see* Xylókastro
Xin *see* Xinjiang Uygur Zizhiqu
161 R10 **Xin'anjiang Shuiku** ⊞ SE China
Xin'anzhen *see* Xinyi
163 Q7 **Xin Barag Youqi** *var.* Altan Emel. Nei Mongol Zizhiqu, N China
163 R7 **Xin Barag Zuoqi** *var.* Amgalang. Nei Mongol Zizhiqu, N China
163 W12 **Xinbin** Liaoning, NE China
161 O7 **Xincai** Henan, C China
159 V8 **Xincheng** *var.* Yinchuanzhan. Ningxia, N China
161 O13 **Xinfeng** Jiangxi, S China
161 O14 **Xinfengjiang Shuiku** ⊞ S China
163 T13 **Xingcheng** Liaoning, NE China
82 E11 **Xinge** Lunda Norte, NE Angola
161 P12 **Xingguo** Jiangxi, S China
159 S11 **Xinghai** Qinghai, C China
161 R7 **Xinghua** Jiangsu, E China
Xingkai Hu *see* Khanka, Lake
161 P13 **Xingning** Guangdong, S China
160 I13 **Xingren** Guizhou, S China
161 O4 **Xingtai** Hebei, E China
59 J14 **Xingu, Rio** ≈ C Brazil
159 P6 **Xingxingxia** Xinjiang Uygur Zizhiqu, NW China
160 I13 **Xingyi** Guizhou, S China
158 I6 **Xinhe** *var.* Toksu. Xinjiang Uygur Zizhiqu, NW China
Xin Hot *see* Abag Qi
159 T10 **Xining** *var.* Hsining, Hsi-ning, Sining. *province capital* Qinghai, C China
161 O4 **Xinji** *prev.* Shulu. Hebei, E China
161 P10 **Xinjian** Jiangxi, S China
Xinjiang *see* Xinjiang Uygur Zizhiqu
162 D8 **Xinjiang Uygur Zizhiqu** *var.* Sinkiang, Sinkiang Uighur Autonomous Region, Xin, Xinjiang. ◈ *autonomous region* NW China
160 H9 **Xinjin** Sichuan, C China
Xinjin *see* Pulandian
163 U12 **Xinmin** Liaoning, NE China
160 M12 **Xinning** Hunan, S China
Xinpu *see* Lianyungang
161 P5 **Xinwen** *prev.* Suncun. Shandong, E China
Xin Xian *see* Xinzhou
161 N6 **Xinxiang** Henan, C China
161 O8 **Xinyang** *var.* Hsin-yang, Sinyang. Henan, C China
161 Q6 **Xinyi** *var.* Xin'anzhen. Jiangsu, E China
161 Q6 **Xinyi He** ≈ E China
161 O11 **Xinyu** Jiangxi, S China
158 I5 **Xinyuan** *var.* Künes. Xinjiang Uygur Zizhiqu, NW China
Xinyuan *see* Tianjun
162 M14 **Xinzhao Shan** ▲ N China
161 N3 **Xinzhou** *var.* Xin Xian. Shanxi, C China
104 H4 **Xinzo de Limia** Galicia, NW Spain
Xions *see* Książ Wielkopolski
161 O7 **Xiping** Henan, C China
159 T11 **Xiqing Shan** ▲ C China
59 N16 **Xique-Xique** Bahia, E Brazil
115 E14 **Xirovoúni** ▲ N Greece
Xishanzui *see* Urad Qianqi
160 J11 **Xishui** Guizhou, S China
161 O9 **Xishui** Hubei, C China
163 R10 **Xi Ujimqin Qi** *var.* Bayan Ul Hot. Nei Mongol Zizhiqu, N China
160 K11 **Xiushan** Sichuan, C China
161 O10 **Xiu Shui** ≈ S China
158 J16 **Xixabangma Feng** ▲ W China
160 M7 **Xixia** Henan, C China
Xixón *see* Gijón
Xixona *see* Jijona
Xizang *see* Xizang Zizhiqu
Xizang Gaoyuan *see* Qingzang Gaoyuan
160 E9 **Xizang Zizhiqu** *var.* Thibet, Tibetan Autonomous Region, Xizang, *Eng.* Tibet. ◈ *autonomous region* W China
163 U14 **Xizhong Dao** *island* N China
Xolotlán *see* Managua, Lago de
159 N9 **Xorkol** Xinjiang Uygur Zizhiqu, NW China
41 X14 **Xpujil** Quintana Roo, E Mexico
Xuancheng *see* Xuanzhou
167 T9 **Xuân Đuc** Quang Binh, C Vietnam
160 L9 **Xuan'en** Hubei, C China
160 K8 **Xuanhan** Sichuan, C China
161 O2 **Xuanhua** Hebei, E China
161 P4 **Xuanhui He** ≈ E China
161 Q8 **Xuanzhou** *var.* Xuancheng. Anhui, E China
161 N7 **Xuchang** Henan, C China
137 X10 **Xudat** *Rus.* Khudat. NE Azerbaijan
81 M16 **Xuddur** *var.* Hudur, *It.* Oddur. Bakool, SW Somalia
80 O13 **Xudun** Nugaal, N Somalia
160 L11 **Xuefeng Shan** ▲ S China
42 F2 **Xunantunich** *ruins* Cayo, W Belize
163 W6 **Xun He** ≈ NE China
160 L7 **Xun He** ≈ C China
160 L14 **Xun Jiang** ≈ S China
163 W5 **Xunke** Heilongjiang, NE China
161 P13 **Xunwu** Jiangxi, S China
161 O3 **Xushui** Hebei, E China
160 L16 **Xuwen** Guangdong, S China
160 I11 **Xuyong** *var.* Yongning. Sichuan, C China
161 P6 **Xuzhou** *var.* Hsu-chou, Suchow, Tongshan; *prev.* T'ung-shan. Jiangsu, E China
114 K13 **Xylaganí** *var.* Xilaganí. Anatolikí Makedonía kai Thráki, NE Greece
115 F19 **Xylókastro** *var.* Xilokastro. Pelopónnisos, S Greece

Y

160 H9 **Ya'an** *var.* Yaan. Sichuan, C China
182 L10 **Yaapeet** Victoria, SE Australia
79 D15 **Yabassi** Littoral, W Cameroon
81 J15 **Yabēlo** Oromo, C Ethiopia
114 H9 **Yablanitsa** Lovech Oblast, W Bulgaria
43 N7 **Yablis** Región Autónoma Atlántico Norte, NE Nicaragua
123 O14 **Yablonovyy Khrebet** ▲ S Russian Federation
162 J14 **Yabrai Shan** ▲ NE China
45 U6 **Yabucoa** E Puerto Rico
160 J11 **Yachi He** ≈ S China
32 H10 **Yacolt** Washington, NW USA
54 M10 **Yacuaray** Amazonas, S Venezuela
57 M22 **Yacuiba** Tarija, S Bolivia
57 K16 **Yacuma, Río** ≈ C Bolivia
155 H16 **Yādgīr** Karnātaka, C India
21 R8 **Yadkin River** ≈ North Carolina, SE USA
21 R9 **Yadkinville** North Carolina, SE USA
129 P3 **Yadrin** Chuvashskaya Respublika, W Russian Federation
165 O16 **Yaeyama-shotō** *var.* Yaegama-shotō. *island group* SW Japan
75 O8 **Yafran** NW Libya
165 S2 **Yagashiri-tō** *island* NE Japan
65 H21 **Yaghan Basin** *undersea feature* SE Pacific Ocean
123 S9 **Yagodnoye** Magadanskaya Oblast', E Russian Federation
Yagotin *see* Yahotyn
78 G12 **Yagoua** Extrême-Nord, NE Cameroon
159 Q11 **Yagradagzê Shan** ▲ C China
Yaguachi *see* Yaguachi Nuevo
56 B7 **Yaguachi Nuevo** *var.* Yaguachi. Guayas, W Ecuador
Yaguarón, Río *see* Jaguarão, Rio
117 Q11 **Yahorlyts'kyy Lyman** *bay* S Ukraine
117 Q5 **Yahotyn** *Rus.* Yagotin. Kyyivs'ka Oblast', N Ukraine
40 L12 **Yahualica** Jalisco, SW Mexico
79 L17 **Yahuma** Orientale, N Dem. Rep. Congo (Zaire)
136 K15 **Yahyalı** Kayseri, C Turkey
167 N15 **Yai, Khao** ▲ SW Thailand
164 M14 **Yaizu** Shizuoka, Honshū, S Japan
160 G9 **Yajiang** Sichuan, C China
119 O14 **Yakawlyevichi** *Rus.* Yakovlevichi. Vitsyebskaya Voblasts', NE Belarus
163 S6 **Yakeshi** Nei Mongol Zizhiqu, N China
32 I9 **Yakima** Washington, NW USA
32 J10 **Yakima River** ≈ Washington, NW USA
114 G7 **Yakimovo** Montana, NW Bulgaria
Yakkabag *see* Yakkabogh
147 N12 **Yakkabogh** *Rus.* Yakkabag. Qashqadaryo Wiloyati, S Uzbekistan
148 L12 **Yakmach** Baluchistān, SW Pakistan
77 O12 **Yako** W Burkina
39 W13 **Yakobi Island** *island* Alexander Archipelago, Alaska, USA
79 K16 **Yakoma** Equateur, N Dem. Rep. Congo (Zaire)
114 H11 **Yakoruda** Blagoevgrad, SW Bulgaria
Yakovlevichi *see* Yakawlyevichi
129 T2 **Yakshur-Bod'ya** Udmurtskaya Respublika, NW Russian Federation
165 Q5 **Yakumo** Hokkaidō, NE Japan
164 B17 **Yaku-shima** *island* Nansei-shotō, SW Japan
39 V12 **Yakutat** Alaska, USA
39 U12 **Yakutat Bay** *inlet* Alaska, USA
Yakutia/Yakutiya/Yakutiya, Respublika *see* Sakha (Yakutiya), Respublika
123 Q10 **Yakutsk** Respublika Sakha (Yakutiya), NE Russian Federation
167 O17 **Yala** Yala, SW Thailand
182 D6 **Yalata** South Australia
31 S9 **Yale** Michigan, N USA
180 I11 **Yalgoo** Western Australia
114 O12 **Yalıköy** İstanbul, NW Turkey
79 L14 **Yalinga** Haute-Kotto, C Central African Republic
119 M17 **Yalizava** *Rus.* Yelizovo. Mahilyowskaya Voblasts', E Belarus
44 L13 **Yallahs Hill** ▲ E Jamaica
22 L3 **Yalobusha River** ≈ Mississippi, S USA
79 H15 **Yaloké** Ombella-Mpoko, W Central African Republic
160 E7 **Yalong Jiang** ≈ C China
136 E11 **Yalova** Yalova, NW Turkey
136 E11 **Yalova** ◈ *province* NW Turkey
Yaloveny *see* Ialoveni
Yalpug *see* Ialpug
Yalpug, Ozero *see* Yalpuh, Ozero
117 N12 **Yalpuh, Ozero** *Rus.* Ozero Yalpug. ◎ SW Ukraine
117 T14 **Yalta** Respublika Krym, S Ukraine
163 W12 **Yalu** *Chin.* Yalu Jiang, *Jap.* Oryokko, *Kor.* Amnok-kang. ≈ China/North Korea
Yalu Jiang *see* Yalu
136 F14 **Yalvaç** İsparta, SW Turkey
165 R9 **Yamada** Iwate, Honshū, C Japan
165 D14 **Yamaga** Kumamoto, Kyūshū, SW Japan
165 P10 **Yamagata** Yamagata, Honshū, C Japan
165 P9 **Yamagata** *off.* Yamagata-ken. ◈ *prefecture* Honshū, C Japan
164 C16 **Yamagawa** Kagoshima, Kyūshū, SW Japan
164 E13 **Yamaguchi** *var.* Yamaguti. Yamaguchi, Honshū, SW Japan
164 E13 **Yamaguchi** *off.* Yamaguchi-ken, *var.* Yamaguti. ◈ *prefecture* Honshū, SW Japan
Yamaguti *see* Yamaguchi
127 X5 **Yamalo-Nenetskiy Avtonomnyy Okrug** ◈ *autonomous district* N Russian Federation
122 J7 **Yamal, Poluostrov** *peninsula* N Russian Federation
165 N13 **Yamanashi** *off.* Yamanashi-ken, *var.* Yamanasi. ◈ *prefecture* Honshū, S Japan
Yamanasi *see* Yamanashi
Yamanīyah, Al Jumhūrīyah al *see* Yemen
129 W5 **Yamantau** ▲ W Russian Federation
Yamasaki *see* Yamazaki
15 P12 **Yamaska** ≈ Quebec, SE Canada
192 G4 **Yamato Ridge** *undersea feature* S Sea of Japan
164 I13 **Yamazaki** *var.* Yamasaki. Hyōgo, Honshū, SW Japan
183 V5 **Yamba** New South Wales, SE Australia
81 D16 **Yambio** *var.* Yambiyo. Western Equatoria, S Sudan
Yambiyo *see* Yambio
114 L10 **Yambol** *Turk.* Yanboli. Yambol, E Bulgaria
114 M11 **Yambol** ◈ *province* E Bulgaria
79 M17 **Yambuya** Orientale, N Dem. Rep. Congo (Zaire)
171 T15 **Yamdena, Pulau** *prev.* Jamdena. *island* Kepulauan Tanimbar, E Indonesia
165 O14 **Yame** Fukuoka, Kyūshū, SW Japan
166 M6 **Yamethin** Mandalay, C Burma
186 C6 **Yaminbot** East Sepik, NW PNG
181 U9 **Yamma Yamma, Lake** ◎ Queensland, C Australia
76 M16 **Yamoussoukro** ● (Ivory Coast) C Ivory Coast
37 P3 **Yampa River** ≈ Colorado, C USA
117 S2 **Yampil'** Sums'ka Oblast', NE Ukraine
116 M8 **Yampil'** Vinnyts'ka Oblast', C Ukraine
123 T9 **Yamsk** Magadanskaya Oblast', E Russian Federation
152 J8 **Yamuna** *prev.* Jumna. ≈ N India
152 I9 **Yamunānagar** Haryāna, N India
Yamundá *see* Nhamundá, Rio
145 U8 **Yamyshevo** Pavlodar, NE Kazakhstan
159 N16 **Yamzho Yumco** ◎ W China
123 Q8 **Yana** ≈ NE Russian Federation
186 H9 **Yanaba Island** *island* SE PNG
155 L16 **Yanam** *var.* Yanaon. Pondicherry, E India
160 L5 **Yan'an** *var.* Yanan. Shaanxi, C China
Yanaon *see* Yanam
129 U3 **Yanaul** Respublika Bashkortostan, W Russian Federation
118 O12 **Yanavichy** *Rus.* Yanovichi. Vitsyebskaya Voblasts', NE Belarus
Yanboli *see* Yambol
140 K8 **Yanbu' al Baḩr** Al Madīnah, W Saudi Arabia
21 T8 **Yanceyville** North Carolina, SE USA
161 R7 **Yancheng** Jiangsu, E China
159 W8 **Yanchi** Ningxia, N China
160 L5 **Yanchuan** Shaanxi, C China
183 O10 **Yanco Creek** *seasonal river* New South Wales, SE Australia
183 O6 **Yanda Creek** *seasonal river* New South Wales, SE Australia
182 K4 **Yandama Creek** *seasonal river* New South Wales/South Australia
161 S11 **Yandang Shan** ▲ SE China
Yandua *see* Yadua
159 O6 **Yandun** Xinjiang Uygur Zizhiqu, W China
76 L13 **Yanfolila** Sikasso, SW Mali
79 M18 **Yangambi** Orientale, N Dem. Rep. Congo (Zaire)
158 M15 **Yangbajain** Xizang Zizhiqu, W China
Yangchow *see* Yangzhou
160 M15 **Yangchun** Guangdong, S China
161 N2 **Yanggao** Shanxi, C China
Yanggeta *see* Yaqeta
Yangiabad *see* Yangiobod
Yangibazar *see* Dzhany-Bazar, Kyrgyzstan
Yangi-Bazar *see* Kofarnihon, Tajikistan
Yangiklshak *see* Yangiqishloq
146 M13 **Yangi-Nishon** *Rus.* Yang-Nishan. Qashqadaryo Wiloyati, S Uzbekistan
147 Q9 **Yangiobod** *Rus.* Yangiabad. Toshkent Wiloyati, E Uzbekistan
147 O10 **Yangiqishloq** *Rus.* Yangiklshak. Jizzakh Wiloyati, C Uzbekistan
147 P11 **Yangiyer** Sirdaryo Wiloyati, E Uzbekistan
147 P9 **Yangiyŭl** *Rus.* Yangiyul'. Toshkent Wiloyati, E Uzbekistan
160 M15 **Yangjiang** Guangdong, S China
Yangku *see* Taiyuan
Yang-Nishan *see* Yangi-Nishon
166 L8 **Yangon** *Eng.* Rangoon. ● (Burma) Yangon, S Burma
166 M8 **Yangon** *Eng.* Rangoon. ◈ *division* SW Burma
160 K17 **Yangpu Gang** *harbor* Hainan, S China
161 N4 **Yangquan** Shanxi, C China
161 N13 **Yangshan** Guangdong, S China
167 U12 **Yang Sin, Chu** ▲ S Vietnam
Yangtze *see* Chang Jiang, C China
Yangtze Kiang *see* Chang Jiang
161 R7 **Yangzhou** *var.* Yangchow. Jiangsu, E China
160 L5 **Yan He** ≈ C China
163 Y10 **Yanji** Jilin, NE China
Yanji *see* Longjing
29 Q12 **Yankton** South Dakota, N USA
Yannina *see* Ioánnina
123 Q7 **Yano-Indigirskaya Nizmennost'** *plain* NE Russian Federation
Yanovichi *see* Yanavichy
155 K24 **Yan Oya** ≈ N Sri Lanka
158 K6 **Yanqi** *var.* Yanqi Huizu Zizhixian. Xinjiang Uygur Zizhiqu, NW China
Yanqi Huizu Zizhixian *see* Yanqi
161 P2 **Yan Shan** ▲ E China
161 Q10 **Yanshan** Jiangxi, S China
160 H14 **Yanshan** *prev.* Hekou. Yunnan, SW China
163 X8 **Yanshou** Heilongjiang, NE China
123 Q7 **Yanskiy Zaliv** *bay* N Russian Federation
183 O4 **Yantabulla** New South Wales, SE Australia
161 R4 **Yantai** *var.* Yan-t'ai; *prev.* Chefoo, Chih-fu. Shandong, E China
118 A13 **Yantarnyy** *Ger.* Palmnicken. Kaliningradskaya Oblast', W Russian Federation
114 J9 **Yantra** Gabrovo, N Bulgaria
114 K9 **Yantra** ≈ N Bulgaria
160 G11 **Yanyuan** Sichuan, C China
161 P5 **Yanzhou** Shandong, E China
79 E16 **Yaoundé** *var.* Yaunde. ● (Cameroon) Centre, S Cameroon
188 I14 **Yap** ◇ *state* W Micronesia
188 F16 **Yap** *island* Caroline Islands, W Micronesia
57 M18 **Yapacani, Río** ≈ C Bolivia
171 W14 **Yapa Kopra** Irian Jaya, E Indonesia
Yapan *see* Yapen, Selat
Yapanskoye More *see* Japan, Sea of
77 P15 **Yapei** N Ghana
12 M10 **Yapeitso, Mont** ▲ Quebec, E Canada
171 W12 **Yapen, Pulau** *prev.* Japen. *island* E Indonesia
171 W12 **Yapen, Selat** *var.* Yapan. *strait* Irian Jaya, E Indonesia
61 E15 **Yapeyú** Corrientes, NE Argentina
136 I11 **Yapraklı** Çankırı, N Turkey
174 M3 **Yap Trench** *var.* Yap Trough. *undersea feature* SE Philippine Sea
Yap Trough *see* Yap Trench
Yapurá *see* Caquetá, Río, Brazil/Colombia
Yapurá *see* Japurá, Rio, Brazil/Colombia
197 I12 **Yaqaga** *island* N Fiji
197 H12 **Yaqeta** *prev.* Yanggeta. *island* Yasawa Group, NW Fiji
40 G6 **Yaqui** Sonora, NW Mexico
32 E12 **Yaquina Bay** *bay* Oregon, NW USA
40 G6 **Yaqui, Río** ≈ NW Mexico
54 K5 **Yaracuy** *off.* Estado Yaracuy. ◈ *state* NW Venezuela
146 E13 **Yaradzhi** *Turkm.* Yarajy. Akhalskiy Velayat, C Turkmenistan
Yarajy *see* Yaradzhi
127 Q15 **Yaransk** Kirovskaya Oblast', NW Russian Federation
136 F17 **Yardımcı Burnu** *headland* SW Turkey
97 Q19 **Yare** ≈ E England, UK
127 S9 **Yarega** Respublika Komi, NW Russian Federation
116 I7 **Yaremcha** Ivano-Frankivs'ka Oblast', W Ukraine
189 Q9 **Yaren** SW Nauru
127 Q10 **Yarensk** Arkhangel'skaya Oblast', NW Russian Federation
155 F16 **Yargatti** Karnātaka, W India
164 M12 **Yariga-take** ▲ Honshū, S Japan
141 O15 **Yarīm** W Yemen
54 F14 **Yarí, Río** ≈ SW Colombia
54 K5 **Yaritagua** Yaracuy, N Venezuela
Yarkand *see* Yarkant He
Yarkant *see* Shache
158 E9 **Yarkant He** *var.* Yarkand. ≈ NW China
149 U3 **Yarkhūn** ≈ NW Pakistan
Yarlung Zangbo Jiang *see* Brahmaputra
116 L6 **Yarmolyntsi** Khmel'nyts'ka Oblast', W Ukraine
163 T11 **Yar Moron** ≈ N China
13 O16 **Yarmouth** Nova Scotia, SE Canada
Yarmouth *see* Great Yarmouth
Yaroslav *see* Jarosław
126 L15 **Yaroslavl'** Yaroslavskaya Oblast', W Russian Federation
126 K14 **Yaroslavskaya Oblast'** ◈ *province* W Russian Federation
123 N11 **Yaroslavskiy** Respublika Sakha (Yakutiya), NE Russian Federation
183 P13 **Yarram** Victoria, SE Australia
183 O11 **Yarrawonga** Victoria, SE Australia
182 L4 **Yarriarraburra Swamp** *wetland* New South Wales, SE Australia
122 I8 **Yar-Sale** Yamalo-Nenetskiy Avtonomnyy Okrug, N Russian Federation
122 K11 **Yartsevo** Krasnoyarskiy Kray, C Russian Federation
128 I4 **Yartsevo** Smolenskaya Oblast', W Russian Federation
54 E8 **Yarumal** Antioquia, NW Colombia
187 W14 **Yasawa Group** *island group* NW Fiji
77 V12 **Yashi** Katsina, N Nigeria
77 S14 **Yashikera** Kwara, W Nigeria
147 T14 **Yashilkŭl** *Rus.* Ozero Yashil'kul'. ◎ SE Tajikistan
Yashil'kul', Ozero *see* Yashilkŭl
165 P9 **Yashima** Akita, Honshū, C Japan
129 P13 **Yashkul'** Respublika Kalmykiya, SW Russian Federation
146 F13 **Yashlyk** Akhalskiy Velayat, C Turkmenistan
Yasinovataya *see* Yasynuvata
114 N10 **Yasna Polyana** Burgas, SE Bulgaria
167 R10 **Yasothon** Yasothon, E Thailand
183 R10 **Yass** New South Wales, SE Australia
Yassy *see* Iaşi
164 H12 **Yasugi** Shimane, Honshū, SW Japan
143 N10 **Yāsūj** *var.* Yesuj; *prev.* Tal-e Khosravī. Kohkīlūyeh va Būyer Aḩmadī, C Iran
136 M11 **Yasun Burnu** *headland* N Turkey
117 X8 **Yasynuvata** *Rus.* Yasinovataya. Donets'ka Oblast', SE Ukraine
136 C15 **Yatağan** Muğla, SW Turkey
165 Q7 **Yatate-tōge** *pass* Honshū, C Japan
187 Q17 **Yaté** Province Sud, S New Caledonia
27 P6 **Yates Center** Kansas, C USA
185 B21 **Yates Point** *headland* South Island, NZ
9 N9 **Yathkyed Lake** ◎ Nunavut, NE Canada
171 T16 **Yatoke** Pulau Babar, E Indonesia
79 M18 **Yatolema** Orientale, N Dem. Rep. Congo (Zaire)
164 C15 **Yatsushiro** *var.* Yatusiro. Kumamoto, Kyūshū, SW Japan
164 C15 **Yatsushiro-kai** *bay* SW Japan
138 F11 **Yatta** *var.* Yuta. S West Bank
81 J20 **Yatta Plateau** *plateau* SE Kenya
Yatusiro *see* Yatsushiro
57 F17 **Yauca, Río** ≈ SW Peru
45 S6 **Yauco** W Puerto Rico
Yaunde *see* Yaoundé
Yavan *see* Yovon
Yavarí *see* Javari, Rio
56 G9 **Yavari Mirim, Río** ≈ NE Peru
40 G7 **Yavaros** Sonora, NW Mexico
154 I13 **Yavatmāl** Mahārāshtra, C India
54 M9 **Yaví, Cerro** ▲ C Venezuela
43 W16 **Yaviza** Darién, SE Panama
138 F10 **Yavne** Central, W Israel
116 H5 **Yavoriv** *Pol.* Jaworów, *Rus.* Yavorov. L'vivs'ka Oblast', NW Ukraine
Yavorov *see* Yavoriv
164 F14 **Yawatahama** Ehime, Shikoku, SW Japan
Ya Xian *see* Sanya
136 L17 **Yayladaği** Hatay, S Turkey
127 V13 **Yayva** Permskaya Oblast', NW Russian Federation
127 V12 **Yayva** ≈ NW Russian Federation
143 Q9 **Yazd** *var.* Yezd. Yazd, C Iran
143 Q8 **Yazd** *off.* Ostān-e Yazd, *var.* Yezd. ◈ *province* C Iran
Yazgulemskiy Khrebet *see* Yazgulom, Qatorkŭhi
147 S13 **Yazgulom, Qatorkŭhi** *Rus.* Yazgulemskiy Khrebet. ▲ S Tajikistan
22 K5 **Yazoo City** Mississippi, S USA
22 K5 **Yazoo River** ≈ Mississippi, S USA
129 Q5 **Yazykovo** Ul'yanovskaya Oblast', W Russian Federation
109 U4 **Ybbs** Niederösterreich, NE Austria
109 U4 **Ybbs** ≈ C Austria
95 G22 **Yding Skovhøj** *hill* C Denmark
115 G20 **Ýdra** *var.* Ídhra, Idra. Ýdra, S Greece
115 G21 **Ýdra** *var.* Ídhra. *island* S Greece
115 G20 **Ýdras, Kólpos** *strait* S Greece
167 N10 **Ye** Mon State, S Myanmar
183 O12 **Yea** Victoria, SE Australia
78 I5 **Yebbi-Bou** Borkou-Ennedi-Tibesti, N Chad
158 F9 **Yecheng** *var.* Kargilik. Xinjiang Uygur Zizhiqu, NW China
105 R11 **Yecla** Murcia, SE Spain
40 H6 **Yécora** Sonora, NW Mexico
Yedintsy *see* Edineţ
126 J13 **Yefimovskiy** Leningradskaya Oblast', NW Russian Federation
128 K6 **Yefremov** Tul'skaya Oblast', W Russian Federation
Yégainnyin *see* Henan
137 U12 **Yeghegis** *Rus.* Yekhegis. ≈ C Armenia
145 T10 **Yegindybulak** *Kaz.* Egindibulaq. Karaganda, C Kazakhstan
128 L4 **Yegor'yevsk** Moskovskaya Oblast', W Russian Federation
Yehuda, Haré *see* Judaean Hills
81 E15 **Yei** ≈ S Sudan
161 P8 **Yeji** *var.* Yejiaji. Anhui, E China
Yejiaji *see* Yeji
122 G10 **Yekaterinburg** *prev.* Sverdlovsk. Sverdlovskaya Oblast', C Russian Federation
Yekaterinodar *see* Krasnodar
Yekaterinoslav *see* Dnipropetrovs'k
123 R13 **Yekaterinoslavka** Amurskaya Oblast', SE Russian Federation
129 O7 **Yekaterinovka** Saratovskaya Oblast', W Russian Federation
76 K16 **Yekepa** NE Liberia
129 T3 **Yelabuga** Respublika Tatarstan, W Russian Federation
Yela Island *see* Rossel Island
129 O8 **Yelan'** Volgogradskaya Oblast', SW Russian Federation
117 Q9 **Yelanets'** *Rus.* Yelanets. Mykolayivs'ka Oblast', S Ukraine
123 S13 **Yel'ban'** Khabarovskiy Kray, E Russian Federation
128 L7 **Yelets** Lipetskaya Oblast', W Russian Federation
127 W4 **Yeletskiy** Respublika Komi, NW Russian Federation
76 J11 **Yélimané** Kayes, W Mali
Yelisavetpol *see* Gäncä
Yelizavetgrad *see* Kirovohrad

◆ Country ● Country Capital ◇ Dependent Territory ○ Dependent Territory Capital ◈ Administrative Region ✕ International Airport ▲ Mountain ▲ Mountain Range Volcano ≈ River ◎ Lake ⊞ Reservoir

123 T12 Yelizavety, Mys headland SE Russian Federation
Yelizovo see Yelizava
129 S5 Yelkhovka Samarskaya Oblast', W Russian Federation
96 M1 Yell island NE Scotland, UK
155 E17 Yellāpur Karnātaka, W India
11 U17 Yellow Grass Saskatchewan, S Canada
Yellowhammer State see Alabama
11 O15 Yellowhead Pass pass Alberta/British Columbia, SW Canada
8 K10 Yellowknife territory capital Northwest Territories, W Canada
8 K9 Yellowknife ∽ Northwest Territories, NW Canada
23 P8 Yellow River ∽ Alabama/Florida, S USA
30 I4 Yellow River ∽ Wisconsin, N USA
30 J6 Yellow River ∽ Wisconsin, N USA
30 K7 Yellow River ∽ Wisconsin, N USA
Yellow River see Huang He
157 V8 Yellow Sea Chin. Huang Hai, Kor. Hwang-Hae. sea E Asia
33 S13 Yellowstone Lake ◎ Wyoming, C USA
33 T13 Yellowstone National Park national park Wyoming, NW USA
33 Y8 Yellowstone River ∽ Montana/Wyoming, NW USA
96 L1 Yell Sound strait N Scotland, UK
27 U9 Yellville Arkansas, C USA
122 K10 Yeloguy ∽ C Russian Federation
146 J14 Yëloten prev. Iolotan', Turkm. Yolöten. Maryyskiy Velayat, S Turkmenistan
119 M20 Yel'sk Rus. Yel'sk. Homyel'skaya Voblasts', SE Belarus
77 T13 Yelwa Kebbi, W Nigeria
21 R15 Yemassee South Carolina, SE USA
141 O15 Yemen off. Republic of Yemen, Ar. Al Jumhūrīyah al Yamanīyah, Al Yaman. ◆ republic SW Asia
116 M4 Yemil'chyne Zhytomyrs'ka Oblast', N Ukraine
126 M10 Yemtsa Arkhangel'skaya Oblast', NW Russian Federation
126 M10 Yemtsa ∽ NW Russian Federation
127 R10 Yemva prev. Zheleznodorozhnyy. Respublika Komi, NW Russian
77 U17 Yenagoa Bayelsa, S Nigeria
117 X7 Yenakiyeve Rus. Yenakiyevo; prev. Ordzhonikidze, Rykovo. Donets'ka Oblast', E Ukraine
Yenakiyevo see Yenakiyeve
166 L6 Yenangyaung Magwe, W Myanmar
167 S5 Yên Bai Yên Bai, N Vietnam
183 P9 Yenda New South Wales, SE Australia
77 Q14 Yendi NE Ghana
158 E8 Yengisar Xinjiang Uygur Zizhiqu, NW China
121 R1 Yenierenköy var. Yialousa, Gk. Agialoúsa. NE Cyprus
Yenipazar see Novi Pazar
136 E12 Yenişehir Bursa, NW Turkey
Yenisei Bay see Yeniseyskiy Zaliv
122 K12 Yeniseysk Krasnoyarskiy Kray, C Russian Federation
197 W10 Yeniseyskiy Zaliv var. Yenisei Bay. bay N Russian Federation
129 Q12 Yenotayevka Astrakhanskaya Oblast', SW Russian Federation
126 L4 Yenozero, Ozero ◎ NW Russian Federation
Yenping see Nanping
39 Q11 Yentna River ∽ Alaska, USA
180 M10 Yeo, Lake salt lake Western Australia
183 R7 Yeoval New South Wales, SE Australia
97 K23 Yeovil SW England, UK
40 H6 Yepachic Chihuahua, N Mexico
181 Y8 Yeppoon Queensland, E Australia
128 M5 Yeraktur Ryazanskaya Oblast', W Russian Federation
Yeraliyev see Kuryk
146 F12 Yerbent Akhalskiy Velayat, C Turkmenistan
123 N11 Yerbogachen Irkutskaya Oblast', C Russian Federation
137 T12 Yerevan Eng. Erivan. ● (Armenia) C Armenia
137 U12 Yerevan ✕ C Armenia
145 R9 Yereymentau var. Jermentau, Yermentau, Kaz. Ereymentaū. Akmola, C Kazakhstan
129 O12 Yergeni hill range SW Russian Federation
Yeriho see Jericho
35 R6 Yerington Nevada, W USA
136 J13 Yerköy Yozgat, C Turkey
114 L13 Yerlisu Edirne, NW Turkey
Yermak see Aksu
145 R9 Yermentau Kaz. Ereymentaū, Jermentau. Akmola, C Kazakhstan
145 R9 Yermentau, Gory ⛰ C Kazakhstan
127 R5 Yermitsa Respublika Komi, NW Russian Federation
35 V14 Yermo California, W USA
123 P13 Yerofey Pavlovich Amurskaya Oblast', SE Russian Federation
99 F15 Yerseke Zeeland, SW Netherlands
129 Q8 Yershov Saratovskaya Oblast', W Russian Federation
127 P9 Yërtom Respublika Komi, NW Russian Federation
56 D13 Yerupaja, Nevado ▲ C Peru
Yerushalayim see Jerusalem
105 R4 Yesa, Embalse de ⊞ NE Spain
145 V15 Yesik Kaz. Esik; prev. Issyk. Almaty, SE Kazakhstan
145 O8 Yesil' Kaz. Esil. Akmola, C Kazakhstan
136 K15 Yeşilhisar Kayseri, C Turkey
136 L11 Yeşilırmak anc. Iris. ∽ N Turkey
37 U12 Yeso New Mexico, SW USA
Yeso see Hokkaidō
129 N15 Yessentuki Stavropol'skiy Kray, SW Russian Federation
122 M9 Yessey Evenkiyskiy Avtonomnyy Okrug, N Russian Federation
105 P12 Yeste Castilla-La Mancha, C Spain
Yesuj see Yāsūj
183 T4 Yetman New South Wales, SE Australia
76 L4 Yetti physical region N Mauritania
166 M4 Ye-u Sagaing, C Myanmar
102 H9 Yeu, Île d' island NW France
Yevlakh see Yevlax
137 W11 Yevlax Rus. Yevlakh. C Azerbaijan
117 S13 Yevpatoriya Respublika Krym, S Ukraine
128 K12 Yeya ∽ SW Russian Federation
158 I10 Yeyik Xinjiang Uygur Zizhiqu, W China
128 K12 Yeysk Krasnodarskiy Kray, SW Russian Federation
Yezd see Yazd
Yezerishche see Yezyaryshcha
Yezo see Hokkaidō
118 N11 Yezyaryshcha Rus. Yezerishche. Vitsyebskaya Voblasts', NE Belarus
Yialí see Gyalí
Yialousa see Yenierenköy
163 V7 Yi'an Heilongjiang, NE China
Yiannitsá see Giannitsá
160 I10 Yibin Sichuan, C China
158 K13 Yibug Caka ◎ W China
160 M9 Yichang Hubei, C China
160 L5 Yichuan Shaanxi, C China
157 W3 Yichun Heilongjiang, NE China
163 X6 Yichun var. I-ch'un. Heilongjiang, NE China
161 O11 Yichun Jiangxi, S China
Yidu see Qingzhou
188 C15 Yigo NE Guam
161 Q5 Yi He ∽ E China
163 X8 Yilan Heilongjiang, NE China
136 C9 Yıldız Dağları ⛰ NW Turkey
136 L13 Yıldızeli Sivas, N Turkey
163 U4 Yilehuli Shan ⛰ NE China
163 S7 Yimin He ∽ NE China
159 W8 Yinchuan var. Yinch'uan, Yin-ch'uan, Yinchwan. Ningxia, N China
Yinchuanzhan see Xincheng
Yinchwan see Yinchuan
Yindu He see Indus
161 N14 Yingde Guangdong, S China
161 O7 Ying He ∽ C China
163 U13 Yingkou var. Ying-k'ou, Yingkow; prev. Newchwang, Niuchwang. Liaoning, NE China
Yingkow see Yingkou
161 P9 Yingshan Hubei, C China
Yingshan see Guangshui
161 Q10 Yingtan Jiangxi, S China
Yin-hsien see Ningbo
158 H5 Yining var. I-ning, Uigh. Gulja, Kuldja. Xinjiang Uygur Zizhiqu, NW China
160 K11 Yinjiang Guizhou, S China
166 L4 Yinmabin Sagaing, C Myanmar
163 N13 Yin Shan ⛰ N China
Yin-tu Ho see Indus
159 P15 Yi'ong Zangbo ∽ W China
Yioúra see Gyáros
81 J14 Yirga 'Alem It. Irgalem. Southern, S Ethiopia
61 E19 Yí, Río ∽ C Uruguay
81 E14 Yirol El Buhayrat, S Sudan
Yirshi see Yirxie
163 S8 Yirxie prev. Yirshi. Nei Mongol Zizhiqu, N China
161 Q5 Yishui Shandong, E China
Yisrael/Yisra'el see Israel
Yíthion see Gýtheio
Yitiaoshan see Jingtai
163 W10 Yitong Jilin, NE China
159 P5 Yiwu var. Aratürük. Xinjiang Uygur Zizhiqu, NW China
163 U12 Yiwulü Shan ⛰ N China
163 T12 Yi Xian Liaoning, NE China
161 N10 Yiyang Hunan, S China
161 Q10 Yiyang Jiangxi, S China
161 N13 Yizhang Hunan, S China
93 K19 Yläne Länsi-Suomi, W Finland
93 L14 Yli-Ii Oulu, C Finland
93 L14 Ylikiiminki Oulu, C Finland
92 N13 Yli-Kitka ◎ NE Finland
93 K17 Ylistaro Länsi-Suomi, W Finland
92 K13 Ylitornio Lappi, NW Finland
93 L15 Ylivieska Oulu, W Finland
93 L18 Ylöjärvi Länsi-Suomi, W Finland
95 N17 Yngaren ◎ C Sweden
25 T12 Yoakum Texas, SW USA
77 X13 Yobe ◈ state NE Nigeria
165 R3 Yobetsu-dake ⊼ Hokkaidō, NE Japan
80 L11 Yoboki C Djibouti
22 M4 Yockanookany River ∽ Mississippi, S USA
22 L2 Yocona River ∽ Mississippi, S USA
171 Y15 Yodom Irian Jaya, E Indonesia
169 Q16 Yogyakarta prev. Djokjakarta, Jogjakarta, Jokyakarta. Jawa, C Indonesia
169 P17 Yogyakarta off. Daerah Istimewa Yogyakarta, var. Djokjakarta, Jogjakarta, Jokyakarta. ◈ autonomous district S Indonesia
165 Q3 Yoichi Hokkaidō, NE Japan
42 G6 Yojoa, Lago de ◎ NW Honduras
79 G16 Yokadouma Est, SE Cameroon
Yōkaiti see Yōkaichi
164 K13 Yokkaichi var. Yokkaiti. Mie, Honshū, SW Japan
Yokkaiti see Yokkaichi
79 E15 Yoko Centre, C Cameroon
165 V15 Yokoate-jima island Nansei-shotō, SW Japan
165 R6 Yokohama Aomori, Honshū, C Japan
165 O14 Yokosuka Kanagawa, Honshū, S Japan
164 G12 Yokota Shimane, Honshū, SW Japan
165 Q9 Yokote Akita, Honshū, C Japan
77 Y14 Yola Adamawa, E Nigeria
79 L19 Yolombo Equateur, C Dem. Rep. Congo (Zaire)
Yolöten see Yëloten
165 Y15 Yome-jima island Ogasawara-shotō, SE Japan
76 K16 Yomou Guinée-Forestière, SE Guinea
171 Y15 Yomuka Irian Jaya, E Indonesia
188 C16 Yona E Guam
164 H12 Yonago Tottori, Honshū, SW Japan
165 N16 Yonaguni Okinawa, SW Japan
165 N16 Yonaguni-jima island Nansei-shotō, SW Japan
165 T16 Yonaha-dake ▲ Okinawa, SW Japan
163 X14 Yonan SW North Korea
165 P10 Yonezawa Yamagata, Honshū, C Japan
161 Q12 Yong'an var. Yongan. Fujian, SE China
159 T9 Yongchang Gansu, N China
161 P7 Yongcheng Henan, C China
163 Z15 Yŏngch'ŏn Jap. Eisen. SE South Korea
160 J10 Yongchuan Chongqing Shi, C China
159 U10 Yongdeng Gansu, C China
131 W9 Yongding He ∽ E China
161 P11 Yongfeng Jiangxi, S China
158 L5 Yongfengqu Xinjiang Uygur Zizhiqu, W China
160 L13 Yongfu Guangxi Zhuangzu Ziziqu, S China 24.57
163 X13 Yŏnghŭng E North Korea
159 U10 Yongjing Gansu, C China
163 Y15 Yŏngju Jap. Eishū. C South Korea
Yongning see Xuyong
160 E12 Yongping Yunnan, SW China
160 G12 Yongren Yunnan, SW China
160 L10 Yongshun var. Lingxi. Hunan, S China
161 P10 Yongxiu var. Tujiabu. Jiangxi, S China
160 M12 Yongzhou Hunan, S China
18 K14 Yonkers New York, NE USA
103 Q7 Yonne ◈ department C France
103 P6 Yonne ∽ C France
54 H9 Yopal var. El Yopal. Casanare, C Colombia
158 E8 Yopurga var. Yukuriawat. Xinjiang Uygur Zizhiqu, NW China
180 J12 York Western Australia
97 M16 York anc. Eboracum, Eburacum. N England, UK
23 N5 York Alabama, S USA
29 Q15 York Nebraska, C USA
18 G16 York Pennsylvania, NE USA
21 R11 York South Carolina, SE USA
14 J13 York ∽ Ontario, SE Canada
15 X6 York ∽ Quebec, SE Canada
181 V1 York, Cape headland Queensland, NE Australia
182 I9 Yorke Peninsula peninsula South Australia
182 I9 Yorketown South Australia
18 P9 York Harbor Maine, NE USA
21 X6 York River ∽ Virginia, NE USA
97 M16 Yorkshire cultural region N England, UK
97 L16 Yorkshire Dales physical region N England, UK
11 V16 Yorkton Saskatchewan, S Canada
25 T12 Yorktown Texas, SW USA
21 X6 Yorktown Virginia, NE USA
30 M11 Yorkville Illinois, N USA
42 I5 Yoro Yoro, C Honduras
42 H5 Yoro ◈ department N Honduras
165 T16 Yoron-jima island Nansei-shotō, SW Japan
77 N13 Yorosso Sikasso, S Mali
35 R8 Yosemite National Park national park California, W USA
129 Q3 Yoshkar-Ola Respublika Mariy El, W Russian Federation
Yosino Gawa see Yoshino-gawa
171 Y16 Yos Sudarso, Pulau var. Pulau Dolak, Pulau Kolepom; prev. Jos Sudarso. island E Indonesia
163 Y17 Yŏsu Jap. Reisui. S South Korea
165 R4 Yotei-zan ▲ Hokkaidō, NE Japan
97 D21 Youghal Ir. Eochaill. S Ireland
97 D21 Youghal Bay Ir. Cuan Eochaille. inlet S Ireland
18 C15 Youghiogheny River ∽ Pennsylvania, NE USA
160 K14 You Jiang ∽ S China
183 Q9 Young New South Wales, SE Australia
11 T15 Young Saskatchewan, S Canada
61 E18 Young Río Negro, W Uruguay
182 G5 Younghusband, Lake salt lake South Australia
182 J10 Younghusband Peninsula peninsula South Australia
184 Q10 Young Nicks Head headland North Island, NZ
185 D20 Young Range ⛰ South Island, NZ
191 Q15 Young's Rock island Pitcairn Island, Pitcairn Islands
11 R16 Youngstown Alberta, SW Canada
31 V12 Youngstown Ohio, N USA
159 N9 Youshashan Qinghai, C China
Youth, Isle of see Juventud, Isla de la
77 N11 Youvarou Mopti, C Mali
160 K10 Youyang Sichuan, C China
163 Y7 Youyi Heilongjiang, NE China
147 P13 Yovon Rus. Yavan. SW Tajikistan
136 J13 Yozgat Yozgat, C Turkey
136 K13 Yozgat ◈ province C Turkey
62 O6 Ypacaraí var. Ypacaray. Central, S Paraguay
Ypacaray see Ypacaraí
62 P5 Ypané, Río ∽ C Paraguay
Ypres see Ieper
114 I13 Ypsário var. Ipsario. ▲ Thásos, E Greece
31 R10 Ypsilanti Michigan, N USA
34 M1 Yreka California, W USA
Yrendagüé see General Eugenio A. Garay
186 G5 Ysabel Channel channel N PNG
14 K8 Yser, Lac ◎ Quebec, SE Canada
147 Y8 Yshtyk Issyk-Kul'skaya Oblast', E Kyrgyzstan
Yssel see IJssel
103 Q12 Yssingeaux Haute-Loire, C France
95 K23 Ystad Skåne, S Sweden
Ysyk-Köl see Balykchy, Kyrgyzstan
Ysyk-Köl see Issyk-Kul', Ozero, Kyrgyzstan
Ysyk-Köl Oblasty see Issyk-Kul'skaya Oblast'
96 L8 Ythan ∽ NE Scotland, UK
Y Trallwng see Welshpool
94 C13 Ytre Arna Hordaland, S Norway
94 B12 Ytre Sula island S Norway
93 G17 Ytterhogdal Jämtland, C Sweden
Yu see Henan
Yuan Jiang see Red River
161 S13 Yüanlin Jap. Inrin. C Taiwan
161 N3 Yuanping Shanxi, C China
161 O11 Yuan Shui ∽ S China
35 O6 Yuba City California, W USA
35 O6 Yuba River ∽ California, W USA
80 H13 Yubdo Oromo, C Ethiopia
165 U3 Yübetsu Hokkaidō, NE Japan
Yübetsu-gawa see Yabetsu-gawa
41 X12 Yucatán ◈ state SE Mexico
47 O3 Yucatan Basin var. Yucatan Deep. undersea feature N Caribbean Sea
Yucatán, Canal de see Yucatan Channel
41 Y10 Yucatan Channel Sp. Canal de Yucatán. channel Cuba/Mexico
Yucatan Deep see Yucatan Basin
Yucatan Peninsula see Yucatán, Península de
41 X13 Yucatán, Península de Eng. Yucatan Peninsula. peninsula Guatemala/Mexico
36 I11 Yucca Arizona, SW USA
35 V15 Yucca Valley California, W USA
161 P4 Yucheng Shandong, E China
161 N4 Yuci Shanxi, C China
131 X5 Yudoma ∽ E Russian Federation
161 P12 Yudu Jiangxi, C China
Yue see Guangdong
160 M12 Yuecheng Ling ⛰ S China
181 P7 Yuendumu Northern Territory, N Australia
160 H10 Yuexi Sichuan, C China
161 N10 Yueyang Hunan, S China
127 U14 Yug Permskaya Oblast', NW Russian Federation
127 P13 Yug ∽ NW Russian Federation
123 R10 Yugorenok Respublika Sakha (Yakutiya), NE Russian Federation
122 H9 Yugorsk Khanty-Mansiyskiy Avtonomnyy Okrug, C Russian Federation
122 H7 Yugorskiy Poluostrov peninsula NW Russian Federation
112 M13 Yugoslavia off. Federal Republic of Yugoslavia, SCr. Jugoslavija, Savezna Republika Jugoslavija. ◆ federal republic SE Europe
146 K14 Yugo-Vostochnyye Garagumy prev. Yugo-Vostochnyye Karakumy. desert E Turkmenistan
Yugo-Vostochnyye Karakumy see Yugo-Vostochnyye Garagumy
161 S10 Yuhuan Dao island SE China
160 L14 Yu Jiang ∽ S China
123 S7 Yukagirskoye Ploskogor'ye plateau NE Russian Federation
118 L11 Yukhavichy Rus. Yukhovichi. Vitsyebskaya Voblasts', N Belarus
128 J4 Yukhnov Kaluzhskaya Oblast', W Russian Federation
Yukhovichi see Yukhavichy
79 J20 Yuki var. Yuki Kengunda. Bandundu, W Dem. Rep. Congo (Zaire)
Yuki Kengunda see Yuki
26 M10 Yukon Oklahoma, C USA
(0) F4 Yukon ∽ Canada/USA
Yukon see Yukon Territory
39 S7 Yukon Flats salt flat Alaska, USA
8 F8 Yukon Territory var. Yukon, Fr. Territoire du Yukon. ◈ territory NW Canada
137 T16 Yüksekova Hakkâri, SE Turkey
123 N10 Yukta Evenkiyskiy Avtonomnyy Okrug, C Russian Federation
165 O13 Yukuhashi var. Yukuhasi. Fukuoka, Kyūshū, SW Japan
Yukuhasi see Yukuhashi
Yukuriawat see Yopurga
127 O9 Yula ∽ NW Russian Federation
181 P8 Yulara Northern Territory, N Australia
129 W6 Yuldybayevo Respublika Bashkortostan, W Russian Federation
23 W8 Yulee Florida, SE USA
158 K7 Yuli var. Lopnur. Xinjiang Uygur Zizhiqu, NW China
161 T14 Yüli C Taiwan
160 L15 Yulin Guangxi Zhuangzu Zizhiqu, S China
160 L4 Yulin Shaanxi, C China
161 T14 Yüli Shan ▲ E Taiwan
160 F11 Yulongxue Shan ▲ SW China
36 H14 Yuma Arizona, SW USA
37 W3 Yuma Colorado, C USA
54 K5 Yumare Yaracuy, N Venezuela
63 G14 Yumbel Bío Bío, C Chile
79 N19 Yumbi Maniema, E Dem. Rep. Congo (Zaire)
159 R8 Yumen var. Laojunmiao, Yümen. Gansu, N China
159 Q7 Yumenzhen Gansu, N China
158 J3 Yumin Xinjiang Uygur Zizhiqu, NW China
Yun see Yunnan
136 G14 Yunak Konya, W Turkey
45 O8 Yuna, Río ∽ E Dominican Republic
38 I17 Yunaska Island island Aleutian Islands, Alaska, USA
160 M6 Yuncheng Shanxi, C China
57 L18 Yungas physical region E Bolivia
Yungki see Jilin
Yung-ning see Nanning
160 I12 Yun Gui Gaoyuan plateau SW China
Yunjinghong see Jinghong
160 M15 Yunkai Dashan ⛰ S China
Yunki see Jilin
160 E11 Yun Ling ⛰ SW China
161 N9 Yunmeng Hubei, C China
157 N14 Yunnan var. Yun, Yunnan Sheng, Yünnan, Yun-nan. ◈ province SW China
Yunnan see Kunming
Yunnan Sheng see Yunnan
165 P15 Yunomae Kumamoto, Kyūshū, SW Japan
161 N8 Yun Shui ∽ C China
182 J7 Yunta South Australia
161 Q14 Yunxiao Fujian, SE China
160 K9 Yunyang Sichuan, C China
193 S9 Yupanqui Basin undersea feature E Pacific Ocean
Yuratishki see Yuratsishki
119 I15 Yuratsishki Pol. Juraciszki, Rus. Yuratishki. Hrodzyenskaya Voblasts', W Belarus
Yurev see Tartu
122 J12 Yurga Kemerovskaya Oblast', S Russian Federation
56 E10 Yurimaguas Loreto, N Peru
129 P3 Yurino Respublika Mariy El, W Russian Federation
41 N13 Yuriria Guanajuato, C Mexico
127 T13 Yurla Komi-Permyatskiy Avtonomnyy Okrug, NW Russian Federation
Yuruá, Río see Juruá, Rio
114 M13 Yürük Tekirdağ, NW Turkey
158 G10 Yurungkax He ∽ W China
127 Q14 Yur'ya var. Jarja. Kirovskaya Oblast', NW Russian Federation
Yur'yev see Tartu
127 N16 Yur'yevets Ivanovskaya Oblast', W Russian Federation
128 M3 Yur'yev-Pol'skiy Vladimirskaya Oblast', W Russian Federation
117 V7 Yur"yivka Dnipropetrovs'ka Oblast', E Ukraine
42 I7 Yuscarán El Paraíso, S Honduras
161 P12 Yu Shan ⛰ S China
126 I7 Yushkozero Respublika Kareliya, NW Russian Federation
159 R13 Yushu Qinghai, C China
129 P12 Yusta Respublika Kalmykiya, SW Russian Federation
126 I10 Yustozero Respublika Kareliya, NW Russian Federation
137 Q11 Yusufeli Artvin, NE Turkey
164 F14 Yusuhara Kōchi, Shikoku, SW Japan
127 T14 Yus'va Permskaya Oblast', NW Russian Federation
Yuta see Yatta
161 P2 Yutian Hebei, E China
158 H10 Yutian var. Keriya. Xinjiang Uygur Zizhiqu, NW China
62 K5 Yuto Jujuy, NW Argentina
62 P7 Yuty Caazapá, S Paraguay
160 G13 Yuxi Yunnan, SW China
161 O2 Yuxian prev. Yu Xian. Hebei, E China
165 Q9 Yuzawa Akita, Honshū, C Japan
127 N16 Yuzha Ivanovskaya Oblast', W Russian Federation
Yuzhno-Alichurskiy Khrebet see Alichuri Janubí, Qatorkŭhi
Yuzhno-Kazakhstanskaya Oblast' see Yuzhnyy Kazakhstan
123 T13 Yuzhno-Sakhalinsk Jap. Toyohara; prev. Vladimirovka. Ostrov Sakhalin, Sakhalinskaya Oblast', SE Russian Federation
129 P14 Yuzhno-Sukhokumsk Respublika Dagestan, SW Russian Federation
145 Z10 Yuzhnyy Altay, Khrebet ⛰ E Kazakhstan
Yuzhnyy Bug see Pivdennyy Buh
145 O15 Yuzhnyy Kazakhstan off. Yuzhno-Kazakhstanskaya Oblast', Eng. South Kazakhstan, Kaz. Ongtüstik Qazaqstan Oblysy; prev. Chimkentskaya Oblast'. ◈ province S Kazakhstan
123 U10 Yuzhnyy, Mys headland E Russian Federation
129 W6 Yuzhnyy Ural var. Southern Urals. ⛰ W Russian Federation
159 V10 Yuzhong Gansu, C China
Yuzhou see Chongqing
103 N5 Yvelines ◈ department N France
108 B9 Yverdon var. Yverdon-les-Bains, Ger. Iferten; anc. Eborodunum. Vaud, W Switzerland
Yverdon-les-Bains see Yverdon
102 M3 Yvetot Seine-Maritime, N France
Yylanly see Il'yaly

Z

147 T12 Zaalayskiy Khrebet Taj. Qatorkŭhi Pasi Oloy. ⛰ Kyrgyzstan/Tajikistan
Zaamin see Zomin
Zaandam see Zaanstad
98 I10 Zaanstad prev. Zaandam. Noord-Holland, C Netherlands
Zabadani see Az Zabdānī
119 L18 Zabalatstsye Rus. Zabolot'ye. Homyel'skaya Voblasts', SE Belarus
112 L9 Žabalj Ger. Josefsdorf, Hung. Zsablya; prev. Józseffalva;. Serbia, N Yugoslavia
Zāb aş Şaghīr, Nahraz see Little Zab
123 P14 Zabaykal'sk Chitinskaya Oblast', S Russian Federation
Zāb-e Kuchek, Rūdkhāneh-ye see Little Zab
Zabeln see Sabile
Zabéré see Zabré
Zabern see Saverne
141 N16 Zabīd W Yemen
141 O16 Zabīd, Wādī dry watercourse SW Yemen
Žabinka see Zhabinka
Ząbkowice see Ząbkowice Śląskie
111 G15 Ząbkowice Śląskie var. Ząbkowice, Ger. Frankenstein, Frankenstein in Schlesien. Dolnośląskie, SW Poland
110 P10 Zabłudów Podlaskie, NE Poland
112 D8 Zabok Krapina-Zagorje, N Croatia
143 W9 Zābol var. Shahr-i-Zabul, Zabul; prev. Nasratabad. Sīstān va Balūchestān, E Iran
Zābol see Zābul
143 W13 Zābolī Sīstān va Balūchestān, SE Iran
Zabolot'ye see Zabalatstsye
77 Q13 Zabré var. Zabéré. S Burkina
111 G17 Zábřeh Ger. Hohenstadt. Olomoucký Kraj, E Czech Republic
111 J16 Zabrze Ger. Hindenburg, Hindenburg in Oberschlesien. Śląskie, S Poland
149 O7 Zābul Per. Zābol. ◈ province SE Afghanistan
Zabul see Zābol
42 E6 Zacapa Zacapa, E Guatemala
42 A3 Zacapa off. Departamento de Zacapa. ◈ department E Guatemala
40 M14 Zacapú Michoacán de Ocampo, SW Mexico
41 V14 Zacatal Campeche, SE Mexico
40 M11 Zacatecas Zacatecas, C Mexico
40 L10 Zacatecas ◈ state C Mexico
42 F8 Zacatecoluca La Paz, S El Salvador
41 P15 Zacatepec Morelos, S Mexico
41 Q13 Zacatlán Puebla, S Mexico
144 F8 Zachagansk Zapadnyy Kazakhstan, NW Kazakhstan
115 D20 Zacháro var. Zaharo, Zakháro. Dytikí Elláda, S Greece
22 J8 Zachary Louisiana, S USA
117 U6 Zachepylivka Kharkivs'ka Oblast', E Ukraine
Zachist'ye see Zachystsye
110 E9 Zachodniopomorskie ◈ province NW Poland
119 L14 Zachystsye Rus. Zachist'ye. Minskaya Voblasts', NW Belarus
40 L13 Zacoalco var. Zacoalco de Torres. Jalisco, SW Mexico
Zacoalco de Torres see Zacoalco
41 P13 Zacualtipán Hidalgo, C Mexico
112 C12 Zadar It. Zara; anc. Iader. Zadar, W Croatia
112 C12 Zadar off. Zadarsko-Kninska Županija prev. Zadar-Knin. ◈ province SW Croatia
Zadar-Knin see Zadar
166 M14 Zadetkyi Kyun var. St. Matthew's Island. island Mergui Archipelago, S Myanmar
67 Q9 Zadié var. Djadié. ∽ NE Gabon
159 Q13 Zadoi Qinghai, C China
128 L7 Zadonsk Lipetskaya Oblast', W Russian Federation
75 X8 Za'farâna E Egypt
149 W7 Zafarwāl Punjab, E Pakistan
121 Q1 Zafer Burnu var. Cape Andreas, Cape Apostolas Andreas, Gk. Akrotíri Apostólou Andréa. headland NE Cyprus
107 J23 Zafferano, Capo headland Sicilia, Italy, C Mediterranean Sea
114 M7 Zafirovo Silistra, NE Bulgaria
115 L23 Zaforá island Kykládes, Greece, Aegean Sea
104 J12 Zafra Extremadura, W Spain
110 E13 Żagań var. Zagań, Żegań, Ger. Sagan. Lubuskie, W Poland
118 F10 Žagarė Pol. Żagory. Joniškis, N Lithuania
75 W7 Zagazig var. Az Zaqāzīq. N Egypt
74 M5 Zaghouan var. Zaghwān. NE Tunisia
Zaghwān see Zaghouan
115 G16 Zagorá Thessalía, C Greece
Zagorod'ye see Zaharoddzye
Żagory see Žagarė
Zágráb see Zagreb
112 E8 Zagreb Ger. Agram, Hung. Zágráb. ● (Croatia) Zagreb, N Croatia
112 E8 Zagreb prev. Grad Zagreb. ◈ province NC Croatia
142 L7 Zāgros, Kūhhā-ye Eng. Zagros Mountains. ⛰ W Iran
Zagros Mountains see Zāgros, Kūhhā-ye
112 O12 Žagubica Serbia, E Yugoslavia
111 L22 Zagyva ∽ N Hungary
Zaharo see Zacháro

◆ Country ● Country Capital ◇ Dependent Territory ○ Dependent Territory Capital ◈ Administrative Region ✕ International Airport ▲ Mountain ⛰ Mountain Range ⊼ Volcano ∽ River ◎ Lake ⊞ Reservoir

119 G19 **Zaharoddzye** *Rus.* Zagorod'ye. *physical region* SW Belarus
143 W11 **Zāhedān** *var.* Zahidan; *prev.* Duzdab. Sīstān va Balūchestān, SE Iran
Zahidan *see* Zāhedān
Zaḩlah *see* Zahlé
138 H7 **Zahlé** *var.* Zaḩlah. C Lebanon
Zähmet *see* Zakhmet
111 O20 **Záhony** Szabolcs-Szatmár-Bereg, NE Hungary
141 N13 **Zahrān** 'Asīr, S Saudi Arabia
139 R12 **Zahrat al Baţn** *hill range* S Iraq
120 H11 **Zahrez Chergui** *var.* Zahrez Chergúi. *marsh* N Algeria
129 S4 **Zainsk** Respublika Tatarstan, W Russian Federation
82 A10 **Zaire** *prev.* Congo. ◈ *province* NW Angola
Zaire *see* Congo (Democratic Republic of)
Zaire *see* Congo (river)
112 P13 **Zaječar** Serbia, E Yugoslavia
83 L18 **Zaka** Masvingo, E Zimbabwe
122 M14 **Zakamensk** Respublika Buryatiya, S Russian Federation
116 G7 **Zakarpats'ka Oblast'** ***Eng.*** Transcarpathian Oblast, ***Rus.*** Zakarpatskaya Oblast'. ◈ *province* W Ukraine
Zakarpatskaya Oblast' *see* Zakarpats'ka Oblast'
Zakataly *see* Zaqatala
Zakháro *see* Zacháro
Zakhidnyy Buh/Zakhodni Buh *see* Bug
146 J14 **Zakhmet** ***Turkm.*** Zähmet. Maryyskiy Velayat, C Turkmenistan
139 Q1 **Zākhō** *var.* Zākhū. N Iraq
Zākhū *see* Zākhō
Zákinthos *see* Zákynthos
111 L18 **Zakopane** Małopolskie, S Poland
78 J12 **Zakouma** Salamat, S Chad
115 L25 **Zákros** Kríti, Greece, E Mediterranean Sea
115 C19 **Zákynthos** *var.* Zákinthos. Zákynthos, W Greece
115 C20 **Zákynthos** *var.* Zákinthos, ***It.*** Zante. *island* Iónioi Nísoi, Greece, C Mediterranean Sea
115 C19 **Zakýnthou, Porthmós** *strait* SW Greece
111 G24 **Zala** *off.* Zala Megye. ◈ *county* W Hungary
111 G24 **Zala** ≈ W Hungary
138 M4 **Zalābiyah** Dayr az Zawr, C Syria
111 G24 **Zalaegerszeg** Zala, W Hungary
104 K11 **Zalamea de la Serena** Extremadura, W Spain
104 J13 **Zalamea la Real** Andalucía, S Spain
163 U7 **Zalantun** *var.* Butha Qi. Nei Mongol Zizhiqu, N China
111 G23 **Zalaszentgrót** Zala, SW Hungary
Zalatna *see* Zlatna
116 G9 **Zalău** ***Ger.*** Waltenberg, ***Hung.*** Zilah; *prev.* ***Ger.*** Zillenmarkt. Sălaj, NW Romania
109 V10 **Žalec** ***Ger.*** Sachsenfeld. C Slovenia
117 S9 **Zalenodol's'k** Dnipropetrovs'ka Oblast', E Ukraine
110 K8 **Zalewo** ***Ger.*** Saalfeld. Warmińsko-Mazurskie, NE Poland
141 N9 **Ẕalim** Makkah, W Saudi Arabia
80 A11 **Zalingei** *var.* Zalinje. Western Darfur, W Sudan
Zalinje *see* Zalingei
116 K7 **Zalishchyky** Ternopil's'ka Oblast', W Ukraine
Zallah *see* Zillah
98 J13 **Zaltbommel** Gelderland, C Netherlands
126 H15 **Zaluch'ye** Novgorodskaya Oblast', NW Russian Federation
Zamak *see* Zamakh
141 Q14 **Zamakh** *var.* Zamak. N Yemen
136 K15 **Zamantı Irmağı** ≈ C Turkey
Zambesi/Zambeze *see* Zambezi
83 G14 **Zambezi** North Western, W Zambia
83 K15 **Zambezi** *var.* Zambesi, ***Port.*** Zambeze. ≈ S Africa
83 O15 **Zambézia** *off.* Província da Zambézia. ◈ *province* C Mozambique
83 I14 **Zambia** *off.* Republic of Zambia; *prev.* Northern Rhodesia. ◆ *republic* S Africa
171 O8 **Zamboanga** *off.* Zamboanga City. Mindanao, S Philippines
54 E5 **Zambrano** Bolívar, N Colombia
110 N10 **Zambrów** Łomża, E Poland
83 L14 **Zambué** Tete, NW Mozambique
77 T13 **Zamfara** ≈ NW Nigeria
56 C9 **Zamora** Zamora Chinchipe, S Ecuador
104 K6 **Zamora** Castilla-León, NW Spain
104 K5 **Zamora** ◈ *province* Castilla-León, NW Spain
Zamora *see* Barinas
56 A13 **Zamora Chinchipe** ◈ *province* S Ecuador
40 M13 **Zamora de Hidalgo** Michoacán de Ocampo, SW Mexico
111 P15 **Zamość** ***Rus.*** Zamoste. Lubelskie, E Poland
Zamoste *see* Zamość
160 G7 **Zamtang** *prev.* Gamda. Sichuan, C China
75 O8 **Zamzam, Wādī** *dry watercourse* NW Libya
79 F20 **Zanaga** La Lékoumou, S Congo
41 T16 **Zanatepec** Oaxaca, SE Mexico
105 P9 **Záncara** ≈ C Spain
Zancle *see* Messina
158 G14 **Zanda** Xizang Zizhiqu, W China
98 H10 **Zandvoort** Noord-Holland, W Netherlands
39 P8 **Zane Hills** *hill range* Alaska, USA
31 T13 **Zanesville** Ohio, N USA
Zanga *see* Hrazdan
142 L4 **Zanjān** *var.* Zenjan, Zinjan. Zanjān, NW Iran
142 L4 **Zanjān** *off.* Ostān-e Zanjān, *var.* Zenjan, Zinjan. ◈ *province* NW Iran
Zante *see* Zákynthos
81 J22 **Zanzibar** Zanzibar, E Tanzania
81 J22 **Zanzibar** ◈ *region* E Tanzania
81 J22 **Zanzibar** ***Swa.*** Unguja. *island* E Tanzania
81 J22 **Zanzibar Channel** *channel* E Tanzania
165 P10 **Zaō-san** ▲ Honshū, C Japan
161 N8 **Zaoyang** Hubei, C China
161 Q6 **Zaozhuang** Shandong, E China
28 L4 **Zap** North Dakota, N USA
112 L13 **Zapadna Morava** ***Ger.*** Westliche Morava. ≈ C Yugoslavia
126 H16 **Zapadnaya Dvina** Tverskaya Oblast', W Russian Federation
Zapadnaya Dvina *see* Western Dvina
122 I9 **Zapadno-Sibirskaya Ravnina** ***Eng.*** West Siberian Plain. *plain* C Russian Federation
Zapadnyy Bug *see* Bug
144 E9 **Zapadnyy Kazakhstan** *off.* Zapadno-Kazakhstanskaya Oblast', ***Eng.*** West Kazakhstan, ***Kaz.*** Batys Qazaqstan Oblysy; *prev.* Ural'skaya Oblast'. ◈ *province* NW Kazakhstan
122 K13 **Zapadnyy Sayan** ***Eng.*** Western Sayans. ▲▲ S Russian Federation
63 H15 **Zapala** Neuquén, W Argentina
62 I4 **Zapaleri, Cerro** *var.* Cerro Sapaleri. ▲ N Chile
25 Q16 **Zapata** Texas, SW USA
44 D5 **Zapata, Península de** *peninsula* W Cuba
61 G19 **Zapicán** Lavalleja, S Uruguay
65 J19 **Zapiola Ridge** *undersea feature* SW Atlantic Ocean
65 L19 **Zapiola Seamount** *undersea feature* S Atlantic Ocean
126 I2 **Zapolyarnyy** Murmanskaya Oblast', NW Russian Federation
117 U8 **Zaporizhzhya** ***Rus.*** Zaporozh'ye; *prev.* Aleksandrovsk. Zaporiz'ka Oblast', SE Ukraine
Zaporizhzhya *see* Zaporiz'ka Oblast'
117 U9 **Zaporiz'ka Oblast'** *var.* Zaporizhzhya, ***Rus.*** Zaporozhskaya Oblast'. ◈ *province* SE Ukraine
Zaporozhskaya Oblast' *see* Zaporiz'ka Oblast'
Zaporozh'ye *see* Zaporizhzhya
40 L14 **Zapotiltic** Jalisco, SW Mexico
158 G13 **Zapug** Xizang Zizhiqu, W China
137 V10 **Zaqatala** ***Rus.*** Zakataly. NW Azerbaijan
159 P13 **Zaqên** Qinghai, W China
159 Q13 **Za Qu** ≈ C China
136 M13 **Zara** Sivas, C Turkey
Zara *see* Zadar
Zarafshan *see* Zarafshon
147 P12 **Zarafshan** ***Rus.*** Zeravshan. W Tajikistan
146 L9 **Zarafshon** ***Rus.*** Zarafshan. Nawoiy Wiloyati, N Uzbekistan
Zarafshon *see* Zeravshan
147 O12 **Zarafshon, Qatorkŭhi** ***Rus.*** Zeravshanskiy Khrebet, ***Uzb.*** Zarafshon Tizmasi. ▲▲ Tajikistan/Uzbekistan
Zarafshon Tizmasi *see* Zarafshon, Qatorkŭhi
54 E7 **Zaragoza** Antioquia, N Colombia
40 I5 **Zaragoza** Chihuahua, N Mexico
41 N6 **Zaragoza** Coahuila de Zaragoza, NE Mexico
41 O10 **Zaragoza** Nuevo León, NE Mexico
105 R5 **Zaragoza** ***Eng.*** Saragossa; *anc.* Caesaraugusta, Salduba. Aragón, NE Spain
105 R6 **Zaragoza** ◈ *province* Aragón, NE Spain
105 R5 **Zaragoza** ✕ Aragón, NE Spain
143 S10 **Zarand** Kermān, C Iran
148 J9 **Zaranj** Nīmrūz, SW Afghanistan
118 I11 **Zarasai** Zarasai, E Lithuania
62 N12 **Zárate** *prev.* General José F.Uriburu. Buenos Aires, E Argentina
105 Q2 **Zarautz** *var.* Zarauz. País Vasco, N Spain
Zarauz *see* Zarautz
Zaravecchia *see* Biograd na Moru
Zarāyīn *see* Zarēn
128 L4 **Zaraysk** Moskovskaya Oblast', W Russian Federation
55 N6 **Zaraza** Guárico, N Venezuela
Zarbdar *see* Zarbdor
147 P11 **Zarbdor** ***Rus.*** Zarbdar. Jizzakh Wiloyati, C Uzbekistan
142 M8 **Zard Kūh** ▲ SW Iran
126 I5 **Zarechensk** Murmanskaya Oblast', NW Russian Federation
149 Q7 **Zareh Sharan** Paktīkā, E Afghanistan
39 Y14 **Zarembo Island** *island* Alexander Archipelago, Alaska, USA
139 V4 **Zarēn** *var.* Zarāyīn. E Iraq
149 Q7 **Zarghūn Shahr** *var.* Katawaz. Paktīkā, SE Afghanistan
77 V13 **Zaria** Kaduna, C Nigeria
116 K2 **Zarichne** Rivnens'ka Oblast', NW Ukraine
122 J13 **Zarinsk** Altayskiy Kray, S Russian Federation
116 J12 **Zărneşti** ***Hung.*** Zernest. Braşov, C Romania
115 J25 **Zarós** Kríti, Greece, E Mediterranean Sea
100 O9 **Zarow** ≈ NE Germany
Zarqa/Zarqā', Muḩāfaẓat az *see* Az Zarqā'
111 G20 **Záruby** ▲ W Slovakia
56 B8 **Zaruma** El Oro, SW Ecuador
110 E13 **Żary** ***Ger.*** Sorau, Sorau in der Niederlausitz. Lubuskie, W Poland
54 D10 **Zarzal** Valle del Cauca, W Colombia
42 I7 **Zarzalar, Cerro** ▲ S Honduras
152 I5 **Zāskār** ≈ NE India
152 I5 **Zāskār Range** ▲▲ NE India
119 K15 **Zaslawye** Minskaya Voblasts', C Belarus
116 K7 **Zastavna** Chernivets'ka Oblast', W Ukraine
111 B16 **Žatec** ***Ger.*** Saaz. Ústecký Kraj, NW Czech Republic
Zaumgarten *see* Chrzanów
146 G10 **Zaungukskiye Garagumy** ***Turkm.*** Üngüz Angyrsyndaky Garagum. *desert* N Turkmenistan
25 X9 **Zavalla** Texas, SW USA
99 H18 **Zaventem** Vlaams Brabant, C Belgium
99 H18 **Zaventem** ✕ (Brussel/Bruxelles) Vlaams Brabant, C Belgium
Zavertse *see* Zawiercie
114 L7 **Zavet** Razgrad, NE Bulgaria
129 O12 **Zavetnoye** Rostovskaya Oblast', SW Russian Federation
156 M3 **Zavhan Gol** ≈ W Mongolia
112 H12 **Zavidovići** Federacija Bosna I Hercegovina, N Bosnia and Herzegovina
123 R13 **Zavitinsk** Amurskaya Oblast', SE Russian Federation
Zawia *see* Az Zāwiyah
111 K15 **Zawiercie** ***Rus.*** Zavertse. Śląskie, S Poland
75 P11 **Zawīlah** *var.* Zuwaylah, ***It.*** Zueila. C Libya
138 I4 **Zāwīyah, Jabal az** ▲▲ NW Syria
109 Y3 **Zaya** ≈ NE Austria
166 M8 **Zayatkyi** Pegu, C Myanmar
145 Y11 **Zaysan** Vostochnyy Kazakhstan, E Kazakhstan
Zaysan Köl *see* Zaysan, Ozero
145 Y11 **Zaysan, Ozero** ***Kaz.*** Zaysan Köl. ◎ E Kazakhstan
159 R16 **Zayü** *var.* Gyigang. Xizang Zizhiqu, W China
Zayyq *see* Ural
44 F6 **Zaza** ≈ C Cuba
116 K5 **Zbarazh** Ternopil's'ka Oblast', W Ukraine
116 J5 **Zboriv** Ternopil's'ka Oblast', W Ukraine
111 F18 **Zbraslav** Brněnský Kraj, SE Czech Republic
116 K6 **Zbruch** ≈ W Ukraine
Žďár *see* Žďár nad Sázavou
111 F17 **Žďár nad Sázavou** ***Ger.*** Saar in Mähren; *prev.* Žďár. Jihlavský Kraj, C Czech Republic
116 K4 **Zdolbuniv** ***Pol.*** Zdolbunów, ***Rus.*** Zdolbunov. Rivnens'ka Oblast', NW Ukraine
Zdolbunov/Zdolbunów *see* Zdolbuniv
110 J13 **Zduńska Wola** Sieradz, C Poland
117 O4 **Zdvizh** ≈ N Ukraine
Zdzięciół *see* Dzyatlava
111 I16 **Zdzieszowice** ***Ger.*** Odertal. Opolskie, S Poland
Zealand *see* Sjælland
188 K6 **Zealandia Bank** *undersea feature* C Pacific Ocean
63 H20 **Zeballos, Monte** ▲ S Argentina
83 K20 **Zebediela** Northern, NE South Africa
113 L18 **Zebë, Mal** *var.* Mali i Zebës. ▲ NE Albania
Zebës, Mali i *see* Zebë, Mal
21 V9 **Zebulon** North Carolina, SE USA
112 K8 **Žednik** ***Hung.*** Bácsjózseffalva. Serbia, N Yugoslavia
99 C15 **Zeebrugge** West-Vlaanderen, NW Belgium
183 N16 **Zeehan** Tasmania, SE Australia
99 L14 **Zeeland** Noord-Brabant, SE Netherlands
29 N7 **Zeeland** North Dakota, N USA
99 E14 **Zeeland** ◈ *province* SW Netherlands
83 I21 **Zeerust** North-West, N South Africa
98 K10 **Zeewolde** Flevoland, C Netherlands
138 G8 **Ẕefat** *var.* Safed, Tsefat, ***Ar.*** Safad. Northern, N Israel
Żegań *see* Żagań
Zehden *see* Cedynia
100 O11 **Zehdenick** Brandenburg, NE Germany
Zē-i Bādīnān *see* Great Zab
Zeiden *see* Codlea
146 M14 **Zeidskoye Vodokhranilishche** ▣ E Turkmenistan
Zē-i Kōya *see* Little Zab
181 P7 **Zeil, Mount** ▲ Northern Territory, C Australia
98 J12 **Zeist** Utrecht, C Netherlands
101 M16 **Zeitz** Sachsen-Anhalt, E Germany
159 T11 **Zêkog** Qinghai, C China
Zelaya Norte *see* Atlántico Norte, Región Autónoma
Zelaya Sur *see* Atlántico Sur, Región Autónoma
99 F17 **Zele** Oost-Vlaanderen, NW Belgium
110 N12 **Żelechów** Lubelskie, E Poland
113 H14 **Zelena Glava** ▲ SE Bosnia and Herzegovina
113 I14 **Zelengora** ▲▲ S Bosnia and Herzegovina
126 I5 **Zelenoborskiy** Murmanskaya Oblast', NW Russian Federation
129 R3 **Zelenodol'sk** Respublika Tatarstan, W Russian Federation
126 G12 **Zelenogorsk** ***Fin.*** Terijoki. Leningradskaya Oblast', NW Russian Federation
128 K3 **Zelenograd** Moskovskaya Oblast', W Russian Federation
118 B13 **Zelenogradsk** ***Ger.*** Cranz, Kranz. Kaliningradskaya Oblast', W Russian Federation
129 O15 **Zelenokumsk** Stavropol'skiy Kray, SW Russian Federation
165 X4 **Zelënyy, Ostrov** *var.* Shibotsu-jima. *island* NE Russian Federation
Železna Kapela *see* Eisenkappel
Železna Vrata *see* Demir Kapija
112 L11 **Železniki** Serbia, N Yugoslavia
98 N12 **Zelhem** Gelderland, E Netherlands
113 N18 **Želino** NW FYR Macedonia
113 M14 **Željin** ▲▲ C Yugoslavia
101 K17 **Zella-Mehlis** Thüringen, C Germany
109 P7 **Zell am See** *var.* Zell-am-See. Salzburg, S Austria
109 N7 **Zell am Ziller** Tirol, W Austria
Zelle *see* Celle
109 W2 **Zellerndorf** Niederösterreich, NE Austria
109 U7 **Zeltweg** Steiermark, S Austria
119 G17 **Zel'va** ***Pol.*** Zelwa. Hrodzyenskaya Voblasts', W Belarus
118 H13 **Želva** Ukmergė, C Lithuania
Zelwa *see* Zel'va
99 E14 **Zelzate** *var.* Selzaete. Oost-Vlaanderen, NW Belgium
118 E11 **Žemaičių Aukštumas** *physical region* W Lithuania
118 C12 **Žemaičių Naumiestis** Šilutė, SW Lithuania
Zembin *see* Zyembin
129 N6 **Zemetchino** Penzenskaya Oblast', W Russian Federation
79 M15 **Zémio** Haut-Mbomou, E Central African Republic
41 R16 **Zempoaltepec, Cerro** ▲ SE Mexico
99 G17 **Zemst** Vlaams Brabant, C Belgium
112 L11 **Zemun** Serbia, N Yugoslavia
Zendajan *see* Zendeh Jan
148 J5 **Zendeh Jan** *var.* Zendajan, Zindajān. Herāt, NW Afghanistan
Zengg *see* Senj
112 H12 **Zenica** Federacija Bosna I Hercegovina, C Bosnia and Herzegovina
Zenjan *see* Zanjān
Zen'kov *see* Zin'kiv
Zenshū *see* Chŏnju
Zenta *see* Senta
Zentûzi *see* Zentsûji
82 B11 **Zenza do Itombe** Cuanza Norte, NW Angola
112 H12 **Žepče** Federacija Bosna I Hercegovina, N Bosnia and Herzegovina
23 W12 **Zephyrhills** Florida, SE USA
192 L9 **Zephyr Reef** *reef* Pacific Ocean
158 F9 **Zepu** *var.* Poskam. Xinjiang Uygur Zizhiqu, NW China
147 Q12 **Zeravshan** ***Taj./Uzb.*** Zarafshon. ≈ Tajikistan/Uzbekistan
Zeravshan *see* Zarafshon
Zeravshanskiy Khrebet *see* Zarafshon, Qatorkŭhi
101 M14 **Zerbst** Sachsen-Anhalt, E Germany
145 P8 **Zerenda** Severnyy Kazakhstan, N Kazakhstan
110 H12 **Żerków** Wielkopolskie, C Poland
108 E11 **Zermatt** Valais, SW Switzerland
Zernest *see* Zărneşti
108 J9 **Zernez** Graubünden, SE Switzerland
128 L12 **Zernograd** Rostovskaya Oblast', SW Russian Federation
Zestafoni *see* Zestap'oni
137 S9 **Zestap'oni** ***Rus.*** Zestafoni. C Georgia
98 H12 **Zestienhoven** ✕ (Rotterdam) Zuid-Holland, SW Netherlands
113 J16 **Zeta** ≈ SW Yugoslavia
8 L6 **Zeta Lake** ◎ Victoria Island, Nunavut, N Canada
98 L12 **Zetten** Gelderland, SE Netherlands
101 M17 **Zeulenroda** Thüringen, C Germany
100 H10 **Zeven** Niedersachsen, NW Germany
98 M12 **Zevenaar** Gelderland, SE Netherlands
99 H14 **Zevenbergen** Noord-Brabant, S Netherlands
131 X6 **Zeya** ≈ SE Russian Federation
Zeya Reservoir *see* Zeyskoye Vodokhranilishche
143 T11 **Zeynalābād** Kermān, C Iran
123 R12 **Zeyskoye Vodokhranilishche** ***Eng.*** Zeya Reservoir. ▣ SE Russian Federation
104 H8 **Zêzere, Rio** ≈ C Portugal
Zgerzh *see* Zgierz
138 H6 **Zgharta** N Lebanon
110 K12 **Zgierz** ***Ger.*** Neuhof, ***Rus.*** Zgerzh. Łódź, C Poland
111 E14 **Zgorzelec** ***Ger.*** Görlitz. Dolnośląskie, SW Poland
Zhabdün *see* Zhongba
119 F19 **Zhabinka** ***Pol.*** Żabinka, ***Rus.*** Zhabinka. Brestskaya Voblasts', SW Belarus
Zhaggo *see* Luhuo
159 R15 **Zhag'yab** Xizang Zizhiqu, W China
144 L9 **Zhailma** ***Kaz.*** Zhayylma. Kostanay, N Kazakhstan
145 V16 **Zhalanash** Almaty, SE Kazakhstan
Zhalashash *see* Dzhalagash
145 S7 **Zhalauly, Ozero** ◎ NE Kazakhstan
144 E9 **Zhalpaktal** *prev.* Furmanovo. Zapadnyy Kazakhstan, W Kazakhstan
119 G16 **Zhaludok** ***Rus.*** Zheludok. Hrodzyenskaya Voblasts', W Belarus
Zhaman-Akkol', Ozero *see* Akkol', Ozero
Zhambyl *see* Taraz
145 Q14 **Zhambyl** *off.* Zhambylskaya Oblast', ***Kaz.*** Zhambyl Oblysy; *prev.* Dzhambulskaya Oblast'. ◈ *province* S Kazakhstan
Zhambyl Oblysy/Zhambylskaya Oblast' *see* Zhambyl
Zhamo *see* Bomi
145 S12 **Zhamshy** ≈ C Kazakhstan
144 M15 **Zhanadar'ya** Kzylorda, S Kazakhstan
145 O15 **Zhanakorgan** ***Kaz.*** Zhangaqorghan. Kzylorda, S Kazakhstan
159 N16 **Zhanang** Xizang Zizhiqu, W China
145 T12 **Zhanaortalyk** Zhezkazgan, C Kazakhstan
144 F15 **Zhanaozen** ***Kaz.*** Zhangaözen, *prev.* Novyy Uzen'. Mangistau, W Kazakhstan
145 Q16 **Zhanatas** Zhambyl, S Kazakhstan
Zhangaözen *see* Zhanaozen
Zhangaqazaly *see* Ayteke Bi
Zhangaqorghan *see* Zhanakorgan
161 O2 **Zhangbei** Hebei, E China
Zhangdian *see* Zibo
163 X9 **Zhangguangcai Ling** ▲▲ NE China
145 W10 **Zhangiztobe** Vostochnyy Kazakhstan, E Kazakhstan
159 W11 **Zhangjiachuan** Gansu, N China
160 L10 **Zhangjiajie** *var.* Dayong. Hunan, S China
161 O2 **Zhangjiakou** *var.* Changkiakow, Zhang-chia-k'ou, ***Eng.*** Kalgan; *prev.* Wanchuan. Hebei, E China
161 Q13 **Zhangping** Fujian, SE China
161 Q13 **Zhangpu** Fujian, SE China
163 U11 **Zhangwu** Liaoning, NE China
159 S8 **Zhangye** Gansu, N China
161 Q13 **Zhangzhou** Fujian, SE China
163 W6 **Zhan He** ≈ NE China
Zhänibek *see* Dzhanybek
160 L16 **Zhanjiang** *var.* Chanchiang, Chan-chiang, ***Cant.*** Tsamkong, ***Fr.*** Fort-Bayard. Guangdong, S China
Zhansügirov *see* Dzhansugurov
163 V8 **Zhaodong** Heilongjiang, NE China
Zhaoge *see* Qixian
160 H11 **Zhaojue** Sichuan, C China
161 N14 **Zhaoqing** Guangdong, S China
158 H5 **Zhaosu** *var.* Mongolküre. Xinjiang Uygur Zizhiqu, NW China
160 H11 **Zhaotong** Yunnan, SW China
163 V9 **Zhaoyuan** Heilongjiang, NE China
163 V9 **Zhaozhou** Heilongjiang, NE China
145 X13 **Zharbulak** Vostochnyy Kazakhstan, E Kazakhstan
158 J15 **Zhari Namco** ◎ W China
144 I12 **Zharkamys** ***Kaz.*** Zharqamys. Aktyubinsk, W Kazakhstan
145 W15 **Zharkent** *prev.* Panfilov. Almaty, SE Kazakhstan
126 H17 **Zharkovskiy** Tverskaya Oblast', W Russian Federation
145 W11 **Zharma** Vostochnyy Kazakhstan, E Kazakhstan
144 F14 **Zharmysh** Mangistau, SW Kazakhstan
Zharqamys *see* Zharkamys
118 L13 **Zhary** ***Rus.*** Zhary. Vitsyebskaya Voblasts', N Belarus
Zhaslyk *see* Jasliq
158 J14 **Zhaxi Co** ◎ W China
Zhayylma *see* Zhailma
Zhdanov *see* Beylăqan, Azerbaijan
Zhdanov *see* Mariupol', Ukraine
Zhe *see* Zhejiang
161 R10 **Zhejiang** *var.* Che-chiang, Chekiang, Zhe, Zhejiang Sheng. ◈ *province* SE China
Zhejiang Sheng *see* Zhejiang
145 S7 **Zhelezinka** Pavlodar, N Kazakhstan
119 C14 **Zheleznodorozhnyy** ***Ger.*** Gerdauen. Kaliningradskaya Oblast', W Russian Federation
Zheleznodorozhnyy *see* Yemva
128 J7 **Zheleznogorsk** Kurskaya Oblast', W Russian Federation
129 N15 **Zheleznovodsk** Stavropol'skiy Kray, SW Russian Federation
Zhëltyye Vody *see* Zhovti Vody
Zheludok *see* Zhaludok
Zhem *see* Emba
160 K7 **Zhenba** Shaanxi, C China
160 I13 **Zhenfeng** Guizhou, S China
Zhengjiatun *see* Shuangliao
159 X10 **Zhengning** Gansu, N China
163 Q12 **Zhengxiangbai Qi** Nei Mongol Zizhiqu, N China
161 N6 **Zhengzhou** *var.* Ch'eng-chou, Chengchow; *prev.* Chenghsien. Henan, C China
161 R8 **Zhenjiang** *var.* Chenkiang. Jiangsu, E China
163 U9 **Zhenlai** Jilin, NE China
160 I11 **Zhenxiong** Yunnan, SW China
160 K11 **Zhenyuan** *prev.* Wuyang. Guizhou, S China
161 R11 **Zherong** Fujian, SE China
Zhetiqara *see* Dzhetygara
144 F15 **Zhetybay** Mangistau, SW Kazakhstan
145 P17 **Zhetysay** *var.* Dzhetysay. Yuzhnyy Kazakhstan
160 M11 **Zhexi Shuiku** ▣ C China
145 O12 **Zhezdy** Zhezkazgan, C Kazakhstan
145 O12 **Zhezkazgan** ***Kaz.*** Zhezqazghan; *prev.* Dzhezkazgan. Zhezkazgan, C Kazakhstan
Zhezqazghan *see* Zhezkazgan
160 M9 **Zhicheng** Hubei, C China
Zhidachov *see* Zhydachiv
159 Q12 **Zhidoi** Qinghai, C China
122 M13 **Zhigalovo** Irkutskaya Oblast', S Russian Federation
129 R6 **Zhigulevsk** Samarskaya Oblast', W Russian Federation
118 D13 **Zhilino** ***Ger.*** Schillen. Kaliningradskaya Oblast', W Russian Federation
129 O8 **Zhirnovsk** Volgogradskaya Oblast', SW Russian Federation
Zhitarovo *see* Vetren
Zhitkovichi *see* Zhytkavichy
129 P10 **Zhitkur** Volgogradskaya Oblast', SW Russian Federation
Zhitomir *see* Zhytomyr
Zhitomirskaya Oblast' *see* Zhytomyrs'ka Oblast'
128 J5 **Zhizdra** Kaluzhskaya Oblast', W Russian Federation
119 N18 **Zhlobin** Homyel'skaya Voblasts', SE Belarus
Zhmerinka *see* Zhmerynka
116 M7 **Zhmerynka** ***Rus.*** Zhmerinka. Vinnyts'ka Oblast', C Ukraine
149 R9 **Zhob** *var.* Fort Sandeman. Baluchistān, SW Pakistan
149 R8 **Zhob** ≈ C Pakistan
144 I10 **Zhobda** *prev.* Novoalekseyevka. Aktyubinsk, W Kazakhstan
Zhodino *see* Zhodzina
119 L15 **Zhodzina** ***Rus.*** Zhodino. Minskaya Voblasts', C Belarus
123 Q5 **Zhokhova, Ostrov** *island* Novosibirskiye Ostrova, NE Russian Federation
Zholkev/Zholkva *see* Zhovkva
Zholsaly *see* Dzhusaly
Zhondor *see* Jondor
158 I15 **Zhongba** *var.* Zhabdün. Xizang Zizhiqu, W China
160 F11 **Zhongdian** Yunnan, SW China
Zhonghua Renmin Gongheguo *see* China
159 V9 **Zhongning** Ningxia, N China
161 N15 **Zhongshan** Guangdong, S China
195 X7 **Zhongshan** *Chinese research station* Antarctica
160 M6 **Zhongtiao Shan** ▲▲ C China
159 V9 **Zhongwei** Ningxia, N China
160 K9 **Zhongxian** *var.* Zhong Xian. Chongqing Shi, C China
161 N9 **Zhongxiang** Hubei, C China
161 O7 **Zhoukou** *var.* Zhoukouzhen. Henan, C China
Zhoukouzhen *see* Zhoukou
161 S9 **Zhoushan** Zhejiang, S China
161 S9 **Zhoushan Qundao** ***Eng.*** Zhoushan Islands. *island group* SE China
116 I5 **Zhovkva** ***Pol.*** Żółkiew, ***Rus.*** Zholkev, Zholkva; *prev.* Nesterov. L'vivs'ka Oblast', NW Ukraine
117 S7 **Zhovti Vody** ***Rus.*** Zhëltyye Vody. Dnipropetrovs'ka Oblast', E Ukraine
117 Q10 **Zhovtneve** ***Rus.*** Zhovtnevoye. Mykolayivs'ka Oblast', S Ukraine
Zhovtnevoye *see* Zhovtneve
114 K9 **Zhrebchevo, Yazovir** ▣ C Bulgaria
163 V13 **Zhuanghe** Liaoning, NE China
159 W11 **Zhuanglang** Gansu, C China
145 P15 **Zhuantobe** ***Kaz.*** Zhūantöbe. Yuzhnyy Kazakhstan, S Kazakhstan
161 Q5 **Zhucheng** Shandong, E China
159 V12 **Zhugqu** Gansu, C China
161 N15 **Zhuhai** Guangdong, S China
Zhuizishan *see* Weichang
Zhuji *see* Shangqiu
128 I5 **Zhukovka** Bryanskaya Oblast', W Russian Federation
161 O3 **Zhuozhou** *prev.* Zhuo Xian. Hebei, E China
162 L14 **Zhuozi Shan** ▲ N China
Zhuravichi *see* Zhuravichy
119 O17 **Zhuravichy** ***Rus.*** Zhuravichi. Homyel'skaya Voblasts', SE Belarus
145 Q8 **Zhuravlevka** Akmola, N Kazakhstan
117 Q4 **Zhurivka** Kyyivs'ka Oblast', N Ukraine
144 J11 **Zhuryn** Aktyubinsk, W Kazakhstan
145 T15 **Zhusandala, Step'** *grassland* SE Kazakhstan
160 L8 **Zhushan** Hubei, C China
161 N11 **Zhuzhou** Hunan, S China
116 I6 **Zhydachiv** ***Pol.*** Żydaczów, ***Rus.*** Zhidachov. L'vivs'ka Oblast', NW Ukraine
Zhympīty *see* Dzhambeyty
119 K19 **Zhytkavichy** ***Rus.*** Zhitkovichi. Homyel'skaya Voblasts', SE Belarus
117 N4 **Zhytomyr** ***Rus.*** Zhitomir. Zhytomyrs'ka Oblast', NW Ukraine
Zhytomyr *see* Zhytomyrs'ka Oblast'
116 M4 **Zhytomyrs'ka Oblast'** *var.* Zhytomyr, ***Rus.*** Zhitomirskaya Oblast'. ◈ *province* N Ukraine
153 U15 **Zia** ✕ (Dhaka) Dhaka, C Bangladesh
111 J20 **Žiar nad Hronom** *var.* Svätý Kríž nad Hronom, ***Ger.*** Heiligenkreuz, ***Hung.*** Garamszentkereszt. Banskobystrický Kraj, C Slovakia
161 Q4 **Zibo** *var.* Zhangdian. Shandong, E China

◆ Country ● Country Capital ◇ Dependent Territory ○ Dependent Territory Capital ◈ Administrative Region ✕ International Airport ▲ Mountain ▲▲ Mountain Range Volcano ≈ River ◎ Lake ▣ Reservoir

160 L4 **Zichang** *prev.* Wayaobu. Shaanxi, C China
Zichenau *see* Ciechanów
111 G15 **Ziębice** *Ger.* Münsterberg in Schlesien. Dolnośląskie, SW Poland
Ziebingen *see* Cybinka
Ziegenhais *see* Głuchołazy
110 E12 **Zielona Góra** *Ger.* Grünberg, Grünberg in Schlesien, Grüneberg. Lubuskie, W Poland
99 F14 **Zierikzee** Zeeland, SW Netherlands
160 I10 **Zigong** *var.* Tzekung. Sichuan, C China
76 G12 **Ziguinchor** SW Senegal
41 N16 **Zihuatanejo** Guerrero, S Mexico
Zilah *see* Zalău
129 W7 **Zilair** Respublika Bashkortostan, W Russian Federation
136 L12 **Zile** Tokat, N Turkey
111 J18 **Žilina** *Ger.* Sillein, *Hung.* Zsolna. Žilinský Kraj, N Slovakia
111 J19 **Žilinský Kraj** ⬖ *region* N Slovakia
75 Q9 **Zillah** *var.* Zallah. C Libya
Zillenmarkt *see* Zalău
109 N7 **Ziller** ∾ W Austria
Zillertal Alps *see* Zillertaler Alpen
109 N8 **Zillertaler Alpen** *Eng.* Zillertal Alps, *It.* Alpi Aurine. ⛰ Austria/Italy
118 K10 **Zilupe** *Ger.* Rosenhof. Ludza, E Latvia
41 O13 **Zimapán** Hidalgo, C Mexico
83 I16 **Zimba** Southern, S Zambia
83 J17 **Zimbabwe** *off.* Republic of Zimbabwe; *prev.* Rhodesia. ◆ *republic* S Africa
116 H10 **Zimbor** *Hung.* Magyarzsombor. Sălaj, NW Romania
Zimmerbude *see* Svetlyy
116 J15 **Zimnicea** Teleorman, S Romania
114 L9 **Zimnitsa** Yambol, E Bulgaria
129 N12 **Zimovniki** Rostovskaya Oblast', SW Russian Federation
Zindajân *see* Zendeh Jan
77 V12 **Zinder** Zinder, S Niger
77 W11 **Zinder** ⬖ *department* S Niger
77 P12 **Ziniaré** C Burkina
Zinjan *see* Zanjān
141 P16 **Zinjibār** SW Yemen
117 T4 **Zin'kiv** *var.* Zen'kov. Poltavs'ka Oblast', NE Ukraine
Zinov'yevsk *see* Kirovohrad
Zintenhof *see* Sindi
31 N10 **Zion** Illinois, N USA
54 F10 **Zipaquirá** Cundinamarca, C Colombia
Zipser Neudorf *see* Spišská Nová Ves
111 H23 **Zirc** Veszprém, W Hungary
113 D14 **Žirje** *It.* Zuri. *island* S Croatia
Zirknitz *see* Cerknica
108 M7 **Zirl** Tirol, W Austria
101 K20 **Zirndorf** Bayern, SE Germany
160 M11 **Zi Shui** ∾ C China
109 Y3 **Zistersdorf** Niederösterreich, NE Austria
41 O14 **Zitácuaro** Michoacán de Ocampo, SW Mexico
101 Q16 **Zittau** Sachsen, E Germany
112 I12 **Živinice** Federacija Bosna I Hercegovina, E Bosnia and Herzegovina
Ziwa Magharibi *see* Kagera
81 J14 **Ziway Hāyk'** ◎ C Ethiopia
161 N12 **Zixing** Hunan, S China
129 W7 **Ziyanchurino** Orenburgskaya Oblast', W Russian Federation
160 K8 **Ziyang** Shaanxi, C China
111 I20 **Zlaté Moravce** *Hung.* Aranyosmarót. Nitriansky Kraj, SW Slovakia
112 K13 **Zlatibor** ⛰ W Yugoslavia
114 L9 **Zlati Voyvoda** Sliven, E Bulgaria
116 G11 **Zlatna** *Ger.* Kleinschlatten, *Hung.* Zalatna; *prev. Ger.* Goldmarkt. Alba, C Romania
114 I8 **Zlatna Panega** Lovech, N Bulgaria
114 N8 **Zlatni Pyasŭtsi** Dobrich, NE Bulgaria
122 F11 **Zlatoust** Chelyabinskaya Oblast', C Russian Federation
111 M19 **Zlatý Stôl** *Ger.* Goldener Tisch, *Hung.* Aranyosasztal. ▲ C Slovakia
113 P18 **Zletovo** NE FYR Macedonia
111 H18 **Zlín** *prev.* Gottwaldov. Zlínský Kraj, SE Czech Republic
113 H19 **Zlínský Kraj** ⬖ *region* E Czech Republic
75 O7 **Zlīṭan** W Libya
110 F9 **Złocieniec** *Ger.* Falkenburg in Pommern. Zachodniopomorskie, NW Poland
110 J13 **Złoczew** Sieradz, S Poland
Złoczów *see* Zolochiv
111 F14 **Złotoryja** *Ger.* Goldberg. Dolnośląskie, W Poland
110 G9 **Złotów** Wielkopolskie, NW Poland
110 G13 **Żmigród** *Ger.* Trachenberg. Dolnośląskie, SW Poland
128 J6 **Zmiyevka** Orlovskaya Oblast', W Russian Federation
117 V5 **Zmiyiv** Kharkivs'ka Oblast', E Ukraine
Zna *see* Tsna
Znaim *see* Znojmo
128 M7 **Znamenka** Tambovskaya Oblast', W Russian Federation
Znamenka *see* Znam"yanka
119 C14 **Znamensk** *Ger.* Wehlau. Kaliningradskaya Oblast', W Russian Federation
117 R7 **Znam"yanka** *Rus.* Znamenka. Kirovohrads'ka Oblast', C Ukraine
110 H10 **Żnin** Kujawsko-pomorskie, C Poland
111 F19 **Znojmo** *Ger.* Znaim. Brněnský Kraj, S Czech Republic
79 N16 **Zobia** Orientale, N Dem. Rep. Congo (Zaire)
83 N15 **Zóbuè** Tete, NW Mozambique
98 G12 **Zoetermeer** Zuid-Holland, W Netherlands
108 E7 **Zofingen** Aargau, N Switzerland
159 R15 **Zogang** *var.* Wangda. Xizang Zizhiqu, W China
106 E7 **Zogno** Lombardia, N Italy
142 M10 **Zohreh, Rūd-e** ∾ SW Iran
160 H7 **Zoigê** Sichuan, C China
Zółkiew *see* Zhovkva
108 D8 **Zollikofen** Bern, W Switzerland
Zolochev *see* Zolochiv
117 U4 **Zolochiv** *Rus.* Zolochev. Kharkivs'ka Oblast', E Ukraine
116 J5 **Zolochiv** *Pol.* Złoczów, *Rus.* Zolochev. L'vivs'ka Oblast', W Ukraine
117 X7 **Zolote** *Rus.* Zolotoye. Luhans'ka Oblast', E Ukraine
117 Q6 **Zolotonosha** Cherkas'ka Oblast', C Ukraine
Zolotoye *see* Zolote
Zólyom *see* Zvolen
83 N15 **Zomba** Southern, S Malawi
Zombor *see* Sombor
99 D17 **Zomergem** Oost-Vlaanderen, NW Belgium
147 P11 **Zomin** *Rus.* Zaamin. Jizzakh Wiloyati, C Uzbekistan
79 I15 **Zongo** Equateur, N Dem. Rep. Congo (Zaire)
136 G10 **Zonguldak** Zonguldak, NW Turkey
136 H10 **Zonguldak** ⬖ *province* NW Turkey
99 K17 **Zonhoven** Limburg, NE Belgium
142 J2 **Zonūz** Āzarbāyjān-e Khāvarī, NW Iran
103 Y16 **Zonza** Corse, France, C Mediterranean Sea
Zoppot *see* Sopot
Zorgho *see* Zorgo
77 Q13 **Zorgo** *var.* Zorgho. C Burkina
104 K10 **Zorita** Extremadura, W Spain
147 U14 **Zorkŭl** *Rus.* Ozero Zorkul'. ◎ SE Tajikistan
Zorkul', Ozero *see* Zorkŭl
56 A8 **Zorritos** Tumbes, N Peru
111 J16 **Żory** *var.* Zory, *Ger.* Sohrau. Śląskie, S Poland
76 K15 **Zorzor** N Liberia
99 E18 **Zottegem** Oost-Vlaanderen, NW Belgium
77 R15 **Zou** ∾ S Benin
78 H6 **Zouar** Borkou-Ennedi-Tibesti, N Chad
76 J6 **Zouérat** *var.* Zouérate, Zouîrât. Tiris Zemmour, N Mauritania
Zouérate *see* Zouérat
Zoug *see* Zug
Zouîrât *see* Zouérat
76 M16 **Zoukougbeu** C Ivory Coast
98 M5 **Zoutkamp** Groningen, NE Netherlands
99 J18 **Zoutleeuw** *Fr.* Leau. Vlaams Brabant, C Belgium
112 L9 **Zrenjanin** *prev.* Petrovgrad, Veliki Bečkerek, *Ger.* Grossbetschkerek, *Hung.* Nagybecskerek. Serbia, N Yugoslavia
112 E10 **Zrinska Gora** ⛰ C Croatia
Zsablya *see* Žabalj
101 N16 **Zschopau** ∾ E Germany
Zsebely *see* Jebel
Zsibó *see* Jibou
Zsil/Zsily *see* Jiu
Zsilyvajdevulkán *see* Vulcan
Zsolna *see* Žilina
Zsombolya *see* Jimbolia
Zsupanya *see* Županja
55 N7 **Zuata** Anzoátegui, NE Venezuela
105 N14 **Zubia** Andalucía, S Spain
65 P16 **Zubov Seamount** *undersea feature* E Atlantic Ocean
126 I16 **Zubtsov** Tverskaya Oblast', W Russian Federation
108 M8 **Zuckerhütl** ▲ SW Austria
Zueila *see* Zawīlah
76 M16 **Zuénoula** C Ivory Coast
105 S5 **Zuera** Aragón, NE Spain
141 V13 **Ẓufār** *Eng.* Dhofar. *physical region* SW Oman
108 G8 **Zug** *Fr.* Zoug. Zug, C Switzerland
108 G8 **Zug** *Fr.* Zoug. ⬖ *canton* C Switzerland
137 R9 **Zugdidi** W Georgia
108 G8 **Zuger See** ◎ NW Switzerland
101 K25 **Zugspitze** ▲ S Germany
99 E15 **Zuid-Beveland** *var.* South Beveland. *island* SW Netherlands
98 K10 **Zuidelijk-Flevoland** *polder* C Netherlands
Zuider Zee *see* IJsselmeer
98 G12 **Zuid-Holland** *Eng.* South Holland. ⬖ *province* W Netherlands
98 N5 **Zuidhorn** Groningen, NE Netherlands
98 O6 **Zuidlaardermeer** ◎ NE Netherlands
98 O6 **Zuidlaren** Drenthe, NE Netherlands
99 K14 **Zuid-Willemsvaart Kanaal** *canal* S Netherlands
98 N8 **Zuidwolde** Drenthe, NE Netherlands
Zuitaizi *see* Kangxian
105 O14 **Zújar** Andalucía, S Spain
104 L11 **Zújar** ∾ W Spain
104 L11 **Zújar, Embalse del** ⊠ W Spain
80 J9 **Zula** E Eritrea
54 G6 **Zulia** *off.* Estado Zulia. ⬖ *state* NW Venezuela
Zullapara *see* Sinchaingbyin
Züllichau *see* Sulechów
105 P3 **Zumárraga** País Vasco, N Spain
112 D8 **Žumberačko Gorje** *var.* Gorjanči, Uskocke Planine, Žumberak, *Ger.* Uskokengebirge; *prev.* Sichelburger Gebirge. ▲ Croatia/Slovenia *see also* Gorjanci
Žumberak *see* Gorjanci/Žumberačko Gorje
194 K7 **Zumberge Coast** *coastal feature* Antarctica
Zumbo *see* Vila do Zumbo
29 W10 **Zumbro Falls** Minnesota, N USA
29 W10 **Zumbro River** ∾ Minnesota, N USA
29 W10 **Zumbrota** Minnesota, N USA
99 H15 **Zundert** Noord-Brabant, S Netherlands
Zungaria *see* Dzungaria
77 U14 **Zungeru** Niger, C Nigeria
37 O11 **Zuni** New Mexico, SW USA
37 P11 **Zuni Mountains** ⛰ New Mexico, SW USA
160 J11 **Zunyi** Guizhou, S China
160 J15 **Zuo Jiang** ∾ China/Vietnam
108 J9 **Zuoz** Graubünden, SE Switzerland
112 I10 **Županja** *Hung.* Zsupanya. Vukovar-Srijem, E Croatia
113 M17 **Žur** Serbia, S Yugoslavia
129 T2 **Zura** Udmurtskaya Respublika, NW Russian Federation
139 V8 **Zurbāṭīyah** E Iraq
Zuri *see* Žirje
108 F7 **Zürich** *Eng./Fr.* Zurich, *It.* Zurigo. Zürich, N Switzerland
108 G6 **Zürich** *Eng./Fr.* Zurich. ⬖ *canton* N Switzerland
Zurich, Lake *see* Zürichsee
108 G7 **Zürichsee** *Eng.* Lake Zurich. ◎ NE Switzerland
Zurigo *see* Zürich
149 V1 **Zŭrkŭl** *Pash.* Sarī Qūl, *Rus.* Ozero Zurkul'. ◎ Afghanistan/Tajikistan *see also* Sarī Qūl
Zurkul', Ozero *see* Sarī Qūl/Zŭrkŭl
110 K10 **Żuromin** Mazowieckie, N Poland
108 J8 **Zürs** Vorarlberg, W Austria
77 T13 **Zuru** Kebbi, W Nigeria
108 F6 **Zurzach** Aargau, N Switzerland
101 J22 **Zusam** ∾ S Germany
98 M11 **Zutphen** Gelderland, E Netherlands
75 N7 **Zuwārah** NW Libya
Zuwaylah *see* Zawīlah
127 R14 **Zuyevka** Kirovskaya Oblast', NW Russian Federation
161 N10 **Zuzhou** Hunan, S China
Zvenigorodka *see* Zvenyhorodka
117 P6 **Zvenyhorodka** *Rus.* Zvenigorodka. Cherkas'ka Oblast', C Ukraine
123 N12 **Zvezdnyy** Irkutskaya Oblast', C Russian Federation
83 K18 **Zvishavane** *prev.* Shabani. Matabeleland South, S Zimbabwe
111 J20 **Zvolen** *Ger.* Altsohl, *Hung.* Zólyom. Banskobystrický Kraj, C Slovakia
112 J12 **Zvornik** E Bosnia and Herzegovina
98 M5 **Zwaagwesteinde** *Fris.* De Westerein. Friesland, N Netherlands
98 H10 **Zwanenburg** Noord-Holland, C Netherlands
98 L8 **Zwarte Meer** ◎ N Netherlands
98 M9 **Zwarte Water** ∾ N Netherlands
98 M8 **Zwartsluis** Overijssel, E Netherlands
76 L17 **Zwedru** *var.* Tchien. E Liberia
98 O8 **Zweeloo** Drenthe, NE Netherlands
101 E20 **Zweibrücken** *Fr.* Deux-Ponts; *Lat.* Bipontium. Rheinland-Pfalz, SW Germany
108 D9 **Zweisimmen** Fribourg, W Switzerland
101 M15 **Zwenkau** Sachsen, E Germany
109 V3 **Zwettl** Wien, NE Austria
109 T3 **Zwettl an der Rodl** Oberösterreich, N Austria
99 D18 **Zwevegem** West-Vlaanderen, W Belgium
101 M17 **Zwickau** Sachsen, E Germany
101 O21 **Zwiesel** Bayern, SE Germany
98 H13 **Zwijndrecht** Zuid-Holland, SW Netherlands
101 N16 **Zwikauer Mulde** ∾ E Germany
Zwischenwässern *see* Medvode
Zwittau *see* Svitavy
110 N13 **Zwoleń** Mazowieckie, SE Poland
98 M9 **Zwolle** Overijssel, E Netherlands
22 G6 **Zwolle** Louisiana, S USA
110 K12 **Żychlin** Łodzkie, C Poland
Żydaczów *see* Zhydachiv
119 L14 **Zyembin** *Rus.* Zembin. Minskaya Voblasts', C Belarus
Zyôetu *see* Jôetsu
110 L12 **Żyrardów** Mazowieckie, C Poland
123 S8 **Zyryanka** Respublika Sakha (Yakutiya), NE Russian Federation
145 Y9 **Zyryanovsk** Vostochnyy Kazakhstan, E Kazakhstan
111 J17 **Żywiec** *Ger.* Bäckermühle Schulzenmühle. Śląskie, S Poland

◆ Country ● Country Capital ◇ Dependent Territory ○ Dependent Territory Capital ⬖ Administrative Region ✕ International Airport ▲ Mountain ⛰ Mountain Range ⩕ Volcano ∾ River ◎ Lake ⊠ Reservoir

Picture Credits

Dorling Kindersley *would like to express their thanks to the following individuals, companies, and institutions for their help in preparing this atlas.*

Earth Resource Mapping Ltd., Egham, Surrey
Brian Groombridge, World Conservation Monitoring Centre, Cambridge
The British Library, London
British Library of Political and Economic Science, London
The British Museum, London
The City Business Library, London
King's College, London
National Meteorological Library and Archive, Bracknell
The Printed Word, London
The Royal Geographical Society, London
University of London Library
Paul Beardmore
Philip Boyes
Hayley Crockford
Alistair Dougal
Reg Grant
Louise Keane
Zoe Livesley
Laura Porter
Jeff Eidenshink
Chris Hornby
Rachelle Smith
Ray Pinchard
Robert Meisner
Fiona Strawbridge

Every effort has been made to trace the copyright holders and we apologize in advance for any unintentional omissions. We would be pleased to insert the appropriate acknowledgment in any subsequent edition of this publication.

Adams Picture Library: 86CLA; **G Andrews:** 186CR; **Ardea London Ltd:** K Ghana 150C; M Iljima 132TC; R Waller 148TR; Art Directors **Aspect Picture Library:** P Carmichael 160TR; 131CR(below); G Tompkinson 190TRB; **Axiom:** C Bradley 148CA, 158CA; J Holmes xivCRA, xxivBCR, xxviiCRB, 150TCR, 165C(below), 166TL, J Morris 75TL, 77CRB, J Spaull 134BL; **Bridgeman Art Library, London / New York:** Collection of the Earl of Pembroke, Wilton House xxBC; **The J. Allan Cash Photolibrary:** xlBR, xliiCLA, xlivCL, 10BC, 60CL, 69CLB, 70CL, 72CLB, 75BR, 76BC, 87BL, 109BR, 138BCL, 141TL, 154CR, 178BR, 181TR; **Bruce Coleman Ltd:** 86BC, 98CL, 100TC; S Alden 192BC(below); Atlantide xxviTCR, 138BR; E Bjurstrom 141BR; S Bond 96CRB; T Buchholz xvCL, 92TR, 123TCL; J Burton xxiiiC; J Cancalosi 181TRB; B J Coates xxvBL, 192CL; B Coleman 63TL; B & C Colhoun 2TR, 36CB; A Compost xxiiiCBR; Dr S Coyne 45TL; G Cubitt xviTCL, 169BR, 178TR, 184TR; P Davey xxviiCLB, 121TL(below); N Devore 189CBL; S J Doylee xxiiCRR; H Flygare xviiCRA; M P L Fogden 17C(above) ; Jeff Foott Productions xxiiiCRB, 11CRA; M Freeman 91BRA; P van Gaalen 86TR; G Gualco 140C; B Henderson 194CR; Dr C Henneghien 69C; HPH Photography, H Van den Berg 69CR; C Hughes 69BCL; C James xxxixTC; J Johnson 39CR, 197TR; J Jurka 91CA; S C Kaufman 28C; S J Krasemann 33TR; H Lange 10TRB, 68CA; C Lockwood 32BC; L C Marigo xxiiBC, xxviiCLA, 49CRA, 59BR; M McCoy 187TR; D Meredith 3CR; J Murray xvCR, 179BR; Orion Press 165CR(above); Orion Services & Trading Co. Inc. 164CR; C Ott 17BL; Dr E Pott 9TR, 40CL, 87C, 93TL, 194CLB; F Prenzel 186BC, 193BC; M Read 42BR, 43CRB; H Reinhard xxiiCR, xxviiTR, 194BR; L Lee Rue III 151BCL; J Shaw xixTL; K N Swenson 194BC; P Terry 115CR; N Tomalin 54BCL; P Ward 78TC; S Widstrand 57TR; K Wothe 91C, 173TCL; J T Wright 127BR; **Colorific:** Black Star / L Mulvehil 156CL; Black Star / R Rogers 57BR; Black Star / J Rupp 161BCR; Camera Tres / C. Meyer 59BRA; R Caputo / Matrix 78CL; J. Hill 117CLB; M Koene 55TR; G Satterley xliiCLAR; M Yamashita 156BL, 167CR(above); **Comstock:** 108CRB; Corbis UK Ltd: 170TR, 170BL; **D Cousens:** 147 CRA; **Sue Cunningham Photographic:** 51CR; S Alden 192BC(below) **James Davis Travel Photography:** xxxviTCB, xxxviTR, xxxviCL, 13CA, 19BC, 49TLB, 56BCR, 57CLA, 61BCL, 93BC, 94TC, 102TR, 120CB, 158BC, 179CRA, 191BR; **G Dunnet:** 124CA; **Environmental Picture Library:** Chris Westwood 126C; **Eye Ubiquitous:** xlCA; L. Fordyce 12CLA; L Johnstone 6CRA, 28BLA, 30CB; S. Miller xxiCA; M Southern 73BLA; **Chris Fairclough Colour Library:** xliBR; **Ffotograff:** N. Tapsell 158CL **FLPA -Images of nature:** 123TR; **Geoscience Features:** xviBCR, xviBR, 102CL, 108BC, 122BR; Solar Film 64TC; **gettyone stone**: 131BC, 133BR, 164CR(above); G Johnson 130BL; R Passmore 120TR; D Austen 187CL; G Allison 186CL; L Ulrich 17TL; M Vines 17BL; R Wells 193BL; **Robert Harding Picture Library:** xviiTC, xxivCR, xxxC, xxxvTC, 2TLB, 3CA, 15CRB, 15CR, 37BC, 38CRA, 50BL, 95BR, 99CR, 114CR, 122BL, 131CLA, 142CB, 143TL, 147TR, 168TR, 168CA, 166BR; P G. Adam 13TCB; D Atchison-Jones 70BLA; J Bayne 72BCL; B Schuster 80CR; C Bowman 50BR, 53CA, 62CL, 70CRL; C Campbell xxiBC; G Corrigan 159CRB, 161CRB; P Craven xxxvBL; R Cundy 69BR; Delu 79BC; A Durand 111BR; Financial Times 142BR; R Frerck 51BL; T Gervis 3BCL, 7CR; I Griffiths xxxCL, 77TL; T Hall 166CRA; D Harney 142CA; S Harris xliiiBCL; G Hellier xvCRB, 135BL; F Jackson 137BCR; Jacobs xxxviiTL; P Koch 139TR; F Joseph Land 122TR; Y Marcoux 9BR; S Massif xvBC; A Mills 88CLB; L Murray 114TR; R Rainford xlivBL; G Renner 74CB, 194C; C Rennie 48CL, 116BR; R Richardson 118CL; P Van Riel 48BR; E Rooney 124TR; Sassoon xxivCL, 148CLB; P Scholey 176TR; M Short 137TL; E Simanor xxviiCR; V Southwell 139CR; J Strachan 42TR, 111BL, 132BCR; C Tokeley 131CLA; A C Waltham 161C; T Waltham xviiBL, xxiiCLLL, 138CRB; Westlight 37CR; N Wheeler 139BL; A Williams xxxviiiBR, xlTR; A Woolfitt 95BRA; Paul Harris: 168TC; **Hutchison Library:** 131CR (above) 6BL; P. Collomb 137CR; C. Dodwell 130TR; S Errington 70BCL; P. Hellyer 142BC; J. Horner xxxiTC; R. Ian Lloyd 134CRA; N. Durrell McKenna xxviBCR; J.Nowell 135CLB, 143TC; A Zvoznikov xxiiCL; **Image Bank:** 87BR; J Banagan 190BCA; A Becker xxivBCL; M Khansa 121CR, M Isy-Schwart 193CR(above), 191CL; Khansa K Forest 163TR; Lomeo xxivTCR; T Madison 170TL(below); C Molyneux xxiiCRRR; C Navajas xviiiTR; Ocean Images Inc. 192CLB; J van Os xviiTCR; S Proehl 6CL; T Rakke xixTC, 64CL; M Reitz 196CA; M Romanelli 166CL(below); G A Rossi 151BCR, 176BLA; B Roussel 109TL; S Satushek xviiBCR; Stock Photos / J M Spielman xxivTRL; **Images Colour Library:** xxiiCLL, xxxixTR, xliCR, xliiiBL, 3BR, 19BR, 37TL, 44TL, 62TC, 91BR, 102CLB, 103CR, 150CL, 180CA; 164BC, 165TL; **Impact Photos:** J & G Andrews 186BL; C. Bluntzer 156BR; Cosmos / G. Buthaud 65BC; S Franklin 126BL; A. le Garsmeur 131C; A Indge xxviiTC; C Jones xxxiCB, 70BL; V. Nemirousky 137BR; J Nicholl 76TCR; C. Penn 187C(below); G Sweeney xviiBR, 196CB, 196TR, J & G Andrews 186TR; **JVZ Picture Library:** T Nilson 135TC; **Frank Lane Picture Agency:** xxiTCR, xxiiiBL, 93TR; A Christiansen 58CRA; J Holmes xivBL; S. McCutcheon 3C; Silvestris 173TCR; D Smith xxiiBCL; W Wisniewsli 195BR; **Leeds Castle Foundation:** xxxviiBC; **Magnum:** Abbas 83CR, 136CA; S Franklin 134CRB; D Hurn 4BCL; P. Jones-Griffiths 191BL; H Kubota xviBCL, 156CLB; F Maver xviBL; S McCurry 73CL, 133BCR; G. Rodger 74TR; C Steele Perkins 72BL; **Mountain Camera / John Cleare:** 153TR; C Monteath 153CR; **Nature Photographers:** E.A. Janes 112CL; **Natural Science Photos:** M Andera 110C; **Network Photographers Ltd.:** C Sappa / Rapho 119BL; **N.H.P.A.:** N. J. Dennis xxiiiCL; D Heuchlin xxiiiCLA; S Krasemann 15BL, 25BR, 38TC; K Schafer 49CB; R Tidman 160CLB; D Tomlinson 145CR; M Wendler 48TR; **Nottingham Trent University:** T Waltham xivCL, xvBR; **Novosti:** 144BLA; **Oxford Scientific Films:** D Allan xxiiTR; H R Bardarson xviiiBC; D Bown xxiiiCBLL; M Brown 140BL; M Colbeck 147CAR; W Faidley 3TL; L Gould xxiiiTRB; D Guravich xxiiiTR; P Hammerschmidy / Okapia 87CLA; M Hill 57TL, 195TR; C Menteath ; J Netherton 2CRB; S Osolinski 82CA; R Packwood 72CA; M Pitts 179TC; N Rosing xxiiiCBL, 9TR, 197BR; D Simonson 57C; Survival Anglia / C Catton 137TR; R Toms xxiiiBR; K Wothe xxiBL, xviiCLA; **Panos Pictures:** B Aris 133C; P Barker xxivBR; T Bolstao 153BR; N Cooper 82CB, 153TC; J-L Dugast 166C(below), 167BR; J Hartley 73CA, 90CL; J Holmes 149BC; J Morris 76CLB; M Rose 146TR; D Sansoni 155CL; C Stowers 163TL; **Edward Parker:** 49TL, 49CLB; **Pictor International:** xivBR, xvBRA, xixTCL, xxCL, 3CLA, 17BR, 20TR, 20CRB, 23BCA, 23CL, 26CB, 27BC, 30CA, 33TRB, 34BC, 34BR, 34CR, 38CB, 38CL, 43CL, 63BR, 65TC, 82CL, 83CLB, 99BR, 107CLA, 166TR, 171CL(above), 180CLB, 185TL; **Pictures Colour Library:** xxiBCL, xxiiBR, xxviBCL, 6BR, 15TR, 8TR, 16CL(above), 19TL, 20BL, 24C, 24CLA, 27TR, 32TRB, 36BC, 41CA, 43CRA, 68BL, 90TCB, 94BL, 99BL, 106CA, 107CLB, 107CR, 107BR, 117BL, 164BC, 192BL, K Forest 165TL(below); **Planet Earth Pictures:** 193CR(below); D Barrett 148CB, 184CA; R Coomber 16BL; G Douwma 172BR; E Edmonds 173BR; J Lythgoe 196BL; A Mounter 172CR; M Potts 6CA; P Scoones xxTR; J Walencik 110TR; J Waters 53BCL; **Popperfoto:** Reuters / J Drake xxxiiCLA; **Rex Features:** 165CR; Antelope xxxiiCLB; M Friedel xxiCR; I McIlgorm xxxCBR; J Shelley xxxCR; Sipa Press xxxCR; Sipa Press / Alix xxxCBL; Sipa Press / Chamussy 176BL; **Robert Harding Picture Library:** C. Tokeley 131TL; J Strachan 132BL; Franz Joseph Land 122TR; Franz Joseph Land 364/7088 123BL, 169C(above), 170C(above), 168CL, Tony Waltham 186CR(below), Y Marcoux 9BR; **Russia & Republics Photolibrary:** M Wadlow 118CR, 119CL, 124BC, 124CL, 125TL, 125BR, 126TCR; **Science Photo Library:** Earth Satellite Corporation xixTRB, xxxiCR, 49BCL; F Gohier xiCR; J Heseltine xviTCB; K Kent xvBLA; P Menzell xvBL; N.A.S.A. xBC; D Parker xivBC; University of Cambridge Collection Air Pictures 87CLB; RJ Wainscoat / P Arnold, Inc. xiBC; D Weintraub xiBL; **South American Pictures:** 57BL, 62TR; R Francis 52BL; Guyana Space Centre 50TR; T Morrison 49CRB, 49BL, 50CR, 52TR, 54TR, 60BL, 61C; **Southampton Oceanography:** xviiiBL; **Sovofoto / Eastfoto:** xxxiiCBR; **Spectrum Colour Library:** 50BC, 160BC; J King 145BR; **Frank Spooner Pictures:** Gamma-Liason/Vogel 131CL(above); 26CRB; E. Baitel xxxiiBC; Bernstein xxxiCL; Contrast 112CR; Diard / Photo News 113CL; Liaison / C. Hires xxxiiTCB; Liaison / Nickelsberg xxxiiTR; Marleen 113TL; Novosti 116CA; P. Piel xxxCA; N Quidu 135CL; H Stucke 188CLB, 190CA; Torrengo / Figaro 78BR; A Zamur 113BL; **Still Pictures:** C Caldicott 77TC; A Crump 189CL; M & C Denis-Huot xxiiBL, 78CR, 81BL; M Edwards xxiCRL, 53BL, 64CR, 69BLA, 155BR; J Frebet 53CLB; H Giradet 53TC; E Parker 52CL; M Gunther 121BC; **Tony Stone Images:** xxviTR, 4CA, 7BL, 7CL, 13CRB, 39BR, 58C, 97BC, 101BR, 106TR, 109CL, 109CRB, 164CLB, 165C,180CB, 181BR, 188BC, 192TR; G Allison 18TR, 31CRB, 187CRB; D Armand 14TCB; D Austen 180TR, 186CL, 187CL; J Beatty 74CL; O Benn xxviBR; K Biggs xxiTL; R Bradbury 44BR; R A Butcher xxviTL; J Callahan xxviiCRA; P Chesley 185BCL, 188C; W Clay 30BL, 31CRA; J Cornish 96BL, 107TL; C Condina 41CB; T Craddock xxivTR; P Degginger 36CLB; Demetrio 5BR; N DeVore xxivBC; A Diesendruck 60BR; S Egan 87CRA, 96BR; R Elliot xxiiBCR; S Elmore 19C; J Garrett 73CR; S Grandadam 14BR; R Grosskopf 28BL; D Hanson 104BC; C Harvey 69TL; G Hellier 110BL, 165CR; S Huber 103CRB; D Hughs xxxiBR; A Husmo 91TR; G Irvine 31BC; J Jangoux 58CL; D Johnston xviiTR; A Kehr 113C; R Koskas xviTR; J Lamb 96CRA; J Lawrence 75CRA; L Lefkowitz 7CA; M Lewis 45CLA; S Mayman 55BR; Murray & Associates 45CR; G Norways 104CA; N Parfitt xxviiCL, 68TCR, 81TL; R Passmore 121TR; N Press xviBCA; E Pritchard 88CA, 90CLR; T Raymond 21BL, 29TR; L Resnick 74BR; M Rogers 80BR; A Sacks 28TCB; C Saule 90CR; S Schulhof xxivTC; P Seaward 34CL; M Segal 32BL; V Shenai 152CL; R Sherman 26CL; H Sitton 136CR; R Smith xxvBLA, 56C; S Studd 108CLA; H Strand 49BR, 63TR; P Tweedie 177CR; L Ulrich 17BL; M Vines 17TC; A B Wadham 60CR; J Warden 63CLB; R Wells 23CRA, 193BL; G Yeowell 34BL; **Telegraph Colour Library:** 61CRB, 61TCR, 157TL; R Antrobus xxxixBR; J Sims 26BR; **Topham Picturepoint:** xxxiCBL, 162BR, 168TR, 168BC; **Travel Ink:** A Cowin 88TR; **Trip:** 140BR, 144CA, 155CRA; B Ashe 159TR; D Cole 190BCL, 190CR; D Davis 89BL; I Deineko xxxiTR; J Dennis 22BL; Dinodia 154CL; Eye Ubiquitous / L Fordyce 2CLB; A Gasson 149CR; W Jacobs 43TL, 54BL, 177BC, 178CLA, 185BCR, 186BL; P Kingsbury 112C; K Knight 177BR; V Kolpakov 147BL; T Noorits 87TL, 119BR, 146CL; R Power 41TR; N Ray 166BL, 168TC; C Rennie 116CLB; V Sidoropolev 145TR; E Smith 183BC, 183TL; **Woodfin Camp & Associates:** 92BLR; **World Pictures:** xvCRA, xviiCRA, 9CRB, 22CL, 23BC, 24BL, 35BL, 40TR, 51TR, 71BR, 80TCR, 82TR, 83BL, 86BCR, 96TC, 98BL, 100CR, 101CR, 103BC, 105TC, 157BL, 161BCL, 162CLB, 172CLB, 172BC, 179BL, 182CB, 183C, 184CL, 185CR; 121BR, 121TT; **Zefa Picture Library:** xviBLR, xviiBCL, xviiiCL, 3CL, 8BC, 8CT, 9CR, 13BC, 14TC, 16TR, 21TL, 22CRB, 25BL, 32TCR, 36BCR, 59BCL, 65TCL, 69CLA, 79TL, 81BR, 87CRB, 92C, 98C, 99TL, 100BL, 107TR, 118CRB, 120BL; 122C(below), 124CLA, 164BR, 183TR; Anatol 113BR; Barone 114BL; Brandenburg 5C; A J Brown 44TR; H J Clauss 55CLB; Damm 71BC; Evert 92BL; W Felger 3BL; J Fields 189CRA; R Frerck 4BL; G Heil 56BR; K Heibig 115BR; Heilman 28BC; Hunter 8C; Kitchen 10TR, 8CL, 8BL, 9TR; Dr H Kramarz 7BLA, 123CR(below); Mehlio 155BL; J F Raga 24TR; Rossenbach 105BR; Streichan 89TL; T Stewart 13TR, 19CR; Sunak 54BR, 162TR; D H Teuffen 95TL; B Zaunders 40BC. **Additional Photography:** Geoff Dann; Rob Reichenfeld; H Taylor; Jerry Young.

NORTH AMERICA

CANADA
PAGES 8–15

UNITED STATES OF AMERICA
PAGES 16–39

MEXICO
PAGES 40–41

BELIZE
PAGES 42–43

COSTA RICA
PAGES 42–43

EL SALVADOR
PAGES 42–43

GUATEMALA
PAGES 42–43

HONDURAS
PAGES 42–43

GRENADA
PAGES 44–45

HAITI
PAGES 44–45

JAMAICA
PAGES 44–45

ST KITTS & NEVIS
PAGES 44–45

ST LUCIA
PAGES 44–45

ST VINCENT & THE GRENADINES
PAGES 44–45

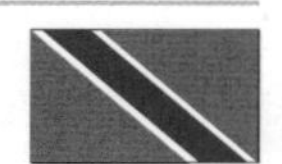
TRINIDAD & TOBAGO
PAGES 44–45

SOUTH AME

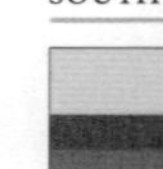
COLOMBIA
PAGES 54–55

URUGUAY
PAGES 60–61

CHILE
PAGES 62–63

PARAGUAY
PAGES 62–63

AFRICA

ALGERIA
PAGES 74–75

EGYPT
PAGES 74–75

LIBYA
PAGES 74–75

MOROCCO
PAGES 74–75

TUNIS
PAGES 7

LIBERIA
PAGES 76–77

MALI
PAGES 76–77

MAURITANIA
PAGES 76–77

NIGER
PAGES 76–77

NIGERIA
PAGES 76–77

SENEGAL
PAGES 76–77

SIERRA LEONE
PAGES 76–77

TOGO
PAGES 76–7

BURUNDI
PAGES 80–81

DJIBOUTI
PAGES 80–81

ERITREA
PAGES 80–81

ETHIOPIA
PAGES 80–81

KENYA
PAGES 80–81

RWANDA
PAGES 80–81

SOMALIA
PAGES 80–81

SUDAN
PAGES 80–81

SOUTH AFRICA
PAGES 82–83

SWAZILAND
PAGES 82–83

ZAMBIA
PAGES 82–83

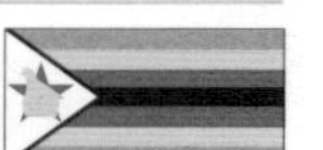
ZIMBABWE
PAGES 82–83

EUROPE

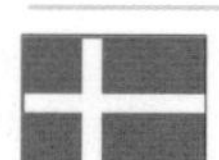
DENMARK
PAGES 92–93

FINLAND
PAGES 92–93

ICELAND
PAGES 92–93

NORWAY
PAGES 92–95

MONACO
PAGES 102–103

ANDORRA
PAGES 104–105

PORTUGAL
PAGES 104–105

SPAIN
PAGES 104–105

ITALY
PAGES 106–107

SAN MARINO
PAGES 106–107

VATICAN CITY
PAGES 106–107

AUSTRIA
PAGES 108–109

BOSNIA & HERZEGOVINA
PAGES 112–113

CROATIA
PAGES 112–113

MACEDONIA
PAGES 112–113

YUGOSLAVIA
PAGES 112–113

BULGARIA
PAGES 114–115

GREECE
PAGES 114–115

MOLDOVA
PAGES 116–117

ROMANIA
PAGES 116–117

ASIA

ARMENIA
PAGES 136–137

AZERBAIJAN
PAGES 136–137

GEORGIA
PAGES 136–137

TURKEY
PAGES 136–137/114–115

IRAQ
PAGES 138–139

ISRAEL
PAGES 138–139

JORDAN
PAGES 138–139

LEBANON
PAGES 138–139

IRAN
PAGES 142–143

KAZAKHSTAN
PAGES 144–145

KYRGYZSTAN
PAGES 146–147

TAJIKISTAN
PAGES 146–147

TURKMENISTAN
PAGES 146–147

UZBEKISTAN
PAGES 146–147

AFGHANISTAN
PAGES 148–149

PAKISTAN
PAGES 148–151

SOUTH KOREA
PAGES 156–157/162–163

TAIWAN
PAGES 160–161

JAPAN
PAGES 164–165

MYANMAR
PAGES 166–167

CAMBODIA
PAGES 166–167

LAOS
PAGES 166–167

PHILIPPINES
PAGES 166–167

THAILAND
PAGES 166–167

AUSTRALASIA & OCEANIA

MAURITIUS
PAGES 172–173

SEYCHELLES
PAGES 172–173

AUSTRALIA
PAGES 180–183

NEW ZEALAND
PAGES 184–185

PAPUA NEW GUINEA
PAGES 186–187

FIJI
PAGES 186–187

SOLOMON ISLANDS
PAGES 186–187

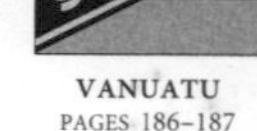
VANUATU
PAGES 186–187